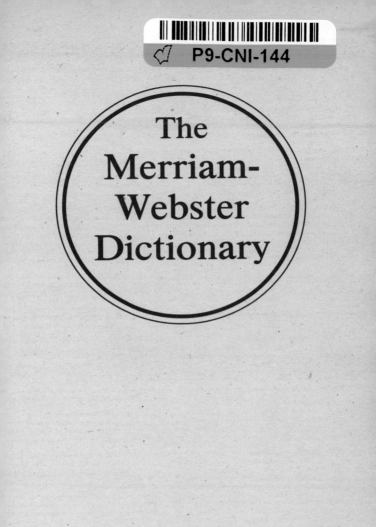

The
Merriam-
Webster
Dictionary

The Merriam-Webster Dictionary

Merriam-Webster, Incorporated
Springfield, Massachusetts

A GENUINE MERRIAM-WEBSTER

The name *Webster* alone is no guarantee of excellence. It is used by a number of publishers and may serve mainly to mislead an unwary buyer.

Merriam-Webster™ is the name you should look for when you consider the purchase of dictionaries or other fine reference books. It carries the reputation of a company that has been publishing since 1831 and is your assurance of quality and authority.

PREFACE

This new edition of *The Merriam-Webster Dictionary* is the sixth in a line of Merriam-Webster paperback dictionaries which began in 1947. It is based on and preserves the best aspects of preceding editions, but it also offers much that is new, drawing specifically on *Merriam-Webster's Collegiate Dictionary, Eleventh Edition*. Every entry and every section has been reexamined and revised in light of the most current information available. Definitions have been based on examples of actual use found in the Merriam-Webster citation files, which now contain more than 15,000,000 examples of English words in context from a wide range of printed sources, and more than 75 million words available through electronic searching. The editors of this book have created it with the same careful, serious attention that has gone into every Merriam-Webster dictionary.

The 65,000 entries in this dictionary give coverage to the most frequently used words in the language. The heart of the dictionary is the A-Z vocabulary section, where readers will find information about meaning, spelling, pronunciation, etymology, and synonyms. This section is followed by others that users have long found useful: the section Foreign Words and Phrases covers words and phrases from other languages that often occur in English texts but have not become part of the English vocabulary; the section Biographical Names identifies individuals from history and contemporary culture, as well as biblical, legendary, and mythological characters; the section Geographical Names identifies places of importance in the United States and the world, along with current population figures.

The Merriam-Webster Dictionary has been created by a company that has been publishing dictionaries for more than 150 years. It has been edited by an experienced staff of lexicographers, who believe it will serve well those who want a concise and handy guide to the English language of today.

EXPLANATORY NOTES

The dictionary contains so much information, that it is necessary to condense much of it to accommodate the limitations of the printed page. This section provides information on the conventions used throughout the dictionary, from the styling of entries and pronunciation to how we present information on usage and meaning. An understanding of the information contained in these notes will make the dictionary both easier and more rewarding to use.

ENTRIES

A boldface letter or a combination of such letters, including punctuation marks and diacritics where needed, that is set flush with the left-hand margin of each column of type is a main entry. The main entry may consist of letters set solid, of letters joined by a hyphen or a diagonal, or of letters separated by one or more spaces:

alone·. . . *adj*
avant–garde . . . *n*
and/or . . . *conj*
assembly language . . . *n*
av·a·lanche . . . *n*

The material in lightface type that follows each main entry on the same line and on succeeding indented lines presents information about the main entry.

The main entries follow one another in alphabetical order letter by letter: *bill of attainder* follows *billion; Day of Atonement* follows *daylight saving time.* Those containing an Arabic numeral are alphabetized as if the numeral were spelled out: *4-H* comes between *fourfold* and *Four Hundred; 3-D* comes between *three* and *three-dimensional.* Those that often begin with the abbreviation *St.* in common usage have the abbreviation spelled out: *Saint Valentine's Day.* Main entries that begin with *Mc* are alphabetized just as they are spelled.

A pair of guide words is printed at the top of each page. These indicate that the entries falling alphabetically between the words at the top of the outer column of each page are found on that page.

The guide words are usually the alphabetically first and the alphabetically last entries on the page:

animosity • another

Occasionally the last printed entry is not the alphabetically last entry. On page 171, for example, *cropper* is the last main entry, but *cropping,* an inflected form at *crop,* is the alphabetically last entry and is therefore the second guide word. The alphabetically last entry is not used, however, if it follows alphabetically the first guide word on the succeeding page. Thus on page 209 *distressful* is not a guide word because it follows alphabetically the entry *distress* which is the first guide word on page 210.

Any boldface word—a main entry with definition, a variant, an inflected form, a defined or undefined run-on, or a run-in entry—may be used as a guide word.

When one main entry has exactly the same written form as another, the two are distinguished by superscript numerals preceding each word:

^{1}melt . . . *vb*
^{2}melt *n*
^{1}pine . . . *n*
^{2}pine *vb*

Full words come before parts of words made up of the same letters; solid compounds come before hyphenated compounds; hyphenated compounds come before open compounds; and lowercase entries come before those with an initial capital:

²**super** *n*
super- . . . *prefix*
run·down . . . *n*
run–down . . . *adj*
run down *vb*
dutch . . . *adv*
Dutch . . . *n*

The centered dots within entry words indicate division points at which a hyphen may be put at the end of a line of print or writing. Thus the noun *cap·puc·ci·no* may be ended on one line and continued on the next in this manner:

cap-
puccino

cappuc-
cino

cappucci-
no

Centered dots are not shown after a single initial letter or before a single terminal letter because typesetters seldom cut off a single letter:

abyss . . . *n*
flighty . . . *adj*
idea . . . *n*

Nor are they usually shown at the second and succeeding homographs unless they differ among themselves:

¹**sig·nal** . . . *n*
²**signal** *vb*
³**signal** *adj*
but
¹**min·ute** . . . *n*
²**mi·nute** . . . *adj*

There are acceptable alternative end-of-line divisions just as there are acceptable variant spellings and pronunciations, but no more than one division is shown for any entry in this dictionary.

A double hyphen at the end of a line in this dictionary (as in the definition at **cod**) stands for a hyphen that is retained when the word is written as a unit on one line. This kind of fixed hyphen is always represented in boldface words in this dictionary with an en dash, longer than an ordinary hyphen.

When a main entry is followed by the word *or* and another spelling, the two spellings are equal variants. Both are standard, and either one may be used according to personal inclination:

ocher *or* **ochre**

If two variants joined by *or* are out of alphabetical order, they remain equal variants. The one printed first is, however, slightly more common than the second:

¹**plow** *or* **plough**

When another spelling is joined to the main entry by the word *also*, the spelling after *also* is a secondary variant and occurs less frequently than the first:

absinthe *also* **absinth**

Secondary variants belong to standard usage and may be used according to personal inclination. Once the word *also* is used to signal a secondary variant, all following secondary variants are joined by *or*:

²**wool·ly** *also* **wool·ie** *or* **wooly**

Variants whose spelling puts them alphabetically more than a column away from the main entry are entered at their own alphabetical places as well as at the main entry:

²**gage** *var of* GAUGE
. . .
¹**gauge** *also* **gage**

Variants having a usage label appear only at their own alphabetical places:

me·tre . . . *chiefly Brit var of* METER

To show all the stylings that are found for English compounds would require space that can be better used for other information. So this dictionary limits itself to a single styling for a compound:

peace·mak·er
pell–mell
boom box

When a compound is widely used and one styling predominates, that styling is shown. When a compound is uncommon or when the evidence indicates that two or three stylings are approximately equal in frequency, the styling shown is based on the comparison of other similar compounds.

A main entry may be followed by

one or more derivatives or by a homograph with a different functional label. These are run-on entries. Each is introduced by a long dash and each has a functional label. They are not defined, however, since their meanings are readily understood from the meaning of the root word:

   fear·less . . . *adj* . . . — **fear·less·ly**
   adv — **fear·less·ness** *n*
   hic·cup . . . *n* . . . — **hiccup** *vb*

A main entry may be followed by one or more phrases containing the entry word or an inflected form of it. These are also run-on entries. Each is introduced by a long dash but there is no functional label. They are, however, defined since their meanings are more than the sum of the meanings of their elements:

   ¹**set** . . . *vb* . . . — **set sail** : . . .
   ¹**hand** . . . *n* . . . — **at hand** : . . .

Defined phrases of this sort are run on at the entry defining the first major word in the phrase. When there are variants, however, the run-on appears at the entry defining the first major invariable word in the phrase:

   ¹**seed** . . . *n* . . . — **go to seed** *or* **run to seed** 1 : . . .

Boldface words that appear within parentheses (as **co·ca** at **co·caine** and **jet engine** and **jet propulsion** at **jet–propelled**) are run-in entries.

Attention is called to the definition of *vocabulary entry* on page 811. The term *dictionary entry* includes all vocabulary entries as well as all boldface entries in the back sections headed "Foreign Words & Phrases," "Biographical Names," and "Geographical Names."

PRONUNCIATION

The matter between a pair of reversed slashes \ \ following the entry word indicates the pronunciation. The symbols used are explained in the chart at the end of this section.

A hyphen is used in the pronunciation to show syllabic division. These hyphens sometimes coincide with the centered dots in the entry word that indicate end-of-line division:

   ab·sen·tee \ˌab-sən-'tē\

Sometimes they do not:

   met·ric \'me-trik\

A high-set mark ' indicates major (primary) stress or accent; a low-set mark ˌ indicates minor (secondary) stress or accent:

   heart·beat \'härt-ˌbēt\

The stress mark stands at the beginning of the syllable that receives the stress.

A syllable with neither a high-set mark nor a low-set mark is unstressed:

   ¹**struc·ture** \'strək-chər\

The presence of variant pronunciations indicates that not all educated

speakers pronounce words the same way. A second-place variant is not to be regarded as less acceptable than the pronunciation that is given first. It may, in fact, be used by as many educated speakers as the first variant, but the requirements of the printed page are such that one must precede the other:

   apri·cot \'a-prə-ˌkät, 'ā-\
   for·head \'fȯr-əd, 'fȯr-ˌhed\

Symbols enclosed by parentheses represent elements that are present in the pronunciation of some speakers but are absent from the pronunciation of other speakers, or elements that are present in some but absent from other utterances of the same speaker:

   ¹**om·ni·bus** \'äm-ni-(ˌ)bəs\
   ad·di·tion·al \ə-'di-sh(ə-)nəl\

Thus, the above parentheses indicate that some people say \'äm-ni-ˌbəs\ and others say \'äm-ni-bəs\; some \ə-'di-shə-nəl\, others \ə-'di-shnəl\.

When a main entry has less than a full pronunciation, the missing part is to be supplied from a pronunciation in a preceding entry or within the same pair of reversed slashes:

cham·pi·on·ship \-₁ship\
pa·la·ver \pə-'la-vər, -'lä-\

The pronunciation of the first three syllables of *championship* is found at the main entry *champion*. The hyphens before and after \'lä\ in the pronunciation of *palaver* indicate that both the first and the last parts of the pronunciation are to be taken from the immediately preceding pronunciation.

In general, no pronunciation is indicated for open compounds consisting of two or more English words that have own-place entry:

witch doctor *n*

Only the first entry in a sequence of numbered homographs is given a pro-nunciation if their pronunciations are the same:

¹**re·ward** \ri-'word\ *vb*
²**reward** *n*

The absent but implied pronunciation of derivatives and compounds run on after a main entry is a combination of the pronunciation at the main entry and the pronunciation of the other element as given at its alphabetical place in the vocabulary:

— **quick·ness** *n*
— **hold out**

Thus, the pronunciation of *quickness* is the sum of the pronunciations given at *quick* and *-ness;* that of *hold out*, the sum of the pronunciations of the two elements that make up the phrase.

FUNCTIONAL LABELS

An italic label indicating a part of speech or another functional classification follows the pronunciation or, if no pronunciation is given, the main entry. The eight traditional parts of speech are indicated as follows:

bold . . . *adj*
forth·with . . . *adv*
¹**but** . . . *conj*
ge·sund·heit . . . *interj*
bo·le·ro . . . *n*
²**un·der** . . . *prep*
¹**it** . . . *pron*
slap . . . *vb*

Other italicized labels used to indicate functional classifications that are not traditional parts of speech include:

AT *abbr*
self- *comb form*
un- . . . *prefix*
-ial *adj suffix*
²**-ly** *adv suffix*
²**-er** . . . *n suffix*
-ize . . . *vb suffix*
Fe *symbol*
may . . . *verbal auxiliary*

Functional labels are sometimes combined:

afloat . . . *adj or adv*

INFLECTED FORMS

NOUNS

The plurals of nouns are shown in this dictionary when suffixation brings about a change of final *-y* to *-i-*, when the noun ends in a consonant plus *-o* or in *-ey*, when the noun ends in *-oo*, when the noun has an irregular plural or an uninflected plural or a foreign plural, when the noun is a compound that pluralizes any element but the last, when a final consonant is doubled, when the noun has variant plurals, and when it is believed that the dictionary user might have reasonable doubts about the spelling of the plural or when the plural is spelled in a way contrary to what is expected:

²spy *n, pl* spies
si·lo . . . *n, pl* silos
val·ley . . . *n, pl* valleys
²shampoo *n, pl* shampoos
mouse . . . *n, pl* mice
moose . . . *n, pl* moose
cri·te·ri·on . . . *n, pl* -ria
son—in—law . . . *n, pl* sons—in—law
¹quiz . . . *n, pl* quiz·zes
¹fish . . . *n, pl* fish *or* fishes
pi . . . *n, pl* pis
³dry *n, pl* drys

Cutback inflected forms are used when the noun has three or more syllables:

ame·ni·ty . . . *n, pl* -ties

The plurals of nouns are usually not shown when the base word is unchanged by suffixation, when the noun is a compound whose second element is readily recognizable as a regular free form entered at its own place, or when the noun is unlikely to occur in the plural:

night . . . *n*
fore·foot . . . *n*
mo·nog·a·my . . . *n*

Nouns that are plural in form and that are regularly construed as plural are labeled *n pl:*

munch·ies . . . *n pl*

Nouns that are plural in form but that are not always construed as plurals are appropriately labeled:

lo·gis·tics . . . *n sing or pl*

VERBS

The principal parts of verbs are shown in this dictionary when suffixation brings about a doubling of a final consonant or an elision of a final *-e* or a change of final *-y* to *-i-*, when final *-c* changes to *-ck* in suffixation, when the verb ends in *-ey*, when the inflection is irregular, when there are variant inflected forms, and when it is believed that the dictionary user might have reasonable doubts about the spelling of an inflected form or when the inflected form is spelled in a way contrary to what is expected:

²snag *vb* snagged; snag·ging
¹move . . . *vb* moved; mov·ing
¹cry . . . *vb* cried; cry·ing
¹frol·ic . . . *vb* frol·icked; frol·ick·ing
sur·vey . . . *vb* sur·veyed; sur·vey·ing
¹drive . . . *vb* drove . . . driv·en . . . driv·ing
²bus *vb* bused *or* bussed; bus·ing *or* bus·sing
²visa *vb* vi·saed . . . vi·sa·ing
²chagrin *vb* cha·grined . . . cha·grin·ing

The principal parts of a regularly inflected verb are shown when it is desirable to indicate the pronunciation of one of the inflected forms:

learn . . . *vb* learned \'lərnd, 'lərnt\; learn·ing

¹al·ter \'ȯl·tər\ *vb* al·tered; al·ter·ing \-t(ə-)riŋ\

Cutback inflected forms are usually used when the verb has three or more syllables, when it is a two-syllable word that ends in *-l* and has variant spellings, and when it is a compound whose second element is readily recognized as an irregular verb:

elim·i·nate . . . *vb* -nat·ed; -nat·ing
²quarrel *vb* -reled *or* -relled; -rel·ing *or* -rel·ling
¹re·take . . . *vb* -took . . . -tak·en . . . -tak·ing

The principal parts of verbs are usually not shown when the base word is unchanged by suffixation or when the verb is a compound whose second element is readily recognizable as a regular free form entered at its own place:

¹jump . . . *vb*
pre·judge . . . *vb*

Another inflected form of English verbs is the third person singular of the present tense, which is regularly formed by the addition of *-s* or *-es* to the base form of the verb. This inflected form is not shown except at a handful of entries (as *have* and *do*) for which it is in some way unusual.

ADJECTIVES & ADVERBS

The comparative and superlative forms of adjectives and adverbs are shown in this dictionary when suffixation brings about a doubling of a final consonant or an elision of a final -e or a change of final -y to -i-, when the word ends in -ey, when the inflection is irregular, and when there are variant inflected forms:

>¹red . . . adj red·der; red·dest
>¹tame . . . adj tam·er; tam·est
>¹kind·ly . . . adj kind·li·er; -est
>hors·ey also horsy . . . adj hors·i·er; -est
>¹good . . . adj bet·ter . . . best
>¹far . . . adv far·ther . . . or fur·ther . . . far·thest or fur·thest

The superlative forms of adjectives and adverbs of two or more syllables are usually cut back:

>³fancy adj fan·ci·er; -est
>¹ear·ly . . . adv ear·li·er; -est

The comparative and superlative forms of regularly inflected adjectives and adverbs are shown when it is desirable to indicate the pronunciation of the inflected forms:

>¹young \'yəŋ\ adj youn·ger \'yəŋ-gər\ youn·gest \'yəŋ-gəst\

The inclusion of inflected forms in -er and -est at adjective and adverb entries means nothing more about the use of more and most with these adjectives and adverbs than that their comparative and superlative degrees may be expressed in either way: lazier or more lazy; laziest or most lazy.

At a few adjective entries only the superlative form is shown:

>²mere adj, superlative mer·est

The absence of the comparative form indicates that there is no evidence of its use.

The comparative and superlative forms of adjectives and adverbs are usually not shown when the base word is unchanged by suffixation, when the inflected forms of the word are identical with those of a preceding homograph, or when the word is a compound whose second element is readily recognizable as a regular free form entered at its own place:

>¹near adv
>³good adv
>un·wor·thy . . . adj

Inflected forms are not shown at undefined run-ons.

CAPITALIZATION

Most entries in this dictionary begin with a lowercase letter. A few of these have an italicized label often cap, which indicates that the word is as likely to be capitalized as not and that it is as acceptable with an uppercase initial as it is with one in lowercase. Some entries begin with an uppercase letter, which indicates that the word is usually capitalized. The absence of an initial capital or of an often cap label indicates that the word is not ordinarily capitalized:

>salm·on . . . n
>gar·gan·tuan . . . adj, often cap
>Mo·hawk . . . n

The capitalization of entries that are open or hyphenated compounds is similarly indicated by the form of the entry or by an italicized label:

>dry goods . . . n pl
>french fry n, often cap 1st F
>un—Amer·i·can . . . adj
>Par·kin·son's disease . . . n
>lazy Su·san . . . n
>Jack Frost n

A word that is capitalized in some senses and lowercase in others shows variations from the form of the main entry by the use of italicized labels at the appropriate senses:

>Trin·i·ty . . . n . . . 2 not cap
>To·ry . . . n . . . 3 often not cap
>ti·tan . . . n 1 cap
>re·nais·sance . . . n . . . 1 cap . . . 2 often cap

ETYMOLOGY

This dictionary gives the etymologies for a number of the vocabulary entries. These etymologies are inside square brackets preceding the definition. Meanings given in roman type within these brackets are not definitions of the entry, but are meanings of the Middle English, Old English, or non-English words within the brackets.

The etymology gives the language from which words borrowed into English have come. It also gives the form of the word in that language or a representation of the word in our alphabet if the form in that language differs from that in English:

phi·lo·den·dron . . . [NL, fr. Gk, neut. of *philodendros* loving trees . . .]

¹sav·age . . . [ME *sauvage*, fr. MF, fr.

ML *salvaticus*, alter. of L *silvaticus* of the woods, wild . . .]

An etymology beginning with the name of a language (including ME or OE) and not giving the foreign (or Middle English or Old English) form indicates that this form is the same as the form of the entry word:

le·gume . . . [F]

¹jour·ney . . . [ME, fr. OF . . .]

An etymology beginning with the name of a language (including ME or OE) and not giving the foreign (or Middle English or Old English) meaning indicates that this meaning is the same as the meaning expressed in the first definition in the entry:

ug·ly . . . *adj* . . . [ME, fr. ON *uggligr* . . .] **1** : FRIGHTFUL, DIRE

USAGE

Three types of status labels are used in this dictionary—temporal, regional, and stylistic—to signal that a word or a sense of a word is not part of the standard vocabulary of English.

The temporal label *obs* for "obsolete" means that there is no evidence of use since 1755:

³post *n* **1** *obs*

The label *obs* is a comment on the word being defined. When a thing, as distinguished from the word used to designate it, is obsolete, appropriate orientation is usually given in the definition:

cat·a·pult . . . *n* **1** : an ancient military machine for hurling missiles

The temporal label *archaic* means that a word or sense once in common use is found today only sporadically or in special contexts:

¹mete . . . *vb* . . . **1** *archaic*

¹thou . . . *pron, archaic*

A word or sense limited in use to a specific region of the U.S. has an appropriate label. The adverb *chiefly* precedes a label when the word has some currency outside the specified

region, and a double label is used to indicate considerable currency in each of two specific regions:

²wash *n* . . . **8** *West*

do·gie . . . *n, chiefly West*

crul·ler . . . *n* . . . **2** *Northern & Midland*

Words current in all regions of the U.S. have no label.

A word or sense limited in use to one of the other countries of the English-speaking world has an appropriate regional label:

chem·ist . . . *n* . . . **2** *Brit*

loch . . . *n, Scot*

²wireless *n* . . . **2** *chiefly Brit*

The label *dial* for "dialect" indicates that the pattern of use of a word or sense is too complex for summary labeling: it usually includes several regional varieties of American English or of American and British English:

²mind *vb* **1** *chiefly dial*

The stylistic label *slang* is used with words or senses that are especially appropriate in contexts of extreme informality:

³can . . . *vb* . . . **2** *slang*

²grand *n* . . . *slang*

There is no satisfactory objective test for slang, especially with reference to a word out of context. No word, in fact, is invariably slang, and many standard words can be given slang applications.

The stylistic labels *offensive* and *disparaging* are used for those words or senses that in common use are intended to hurt or that are likely to give offense even when they are used without such an intent:

dumb . . . *adj* 1 *often offensive*
half–breed . . . *n, often disparaging*

Definitions are sometimes followed by verbal illustrations that show a typical use of the word in context. These illustrations are enclosed in angle brackets, and the word being illustrated is usually replaced by a lightface swung dash. The swung dash stands for the boldface entry word, and it may be followed by an italicized suffix:

¹jump . . . *vb* . . . 5 . . . ⟨∼ town⟩
all–around . . . *adj* 1 . . . ⟨best ∼ performance⟩
¹can·on . . . *n* . . . 3 . . . ⟨the ∼s of good taste⟩
en·joy . . . *vb* . . . 2 . . . ⟨∼ed the concert⟩

The swung dash is not used when the form of the boldface entry word is changed in suffixation, and it is not used for compounds:

²deal *vb* . . . 2 . . . ⟨*dealt* him a blow⟩
drum up *vb* 1 . . . ⟨*drum up* business⟩

Definitions are sometimes followed by usage notes that give supplementary information about such matters as idiom, syntax, and semantic relationship. A usage note is introduced by a lightface dash:

²cry *n* . . . 5 . . . — usu. used in the phrase *a far cry*
²drum *vb* . . . 4 . . . — usu. used with *out*
¹jaw . . . *n* . . . 2 . . . — usu. used in pl.
¹ada·gio . . . *adv or adj* . . . — used as a direction in music
hajji . . . *n* . . . — often used as a title

Sometimes a usage note is used in place of a definition. Some function words (as conjunctions and prepositions) have chiefly grammatical meaning and little or no lexical meaning; most interjections express feelings but are otherwise untranslatable into lexical meaning; and some other words (as honorific titles) are more amenable to comment than to definition:

or . . . *conj* — used as a function word to indicate an alternative
¹at . . . *prep* 1 — used to indicate a point in time or space
auf Wie·der·seh·en . . . *interj* . . . — used to express farewell
sir . . . *n* . . . 2 — used as a usu. respectful form of address

SENSE DIVISION

A boldface colon is used in this dictionary to introduce a definition:

equine . . . *adj* . . . : of or relating to the horse

It is also used to separate two or more definitions of a single sense:

no·ti·fy . . . *vb* . . . 1 : to give notice of : report the occurrence of

Boldface Arabic numerals separate the senses of a word that has more than one sense:

add . . . *vb* 1 : to join to something else so as to increase in number or amount 2 : to say further . . . 3 : to combine (numbers) into one sum

A particular semantic relationship between senses is sometimes suggested by the use of one of the two italic sense dividers *esp* or *also*.

The sense divider *esp* (for *especially*) is used to introduce the most common meaning included in the more general preceding definition:

crys·tal . . . *n* . . . 2 : something resembling crystal (as in transparency); *esp* : a clear colorless glass of superior quality

The sense divider *also* is used to introduce a meaning related to the preceding sense by an easily understood extension of that sense:

chi·na . . . *n* : porcelain ware; *also* : domestic pottery in general

The order of senses is historical: the sense known to have been first used in English is entered first. This is not to be taken to mean, however, that each sense of a multisense word developed from the immediately preceding sense. It is altogether possible that sense 1 of a word has given rise to sense 2 and sense 2 to sense 3, but frequently sense 2 and sense 3 may have developed independently of one another from sense 1.

When an italicized label follows a boldface numeral, the label applies only to that specific numbered sense.

It does not apply to any other boldface numbered senses:

craft . . . *n* . . . **3** *pl usu* **craft**
¹fa·ther . . . *n* . . . **2** *cap* . . . **5** *often cap*
dul·ci·mer . . . *n* . . . **2** *or* **dul·ci·more**
\-₁mōr\
²lift *n* . . . **5** *chiefly Brit*

At *craft* the *pl* label applies to sense 3 but to none of the other numbered senses. At *father* the *cap* label applies only to sense 2 and the *often cap* label only to sense 5. At *dulcimer* the variant spelling and pronunciation apply only to sense 2, and the *chiefly Brit* label at *lift* applies only to sense 5.

CROSS-REFERENCE

Four different kinds of cross-references are used in this dictionary: directional, synonymous, cognate, and inflectional. In each instance the cross-reference is readily recognized by the lightface small capitals in which it is printed.

A cross-reference following a lightface dash and beginning with *see* is a directional cross-reference. It directs the dictionary user to look elsewhere for further information:

eu·ro . . . *n* . . . —see MONEY table

A cross-reference following a boldface colon is a synonymous cross-reference. It may stand alone as the only definition for an entry or for a sense of an entry; it may follow an analytical definition; it may be one of two or more synonymous cross-references separated by commas:

pa·pa . . . *n* : FATHER
¹par·tic·u·lar . . . *adj* . . . **4** : attentive to details : PRECISE
²main *adj* **1** : CHIEF, PRINCIPAL
¹fig·ure . . . *n* . . . **6** : SHAPE, FORM, OUTLINE

A synonymous cross-reference indicates that an entry, a definition at the entry, or a specific sense at the entry cross-referred to can be substituted as a definition for the entry or the sense in which the cross-reference appears.

A cross-reference following an italic *var of* ("variant of") is a cognate cross-reference:

pick·a·back . . . *var of* PIGGYBACK

Occasionally a cognate cross-reference has a limiting label preceding *var of* as an indication that the variant is not standard American English:

aero·plane . . . *chiefly Brit var of* AIRPLANE

A cross-reference following an italic label that identifies an entry as an inflected form (as of a noun or verb) is an inflectional cross-reference:

calves *pl of* CALF
woven *past part of* WEAVE

Inflectional cross-references appear only when the inflected form falls at least a column away from the entry cross-referred to.

SYNONYMS

A bold italic Synonyms preceded by a small black diamond figure near the end of an entry introduces words that are synonymous with the word being defined:

> **alone** . . . *adj* . . . ♦ *Synonyms* LONE-LY, LONESOME, LONE, SOLITARY

Synonyms are not definitions although they may often be substituted for each other in context.

COMBINING FORMS, PREFIXES, & SUFFIXES

An entry that begins or ends with a hyphen is a word element that forms part of an English compound:

> **-wise** . . . *adv comb form* . . . ⟨slant-*wise*⟩
>
> **ex-** . . . *prefix* . . . **2** . . . ⟨*ex*-president⟩
>
> **-let** *n suffix* **1** . . . ⟨book*let*⟩

Combining forms, prefixes, and suffixes are entered in this dictionary for two reasons: to make understandable the meaning of many undefined run-ons and to make recognizable the meaningful elements of words that are not entered in the dictionary.

LISTS OF UNDEFINED WORDS

Many words that begin with the prefixes or combining forms *anti-*, *in-*, *non-*, *over-*, *re-*, *self-*, *semi-*, *sub-*, *super-*, and *un-* are self-explanatory combinations of the prefix or combining form and a word entered elsewhere in the dictionary, and they are listed undefined at the bottom of the page or spread on which they would normally appear if defined.

ABBREVIATIONS & SYMBOLS

Abbreviations and symbols for chemical elements or combining forms are included as main entries in the vocabulary:

> **RSVP** *abbr* . . . please reply
>
> **Ca** *symbol* calcium

Abbreviations have been normalized to one form. In practice, however, there is considerable variation in the use of periods and in capitalization (as *vhf*, *v.h.f.*, *VHF*, and *V.H.F.*), and stylings other than those given in this dictionary are often acceptable.

ABBREVIATIONS IN THIS WORK

ab	about	*masc*	masculine
abbr	abbreviation	*MD*	Middle Dutch
abl	ablative	*ME*	Middle English
acc	accusative	*MexSp*	Mexican Spanish
A.D.	anno Domini	*MF*	Middle French
adj	adjective	*MGk*	Middle Greek
adv	adverb	*mi*	miles
alter	alteration	*ML*	Medieval Latin
Am, Amer	American	*modif*	modification
AmerF	American French	*MS*	manuscript
AmerInd	American Indian	*Mt*	Mount
AmerSp	American Spanish	*n*	noun
Ar	Arabic	*neut*	neuter
Aram	Aramaic	*NewEng*	New England
B.C.	before Christ	*NGk*	New Greek
Brit	British	*NHeb*	New Hebrew
C	Celsius	*NL*	New Latin
ca	circa	*No*	North
Calif	California	*Norw*	Norwegian
Canad	Canadian	*n pl*	noun plural
CanF	Canadian French	*obs*	obsolete
cap	capital, capitalized	*OE*	Old English
Celt	Celtic	*OF*	Old French
cen	central	*OIt*	Old Italian
cent	century	*ON*	Old Norse
Chin	Chinese	*OPer*	Old Persian
comb	combining	*orig*	originally
compar	comparative	*part*	participle
conj	conjunction	*Per*	Persian
D	Dutch	*perh*	perhaps
Dan	Danish	*Pg*	Portuguese
dat	dative	*pl*	plural
deriv	derivative	*Pol*	Polish
dial	dialect	*pp*	past participle
dim	diminutive	*prep*	preposition
E	English	*pres*	present, president
Egypt	Egyptian	*prob*	probably
Eng	English	*pron*	pronoun, pronunciation
esp	especially	*prp*	present participle
est	estimated	*pseud*	pseudonym
F	Fahrenheit, French	*r*	reigned
fem	feminine	*Russ*	Russian
fl	flourished	*Sc*	Scotch, Scots
fr	from	*Scand*	Scandinavian
ft	feet	*ScGael*	Scottish Gaelic
G, Ger	German	*Scot*	Scottish
Gk	Greek	*sing*	singular
Gmc	Germanic	*Skt*	Sanskrit
Heb	Hebrew	*Slav*	Slavic
Hung	Hungarian	*So*	South
Icel	Icelandic	*Sp, Span*	Spanish
imit	imitative	*St*	Saint
imper	imperative	*superl*	superlative
interj	interjection	*Sw*	Swedish
Ir	Irish	*syn*	synonym, synonymy
irreg	irregular	*trans*	translation
It, Ital	Italian	*Turk*	Turkish
Jp	Japanese	*US*	United States
K	Kelvin	*USSR*	Union of Soviet Socialist Republics
km	kilometers		
L	Latin	*usu*	usually
LaF	Louisiana French	*var*	variant
LG	Low German	*vb*	verb
LGk	Late Greek	*vi*	verb intransitive
LHeb	Late Hebrew	*VL*	Vulgar Latin
lit	literally	*vt*	verb transitive
LL	Late Latin	*W*	Welsh
m	meters		

PRONUNCIATION SYMBOLS

ə	abut, collect, suppose	ȯi	toy
ˈə, ˌə	humdrum	p	pepper, lip
ᵊ	(in ᵊl, ᵊn) battle, cotton; (in lᵊ, mᵊ, rᵊ) French table, prisme, titre	r	rarity
		s	source, less
		sh	shy, mission
ər	operation, further	t	tie, attack
a	map, patch	th	thin, ether
ā	day, fate	t͟h	then, either
ä	bother, cot, father	ü	boot, few \ˈfyü\
är	car, heart	u̇	put, pure \ˈpyu̇r\
au̇	now, out	u̇r	boor, tour
b	baby, rib	ᵫ	French rue, German füllen, fühlen
ch	chin, catch		
d	did, adder	v	vivid, give
e	set, red	w	we, away
er	bare, fair	y	yard, cue \ˈkyü\
ē	beat, easy	ʸ	indicates that a preceding \l\, \n\, or \w\ is modified by having the tongue approximate the position for \y\, as in French digne \dēnʸ\
f	fifty, cuff		
g	go, big		
h	hat, ahead		
hw	whale		
i	tip, banish	z	zone, raise
ir	near, deer	zh	vision, pleasure
ī	site, buy	\	slant line used in pairs to mark the beginning and end of a transcription: \ˈpen\
j	job, edge		
k	kin, cook		
k͟	German Bach, Scots loch	ˈ	mark at the beginning of a syllable that has primary (strongest) stress: \ˈshə-fəl-ˌbȯrd\
l	lily, cool		
m	murmur, dim		
n	nine, own	ˌ	mark at the beginning of a syllable that has secondary (next-strongest) stress: \ˈshə-fəl-ˌbȯrd\
ⁿ	indicates that a preceding vowel is pronounced through both nose and mouth, as in French bon \bōⁿ\		
		-	mark of a syllable division in pronunciations (the mark of end-of-line division in boldface entries is a centered dot ·)
ŋ	sing, singer, finger, ink		
ō	bone, hollow		
ȯ	saw	( )	indicate that what is symbolized between sometimes occurs and sometimes does not occur in the pronunciation of the word: bakery \ˈbā-k(ə-)rē\ = \ˈbā-kə-rē, ˈbā-krē\
ȯr	boar, port		
œ	French bœuf, feu, German Hölle, Höhle		

A

¹a \'ā\ *n, pl* **a's** *or* **as** \'āz\ *often cap* **1** : the 1st letter of the English alphabet **2** : a grade rating a student's work as superior

²a \ə, (¹)ā\ *indefinite article* : ONE, SOME — used to indicate an unspecified or unidentified individual ⟨there's ∼ man outside⟩

³a *abbr, often cap* **1** absent **2** acre **3** alto **4** answer **5** are **6** area

AA *abbr* **1** Alcoholics Anonymous **2** antiaircraft **3** associate in arts

AAA *abbr* American Automobile Association

A and M *abbr* agricultural and mechanical

A and R *abbr* artists and repertory

aard·vark \'ärd-,värk\ *n* [obs. Afrikaans, fr. Afrikaans *aard* earth + *vark* pig] : a large burrowing African mammal that feeds on ants and termites with its long sticky tongue

¹**ab** \'ab\ *n* : an abdominal muscle

²**ab** *abbr* about

AB *abbr* **1** able-bodied seaman **2** airman basic **3** [NL *artium baccalaureus*] bachelor of arts

ABA *abbr* American Bar Association

aback \ə-'bak\ *adv* : by surprise ⟨taken ∼⟩

aba·cus \'a-bə-kəs\ *n, pl* **aba·ci** \-,sī, -,kē\ *or* **aba·cus·es** : an instrument for making calculations by sliding counters along rods or grooves

¹**abaft** \ə-'baft\ *prep* : to the rear of

²**abaft** *adv* : toward or at the stern : AFT

ab·a·lo·ne \,a-bə-'lō-nē, 'a-bə-,\ *n* : any of a genus of large edible sea mollusks with a flattened slightly spiral shell with holes along the edge

¹**aban·don** \ə-'ban-dən\ *vb* [ME *abandounen,* fr. AF *abanduner,* fr. (*mettre*) *a bandun* to hand over, put in someone's control] : to give up completely : FORSAKE, DESERT — **aban·don·ment** *n*

²**abandon** *n* : a thorough yielding to natural impulses; *esp* : EXUBERANCE

aban·doned \ə-'ban-dənd\ *adj* : morally unrestrained ♦ **Synonyms** PROFLIGATE, DISSOLUTE, REPROBATE

abase \ə-'bās\ *vb* **abased; abas·ing** : HUMBLE, DEGRADE.— **abase·ment** *n*

abash \ə-'bash\ *vb* : to destroy the composure of : EMBARRASS — **abash·ment** *n*

abate \ə-'bāt\ *vb* **abat·ed; abat·ing 1** : to put an end to ⟨∼ a nuisance⟩ **2** : to decrease in amount, number, or degree

abate·ment \ə-'bāt-mənt\ *n* **1** : DECREASE **2** : an amount abated; *esp* : a deduction from a tax

ab·at·toir \'a-bə-,twär\ *n* [F] : SLAUGHTERHOUSE

ab·ba·cy \'a-bə-sē\ *n, pl* **-cies** : the office or term of office of an abbot or abbess

ab·bé \a-'bā, 'a-,\ *n* : a member of the French secular clergy — used as a title

ab·bess \'a-bəs\ *n* : the superior of a convent for nuns

ab·bey \'a-bē\ *n, pl* **abbeys 1** : MONASTERY **2** : CONVENT **3** : an abbey church

ab·bot \'a-bət\ *n* [ME *abbod,* fr. OE, fr. LL *abbat-, abbas,* fr. LGk *abbas,* fr. Aramaic *abbā* father] : the superior of a monastery for men

abbr *abbr* abbreviation

ab·bre·vi·ate \ə-'brē-vē-,āt\ *vb* **-at·ed; -at·ing** : SHORTEN, CURTAIL; *esp* : to reduce to an abbreviation

ab·bre·vi·a·tion \ə-,brē-vē-'ā-shən\ *n* **1** : the act or result of abbreviating **2** : a shortened form of a word or phrase used for brevity esp. in writing

¹**ABC** \,ā-(,)bē-'sē\ *n, pl* **ABC's** *or* **ABCs** \-'sēz\ **1** : ALPHABET — usu. used in pl. **2** : RUDIMENTS — usu. used in pl.

²**ABC** *abbr* American Broadcasting Company

Ab·di·as \ab-'dī-əs\ *n* : OBADIAH

ab·di·cate \'ab-di-,kāt\ *vb* **-cat·ed; -cat·ing** : to give up (as a throne) formally — **ab·di·ca·tion** \,ab-di-'kā-shən\ *n*

ab·do·men \'ab-də-mən, ab-'dō-\ *n* **1** : the cavity in or area of the body between the chest and the pelvis **2** : the part of the body posterior to the thorax in an arthropod — **ab·dom·i·nal** \ab-'dä-mə-n°l\ *adj* — **ab·dom·i·nal·ly** *adv*

ab·duct \ab-'dəkt\ *vb* : to take away (a person) by force : KIDNAP — **ab·duc·tion** \-'dək-shən\ *n* — **ab·duc·tor** \-tər\ *n*

abeam \ə-'bēm\ *adv or adj* : on a line at right angles to a ship's keel

abed \ə-'bed\ *adv or adj* : in bed

Abe·na·ki \,a-bə-'nä-kē\ *also* **Ab·na·ki** \ab-'nä-kē\ *n, pl* **Abenaki** *or* **Abenakis** *also* **Abnaki** *or* **Abnakis** : a member of a group of American Indian peoples of northern New England and southern Quebec

ab·er·ra·tion \,a-bə-'rā-shən\ *n* **1** : deviation esp. from a moral standard or normal state **2** : failure of a mirror or lens to produce exact point-to-point correspondence between an object and its image **3** : unsoundness of mind : DERANGEMENT — **ab·er·rant** \a-'ber-ənt\ *adj*

abet \ə-'bet\ *vb* **abet·ted; abet·ting** [ME *abetten,* fr. AF *abeter,* fr. *beter* to bait] **1** : INCITE, ENCOURAGE **2** : to assist or support in the achievement of a purpose ⟨∼ a fugitive⟩ — **abet·tor** *or* **abet·ter** \-'be-tər\ *n*

abey·ance \ə-'bā-əns\ *n* : a condition of suspended activity — **abey·ant** \-ənt\ *adj*

ab·hor \əb-'hȯr, ab-\ *vb* **ab·horred; ab·hor·ring** [ME *abhorren,* fr. L *abhorrēre,* fr. *ab-* + *horrēre* to shudder] : LOATHE, DETEST — **ab·hor·rence** \-əns\ *n*

ab·hor·rent \-ənt\ *adj* : LOATHSOME, DETESTABLE ⟨∼ crimes⟩

abide \ə-'bīd\ *vb* **abode** \-'bōd\ *or* **abid·ed; abid·ing 1** : BEAR, ENDURE **2** : DWELL, REMAIN, LAST — **abide by** : to conform or acquiesce to ⟨*abide by* the law⟩

abil·i·ty \ə-'bi-lə-tē\ *n, pl* **-ties** : the quality of being able : POWER, SKILL

-ability *also* **-ibility** *n suffix* : capacity, fitness, or tendency to act or be acted on in a (specified) way ⟨flamm*ability*⟩

ab·ject \'ab-,jekt, ab-'jekt\ *adj* : low in spirit, hope, or state ⟨∼ poverty⟩ — **ab·jec·tion** \ab-'jek-shən\ *n* — **ab·ject·ly** *adv* — **ab·ject·ness** *n*

ab·jure \ab-'jùr\ *vb* **ab·jured; ab·jur·ing** 1 : to renounce solemnly : RECANT 2 : to abstain from — **ab·ju·ra·tion** \,ab-jə-'rā-shən\ *n*

abl *abbr* ablative

ab·late \a-'blāt\ *vb* **ab·lat·ed; ab·lat·ing** : to remove or become removed esp. by cutting, abrading, or vaporizing

ab·la·tion \a-'blā-shən\ *n* 1 : surgical cutting and removal 2 : loss of a part (as the outside of a nose cone) by melting or vaporization

ab·la·tive \'ab-lə-tiv\ *adj* : of, relating to, or constituting a grammatical case (as in Latin) expressing typically the relation of separation and source — **ablative** *n*

ablaze \ə-'blāz\ *adj or adv* : being on fire : BLAZING

able \'ā-bəl\ *adj* **abler** \-b(ə-)lər\; **ablest** \-b(ə-)ləst\ [ME, fr. AF, fr. L *habilis* apt, fr. *habēre* to hold, possess] 1 : having sufficient power, skill, or resources to accomplish an object 2 : marked by skill or efficiency — **ably** \-blē\ *adv*

-able *also* **-ible** *adj suffix* 1 : capable of, fit for, or worthy of (being so acted upon or toward) ⟨break*able*⟩ ⟨collect*ible*⟩ 2 : tending, given, or liable to ⟨knowledge*able*⟩ ⟨perish*able*⟩

able–bod·ied \,ā-bəl-'bä-dēd\ *adj* : having a sound strong body

abloom \ə-'blüm\ *adj* : BLOOMING

ab·lu·tion \ə-'blü-shən, a-\ *n* : the washing of one's body or part of it

ABM \,ā-(,)bē-'em\ *n, pl* **ABM's** *or* **ABMs** : ANTIBALLISTIC MISSILE

Abnaki *var of* ABENAKI

ab·ne·gate \'ab-ni-,gāt\ *vb* **-gat·ed; -gat·ing** 1 : DENY, RENOUNCE 2 : SURRENDER, RELINQUISH ⟨∼ her powers⟩ — **ab·ne·ga·tion** \,ab-ni-'gā-shən\ *n*

ab·nor·mal \ab-'nòr-məl\ *adj* : deviating from the normal or average — **ab·nor·mal·i·ty** \,ab-nòr-'ma-lə-tē\ *n* — **ab·nor·mal·ly** *adv*

¹**aboard** \ə-'bòrd\ *adv* 1 : ALONGSIDE 2 : on, onto, or within a car, ship, or aircraft 3 : in or into a group or association ⟨welcome new workers ∼⟩

²**aboard** *prep* : ON, ONTO, WITHIN

abode \ə-'bōd\ *n* 1 : STAY, SOJOURN 2 : HOME, RESIDENCE

abol·ish \ə-'bä-lish\ *vb* : to do away with : ANNUL ⟨∼ slavery⟩ — **ab·o·li·tion** \,a-bə-'li-shən\ *n*

ab·o·li·tion·ism \,a-bə-'li-shə-,ni-zəm\ *n* : advocacy of the abolition of slavery — **ab·o·li·tion·ist** \-'li-sh(ə-)nist\ *n or adj*

A–bomb \'ā-,bäm\ *n* : ATOMIC BOMB — **A–bomb** *vb*

abom·i·na·ble \ə-'bä-mə-nə-bəl\ *adj* : ODIOUS, LOATHSOME, DETESTABLE

abominable snow·man \-'snō-mən, -,man\ *n, often cap A&S* : a mysterious creature with human or apelike characteristics reported to exist in the high Himalayas

abom·i·nate \ə-'bä-mə-,nāt\ *vb* **-nat·ed; -nat·ing** [L *abominari*, lit., to deprecate as an ill omen, fr. *ab-* away + *omen* omen] : LOATHE, DETEST

abom·i·na·tion \ə-,bä-mə-'nā-shən\ *n* 1 : something abominable 2 : DISGUST, LOATHING

ab·orig·i·nal \,a-bə-'ri-jə-nəl\ *adj* : ORIGINAL, INDIGENOUS, PRIMITIVE

ab·orig·i·ne \,a-bə-'ri-jə-nē\ *n* : a member of the original race of inhabitants of a region : NATIVE

aborn·ing \ə-'bòr-niŋ\ *adv* : while being born or produced

¹**abort** \ə-'bòrt\ *vb* 1 : to cause or undergo abortion 2 : to terminate prematurely ⟨∼ a spaceflight⟩ — **abor·tive** \-'bòr-tiv\ *adj*

²**abort** *n* : the premature termination of a mission of or a procedure relating to an aircraft or spacecraft

abor·tion \ə-'bòr-shən\ *n* : the spontaneous or induced termination of a pregnancy after, accompanied by, resulting in, or closely followed by the death of the embryo or fetus

abor·tion·ist \-sh(ə-)nist\ *n* : one who induces abortions

abound \ə-'baùnd\ *vb* 1 : to be plentiful : TEEM 2 : to be fully supplied

¹**about** \ə-'baùt\ *adv* 1 : reasonably close to; *also* : on the verge of ⟨∼ to join the army⟩ 2 : on all sides 3 : NEARBY

²**about** *prep* 1 : on every side of 2 : near to 3 : CONCERNING

about–face \-'fās\ *n* : a reversal of direction or attitude — **about–face** *vb*

¹**above** \ə-'bəv\ *adv* 1 : in the sky; *also* : in or to heaven 2 : in or to a higher place; *also* : higher on the same page or on a preceding page

²**above** *prep* 1 : in or to a higher place than : OVER ⟨storm clouds ∼ the bay⟩ 2 : superior to ⟨he thought her far above him⟩ 3 : more than : EXCEEDING 4 : as distinct from ⟨∼ the noise⟩

above·board \-,bòrd\ *adv or adj* : without concealment or deception : OPENLY

abp *abbr* archbishop

abr *abbr* abridged; abridgment

ab·ra·ca·dab·ra \,a-brə-kə-'da-brə\ *n* 1 : a magical charm or incantation against calamity 2 : GIBBERISH

abrade \ə-'brād\ *vb* **abrad·ed; abrad·ing** 1 : to wear away by friction 2 : to wear down in spirit : IRRITATE — **abra·sion** \-'brā-zhən\ *n*

¹**abra·sive** \ə-'brā-siv\ *n* : a substance (as pumice) for abrading, smoothing, or polishing

²**abrasive** *adj* : tending to abrade : causing irritation ⟨∼ relationships⟩ — **abra·sive·ly** *adv* — **abra·sive·ness** *n*

abreast \ə-'brest\ *adv or adj* 1 : side by

side **2** : up to a standard or level esp. of knowledge ⟨kept ∼ of the news⟩

abridge \ə-'brij\ vb **abridged; abridging** [ME abregen, fr. AF abreger, fr. LL abbreviare, fr. L ad to + brevis short] : to lessen in length or extent : SHORTEN — **abridg·ment** or **abridge·ment** n

abroad \ə-'bród\ adv or adj **1** : over a wide area **2** : away from one's home **3** : outside one's country

ab·ro·gate \'a-brə-ˌgāt\ vb **-gat·ed; -gat·ing** : ANNUL, REVOKE — **ab·ro·ga·tion** \ˌa-brə-'gā-shən\ n

abrupt \ə-'brəpt\ adj **1** : broken or as if broken off **2** : SUDDEN, HASTY ⟨an ∼ turn⟩ **3** : so quick as to seem rude ⟨an ∼ reply⟩ **4** : DISCONNECTED **5** : STEEP — **abrupt·ly** adv

abs abbr absolute

ab·scess \'ab-ˌses\ n, pl **ab·scess·es** [L abscessus, lit., act of going away, fr. abscedere to go away, fr. abs-, ab- away + cedere to go] : a localized collection of pus surrounded by inflamed tissue — **ab·scessed** \-ˌsest\ adj

ab·scis·sa \ab-'si-sə\ n, pl **abscissas** also **ab·scis·sae** \-'si-(ˌ)sē\ : the horizontal coordinate of a point in a plane coordinate system obtained by measuring parallel to the x-axis

ab·scis·sion \ab-'si-zhən\ n **1** : the act or process of cutting off **2** : the natural separation of flowers, fruits, or leaves from plants — **ab·scise** \ab-'sīz\ vb

ab·scond \ab-'skänd\ vb : to depart secretly and hide oneself

ab·sence \'ab-səns\ n **1** : the state or time of being absent **2** : WANT, LACK **3** : INATTENTION

¹**ab·sent** \'ab-sənt\ adj **1** : not present **2** : LACKING **3** : INATTENTIVE

²**ab·sent** \ab-'sent\ vb : to keep (oneself) away

³**ab·sent** \'ab-sənt\ prep : in the absence of : WITHOUT

ab·sen·tee \ˌab-sən-'tē\ n : one that is absent or keeps away

absentee ballot n : a ballot submitted (as by mail) in advance of an election by a voter who is unable to be present at the polls

ab·sen·tee·ism \ˌab-sən-'tē-ˌi-zəm\ n : chronic absence (as from work or school)

ab·sent-mind·ed \ˌab-sənt-'mīn-dəd\ adj : unaware of one's surroundings or actions : INATTENTIVE — **ab·sent-mind·ed·ly** adv — **ab·sent-mind·ed·ness** n

ab·sinthe also **ab·sinth** \'ab-ˌsinth\ n [F] : a liqueur flavored esp. with wormwood and anise

ab·so·lute \'ab-sə-ˌlüt, ˌab-sə-'lüt\ adj **1** : free from imperfection or mixture **2** : free from control, restriction, or qualification ⟨∼ power⟩ **3** : lacking grammatical connection with any other word in a sentence ⟨∼ construction⟩ **4** : POSITIVE ⟨∼ proof⟩ **5** : relating to the fundamental units of length, mass, and time **6** : FUNDAMENTAL, ULTIMATE — **ab·so·lute·ly** adv

absolute pitch n **1** : the position of a tone in a standard scale independently determined by its rate of vibration **2** : the ability to sing a note asked for or to name a note heard

absolute value n : a nonnegative number equal to a given real number with any negative sign removed

absolute zero n : a theoretical temperature marked by a complete absence of heat and motion and equivalent to exactly -273.15°C or -459.67°F

ab·so·lu·tion \ˌab-sə-'lü-shən\ n : the act of absolving; esp : a remission of sins pronounced by a priest in the sacrament of reconciliation

ab·so·lut·ism \'ab-sə-ˌlü-ˌti-zəm\ n **1** : the theory that a ruler or government should have unlimited power **2** : government by an absolute ruler or authority

ab·solve \əb-'zälv, -'sälv\ vb **ab·solved; ab·solv·ing** : to set free from an obligation or the consequences of guilt

ab·sorb \əb-'sórb, -'zórb\ vb **1** : to take in and make part of an existent whole **2** : to suck up or take in in the manner of a sponge **3** : to engage (one's attention) : ENGROSS **4** : to receive without recoil or echo ⟨a ceiling that ∼s sound⟩ **5** : ASSUME, BEAR ⟨∼ all costs⟩ **6** : to transform (radiant energy) into a different form esp. with a resulting rise in temperature — **ab·sorb·ing** adj — **ab·sorb·ing·ly** adv

ab·sor·bent also **ab·sor·bant** \əb-'sór-bənt, -'zór-\ adj : able to absorb ⟨∼ cotton⟩ — **ab·sor·ben·cy** \-bən-sē\ n — **absorbent** also **absorbant** n

ab·sorp·tion \əb-'sórp-shən, -'zórp-\ n **1** : a process of absorbing or being absorbed **2** : concentration of attention — **ab·sorp·tive** \-tiv\ adj

ab·stain \əb-'stān\ vb : to refrain from an action or practice — **ab·stain·er** n — **ab·sten·tion** \-'sten-chən\ n

ab·ste·mi·ous \ab-'stē-mē-əs\ adj : sparing in use of food or drink : TEMPERATE — **ab·ste·mi·ous·ly** adv — **ab·ste·mi·ous·ness** n

ab·sti·nence \'ab-stə-nəns\ n : voluntary refraining esp. from eating certain foods, drinking liquor, or engaging in sexual intercourse — **ab·sti·nent** \-nənt\ adj

abstr abbr abstract

¹**ab·stract** \ab-'strakt, 'ab-ˌstrakt\ adj **1** : considered apart from a particular instance **2** : expressing a quality apart from an object ⟨whiteness is an ∼ word⟩ **3** : having only intrinsic form with little or no pictorial representation ⟨∼ painting⟩ — **ab·stract·ly** adv — **ab·stract·ness** n

²**ab·stract** \'ab-ˌstrakt; 2 also ab-'strakt\ n, **1** : SUMMARY, EPITOME **2** : an abstract thing or state

³**ab·stract** \ab-'strakt, 'ab-ˌstrakt; 2 usu 'ab-ˌstrakt\ vb **1** : REMOVE, SEPARATE **2** : to make an abstract of : SUMMARIZE **3** : to draw away the attention of **4** : STEAL — **ab·stract·ed·ly** \ab-'strak-təd-lē, 'ab-ˌstrak-\ adv

abstract expressionism *n* : art that expresses the artist's attitudes and emotions through abstract forms — **abstract expressionist** *n*

ab·strac·tion \ab-'strak-shən\ *n* 1 : the act of abstracting : the state of being abstracted 2 : an abstract idea 3 : an abstract work of art

ab·struse \ab-'strüs\ *adj* : hard to understand : RECONDITE — **ab·struse·ly** *adv* — **ab·struse·ness** *n*

ab·surd \əb-'sərd, -'zərd\ *adj* [MF *absurde*, fr. L *absurdus*, fr. *ab-* from + *surdus* deaf, stupid] 1 : RIDICULOUS, UNREASONABLE — **ab·sur·di·ty** \-'sər-də-tē, -'zər-\ *n* — **ab·surd·ly** *adv*

abun·dant \ə-'bən-dənt\ *adj* [ME, fr. AF, fr. L *abundant-, abundans*, prp. of *abundare* to abound, fr. *ab-* from + *unda* wave] : more than enough : amply sufficient ✦ **Synonyms** COPIOUS, PLENTIFUL, AMPLE, BOUNTIFUL — **abun·dance** \-dəns\ *n* — **abun·dant·ly** *adv*

¹**abuse** \ə-'byüs\ *n* 1 : a corrupt practice 2 : MISUSE ⟨drug ∼⟩ 3 : coarse and insulting speech 4 : MISTREATMENT ⟨child ∼⟩

²**abuse** \ə-'byüz\ *vb* **abused; abus·ing** 1 : to put to a wrong use : MISUSE 2 : to use excessively ⟨∼ alcohol⟩ 3 : MISTREAT 4 : to attack in words : REVILE — **abus·er** *n* — **abu·sive** \-'byü-siv\ *adj* — **abu·sive·ly** *adv* — **abu·sive·ness** *n*

abut \ə-'bət\ *vb* **abut·ted; abut·ting** : to touch along a border : border on

abut·ment \ə-'bət-mənt\ *n* : the part of a structure (as a bridge) that supports weight or withstands lateral pressure

abut·ter \ə-'bə-tər\ *n* : one that abuts; *esp* : the owner of a contiguous property

abuzz \ə-'bəz\ *adj* : filled or resounding with activity or excitement ⟨an office ∼ with rumors⟩

abys·mal \ə-'biz-məl\ *adj* 1 : immeasurably deep : BOTTOMLESS 2 : absolutely wretched ⟨∼ living conditions of the poor⟩ — **abys·mal·ly** *adv*

abyss \ə-'bis\ *n* 1 : the bottomless pit in old accounts of the universe 2 : an immeasurable depth

abys·sal \ə-'bi-səl\ *adj* : of or relating to the bottom waters of the ocean depths

ac *abbr* account

-ac *n suffix* : one affected with ⟨hypochondriac⟩

Ac *symbol* actinium

AC *abbr* 1 air-conditioning 2 alternating current 3 [L *ante Christum*] before Christ 4 [L *ante cibum*] before meals 5 area code

aca·cia \ə-'kā-shə\ *n* : any of a genus of leguminous trees or shrubs with round white or yellow flower clusters and often feathery leaves

acad *abbr* academic; academy

ac·a·deme \'a-kə-ˌdēm, ˌa-kə-'\ *n* : SCHOOL; *also* : academic environment

¹**ac·a·dem·ic** \ˌa-kə-'de-mik\ *n* : a person who is academic in background, outlook, or methods

²**academic** *adj* 1 : of, relating to, or associated with schools or colleges 2 : literary or general rather than technical 3 : theoretical rather than practical — **ac·a·dem·i·cal·ly** \-mi-k(ə-)lē\ *adv*

ac·a·de·mi·cian \ˌa-kə-də-'mi-shən, ə-ˌkadə-\ *n* 1 : a member of a society of scholars or artists 2 : ACADEMIC

ac·a·dem·i·cism \ˌa-kə-'de-mə-ˌsi-zəm\ *also* **acad·e·mism** \ə-'ka-də-ˌmi-zəm\ *n* 1 : a formal academic quality 2 : purely speculative thinking

acad·e·my \ə-'ka-də-mē\ *n, pl* **-mies** [Gk *Akadēmeia*, school of philosophy founded by Plato, fr. *Akadēmeia*, gymnasium where Plato taught, fr. *Akadēmos* Greek mythological hero] 1 : a school above the elementary level; *esp* : a private high school 2 : a society of scholars or artists

acan·thus \ə-'kan-thəs\ *n, pl* **acanthus** 1 : any of a genus of prickly herbs of the Mediterranean region 2 : an ornamentation (as on a column) representing the leaves of the acanthus

a cap·pel·la *also* **a ca·pel·la** \ˌä-kə-'pe-lə\ *adv or adj* [It *a cappella* in chapel style] : without instrumental accompaniment

acc *abbr* accusative

ac·cede \ak-'sēd\ *vb* **ac·ced·ed; ac·ced·ing** 1 : to become a party to an agreement 2 : to express approval 3 : to enter upon an office ✦ **Synonyms** AGREE, ACQUIESCE, ASSENT, CONSENT, SUBSCRIBE

ac·cel·er·ate \ik-'se-lə-ˌrāt, ak-\ *vb* **-at·ed; -at·ing** 1 : to bring about earlier 2 : to speed up : QUICKEN — **ac·cel·er·a·tion** \-ˌse-lə-'rā-shən\ *n*

ac·cel·er·a·tor \ik-'se-lə-ˌrā-tər, ak-\ *n* 1 : one that accelerates 2 : a pedal for controlling the speed of a motor-vehicle engine 3 : an apparatus for imparting high velocities to charged particles

ac·cel·er·om·e·ter \ik-ˌse-lə-'rä-mə-tər, ak-\ *n* : an instrument for measuring acceleration or vibrations

¹**ac·cent** \'ak-ˌsent, ak-'sent\ *vb* : STRESS, EMPHASIZE

²**ac·cent** \'ak-ˌsent\ *n* 1 : prominence given to one syllable of a word esp. by stress 2 : a distinctive manner of pronunciation ⟨a foreign ∼⟩ 3 : a mark (as ´, `, ˆ) over a vowel used usu. to indicate a difference in pronunciation from a vowel not so marked — **ac·cen·tu·al** \ak-'sen-chə-wəl\ *adj*

ac·cen·tu·ate \ak-'sen-chə-ˌwāt\ *vb* **-at·ed; -at·ing** : STRESS, EMPHASIZE — **ac·cen·tu·a·tion** \-ˌsen-chə-'wā-shən\ *n*

ac·cept \ik-'sept, ak-\ *vb* 1 : to receive willingly 2 : to agree to 3 : to assume an obligation to pay

ac·cept·able \ik-'sep-tə-bəl, ak-\ *adj* : capable or worthy of being accepted — **ac·cept·abil·i·ty** \ik-ˌsep-tə-'bi-lə-tē, ak-\ *n*

ac·cep·tance \ik-'sep-təns, ak-\ *n* 1 : the act of accepting 2 : the state of being accepted or acceptable 3 : an accepted bill of exchange

ac·cep·ta·tion \ˌak-ˌsep-'tā-shən\ *n* : the generally understood meaning of a word

¹**ac·cess** \'ak-ˌses\ *n* 1 : capacity to enter

or approach   **2** : a way of approach : EN-
TRANCE

²access \vb\ : to get at : gain access to

ac·ces·si·ble \ik-'se-sə-bəl, ak-, ek-\ *adj*
1 : capable of being reached ⟨∼ by
train⟩   **2** : capable of being used or seen
⟨∼ archives⟩   **3** : capable of being understood ⟨an ∼ film⟩ — **ac·ces·si·bil·i-
ty** \-ˌse-sə-'bi-lə-tē\ *n*

ac·ces·sion \ik-'se-shən, ak-\ *n* **1** : increase by something added   **2** : something added   **3** : the act of coming to a
high office or position

ac·ces·so·ry *also* **ac·ces·sa·ry** \ik-'se-
sə-rē, ak-\ *n, pl* **-ries** **1** : a person who
though not present abets or assists in the
commission of an offense   **2** : something
helpful but not essential ◆ **Synonyms**
APPURTENANCE, ADJUNCT, APPENDAGE,
APPENDIX — **accessory** *adj*

ac·ci·dent \'ak-sə-dənt\ *n* **1** : an event
occurring by chance or unintentionally
2 : CHANCE ⟨met by ∼⟩   **3** : a nonessential property

¹ac·ci·den·tal \ˌak-sə-'den-t³l\ *adj* **1**
: happening unexpectedly or by chance
2 : happening without intent or through
carelessness ◆ **Synonyms** CASUAL, FOR-
TUITOUS, INCIDENTAL, CHANCE — **ac·ci-
den·tal·ly** \-'den-t³l-ē\ *also* **ac·ci·dent·ly**
\-'dent-lē\ *adv*

²accidental *n* : a musical note foreign to a
key indicated by a signature

ac·claim \ə-'klām\ *vb* **1** : APPLAUD,
PRAISE   **2** : to declare by acclamation
◆ **Synonyms** EXTOL, LAUD, COMMEND,
HAIL — **acclaim** *n*

ac·cla·ma·tion \ˌa-klə-'mā-shən\ *n* **1**
: loud eager applause   **2** : an overwhelming affirmative vote by shouting or applause rather than by ballot

ac·cli·mate \'a-klə-ˌmāt, ə-'klī-mət\ *vb*
-mat·ed; -mat·ing : to accustom or become accustomed to a new climate or situation — **ac·cli·ma·tion** \ˌa-klə-'mā-
shən, -ˌklī-\ *n*

ac·cli·ma·tise *Brit var of* ACCLIMATIZE

ac·cli·ma·tize \ə-'klī-mə-ˌtīz\ *vb* **-tized;
-tiz·ing** : ACCLIMATE — **ac·cli·ma·ti·za-
tion** \-ˌklī-mə-tə-'zā-shən\ *n*

ac·cliv·i·ty \ə-'kli-və-tē\ *n, pl* **-ties** : an ascending slope

ac·co·lade \'a-kə-ˌlād\ *n* [F, fr. *accoler* to
embrace, ultim. fr. L *ad-* to + *collum*
neck] : an expression of praise : AWARD

ac·com·mo·date \ə-'kä-mə-ˌdāt\ *vb* **-dat-
ed; -dat·ing** **1** : to make fit or suitable
: ADAPT, ADJUST   **2** : HARMONIZE, REC-
ONCILE   **3** : to provide with something
needed   **4** : to hold without crowding   **5**
: to undergo visual accommodation

ac·com·mo·dat·ing *adj* : OBLIGING

ac·com·mo·da·tion \ə-ˌkä-mə-'dā-shən\
n **1** : something supplied to satisfy a
need; *esp* : LODGINGS — usu. used in pl.
2 : the act of accommodating : ADJUST-
MENT   **3** : the automatic adjustment of
the eye for seeing at different distances

ac·com·pa·ni·ment \ə-'kəm-pə-nē-mənt,
-'kəmp-nē-\ *n* : something that accompanies another; *esp* : subordinate music to
support a principal voice or instrument

ac·com·pa·ny \-nē\ *vb* **-nied; -ny·ing** **1**
: to go or occur with : ATTEND   **2** : to
play an accompaniment for — **ac·com-
pa·nist** \-nist\ *n*

ac·com·plice \ə-'käm-pləs, -'kəm-\ *n* : an
associate in wrongdoing

ac·com·plish \ə-'käm-plish, -'kəm-\ *vb*
: to bring to completion ◆ **Synonyms**
ACHIEVE, EFFECT, EXECUTE, PERFORM
— **ac·com·plish·er** *n*

ac·com·plished \-plisht\ *adj* **1** : EX-
PERT, SKILLED ⟨an ∼ pianist⟩   **2** : established beyond doubt ⟨an ∼ fact⟩

ac·com·plish·ment \ə-'käm-plish-mənt,
-'kəm-\ *n* **1** : COMPLETION   **2** : something completed or effected   **3** : an acquired excellence or skill

¹ac·cord \ə-'kȯrd\ *vb* [ME, fr. AF *acorder*,
fr. VL **accordare*, fr. L *ad-* to + *cord-, cor*
heart] **1** : GRANT, CONCEDE   **2** : AGREE,
HARMONIZE — **ac·cor·dant** \-'kȯr-d³nt\
adj

²accord *n* **1** : AGREEMENT, HARMONY   **2**
: willingness to act ⟨gave of their own
∼⟩

ac·cor·dance \ə-'kȯr-d³ns\ *n* **1** : AC-
CORD   **2** : the act of granting

ac·cord·ing·ly \ə-'kȯr-diŋ-lē\ *adv* **1** : in
accordance   **2** : CONSEQUENTLY, SO

according to *prep* **1** : in conformity with
⟨paid *according to* ability⟩   **2** : as stated
or attested by ⟨*according to* you⟩

¹ac·cor·di·on \ə-'kȯr-dē-ən\ *n* [G *Akkor-
dion*, fr. *Akkord* chord] : a portable keyboard instrument with a keyboard and
reeds — **ac·cor·di·on·ist** \-ə-nist\ *n*

²accordion *adj* : folding like the bellows of
an accordion ⟨∼ pleats⟩

ac·cost \ə-'kȯst\ *vb* [MF *accoster*, ultim.
fr. L *ad-* to + *costa* rib, side] : to approach
and speak to esp. aggressively

¹ac·count \ə-'kau̇nt\ *n* **1** : a statement of
business transactions   **2** : a formal business arrangement for regular dealings or
services   **3** : a statement of reasons, causes, or motives   **4** : VALUE, IMPORTANCE
5 : a sum of money deposited in a bank
and subject to withdrawal by the depositor — **on account of** : BECAUSE OF —
on no account : under no circumstances — **on one's own account** : on
one's own behalf

²account *vb* **1** : CONSIDER ⟨I ∼ him
lucky⟩   **2** : to give an explanation — used
with *for*

ac·count·able \ə-'kau̇n-tə-bəl\ *adj* **1**
: ANSWERABLE, RESPONSIBLE   **2** : EXPLI-
CABLE — **ac·count·abil·i·ty** \-ˌkau̇n-tə-
'bi-lə-tē\ *n*

ac·coun·tant \ə-'kau̇n-t³nt\ *n* : a person
skilled in accounting — **ac·coun·tan·cy**
\-t³n-sē\ *n*

account executive *n* : a business executive in charge of a client's account

ac·count·ing \ə-'kau̇n-tiŋ\ *n* : the art or
system of keeping and analyzing financial
records

ac·cou·tre *or* **ac·cou·ter** \ə-'kü-tər\ *vb*
-cou·tred *or* **-cou·tered; -cou·tring** *or*
-cou·ter·ing \-'kü-t(ə-)riŋ\ : EQUIP, OUT-
FIT

ac·cou·tre·ment *or* **ac·cou·ter·ment** \ə-'kü-trə-mənt, -'kü-tər-\ *n* [F] **1** : an accessory item — usu. used in pl. **2** : an identifying characteristic

ac·cred·it \ə-'kre-dət\ *vb* **1** : to endorse or approve officially **2** : CREDIT — **ac·cred·i·ta·tion** \-,kre-də-'tā-shən\ *n*

ac·cre·tion \ə-'krē-shən\ *n* **1** : growth or enlargement esp. by addition from without **2** : a product of accretion

accretion disk *n* : a disk of usu. gaseous matter surrounding and gradually accumulating onto a massive celestial object

ac·crue \ə-'krü\ *vb* **ac·crued; ac·cru·ing** **1** : to come by way of increase **2** : to be added by periodic growth — **ac·cru·al** \-əl\ *n*

acct *abbr* account; accountant

ac·cul·tur·a·tion \ə-,kəl-chə-'rā-shən\ *n* : cultural modification of an individual or group by borrowing and adapting traits from another culture

ac·cu·mu·late \ə-'kyü-myə-,lāt\ *vb* **-lat·ed; -lat·ing** [L *accumulare*, fr. *ad-* to + *cumulare* to heap up] : to heap or pile up ♦ *Synonyms* AMASS, GATHER, COLLECT, STOCKPILE — **ac·cu·mu·la·tion** \-,kyü-myə-'lā-shən\ *n* — **ac·cu·mu·la·tive** \-'kyü-myə-,lā-tiv\ *adj* — **ac·cu·mu·la·tor** \-'kyü-myə-,lā-tər\ *n*

ac·cu·rate \'a-kyə-rət\ *adj* : free from error : EXACT, PRECISE — **ac·cu·ra·cy** \-rə-sē\ *n* — **ac·cu·rate·ly** *adv* — **ac·cu·rate·ness** *n*

ac·cursed \ə-'kərst, -'kər-səd\ *or* **ac·curst** \ə-'kərst\ *adj* **1** : being under a curse **2** : DAMNABLE, EXECRABLE

ac·cus·al \ə-'kyü-zəl\ *n* : ACCUSATION

ac·cu·sa·tive \ə-'kyü-zə-tiv\ *adj* : of, relating to, or being a grammatical case marking the direct object of a verb or the object of a preposition — **accusative** *n*

ac·cu·sa·to·ry \ə-'kyü-zə-,tȯr-ē\ *adj* : expressing accusation ⟨an ∼ tone⟩

ac·cuse \ə-'kyüz\ *vb* **ac·cused; ac·cus·ing** : to charge with an offense : BLAME — **ac·cu·sa·tion** \,a-kyə-'zā-shən\ *n* — **ac·cus·er** *n*

ac·cused \ə-'kyüzd\ *n, pl* **accused** : the defendant in a criminal case

ac·cus·tom \ə-'kəs-təm\ *vb* : to make familiar through use or experience

ac·cus·tomed \ə-'kəs-təmd\ *adj* : USUAL, CUSTOMARY ⟨with ∼ grace⟩; *also* : being in the habit ⟨∼ed to winning⟩

¹ace \'ās\ *n* [ME *as* a die face marked with one spot, fr. AF, fr. L, unit, a copper coin] **1** : a playing card bearing a single large pip in its center **2** : a point (as in tennis) won on a serve that goes untouched **3** : a golf score of one stroke on a hole **4** : a combat pilot who has downed five or more enemy planes **5** : one that excels **6** : the best pitcher on a baseball team

²ace *vb* **aced; ac·ing** **1** : to score an ace against (an opponent) or on (a golf hole) **2** : to defeat decisively **3** : to perform extremely well in or on ⟨*aced* the quiz⟩

³ace *adj* : of first rank or quality

ACE in·hib·i·tor \'ā-,sē-'ē-in-'hi-bə-tər, 'ās-\ *n* : any of a group of drugs that

lower blood pressure by relaxing the arteries

acer·bic \ə-'sər-bik, a-\ *adj* : acid in temper, mood, or tone ⟨∼ wit⟩

acer·bi·ty \ə-'sər-bə-tē\ *n, pl* **-ties** : SOURNESS, BITTERNESS

acet·amin·o·phen \ə-,sē-tə-'mi-nə-fən\ *n* : a crystalline compound used in chemical synthesis and in medicine to relieve pain and fever

ace·tate \'a-sə-,tāt\ *n* **1** : a salt or ester of acetic acid **2** : a textile fiber made from cellulose and acetic acid; *also* : a fabric or plastic made of this fiber

ace·tic acid \ə-'sē-tik-\ *n* : a colorless pungent liquid acid that is the chief acid of vinegar and is used esp. in making chemical compounds

ace·tone \'a-sə-,tōn\ *n* : a volatile flammable fragrant liquid compound used in making other chemical compounds and as a solvent

ace·tyl·cho·line \ə-,sē-t³l-'kō-,lēn\ *n* : a compound that is released at nerve endings of the autonomic nervous system and is active in the transmission of nerve impulses

acet·y·lene \ə-'se-t³l-ən, -t³l-,ēn\ *n* : a colorless flammable gas used as a fuel (as in welding and soldering)

ace·tyl·sal·i·cyl·ic acid \ə-'sē-t³l-,sa-lə-,si-lik-\ *n* : ASPIRIN 1

ache \'āk\ *vb* **ached; ach·ing** **1** : to suffer a usu. dull persistent pain ⟨an *aching* back⟩ **2** : LONG, YEARN ⟨*aching* to go home⟩ — **ache** *n* — **ach·ing·ly** \'ā-kiŋ-lē\ *adv*

achieve \ə-'chēv\ *vb* **achieved; achiev·ing** [ME *acheven*, fr. AF *achever* to finish, fr. *a-* to (fr. L *ad-*) + *chef* end, head, fr. L *caput*] : to gain by work or effort ♦ *Synonyms* ACCOMPLISH, ATTAIN, REALIZE — **achiev·able** \-'chē-və-bəl\ *adj* — **achieve·ment** *n* — **achiev·er** *n*

Achil·les' heel \ə-,ki-lēz-\ *n* [fr. the story that the Greek warrior Achilles was vulnerable only in the heel] : a vulnerable point

Achil·les tendon \ə-,ki-lēz-\ *n* : the tendon joining the muscles in the calf of the leg to the bone of the heel

ach·ro·mat·ic \,a-krə-'ma-tik\ *adj* : giving an image almost free from extraneous colors ⟨∼ lens⟩

achy \'ā-kē\ *adj* **ach·i·er; ach·i·est** : afflicted with aches — **ach·i·ness** *n*

¹ac·id \'a-səd\ *adj* **1** : sour or biting to the taste; *also* : sharp or sour in manner **2** : of or relating to an acid — **acid·i·ty** \ə-'si-də-tē\ *n* — **acid·ly** *adv*

²acid *n* **1** : a sour substance **2** : a usu. water-soluble chemical compound that has a sour taste, reacts with a base to form a salt, and reddens litmus **3** : LSD — **acid·ic** \ə-'si-dik\ *adj*

acid·i·fy \ə-'si-də-,fī\ *vb* **-fied; -fy·ing** **1** : to make or become acid **2** : to change into an acid — **acid·i·fi·ca·tion** \-,si-də-fə-'kā-shən\ *n*

ac·i·do·sis \,a-sə-'dō-səs\ *n, pl* **-do·ses** \-,sēz\ : an abnormal state of reduced alkalinity of the blood and body tissues

acid precipitation n : precipitation with above normal acidity that is caused esp. by atmospheric pollutants

acid rain n : acid precipitation in the form of rain

acid test n : a severe or crucial test

acid·u·lous \ə-'si-jə-ləs\ adj : somewhat acid or harsh in taste or manner

ack abbr acknowledge; acknowledgment

ac·knowl·edge \ik-'nä-lij, ak-\ vb **-edged; -edg·ing 1** : to recognize the rights or authority of **2** : to admit as true **3** : to express thanks for; also : to report receipt of ⟨~ a letter⟩ **4** : to recognize as valid — **ac·knowl·edg·ment** or **ac·knowl·edge·ment** n

ACL \ā-ˌsē-'el\ n : ANTERIOR CRUCIATE LIGAMENT

ACLU abbr American Civil Liberties Union

ac·me \'ak-mē\ n [Gk akmē] : the highest point

ac·ne \'ak-nē\ n [Gk aknē, MS var. of akmē, lit., point] : a skin disorder marked by inflammation of skin glands and hair follicles and by pimple formation esp. on the face

ac·o·lyte \'a-kə-ˌlīt\ n **1** : one who assists a member of the clergy in a liturgical service **2** : FOLLOWER

ac·o·nite \'a-kə-ˌnīt\ n **1** : MONKSHOOD **2** : the dried root of a common Eurasian monkshood used formerly as a drug

acorn \'ā-ˌkȯrn, -kərn\ n : the nut of the oak

acorn squash n : an acorn-shaped dark green winter squash with a ridged surface and yellow to orange flesh

acous·tic \ə-'kü-stik\ or **acous·ti·cal** \-sti-kəl\ adj **1** : of or relating to the sense or organs of hearing, to sound, or to the science of sounds **2** : deadening sound ⟨~ tile⟩ **3** : operated by or utilizing sound waves **4** : having a sound that is not electronically modified ⟨~ guitar⟩ — **acous·ti·cal·ly** \-k(ə-)lē\ adv

acous·tics \ə-'kü-stiks\ n sing or pl **1** : the science of sound **2** : the qualities in a room that make it easy or hard for a person in it to hear distinctly

ac·quaint \ə-'kwānt\ vb [ME, ultim. fr. L ad- + cognoscere to know] **1** : to cause to know personally **2** : INFORM

ac·quain·tance \ə-'kwān-t°ns\ n **1** : personal knowledge **2** : a person with whom one is acquainted — **ac·quain·tance·ship** n

acquaintance rape n : rape committed by someone known to the victim

ac·qui·esce \ˌa-kwē-'es\ vb **-esced; -esc·ing** : to accept, comply, or submit without open opposition ♦ Synonyms CONSENT, AGREE, ASSENT, ACCEDE — **ac·qui·es·cence** \-'e-s°ns\ n — **ac·qui·es·cent** \-s°nt\ adj — **ac·qui·es·cent·ly** adv

ac·quire \ə-'kwī-(ə)r\ vb **ac·quired; ac·quir·ing** : to gain possession of : GET — **ac·quir·able** \-ˌkwī-rə-bəl\ adj

acquired adj **1** : gained by or as a result of effort or experience **2** : caused by environmental forces and not passed from parent to offspring in the genes ⟨~ characteristics⟩

acquired immune deficiency syndrome n : AIDS

acquired immunodeficiency syndrome n : AIDS

ac·quire·ment \ə-'kwī(-ə)r-mənt\ n **1** : ATTAINMENT, ACCOMPLISHMENT **2** : the act of acquiring

ac·qui·si·tion \ˌa-kwə-'zi-shən\ n **1** : ACQUIREMENT **2** : something acquired

ac·quis·i·tive \ə-'kwi-zə-tiv\ adj : eager to acquire : GREEDY — **ac·quis·i·tive·ly** adv — **ac·quis·i·tive·ness** n

ac·quit \ə-'kwit\ vb **ac·quit·ted; ac·quit·ting 1** : to pronounce not guilty **2** : to conduct (oneself) usu. satisfactorily — **ac·quit·tal** \ə-'kwi-t°l\ n

acre \'ā-kər\ n **1** pl : LANDS, ESTATE **2** — see WEIGHT table

acre·age \'ā-k(ə-)rij\ n : area in acres

ac·rid \'a-krəd\ adj **1** : sharp and biting in taste or odor **2** : deeply bitter : CAUSTIC — **ac·rid·i·ty** \a-'kri-də-tē\ n — **ac·rid·ness** n

ac·ri·mo·ny \'a-krə-ˌmō-nē\ n, pl **-nies** : harsh or biting sharpness of language or feeling — **ac·ri·mo·ni·ous** \ˌa-krə-'mō-nē-əs\ adj — **ac·ri·mo·ni·ous·ly** adv — **ac·ri·mo·ni·ous·ness** n

ac·ro·bat \'a-krə-ˌbat\ n [F acrobate, fr. Gk akrobatēs, fr. akros topmost + bainein to go] : a performer of gymnastic feats — **ac·ro·bat·ic** \ˌa-krə-'ba-tik\ adj — **ac·ro·bat·i·cal·ly** \-ti-k(ə-)lē\ adv

ac·ro·bat·ics \ˌa-krə-'ba-tiks\ n sing or pl : the performance of an acrobat

ac·ro·nym \'a-krə-ˌnim\ n : a word (as radar) or abbreviation (as FBI) formed from the initial letter or letters of each of the successive parts or major parts of a compound term

ac·ro·pho·bia \ˌa-krə-'fō-bē-ə\ n : abnormal dread of being in a high place : fear of heights

acrop·o·lis \ə-'krä-pə-ləs\ n [Gk akropolis, fr. akros topmost + polis city] : the upper fortified part of an ancient Greek city

¹across \ə-'krȯs\ adv **1** : to or on the opposite side **2** : so as to be understandable ⟨get the point ~⟩

²across prep **1** : to or on the opposite side of ⟨ran ~ the street⟩ **2** : on so as to cross or pass at an angle ⟨a log ~ the road⟩

across-the-board adj **1** : placed to win if a competitor wins, places, or shows ⟨an ~ bet⟩ **2** : including all classes or categories ⟨an ~ wage increase⟩

acros·tic \ə-'krȯs-tik\ n : a composition usu. in verse in which the initial or final letters of the lines taken in order form a word or phrase — **acrostic** adj

acryl·ic \ə-'kri-lik\ n **1** : ACRYLIC RESIN **2** : a paint in which the vehicle is acrylic resin **3** : a quick-drying synthetic textile fiber

acrylic resin n : a glassy thermoplastic used for cast and molded parts or as coatings and adhesives

act • adapt

8

¹act \'akt\ *n* **1** : a thing done : DEED **2** : STATUTE, DECREE **3** : a main division of a play; *also* : an item on a variety program **4** : an instance of insincere behavior : PRETENSE

²act *vb* **1** : to perform by action esp. on the stage; *also* : FEIGN, SIMULATE, PRETEND **2** : to take action **3** : to conduct oneself : BEHAVE **4** : to perform a specified function **5** : to produce an effect

³act *abbr* **1** active **2** actual

ACT *abbr* Australian Capital Territory

actg *abbr* acting

ACTH \ˌā-ˌ)sē-ˌ)tē-ˈāch\ *n* : a protein hormone of the pituitary gland that stimulates the adrenal cortex

act·ing \'ak-tiŋ\ *adj* : doing duty temporarily or for another ⟨~ president⟩

ac·tin·i·um \ak-ˈti-nē-əm\ *n* : a radioactive metallic chemical element

ac·tion \'ak-shən\ *n* **1** : a legal proceeding **2** : the manner or method of performing **3** : ACTIVITY **4** : ACT, DEED **5** : the accomplishment of a thing usu. over a period of time, in stages, or with the possibility of repetition **6** *pl* : CONDUCT **7** : COMBAT, BATTLE **8** : the events of a literary plot **9** : an operating mechanism ⟨the ~ of a gun⟩; *also* : the way it operates ⟨stiff ~⟩

ac·tion·able \'ak-sh(ə-)nə-bəl\ *adj* : affording ground for an action or suit at law — **ac·tion·ably** \-blē\ *adv*

ac·ti·vate \'ak-tə-ˌvāt\ *vb* -**vat·ed**; -**vat·ing** **1** : to spur into action; *also* : to make active, reactive, or radioactive **2** : to treat (as carbon) so as to improve adsorptive properties **3** : to set up (a military unit) formally; *also* : to call to active duty — **ac·ti·va·tion** \ˌak-tə-ˈvā-shən\ *n* — **ac·ti·va·tor** \'ak-tə-ˌvā-tər\ *n*

ac·tive \'ak-tiv\ *adj* **1** : causing or involving action or change **2** : asserting that the grammatical subject performs the action represented by the verb ⟨~ voice⟩ **3** : BRISK, LIVELY **4** : erupting or likely to erupt ⟨~ volcano⟩ **5** : presently in operation or use **6** : tending to progress or to cause degeneration ⟨~ tuberculosis⟩ — **active** *n* — **ac·tive·ly** *adv* — **ac·tive·ness** *n*

ac·tive–ma·trix \'ak-tiv-ˌmā-triks\ *adj* : of, relating to, or being an LCD in which each pixel is individually controlled

ac·tive·wear \'ak-tiv-ˌwer\ *n* : clothing designed for recreation or informal wear

ac·tiv·ism \'ak-ti-ˌvi-zəm\ *n* : a doctrine or practice that emphasizes vigorous action for political ends — **ac·tiv·ist** \-vist\ *n or adj*

ac·tiv·i·ty \ak-ˈti-və-tē\ *n, pl* -**ties** **1** : the quality or state of being active **2** : forceful or energetic action **3** : an occupation in which one is engaged

ac·tor \'ak-tər\ *n* : a person who acts in a play or motion picture

ac·tress \'ak-trəs\ *n* : a woman who is an actor

Acts \'akts\ *or* **Acts of the Apostles** *n* — see BIBLE table

ac·tu·al \'ak-chə-wəl, -shə-\ *adj* : really

existing : REAL — **ac·tu·al·i·ty** \ˌak-chə-ˈwa-lə-tē, -shə-\ *n* — **ac·tu·al·i·za·tion** \ˌak-chə-wə-lə-ˈzā-shən, -shə-\ *n* — **ac·tu·al·ize** \'ak-chə-wə-ˌlīz, -shə-\ *vb*

ac·tu·al·ly \'ak-chə-wə-lē, -shə-\ *adv* : in fact or in truth : REALLY

ac·tu·ary \'ak-chə-ˌwer-ē, -shə-\ *n, pl* -**ar·ies** : a person who calculates insurance risks and premiums — **ac·tu·ar·i·al** \ˌak-chə-ˈwer-ē-əl, -shə-\ *adj*

ac·tu·ate \'ak-chə-ˌwāt\ *vb* -**at·ed**; -**at·ing** **1** : to put into action **2** : to move to action — **ac·tu·a·tion** \ˌak-chə-ˈwā-shən, -shə-\ *n* — **ac·tu·a·tor** \'ak-chə-ˌwā-tər, -shə-\ *n*

act up *vb* **1** : MISBEHAVE **2** : to function improperly

acu·ity \ə-ˈkyü-ə-tē\ *n, pl* -**ities** : keenness of perception

acu·men \ə-ˈkyü-mən\ *n* : mental keenness and penetration ✦ *Synonyms* DISCERNMENT, INSIGHT, PERCIPIENCE, PERSPICACITY

acu·pres·sure \'a-kyu̇-ˌpre-shər\ *n* : a finger massage of those points on the body stimulated in acupuncture

acu·punc·ture \-ˌpəŋk-chər\ *n* : an orig. Chinese practice of inserting thin needles through the skin at specific points esp. to cure disease or relieve pain — **acu·punc·tur·ist** \ˌa-kyu̇-ˈpəŋk-chə-rist\ *n*

acute \ə-ˈkyüt\ *adj* **acut·er**; **acut·est** [ME, fr. L *acutus*, pp. of *acuere* to sharpen, fr. *acus* needle] **1** : SHARP, POINTED **2** : containing less than 90 degrees ⟨an ~ angle⟩ **3** : sharply perceptive; *esp* : mentally keen **4** : SEVERE ⟨~ distress⟩; *also* : having a sudden onset, sharp rise, and short duration ⟨~ inflammation⟩ **5** : of, marked by, or being an accent mark having the form ´ — **acute·ly** *adv* — **acute·ness** *n*

acy·clo·vir \ˌ)ā-ˈsī-klō-ˌvir\ *n* : a drug used esp. to treat the genital form of herpes simplex

ad \'ad\ *n* : ADVERTISEMENT

AD *abbr* **1** after date **2** [L *anno Domini*] in the year of our Lord — often printed in small capitals and often punctuated **3** assistant director **4** athletic director

ad·age \'a-dij\ *n* : an old familiar saying : PROVERB, MAXIM

¹ada·gio \ə-ˈdä-j(ē-ˌ)ō, -zh(ē-ˌ)ō\ *adv or adj* [It] : at a slow tempo — used as a direction in music

²adagio *n, pl* -**gios** **1** : an adagio movement **2** : a ballet duet or trio displaying feats of lifting and balancing

¹ad·a·mant \'a-də-mənt, -ˌmant\ *n* [ME, fr. AF, fr. L *adamant-, adamas* hardest metal, diamond, fr. Gk] : a stone believed to be impenetrably hard — **ad·a·man·tine** \ˌa-də-ˈman-ˌtēn, -ˌtin\ *adj*

²adamant *adj* : INFLEXIBLE, UNYIELDING — **ad·a·man·cy** \'a-də-mən-sē\ *n* — **ad·a·mant·ly** *adv*

Ad·am's apple \'a-dəmz-\ *n* : the projection in front of the neck formed by the largest cartilage of the larynx

adapt \ə-ˈdapt\ *vb* **1** : to make suitable or fit (as for a new use or for a different situation) **2** : to adjust to environmental conditions ✦ *Synonyms* ADJUST, ACCOMMODATE, CONFORM — **adapt·abil·i·ty** \ə-ˌdap-tə-ˈbi-lə-tē\ *n* — **adapt·able** *adj* — **ad·ap·ta·tion** \ˌa-ˌdap-ˈtā-shən\ *n* — **ad·ap·ta·tion·al** \-sh(ə-)nəl\ *adj* — **adap·tive** \ə-ˈdap-tiv\ *adj* — **ad·ap·tiv·i·ty** \ˌa-ˌdap-ˈti-və-tē\ *n*

adapt·er *also* **adap·tor** \ə-ˈdap-tər\ *n* **1** : one that adapts **2** : a device for connecting two dissimilar parts of an apparatus **3** : an attachment for adapting apparatus for uses not orig. intended

adaptive optics *n sing or pl* : a telescopic system that improves image resolution by compensating for distortions from atmospheric turbulence

ADC *abbr* **1** aide-de-camp **2** Aid to Dependent Children

add \ˈad\ *vb* **1** : to join to something else so as to increase in number or amount **2** : to say further ⟨let me ∼ this⟩ **3** : to combine (numbers) into one sum

ADD *abbr* attention deficit disorder

ad·dend \ˈa-ˌdend\ *n* : a number to be added to another

ad·den·dum \ə-ˈden-dəm\ *n, pl* **-da** \-də\ [L] : something added; *esp* : a supplement to a book

¹**ad·der** \ˈa-dər\ *n* [ME, alter. (by false division of *a naddre*) of *naddre*, fr. OE *næddre*] **1** : a poisonous European viper or a related snake **2** : any of various harmless No. American snakes (as the hognose snake)

²**add·er** \ˈa-dər\ *n* : one that adds; *esp* : a device that performs addition

¹**ad·dict** \ə-ˈdikt\ *vb* **1** : to devote or surrender (oneself) to something habitually or excessively **2** : to cause addiction to a substance in (as a person) — **ad·dic·tive** \-ˈdik-tiv\ *adj*

²**ad·dict** \ˈa-(ˌ)dikt\ *n* : one who is addicted esp. to a substance

ad·dic·tion \ə-ˈdik-shən\ *n* **1** : the quality or state of being addicted **2** : compulsive need for and use of a habit-forming substance (as heroin, nicotine, or alcohol) characterized by well-defined physiological symptoms upon withdrawal; *also* : persistent compulsive use of a substance known by the user to be harmful

ad·di·tion \ə-ˈdi-shən\ *n* **1** : the act or process of adding; *also* : something added **2** : the operation of combining numbers to obtain their sum ✦ *Synonyms* ACCRETION, INCREMENT, ACCESSION, AUGMENTATION

ad·di·tion·al \ə-ˈdi-sh(ə-)nəl\ *adj* : coming by way of addition : ADDED, EXTRA

ad·di·tion·al·ly \ə-ˈdi-sh(ə-)nə-lē\ *adv* : in or by way of addition : FURTHERMORE

¹**ad·di·tive** \ˈa-də-tiv\ *adj* **1** : of, relating to, or characterized by addition **2** : produced by addition — **ad·di·tiv·i·ty** \ˌa-də-ˈti-və-tē\ *n*

²**additive** *n* : a substance added to another in small quantities to effect a desired change in properties ⟨food ∼s⟩

ad·dle \ˈa-dᵊl\ *vb* **ad·dled; ad·dling** **1** : to throw into confusion : MUDDLE **2** : to become rotten ⟨*addled* eggs⟩

addn *abbr* addition

addnl *abbr* additional

add–on \ˈad-ˌon, -ˌän\ *n* : something (as a feature or accessory) added esp. as an enhancement

¹**ad·dress** \ə-ˈdres\ *vb* **1** : to direct the attention of (oneself) **2** : to direct one's remarks to : deliver an address to **3** : to mark directions for delivery on **4** : to identify (as a memory location) by an address

²**ad·dress** \ə-ˈdres, ˈa-ˌdres\ *n* **1** : skillful management **2** : a formal speech : LECTURE **3** : the place where a person or organization may be communicated with **4** : the directions for delivery placed on mail; *also* : the designation of a computer account from which one can send or receive e-mail **5** : a location (as in a computer's memory) where particular data is stored; *also* : URL

ad·dress·ee \ˌa-ˌdre-ˈsē, ə-ˌdre-ˈsē\ *n* : one to whom something is addressed

ad·duce \ə-ˈdüs, -ˈdyüs\ *vb* **ad·duced; ad·duc·ing** : to offer as argument, reason, or proof ✦ *Synonyms* ADVANCE, ALLEGE, CITE, SUBMIT — **ad·duc·er** *n*

-ade *n suffix* **1** : act : action ⟨block*ade*⟩ **2** : product; *esp* : sweet drink ⟨lime*ade*⟩

ad·e·nine \ˈa-də-ˌnēn\ *n* : a purine base that codes genetic information in the molecular chain of DNA and RNA

ad·e·noid \ˈa-də-ˌnoid, ˈad-ˌnoid\ *n* : an enlarged mass of tissue near the opening of the nose into the throat — usu. used in pl. — **adenoid** *or* **ad·e·noi·dal** \ˌa-də-ˈnoi-dᵊl\ *adj*

aden·o·sine tri·phos·phate \ə-ˈde-nə-ˌsēn-trī-ˈfäs-ˌfāt\ *n* : ATP

ad·e·no·vi·rus \ˌa-dᵊn-ō-ˈvī-rəs\ *n* : any of a family of viruses causing infections of the respiratory tract, conjunctiva, and gastrointestinal tract

¹**ad·ept** \ˈa-ˌdept\ *n* : EXPERT

²**ad·ept** \ə-ˈdept\ *adj* : highly skilled : EXPERT — **adept·ly** *adv* — **adept·ness** *n*

ad·e·quate \ˈa-di-kwət\ *adj* : equal to or sufficient for a specific requirement — **ad·e·qua·cy** \-kwə-sē\ *n* — **ad·e·quate·ly** *adv* — **ad·e·quate·ness** *n*

ad·here \ad-ˈhir\ *vb* **ad·hered; ad·her·ing** **1** : to give support : maintain loyalty **2** : to stick fast : CLING — **ad·her·ence** \-ˈhir-əns\ *n* — **ad·her·ent** \-ənt\ *adj or n*

ad·he·sion \ad-ˈhē-zhən\ *n* **1** : the act or state of adhering **2** : the union of bodily tissues abnormally grown together after inflammation; *also* : the newly formed uniting tissue **3** : the molecular attraction between the surfaces of bodies in contact

¹**ad·he·sive** \-ˈhē-siv, -ziv\ *adj* **1** : tending to adhere : STICKY **2** : prepared for adhering

²**adhesive** *n* : an adhesive substance

adhesive tape *n* : tape coated on one side with an adhesive mixture; *esp* : one used for covering wounds

¹**ad hoc** \ˈad-ˈhäk, -ˈhōk\ *adv* [L, for this] : for the case at hand apart from other applications

²**ad hoc** *adj* : concerned with or formed for a particular purpose ⟨an *ad hoc* committee⟩ ⟨*ad hoc* solutions⟩

adi·a·bat·ic \ˌa-dē-ə-'ba-tik\ *adj* : occurring without loss or gain of heat — **adi·a·bat·i·cal·ly** \-ti-k(ə-)lē\ *adv*

adieu \ə-'dü, -'dyü\ *n*, *pl* **adieus** *or* **adieux** \ə-'düz, -'dyüz\ : FAREWELL — often used interjectionally

ad in·fi·ni·tum \ˌad-ˌin-fə-'nī-təm\ *adv or adj* : without end or limit

ad in·ter·im \ad-'in-tə-rəm, -ˌrim\ *adv* : for the intervening time — **ad interim** *adj*

adi·os \ˌa-dē-'ōs, ˌä-\ *interj* [Sp *adiós*, lit., to God] — used to express farewell

ad·i·pose \'a-də-ˌpōs\ *adj* : of or relating to animal fat : FATTY

adj *abbr* **1** adjective **2** adjutant

ad·ja·cent \ə-'jā-sᵊnt\ *adj* : situated near or next ◆ **Synonyms** ADJOINING, CONTIGUOUS, ABUTTING, JUXTAPOSED, CONTERMINOUS — **ad·ja·cent·ly** *adv*

ad·jec·tive \'a-jik-tiv\ *n* : a word that typically serves as a modifier of a noun — **ad·jec·ti·val** \ˌa-jik-'tī-vəl\ *adj* — **ad·jec·ti·val·ly** *adv*

ad·join \ə-'jȯin\ *vb* : to be situated next to

ad·join·ing *adj* : touching or bounding at a point or line

ad·journ \ə-'jərn\ *vb* **1** : to suspend indefinitely or until a stated time **2** : to transfer to another place — **ad·journ·ment** *n*

ad·judge \ə-'jəj\ *vb* **ad·judged; ad·judg·ing** **1** : JUDGE, ADJUDICATE **2** : to hold or pronounce to be : DEEM **3** : to award by judicial decision

ad·ju·di·cate \ə-'jü-di-ˌkāt\ *vb* **-cat·ed; -cat·ing** : to settle judicially — **ad·ju·di·ca·tion** \ə-ˌjü-di-'kā-shən\ *n*

ad·junct \'a-ˌjəŋkt\ *n* : something joined or added to another but not essentially a part of it ◆ **Synonyms** APPENDAGE, APPURTENANCE, ACCESSORY, APPENDIX — **adjunct** *adj*

ad·jure \ə-'ju̇r\ *vb* **ad·jured; ad·jur·ing** : to command solemnly : urge earnestly ◆ **Synonyms** BEG, BESEECH, IMPLORE — **ad·ju·ra·tion** \ˌa-jə-'rā-shən\ *n*

ad·just \ə-'jəst\ *vb* **1** : to bring to agreement : SETTLE **2** : to cause to conform : ADAPT, FIT **3** : REGULATE ⟨~ a watch⟩ — **ad·just·able** *adj* — **ad·just·er** *also* **ad·jus·tor** \ə-'jəs-tər\ *n* — **ad·just·ment** \ə-'jəst-mənt\ *n*

ad·ju·tant \'a-jə-tənt\ *n* : one who assists; *esp* : an officer who assists a commanding officer by handling correspondence and keeping records

ad·ju·vant \'a-jə-vənt\ *n* : one that helps or facilitates; *esp* : something that enhances the effectiveness of medical treatment — **adjuvant** *adj*

¹**ad–lib** \'ad-'lib\ *vb* **ad–libbed; ad–lib·bing** : IMPROVISE — **ad–lib** *n*

²**ad–lib** *adj* : spoken, composed, or performed without preparation

ad lib \'ad-'lib\ *adv* [NL *ad libitum*] **1** : at one's pleasure **2** : without limit

adm *abbr* administration; administrative

ADM *abbr* admiral

ad·man \'ad-ˌman\ *n* : one who writes, solicits, or places advertisements

admin *abbr* administration; administrative

ad·min·is·ter \ad-'mi-nə-stər\ *vb* **1** : MANAGE, SUPERINTEND **2** : to mete out : DISPENSE ⟨~ punishment⟩ **3** : to give ritually or remedially ⟨~ quinine for malaria⟩ **4** : to perform the office of administrator — **ad·min·is·tra·ble** \-strə-bəl\ *adj* — **ad·min·is·trant** \-strənt\ *n*

ad·min·is·tra·tion \ad-ˌmi-nə-'strā-shən\ *n* **1** : the act or process of administering **2** : MANAGEMENT **3** : the officials directing the government of a country **4** : the term of office of an administrative officer or body — **ad·min·is·tra·tive** \ad-'mi-nə-ˌstrā-tiv\ *adj* — **ad·min·is·tra·tive·ly** *adv*

ad·min·is·tra·tor \ad-'mi-nə-ˌstrā-tər\ *n* : one that administers; *esp* : one who settles an intestate estate

ad·mi·ra·ble \'ad-m(ə-)rə-bəl\ *adj* : worthy of admiration : EXCELLENT — **ad·mi·ra·bil·i·ty** \ˌad-m(ə-)rə-'bi-lə-tē\ *n* — **ad·mi·ra·ble·ness** *n* — **ad·mi·ra·bly** \-blē\ *adv*

ad·mi·ral \'ad-m(ə-)rəl\ *n* [ME, ultim. fr. Ar *amīr-al-* commander of the (as in *amīr-al-baḥr* commander of the sea)] : a commissioned officer in the navy ranking next below a fleet admiral

ad·mi·ral·ty \'ad-m(ə-)rəl-tē\ *n* **1** *cap* : a British government department formerly having authority over naval affairs **2** : the court having jurisdiction over questions of maritime law

ad·mire \ad-'mī(-ə)r\ *vb* **ad·mired; ad·mir·ing** [MF *admirer*, fr. L *admirari*, fr. *ad-* to + *mirari* to wonder] : to regard with high esteem — **ad·mi·ra·tion** \ˌad-mə-'rā-shən\ *n* — **ad·mir·er** *n* — **ad·mir·ing·ly** \-'mī-riŋ-lē\ *adv*

ad·mis·si·ble \əd-'mi-sə-bəl\ *adj* : that can be or is worthy to be admitted or allowed : ALLOWABLE ⟨~ evidence⟩ — **ad·mis·si·bil·i·ty** \-ˌmi-sə-'bi-lə-tē\ *n*

ad·mis·sion \əd-'mi-shən\ *n* **1** : the act of admitting **2** : the privilege of being admitted **3** : a fee paid for admission **4** : the granting of an argument **5** : the acknowledgment of a fact

ad·mit \əd-'mit\ *vb* **ad·mit·ted; ad·mit·ting** **1** : PERMIT, ALLOW **2** : to recognize as genuine or valid **3** : to allow to enter ⟨*admitted* to the club⟩ **4** : to accept into a hospital as an inpatient

ad·mit·tance \əd-'mi-tᵊns\ *n* : the act or process of admitting : permission to enter

ad·mit·ted·ly \əd-'mi-təd-lē\ *adv* **1** : as has been or must be admitted **2** : it must be admitted

ad·mix \ad-'miks\ *vb* : to mix in

ad·mix·ture \ad-'miks-chər\ *n* **1** : something added in mixing **2** : MIXTURE

ad·mon·ish \ad-'mä-nish\ *vb* : to warn gently; : reprove with a warning ◆ **Synonyms** CHIDE, REPROACH, REBUKE, REPRIMAND, REPROVE — **ad·mon·ish·er** *n* — **ad·mon·ish·ing·ly** *adv* — **ad·mon-**

ish·ment *n* — ad·mo·ni·tion \ˌad-mə-'ni-shən\ *n* — ad·mon·i·to·ry \ad-'mä-nə-ˌtȯr-ē\ *adj*

ad nau·se·am \ad-'nȯ-zē-əm\ *adv* [L] : to a sickening or excessive degree

ado \ə-'dü\ *n* **1** : heightened fuss or concern **2** : TROUBLE

ado·be \ə-'dō-bē\ *n* **1** : sun-dried brick; *also* : clay for making such bricks **2** : a structure made of adobe bricks

ad·o·les·cence \ˌa-də-'le-sᵊns\ *n* : the process or period of growth between childhood and maturity — ad·o·les·cent \-sᵊnt\ *adj or n*

adopt \ə-'däpt\ *vb* **1** : to take (a child of other parents) as one's own child **2** : to take up and practice as one's own **3** : to accept formally and put into effect — adopt·able \ə-'däp-tə-bəl\ *adj* — adopt·er *n* — adop·tion \-'däp-shən\ *n*

adop·tive \ə-'däp-tiv\ *adj* : made or acquired by adoption ⟨the ~ father⟩ — adop·tive·ly *adv*

ador·able \ə-'dȯr-ə-bəl\ *adj* **1** : worthy of adoration **2** : extremely charming ⟨an ~ child⟩ — ador·able·ness *n* — ador·ably \-blē\ *adv*

adore \ə-'dȯr\ *vb* adored; ador·ing [ME *adouren*, fr. AF *aurer, adourer*, fr. L *adorare*, fr. *ad-* + *orare* to speak, pray] **1** : WORSHIP **2** : to regard with loving admiration ⟨~s his wife⟩ **3** : to be extremely fond of ⟨~s pecan pie⟩ — ad·o·ra·tion \ˌa-də-'rā-shən\ *n*

adorn \ə-'dȯrn\ *vb* : to enhance the appearance of esp. with ornaments ⟨blouses ~ed with sequins⟩ — adorn·ment *n*

ad·re·nal \ə-'drē-nᵊl\ *adj* : of, relating to, or being a pair of endocrine organs (ad·renal glands) that are located near the kidneys and produce several hormones and esp. epinephrine

adren·a·line \ə-'dre-nə-lən\ *n* : EPINEPH·RINE

adrift \ə-'drift\ *adv or adj* **1** : afloat without motive power or moorings **2** : without guidance or purpose

adroit \ə-'drȯit\ *adj* [F, fr. OF, fr. *a-* to + *droit* right] **1** : dexterous with one's hands **2** : SHREWD, RESOURCEFUL ◆ Synonyms CANNY, CLEVER, CUNNING, INGENIOUS — adroit·ly *adv* — adroit·ness *n*

ad·sorb \ad-'sȯrb, -'zȯrb\ *vb* : to take up (as molecules of gases) and hold on the surface of a solid or liquid — ad·sorp·tion \-'sȯrp-shən, -'zȯrp-\ *n*

ad·u·la·tion \ˌa-jə-'lā-shən\ *n* : excessive admiration or flattery — ad·u·late \'a-jə-ˌlāt\ *vb* — ad·u·la·tor \-ˌlā-tər\ *n* — ad·u·la·to·ry \-lə-ˌtȯr-ē\ *adj*

¹adult \ə-'dəlt, 'a-ˌ\ *adj* [L *adultus*, pp. of *adolescere* to grow up, fr. *ad-* to + *alescere* to grow] : fully developed and mature — adult·hood *n*

²adult *n* : one that is adult; *esp* : a human being after an age (as 18) specified by law

adul·ter·ant \ə-'dəl-tə-rənt\ *n* : something used to adulterate another

adul·ter·ate \ə-'dəl-tə-ˌrāt\ *vb* -at·ed; -at·ing [L *adulterare*, fr. *ad-* to + *alter* other] : to make impure by mixing in a foreign

or inferior substance — adul·ter·a·tion \-ˌdəl-tə-'rā-shən\ *n*

adul·tery \ə-'dəl-t(ə-)rē\ *n, pl* -ter·ies : sexual unfaithfulness of a married person — adul·ter·er \-tər-ər\ *n* — adul·ter·ess \-t(ə-)rəs\ *also* adul·tress \-trəs\ *n* — adul·ter·ous \-t(ə-)rəs\ *adj*

ad·um·brate \'a-dəm-ˌbrāt\ *vb* -brat·ed; -brat·ing **1** : to foreshadow vaguely : INTIMATE **2** : to suggest or disclose partially **3** : SHADE, OBSCURE — ad·um·bra·tion \ˌa-dəm-'brā-shən\ *n*

adv *abbr* **1** adverb **2** advertisement

ad va·lor·em \ˌad-və-'lȯr-əm\ *adj* [L, according to the value] : imposed at a percentage of the value ⟨an *ad valorem* tax⟩

¹ad·vance \əd-'vans\ *vb* ad·vanced; ad·vanc·ing **1** : to assist the progress of ⟨~ a cause⟩ **2** : to bring or move forward ⟨~ a pawn⟩ **3** : to promote in rank **4** : to make earlier in time **5** : PROPOSE **6** : LEND **7** : to raise in rate : INCREASE — ad·vance·ment *n*

²advance *n* **1** : a forward movement **2** : IMPROVEMENT **3** : a rise esp. in price or value **4** : OFFER — in advance : BE·FOREHAND

³advance *adj* : made, sent, or furnished ahead of time ⟨~ payment⟩

ad·van·tage \əd-'van-tij\ *n* **1** : superiority of position **2** : BENEFIT, GAIN **3** : the 1st point won in tennis after deuce — ad·van·ta·geous \ˌad-ˌvan-'tā-jəs\ *adj* — ad·van·ta·geous·ly *adv*

ad·vent \'ad-ˌvent\ *n* **1** *cap* : a penitential period beginning four Sundays before Christmas **2** *cap* : the coming of Christ **3** : a coming into being or use

ad·ven·ti·tious \ˌad-vən-'ti-shəs\ *adj* **1** : ACCIDENTAL, INCIDENTAL **2** : arising or occurring sporadically or in other than the usual location ⟨~ buds⟩ — ad·ven·ti·tious·ly *adv*

¹ad·ven·ture \əd-'ven-chər\ *n* **1** : a risky undertaking **2** : a remarkable and exciting experience — ad·ven·tur·ous \-ch(ə-)rəs\ *adj*

²adventure *vb* -ven·tured; -ven·tur·ing \-'ven-ch(ə-)riŋ\ **1** : RISK, HAZARD ⟨~ their capital in foreign trade⟩ **2** : to engage in adventure

ad·ven·tur·er \əd-'ven-ch(ə-)rər\ *n* **1** : a person who engages in new and risky undertakings **2** : a person who follows a military career for adventure or profit **3** : a person who tries to gain wealth by questionable means

ad·ven·ture·some \əd-'ven-chər-səm\ *adj* : inclined to take risks

ad·ven·tur·ess \əd-'ven-ch(ə-)rəs\ *n* : a female adventurer

ad·verb \'ad-ˌvərb\ *n* : a word that typically serves as a modifier of a verb, an adjective, or another adverb — ad·ver·bi·al \ad-'vər-bē-əl\ *adj* — ad·ver·bi·al·ly *adv*

¹ad·ver·sary \'ad-vər-ˌser-ē\ *n, pl* -sar·ies : FOE

²adversary *adj* : involving antagonistic parties or interests

ad·verse \ad-'vərs, 'ad-ˌvərs\ *adj* **1** : acting against or in a contrary direction ⟨~

winds⟩ **2** : UNFAVORABLE ⟨~ criticism⟩ — **ad·verse·ly** *adv*

ad·ver·si·ty \ad-ˈvər-sə-tē\ *n, pl* **-ties** : hard times : MISFORTUNE

ad·vert \ad-ˈvərt\ *vb* : REFER ⟨~ to a previous remark⟩

ad·ver·tise \ˈad-vər-ˌtīz\ *vb* **-tised; -tis·ing** **1** : INFORM, NOTIFY **2** : to call public attention to esp. in order to sell — **ad·ver·tis·er** *n*

ad·ver·tise·ment \ˌad-vər-ˈtīz-mənt; əd-ˈvər-təs-mənt\ *n* **1** : the act of advertising **2** : a public notice intended to advertise something

ad·ver·tis·ing \ˈad-vər-ˌtī-ziŋ\ *n* : the business of preparing advertisements

ad·vice \əd-ˈvīs\ *n* **1** : recommendation with regard to a course of action : COUNSEL **2** : INFORMATION, REPORT

ad·vis·able \əd-ˈvī-zə-bəl\ *adj* : proper to be done : EXPEDIENT ⟨~ to stay fit⟩ — **ad·vis·abil·i·ty** \-ˌvī-zə-ˈbi-lə-tē\ *n*

ad·vise \əd-ˈvīz\ *vb* **ad·vised; ad·vis·ing** **1** : to give advice to : COUNSEL **2** : INFORM, NOTIFY **3** : CONSULT, CONFER ⟨~ with your friends⟩ — **ad·vis·er** *also* **ad·vi·sor** \-ˈvī-zər\ *n*

ad·vised \əd-ˈvīzd\ *adj* : thought out : CONSIDERED ⟨well-*advised*⟩ — **ad·vis·ed·ly** \-ˈvī-zəd-lē\ *adv*

ad·vise·ment \əd-ˈvīz-mənt\ *n* **1** : careful consideration ⟨take the matter under ~⟩ **2** : the act of advising

ad·vi·so·ry \əd-ˈvi-zə-rē\ *adj* **1** : having or exercising power to advise **2** : containing or giving advice

[1]ad·vo·cate \ˈad-və-kət, -ˌkāt\ *n* [ultim. fr. L *advocare* to summon, fr. *ad-* to + *vocare* to call] **1** : one who pleads another's cause **2** : one who argues or pleads for a cause or proposal — **ad·vo·ca·cy** \-və-kə-sē\ *n*

[2]ad·vo·cate \-ˌkāt\ *vb* **-cat·ed; -cat·ing** : to plead in favor of — **ad·vo·ca·tion** \ˌad-və-ˈkā-shən\ *n*

advt *abbr* advertisement

adze *also* **adz** \ˈadz\ *n* : a tool with a curved blade set at right angles to the handle that is used in shaping wood

AEC *abbr* Atomic Energy Commission

ae·gis \ˈē-jəs\ *n* **1** : SHIELD, PROTECTION ⟨under the ~ of the constitution⟩ **2** : PATRONAGE, SPONSORSHIP ⟨under the ~ of the museum⟩

ae·o·li·an harp \ē-ˈō-lē-ən-\ *n* : a box with strings that produce musical sounds when the wind blows on them

ae·on *or* **eon** \ˈē-ən, -ˌän\ *n* : an indefinitely long time : AGE

aer·ate \ˈer-ˌāt\ *vb* **aer·at·ed; aer·at·ing** **1** : to supply, impregnate, or combine with a gas and esp. air **2** : to supply (blood) with oxygen by respiration — **aer·a·tion** \ˌer-ˈā-shən\ *n* — **aer·a·tor** \ˈer-ˌā-tər\ *n*

[1]ae·ri·al \ˈer-ē-əl\ *adj* **1** : inhabiting, occurring in, or done in the air **2** : AIRY **3** : of or relating to aircraft

[2]aer·i·al \ˈer-ē-əl\ *n* : ANTENNA 2

ae·ri·al·ist \ˈer-ē-ə-list\ *n* : a performer of feats above the ground esp. on a trapeze

ae·rie \ˈer-ē, ˈir-ē\ *n* : a highly placed nest (as of an eagle)

aer·o·bat·ics \ˌer-ə-ˈba-tiks\ *n sing or pl* : spectacular flying feats and maneuvers

aer·o·bic \ˌer-ˈrō-bik\ *adj* **1** : living or active only in the presence of oxygen ⟨~ bacteria⟩ **2** : involving or increasing oxygen consumption; *also* : of or relating to aerobics — **aer·o·bi·cal·ly** \-bi-k(ə-)lē\ *adv*

aer·o·bics \-biks\ *n sing or pl* : strenuous exercises that produce a marked temporary increase in respiration and heart rate; *also* : a system of physical conditioning involving these

aero·drome \ˈer-ə-ˌdrōm\ *n, chiefly Brit* : AIRPORT

aero·dy·nam·ics \ˌer-ō-dī-ˈna-miks\ *n* : the science dealing with the forces acting on bodies in motion in a gas (as air) — **aero·dy·nam·ic** \-mik\ *also* **aero·dy·nam·i·cal** \-mi-kəl\ *adj* — **aero·dy·nam·i·cal·ly** \-mi-k(ə-)lē\ *adv*

aero·naut \ˈer-ə-ˌnȯt\ *n* [F *aéronaute,* ultim. fr. Gk *aēr* air + *nautēs* sailor] : one who operates or travels in an airship or balloon

aero·nau·tics \ˌer-ə-ˈnȯ-tiks\ *n* : the science of aircraft operation — **aero·nau·ti·cal** \-ti-kəl\ *also* **aero·nau·tic** \-tik\ *adj*

aero·pho·bia \ˌer-ō-ˈfō-bē-ə\ *n* : fear or strong dislike of flying

aero·plane \ˈer-ə-ˌplān\ *chiefly Brit var of* AIRPLANE

aero·sol \ˈer-ə-ˌsäl, -ˌsȯl\ *n* **1** : a suspension of fine solid or liquid particles in a gas; *also, pl* : the particles themselves **2** : a substance (as an insecticide) dispensed from a pressurized container as an aerosol

aero·space \ˈer-ō-ˌspās\ *n* : the earth's atmosphere and the space beyond — **aerospace** *adj*

aery \ˈer-ē\ *adj* **aer·i·er; -est** : having an aerial quality : ETHEREAL ⟨~ visions⟩

aes·thete *also* **es·thete** \ˈes-ˌthēt\ *n* : a person having or affecting sensitivity to beauty esp. in art

aes·thet·ic *also* **es·thet·ic** \es-ˈthe-tik\ *adj* **1** : of or relating to aesthetics : ARTISTIC **2** : appreciative of the beautiful — **aes·thet·i·cal·ly** *also* **es·thet·i·cal·ly** \-ti-k(ə-)lē\ *adv*

aes·thet·ics *also* **es·thet·ics** \-tiks\ *n* : a branch of philosophy dealing with the nature, creation, and appreciation of beauty

ae·ti·ol·o·gy *chiefly Brit var of* ETIOLOGY

AF *abbr* **1** air force **2** audio frequency

[1]afar \ə-ˈfär\ *adv* : from, at, or to a great distance

[2]afar *n* : a great distance

AFB *abbr* air force base

AFC *abbr* **1** American Football Conference **2** automatic frequency control

AFDC *abbr* Aid to Families with Dependent Children

af·fa·ble \ˈa-fə-bəl\ *adj* : courteous and agreeable in conversation — **af·fa·bil·i·ty** \ˌa-fə-ˈbi-lə-tē\ *n* — **af·fa·bly** \ˈa-fə-blē\ *adv*

af·fair \ə-ˈfer\ *n* [ME *afere*, fr. AF fr. *afaire*, fr. *a faire* to do] **1** : something that relates to or involves one : CONCERN **2** : a romantic or sexual attachment of limited duration

¹af·fect \ə-ˈfekt, a-\ *vb* **1** : to be fond of using or wearing **2** : SIMULATE, ASSUME, PRETEND

²affect *vb* : to produce an effect on : INFLUENCE

³af·fect \ˈa-ˌfekt\ *n* : EMOTION; *also* : an observable display of emotion ⟨an expressionless ~⟩

af·fec·ta·tion \ˌa-ˌfek-ˈtā-shən\ *n* : an attitude or behavior that is assumed by a person but not genuinely felt

af·fect·ed \a-ˈfek-təd\ *adj* **1** : given to or marked by affectation **2** : artificially assumed to impress others — **af·fect·ed·ly** *adv*

af·fect·ing \a-ˈfek-tiŋ\ *adj* : arousing pity, sympathy, or sorrow ⟨an ~ story⟩ — **af·fect·ing·ly** *adv*

af·fec·tion \ə-ˈfek-shən\ *n* : tender attachment — **af·fec·tion·ate** \-sh(ə-)nət\ *adj* — **af·fec·tion·ate·ly** *adv*

af·fec·tive \a-ˈfek-tiv\ *adj* : relating to, influencing, or expressing an emotion or feeling : EMOTIONAL ⟨an ~ disorder⟩

af·fer·ent \ˈa-fə-rənt, -ˌfer-ənt\ *adj* : bearing or conducting inward toward a more central part and esp. a nerve center (as the central nervous system)

af·fi·ance \ə-ˈfī-əns\ *vb* **-anced; -anc·ing** : BETROTH, ENGAGE

af·fi·da·vit \ˌa-fə-ˈdā-vət\ *n* [ML, he has made an oath] : a sworn statement in writing

¹af·fil·i·ate \ə-ˈfi-lē-ˌāt\ *vb* **-at·ed; -at·ing** : to associate as a member or branch — **af·fil·i·a·tion** \-ˌfi-lē-ˈā-shən\ *n*

²af·fil·i·ate \ə-ˈfi-lē-ət\ *n* : an affiliated person or organization

af·fin·i·ty \ə-ˈfi-nə-tē\ *n, pl* **-ties** **1** : KINSHIP, RELATIONSHIP **2** : attractive force : ATTRACTION, SYMPATHY

affinity card *n* : a credit card issued in affiliation with an organization (as a charity or an airline) the use of which benefits the organization or possessor of the card

af·firm \ə-ˈfərm\ *vb* **1** : CONFIRM **2** : to assert positively **3** : to make a solemn and formal declaration or assertion in place of an oath ✦ *Synonyms* AVER, AVOW, AVOUCH, DECLARE, ASSERT — **af·fir·ma·tion** \ˌa-fər-ˈmā-shən\ *n*

¹af·fir·ma·tive \ə-ˈfər-mə-tiv\ *adj* : asserting that the fact is so : POSITIVE

²affirmative *n* **1** : an expression of affirmation or assent **2** : the side that upholds the proposition stated in a debate

affirmative action *n* : an active effort to improve the employment or educational opportunities of members of minority groups and women

¹af·fix \ə-ˈfiks\ *vb* : ATTACH, ADD

²af·fix \ˈa-ˌfiks\ *n* : one or more sounds or letters attached to the beginning or end of a word that produce a derivative word or an inflectional form

af·fla·tus \ə-ˈflā-təs\ *n* : divine inspiration

af·flict \ə-ˈflikt\ *vb* : to cause pain and distress to ✦ *Synonyms* RACK, TRY, TORMENT, TORTURE — **af·flic·tion** \-ˈflik-shən\ *n*

af·flic·tive \ə-ˈflik-tiv\ *adj* : causing affliction : DISTRESSING ⟨~ emotions⟩ — **af·flic·tive·ly** *adv*

af·flu·ence \ˈa-ˌflü-ən(t)s, a-ˈflü-\ *n* : abundant supply; *also* : WEALTH, RICHES — **af·flu·ent** \-ənt\ *adj*

af·ford \ə-ˈfȯrd\ *vb* **1** : to manage to bear or bear the cost of without serious harm or loss **2** : PROVIDE, FURNISH ⟨the roof ~ed a fine view⟩

af·for·es·ta·tion \a-ˌfȯr-ə-ˈstā-shən\ *n* : the act or process of establishing a forest — **af·for·est** \a-ˈfȯr-əst, -ˈfär-\ *vb*

af·fray \ə-ˈfrā\ *n* : FIGHT, FRAY

af·fright \ə-ˈfrīt\ *vb, archaic* : FRIGHTEN, ALARM — **affright** *n*

af·front \ə-ˈfrənt\ *vb* **1** : INSULT **2** : CONFRONT ⟨~ death⟩ — **affront** *n*

af·ghan \ˈaf-ˌgan\ *n* **1** *cap* : a native or inhabitant of Afghanistan **2** : a blanket or shawl of colored wool knitted or crocheted in sections — **Afghan** *or* **Afghani** \af-ˈga-nē, -ˈgä-\ *adj*

Afghan hound *n* : any of a breed of tall slim swift hunting dogs with a coat of silky thick hair and a long silky top-knot

af·gha·ni \af-ˈga-nē\ *n* — see MONEY table

afi·cio·na·do \ə-ˌfish(ē-)ə-ˈnä-dō, -sē-ə-\ *n, pl* **-dos** [Sp, fr. pp. of *aficionar* to inspire affection] : DEVOTEE, FAN

afield \ə-ˈfēld\ *adv or adj* **1** : to, in, or on the field **2** : away from home **3** : out of the way : ASTRAY

afire \ə-ˈfī(-ə)r\ *adj or adv* : being on fire : BURNING

AFL *abbr* American Football League

aflame \ə-ˈflām\ *adj or adv* : FLAMING

AFL–CIO *abbr* American Federation of Labor and Congress of Industrial Organizations

afloat \ə-ˈflōt\ *adj or adv* **1** : borne on or as if on the water **2** : CIRCULATING ⟨rumors were ~⟩ **3** : ADRIFT

aflut·ter \ə-ˈflə-tər\ *adj* **1** : FLUTTERING **2** : nervously excited ⟨~ at the news⟩

afoot \ə-ˈfu̇t\ *adv or adj* **1** : on foot **2** : in action : in progress

afore·men·tioned \ə-ˈfȯr-ˈmen-chənd\ *adj* : mentioned previously

afore·said \-ˌsed\ *adj* : said or named before

afore·thought \-ˌthȯt\ *adj* : PREMEDITATED ⟨with malice ~⟩

a for·ti·o·ri \ˌä-ˌfȯr-tē-ˈȯr-ē\ *adv* [NL, lit., from the stronger (argument)] : with even greater reason

afoul of \ə-ˈfau̇l-əv\ *prep* **1** : in or into conflict with **2** : in or into collision or entanglement with

Afr *abbr* Africa; African

afraid \ə-ˈfrād\ *adj* **1** : FRIGHTENED, FEARFUL **2** : filled with concern or regret ⟨~ I won't be able to go⟩

A-frame \ˈā-ˌfrām\ *n* : a building having triangular front and rear walls with the roof reaching to the ground

afresh \ə-'fresh\ *adv* : ANEW, AGAIN

Af·ri·can \'a-fri-kən\ *n* **1** : a native or inhabitant of Africa **2** : a person of African ancestry — **African** *adj*

Af·ri·can–Amer·i·can \-ə-'mer-ə-kən\ *n* : an American of African and esp. of black African descent — **African–American** *adj*

Af·ri·can·ized bee \'a-frə-kə-ˌnīzd-\ *n* : a highly aggressive hybrid honeybee accidentally produced from Brazilian and African stocks that has spread from So. America into Mexico and the southern U.S.

Africanized honeybee *n* : AFRICANIZED BEE

African violet *n* : a tropical African plant widely grown indoors for its velvety fleshy leaves and showy purple, pink, or white flowers

Af·ri·kaans \ˌa-fri-'käns\ *n* : a language developed from 17th century Dutch that is one of the official languages of the Republic of So. Africa

Afro *n, pl* **Afros** : a hairstyle of tight curls in a full evenly rounded shape

Af·ro–Amer·i·can \ˌa-frō-ə-'mer-ə-kən\ *n* : AFRICAN–AMERICAN — **Afro–American** *adj*

aft \'aft\ *adv* : near, toward, or in the stern of a ship or the tail of an aircraft

AFT *abbr* American Federation of Teachers

¹af·ter \'af-tər\ *adv* : AFTERWARD, SUBSEQUENTLY

²after *prep* **1** : behind in place **2** : later than ⟨~ dinner⟩ **3** : in pursuit or search of ⟨he's ~ your job⟩

³after *conj* : following the time when ⟨we will come ~ we make plans⟩

⁴after *adj* **1** : LATER ⟨in ~ years⟩ **2** : located toward the rear

af·ter·birth \'af-tər-ˌbərth\ *n* : the placenta and membranes of the fetus that are expelled after childbirth

af·ter·burn·er \-ˌbər-nər\ *n* : a device incorporated in the tail pipe of a turbojet engine for injecting fuel into the hot exhaust gases and burning it to provide extra thrust

af·ter·care \-ˌker\ *n* : the care, nursing, or treatment of a convalescent patient

af·ter·deck \-ˌdek\ *n* : the rear half of the deck of a ship

af·ter·ef·fect \-ə-ˌfekt\ *n* : an effect that follows its cause after an interval

af·ter·glow \-ˌglō\ *n* : a glow remaining where a light has disappeared

af·ter·im·age \-ˌim-ij\ *n* : a usu. visual sensation continuing after the stimulus causing it has ended

af·ter·life \-ˌlīf\ *n* : an existence after death

af·ter·math \-ˌmath\ *n* **1** : a second-growth crop esp. of hay **2** : CONSEQUENCES, EFFECTS ♦ *Synonyms* AFTEREFFECT, UPSHOT, RESULT, OUTCOME

af·ter·noon \ˌaf-tər-'nün\ *n* : the time between noon and evening

af·ter·shave \'af-tər-ˌshāv\ *n* : a usu. scented lotion for the face after shaving

af·ter·taste \-ˌtāst\ *n* : a sensation (as of flavor) continuing after the stimulus causing it has ended

af·ter·tax \'af-tər-'taks\ *adj* : remaining after payment of taxes and esp. of income tax ⟨an ~ profit⟩

af·ter·thought \-ˌthȯt\ *n* : an idea occurring later

af·ter·ward \-wərd\ *or* **af·ter·wards** \-wərdz\ *adv* : at a later time

Ag *symbol* [L *argentum*] silver

AG *abbr* **1** adjutant general **2** attorney general

again \ə-'gen, -'gin\ *adv* **1** : once more : ANEW ⟨come see us ~⟩ **2** : on the other hand ⟨we may, and ~ we may not⟩ **3** : in addition : BESIDES

against \ə-'genst\ *prep* **1** : in opposition to **2** : directly opposite to : FACING **3** : as defense from **4** : so as to touch or strike ⟨threw him ~ the wall⟩; *also* : TOUCHING

¹aga·pe \ä-'gä-pā, 'ä-gə-ˌpā\ *n* [LL, fr. Gk *agapē*, lit., love] : unselfish unconditional love for another

²agape \ə-'gāp\ *adj or adv* : having the mouth open in wonder or surprise : GAPING

agar \'ä-gär\ *n* **1** : a jellylike substance extracted from a red alga and used esp. as a gelling and stabilizing agent in foods **2** : a culture medium containing agar

agar–agar \ˌä-gär-'ä-ˌgär\ *n* : AGAR

ag·ate \'a-gət\ *n* **1** : a striped or clouded quartz **2** : a playing marble of agate or of glass

aga·ve \ə-'gä-vē\ *n* : any of a genus of spiny-leaved plants (as a century plant) related to the amaryllis

agcy *abbr* agency

¹age \'āj\ *n* **1** : the length of time during which a being or thing has lived or existed **2** : the time of life at which some particular qualification is achieved; *esp* : MAJORITY **3** : the latter part of life **4** : a long time **5** : a period in history

²age *vb* **aged; ag·ing** *or* **age·ing** **1** : to grow old or cause to grow old **2** : to become or cause to become mature or mellow

-age *n suffix* **1** : aggregate : collection ⟨track*age*⟩ **2** : action : process ⟨haul*age*⟩ **3** : cumulative result of ⟨break*age*⟩ **4** : rate of ⟨dos*age*⟩ **5** : house or place of ⟨orphan*age*⟩ **6** : state : rank ⟨vassal*age*⟩ **7** : fee : charge ⟨post*age*⟩

aged \'ā-jəd *for 1*; 'ājd *for 2*\ *adj* **1** : of advanced age **2** : having attained a specified age ⟨a man ~ 40 years⟩

age·ism \'ā-ˌji-zəm\ *n* : discrimination against persons of a particular age and esp. the elderly — **age·ist** \-jist\ *n*

age·less \'āj-ləs\ *adj* **1** : not growing old or showing the effects of age **2** : TIMELESS, ETERNAL ⟨~ truths⟩

agen·cy \'ā-jən-sē\ *n, pl* **-cies** **1** : one through which something is accomplished : INSTRUMENTALITY **2** : the office or function of an agent **3** : an establishment doing business for another **4** : an administrative division (as of a government) ✦ *Synonyms* MEANS, MEDI-UM, VEHICLE

agen·da \ə-'jen-də\ n : a list of things to be done : PROGRAM

agent \'ā-jənt\ n 1 : one that acts 2 : MEANS, INSTRUMENT 3 : a person acting or doing business for another 4 : a computer program designed to automate certain tasks (as gathering information online) ✦ *Synonyms* ATTORNEY, DEPUTY, PROXY, DELEGATE

Agent Orange n : an herbicide widely used in the Vietnam War that is composed of 2,4-D and 2,4,5-T and contains a toxic contaminant

agent pro·vo·ca·teur \'ä-,zhäⁿ-prō-,vä-kə-'tər, 'ä-jənt-\ n, pl **agents provocateurs** \'ä-,zhäⁿ-prō-,väk-ə-'tər, 'ä-jənts-prō-\ [F] : a person hired to infiltrate a group and incite its members to illegal action

age of consent : the age at which one is legally competent to give consent esp. to marriage or to sexual intercourse

age–old \'āj-'ōld\ adj : having existed for ages : ANCIENT

ag·er·a·tum \,a-jə-'rā-təm\ n, pl **-tums** also **-tum** : any of a genus of tropical American plants that are related to the daisies and have small showy heads of usu. blue or white flowers

age spots n pl : benign flat spots of dark pigmentation on the skin occurring esp. among older people

Ag·ge·us \'a-'gē-əs\ n : HAGGAI

¹**ag·glom·er·ate** \ə-'glä-mə-,rāt\ vb **-at·ed; -at·ing** [L *agglomerare* to heap up, join, fr. *ad-* to + *glomer-, glomus* ball] : to gather into a mass : CLUSTER — **ag·glom·er·a·tion** \-,glä-mə-'rā-shən\ n

²**ag·glom·er·ate** \-rət\ n : rock composed of volcanic fragments

ag·glu·ti·nate \ə-'glü-t⁵n-,āt\ vb **-nat·ed; -nat·ing** 1 : to cause to adhere : gather into a group or mass 2 : to cause (as red blood cells or bacteria) to collect into clumps — **ag·glu·ti·na·tion** \-,glü-t⁵n-'ā-shən\ n

ag·gran·dise Brit var of AGGRANDIZE

ag·gran·dize \ə-'gran-,dīz, 'a-grən-\ vb **-dized; -diz·ing** : to make great or greater ⟨~ an estate⟩ — **ag·gran·dize·ment** \ə-'gran-dəz-mənt, -,dīz-; ,a-grən-'dīz-\ n

ag·gra·vate \'a-grə-,vāt\ vb **-vat·ed; -vat·ing** 1 : to make more severe : INTENSIFY 2 : IRRITATE — **ag·gra·va·tion** \,a-grə-'vā-shən\ n

¹**ag·gre·gate** \'a-gri-gət\ adj : formed by the gathering of units into one mass

²**ag·gre·gate** \-,gāt\ vb **-gat·ed; -gat·ing** : to collect into one mass

³**ag·gre·gate** \-gət\ n : a mass or body of units or parts somewhat loosely associated with one another; also : the whole amount

ag·gre·ga·tion \,a-gri-'gā-shən\ n 1 : a group, body, or mass composed of many distinct parts 2 : the collecting of units or parts into a mass or whole

ag·gres·sion \ə-'gre-shən\ n 1 : an un-

provoked attack 2 : the practice of making attacks 3 : hostile, injurious, or destructive behavior or outlook esp. when caused by frustration — **ag·gres·sor** \-'gre-sər\ n

ag·gres·sive \ə-'gre-siv\ adj 1 : tending toward or exhibiting aggression; esp : marked by combative readiness 2 : marked by driving energy or initiative : ENTERPRISING 3 : more intensive or comprehensive esp. in dosage or extent — **ag·gres·sive·ly** adv — **ag·gres·sive·ness** n

ag·grieve \ə-'grēv\ vb **ag·grieved; ag·griev·ing** 1 : to cause grief to 2 : to inflict injury on : WRONG

ag·gro \'a-,grō\ adj : aggressive or aggressively daring in style or manner ⟨~ music⟩ ⟨~ surfing⟩

aghast \ə-'gast\ adj : struck with amazement or horror

ag·ile \'a-jəl\ adj : able to move quickly and easily — **ag·ile·ly** adv — **agil·i·ty** \ə-'ji-lə-tē\ n

ag·i·ta \'a-jə-tə\ n [southern It dial. pron. of It *acido*, lit., heartburn, acid] : a feeling of agitation or anxiety

ag·i·tate \'a-jə-,tāt\ vb **-tat·ed; -tat·ing** 1 : to move with an irregular rapid motion 2 : to stir up : EXCITE 3 : to discuss earnestly 4 : to attempt to arouse public feeling — **ag·i·ta·tion** \,a-jə-'tā-shən\ n — **ag·i·ta·tor** \'a-jə-,tā-tər\ n

ag·it·prop \'a-jət-,präp\ n [Russ] : political propaganda promulgated esp. through the arts

agleam \ə-'glēm\ adj : GLEAMING ⟨eyes ~ with tears⟩

aglit·ter \ə-'gli-tər\ adj : GLITTERING

aglow \ə-'glō\ adj : GLOWING

ag·nos·tic \ag-'näs-tik\ adj [Gk *agnōstos* unknown, unknowable, fr. *a-* un- + *gnōstos* known] : of or relating to the belief that the existence of any ultimate reality (as God) is unknown and prob. unknowable — **agnostic** n — **ag·nos·ti·cism** \-'näs-tə-,si-zəm\ n

ago \ə-'gō\ adj or adv : earlier than the present time ⟨10 years ~⟩

agog \ə-'gäg\ adj [MF *en gogues* in mirth] : full of excitement : EAGER

a–go–go \ä-'gō-,gō\ adj [*Whisky à Gogo*, café and disco in Paris, France, fr. F *à gogo* galore] : GO-GO

ag·o·nise Brit var of AGONIZE

ag·o·nize \'a-gə-,nīz\ vb **-nized; -niz·ing** : to suffer or cause to suffer agony — **ag·o·niz·ing·ly** adv

ag·o·ny \'a-gə-nē\ n, pl **-nies** [ME *agonie*, fr. L *agonia*, fr. Gk *agōnia* struggle, anguish, fr. *agōn* gathering, contest for a prize] : extreme pain of mind or body ✦ *Synonyms* SUFFERING, DISTRESS, MISERY

ago·ra \,ä-gə-'rä\ n, pl **ago·rot** \-'rōt\ — see *shekel* at MONEY table

ag·o·ra·pho·bia \,a-gə-rə-'fō-bē-ə\ n : abnormal fear of being in a helpless, embarrassing, or inescapable situation characterized esp. by avoidance of open or public places — **ag·o·ra·pho·bic** \-'fō-bik, -'fä-\ adj or n

agr *abbr* agricultural; agriculture

agrar·i·an \ə-ˈgrer-ē-ən\ *adj* **1** : of or relating to land or its ownership ⟨~ reforms⟩ **2** : of or relating to farmers or farming interests — **agrarian** *n* — **agrar·i·an·ism** *n*

agree \ə-ˈgrē\ *vb* **agreed; agree·ing 1** : ADMIT, CONCEDE ⟨~s that he was wrong⟩ **2** : to be similar : CORRESPOND ⟨both copies ~⟩ **3** : to express agreement or approval **4** : to be in harmony **5** : to settle by common consent **6** : to be fitting or healthful : SUIT ⟨this climate ~s with her⟩

agree·able \ə-ˈgrē-ə-bəl\ *adj* **1** : PLEASING, PLEASANT ⟨an ~ fragrance⟩ **2** : ready to consent ⟨I'm ~ to their proposal⟩ **3** : being in harmony : CONSONANT — **agree·able·ness** *n* — **agree·ably** \-blē\ *adv*

agree·ment \ə-ˈgrē-mənt\ *n* **1** : harmony of opinion or action **2** : mutual understanding or arrangement; *also* : a document containing such an arrangement

ag·ri·busi·ness \ˈa-grə-ˌbiz-nəs, -nəz\ *n* : an industry engaged in the manufacture and sale of farm equipment and supplies and in the production, processing, storage, and sale of farm commodities

agric *abbr* agricultural; agriculture

ag·ri·cul·ture \ˈa-gri-ˌkəl-chər\ *n* : FARMING, HUSBANDRY — **ag·ri·cul·tur·al** \ˌa-gri-ˈkəl-ch(ə-)rəl\ *adj* — **ag·ri·cul·tur·ist** \-ch(ə-)rist\ *or* **ag·ri·cul·tur·al·ist** \-ch(ə-)rə-list\ *n*

agron·o·my \ə-ˈgrä-nə-mē\ *n* : a branch of agriculture that deals with the raising of crops and the care of the soil — **ag·ro·nom·ic** \ˌa-grə-ˈnä-mik\ *adj* — **agron·o·mist** \ə-ˈgrä-nə-mist\ *n*

aground \ə-ˈgraůnd\ *adv or adj* : on or onto the bottom or shore ⟨ran ~⟩

agt *abbr* agent

ague \ˈā-gyü\ *n* : a fever (as malaria) with recurrent chills and sweating

ahead \ə-ˈhed\ *adv or adj* **1** : in or toward the front **2** : into or for the future ⟨plan ~⟩ **3** : in or toward a more advantageous position

ahead of *prep* **1** : in front or advance of **2** : in excess of : ABOVE

ahoy \ə-ˈhói\ *interj* — used in hailing ⟨ship ~⟩

AI *abbr* artificial intelligence

¹aid \ˈād\ *vb* : to provide with what is useful in achieving an end : ASSIST

²aid *n* **1** : ASSISTANCE **2** : ASSISTANT

AID *abbr* Agency for International Development

aide \ˈād\ *n* : a person who acts as an assistant; *esp* : a military officer assisting a superior

aide–de–camp \ˌād-di-ˈkamp, -ˈkäⁿ\ *n, pl* **aides–de–camp** \ˌādz-di-\ [F] : AIDE

AIDS \ˈādz\ *n* [*acquired immunodeficiency syndrome*] : a serious disease of the human immune system that is characterized by severe reduction in the numbers of helper T cells and increased vulnerability to life-threatening illnesses and that is caused by infection with HIV commonly transmitted in infected blood esp. during illicit intravenous drug use and in bodily secretions (as semen) during sexual intercourse

AIDS–related complex *n* : a group of symptoms (as fever, weight loss, and lymphadenopathy) that is associated with the presence of antibodies to HIV and is followed by the development of AIDS in a certain proportion of cases

AIDS virus *n* : HIV

ai·grette \ā-ˈgret, ˈā-,\ *n* [F, plume, egret] : a plume or decorative tuft for the head

ail \ˈāl\ *vb* **1** : to be the matter with : TROUBLE **2** : to be unwell

ai·lan·thus \ā-ˈlan-thəs\ *n* : any of a genus of Asian trees or shrubs with pinnate leaves and ill-scented greenish flowers; *esp* : TREE OF HEAVEN

ai·le·ron \ˈā-lə-ˌrän\ *n* : a movable part of an airplane wing used in banking

ail·ment \ˈāl-mənt\ *n* : a bodily disorder

¹aim \ˈām\ *vb* [ME, fr. AF *aesmer* & *esmer*; AF *aesmer*, fr. *a-* to (fr. L *ad-*) + *esmer* to estimate, fr. L *aestimare*] **1** : to point a weapon at an object **2** : to direct one's efforts : ASPIRE **3** : to direct to or toward a specified object or goal

²aim *n* **1** : the pointing of a weapon at an object **2** : the ability to hit a target **3** : OBJECT, PURPOSE ⟨my ~ is to win⟩ — **aim·less** \-ləs\ *adj* — **aim·less·ly** *adv* — **aim·less·ness** *n*

AIM *abbr* American Indian Movement

ain't \ˈānt\ **1** : are not **2** : is not **3** : am not — though disapproved by many and more common in less educated speech, used in both speech and writing to catch attention and to gain emphasis

Ai·nu \ˈī-nü\ *n, pl* **Ainu** *or* **Ainus 1** : a member of an indigenous people of northern Japan **2** : the language of the Ainu people

¹air \ˈer\ *n* **1** : the gaseous mixture surrounding the earth **2** : a light breeze **3** : MELODY, TUNE **4** : the outward appearance of a person or thing : MANNER **5** : an artificial manner **6** : COMPRESSED AIR ⟨~ sprayer⟩ **7** : AIRCRAFT ⟨traveled by ~⟩ **8** : AVIATION ⟨~ safety⟩ **9** : the medium of transmission of radio waves; *also* : RADIO, TELEVISION

²air *vb* **1** : to expose to the air **2** : to expose to public view

air bag *n* : a bag designed to inflate automatically to protect automobile occupants in case of collision

air·boat \ˈer-ˌbōt\ *n* : a shallow-draft boat driven by an airplane propeller

air·borne \-ˌbórn\ *adj* : done or being in the air

air brake *n* **1** : a brake operated by a piston driven by compressed air **2** : a surface projected into the airflow to lower an airplane's speed

air·brush \ˈer-ˌbrəsh\ *n* : a device for applying a fine spray (as of paint) by compressed air — **airbrush** *vb*

air con·di·tion·er \ˌer-kən-ˈdi-sh(ə-)nər\ *n* : an apparatus for filtering air and controlling its humidity and temperature — **air–con·di·tion** \-ˈdi-shən\ *vb*

air·craft \'er-,kraft\ *n, pl* **aircraft** : a vehicle for traveling through the air

aircraft carrier *n* : a warship with a deck on which airplanes can be launched and landed

air·drop \'er-,dräp\ *n* : delivery of cargo or personnel by parachute from an airplane in flight — **air·drop** *vb*

Aire·dale terrier \'er-,dāl-\ *n* : any of a breed of large terriers with a hard wiry coat

air·fare \'er-,fer\ *n* : fare for travel by airplane

air·field \-,fēld\ *n* : AIRPORT

air·flow \-,flō\ *n* : the motion of air relative to a body in it

air·foil \-,fȯi(-ə)l\ *n* : an airplane surface designed to produce reaction forces from the air through which it moves

air force *n* : the military organization of a nation for air warfare

air·frame \'er-,frām\ *n* : the structure of an aircraft, rocket, or missile without the power plant; *also* : AIRCRAFT

air·freight \-'frāt\ *n* : freight transport by aircraft in volume; *also* : the charge for this service

air gun *n* **1** : a gun operated by compressed air **2** : a hand tool that works by compressed air; *esp* : AIRBRUSH

air·head \'er-,hed\ *n* : a mindless or stupid person

air lane *n* : AIRWAY 1

air·lift \'er-,lift\ *n* : transportation (as of supplies or passengers) by aircraft — **airlift** *vb*

air·line \-,līn\ *n* : a transportation system using airplanes

air·lin·er \-,lī-nər\ *n* : a large passenger airplane operated by an airline

air lock *n* : an airtight chamber separating areas of different pressure

air·mail \'er-,māl\ *n* : the system of transporting mail by aircraft; *also* : mail so transported — **airmail** *vb*

air·man \-mən\ *n* **1** : AVIATOR, PILOT **2** : an enlisted man in the air force in one of the three ranks below sergeant

airman basic *n* : an enlisted man of the lowest rank in the air force

airman first class *n* : an enlisted man in the air force with a rank just below that of sergeant

air mass *n* : a large horizontally homogeneous body of air

air·mo·bile \'er-,mō-bəl, -,bēl\ *adj* : of, relating to, or being a military unit whose members are transported to combat areas usu. by helicopter

air·plane \-,plān\ *n* : a powered heavier-than-air aircraft that has fixed wings from which it derives lift

air·play \-,plā\ *n* : the playing of a musical recording on the air by a radio station

air pocket *n* : a condition of the atmosphere (as a local downdraft) that causes an airplane to drop suddenly

air police *n* : the military police of an air force

air·port \'er-,pȯrt\ *n* : a place from which aircraft operate that usu. has paved runways and a terminal

air rage *n* : an airline passenger's uncontrolled anger that is usu. expressed in aggressive or violent behavior

air raid *n* : an attack by armed airplanes on a surface target

air·ship \'er-,ship\ *n* : a lighter-than-air aircraft having propulsion and steering systems

air·sick \-,sik\ *adj* : affected with motion sickness associated with flying — **air·sick·ness** *n*

air·space \-,spās\ *n* : the space above a nation and under its jurisdiction

air·speed \-,spēd\ *n* : the speed of an object (as an airplane) with relation to the surrounding air

air·strip \-,strip\ *n* : a runway without normal airport facilities

air·tight \'er-'tīt\ *adj* **1** : so tightly sealed that no air can enter or escape **2** : leaving no opening for attack

air–to–air *adj* : launched from one airplane in flight at another; *also* : involving aircraft in flight

air·waves \'er-,wāvz\ *n pl* : AIR 9

air·way \-,wā\ *n* **1** : a regular route for airplanes **2** : AIRLINE

air·wor·thy \-,wər-thē\ *adj* : fit for operation in the air ⟨an ~ plane⟩ — **air·wor·thi·ness** *n*

airy \'er-ē\ *adj* **air·i·er; -est 1** : LOFTY ⟨~ perches⟩ **2** : lacking in reality : EMPTY **3** : DELICATE **4** : BREEZY

aisle \'ī(-ə)l\ *n* [ME *ile*, fr. AF *ele*, lit., wing, fr. L *ala*] **1** : the side of a church nave separated by piers from the nave proper **2** : a passage between sections of seats

ajar \ə-'jär\ *adj or adv* : partly open

AK *abbr* Alaska

aka *abbr* also known as

AKC *abbr* American Kennel Club

akim·bo \ə-'kim-bō\ *adj or adv* : having the hand on the hip and the elbow turned outward

akin \ə-'kin\ *adj* **1** : related by blood **2** : similar in kind

Al *symbol* aluminum

AL *abbr* **1** Alabama **2** American League **3** American Legion

¹-al *adj suffix* : of, relating to, or characterized by ⟨direction*al*⟩

²-al *n suffix* : action : process ⟨rehears*al*⟩

Ala *abbr* Alabama

al·a·bas·ter \'a-lə-,bas-tər\ *n* **1** : a compact fine-textured usu. white and translucent gypsum often carved into objects (as vases) **2** : a hard translucent calcite

à la carte \,a-lə-'kärt, ,ä-\ *adv or adj* [F] : with a separate price for each item on the menu

alac·ri·ty \ə-'la-krə-tē\ *n* : cheerful readiness : BRISKNESS

à la mode \,a-lə-'mōd, ,ä-\ *adj* [F, according to the fashion] **1** : FASHIONABLE, STYLISH **2** : topped with ice cream

¹alarm \ə-'lärm\ *also* **ala·rum** \ə-'lär-əm, -'ler-\ *n* [ME *alarme*, fr. MF, fr. OIt *all'arme*, lit., to arms] **1** : a warning signal or device **2** : the terror caused by sudden danger

²**alarm** *also* **alarum** *vb* **1** : to warn of danger **2** : FRIGHTEN

alarm·ist \ə-'lär-mist\ *n* : a person who alarms others esp. needlessly

alas \ə-'las\ *interj* — used to express unhappiness, pity, or concern

al·ba·core \'al-bə-ˌkȯr\ *n, pl* **-core** *or* **-cores** : a large tuna that is a source of canned tuna

Al·ba·nian \al-'bā-nē-ən\ *n* : a native or inhabitant of Albania

al·ba·tross \'al-bə-ˌtrȯs, -ˌträs\ *n, pl* **-tross** *or* **-tross·es** : any of a family of large web-footed seabirds

al·be·do \al-'bē-(ˌ)dō\ *n, pl* **-dos** : the fraction of incident radiation that is reflected by a body or surface

al·be·it \ȯl-'bē-ət, al-\ *conj* : even though : ALTHOUGH

al·bi·no \al-'bī-nō\ *n, pl* **-nos** : a person or animal lacking coloring matter in the skin, hair, and eyes — **al·bi·nism** \'al-bə-ˌni-zəm\ *n*

al·bum \'al-bəm\ *n* **1** : a book with blank pages used for making a collection (as of stamps or photographs) **2** : one or more recordings (as on tape or disk) produced as a single unit

al·bu·men \al-'byü-mən\ *n* **1** : the white of an egg **2** : ALBUMIN

al·bu·min \al-'byü-mən\ *n* : any of numerous water-soluble proteins of blood, milk, egg white, and plant and animal tissues

al·bu·min·ous \al-'byü-mə-nəs\ *adj* : containing or resembling albumen or albumin

al·bu·ter·ol \al-'byü-tə-ˌrȯl, -ˌrōl\ *n* : a drug used as an aerosol or in tablet form to treat asthma

alc *abbr* alcohol

al·cal·de \al-'käl-dē\ *n* : the chief administrative and judicial officer of a Spanish or Spanish-American town

al·ca·zar \ˈkä-zər, -ˈka-\ *n* [Sp *alcázar*, fr. Ar *al-qaṣr* the castle] : a Spanish fortress or palace

al·che·my \'al-kə-mē\ *n* : medieval chemistry chiefly concerned with efforts to turn base metals into gold — **al·che·mist** \'al-kə-mist\ *n*

al·co·hol \'al-kə-ˌhȯl\ *n* [NL, fr. ML, powdered antimony, fr. Sp, fr. Ar *al-kuḥul* the powdered antimony] **1** : a colorless flammable liquid that is the intoxicating agent in fermented and distilled liquors **2** : any of various carbon compounds similar to alcohol **3** : beverages containing alcohol

¹**al·co·hol·ic** \ˌal-kə-'hȯ-lik, -'hä-\ *adj* **1** : of, relating to, caused by, or containing alcohol **2** : affected with alcoholism — **al·co·hol·i·cal·ly** \-li-k(ə-)lē\ *adv*

²**alcoholic** *n* : a person affected with alcoholism

al·co·hol·ism \'al-kə-ˌhȯ-ˌli-zəm\ *n* : continued excessive and usu. uncontrollable use of alcoholic drinks; *also* : a complex chronic psychological and nutritional disorder associated with such use

al·cove \'al-ˌkōv\ *n* **1** : a nook or small recess opening off a larger room **2** : a niche or arched opening (as in a wall)

ald *abbr* alderman

al·der \'ȯl-dər\ *n* : any of a genus of trees or shrubs related to the birches and growing in wet areas

al·der·man \'ȯl-dər-mən\ *n* : a member of a city legislative body

ale \'āl\ *n* : an alcoholic beverage brewed from malt and hops that is usu. more bitter than beer

ale·a·tor·ic \ˌā-lē-ə-'tȯr-ik\ *adj* : characterized by chance or random elements ⟨~ music⟩

ale·a·to·ry \'ā-lē-ə-ˌtȯr-ē\ *adj* : ALEATORIC

alee \ə-'lē\ *adv* : on or toward the lee

ale·house \'āl-ˌhaus\ *n* : a place where ale is sold to be drunk on the premises

¹**alert** \ə-'lərt\ *adj* [It *all' erta*, lit., on the ascent] **1** : watchful against danger **2** : quick to perceive and act — **alert·ly** *adv* — **alert·ness** *n*

²**alert** *n* **1** : ALARM 1 **2** : the period during which an alert is in effect

³**alert** *vb* **1** : WARN **2** : to make aware of

Aleut \ˌa-lē-'üt, ə-'lüt\ *n* **1** : a member of a people of the Aleutian and Shumagin islands and the western part of Alaska Peninsula **2** : the language of the Aleuts

ale·wife \'āl-ˌwīf\ *n, pl* **ale·wives** \-ˌwīvz\ : a food fish related to the herring that is abundant esp. along the Atlantic coast

Al·ex·an·dri·an \ˌa-lig-'zan-drē-ən\ *adj* **1** : HELLENISTIC **2** : of or relating to Alexander the Great

al·ex·an·drine \-'zan-drən\ *n, often cap* : a line of six iambic feet

al·fal·fa \al-'fal-fə\ *n* : a leguminous plant widely grown for hay and forage

al·fres·co \al-'fres-kō\ *adj or adv* [It] : taking place in the open air

alg *abbr* algebra

al·ga \'al-gə\ *n, pl* **al·gae** \'al-(ˌ)jē\ : any of a group of lower plants having chlorophyll but no vascular system and including seaweeds and related freshwater plants — **al·gal** \-gəl\ *adj*

al·ge·bra \'al-jə-brə\ *n* [ML, fr. Ar *al-jabr*] : a generalization of arithmetic in which letters representing numbers are combined according to the rules of arithmetic — **al·ge·bra·ic** \ˌal-jə-'brā-ik\ *adj* — **al·ge·bra·i·cal·ly** \-'brā-ə-k(ə-)lē\ *adv*

Al·gon·qui·an \al-'gän-kwē-ən, -'gän-\ *or* **Al·gon·quin** \-kwən\ *n,* **1** *usu* Algonquin : a member of an American Indian people of the Ottawa River valley **2** *usu* Algonquian : a family of American Indian languages of eastern and central No. America

al·go·rithm \'al-gə-ˌri-thəm\ *n* : a procedure for solving a problem esp. in mathematics or computing — **al·go·rith·mic** \ˌal-gə-'rith-mik\ *adj* — **al·go·rith·mi·cal·ly** \-mi-k(ə-)lē\ *adv*

¹**alias** \'ā-lē-əs, 'āl-yəs\ *adv* [L, otherwise, fr. *alius* other] : otherwise called

²**alias** *n* : an assumed name

¹**al·i·bi** \'a-lə-ˌbī\ *n* [L, elsewhere, fr. *alius* other] **1** : a plea offered by an accused person of not having been at the scene of an offense **2** : an excuse (as for failure)

²**alibi** *vb* **-bied; -bi·ing** **1** : to furnish an excuse for **2** : to offer an excuse

¹**alien** \'ā-lē-ən, 'āl-yən\ *adj* **1** : belonging to another : FOREIGN **2** : EXOTIC 1

²**alien** *n* **1** : a foreign-born resident who has not been naturalized **2** : EXTRATER-RESTRIAL

alien·able \'āl-yə-nə-bəl, 'ā-lē-ə-nə-\ *adj* : transferable to the ownership of another ⟨~ property⟩

alien·ate \'ā-lē-ə-‚nāt, 'āl-yə-\ *vb* **-at·ed; -at·ing** **1** : to make hostile : ESTRANGE **2** : to transfer (property) to another — **alien·ation** \‚ā-lē-ə-'nā-shən, ‚āl-yə-\ *n*

alien·ist \'ā-lē-ə-nist, 'āl-yə-\ *n* : PSYCHIA-TRIST

¹**alight** \ə-'līt\ *vb* **alight·ed** *also* **alit** \ə-'lit\; **alight·ing** **1** : to get down (as from a vehicle) **2** : to come to rest from the air ✦ ***Synonyms*** SETTLE, LAND, PERCH

²**alight** *adj* : lighted up

align *also* **aline** \ə-'līn\ *vb* **1** : to bring into line **2** : to array on the side of or against a cause — **align·er** *n* — **alignment** *also* **aline·ment** *n*

¹**alike** \ə-'līk\ *adv* : EQUALLY ⟨denounced by teachers and students ~⟩

²**alike** *adj* : LIKE ⟨~ in their beliefs⟩ ✦ ***Synonyms*** AKIN, ANALOGOUS, SIMILAR, COMPARABLE

al·i·ment \'a-lə-mənt\ *n* : NOURISHMENT 1 — **aliment** *vb*

al·i·men·ta·ry \‚a-lə-'men-t(ə-)rē\ *adj* : of, relating to, or functioning in nourishment or nutrition

alimentary canal *n* : the tube that extends from the mouth to the anus and functions in the digestion and absorption of food and the elimination of residues

al·i·mo·ny \'a-lə-‚mō-nē\ *n, pl* **-nies** [L *alimonia* sustenance, fr. *alere* to nourish] : an allowance made to one spouse by the other for support pending or after legal separation or divorce

A–line \'ā-‚līn\ *adj* : having a flared bottom and a close-fitting top ⟨an ~ skirt⟩

alive \ə-'līv\ *adj* **1** : having life **2** : being in force or operation **3** : SENSITIVE ⟨~ to the danger⟩ **4** : ALERT, BRISK **5** : ANIMATED ⟨streets ~ with traffic⟩ — **alive·ness** *n*

alk *abbr* alkaline

al·ka·li \'al-kə-‚lī\ *n, pl* **-lies** *or* **-lis** **1** : a substance (as a hydroxide) that has a bitter taste and neutralizes acids **2** : a mixture of salts in the soil of some dry regions in such amount as to make ordinary farming impossible — **al·ka·line** \-kə-lən, -‚līn\ *adj* — **al·ka·lin·i·ty** \‚al-kə-'li-nə-tē\ *n*

al·ka·loid \'al-kə-‚lȯid\ *n* : any of various usu. basic and bitter organic compounds found esp. in seed plants

al·kane \'al-‚kān\ *n* : a hydrocarbon in which each carbon atom is bonded to 4 other atoms

al·kyd \'al-kəd\ *n* : any of numerous synthetic resins used esp. for protective coatings and in paint

¹**all** \'ȯl\ *adj* **1** : the whole of ⟨sat up ~ night⟩ **2** : every member of : EVERY

⟨~ manner of problems⟩ **4** : any whatever ⟨beyond ~ doubt⟩ **5** : nothing but ⟨~ ears⟩ **6** : being more than one person or thing ⟨who ~ is coming⟩

²**all** *adv* **1** : WHOLLY ⟨sat ~ alone⟩ **2** : selected as the best — used in combination ⟨*all*-state champs⟩ **3** : so much ⟨~ the better for it⟩ **4** : for each side ⟨the score is two ~⟩

³**all** *pron sing or pl* **1** : the whole number, quantity, or amount ⟨~ of it is gone⟩ **2** : EVERYBODY, EVERYTHING ⟨~ are members⟩ ⟨that is ~⟩

⁴**all** *n* : the whole of one's resources ⟨gave his ~⟩

Al·lah \'ä-lə, 'a-; 'ä-‚lä, ä-'lä\ *n* [Ar *allāh*] : GOD 1 — used in Islam

all along *adv* : all the time ⟨knew it *all along*⟩

all–Amer·i·can \‚ȯl-ə-'mer-ə-kən\ *adj* **1** : selected as the best in the U.S. **2** : composed wholly of American elements **3** : typical of the U.S. — **all–American** *n*

all–around \‚ȯl-ə-'raȯnd\ *adj* **1** : considered in all aspects ⟨best ~ performance⟩ **2** : competent in many fields : VERSATILE ⟨an ~ athlete⟩

al·lay \ə-'lā\ *vb* **1** : ALLEVIATE **2** : CALM ✦ ***Synonyms*** LIGHTEN, RELIEVE, EASE, ASSUAGE

all clear *n* : a signal that a danger has passed

al·lege \ə-'lej\ *vb* **al·leged; al·leg·ing** **1** : to assert without proof **2** : to offer as a reason — **al·le·ga·tion** \‚a-li-'gā-shən\ *n* — **al·leged** \ə-'lejd, -'le-jəd\ *adj* — **al·leg·ed·ly** \ə-'le-jəd-lē\ *adv*

al·le·giance \ə-'lē-jəns\ *n* **1** : loyalty owed by a citizen to a government **2** : loyalty to a person or cause

al·le·go·ry \'a-lə-‚gȯr-ē\ *n, pl* **-ries** : the expression through symbolism of truths or generalizations about human experience — **al·le·gor·i·cal** \‚a-lə-'gȯr-i-kəl\ *adj* — **al·le·gor·i·cal·ly** \-k(ə-)lē\ *adv*

¹**al·le·gro** \ə-'le-grō, -'lā-\ *n, pl* **-gros** : an allegro movement

²**allegro** *adv or adj* [It, merry] : at a brisk lively tempo — used as a direction in music

al·lele \ə-'lēl\ *n* : any of the alternative forms of a gene that may occur at a given site on a chromosome — **al·le·lic** \-'lē-lik, -'le-\ *adj*

al·le·lu·ia \‚a-lə-'lü-yə\ *interj* : HALLELUJAH

Al·len wrench \'a-lən-\ *n* [*Allen* Manufacturing Company, Hartford, Conn.] : an L-shaped hexagonal metal bar of which either end fits the socket of a screw or bolt

al·ler·gen \'a-lər-jən\ *n* : something that causes allergy — **al·ler·gen·ic** \‚a-lər-'je-nik\ *adj*

al·ler·gist \'a-lər-jist\ *n* : a specialist in allergies

al·ler·gy \'a-lər-jē\ *n, pl* **-gies** [G *Allergie*, fr. Gk *allos* other + *ergon* work] : exaggerated or abnormal reaction (as by sneezing) to substances or situations harmless to most people — **al·ler·gic** \ə-'lər-jik\ *adj*

al·le·vi·ate \ə-'lē-vē-ˌāt\ *vb* **-at·ed; -at·ing** : RELIEVE, LESSEN ⟨~ pain⟩ ◆ *Synonyms* LIGHTEN, MITIGATE, ALLAY — **al·le·vi·a·tion** \ə-ˌlē-vē-'ā-shən\ *n*

al·ley \'a-lē\ *n, pl* **alleys** **1** : a garden or park walk **2** : a place for bowling ·**3** : a narrow passageway esp. between buildings

al·ley–oop \ˌa-lē-'yüp\ *n* : a basketball play in which a player catches a pass above the basket and immediately dunks the ball

al·ley·way \'a-lē-ˌwā\ *n* : ALLEY 3

all–fired \'ȯl-ˌfī(-ə)rd\ *adv* : EXTREMELY, EXCESSIVELY ⟨~ stubborn⟩

All·hal·lows \ȯl-'ha-lōz\ *n, pl* **Allhallows** : ALL SAINTS' DAY

all hours *n pl* : a very late time ⟨stayed up until *all hours*⟩

al·li·ance \ə-'lī-əns\ *n* : a union to promote common interests ◆ *Synonyms* LEAGUE, COALITION, CONFEDERACY, FEDERATION

al·li·ga·tor \'a-lə-ˌgā-tər\ *n* [Sp *el lagarto* the lizard] : either of two large shortlegged reptiles resembling crocodiles but having a shorter and broader snout

alligator pear *n* : AVOCADO

al·lit·er·ate \ə-'li-tə-ˌrāt\ *vb* **-at·ed; -at·ing** **1** : to form an alliteration **2** : to arrange so as to make alliteration

al·lit·er·a·tion \ə-ˌli-tə-'rā-shən\ *n* : the repetition of initial sounds in adjacent words or syllables — **al·lit·er·a·tive** \-'li-tə-ˌrā-tiv\ *adj*

al·lo·cate \'a-lə-ˌkāt\ *vb* **-cat·ed; -cat·ing** : ALLOT, ASSIGN — **al·lo·ca·tion** \ˌa-lə-'kā-shən\ *n*

al·lot \ə-'lät\ *vb* **al·lot·ted; al·lot·ting** : to distribute as a share ◆ *Synonyms* ASSIGN, APPORTION, ALLOCATE — **al·lot·ment** *n*

all–out \'ȯl-'au̇t\ *adj* : made with maximum effort

¹all over *adv* : EVERYWHERE

²all over *prep* **1** : in eagerly affectionate, attentive, or aggressive pursuit **2** : in or into a state marked by excessive criticism

al·low \ə-'lau̇\ *vb* **1** : to assign as a share ⟨~ time for rest⟩ **2** : to count as a deduction **3** : to make allowance ⟨~ for expansion⟩ **4** : ADMIT, CONCEDE ⟨~ed that the situation was serious⟩ **5** : PERMIT ⟨~s the dog to roam⟩ — **al·low·able** *adj*

al·low·ance \-əns\ *n* **1** : an allotted share **2** : money given regularly for expenses **3** : a taking into account of extenuating circumstances

al·loy \'a-ˌlȯi, ə-'lȯi\ *n* **1** : a substance composed of metals melted together **2** : an admixture that lessens value — **al·loy** \ə-'lȯi, 'a-ˌlȯi\ *vb*

all right *adv* **1** — used interjectionally esp. to express agreement or resignation or to indicate the resumption of a discussion ⟨*all right*, let's go⟩ **2** : beyond doubt **3** : SATISFACTORILY ⟨does *all right* in school⟩ — **all right** *adj*

All Saints' Day *n* : a Christian feast on November 1 in honor of all the saints

All Souls' Day *n* : a day of prayer observed by some Christian churches on November 2 for the souls of the faithful departed

all·spice \'ȯl-ˌspīs\ *n* : the berry of a West Indian tree related to the European myrtle; *also* : the mildly pungent and aromatic spice made from it

all–star \'ȯl-ˌstär\ *n* : a member of a team of star performers — **all–star** *adj*

all–ter·rain vehicle *n* : a small motor vehicle with three or four wheels for use on a wide range of terrain

all told *adv* : with everything or everyone counted ⟨expecting eight guests *all told*⟩

al·lude \ə-'lüd\ *vb* **al·lud·ed; al·lud·ing** [L *alludere*, lit., to play with] : to refer indirectly — **al·lu·sion** \-'lü-zhən\ *n* — **al·lu·sive** \-'lü-siv\ *adj* — **al·lu·sive·ly** *adv* — **al·lu·sive·ness** *n*

al·lure \ə-'lu̇r\ *vb* **al·lured; al·lur·ing** : CHARM, ENTICE — **allure** *n* — **al·lur·ing·ly** *adv*

al·lu·vi·um \ə-'lü-vē-əm\ *n, pl* **-vi·ums** *or* **-via** \-vē-ə\ : soil material (as clay) deposited by running water — **al·lu·vi·al** \-vē-əl\ *adj or n*

all–wheel \'ȯl-ˌwēl\ *adj* : acting independently on or by means of all four wheels of a vehicle

al·ly \ə-'lī, 'a-ˌlī\ *vb* **al·lied; al·ly·ing** : to enter into an alliance — **al·ly** \'a-ˌlī, ə-'lī\ *n*

-ally *adv suffix* : ²-LY ⟨specific*ally*⟩

al·ma ma·ter \ˌal-mə-'mä-tər\ *n* [L, fostering mother] **1** : an educational institute that one has attended **2** : the song or hymn of an alma mater

al·ma·nac \'ȯl-mə-ˌnak, 'al-\ *n* **1** : a publication esp. of astronomical and meteorological data **2** : a usu. annual publication of miscellaneous information

al·man·dite \'al-mən-ˌdīt\ *n* : a deep red garnet

al·mighty \ȯl-'mī-tē\ *adj* **1** *often cap* : having absolute power over all ⟨*Almighty* God⟩ **2** : relatively unlimited in power — **al·might·i·ness** *n*

Almighty *n* : GOD 1

al·mond \'ä-mənd, 'a-\ *n* : a small tree related to the peach; *also* : the edible nutlike kernel of its fruit

al·mo·ner \'al-mə-nər, 'ä-mə-\ *n* : a person who distributes alms

al·most \'ȯl-ˌmōst, ȯl-'mōst\ *adv* : very nearly but not exactly

alms \'ämz, 'älmz\ *n, pl* **alms** [ME *almesse, almes,* fr. OE *ælmesse, ælms,* fr. L *eleemosyna* alms, fr. Gk *eleēmosynē* pity, alms, fr. *eleēmōn* merciful, fr. *eleos* pity] : something given freely to relieve the poor

alms·house \-ˌhau̇s\ *n* : POORHOUSE

al·oe \'a-lō\ *n* **1** : any of a large genus of succulent chiefly southern African plants related to the lilies **2** *pl* : the dried juice of the leaves of an aloe used esp. formerly as a laxative

aloe vera \-'ver-ə, -'vir-\ *n* : an aloe with leaves that yield a jellylike emollient extract used esp. in cosmetics; *also* : this extract

aloft \ə-ˈlóft\ *adv* **1** : high in the air **2** : in flight

alo·ha \ə-ˈlō-ə, ä-ˈlō-hä\ *interj* [Hawaiian] — used to greet or bid farewell

alone \ə-ˈlōn\ *adj* **1** : separated from others **2** : not including anyone or anything else : ONLY ⟨she ~ knows why⟩ ♦ **Synonyms** LONELY, LONESOME, LONE, SOLITARY, **alone** *adv*

¹**along** \ə-ˈlóŋ\ *prep* **1** : in a line matching the direction of ⟨sail ~ the coast⟩ **2** : at a point on or during ⟨stopped ~ the way⟩

²**along** *adv* **1** : FORWARD, ON ⟨move ~⟩ **2** : as a companion ⟨bring her ~⟩ **3** : at an advanced point ⟨plans are far ~⟩

along·shore \ə-ˈlóŋ-ˈshòr\ *adv or adj* : along the shore or coast ⟨walked ~⟩

¹**along·side** \-ˌsīd\ *adv* : along or by the side

²**alongside** *prep* **1** : along or by the side of **2** : in association with

alongside of *prep* : ALONGSIDE

aloof \ə-ˈlüf\ *adj* : removed or distant physically or emotionally — **aloof·ly** *adv* — **aloof·ness** *n*

al·o·pe·cia \ˌa-lə-ˈpē-sh(ē-)ə\ *n* : BALDNESS

aloud \ə-ˈlaùd\ *adv* : with the speaking voice ⟨read ~⟩

alp \ˈalp\ *n* : a high rugged mountain

al·pac·a \al-ˈpa-kə\ *n* : a domesticated mammal esp. of Peru that is related to the llama; *also* : its woolly hair or a thin cloth made from this hair

al·pha \ˈal-fə\ *n* **1** : the 1st letter of the Greek alphabet — A or α **2** : something first : BEGINNING

al·pha·bet \ˈal-fə-ˌbet\ *n* : the set of letters or characters used in writing a language

al·pha·bet·i·cal \ˌal-fə-ˈbe-ti-kəl\ *or* **al·pha·bet·ic** \-ˈbe-tik\ *adj* **1** : arranged in the order of the letters of the alphabet **2** : of or employing an alphabet — **al·pha·bet·i·cal·ly** \-ti-k(ə-)lē\ *adv*

al·pha·bet·ize \ˈal-fə-bə-ˌtīz\ *vb* **-ized**; **-iz·ing** : to arrange in alphabetical order — **al·pha·bet·iz·er** *n*

al·pha·nu·mer·ic \ˌal-fə-nù-ˈmer-ik, -nyù-\ *adj* : consisting of letters and numbers and often other symbols ⟨an ~ code⟩; *also* : being a character in an alphanumeric system

alpha particle *n* : a positively charged particle identical with the nucleus of a helium atom that is ejected at high speed in certain radioactive transformations

alpha rhythm *n* : ALPHA WAVE

alpha wave *n* : an electrical rhythm of the brain often associated with a state of wakeful relaxation

Al·pine \ˈal-ˌpīn\ *adj* **1** : relating to, located in, or resembling the Alps **2** *often not cap* : of, relating to, or growing on upland slopes above timberline **3** : of or relating to competitive ski events consisting of slalom and downhill racing

al·ready \ól-ˈre-dē\ *adv* : by this time : PREVIOUSLY

al·right \ól-ˈrīt\ *adv* : ALL RIGHT

al·so \ˈól-sō\ *adv* : in addition : TOO

al·so-ran \-ˌran\ *n* **1** : a horse or dog that finishes out of the money in a race **2** : a contestant that does not win

alt *abbr* **1** alternate **2** altitude

Alta *abbr* Alberta

al·tar \ˈól-tər\ *n* **1** : a structure on which sacrifices are offered or incense is burned **2** : a table used as a center of ritual or worship

altar server *n* : a boy or girl who assists the celebrant at a church service

¹**al·ter** \ˈól-tər\ *vb* **al·tered**; **al·ter·ing** \-t(ə-)riŋ\ **1** : to make or become different **2** : CASTRATE, SPAY — **al·ter·able** \ˈól-tə-rə-bəl\ *adj* — **al·ter·a·tion** \ˌól-tə-ˈrā-shən\ *n*

²**alter** *abbr* alteration

al·ter·ca·tion \ˌól-tər-ˈkā-shən\ *n* : a noisy or angry dispute

al·ter ego \ˌól-tər-ˈē-gō\ *n* [L, lit., second I] : a second self; *esp* : a trusted friend

al·ter·i·ty \ól-ˈter-ə-tē\ *n* : the quality or state of being radically alien to the conscious self or a particular cultural orientation

¹**al·ter·nate** \ˈól-tər-nət, ˈal-\ *adj* **1** : arranged or succeeding by turns **2** : every other **3** : being an alternative ⟨an ~ route⟩ — **al·ter·nate·ly** *adv*

²**al·ter·nate** \-ˌnāt\ *vb* **-nat·ed**; **-nat·ing** : to occur or cause to occur by turns — **al·ter·na·tion** \ˌól-tər-ˈnā-shən, ˌal-\ *n*

³**alternate** *n* : SUBSTITUTE

alternating current *n* : an electric current that reverses its direction at regular intervals

al·ter·na·tive \ól-ˈtər-nə-tiv, al-\ *adj* **1** : offering a choice ⟨several ~ plans⟩ **2** : different from the usual or conventional — **alternative** *n*

alternative medicine *n* : any of various systems of healing (as homeopathy) not typically practiced in conventional Western medicine

al·ter·na·tor \ˈól-tər-ˌnā-tər, ˈal-\ *n* : an electric generator for producing alternating current

al·though *also* **al·tho** \ól-ˈthō\ *conj* : in spite of the fact that : even though

al·tim·e·ter \al-ˈti-mə-tər, ˈal-tə-ˌmē-tər\ *n* : an instrument for measuring altitude

al·ti·tude \ˈal-tə-ˌtüd, -ˌtyüd\ *n* **1** : angular distance above the horizon **2** : vertical distance : HEIGHT **3** : the perpendicular distance in a geometric figure from the vertex to the base, from the vertex of an angle to the side opposite, or from the base to a parallel side or face

al·to \ˈal-tō\ *n, pl* **altos** [It, lit., high, fr. L *altus*] : the lower female voice part in a 4-part chorus; *also* : a singer having this voice or part

¹**al·to·geth·er** \ˌól-tə-ˈge-thər\ *adv* **1** : WHOLLY ⟨stopped raining ~⟩ **2** : in all ⟨spent $100 ~⟩ **3** : on the whole ⟨~ their efforts were successful⟩

²**altogether** *n* : NUDE ⟨posed in the ~⟩

al·tru·ism \ˈal-trü-ˌi-zəm\ *n* [F *altruisme*, fr. *autrui* other people, fr. OF, oblique case form of *autre* other, fr. L *alter*] : unselfish interest in the welfare of others —

al·tru·ist \-ist\ *n* — **al·tru·is·tic** \,al-trü-'is-tik\ *adj* — **al·tru·is·ti·cal·ly** \-ti-k(ə-)lē\ *adv*

al·um \'a-ləm\ *n* : either of two colorless crystalline aluminum-containing compounds used esp. as an emetic or as an astringent and styptic

alu·mi·na \ə-'lü-mə-nə\ *n* : the oxide of aluminum occurring in nature as corundum and in bauxite

al·u·min·i·um \,al-yə-'mi-nē-əm\ *n*, *chiefly Brit* : ALUMINUM

alu·mi·nize \ə-'lü-mə-,nīz\ *vb* **-nized; -niz·ing** : to treat with aluminum

alu·mi·num \ə-'lü-mə-nəm\ *n* : a silver-white malleable ductile light metallic element that is the most abundant metal in the earth's crust

aluminum oxide *n* : ALUMINA

alum·na \ə-'ləm-nə\ *n, pl* **-nae** \-(,)nē\ : a woman graduate or former student of a college or school

alum·nus \ə-'ləm-nəs\ *n, pl* **-ni** \-,nī\ [L, foster son, pupil, fr. *alere* to nourish] : a graduate or former student of a college or school

al·ways \'ȯl-wēz, -wəz, -(,)wāz\ *adv* **1** : at all times : INVARIABLY **2** : FOREVER

Alz·hei·mer's disease \'älts-,hī-mərz-, 'alts-\ *n* : a degenerative brain disease of unknown cause that is characterized esp. by progressive mental deterioration and memory loss

am *pres 1st sing of* BE

¹Am *abbr* America; American

²Am *symbol* americium

¹AM \'ā-,em\ *n* : a broadcasting system using amplitude modulation; *also* : a radio receiver for broadcasts made by such a system

²AM *abbr* **1** ante meridiem — often not cap. and often punctuated **2** [NL *artium magister*] master of arts

AMA *abbr* American Medical Association

amah \'ä-(,)mä\ *n* : a female servant in eastern Asia; *esp* : a Chinese nurse

amain \ə-'mān\ *adv, archaic* : with full force or speed

amal·gam \ə-'mal-gəm\ *n* **1** : an alloy of mercury with another metal used in making dental cements **2** : a mixture of different elements

amal·gam·ate \ə-'mal-gə-,māt\ *vb* **-at·ed; -at·ing** : to unite or merge into one body — **amal·gam·a·tion** \-,mal-gə-'mā-shən\ *n*

aman·u·en·sis \ə-,man-yə-'wen-səs\ *n; pl* **-en·ses** \-,sēz\ : one employed to write from dictation or to copy what another has written : SECRETARY

am·a·ranth \'a-mə-,ranth\ *n* **1** : any of a large genus of coarse herbs sometimes grown for their showy flowers **2** : a flower that never fades

am·a·ran·thine \,a-mə-'ran-thən, -,thīn\ *adj* **1** : relating to or resembling an amaranth **2** : UNDYING

am·a·ryl·lis \,a-mə-'ri-ləs\ *n* : any of various plants related to the lilies; *esp* : an autumn-flowering South African bulbous

herb widely grown for its large showy red to whitish flowers

amass \ə-'mas\ *vb* : ACCUMULATE

am·a·teur \'a-mə-(,)tər, -,tür, -,tyür, -,chür, -chər\ *n* [F, fr. L *amator* lover, fr. *amare* to love] **1** : a person who engages in a pursuit for pleasure and not as a profession **2** : a person who is not expert — **am·a·teur·ish** \,a-mə-'tər-ish, -'tür-, -'tyür-, -'chür-, -'chər-\ *adj* — **am·a·teur·ism** \'a-mə-(,)tər-i-zəm, -,tür-, -,tyür-, -,chür-, -,chər-\ *n*

am·a·tive \'a-mə-tiv\ *adj* : indicative of love : AMOROUS — **am·a·tive·ly** *adv* — **am·a·tive·ness** *n*

am·a·to·ry \'a-mə-,tȯr-ē\ *adj* : of or expressing sexual love

amaze \ə-'māz\ *vb* **amazed; amaz·ing** : to fill with wonder : ASTOUND **♦ Synonyms** ASTONISH, SURPRISE, DUMBFOUND — **amaze·ment** *n* — **amaz·ing·ly** *adv*

am·a·zon \'a-mə-,zän, -zən\ *n* **1** *cap* : a member of a race of female warriors of Greek mythology **2** : a tall strong often masculine woman — **am·a·zo·ni·an** \,a-mə-'zō-nē-ən\ *adj, often cap*

amb *abbr* ambassador

am·bas·sa·dor \am-'ba-sə-dər\ *n* : a representative esp. of a government — **am·bas·sa·do·ri·al** \-,ba-sə-'dȯr-ē-əl\ *adj* — **am·bas·sa·dor·ship** *n*

am·ber \'am-bər\ *n* : a yellowish or brownish fossil resin used esp. for ornamental objects; *also* : the color of this resin

am·ber·gris \'am-bər-,gris, -,grēs\ *n* : a waxy substance from the sperm whale used in making perfumes

am·bi·dex·trous \,am-bi-'dek-strəs\ *adj* : using both hands with equal ease — **am·bi·dex·trous·ly** *adv*

am·bi·ence *or* **am·bi·ance** \'am-bē-əns, äⁿ-'byäⁿs\ *n* : a pervading atmosphere

¹am·bi·ent \'am-bē-ənt\ *adj* : existing on all sides

²ambient *n* : music intended to serve as an unobtrusive accompaniment to other activities

am·big·u·ous \am-'bi-gyə-wəs\ *adj* : capable of being understood in more than one way — **am·bi·gu·i·ty** \,am-bə-'gyü-ə-tē\ *n* — **am·big·u·ous·ly** *adv*

am·bi·tion \am-'bi-shən\ *n* [ME, fr. MF or L; MF, fr. L *ambition-, ambitio*, lit., act of soliciting for votes, fr. *ambire* to go around] : eager desire for success or power

am·bi·tious \-shəs\ *adj* : characterized by ambition — **am·bi·tious·ly** *adv* — **am·bi·tious·ness** *n*

am·biv·a·lence \am-'bi-və-ləns\ *n* : simultaneous attraction toward and repulsion from a person, object, or action — **am·biv·a·lent** \-lənt\ *adj*

¹am·ble \'am-bəl\ *vb* **am·bled; am·bling** \-b(ə-)liŋ\ : to go at or in an amble

²amble *n* : an easy gait esp. of a horse

am·bro·sia \am-'brō-zh(ē-)ə\ *n* : the food of the Greek and Roman gods — **am·bro·sial** \-zh(ē-)əl\ *adj*

am·bu·lance \'am-byə-ləns\ n : a vehicle equipped for carrying the injured or sick

am·bu·lant \'am-byə-lənt\ adj : AMBULATORY

¹**am·bu·la·to·ry** \'am-byə-lə-₁tōr-ē\ adj **1** : of, relating to, or adapted to walking **2** : able to walk or move about

²**ambulatory** n, pl **-ries** : a sheltered place (as in a cloister) for walking

am·bus·cade \'am-bə-₁skād\ n : AMBUSH

am·bush \'am-₁bùsh\ n : a trap in which concealed persons wait to attack by surprise — **ambush** vb

amdt abbr amendment

ameba, ameboid var of AMOEBA, AMOEBOID

ame·lio·rate \ə-'mēl-yə-₁rāt\ vb **-rat·ed; -rat·ing** : to make or grow better : IMPROVE — **ame·lio·ra·tion** \-₁mēl-yə-'rā-shən\ n

amen \(₁)ā-'men, (₁)ä-\ interj — used esp. at the end of prayers to affirm or express approval

ame·na·ble \ə-'mē-nə-bəl, -'me-\ adj **1** : ANSWERABLE ⟨~ to the law⟩ **2** : COMPLIANT

amend \ə-'mend\ vb **1** : to change for the better : IMPROVE **2** : to alter formally in phraseology — **amend·able** \-'men-də-bəl\ adj

amend·ment \ə-'mend-mənt\ n **1** : correction of faults **2** : the process of amending a parliamentary motion or a constitution; also : the alteration so proposed or made

amends \ə-'mendz\ n sing or pl : compensation for injury or loss

ame·ni·ty \ə-'me-nə-tē, -'mē-\ n, pl **-ties 1** : AGREEABLENESS **2** : a gesture observed in social relationships **3** : something that serves as a comfort or convenience

Amer abbr America; American

amerce \ə-'mərs\ vb **amerced; amerc·ing 1** : to penalize by a fine determined by the court **2** : PUNISH — **amerce·ment** n

Amer·i·ca·na \ə-₁mer-ə-'kä-nə, -'kä-\ n pl : materials concerning or characteristic of America, its civilization, or its culture

American Indian n : a member of any of the aboriginal peoples of No. and So. America except the Eskimos

Amer·i·can·ism \ə-'mer-ə-kə-₁ni-zəm\ n **1** : a characteristic feature of English as used in the U.S. **2** : attachment or loyalty to the traditions, interests, or ideals of the U.S. **3** : a custom or trait peculiar to the U.S. or to Americans

Amer·i·can·ize \ə-'mer-ə-kə-₁nīz\ vb : to make or become American — **Amer·i·can·i·za·tion** \ə-₁mer-ə-kə-nə-'zā-shən\ n

Amer·i·can·ness \ə-'mer-ə-kən-nəs\ n : the quality or state of being American

American plan n : a hotel plan whereby the daily rates cover the cost of room and three meals

American Sign Language n : a sign language for the deaf in which meaning is conveyed by a system of hand gestures and placement

amer·i·ci·um \₁am-ə-'rish-ē-əm, -'ris-\ n : a radioactive metallic chemical element produced artificially from plutonium

AmerInd abbr American Indian

Am·er·in·di·an \₁a-mə-'rin-dē-ən\ n : AMERICAN INDIAN — **Amerindian** adj

am·e·thyst \'a-mə-thəst\ n [ME amatiste, fr. AF & L; AF, fr. L amethystus, fr. Gk amethystos, lit., remedy against drunkenness, fr. a- not + methyein to be drunk, fr. methy wine] : a gemstone consisting of clear purple or bluish-violet quartz

ami·a·ble \'ā-mē-ə-bəl\ adj **1** : AGREEABLE ⟨an ~ comedy⟩ **2** : having a friendly and sociable disposition — **ami·a·bil·i·ty** \₁ā-mē-ə-'bi-lə-tē\ n — **ami·a·ble·ness** n — **ami·a·bly** \'ā-mē-ə-blē\ adv

am·i·ca·ble \'a-mi-kə-bəl\ adj : FRIENDLY, PEACEABLE ⟨an ~ settlement of differences⟩ — **am·i·ca·bil·i·ty** \₁a-mi-kə-'bi-lə-tē\ n — **am·i·ca·bly** \'a-mi-kə-blē\ adv

amid \ə-'mid\ or **amidst** \-'midst\ prep : in or into the middle of : AMONG

amid·ships \ə-'mid-₁ships\ adv : in or near the middle of a ship

ami·no acid \ə-'mē-nō-\ n : any of numerous nitrogen-containing acids that include some which are used by cells to build proteins

amir var of EMIR

¹**amiss** \ə-'mis\ adv **1** : WRONGLY **2** : ASTRAY ⟨something had gone ~⟩ **3** : IMPERFECTLY

²**amiss** adj **1** : WRONG **2** : out of place

am·i·ty \'a-mə-tē\ n, pl **-ties** : FRIENDSHIP; esp : friendly relations between nations

am·me·ter \'a-₁mē-tər\ n : an instrument for measuring electric current esp. in amperes

am·mo \'a-mō\ n : AMMUNITION

am·mo·nia \ə-'mō-nyə\ n [NL, fr. L sal ammoniacus sal ammoniac (ammonium chloride), lit., salt of Ammon, fr. Gk ammōniakos of Ammon, fr. Ammōn Ammon, an Egyptian god near one of whose temples it was extracted] **1** : a colorless gaseous compound of nitrogen and hydrogen used in refrigeration and in the making of fertilizers and explosives **2** : a solution (**ammonia water**) of ammonia in water

am·mo·ni·um \ə-'mō-nē-əm\ n : an ion or chemical group derived from ammonia by combination with hydrogen

ammonium chloride n : a white crystalline volatile salt used in batteries and as an expectorant

am·mu·ni·tion \₁am-yə-'ni-shən\ n **1** : projectiles fired from guns **2** : explosive items used in war **3** : material for use in attack or defense

Amn abbr airman

am·ne·sia \am-'nē-zhə\ n **1** : abnormal loss of memory **2** : the selective overlooking of events or acts not favorable to one's purpose — **am·ne·si·ac** \-zhē-₁ak, -zē-\ or **am·ne·sic** \-zik, -sik\ adj or n

am·nes·ty \'am-nə-stē\ n, pl **-ties** : an act

granting a pardon to a group of individuals — **amnesty** *vb*

am·ni·o·cen·te·sis \,am-nē-ō-,sen-'tē-səs\ *n, pl* **-te·ses** \-,sēz\ : the surgical insertion of a hollow needle through the abdominal wall and uterus of a pregnant female esp. to obtain fluid used to check the fetus for chromosomal abnormality and to determine sex

am·ni·ot·ic fluid \,am-nē-'ä-tik-\ *n* : the watery fluid in which the embryo or fetus is immersed

amoe·ba *also* **ame·ba** \ə-'mē-bə\ *n, pl* **-bas** *or* **-bae** \-(,)bē\ : any of various tiny one-celled protozoans that lack permanent cell organs and occur esp. in water and soil — **amoe·bic** \-bik\ *adj*

amoe·boid *also* **ame·boid** \-,bȯid\ *adj* : resembling an amoeba esp. in moving or readily changing shape

amok \ə-'mək, -'mäk\ *or* **amuck** \-'mək\ *adv* : in a violent, frenzied, or uncontrolled manner ⟨run ∼⟩

among \ə-'məŋ\ *also* **amongst** \-'məŋst\ *prep* **1** : in or through the midst of **2** : in the number, class, or company of **3** : in shares to each of **4** : by common action of

amon·til·la·do \ə-,män-tə-'lä-dō\ *n, pl* **-dos** [Sp] : a medium dry sherry

amor·al \ā-'mȯr-əl\ *adj* **1** : neither moral nor immoral; *esp* : being outside the sphere to which moral judgments apply **2** : lacking moral sensibility — **amor·al·ly** *adv*

am·o·rous \'a-mə-rəs\ *adj* **1** : inclined to love **2** : being in love **3** : of or indicative of love — **am·o·rous·ly** *adv* — **am·o·rous·ness** *n*

amor·phous \ə-'mȯr-fəs\ *adj* **1** : SHAPELESS, FORMLESS **2** : not crystallized

am·or·tize \'a-mər-,tīz, ə-'mȯr-\ *vb* **-tized; -tiz·ing** : to extinguish (as a mortgage) usu. by payment on the principal at the time of each periodic interest payment — **amor·ti·za·tion** \,a-mər-tə-'zā-shən, ə-,mȯr-\ *n*

Amos \'ā-məs\ — see BIBLE table

¹**amount** \ə-'maunt\ *vb* **1** : to be equivalent **2** : to reach a total : add up

²**amount** *n* **1** : the total number or quantity **2** : a principal sum plus the interest on it

amour \ə-'mur, ä-, a-\ *n* **1** : a love affair esp. when illicit **2** : LOVER

amour pro·pre \,a-,mur-'prȯprª, ä-, -'prȯprª\ *n* [F] : SELF-ESTEEM

¹**amp** \'amp\ *n* **1** : AMPERE **2** : AMPLIFIER; *also* : a unit consisting of an electronic amplifier and a loudspeaker

²**amp** *vb* : EXCITE, ENERGIZE ⟨tried to ∼ up the crowd⟩

am·per·age \'am-p(ə-)rij\ *n* : the strength of a current of electricity expressed in amperes

am·pere \'am-,pir\ *n* : a unit of electric current equivalent to a steady current produced by one volt applied across a resistance of one ohm

am·per·sand \'am-pər-,sand\ *n* [alter. of *and per se and*, spoken form of the phrase *& per se and*, lit., (the character) *&* by itself (stands for the word) *and*] : a character *&* used for the word *and*

am·phet·amine \am-'fe-tə-,mēn, -mən\ *n* : a compound or one of its derivatives that stimulates the central nervous system and is used esp. to treat hyperactive children and to suppress appetite

am·phib·i·an \am-'fi-bē-ən\ *n* **1** : an amphibious organism; *esp* : any of a class of vertebrate animals (as frogs and salamanders) intermediate between fishes and reptiles **2** : an airplane that can land on and take off from either land or water

am·phib·i·ous \am-'fi-bē-əs\ *adj* [Gk *amphibios*, lit., living a double life, fr. *amphi-* + *bios* mode of life] **1** : able to live both on land and in water **2** : adapted for both land and water **3** : made by joint action of land, sea, and air forces invading from the water; *also* : trained for such action

am·phi·bole \'am-fə-,bōl\ *n* : any of a group of rock-forming minerals of similar crystal structure

am·phi·the·ater \'am-fə-,thē-ə-tər\ *n* **1** : an oval or circular structure with rising tiers of seats around an arena **2** : a very large auditorium

am·pho·ra \'am-fə-rə\ *n, pl* **-rae** \-,rē\ *or* **-ras** : an ancient Greek jar or vase with two handles that rise almost to the level of the mouth

am·ple \'am-pəl\ *adj* **am·pler** \-plər\; **am·plest** \-pləst\ **1** : LARGE, CAPACIOUS **2** : enough to satisfy : ABUNDANT — **am·ply** \-plē\ *adv*

am·pli·fy \'am-plə-,fī\ *vb* **-fied; -fy·ing 1** : to expand by extended treatment **2** : to increase in magnitude or strength; *esp* : to make louder — **am·pli·fi·ca·tion** \,am-plə-fə-'kā-shən\ *n* — **am·pli·fi·er** \'am-plə-,fī(-ə)r\ *n*

am·pli·tude \-,tüd, -,tyüd\ *n* **1** : ample extent : FULLNESS **2** : the extent of a vibratory movement (as of a pendulum) **3** : the height or depth of an oscillation (as of an alternating current or a radio wave) compared to its average value

amplitude modulation *n* : modulation of the amplitude of a radio carrier wave in accordance with the strength of the signal; *also* : a broadcasting system using such modulation

am·poule *or* **am·pule** *also* **am·pul** \'am-,pyül, -,pül\ *n* : a small sealed bulbous glass vessel used to hold a solution for hypodermic injection

am·pu·tate \'am-pyə-,tāt\ *vb* **-tat·ed; -tat·ing** : to cut off ⟨∼ a leg⟩ — **am·pu·ta·tion** \,am-pyə-'tā-shən\ *n*

am·pu·tee \,am-pyə-'tē\ *n* : one who has had a limb amputated

AMSLAN *abbr* American Sign Language

amt *abbr* amount

amuck *var of* AMOK

am·u·let \'am-yə-lət\ *n* : an ornament worn as a charm against evil

amuse \ə-'myüz\ *vb* **amused; amus·ing** : to entertain in a light or playful manner : DIVERT — **amuse·ment** *n* — **amusing** *adj* — **amus·ing·ly** *adv*

amusement park *n* : a commercially operated park having various devices (as a roller coaster) for entertainment and booths for selling refreshments

AM·VETS \'am-ˌvets\ *abbr* American Veterans (of World War II)

am·y·lase \'a-mə-ˌlās, -ˌlāz\ *n* : any of several enzymes that accelerate the breakdown of starch and glycogen

an \ən, (ˈ)an\ *indefinite article* : A — used before words beginning with a vowel sound

¹-an *or* **-ian** *also* **-ean** *n suffix* **1** : one that belongs to ⟨American⟩ ⟨crustacean⟩ **2** : one skilled in or specializing in ⟨phonetician⟩

²-an *or* **-ian** *also* **-ean** *adj suffix* **1** : of or belonging to ⟨American⟩ **2** : characteristic of : resembling ⟨Mozartean⟩

AN *abbr* airman (Navy)

an·a·bol·ic steroid \ˌa-nə-ˈbä-lik-\ *n* : any of a group of synthetic steroid hormones sometimes abused by athletes in training to increase the size and strength of their muscles

anach·ro·nism \ə-ˈna-krə-ˌni-zəm\ *n* **1** : the error of placing a person or thing in the wrong period **2** : one that is chronologically out of place — **anach·ro·nis·tic** \ə-ˌna-krə-ˈnis-tik\ *adj* — **anach·ro·nous** \-ˈna-krə-nəs\ *adj*

an·a·con·da \ˌa-nə-ˈkän-də\ *n* : a large So. American snake that suffocates and kills its prey by constriction

anad·ro·mous \ə-ˈna-drə-məs\ *adj* : ascending rivers from the sea for breeding ⟨shad are ∼⟩

anae·mia, anae·mic *chiefly Brit var of* ANEMIA, ANEMIC

an·aer·obe \'a-nə-ˌrōb\ *n* : an anaerobic organism

an·aer·o·bic \ˌa-nə-ˈrō-bik\ *adj* : living, active, occurring, or existing in the absence of free oxygen

an·aes·the·sia, an·aes·thet·ic *chiefly Brit var of* ANESTHESIA, ANESTHETIC

ana·gram \'a-nə-ˌgram\ *n* : a word or phrase made by transposing the letters of another word or phrase

¹anal \'ā-nᵊl\ *adj* **1** : of, relating to, situated near, or involving the anus **2** : of, relating to, or characterized by the stage of psychosexual development in psychoanalytic theory during which one is concerned esp. with feces **3** : of, relating to, or characterized by personality traits (as frugality and neatness) considered typical of fixation at the anal stage of development — **anal·ly** *adv*

²anal *abbr* **1** analogy **2** analysis; analytic

an·al·ge·sia \ˌa-nᵊl-ˈjē-zhə\ *n* : insensibility to pain — **an·al·ge·sic** \-ˈjē-zik, -sik\ *adj*

an·al·ge·sic \-ˈjē-zik, -sik\ *n* : an agent for producing analgesia

analog computer *n* : a computer that operates with numbers represented by directly measurable quantities (as voltages)

anal·o·gous \ə-ˈna-lə-gəs\ *adj* : similar in one or more respects — **anal·o·gous·ly** *adv*

an·a·logue *or* **an·a·log** \'a-nə-ˌlȯg, -ˌläg\ *n* **1** : something that is analogous to something else **2** : an organ similar in function to one of another animal or plant but different in structure or origin

anal·o·gy \ə-ˈna-lə-jē\ *n, pl* **-gies** **1** : inference that if two or more things agree in some respects they will probably agree in others **2** : a likeness in one or more ways between things otherwise unlike — **an·a·log·i·cal** \ˌa-nə-ˈlä-ji-kəl\ *adj* — **an·a·log·i·cal·ly** \-k(ə-)lē\ *adv*

anal–re·ten·tive \ˈā-nᵊl-ri-ˈten-tiv\ *adj* : ANAL 3

an·a·lyse *chiefly Brit var of* ANALYZE

anal·y·sis \ə-ˈna-lə-səs\ *n, pl* **-y·ses** \-ˌsēz\ [NL, fr. Gk, fr. *analyein* to break up, fr. *ana-* up + *lyein* to loosen] **1** : separation of a thing into the parts or elements of which it is composed **2** : an examination of a thing to determine its parts or elements; *also* : a statement showing the results of such an examination **3** : PSYCHOANALYSIS — **an·a·lyst** \'a-nə-list\ *n* — **an·a·lyt·ic** \ˌa-nə-ˈli-tik\ *or* **an·a·lyt·i·cal** \-ti-kəl\ *adj* — **an·a·lyt·i·cal·ly** *adv*

an·a·lyte \'a-nə-ˌlīt\ *n* : a chemical substance that is the subject of chemical analysis

an·a·lyze \'a-nə-ˌlīz\ *vb* **-lyzed; -lyz·ing** : to make an analysis of

an·a·pest \'a-nə-ˌpest\ *n* : a metrical foot of two unaccented syllables followed by one accented syllable — **an·a·pes·tic** \ˌa-nə-ˈpes-tik\ *adj or n*

an·ar·chism \'a-nər-ˌki-zəm\ *n* : the theory that all government is undesirable — **an·ar·chist** \-kist\ *n or adj* — **an·ar·chis·tic** \ˌa-nər-ˈkis-tik\ *adj*

an·ar·chy \'a-nər-kē\ *n* **1** : a social structure without government or law and order **2** : utter confusion — **an·ar·chic** \a-ˈnär-kik\ *adj* — **an·ar·chi·cal·ly** \-ki-k(ə-)lē\ *adv*

anas·to·mo·sis \ə-ˌnas-tə-ˈmō-səs\ *n, pl* **-mo·ses** \-ˌsēz\ **1** : the union of parts or branches (as of blood vessels) **2** : NETWORK

anat *abbr* anatomical; anatomy

anath·e·ma \ə-ˈna-thə-mə\ *n* **1** : a solemn curse **2** : a person or thing accursed; *also* : one intensely disliked

anath·e·ma·tize \-ˌtīz\ *vb* **-tized; -tiz·ing** : to pronounce an anathema against : CURSE

anat·o·mise *Brit var of* ANATOMIZE

anat·o·mize \ə-ˈna-tə-ˌmīz\ *vb* **-mized; -miz·ing** : to dissect so as to examine the structure and parts; *also* : ANALYZE

anat·o·my \ə-ˈna-tə-mē\ *n, pl* **-mies** [LL *anatomia* dissection, fr. Gk *anatomē*, fr. *anatemnein* to dissect, fr. *ana-* up + *temnein* to cut] **1** : a branch of science dealing with the structure of organisms **2** : structural makeup esp. of an organism or any of its parts **3** : a separating into parts for detailed study : ANALYSIS — **an·a·tom·i·cal** \ˌa-nə-ˈtä-mi-kəl\ *or* **an·a·tom·ic** \-mik\ *adj* — **an·a·tom·i·cal·ly** \-mi-k(ə-)lē\ *adv* — **anat·o·mist** \ə-ˈna-tə-mist\ *n*

anc *abbr* ancient

-ance *n suffix* **1** : action or process ⟨further*ance*⟩ : instance of an action or process ⟨perform*ance*⟩ **2** : quality or state : instance of a quality or state ⟨protuber*ance*⟩ **3** : amount or degree ⟨conduct*ance*⟩

an·ces·tor \'an-ˌses-tər\ *n* [ME *ancestre*, fr. AF, fr. L *antecessor* predecessor, fr. *antecedere* to go before, fr. *ante-* before + *cedere* to go] : one from whom an individual is descended

an·ces·tress \'an-ˌses-trəs\ *n* : a female ancestor

an·ces·try \'an-ˌses-trē\ *n* **1** : line of descent : LINEAGE **2** : ANCESTORS — **an·ces·tral** \an-'ses-trəl\ *adj*

an·cho \'än-chō\ *n, pl* **anchos** : a poblano chili pepper esp. when mature and dried to a reddish black

¹an·chor \'aŋ-kər\ *n* **1** : a heavy metal device attached to a ship that catches hold of the bottom and holds the ship in place **2** : something that serves to hold an object firmly **3** : ANCHORPERSON **4** : a large store that attracts customers and other businesses to a shopping mall

²anchor *vb* : to hold or become held in place by or as if by an anchor

an·chor·age \'aŋ-k(ə-)rij\ *n* : a place suitable for ships to anchor

an·cho·rite \'aŋ-kə-ˌrīt\ *n* : HERMIT

an·chor·man \'aŋ-kər-ˌman\ *n* **1** : the member of a team who competes last **2** : an anchorperson who is a man

an·chor·per·son \-ˌpər-sən\ *n* : a broadcaster who reads the news and introduces the reports of other broadcasters

an·chor·wom·an \-ˌwu̇-mən\ *n* **1** : a woman who competes last **2** : an anchorperson who is a woman

an·cho·vy \'an-ˌchō-vē, an-'chō-\ *n, pl* **-vies** *or* **-vy** : any of a family of small herringlike fishes often used as food

an·cien ré·gime \äⁿs-yaⁿ-rā-'zhēm\ *n* **1** : the political and social system of France before the Revolution of 1789 **2** : a system no longer prevailing

¹an·cient \'än-shənt\ *adj* **1** : having existed for many years ⟨~ customs⟩ **2** : belonging to times long past; *esp* : belonging to the period before the Middle Ages

²ancient *n* **1** : an aged person **2** *pl* : the peoples of ancient Greece and Rome; *esp* : the classical authors of Greece and Rome

an·cil·lary \'an-sə-ˌler-ē\ *adj* **1** : SUBORDINATE, SUBSIDIARY ⟨a factory's ~ plants⟩ **2** : AUXILIARY, SUPPLEMENTARY ⟨~ evidence⟩ — **ancillary** *n*

-ancy *n suffix* : quality or state ⟨flamboy*ancy*⟩

and \ənd, (ˈ)and\ *conj* **1** — used to indicate connection or addition esp. of items within the same class or type or to join words or phrases of the same grammatical rank or function **2** — used to join one finite verb to another so that together they are equivalent to an infinitive of purpose ⟨come ~ see me⟩

¹an·dan·te \än-'dän-ˌtā, -tē\ *adv or adj* [It, lit., going, prp. of *andare* to go] : moderately slow — used as a direction in music

²andante *n* : an andante movement

and·iron \'an-ˌdī(-ə)rn\ *n* : one of a pair of metal supports for firewood in a fireplace

and/or \'and-'ȯr\ *conj* — used to indicate that either *and* or *or* may apply ⟨men ~ women means men *and* women or men *or* women⟩

an·dro·gen \'an-drə-jən\ *n* : a male sex hormone (as testosterone)

an·drog·y·nous \an-'drä-jə-nəs\ *adj* **1** : having the characteristics of both male and female **2** : suitable for either sex ⟨~ clothing⟩ — **an·drog·y·ny** \-nē\ *n*

an·droid \'an-ˌdrȯid\ *n* : a mobile robot usu. with a human form

an·ec·dot·al \ˌa-nik-'dō-tᵊl\ *adj* **1** : relating to or consisting of anecdotes **2** : based on reports of an unscientific nature — **an·ec·dot·al·ly** *adv*

an·ec·dote \'an-ik-ˌdōt\ *n, pl* **-dotes** *also* **-dota** \ˌa-nik-'dō-tə\ [F, fr. Gk *anekdota* unpublished items, fr. *a-* not + *ekdidonai* to publish] : a brief story of an interesting, amusing, or biographical incident

ane·mia \ə-'nē-mē-ə\ *n* **1** : a condition in which blood is deficient in quantity, in red blood cells, or in hemoglobin and which is marked by pallor, weakness, and irregular heart action **2** : lack of vitality — **ane·mic** \ə-'nē-mik\ *adj*

an·e·mom·e·ter \ˌa-nə-'mä-mə-tər\ *n* : an instrument for measuring the force or speed of the wind

anem·o·ne \ə-'ne-mə-nē\ *n* : any of a large genus of herbs related to the buttercups that have showy flowers without petals but with conspicuous often colored sepals

anent \ə-'nent\ *prep* : CONCERNING

an·es·the·sia \ˌa-nəs-'thē-zhə\ *n* : loss of bodily sensation

an·es·the·si·ol·o·gy \-ˌthē-zē-'ä-lə-jē\ *n* : a branch of medical science dealing with anesthesia and anesthetics — **an·es·the·si·ol·o·gist** \-jist\ *n*

¹an·es·thet·ic \ˌa-nəs-'the-tik\ *adj* : of, relating to, or capable of producing anesthesia

²anesthetic *n* : an agent that produces anesthesia

anes·the·tist \ə-'nes-thə-tist\ *n* : one who administers anesthetics

anes·the·tize \ə-'nes-thə-ˌtīz\ *vb* **-tized; -tiz·ing** : to subject to anesthesia

an·eu·rysm *also* **an·eu·rism** \'an-yə-ˌri-zəm\ *n* : an abnormal blood-filled bulge of a blood vessel

anew \ə-'nü, -'nyü\ *adv* **1** : over again ⟨begin ~⟩ **2** : in a new form ⟨this film tells the story ~⟩

an·gel \'än-jəl\ *n* [ME, fr. OE *engel* & AF *angele*, both fr. L *angelus*, fr. Gk *angelos*, lit., messenger] **1** : a spiritual being superior to man **2** : an attendant spirit **3** : a winged figure of human form in art **4** : MESSENGER, HARBINGER ⟨~ of death⟩ **5** : a person held to resemble an angel **6** : a financial backer — **an·gel·ic**

\an-'je-lik\ *or* **an·gel·i·cal** \-li-kəl\ *adj* — **an·gel·i·cal·ly** \-k(ə-)lē\ *adv*

an·gel·fish \'ān-jəl-ˌfish\ *n* : any of several brightly colored tropical fishes that are flattened from side to side

an·gel·i·ca \an-'je-li-kə\ *n* : a biennial herb related to the carrot whose roots and fruit furnish a flavoring oil

¹an·ger \'aŋ-gər\ *vb* : to make angry

²anger *n* [ME, affliction, anger, fr. ON *angr* grief] : a strong feeling of displeasure ♦ **Synonyms** WRATH, IRE, RAGE, FURY, INDIGNATION

an·gi·na \an-'jī-nə\ *n* : a disorder (as of the heart) marked by attacks of intense pain; *esp* : ANGINA PECTORIS — **an·gi·nal** \an-'jī-nᵊl\ *adj*

angina pec·to·ris \-'pek-t(ə-)rəs\ *n* : a heart disease marked by brief attacks of sharp chest pain caused by deficient oxygenation of heart muscles

an·gio·gen·e·sis \ˌan-jē-ō-'je-nə-səs\ *n* : the formation of blood vessels — **an·gio·gen·ic** \-'je-nik\ *adj*

an·gio·gram \'an-jē-ə-ˌgram\ *n* : a radiograph made by angiography

an·gi·og·ra·phy \ˌan-jē-'ä-grə-fē\ *n* : the use of radiography to make blood vessels visible after injection of a substance opaque to radiation

an·gio·plas·ty \'an-jē-ə-ˌplas-tē\ *n* : surgical repair of a blood vessel esp. by using an inflatable catheter to unblock arteries clogged by atherosclerotic deposits

an·gio·sperm \-ˌspərm\ *n* : FLOWERING PLANT

¹an·gle \'aŋ-gəl\ *n* **1** : a sharp projecting corner **2** : the figure formed by the meeting of two lines in a point **3** : a point of view **4** : a special technique or plan : GIMMICK — **an·gled** *adj*

²angle *vb* **an·gled; an·gling** \-g(ə-)liŋ\ : to turn, move, or direct at an angle

³angle *vb* **an·gled; an·gling** \-g(ə-)liŋ\ : to fish with a hook and line — **an·gler** \-glər\ *n* — **an·gling** \-gliŋ\ *n*

an·gle·worm \'aŋ-gəl-ˌwərm\ *n* : EARTHWORM

An·gli·can \'aŋ-gli-kən\ *adj* **1** : of or relating to the established episcopal Church of England **2** : of or relating to England or the English nation — **Anglican** *n* — **An·gli·can·ism** \-kə-ˌni-zəm\ *n*

an·gli·cize \'aŋ-glə-ˌsīz\ *vb* **-cized; -cizing** *often cap* **1** : to make English (as in habits, speech, character, or outlook) **2** : to borrow (a foreign word or phrase) into English without changing form or spelling and sometimes without changing pronunciation — **an·gli·ci·za·tion** \ˌaŋ-glə-sə-'zā-shən\ *n, often cap*

An·glo \'aŋ-glō\ *n, pl* **Anglos** : a non-Hispanic white inhabitant of the U.S.; *esp* : one of English origin and descent

An·glo·cen·tric \ˌaŋ-glō-'sen-trik\ *adj* : centered on or favoring England or things English

An·glo–French \ˌaŋ-glō-'french\ *n* : the French language used in medieval England

An·glo·phile \'aŋ-glə-ˌfī(-ə)l\ *also* **An-**glo·phil** \-ˌfil\ *n* : one who greatly admires England and things English

An·glo·phobe \'aŋ-glə-ˌfōb\ *n* : one who is averse to England and things English

An·glo–Sax·on \ˌaŋ-glō-'sak-sən\ *n* **1** : a member of any of the Germanic peoples who invaded England in the 5th century A.D. **2** : a member of the English people **3** : Old English — **Anglo–Saxon** *adj*

an·go·ra \aŋ-'gór-ə, an-\ *n* **1** : yarn or cloth made from the hair of an Angora goat or rabbit **2** *cap* : any of a breed of cats, goats, or rabbits with a long silky coat

an·gry \'aŋ-grē\ *adj* **an·gri·er; -est** : feeling or showing anger ♦ **Synonyms** ENRAGED, WRATHFUL, IRATE, INDIGNANT, MAD — **an·gri·ly** \-grə-lē\ *adv*

angst \'äŋst\ *n* [G] : a feeling of anxiety

ang·strom \'aŋ-strəm\ *n* : a unit of length equal to one ten-billionth of a meter

an·guish \'aŋ-gwish\ *n* : extreme pain or distress esp. of mind — **an·guished** \-gwisht\ *adj*

an·gu·lar \'aŋ-gyə-lər\ *adj* **1** : sharp-cornered **2** : having one or more angles **3** : being thin and bony — **an·gu·lar·i·ty** \ˌaŋ-gyə-'ler-ə-tē\ *n*

An·gus \'aŋ-gəs\ *n* : any of a breed of usu. black hornless beef cattle originating in Scotland

an·hy·drous \an-'hī-drəs\ *adj* : free from water

an·i·line \'a-nᵊl-ən\ *n* : an oily poisonous liquid used in making dyes, medicines, and explosives

an·i·mad·vert \ˌa-nə-ˌmad-'vərt\ *vb* : to remark critically : express censure — **an·i·mad·ver·sion** \-'vər-zhən\ *n*

¹an·i·mal \'a-nə-məl\ *n* **1** : any of a kingdom of living things typically differing from plants in capacity for active movement, in rapid response to stimulation, and in lack of cellulose cell walls **2** : a lower animal as distinguished from human beings; *also* : MAMMAL

²animal *adj* **1** : of, relating to, or derived from animals **2** : of or relating to the physical as distinguished from the mental or spiritual ♦ **Synonyms** CARNAL, FLESHLY, SENSUAL

an·i·mal·cule \ˌa-nə-'mal-kyül\ *n* : a tiny animal usu. invisible to the naked eye

¹an·i·mate \'a-nə-mət\ *adj* : having life

²an·i·mate \-ˌmāt\ *vb* **-mat·ed; -mat·ing** **1** : to impart life to **2** : to give spirit and vigor to **3** : to make appear to move ⟨~ a cartoon for motion pictures⟩ — **an·i·mat·ed** *adj* — **an·i·mat·ed·ly** *adv*

an·i·ma·tion \ˌa-nə-'mā-shən\ *n* **1** : VIVACITY, LIVELINESS **2** : a motion picture made from a series of drawings simulating motions by means of slight progressive changes

an·i·ma·tron·ic \ˌa-nə-mə-'trä-nik\ *adj* : of, relating to, or being an electrically animated mechanical figure (as a puppet)

an·i·mism \'a-nə-ˌmi-zəm\ *n* : attribution of conscious life to objects in and phenomena of nature or to inanimate objects — **an·i·mist** \-mist\ *n* — **an·i·mis·tic** \ˌa-nə-'mis-tik\ *adj*

an·i·mos·i·ty \ˌa-nə-'mä-sə-tē\ *n, pl* **-ties** : ILL WILL, RESENTMENT

an·i·mus \'a-nə-məs\ *n* : deep-seated resentment and hostility

an·ion \'a-ˌnī-ən, -ˌnī-ˌän\ *n* : a negatively charged ion

an·ise \'a-nəs\ *n* : an herb related to the carrot with aromatic seeds (**aniseed** \-ˌsēd\) used in flavoring

an·is·ette \ˌa-nə-'set, -'zet\ *n* [F] : a usu. colorless sweet liqueur flavored with aniseed

ankh \'äŋk\ *n* : a cross having a loop for its upper vertical arm and serving esp. in ancient Egypt as an emblem of life

an·kle \'aŋ-kəl\ *n* : the joint or region between the foot and the leg

an·kle·bone \'aŋ-kəl-ˌbōn\ *n* : the bone that in human beings bears the weight of the body and with the tibia and fibula forms the ankle joint

an·klet \'aŋ-klət\ *n* **1** : something (as an ornament) worn around the ankle **2** : a short sock reaching slightly above the ankle

ann *abbr* **1** annals **2** annual

an·nals \'a-n°lz\ *n pl* **1** : a record of events in chronological order **2** : historical records — **an·nal·ist** \-n°l-ist\ *n*

an·neal \ə-'nēl\ *vb* **1** : to make (as glass or steel) less brittle by heating and then cooling : STRENGTHEN, TOUGHEN

¹**an·nex** \ə-'neks, 'a-ˌneks\ *vb* **1** : to attach as an addition **2** : to incorporate (as a territory) within a political domain — **an·nex·a·tion** \ˌa-ˌnek-'sā-shən\ *n*

²**an·nex** \'a-ˌneks, -niks\ *n* : a subsidiary or supplementary structure

an·nexe *chiefly Brit var of* ANNEX

an·ni·hi·late \ə-'nī-ə-ˌlāt\ *vb* **-lat·ed; -lat·ing** : to destroy completely — **an·ni·hi·la·tion** \-ˌnī-ə-'lā-shən\ *n*

an·ni·ver·sa·ry \ˌa-nə-'vər-sə-rē\ *n, pl* **-ries** : the annual return of the date of a notable event and esp. a wedding

an·no Do·mi·ni \ˌa-nō-'dä-mə-nē, -'dō-, -ˌnī\ *adv, often cap A* [ML, in the year of the Lord] — used to indicate that a time division falls within the Christian era

an·no·tate \'a-nə-ˌtāt\ *vb* **-tat·ed; -tat·ing** : to furnish with notes — **an·no·ta·tion** \ˌa-nə-'tā-shən\ *n* — **an·no·ta·tor** \'a-nə-ˌtā-tər\ *n*

an·nounce \ə-'naůns\ *vb* **an·nounced; an·nounc·ing** **1** : to make known publicly **2** : to give notice of the arrival or presence of — **an·nounce·ment** *n*

an·nounc·er \ə-'naůn-sər\ *n* : a person who introduces radio or television programs, makes commercial announcements, or gives station identification

an·noy \ə-'nȯi\ *vb* : to disturb or irritate esp. by repeated acts : VEX ♦ *Synonyms* IRK, BOTHER, PESTER, TEASE, HARASS — **an·noy·ing·ly** *adv*

an·noy·ance \ə-'nȯi-əns\ *n* **1** : the act of annoying **2** : the state of being annoyed **3** : NUISANCE ⟨the delay was a minor ∼⟩

¹**an·nu·al** \'an-yə-wəl\ *adj* **1** : covering the period of a year ⟨∼ rainfall⟩ **2** : occurring once a year : YEARLY **3** : complet-

ing the life cycle in one growing season ⟨∼ plants⟩ — **an·nu·al·ly** *adv*

²**annual** *n* **1** : a publication appearing once a year **2** : an annual plant

annual ring *n* : the layer of wood produced by a single year's growth of a woody plant

an·nu·i·tant \ə-'nü-ə-tənt, -'nyü-\ *n* : a beneficiary of an annuity

an·nu·i·ty \ə-'nü-ə-tē, -'nyü-\ *n, pl* **-i·ties** : an amount payable annually; *also* : the right to receive such a payment

an·nul \ə-'nəl\ *vb* **an·nulled; an·nul·ling** : to make legally void — **an·nul·ment** *n*

an·nu·lar \'an-yə-lər\ *adj* : ring-shaped

an·nun·ci·ate \ə-'nən-sē-ˌāt\ *vb* **-at·ed; -at·ing** : ANNOUNCE

an·nun·ci·a·tion \ə-ˌnən-sē-'ā-shən\ *n* **1** *cap* : March 25 observed as a church festival commemorating the announcement of the Incarnation **2** : ANNOUNCEMENT

an·nun·ci·a·tor \ə-'nən-sē-ˌā-tər\ *n* : one that annunciates; *specif* : a usu. electrically controlled signal board or indicator

an·ode \'a-ˌnōd\ *n* **1** : the positive electrode of an electrolytic cell **2** : the negative terminal of a battery **3** : the electron-collecting electrode of an electron tube — **an·od·ic** \a-'nä-dik\ *also* **an·od·al** \-'nō-d°l\ *adj*

an·od·ize \'a-nə-ˌdīz\ *vb* **-ized; -iz·ing** : to subject (a metal) to electrolytic action as the anode of a cell in order to coat with a protective or decorative film

an·o·dyne \'a-nə-ˌdīn\ *n* : something that relieves pain : a soothing agent

anoint \ə-'nȯint\ *vb* **1** : to apply oil to esp. as a sacred rite **2** : CONSECRATE — **anoint·ment** *n*

anom·a·lous \ə-'nä-mə-ləs\ *adj* : deviating from a general rule : ABNORMAL

anom·a·ly \ə-'nä-mə-lē\ *n, pl* **-lies** : something anomalous : IRREGULARITY

¹**anon** \ə-'nän\ *adv* : SOON

²**anon** *abbr* anonymous; anonymously

anon·y·mous \ə-'nä-nə-məs\ *adj* : of unknown or undeclared origin or authorship — **an·o·nym·i·ty** \ˌa-nə-'ni-mə-tē\ *n* — **anon·y·mous·ly** *adv*

anoph·e·les \ə-'nä-fə-ˌlēz\ *n* [NL, genus name, fr. Gk *anōphelēs* useless, fr. *a-* not + *ophelos* advantage, help] : any of a genus of mosquitoes that includes all mosquitoes which transmit malaria to human beings

an·o·rec·tic \ˌa-nə-'rek-tik\ *adj* : ANOREXIC — **anorectic** *n*

an·orex·ia \ˌa-nə-'rek-sē-ə\ *n* **1** : loss of appetite esp. when prolonged **2** : ANOREXIA NERVOSA

anorexia ner·vo·sa \-nər-'vō-sə\ *n* : a serious disorder in eating behavior marked esp. by a pathological fear of weight gain leading to faulty eating patterns, malnutrition, and usu. excessive weight loss

an·orex·ic \ˌa-nə-'rek-sik\ *adj* **1** : lacking or causing loss of appetite **2** : affected with or as if with anorexia nervosa — **anorexic** *n*

¹**an·oth·er** \ə-'nə-thər\ *adj* **1** : some other ⟨do it ∼ time⟩ **2** : being one in addition : one more ⟨∼ piece of pie⟩

²**another** *pron* **1** : an additional one : one more **2** : one that is different from the first or present one

ans *abbr* answer

¹**an·swer** \'an-sər\ *n* **1** : something spoken or written in reply to a question **2** : a solution of a problem

²**answer** *vb* **1** : to speak or write in reply to **2** : to be responsible **3** : to be adequate — **an·swer·er** *n*

an·swer·able \'an-sə-rə-bəl\ *adj* **1** : subject to taking blame or responsibility **2** : capable of being refuted

answering machine *n* : a machine that receives telephone calls by playing a recorded message and usu. by recording messages from callers

answering service *n* : a commercial service that answers telephone calls for its clients

¹**ant** \'ant\ *n* : any of a family of small social insects related to the bees and living in communities usu. in earth or wood

²**ant** *abbr* antonym

Ant *abbr* Antarctica

ant- — see ANTI-

¹**-ant** *n suffix* **1** : one that performs or promotes (a specified action) ⟨cool*ant*⟩ **2** : thing that is acted upon (in a specified manner) ⟨inhal*ant*⟩

²**-ant** *adj suffix* **1** : performing (a specified action) or being (in a specified condition) ⟨propell*ant*⟩ **2** : promoting (a specified action or process) ⟨expector*ant*⟩

ant·ac·id \ant-'a-səd\ *n* : an agent that counteracts acidity — **antacid** *adj*

an·tag·o·nism \an-'ta-gə-ˌni-zəm\ *n* **1** : active opposition or hostility **2** : opposition in physiological action — **an·tag·o·nis·tic** \-ˌta-gə-'nis-tik\ *adj*

an·tag·o·nist \-nist\ *n* : ADVERSARY, OPPONENT

an·tag·o·nize \an-'ta-gə-ˌnīz\ *vb* **-nized; -niz·ing** : to provoke the hostility of

ant·arc·tic \ant-'ärk-tik, -'är-tik\ *adj, often cap* : of or relating to the south pole or the region near it

antarctic circle *n, often cap A&C* : the parallel of latitude that is approximately 66½ degrees south of the equator

¹**an·te** \'an-tē\ *n* : a poker stake put up before the deal to build the pot; *also* : an amount paid : PRICE

²**ante** *vb* **an·ted; an·te·ing** **1** : to put up (an ante) **2** : PAY

ant·eat·er \'ant-ˌē-tər\ *n* : any of several mammals (as an aardvark) that feed mostly on ants or termites

an·te·bel·lum \ˌan-ti-'be-ləm\ *adj* : existing before a war; *esp* : existing before the U.S. Civil War of 1861-65

an·te·ced·ent \ˌan-tə-'sē-dənt\ *n* **1** : a noun, pronoun, phrase, or clause referred to by a personal or relative pronoun **2** : a preceding event or cause **3** *pl* : the significant conditions of one's earlier life **4** *pl* : ANCESTORS — **antecedent** *adj*

an·te·cham·ber \'an-ti-ˌchām-bər\ *n* : ANTEROOM

an·te·date \'an-ti-ˌdāt\ *vb* **1** : to date (a paper) as of an earlier day than that on

which the actual writing or signing is done **2** : to precede in time

an·te·di·lu·vi·an \ˌan-ti-də-'lü-vē-ən, -dī-\ *adj* **1** : of the period before the biblical flood **2** : ANTIQUATED

an·te·lope \'an-tə-ˌlōp\ *n, pl* **-lope** or **-lopes** [ME, fabulous heraldic beast, prob. fr. MF *antelop* savage animal with sawlike horns, fr. ML *anthalopus*, fr. LGk *antholops*] **1** : any of various deerlike ruminant mammals that chiefly inhabit Africa and have a slender build and horns extending upward and backward **2** : PRONGHORN

an·te me·ri·di·em \'an-ti-mə-'ri-dē-əm\ *adj* [L] : being before noon

an·ten·na \an-'te-nə\ *n, pl* **-nae** \-(ˌ)nē\ or **-nas** [ML, fr. L, sail yard] **1** : one of the long slender paired segmented sensory organs on the head of an arthropod (as an insect or crab) **2** *pl usu* **-nas** : a metallic device (as a rod or wire) for sending out or receiving radio waves

an·te·pe·nult \ˌan-ti-'pē-ˌnəlt\ *also* **an·te·pen·ul·ti·ma** \-pi-'nəl-tə-mə\ *n* : the 3d syllable of a word counting from the end — **an·te·pen·ul·ti·mate** \-pi-'nəl-tə-mət\ *adj or n*

an·te·ri·or \an-'tir-ē-ər\ *adj* **1** : situated before or toward the front **2** : situated near or nearer to the head **3** : coming before in time ♦ *Synonyms* PRECEDING, PREVIOUS, PRIOR, ANTECEDENT

anterior cruciate ligament *n* : a cross-shaped ligament of the knee that connects the tibia and femur

an·te·room \'an-ti-ˌrüm, -ˌrùm\ *n* : a room forming the entrance to another and often used as a waiting room

an·them \'an-thəm\ *n* **1** : a sacred vocal composition **2** : a song or hymn of praise or gladness

an·ther \'an-thər\ *n* : the part of a stamen of a seed plant that produces and contains pollen

ant·hill \'ant-ˌhil\ *n* : a mound thrown up by ants or termites in digging their nest

an·thol·o·gy \an-'thä-lə-jē\ *n, pl* **-gies** [NL *anthologia* collection of epigrams, fr. MGk, fr. Gk, flower gathering, fr. *anthos* flower + *logia* collecting, fr. *legein* to gather] : a collection of literary selections — **an·thol·o·gist** \-jist\ *n* — **an·thol·o·gize** \-ˌjīz\ *vb*

an·thra·cite \'an-thrə-ˌsīt\ *n* : a hard glossy coal that burns without much smoke

an·thrax \'an-ˌthraks\ *n* : an infectious and usu. fatal bacterial disease of warm-blooded animals (as cattle and sheep) that is transmissible to humans; *also* : a bacterium causing anthrax

an·thro·po·cen·tric \ˌan-thrə-pə-'sen-trik\ *adj* : interpreting or regarding the world in terms of human values and experiences

an·thro·poid \'an-thrə-ˌpóid\ *n* **1** : any of several large tailless apes (as a gorilla) **2** : a person resembling an ape — **anthropoid** *adj*

an·thro·pol·o·gy \ˌan-thrə-'pä-lə-jē\ *n* : the science of human beings and esp. of their physical characteristics, their origin and ancestry, their environment and social relations, and their culture — **an·thro·po·log·i·cal** \-pə-'lä-ji-kəl\ adj — **an·thro·pol·o·gist** \-'pä-lə-jist\ n

an·thro·po·mor·phism \,an-thrə-pə-'mor-,fi-zəm\ n : an interpretation of what is not human or personal in terms of human or personal characteristics : HUMANIZATION — **an·thro·po·mor·phic** \-fik\ adj

an·ti \'an-,tī, -tē\ n, pl **antis** : one who is opposed

anti- \an-ti, -tē, -,tī\ or **ant-** or **anth-** prefix **1** : opposite in kind, position, or action **2** : opposing : hostile toward **3** : counteractive **4** : preventive of : curative of

an·ti·abor·tion \,an-tē-ə-'bor-shən, ,an-,tī-\ adj : opposed to abortion — **an·ti·abor·tion·ist** \-shə-nist\ n

an·ti·bal·lis·tic missile \,an-ti-bə-'lis-tik-, ,an-,tī-\ n : a missile for intercepting and destroying ballistic missiles

an·ti·bi·ot·ic \-bī-'ä-tik, -bē-\ n : a substance produced by or derived by chemical alteration of a substance produced by a microorganism (as a fungus or bacterium) that in dilute solution inhibits or kills another microorganism — **antibiotic** adj

an·ti·body \'an-ti-,bä-dē\ n : any of a large number of proteins of high molecular weight produced normally by specialized B cells after stimulation by an antigen and acting specifically against the antigen in an immune response

¹an·tic \'an-tik\ n [It antico ancient thing or person, fr. antico ancient, fr. L antiquus] : an often wildly playful or funny act or action

²antic adj, **1** archaic : GROTESQUE **2** : PLAYFUL

an·ti·can·cer \,an-ti-'kan-sər, ,an-,tī-\ adj : used against or tending to arrest or prevent cancer ⟨~ drugs⟩

An·ti·christ \'an-ti-,krīst\ n **1** : one who denies or opposes Christ **2** : a false Christ

an·tic·i·pate \an-'ti-sə-,pāt\ vb -pat·ed; -pat·ing **1** : to foresee and provide for beforehand ⟨~s problems⟩ **2** : to look forward to — **an·tic·i·pa·tion** \-,ti-sə-'pā-shən\ n — **an·tic·i·pa·to·ry** \-'ti-sə-pə-,tor-ē\ adj

an·ti·cli·max \,an-ti-'klī-,maks\ n : something (as the ending of a story) that is strikingly less important or dramatic than expected — **an·ti·cli·mac·tic** \-klī-'mak-tik\ adj

an·ti·cline \'an-ti-,klīn\ n : an arch of layers of rock in the earth's crust

an·ti·co·ag·u·lant \,an-ti-kō-'a-gyə-lənt\ n : a substance that hinders the clotting of blood — **anticoagulant** adj

an·ti·cy·clone \,an-ti-'sī-,klōn\ n : a system of winds that rotates about a center of high atmospheric pressure — **an·ti·cy·clon·ic** \-sī-'klä-nik\ adj

an·ti·de·pres·sant \,an-ti-di-'pres-ᵊnt, ,an-,tī-\ n : a drug used to relieve psychic depression — **antidepressant** adj

an·ti·dote \'an-ti-,dōt\ n : a remedy to counteract the effects of poison

an·ti·drug \'an-,tī-,drəg\ adj : acting against or opposing illicit drugs

an·ti·fer·til·i·ty \,an-ti-fər-'ti-lə-tē\ adj : tending to reduce or destroy fertility : CONTRACEPTIVE ⟨~ agents⟩

an·ti·freeze \'an-ti-,frēz\ n : a substance added to a liquid to lower its freezing temperature

an·ti·fun·gal \,an-tē-'fən-gəl, ,an-,tī-\ n : FUNGICIDE — **antifungal** adj

an·ti·gen \'an-ti-jən\ n : any substance (as a toxin) foreign to the body that induces an immune response — **an·ti·gen·ic** \,an-ti-'je-nik\ adj — **an·ti·ge·nic·i·ty** \-jə-'ni-sə-tē\ n

an·ti·grav·i·ty \,an-ti-'gra-və-tē, ,an-,tī-\ adj : reducing or canceling the effect of gravity

an·ti·he·ro \'an-ti-,hē-rō, 'an-,tī-\ n : a protagonist who is notably lacking in heroic qualities (as courage)

an·ti·his·ta·mine \,an-ti-'his-tə-,mēn, ,an-,tī-, -mən\ n : any of various drugs used in treating allergies and colds — **antihistamine** adj

an·ti·hy·per·ten·sive \-,hī-pər-'ten-siv\ n : a substance that is effective against high blood pressure — **antihypertensive** adj

an·ti·in·flam·ma·to·ry \-in-'fla-mə-,tor-ē\ adj : counteracting inflammation — **anti-inflammatory** n

an·ti·in·tel·lec·tu·al \,in-tə-'lek-chə-wəl\ adj : opposing or hostile to intellectuals or to an intellectual view or approach

an·ti·lock \,an-ti-,läk, 'an-,tī-\ adj : being a braking system designed to prevent the wheels from locking

an·ti·log·a·rithm \,an-ti-'ló-gə-,ri-thəm, ,an-,tī-, -'lä-\ n : the number corresponding to a given logarithm ⟨if the logarithm in base x of a equals b then the antilogarithm in base x of b equals a⟩

an·ti·ma·cas·sar \,an-ti-mə-'ka-sər\ n : a cover to protect the back or arms of furniture

an·ti·mat·ter \'an-ti-,ma-tər, 'an-,tī-\ n : matter composed of antiparticles

an·ti·mo·ny \'an-tə-,mō-nē\ n : a brittle silvery white metallic chemical element used esp. in alloys

an·ti·neu·tron \,an-ti-'nü-,trän, ,an-,tī-, -'nyü-\ n : the antiparticle of the neutron

antiaging	antibacterial	anticommunist	anti-imperialism
anti-AIDS	anticapitalist	antidemocratic	anti-imperialist
antiaircraft	anti-Catholic	antidiscrimination	antiknock
antialcohol	anticholesterol	antiestablishment	antilabor
anti-American	anticlerical	antifascist	antimalarial
antianxiety	anticolonial	antigovernment	antimicrobial
antiapartheid	anticommunism	anti-HIV	antinausea

an·ti·no·mi·an \,an-ti-ˈnō-mē-ən\ *n* : one who denies the validity of moral laws

an·tin·o·my \an-ˈti-nə-mē\ *n, pl* **-mies** : a contradiction between two seemingly true statements

an·ti·nov·el \ˈan-ti-,nä-vəl, ˈan-,tī-\ *n* : a work of fiction that lacks all or most of the traditional features of the novel

an·ti·nu·cle·ar \,an-ti-ˈnü-klē-ər, -ˈnyü-\ *adj* : opposing the use or production of nuclear power

an·ti·ox·i·dant \,an-tē-ˈäk-sə-dənt, ,an-,tī-\ *n* : a substance that inhibits oxidation — **antioxidant** *adj*

an·ti·par·ti·cle \ˈan-ti-,pär-ti-kəl, ˈan-,tī-\ *n* : a subatomic particle identical to another subatomic particle in mass but opposite to it in electric and magnetic properties

an·ti·pas·to \,an-ti-ˈpas-tō, ,än-ti-ˈpäs-\ *n, pl* **-ti** \-(,)tē\ : any of various typically Italian hors d'oeuvres

an·tip·a·thy \an-ˈti-pə-thē\ *n, pl* **-thies** 1 : settled aversion or dislike 2 : an object of aversion — **an·ti·pa·thet·ic** \,an-ti-pə-ˈthe-tik\ *adj*

an·ti·per·son·nel \,an-ti-,pər-sə-ˈnel, ,an-,tī-\ *adj* : designed for use against military personnel 〈~ mine〉

an·ti·per·spi·rant \-ˈpər-spə-rənt\ *n* : a preparation used to reduce perspiration

an·tiph·o·nal \an-ˈti-fə-nᵊl\ *adj* : performed by two alternating groups — **an·tiph·o·nal·ly** *adv*

an·ti·pode \ˈan-tə-,pōd\ *n, pl* **an·tip·o·des** \an-ˈti-pə-,dēz\ [ME *antipodes*, pl., persons dwelling at opposite points on the globe, fr. L, fr. Gk, fr. pl. of *antipod-, antipous* with feet opposite, fr. *anti-* against + *pod-, pous* foot] : the parts of the earth diametrically opposite — usu. used in pl. — **an·tip·o·dal** \an-ˈti-pə-dᵊl\ *adj* — **an·tip·o·de·an** \(,)an-,ti-pə-ˈdē-ən\ *adj*

an·ti·pol·lu·tion \,an-ti-pə-ˈlü-shən\ *adj* : designed to prevent, reduce, or eliminate pollution 〈~ laws〉

an·ti·pope \ˈan-ti-,pōp\ *n* : one elected or claiming to be pope in opposition to the pope canonically chosen

an·ti·pro·ton \,an-ti-ˈprō-,tän\ *n* : the antiparticle of the proton

an·ti·psy·chot·ic \,an-tē-sī-ˈkä-tik\ *n* : any of the powerful tranquilizers used to treat psychosis — **antipsychotic** *adj*

an·ti·quar·i·an \,an-tə-ˈkwer-ē-ən\ *adj* 1 : of or relating to antiquities 2 : dealing in old books — **antiquarian** *n* — **an·ti·quar·i·an·ism** *n*

an·ti·quary \ˈan-tə-,kwer-ē\ *n, pl* **-quar·ies** : a person who collects or studies antiquities

an·ti·quat·ed \ˈan-tə-,kwä-təd\ *adj* : OUT-OF-DATE, OLD-FASHIONED

¹**an·tique** \an-ˈtēk\ *n* : an object made in a bygone period

²**antique** *adj* 1 : belonging to antiquity 2 : OLD-FASHIONED 3 : of a bygone style or period

³**antique** *vb* **-tiqued; -tiqu·ing** 1 : to finish or refinish in antique style : give an appearance of age to 2 : to shop around for antiques — **an·tiqu·er** *n*

an·tiq·ui·ty \an-ˈti-kwə-tē\ *n, pl* **-ties** 1 : ancient times 2 : great age 3 *pl* : relics of ancient times 4 *pl* : matters relating to ancient culture

an·ti·re·tro·vi·ral \,an-tē-ˈre-trō-,vī-rəl, ,an-,tī-\ *adj* : effective against retroviruses 〈~ drugs〉 — **antiretroviral** *n*

antis *pl of* ANTI

an·ti–Sem·i·tism \,an-ti-ˈse-mə-,ti-zəm, ,an-,tī-\ *n* : hostility toward Jews as a religious or social minority — **an·ti–Sem·ite** \-ˈse-,mīt\ *n* — **an·ti–Se·mit·ic** \-sə-ˈmi-tik\ *adj*

an·ti·sep·tic \,an-tə-ˈsep-tik\ *adj* 1 : killing or checking the growth of germs that cause decay or infection 2 : scrupulously clean : ASEPTIC 3 : coldly impersonal 〈an ~ greeting〉 — **antiseptic** *n* — **an·ti·sep·ti·cal·ly** *adv*

an·ti·se·rum \ˈan-ti-,sir-əm, ˈan-,tī-\ *n* : a serum containing antibodies

an·ti·so·cial \,an-ti-ˈsō-shəl\ *adj* 1 : disliking the society of others 2 : contrary or hostile to the well-being of society 〈crime is ~〉; *esp* : deviating sharply from the social norm — **an·ti·so·cial·ly** *adv*

an·tith·e·sis \an-ˈti-thə-səs\ *n, pl* **-e·ses** \-,sēz\ 1 : the opposition or contrast of ideas 2 : the direct opposite

an·ti·thet·i·cal \,an-tə-ˈthe-ti-kəl\ *also* **an·ti·thet·ic** \-tik\ *adj* : constituting or marked by antithesis — **an·ti·thet·i·cal·ly** \-ti-k(ə-)lē\ *adv*

an·ti·tox·in \,an-ti-ˈtäk-sən\ *n* : an antibody that is able to neutralize a particular toxin or disease-causing agent; *also* : an antiserum containing an antitoxin

an·ti·trust \,an-ti-ˈtrəst\ *adj* : of or relating to legislation against trusts; *also* : consisting of laws to protect trade and commerce from unlawful restraints and monopolies or unfair business practices

an·ti·ven·in \-ˈve-nən\ *n* : an antitoxin to a venom; *also* : a serum containing such antitoxin

ant·ler \ˈant-lər\ *n* [ME *aunteler*, fr. AF *antiler*, fr. VL *anteocularis located before the eye, fr. L *ante-* before + *oculus* eye] : one of the paired deciduous solid bone processes on the head of a deer; *also* : a branch of this — **ant·lered** \-lərd\ *adj*

ant lion *n* : any of various insects having a long-jawed larva that digs a conical pit in which it lies in wait for insects (as ants) on which it feeds

an·to·nym \ˈan-tə-,nim\ *n* : a word of opposite meaning

ant·sy \ˈant-sē\ *adj* 1 : RESTLESS, IMPATIENT 〈~ children〉 2 : APPREHENSIVE 〈~ investors〉

anus \ˈā-nəs\ *n* [L] : the lower or posterior opening of the alimentary canal

antipoverty	antistatic	antitank	antiviral
antislavery	antisubmarine	antitumor	antiwar
antispasmodic			

an·vil \'an-vəl\ *n* **1** : a heavy iron block on which metal is shaped **2** : INCUS

anx·i·ety \aŋ-'zī-ə-tē\ *n, pl* **-et·ies** **1** : painful uneasiness of mind usu. over an anticipated ill **2** : abnormal apprehension and fear often accompanied by physiological signs (as sweating and increased pulse), by doubt about the nature and reality of the threat itself, and by self-doubt

anx·ious \'aŋk-shəs\ *adj* **1** : uneasy in mind : WORRIED ⟨∼ parents⟩ **2** : earnestly wishing : EAGER ⟨∼ to leave⟩ — **anx·ious·ly** *adv*

¹any \'e-nē\ *adj* **1** : one chosen at random **2** : of whatever number or quantity

²any *pron* **1** : any one or ones ⟨take ∼ of the books you like⟩ **2** : any amount ⟨∼ of the money not used is to be returned⟩

³any *adv* : to any extent or degree : AT ALL ⟨could not walk ∼ farther⟩

any·body \-,bä-dē, -bə-\ *pron* : ANYONE

any·how \-,haú\ *adv* **1** : in any way **2** : NEVERTHELESS; *also* : in any case

any·more \,e-nē-'mór\ *adv* **1** : any longer ⟨won't bother you ∼⟩ **2** : at the present time

any·one \'e-nē-(,)wən\ *pron* : any person

any·place \-,plās\ *adv* : ANYWHERE 1

any·thing \-,thiŋ\ *pron* : any thing whatever

any·time \'e-nē-,tīm\ *adv* : at any time whatever

any·way \-,wā\ *adv* : ANYHOW

any·where \-,hwer\ *adv* **1** : in or to any place **2** : to any extent ⟨not ∼ near done⟩

any·wise \-,wīz\ *adv* : in any way whatever

A–OK \,ā-ō-'kā\ *adv or adj* : very definitely OK

A1 \'ā-'wən\ *adj* : of the finest quality

aor·ta \ā-'òr-tə\ *n, pl* **-tas** *or* **-tae** \-,tē\ : the main artery that carries blood from the heart — **aor·tic** \-tik\ *adj*

ap *abbr* **1** apostle **2** apothecaries'

AP *abbr* **1** American plan **2** Associated Press

apace \ə-'pās\ *adv* : SWIFTLY

Apache \ə-'pa-chē\ *n, pl* **Apache** *or* **Apach·es** \-'pa-chēz, -'pa-shəz\ : a member of an American Indian people of the southwestern U.S.; *also* : any of the languages of the Apache people — **Apach·e·an** \ə-'pa-chē-ən\ *adj or n*

apanage *var of* APPANAGE

apart \ə-'pärt\ *adv* **1** : separately in place or time **2** : ASIDE **3** : in two or more parts : to pieces

apart·heid \ə-'pär-,tāt, -,tīt\ *n* [Afrikaans] : a policy of racial segregation formerly practiced in the Republic of So. Africa

apart·ment \ə-'pärt-mənt\ *n* : a room or set of rooms occupied as a dwelling; *also* : a building divided into individual dwelling units

ap·a·thy \'a-pə-thē\ *n* **1** : lack of emotion **2** : lack of interest : INDIFFERENCE — **ap·a·thet·ic** \,a-pə-'the-tik\ *adj* — **ap·a·thet·i·cal·ly** \-ti-k(ə-)lē\ *adv*

ap·a·tite \'a-pə-,tīt\ *n* : any of a group of minerals that are phosphates of calcium

and occur esp. in phosphate rock and in bones and teeth

apato·sau·rus \ə-,pa-tə-'sòr-əs\ *n* : BRONTOSAURUS

APB *abbr* all points bulletin

¹ape \'āp\ *n* **1** : any of the larger tailless primates (as a baboon or gorilla); *also* : MONKEY **2** : MIMIC, IMITATOR; *also* : a large uncouth person

²ape *vb* **aped; ap·ing** : IMITATE, MIMIC

ape–man \'āp-,man\ *n* : a primate intermediate in character between Homo sapiens and the higher apes

aper·çu \,a-pər-'sü\ *n, pl* **aperçus** \-'süz\ : an immediate impression; *esp* : INSIGHT

aper·i·tif \ä-,per-ə-'tēf\ *n* : an alcoholic drink taken as an appetizer

ap·er·ture \'a-pər-,chúr, -chər\ *n* : OPENING, HOLE

apex \'ā-,peks\ *n, pl* **apex·es** *or* **api·ces** \'ā-pə-,sēz, 'a-\ : the highest point : PEAK

apha·sia \ə-'fā-zh(ē-)ə\ *n* : loss or impairment of the power to use or comprehend words — **apha·sic** \-zik\ *adj or n*

aph·elion \a-'fēl-yən\ *n, pl* **-elia** \-yə\ [NL, fr. *apo-* away from + Gk *hēlios* sun] : the point in an object's orbit most distant from the sun

aphid \'ā-fəd\ *n* : any of numerous small insects that suck the juices of plants

aphis \'ā-fəs, 'a-\ *n, pl* **aphi·des** \-fə-,dēz\ : APHID

aph·o·rism \'a-fə-,ri-zəm\ *n* : a short saying stating a general truth : MAXIM — **aph·o·ris·tic** \,a-fə-'ris-tik\ *adj*

aph·ro·di·si·ac \,a-frə-'di-zē-,ak, -'dē-zē-\ *n* : an agent that excites sexual desire — **aphrodisiac** *adj*

api·ary \'ā-pē-,er-ē\ *n, pl* **-ar·ies** : a place where bees are kept — **api·a·rist** \-pē-ə-rist\ *n*

api·cal \'ā-pi-kəl, 'a-\ *adj* : of, relating to, or situated at an apex — **api·cal·ly** \-k(ə-)lē\ *adv*

apiece \ə-'pēs\ *adv* : for each one

aplen·ty \ə-'plen-tē\ *adj* : being in plenty or abundance

aplomb \ə-'pläm, -'pləm\ *n* [F, lit., perpendicularity, fr. MF, fr. *a plomb*, lit., according to the plummet] : complete composure or self-assurance

APO *abbr* army post office

Apoc *abbr* **1** Apocalypse **2** Apocrypha

apoc·a·lypse \ə-'pä-kə-,lips\ *n* **1** : a writing prophesying a cataclysm in which evil forces are destroyed **2** *cap* — see BIBLE table — **apoc·a·lyp·tic** \-,pä-kə-'lip-tik\ *also* **apoc·a·lyp·ti·cal** \-ti-kəl\ *adj*

Apoc·ry·pha \ə-'pä-krə-fə\ *n* **1** *not cap* : writings of dubious authenticity **2** : books included in the Septuagint and Vulgate but excluded from the Jewish and Protestant canons of the Old Testament — see BIBLE table **3** : early Christian writings not included in the New Testament

apoc·ry·phal \-fəl\ *adj* **1** : not canonical : SPURIOUS **2** *often cap* : of or resembling the Apocrypha — **apoc·ry·phal·ly** *adv* — **apoc·ry·phal·ness** *n*

apo·gee \'a-pə-(,)jē\ *n* [F *apogée*, fr. NL *apogaeum*, fr. Gk *apogaion*, fr. *apo* away from + **gē, gaia** earth] : the point at which an orbiting object is farthest from the body being orbited

apo·lit·i·cal \ˌā-pə-ˈli-ti-kəl\ adj 1 : having an aversion for or no interest in political affairs 2 : having no political significance — **apo·lit·i·cal·ly** \-k(ə-)lē\ adv

apol·o·get·ic \ə-ˌpä-lə-ˈje-tik\ adj : expressing apology — **apol·o·get·i·cal·ly** \-ti-k(ə-)lē\ adv

apol·o·gia \ˌa-pə-ˈlō-j(ē-)ə\ n : APOLOGY; *esp* : an argument in support or justification

apol·o·gise *Brit var of* APOLOGIZE

apol·o·gize \ə-ˈpä-lə-ˌjīz\ vb **-gized; -gizing** : to make an apology : express regret — **apol·o·gist** \-jist\ n

apol·o·gy \ə-ˈpä-lə-jē\ n, pl **-gies** 1 : a formal justification : DEFENSE 2 : an expression of regret for a wrong

apo·plexy \ˈa-pə-ˌplek-sē\ n : STROKE 3 — **apo·plec·tic** \ˌa-pə-ˈplek-tik\ adj

ap·o·pto·sis \ˌa-pəp-ˈtō-səs, -pə-ˈtō-\ n, pl **-pto·ses** \-ˌsēz\ : a genetically directed process of cell self-destruction

aport \ə-ˈpȯrt\ adv : on or toward the left side of a ship

apos·ta·sy \ə-ˈpäs-tə-sē\ n, pl **-sies** : a renunciation or abandonment of a former loyalty (as to a religion) — **apos·tate** \ə-ˈpäs-ˌtāt, -tət\ adj or n

a pos·te·ri·o·ri \ˌä-pō-ˌstir-ē-ˈȯr-ē\ adj [L, lit., from the latter] : relating to or derived by reasoning from observed facts — **a posteriori** adv

apos·tle \ə-ˈpä-səl\ n 1 : one of the group composed of Jesus' 12 original disciples and Paul 2 : the first prominent missionary to a region or group 3 : a person who initiates or first advocates a great reform — **apos·tle·ship** n

ap·os·tol·ic \ˌa-pə-ˈstä-lik\ adj 1 : of or relating to an apostle or to the New Testament apostles 2 : of or relating to a succession of spiritual authority from the apostles 3 : PAPAL

¹**apos·tro·phe** \ə-ˈpäs-trə-(ˌ)fē\ n : the rhetorical addressing of a usu. absent person or a usu. personified thing (as in "O grave, where is thy victory?")

²**apostrophe** n : a punctuation mark ' used esp. to indicate the possessive case or the omission of a letter or figure

apos·tro·phise *Brit var of* APOSTROPHIZE

apos·tro·phize \ə-ˈpäs-trə-ˌfīz\ vb **-phized; -phiz·ing** : to address as if present or capable of understanding

apothecaries' weight n : a system of weights based on the troy pound and ounce and used chiefly by pharmacists — see WEIGHT table

apoth·e·cary \ə-ˈpä-thə-ˌker-ē\ n, pl **-caries** [ME *apothecarie*, fr. ML *apothecarius*, fr. LL, shopkeeper, fr. L *apotheca* storehouse, fr. Gk *apothēkē*, fr. *apotithenai* to put away] : DRUGGIST

ap·o·thegm \ˈa-pə-ˌthem\ n : APHORISM

apo·the·o·sis \ə-ˌpä-thē-ˈō-səs, ˌa-pə-ˈthē-ə-səs\ n, pl **-o·ses** \-ˌsēz\ 1 : DEIFICATION 2 : the perfect example

¹**app** \ˈap\ n : APPLICATION 6

²**app** *abbr* 1 apparatus 2 appendix

ap·pall *also* **ap·pal** \ə-ˈpȯl\ vb **ap·palled; ap·pall·ing** : to overcome with horror : DISMAY

Ap·pa·loo·sa \ˌa-pə-ˈlü-sə\ n : any of a breed of saddle horses developed in western No. America and usu. having a white or solid-colored coat with small spots

ap·pa·nage *also* **a·pa·nage** \ˈa-pə-nij\ n 1 : provision (as a grant of land) made by a sovereign or legislative body for dependent members of the royal family 2 : a rightful adjunct

ap·pa·ra·tus \ˌa-pə-ˈra-təs, -ˈrā-\ n, pl **-tus·es** or **-tus** [L] 1 : a set of materials or equipment for a particular use 2 : a complex machine or device : MECHANISM 3 : the organization of a political party or underground movement

¹**ap·par·el** \ə-ˈper-əl\ vb **-eled** or **-elled; -el·ing** or **-el·ling** 1 : CLOTHE 2 : ADORN

²**apparel** n : CLOTHING, DRESS

ap·par·ent \ə-ˈper-ənt\ adj 1 : open to view : VISIBLE 2 : EVIDENT, OBVIOUS 3 : appearing as real or true : SEEMING

ap·par·ent·ly \-lē\ adv : it seems apparent

ap·pa·ri·tion \ˌa-pə-ˈri-shən\ n : a supernatural appearance : GHOST

ap·peal \ə-ˈpēl\ vb 1 : to take steps to have (a case) reheard in a higher court 2 : to plead for help, corroboration, or decision 3 : to arouse a sympathetic response — **appeal** n

ap·pear \ə-ˈpir\ vb 1 : to become visible 2 : to come formally before an authority 3 : SEEM 4 : to become evident 5 : to come before the public

ap·pear·ance \ə-ˈpir-əns\ n 1 : outward aspect : LOOK 2 : the act of appearing 3 : PHENOMENON

ap·pease \ə-ˈpēz\ vb **ap·peased; ap·peas·ing** 1 : to cause to subside : ALLAY 2 : PACIFY, CONCILIATE; *esp* : to buy off by concessions — **ap·pease·ment** n — **ap·peas·able** \-ˈpē-zə-bəl\ adj

ap·pel·lant \ə-ˈpe-lənt\ n : one who appeals esp. from a judicial decision

ap·pel·late \ə-ˈpe-lət\ adj : having power to review decisions of a lower court

ap·pel·la·tion \ˌa-pə-ˈlā-shən\ n : NAME, DESIGNATION

ap·pel·lee \ˌa-pə-ˈlē\ n : one against whom an appeal is taken

ap·pend \ə-ˈpend\ vb : to attach esp. as something additional : AFFIX

ap·pend·age \ə-ˈpen-dij\ n 1 : something appended to a principal or greater thing 2 : a projecting part (as an antenna) of an animal or plant body; *esp* : an arm, leg, or similar part ♦ *Synonyms* ACCESSORY, ADJUNCT, APPENDIX, APPURTENANCE

ap·pen·dec·to·my \ˌa-pən-ˈdek-tə-mē\ n, pl **-mies** : surgical removal of the intestinal appendix

ap·pen·di·ci·tis \ə-ˌpen-də-ˈsī-təs\ n : inflammation of the intestinal appendix

ap·pen·dix \ə-ˈpen-diks\ n, pl **-dix·es** or

-di·ces \-də-ˌsēz\ [L] 1 : supplementary matter added at the end of a book 2 : a narrow blind tube usu. about three or four inches long that extends from the cecum in the lower right-hand part of the abdomen

ap·per·tain \ˌa-pər-ˈtān\ vb : to belong as a rightful part or privilege

ap·pe·tis·er, ap·pe·tis·ing Brit var of AP-PETIZER, APPETIZING

ap·pe·tite \ˈa-pə-ˌtīt\ n [ME apetit, fr. AF, fr. L appetitus, fr. appetere to strive after, fr. ad- to + petere to go to] 1 : natural desire for satisfying some want or need esp. for food 2 : TASTE, PREFERENCE

ap·pe·tiz·er \ˈa-pə-ˌtī-zər\ n : a food or drink taken just before a meal to stimulate the appetite

ap·pe·tiz·ing \-ziŋ\ adj : tempting to the appetite — **ap·pe·tiz·ing·ly** adv

appl abbr applied

ap·plaud \ə-ˈplȯd\ vb : to show approval esp. by clapping

ap·plause \ə-ˈplȯz\ n : approval publicly expressed (as by clapping)

ap·ple \ˈa-pəl\ n : a rounded fruit with firm white flesh and a seedy core; also : a tree that bears this fruit

ap·ple·jack \-ˌjak\ n : a liquor distilled from fermented cider

ap·plet \ˈa-plət\ n : a short computer program esp. for performing a simple specific task

ap·pli·ance \ə-ˈplī-əns\ n 1 : INSTRUMENT, DEVICE 2 : a piece of household equipment (as a stove or toaster) operated by gas or electricity

ap·pli·ca·ble \ˈa-pli-kə-bəl, ə-ˈpli-kə-\ adj : capable of being applied : RELEVANT — **ap·pli·ca·bil·i·ty** \ˌa-pli-kə-ˈbi-lə-tē, ə-ˌpli-kə-\ n

ap·pli·cant \ˈa-pli-kənt\ n : one who applies ⟨a job ~⟩

ap·pli·ca·tion \ˌa-plə-ˈkā-shən\ n 1 : the act of applying 2 : assiduous attention 3 : REQUEST; also : a form used in making a request 4 : something placed or spread on a surface 5 : capacity for use 6 : a program (as a word processor) that performs one of a computer's major tasks

ap·pli·ca·tor \ˈa-plə-ˌkā-tər\ n : a device for applying a substance (as medicine or polish)

ap·plied \ə-ˈplīd\ adj : put to practical use ⟨~ art⟩

ap·pli·qué \ˌa-plə-ˈkā\ n [F] : a fabric decoration cut out and fastened to a larger piece of material — **appliqué** vb

ap·ply \ə-ˈplī\ vb **ap·plied; ap·ply·ing** 1 : to put to practical use 2 : to place in contact : put or spread on a surface 3 : to employ with close attention 4 : to have reference or connection 5 : to submit a request

ap·point \ə-ˈpȯint\ vb 1 : to fix or set officially ⟨~ a day for trial⟩ 2 : to name officially 3 : to fit out : EQUIP

ap·poin·tee \ə-ˌpȯin-ˈtē, ˌa-\ n : a person appointed

ap·point·ive \ə-ˈpȯin-tiv\ adj : subject to appointment

ap·point·ment \ə-ˈpȯint-mənt\ n 1 : the act of appointing 2 : an arrangement for a meeting 3 pl : FURNISHINGS, EQUIPMENT 4 : a nonelective office or position

ap·por·tion \ə-ˈpȯr-shən\ vb : to distribute proportionately : ALLOT — **ap·por·tion·ment** n

ap·po·site \ˈa-pə-zət\ adj : APPROPRIATE, RELEVANT — **ap·po·site·ly** adv — **ap·po·site·ness** n

ap·po·si·tion \ˌa-pə-ˈzi-shən\ n : a grammatical construction in which a noun or pronoun is followed by another that has the same referent (as the poet and Burns in "a biography of the poet Burns")

ap·pos·i·tive \ə-ˈpä-zə-tiv, a-\ adj : of, relating to, or standing in grammatical apposition — **appositive** n

ap·praise \ə-ˈprāz\ vb **ap·praised; ap·prais·ing** : to set a value on — **ap·prais·al** \-ˈprā-zəl\ n — **ap·prais·er** n

ap·pre·cia·ble \ə-ˈprē-shə-bəl\ adj : large enough to be recognized and measured — **ap·pre·cia·bly** adv

ap·pre·ci·ate \ə-ˈprē-shē-ˌāt\ vb **-at·ed; -at·ing** 1 : to value justly 2 : to be aware of 3 : to be grateful for 4 : to increase in value — **ap·pre·ci·a·tion** \-ˌprē-shē-ˈā-shən\ n

ap·pre·cia·tive \ə-ˈprē-shə-tiv, -shē-ˌāt-\ adj : having or showing appreciation — **ap·pre·cia·tive·ly** adv

ap·pre·hend \ˌa-pri-ˈhend\ vb 1 : ARREST 2 : to become aware of 3 : to look forward to with dread 4 : UNDERSTAND — **ap·pre·hen·sion** \-ˈhen-chən\ n

ap·pre·hen·sive \-ˈhen-siv\ adj : viewing the future with anxiety — **ap·pre·hen·sive·ly** adv — **ap·pre·hen·sive·ness** n

¹**ap·pren·tice** \ə-ˈpren-təs\ n 1 : a person learning a craft under a skilled worker 2 : BEGINNER — **ap·pren·tice·ship** n

²**apprentice** vb **-ticed; -tic·ing** : to bind or set at work as an apprentice

ap·prise \ə-ˈprīz\ vb **ap·prised; ap·pris·ing** : INFORM ⟨apprised him of his rights⟩

ap·proach \ə-ˈprōch\ vb 1 : to move nearer to ⟨~ the bench⟩ 2 : to be almost the same as 3 : to make advances to esp. for the purpose of creating a desired result 4 : to take preliminary steps toward ⟨~ the subject carefully⟩ — **approach** n — **ap·proach·able** adj

ap·pro·ba·tion \ˌa-prə-ˈbā-shən\ n : APPROVAL

¹**ap·pro·pri·ate** \ə-ˈprō-prē-ˌāt\ vb **-at·ed; -at·ing** 1 : to take possession of 2 : to set apart for a particular use

²**ap·pro·pri·ate** \ə-ˈprō-prē-ət\ adj : fitted to a purpose or use : SUITABLE ♦ **Synonyms** PROPER, FIT, APT, BEFITTING — **ap·pro·pri·ate·ly** adv — **ap·pro·pri·ate·ness** n

ap·pro·pri·a·tion \ə-ˌprō-prē-ˈā-shən\ n : something (as money) set aside by formal action for a specific use

ap·prov·al \ə-ˈprü-vəl\ n : an act of approving — **on approval** : subject to a prospective buyer's acceptance or refusal

ap·prove \ə-'prüv\ *vb* **ap·proved; ap·prov·ing** **1** : to have or express a favorable opinion of **2** : to accept as satisfactory : RATIFY ⟨~ the treaty⟩

approx *abbr* approximate; approximately

¹ap·prox·i·mate \ə-'präk-sə-mət\ *adj* : nearly correct or exact ⟨an ~ count⟩ — **ap·prox·i·mate·ly** *adv*

²ap·prox·i·mate \-ˌmāt\ *vb* **-mat·ed; -mat·ing** : to come or bring near or close — **ap·prox·i·ma·tion** \ə-ˌpräk-sə-'mā-shən\ *n*

appt *abbr* appoint; appointed; appointment

ap·pur·te·nance \ə-'pərt-nəns, -'pər-tə-nəns\ *n* : something that belongs to or goes with another thing ♦ **Synonyms** ACCESSORY, ADJUNCT, APPENDAGE, APPENDIX — **ap·pur·te·nant** \ə-'pərt-nənt, -'pər-tə-nənt\ *adj*

Apr *abbr* April

APR *abbr* annual percentage rate

apri·cot \'a-prə-ˌkät, 'ā-\ *n* [alter. of earlier *abrecock,* ultim. fr. Ar *al-birqūq,* ultim. fr. L (*persicum*) *praecox,* lit., early-ripening (peach)] : an oval orange-colored fruit resembling the related peach and plum in flavor; *also* : a tree bearing apricots

April \'ā-prəl\ *n* [ME, fr. AF & L; AF *avrill,* fr. L *Aprilis*] : the 4th month of the year

a pri·o·ri \ˌä-prē-'ȯr-ē\ *adj* [L, from the former] **1** : characterized by or derived by reasoning from self-evident propositions **2** : independent of experience — **a priori** *adv*

apron \'ā-prən\ *n* [ME, alter. (fr. misdivision of *a napron*) of *napron,* fr. MF *naperon,* dim. of *nape* cloth, modif. of L *mappa* napkin] **1** : a garment tied over the front of the body to protect the clothes **2** : a paved area for parking or handling airplanes — **aproned** *adj*

¹ap·ro·pos \ˌa-prə-'pō, 'a-prə-ˌpō\ *adv* [F *à propos,* lit., to the purpose] **1** : OPPORTUNELY **2** : in passing : INCIDENTALLY

²apropos *adj* : being to the point

apropos of *prep* : with regard to

apse \'aps\ *n* : a projecting usu. semicircular and vaulted part of a building (as a church)

¹apt \'apt\ *adj* **1** : well adapted : SUITABLE **2** : having an habitual tendency : LIKELY **3** : quick to learn — **apt·ly** *adv* — **apt·ness** \'apt-nəs\ *n*

²apt *abbr* **1** apartment **2** aptitude

ap·ti·tude \'ap-tə-ˌtüd, -ˌtyüd\ *n* **1** : natural ability : TALENT **2** : capacity for learning **3** : APPROPRIATENESS

aqua \'a-kwə, 'ä-\ *n* : a light greenish blue color

aqua·cul·ture \'a-kwə-ˌkəl-chər, 'ä-\ *n* : the cultivation of aquatic organisms (as fish or shellfish) for human use esp. as food — **aqua·cul·tur·ist** \-chə-rist\ *n*

aqua·ma·rine \ˌa-kwə-mə-'rēn, ˌä-\ *n* **1** : a bluish green gem **2** : a pale blue to light greenish blue

aqua·naut \'a-kwə-ˌnȯt, 'ä-\ *n* : a person

who lives in an underwater shelter for an extended period

aqua·plane \-ˌplān\ *n* : a board towed behind a motorboat and ridden by a person standing on it — **aquaplane** *vb*

aqua re·gia \ˌa-kwə-'rē-j(ē-)ə\ *n* [NL, lit., royal water] : a mixture of nitric and hydrochloric acids that dissolves gold or platinum

aquar·i·um \ə-'kwer-ē-əm\ *n, pl* **-i·ums** *or* **-ia** \-ē-ə\ **1** : a container (as a glass tank) in which living aquatic animals or plants are kept **2** : a place where aquatic animals and plants are kept and shown

Aquar·i·us \ə-'kwer-ē-əs\ *n* [L, lit., water carrier] **1** : a zodiacal constellation between Capricorn and Pisces usu. pictured as a man pouring water **2** : the 11th sign of the zodiac in astrology; *also* : one born under this sign

¹aquat·ic \ə-'kwä-tik, -'kwa-\ *adj* **1** : growing or living in or frequenting water **2** : performed in or on water

²aquatic *n* : an aquatic animal or plant

aqua·vit \'ä-kwə-ˌvēt\ *n* : a clear liquor flavored with caraway seeds

aqua vi·tae \ˌa-kwə-'vī-tē, ˌä-\ *n* [ME, fr. ML, lit., water of life] : a strong alcoholic liquor (as brandy)

aq·ue·duct \'a-kwə-ˌdəkt\ *n* **1** : a conduit for carrying running water **2** : a structure carrying a canal over a river or hollow **3** : a passage in a bodily part

aque·ous \'ā-kwē-əs, 'a-\ *adj* **1** : WATERY **2** : made of, by, or with water

aqueous humor *n* : a clear fluid occupying the space between the lens and the cornea of the eye

aqui·fer \'ā-kwə-fər, 'a-\ *n* : a water-bearing stratum of permeable rock, sand, or gravel

aq·ui·line \'a-kwə-ˌlīn, -lən\ *adj* **1** : of or resembling an eagle **2** : hooked like an eagle's beak ⟨an ~ nose⟩

ar *abbr* arrival; arrive

Ar *symbol* argon

AR *abbr* Arkansas

-ar *adj suffix* : of or relating to ⟨molecular⟩ : being ⟨spectacular⟩ : resembling ⟨oracular⟩

Ar·ab \'a-rəb\ *n* **1** : a member of a Semitic people of the Arabian peninsula in southwestern Asia **2** : a member of an Arabic-speaking people — **Arab** *adj* — **Ara·bi·an** \ə-'rā-bē-ən\ *adj or n*

ar·a·besque \ˌa-rə-'besk\ *n* : a design of interlacing lines forming figures of flowers, foliage, and sometimes animals — **arabesque** *adj*

¹Ar·a·bic \'a-rə-bik\ *n* : a Semitic language of southwestern Asia and northern Africa

²Arabic *adj* **1** : of or relating to the Arabs, Arabic, or the Arabian peninsula in southwestern Asia **2** : expressed in or making use of Arabic numerals

Arabic numeral *n* : any of the number symbols 0, 1, 2, 3, 4, 5, 6, 7, 8, 9

ar·a·ble \'a-rə-bəl\ *adj* : fit for or used for the growing of crops ⟨~ land⟩

arach·nid \ə-'rak-nəd\ *n* : any of a class of usu. 8-legged arthropods comprising the spiders, scorpions, mites, and ticks — **arachnid** *adj*

Ar·a·ma·ic \ˌa-rə-ˈmā-ik\ *n* : an ancient Semitic language

ar·a·mid \ˈa-rə-məd, -ˌmid\ *n* : any of several light but very strong heat-resistant synthetic materials used esp. in textiles and plastics

Arap·a·ho *or* **Arap·a·hoe** \ə-ˈra-pə-ˌhō\ *n, pl* **-ho** *or* **-hos** *or* **-hoe** *or* **-hoes** : a member of an American Indian people of the western U.S.

ar·bi·ter \ˈär-bə-tər\ *n* : one having power to decide : JUDGE

ar·bi·trage \ˈär-bə-ˌträzh\ *n* [F, fr. MF, arbitration] : the purchase and sale of the same or equivalent securities in different markets in order to profit from price discrepancies

ar·bi·tra·geur \ˌär-bə-(ˌ)trä-ˈzhər\ *or* **ar·bi·trag·er** \ˈär-bə-ˌträ-zhər\ *n* : one who practices arbitrage

ar·bit·ra·ment \är-ˈbi-trə-mənt\ *n* 1 : the act of deciding a dispute 2 : the judgment given by an arbitrator

ar·bi·trary \ˈär-bə-ˌtrer-ē\ *adj* 1 : AUTOCRATIC, DESPOTIC 2 : determined by will or caprice : selected at random — **ar·bi·trari·ly** \ˌär-bə-ˈtrer-ə-lē\ *adv* — **ar·bi·trari·ness** \ˈär-bə-ˌtrer-ē-nəs\ *n*

ar·bi·trate \ˈär-bə-ˌtrāt\ *vb* **-trat·ed; -trat·ing** 1 : to act as arbitrator 2 : to act on as arbitrator 3 : to submit for decision to an arbitrator — **ar·bi·tra·tion** \ˌär-bə-ˈtrā-shən\ *n*

ar·bi·tra·tor \ˈär-bə-ˌtrā-tər\ *n* : one chosen to settle differences between two parties in a controversy

ar·bor \ˈär-bər\ *n* [ME *erber, herber* garden, fr. AF, fr. *herbe* herb, grass] : a shelter formed of or covered with vines or branches

ar·bo·re·al \är-ˈbȯr-ē-əl\ *adj* 1 : of, relating to, or resembling a tree 2 : living in trees ⟨~ monkeys⟩

ar·bo·re·tum \ˌär-bə-ˈrē-təm\ *n, pl* **-re·tums** *or* **-re·ta** \-tə\ [L, plantation of trees, fr. *arbor* tree] : a place where trees and plants are grown for scientific and educational purposes

ar·bor·vi·tae \ˌär-bər-ˈvī-tē\ *n* : any of various evergreen trees and shrubs with scalelike leaves that are related to the cypresses

ar·bour *chiefly Brit var of* ARBOR

ar·bu·tus \är-ˈbyü-təs\ *n* : TRAILING ARBUTUS

¹**arc** \ˈärk\ *n* 1 : a sustained luminous discharge of electricity (as between two electrodes) 2 : a continuous portion of a curved line (as part of the circumference of a circle)

²**arc** *vb* **arced** \ˈärkt\; **arc·ing** \ˈär-kiŋ\ : to form an electric arc

ARC *abbr* 1 AIDS-related complex 2 American Red Cross

ar·cade \är-ˈkād\ *n* 1 : an arched or covered passageway; *esp* : one lined with shops 2 : a row of arches with their supporting columns 3 : an amusement center having coin-operated games

ar·cane \är-ˈkān\ *adj* : SECRET, MYSTERIOUS

¹**arch** \ˈärch\ *n* 1 : a curved structure spanning an opening (as a door) 2 : something resembling an arch 3 : ARCHWAY

²**arch** *vb* 1 : to cover with an arch 2 : to form or bend into an arch

³**arch** *adj* 1 : CHIEF, EMINENT ⟨my ~ enemy⟩ 2 : ROGUISH, MISCHIEVOUS; *also* : deliberately playful or impudent ⟨~ comments⟩ — **arch·ly** *adv* — **arch·ness** *n*

⁴**arch** *abbr* architect; architectural; architecture

ar·chae·ol·o·gy *or* **ar·che·ol·o·gy** \ˌär-kē-ˈä-lə-jē\ *n* : the study of past human life as revealed by relics left by ancient peoples — **ar·chae·o·log·i·cal** \-ə-ˈlä-ji-kəl\ *adj* — **ar·chae·ol·o·gist** \-ˈä-lə-jist\ *n*

ar·cha·ic \är-ˈkā-ik\ *adj* 1 : having the characteristics of the language of the past and surviving chiefly in specialized uses ⟨~ words⟩ 2 : belonging to an earlier time : ANTIQUATED — **ar·cha·i·cal·ly** \-i-k(ə-)lē\ *adv*

arch·an·gel \ˈär-ˌkān-jəl\ *n* : a chief angel

arch·bish·op \ärch-ˈbi-shəp\ *n* : a bishop of high rank

arch·bish·op·ric \-shə-(ˌ)prik\ *n* : the jurisdiction or office of an archbishop

arch·con·ser·va·tive \(ˌ)ärch-kən-ˈsər-və-tiv\ *n* : an extreme conservative — **archconservative** *adj*

arch·dea·con \-ˈdē-kən\ *n* : a church official who assists a diocesan bishop in ceremonial or administrative functions

arch·di·o·cese \-ˈdī-ə-səs, -ˌsēz\ *n* : the diocese of an archbishop

arch·duke \-ˈdük, -ˈdyük\ *n* 1 : a sovereign prince 2 : a prince of the imperial family of Austria

Ar·che·an \är-ˈkē-ən\ *adj* : of, relating to, or being the earliest eon of geologic history — **Archean** *n*

arch·en·e·my \ärch-ˈe-nə-mē\ *n, pl* **-mies** : a principal enemy

Ar·cheo·zo·ic \ˌär-kē-ə-ˈzō-ik\ *adj* : ARCHEAN — **Archeozoic** *n*

ar·chery \ˈär-chə-rē\ *n* : the art or practice of shooting with bow and arrows — **ar·cher** \ˈär-chər\ *n*

ar·che·type \ˈär-ki-ˌtīp\ *n* : the original pattern or model of all things of the same type — **ar·che·typ·al** \ˌär-kə-ˈtī-pəl\ *adj*

arch·fiend \ˈärch-ˈfēnd\ *n* : a chief fiend; *esp* : SATAN

ar·chi·epis·co·pal \ˌär-kē-ə-ˈpis-kə-pəl\ *adj* : of or relating to an archbishop

ar·chi·man·drite \ˌär-kə-ˈman-ˌdrīt\ *n* : a dignitary in an Eastern church ranking below a bishop

ar·chi·pel·a·go \ˌär-kə-ˈpe-lə-ˌgō, ˌär-chə-\ *n, pl* **-goes** *or* **-gos** : a group of islands

ar·chi·tect \ˈär-kə-ˌtekt\ *n* : a person who plans buildings and oversees their construction : a person who designs and guides a plan or undertaking

ar·chi·tec·ture \ˈär-kə-ˌtek-chər\ *n* 1 : the art or science of planning and building structures **2** : a method or style of building **3** : the manner in which the elements (as of a design) or components (of a computer) are arranged or organized — **ar·chi·tec·tur·al** \ˌär-kə-'tek-chə-rəl, -'tek-shrəl\ *adj* — **ar·chi·tec·tur·al·ly** *adv*

ar·chi·trave \'är-kə-ˌträv\ *n* : the supporting horizontal member just above the columns in a building in the classical style of architecture

ar·chive \'är-ˌkīv\ *n* **1** : a place for keeping public records; *also* : public records — often used in pl. **2** : a repository esp. of information

ar·chi·vist \'är-kə-vist, -ˌkī-\ *n* : a person in charge of archives

ar·chon \'är-ˌkän, -kən\ *n* : a chief magistrate of ancient Athens

arch·ri·val \'ärch-'rī-vəl\ *n* : a principal rival

arch·way \'ärch-ˌwä\ *n* : a passageway under an arch; *also* : an arch over a passage

arc lamp *n* : a gas-filled electric lamp that produces light when a current arcs between incandescent electrodes

¹arc·tic \'ärk-tik, 'är-tik\ *adj* [ME *artik*, fr. L *arcticus*, fr. Gk *arktikos*, fr. *arktos* bear, Ursa Major, north] **1** *often cap* : of or relating to the north pole or the region near it **2** : FRIGID

²arc·tic \'är-tik, 'ärk-tik\ *n* : a rubber overshoe that reaches to the ankle or above

arctic circle *n, often cap A&C* : the parallel of latitude that is approximately 66½ degrees north of the equator

-ard *also* **-art** *n suffix* : one that is characterized by performing some action, possessing some quality, or being associated with some thing esp. conspicuously or excessively ⟨brag*art*⟩ ⟨dull*ard*⟩

ar·dent \'är-dˀnt\ *adj* **1** : characterized by warmth of feeling : PASSIONATE **2** : FIERY, HOT ⟨an ~ sun⟩ **3** : GLOWING ⟨~ eyes⟩ — **ar·dent·ly** *adv*

ar·dor \'är-dər\ *n* **1** : warmth of feeling : ZEAL **2** : sexual excitement

ar·dour *chiefly Brit var of* ARDOR

ar·du·ous \'är-jə-wəs, -dyü-wəs\ *adj* : DIFFICULT, LABORIOUS — **ar·du·ous·ly** *adv* — **ar·du·ous·ness** *n*

¹are *pres 2d sing or pres pl of* BE

²are \'er\ *n* — see METRIC SYSTEM table

ar·ea \'er-ē-ə\ *n* **1** : a flat surface or space **2** : the amount of surface included (as within the lines of a geometric figure) **3** : range or extent of some thing or concept : FIELD **4** : REGION

area code *n* : a usu. 3-digit number that identifies each telephone service area in a country (as the U.S. or Canada)

are·na \ə-'rē-nə\ *n* [L *harena, arena* sand, sandy place] **1** : an enclosed area used for public entertainment **2** : a sphere of activity or competition

ar·gen·tite \'är-jən-ˌtīt\ *n* : a dark gray or black mineral of metallic luster that is an important ore of silver

ar·gon \'är-ˌgän\ *n* [Gk, neut. of *argos* idle, lazy, fr. *a-* not + *ergon* work; fr. its relative inertness] : a colorless odorless

gaseous chemical element found in the air and used for filling electric lamps

ar·go·sy \'är-gə-sē\ *n, pl* **-sies 1** : a large merchant ship **2** : FLEET

ar·got \'är-gət, -ˌgō\ *n* : the language of a particular group or class

argu·able \'är-gyü-ə-bəl\ *adj* : open to argument, dispute, or question

ar·gu·ably \'är-gyü-(ə-)blē\ *adv* : as may be argued or shown by argument

ar·gue \'är-gyü\ *vb* **ar·gued; ar·gu·ing 1** : to give reasons for or against something **2** : to contend in words : DISPUTE **3** : DEBATE **4** : to persuade by giving reasons

ar·gu·ment \'är-gyə-mənt\ *n* **1** : a reason offered in proof **2** : discourse intended to persuade **3** : QUARREL

ar·gu·men·ta·tion \ˌär-gyə-mən-'tä-shən\ *n* : the art of formal discussion

ar·gu·men·ta·tive \ˌär-gyə-'men-tə-tiv\ *adj* : inclined to argue

ar·gyle *also* **ar·gyll** \'är-ˌgī(-ə)l\ *n, often cap* : a geometric knitting pattern of varicolored diamonds on a single background color; *also* : a sock knit in this pattern

aria \'är-ē-ə\ *n* : an accompanied elaborate vocal solo forming part of a larger work

ar·id \'a-rəd\ *adj* : very dry; *esp* : having insufficient rainfall to support agriculture — **arid·i·ty** \ə-'ri-də-tē\ *n*

Ar·i·es \'er-ˌēz, -ē-ˌēz\ *n* [L, lit., ram] **1** : a zodiacal constellation between Pisces and Taurus pictured as a ram **2** : the 1st sign of the zodiac in astrology; *also* : one born under this sign

aright \ə-'rīt\ *adv* : RIGHT, CORRECTLY

arise \ə-'rīz\ *vb* **arose** \-'rōz\; **aris·en** \-'ri-zˀn\; **aris·ing** \-'rī-ziŋ\ **1** : to get up **2** : ORIGINATE **3** : ASCEND ♦ **Synonyms** RISE, DERIVE, SPRING, ISSUE

ar·is·toc·ra·cy \ˌa-rə-'stä-krə-sē\ *n, pl* **-cies 1** : government by a noble or privileged class; *also* : a state so governed **2** : the governing class of an aristocracy **3** : UPPER CLASS — **aris·to·crat** \ə-'ris-tə-ˌkrat\ *n* — **aris·to·crat·ic** \ə-ˌris-tə-'kra-tik\ *adj*

arith *abbr* arithmetic; arithmetical

arith·me·tic \ə-'rith-mə-ˌtik\ *n* **1** : a branch of mathematics that deals with computations usu. with nonnegative real numbers **2** : COMPUTATION, CALCULATION — **ar·ith·met·ic** \ˌer-ith-'me-tik\ *or* **ar·ith·met·i·cal** \-i-kəl\ *adj* — **arith·met·i·cal·ly** \-ti-k(ə-)lē\ *adv* — **arith·me·ti·cian** \ə-ˌrith-mə-'ti-shən\ *n*

arithmetic mean *n* : the sum of a set of numbers divided by the number of numbers in the set

Ariz *abbr* Arizona

ark \'ärk\ *n* **1** : a boat held to resemble that of Noah's at the time of the Flood **2** : the sacred chest in a synagogue representing to Hebrews the presence of God; *also* : the repository for the scrolls of the Torah

Ark *abbr* Arkansas

¹arm \'ärm\ *n* [ME, fr. OE *earm*] **1** : a human upper limb and esp. the part between the shoulder and wrist; *also* : a corresponding limb of a 2-footed vertebrate

2 : something resembling an arm in shape or position ⟨an ∼ of a chair⟩ ⟨the eight ∼s of an octopus⟩ **3** : POWER, MIGHT ⟨the ∼ of the law⟩ — **armed** \'ärmd\ — **arm·less** adj

²**arm** vb [ME, fr. AF armer, fr. L armare, fr. arma weapons, tools] : to furnish with weapons

³**arm** n **1** : WEAPON **2** : a branch of the military forces **3** pl : the hereditary heraldic devices of a family

ar·ma·da \är-'mä-də, -'mä-\ n : a fleet of warships

ar·ma·dil·lo \,är-mə-'di-lō\ n, pl **-los** [Sp, fr. dim. of armado armed one] : any of several small burrowing mammals with the head and body protected by an armor of bony plates

Ar·ma·ged·don \,är-mə-'ge-d³n\ n : a final conclusive battle between the forces of good and evil; also : the site or time of this

ar·ma·ment \'är-mə-mənt\ n **1** : military strength **2** : arms and equipment (as of a tank or combat unit) **3** : the process of preparing for war

ar·ma·ture \'är-mə-,chu̇r, -chər\ n **1** : a protective covering or structure (as the spines of a cactus) **2** : the rotating part of an electric generator or motor; also : the movable part in an electromagnetic device (as a loudspeaker)

arm·chair \'ärm-,cher\ n : a chair with armrests

armed forces n pl : the combined military, naval, and air forces of a nation

Ar·me·nian \är-'mē-nē-ən\ n **1** : a native or inhabitant of Armenia **2** : the Indo-European language of the Armenians

arm·ful \'ärm-,fu̇l\ n, pl **armfuls** or **armsful** \'ärmz-,fu̇l\ : as much as the arm or arms can hold

arm·hole \'ärm-,hōl\ n : an opening for the arm in a garment

ar·mi·stice \'är-mə-stəs\ n : temporary suspension of hostilities by mutual agreement : TRUCE

arm·let \'ärm-lət\ n : a band worn around the upper arm

ar·mor \'är-mər\ n **1** : protective covering **2** : armored forces and vehicles — **ar·mored** \-mərd\ adj

ar·mor·er \'är-mər-ər\ n **1** : a person who makes arms and armor **2** : a person who services firearms

ar·mo·ri·al \är-'mȯr-ē-əl\ adj : of or bearing heraldic arms

ar·mory \'är-mə-rē\ n, pl **ar·mor·ies** **1** : a place where arms are stored **2** : a factory where arms are made

ar·mour, ar·moury chiefly Brit var of ARMOR, ARMORY

arm·pit \'ärm-,pit\ n : the hollow under the junction of the arm and shoulder

arm·rest \-,rest\ n : a support for the arm

ar·my \'är-mē\ n, pl **armies** **1** : a body of men organized for war **2** often cap : the complete military organization of a country for land warfare **3** : a great number **4** : a body of persons organized to advance a cause

army ant n : any of various nomadic social ants

ar·my·worm \'är-mē-,wərm\ n : any of numerous moths whose larvae move about destroying crops

aro·ma \ə-'rō-mə\ n : a usu. pleasing odor : FRAGRANCE — **ar·o·mat·ic** \,ar-ə-'ma-tik\ adj

aro·ma·ther·a·py \ə-,rō-mə-'ther-ə-pē\ n : massage with a preparation of fragrant oils extracted from herbs, flowers, and fruits

arose past of ARISE

¹**around** \ə-'rau̇nd\ adv **1** : in a circle or in circumference ⟨a tree five feet ∼⟩ **2** : in or along a circuit ⟨the road goes ∼ by the lake⟩ **3** : on all sides ⟨nothing for miles ∼⟩ **4** : NEARBY ⟨wait ∼ awhile⟩ **5** : from one place to another ⟨travels ∼ on business⟩ **6** : in an opposite direction ⟨turn ∼⟩ **7** — used with some verbs to indicate continued action ⟨joking ∼⟩ **8** : APPROXIMATELY ⟨cost ∼ $5⟩

²**around** prep **1** : SURROUNDING ⟨trees ∼ the house⟩ **2** : to or on another side of ⟨∼ the corner⟩ **3** : NEAR ⟨stayed right ∼ home⟩ **4** : along the circuit of ⟨go ∼ the world⟩

arouse \ə-'rau̇z\ vb **aroused**; **arous·ing** **1** : to awaken from sleep **2** : to stir up : EXCITE — **arous·al** \-'rau̇-zəl\ n

ar·peg·gio \är-'pe-jē-,ō, -'pe-jō\ n, pl **-gios** [It fr. arpeggiare to play on the harp, fr. arpa harp] : a chord whose notes are performed in succession and not simultaneously

arr abbr **1** arranged **2** arrival; arrive

ar·raign \ə-'rān\ vb **1** : to call before a court to answer to an indictment **2** : to accuse of wrong or imperfection — **ar·raign·ment** n

ar·range \ə-'rānj\ vb **ar·ranged**; **ar·rang·ing** **1** : to put in order **2** : PLAN ⟨∼ an interview⟩ **3** : to adapt (a musical composition) to voices or instruments other than those for which it was orig. written **4** : to come to an agreement about : SETTLE — **ar·range·ment** n — **ar·rang·er** n

ar·rant \'a-rənt\ adj : being notoriously without moderation : EXTREME

ar·ras \'a-rəs\ n, pl **arras** **1** : TAPESTRY **2** : a wall hanging or screen of tapestry

¹**ar·ray** \ə-'rā\ vb **1** : to dress esp. splendidly **2** : to arrange in order (as in an array)

²**array** n **1** : a regular arrangement **2** : rich apparel **3** : a large or varied group

ar·rears \ə-'rirz\ n pl **1** : a state of being behind in the discharge of obligations ⟨in ∼ with the rent⟩ **2** : overdue debts

¹**ar·rest** \ə-'rest\ vb **1** : STOP, CHECK **2** : to take into legal custody

²**arrest** n **1** : the act of stopping; also : the state of being stopped **2** : the taking into custody by legal authority

ar·rhyth·mia \ā-'rith-mē-ə\ n : an alteration of the heartbeat's rhythm

ar·riv·al \ə-'rī-vəl\ n **1** : the act of arriving **2** : one that arrives

ar·rive \ə-'rīv\ vb **ar·rived**; **ar·riv·ing** **1**

: to reach a destination　**2** : to make an appearance ⟨the guests have *arrived*⟩　**3** : to attain success

ar·ro·gant \\'er-ə-gənt\\ *adj* : offensively exaggerating one's own importance — **ar·ro·gance** \\-gəns\\ *n* — **ar·ro·gant·ly** *adv*

ar·ro·gate \\-,gāt\\ *vb* **-gat·ed; -gat·ing** : to claim or seize without justification as one's right — **ar·ro·ga·tion** \\,ar-ə-'gā-shən\\ *n*

ar·row \\'er-ō\\ *n* **1** : a missile shot from a bow and usu. having a slender shaft, a pointed head, and feathers at the butt　**2** : a pointed mark used to indicate direction

ar·row·head \\'er-ō-,hed\\ *n* : the pointed end of an arrow

ar·row·root \\-,rüt, -,rut\\ *n* : an edible starch from the roots of any of several tropical American plants; *also* : a plant yielding arrowroot

ar·royo \\ə-'roi-ə, -ō\\ *n, pl* **-royos** [Sp] **1** : a watercourse in a dry region　**2** : a water-carved gully or channel

ar·se·nal \\'ärs-nəl, 'är-sə-nəl\\ *n* [ultim. fr. Ar *dār ṣinā'a* house of manufacture] **1** : a place for making and storing arms and military equipment　**2** : STORE, REPERTOIRE

ar·se·nic \\'ärs-nik, 'är-sə-nik\\ *n* **1** : a solid brittle poisonous chemical element of grayish metallic luster　**2** : a very poisonous oxygen compound of arsenic used in making insecticides

ar·son \\'är-s°n\\ *n* : the willful or malicious burning of property — **ar·son·ist** \\-ist\\ *n*

¹art \\'ärt\\ *n* **1** : skill acquired by experience or study　**2** : a branch of learning; *esp* : one of the humanities　**3** : an occupation requiring knowledge or skill　**4** : the use of skill and imagination in the production of things of beauty; *also* : works so produced　**5** : ARTFULNESS

²art *adj* : produced as an artistic effort ⟨an ~ film⟩

³art *abbr* **1** article　**2** artificial　**3** artillery

-art — see -ARD

ar·te·fact *chiefly Brit var of* ARTIFACT

ar·te·ri·al \\är-'tir-ē-əl\\ *adj* **1** : of or relating to an artery; *also* : relating to or being the oxygenated blood found in most arteries　**2** : of, relating to, or being a route for through traffic

ar·te·ri·ole \\är-'tir-ē-,ōl\\ *n* : any of the small terminal branches of an artery that ends in capillaries — **ar·te·ri·o·lar** \\-,tir-ē-'ō-lər\\ *adj*

ar·te·rio·scle·ro·sis \\är-,tir-ē-ō-sklə-'rō-səs\\ *n* : a chronic disease in which arterial walls are abnormally thickened and hardened — **ar·te·rio·scle·rot·ic** \\-'rä-tik\\ *adj or n*

ar·tery \\'är-tə-rē\\ *n, pl* **-ter·ies** **1** : one of the tubular vessels that carry blood from the heart　**2** : a main channel of transportation or communication

ar·te·sian well \\är-'tē-zhən-\\ *n* : a well from which the water flows to the surface by natural pressure; *also* : a deep well

art·ful \\'ärt-fəl\\ *adj* **1** : performed with, showing, or using art or skill　**2** : CRAFTY — **art·ful·ly** *adv* — **art·ful·ness** *n*

ar·thri·tis \\är-'thrī-təs\\ *n, pl* **-thri·ti·des** \\-'thri-tə-,dēz\\ : inflammation of the joints — **ar·thrit·ic** \\-'thri-tik\\ *adj or n*

ar·thro·pod \\'är-thrə-,päd\\ *n* : any of a phylum of invertebrate animals comprising those (as insects, spiders, or crabs) with segmented bodies and jointed limbs — **arthropod** *adj*

ar·thros·co·py \\är-'thräs-kə-pē\\ *n, pl* **-pies** : visual examination of the interior of a joint (as the knee) with a special surgical instrument; *also* : surgery on a joint using arthroscopy — **ar·thro·scope** \\'är-thrə-,skōp\\ *n* — **ar·thro·scop·ic** \\,är-thrə-'skä-pik\\ *adj*

ar·ti·choke \\'är-tə-,chōk\\ *n* [It dial. *articiocco*, ultim. fr. Ar *al-khurshūf*] : a tall thistlelike herb related to the daisies; *also* : its edible flower head

ar·ti·cle \\'är-ti-kəl\\ *n* [ME, fr. AF, fr. L *articulus* joint, division, dim. of *artus* joint, limb] **1** : a distinct part of a written document　**2** : a nonfictional prose composition forming an independent part of a publication　**3** : a word (as *an, the*) used with a noun to limit or give definiteness to its application　**4** : a member of a class of things; *esp* : COMMODITY

ar·tic·u·lar \\är-'ti-kyə-lər\\ *adj* : of or relating to a joint ⟨~ cartilage⟩

¹ar·tic·u·late \\är-'ti-kyə-lət\\ *adj* **1** : divided into meaningful parts : INTELLIGIBLE　**2** : able to speak; *also* : expressing oneself readily and effectively ⟨an ~ orator⟩　**3** : JOINTED — **ar·tic·u·late·ly** *adv* — **ar·tic·u·late·ness** *n*

²ar·tic·u·late \\-,lāt\\ *vb* **-lat·ed; -lat·ing** **1** : to utter distinctly　**2** : to unite by or as if by joints — **ar·tic·u·la·tion** \\-,ti-kyə-'lā-shən\\ *n*

ar·ti·fact \\'är-tə-,fakt\\ *n* : something made or modified by humans usu. for a purpose; *esp* : an object remaining from another time or culture ⟨prehistoric ~s⟩

ar·ti·fice \\'är-tə-fəs\\ *n* **1** : TRICK; *also* : TRICKERY　**2** : an ingenious device; *also* : INGENUITY

ar·ti·fi·cer \\är-'ti-fə-sər, 'är-tə-fə-sər\\ *n* : a skilled worker

ar·ti·fi·cial \\,är-tə-'fi-shəl\\ *adj* **1** : produced by art rather than nature; *also* : made by humans to imitate nature　**2** : not genuine : FEIGNED — **ar·ti·fi·ci·al·i·ty** \\-,fi-shē-'a-lə-tē\\ *n* — **ar·ti·fi·cial·ly** *adv* — **ar·ti·fi·cial·ness** *n*

artificial insemination *n* : introduction of semen into the uterus or oviduct by other than natural means

artificial intelligence *n* : the capability of a machine and esp. a computer to imitate intelligent human behavior

artificial respiration *n* : the rhythmic forcing of air into and out of the lungs of a person whose breathing has stopped

ar·til·lery \\är-'ti-lə-rē\\ *n, pl* **-ler·ies** **1** : crew-served mounted firearms (as guns)　**2** : a branch of the army armed with artillery — **ar·til·ler·ist** \\-rist\\ *n*

ar·ti·san \'är-tə-zən, -sən\ *n* : a worker who practices a trade or handicraft

art·ist \'ärt-ist\ *n* **1** : one who practices an art; *esp* : one who creates objects of beauty **2** : ARTISTE

ar·tiste \är-'tēst\ *n* : a skilled public performer

ar·tis·tic \är-'tis-tik\ *adj* : showing taste and skill — **ar·tis·ti·cal·ly** \-ti-k(ə-)lē\ *adv*

art·ist·ry \'ärt-ə-strē\ *n* : artistic quality or ability

art·less \'ärt-ləs\ *adj* **1** : lacking art or skill **2** : free from artificiality : NATURAL **3** : free from guile : SINCERE — **art·less·ly** *adv* — **art·less·ness** *n*

art nou·veau \,är-nü-'vō, ,ärt-\ *n, often cap A&N* [F, lit., new art] : a late 19th century design style characterized by sinuous lines and leaf-shaped forms

art·work \'ärt-,wərk\ *n* : an artistic production or work

arty \'är-tē\ *adj* **art·i·er; -est** : showily or pretentiously artistic — **art·i·ly** \'ärt-ə-lē\ *adv* — **art·i·ness** *n*

aru·gu·la \ə-'rü-gə-lə\ *n* : a yellowish-flowered herb related to the mustards with edible leaves used esp. in salads

ar·um \'a-rəm\ *n* : any of a family of plants (as the jack-in-the-pulpit or a skunk cabbage) with flowers in a fleshy enclosed spike

ARV *abbr* American Revised Version

¹-ary *n suffix* : thing or person belonging to or connected with ⟨function*ary*⟩

²-ary *adj suffix* : of, relating to, or connected with ⟨budget*ary*⟩

Ary·an \'a-rē-ən, 'er-e-; 'är-yən\ *adj* **1** : INDO-EUROPEAN **2** : NORDIC — **Aryan** *n*

¹as \əz, (,)az\ *adv* **1** : to the same degree or amount : EQUALLY ⟨~ green as grass⟩ **2** : for instance ⟨various trees, ~ oak or pine⟩ **3** : when considered in a specified relation ⟨my opinion ~ distinguished from his⟩

²as *conj* **1** : in the same amount or degree in which ⟨green ~ grass⟩ **2** : in the same way that ⟨farmed ~ his father before him had farmed⟩ **3** : WHILE, WHEN ⟨spoke to me ~ I was leaving⟩ **4** : THOUGH ⟨improbable ~ it seems⟩ **5** : SINCE, BECAUSE ⟨~ I'm not wanted, I'll go⟩ **6** : that the result is ⟨so guilty ~ to leave no doubt⟩

³as *pron* : THAT — used after *same* or *such* ⟨it's the same price ~ before⟩ **2** : a fact that ⟨he's rich, ~ you know⟩

⁴as *prep* : in the capacity or character of ⟨this will serve ~ a substitute⟩

As *symbol* arsenic

AS *abbr* **1** American Samoa **2** Anglo-Saxon **3** associate in science

asa·fet·i·da *or* **asa·foe·ti·da** \,a-sə-'fe-tə-dē, -'fē-\ *n* : an ill-smelling plant gum formerly used in medicine

ASAP *abbr* as soon as possible

as·bes·tos \as-'bes-təs, az-\ *n* : a noncombustible grayish mineral that occurs in fibrous form and has been used as a fireproof material

as·cend \ə-'send\ *vb* **1** : to move upward : MOUNT, CLIMB **2** : to succeed to : OCCUPY ⟨he ~ed the throne⟩

as·cen·dan·cy *also* **as·cen·den·cy** \ə-'sen-dən-sē\ *n* : controlling influence : DOMINATION

¹as·cen·dant *also* **as·cen·dent** \ə-'sen-dənt\ *n* : a dominant position

²ascendant *also* **ascendent** *adj* **1** : moving upward **2** : DOMINANT

as·cen·sion \ə-'sen-chən\ *n* : the act or process of ascending

Ascension Day *n* : the Thursday 40 days after Easter observed in commemoration of Christ's ascension into heaven

as·cent \ə-'sent\ *n* **1** : the act of mounting upward : CLIMB **2** : degree of upward slope

as·cer·tain \,a-sər-'tān\ *vb* : to learn with certainty — **as·cer·tain·able** *adj*

as·cet·ic \ə-'se-tik\ *adj* : practicing self= denial esp. for spiritual reasons : AUSTERE — **ascetic** *n* — **as·cet·i·cism** \-'se-tə-,si-zəm\ *n*

ASCII \'as-kē\ *n* [*A*merican *S*tandard *C*ode for *I*nformation *I*nterchange] : a computer code for representing alphanumeric information

ascor·bic acid \ə-'skȯr-bik-\ *n* : VITAMIN C

as·cot \'as-kət, -,kät\ *n* [*Ascot* Heath, racetrack near Ascot, England] : a broad neck scarf that is looped under the chin

as·cribe \ə-'skrīb\ *vb* **as·cribed; as·crib·ing** : to refer to a supposed cause, source, or author : ATTRIBUTE — **as·crib·able** *adj* — **as·crip·tion** \-'skrip-shən\ *n*

asep·tic \ā-'sep-tik\ *adj* : free or freed from disease-causing germs

asex·u·al \ā-'sek-shə-wəl\ *adj* **1** : lacking sex or functional sex organs **2** : occurring or formed without the production and union of two kinds of gametes ⟨~ reproduction⟩ **3** : devoid of sexuality — **asex·u·al·ly** *adv*

as for *prep* : with regard to : CONCERNING ⟨*as for* the others, they were late⟩

¹ash \'ash\ *n* **1** : any of a genus of trees related to the olive and having winged seeds and bark with grooves and ridges **2** : the tough elastic wood of an ash

²ash *n* **1** : the solid matter left when material is burned **2** : fine mineral particles from a volcano **3** *pl* : the remains of the dead human body after cremation or disintegration

ashamed \ə-'shāmd\ *adj* **1** : feeling shame **2** : restrained by anticipation of shame ⟨~ to say anything⟩ — **asham·ed·ly** \-'shā-məd-lē\ *adv*

ash·en \'a-shən\ *adj* : resembling ashes (as in color); *esp* : deadly pale

ash·lar \'ash-lər\ *n* : hewn or squared stone; *also* : masonry of such stone

ashore \ə-'shȯr\ *adv* : on or to the shore

as how *conj* : THAT ⟨allowed *as how* she was glad to be here⟩

ash·ram \'äsh-rəm\ *n* : a religious retreat esp. of a Hindu sage

ash·tray \'ash-,trā\ *n* : a receptacle for tobacco ashes

Ash Wednesday n : the 1st day of Lent

ashy \'a-shē\ adj **ash·i·er; -est** : ASHEN

Asian \'ā-zhən\ adj : of, relating to, or characteristic of the continent of Asia or its people — **Asian** n

¹**aside** \ə-'sīd\ adv **1** : to or toward the side **2** : out of the way : AWAY ⟨putting ~ savings⟩

²**aside** n : an actor's words heard by the audience but supposedly not by other characters on stage

aside from prep **1** : BESIDES ⟨aside from being pretty, she's intelligent⟩ **2** : with the exception of ⟨aside from one D his grades are excellent⟩

as if conj **1** : as it would be if ⟨it's as if nothing had changed⟩ **2** : as one would if ⟨he acts as if he'd never been away⟩ **3** : THAT ⟨it seems as if nothing ever happens around here⟩

as·i·nine \'a-sə-ˌnīn\ adj [L asininus, fr. asinus ass] : STUPID, FOOLISH — **as·i·nin·i·ty** \ˌa-sə-'ni-nə-tē\ n

ask \'ask\ vb **asked** \'askt\; **ask·ing 1** : to call on for an answer ⟨she ~ed him about his trip⟩ **2** : UTTER ⟨~ a question⟩ **3** : to make a request of ⟨~ him for help⟩ **4** : to make a request for ⟨~ help of her⟩ **5** : to set as a price ⟨~ed $800 for the car⟩ **6** : INVITE

askance \ə-'skans\ adv **1** : with a side glance **2** : with distrust

askew \ə-'skyü\ adv or adj : out of line : AWRY

ASL abbr American Sign Language

¹**aslant** \ə-'slant\ adv or adj : in a slanting direction

²**aslant** prep : over or across in a slanting direction

asleep \ə-'slēp\ adv or adj **1** : in or into a state of sleep **2** : DEAD **3** : NUMB **4** : INACTIVE

as long as conj **1** : provided that ⟨do as you like as long as you get home on time⟩ **2** : INASMUCH AS, SINCE ⟨as long as you're up, turn on the light⟩

aso·cial \(ˌ)ā-'sō-shəl\ adj : ANTISOCIAL

as of prep : AT, DURING, FROM, ON ⟨takes effect as of July 1⟩

asp \'asp\ n : a small poisonous African snake

as·par·a·gus \ə-'sper-ə-gəs\ n : a tall branching perennial herb related to the lilies; also : its edible young stalks

as·par·tame \'as-pər-ˌtām, ə-'spär-\ n : a crystalline low-calorie sweetener

ASPCA abbr American Society for the Prevention of Cruelty to Animals

as·pect \'as-ˌpekt\ n **1** : a position facing a particular direction **2** : APPEARANCE, LOOK **3** : PHASE

as·pen \'as-pən\ n : any of several poplars with leaves that flutter in the slightest breeze

as per \'az-ˌpər\ prep : in accordance with ⟨as per instructions⟩

as·per·i·ty \a-'sper-ə-tē\ n, pl **-ties 1** : ROUGHNESS **2** : harshness of temper

as·per·sion \ə-'spər-zhən\ n : a slanderous or defamatory remark

as·phalt \'as-ˌfȯlt\ also **as·phal·tum** \as-'fȯl-təm\ n : a dark substance found in natural beds or obtained as a residue in petroleum refining and used esp. in paving streets

asphalt jungle n : a big city or a specified part of a big city

as·pho·del \'as-fə-ˌdel\ n : any of several Old World herbs related to the lilies and bearing flowers in long erect spikes

as·phyx·ia \as-'fik-sē-ə\ n : a lack of oxygen or excess of carbon dioxide in the body that results in unconsciousness and often death and is usu. caused by interruption of breathing

as·phyx·i·ate \-sē-ˌāt\ vb **-at·ed; -at·ing** : SUFFOCATE — **as·phyx·i·a·tion** \-ˌfik-sē-'ā-shən\ n

as·pic \'as-pik\ n [F, lit., asp] : a savory meat jelly

as·pi·rant \'as-pə-rənt, ə-'spī-rənt\ n : one who aspires ♦ **Synonyms** CANDIDATE, APPLICANT, SEEKER

¹**as·pi·rate** \'as-pə-rət\ n **1** : an independent sound \h\ or a character (as the letter h) representing it **2** : a consonant having aspiration as its final component

²**as·pi·rate** \'as-pə-ˌrāt\ vb **-rat·ed; -rat·ing** : to draw, remove, or take up or into by suction

as·pi·ra·tion \ˌas-pə-'rā-shən\ n **1** : the pronunciation or addition of an aspirate; also : the aspirate or its symbol **2** : a drawing of something in, out, up, or through by or as if by suction **3** : a strong desire to achieve something noble; also : an object of this desire

as·pire \ə-'spī(-ə)r\ vb **as·pired; as·pir·ing 1** : to seek to attain or accomplish a particular goal **2** : to rise aloft

as·pi·rin \'as-pə-rən\ n, pl **aspirin** or **as·pirins 1** : a white crystalline drug used to relieve pain and fever **2** : a tablet of aspirin

as regards also **as respects** prep : in regard to : with respect to

ass \'as\ n **1** : any of several long-eared mammals smaller than the related horses; esp : one of Africa ancestral to the donkey **2** : a stupid person

as·sail \ə-'sāl\ vb : to attack violently — **as·sail·able** adj — **as·sail·ant** n

as·sas·sin \ə-'sa-sᵊn\ n [ML assassinus, fr. Ar ḥashshāshīn, pl. of ḥashshāsh worthless person, lit., hashish-user, fr. ḥashīsh hashish] : a murderer esp. for hire or fanatical reasons

as·sas·si·nate \ə-'sa-sə-ˌnāt\ vb **-nat·ed; -nat·ing** : to murder by sudden or secret attack — **as·sas·si·na·tion** \-ˌsa-sə-'nā-shən\ n

as·sault \ə-'sȯlt\ n **1** : a violent attack **2** : an unlawful attempt or threat to do harm to another — **assault** vb — **as·sault·ive** \ə-'sȯl-tiv\ adj

assault rifle n : a military automatic rifle with a large-capacity magazine

¹**as·say** \'a-ˌsā, a-'sā\ n : analysis to determine the quantity of one or more components present in a sample (as of an ore or drug)

²**as·say** \a-'sā, 'a-ˌsā\ vb **1** : TRY, AT-

TEMPT **2** : to subject (as an ore or drug) to an assay **3** : JUDGE 3

as·sem·blage \ə-'sem-blij, 3 & 4 also ˌas-ˌäm-'bläzh\ n **1** : a collection of persons or things : GATHERING **2** : the act of assembling **3** : an artistic composition made from scraps, junk, and odds and ends **4** : the art of making assemblages

as·sem·ble \ə-'sem-bəl\ vb **-bled; -bling 1** : to collect into one place : CONGREGATE **2** : to fit together the parts of **3** : to meet together : CONVENE

as·sem·bly \ə-'sem-blē\ n, pl **-blies 1** : a gathering of persons : MEETING **2** cap : a legislative body; esp : the lower house of a legislature **3** : a signal for troops to assemble **4** : the fitting together of parts (as of a machine)

assembly language n : a computer language consisting of mnemonic codes corresponding to machine-language instructions

as·sem·bly–line \ə-'sem-blē-ˌlīn\ adj : made by or as if by an assembly line; esp : lacking originality or creativity

assembly line n : an arrangement of machines, equipment, and workers in which work passes from operation to operation in a direct line

as·sem·bly·man \ə-'sem-blē-mən\ n : a member of a legislative assembly

as·sem·bly·wom·an \-ˌwu̇-mən\ n : a woman who is a member of a legislative assembly

as·sent \ə-'sent\ vb : AGREE, CONCUR — **assent** n

as·sert \ə-'sərt\ vb **1** : to state positively **2** : to demonstrate the existence of ♦ **Synonyms** DECLARE, AFFIRM, PROTEST, AVOW, CLAIM — **as·ser·tive** \-'sər-tiv\ adj — **as·ser·tive·ly** adv — **as·ser·tive·ness** n

as·ser·tion \ə-'sər-shən\ n : a positive statement

as·sess \ə-'ses\ vb **1** : to fix the rate or amount of **2** : to impose (as a tax) at a specified rate **3** : to evaluate for taxation — **as·sess·ment** n — **as·ses·sor** \-'se-sər\ n

as·set \'a-ˌset\ n **1** pl : the entire property of a person or company that may be used to pay debts **2** : ADVANTAGE, RESOURCE ⟨my wit is my chief ∼⟩

as·sev·er·ate \ə-'se-və-ˌrāt\ vb **-at·ed; -at·ing** : to assert earnestly — **as·sev·er·a·tion** \-ˌse-və-'rā-shən\ n

as·sid·u·ous \ə-'si-jə-wəs\ adj : steadily attentive : DILIGENT — **as·si·du·i·ty** \ˌa-sə-'dü-ə-tē, -'dyü-\ n — **as·sid·u·ous·ly** adv — **as·sid·u·ous·ness** n

as·sign \ə-'sīn\ vb **1** : to transfer (property) to another **2** : to appoint to or as a duty ⟨∼ a lesson⟩ **3** : FIX, SPECIFY ⟨∼ a limit⟩ **4** : ASCRIBE ⟨∼ a reason⟩ — **as·sign·able** adj

as·sig·na·tion \ˌa-sig-'nā-shən\ n : an appointment for a meeting; esp : TRYST

assigned risk n : a poor risk (as an accident-prone motorist) that an insurance company is forced to insure by state law

as·sign·ment \ə-'sīn-mənt\ n **1** : the act of assigning **2** : something assigned

as·sim·i·late \ə-'si-mə-ˌlāt\ vb **-lat·ed; -lat·ing 1** : to take up and absorb as nourishment; also : to absorb into a cultural tradition **2** : COMPREHEND **3** : to make or become similar — **as·sim·i·la·tion** \-ˌsi-mə-'lā-shən\ n

¹as·sist \ə-'sist\ vb : HELP, AID — **as·sis·tance** \-'sis-təns\ n

²assist n **1** : an act of assistance **2** : the action of a player who enables a teammate to make a putout (as in baseball) or score a goal (as in hockey or basketball)

as·sis·tant \ə-'sis-tənt\ n : a person who assists : HELPER

as·sis·ted living \ə-'sis-təd-\ n : a system of housing and limited care for senior citizens who need assistance with daily activities but do not require care in a nursing home

as·sis·tive \ə-'sis-tiv\ adj : providing aid or assistance ⟨∼ technology⟩

as·size \ə-'sīz\ n [ME assise, fr. AF, session, legal action, fr. asseer, asseoir to seat, fr. VL *assedēre, fr. L assidēre to sit beside] **1** : a judicial inquest **2** pl : the former regular sessions of superior courts in English counties

assn abbr association

assoc abbr associate; associated; association

¹as·so·ci·ate \ə-'sō-shē-ˌāt, -sē-\ vb **-at·ed; -at·ing 1** : to join in companionship or partnership **2** : to connect in thought

²as·so·ci·ate \-shē-ət, -sē-; -shət\ n **1** : a fellow worker : PARTNER **2** : COMPANION **3** often cap : a degree conferred esp. by a junior college ⟨∼ in arts⟩ — **associate** adj

as·so·ci·a·tion \ə-ˌsō-shē-'ā-shən, -sē-\ n **1** : the act of associating **2** : an organization of persons : SOCIETY

as·so·cia·tive \ə-'sō-shē-ˌā-tiv, -sē-; -shə-tiv\ adj **1** : of, relating to, or involved in association esp. of ideas or images **2** : of, having, or being the property of producing the same mathematical value regardless of how an expression's elements are grouped as long as their order is the same

as·so·nance \'a-sə-nəns\ n : repetition of vowels esp. as an alternative to rhyme in verse — **as·so·nant** \-nənt\ adj or n

as soon as conj : immediately at or shortly after the time that ⟨we'll start as soon as they arrive⟩

as·sort \ə-'sȯrt\ vb **1** : to distribute into like groups : CLASSIFY **2** : HARMONIZE

as·sort·ed \-'sȯr-təd\ adj : consisting of various kinds

as·sort·ment \-'sȯrt-mənt\ n : a collection of assorted things or persons

asst abbr assistant

as·suage \ə-'swāj\ vb **as·suaged; as·suag·ing 1** : to make (as pain or grief) less : EASE **2** : SATISFY ♦ **Synonyms** ALLEVIATE, RELIEVE, LIGHTEN, MITIGATE

as·sume \ə-'süm\ vb **as·sumed; as·sum·ing 1** : to take upon oneself **2** : to pretend to have or be **3** : to take as granted or true though not proved

as·sump·tion \ə-'səmp-shən\ n **1** : the taking up of a person into heaven **2** cap : August 15 observed in commemoration of the Assumption of the Virgin Mary **3** : a taking upon oneself **4** : PRETENSION **5** : SUPPOSITION

as·sur·ance \ə-'shür-əns\ n, **1** : PLEDGE **2** chiefly Brit : INSURANCE **3** : SECURITY **4** : SELF-CONFIDENCE; also : AUDACITY

as·sure \ə-'shür\ vb as·sured; as·sur·ing **1** : INSURE **2** : to give confidence to **3** : to state confidently to **4** : to make certain the coming or attainment of

as·sured \ə-'shürd\ n, pl **assured** or **as·sureds** : INSURED

as·ta·tine \'as-tə-ˌtēn\ n : an unstable radioactive chemical element

as·ter \'as-tər\ n : any of various mostly fall-blooming leafy-stemmed composite herbs with daisylike purple, white, pink, or yellow flower heads

as·ter·isk \'as-tə-ˌrisk\ n [L asteriscus, fr. Gk asteriskos, lit., little star, dim. of astēr star] : a character * used as a reference mark or as an indication of the omission of letters or words

astern \ə-'stərn\ adv or adj **1** : in, at, or toward the stern **2** : BACKWARD

as·ter·oid \'as-tə-ˌrȯid\ n : any of the numerous small celestial bodies found esp. between Mars and Jupiter

asth·ma \'az-mə\ n : a chronic lung disorder marked by recurrent episodes of labored breathing, a feeling of tightness in the chest, and coughing — **asth·mat·ic** \az-'ma-tik\ adj or n

as though conj : AS IF

astig·ma·tism \ə-'stig-mə-ˌti-zəm\ n : a defect in a lens or an eye causing improper focusing and blurred vision — **as·tig·mat·ic** \ˌas-tig-'ma-tik\ adj

astir \ə-'stər\ adj **1** : being in action : MOVING **2** : being out of bed

as to prep **1** : ABOUT, CONCERNING ⟨uncertain as to what went on⟩ **2** : ACCORDING TO ⟨graded as to size⟩

as·ton·ish \ə-'stä-nish\ vb : to strike with sudden and usu. great wonder : AMAZE — **as·ton·ish·ing·ly** adv — **as·ton·ish·ment** n

as·tound \ə-'staund\ vb : to fill with bewilderment or wonder — **as·tound·ing·ly** adv

¹**astrad·dle** \ə-'stra-dᵊl\ adv : on or above and extending onto both sides

²**astraddle** prep : ASTRIDE

as·tra·khan \'as-trə-kən, -ˌkan\ n, often cap **1** : karakul of Russian origin **2** : a cloth with a usu. wool, curled, and looped pile resembling karakul

as·tral \'as-trəl\ adj : of, relating to, or coming from the stars

astray \ə-'strā\ adv or adj **1** : off the right path or route **2** : into error

¹**astride** \ə-'strīd\ adv **1** : with one leg on each side **2** : with legs apart

²**astride** prep : with one leg on each side of

¹**as·trin·gent** \ə-'strin-jənt\ adj : able or tending to shrink body tissues — **as·trin·gen·cy** \-jən-sē\ n

²**astringent** n : an astringent agent or substance

astrol abbr astrologer; astrology

as·tro·labe \'as-trə-ˌlāb\ n : an instrument formerly used for observing the positions of celestial bodies

as·trol·o·gy \ə-'strä-lə-jē\ n : divination based on the supposed influence of the stars upon human events — **as·trol·o·ger** \-jər\ n — **as·tro·log·i·cal** \ˌas-trə-'lä-ji-kəl\ adj — **as·tro·log·i·cal·ly** \-kə-lē\ adv

astron abbr astronomer; astronomy

as·tro·naut \'as-trə-ˌnȯt\ n : a traveler in a spacecraft

as·tro·nau·tics \ˌas-trə-'nȯ-tiks\ n : the science of the construction and operation of spacecraft — **as·tro·nau·tic** \-tik\ or **as·tro·nau·ti·cal** \-ti-kəl\ adj

as·tro·nom·i·cal \ˌas-trə-'nä-mi-kəl\ also **as·tro·nom·ic** \-mik\ adj **1** : of or relating to astronomy **2** : extremely large ⟨an ∼ amount of money⟩

astronomical unit n : a unit of length used in astronomy equal to the mean distance of the earth from the sun or about 93 million miles (150 million kilometers)

as·tron·o·my \ə-'strä-nə-mē\ n, pl **-mies** : the science of objects and matter beyond the earth's atmosphere — **as·tron·o·mer** \-mər\ n

as·tro·phys·ics \ˌas-trə-'fi-ziks\ n : astronomy dealing esp. with the physical properties and dynamic processes of celestial objects — **as·tro·phys·i·cal** \-zi-kəl\ adj — **as·tro·phys·i·cist** \-'fi-zə-sist\ n

as·tute \ə-'stüt, -'styüt, a-\ adj [L astutus, fr. astus craft] : shrewdly discerning; also : WILY — **as·tute·ly** adv — **as·tute·ness** n

asun·der \ə-'sən-dər\ adv or adj **1** : into separate pieces ⟨torn ∼⟩ **2** : separated in position from each other

ASV abbr American Standard Version

¹**as well as** conj : and in addition : and moreover ⟨brave as well as loyal⟩

²**as well as** prep : in addition to : BESIDES ⟨the coach, as well as the team, is ready⟩

asy·lum \ə-'sī-ləm\ n [ME, fr. L, fr. Gk asylon, neut. of asylos inviolable, fr. a- not + sylon right of seizure] **1** : a place of refuge **2** : protection given to esp. political fugitives **3** : an institution for the care of the needy or sick and esp. of the insane

asym·met·ri·cal \ˌā-sə-'me-tri-kəl\ or **asym·met·ric** \-trik\ adj : not symmetrical — **asym·met·ri·cal·ly** \-tri-kə-lē\ adv — **asym·me·try** \(ˌ)ā-'si-mə-trē\ n

asymp·tom·at·ic \ˌā-ˌsimp-tə-'ma-tik\ adj : presenting no symptoms of disease ⟨an ∼ infection⟩

as·ymp·tote \'a-səmp-ˌtōt\ n : a straight line that is approached ever more closely by a curve that never coincides with it — **as·ymp·tot·ic** \ˌa-səmp-'tä-tik\ adj — **as·ymp·tot·i·cal·ly** \-ti-k(ə-)lē\ adv

¹**at** \ət, (ˈ)at\ prep **1** — used to indicate a point in time or space ⟨be here ∼ 3 o'clock⟩ **2** — used to indicate a goal

⟨swung ∼ the ball⟩ **3** — used to indicate position or condition ⟨∼ rest⟩ **4** — used to indicate means, cause, or manner ⟨sold ∼ auction⟩

²at also **at** \'ät\ n, pl at also **att** — see kip at MONEY table

At symbol astatine

AT abbr automatic transmission

at all adv : in any way : in any circumstances ⟨not at all likely⟩

at·a·vism \'a-tə-ˌvi-zəm\ n : appearance in an individual of a character typical of an ancestral form; also : such an individual or character — **at·a·vis·tic** \ˌa-tə-'vis-tik\ adj

atax·ia \ə-'tak-sē-ə\ n : an inability to coordinate muscular movements

ate past of EAT

¹-ate n suffix **1** : one acted upon (in a specified way) ⟨distillate⟩ **2** : chemical compound or complex derived from a (specified) compound or element ⟨acetate⟩

²-ate n suffix **1** : office : function : rank : group of persons holding a (specified) office or rank ⟨episcopate⟩ **2** : state : dominion : jurisdiction ⟨emirate⟩

³-ate adj suffix **1** : acted on (in a specified way) : being in a (specified) state ⟨temperate⟩ ⟨degenerate⟩ **2** : marked by having ⟨vertebrate⟩

⁴-ate vb suffix : cause to be modified or affected by ⟨pollinate⟩ : cause to become ⟨activate⟩ : furnish with ⟨aerate⟩

ate·lier \ˌa-tᵊl-'yā\ n **1** : an artist's or designer's studio **2** : WORKSHOP

athe·ist \'ā-thē-ist\ n : one who denies the existence of God — **athe·ism** \-ˌi-zəm\ n — **athe·is·tic** \ˌā-thē-'is-tik\ adj

ath·e·nae·um or **ath·e·ne·um** \ˌa-thə-'nē-əm\ n : LIBRARY 1

ath·ero·scle·ro·sis \ˌa-thə-rō-sklə-'rō-səs\ n : arteriosclerosis characterized by the deposition of fatty substances in and the hardening of the inner layer of the arteries — **ath·ero·scle·rot·ic** \-'rä-tik\ adj

athirst \ə-'thərst\ adj, **1** archaic : THIRSTY **2** : EAGER, LONGING

ath·lete \'ath-ˌlēt\ n [ME, fr. L athleta, fr. Gk athlētēs, fr. athlein to contend for a prize, fr. athlon prize, contest] : a person who is trained to compete in athletics

athlete's foot n : ringworm of the feet

ath·let·ic \ath-'le-tik\ adj **1** : of or relating to athletes or athletics **2** : VIGOROUS, ACTIVE **3** : STURDY, MUSCULAR — **ath·let·i·cal·ly** \-ti-kə-lē\ adv — **ath·let·i·cism** \-tə-ˌsi-zəm\ n

ath·let·ics \ath-'le-tiks\ n sing or pl : exercises and games requiring physical skill, strength, and endurance

athletic supporter n : an elastic pouch used to support the male genitals and worn esp. during athletic activity

¹athwart \ə-'thwȯrt\ prep **1** : ACROSS **2** : in opposition to

²athwart adv : obliquely across

atilt \ə-'tilt\ adv or adj **1** : in a tilted position **2** : with lance in hand

-ation n suffix : action or process ⟨flirtation⟩ : something connected with an action or process ⟨discoloration⟩

Atl abbr Atlantic

at–large \'at-'lärj\ adj : of or being a political representative who is elected to serve an entire area rather than one of its subdivisions

at·las \'at-ləs\ n : a book of maps

atm abbr atmosphere; atmospheric

ATM n : a computerized electronic machine that performs basic banking functions

at·mo·sphere \'at-mə-ˌsfir\ n **1** : the gaseous envelope of a celestial body; esp : the mass of air surrounding the earth **2** : a surrounding influence **3** : a unit of pressure equal to the pressure of air at sea level or about 14.7 pounds per square inch (10 newtons per square centimeter) **4** : an intriguing or singular tone, effect, or appeal — **at·mo·spher·ic** \ˌat-mə-'sfir-ik, -'sfer-\ adj — **at·mo·spher·i·cal·ly** \-i-k(ə-)lē\ adv

at·mo·sphe·rics \ˌat-mə-'sfir-iks, -'sfer-\ n pl : radio noise from atmospheric electrical phenomena

atoll \'a-ˌtȯl, -ˌtäl, 'ā-\ n : a coral island consisting of a reef surrounding a lagoon

at·om \'a-təm\ n [ME, fr. L atomus, fr. Gk atomos, fr. atomos indivisible, fr. a- not + temnein to cut] **1** : a tiny particle : BIT **2** : the smallest particle of a chemical element that can exist alone or in combination

atom·ic \ə-'tä-mik\ adj **1** : of or relating to atoms; also : NUCLEAR 2 ⟨∼ energy⟩ **2** : extremely small

atomic bomb n : a very destructive bomb utilizing the energy released by splitting the atom

atomic clock n : a very precise clock regulated by the natural vibration of atoms or molecules (as of cesium)

atomic number n : the number of protons in the nucleus of an element

atomic weight n : the mass of one atom of an element

at·om·ise, at·om·is·er Brit var of ATOMIZE, ATOMIZER

at·om·ize \'a-tə-ˌmīz\ vb **-ized; -iz·ing** : to reduce to minute particles

at·om·iz·er \'a-tə-ˌmī-zər\ n : a device for dispensing a liquid (as perfume) as a mist

atom smasher n : ACCELERATOR 3

aton·al \ā-'tō-nᵊl\ adj : marked by avoidance of traditional musical tonality — **ato·nal·i·ty** \ˌā-tō-'na-lə-tē\ n — **aton·al·ly** \ā-'tō-nə-lē\ adv

atone \ə-'tōn\ vb **atoned; aton·ing** **1** : to make amends **2** : EXPIATE

atone·ment \ə-'tōn-mənt\ n **1** : the reconciliation of God and mankind through the death of Jesus Christ **2** : reparation for an offense : SATISFACTION

¹atop \ə-'täp\ adv or adj : on, to, or at the top

²atop prep : on top of

ATP \ˌā-ˌtē-'pē\ n [adenosine triphosphate] : a compound that occurs widely in living tissue and supplies energy for many cellular processes by undergoing enzymatic hydrolysis

atri·um \'ā-trē-əm\ n, pl **atria** \-trē-ə\ also

atri·ums 1 : the central room of a Roman house; *also* : an open patio or court in the center of a building (as a hotel) 2 : an anatomical cavity or passage; *esp* : one of the chambers of the heart that receives blood from the veins — **atri·al** \-əl\ *adj*

atro·cious \ə-'trō-shəs\ *adj* 1 : savagely brutal, cruel, or wicked 2 : very bad : ABOMINABLE — **atro·cious·ly** *adv* — **atro·cious·ness** *n*

atroc·i·ty \ə-'trä-sə-tē\ *n, pl* **-ties** 1 : ATROCIOUSNESS 2 : an atrocious act or object ⟨the *atrocities* of war⟩

at·ro·phy \'a-trə-fē\ *n, pl* **-phies** : decrease in size or wasting away of a bodily part or tissue — **atrophy** *vb*

at·ro·pine \'a-trə-ˌpēn\ *n* : a drug from belladonna and related plants used esp. to relieve spasms and to dilate the pupil of the eye

¹**att** *var of* AT

²**att** *abbr* 1 attached 2 attention 3 attorney

at·tach \ə-'tach\ *vb* 1 : to seize legally in order to force payment of a debt 2 : to bind by personal ties 3 : FASTEN, CONNECT 4 : to be fastened or connected

at·ta·ché \ˌa-ˌta-'shā, ˌa-ˌta-, ˌa-tə-\ *n* [F] : a technical expert on the diplomatic staff of an ambassador

at·ta·ché case \ə-'ta-shā-, ˌa-tə-'shā-\ *n* : a small thin suitcase used esp. for carrying business papers; *also* : BRIEFCASE

at·tach·ment \ə-'tach-mənt\ *n* 1 : legal seizure of property 2 : connection by ties of affection and regard 3 : a device attached to a machine or implement 4 : a connection by which one thing is attached to another

¹**at·tack** \ə-'tak\ *vb* 1 : to set upon with force or words : ASSAIL, ASSAULT 2 : to set to work on

²**attack** *n* 1 : an offensive action 2 : a fit of sickness 3 : a scoring action in a game

³**attack** *adj* : designed, planned, or used for a military attack

at·tain \ə-'tān\ *vb* 1 : ACHIEVE, ACCOMPLISH 2 : to arrive at : REACH — **at·tain·abil·i·ty** \-ˌtā-nə-'bi-lə-tē\ *n* — **at·tain·able** *adj*

at·tain·der \ə-'tān-dər\ *n* : extinction of the civil rights of a person upon sentence of death or outlawry

at·tain·ment \ə-'tān-mənt\ *n* 1 : the act of attaining 2 : ACCOMPLISHMENT

at·taint \ə-'tānt\ *vb* : to condemn to loss of civil rights

at·tar \'a-tər\ *n* [Pers *'aṭir* perfumed, fr. Ar, fr. *'iṭr* perfume] : a fragrant floral oil

at·tempt \ə-'tempt\ *vb* : to make an effort toward : TRY — **attempt** *n*

at·tend \ə-'tend\ *vb* 1 : to look after : TEND 2 : to be present with 3 : to be present at 4 : to apply oneself 5 : to pay attention 6 : to direct one's attention

at·ten·dance \ə-'ten-dəns\ *n* 1 : the act or fact of attending : the number of persons present; *also* : the number of times a person attends

¹**at·ten·dant** \ə-'ten-dənt\ *n* : one that attends another to render a service

²**attendant** *adj* : ACCOMPANYING ⟨∼ circumstances⟩

at·ten·tion \ə-'ten-chən\ *n* 1 : the act or state of applying the mind to an object 2 : CONSIDERATION 3 : an act of courtesy 4 : a position of readiness assumed in command by a soldier — **at·ten·tive** \-'ten-tiv\ *adj* — **at·ten·tive·ly** *adv* — **at·ten·tive·ness** *n*

attention deficit disorder *n* : a behavioral syndrome esp. of children that is marked by hyperactivity, impulsive behavior, and inattention

attention–deficit/hyperactivity disorder *n* : ATTENTION DEFICIT DISORDER

attention span *n* : the length of time during which one is able to concentrate or remain interested

at·ten·u·ate \ə-'ten-yə-ˌwāt\ *vb* **-at·ed; -at·ing** 1 : to make or become thin 2 : WEAKEN ⟨sorrows ∼ with time⟩ — **at·ten·u·ate** \-wət\ *adj* — **at·ten·u·a·tion** \-ˌten-yə-'wā-shən\ *n*

at·test \ə-'test\ *vb* 1 : to certify as genuine by signing as a witness 2 : MANIFEST ⟨her record ∼s her integrity⟩ 3 : TESTIFY ⟨∼ to a belief⟩ — **at·tes·ta·tion** \ˌa-ˌtes-'tā-shən\ *n*

at·tic \'a-tik\ *n* : the space or room in a building immediately below the roof

¹**at·tire** \ə-'tī(-ə)r\ *vb* **at·tired; at·tir·ing** : to put garments on : DRESS, ARRAY

²**attire** *n* : DRESS, CLOTHES

at·ti·tude \'a-tə-ˌtüd, -ˌtyüd\ *n* 1 : POSTURE 2 : a mental position or feeling with regard to a fact or state 3 : the position of something in relation to something else 4 : a negative or hostile state of mind 5 : a cocky or arrogant manner

at·ti·tu·di·nise *Brit var of* ATTITUDINIZE

at·ti·tu·di·nize \ˌa-tə-'tüd-ə-ˌnīz, -'tyü-\ *vb* **-nized; -niz·ing** : to assume an affected mental attitude : POSE

attn *abbr* attention

at·tor·ney \ə-'tər-nē\ *n, pl* **-neys** : a legal agent qualified to act for persons in legal proceedings

attorney general *n, pl* **attorneys general** *or* **attorney generals** : the chief legal representative and adviser of a nation or state

at·tract \ə-'trakt\ *vb* 1 : to draw to or toward oneself : cause to approach 2 : to draw by emotional or aesthetic appeal

♦ **Synonyms** CHARM, FASCINATE, ALLURE, CAPTIVATE, ENCHANT — **at·trac·tive** \-'trak-tiv\ *adj* — **at·trac·tive·ly** *adv* — **at·trac·tive·ness** *n*

at·trac·tant \ə-'trak-tənt\ *n* : a substance (as a pheromone) that attracts specific animals (as insects)

at·trac·tion \ə-'trak-shən\ *n* 1 : the act or power of attracting; *esp* : personal charm 2 : an attractive quality, object, or feature 3 : a force tending to draw particles together

attrib *abbr* attributive

¹**at·tri·bute** \'a-trə-ˌbyüt\ *n* 1 : an inherent characteristic 2 : a word ascribing a quality; *esp* : ADJECTIVE

²**at·trib·ute** \ə-'tri-ˌbyüt, -byət\ *vb* **-ut·ed;**

-ut·ing 1 : to explain as to cause or origin ⟨~ the illness to fatigue⟩ **2** : to regard as a characteristic ✦ *Synonyms* AS-CRIBE, CREDIT, CHARGE, IMPUTE — **at·trib·ut·able** *adj* — **at·tri·bu·tion** \ˌa-trə-'byü-shən\ *n*

at·trib·u·tive \ə-'trib-yə-tiv\ *adj* : joined directly to a modified noun without a linking verb ⟨*red* in *red hair* is an ~ adjective⟩ — **attributive** *n* — **at·trib·u·tive·ly** *adv*

at·tri·tion \ə-'tri-shən\ *n* **1** : the act of wearing away or as if by rubbing **2** : a reduction in numbers as a result of resignation, retirement, or death

at·tune \ə-'tün, -'tyün\ *vb* : to bring into harmony : TUNE — **at·tune·ment** *n*

atty *abbr* attorney

ATV \ˌā-ˌtē-'vē\ *n* : ALL-TERRAIN VEHICLE

atyp·i·cal \ā-'ti-pi-kəl\ *adj* : not typical : IRREGULAR — **atyp·i·cal·ly** \-k(ə-)lē\ *adv*

Au *symbol* [L *aurum*] gold

au·burn \'ȯ-bərn\ *adj* : reddish brown — **auburn** *n*

au cou·rant \ˌō-kù-'ränⁿ\ *adj* [F, lit., in the current] : UP-TO-DATE, STYLISH

¹auc·tion \'ȯk-shən\ *n* [L *auction-, auctio,* fr. *augēre* to increase] : public sale of property to the highest bidder

²auction *vb* **auc·tioned; auc·tion·ing** \-shə-niŋ\ : to sell at auction

auc·tion·eer \ˌȯk-shə-'nir\ *n* : an agent who conducts an auction

aud *abbr* audit; auditor

au·da·cious \ȯ-'dā-shəs\ *adj* **1** : DARING, BOLD **2** : INSOLENT — **au·da·cious·ly** *adv* — **au·da·cious·ness** *n* — **au·dac·i·ty** \-'da-sə-tē\ *n*

¹au·di·ble \'ȯ-də-bəl\ *adj* : capable of being heard — **au·di·bil·i·ty** \ˌȯ-də-'bi-lə-tē\ *n* — **au·di·bly** \'ȯ-də-blē\ *adv*

²audible *n* : a play called at the line of scrimmage — **audible** *vb*

au·di·ence \'ȯ-dē-əns\ *n* **1** : a formal interview **2** : an opportunity of being heard **3** : an assembly of listeners or spectators

¹au·dio \'ȯ-dē-ˌō\ *adj* **1** : of or relating to frequencies (as of radio waves) corresponding to those of audible sound waves **2** : of or relating to sound or its reproduction and esp. high-fidelity reproduction **3** : relating to or used in the transmission or reception of sound

²audio *n* **1** : the transmission, reception, or reproduction of sound **2** : the section of television or motion-picture equipment that deals with sound

au·di·ol·o·gy \ˌȯ-dē-'ä-lə-jē\ *n* : a branch of science dealing with hearing and esp. with the treatment of individuals having trouble with hearing — **au·di·o·log·i·cal** \-ə-'lä-ji-kəl\ *adj* — **au·di·ol·o·gist** \-'ä-lə-jist\ *n*

au·dio·phile \'ȯ-dē-ō-ˌfī(-ə)l\ *n* : one who is enthusiastic about high-fidelity sound reproduction

au·dio·tape \'ȯ-dē-ō-ˌtāp\ *n* : a tape recording of sound

au·dio·vi·su·al \ˌȯ-dē-ō-'vi-zhə-wəl\ *adj* : of, relating to, or making use of both hearing and sight

au·dio·vi·su·als \-wəlz\ *n pl* : audiovisual teaching materials (as videotapes)

¹au·dit \'ȯ-dət\ *n* : a formal examination and verification of financial accounts

²audit *vb* **1** : to perform an audit on or for **2** : to attend (a course) without expecting formal credit

¹au·di·tion \ȯ-'di-shən\ *n* **1** : HEARING **2** : a trial performance to appraise an entertainer's merits

²audition *vb* **-tioned; -tion·ing** \-'di-shə-niŋ\ : to give an audition to; *also* : to give a trial performance

au·di·tor \'ȯ-də-tər\ *n* **1** : LISTENER **2** : a person who audits

au·di·to·ri·um \ˌȯ-də-'tȯr-ē-əm\ *n, pl* **-ri·ums** *or* **-ria** \-rē-ə\ **1** : the part of a public building where an audience sits **2** : a hall or building used for public gatherings

au·di·to·ry \'ȯ-də-ˌtȯr-ē\ *adj* : of or relating to hearing or to the sense or organs of hearing ⟨~ stimuli⟩

auditory tube *n* : EUSTACHIAN TUBE

auf Wie·der·seh·en \aủf-'vē-dər-ˌzān\ *interj* [G] — used to express farewell

Aug *abbr* August

au·ger \'ȯ-gər\ *n* : a tool for boring

aught \'ȯt, 'ät\ *n* : ZERO, CIPHER

aug·ment \ȯg-'ment\ *vb* : ENLARGE, INCREASE — **aug·men·ta·tion** \ˌȯg-mən-'tā-shən\ *n*

au gra·tin \ō-'gra-t⁰n, ȯ-, -'grä-\ *adj* [F, lit., with the burnt scrapings from the pan] : covered with bread crumbs or grated cheese and browned

¹au·gur \'ȯ-gər\ *n* : DIVINER, SOOTHSAYER

²augur *vb* **1** : to foretell esp. from omens **2** : to give promise of : PRESAGE

au·gu·ry \'ȯ-gyə-rē, -gə-\ *n, pl* **-ries 1** : divination from omens **2** : OMEN, PORTENT

au·gust \ȯ-'gəst\ *adj* : marked by majestic dignity or grandeur — **au·gust·ly** *adv* — **au·gust·ness** *n*

Au·gust \'ȯ-gəst\ *n* [ME, fr. OE, fr. L *Augustus,* fr. *Augustus* Caesar] : the 8th month of the year

au jus \ō-'zhü, -'zhüs, -ˌjüs; ō-zhuͤ\ *adj* [F] : served in the juice obtained from roasting

auk \'ȯk\ *n* : any of several stocky black-and-white diving seabirds that breed in colder parts of the northern hemisphere

auld \'ȯl, 'ȯld, 'äl, 'äld\ *adj, chiefly Scot* : OLD

aunt \'ant, 'änt\ *n* **1** : the sister of one's father or mother **2** : the wife of one's uncle

aunt·ie \'an-tē, 'än-\ *n* : AUNT

au pair \ō-'per\ *n* [F, on even terms] : a usu. young foreign person who does domestic work for a family in return for room and board and to learn the family's language

au·ra \'ȯr-ə\ *n* **1** : a distinctive atmosphere surrounding a given source **2** : a luminous radiation

au·ral \'ȯr-əl\ *adj* : of or relating to the ear or to the sense of hearing

aurar *pl of* EYRIR

au·re·ole \'òr-ē-,ōl\ *or* **au·re·o·la** \ò-'rē-ə-lə\ *n* : HALO, NIMBUS

au re·voir \,ō-rə-'vwär\ *n* [F, lit., till seeing again] : GOOD-BYE

au·ri·cle \'òr-i-kəl\ *n* : an atrium of the heart

au·ric·u·lar \ò-'ri-kyə-lər\ *adj* **1** : told privately ⟨∼ confession⟩ **2** : known or recognized by the sense of hearing

au·ro·ra \ə-'ròr-ə\ *n, pl* **auroras** *or* **au·ro·rae** \-(,)ē\ : a luminous phenomenon of streamers or arches of light appearing in the upper atmosphere esp. of a planet's polar regions — **au·ro·ral** \-əl\ *adj*

aurora aus·tra·lis \ò-'strā-ləs\ *n* : an aurora that occurs in earth's southern hemisphere

aurora bo·re·al·is \-,bòr-ē-'a-ləs\ *n* : an aurora that occurs in earth's northern hemisphere

AUS *abbr* Army of the United States

aus·pice \'ò-spəs\ *n, pl* **aus·pic·es** \-spə-səz, -,sēz\ [L *auspicium*, fr. *auspic-, auspex* diviner by birds, fr. *avis* bird + *specere* to look, look at] **1** : observation of birds by an augur **2** *pl* : kindly patronage and protection **3** : a prophetic sign or omen

aus·pi·cious \ò-'spi-shəs\ *adj* **1** : promising success : PROPITIOUS **2** : FORTUNATE, PROSPEROUS ⟨an ∼ year⟩ — **aus·pi·cious·ly** *adv* — **aus·pi·cious·ness** *n*

aus·tere \ò-'stir\ *adj* **1** : STERN, SEVERE, STRICT **2** : ABSTEMIOUS **3** : UNADORNED ⟨∼ style⟩ — **aus·tere·ly** *adv* — **aus·ter·i·ty** \-'ster-ə-tē\ *n*

aus·tral \'òs-trəl\ *adj* : SOUTHERN

Aus·tro·ne·sian \,òs-trə-'nē-zhən\ *adj* : of, relating to, or constituting a family of languages spoken in the area extending from Madagascar eastward through the Malay Peninsula to Hawaii and Easter Island

auth *abbr* **1** authentic **2** author **3** authorized

au·then·tic \ə-'then-tik, ò-\ *adj* : GENUINE, REAL — **au·then·ti·cal·ly** \-ti-k(ə-)lē\ *adv* — **au·then·tic·i·ty** \ò-,then-'ti-sə-tē\ *n*

au·then·ti·cate \ə-'then-ti-,kāt, ò-\ *vb* **-cat·ed; -cat·ing** : to prove genuine — **au·then·ti·ca·tion** \-,then-ti-'kā-shən\ *n*

au·thor \'ò-thər\ *n* [ME *auctour*, fr. AF *auctor, autor*, fr. L *auctor* originator, author, fr. *augēre* to increase] **1** : one that originates or creates **2** : one that writes or composes a literary work

au·thor·ess \'ò-thə-rəs\ *n* : a woman author

au·tho·ri·sa·tion, au·tho·rise *Brit var of* AUTHORIZATION, AUTHORIZE

au·thor·i·tar·i·an \ò-,thär-ə-'ter-ē-ən, ə-, -,thòr-\ *adj* **1** : characterized by or favoring the principle of blind obedience to authority **2** : characterized by or favoring concentration of political power in an authority not responsible to the people — **authoritarian** *n*

au·thor·i·ta·tive \ə-'thär-ə-,tā-tiv, ò-, -'thòr-\ *adj* : supported by, proceeding from, or being an authority — **au·thor·i·ta·tive·ly** *adv* — **au·thor·i·ta·tive·ness** *n*

au·thor·i·ty \ə-'thär-ə-tē, ò-, -'thòr-\ *n, pl* **-ties** **1** : a citation used in support of a statement or in defense of an action; *also* : the source of such a citation **2** : one appealed to as an expert **3** : power to influence thought or behavior **4** : freedom granted : RIGHT **5** : persons in command; *esp* : GOVERNMENT **6** : convincing force

au·tho·rize \'ò-thə-,rīz\ *vb* **-rized; -riz·ing** **1** : SANCTION ⟨custom *authorized* by time⟩ **2** : to give legal power to — **au·tho·ri·za·tion** \ò-thə-rə-'zā-shən\ *n*

au·thor·ship \'ò-thər-,ship\ *n* **1** : the state of being an author **2** : the source of a piece of writing, music, or art

au·tism \'ò-,ti-zəm\ *n* : a disorder that appears by age three and is characterized esp. by impaired ability to communicate with others and form normal social relationships and by repetitive patterns of behavior — **au·tis·tic** \ò-'tis-tik\ *adj*

¹au·to \'ò-tō\ *n, pl* **autos** : AUTOMOBILE

²auto *abbr* automatic

au·to·bahn \'ò-tō-,bän, 'au̇-\ *n* : a German, Swiss, or Austrian expressway

au·to·bi·og·ra·phy \,ò-tə-bī-'ä-grə-fē\ *n* : the biography of a person narrated by that person — **au·to·bi·og·ra·pher** \-fər\ *n* — **au·to·bi·o·graph·i·cal** \-,bī-ə-'gra-fi-kəl\ *adj* — **au·to·bi·o·graph·i·cal·ly** \-k(ə-)lē\ *adv*

au·toch·tho·nous \ò-'täk-thə-nəs\ *adj* : INDIGENOUS, NATIVE ⟨an ∼ people⟩

au·to·clave \'ò-tō-,klāv\ *n* : an apparatus (as for sterilizing) using superheated high-pressure steam

au·toc·ra·cy \ò-'tä-krə-sē\ *n, pl* **-cies** : government by one person having unlimited power — **au·to·crat** \'ò-tə-,krat\ *n* — **au·to·crat·ic** \,ò-tə-'kra-tik\ *adj* — **au·to·crat·i·cal·ly** \-ti-k(ə-)lē\ *adv*

au·to·ex·po·sure \,ò-tō-ik-'spō-zhər\ *n* : a camera system that automatically adjusts the exposure according to ambient light

¹au·to·graph \'ò-tə-,graf\ *n* **1** : an original manuscript **2** : a person's signature written by hand

²autograph *vb* : to write one's signature on

au·to·im·mune \,ò-tō-i-'myün\ *adj* : of, relating to, or caused by antibodies or lymphocytes that attack molecules, cells, or tissues of the organism producing them ⟨∼ diseases⟩ — **au·to·im·mu·ni·ty** \-i-'myü-nə-tē\ *n*

au·to·mate \'ò-tə-,māt\ *vb* **-mat·ed; -mat·ing** **1** : to operate automatically using mechanical or electronic devices **2** : to convert to automatic operation — **au·to·ma·tion** \ò-tə-'mā-shən\ *n*

automated teller machine *n* : ATM

¹au·to·mat·ic \,ò-tə-'ma-tik\ *adj* **1** : INVOLUNTARY **2** : made so that certain parts act in a desired manner at the proper time : SELF-ACTING — **au·to·mat·i·cal·ly** \-ti-k(ə-)lē\ *adv*

²automatic *n* : an automatic device; *esp* : an automatic firearm

automatic teller *n* : ATM

automatic teller machine *n* : ATM

au·tom·a·ton \ȯ-'tä-mə-tən, -,tän\ *n, pl* **-atons** *or* **-a·ta** \-ə-tə, -ə-,tä\ **1** : an automatic machine; *esp* : ROBOT **2** : an individual who acts mechanically

au·to·mo·bile \'ȯ-tə-mō-,bēl, ,ȯ-tə-mə-'bēl\ *n* : a usu. 4-wheeled automotive vehicle for passenger transportation

au·to·mo·tive \,ȯ-tə-'mō-tiv\ *adj* **1** : of or relating to automobiles, trucks, or buses **2** : SELF-PROPELLED

au·to·nom·ic nervous system \,ȯ-tə-'nä-mik-\ *n* : a part of the vertebrate nervous system that governs involuntary actions and that consists of the sympathetic nervous system and the parasympathetic nervous system

au·ton·o·mous \ȯ-'tä-nə-məs\ *adj* : having the right or power of self-government — **au·ton·o·mous·ly** *adv* — **au·ton·o·my** \-mē\ *n*

au·top·sy \'ȯ-,täp-sē, 'ȯ-təp-\ *n, pl* **-sies** [Gk *autopsia* act of seeing with one's own eyes, fr. *autos* self + *opsis* sight] : examination of a dead body usu. with dissection sufficient to determine the cause of death or extent of change produced by disease — **autopsy** *vb*

au·tumn \'ȯ-təm\ *n* : the season between summer and winter — **au·tum·nal** \ȯ-'təm-nəl\ *adj*

aux *abbr* auxiliary

¹aux·il·ia·ry \ȯg-'zil-yə-rē, -'zi-lə-rē\ *adj* **1** : providing help **2** : functioning in a subsidiary capacity **3** : accompanying a verb form to express person, number, mood, or tense ⟨~ verbs⟩

²auxiliary *n, pl* **-ries** **1** : an auxiliary person, group, or device **2** : an auxiliary verb

aux·in \'ȯk-sən\ *n* : a plant hormone that stimulates growth in length

av *abbr* **1** avenue **2** average **3** avoirdupois

AV *abbr* **1** ad valorem **2** audiovisual **3** Authorized Version

¹avail \ə-'vāl\ *vb* : to be of use or advantage : HELP, BENEFIT

²avail *n* : USE ⟨effort was of no ~⟩

avail·able \ə-'vā-lə-bəl\ *adj* **1** : USABLE ⟨~ resources⟩ **2** : ACCESSIBLE ⟨~ in any drugstore⟩ — **avail·abil·i·ty** \,vā-lə-'bi-lə-tē\ *n*

av·a·lanche \'a-və-,lanch\ *n* : a mass of snow, ice, earth, or rock sliding down a mountainside

avant–garde \,ä-,vän-'gärd, -,vänt-\ *n* [F, vanguard] : those esp. in the arts who create or apply new or experimental ideas and techniques — **avant–garde** *adj*

av·a·rice \'a-və-rəs\ *n* : excessive desire for wealth : GREED — **av·a·ri·cious** \,a-və-'ri-shəs\ *adj*

avast \ə-'vast\ *vb imper* — a nautical command to stop or cease

av·a·tar \'a-və-,tär\ *n* [Skt *avatāra* descent] : INCARNATION

avaunt \ə-'vȯnt\ *adv* : AWAY, HENCE

avdp *abbr* avoirdupois

ave *abbr* avenue

Ave Ma·ria \,ä-,vä-mə-'rē-ə\ *n* : HAIL MARY

avenge \ə-'venj\ *vb* **avenged; aveng·ing** : to take vengeance for — **aveng·er** *n*

av·e·nue \'a-və-,nü, -,nyü\ *n* **1** : a way or route to a place or goal : PATH **2** : a broad street

aver \ə-'vər\ *vb* **averred; aver·ring** : ALLEGE, ASSERT; *also* : DECLARE

¹av·er·age \'a-və-rij, 'a-vrij\ *n* [earlier, proportionally distributed charge for damage at sea, modif. of MF *avarie* damage to ship or cargo, fr. It *avaria*, fr. Ar *'awārīyah* damaged merchandise] **1** : ARITHMETIC MEAN **2** : a ratio of successful tries to total tries esp. in athletics ⟨batting ~ of .303⟩

²average *adj* **1** : equaling or approximating an arithmetic mean **2** : being about midway between extremes **3** : not out of the ordinary : COMMON

³average *vb* **av·er·aged; av·er·ag·ing** **1** : to be at or come to an average **2** : to be, do, or get usually **3** : to find the average of

averse \ə-'vərs\ *adj* : having an active feeling of dislike or reluctance ⟨~ to exercise⟩

aver·sion \ə-'vər-zhən\ *n* **1** : a feeling of repugnance for something with a desire to avoid it **2** : something decidedly disliked

avert \ə-'vərt\ *vb* **1** : to turn aside or away ⟨~ the eyes⟩ **2** : to ward off

avg *abbr* average

avi·an \'ā-vē-ən\ *adj* [L *avis* bird] : of, relating to, or derived from birds

avi·ary \'ā-vē-,er-ē\ *n, pl* **-ar·ies** : a place for keeping birds confined

avi·a·tion \,ā-vē-'ā-shən, ,a-\ *n* **1** : the operation of heavier-than-air aircraft **2** : aircraft manufacture, development, and design

avi·a·tor \'ā-vē-,ā-tər, 'a-\ *n* : an airplane pilot

avi·a·trix \,ā-vē-'ā-triks, ,a-\ *n, pl* **-trix·es** \-trik-səz\ *or* **-tri·ces** \-trə-,sēz\ : a woman airplane pilot

av·id \'a-vəd\ *adj* **1** : craving eagerly : GREEDY **2** : enthusiastic in pursuit of an interest — **avid·i·ty** \ə-'vi-də-tē, a-\ *n* — **av·id·ly** *adv* — **av·id·ness** *n*

avi·on·ics \,ā-vē-'ä-niks, ,a-\ *n pl* : electronics designed for use in aerospace vehicles — **avi·on·ic** \-nik\ *adj*

avo \'a-(,)vü\ *n, pl* **avos** — see *pataca* at MONEY table

av·o·ca·do \,a-və-'kä-dō, ,ä-\ *n, pl* **-dos** *also* **-does** [modif. of Sp *aguacate,*, fr. Nahuatl *āhuacatl,* avocado, testicle] : a pulpy green- to purple-skinned nutty-flavored fruit of a tropical American tree; *also* : this tree

av·o·ca·tion \,a-və-'kā-shən\ *n* : HOBBY

av·o·cet \'a-və-,set\ *n* : any of several long-legged shorebirds with webbed feet and slender upward-curving bills

avoid \ə-'vȯid\ *vb* **1** : to keep away from : SHUN **2** : to prevent the occurrence of **3** : to refrain from — **avoid·able** *adj* — **avoid·ably** *adv* — **avoid·ance** \ə-'vȯi-dəns\ *n*

av·oir·du·pois \ˌa-vər-də-ˈpȯiz\ *n* [ME *avoir de pois* goods sold by weight, fr. AF, lit., goods of weight] 1 : AVOIRDUPOIS WEIGHT 2 : WEIGHT, HEAVINESS; *esp* : personal weight

avoirdupois weight *n* : a system of weights based on a pound of 16 ounces and an ounce of 16 drams (28 grams) — see WEIGHT table

avouch \ə-ˈvau̇ch\ *vb* 1 : to declare positively : AVER 2 : to vouch for

avow \ə-ˈvau̇\ *vb* : to declare openly — **avow·al** \-ˈvau̇(-ə)l\ *n*

avun·cu·lar \ə-ˈvəŋ-kyə-lər\ *adj* : of, relating to, or resembling an uncle

await \ə-ˈwāt\ *vb* : to wait for : EXPECT

¹awake \ə-ˈwāk\ *vb* **awoke** \-ˈwōk\ *also* **awaked** \-ˈwākt\; **awo·ken** \-ˈwō-kən\ *or* **awaked** *also* **awoke**; **awak·ing** : to bring back to consciousness : wake up

²awake *adj* : not asleep; *also* : ALERT

awak·en \ə-ˈwā-kən\ *vb* **awak·ened**; **awak·en·ing** \-ˈwā-kə-niŋ\ : AWAKE

¹award \ə-ˈwȯrd\ *vb* 1 : to give by judicial decision \~ damages\ 2 : to give in recognition of merit or achievement

²award *n* 1 : a final decision : JUDGMENT 2 : something awarded : PRIZE

aware \ə-ˈwer\ *adj* : having perception or knowledge : CONSCIOUS, INFORMED — **aware·ness** *n*

awash \ə-ˈwȯsh, -ˈwäsh\ *adj* 1 : washed by waves or tide 2 : AFLOAT 3 : FLOODED

¹away \ə-ˈwā\ *adv* 1 : from this or that place \go \~\ 2 : out of the way 3 : in another direction \turn \~\ 4 : out of existence \fade \~\ 5 : from one's possession \give \~\ 6 : without interruption \chatter \~\ 7 : at a distance in space or time \far \~\ \\~ back in 1910\

²away *adj* 1 : ABSENT 2 : distant in space or time \a lake 10 miles \~\

¹awe \ˈȯ\ *n* 1 : profound and reverent dread of the supernatural 2 : respectful fear inspired by authority

²awe *vb* **awed**; **aw·ing** : to inspire with awe

aweigh \ə-ˈwā\ *adj* : just clear of the bottom \anchors \~\

awe·some \ˈȯ-səm\ *adj* 1 : expressive of awe \\~ tribute\ 2 : inspiring awe

awe·struck \-ˌstrək\ *also* **awe·strick·en** \-ˌstri-kən\ *adj* : filled with awe

aw·ful \ˈȯ-fəl\ *adj* 1 : inspiring awe 2 : extremely disagreeable 3 : very great \an \~ lot of money\ — **aw·ful·ly** *adv*

awhile \ə-ˈhwī(-ə)l\ *adv* : for a while

awhirl \ə-ˈhwərl\ *adj* : being in a whirl

awk·ward \ˈȯ-kwərd\ *adj* 1 : CLUMSY \\~ with needle and thread\ 2 : UNGRACEFUL \\~ writing\ 3 : difficult to explain : EMBARRASSING 4 : difficult to deal with — **awk·ward·ly** *adv* — **awk·ward·ness** *n*

awl \ˈȯl\ *n* : a pointed instrument for making small holes

aw·ning \ˈȯ-niŋ\ *n* : a rooflike cover (as of canvas) extended over or in front of a place as a shelter

AWOL \ˈā-ˌwȯl, ˌā-ˌdə-bəl-yü-ˌō-ˈel\ *n* : a person who is absent without leave — **AWOL** *adj or adv*

awry \ə-ˈrī\ *adv or adj* 1 : ASKEW 2 : AMISS

ax *or* **axe** \ˈaks\ *n* : a chopping or cutting tool with an edged head fitted parallel to a handle

ax·i·al \ˈak-sē-əl\ *adj* 1 : of, relating to, or functioning as an axis 2 : situated around, in the direction of, on, or along an axis — **ax·i·al·ly** *adv*

ax·i·om \ˈak-sē-əm\ *n* [L *axioma*, fr. Gk *axiōma*, lit., something worthy, fr. *axioun* to think worthy, fr. *axios* worth, worthy] 1 : a statement generally accepted as true : MAXIM 2 : a proposition regarded as a self-evident truth — **ax·i·om·at·ic** \ˌak-sē-ə-ˈma-tik\ *adj* — **ax·i·om·at·i·cal·ly** \-ti-k(ə-)lē\ *adv*

ax·is \ˈak-səs\ *n, pl* **ax·es** \-ˌsēz\ 1 : a straight line around which a body rotates 2 : a straight line or structure with respect to which a body or figure is symmetrical 3 : one of the reference lines of a system of coordinates 4 : an alliance between major powers

ax·le \ˈak-səl\ *n* : a shaft on which a wheel revolves

ax·on \ˈak-ˌsän\ *n* : the long thin usu. unbranched part of a nerve cell that usu. conducts impulses away from the cell body

ayah \ˈī-ə\ *n* [Hindi & Urdu *āyā*, fr. Pg *aia*, fr. L *avia* grandmother] : a nurse or maid native to India

aya·tol·lah \ˌī-ə-ˈtō-lə\ *n* [Pers *āyatollāh*, lit., sign of God, fr. Ar *aya* sign, miracle + *allāh* God] : an Islamic religious leader — used as a title of respect

¹aye *also* **ay** \ˈā\ *adv* : ALWAYS, EVER

²aye *also* **ay** \ˈī\ *adv* : YES

³aye *also* **ay** \ˈī\ *n, pl* **ayes** : an affirmative vote

AZ *abbr* Arizona

aza·lea \ə-ˈzāl-yə\ *n* : any of numerous rhododendrons with funnel-shaped blossoms and usu. deciduous leaves

az·i·do·thy·mi·dine \ə-ˌzi-dō-ˈthī-mə-ˌdēn\ *n* : AZT

az·i·muth \ˈa-zə-məth\ *n* : horizontal direction expressed as an angular distance from a fixed point

AZT \ˌā-(ˌ)zē-ˈtē\ *n* : an antiviral drug used to treat AIDS

Az·tec \ˈaz-ˌtek\ *n* : a member of a Nahuatl-speaking people that founded the Mexican empire and were conquered by Hernan Cortes in 1519 — **Az·tec·an** *adj*

azure \ˈa-zhər\ *n* : the blue of the clear sky — **azure** *adj*

B

¹**b** \'bē\ *n, pl* **b's** *or* **bs** \'bēz\ *often cap* **1** : the 2d letter of the English alphabet **2** : a grade rating a student's work as good

²**b** *abbr, often cap* **1** bachelor **2** bass **3** bishop **4** book **5** born

B *symbol* boron

Ba *symbol* barium

BA *abbr* **1** bachelor of arts **2** batting average

bab·ble \'ba-bəl\ *vb* **bab·bled; bab·bling** **1** : to talk meaningless or excessively **2** : to utter meaningless sounds — **babble** *n* — **bab·bler** \-b(ə-)lər\ *n*

babe \'bāb\ *n,* **1** : BABY **2** *slang* : GIRL, WOMAN

ba·bel \'bā-bəl, 'ba-\ *n, often cap* [fr. the Tower of *Babel,* Gen 11:4–9] : a place or scene of noise and confusion; *also* : a confused sound ❖ *Synonyms* HUBBUB, RACKET, DIN, UPROAR, CLAMOR

ba·boon \ba-'bün\ *n* [ME *babewin,* fr. MF *babouin,* fr. *baboue* grimace] : any of several large apes of Asia and Africa with doglike muzzles

ba·bush·ka \bə-'büsh-kə, -'bush-\ *n* [Russ, grandmother, dim. of *baba* old woman] : a kerchief for the head

¹**ba·by** \'bā-bē\ *n, pl* **babies** **1** : a very young child : INFANT **2** : the youngest or smallest of a group **3** : a childish person — **baby** *adj* — **ba·by·hood** *n* — **ba·by·ish** *adj*

²**baby** *vb* **ba·bied; ba·by·ing** : to tend or treat with excessive care

baby boom *n* : a marked rise in birthrate — **baby boom·er** \-'bü-mər\ *n*

baby's breath *n* : any of a genus of herbs that are related to the pinks and have small delicate flowers

ba·by·sit \'bā-bē-ˌsit\ *vb* **-sat** \-ˌsat\; **-sit·ting** : to care for children usu. during a short absence of the parents — **ba·by·sit·ter** *n*

bac·ca·lau·re·ate \ˌba-kə-'lòr-ē-ət\ *n* **1** : the degree of bachelor conferred by colleges and universities **2** : a sermon delivered to a graduating class

bac·ca·rat \ˌbä-kə-'rä, ˌba-\ *n* : a card game in which three hands are dealt and players may bet either or both hands against the dealer's

bac·cha·nal \'bä-kə-nᵊl, ˌba-kə-'nal, ˌbä-kə-'näl\ *n* **1** : ORGY **2** : REVELER

bac·cha·na·lia \ˌba-kə-'näl-yə\ *n, pl* **bac·chanalia** : a drunken orgy — **bac·cha·na·lian** \-'nāl-yən\ *adj or n*

bach·e·lor \'bach-lər, 'ba-chə-lər\ *n* **1** : a person who has received the usu. lowest degree conferred by a 4-year college **2** : an unmarried man — **bach·e·lor·hood** *n*

bach·e·lor·ette \ˌbach-lə-'ret, ˌba-chə-\ *n* : an unmarried woman

bachelor's button *n* : a European plant related to the daisies and having usu. blue, pink, or white flower heads

ba·cil·lus \bə-'si-ləs\ *n, pl* **-li** \-ˌlī\ [NL, fr.

ML, small staff, dim. of L *baculus* staff] : any of a genus of rod-shaped bacteria; *also* : a disease-producing bacterium — **bac·il·lary** \'ba-sə-ˌler-ē\ *adj*

¹**back** \'bak\ *n* **1** : the rear or dorsal part of the human body; *also* : the corresponding part of a lower animal **2** : the part or surface opposite the front **3** : a player in the backfield in football — **back·less** \-ləs\ *adj*

²**back** *adv* **1** : to, toward, or at the rear **2** : AGO **3** : so as to be restrained or retarded **4** : to, toward, or in a former place or state **5** : in return or reply

³**back** *adj* **1** : located at or in the back; *also* : REMOTE **2** : OVERDUE ⟨~ rent⟩ **3** : moving or operating backward **4** : not current ⟨~ issues of a magazine⟩

⁴**back** *vb* **1** : SUPPORT, UPHOLD **2** : to go or cause to go backward or in reverse **3** : to furnish with a back : form the back of — **back·er** *n*

back·ache \'bak-ˌāk\ *n* : a pain in the lower back

back–bench·er \-'ben-chər\ *n* : a rank-and-file member of a British legislature

back·bite \-ˌbīt\ *vb* **-bit** \-ˌbit\; **-bit·ten** \-ˌbi-tᵊn\; **-bit·ing** \-ˌbī-tiŋ\ : to say mean or spiteful things about someone who is absent — **back·bit·er** *n*

back·board \-ˌbórd\ *n* : a board placed at or serving as the back of something

back·bone \-ˌbōn\ *n* **1** : the bony column in the back of a vertebrate that is the chief support of the trunk and consists of a jointed series of vertebrae enclosing and protecting the spinal cord **2** : firm resolute character **3** : the primary high-speed hardware and transmission lines of a telecommunication network

back·drop \'bak-ˌdräp\ *n* : a painted cloth hung across the rear of a stage

back·field \-ˌfēld\ *n* : the football players whose positions are behind the line

¹**back·fire** \-ˌfī(-ə)r\ *n* : a loud noise caused by the improperly timed explosion of fuel in the cylinder of an internal combustion engine

²**backfire** *vb* **1** : to make or undergo a backfire **2** : to have a result opposite to what was intended

back·flip \-ˌflip\ *n* : a backward somersault esp. in the air

back·gam·mon \'bak-ˌga-mən\ *n* : a game played with pieces on a double board in which the moves are determined by throwing dice

back·ground \'bak-ˌgraúnd\ *n* **1** : the scenery behind something **2** : the setting within which something takes place; *also* : the sum of a person's experience, training, and understanding

back·hand \'bak-ˌhand\ *n* : a stroke (as in tennis) made with the back of the hand turned in the direction of movement; *also* : the side on which such a stroke is made — **back·hand** *vb*

back·hand·ed \'bak-ˌhan-dəd\ *adj* **1** : INDIRECT, DEVIOUS; *esp* : SARCASTIC ⟨a ∼ compliment⟩ **2** : using or made with a backhand

back·hoe \'bak-ˌhō\ *n* : an excavating machine having a bucket that is drawn toward the machine

back·ing \'ba-kiŋ\ *n* **1** : something forming a back **2** : SUPPORT, AID; *also* : a body of supporters

back·lash \'bak-ˌlash\ *n* **1** : a sudden violent backward movement or reaction **2** : a strong adverse reaction

¹back·log \-ˌlȯg, -ˌläg\ *n* **1** : a large log at the back of a hearth fire **2** : an accumulation of tasks unperformed or materials not processed

²backlog *vb* : to accumulate in reserve

back of *prep* : BEHIND

back order *n* : a business order yet to be fulfilled because stock is unavailable — **back-order** *vb*

back out *vb* : to withdraw esp. from a commitment or contest

¹back·pack \'bak-ˌpak\ *n* : a camping pack supported by an aluminum frame and carried on the back

²backpack *vb* : to hike with a backpack — **back·pack·er** *n*

back·ped·al \'bak-ˌpe-dᵊl\ *vb* : RETREAT

back·rest \-ˌrest\ *n* : a rest for the back

back·side \-ˌsīd\ *n* : BUTTOCKS

back·slap \-ˌslap\ *vb* : to display excessive cordiality — **back·slap·per** *n*

back·slide \-ˌslīd\ *vb* **-slid** \-ˌslid\; **-slid** *or* **-slid·den** \-ˌsli-dᵊn\; **-slid·ing** \-ˌslī-diŋ\ : to lapse morally or in religious practice — **back·slid·er** *n*

back·space \-ˌspās\ *vb* : to move back a space in a text with the press of a key — **backspace** *n*

back·spin \-ˌspin\ *n* : a backward rotary motion of a ball

¹back·stage \'bak-ˌstāj\ *adj* **1** : relating to or occurring in the area behind a stage **2** : of or relating to the private lives of theater people **3** : of or relating to the inner working or operation

²back·stage \'bak-ˈstāj\ *adv* **1** : in or to a backstage area **2** : SECRETLY ⟨worked ∼ to gain support⟩

back·stairs \-ˌsterz\ *adj* : SECRET, FURTIVE; *also* : SORDID, SCANDALOUS

¹back·stop \-ˌstäp\ *n* : something serving as a stop behind something else; *esp* : a screen or fence to keep a ball from leaving the field of play

²backstop *vb* **1** : SUPPORT **2** : to serve as a backstop to

back·sto·ry \-ˌstȯr-ē\ *n* : a story that tells what led up to the main story or plot (as of a film)

back·stretch \'bak-ˈstrech\ *n* : the side opposite the homestretch on a racecourse

back·stroke \-ˌstrōk\ *n* : a swimming stroke executed on the back — **back·strok·er** \-ˌstrō-kər\ *n*

back talk *n* : impudent, insolent, or argumentative replies

back·track \'bak-ˌtrak\ *vb* **1** : to retrace one's course **2** : to reverse a position or stand

back·up \-ˌəp\ *n* **1** : one that serves as a substitute or alternative **2** : a copy of computer data — **back up** *vb*

¹back·ward \'bak-wərd\ *or* **back·wards** \-wərdz\ *adv* **1** : toward the back **2** : with the back foremost ⟨ride ∼⟩ **3** : in a reverse or contrary direction or way ⟨count ∼⟩ **4** : toward the past; *also* : toward a worse state

²backward *adj* **1** : directed, turned, or done backward **2** : DIFFIDENT, SHY **3** : retarded in development — **back·ward·ly** *adv* — **back·ward·ness** *n*

back·wash \'bak-ˌwȯsh, -ˌwäsh\ *n* : a backward flow or movement (as of water or air) produced by a propelling force (as the motion of oars)

back·wa·ter \-ˌwȯ-tər, -ˌwä-\ *n* **1** : water held or turned back in its course **2** : an isolated or backward place or condition

back·woods \-ˈwu̇dz\ *n pl* **1** : wooded or partly cleared areas far from cities **2** : a remote or isolated place

ba·con \'bā-kən\ *n* : salted and smoked meat from the sides or back of a pig

bacteria *pl of* BACTERIUM

bac·te·ri·cid·al \bak-ˌtir-ə-ˈsī-dᵊl\ *adj* : destroying bacteria — **bac·te·ri·cide** \-ˈtir-ə-ˌsīd\ *n*

bac·te·ri·ol·o·gy \bak-ˌtir-ē-ˈä-lə-jē\ *n* **1** : a science dealing with bacteria **2** : bacterial life and phenomena — **bac·te·ri·o·log·ic** \-ə-ˈlä-jik\ *or* **bac·te·ri·o·log·i·cal** \-ə-ˈlä-ji-kəl\ *adj* — **bac·te·ri·ol·o·gist** \-ˈä-lə-jist\ *n*

bac·te·rio·phage \bak-ˈtir-ē-ə-ˌfāj\ *n* : any of various viruses that attack specific bacteria

bac·te·ri·um \bak-ˈtir-ē-əm\ *n, pl* **-ria** \-ē-ə\ [NL, fr. Gk *baktērion* staff] : any of a group of single-celled microorganisms including some that cause disease and others that are valued esp. for their chemical effects (as fermentation) — **bac·te·ri·al** \-ē-əl\ *adj*

bad \'bad\ *adj* **worse** \'wərs\; **worst** \'wərst\ **1** : below standard : POOR; *also* : UNFAVORABLE ⟨a ∼ report⟩ **2** : SPOILED, DECAYED : WICKED; *also* : not well-behaved : NAUGHTY **4** : DISAGREEABLE ⟨a ∼ taste⟩; *also* : HARMFUL **5** : DEFECTIVE, FAULTY ⟨∼ wiring⟩; *also* : not valid ⟨a ∼ check⟩ **6** : UNWELL, ILL **7** : SORRY, REGRETFUL ⟨feels ∼ about forgetting to call⟩ ♦ **Syn·onyms** EVIL, WRONG, IMMORAL, INIQUITOUS — **bad·ly** *adv* — **bad·ness** *n*

bade *past and past part of* BID

badge \'baj\ *n* : a device or token usu. worn as a sign of status

¹bad·ger \'ba-jər\ *n* : any of several sturdy burrowing mammals with long claws on their forefeet

²badger *vb* : to harass or annoy persistently

ba·di·nage \ˌba-də-ˈnäzh\ *n* [F] : playful talk back and forth : BANTER

bad·land \'bad-ˌland\ *n* : a region marked by intricate erosional sculpturing and scanty vegetation — usu. used in pl.

bad·min·ton \'bad-ˌmi-tᵊn, -ˌmin-tᵊn\ *n* : a court game played with light rackets and a shuttlecock volleyed over a net

bad-mouth \'bad-,maůth\ *vb* : to criticize severely

Bae-de-ker \'bā-di-kər, 'be-\ *n* : GUIDEBOOK

¹**baf-fle** \'ba-fəl\ *vb* **baf-fled; baf-fling** \-f(ə)liŋ\ : FRUSTRATE, THWART, FOIL; *also* : PERPLEX — **baf-fle-ment** *n*

²**baffle** *n* : a device (as a wall or screen) to deflect, check, or regulate flow (as of liquid or sound) — **baf-fled** \'ba-fəld\ *adj*

¹**bag** \'bag\ *n* **1** : a flexible usu. closable container (as for storing or carrying) **2** : something that bulges and sags like a bag ⟨∼s under the eyes⟩

²**bag** *vb* **bagged; bag-ging 1** : DISTEND, BULGE **2** : to put in a bag **3** : to get possession of; *esp* : to take in hunting ✦ **Synonyms** TRAP, SNARE, CATCH, CAPTURE, COLLAR

ba-gasse \bə-'gas\ *n* [F] : plant residue (as of sugarcane) left after a product (as juice) has been extracted

bag-a-telle \,ba-gə-'tel\ *n* [F] : TRIFLE 1

ba-gel \'bā-gəl\ *n* [Yiddish *beygl*] : a firm doughnut-shaped roll usu. made by boiling and then baking

bag-gage \'ba-gij\ *n* **1** : the traveling bags and personal belongings of a traveler : LUGGAGE **2** : intangible things that get in the way ⟨emotional ∼⟩

bag-gies \'ba-gēz\ *n pl* : baggy pants or shorts

bag-gy \'ba-gē\ *adj* **bag-gi-er; -est** : puffed out or hanging like a bag — **bag-gi-ly** \-gə-lē\ *adv* — **bag-gi-ness** \-gē-nəs\ *n*

bag-man \'bag-mən\ *n* : a person who collects or distributes illicitly gained money on behalf of another

ba-gnio \'ban-yō\ *n, pl* **bagnios** [It *bagno*, lit., public bath] : BROTHEL

bag of waters *n* : a double-walled fluid-filled sac that encloses and protects the fetus in the womb and that breaks releasing its fluid during the process of birth

bag-pipe \'bag-,pīp\ *n* : a musical wind instrument consisting of a bag, a tube with valves, and sounding pipes — often used in pl. — **bag-pip-er** \-,pī-pər\ *n*

ba-guette \ba-'get\ *n* [F, lit., rod] **1** : a gem having the shape of a narrow rectangle; *also* : the shape itself **2** : a long thin loaf of French bread

baht \'bät\ *n, pl* **baht** *also* **bahts** — see MONEY table

¹**bail** \'bāl\ *n* : a container for ladling water out of a boat

²**bail** *vb* : to dip and throw out water from a boat — **bail-er** *n*

³**bail** *n* : security given to guarantee a prisoner's appearance when legally required; *also* : one giving such security or the release secured

⁴**bail** *vb* : to release under bail; *also* : to procure the release of by giving bail — **bail-able** \'bā-lə-bəl\ *adj*

⁵**bail** *n* : the arched handle (as of a pail or kettle)

bai-liff \'bā-ləf\ *n* **1** : an aide of a British sheriff who serves writs and makes arrests; *also* : a minor officer of a U.S.

court **2** : an estate or farm manager esp. in Britain : STEWARD

bai-li-wick \'bā-li-,wik\ *n* : one's special province or domain ✦ **Synonyms** TERRITORY, FIELD, SPHERE

bail-out \'bā-,laůt\ *n* : a rescue from financial distress

bairn \'bern\ *n, chiefly Scot* : CHILD

¹**bait** \'bāt\ *vb* **1** : to persecute by continued attacks **2** : to harass with dogs usu. for sport ⟨∼ a bear⟩ **3** : to furnish (as a hook) with bait **4** : ALLURE, ENTICE **5** : to give food and drink to (as an animal) ✦ **Synonyms** BADGER, HECKLE, HOUND

²**bait** *n* **1** : a lure for catching animals (as fish) **2** : LURE, TEMPTATION ✦ **Synonyms** SNARE, TRAP, DECOY, COME-ON, ENTICEMENT

bait-fish \'bāt-,fish\ *n* : a small fish that attracts and is a food source for a larger fish; *also* : a fish used for bait

bai-za \'bī-(,)zä\ *n, pl* **baiza** *or* **baizas** — see *rial* at MONEY table

baize \'bāz\ *n* : a coarse feltlike fabric

¹**bake** \'bāk\ *vb* **baked; bak-ing 1** : to cook or become cooked in dry heat esp. in an oven **2** : to dry and harden by heat ⟨∼ bricks⟩ — **bak-er** *n*

²**bake** *n* : a social gathering featuring baked food

baker's dozen *n* : THIRTEEN

bak-ery \'bā-k(ə-)rē\ *n, pl* **-er-ies** : a place for baking or selling baked goods

bake sale *n* : a fund-raising event at which usu. homemade foods are sold

bake-shop \'bāk-,shäp\ *n* : BAKERY

bake-ware \-,wer\ *n* : dishes used for baking and serving food

baking powder *n* : a powder that consists of a carbonate, an acid, and a starch and that makes the dough rise in baking cakes and biscuits

baking soda *n* : SODIUM BICARBONATE

bak-sheesh \'bak-,shēsh\ *n* : payment (as a tip or bribe) to expedite service

bal *abbr* balance

bal-a-lai-ka \,ba-lə-'lī-kə\ *n* [Russ] : a triangular 3-stringed instrument of Russian origin played by plucking or strumming

¹**bal-ance** \'ba-ləns\ *n* [ME, fr. AF, fr. VL *bilancia*, fr. LL *bilanc-, bilanx* having two scalepans, fr. L *bi* two + *lanc-, lanx* plate] **1** : a weighing device : SCALE **2** : a weight, force, or influence counteracting the effect of another **3** : an oscillating wheel used to regulate a timepiece **4** : a state of equilibrium **5** : REMAINDER, REST; *esp* : an amount in excess esp. on the credit side of an account — **bal-anced** \-lənst\ *adj*

²**balance** *vb* **bal-anced; bal-anc-ing 1** : to compute the balance of an account **2** : to arrange so that one set of elements equals another; *also* : to equal or equalize in weight, number, or proportions **3** : WEIGH **4** : to bring or come to a state or position of balance; *also* : to bring into harmony or proportion

bal-boa \bal-'bō-ə\ *n* — see MONEY table

bal-brig-gan \bal-'bri-gən\ *n* : a knitted cotton fabric used esp. for underwear

bal·co·ny \'bal-kə-nē\ *n, pl* **-nies** **1** : a platform projecting from the side of a building and enclosed by a railing **2** : a gallery inside a building

bald \'bȯld\ *adj* **1** : lacking a natural or usual covering (as of hair) **2** : UNADORNED, PLAIN ⟨the ~ truth⟩ **♦ Synonyms** BARE, BARREN, NAKED, NUDE — **bald·ly** *adv* — **bald·ness** *n*

bal·da·chin \'bȯl-də-kən, 'bal-\ *or* **bal·da·chi·no** \ˌbal-də-'kē-nō\ *n, pl* **-chins** *or* **-chinos** : a canopylike structure over an altar

bald cypress *n* : either of two coniferous trees of southern U.S. swamps; *also* : their hard red wood

bald eagle *n* : a large brown eagle of No. America that when mature has white head and neck feathers and a white tail

bal·der·dash \'bȯl-dər-ˌdash\ *n* : NONSENSE

bald·ing \'bȯl-diŋ\ *adj* : becoming bald

bal·dric \'bȯl-drik\ *n* : a belt worn over the shoulder to carry a sword or bugle

¹bale \'bāl\ *n* : a large or closely packed bundle

²bale *vb* **baled; bal·ing** : to pack in a bale — **bal·er** *n*

ba·leen \bə-'lēn\ *n* : a horny substance attached in plates to the upper jaw of some large whales (**baleen whales**)

bale·ful \'bāl-fəl\ *adj* : DEADLY, HARMFUL; *also* : OMINOUS **♦ Synonyms** SINISTER, MALEFIC, MALEFICENT, MALIGN

¹balk \'bȯk\ *n* **1** : HINDRANCE, CHECK, SETBACK **2** : an illegal motion of the pitcher in baseball while in position

²balk *vb* **1** : BLOCK, THWART **2** : to stop short and refuse to go on **3** : to commit a balk in sports **♦ Synonyms** FRUSTRATE, BAFFLE, FOIL, THWART — **balky** \'bȯ-kē\ *adj*

¹ball \'bȯl\ *n* **1** : a rounded body or mass (as an object used in a game or as a missile); *also* : a roundish protuberant part of the body ⟨the ~ of the foot⟩ **2** : a game played with a ball **3** : a pitched baseball that misses the strike zone and is not swung at by the batter **4** : a hit or thrown ball in various games ⟨foul ~⟩ — **on the ball** : COMPETENT, KNOWLEDGEABLE, ALERT

²ball *vb* : to form into a ball

³ball *n* : a large formal dance

bal·lad \'ba-ləd\ *n* **1** : a narrative poem of strongly marked rhythm suitable for singing **2** : a simple song : AIR **3** : a slow romantic song

bal·lad·eer \ˌba-lə-'dir\ *n* : a singer of ballads

¹bal·last \'ba-ləst\ *n* **1** : heavy material used to stabilize a ship or control a balloon's ascent **2** : crushed stone laid in a railroad bed or used in making concrete

²ballast *vb* : to provide with ballast **♦ Synonyms** BALANCE, STABILIZE, STEADY

ball bearing *n* : a bearing in which the revolving part turns upon steel balls that roll easily in a groove; *also* : one of the balls in such a bearing

ball·car·ri·er \'bȯl-ˌker-ē-ər\ *n* : the foot-

ball player carrying the ball in an offensive play

ball·er \'bȯ-lər\ *n* : an implement for shaping food into a ball ⟨melon ~⟩

bal·le·ri·na \ˌba-lə-'rē-nə\ *n* : a female ballet dancer

bal·let \'ba-ˌlā, ba-'lā\ *n* **1** : dancing in which fixed poses and steps are combined with light flowing movements often to convey a story; *also* : a theatrical art form using ballet dancing **2** : a company of ballet dancers

bal·let·o·mane \ba-'le-tə-ˌmān\ *n* : a devotee of ballet

bal·lis·tic missile \bə-'lis-tik-\ *n* : a missile that is guided during ascent and that falls freely during descent

bal·lis·tics \-tiks\ *n sing or pl* **1** : the science of the motion of projectiles (as bullets) in flight **2** : the flight characteristics of a projectile — **ballistic** *adj*

ball of fire : an unusually energetic person

¹bal·loon \bə-'lün\ *n* **1** : a bag filled with gas or heated air so as to rise and float in the atmosphere usu. carrying a suspended load **2** : an inflatable bag used as a toy or decoration — **bal·loon·ist** *n*

²balloon *vb* **1** : to swell or puff out **2** : to travel in a balloon **3** : to increase rapidly

¹bal·lot \'ba-lət\ *n* [It *ballotta* small ball used in secret voting, fr. It dial., dim. of *balla* ball] **1** : a piece of paper used to cast a vote **2** : the action or a system of voting; *also* : the right to vote

²ballot *vb* : to decide by ballot : VOTE

¹ball·park \'bȯl-ˌpark\ *n* : a park in which ball games are played

²ballpark *adj* : approximately correct ⟨~ estimate⟩

ball·point \'bȯl-ˌpȯint\ *n* : a pen whose writing point is a small rotating metal ball that inks itself from an inner container

ball·room \'bȯl-ˌrüm, -ˌrùm\ *n* : a large room for dancing

ballroom dance *n* : any of various dances (as the tango, two-step, and waltz) in which couples perform set moves

bal·ly·hoo \'ba-lē-ˌhü\ *n, pl* **-hoos** : extravagant statements and claims made for publicity — **ballyhoo** *vb*

balm \'bäm, 'bälm\ *n* **1** : a fragrant healing or soothing lotion or ointment **2** : any of several spicy fragrant herbs of the mint family **3** : something that comforts or soothes

balmy \'bä-mē, 'bäl-\ *adj* **balm·i·er; -est** **1** : gently soothing : MILD **2** : FOOLISH, ABSURD **♦ Synonyms** SOFT, BLAND, MILD, GENTLE — **balm·i·ness** *n*

ba·lo·ney \bə-'lō-nē\ *n* : NONSENSE

bal·sa \'bȯl-sə\ *n* : the extremely light strong wood of a tropical American tree; *also* : the tree

bal·sam \'bȯl-səm\ *n* **1** : a fragrant aromatic and usu. resinous substance oozing from various plants; *also* : a preparation containing or smelling like balsam **2** : a balsam-yielding tree (as balsam fir) **3** : a

common garden ornamental plant —
bal·sam·ic \bȯl-ˈsa-mik\ *adj*

balsam fir *n* : a resinous No. American evergreen tree that is widely used for pulpwood and as a Christmas tree

balsamic vinegar *n* : an aged Italian vinegar made from white grapes

Balt \ˈbȯlt\ *n* : a native or inhabitant of Lithuania, Latvia, or Estonia

Bal·ti·more oriole \ˈbȯl-tə-ˌmȯr-\ *n* : a common American oriole in which the male is brightly colored with orange, black, and white

bal·us·ter \ˈba-lə-stər\ *n* [F *balustre*, fr. It *balaustro*, fr. L *balaustium*; fr. its shape] : an upright support for a rail (as of a staircase)

bal·us·trade \ˈba-lə-ˌsträd\ *n* : a row of balusters topped by a rail

bam·boo \bam-ˈbü\ *n, pl* **bamboos** : any of various woody mostly tall tropical grasses including some with strong hollow stems used for building, furniture, or utensils

bamboo curtain *n, often cap B&C* : a political, military, and ideological barrier in eastern Asia

bam·boo·zle \bam-ˈbü-zəl\ *vb* **-boo·zled; -boo·zling** : TRICK, HOODWINK

¹**ban** \ˈban\ *vb* **banned; ban·ning** : PROHIBIT, FORBID

²**ban** *n* **1** : CURSE **2** : a legal or formal prohibition ⟨a ~ on beef imports⟩

³**ban** \ˈbän\ *n, pl* **ba·ni** \ˈbä-nē\ — see *leu* at MONEY table

ba·nal \bə-ˈnäl, -ˈnal; ˈbä-nᵊl\ *adj* [F] : COMMONPLACE, TRITE — **ba·nal·i·ty** \bā-ˈna-lə-tē\ *n*

ba·nana \bə-ˈna-nə\ *n* : a treelike tropical plant bearing thick clusters of yellow or reddish finger-shaped fruit; *also* : this fruit

¹**band** \ˈband\ *n* **1** : something that binds, ties, or goes around **2** : a strip or stripe that can be distinguished (as by color or texture) from nearby matter **3** : a range of wavelengths (as in radio)

²**band** *vb* **1** : to tie up, finish, or enclose with a band **2** : to gather together or unite esp. for some common end — **band·er** *n*

³**band** *n* : a group of persons, animals, or things; *esp* : a group of musicians organized for playing together

¹**ban·dage** \ˈban-dij\ *n* : a strip of material used esp. in dressing wounds

²**bandage** *vb* **ban·daged; ban·dag·ing** : to dress or cover with a bandage

Band–Aid \ˈban-ˈdād\ *adj* : offering, making use of, or serving as a temporary or expedient remedy or solution

ban·dan·na or **ban·dana** \ban-ˈda-nə\ *n* : a large colored figured handkerchief

B and B *abbr* bed-and-breakfast

band·box \ˈband-ˌbäks\ *n* : a usu. cylindrical box for carrying clothing

band·ed \ˈban-dəd\ *adj* : having or marked with bands

ban·de·role or **ban·de·rol** \ˈban-də-ˌrōl\ *n* : a long narrow forked flag or streamer

ban·dit \ˈban-dət\ *n* [It *bandito*, fr. *bandire* to banish] **1** *pl also* **ban·dit·ti** \ban-ˈdi-tē\ : an outlaw who lives by plunder; *esp* : a member of a band of marauders **2** : ROBBER — **ban·dit·ry** \ˈban-də-trē\ *n*

ban·do·lier or **ban·do·leer** \ˌban-də-ˈlir\ *n* : a belt slung over the shoulder esp. to carry ammunition

band saw *n* : a saw in the form of an endless steel belt running over pulleys

band·stand \ˈband-ˌstand\ *n* : a usu. roofed platform on which a band or orchestra performs outdoors

b and w *abbr* black and white

band·wag·on \ˈband-ˌwa-gən\ *n* **1** : a wagon carrying musicians in a parade **2** : a movement that attracts growing support

band·width \-ˈwidth\ *n* : the capacity for data transfer of an electronic communication system

¹**ban·dy** \ˈban-dē\ *vb* **ban·died; ban·dy·ing** **1** : to exchange (as blows or quips) esp. in rapid succession **2** : to use in a glib or offhand way

²**bandy** *adj* : curved outward ⟨~ legs⟩

bane \ˈbān\ *n* **1** : POISON **2** : WOE, HARM; *also* : a source of this — **bane·ful** *adj*

¹**bang** \ˈbaŋ\ *vb* **1** : BUMP ⟨fell and ~ed his knee⟩ **2** : to strike, thrust, or move usu. with a loud noise

²**bang** *n* **1** : a resounding blow **2** : a sudden loud noise

³**bang** *adv* : DIRECTLY, RIGHT ⟨ran ~ up against more trouble⟩

⁴**bang** *n* : a fringe of hair cut short (as across the forehead) — usu. used in pl.

⁵**bang** *vb* : to cut (as hair) to produce bangs

ban·gle \ˈbaŋ-gəl\ *n* **1** : BRACELET **2** : a loose-hanging ornament

bang–up \ˈbaŋ-ˌəp\ *adj* : FIRST-RATE, EXCELLENT ⟨a ~ job⟩

bani *pl of* ³BAN

ban·ish \ˈba-nish\ *vb* **1** : to require by authority to leave a country **2** : to drive out : EXPEL ♦ *Synonyms* EXILE, OSTRACIZE, DEPORT, RELEGATE — **ban·ish·ment** *n*

ban·is·ter \ˈba-nə-stər\ *n* **1** : a handrail with its supporting posts **2** : HANDRAIL **3** : BALUSTER

ban·jo \ˈban-jō\ *n, pl* **banjos** *also* **banjoes** : a musical instrument with a long neck, a drumlike body, and usu. five strings — **ban·jo·ist** \-ist\ *n*

¹**bank** \ˈbaŋk\ *n* **1** : a piled-up mass (as of cloud or earth) **2** : an undersea elevation **3** : rising ground bordering a lake, river, or sea **4** : the sideways slope of a surface along a curve or of a vehicle as it rounds a curve

²**bank** *vb* **1** : to form a bank about **2** : to cover (as a fire) with fuel to keep inactive **3** : to build (a curve) with the roadbed or track inclined laterally upward from the inside edge **4** : to pile or heap in a bank; *also* : to arrange in a tier **5** : to incline (an airplane) laterally

³**bank** *n* [ME, fr. MF or It; MF *banque*, fr.

It *banca*, lit., bench, of Gmc origin] **1** : an establishment concerned esp. with the custody, loan, exchange, or issue of money, the extension of credit, and the transmission of funds **2** : a stock of or a place for holding something in reserve ⟨a blood ∼⟩

4bank *vb* **1** : to conduct the business of a bank **2** : to deposit money or have an account in a bank — **bank·er** *n* — **bank·ing** *n*

5bank *n* : a group of objects arranged close together (as in a row or tier) ⟨a ∼ of file drawers⟩

bank·book \'baŋk-ˌbuk\ *n* : the depositor's book in which a bank records deposits and withdrawals

bank-card \-ˌkärd\ *n* : a card (as a credit card or an ATM card) issued by a bank

bank·note \-ˌnōt\ *n* : a promissory note issued by a bank and circulating as money

bank·roll \-ˌrōl\ *n* : supply of money : FUNDS

1bank·rupt \'baŋk-(ˌ)rəpt\ *n* [modif. of MF *banquerote* bankruptcy, fr. It *bancarotta*, fr. *banca* bank + *rotta* broken] : an insolvent person; *esp* : one whose property is turned over by court action to a trustee to be handled for the benefit of his creditors — **bankrupt** *vb*

2bankrupt *adj* **1** : reduced to financial ruin; *esp* : legally declared a bankrupt **2** : wholly lacking in or deprived of some essential ⟨morally ∼⟩ — **bank·rupt·cy** \'baŋk-(ˌ)rəpt-sē\ *n*

1ban·ner \'ba-nər\ *n* **1** : a piece of cloth attached to a staff and used by a leader as his standard **2** : FLAG **3** : an advertisement that runs usu. across the top of a Web page

2banner *adj* : distinguished from all others esp. in excellence ⟨a ∼ year⟩

ban·nock \'ba-nək\ *n* : a flat oatmeal or barley cake usu. cooked on a griddle

banns \'banz\ *n pl* : public announcement esp. in church of a proposed marriage

ban·quet \'baŋ-kwət\ *n* [MF, fr. It *banchetto*, fr. dim. of *banca* bench] : a ceremonial dinner — **banquet** *vb*

ban·quette \baŋ-'ket\ *n* : a long upholstered bench esp. along a wall

ban·shee \'ban-shē\ *n* [Ir *bean sídhe* & ScGael *bean sith*, lit., woman of fairyland] : a female spirit in Gaelic folklore whose wailing warns a family that one of them will soon die

ban·tam \'ban-təm\ *n* **1** : any of numerous small domestic fowls that are often miniatures of standard breeds **2** : a small but pugnacious person

1ban·ter \'ban-tər\ *vb* : to speak to in a witty and teasing manner

2banter *n* : good-natured witty joking

Ban·tu \'ban-ˌtü\ *n, pl* **Bantu** *or* **Bantus** **1** : a group of languages spoken in central and southern Africa **2** : a member of a group of African peoples who speak Bantu

ban·yan \'ban-yən\ *n* : a large tropical Asian tree whose aerial roots grow downward to the ground and form new trunks

ban·zai \bän-'zī\ *n* : a Japanese cheer or cry of triumph

bao·bab \'bau̇-ˌbab, 'bā-ə-\ *n* : a tropical African tree with short swollen trunk and sour edible fruits resembling gourds

bap·tism \'bap-ˌti-zəm\ *n* **1** : a Christian sacrament signifying spiritual rebirth and symbolized by the ritual use of water **2** : an act of baptizing — **bap·tis·mal** \bap-'tiz-məl\ *adj*

baptismal name *n* : GIVEN NAME

Bap·tist \'bap-tist\ *n* : a member of any of several Protestant denominations emphasizing baptism by immersion of believers only

bap·tis·tery *or* **bap·tis·try** \'bap-tə-strē\ *n, pl* **-ter·ies** *or* **-tries** : a place esp. in a church used for baptism

bap·tize \bap-'tīz, 'bap-ˌtīz\ *vb* **bap·tized; bap·tiz·ing** [ME, fr. AF *baptiser*, fr. L *baptizare*, fr. Gk *baptizein* to dip, baptize, fr. *baptein* to dip] **1** : to administer baptism to; *also* : CHRISTEN **2** : to purify esp. by an ordeal

1bar \'bär\ *n* **1** : a long narrow piece of material (as wood or metal) used esp. for a lever, fastening, or support **2** : BARRIER, OBSTACLE **3** : the railing in a law court at which prisoners are stationed; *also* : the legal profession or the whole body of lawyers **4** : a stripe, band, or line much longer than wide **5** : a counter at which food or esp. drink is served; *also* : BARROOM **6** : a vertical line across the musical staff

2bar *vb* **barred; bar·ring** **1** : to fasten, confine, or obstruct with or as if with a bar or bars **2** : to mark with bars : STRIPE **3** : to shut or keep out : EXCLUDE **4** : FORBID, PREVENT

3bar *prep* : EXCEPT ⟨the most popular actor, ∼ none⟩

4bar *abbr* barometer; barometric

Bar *abbr* Baruch

barb \'bärb\ *n* **1** : a sharp projection extending backward (as from the point of an arrow) **2** : a biting critical remark — **barbed** \'bärbd\ *adj* — **barb·less** \'bärb-ləs\ *adj*

bar·bar·ian \bär-'ber-ē-ən\ *adj* **1** : of, relating to, or being a land, culture, or people alien to and usu. believed to be inferior to another's **2** : lacking refinement, learning, or artistic or literary culture — **barbarian** *n* — **bar·bar·i·an·ism** \-ē-ə-ˌni-zəm\ *n*

bar·bar·ic \bär-'ber-ik\ *adj* **1** : BARBARIAN **2** : marked by a lack of restraint : WILD **3** : PRIMITIVE, UNSOPHISTICATED

bar·ba·rism \'bär-bə-ˌri-zəm\ *n* **1** : the social condition of barbarians; *also* : the use or display of barbarian or barbarous acts, attitudes, or ideas **2** : a word or expression that offends standards of correctness or purity

bar·ba·rous \'bär-bə-rəs\ *adj* **1** : lacking culture or refinement **2** : using linguistic barbarisms **3** : mercilessly harsh or cruel — **bar·bar·i·ty** \bär-'ber-ə-tē\ *n* — **bar·ba·rous·ly** *adv* — **bar·ba·rous·ness** *n*

¹bar·be·cue \'bär-bi-ˌkyü\ vb -cued; -cu·ing 1 : to cook on a rack or revolving spit over or before a source of heat 2 : to cook in a highly seasoned vinegar sauce

²barbecue n : a social gathering at which barbecued food is served

bar·bell \'bär-ˌbel\ n : a bar with adjustable weights attached to each end used for exercise and in weight-lifting competition

bar·ber \'bär-bər\ n [ME, fr. AF barboor, fr. barbe beard, fr. L barba] : one whose business is cutting and dressing hair and shaving and trimming beards

bar·ber·ry \'bär-ˌber-ē\ n : any of a genus of spiny shrubs bearing yellow flowers and oblong red berries

bar·bi·tu·rate \bär-'bi-chə-rət\ n : any of various compounds (as a salt or ester) formed from an organic acid (bar·bi·tu·ric acid \ˌbär-bə-'tür-ik-, -'tyür-\); esp : one used as a sedative or hypnotic

bar·ca·role or bar·ca·rolle \'bär-kə-ˌrōl\ n : a Venetian boat song characterized by a beat suggesting a rowing rhythm; also : a piece of music imitating this

bar chart n : BAR GRAPH

bar code n : a set of printed and variously spaced bars and sometimes numerals that is designed to be scanned to provide information about the object it labels — bar·cod·ed \'bär-ˌkō-dəd\ adj — bar coding n

bard \'bärd\ n : POET

¹bare \'ber\ adj bar·er; bar·est 1 : NAKED 2 : UNCONCEALED, EXPOSED 3 : EMPTY 4 : leaving nothing to spare : MERE 5 : PLAIN, UNADORNED ⟨the ~ facts⟩ ♦ Synonyms NUDE, BALD — bare·ness n

²bare vb bared; bar·ing : to make or lay bare : UNCOVER

bare·back \-ˌbak\ or bare·backed \-ˌbakt\ adv or adj : without a saddle

bare·faced \-'fāst\ adj 1 : having the face uncovered; esp : BEARDLESS 2 : not concealed : OPEN — bare·faced·ly \-'fā-səd-lē, -'fāst-lē\ adv

bare·foot \-ˌfút\ or bare·foot·ed \-'fú-təd\ adv or adj : with bare feet

bare–hand·ed \-'han-dəd\ adv or adj 1 : without gloves 2 : without tools or weapons

bare·head·ed \-'he-dəd\ adv or adj : without a hat

bare·ly \'ber-lē\ adv 1 : PLAINLY, MEAGERLY ⟨a ~ furnished room⟩ 2 : by a narrow margin : only just ⟨~ enough money⟩

bar·fly \'bär-ˌflī\ n : a drinker who frequents bars

¹bar·gain \'bär-gən\ n 1 : AGREEMENT 2 : an advantageous purchase 3 : a transaction, situation, or event regarded in the light of its results

²bargain vb 1 : to negotiate over the terms of an agreement; also : to come to terms 2 : BARTER

bar·gain–base·ment \ˌbär-gən-'bās-mənt\ adj : markedly inexpensive

¹barge \'bärj\ n 1 : a broad flat-bottomed boat usu. moved by towing 2 : a motorboat supplied to a flagship (as for an admiral) 3 : a ceremonial boat elegantly furnished — barge·man \-mən\ n

²barge vb barged; barg·ing 1 : to carry by barge 2 : to move or thrust oneself clumsily or rudely

bar graph n : a graphic technique for comparing amounts by rectangles whose lengths are proportional to the amounts they represent

ba·ris·ta \bə-'rēs-tə\ n : a person who makes and serves coffee to the public

bari·tone \'ber-ə-ˌtōn\ n [F baryton or It baritono, fr. Gk barytonos deep sounding, fr. barys heavy + tonos tone] 1 : a male voice between bass and tenor; also : a man with such a voice

bar·i·um \'ber-ē-əm\ n : a silver-white metallic chemical element that occurs only in combination

¹bark \'bärk\ vb 1 : to make the short loud cry of a dog 2 : to speak or utter in a curt loud tone : SNAP

²bark n : the sound made by a barking dog

³bark n : the tough corky outer covering of a woody stem or root

⁴bark vb 1 : to strip the bark from 2 : to rub the skin from : ABRADE

⁵bark n : a ship of three or more masts with the aft mast fore-and-aft rigged and the others square-rigged

bar·keep \'bär-ˌkēp\ also bar·keep·er \-ˌkē-pər\ n : BARTENDER

bark·er \'bär-kər\ n : a person who stands at the entrance esp. to a show and tries to attract customers to it

bar·ley \'bär-lē\ n : a cereal grass with seeds used as food and in making malt liquors; also : its seed

bar mitz·vah \ˌbär-'mits-və\ n, often cap B&M [Heb bar miṣwāh, lit., son of the (divine) law] 1 : a Jewish boy who at the age of 13 years of age assumes religious responsibilities 2 : the ceremony recognizing a boy as a bar mitzvah

barn \'bärn\ n [ME bern, fr. OE bereærn, fr. bere barley + ærn house, store] : a building used esp. for storing hay and grain and for housing livestock or farm equipment

bar·na·cle \'bär-ni-kəl\ n : any of numerous small marine crustaceans free-swimming when young but permanently fixed (as to rocks, whales, or ships) when adult

barn·storm \'bärn-ˌstórm\ vb : to travel through the country making brief stops to entertain (as with shows or flying stunts) or to campaign for political office

barn·yard \-ˌyärd\ n : a usu. fenced area adjoining a barn

baro·graph \'ber-ə-ˌgraf\ n : a recording barometer

ba·rom·e·ter \bə-'räm-ə-tər\ n : an instrument for measuring atmospheric pressure — baro·met·ric \ˌbär-ə-'me-trik\ adj

bar·on \'ber-ən\ n : a member of the lowest grade of the British peerage — ba·ro·ni·al \bə-'rō-nē-əl\ adj — bar·ony \'ber-ə-nē\ n

bar·on·age \'ber-ə-nij\ n : PEERAGE

bar·on·ess \'ber-ə-nəs\ *n* **1** : the wife or widow of a baron **2** : a woman holding a baronial title in her own right

bar·on·et \'ber-ə-nət\ *n* : a man holding a rank of honor below a baron but above a knight — **bar·on·et·cy** \-sē\ *n*

ba·roque \bə-'rōk, -'räk\ *adj* : marked by the use of complex forms, bold ornamentation, and the juxtapositioning of contrasting elements

ba·rouche \bə-'rüsh\ *n* [G *Barutsche,* fr. It *biroccio,* ultim. fr. LL *birotus* two-wheeled, fr. L *bi-* two + *rota* wheel] : a 4-wheeled carriage with a high driver's seat in front and a folding top

bar·racks \'ber-əks\ *n sing or pl* : a building or group of buildings for lodging soldiers

bar·ra·cu·da \ˌber-ə-'kü-də\ *n, pl* **-da** *or* **-das** : any of several large slender predaceous sea fishes including some used for food

bar·rage \bə-'räzh, -'räj\ *n* : a heavy concentration of fire (as of artillery)

barred \'bärd\ *adj* : STRIPED

¹bar·rel \'ber-əl\ *n* **1** : a round bulging cask with flat ends of equal diameter **2** : the amount contained in a barrel **3** : a cylindrical or tubular part ⟨gun ∼⟩ — **bar·reled** \-əld\ *adj*

²barrel *vb* **-reled** *or* **-relled; -rel·ing** *or* **-rel·ling** **1** : to pack in a barrel **2** : to travel at high speed

bar·rel·head \-ˌhed\ *n* : the flat end of a barrel — **on the barrelhead** : asking for or granting no credit ⟨paid cash *on the barrelhead*⟩

barrel roll *n* : an airplane maneuver in which a complete revolution about the longitudinal axis is made

¹bar·ren \'ber-ən\ *adj* **1** : STERILE, UNFRUITFUL **2** : unproductive of results ⟨a ∼ scheme⟩ **3** : lacking interest or charm **4** : lacking inspiration or ideas — **bar·ren·ness** \-nəs\ *n*

²barren *n* : a tract of barren land

bar·rette \bä-'ret, bə-\ *n* : a clasp or bar for holding the hair in place

¹bar·ri·cade \'ber-ə-ˌkād, ˌber-ə-'kād\ *vb* **-cad·ed; -cad·ing** : to block, obstruct, or fortify with a barricade

²barricade *n* [F, fr. MF, fr. *barriquer* to barricade, fr. *barrique* barrel] **1** : a hastily thrown-up obstruction or fortification **2** : BARRIER, OBSTACLE

bar·ri·er \'ber-ē-ər\ *n* : something that separates, demarcates, or serves as a barricade ⟨racial ∼s⟩

barrier island *n* : a long broad sandy island lying parallel to a shore

barrier reef *n* : a coral reef roughly parallel to a shore and separated from it usu. by a lagoon

bar·ring \'bär-iŋ\ *prep* : excluding by exception : EXCEPTING

bar·rio \'bär-ē-ˌō, 'ber-\ *n, pl* **-ri·os** **1** : a district of a city or town in a Spanish-speaking country **2** : a Spanish-speaking quarter in a U.S. city

bar·ris·ter \'ber-ə-stər\ *n* : a British counselor admitted to plead in the higher courts

bar·room \'bär-ˌrüm, -ˌrum\ *n* : a room or establishment whose main feature is a bar for the sale of liquor

¹bar·row \'ber-ō\ *n* : a large burial mound of earth and stones

²barrow *n* **1** : WHEELBARROW **2** : a cart with a boxlike body and two shafts for pushing it

Bart *abbr* baronet

bar·tend·er \'bär-ˌten-dər\ *n* : a person who serves liquor at a bar

bar·ter \'bär-tər\ *vb* : to trade by exchange of goods — **barter** *n* — **bar·ter·er** *n*

Ba·ruch \'bär-ˌük, bə-'rük\ *n* — see BIBLE table

bas·al \'bā-səl\ *adj* **1** : situated at or forming the base **2** : BASIC

basal metabolism *n* : the turnover of energy in a fasting and resting organism using energy solely to maintain vital cellular activity, respiration, and circulation as measured by the rate at which heat is given off

ba·salt \bə-'sȯlt, 'bā-ˌsȯlt\ *n* : a dark fine-grained igneous rock — **ba·sal·tic** \bə-'sȯl-tik\ *adj*

¹base \'bās\ *n, pl* **bas·es** \'bā-səz\ **1** : BOTTOM, FOUNDATION **2** : a side or face on which a geometrical figure stands; *also* : the length of a base **3** : a main ingredient or fundamental part **4** : the point of beginning of an act or operation **5** : a place on which a force depends for supplies **6** : a number (as 5 in 5⁷) that is raised to a power; *esp* : a number that when raised to a power equal to the logarithm of a number yields the number itself ⟨the logarithm of 100 to ∼ 10 is 2 since 10² = 100⟩ **7** : the number of units in a given digit's place of a number system that is required to give the numeral 1 in the next higher place ⟨the decimal system uses a ∼ of 10⟩; *also* : such a system using an indicated base ⟨convert from ∼ 10 to ∼ 2⟩ **8** : any of the four stations at the corners of a baseball diamond **9** : a chemical compound (as lime or ammonia) that reacts with an acid to form a salt, has a bitter taste, and turns litmus blue **♦ Synonyms** BASIS, GROUND, GROUNDWORK, FOOTING, FOUNDATION — **base·less** *adj*

²base *vb* **based; bas·ing** **1** : to form or serve as a base for **2** : ESTABLISH

³base *adj* **1** : of low value and inferior quality : DEBASED, ALLOYED **2** : CONTEMPTIBLE, IGNOBLE **3** : MENIAL, DEGRADING **♦ Synonyms** LOW, VILE, DESPICABLE, WRETCHED — **base·ly** *adv* — **base·ness** *n*

base·ball \'bās-ˌbȯl\ *n* : a game played with a bat and ball by two teams on a field with four bases arranged in a diamond; *also* : the ball used in this game

baseball cap *n* : a cap of the kind worn by baseball players that has a rounded crown and a long visor

base·board \-ˌbȯrd\ *n* : a line of boards or molding covering the joint of a wall and the adjoining floor

base-born \-'bȯrn\ *adj* **1** : MEAN, IGNO-

BLE **2** : of humble birth **3** : of illegitimate birth

base exchange *n* : a post exchange at a naval or air force base

base hit *n* : a hit in baseball that enables the batter to reach base safely with no error made and no base runner forced out

BASE jumping \'bās-\ *n* [*b*uilding, *a*ntenna, *s*pan, *e*arth] : the activity of parachuting from a high structure or cliff

base·line \'bās-ˌlīn\ *n* **1** : a line serving as a basis esp. to calculate or locate something **2** : the area within which a baseball player must keep when running between bases

base·ment \-mənt\ *n* **1** : the part of a building that is wholly or partly below ground level **2** : the lowest or fundamental part of something

base on balls *n* : an advance to first base given to a baseball player who receives four balls

base runner *n* : a baseball player who is on base or is attempting to reach a base

¹bash \'bash\ *vb* **1** : to strike violently : HIT **2** : to smash by a blow **3** : to attack physically or verbally

²bash *n* **1** : a heavy blow **2** : a festive social gathering : PARTY

bash·ful \'bash-fəl\ *adj* : inclined to shrink from public attention — **bash·ful·ly** \-fə-lē\ *adv* — **bash·ful·ness** *n*

ba·sic \'bā-sik\ *adj* **1** : of, relating to, or forming the base or essence : FUNDAMENTAL **2** : concerned with fundamental scientific principles : not applied **3** : of, relating to, or having the character of a chemical base ✦ *Synonyms* UNDERLYING, BASAL, PRIMARY — **ba·sic·i·ty** \bā-ˈsi-sə-tē\ *n*

BA·SIC \'bā-sik\ *n* [*B*eginner's *A*ll-purpose *S*ymbolic *I*nstruction *C*ode] : a simplified language for programming a computer

ba·si·cal·ly \'bā-si-k(ə-)lē\ *adv* **1** : at a basic level **2** : for the most part **3** : in a basic manner

ba·sil \'bā-zəl, 'bā-, -səl\ *n* : any of several mints with fragrant leaves used in cooking; *also* : the leaves

ba·sil·i·ca \bə-ˈsi-li-kə, -ˈzi-\ *n* [L, fr. Gk *basilikē*, fr. fem. of *basilikos* royal, fr. *basileus* king] **1** : an early Christian church building consisting of nave and aisles with clerestory and apse **2** : a Roman Catholic church given ceremonial privileges

bas·i·lisk \'ba-sə-ˌlisk, 'ba-zə-\ *n* [ME, fr. L *basiliscus*, fr. Gk *basiliskos*, fr. dim. of *basileus* king] : a legendary reptile with fatal breath and glance

ba·sin \'bā-sⁿn\ *n* **1** : an open usu. circular vessel with sloping sides for holding liquid (as water) **2** : a hollow or enclosed place containing water; *also* : the region drained by a river

ba·sis \'bā-səs\ *n, pl* **ba·ses** \-ˌsēz\ **1** : FOUNDATION, BASE **2** : a fundamental principle

bask \'bask\ *vb* **1** : to expose oneself to comfortable heat **2** : to enjoy something

warmly comforting ⟨~*ing* in his friends' admiration⟩

bas·ket \'bas-kət\ *n* : a container made of woven material (as twigs or grasses); *also* : any of various lightweight usu. wood containers — **bas·ket·ful** *n*

bas·ket·ball \-ˌbȯl\ *n* : a game played on a court by two teams who try to throw an inflated ball through a raised goal; *also* : the ball used in this game — **bas·ket·ball·er** \-ˌbȯ-lər\ *n*

basket case *n* **1** : a person who has all four limbs amputated **2** : a person who is mentally incapacitated or worn out (as from nervous tension)

basket weave *n* : a textile weave resembling the checkered pattern of a plaited basket

bas·ma·ti rice \ˌbäz-ˈmä-tē-\ *n* : an aromatic long-grain rice originating in southern Asia

bas mitzvah *var of* BAT MITZVAH

Basque \'bask\ *n* **1** : a member of a people inhabiting a region bordering on the Bay of Biscay in northern Spain and southwestern France **2** : the language of the Basque people — **Basque** *adj*

bas–re·lief \ˌbä-ri-ˈlēf\ *n* [F] : a sculpture in relief with the design raised very slightly from the background

¹bass \'bas\ *n, pl* **bass** *or* **bass·es** : any of numerous sport and food bony fishes (as a striped bass)

²bass \'bās\ *adj* : of low pitch

³bass \'bās\ *n* **1** : a deep sound or tone **2** : the lower half of the musical pitch range **3** : the lowest part in a 4-part chorus; *also* : a singer having this voice or part

bas·set hound \'ba-sət-\ *n* : any of an old breed of short-legged hunting dogs of French origin having very long ears and a short smooth coat

bas·si·net \ˌba-sə-ˈnet\ *n* : a baby's bed that resembles a basket and often has a hood over one end

bas·so \'ba-sō, 'bä-\ *n, pl* **bassos** *or* **bas·si** \'bä-ˌsē\ [It] : a bass singer

bas·soon \bə-ˈsün\ *n* : a musical wind instrument lower in pitch than the oboe

bass·wood \'bas-ˌwu̇d\ *n* : any of several New World lindens or their wood

bast \'bast\ *n* : BAST FIBER

¹bas·tard \'bas-tərd\ *n* **1** : an illegitimate child **2** : an offensive or disagreeable person

²bastard *adj* **1** : ILLEGITIMATE **2** : of an inferior or nontypical kind, size, or form; *also* : SPURIOUS — **bas·tardy** *n*

bas·tard·ise *Brit var of* BASTARDIZE

bas·tard·ize \'bas-tər-ˌdīz\ *vb* **-ized; -iz·ing** : to reduce from a higher to a lower state : DEBASE

¹baste \'bāst\ *vb* **bast·ed; bast·ing** : to sew with long stitches so as to keep temporarily in place

²baste *vb* **bast·ed; bast·ing** : to moisten (as meat) at intervals with liquid while cooking

bast fiber *n* : a strong woody plant fiber obtained chiefly from phloem and used esp. in making ropes

bas·ti·na·do \ˌbas-tə-ˈnā-dō, -ˈnä-\ *or* **bas·ti·nade** \ˌbas-tə-ˈnād, -ˈnäd\ *n, pl* **-na·does** *or* **-nades** 1 : a blow or beating esp. with a stick 2 : a punishment consisting of beating the soles of the feet

bas·tion \ˈbas-chən\ *n* : a projecting part of a fortification; *also* : a fortified position

¹**bat** \ˈbat\ *n* 1 : a stout stick : CLUB 2 : a sharp blow 3 : an implement (as of wood) used to hit a ball (as in baseball) 4 : a turn at batting — usu. used in the phrase *at bat*

²**bat** *vb* **bat·ted; bat·ting** : to hit with or as if with a bat

³**bat** *n* : any of an order of night-flying mammals with forelimbs modified to form wings

⁴**bat** *vb* **bat·ted; bat·ting** : WINK, BLINK

batch \ˈbach\ *n* 1 : a quantity (as of bread) baked at one time 2 : a quantity of material for use at one time or produced at one operation

bate \ˈbāt\ *vb* **bat·ed; bat·ing** : MODERATE, REDUCE

bath \ˈbath, ˈbäth\ *n, pl* **baths** \ˈbathz, ˈbaths, ˈbäthz, ˈbäths\ 1 : a washing of the body 3 : water for washing the body 3 : a liquid in which objects are immersed so that it can act on them 4 : BATHROOM 5 : a financial loss ⟨took a ∼ in the market⟩

bathe \ˈbāth\ *vb* **bathed; bath·ing** 1 : to wash in liquid and esp. water; *also* : to apply water or a medicated liquid to ⟨*bathed* her eyes⟩ 2 : to take a bath; *also* : to take a swim 3 : to wash along, over, or against so as to wet 4 : to suffuse with or as if with light — **bath·er** *n*

bath·house \ˈbath-ˌhaus, ˈbäth-\ *n* 1 : a building equipped for bathing 2 : a building containing dressing rooms for bathers

bathing suit *n* : SWIMSUIT

ba·thos \ˈbā-ˌthäs\ *n* [Gk, lit., depth] 1 : the sudden appearance of the commonplace in otherwise elevated matter or style 2 : insincere or overdone pathos — **ba·thet·ic** \bə-ˈthe-tik\ *adj*

bath·robe \ˈbath-ˌrōb, ˈbäth-\ *n* : a loose often absorbent robe worn before and after bathing or as a dressing gown

bath·room \-ˌrüm, -ˌrum\ *n* : a room containing a bathtub or shower and usu. a sink and toilet

bath·tub \-ˌtəb\ *n* : a usu. fixed tub for bathing

ba·tik \bə-ˈtēk, ˈba-tik\ *n* [Javanese *batik*] 1 : an Indonesian method of hand-printing textiles by coating with wax the parts not to be dyed; *also* : a design so executed 2 : a fabric printed by batik

ba·tiste \bə-ˈtēst\ *n* : a fine sheer fabric of plain weave

bat·man \ˈbat-mən\ *n* : an orderly of a British military officer

bat mitz·vah \bät-ˈmits-və\ *also* **bas mitz·vah** \bäs-\ *n, often cap B&M* [Heb *bath miṣwāh*, lit., daughter of the (divine) law] 1 : a Jewish girl who at about 13 years of age assumes religious responsi-

bilities 2 : the ceremony recognizing a girl as a bat mitzvah

ba·ton \bə-ˈtän\ *n* : STAFF, ROD; *esp* : a stick with which the leader directs an orchestra or band

bats·man \ˈbats-mən\ *n* : a batter esp. in cricket

bat·tal·ion \bə-ˈtal-yən\ *n* 1 : a large body of troops organized to act together : ARMY 2 : a military unit composed of a headquarters and two or more units (as companies)

¹**bat·ten** \ˈba-tᵊn\ *vb* 1 : to grow or make fat 2 : THRIVE

²**batten** *n* : a strip of wood used esp. to seal or strengthen a joint

³**batten** *vb* : to fasten with battens

¹**bat·ter** \ˈba-tər\ *vb* : to beat or damage with repeated blows

²**batter** *n* : a soft mixture (as for cake) basically of flour and liquid

³**batter** *n* : one that bats; *esp* : the player whose turn it is to bat

battering ram *n* 1 : an ancient military machine for battering down walls 2 : a heavy metal bar with handles used to batter down doors

bat·tery \ˈba-tə-rē\ *n, pl* **-ter·ies** 1 : BEATING; *esp* : unlawful beating or use of force on a person 2 : a grouping of artillery pieces for tactical purposes; *also* : the guns of a warship 3 : a group of electric cells for furnishing electric current; *also* : a single electric cell (a flashlight ∼) 4 : a number of similar items grouped or used as a unit ⟨a ∼ of tests⟩ 5 : the pitcher and catcher of a baseball team

bat·ting \ˈba-tiŋ\ *n* : layers or sheets of cotton or wool (as for lining quilts)

batting cage *n* : a screen around the back and sides of the home plate area to stop baseballs during practice

¹**bat·tle** \ˈba-tᵊl\ *n* [ME *batel*, fr. AF *bataille* battle, battalion, fr. LL *battalia* combat, alter. of *battualia* fencing exercises, fr. L *battuere* to beat] : a general military engagement; *also* : an extended contest or controversy

²**battle** *vb* **bat·tled; bat·tling** : to engage in battle : CONTEND, FIGHT

bat·tle-ax *or* **battle-axe** \ˈba-tᵊl-ˌaks\ *n* 1 : a long-handled ax formerly used as a weapon 2 : a quarrelsome domineering woman

battle fatigue *n* : COMBAT FATIGUE

bat·tle·field \ˈba-tᵊl-ˌfēld\ *n* : a place where a battle is fought

bat·tle·ment \-mənt\ *n* : a decorative or defensive parapet on top of a wall

bat·tle·ship \-ˌship\ *n* : a warship of the most heavily armed and armored class

bat·tle·wag·on \-ˌwa-gən\ *n* : BATTLESHIP

bat·ty \ˈba-tē\ *adj* **bat·ti·er; -est** : CRAZY, FOOLISH

bau·ble \ˈbȯ-bəl\ *n* : TRINKET

baud \ˈbȯd, *Brit* ˈbōd\ *n, pl* **baud** *also* **bauds** : a unit of data transmission speed

baulk *chiefly Brit var of* BALK

baux·ite \ˈbȯk-ˌsīt\ *n* : a clayey mixture that is the chief ore of aluminum

bawd \'bȯd\ n 1 : MADAM 2 2 : PROSTI-TUTE

bawdy \'bȯ-dē\ adj **bawd·i·er; -est** : OB-SCENE, LEWD — **bawd·i·ly** \'bȯ-də-lē\ adv — **bawd·i·ness** \-dē-nəs\ n

¹**bawl** \'bȯl\ vb : to cry or cry out loudly; also : to scold harshly

²**bawl** n : a long loud cry : BELLOW

¹**bay** \'bā\ adj : reddish brown

²**bay** n 1 : a bay-colored animal 2 : a reddish brown color

³**bay** n 1 : a section or compartment of a building or vehicle 2 : a compartment projecting outward from the wall of a building and containing a window (**bay window**)

⁴**bay** vb : to bark with deep long tones

⁵**bay** n 1 : the position of one unable to escape and forced to face danger 2 : a baying of dogs

⁶**bay** n : an inlet of a body of water (as the sea) usu. smaller than a gulf

⁷**bay** n : LAUREL; also : a shrub or tree resembling the laurel

bay·ber·ry \'bā-ˌber-ē\ n : a hardy deciduous shrub of coastal eastern No. America bearing small hard berries coated with a white wax used for candles; also : its fruit

bay leaf n : the dried leaf of the European laurel used in cooking

¹**bay·o·net** \'bā-ə-nət, ˌbā-ə-'net\ n : a daggerlike weapon made to fit on the muzzle end of a rifle

²**bayonet** vb **-net·ed** also **-net·ted; -net·ing** also **-net·ting** : to use or stab with a bayonet

bay·ou \'bī-yü, -ō\ n [Louisiana French, fr. Choctaw bayuk] : a marshy or sluggish body of water

bay rum n : a fragrant liquid used esp. as a cologne or after-shave lotion

ba·zaar \bə-'zär\ n 1 : a group of shops : MARKETPLACE 2 : a fair for the sale of articles usu. for charity

ba·zoo·ka \bə-'zü-kə\ n [bazooka (a crude musical instrument made of pipes and a funnel)] : a weapon consisting of a tube that launches an explosive rocket able to pierce armor

¹**BB** \'bē-(ˌ)bē\ n : a small round shot pellet

²**BB** abbr : base on balls

BBB abbr Better Business Bureau

BBC abbr British Broadcasting Corporation

bbl abbr barrel; barrels

BC abbr 1 before Christ — often printed in small capitals and often punctuated 2 British Columbia

B cell n [bone-marrow-derived cell] : any of the lymphocytes that secrete antibodies when mature

B complex n : VITAMIN B COMPLEX

bd abbr 1 board 2 bound

bdl or **bdle** abbr bundle

bdrm abbr bedroom

be \'bē\ vb, past 1st & 3d sing **was** \'wəz, 'wäz\; 2d sing **were** \'wər\; pl **were**; past subjunctive **were**; past part **been** \'bin\; pres part **be·ing** \'bē-iŋ\; pres 1st sing **am** \əm, 'am\; 2d sing **are** \ər, 'är\; 3d sing **is** \'iz, əz\; pl **are**; pres subjunctive **be** 1 : to equal in meaning or symbolically (God is

love); also : to have a specified qualification or relationship (leaves are green) (this fish is a trout) 2 : to have objective existence (I think, therefore I am); also : to have or occupy a particular place (here is your pen) 3 : to take place : OCCUR (the meeting is tonight) 4 — used with the past participle of transitive verbs as a passive voice auxiliary (the door was opened) 5 — used as the auxiliary of the present participle in expressing continuous action (he is sleeping) 6 — used as an auxiliary with the past participle of some intransitive verbs to form archaic perfect tenses 7 — used as an auxiliary with to and the infinitive to express futurity, prearrangement, or obligation (you are to come when called)

Be symbol beryllium

¹**beach** \'bēch\ n : a sandy or gravelly part of the shore of an ocean or lake

²**beach** vb : to run or drive ashore

beach buggy n : DUNE BUGGY

beach·comb·er \'bēch-ˌkō-mər\ n : a person who searches along a shore for something of use or value

beach·head \'bēch-ˌhed\ n : a small area on an enemy-held shore occupied in the initial stages of an invasion

bea·con \'bē-kən\ n 1 : a signal fire 2 : a guiding or warning signal (as a lighthouse) 3 : a radio transmitter emitting signals for guidance of aircraft

¹**bead** \'bēd\ n [ME bede prayer, prayer bead, fr. OE bed, gebed prayer] 1 pl : a series of prayers and meditations made with a rosary 2 : a small piece of material pierced for threading on a line (as in a rosary) 3 : a small globular body 4 : a narrow projecting rim or band — **beading** n — **beady** adj

²**bead** vb : to form into a bead

bea·dle \'bē-dᵊl\ n : a usu. English parish officer whose duties include keeping order in church

bea·gle \'bē-gəl\ n : a small short-legged smooth-coated hound

beak \'bēk\ n : the bill of a bird and esp. of a bird of prey; also : a pointed projecting part — **beaked** \'bēkt\ adj

bea·ker \'bē-kər\ n 1 : a large widemouthed drinking cup 2 : a widemouthed thin-walled laboratory vessel

¹**beam** \'bēm\ n 1 : a large long piece of timber or metal 2 : the bar of a balance from which the scales hang 3 : the breadth of a ship at its widest part 4 : a ray or shaft of light 5 : a collection of nearly parallel rays (as X-rays) or particles (as electrons) 6 : a constant radio signal transmitted for the guidance of pilots; also : the course indicated by this signal

²**beam** vb 1 : to send out light 2 : BROADCAST 3 : to transmit (data) electronically 4 : to smile with joy

¹**bean** \'bēn\ n : the edible seed borne in pods by some leguminous plants; also : a plant or a pod bearing beans

²**bean** vb : to strike on the head with an object

bean·bag \'bēn-₁bag\ n : a cloth bag partially filled typically with dried beans and used as a toy

bean·ball \'bēn-₁bȯl\ n : a pitch thrown at a batter's head

bean curd n : TOFU

bean·ie \'bē-nē\ n : a small round tight-fitting skullcap

beano \'bē-nō\ n, pl **beanos** : BINGO

¹**bear** \'ber\ n, pl **bears** 1 or pl **bear** : any of a family of large heavy mammals with shaggy hair and small tails 2 : a gruff or sullen person 3 : one who sells (as securities) in expectation of a price decline — **bear·ish** adj

²**bear** vb **bore** \'bȯr\; **borne** \'bȯrn\ also **born** \'bȯrn\; **bear·ing** 1 : CARRY 2 : to be equipped with 3 : to give as testimony ⟨~ witness to the facts of the case⟩ 4 : to give birth to; also : PRODUCE, YIELD ⟨a tree that ~s regularly⟩ 5 : ENDURE, SUSTAIN ⟨~ pain⟩ ⟨bore the weight on piles⟩; also : to exert pressure or influence 6 : to go in an indicated direction ⟨~ to the right⟩ — **bear·able** adj — **bear·er** n

¹**beard** \'bird\ n 1 : the hair that grows on the face of a man 2 : a growth of bristly hairs (as on a goat's chin) — **beard·ed** \'bir-dəd\ adj — **beard·less** adj

²**beard** vb : to confront boldly

bearing n 1 : manner of carrying oneself : COMPORTMENT 2 : a supporting object, purpose, or point 3 : a machine part in which another part (as an axle or pin) turns 4 : an emblem in a coat of arms 5 : the position or direction of one point with respect to another or to the compass; also : a determination of position 6 pl : comprehension of one's situation 7 : connection with or influence on something; also : SIGNIFICANCE

bear market n : a market in which securities or commodities are persistently declining in value

bear·skin \'ber-₁skin\ n : an article (as a hat) made of the skin of a bear

beast \'bēst\ n 1 : ANIMAL 1; esp : a 4-footed mammal 2 : a contemptible person

¹**beast·ly** \'bēst-lē\ adj **beast·li·er; -est** 1 : BESTIAL 2 : ABOMINABLE, DISAGREEABLE — **beast·li·ness** \-nəs\ n

²**beastly** adv : VERY ⟨a ~ cold day⟩

¹**beat** \'bēt\ vb **beat; beat·en** \'bē-t²n\ or **beat; beat·ing** 1 : to strike repeatedly 2 : TREAD 3 : to affect or alter by beating ⟨~ metal into sheets⟩ 4 : to sound (as an alarm) on a drum 5 : OVERCOME; also : SURPASS 6 : to act or arrive before ⟨~ his brother home⟩ 7 : THROB — **beat·er** n

²**beat** n 1 : a single stroke or blow esp. of a series; also : PULSATION 2 : a rhythmic stress in poetry or music or the rhythmic effect of these 3 : a regularly traversed course

³**beat** adj 1 : EXHAUSTED 2 : of or relating to beatniks

⁴**beat** n : BEATNIK

be·atif·ic \₁bē-ə-'ti-fik\ adj : giving or indicative of great joy or bliss

be·at·i·fy \bē-'a-tə-₁fī\ vb **-fied; -fy·ing** 1 : to make supremely happy 2 : to declare to have attained the blessedness of heaven and authorize the title "Blessed" for — **be·at·i·fi·ca·tion** \-₁a-tə-fə-'kā-shən\ n

be·at·i·tude \bē-'a-tə-₁tüd, -₁tyüd\ n 1 : a state of utmost bliss 2 : any of the declarations made in the Sermon on the Mount (Mt 5:3–12) beginning "Blessed are"

beat·nik \'bēt-nik\ n : a usu. young and artistic person who rejects the mores of established society

beau \'bō\ n, pl **beaux** \'bōz\ or **beaus** [F, fr. beau beautiful, fr. L bellus pretty] 1 : a man of fashion : DANDY 2 : SUITOR, LOVER

beau geste \bō-'zhest\ n, pl **beaux gestes** or **beau gestes** \bō-'zhest\ [F] : a graceful or magnanimous gesture

beau ide·al \₁bō-ī-'dē(-ə)l\ n, pl **beau ideals** [F] : the perfect type or model

Beau·jo·lais \₁bō-zhō-'lā\ n : a light fruity red wine

beau monde \bō-'mänd, -'mō⁼d\ n, pl **beau mondes** \-'mänz, -'mändz\ or **beaux mondes** \bō-'mō⁼d\ [F] : the world of high society and fashion

beau·te·ous \'byü-tē-əs\ adj : BEAUTIFUL — **beau·te·ous·ly** adv

beau·ti·cian \byü-'ti-shən\ n : COSMETOLOGIST

beau·ti·ful \'byü-ti-fəl\ adj : characterized by beauty : LOVELY ✦ **Synonyms** PRETTY, FAIR, COMELY — **beau·ti·ful·ly** \-f(ə-)lē\ adv

beautiful people n pl, often cap B&P : wealthy or famous people whose lifestyle is usu. expensive and well-publicized

beau·ti·fy \'byü-tə-₁fī\ vb **-fied; -fy·ing** : to make more beautiful — **beau·ti·fi·ca·tion** \₁byü-tə-fə-'kā-shən\ n — **beau·ti·fi·er** n

beau·ty \'byü-tē\ n, pl **beauties** : qualities that give pleasure to the senses or exalt the mind : LOVELINESS; also : something having such qualities

beauty shop n : an establishment where hairdressing, facials, and manicures are done

beaux arts \bō-'zär\ n pl [F] : FINE ARTS

bea·ver \'bē-vər\ n, pl **beavers** : a large fur-bearing herbivorous rodent that builds dams and underwater houses of mud and sticks; also : its fur

be·calm \bi-'käm, -'kälm\ vb : to keep (as a ship) motionless by lack of wind

be·cause \bi-'kȯz, -'kəz\ conj : for the reason that ⟨ran away ~ they were afraid⟩

because of prep : by reason of

beck \'bek\ n : a beckoning gesture; also : SUMMONS

beck·on \'be-kən\ vb : to summon or signal esp. by a nod or gesture; also : ATTRACT

be·cloud \bi-'klaůd\ vb : OBSCURE

be·come \bi-'kəm\ vb **-came** \-'kām\; **-come; -com·ing** 1 : to come to be ⟨~ tired⟩ 2 : to suit or be suitable to ⟨her dress ~s her⟩

be·com·ing *adj* : SUITABLE, FIT; *also* : ATTRACTIVE — **be·com·ing·ly** *adv*

¹**bed** \'bed\ *n* **1** : an article of furniture to sleep on **2** : a plot of ground prepared for plants **3** : FOUNDATION, BOTTOM **4** : LAYER, STRATUM

²**bed** *vb* **bed·ded; bed·ding 1** : to put or go to bed **2** : to fix in a foundation : EMBED **3** : to plant in beds **4** : to lay or lie flat or in layers

bed–and–breakfast *n* : an establishment offering lodging and breakfast

be·daub \bi-'dob\ *vb* : SMEAR

be·daz·zle \bi-'da-zəl\ *vb* : to confuse by or as if by a strong light; *also* : FASCINATE — **be·daz·zle·ment** *n*

bed·bug \'bed-ˌbəg\ *n* : a wingless bloodsucking bug infesting houses and esp. beds

bed·clothes \'bed-ˌklō‍thz\ *n pl* : materials for making up a bed

bed·ding \'be-diŋ\ *n* **1** : BEDCLOTHES **2** : FOUNDATION

be·deck \bi-'dek\ *vb* : ADORN

be·dev·il \bi-'de-vəl\ *vb* **1** : HARASS, TORMENT **2** : CONFUSE, MUDDLE

be·dew \bi-'dü, -'dyü\ *vb* : to wet with or as if with dew

bed·fast \'bed-ˌfast\ *adj* : BEDRIDDEN

bed·fel·low \-ˌfe-lō\ *n* **1** : one sharing the bed of another **2** : a close associate : ALLY

be·di·zen \bi-'dī-z³n, -'di-\ *vb* : to dress or adorn with showy or vulgar finery

bed·lam \'bed-ləm\ *n* [*Bedlam,* popular name for the Hospital of St. Mary of Bethlehem, London, an insane asylum, fr. ME *Bedlem* Bethlehem] **1** *often cap* : an insane asylum **2** : a scene of uproar and confusion

bed·ou·in *also* **bed·u·in** \'be-də-wən\ *n, pl* **bedouin** *or* **bedouins** *also* **beduin** *or* **beduins** *often cap* [ME *Bedoyne,* fr. MF *bedoïn,* fr. Ar *badawī* desert dweller] : a nomadic Arab of the Arabian, Syrian, or No. African deserts

bed·pan \'bed-ˌpan\ *n* : a shallow vessel used by a bedridden person for urination or defecation

bed·post \-ˌpōst\ *n* : the post of a bed

be·drag·gled \bi-'dra-gəld\ *adj* : soiled and disordered as if by being drenched

bed·rid·den \'bed-ˌri-d³n\ *adj* : kept in bed by illness or weakness

¹**bed·rock** \-'räk\ *n* : the solid rock underlying surface materials (as soil)

²**bedrock** *adj* : solidly fundamental, basic, or reliable ⟨traditional ~ values⟩

bed·roll \'bed-ˌrōl\ *n* : bedding rolled up for carrying

bed·room \-ˌrüm, -ˌrum\ *n* : a room containing a bed and used esp. for sleeping

bed·side \-ˌsīd\ *n* : the place beside a bed esp. of a sick or dying person

bed·sore \-ˌsor\ *n* : an ulceration of tissue deprived of adequate blood supply by prolonged pressure

bed·spread \-ˌspred\ *n* : a usu. ornamental cloth cover for a bed

bed·stead \-ˌsted\ *n* : the framework of a bed

bed·time \-ˌtīm\ *n* : time for going to bed

bed–wet·ting \-ˌwe-tiŋ\ *n* : involuntary discharge of urine esp. in bed during sleep — **bed–wet·ter** *n*

¹**bee** \'bē\ *n* : any of numerous 4-winged insects (as honeybees or bumblebees) that feed on nectar and pollen and that sometimes produce honey or have a painful sting

²**bee** *n* : a gathering of people for a specific purpose ⟨a quilting ~⟩

beech \'bēch\ *n, pl* **beech·es** *or* **beech** : any of a genus of hardwood trees with smooth gray bark and small sweet triangular nuts; *also* : its wood — **beech·en** \'bē-chən\ *adj*

beech·nut \'bēch-ˌnət\ *n* : the nut of a beech

¹**beef** \'bēf\ *n, pl* **beefs** \'bēfs\ *or* **beeves** \'bēvz\ **1** : the flesh of a steer, cow, or bull; *also* : the dressed carcass of a beef animal **2** : a steer, cow, or bull esp. when fattened for food **3** : MUSCLE, BRAWN **4** *pl* **beefs** : COMPLAINT

²**beef** *vb* **1** : STRENGTHEN — usu. used with *up* ⟨~ed up security⟩ **2** : COMPLAIN

beef·eat·er \'bē-ˌfē-tər\ *n* : a yeoman of the guard of an English monarch

beef·steak \-ˌstāk\ *n* : a slice of beef suitable for broiling or frying

beefy \'bē-fē\ *adj* **beef·i·er; -est** : THICKSET, BRAWNY

bee·hive \'bē-ˌhīv\ *n* : HIVE 1, HIVE 3

bee·keep·er \-ˌkē-pər\ *n* : a person who raises bees — **bee·keep·ing** *n*

bee·line \-ˌlīn\ *n* : a straight direct course

been *past part of* BE

beep·er \'bē-pər\ *n* : PAGER; *esp* : one that beeps

beer \'bir\ *n* : an alcoholic beverage brewed from malt and hops — **beery** *adj*

beer belly *n* : POTBELLY

bees·wax \'bēz-ˌwaks\ *n* : WAX 1

beet \'bēt\ *n* : a garden plant with edible leaves and a thick sweet root used as a vegetable, as a source of sugar, or as forage; *also* : its root

¹**bee·tle** \'bē-t³l\ *n* : any of an order of insects having four wings of which the stiff outer pair covers the membranous inner pair when not in flight

²**beetle** *vb* **bee·tled; bee·tling** : to jut out : PROJECT

be·fall \bi-'fol\ *vb* **-fell** \-'fel\; **-fall·en** \-'fô-lən\ : to happen to : OCCUR

be·fit \bi-'fit\ *vb* : to be suitable to

be·fog \bi-'fog, -'fäg\ *vb* : OBSCURE; *also* : CONFUSE

¹**be·fore** \bi-'for\ *adv or adj* **1** : in front **2** : EARLIER

²**before** *prep* **1** : in front of ⟨stood ~ him⟩ **2** : earlier than ⟨got there ~ me⟩ **3** : in a more important category than ⟨put quality ~ quantity⟩

³**before** *conj* **1** : earlier than the time that ⟨he got here ~ I did⟩ **2** : more willingly than ⟨she'd starve ~ she'd steal⟩

be·fore·hand \bi-'for-ˌhand\ *adv or adj* : in advance

be·foul \bi-'fau̇(-ə)l\ *vb* : SOIL

be·friend \bi-'frend\ *vb* : to act as friend to

be·fud·dle \bi-'fə-d³l\ *vb* : MUDDLE, CONFUSE

beg \'beg\ *vb* **begged; beg·ging 1** : to ask as a charity; *also* : ENTREAT **2** : EVADE; *also* : assume as established, settled, or proved ⟨~ the question⟩

be·get \bi-'get\ *vb* **-got** \-'gät\; **-got·ten** \-'gä-t³n\ *or* **-got; -get·ting** : to become the father of : SIRE

¹beg·gar \'be-gər\ *n* : one that begs; *esp* : a person who begs as a way of life

²beggar *vb* : IMPOVERISH

beg·gar·ly \'be-gər-lē\ *adj* **1** : contemptibly mean or inadequate **2** : marked by unrelieved poverty ⟨a ~ life⟩

beg·gary \'be-gə-rē\ *n* : extreme poverty

be·gin \bi-'gin\ *vb* **be·gan** \-'gan\; **be·gun** \-'gən\; **be·gin·ning 1** : to do the first part of an action : COMMENCE **2** : to come into being : ARISE; *also* : FOUND **3** : ORIGINATE, INVENT — **be·gin·ner** *n*

beg off *vb* : to ask to be excused from something

be·gone \bi-'gòn\ *vb* : to go away : DEPART — used esp. in the imperative

be·go·nia \bi-'gōn-yə\ *n* : any of a genus of tropical herbs widely grown for their showy leaves and waxy flowers

be·grime \bi-'grīm\ *vb* **be·grimed; be·grim·ing** : to make dirty

be·grudge \bi-'grəj\ *vb* **1** : to give or concede reluctantly **2** : to be reluctant to grant or allow — **be·grudg·ing·ly** \-'grə-jiŋ-lē\ *adv*

be·guile \-'gī(-ə)l\ *vb* **be·guiled; be·guil·ing 1** : DECEIVE **2** : to while away **3** : to engage the interest of by guile

be·guine \bi-'gēn\ *n* [AmerF *béguine,* fr. F *béguin* flirtation] : a vigorous popular dance of the islands of Saint Lucia and Martinique

be·gum \'bā-gəm, 'bē-\ *n* : a Muslim woman of high rank

be·half \bi-'haf, -'häf\ *n* : BENEFIT, SUPPORT, DEFENSE

be·have \bi-'hāv\ *vb* **be·haved; be·hav·ing 1** : to bear, comport, or conduct oneself in a particular and esp. a proper way **2** : to act, function, or react in a particular way

be·hav·ior \bi-'hā-vyər\ *n* : way of behaving; *esp* : personal conduct — **be·hav·ior·al** \-vyə-rəl\ *adj* — **be·hav·ior·al·ly** \-rə-lē\ *adv*

be·hav·ior·ism \bi-'hā-vyə-ˌri-zəm\ *n* : a school of psychology concerned with the objective evidence of behavior without reference to conscious experience

be·hav·ior·ist \-vyə-rist\ *n* **1** : a person who supports behaviorism **2** : a person who studies behavior

be·hav·iour, be·hav·iour·ism *chiefly Brit var of* BEHAVIOR, BEHAVIORISM

be·head \bi-'hed\ *vb* : to cut off the head of

be·he·moth \bi-'hē-məth, 'bē-ə-ˌmäth\ *n* : a huge powerful animal described in Job 40:15–24; *also* : something of monstrous size or power

be·hest \bi-'hest\ *n* **1** : COMMAND **2** : an urgent prompting

¹be·hind \bi-'hīnd\ *adv or adj* **1** : BACK, BACKWARD ⟨look ~⟩ **2** : LATE, SLOW

²behind *prep* **1** : in or to a place or situation in back of or to the rear of ⟨look ~ you⟩ ⟨the staff stayed ~ the troops⟩ **2** : inferior to (as in rank) : BELOW ⟨three games ~ the first-place team⟩ **3** : in support of : SUPPORTING ⟨we're ~ you all the way⟩

be·hind·hand \bi-'hīnd-ˌhand\ *adj* : being in arrears ✦ *Synonyms* TARDY, LATE, OVERDUE, BELATED

be·hold \bi-'hōld\ *vb* **-held** \-'held\; **-hold·ing 1** : to have in sight : SEE **2** — used imperatively to direct the attention ✦ *Synonyms* VIEW, OBSERVE, NOTICE, ESPY — **be·hold·er** *n*

be·hold·en \bi-'hōl-dən\ *adj* : OBLIGATED, INDEBTED

be·hoove \bi-'hüv\ *vb* **be·hooved; be·hoov·ing** : to be necessary, proper, or advantageous for

be·hove *chiefly Brit var of* BEHOOVE

beige \'bāzh\ *n* : a pale dull yellowish brown — **beige** *adj*

be·ing \'bē-iŋ\ *n* **1** : EXISTENCE; *also* : LIFE **2** : the qualities or constitution of an existent thing **3** : a living thing; *esp* : PERSON

be·la·bor \bi-'lā-bər\ *vb* : to assail (as with words) tiresomely or at length

be·la·bour *chiefly Brit var of* BELABOR

be·lat·ed \bi-'lā-təd\ *adj* : DELAYED, LATE

be·lay \bi-'lā\ *vb* **1** : to wind (a rope) around a pin or cleat in order to hold secure **2** : QUIT, STOP — used in the imperative

belch \'belch\ *vb* **1** : to expel (gas) from the stomach through the mouth **2** : to gush forth ⟨a volcano ~*ing* lava⟩ — **belch** *n*

bel·dam *or* **bel·dame** \'bel-dəm\ *n* [ME *beldam* grandmother, fr. AF *bel* beautiful + ME *dam* lady, mother] : an old woman

be·lea·guer \bi-'lē-gər\ *vb* **1** : BESIEGE **2** : HARASS ⟨~*ed* parents⟩

bel·fry \'bel-frē\ *n, pl* **belfries** : a tower for a bell (as on a church); *also* : the part of the tower in which the bell hangs

Belg *abbr* Belgian; Belgium

Bel·gian endive \'bel-jən\ *n* : the blanched shoot of chicory

Belgian waffle *n* : a waffle having large depressions and usu. topped with fruit and whipped cream

be·lie \bi-'lī\ *vb* **-lied; -ly·ing 1** : MISREPRESENT **2** : to show (something) to be false **3** : to run counter to

be·lief \bə-'lēf\ *n* **1** : CONFIDENCE, TRUST **2** : something (as a tenet or creed) believed ✦ *Synonyms* CONVICTION, OPINION, PERSUASION, SENTIMENT

be·lieve \bə-'lēv\ *vb* **be·lieved; be·liev·ing 1** : to have religious convictions **2** : to have a firm conviction about something : accept as true **3** : to hold as an opinion : SUPPOSE — **be·liev·able** \-'lē-və-bəl\ *adj* — **be·liev·ably** \-blē\ *adv* — **be·liev·er** *n*

be·like \bi-'līk\ *adv, archaic* : PROBABLY

be·lit·tle \bi-'li-t³l\ *vb* **-lit·tled; -lit·tling** : to make seem little or less; *also* : DIS-PARAGE

¹bell \'bel\ *n* **1** : a hollow metallic device that makes a ringing sound when struck **2** : the sounding or stroke of a bell (as on shipboard to tell the time); *also* : time so indicated **3** : something with the flared form of a typical bell

²bell *vb* : to provide with a bell

bel·la·don·na \be-lə-'dä-nə\ *n* [It. lit., beautiful lady] : a medicinal extract (as atropine) from a poisonous European herb related to the potato; *also* : this herb

bell–bot·toms \'bel-'bä-təmz\ *n pl* : pants with wide flaring bottoms — **bell–bot·tom** *adj*

bell·boy \'bel-,bȯi\ *n* : BELLHOP

belle \'bel\ *n* : an attractive and popular girl or woman

belles let·tres \bel-'letrᵊ\ *n pl* [F] : literature that is an end in itself and not practical or purely informative — **bel·le·tris·tic** \,be-lə-'tris-tik\ *adj*

bell·hop \'bel-,häp\ *n* : a hotel or club employee who takes guests to rooms, carries luggage, and runs errands

bel·li·cose \'be-li-,kōs\ *adj* : WARLIKE, PUGNACIOUS ✦ *Synonyms* BELLIGERENT, QUARRELSOME, COMBATIVE, CONTENTIOUS — **bel·li·cos·i·ty** \,be-li-'kä-sə-tē\ *n*

bel·lig·er·en·cy \bə-'li-jə-rən-sē\ *n* **1** : the status of a nation engaged in war **2** : BELLIGERENCE, TRUCULENCE

bel·lig·er·ent \-rənt\ *adj* **1** : waging war **2** : aggressively self-assertive ✦ *Synonyms* BELLICOSE, PUGNACIOUS, COMBATIVE, CONTENTIOUS, WARLIKE — **bel·lig·er·ence** \-rəns\ *n* — belligerent *n* — **bel·lig·er·ent·ly** *adv*

bel·low \'be-lō\ *vb* **1** : to make the deep hollow sound characteristic of a bull **2** : to shout in a deep voice — **bellow** *n*

bel·lows \-lōz, -ləz\ *n sing or pl* : a closed device with sides that can be spread apart and then pressed together to draw in air and expel it through a tube

bell·weth·er \'bel-'we-thər, -,we-\ *n* : one that takes the lead or initiative; *also* : an indicator of trends

¹bel·ly \'be-lē\ *n, pl* **bellies** [ME *bely* bellows, belly, fr. OE *belg* bag, skin] **1** : ABDOMEN 1; *also* : POTBELLY **2** : the underpart of an animal's body

²belly *vb* **bel·lied; bel·ly·ing** : BULGE

¹bel·ly·ache \'be-lē-,āk\ *n* : pain in the abdomen : STOMACHACHE

²bellyache *vb* : COMPLAIN

belly button *n* : the human navel

belly dance *n* : a usu. solo dance emphasizing movement of the belly — **belly dance** *vb* — **belly dancer** *n*

belly laugh *n* : a deep hearty laugh

be·long \bi-'lȯŋ\ *vb* **1** : to be suitable or appropriate; *also* : to be properly situated ⟨shoes ∼ in the closet⟩ **2** : to be the property ⟨this ∼s to me⟩; *also* : to be attached (as through birth or membership) ⟨∼ to a club⟩ **3** : to form an attribute or part ⟨this wheel ∼s to the cart⟩ **4** : to be

classified ⟨whales ∼ among the mammals⟩

be·long·ings \-'lȯŋ-iŋz\ *n pl* : GOODS, EFFECTS, POSSESSIONS

be·loved \bi-'ləvd, -'lə-vəd\ *adj* : dearly loved — **beloved** *n*

¹be·low \bi-'lō\ *adv* **1** : in or to a lower place or rank **2** : on earth **3** : in hell

²below *prep* **1** : lower than ⟨∼ sea level⟩ **2** : inferior to (as in rank)

be·low·decks \bi-,lō-'deks, -'lō-,deks\ *adv* : inside the superstructure of a boat or down to a lower deck

¹belt \'belt\ *n* **1** : a strip (as of leather) worn about the waist **2** : a flexible continuous band to communicate motion or convey material **3** : a region marked by some distinctive feature; *esp* : one suited to a particular crop

²belt *vb* **1** : to encircle or secure with a belt **2** : to beat with or as if with a belt **3** : to mark with an encircling band **4** : to sing loudly

³belt *n* **1** : a jarring blow : WHACK **2** : DRINK ⟨a ∼ of whiskey⟩

belt·er \'bel-tər\ *n* : a singer with a powerful voice

belt–tightening *n* : a reduction in spending

belt·way \'belt-,wā\ *n* : a highway around a city

be·lu·ga \bə-'lü-gə\ *n* [Russ] **1** : a large white sturgeon of the Black Sea, Caspian Sea, and their tributaries that is a source of caviar; *also* : caviar from beluga roe **2** : a whale of arctic and subarctic waters that is white when mature

bel·ve·dere \'bel-və-,dir\ *n* [It. lit., beautiful view] : a structure (as a summerhouse) designed to command a view

be·mire \bi-'mī(-ə)r\ *vb* : to cover or soil with or sink in mire

be·moan \bi-'mōn\ *vb* : LAMENT, DEPLORE ✦ *Synonyms* BEWAIL, GRIEVE, MOAN, WEEP

be·muse \bi-'myüz\ *vb* : BEWILDER, CONFUSE

¹bench \'bench\ *n* **1** : a long seat for two or more persons **2** : the seat of a judge in court; *also* : the office or dignity of a judge **3** : COURT; *also* : JUDGES **4** : a table for holding work and tools ⟨a carpenter's ∼⟩

²bench \'bench\ *vb* **1** : to furnish with benches **2** : to seat on a bench **3** : to remove from or keep out of a game

¹bench·mark \'bench-,märk\ *n* **1** *usu* **bench mark** : a mark on a permanent object serving as an elevation reference in topographical surveys **2** : a point of reference for measurement; *also* : STANDARD

²benchmark *vb* : to study (as a competitor's business practices) in order to improve one's own performance

bench press *n* : an exercise in which a weight is raised by a person lying on a bench — **bench–press** *vb*

bench warrant *n* : a warrant issued by a presiding judge or by a court against a person guilty of contempt or indicted for a crime

¹bend \'bend\ *vb* **bent** \'bent\; **bend·ing** **1** : to draw (as a bow) taut **2** : to curve or cause a change of shape in ⟨~ a bar⟩ **3** : to make fast **4** : SECURE **4** : DEFLECT **5** : to turn in a certain direction ⟨bent his steps toward town⟩ **6** : APPLY ⟨bent themselves to the task⟩ **7** : SUBDUE **8** : to curve downward **9** : YIELD, SUBMIT

²bend *n* **1** : an act or process of bending **2** : something bent; *esp* : CURVE **3** *pl* : a painful and sometimes fatal disorder caused by release of gas bubbles in the tissues upon too rapid decrease in air pressure after a stay in a compressed atmosphere

³bend *n* : a knot by which a rope is fastened (as to another rope)

bend·er \'ben-dər\ *n* : SPREE ⟨hungover after a weekend ~⟩

¹be·neath \bi-'nēth\ *adv* : BELOW ⟨the mountains and the town ~⟩ ♦ *Synonyms* UNDER, UNDERNEATH

²beneath *prep* **1** : BELOW, UNDER ⟨stood ~ a tree⟩ **2** : unworthy of ⟨considered such behavior ~ her⟩ **3** : concealed by ⟨a warm heart ~ a gruff manner⟩

bene·dic·tion \,be-nə-'dik-shən\ *n* : the invocation of a blessing esp. at the close of a public worship service

ben·e·fac·tion \'fak-shən\ *n* : a charitable donation ♦ *Synonyms* CONTRIBUTION, ALMS, BENEFICENCE, OFFERING

ben·e·fac·tor \'ben-ə-,fak-tər\ *n* : one that confers a benefit and esp. a benefaction

ben·e·fac·tress \-,fak-trəs\ *n* : a woman who is a benefactor

ben·e·fice \'be-nə-fəs\ *n* : an ecclesiastical office to which the revenue from an endowment is attached

be·nef·i·cence \bə-'ne-fə-səns\ *n* **1** : beneficent quality **2** : BENEFACTION

be·nef·i·cent \-sənt\ *adj* : doing or producing good (as by acts of kindness or charity); *also* : BENEFICIAL

ben·e·fi·cial \,be-nə-'fi-shəl\ *adj* : being of benefit or help : HELPFUL ♦ *Synonyms* ADVANTAGEOUS, PROFITABLE, FAVORABLE, PROPITIOUS — **ben·e·fi·cial·ly** *adv*

ben·e·fi·cia·ry \,be-nə-'fi-shē-,er-ē, -'fi-shə-rē\ *n, pl* **-ries** : one that receives a benefit (as the income of a trust or the proceeds of an insurance)

¹ben·e·fit \'be-nə-,fit\ *n* **1** : ADVANTAGE ⟨the ~s of exercise⟩ **2** : useful aid : HELP; *also* : material aid or service provided or due (as in sickness or unemployment) as a right in addition to regular pay **3** : a performance or event to raise funds

²benefit *vb* **-fit·ed** \-,fi-təd\ *also* **-fit·ted**; **-fit·ing** *also* **-fit·ting** **1** : to be useful or profitable to **2** : to receive benefit

be·nev·o·lence \bə-'ne-və-ləns\ *n* **1** : charitable nature **2** : an act of kindness : CHARITY — **be·nev·o·lent** \-lənt\ *adj* — **be·nev·o·lent·ly** *adv*

be·night·ed \bi-'nī-təd\ *adj* **1** : overtaken by darkness or night **2** : living in ignorance

be·nign \bi-'nīn\ *adj* [ME *benigne*, fr. AF, fr. L *benignus*] **1** : of a gentle disposition; *also* : showing kindness **2** : of a mild kind; *esp* : not malignant ⟨~ tumors⟩ ♦ *Synonyms* BENIGNANT, KIND, KINDLY, GOOD-HEARTED — **be·nig·ni·ty** \-'nig-nə-tē\ *n* — **be·nign·ly** *adv*

be·nig·nant \-'nig-nənt\ *adj* : BENIGN 1 ♦ *Synonyms* KIND, KINDLY, GOOD-HEARTED

ben·i·son \'be-nə-sən, -zən\ *n* : BLESSING, BENEDICTION

¹bent \'bent\ *n* **1** : strong inclination or interest; *also* : TALENT **2** : power of endurance ♦ *Synonyms* TALENT, APTITUDE, GIFT, FLAIR, KNACK, GENIUS

²bent *adj* **1** : changed by bending : CROOKED ⟨~ branches⟩ **2** : strongly inclined : DETERMINED ⟨~ on going⟩

bent grass *n* : any of a genus of stiff velvety grasses used esp. for lawns and pastures

ben·thic \'ben-thik\ *adj* : of, relating to, or occurring at the bottom of a body of water

ben·ton·ite \'ben-tə-,nīt\ *n* : an absorptive clay used esp. as a filler (as in paper)

bent·wood \'bent-,wud\ *adj* : made of wood bent into shape ⟨a ~ rocker⟩

be·numb \bi-'nəm\ *vb* **1** : DULL, DEADEN **2** : to make numb esp. by cold

ben·zene \'ben-,zēn\ *n* : a colorless volatile flammable liquid hydrocarbon used in organic synthesis and as a solvent — **ben·ze·noid** \-zə-,nȯid\ *adj or n*

ben·zine \'ben-,zēn\ *n* : any of various flammable petroleum distillates used as solvents or as motor fuels

ben·zo·ate \'ben-zə-,wāt\ *n* : a salt or ester of benzoic acid

ben·zo·ic acid \ben-'zō-ik-\ *n* : a white crystalline acid used as a preservative and antiseptic and in synthesizing chemicals

ben·zo·in \'ben-zə-wən, -,zȯin\ *n* : a balsamic resin from trees of southern Asia used esp. in medicine and perfumes

be·queath \bi-'kwēth, -'kwēth\ *vb* [ME *bequethen*, fr. OE *becwethan*, fr. *be-* + *cwethan* to say] **1** : to leave by will **2** : to hand down

be·quest \bi-'kwest\ *n* **1** : the action of bequeathing **2** : something bequeathed : LEGACY

be·rate \-'rāt\ *vb* : to scold harshly

Ber·ber \'bər-bər\ *n* : a member of any of various peoples living in northern Africa west of Tripoli

ber·ceuse \ber-'sœz, -'süz\ *n, pl* **berceuses** *same or* -'sü-zəz\ [F, fr. *bercer* to rock] **1** : LULLABY **2** : a musical composition that resembles a lullaby

¹be·reaved \bi-'rēvd\ *adj* : suffering the death of a loved one — **be·reave·ment** *n*

²bereaved *n, pl* **bereaved** : one who is bereaved

be·reft \-'reft\ *adj* **1** : deprived of or lacking something — usu. used with *of* **2** : BEREAVED ⟨a ~ mother⟩

be·ret \bə-'rā\ *n* : a round soft cap with no visor

berg \'bərg\ *n* : ICEBERG

beri·beri \ˌber-ē-ˈber-ē\ *n* : a deficiency disease marked by weakness, wasting, and nerve damage and caused by lack of thiamine

berke·li·um \ˈbər-klē-əm\ *n* : an artificially produced radioactive chemical element

berm \ˈbərm\ *n* : a narrow shelf or path at the top or bottom of a slope; *also* : a mound or bank of earth

Bermuda grass *n* : a creeping grass often used for lawns and pastures

Ber·mu·das \bər-ˈmyü-dəz\ *n pl* : BERMUDA SHORTS

Bermuda shorts *n pl* : knee-length walking shorts

ber·ry \ˈber-ē\ *n, pl* **berries** **1** : a small pulpy fruit (as a strawberry) **2** : a simple fruit (as a grape, tomato, or cucumber) with the wall of the ripened ovary thick and pulpy **3** : the dry seed of some plants (as coffee)

ber·serk \bər-ˈsərk, -ˈzərk\ *adj* [ON *berserkr* warrior frenzied in battle, prob. fr. *ber-* bear + *serkr* shirt] : FRENZIED, CRAZED — **berserk** *adv*

¹berth \ˈbərth\ *n* **1** : adequate distance esp. for a ship to maneuver **2** : the place where a ship is anchored or a vehicle rests **3** : ACCOMMODATIONS **4** : JOB, POSITION ✦ **Synonyms** POST, SITUATION, OFFICE, APPOINTMENT

²berth *vb* **1** : to bring or come into a berth **2** : to allot a berth to

ber·yl \ˈber-əl\ *n* : a hard silicate mineral occurring as colorless hexagonal crystals when pure

be·ryl·li·um \bə-ˈri-lē-əm\ *n* : a light strong metallic chemical element used as a hardener in alloys

be·seech \bi-ˈsēch\ *vb* **-sought** \-ˈsȯt\ *or* **-seeched; -seech·ing** : to beg urgently : ENTREAT ✦ **Synonyms** IMPLORE, PLEAD, SUPPLICATE, IMPORTUNE

be·seem \bi-ˈsēm\ *vb, archaic* : BEFIT

be·set \-ˈset\ *vb* **-set; -set·ting** **1** : TROUBLE, HARASS **2** : ASSAIL; *also* : SURROUND

be·set·ting *adj* : persistently present

¹be·side \bi-ˈsīd\ *prep* **1** : by the side of ⟨sit ~ me⟩ **2** : BESIDES **3** : not relevant to ⟨~ the point⟩

²beside *adv, archaic* : BESIDES

¹be·sides \bi-ˈsīdz\ *prep* **1** : other than ⟨no one ~ us⟩ **2** : together with

²besides *adv* **1** : as well : ALSO **2** : MOREOVER

be·siege \bi-ˈsēj\ *vb* : to lay siege to; *also* : to press with requests — **be·sieg·er** *n*

be·smear \-ˈsmir\ *vb* : SMEAR

be·smirch \-ˈsmərch\ *vb* : SMIRCH, SOIL

be·som \ˈbē-zəm\ *n* : BROOM

be·sot \bi-ˈsät\ *vb* **be·sot·ted; be·sot·ting** **1** : INFATUATE **2** : to make dull esp. by drinking

be·spat·ter \-ˈspa-tər\ *vb* : SPATTER

be·speak \bi-ˈspēk\ *vb* **-spoke** \-ˈspōk\; **-spo·ken** \-ˈspō-kən\; **-speak·ing** **1** : PREARRANGE **2** : ADDRESS **3** : REQUEST **4** : INDICATE, SIGNIFY **5** : FORETELL

be·sprin·kle \-ˈspriŋ-kəl\ *vb* : SPRINKLE

¹best \ˈbest\ *adj, superlative of* GOOD **1** : excelling all others **2** : most productive (as of good or satisfaction) **3** : LARGEST, MOST

²best *adv, superlative of* WELL **1** : in the best way **2** : MOST

³best *n* : something that is best

⁴best *vb* : to get the better of : OUTDO

bes·tial \ˈbes-chəl\ *adj* **1** : of or relating to beasts **2** : resembling a beast esp. in brutality or lack of intelligence

bes·ti·al·i·ty \ˌbes-chē-ˈa-lə-tē, ˌbēs-\ *n, pl* **-ties** **1** : the condition or status of a lower animal **2** : display or gratification of bestial traits or impulses **3** : sexual relations between a human being and a lower animal

bes·ti·ary \ˈbes-chē-ˌer-ē\ *n, pl* **-ar·ies** : a medieval allegorical or moralizing work on the appearance and habits of animals

be·stir \bi-ˈstər\ *vb* : to rouse to action

best man *n* : the principal groomsman at a wedding

be·stow \bi-ˈstō\ *vb* **1** : PUT, PLACE, STOW **2** : to present as a gift — **be·stow·al** *n* — **be·stow·er** *n*

be·stride \bi-ˈstrīd\ *vb* **-strode** \-ˈstrōd\; **-strid·den** \-ˈstri-dᵊn\; **-strid·ing** : to ride, sit, or stand astride

¹bet \ˈbet\ *n* **1** : something that is wagered, risked, or pledged usu. between two parties on the outcome of a contest; *also* : the making of such a bet **2** : OPTION ⟨the back road is your best ~⟩

²bet *vb* **bet** *also* **bet·ted; bet·ting** **1** : to stake on the outcome of an issue or a contest ⟨~ $2 on the race⟩ **2** : to make a bet with **3** : to lay a bet

³bet *abbr* between

be·ta \ˈbā-tə\ *n* **1** : the 2d letter of the Greek alphabet — B or β **2** : a nearly complete form of a new product (as software)

beta–block·er \-ˌblä-kər\ *n* : any of a group of drugs that decrease the rate and force of heart contractions and lower high blood pressure

be·ta–car·o·tene \-ˈker-ə-ˌtēn\ *n* : an isomer of carotene found in dark green and dark yellow vegetables and fruits

be·take \bi-ˈtāk\ *vb* **-took** \-ˈtúk\; **-tak·en** \-ˈtā-kən\; **-tak·ing** : to cause (oneself) to go

beta particle *n* : a high-speed electron; *esp* : one emitted by a radioactive nucleus

beta ray *n* **1** : BETA PARTICLE **2** : a stream of beta particles

beta test *n* : a field test of the beta version of a product esp. by outside testers and prior to commercial release — **beta test** *vb*

be·tel \ˈbē-tᵊl\ *n* : a climbing pepper of southern Asia whose leaves are chewed together with lime and betel nut as a stimulant

betel nut *n* : the astringent seed of an Asian palm that is chewed with betel leaves

bête noire \ˌbet-ˈnwär, ˌbāt-\ *n, pl* **bêtes noires** *same or* -ˈnwärz\ [F, lit., black beast] : a person or thing strongly disliked or avoided

beth·el \'be-thəl\ n [Heb *bēth'ēl* house of God] : a place of worship esp. for seamen

be·think \bi-'thiŋk\ vb **-thought** \-'thȯt\; **-think·ing** : REMEMBER; *also* : PONDER

be·tide \bi-'tīd\ vb : to happen to

be·times \bi-'tīmz\ adv : in good time : EARLY ✦ *Synonyms* SOON, SEASONABLY, TIMELY

be·to·ken \bi-'tō-kən\ vb **1** : PRESAGE **2** : to give evidence of ✦ *Synonyms* INDICATE, ATTEST, BESPEAK, TESTIFY

be·tray \bi-'trā\ vb **1** : to lead astray; *esp* : SEDUCE **2** : to deliver to an enemy **3** : ABANDON **4** : to prove unfaithful to **5** : to reveal unintentionally; *also* : SHOW, INDICATE ✦ *Synonyms* MISLEAD, DELUDE, DECEIVE, BEGUILE — **be·tray·al** n — **be·tray·er** n

be·troth \bi-'trōth, -'tròth\ vb : to promise to marry — **be·troth·al** n

be·trothed n : the person to whom one is betrothed

¹bet·ter \'be-tər\ adj, *comparative of* GOOD **1** : greater than half **2** : improved in health **3** : more attractive, favorable, or commendable **4** : more advantageous or effective ⟨a ~ solution⟩ **5** : improved in accuracy or performance

²better vb **1** : to make or become better **2** : SURPASS, EXCEL

³better adv, *comparative of* WELL **1** : in a superior manner **2** : to a higher or greater degree; *also* : MORE

⁴better n **1** : something better; *also* : a superior esp. in merit or rank **2** : ADVANTAGE

⁵better *verbal auxiliary* : had better ⟨you ~ hurry⟩

better half n : SPOUSE

bet·ter·ment \'be-tər-mənt\ n : IMPROVEMENT

bet·tor or **bet·ter** \'be-tər\ n : one that bets

¹be·tween \bi-'twēn\ prep **1** : by the common action of ⟨earned $10,000 ~ the two of them⟩ **2** : in the interval separating ⟨an alley ~ two buildings⟩; *also* : in intermediate relation to **3** : in point of comparison of ⟨choose ~ two cars⟩

²between adv : in an intervening space or interval

be·twixt \bi-'twikst\ adv or prep : BETWEEN

¹bev·el \'be-vəl\ n **1** : a device for adjusting the slant of the surfaces of a piece of work **2** : the angle or slant that one surface or line makes with another when not at right angles

²bevel vb **-eled** or **-elled**; **-el·ing** or **-el·ling 1** : to cut or shape to a bevel **2** : INCLINE, SLANT

bev·er·age \'bev-rij\ n : a drinkable liquid

bevy \'be-vē\ n, pl **bev·ies 1** : a large group or collection **2** : a group of animals and esp. quail

be·wail \bi-'wāl\ vb : LAMENT ✦ *Synonyms* DEPLORE, BEMOAN, GRIEVE, MOAN, WEEP

be·ware \-'wer\ vb : to be on one's guard : be wary of

be·wil·der \bi-'wil-dər\ vb : PERPLEX, CONFUSE ✦ *Synonyms* MYSTIFY, DISTRACT, PUZZLE — **be·wil·der·ment** n

be·witch \-'wich\ vb **1** : to affect by witchcraft **2** : CHARM, FASCINATE ✦ *Synonyms* ENCHANT, ATTRACT, CAPTIVATE — **be·witch·ment** n

bey \'bā\ n **1** : a former Turkish provincial governor **2** : the former native ruler of Tunis or Tunisia

¹be·yond \bē-'änd\ adv **1** : FARTHER ⟨extends to the river and ~⟩ **2** : BESIDES

²beyond prep **1** : on or to the farther side of **2** : out of the reach or sphere of **3** : BESIDES

be·zel \'bē-zəl, 'be-\ n **1** : a rim that holds a transparent covering (as on a watch) **2** : the faceted part of a cut gem that rises above the setting

bf abbr boldface

BG or **B Gen** abbr brigadier general

Bh symbol bohrium

bhang \'baŋ\ n [Hindi *bhāṅg*] : HEMP; *also* : a mildly intoxicating preparation made from hemp leaves

Bi symbol bismuth

BIA abbr Bureau of Indian Affairs

bi·an·nu·al \(ˌ)bī-'an-yə-wəl\ adj : occurring twice a year — **bi·an·nu·al·ly** adv

¹bi·as \'bī-əs\ n **1** : a line diagonal to the grain of a fabric **2** : PREJUDICE, BENT

²bias adv : on the bias : DIAGONALLY ⟨cut cloth ~⟩

³bias vb **bi·ased** or **bi·assed**; **bi·as·ing** or **bi·as·sing** : PREJUDICE

bi·ath·lon \bī-'ath-lən, -ˌlän\ n : a composite athletic contest consisting of cross-country skiing and target shooting with a rifle

¹bib \'bib\ n : a cloth or plastic shield tied under the chin to protect the clothes while eating

²bib abbr Bible; biblical

bi·be·lot \'bē-bə-ˌlō\ n, pl **bibelots** \same or -ˌlōz\ : a small household ornament or decorative object

bi·ble \'bī-bəl\ n [ME, fr. OF, fr. ML *biblia*, fr. Gk, pl. of *biblion* book, dim. of *byblos* papyrus, book, fr. *Byblos*, ancient Phoenician city from which papyrus was exported] **1** *cap* : the sacred scriptures of Christians comprising the Old and New Testaments **2** *cap* : the sacred scriptures of Judaism; *also* : those of some other religion **3** : a publication that is considered authoritative for its subject — **bib·li·cal** \'bi-bli-kəl\ adj

☞ the BIBLE table is on page 68

bib·li·og·ra·phy \ˌbi-blē-'ä-grə-fē\ n, pl **-phies 1** : the history or description of writings or publications **2** : a list of writings (as on a subject or of an author) — **bib·li·og·ra·pher** \-fər\ n — **bib·lio·graph·ic** \-ə-'gra-fik\ *also* **bib·li·o·graph·i·cal** \-fi-kəl\ adj

bib·lio·phile \'bi-blē-ə-ˌfī(-ə)l\ n : a lover of books

bib·u·lous \'bi-byə-ləs\ adj **1** : highly absorbent **2** : fond of alcoholic beverages

bi·cam·er·al \'bī-'ka-mə-rəl\ adj : having or consisting of two legislative branches

bicarb \(ˌ)bī-'kärb, 'bī-ˌ\ n : SODIUM BICARBONATE

BOOKS OF THE BIBLE

HEBREW BIBLE

LAW	PROPHETS		WRITINGS
Genesis	Joshua	Obadiah	Psalms
Exodus	Judges	Jonah	Proverbs
Leviticus	1 & 2 Samuel	Micah	Job
Numbers	1 & 2 Kings	Nahum	Song of Songs
Deuteronomy	Isaiah	Habakkuk	Ruth
	Jeremiah	Zephaniah	Lamentations
	Ezekiel	Haggai	Ecclesiastes
	Hosea	Zechariah	Esther
	Joel	Malachi	Daniel
	Amos		Ezra
			Nehemiah
			1 & 2 Chronicles

CHRISTIAN CANON——OLD TESTAMENT

ROMAN CATHOLIC	PROTESTANT	ROMAN CATHOLIC	PROTESTANT
Genesis	Genesis	Wisdom	
Exodus	Exodus	Sirach	
Leviticus	Leviticus	Isaiah	Isaiah
Numbers	Numbers	Jeremiah	Jeremiah
Deuteronomy	Deuteronomy	Lamentations	Lamentations
Joshua	Joshua	Baruch	
Judges	Judges	Ezekiel	Ezekiel
Ruth	Ruth	Daniel	Daniel
1 & 2 Samuel	1 & 2 Samuel	Hosea	Hosea
1 & 2 Kings	1 & 2 Kings	Joel	Joel
1 & 2 Chronicles	1 & 2 Chronicles	Amos	Amos
Ezra	Ezra	Obadiah	Obadiah
Nehemiah	Nehemiah	Jonah	Jonah
Tobit		Micah	Micah
Judith		Nahum	Nahum
Esther	Esther	Habakkuk	Habakkuk
Job	Job	Zephaniah	Zephaniah
Psalms	Psalms	Haggai	Haggai
Proverbs	Proverbs	Zechariah	Zechariah
Ecclesiastes	Ecclesiastes	Malachi	Malachi
Song of Songs	Song of Solomon	1 & 2 Maccabees	

PROTESTANT APOCRYPHA

1 & 2 Esdras	Baruch
Tobit	Prayer of Azariah and the Song
Judith	of the Three Holy Children
Additions to Esther	Susanna
Wisdom of Solomon	Bel and the Dragon
Ecclesiasticus or the Wisdom of Jesus	The Prayer of Manasses
Son of Sirach	1 & 2 Maccabees

CHRISTIAN CANON——NEW TESTAMENT

Matthew	Ephesians	James
Mark	Philippians	1 & 2 Peter
Luke	Colossians	1, 2, 3 John
John	1 & 2 Thessalonians	Jude
Acts of the Apostles	1 & 2 Timothy	Revelation *or*
Romans	Titus	Apocalypse
1 & 2 Corinthians	Philemon	
Galatians	Hebrews	

bi·car·bon·ate \(ˌ)bī-'kär-bə-ˌnāt, -nət\ *n* : an acid carbonate

bicarbonate of soda : SODIUM BICARBONATE

bi·cen·te·na·ry \ˌbī-sen-'te-nə-rē, bī-'sen-t⁰n-ˌer-ē\ *n* : BICENTENNIAL — **bicentenary** *adj*

bi·cen·ten·ni·al \ˌbī-sen-'te-nē-əl\ *n* : a 200th anniversary or its celebration — **bicentennial** *adj*

bi·ceps \'bī-ˌseps\ *n, pl* biceps *also* biceps·es [NL, fr. L, two-headed, fr. *bi-* two + *caput* head] : a muscle (as in the front of the upper arm) having two points of origin

¹**bick·er** \'bi-kər\ *n* : ALTERCATION

²**bicker** *vb* : to engage in a petty quarrel

bi·coast·al \bī-'kōs-t⁰l\ *adj* : living or working on both the east and west coasts of the U.S.

bi·con·cave \ˌbī-(ˌ)kän-'kāv, (ˌ)bī-'kän-ˌkāv\ *adj* : concave on both sides

bi·con·vex \ˌbī-(ˌ)kän-'veks, (ˌ)bī-'kän-ˌveks\ *adj* : convex on both sides

bi·cus·pid \bī-'kəs-pəd\ *n* : PREMOLAR

¹**bi·cy·cle** \'bī-ˌsi-kəl\ *n* : a light 2-wheeled vehicle with a saddle, pedals, and handlebars for steering

²**bicycle** *vb* **-cy·cled; -cy·cling** \-ˌsi-k(ə-)liŋ, -ˌsī-\ : to ride a bicycle — **bi·cy·cler** \-k(ə-)lər\ *n* — **bi·cy·clist** \-k(ə-)list\ *n*

¹**bid** \'bid\ *vb* **bade** \'bad, 'bād\ *or* **bid; bidden** \'bi-d⁰n\ *or* **bid** *also* **bade; bidding** 1 : COMMAND, ORDER 2 : INVITE 3 : to give expression to ⟨*bade* a tearful farewell⟩ 4 : to make a bid : OFFER — **bid·der** *n*

²**bid** *n* 1 : the act of one who bids; *also* : an offer for something 2 : INVITATION 3 : an announcement in a card game of what a player proposes to accomplish 4 : an attempt to win or gain ⟨a ~ for mayor⟩

bid·da·ble \'bi-də-bəl\ *adj* 1 : OBEDIENT, DOCILE 2 : capable of being bid

bid·dy \'bi-dē\ *n, pl* biddies : HEN; *also* : a young chicken

bide \'bīd\ *vb* **bode** \'bōd\ *or* **bid·ed; bided; bid·ing** 1 : to wait for 2 : WAIT, TARRY 3 : DWELL

bi·det \bi-'dā\ *n* : a bathroom fixture used esp. for bathing the external genitals and the anal region

bi·di·rec·tion·al \ˌbī-də-'rek-sh(ə-)nəl\ *adj* : involving, moving, or taking place in two usu. opposite directions — **bi·di·rec·tion·al·ly** *adv*

bi·en·ni·al \bī-'e-nē-əl\ *adj* 1 : taking place once in two years 2 : lasting two years 3 : producing leaves the first year and fruiting and dying the second year — **biennial** *n* — **bi·en·ni·al·ly** *adv*

bi·en·ni·um \bī-'e-nē-əm\ *n, pl* **-niums** *or* **-nia** \-ə\ [L, fr. *bi-* two + *annus* year] : a period of two years

bier \'bir\ *n* : a stand bearing a coffin or corpse

bi·fo·cal \'bī-ˌfō-kəl\ *adj* : having two focal lengths

bifocals \-kəlz\ *n pl* : eyeglasses with lenses that have one part that corrects for near vision and one for distant vision

bi·fold \'bī-ˌfōld\ *adj* : designed to fold twice ⟨~ doors⟩

bi·fur·cate \'bī-fər-ˌkāt, bī-'fər-\ *vb* **-cat·ed; -cat·ing** : to divide into two branches or parts — **bi·fur·ca·tion** \ˌbī-fər-'kā-shən\ *n*

big \'big\ *adj* **big·ger; big·gest** 1 : large in size, amount, or scope 2 : PREGNANT; *also* : SWELLING 3 : IMPORTANT, IMPOSING 4 : NOBLE, GENEROUS 5 : POPULAR — **big·ness** *n* — **big on** : strongly favoring or liking

big·a·my \'bi-gə-mē\ *n* : the act of marrying one person while still legally married to another — **big·a·mist** \-mist\ *n* — **big·a·mous** \-məs\ *adj*

big bang theory *n* : a theory in astronomy: the universe originated in an explosion (**big bang**) from a single point of nearly infinite energy density

big brother *n* 1 : an older brother 2 : a man who befriends a delinquent or friendless boy 3 *cap both Bs* : the leader of an authoritarian state or movement

big cheese *n* : ³BOSS

big crunch *n* : a hypothetical event in which all matter in the universe collapses to a single point of nearly infinite energy density

Big Dipper *n* : the seven principal stars of Ursa Major in a form resembling a dipper

big·foot \'big-ˌfut\ *n* : SASQUATCH

big·horn sheep \'big-ˌhörn\ *n* : a wild sheep of mountainous western No. America

bight \'bīt\ *n* 1 : a curve in a coast; *also* : the bay formed by such a curve 2 : a slack part in a rope

big-name \'big-'nām\ *adj* : widely popular ⟨a ~ performer⟩ — **big name** *n*

big·ot \'bi-gət\ *n* : one who regards or treats members of a group with hatred and intolerance ♦ **Synonyms** FANATIC, ENTHUSIAST, ZEALOT — **big·ot·ed** \-gə-təd\ *adj* — **big·ot·ry** \-trē\ *n*

big screen *n* : the motion picture medium as contrasted to television

big shot \'big-ˌshät\ *n* : an important person

big time \-ˌtīm\ *n* 1 : a high-paying vaudeville circuit requiring only two performances a day 2 : the top rank of an activity or enterprise — **big–tim·er** *n*

big top *n* 1 : the main tent of a circus 2 : CIRCUS

big·wig \'big-ˌwig\ *n* : BIG SHOT

bike \'bīk\ *n* 1 : BICYCLE 2 : MOTORCYCLE

bik·er *n* : MOTORCYCLIST; *esp* : one who is a member of an organized gang

bike·way \'bīk-ˌwā\ *n* : a thoroughfare for bicycles

bi·ki·ni \bə-'kē-nē\ *n* [F, fr. *Bikini*, atoll in the Marshall Islands] : a woman's brief 2-piece bathing suit

bi·lat·er·al \bī-'la-tə-rəl\ *adj* 1 : having or involving two sides 2 : affecting reciprocally two sides or parties — **bi·lat·er·al·ism** \-tə-rə-ˌli-zəm\ *n* — **bi·lat·er·al·ly** *adv*

bile \'bī(-ə)l\ *n* 1 : a bitter greenish fluid secreted by the liver that aids in the digestion of fats 2 : an ill-humored mood

bilge \'bilj\ *n* 1 : the part of a ship that lies between the bottom and the point where the sides go straight up 2 : stale or worthless remarks or ideas

bi·lin·gual \bī-'liŋ-gwəl\ *adj* : expressed in, knowing, or using two languages

bil·ious \'bil-yəs\ *adj* 1 : marked by or suffering from disordered liver function 2 : IRRITABLE, ILL-TEMPERED — **bil·ious·ness** *n*

bilk \'bilk\ *vb* : CHEAT, SWINDLE

¹bill \'bil\ *n* : the jaws of a bird together with their horny covering; *also* : a mouthpart (as of a turtle) resembling these — **billed** \'bild\ *adj*

²bill *vb* : to caress fondly

³bill *n* 1 : an itemized statement of particulars; *also* : INVOICE 2 : a written document or note 3 : a printed advertisement (as a poster) announcing an event 4 : a draft of a law presented to a legislature for enactment 5 : a written statement of a legal wrong suffered or of some breach of law 6 : a piece of paper money

⁴bill *vb* 1 : to enter in or prepare a bill; *also* : to submit a bill or account to 2 : to advertise by bills or posters

bill·board \-ˌbȯrd\ *n* : a flat surface on which advertising bills are posted

¹bil·let \'bil-ət\ *n* 1 : an order requiring a person to provide lodging for a soldier; *also* : quarters assigned by or as if by such an order 2 : POSITION, APPOINTMENT

²billet *vb* : to assign lodging to by billet

bil·let-doux \ˌbi-lā-'dü\ *n, pl* **billets-doux** *same or* -'düz\ [F *billet doux,* lit., sweet letter] : a love letter

bill·fold \'bil-ˌfōld\ *n* : WALLET

bil·liards \'bil-yərdz\ *n* : any of several games played on an oblong table by driving balls against each other or into pockets with a cue

bil·lings·gate \'bil-iŋz-ˌgāt, *Brit usu* -git\ *n* [*Billingsgate,* old gate and fish market, London, England] : coarsely abusive language

bil·lion \'bil-yən\ *n,* 1 : a thousand millions 2 *Brit* : a million millions — **billion** *adj* — **bil·lionth** \-yənth\ *adj or n*

bill of attainder : a legislative act that imposes punishment without a trial

bill of health : a usu. favorable report following an examination

bill of sale : a legal document transferring ownership of goods

¹bil·low \'bil-lō\ *n* 1 : WAVE; *esp* : a great wave 2 : a rolling mass (as of fog or flame) like a great wave — **bil·lowy** \'bil-lə-wē\ *adj*

²billow *vb* : to rise and roll in waves; *also* : to swell out ⟨*~ing* sails⟩

bil·ly \'bil-lē\ *n, pl* **billies** : BILLY CLUB

billy club *n* : a heavy usu. wooden club; *esp* : a police officer's club

bil·ly goat \'bil-lē-\ *n* : a male goat

bi·met·al \'bī-ˌme-t⁸l\ *adj* : BIMETALLIC — **bimetal** *n*

bi·me·tal·lic \ˌbī-mə-'ta-lik\ *adj* : made of two different metals — often used of de-

vices having a bonded expansive part — **bimetallic** *n*

bi·met·al·lism \bī-'me-t⁸l-ˌi-zəm\ *n* : the use of two metals at fixed ratios to form a standard of value for a monetary system

¹bi·month·ly \bī-'mənth-lē\ *adj* : occurring every two months 2 : occurring twice a month : SEMIMONTHLY — **bimonthly** *adv*

²bimonthly *n* : a bimonthly publication

bin \'bin\ *n* : a box, crib, or enclosure used for storage

bi·na·ry \'bī-nə-rē, -ˌner-ē\ *adj* 1 : consisting of two things or parts 2 : relating to, being, or belonging to a system of numbers having 2 as its base ⟨the ~ digits 0 and 1⟩ 3 : involving a choice between or condition of two alternatives only (as on-off, yes-no) — **binary** *n*

binary star *n* : a system of two stars revolving around each other

binary system *n* : BINARY STAR

bin·au·ral \bī-'nȯr-əl\ *adj* : of or relating to sound reproduction involving the use of two separated microphones and two transmission channels to achieve a stereophonic effect

bind \'bīnd\ *vb* **bound** \'baùnd\; **binding** 1 : TIE; *also* : to restrain as if by tying 2 : to put under an obligation; *also* : to constrain with legal authority 3 : BANDAGE 4 : to unite into a mass 5 : to compel as if by a pledge ⟨a handshake ~s the deal⟩ 6 : to strengthen or decorate with a band 7 : to fasten together and enclose in a cover ⟨~ books⟩ 8 : to exert a tying, restraining, or compelling effect — **bind·er** *n*

bind·ing \'bīn-diŋ\ *n* : something (as a ski fastening, a cover, or an edging fabric) used to bind

bin·dle \'bin-d⁹l\ *n* : a bundle of clothes or bedding

¹binge \'binj\ *n* 1 : SPREE 2 : an act of excessive consumption (as of food)

²binge *vb* **binged; binge·ing** *or* **bing·ing** : to go on a binge — **bing·er** *n*

bin·go \'biŋ-gō\ *n, pl* **bingos** : a game of chance played with cards having numbered squares corresponding to numbered balls drawn at random and won by covering five squares in a row

bin·na·cle \'bi-ni-kəl\ *n* [alter. of ME *bitakle,* fr. Pg or Sp; Pg *bitácola* & Sp *bitácula,* fr. L *habitaculum* dwelling place, fr. *habitare* to inhabit] : a container holding a ship's compass

¹bin·oc·u·lar \bī-'nä-kyə-lər, bə-\ *adj* : of, relating to, or adapted to the use of both eyes — **bin·oc·u·lar·ly** *adv*

²bin·oc·u·lar \bə-'nä-kyə-lər, bī-\ *n* 1 : a binocular optical instrument (as a microscope) 2 : a hand-held optical instrument composed of two telescopes and a focusing device — usu. used in pl.

bi·no·mi·al \bī-'nō-mē-əl\ *n* 1 : a mathematical expression consisting of two terms connected by the sign plus (+) or minus (−) 2 : a biological species name consisting of two terms — **binomial** *adj*

bio·chem·is·try \ˌbī-ō-'ke-mə-strē\ *n* : chemistry that deals with the chemical compounds and processes occurring in living things — **bio·chem·i·cal** \-mi-kəl\ *adj or n* — **bio·chem·i·cal·ly** \-k(ə-)lē\ *adv* — **bio·chem·ist** \-'mist\ *n*

bio·de·grad·able \-di-'grā-də-bəl\ *adj* : capable of being broken down esp. into innocuous products by the actions of living things (as microorganisms) ⟨a ~ detergent⟩ — **bio·de·grad·abil·i·ty** \-grā-də-ˌbi-lə-tē\ *n* — **bio·deg·ra·da·tion** \-ˌde-grə-'dā-shən\ *n* — **bio·de·grade** \-di-'grād\ *vb*

bio·di·ver·si·ty \-də-'vər-sə-tē, -dī-\ *n* : biological diversity in an environment as indicated by numbers of different species of plants and animals

bio·en·gi·neer·ing \-ˌen-jə-'nir-iŋ\ *n* **1** : the application of engineering principles to medicine and biology **2** : GENETIC ENGINEERING

bio·eth·ics \-'e-thiks\ *n* : the ethics of biological research and its applications esp. in medicine — **bio·eth·i·cal** \-'e-thi-kəl\ *adj* — **bio·eth·i·cist** \-'e-thə-sist\ *n*

bio·feed·back \-'fēd-ˌbak\ *n* : the technique of making unconscious or involuntary bodily processes (as heartbeats or brain waves) perceptible to the senses (as by use of an oscilloscope) in order to manipulate them by conscious mental control

biog *abbr* biographer; biographical; biography

bio·ge·og·ra·phy \ˌbī-ō-jē-'ä-grə-fē\ *n* : a science that deals with the geographical distribution of plants and animals — **bio·ge·og·ra·pher** *n*

bi·og·ra·phy \bī-'ä-grə-fē, bē-\ *n, pl* **-phies** : a written history of a person's life; *also* : such writings in general — **bi·og·ra·pher** *n* — **bio·graph·i·cal** \ˌbī-ə-'gra-fi-kəl\ *also* **bio·graph·ic** \-'fik\ *adj*

bio·in·for·mat·ics \ˌbī-ō-in-fər-'ma-tiks\ *n* : the storage, classification, and analysis of biological information using computers

biol *abbr* biologic; biological; biologist; biology

bi·o·log·i·cal \ˌbī-ə-'lä-ji-kəl\ *also* **bi·o·log·ic** \-jik\ *adj* **1** : of, relating to, or produced by biology or life and living processes **2** : connected by direct genetic relationship rather than by adoption or marriage ⟨her ~ father⟩ — **bi·o·log·i·cal·ly** \-ji-k(ə-)lē\ *adv*

biological clock *n* : an inherent timing mechanism in a living system that is inferred to exist in order to explain the timing of various physiological and behavioral states and processes

biological warfare *n* : warfare in which harmful living organisms (**biological weapons**) are used against an enemy esp. to cause large-scale death or disease

bi·ol·o·gy \bī-'ä-lə-jē\ *n* [G *Biologie*, fr. Gk *bios* mode of life + *logos* word, discourse] **1** : a science that deals with living beings and life processes **2** : the life processes of an organism or group — **bi·ol·o·gist** \bī-'ä-lə-jist\ *n*

bio·mass \'bī-ō-ˌmas\ *n* **1** : the amount

of living matter (as in a unit area) **2** : plant materials and animal waste used esp. as fuel

bio·med·i·cal \ˌbī-ō-'me-di-kəl\ *adj* : of, relating to, or involving biological, medical, and physical science

bi·on·ic \bī-'ä-nik\ *adj* : having normal biological capability or performance enhanced by or as if by electronic or mechanical devices

bio·phys·ics \ˌbī-ō-'fi-ziks\ *n* : a branch of science concerned with the application of physical principles and methods to biological problems — **bio·phys·i·cal** \-zi-kəl\ *adj* — **bio·phys·i·cist** \-'fi-zə-sist\ *n*

bio·pic \'bī-ō-ˌpik\ *n* : a biographical movie

bi·op·sy \'bī-ˌäp-sē\ *n, pl* **-sies** : the removal of tissue, cells, or fluids from the living body for examination

bio·rhythm \'bī-ō-ˌri-thəm\ *n* : an innately determined rhythmic biological process (as sleep); *also* : the internal mechanism controlling such a process

bio·sci·ence \-'sī-əns\ *n* : BIOLOGY 1; *also* : LIFE SCIENCE

bio·sphere \'bī-ə-ˌsfir\ *n* **1** : the part of the world in which life can exist **2** : living organisms together with their environment

bio·tech \'bī-ō-ˌtek\ *n* : BIOTECHNOLOGY

bio·tech·nol·o·gy \ˌbī-ō-tek-'nä-lə-jē\ *n* : the manipulation (as through genetic engineering) of living organisms to produce useful products; *also* : biological science so applied

bio·ter·ror·ism \-'ter-ər-ˌi-zəm\ *n* : terrorism involving the use of biological weapons — **bio·ter·ror·ist** \-ist\ *adj or n*

bi·ot·ic \bī-'ä-tik\ *adj* : of, relating to, or caused by living organisms

bi·o·tin \'bī-ə-tən\ *n* : a vitamin of the vitamin B complex found esp. in yeast, liver, and egg yolk and active in growth promotion

bi·o·tite \'bī-ə-ˌtīt\ *n* : a dark mica containing iron, magnesium, potassium, and aluminum

bi·par·ti·san \bī-'pär-tə-zən\ *adj* : marked by or involving cooperation, agreement, and compromise between two major political parties — **bi·par·ti·san·ship** \-ˌship\

bi·par·tite \-'pär-ˌtīt\ *adj* **1** : being in two parts **2** : shared by two ⟨~ treaty⟩

bi·ped \'bī-ˌped\ *n* : a 2-footed animal — **bi·ped·al** \(ˌ)bī-'pe-dəl\ *adj*

bi·plane \'bī-ˌplān\ *n* : an aircraft with two wings placed one above the other

bi·po·lar \bī-'pō-lər\ *adj* : having or involving the use of two poles — **bi·po·lar·i·ty** \ˌbī-pō-'ler-ə-tē\ *n*

bipolar disorder *n* : any of several psychological disorders of mood characterized usu. by alternating episodes of depression and mania

bi·ra·cial \bī-'rā-shəl\ *adj* : of, relating to, or involving members of two races

¹**birch** \'bərch\ *n* **1** : any of a genus of mostly short-lived deciduous shrubs and trees with membranous outer bark and pale close-grained wood; *also* : this wood

2 : a birch rod or bundle of twigs for flogging — **birch** or **birch·en** \'bər-chən\ adj

²birch vb : WHIP, FLOG

¹bird \'bərd\ n : any of a class of warm-blooded egg-laying vertebrates having the body feathered and the forelimbs modified to form wings

²bird vb : to observe or identify wild birds in their native habitat — **bird·er** n

bird·bath \'bərd-,bath, -,bäth\ n : a usu. ornamental basin set up for birds to bathe in

bird·house \-,haùs\ n : an artificial nesting place for birds; also : AVIARY

bird·ie \'bər-dē\ n : a score of one under par on a hole in golf

bird·lime \-,līm\ n : a sticky substance smeared on twigs to snare small birds

bird of paradise : any of numerous brilliantly colored plumed birds of the New Guinea area

bird of prey : a carnivorous bird that feeds wholly or chiefly on carrion or on meat taken by hunting

bird·seed \'bərd-,sēd\ n : a mixture of small seeds (as of hemp or millet) used for feeding birds

bird's-eye \'bərdz-,ī\ adj **1** : marked with spots resembling birds' eyes ⟨~ maple⟩ **2** : seen from above as if by a flying bird ⟨~ view⟩; also : CURSORY

bi·ret·ta \bə-'re-tə\ n : a square cap with three ridges on top worn esp. by Roman Catholic clergymen

birr \'bir, 'bər\ n, pl **birr** — see MONEY table

¹birth \'bərth\ n **1** : the act or fact of being born or of bringing forth young **2** : LINEAGE, DESCENT **3** : ORIGIN, BEGINNING — **birth** vb

²birth adj : BIOLOGICAL 2 ⟨~ parents⟩

birth canal n : the channel formed by the cervix, vagina, and vulva through which the fetus passes during birth

birth control n : control of the number of children born esp. by preventing or lessening the frequency of conception

birth·day \'bərth-,dā\ n : the day or anniversary of one's birth

birth defect n : a physical or biochemical defect present at birth and inherited or environmentally induced

birth·mark \'bərth-,märk\ n : an unusual mark or blemish on the skin at birth

birth·place \-,plās\ n : place of birth or origin

birth·rate \-,rāt\ n : the number of births per number of individuals in a given area or group during a given time

birth·right \-,rīt\ n : a right, privilege, or possession to which one is entitled by birth ♦ **Synonyms** LEGACY, PATRIMONY, HERITAGE, INHERITANCE

birth·stone \-,stōn\ n : a gemstone associated symbolically with the month of one's birth

bis·cuit \'bis-kət\ n, [ME bisquite, fr. AF besquit, fr. (pain) besquit twice-cooked bread] **1** : a crisp flat cake; esp, Brit : CRACKER 2 **2** : a small quick bread

made from dough that has been rolled and cut or dropped from a spoon

bi·sect \'bī-,sekt\ vb : to divide into two usu. equal parts; also : CROSS, INTERSECT — **bi·sec·tion** \'bī-,sek-shən\ n — **bi·sec·tor** \-tər\ n

bi·sex·u·al \bī-'sek-shə-wəl\ adj **1** : possessing characters of or having sexual desire for both sexes **2** : of, relating to, or involving both sexes — **bisexual** n — **bi·sex·u·al·i·ty** \,bī-,sek-shə-'wal-ə-tē\ n

bish·op \'bi-shəp\ n [ME bisshop, fr. OE bisceop, fr. LL episcopus, fr. Gk episkopos, lit., overseer, fr. epi- on, over + skeptesthai to look] **1** : a member of the clergy ranking above a priest and typically governing a diocese **2** : any of various Protestant church officials who superintend other clergy **3** : a chess piece that can move diagonally across any number of adjoining unoccupied squares

bish·op·ric \'bi-shə-prik\ n **1** : DIOCESE **2** : the office of bishop

bis·muth \'biz-məth\ n : a heavy brittle grayish white metallic chemical element used in alloys and medicine

bi·son \'bī-s⁸n, -z⁸n\ n, pl **bison** : BUFFALO 2

bisque \'bisk\ n : a thick cream soup

bis·tro \'bēs-trō, 'bis-\ n, pl **bistros** [F] **1** : a small or unpretentious restaurant **2** : BAR; also : NIGHTCLUB

¹bit \'bit\ n **1** : the biting or cutting edge or part of a tool **2** : the part of a bridle that is placed in a horse's mouth

²bit n **1** : a morsel of food; also : a small piece or quantity of something **2** : a small coin; also : a unit of value equal to 12½ cents **3** : something small or trivial **4** : an indefinite usu. small degree or extent ⟨a ~ tired⟩

³bit n [binary digit] : a unit of computer information equivalent to the result of a choice between two alternatives; also : its physical representation

¹bitch \'bich\ n **1** : a female canine; esp : a female dog **2** : a malicious, spiteful, or overbearing woman

²bitch vb : COMPLAIN

¹bite \'bīt\ vb **bit** \'bit\; **bit·ten** \'bi-t⁸n\ also **bit**; **bit·ing** \'bī-tiŋ\ **1** : to grip with teeth or jaws; also : to wound or sting with or as if with fangs **2** : to cut or pierce with or as if with an edged instrument **3** : to cause to smart or sting **4** : CORRODE **5** : to take bait

²bite n **1** : the act or manner of biting **2** : FOOD **3** : a wound made by biting; also : a penetrating effect

bite–size \'bīt-,sīz\ adj **1** : of a size that can be eaten in one bite **2** : being or made small or brief esp. so as to be easily manageable

biting adj : SHARP, CUTTING

bit·map \'bit-,map\ n : an array of binary data representing a bitmapped image or display

bit·mapped \'bit-,mapt\ adj : of, relating to, or being a digital image or display for which an array of binary data specifies the value of each pixel

bit·ter \'bi-tər\ *adj* **1** : being or inducing the one of the basic taste sensations that is acrid, astringent, or disagreeable and is suggestive of hops **2** : marked by intensity or severity (as of distress or hatred) **3** : extremely harsh or cruel — **bit·ter·ly** *adv* — **bit·ter·ness** *n*

bit·tern \'bi-tərn\ *n* : any of various small or medium-sized herons

bit·ters \'bi-tərz\ *n sing or pl* : a usu. alcoholic solution of bitter and often aromatic plant products used in mixing drinks and as a mild tonic

¹bit·ter·sweet \'bi-tər-ˌswēt\ *n* **1** : a poisonous nightshade with purple flowers and reddish berries **2** : a woody vine with yellow capsules that open when ripe to show scarlet seed covers

²bittersweet *adj* : being at once both bitter and sweet

bi·tu·mi·nous coal \bə-'tü-mə-nəs-, bī-, -'tyü-\ *n* : a coal that when heated yields considerable volatile waste matter

bi·valve \'bī-ˌvalv\ *n* : any of a class of mollusks (as clams or scallops) of two separate parts that open and shut — **bi·valve** *adj*

¹biv·ouac \'bi-və-ˌwak\ *n* [F, fr. LG *biwacht*, fr. *bi* at + *wacht* guard] : a temporary encampment or shelter

²bivouac *vb* **-ouacked; -ouack·ing** : to form a bivouac : CAMP

¹bi·week·ly \ˌbī-'wē-klē\ *adj* **1** : occurring twice a week **2** : occurring every two weeks : FORTNIGHTLY — **biweekly** *adv*

²biweekly *n* : a biweekly publication

bi·year·ly \-'yir-lē\ *adj* **1** : BIANNUAL **2** : BIENNIAL

bi·zarre \bə-'zär\ *adj* : ODD, ECCENTRIC, FANTASTIC ⟨~ costumes⟩ — **bi·zarre·ly** *adv*

bi·zar·ro \bə-'zär-ō\ *adj* : characterized by a bizarre, fantastic, or unconventional approach

bk *abbr* **1** bank **2** book

Bk *symbol* berkelium

bkg *abbr* banking

bkgd *abbr* background

bks *abbr* barracks

bkt *abbr* **1** basket **2** bracket

bl *abbr* **1** bale **2** barrel **3** blue

blab \'blab\ *vb* **blabbed; blab·bing** : TATTLE, GOSSIP

¹black \'blak\ *adj* **1** : of the color black; *also* : very dark **2** : SWARTHY **3** : of or relating to various groups of dark-skinned people **4** : of or relating to the African-American people or their culture **5** : SOILED, DIRTY **6** : lacking light ⟨a ~ night⟩ **7** : WICKED, EVIL ⟨~ magic⟩ **8** : DISMAL, GLOOMY ⟨a ~ outlook⟩ **9** : SULLEN ⟨a ~ mood⟩ — **black·ish** *adj* — **black·ly** *adv* — **black·ness** *n*

²black *n* **1** : a black pigment or dye; *also* : something (as clothing) that is black **2** : the characteristic color of soot or coal **3** : a person of a dark-skinned race **4** : AFRICAN-AMERICAN

³black *vb* : BLACKEN

black·a·moor \'bla-kə-ˌmùr\ *n* : a dark-skinned person

black–and–blue \ˌbla-kən-'blü\ *adj* : darkly discolored from blood effused by bruising

black–and–white \ˌbla-kən-'hwīt\ *n* : SQUAD CAR

black·ball \'blak-ˌbòl\ *vb* **1** : to vote against; *esp* : to exclude from membership by casting a negative vote **2** : OSTRACIZE — **black·ball** *n*

black bass *n* : any of several freshwater sunfishes native to eastern and central No. America

black bear *n* : a usu. black-furred bear of No. American forests

¹black belt \'blak-ˌbelt\ *n, often cap both Bs* : an area densely populated by blacks

²black belt \-'belt\ *n* : one who holds the rating of expert (as in judo or karate); *also* : the rating itself

black·ber·ry \-ˌber-ē\ *n* : the usu. black or purple juicy but seedy edible fruit of various brambles; *also* : a plant bearing this fruit

black·bird \-ˌbərd\ *n* : any of various birds (as the red-winged blackbird) of which the male is largely or wholly black

black·board \-ˌbòrd\ *n* : a smooth usu. dark surface used for writing or drawing on with chalk

black·body \-'bä-dē\ *n* : a body or surface that completely absorbs incident radiation with no reflection

black box *n* **1** : a usu. complicated electronic device whose components and workings are unknown or mysterious to the user **2** : a device used in aircraft to record cockpit conversations and flight data

black death *n* : an epidemic of bacterial plague and esp. bubonic plague that spread rapidly in Europe and Asia in the 14th century

black·en \'bla-kən\ *vb* **black·ened; black·en·ing** **1** : to make or become black **2** : DEFAME, SULLY ⟨~ed her reputation⟩

black·ened *adj* : coated with spices and quickly seared in a very hot skillet ⟨~ swordfish⟩

black eye *n* : a discoloration of the skin around the eye from bruising

black–eyed Su·san \ˌblak-ˌīd-'sü-zªn\ *n* : a coarse No. American plant that is related to the daisies and has deep yellow to orange flower heads with dark conical centers

Black·foot \'blak-ˌfùt\ *n, pl* **Black·feet** *or* **Blackfoot** : a member of an American Indian people of Montana, Alberta, and Saskatchewan

black·guard \'bla-gərd, -ˌgärd\ *n* : SCOUNDREL, RASCAL

black·head \'blak-ˌhed\ *n* : a small usu. dark oily mass plugging the outlet of a skin gland

black hole *n* : a celestial object with a gravitational field so strong that light cannot escape from it

black·ing \'bla-kiŋ\ *n* : a substance applied to something to make it black

¹black·jack \'blak-ˌjak\ *n* **1** : a leather-covered club with a flexible handle **2** : a card game in which the object is to be dealt cards having a higher count than the dealer but not exceeding 21

²**blackjack** *vb* : to hit with or as if with a blackjack

black light *n* : invisible ultraviolet light

black·list \'blak-ˌlist\ *n* : a list of persons who are disapproved of and are to be punished or boycotted — **blacklist** *vb*

black·mail \'blak-ˌmāl\ *n* : extortion by threats esp. of public exposure; *also* : something so extorted — **blackmail** *vb* — **black·mail·er** *n*

black market *n* : illicit trade in goods; *also* : a place where such trade is carried on

Black Mass *n* : a travesty of the Christian Mass ascribed to worshipers of Satan

Black Muslim *n* : a member of a chiefly black group that professes Islamic religious belief

black nationalist *n, often cap B&N* : a member of a group of militant blacks who advocate separatism from whites and the formation of self-governing black communities — **black nationalism** *n, often cap B&N*

black–on–black *adj* : involving a black person against another black person 〈∼ crime〉

black·out \'blak-ˌaút\ *n* **1** : a period of darkness due to electrical power failure **2** : a transitory loss or dulling of vision or consciousness **3** : the prohibition or restriction of the telecasting of a sports event — **black out** *vb*

black pepper *n* : a spice that consists of the dried berry of a pepper plant ground with the black husk still on

black power *n* : the mobilization of the political and economic power of black Americans esp. to compel respect for their rights and improve their condition

black sheep *n* : a member of a group who is disreputable or not regarded favorably

black·smith \'blak-ˌsmith\ *n* : a person who forges iron — **black·smith·ing** *n*

black·strap molasses \'blak-ˌstrap-\ *n* : a thick dark molasses obtained from successive processing of raw sugar

black·thorn \-ˌthȯrn\ *n* : a European thorny plum

black–tie \'blak-'tī\ *adj* : characterized by or requiring semiformal evening clothes consisting of a usu. black tie and tuxedo for men and a formal dress for women

black·top \'blak-ˌtäp\ *n* : a dark tarry material (as asphalt) used esp. for surfacing roads — **blacktop** *vb*

black widow *n* : a venomous New World spider having the female black with an hourglass-shaped red mark on the underside of the abdomen

blad·der \'bla-dər\ *n* : a sac in which liquid or gas is stored; *esp* : one in a vertebrate into which urine passes from the kidneys

¹**blade** \'blād\ *n* **1** : a leaf of a plant and esp. of a grass; *also* : the flat part of a leaf as distinguished from its stalk **2** : something (as the flat part of an oar or an arm of a propeller) resembling the blade of a leaf **3** : the cutting part of an instrument or tool **4** : SWORD; *also* : SWORDSMAN **5** : a dashing fellow 〈a gay ∼〉 **6** : the runner of an ice skate — **blad·ed** \'blā-dəd\ *adj*

²**blade** *vb* **blad·ed; blad·ing** : to skate on in-line skates — **blad·er** \'blā-dər\ *n*

blain \'blān\ *n* : an inflammatory swelling or sore

¹**blame** \'blām\ *vb* **blamed; blam·ing** [ME, fr. AF *blamer, blasmer,* fr. L *blasphemare* to blaspheme, fr. Gk *blasphēmein*] **1** : to find fault with **2** : to hold responsible or responsible for ♦ **Synonyms** CENSURE, DENOUNCE, CONDEMN, CRITICIZE — **blam·able** *adj*

²**blame** *n* **1** : CENSURE, REPROOF **2** : responsibility for fault or error ♦ **Synonyms** GUILT, FAULT, CULPABILITY, ONUS — **blame·less** *adj* — **blame·less·ly** *adv* — **blame·less·ness** *n*

blame·wor·thy \-ˌwȯr-thē\ *adj* : deserving blame — **blame·wor·thi·ness** *n*

blanch \'blanch\ *vb* : to make or become white or pale : BLEACH

blanc·mange \blə-'mänj, -'mä⁻zh\ *n* : a dessert made from gelatin or a starchy substance and milk usu. sweetened and flavored

bland \'bland\ *adj* **1** : smooth in manner : SUAVE 〈a ∼ smile〉 **2** : gently soothing 〈a ∼ diet〉; *also* : INSIPID ♦ **Synonyms** GENTLE, MILD, SOFT, BALMY — **bland·ly** *adv* — **bland·ness** *n*

blan·dish·ment \'blan-dish-mənt\ *n* : flattering or coaxing speech or action : CAJOLERY

¹**blank** \'blaŋk\ *adj* **1** : showing or causing an appearance of dazed dismay; *also* : EXPRESSIONLESS **2** : free from writing or marks; *also* : having spaces to be filled in **3** : DULL, EMPTY 〈∼ moments〉 **4** : ABSOLUTE, DOWNRIGHT 〈a ∼ refusal〉 **5** : not shaped in final form — **blank·ly** *adv* — **blank·ness** *n*

²**blank** *n* **1** : an empty space **2** : a form with spaces for the entry of data **3** : an unfinished form (as of a key) **4** : a cartridge with propellant and a seal but no projectile

³**blank** *vb* **1** : to cover or close up : OBSCURE **2** : to keep from scoring

blank check *n* **1** : a signed check with the amount unspecified **2** : complete freedom of action

¹**blan·ket** \'blaŋ-kət\ *n* **1** : a heavy woven often woolen covering **2** : a covering layer 〈a ∼ of snow〉

²**blanket** *vb* : to cover with a blanket

³**blanket** *adj* : covering a group or class 〈∼ insurance〉; *also* : applicable in all instances 〈∼ rules〉

blank verse *n* : unrhymed iambic pentameter

blare \'bler\ *vb* **blared; blar·ing** : to sound loud and harsh; *also* : to proclaim loudly — **blare** *n*

blar·ney \'blär-nē\ *n* [*Blarney stone,* a stone in Blarney Castle, near Cork, Ireland, held to bestow skill in flattery on those who kiss it] : skillful flattery : BLANDISHMENT

bla·sé \blä-ˈzā\ *adj* [F] : apathetic to pleasure or excitement as a result of excessive indulgence; *also* : SOPHISTICATED

blas·pheme \blas-ˈfēm, ˈblas-,\ *vb* **blasphemed; blas·phem·ing 1** : to speak of or address with irreverence **2** : to utter blasphemy — **blas·phem·er** *n*

blas·phe·my \ˈblas-fə-mē\ *n, pl* **-mies 1** : the act of expressing lack of reverence for God **2** : irreverence toward something considered sacred — **blas·phe·mous** \-məs\ *adj*

¹blast \ˈblast\ *n* **1** : a violent gust of wind; *also* : its effect **2** : sound made by a wind instrument **3** : a current of air forced at high pressure through a hole in a furnace (**blast furnace**) **4** : a sudden withering esp. of plants : BLIGHT **5** : EXPLOSION; *also* : the shock wave of an explosion

²blast *vb* : to shatter by or as if by an explosive

blast off *vb* : TAKE OFF 4 — used esp. of rocket-propelled vehicles — **blast·off** \ˈblast-ˌôf\ *n*

bla·tant \ˈblā-tᵊnt\ *adj* : offensively obtrusive : vulgarly showy ✦ **Synonyms** VOCIFEROUS, BOISTEROUS, CLAMOROUS, OBSTREPEROUS — **bla·tan·cy** \-tᵊn-sē\ *n* — **bla·tant·ly** *adv*

blath·er \ˈbla-thər\ *vb* : to talk foolishly at length — **blather** *n*

blath·er·skite \ˈbla-thər-ˌskīt\ *n* : a person who blathers

¹blaze \ˈblāz\ *n* **1** : FIRE **2** : intense direct light accompanied by heat **3** : something (as a dazzling display or sudden outburst) suggesting fire ⟨a ~ of autumn leaves⟩ ✦ **Synonyms** GLARE, GLOW, FLAME

²blaze *vb* **blazed; blaz·ing 1** : to burn brightly; *also* : to flare up **2** : to be conspicuously bright : GLITTER

³blaze *vb* **blazed; blaz·ing** : to make public or conspicuous

⁴blaze *n* **1** : a usu. white stripe on the face of an animal **2** : a trail marker; *esp* : one made on a tree

⁵blaze *vb* **blazed; blaz·ing** : to mark (as a tree or trail) with blazes

blaze orange *n* : a very bright orange used in clothing for visibility

blaz·er \ˈblā-zər\ *n* : a sports jacket often with notched collar and pockets that are stitched on

¹bla·zon \ˈblā-zᵊn\ *n* **1** : COAT OF ARMS **2** : ostentatious display

²blazon *vb* **1** : to publish widely : PROCLAIM **2** : DECK, ADORN

bldg *abbr* building

bldr *abbr* builder

¹bleach \ˈblēch\ *vb* : WHITEN, BLANCH

²bleach *n* : a preparation used in bleaching

bleach·ers \ˈblē-chərz\ *n sing or pl* : a usu. uncovered stand of tiered seats for spectators

bleak \ˈblēk\ *adj* **1** : desolately barren and often windswept **2** : lacking warm or cheering qualities — **bleak·ly** *adv* — **bleak·ness** *n*

blear \ˈblir\ *adj* : dim with water or tears ⟨~ eyes⟩

bleary \ˈblir-ē\ *adj* **1** : dull or dimmed

esp. from fatigue or sleep **2** : poorly outlined or defined ⟨a ~ view⟩

bleat \ˈblēt\ *n* : the cry of a sheep or goat or a sound like it — **bleat** *vb*

bleed \ˈblēd\ *vb* **bled** \ˈbled\; **bleed·ing 1** : to lose or shed blood **2** : to be wounded; *also* : to feel pain or distress **3** : to flow or ooze from a wounded surface; *also* : to draw fluid from ⟨~ a tire⟩ **4** : to extort money from

bleed·er \ˈblē-dər\ *n* : one that bleeds; *esp* : HEMOPHILIAC

bleeding heart *n* **1** : a garden plant related to the poppies that has usu. deep pink or white drooping heart-shaped flowers **2** : a person who shows extravagant sympathy esp. for an object of alleged persecution

¹blem·ish \ˈble-mish\ *vb* : to spoil by a flaw : MAR

²blemish *n* : a noticeable flaw

¹blench \ˈblench\ *vb* [ME, to deceive, blench, fr. OE *blencan* to deceive] : FLINCH, QUAIL ✦ **Synonyms** SHRINK, RECOIL, WINCE, START

²blench *vb* : to grow or make pale

¹blend \ˈblend\ *vb* **blend·ed; blend·ing 1** : to mix thoroughly **2** : to prepare (as coffee) by mixing different varieties **3** : to combine into an integrated whole **4** : HARMONIZE ✦ **Synonyms** FUSE, MERGE, MINGLE, COALESCE — **blend·er** *n*

²blend *n* : a product of blending ✦ **Synonyms** COMPOUND, COMPOSITE, ALLOY, MIXTURE

blended family *n* : a family that includes children of a previous marriage of one spouse or both

bless \ˈbles\ *vb* **blessed** \ˈblest\ *also* **blest** \ˈblest\; **bless·ing** [ME, fr. OE *blētsian*, fr. *blōd* blood; fr. the use of blood in consecration] **1** : to consecrate by religious rite or word **2** : to sanctify with the sign of the cross **3** : to invoke divine care for **4** : PRAISE, GLORIFY **5** : to confer happiness upon

bless·ed \ˈble-səd\ *also* **blest** \ˈblest\ *adj* **1** : HOLY **2** : BEATIFIED **3** : DELIGHTFUL — **bless·ed·ly** *adv* — **bless·ed·ness** *n*

bless·ing \ˈble-siŋ\ *n* **1** : the act or words of one who blesses; *also* : APPROVAL **2** : a thing conducive to happiness **3** : grace said at a meal

blew *past of* BLOW

¹blight \ˈblīt\ *n* **1** : a plant disease or injury marked esp. by withering and death of parts; *also* : an organism causing blight **2** : an impairing or frustrating influence; *also* : a deteriorated condition ⟨urban ~⟩

²blight *vb* : to affect with or suffer from blight

blimp \ˈblimp\ *n* : an airship that maintains its form by pressure of contained gas

¹blind \ˈblīnd\ *adj* **1** : lacking or grossly deficient in ability to see; *also* : intended for blind persons **2** : not based on reason, evidence, or knowledge ⟨~ faith⟩ **3** : not intelligently controlled or directed

⟨~ chance⟩ **4** : performed solely by using aircraft instruments ⟨a ~ landing⟩ **5** : hard to discern or make out : HIDDEN ⟨a ~ seam⟩ **6** : lacking an opening or outlet ⟨a ~ alley⟩ — **blind·ly** adv — **blind·ness** \'blīnd-nəs\ n

²**blind** vb **1** : to make blind **2** : DAZZLE **3** : DARKEN; also : HIDE

³**blind** n **1** : something (as a shutter) to hinder vision or keep out light **2** : a place of concealment **3** : SUBTERFUGE

blind date n : a date between persons who have not previously met; also : either of these persons

blind·er \'blīn-dər\ n : either of two flaps on a horse's bridle to prevent it from seeing to the side

blind·fold \'blīnd-ˌfōld\ vb : to cover the eyes of with or as if with a bandage — **blindfold** n

¹**blink** \'bliŋk\ vb **1** : WINK **2** : TWINKLE **3** : EVADE, IGNORE

²**blink** n **1** : GLIMMER, SPARKLE **2** : a usu. involuntary shutting and opening of the eye

blink·er \'bliŋ-kər\ n : a blinking light used as a signal

blin·tze \'blint-sə\ or **blintz** \'blints\ n [Yiddish blintse] : a thin rolled pancake with a filling usu. of cream cheese

blip \'blip\ n **1** : a spot on a radar screen **2** : ABERRATION 1

bliss \'blis\ n : complete happiness : JOY ◆ Synonyms BEATITUDE, BLESSEDNESS — **bliss·ful** \-fəl\ adj — **bliss·ful·ly** adv

¹**blis·ter** \'blis-tər\ n **1** : a raised area of skin containing watery fluid; also : an agent that causes blisters **2** : something (as a raised spot in paint) suggesting a blister **3** : a disease of plants marked by large raised patches on the leaves

²**blister** vb : to develop a blister; also : to cause blisters

blithe \'blīth, 'blīth\ adj **blith·er; blith·est** : happily lighthearted ◆ Synonyms MERRY, JOVIAL, JOLLY, JOCUND — **blithe·ly** adv — **blithe·some** \-səm\ adj

blitz \'blits\ n **1** : an intensive series of air raids **2** : a fast intensive campaign **3** : a rush of the passer by the defensive linebackers in football — **blitz** vb

blitz·krieg \-ˌkrēg\ n [G, fr. Blitz lightning + Krieg war] : a sudden violent enemy attack

bliz·zard \'bli-zərd\ n : a long severe snowstorm

blk abbr **1** black **2** block

bloat \'blōt\ vb : to swell by or as if by filling with water or air

blob \'bläb\ n : a small lump or drop of a thick consistency

bloc \'bläk\ n [F, lit., block] : a combination of individuals or groups (as nations) working for a common purpose

¹**block** \'bläk\ n **1** : a solid piece of substantial material (as wood or stone) **2** : HINDRANCE, OBSTRUCTION; also : interruption of normal function of body or mind ⟨heart ~⟩ **3** : a frame enclosing one or more pulleys and having a hook or strap by which it may be attached **4** : a piece of material with a hand-cut design

on its surface from which copies are to be made **5** : a large building divided into separate units (as apartments or offices) **6** : a row of houses or shops **7** : a city square; also : the distance along one of the sides of such a square **8** : a quantity of things considered as a unit ⟨a ~ of seats⟩

²**block** vb **1** : OBSTRUCT, CHECK **2** : to outline roughly ⟨~ out a design⟩ **3** : to provide or support with a block ◆ Synonyms BAR, IMPEDE, HINDER, OBSTRUCT

block·ade \blä-'kād\ n : the isolation of a place usu. by troops or ships — **blockade** vb — **block·ad·er** n

block·age \'blä-kij\ n : an act or instance of obstructing : the state of being blocked

block·bust·er \'bläk-ˌbəs-tər\ n : one that is very large, successful, expensive, or extravagant ⟨a ~ movie⟩

block·head \'bläk-ˌhed\ n : DOLT, DUNCE

block·house \-ˌhaus\ n : a small strong building used as a shelter (as from enemy fire) or observation post

¹**blond** or **blonde** \'bländ\ adj : fair in complexion; also : of a light or bleached color ⟨~ mahogany⟩ — **blond·ish** \'blän-dish\ adj

²**blond** or **blonde** n : a person having blond hair

blood \'bləd\ n **1** : a usu. red liquid that circulates in the heart, arteries, and veins of animals **2** : LIFEBLOOD; also : LIFE **3** : LINEAGE, STOCK **4** : KINSHIP; also : KINDRED **5** : the taking of life **6** : TEMPER, PASSION **7** : DANDY 1 — **blood·less** adj — **blood·y** adj

blood·bath \'bləd-ˌbath, -ˌbäth\ n : MASSACRE

blood count n : the determination of the number of blood cells in a specific volume of blood; also : the number of cells so determined

blood-cur·dling \'bləd-ˌkərd-liŋ, -ˌkər-dᵊl-iŋ\ adj : arousing fright or horror

blood·ed \'blə-dəd\ adj **1** : having blood of a specified kind ⟨warm-blooded animals⟩ **2** : entirely or largely purebred ⟨~ horses⟩

blood group n : one of the classes into which human beings can be separated by the presence or absence in their blood of specific antigens

blood·hound \'bləd-ˌhaund\ n : any of a breed of large powerful hounds with long drooping ears, a wrinkled face, and keen sense of smell

blood·let·ting \-ˌle-tiŋ\ n **1** : PHLEBOTOMY **2** : BLOODSHED

blood·line \-ˌlīn\ n : a sequence of direct ancestors esp. in a pedigree

blood·lust \-ˌləst\ n : desire for bloodshed

blood·mo·bile \-mō-ˌbēl\ n : a motor vehicle equipped for collecting blood from donors

blood poisoning n : invasion of the bloodstream by virulent microorganisms from a focus of infection accompanied esp. by chills, fever, and prostration

blood pressure n : pressure of the blood on the walls of blood vessels and esp. arteries

blood·root \'bləd-ˌrüt, -ˌrüt\ *n* : a plant related to the poppy that has a red root and sap, a solitary leaf, and a white flower in early spring

blood·shed \-ˌshed\ *n* : wounding or taking of life : CARNAGE, SLAUGHTER

blood·shot \-ˌshät\ *adj* : inflamed to redness ⟨~ eyes⟩

blood·stain \-ˌstān\ *n* : a discoloration caused by blood — **blood·stained** \-ˌstānd\ *adj*

blood·stone \-ˌstōn\ *n* : a green quartz sprinkled with red spots

blood·stream \-ˌstrēm\ *n* : the flowing blood in a circulatory system

blood·suck·er \-ˌsə-kər\ *n* : an animal that sucks blood; *esp* : LEECH — **blood·suck·ing** *adj*

blood test *n* : a test of the blood (as to detect disease-causing agents)

blood thinner *n* : a drug used to prevent the clotting of blood

blood·thirsty \'bləd-ˌthər-stē\ *adj* : eager to shed blood — **blood·thirst·i·ly** \-ˌthər-stə-lē\ *adv* — **blood·thirst·i·ness** \-stē-nəs\ *n*

blood type *n* : BLOOD GROUP — **blood·typ·ing** *n*

blood vessel *n* : a vessel (as a vein or artery) in which blood circulates in the body

Bloody Mary \-'mer-ē\ *n, pl* **Bloody Marys** : a drink made essentially of vodka and tomato juice

¹**bloom** \'blüm\ *n* **1** : FLOWER 1; *also* : flowers or amount of flowers (as of a plant) **2** : the period or state of flowering **3** : a state or time of beauty and vigor **4** : a powdery coating esp. on fruits and leaves **5** : rosy color; *also* : an appearance of freshness or health — **bloomy** *adj*

²**bloom** *vb* **1** : to produce or yield flowers **2** : MATURE **3** : to glow esp. with healthy color ♦ **Synonyms** FLOWER, BLOSSOM

bloo·mers \'blü-mərz\ *n pl* [Amelia *Bloomer* †1894 Am. reformer] : a woman's garment of short loose pants gathered at the knee

bloop·er \'blü-pər\ *n* **1** : a fly ball hit barely beyond a baseball infield **2** : an embarrassing public blunder

¹**blos·som** \'blä-səm\ *n* **1** : the flower of a plant **2** : the period or state of flowering

²**blossom** *vb* : FLOWER, BLOOM

¹**blot** \'blät\ *n* **1** : SPOT, STAIN ⟨ink ~s⟩ **2** : BLEMISH ♦ **Synonyms** STIGMA, BRAND, SLUR

²**blot** *vb*, **blot·ted; blot·ting** **1** : SPOT, STAIN **2** : OBSCURE, ECLIPSE ⟨~ out the sun⟩ **3** *obs* : MAR; *esp* : DISGRACE **4** : to dry or remove with or as if with an absorbing material **5** : to make a blot

blotch \'bläch\ *n* : a usu. large and irregular spot or mark (as of ink or color) — **blotch·y** *adj*

blot·ter \'blä-tər\ *n* **1** : a piece of blotting paper **2** : a book for preliminary records (as of sales or arrests)

blot·ting paper *n* : a spongy paper used to absorb ink

blouse \'blau̇s, 'blau̇z\ *n* **1** : a loose outer garment like a smock **2** : a usu. loose garment reaching from the neck to about the waist

¹**blow** \'blō\ *vb* **blew** \'blü\; **blown** \'blōn\; **blow·ing** **1** : to be in motion; *esp* : to move forcibly ⟨the wind *blew*⟩ **2** : to send forth a current of gas (as air) **3** : to act on with a current of gas or vapor; *esp* : to drive with such a current **4** : to clear with a current of air **5** : to sound or cause to sound ⟨~ a horn⟩ **6** : PANT, GASP; *also* : to expel moist air in breathing ⟨the whale *blew*⟩ **7** : BOAST; *also* : BLUSTER **8** : ERUPT, EXPLODE **9** : MELT — used of an electrical fuse **10** : to shape or form by blown or injected air ⟨~ glass⟩ **11** : to shatter or destroy by or as if by explosion **12** : to make breathless by exertion **13** : to spend recklessly **14** : BOTCH ⟨*blew* her lines⟩ — **blow·er** *n*

²**blow** *n* **1** : a usu. strong blowing of air **2** : GALE **3** : BOASTING, BRAG **3** : an act or instance of blowing

³**blow** *vb* **blew** \'blü\; **blown** \'blōn\; **blow·ing** : FLOWER, BLOOM

⁴**blow** *n* **1** : a forcible stroke ⟨a ~ to the head⟩ **2** : COMBAT ⟨come to ~s⟩ **3** : a severe and usu. unexpected calamity

blow-by-blow *adj* : minutely detailed ⟨~ account⟩

blow-dry \-ˌdrī\ *vb* : to dry and usu. style hair with a blow-dryer

blow-dryer \-ˌdrī-(ə)r\ *n* : a hand-held hair dryer

blow·fly \'blō-ˌflī\ *n* : any of a family of dipteran flies (as a bluebottle) that deposit their eggs or maggots on meat or in wounds

blow·gun \-ˌgən\ *n* : a tube from which an arrow or a dart may be shot by the force of the breath

blow·out \'blō-ˌau̇t\ *n* **1** : a bursting of something (as a tire) because of pressure of the contents (as air) **2** : a depression created by the wind in sand or soil

blow·sy *also* **blow·zy** \'blau̇-zē\ *adj* : DISHEVELED, SLOVENLY

blow·torch \'blō-ˌtȯrch\ *n* : a small portable burner whose flame is made hotter by a blast of air or oxygen

blow·up \'blō-ˌəp\ *n* **1** : EXPLOSION **2** : an outburst of temper **3** : a photographic enlargement

blowy \'blō-ē\ *adj* : WINDY

BLT \ˌbē-ˌel-'tē\ *n* : a bacon, lettuce, and tomato sandwich

¹**blub·ber** \'blə-bər\ *vb* : to cry noisily

²**blubber** *n* **1** : the fat of large sea mammals (as whales) **2** : a noisy crying

¹**blud·geon** \'blə-jən\ *n* : a short often loaded club

²**bludgeon** *vb* : to strike with or as if with a bludgeon

¹**blue** \'blü\ *adj* **blu·er; blu·est** [ME, fr. AF *blef, blew*, of Gmc origin] **1** : of the color blue; *also* : BLUISH **2** : MELANCHOLY; *also* : DEPRESSING **3** : PURITANICAL **4** : INDECENT — **blue·ness** *n*

²**blue** *n* **1** : a color between green and violet in the spectrum : the color of the clear

daytime sky **2** : something (as clothing or the sky) that is blue

blue baby *n* : a baby with bluish skin due to faulty circulation caused by a heart defect

blue·bell \-,bel\ *n* : any of various plants with blue bell-shaped flowers

blue·ber·ry \'blü-,ber-ē, -bə-rē\ *n* : the edible blue or blackish berry of various shrubs of the heath family; *also* : one of these shrubs

blue·bird \-,bərd\ *n* : any of three small No. American thrushes that are blue above and reddish-brown or pale blue below

blue·bon·net \'blü-,bä-nət\ *n* : either of two low-growing annual lupines of Texas with silky foliage and blue flowers

blue·bot·tle \'blü-,bä-t³l\ *n* : any of several blowflies with iridescent blue bodies or abdomens

blue cheese *n* : cheese having veins of greenish-blue mold

blue·col·lar \'blü-'kä-lər\ *adj* : of, relating to, or being the class of workers whose duties call for work clothes

blue·fish \-,fish\ *n* : a marine sport and food fish that is bluish above and silvery below

blue·grass \-,gras\ *n* **1** : KENTUCKY BLUEGRASS **2** : country music played on stringed instruments having free improvisation and close harmonies

blue jay \-,jā\ *n* : a crested bright blue No. American jay

blue jeans *n pl* : pants usu. made of blue denim

blue·nose \'blü-,nōz\ *n* : a person who advocates a rigorous moral code

blue·point \-,point\ *n* : a small oyster typically from the south shore of Long Island, New York

blue·print \-,print\ *n* **1** : a photographic print in white on a blue ground used esp. for copying mechanical drawings and architects' plans **2** : a detailed plan of action — **blueprint** *vb*

blues \'blüz\ *n pl* **1** : MELANCHOLY **2** : music in a style marked by recurrent minor intervals and melancholy lyrics

blue screen *n* : a technique in which a subject is filmed in front of a blue background so as to allow the creation of a composite with other footage

blue·stock·ing \'blü-,stä-kiŋ\ *n* : a woman having intellectual interests

blu·et \'blü-ət\ *n* : a low No. American herb with dainty bluish flowers

blue whale *n* : a very large baleen whale that may reach a weight of 150 tons (135 metric tons) and a length of 100 feet (30 meters)

¹**bluff** \'bləf\ *adj* **1** : having a broad flattened front **2** : rising steeply with a broad flat front **3** : OUTSPOKEN, FRANK
  ♦ **Synonyms** ABRUPT, BLUNT, BRUSQUE, CURT, GRUFF

²**bluff** *n* : a high steep bank : CLIFF

³**bluff** *vb* : to frighten or deceive by pretense or a mere show of strength

⁴**bluff** *n* : an act or instance of bluffing; *also* : one who bluffs

blu·ing *or* **blue·ing** \'blü-iŋ\ *n* : a preparation used in laundering to counteract yellowing of white fabrics

blu·ish \'blü-ish\ *adj* : somewhat blue

¹**blun·der** \'blən-dər\ *vb* **1** : to move clumsily or unsteadily **2** : to make a stupid or needless mistake

²**blunder** *n* : an avoidable and usu. serious mistake

blun·der·buss \'blən-dər-,bəs\ *n* [obs. D *donderbus*, fr. D *donder* thunder + obs. D *bus* gun] : an obsolete short-barreled firearm with a flaring muzzle

¹**blunt** \'blənt\ *adj* **1** : not sharp : DULL **2** : lacking in tact : BLUFF ⟨~ criticism⟩
  ♦ **Synonyms** BRUSQUE, CURT, GRUFF, ABRUPT, CRUSTY — **blunt·ly** *adv* — **blunt·ness** *n*

²**blunt** *vb* : to make or become dull

¹**blur** \'blər\ *n* **1** : a smear or stain that obscures **2** : something vaguely perceived; *esp* : something moving too quickly to be clearly perceived — **blur·ry** \-ē\ *adj*

²**blur** *vb* **blurred**; **blur·ring** : DIM, CLOUD, OBSCURE

blurb \'blərb\ *n* : a short publicity notice (as on a book jacket)

blurt \'blərt\ *vb* : to utter suddenly and impulsively

blush \'bləsh\ *n* **1** : a reddening of the face (as from modesty or confusion) : FLUSH **2** : a cosmetic used to tint the face pink — **blush** *vb* — **blush·ful** *adj*

blus·ter \'bləs-tər\ *vb* **1** : to blow in stormy noisy gusts **2** : to talk or act with noisy swaggering threats — **bluster** *n* — **blus·tery** \-tə-rē\ *adj*

blvd *abbr* boulevard

B lymphocyte *n* : B CELL

BM *abbr* bowel movement

B movie *n* : a cheaply produced motion picture

BO *abbr* **1** best offer **2** body odor **3** box office **4** branch office

boa \'bō-ə\ *n* **1** : a large snake (as the **boa con·stric·tor** \-kən-'strik-tər\ or the related anaconda) that suffocates and kills its prey by constriction **2** : a fluffy scarf usu. of fur or feathers

boar \'bōr\ *n* : a male swine; *also* : WILD BOAR

¹**board** \'bōrd\ *n* **1** : the side of a ship **2** : a thin flat length of sawed lumber; *also* : material (as cardboard) or a piece of material formed as a thin flat firm sheet **3** *pl* : STAGE **1** **4** : a table spread with a meal; *also* : daily meals esp. when furnished for pay **5** : a table at which a council or magistrates sit **6** : a group or association of persons organized for a special responsibility (as the management of a business or institution); *also* : an organized commercial exchange **7** : a sheet of insulating material carrying circuit elements and inserted in an electronic device **8** : BULLETIN BOARD

²**board** *vb* **1** : to go or put aboard ⟨~ a boat⟩ **2** : to cover with boards **3** : to provide or be provided with meals and often lodging — **board·er** *n*

board game *n* : a game of strategy (as

checkers or chess) played by moving pieces on a board

board·ing·house \'bȯr-diŋ-ˌhau̇s\ n : a house at which persons are boarded

board·walk \'bȯrd-ˌwȯk\ n : a promenade (as of planking) along a beach

boast \'bōst\ vb **1** : to praise oneself **2** : to mention or assert with excessive pride **3** : to prize as a possession; also : HAVE ⟨the house ~s a fireplace⟩ — **boast** n — **boast·ful** \-fəl\ adj — **boast·ful·ly** adv

boat \'bōt\ n : a small vessel for travel on water, also : SHIP — **boat** vb

boat·er \'bō-tər\ n **1** : one that travels in a boat **2** : a stiff straw hat

boat·man \'bōt-mən\ n : a man who operates, works on, or deals in boats

boat people n pl : refugees fleeing by boat

boat·swain or **bo·sun** \'bō-sᵊn\ n : a subordinate officer of a ship in charge of the hull and related equipment

¹bob \'bäb\ vb **bobbed**; **bob·bing 1** : to move up and down jerkily or repeatedly **2** : to emerge, arise, or appear suddenly or unexpectedly

²bob n : a bobbing movement

³bob n **1** : a knob, knot, twist, or curl esp. of ribbons, yarn, or hair **2** : a short haircut of a woman or child **3** : FLOAT 2 **4** : a weight hanging from a line

⁴bob vb **bobbed**; **bob·bing** : to cut hair in a bob

⁵bob n, pl **bob** slang Brit : SHILLING

bob·bin \'bä-bən\ n : a cylinder or spindle for holding or dispensing thread (as in a sewing machine)

bob·ble \'bä-bəl\ vb **bob·bled**; **bob·bling** : FUMBLE — **bobble** n

bob·by \'bä-bē\ n, pl **bobbies** [Bobby, nickname for Sir Robert Peel, who organized the London police force] Brit : a police officer

bobby pin n : a flat wire hairpin with prongs that press close together

bob·cat \'bäb-ˌkat\ n : a small usu. rusty-colored No. American lynx

bob·o·link \'bä-bə-ˌliŋk\ n : an American migratory songbird related to the meadowlarks

bob·sled \'bäb-ˌsled\ n **1** : a short sled usu. used as one of a joined pair **2** : a racing sled with two pairs of runners, a steering wheel, and a hand brake — **bobsled** vb

bob·white \(ˌ)bäb-'hwīt\ n : any of a genus of quail; esp : a popular game bird of eastern and central No. America

boc·cie or **boc·ci** or **boc·ce** \'bä-chē\ n : Italian lawn bowling played on a long narrow court

bock \'bäk\ n : a strong dark beer usu. sold in early spring

bod \'bäd\ n : BODY

¹bode \'bōd\ vb **bod·ed**; **bod·ing** : to indicate by signs : PRESAGE

²bode past of BIDE

bo·de·ga \bō-'dä-gə\ n [Sp, fr. L apotheca storehouse] : a usu. small store specializing in Hispanic groceries

bod·ice \'bä-dəs\ n [alter. of bodies, pl. of body] : the usu. close-fitting part of a dress above the waist

bodi·less \'bä-di-ləs\ adj : lacking a body or material form

¹bodi·ly \'bä-dᵊl-ē\ adj : of or relating to the body ⟨~ contact⟩ ⟨~ organs⟩

²bodily adv **1** : in the flesh **2** : as a whole ⟨lifted the crate up ~⟩

bod·kin \'bäd-kən\ n **1** : DAGGER **2** : a pointed implement for punching holes in cloth **3** : a blunt needle for drawing tape or ribbon through a loop or hem

body \'bä-dē\ n, pl **bod·ies 1** : the physical whole of a living or dead organism; also : the trunk or main mass of an organism as distinguished from its appendages **2** : a human being : PERSON **3** : the main part of something **4** : a mass of matter distinct from other masses **5** : GROUP **6** : VISCOSITY, FIRMNESS **7** : richness of flavor — used esp. of wines — **bod·ied** \'bä-dēd\ adj

body·build·ing \'bä-dē-ˌbil-diŋ\ n : the developing of the body through exercise and diet — **body·build·er** \-dər\ n

body English n : bodily motions made in a usu. unconscious effort to influence the movement of a propelled object (as a ball)

body·guard \'bä-dē-ˌgärd\ n : a personal guard; also : RETINUE

body language n : movements (as with the hands) or posture used as a means of communication

body stocking n : a sheer close-fitting one-piece garment for the torso that often has sleeves and legs

body·work \'bä-dē-ˌwərk\ n : the making or repairing of vehicle bodies

Boer \'bȯr, 'bu̇r\ n [D, lit., farmer] : a South African of Dutch or Huguenot descent

¹bog \'bäg, 'bȯg\ n : wet, spongy, poorly drained, and usu. acid ground — **bog·gy** adj

²bog vb **bogged**; **bog·ging** : to sink into or as if into a bog

bo·gey also **bo·gie** or **bo·gy** \'bu̇-gē, 'bō- for 1; 'bō- for 2\ n, pl **bogeys** also **bogies 1** : SPECTER, HOBGOBLIN; also : a source of fear or annoyance **2** : a score of one over par on a hole in golf

bo·gey·man \'bu̇-gē-ˌman, 'bō-, 'bu̇-\ n : an imaginary monster used in threatening children

bog·gle \'bä-gəl\ vb **bog·gled**; **bog·gling** : to overwhelm or be overwhelmed with fright or amazement

bo·gus \'bō-gəs\ adj : SPURIOUS, SHAM

Bo·he·mi·an \bō-'hē-mē-ən\ n **1** : a native or inhabitant of Bohemia **2** often not cap : VAGABOND, WANDERER **3** often not cap : a person (as a writer or artist) living an unconventional life — **bohemian** adj, often cap

bohr·i·um \'bȯr-ē-əm\ n : an artificially produced radioactive chemical element

¹boil \'bȯi(-ə)l\ n : an inflamed swelling on the skin containing pus

²boil vb **1** : to heat or become heated to a

temperature (**boil·ing point**) at which vapor is formed and rises in bubbles ⟨water ~s and changes to steam⟩; *also* : to act on or be acted on by a boiling liquid ⟨~ eggs⟩ **2** : to be in a state of seething agitation

³**boil** *n* **1** : the act or state of boiling **2** : a boiled dish (as of seafood) **3** : a gathering where boiled food is served

boil·er \'bȯi-lər\ *n* **1** : a container in which something is boiled **2** : a strong vessel used in making steam **3** : a tank holding hot water

boil·er·mak·er \'bȯi-lər-ˌmā-kər\ *n* : whiskey with a beer chaser

bois·ter·ous \'bȯi-st(ə-)rəs\ *adj* : noisily turbulent or exuberant — **bois·ter·ous·ly** *adv*

bok choy \'bäk-'chȯi\ *n* : a Chinese vegetable related to the mustards that forms a loose head of green leaves with long thick white stalks

bo·la \'bō-lə\ *or* **bo·las** \-ləs\ *n, pl* **bolas** \-ləz\ *also* **bo·las·es** [AmerSp *bolas,* fr. Sp *bola* ball] : a cord with weights attached to the ends for hurling at and entangling an animal

bold \'bōld\ *adj* **1** : COURAGEOUS, INTREPID **2** : IMPUDENT **3** : STEEP **4** : ADVENTUROUS, FREE ⟨a ~ thinker⟩ ♦ *Synonyms* DAUNTLESS, BRAVE, VALIANT — **bold·ly** *adv* — **bold·ness** \'bōld-nəs\ *n*

bold·face \'bōld-ˌfās\ *n* : a heavy-faced type; *also* : printing in boldface — **bold·faced** \-'fāst\ *adj*

bole \'bōl\ *n* : the trunk of a tree

bo·le·ro \bə-'ler-ō\ *n, pl* **-ros** **1** : a Spanish dance or its music **2** : a short loose jacket open at the front

bo·li·var \bə-'lē-ˌvär, 'bä-lə-vər\ *n, pl* **-va·res** \ˌbä-lə-'vär-ˌās, ˌbō-\ *or* **-vars** — see MONEY table

Bo·liv·i·an \bə-'li-vē-ən\ *n* : a native or inhabitant of Bolivia — **Bolivian** *adj*

bo·li·vi·a·no \bə-ˌli-vē-'ä-(ˌ)nō\ *n, pl* **-nos** — see MONEY table

boll \'bōl\ *n* : a seed pod (as of cotton)

boll weevil *n* : a small usu. grayish or brown weevil that infests the cotton plant both as a larva and as an adult

boll·worm \'bōl-ˌwərm\ *n* : any of several moths and esp. the corn earworm whose larvae feed on cotton bolls

bo·lo·gna \bə-'lō-nē\ *n* [short for *Bologna sausage,* fr. *Bologna,* Italy] : a large smoked sausage of beef, veal, and pork

Bol·she·vik \'bōl-shə-ˌvik\ *n, pl* **Bolsheviks** *also* **Bol·she·vi·ki** \ˌbōl-shə-'vi-kē\ [Russ *bol'shevik,* fr. *bol'shii* larger] **1** : a member of the party that seized power in Russia in the revolution of November 1917 **2** : COMMUNIST — **Bolshevik** *adj*

bol·she·vism \'bōl-shə-ˌvi-zəm\ *n, often cap* : the doctrine or program of the Bolsheviks advocating violent overthrow of capitalism

¹**bol·ster** \'bōl-stər\ *n* : a long pillow or cushion

²**bolster** *vb* : to support with or as if with a bolster; *also* : REINFORCE

¹**bolt** \'bōlt\ *n* **1** : a missile (as an arrow) for a crossbow or catapult **2** : a flash of lightning : THUNDERBOLT **3** : a sliding bar used to fasten a door **4** : a roll of cloth or wallpaper of specified length **5** : a rod with a head at one end and a screw thread at the other used with a nut to fasten objects together **6** : a metal cylinder that drives the cartridge into the chamber of a firearm

²**bolt** *vb* **1** : to move suddenly (as in fright or hurry) : START, DASH **2** : to break away (as from association) ⟨~ from a political platform⟩ **3** : to produce seed prematurely **4** : to secure or fasten with a bolt **5** : to swallow hastily or without chewing

³**bolt** *n* : an act of bolting

bo·lus \'bō-ləs\ *n, pl* **bo·lus·es** **1** : a large pill **2** : a soft mass of chewed food

¹**bomb** \'bäm\ *n* **1** : a fused explosive device designed to detonate under specified conditions (as impact) **2** : an aerosol or foam dispenser (as of insecticide or hair spray) : SPRAY CAN **3** : FAILURE, FLOP **4** : a long pass, shot, or hit

²**bomb** *vb* **1** : to attack with bombs **2** : FAIL ⟨~ed at the audition⟩

bom·bard \bäm-'bärd\ *vb* **1** : to attack esp. with artillery or bombers **2** : to assail persistently **3** : to subject to the impact of rapidly moving particles (as electrons) — **bom·bard·ment** *n*

bom·bar·dier \ˌbäm-bər-'dir\ *n* : a bomber-crew member who releases the bombs

bom·bast \'bäm-ˌbast\ *n* [ME, cotton padding, fr. MF *bombace,* fr. ML *bombax* cotton, alter. of L *bombyx* silkworm, silk, fr. Gk] : pretentious wordy speech or writing — **bom·bas·tic** \bäm-'bas-tik\ *adj* — **bom·bas·ti·cal·ly** \-ti-k(ə-)lē\ *adv*

bom·ba·zine \ˌbäm-bə-'zēn\ *n* **1** : a twilled fabric with silk warp and worsted filling **2** : a silk fabric in twill weave dyed black

bomb·er \'bä-mər\ *n* : one that bombs; *esp* : an airplane for dropping bombs

bomb·proof \'bäm-ˌprüf\ *adj* : safe against the explosive force of bombs

bomb·shell \'bäm-ˌshel\ *n* **1** : BOMB 1 **2** : one that stuns, amazes, or completely upsets

bona fide \'bō-nə-ˌfīd, 'bä-; ˌbō-nə-'fī-dē, -də\ *adj* [L, in good faith] **1** : made in good faith ⟨a *bona fide* agreement⟩ **2** : GENUINE, REAL ⟨a *bona fide* bargain⟩

bo·nan·za \bə-'nan-zə\ *n* [Sp, lit., calm sea, fr. ML *bonacia,* alter. of L *malacia,* fr. Gk *malakia,* lit., softness, fr. *malakos* soft] **1** : something yielding a rich return **2** : EXTRAVAGANZA

bon·bon \'bän-ˌbän\ *n* : a candy with a creamy center and a soft covering (as of chocolate)

¹**bond** \'bänd\ *n* **1** : FETTER **2** : a binding or uniting force or tie ⟨~s of friendship⟩ **3** : an agreement or obligation often made binding by a pledge of money or goods **4** : a person who acts as surety

for another **5** : an interest-bearing certificate of public or private indebtedness **6** : the state of goods subject to supervision pending payment of taxes or duties due

²**bond** *vb* **1** : to assure payment of duties or taxes on (goods) by giving a bond **2** : to insure against losses caused by the acts of ⟨~ a bank teller⟩ **3** : to make or become firmly united as if by bonds ⟨~ iron to copper⟩ **4** : to form a close relationship ⟨~ed with her stepmother⟩

bond·age \'bän-dij\ *n* : SLAVERY, SERVITUDE

bond·hold·er \'bänd-,hōl-dər\ *n* : one that owns a government or corporation bond

bond·ing \'bän-diŋ\ *n* **1** : the formation of a close personal relationship esp. through frequent or constant association **2** : the attaching of a material (as porcelain) to a tooth surface esp. for cosmetic purposes

bond·man \'bänd-mən\ *n* : SLAVE, SERF

¹**bonds·man** \'bändz-mən\ *n* : SURETY 3

²**bondsman** *var of* BONDMAN

bond·wom·an \'bänd-,wu̇-mən\ *n* : a female slave or serf

¹**bone** \'bōn\ *n* **1** : a hard largely calcareous tissue forming most of the skeleton of a vertebrate animal; *also* : one of the pieces of bone making up a vertebrate skeleton **2** : a hard animal substance (as ivory or baleen) similar to true bone **3** : something made of bone — **bone·less** *adj* — **bony** *also* **bon·ey** \'bō-nē\ *adj*

²**bone** *vb* **boned; bon·ing** : to free from bones ⟨~ a chicken⟩

bone black *n* : the black carbon residue from calcined bones used esp. as a pigment

bone marrow *n* : MARROW

bone·meal \'bōn-,mēl\ *n* : crushed or ground bone used esp. as fertilizer or feed

bon·er \'bō-nər\ *n* : a stupid and ridiculous blunder

bone up *vb* **1** : CRAM **3** **2** : to refresh one's memory ⟨boned up on the speech before giving it⟩

bon·fire \'bän-,fī(-ə)r\ *n* [ME *bonefire* a fire of bones, fr. *bone* bone + *fire*] : a large fire built in the open air

bon·go \'bäŋ-gō\ *n, pl* **bongos** *also* **bon·goes** [AmerSp *bongó*] : one of a pair of small tuned drums played with the hands

bon·ho·mie \,bä-nə-'mē\ *n* [F *bonhomie*, fr. *bonhomme* good-natured man, fr. *bon* good + *homme* man] : good-natured easy friendliness

bo·ni·to \bə-'nē-tō\ *n, pl* **-tos** *or* **-to** : any of several medium-sized tunas

bon mot \bōⁿ-'mō\ *n, pl* **bons mots** *same*\ *or* **bon mots** *same*\ [F, lit., good word] : a clever remark

bon·net \'bä-nət\ *n* : a covering (as a cap) for the head; *esp* : a hat for a woman or infant tied under the chin

bon·ny \'bä-nē\ *adj*, **bon·ni·er; -est** *chiefly Brit* : ATTRACTIVE, FAIR; *also* : FINE, EXCELLENT

bon·sai \bōn-'sī, 'bän-,\ *n, pl* **bonsai** [Jp] : a potted plant (as a tree) dwarfed and trained to an artistic shape; *also* : the art of growing such a plant

bo·nus \'bō-nəs\ *n* : something in addition to what is expected

bon vi·vant \,bän-vē-'vänt, ,bōⁿ-vē-'väⁿ\ *n, pl* **bons vivants** \,bän-vē-'vänts, ,bōⁿ-vē-'väⁿ\ *or* **bon vivants** *same*\ [F, lit., good liver] : a person having cultivated, refined, and sociable tastes esp. in food and drink

bon voy·age \,bōⁿ-,vȯi-'äzh, ,bän-; ,bōⁿ-,vwä-'yäzh\ *n* : FAREWELL — often used as an interjection

bony fish *n* : any of a class of fishes (as eels or sturgeons) with a bony rather than a cartilaginous skeleton

bonze \'bänz\ *n* : a Buddhist monk

boo \'bü\ *n, pl* **boos** : a shout of disapproval or contempt — **boo** *vb*

boo·by \'bü-bē\ *n, pl* **boobies** : an awkward foolish person — **DOPE**

booby hatch *n* : a psychiatric hospital

booby prize *n* : an award for the poorest performance in a contest

booby trap *n* : a trap for the unwary; *esp* : a concealed explosive device set to go off when some harmless-looking object is touched — **booby–trap** *vb*

boo·dle \'bü-d²l\ *n* **1** : bribe money **2** : a large amount of money

¹**book** \'bu̇k\ *n* **1** : a set of sheets bound into a volume **2** : a long written or printed narrative or record **3** : a major division of a long literary work **4** *cap* : BIBLE — **in one's book** : in one's own opinion

²**book** *vb* **1** : to engage, reserve, or schedule by or as if by writing in a book ⟨~ seats on a plane⟩ **2** : to enter charges against in a police register

book·case \-,kās\ *n* : a piece of furniture consisting of shelves to hold books

book·end \-,end\ *n* : a support to hold up a row of books

book·ie \'bu̇-kē\ *n* : BOOKMAKER

book·ish \'bu̇-kish\ *adj* **1** : fond of books and reading **2** : inclined to rely unduly on book knowledge

book·keep·er \'bu̇k-,kē-pər\ *n* : a person who records the accounts or transactions of a business — **book·keep·ing** *n*

book·let \'bu̇k-lət\ *n* : PAMPHLET

book·mak·er \'bu̇k-,mā-kər\ *n* : a person who determines odds and receives and pays off bets — **book·mak·ing** *n*

book·mark \-,märk\ *or* **book·mark·er** \-,mär-kər\ *n* **1** : a marker for finding a place in a book **2** : a shortcut to a previously viewed location (as a Web site) on a computer — **bookmark** *vb*

book·mo·bile \'bu̇k-mō-,bēl\ *n* : a truck that serves as a traveling library

book·plate \'bu̇k-,plāt\ *n* : a label pasted in a book to show who owns it

book·sell·er \'bu̇k-,se-lər\ *n* : one that sells books; *esp* : the proprietor of a bookstore

book·shelf \-,shelf\ *n* : a shelf for books

book·worm \'bu̇k-,wərm\ *n* : a person unusually devoted to reading and study

¹**boom** \'büm\ *vb* **1** : to make a deep hol-

low sound : RESOUND **2** : to grow or cause to grow rapidly esp. in number, value, esteem, or importance

²boom *n* **1** : a booming sound or cry **2** : a rapid expansion or increase esp. of economic activity

³boom *n* [D, tree, beam] **1** : a long spar used to extend the bottom of a sail **2** : a line of floating timbers used to obstruct passage or catch floating objects **3** : a beam projecting from the upright pole of a derrick to support or guide the object lifted **4** : a long usu. horizontal supporting arm (as for a microphone)

boom box *n* : a large portable radio and often tape or CD player

boo·mer·ang \'bü-mə-ˌraŋ\ *n* [Dharuk (an Australian aboriginal language) *bumarin*] : a bent or angular club that can be so thrown as to return near the starting point

boom·ing \'bü-miŋ\ *adj* **1** : making a loud deep sound ⟨a ~ voice⟩ **2** : powerfully executed ⟨hit a ~ serve⟩

¹boon \'bün\ *n* [ME *bone* prayer, request, the favor requested, fr. ON *bōn* request] : BENEFIT, BLESSING ✦ *Synonyms* FAVOR, GIFT, LARGESS, PRESENT

²boon *adj* [ME *bon*, fr. AF, good] : CONVIVIAL ⟨a ~ companion⟩

boon·docks \'bün-ˌdäks\ *n pl* [Tagalog (language of the Philippines) *bundok* mountain] **1** : rough country filled with dense brush **2** : a rural area

boon·dog·gle \'bün-ˌdä-gəl, -ˌdȯ-\ *n* : a useless or wasteful project or activity

boor \'bu̇r\ *n* **1** : YOKEL **2** : a rude or insensitive person ✦ *Synonyms* CHURL, LOUT, CLOWN, CLODHOPPER — **boor·ish** *adj*

boost \'büst\ *vb* **1** : to push up from below **2** : INCREASE, RAISE ⟨~ prices⟩ **3** : AID, PROMOTE ⟨voted a bonus to ~ morale⟩ — **boost** *n* — **boost·er** *n*

¹boot \'büt\ *n, chiefly dial* : something to equalize a trade — **to boot** : BESIDES

²boot *vb, archaic* : AVAIL, PROFIT

³boot *n*. **1** : a covering for the foot and leg **2** : a protective sheath (as of a flower) **3** *Brit* : an automobile trunk **4** : KICK; *also* : a discharge from employment **5** : a navy or marine corps trainee

⁴boot *vb* **1** : KICK **2** : to eject or discharge summarily **3** : to load or become loaded into a computer from a disk **4** : to start or become ready for use esp. by booting a program ⟨~ up the computer⟩

boot·black \'büt-ˌblak\ *n* : a person who shines shoes

boot camp *n* **1** : a navy or marine corps training camp **2** : a facility with a rigorous disciplinary program for young offenders

boo·tee *or* **boo·tie** \'bü-tē\ *n* : an infant's knitted or crocheted sock

booth \'büth\ *n, pl* **booths** \'büthz, 'büths\ **1** : a small enclosed stall (as at a fair) **2** : a small enclosure giving privacy for a person ⟨voting ~⟩ ⟨telephone ~⟩ **3** : a restaurant accommodation having a table between backed benches

boot·leg \'büt-ˌleg\ *vb* : to make, transport, or sell (as liquor) illegally — **bootleg** *adj or n* — **boot·leg·ger** *n*

boot·less \'büt-ləs\ *adj* : USELESS ✦ *Synonyms* FUTILE, VAIN, ABORTIVE, FRUITLESS — **boot·less·ly** *adv* — **boot·less·ness** *n*

¹boo·ty \'bü-tē\ *n, pl* **booties** : PLUNDER, SPOIL

²booty *also* **boo·tie** \'bü-tē\ *n, pl* **booties** *slang* : BUTTOCKS

¹booze \'büz\ *vb* **boozed; booz·ing** : to drink liquor to excess — **booz·er** *n*

²booze *n* : intoxicating liquor — **boozy** *adj*

bop \'bäp\ *vb* **bopped; bop·ping** : HIT, SOCK — **bop** *n*

BOQ *abbr* bachelor officers' quarters

bor *abbr* borough

bo·rate \'bȯr-ˌāt\ *n* : a salt or ester of boric acid

bo·rax \'bȯr-ˌaks\ *n* : a crystalline borate of sodium that occurs as a mineral and is used as a flux and cleanser

bor·del·lo \bȯr-'de-lō\ *n, pl* **-los** [It] : BROTHEL

¹bor·der \'bȯr-dər\ *n* **1** : EDGE, MARGIN **2** : BOUNDARY, FRONTIER ✦ *Synonyms* RIM, BRIM, BRINK, FRINGE, PERIMETER

²border *vb* **bor·dered; bor·der·ing 1** : to put a border on **2** : ADJOIN **3** : VERGE

border collie *n, often cap B* : any of a British breed of medium-sized long-haired sheepdogs

bor·der·land \'bȯr-dər-ˌland\ *n* **1** : territory at or near a border **2** : an outlying or intermediate region often not clearly defined

bor·der·line \-ˌlīn\ *adj* : being in an intermediate position or state; *esp* : not quite up to what is standard or expected ⟨~ intelligence⟩

¹bore \'bȯr\ *vb* **bored; bor·ing 1** : to make a hole in with or as if with a drill **2** : to make (as a well) by boring or digging away material ✦ *Synonyms* PERFORATE, DRILL, PRICK, PUNCTURE — **bor·er** *n*

²bore *n* **1** : a hole made by or as if by boring **2** : a cylindrical cavity **3** : the diameter of a hole or tube; *esp* : the interior diameter of a gun barrel or engine cylinder

³bore *past of* BEAR

⁴bore *n* : a tidal flood with a high abrupt front

⁵bore *n* : one that causes boredom

⁶bore *vb* **bored; bor·ing** : to weary with tedious dullness

bo·re·al \'bȯr-ē-əl\ *adj* : of, relating to, or located in northern regions

bore·dom \'bȯr-dəm\ *n* : the condition of being bored

bo·ric acid \'bȯr-ik-\ *n* : a white crystalline weak acid that contains boron and is used esp. as an antiseptic

born \'bȯrn\ *adj* **1** : brought into life by birth **2** : NATIVE ⟨American-*born*⟩ **3** : having special natural abilities or character from birth ⟨a ~ leader⟩

born–again *adj* : having experienced a revival of a personal faith or conviction ⟨a ~ believer⟩ ⟨a ~ liberal⟩

borne *past part of* BEAR

bo·ron \'bōr-ˌän\ *n* : a chemical element that occurs in nature only in combination (as in borax)

bor·ough \'bər-ō\ *n* [ME *burgh*, fr. OE *burg* fortified town] **1** : a British town that sends one or more members to Parliament; *also* : an incorporated British urban area **2** : an incorporated town or village in some U.S. states; *also* : any of the five political divisions of New York City **3** : a civil division of the state of Alaska corresponding to a county in most other states

bor·row \'bär-ō\ *vb* **1** : to take or receive (something) temporarily and with intent to return ⟨∼ed my car⟩ **2** : to take into possession or use from another source : DERIVE, APPROPRIATE ⟨∼ a metaphor⟩

borscht \'bȯrsht\ *or* **borsch** \'bȯrsh\ *n* [Yiddish *borsht* & Ukrainian & Russ *borshch*] : a soup made mainly from beets

bosh \'bäsh\ *n* [Turk *boş* empty] : foolish talk or action : NONSENSE

bosky \'bäs-kē\ *adj* : covered with trees or shrubs

¹bos·om \'bu̇-zəm, 'bü-\ *n* **1** : the front of the human chest; *esp* : the female breasts **2** : the seat of secret thoughts and feelings **3** : the part of a garment covering the breast — **bos·omed** \-zəmd\ *adj*

²bosom *adj* : CLOSE, INTIMATE

¹boss \'bäs, 'bȯs\ *n* : a knoblike ornament : STUD

²boss *vb* : to ornament with bosses

³boss \'bȯs\ *n* **1** : one (as a foreman or manager) exercising control or supervision **2** : a politician who controls votes or dictates policies — **bossy** *adj*

⁴boss \'bȯs\ *vb* : to act as or in the manner of a boss

bosun *var of* BOATSWAIN

bot *abbr* botanical; botanist; botany

bot·a·ny \'bät-ə-nē, 'bät-nē\ *n, pl* **-nies** : a branch of biology dealing with plants and plant life **2** : plant life (as of a given region); *also* : the biology of a plant or plant group — **bo·tan·i·cal** \bə-'ta-ni-kəl\ *adj or n* — **bo·tan·i·cal·ly** \-k-lē\ *adv* — **bot·a·nist** *n* — **bot·a·nize** \'bät-ə-ˌnīz\ *vb*

botch \'bäch\ *vb* : to foul up hopelessly : BUNGLE — **botch** *n*

¹both \'bōth\ *pron* : both ones : the one as well as the other

²both *conj* — used as a function word to indicate and stress the inclusion of each of two or more things specified by coordinated words, phrases, or clauses ⟨∼ New York and London⟩

³both *adj* : being the two : affecting the one and the other

both·er \'bä-thər\ *vb* **1** : PESTER, TROUBLE ⟨was ∼ed by bees⟩ **2** : to concern oneself : make an effort ⟨didn't ∼ asking⟩ ✦ *Synonyms* VEX, ANNOY, IRK, PROVOKE — **bother** *n* — **both·er·some** \-səm\ *adj*

¹bot·tle \'bä-tᵊl\ *n* **1** : a container (as of glass) with a narrow neck and usu. no

handles **2** : the quantity held by a bottle **3** : intoxicating liquor

²bottle *vb* **bot·tled**; **bot·tling** **1** : to confine as if in a bottle : RESTRAIN ⟨*bottled* up his anger⟩ **2** : to put into a bottle

bot·tle·neck \'bä-tᵊl-ˌnek\ *n* **1** : a narrow passage or point of congestion **2** : something that obstructs or impedes

¹bot·tom \'bä-təm\ *n* **1** : an under or supporting surface; *also* : BUTTOCKS **2** : the surface on which a body of water lies **3** : the lowest part or place; *also* : an inferior or position ⟨start at the ∼⟩ **4** : BOTTOMLAND **5** : BASIS, SOURCE ⟨get to the ∼ of this mystery⟩ **6** : a quark with a charge of -⅓ and a measured energy of approximately 5 billion electron volts — **bottom** *adj* — **bot·tom·less** *adj*

²bottom *vb* **1** : to furnish with a bottom **2** : to reach the bottom **3** : to reach a point where a decline is halted or reversed — usu. used with *out*

bot·tom·land \'bä-təm-ˌland\ *n* : low land along a river

bottom line *n* **1** : the essential point : CRUX **2** : the final result : OUTCOME

bot·u·lism \'bä-chə-ˌli-zəm\ *n* : an acute paralytic disease caused by a bacterial toxin (**bot·u·li·num toxin** \ˌbä-chə-'lī-nəm-\) esp. in tainted food

bou·doir \'bü-ˌdwär, 'bü-, ˌbü-', ˌbü-'\ *n* [F, fr. *bouder* to pout] : a woman's dressing room or bedroom

bouf·fant \bü-'fänt, 'bü-ˌfänt\ *adj* [F] : puffed out ⟨∼ hairdos⟩

bough \'bau̇\ *n* : a usu. large or main branch of a tree

bought *past and past part of* BUY

bouil·la·baisse \ˌbü-yə-'bās\ *n* [F] : a highly seasoned fish stew made with at least two kinds of fish

bouil·lon \'bü-ˌyän, 'bu̇l-ˌyän, -yən\ *n* : a clear soup made usu. from beef

boul·der *also* **bowl·der** \'bōl-dər\ *n* : a large detached rounded or worn mass of rock — **boul·dered** \-dərd\ *adj*

bou·le·vard \'bu̇-lə-ˌvärd, 'bü-\ *n* [F, modif. of MD *bolwerc* bulwark] : a broad often landscaped thoroughfare

bounce \'bau̇ns\ *vb* **bounced**; **bounc·ing** **1** : to cause to rebound ⟨∼ a ball⟩ **2** : to rebound after striking **3** : to issue (a check) from an account with insufficient funds — **bounce** *n* — **bouncy** \'bau̇n-sē\ *adj*

bounc·er \'bau̇n-sər\ *n* : a person employed in a public place to remove disorderly persons

¹bound \'bau̇nd\ *adj* : intending to go

²bound *n* : LIMIT, BOUNDARY — **bound·less** *adj* — **bound·less·ness** *n*

³bound *vb* **1** : to set limits to **2** : to form the boundary of **3** : to name the boundaries of

⁴bound *past and past part of* BIND

⁵bound *adj* **1** : constrained by or as if by bonds : CONFINED, OBLIGED **2** : enclosed in a binding or cover **3** : RESOLVED, DETERMINED; *also* : SURE

⁶bound *n* **1** : LEAP, JUMP **2** : REBOUND, BOUNCE

⁷**bound** vb : SPRING, BOUNCE

bound·ary \'baùn-drē\ n, pl **-aries** : something that marks or fixes a limit or extent (as of territory) ◆ **Synonyms** BORDER, FRONTIER, MARCH

bound·en \'baùn-dən\ adj : BINDING

boun·te·ous \'baùn-tē-əs\ adj 1 : GENEROUS 2 : ABUNDANT — **boun·te·ous·ly** adv — **boun·te·ous·ness** n

boun·ti·ful \'baùn-ti-fəl\ adj 1 : giving freely 2 : PLENTIFUL — **boun·ti·ful·ly** adv — **boun·ti·ful·ness** n

boun·ty \'baùn-tē\ n, pl **bounties** [ME bounte goodness, fr. AF bunté, fr. L bonitas, fr. bonus good] 1 : GENEROSITY 2 : something given liberally 3 : a reward, premium, or subsidy given usu. for doing something

bou·quet \bō-'kā, bü-\ n [F, fr. MF, thicket, bunch of flowers, fr. OF (dial. of Normandy and Picardy) bosquet thicket, fr. bosc forest] 1 : flowers picked and fastened together in a bunch 2 : a distinctive aroma (as of wine) ◆ **Synonyms** SCENT, FRAGRANCE, PERFUME, REDOLENCE

bour·bon \'bər-bən\ n : a whiskey distilled from a corn mash

bour·geois \'bùrzh-ˌwä, bùrzh-'wä\ n, pl **bourgeois** \same or -ˌwäz, -'wäz\ [MF, fr. OF burgeis townsman, fr. burc, borg town, fr. L burgus fortified place, of Gmc origin] : a middle-class person — **bourgeois** adj

bour·geoi·sie \ˌbùrzh-ˌwä-'zē\ n : a social order dominated by bourgeois

bourne also **bourn** \'bōrn, 'bùrn\ n : BOUNDARY; also : DESTINATION

bourse \'bùrs\ n : a European stock exchange

bout \'baùt\ n 1 : CONTEST, MATCH 2 : OUTBREAK, ATTACK ⟨a ~ of measles⟩ 3 : SESSION

bou·tique \bü-'tēk\ n : a small fashionable specialty shop

bou·ton·niere \ˌbü-t³n-'iər\ n : a flower or bouquet worn in a buttonhole

¹**bo·vine** \'bō-ˌvīn, -ˌvēn\ adj 1 : of or relating to bovines 2 : having qualities (as placidity or dullness) characteristic of oxen or cows

²**bovine** n : any of a group of mammals including oxen, buffalo, and their close relatives

bovine spon·gi·form encephalopathy \-'spən-ji-ˌfórm-\ n : MAD COW DISEASE

¹**bow** \'baù\ vb 1 : SUBMIT, YIELD 2 : to bend the head or body (as in submission, courtesy, or assent) 3 : DEBUT ⟨the play ~s next month⟩

²**bow** n : an act or posture of bowing

³**bow** \'bō\ n 1 : BEND, ARCH; esp : RAINBOW 2 : a weapon for shooting arrows; also : ARCHER 3 : a knot formed by doubling a line into two or more loops 4 : a wooden rod strung with horsehairs for playing an instrument of the violin family

⁴**bow** \'bō\ vb 1 : BEND, CURVE 2 : to play (an instrument) with a bow

⁵**bow** \'baù\ n : the forward part of a ship — **bow** adj

bowd·ler·ise Brit var of BOWDLERIZE

bowd·ler·ize \'bōd-lə-ˌrīz, 'baùd-\ vb **-ized; -iz·ing** : to expurgate by omitting parts considered vulgar

bow·el \'baù-(ə)l\ n 1 : INTESTINE; also : one of the divisions of the intestine — usu. used in pl. 2 pl : the inmost parts ⟨the ~s of the earth⟩

bow·er \'baù-(ə)r\ n : a shelter of boughs or vines : ARBOR

¹**bowl** \'bōl\ n 1 : a concave vessel used to hold liquids 2 : a drinking vessel 3 : a bowl-shaped part or structure — **bowl·ful** \-ˌfül\ n

²**bowl** n 1 : a ball for rolling on a level surface in bowling 2 : a cast of the ball in bowling

³**bowl** vb 1 : to play a game of bowling; also : to roll a ball in bowling 2 : to travel (as in a vehicle) rapidly and smoothly 3 : to strike or knock down with a moving object

bowlder var of BOULDER

bow-legged \'bō-ˌle-gəd\ adj : having legs that bow outward at or below the knee — **bow-leg** \'bō-ˌleg\ n

¹**bowl·er** \'bō-lər\ n : a person who bowls

²**bowl·er** \'bō-lər\ n : DERBY 3

bow·line \'bō-lən, -ˌlīn\ n : a knot used to form a loop that neither slips nor jams

bowl·ing \'bō-liŋ\ n : any of various games in which balls are rolled on a green or alley at an object or a group of objects

bow·man \'bō-mən\ n : ARCHER

bow·sprit \'baù-ˌsprit\ n : a spar projecting forward from the prow of a ship

bow·string \'bō-ˌstriŋ\ n : the cord connecting the two ends of a shooting bow

¹**box** \'bäks\ n, pl **box** or **box·es** : an evergreen shrub or small tree used esp. for hedges

²**box** n 1 : a rigid typically rectangular receptacle often with a cover; also : the quantity held by a box 2 : a small compartment (as for a group of theater patrons); also : a boxlike receptacle or division 3 : a usu. rectangular space demarcated for a particular purpose ⟨the batter's ~⟩ 4 : PREDICAMENT — **boxy** \'bäk-sē\ adj

³**box** vb : to enclose in or as if in a box

⁴**box** n : a punch or slap esp. on the ear

⁵**box** vb 1 : to strike with the hand 2 : to engage in boxing with

box·car \'bäks-ˌkär\ n : a roofed freight car usu. with sliding doors in the sides

box cutter n : a small cutting tool with a retractable razor blade

¹**box·er** \'bäk-sər\ n 1 : a person who engages in boxing 2 pl : BOXER SHORTS

²**boxer** n : any of a German breed of compact medium-sized dogs with a short usu. fawn or brindled coat

boxer shorts n pl : men's loose-fitting shorts worn as underwear

box·ing \'bäk-siŋ\ n : the sport of fighting with the fists

box office n : an office (as in a theater) where admission tickets are sold

box turtle n : any of several No. American land turtles able to withdraw completely into their shell

box·wood \'bäks-ˌwud\ n : the tough hard wood of the box; *also* : a box tree or shrub

boy \'boi\ n **1** : a male child : YOUTH **2** : SON — **boy·hood** \-ˌhud\ n — **boy·ish** adj — **boy·ish·ly** adv — **boy·ish·ness** n

boy·cott \'boi-ˌkät\ vb [Charles C. *Boycott* †1897 Eng. land agent in Ireland who was ostracized for refusing to reduce rents] : to refrain from having any dealings with — **boycott** n

boy·friend \'boi-ˌfrend\ n **1** : a male friend **2** : a frequent or regular male companion in a romantic relationship

Boy Scout n : a member of any of various national scouting programs (as the Boy Scouts of America)

boy·sen·ber·ry \'boi-zᵊn-ˌber-ē, 'bois-\ n : a large reddish-black fruit with a raspberry flavor; *also* : the hybrid bramble bearing it developed by crossing blackberries and raspberries

bo·zo \'bō-ˌzō\ n, pl **bozos** : a foolish or incompetent person

bp abbr **1** bishop **2** birthplace

BP abbr **1** batting practice **2** blood pressure **3** boiling point

bpl abbr birthplace

BPOE abbr Benevolent and Protective Order of Elks

br abbr **1** branch **2** brass **3** brown

¹Br abbr Britain; British

²Br symbol bromine

BR abbr bedroom

bra \'brä\ n : BRASSIERE

¹brace \'brās\ vb, **braced; brac·ing 1** archaic : to make fast : BIND **2** : to tighten preparatory to use; *also* : to get ready for : prepare oneself **3** : INVIGORATE **4** : to furnish or support with a brace; *also* : STRENGTHEN **5** : to set firmly **6** : to gain courage or confidence

²brace n, pl **brac·es 1** or pl **brace** : two of a kind ⟨a ~ of dogs⟩ **2** : a crankshaped device for turning a bit **3** : something (as a tie, prop, or clamp) that distributes, directs, or resists pressure or weight **4** pl : SUSPENDERS **5** : an appliance for supporting a body part (as the shoulders) **6** pl : a dental appliance used to exert pressure to straighten misaligned teeth **7** : one of two marks { } used to connect words or items to be considered together

brace·let \'brā-slət\ n [ME, fr. MF, dim. of *bras* arm, fr. L *bracchium*, fr. Gk *brachiôn*] : an ornamental band or chain worn around the wrist

bra·ce·ro \brä-'ser-ō\ n, pl **-ros** : a Mexican laborer admitted to the U.S. esp. for seasonal farm work

brack·en \'bra-kən\ n : a large coarse fern; *also* : a growth of such ferns

¹brack·et \'bra-kət\ n **1** : a projecting framework or arm designed to support weight; *also* : a shelf on such framework **2** : one of a pair of punctuation marks [ ] used esp. to enclose interpolated matter **3** : a continuous section of a series; *esp* : one of a graded series of income groups

²bracket vb **1** : to furnish or fasten with brackets **2** : to place within brackets; *also* : to separate or group with or as if with brackets

brack·ish \'bra-kish\ adj : somewhat salty — **brack·ish·ness** n

bract \'brakt\ n : an often modified leaf on or at the base of a flower stalk

brad \'brad\ n : a slender nail with a small head

brae \'brā\ n, chiefly Scot : a hillside esp. along a river

brag \'brag\ vb **bragged; brag·ging** : to talk or assert boastfully — **brag** n — **brag·ger** n

brag·ga·do·cio \ˌbra-gə-'dō-shē-ˌō, -sē-, -chē-\ n, pl **-cios 1** : BRAGGART, BOASTER **2** : empty boasting **3** : arrogant pretension : COCKINESS

brag·gart \'bra-gərt\ n : one who brags

Brah·man or **Brah·min** \'brä-mən for 1; 'brä-, 'brā-, 'bra- for 2\ n **1** : a Hindu of the highest caste traditionally assigned to the priesthood **2** : any of a breed of large vigorous humped cattle developed in the southern U.S. from Indian stock **3** usu **Brahmin** : a person of high social standing and cultivated intellect and taste

Brah·man·ism \'brä-mə-ˌni-zəm\ n : orthodox Hinduism

¹braid \'brād\ vb **1** : to form (strands) into a braid : PLAIT; *also* : to make from braids **2** : to ornament with braid

²braid n **1** : a length of braided hair **2** : a cord or ribbon of three or more interwoven strands; *esp* : a narrow ornamental one

braille \'brāl\ n, often cap : a system of writing for the blind that uses characters made up of raised dots

¹brain \'brān\ n **1** : the part of the vertebrate central nervous system enclosed in the skull and continuous with the spinal cord that is composed of neurons and supporting structures and is the center of thought and nervous system control; *also* : a centralized mass of nerve tissue in an invertebrate **2** : INTELLECT, INTELLIGENCE — often used in pl. — **brained** \'brānd\ adj — **brain·less** adj — **brainy** adj

²brain vb **1** : to kill by smashing the skull **2** : to hit on the head

brain·child \'brān-ˌchī(-ə)ld\ n : a product of one's creative imagination

brain death n : final cessation of activity in the central nervous system esp. as indicated by a flat electroencephalogram — **brain-dead** \-ˌded\ adj

brain drain n : the departure of educated or professional people from one country, sector, or field to another usu. for better pay or living conditions

brain·storm \-ˌstorm\ n : a sudden inspiration or idea — **brainstorm** vb

brain-teas·er \-ˌtē-zər\ n : a challenging puzzle

brain·wash·ing \'brān-ˌwò-shiŋ, -ˌwä-\ n **1** : a forcible indoctrination to induce someone to give up basic political, social, or religious beliefs and attitudes and to accept contrasting regimented ideas **2** : persuasion by propaganda or salesmanship — **brain·wash** vb

brain wave n **1** : BRAINSTORM **2** : rhythmic fluctuations of voltage between parts of the brain; also : a current produced by brain waves

braise \'brāz\ vb **braised; brais·ing** : to cook slowly in fat and little moisture in a closed pot

¹brake \'brāk\ n : a common bracken fern

²brake n : rough or wet land heavily overgrown (as with thickets or reeds)

³brake n : a device for slowing or stopping motion esp. by friction — **brake·less** adj

⁴brake vb **braked; brak·ing** **1** : to slow or stop by or as if by a brake **2** : to apply a brake

brake·man \'brāk-mən\ n : a train crew member who inspects the train and assists the conductor

bram·ble \'bram-bəl\ n : any of a large genus of prickly shrubs (as a blackberry) related to the roses; also : any rough prickly shrub or vine — **bram·bly** \-b(ə-)lē\ adj

bran \'bran\ n : the edible broken husks of cereal grain sifted from flour or meal

¹branch \'branch\ n [ME, fr. AF branche, fr. LL branca paw] **1** : a natural subdivision (as a bough or twig) of a plant stem **2** : a division (as of an antler or a river) related to a whole like a plant branch to its stem **3** : a discrete element of a complex system (the executive ∼); esp : a division of a family descended from one ancestor — **branched** \'brancht\ adj

²branch vb **1** : to develop branches **2** : DIVERGE **3** : to extend activities (the business is ∼ing out)

¹brand \'brand\ n **1** : a piece of charred or burning wood **2** : a mark made (as by burning) usu. to identify; also : a mark of disgrace : STIGMA **3** : a class of goods identified as the product of a particular firm or producer **4** : a distinctive kind (my own ∼ of humor)

²brand vb **1** : to mark with a brand **2** : STIGMATIZE (was ∼ed a traitor)

bran·dish \'bran-dish\ vb : to shake or wave menacingly (∼ a knife) ◆ **Synonyms** FLOURISH, FLASH, FLAUNT

brand–new \'bran-'nü, -'nyü\ adj : conspicuously new and unused

bran·dy \'bran-dē\ n, pl **brandies** [short for brandywine, fr. D brandewijn, fr. MD brantwijn, fr. brant distilled + wijn wine] : a liquor distilled from wine or fermented fruit juice — **brandy** vb

brash \'brash\ adj **1** : IMPETUOUS, AUDACIOUS **2** : aggressively self-assertive — **brash·ly** adv — **brash·ness** n

brass \'bras\ n **1** : an alloy of copper and zinc; also : an object of brass **2** : brazen self-assurance **3** : persons of high rank (as in the military) — **brassy** adj

bras·siere \brə-'zir\ n : a woman's close-fitting undergarment designed to support the breasts

brat \'brat\ n : an ill-behaved child — **brat·ti·ness** n — **brat·ty** adj

bra·va·do \brə-'vä-dō\ n, pl **-does** or **-dos** **1** : blustering swaggering conduct **2** : a show of bravery

¹brave \'brāv\ adj **brav·er; brav·est** [MF, fr. It & Sp bravo courageous, wild, prob. fr. L barbarus barbarous] **1** : showing courage **2** : EXCELLENT, SPLENDID ◆ **Synonyms** BOLD, INTREPID, COURAGEOUS, VALIANT — **brave·ly** adv

²brave vb **braved; brav·ing** : to face or endure bravely

³brave n : an American Indian warrior

brav·ery \'brā-və-rē\ n, pl **-er·ies** : COURAGE

bra·vo \'brä-vō\ n, pl **bravos** : a shout of approval — often used as an interjection in applauding

bra·vu·ra \brə-'vyùr-ə, -'vùr-\ n **1** : a florid brilliant musical style **2** : self-assured brilliant performance — **bravura** adj

brawl \'bról\ n : a noisy quarrel ◆ **Synonyms** FRACAS, ROW, RUMPUS, SCRAP, FRAY, MELEE — **brawl** vb — **brawl·er** n

brawn \'brón\ n : strong muscles; also : muscular strength — **brawn·i·ness** n — **brawny** adj

bray \'brā\ n : the characteristic harsh cry of a donkey — **bray** vb

braze \'brāz\ vb **brazed; braz·ing** : to solder with an alloy (as brass) that melts at a lower temperature than the metals being joined — **braz·er** n

¹bra·zen \'brā-z²n\ adj **1** : made of brass **2** : sounding harsh and loud **3** : of the color of brass **4** : marked by contemptuous boldness (a ∼ rebuff) — **bra·zen·ly** adv — **bra·zen·ness** n

²brazen vb : to face boldly or defiantly

¹bra·zier \'brā-zhər\ n : a worker in brass

²brazier n **1** : a vessel holding burning coals (as for heating) **2** : a device on which food is grilled

Bra·zil nut \brə-'zil-\ n : a triangular oily edible nut borne in large capsules by a tall So. American tree; also : the tree

¹breach \'brēch\ n **1** : a breaking of a law, obligation, tie (as of friendship), or standard (as of conduct) **2** : an interruption or opening made by or as if by breaking through ◆ **Synonyms** VIOLATION, TRANSGRESSION, INFRINGEMENT, TRESPASS

²breach vb **1** : to make a breach in **2** : to leap out of water (whales ∼ing)

¹bread \'bred\ n **1** : baked food made basically of flour or meal **2** : FOOD

²bread vb : to cover with bread crumbs

bread·bas·ket \'bred-ˌbas-kət\ n : a major cereal-producing region

bread·fruit \-ˌfrüt\ n : a round usu. seedless fruit resembling bread in color and texture when baked; also : a tall tropical tree related to the mulberry and bearing breadfruit

bread·stuff \-ˌstəf\ n : GRAIN, FLOUR

breadth \'bredth, 'bretth\ n **1** : WIDTH **2** : comprehensive quality : SCOPE (her ∼ of knowledge)

bread·win·ner \'bred-ˌwi-nər\ *n* : a member of a family whose wages supply its livelihood

¹break \'brāk\ *vb* **broke** \'brōk\; **bro·ken** \'brō-kən\; **break·ing 1** : to separate into parts usu. suddenly or violently; *also* : to render inoperable ⟨*broke* his watch⟩ **2** : TRANSGRESS ⟨~ a law⟩ **3** : to force a way into, out of, or through **4** : to disrupt the order or unity of ⟨~ ranks⟩ ⟨~ up a gang⟩; *also* : to bring to submission or helplessness **5** : EXCEED, SURPASS ⟨~ a record⟩ **6** : RUIN **7** : to make known ⟨~ the bad news⟩ **8** : HALT, INTERRUPT; *also* : to act or change abruptly (as a course or activity) **9** : to come esp. suddenly into being or notice ⟨as day ~s⟩ **10** : to fail under stress **11** : HAPPEN, DEVELOP ⟨report news as it ~s⟩ — **break·able** *adj or n* — **break into 1** : to begin with a sudden throwing off of restraint ⟨*broke into* tears⟩ **2** : to make entry or entrance into ⟨*break into* show business⟩

²break *n* **1** : an act of breaking **2** : a result of breaking; *esp* : an interruption of continuity ⟨coffee ~⟩ ⟨a ~ for the commercial⟩ **3** : a stroke of luck

break·age \'brā-kij\ *n* **1** : loss due to things broken **2** : the action of breaking **3** : articles or amount broken

break·down \'brāk-ˌdau̇n\ *n* **1** : functional failure; *esp* : a physical, mental, or nervous collapse **2** : DISINTEGRATION **3** : DECOMPOSITION **4** : ANALYSIS, CLASSIFICATION — **break down** *vb*

break·er \'brā-kər\ *n* **1** : one that breaks **2** : a wave that breaks into foam (as against the shore)

break·fast \'brek-fəst\ *n* : the first meal of the day — **breakfast** *vb*

break in *vb* **1** : to enter a building by force **2** : INTERRUPT; *also* : INTRUDE **3** : TRAIN — **break–in** \'brāk-ˌin\ *n*

break·neck \'brāk-ˈnek\ *adj* : very fast or dangerous ⟨~ speed⟩

break out *vb* **1** : to develop or erupt suddenly or with force **2** : to develop a skin rash

break·through \'brāk-ˌthrü\ *n* **1** : an act or instance of breaking through an obstruction or defensive line **2** : a sudden advance in knowledge or technique ⟨a scientific ~⟩

break·up \-ˌəp\ *n* **1** : DISSOLUTION **2** : a division into smaller units — **break up** *vb*

break·wa·ter \'brāk-ˌwȯ-tər, -ˌwä-\ *n* : a structure protecting a harbor or beach from the force of waves

bream \'brim, 'brēm\ *n, pl* **bream** *or* **breams** : any of various small freshwater sunfishes

breast \'brest\ *n* **1** : either of the pair of mammary glands extending from the front of the chest esp. in pubescent and adult human females **2** : the front part of the body between the neck and the abdomen **3** : the seat of emotion and thought

breast·bone \'brest-ˌbōn\ *n* : STERNUM

breast–feed \-ˌfēd\ *vb* : to feed (a baby) from a mother's breast

breast·plate \-ˌplāt\ *n* : a metal plate of armor for the breast

breast·stroke \-ˌstrōk\ *n* : a swimming stroke executed by extending both arms forward and then sweeping them back with palms out while kicking backward and outward with both legs

breast·work \-ˌwərk\ *n* : a temporary fortification

breath \'breth\ *n* **1** : the act or power of breathing **2** : a slight breeze **3** : air inhaled or exhaled in breathing **4** : spoken sound **5** : SPIRIT — **breath·less** *adj* — **breath·less·ly** *adv* — **breath·less·ness** *n* — **breathy** \'bre-thē\ *adj*

breathe \'brēth\ *vb* **breathed**; **breath·ing 1** : to inhale and exhale **2** : LIVE **3** : to halt for rest **4** : to utter softly or secretly — **breath·able** *adj*

breath·er \'brē-thər\ *n* **1** : one that breathes **2** : a short rest

breath·tak·ing \'breth-ˌtā-kiŋ\ *adj* **1** : making one out of breath **2** : EXCITING, THRILLING ⟨~ beauty⟩ — **breath·tak·ing·ly** *adv*

brec·cia \'bre-chē-ə, -chə\ *n* : a rock composed of sharp fragments held in fine-grained material

breech \'brēch\ *n* **1** *pl* \usu 'bri-chəz\ : pants ending near the knee **2** : BUTTOCKS, RUMP **3** : the part of a firearm at the rear of the barrel

¹breed \'brēd\ *vb* **bred** \'bred\; **breed·ing 1** : BEGET; *also* : ORIGINATE **2** : to propagate sexually; *also* : MATE **3** : BRING UP, NURTURE **4** : to produce (fissionable material) from material that is not fissionable ♦ **Synonyms** GENERATE, REPRODUCE, PROCREATE, PROPAGATE — **breed·er** *n*

²breed *n* **1** : a strain of similar and presumably related plants or animals usu. developed in domestication **2** : KIND, SORT, CLASS

breeding *n* **1** : ANCESTRY **2** : training in polite social interaction **3** : sexual propagation of plants or animals

¹breeze \'brēz\ *n* **1** : a light wind **2** : CINCH, SNAP — **breeze·less** *adj*

²breeze *vb* **breezed**; **breez·ing** : to progress quickly and easily

breeze·way \'brēz-ˌwā\ *n* : a roofed open passage connecting two buildings (as a house and garage)

breezy \'brē-zē\ *adj* **1** : swept by breezes **2** : briskly informal ⟨~ prose⟩ — **breez·i·ly** \'brē-zə-lē\ *adv* — **breez·i·ness** \-zē-nəs\ *n*

breth·ren \'breth-rən, 'bre-thə-; 'brethərn\ *pl of* BROTHER — used esp. in formal or solemn address

Brethren *n pl* : members of one of several Protestant denominations originating chiefly in a German religious movement and stressing personal religious experience

bre·via·ry \'brē-vyə-rē, -vē-ˌer-ē\ *n, pl* **-ries** *often cap* : a book of prayers, hymns, psalms, and readings used by Roman Catholic priests

brev·i·ty \'bre-və-tē\ *n, pl* **-ties** 1 : shortness or conciseness of expression 2 : shortness of duration

brew \'brü\ *vb* 1 : to prepare (as beer) by steeping, boiling, and fermenting 2 : to prepare (as tea) by steeping in hot water — **brew** *n* — **brew·er** *n* — **brew·ery** \'brü-ə-rē, 'brù(-ə)r-ē\ *n*

¹**bri·ar** *also* **bri·er** \'brī-ər\ *n* : a plant (as a bramble or rose) with a thorny or prickly usu. woody stem; *also* : a mass or twig of these — **bri·ary** \'brī-ər-ē\ *adj*

²**briar** *n* : a tobacco pipe made from the root or stem of a European heath

¹**bribe** \'brīb\ *n* [ME, morsel given to a beggar, bribe, fr. AF, morsel] : something (as money or a favor) given or promised to a person to influence conduct

²**bribe** *vb* **bribed; brib·ing** : to influence by offering a bribe — **brib·able** *adj* — **brib·er** *n* — **brib·ery** \'brī-bə-rē\ *n*

bric-a-brac \'bri-kə-ˌbrak\ *n pl* [F] : small ornamental articles

¹**brick** \'brik\ *n* : a block molded from moist clay and hardened by heat used esp. for building

²**brick** *vb* : to close, cover, or pave with bricks

brick·bat \'brik-ˌbat\ *n* 1 : a piece of a hard material (as a brick) esp. when thrown as a missile 2 : an uncomplimentary remark

brick·lay·er \'brik-ˌlā-ər\ *n* : a person who builds or paves with bricks — **brick·lay·ing** *n*

¹**brid·al** \'brī-dᵊl\ *n* [ME *bridale*, fr. OE *brȳdealu*, fr. *brȳd* bride + *ealu* ale] : MARRIAGE, WEDDING

²**bridal** *adj* : of or relating to a bride or a wedding

bride \'brīd\ *n* : a woman just married or about to be married

bride·groom \'brīd-ˌgrüm, -ˌgrùm\ *n* : a man just married or about to be married

brides·maid \'brīdz-ˌmād\ *n* : a woman who attends a bride at her wedding

¹**bridge** \'brij\ *n* 1 : a structure built over a depression or obstacle for use as a passageway 2 : something (as the upper part of the nose) resembling a bridge in form or function 3 : a curved piece raising the strings of a musical instrument 4 : the forward part of a ship's superstructure from which it is navigated 5 : an artificial replacement for missing teeth

²**bridge** *vb* **bridged; bridg·ing** : to build a bridge over — **bridge·able** *adj*

³**bridge** *n* : a card game for four players developed from whist

bridge·head \-ˌhed\ *n* : an advanced position seized in enemy territory

bridge·work \-ˌwərk\ *n* : dental bridges

¹**bri·dle** \'brī-dᵊl\ *n* 1 : headgear with which a horse is controlled 2 : CURB, RESTRAINT

²**bridle** *vb* **bri·dled; bri·dling** 1 : to put a bridle on; *also* : to restrain with or as if with a bridle 2 : to show hostility or scorn usu. by tossing the head

Brie \'brē\ *n* : a soft cheese with a whitish rind and a pale yellow interior

¹**brief** \'brēf\ *adj* 1 : short in duration or extent 2 : CONCISE; *also* : CURT — **briefly** *adv* — **brief·ness** *n*

²**brief** *n* 1 : a concise statement or document; *esp* : one summarizing a law client's case or a legal argument 2 *pl* : short snug underpants

³**brief** *vb* : to give final instructions or essential information to

brief·case \'brēf-ˌkās\ *n* : a flat flexible case for carrying papers

brier *var of* BRIAR

¹**brig** \'brig\ *n* : a 2-masted square-rigged sailing ship

²**brig** *n* : the place of confinement for offenders on a naval ship

³**brig** *abbr* brigade

bri·gade \bri-'gād\ *n* 1 : a military unit composed of a headquarters, one or more units of infantry or armored forces, and supporting units 2 : a group organized for a particular purpose (as fire fighting)

brig·a·dier general \'bri-gə-ˌdir-\ *n* : a commissioned officer (as in the army) ranking next below a major general

brig·and \'bri-gənd\ *n* : BANDIT — **brig·and·age** \-gən-dij\ *n*

brig·an·tine \'bri-gən-ˌtēn\ *n* : a 2-masted square-rigged ship with a fore-and-aft mainsail

Brig Gen *abbr* brigadier general

bright \'brīt\ *adj* 1 : SHINING, RADIANT 2 : ILLUSTRIOUS, GLORIOUS 3 : INTELLIGENT, CLEVER; *also* : LIVELY, CHEERFUL ✦ *Synonyms* BRILLIANT, LUSTROUS, BEAMING — **bright** *adv* — **bright·ly** *adv* — **bright·ness** *n*

bright·en \'brī-tᵊn\ *vb* : to make or become bright or brighter — **bright·en·er** *n*

¹**bril·liant** \'bril-yənt\ *adj* [F *brillant*, prp. of *briller* to shine, fr. It *brillare*] 1 : very bright 2 : STRIKING, DISTINCTIVE 3 : very intelligent ✦ *Synonyms* RADIANT, LUSTROUS, BEAMING, LUCID, BRIGHT, LAMBENT — **bril·liance** \-yəns\ *n* — **bril·lian·cy** \-yən-sē\ *n* — **bril·liant·ly** *adv*

²**brilliant** *n* : a gem cut in a particular form with many facets

¹**brim** \'brim\ *n* : EDGE, RIM ✦ *Synonyms* BRINK, BORDER, VERGE, FRINGE — **brim·less** *adj*

²**brim** *vb* **brimmed; brim·ming** : to be or become full often to overflowing

brim·ful \-'fùl\ *adj* : full to the brim

brim·stone \'brim-ˌstōn\ *n* : SULFUR

brin·dled \'brin-dᵊld\ *adj* : having dark streaks or flecks on a gray or tawny ground ⟨a ~ Great Dane⟩

brine \'brīn\ *n* 1 : water saturated with salt 2 : OCEAN — **brin·i·ness** *n* — **briny** \'brī-nē\ *adj*

bring \'briŋ\ *vb* **brought** \'brȯt\; **bringing** \'briŋ-iŋ\ 1 : to cause to come with one 2 : INDUCE, PERSUADE, LEAD 3 : PRODUCE, EFFECT 4 : to sell for ⟨~ a good price⟩ — **bring·er** *n*

bring about *vb* : to cause to take place

bring up *vb* 1 : to give a parent's fostering care to **2** : to come or bring to a sudden halt **3** : to call to notice

brink \'briŋk\ n **1** : an edge at the top of a steep place **2** : the point of onset

brio \'brē-ō\ n : VIVACITY, SPIRIT

bri·quette or **bri·quet** \bri-'ket\ n : a compacted often brick-shaped mass of fine material ⟨a charcoal ∼⟩

bris also **briss** \'bris\ n : the Jewish rite of circumcision

brisk \'brisk\ adj **1** : ALERT, LIVELY **2** : INVIGORATING ⟨∼ weather⟩ **3** : highly active ⟨a ∼ business⟩ ♦ **Synonyms** AGILE, SPRY, NIMBLE — **brisk·ly** adv — **brisk·ness** n

bris·ket \'bris-kət\ n : the breast or lower chest of a quadruped; also : a cut of beef from the brisket

bris·ling \'briz-liŋ, 'bris-\ n : SPRAT 1

¹bris·tle \'bri-səl\ n : a short stiff coarse hair — **bris·tle·like** \'bri-səl-,līk\ adj — **bris·tly** adj

²bristle vb **bris·tled; bris·tling 1** : to stand stiffly erect **2** : to show angry defiance ⟨bristled at the charges⟩ **3** : to appear as if covered with bristles

Brit abbr British

Bri·tan·nic \bri-'ta-nik\ adj : BRITISH

britch·es \'bri-chəz\ n pl : BREECHES, TROUSERS

Brit·ish \'bri-tish\ n pl : the people of Great Britain or the Commonwealth — **British** adj — **Brit·ish·ness** n

British thermal unit n : the quantity of heat needed to raise the temperature of one pound of water one degree Fahrenheit

Brit·on \'bri-tⁿn\ n **1** : a member of a people inhabiting Britain before the Anglo-Saxon invasion **2** : a native or inhabitant of Great Britain

brit·tle \'bri-tⁿl\ adj **brit·tler; brit·tlest** : easily broken : FRAGILE ♦ **Synonyms** CRISP, CRUMBLY, FRIABLE — **brit·tle·ness** n

bro \'brō\ n, pl **bros 1** : BROTHER 1 **2** : SOUL BROTHER

¹broach \'brōch\ n : a pointed tool

²broach vb **1** : to pierce (as a cask) in order to draw the contents **2** : to open up (a subject) for discussion

broad \'brȯd\ adj **1** : WIDE **2** : SPACIOUS ⟨the ∼ plains⟩ **3** : CLEAR, OPEN ⟨∼ daylight⟩ **4** : OBVIOUS ⟨a ∼ hint⟩ **5** : COARSE, CRUDE ⟨∼ stories⟩ **6** : tolerant in outlook **7** : GENERAL ⟨a ∼ rule⟩ **8** : dealing with essential points — **broad·ly** adv — **broad·ness** n

broad·band \'brȯd-,band\ n : a system of high-speed telecommunication in which a frequency range is divided into multiple independent channels for simultaneous transmission of signals

¹broad·cast \'brȯd-,kast\ vb **broadcast** also **broad·cast·ed; broad·cast·ing 1** : to scatter or sow broadcast **2** : to make widely known **3** : to transmit a broadcast — **broad·cast·er** n

²broadcast adv : to or over a wide area

³broadcast n **1** : the transmission of sound or images by radio or television **2** : a single radio or television program

broad·cloth \-,klȯth\ n **1** : a smooth dense woolen cloth **2** : a fine soft cloth of cotton, silk, or synthetic fiber

broad·en \'brȯ-dⁿn\ vb : WIDEN

broad·loom \-,lüm\ adj : woven on a wide loom esp. in a solid color

broad–mind·ed \-'mīn-dəd\ adj : tolerant of varied opinions — **broad–mind·ed·ly** adv — **broad–mind·ed·ness** n

¹broad·side \-,sīd\ n **1** : a sheet of paper printed usu. on one side (as an advertisement) **2** : all of the guns on one side of a ship; also : their simultaneous firing **3** : a volley of abuse or denunciation

²broadside adv **1** : with one side forward : SIDEWAYS **2** : from the side ⟨the car was hit ∼⟩

broad–spectrum adj : effective against a wide range of organisms ⟨∼ antibiotics⟩

broad·sword \'brȯd-,sȯrd\ n : a broad-bladed sword

broad·tail \-,tāl\ n : a karakul esp. with flat and wavy fur

bro·cade \brō-'kād\ n : a usu. silk fabric with a raised design

broc·co·li \'brä-kə-lē\ n [It, pl. of broccolo flowering top of a cabbage, dim. of brocco small nail, sprout, fr. L broccus projecting] : the stems and immature usu. green or purple flower heads of either of two garden vegetable plants closely related to the cabbage; also : either of the plants

bro·chette \brō-'shet\ n : SKEWER

bro·chure \brō-'shùr\ n [F, fr. brocher to sew, fr. MF, to prick, fr. OF brochier, fr. broche pointed tool] : PAMPHLET, BOOKLET

bro·gan \'brō-gən, brō-'gan\ n : a heavy shoe

brogue \'brōg\ n : a dialect or regional pronunciation; esp : an Irish accent

broil \'brȯi(-ə)l\ vb : to cook by exposure to radiant heat : GRILL — **broil** n

broil·er \'brȯi-lər\ n **1** : a utensil for broiling **2** : a young chicken fit for broiling

broil·ing \'brȯi-(ə)-liŋ\ adj : extremely hot ⟨a ∼ sun⟩

¹broke \'brōk\ past of BREAK

²broke adj : PENNILESS

¹bro·ken \'brō-kən\ past part of BREAK

²broken adj **1** : SHATTERED ⟨∼ glass⟩ **2** : having gaps or breaks : INTERRUPTED, DISRUPTED **3** : SUBDUED, CRUSHED ⟨a ∼ spirit⟩ **4** : BANKRUPT **5** : imperfectly spoken ⟨∼ English⟩ — **bro·ken·ly** adv

bro·ken·heart·ed \,brō-kən-'här-təd\ adj : overcome by grief or despair

bro·ker \'brō-kər\ n : an agent who negotiates contracts of purchase and sale — **broker** vb

bro·ker·age \'brō-kə-rij\ n **1** : the business of a broker **2** : the fee or commission charged by a broker

bro·me·li·ad \brō-'mē-lē-,ad\ n : any of several tropical American ornamental plants related to the pineapple that usu. grow on trees

bro·mide \'brō-,mīd\ n : a compound of bromine and another element or chemical group including some (as potassium bromide) used as sedatives

bro·mid·ic \brō-'mi-dik\ adj : TRITE, UNORIGINAL

bro·mine \'brō-,mēn\ n [F brome bromine, fr. Gk brōmos stink] : a deep red liquid corrosive chemical element that gives off an irritating vapor

bronc \'bräŋk\ n : an unbroken or partly broken range horse of western No. America; also : MUSTANG

bron·chi·al \'bräŋ-kē-əl\ adj : of, relating to, or affecting the bronchi or their branches

bron·chi·tis \brän-'kī-təs, bräŋ-\ n : inflammation of the bronchi and their branches — **bron·chit·ic** \-'ki-tik\ adj

bron·chus \'bräŋ-kəs\ n, pl **bron·chi** \'bräŋ-,kī, -,kē\ : either of the main divisions of the trachea each leading to a lung

bron·co \'bräŋ-kō\ n, pl **broncos** [MexSp, fr. Sp, rough, wild] : BRONC

bron·to·sau·rus \,brän-tə-'sôr-əs\ also **bron·to·saur** \'brän-tə-,sôr\ n [NL, fr. Gk brontē thunder + sauros lizard] : any of a genus of large 4-footed sauropod dinosaurs of the Jurassic

Bronx cheer \'bräŋks-\ n : RASPBERRY 2

¹**bronze** \'bränz\ vb **bronzed**; **bronz·ing** : to give the appearance of bronze to

²**bronze** n 1 : an alloy of copper and tin and sometimes other elements; also : something made of bronze 2 : a yellowish brown color — **bronzy** \'brän-zē\ adj

brooch \'brōch, 'brüch\ n : an ornamental clasp or pin

¹**brood** \'brüd\ n : a family of young animals or children and esp. of birds

²**brood** adj : kept for breeding ⟨a ~ mare⟩

³**brood** vb 1 : to sit on eggs to hatch them; also : to shelter (hatched young) with the wings 2 : to think anxiously or gloomily about something — **brood·ing·ly** adv

brood·er \'brü-dər\ n 1 : one that broods 2 : a heated structure for raising young birds

¹**brook** \'brük\ n : a small natural stream

²**brook** vb : TOLERATE, BEAR ⟨would ~ no interference with his plan⟩

brook·let \'brü-klət\ n : a small brook

brook trout n : a common speckled coldwater char of No. America

broom \'brüm, 'brüm\ n 1 : any of several shrubs of the legume family with long slender branches and usu. yellow flowers 2 : an implement with a long handle (**broom·stick** \-,stik\) used for sweeping

broth \'broth\ n, pl **broths** \'broths, 'brothz\ 1 : liquid in which meat or sometimes vegetable food has been cooked 2 : a fluid culture medium

broth·el \'brä-thəl, 'brȯ-\ n : a house of prostitution

broth·er \'brə-thər\ n, pl **brothers** also **breth·ren** \'breth-rən, 'bre-thə-; 'bre-thərn\ 1 : a male having one or both parents in common with another individual 2 : a man who is a religious but not a priest 3 : KINSMAN; also : SOUL BROTH-

ER — **broth·er·li·ness** \-lē-nəs\ n — **broth·er·ly** adj

broth·er·hood \'brə-thər-,hùd\ n 1 : the state of being brothers or a brother 2 : ASSOCIATION, FRATERNITY 3 : the whole body of persons in a business or profession

broth·er–in–law \'brə-thə-rən-,lò, 'brə-thərn-,lò\ n, pl **brothers–in–law** \'brə-thər-zən-\ : the brother of one's spouse; also : the husband of one's sister or of one's spouse's sister

brougham \'brü(-ə)m, 'brō(-ə)m\ n : a light closed horse-drawn carriage with the driver outside in front

brought past and past part of BRING

brou·ha·ha \'brü-,hä-,hä\ n : HUBBUB, UPROAR

brow \'braù\ n 1 : the eyebrow or the ridge on which it grows; also : FOREHEAD 2 : the projecting upper part of a steep place

brow·beat \'braù-,bēt\ vb **-beat**; **-beat·en** \-'bē-t²n\ or **-beat**; **-beat·ing** : to intimidate by sternness or arrogance

¹**brown** \'braùn\ adj : of the color brown; also : of dark or tanned complexion

²**brown** n : a color like that of coffee or chocolate that is a blend of red and yellow darkened by black — **brown·ish** adj

³**brown** vb : to make or become brown

brown bag·ging \-'ba-giŋ\ n : the practice of carrying one's lunch usu. in a brown bag — **brown bag·ger** n

brown bear n : any of various large typically brown-furred bears including the grizzly bear

brown·ie \'braù-nē\ n 1 : a legendary cheerful elf who performs good deeds at night 2 cap : a member of a program of the Girl Scouts for girls in the first through third grades 3 : a small square or rectangle of chocolate cake

brown·nose \'braùn-,nōz\ vb : to ingratiate oneself with — **brownnose** n

brown·out \'braù-,naùt\ n : a period of reduced voltage of electricity caused esp. by high demand and resulting in reduced illumination

brown rice n : hulled but unpolished rice that retains most of the bran layers

brown·stone \'braùn-,stōn\ n : a dwelling faced with reddish-brown sandstone

¹**browse** \'braùz\ vb **browsed**; **brows·ing** 1 : to feed on browse; also : GRAZE 2 : to read or look over something in a casual way 3 : to access (a network) with a browser

²**browse** n : tender shoots, twigs, and leaves fit for food for cattle

brows·er \'braù-zər\ n : a computer program for accessing sites or information on a network (as the World Wide Web)

bru·in \'brü-ən\ n : BEAR

¹**bruise** \'brüz\ vb **bruised**; **bruis·ing** 1 : to inflict a bruise on; also : to become bruised 2 : to break down (as leaves or berries) by pounding

²**bruise** n : a surface injury to flesh : CONTUSION

bruis·er \'brü-zər\ *n* : a big husky man

bruit \'brüt\ *vb* : to make widely known by common report ⟨word of his dismissal was ~*ed* about⟩

brunch \'brənch\ *n* : a meal that combines a late breakfast and an early lunch

bru·net *or* **bru·nette** \brü-'net\ *adj* [F *brunet*, masc., *brunette*, fem., brownish, fr. OF, fr. *brun* brown, of Gmc origin] : having brown or black hair and usu. a relatively dark complexion — **brunet** *or* **brunette** *n*

brunt \'brənt\ *n* : the main shock, force, or stress esp. of an attack; *also* : the greater burden

bru·schet·ta \brü-'she-tə, -'ske-\ *n* : an appetizer of grilled bread with toppings

¹**brush** \'brəsh\ *n* 1 : BRUSHWOOD 2 : scrub vegetation or land covered with it

²**brush** *n* 1 : a device composed of bristles set in a handle and used esp. for cleaning or painting 2 : a bushy tail (as of a fox) 3 : an electrical conductor that makes contact between a stationary and a moving part (as of a motor) 4 : a quick light touch in passing

³**brush** *vb* 1 : to treat (as in cleaning or painting) with a brush 2 : to remove with or as if with a brush; *also* : to dismiss in an offhand manner 3 : to touch gently in passing

⁴**brush** *n* : SKIRMISH ⟨a ~ with the law⟩ ♦ **Synonyms** ENCOUNTER, RUN-IN

brush fire *n* 1 : a fire involving low-growing plants 2 : a minor conflict or crisis

brush–off \'brəsh-ˌȯf\ *n* : a curt offhand dismissal

brush up *vb* : to renew one's skill

brush·wood \'brəsh-ˌwùd\ *n* 1 : small branches of wood esp. when cut 2 : a thicket of shrubs and small trees

brusque \'brəsk\ *adj* [F *brusque*, fr. It *brusco*, fr. ML *bruscus* a plant with stiff twigs used for brooms] : CURT, BLUNT, ABRUPT ⟨a ~ answer⟩ ♦ **Synonyms** GRUFF, BLUFF, CRUSTY, SHORT — **brusque·ly** *adv*

brus·sels sprout \ˌbrəs-əlz-\ *n, often cap B* : one of the edible green heads borne on the stalk of a plant closely related to the cabbage; *also, pl* : this plant

bru·tal \'brü-t⁰l\ *adj* 1 : befitting a brute : UNFEELING, CRUEL 2 : HARSH, SEVERE ⟨~ weather⟩ 3 : unpleasantly accurate — **bru·tal·i·ty** \brü-'ta-lə-tē\ *n* — **bru·tal·ly** *adv*

bru·tal·ise *Brit var of* BRUTALIZE

bru·tal·ize \'brü-t⁰l-ˌīz\ *vb* **-ized; -iz·ing** 1 : to make brutal 2 : to treat brutally

¹**brute** \'brüt\ *adj* [ME, fr. MF *brut* rough, fr. L *brutus* brutish, lit., heavy] 1 : of or relating to beasts 2 : BRUTAL 3 : UNREASONING; *also* : purely physical ⟨~ strength⟩

²**brute** *n* 1 : BEAST 1 2 : a brutal person

brut·ish \'brü-tish\ *adj* 1 : BRUTE 1 2 : strongly sensual; *also* : showing little intelligence

BS *abbr* bachelor of science

BSA *abbr* Boy Scouts of America

bskt *abbr* basket

Bt *abbr* baronet

btry *abbr* battery

Btu *abbr* British thermal unit

bu *abbr* bushel

¹**bub·ble** \'bə-bəl\ *n* 1 : a globule of gas in a liquid 2 : a thin film of liquid filled with gas 3 : something lacking firmness or solidity — **bub·bly** *adj*

²**bubble** *vb* **bub·bled; bub·bling** : to form, rise in, or give off bubbles

bub·kes \'bəp-kəs, 'bùp-\ *n pl* [Yiddish] : the least amount ⟨didn't win ~⟩

bu·bo \'bü-bō, 'byü-\ *n, pl* **buboes** : an inflammatory swelling of a lymph gland — **bu·bon·ic plague** \bü-'bä-nik-, byü-\ *n* : plague caused by a bacterium transmitted to human beings by flea bites and marked esp. by chills and fever and by buboes usu. in the groin

buc·ca·neer \ˌbə-kə-'nir\ *n* : PIRATE

¹**buck** \'bək\ *n, pl* **bucks** 1 *or pl* **buck** : a male animal (as a deer or antelope) 2 : DANDY 3 : DOLLAR

²**buck** *vb* 1 : to spring with an arching leap ⟨a ~*ing* horse⟩ 2 : to charge against something; *also* : to strive for advancement sometimes without regard to ethical behavior

buck·board \-ˌbȯrd\ *n* : a 4-wheeled horse-drawn wagon with a floor of long springy boards

buck·et \'bə-kət\ *n* 1 : PAIL 2 : an object resembling a bucket in collecting, scooping, or carrying something — **buck·et·ful** *n*

bucket seat *n* : a low separate seat for one person (as in an automobile)

buck·eye \'bək-ˌkī\ *n* : any of various trees or shrubs related to the horse chestnut; *also* : the large nutlike seed of such a shrub or tree

buck fever *n* : nervous excitement of an inexperienced hunter at the sight of game

¹**buck·le** \'bə-kəl\ *n* : a clasp (as on a belt) for two loose ends

²**buckle** *vb* **buck·led; buck·ling** 1 : to fasten with a buckle 2 : to apply oneself with vigor 3 : to crumple up : BEND, COLLAPSE

³**buckle** *n* : BEND, FOLD, KINK

buck·ler \'bə-klər\ *n* : SHIELD

buck·ram \'bə-krəm\ *n* : a coarse stiff cloth used esp. for binding books

buck·saw \'bək-ˌsȯ\ *n* : a saw set in a usu. H-shaped frame for sawing wood

buck·shot \'bək-ˌshät\ *n* : lead shot that is from .24 to .33 inch (about 6.1 to 8.4 millimeters) in diameter

buck·skin \-ˌskin\ *n* 1 : the skin of a buck 2 : a soft usu. suede-finished leather — **buckskin** *adj*

buck·tooth \-'tüth\ *n* : a large protruding front tooth — **buck–toothed** \-'tütht\ *adj*

buck·wheat \-ˌhwēt\ *n* : either of two plants grown for their triangular seeds which are used as a cereal grain; *also* : these seeds

bu·col·ic \byü-'kä-lik\ *adj* [L *bucolicus*, fr. Gk *boukolikos*, fr. *boukolos* cowherd] : PASTORAL, RURAL

¹bud \'bəd\ *n* **1** : an undeveloped plant shoot (as of a leaf or a flower); *also* : a partly opened flower **2** : an asexual reproductive structure that detaches from the parent and forms a new individual **3** : something not yet fully developed ⟨nipped in the ∼⟩

²bud *vb* **bud·ded; bud·ding** **1** : to form or put forth buds; *also* : to reproduce by asexual buds **2** : to be or develop like a bud **3** : to reproduce a desired variety (as of peach) by inserting a bud in a plant of a different variety

Bud·dhism \'bü-ˌdi-zəm, 'bù-\ *n* : a religion of eastern and central Asia growing out of the teachings of Gautama Buddha — **Bud·dhist** \'bü-dist, 'bù-\ *n or adj*

bud·dy \'bə-dē\ *n, pl* **buddies** **1** : COMPANION; *also* : FRIEND **2** : FELLOW

budge \'bəj\ *vb* **budged; budg·ing** : MOVE, SHIFT; *also* : YIELD

bud·ger·i·gar \'bə-jə-rē-ˌgar\ *n* : a small brightly colored Australian parrot often kept as a pet

¹bud·get \'bə-jət\ *n* [ME *bowgette*, fr. MF *bougette*, dim. of *bouge* leather bag, fr. L *bulga*] **1** : STOCK, SUPPLY **2** : a financial report containing estimates of income and expenses; *also* : a plan for coordinating income and expenses **3** : the amount of money available for a particular use — **bud·get·ary** \'bə-jə-ˌter-ē\ *adj*

²budget *vb* **1** : to allow for in a budget **2** : to draw up a budget

³budget *adj* : INEXPENSIVE

bud·gie \'bə-jē\ *n* : BUDGERIGAR

¹buff \'bəf\ *n* **1** : a yellow to orange yellow color **2** : FAN, ENTHUSIAST

²buff *adj* : of the color buff

³buff *vb* : POLISH, SHINE

buf·fa·lo \'bə-fə-ˌlō\ *n, pl* **-lo** *or* **-los** **-los** **1** : WATER BUFFALO **2** : a large shaggy-maned No. American wild bovine mammal that has short horns and heavy forequarters with a large muscular hump

buffalo soldier *n* : an African-American soldier serving in the western U.S. after the Civil War

¹buf·fer \'bə-fər\ *n* : something or someone that protects or shields (as from physical damage or a financial blow)

²buffer *n* : one that buffs

¹buf·fet \'bə-fət\ *n* : BLOW, SLAP

²buffet *vb* **1** : to strike with the hand; *also* : to pound repeatedly **2** : to struggle against or on ✦ **Synonyms** BEAT, BATTER, DRUB, PUMMEL, THRASH

³buf·fet \ˌbə-'fā, bü-\ *n* **1** : SIDEBOARD **2** : a counter for refreshments; *also* : a meal at which people serve themselves informally

buff leather *n* : a strong supple oil-tanned leather

buf·foon \ˌ(ˌ)bə-'fün\ *n* [MF *bouffon*, fr. It *buffone*] : CLOWN **2** — **buf·foon·ery** \-'fü-nə-rē\ *n* — **buf·foon·ish** \-'fü-nish\ *adj*

¹bug \'bəg\ *n* **1** : an insect or other creeping or crawling invertebrate animal; *esp* : an insect pest (as the cockroach or bedbug **2** : any of an order of insects with sucking mouthparts and incomplete metamorphosis that includes many plant pests **3** : an unexpected flaw or imperfection ⟨a ∼ in a computer program⟩ **4** : a disease-producing germ; *also* : a disease caused by it **5** : a concealed listening device — **bug·gy** \'bə-gē\ *adj*

²bug *vb* **bugged; bug·ging** **1** : BOTHER, ANNOY **2** : to plant a concealed microphone in

³bug *vb*, **bugged; bug·ging** *of the eyes* : PROTRUDE, BULGE

bug·a·boo \'bə-gə-ˌbü\ *n, pl* **-boos** : BOGEY 1

bug·bear \'bəg-ˌber\ *n* : BOGEY 1; *also* : a source of dread

bug·gy \'bə-gē\ *n, pl* **buggies** : a light horse-drawn carriage; *also* : a carriage for a baby

bu·gle \'byü-gəl\ *n* [ME, buffalo, instrument made of buffalo horn, bugle, fr. AF, fr. L *buculus*, dim. of *bos* head of cattle] : a valveless brass instrument resembling a trumpet and used esp. for military calls — **bu·gler** *n*

bug out *vb* **1** : to flee in panic **2** : to depart in a hurry

¹build \'bild\ *vb* **built** \'bilt\; **build·ing** **1** : to form or have formed by ordering and uniting materials ⟨∼ a house⟩; *also* : to bring into being or develop **2** : to produce or create gradually ⟨∼ an argument on facts⟩ **3** : INCREASE, ENLARGE; *also* : ENHANCE **4** : to engage in building — **build·er** *n*

²build *n* : form or mode of structure; *esp* : PHYSIQUE

build·ing \'bil-diŋ\ *n* **1** : a usu. roofed and walled structure (as a house) for permanent use **2** : the art or business of constructing buildings

build·up \'bild-ˌəp\ *n* : the act or process of building up; *also* : something produced by this

built–in \'bilt-'in\ *adj* **1** : forming an integral part of a structure **2** : INHERENT

bulb \'bəlb\ *n* **1** : an underground resting stage of a plant (as a lily or an onion) consisting of a short stem base bearing one or more buds enclosed in overlapping leaves; *also* : a fleshy plant structure (as a tuber) resembling a bulb **2** : a plant having or growing from a bulb **3** : a rounded more or less bulb-shaped object or part (as for an electric lamp) — **bul·bous** \'bəl-bəs\ *adj*

¹bulge \'bəlj\ *vb* **bulged; bulg·ing** : to become or cause to become protuberant

²bulge *n* : a swelling projecting part

bu·li·mia \bü-'lē-mē-ə, byü-, -'li-\ *n* **1** : an abnormal and constant craving for food **2** : a serious eating disorder chiefly of females that is characterized by compulsive overeating usu. followed by self-induced vomiting or laxative or diuretic abuse — **bu·lim·ic** \-'lē-mik, -'li-\ *adj or n*

¹bulk \'bəlk\ *n* **1** : MAGNITUDE, VOLUME **2** : material that forms a mass in the intestine; *esp* : FIBER 2 **3** : a large mass **4** : the major portion

²bulk *vb* **1** : to cause to swell or bulge **2** : to appear as a factor : LOOM

bulk·head \'bəlk-,hed\ *n* **1** : a partition separating compartments **2** : a structure built to cover a shaft or a cellar stairway

bulky \'bəl-kē\ *adj* **bulk·i·er; -est** : having large bulk; *esp* : being large and unwieldy

¹bull \'bul\ *n* **1** : a male bovine animal; *also* : a usu. adult male of various large animals (as the moose, elephant, or whale) **2** : one who buys securities or commodities in expectation of a price increase — **bull·ish** *adj*

²bull *adj* **1** : of, relating to, or suggestive of a bull : MALE **2** : large of its kind ⟨a ~ lathe⟩

³bull *n* [ME *bulle*, fr. ML *bulla*, fr. L, bubble, amulet] **1** : a papal letter **2** : DECREE

⁴bull *n, slang* : NONSENSE

⁵bull *abbr* bulletin

¹bull·dog \'bul-,dȯg\ *n* : any of a breed of compact muscular short-haired dogs of English origin

²bulldog *vb* : to throw (a steer) by seizing the horns and twisting the neck

bull·doze \-,dōz\ *vb* **1** : to move, clear, or level with a tractor-driven machine (**bull·doz·er**) having a broad blade for pushing **2** : to force as if by using a bulldozer

bul·let \'bul-lət\ *n* [MF *boulette* small ball & *boulet* missile, dims. of *boule* ball, fr. L *bulla* bubble] : a missile to be shot from a firearm

bul·le·tin \'bul-lə-t²n\ *n* **1** : a brief public report intended for immediate release on a matter of public interest **2** : a periodical publication (as of a college)

bulletin board *n* **1** : a board for posting notices **2** : a public forum on a computer network in which users write or read messages or download files

bul·let·proof \'bul-lət-,prüf\ *adj* **1** : impenetrable to bullets **2** : not subject to correction, alteration, or modification **3** : INVINCIBLE

bull·fight \'bul-,fīt\ *n* : a spectacle in which people ceremonially fight with and usu. kill bulls in an arena — **bull·fight·er** *n*

bull·frog \-,frȯg, -,fräg\ *n* : a large deep-voiced frog

bull·head \-,hed\ *n* : any of several common large-headed freshwater catfishes of the U.S.

bull·head·ed \-'he-dəd\ *adj* : stupidly stubborn : HEADSTRONG

bul·lion \'bul-yən\ *n* : gold or silver esp. in bars or ingots

bull market *n* : a market in which securities or commodities are persistently rising in value

bull·ock \'bul-lək\ *n* : a young bull; *also* : STEER

bull pen *n* : a place on a baseball field where pitchers warm up; *also* : the relief pitchers of a baseball team

bull session *n* : an informal discussion

bull's-eye \'bulz-,ī\ *n, pl* **bull's-eyes** : the center of a target; *also* : a shot that hits the bull's<->eye

¹bul·ly \'bul-lē\ *n, pl* **bullies** : a person habitually cruel to others who are weaker

²bully *adj* : EXCELLENT, FIRST-RATE — often used interjectionally ⟨~ for you⟩

³bully *vb* **bul·lied; bul·ly·ing** : to behave as a bully toward : DOMINEER ✦ **Synonyms** BROWBEAT, INTIMIDATE, HECTOR

bul·rush \'bul-,rəsh\ *n* : any of several large rushes or sedges of wetlands

bul·wark \'bul-(,)wərk, -,wȯrk; 'bəl-(,)wərk\ *n* **1** : a wall-like defensive structure **2** : a strong support or protection

¹bum \'bəm\ *adj* **1** : of poor quality ⟨~ advice⟩ **2** : disabled by damage or injury ⟨a ~ knee⟩

²bum *vb* **bummed; bum·ming 1** : to spend time unemployed and wandering; *also* : LOAF **2** : to obtain by begging

³bum *n* **1** : LOAFER **2** : one whose time is devoted to a recreational activity ⟨a ski ~⟩ **3** : TRAMP 1

bum·ble \'bəm-bəl\ *vb* **bum·bled; bum·bling 1** : to speak in a stuttering and faltering manner **2** : to proceed unsteadily **3** : BUNGLE

bum·ble·bee \'bəm-bəl-,bē\ *n* : any of numerous large hairy social bees

bum·mer \'bə-mər\ *n* **1** : an unpleasant experience **2** : FAILURE

¹bump \'bəmp\ *n* **1** : a local bulge; *esp* : a swelling of tissue **2** : a sudden forceful blow or impact — **bumpy** *adj*

²bump *vb* **1** : to strike or knock forcibly; *also* : to move by or as if by bumping **2** : to collide with

¹bum·per \'bəm-pər\ *n* **1** : a cup or glass filled to the brim **2** : something unusually large — **bumper** *adj*

²bump·er \'bəm-pər\ *n* : a device for absorbing shock or preventing damage; *esp* : a usu. metal bar at either end of an automobile

bump·kin \'bəmp-kən\ *n* : an awkward and unsophisticated country person

bump·tious \'bəmp-shəs\ *adj* : obtusely and often noisily self-assertive

bun \'bən\ *n* : a sweet biscuit or roll

¹bunch \'bənch\ *n* **1** : SWELLING **2** : CLUSTER, GROUP — **bunchy** *adj*

²bunch *vb* : to form into a group or bunch

bun·co *or* **bun·ko** \'bəŋ-kō\ *n, pl* **buncos** *or* **bunkos** : a swindling scheme — **bunco** *vb*

¹bun·dle \'bən-d²l\ *n* **1** : several items bunched and fastened together; *also* : something wrapped for carrying **2** : a considerable amount : LOT **3** : a small band of mostly parallel nerve or muscle fibers **4** : a package offering related products or services at a single price

²bundle *vb* **bun·dled; bun·dling** : to gather or tie in a bundle

bundling *n* : a former custom of a courting couple's occupying the same bed without undressing

bung \'bəŋ\ *n* : the stopper in the bunghole of a cask

bun·ga·low \'bəŋ-gə-,lō\ *n* [Hindi & Urdu *banglā*, lit., (house) in the Bengal style] : a one-storied house with a low-pitched roof

bun·gee cord \'bən-jē-\ *n* : a long elastic cord used esp. as a fastening or shock-absorbing device

bungee jump vb : to jump from a height while attached to a bungee cord — **bungee jumper** n

bung·hole \'bəŋ-ˌhōl\ n : a hole for emptying or filling a cask

bun·gle \'bəŋ-gəl\ vb **bun·gled; bun·gling** : to do badly : BOTCH — **bungle** n — **bun·gler** n

bun·ion \'bən-yən\ n : an inflamed swelling of the first joint of the big toe

¹**bunk** \'bəŋk\ n : BED; esp : a built-in bed that is often one of a tier

²**bunk** n : BUNKUM, NONSENSE

bunk bed n : one of two single beds usu. placed one above the other

bun·ker \'bəŋ-kər\ n **1** : a bin or compartment for storage (as for coal on a ship) **2** : a protective embankment or dugout **3** : a sand trap or embankment constituting a hazard on a golf course

bun·kum or **bun·combe** \'bəŋ-kəm\ n [Buncombe County, N.C.; fr. a remark made by its congressman, who defended an irrelevant speech by claiming that he was speaking to Buncombe] : insincere or foolish talk

bun·ny \'bə-nē\ n, pl **-nies** : RABBIT

bunny slope n : a gentle incline used by novice skiers — called also **bunny hill**

Bun·sen burner \'bən-sən-\ n : a gas burner usu. consisting of a straight tube with air holes at the bottom

¹**bunt** \'bənt\ vb **1** : ¹BUTT **2** : to push or tap a baseball lightly without swinging the bat

²**bunt** n : an act or instance of bunting; also : a bunted ball

¹**bun·ting** \'bən-tiŋ\ n : any of numerous small stout-billed finches

²**bunting** n : a thin fabric used esp. for flags; also : FLAGS

¹**buoy** \'bü-ē, 'bȯi\ n **1** : a floating object anchored in water to mark something (as a channel) **2** : a float consisting of a ring of buoyant material to support a person who has fallen into the water

²**buoy** vb **1** : to mark by a buoy **2** : to keep afloat **3** : to raise the spirits of

buoy·an·cy \'bȯi-ən-sē, 'bü-yən-\ n **1** : the tendency of a body to float or rise when submerged in a fluid **2** : the power of a fluid to exert an upward force on a body placed in it **3** : resilience of spirit — **buoy·ant** \-ənt, -yənt\ adj

¹**bur** var of BURR

²**bur** abbr bureau

burbs \'bərbz\ n pl : SUBURBS

¹**bur·den** \'bər-dᵊn\ n **1** : LOAD; also : CARE, RESPONSIBILITY **2** : something oppressive : ENCUMBRANCE **3** : CARGO; also : capacity for cargo

²**burden** vb : LOAD, OPPRESS — **bur·den·some** \-səm\ adj

³**burden** n **1** : REFRAIN, CHORUS **2** : a main theme or idea : GIST

bur·dock \'bər-ˌdäk\ n : any of a genus of coarse composite herbs with globe-shaped flower heads surrounded by prickly bracts

bu·reau \'byùr-ō\ n, pl **bureaus** also **bu·reaux** \-ōz\ [F, desk, cloth covering for desks, fr. OF burel woolen cloth, ultim. fr. L burra shaggy cloth] **1** : a chest of drawers **2** : an administrative unit (as of a government department) **3** : a branch of a publication or wire service in an important news center

bu·reau·cra·cy \byù-'rä-krə-sē\ n, pl **-cies 1** : a body of appointive government officials **2** : government marked by specialization of functions under fixed rules and a hierarchy of authority; also : an unwieldy administrative system burdened with excessive complexity and lack of flexibility — **bu·reau·crat** \'byùr-ə-ˌkrat\ n — **bu·reau·crat·ic** \ˌbyùr-ə-'kra-tik\ adj

bur·geon \'bər-jən\ vb : to put forth fresh growth (as from buds) : grow vigorously : FLOURISH

burgh \'bər-ō\ n : a Scottish town

bur·gher \'bər-gər\ n **1** : TOWNSMAN **2** : a prosperous solid citizen

bur·glary \'bər-glə-rē\ n, pl **-glar·ies** : forcible entry into a building esp. at night with the intent to commit a crime (as theft) — **bur·glar** \-glər\ n — **bur·glar·ize** \'bər-glə-ˌrīz\ vb

bur·gle \'bər-gəl\ vb **bur·gled; bur·gling** : to commit burglary on

bur·go·mas·ter \'bər-gə-ˌmas-tər\ n : the chief magistrate of a town in some European countries

bur·gun·dy \'bər-gən-dē\ n, pl **-dies** often cap **1** : a red or white table wine from the Burgundy region of France **2** : a blended red wine

buri·al \'ber-ē-əl\ n : the act or process of burying

bur·ka or **bur·qa** \'bùr-kə\ n : a loose garment that covers the face and body and is worn in public by certain Muslim women

burl \'bərl\ n : a hard woody often flattened hemispherical outgrowth on a tree

bur·lap \'bər-ˌlap\ n : a coarse fabric usu. of jute or hemp used esp. for bags

¹**bur·lesque** \(ˌ)bər-'lesk\ n [burlesque, adj., comic, droll, fr. F, fr. It burlesco, fr. burla joke, fr. Sp] **1** : a witty or derisive literary or dramatic imitative work **2** : broadly humorous theatrical entertainment consisting of several items (as songs, skits, or dances)

²**burlesque** vb **bur·lesqued; bur·lesqu·ing** : to make ludicrous by burlesque ◆ **Synonyms** CARICATURE, PARODY, TRAVESTY

bur·ly \'bər-lē\ adj **bur·li·er; -est** : strongly and heavily built : HUSKY ◆ **Synonyms** MUSCULAR, BRAWNY, BEEFY, HEFTY

¹**burn** \'bərn\ vb **burned** \'bərnd, 'bərnt\ or **burnt** \'bərnt\; **burn·ing 1** : to be on fire **2** : to feel or look as if on fire **3** : to alter or become altered by or as if by the action of fire or heat **4** : to use as fuel ⟨~ coal⟩; also : to destroy by fire ⟨~ trash⟩ **5** : to cause or make by fire ⟨~ a hole⟩; also : to affect as if by heat **6** : to record digital data or music on (an optical disk) using a laser ⟨~ a CD⟩

²**burn** n : an injury or effect produced by or as if by burning

burn·er \'bər-nər\ n : the part of a fuel-burning or heat-producing device where the flame or heat is produced

bur·nish \'bər-nish\ vb : to make shiny esp. by rubbing : POLISH — **bur·nish·er** n — **bur·nish·ing** adj or n

bur·noose or **bur·nous** \(ˌ)bər-'nüs\ n : a hooded cloak worn esp. by Arabs

burn·out \'bərn-ˌaut\ n 1 : the cessation of operation of a jet or rocket engine 2 : exhaustion of one's physical or emotional strength; also : a person suffering from burnout

burp \'bərp\ n : an act of belching — **burp** vb

burp gun n : a small submachine gun

burr \'bər\ n 1 usu **bur** : a rough or prickly envelope of a fruit; also : a plant that bears burs 2 : roughness left in cutting or shaping metal 3 : a trilled \r\ as used by some speakers in northern England and Scotland 4 : WHIR — **bur·ry** adj

bur·ri·to \bə-'rē-tō\ n [AmerSp, fr. Sp, little donkey, dim. of burro] : a flour tortilla rolled around a filling and baked

bur·ro \'bər-ō, 'bùr-\ n, pl **burros** [Sp] : a usu. small donkey

¹**bur·row** \'bər-ō\ n : a hole in the ground made by an animal (as a rabbit)

²**burrow** vb 1 : to form by tunneling; also : to make a burrow 2 : to progress by or as if by digging — **bur·row·er** n

bur·sar \'bər-sər\ n : a treasurer esp. of a college

bur·si·tis \(ˌ)bər-'sī-təs\ n : inflammation of the serous sac (**bur·sa** \'bər-sə\) of a joint (as the elbow or shoulder)

¹**burst** \'bərst\ vb **burst** or **burst·ed**; **burst·ing** 1 : to fly apart or into pieces 2 : to show one's feelings suddenly; also : PLUNGE ⟨~ into song⟩ 3 : to enter or emerge suddenly : SPRING 4 : to be filled to the breaking point

²**burst** n 1 : a sudden outbreak : SPURT 2 : EXPLOSION 3 : result of bursting

bury \'ber-ē\ vb **bur·ied**; **bury·ing** 1 : to deposit in the earth; also : to inter with funeral ceremonies 2 : CONCEAL, HIDE 3 : SUBMERGE, ENGROSS — usu. used with in ⟨buried himself in work⟩

¹**bus** \'bəs\ n, pl **bus·es** also **bus·ses** [short for omnibus, fr. F, fr. L, for all, dat. pl. of omnis all] : a large motor vehicle for carrying passengers

²**bus** vb **bused** or **bussed**; **bus·ing** or **bus·sing** 1 : to travel or transport by bus 2 : to work as a busboy

³**bus** abbr business

bus·boy \'bəs-ˌbòi\ n : a waiter's helper

bus·by \'bəz-bē\ n, pl **busbies** : a military full-dress fur hat

bush \'bùsh\ n 1 : SHRUB 2 : rough uncleared country 3 : a thick tuft ⟨a ~ of hair⟩ — **bushy** adj

bushed \'bùsht\ adj : TIRED, EXHAUSTED

bush·el \'bù-shəl\ n — see WEIGHT table

bush·ing \'bù-shiŋ\ n : a usu. removable cylindrical lining for an opening of a mechanical part to limit the size of the opening, resist wear, or serve as a guide

bush·mas·ter \'bùsh-ˌmas-tər\ n : a large venomous pit viper of Central and So. America

bush·whack \-ˌhwak\ vb 1 : AMBUSH 2 : to clear a path through esp. by chopping down bushes and branches — **bush·whack·er** n

busi·ness \'biz-nəs, -nəz\ n 1 : OCCUPATION; also : TASK, MISSION 2 : a commercial or industrial enterprise; also : TRADE ⟨~ is good⟩ 3 : AFFAIR, MATTER 4 : personal concern

busi·ness·man \-ˌman\ n : a man engaged in business esp. as an executive

busi·ness·per·son \-ˌpər-sᵊn\ n : a businessman or businesswoman

busi·ness·wom·an \-ˌwù-mən\ n : a woman engaged in business esp. as an executive

bus·kin \'bəs-kən\ n 1 : a laced boot reaching halfway to the knee 2 : tragic drama

buss \'bəs\ n : KISS — **buss** vb

¹**bust** \'bəst\ n [F buste, fr. It busto, fr. L bustum tomb] 1 : sculpture representing the upper part of the human figure 2 : the part of the human torso between the neck and the waist; esp : the breasts of a woman

²**bust** vb **bust·ed** also **bust**; **bust·ing** 1 : BREAK, SMASH; also : BURST 2 : to ruin financially 3 : TAME 4 : DEMOTE 5 slang : ARREST; also : RAID

³**bust** n 1 : a drinking session 2 : a complete failure : FLOP 3 : a business depression 4 : PUNCH, SOCK 5 slang : a police raid; also : ARREST

¹**bus·tle** \'bə-səl\ vb **bus·tled**; **bus·tling** : to move or work in a brisk busy manner

²**bustle** n : briskly energetic activity

³**bustle** n : a pad or frame worn to support the fullness at the back of a woman's skirt

busy \'bi-zē\ adj **busi·er; -est** 1 : engaged in action : not idle 2 : being in use ⟨~ telephones⟩ 3 : full of activity ⟨~ streets⟩ 4 : MEDDLING — **busi·ly** \'bi-zə-lē\ adv

²**busy** vb **bus·ied**; **busy·ing** : to make or keep busy : OCCUPY

busy·body \'bi-zē-ˌbä-dē\ n : MEDDLER

busy·work \-ˌwərk\ n : work that appears productive but only keeps one occupied

¹**but** \'bət\ conj 1 : except for the fact ⟨would have protested ~ that he was afraid⟩ 2 : THAT ⟨there's no doubt ~ he won⟩ 3 : without the certainty that ⟨never rains ~ it pours⟩ 4 : on the contrary ⟨not one, ~ two job offers⟩ 5 : YET ⟨poor ~ proud⟩ 6 : with the exception of ⟨none ~ the strongest attempt it⟩

²**but** prep : other than : EXCEPT ⟨this letter is nothing ~ an insult⟩; also : with the exception of ⟨no one here ~ me⟩

bu·tane \'byü-ˌtān\ n : either of two gaseous hydrocarbons used as a fuel

butch \'bùch\ adj : notably masculine in appearance or manner

¹**butch·er** \'bù-chər\ n [ME bocher, fr. AF, fr. buc he-goat] 1 : one who slaughters animals or dresses their flesh; also : a

dealer in meat **2** : one that kills brutally or needlessly **3** : one that botches — **butch·ery** \-chə-rē\ n

²**butcher** vb **1** : to slaughter and dress for meat ⟨∼ hogs⟩ **2** : to kill barbarously **3** : BOTCH

but·ler \'bət-lər\ n [ME buteler, fr. AF butiller, † fr. OF botele bottle] : the chief male servant of a household

¹**butt** \'bət\ vb : to strike with the head or horns

²**butt** n : a blow or thrust with the head or horns

³**butt** n : a large cask

⁴**butt** n **1** : TARGET **2** : an object of abuse or ridicule

⁵**butt** n **1** : BUTTOCKS **2** : a large, thicker, or bottom end of something

⁶**butt** vb **1** : ABUT — used with on or against **2** : to place or join edge to edge without overlapping

butte \'byüt\ n : an isolated steep hill

¹**but·ter** \'bə-tər\ n [ME butere, fr. L butyrum butter, fr. Gk boutyron, fr. bous cow + tyros cheese] **1** : a solid edible emulsion of fat obtained from cream by churning **2** : a substance resembling butter — **but·tery** adj

²**butter** vb : to spread with or as if with butter

but·ter–and–eggs \ˌbə-tər-ən-'negz\ n sing or pl : a common perennial herb related to the snapdragon that has showy yellow and orange flowers

butter bean n **1** : LIMA BEAN **2** : WAX BEAN **3** : a green shell bean

but·ter·cream \'bə-tər-ˌkrēm\ n : a sweet butter-based mixture used esp. as a filling or frosting

but·ter·cup \'bə-tər-ˌkəp\ n : any of a genus of herbs having usu. yellow flowers with five petals and sepals

but·ter·fat \-ˌfat\ n : the natural fat of milk and chief constituent of butter

but·ter·fin·gered \-ˌfin-gərd\ adj : likely to let things fall or slip through the fingers — **but·ter·fin·gers** \-gərz\ n sing or pl

but·ter·fly \-ˌflī\ n : any of a group of slender day-flying insects with broad often brightly-colored wings

but·ter·milk \-ˌmilk\ n : the liquid remaining after butter is churned

but·ter·nut \-ˌnət\ n : the sweet egg-shaped nut of an American tree related to the walnut; also : this tree

butternut squash n : a smooth buff-colored cylindrical winter squash

but·ter·scotch \-ˌskäch\ n : a candy made from brown sugar, corn syrup, and water; also : the flavor of such candy

but·tock \'bə-tək\ n **1** : the back of a hip that forms one of the fleshy parts on which a person sits **2** pl : the seat of the body : RUMP

¹**but·ton** \'bə-t²n\ n **1** : a small knob secured to an article (as of clothing) and used as a fastener by passing it through a buttonhole or loop **2** : something that resembles a button **3** : PUSH BUTTON **4** : a hidden sensitivity that can be manipu-

lated to produce a desired response **5** : a usu. box-shaped computer icon that initiates a software function

²**button** vb : to close or fasten with or as if with buttons

¹**but·ton·hole** \'bə-t²n-ˌhōl\ n : a slit or loop for a button to pass through

²**buttonhole** vb : to detain in conversation by or as if by holding on to the outer garments of

¹**but·tress** \'bə-trəs\ n [ME butres, fr. AF (arche) boteraz thrusting (arch), ultim. fr. buter to thrust] **1** : a projecting structure to support a wall **2** : PROP, SUPPORT

²**buttress** vb : PROP, SUPPORT

bu·tut \bü-'tüt\ n, pl bututs or butut — see dalasi at MONEY table

bux·om \'bək-səm\ adj : healthily plump; esp : full-bosomed

¹**buy** \'bī\ vb bought \'bòt\; buy·ing **1** : to obtain for a price : PURCHASE; also : BRIBE **2** : to accept as true — **buy·er** n

²**buy** n **1** : PURCHASE 1, 2 **2** : an exceptional value : BARGAIN

¹**buzz** \'bəz\ vb **1** : to make a buzz **2** : to fly fast and close to

²**buzz** n **1** : a low humming sound **2** : RUMOR, GOSSIP

buz·zard \'bə-zərd\ n : any of various usu. large birds of prey and esp. the turkey vulture

buzz·er \'bə-zər\ n : a device that signals with a buzzing sound

buzz saw n : CIRCULAR SAW

buzz·word \'bəz-ˌwərd\ n : a voguish word or phrase often from technical jargon

BVM abbr Blessed Virgin Mary

BWI abbr British West Indies

bx abbr box

BX abbr base exchange

¹**by** \'bī, bə\ prep **1** : NEAR ⟨stood ∼ the window⟩ **2** : through or through the medium of : VIA ⟨left ∼ the door⟩ **3** : PAST ⟨drove ∼ the house⟩ **4** : DURING, AT ⟨studied ∼ night⟩ **5** : no later than ⟨get here ∼ 3 p.m.⟩ **6** : through the means or direct agency of ⟨∼ force⟩ **7** : in conformity with; also : ACCORDING TO ⟨did it ∼ the book⟩ **8** : with respect to ⟨a doctor ∼ profession⟩ **9** : to the amount or extent of ⟨won ∼ a nose⟩ **10** — used to express relationship in multiplication, in division, and in measurements ⟨divide a ∼ b⟩ ⟨multiply ∼ 6⟩ ⟨15 feet ∼ 20 feet⟩

²**by** \'bī\ adv **1** : near at hand; also : IN ⟨stop ∼⟩ **2** : PAST ⟨saw him go ∼⟩ **3** : ASIDE, APART

bye \'bī\ n : a position of a participant in a tournament who advances to the next round without playing

by–elec·tion also **bye–election** \'bī-ə-ˌlek-shən\ n : a special election held between regular elections in order to fill a vacancy

by·gone \'bī-ˌgòn\ adj : gone by : PAST — **bygone** n

by·law also **bye·law** \'bī-ˌlò\ n : a rule adopted by an organization for managing its internal affairs

by–line \'bī-,līn\ *n* : a line at the beginning of a news story or magazine article giving the writer's name

BYO *abbr* bring your own

BYOB *abbr* bring your own beer; bring your own booze; bring your own bottle

¹**by-pass** \'bī-,pas\ *n* : a passage to one side or around a blocked or congested area; *also* : a surgical procedure establishing this ⟨a coronary ∼⟩

²**bypass** *vb* : to avoid by means of a bypass

by-path \-,path, -,päth\ *n* : BYWAY

by-play \'bī-,plā\ *n* : action engaged in on the side (as of a stage) while the main action proceeds

by–prod·uct \-,prä-(,)dəkt\ *n* : a sometimes unexpected product or result produced in addition to the main product or result

by·stand·er \-,stan-dər\ *n* : one present but not participating ♦ **Synonyms** ON-LOOKER, WITNESS, SPECTATOR, EYEWIT-NESS

byte \'bīt\ *n* : a unit of computer information consisting of a group of 8 bits

by·way \'bī-,wā\ *n* 1 : a little-traveled side road 2 : a secondary aspect

by·word \-,wərd\ *n* 1 : PROVERB 2 : one that is noteworthy or notorious

Byz·an·tine \'biz-ᵊn-,tēn, 'bī-, -,tīn; bə-'zan-, bī-\ *adj* 1 : of, relating to, or characteristic of the ancient city of Byzantium or the Byzantine Empire 2 *often not cap* : intricately involved and often devious

C

¹**c** \'sē\ *n, pl* **c's** *or* **cs** \'sēz\ *often cap* 1 : the 3d letter of the English alphabet 2 *slang* : a sum of $100 3 : a grade rating a student's work as fair

²**c** *abbr, often cap* 1 calorie 2 carat 3 Celsius 4 cent 5 centigrade 6 centimeter 7 century 8 chapter 9 circa 10 cocaine 11 copyright

C *symbol* carbon

ca *abbr* circa

Ca *symbol* calcium

CA *abbr* 1 California 2 chartered accountant 3 chief accountant 4 chronological age

cab \'kab\ *n* 1 : a light closed horse-drawn carriage 2 : TAXICAB 3 : the covered compartment for the engineer and controls of a locomotive; *also* : a similar compartment (as on a truck) — **cab** *vb*

CAB *abbr* Civil Aeronautics Board

ca·bal \kə-'bäl, -'bal\ *n* [F *cabale*, fr. ML *cabbala* cabala, fr. Heb *qabbālāh*, lit., received (lore)] 1 : a secret group of plotters or political conspirators 2 : CLUB, GROUP ⟨a ∼ of artists⟩

cabala *var of* KABALLAH

ca·bana \kə-'ban-yə, -'ba-nə\ *n* : a shelter at a beach or swimming pool

cab·a·ret \,ka-bə-'rā\ *n* : NIGHTCLUB

cab·bage \'ka-bij\ *n* [ME *caboche*, fr. MF dial., lit., head, noggin] : a vegetable related to the mustard with a dense head of leaves

cab·bie *or* **cab·by** \'ka-bē\ *n, pl* **cabbies** : a driver of a cab

cab·er·net sau·vi·gnon \,ka-bər-'nā-sō-vē-'nyōⁿ\ *n* : a dry red wine made from a single variety of black grape

cab·in \'ka-bən\ *n* 1 : a private room on a ship; *also* : a compartment below deck on a boat for passengers or crew 2 : an aircraft or spacecraft compartment for passengers, crew, or cargo 3 : a small simple one-story house

cabin boy *n* : a boy working as servant on a ship

cabin class *n* : a class of accommodations on a passenger ship superior to tourist class and inferior to first class

cabin cruiser *n* : CRUISER 3

cab·i·net \'kab-nit\ *n* 1 : a case or cupboard for holding or displaying articles 2 : the advisory council of a head of state (as a president or sovereign)

cab·i·net·mak·er \-,mā-kər\ *n* : a woodworker who makes fine furniture — **cab·i·net·mak·ing** *n*

cab·i·net·work \-,wərk\ *n* : the finished work of a cabinetmaker

¹**ca·ble** \'kā-bəl\ *n* 1 : a very strong rope, wire, or chain 2 : a bundle of insulated wires usu. twisted around a central core 3 : CABLEGRAM 4 : CABLE TELEVISION

²**cable** *vb* **ca·bled; ca·bling** : to telegraph by cable

cable car *n* : a vehicle moved by an endless cable

ca·ble·cast \'kā-bəl-,kast\ *n* : a cable television transmission — **cablecast** *vb*

ca·ble·gram \'kā-bəl-,gram\ *n* : a message sent by a submarine telegraph cable

cable modem *n* : a modem for connecting a computer to a network over a cable television line

cable television *n* : a system of television reception in which signals from distant stations are sent by cable to the receivers of paying subscribers

cab·o·chon \'ka-bə-,shän\ *n* : a gem or bead cut in convex form and highly polished but not given facets; *also* : this style of cutting — **cabochon** *adv*

ca·boose \kə-'büs\ *n* : a car usu. at the rear of a freight train for the use of the train crew and railroad workers

cab·ri·o·let \,ka-brē-ə-'lā\ *n* [F] 1 : a light 2-wheeled one-horse carriage 2 : a convertible coupe

cab·stand \'kab-,stand\ *n* : a place where cabs wait for passengers

ca·cao \kə-'kaù, -'kā-ō\ *n, pl* **cacaos** [Sp, fr. Nahuatl *cacahuatl*] : a So. American tree whose seeds (**cacao beans**) are the source of cocoa and chocolate; *also* : its dried fatty seeds

cac·cia·to·re \ˌkä-chə-ˈtȯr-ē\ *adj* [It] : cooked with tomatoes and herbs ⟨chicken ∼⟩

cache \ˈkash\ *n* [F] : a hiding place esp. for preserving provisions; *also* : something hidden or stored in a cache — **cache** *vb*

ca·chet \ka-ˈshā\ *n* [F] **1** : a seal used esp. as a mark of official approval **2** : a feature or quality conferring prestige; *also* : PRESTIGE **3** : a design, inscription, or advertisement printed or stamped on mail

cack·le \ˈka-kəl\ *vb* **cack·led; cack·ling 1** : to make the sharp broken cry characteristic of a hen **2** : to laugh or chatter noisily — **cackle** *n* — **cack·ler** *n*

ca·coph·o·ny \ka-ˈkä-fə-nē\ *n, pl* **-nies** : harsh or discordant sound — **ca·coph·o·nous** \-nəs\ *adj*

cac·tus \ˈkak-təs\ *n, pl* **cac·ti** \-ˌtī\ *or* **cac·tus·es** *also* **cactus** : any of a large family of drought-resistant flowering plants with succulent stems and with leaves replaced by scales or prickles

cad \ˈkad\ *n* : a man who deliberately disregards another's feelings — **cad·dish** \ˈka-dish\ *adj* — **cad·dish·ly** *adv* — **cad·dish·ness** *n*

ca·dav·er \kə-ˈda-vər\ *n* : a dead body

ca·dav·er·ous \kə-ˈda-və-rəs\ *adj* : suggesting a corpse esp. in gauntness or pallor ♦ *Synonyms* WASTED, EMACIATED, GAUNT — **ca·dav·er·ous·ly** *adv*

cad·die *or* **cad·dy** \ˈka-dē\ *n, pl* **caddies** [Sc, errand boy, modif. of F *cadet* military cadet] : a person who assists a golfer esp. by carrying the clubs — **caddie** *or* **caddy** *vb*

cad·dy \ˈka-dē\ *n, pl* **caddies** [Malay *kati* a unit of weight] : a small box, can, or chest; *esp* : one to keep tea in

ca·dence \ˈkād-ᵊns\ *n* : the measure or beat of a rhythmical flow : RHYTHM — **ca·denced** \-ᵊnst\ *adj*

ca·den·za \kə-ˈden-zə\ *n* [It] : a brilliant sometimes improvised passage usu. toward the close of a musical composition

ca·det \kə-ˈdet\ *n* [F, fr. Occitan (Gascony) *capdet* chief, fr. L *capitellum*, fr. L *caput* head] **1** : a younger son or brother **2** : a student in a service academy

Ca·dette \kə-ˈdet\ *n* : a member of a Girl Scout program for girls in sixth through ninth grades

cadge \ˈkaj\ *vb* **cadged; cadg·ing** : SPONGE, BEG ⟨∼ a free meal⟩ — **cadg·er** *n*

cad·mi·um \ˈkad-mē-əm\ *n* : a bluish-white metallic chemical element used esp. in protective platings

cad·re \ˈka-ˌdrā, ˈkä-, -drē\ *n* [F] **1** : FRAMEWORK **2** : a central unit esp. of trained personnel able to assume control and train others **3** : a group of indoctrinated leaders active in promoting the interests of a revolutionary party

ca·du·ceus \kə-ˈdü-sē-əs, -ˈdyü-, -shəs\ *n, pl* **-cei** \-sē-ˌī\ [L] **1** : the staff of a herald; *esp* : a representation of a staff with

two entwined snakes and two wings at the top **2** : an insignia bearing a caduceus and symbolizing a physician

cae·cum *var of* CECUM

Cae·sar \ˈsē-zər\ *n* **1** : any of the Roman emperors succeeding Augustus Caesar — used as a title **2** *often not cap* : a powerful ruler : AUTOCRAT, DICTATOR; *also* : the civil or temporal power

caesarean *also* **caesarian** *var of* CESAREAN

cae·si·um *chiefly Brit var of* CESIUM

cae·su·ra \si-ˈzhùr-ə\ *n, pl* **-suras** *or* **-su·rae** \-ˈzhùr-(ˌ)ē\ : a break in the flow of sound usu. in the middle of a line of verse

ca·fé \ka-ˈfā\ *n* [F, lit., coffee] **1** : RESTAURANT **2** : BARROOM **3** : NIGHTCLUB

ca·fé au lait \(ˌ)ka-ˌfā-ō-ˈlā\ *n* : coffee with hot milk in about equal parts

caf·e·te·ria \ˌka-fə-ˈtir-ē-ə\ *n* [AmerSp *cafetería* coffeehouse] : a restaurant in which the customers serve themselves or are served at a counter

caf·feine \ka-ˈfēn, ˈka-ˌfēn\ *n* : a stimulating alkaloid found esp. in coffee and tea

caf·fein·at·ed \ˈka-fə-ˌnā-təd\ *adj* **1** : stimulated by or as if by caffeine **2** : containing caffeine

caf·fe lat·te \ˈkä-fā-ˈlä-tā\ *n* [It] : espresso mixed with hot or steamed milk

caf·tan \kaf-ˈtan, ˈkaf-ˌtan\ *n* [Russ *kaftan*, fr. Turk, fr. Pers *qaftān*] : an ankle-length garment with long sleeves worn in countries of the eastern Mediterranean

¹**cage** \ˈkāj\ *n* **1** : an openwork enclosure for confining an animal **2** : something resembling a cage

²**cage** *vb* **caged; cag·ing** : to put or keep in or as if in a cage

ca·gey *also* **ca·gy** \ˈkā-jē\ *adj* **ca·gi·er; -est** : wary of being trapped or deceived : SHREWD ⟨a ∼ dealer⟩ — **ca·gi·ly** \-jə-lē\ *adv* — **ca·gi·ness** \-jē-nəs\ *n*

CAGS *abbr* Certificate of Advanced Graduate Study

ca·hoot \kə-ˈhüt\ *n* : PARTNERSHIP, LEAGUE — usu. used in pl. ⟨officials in ∼s with the underworld⟩

cai·man *also* **cayman** \ˈkā-mən; kā-ˈman, kī-\ *n* : any of several Central and So. American reptiles closely related to alligators and crocodiles

cairn \ˈkarn\ *n* : a heap of stones serving as a memorial or a landmark

cais·son \ˈkā-ˌsän, ˈkäs-ᵊn\ *n* **1** : a usu. 2-wheeled vehicle for artillery ammunition **2** : a watertight chamber used in underwater construction work or as a foundation

caisson disease *n* : ²BEND 3

cai·tiff \ˈkā-təf\ *adj* [ME *caitif*, fr. AF *caitif, chaitif* wretched, despicable, fr. L *captivus* captive] : being base, cowardly, or despicable — **caitiff** *n*

ca·jole \kə-ˈjōl\ *vb* **ca·joled; ca·jol·ing** [F *cajoler*] : to persuade or coax esp. with flattery or false promises — **ca·jole·ment** *n* — **ca·jol·ery** \-ˈjō-lə-rē\ *n*

Ca·jun \ˈkā-jən\ *n* : a Louisianian descended from French-speaking immigrants from Acadia (Nova Scotia) — **Cajun** *adj*

¹**cake** \'kāk\ *n* **1** : a baked or fried bread-like food usu. in a small flat shape **2** : a sweet baked food made from batter or dough usu. containing flour, sugar, short-ening, and a leaven (as baking powder) **3** : a hardened or compacted substance ⟨a ∼ of soap⟩ **4** : something easily done ⟨the quiz was ∼⟩

²**cake** *vb* **caked; cak·ing 1** : ENCRUST **2** : to form or harden into a cake

cake-walk \'kāk-ˌwȯk\ *n* **1** : a stage dance typically involving a high prance with backward tilt **2** : a one-sided con-test or an easy task

cal *abbr* **1** calendar **2** caliber

Cal *abbr* **1** California **2** calorie

cal·a·bash \'ka-lə-ˌbash\ *n* : the fruit of a gourd; *also* : a utensil made from its hard shell

cal·a·boose \'ka-lə-ˌbüs\ *n* [Sp *calabozo* dungeon] : JAIL

ca·la·di·um \kə-'lā-dē-əm\ *n* : any of a genus of tropical American ornamental plants related to the arums

cal·a·mari \ˌkä-lə-'mär-ē\ *n* [It] : squid used as food

cal·a·mine \'ka-lə-ˌmīn\ *n* : a lotion of ox-ides of zinc and iron

ca·lam·i·ty \kə-'la-mə-tē\ *n, pl* **-ties 1** : great distress or misfortune **2** : an event causing great harm or loss and af-fliction : DISASTER ⟨an economic ∼⟩ — **ca·lam·i·tous** \-təs\ *adj* — **ca·lam·i·tous·ly** *adv* — **ca·lam·i·tous·ness** *n*

calc *abbr* calculated; calculated

cal·car·e·ous \kal-'kar-ē-əs\ *adj* : resem-bling calcium carbonate in hardness; *also* : containing calcium or calcium carbon-ate

cal·cif·er·ous \kal-'si-fə-rəs\ *adj* : pro-ducing or containing calcium carbonate

cal·ci·fy \'kal-sə-ˌfī\ *vb* **-fied; -fy·ing** : to make or become calcareous — **cal·ci·fi·ca·tion** \ˌkal-sə-fə-'kā-shən\ *n*

cal·ci·mine \'kal-sə-ˌmīn\ *n* : a thin water paint used esp. on plastered surfaces — **calcimine** *vb*

cal·cine \kal-'sīn\ *vb* **cal·cined; cal·cin·ing** : to heat to a high temperature but without fusing to drive off volatile matter and often to reduce to powder — **cal·ci·na·tion** \ˌkal-sə-'nā-shən\ *n*

cal·cite \'kal-ˌsīt\ *n* : a crystalline mineral consisting of calcium carbonate — **cal·cit·ic** \kal-'si-tik\ *adj*

cal·ci·um \'kal-sē-əm\ *n* : a silver-white soft metallic chemical element occurring only in combination

calcium carbonate *n* : a substance found in nature as limestone and marble and in plant ashes, bones, and shells

cal·cu·late \'kal-kyə-ˌlāt\ *vb* **-lat·ed; -lat·ing** [L *calculare*, fr. *calculus* pebble (used in reckoning)] **1** : to determine by math-ematical processes : COMPUTE **2** : to reckon by exercise of practical judgment : ESTIMATE **3** : to design or adapt for a purpose **4** : COUNT, RELY — **cal·cu·la·ble** \-lə-bəl\ *adj* — **cal·cu·la·tor** \-ˌlā-tər\ *n*

cal·cu·lat·ed \-ˌlā-təd\ *adj* **1** : under-taken after estimating the chance of suc-cess or failure ⟨a ∼ risk⟩ **2** : planned purposefully : DELIBERATE ⟨a ∼ strate-gy⟩

cal·cu·lat·ing \-ˌlā-tiŋ\ *adj* : marked by shrewd consideration esp. of self-interest — **cal·cu·lat·ing·ly** *adv*

cal·cu·la·tion \ˌkal-kyə-'lā-shən\ *n* **1** : the process or an act of calculating **2** : the result of an act of calculating **3** : studied care; *also* : cold heartless plan-ning to promote self-interest

cal·cu·lus \'kal-kyə-ləs\ *n, pl* **-li** \-ˌlī\ *also* **-lus·es** [L, pebble (used in reckoning)] **1** : a method of computation or calcula-tion in a special notation (as of logic) **2** : a branch of mathematics concerned with the rate of change of functions and with methods of finding lengths, areas, and volumes **3** : a concretion usu. of mineral salts esp. in hollow organs or ducts

cal·de·ra \kal-'der-ə, kȯl-, -'dir-\ *n* [Sp, lit., cauldron] : a large crater usu. formed by the collapse of a volcanic cone

cal·dron *var of* CAULDRON

¹**cal·en·dar** \'ka-lən-dər\ *n* **1** : an arrange-ment of time into days, weeks, months, and years; *also* : a sheet or folder contain-ing such an arrangement for a period **2** : an orderly list

²**calendar** *vb* : to enter in a calendar

¹**cal·en·der** \'ka-lən-dər\ *vb* : to press (as cloth or paper) between rollers or plates so as to make smooth or glossy or to thin into sheets

²**calender** *n* : a machine for calendering

ca·lends \'ka-ləndz, 'kā-\ *n sing or pl* : the first day of the ancient Roman month

ca·len·du·la \kə-'len-jə-lə\ *n* : any of a genus of yellow-flowered herbs related to the daisies

¹**calf** \'kaf, 'käf\ *n, pl* **calves** \'kavz, 'kȧvz\ **1** : the young of the domestic cow; *also* : the young of various large mammals (as the elephant or whale) **2** : CALFSKIN

²**calf** *n, pl* **calves** \'kavz, 'kȧvz\ : the fleshy back of the leg below the knee

calf·skin \'kaf-ˌskin, 'käf-\ *n* : leather made of the skin of a calf

cal·i·ber *or* **cal·i·bre** \'ka-lə-bər\ *n* [MF *calibre*, fr. It *calibro*, fr. Ar *qālib* shoe-maker's last] **1** : degree of mental capac-ity, excellence, or importance **2** : the di-ameter of a projectile **3** : the diameter of the bore of a gun

cal·i·brate \'ka-lə-ˌbrāt\ *vb* **-brat·ed; -brat·ing** : to adjust precisely

cal·i·bra·tion \ˌka-lə-'brā-shən\ *n* : a set of graduated marks indicating values or positions — usu. used in pl.

cal·i·co \'ka-li-ˌkō\ *n, pl* **-coes** *or* **-cos 1** : printed cotton fabric **2** : a mottled or spotted animal — **calico** *adj*

Calif *abbr* California

Cal·i·for·nia poppy \ˌka-lə-'fȯr-nyə-\ *n* : a widely cultivated herb with usu. yel-low or orange flowers that is related to the poppies

cal·i·for·ni·um \ˌka-lə-'fȯr-nē-əm\ *n* : an

artificially prepared radioactive chemical element

cal·i·per \'ka-lə-pər\ n 1 : any of various instruments having two arms, legs, or jaws used esp. to measure diameter or thickness — usu. used in pl. 2 : a device for pressing a frictional material against the sides of a rotating wheel or disk

ca·liph \'kā-ləf, 'ka-\ n : a successor of Muhammad as head of Islam — used as a title — **ca·liph·ate** \-lə-,fāt, -fət\ n

cal·is·then·ics \,ka-ləs-'the-niks\ n sing or pl [Gk kalos beautiful + sthenos strength] : bodily exercises usu. done without apparatus — **cal·is·then·ic** adj

calk \'kòk\ var of CAULK

¹call \'kòl\ vb 1 : SHOUT, CRY; also : to utter a characteristic note or cry 2 : to utter in a loud clear voice ⟨~ed out my name⟩ 3 : to announce authoritatively 4 : SUMMON ⟨was ~ed to testify⟩ 5 : to make a request or demand ⟨~ for an investigation⟩ 6 : to halt (as a baseball game) because of unsuitable conditions 7 : to demand payment of (a loan); also : to demand surrender of (as a bond) for redemption 8 : to get or try to get in communication by telephone 9 : to make a brief visit 10 : to speak of or address by name : give a name to 11 : to estimate or consider for practical purposes ⟨~ it ten miles⟩ 12 : to temporarily transfer control of computer processing to (as a subroutine or procedure) — **call·er** n

²call n 1 : SHOUT 2 : the cry of an animal (as a bird) 3 : a request or a command to come or assemble : INVITATION, SUMMONS 4 : DEMAND, CLAIM; also : REQUEST 5 : a brief usu. formal visit 6 : an act of calling on the telephone 7 : DECISION ⟨a tough ~⟩ 8 : a temporary transfer of control of computer processing to a particular set of instructions

cal·la lily \'ka-lə-\ n : a plant related to the arums and grown for its large white lily-like bract that surrounds a fleshy spike of small yellow flowers

call·back \'kòl-,bak\ n : a calling back; esp : RECALL 5

call–board \-,bòrd\ n : a board for posting notices (as of rehearsal calls)

call down vb : REPRIMAND

call girl n : a prostitute with whom appointments are made by phone

cal·lig·ra·phy \kə-'li-grə-fē\ n : artistic or elegant handwriting; also : the art of producing such writing — **cal·lig·ra·pher** \-fər\ n — **cal·li·graph·ic** \,ka-lə-'graf-ik\ adj

call–in \'kòl-,in\ adj : allowing listeners to engage in broadcast telephone conversations ⟨a ~ show⟩

call in vb 1 : to order to return or be returned 2 : to summon to one's aid 3 : to report by telephone

call·ing \'kò-liŋ\ n 1 : a strong inner impulse toward a particular course of action 2 : the activity in which one customarily engages as an occupation

cal·li·ope \kə-'lī-ə-(,)pē, 'ka-lē-,ōp\ n [fr. Calliope, chief of the Muses, fr. L, fr. Gk Kalliopē] : a keyboard musical instrument similar to an organ and made up of a series of whistles

cal·li·per chiefly Brit var of CALIPER

call number n : a combination of characters assigned to a library book to indicate its place on a shelf

call off vb : CANCEL ⟨called off the trip⟩

cal·los·i·ty \ka-'lä-sə-tē\ n, pl -ties 1 : the quality or state of being callous 2 : CALLUS 1

¹cal·lous \'ka-ləs\ adj 1 : being thickened and hardened ⟨~ skin⟩ 2 : feeling no emotion or sympathy — **cal·lous·ly** adv — **cal·lous·ness** n

²callous vb : to make callous

cal·low \'ka-lō\ adj [ME calu bald, fr. OE] : lacking adult sophistication ⟨a ~ youth⟩ — **cal·low·ness** n

call–up \'kò-,ləp\ n : an order to report for active military service

call up vb : to summon for active military duty

cal·lus \'ka-ləs\ n 1 : a callous area on skin or bark 2 : tissue that is converted into bone in the healing of a bone fracture — **callus** vb

call–waiting n : a telephone service by which during a call in progress an incoming call is signaled (as by a click)

¹calm \'käm, 'kälm\ n 1 : a period or a condition free from storms, high winds, or rough water 2 : complete or almost complete absence of wind 3 : a state of tranquillity

²calm vb : to make or become calm

³calm adj : marked by calm : STILL, UNRUFFLED — **calm·ly** adv — **calm·ness** n

cal·o·mel \'ka-lə-məl, -,mel\ n : a chloride of mercury used esp. as a fungicide

ca·lor·ic \kə-'lör-ik\ adj 1 : of or relating to heat 2 : of, relating to, or containing calories — **ca·lo·ric·al·ly** \-i-k(ə-)lē\ adv

cal·o·rie also **cal·o·ry** \'ka-lə-rē\ n, pl -ries : a unit for measuring heat; esp : one for measuring the value of foods for producing heat and energy in the human body equivalent to the amount of heat required to raise the temperature of one kilogram of water one degree Celsius

cal·o·rim·e·ter \,ka-lə-'ri-mə-tər\ n : an apparatus for measuring quantities of heat — **cal·o·rim·e·try** \-trē\ n

cal·u·met \'kal-yə-,met, -mət\ n : an American Indian ceremonial pipe

ca·lum·ni·ate \kə-'ləm-nē-,āt\ vb -at·ed; -at·ing : to make false and malicious statements about ♦ *Synonyms* DEFAME, MALIGN, LIBEL, SLANDER, TRADUCE — **ca·lum·ni·a·tion** \-,ləm-nē-'ā-shən\ n — **ca·lum·ni·a·tor** \-'ləm-nē-,ā-tər\ n

cal·um·ny \'ka-ləm-nē\ n, pl -nies : false and malicious accusation — **ca·lum·ni·ous** \kə-'ləm-nē-əs\ adj

calve \'kav, 'käv\ vb calved; calv·ing : to give birth to a calf

calves pl of CALF

Cal·vin·ism \'kal-və-,ni-zəm\ n : the theological system of John Calvin and his followers — **Cal·vin·ist** \-nist\ *n or adj* — **Cal·vin·is·tic** \,kal-və-'nis-tik\ *adj*

ca·lyp·so \kə-'lip-sō\ *n, pl* **-sos** : a style of music originating in the British West Indies and having lyrics that usu. satirize local personalities and events

ca·lyx \'kā-liks, 'ka-\ *n, pl* **ca·lyx·es** or **ca·ly·ces** \'kā-lə-,sēz, 'ka-\ : the usu. green or leaflike outer part of a flower consisting of sepals

cal·zo·ne \kal-'zōn, -'zō-nē\ *n* : a baked or fried turnover of pizza dough stuffed with cheese and various fillings

¹cam \'kam\ *n* : a rotating or sliding piece in a mechanical linkage by which rotary motion is transformed into linear motion or vice versa

²cam *n* : CAMERA

ca·ma·ra·de·rie \,käm-'rä-də-rē, ,kam-, -'ra-\ *n* [F] : friendly feeling and goodwill among comrades

cam·bi·um \'kam-bē-əm\ *n, pl* **-bi·ums** or **-bia** \-bē-ə\ : a thin cellular layer between xylem and phloem of most higher plants from which new tissues develop — **cam·bi·al** \-əl\ *adj*

Cam·bri·an \'kam-brē-ən, 'käm-\ *adj* : of, relating to, or being the earliest period of the Paleozoic era — **Cambrian** *n*

cam·bric \'kām-brik\ *n* : a fine thin white linen or cotton fabric

cam·cord·er \'kam-,kȯr-dər\ *n* : a small portable combined camera and VCR

came *past of* COME

cam·el \'ka-məl\ *n* : either of two large hoofed cud-chewing mammals used esp. in desert regions of Asia and Africa for carrying and riding

camel hair *also* **camel's hair** *n* **1** : the hair of a camel or a substitute for it **2** : cloth made of camel hair or of camel hair and wool

ca·mel·lia \kə-'mēl-yə\ *n* : any of a genus of shrubs and trees related to the tea plant and grown in warm regions and greenhouses for their showy roselike flowers

Cam·em·bert \'ka-məm-,ber\ *n* : a soft cheese with a grayish rind and yellow interior

cam·eo \'ka-mē-,ō\ *n, pl* **-eos** **1** : a gem carved in relief; *also* : a small medallion with a profiled head in relief **2** : a brief appearance esp. by a well-known actor in a play or movie

cam·era \'kam-rə, 'ka-mər-ə\ *n* : a device with a lightproof chamber fitted with a lens through which the image of an object is projected onto a surface for recording (as on film) or for conversion into electrical signals (as for television broadcast) — **cam·era·man** \-,man, -mən\ *n* — **cam·era·wom·an** *n*

cam·i·sole \'ka-mə-,sōl\ *n* : a short sleeveless garment for women

camomile *var of* CHAMOMILE

cam·ou·flage \'ka-mə-,fläzh, -,fläj\ *n* [F] **1** : the disguising of military equipment with paint, nets, or foliage; *also* : the disguise itself **2** : deceptive behavior — **camouflage** *vb*

¹camp \'kamp\ *n* **1** : a place where tents or buildings are erected for usu. temporary shelter **2** : a collection of tents or other shelters **3** : a program offering recreational activities (as boating and hiking) for a limited time ⟨summer ∼⟩ **4** : a body of persons encamped **5** : a training session for athletes outside of the regular season — **camp·ground** \-,graund\ *n* — **camp·site** \-,sīt\ *n*

²camp *vb* **1** : to make or occupy a camp **2** : to live in a camp or outdoors

³camp *n* **1** : exaggerated effeminate mannerisms **2** : something so outrageous, inappropriate, or theatrical as to be considered amusing — **camp** *adj* — **camp·i·ly** \'kam-pə-lē\ *adv* — **camp·i·ness** \-pē-nəs\ *n* — **campy** \-pē\ *adj*

⁴camp *vb* : to engage in camp : exhibit the qualities of camp

cam·paign \kam-'pān\ *n* **1** : a series of military operations forming one distinct stage in a war **2** : a series of activities designed to bring about a particular result ⟨advertising ∼⟩ — **campaign** *vb* — **cam·paign·er** *n*

cam·pa·ni·le \,kam-pə-'nē-lē\ *n, pl* **-ni·les** or **-ni·li** \-'nē-lē\ : a usu. freestanding bell tower

cam·pa·nol·o·gy \,kam-pə-'nä-lə-jē\ *n* : the art of bell ringing — **cam·pa·nol·o·gist** \-jist\ *n*

camp·er \'kam-pər\ *n* **1** : one who camps **2** : a portable dwelling (as a specially equipped vehicle) for use during casual travel and camping

Camp Fire Girl *n* : a member of a national organization of girls from ages 5 to 18

camp follower *n* **1** : a civilian (as a prostitute) who follows a military unit to attend or exploit its personnel **2** : a follower of a group who is not an adherent; *esp* : a politician who joins a movement solely for personal gain

cam·phor \'kam-fər\ *n* : a gummy volatile aromatic compound obtained from an evergreen Asian tree (**camphor tree**) and used esp. in medicine

camp meeting *n* : a series of evangelistic meetings usu. held outdoors

camp·o·ree \,kam-pə-'rē\ *n* : a gathering of Boy Scouts or Girl Scouts from a given geographic area

cam·pus \'kam-pəs\ *n* [L, plain] : the grounds and buildings of a college or school; *also* : grounds resembling a campus ⟨hospital ∼⟩

cam·shaft \'kam-,shaft\ *n* : a shaft to which a cam is fastened

¹can \kən, 'kan\ *vb, past* **could** \kəd, 'kud\; *pres sing & pl* **can** **1** : be able to **2** : may perhaps ⟨∼ he still be alive⟩ **3** : be permitted by conscience or feeling to ⟨you ∼ hardly blame her⟩ **4** : have permission to ⟨you ∼ go now⟩

²can \'kan\ *n* **1** : a usu. cylindrical container or receptacle ⟨garbage ∼⟩ ⟨coffee ∼⟩ **2** : JAIL **3** : TOILET

³can \'kan\ *vb*, **canned; can·ning** **1** : to put in a can : preserve by sealing in airtight cans or jars **2** *slang* : to discharge from employment **3** *slang* : to put a stop or an end to — **can·ner** *n*

Can *or* **Canad** *abbr* Canada; Canadian

Can·a·da goose \'ka-nə-də\ *n* : a common wild goose of No. America

ca·naille \kə-'nī, -'nāl\ *n* [F, fr. It *canaglia*, fr. *cane* dog] : RABBLE, RIFFRAFF

ca·nal \kə-'nal\ *n* **1** : a tubular passage in the body : DUCT **2** : an artificial waterway (as for boats or irrigation)

can·a·lize \'kan-³l-,īz\ *vb* **-lized; -liz·ing** **1** : to provide with a canal or make into or like a channel **2** : to provide with an outlet; *esp* : to direct into preferred channels — **ca·nal·i·za·tion** \,kan-³l-ə-'zā-shən\ *n*

can·a·pé \'ka-nə-pē, -,pā\ *n* [F, lit., sofa, fr. ML *canopeum, canapeum* mosquito net] : a piece of bread or toast or a cracker topped with a savory food

ca·nard \kə-'närd\ *n* : a false or unfounded report, story or belief

ca·nary \kə-'ner-ē\ *n, pl* **ca·nar·ies** [fr. the *Canary* islands] **1** : a usu. sweet wine similar to Madeira **2** : a usu. yellow or greenish finch often kept in a cage as a pet

ca·nas·ta \kə-'nas-tə\ *n* [Sp, lit., basket] : rummy played with two full decks of cards plus four jokers

canc *abbr* canceled

can-can \'kan-,kan\ *n* : a woman's dance of French origin characterized by high kicking

¹can·cel \'kan-səl\ *vb* **-celed** *or* **-celled; -cel·ing** *or* **-cel·ling** [ME *cancellen*, fr. AF *canceller, chanceller*, fr. LL *cancellare*, fr. L, to make like a lattice, fr. *cancelli* lattice] **1** : to destroy the force or validity of : ANNUL **2** : to match in force or effect : OFFSET **3** : to cross out : DELETE **4** : to remove (a common divisor) from a numerator and denominator; *also* : to remove (equivalents) on opposite sides of an equation or account **5** : to mark (a postage stamp or check) so that it cannot be reused **6** : to neutralize each other's strength or effect — **can·cel·la·tion** \,kan-sə-'lā-shən\ *n* — **can·cel·er** *or* **can·cel·ler** *n*

²cancel *n* **1** : CANCELLATION **2** : a deleted part

can·cer \'kan-sər\ *n* [L, lit., crab] **1** *cap* : a zodiacal constellation between Gemini and Leo usu. pictured as a crab **2** *cap* : the 4th sign of the zodiac in astrology; *also* : one born under this sign **3** : a malignant tumor that tends to spread in the body; *also* : an abnormal state marked by such tumors **4** : a malignant evil that spreads destructively — **can·cer·ous** \-sə-rəs\ *adj* — **can·cer·ous·ly** *adv*

can·de·la·bra \,kan-də-'lä-brə, -'la-\ *n* : an ornamental branched candlestick or lamp with several lights

can·de·la·brum \-brəm\ *n, pl* **-bra** *also* **-brums** : CANDELABRA

can·did \'kan-dəd\ *adj* **1** : FRANK, STRAIGHTFORWARD \a ~ critique\ **2** : relating to photography of subjects acting naturally or spontaneously without

being posed — **can·did·ly** *adv* — **can·did·ness** *n*

can·di·da·cy \'kan-də-də-sē\ *n, pl* **-cies** : the state of being a candidate

can·di·date \'kan-də-,dāt, 'ka-nə-, -dət\ *n* [L *candidatus*, fr. *candidatus* clothed in white, fr. *candidus* white; fr. the white toga worn by office seekers in ancient Rome] : one who seeks or is proposed for an office, honor, or membership \a ~ for governor\

can·di·da·ture \'kan-də-də-,chùr, 'ka-nə-\ *n, chiefly Brit* : CANDIDACY

can·died \'kan-dēd\ *adj* : preserved in or encrusted with sugar

¹can·dle \'kan-d³l\ *n* : a usu. slender mass of tallow or wax molded around a wick that is burned to give light

²candle *vb* **can·dled; can·dling** : to examine (as eggs) by holding between the eye and a light — **can·dler** *n*

can·dle·light \'kan-d³l-līt\ *n* **1** : the light of a candle; *also* : any soft artificial light **2** : the time when candles are lit : TWILIGHT

can·dle·lit \-,lit\ *adj* : illuminated by candlelight \a ~ dinner\

Can·dle·mas \'kan-d³l-məs\ *n* : February 2 observed as a church festival in commemoration of the presentation of Christ in the temple

can·dle·stick \-,stik\ *n* : a holder with a socket for a candle

can·dle·wick \-,wik\ *n* : a soft cotton yarn; *also* : embroidery made with this yarn usu. in tufts

can·dor \'kan-dər\ *n* : FRANKNESS, OUTSPOKENNESS

can·dour *chiefly Brit var of* CANDOR

C and W *abbr* country and western

¹can·dy \'kan-dē\ *n, pl* **candies** [ME *sugre candy*, fr. MF *sucre candi*, fr. OF *sucre* sugar + Ar *qandī* candied, fr. *qand* crystallized sugar] **1** : a confection made from sugar often with flavoring and filling **2** : something that appeals in a light or frivolous way

²candy *vb* **can·died; can·dy·ing** : to encrust in sugar often by cooking in a syrup

candy strip·er \-'strī-pər\ *n* : a teenage volunteer worker at a hospital

¹cane \'kān\ *n* **1** : a slender hollow or pithy stem (as of a reed or bramble) **2** : a tall woody grass or reed (as sugarcane or sorghum) **3** : a walking stick; *also* : a rod for flogging

²cane *vb* **caned; can·ing** **1** : to beat with a cane **2** : to weave or make with cane — **can·er** *n*

cane·brake \'kān-,brāk\ *n* : a thicket of cane

¹ca·nine \'kā-,nīn\ *n* **1** : a pointed tooth between the outer incisor and the first premolar **2** : a canine mammal (as a domestic dog)

²canine *adj* [L *caninus*, fr. *canis* dog] : of or relating to dogs or to the family to which they belong

can·is·ter \'ka-nə-stər\ *n* : an often cylindrical container

can·ker \'kaŋ-kər\ *n* : a spreading sore

that eats into tissue — **can·ker·ous** \-kə-rəs\ *adj*

can·ker·worm \-ˌwərm\ *n* : either of two moths and esp. their larvae that are pests of fruit and shade trees

can·na \'ka-nə\ *n* : any of a genus of tropical herbs with large leaves and racemes of bright-colored flowers

can·na·bis \'ka-nə-bəs\ *n* : any of the psychoactive preparations (as marijuana) or chemicals (as THC) derived from hemp; *also* : HEMP

canned \'kand\ *adj* : prepared in standardized form for general use or wide distribution ⟨~ music⟩

can·nery \'ka-nə-rē\ *n, pl* **-ner·ies** : a factory for the canning of foods

can·ni·bal \'ka-nə-bəl\ *n* [NL *Canibalis* a member of a Caribbean Indian people, fr. Sp *Caníbal*] : one that eats the flesh of its own kind — **can·ni·bal·ism** \-bə-ˌli-zəm\ *n* — **can·ni·bal·is·tic** \-bə-'lis-tik\ *adj*

can·ni·bal·ise *Brit var of* CANNIBALIZE

can·ni·bal·ize \'ka-nə-bə-ˌlīz\ *vb* **-ized; -iz·ing** 1 : to take usable parts from (as an inoperative machine) to construct or repair another machine 2 : to practice cannibalism

can·non \'ka-nən\ *n, pl* **cannons** *or* **cannon** [ME *canon*, fr. AF, fr. It *cannone*, lit., large tube, fr. *canna* reed, tube, fr. L cane, reed] : a large heavy gun; *esp* : one mounted on a carriage

can·non·ade \ˌka-nə-'nād\ *n* : a heavy fire of artillery — **cannonade** *vb*

can·non·ball \'ka-nən-ˌbȯl\ *n* : a usu. round solid missile for a cannon

can·non·eer \ˌka-nə-'nir\ *n* : an artillery gunner

can·not \'ka-ˌnät; kə-'nät\ : can not — **cannot but** : to be unable to do otherwise than ⟨we *cannot but* wonder why⟩

can·nu·la \'kan-yə-lə\ *n, pl* **-las** *or* **-lae** \-ˌlē\ : a small tube for insertion into a body cavity or into a duct or vessel

can·ny \'ka-nē\ *adj* **can·ni·er; -est** : PRUDENT, SHREWD — **can·ni·ly** \'ka-ⁿl-ē\ *adv* — **can·ni·ness** \'ka-nē-nəs\ *n*

ca·noe \kə-'nü\ *n* : a light narrow boat with sharp ends and curved sides that is usu. propelled by paddles — **canoe** *vb* — **ca·noe·ist** *n*

ca·no·la \kə-'nō-lə\ *n* : a rape plant producing seeds that are low in a toxic acid and yield an edible oil (**canola oil**) high in monounsaturated fatty acids; *also* : this oil

¹**can·on** \'ka-nən\ *n* 1 : a regulation decreed by a church council; *also* : a provision of canon law 2 : an official or authoritative list (as of works of literature) 3 : an accepted principle ⟨the ~s of good taste⟩

²**canon** *n* : a member of the clergy on the staff of a cathedral

ca·non·i·cal \kə-'nä-ni-kəl\ *adj* 1 : of, relating to, or forming a canon 2 : conforming to a general rule or acceptable procedure : ORTHODOX 3 : of or relating to a canon of a cathedral — **ca·non·i·cal·ly** \-k(ə-)lē\ *adv*

can·on·ize \'ka-nə-ˌnīz\ *vb* **can·on·ized** \-ˌnīzd\; **can·on·iz·ing** 1 : to declare (a deceased person) an officially recognized saint 2 : GLORIFY, EXALT — **can·on·i·za·tion** \ˌka-nə-nə-'zā-shən\ *n*

canon law *n* : the law governing a church

can·o·py \'ka-nə-pē\ *n, pl* **-pies** [ME *canope*, fr. ML *canopeum* mosquito net, fr. L *conopeum*, fr. Gk *kōnōpion*, fr. *kōnōps* mosquito] 1 : an overhanging cover, shelter, or shade 2 : the uppermost spreading layer of a forest 3 : a transparent cover for an airplane cockpit 4 : the fabric part of a parachute — **canopy** *vb*

¹**cant** \'kant\ *vb* : to give a slant to

²**cant** *n* 1 : an oblique or slanting surface 2 : TILT, SLANT

³**cant** *vb* 1 : to beg in a whining manner 2 : to talk hypocritically

⁴**cant** *n* 1 : the special idiom of a profession or trade : JARGON 2 : insincere speech; *esp* : insincerely pious words or statements

Cant *abbr* Canticle of Canticles

can·ta·bi·le \kän-'tä-bə-ˌlā\ *adv or adj* [It] : in a singing manner — used as a direction in music

can·ta·loupe *also* **can·ta·loup** \'kant-ⁿl-ˌōp\ *n* : MUSKMELON; *esp* : one with orange flesh and rough skin

can·tan·ker·ous \kan-'taŋ-kə-rəs\ *adj* : difficult to deal with : ILL-NATURED ⟨a ~ mule⟩ — **can·tan·ker·ous·ly** *adv* — **can·tan·ker·ous·ness** *n*

can·ta·ta \kən-'tä-tə\ *n* [It] : a choral composition usu. sung to instrumental accompaniment

can·teen \kan-'tēn\ *n* [F *cantine* bottle case, canteen (store), fr. It *cantina* wine cellar] 1 : a flask for carrying liquids 2 : a place of recreation and entertainment for military personnel 3 : a small cafeteria or counter at which snacks are served

can·ter \'kan-tər\ *n* : a horse's 3-beat gait resembling but smoother and slower than a gallop — **canter** *vb*

Can·ter·bury bell \'kant-ər-ˌber-ē-\ *n* : any of several plants related to the bluebell that are cultivated for their showy flowers

can·ti·cle \'kan-ti-kəl\ *n* : SONG; *esp* : any of several liturgical songs taken from the Bible

Canticle of Canticles *n* : SONG OF SONGS

¹**can·ti·le·ver** \'kant-ⁿl-ˌē-vər\ *n* : a projecting beam or structure supported only at one end; *also* : either of a pair of such structures projecting toward each other so that when joined they form a bridge

²**cantilever** *vb* 1 : to support by a cantilever ⟨a ~ed shelf⟩ 2 : to build as a cantilever 3 : to project as a cantilever

can·tle \'kant-ⁿl\ *n* : the upwardly projecting rear part of a saddle

can·to \'kan-ˌtō\ *n, pl* **cantos** [It, fr. L *cantus* song] : one of the major divisions of a long poem

can·ton \'kant-ⁿn, 'kan-ˌtän\ *n* : a small territorial division of a country; *esp* : one of the political divisions of Switzerland — **can·ton·al** \\'kant-ᵊn-ᵊl, kan-'tän-ᵊl\\ *adj*

can·ton·ment \\kan-'tōn-mənt, -'tän-\\ *n* : usu. temporary quarters for troops

can·tor \\'kan-tər\\ *n* **1** : a choir leader **2** : a synagogue official who sings liturgical music and leads the congregation in prayer

can·vas *also* **can·vass** \\'kan-vəs\\ *n* **1** : a strong cloth formerly much used for making tents and sails **2** : a set of sails **3** : a group of tents **4** : a piece of cloth prepared as a surface for a painting; *also* : a painting on this surface **5** : the canvas-covered floor of a boxing or wrestling ring

can·vas·back \\'kan-vəs-ˌbak\\ *n* : a No. American wild duck with red head and gray back

¹can·vass *also* **can·vas** \\'kan-vəs\\ *vb* **can·vassed; can·vas·sing** : to go through (a district) or to (persons) to solicit votes or orders for goods or to determine public opinion or sentiment — **can·vass·er** *n*

²canvass *n* : an act or instance of canvassing

can·yon \\'kan-yən\\ *n* : a deep narrow valley with high steep sides

¹cap \\'kap\\ *n* **1** : a covering for the head esp. with a visor and no brim; *also* : something resembling such a covering esp. on a tip, knob or end ⟨a bottle ∼⟩ **2** : a container holding an explosive charge (as for a toy gun) **3** : an upper limit (as on expenditures)

²cap *vb* **capped; cap·ping 1** : to provide or protect with a cap **2** : to form a cap over : CROWN **3** : OUTDO, SURPASS **4** : to bring to a conclusion ⟨∼ off dinner with coffee⟩

³cap *abbr* **1** capacity **2** capital **3** capitalize; capitalized

CAP *abbr* Civil Air Patrol

ca·pa·ble \\'kā-pə-bəl\\ *adj* : having ability, capacity, or power to do something : ABLE, COMPETENT — **ca·pa·bil·i·ty** \\ˌkā-pə-'bi-lə-tē\\ *n* — **ca·pa·bly** *adv*

ca·pa·cious \\kə-'pā-shəs\\ *adj* : able to contain much — **ca·pa·cious·ly** *adv* — **ca·pa·cious·ness** *n*

ca·pac·i·tance \\kə-'pa-sə-təns\\ *n* : the property of an electric nonconductor that permits the storage of energy

ca·pac·i·tor \\kə-'pa-sə-tər\\ *n* : an electronic device for temporary storage of electrical energy

¹ca·pac·i·ty \\kə-'pa-sə-tē\\ *n, pl* **-ties 1** : legal qualification or fitness ⟨∼ to stand trial⟩ **2** : the ability to contain, receive, or accommodate ⟨seating ∼⟩ **3** : the maximum amount or number that can be contained — see METRIC SYSTEM table, WEIGHT table **4** : ABILITY **5** : position or character assigned or assumed

²capacity *adj* : equaling maximum capacity ⟨a ∼ crowd⟩

cap–a–pie *or* **cap–à–pie** \\ˌka-pə-'pē\\ *adv* [MF] : from head to foot : at all points

ca·par·i·son \\kə-'par-ə-sən\\ *n* **1** : an ornamental covering for a horse **2** : TRAPPINGS, ADORNMENT — **caparison** *vb*

¹cape \\'kāp\\ *n* **1** : a point of land jutting out into water **2** *often cap* : CAPE COD COTTAGE

²cape *n* : a sleeveless garment hanging from the neck over the shoulders — **caped** *adj*

Cape Cod cottage \\'kāp-'käd-\\ *n* : a compact rectangular dwelling of one or one-and-a-half stories usu. with a steep gable roof

¹ca·per \\'kā-pər\\ *n* : the greenish flower bud or young berry of a Mediterranean shrub pickled for use as a relish; *also* : this shrub

²caper *vb* **ca·pered; ca·per·ing** : to leap about in a playful manner

³caper *n* **1** : a frolicsome leap **2** : a capricious escapade **3** : an illegal or questionable act

cape·skin \\'kāp-ˌskin\\ *n* : a light flexible leather made from sheepskins

cap·ful \\'kap-ˌfül\\ *n, pl* **cap·fuls** *also* **caps·ful** \\'kaps-\\ : as much as a cap will hold

cap·il·lar·i·ty \\ˌka-pə-'lar-ə-tē\\ *n, pl* **-ties** : the action by which the surface of a liquid where it is in contact with a solid (as in a slender tube) is raised or lowered depending on the relative attraction of the molecules of the liquid for each other and for those of the solid

¹cap·il·lary \\'ka-pə-ˌler-ē\\ *adj* **1** : resembling a hair **2** : having a very small bore ⟨∼ tube⟩ **3** : of or relating to capillaries or to capillarity

²capillary *n, pl* **-lar·ies** : any of the tiny thin-walled blood vessels that carry blood between the smallest arteries and their corresponding veins

¹cap·i·tal \\'ka-pət-ᵊl\\ *n* : the top part or piece of an architectural column

²capital *adj* **1** : conforming to the series A, B, C rather than a, b, c ⟨∼ letters⟩ ⟨∼ G⟩ **2** : punishable by death ⟨a ∼ crime⟩ **3** : most serious ⟨a ∼ error⟩ **4** : first in importance or position : CHIEF; *also* : being the seat of government ⟨the ∼ city⟩ **5** : of or relating to capital ⟨∼ expenditures⟩; *esp* : relating to or being assets that add to the long-term net worth of a corporation **6** : FIRST-RATE, EXCELLENT

³capital *n* **1** : accumulated wealth esp. as used to produce more wealth **2** : the total face value of shares of stock issued by a company **3** : persons holding capital **4** : ADVANTAGE, GAIN **5** : a letter larger than the ordinary small letter and often different in form **6** : the capital city of a state, province or country; *also* : a city preeminent in some activity ⟨the fashion ∼⟩

capital gain *n* : the increase in value of an asset (as stock or real estate) between the time it is bought and the time it is sold

capital goods *n pl* : machinery, tools, factories, and commodities used in the production of goods

cap·i·tal·ise *Brit var of* CAPITALIZE

cap·i·tal·ism \'ka-pət-°l-ˌi-zəm\ *n* : an economic system characterized by private or corporate ownership of capital goods and by prices, production, and distribution of goods that are determined mainly by competition in a free market

¹**cap·i·tal·ist** \-ist\ *n* 1 : a person who has capital esp. invested in business 2 : a person of great wealth : PLUTOCRAT 3 : a believer in capitalism

²**capitalist** *or* **cap·i·tal·is·tic** \ˌka-pət-°l-'is-tik\ *adj* 1 : owning capital 2 : practicing or advocating capitalism 3 : marked by capitalism — **cap·i·tal·is·ti·cal·ly** \-ti-k(ə-)lē\ *adv*

cap·i·tal·iza·tion \ˌka-pət-°l-ə-'zā-shən\ *n* 1 : the act or process of capitalizing 2 : the total amount of money used as capital in a business

cap·i·tal·ize \'ka-pət-°l-ˌīz\ *vb* -**ized; -iz·ing** 1 : to write or print with an initial capital or in capitals 2 : to convert into or use as capital 3 : to supply capital for 4 : to gain by turning something to advantage : PROFIT

cap·i·tal·ly \'ka-pət-°l-ē\ *adv* : ADMIRABLY, EXCELLENTLY

cap·i·ta·tion \ˌka-pə-'tā-shən\ *n* : a direct uniform tax levied on each person

cap·i·tol \'ka-pət-°l\ *n* : the building in which a legislature holds its sessions

ca·pit·u·late \kə-'pi-chə-ˌlāt\ *vb* -**lat·ed; -lat·ing** 1 : to surrender esp. on conditions agreed upon 2 : to cease resisting : ACQUIESCE ♦ *Synonyms* SUBMIT, YIELD, SUCCUMB, CAVE, DEFER — **ca·pit·u·la·tion** \-ˌpi-chə-'lā-shən\ *n*

ca·pon \'kā-ˌpän, -pən\ *n* : a castrated male chicken

cap·puc·ci·no \ˌka-pə-'chē-nō, ˌkä-\ *n* [It, lit., Capuchin; fr. the likeness of its color to that of a Capuchin's habit] : espresso mixed with foamy hot milk or cream and often flavored with cinnamon

ca·pric·cio \kə-'prē-chē-ˌō, -chō\ *n, pl* -**cios** [It, lit., whim, prank] : an instrumental piece in free form usu. lively in tempo and brilliant in style

ca·price \kə-'prēs\ *n* [F, fr. It *capriccio*] 1 : a sudden whim or fancy 2 : an inclination to do things impulsively 3 : CAPRICCIO — **ca·pri·cious** \-'pri-shəs\ *adj* — **ca·pri·cious·ly** *adv* — **ca·pri·cious·ness** *n*

Cap·ri·corn \'ka-pri-ˌkórn\ *n* 1 : a zodiacal constellation between Sagittarius and Aquarius usu. pictured as a goat 2 : the 10th sign of the zodiac in astrology; *also* : one born under this sign

cap·ri·ole \'ka-prē-ˌōl\ *n* : ³CAPER 1; *also* : an upward leap of a horse with a backward kick at the height of the leap — **capriole** *vb*

caps *abbr* 1 capitals 2 capsule

cap·sa·i·cin \kap-'sā-ə-sən\ *n* : a colorless compound found in various capsicums that gives hot peppers their hotness

cap·si·cum \'kap-si-kəm\ *n* : PEPPER 2

cap·size \'kap-ˌsīz, kap-'sīz\ *vb* **cap·sized; cap·siz·ing** : UPSET, OVERTURN

cap·stan \'kap-stən, -ˌstan\ *n* 1 : a machine for moving or raising heavy weights

that consists of a vertical drum which can be rotated and around which cable is turned 2 : a rotating shaft that drives recorder tape

cap·su·lar \'kap-sə-lər\ *adj* : of, relating to, or resembling a capsule

cap·su·lat·ed \-ˌlā-təd\ *adj* : enclosed in a capsule

¹**cap·sule** \'kap-səl, -sül\ *n* 1 : a membrane or sac enclosing a body part (as of a joint) 2 : a case bearing spores or seeds 3 : a shell usu. of gelatin that is used for packaging something (as a drug); *also* : such a shell together with its contents 4 : a small pressurized compartment or vehicle (as for space flight)

²**capsule** *adj* 1 : very brief 2 : very compact

Capt *abbr* captain

¹**cap·tain** \'kap-tən\ *n* 1 : a commander of a body of troops 2 : a commissioned officer in the army, air force, or marine corps ranking next below a major 3 : an officer in charge of a ship 4 : a commissioned officer in the navy ranking next below a rear admiral or a commodore 5 : a leader of a side or team 6 : a dominant figure — **cap·tain·cy** *n*

²**captain** *vb* : to be captain of : LEAD

cap·tion \'kap-shən\ *n* 1 : a heading esp. of an article or document : TITLE 2 : the explanatory matter accompanying an illustration 3 : a motion-picture subtitle — **cap·tion** *vb*

cap·tious \'kap-shəs\ *adj* : marked by an inclination to find fault — **cap·tious·ly** *adv* — **cap·tious·ness** *n*

cap·ti·vate \'kap-tə-ˌvāt\ *vb* -**vat·ed; -vat·ing** : to attract and hold irresistibly by some special charm or art — **cap·ti·va·tion** \ˌkap-tə-'vā-shən\ *n* — **cap·ti·va·tor** \'kap-tə-ˌvā-tər\ *n*

cap·tive \'kap-tiv\ *adj* 1 : made prisoner esp. in war 2 : kept within bounds : CONFINED 3 : held under control — **captive** *n* — **cap·tiv·i·ty** \kap-'ti-və-tē\ *n*

cap·tor \'kap-tər\ *n* : one that captures

¹**cap·ture** \'kap-chər\ *n* 1 : the act of capturing 2 : one that has been captured

²**capture** *vb* **cap·tured; cap·tur·ing** 1 : to take captive : WIN, GAIN ⟨∼ the crown⟩ 2 : to preserve in a relatively permanent form ⟨∼ the moment on film⟩

Ca·pu·chin \'ka-pyə-shən\ *n* : a member of an austere branch of the order of St. Francis of Assisi engaged in missionary work and preaching

car \'kär\ *n* 1 : a vehicle moving on wheels 2 : the compartment of an elevator 3 : the part of a balloon or airship that carries passengers or equipment

car·a·cole \'kar-ə-ˌkōl\ *n* : a half turn to right or left executed by a mounted horse — **caracole** *vb*

car·a·cul \'kar-ə-kəl\ *n* : the pelt of a karakul lamb after the curl begins to loosen

ca·rafe \kə-'raf, -'räf\ *n* 1 : a bottle with a flaring lip used esp. to hold wine 2 : a usu. glass pitcher for pouring coffee

car·am·bo·la \ˌkar-əm-ˈbō-lə\ *n*   1 : a 5-angled green to yellow edible tropical fruit of star-shaped cross section   2 : a tropical Asian tree widely cultivated for carambolas

car·a·mel \ˈkar-ə-məl, ˈkär-məl\ *n*   1 : an amorphous substance obtained by heating sugar and used for flavoring and coloring   2 : a firm chewy candy

car·a·pace \ˈkar-ə-ˌpās\ *n* : a protective case or shell on the back of some animals (as turtles or crabs)

¹car·at *var of* KARAT

²car·at \ˈkar-ət\ *n* : a unit of weight for precious stones equal to 200 milligrams

car·a·van \ˈkar-ə-ˌvan\ *n*   1 : a group of travelers journeying together through desert or hostile regions   2 : a group of vehicles traveling in a file

car·a·van·sa·ry \ˌkar-ə-ˈvan-sə-rē\ *or* **car·a·van·se·rai** \-sə-ˌrī\ *n, pl* **-ries** *or* **-rais** *or* **-rai** [Pers *kārvānsarāī*, fr. *kārvān* caravan + *sarāī* palace, inn] : an inn in eastern countries where caravans rest at night   2 : HOTEL, INN

car·a·vel \ˈkar-ə-ˌvel\ *n* : a small 15th and 16th century ship with a broad bow, high narrow poop, and usu. three masts

car·a·way \ˈkar-ə-ˌwā\ *n* : an aromatic herb related to the carrot with fruits (**caraway seed**) used in seasoning and medicine; *also* : its fruit

car·bide \ˈkär-ˌbīd\ *n* : a compound of carbon with another element

car·bine \ˈkär-ˌbēn, -ˌbīn\ *n* : a short-barreled lightweight rifle

car·bo·hy·drate \ˌkär-bō-ˈhī-ˌdrāt, -drət\ *n* : any of various compounds composed of carbon, hydrogen, and oxygen (as sugars and starches)

car·bol·ic acid \ˌkär-ˈbä-lik-\ *n* : PHENOL

car·bon \ˈkär-bən\ *n*   1 : a nonmetallic chemical element occurring in nature esp. as diamond and graphite and as a constituent of coal, petroleum, and limestone   2 : a sheet of carbon paper; *also* : CARBON COPY 1 — **car·bon·less** \-ləs\ *adj*

car·bo·na·ceous \ˌkär-bə-ˈnā-shəs\ *adj* : relating to, containing, or composed of carbon

¹car·bon·ate \ˈkär-bə-ˌnāt, -nət\ *n* : a salt or ester of carbonic acid

²car·bon·ate \-ˌnāt\ *vb* **-at·ed; -at·ing** : to combine or infuse with carbon dioxide ⟨*carbonated* beverages⟩ — **car·bon·ation** \ˌkär-bə-ˈnā-shən\ *n*

carbon black *n* : any of various black substances consisting chiefly of carbon and used esp. as pigments

carbon copy *n*   1 : a copy made by carbon paper   2 : DUPLICATE

carbon dating *n* : the determination of the age of old material (as an archaeological specimen) by its content of carbon 14

carbon dioxide *n* : a heavy colorless gas that does not support combustion and is formed in animal respiration and in the combustion and decomposition of organic substances

carbon 14 *n* : a heavy radioactive form of carbon used esp. in dating old materials (as archaeological specimens)

car·bon·ic acid \kär-ˈbä-nik-\ *n* : a weak acid that decomposes readily into water and carbon dioxide

car·bon·if·er·ous \ˌkär-bə-ˈni-fə-rəs\ *adj*   1 : producing or containing carbon or coal   2 *cap* : of, relating to, or being the period of the Paleozoic era between the Devonian and the Permian — **Carboniferous** *n*

carbon monoxide *n* : a colorless odorless very poisonous gas formed by the incomplete burning of carbon

carbon paper *n* : a thin paper coated with a pigment and used for making copies

carbon tet·ra·chlo·ride \-ˌte-trə-ˈklōr-ˌīd\ *n* : a colorless nonflammable toxic liquid used esp. as a solvent

carbon 12 *n* : the most abundant isotope of carbon having a nucleus of 6 protons and 6 neutrons and used as a standard for measurements of atomic weight

car·boy \ˈkär-ˌbȯi\ *n* [Pers *qarāba*, fr. Ar *qarrāba* demijohn] : a large container for liquids

car·bun·cle \ˈkär-ˌbəŋ-kəl\ *n* : a painful inflammation of the skin and underlying tissue that discharges pus from several openings

car·bu·re·tor \ˈkär-bə-ˌrā-tər, -byə-\ *n* : an apparatus for premixing vaporized fuel and air and supplying the mixture to an internal combustion engine

car·bu·ret·tor *also* **car·bu·ret·ter** \ˌkär-byə-ˈre-tər, ˈkär-byə-ˌ\ *chiefly Brit var of* CARBURETOR

car·case *Brit var of* CARCASS

car·cass \ˈkär-kəs\ *n* : a dead body; *esp* : one of an animal dressed for food

car·cin·o·gen \kär-ˈsi-nə-jən\ *n* : a substance or agent causing cancer — **car·ci·no·gen·ic** \ˌkärs-ᵊn-ō-ˈje-nik\ *adj* — **car·ci·no·ge·nic·i·ty** \-jə-ˈni-sə-tē\ *n*

car·ci·no·ma \ˌkärs-ᵊn-ˈō-mə\ *n, pl* **-mas** *also* **-ma·ta** \-tə\ : a malignant tumor of epithelial origin — **car·ci·no·ma·tous** \-təs\ *adj*

¹card \ˈkärd\ *vb* : to comb with a card : cleanse and untangle before spinning — **card·er** *n*

²card *n* : an instrument for combing fibers (as wool or cotton)

³card *n*   1 : PLAYING CARD   2 *pl* : a game played with playing cards; *also* : card playing   3 : an emotional issue used to one's advantage (as in a political campaign)   4 : a usu. clownishly amusing person : WAG   5 : a flat stiff usu. small piece of paper, cardboard, or plastic often bearing pictures or information   6 : PROGRAM; *esp* : a sports program — **in the cards** : INEVITABLE

⁴card *vb*   1 : to list or schedule on a card   2 : SCORE   3 : to ask for identification (as at a bar)

⁵card *abbr* cardinal

car·da·mom \ˈkär-də-məm\ *n* : the aromatic capsular fruit of an Indian herb related to the ginger whose seeds are used as a spice or condiment and in medicine; *also* : this plant

card·board \'kärd-ˌbȯrd\ n : a material thicker than paper and made from cellulose fiber

card–car·ry·ing \'kärd-ˌkar-ē-iŋ\ adj : being a regularly enrolled member of an organization (as a political party)

card catalog n : a catalog (as of books) in which the entries are arranged systematically on cards

car·di·ac \'kär-dē-ˌak\ adj [L *cardiacus*, fr. Gk *kardiakos*, fr. *kardia* heart] **1** : of, relating to, or located near the heart **2** : of, relating to, or affected with heart disease ⟨∼ patients⟩

car·di·gan \'kär-di-gən\ n : a sweater or jacket usu. without a collar and with a full-length opening in the front

¹car·di·nal \'kärd-nəl, 'kär-d³n-əl\ n **1** : an ecclesiastical official of the Roman Catholic Church ranking next below the pope **2** : a crested No. American finch that is nearly completely red in the male

²cardinal adj [ME, fr. LL *cardinalis*, fr. L serving as a hinge, fr. *cardo* hinge] **1** : of basic importance : CHIEF, MAIN, PRIMARY **2** : very serious ⟨a ∼ sin⟩ — **car·di·nal·ly** adv

car·di·nal·ate \'kärd-nə-lət, -'kär-d³n-ə-let, -ˌlāt\ n : the office, rank, or dignity of a cardinal

cardinal flower n : a No. American plant that bears a spike of brilliant red flowers

cardinal number n : a number (as 1, 5, 82, 357) that is used in simple counting and answers the question "how many?" — compare ORDINAL NUMBER

cardinal point n : one of the four principal compass points north, south, east, and west

car·dio \'kär-dē-ō\ adj : CARDIOVASCULAR 2

car·di·ol·o·gy \ˌkär-dē-'ä-lə-jē\ n : the study of the heart and its action and diseases — **car·di·ol·o·gist** \-jist\ n

car·dio·pul·mo·nary resuscitation \ˌkär-dē-ō-'pu̇l-mə-ˌner-ē-\ n : a procedure to restore normal breathing after cardiac arrest that includes the clearance of air passages to the lungs, mouth-to-mouth method of artificial respiration, and heart massage by the exertion of pressure on the chest

car·dio·vas·cu·lar \-'vas-kyə-lər\ adj **1** : of or relating to the heart and blood vessels **2** : causing a temporary increase in heart rate ⟨a ∼ workout⟩

card–sharp \-ˌshärp\ or **card·sharp·er** \'kärd-ˌshär-pər\ n : a cheater at cards

¹care \'ker\ n **1** : a disquieted state of uncertainty and responsibility : ANXIETY **2** : watchful attention : HEED **3** : CHARGE, SUPERVISION ⟨under a doctor's ∼⟩ **4** : a person or thing that is an object of anxiety or solicitude

²care vb **cared; car·ing 1** : to feel anxiety **2** : to feel interest **3** : to give care **4** : to have a liking, fondness, taste, or inclination **5** : to be concerned about ⟨∼ what happens⟩

CARE abbr Cooperative for American Relief to Everywhere

ca·reen \kə-'rēn\ vb **1** : to put (a ship or boat) on a beach esp. in order to clean or repair its hull **2** : to sway from side to side **3** : CAREER

¹ca·reer \kə-'rir\ n [MF *carrière*, fr. Old Occitan *carriera* street, fr. ML *carraria* road for vehicles, fr. L *carrus* car] **1** : COURSE, PASSAGE; *also* : speed in a course ⟨ran at full ∼⟩ **2** : an occupation or profession followed as a life's work

²career vb : to go at top speed esp. in a headlong manner

care·free \'ker-ˌfrē\ adj : free from care or worry

care·ful \-fəl\ adj **care·ful·ler; care·ful·lest 1** : using or taking care : VIGILANT **2** : marked by solicitude, caution, or prudence — **care·ful·ly** adv — **care·ful·ness** n

care·giv·er \-ˌgi-vər\ n : a person who provides direct care (as for children, elderly people, or the chronically ill)

care·less \-ləs\ adj **1** : free from care : UNTROUBLED **2** : UNCONCERNED, INDIFFERENT ⟨∼ of the consequences⟩ **3** : not taking care **4** : not showing or receiving care — **care·less·ly** adv — **care·less·ness** n

care package n : a package of useful or pleasurable items given as a gift to another

¹ca·ress \kə-'res\ vb : to touch or stroke tenderly or lovingly — **ca·ress·er** n

²caress n : a tender or loving touch or embrace

car·et \'ker-ət\ n [L, there is lacking, fr. *carēre* to lack, be without] : a mark ^ used to indicate the place where something is to be inserted

care·tak·er \'ker-ˌtā-kər\ n **1** : one in charge usu. as occupant in place of an absent owner **2** : one temporarily fulfilling the functions of an office

care·worn \-ˌwȯrn\ adj : showing the effects of grief or anxiety

car·fare \'kär-ˌfer\ n : passenger fare (as on a streetcar or bus)

car·go \'kär-gō\ n, pl **cargoes** or **cargos** : the goods carried in a ship, airplane, or vehicle : FREIGHT

Ca·rib·be·an \ˌker-ə-'bē-ən, kə-'ri-bē-ən\ adj : of or relating to the eastern and southern West Indies or the Caribbean Sea

car·i·bou \'ker-ə-ˌbü\ n, pl **caribou** or **caribous** : a large circumpolar gregarious deer of northern taiga and tundra that usu. has large branched antlers usu. in both sexes — used esp. for one of the New World

car·i·ca·ture \'ker-i-kə-ˌchu̇r\ n **1** : distorted representation to produce a ridiculous effect **2** : a representation esp. in literature or art having the qualities of caricature — **caricature** vb — **car·i·ca·tur·ist** \-ist\ n

car·ies \'ker-ēz\ n, pl **caries** : tooth decay

car·il·lon \'ker-ə-ˌlän\ n : a set of tuned bells sounded by hammers, controlled from a keyboard

car·i·ous \'ker-ē-əs\ *adj* : affected with caries

car·jack·ing \'kär-ja-kiŋ\ *n* : the theft of an automobile by force or intimidation — **car·jack·er** *n*

car·load \'kär-ˌlōd\ *n* : a load that fills a car

car·mi·na·tive \kär-'mi-nə-tiv\ *adj* : expelling gas from the stomach or intestines — **carminative** *n*

car·mine \'kär-mən, -ˌmīn\ *n* : a vivid red

car·nage \'kär-nij\ *n* : great destruction of life : SLAUGHTER

car·nal \'kär-n²l\ *adj* [ME, fr. LL *carnalis*, fr. L *carn-, caro* flesh] **1** : of or relating to the body **2** : relating to or given to sensual pleasures and appetites — **car·nal·i·ty** \kär-'na-lə-tē\ *n* — **car·nal·ly** *adv*

car·na·tion \kär-'nā-shən\ *n* : a cultivated pink of any of numerous usu. double-flowered varieties derived from an Old World species

car·nau·ba wax \kär-'nȯ-bə-, -'naủ-; ˌkär-nə-'ü-bə-\ *n* : a brittle yellowish wax from a Brazilian palm that is used esp. in polishes

car·ne·lian \kär-'nēl-yən\ *n* : a hard red chalcedony used as a gem

car·ni·val \'kär-nə-vəl\ *n* [It *carnevale*, alter. of *carnelevare*, lit., removal of meat] **1** : a season of merrymaking just before Lent **2** : a boisterous merrymaking **3** : a traveling enterprise offering amusements **4** : an organized program of entertainment

car·ni·val·esque \ˌkär-nə-və-'lesk\ *adj* : suggestive of a carnival

car·niv·o·ra \kär-'ni-və-rə\ *n pl* : carnivorous mammals

car·ni·vore \'kär-nə-ˌvȯr\ *n* : a flesh-eating animal; *esp* : any of an order of mammals (as dogs, cats, bears, minks, and seals) feeding mostly on animal flesh

car·niv·o·rous \kär-'ni-və-rəs\ *adj* **1** : feeding on animal tissues **2** : of or relating to the carnivores — **car·niv·o·rous·ly** *adv* — **car·niv·o·rous·ness** *n*

car·ny *or* **car·ney** *or* **car·nie** \'kär-nē\ *n, pl* **carnies** *or* **carneys 1** : CARNIVAL 3 **2** : one who works with a carnival

car·ol \'ker-əl\ *n* : a song of joy or devotion — **carol** *vb* — **car·ol·er** *or* **car·ol·ler** *n*

car·om \'ker-əm\ *n* **1** : a shot in billiards in which the cue ball strikes two other balls **2** : a rebounding esp. at an angle — **carom** *vb*

car·o·tene \'ker-ə-ˌtēn\ *n* : any of several orange to red pigments (as beta-carotene) formed esp. in plants and used as a source of vitamin A

ca·rot·en·oid \kə-'rä-tə-ˌnȯid\ *n* : any of various usu. yellow to red pigments (as carotenes) found widely in plants and animals

ca·rot·id \kə-'rä-təd\ *adj* : of, relating to, or being the chief artery or pair of arteries that pass up the neck and supply the head — **carotid** *n*

ca·rous·al \kə-'raủ-zəl\ *n* : CAROUSE

ca·rouse \kə-'raủz\ *n* [MF *carrousse,* fr. *carous,* adv., all out (in *boire carous* to empty the cup), fr. G *garaus*] : a drunken revel — **carouse** *vb* — **ca·rous·er** *n*

car·ou·sel *also* **car·rou·sel** \ˌker-ə-'sel, 'kar-ə-ˌsel\ *n* **1** : MERRY-GO-ROUND **2** : a circular conveyor

¹carp \'kärp\ *vb* : to find fault : CAVIL, COMPLAIN — **carp** *n* — **carp·er** *n*

²carp *n, pl* **carp** *or* **carps** : a large variable Asian freshwater fish of sluggish waters often raised for food

¹car·pal \'kär-pəl\ *adj* : of or relating to the wrist or the bones of the wrist

²carpal *n* : a carpal element or bone

carpal tunnel syndrome *n* : a condition characterized esp. by weakness, pain, and disturbances of sensation (as numbness) in the hand and fingers and caused by compression of a nerve in the wrist

car·pe di·em \'kär-pe-'dē-ˌem, -'dī-\ *n* [L, lit., pluck the day] : enjoyment of the present without concern for the future

car·pel \'kär-pəl\ *n* : one of the highly modified leaves that together form the ovary of a flower of a seed plant

car·pen·ter \'kär-pən-tər\ *n* : one who builds or repairs wooden structures — **carpenter** *vb* — **car·pen·try** \-trē\ *n*

car·pet \'kär-pət\ *n* : a heavy fabric used as a floor covering — **carpet** *vb*

car·pet·bag \-ˌbag\ *n* : a traveling bag common in the 19th century

car·pet·bag·ger \-ˌba-gər\ *n* : a Northerner in the South after the American Civil War usu. seeking private gain under the reconstruction governments

car·pet·ing \'kär-pə-tiŋ\ *n* : material for carpets; *also* : CARPETS

car pool *n* : an arrangement in which a group of people commute together by car; *also* : a group having this arrangement — **car·pool** \-ˌpül\ *vb*

car·port \'kär-ˌpȯrt\ *n* : an open-sided automobile shelter

car·pus \'kär-pəs\ *n* : the wrist or its bones

car·ra·geen·an *or* **car·ra·geen·in** \ˌker-ə-'gē-nən\ *n* : a colloid extracted esp. from a dark purple branching seaweed and used in foods esp. to stabilize and thicken them

car·rel \'ker-əl\ *n* : a table often partitioned or enclosed for individual study in a library

car·riage \'ker-ij\ *n,* **1** : the act of carrying **2** : manner of holding the body **3** : a wheeled vehicle **4** *Brit* : a railway passenger coach **5** : a movable part of a machine for supporting some other moving part ⟨a typewriter ∼⟩

carriage trade *n* : trade from well-to-do or upper-class people

car·ri·er \'ker-ē-ər\ *n* **1** : one that carries **2** : a person or organization in the transportation business **3** : AIRCRAFT CARRIER **4** : one whose system carries the causative agents of a disease but who is immune to the disease **5** : an individual having a gene for a trait or condition that is not expressed outwardly **6** : an electromagnetic wave whose amplitude or frequency is varied in order to convey a radio or television signal

carrier pigeon *n* : a pigeon used esp. to carry messages

car·ri·on \'ker-ē-ən\ *n* : dead and decaying flesh

car·rot \'ker-ət\ *n* : the elongated usu. orange root of a common garden plant that is eaten as a vegetable; *also* : this plant

carrousel *var of* CAROUSEL

¹**car·ry** \ka-rē, 'ker-ē\ *vb* **car·ried; carrying** [ME *carien,* fr. AF *carier,* fr. *carre* vehicle, fr. L *carrus*] **1** : to move while supporting : TRANSPORT, CONVEY, TAKE **2** : to influence by mental or emotional appeal **3** : to get possession or control of : CAPTURE, WIN **4** : to transfer from one place (as a column) to another ⟨∼ a number in adding⟩ **5** : to have or wear on one's person; *also* : to bear within one **6** : INVOLVE, IMPLY **7** : to hold or bear (oneself) in a specified way **8** : to keep in stock for sale **9** : to sustain the weight or burden of : SUPPORT **10** : to prolong in space, time, or degree **11** : to keep on one's books as a debtor **12** : to succeed in (an election) **13** : to win adoption (as in a legislature) **14** : PUBLISH, PRINT **15** : to reach or penetrate to a distance

²**carry** *n* **1** : the range of a gun or projectile or of a struck or thrown ball **2** : PORTAGE **3** : an act or method of carrying ⟨fireman's ∼⟩

car·ry·all \-,ȯl\ *n* : a capacious bag or case

carry away *vb* : to arouse to a high and often excessive degree of emotion

carrying charge *n* : a charge added to the price of merchandise sold on the installment plan

car·ry-on \-,ȯn, -,än\ *n* : a piece of luggage suitable for being carried aboard an airplane by a passenger — **carry-on** *adj*

carry on *vb* **1** : CONDUCT, MANAGE **2** : to behave in a foolish, excited, or improper manner **3** : to continue in spite of hindrance or discouragement

carry out *vb* **1** : to bring to a successful conclusion **2** : to put into execution

car·sick \'kär-,sik\ *adj* : affected with motion sickness esp. in an automobile — **car sickness** *n*

¹**cart** \'kärt\ *n* **1** : a heavy 2-wheeled wagon **2** : a small wheeled vehicle

²**cart** *vb* : to convey in or as if in a cart — **cart·er** *n*

cart·age \'kär-tij\ *n* : the act of or rate charged for carting

carte blanche \'kärt-'blänsh\ *n, pl* **cartes blanches** *same or* -'blän-shəz\ [F, lit., blank document] : full discretionary power

car·tel \kär-'tel\ *n* : a combination of independent business enterprises designed to limit competition ♦ *Synonyms* POOL, SYNDICATE, MONOPOLY, TRUST

car·ti·lage \'kär-tə-lij\ *n* : a usu. translucent somewhat elastic tissue that composes most of the skeleton of young vertebrate embryos and later is mostly converted to bone in higher vertebrates

— **car·ti·lag·i·nous** \,kär-tə-'la-jə-nəs\ *adj*

cartilaginous fish *n* : any of a class of fishes (as a shark or ray) having the skeleton wholly or largely composed of cartilage

car·tog·ra·phy \kär-'tä-grə-fē\ *n* : the making of maps — **car·tog·ra·pher** *n* — **car·to·graph·ic** \,kär-tə-'gra-fik\ *adj*

car·ton \'kär-t²n\ *n* : a cardboard box or container

car·toon \kär-'tün\ *n* **1** : a preparatory sketch (as for a painting) **2** : a drawing intended as humor, caricature, or satire **3** : COMIC STRIP — **cartoon** *vb* — **cartoon·ist** *n*

car·tridge \'kär-trij\ *n* **1** : a tube containing a complete charge for a firearm **2** : a container of material for insertion into an apparatus **3** : a small case containing a phonograph needle and transducer that is attached to a tonearm **4** : a case containing a magnetic tape or disk **5** : a case for holding integrated circuits containing a computer program

cart·wheel \'kärt-,hwēl\ *n* **1** : a large coin (as a silver dollar) **2** : a lateral handspring with arms and legs extended

carve \'kärv\ *vb* **carved; carv·ing 1** : to cut with care or precision : shape by cutting **2** : to cut into pieces or slices **3** : to slice and serve meat at table — **carv·er** *n*

cary·at·id \,ker-ē-'a-təd\ *n, pl* **-ids** *or* **-i·des** \-'a-tə-,dēz\ : a sculptured draped female figure used as an architectural column

CAS *abbr* certificate of advanced study

ca·sa·ba \kə-'sä-bə\ *n* : any of several muskmelons with a yellow rind and sweet flesh

¹**cas·cade** \,kas-'kād\ *n* **1** : a steep usu. small waterfall **2** : something arranged in a series or succession of stages so that each stage derives from or acts upon the product of the preceding

²**cas·cade** *vb* **cas·cad·ed; cas·cad·ing** : to fall, pass, or connect in or as if in a cascade

cas·cara \ka-'ska-rə\ *n* : the dried bark of a small Pacific coastal tree of the U.S. and southern Canada used as a laxative; *also* : this tree

¹**case** \'kās\ *n* [ME *cas,* fr. AF, fr. L *casus* fall, chance, fr. *cadere* to fall] **1** : a particular instance or situation **2** : an inflectional form of a noun, pronoun, or adjective indicating its grammatical relation to other words; *also* : such a relation whether indicated by inflection or not **3** : what actually exists or happens : FACT **4** : a suit or action in law : CAUSE **5** : a convincing argument **6** : an instance of disease or injury; *also* : PATIENT **7** : INSTANCE, EXAMPLE — **in case** : as a precaution — **in case of** : in the event of

²**case** *n* [ME *cas,* fr. AF *case, chase,* fr. L *capsa*] **1** : a box or container for holding something; *also* : a box with its contents **2** : an outer covering **3** : a divided tray for holding printing type **4** : CASING 2

³**case** *vb* **cased; cas·ing 1** : to enclose in

or cover with a case　**2** : to inspect esp. with intent to rob

ca·sein \'kā-ˌsēn, kā-'\ *n* : any of several phosphorus-containing proteins occurring in or produced from milk

case·ment \'kās-mənt\ *n* : a window that opens like a door

case·work \-ˌwərk\ *n* : social work that involves the individual person or family — **case·work·er** *n*

¹**cash** \'kash\ *n* [MF or It; MF *casse* money box, fr. It *cassa*, fr. L *capsa* chest, case]　**1** : ready money　**2** : money or its equivalent paid at the time of purchase or delivery

²**cash** *vb* : to pay or obtain cash for

ca·shew \'ka-shū, kə-'shū\ *n* : an edible kidney-shaped nut of a tropical American tree related to the sumacs; *also* : the tree

¹**ca·shier** \ka-'shir\ *vb* : to dismiss from service; *esp* : to dismiss in disgrace

²**cash·ier** \ka-'shir\ *n*　**1** : a bank official responsible for moneys received and paid out　**2** : a person who receives and records payments

cashier's check *n* : a check drawn by a bank upon its own funds and signed by its cashier

cash in *vb*　**1** : to convert into cash ⟨*cash in* bonds⟩　**2** : to settle accounts and withdraw from a gambling game or business deal　**3** : to obtain financial profit or advantage

cash·less \'kash-ləs\ *adj* : relying on monetary transactions that use electronic means rather than cash

cash·mere \'kazh-ˌmir, 'kash-\ *n* : fine wool from the undercoat of an Indian goat (**cashmere goat**) or a yarn spun of this; *also* : a soft twilled fabric orig. woven from this yarn

cash out *vb* : to convert noncash assets into cash

cash register *n* : a business machine that usu. has a money drawer, indicates each sale, and records the money received

cash–strapped \'kash-ˌstrapt\ *adj* : lacking sufficient money

cas·ing \'kā-siŋ\ *n*　**1** : something that encases　**2** : the frame of a door or window

ca·si·no \kə-'sē-nō\ *n, pl* **-nos** [It, fr. *casa* house]　**1** : a building or room for social amusements; *esp* : one used for gambling　**2** *also* **cas·si·no** : a card game in which players win cards by matching those on the table

cask \'kask\ *n* : a barrel-shaped container usu. for liquids; *also* : the quantity held by such a container

cas·ket \'kas-kət\ *n*　**1** : a small box (as for jewels)　**2** : COFFIN

casque \'kask\ *n* : HELMET

cas·sa·va \kə-'sä-və\ *n* : any of several tropical spurges with rootstocks yielding a nutritious starch from which tapioca is prepared; *also* : the rootstock or its starch

cas·se·role \'ka-sə-ˌrōl\ *n*　**1** : a dish in which food may be baked and served　**2** : food cooked and served in a casserole

cas·sette *also* **ca·sette** \kə-'set\ *n*　**1** : a lightproof container for photographic plates or film　**2** : a plastic case containing magnetic tape

cas·sia \'ka-shə\ *n*　**1** : a dried coarse cinnamon bark　**2** : any of a genus of leguminous herbs, shrubs, and trees of warm regions including several which yield senna

cas·sit·er·ite \kə-'si-tə-ˌrīt\ *n* : a dark mineral that is the chief tin ore

cas·sock \'ka-sək\ *n* : an ankle-length garment worn esp. by Roman Catholic and Anglican clergy

cas·so·wary \'ka-sə-ˌwer-ē\ *n, pl* **-war·ies** : any of a genus of large flightless birds closely related to the emu

¹**cast** \'kast\ *vb* **cast; cast·ing**　**1** : THROW, FLING　**2** : DIRECT ⟨~ a glance⟩　**3** : to deposit (a ballot) formally　**4** : to throw off, out, or away : DISCARD, SHED　**5** : COMPUTE; *esp* : to add up　**6** : to assign the parts of (a play) to actors; *also* : to assign to a role or part　**7** : to shape (a substance) by pouring in liquid or plastic form into a mold and letting harden without pressure　**8** : to make (as a knot or stitch) by looping or catching up

²**cast** *n*　**1** : THROW, FLING　**2** : a throw of dice　**3** : the set of actors in a dramatic production　**4** : something formed in or as if in a mold; *also* : a rigid surgical casing (as for protecting and supporting a fractured bone)　**5** : TINGE, HUE　**6** : APPEARANCE, LOOK ⟨features of delicate ~⟩　**7** : something thrown out or off, shed, or expelled ⟨worm ~s⟩

cas·ta·net \ˌkas-tə-'net\ *n* [Sp *castañeta*, fr. *castaña* chestnut, fr. L *castanea*] : a rhythm instrument consisting of two small wooden, ivory, or plastic shells held in the hand and clicked together

cast·away \'kas-tə-ˌwā\ *adj*　**1** : thrown away : REJECTED　**2** : cast adrift or ashore as a survivor of a shipwreck — **castaway** *n*

caste \'kast\ *n* [Pg *casta*, lit., race, lineage, fr. fem. of *casto* pure, chaste, fr. L *castus*]　**1** : one of the hereditary social classes in Hinduism　**2** : a division of a society based on wealth, inherited rank, or occupation　**3** : social position : PRESTIGE　**4** : a system of rigid social stratification

cas·tel·lat·ed \'kas-tə-ˌlā-təd\ *adj* : having battlements like a castle

cast·er \'kas-tər\ *n* **1** *or* **cas·tor** : a small container to hold salt or pepper at the table　**2** : a small wheel that turns freely and is used to support and move furniture, trucks, and equipment

cas·ti·gate \'kas-tə-ˌgāt\ *vb* **-gat·ed; -gat·ing** : to punish or criticize severely — **cas·ti·ga·tion** \ˌkas-tə-'gā-shən\ *n* — **cas·ti·ga·tor** \'kas-tə-ˌgā-tər\ *n*

cast·ing \'kas-tiŋ\ *n*　**1** : CAST 7　**2** : something cast in a mold

casting vote *n* : a deciding vote cast by a presiding officer to break a tie

cast iron *n* : a hard brittle alloy of iron, carbon, and silicon cast in a mold

cas·tle \'ka-səl\ *n*　**1** : a large fortified building or set of buildings　**2** : a large or imposing house　**3** : ³ROOK

castle in the air : an impracticable project

cast–off \'kast-,òf\ *adj* : thrown away or aside — **cast-off** *n*

cas·tor oil \'kas-tər-\ *n* : a thick yellowish oil extracted from the poisonous seeds of an herb (**castor–oil plant**) and used as a lubricant and purgative

cas·trate \'kas-,trāt\ *vb* **cas·trat·ed; cas·trat·ing** : to deprive of sex glands and esp. testes — **cas·tra·tion** \kas-'trā-shən\ *n* — **cas·tra·tor** \-ər\ *n*

ca·su·al \'ka-zhə-wəl\ *adj* 1 : resulting from or occurring by chance 2 : OCCASIONAL, INCIDENTAL ⟨~ employment⟩ 3 : OFFHAND, NONCHALANT ⟨a ~ approach to cooking⟩ 4 : designed for informal use ⟨~ clothing⟩ — **ca·su·al·ly** *adv* — **ca·su·al·ness** *n*

ca·su·al·ty \'ka-zhəl-tē, 'ka-zhə-wəl-\ *n, pl* **-ties** 1 : serious or fatal accident 2 : a military person lost through death, injury, sickness, or capture or through being missing in action 3 : a person or thing injured, lost, or destroyed

ca·su·ist·ry \'ka-zhə-wə-strē\ *n, pl* **-ries** : specious argument : RATIONALIZATION — **ca·su·ist** \-wist\ *n* — **ca·su·is·tic** \,ka-zhə-'wis-tik\ *or* **ca·su·is·ti·cal** \-ti-kəl\ *adj*

ca·sus bel·li \,kä-səs-'be-,lē, ,kä-səs-'be-,lī\ *n, pl* **ca·sus belli** \,kä-,süs-, ,kä-\ [NL, occasion of war] : a cause or pretext for a declaration of war

¹**cat** \'kat\ *n* 1 : a carnivorous mammal long domesticated as a pet and for catching rats and mice 2 : any of a family of animals (as the lion, lynx, or leopard) including the domestic cat 3 : a malicious woman 4 : GUY

²**cat** *abbr* catalog

ca·tab·o·lism \kə-'ta-bə-,li-zəm\ *n* : destructive metabolism involving the release of energy and resulting in the breakdown of complex materials — **cat·a·bol·ic** \,ka-tə-'bä-lik\ *adj*

cat·a·clysm \'ka-tə-,kli-zəm\ *n* : a violent change or upheaval — **cat·a·clys·mal** \,ka-tə-'kliz-məl\ *or* **cat·a·clys·mic** \-'kliz-mik\ *adj*

cat·a·comb \'ka-tə-,kōm\ *n* : an underground burial place with galleries and recesses for tombs

cat·a·falque \'ka-tə-,falk, -,fòlk, -,fòk\ *n* : an ornamental structure sometimes used in solemn funerals to hold the body

cat·a·lep·sy \'ka-tə-,lep-sē\ *n, pl* **-sies** : a trancelike state characterized esp. by loss of voluntary motion — **cat·a·lep·tic** \,ka-tə-'lep-tik\ *adj or n*

¹**cat·a·log** *or* **cat·a·logue** \'ka-tə-,lòg\ *n* 1 : LIST, REGISTER 2 : a systematic list of items with descriptive details; *also* : a book containing such a list

²**catalog** *or* **catalogue** *vb* **-loged** *or* **-logued; -log·ing** *or* **-logu·ing** 1 : to make a catalog of 2 : to enter in a catalog — **cat·a·log·er** *or* **cat·a·logu·er** *n*

ca·tal·pa \kə-'tal-pə\ *n* : any of a genus of broad-leaved trees with showy flowers and long slim pods

ca·tal·y·sis \kə-'ta-lə-səs\ *n, pl* **-y·ses** \-,sēz\ : a change and esp. increase in the rate of a chemical reaction brought about by a substance (**cat·a·lyst** \'ka-tə-list\) that is itself unchanged at the end of the reaction — **cat·a·lyt·ic** \,ka-tə-'li-tik\ *adj* — **cat·a·lyt·i·cal·ly** \-ti-k(ə-)lē\ *adv*

catalytic converter *n* : an automobile exhaust-system component in which a catalyst changes harmful gases into mostly harmless products

cat·a·lyze \'ka-tə-,līz\ *vb* **-lyzed; -lyz·ing** : to bring about the catalysis of (a chemical reaction)

cat·a·ma·ran \,ka-tə-mə-'ran\ *n* [Tamil (a language of southern India) *kaṭṭumaram*, fr. *kaṭṭu* to tie + *maram* tree] : a boat with twin hulls

cat·a·mount \'ka-tə-,maùnt\ *n* : COUGAR; *also* : LYNX

cat·a·pult \'ka-tə-,pəlt, -,pùlt\ *n* 1 : an ancient military machine for hurling missiles 2 : a device for launching an airplane (as from an aircraft carrier) — **catapult** *vb*

cat·a·ract \'ka-tə-,rakt\ *n* 1 : a cloudiness of the lens of the eye obstructing vision 2 : a large waterfall; *also* : steep rapids in a river

ca·tarrh \kə-'tär\ *n* : inflammation of a mucous membrane esp. of the nose and throat — **ca·tarrh·al** \-əl\ *adj*

ca·tas·tro·phe \kə-'tas-trə-(,)fē\ *n* [Gk *katastrophē*, fr. *katastrephein* to overturn, fr. *kata-* down + *strephein* to turn] 1 : a great disaster or misfortune 2 : utter failure — **cat·a·stroph·ic** \,ka-tə-'strä-fik\ *adj* — **cat·a·stroph·i·cal·ly** \-fi-k(ə-)lē\ *adv*

cat·a·ton·ic \,ka-tə-'tä-nik\ *adj* : of, relating to, or marked by schizophrenia characterized esp. by stupor, negativism, rigidity, purposeless excitement, and bizarre posturing — **catatonic** *n*

cat·bird \'kat-,bərd\ *n* : an American songbird with a catlike mewing call

cat·boat \'kat-,bōt\ *n* : a single-masted sailboat with a single large sail extended by a long boom

cat·call \-,kòl\ *n* : a loud cry made esp. to express disapproval — **catcall** *vb*

¹**catch** \'kach, 'kech\ *vb* **caught** \'kòt\; **catch·ing** [ME *cacchen*, fr. AF *cacher, chacher, chacer* to hunt, ultim. fr. L *captare* to chase] 1 : to capture esp. after pursuit 2 : TRAP 3 : to discover unexpectedly ⟨*caught* in the act⟩ 4 : to become suddenly aware of 5 : to take hold of : SNATCH ⟨~ at a straw⟩ 6 : INTERCEPT 7 : to get entangled 8 : to become affected with or by ⟨~ fire⟩ ⟨~ cold⟩ 9 : to seize and hold firmly; *also* : FASTEN 10 : OVERTAKE 11 : to be in time for ⟨~ a train⟩ 12 : to take in and retain 13 : to look at or listen to

²**catch** *n* 1 : something caught 2 : the act of catching; *also* : a game consisting of throwing and catching a ball 3 : something that catches or checks or holds immovable ⟨a door ~⟩ 4 : one worth catching esp. as a mate 5 : FRAGMENT,

SNATCH **6** : a concealed difficulty or complication

catch·all \'kach-₁ol, 'kech-\ *n* : something to hold a variety of odds and ends

catch–as–catch–can *adj* : using any means available

catch·er \'ka-chər, 'ke-\ *n* : one that catches; *esp* : a player positioned behind home plate in baseball

catch·ing *adj* **1** : INFECTIOUS, CONTAGIOUS **2** : ALLURING, CATCHY

catch·ment \'kach-mənt, 'kech-\ *n* **1** : something that catches water **2** : the action of catching water

catch on *vb* **1** : UNDERSTAND **2** : to become popular

catch·pen·ny \'kach-₁pe-nē, 'kech-\ *adj* : using sensationalism or cheapness for appeal ⟨a ~ newspaper⟩

catch·phrase \-₁frāz\ *n* : a word or expression frequently used to represent or characterize a person, group, idea, or point of view

catch–22 \-₁twen-tē-'tü\ *n, pl* **catch–22's** *or* **catch–22s** *often cap C* [fr. *Catch-22*, a paradoxical rule found in the novel *Catch-22* (1961) by Joseph Heller] : a problematic situation for which the only solution is denied by a circumstance inherent in the problem or by a rule; *also* : the circumstance or rule that denies a solution

catchup *var of* KETCHUP

catch up *vb* : to travel or work fast enough to overtake or complete

catch·word \'kach-₁wərd, 'kech-\ *n* **1** : GUIDE WORD **2** : CATCHPHRASE

catchy \'ka-chē, 'ke-\ *adj* **catch·i·er; -est 1** : likely to catch the interest or attention **2** : TRICKY ⟨a ~ question⟩

cat·e·chism \'ka-tə-₁ki-zəm\ *n* : a summary or test (as of religious doctrine) usu. in the form of questions and answers — **cat·e·chist** \-₁kist\ *n* — **cat·e·chize** \-₁kīz\ *vb*

cat·e·chu·men \₁ka-tə-'kyü-mən\ *n* : a religious convert receiving training before baptism

cat·e·gor·i·cal \₁ka-tə-'gòr-i-kəl\ *adj* **1** : ABSOLUTE, UNQUALIFIED ⟨a ~ denial⟩ **2** : of, relating to, or constituting a category — **cat·e·gor·i·cal·ly** \-i-k(ə-)lē\ *adv*

cat·e·go·rise *Brit var of* CATEGORIZE

cat·e·go·rize \'ka-ti-gə-₁rīz\ *vb* **-rized; -riz·ing** : to put into a category : CLASSIFY — **cat·e·go·ri·za·tion** \₁ka-ti-gə-rə-'zā-shən\ *n*

cat·e·go·ry \'ka-tə-₁gòr-ē\ *n, pl* **-ries** : a division used in classification; *also* : CLASS, GROUP, KIND

ca·ter \'kā-tər\ *vb* [obs. *cater* buyer of provisions, fr. ME *catour*, short for *acatour*, fr. AF, fr. *acater*, *achater* to buy] **1** : to provide a supply of food **2** : to supply what is wanted — **ca·ter·er** *n*

catercorner *or* **cater–cornered** *var of* KITTY-CORNER

cat·er·pil·lar \'ka-tər-₁pi-lər\ *n* [ME *catyrpel*, fr. OF *catepelose*, lit., hairy cat] : a wormlike often hairy insect larva esp. of a butterfly or moth

cat·er·waul \'ka-tər-₁wòl\ *vb* : to make a harsh cry — **caterwaul** *n*

cat·fish \'kat-₁fish\ *n* : any of an order of chiefly freshwater stout-bodied fishes with slender tactile processes around the mouth

cat·gut \-₁gət\ *n* : a tough cord made usu. from sheep intestines

ca·thar·sis \kə-'thär-səs\ *n, pl* **ca·thar·ses** \-₁sēz\ **1** : an act of purging or purification **2** : elimination of a complex by bringing it to consciousness and affording it expression

¹ca·thar·tic \kə-'thär-tik\ *adj* : of, relating to, or producing catharsis

²cathartic *n* : PURGATIVE

ca·the·dral \kə-'thē-drəl\ *n* : the principal church of a diocese

cath·e·ter \'ka-thə-tər\ *n* : a tube for insertion into a bodily passage or cavity usu. for injecting or drawing off material or for keeping a passage open

cath·e·ter·i·za·tion \₁ka-thə-tə-rə-'zā-shən\ *n* : the use of or introduction of a catheter — **cath·e·ter·ize** \'ka-thə-tə-₁rīz\ *vb*

cath·ode \'ka-₁thōd\ *n* **1** : the negative electrode of an electrolytic cell **2** : the positive terminal of a battery **3** : the electron-emitting electrode of an electron tube — **cath·od·al** \'ka-₁thō-dᵊl\ *adj* — **ca·thod·ic** \ka-'thä-dik\ *adj*

cathode–ray tube *n* : a vacuum tube in which a beam of electrons is projected on a phosphor-coated screen to produce a luminous spot

cath·o·lic \'kath-lik, 'ka-thə-\ *adj* [ME *catholik* relating to the church universal, ultim. fr. Gk *katholikos* universal, general, fr. *katholou* in general] **1** *cap* : of or relating to Catholics and esp. Roman Catholics **2** : GENERAL, UNIVERSAL

Cath·o·lic \'kath-lik, 'ka-thə-\ *n* : a member of a church claiming historical continuity from the ancient undivided Christian church; *esp* : a member of the Roman Catholic Church — **Ca·thol·i·cism** \kə-'thä-lə-₁si-zəm\ *n*

cath·o·lic·i·ty \₁ka-thə-'li-sə-tē\ *n, pl* **-ties 1** *cap* : the character of being in conformity with a Catholic church **2** : liberality of sentiments or views **3** : comprehensive range

cat·ion \'kat-₁ī-ən\ *n* : the ion in an electrolyte that migrates to the cathode; *also* : a positively charged ion

cat·kin \'kat-kən\ *n* : a long flower cluster (as of a willow) bearing crowded unisexual and prominent bracts

cat·like \-₁līk\ *adj* : resembling a cat or its behavior; *esp* : STEALTHY

cat·nap \-₁nap\ *n* : a very short light nap — **catnap** *vb*

cat·nip \-₁nip\ *n* : an aromatic mint that is esp. attractive to cats

cat–o'–nine–tails \₁ka-tə-'nīn-₁tālz\ *n, pl* **cat–o'–nine–tails** : a whip made of usu. nine knotted cords fastened to a handle

CAT scan \'kat-\ *n* [computerized *a*xial *t*omography] : an image made by computed tomography

CAT scanner *n* : a medical instrument consisting of integrated X-ray and computing equipment that is used to make CAT scans

cat's cradle *n* : a game played with a string looped on the fingers in such a way as to resemble a small cradle

cat's–eye \'kats-ˌī\ *n, pl* **cat's–eyes** : any of various iridescent gems

cat's–paw \-ˌpo̅\ *n, pl* **cat's–paws** : a person used by another as a tool

cat·suit \'kat-ˌsūt\ *n* : a close-fitting one-piece garment that covers the torso and the legs

catsup *var of* KETCHUP

cat·tail \'kat-ˌtāl\ *n* : any of a genus of tall reedlike marsh plants with furry brown spikes of tiny flowers

cat·tle \'ka-t³l\ *n pl* : LIVESTOCK; *esp* : domestic bovines (as cows, bulls, or calves) — **cat·tle·man** \-mən, -ˌman\ *n*

cat·ty \'ka-tē\ *adj* **cat·ti·er, -est** : slyly spiteful — **cat·ti·ly** \'ka-tə-lē\ *adv* — **cat·ti·ness** *n*

catty–corner *or* **catty–cornered** *var of* KITTY-CORNER

CATV *abbr* community antenna television

cat·walk \'kat-ˌwȯk\ *n* : a narrow walk (as along a bridge)

Cau·ca·sian \ko̅-'kā-zhən\ *adj* : of or relating to the white race of humankind — **Caucasian** *n* — **Cau·ca·soid** \'ko̅-kə-ˌsȯid\ *adj or n*

cau·cus \'ko̅-kəs\ *n* : a meeting of a group of persons belonging to the same political party or faction usu. to decide upon policies and candidates — **caucus** *vb*

cau·dal \'ko̅-d³l\ *adj* : of, relating to, or located near the tail or the hind end of the body — **cau·dal·ly** *adv*

cau·di·llo \kau̇-'thē-(ˌ)yȯ, -'thēl-\ *n, pl* **-llos** : a Spanish or Latin-American military dictator

caught \'ko̅t\ *past and past part of* CATCH

caul \'ko̅l\ *n* : the inner fetal membrane of higher vertebrates esp. when covering the head at birth

caul·dron \'ko̅l-drən\ *n* : a large kettle

cau·li·flow·er \'ko̅-li-ˌflau̇(-ə)r\ *n* [It *cavolfiore*, fr. *cavolo* cabbage + *fiore* flower] : a garden plant closely related to cabbage and grown for its compact edible head of undeveloped flowers; *also* : this head used as a vegetable

cauliflower ear *n* : an ear deformed from injury and excessive growth of scar tissue

¹**caulk** *or* **calk** \'ko̅k\ *vb* [ME, fr. AF *cauker, calcher* to trample, fr. L *calcare*, fr. *calx* heel] : to stop up and make tight against leakage (as a boat or its seams) — **caulk·er** *n*

²**caulk** *or* **calk** *also* **caulk·ing** *or* **calk·ing** *n* : material used to caulk

caus·al \'ko̅-zəl\ *adj* **1** : expressing or indicating cause **2** : relating to or acting as a cause — **cau·sal·i·ty** \ko̅-'za-lə-tē\ *n* — **caus·al·ly** *adv*

cau·sa·tion \ko̅-'zā-shən\ *n* **1** : the act or process of causing **2** : the means by which an effect is produced

¹**cause** \'ko̅z\ *n* **1** : REASON, MOTIVE **2** : something that brings about a result; *esp* : a person or thing that is the agent of bringing something about **3** : a suit or action in court : CASE **4** : a question or matter to be decided **5** : a principle or movement earnestly supported — **cause·less** *adj*

²**cause** *vb* **caused; caus·ing** : to be the cause or occasion of — **caus·a·tive** \'ko̅-zə-tiv\ *adj* — **caus·er** *n*

cause cé·lè·bre \ˌko̅z-sā-'lebr³, ˌko̅z-\ *n, pl* **causes célèbres** *same*\ [F, lit., celebrated case] **1** : a legal case that excites widespread interest **2** : a notorious person, thing, incident, or episode

cau·se·rie \ˌko̅z-'rē, ˌko̅-zə-\ *n* [F] **1** : an informal conversation : CHAT **2** : a short informal essay

cause·way \'ko̅z-ˌwā\ *n* : a raised way or road across wet ground or water

¹**caus·tic** \'ko̅-stik\ *adj* **1** : CORROSIVE **2** : SHARP, INCISIVE \~ wit\

²**caustic** *n* **1** : a substance that burns or destroys organic tissue by chemical action **2** : SODIUM HYDROXIDE

cau·ter·ize \'ko̅-tə-ˌrīz\ *vb* **-ized; -iz·ing** : to burn or sear usu. to prevent infection or bleeding — **cau·ter·i·za·tion** \ˌko̅-tə-rə-'zā-shən\ *n*

¹**cau·tion** \'ko̅-shən\ *n* **1** : ADMONITION, WARNING **2** : prudent forethought to minimize risk **3** : one that astonishes — **cau·tion·ary** \-shə-ˌner-ē\ *adj*

²**caution** *vb* : to advise caution to

cau·tious \'ko̅-shəs\ *adj* : marked by or given to caution : CAREFUL — **cau·tious·ly** *adv* — **cau·tious·ness** *n*

cav *abbr* **1** cavalry **2** cavity

cav·al·cade \ˌka-vəl-'kād\ *n* **1** : a procession of riders or carriages; *also* : a procession of vehicles **2** : a dramatic sequence or procession

¹**cav·a·lier** \ˌka-və-'lir\ *n* [MF, fr. It *cavaliere*, fr. Old Occitan *cavalier*, fr. LL *caballarius* horseman, fr. L *caballus* horse] **1** : a mounted soldier : KNIGHT **2** *cap* : an adherent of Charles I of England **3** : GALLANT

²**cavalier** *adj* **1** : DEBONAIR **2** : DISDAINFUL, HAUGHTY \a \~ attitude toward money\ — **cav·a·lier·ly** *adv*

cav·al·ry \'ka-vəl-rē\ *n, pl* **-ries** : troops mounted on horseback or moving in motor vehicles — **cav·al·ry·man** \-mən, -ˌman\ *n*

¹**cave** \'kāv\ *n* : a natural underground chamber open to the surface

²**cave** *vb* **caved; cav·ing** **1** : to collapse or cause to collapse **2** : to cease to resist : SUBMIT — usu. used with *in*

ca·ve·at \'ka-vē-ˌät, -ˌat; 'kä-vē-ˌät\ *n* [L, let him beware] : WARNING

caveat emp·tor \-'emp-tər, -ˌtȯr\ *n* [NL, let the buyer beware] : a principle in commerce: without a warranty the buyer takes a risk

cave–in \'kā-ˌvin\ *n* **1** : the action of caving in **2** : a place where earth has caved in

cave·man \'kāv-ˌman\ *n* **1** : a cave

dweller esp. of the Stone Age **2** : a man who acts in a rough or crude manner

cav·ern \'ka-vərn\ *n* : CAVE; *esp* : one of large or unknown size — **cav·ern·ous** *adj* — **cav·ern·ous·ly** *adv*

cav·i·ar *also* **cav·i·are** \'ka-vē-,är, 'kä-\ *n* : the salted roe of a large fish (as sturgeon) used as an appetizer

cav·il \'ka-vəl\ *vb* **-iled** *or* **-illed; -il·ing** *or* **-il·ling** : to make frivolous objections or raise trivial objections to — **cavil** *n* — **cav·il·er** *or* **cav·il·ler** *n*

cav·ing \'kā-viŋ\ *n* : the sport of exploring caves : SPELUNKING

cav·i·ta·tion \,ka-və-'tā-shən\ *n* : the formation of partial vacuums in a liquid by a swiftly moving solid body (as a propeller) or by high-intensity sound waves

cav·i·ty \'ka-və-tē\ *n, pl* **-ties** **1** : an unfilled space within a mass : a hollow place **2** : an area of decay in a tooth

ca·vort \kə-'vȯrt\ *vb* : PRANCE, CAPER

ca·vy \'kā-vē\ *n, pl* **cavies** : GUINEA PIG 1

caw \'kȯ\ *vb* : to utter the harsh call of the crow or a similar cry — **caw** *n*

cay \'kē, 'kā\ *n* : ⁴KEY

cay·enne pepper \,kī-'en-, ,kā-\ *n* : a condiment consisting of ground dried fruits or seeds of a hot pepper

cayman *var of* CAIMAN

Ca·yu·ga \kā-'ü-gə, kī-\ *n, pl* **Cayuga** *or* **Cayugas** : a member of an American Indian people of New York

Cay·use \'kī-,yüs, kī-'\ *n,* **1** *pl* **Cayuse** *or* **Cayuses** : a member of an American Indian people of Oregon and Washington **2** *pl* **cayuses,** *not cap West* : a native range horse

Cb *symbol* columbium

CB \'sē-'bē\ *n* : CITIZENS BAND; *also* : the radio set used for citizens-band communications

CBC *abbr* Canadian Broadcasting Corporation

CBD *abbr* cash before delivery

CBS *abbr* Columbia Broadcasting System

CBW *abbr* chemical and biological warfare

cc *abbr* cubic centimeter

CC *abbr* **1** carbon copy **2** community college **3** country club

CCD \,sē-,sē-'dē\ *n* : CHARGE-COUPLED DEVICE

CCTV *abbr* closed-circuit television

CCU *abbr* **1** cardiac care unit **2** coronary care unit **3** critical care unit

ccw *abbr* counterclockwise

cd *abbr* cord

Cd *symbol* cadmium

¹CD \,sē-'dē\ *n* : CERTIFICATE OF DEPOSIT

²CD *n* : a small optical disk usu. containing recorded music or computer data; *also* : the content of a CD

³CD *abbr* Civil Defense

CDR *abbr* commander

CD-ROM \,sē-,dē-'räm\ *n* : a CD containing computer data that cannot be altered

CDT *abbr* central daylight (saving) time

Ce *symbol* cerium

CE *abbr* **1** chemical engineer **2** civil engineer **3** Corps of Engineers

cease \'sēs\ *vb* **ceased; ceas·ing** : to come or bring to an end : STOP

cease–fire \'sēs-'fi(-ə)r\ *n* : a suspension of active hostilities

cease·less \'sēs-ləs\ *adj* : being without pause or stop : CONTINUOUS — **cease·less·ly** *adv* — **cease·less·ness** *n*

ce·cum *also* **cae·cum** \'sē-kəm\ *n, pl* **ce·ca** \-kə\ : the blind pouch at the beginning of the large intestine into which the small intestine opens — **ce·cal** *also* **cae·cal** \-kəl\ *adj*

ce·dar \'sē-dər\ *n* : any of numerous coniferous trees (as a juniper) noted for their fragrant durable wood; *also* : this wood

cede \'sēd\ *vb* **ced·ed; ced·ing** **1** : to yield or give up esp. by treaty **2** : ASSIGN, TRANSFER — **ced·er** *n*

ce·di \'sä-dē\ *n* — see MONEY table

ce·dil·la \si-'di-lə\ *n* : a mark placed under the letter *c* (as ç) to show that the *c* is to be pronounced like *s*

ceil·ing \'sē-liŋ\ *n* **1** : the overhead inside lining of a room **2** : the height above the ground of the base of the lowest layer of clouds when over half of the sky is obscured **3** : the greatest height at which an airplane can operate efficiently **4** : a prescribed upper limit ⟨price ∼⟩

cel·an·dine \'se-lən-,dīn, -,dēn\ *n* : a yellow-flowered herb related to the poppies

cel·e·brant \'se-lə-brənt\ *n* : one who celebrates; *esp* : a priest officiating at the Eucharist

cel·e·brate \'se-lə-,brāt\ *vb* **-brat·ed; -brat·ing** **1** : to perform (as a sacrament) with appropriate rites **2** : to honor (as a holiday) by solemn ceremonies or by refraining from ordinary business **3** : to observe a notable occasion with festivities **4** : EXTOL — **cel·e·bra·tion** \,se-lə-'brā-shən\ *n* — **cel·e·bra·tor** \'se-lə-,brā-tər\ *n* — **cel·e·bra·to·ry** \-brə-,tȯr-ē, ,se-lə-'brā-tə-rē\ *adj*

celebrated *adj* : widely known and often referred to ⟨a ∼ author⟩ ✦ **Synonyms** DISTINGUISHED, RENOWNED, NOTED, FAMOUS, ILLUSTRIOUS, NOTORIOUS

ce·leb·ri·ty \sə-'le-brə-tē\ *n, pl* **-ties** **1** : the state of being celebrated : RENOWN **2** : a celebrated person

ce·ler·i·ty \sə-'ler-ə-tē\ *n* : SPEED, RAPIDITY

cel·ery \'se-lə-rē\ *n, pl* **-er·ies** : a European herb related to the carrot and widely grown for the crisp edible stems of its leaves

celery cabbage *n* : CHINESE CABBAGE 2

ce·les·ta \sə-'les-tə\ *or* **ce·leste** \sə-'lest\ *n* : a keyboard instrument with hammers that strike steel plates

ce·les·tial \sə-'les-chəl\ *adj* **1** : HEAVENLY, DIVINE **2** : of or relating to the sky — **ce·les·tial·ly** *adv*

celestial navigation *n* : navigation by observation of the positions of stars

celestial sphere *n* : an imaginary sphere of infinite radius against which the celestial bodies appear to be projected

cel·i·ba·cy \'se-lə-bə-sē\ *n* **1** : the state of being unmarried; *esp* : abstention by vow from marriage **2** : abstention from sexual intercourse

cel·i·bate \'se-lə-bət\ *n* : one who lives in celibacy — **celibate** *adj*

cell \'sel\ *n* **1** : a small room (as in a convent or prison) usu. for one person; *also* : a small compartment, cavity, or bounded space **2** : a tiny mass of protoplasm that usu. contains a nucleus, is enclosed by a membrane, and forms the smallest structural unit of living matter capable of functioning independently **3** : a container holding an electrolyte either for generating electricity or for use in electrolysis **4** : a single unit in a device for converting radiant energy into electrical energy — **celled** \'seld\ *adj*

cel·lar \'se-lər\ *n* **1** : BASEMENT 1 **2** : the lowest place in the standings (as in an athletic league) **3** : a stock of wines

cel·lar·ette *or* **cel·lar·et** \,se-lə-'ret\ *n* : a case or cabinet for a few bottles of wine or liquor

cell body *n* : the nucleus-containing central part of a neuron exclusive of its processes

cel·lo \'che-lō\ *n, pl* **cellos** : a bass member of the violin family tuned an octave below the viola — **cel·list** \-list\ *n*

cel·lo·phane \'se-lə-,fān\ *n* : a thin transparent material made from cellulose and used as a wrapping

cell phone *n* : a portable cordless telephone for use in a cellular system

cel·lu·lar \'sel-yə-lər\ *adj* **1** : of, relating to, or consisting of cells 〈∼ proteins〉 **2** : of, relating to, or being a radiotelephone system in which a geographical area is divided into small sections each served by a transmitter of limited range

cel·lu·lite \'sel-yə-,līt\ *n* : deposits of lumpy fat within connective tissue (as in the thighs, hips, and buttocks)

cel·lu·lose \'sel-yə-,lōs\ *n* : a complex carbohydrate of the cell walls of plants used esp. in making paper or rayon — **cel·lu·los·ic** \,sel-yə-'lō-sik\ *adj or n*

Cel·si·us \'sel-sē-əs\ *adj* : relating to or having a scale for measuring temperature on which the interval between the triple point and the boiling point of water is divided into 99.99 degrees with 0.01° being the triple point and 100.00° the boiling point; *also* : CENTIGRADE

Celt \'kelt, 'selt\ *n* : a member of any of a group of peoples (as the Irish or Welsh) of western Europe — **Celt·ic** *adj*

cem·ba·lo \'chem-bə-,lō\ *n, pl* **-ba·li** \-,lē\ *or* **-balos** [It] : HARPSICHORD

¹ce·ment \si-'ment\ *n* **1** : CONCRETE; *also* : a powder that is produced from a burned mixture chiefly of clay and limestone and that is used in mortar and concrete **2** : a binding element or agency **3** : CEMENTUM; *also* : a substance for filling cavities in teeth

²cement *vb* **1** : to unite by or as if by cement **2** : to cover with concrete — **ce·ment·er** *n*

ce·men·tum \si-'men-təm\ *n* : a specialized external bony layer covering the dentin of the part of a tooth normally within the gum

cem·e·tery \'se-mə-,ter-ē\ *n, pl* **-ter·ies** [ME *cimitery*, fr. AF *cimiterie*, fr. LL *coemeterium*, fr. Gk *koimētērion* sleeping chamber, burial place, fr. *koiman* to put to sleep] : a burial ground : GRAVEYARD

cen·o·bite \'se-nə-,bīt\ *n* : a member of a religious group living together in a monastic community — **cen·o·bit·ic** \,se-nə-'bi-tik\ *adj*

ceno·taph \'se-nə-,taf\ *n* [F *cénotaphe*, fr. L *cenotaphium*, fr. Gk *kenotaphion*, fr. *kenos* empty + *taphos* tomb] : a tomb or a monument erected in honor of a person whose body is elsewhere

Ce·no·zo·ic \,sē-nə-'zō-ik, ,se-\ *adj* : of, relating to, or being the era of geologic history that extends from about 65 million years ago to the present — **Cenozoic** *n*

cen·ser \'sen-sər\ *n* : a vessel for burning incense (as in a religious ritual)

¹cen·sor \'sen-sər\ *n* **1** : a person who inspects printed matter or motion pictures with power to suppress anything objectionable **2** : one of two early Roman magistrates whose duties included taking the census — **cen·so·ri·al** \sen-'sȯr-ē-əl\ *adj*

²censor *vb* : to subject to censorship

cen·so·ri·ous \sen-'sȯr-ē-əs\ *adj* : marked by or given to censure : CRITICAL — **cen·so·ri·ous·ly** *adv* — **cen·so·ri·ous·ness** *n*

cen·sor·ship \'sen-sər-,ship\ *n* **1** : the action of a censor esp. in stopping the transmission or publication of matter considered objectionable **2** : the office of a Roman censor

¹cen·sure \'sen-chər\ *n* **1** : the act of blaming or condemning sternly **2** : an official reprimand

²censure *vb* **cen·sured; cen·sur·ing** : to find fault with and criticize as blameworthy — **cen·sur·able** *adj* — **cen·sur·er** *n*

cen·sus \'sen-səs\ *n* **1** : a periodic governmental count of population **2** : COUNT, TALLY — **census** *vb*

¹cent \'sent\ *n* [F, hundred, fr. L *centum*] **1** : a monetary unit equal to ¹⁄₁₀₀ of a basic unit of value — see *birr, dollar, euro, gulden, leone, lilangeni, lira, nakfa, pound, rand, rupee, shilling* at MONEY table **2** : a coin, token, or note representing one cent **3** : a former monetary unit equal to ¹⁄₁₀₀ Dutch gulden

²cent *abbr* **1** centigrade **2** central **3** century

cen·tas \'sen-,täs\ *n, pl* **cen·tai** \-,tī\ *or* **cen·tu** \-,tü\ — see *litas* at MONEY table

cen·taur \'sen-,tȯr\ *n* : any of a race of creatures in Greek mythology half man and half horse

¹cen·ta·vo \sen-'tä-(,)vō\ *n, pl* **-vos** — see *boliviano, colón, cordoba, lempira, peso, quetzal, sucre* at MONEY table

²cen·ta·vo \-'tä-(,)vü, -(,)vō\ *n, pl* **-vos 1** — see *escudo, metical, real* at MONEY table **2** : a former monetary unit equal to ¹⁄₁₀₀ Portuguese escudo

cen·te·nar·i·an \ˌsen-tə-ˈner-ē-ən\ *n* : a person who is 100 or more years old

cen·te·na·ry \sen-ˈte-nə-rē, ˈsen-tə-ˌner-ē\ *n, pl* **-ries** : CENTENNIAL — **centenary** *adj*

cen·ten·ni·al \sen-ˈte-nē-əl\ *n* : a 100th anniversary or its celebration — **centennial** *adj*

¹**cen·ter** \ˈsen-tər\ *n* **1** : the point that is equally distant from all points on the circumference of a circle or surface of a sphere; *also* : MIDDLE 1 **2** : the point about which an activity concentrates or from which something originates **3** : a region of concentrated population **4** : a middle part **5** *often cap* : political figures holding moderate views esp. between those of conservatives and liberals **6** : a player occupying a middle position (as in football or basketball)

²**center** *vb* **1** : to place or fix at or around a center or central area **2** : to give a central focus or basis : CONCENTRATE **3** : to have a center : FOCUS

cen·ter·board \ˈsen-tər-ˌbórd\ *n* : a retractable keel used esp. in sailboats

cen·ter·piece \-ˌpēs\ *n* **1** : an object in a central position; *esp* : an adornment in the center of a table **2** : one that is of central importance or interest in a larger whole

cen·tes·i·mal \sen-ˈte-sə-məl\ *adj* : marked by or relating to division into hundredths

¹**cen·tes·i·mo** \chen-ˈte-zə-ˌmō\ *n, pl* **-mi** \-ˌ(ˌ)mē\ : a former monetary unit equal to ¹⁄₁₀₀ Italian lira

²**cen·tes·i·mo** \sen-ˈte-sə-ˌmō\ *n, pl* **-mos** — see *balboa, peso* at MONEY table

cen·ti·grade \ˈsen-tə-ˌgrād, ˈsän-\ *adj* : relating to, conforming to, or having a thermometer scale on which the interval between the freezing and boiling points of water is divided into 100 degrees with 0° representing the freezing point and 100° the boiling point ⟨10° ∼⟩ — compare CELSIUS

cen·ti·gram \-ˌgram\ *n* — see METRIC SYSTEM table

cen·ti·li·ter \ˈsen-ti-ˌlē-tər\ *n* — see METRIC SYSTEM table

cen·time \ˈsän-ˌtēm\ *n* **1** : a former monetary unit of any of several countries (as Belgium, France, and Luxembourg) equal to ¹⁄₁₀₀ franc **2** — see *dinar, dirham, franc, gourde* at MONEY table

cen·ti·me·ter \ˈsen-tə-ˌmē-tər, ˈsän-\ *n* — see METRIC SYSTEM table

centimeter–gram–second *adj* : of, relating to, or being a system of units based on the centimeter as the unit of length, the gram as the unit of mass, and the second as the unit of time

cen·ti·mo \ˈsen-tə-ˌmō\ *n, pl* **-mos** **1** — see *bolivar, colón, dobra, guarani, sol* at MONEY table **2** : a former monetary unit equal to ¹⁄₁₀₀ peseta

cen·ti·pede \ˈsen-tə-ˌpēd\ *n* [L *centipeda*, fr. *centum* hundred + *pes* foot] : any of a class of long flattened segmented arthropods with one pair of legs on each seg-

ment except the first which has a pair of poison fangs

¹**cen·tral** \ˈsen-trəl\ *adj* **1** : constituting a center **2** : ESSENTIAL, PRINCIPAL ⟨the novel's ∼ character⟩ **3** : situated at, in, or near the center **4** : centrally placed and superseding separate units ⟨∼ heating⟩ — **cen·tral·ly** *adv*

²**central** *n* : a central controlling office

cen·tral·ise *Brit var of* CENTRALIZE

cen·tral·ize \ˈsen-trə-ˌlīz\ *vb* **-ized; -izing** : to bring to a central point or under central control — **cen·tral·i·za·tion** \ˌsen-trə-lə-ˈzā-shən\ *n* — **cen·tral·iz·er** \ˈsen-trə-ˌlī-zər\ *n*

central nervous system *n* : the part of the nervous system which integrates nervous function and activity and which in vertebrates consists of the brain and spinal cord

cen·tre *chiefly Brit var of* CENTER

cen·trif·u·gal \sen-ˈtri-fyə-gəl, -fi-\ *adj* [NL *centrifugus*, fr. *centr-* center + L *fugere* to flee] **1** : proceeding or acting in a direction away from a center or axis **2** : using or acting by centrifugal force

centrifugal force *n* : the apparent force felt by an object moving in a curved path and acting outward from a center of rotation

cen·tri·fuge \ˈsen-trə-ˌfyüj\ *n* : a machine using centrifugal force (as for separating substances of different densities or for removing moisture)

cen·trip·e·tal \sen-ˈtri-pə-t⁰l\ *adj* [NL *centripetus*, fr. *centr-* center + L *petere* seek] : proceeding or acting in a direction toward a center or axis

centripetal force *n* : the force needed to keep an object revolving about a point moving in a circular path

cen·trist \ˈsen-trist\ *n* **1** *often cap* : a member of a center party **2** : one who holds moderate views

cen·tu·ri·on \sen-ˈtùr-ē-ən, -ˈtyùr-\ *n* : an officer commanding a Roman century

cen·tu·ry \ˈsen-chə-rē\ *n, pl* **-ries** **1** : a subdivision of a Roman legion **2** : a group or sequence of 100 like things **3** : a period of 100 years

century plant *n* : a Mexican agave maturing and flowering only once in many years and then dying

CEO \ˌsē-(ˌ)ē-ˈō\ *n* : the executive with the chief decision-making authority in an organization or business

ce·phal·ic \sə-ˈfa-lik\ *adj* **1** : of or relating to the head **2** : directed toward or situated on or in or near the head

ce·ram·ic \sə-ˈra-mik\ *n* **1** *pl* : the art or process of making articles from a nonmetallic mineral (as clay) by firing **2** : a product produced by ceramics — **ceramic** *adj*

ce·ra·mist \sə-ˈra-mist\ *or* **ce·ram·i·cist** \sə-ˈra-mə-sist\ *n* : one who engages in ceramics

¹**ce·re·al** \ˈsir-ē-əl\ *adj* [L *cerealis*, fr. *Ceres*, the Roman goddess of agriculture] : relating to grain or to the plants that produce it; *also* : made of grain

²**cereal** *n* **1** : a grass (as wheat) yielding grain suitable for food; *also* : its grain **2** : a food and esp. a breakfast food prepared from the grain of a cereal

cer·e·bel·lum \ˌser-ə-ˈbe-ləm\ *n, pl* **-bellums** *or* **-bel·la** \-lə\ [ML, fr. L, dim. of *cerebrum* brain] : a part of the brain that projects over the medulla and is concerned esp. with coordination of muscular action and with bodily balance — **cer·e·bel·lar** \-lər\ *adj*

ce·re·bral \sə-ˈrē-brəl, ˈser-ə-\ *adj* **1** : of or relating to the brain, intellect, or cerebrum **2** : appealing to or involving the intellect — **ce·re·bral·ly** *adv*

cerebral cortex *n* : the surface layer of gray matter of the cerebrum that functions chiefly in coordination of sensory and motor information

cerebral palsy *n* : a disorder caused by brain damage usu. before, during, or shortly after birth and marked esp. by defective muscle control

cer·e·brate \ˈser-ə-ˌbrāt\ *vb* **-brat·ed; -brat·ing** : THINK — **cer·e·bra·tion** \ˌser-ə-ˈbrā-shən\ *n*

ce·re·brum \sə-ˈrē-brəm, ˈser-ə-\ *n, pl* **-brums** *or* **-bra** \-brə\ [L, brain] : the enlarged front and upper part of the brain that contains the higher nervous centers

cere·ment \ˈser-ə-mənt, ˈsir-mənt\ *n* : a shroud for the dead

¹**cer·e·mo·ni·al** \ˌser-ə-ˈmō-nē-əl\ *adj* : of, relating to, or forming a ceremony; *also* : stressing careful attention to form and detail — **cer·e·mo·ni·al·ly** *adv*

²**ceremonial** *n* : a ceremonial act or system : RITUAL, FORM

cer·e·mo·ni·ous \ˌser-ə-ˈmō-nē-əs\ *adj* **1** : devoted to forms and ceremony **2** : CEREMONIAL **3** : according to formal usage or procedure **4** : marked by ceremony — **cer·e·mo·ni·ous·ly** *adv* — **cer·e·mo·ni·ous·ness** *n*

cer·e·mo·ny \ˈser-ə-ˌmō-nē\ *n, pl* **-nies** **1** : a formal act or series of acts prescribed by law, ritual, or convention **2** : a conventional act of politeness **3** : a mere outward form with no deeper significance **4** : FORMALITY

ce·re·us \ˈsir-ē-əs\ *n* : any of various cacti of the western U.S. and tropical America

ce·rise \sə-ˈrēs\ *n* [F, lit., cherry] : a moderate red color

ce·ri·um \ˈsir-ē-əm\ *n* : a malleable metallic chemical element used esp. in alloys

cer·met \ˈsər-ˌmet\ *n* : a strong alloy of a heat-resistant compound and a metal used esp. for turbine blades

cert *abbr* certificate; certification; certified; certify

¹**cer·tain** \ˈsər-tᵊn\ *adj* **1** : FIXED, SETTLED **2** : of a specific but unspecified character ⟨∼ people in authority⟩ **3** : DEPENDABLE, RELIABLE **4** : INDISPUTABLE, UNDENIABLE **5** : assured in mind or action — **cer·tain·ly** *adv*

²**certain** *pron* : certain ones

cer·tain·ty \-tē\ *n, pl* **-ties** **1** : something that is certain **2** : the quality or state of being certain

cer·tif·i·cate \sər-ˈti-fi-kət\ *n* **1** : a document testifying to the truth of a fact **2** : a document testifying that one has fulfilled certain requirements (as of a course) **3** : a document giving evidence of ownership or debt ⟨a stock ∼⟩

certificate of deposit : a money-market bond redeemable without penalty only on maturity

cer·ti·fi·ca·tion \ˌsər-tə-fə-ˈkā-shən\ *n* **1** : the act of certifying : the state of being certified **2** : a certified statement

certified mail *n* : first class mail for which proof of delivery may be secured but no indemnity value is claimed

certified public accountant *n* : an accountant who has met the requirements of a state law and has been granted a certificate

cer·ti·fy \ˈsər-tə-ˌfī\ *vb* **-fied; -fy·ing** **1** : VERIFY, CONFIRM **2** : to endorse officially **3** : to guarantee (a bank check) as good by a statement to that effect stamped on its face **4** : to recognize as having met specific qualifications within a field ⟨*certified* teachers⟩ ◆ **Synonyms** ACCREDIT, APPROVE, SANCTION, ENDORSE — **cer·ti·fi·able** \-ə-bəl\ *adj* — **cer·ti·fi·ably** \-blē\ *adv* — **cer·ti·fi·er** *n*

cer·ti·tude \ˈsər-tə-ˌtüd, -ˌtyüd\ *n* : the state of being or feeling certain

ce·ru·le·an \sə-ˈrü-lē-ən\ *adj* : AZURE

ce·ru·men \sə-ˈrü-mən\ *n* : EARWAX

cer·vi·cal \ˈsər-vi-kəl\ *adj* : of or relating to a neck or cervix

cervical cap *n* : a contraceptive device in the form of a thimble-shaped molded cap that fits snugly over the uterine cervix and blocks sperm from entering the uterus

cer·vix \ˈsər-viks\ *n, pl* **cer·vi·ces** \-və-ˌsēz\ *or* **cer·vix·es** **1** : NECK; *esp* : the back part of the neck **2** : a constricted portion of an organ or part; *esp* : the narrow outer end of the uterus

ce·sar·e·an *or* **cae·sar·e·an** *also* **ce·sar·i·an** *or* **cae·sar·i·an** \si-ˈzer-ē-ən\ *n, often cap* : CESAREAN SECTION — **cesarean** *or* **caesarean** *also* **cesarian** *or* **caesarian** *adj*

cesarean section *also* **caesarean section** *n, often cap* C [fr. the legendary association of such a delivery with the Roman cognomen *Caesar*] : surgical incision of the walls of the abdomen and uterus for delivery of offspring

ce·si·um \ˈsē-zē-əm\ *n* : a silver-white soft ductile chemical element

ces·sa·tion \se-ˈsā-shən\ *n* : a temporary or final ceasing (as of action)

ces·sion \ˈse-shən\ *n* : a yielding (as of rights) to another

cess·pool \ˈses-ˌpül\ *n* **1** : an underground pit or tank for receiving household sewage **2** : a filthy or corrupt situation

ce·ta·cean \si-ˈtā-shən\ *n* : any of an order of aquatic mostly marine mammals that includes whales, porpoises, dolphins, and related forms — **cetacean** *adj*

cf *abbr* [L *confer*] compare

Cf *symbol* californium

CF *abbr* cystic fibrosis

CFC *abbr* chlorofluorocarbon

cg *abbr* centigram

CG **1** coast guard **2** commanding general

cgs *abbr* centimeter-gram-second

ch *abbr* **1** chain **2** champion **3** chapter **4** church

CH *abbr* **1** clearinghouse **2** courthouse **3** customhouse

Cha·blis \sha-ˈblē, shə-, shä-; ˈsha-ˌblē\ *n, pl* **Cha·blis** \-ˈblēz, -ˌ(ˌ)blēz\ **1** : a dry sharp white Burgundy wine **2** : a white California wine

cha–cha \ˈchä-ˌchä\ *n* : a fast rhythmic ballroom dance of Latin American origin

chafe \ˈchāf\ *vb* **chafed; chaf·ing 1** : IRRITATE, VEX **2** : FRET **3** : to warm by rubbing **4** : to rub so as to wear away; *also* : to make sore by rubbing

cha·fer \ˈchā-fər\ *n* : any of various scarab beetles

¹chaff \ˈchaf\ *n* **1** : debris (as husks) separated from grain in threshing **2** : something comparatively worthless — **chaffy** *adj*

²chaff *n* : light jesting talk : BANTER

³chaff *vb* : to tease good-naturedly

chaf·fer \ˈcha-fər\ *vb* : BARGAIN, HAGGLE — **chaf·fer·er** *n*

chaf·finch \ˈcha-ˌfinch\ *n* : a common European finch with a cheerful song

chaf·ing dish \ˈchā-fiŋ-\ *n* : a utensil for cooking food at the table

cha·grin \shə-ˈgrin\ *n* : mental uneasiness or annoyance caused by failure, disappointment, or humiliation

²chagrin *vb* **cha·grined** \-ˈgrind\; **cha·grin·ing** : to cause to feel chagrin

¹chain \ˈchān\ *n* [ME *cheyne*, fr. AF *chaene*, fr. L *catena*] **1** : a flexible series of connected links **2** : a chainlike surveying instrument; *also* : a unit of length equal to 66 feet (about 20 meters) **3** *pl* : BONDS, FETTERS **4** : a series of things linked together ⟨mountain ∼s⟩; *also* : a group of usu. identical enterprises with a single owner ⟨fast-food ∼s⟩ ♦ **Synonyms** TRAIN, STRING, SEQUENCE, SUCCESSION, SERIES

²chain *vb* : to fasten, bind, or connect with a chain; *also* : FETTER

chain gang *n* : a gang of convicts chained together

chain letter *n* : a letter sent to several persons with a request that each send copies to an equal number of persons

chain mail *n* : flexible armor of interlocking metal rings

chain reaction *n* **1** : a series of events in which each event initiates the succeeding one **2** : a chemical or nuclear reaction yielding products that cause further reactions of the same kind

chain saw *n* : a portable power saw that has teeth linked together to form an endless chain — **chain·saw** \ˈchān-ˌsȯ\ *vb*

chain–smoke \ˈchān-ˈsmōk\ *vb* : to smoke esp. cigarettes continuously

¹chair \ˈcher\ *n* [ME *chaiere*, fr. AF, fr. L *cathedra*, fr. Gk *kathedra*, fr. *kata-* down + *hedra* seat] **1** : a seat with a back for one person **2** : ELECTRIC CHAIR **3** : an official seat; *also* : an office or position of authority or dignity **4** : CHAIRMAN

²chair *vb* : to act as chairman of

chair·lift \ˈcher-ˌlift\ *n* : a motor-driven conveyor for skiers consisting of seats hung from a moving cable

chair·man \-mən\ *n* : the presiding officer of a meeting, committee, or event — **chair·man·ship** *n*

chair·per·son \-ˌpər-sən\ *n* : CHAIRMAN

chair·wom·an \-ˌwu̇-mən\ *n* : a woman who serves as chairman

chaise \ˈshāz\ *n* : a 2-wheeled horse-drawn carriage with a folding top

chaise longue \ˈshāz-ˈlȯŋ\ *n, pl* **chaise longues** *same or* -ˈlȯŋz\ [F, lit., long chair] : a long reclining chair

chaise lounge \-ˈlau̇nj\ *n* : CHAISE LONGUE

chal·ced·o·ny \kal-ˈse-d°n-ē\ *n, pl* **-nies** : a translucent quartz of various colors

chal·co·py·rite \ˌkal-kə-ˈpī-ˌrīt\ *n* : a yellow mineral constituting an important copper ore

cha·let \sha-ˈlā\ *n* **1** : a herdsman's cabin in the Swiss mountains **2** : a building in the style of a Swiss cottage with a wide roof overhang

chal·ice \ˈcha-ləs\ *n* : a drinking cup; *esp* : the eucharistic cup

¹chalk \ˈchȯk\ *n* **1** : a soft limestone **2** : chalk or chalky material esp. when used as a crayon — **chalky** *adj*

²chalk *vb* **1** : to rub or mark with chalk **2** : to record with or as if with chalk — usu. used with *up*

chalk·board \ˈchȯk-ˌbȯrd\ *n* : BLACKBOARD

chalk up *vb* **1** : ASCRIBE, CREDIT **2** : ATTAIN, ACHIEVE ⟨*chalk up* a victory⟩

¹chal·lenge \ˈcha-lənj\ *vb* **chal·lenged; chal·leng·ing** [ME *chalengen* to accuse, fr. AF *chalenger*, fr. L *calumniari* to accuse falsely, fr. *calumnia* calumny] **1** : to order to halt and prove identity **2** : to take exception to : DISPUTE ⟨∼ a ruling⟩ **3** : to issue an invitation to compete ⟨*challenged* me to another game⟩ **4** : to stimulate by presenting difficulties ⟨a job that ∼s her⟩ — **chal·leng·er** *n*

²challenge *n* **1** : a summons to a duel **2** : an invitation to compete in a sport **3** : a calling into question **4** : an exception taken to a juror **5** : a sentry's command to halt and prove identity **6** : a stimulating or interesting task or problem

challenged *adj* : presented with difficulties (as by a disability)

chal·lis \ˈsha-lē\ *n, pl* **chal·lises** \-lēz\ : a lightweight clothing fabric of wool, cotton, or synthetic yarns

cham·ber \ˈchām-bər\ *n* **1** : ROOM; *esp* : BEDROOM **2** : an enclosed space or cavity **3** : a hall for meetings of a legislative body **4** : a judge's consultation room — usu. used in pl. **5** : a legislative or judicial body; *also* : a council for a business purpose **6** : the part of a firearm that holds the cartridge or powder charge during firing — **cham·bered** \-bərd\ *adj*

cham·ber·lain \'chām-bər-lən\ *n* **1** : a chief officer in the household of a king or nobleman **2** : TREASURER

cham·ber·maid \-ˌmād\ *n* : a maid who takes care of bedrooms

chamber music *n* : music intended for performance by a few musicians before a small audience

chamber of commerce : an association of businesspeople for promoting commercial and industrial interests in the community

cham·bray \'sham-ˌbrā\ *n* : a lightweight clothing fabric of white and colored threads

cha·me·leon \kə-'mēl-yən\ *n* [ME *camelion*, fr. MF, fr. L *chamaeleon*, fr. Gk *chamaileōn*, fr. *chamai* on the ground + *leōn* lion] : a small lizard whose skin changes color esp. according to its surroundings

¹cham·fer \'cham-fər\ *vb* **1** : to cut a furrow in (as a column) : GROOVE **2** : to make a chamfer on : BEVEL

²chamfer *n* : a beveled edge

cham·ois \'sha-mē\ *n, pl* **cham·ois** *same or* -mēz\ **1** : a small goatlike ruminant mammal of Europe and the Caucasus region of Russia **2** *also* **cham·my** \'sha-mē\ : a soft leather made esp. from the skin of the sheep or goat **3** : a cotton fabric made in imitation of chamois leather

cham·o·mile *or* **cam·o·mile** \'ka-mə-ˌmī(-ə)l, -ˌmēl\ *n* : any of a genus of strong-scented herbs related to the daisies and having flower heads that yield a bitter substance used esp. in tonics and teas

¹champ \'champ, 'chämp\ *vb* **1** : to chew noisily **2** : to show impatience of delay or restraint

²champ \'champ\ *n* : CHAMPION

cham·pagne \sham-'pān\ *n* : a white effervescent wine

¹cham·pi·on \'cham-pē-ən\ *n* **1** : a militant advocate or defender **2** : one that wins first prize or place in a contest **3** : one that is acknowledged to be better than all others

²champion *vb* : to protect or fight for as a champion ∗ **Synonyms** BACK, ADVOCATE, UPHOLD, SUPPORT

cham·pi·on·ship \-ˌship\ *n* **1** : the position or title of a champion **2** : the act of championing : DEFENSE **3** : a contest held to determine a champion

¹chance \'chans\ *n* **1** : something that happens without apparent cause **2** : the unpredictable element in existence : LUCK, FORTUNE **3** : OPPORTUNITY **4** : the likelihood of a particular outcome in an uncertain situation : PROBABILITY **5** : RISK **6** : a raffle ticket — **chance** *adj* — **by chance** : in the haphazard course of events

²chance *vb* **chanced; chanc·ing 1** : to take place by chance : HAPPEN **2** : to come casually and unexpectedly — used with *upon* **3** : to leave to chance **4** : to accept the risk of

chan·cel \'chan-səl\ *n* : the part of a church including the altar and choir

chan·cel·lery *or* **chan·cel·lory** \'chan-sə-lə-rē\ *n, pl* **-ler·ies** *or* **-lor·ies 1** : the position or office of a chancellor **2** : the building or room where a chancellor works **3** : the office or staff of an embassy or consulate

chan·cel·lor \'chan-sə-lər\ *n* **1** : a high state official in various countries **2** : the head of a university **3** : a judge in the equity court in various states of the U.S. **4** : the chief minister of state in some European countries — **chan·cel·lor·ship** *n*

chan·cery \'chan-sə-rē\ *n, pl* **-cer·ies 1** : a record office for public or diplomatic archives **2** : any of various courts of equity in the U.S. and Britain **3** : a chancellor's court or office **4** : the office of an embassy **5** : the business office of a diocese

chan·cre \'shaŋ-kər\ *n* [F, fr. OF, fr. L *cancer*] : a primary sore or ulcer at the site of entry of an infective agent (as of syphilis)

chan·croid \'chaŋ-ˌkrȯid\ *n* : a sexually transmitted disease caused by a bacterium and characterized by chancres that differ from those of syphilis in lacking hardened margins

chancy \'chan-sē\ *adj* **chanc·i·er; -est 1** *Scot* : AUSPICIOUS **2** : RISKY

chan·de·lier \ˌshan-də-'lir\ *n* : a branched lighting fixture suspended from a ceiling

chan·dler \'chand-lər\ *n* [ME *chandeler* a maker or seller of candles, fr. AF, fr. *chandele* candle, fr. L *candela*] : a dealer in provisions and supplies of a specified kind ⟨ship's ∼⟩ — **chan·dlery** *n*

¹change \'chānj\ *vb* **changed; chang·ing 1** : to make or become different : ALTER **2** : to replace with another **3** : to give or receive an equivalent sum in notes or coins of usu. smaller denominations or of another currency **4** : to put fresh clothes or covering on ⟨∼ a bed⟩ **5** : to put on different clothes **6** : EXCHANGE — **change·able** *adj* — **changer** *n*

²change *n* **1** : the act, process, or result of changing **2** : a fresh set of clothes **3** : money given in exchange for other money of higher denomination **4** : money returned when a payment exceeds the sum due **5** : coins esp. of small denominations — **change·ful** *adj*

change·ling \'chānj-liŋ\ *n* : a child secretly exchanged for another in infancy

change of life : MENOPAUSE

change·over \'chānj-ˌō-vər\ *n* : CONVERSION, TRANSITION

change ringing *n* : the art or practice of ringing a set of tuned bells in continually varying order

¹chan·nel \'cha-nᵊl\ *n* **1** : the bed of a stream **2** : the deeper part of a waterway **3** : STRAIT **4** : a means of passage or transmission **5** : a range of frequencies of sufficient width for a single radio or television transmission **6** : a usu. tubular enclosed passage : CONDUIT **7** : a long gutter, groove, or furrow

²**channel** vb **-neled** or **-nelled; -neling** or **-nel·ling 1** : to make a channel in **2** : to direct into or through a channel

chan·nel·ize \'cha-nə-ˌlīz\ vb **-ized; -iz·ing** : CHANNEL — **chan·nel·i·za·tion** \ˌcha-nə-lə-'zā-shən\ n

chan·son \shäⁿ-'sōⁿ\ n, pl **chan·sons** \same or -'sōⁿz\ : SONG; esp : a cabaret song

¹**chant** \'chant\ vb **1** : SING; esp : to sing a chant **2** : to utter or recite in the manner of a chant **3** : to celebrate or praise in song — **chant·er** n

²**chant** n **1** : a repetitive melody in which several words are sung to one tone : SONG; esp : a liturgical melody **2** : a manner of singing or speaking in musical monotones

chan·te·relle \ˌshan-tə-'rel\ n : a fragrant edible mushroom

chan·teuse \shäⁿ-'tœrz, shan-'tüz\ n, pl **chan·teuses** \same or -'tœr-zəz, -'tü-zəz\ [F] : a woman who is a concert or night-club singer

chan·tey or **chan·ty** \'shan-tē, 'chan-\ n, pl **chanteys** or **chanties** : a song sung by sailors in rhythm with their work

chan·ti·cleer \ˌchan-tə-'klir, ˌshan-\ n : ROOSTER

Chanukah var of HANUKKAH

cha·os \'kā-ˌäs\ n **1** often cap : the confused unorganized state existing before the creation of distinct forms **2** : the inherent unpredictability in the behavior of a complex natural system (as the atmosphere or the beating heart) **3** : complete disorder ♦ **Synonyms** CONFUSION, JUMBLE, SNARL, MUDDLE, DISARRAY — **cha·ot·ic** \kā-'ä-tik\ adj — **cha·ot·i·cal·ly** \-ti-k(ə-)lē\ adv

chaos theory n : a branch of mathematical and physical theory concerned with chaotic systems

¹**chap** \'chap\ vb **chapped; chap·ping** : to dry and crack open usu. from wind and cold ⟨chapped lips⟩

²**chap** n : a jaw with its fleshy covering — usu. used in pl.

³**chap** n, chiefly Brit : FELLOW

⁴**chap** abbr chapter

chap·ar·ral \ˌsha-pə-'ral\ n **1** : a dense impenetrable thicket of shrubs or dwarf trees **2** : an ecological community esp. of southern California composed of shrubby plants

chap·book \'chap-ˌbůk\ n : a small book of ballads, tales, or tracts

cha·peau \sha-'pō\ n, pl **cha·peaus** \-'pōz\ or **cha·peaux** \-'pō, -'pōz\ [MF] : HAT

cha·pel \'cha-pəl\ n [ME, fr. AF chapele, fr. ML cappella, fr. LL cappa cloak; fr. the cloak of St. Martin of Tours preserved as a sacred relic in a chapel built for that purpose] **1** : a private or subordinate place of worship **2** : an assembly at an educational institution usu. including devotional exercises **3** : a place of worship used by a Christian group other than an established church

¹**chap·er·one** or **chap·er·on** \'sha-pə-ˌrōn\ n [F chaperon, lit., hood, fr. MF,

head covering, fr. chape cape, fr. LL cappa] **1** : a person (as a matron) who accompanies young unmarried women in public for propriety **2** : an older person who accompanies young people at a social gathering to ensure proper behavior

²**chaperone** or **chaperon** vb **-oned; -oning 1** : ESCORT, GUIDE **2** : to act as a chaperone to or for ⟨~ a dance⟩ ⟨~ teenagers⟩ — **chap·er·on·age** \-ˌrō-nij\ n

chap·fall·en \'chap-ˌfȯ-lən, 'chäp-\ adj **1** : having the lower jaw hanging loosely **2** : DEJECTED, DEPRESSED

chap·lain \'cha-plən\ n **1** : a member of the clergy officially attached to a special group (as the army) **2** : a person chosen to conduct religious exercises (as for a club) — **chap·lain·cy** \-sē\ n

chap·let \'cha-plət\ n **1** : a wreath for the head **2** : a string of beads : NECKLACE

chap·man \'chap-mən\ n, Brit : an itinerant dealer : PEDDLER

chaps \'shaps, 'chaps\ n pl [MexSp chaparreras] : leather leggings resembling pants without a seat that are worn esp. by western ranch hands

chap·ter \'chap-tər\ n **1** : a main division of a book **2** : a body of canons (as of a cathedral) **3** : a local branch of a society or fraternity

¹**char** \'chär\ n, pl **char** or **chars** : any of a genus of trouts (as the common brook trout) with small scales

²**char** vb **charred; char·ring 1** : to burn or become burned to charcoal **2** : SCORCH

³**char** vb **charred; char·ring** : to work as a cleaning woman

char·ac·ter \'ker-ik-tər\ n [ME caracter, fr. L character mark, distinctive quality, fr. Gk charaktēr, fr. charassein to scratch, engrave] **1** : a graphic symbol (as a letter) used in writing or printing **2** : a symbol that represents information; also : a representation of such a character that may be accepted by a computer **3** : a distinguishing feature : ATTRIBUTE **4** : the complex of mental and ethical traits marking a person or a group **5** : a person marked by conspicuous often peculiar traits **6** : one of the persons in a novel or play **7** : REPUTATION **8** : moral excellence

¹**char·ac·ter·is·tic** \ˌker-ik-tə-'ris-tik\ n : a distinguishing trait, quality, or property

²**characteristic** adj : serving to mark individual character ♦ **Synonyms** INDIVIDUAL, PECULIAR, DISTINCTIVE — **char·ac·ter·is·ti·cal·ly** \-ti-k(ə-)lē\ adv

char·ac·ter·ize \'ker-ik-tə-ˌrīz\ vb **-ized; -iz·ing 1** : to describe the character of **2** : to be characteristic of — **char·ac·ter·i·za·tion** \ˌker-ik-tə-rə-'zā-shən\ n

cha·rades \shə-'rādz\ n sing or pl : a game in which some of the players try to guess a word or phrase from the actions of another player who may not speak

char·coal \'chär-ˌkōl\ n **1** : a porous carbon prepared from vegetable or animal substances **2** : a piece of fine charcoal used in drawing; *also* : a drawing made with charcoal

chard \'chärd\ *n* : SWISS CHARD

char·don·nay \ˌshär-d⁸n-'ā\ *n, often cap* [F] : a dry white wine made from a single variety of white grape

¹**charge** \'chärj\ *n* **1** : a quantity (as of fuel or ammunition) required to fill something to capacity **2** : a store or accumulation of force **3** : an excess or deficiency of electrons in a body **4** : THRILL, KICK **5** : a task or duty imposed **6** : CARE, RESPONSIBILITY **7** : one given into another's care **8** : instructions from a judge to a jury **9** : COST, EXPENSE, PRICE; *also* : a debit to an account **10** : ACCUSATION, INDICTMENT **11** : ATTACK, ASSAULT

²**charge** *vb* **charged; charg·ing 1** : to load or fill to capacity **2** : to give an electric charge to; *also* : to restore the activity of (a storage battery) by means of an electric current **3** : to impose a task or responsibility on **4** : COMMAND, ORDER **5** : ACCUSE **6** : to rush against : rush forward in assault **7** : to make liable for payment; *also* : to record a debt or liability against **8** : to fix as a price — **charge·able** *adj*

charge–coupled device *n* : a semiconductor device used esp. as an optical sensor

char·gé d'af·faires \shär-ˌzhä-də-'fer\ *n, pl* **char·gés d'affaires** \-ˌzhä-, -ˌzhäz-\ [F] : a diplomat who substitutes for an ambassador or minister

¹**char·ger** \'chär-jər\ *n* : a large platter

²**charg·er** *n* **1** : a device or a worker that charges something **2** : WARHORSE 1

char·i·ot \'cher-ē-ət\ *n* : a 2-wheeled horse-drawn vehicle of ancient times used esp. in war and in races — **char·i·o·teer** \ˌcher-ē-ə-'tir\ *n*

cha·ris·ma \kə-'riz-mə\ *n* : a personal quality of leadership arousing popular loyalty or enthusiasm — **char·is·mat·ic** \ˌkar-əz-'ma-tik\ *adj*

char·i·ta·ble \'cher-ə-tə-bəl\ *adj* **1** : liberal in giving to needy people **2** : merciful or lenient in judging others ♦ **Synonyms** BENEVOLENT, PHILANTHROPIC, ALTRUISTIC, HUMANITARIAN — **char·i·ta·ble·ness** *n* — **char·i·ta·bly** \-blē\ *adv*

char·i·ty \'cher-ə-tē\ *n, pl* **-ties 1** : goodwill toward or love of humanity **2** : an act or feeling of generosity **3** : the giving of aid to the poor; *also* : ALMS **4** : an institution engaged in relief of the poor **5** : leniency in judging others ♦ **Synonyms** MERCY, CLEMENCY, LENITY

char·la·tan \'shär-lə-tən\ *n* : a person making usu. showy pretenses to knowledge or ability : FRAUD, FAKER

Charles·ton \'chärl-stən\ *n* : a lively dance in which the knees are swung in and out and the heels are turned sharply outward on each step

char·ley horse \'chär-lē-ˌhors\ *n* : a muscular pain, cramping, or stiffness from a strain or bruise

¹**charm** \'chärm\ *n* [ME *charme*, fr. AF, fr. L *carmen* song, fr. *canere* to sing] **1** : a practice or expression believed to have magic power **2** : something worn about the person to ward off evil or bring good fortune : AMULET **3** : a trait that fascinates or allures **4** : physical grace or attraction **5** : a small ornament worn on a bracelet or chain **6** : a quark with a charge of +⅔ and a measured energy of approximately 1.5 billion electron volts

²**charm** *vb* **1** : to affect by or as if by a magic spell **2** : to protect by or as if by charms **3** : FASCINATE, ENCHANT ♦ **Synonyms** ALLURE, CAPTIVATE, BEWITCH, ATTRACT — **charm·er** *n*

charmed \'chärmd\ *adj* : extremely lucky or prosperous ⟨a ~ life⟩

charm·ing \'chär-min\ *adj* : PLEASING, DELIGHTFUL — **charm·ing·ly** *adv*

char·nel house \'chär-n⁸l-\ *n* : a building or chamber in which bodies or bones are deposited

¹**chart** \'chärt\ *n* **1** : MAP **2** : a sheet giving information in the form of a table, list, or diagram; *also* : GRAPH

²**chart** *vb* **1** : PLAN ⟨~ a course⟩ **2** : to make a chart of **3** : CHRONICLE ⟨~ed his adventures⟩

¹**char·ter** \'chär-tər\ *n* **1** : an official document granting rights or privileges (as to a colony, town, or college) from a sovereign or a governing body **2** : CONSTITUTION **3** : a written instrument from a society creating a branch **4** : a mercantile lease of a ship

²**charter** *vb* **1** : to grant a charter to **2** *Brit* : CERTIFY ⟨~ed engineer⟩ **3** : to hire, rent, or lease for temporary use ⟨~ a bus⟩ — **char·ter·er** *n*

charter member *n* : an original member of an organization

char·treuse \shär-'trüz, -'trüs\ *n* : a brilliant yellow green

char·wom·an \'chär-ˌwu̇-mən\ *n* : a cleaning woman esp. in large buildings

chary \'cher-ē\ *adj* **chari·er; -est** [ME, sorrowful, dear, fr. OE *cearig* sorrowful, fr. *caru* sorrow] **1** : CAUTIOUS, CIRCUMSPECT **2** : SPARING — **char·i·ly** \-ə-lē\ *adv*

¹**chase** \'chās\ *n* **1** : PURSUIT; *also* : HUNTING **2** : QUARRY **3** : a tract of unenclosed land used as a game preserve

²**chase** *vb* **chased; chas·ing 1** : to follow rapidly : PURSUE **2** : HUNT **3** : to seek out ⟨*chasing* down clues⟩ **4** : to cause to depart or flee : drive away **5** : RUSH, HASTEN

³**chase** *vb* **chased; chas·ing** : to decorate (a metal surface) by embossing or engraving

⁴**chase** *n* : FURROW, GROOVE

chas·er \'chā-sər\ *n* **1** : one that chases **2** : a mild drink (as beer) taken after hard liquor

chasm \'ka-zəm\ *n* : GORGE 2

chas·sis \'cha-sē, 'sha-sē\ *n, pl* **chas·sis** \-sēz\ : the supporting frame of a structure (as an automobile or television set)

chaste \'chāst\ *adj* **chast·er; chast·est**

1 : innocent of unlawful sexual intercourse : VIRTUOUS, PURE **2 :** CELIBATE **3 :** pure in thought : MODEST **4 :** severe or simple in design — **chaste·ly** adv — **chaste·ness** n

chas·ten \'chā-s⁸n\ vb : to correct through punishment or suffering : DISCIPLINE; also : PURIFY — **chas·ten·er** n

chas·tise \chas-'tīz\ vb **chas·tised; chas·tis·ing** [ME chastisen, alter. of chasten] **1 :** to punish esp. bodily **2 :** to censure severely : CASTIGATE — **chas·tise·ment** \-mənt, 'chas-təz-\ n

chas·ti·ty \'chas-tə-tē\ n : the quality or state of being chaste; esp : sexual purity

cha·su·ble \'cha-zə-bəl, -sə-\ n : the outer vestment of the priest at mass

chat \'chat\ n **1 :** light familiar informal talk **2 :** online discussion in a chat room — **chat** vb

châ·teau \sha-'tō\ n, pl **châ·teaus** \-'tōz\ or **châ·teaux** \-'tō, -'tōz\ [F, fr. OF chastel, fr. L castellum castle, dim. of castra camp] **1 :** a feudal castle in France **2 :** a large country house **3 :** a French vineyard estate

chat·e·laine \'shat-tə-'lān\ n **1 :** the mistress of a chateau **2 :** a clasp or hook for a watch, purse, or keys

chat room n : a real-time online interactive discussion group

chat·tel \'cha-t⁹l\ n **1 :** an item of tangible property other than real estate **2 :** SLAVE, BONDMAN

chat·ter \'cha-tər\ vb **1 :** to utter speech-like but meaningless sounds **2 :** to talk idly, incessantly, or fast **3 :** to click repeatedly or uncontrollably — **chatter** n — **chat·ter·er** n

chat·ter·box \'cha-tər-,bäks\ n : one who talks incessantly

chat·ty \'cha-tē\ adj **chat·ti·er; -est** : TALKATIVE — **chat·ti·ly** \-tə-lē\ adv — **chat·ti·ness** \-tē-nəs\ n

¹chauf·feur \'shō-fər, shō-'fər\ n [F, lit., stoker, fr. chauffer to heat] : a person employed to drive an automobile

²chauffeur vb **1 :** to do the work of a chauffeur **2 :** to transport in the manner of a chauffeur ⟨~ed the kids to school⟩

chaunt var of CHANT

chau·vin·ism \'shō-və-,ni-zəm\ n [F chauvinisme, fr. Nicolas Chauvin, fictional soldier of excessive patriotism and devotion to Napoleon] **1 :** excessive or blind patriotism **2 :** an attitude of superiority toward members of the opposite sex — **chau·vin·ist** \-nist\ n or adj — **chau·vin·is·tic** \,shō-və-'nis-tik\ adj — **chau·vin·is·ti·cal·ly** \-ti-k(ə-)lē\ adv

cheap \'chēp\ adj **1 :** INEXPENSIVE **2 :** costing little effort to obtain ⟨~ tickets⟩ **3 :** worth little : SHODDY, TAWDRY ⟨~ workmanship⟩ **4 :** worthy of scorn **5 :** STINGY — **cheap** adv — **cheap·ly** adv — **cheap·ness** n

cheap·en \'chē-pən\ vb **1 :** to make or become cheap or cheaper in price or value **2 :** to make tawdry

cheap·skate \'chēp-,skāt\ n : a miserly or stingy person; esp : one who tries to avoid paying a fair share of costs

¹cheat \'chēt\ vb **1 :** to deprive of something through fraud or deceit ⟨~ed workers of their pay⟩ **2 :** to practice fraud or trickery **3 :** to violate rules dishonestly ⟨~ at cards⟩ **4 :** to be sexually unfaithful — **cheat·er** n

²cheat n **1 :** the act of deceiving : FRAUD, DECEPTION **2 :** one that cheats : a dishonest person

¹check \'chek\ n **1 :** exposure of a chess king to an attack **2 :** a sudden stoppage of progress **3 :** a sudden pause or break **4 :** something that stops or restrains **5 :** a standard for testing or evaluation **6 :** EXAMINATION, INVESTIGATION **7 :** the act of testing or verifying **8 :** a written order to a bank to pay money **9 :** a ticket or token showing ownership or identity **10 :** a slip indicating an amount due **11 :** a pattern in squares; also : a fabric in such a pattern **12 :** a mark typically ✓ placed beside an item to show that it has been noted **13 :** CRACK, SPLIT

²check vb **1 :** to put (a chess king) in check **2 :** to slow down or stop : BRAKE **3 :** to restrain the action or force of : CURB **4 :** to compare with a source, original, or authority : VERIFY **5 :** to inspect or test for satisfactory condition **6 :** to mark with a check as examined **7 :** to consign for shipment for one holding a passenger ticket **8 :** to mark into squares **9 :** to leave or accept for safekeeping in a checkroom **10 :** to prove to be consistent or truthful **11 :** CRACK, SPLIT

check·book \'chek-,bůk\ n : a book containing blank checks

¹check·er \'che-kər\ n : a piece in the game of checkers

²checker vb **1 :** to variegate with different colors or shades **2 :** to vary with contrasting elements ⟨a ~ed career⟩ **3 :** to mark into squares

³checker n : one that checks; esp : an employee who checks out purchases in a store

check·er·ber·ry \'che-kər-,ber-ē\ n : WINTERGREEN 1; also : the spicy red fruit of this plant

check·er·board \-,bōrd\ n : a board of 64 squares of alternate colors used in various games

check·ered \'che-kərd\ adj : marked by inconsistent fortune or recurring problems ⟨his ~ past⟩

check·ers \'che-karz\ n : a checkerboard game for 2 players each with 12 pieces

check in vb : to report one's presence or arrival (as at a hotel)

check·list \'chek-,list\ n : a list of things to be checked or done; also : a comprehensive list

check·mate \'chek-,māt\ vb [ME chekmaten, fr. chekmate, interj. used to announce checkmate, fr. AF eschec mat, fr. Ar shāh māt, fr. Pers, lit., the king is left unable to escape] **1 :** to thwart completely : DEFEAT, FRUSTRATE **2 :** to attack (an opponent's king) in chess so that escape is impossible — **checkmate** n

check·off \'chek-,òf\ *n* : the deduction of union dues from a worker's paycheck by the employer

check·out \'chek-,aùt\ *n* **1** : the action or an instance of checking out **2** : a counter at which checking out is done **3** : the process of examining and testing something as to readiness for intended use

check out *vb* **1** : to settle one's account (as at a hotel) and leave **2** : to total or have totaled the cost of purchases in a store and to make or receive payment for them

check·point \'chek-,pòint\ *n* : a point at which a check is performed

check·room \-,rüm, -,rùm\ *n* : a room at which baggage, parcels, or clothing is left for safekeeping

checks and balances *n pl* : a system allowing each branch of a government to restrict the actions of another branch (as by a veto)

check·up \'chek-,əp\ *n* : EXAMINATION; *esp* : a general physical examination

ched·dar \'che-dər\ *n, often cap* : a hard mild to sharp white or yellow cheese of smooth texture

cheek \'chēk\ *n* **1** : the fleshy side part of the face **2** : IMPUDENCE, BOLDNESS, AUDACITY **3** : BUTTOCK 1 — **cheeked** \'chēkt\ *adj*

cheek·bone \'chēk-,bōn\ *n* : the bone or bony ridge below the eye

cheeky \'chē-kē\ *adj* **cheek·i·er; -est** : IMPUDENT, SAUCY — **cheek·i·ly** \-kə-lē\ *adv* — **cheek·i·ness** \-kē-nəs\ *n*

cheep \'chēp\ *vb* : to utter faint shrill sounds : PEEP — **cheep** *n*

¹**cheer** \'chir\ *n* [ME *chere* face, cheer, fr. AF, face, fr. ML *cara*, prob. fr. Gk *kara* head, face] **1** : state of mind or heart : SPIRIT **2** : ANIMATION, GAIETY **3** : hospitable entertainment : WELCOME **4** : food and drink for a feast **5** : something that gladdens **6** : a shout of applause or encouragement

²**cheer** *vb* **1** : to give hope or courage to : COMFORT **2** : to make glad **3** : to urge on esp. by shouts **4** : to applaud with shouts **5** : to grow or be cheerful — usu. used with *up* — **cheer·er** *n*

cheer·ful \'chir-fəl\ *adj* **1** : having or showing good spirits **2** : conducive to good spirits : pleasant and bright — **cheer·ful·ly** *adv* — **cheer·ful·ness** *n*

cheer·lead·er \'chir-,lē-dər\ *n* : a person who directs organized cheering esp. at a sports event — **cheer·lead·ing** *n*

cheer·less \'chir-ləs\ *adj* : BLEAK, DISPIRITING ⟨a ~ office⟩ — **cheer·less·ly** *adv* — **cheer·less·ness** *n*

cheery \'chir-ē\ *adj* **cheer·i·er; -est** : CHEERFUL ⟨~ music⟩ — **cheer·i·ly** \-ə-lē\ *adv* — **cheer·i·ness** \-ē-nəs\ *n*

cheese \'chēz\ *n* : the curd of milk usu. pressed into cakes and cured for use as food

cheese·burg·er \-,bər-gər\ *n* : a hamburger topped with cheese

cheese·cake \-,kāk\ *n* **1** : a dessert consisting of a creamy filling usu. containing

cheese baked in a shell **2** : photographs of shapely scantily clad women

cheese·cloth \-,klòth\ *n* : a lightweight coarse cotton gauze

cheese·par·ing \-,per-iŋ\ *n* : miserly economizing — **cheeseparing** *adj*

cheese·steak \-,stāk\ *n* : a sandwich of thinly sliced beef topped with melted cheese

cheesy \'chē-zē\ *adj* **chees·i·er; -est** **1** : resembling, suggesting, or containing cheese **2** : CHEAP **3** ⟨~ motels⟩

chee·tah \'chē-tə\ *n* [Hindi *cītā* leopard, fr. Skt *citraka*, fr. *citra* bright, variegated] : a large long-legged swift-moving spotted cat of Africa and southwestern Asia

chef \'shef\ *n* : COOK; *esp* : one who manages a kitchen (as of a restaurant)

chef d'oeu·vre \shā-'dœvr°\ *n, pl* **chefs d'oeuvre** *same*\ : MASTERPIECE

chem *abbr* chemical; chemist; chemistry

¹**chem·i·cal** \'ke-mi-kəl\ *adj* **1** : of, relating to, used in, or produced by chemistry ⟨~ reactions⟩ **2** : acting or operated or produced by chemicals — **chem·i·cal·ly** \-k(ə-)lē\ *adv*

²**chemical** *n* **1** : a substance obtained by a chemical process or producing a chemical effect **2** : DRUG

chemical engineering *n* : engineering dealing with the industrial application of chemistry — **chemical engineer** *n*

chemical warfare *n* : warfare using incendiary mixtures, smokes, or irritant, burning, or asphyxiating gases

chemical weapon *n* : a weapon used in chemical warfare

che·mise \shə-'mēz\ *n* **1** : a woman's one-piece undergarment **2** : a loose straight-hanging dress

chem·ist \'ke-mist\ *n,* **1** : one trained in chemistry **2** *Brit* : PHARMACIST

chem·is·try \'ke-mə-strē\ *n, pl* **-tries 1** : the science that deals with the composition, structure, and properties of substances and of the changes they undergo **2** : chemical composition or properties ⟨the ~ of gasoline⟩ **3** : a strong mutual attraction; *also* : harmonious interaction among people (as on a team)

che·mo \'kē-mō\ *n* : CHEMOTHERAPY

che·mo·ther·a·py \,kē-mō-'ther-ə-pē\ *n* : the use of chemicals in the treatment or control of disease — **che·mo·ther·a·peu·tic** \-,ther-ə-'pyü-tik\ *adj*

che·nille \shə-'nēl\ *n* [F, lit., caterpillar, fr. OF, fr. L *canicula*, dim. of *canis* dog] : a fabric with a deep fuzzy pile often used for bedspreads and rugs

cheque *chiefly Brit var of* ¹CHECK 7

che·quer *chiefly Brit var of* CHECKER

cher·ish \'cher-ish\ *vb* **1** : to hold dear : treat with care and affection **2** : to keep deeply in mind ⟨~ a memory⟩ — **cher·ish·able** *adj* — **cher·ish·er** *n*

Cher·o·kee \'cher-ə-(,)kē\ *n, pl* **Cherokee** *or* **Cherokees** : a member of an American Indian people orig. of Tennessee and No. Carolina; *also* : their language

che·root \shə-'rüt\ *n* : a cigar cut square at both ends

cher·ry \'cher-ē\ *n, pl* **cherries** [ME *chery*, fr. AF *cherise, cirice* (taken as a plural), fr. LL *ceresia*, fr. L *cerasus* cherry tree, fr. Gk *kerasos*] **1** : the small fleshy pale yellow to deep blackish red fruit of a tree related to the roses; *also* : the tree or its wood **2** : a moderate red

chert \'chərt, 'chat\ *n* : a rock resembling flint and consisting essentially of fine crystalline quartz and fibrous chalcedony — **cherty** *adj*

cher·ub \'cher-əb\ *n* **1** *pl* **cher·u·bim** \'cher-ə-,bim\ : an angel of the 2d highest rank **2** *pl* **cherubs** : a chubby rosy person — **che·ru·bic** \chə-'rü-bik\ *adj*

chess \'ches\ *n* : a game for 2 played on a chessboard with each player having 16 pieces — **chess·man** \-,man, -mən\ *n*

chess·board \'ches-,bórd\ *n* : a checkerboard used in the game of chess

chest \'chest\ *n* **1** : a box, case, or boxlike receptacle for storage or shipping **2** : the part of the body enclosed by the ribs and sternum — **chest·ed** \'ches-təd\ *adj* — **chest·ful** \'ches-,fül\ *n*

ches·ter·field \'ches-tər-,fēld\ *n* : an overcoat with a velvet collar

chest·nut \'ches-(,)nət\ *n* **1** : the edible nut of any of a genus of trees related to the beeches and oaks; *also* : this tree or its wood **2** : a grayish to reddish brown **3** : an old joke or story

chet·rum \'che-trəm\ *n, pl* **chetrums** *or* **chetrum** — see *ngultrum* at MONEY table

che·val glass \shə-'val-\ *n* : a full-length mirror that may be tilted in a frame

che·va·lier \,she-və-'lir, shə-'val-,yā\ *n* : a member of one of various orders of knighthood or of merit

chev·i·ot \'she-vē-ət\ *n, often cap* **1** : a twilled fabric with a rough nap **2** : a sturdy soft-finished cotton fabric

chev·ron \'she-vrən\ *n* : a sleeve badge of one or more V-shaped or inverted V-shaped stripes worn to indicate rank or service (as in the armed forces)

¹chew \'chü\ *vb* : to crush or grind with the teeth — **chew·able** *adj* — **chew·er** *n* — **chewy** \'chü-ē\ *adj* — **chew on** : to think about : PONDER ⟨*chew on* the proposals⟩ — **chew the fat** : to make conversation : CHAT

²chew *n* **1** : an act of chewing **2** : something for chewing

Chey·enne \shī-'an, -'en\ *n, pl* **Cheyenne** *or* **Cheyennes** [AmerF, fr. Dakota *šahíyena*] : a member of an American Indian people of the western plains of the U.S.; *also* : their language

chg *abbr* **1** change **2** charge

chi \'kī\ *n* : the 22d letter of the Greek alphabet — X or χ

Chi·an·ti \kē-'än-tē, -'an-\ *n* : a dry usu. red wine

chiar·oscu·ro \kē-,är-ə-'skūr-ō, -,skyūr-\ *n, pl* **-ros** [It, fr. *chiaro* clear, light + *oscuro* obscure, dark] **1** : pictorial representation in terms of light and shade without regard to color **2** : the arrangement or treatment of light and dark parts in a pictorial work of art

¹chic \'shēk\ *n* : STYLISHNESS

²chic *adj* : cleverly stylish : SMART; *also* : currently fashionable

Chi·ca·na \chi-'kä-nə *also* shi-\ *n* : an American woman or girl of Mexican descent — **Chicana** *adj*

chi·cane \shi-'kān\ *n* : CHICANERY

chi·ca·nery \-'kā-nə-rē\ *n, pl* **-ner·ies** : TRICKERY, DECEPTION

Chi·ca·no \chi-'kä-nō\ *n, pl* **-nos** : a usu. male American of Mexican descent — **Chicano** *adj*

chi·chi \'shē-(,)shē, 'chē-(,)chē\ *adj* [F] **1** : SHOWY, FRILLY **2** : ARTY, PRECIOUS **3** : CHIC — **chichi** *n*

chick \'chik\ *n* **1** : a young chicken; *also* : a young bird **2** *slang* : GIRL, WOMAN

chick·a·dee \'chi-kə-(,)dē\ *n* : any of several small grayish American birds with black or brown caps

Chick·a·saw \'chi-kə-,só\ *n, pl* **Chickasaw** *or* **Chickasaws** : a member of an American Indian people of Mississippi and Alabama

¹chick·en \'chi-kən\ *n* **1** : a common domestic fowl esp. when young; *also* : its flesh used as food **2** : COWARD

²chicken *adj* **1** : COWARDLY **2** *slang* : insistent on petty esp. military discipline

chicken feed *n, slang* : an insignificant sum of money

chick·en-heart·ed \,chi-kən-'här-təd\ *adj* : TIMID, COWARDLY

chicken out *vb* : to lose one's courage

chicken pox *n* : an acute contagious viral disease esp. of children characterized by a low fever and blisters

chicken wire *n* : a light wire netting of hexagonal mesh

chick·pea \'chik-,pē\ *n* : an Asian herb of the legume family cultivated for its short pods with one or two edible seeds; *also* : its seed

chick·weed \'chik-,wēd\ *n* : any of several low-growing small-leaved weeds related to the pinks

chi·cle \'chi-kəl\ *n* : a gum from the latex of a tropical tree used as the chief ingredient of chewing gum

chic·o·ry \'chi-kə-rē\ *n, pl* **-ries** : a usu. blue-flowered herb related to the daisies and grown for its root and for use in salads; *also* : its dried ground root used to flavor or adulterate coffee

chide \'chīd\ *vb* **chid** \'chid\ *or* **chid·ed** \'chī-dəd\; **chid** *or* **chid·den** \'chid-³n\ *or* **chided**; **chid·ing** : to speak disapprovingly to ♦ *Synonyms* REPROACH, REPROVE, REPRIMAND, ADMONISH, SCOLD, REBUKE

¹chief \'chēf\ *adj* **1** : highest in rank **2** : most important ♦ *Synonyms* PRINCIPAL, MAIN, LEADING, MAJOR — **chief·ly** *adv*

²chief *n* **1** : the leader of a body or organization : HEAD **2** : the principal or most valuable part — **chief·dom** *n*

chief master sergeant *n* : a noncommissioned officer of the highest rank in the air force

chief of staff 1 : the ranking officer of a

staff in the armed forces **2** : the ranking office of the army or air force

chief of state : the formal head of a national state as distinguished from the head of the government

chief petty officer *n* : an enlisted man in the navy ranking next below a senior chief petty officer

chief·tain \'chēf-tən\ *n* : a chief esp. of a band, tribe, or clan — **chief·tain·cy** \-sē\ *n* — **chief·tain·ship** *n*

chief warrant officer *n* : a warrant officer of senior rank

chif·fon \shi-'fän, 'shi-,\ *n* [F, lit., rag, fr. *chiffe* old rag] : a sheer fabric esp. of silk

chif·fo·nier \,shi-fə-'nir\ *n* : a high narrow chest of drawers

chig·ger \'chi-gər\ *n* : a bloodsucking larval mite that causes intense itching

chi·gnon \'shēn-,yän\ *n* [F, fr. MF *chaignon* chain, collar, nape] : a knot of hair worn at the back of the head

Chi·hua·hua \chə-'wä-,wä\ *n* : any of a breed of very small large-eared dogs that originated in Mexico

chil·blain \'chil-,blān\ *n* : a sore or inflamed swelling (as on the feet or hands) caused by exposure to cold

child \'chī(-ə)ld\ *n, pl* **chil·dren** \'chil-drən\ **1** : an unborn or recently born person **2** : a young person between the periods of infancy and youth **3** : a male or female offspring : SON, DAUGHTER **4** : one strongly influenced by another or by a place or state of affairs — **child·ish** *adj* — **child·ish·ly** *adv* — **child·ish·ness** *n* — **child·less** *adj* — **child·less·ness** *n* — **child·like** *adj*

child·bear·ing \'chīld-,ber-iŋ\ *n* : CHILDBIRTH — **childbearing** *adj*

child·birth \-,bərth\ *n* : the act or process of giving birth to offspring

child·hood \-,hüd\ *n* : the state or time of being a child

¹child·proof \-,prüf\ *adj* **1** : made to prevent opening or use by children ⟨~ lighters⟩ **2** : made safe for children

²childproof *vb* : to make childproof ⟨~ a house⟩

child's play *n* : a simple task or act

chili *also* **chile** *or* **chil·li** \'chi-lē\ *n, pl* **chil·ies** *also* **chil·es** *or* **chilis** *or* **chil·lies** **1** : any of various pungent peppers related to the tomato **2** : a thick sauce of meat and chilies **3** : CHILI CON CARNE

chili con car·ne \chə-lē-kän-'kär-nē\ *n* [AmerSp *chile con carne* chili with meat] : a spiced stew of ground beef and chilies or chili powder usu. with beans

chili powder *n* : a seasoning made of ground chilies and other spices

chili sauce *n* : a spiced tomato sauce usu. made with red and green peppers

¹chill \'chil\ *n* **1** : a feeling of coldness accompanied by shivering **2** : moderate coldness **3** : a check to enthusiasm or warmth of feeling

²chill *adj* **1** : moderately cold **2** : COLD, RAW **3** : DISTANT, FORMAL ⟨a ~ reception⟩ **4** : DEPRESSING, DISPIRITING

³chill *vb* **1** : to make or become cold or

chilly **2** : to make cool esp. without freezing **3** : RELAX — **chill·er** *n*

chill·ing \'chi-liŋ\ *adj* : gravely disturbing or frightening ⟨a ~ scene⟩

chilly \'chi-lē\ *adj* **chill·i·er; -est** **1** : noticeably cold **2** : unpleasantly affected by cold **3** : lacking warmth of feeling ⟨a ~ reception⟩ — **chill·i·ness** *n*

chimaera *chiefly Brit var of* CHIMERA

¹chime \'chīm\ *n* **1** : a set of bells musically tuned **2** : the sound of a set of bells — usu. used in pl. **3** : a musical sound suggesting bells

²chime *vb* **chimed; chim·ing** **1** : to make bell-like sounds **2** : to indicate (as the time of day) by chiming **3** : to be or act in accord : be in harmony

chime in *vb* : to break into or join in a conversation

chi·me·ra \kī-'mir-ə, kə-\ *n* [L *chimaera*, fr. Gk *chimaira* she-goat, chimera] **1** : an imaginary monster made up of incongruous parts **2** : an illusion or fabrication of the mind; *esp* : an impossible dream

chi·me·ri·cal \kī-'mer-i-kəl\ *also* **chi·me·ric** \-ik\ *adj* **1** : FANTASTIC, IMAGINARY **2** : inclined to fantastic schemes

chim·ney \'chim-nē\ *n, pl* **chimneys** **1** : a vertical structure extending above the roof of a building for carrying off smoke **2** : a glass tube around a lamp flame

chimp \'chimp\ *n* : CHIMPANZEE

chim·pan·zee \,chim-,pan-'zē, chim-'pan-zē\ *n* : an African ape related to the much larger gorilla

¹chin \'chin\ *n* : the part of the face below the lower lip including the prominence of the lower jaw — **chin·less** *adj*

²chin *vb* **chinned; chin·ning** : to raise (oneself) while hanging by the hands until the chin is level with the support

chi·na \'chī-nə\ *n* : porcelain ware; *also* : domestic pottery in general

Chi·na·town \'chī-nə-,taún\ *n* : the Chinese quarter of a city

chinch bug \'chinch-\ *n* : a small black and white bug destructive to cereal grasses

chin·chil·la \chin-'chi-lə\ *n* **1** : either of two small So. American rodents with soft pearl-gray fur; *also* : this fur **2** : a heavy long-napped woolen cloth

chine \'chīn\ *n* : BACKBONE, SPINE; *also* : a cut of meat including all or part of the backbone

Chi·nese \chī-'nēz, -'nēs\ *n, pl* **Chinese** **1** : a native or inhabitant of China **2** : any of a group of related languages of China — **Chinese** *adj*

Chinese cabbage *n* **1** : BOK CHOY **2** : an Asian garden plant related to the cabbage and widely grown in the U.S. for its tight elongate cylindrical heads of pale green to cream-colored leaves

Chinese checkers *n* : a game in which each player in turn transfers a set of marbles from a home point to the opposite point of a pitted 6-pointed star

Chinese gooseberry *n* : a subtropical vine that bears kiwifruit; *also* : KIWIFRUIT

Chinese lantern *n* : a collapsible translucent cover for a light

¹chink \'chiŋk\ *n* : a small crack or fissure

²chink *vb* : to fill the chinks of : stop up

³chink *n* : a slight sharp metallic sound

⁴chink *vb* : to make a slight sharp metallic sound

chi·no \'chē-nō\ *n, pl* **chinos 1** : a usu. khaki cotton twill **2** *pl* : an article of clothing made of chino

Chi·nook \sha-'nùk, cha-, -'nùk\ *n, pl* **Chinook** *or* **Chinooks** : a member of an American Indian people of Oregon

chintz \'chints\ *n* : a usu. glazed printed cotton cloth

chintzy \'chint-sē\ *adj* **chintz·i·er; -est 1** : decorated with or as if with chintz **2** : GAUDY, CHEAP **3** : STINGY — **chintz·i·ness** *n*

chin–up \'chin-,əp\ *n* : the act of chinning oneself

¹chip \'chip\ *n,* **1** : a small usu. thin and flat piece (as of wood) cut or broken off **2** : a thin crisp morsel of food **3** : a counter used in games (as poker) **4** *pl, slang* : MONEY **5** : a flaw left after a chip is broken off **6** : INTEGRATED CIRCUIT **7** : a very small slice of silicon containing electronic circuits — **chip off the old block** : a child that resembles his or her parent

²chip *vb* **chipped; chip·ping 1** : to cut or break chips from **2** : to break off in small pieces at the edges **3** : to play a chip shot

chip in *vb* : CONTRIBUTE

chip·munk \'chip-,məŋk\ *n* [earlier *chitmunk,* prob. fr. Ojibwa *ačitamo·n?* red squirrel] : any of a genus of small striped No. American and Asian rodents closely related to the squirrels and marmots

chi·pot·le \chə-'pōt-lā\ *n* : a smoked and usu. dried jalapeño pepper

chipped beef \'chipt-\ *n* : smoked dried beef sliced thin

¹chip·per \'chi-pər\ *n* : one that chips

²chipper *adj* : LIVELY, CHEERFUL

Chip·pe·wa \'chi-pə-,wȯ, -,wä, -,wä, -wə\ *n, pl* **Chippewa** *or* **Chippewas** : OJIBWA

chip shot *n* : a short usu. low shot to the green in golf

chi·rog·ra·phy \kī-'rä-grə-fē\ *n* : HANDWRITING, PENMANSHIP — **chi·ro·graph·ic** \,kī-rə-'gra-fik\ *adj*

chi·rop·o·dy \kə-'rä-pə-dē, shə-\ *n* : PODIATRY — **chi·rop·o·dist** \-dist\ *n*

chi·ro·prac·tic \'kī-rə-,prak-tik\ *n* : a system of therapy based esp. on manipulation of body structures — **chi·ro·prac·tor** \-tər\ *n*

chirp \'chərp\ *n* : a short sharp sound characteristic of a small bird or cricket — **chirp** *vb* — **chirpy** \'chər-pē\ *adj*

¹chis·el \'chi-zəl\ *n* : a metal tool with a sharpened edge at one end used to chip, carve, or cut into a solid material (as wood or stone)

²chisel *vb* **-eled** *or* **-elled; -el·ing** *or* **-el·ling 1** : to work with or as if with a chisel **2** : to obtain by shrewd often unfair methods; *also* : CHEAT — **chis·el·er** *n*

¹chit \'chit\ *n* [ME *chitte* kitten, cub] **1** : CHILD **2** : a pert young woman

²chit *n* [Hindi *ciṭṭhī* letter, note] : a signed voucher for a small debt

chit·chat \'chit-,chat\ *n* : casual or trifling conversation — **chitchat** *vb*

chi·tin \'kī-t²n\ *n* : a sugar polymer that forms part of the hard outer integument esp. of insects — **chi·tin·ous** *adj*

chit·ter·lings *or* **chit·lins** \'chit-lənz\ *n pl* : the intestines of hogs esp. when prepared as food

chi·val·ric \shə-'val-rik\ *adj* : relating to chivalry : CHIVALROUS

chiv·al·rous \'shi-vəl-rəs\ *adj* **1** : of or relating to chivalry **2** : marked by honor, courtesy, and generosity **3** : marked by especial courtesy to women — **chiv·al·rous·ly** *adv* — **chiv·al·rous·ness** *n*

chiv·al·ry \'shi-vəl-rē\ *n, pl* **-ries 1** : mounted men-at-arms **2** : the system or practices of knighthood **3** : the spirit or character of the ideal knight

chive \'chīv\ *n* : an herb related to the onion that has slender leaves used for flavoring; *also* : its leaves

chla·myd·ia \klə-'mi-dē-ə\ *n, pl* **-i·ae** \-dē-,ē\ **1** : any of a genus of bacteria that cause various diseases of the eye and urogenital tract **2** : a disease or infection caused by chlamydiae

chlo·ral hydrate \'klȯr-əl-\ *n* : a white crystalline compound used as a hypnotic and sedative

chlor·dane \'klȯr-,dān\ *n* : a highly chlorinated persistent insecticide

chlo·ride \'klȯr-,īd\ *n* : a compound of chlorine with another element or group

chlo·ri·nate \'klȯr-ə-,nāt\ *vb* **-nat·ed; -nat·ing** : to treat or combine with chlorine or a chlorine compound — **chlo·ri·na·tion** \,klȯr-ə-'nā-shən\ *n* — **chlo·ri·na·tor** \'klȯr-ə-,nā-tər\ *n*

chlo·rine \'klȯr-,ēn\ *n* : a nonmetallic chemical element that is found alone as a strong-smelling greenish-yellow irritating gas and is used as a bleach, oxidizing agent, and disinfectant

chlorine monoxide \-\ *n* : a reactive radical that plays a major role in stratospheric ozone depletion

chlo·rite \'klȯr-,īt\ *n* : a usu. green mineral found with and resembling mica

chlo·ro·flu·o·ro·car·bon \,klȯr-ə-'flȯr-ə-,kär-bən, -'flȯr-\ *n* : any of several gaseous compounds that contain carbon, chlorine, fluorine, and sometimes hydrogen and are used esp. as solvents, refrigerants, and aerosol propellants

¹chlo·ro·form \'klȯr-ə-,fȯrm\ *n* : a colorless heavy fluid with etherlike odor used as a solvent

²chloroform *vb* : to treat with chloroform to produce anesthesia or death

chlo·ro·phyll \-,fil\ *n* : the green coloring matter of plants that functions in photosynthesis

chlo·ro·plast \'klȯr-ə-,plast\ *n* : a cytoplasmic organelle that contains chlorophyll and is the site of photosynthesis

chm *abbr* chairman

chock \'chäk\ *n* : a wedge for steadying something or for blocking the movement of a wheel — **chock** *vb*

chock-a-block \'chäk-ə-ˌbläk\ *adj* : very full : CROWDED

chock–full \'chɔk-'fúl, 'chäk-\ *adj* : full to the limit : CRAMMED

choc·o·late \'chä-k(ə-)lət, 'chô-\ *n* [Sp, fr. Nahuatl *chocōlātl*] **1** : a food prepared from ground roasted cacao beans; *also* : a drink prepared from this **2** : a candy made of or with a coating of chocolate **3** : a dark brown color — **choc·o·laty** or **choc·o·lat·ey** \-k(ə-)lə-tē\ *adj*

Choc·taw \'chäk-ˌtó\ *n, pl* **Choctaw** or **Choctaws** : a member of an American Indian people of Mississippi, Alabama, and Louisiana; *also* : their language

¹choice \'chòis\ *n* **1** : the act of choosing : SELECTION **2** : the power or opportunity of choosing : OPTION **3** : the best part **4** : a person or thing selected **5** : a variety offered for selection

²choice *adj* **choic·er; choic·est 1** : worthy of being chosen **2** : selected with care **3** : of high quality

choir \'kwī(-ə)r\ *n* **1** : an organized company of singers (as in a church service) **2** : the part of a church occupied by the singers or by the clergy

choir·boy \'kwī-(-ə)r-ˌbòi\ *n* : a boy member of a choir

choir·mas·ter \-ˌmas-tər\ *n* : the director of a choir (as in a church)

¹choke \'chōk\ *vb* **choked; chok·ing 1** : to hinder breathing (as by obstructing the trachea) : STRANGLE **2** : to check the growth or action of **3** : CLOG, OBSTRUCT **4** : to enrich the fuel mixture of (a motor) by restricting the carburetor air intake **5** : to perform badly in a critical situation

²choke *n* **1** : the act of choking **2** : a narrowing in size toward the muzzle in the bore of a gun **3** : a valve for choking a gasoline engine

choke hold *n* **1** : a hold that involves strong choking pressure **2** : absolute control

chok·er \'chō-kər\ *n* : something (as a necklace) worn tightly around the neck

cho·ler \'kä-lər, 'kō-\ *n* : a tendency toward anger : IRASCIBILITY

chol·era \'kä-lə-rə\ *n* : any of several bacterial diseases usu. marked by severe vomiting and dysentery

cho·ler·ic \'kä-lə-rik, kə-'ler-ik\ *adj* **1** : IRASCIBLE **2** : ANGRY, IRATE

cho·les·ter·ol \kə-'les-tə-ˌról\ *n* : a physiologically important waxy steroid alcohol found in animal tissues and in high concentrations implicated as a cause of arteriosclerosis

chomp \'chämp, 'chómp\ *vb* : to chew or bite on something heavily

chon \'chän\ *n, pl* **chon** — see *won* at MONEY table

choose \'chüz\ *vb* **chose** \'chōz\; **chosen** \'chō-z³n\; **choos·ing** \'chü-ziŋ\ **1** : to select esp. after consideration **2**

: DECIDE **3** : to have a preference for — **choos·er** *n*

choosy or **choos·ey** \'chü-zē\ *adj* **choos·i·er; -est** : very particular in making choices

¹chop \'chäp\ *vb* **chopped; chop·ping 1** : to cut by repeated blows **2** : to cut into small pieces : MINCE **3** : to strike (a ball) with a short quick downward stroke

²chop *n* **1** : a sharp downward blow or stroke **2** : a small cut of meat often including part of a rib **3** : a short abrupt motion (as of a wave)

³chop *n* **1** : an official seal or stamp **2** : a mark on goods to indicate quality or kind; *also* : QUALITY, GRADE

chop·house \'chäp-ˌhaús\ *n* : RESTAURANT

chop·per \'chä-pər\ *n,* **1** : one that chops **2** *pl, slang* : TEETH **3** : HELICOPTER

chop·pi·ness \'chä-pē-nəs\ *n* : the quality or state of being choppy

¹chop·py \'chä-pē\ *adj* **chop·pi·er; -est 1** : rough with small waves **2** : JERKY, DISCONNECTED — **chop·pi·ly** \-pə-lē\ *adv*

²choppy *adj* **chop·pi·er; -est** : CHANGEABLE, VARIABLE ⟨a ~ wind⟩

chops \'chäps\ *n pl* **1** : the fleshy covering of the jaws **2** : expertise in a particular field or activity ⟨acting ~⟩

chop·stick \'chäp-ˌstik\ *n* : one of a pair of sticks used chiefly in Asian countries for lifting food to the mouth

chop su·ey \chäp-'sü-ē\ *n, pl* **chop sueys** : a dish made of vegetables (as bean sprouts, bamboo shoots, water chestnuts, onions, mushrooms) and meat or fish and served with rice

cho·ral \'kòr-əl\ *adj* : of, relating to, or sung by a choir or chorus or in chorus — **cho·ral·ly** *adv*

cho·rale \kə-'ral, -'räl\ *n* **1** : a hymn or psalm sung in church; *also* : a harmonization of a traditional melody **2** : CHORUS, CHOIR

¹chord \'kòrd\ *n* [alter. of ME *cord,* short for *accord*] : three or more musical tones sounded simultaneously

²chord *n* **1** : CORD 2 **2** : a straight line joining two points on a curve

chore \'chòr\ *n* [ME *char* turn, piece of work, fr. OE *chierr*] **1** *pl* : the daily light work of a household or farm **2** : a routine task or job **3** : a difficult or disagreeable task

cho·rea \kə-'rē-ə\ *n* : any of various nervous disorders marked by spasmodic uncontrolled movements

cho·re·og·ra·phy \ˌkòr-ē-'ä-grə-fē\ *n, pl* **-phies** : the art of composing and arranging dances and esp. ballets — **cho·reo·graph** \'kòr-ē-ə-ˌgraf\ *vb* — **cho·re·og·ra·pher** \ˌkór-ē-'ä-grə-fər\ *n* — **cho·reo·graph·ic** \ˌkòr-ē-ə-'gra-fik\ *adj* — **cho·reo·graph·i·cal·ly** \-fi-k(ə-)lē\ *adv*

cho·ris·ter \'kòr-ə-stər\ *n* : a singer in a choir

chor·tle \'chòr-t³l\ *vb* **chor·tled; chor-**

tling : to laugh or chuckle esp. in satisfaction or exultation — **chortle** n

¹**chorus** \'kór-əs\ n 1 : an organized company of singers : CHOIR 2 : a group of dancers and singers (as in a musical comedy) 3 : a part of a song repeated at intervals 4 : a composition to be sung by a chorus; also : group singing 5 : sounds uttered by a number of persons or animals together ⟨a ∼ of boos⟩

²**chorus** vb : to sing or utter in chorus

chose past of CHOOSE

cho·sen \'chō-z²n\ adj : selected or marked for special favor or privilege

chou·croute \shü-'krüt\ n 1 : SAUERKRAUT 2 or **choucroute gar·nie** \-gär-'nē\ : sauerkraut cooked and served with meat

¹**chow** \'chaù\ n : FOOD

²**chow** vb : EAT — often used with down

³**chow** n : CHOW CHOW

chow–chow \'chaù-,chaù\ n : chopped mixed pickles in mustard sauce

chow chow \'chaù-,chaù\ n : any of a breed of thick-coated muscular dogs of Chinese origin with a blue-black tongue and a short tail curled close to the back

chow·der \'chaù-dər\ n : a soup or stew made from seafood or vegetables and containing milk or tomatoes

chow mein \'chaù-'mān\ n : a seasoned stew of shredded or diced meat, mushrooms, and vegetables that is usu. served with fried noodles

chrism \'kri-zəm\ n : consecrated oil used esp. in baptism, confirmation, and ordination

Christ \'krīst\ n [ME Crist, fr. OE, fr. L Christus, fr. Gk Christos, lit., anointed] : Jesus esp. as the Messiah — **Christ·like** adj — **Christ·ly** adj

chris·ten \'kri-s²n\ vb 1 : BAPTIZE 2 : to name at baptism 3 : to name or dedicate (as a ship) by a ceremony suggestive of baptism — **chris·ten·ing** n

Chris·ten·dom \'kri-s²n-dəm\ n 1 : CHRISTIANITY 2 : the part of the world in which Christianity prevails

¹**Chris·tian** \'kris-chən\ n : an adherent of Christianity

²**Christian** adj 1 : of or relating to Christianity 2 : based on or conforming with Christianity 3 : of or relating to a Christian 4 : professing Christianity

Chris·ti·an·i·ty \,kris-chē-'a-nə-tē\ n : the religion derived from Jesus Christ, based on the Bible as sacred scripture, and professed by Christians

Chris·tian·ize \'kris-chə-,nīz\ vb -ized; -iz·ing : to make Christian

Christian name n : GIVEN NAME

Christian Science n : a religion and system of healing founded by Mary Baker Eddy and taught by the Church of Christ, Scientist — **Christian Scientist** n

chris·tie or **chris·ty** \'kris-tē\ n, pl **chris·ties** : a skiing turn made by shifting body weight forward and skidding into a turn with parallel skis

Christ·mas \'kris-məs\ n : December 25 celebrated as a church festival in commemoration of the birth of Christ and observed as a legal holiday

Christmas club n : a savings account in which regular deposits are made to provide money for Christmas shopping

Christ·mas·tide \'kris-məs-,tīd\ n : the season of Christmas

chro·mat·ic \krō-'ma-tik\ adj 1 : of or relating to color 2 : proceeding by half steps of the musical scale — **chro·mat·i·cism** \-tə-,si-zəm\ n

chro·mato·graph \krō-'ma-tə-,graf\ n : an instrument used in chromatography

chro·ma·tog·ra·phy \,krō-mə-'tä-grə-fē\ n : the separation of a complex mixture into its component compounds as a result of the different rates at which the compounds travel through or over a stationary substance due to differing affinities for the substance — **chro·mato·graph·ic** \krō-,ma-tə-'gra-fik\ adj — **chro·mato·graph·i·cal·ly** \-fi-k(ə-)lē\ adv

chrome \'krōm\ n 1 : CHROMIUM 2 : a chromium pigment 3 : something plated with an alloy of chromium

chro·mi·um \'krō-mē-əm\ n : a bluish white metallic element used esp. in alloys and chrome plating

chro·mo·some \'krō-mə-,sōm, -,zōm\ n [G Chromosom, fr. Gk chrōma color, pigment + sōma body] : any of the rod-shaped or threadlike DNA-containing structures of cellular organisms that contain most or all of the genes of the organism — **chro·mo·som·al** \,krō-mə-'sō-məl, -'zō-\ adj

chro·mo·sphere \'krō-mə-,sfir\ n : the lower part of a star's atmosphere

chron abbr 1 chronicle 2 chronological; chronology

Chron abbr Chronicles

chron·ic \'krä-nik\ adj : marked by long duration or frequent recurrence ⟨a ∼ disease⟩; also : HABITUAL ⟨a ∼ grumbler⟩ — **chron·i·cal·ly** \-ni-k(ə-)lē\ adv

chronic fatigue syndrome n : a disorder of unknown cause that is characterized by persistent profound fatigue

¹**chron·i·cle** \'krä-ni-kəl\ n : HISTORY, NARRATIVE

²**chronicle** vb -cled; -cling : to record in or as if in a chronicle — **chron·i·cler** n

Chronicles n — see BIBLE table

chro·no·graph \'krä-nə-,graf\ n : an instrument for measuring and recording time intervals with accuracy — **chro·no·graph·ic** \,krä-nə-'gra-fik\ adj — **chro·nog·ra·phy** \krə-'nä-grə-fē\ n

chro·nol·o·gy \krə-'nä-lə-jē\ n, pl -gies 1 : the science that deals with measuring time and dating events 2 : a chronological list or table 3 : arrangement of events in the order of their occurrence — **chron·o·log·i·cal** \,krän-ºl-'ä-ji-kəl\ adj — **chron·o·log·i·cal·ly** \-k(ə-)lē\ adv — **chro·nol·o·gist** \krə-'nä-lə-jist\ n

chro·nom·e·ter \krə-'nä-mə-tər\ n : a very accurate timepiece

chrys·a·lid \'kri-sə-ləd\ n : CHRYSALIS

chrys·a·lis \'kri-sə-ləs\ n, pl **chry·sal·i·des** \kri-'sa-lə-,dēz\ or **chrys·a·lis·es**

: an insect pupa in a firm case without a cocoon

chry·san·the·mum \kri-'san-thə-məm\ *n* [L, fr. Gk *chrysanthemon*, fr. *chrysos* gold + *anthemon* flower] : any of various plants related to the daisies including some grown for their showy brightly colored flowers or for medicinal products or insecticides; *also* : a flower of a chrysanthemum

chub \'chəb\ *n*, *pl* chub *or* chubs : any of various small freshwater fishes related to the carp

chub·by \'chə-bē\ *adj* chub·bi·er; -est : PLUMP ⟨a ~ face⟩ — **chub·bi·ness** *n*

¹chuck \'chək\ *vb* **1** : to give a pat or tap **2** : TOSS **3** : DISCARD; *also* : EJECT **4** : to have done with ⟨~ed his job⟩

²chuck *n* : a light pat under the chin **2** : TOSS

³chuck *n* **1** : a cut of beef including most of the neck and the parts around the shoulder blade and the first three ribs **2** : a device for holding work or a tool in a machine (as a lathe)

chuck·hole \'chək-ˌhōl\ *n* : POTHOLE

chuck·le \'chə-kəl\ *vb* **chuck·led; chuck·ling** : to laugh in a quiet hardly audible manner — **chuckle** *n*

chuck wagon *n* : a wagon equipped with a stove and food supplies

¹chug \'chəg\ *n* **1** : a dull explosive sound made by or as if by a laboring engine

²chug *vb* **chugged; chug·ging** : to move or go with chugs

chuk·ka \'chə-kə\ *n* : a usu. ankle-length leather boot

chuk·ker \'chə-kər\ *also* **chuk·ka** \'chə-kə\ *n* : a playing period of a polo game

¹chum \'chəm\ *n* : a close friend

²chum *vb* **chummed; chum·ming 1** : to room together **2** : to be a close friend

chum·my \'chə-mē\ *adj* **chum·mi·er; -est** : quite friendly — **chum·mi·ly** \-mə-lē\ *adv* — **chum·mi·ness** \-mē-nəs\ *n*

chump \'chəmp\ *n* : FOOL, BLOCKHEAD

chunk \'chəŋk\ *n* **1** : a short thick piece **2** : a sizable amount

chunky \'chən-kē\ *adj* **chunk·i·er; -est 1** : STOCKY **2** : containing chunks

church \'chərch\ *n* [ME *chirche*, fr. OE *cirice*, ultim. fr. LGk *kyriakon*, fr. Gk, neut. of *kyriakos* of the lord, fr. *kyrios* lord, master] **1** : a building esp. for Christian public worship **2** *often cap* : the whole body of Christians **3** : DENOMINATION **4** : CONGREGATION **5** : public divine worship

church·go·er \'chərch-ˌgō-ər\ *n* : one who habitually attends church — **church·go·ing** *adj or n*

church·less \'chərch-ləs\ *adj* : not affiliated with a church

church·man \'chərch-mən\ *n* **1** : CLERGYMAN **2** : a member of a church

church·war·den \'chərch-ˌwȯr-dᵊn\ *n* : WARDEN **5**

church·yard \-ˌyärd\ *n* : a yard that belongs to a church and is often used as a burial ground

churl \'chərl\ *n* **1** : a medieval peasant **2**

: RUSTIC **3** : a rude ill-bred person — **churl·ish** *adj* — **churl·ish·ly** *adv* — **churl·ish·ness** *n*

¹churn \'chərn\ *n* : a container in which milk or cream is agitated in making butter

²churn *vb* **1** : to stir in a churn; *also* : to make (butter) by such stirring **2** : to shake around violently

churn out *vb* : to produce mechanically or in large quantity

chute \'shüt\ *n* **1** : an inclined surface, trough, or passage down or through which something may pass ⟨a coal ~⟩ ⟨a mail ~⟩ **2** : PARACHUTE

chut·ney \'chət-nē\ *n*, *pl* **chutneys** : a thick sauce containing fruits, vinegar, sugar, and spices

chutz·pah \'hut-spə, 'kut-, -ˌ)spä\ *n* : supreme self-confidence

CIA *abbr* Central Intelligence Agency

cía *abbr* [Sp *compañía*] company

ciao \'chau\ *interj* — used to express greeting or farewell

ci·ca·da \sə-'kā-də\ *n* : any of a family of stout-bodied insects related to the aphids and having wide blunt heads and large transparent wings

ci·ca·trix \'si-kə-ˌtriks\ *n*, *pl* **ci·ca·tri·ces** \ˌsi-kə-'trī-ˌsēz\ [L] : a scar resulting from formation and contraction of fibrous tissue in a wound

ci·ce·ro·ne \ˌsi-sə-'rō-nē, ˌchē-chə-\ *n*, *pl* **-ni** \-ˌ)nē\ : a guide who conducts sightseers

CID *abbr* Criminal Investigation Department

ci·der \'sī-dər\ *n* : juice pressed from fruit (as apples) and used as a beverage, vinegar, or flavoring

cie *abbr* [F *compagnie*] company

ci·gar \si-'gär\ *n* [Sp *cigarro*] : a roll of tobacco for smoking

cig·a·rette \ˌsi-gə-'ret, 'si-gə-ˌret\ *n* [F, dim. of *cigare* cigar] : a slender roll of cut tobacco enclosed in paper for smoking

cig·a·ril·lo \ˌsi-gə-'ri-lō, -'rē-ō\ *n*, *pl* **-los** [Sp] **1** : a very small cigar **2** : a cigarette wrapped in tobacco rather than paper

ci·lan·tro \si-'län-trō, -'lan-\ *n* : leaves of coriander used as a flavoring or garnish; *also* : the coriander plant

cil·i·ate \'si-lē-ˌāt\ *n* : any of a group of protozoans characterized by cilia

cil·i·um \'si-lē-əm\ *n*, *pl* **cil·ia** \-lē-ə\ **1** : a minute short hairlike process; *esp* : one of a cell **2** : EYELASH

C in C *abbr* commander in chief

cinch \'sinch\ *n* **1** : a girth for a pack or saddle **2** : a sure or an easy thing — **cinch** *vb*

cin·cho·na \siŋ-'kō-nə\ *n* : any of a genus of So. American trees related to the madder; *also* : the bitter quinine-containing bark of a cinchona

cinc·ture \'siŋk-chər\ *n* : BELT, SASH

cin·der \'sin-dər\ *n* **1** : SLAG **2** *pl* : ASHES **3** : a hot piece of partly burned wood or coal **4** : a fragment of lava from an erupting volcano — **cin·dery** *adj*

cinder block *n* : a building block made of cement and coal cinders

cin·e·ma \'si-nə-mə\ n 1 : a motion-picture theater 2 : MOVIES — **cin·e·mat·ic** \si-nə-'ma-tik\ adj

cin·e·ma·theque \si-nə-mə-'tek\ n : a small movie house specializing in avant-garde films

cin·e·ma·tog·ra·phy \si-nə-mə-'tä-grə-fē\ n : motion-picture photography — **cin·e·ma·tog·ra·pher** n — **cin·e·mat·o·graph·ic** \-mat-ə-'gra-fik\ adj

cine·phile \'si-nə-ˌfī(-ə)l\ n : a lover of motion pictures

cin·e·plex \'si-nə-ˌpleks\ n : a complex that houses several movie theaters

cin·er·ar·i·um \si-nə-'rer-ē-əm\ n, pl **-ia** \-ē-ə\ : a place to receive the ashes of the cremated dead — **cin·er·ary** \'si-nə-ˌrer-ē\ adj

cin·na·bar \'si-nə-ˌbär\ n 1 : a red mineral that is the only important ore of mercury 2 : a deep vivid red

cin·na·mon \'si-nə-mən\ n : a spice prepared from the highly aromatic bark of any of several Asian trees related to the true laurel; also : a tree that yields cinnamon

cinque·foil \'siŋk-ˌfȯi(-ə)l, 'saŋk-\ n : any of a genus of plants related to the roses with leaves having five lobes

¹**ci·pher** \'sī-fər\ n [ME, fr. ML cifra, fr. Ar ṣifr empty, zero] 1 : ZERO, NAUGHT 2 : a method of secret writing

²**cipher** vb : to compute arithmetically

cir or **circ** abbr circular

cir·ca \'sər-kə\ prep : ABOUT ⟨~ 1600⟩

cir·ca·di·an \sər-'kā-dē-ən\ adj : being, having, characterized by, or occurring in approximately 24-hour intervals (as of biological activity)

¹**cir·cle** \'sər-kəl\ n 1 : a closed curve every point of which is equally distant from a fixed point within it 2 : something circular 3 : an area of action or influence 4 : CYCLE 5 : a group bound by a common tie ⟨sewing ~⟩

²**circle** vb **cir·cled**; **cir·cling** 1 : to enclose in a circle 2 : to move or revolve around; also : to move in a circle

cir·clet \'sər-klət\ n : a small circle; esp : a circular ornament

cir·cuit \'sər-kət\ n 1 : a boundary around an enclosed space 2 : a course around a periphery 3 : a regular tour (as by a judge) around an assigned territory 4 : the complete path of an electric current; also : an assemblage of electronic components 5 : LEAGUE; also : a chain of theaters

circuit board n : BOARD 7

circuit breaker n : a switch that automatically interrupts the current of an overloaded circuit

circuit court n : a court that sits at two or more places within one judicial district

cir·cu·i·tous \sər-'kyü-ə-təs\ adj 1 : having a circular or winding course 2 : not being forthright or direct in language or action

cir·cuit·ry \'sər-kə-trē\ n, pl **-ries** : the plan or the components of an electric circuit

cir·cu·i·ty \sər-'kyü-ə-tē\ n, pl **-ities** : INDIRECTION

¹**cir·cu·lar** \'sər-kyə-lər\ adj 1 : having the form of a circle : ROUND 2 : moving in or around a circle 3 : CIRCUITOUS 4 : intended for circulation ⟨a ~ letter⟩ — **cir·cu·lar·i·ty** \ˌsər-kyə-'ler-ə-tē\ n

²**circular** n : a paper (as a leaflet) intended for wide distribution

cir·cu·lar·ise Brit var of CIRCULARIZE

cir·cu·lar·ize \'sər-kyə-lə-ˌrīz\ vb **-ized**; **-iz·ing** 1 : to send circulars to 2 : to poll by questionnaire 3 : to make circular

circular saw n : a power saw with a round cutting blade

cir·cu·late \'sər-kyə-ˌlāt\ vb **-lat·ed**; **-lat·ing** 1 : to move or cause to move in a circle, circuit, or orbit 2 : to pass from place to place or from person to person — **cir·cu·la·tion** \ˌsər-kyə-'lā-shən\ n

cir·cu·la·to·ry \'sər-kyə-lə-ˌtȯr-ē\ adj : of or relating to circulation or the circulatory system

circulatory system n : the system of blood, blood vessels, lymphatic vessels, and heart concerned with the circulation of the blood and lymph

cir·cum·am·bu·late \ˌsər-kəm-'am-byə-ˌlāt\ vb **-lat·ed**; **-lat·ing** : to circle on foot esp. as part of a ritual

cir·cum·cise \'sər-kəm-ˌsīz\ vb **-cised**; **-cis·ing** [ME, fr. L circumcisus, pp. of circumcidere, lit., to cut around, fr. circum around + caedere to cut] : to cut off the foreskin of — **cir·cum·ci·sion** \ˌsər-kəm-'si-zhən\ n

cir·cum·fer·ence \sər-'kəm-f(ə-)rəns\ n 1 : the perimeter of a circle 2 : the external boundary or surface of a figure or object

cir·cum·flex \'sər-kəm-ˌfleks\ n : the mark ˆ over a vowel

cir·cum·lo·cu·tion \ˌsər-kəm-lō-'kyü-shən\ n : the use of unnecessary words in expressing an idea

cir·cum·lu·nar \-'lü-nər\ adj : revolving about or surrounding the moon

cir·cum·nav·i·gate \-'na-və-ˌgāt\ vb : to go completely around (as the earth) esp. by water — **cir·cum·nav·i·ga·tion** \-ˌna-və-'gā-shən\ n

cir·cum·po·lar \-'pō-lər\ adj 1 : continually visible above the horizon ⟨a ~ star⟩ 2 : surrounding or found near a pole of the earth ⟨a ~ current⟩

cir·cum·scribe \'sər-kəm-ˌskrīb\ vb 1 : to constrict the range or activity of 2 : to draw a line around — **cir·cum·scrip·tion** \ˌsər-kəm-'skrip-shən\ n

cir·cum·spect \'sər-kəm-ˌspekt\ adj : careful to consider all circumstances and consequences : PRUDENT — **cir·cum·spec·tion** \ˌsər-kəm-'spek-shən\ n

cir·cum·stance \'sər-kəm-ˌstans\ n 1 : a fact or event that must be considered along with another fact or event 2 : surrounding conditions 3 : CHANCE, FATE 4 pl : situation with regard to wealth 5 : CEREMONY

cir·cum·stan·tial \ˌsər-kəm-'stan-chəl\

adj **1** : consisting of or depending on circumstances **2** : INCIDENTAL **3** : containing full details — **cir·cum·stan·tial·ly** *adv*

cir·cum·vent \ˌsər-kəm-ˈvent\ *vb* : to check or defeat esp. by stratagem — **cir·cum·ven·tion** \ˈvent-shən\ *n*

cir·cus \ˈsər-kəs\ *n* **1** : a usu. traveling show that features feats of physical skill, wild animal acts, and performances by clowns **2** : a circus performance; *also* : the equipment, livestock, and personnel of a circus

cirque \ˈsərk\ *n* : a deep steep-walled mountain basin usu. forming the blunt end of a valley

cir·rho·sis \sə-ˈrō-səs\ *n, pl* **-rho·ses** \-ˌsēz\ [NL, fr. Gk *kirrhos* orange-colored] : fibrosis of the liver — **cir·rhot·ic** \-ˈrä-tik\ *adj or n*

cir·rus \ˈsir-əs\ *n, pl* **cir·ri** \ˈsir-ˌī\ : a wispy white cloud usu. of minute ice crystals at high altitudes

cis·lu·nar \(ˌ)sis-ˈlü-nər\ *adj* : lying between the earth and the moon or the moon's orbit

cis·sy *Brit var of* SISSY

cis·tern \ˈsis-tərn\ *n* : an often underground tank for storing water

cit *abbr* **1** citation; cited **2** citizen

cit·a·del \ˈsi-tə-dəl, -ˌdel\ *n* **1** : a fortress commanding a city **2** : STRONGHOLD

ci·ta·tion \sī-ˈtā-shən\ *n* **1** : an official summons to appear (as before a court) **2** : QUOTATION **3** : a formal statement of the achievements of a person; *also* : a specific reference in a military dispatch to meritorious performance of duty

cite \ˈsīt\ *vb* **cit·ed; cit·ing** **1** : to summon to appear before a court **2** : QUOTE **3** : to refer to esp. in commendation or praise

cit·i·fied \ˈsi-ti-ˌfīd\ *adj* : of, relating to, or characterized by an urban style of living

cit·i·zen \ˈsi-tə-zən\ *n* **1** : an inhabitant of a city or town **2** : a person who owes allegiance to a government and is entitled to its protection — **cit·i·zen·ship** *n*

cit·i·zen·ry \-rē\ *n, pl* **-ries** : a whole body of citizens

citizens band *n* : a range of radio frequencies set aside for private radio communications

cit·ric acid \ˈsi-trik-\ *n* : a sour organic acid obtained from lemon and lime juices or by fermentation of sugars and used chiefly as a flavoring

cit·ron \ˈsi-trən\ *n* **1** : the oval lemonlike fruit of a citrus tree; *also* : the tree **2** : a small hard-fleshed watermelon used esp. in pickles and preserves

cit·ro·nel·la \ˌsi-trə-ˈne-lə\ *n* : a lemon-scented oil obtained from a fragrant grass of southern Asia and used in perfumes and as an insect repellent

cit·rus \ˈsi-trəs\ *n, pl* **citrus** *or* **cit·rus·es** : any of a genus of often thorny evergreen trees or shrubs grown in warm regions for their fruits (as the orange, lemon, lime, and grapefruit); *also* : the fruit

city \ˈsi-tē\ *n, pl* **cit·ies** [ME *citie* large or small town, fr. AF *cité*, fr. ML *civitas*, fr.

L, citizenship, state, city of Rome, fr. *civis* citizen] **1** : an inhabited place larger or more important than a town **2** : a municipality in the U.S. governed under a charter granted by the state; *also* : an incorporated municipal unit of the highest class in Canada

city manager *n* : an official employed by an elected council to direct the administration of a city government

city–state \ˈsi-tē-ˌstāt\ *n* : an autonomous state consisting of a city and surrounding territory

civ *abbr* **1** civil; civilian **2** civilization

civ·et \ˈsi-vət\ *n* : a yellowish strong-smelling substance obtained from a cat-like Old World mammal (**civet cat**) and used in making perfumes

civ·ic \ˈsi-vik\ *adj* : of or relating to a city, citizenship, or civil affairs

civ·ics \-viks\ *n* : a social science dealing with the rights and duties of citizens

civ·il \ˈsi-vəl\ *adj* **1** : of or relating to citizens or to the state as a political body **2** : COURTEOUS, POLITE **3** : of or relating to legal proceedings in connection with private rights and obligations ⟨the ~ code⟩ **4** : of or relating to the general population : not military or ecclesiastical

civil defense *n* : protective measures and emergency relief activities conducted by civilians in case of enemy attack or natural disaster

civil disobedience *n* : refusal to obey governmental commands esp. as a nonviolent means of protest

civil engineer *n* : an engineer whose training or occupation is in the design and construction esp. of public works (as roads or harbors) — **civil engineering** *n*

ci·vil·ian \sə-ˈvil-yən\ *n* : a person not on active duty in a military, police, or fire-fighting force

civ·i·li·sa·tion, **civ·i·lise** *chiefly Brit var of* CIVILIZATION, CIVILIZE

ci·vil·i·ty \sə-ˈvi-lə-tē\ *n, pl* **-ties** **1** : POLITENESS, COURTESY **2** : a polite act or expression

civ·i·li·za·tion \ˌsi-və-lə-ˈzā-shən\ *n* **1** : a relatively high level of cultural and technological development **2** : the culture characteristic of a time or place — **civ·i·li·za·tion·al** \-shə-nᵊl\ *adj*

civ·i·lize \ˈsi-və-ˌlīz\ *vb* **-lized; -liz·ing** **1** : to raise from a primitive state to an advanced and ordered stage of cultural development **2** : REFINE — **civ·i·lized** *adj*

civil liberty *n* : freedom from arbitrary governmental interference specifically by denial of governmental power — usu. used in pl.

civ·il·ly \ˈsi-vəl-lē\ *adv* **1** : in terms of civil rights, matters, or law ⟨~ dead⟩ **2** : in a civil manner : POLITELY

civil rights *n pl* : the nonpolitical rights of a citizen; *esp* : those guaranteed by the 13th and 14th amendments to the Constitution and by acts of Congress

civil servant *n* : a member of a civil service

civil service *n* : the administrative service of a government

civil war *n* : a war between opposing groups of citizens of the same country

civ·vies \'si-vēz\ *n pl* : civilian clothes as distinguished from a military uniform

CJ *abbr* chief justice

ck *abbr* **1** cask **2** check

cl *abbr* **1** centiliter **2** class

Cl *symbol* chlorine

¹**clack** \'klak\ *vb* **1** : CHATTER, PRATTLE **2** : to make or cause to make a clatter

²**clack** *n* **1** : rapid continuous talk : CHATTER **2** : a sound of clacking ⟨the ～ of a typewriter⟩

clad \'klad\ *adj* **1** : CLOTHED, COVERED **2** : being or consisting of coins made of outer layers of one metal bonded to a core of a different metal

¹**claim** \'klām\ *vb* [ME, fr. AF *claimer*, *clamer*, fr. L *clamare* to cry out, shout] **1** : to ask for as one's own; *also* : to take as the rightful owner **2** : to call for : REQUIRE **3** : to state as a fact : MAINTAIN

²**claim** *n* **1** : a demand for something due ⟨an insurance ～⟩ **2** : a right to something usu. in another's possession **3** : an assertion open to challenge **4** : something claimed (as a tract of land)

claim·ant \'klā-mənt\ *n* : a person making a claim

clair·voy·ant \klar-'vói-ənt\ *adj* [F, fr. *clair* clear + *voyant* seeing] **1** : able to see beyond the range of ordinary perception **2** : having the power of discerning objects not present to the senses — **clair·voy·ance** \-əns\ *n* — **clairvoyant** *n*

clam \'klam\ *n* **1** : any of numerous bivalve mollusks including many that are edible **2** : DOLLAR

clam·bake \-,bāk\ *n* : a party or gathering (as at the seashore) at which food is cooked usu. on heated rocks covered by seaweed

clam·ber \'klam-bər\ *vb* : to climb awkwardly — **clam·ber·er** *n*

clam·my \'kla-mē\ *adj* **clam·mi·er; -est** : being damp, soft, sticky, and usu. cool — **clam·mi·ness** *n*

clam·or \'kla-mər\ *n* **1** : a noisy shouting **2** : a loud continuous noise **3** : insistent public expression (as of support or protest) — **clamor** *vb* — **clam·or·ous** *adj*

clam·our *chiefly Brit var of* CLAMOR

¹**clamp** \'klamp\ *n* : a device that holds or presses parts together firmly

²**clamp** *vb* : to fasten with or as if with a clamp

clamp down *vb* : to impose restrictions : become repressive — **clamp·down** \'klamp-,daún\ *n*

clam·shell \'klam-,shel\ *n* **1** : the shell of a clam **2** : a bucket or grapnel (as on a dredge) having two hinged jaws

clam up *vb* : to become silent

clan \'klan\ *n* [ME, fr. ScGael *clann* offspring, clan, fr. Old Irish *cland* plant, offspring, fr. L *planta* plant] : a group (as in the Scottish Highlands) made up of households whose heads claim descent from a common ancestor — **clan·nish** *adj* — **clan·nish·ness** *n*

clan·des·tine \klan-'des-tən\ *adj* : held in or conducted with secrecy

clang \'klaŋ\ *n* : a loud metallic ringing sound — **clang** *vb*

clan·gor \'klaŋ-ər, -gər\ *n* : a resounding clang or medley of clangs

clan·gour *chiefly Brit var of* CLANGOR

clank \'klaŋk\ *n* : a sharp brief metallic ringing sound — **clank** *vb*

¹**clap** \'klap\ *vb* **clapped; clap·ping** **1** : to strike noisily **2** : APPLAUD

²**clap** *n* **1** : a loud noisy crash **2** : the noise made by clapping the hands

³**clap** *n* : GONORRHEA

clap·board \'kla-bərd, -,bórd; 'klap-,bórd\ *n* : a narrow board thicker at one edge than the other used for siding — **clap·board** *vb*

clap·per \'kla-pər\ *n* : one that claps; *esp* : the tongue of a bell

clap·trap \'klap-,trap\ *n* : pretentious nonsense

claque \'klak\ *n* [F, fr. *claquer* to clap] **1** : a group hired to applaud at a performance **2** : a group of sycophants

clar·et \'kler-ət\ *n* [ME, fr. AF *(vin)* claret clear wine] : a dry red wine

clar·i·fy \'kler-ə-,fī\ *vb* **-fied; -fy·ing** : to make or become clear — **clar·i·fi·ca·tion** \,kler-ə-fə-'kā-shən\ *n*

clar·i·net \,kler-ə-'net\ *n* : a single-reed woodwind instrument in the form of a cylindrical tube with a moderately flaring end — **clar·i·net·ist** *or* **clar·i·net·tist** \-'ne-tist\ *n*

clar·i·on \'kler-ē-ən\ *adj* : brilliantly clear ⟨a ～ call⟩

clar·i·ty \'kler-ə-tē\ *n* : CLEARNESS

¹**clash** \'klash\ *vb* **1** : to make or cause to make a clash **2** : CONFLICT, COLLIDE

²**clash** *n* **1** : a noisy usu. metallic sound of collision **2** : a hostile encounter **3** : a sharp conflict ⟨a ～ of opinions⟩

clasp \'klasp\ *n* **1** : a device (as a hook) for holding objects or parts together **2** : EMBRACE, GRASP — **clasp** *vb*

¹**class** \'klas\ *n* [F *classe*, fr. L *classis* group called to military service, fleet, class] **1** : a group of students meeting regularly in a course; *also* : a group graduating together **2** : a course of instruction; *also* : the period when such a course is taught **3** : social rank; *also* : high quality **4** : a group of the same general status or nature; *esp* : a major category in biological classification that is above the order and below the phylum **5** : a division or rating based on grade or quality — **class·less** *adj*

²**class** *vb* : CLASSIFY

class action *n* : a legal action undertaken in behalf of the plaintiffs and all others having an identical interest in the alleged wrong

¹**clas·sic** \'kla-sik\ *adj* **1** : serving as a standard of excellence; *also* : TRADITIONAL **2** : CLASSICAL **3** : notable esp. as the best example **4** : AUTHENTIC ⟨a ～ folk dance⟩

²**classic** n **1** : a work of enduring excellence and esp. of ancient Greece or Rome; *also* : its author **2** : a traditional event ⟨a football ~⟩

clas·si·cal \'kla-si-kəl\ adj **1** : CLASSIC **2** : of or relating to the ancient Greek and Roman classics **3** : of or relating to a form or system of primary significance before modern times ⟨~ economics⟩ **4** : concerned with a general study of the arts and sciences — **clas·si·cal·ly** \-k(ə-)lē\ adv

clas·si·cism \'kla-sə-ˌsi-zəm\ n **1** : the principles or style of the literature or art of ancient Greece and Rome **2** : adherence to traditional standards believed to be universally valid — **clas·si·cist** \-sist\ n

clas·si·fied \'kla-sə-ˌfīd\ adj : withheld from general circulation for reasons of national security

clas·si·fieds \-ˌfīdz\ n pl : advertisements grouped by subject

clas·si·fy \'kla-sə-ˌfī\ vb **-fied; -fy·ing** : to arrange in or assign to classes — **clas·si·fi·able** adj — **clas·si·fi·ca·tion** \ˌkla-sə-fə-'kā-shən\ n — **clas·si·fi·er** n

class·mate \'klas-ˌmāt\ n : a member of the same class (as in a college)

class·room \-ˌrüm-, -ˌrum\ n : a place where classes meet

classy \'kla-sē\ adj **class·i·er; -est** : ELEGANT, STYLISH ⟨a ~ clientele⟩ — **class·i·ness** n

clat·ter \'kla-tər\ n : a rattling sound ⟨the ~ of dishes⟩ — **clatter** vb

clause \'klóz\ n **1** : a group of words having its own subject and predicate but forming only part of a compound or complex sentence **2** : a separate part of an article or document

claus·tro·pho·bia \ˌkló-strə-'fō-bē-ə\ n : abnormal dread of being in closed or narrow spaces — **claus·tro·pho·bic** \-bik\ adj

clav·i·chord \'kla-və-ˌkórd\ n : an early keyboard instrument in use before the piano

clav·i·cle \'kla-vi-kəl\ n [F *clavicule*, fr. NL *clavicula*, fr. L, dim. of L *clavis* key] : COLLARBONE

cla·vier \klə-'vir; 'klā-vē-ər\ n **1** : the keyboard of a musical instrument **2** : an early keyboard instrument

¹**claw** \'kló\ n **1** : a sharp usu. curved nail on the toe of an animal **2** : a sharp curved process (as on the foot of an insect); *also* : a pincerlike organ at the end of a limb of some arthropods (as a lobster) — **clawed** \'klód\ adj

²**claw** vb : to rake, seize, or dig with or as if with claws

clay \'klā\ n **1** : an earthy material that is plastic when moist but hard when fired and is used in making pottery; *also* : finely divided soil consisting largely of such clay **2** : EARTH, MUD **3** : a plastic substance used for modeling **4** : the mortal human body — **clay·ey** \'klā-ē\ adj

clay·more \'klā-ˌmór\ n : a large 2-edged sword formerly used by Scottish Highlanders

clay pigeon n : a saucer-shaped target thrown from a trap in trapshooting

¹**clean** \'klēn\ adj **1** : free from dirt, disease, or pollution ⟨~ air⟩ **2** : PURE ⟨the ~ thrill of one's first flight⟩; *also* : HONORABLE **3** : THOROUGH ⟨made a ~ sweep⟩ **4** : TRIM ⟨a ~ edge⟩ ⟨a ship with ~ lines⟩; *also* : EVEN **5** : habitually neat — **clean** adv — **clean·ly** \'klēn-lē\ adv — **clean·ness** \'klēn-nəs\ n

²**clean** vb : to make or become clean — **clean·able** \'klē-nə-bəl\ adj — **clean·er** n

clean–cut \'klēn-'kət\ adj **1** : cut so that the surface or edge is smooth and even **2** : sharply defined or outlined **3** : giving an effect of wholesomeness

clean·ly \'klen-lē\ adj **clean·li·er; -est 1** : careful to keep clean **2** : habitually kept clean — **clean·li·ness** n

clean room \'klēn-ˌrüm, -ˌrum\ n : an uncontaminated room maintained for the manufacture or assembly of objects (as precision parts)

cleanse \'klenz\ vb **cleansed; cleans·ing** : to make clean — **cleans·er** n

¹**clean–up** \'klēn-ˌəp\ n **1** : an act or instance of cleaning **2** : a very large profit

²**cleanup** adj : being 4th in the batting order of a baseball team — **cleanup** adv

clean up vb : to make a spectacular business profit

¹**clear** \'klir\ adj [ME *clere*, fr. AF *cler*, fr. L *clarus*] **1** : BRIGHT, LUMINOUS; *also* : UNTROUBLED, SERENE **2** : CLOUDLESS **3** : CLEAN, PURE; *also* : TRANSPARENT **4** : easily heard, seen, or understood **5** : capable of sharp discernment; *also* : free from doubt **6** : INNOCENT ⟨a ~ conscience⟩ **7** : free from restriction, obstruction, or entanglement — **clear** adv — **clear·ness** n

²**clear** vb **1** : to make or become clear **2** : to go away : DISPERSE **3** : to free from accusation or blame; *also* : to certify as trustworthy **4** : EXPLAIN **5** : to get free from obstruction **6** : SETTLE **7** : NET ⟨~ed a profit⟩ **8** : to get rid of : REMOVE **9** : to jump or go by without touching; *also* : PASS ⟨the bill ~ed the legislature⟩

³**clear** n : a clear space or part

clear·ance \'klir-əns\ n **1** : an act or process of clearing **2** : the distance by which one object clears another **3** : AUTHORIZATION

clear–cut \'klir-'kət\ adj **1** : sharply outlined **2** : DEFINITE, UNEQUIVOCAL ⟨a ~ victory⟩

clear–cut·ting \-ˌkə-tiŋ\ n : removal of all the trees in a stand of timber — **clear-cut** \-ˌkət\ vb

clear·head·ed \-'he-dəd\ adj : having a clear understanding : PERCEPTIVE

clear·ing \'klir-iŋ\ n **1** : a tract of land cleared of wood and brush **2** : the passage of checks and claims through a clearinghouse

clear·ing·house \-ˌhaús\ n : an institution maintained by banks for making an exchange of checks and claims held by each bank against other banks; *also* : an informal channel for information or assistance

clear·ly \\'klir-lē\\ *adv* **1** : in a clear manner **2** : it is clear

cleat \\'klēt\\ *n* : a piece of wood or metal fastened on or projecting from something to give strength, provide a grip, or prevent slipping

cleav·age \\'klē-vij\\ *n* **1** : a splitting apart : SPLIT **2** : the depression between a woman's breasts esp. when exposed by a low-cut dress

¹**cleave** \\'klēv\\ *vb* **cleaved** \\'klēvd\\ *or* **clove** \\'klōv\\; **cleaved; cleav·ing** : ADHERE, CLING

²**cleave** *vb* **cleaved** \\'klēvd\\ *also* **cleft** \\'kleft\\ *or* **clove** \\'klōv\\; **cleaved** *also* **cleft** *or* **clo·ven** \\'klō-vən\\; **cleav·ing** **1** : to divide by force : split asunder **2** : DIVIDE

cleav·er \\'klē-vər\\ *n* : a heavy chopping knife for cutting meat

clef \\'klef\\ *n* : a sign placed on the staff in music to show what pitch is represented by each line and space

cleft \\'kleft\\ *n* : FISSURE, CRACK

cleft lip *n* : a birth defect in which the upper lip is vertically split

cleft palate *n* : a split in the roof of the mouth that appears as a birth defect

clem·a·tis \\'kle-mə-təs; kli-'ma-təs\\ *n* : any of a genus of vines or herbs related to the buttercups that have showy usu. white or purple flowers

clem·en·cy \\'kle-mən-sē\\ *n, pl* **-cies** **1** : disposition to be merciful **2** : mildness of weather

clem·ent \\'kle-mənt\\ *adj* **1** : MERCIFUL, LENIENT ⟨a ~ judge⟩ **2** : TEMPERATE, MILD ⟨~ weather for this time of year⟩

clem·en·tine \\'kle-mən-ˌtēn\\ *n* : a small citrus fruit that is probably a hybrid between a tangerine and an orange

clench \\'klench\\ *vb* **1** : CLINCH **2** : to hold fast **3** : to set or close tightly

clere·sto·ry \\'klir-ˌstȯr-ē\\ *n* : an outside wall of a room or building that rises above an adjoining roof and contains windows

cler·gy \\'klər-jē\\ *n* : a body of religious officials authorized to conduct services

cler·gy·man \\-mən\\ *n* : a member of the clergy

cler·gy·per·son \\-ˌpər-s°n\\ *n* : a member of the clergy

cler·ic \\'kler-ik\\ *n* : a member of the clergy

cler·i·cal \\'kler-i-kəl\\ *adj* **1** : of or relating to the clergy **2** : of or relating to a clerk

cler·i·cal·ism \\'kler-i-kə-ˌli-zəm\\ *n* : a policy of maintaining or increasing the power of a religious hierarchy

clerk \\'klərk, *Brit* 'klärk\\ *n* **1** : CLERIC **2** : an official responsible for correspondence, records, and accounts; *also* : a person employed to perform general office work **3** : a store salesperson — **clerk** *vb* — **clerk·ship** *n*

clev·er \\'kle-vər\\ *adj* **1** : showing skill or resourcefulness **2** : marked by wit or ingenuity — **clev·er·ly** *adv* — **clev·er·ness** *n*

clev·is \\'kle-vəs\\ *n* : a U-shaped shackle used for fastening

¹**clew** \\'klü\\ *n* **1** : CLUE **2** : a metal loop on a lower corner of a sail

²**clew** *vb* : to haul (a sail) up or down by ropes through the clews

cli·ché \\kli-'shā\\ *n* [F] : a trite phrase or expression — **cli·chéd** \\-'shād\\ *adj*

¹**click** \\'klik\\ *vb* **1** : to make or cause to make a click **2** : to fit or work together smoothly **3** : to select or make a selection on a computer by pressing a button on a control device (as a mouse) — **click·able** \\'kli-kə-bəl\\ *adj*

²**click** *n* **1** : a slight sharp noise **2** : an instance of clicking ⟨a mouse ~⟩

click·er \\'kli-kər\\ *n* : REMOTE CONTROL 2

cli·ent \\'klī-ənt\\ *n* **1** : DEPENDENT **2** : a person who engages the professional services of another; *also* : PATRON, CUSTOMER **3** : a computer in a network that uses the services (as access to files) provided by a server

cli·en·tele \\ˌklī-ən-'tel, ˌklē-\\ *n* : a body of clients and esp. customers

cliff \\'klif\\ *n* : a high steep face of rock, earth, or ice

cliff–hang·er \\-ˌhaŋ-ər\\ *n* **1** : an adventure serial or melodrama usu. presented in installments each of which ends in suspense **2** : a contest whose outcome is in doubt up to the very end

cli·mac·ter·ic \\klī-'mak-tə-rik\\ *n* **1** : a major turning point or critical stage **2** : MENOPAUSE; *also* : a corresponding period in the male

cli·mate \\'klī-mət\\ *n* [ME *climat*, fr. MF, fr. LL *clima*, fr. Gk *klima* inclination, latitude, climate, fr. *klinein* to lean] **1** : a region having specific climatic conditions **2** : the average weather conditions at a place over a period of years **3** : the prevailing set of conditions (as temperature and humidity) indoors **4** : a prevailing atmosphere or environment ⟨the ~ of opinion⟩ — **cli·mat·ic** \\klī-'ma-tik\\ *adj* — **cli·mat·i·cal·ly** \\-ti-k(ə-)lē\\ *adv*

cli·ma·tol·o·gy \\ˌklī-mə-'tä-lə-jē\\ *n* : the science that deals with climates — **cli·ma·to·log·i·cal** \\-mə-tə-'lä-ji-kəl\\ *adj* — **cli·ma·to·log·i·cal·ly** \\-k(ə-)lē\\ *adv* — **cli·ma·tol·o·gist** \\-mə-'tä-lə-jist\\ *n*

¹**cli·max** \\'klī-ˌmaks\\ *n* [L, fr. Gk *klimax*, lit., ladder, fr. *klinein* to lean] **1** : a series of ideas or statements so arranged that they increase in force and power from the first to the last; *also* : the last member of such a series **2** : the highest point **3** : ORGASM — **cli·mac·tic** \\klī-'mak-tik\\ *adj*

²**climax** *vb* : to come or bring to a climax

¹**climb** \\'klīm\\ *vb* **1** : to rise to a higher point **2** : to go up or down esp. by use of hands and feet; *also* : to ascend in growing — **climb·er** *n*

²**climb** *n* **1** : a place where climbing is necessary **2** : the act of climbing : ascent by climbing

clime \\'klīm\\ *n* : CLIMATE

¹**clinch** \'klinch\ *vb* **1** : to turn over or flatten the end of something sticking out ⟨∼ a nail⟩; *also* : to fasten by clinching **2** : to make final : SETTLE **3** : to hold a boxing opponent **2** : to hold fast or firmly
²**clinch** *n* **1** : a fastening by means of a clinched nail, rivet, or bolt **2** : an act or instance of clinching in boxing
clinch·er \'klin-chər\ *n* : one that clinches; *esp* : a decisive fact, argument, act, or remark
cling \'kliŋ\ *vb* **clung** \'kləŋ\; **cling·ing 1** : to adhere as if glued; *also* : to hold or hold on tightly **2** : to have a strong emotional attachment — **clingy** \'kliŋ-ē\ *adj*
cling·stone \'kliŋ-ˌstōn\ *n* : any of various fruits (as some peaches) whose flesh adheres strongly to the pit
clin·ic \'kli-nik\ *n* **1** : a medical class in which patients are examined and discussed **2** : a group meeting for teaching a certain skill and working on individual problems ⟨a reading ∼⟩ **3** : a facility (as of a hospital) for diagnosis and treatment of outpatients
clin·i·cal \'kli-ni-kəl\ *adj* **1** : of, relating to, or typical of a clinic; *esp* : involving direct observation of the patient ⟨∼ studies⟩ **2** : scientifically dispassionate — **clin·i·cal·ly** \-k(ə-)lē\ *adv*
cli·ni·cian \kli-'ni-shən\ *n* : a person qualified in the clinical practice of medicine, psychiatry, or psychology as distinguished from one specializing in laboratory or research techniques or in theory
¹**clink** \'kliŋk\ *vb* : to make or cause to make a sharp short metallic sound
²**clink** *n* : a clinking sound
clin·ker \'kliŋ-kər\ *n* : stony matter fused together : SLAG
¹**clip** \'klip\ *vb* **clipped**; **clip·ping** : to fasten with a clip
²**clip** *n* **1** : a device that grips, clasps, or hooks **2** : a cartridge holder for a rifle
³**clip** *vb* **clipped**; **clip·ping 1** : to cut or cut off with shears **2** : CURTAIL, DIMINISH **3** : HIT, PUNCH **4** : to illegally block (an opponent) in football
⁴**clip** *n* **1** : a 2-bladed instrument for cutting esp. the nails **2** : a sharp blow **3** : a rapid pace
clip art *n* : ready-made usu. copyright-free illustrations
clip·board \'klip-ˌbȯrd\ *n* **1** : a small writing board with a spring clip at the top for holding papers **2** : a section of computer memory that temporarily stores data esp. to facilitate its movement or duplication
clip joint *n, slang* : an establishment (as a nightclub) that makes a practice of defrauding its customers
clip·per \'kli-pər\ *n* **1** : an implement for clipping esp. the hair or nails — usu. used in pl. **2** : a fast sailing ship
clip·ping \'kli-piŋ\ *n* : a piece clipped from something (as a newspaper)
clique \'klēk, 'klik\ *n* [F] : a small exclusive group of people : COTERIE — **cliqu·ey** \'klē-kē, 'kli-\ *adj* — **cliqu·ish** \-kish\ *adj*

cli·to·ris \'kli-tə-rəs\ *n, pl* **cli·to·ris·es** : a small erectile organ at the anterior or ventral part of the vulva homologous to the penis — **cli·to·ral** \-rəl\ *adj*
clk *abbr* clerk
clo *abbr* clothing
¹**cloak** \'klōk\ *n* **1** : a loose outer garment **2** : something that conceals
²**cloak** *vb* : to cover or hide with a cloak
cloak–and–dagger *adj* : involving or suggestive of espionage
clob·ber \'klä-bər\ *vb* **1** : to pound mercilessly; *also* : to hit with force : SMASH **2** : to defeat overwhelmingly
cloche \'klōsh\ *n* [F, lit., bell] : a woman's small close-fitting hat
¹**clock** \'kläk\ *n* : a timepiece not intended to be carried on the person
²**clock** *vb* **1** : to time (a person or a performance) by a timing device **2** : to register (as speed) on a mechanical recording device — **clock·er** *n*
³**clock** *n* : an ornamental figure on a stocking or sock
clock·wise \'kläk-ˌwīz\ *adv* : in the direction in which the hands of a clock move — **clockwise** *adj*
clock·work \-ˌwərk\ *n* **1** : the machinery that runs a mechanical device (as a clock or toy) **2** : the precision or regularity associated with a clock
clod \'kläd\ *n* **1** : a lump esp. of earth or clay **2** : a dull or insensitive person
clod·hop·per \-ˌhä-pər\ *n* **1** : an uncouth rustic **2** : a large heavy shoe
¹**clog** \'kläg\ *n* **1** : a weight attached esp. to an animal to impede motion **2** : a thick-soled shoe
²**clog** *vb* **clogged**; **clog·ging 1** : to impede with a clog : HINDER **2** : to obstruct passage through **3** : to become filled with extraneous matter
cloi·son·né \ˌklȯi-zə-'nā\ *adj* : a colored decoration made of enamels poured into the divided areas in a design outlined with wire or metal strips
¹**clois·ter** \'klȯi-stər\ *n* [ME *cloistre*, fr. AF, fr. ML *claustrum*, fr. L, bar, bolt, fr. *claudere* to close] **1** : a monastic establishment **2** : a covered usu. colonnaded passage on the side of a court — **clois·tral** \-strəl\ *adj*
²**cloister** *vb* : to shut away from the world
clone \'klōn\ *n* [Gk *klōn* twig, slip] **1** : the collection of genetically identical cells or organisms produced asexually from a single ancestral cell or organism; *also* : an individual grown from a single cell and genetically identical to it ⟨a sheep ∼⟩ **2** : a group of replicas of a biological molecule (as DNA) **3** : one that appears to be a copy of an original form — **clon·al** \'klō-nᵊl\ *adj* — **clone** *vb*
clop \'kläp\ *n* : a sound made by or as if by a hoof or wooden shoe against pavement — **clop** *vb*
¹**close** \'klōz\ *vb* **closed**; **clos·ing 1** : to bar passage through : SHUT **2** : to suspend the operations (as of a school) **3** : END, TERMINATE **4** : to bring together the parts or edges of; *also* : to fill up **5**

: GRAPPLE ⟨~ with the enemy⟩ **6** : to enter into an agreement — **clos·able** or **close·able** adj

²**close** \'klōz\ n : CONCLUSION, END

³**close** \'klōs\ adj **clos·er; clos·est** **1** : having no openings **2** : narrowly restricting or restricted **3** : limited to a privileged class **4** : SECLUDED; also : SECRETIVE **5** : RIGOROUS ⟨keep ~ watch⟩ **6** : SULTRY, STUFFY **7** : STINGY **8** : having little space between items or units **9** : fitting tightly; also : SHORT ⟨~ haircut⟩ **10** : NEAR ⟨at ~ range⟩ **11** : INTIMATE ⟨~ friends⟩ **12** : ACCURATE **13** : decided by a narrow margin ⟨a ~ game⟩ — **close** adv — **close·ly** adv — **close·ness** n

closed–circuit \'klōzd-'sər-kət\ adj : used in, shown on, or being a television installation in which the signal is transmitted by wire to a limited number of receivers

closed shop n : an establishment having only members of a labor union on the payroll

close·fist·ed \'klōz-'fis-təd, 'klōs-\ adj : STINGY

close–knit \'klōs-'nit\ adj : closely bound together by social, cultural, economic, or political ties

close–mouthed \'klōz-'maủthd, 'klōs-'maủtht\ adj : cautious or reticent in speaking

close·out \'klōz-,aủt\ n : a sale of a business's entire stock at low prices

close out vb **1** : to dispose of by a closeout **2** : to dispose of a business : SELL OUT

clos·er \'klō-zər\ n : one that closes; esp : a relief pitcher who specializes in finishing games

¹**clos·et** \'klä-zət, 'klō-\ n **1** : a small room for privacy **2** : a small compartment for household utensils or clothing **3** : a state or condition of secrecy ⟨came out of the ~⟩

²**closet** vb : to take into a private room for an interview

close–up \'klōs-,əp\ n **1** : a photograph or movie shot taken at close range **2** : an intimate view or examination

clo·sure \'klō-zhər\ n **1** : an act of closing : the condition of being closed **2** : something that closes **3** : CLOTURE

clot \'klät\ n : a mass formed by a portion of liquid (as blood) thickening and sticking together — **clot** vb

cloth \'klóth\ n, pl **cloths** \'klóthz, 'klóths\ **1** : a pliable fabric made usu. by weaving or knitting natural or synthetic fibers and filaments **2** : TABLECLOTH **3** : distinctive dress of the clergy; also : CLERGY

clothe \'klōth\ vb **clothed** or **clad** \'klad\; **cloth·ing** **1** : DRESS; also : to provide with clothes **2** : to express by suitably significant language ⟨policies clothed in rhetoric⟩

clothes \'klōthz, 'klōz\ n pl **1** : CLOTHING **2** : BEDCLOTHES

clothes·horse \-,hórs\ n **1** : a frame on which to hang clothes **2** : a conspicuously dressy person

¹**clothes·line** \-,līn\ n : a rope or cord on which clothes are hung to dry

²**clothesline** vb : to knock down by catching by the neck with one's outstretched arm

clothes moth n : any of several small pale moths whose larvae eat wool, fur, and feathers

clothes·pin \'klōthz-,pin, 'klōz-\ n : a device for fastening clothes on a line

clothes·press \-,pres\ n : a receptacle for clothes

cloth·ier \'klōth-yər, 'klō-thē-ər\ n : a maker or seller of clothing

cloth·ing \'klō-thin\ n : garments in general

clo·ture \'klō-chər\ n : the closing or limitation (as by calling for a vote) of debate in a legislative body

¹**cloud** \'klaủd\ n [ME, rock, cloud, fr. OE clūd] **1** : a visible mass of particles of condensed vapor (as water or ice) suspended in the atmosphere **2** : a usu. visible mass of minute airborne particles; also : a mass of obscuring matter in interstellar space **3** : CROWD, SWARM ⟨a ~ of mosquitoes⟩ **4** : something having a dark or threatening aspect ⟨a ~ of suspicion⟩ **5** : something that obscures or blemishes ⟨a ~ of ambiguity⟩ — **cloud·i·ness** \'klaủ-dē-nəs\ n — **cloud·less** adj — **cloudy** adj

²**cloud** vb **1** : to darken or hide with or as if with a cloud **2** : OBSCURE ⟨~ed in mystery⟩ **3** : TAINT, SULLY ⟨a ~ed reputation⟩

cloud·burst \-,bərst\ n : a sudden heavy rainfall

cloud·let \-lət\ n : a small cloud

cloud nine n : a feeling of extreme well-being or elation — usu. used with on

¹**clout** \'klaủt\ n **1** : a blow esp. with the hand **2** : PULL, INFLUENCE

²**clout** vb : to hit forcefully

¹**clove** \'klōv\ n : one of the small bulbs that grows at the base of the scales of a large bulb ⟨a ~ of garlic⟩

²**clove** past of CLEAVE

³**clove** n [ME clowe, fr. AF clou (de girofle), lit., nail of clove, fr. L clavus nail] : the dried flower bud of a tropical tree used esp. as a spice

clo·ven \'klō-vən\ past part of CLEAVE

cloven foot n : CLOVEN HOOF — **cloven–foot·ed** \-'fủ-təd\ adj

cloven hoof n : a foot (as of a sheep) with the front part divided into two parts — **cloven–hoofed** \-'hủft, -'hủvd\ adj

clo·ver \'klō-vər\ n : any of a genus of leguminous herbs with usu. 3-parted leaves and dense flower heads

clo·ver·leaf \-,lēf\ n, pl **cloverleafs** \-,lēfs\ or **clo·ver·leaves** \-,lēvz\ : an interchange between two major highways that from above resembles a 4-leaf clover

¹**clown** \'klaủn\ n **1** : BOOR **2** : a fool or comedian in an entertainment (as a circus) **3** : a person given to joking and buf-

foonery — **clown·ish** *adj* — **clown·ish·ly** *adv* — **clown·ish·ness** *n*

²**clown** *vb* : to act like a clown

cloy \'klòi\ *vb* : to disgust or nauseate with excess of something orig. pleasing — **cloy·ing·ly** *adv*

clr *abbr* clear

¹**club** \'kləb\ *n* **1** : a heavy wooden stick or staff used as a weapon; *also* : BAT **2** : any of a suit of playing cards marked with a black figure resembling a clover leaf **3** : a group of persons associated for a common purpose; *also* : the meeting place of such a group **4** : CLUB SANDWICH

²**club** *vb* **clubbed; club·bing 1** : to strike with a club **2** : to unite or combine for a common cause **3** : to patronize nightclubs

club·foot \'kləb-'fút\ *n* : a misshapen foot twisted out of position from birth; *also* : this deformed condition — **club·foot·ed** \-'fú-təd\ *adj*

club·house \'kləb-,haús\ *n* **1** : a house occupied by a club **2** : locker rooms used by an athletic team **3** : a building at a golf course with locker rooms and usu. a pro shop and a restaurant

club sandwich *n* : a sandwich of three slices of bread with two layers of meat (as turkey) and lettuce, tomato, and mayonnaise

club soda *n* : SODA WATER

cluck \'klək\ *n* : the call of a hen esp. to her chicks — **cluck** *vb*

¹**clue** \'klü\ *n* **1** : something that guides through an intricate procedure or maze; *esp* : a piece of evidence leading to the solution of a problem **2** : IDEA, NOTION 〈has no ~ what he's doing〉

²**clue** *vb* **clued; clue·ing** *or* **clu·ing** : to provide with a clue; *also* : to give information to 〈~ me in〉

¹**clump** \'kləmp\ *n* **1** : a group of things clustered together **2** : a heavy tramping sound

²**clump** *vb* : to tread clumsily and noisily

clum·sy \'kləm-zē\ *adj* **clum·si·er; -est 1** : lacking dexterity, nimbleness, or grace **2** : not tactful or subtle — **clum·si·ly** \-zə-lē\ *adv* — **clum·si·ness** \-zē-nəs\ *n*

clung *past and past part of* CLING

clunk·er \'klən-kər\ *n* **1** : a dilapidated automobile **2** : a notable failure

¹**clus·ter** \'kləs-tər\ *n* : GROUP, BUNCH

²**cluster** *vb* : to grow or gather in a cluster

¹**clutch** \'kləch\ *vb* : to grasp with or as if with the hand

²**clutch** *n* **1** : the claws or a hand in the act of grasping; *also* : CONTROL, POWER **2** : a device for gripping an object **3** : a coupling used to connect and disconnect a driving and a driven part of a mechanism; *also* : a lever or pedal operating such a coupling **4** : a crucial situation

³**clutch** *adj* : made, done, or successful in a crucial situation

⁴**clutch** *n* **1** : a nest or batch of eggs; *also* : a brood of chicks **2** : GROUP, BUNCH

¹**clut·ter** \'klə-tər\ *vb* : to fill or cover with a disorderly scattering of things

²**clutter** *n* : a crowded mass

cm *abbr* centimeter

Cm *symbol* curium

CM *abbr* [Commonwealth of the Northern Mariana Islands] Northern Mariana Islands

cmdr *abbr* commander

cml *abbr* commercial

CMSgt *abbr* chief master sergeant

CNO *abbr* chief of naval operations

CNS *abbr* central nervous system

co *abbr* **1** company **2** county

Co *symbol* cobalt

CO *abbr* **1** Colorado **2** commanding officer **3** conscientious objector

c/o *abbr* care of

¹**coach** \'kōch\ *n* [MF *coche,* ultim. fr. Hung *kocsi (szekér),* lit., (wagon) of Kocs (town in Hungary)] **1** : a large closed 4-wheeled carriage with an elevated outside front seat for the driver **2** : a railroad passenger car esp. for day travel **3** : BUS **4** : a private tutor; *also* : one who instructs or trains 〈an acting ~〉 〈a soccer ~〉

²**coach** *vb* : to instruct, direct, or prompt as a coach

coach·man \-mən\ *n* : a man who drives a coach or carriage

co·ad·ju·tor \,kō-ə-'jü-tər, kō-'a-jə-tər\ *n* : ASSISTANT; *esp* : an assistant bishop having the right of succession

co·ag·u·lant \kō-'a-gyə-lənt\ *n* : something that produces coagulation

co·ag·u·late \-,lāt\ *vb* **-lat·ed; -lat·ing** : CLOT — **co·ag·u·la·tion** \kō-,a-gyə-'lā-shən\ *n*

¹**coal** \'kōl\ *n* **1** : EMBER **2** : a black solid combustible mineral used as fuel

²**coal** *vb* **1** : to supply with coal **2** : to take in coal

co·a·lesce \,kō-ə-'les\ *vb* **co·a·lesced; co·a·lesc·ing** : to grow together; *also* : FUSE ✦ **Synonyms** MERGE, BLEND, MINGLE, MIX — **co·a·les·cence** \-'ns\ *n*

coal·field \'kōl-,fēld\ *n* : a region rich in coal deposits

coal gas *n* : gas from coal; *esp* : gas distilled from bituminous coal and used for heating

co·a·li·tion \,kō-ə-'li-shən\ *n* : UNION; *esp* : a temporary union for a common purpose — **co·a·li·tion·ist** *n*

coal oil *n* : KEROSENE

coal tar *n* : tar distilled from bituminous coal and used in dyes and drugs

co·an·chor \'kō-'aŋ-kər\ *n* : a newscaster who shares the duties of head broadcaster

coarse \'kòrs\ *adj* **coars·er; coars·est 1** : of ordinary or inferior quality **2** : composed of large parts or particles 〈~ sand〉 **3** : CRUDE 〈~ manners〉 **4** : ROUGH, HARSH — **coarse·ly** *adv* — **coarse·ness** *n*

coars·en \'kòr-sᵊn\ *vb* : to make or become coarse

¹**coast** \'kōst\ *n* [ME *cost,* fr. AF *coste,* fr. L *costa* rib, side] **1** : SEASHORE **2** : a slide down a slope **3** : the immediate area of view — used in the phrase *the coast is clear* — **coast·al** *adj*

²**coast** vb **1** : to sail along the shore **2** : to move (as downhill on a sled) without effort

coast·er n **1** : one that coasts **2** : a shallow container or a plate or mat to protect a surface

coaster brake n : a brake in the hub of the rear wheel of a bicycle

coast guard n : a military force employed in guarding or patrolling a coast — **coast·guards·man** \'kōst-ˌgärdz-mən\ n

coast·line \'kōst-ˌlīn\ n : the outline or shape of a coast

¹**coat** \'kōt\ n **1** : an outer garment for the upper part of the body **2** : an external growth (as of fur or feathers) on an animal **3** : a covering layer ⟨a ~ of paint⟩ — **coat·ed** \'kō-təd\ adj

²**coat** vb : to cover usu. with a finishing or protective coat

coat·ing \'kō-tiŋ\ n : COAT, COVERING

coat of arms : the heraldic bearings (as of a person) usu. depicted on an escutcheon

coat of mail : a garment of metal scales or rings worn as armor

co·au·thor \'kō-'ȯ-thər\ n : a joint or associate author — **coauthor** vb

coax \'kōks\ vb : WHEEDLE; also : to gain by gentle urging or flattery

co·ax·i·al \'kō-'ak-sē-əl\ adj : having coincident axes — **co·ax·i·al·ly** adv

coaxial cable n : a cable that consists of a tube of electrically conducting material surrounding a central conductor

cob \'käb\ n **1** : a male swan **2** : CORN-COB **3** : a short-legged stocky horse

co·balt \'kō-ˌbȯlt\ n [G Kobalt, alter. of Kobold, lit., goblin; fr. its occurrence in silver ore, believed to be due to goblins] : a tough shiny silver-white magnetic metallic chemical element found with iron and nickel

cob·ble \'kä-bəl\ vb **cob·bled; cob·bling** : to make or put together roughly or hastily ⟨~ together a solution⟩

cob·bler \'kä-blər\ n **1** : a mender or maker of shoes **2** : a deep-dish fruit pie with a thick crust

cob·ble·stone \'kä-bəl-ˌstōn\ n : a naturally rounded stone larger than a pebble and smaller than a boulder

co·bra \'kō-brə\ n [Pg cobra (de capello), lit., hooded snake] : any of several venomous snakes of Asia and Africa that when excited expand the skin of the neck into a broad hood

cob·web \'käb-ˌweb\ n [ME coppeweb, fr. coppe spider, fr. OE ātorcoppe] **1** : SPIDERWEB; also : a thread spun by a spider or insect larva **2** : something flimsy or entangling — **cob·web·by** \-ˌwe-bē\ adj

co·caine \kō-'kān, 'kō-ˌkān\ n : a drug obtained from the leaves of a So. American shrub (**co·ca** \'kō-kə\) that can result in severe psychological dependence and is sometimes used in medicine as a local anesthetic and illegally as a stimulant of the central nervous system

coc·cus \'kä-kəs\ n, pl **coc·ci** \'käk-ˌsī\ : a spherical bacterium

coc·cyx \'käk-siks\ n, pl **coc·cy·ges** \'käk-sə-ˌjēz\ also **coc·cyx·es** \'käk-sik-səz\ : the end of the spinal column beyond the sacrum esp. in humans

co·chi·neal \'kä-chə-ˌnēl\ n : a red dye made from the dried bodies of females of a tropical American insect (**cochineal insect**)

co·chlea \'kō-klē-ə, 'kä-\ n, pl **co·chle·as** or **co·chle·ae** \-klē-ˌē, -ˌī\ : the usu. spiral part of the inner ear containing nerve endings which carry information about sound to the brain — **co·chle·ar** \-klē-ər\ adj

¹**cock** \'käk\ n **1** : the adult male of a bird and esp. of the common domestic chicken **2** : VALVE, FAUCET **3** : LEADER **4** : the hammer of a firearm; also : the position of the hammer when ready for firing

²**cock** vb **1** : to draw back the hammer of a firearm **2** : to set or draw back in readiness for some action ⟨~ your arm to throw⟩ **3** : to turn or tilt usu. to one side ⟨~ one's head⟩

³**cock** n : a small pile (as of hay)

cock·ade \kä-'kād\ n : an ornament worn on the hat as a badge

cock·a·tiel \ˌkä-kə-'tēl\ n : a small crested gray parrot often kept as a cage bird

cock·a·too \'kä-kə-ˌtü\ n, pl **-toos** [D kaketoe, fr. Malay kakatua] : any of various large noisy crested parrots chiefly of Australia

cock·a·trice \'kä-kə-trəs, -ˌtrīs\ n : a legendary serpent with a deadly glance

cock·crow \'käk-ˌkrō\ n : DAWN

cocked hat \'käkt-\ n : a hat with the brim turned up on two or three sides

cock·er·el \'kä-kə-rəl\ n : a young male domestic chicken

cock·er spaniel \'kä-kər-\ n [cocking woodcock hunting] : any of a breed of small spaniels with long ears, square muzzle, and silky coat

cock·eyed \'kä-'kīd\ adj **1** : turned or tilted to one side **2** : slightly crazy : FOOLISH

cock·fight \'käk-ˌfīt\ n : a contest of gamecocks usu. fitted with metal spurs

¹**cock·le** \'kä-kəl\ n : any of several weedy plants related to the pinks

²**cockle** n : a bivalve mollusk with a heart= shaped shell

cock·le·shell \-ˌshel\ n **1** : the shell of a cockle **2** : a light flimsy boat

cock·ney \'käk-nē\ n, pl **cockneys** : a native of London and esp. of the East End of London; also : the dialect of a cockney

cock·pit \'käk-ˌpit\ n **1** : a pit for cockfights **2** : a space or compartment in a vehicle from which it is steered, piloted, or driven

cock·roach \'käk-ˌrōch\ n [Sp cucaracha] : any of an order or suborder of active nocturnal insects including some which infest houses and ships

cock·sure \'käk-'shùr\ adj **1** : perfectly sure : CERTAIN **2** : COCKY

cock·tail \'käk-ˌtāl\ n **1** : an iced drink made of liquor and flavoring ingredients **2** : an appetizer (as tomato juice) served as a first course of a meal

cocky \'kä-kē\ *adj* **cock·i·er; -est** : marked by overconfidence : PERT, CONCEITED — **cock·i·ly** \-kə-lē\ *adv* — **cock·i·ness** \-kē-nəs\ *n*

co·coa \'kō-kō\ *n* **1** : CACAO **2** : chocolate deprived of some of its fat and powdered; *also* : a drink made of this heated with water or milk

cocoa butter *n* : a pale vegetable fat obtained from cacao beans

co·co·nut \'kō-kə-(,)nət\ *n* : a large edible hard-shelled fruit produced by a tall tropical palm (**coconut palm**)

co·coon \kə-'kün\ *n* **1** : a case usu. of silk formed by some insect larvae for protection during the pupal stage **2** : something that offers protection or isolation

cod \'käd\ *n, pl* **cod** *also* **cods** : a bottom-dwelling bony fish of the North Atlantic that is an important food fish; *also* : a related fish of the Pacific Ocean

COD *abbr* **1** cash on delivery **2** collect on delivery

co·da \'kō-də\ *n* : a closing section in a musical composition that is formally distinct from the main structure

cod·dle \'kä-d°l\ *vb* **cod·dled; cod·dling 1** : to cook slowly in water below the boiling point **2** : PAMPER

¹code \'kōd\ *n* [ME, fr. MF, fr. L *caudex, codex* trunk of a tree, document formed orig. from wooden tablets] **1** : a systematic statement of a body of law **2** : a system of principles or rules ⟨moral ∼⟩ **3** : a system of signals **4** : a system of symbols (as in secret communication) with special meanings **5** : GENETIC CODE

²code *vb* **cod·ed; cod·ing** : to put into the form or symbols of a code

co·deine \'kō-,dēn\ *n* : a narcotic drug obtained from opium and used esp. as an analgesic and cough suppressant

co·dex \'kō-,deks\ *n, pl* **co·di·ces** \'kō-də-,sēz, 'kä-\ : a manuscript book (as of the Scriptures or classics)

cod·fish \'käd-,fish\ *n* : COD

cod·ger \'kä-jər\ *n* : an odd or cranky and usu. elderly fellow

cod·i·cil \'kä-də-səl, -,sil\ *n* : a legal instrument modifying an earlier will

cod·i·fy \'kä-də-,fī, 'kō-\ *vb* **-fied; -fy·ing** : to arrange in a systematic form — **cod·i·fi·ca·tion** \,kä-də-fə-'kā-shən, ,kō-\ *n*

co·ed \'kō-,ed\ *n* : a female student in a coeducational institution — **coed** *adj*

co·ed·u·ca·tion \,kō-,e-jə-'kā-shən\ *n* : the education of male and female students at the same institution — **co·ed·u·ca·tion·al** \-shə-nəl\ *adj* — **co·ed·u·ca·tion·al·ly** *adv*

co·ef·fi·cient \,kō-ə-'fi-shənt\ *n* **1** : a constant factor as distinguished from a variable in a mathematical term **2** : a number that serves as a measure of some property (as of a substance, device, or process)

coe·len·ter·ate \si-'len-tə-,rāt, -rət\ *n* : any of a phylum of radially symmetrical invertebrate animals including the corals, sea anemones, and jellyfishes

co·equal \kō-'ē-kwəl\ *adj* : equal with another — **coequal** *n* — **co·equal·i·ty** \,kō-ē-'kwä-lə-tē\ *n* — **co·equal·ly** *adv*

co·erce \kō-'ərs\ *vb* **co·erced; co·erc·ing 1** : RESTRAIN, REPRESS **2** : COMPEL **3** : ENFORCE — **co·er·cion** \-'ər-zhən, -shən\ *n* — **co·er·cive** \-'ər-siv\ *adj*

co·e·val \kō-'ē-vəl\ *adj* : of the same age — **coeval** *n*

co·ex·ist \,kō-ig-'zist\ *vb* **1** : to exist together or at the same time **2** : to live in peace with each other — **co·ex·is·tence** \-'zis-təns\ *n*

co·ex·ten·sive \,kō-ik-'sten-siv\ *adj* : having the same scope or extent in space or time

C of C *abbr* Chamber of Commerce

cof·fee \'ko-fē\ *n* [It & Turk; It *caffè,* fr. Turk *kahve,* fr. Ar *qahwah*] : a drink made from the roasted and ground seeds of a fruit of a tropical shrub or tree; *also* : these seeds (**coffee beans**) or a plant producing them

cof·fee·house \-,haus\ *n* : a place where refreshments (as coffee) are sold

coffee klatch \-,klach\ *n* : KAFFEEKLATSCH

cof·fee·pot \-,pät\ *n* : a pot for brewing or serving coffee

coffee shop *n* : a small restaurant

coffee table *n* : a low table customarily placed in front of a sofa

cof·fer \'ko-fər\ *n* : a chest or box used esp. for valuables

cof·fer·dam \-,dam\ *n* : a watertight enclosure from which water is pumped to expose the bottom of a body of water and permit construction

cof·fin \'ko-fən\ *n* : a box or chest for burying a corpse

C of S *abbr* chief of staff

¹cog \'käg\ *n* : a tooth on the rim of a wheel or gear — **cogged** \'kägd\ *adj*

²cog *abbr* cognate

co·gen·er·a·tion \,kō-je-nə-'rā-shən\ *n* : the simultaneous generation of electricity and heat from the same fuel

co·gent \'kō-jənt\ *adj* : having power to compel or constrain : CONVINCING ⟨a ∼ argument⟩ — **co·gen·cy** \-jən-sē\ *n*

cog·i·tate \'kä-jə-,tāt\ *vb* **-tat·ed; -tat·ing** : THINK, PONDER — **cog·i·ta·tion** \,kä-jə-'tā-shən\ *n* — **cog·i·ta·tive** \'kä-jə-,tā-tiv\ *adj*

co·gnac \'kōn-,yak\ *n* : a French brandy

cog·nate \'käg-,nāt\ *adj* **1** : of the same or similar nature **2** : RELATED; *esp* : related by descent from the same ancestral language — **cognate** *n*

cog·ni·tive \'käg-nə-tiv\ *adj* : of, relating to, or being conscious intellectual activity (as thinking, remembering, reasoning, or using language) — **cog·ni·tion** \käg-'ni-shən\ *n* — **cog·ni·tive·ly** *adv*

cog·ni·zance \'käg-nə-zəns\ *n* **1** : apprehension by the mind : AWARENESS **2** : NOTICE, HEED — **cog·ni·zant** \'käg-nə-zənt\ *adj*

cog·no·men \käg-'nō-mən, 'käg-nə-\ *n, pl* **cognomens** *or* **cog·no·mi·na** \käg-'nä-mə-nə, -'nō-\ : NAME; *esp* : NICKNAME

co·gno·scen·te \ˌkän-yə-ˈshen-tē\ n, pl **-scen·ti** \-tē\ [obs. It] : CONNOISSEUR

cog·wheel \ˈkäg-ˌhwēl\ n : a wheel with cogs or teeth

co·hab·it \kō-ˈha-bət\ vb : to live together as a couple — **co·hab·i·ta·tion** \-ˌha-bə-ˈtā-shən\ n

co·here \kō-ˈhir\ vb **co·hered; co·her·ing** : to stick together

co·her·ent \kō-ˈhir-ənt\ adj **1** : having the quality of cohering **2** : logically consistent ⟨a ~ explanation⟩ — **co·her·ence** \-əns\ n — **co·her·ent·ly** adv

co·he·sion \kō-ˈhē-zhən\ n **1** : a sticking together **2** : molecular attraction by which the particles of a body are united — **co·he·sive** \-siv\ adj — **co·he·sive·ly** adv — **co·he·sive·ness** n

co·ho \ˈkō-ˌhō\ n, pl **cohos** or **coho** : a rather small Pacific salmon with light-colored flesh

co·hort \ˈkō-ˌhórt\ n **1** : a group of warriors or followers **2** : COMPANION, ACCOMPLICE

coif \ˈkóif; 2 usu ˈkwäf\ n **1** : a close-fitting hat **2** : COIFFURE

coif·feur \kwä-ˈfər\ n [F] : HAIRDRESSER

coif·feuse \kwä-ˈfərz, -ˈfəz, -ˈfüz, -ˈfyüz\ n : a female hairdresser

coif·fure \kwä-ˈfyúr\ n : a manner of arranging the hair

¹**coil** \ˈkói(-ə)l\ vb : to wind in a spiral shape

²**coil** n : a series of rings or loops (as of coiled rope, wire, or pipe) : RING, LOOP

¹**coin** \ˈkóin\ n [ME, wedge, corner, image on a coin, fr. AF *coing*, fr. L *cuneus* wedge] **1** : a piece of metal issued by government authority as money **2** : metal money

²**coin** vb **1** : to make (a coin) esp. by stamping : MINT **2** : CREATE, INVENT ⟨~ a phrase⟩ — **coin·er** n

coin·age \ˈkói-nij\ n **1** : the act or process of coining **2** : COINS

co·in·cide \ˌkō-ən-ˈsīd, ˈkō-ən-ˌsīd\ vb **-cid·ed; -cid·ing 1** : to occupy the same place in space or time **2** : to correspond or agree exactly

co·in·ci·dence \kō-ˈin-sə-dəns\ n **1** : exact agreement **2** : occurrence together apparently without reason; *also* : an event that so occurs

co·in·ci·dent \kō-ˈin-sə-dənt\ adj **1** : of similar nature **2** : occupying the same space or time — **co·in·ci·den·tal** \kō-ˌin-sə-ˈden-t³l\ adj

co·i·tus \ˈkō-ə-təs\ n [L, fr. *coire* to come together] : SEXUAL INTERCOURSE 1 — **co·i·tal** \-t³l\ adj

¹**coke** \ˈkōk\ n : a hard gray porous fuel made by heating soft coal to drive off most of its volatile material

²**coke** n : COCAINE

¹**col** abbr **1** colonial; colony **2** column

²**col** or **coll** abbr **1** collect, collected, collection **2** college, collegiate

Col abbr **1** colonel **2** Colorado **3** Colossians

COL abbr **1** colonel **2** cost of living

co·la \ˈkō-lə\ n : a carbonated soft drink usu. containing sugar, caffeine, caramel, and special flavoring

col·an·der \ˈkə-lən-dər, ˈkä-\ n : a perforated utensil for draining food

¹**cold** \ˈkōld\ adj **1** : having a low or decidedly subnormal temperature **2** : lacking warmth of feeling **3** : suffering or uncomfortable from lack of warmth — **cold·ly** adv — **cold·ness** n — **in cold blood** : with premeditation : DELIBERATELY

²**cold** n **1** : a condition marked by low temperature; *also* : cold weather **2** : a chilly feeling **3** : a bodily disorder popularly associated with chilling; *esp* : COMMON COLD

³**cold** adv **1** : TOTALLY, FINALLY ⟨stopped them ~⟩ **2** : without notice or preparation

cold-blood·ed \ˈkōld-ˈblə-dəd\ adj **1** : lacking normal human feelings **2** : having a body temperature not internally regulated but close to that of the environment **3** : sensitive to cold

cold cuts n pl : sliced assorted cold cooked meats

cold feet n pl : doubt or fear that prevents action

cold front n : an advancing edge of a cold air mass

cold shoulder n : cold or unsympathetic behavior — **cold-shoul·der** vb

cold sore n : a group of fluid-filled blisters appearing in or about the mouth in the oral form of herpes simplex

cold sweat n : concurrent perspiration and chill usu. associated with fear, pain, or shock

¹**cold turkey** n : abrupt complete cessation of the use of an addictive drug

²**cold turkey** adv **1** : without a period of adjustment **2** : without preparation

cold war n : a conflict characterized by the use of means short of sustained overt military action

cole·slaw \ˈkōl-ˌslò\ n [D *koolsla*, fr. *kool* cabbage + *sla* salad] : a salad made of raw cabbage

col·ic \ˈkä-lik\ n **1** : sharp sudden abdominal pain **2** : a condition marked by recurrent episodes of crying and irritability in an otherwise healthy infant — **col·icky** \ˈkä-li-kē\ adj

col·i·se·um \ˌkä-lə-ˈsē-əm\ n : a large structure esp. for athletic contests

co·li·tis \kō-ˈlī-təs\ n : inflammation of the colon

col·lab·o·rate \kə-ˈla-bə-ˌrāt\ vb **-rat·ed; -rat·ing 1** : to work jointly with others (as in writing a book) **2** : to cooperate with an enemy force occupying one's country — **col·lab·o·ra·tion** \-ˌla-bə-ˈrā-shən\ n — **col·lab·o·ra·tive** \-ˈla-bə-ˌrā-tiv, -b(ə-)rə-\ adj — **col·lab·o·ra·tor** \-ˈla-bə-ˌrā-tər\ n

col·lage \kə-ˈläzh\ n [F, lit., gluing] : an artistic composition of fragments (as of printed matter) pasted on a surface; *also* : a work that combines various elements into a cohesive whole

col·la·gen \ˈkä-lə-jən\ n : any of a group

of fibrous proteins widely found in vertebrate connective tissue

¹col·lapse \kə-'laps\ *vb* col·lapsed; col·laps·ing **1** : to shrink together abruptly **2** : DISINTEGRATE; *also* : to fall in : give way **3** : to break down physically or mentally; *esp* : to fall helpless or unconscious **4** : to fold down compactly — col·laps·ible *adj*

²collapse *n* : BREAKDOWN

¹col·lar \'kä-lər\ *n* **1** : a band, strip, or chain worn around the neck or the neckline of a garment **2** : something resembling a collar — col·lar·less *adj*

²collar *vb* : to seize by the collar; *also* : ARREST, GRAB ⟨~ a fugitive⟩

col·lar·bone \-ˌbōn\ *n* : the bone of the shoulder that joins the breastbone and the shoulder blade

col·lard \'kä-lərd\ *n* : a stalked smooth-leaved kale — usu. used in pl.

col·late \kə-'lāt, 'kä-ˌlāt, 'kō-\ *vb* col·lat·ed; col·lat·ing **1** : to compare (as two texts) carefully and critically **2** : to assemble in proper order

¹col·lat·er·al \kə-'la-tə-rəl\ *adj* **1** : associated but of secondary importance **2** : descended from the same ancestors but not in the same line **3** : PARALLEL **4** : of, relating to, or being collateral used as security; *also* : guaranteed by collateral

²collateral *n* : property (as stocks) used as security for the repayment of a loan

col·la·tion \kä-'lā-shən, kō-\ *n* **1** : a light meal **2** : the act, process, or result of collating

col·league \'kä-ˌlēg\ *n* : an associate esp. in a profession

¹col·lect \'kä-likt, -ˌlekt\ *n* : a short prayer comprising an invocation, petition, and conclusion

²col·lect \kə-'lekt\ *vb* **1** : to bring or come together into one body or place : GATHER **2** : to accumulate (as coins) as a hobby **3** : to gain control of ⟨~ his thoughts⟩ **4** : to receive payment of — col·lect·ible *or* col·lect·able *adj or n* — col·lec·tor \-'lek-tər\ *n*

³col·lect \kə-'lekt\ *adv or adj* : to be paid for by the receiver

col·lect·ed \kə-'lek-təd\ *adj* **1** : gathered together ⟨his ~ poems⟩ **2** : SELF-POSSESSED, CALM

col·lec·tion \kə-'lek-shən\ *n* **1** : the act or process of collecting ⟨garbage ~⟩ **2** : something collected ⟨a stamp ~⟩ **3** : GROUP, AGGREGATE

¹col·lec·tive \kə-'lek-tiv\ *adj* **1** : of, relating to, or denoting a group of individuals considered as a whole **2** : involving all members of a group as distinct from its individuals ⟨~ action⟩ **3** : shared or assumed by all members of the group ⟨a ~ groan⟩ — col·lec·tive·ly *adv*

²collective *n* **1** : GROUP **2** : a cooperative unit or organization

collective bargaining *n* : negotiation between an employer and a labor union

col·lec·tiv·ise *chiefly Brit var of* COLLECTIVIZE

col·lec·tiv·ism \kə-'lek-ti-ˌvi-zəm\ *n* : a political or economic theory advocating collective control esp. over production and distribution

col·lec·tiv·ize \-ˌvīz\ *vb* -ized; -iz·ing : to organize under collective control — col·lec·tiv·i·za·tion \-ˌlek-ti-və-'zā-shən\ *n*

col·leen \kä-'lēn, 'kä-ˌlēn\ *n* : an Irish girl

col·lege \'kä-lij\ *n* [ME, endowed body of clergy or scholars, fr. AF, fr. L *collegium* society, fr. *collega* colleague, fr. *com-* with + *legare* to depute] **1** : a building used for an educational or religious purpose **2** : an institution of higher learning or division of a university granting a bachelor's degree; *also* : an institution offering instruction esp. in a vocational or technical field ⟨barber ~⟩ **3** : an organized body of persons having common interests or duties ⟨~ of cardinals⟩ — col·le·giate \kə-'lē-jət\ *adj*

col·le·gi·al·i·ty \kə-ˌlē-jē-'a-lə-tē\ *n* : the relationship of colleagues

col·le·gian \kə-'lē-jən\ *n* : a college student or recent college graduate

col·le·gi·um \kə-'le-gē-əm, -'lā-\ *n, pl* -gia \-gē-ə\ *or* -gi·ums : a group in which each member has approximately equal power

col·lide \kə-'līd\ *vb* col·lid·ed; col·lid·ing **1** : to come together with solid impact **2** : to come into conflict : CLASH

col·lid·er \kə-'lī-dər\ *n* : a particle accelerator in which two beams of particles are made to collide

col·lie \'kä-lē\ *n* : any of a breed of large dogs developed in Scotland for herding sheep that occur in rough-coated and smooth-coated varieties

col·lier \'käl-yər\ *n* **1** : a coal miner **2** : a ship for carrying coal

col·liery \'käl-yə-rē\ *n, pl* -lier·ies : a coal mine and its associated buildings

col·li·mate \'kä-lə-ˌmāt\ *vb* -mat·ed; -mat·ing : to make (as light rays) parallel

col·li·sion \kə-'li-zhən\ *n* : an act or instance of colliding

col·lo·ca·tion \ˌkä-lə-'kä-shən\ *n* : the act or result of placing or arranging together; *esp* : a noticeable arrangement or conjoining of linguistic elements (as words)

col·loid \'kä-ˌlȯid\ *n* : a substance in the form of submicroscopic particles that when in solution or suspension do not settle out; *also* : such a substance together with the medium in which it is dispersed — col·loi·dal \kə-'lȯi-d°l\ *adj*

colloq *abbr* colloquial

col·lo·qui·al \kə-'lō-kwē-əl\ *adj* : of, relating to, or characteristic of conversation and esp. of familiar and informal conversation

col·lo·qui·al·ism \-'lō-kwē-ə-ˌli-zəm\ *n* : a colloquial expression

col·lo·qui·um \kə-'lō-kwē-əm\ *n, pl* -qui·ums *or* -quia \-ə\ : CONFERENCE, SEMINAR

col·lo·quy \'kä-lə-kwē\ *n, pl* -quies : a usu. formal conversation or conference

col·lu·sion \kə-'lü-zhən\ *n* : secret agreement or cooperation for an illegal or deceitful purpose — col·lu·sive \-siv\ *adj*

Colo *abbr* Colorado

co·logne \kə-'lōn\ *n* [*Cologne*, Germany]

: a perfumed liquid — **co·logned** \-ˈlōnd\ adj

Co·lom·bi·an \kə-ˈləm-bē-ən\ n : a native or inhabitant of Colombia — **Colombian** adj

¹**co·lon** \ˈkō-lən\ n, pl **colons** or **co·la** \-lə\ : the part of the large intestine extending from the cecum to the rectum — **co·lon·ic** \kō-ˈlä-nik\ adj

²**colon** n, pl **colons** : a punctuation mark : used esp. to direct attention to following matter (as a list)

co·lón also **co·lone** \kə-ˈlōn\ n, pl **co·lones** \-ˈlō-ˌnās\ — see MONEY table

col·o·nel \ˈkər-nᵊl\ n [alter. of coronel, fr. MF, fr. It colonnello column of soldiers, colonel, ultim. fr. L columna column] : a commissioned officer (as in the army) ranking next below a brigadier general

¹**co·lo·nial** \kə-ˈlō-nē-əl\ adj 1 : of, relating to, or characteristic of a colony; also : possessing or composed of colonies 2 often cap : of or relating to the original 13 colonies forming the U.S.

²**colonial** n 1 : a member or inhabitant of a colony 2 : a house built in the style of the American colonial period

co·lo·nial·ism \-ˌi-zəm\ n : control by one power over a dependent area or people; also : a policy advocating or based on such control — **co·lo·nial·ist** \-list\ n or adj

col·o·nise Brit var of COLONIZE

col·o·nist \ˈkä-lə-nist\ n 1 : COLONIAL 2 : one that colonizes or settles in a new country

col·o·nize \ˈkä-lə-ˌnīz\ vb -nized; -nizing 1 : to establish a colony in or on 2 : SETTLE — **col·o·ni·za·tion** \ˌkä-lə-nə-ˈzā-shən\ n — **col·o·niz·er** n

col·on·nade \ˌkä-lə-ˈnād\ n : an evenly spaced row of columns usu. supporting the base of a roof structure

co·lo·nos·co·py \ˌkō-lə-ˈnäs-kə-pē\ n, pl -pies : endoscopic examination of the colon — **co·lon·o·scope** \kō-ˈlä-nə-ˌskōp\ n

col·o·ny \ˈkä-lə-nē\ n, pl -nies 1 : a body of people living in a new territory; also : the territory inhabited by these people 2 : a localized population of organisms ⟨a ∼ of bees⟩ 3 : a group with common interests situated in close association ⟨a writers' ∼⟩; also : the area occupied by such a group

col·o·phon \ˈkä-lə-fən, -ˌfän\ n 1 : an inscription placed at the end of a book with facts relative to its production 2 : a distinctive symbol used by a printer or publisher

¹**col·or** \ˈkə-lər\ n 1 : a phenomenon of light (as red or blue) or visual perception that enables one to differentiate otherwise identical objects; also : a hue as contrasted with black, white, or gray 2 : APPEARANCE 3 : complexion tint 4 pl : FLAG; also : military service ⟨a call to the ∼s⟩ 5 : VIVIDNESS, INTEREST — **col·or·ful** adj — **col·or·less** adj

²**color** vb 1 : to give color to; also : to change the color of 2 : BLUSH

Col·o·ra·do potato beetle \ˌkä-lə-ˈra-dō-, -ˈrä-\ n : a black-and-yellow striped beetle that feeds on the leaves of the potato

col·or·ation \ˌkə-lə-ˈrā-shən\ n : use or arrangement of colors

col·or·a·tu·ra \ˌkə-lə-rə-ˈtu̇r-ə, -ˈtyu̇r-\ n 1 : elaborate ornamentation in vocal music 2 : a soprano specializing in coloratura

col·or–blind \ˈkə-lər-ˌblīnd\ adj 1 : partially or totally unable to distinguish one or more chromatic colors 2 : not influenced by differences of race — **color blindness** n

co·lo·rec·tal \ˌkō-lō-ˈrek-tᵊl\ adj : relating to or affecting the colon and rectum ⟨∼ cancer⟩

col·ored \ˈkə-lərd\ adj 1 : having color 2 : SLANTED, BIASED

col·or·fast \ˈkə-lər-ˌfast\ adj : having color that does not fade or run — **col·or·fast·ness** n

col·or·ize \ˈkə-lə-ˌrīz\ vb -ized; -iz·ing : to add color to by means of a computer — **col·or·i·za·tion** \ˌkə-lə-rə-ˈzā-shən\ n

co·los·sal \kə-ˈlä-səl\ adj : of very great size or degree ⟨a ∼ feat⟩

Co·los·sians \kə-ˈlä-shənz\ n — see BIBLE table

co·los·sus \kə-ˈlä-səs\ n, pl **co·los·si** \-ˌsī\ [L] : a gigantic statue; also : something of immense size or power

col·our chiefly Brit var of COLOR

col·por·teur \ˈkäl-ˌpȯr-tər\ n [F] : a peddler of religious books

colt \ˈkōlt\ n : FOAL; also : a young male horse, ass, or zebra — **colt·ish** adj

col·um·bine \ˈkä-ləm-ˌbīn\ n [ME, fr. AF, fr. ML columbina, fr. L, fem. of columbinus dovelike, fr. columba dove] : any of a genus of plants with showy spurred flowers that are related to the buttercups

co·lum·bi·um \kə-ˈləm-bē-əm\ n : NIOBIUM

Columbus Day \kə-ˈləm-bəs-\ n : the 2d Monday in October or formerly October 12 observed as a legal holiday in many states in commemoration of the landing of Columbus

col·umn \ˈkä-ləm\ n 1 : one of two or more vertical sections of a printed page; also : one in a usu. regular series of articles (as in a newspaper) 2 : a supporting pillar; esp : one consisting of a usu. round shaft, a capital, and a base 3 : something resembling a column ⟨a ∼ of water⟩ 4 : a long row (as of soldiers) 5 : a statistical category tracked vertically (as on a spreadsheet) — **co·lum·nar** \kə-ˈləm-nər\ adj

col·um·nist \ˈkä-ləm-nist\ n : a person who writes a newspaper or magazine column

com abbr 1 comedy; comic 2 comma 3 commercial organization

co·ma \ˈkō-mə\ n : a state of deep unconsciousness caused by disease, injury, or poison — **co·ma·tose** \ˈkō-mə-ˌtōs, ˈkä-\ adj

Co·man·che \kə-ˈman-chē\ n, pl **Co-**

manche *or* **Comanches** : a member of an American Indian people ranging from Wyoming and Nebraska south into New Mexico and Texas

¹comb \'kōm\ *n* **1** : a toothed instrument for arranging the hair or for separating and cleaning textile fibers **2** : a fleshy crest on the head of a fowl **3** : HONEYCOMB

²comb *vb* **1** : to pass a comb through **2** : to search through systematically

³comb *abbr* combination; combining

com·bat \käm-'bat, 'käm-,bat\ *vb* **-bat·ed** *or* **-bat·ted; -bat·ing** *or* **-bat·ting** **1** : FIGHT, CONTEND **2** : to struggle against : OPPOSE — **combat** \'käm-,bat\ *n* — **com·bat·ant** \kəm-'ba-tᵊnt, 'käm-bə-tənt\ *n* — **com·bat·ive** \kəm-'ba-tiv\ *adj*

combat fatigue *n* : a traumatic psychological reaction occurring under wartime conditions (as combat) that cause intense stress

comb·er \'kō-mər\ *n* **1** : one that combs **2** : a long curling wave of the sea

com·bi·na·tion \,käm-bə-'nā-shən\ *n* **1** : a result or product of combining **2** : a sequence of letters or numbers chosen in setting a lock **3** : the act or process of combining; *also* : the quality or state of being combined

¹com·bine \kəm-'bīn\ *vb* **com·bined; com·bin·ing** : to become one : UNITE

²com·bine \'käm-,bīn\ *n* **1** : a combination esp. of business or political interests **2** : a machine that harvests and threshes grain while moving over a field

comb·ings \'kō-miŋz\ *n pl* : loose hairs or fibers removed by a comb

combining form *n* : a linguistic form that occurs only in compounds or derivatives

com·bo \'käm-bō\ *n, pl* **combos** : a small jazz or dance band

comb-over \'kōm-,ō-vər\ *n* : a hairstyle in which hair from the side of the head is combed over a bald spot

com·bus·ti·ble \kəm-'bəs-tə-bəl\ *adj* **1** : capable of being burned **2** : easily excited — **com·bus·ti·bil·i·ty** \-,bəs-tə-'bi-lə-tē\ *n* — **combustible** *n*

com·bus·tion \kəm-'bəs-chən\ *n* **1** : an act or instance of burning **2** : slow oxidation (as in the animal body)

comdg *abbr* commanding

comdr *abbr* · commander

comdt *abbr* commandant

come \'kəm\ *vb* **came** \'kām\; **come; com·ing** \'kə-miŋ\ **1** : APPROACH **2** : ARRIVE **3** : to reach the point of being or becoming 〈∼ to a boil〉 **4** : AMOUNT 〈the bill *came* to $10〉 **5** : to take place **6** : ORIGINATE, ARISE 〈wine ∼s from grapes〉 **7** : to be available 〈∼s in three sizes〉 **8** : REACH, EXTEND 〈grass that ∼s to our knees〉 — **come across** **1** : to make a specified impression 〈*came across* as rude〉 **2** : to find esp. by chance 〈*came across* an intriguing story〉 — **come clean** : CONFESS — **come into** : ACQUIRE, ACHIEVE — **come of age** : MATURE — **come to grips with** : to meet or deal with frankly — **come to**

pass : HAPPEN — **come to terms** : to reach an agreement

come·back \'kəm-,bak\ *n* **1** : RETORT **2** : a return to a former position or condition — **come back** *vb*

co·me·di·an \kə-'mē-dē-ən\ *n* **1** : an actor in comedy **2** : a comic person; *esp* : an entertainer specializing in comedy

co·me·di·enne \-,mē-dē-'en\ *n* : a woman who is a comedian

come·down \'kəm-,daún\ *n* : a descent in rank or dignity

com·e·dy \'kä-mə-dē\ *n, pl* **-dies** [ME, narrative that ends happily, fr. ML *comoedia*, fr. L, play with a happy ending, fr. Gk *kōmōidia*, fr. *kōmos* revel + *aeidein* to sing] **1** : a light amusing play with a happy ending **2** : a literary work treating a comic theme or written in a comic style **3** : humorous entertainment — **co·me·dic** \kə-'mē-dik\ *adj*

come·ly \'kəm-lē\ *adj* **come·li·er; -est** : ATTRACTIVE, HANDSOME — **come·li·ness** *n*

come off *vb* **1** : APPEAR, SEEM 〈*comes off* as crass〉 **2** : SUCCEED **3** : to have recently ended 〈is *coming off* surgery〉

come-on \'kə-,món, -,män\ *n* : INDUCEMENT, LURE

come out *vb* **1** : to come into public view **2** : to declare oneself **3** : TURN OUT 6 〈everything *came out* all right〉 — **come out with** : SAY 1

com·er \'kə-mər\ *n* **1** : one that comes 〈all ∼s〉 **2** : a promising beginner

¹co·mes·ti·ble \kə-'mes-tə-bəl\ *adj* : EDIBLE

²comestible *n* : FOOD — usu. used in pl.

com·et \'kä-mət\ *n* [ME *comete*, fr. OE *cometa*, fr. L, fr. Gk *komētēs*, lit., longhaired, fr. *komē* hair] : a small bright celestial body that develops a long tail when near the sun

come to *vb* : to regain consciousness

come·up·pance \,kə-'mə-pəns\ *n* : a deserved rebuke or penalty

com·fit \'kəm-fət\ *n* : a candied fruit or nut

¹com·fort \'kəm-fərt\ *vb* **1** : to give strength and hope to **2** : CONSOLE

²comfort *n* **1** : CONSOLATION **2** : freedom from pain, trouble, or anxiety; *also* : something that gives such freedom

com·fort·able \'kəm-fər-tə-bəl, 'kəmftər-\ *adj* **1** : providing comfort or security **2** : feeling at ease — **com·fort·ably** \-blē\ *adv*

com·fort·er \'kəm-fər-tər\ *n* **1** : one that comforts **2** : QUILT

com·frey \'kəm-frē\ *n, pl* **comfreys** : any of a genus of perennial herbs that have coarse hairy leaves and are often used in herbal remedies

com·fy \'kəm-fē\ *adj* : COMFORTABLE

¹com·ic \'kä-mik\ *adj* **1** : relating to comedy or comic strips **2** : provoking laughter or amusement ◆ *Synonyms* LAUGHABLE, FUNNY, FARCICAL — **com·i·cal** *adj*

²comic *n* **1** : COMEDIAN **2** *pl* : the part of a newspaper devoted to comic strips

comic book *n* : a magazine containing sequences of comic strips

comic strip *n* : a group of cartoons in narrative sequence

coming *adj* 1 : APPROACHING, NEXT 2 : gaining importance ⟨the ~ trend⟩

co·mi·ty \'kä-mə-tē, 'kō-\ *n, pl* **-ties** : friendly civility : COURTESY

coml *abbr* commercial

comm *abbr* 1 command; commander 2 commerce; commercial 3 commission; commissioner 4 committee 5 common 6 commonwealth

com·ma \'kä-mə\ *n* : a punctuation mark, used esp. as a mark of separation within the sentence

¹**com·mand** \kə-'mand\ *vb* 1 : to direct authoritatively : ORDER 2 : DOMINATE, CONTROL, GOVERN 3 : to overlook from a strategic position

²**command** *n* 1 : an order given 2 : ability to control : MASTERY 3 : the act of commanding 4 : a signal that actuates a device (as a computer); *also* : the activation of a device by means of a signal 5 : a body of troops under a commander; *also* : an area or position that one commands 6 : a position of highest authority

com·man·dant \'kä-mən-ˌdant, -ˌdänt\ *n* : an officer in command

com·man·deer \ˌkä-mən-'dir\ *vb* : to take possession of by force

com·mand·er \kə-'man-dər\ *n* 1 : LEADER, CHIEF; *esp* : an officer commanding an army or subdivision of an army 2 : a commissioned officer in the navy ranking next below a captain

commander in chief : the supreme commander of the armed forces

com·mand·ment \kə-'mand-mənt\ *n* : COMMAND, ORDER; *esp* : any of the Ten Commandments

command module *n* : a space vehicle module designed to carry the crew and reentry equipment

com·man·do \kə-'man-dō\ *n, pl* **-dos** or **-does** : a member of a military unit trained for surprise raids

command sergeant major *n* : a noncommissioned officer in the army ranking above a sergeant major

com·mem·o·rate \kə-'me-mə-ˌrāt\ *vb* **-rat·ed; -rat·ing** 1 : to call or recall to mind 2 : to serve as a memorial of — **com·mem·o·ra·tion** \-ˌme-mə-'rā-shən\ *n*

com·mem·o·ra·tive \kə-'mem-rə-tiv, -'me-mə-ˌrā-tiv\ *adj* : intended to commemorate an event ⟨a ~ stamp⟩

com·mence \kə-'mens\ *vb* **com·menced; com·menc·ing** : BEGIN, START

com·mence·ment \-mənt\ *n* 1 : the act or time of a beginning 2 : the graduation exercises of a school or college

com·mend \kə-'mend\ *vb* 1 : to commit to one's care 2 : RECOMMEND 3 : PRAISE — **com·mend·able** \-'men-də-bəl\ *adj* — **com·mend·ably** \-blē\ *adv* — **com·men·da·tion** \ˌkä-mən-'dā-shən, -ˌmen-\ *n* — **com·mend·er** *n*

com·men·su·ra·ble \kə-'men-sə-rə-bəl\ *adj* : having a common measure or a common divisor

com·men·su·rate \kə-'men-sə-rət, -'men-chə-\ *adj* : equal in measure or extent; *also* : PROPORTIONAL, CORRESPONDING ⟨a job ~ with her abilities⟩

com·ment \'kä-ˌment\ *n* 1 : an expression of opinion 2 : an explanatory, illustrative, or critical note or observation : REMARK — **comment** *vb*

com·men·tary \'kä-mən-ˌter-ē\ *n, pl* **-tar·ies** : a systematic series of comments

com·men·ta·tor \-ˌtā-tər\ *n* : one who comments; *esp* : a person who discusses news events on radio or television

com·merce \'kä-(ˌ)mərs\ *n* : the buying and selling of commodities : TRADE

¹**com·mer·cial** \kə-'mər-shəl\ *adj* : having to do with commerce; *also* : designed for profit or for mass appeal — **com·mer·cial·ly** *adv*

²**commercial** *n* : an advertisement broadcast on radio or television

com·mer·cial·ise *Brit var of* COMMERCIALIZE

com·mer·cial·ism \kə-'mər-shə-ˌli-zəm\ *n* 1 : a spirit, method, or practice characteristic of business 2 : excessive emphasis on profit

com·mer·cial·ize \-ˌlīz\ *vb* **-ized; -iz·ing** 1 : to manage on a business basis for profit 2 : to exploit for profit

com·mi·na·tion \ˌkä-mə-'nā-shən\ *n* : DENUNCIATION — **com·mi·na·to·ry** \'kä-mə-nə-ˌtȯr-ē\ *adj*

com·min·gle \kə-'miŋ-gəl\ *vb* : MINGLE, BLEND

com·mis·er·ate \kə-'mi-zə-ˌrāt\ *vb* **-at·ed; -at·ing** : to feel or express pity : SYMPATHIZE — **com·mis·er·a·tion** \-ˌmi-zə-'rā-shən\ *n*

com·mis·sar \'kä-mə-ˌsär\ *n* [Russ *komissar*] : a Communist party official

com·mis·sar·i·at \ˌkä-mə-'ser-ē-ət\ *n* 1 : a system for supplying troops with food 2 : a department headed by a commissar

com·mis·sary \'kä-mə-ˌser-ē\ *n, pl* **-sar·ies** : a store for equipment and provisions esp. for military personnel

¹**com·mis·sion** \kə-'mi-shən\ *n* 1 : a warrant granting certain powers and imposing certain duties 2 : a certificate conferring military rank and authority 3 : authority to act as agent for another; *also* : something to be done by an agent 4 : a body of persons charged with performing a duty 5 : the doing of some act ⟨~ of a crime⟩; *also* : the thing done 6 : the allowance made to an agent for transacting business for another

²**commission** *vb* 1 : to give a commission to 2 : to order to be made ⟨~ a portrait⟩ 3 : to put (a ship) into a state of readiness for service

commissioned officer *n* : an officer of the armed forces holding rank by a commission from the president

com·mis·sion·er \kə-'mi-shə-nər\ *n* 1 : a member of a commission 2 : an official in charge of a department of public service ⟨a police ∼⟩ **3** : the administrative head of a professional sport — **com·mis·sion·er·ship** *n*

com·mit \kə-'mit\ *vb* **com·mit·ted; com·mit·ting** **1** : to put into charge or trust : ENTRUST **2** : to put in a prison or mental institution **3** : TRANSFER, CONSIGN **4** : to carry into action : PERPETRATE ⟨∼ a crime⟩ **5** : to pledge or assign to some particular course or use — **com·mit·ment** *n* — **com·mit·tal** *n*

com·mit·tee \kə-'mi-tē\ *n* : a body of persons selected to consider and act or report on some matter — **com·mit·tee·man** \-mən\ *n* — **com·mit·tee·wom·an** \-ˌwu̇-mən\ *n*

commo *abbr* commodore

com·mode \kə-'mōd\ *n* [F, fr. *commode*, adj., suitable, convenient, fr. L *commodus*, fr. *com-* with + *modus* measure] **1** : a movable washstand with cupboard below **2** : TOILET 3

com·mo·di·ous \kə-'mō-dē-əs\ *adj* : comfortably spacious : ROOMY

com·mod·i·ty \kə-'mä-də-tē\ *n, pl* **-ties** **1** : a product of agriculture or mining **2** : an article of commerce **3** : something useful or valued ⟨that valuable ∼ patience⟩

com·mo·dore \'kä-mə-ˌdȯr\ *n* **1** : a commissioned officer in the navy ranking next below a rear admiral **2** : an officer commanding a group of merchant ships **3** : the chief officer of a yacht club

¹com·mon \'kä-mən\ *adj* **1** : belonging to or serving the community : PUBLIC **2** : shared by a number in a group **3** : widely or generally known, found, or observed ⟨∼ knowledge⟩ **4** : FAMILIAR : VERNACULAR **3** ⟨∼ names of plants⟩ **5** : not above the average esp. in social status ◆ *Synonyms* UNIVERSAL, GENERAL, GENERIC — **com·mon·ly** *adv*

²common *n* **1** *pl* : the common people **2** *pl* : a dining hall **3** *pl, cap* : the lower house of the British and Canadian parliaments **4** : a piece of land subject to common use — **in common** : shared together

com·mon·al·ty \'kä-mə-nᵊl-tē\ *n, pl* **-ties** : the common people

common cold *n* : a contagious respiratory disease caused by a virus and characterized by a sore, swollen, and inflamed nose and throat, usu. by much mucus, and by coughing and sneezing

common denominator *n* **1** : a common multiple of the denominators of a group of fractions **2** : a common trait or theme

common divisor *n* : a number or expression that divides two or more numbers or expressions without remainder

com·mon·er \'kä-mə-nər\ *n* : one of the common people : a person having no rank of nobility

common fraction *n* : a fraction (as ½ or ¾) in which the numerator and denominator are both integers and are separated by a horizontal or slanted line

common law *n* : a group of legal practices and traditions based on judges' decisions and social customs and usu. having

the same force as laws passed by legislative bodies

common logarithm *n* : a logarithm whose base is 10

common market *n* : an economic association formed to remove trade barriers among members

common multiple *n* : a multiple of each of two or more numbers or expressions

¹com·mon·place \'kä-mən-ˌplās\ *n* : something that is ordinary or trite

²commonplace *adj* : ORDINARY

common sense *n* : ordinary good sense and judgment — **com·mon·sen·si·cal** \ˌkä-mən-'sen-si-kəl\ *adj*

com·mon·weal \'kä-mən-ˌwēl\ *n,* **1** *archaic* : COMMONWEALTH **2** : the general welfare

com·mon·wealth \-ˌwelth\ *n* **1** : the body of people politically organized into a state **2** : STATE; *also* : an association or federation of autonomous states

com·mo·tion \kə-'mō-shən\ *n* **1** : DISTURBANCE, UPRISING **2** : AGITATION

com·mu·nal \kə-'myü-nᵊl, 'käm-yə-nᵊl\ *adj* **1** : of or relating to a commune or community **2** : marked by collective ownership and use of property **3** : shared or used in common

¹com·mune \kə-'myün\ *vb* **com·muned; com·mun·ing** : to communicate intimately ⟨∼ with nature⟩

²com·mune \'käm-ˌyün; kə-'myün\ *n* **1** : the smallest administrative district in some European countries **2** : a community organized on a communal basis

com·mu·ni·ca·ble \kə-'myü-ni-kə-bəl\ *adj* : capable of being communicated ⟨∼ diseases⟩ — **com·mu·ni·ca·bil·i·ty** \-ˌmyü-ni-kə-'bi-lə-tē\ *n*

com·mu·ni·cant \-'myü-ni-kənt\ *n* **1** : a church member entitled to receive Communion **2** : one that communicates; *esp* : INFORMANT

com·mu·ni·cate \kə-'myü-nə-ˌkāt\ *vb* **-cat·ed; -cat·ing** **1** : to make known **2** : to pass from one to another : TRANSMIT **3** : to receive Communion **4** : to be in communication **5** : JOIN, CONNECT — **com·mu·ni·ca·tor** \-ˌkā-tər\ *n*

com·mu·ni·ca·tion \kə-ˌmyü-nə-'kā-shən\ *n* **1** : an act of transmitting **2** : MESSAGE **3** : exchange of information or opinions **4** : a means of communicating — **com·mu·ni·ca·tive** \-'myü-nə-ˌkä-tiv, -ni-kə-tiv\ *adj*

com·mu·nion \kə-'myü-nyən\ *n* **1** : a sharing of something with others **2** *cap* : a Christian sacrament in which bread and wine are consumed as the substance or symbols of Christ's body and blood in commemoration of the death of Christ **3** : intimate fellowship or rapport **4** : a body of Christians having a common faith and discipline

com·mu·ni·qué \kə-'myü-nə-ˌkā, -ˌmyü-nə-'kā\ *n* : BULLETIN 1

com·mu·nism \'käm-yə-ˌni-zəm\ *n* **1** : social organization in which goods are held in common **2** : a theory of social organization advocating common ownership of means of production and a distribution of products of industry based on need **3** *cap* : a political doctrine based on revolutionary Marxist socialism that was the official ideology of the U.S.S.R. and some other countries; *also* : a system of government in which one party controls state-owned means of production — **com·mu·nist** \-nist\ *n or adj, often cap* — **com·mu·nis·tic** \ˌkäm-yə-ˈnis-tik\ *adj, often cap*

com·mu·ni·ty \kə-ˈmyü-nə-tē\ *n, pl* **-ties** **1** : a body of people living in the same place under the same laws; *also* : a natural population of plants and animals that interact ecologically and live in one place (as a pond) **2** : society at large **3** : joint ownership 〈~ of goods〉 **4** : SIMILARITY, LIKENESS 〈~ of interests〉

community college *n* : a 2-year government-supported college that offers an associate degree

community property *n* : property held jointly by husband and wife

com·mu·ta·tion \ˌkäm-yə-ˈtā-shən\ *n* : substitution of one form of payment or penalty for another

com·mu·ta·tive \ˈkäm-yə-ˌtā-tiv, kə-ˈmyü-tə-\ *adj* : of, having, or being the property that the result obtained using a mathematical operation on any two elements of a set does not differ with the order in which the elements are used 〈*a* x *b* = *b* x *a* because multiplication is ~〉 — **com·mu·ta·tiv·i·ty** \kə-ˌmyü-tə-ˈti-və-tē, ˌkäm-yə-tə-\ *n*

com·mu·ta·tor \ˈkäm-yə-ˌtā-tər\ *n* : a device (as on a generator or motor) for changing the direction of electric current

¹com·mute \kə-ˈmyüt\ *vb* **com·mut·ed; com·mut·ing** **1** : EXCHANGE **2** : to revoke (a sentence) and impose a milder penalty **3** : to travel back and forth regularly — **com·mut·er** *n*

²commute *n* : a trip made in commuting

comp *abbr* **1** comparative; compare **2** compensation **3** compiled; compiler **4** composition; compositor **5** compound **6** comprehensive **7** comptroller

¹com·pact \kəm-ˈpakt, ˈkäm-ˌpakt\ *adj* **1** : SOLID, DENSE **2** : BRIEF, SUCCINCT **3** : occupying a small volume by efficient use of space 〈~ camera〉 — **com·pact·ly** *adv* — **com·pact·ness** *n*

²compact *vb* : to pack together : COMPRESS — **com·pac·tor** \kəm-ˈpak-tər, ˈkäm-ˌpak-\ *n*

³com·pact \ˈkäm-ˌpakt\ *n* **1** : a small case for cosmetics **2** : a small automobile

⁴com·pact \ˈkäm-ˌpakt\ *n* : AGREEMENT, COVENANT

compact disc \ˈkäm-ˌpakt-\ *n* : CD

com·pa·dre \kəm-ˈpä-drā\ *n* : a close friend : BUDDY

¹com·pan·ion \kəm-ˈpan-yən\ *n* [ME *compainoun*, fr. AF *cumpaing, cumpaignun*, fr. LL *companion-, companio*, fr. L *com-* together + *panis* bread] **1** : an intimate friend or associate : COMRADE **2** : one that is closely connected with something similar **3** : a celestial body that appears close to another but that may not be asso-

ciated with it in space — **com·pan·ion·able** *adj* — **com·pan·ion·ship** *n*

²companion *n* : COMPANIONWAY

com·pan·ion·way \-ˌwā\ *n* : a ship's stairway from one deck to another

com·pa·ny \ˈkəm-pə-nē\ *n, pl* **-nies** **1** : association with others : FELLOWSHIP; *also* : COMPANIONS **2** : GUESTS **3** : a group of persons or things **4** : an infantry unit consisting of two or more platoons and normally commanded by a captain **5** : a group of musical or dramatic performers **6** : the officers and crew of a ship **7** : an association of persons for carrying on a business ♦ *Synonyms* PARTY, BAND, TROOP, TROUPE, CORPS, OUTFIT

com·pa·ra·ble \ˈkäm-pə-rə-bəl, -prə-\ *adj* : capable of being compared 〈singers of ~ talent〉 ♦ *Synonyms* PARALLEL, SIMILAR, LIKE, ALIKE, CORRESPONDING — **com·pa·ra·bil·i·ty** \ˌkäm-pə-rə-ˈbi-lə-tē\ *n*

¹com·par·a·tive \kəm-ˈper-ə-tiv\ *adj* **1** : of, relating to, or constituting the degree of grammatical comparison that denotes increase in quality, quantity, or relation **2** : RELATIVE 〈a ~ stranger〉 — **par·a·tive·ly** *adv*

²comparative *n* : the comparative degree or form in a language

¹com·pare \kəm-ˈper\ *vb* **com·pared; com·par·ing** **1** : to represent as similar : LIKEN **2** : to examine for likenesses and differences **3** : to inflect or modify (an adjective or adverb) according to the degrees of comparison

²compare *n* : the possibility of comparing 〈beauty beyond ~〉

com·par·i·son \kəm-ˈper-ə-sən\ *n* **1** : the act of comparing **2** : change in the form of an adjective or adverb to show different levels of quality, quantity, or relation

com·part·ment \kəm-ˈpärt-mənt\ *n* **1** : a separate division **2** : a section of an enclosed space : ROOM

com·part·men·tal·ise Brit var of COMPARTMENTALIZE

com·part·men·tal·ize \kəm-ˌpärt-ˈmen-t³l-ˌīz\ *vb* **-ized; -iz·ing** : to separate into compartments

¹com·pass \ˈkəm-pəs, ˈkäm-\ *vb* [ME, fr. AF *cumpasser* to measure, fr. VL **compassare* to pace off, fr. L *com-* + *passus* pace] **1** : CONTRIVE, PLOT **2** : ENCIRCLE, ENCOMPASS **3** : BRING ABOUT, ACHIEVE

²compass *n* **1** : BOUNDARY, CIRCUMFERENCE **2** : an enclosed space **3** : RANGE, SCOPE **4** : a device for determining direction by means of a magnetic needle swinging freely and pointing to the magnetic north; *also* : a nonmagnetic device that indicates direction **5** : an instrument for drawing circles or transferring measurements consisting of two legs joined by a pivot

com·pas·sion \kəm-ˈpa-shən\ *n* : sympathetic feeling : PITY, MERCY — **com·pas·sion·ate** \-shə-nət\ *adj* — **com·pas·sion·ate·ly** *adv*

com·pat·i·ble \kəm-ˈpa-tə-bəl\ *adj* : able to exist or act together harmoniously ⟨~ colors⟩ ⟨~ drugs⟩ ✦ *Synonyms* CONSONANT, CONGENIAL, SYMPATHETIC — **com·pat·i·bil·i·ty** \-ˌpa-tə-ˈbi-lə-tē\ *n*

com·pa·tri·ot \kəm-ˈpā-trē-ət, -ˌät\ *n* : a fellow countryman

com·peer \ˈkäm-ˌpir\ *n* : EQUAL, PEER

com·pel \kəm-ˈpel\ *vb* **com·pelled; com·pel·ling** : to drive or urge with force

com·pen·di·ous \kəm-ˈpen-dē-əs\ *adj* : concise and comprehensive; *also* : COMPREHENSIVE ⟨a ~ almanac⟩

com·pen·di·um \kəm-ˈpen-dē-əm\ *n, pl* **-di·ums** *or* **-dia** \-ə\ **1** : a brief summary of a larger work or of a field of knowledge **2** : COLLECTION

com·pen·sate \ˈkäm-pən-ˌsāt\ *vb* **-sat·ed; -sat·ing 1** : to be equivalent to : make up for **2** : PAY, REMUNERATE ✦ *Synonyms* BALANCE, OFFSET, COUNTERBALANCE, COUNTERPOISE — **com·pen·sa·tion** \ˌkäm-pən-ˈsā-shən\ *n* — **com·pen·sa·to·ry** \kəm-ˈpen-sə-ˌtȯr-ē\ *adj*

com·pete \kəm-ˈpēt\ *vb* **com·pet·ed; com·pet·ing** : CONTEND, VIE ⟨~ for the title⟩ ⟨~ for customers⟩

com·pe·tence \ˈkäm-pə-təns\ *n* **1** : adequate means for subsistence **2** : FITNESS, ABILITY

com·pe·ten·cy \-tən-sē\ *n, pl* **-cies** : COMPETENCE

com·pe·tent \-tənt\ *adj* : CAPABLE, FIT, QUALIFIED ⟨a ~ mechanic⟩ ⟨a ~ juror⟩

com·pe·ti·tion \ˌkäm-pə-ˈti-shən\ *n* **1** : the act of competing : RIVALRY **2** : CONTEST, MATCH; *also* : one's competitors — **com·pet·i·tive** \kəm-ˈpe-tə-tiv\ *adj* — **com·pet·i·tive·ly** *adv* — **com·pet·i·tive·ness** *n*

com·pet·i·tor \kəm-ˈpe-tə-tər\ *n* : one that competes : RIVAL

com·pile \kəm-ˈpī(-ə)l\ *vb* **com·piled; com·pil·ing** [ME, fr. AF *compiler*, fr. L *compilare* to plunder] **1** : to compose out of materials from other documents **2** : to collect and edit into a volume **3** : to translate (a computer program) with a compiler **4** : to build up gradually ⟨~ a record of four wins and two losses⟩ — **com·pi·la·tion** \ˌkäm-pə-ˈlā-shən\ *n*

com·pil·er \kəm-ˈpī-lər\ *n* **1** : one that compiles **2** : a computer program that translates any program correctly written in a specific programming language into machine language

com·pla·cence \kəm-ˈplā-s°ns\ *n* : COMPLACENCY — **com·pla·cent** \-s°nt\ *adj* — **com·pla·cent·ly** *adv*

com·pla·cen·cy \-s°n-sē\ *n, pl* **-cies** : SATISFACTION; *esp* : SELF-SATISFACTION

com·plain \kəm-ˈplān\ *vb* **1** : to express grief, pain, or discontent **2** : to make a formal accusation — **com·plain·ant** *n* — **com·plain·er** *n*

com·plaint \kəm-ˈplānt\ *n* **1** : expression of grief, pain, or dissatisfaction **2** : a bodily ailment or disease **3** : a formal accusation against a person

com·plai·sance \kəm-ˈplā-s°ns, ˌkäm-plā-ˈzans\ *n* [F] : disposition to please — **com·plai·sant** \-s°nt, -ˈzant\ *adj* — **com·plai·sant·ly** *adv*

com·pleat \kəm-ˈplēt\ *adj* : PROFICIENT

com·plect·ed \kəm-ˈplek-təd\ *adj* : having a specified facial complexion ⟨dark-complected⟩

¹**com·ple·ment** \ˈkäm-plə-mənt\ *n* **1** : something that fills up or completes; *also* : the full quantity, number, or amount that makes a thing complete **2** : an added word by which a predicate is made complete **3** : a group of proteins in blood that combines with antibodies to destroy antigens — **com·ple·men·ta·ry** \ˌkäm-plə-ˈmen-t(ə-)rē\ *adj*

²**com·ple·ment** \-ˌment\ *vb* : to be complementary to : fill out

complementary medicine *n* : ALTERNATIVE MEDICINE

¹**com·plete** \kəm-ˈplēt\ *adj* **com·plet·er; -est 1** : having all parts or elements **2** : brought to an end **3** : fully carried out; *also* : ABSOLUTE **2** ⟨~ silence⟩ — **com·plete·ly** *adv* — **com·plete·ness** *n* — **com·ple·tion** \-ˈplē-shən\ *n*

²**complete** *vb* **com·plet·ed; com·plet·ing 1** : FINISH, CONCLUDE **2** : to make whole or perfect ⟨the hat ~s the outfit⟩

com·plet·ist \kəm-ˈplē-tist\ *n* : one who wants to make something (as a collection) complete

¹**com·plex** \ˈkäm-ˌpleks\ *n* **1** : a whole made up of or involving intricately interrelated elements **2** : a group of repressed desires and memories that exert a dominating influence on one's personality and behavior ⟨a guilt ~⟩

²**com·plex** \käm-ˈpleks, ˈkäm-ˌpleks\ *adj* **1** : composed of two or more parts **2** : consisting of a main clause and one or more subordinate clauses ⟨~ sentence⟩ **3** : hard to separate, analyze, or solve — **com·plex·i·ty** \käm-ˈplek-sə-tē\ *n* — **com·plex·ly** *adv*

complex fraction *n* : a fraction with a fraction or mixed number in the numerator or denominator or both

com·plex·ion \kəm-ˈplek-shən\ *n* **1** : the hue or appearance of the skin esp. of the face **2** : overall appearance — **com·plex·ioned** \-shənd\ *adj*

complex number *n* : a number of the form $a + b \sqrt{-1}$ where a and b are real numbers

com·pli·ance \kəm-ˈplī-əns\ *n* **1** : the act of complying to a demand or proposal **2** : a disposition to yield — **com·pli·ant** \-ənt\ *adj*

com·pli·cate \ˈkäm-plə-ˌkāt\ *vb* **-cat·ed; -cat·ing** : to make or become complex or intricate

com·pli·cat·ed \ˈkäm-plə-ˌkā-təd\ *adj* **1** : consisting of parts intricately combined **2** : difficult to analyze, understand, or explain — **com·pli·cat·ed·ly** *adv*

com·pli·ca·tion \ˌkäm-plə-ˈkā-shən\ *n* **1** : the quality or state of being complicated; *also* : a complex feature **2** : a disease or condition that develops during and affects the course of a primary disease or condition

com·plic·i·ty \kəm-'pli-sə-tē\ n, pl **-ties** : the state of being an accomplice

[1]**com·pli·ment** \'käm-plə-ment\ n **1** : an expression of approval or admiration; esp : a flattering remark **2** pl : best wishes : REGARDS

[2]**com·pli·ment** \-,ment\ vb : to pay a compliment to

com·pli·men·ta·ry \,käm-plə-'men-t(ə-)rē\ adj **1** : containing or expressing a compliment **2** : given free as a courtesy ⟨~ ticket⟩

com·ply \kəm-'plī\ vb **com·plied**; **com·ply·ing** : CONFORM, YIELD

[1]**com·po·nent** \kəm-'pō-nənt, 'käm-,pō-\ n : a component part ✦ Synonyms INGREDIENT, ELEMENT, FACTOR, CONSTITUENT

[2]**component** adj : serving to form a part of : CONSTITUENT

com·port \kəm-'pōrt\ vb **1** : AGREE, ACCORD ⟨actions that ~ with policy⟩ **2** : CONDUCT ⟨~ oneself with dignity⟩ ✦ Synonyms BEHAVE, ACQUIT, DEPORT — **com·port·ment** n

com·pose \kəm-'pōz\ vb **com·posed**; **com·pos·ing** **1** : to form by putting together : FASHION **2** : to produce (as pages of type) by composition **3** : ADJUST, ARRANGE **4** : CALM, QUIET **5** : to practice composition ⟨~ music⟩ — **com·pos·er** n

[1]**com·pos·ite** \käm-'pä-zət\ adj **1** : made up of distinct parts or elements **2** : of, relating to, or being a large family of flowering plants (as a daisy or aster) that bear many small flowers united into compact heads resembling single flowers

[2]**composite** n **1** : something composite **2** : a plant of the composite family ✦ Synonyms BLEND, COMPOUND, MIXTURE, AMALGAMATION

com·po·si·tion \,käm-pə-'zi-shən\ n **1** : the act or process of composing; esp : arrangement esp. in artistic form **2** : the arrangement or production of type for printing **3** : general makeup **4** : a product of mixing various elements or ingredients **5** : a literary, musical, or artistic product; esp : ESSAY

com·po·si·tion·ist \-'zi-shə-nist\ n : a teacher of writing

com·pos·i·tor \kəm-'pä-zə-tər\ n : one who sets type

com·post \'käm-,pōst\ n : a fertilizing material consisting largely of decayed organic matter — **compost** vb

com·po·sure \kəm-'pō-zhər\ n : CALMNESS, SELF-POSSESSION

com·pote \'käm-,pōt\ n **1** : fruits cooked in syrup **2** : a bowl (as of glass) with a base and stem for serving esp. fruit or compote

[1]**com·pound** \käm-'paund, 'käm-,\ vb [ME compounen, fr. AF *cumpundre, fr. L componere, fr. com- together + ponere to put] **1** : COMBINE **2** : to form by combining parts ⟨~ a medicine⟩ **3** : SETTLE ⟨~ a dispute⟩; also : to refrain from prosecuting (an offense) in return for a

consideration **4** : to increase (as interest) by an amount that can itself vary; also : to add to

[2]**com·pound** \'käm-,paund\ adj **1** : made up of individual parts **2** : composed of united similar parts esp. of a kind usu. independent ⟨a ~ plant ovary⟩ **3** : formed by the combination of two or more otherwise independent elements ⟨~ sentence⟩

[3]**com·pound** \'käm-,paund\ n **1** : a word consisting of parts that are words **2** : something formed from a union of elements or parts; esp : a distinct substance formed by the union of two or more chemical elements ✦ Synonyms MIXTURE, COMPOSITE, BLEND, ADMIXTURE, ALLOY

[4]**com·pound** \'käm-,paund\ n [by folk etymology fr. Malay kampung group of buildings, village] : an enclosure containing buildings

compound interest n : interest computed on the sum of an original principal and accrued interest

com·pre·hend \,käm-pri-'hend\ vb **1** : UNDERSTAND **2** : INCLUDE — **com·pre·hen·si·ble** \-'hen-sə-bəl\ adj — **com·pre·hen·sion** \-'hen-chən\ n

com·pre·hen·sive \,käm-pri-'hen-siv\ adj : covering completely or broadly ⟨~ insurance⟩ — **com·pre·hen·sive·ly** adv — **com·pre·hen·sive·ness** n

[1]**com·press** \kəm-'pres\ vb **1** : to squeeze together **2** : to reduce in size as if by squeezing ✦ Synonyms CONSTRICT, CONTRACT, SHRINK — **com·pres·sor** \-'pre-sər\ n

[2]**com·press** \'käm-,pres\ n : a folded pad or cloth used to press upon a body part

compressed air n : air under pressure greater than that of the atmosphere

com·pres·sion \kəm-'pre-shən\ n **1** : the act or process of compressing **2** : the process of compressing the fuel mixture in an internal combustion engine **3** : conversion (as of data) in order to reduce the space occupied or the bandwidth required

com·prise \kəm-'prīz\ vb **com·prised**; **com·pris·ing** **1** : INCLUDE, CONTAIN **2** : to be made up of **3** : COMPOSE, CONSTITUTE

[1]**com·pro·mise** \'käm-prə-,mīz\ n : a settlement of differences reached by mutual concessions

[2]**compromise** vb **-mised; -mis·ing** **1** : to settle by compromise **2** : to expose to suspicion or loss of reputation

comp·trol·ler \kən-'trō-lər, 'kämp-,trō-\ n : an official who audits and supervises expenditures and accounts

com·pul·sion \kəm-'pəl-shən\ n **1** : an act of compelling **2** : a force that compels **3** : an irresistible persistent impulse to perform an act ✦ Synonyms CONSTRAINT, FORCE, VIOLENCE, DURESS — **com·pul·sive** \-siv\ adj — **com·pul·sive·ly** adv — **com·pul·so·ry** \-sə-rē\ adj

com·punc·tion \kəm-'pəŋk-shən\ n : anxiety arising from guilt : REMORSE

com·pute \kəm-'pyüt\ vb **com·put·ed; com·put·ing** : CALCULATE, RECKON — **com·pu·ta·tion** \ˌkäm-pyü-'tā-shən\ n — **com·pu·ta·tion·al** adj

computed tomography n : radiography in which a three-dimensional image of a body structure is constructed by computer from a series of plane cross-sectional images made along an axis

com·put·er \kəm-'pyü-tər\ n : a programmable electronic device that can store, retrieve, and process data

com·put·er·ise chiefly Brit var of COMPUTERIZE

com·put·er·ize \kəm-'pyü-tə-ˌrīz\ vb **-ized; -iz·ing 1** : to carry out, control, or produce by means of a computer **2** : to provide with computers **3** : to store in a computer; also : put into a form that a computer can use — **com·put·er·i·za·tion** \-ˌpyü-tə-rə-'zā-shən\ n

computerized axial tomography n : COMPUTED TOMOGRAPHY

com·rade \'käm-ˌrad\ n [MF camarade group sleeping in one room, roommate, companion, fr. Sp camarada, fr. cámara room, fr. LL camera] : COMPANION, ASSOCIATE — **com·rade·ly** adj — **com·rade·ship** n

¹**con** \'kän\ vb **conned; con·ning 1** : MEMORIZE **2** : STUDY

²**con** adv : in opposition : AGAINST

³**con** n : an opposing argument, person, or position ⟨pros and ~s⟩

⁴**con** vb **conned; con·ning 1** : SWINDLE **2** : PERSUADE, CAJOLE

⁵**con** n : CONVICT

conc abbr concentrated

con·cat·e·nate \kän-'ka-tə-ˌnāt\ vb **-nat·ed; -nat·ing** : to link together in a series or chain — **con·cat·e·na·tion** \(ˌ)kän-ˌka-tə-'nā-shən\ n

con·cave \kän-'kāv, 'kän-ˌ\ adj : curved or rounded inward like the inside of a bowl — **con·cav·i·ty** \kän-'ka-və-tē\ n

con·ceal \kən-'sēl\ vb : to place out of sight : HIDE — **con·ceal·er** n — **con·ceal·ment** n

con·cede \kən-'sēd\ vb **con·ced·ed; con·ced·ing 1** : to admit to be true **2** : GRANT, YIELD ✦ Synonyms ALLOW, ACKNOWLEDGE, AVOW, CONFESS

con·ceit \kən-'sēt\ n **1** : excessively high opinion of one's self or ability : VANITY **2** : an elaborate or strained metaphor — **con·ceit·ed** adj — **con·ceit·ed·ly** adv — **con·ceit·ed·ness** n

con·ceive \kən-'sēv\ vb **con·ceived; con·ceiv·ing 1** : to become pregnant or pregnant with ⟨~ a child⟩ **2** : to form an idea of : THINK, IMAGINE — **con·ceiv·able** \-'sē-və-bəl\ adj — **con·ceiv·ably** \-blē\ adv

con·cel·e·brant \kən-'se-lə-brənt\ n : one that jointly participates in celebrating the Eucharist

¹**con·cen·trate** \'kän-sən-ˌtrāt\ vb **-trat·ed; -trat·ing 1** : to gather into one body, mass, or force **2** : to make less dilute **3** : to fix one's powers, efforts, or attentions

²**concentrate** n : something concentrated

con·cen·tra·tion \ˌkän-sən-'trā-shən\ n **1** : the act or process of concentrating : the state of being concentrated; esp : direction of attention on a single object **2** : the amount of a component in a given area or volume

concentration camp n : a camp where persons (as prisoners of war or political prisoners) are confined

con·cen·tric \kən-'sen-trik\ adj **1** : having a common center ⟨~ circles⟩ **2** : COAXIAL

¹**con·cept** \'kän-ˌsept\ n : THOUGHT, NOTION, IDEA — **con·cep·tu·al** \kän-'sep-chə-wəl\ adj — **con·cep·tu·al·ly** adv

²**concept** adj **1** : organized around a main idea or theme ⟨a ~ album⟩ **2** : created to illustrate a concept ⟨a ~ car⟩

con·cep·tion \kən-'sep-shən\ n **1** : the process of conceiving or being conceived **2** : the power to form or understand ideas or concepts **3** : IDEA, CONCEPT **4** : the originating of something

con·cep·tu·al·ise Brit var of CONCEPTUALIZE

con·cep·tu·al·ize \-'sep-chə-wə-ˌlīz\ vb **-ized; -iz·ing** : to form a conception of

¹**con·cern** \kən-'sərn\ vb **1** : to relate to **2** : to be the business of : INVOLVE **3** : ENGAGE, OCCUPY

²**concern** n **1** : INTEREST, ANXIETY **2** : AFFAIR, MATTER **3** : a business organization ✦ Synonyms CARE, WORRY, DISQUIET, UNEASE

con·cerned \-'sərnd\ adj **1** : ANXIOUS, UNEASY ⟨~ for their safety⟩ **2** : INVOLVED

con·cern·ing \-'sər-niŋ\ prep : relating to : REGARDING

con·cern·ment \kən-'sərn-mənt\ n **1** : something in which one is concerned **2** : IMPORTANCE, CONSEQUENCE

¹**con·cert** \'kän-(ˌ)sərt\ n **1** : agreement in a plan or design **2** : a public performance (as of music)

²**con·cert** \kən-'sərt\ vb : to plan together

con·cert·ed \kən-'sər-təd\ adj : mutually agreed on; also : performed in unison

con·cer·ti·na \ˌkän-sər-'tē-nə\ n : an instrument of the accordion family

concertina wire n : a coiled wire with sharp points for use as an obstacle

con·cert·mas·ter \'kän-sərt-ˌmas-tər\ or **con·cert·meis·ter** \-ˌmī-stər\ n : the leader of the first violins of an orchestra and assistant to the conductor

con·cer·to \kən-'cher-tō\ n, pl **-ti** \-(ˌ)tē\ or **-tos** [It] : a piece for one or more solo instruments and orchestra in three movements

con·ces·sion \kən-'se-shən\ n **1** : an act of conceding or yielding **2** : something yielded **3** : a grant by a government of land or of a right to use it **4** : a grant of a portion of premises for some specific purpose; also : the activities or enterprise carried on — **con·ces·sion·ary** \-'se-shə-ˌner-ē\ adj

con·ces·sion·aire \kən-ˌse-shə-'ner\ n : one that owns or operates a concession

conch \'käŋk, 'känch\ *n, pl* **conchs** \'käŋks\ *or* **conch·es** \'kän-chəz\ : a large spiral-shelled marine gastropod mollusk; *also* : its shell

con·cierge \kōⁿ-'syerzh\ *n, pl* **con·cierges** *same or* -'syer-zhəz\ [F] **1** : a resident in an apartment building who performs services for the tenants **2** : a usu. multilingual hotel staff member who usu. handles mail and reservations

con·cil·i·ate \kən-'si-lē-,āt\ *vb* **-at·ed; -at·ing 1** : to bring into agreement : RECONCILE **2** : to gain the goodwill of — **con·cil·i·a·tion** \-,si-lē-'ā-shən\ *n* — **con·cil·i·a·tor** \-'si-lē-,ā-tər\ *n* — **con·cil·ia·to·ry** \-'si-lē-ə-,tōr-ē\ *adj*

con·cise \kən-'sīs\ *adj* : expressing much in few words : BRIEF — **con·cise·ly** *adv* — **con·cise·ness** *n*

con·clave \'kän-,klāv\ *n* [ME, fr. ML, fr. L, room that can be locked, fr. *com-* together + *clavis* key] : a private gathering; *also* : CONVENTION

con·clude \kən-'klüd\ *vb* **con·clud·ed; con·clud·ing 1** : to bring to a close : END **2** : DECIDE, JUDGE **3** : to bring about as a result ✦ *Synonyms* CLOSE, FINISH, TERMINATE, COMPLETE, HALT

con·clu·sion \kən-'klü-zhən\ *n* **1** : the logical consequence of a reasoning process **2** : TERMINATION, END **3** : OUTCOME, RESULT — **con·clu·sive** \-siv\ *adj* — **con·clu·sive·ly** *adv* — **con·clu·sive·ness** *n*

con·coct \kən-'käkt, kän-\ *vb* **1** : to prepare by combining raw materials **2** : DEVISE — **con·coc·tion** \-'käk-shən\ *n*

con·com·i·tant \-'kä-mə-tənt\ *adj* : ACCOMPANYING, ATTENDING — **concomitant** *n*

con·cord \'kän-,kord, 'käŋ-\ *n* : AGREEMENT, HARMONY

con·cor·dance \kən-'kor-d²ns\ *n* **1** : an alphabetical index of words in a book or in an author's works with the passages in which they occur **2** : AGREEMENT, COVENANT

con·cor·dant \-d²nt\ *adj* : HARMONIOUS, AGREEING

con·cor·dat \kən-'kor-,dat\ *n* : CONCORDANCE 2

con·course \'kän-,kōrs\ *n* **1** : a spontaneous coming together : GATHERING **2** : an open space or hall (as in a bus terminal) where crowds gather

¹con·crete \'kän-,krēt, kän-'krēt\ *adj* **1** : naming a real thing or class of things : not abstract **2** : not theoretical : ACTUAL **3** : made of or relating to concrete

²con·crete \'kän-,krēt, kän-'krēt\ *vb* **con·cret·ed; con·cret·ing 1** : SOLIDIFY **2** : to cover with concrete

³con·crete \'kän-,krēt, kän-'krēt\ *n* : a hard building material made by mixing cement, sand, and gravel with water

con·cre·tion \kän-'krē-shən\ *n* : a hard mass esp. when formed abnormally in the body

con·cu·bine \'käŋ-kyu-,bīn\ *n* [ME, fr. AF, fr. L *concubina,* fr. *com-* with + *cubare* to lie] : a woman who is not legally a wife but lives with a man and sometimes has a recognized position in his household; *also* : MISTRESS — **con·cu·bi·nage** \kän-'kyü-bə-nij\ *n*

con·cu·pis·cence \kän-'kyü-pə-səns\ *n* : ardent sexual desire : LUST

con·cur \kən-'kər\ *vb* **con·curred; con·cur·ring 1** : to act together **2** : AGREE **3** : COINCIDE ✦ *Synonyms* UNITE, COMBINE, COOPERATE, BAND, JOIN

con·cur·rence \-'kər-əns\ *n* **1** : agreement in action or opinion **2** : occurrence together : CONJUNCTION

con·cur·rent \-'kər-ənt\ *adj* **1** : happening or operating at the same time **2** : joint and equal in authority

con·cus·sion \kən-'kə-shən\ *n* **1** : a hard blow or collision; *also* : bodily injury (as to the brain) resulting from a sudden jar **2** : AGITATION, SHAKING

con·demn \kən-'dem\ *vb* **1** : to declare to be wrong **2** : to convict of guilt **3** : to sentence judicially **4** : to pronounce unfit for use ⟨~ a building⟩ **5** : to declare forfeited or taken for public use ✦ *Synonyms* DENOUNCE, CENSURE, BLAME, CRITICIZE, REPREHEND — **con·dem·na·tion** \,kän-,dem-'nā-shən\ *n* — **con·dem·na·to·ry** \kən-'dem-nə-,tōr-ē\ *adj*

con·den·sate \'kän-dən-,sāt, kən-'den-\ *n* : a product of condensation

con·dense \kən-'dens\ *vb* **con·densed; con·dens·ing 1** : to make or become more compact or dense : CONCENTRATE **2** : to change from vapor to liquid ✦ *Synonyms* CONTRACT, SHRINK, COMPRESS, CONSTRICT — **con·den·sa·tion** \,kän-den-'sā-shən\ *n*

con·dens·er \kən-'den-sər\ *n* **1** : one that condenses **2** : CAPACITOR

con·de·scend \,kän-di-'send\ *vb* : to assume an air of superiority — **con·de·scend·ing·ly** \-'sen-diŋ-lē\ *adv* — **con·de·scen·sion** \-'sen-chən\ *n*

con·dign \kən-'dīn, 'kän-,dīn\ *adj* : DESERVED, APPROPRIATE ⟨~ punishment⟩

con·di·ment \'kän-də-mənt\ *n* : something used to make food savory; *esp* : a pungent seasoning (as pepper)

¹con·di·tion \kən-'di-shən\ *n* **1** : something essential to the occurrence of some other thing **2** : state of being **3** : social status **4** *pl* : state of affairs : CIRCUMSTANCES **5** : a bodily state in which something is wrong ⟨a heart ~⟩ **6** : a state of health, fitness, or working order ⟨in good ~⟩

²condition *vb* **1** : to put into proper condition for action or use **2** : to adapt, modify, or mold to respond in a particular way **3** : to modify so that an act or response previously associated with one stimulus becomes associated with another

con·di·tion·al \kən-'di-shə-nəl\ *adj* : containing, implying, or depending on a condition — **con·di·tion·al·ly** *adv*

con·di·tioned \-'di-shənd\ *adj* : determined or established by conditioning

con·di·tion·er \-'di-shə-nər\ *n* : a preparation used to improve the condition of hair

con·do \'kän-(ˌ)dō\ n : CONDOMINIUM 3

con·dole \kən-'dōl\ vb **con·doled; con·dol·ing** : to express sympathetic sorrow — **con·do·lence** \kən-'dō-ləns\ n

con·dom \'kän-dəm, 'kən-\ n : a usu. rubber sheath worn over the penis (as to prevent pregnancy or venereal infection during sexual intercourse)

con·do·min·i·um \ˌkän-də-'mi-nē-əm\ n, pl **-ums** 1 : joint sovereignty (as by two or more nations) 2 : a politically dependent territory under condominium 3 : individual ownership of a unit (as an apartment) in a multiunit structure; also : a fancy dish or sweet; also : CANDY — **con·fect** \kən-'fekt\ vb

con·done \kən-'dōn\ vb **con·doned; con·don·ing** : to overlook or forgive esp. by treating (an offense) as harmless or trivial ✦ **Synonyms** EXCUSE, PARDON, FORGIVE, REMIT — **con·do·na·tion** \ˌkän-də-'nā-shən\ n

con·dor \'kän-dər, -ˌdor\ n [Sp cóndor, fr. Quechua kuntur] : a very large American vulture of the high Andes; also : a related nearly extinct vulture of southern California now resident only in captivity

con·duce \kən-'düs, -'dyüs\ vb **conduced; con·duc·ing** : to lead or contribute to a particular result — **con·ducive** adj

¹**con·duct** \'kän-(ˌ)dəkt\ n 1 : MANAGEMENT, DIRECTION 2 : BEHAVIOR

²**con·duct** \kən-'dəkt\ vb 1 : GUIDE, ESCORT 2 : MANAGE, DIRECT 3 : to act as a medium for conveying or transmitting 4 : BEHAVE — **con·duc·tion** \-'dək-shən\ n

con·duc·tance \kən-'dək-təns\ n : the readiness with which a conductor transmits an electric current

con·duc·tive \kən-'dək-tiv\ adj : having the power to conduct (as heat or electricity) — **con·duc·tiv·i·ty** \ˌkän-ˌdək-'ti-və-tē\ n

con·duc·tor \kən-'dək-tər\ n 1 : one that conducts; esp : a material that permits an electric current to flow easily 2 : a collector of fares in a public conveyance 3 : the leader of a musical ensemble

con·duit \'kän-ˌdü-ət, ˌdyü-, -dwət\ n 1 : a channel for conveying fluid 2 : a tube or trough for protecting electric wires or cables 3 : a means of transmitting or distributing

con·dyle \'kän-ˌdī(-ə)l, -d°l\ n : an articular prominence of a bone — **con·dy·lar** \-də-lər\ adj

cone \'kōn\ n 1 : the scaly usu. ovate fruit of trees of most conifers 2 : a solid figure formed by rotating a right triangle about one of its legs 3 : a solid figure that slopes evenly to a point from a usu. circular base 4 : any of the conical light-sensitive receptor cells of the retina that function in color vision 5 : something shaped like a cone

cone·flow·er \'kōn-ˌflau̇(-ə)r\ n : any of several composite plants having cone-shaped flower disks

Con·es·to·ga wagon \ˌkä-nə-'stō-gə-\ n : a broad-wheeled covered wagon used esp. for transporting freight across the prairies

co·ney or **co·ny** \'kō-nē\ n, pl **coneys** or **conies** 1 : RABBIT; also : its fur 2 : PIKA

conf abbr 1 conference 2 confidential

con·fab \'kän-ˌfab, kən-'fab\ n : CONFABULATION 1

con·fab·u·la·tion \kən-ˌfab-yə-'lā-shən\ n 1 : CHAT; also : CONFERENCE 2 : a filling in of gaps in memory by fabrication — **con·fab·u·late** \-'fa-byə-ˌlāt\ vb

con·fec·tion \kən-'fek-shən\ n 1 : something put together from varied material 2 : a fancy dish or sweet; also : CANDY — **con·fect** \kən-'fekt\ vb

con·fec·tion·er \-sh(ə-)nər\ n : a maker of or dealer in confections

con·fec·tion·ery \-shə-ˌner-ē\ n, pl **-er·ies** 1 : sweet foods 2 : a confectioner's place of business

Confed abbr Confederate

con·fed·er·a·cy \kən-'fe-də-rə-sē\ n, pl **-cies** 1 : LEAGUE, ALLIANCE 2 cap : the 11 southern states that seceded from the U.S. in 1860 and 1861

¹**con·fed·er·ate** \kən-'fe-də-rət\ adj 1 : united in a league : ALLIED 2 cap : of or relating to the Confederacy

²**confederate** n 1 : ALLY, ACCOMPLICE 2 cap : an adherent of the Confederacy

³**con·fed·er·ate** \-'fe-də-ˌrāt\ vb **-at·ed; -at·ing** : to unite in a confederacy

con·fed·er·a·tion \kən-ˌfe-də-'rā-shən\ n 1 : an act of confederating; ALLIANCE 2 : LEAGUE

con·fer \kən-'fər\ vb **con·ferred; con·fer·ring** 1 : GRANT, BESTOW 2 : to exchange views : CONSULT — **con·fer·ee** \ˌkän-fə-'rē\ n

con·fer·ence \'kän-f(ə-)rəns\ n 1 : an interchange of views; also : a meeting for this purpose 2 : an association of athletic teams

con·fer·enc·ing \'kän-f(ə-)rən-siŋ\ n : the holding of conferences esp. by means of electronic devices

con·fess \kən-'fes\ vb 1 : to acknowledge or disclose one's misdeed, fault, or sin 2 : to acknowledge one's sins to God or to a priest 3 : to receive the confession of (a penitent) ✦ **Synonyms** ADMIT, OWN, AVOW, CONCEDE, GRANT

con·fessed·ly \-'fe-səd-lē\ adv : by confession : ADMITTEDLY

con·fes·sion \-'fe-shən\ n 1 : an act of confessing (as in the sacrament of penance) 2 : an acknowledgment of guilt 3 : a formal statement of religious beliefs 4 : a religious body having a common creed — **con·fes·sion·al** adj

con·fes·sion·al \-'fe-shə-nəl\ n : a place where a priest hears confessions

con·fes·sor \kən-'fe-sər\ n 1 : one that confesses 2 : a priest who hears confessions

con·fet·ti \kən-'fe-tē\ n [It, pl. of confetto sweetmeat, fr. ML confectum, fr. L, neut. of confectus, pp. of conficere to prepare] : bits of colored paper or ribbon for throwing (as at weddings)

con·fi·dant \'kän-fə-ˌdänt, -ˌdant\ *n* : one to whom secrets are confided

con·fi·dante \-ˌdänt, -ˌdant\ *n* : CONFIDANT; *esp* : one who is a woman

con·fide \kən-'fīd\ *vb* **con·fid·ed; con·fid·ing 1** : to have or show faith : TRUST ⟨~ in a friend⟩ **2** : to tell confidentially ⟨~ a secret⟩ **3** : ENTRUST

¹con·fi·dence \'kän-fə-dəns\ *n* **1** : TRUST, RELIANCE **2** : SELF-ASSURANCE, BOLDNESS **3** : a state of trust or intimacy **4** : SECRET **2** — **con·fi·dent** \-dənt\ *adj* — **con·fi·dent·ly** *adv*

²confidence *adj* : of or relating to swindling by false promises ⟨a ~ game⟩

con·fi·den·tial \ˌkän-fə-'den-shəl\ *adj* **1** : SECRET, PRIVATE ⟨~ information⟩ **2** : entrusted with confidences ⟨~ clerk⟩ — **con·fi·den·ti·al·i·ty** \-ˌden-shē-'a-lə-tē\ *n* — **con·fi·den·tial·ly** \-'den-shə-lē\ *adv*

con·fig·u·ra·tion \kən-ˌfi-gyə-'rā-shən\ *n* : structural arrangement of parts : SHAPE

con·fig·ure \kən-'fi-gyər\ *vb* **-ured; -ur·ing** : to set up for operation esp. in a particular way

con·fine \kən-'fīn\ *vb* **con·fined; con·fin·ing 1** : to hold within a location; *also* : IMPRISON **2** : to keep within limits ⟨will ~ my remarks to one subject⟩ — **con·fine·ment** *n* — **con·fin·er** *n*

con·fines \'kän-ˌfīnz\ *n pl* : BOUNDS, BORDERS

con·firm \kən-'fərm\ *vb* **1** : to give approval to : RATIFY **2** : to make firm or firmer **3** : to administer the rite of confirmation to **4** : VERIFY, CORROBORATE — **con·fir·ma·to·ry** \-'fər-mə-ˌtór-ē\ *adj*

con·fir·ma·tion \ˌkän-fər-'mā-shən\ *n* **1** : a religious ceremony admitting a person to full membership in a church or synagogue **2** : an act of ratifying or corroborating; *also* : PROOF

con·fis·cate \'kän-fə-ˌskāt\ *vb* **-cat·ed; -cat·ing** [L *confiscare,* fr. *com-* with + *fiscus* treasury] : to take possession of by or as if by public authority — **con·fis·ca·tion** \ˌkän-fə-'skā-shən\ *n* — **con·fis·ca·to·ry** \kən-'fis-kə-ˌtór-ē\ *adj*

con·fit \kōn-'fē\ *n* : a garnish of fruit or vegetables cooked in a seasoned liquid

con·fla·gra·tion \ˌkän-flə-'grā-shən\ *n* : FIRE; *esp* : a large disastrous fire

¹con·flict \'kän-ˌflikt\ *n* **1** : WAR **2** : a clash between hostile or opposing elements, ideas, or forces

²con·flict \kən-'flikt\ *vb* : to show opposition or irreconcilability : CLASH

con·flu·ence \'kän-ˌflü-əns, kən-'flü-\ *n* **1** : a coming together at one point **2** : the meeting or place of meeting of two or more streams — **con·flu·ent** \-ənt\ *adj*

con·flux \'kän-ˌfləks\ *n* : CONFLUENCE

con·form \kən-'fórm\ *vb* **1** : to be similar or identical; *also* : AGREE **2** : to obey customs or standards; *also* : COMPLY — **con·form·able** *adj* — **con·form·ist** \-'fór-mist\ *n*

con·for·mance \kən-'fór-məns\ *n* : CONFORMITY

con·for·ma·tion \ˌkän-fór-'mā-shən\ *n* : a forming into a whole by arranging parts

con·for·mi·ty \kən-'fór-mə-tē\ *n, pl* **-ties 1** : HARMONY, AGREEMENT **2** : COMPLIANCE, OBEDIENCE

con·found \kən-'faùnd, kän-\ *vb* **1** : to throw into disorder or confusion **2** : CONFUSE **2** ✦ **Synonyms** BEWILDER, PUZZLE, PERPLEX, BEFOG

con·fra·ter·ni·ty \ˌkän-frə-'tər-nə-tē\ *n* : a society devoted esp. to a religious or charitable cause

con·frere \'kän-ˌfrer, 'kō^n-\ *n* : COLLEAGUE, COMRADE

con·front \kən-'frənt\ *vb* **1** : to face esp. in challenge : OPPOSE; *also* : to deal unflinchingly with ⟨~ed the issue⟩ **2** : to cause to face or meet — **con·fron·ta·tion** \ˌkän-frən-'tā-shən\ *n* — **con·fron·ta·tion·al** \-shə-n°l\ *adj*

Con·fu·cian \kən-'fyü-shən\ *adj* : of or relating to the Chinese philosopher Confucius or his teachings — **Con·fu·cian·ism** \-shə-ˌni-zəm\ *n*

con·fuse \kən-'fyüz\ *vb* **con·fused; con·fus·ing 1** : to make mentally unclear or uncertain; *also* : to disturb the composure of **2** : to mix up : JUMBLE ✦ **Synonyms** MUDDLE, BEFUDDLE, ADDLE, FLUSTER — **con·fus·ed·ly** \-'fyü-zəd-lē\ *adv* — **con·fus·ing·ly** \-'fyü-ziŋ-lē\ *adv*

con·fu·sion \-'fyü-zhən\ *n* **1** : an act or instance of confusing **2** : the quality or state of being confused

con·fute \kən-'fyüt\ *vb* **con·fut·ed; con·fut·ing** : to overwhelm by argument : REFUTE — **con·fu·ta·tion** \ˌkän-fyü-'tā-shən\ *n*

cong *abbr* congress; congressional

con·ga \'käŋ-gə\ *n* : a Cuban dance of African origin performed by a group usu. in single file

con·geal \kən-'jēl\ *vb* **1** : FREEZE **2** : to make or become hard or thick

con·gee \'kän-jē\ *n* : porridge made from rice

con·ge·ner \'kän-jə-nər\ *n* : one related to another; *esp* : a plant or animal of the same taxonomic genus as another — **con·ge·ner·ic** \ˌkän-jə-'ner-ik\ *adj*

con·ge·nial \kən-'jē-nyəl\ *adj* **1** : KINDRED, SYMPATHETIC ⟨~ companions⟩ **2** : suited to one's taste or nature : AGREEABLE — **con·ge·ni·al·i·ty** \-ˌjē-nē-'a-lə-tē\ *n* — **con·ge·nial·ly** *adv*

con·gen·i·tal \kən-'je-nə-t°l\ *adj* : existing at or dating from birth ⟨~ deafness⟩ ✦ **Synonyms** INBORN, INNATE, NATURAL

con·ger eel \'kän-gər-\ *n* : a large edible marine eel of the Atlantic

con·ge·ries \'kän-jə-(ˌ)rēz\ *n, pl* **congeries** : AGGREGATION, COLLECTION

con·gest \kən-'jest\ *vb* **1** : to cause excessive fullness of the blood vessels of (as a lung) **2** : to obstruct by overcrowding — **con·ges·tion** \-'jes-chən\ *n* — **con·ges·tive** \-'jes-tiv\ *adj*

congestive heart failure *n* : heart failure in which the heart is unable to keep enough blood circulating in the tissues or is unable to pump out the blood returned to it by the veins

¹**con·glom·er·ate** \kən-ˈglä-mə-rət\ *adj* [L *conglomerare* to roll together, fr. *com-* together + *glomerare* to wind into a ball, fr. *glomer-, glomus* ball] : made up of parts from various sources

²**con·glom·er·ate** \-ˌrāt\ *vb* **-at·ed; -at·ing** : to form into a mass — **con·glom·er·a·tion** \-ˌglä-mə-ˈrā-shən\ *n*

³**con·glom·er·ate** \-rət\ *n* **1** : a mass formed of fragments from various sources; *esp* : a rock composed of fragments varying from pebbles to boulders held together by a cementing material **2** : a widely diversified corporation

con·grat·u·late \kən-ˈgra-chə-ˌlāt\ *vb* **-lat·ed; -lat·ing** : to express sympathetic pleasure to on account of success or good fortune : FELICITATE — **con·grat·u·la·tion** \-ˌgra-chə-ˈlā-shən\ *n* — **con·grat·u·la·to·ry** \-ˈgra-chə-lə-ˌtōr-ē\ *adj*

con·gre·gate \ˈkäŋ-gri-ˌgāt\ *vb* **-gat·ed; -gat·ing** [ME, fr. L *congregatus*, pp. of *congregare*, fr. *com-* together + *greg-, grex* flock] : ASSEMBLE

con·gre·ga·tion \ˌkäŋ-gri-ˈgā-shən\ *n* **1** : an assembly of persons met esp. for worship; *also* : a group that habitually so meets **2** : a religious community or order **3** : the act or an instance of congregating

con·gre·ga·tion·al \-shə-nəl\ *adj* **1** : of or relating to a congregation **2** *cap* : observing the faith and practice of certain Protestant churches which recognize the independence of each congregation in church matters — **con·gre·ga·tion·al·ism** \-nə-ˌli-zəm\ *n, often cap* — **con·gre·ga·tion·al·ist** \-list\ *n, often cap*

con·gress \ˈkäŋ-grəs\ *n* **1** : an assembly esp. of delegates for discussion and usu. action on some question **2** : the body of senators and representatives constituting a nation's legislature — **con·gres·sio·nal** \kən-ˈgre-shə-nəl\ *adj*

con·gress·man \ˈkäŋ-grəs-mən\ *n* : a member of a congress

con·gress·wom·an \-ˌwu̇-mən\ *n* : a woman who is a member of a congress

con·gru·ence \kən-ˈgrü-əns, ˈkäŋ-grü-\ *n* : the quality of agreeing or coinciding : CONGRUITY — **con·gru·ent** \kən-ˈgrü-ənt, ˈkäŋ-grü-\ *adj*

con·gru·en·cy \-sē\ *n, pl* **-cies** : CONGRUENCE

con·gru·ity \kän-ˈgrü-ə-tē\ *n, pl* **-ities** : correspondence between things — **con·gru·ous** \ˈkäŋ-grü-əs\ *adj*

con·ic \ˈkä-nik\ *adj* **1** : of or relating to a cone **2** : CONICAL

con·i·cal \ˈkä-ni-kəl\ *adj* : resembling a cone esp. in shape

co·ni·fer \ˈkä-nə-fər, ˈkō-\ *n* : any of an order of shrubs or trees (as the pines) that usu. are evergreen and bear cones — **co·nif·er·ous** \kō-ˈni-fə-rəs\ *adj*

conj *abbr* conjunction

con·jec·ture \kən-ˈjek-chər\ *n* : GUESS, SURMISE — **con·jec·tur·al** \-chə-rəl\ *adj* — **conjecture** *vb*

con·join \kən-ˈjȯin\ *vb* : to join together — **con·joint** \-ˈjȯint\ *adj*

con·ju·gal \ˈkän-ji-gəl\ *adj* : of or relating to marriage : MATRIMONIAL

¹**con·ju·gate** \ˈkän-ji-gət, -jə-ˌgāt\ *adj* **1** : united esp. in pairs : COUPLED **2** : of kindred origin and meaning ⟨*sing* and *song* are ~⟩ — **con·ju·gate·ly** *adv*

²**con·ju·gate** \-jə-ˌgāt\ *vb* **-gat·ed; -gat·ing 1** : INFLECT ⟨~ a verb⟩ **2** : to join together : COUPLE

con·ju·ga·tion \ˌkän-jə-ˈgā-shən\ *n* **1** : an arrangement of the inflectional forms of a verb **2** : the act of conjugating : the state of being conjugated

con·junct \kän-ˈjəŋkt\ *adj* : JOINED, UNITED

con·junc·tion \kən-ˈjəŋk-shən\ *n* **1** : COMBINATION **2** : occurrence at the same time **3** : a word that joins together sentences, clauses, phrases, or words

con·junc·ti·va \ˌkän-jəŋk-ˈtī-və\ *n, pl* **-vas** *or* **-vae** \-ˌ)vē\ : the mucous membrane lining the inner surface of the eyelids and continuing over the forepart of the eyeball

con·junc·tive \kən-ˈjəŋk-tiv\ *adj* **1** : CONNECTIVE **2** : CONJUNCT ⟨the ~ operation of different factors⟩ **3** : being or functioning like a conjunction

con·junc·ti·vi·tis \kən-ˌjəŋk-ti-ˈvī-təs\ *n* : inflammation of the conjunctiva

con·junc·ture \kən-ˈjəŋk-chər\ *n* **1** : CONJUNCTION, UNION **2** : JUNCTURE **3**

con·jun·to \kȯn-ˈhün-tō\ *n* : Mexican-American music influenced by the music of German immigrants to Texas

con·jure \ˈkän-jər, ˈkən- *for* 1, 2; kən-ˈju̇r *for* 3\ *vb* **con·jured; con·jur·ing 1** : to implore earnestly or solemnly **2** : to practice magic; *esp* : to summon (as a devil) by sorcery **3** : to practice sleight of hand — **con·ju·ra·tion** \ˌkän-jü-ˈrā-shən, ˌkən-\ *n* — **con·jur·er** *or* **con·ju·ror** \ˈkän-jər-ər, ˈkən-\ *n*

conk \ˈkäŋk\ *vb* : BREAK DOWN; *esp* : STALL ⟨the motor ~ed out⟩

Conn *abbr* Connecticut

con·nect \kə-ˈnekt\ *vb* **1** : JOIN, LINK **2** : to associate in one's mind **3** : to establish a communications connection ⟨~ to the Internet⟩ — **con·nect·able** *adj* — **con·nec·tor** *n*

con·nec·tion \kə-ˈnek-shən\ *n* **1** : JUNCTION, UNION **2** : logical relationship : COHERENCE; *esp* : relation of a word to other words in a sentence **3** : family relationship **4** : BOND, LINK **5** : a person related by blood or marriage **6** : relationship in social affairs or in business **7** : an association of persons; *esp* : a religious denomination **8** : a means of communication or transport ⟨a telephone ~⟩

¹**con·nec·tive** \kə-ˈnek-tiv\ *adj* : serving to connect — **con·nec·tiv·i·ty** \ˌkä-ˌnek-ˈti-və-tē\ *n*

²**connective** *n* : a word (as a conjunction) that connects words or word groups

connective tissue *n* : a tissue (as bone or cartilage) that forms a supporting framework for the body or its parts

con·nex·ion *chiefly Brit var of* CONNECTION

con·ning tower \'kä-niŋ-\ *n* : a raised structure on the deck of a submarine

con·nip·tion \kə-'nip-shən\ *n* : a fit of rage, hysteria, or alarm

con·nive \kə-'nīv\ *vb* **con·nived; con·niv·ing** [F or L; F *conniver*, fr. L *convēre* to close the eyes, connive] **1** : to pretend ignorance of something one ought to oppose as wrong **2** : to cooperate secretly : give secret aid — **con·niv·ance** *n* — **con·niv·er** *n*

con·nois·seur \,kä-nə-'sər\ *n* : a critical judge in matters of art or taste

con·no·ta·tion \,kä-nə-'tā-shən\ *n* : a meaning in addition to or apart from the thing explicitly named or described by a word

con·no·ta·tive \'kä-nə-,tā-tiv, kə-'nō-tə-\ *adj* **1** : connoting or tending to connote **2** : relating to connotation

con·note \kə-'nōt\ *vb* **con·not·ed; con·not·ing** : to suggest or mean as a connotation

con·nu·bi·al \kə-'nü-bē-əl, -'nyü-\ *adj* : of or relating to marriage : CONJUGAL

con·quer \'käŋ-kər\ *vb* **1** : to gain by force of arms : WIN **2** : to get the better of : OVERCOME ♦ *Synonyms* DEFEAT, SUBJUGATE, SUBDUE, OVERTHROW, VANQUISH — **con·quer·or** \-ər\ *n*

con·quest \'kän-,kwest, 'käŋ-\ *n* **1** : an act of conquering : VICTORY **2** : something conquered

con·quis·ta·dor \kón-'kēs-tə-,dór, kän-'kwis-\, *n, pl* **-do·res** \-,kēs-tə-'dór-ēz, -,kwis-\ *or* **-dors** : CONQUEROR; *esp* : a leader in the Spanish conquest of the Americas in the 16th century

cons *abbr* consonant

con·san·guin·i·ty \,kän-,san-'gwi-nə-tē, -,saŋ-\ *n, pl* **-ties** : blood relationship — **con·san·guin·e·ous** \-'nē-əs\ *adj*

con·science \'kän-chəns\ *n* : consciousness of the moral right and wrong of one's own acts or motives — **con·science·less** *adj*

con·sci·en·tious \,kän-chē-'en-chəs\ *adj* : guided by one's own sense of right and wrong ♦ *Synonyms* SCRUPULOUS, HONORABLE, HONEST, UPRIGHT, JUST — **con·sci·en·tious·ly** *adv*

conscientious objector *n* : a person who refuses to serve in the armed forces or to bear arms on moral or religious grounds

¹con·scious \'kän-chəs\ *adj* **1** : AWARE **2** : known or felt by one's inner self **3** : mentally awake or alert : not asleep or unconscious **4** : done with awareness or purpose ⟨a ~ decision⟩ — **con·scious·ly** *adv* — **con·scious·ness** *n*

²conscious *n* : the upper level of mental life of which a person is aware : CONSCIOUSNESS

con·script \kən-'skript\ *vb* : to enroll by compulsion for military or naval service — **con·script** \'kän-,skript\ *n* — **con·scrip·tion** \kən-'skrip-shən\ *n*

con·se·crate \'kän-sə-,krāt\ *vb* **-crat·ed; -crat·ing** [ME, fr. L *consecratus*, pp. of *consecrare*, fr. *com-* together + *sacrare* to

set aside as sacred, fr. *sacer* sacred] **1** : to induct (as a bishop) into an office with a religious rite **2** : to make or declare sacred ⟨~ a church⟩ **3** : to devote solemnly to a purpose — **con·se·cra·tion** \,kän-sə-'krā-shən\ *n*

con·sec·u·tive \kən-'se-kyə-tiv\ *adj* : following in regular order : SUCCESSIVE — **con·sec·u·tive·ly** *adv*

con·sen·su·al \kən-'sen-chə-wəl\ *adj* : involving or based on mutual consent

con·sen·sus \kən-'sen-səs\ *n* **1** : agreement in opinion, testimony, or belief **2** : collective opinion

¹con·sent \kən-'sent\ *vb* : to give assent or approval

²consent *n* : approval or acceptance of something done or proposed by another

con·se·quence \'kän-sə-,kwens\ *n* **1** : RESULT **2** : IMPORTANCE ♦ *Synonyms* EFFECT, OUTCOME, AFTERMATH, UPSHOT

con·se·quent \-kwənt, -,kwent\ *adj* : following as a result or effect

con·se·quen·tial \,kän-sə-'kwen-chəl\ *adj* **1** : having significant consequences **2** : showing self-importance

con·se·quent·ly \'kän-sə-,kwent-lē, -kwənt-\ *adv* : as a result : ACCORDINGLY

con·ser·van·cy \kən-'sər-vən-sē\ *n, pl* **-cies** : an organization or area designated to conserve natural resources

con·ser·va·tion \,kän-sər-'vā-shən\ *n* : PRESERVATION; *esp* : planned management of natural resources

con·ser·va·tion·ist \-shə-nist\ *n* : a person who advocates conservation esp. of natural resources

con·ser·va·tism \kən-'sər-və-,ti-zəm\ *n* : disposition to keep to established ways : opposition to change

¹con·ser·va·tive \kən-'sər-və-tiv\ *adj* **1** : PRESERVATIVE **2** : disposed to maintain existing views, conditions, or institutions **3** : MODERATE, CAUTIOUS ⟨a ~ investment⟩ — **con·ser·va·tive·ly** *adv*

²conservative *n* : a person who is conservative esp. in politics

con·ser·va·tor \kən-'sər-və-tər, 'kän-sər-,vā-\ *n* **1** : PROTECTOR, GUARDIAN **2** : one named by a court to protect the interests of an incompetent (as a child)

con·ser·va·to·ry \kən-'sər-və-,tōr-ē\ *n, pl* **-ries** **1** : GREENHOUSE **2** : a place of instruction in one of the fine arts (as music)

¹con·serve \kən-'sərv\ *vb* **con·served; con·serv·ing** : to keep from losing or wasting : PRESERVE

²con·serve \'kän-,sərv\ *n* **1** : CONFECTION **2**; *esp* : a candied fruit **2** : PRESERVE; *esp* : one prepared from a mixture of fruits

con·sid·er \kən-'si-dər\ *vb* [ME, fr. AF *considerer*, fr. L *considerare* to observe, think about, fr. *com-* together + *sidus, sidus* heavenly body] **1** : THINK, PONDER **2** : HEED, REGARD **3** : JUDGE, BELIEVE — **con·sid·ered** *adj*

con·sid·er·able \-'si-dər-ə-bəl, -'si-drə-bəl\ *adj* **1** : IMPORTANT **2** : large in extent, amount, or degree — **con·sid·er·ably** \-blē\ *adv*

con·sid·er·ate \kən-'si-də-rət\ adj : observant of the rights and feelings of others ✦ **Synonyms** THOUGHTFUL, ATTENTIVE

con·sid·er·ation \kən-ˌsi-də-'rā-shən\ n 1 : careful thought : DELIBERATION 2 : a matter taken into account 3 : thoughtful attention 4 : JUDGMENT, OPINION 5 : RECOMPENSE

con·sid·er·ing \-'si-d(ə-)riŋ\ prep : in view of : taking into account ⟨did well ~ his limitations⟩

con·sign \kən-'sīn\ vb 1 : ENTRUST, COMMIT 2 : to deliver formally 3 : to send (goods) to an agent for sale — **con·sign·ee** \ˌkän-sə-'nē, -ˌsī-; kən-ˌsī-\ n — **con·sign·or** \ˌkän-sə-'nȯr, -ˌsī-; kən-ˌsī-\ n

con·sign·ment \kən-'sīn-mənt\ n : something consigned esp. in a single shipment

con·sil·ience \kən-'sil-yəns\ n : the linking together of principles from different disciplines when forming a comprehensive theory

con·sist \kən-'sist\ vb 1 : to be inherent : LIE — usu. used with in 2 : to be composed or made up — usu. used with of

con·sis·tence \kən-'sis-təns\ n : CONSISTENCY

con·sis·ten·cy \-tən-sē\ n, pl -cies 1 : COHESIVENESS, FIRMNESS 2 : agreement or harmony in parts or of different things 3 : UNIFORMITY ⟨~ of behavior⟩ — **con·sis·tent** \-tənt\ adj — **con·sis·tent·ly** adv

con·sis·to·ry \kən-'sis-tə-rē\ n, pl -ries : a solemn assembly (as of Roman Catholic cardinals)

consol abbr consolidated

¹**con·sole** \'kän-ˌsōl\ n [F] 1 : the desk-like part of an organ at which the organist sits 2 : the combination of displays and controls of a device or system 3 : a cabinet for a radio or television set resting directly on the floor 4 : a small storage cabinet between bucket seats in an automobile

²**con·sole** \kən-'sōl\ vb **con·soled**; **con·sol·ing** : to soothe the grief of : COMFORT, SOLACE — **con·so·la·tion** \ˌkän-sə-'lā-shən\ n — **con·so·la·to·ry** \kən-'sō-lə-ˌtȯr-ē, -'sä-\ adj

con·sol·i·date \kən-'sä-lə-ˌdāt\ vb -dat·ed; -dat·ing 1 : to unite or become united into one whole : COMBINE 2 : to make firm or secure 3 : to form into a compact mass — **con·sol·i·da·tion** \-ˌsä-lə-'dā-shən\ n — **con·sol·i·da·tor** \-'sä-lə-ˌdā-tər\ n

con·som·mé \ˌkän-sə-'mā\ n [F] : a clear soup made from well-seasoned stock

con·so·nance \'kän-sə-nəns\ n 1 : AGREEMENT, HARMONY 2 : repetition of consonants esp. as an alternative to rhyme in verse

¹**con·so·nant** \-nənt\ adj : having consonance, harmony, or agreement ✦ **Synonyms** CONSISTENT, COMPATIBLE, CONGRUOUS, CONGENIAL, SYMPATHETIC — **con·so·nant·ly** adv

²**consonant** n 1 : a speech sound (as \p\, \g\, \n\, \l\, \s\, \r\) characterized by constriction or closure at one or more points

in the breath channel 2 : a letter other than a, e, i, o, and u — **con·so·nan·tal** \ˌkän-sə-'nan-t°l\ adj

¹**con·sort** \'kän-ˌsȯrt\ n 1 : a ship accompanying another 2 : SPOUSE, MATE

²**con·sort** \kən-'sȯrt\ vb 1 : to keep company 2 : ACCORD, HARMONIZE

con·sor·tium \kən-'sȯr-shəm; -shē-əm, -tē-\ n, pl -**sor·tia** \-shə-; -shē-ə, -tē-\ [L, fellowship] : an agreement or combination (as of companies) formed to undertake a large enterprise

con·spec·tus \kən-'spek-təs\ n 1 : a brief survey or summary 2 : SUMMARY

con·spic·u·ous \kən-'spi-kyə-wəs\ adj : attracting attention : PROMINENT, STRIKING ✦ **Synonyms** NOTICEABLE, REMARKABLE, OUTSTANDING — **con·spic·u·ous·ly** adv

con·spir·a·cy \kən-'spir-ə-sē\ n, pl -cies : an agreement among conspirators : PLOT

con·spir·a·tor \kən-'spir-ə-tər\ n : one who conspires — **con·spir·a·to·ri·al** \-ˌspir-ə-'tȯr-ē-əl\ adj

con·spire \kən-'spī(-ə)r\ vb **conspired**; **con·spir·ing** [ME, fr. AF conspirer, fr. L conspirare to be in harmony, conspire, fr. com- together + spirare to breathe] : to plan secretly an unlawful act : PLOT

const abbr 1 constant 2 constitution; constitutional

con·sta·ble \'kän-stə-bəl, 'kən-\ n [ME conestable, fr. AF, fr. LL comes stabuli, lit., officer of the stable] : a public officer responsible for keeping the peace

con·stab·u·lary \kən-'sta-byə-ˌler-ē\ n, pl -lar·ies 1 : the police of a particular district or country 2 : a police force organized like the military

con·stan·cy \'kän-stən-sē\ n, pl -cies 1 : firmness of mind 2 : STABILITY

¹**con·stant** \-stənt\ adj 1 : STEADFAST, FAITHFUL 2 : FIXED, UNCHANGING ⟨a ~ flow⟩ 3 : continually recurring : REGULAR ⟨a ~ annoyance⟩ — **con·stant·ly** adv

²**constant** n : something unchanging

con·stel·la·tion \ˌkän-stə-'lā-shən\ n 1 : any of 88 groups of stars forming patterns 2 : a group of usu. related persons, qualities, or things

con·ster·na·tion \ˌkän-stər-'nā-shən\ n : amazed dismay and confusion

con·sti·pa·tion \ˌkän-stə-'pā-shən\ n : abnormally difficult or infrequent bowel movements — **con·sti·pate** \'kän-stə-ˌpāt\ vb

con·stit·u·en·cy \kən-'sti-chə-wən-sē\ n, pl -cies : a body of constituents; also : an electoral district

¹**con·stit·u·ent** \-wənt\ n 1 : a person entitled to vote for a representative for a district 2 : a component part

²**constituent** adj 1 : COMPONENT ⟨~ parts⟩ 2 : having power to create a government or frame or amend a constitution

con·sti·tute \'kän-stə-ˌtüt, -ˌtyüt\ vb -tut·ed; -tut·ing 1 : to appoint to an office or duty **2** : SET UP, ESTABLISH ⟨∼ a law⟩ **3** : MAKE UP, COMPOSE

con·sti·tu·tion \ˌkän-stə-ˈtü-shən, -ˈtyü-\ *n* **1** : an established law or custom **2** : the physical makeup of the individual **3** : the structure, composition, or makeup of something ⟨∼ of the sun⟩ **4** : the basic law in a politically organized body; *also* : a document containing such law

¹**con·sti·tu·tion·al** \-shə-nəl\ *adj* **1** : of or relating to the constitution of body or mind **2** : being in accord with the constitution of a state or society; *also* : of or relating to such a constitution — **con·sti·tu·tion·al·ly** *adv*

²**constitutional** *n* : an exercise (as a walk) taken for one's health

con·sti·tu·tion·al·i·ty \-ˌtü-shə-ˈna-lə-tē, -ˌtyü-\ *n* : the quality or state of being constitutional

con·sti·tu·tive \ˈkän-stə-ˌtü-tiv, -ˌtyü-, kən-ˈsti-chə-tiv\ *adj* **1** : CONSTRUCTIVE **2** : CONSTITUENT, ESSENTIAL

constr *abbr* construction

con·strain \kən-ˈstrān\ *vb* **1** : COMPEL, FORCE **2** : CONFINE **3** : RESTRAIN

con·straint \-ˈstrānt\ *n* **1** : COMPULSION; *also* : RESTRAINT **2** : repression of one's natural feelings

con·strict \kən-ˈstrikt\ *vb* : to draw together : SQUEEZE — **con·stric·tion** \-ˈstrik-shən\ *n* — **con·stric·tive** \-ˈstrik-tiv\ *adj*

con·stric·tor \kən-ˈstrik-tər\ *n* : a snake that coils around and compresses its prey

con·struct \kən-ˈstrəkt\ *vb* : BUILD, MAKE — **con·struc·tor** \-ˈstrək-tər\ *n*

con·struc·tion \kən-ˈstrək-shən\ *n* **1** : INTERPRETATION **2** : the art, process, or manner of building; *also* : something built, created, or established : STRUCTURE **3** : syntactical arrangement of words in a sentence — **con·struc·tive** \-tiv\ *adj*

con·struc·tion·ist \-shə-nist\ *n* : a person who construes a legal document (as the U.S. Constitution) in a specific way ⟨a strict ∼⟩

con·strue \kən-ˈstrü\ *vb* **con·strued; con·stru·ing 1** : to analyze the mutual relations of words in a sentence; *also* : TRANSLATE, INTERPRET — **con·stru·able** *adj* — **con·stru·al** \-ˈstrü-əl\ *n*

con·sub·stan·ti·a·tion \ˌkän-səb-ˌstan-chē-ˈā-shən\ *n* : the actual substantial presence and combination of the body and blood of Christ with the eucharistic bread and wine

con·sul \ˈkän-səl\ *n* **1** : a chief magistrate of the Roman republic **2** : an official appointed by a government to reside in a foreign country to care for the commercial interests of the appointing government's citizens — **con·sul·ar** \-sə-lər\ *adj* — **con·sul·ate** \-lət\ *n* — **con·sul·ship** *n*

con·sult \kən-ˈsəlt\ *vb* **1** : to ask the advice or opinion of **2** : CONFER — **con·sul·tant** \-ˈsəl-tənt\ *n* — **con·sul·ta·tion** \ˌkän-səl-ˈtā-shən\ *n*

con·sume \kən-ˈsüm\ *vb* **con·sumed; con·sum·ing 1** : DESTROY ⟨*consumed* by fire⟩ **2** : to spend wastefully **3** : to eat up : DEVOUR **4** : to absorb the attention of : ENGROSS — **con·sum·able** *adj* — **con·sum·er** *n*

con·sum·er·ism \kən-ˈsü-mə-ˌri-zəm\ *n* : the promotion of consumers' interests (as against false advertising)

¹**con·sum·mate** \ˈkän-sə-mət, kən-ˈsə-\ *adj* : PERFECT ⟨a ∼ team player⟩ ◆ *Synonyms* FINISHED, ACCOMPLISHED

²**con·sum·mate** \ˈkän-sə-ˌmāt\ *vb* **-mat·ed; -mat·ing** : to make complete : FINISH, ACHIEVE — **con·sum·ma·tion** \ˌkän-sə-ˈmā-shən\ *n*

con·sump·tion \kən-ˈsəmp-shən\ *n* **1** : progressive bodily wasting away; *also* : TUBERCULOSIS **2** : the act of consuming or using up **3** : the use of economic goods

¹**con·sump·tive** \-ˈsəmp-tiv\ *adj* **1** : tending to consume **2** : relating to or affected with consumption

²**consumptive** *n* : a person who has consumption

cont *abbr* **1** containing **2** contents **3** continent; continental **4** continued **5** control

¹**con·tact** \ˈkän-ˌtakt\ *n* **1** : a touching or meeting of bodies **2** : ASSOCIATION, RELATIONSHIP; *also* : CONNECTION, COMMUNICATION **3** : a person serving as a go-between or source of information **4** : CONTACT LENS

²**contact** *vb* **1** : to come or bring into contact : TOUCH **2** : to get in communication with

contact lens *n* : a thin lens fitting over the cornea usu. to correct vision

con·ta·gion \kən-ˈtā-jən\ *n* [ME, fr. L *contagio*, fr. *contingere* to have contact with, pollute, fr. *com-* together + *tangere* to touch] **1** : a contagious disease; *also* : the transmission of such a disease **2** : a disease-producing agent (as a virus) **3** : transmission of an influence on the mind or emotions

con·ta·gious \-jəs\ *adj* **1** : able to be passed by contact between individuals ⟨colds are ∼⟩ ⟨∼ disease⟩; *also* : capable of passing on a contagious disease **2** : communicated or transmitted like a contagious disease; *esp* : exciting similar emotion or conduct in others

con·tain \kən-ˈtān\ *vb* **1** : RESTRAIN **2** : to have within : HOLD **3** : COMPRISE, INCLUDE — **con·tain·able** \-ˈtā-nə-bəl\ *adj* — **con·tain·ment** \-ˈtān-mənt\ *n*

con·tain·er \kən-ˈtā-nər\ *n* : RECEPTACLE

con·tam·i·nant \kən-ˈta-mə-nənt\ *n* : something that contaminates

con·tam·i·nate \kən-ˈta-mə-ˌnāt\ *vb* **-nat·ed; -nat·ing** : to soil, stain, or infect by contact or association — **con·tam·i·na·tion** \-ˌta-mə-ˈnā-shən\ *n*

contd *abbr* continued

con·temn \kən-'tem\ *vb* : to view or treat with contempt : DESPISE

con·tem·plate \'kän-təm-ˌplāt\ *vb* **-plat·ed; -plat·ing** [L *contemplari,* fr. *com-* with + *templum* space marked out for observation of auguries] **1** : to view or consider with continued attention **2** : INTEND — **con·tem·pla·tion** \ˌkän-təm-'plā-shən\ *n* — **con·tem·pla·tive** \kən-'tem-plə-tiv, 'kän-təm-ˌplā-\ *adj* : CONTEMPORARY I

con·tem·po·ra·ne·ous \kən-ˌtem-pə-'rā-nē-əs\ *adj* : CONTEMPORARY I

con·tem·po·rary \kən-'tem-pə-ˌrer-ē\ *adj* **1** : occurring or existing at the same time **2** : marked by characteristics of the present period — **contemporary** *n*

con·tempt \kən-'tempt\ *n* **1** : the act of despising **2** : the state of mind of one who despises **2** : the state of being despised **3** : disobedience to or open disrespect of a court or legislature

con·tempt·ible \kən-'temp-tə-bəl\ *adj* : deserving contempt : DESPICABLE — **con·tempt·ibly** \-blē\ *adv*

con·temp·tu·ous \-'temp-chə-wəs\ *adj* : feeling or expressing contempt — **con·temp·tu·ous·ly** *adv*

con·tend \kən-'tend\ *vb* **1** : to strive against rivals or difficulties **2** : ARGUE **3** : MAINTAIN, ASSERT — **con·tend·er** *n*

¹con·tent \kən-'tent\ *adj* : SATISFIED

²content *vb* : SATISFY; *esp* : to limit (oneself) in requirements or actions

³content *n* : CONTENTMENT ⟨ate to his heart's ∼⟩

⁴con·tent \'kän-ˌtent\ *n* **1** : something contained ⟨∼s of a room⟩ **2** : subject matter or topics treated (as in a book) **3** : material (as text or music) offered by a Web site **4** : MEANING, SIGNIFICANCE **5** : the amount of material contained

con·tent·ed \kən-'ten-təd\ *adj* : SATISFIED — **con·tent·ed·ly** *adv* — **con·tent·ed·ness** *n*

con·ten·tion \kən-'ten-chən\ *n* **1** : CONTEST, STRIFE **2** : an idea or point for which a person argues — **con·ten·tious** \-chəs\ *adj* — **con·ten·tious·ly** *adv*

con·tent·ment \kən-'tent-mənt\ *n* : ease of mind

con·ter·mi·nous \kän-'tər-mə-nəs\ *adj* : having the same or a common boundary — **con·ter·mi·nous·ly** *adv*

¹con·test \kən-'test\ *vb* **1** : to engage in a struggle or competition : COMPETE, VIE **2** : CHALLENGE, DISPUTE ⟨∼ the accusations⟩ — **con·tes·tant** \-'tes-tənt\ *n*

²con·test \'kän-ˌtest\ *n* : STRUGGLE, COMPETITION

con·text \'kän-ˌtekst\ *n* [ME, fr. L *contextus* connection of words, coherence, fr. *contexere* to weave together] : the parts of a discourse that surround a word or passage and help to explain its meaning; *also* : the circumstances surrounding an act or event ⟨the ∼ of the war⟩ — **con·tex·tu·al·ly** *adv*

con·tig·u·ous \kən-'ti-gyə-wəs\ *adj* : being in contact : TOUCHING; *also* : NEXT, ADJOINING — **con·ti·gu·i·ty** \ˌkän-tə-'gyü-ə-tē\ *n*

con·ti·nence \'kän-tə-nəns\ *n* **1** : SELF-RESTRAINT; *esp* : a refraining from sexual intercourse **2** : the ability to retain urine or feces voluntarily

¹con·ti·nent \'kän-tə-nənt\ *adj* : exercising continence

²continent *n* **1** : any of the great divisions of land on the globe **2** *cap* : the continent of Europe

¹con·ti·nen·tal \ˌkän-tə-'nen-t⁹l\ *adj* **1** : of or relating to a continent; *esp, often cap* : of or relating to the continent of Europe **2** *often cap* : of or relating to the colonies later forming the U.S. **3** : of or relating to cuisine based on classical European cooking

²continental *n* **1** *often cap* : a soldier in the Continental army **2** : EUROPEAN

continental drift *n* : a slow movement of the continents over a fluid layer deep within the earth

continental shelf *n* : a shallow submarine plain forming a border to a continent

continental slope *n* : a comparatively steep slope from a continental shelf to the ocean floor

con·tin·gen·cy \kən-'tin-jən-sē\ *n, pl* **-cies** : a chance or possible event

¹con·tin·gent \-jənt\ *adj* **1** : liable but not certain to happen : POSSIBLE **2** : happening by chance : not planned **3** : dependent on something that may or may not occur **4** : CONDITIONAL ✦ *Synonyms* ACCIDENTAL, CASUAL, INCIDENTAL, ODD

²contingent *n* : a quota (as of troops) supplied from an area or group

con·tin·u·al \kən-'tin-yə-wəl\ *adj* **1** : CONTINUOUS, UNBROKEN **2** : steadily recurring — **con·tin·u·al·ly** *adv*

con·tin·u·ance \-yə-wəns\ *n* **1** : unbroken succession **2** : the extent of continuing : DURATION **3** : adjournment of legal proceedings

con·tin·u·a·tion \kən-ˌtin-yə-'wā-shən\ *n* **1** : extension or prolongation of a state or activity **2** : resumption after an interruption; *also* : something that carries on after a pause or break

con·tin·ue \kən-'tin-yü\ *vb* **-tin·ued; -tinu·ing** **1** : to maintain without interruption **2** : ENDURE, LAST ⟨the tradition ∼s⟩ **3** : to remain in a place or condition ⟨∼ at this job⟩ **4** : to resume (as a story) after an intermission **5** : EXTEND ⟨∼ a subscription⟩; *also* : to persist in ⟨will ∼ to remind you⟩ **6** : to allow to remain **7** : to keep (a legal case) on the calendar or undecided

con·ti·nu·i·ty \ˌkän-tə-'nü-ə-tē, -'nyü-\ *n, pl* **-ties** **1** : the state of being continuous **2** : something (as a film script) that has or provides continuity

con·tin·u·ous \kən-'tin-yə-wəs\ *adj* : continuing without interruption — **con·tin·u·ous·ly** *adv*

con·tin·u·um \-yə-wəm\ *n, pl* **-ua** \-yə-wə\ *also* **-u·ums** : something that is the same throughout or consists of a series of variations or of a sequence of things in regular order

con·tort \kən-ˈtȯrt\ *vb* : to twist out of shape ⟨a ~*ed* face⟩ ⟨~ the truth⟩ — **con·tor·tion** \-ˈtȯr-shən\ *n*

con·tor·tion·ist \-ˈtȯr-shə-nist\ *n* : an acrobat able to twist the body into unusual postures

con·tour \ˈkän-ˌtu̇r\ *n* [F, fr. It *contorno* fr. *contornare* to round off, fr. ML, to turn around, fr. L *com-* together + *tornare* to turn on a lathe, fr. *tornus* lathe] 1 : OUTLINE 2 : SHAPE, FORM — often used in pl. ⟨the ~s of a statue⟩

contr *abbr* contract; contraction

con·tra·band \ˈkän-trə-ˌband\ *n* : goods legally prohibited in trade; *also* : smuggled goods

con·tra·cep·tion \ˌkän-trə-ˈsep-shən\ *n* : intentional prevention of conception and pregnancy — **con·tra·cep·tive** \-ˈsep-tiv\ *adj or n*

¹**con·tract** \ˈkän-ˌtrakt\ *n* 1 : a binding agreement; *also* : a document stating its terms 2 : an undertaking to win a specified number of tricks in bridge — **con·tract** *adj* — **con·trac·tu·al** \kən-ˈtrak-chə-wəl\ *adj* — **con·trac·tu·al·ly** *adv*

²**con·tract** \kən-ˈtrakt, 2 *usu* ˈkän-ˌtrakt\ *vb* 1 : to become affected with ⟨~ a disease⟩ 2 : to establish or undertake by contract 3 : SHRINK, LESSEN; *esp* : to draw together esp. so as to shorten ⟨~ a muscle⟩ 4 : to shorten (a word) by omitting letters or sounds in the middle — **con·tract·ible** \kən-ˈtrak-tə-bəl, ˈkän-ˌ\ *adj* — **con·trac·tion** \kən-ˈtrak-shən\ *n* — **con·trac·tor** \ˈkän-ˌtrak-tər, kən-ˈtrak-\ *n*

con·trac·tile \kən-ˈtrak-tᵊl\ *adj* : able to contract — **con·trac·til·i·ty** \ˌkän-ˌtrak-ˈti-lə-tē\ *n*

con·tra·dict \ˌkän-trə-ˈdikt\ *vb* : to assert the contrary of : deny the truth of ⟨~ a rumor⟩ — **con·tra·dic·tion** \-ˈdik-shən\ *n* — **con·tra·dic·to·ry** \-ˈdik-tə-rē\ *adj*

con·tra·dis·tinc·tion \ˌkän-trə-dis-ˈtiŋk-shən\ *n* : distinction by contrast

con·trail \ˈkän-ˌtrāl\ *n* : a streak of condensed water vapor created by an airplane or rocket at high altitudes

con·tra·in·di·cate \ˌkän-trə-ˈin-də-ˌkāt\ *vb* : to make (a treatment or procedure) inadvisable — **con·tra·in·di·ca·tion** \-ˌin-də-ˈkā-shən\ *n*

con·tral·to \kən-ˈtral-tō\ *n, pl* **-tos** : the lowest female voice; *also* : a singer having such a voice

con·trap·tion \kən-ˈtrap-shən\ *n* : CONTRIVANCE, DEVICE

con·tra·pun·tal \ˌkän-trə-ˈpən-tᵊl\ *adj* : of or relating to counterpoint

con·tra·ri·ety \ˌkän-trə-ˈrī-ə-tē\ *n, pl* **-eties** : the state of being contrary : DISAGREEMENT, INCONSISTENCY

con·trari·wise \ˈkän-ˌtrer-ē-ˌwīz, kən-ˈtrer-\ *adv* 1 : on the contrary 2 : VICE VERSA

con·trary \ˈkän-ˌtrer-ē; 4 *often* kən-ˈtrer-ē\ *adj* 1 : opposite in nature or position 2 : COUNTER, OPPOSED 3 : UNFAVORABLE — used of wind or weather 4 : unwilling to accept control or advice —

con·trar·i·an \kən-ˈtrer-ē-ən, kän-\ *n or adj* — **con·trari·ly** \ˈkän-ˌtrer-ə-lē, kən-ˈtrer-\ *adv* — **con·trary** *n is* ˈkän-ˌtrer-ē, *adv is like adj*\ *n or adv*

¹**con·trast** \kən-ˈtrast\ *vb* [F *contraster*, fr. MF, to oppose, resist, fr. VL **contrastare*, fr. L *contra-* against + *stare* to stand] 1 : to show differences when compared 2 : to compare in such a way as to show differences

²**con·trast** \ˈkän-ˌtrast\ *n* 1 : diversity of adjacent parts in color, emotion, tone, or brightness ⟨the ~ of a photograph⟩ 2 : unlikeness as shown when things are compared : DIFFERENCE

con·tra·vene \ˌkän-trə-ˈvēn\ *vb* **-vened; -ven·ing** 1 : to go or act contrary to ⟨~ a law⟩ 2 : CONTRADICT ⟨~ a claim⟩

con·tre·temps \ˈkän-trə-ˌtäⁿ, kōⁿ-trə-ˈtäⁿ\ *n, pl* **con·tre·temps** \-ˌtäⁿ, -ˈtäⁿz\ [F] : an inopportune or embarrassing occurrence

contrib *abbr* contribution; contributor

con·trib·ute \kən-ˈtri-byət\ *vb* **-ut·ed; -ut·ing** : to give along with others (as to a fund); *also* : HELP, ASSIST — **con·tri·bu·tion** \ˌkän-trə-ˈbyü-shən\ *n* — **con·trib·u·tor** \kən-ˈtri-byə-tər\ *n* — **con·trib·u·to·ry** \-byə-ˌtȯr-ē\ *adj*

con·trite \ˈkän-ˌtrīt, kən-ˈtrīt\ *adj* : PENITENT, REPENTANT — **con·trite·ly** *adv* — **con·tri·tion** \kən-ˈtri-shən\ *n*

con·triv·ance \kən-ˈtrī-vəns\ *n* 1 : a mechanical device 2 : SCHEME, PLAN

con·trive \kən-ˈtrīv\ *vb* **con·trived; con·triv·ing** 1 : PLAN, DEVISE 2 : FRAME, MAKE 3 : to bring about with difficulty — **con·triv·er** *n*

con·trived \-ˈtrīvd\ *adj* : lacking in natural quality ⟨a ~ plot⟩

¹**con·trol** \kən-ˈtrōl\ *vb* **con·trolled; con·trol·ling** [ME *controllen* to verify, fr. AF *countrerouler*, fr. *countrerole* copy of an account, audit, fr. ML *contrarotulus*, fr. L *contra* against + ML *rotulus* roll] 1 : to exercise restraining or directing influence over : REGULATE 2 : DOMINATE, RULE — **con·trol·la·ble** \-ˈtrō-lə-bəl\ *adj*

²**control** *n* 1 : power to direct or regulate 2 : RESERVE, RESTRAINT 3 : a device for regulating a mechanism

con·trol·ler \kən-ˈtrō-lər, ˈkän-ˌtrō-lər\ *n* 1 : COMPTROLLER 2 : a person or thing that controls ⟨an air traffic ~⟩ ⟨a game ~⟩

con·tro·ver·sy \ˈkän-trə-ˌvər-sē\ *n, pl* **-sies** : a clash of opposing views : DISPUTE — **con·tro·ver·sial** \ˌkän-trə-ˌvər-shəl, -sē-əl\ *adj*

con·tro·vert \ˈkän-trə-ˌvərt, ˌkän-trə-ˈvərt\ *vb* : DENY, CONTRADICT — **con·tro·vert·ible** *adj*

con·tu·ma·cious \ˌkän-tü-ˈmā-shəs, -tyü-\ *adj* : stubbornly disobedient ♦ *Synonyms* REBELLIOUS, INSUBORDINATE, SEDITIOUS — **con·tu·ma·cy** \kən-ˈtü-mə-sē, -ˈtyü-; ˈkän-tyə-\ *n* — **con·tu·ma·cious·ly** *adv*

con·tu·me·ly \kən-ˈtü-mə-lē, -ˈtyü-; ˈkän-tə-ˌmē-lē, -tyə-\ *n, pl* **-lies** : contemptuous treatment : INSULT

con·tu·sion \kən-'tü-zhən, -'tyü-\ n : BRUISE — **con·tuse** \-'tüz, -'tyüz\ vb

co·nun·drum \kə-'nən-drəm\ n : RIDDLE

conv abbr 1 convention 2 convertible

con·va·lesce \ˌkän-və-'les\ vb **-lesced**; **-lesc·ing** : to recover health gradually — **con·va·les·cence** \-'le-sᵊns\ n — **con·va·les·cent** \-sᵊnt\ adj or n

con·vec·tion \kən-'vek-shən\ n : circulatory motion in a fluid due to warmer portions rising and cooler denser portions sinking; also : the transfer of heat by such motion — **con·vec·tion·al** \-shə-nəl\ adj — **con·vec·tive** \-'vek-tiv\ adj

convection oven n : an oven with a fan that circulates hot air uniformly and continuously around the food

con·vene \kən-'vēn\ vb **con·vened**; **con·ven·ing** : ASSEMBLE, MEET

con·ve·nience \kən-'vē-nyəns\ n 1 : SUITABLENESS 2 : a laborsaving device 3 : a suitable time ⟨at your ∼⟩ 4 : personal comfort : EASE

convenience store n : a small market that is open long hours

con·ve·nient \-nyənt\ adj 1 : suited to personal comfort or ease 2 : placed near at hand — **con·ve·nient·ly** adv

con·vent \'kän-vənt, -ˌvent\ n [ME covent, fr. AF, fr. ML conventus, fr. L, assembly, fr. convenire to come together] : a local community or house of a religious order esp. of nuns — **con·ven·tu·al** \kän-'ven-chə-wəl\ adj

con·ven·ti·cle \kən-'ven-ti-kəl\ n : MEETING; esp : a secret meeting for worship

con·ven·tion \kən-'ven-chən\ n 1 : an agreement esp. between states on a matter of common concern 2 : MEETING, ASSEMBLY 3 : an assembly of persons convened for some purpose 4 : generally accepted custom, practice, or belief

con·ven·tion·al \-chə-nəl\ adj 1 : sanctioned by general custom 2 : COMMONPLACE, ORDINARY — **con·ven·tion·al·i·ty** \-ˌven-chə-'na-lə-tē\ n — **con·ven·tion·al·ize** \-'ven-chə-nə-ˌlīz\ vb — **con·ven·tion·al·ly** adv

con·verge \kən-'vərj\ vb **con·verged**; **con·verg·ing** : to approach one common center or single point ⟨converging paths⟩ — **con·ver·gence** \kən-'vər-jəns\ n — **con·ver·gent** \-jənt\ adj

con·ver·sant \kən-'vər-sᵊnt\ adj : having knowledge and experience — used with with

con·ver·sa·tion \ˌkän-vər-'sā-shən\ n : an informal talking together — **con·ver·sa·tion·al** \-shə-nᵊl\ adj — **con·ver·sa·tion·al·ly** adv

con·ver·sa·tion·al·ist \-shə-nᵊl-ist\ n : a person who converses a great deal or who excels in conversation

¹**con·verse** \'kän-ˌvərs\ n : CONVERSATION

²**con·verse** \kən-'vərs\ vb **con·versed**; **con·vers·ing** : to engage in conversation

³**con·verse** \'kän-ˌvərs\ n : a statement related to another statement by having its hypothesis and conclusion or its subject and predicate reversed or interchanged

⁴**con·verse** \kən-'vərs, 'kän-ˌvers\ adj : reversed in order or relation — **con·verse·ly** adv

con·ver·sion \kən-'vər-zhən\ n 1 : a change in nature or form 2 : an experience associated with a decisive adoption of religion

¹**con·vert** \kən-'vərt\ vb 1 : to turn from one belief or party to another 2 : TRANSFORM, CHANGE 3 : MISAPPROPRIATE 4 : EXCHANGE — **con·vert·er** or **con·ver·tor** \-'vər-tər\ n

²**con·vert** \'kän-ˌvərt\ n : a person who has undergone religious conversion

¹**con·vert·ible** \kən-'vər-tə-bəl\ adj : capable of being converted

²**convertible** n : an automobile with a top that may be lowered or removed

con·vex \kän-'veks, 'kän-ˌveks\ adj : curved or rounded outward like the exterior of a sphere or circle — **con·vex·i·ty** \kän-'vek-sə-tē\ n

con·vey \kən-'vā\ vb 1 : CARRY, TRANSPORT ⟨a river ∼ing logs⟩ 2 : TRANSFER, COMMUNICATE ⟨∼ a message⟩ — **con·vey·or** also **con·vey·er** \-ər\ n

con·vey·ance \-'vā-əns\ n 1 : the act of conveying 2 : a legal paper transferring ownership of property 3 : VEHICLE

¹**con·vict** \kən-'vikt\ vb : to prove or find guilty

²**con·vict** \'kän-ˌvikt\ n : a person serving a prison sentence

con·vic·tion \kən-'vik-shən\ n 1 : the act of convicting esp. in a court 2 : the state of being convinced : BELIEF

con·vince \kən-'vins\ vb **con·vinced**; **con·vinc·ing** : to bring (as by argument) to belief or action — **con·vinc·ing** adj — **con·vinc·ing·ly** adv

con·viv·ial \kən-'vi-vē-əl\ adj [LL convivialis, fr. L convivium banquet, fr. com- together + vivere to live] : enjoying companionship and the pleasures of feasting and drinking : JOVIAL, FESTIVE — **con·viv·i·al·i·ty** \-ˌvi-vē-'a-lə-tē\ n — **con·viv·ial·ly** adv

con·vo·ca·tion \ˌkän-və-'kā-shən\ n 1 : a ceremonial assembly (as of the clergy) 2 : the act of convoking

con·voke \kən-'vōk\ vb **con·voked**; **con·vok·ing** : to call together to a meeting

con·vo·lut·ed \'kän-və-ˌlü-təd\ adj 1 : folded in curved or tortuous windings 2 : INVOLVED, INTRICATE

con·vo·lu·tion \ˌkän-və-'lü-shən\ n : a tortuous or winding structure; esp : one of the ridges of the brain

¹**con·voy** \'kän-ˌvȯi, kən-'vȯi\ vb : to accompany for protection

²**con·voy** \'kän-ˌvȯi\ n 1 : one that convoys; esp : a protective escort (as for ships) 2 : the act of convoying 3 : a group of moving vehicles

con·vulse \kən-'vəls\ vb **con·vulsed**; **con·vuls·ing** : to agitate violently

con·vul·sion \kən-'vəl-shən\ n 1 : an abnormal and violent involuntary contraction or series of contractions of muscle 2

: a violent disturbance — **con·vul·sive** \-siv\ adj — **con·vul·sive·ly** adv

cony var of CONEY

coo \'kü\ n : a soft low sound made by doves or pigeons; also : a sound like this — **coo** vb

COO abbr chief operating officer

¹**cook** \'kuk\ n : a person who prepares food for eating

²**cook** vb 1 : to prepare food for eating 2 : to subject to heat or fire 3 : CONCOCT, FABRICATE — usu. used with up ⟨~ up a scheme⟩ — **cook·er** n — **cook·ware** \-,wer\ n

cook·book \-,buk\ n : a book of cooking directions and recipes

cook·ery \'ku-kə-rē\ n, pl **-er·ies** : the art or practice of cooking

cook·ie or **cooky** \'ku-kē\ n, pl **cook·ies** [D koekje, dim. of koek cake] 1 : a small sweet flat cake 2 cookie : a file containing information about a Web site user created and read by a Web site server and stored on the user's computer

cookie-cutter adj : marked by a lack of originality or distinction ⟨~ malls⟩

cook·out \'kuk-,aut\ n : an outing at which a meal is cooked and served in the open

¹**cool** \'kül\ adj, 1 : moderately cold 2 : not excited : CALM 3 : not friendly 4 : IMPUDENT 5 : protecting from heat 6 slang : very good 7 slang : FASHIONABLE ♦ **Synonyms** UNFLAPPABLE, COMPOSED, COLLECTED, UNRUFFLED, NONCHALANT — **cool·ly** adv — **cool·ness** n

²**cool** vb : to make or become cool

³**cool** n 1 : a cool time or place 2 : INDIFFERENCE; also : SELF-ASSURANCE, COMPOSURE ⟨kept his ~⟩

cool·ant \'kü-lənt\ n : a usu. fluid cooling agent

cool·er \'kü-lər\ n 1 : a container for keeping food or drink cool 2 : JAIL, PRISON 3 : a tall iced drink

coo·lie \'kü-lē\ n [Hindi & Urdu qulī] : an unskilled laborer usu. in or from the Far East

coon \'kün\ n : RACCOON

coon·hound \-,haund\ n : a sporting dog trained to hunt raccoons

coon·skin \-,skin\ n : the pelt of a raccoon; also : something (as a cap) made of this

¹**coop** \'küp, 'kup\ n : a small enclosure or building usu. for poultry

²**coop** vb : to confine in or as if in a coop — usu. used with up

co-op \'kō-,äp\ n : COOPERATIVE

coo·per \'kü-pər, 'ku-\ n : one who makes or repairs barrels or casks — **cooper** vb — **coo·per·age** \-pə-rij\ n

co·op·er·ate \kō-'ä-pə-,rāt\ vb : to act jointly or in compliance with others — **co·op·er·a·tion** \-,ä-pə-'rā-shən\ n — **co·op·er·a·tor** \-'ä-pə-,rā-tər\ n

¹**co·op·er·a·tive** \kō-'ä-prə-tiv, -'ä-pə-,rā-\ adj 1 : willing to work with others 2 : of or relating to an association formed to enable its members to buy or sell to better advantage by eliminating middlemen's profits

²**cooperative** n : a cooperative association

co-opt \kō-'äpt\ vb 1 : to choose or elect as a colleague 2 : ABSORB, ASSIMILATE; also : TAKE OVER ⟨a style ~ed by advertisers⟩

¹**co·or·di·nate** \kō-'or-də-nət\ adj 1 : equal in rank or order 2 : of equal rank in a compound sentence ⟨~ clause⟩ 3 : joining words or word groups of the same rank — **co·or·di·nate·ly** adv

²**co·or·di·nate** \-'or-də-,nāt\ vb **-nat·ed; -nat·ing** 1 : to make or become coordinate ⟨~ our schedules⟩ 2 : to work or act together harmoniously ⟨a coordinated wardrobe⟩ — **co·or·di·na·tion** \-,or-də-'nā-shən\ n — **co·or·di·na·tor** \-'or-də-'nā-tər\ n

³**co·or·di·nate** \-'or-də-nət\ n 1 : one of a set of numbers used in specifying the location of a point on a surface or in space 2 pl : articles (as of clothing) designed to be used together and to attain their effect through pleasing contrast

coot \'küt\ n 1 : a dark-colored ducklike bird related to the rails 2 : any of several No. American sea ducks 3 : a harmless simple person

coo·tie \'kü-tē\ n : a body louse

¹**cop** \'käp\ n : POLICE OFFICER

²**cop** vb, 1 slang : STEAL ⟨~ a glance⟩ 2 slang : ADMIT — used with to ⟨~ to the charges⟩ 3 : ADOPT ⟨~ an attitude⟩

co-pay \'kō-'pā\ n : CO-PAYMENT

co-pay·ment \'kō-,pā-mənt, ,kō-'\ n : a fixed fee required of a patient by a health insurer (as an HMO) at the time of each outpatient service or filling of a prescription

¹**cope** \'kōp\ n : a long cloaklike ecclesiastical vestment

²**cope** vb **coped; cop·ing** : to struggle to overcome problems or difficulties ⟨~ with tragedy⟩

copi·er \'kä-pē-ər\ n : one that copies; esp : a machine for making copies

co·pi·lot \'kō-,pī-lət\ n : an assistant pilot of an aircraft or spacecraft

cop·ing \'kō-pin\ n : the top layer of a wall

co·pi·ous \'kō-pē-əs\ adj : LAVISH, ABUNDANT ⟨a ~ harvest⟩ — **co·pi·ous·ly** adv — **co·pi·ous·ness** n

cop-out \'käp-,aut\ n : an excuse for copping out; also : an act of copping out

cop out vb : to back out (as of an unwanted responsibility)

cop·per \'kä-pər\ n 1 : a malleable reddish metallic chemical element that is one of the best conductors of heat and electricity 2 : a coin or token made of copper — **cop·pery** adj

cop·per·head \'kä-pər-,hed\ n : a largely coppery brown pit viper esp. of the eastern and central U.S.

cop·pice \'kä-pəs\ n : THICKET

co·pra \'kō-prə\ n : dried coconut meat yielding coconut oil

copse \'käps\ n : THICKET

cop·ter \'käp-tər\ n : HELICOPTER

cop·u·la \'kä-pyə-lə\ n : LINKING VERB — **cop·u·la·tive** \-lə-tiv, -,lā-\ adj

cop·u·late \'kä-pyə-ˌlāt\ vb **-lat·ed; -lat·ing** : to engage in sexual intercourse — **cop·u·la·tion** \ˌkä-pyə-'lā-shən\ n — **cop·u·la·to·ry** \'kä-pyə-lə-ˌtör-ē\ adj

¹copy \'kä-pē\ n, pl **cop·ies** **1** : an imitation or reproduction of an original work **2** : material to be set in type **3** : DUPLICATE ♦ *Synonyms* DUPLICATE, REPRODUCTION, FACSIMILE, REPLICA

²copy vb **cop·ied; copy·ing** **1** : to make a copy of **2** : IMITATE — **copy·ist** n

copy·book \'kä-pē-ˌbuk\ n : a book formerly used to teach handwriting containing examples to be copied

copy·boy \-ˌbȯi\ n : a person who carries copy and runs errands (as in a newspaper office)

copy·cat \-ˌkat\ n : a slavish imitator

copy·desk \-ˌdesk\ n : the desk at which newspaper copy is edited

copy editor n : one who edits or prepares copy (as headlines) esp. for a newspaper

copy·read·er \-ˌrē-dər\ n : COPY EDITOR

¹copy·right \-ˌrīt\ n : the sole right to reproduce, publish, sell, or distribute a literary or artistic work

²copyright vb : to secure a copyright on

copy·writ·er \'kä-pē-ˌrī-tər\ n : a writer of advertising copy

co·quet or **co·quette** \kō-'ket\ vb **co·quet·ted; co·quet·ting** : FLIRT — **co·quet·ry** \'kō-kə-trē, kō-'ke-trē\ n

co·quette \kō-'ket\ n [F, fem. of *coquet*, flirtatious man, dim. of *coq* cock] : FLIRT — **co·quett·ish** adj

cor abbr corner

Cor abbr Corinthians

cor·a·cle \'kȯr-ə-kəl\ n [W *corwgl*] : a boat made of a frame covered usu. with hide or tarpaulin

cor·al \'kȯr-əl\ n **1** : a stony or horny material that forms the skeleton of colonies of tiny sea polyps and includes a red form used in jewelry; *also* : a coral-forming polyp or polyp colony **2** : a deep pink color — **coral** adj

coral snake n : any of several venomous chiefly tropical New World snakes brilliantly banded in red, black, and yellow or white

cor·bel \'kȯr-bəl\ n : a bracket-shaped architectural member that projects from a wall and supports a weight

¹cord \'kȯrd\ n **1** : a usu. heavy string consisting of several strands woven or twisted together **2** : a long slender anatomical structure (as a tendon or nerve) **3** : a small flexible insulated electrical cable used to connect an appliance with a receptacle **4** : a cubic measure used esp. for firewood and equal to a stack 4×4×8 feet **5** : a rib or ridge on cloth

²cord vb **1** : to tie or furnish with a cord **2** : to pile (wood) in cords

cord·age \'kȯr-dij\ n : ROPES, CORDS; *esp* : ropes in the rigging of a ship

¹cor·dial \'kȯr-jəl\ adj [ME, fr. ML *cordialis*, fr. L *cord-, cor* heart] : warmly receptive or welcoming : HEARTFELT, HEARTY — **cor·di·al·i·ty** \ˌkȯr-jē-'a-lə-tē, kȯr-'ja-\ n — **cor·dial·ly** adv

²cordial n **1** : a stimulating medicine or drink **2** : LIQUEUR

cor·dil·le·ra \ˌkȯr-dəl-'yer-ə, -də-'ler-\ n [Sp] : a series of parallel mountain ranges

cord·less \'kȯrd-ləs\ adj : having no cord; *esp* : powered by a battery ⟨a ∼ phone⟩ — **cord·less** n

cór·do·ba \'kȯr-də-bə, -və\ n — see MONEY table

cor·don \'kȯr-dᵊn\ n **1** : an ornamental cord or ribbon **2** : an encircling line (as of troops or police) — **cordon** vb

cor·do·van \'kȯr-də-vən\ n : a soft fine-grained leather

cor·du·roy \'kȯr-də-ˌrȯi\ n, pl **-roys** : a heavy ribbed fabric; *also, pl* : pants of this material

cord·wain·er \'kȯrd-ˌwā-nər\ n : SHOEMAKER

¹core \'kȯr\ n **1** : the central usu. inedible part of some fruits (as the apple); *also* : an inmost part of something **2** : GIST, ESSENCE

²core vb **cored; cor·ing** : to take out the core of — **cor·er** n

CORE \'kȯr\ abbr Congress of Racial Equality

co·re·op·sis \ˌkȯr-ē-'äp-səs\ n, pl **coreopsis** : any of a genus of widely cultivated composite herbs with showy often yellow flower heads

co·re·spon·dent \ˌkō-ri-'spän-dənt\ n : a person named as guilty of adultery with the defendant in a divorce suit

co·ri·an·der \'kȯr-ē-ˌan-dər\ n : an herb related to the carrot; *also* : its aromatic dried fruit used as a flavoring

Cor·in·thi·ans \kə-'rin-thē-ənz\ n — see BIBLE table

¹cork \'kȯrk\ n **1** : the tough elastic bark of a European oak (**cork oak**) used esp. for stoppers and insulation; *also* : a stopper of this **2** : a tissue of a woody plant making up most of the bark — **corky** adj

²cork vb : to furnish with or stop up with cork or a cork ⟨∼ a bottle⟩

cork·screw \'kȯrk-ˌskrü\ n : a device for drawing corks from bottles

corm \'kȯrm\ n : a solid bulblike underground part of a stem (as of the crocus or gladiolus)

cor·mo·rant \'kȯr-mə-rənt, -ˌrant\ n [ME *cormeraunt*, fr. MF *cormorant*, fr. OF *cormareng*, fr. *corp* raven + *marenc* of the sea, fr. L *marinus*] : any of various dark-colored water birds with a long neck, hooked bill, and distensible throat pouch

¹corn \'kȯrn\ n **1** : the seeds of a cereal grass and esp. of the chief cereal crop of a region (as wheat in Britain and Indian corn in the U.S.); *also* : a cereal grass **2** : sweet corn served as a vegetable

²corn vb : to salt (as beef) in brine and preservatives

³corn n : a local hardening and thickening of skin (as on a toe)

¹corn·ball \'kȯrn-ˌbȯl\ n : an unsophisticated person; *also* : something cornig

²cornball adj : CORNY ⟨∼ humor⟩

corn bread n : bread made with cornmeal

corn·cob \-ˌkäb\ *n* : the woody core on which the kernels of Indian corn are arranged

corn·crib \-ˌkrib\ *n* : a crib for storing ears of Indian corn

cor·nea \'kȯr-nē-ə\ *n* : the transparent part of the coat of the eyeball covering the iris and the pupil — **cor·ne·al** *adj*

corn ear·worm \-'ir-ˌwərm\ *n* : a moth whose larva is destructive esp. to Indian corn

¹**cor·ner** \'kȯr-nər\ *n* [ME, fr. AF *cornere*, fr. *corne* horn, corner, fr. L *cornu* horn, point] **1** : the point or angle formed by the meeting of lines, edges, or sides **2** : the place where two streets come together **3** : a quiet secluded place **4** : a position from which retreat or escape is impossible **5** : control of enough of the available supply (as of a commodity) to permit manipulation of the price — **cornered** *adj* — **around the corner** : IMMINENT ⟨has a birthday just *around the corner*⟩

²**cor·ner** *vb* **1** : to drive into a corner **2** : to get a corner on ⟨~ the wheat market⟩ **3** : to turn a corner

cor·ner·stone \'kȯr-nər-ˌstōn\ *n* **1** : a stone forming part of a corner in a wall; *esp* : such a stone laid at a formal ceremony **2** : something of basic importance

cor·net \kȯr-'net\ *n* : a brass band instrument resembling the trumpet

corn flour *n, Brit* : CORNSTARCH

corn·flow·er \'kȯrn-ˌflau̇(-ə)r\ *n* : BACHELOR'S BUTTON

cor·nice \'kȯr-nəs\ *n* : the horizontal projecting part crowning the wall of a building

corn·meal \'kȯrn-ˌmēl\ *n* : meal ground from corn

corn·row \-ˌrō\ *n* : a section of hair braided flat to the scalp in rows — **cornrow** *vb*

corn·stalk \-ˌstȯk\ *n* : a stalk of Indian corn

corn·starch \-ˌstärch\ *n* : a starch made from corn and used in cookery as a thickening agent

corn syrup *n* : a sweet syrup obtained from cornstarch

cor·nu·co·pia \ˌkȯr-nə-'kō-pē-ə, -nyə-\ *n* [LL, fr. L *cornu copiae* horn of plenty] **1** : a horn-shaped container filled with fruits and grain emblematic of abundance **2** : ABUNDANCE

corny \'kȯr-nē\ *adj* **corn·i·er; -est** : tiresomely simple or sentimental

co·rol·la \kə-'rä-lə, -'rō-\ *n* : the petals of a flower

cor·ol·lary \'kȯr-ə-ˌler-ē\ *n, pl* **-lar·ies 1** : a deduction from a proposition already proved true **2** : CONSEQUENCE, RESULT

co·ro·na \kə-'rō-nə\ *n* **1** : a colored circle often seen around and close to a luminous body (as the sun or moon) **2** : the outermost part of the atmosphere of a star (as the sun) — **co·ro·nal** \'kȯr-ə-nᵊl, kə-'rō-nᵊl\ *adj*

cor·o·nal \'kȯr-ə-nᵊl\ *n* : a circlet for the head

¹**cor·o·nary** \'kȯr-ə-ˌner-ē\ *adj* : of or relating to the heart or its blood vessels

²**coronary** *n, pl* **-nar·ies 1** : a coronary blood vessel **2** : CORONARY THROMBOSIS; *also* : HEART ATTACK

coronary thrombosis *n* : the blocking by a thrombus of one of the arteries supplying the heart tissues

cor·o·na·tion \ˌkȯr-ə-'nā-shən\ *n* : the act or ceremony of crowning a monarch

cor·o·ner \'kȯr-ə-nər\ *n* [ME, an officer of the crown, fr. AF, fr. *corone* crown, fr. L *corona*] : a public official who investigates causes of deaths possibly not due to natural causes

cor·o·net \ˌkȯr-ə-'net\ *n* **1** : a small crown **2** : an ornamental band worn around the temples

corp *abbr* **1** corporal **2** corporation

¹**cor·po·ral** \'kȯr-p(ə-)rəl\ *adj* : of or relating to the body ⟨~ punishment⟩

²**corporal** *n* : a noncommissioned officer (as in the army) ranking next below a sergeant

cor·po·rate \'kȯr-p(ə-)rət\ *adj* **1** : INCORPORATED; *also* : belonging to an incorporated body **2** : of or relating to large-scale business ⟨~ mergers⟩ **3** : combined into one body

cor·po·ra·tion \ˌkȯr-pə-'rā-shən\ *n* **1** : the municipal authorities of a town or city **2** : a legal creation authorized to act with the rights and liabilities of a person; *also* : COMPANY

cor·po·rat·ize \'kȯr-pə-rə-ˌtīz\ *vb* **ized; -iz·ing** : to subject to corporate control ⟨~ education⟩

cor·po·re·al \kȯr-'pȯr-ē-əl\ *adj.* **1** : PHYSICAL, MATERIAL **2** *archaic* : BODILY — **cor·po·re·al·i·ty** \-ˌpȯr-ē-'a-lə-tē\ *n* — **cor·po·re·al·ly** *adv*

corps \'kȯr\ *n, pl* **corps** \'kȯrz\ [F, fr. OF *cors*, fr. L *corpus* body] **1** : an organized subdivision of a country's military forces **2** : a group acting under common direction

corpse \'kȯrps\ *n* : a dead body

corps·man \'kȯr-mən, 'kȯrz-\ *n* : an enlisted man trained to give first aid

cor·pu·lence \'kȯr-pyə-ləns\ *n* : excessive fatness : OBESITY

cor·pu·lent \-lənt\ *adj* : OBESE

cor·pus \'kȯr-pəs\ *n, pl* **cor·po·ra** \-pə-rə\ [ME, fr. L] **1** : BODY; *esp* : CORPSE **2** : a body of writings or works

cor·pus·cle \'kȯr-pə-səl, -ˌpə-\ *n* **1** : a minute particle **2** : a living cell (as in blood or cartilage) not aggregated into continuous tissues — **cor·pus·cu·lar** \'kȯr-'pəs-kyə-lər\ *adj*

cor·pus de·lic·ti \ˌkȯr-pəs-di-'lik-ˌtī, -tē\ *n, pl* **corpora delicti** [NL, lit., body of the crime] **1** : the substantial fact proving that a crime has been committed **2** : the body of a victim of murder

corr *abbr* **1** correct; corrected; correction **2** correspondence; correspondent; corresponding

cor·ral \kə-'ral\ *n* [Sp] : an enclosure for confining or capturing animals; *also* : an enclosure of wagons for defending a camp — **corral** *vb*

¹**cor·rect** \kə-ˈrekt\ *vb* **1** : to make right ⟨~ an error⟩ **2** : REPROVE, CHASTISE ⟨~ed the child⟩ — **cor·rect·able** \-ˈrek-tə-bəl\ *adj* — **cor·rec·tion** \-ˈrek-shən\ *n* — **cor·rec·tion·al** \-ˈrek-sh(ə-)nəl\ *adj* — **cor·rec·tive** \-ˈrek-tiv\ *adj*

²**correct** *adj* **1** : conforming to a conventional standard ⟨~ behavior⟩ **2** : agreeing with fact or truth ⟨a ~ answer⟩ **3** : conforming to the standards of a specific ideology ⟨environmentally ~⟩ — **cor·rect·ly** *adv* — **cor·rect·ness** *n*

cor·re·late \ˈkȯr-ə-ˌlāt\ *vb* **-lat·ed; -lat·ing** : to connect in a systematic way : establish the mutual relations of — **cor·re·late** \-lət, -ˌlāt\ *n* — **cor·re·la·tion** \ˌkȯr-ə-ˈlā-shən\ *n*

cor·rel·a·tive \kə-ˈre-lə-tiv\ *adj* **1** : reciprocally related **2** : regularly used together (as *either* and *or*) — **correlative** *n* — **cor·rel·a·tive·ly** *adv*

cor·re·spond \ˌkȯr-ə-ˈspänd\ *vb* **1** : to be in agreement : SUIT, MATCH **2** : to communicate by letter — **cor·re·spond·ing·ly** *adv*

cor·re·spon·dence \-ˈspän-dəns\ *n* **1** : agreement between particular things **2** : communication by letters; *also* : the letters exchanged

¹**cor·re·spon·dent** \-dənt\ *adj* **1** : SIMILAR **2** : FITTING, CONFORMING

²**correspondent** *n* **1** : something that corresponds **2** : a person with whom one communicates by letter **3** : a person employed to contribute news regularly from a place ⟨a war ~⟩

cor·ri·dor \ˈkȯr-ə-dər, -ˌdȯr\ *n* **1** : a passageway into which compartments or rooms open (as in a hotel or school) **2** : a narrow strip of land esp. through foreign-held territory **3** : a densely populated strip of land including two or more major cities **4** : an area identified by a common characteristic or purpose ⟨a ~ of liberalism⟩

cor·ri·gen·dum \ˌkȯr-ə-ˈjen-dəm\ *n, pl* **-da** \-də\ [L] : an error in a printed work discovered after printing and shown with its correction on a separate sheet

cor·ri·gi·ble \ˈkȯr-ə-jə-bəl\ *adj* : CORRECTABLE

cor·rob·o·rate \kə-ˈrä-bə-ˌrāt\ *vb* **-rat·ed; -rat·ing** [L *corroborare*, fr. *robur* strength] : to support with evidence : CONFIRM — **cor·rob·o·ra·tion** \-ˌrä-bə-ˈrä-shən\ *n* — **cor·rob·o·ra·tive** \-ˈrä-bə-ˌrā-tiv, -ˈrä-brə-\ *adj* — **cor·rob·o·ra·to·ry** \-ˈrä-brə-ˌtȯr-ē\ *adj*

cor·rode \kə-ˈrōd\ *vb* **cor·rod·ed; cor·rod·ing** : to wear or be worn away gradually (as by chemical action) — **cor·ro·sion** \-ˈrō-zhən\ *n* — **cor·ro·sive** \-ˈrō-siv\ *adj or n*

cor·ru·gate \ˈkȯr-ə-ˌgāt\ *vb* **-gat·ed; -gat·ing** : to form into wrinkles or ridges and grooves — **cor·ru·gat·ed** *adj* — **cor·ru·ga·tion** \ˌkȯr-ə-ˈgā-shən\ *n*

¹**cor·rupt** \kə-ˈrəpt\ *vb* **1** : to make evil : DEPRAVE; *esp* : BRIBE **2** : ROT, SPOIL —

cor·rupt·ible *adj* — **cor·rup·tion** \-ˈrəp-shən\ *n*

²**corrupt** *adj* : morally degenerate; *also* : characterized by improper conduct ⟨~ officials⟩

cor·sage \kȯr-ˈsäzh, -ˈsäj\ *n* [F, bust, bodice, fr. OF, bust, fr. *cors* body, fr. L *corpus*] **1** : the waist or bodice of a dress **2** : a bouquet to be worn or carried

cor·sair \ˈkȯr-ˌser\ *n* : PIRATE

cor·set \ˈkȯr-sət\ *n* : a stiffened undergarment worn for support or to give shape to the waist and hips

cor·tege *also* **cor·tège** \kȯr-ˈtezh, ˈkȯr-ˌtezh\ *n* [F] : PROCESSION; *esp* : a funeral procession

cor·tex \ˈkȯr-ˌteks\ *n, pl* **cor·ti·ces** \ˈkȯr-tə-ˌsēz\ *or* **cor·tex·es** : an outer or covering layer of an organism or one of its parts ⟨the adrenal ~⟩ ⟨~ of a plant stem⟩; *esp* : CEREBRAL CORTEX — **cor·ti·cal** \ˈkȯr-ti-kəl\ *adj*

cor·ti·co·ste·roid \ˌkȯr-ti-kō-ˈstir-ˌȯid, -ˈster-\ *n* : any of various steroids made in the adrenal cortex and used medically as anti-inflammatory agents

cor·ti·sone \ˈkȯr-tə-ˌsōn, -ˌzōn\ *n* : a corticosteroid used esp. in treating rheumatoid arthritis

co·run·dum \kə-ˈrən-dəm\ *n* : a very hard aluminum-containing mineral used as an abrasive or as a gem

cor·us·cate \ˈkȯr-ə-ˌskāt\ *vb* **-cat·ed; -cat·ing** : FLASH, SPARKLE — **cor·us·ca·tion** \ˌkȯr-ə-ˈskā-shən\ *n*

cor·vette \kȯr-ˈvet\ *n* **1** : a naval sailing ship smaller than a frigate **2** : an armed escort ship smaller than a destroyer

co·ry·za \kə-ˈrī-zə\ *n* : an inflammatory disorder of the upper respiratory tract; *esp* : COMMON COLD

cos *abbr* cosine

COS *abbr* **1** cash on shipment **2** chief of staff

co·sig·na·to·ry \kō-ˈsig-nə-ˌtȯr-ē\ *n* : a joint signer

co·sign·er \ˈkō-ˌsī-nər\ *n* : COSIGNATORY; *esp* : a joint signer of a promissory note

co·sine \ˈkō-ˌsīn\ *n* : the trigonometric function that is the ratio between the side next to an acute angle in a right triangle and the hypotenuse

¹**cos·met·ic** \käz-ˈme-tik\ *adj* [Gk *kosmētikos* skilled in adornment, fr. *kosmein* to arrange, adorn, fr. *kosmos* order, ornament, universe] **1** : intended to beautify the hair or complexion **2** : correcting physical defects esp. to improve appearance ⟨~ dentistry⟩ **3** : SUPERFICIAL — **cos·met·i·cal·ly** \-ti-k(ə-)lē\ *adv*

²**cosmetic** *n* : a cosmetic preparation

cos·me·tol·o·gist \ˌkäz-mə-ˈtä-lə-jist\ *n* : one who gives beauty treatments — **cos·me·tol·o·gy** \-jē\ *n*

cos·mic \ˈkäz-mik\ *also* **cos·mi·cal** \-mi-kəl\ *adj* **1** : of or relating to the cosmos **2** : VAST, GRAND **3** : of or relating to spiritual or metaphysical ideas ⟨a ~ thinker⟩ — **cos·mi·cal·ly** *adv*

cosmic ray *n* : a stream of very penetrating atomic nuclei that enter the earth's atmosphere from outer space

cos·mog·o·ny \käz-'mä-gə-nē\ *n, pl* **-nies** : the origin or creation of the world or universe

cos·mol·o·gy \-'mä-lə-jē\ *n, pl* **-gies** : a branch of astronomy dealing with the origin and structure of the universe — **cos·mo·log·i·cal** \käz-mə-'lä-ji-kəl\ *adj* — **cos·mol·o·gist** \käz-'mä-lə-jist\ *n*

cos·mo·naut \'käz-mə-,nót\ *n* : a Soviet or Russian astronaut

cos·mo·pol·i·tan \käz-mə-'pä-lə-tən\ *adj* : belonging to all the world : not local
◆ *Synonyms* UNIVERSAL, GLOBAL, CATHOLIC — **cosmopolitan** *n*

cos·mos \'käz-məs, 1 *also* -mōs, -mäs\ *n* **1** : UNIVERSE **2** : a tall garden herb related to the daisies

co·spon·sor \'kō-,spän-sər, -'spän-\ *n* : a joint sponsor — **cosponsor** *vb*

Cos·sack \'kä-,sak, -sək\ *n* [Pol & Ukrainian *kozak*, of Turkic origin] : a member of one of several autonomous communities drawn from various ethnic groups in southern Russia; *also* : a mounted soldier from one of these communities

¹**cost** \'kóst\ *n* **1** : the amount paid or charged for something : PRICE **2** : the loss or penalty incurred in gaining something **3** *pl* : expenses incurred in a law suit — **at all costs** : regardless of consequences ⟨win *at all costs*⟩

²**cost** *vb* **cost; cost·ing 1** : to require a specified amount in payment **2** : to cause to pay, suffer, or lose

co·star \'kō-,stär\ *n* : one of two leading players in a motion picture or play — **co·star** *vb*

cos·tive \'käs-tiv\ *adj* : affected with or causing constipation

cost·ly \'kóst-lē\ *adj* **cost·li·er; -est 1** : of great cost or value ⟨~ gems⟩ **2** : done at great expense or sacrifice ⟨a ~ error⟩
◆ *Synonyms* DEAR, VALUABLE, EXPENSIVE — **cost·li·ness** *n*

cos·tume \'käs-,tüm, -,tyüm\ *n* [F, fr. It, custom, dress, fr. L *consuetudo* custom] **1** : the style of attire characteristic of a period or country **2** : a special or fancy dress ⟨Halloween ~s⟩ — **cos·tum·er** \'käs-,tü-mər, -,tyü-\ *n*

costume jewelry *n* : inexpensive jewelry

cosy *chiefly Brit var of* COZY

¹**cot** \'kät\ *n* : a small house : COTTAGE

²**cot** *n* : a small often collapsible bed

cote \'kōt, 'kät\ *n* : a small shed or coop (as for sheep or doves)

co·te·rie \'kō-tə-,rē, ,kō-tə-'rē\ *n* [F] : an intimate often exclusive group of persons with a common interest

co·ter·mi·nous \,kō-'tər-mə-nəs\ *adj* : having the same scope or duration

co·til·lion \kō-'til-yən, kə-\ *n* : a formal ball

cot·tage \'kä-tij\ *n* : a small house — **cot·tag·er** *n*

cottage cheese *n* : a soft uncured cheese made from soured skim milk

cot·tar *or* **cot·ter** \'kä-tər\ *n* : a peasant or

farm laborer occupying a cottage and often a small holding

cotter pin *n* : a metal strip bent into a pin whose ends can be spread apart after insertion through a hole or slot

cot·ton \'kä-t²n\ *n* [ME *coton*, fr. AF *cotun*, fr. Ar *quṭun*] **1** : a soft fibrous usu. white substance composed of hairs attached to the seeds of various tropical plants related to the mallow; *also* : this plant **2** : thread or cloth made of cotton — **cot·tony** *adj*

cotton candy *n* : a candy made of spun sugar

cot·ton·mouth \'kä-t²n-,maúth\ *n* : WATER MOCCASIN

cot·ton·seed \-,sēd\ *n* : the seed of the cotton plant yielding a protein-rich meal and a fatty oil (**cottonseed oil**) used esp. in cooking

cot·ton·tail \-,tāl\ *n* : a No. American rabbit with a white-tufted tail

cot·ton·wood \-,wúd\ *n* : a poplar having seeds with cottony hairs

cot·y·le·don \,kä-tə-'lē-d²n\ *n* : the first leaf or one of the first pair or whorl of leaves developed by a seed plant

¹**couch** \'kaúch\ *vb* **1** : to lie or place on a couch **2** : to phrase in a specified manner ⟨proposals ~ed in jargon⟩

²**couch** *n* : a piece of furniture (as a bed or sofa) that one can sit or lie on

couch·ant \'kaú-chənt\ *adj* : lying down with the head raised ⟨coat of arms with lion ~⟩

couch potato *n* : one who spends a great deal of time watching television

cou·gar \'kü-gər\ *n, pl* **cougars** *also* **cougar** [F *couguar*, fr. NL *cuguacuarana*, modif. of Tupi (a Brazilian Indian language) *siwasuarána*, fr. *siwásu* deer + *-ran* resembling] : a large powerful tawny brown wild American cat

cough \'kóf\ *vb* : to force air from the lungs with short sharp noises; *also* : to expel by coughing — **cough** *n*

could \kəd, 'kúd\ *past of* CAN — used as an auxiliary in the past or as a polite or less forceful alternative to *can* in the present

cou·lee \'kü-lē\ *n* **1** : a small stream **2** : a dry streambed **3** : GULLY

cou·lomb \'kü-,läm, -,lōm\ *n* : a unit of electric charge equal to the electricity transferred by a current of one ampere in one second

coun·cil \'kaún-səl\ *n* **1** : ASSEMBLY, MEETING **2** : an official body of lawmakers ⟨city ~⟩ — **coun·cil·lor** *or* **coun·cil·or** \-sə-lər\ *n* — **coun·cil·man** \-səl-mən\ *n* — **coun·cil·wom·an** \-,wú-mən\ *n*

¹**coun·sel** \'kaún-səl\ *n* **1** : ADVICE **2** : a plan of action **3** : deliberation together **4** *pl* **counsel** : LAWYER

²**counsel** *vb* **-seled** *or* **-selled; -sel·ing** *or* **-sel·ling 1** : ADVISE **2** : CONSULT

coun·sel·or *or* **coun·sel·lor** \'kaún-sə-lər\ *n* **1** : ADVISER **2** : LAWYER **3** : one who has supervisory duties at a summer camp

¹**count** \'kaůnt\ *vb* [ME, fr. AF *cunter, counter,* fr. L *computare,* fr. *com-* with + *putare* to consider] **1** : to name or indicate one by one in order to find the total number **2** : to recite numbers in order **3** : CONSIDER, ACCOUNT **4** : RELY ⟨you can ~ on me⟩ **5** : to be of value or account ⟨~s toward your grade⟩ — **count·able** *adj*

²**count** *n* **1** : the act of counting; *also* : the total obtained by counting **2** : a particular charge in an indictment or legal declaration ⟨two ~s of murder⟩

³**count** *n* [ME, fr. AF *cunte,* fr. LL *comes,* fr. L companion, one of the imperial court, fr. *com-* with + *ire* to go] : a European nobleman whose rank corresponds to that of a British earl

count·down \'kaůnt-ˌdaůn\ *n* : a backward counting in fixed units (as seconds) to indicate the time remaining before an event (as the launching of a rocket) — **count down** *vb*

¹**coun·te·nance** \'kaůn-tᵊn-əns\ *n* **1** : the human face **2** : FAVOR, APPROVAL

²**countenance** *vb* **-nanced; -nanc·ing** : SANCTION, TOLERATE

¹**count·er** \'kaůn-tər\ *n* **1** : a piece (as of metal or plastic) used in reckoning or in games **2** : a level surface over which business is transacted, food is served, or work is conducted

²**count·er** *n* : a device for recording a number or amount

³**coun·ter** *vb* : to act in opposition to.

⁴**coun·ter** *adv* : in an opposite direction : CONTRARY

⁵**coun·ter** *n* **1** : OPPOSITE, CONTRARY **2** : an answering or offsetting force or blow

⁶**coun·ter** *adj* : CONTRARY, OPPOSITE

coun·ter·act \ˌkaůn-tər-'akt\ *vb* : to lessen the force of : OFFSET — **coun·ter·ac·tive** \-'ak-tiv\ *adj*

coun·ter·at·tack \'kaůn-tər-ə-ˌtak\ *n* : an attack made to oppose an enemy's attack — **counterattack** *vb*

¹**coun·ter·bal·ance** \'kaůn-tər-ˌba-ləns\ *n* : a weight or influence that balances another

²**counterbalance** \ˌkaůn-tər-'ba-ləns\ *vb* : to oppose with equal weight or influence

coun·ter·claim \'kaůn-tər-ˌklām\ *n* : an opposing claim esp. in law

coun·ter·clock·wise \ˌkaůn-tər-'kläk-ˌwīz\ *adv* : in a direction opposite to that in which the hands of a clock rotate — **counterclockwise** *adj*

coun·ter·cul·ture \'kaůn-tər-ˌkəl-chər\ *n* : a culture with values and mores that run counter to those of established society

coun·ter·es·pi·o·nage \ˌkaůn-tər-'es-pē-ə-ˌnäzh, -nij\ *n* : activities intended to discover and defeat enemy espionage

¹**coun·ter·feit** \'kaůn-tər-ˌfit\ *adj* : SHAM, SPURIOUS; *also* : FORGED ⟨~ money⟩

²**counterfeit** *vb* **1** : to copy or imitate in order to deceive **2** : PRETEND, FEIGN — **coun·ter·feit·er** *n*

³**counterfeit** *n* : something counterfeit : FORGERY ♦ **Synonyms** FRAUD, SHAM, FAKE, IMPOSTURE, DECEIT, DECEPTION

coun·ter·in·sur·gen·cy \ˌkaůn-tər-in-'sər-jən-sē\ *n* : military activity designed to deal with insurgents

coun·ter·in·tel·li·gence \-in-'te-lə-jəns\ *n* : organized activities of an intelligence service designed to counter the activities of an enemy's intelligence service

coun·ter·in·tu·i·tive \-in-'tü-ə-tiv, -'tyü-\ *adj* : contrary to what would intuitively be expected

count·er·man \'kaůn-tər-ˌman, -mən\ *n* : one who tends a counter

coun·ter·mand \'kaůnt-ər-ˌmand\ *vb* : to withdraw (an order already given) by a contrary order

coun·ter·mea·sure \-ˌme-zhər\ *n* : an action or device designed to counter another

coun·ter·of·fen·sive \-ə-ˌfen-siv\ *n* : a large-scale counterattack

coun·ter·pane \-ˌpān\ *n* : BEDSPREAD

coun·ter·part \-ˌpärt\ *n* : a person or thing very closely like or corresponding to another person or thing

coun·ter·point \-ˌpóint\ *n* : music in which one melody is accompanied by one or more other melodies all woven into a harmonious whole

coun·ter·poise \-ˌpóiz\ *n* : COUNTERBALANCE

coun·ter·rev·o·lu·tion \ˌkaůn-tər-ˌre-və-'lü-shən\ *n* : a revolution opposed to a current or earlier one — **coun·ter·rev·o·lu·tion·ary** \-shə-ˌner-ē\ *adj or n*

coun·ter·sign \'kaůn-tər-ˌsīn\ *n* **1** : a confirmatory signature added to a writing already signed by another person **2** : a military secret signal that must be given by a person who wishes to pass a guard — **countersign** *vb*

coun·ter·sink \-ˌsiŋk\ *vb* **-sunk** \-ˌsəŋk\; **-sink·ing** **1** : to form a funnel-shaped enlargement at the outer end of a drilled hole **2** : to set the head of (as a screw) at or below the surface — **countersink** *n*

coun·ter·spy \-ˌspī\ *n* : a spy engaged in counterespionage

coun·ter·ten·or \-ˌte-nər\ *n* : a tenor with an unusually high range

coun·ter·vail \ˌkaůn-tər-'vāl\ *vb* : COUNTERACT

coun·ter·weight \'kaůn-tər-ˌwāt\ *n* : COUNTERBALANCE

count·ess \'kaůn-təs\ *n* **1** : the wife or widow of a count or an earl **2** : a woman holding the rank of a count or an earl in her own right

count·ing·house \'kaůn-tiŋ-ˌhaůs\ *n* : a building or office for keeping books and conducting business

count·less \'kaůnt-ləs\ *adj* : INNUMERABLE

coun·tri·fied *also* **coun·try·fied** \'kən-tri-ˌfīd\ *adj* **1** : RURAL, RUSTIC **2** : UNSOPHISTICATED **3** : played or sung in the manner of country music

¹**coun·try** \'kən-trē\ *n, pl* **countries** [ME *contree,* fr. AF *cuntree, contré,* fr. ML *contrata,* fr. L *contra* against, on the opposite side] **1** : REGION, DISTRICT **2** : FATHERLAND **3** : a nation or its territory **4**

: rural regions as opposed to towns and cities **5** : COUNTRY MUSIC

²country *adj* **1** : RURAL **2** : of or relating to country music ⟨a ∼ singer⟩

country and western *n* : COUNTRY MUSIC

country club *n* : a suburban club for social life and recreation; *esp* : one having a golf course —,**country–club** *adj*

coun·try–dance \'kən-trē-,dans\ *n* : an English dance in which partners face each other esp. in rows

coun·try·man \'kən-trē-mən, 2 often -,man\ *n* **1** : an inhabitant of a specified country **2** : COMPATRIOT **3** : one raised or living in the country : RUSTIC

country music *n* : music derived from or imitating the folk style of the southern U.S. or of the Western cowboy

coun·try·side \'kən-trē-,sīd\ *n* : a rural area or its people

coun·ty \'kaùn-tē\ *n, pl* **counties** **1** : the domain of a count **2** : a territorial division of a country or state for purposes of local government

coup \'kü\ *n, pl* **coups** \'küz\ [F, blow, stroke] **1** : a brilliant sudden stroke or stratagem **2** : COUP D'ÉTAT

coup de grace \,kü-də-'gräs\ *n, pl* **coups de grace** *same*\ [F *coup de grâce*, lit., stroke of mercy] : DEATHBLOW; *also* : a final decisive stroke or event

coup d'état \,kü-də-'tä\ *n, pl* **coups d'é·tat** *same or* -'täz\ [F, lit., stroke of state] : a sudden violent overthrow of a government by a small group

cou·pé *or* **coupe** \kü-'pā, 2 often 'küp\ *n* [F *coupé*, fr. *couper* to cut] **1** : a closed horse-drawn carriage for two persons inside with an outside seat for the driver **2** *usu* **coupe** : a 2-door automobile with an enclosed back

¹cou·ple \'kə-pəl\ *n* **1** : two persons married, engaged, or otherwise romantically paired **2** : PAIR **3** : BOND, TIE **4** : an indefinite small number : FEW ⟨a ∼ of days ago⟩

²couple *vb* **cou·pled; cou·pling** : to link together

cou·plet \'kə-plət\ *n* : two successive rhyming lines of verse

cou·pling \'kə-pliŋ (*usual for 2*), -pə-liŋ\ *n* **1** : CONNECTION **2** : a device for connecting two parts or things

cou·pon \'kü-,pän, 'kyü-\ *n* **1** : a statement attached to a bond showing interest due and designed to be cut off and presented for payment **2** : a form surrendered in order to obtain an article, service, or accommodation **3** : a printed document or slip used to submit orders or inquiries or to obtain a discount on merchandise or services

cour·age \'kər-ij\ *n* : ability to conquer fear or despair : BRAVERY, VALOR — **cou·ra·geous** \kə-'rā-jəs\ *adj* — **cou·ra·geous·ly** *adv*

cou·ri·er \'kur-ē-ər, 'kər-ē-\ *n* : one who bears messages or information esp. for the diplomatic or military services

¹course \'kórs\ *n* **1** : PROGRESS, PASSAGE;

also : direction of progress **2** : the ground or path over which something moves **3** : method of procedure : CONDUCT, BEHAVIOR **4** : an ordered series of acts or proceedings : sequence of events **5** : a series of instruction periods dealing with a subject **6** : the series of studies leading to graduation from a school or college **7** : the part of a meal served at one time — **of course** : as might be expected

²course *vb* **coursed; cours·ing** **1** : to hunt with dogs **2** : to run or go speedily

cours·er \'kòr-sər\ *n* : a swift or spirited horse

¹court \'kòrt\ *n* [ME, fr. AF, fr. L *cohort-, cohors* enclosure, group, retinue, cohort] **1** : the residence of a sovereign or similar dignitary **2** : a sovereign's formal assembly of officials and advisers as a governing power **3** : an assembly of the retinue of a sovereign **4** : an open space enclosed by a building or buildings **5** : a space walled or marked off for playing a game (as tennis or basketball) **6** : the place where justice is administered; *also* : a judicial body or a meeting of a judicial body **7** : attention intended to win favor

²court *vb* **1** : to try to gain the favor of **2** : WOO **3** : ATTRACT, TEMPT

cour·te·ous \'kər-tē-əs\ *adj* : marked by respect for others : CIVIL, POLITE — **cour·te·ous·ly** *adv*

cour·te·san \'kòr-tə-zən, -,zan\ *n* : PROSTITUTE

cour·te·sy \'kər-tə-sē\ *n, pl* **-sies** **1** : courteous behavior : POLITENESS **2** : a favor courteously performed

court·house \'kòrt-,haús\ *n* : a building in which courts of law are held or county offices are located

court·ier \'kòr-tē-ər\ *n* : a person in attendance at a royal court

court·ly \'kòrt-lē\ *adj* **court·li·er; -est** : REFINED, ELEGANT, POLITE ♦ *Synonyms* GALLANT, GRACIOUS — **court·li·ness** *n*

court–mar·tial \'kòrt-,mär-shəl\ *n, pl* **courts–martial** : a military or naval court for trial of offenses against military or naval law; *also* : a trial by this court — **court–martial** *vb*

court·room \-,rüm, -,rùm\ *n* : a room in which a court of law is held

court·ship \-,ship\ *n* : the act of courting : WOOING

court·yard \-,yärd\ *n* : an enclosure next to a building

cous·cous \'küs-,küs\ *n* : a No. African dish of steamed semolina usu. served with meat or vegetables; *also* : the semolina itself

cous·in \'kə-zən\ *n* [ME *cosin*, fr. AF, fr. L *consobrinus*, fr. *com-* with + *sobrinus* second cousin, fr. *soror* sister] : a child of one's uncle or aunt

cou·ture \kü-'tùr, -'tuer\ *n* [F] : the business of designing custom-made women's clothing; *also* : the designers and establishments engaged in this business

cou·tu·ri·er \kü-'tu̇r-ē-ər, -ē-ˌā\ *n* [F, dressmaker] : the owner of an establishment engaged in couture

cove \'kōv\ *n* : a small sheltered inlet or bay

co·ven \'kə-vən\ *n* : an assembly or band of witches

cov·e·nant \'kə-və-nənt\ *n* : a formal binding agreement : COMPACT — **cov·e·nant** \-nənt, -ˌnant\ *vb*

¹**cov·er** \'kə-vər\ *vb* 1 : to bring or hold within range of a firearm 2 : PROTECT, GUARD ⟨~ed by insurance⟩ ⟨~ than base⟩ 3 : HIDE, CONCEAL ⟨~ up a crime⟩ 4 : to place something over or upon 5 : INCLUDE, COMPRISE 6 : to have as one's field of activity ⟨one salesman ~s the state⟩ 7 : to buy (stocks) in order to have them for delivery on a previous short sale

²**cover** *n* 1 : something that protects or shelters 2 : LID, TOP 3 : CASE, BINDING 4 : TABLECLOTH 5 : a cloth used on a bed 6 : SCREEN, DISGUISE 7 : an envelope or wrapper for mail

cov·er·age \'kə-və-rij\ *n* 1 : the act or fact of covering 2 : the total group covered : SCOPE

cov·er·all \'kə-vər-ˌȯl\ *n* : a one-piece outer garment worn to protect one's clothes — usu. used in pl.

cover charge *n* : a charge made by a restaurant or nightclub in addition to the charge for food and drink

cover crop *n* : a crop planted to prevent soil erosion and to provide humus

cov·er·let \'kə-vər-lət\ *n* : BEDSPREAD

¹**co·vert** \'kō-ˌvərt, 'kə-vərt\ *adj* 1 : HIDDEN, SECRET ⟨a ~ operation⟩ 2 : SHELTERED — **co·vert·ly** *adv*

²**co·vert** \'kə-vərt, 'kō-\ *n* 1 : a secret or sheltered place; *esp* : a thicket sheltering game 2 : a feather covering the bases of the quills of the wings and tail of a bird

cov·er-up \'kə-vər-ˌəp\ *n* 1 : a device for masking or concealing 2 : a usu. concerted effort to keep an illegal or unethical act or situation from being made public

cov·et \'kə-vət\ *vb* : to desire enviously (what belongs to another) — **cov·et·ous** *adj* — **cov·et·ous·ness** *n*

cov·ey \'kə-vē\ *n, pl* **coveys** [ME, fr. AF *covee* sitting of eggs, fr. *cover* to sit on, brood over, fr. L *cubare* to lie] 1 : a bird with her brood of young 2 : a small flock (as of quail) 3 : GROUP 1

¹**cow** \'kau̇\ *n* 1 : the mature female of cattle or of an animal (as the moose, elephant, or whale) of which the male is called *bull* 2 : any domestic bovine animal irrespective of sex or age

²**cow** *vb* : INTIMIDATE, DAUNT, OVERAWE

cow·ard \'kau̇-(ə)rd\ *n* [ME, fr. AF *cuard*, fr. *cue, coe* tail, fr. L *cauda*] : one who lacks courage or shows shameful fear or timidity — **coward** *adj* — **cow·ard·ice** \'kau̇-ər-dəs\ *n* — **cow·ard·ly** *adv or adj*

cow·bird \'kau̇-ˌbərd\ *n* : a small No. American blackbird that lays its eggs in the nests of other birds

cow·boy \-ˌbȯi\ *n* : one (as a mounted ranch hand) who tends cattle or horses

cow·er \'kau̇(-ə)r\ *vb* : to shrink or crouch down from fear or cold : QUAIL

cow·girl \'kau̇-ˌgərl\ *n* : a girl or woman who tends cattle or horses

cow·hand \'kau̇-ˌhand\ *n* : COWBOY

cow·herd \-ˌhərd\ *n* : one who tends cows

cow·hide \-ˌhīd\ *n* 1 : the hide of a cow; *also* : leather made from it 2 : a coarse whip of braided rawhide

cowl \'kau̇l\ *n* : a monk's hood

cow·lick \'kau̇-ˌlik\ *n* : a turned-up tuft of hair that resists control

cowl·ing \'kau̇-liŋ\ *n* : a usu. metal covering for the engine or another part of an airplane

cow·man \'kau̇-mən, -ˌman\ *n* : COWBOY; *also* : a cattle owner or rancher

co·work·er \'kō-ˌwər-kər\ *n* : a fellow worker

cow·poke \'kau̇-ˌpōk\ *n* : COWBOY

cow pony *n* : a strong and agile horse trained for herding cattle

cow·pox \'kau̇-ˌpäks\ *n* : a mild disease of the cow that when communicated to humans protects against smallpox

cow·punch·er \-ˌpən-chər\ *n* : COWBOY

cow·slip \'kau̇-ˌslip\ *n* 1 : a yellow-flowered European primrose 2 : MARSH MARIGOLD

cox·comb \'käks-ˌkōm\ *n* : a conceited foolish person : FOP

cox·swain \'käk-sən, -ˌswān\ *n* : the steersman of a ship's boat or a racing shell

coy \'kȯi\ *adj* [ME, quiet, shy, fr. AF *quei, quoi, koi* quiet, fr. L *quietus*] 1 : BASHFUL, SHY 2 : marked by artful playfulness : COQUETTISH — **coy·ly** *adv* — **coy·ness** *n*

coy·ote \'kī-ˌōt, kī-'ō-tē\ *n, pl* **coyotes** *or* **coyote** : a mammal of No. America smaller than the related wolves

coy·pu \'kȯi-ˌpü\ *n* : NUTRIA 2

coz·en \'kə-zᵊn\ *vb* : CHEAT, DEFRAUD — **coz·en·age** \-ij\ *n* — **coz·en·er** *n*

¹**co·zy** \'kō-zē\ *adj* **co·zi·er; -est** : SNUG, COMFORTABLE ⟨a ~ cabin⟩ — **co·zi·ly** \-zə-lē\ *adv* — **co·zi·ness** \-zē-nəs\ *n*

²**cozy** *n, pl* **co·zies** : a padded covering for a vessel (as a teapot) to keep the contents hot

cp *abbr* 1 compare 2 coupon

CP *abbr* 1 cerebral palsy 2 chemically pure 3 command post 4 communist party

CPA *abbr* certified public accountant

CPB *abbr* Corporation for Public Broadcasting

cpd *abbr* compound

CPI *abbr* consumer price index

Cpl *abbr* corporal

CPO *abbr* chief petty officer

CPOM *abbr* master chief petty officer

CPOS *abbr* senior chief petty officer

CPR *abbr* cardiopulmonary resuscitation

CPT *abbr* captain

CPU \ˌsē-ˌpē-'yü\ *n* [central *p*rocessing *u*nit] : the part of a computer that performs its basic operations, manages its components, and exchanges data with memory or peripherals

CQ *abbr* charge of quarters

cr *abbr* credit; creditor

Cr *symbol* chromium

¹crab \'krab\ *n, pl* **crabs** *also* **crab** : any of various crustaceans with a short broad shell and small abdomen

²crab *n* : an ill-natured person

³crab *vb* **crabbed; crab·bing** : COMPLAIN, GROUSE

crab apple *n* : a small often highly colored sour apple; *also* : a tree that produces crab apples

crab·bed \'kra-bəd\ *adj* **1** : MOROSE, PEEVISH ⟨a ~ view of human nature⟩ **2** : CRAMPED, IRREGULAR ⟨~ handwriting⟩

crab·by \'kra-bē\ *adj* **crab·bi·er; -est** : CROSS, ILL-NATURED

crab·grass \'krab-ˌgras\ *n* : a weedy grass with creeping or sprawling stems that root freely at the nodes

crab louse *n* : a louse infesting the pubic region in humans

¹crack \'krak\ *vb* **1** : to break with a sharp sudden sound **2** : to break with or without completely separating into parts **3** : to fail in tone or become harsh ⟨her voice ~*ed*⟩ **4** : to subject (as a petroleum oil) to heat for breaking down into lighter products (as gasoline)

²crack *n* **1** : a sudden sharp noise **2** : a witty or sharp remark **3** : a narrow break or opening : FISSURE **4** : a sharp blow **5** : ATTEMPT, TRY **6** : a potent form of cocaine in small chips used illicitly for smoking

³crack *adj* : extremely proficient

crack·down \'krak-ˌdaún\ *n* : an act or instance of taking sharply disciplinary action ⟨a ~ on gambling⟩ — **crack down** *vb*

crack·er \'kra-kər\ *n* **1** : FIRECRACKER **2** : a dry thin crispy baked bread product made of flour and water

crack·er·jack \-ˌjak\ *n* : something excellent — **crackerjack** *adj*

crack·le \'kra-kəl\ *vb* **crack·led; crack·ling** **1** : to make small sharp snapping noises **2** : to develop fine cracks in a surface — **crackle** *n* — **crack·ly** \-k(ə-)lē\ *adj*

crack·pot \'krak-ˌpät\ *n* : an eccentric person

crack–up \'krak-ˌəp\ *n* : CRASH, WRECK; *also* : BREAKDOWN

crack up *vb* **1** : PRAISE ⟨isn't all it's *cracked up* to be⟩ **2** : to laugh or cause to laugh out loud **3** : to crash a vehicle

¹cra·dle \'krā-dᵊl\ *n* **1** : a baby's bed or cot **2** : a framework or support (as for a telephone receiver) **3** : INFANCY ⟨from ~ to the grave⟩ **4** : a place of origin

²cradle *vb* **cra·dled; cra·dling** **1** : to place in or as if in a cradle **2** : SHELTER, REAR

craft \'kraft\ *n* **1** : ART, SKILL; *also* : an occupation requiring special skill **2** : CUNNING, GUILE **3** *pl usu* **craft** : a boat esp. of small size; *also* : AIRCRAFT, SPACECRAFT

crafts·man \'krafts-mən\ *n* : a skilled artisan — **crafts·man·ship** *n*

crafty \'kraf-tē\ *adj* **craft·i·er; -est** : CUNNING, DECEITFUL, SUBTLE — **craft·i·ly** \-tə-lē\ *adv* — **craft·i·ness** \-tē-nəs\ *n*

crag \'krag\ *n* : a steep rugged cliff or rock — **crag·gy** *adj*

cram \'kram\ *vb* **crammed; cram·ming** **1** : to pack in tight : JAM **2** : to eat greedily **3** : to study rapidly under pressure for an examination

¹cramp \'kramp\ *n* **1** : a sudden painful contraction of muscle **2** : sharp abdominal pain — usu. used in pl.

²cramp *vb* **1** : to affect with a cramp or cramps **2** : to restrain from free action : HAMPER

cran·ber·ry \'kran-ˌber-ē, -bə-rē\ *n* : the red acid berry of any of several trailing plants related to the heaths; *also* : one of these plants

¹crane \'krān\ *n* **1** : any of a family of tall wading birds related to the rails; *also* : any of several herons **2** : a machine for lifting and carrying heavy objects

²crane *vb* **craned; cran·ing** : to stretch one's neck to see better

crane fly *n* : any of a family of long-legged slender dipteran flies that resemble large mosquitoes but do not bite

cranial nerve *n* : any of the nerves that arise in pairs from the lower surface of the brain and pass through openings in the skull to the periphery of the body

cra·ni·um \'krā-nē-əm\ *n, pl* **-ni·ums** *or* **-nia** \-ə\ : SKULL; *esp* : the part enclosing the brain — **cra·ni·al** \-əl\ *adj*

¹crank \'kraŋk\ *n* **1** : a bent part of an axle or shaft or an arm at right angles to the end of a shaft by which circular motion is imparted to or received from it **2** : an eccentric person **3** : a bad-tempered person : GROUCH

²crank *vb* : to start or operate by or as if by turning a crank

crank·case \'kraŋk-ˌkās\ *n* : the housing of a crankshaft

crank out *vb* : to produce in a mechanical manner

crank·shaft \'kraŋk-ˌshaft\ *n* : a shaft turning or driven by a crank

cranky \'kraŋ-kē\ *adj* **crank·i·er; -est** **1** : IRRITABLE **2** : operating uncertainly or imperfectly ⟨a ~ old tractor⟩

cran·ny \'kra-nē\ *n, pl* **crannies** : CREVICE, CHINK

craps \'kraps\ *n* : a gambling game played with two dice

crap·shoot·er \'krap-ˌshü-tər\ *n* : a person who plays craps

¹crash \'krash\ *vb* **1** : to break noisily : SMASH **2** : to damage an airplane in landing **3** : to enter or attend without invitation or without paying ⟨~ a party⟩ **4** : to suffer a sudden major failure usu. with loss of data ⟨my computer ~*ed*⟩

²crash *n* **1** : a loud sound (as of things smashing) **2** : an instance of crashing ⟨a plane ~⟩; *also* : COLLISION **3** : a sudden failure (as of a business)

³crash *adj* : marked by concentrated effort

over the shortest possible time ⟨a ~ diet⟩

⁴crash n : coarse linen fabric used for towels and draperies

crash–land \'krash-ˌland\ vb : to land an aircraft or spacecraft under emergency conditions usu. with damage to the craft — **crash landing** n

crass \'kras\ adj : GROSS, INSENSITIVE ⟨~ ignorance⟩ — **crass·ly** adv — **crass·ness** n

crate \'krāt\ n : a container often of wooden slats — **crate** vb

cra·ter \'krā-tər\ n [L, mixing bowl, crater, fr. Gk kratēr, fr. kerannynai to mix] **1** : the depression around the opening of a volcano **2** : a depression formed by the impact of a meteorite or by the explosion of a bomb or shell

cra·vat \krə-'vat\ n : NECKTIE

crave \'krāv\ vb craved; crav·ing **1** : to ask for earnestly : BEG **2** : to long for : DESIRE

cra·ven \'krā-vən\ adj : COWARDLY — **craven** n — **cra·ven·ly** adv

crav·ing \'krā-viŋ\ n : an urgent or abnormal desire

craw·fish \'krȯ-ˌfish\ n **1** : CRAYFISH 1 **2** : SPINY LOBSTER

¹crawl \'krȯl\ vb **1** : to move slowly by drawing the body along the ground **2** : to advance feebly, cautiously, or slowly **3** : to be swarming with or feel as if swarming with creeping things ⟨a place ~ing with ants⟩ ⟨her flesh ~ed⟩

²crawl n **1** : a very slow pace **2** : a prone speed swimming stroke

cray·fish \'krā-ˌfish\ n **1** : any of numerous freshwater crustaceans usu. much smaller than the related lobsters **2** : SPINY LOBSTER

cray·on \'krā-ˌän, -ən\ n : a stick of chalk or wax used for writing, drawing, or coloring; also : a drawing made with such material — **crayon** vb

¹craze \'krāz\ vb crazed; craz·ing [ME crasen to crush, craze, of Scand origin] : to make or become insane

²craze n : FAD, MANIA

cra·zy \'krā-zē\ adj cra·zi·er; -est **1** : mentally disordered : INSANE **2** : wildly impractical ⟨a ~ plan⟩; also : ERRATIC ⟨~ drivers⟩ — **cra·zi·ly** \-zə-lē\ adv — **cra·zi·ness** \-zē-nəs\ n

CRC abbr Civil Rights Commission

creak \'krēk\ vb : to make a prolonged squeaking or grating sound — **creak** n — **creaky** adj

¹cream \'krēm\ n **1** : the yellowish fat-rich part of milk **2** : a thick smooth sauce, confection, or cosmetic **3** : the choicest part **4** : a pale yellow color — **creamy** adj

²cream vb **1** : to prepare with a cream sauce **2** : to beat or blend into creamy consistency **3** : to defeat decisively

cream cheese n : a cheese made from whole milk enriched with cream

cream·ery \'krē-mə-rē\ n, pl **-er·ies** : an establishment where butter and cheese are made or milk and cream are prepared for sale

crease \'krēs\ n : a mark or line made by or as if by folding — **crease** vb

cre·ate \krē-'āt\ vb cre·at·ed; cre·at·ing : to bring into being : cause to exist : MAKE, PRODUCE — **cre·ative** \-'ā-tiv\ adj — **cre·a·tive·ness** n — **cre·a·tiv·i·ty** \ˌkrē-(ˌ)ā-'ti-və-tē\ n

cre·a·tion \krē-'ā-shən\ n **1** : the act of creating or producing ⟨~ of the world⟩ **2** : something that is created **3** : all created things : WORLD

cre·a·tion·ism \krē-'ā-shə-ˌni-zəm\ n : a doctrine or theory holding that matter, the various forms of life, and the world were created by God out of nothing — **cre·a·tion·ist** \-nist\ n or adj

cre·a·tor \krē-'ā-tər\ n **1** : one that creates : MAKER, AUTHOR **2** cap : GOD 1

crea·ture \'krē-chər\ n : a lower animal; also : a human being

crèche \'kresh\ n [F, manger, crib, fr. OF creche, of Gmc origin] : a representation of the Nativity scene

cre·dence \'krē-dᵊns\ n : mental acceptance as true or real

cre·den·tial \kri-'den-chəl\ n : something that gives a basis for credit or confidence

cre·den·za \kri-'den-zə\ n [It, lit., belief, confidence] : a sideboard, buffet, or bookcase usu. without legs

cred·i·ble \'kre-də-bəl\ adj : TRUSTWORTHY, BELIEVABLE — **cred·i·bil·i·ty** \ˌkre-də-'bil-ə-tē\ n — **cred·i·bly** \'kre-də-blē\ adv

¹cred·it \'kre-dət\ n [MF, fr. It credito, fr. L creditum something entrusted to another, loan, fr. credere to believe, entrust] **1** : the balance (as in a bank) in a person's favor **2** : time given for payment for goods sold on trust **3** : an accounting entry of payment received **4** : BELIEF, FAITH **5** : financial trustworthiness **6** : ESTEEM **7** : a source of honor or distinction **8** : a unit of academic work

²credit vb **1** : BELIEVE **2** : to give credit to

cred·it·able \'kre-də-tə-bəl\ adj : worthy of esteem or praise — **cred·it·ably** \-blē\ adv

credit card n : a card authorizing purchases on credit

cred·i·tor \'kre-də-tər\ n : a person to whom money is owed

cre·do \'krē-dō, 'krā-\ n, pl **credos** [ME, fr. L, I believe] : CREED

cred·u·lous \'kre-jə-ləs\ adj : inclined to believe esp. on slight evidence — **cred·u·lous·ly** adv — **cre·du·li·ty** \kri-'dü-lə-tē, -'dyü-\ n

Cree \'krē\ n, pl **Cree** or **Crees** : a member of an American Indian people of Canada

creed \'krēd\ n [ME crede, fr. OE crēda, fr. L credo I believe, first word of the Apostles' and Nicene Creeds] : a statement of the essential beliefs of a religious faith

creek \'krēk, 'krik\ n, **1** chiefly Brit : a small inlet **2** : a stream smaller than a river and larger than a brook

Creek \'krēk\ n : a member of an American Indian people of Alabama, Georgia, and Florida

creel \'krēl\ n : a wicker basket esp. for carrying fish

creep \'krēp\ vb **crept** \'krept\; **creep·ing 1** : CRAWL **2** : to feel as though insects were crawling on the skin **3** : to spread or grow over a surface like ivy — **creep** n — **creep·er** n

creep·ing \'krē-piŋ\ adj : developing or advancing by imperceptible degrees

creepy \'krē-pē\ adj **creep·i·er; -est** : having or producing a nervous shivery fear

cre·mate \'krē-ˌmāt\ vb **cre·mat·ed; cre·mat·ing** : to reduce (a dead body) to ashes with fire — **cre·ma·tion** \kri-'mā-shən\ n

cre·ma·to·ry \'krē-mə-ˌtȯr-ē, 'krē-\ n, pl **-ries** : a furnace for cremating; also : a structure containing such a furnace

crème or **creme** \'krem, 'krēm\ n, pl **crèmes** or **cremes** \same or 'kremz, 'krēmz\ [F, lit., cream] : a sweet liqueur

cren·el·lat·ed or **cren·el·at·ed** \'kre-nə-lā-təd\ adj : having battlements — **cren·el·la·tion** \ˌkre-nə-'lā-shən\ n

Cre·ole \'krē-ˌōl\ n **1** : a descendant of early French or Spanish settlers of the U.S. Gulf states preserving their speech and culture; also : a person of mixed French or Spanish and black descent speaking a dialect of French or Spanish **2** not cap : a language that has evolved from a pidgin but serves as the native language of a speech community

cre·o·sote \'krē-ə-ˌsōt\ n : an oily liquid obtained by distillation of coal tar and used in preserving wood

crepe or **crêpe** \'krāp\ n : a light crinkled fabric of any of various fibers

crêpe su·zette \ˌkrāp-sü-'zet\ n, pl **crêpes suzette** \same or 'krāps-\ or **crêpe suzettes** \-sü-'zets\ often cap S : a thin folded or rolled pancake in a hot orange-butter sauce that is sprinkled with a liqueur and set ablaze for serving

cre·pus·cu·lar \kri-'pəs-kyə-lər\ adj **1** : of, relating to, or resembling twilight **2** : occurring or active during twilight ⟨~ insects⟩

cre·scen·do \krə-'shen-dō\ adv or adj [It] : increasing in loudness — used as a direction in music — **crescendo** n

cres·cent \'kre-sᵊnt\ n [ME cressant, fr. AF fr. prp. of crestre to grow, increase, fr. L crescere] : the moon at any stage between new moon and first quarter and between last quarter and new moon; also : something shaped like the figure of the crescent moon with a convex and a concave edge — **cres·cen·tic** \kre-'sen-tik\ adj

cress \'kres\ n : any of several salad plants related to the mustards

¹**crest** \'krest\ n **1** : a tuft or process on the head of an animal (as a bird) **2** : a heraldic device **3** : an upper part, edge, or limit ⟨the ~ of a hill⟩ — **crest·ed** \'kres-təd\ adj — **crest·less** adj

²**crest** vb **1** : CROWN **2** : to reach the crest of **3** : to rise to a crest

crest·fall·en \'krest-ˌfȯ-lən\ adj : DISPIRITED, DEJECTED

Cre·ta·ceous \kri-'tā-shəs\ adj : of, relating to, or being the latest period of the Mesozoic era marked by great increase in flowering plants, diversification of mammals, and extinction of the dinosaurs — **Cretaceous** n

cre·tin \'krē-tᵊn\ n [F crétin, fr. F dial. cretin, lit., wretch, innocent victim, fr. L christianus Christian] **1** : one affected with cretinism **2** : a stupid person

cre·tin·ism \-ˌi-zəm\ n : a usu. congenital abnormal condition characterized by physical stunting and mental retardation

cre·tonne \'krē-ˌtän\ n : a strong unglazed cotton cloth for curtains and upholstery

cre·vasse \kri-'vas\ n : a deep fissure esp. in a glacier

crev·ice \'kre-vəs\ n : a narrow fissure

¹**crew** \'krü\ chiefly Brit past of CROW

²**crew** n [ME crue, fr. MF, a reinforcement, lit., increase, fr. croistre to grow, fr. L crescere] **1** : a body of people trained to work together for certain purposes **2** : a group of people who operate a ship, train, aircraft, or spacecraft **3** : the rowers and coxswain of a racing shell; also : the sport of rowing engaged in by a crew — **crew·man** \-mən\ n

crew cut n : a very short bristly haircut

crew·el \'krü-əl\ n : slackly twisted worsted yarn used for embroidery — **crew·el·work** \-ˌwərk\ n

¹**crib** \'krib\ n **1** : a manger for feeding animals **2** : a child's bedstead with high sides **3** : a building or bin for storage (as of grain) **4** : something used for cheating in an exam

²**crib** vb **cribbed; crib·bing 1** : to put in a crib **2** : STEAL, PLAGIARIZE — **crib·ber** n

crib·bage \'kri-bij\ n : a card game usu. played by two players and scored on a board (**cribbage board**)

crib death n : SUDDEN INFANT DEATH SYNDROME

crick \'krik\ n : a painful spasm of muscles (as of the neck)

¹**crick·et** \'kri-kət\ n [ME criket, fr. AF, of imit. origin] : any of a family of leaping insects related to the grasshoppers and noted for the chirping noises of the male

²**cricket** n [MF criquet goal stake in a bowling game] : a game played with a bat and ball by two teams on a field centering upon two wickets each defended by a batsman

cri·er \'krī-(ə)r\ n : one who calls out proclamations and announcements

crime \'krīm\ n : a serious offense against the public law

¹**crim·i·nal** \'kri-mə-nᵊl\ adj **1** : involving or being a crime **2** : relating to crime or its punishment — **crim·i·nal·i·ty** \ˌkri-mə-'na-lə-tē\ n — **crim·i·nal·ly** adv

²**criminal** n : one who has committed a crime

crim·i·nol·o·gy \ˌkri-mə-ˈnä-lə-jē\ n : the scientific study of crime and criminals — **crim·i·no·log·i·cal** \-mə-nə-ˈlä-ji-kəl\ adj — **crim·i·nol·o·gist** \ˌkri-mə-ˈnä-lə-jist\ n

¹**crimp** \ˈkrimp\ vb : to cause to become crinkled, wavy, or bent

²**crimp** n : something (as a curl in hair) produced by or as if by crimping

crim·son \ˈkrim-zən\ n : a deep purplish red color — **crimson** adj

cringe \ˈkrinj\ vb **cringed**; **cring·ing** : to shrink in fear ; WINCE, COWER

crin·kle \ˈkriŋ-kəl\ vb **crin·kled**; **crin·kling** : to form many short bends or curves; also : WRINKLE — **crinkle** n — **crin·kly** \-kə-lē\ adj

crin·o·line \ˈkri-nə-lən\ n **1** : an open-weave cloth used for stiffening and lining **2** : a full stiff skirt or underskirt made of crinoline

¹**crip·ple** \ˈkri-pəl\ n : one that is disabled or deficient in a specified manner ⟨a social ∼⟩

²**cripple** vb **crip·pled**; **crip·pling 1** : to make lame **2** : to make useless or imperfect — **crip·pler** \ˈkri-p(ə-)lər\ n

cri·sis \ˈkrī-səs\ n, pl **cri·ses** \-ˌsēz\ [ME, fr. L, fr. Gk krisis, lit., decision, fr. krinein to decide] **1** : the turning point for better or worse in an acute disease or fever **2** : a decisive or critical moment

crisp \ˈkrisp\ adj **1** : CURLY, WAVY **2** : BRITTLE ⟨a ∼ potato chip⟩ **3** : FIRM, FRESH ⟨∼ lettuce⟩ **4** : being sharp and clear ⟨a ∼ photo⟩ **5** : LIVELY, SPARKLING **6** : FROSTY, SNAPPY; also : INVIGORATING — **crisp** vb — **crisp·ly** adv — **crisp·ness** n — **crispy** adj

¹**criss·cross** \ˈkris-ˌkrós\ vb **1** : to mark with crossed lines **2** : to go or pass back and forth

²**crisscross** adj : marked or characterized by crisscrossing — **crisscross** adv

³**crisscross** n : a pattern formed by crossed lines

crit abbr critical; criticism

cri·te·ri·on \krī-ˈtir-ē-ən\ n, pl **-ria** \-ē-ə\ : a standard on which a judgment may be based

crit·ic \ˈkri-tik\ n **1** : a person who judges literary or artistic works **2** : one inclined to find fault

crit·i·cal \ˈkri-ti-kəl\ adj **1** : being or relating to a condition or disease involving danger of death ⟨∼ care⟩ **2** : being a crisis **3** : inclined to criticize **4** : relating to criticism or critics **5** : requiring careful judgment ⟨∼ thinking⟩ — **crit·i·cal·ly** \-k(ə-)lē\ adv

crit·i·cise Brit var of CRITICIZE

crit·i·cism \ˈkri-tə-ˌsi-zəm\ n **1** : the act of criticizing; esp : CENSURE **2** : a judgment or review **3** : the art of judging works of literature or art

crit·i·cize \ˈkri-tə-ˌsīz\ vb **-cized**; **-cizing 1** : to judge as a critic : EVALUATE **2** : to find fault : express criticism ◆ *Synonyms* BLAME, CENSURE, CONDEMN

cri·tique \krə-ˈtēk\ n : a critical estimate or discussion

crit·ter \ˈkri-tər\ n : CREATURE

croak \ˈkrōk\ n : a hoarse harsh cry (as of a frog) — **croak** vb

croak·er \ˈkrō-kər\ n **1** : an animal that croaks **2** : a fish that produces croaking or grunting noises

Croat \ˈkrō-ˌat\ n : CROATIAN

Cro·atian \krō-ˈā-shən\ n **1** : a native or inhabitant of Croatia **2** : a Slavic language spoken by Croatians — **Croatian** adj

cro·chet \krō-ˈshā\ n : needlework done with a single thread and hooked needle — **crochet** vb

crock \ˈkräk\ n : a thick earthenware pot or jar

crock·ery \ˈkrä-kə-rē\ n : EARTHENWARE

croc·o·dile \ˈkrä-kə-ˌdī(-ə)l\ n [ME & L; ME cocodrille, fr. AF, fr. ML cocodrillus, alter. of L crocodilus, fr. Gk krokodilos lizard, crocodile, fr. krokē shingle, pebble + drilos worm] : any of several thick-skinned long-bodied carnivorous reptiles of tropical and subtropical waters

cro·cus \ˈkrō-kəs\ n, pl **cro·cus·es** also **crocus** or **cro·ci** \-ˌkī\ : any of a large genus of low herbs related to the irises and having brightly colored flowers borne singly in early spring

Crohn's disease \ˈkrōnz\ n : a chronic inflammatory disease of the gastrointestinal tract and esp. the ileum

crois·sant \krō-ˈsänt, krwä-ˈsäⁿ\ n, pl **croissants** \same or -ˈsänts, -ˈsäⁿz\ : a rich crescent-shaped roll

Cro–Magnon \krō-ˈmag-nən, -ˈman-yən\ n : a hominid of a tall erect race known from skeletal remains found in southern France and usu. classified as the same species as present-day humans — **Cro-Magnon** adj

crone \ˈkrōn\ n : HAG

cro·ny \ˈkrō-nē\ n, pl **cronies** : a close friend esp. of long standing

¹**crook** \ˈkruk\ vb : to curve or bend sharply

²**crook** n **1** : a bent or curved implement **2** : a bent or curved part; also : BEND, CURVE **3** : SWINDLER, THIEF

crook·ed \ˈkru-kəd\ adj **1** : having a crook : BENT, CURVED **2** : DISHONEST — **crook·ed·ly** adv — **crook·ed·ness** n

croon \ˈkrün\ vb : to sing or hum in a gentle murmuring voice — **croon·er** n

¹**crop** \ˈkräp\ n **1** : the handle of a whip; also : a short riding whip **2** : a pouch in the throat of many birds and insects where food is received **3** : something (as a plant product) that can be harvested; also : the yield at harvest

²**crop** vb **cropped**; **crop·ping 1** : to remove the tips of : cut off short; also : TRIM **2** : to feed on by cropping **3** : to devote (land) to crops **4** : to appear unexpectedly

crop duster n : a person who uses an airplane to spray crops with insecticidal dusts; also : an airplane so used

crop·land \-ˌland\ n : land devoted to the production of plant crops

crop·per \ˈkrä-pər\ n : a raiser of crops; esp : SHARECROPPER

cro·quet \krō-'kā\ *n* : a game in which mallets are used to drive wooden balls through a series of wickets set out on a lawn

cro·quette \krō-'ket\ *n* [F] : a small often rounded mass of minced meat, fish, or vegetables fried in deep fat

cro·sier *or* **cro·zier** \'krō-zhər\ *n* : a staff carried by bishops and abbots

¹cross \'krós\ *n* 1 : a structure consisting of an upright beam and a crossbar used esp. by the ancient Romans for execution 2 : a figure of the cross on which Christ was crucified used as a Christian symbol 3 : a hybridizing of unlike individuals or strains; *also* : a product of this 4 : a punch delivered with a circular motion over an opponent's lead

²cross *vb* 1 : to lie or place across; *also* : INTERSECT 2 : to cancel by marking a cross on or by lining through 3 : THWART, OBSTRUCT 4 : to go or extend across : TRAVERSE 5 : HYBRIDIZE 6 : to meet and pass on the way

³cross *adj* 1 : lying across 2 : CONTRARY, OPPOSED 3 : marked by bad temper 4 : HYBRID — **cross·ly** *adv*

cross·bar \'krós-,bär\ *n* : a transverse bar or piece

cross·bow \-,bō\ *n* : a short bow mounted crosswise at the end of a wooden stock that shoots short arrows

cross·breed \'krós-,brēd, -'brēd\ *vb* **-bred** \-'bred\; **-breed·ing** : HYBRIDIZE

cross–coun·try \-'kən-trē\ *adj* 1 : extending or moving across a country 2 : proceeding over the countryside (as fields and woods) and not by roads 3 : of or relating to racing or skiing over the countryside instead of over a track or run — **cross–country** *adv*

cross–cur·rent \-'kər-ənt\ *n* 1 : a current running counter to another 2 : a conflicting tendency — usu. used in pl.

¹cross·cut \-,kət\ *vb* : to cut or saw crosswise esp. of the grain of wood

²crosscut *adj* 1 : made or used for crosscutting (a ~ saw) 2 : cut across the grain

³crosscut *n* : something that cuts through transversely

cross–ex·am·ine \,krō-sig-'za-mən\ *vb* : to examine with questions to check the answers to previous questions — **cross–ex·am·i·na·tion** \-,za-mə-'nā-shən\ *n* — **cross–ex·am·in·er** *n*

cross–eyed \'krō-,sīd\ *adj* : having one or both eyes turned inward toward the nose

cross–fer·til·i·za·tion \-,fər-tə-lə-'zā-shən\ *n* 1 : fertilization between sex cells produced by separate individuals or sometimes by individuals of different kinds; *also* : CROSS-POLLINATION 2 : a broadening or productive interchange (as between cultures) — **cross–fer·til·ize** \-'fərt-tə-,līz\ *vb*

cross fire *n* 1 : crossing lines of fire in combat 2 : rapid or angry interchange

cross–hair \'krós-,her\ *n* : a fine wire or thread in the eyepiece of an optical instrument used as a reference line

cross·hatch \'krós-,hach\ *vb* : to mark with two series of parallel lines that intersect — **cross–hatch·ing** *n*

cross·ing \'kró-siŋ\ *n* 1 : a place or structure for crossing something (as a river) 2 : a point of intersection (as of a street and a railroad track)

cross·over \'krós-,ō-vər\ *n* 1 : CROSSING 2 : a member of a political party who votes in the primary of the other party 3 : a broadening of the popular appeal of an artist (as a musician) by a change in the artist's style, genre, or medium 4 : an instance of breaking into another category

cross over *vb* : to achieve broader popularity by a change of medium or style

cross·piece \'krós-,pēs\ *n* : a horizontal member

cross–pol·li·na·tion \,krós-,pä-lə-'nā-shən\ *n* : transfer of pollen from one flower to the stigma of another — **cross–pol·li·nate** \'krós-'pä-lə-,nāt\ *vb*

cross–pur·pose \'krós-'pər-pəs\ *n* : a purpose contrary to another purpose (working at ~s)

cross–ques·tion \-'kwes-chən\ *vb* : CROSS-EXAMINE — **cross–question** *n*

cross–re·fer \,krós-ri-'fər\ *vb* : to refer by a notation or direction from one place to another (as in a book or list) — **cross–ref·er·ence** \'krós-'re-frəns\ *n*

cross·road \'krós-,rōd\ *n* 1 : a road that crosses a main road or runs between main roads 2 : a place where roads meet — usu. used in pl. 3 : a crucial point where a decision must be made — usu. used in pl.

cross section *n* 1 : a section cut across something; *also* : a representation made by or as if by such cutting 2 : a number of persons or things selected from a group that show the general nature of the whole group — **cross–sec·tion·al** *adj*

cross·walk \'krós-,wók\ *n* : a marked path for pedestrians crossing a street

cross·ways \-,wāz\ *adv* : CROSSWISE

cross·wind \-,wind\ *n* : a wind not parallel to a course (as of an airplane)

cross·wise \-,wīz\ *adv* : so as to cross something : ACROSS — **crosswise** *adj*

cross·word \'krós-,wərd\ *n* : a puzzle in which words are put into a pattern of numbered squares in answer to clues

cros·ti·ni \krō-'stē-nē\ *n pl* : small slices of toasted bread served with a topping

crotch \'kräch\ *n* : an angle or area formed by the parting of two legs, branches, or members

crotch·et \'krä-chət\ *n* : an odd notion : WHIM — **crotch·ety** *adj*

crouch \'kraúch\ *vb* 1 : to stoop or bend low 2 : CRINGE, COWER — **crouch** *n*

croup \'krüp\ *n* : laryngitis esp. of infants marked by a hoarse ringing cough and difficult breathing — **croupy** *adj*

crou·pi·er \'krü-pē-ər, -pē-,ā\ *n* [F, lit., rider on the rump of a horse, fr. *croupe* rump] : an employee of a gambling casino who collects and pays bets at a gaming table

crou·ton \'krü-ˌtän\ n [F croûton, dim. of croûte crust] : a small cube of bread toasted or fried crisp

¹crow \'krō\ n 1 : any of various large glossy black birds related to the jays 2 cap : a member of an American Indian people of a region in Montana and Wyoming; also : the language of the Crow people

²crow vb 1 : to make the loud shrill sound characteristic of the cock 2 : to utter a sound expressive of pleasure 3 : EXULT, GLOAT; also : BRAG, BOAST

³crow n : the cry of the cock

crow·bar \'krō-ˌbär\ n : a metal bar usu. wedge-shaped at the end for use as a pry or lever

¹crowd \'kraud\ vb 1 : to press close 2 : to collect in numbers : THRONG 3 : CRAM, STUFF

²crowd n : a large number of people gathered together at random : THRONG

¹crown \'kraun\ n 1 : a mark of victory or honor; esp : the title of a champion in a sport 2 : a royal headdress 3 : the top of the head; also : the part of a hat that covers the top of the head 4 : the highest part (as of a tree or tooth) 5 often cap : sovereign power; also : MONARCH 6 : a formerly used British silver coin — **crowned** \'kraund\ adj

²crown vb 1 : to place a crown on 2 : HONOR 3 : TOP, SURMOUNT 4 : to fit (a tooth) with an artificial crown

crown vetch n : a Eurasian leguminous herb with umbels of pink-and-white flowers and sharp-angled pods

crow's-foot \'krōz-ˌfut\ n, pl **crow's-feet** \-ˌfēt\ : any of the wrinkles around the outer corners of the eyes — usu. used in pl.

crow's nest n : a partly enclosed platform high on a ship's mast for use as a lookout

crozier var of CROSIER

¹CRT \ˌsē-(ˌ)är-'tē\ n, pl **CRTs** or **CRT's** : CATHODE-RAY TUBE; also : a display device incorporating a cathode-ray tube

²CRT abbr carrier route

cru·cial \'krü-shəl\ adj : DECISIVE ⟨a ~ step⟩; also : IMPORTANT, SIGNIFICANT ⟨a ~ question⟩

cru·ci·ate \'krü-shē-ˌāt\ adj : CRUCIFORM

cru·ci·ble \'krü-sə-bəl\ n : a heat-resistant container in which material can be subjected to great heat

cru·ci·fix \'krü-sə-ˌfiks\ n : a representation of Christ on the cross

cru·ci·fix·ion \ˌkrü-sə-'fik-shən\ n 1 cap : the crucifying of Christ 2 : the act of crucifying

cru·ci·form \'krü-sə-ˌfȯrm\ adj : shaped like a cross

cru·ci·fy \'krü-sə-ˌfī\ vb **-fied; -fy·ing** 1 : to put to death by nailing or binding the hands and feet to a cross 2 : MORTIFY 1 3 : TORTURE, PERSECUTE

¹crude \'krüd\ adj **crud·er; crud·est** 1 : not refined : RAW ⟨~ oil⟩ ⟨~ statistics⟩ 2 : lacking grace, taste, tact, or polish : RUDE — **crude·ly** adv — **crude·ness** n — **cru·di·ty** \'krü-də-tē\ n

²crude n : unrefined petroleum

cru·el \'krü-əl\ adj **cru·el·er** or **cru·el·ler; cru·el·est** or **cru·el·lest** [ME, fr. AF, fr. L crudelis, fr. crudus crude] : causing pain and suffering to others — MERCILESS — **cru·el·ly** adv — **cru·el·ty** \-tē\ n

cru·et \'krü-ət\ n : a small usu. glass bottle for vinegar, oil, or sauce

cruise \'krüz\ vb **cruised; cruis·ing** [D .kruisen to make a cross, cruise] 1 : to sail about touching at a series of ports 2 : to travel for enjoyment 3 : to travel about the streets at random 4 : to travel at the most efficient operating speed ⟨the cruising speed of an airplane⟩ 5 : SURF 2 — **cruise** n

cruis·er \'krü-zər\ n 1 : SQUAD CAR 2 : a large fast moderately armored and gunned warship 3 : a motorboat equipped for living aboard

cruis·er·weight \-ˌwāt\ n : a boxer weighing no more than 190 pounds

crul·ler \'krə-lər\ n, 1 : a small sweet cake in the form of a twisted strip fried in deep fat 2 Northern & Midland : an unraised doughnut

¹crumb \'krəm\ n : a small fragment

²crumb vb 1 : to break into crumbs 2 : to cover with crumbs

crum·ble \'krəm-bəl\ vb **crum·bled; crum·bling** : to break into small pieces : DISINTEGRATE — **crum·bly** adj

crum·my also **crumby** \'krə-mē\ adj **crum·mi·er** also **crumb·i·er; -est** : very poor or inferior : LOUSY

crum·pet \'krəm-pət\ n : a small round unsweetened bread cooked on a griddle

crum·ple \'krəm-pəl\ vb **crum·pled; crum·pling** 1 : to crush together : RUMPLE 2 : COLLAPSE

¹crunch \'krənch\ vb : to chew with a grinding noise; also : to grind or press with a crushing noise

²crunch n 1 : an act of or a sound made by crunching 2 : a tight or critical situation — **crunchy** adj

cru·sade \krü-'sād\ n 1 cap : any of the expeditions in the 11th, 12th, and 13th centuries undertaken by Christian countries to take the Holy Land from the Muslims 2 : a reforming enterprise undertaken with zeal — **crusade** vb — **cru·sad·er** n

cruse \'krüz, 'krüs\ n : a jar for water or oil

¹crush \'krəsh\ vb 1 : to squeeze out of shape 2 : HUG, EMBRACE 3 : to grind or pound to small bits 4 : OVERWHELM, SUPPRESS

²crush n 1 : an act of crushing 2 : a violent crowding 3 : INFATUATION

crust \'krəst\ n 1 : the outside part of bread; also : a piece of old dry bread 2 : the cover of a pie 3 : a hard or brittle surface layer — **crust·al** adj

crus·ta·cean \ˌkrəs-'tā-shən\ n : any of a large class of mostly aquatic arthropods (as lobsters or crabs) having a firm crustlike shell — **crustacean** adj

crusty \'krəs-tē\ adj **crust·i·er; -est** 1 : having or being a crust 2 : CROSS, GRUMPY

crutch \'krəch\ *n* : a supporting device; *esp* : a support fitting under the armpit for use by the disabled in walking

crux \'krəks, 'krúks\ *n, pl* **crux·es** [L, cross, torture] **1** : a puzzling or difficult problem **2** : a crucial point

¹cry \'krī\ *vb* **cried; cry·ing 1** : to call out : SHOUT **2** : to proclaim publicly : ADVERTISE **3** : WEEP

²cry *n, pl* **cries 1** : a loud outcry **2** : APPEAL, ENTREATY **3** : a fit of weeping **4** : the characteristic sound uttered by an animal **5** : DISTANCE — usu. used in the phrase *a far cry*

cry·ba·by \'krī-ˌbā-bē\ *n* : one who cries easily or often

cryo·gen·ic \ˌkrī-ə-'je-nik\ *adj* : of or relating to the production of very low temperatures; *also* : involving the use of a very low temperature — **cryo·gen·i·cal·ly** \-ni-k(ə-)lē\ *adv*

cryo·gen·ics \-niks\ *n* : a branch of physics that relates to the production and effects of very low temperatures

cryo·lite \'krī-ə-ˌlīt\ *n* : a usu. white mineral formerly used in making aluminum

crypt \'kript\ *n* : a chamber wholly or partly underground

cryp·tic \'krip-tik\ *adj* : meant to be puzzling or mysterious ⟨~ messages⟩

cryp·to·gram \'krip-tə-ˌgram\ *n* : a communication in cipher or code

cryp·tog·ra·phy \krip-'tä-grə-fē\ *n* : the coding and decoding of secret messages — **cryp·tog·ra·pher** \-fər\ *n*

cryp·to·sys·tem \ˌkrip-tō-'sis-təm\ *n* : a method for coding and decoding messages

crys·tal \'kris-t²l\ *n* [ME *cristal*, fr. AF, fr. L *crystallum*, fr. Gk *krystallos* ice, crystal] **1** : transparent quartz **2** : something resembling crystal (as in transparency); *esp* : a clear colorless glass of superior quality **3** : a body that is formed by solidification of a substance and has a regular repeating arrangement of atoms and often of external plane faces ⟨a salt ~⟩ **4** : the transparent cover of a watch dial

crystal clear *adj* : perfectly or transparently clear

crys·tal·line \'kris-tə-lən\ *adj* **1** : made of or resembling crystal **2** : very clear or sparkling

crys·tal·lise *Brit var of* CRYSTALLIZE

crys·tal·lize \'kris-tə-ˌlīz\ *vb* **-lized; -lizing 1** : to assume or cause to assume a crystalline form **2** : to take or cause to take a definite form — **crys·tal·li·za·tion** \ˌkris-tə-lə-'zā-shən\ *n*

crys·tal·log·ra·phy \ˌkris-tə-'lä-grə-fē\ *n* : the science dealing with the forms and structures of crystals — **crys·tal·log·ra·pher** \-fər\ *n*

cs *abbr* case; cases

Cs *symbol* cesium

CS *abbr* **1** civil service **2** county seat

CSA *abbr* Confederate States of America

C–section \'sē-ˌsek-shən\ *n* : CESAREAN SECTION

CSM *abbr* command sergeant major

CST *abbr* central standard time

ct *abbr* **1** carat **2** cent **3** count **4** county **5** court

CT *abbr* **1** central time **2** Connecticut

ctn *abbr* carton

ctr *abbr* **1** center **2** counter

CT scan \ˌsē-'tē-\ *n* : CAT SCAN

cu *abbr* cubic

Cu *symbol* [L *cuprum*] copper

cub \'kəb\ *n* : a young individual of some animals (as a fox, bear, or lion)

cub·by·hole \'kə-bē-ˌhōl\ *n* : a snug place (as for storing things)

Cu·ban sandwich \'kyü-bən-\ *n* : a usu. grilled and pressed sandwich served on a long split roll

¹cube \'kyüb\ *n* **1** : a solid having 6 equal square sides **2** : the result of raising a number to the third power ⟨the ~ of 3 is 27⟩

²cube *vb* **cubed; cub·ing 1** : to raise to the third power **2** : to form into a cube **3** : to cut into cubes

cube root *n* : a number whose cube is a given number

cu·bic \'kyü-bik\ *also* **cu·bi·cal** *adj* **1** : having the form of a cube **2** : being the volume of a cube whose edge is a specified unit **3** : having length, width, and height

cu·bi·cle \'kyü-bi-kəl\ *n* : a small separate space (as for sleeping, studying, or working)

cubic measure *n* : a unit (as cubic inch) for measuring volume — see METRIC SYSTEM table, WEIGHT table

cubic zir·co·nia \-ˌzər-'kō-nē-ə\ *also* **cubic zirconium** *n* : a synthetic gemstone resembling a diamond made from an oxide of zirconium

cub·ism \'kyü-ˌbi-zəm\ *n* : a style of art characterized by the abstraction of natural forms into fragmented geometric shapes — **cub·ist** \-bist\ *n or adj*

cu·bit \'kyü-bət\ *n* : an ancient unit of length equal to about 18 inches (46 centimeters)

Cub Scout *n* : a member of the program of the Boy Scouts for boys in the first through fifth grades in school

cuck·old \'kə-kəld, 'kú-\ *n* : a man whose wife is unfaithful — **cuckold** *vb*

¹cuck·oo \'kü-kü, 'kú-\ *n, pl* **cuckoos** : a largely grayish brown European bird that lays its eggs in the nests of other birds for them to hatch

²cuckoo *adj* : SILLY, FOOLISH

cu·cum·ber \'kyü-(ˌ)kəm-bər\ *n* : the long fleshy many-seeded fruit of a vine of the gourd family that is grown as a garden vegetable; *also* : this vine

cud \'kəd\ *n* : food brought up into the mouth by some animals (as cows) from the rumen to be chewed again

cud·dle \'kə-d²l\ *vb* **cud·dled; cud·dling** : to lie close : SNUGGLE

cud·gel \'kə-jəl\ *n* : a short heavy club — **cudgel** *vb*

¹cue \'kyü\ *n* **1** : a word, phrase, or action in a play serving as a signal for the next actor to speak or act **2** : HINT — **cue** *vb*

²**cue** *n* : a tapered rod for striking the balls in billiards or pool

cue ball *n* : the ball a player strikes with a cue in billiards or pool

¹**cuff** \\'kəf\\ *n* **1** : a part (as of a sleeve or glove) encircling the wrist **2** : the folded hem of a trouser leg

²**cuff** *vb* : to strike esp. with the open hand : SLAP

³**cuff** *n* : a blow with the hand esp. when open

cui·sine \\kwi-'zēn\\ *n* : style of cooking; *also* : the food prepared

cuke \\'kyük\\ *n* : CUCUMBER

cul–de–sac \\,kəl-di-'sak, ,kül-\\ *n, pl* **culs–de–sac** *same or* ,kəlz-, ,külz-\\ *also* **cul–de–sacs** \\,kəl-də-'saks, ,kül-\\ [F, lit., bottom of the bag] : a street or passage closed at one end

cu·li·nary \\'kə-lə-,ner-ē, 'kyü-\\ *adj* : of or relating to the kitchen or cookery

¹**cull** \\'kəl\\ *vb* : to pick out from a group

²**cull** *n* : something rejected from a group or lot as worthless or inferior

cul·mi·nate \\'kəl-mə-,nāt\\ *vb* **-nat·ed; -nat·ing** : to reach the highest point — **cul·mi·na·tion** \\,kəl-mə-'nā-shən\\ *n*

cu·lotte \\'kü-,lät, ,kyü-, kü-,lät, kyü-\\ *n* [F, breeches, fr. dim. of *cul* backside] : a divided skirt; *also* : a garment having a divided skirt — often used in pl.

cul·pa·ble \\'kəl-pə-bəl\\ *adj* : deserving blame — **cul·pa·bil·i·ty** \\,kəl-pə-'bi-lə-tē\\ *n*

cul·prit \\'kəl-prət\\ *n* [AF *cul.* (abbr. of *culpable* guilty) + *prest, prit* ready (i.e., to prove it), fr. L *praestus*] : one accused or guilty of a crime

cult \\'kəlt\\ *n* **1** : formal religious veneration **2** : a religious system; *also* : its adherents **3** : faddish devotion; *also* : a group of persons showing such devotion — **cult·ish** \\'kəl-tish\\ *adj* — **cult·ist** \\-tist\\ *n*

cul·ti·va·ble \\'kəl-tə-və-bəl\\ *adj* : capable of being cultivated

cul·ti·var \\'kəl-tə-,vär, -ver\\ *n* : a plant variety originating and persisting under cultivation

cul·ti·vate \\'kəl-tə-,vāt\\ *vb* **-vat·ed; -vat·ing** **1** : to prepare for the raising of crops **2** : to foster the growth of by tilling or by labor and care ⟨∼ vegetables⟩ **3** : REFINE, IMPROVE **4** : ENCOURAGE, FURTHER — **cul·ti·va·tion** \\,kəl-tə-'vā-shən\\ *n* — **cul·ti·va·tor** \\'kəl-tə-,vā-tər\\ *n*

cul·ture \\'kəl-chər\\ *n* **1** : TILLAGE, CULTIVATION **2** : the act of developing by education and training **3** : refinement of intellectual and artistic taste **4** : the customary beliefs, social forms, and material traits of a racial, religious, or social group — **cul·tur·al** \\'kəl-chə-rəl\\ *adj* — **cul·tur·al·ly** *adv* — **cul·tured** \\-chərd\\ *adj*

cul·vert \\'kəl-vərt\\ *n* : a drain crossing under a road or railroad

cum *abbr* cumulative

cum·ber \\'kəm-bər\\ *vb* : to weigh down : BURDEN, HINDER

cum·ber·some \\'kəm-bər-səm\\ *adj* : hard to handle or manage because of size or weight — **cum·ber·some·ly** *adv*

cum·brous \\'kəm-brəs\\ *adj* : CUMBERSOME — **cum·brous·ly** *adv* — **cum·brous·ness** *n*

cum·in \\'kə-mən, 'kyü-\\ *n* : the seedlike fruit of a small annual herb related to the carrot that is used as a spice; *also* : this herb

cum·mer·bund \\'kə-mər-,bənd, 'kəm-bər-\\ *n* [Hindi & Urdu *kamarband,* fr. Pers., fr. *kamar* waist + *band* band] : a broad sash worn as a waistband

cu·mu·la·tive \\'kyü-myə-lə-tiv, -,lā-\\ *adj* : increasing in force or value by successive additions

cu·mu·lo·nim·bus \\,kyü-myə-lō-'nim-bəs\\ *n* : an anvil-shaped cumulus cloud extending to great heights

cu·mu·lus \\'kyü-myə-ləs\\ *n, pl* **-li** \\-,lī, -,lē\\ : a dense puffy cloud having a flat base and rounded outlines

cu·ne·i·form \\kyü-'nē-ə-,fòrm\\ *adj* **1** : wedge-shaped **2** : composed of wedge-shaped characters

cun·ni·lin·gus \\,kə-ni-'liŋ-gəs\\ *also* **cun·ni·linc·tus** \\-'liŋk-təs\\ *n* : oral stimulation of the vulva or clitoris

¹**cun·ning** \\'kə-niŋ\\ *adj* **1** : SKILLFUL, DEXTEROUS **2** : marked by wiliness and trickery ⟨∼ schemes⟩ **3** : CUTE ⟨a ∼ kitten⟩ — **cun·ning·ly** *adv*

²**cunning** *n* **1** : SKILL **2** : SLYNESS

¹**cup** \\'kəp\\ *n* **1** : a small bowl-shaped drinking vessel **2** : the contents of a cup **3** : the consecrated wine of the Communion **4** : something resembling a cup : a small bowl or hollow **5** : a half pint — **cup·ful** *n* — **cup·like** \\-,līk\\ *adj*

²**cup** *vb* **cupped; cup·ping** : to curve into the shape of a cup

cup·board \\'kə-bərd\\ *n* : a small closet with shelves for food or dishes

cup·cake \\'kəp-,kāk\\ *n* : a small cake baked in a cuplike mold

cu·pid \\'kyü-pəd\\ *n* : a winged naked figure of an infant often with a bow and arrow that represents the god Cupid

cu·pid·i·ty \\kyü-'pi-də-tē\\ *n, pl* **-ties** : excessive desire for money

cu·po·la \\'kyü-pə-lə, -,lō\\ *n* : a small structure on top of a roof or building

¹**cur** \\'kər\\ *n* : a mongrel dog

²**cur** *abbr* **1** currency **2** current

cu·rate \\'kyúr-ət\\ *n* **1** : a member of the clergy who is in charge of a parish **2** : a member of the clergy who assists a rector or vicar — **cu·ra·cy** \\-ə-sē\\ *n*

cu·ra·tive \\-ə-tiv\\ *adj* : relating to or used in the cure of diseases ⟨∼ therapy⟩ ⟨∼ powers⟩ — **curative** *n*

cu·ra·tor \\'kyúr-,ā-tər, kyü-'rā-\\ *n* : CUSTODIAN; *esp* : one in charge of a place of exhibit (as a museum or zoo)

¹**curb** \\'kərb\\ *n* **1** : a bit that exerts pressure on a horse's jaws **2** : CHECK, RESTRAINT **3** : a raised edging (as of stone or concrete) along a paved street

²**curb** *vb* : to hold in or back : RESTRAIN

curb·ing \\'kər-biŋ\\ *n* **1** : the material for a curb **2** : CURB

curd \'kərd\ *n* : the thick protein-rich part of coagulated milk

cur·dle \'kər-d⁰l\ *vb* **cur·dled; cur·dling** : to form curds; *also* : SPOIL, SOUR

¹**cure** \'kyür\ *n* **1** : spiritual care **2** : recovery or relief from disease **3** : a curative agent : REMEDY **4** : a course or period of treatment

²**cure** *vb* **cured; cur·ing 1** : to restore to health : HEAL, REMEDY; *also* : to become cured **2** : to process for storage or use ⟨~ bacon⟩ — **cur·able** *adj*

cu·ré \kyù-'rā\ *n* [F] : a parish priest

cure–all \'kyür-,ȯl\ *n* : a remedy for all ills : PANACEA

cu·ret·tage \,kyür-ə-'täzh\ *n* : a surgical scraping or cleaning of a body part (as the uterus)

cur·few \'kər-,fyü\ *n* [ME, fr. AF *covrefeu*, signal given to bank the hearth fire, curfew, fr. *coverir* to cover + *fu, feu* fire, fr. L *focus* hearth] : a regulation that specified persons (as children) be off the streets at a set hour of the evening; *also* : the sounding of a signal (as a bell) at this hour

cu·ria \'kyür-ē-ə, 'kür-\ *n, pl* **cu·ri·ae** \'kyür-ē-,ē, 'kür-ē-,ī\ *often cap* : the body of congregations, tribunals, and offices through which the pope governs the Roman Catholic Church

cu·rie \'kyür-ē\ *n* : a unit of radioactivity equal to 37 billion disintegrations per second

cu·rio \'kyür-ē-,ō\ *n, pl* **cu·ri·os** : an object or article valued because it is strange or rare

cu·ri·ous \'kyür-ē-əs\ *adj* **1** : having a desire to investigate and learn **2** : STRANGE, UNUSUAL, ODD ⟨a ~ coincidence⟩ — **cu·ri·os·i·ty** \,kyür-ē-'ä-sə-tē\ *n* — **cu·ri·ous·ness** *n*

cu·ri·ous·ly *adv* **1** : in a curious manner **2** : as is curious

cu·ri·um \'kyür-ē-əm\ *n* : a metallic radioactive element produced artificially

¹**curl** \'kərl\ *vb* **1** : to form into ringlets **2** : CURVE, COIL — **curl·er** *n*

²**curl** *n* **1** : a lock of hair that coils : RINGLET **2** : something having a spiral or twisted form — **curly** *adj*

cur·lew \'kər-lü, 'kərl-yü\ *n, pl* **curlews** *or* **curlew** : any of various long-legged brownish birds that have a down-curved bill and are related to the sandpipers and snipes

curli·cue \'kər-li-,kyü\ *n* : a fancifully curved or spiral figure

cur·rant \'kər-ənt\ *n* **1** : a small seedless raisin **2** : the acid berry of various shrubs related to the gooseberry; *also* : this plant

cur·ren·cy \'kər-ən-sē\ *n, pl* **-cies 1** : general use or acceptance **2** : something that is in circulation as a medium of exchange : MONEY

¹**cur·rent** \'kər-ənt\ *adj* **1** : occurring in or belonging to the present ⟨the ~ crisis⟩ **2** : used as a medium of exchange **3** : generally accepted or practiced

²**current** *n* **1** : the part of a body of fluid moving continuously in a certain direction; *also* : the swiftest part of a stream **2** : a flow of electric charge; *also* : the rate of such flow

cur·ric·u·lum \kə-'ri-kyə-ləm\ *n, pl* **-la** \-lə\ *also* **-lums** [L, running, course, fr. *currere* to run] : the courses offered by an educational institution

¹**cur·ry** \'kər-ē\ *vb* **cur·ried; cur·ry·ing 1** : to clean the coat of (a horse) with a currycomb **2** : to treat (tanned leather) esp. by incorporating oil or grease — **curry favor** : to seek to gain favor by flattery or attention

²**cur·ry** *n, pl* **cur·ries** : a powder of pungent spices used in cooking; *also* : a food seasoned with curry

cur·ry·comb \-,kōm\ *n* : a comb used esp. to curry horses — **currycomb** *vb*

¹**curse** \'kərs\ *n* **1** : a prayer for harm to come upon one **2** : something that is cursed **3** : evil or misfortune coming as if in response to a curse

²**curse** *vb* **cursed; curs·ing 1** : to call on divine power to send injury upon **2** : BLASPHEME ♦ AFFLICT ♦ **Synonyms** EXECRATE, DAMN, ANATHEMATIZE, OBJURGATE

cur·sive \'kər-siv\ *adj* : written with the strokes of the letters joined together and the angles rounded

cur·sor \'kər-sər\ *n* : a visual cue (as a pointer) on a computer screen that indicates position (as for data entry)

cur·so·ry \'kər-sə-rē\ *adj* : rapidly and often superficially done ⟨a ~ reading of the report⟩ — **cur·so·ri·ly** \-rə-lē\ *adv*

curt \'kərt\ *adj* : rudely short or abrupt — **curt·ly** *adv* — **curt·ness** *n*

cur·tail \(,)kər-'tāl\ *vb* : to cut off the end of : SHORTEN — **cur·tail·ment** *n*

cur·tain \'kər-t⁰n\ *n* **1** : a hanging screen that can be drawn back esp. at a window **2** : the screen between the stage and auditorium of a theater — **curtain** *vb*

curt·sy *also* **curt·sey** \'kərt-sē\ *n, pl* **curtsies** *or* **curtseys** : a courteous bow made by women chiefly by bending the knees — **curtsy** *also* **curtsey** *vb*

cur·va·ceous *also* **cur·va·cious** \,kər-'vā-shəs\ *adj* : having curves suggestive of a well-proportioned feminine figure

cur·va·ture \'kər-və-,chůr\ *n* : a measure or amount of curving : BEND

¹**curve** \'kərv\ *vb* **curved; curv·ing** : to bend from a straight line or course

²**curve** *n* **1** : a line esp. when curved **2** : something that bends or curves without angles ⟨a ~ in the road⟩ **3** : a baseball pitch thrown so that it swerves esp. downward and to one side

cur·vet \(,)kər-'vet\ *n* : a prancing leap of a horse — **curvet** *vb*

¹**cush·ion** \'kù-shən\ *n* [ME *cusshin*, fr. AF *cussin, quissin*, fr. VL **coxinus*, fr. L *coxa* hip] **1** : a soft pillow or pad to rest on or against **2** : the springy pad inside the rim of a billiard table **3** : something soft that prevents discomfort or protects against injury

²**cushion** *vb* **1** : to provide (as a seat) with

a cushion **2** : to soften or lessen the force or shock of

cusp \'kəsp\ *n* : a pointed end or part (as of a tooth)

cus-pid \'kəs-pəd\ *n* : a canine tooth

cus-pi-dor \'kəs-pə-ˌdȯr\ *n* : SPITTOON

cus-tard \'kəs-tərd\ *n* : a sweetened cooked mixture of milk and eggs

cus-to-di-al \ˌkəs-'tō-dē-əl\ *adj* : marked by watching and protecting rather than seeking to cure ⟨~ care⟩

cus-to-di-an \ˌkəs-'tō-dē-ən\ *n* : one who has custody (as of a building)

cus-to-dy \'kəs-tə-dē\ *n, pl* **-dies** : immediate charge and control

¹**cus-tom** \'kəs-təm\ *n* **1** : habitual course of action : recognized usage **2** *pl* : taxes levied on imports **3** : business patronage

²**custom** *adj* **1** : made to personal order **2** : doing work only on order

cus-tom-ary \'kəs-tə-ˌmer-ē\ *adj* **1** : based on or established by custom **2** : commonly practiced or observed : HABITUAL — **cus-tom-ari-ly** *adv*

cus-tom-built \ˌkəs-təm-'bilt\ *adj* : built to individual order

cus-tom-er \'kəs-tə-mər\ *n* : BUYER, PURCHASER; *esp* : a regular or frequent buyer

cus-tom-house \'kəs-təm-ˌhaus\ *n* : the building where customs are paid

cus-tom-ise *Brit var of* CUSTOMIZE

cus-tom-ize \'kəs-tə-ˌmīz\ *vb* **-ized; -iz-ing** : to build, fit, or alter according to individual specifications

cus-tom-made \ˌkəs-təm-'mād\ *adj* : made to individual order

¹**cut** \'kət\ *vb* **cut; cut-ting** **1** : to penetrate or divide with a sharp edge : CLEAVE, GASH; *also* : to experience the growth of (a tooth) through the gum **2** : to hurt the feelings of **3** : to strike sharply **4** : SHORTEN, REDUCE **5** : to remove by severing or paring **6** : INTERSECT, CROSS **7** : to divide into parts **8** : to go quickly or change direction abruptly **9** : to cause to stop

²**cut** *n* **1** : something made by cutting : GASH, CLEFT **2** : SHARE **3** : a segment or section of a meat carcass **4** : an excavated channel or roadway **5** : BAND **6** : a sharp stroke or blow **7** : REDUCTION ⟨a ~ in wages⟩ **8** : the shape or manner in which a thing is cut

cut-and-dried \ˌkət-ᵊn-'drīd\ *also* **cut-and-dry** \-'drī\ *adj* : according to a plan, set procedure, or formula

cu-ta-ne-ous \kyù-'tā-nē-əs\ *adj* : of, relating to, or affecting the skin

cut-back \'kət-ˌbak\ *n* : something cut back **2** : REDUCTION

cute \'kyut\ *adj* **cut-er; cut-est** [short for *acute*] **1** : CLEVER, SHREWD **2** : daintily attractive : PRETTY

cu-ti-cle \'kyü-ti-kəl\ *n* **1** : an outer layer (as of skin or a leaf) **2** : dead or horny epidermis esp. around a fingernail — **cu-tic-u-lar** \kyù-'ti-kyə-lər\ *adj*

cut in *vb* **1** : to thrust oneself between others **2** : to interrupt a dancing couple and take one as one's partner

cut-lass \'kət-ləs\ *n* : a short heavy curved sword

cut-ler \'kət-lər\ *n* [ME, fr. AF *cuteler*, fr. LL *cultellarius*, fr. L *cultellus* knife] : one who makes, deals in, or repairs cutlery

cut-lery \'kət-lə-rē\ *n* : edged or cutting tools; *esp* : implements for cutting and eating food

cut-let \'kət-lət\ *n* : a slice of meat (as veal) for broiling or frying

cut-off \'kət-ˌȯf\ *n* **1** : the channel formed when a stream cuts through the neck of an oxbow; *also* : SHORTCUT **2** : a device for cutting off **3** *pl* : shorts orig. made from jeans with the legs cut off at the knees or higher

cut-out \'kət-ˌaut\ *n* : something cut out or prepared for cutting out from something else

cut out *vb* **1** : to determine or assign through necessity ⟨had her work *cut out* for her⟩ **2** : DISCONNECT **3** : to cease operating ⟨the engine *cut out*⟩ **4** : ELIMINATE ⟨*cut out* unnecessary expense⟩

cut-rate \'kət-ˌrāt\ *adj* : relating to or dealing in goods sold at reduced rates

cut-ter \'kət-ər\ *n* **1** : a tool or a machine for cutting **2** : a ship's boat for carrying stores and passengers **3** : a small armed vessel in government service **4** : a light sleigh

¹**cut-throat** \'kət-ˌthrōt\ *n* : MURDERER

²**cutthroat** *adj* **1** : MURDEROUS, CRUEL **2** : RUTHLESS ⟨~ competition⟩

cutthroat trout *n* : a large American trout with a red mark under the jaw

¹**cut-ting** \'kə-tiŋ\ *n* : a piece of a plant able to grow into a new plant

²**cutting** *adj* **1** : SHARP, EDGED **2** : marked by piercing cold **3** : likely to hurt the feelings : SARCASTIC ⟨a ~ remark⟩

cut-tle-fish \'kə-tᵊl-ˌfish\ *n* : any of various marine mollusks having eight arms and two usu. longer tentacles and an internal shell (**cut-tle-bone** \-ˌbōn\) composed of calcium compounds

cut-up \'kət-ˌəp\ *n* : a person who clowns or acts boisterously — **cut up** *vb*

cut-worm \-ˌwərm\ *n* : any of various smooth-bodied moth larvae that feed on plants at night

cw *abbr* clockwise

CWO *abbr* **1** cash with order **2** chief warrant officer

cwt *abbr* hundredweight

-cy \sē\ *n suffix* **1** : action : practice ⟨mendican*cy*⟩ **2** : rank : office ⟨chaplain*cy*⟩ **3** : body : class ⟨constituen*cy*⟩ **4** : state : quality ⟨accura*cy*⟩

cy-an \'sī-ˌan, -ən\ *n* : a greenish blue color

cy-a-nide \'sī-ə-ˌnīd, -nəd\ *n* : a poisonous compound of carbon and nitrogen with another element (as potassium)

cy-ber \'sī-bər\ *adj* : of, relating to, or involving computers or computer networks

cyber- *comb form* : computer : computer network

cy-ber-ca-fe \'sī-bər-ka-ˌfā\ *n* : a small restaurant offering use of computers with Internet access

cy-ber-net-ics \ˌsī-bər-'ne-tiks\ *n* : the science of communication and control theory that is concerned esp. with the comparative study of automatic control systems — **cy·ber·net·ic** *adj*

cy·ber·punk \'sī-bər-ˌpəŋk\ *n* 1 : science fiction dealing with computer-dominated future societies 2 : HACKER 3

cy·ber·sex \'sī-bər-ˌseks\ *n* 1 : online sex-oriented conversations 2 : sex-oriented material available on a computer

cy·ber·space \'sī-bər-ˌspās\ *n* : the online world of the Internet

cy·cla·men \'sī-klə-mən\ *n* : any of a genus of plants related to the primroses and having showy nodding flowers

¹cy·cle \'sī-kəl\ *n* 1 : a period of time occupied by a series of events that repeat themselves regularly and in the same order 2 : a recurring round of operations or events 3 : one complete occurrence of a periodic process (as a vibration or current alternation) 4 : a circular or spiral arrangement 5 : a long period of time : AGE 6 : BICYCLE 7 : MOTORCYCLE — **cy·clic** \'sī-klik, 'si-\ or **cy·cli·cal** \kli-kəl\ *adj* — **cy·cli·cal·ly** \-k(ə-)lē\ *also* **cy·clic·ly** *adv*

²cy·cle \'sī-kəl\ *vb* **cy·cled; cy·cling** : to ride a cycle — **cy·clist** \'sī-klist, -kə-list\ *n*

cy·clone \'sī-ˌklōn\ *n* 1 : a storm or system of winds that rotates about a center of low atmospheric pressure and advances at 20 to 30 miles (about 30 to 50 kilometers) an hour 2 : TORNADO — **cy·clon·ic** \sī-'klä-nik\ *adj*

cy·clo·pe·dia *also* **cy·clo·pae·dia** \ˌsī-klə-'pē-dē-ə\ *n* : ENCYCLOPEDIA

cy·clo·tron \'sī-klə-ˌträn\ *n* : a device for giving high speed to charged particles by magnetic and electric fields

cy·der *Brit var of* CIDER

cyg·net \'sig-nət\ *n* : a young swan

cyl *abbr* cylinder

cyl·in·der \'si-lən-dər\ *n* : the solid figure formed by turning a rectangle about one side as an axis; *also* : a body or space of this form ⟨an engine ~⟩ ⟨a bullet in the ~ of a revolver⟩ — **cy·lin·dri·cal** \sə-'lin-dri-kəl\ *adj*

cym·bal \'sim-bəl\ *n* : a concave brass plate that produces a brilliant clashing sound

cyn·ic \'si-nik\ *n* : one who attributes all actions to selfish motives — **cyn·i·cal** \-ni-kəl\ *adj* — **cyn·i·cal·ly** \-k(ə-)lē\ *adv* — **cyn·i·cism** \si-nə-ˌsi-zəm\ *n*

cy·no·sure \'sī-nə-ˌshu̇r, 'si-\ *n* [MF & L; MF, Ursa Minor, guide, fr. L *cynosura* Ursa Minor, fr. Gk *kynosoura*, fr. *kynos oura*, lit., dog's tail] : a center of attraction

CYO *abbr* Catholic Youth Organization

cy·pher *chiefly Brit var of* CIPHER

cy·press \'sī-prəs\ *n* 1 : any of a genus of scaly-leaved evergreen trees and shrubs 2 : BALD CYPRESS 3 : the wood of a cypress

cyst \'sist\ *n* : an abnormal closed bodily sac usu. containing liquid — **cys·tic** \'sis-tik\ *adj*

cystic fibrosis *n* : a common hereditary disease marked esp. by deficiency of pancreatic enzymes, by respiratory symptoms, and by excessive loss of salt in the sweat

cy·tol·o·gy \sī-'tä-lə-jē\ *n* : a branch of biology dealing with cells — **cy·to·log·i·cal** \ˌsī-tə-'lä-ji-kəl\ *or* **cy·to·log·ic** \-jik\ *adj* — **cy·tol·o·gist** \sī-'tä-lə-jist\ *n*

cy·to·plasm \'sī-tə-ˌpla-zəm\ *n* : the protoplasm of a cell that lies external to the nucleus — **cy·to·plas·mic** \ˌsī-tə-'plaz-mik\ *adj*

cy·to·sine \'sī-tə-ˌsēn\ *n* : a chemical base that is a pyrimidine coding genetic information in DNA and RNA

CZ *abbr* Canal Zone

czar *also* **tsar** *or* **tzar** \'zär, 'tsär\ *n* [NL, fr. Russ *tsar'*, ultim. fr. L *Caesar* Caesar] : the ruler of Russia until 1917; *also* : one having great authority — **czar·ist** *also* **tsar·ist** *or* **tzar·ist** \-ist\ *n or adj*

cza·ri·na \zä-'rē-nə\ *n* : the wife of a czar

Czech \'chek\ *n* 1 : a native or inhabitant of Czechoslovakia or the Czech Republic 2 : the language of the Czechs — **Czech** *adj*

¹d \'dē\ *n, pl* **d's** *or* **ds** \'dēz\ *often cap* 1 : the 4th letter of the English alphabet 2 : a grade rating a student's work as poor 3 : DEFENSE

²d *abbr, often cap* 1 date 2 daughter 3 day 4 dead 5 deceased 6 degree 7 Democrat 8 [L *denarius, denarii*] penny; pence 9 depart; departure 10 diameter

D *symbol* deuterium

DA *abbr* 1 deposit account 2 district attorney 3 don't answer

¹dab \'dab\ *n* 1 : a sudden blow or thrust : POKE; *also* : PECK 2 : a gentle touch or stroke : PAT

²dab *vb* **dabbed; dab·bing** 1 : to strike or touch gently : PAT 2 : to apply lightly or irregularly : DAUB — **dab·ber** *n*

³dab *n* 1 : DAUB 2 : a small amount

dab·ble \'da-bəl\ *vb* **dab·bled; dab·bling** 1 : to wet by splashing : SPATTER 2 : to paddle or play in or as if in water 3 : to work or involve oneself without serious effort — **dab·bler** *n*

da ca·po \dä-'kä-(ˌ)pō\ *adv or adj* [It] : from the beginning — used as a direction in music to repeat

dace \'dās\ *n, pl* **dace** : any of various small No. American freshwater fishes related to the carp

da·cha \'dä-chə\ *n* [Russ] : a Russian country house

dachs·hund \'däks-ˌhúnt\ *n* [G, fr. *Dachs* badger + *Hund* dog] : any of a breed of long-bodied short-legged dogs of German origin

dac·tyl \'dak-tᵊl\ *n* [ME *dactile*, fr. L *dactylus*, fr. Gk *daktylos*, lit., finger; fr. the fact that the three syllables have the first one longest like the joints of the finger] : a metrical foot of one accented syllable followed by two unaccented syllables — **dac·tyl·ic** \dak-'ti-lik\ *adj or n*

dad \'dad\ *n* : FATHER 1

Da·da \'dä-(ˌ)dä\ *n* : a movement in art and literature based on deliberate irrationality and negation of traditional artistic values — **da·da·ism** \-ˌi-zəm\ *n, often cap* — **da·da·ist** \-ˌist\ *n or adj, often cap*

dad·dy \'da-dē\ *n, pl* **daddies** : FATHER 1

dad·dy long·legs \ˌda-dē-'lȯn̄-ˌlegz\ *n, pl* **daddy longlegs** : any of an order of arachnids resembling the true spiders but having small rounded bodies and long slender legs

daemon *var of* DEMON

daf·fo·dil \'da-fə-ˌdil\ *n* : any of various bulbous herbs with usu. large flowers having a trumpetlike center

daf·fy \'da-fē\ *adj* **daf·fi·er; -est** : DAFT

daft \'daft\ *adj* : FOOLISH; *also* : INSANE — **daft·ness** *n*

dag *abbr* dekagram

dag·ger \'da-gər\ *n* 1 : a sharp pointed knife for stabbing 2 : a character † used as a reference mark or to indicate a death date

da·guerre·o·type \də-'ger-(ē-)ə-ˌtīp\ *n* : an early photograph produced on a silver or a silver-covered copper plate

dahl·ia \'dal-yə, 'däl-\ *n* : any of a genus of tuberous herbs related to the daisies and having showy flowers

¹**dai·ly** \'dā-lē\ *adj* 1 : occurring, done, or used every day or every weekday 2 : of or relating to every day ⟨~ visitors⟩ 3 : computed in terms of one day ⟨~ wages⟩ ✦ *Synonyms* DIURNAL, QUOTIDIAN — **dai·li·ness** \-lē-nəs\ *n* — **daily** *adv*

²**daily** *n, pl* **dailies** : a newspaper published every weekday

daily double *n* : a system of betting on races in which the bettor must pick the winners of two stipulated races in order to win

¹**dain·ty** \'dān-tē\ *n, pl* **dainties** [ME *deinte* high esteem, delight, fr. AF *deinté*, fr. L *dignitas* dignity, worth] : something delicious or pleasing to the taste : DELICACY

²**dainty** *adj* **dain·ti·er; -est** 1 : pleasing to the taste 2 : delicately pretty 3 : having or showing delicate taste; *also* : FASTIDIOUS ✦ *Synonyms* CHOICE, DELICATE, EXQUISITE, RARE, RECHERCHÉ — **dain·ti·ly** \-ti-lē\ *adv* — **dain·ti·ness** \-tē-nəs\ *n*

dai·qui·ri \'da-kə-rē, 'dī-\ *n* [*Daiquirí*, Cuba] : a cocktail made usu. of rum, lime juice, and sugar

dairy \'der-ē\ *n, pl* **dair·ies** [ME *deyerie*, fr. *deye* dairymaid, fr. OE *dǣge* kneader of bread] 1 : CREAMERY 2 : a farm specializing in milk production

dairy·ing \'der-ē-iŋ\ *n* : the business of operating a dairy

dairy·maid \-ˌmād\ *n* : a woman employed in a dairy

dairy·man \-mən, -ˌman\ *n* : a person who operates a dairy farm or works in a dairy

da·is \'dā-əs\ *n* : a raised platform usu. above the floor of a hall or large room

dai·sy \'dā-zē\ *n, pl* **daisies** [ME *dayeseye*, fr. OE *dægesēage*, fr. *dæg* day + *ēage* eye] : any of numerous composite plants having flower heads in which the marginal flowers resemble petals

dai·sy–chain \-ˌchān\ *vb* : to link (as computer components) together in series — **daisy chain** *n*

daisy wheel *n* : a disk with spokes bearing type that serves as the printing element of an electric typewriter or printer; *also* : a printer that uses such a disk

Da·ko·ta \də-'kō-tə\ *n, pl* **Dakotas** *also* **Dakota** : a member of an American Indian people of the northern Mississippi valley; *also* : their language

dal *abbr* dekaliter

da·la·si \dä-'lä-sē\ *n, pl* **dalasi** *or* **dalasis** — see MONEY table

dale \'dāl\ *n* : VALLEY

dal·ly \'da-lē\ *vb* **dal·lied; dal·ly·ing** 1 : to act playfully; *esp* : to play amorously 2 : to waste time 3 : LINGER, DAWDLE ✦ *Synonyms* FLIRT, COQUET, TOY, TRIFLE — **dal·li·ance** \-lē-əns\ *n*

dal·ma·tian \dal-'mā-shən\ *n, often cap* : any of a breed of medium-sized dogs having a white short-haired coat with many black or brown spots

¹**dam** \'dam\ *n* : the female parent of an animal and esp. of a domestic animal

²**dam** *n* : a barrier (as across a stream) to stop the flow of water — **dam** *vb*

³**dam** *abbr* dekameter

¹**dam·age** \'da-mij\ *n* 1 : loss or harm due to injury to persons, property, or reputation 2 *pl* : compensation in money imposed by law for loss or injury ⟨bring a suit for ~s⟩

²**damage** *vb* **dam·aged; dam·ag·ing** : to cause damage to ⟨~ the furniture⟩

dam·a·scene \'da-mə-ˌsēn\ *vb* **-scened; -scen·ing** : to ornament (as iron or steel) with wavy patterns or with inlaid work of precious metals

dam·ask \'da-məsk\ *n* 1 : a firm lustrous reversible figured fabric used for household linen 2 : a tough steel having decorative wavy lines

dame \'dām\ *n* 1 : a woman of rank, station, or authority 2 : an elderly woman 3 : WOMAN

damn \'dam\ *vb* [ME *dampnen*, fr. AF *dampner*, fr. L *damnare*, fr. *damnum* damage, loss, fine] 1 : to condemn esp. to hell 2 : CURSE — **damned** *adj*

dam·na·ble \'dam-nə-bəl\ *adj* 1 : liable to or deserving punishment 2 : DETESTABLE ⟨~ weather⟩ — **dam·na·bly** \-blē\ *adv*

dam·na·tion \dam-'nā-shən\ *n* 1 : the act of damning 2 : the state of being damned

¹**damp** \'damp\ *n* 1 : a noxious gas : MOISTURE

²**damp** *vb* : DAMPEN

³**damp** *adj* : MOIST — **damp·ness** *n*

damp·en \'dam-pən\ *vb* 1 : to check or diminish in activity or vigor ⟨~ enthusiasm⟩ 2 : to make or become damp ⟨~ a sponge⟩

damp·er \'dam-pər\ *n* 1 : a dulling or deadening influence ⟨put a ~ on the party⟩ 2 : one that damps; *esp* : a valve or movable plate (as in the flue of a stove, furnace, or fireplace) to regulate the draft

dam·sel \'dam-zəl\ *n* : MAIDEN, GIRL

dam·sel·fly \-,flī\ *n* : any of a group of insects that are closely related to the dragonflies but fold their wings above the body when at rest

dam·son \'dam-zən\ *n* : a plum with acid purple fruit; *also* : its fruit

Dan *abbr* Daniel

¹**dance** \'dans\ *vb* **danced; danc·ing** 1 : to glide, step, or move through a set series of movements usu. to music 2 : to move quickly up and down or about 3 : to perform or take part in as a dancer — **danc·er** *n*

²**dance** *n* 1 : an act or instance of dancing 2 : a social gathering for dancing 3 : a piece of music (as a waltz) by which dancing may be guided 4 : the art of dancing

D & C *n* [*d*ilation *and* *c*urettage] : a surgical procedure that involves stretching the cervix and scraping the inside walls of the uterus (as to test for cancer or to perform an abortion)

dan·de·li·on \'dan-də-,lī-ən, -dē-\ *n* [ME *dendelyoun*, fr. AF *dent de lion*, lit., lion's tooth] : any of a genus of common yellow-flowered composite herbs

dan·der \'dan-dər\ *n* : ANGER, TEMPER

dan·di·fy \'dan-di-,fī\ *vb* **-fied; -fy·ing** : to cause to resemble a dandy

dan·dle \'dan-d³l\ *vb* **dan·dled; dan·dling** : to move up and down in one's arms or on one's knee in affectionate play ◆ Synonyms CARESS, FONDLE, LOVE, PET

dan·druff \'dan-drəf\ *n* : scaly white or grayish flakes of dead skin cells that come off the scalp — **dan·druffy** \-drə-fē\ *adj*

¹**dan·dy** \'dan-dē\ *n, pl* **dandies** 1 : a man unduly attentive to personal appearance 2 : something excellent in its class ◆ Synonyms FOP, COXCOMB, POPINJAY

²**dandy** *adj* **dan·di·er; -est** : very good : FIRST-RATE

Dane \'dān\ *n* 1 : a native or inhabitant of Denmark 2 : GREAT DANE

dan·ger \'dān-jər\ *n* [ME *daunger* control, resistance, peril, fr. AF *dangier*, fr. VL *dominiarium*, fr. L *dominium* ownership] 1 : exposure or liability to injury, harm, or evil 2 : something that may cause injury or harm ◆ Synonyms PERIL, HAZARD, RISK, JEOPARDY

dan·ger·ous \'dān-jə-rəs\ *adj* 1 : HAZARDOUS, PERILOUS ⟨a ~ slope⟩ 2 : able or likely to inflict injury ⟨a ~ man⟩ — **dan·ger·ous·ly** *adv*

dan·gle \'dan-gəl\ *vb* **dan·gled; dan·gling** 1 : to hang loosely esp. with a swinging motion : SWING 2 : to be a hanger-on or dependent 3 : to be left without proper grammatical connection in a sentence ⟨a *dangling* participle⟩ 4 : to keep hanging uncertainly 5 : to offer as an inducement

Dan·iel \'dan-yəl\ *n* — see BIBLE table

Dan·ish \'dā-nish\ *n* : the language of the Danes — **Danish** *adj*

Danish pastry *n* : a pastry made of a rich yeast-raised dough

dank \'dank\ *adj* : disagreeably wet or moist : DAMP — **dank·ness** *n*

dan·seuse \dän-'sərz, -'soz; dän-'süz\ *n* [F] : a female ballet dancer

dap·per \'da-pər\ *adj* 1 : SPRUCE, TRIM 2 : being alert and lively in movement and manners : JAUNTY

dap·ple \'da-pəl\ *vb* **dap·pled; dap·pling** : to mark with different-colored spots

DAR *abbr* Daughters of the American Revolution

¹**dare** \'der\ *vb* **dared; dar·ing** 1 : to have sufficient courage : be bold enough to 2 : CHALLENGE ⟨*dared* him to jump⟩ 3 : to confront boldly

²**dare** *n* : an act or instance of daring : CHALLENGE

dare·dev·il \-,de-vəl\ *n* : a recklessly bold person — **daredevil** *adj*

dar·ing \'der-iŋ\ *n* : venturesome boldness — **daring** *adj* — **dar·ing·ly** *adv*

¹**dark** \'därk\ *adj* 1 : being without light or without much light 2 : not light in color ⟨a ~ suit⟩ 3 : GLOOMY ⟨a ~ outlook⟩ 4 *often cap* : being a period of stagnation or decline ⟨the *Dark* Ages⟩ 5 : SECRETIVE ⟨~ dealings⟩ ◆ Synonyms DIM, DUSKY, MURKY, TENEBROUS — **dark·ly** *adv* — **dark·ness** *n*

²**dark** *n* 1 : absence of light : DARKNESS; *esp* : NIGHT 2 : a dark or deep color — **in the dark** 1 : in secrecy 2 : in ignorance ⟨kept *in the dark* about the plans⟩

dark·en \'där-kən\ *vb* 1 : to make or grow dark or darker 2 : DIM 3 : BESMIRCH, TARNISH 4 : to make or become gloomy or forbidding

dark horse *n* : a contestant or a political figure whose abilities and chances as a contender are not known

dark·ling \'där-kliŋ\ *adj* 1 : DARK ⟨a ~ plain⟩ 2 : MYSTERIOUS

dark·room \'därk-,rüm, -,rum\ *n* : a light-proof room in which photographic materials are processed

¹**dar·ling** \'där-liŋ\ *n* 1 : a dearly loved person 2 : FAVORITE

²**darling** *adj* 1 : dearly loved : FAVORITE 2 : very pleasing : CHARMING

darm·stadt·i·um \,därm-'sta-tē-əm\ *n* : a short-lived radioactive chemical element produced artificially

¹**darn** \'därn\ *vb* : to mend with interlacing stitches — **darn·er** *n*

²**darn** or **darned** \'därnd\ adv : VERY, EXTREMELY ⟨a ~ good job⟩

darning needle n 1 : a needle for darning 2 : DRAGONFLY

¹**dart** \'därt\ n 1 : a small missile with a point on one end and feathers on the other; also, pl : a game in which darts are thrown at a target 2 : something causing a sudden pain 3 : a stitched tapering fold in a garment 4 : a quick movement

²**dart** vb 1 : to throw with a sudden movement 2 : to thrust or move suddenly or rapidly ⟨~ed across the street⟩ 3 : to shoot with a dart containing a usu. tranquilizing drug

dart·er \'där-tər\ n : any of numerous small No. American freshwater fishes related to the perches

Dar·win·ism \'där-wə-̩ni-zəm\ n : a theory explaining the origin and continued existence of new species of plants and animals by means of natural selection acting on chance variations — **Dar·win·ist** \-nist\ n or adj

¹**dash** \'dash\ vb 1 : SMASH 2 : to knock, hurl, or thrust violently 3 : SPLASH, SPATTER 4 : RUIN 5 : DEPRESS, SADDEN 6 : to perform or finish hastily ⟨~ off a letter⟩ 7 : to move with sudden speed ⟨~ed down the hall⟩

²**dash** n 1 : a sudden burst or splash 2 : a stroke of a pen 3 : a punctuation mark — that is used esp. to indicate a break in the thought or structure of a sentence 4 : a small addition ⟨a ~ of salt⟩ 5 : flashy showiness 6 : animation in style and action 7 : a sudden rush or attempt ⟨made a ~ for the door⟩ 8 : a short foot race 9 : DASHBOARD

dash·board \-̩bȯrd\ n : a panel in an automobile or aircraft below the windshield usu. containing dials and controls

dash·er \'da-shər\ n : a device (as in a churn) for agitating something

da·shi·ki \də-'shē-kē\ also **dai·shi·ki** \dī-\ n [modif. of Yoruba (an African language) dàňṣíkí] : a usu. brightly colored loose-fitting pullover garment

dash·ing \'da-shiŋ\ adj 1 : marked by vigorous action 2 : marked by smartness esp. in dress and manners ♦ **Synonyms** STYLISH, CHIC, FASHIONABLE, MODISH, SMART, SWANK

das·tard \'das-tərd\ n 1 : COWARD 2 : a person who acts treacherously — **das·tard·ly** adj

dat abbr dative

da·ta \'dā-tə, 'da-, 'dä-\ n sing or pl [L, pl. of datum] : factual information (as measurements or statistics) used as a basis for reasoning, discussion, or calculation

da·ta·base \-̩bās\ n : a usu. large collection of data organized esp. for rapid search and retrieval (as by a computer) — **database** vb

data processing n : the action or process of supplying a computer with information and having the computer use it to produce a desired result

¹**date** \'dāt\ n [ME, fr. AF, ultim. fr. L dactylus, fr. Gk daktylos, lit., finger] : the oblong edible fruit of a tall palm; also : this palm

²**date** n [ME, fr. AF, fr. LL data, fr. data (as in data Romae given at Rome), fem. of L datus, pp. of dare to give] 1 : the day, month, or year of an event 2 : a statement giving the time of execution or making (as of a coin or check) 3 : the period to which something belongs 4 : APPOINTMENT; esp : a social engagement between two persons that often has a romantic character 5 : a person with whom one has a usu. romantic date — **to date** : up to the present moment

³**date** vb **dat·ed; dat·ing** 1 : to record the date of or on 2 : to determine, mark, or reveal the date, age, or period of 3 : go on a date or dates with ⟨~ed her for a year⟩ 4 : ORIGINATE ⟨~s from ancient times⟩ 5 : EXTEND ⟨dating back to childhood⟩ 6 : to show qualities typical of a past period

dat·ed \'dā-təd\ adj 1 : provided with a date 2 : OLD-FASHIONED ⟨a ~ custom⟩ ♦ **Synonyms** ANTIQUATED, ARCHAIC, OLD HAT, OUTDATED, OUTMODED, PASSÉ

date·less \'dāt-ləs\ adj 1 : ENDLESS 2 : having no date 3 : too ancient to be dated 4 : TIMELESS

date·line \'dāt-̩līn\ n : a line in a publication giving the date and place of composition or issue — **dateline** vb

date rape n : rape committed by the victim's date

da·tive \'dā-tiv\ adj : of, relating to, or constituting a grammatical case marking typically the indirect object of a verb — **dative** n

da·tum \'dā-təm, 'da-, 'dä-\ n, pl **da·ta** \-tə\ or **datums** : a single piece of data : FACT

dau abbr daughter

¹**daub** \'dȯb\ vb 1 : to cover with soft adhesive matter 2 : SMEAR, SMUDGE 3 : to paint crudely — **daub·er** n

²**daub** n 1 : something daubed on : SMEAR 2 : a crude picture

daugh·ter \'dȯ-tər\ n 1 : a female offspring esp. of human beings 2 : a female adopted child 3 : a human female descendant — **daughter** adj — **daugh·ter·less** \-ləs\ adj

daugh·ter–in–law \'dȯ-tə-rən-̩lȯ\ n, pl **daugh·ters–in–law** \-tər-zən-\ : the wife of one's son

daunt \'dȯnt\ vb [ME, fr. AF danter, daunter, fr. L domitare to tame] : to lessen the courage of : INTIMIDATE, OVERWHELM

daunt·ing \'dȯn-tiŋ\ adj : tending to overwhelm or intimidate ⟨a ~ task⟩

daunt·less \-ləs\ adj : FEARLESS, UNDAUNTED ♦ **Synonyms** BRAVE, BOLD, COURAGEOUS, LIONHEARTED — **daunt·less·ly** adv

dau·phin \'dȯ-fən\ n, often cap : the eldest son of a king of France

DAV abbr Disabled American Veterans

dav·en·port \'da-vən-̩pȯrt\ n : a large upholstered sofa

da·vit \'dā-vət, 'da-\ n : a small crane on a

ship used in pairs esp. to raise or lower boats

daw·dle \'dȯ-d°l\ vb **daw·dled; daw·dling 1** : to spend time wastefully or idly **2** : LOITER — **daw·dler** n

¹dawn \'dȯn\ vb **1** : to begin to grow light as the sun rises **2** : to begin to appear or develop **3** : to begin to be understood ⟨the solution ~ed on him⟩

²dawn n **1** : the first appearance of light in the morning **2** : a first appearance : BEGINNING ⟨the ~ of a new era⟩

day \'dā\ n **1** : the period of light between one night and the next; also : DAYLIGHT, DAYTIME **2** : the period of rotation of a planet (as earth) or a moon on its axis : a period of 24 hours beginning at midnight **4** : a specified day or date ⟨wedding ~⟩ **5** : a specified time or period : AGE ⟨in olden ~s⟩ **6** : the conflict or contention of the day **7** : the time set apart by usage or law for work ⟨the 8-hour ~⟩

day·bed \'dā-ˌbed\ n : a couch that can be converted into a bed

day·book \-ˌbu̇k\ n : DIARY, JOURNAL

day·break \-ˌbrāk\ n : DAWN

day care n : supervision of and care for children or disabled adults provided during the day; also : a program offering day care

day·dream \'dā-ˌdrēm\ n : a pleasant reverie — **daydream** vb

day·light \'dā-ˌlīt\ n **1** : the light of day **2** : DAYTIME **3** : DAWN **4** : understanding of something that has been obscure **5** pl : CONSCIOUSNESS; also : WITS **6** : a perceptible space, gap, or difference

daylight saving time n : time usu. one hour ahead of standard time

Day of Atonement : YOM KIPPUR

day school n : a private school without boarding facilities

day student n : a student who attends regular classes at a college or preparatory school but does not live there

day·time \'dā-ˌtīm\ n : the period of daylight

daze \'dāz\ vb **dazed; daz·ing 1** : to stupefy esp. by a blow **2** : DAZZLE — **daze** n — **da·zed·ly** \'dā-zəd-lē\ adv

daz·zle \'da-zəl\ vb **daz·zled; daz·zling 1** : to overpower with light **2** : to impress greatly or confound with brilliance ⟨dazzled by her wit⟩ — **dazzle** n

dB abbr decibel

Db symbol dubnium

d/b/a abbr doing business as

dbl or **dble** abbr double

DC abbr **1** [It da capo] from the beginning **2** direct current **3** District of Columbia **4** doctor of chiropractic

DD abbr **1** days after date **2** demand draft **3** dishonorable discharge **4** doctor of divinity

D–day n [D, abbr. for day] : a day set for launching an operation (as an invasion)

DDS abbr doctor of dental surgery

DDT \ˌdē-ˌdē-ˈtē\ n : a persistent insecticide poisonous to many higher animals

DE abbr Delaware

dea·con \'dē-kən\ n [ME dekene, fr. OE dēacon, fr. LL diaconus, fr. Gk diakonos, lit., servant] : a subordinate officer in a Christian church

dea·con·ess \'dē-kə-nəs\ n : a woman chosen to assist in the church ministry

de·ac·ti·vate \dē-ˈak-tə-ˌvāt\ vb : to make inactive or ineffective

¹dead \'ded\ adj **1** : LIFELESS **2** : DEATHLIKE, DEADLY ⟨in a ~ faint⟩ **3** : NUMB **4** : very tired **5** : UNRESPONSIVE **6** : EXTINGUISHED ⟨~ coals⟩ **7** : INANIMATE, INERT **8** : no longer active or functioning ⟨a ~ battery⟩ **9** : lacking power, significance, or effect ⟨a ~ custom⟩ **10** : OBSOLETE ⟨a ~ language⟩ **11** : lacking in gaiety or animation ⟨a ~ party⟩ **12** : QUIET, IDLE, UNPRODUCTIVE ⟨a ~ capital⟩ **13** : lacking elasticity ⟨a ~ tennis ball⟩ **14** : not circulating : STAGNANT ⟨~ air⟩ **15** : lacking warmth, vigor, or taste ⟨~ wine⟩ **16** : absolutely uniform ⟨~ level⟩ **17** : UNERRING, EXACT ⟨a ~ shot⟩ **18** : ABRUPT ⟨a ~ stop⟩ **19** : COMPLETE ⟨a ~ loss⟩

²dead n, pl **dead 1** : one that is dead — usu. used collectively ⟨the living and the ~⟩ **2** : the time of greatest quiet ⟨the ~ of the night⟩

³dead adv **1** : UTTERLY ⟨~ right⟩ **2** : in a sudden and complete manner ⟨stopped ~⟩ **3** : DIRECTLY ⟨~ ahead⟩

dead·beat \-ˌbēt\ n : a person who persistently fails to pay personal debts or expenses

dead duck n : GONER

dead·en \'de-d°n\ vb **1** : to impair in vigor or sensation : BLUNT ⟨~ pain⟩ **2** : to lessen the luster or spirit of **3** : to make (as a wall) soundproof

dead end n **1** : an end (as of a street) without an exit **2** : a position, situation, or course of action that leads to nothing further — **dead-end** \ˌded-ˈend\ adj

dead heat n : a contest in which two or more contestants tie (as by crossing the finish line simultaneously)

dead horse n : an exhausted topic or issue

dead letter n **1** : something that has lost its force or authority without being formally abolished **2** : a letter that cannot be delivered or returned

dead·line \'ded-ˌlīn\ n : a date or time before which something must be done

dead·lock \'ded-ˌläk\ n **1** : a stoppage of action because neither faction in a struggle will give in **2** : a tie score — **deadlock** vb

¹dead·ly \'ded-lē\ adj **dead·li·er; -est 1** : likely to cause or capable of causing death **2** : HOSTILE, IMPLACABLE **3** : very accurate : UNERRING **4** : tending to deprive of force or vitality ⟨a ~ habit⟩ **5** : suggestive of death **6** : very great : EXTREME — **dead·li·ness** n

²deadly adv **1** : suggesting death ⟨~ pale⟩ **2** : EXTREMELY ⟨~ dull⟩

deadly sin n : one of seven sins of pride, covetousness, lust, anger, gluttony, envy, and sloth held to be fatal to spiritual progress

dead meat *n* : one that is doomed

¹**dead·pan** \'ded-ˌpan\ *adj* : marked by an impassive manner or expression ⟨~ humor⟩ — **deadpan** *vb* — **deadpan** *adv*

²**deadpan** *n* : a completely expressionless face

dead reckoning *n* : the determination of the position of a ship or aircraft solely from the record of the direction and distance of its course

dead·weight \'ded-'wāt\ *n* 1 : the unrelieved weight of an inert mass 2 : a ship's load including the weight of cargo, fuel, crew, and passengers

dead·wood \-ˌwu̇d\ *n* 1 : wood dead on the tree 2 : useless personnel or material

deaf \'def\ *adj* 1 : unable to hear 2 : unwilling to hear or listen ⟨~ to all suggestions⟩ — **deaf·ness** *n*

deaf·en \'de-fən\ *vb* : to make deaf

¹**deal** \'dēl\ *n* 1 : a usu. large or indefinite quantity or degree ⟨a great ~ of support⟩ 2 : the act or right of distributing cards to players in a card game; *also* : HAND

²**deal** *vb* **dealt** \'delt\; **deal·ing** 1 : DISTRIBUTE; *esp* : to distribute playing cards to players in a game 2 : ADMINISTER, DELIVER ⟨*dealt* him a blow⟩ 3 : to concern itself : TREAT ⟨the book ~s with crime⟩ 4 : to take action in regard to something ⟨~ with offenders⟩ 5 : TRADE; *also* : to sell or distribute something as a business ⟨~ in used cars⟩ 6 : to reach a state of acceptance ⟨~ with her child's death⟩ — **deal·er** *n*

³**deal** *n* 1 : BARGAINING, NEGOTIATION 2 : TRANSACTION; *esp* : an agreement by contract 3 : treatment received ⟨a raw ~⟩ 4 : an often secret agreement or arrangement for mutual advantage 5 : BARGAIN

⁴**deal** *n* : wood or a board of fir or pine

deal·er·ship \'dē-lər-ˌship\ *n* : an authorized sales agency ⟨an auto ~⟩

deal·ing \'dē-liŋ\ *n* 1 : a way of acting or of doing business 2 *pl* : friendly or business transactions

dean \'dēn\ *n* [ME *deen,* fr. AF *deien,* fr. LL *decanus,* lit., chief of ten, fr. Gk *dekanos,* fr. *deka* ten] 1 : a clergyman who is head of a group of canons or of joint pastors of a church 2 : the head of a division, faculty, college, or school of a university 3 : a college or secondary school administrator in charge of counseling and disciplining students 4 : DOYEN ⟨the ~ of a diplomatic corps⟩ — **dean·ship** *n*

dean·ery \'dē-nə-rē\ *n, pl* **-er·ies** : the office, jurisdiction, or official residence of a clerical dean

¹**dear** \'dir\ *adj* 1 : highly valued : PRECIOUS 2 : AFFECTIONATE, FOND 3 : EXPENSIVE 4 : HEARTFELT — **dear·ly** *adv* — **dear·ness** *n*

²**dear** *n* : a loved one : DARLING

Dear John \-'jän\ *n* : a letter (as to a soldier) in which a woman breaks off a marital or romantic relationship

dearth \'dərth\ *n* 1 : SCARCITY, FAMINE 2 : an inadequate supply : LACK ⟨a ~ of jobs⟩

death \'deth\ *n* 1 : the end of life 2 : the cause of loss of life 3 : a cause of ruin 4 : the state of being dead 5 : DESTRUCTION, EXTINCTION 6 : SLAUGHTER — **death·like** *adj*

death·bed \-ˌbed\ *n* 1 : the bed in which a person dies 2 : the last hours of life

death·blow \-ˌblō\ *n* : a destructive or killing stroke or event

death grip *n* : an extremely tight grip or hold

death·less \-ləs\ *adj* : IMMORTAL, IMPERISHABLE ⟨~ fame⟩

death·ly \-lē\ *adj* 1 : FATAL 2 : of, relating to, or suggestive of death ⟨a ~ pallor⟩ — **deathly** *adv*

death rattle *n* : a sound produced by air passing through mucus in the lungs and air passages of a dying person

death's—head \'deths-ˌhed\ *n* : a human skull emblematic of death

death·watch \'deth-ˌwäch\ *n* : a vigil kept over the dead or dying

deb \'deb\ *n* : DEBUTANTE

de·ba·cle \di-'bä-kəl, -'ba-\ *also* **dé·bâ·cle** *same or* dā-'bäk\ *n* [F *débâcle*] : DISASTER, FAILURE, ROUT ⟨stock market ~⟩

de·bar \di-'bär\ *vb* : to bar from having or doing something : PRECLUDE

de·bark \di-'bärk\ *vb* : DISEMBARK — **de·bar·ka·tion** \ˌdē-ˌbär-'kā-shən\ *n*

de·base \di-'bās\ *vb* : to lower in character, quality, or value ♦ **Synonyms** DEGRADE, CORRUPT, DEPRAVE — **de·base·ment** *n*

de·bate \di-'bāt\ *vb* **de·bat·ed; de·bat·ing** 1 : to discuss a question by considering opposed arguments 2 : to take part in a debate — **de·bat·able** *adj* — **de·bate** *n* — **de·bat·er** *n*

de·bauch \di-'bȯch\ *vb* : SEDUCE, CORRUPT ♦ **Synonyms** DEBASE, DEMORALIZE, DEPRAVE, PERVERT — **de·bauch·ery** \-'bȯ-chə-rē\ *n*

de·ben·ture \di-'ben-chər\ *n* : BOND; *esp* : one secured by the general credit of the issuer rather than a lien on particular assets

de·bil·i·tate \di-'bi-lə-ˌtāt\ *vb* **-tat·ed; -tat·ing** : to impair the health or strength of ♦ **Synonyms** WEAKEN, DISABLE, ENFEEBLE, UNDERMINE

de·bil·i·ty \di-'bi-lə-tē\ *n, pl* **-ties** : an infirm or weakened state

¹**deb·it** \'de-bət\ *vb* : to enter as a debit : charge with or as a debit

²**debit** *n* 1 : an entry in an account showing money paid out or owed 2 : DISADVANTAGE, SHORTCOMING

debit card *n* : a card by which money may be withdrawn or the cost of purchases paid directly from the holder's bank account

deb·o·nair \ˌde-bə-'ner\ *adj* [ME *debonere,* fr. AF *deboneire,* fr. *de bon aire* of good family or nature] : SUAVE, URBANE; *also* : LIGHTHEARTED

de·bouch \di-'bauch, -'büsh\ vb [F *déboucher,* fr. *dé-* out of + *bouche* mouth] : to come out into an open area : EMERGE

de·brief \di-'brēf\ vb 1 : to question (as a pilot back from a mission) in order to obtain useful information 2 : to review carefully upon completion

de·bris \də-'brē, dā-; 'dā-,brē\ n, pl **debris** \-'brēz, -,brēz\ 1 : the remains of something broken down or destroyed 2 : an accumulation of rock fragments 3 : RUBBISH

debt \'det\ n 1 : SIN, TRESPASS 2 : something owed : OBLIGATION 3 : a condition of owing

debt·or \'de-tər\ n 1 : one guilty of neglect or violation of duty 2 : one that owes a debt

de·bug \(,)dē-'bəg\ vb : to eliminate errors in ⟨~ a computer program⟩

de·bunk \dē-'bəŋk\ vb : to expose the sham or falseness of ⟨~ a legend⟩

¹de·but \'dā-,byü, dā-'byü\ n 1 : a first appearance 2 : a formal entrance into society

²debut vb : to make a debut; *also* : INTRODUCE

deb·u·tante \'de-byu-,tänt\ n : a young woman making her formal entrance into society

dec *abbr* 1 deceased 2 decrease

Dec *abbr* December

de·cade \'de-,kād, de-'kād\ n : a period of 10 years

dec·a·dence \'de-kə-dəns, di-'kā-d²ns\ n : DETERIORATION, DECLINE — **dec·a·dent** \'de-kə-dənt, di-'kā-d²nt\ adj or n

de·caf \'dē-,kaf\ n : decaffeinated coffee

de·caf·fein·at·ed \(,)dē-'ka-fə-nā-təd\ adj : having the caffeine removed ⟨~ coffee⟩

deca·gon \'de-kə-,gän\ n : a plane polygon of 10 angles and 10 sides

de·cal \'dē-,kal\ n : a picture, design, or label made to be transferred (as to glass) from specially prepared paper

de·cal·co·ma·nia \di-,kal-kə-'mā-nē-ə\ n [F *décalcomanie,* fr. *décalquer* to copy by tracing (fr. *calquer* to trace, fr. It *calcare,* lit., to tread, fr. L) + *manie* mania, fr. LL *mania*] : DECAL

Deca·logue \'de-kə-,lóg\ n : TEN COMMANDMENTS

de·camp \di-'kamp\ vb 1 : to break up a camp 2 : to depart suddenly ✦ *Synonyms* ESCAPE, ABSCOND, FLEE

de·cant \di-'kant\ vb : to pour (as wine) from one vessel into another

de·cant·er \di-'kan-tər\ n : an ornamental glass bottle for serving wine

de·cap·i·tate \di-'ka-pə-,tāt\ vb -tat·ed; -tat·ing : BEHEAD — **de·cap·i·ta·tion** \-,ka-pə-'tā-shən\ n — **de·cap·i·ta·tor** \-'ka-pə-,tā-tər\ n

deca·syl·lab·ic \,de-kə-sə-'la-bik\ adj : having or composed of verses having 10 syllables — **decasyllabic** n

de·cath·lon \di-'kath-lən, -,län\ n : a 10-event athletic contest

de·cay \di-'kā\ vb 1 : to decline from a sound or prosperous condition ⟨a ~ing

town⟩ 2 : to cause or undergo decomposition ⟨radium ~s slowly⟩; *esp* : to break down while spoiling : ROT ⟨~ing teeth⟩ — **decay** n

decd *abbr* deceased

de·cease \di-'sēs\ n : DEATH

¹de·ceased \-'sēst\ adj : no longer living; *esp* : recently dead

²deceased n, pl **deceased** : a dead person

de·ce·dent \di-'sē-d²nt\ n : a deceased person

de·ceit \di-'sēt\ n 1 : DECEPTION 2 : TRICK 3 : DECEITFULNESS ✦ *Synonyms* DISSIMULATION, DUPLICITY, GUILE

de·ceit·ful \-fəl\ adj 1 : practicing or tending to practice deceit 2 : MISLEADING, DECEPTIVE ⟨a ~ answer⟩ — **de·ceit·ful·ly** adv — **de·ceit·ful·ness** n

de·ceive \di-'sēv\ vb **de·ceived; de·ceiv·ing** 1 : to cause to believe an untruth 2 : to use or practice deceit ✦ *Synonyms* BEGUILE, BETRAY, DELUDE, MISLEAD — **de·ceiv·er** n

de·cel·er·ate \dē-'se-lə-,rāt\ vb -at·ed; -at·ing : to slow down

De·cem·ber \di-'sem-bər\ n [ME *December,* fr. OE or AF, both fr. L *December* (tenth month), fr. *decem* ten] : the 12th month of the year

de·cen·cy \'dē-s²n-sē\ n, pl -cies 1 : PROPRIETY 2 : conformity to standards of taste, propriety, or quality 3 : standard of propriety — usu. used in pl.

de·cen·ni·al \di-'se-nē-əl\ adj 1 : consisting of 10 years 2 : happening every 10 years ⟨~ census⟩

de·cent \'dē-s²nt\ adj 1 : conforming to standards of propriety, good taste, or morality 2 : modestly clothed 3 : free from immodesty or obscenity 4 : ADEQUATE ⟨~ housing⟩ — **de·cent·ly** adv

de·cen·tral·i·za·tion \dē-,sen-trə-lə-'zā-shən\ n 1 : the distribution of powers from a central authority to regional and local authorities 2 : the redistribution of population and industry from urban centers to outlying areas — **de·cen·tral·ize** \-'sen-trə-,līz\ vb

de·cep·tion \di-'sep-shən\ n 1 : the act of deceiving 2 : the fact or condition of being deceived 3 : FRAUD, TRICK — **de·cep·tive** \-'sep-tiv\ adj — **de·cep·tive·ly** adv — **de·cep·tive·ness** n

deci·bel \'de-sə-,bel, -bəl\ n : a unit for measuring the relative loudness of sounds

de·cide \di-'sīd\ vb **de·cid·ed; de·cid·ing** [ME, fr. L *decidere,* lit., to cut off, fr. *de-* off + *caedere* to cut] 1 : to make a final choice or judgment 2 : to bring to a definitive end ⟨one blow *decided* the fight⟩ 3 : to induce to come to a choice

de·cid·ed \di-'sī-dəd\ adj 1 : UNQUESTIONABLE 2 : FIRM, DETERMINED — **de·cid·ed·ly** adv

de·cid·u·ous \di-'si-jə-wəs\ adj 1 : falling off or out usu. at the end of a period of growth or function ⟨~ leaves⟩ ⟨a ~ tooth⟩ 2 : having deciduous parts ⟨~ trees⟩

deci·gram \'de-sə-,gram\ n — see METRIC SYSTEM table

deci·li·ter \-ˌlē-tər\ n — see METRIC SYSTEM table

¹**dec·i·mal** \ˈde-sə-məl\ adj : based on the number 10 : reckoning by tens

²**decimal** n : any number expressed in base 10; esp : DECIMAL FRACTION

decimal fraction n : a fraction or mixed number in which the denominator is a power of 10 and that is usu. expressed with a decimal point ⟨the *decimal fraction* .25 is equivalent to the common fraction ²⁵⁄₁₀₀⟩

decimal place n : the position of a digit as counted to the right of the decimal point in a decimal fraction

decimal point n : a period, centered dot, or in some countries a comma at the left of a decimal fraction (as .678) less than one or between a whole number and a decimal fraction in a mixed number (as 3.678)

dec·i·mate \ˈde-sə-ˌmāt\ vb **-mat·ed; -mat·ing** 1 : to take or destroy the 10th part of 2 : to cause great destruction or harm to ⟨factories *decimated* by fire⟩

dec·i·me·ter \ˈde-sə-ˌmē-tər\ n — see METRIC SYSTEM table

de·ci·pher \di-ˈsī-fər\ vb 1 : DECODE 2 : to make out the meaning of despite indistinctness — **de·ci·pher·able** adj

de·ci·sion \di-ˈsi-zhən\ n 1 : the act or result of deciding 2 : promptness and firmness in deciding : DETERMINATION

de·ci·sive \-ˈsī-siv\ adj 1 : having the power to decide ⟨the ~ vote⟩ 2 : RESOLUTE, DETERMINED 3 : CONCLUSIVE ⟨a ~ victory⟩ — **de·ci·sive·ly** adv — **de·ci·sive·ness** n

¹**deck** \ˈdek\ n 1 : a floorlike platform of a ship; *also* : something resembling the deck of a ship 2 : a pack of playing cards

²**deck** vb 1 : ARRAY ⟨men ~ed out in suits⟩ 2 : DECORATE 3 : to furnish with a deck 4 : KNOCK DOWN, FLOOR

deck·hand \ˈdek-ˌhand\ n : a sailor who performs manual duties

deck·le edge \ˈdek-əl-\ n : the rough untrimmed edge of paper — **deck·le-edged** \-ˈejd\ adj

de·claim \di-ˈklām\ vb : to speak or deliver in the manner of a formal speech ⟨an actor ~ing his lines⟩ — **dec·la·ma·tion** \ˌde-klə-ˈmā-shən\ n — **de·clam·a·to·ry** \di-ˈkla-mə-ˌtōr-ē\ adj

de·clar·a·tive \di-ˈkler-ə-tiv\ adj : making a declaration ⟨~ sentence⟩

de·clare \di-ˈkler\ vb **de·clared; de·clar·ing** 1 : to make known formally, officially, or explicitly : ANNOUNCE ⟨~ war⟩ 2 : to state emphatically : AFFIRM 3 : to make a full statement of ♦ *Synonyms* BLAZON, BROADCAST, PROCLAIM, PUBLISH — **dec·la·ra·tion** \ˌde-klə-ˈrā-shən\ n — **de·clar·a·to·ry** \di-ˈkler-ə-ˌtōr-ē\ adj — **de·clar·er** n

de·clas·si·fy \dē-ˈkla-sə-ˌfī\ vb : to remove the security classification of ⟨~ documents⟩ — **de·clas·si·fi·ca·tion** \-ˌkla-sə-fə-ˈkā-shən\ n

de·clen·sion \di-ˈklen-chən\ n 1 : the inflectional forms of a noun, pronoun, or adjective 2 : DECLINE, DETERIORATION 3 : DESCENT, SLOPE

¹**de·cline** \di-ˈklīn\ vb **de·clined; de·clin·ing** 1 : to slope downward : DESCEND 2 : DROOP 3 : RECEDE ⟨morale *declined*⟩ 4 : WANE 5 : to withhold consent; *also* : REFUSE, REJECT ⟨~ an invitation⟩ ⟨~ to answer⟩ 6 : INFLECT 2 ⟨~ a noun⟩ — **de·clin·able** adj — **dec·li·na·tion** \ˌde-klə-ˈnā-shən\ n

²**decline** n 1 : a gradual sinking and wasting away 2 : a change to a lower state or level 3 : the time when something is approaching its end ⟨an empire in ~⟩ 4 : a descending slope

de·cliv·i·ty \di-ˈkli-və-tē\ n, pl **-ties** : a steep downward slope

de·code \dē-ˈkōd\ vb : to convert (a coded message) into ordinary language — **de·cod·er** n

dé·col·le·tage \dā-ˌkä-lə-ˈtäzh\ n : the low-cut neckline of a dress

dé·col·le·té \dā-ˌkäl-ˈtā\ adj [F] 1 : wearing a strapless or low-necked gown 2 : having a low-cut neckline

de·com·mis·sion \ˌdē-kə-ˈmi-shən\ vb : to remove from service

de·com·pose \ˌdē-kəm-ˈpōz\ vb 1 : to separate into constituent parts 2 : to break down in decay : ROT — **de·com·po·si·tion** \dēˌkäm-pə-ˈzi-shən\ n

de·com·press \ˌdē-kəm-ˈpres\ vb : to release from pressure or compression — **de·com·pres·sion** \-ˈpre-shən\ n

decompression sickness n : ²BEND 3

de·con·ges·tant \ˌdē-kən-ˈjes-tənt\ n : an agent that relieves congestion (as of mucous membranes)

de·con·struc·tion \ˌdē-kən-ˈstrək-shən\ n : the analysis of something (as language or literature) by the separation and individual examination of its basic elements — **de·con·struct** \-ˈstrəkt\ vb

de·con·tam·i·nate \ˌdē-kən-ˈta-mə-ˌnāt\ vb : to rid of contamination (as radioactive material) — **de·con·tam·i·na·tion** \-ˌta-mə-ˈnā-shən\ n

de·con·trol \ˌdē-kən-ˈtrōl\ vb : to end control of ⟨~ prices⟩ — **decontrol** n

de·cor or **dé·cor** \dā-ˈkór, ˈdā-ˌkór\ n : DECORATION; esp : the style and layout of interior furnishings

dec·o·rate \ˈde-kə-ˌrāt\ vb **-rat·ed; -rat·ing** 1 : to furnish with something ornamental ⟨~ a room⟩ 2 : to award a mark of honor (as a medal) to ⟨*decorated* soldiers⟩ ♦ *Synonyms* ADORN, BEAUTIFY, BEDECK, GARNISH, ORNAMENT

dec·o·ra·tion \ˌde-kə-ˈrā-shən\ n 1 : the act or process of decorating 2 : ORNAMENT 3 : a badge of honor

dec·o·ra·tive \ˈde-kə-rə-tiv\ adj : ORNAMENTAL

dec·o·ra·tor \ˈde-kə-ˌrā-tər\ n : one that decorates; esp : a person who designs or executes interiors and their furnishings

dec·o·rous \ˈde-kə-rəs, di-ˈkór-əs\ adj : PROPER, SEEMLY, CORRECT

de·co·rum \di-ˈkór-əm\ n [L] 1 : conformity to accepted standards of conduct 2 : ORDERLINESS, PROPRIETY

¹**de·coy** \'dē-ˌkȯi, di-'kȯi\ *n* [prob. fr. D *de kooi*, lit., the cage] **1** : something that lures or entices; *esp* : an artificial bird used to attract live birds within shot **2** : something used to draw attention away from another

²**de·coy** \di-'kȯi, 'dē-ˌkȯi\ *vb* : to lure by or as if by a decoy : ENTICE

¹**de·crease** \di-'krēs\ *vb* **de·creased; de·creas·ing** : to grow or cause to grow less : DIMINISH

²**de·crease** \'dē-ˌkrēs\ *n* **1** : the process of decreasing **2** : REDUCTION

¹**de·cree** \di-'krē\ *n* **1** : ORDER, EDICT **2** : a judicial decision

²**decree** *vb* **de·creed; de·cree·ing 1** : COMMAND **2** : to determine or order judicially ♦ *Synonyms* DICTATE, ORDAIN, PRESCRIBE

dec·re·ment \'de-krə-mənt\ *n* **1** : gradual decrease **2** : the quantity lost by diminution or waste

de·crep·it \di-'kre-pət\ *adj* : broken down with age : WORN-OUT — **de·crep·i·tude** \-pə-ˌtüd, -ˌtyüd\ *n*

de·cre·scen·do \ˌdā-krə-'shen-dō\ *adv or adj* : with a decrease in volume — used as a direction in music

de·crim·i·nal·ize \dē-'kri-mə-nə-ˌlīz\ *vb* : to remove or reduce the criminal status of

de·cry \di-'krī\ *vb* : to express strong disapproval of ⟨∼ welfare policies⟩

ded·i·cate \'de-di-ˌkāt\ *vb* **-cat·ed; -cat·ing 1** : to devote to the worship of a divine being esp. with sacred rites **2** : to set apart for a definite purpose **3** : to inscribe or address as a compliment ⟨∼ a novel⟩ — **ded·i·ca·tion** \ˌde-di-'kā-shən\ *n* — **ded·i·ca·tor** \'de-di-ˌkā-tər\ *n* — **ded·i·ca·to·ry** \-kə-ˌtȯr-ē\ *adj*

de·duce \di-'düs, -'dyüs\ *vb* **de·duced; de·duc·ing 1** : to derive by reasoning : INFER **2** : to trace the course of — **de·duc·ible** *adj*

de·duct \di-'dəkt\ *vb* : SUBTRACT — **de·duct·ible** *adj*

de·duc·tion \di-'dək-shən\ *n* **1** : SUBTRACTION **2** : something that is or may be subtracted **3** : the deriving of a conclusion by reasoning : the conclusion so reached — **de·duc·tive** \-'dək-tiv\ *adj* — **de·duc·tive·ly** *adv*

¹**deed** \'dēd\ *n* **1** : something done **2** : FEAT, EXPLOIT **3** : a document containing some legal transfer, bargain, or contract

²**deed** *vb* : to convey or transfer by deed

dee·jay \'dē-ˌjā\ *n* : DISC JOCKEY

deem \'dēm\ *vb* : THINK, JUDGE ♦ *Synonyms* CONSIDER, ACCOUNT, RECKON, REGARD, VIEW

de·em·pha·size \dē-'em-fə-ˌsīz\ *vb* : to reduce in relative importance; *also* : to attach little importance to — **de·em·pha·sis** \-səs\ *n*

¹**deep** \'dēp\ *adj* **1** : extending far down, back, within, or outward ⟨a ∼ well⟩ **2** : having a specified extension downward or backward ⟨3 feet ∼⟩ **3** : difficult to understand; *also* : MYSTERIOUS, OBSCURE

⟨a ∼ dark secret⟩ **4** : WISE **5** : ENGROSSED, INVOLVED ⟨∼ in thought⟩ **6** : INTENSE, PROFOUND ⟨∼ sleep⟩ **7** : dark and rich in color ⟨a ∼ red⟩ **8** : having a low musical pitch or range ⟨a ∼ voice⟩ **9** : situated well within **10** : covered, enclosed, or filled often to a specified degree — **deep·ly** *adv*

²**deep** *adv* **1** : DEEPLY **2** : far on : LATE ⟨∼ in the night⟩

³**deep** *n* **1** : an extremely deep place or part; *esp* : OCEAN **2** : the middle or most intense part ⟨the ∼ of winter⟩

deep·en \'dē-pən\ *vb* : to make or become deep or deeper

deep–freeze \'dēp-'frēz\ *vb* **-froze** \-'frōz\; **-fro·zen** \-'frō-z°n\ : QUICK-FREEZE

deep–fry *vb* : to cook in enough oil to cover the food being fried

deep pocket *n* **1** : one having substantial financial resources **2** *pl* : substantial financial resources

deep–root·ed \'dēp-'rü-təd, -'rů-\ *adj* : deeply implanted or established

deep–sea \'dēp-'sē\ *adj* : of, relating to, or occurring in the deeper parts of the sea ⟨∼ fishing⟩

deep–seat·ed \'dēp-'sē-təd\ *adj* **1** : situated far below the surface **2** : firmly established ⟨∼ convictions⟩

deer \'dir\ *n, pl* **deer** [ME, *deer*, animal, fr. OE *dēor* beast] : any of numerous ruminant mammals with cloven hoofs and usu. antlers esp. in the males

deer·fly \-ˌflī\ *n* : any of numerous small horseflies

deer·skin \-ˌskin\ *n* : leather made from the skin of a deer; *also* : a garment of such leather

deer tick *n* : a tick that transmits the bacterium causing Lyme disease

de–es·ca·late \dē-'es-kə-ˌlāt\ *vb* : to decrease in extent, volume, or scope : LIMIT — **de–es·ca·la·tion** \-ˌes-kə-'lā-shən\ *n*

deet \'dēt\ *n, often all cap* : a colorless oily liquid insect and tick repellent

¹**def** \'def\ *adj* **def·fer; def·fest** *slang* : very good : COOL

²**def** *abbr* **1** defendant **2** definite **3** definition

de·face \di-'fās\ *vb* : to destroy or mar the face or surface of ⟨∼ a desk⟩ — **de·face·ment** *n* — **de·fac·er** *n*

de fac·to \di-'fak-tō, dā-\ *adj or adv* **1** : existing through not formally recognized ⟨a *de facto* recession⟩ **2** : actually exercising power ⟨*de facto* government⟩

de·fal·ca·tion \ˌdē-ˌfal-'kā-shən, -ˌfȯl-; ˌde-fəl-\ *n* : EMBEZZLEMENT

de·fame \di-'fām\ *vb* **de·famed; de·fam·ing** : to injure or destroy the reputation of by libel or slander ♦ *Synonyms* CALUMNIATE, DENIGRATE, LIBEL, MALIGN, SLANDER, VILIFY — **def·a·ma·tion** \ˌde-fə-'mā-shən\ *n* — **de·fam·a·to·ry** \di-'fa-mə-ˌtȯr-ē\ *adj*

de·fault \di-'fȯlt\ *n* **1** : failure to do something required by duty or law; *also* : failure to appear for a legal proceeding **2** : failure to compete in or to finish an appointed contest ⟨lose a race by ~⟩ **3** : a choice made without active consideration due to lack of viable alternatives **4** : a selection made automatically by a computer in the absence of a choice by the user — **default** *vb* — **de·fault·er** *n*

¹de·feat \di-ˈfēt\ *vb* **1** : FRUSTRATE, NULLIFY **2** : to win victory over : BEAT — **de·feat·able** \-ˈfē-tə-bəl\ *adj*

²defeat *n* **1** : FRUSTRATION **2** : an overthrow of an army in battle **3** : loss of a contest

de·feat·ism \-ˈfē-ˌti-zəm\ *n* : acceptance of or resignation to defeat — **de·feat·ist** \-tist\ *n or adj*

def·e·cate \ˈde-fi-ˌkāt\ *vb* **-cat·ed; -cat·ing** **1** : to free from impurity or corruption **2** : to discharge feces from the bowels — **def·e·ca·tion** \ˌde-fi-ˈkā-shən\ *n*

¹de·fect \ˈdē-ˌfekt, di-ˈfekt\ *n* : BLEMISH, FAULT, IMPERFECTION

²de·fect \di-ˈfekt\ *vb* : to desert a cause, party, or nation esp. in order to espouse another — **de·fec·tion** \-ˈfek-shən\ *n* — **de·fec·tor** \-ˈfek-tər\ *n*

de·fec·tive \di-ˈfek-tiv\ *adj* : FAULTY, DEFICIENT — **defective** *n*

de·fence *chiefly Brit var of* DEFENSE

de·fend \di-ˈfend\ *vb* [ME, fr. AF *defendre*, fr. L *defendere*, fr. *de-* from + *-fendere* to strike] **1** : to repel danger or attack from ⟨~ the fort⟩ **2** : to act as attorney for **3** : to oppose the claim of another in a lawsuit : CONTEST **4** : to maintain against opposition ⟨~ an idea⟩ **5** : to try to retain against a challenge ⟨~ed his title⟩ — **de·fend·er** *n*

de·fen·dant \di-ˈfen-dənt\ *n* : a person required to make answer in a legal action or suit

de·fense \di-ˈfens\ *n* **1** : the act of defending : resistance against attack **2** : means, method, or capability of defending **3** : an argument in support **4** : the answer made by the defendant in a legal action **5** : a defending party, group, or team — **de·fense·less** *adj* — **de·fen·si·ble** *adj*

defense mechanism *n* : an often unconscious mental process (as repression) that assists in reaching compromise solutions to personal problems

¹de·fen·sive \di-ˈfen-siv\ *adj* **1** : serving or intended to defend or protect **2** : of or relating to the attempt to keep an opponent from scoring (as in a game) — **de·fen·sive·ly** *adv* — **de·fen·sive·ness** *n*

²defensive *n* : a defensive position

¹de·fer \di-ˈfər\ *vb* **de·ferred; de·fer·ring** [ME *deferren, differren*, fr. MF *differer*, fr. L *differre* to postpone, be different] : POSTPONE, PUT OFF

²defer *vb* **de·ferred; deferring** [ME *deferren, differren*, fr. MF *deferer, defferer*, fr. LL *deferre*, fr. L, to bring down, bring, fr. *de-* down + *ferre* to carry] : to submit or yield to the opinion or wishes of another — **de·fer·ral** \-əl\ *n*

def·er·ence \ˈde-fər-əns\ *n* : courteous, respectful, or ingratiating regard for another's wishes **♦ Synonyms** HONOR,

HOMAGE, OBEISANCE, REVERENCE — **def·er·en·tial** \ˌde-fə-ˈren-chəl\ *adj*

de·fer·ment \di-ˈfər-mənt\ *n* : the act of delaying; *esp* : official postponement of military service

de·fi·ance \di-ˈfī-əns\ *n* **1** : CHALLENGE **2** : disposition to resist or contend

de·fi·ant \-ənt\ *adj* : full of defiance : BOLD, IMPUDENT — **de·fi·ant·ly** *adv*

de·fi·bril·la·tor \dē-ˈfi-brə-ˌlā-tər\ *n* : an electronic device that applies an electric shock to restore the rhythm of a fibrillating heart — **de·fi·bril·late** \-ˌlāt\ *vb* — **de·fi·bril·la·tion** \-ˌfi-brə-ˈlā-shən\ *n*

deficiency disease *n* : a disease (as scurvy or beriberi) caused by a lack of essential dietary elements and esp. a vitamin or mineral

de·fi·cient \di-ˈfi-shənt\ *adj* : lacking in something necessary; *also* : not up to a normal standard — **de·fi·cien·cy** \-shən-sē\ *n*

def·i·cit \ˈde-fə-sət\ *n* : a deficiency in amount; *esp* : an excess of expenditures over revenue

¹de·file \di-ˈfī(-ə)l\ *vb* **de·filed; de·fil·ing** **1** : to make filthy **2** : CORRUPT **3** : to violate the chastity of **4** : to violate the sanctity of : DESECRATE **5** : DISHONOR **♦ Synonyms** CONTAMINATE, POLLUTE, SOIL, TAINT — **de·file·ment** *n*

²de·file \di-ˈfī(-ə)l, ˈdē-ˌfī(-ə)l\ *n* : a narrow passage or gorge

de·fine \di-ˈfīn\ *vb* **de·fined; de·fin·ing** **1** : to set forth the meaning of ⟨~ a word⟩ **2** : to fix or mark the limits of **3** : to clarify in outline or character — **de·fin·able** *adj* — **de·fin·er** *n*

def·i·nite \ˈde-fə-nət\ *adj* **1** : having distinct limits : FIXED **2** : clear in meaning **3** : typically designating an identified or immediately identifiable person or thing ⟨a ~ article⟩ — **def·i·nite·ly** *adv* — **def·i·nite·ness** *n*

def·i·ni·tion \ˌde-fə-ˈni-shən\ *n* **1** : an act of determining or settling **2** : a statement of the meaning of a word or word group; *also* : the action or process of defining **3** : the action or the power of making definite and clear : CLARITY, DISTINCTNESS

de·fin·i·tive \di-ˈfi-nə-tiv\ *adj* **1** : DECISIVE, CONCLUSIVE **2** : authoritative and apparently exhaustive ⟨a ~ edition⟩ **3** : serving to define or specify precisely ⟨~ laws⟩

de·flate \di-ˈflāt\ *vb* **de·flat·ed; de·flat·ing** **1** : to release air or gas from **2** : to reduce in size, importance, or effectiveness; *also* : to reduce from a state of inflation **3** : to become deflated

de·fla·tion \-ˈflā-shən\ *n* **1** : an act or instance of deflating : the state of being deflated **2** : reduction in the volume of available money or credit resulting in a decline of the general price level

de·flect \di-ˈflekt\ *vb* : to turn aside — **de·flec·tion** \-ˈflek-shən\ *n*

de·flo·ra·tion \ˌde-flə-ˈrā-shən\ *n* : rupture of the hymen

de·flow·er \dē-ˈflau̇(-ə)r\ *vb* : to deprive of virginity

de·fog \dē-'fòg, -'fäg\ *vb* : to remove fog or condensed moisture from ⟨∼ a windshield⟩ — **de·fog·ger** *n*

de·fo·li·ant \dē-'fō-lē-ənt\ *n* : a chemical spray or dust used to defoliate plants

de·fo·li·ate \-,āt\ *vb* : to deprive of leaves esp. prematurely — **de·fo·li·a·tion** \dē-,fō-lē-'ā-shən\ *n* — **de·fo·li·a·tor** \dē-'fō-lē-,ā-tər\ *n*

de·for·es·ta·tion \dē-,fòr-ə-'stā-shən\ *n* : the action or process of clearing an area of forests; *also* : the state of having been cleared of forests — **de·for·est** \(,)dē-'fòr-əst, -'fär-\ *vb*

de·form \di-'fòrm\ *vb* **1** : DISFIGURE, DEFACE **2** : to make or become misshapen or changed in shape — **de·for·ma·tion** \dē-,fòr-'mā-shən, ,dē-fər-\ *n*

de·for·mi·ty \di-'fòr-mə-tē\ *n, pl* **-ties** **1** : the state of being deformed **2** : a physical blemish or distortion

de·fraud \di-'fròd\ *vb* : CHEAT

de·fray \di-'frā\ *vb* : to provide for the payment of : PAY — **de·fray·al** *n*

de·frock \(,)dē-'fräk\ *vb* : to deprive (as a priest) of the right to exercise the functions of office

de·frost \di-'fròst\ *vb* **1** : to thaw out **2** : to free from ice — **de·frost·er** *n*

deft \'deft\ *adj* : quick and neat in action — **deft·ly** *adv* — **deft·ness** *n*

de·funct \di-'fəŋkt\ *adj* : DEAD, EXTINCT ⟨a ∼ language⟩

de·fuse \dē-'fyüz\ *vb* **1** : to remove the fuse from (as a bomb) **2** : to make less harmful, potent, or tense

de·fy \di-'fī\ *vb* **de·fied; de·fy·ing** [ME, to renounce faith in, challenge, fr. AF *desfier, defier*, fr. *de-* from + *fier* to entrust, ultim. fr. L *fidere* to trust] **1** : CHALLENGE, DARE **2** : to refuse boldly to obey or to yield to : DISREGARD ⟨∼ the law⟩ **3** : WITHSTAND, BAFFLE ⟨a scene that *defies* description⟩

deg *abbr* degree

de·gas \dē-'gas\ *vb* : to remove gas from

de·gen·er·a·cy \di-'je-nə-rə-sē\ *n, pl* **-cies** **1** : the state of being degenerate **2** : the process of becoming degenerate **3** : PERVERSION

¹de·gen·er·ate \di-'je-nə-rət\ *adj* : fallen or deteriorated from a former, higher, or normal condition — **de·gen·er·a·tion** \-,je-nə-'rā-shən\ *n* — **de·gen·er·a·tive** \-'je-nə-,rā-tiv\ *adj*

²de·gen·er·ate \di-'je-nə-,rāt\ *vb* : to undergo deterioration (as in morality, intelligence, structure, or function)

³de·gen·er·ate \-rət\ *n* : a degenerate person; *esp* : a sexual pervert

de·grad·able \di-'grā-də-bəl\ *adj* : capable of being chemically degraded

de·grade \di-'grād\ *vb* **1** : to reduce from a higher to a lower rank or degree **2** : DEBASE, CORRUPT **3** : DECOMPOSE — **deg·ra·da·tion** \,de-grə-'dā-shən\ *n*

de·gree \di-'grē\ *n* [ME, fr. AF *degré*, fr. VL **degradus*, fr. L *de-* down + *gradus* step, grade] **1** : a step in a series **2** : a rank or grade of official, ecclesiastical, or social position; *also* : the civil condition of a person **3** : the extent, intensity, or scope of something esp. as measured by a graded series **4** : one of the forms or sets of forms used in the comparison of an adjective or adverb **5** : a title conferred upon students by a college, university, or professional school on completion of a program of study **6** : a line or space of the musical staff; *also* : a note or tone of a musical scale **7** : a unit of measure for angles that is equal to an angle with its vertex at the center of a circle and its sides cutting off $\frac{1}{360}$ of the circumference; *also* : a unit of measure for arcs of a circle that is equal to the amount of arc extending $\frac{1}{360}$ of the circumference **8** : any of various units for measuring temperature

de·horn \dē-'hòrn\ *vb* : to deprive of horns

de·hu·man·ize \dē-'hyü-mə-,nīz\ *vb* : to deprive of human qualities, personality, or spirit — **de·hu·man·i·za·tion** \,dē-,hyü-mə-nə-'zā-shən\ *n*

de·hu·mid·i·fy \dē-hyü-'mi-də-,fī\ *vb* : to remove moisture from (as the air) — **de·hu·mid·i·fi·er** *n*

de·hy·drate \dē-'hī-,drāt\ *vb* : to remove water from; *also* : to lose liquid — **de·hy·dra·tion** \,dē-hī-'drā-shən\ *n*

de·hy·dro·ge·na·tion \,dē-(,)hī-,drä-jə-'nā-shən, -drə-\ *n* : the removal of hydrogen from a chemical compound — **de·hy·dro·ge·nate** \,dē-(,)hī-'drä-jə-,nāt, dē-'hī-drə-jə-\ *vb*

de·ice \dē-'īs\ *vb* : to keep free or rid of ice ⟨∼ a lock⟩ — **de·ic·er** *n*

de·i·fy \'dē-ə-,fī, 'dā-\ *vb* **-fied; -fy·ing** **1** : to make a god of **2** : WORSHIP, GLORIFY — **de·i·fi·ca·tion** \,dē-ə-fə-'kā-shən, ,dā-\ *n*

deign \'dān\ *vb* [ME, fr. AF *deigner*, fr. L *dignare, dignari*, fr. *dignus* worthy] : CONDESCEND

de·ion·ize \dē-'ī-ə-,nīz\ *vb* : to remove ions from

de·ism \'dē-,i-zəm, 'dā-\ *n, often cap* : a system of thought advocating natural religion based on human morality and reason rather than divine revelation — **de·ist** \-ist\ *n, often cap* — **de·is·tic** \dē-'is-tik, dā-\ *adj*

de·i·ty \'dē-ə-tē, 'dā-\ *n, pl* **-ties** **1** : DIVINITY **2** **2** *cap* : GOD **3** : a god or goddess

dé·jà vu \,dā-,zhä-'vü\ *n* [F, adj., already seen] : the feeling that one has seen or heard something before

de·ject·ed \di-'jek-təd\ *adj* : low in spirits : SAD — **de·ject·ed·ly** *adv*

de·jec·tion \di-'jek-shən\ *n* : lowness of spirits

de ju·re \dē-'jùr-ē\ *adv or adj* [ML] : by legal right

deka·gram \'de-kə-,gram\ *n* — see METRIC SYSTEM table

deka·li·ter \-,lē-tər\ *n* — see METRIC SYSTEM table

deka·me·ter \-,mē-tər\ *n* — see METRIC SYSTEM table

del *abbr* delegate; delegation

Del *abbr* Delaware

Del·a·ware \'de-lə-,wer\ *n, pl* **Delaware** *or* **Delawares** : a member of an American Indian people orig. of the Delaware valley; *also* : their language

¹**de·lay** \di-'lā\ *n* 1 : the act of delaying : the state of being delayed 2 : the time for which something is delayed

²**delay** *vb* 1 : POSTPONE, PUT OFF 2 : to stop, detain, or hinder for a time 3 : to move or act slowly

de·lec·ta·ble \di-'lek-tə-bəl\ *adj* 1 : highly pleasing : DELIGHTFUL 2 : DELICIOUS

de·lec·ta·tion \,dē-,lek-'tā-shən\ *n* : DELIGHT, PLEASURE, DIVERSION

¹**del·e·gate** \'de-li-gət, -,gāt\ *n* 1 : DEPUTY, REPRESENTATIVE 2 : a member of the lower house of the legislature of Maryland, Virginia, or West Virginia

²**del·e·gate** \-,gāt\ *vb* **-gat·ed; -gat·ing** 1 : to entrust to another ⟨~ authority⟩ 2 : to appoint as one's delegate

del·e·ga·tion \,de-li-'gā-shən\ *n* 1 : the act of delegating 2 : one or more persons chosen to represent others

de·le·git·i·mize \,dē-lə-'ji-tə-,mīz\ *vb* : to diminish or destroy the legitimacy, prestige, or authority of

de·lete \di-'lēt\ *vb* **de·let·ed; de·let·ing** [L *deletus,* pp. of *delēre* to wipe out, destroy] : to eliminate by blotting out, cutting out, or erasing ⟨~ a computer file⟩ — **de·le·tion** \-'lē-shən\ *n*

del·e·te·ri·ous \,de-lə-'tir-ē-əs\ *adj* : HARMFUL, NOXIOUS

delft \'delft\ *n* 1 : a Dutch pottery with an opaque white glaze and predominantly blue decoration 2 : glazed pottery esp. when blue and white

delft·ware \-,wer\ *n* : DELFT

deli \'de-lē\ *n, pl* **del·is** : DELICATESSEN

¹**de·lib·er·ate** \di-'li-bə-,rāt\ *vb* **-at·ed; -at·ing** : to consider carefully — **de·lib·er·a·tion** \-,li-bə-'rā-shən\ *n* — **de·lib·er·a·tive** \-'li-bə-,rā-tiv, -brə-tiv\ *adj* — **de·lib·er·a·tive·ly** *adv*

²**de·lib·er·ate** \di-'li-bə-rət, -'li-brət\ *adj* 1 : determined after careful thought 2 : done or said intentionally 3 : UNHURRIED, SLOW — **de·lib·er·ate·ly** *adv* — **de·lib·er·ate·ness** *n*

del·i·ca·cy \'de-li-kə-sē\ *n, pl* **-cies** 1 : something pleasing to eat and considered rare or luxurious 2 : FINENESS, DAINTINESS; *also* : FRAILTY 3 : nicety or expressiveness of touch 4 : precise perception and discrimination : SENSITIVITY 5 : sensibility in feeling or conduct; *also* : SQUEAMISHNESS 6 : the quality or state of requiring delicate handling

del·i·cate \'de-li-kət\ *adj* 1 : pleasing to the senses of taste or smell esp. in a mild or subtle way 2 : marked by daintiness or charm : EXQUISITE 3 : FASTIDIOUS, SQUEAMISH ⟨a person of ~ tastes⟩ 4 : easily damaged : FRAGILE; *also* : SICKLY 5 : requiring skill or tact 6 : marked by care, skill, or tact 7 : marked by minute precision : very sensitive ⟨a ~ instrument⟩ — **del·i·cate·ly** *adv*

del·i·ca·tes·sen \,de-li-kə-'te-sᵊn\ *n pl* [G, pl. of *Delicatesse* delicacy, fr. F *délicatesse*] 1 : ready-to-eat food products (as cooked meats and prepared salads) 2 *sing, pl* **delicatessens** : a store where delicatessen are sold

de·li·cious \di-'li-shəs\ *adj* : affording great pleasure : DELIGHTFUL; *esp* : very pleasing to the taste or smell — **de·li·cious·ly** *adv* — **de·li·cious·ness** *n*

¹**de·light** \di-'līt\ *n* 1 : great pleasure or satisfaction : JOY 2 : something that gives great pleasure — **de·light·ful** \-fəl\ *adj* — **de·light·ful·ly** *adv*

²**delight** *vb* 1 : to take great pleasure 2 : to satisfy greatly : PLEASE

de·light·ed *adj* : highly pleased : GRATIFIED — **de·light·ed·ly** *adv*

de·lim·it \di-'li-mət\ *vb* : to fix the limits of

de·lin·eate \di-'li-nē-,āt\ *vb* **-eat·ed; -eat·ing** 1 : SKETCH, PORTRAY 2 : to picture in words : DESCRIBE — **de·lin·ea·tion** \-,li-nē-'ā-shən\ *n*

de·lin·quen·cy \di-'liŋ-kwən-sē\ *n, pl* **-cies** : the quality or state of being delinquent

¹**de·lin·quent** \-kwənt\ *n* : a delinquent person

²**delinquent** *adj* 1 : offending by neglect or violation of duty or of law 2 : being overdue in payment

del·i·quesce \,de-li-'kwes\ *vb* **-quesced; -quesc·ing** : MELT, DISSOLVE — **del·i·ques·cent** \-'kwe-sᵊnt\ *adj*

de·lir·i·um \di-'lir-ē-əm\ *n* [L, fr. *delirare* to be crazy, lit., to leave the furrow (in plowing), fr. *de-* from + *lira* furrow] : mental disturbance marked by confusion, disordered speech, and hallucinations; *also* : frenzied excitement — **de·lir·i·ous** \-ē-əs\ *adj* — **de·lir·i·ous·ly** *adv*

delirium tre·mens \-'trē-mənz, -'tre-\ *n* : a violent delirium with tremors that is induced by excessive and prolonged use of alcoholic liquors

de·liv·er \di-'li-vər\ *vb* **-ered; -er·ing** 1 : to set free : SAVE 2 : CONVEY, TRANSFER ⟨~ a letter⟩ 3 : to assist in giving birth or at the birth of; *also* : to give birth to 4 : UTTER, COMMUNICATE 5 : to send to an intended target or destination — **de·liv·er·able** \-'li-v(ə-)rə-bəl\ *adj* — **de·liv·er·ance** \-v(ə-)rəns\ *n* — **de·liv·er·er** *n*

de·liv·ery \di-'li-və-rē\ *n, pl* **-er·ies** : the act of delivering something; *also* : something delivered — **de·liv·ery·man** \-,man\ *n*

dell \'del\ *n* : a small secluded valley

de·louse \dē-'laus\ *vb* : to remove lice from

del·phin·i·um \del-'fi-nē-əm\ *n* : any of a genus of mostly perennial herbs related to the buttercups with tall branching spikes of irregular flowers

del·ta \'del-tə\ *n* 1 : the 4th letter of the Greek alphabet — Δ or δ 2 : something shaped like a capital Δ; *esp* : the triangular silt-formed land at the mouth of a river — **del·ta·ic** \del-'tā-ik\ *adj*

del·toid \'del-ˌtȯid\ *n* : a large triangular muscle that covers the shoulder joint and raises the arm laterally

de·lude \di-'lüd\ *vb* **de·lud·ed; de·lud·ing** : MISLEAD, DECEIVE, TRICK

¹**del·uge** \'del-ˌyüj\ *n* **1** : a flooding of land by water **2** : a drenching rain **3** : a great amount or number ⟨a ~ of mail⟩

²**deluge** *vb* **del·uged; del·ug·ing 1** : INUNDATE, FLOOD **2** : to overwhelm as if with a deluge

de·lu·sion \di-'lü-zhən\ *n* : a deluding or being deluded; *esp* : a persistent false psychotic belief — **de·lu·sion·al** \-'lü-zhə-nəl\ *adj* — **de·lu·sive** \-'lü-siv\ *adj*

de·luxe \di-'lüks, -'lȯks, -'lüks\ *adj* : notably luxurious or elegant

delve \'delv\ *vb* **delved; delv·ing 1** : DIG **2** : to seek laboriously for information

dely *abbr* delivery

Dem *abbr* Democrat; Democratic

de·mag·ne·tize \dē-'mag-nə-ˌtīz\ *vb* : to cause to lose magnetic properties — **de·mag·ne·ti·za·tion** \dē-ˌmag-nə-tə-'zā-shən\ *n*

dem·a·gogue *also* **dem·a·gog** \'de-mə-ˌgäg\ *n* [Gk *dēmagōgos*, fr. *dēmos* people + *agōgos* leading, fr. *agein* to lead] : a person who appeals to the emotions and prejudices of people esp. in order to gain political power — **dem·a·gogu·ery** \-ˌgä-gə-rē\ *n* — **dem·a·gogy** \-ˌgä-gē, -ˌgä-jē\ *n*

¹**de·mand** \di-'mand\ *n* **1** : an act of demanding; *also* : something claimed as due or just **2** : the ability and desire to buy goods or services; *also* : the quantity of goods wanted at a stated price **3** : a seeking or being sought after : urgent need **4** : a pressing need or requirement

²**demand** *vb* **1** : to ask for with authority : claim as due or just **2** : to ask earnestly or in the manner of a command **3** : REQUIRE, NEED ⟨a patient who ~s constant care⟩

de·mar·cate \di-'mär-ˌkāt, 'dē-ˌmär-\ *vb* **-cat·ed; -cat·ing 1** : DELIMIT **2** : to set apart : DISTINGUISH — **de·mar·ca·tion** \ˌdē-ˌmär-'kā-shən\ *n*

dé·marche *or* **de·marche** \dā-'märsh\ *n* : a course of action : MANEUVER

¹**de·mean** \di-'mēn\ *vb* **de·meaned; de·mean·ing** : to behave or conduct (oneself) usu. in a proper manner

²**demean** *vb* **de·meaned; de·mean·ing** : DEGRADE, DEBASE

de·mean·or \di-'mē-nər\ *n* : CONDUCT, BEARING

de·mean·our *Brit var of* DEMEANOR

de·ment·ed \di-'men-təd\ *adj* : MAD, INSANE — **de·ment·ed·ly** *adv*

de·men·tia \di-'men-chə\ *n* **1** : deterioration of cognitive functioning (as in Alzheimer's disease) **2** : INSANITY

de·mer·it \di-'mer-ət\ *n* **1** : FAULT **2** : a mark charged against a person's record for some fault or offense

de·mesne \di-'mān, -'mēn\ *n* **1** : REALM **2** : manorial land actually possessed by the lord and not held by free tenants **3** : ESTATE **4** : REGION

demi·god \'de-mi-ˌgäd\ *n* : a mythological being with more power than a mortal but less than a god

demi·john \'de-mi-ˌjän\ *n* [F *dame-jeanne*, lit., Lady Jane] : a large narrow-necked bottle usu. enclosed in wickerwork

de·mil·i·ta·rize \dē-'mi-lə-tə-ˌrīz\ *vb* : to strip of military forces, weapons, or fortifications — **de·mil·i·tar·i·za·tion** \dē-ˌmi-lə-tə-rə-'zā-shən\ *n*

demi·mon·daine \ˌde-mi-ˌmän-'dān\ *n* : a woman of the demimonde

demi·monde \'de-mi-ˌmänd\ *n* [F *demi-monde*, fr. *demi-* half + *monde* world] **1** : a class of women on the fringes of respectable society supported by wealthy lovers **2** : a distinct isolated group having low reputation or prestige

de·min·er·al·ize \dē-'mi-nə-rə-ˌlīz\ *vb* : to remove the mineral matter from — **de·min·er·al·i·za·tion** \-ˌmi-nə-rə-lə-'zā-shən\ *n*

de·mise \di-'mīz\ *n* **1** : LEASE **2** : transfer of sovereignty to a successor ⟨~ of the crown⟩ **3** : DEATH **4** : loss of status

demi·tasse \'de-mi-ˌtas\ *n* : a small cup of black coffee; *also* : the cup used to serve it

demo \'de-mō\ *n, pl* **demos 1** : DEMONSTRATION **2** : a product used to show performance or merits to prospective buyers **3** : a recording used to show off a song or performer

de·mo·bi·lize \di-'mō-bə-ˌlīz, dē-\ *vb* **1** : DISBAND **2** : to discharge from military service — **de·mo·bi·li·za·tion** \di-ˌmō-bə-lə-'zā-shən, dē-\ *n*

de·moc·ra·cy \di-'mä-krə-sē\ *n, pl* **-cies** [MF *democratie*, fr. LL *democratia*, fr. Gk *dēmokratia*, fr. *dēmos* people + *kratos* strength, power] **1** : government by the people; *esp* : rule of the majority **2** : a government in which the supreme power is held by the people **3** : a political unit that has a democratic government **4** *cap* : the principles and policies of the Democratic party in the U.S. **5** : the common people esp. when constituting the source of political authority **6** : the absence of hereditary or arbitrary class distinctions or privileges

dem·o·crat \'de-mə-ˌkrat\ *n* **1** : one who believes in or practices democracy **2** *cap* : a member of the Democratic party of the U.S.

dem·o·crat·ic \ˌde-mə-'kra-tik\ *adj* **1** : of, relating to, or favoring democracy **2** *often cap* : of or relating to one of the two major political parties in the U.S. associated in modern times with policies of broad social reform and internationalism **3** : relating to or appealing to the common people ⟨~ art⟩ **4** : not snobbish — **dem·o·crat·i·cal·ly** \-ti-k(ə-)lē\ *adv*

de·moc·ra·tize \di-'mä-krə-ˌtīz\ *vb* **-tized; -tiz·ing** : to make democratic

dé·mo·dé \ˌdā-mō-'dā\ *adj* [F] : no longer fashionable : OUT-OF-DATE

de·mo·graph·ics \ˌde-mə-ˈgra-fiks, ˌdē-\ *n pl* : the statistical characteristics of human populations

de·mog·ra·phy \di-ˈmä-grə-fē\ *n* : the statistical study of human populations and esp. their size and distribution and the number of births and deaths — **de·mog·ra·pher** \-fər\ *n* — **de·mo·graph·ic** \ˌde-mə-ˈgra-fik, ˌdē-\ *adj* — **de·mo·graph·i·cal·ly** \-fi-k(ə-)lē\ *adv*

dem·oi·selle \ˌdem-wə-ˈzel\ *n* [F] : a young woman

de·mol·ish \di-ˈmä-lish\ *vb* **1** : to destroy by breaking apart : RAZE **2** : SMASH **3** : to put an end to

de·mo·li·tion \ˌde-mə-ˈli-shən, ˌdē-\ *n* : the act of demolishing; *esp* : destruction by means of explosives

de·mon *or* **dae·mon** \ˈdē-mən\ *n* **1** : an evil spirit : DEVIL **2** *usu daemon* : an attendant power or spirit **3** : one that has unusual drive or effectiveness ⟨a ~ for work⟩

de·mon·e·tize \dē-ˈmä-nə-ˌtīz, -ˈmə-\ *vb* : to stop using as money or as a monetary standard ⟨~ silver⟩ — **de·mon·e·ti·za·tion** \dē-ˌmä-nə-tə-ˈzā-shən, -ˌmə-\ *n*

de·mo·ni·ac \di-ˈmō-nē-ˌak\ *also* **de·mo·ni·a·cal** \ˌdē-mə-ˈnī-ə-kəl\ *adj* **1** : possessed or influenced by a demon **2** : DEMONIC

de·mon·ic \di-ˈmä-nik\ *also* **de·mon·i·cal** \-ni-kəl\ *adj* : DEVILISH, FIENDISH ⟨~ cruelty⟩

de·mon·ize \ˈdē-mə-ˌnīz\ *vb* **-ized; iz·ing** **1** : to convert into a demon **2** : to characterize or treat as evil or harmful

de·mon·ol·o·gy \ˌdē-mə-ˈnä-lə-jē\ *n* **1** : the study of demons **2** : belief in demons

de·mon·stra·ble \di-ˈmän-strə-bəl\ *adj* **1** : capable of being demonstrated **2** : APPARENT, EVIDENT — **de·mon·stra·bly** \-blē\ *adv*

dem·on·strate \ˈde-mən-ˌstrāt\ *vb* **-strat·ed; -strat·ing** **1** : to show clearly **2** : to prove or make clear by reasoning or evidence **3** : to explain esp. with many examples **4** : to show publicly ⟨~ a new car⟩ **5** : to make a public display ⟨~ in protest⟩ — **dem·on·stra·tion** \ˌde-mən-ˈstrā-shən\ *n* — **dem·on·stra·tor** \ˈde-mən-ˌstrā-tər\ *n*

¹**de·mon·stra·tive** \di-ˈmän-strə-tiv\ *adj* **1** : demonstrating as real or true **2** : characterized by demonstration **3** : pointing out the one referred to and distinguishing it from others of the same class ⟨~ pronoun⟩ **4** : marked by display of feeling : EFFUSIVE — **de·mon·stra·tive·ly** *adv* — **de·mon·stra·tive·ness** *n*

²**demonstrative** *n* : a demonstrative word and esp. a pronoun

de·mor·al·ize \di-ˈmȯr-ə-ˌlīz\ *vb* **1** : to corrupt in morals **2** : to weaken in discipline or spirit : DISORGANIZE — **de·mor·al·i·za·tion** \di-ˌmȯr-ə-lə-ˈzā-shən\ *n*

de·mote \di-ˈmōt\ *vb* **de·mot·ed; de·mot·ing** : to reduce to a lower grade or rank — **de·mo·tion** \-ˈmō-shən\ *n*

de·mot·ic \di-ˈmä-tik\ *adj* : COMMON, POPULAR ⟨~ idiom⟩

de·mur \di-ˈmər\ *vb* **de·murred; de·mur·ring** [ME *demuren, demeren* to linger, fr. AF *demurer, demoerer*, fr. L *demorari*, fr. *morari* to linger, fr. *mora* delay] : to take exception : OBJECT — **de·mur** *n*

de·mure \di-ˈmyu̇r\ *adj* **1** : quietly modest : DECOROUS **2** : affectedly modest, reserved, or serious : PRIM ✦ *Synonyms* SHY, BASHFUL, COY, DIFFICULT, RETIRING, UNASSERTIVE — **de·mure·ly** *adv*

de·mur·rer \di-ˈmər-ər\ *n* : a claim by the defendant in a legal action that the plaintiff does not have sufficient grounds to proceed

den \ˈden\ *n* **1** : LAIR **1** **2** : HIDEOUT ⟨a robber's ~⟩; *also* : a place like a hideout or a center of secret activity ⟨opium ~⟩ ⟨a ~ of iniquity⟩ **3** : a cozy private little room

Den *abbr* Denmark

de·nar \ˈde-ˌnär, ˈdä-\ — see MONEY table

de·na·ture \dē-ˈnā-chər\ *vb* **de·na·tured; de·na·tur·ing** : to remove or change the natural qualities of; *esp* : to make (alcohol) unfit for drinking

den·drol·o·gy \den-ˈdrä-lə-jē\ *n* : the study of trees — **den·drol·o·gist** \-jist\ *n*

den·gue \ˈdeŋ-gē, -ˌgā\ *n* [Sp] : an acute infectious disease characterized by headache, severe joint pain, and rash

de·ni \ˈde-ˌnē, ˈdä-\ *n pl* — see *denar* at MONEY table

de·ni·al \di-ˈnī(-ə)l\ *n* **1** : rejection of a request **2** : refusal to admit the truth of a statement or charge; *also* : assertion that something alleged is false **3** : DISAVOWAL **4** : restriction on one's own activity or desires

de·nier \ˈden-yər\ *n* : a unit of fineness for yarn

den·i·grate \ˈde-ni-ˌgrāt\ *vb* **-grat·ed; -grat·ing** [L *denigrare*, fr. *nigrare* to blacken, fr. *niger* black] : to cast aspersions on : DEFAME — **den·i·gra·tion** \ˌde-ni-ˈgrā-shən\ *n*

den·im \ˈde-nəm\ *n* [F *(serge) de Nîmes* serge of Nîmes, France] **1** : a firm durable twilled usu. cotton fabric woven with colored warp and white filling threads **2** *pl* : overalls or pants of usu. blue denim

den·i·zen \ˈde-nə-zən\ *n* : INHABITANT

de·nom·i·nate \di-ˈnä-mə-ˌnāt\ *vb* : to give a name to : DESIGNATE

de·nom·i·na·tion \di-ˌnä-mə-ˈnā-shən\ *n* **1** : an act of denominating **2** : a value or size of a series of related values (as of money) **3** : NAME, DESIGNATION; *esp* : a general name for a category **4** : a religious organization uniting local congregations in a single body — **de·nom·i·na·tion·al** \-shə-nəl\ *adj*

de·nom·i·na·tor \di-ˈnä-mə-ˌnā-tər\ *n* : the part of a fraction that is below the line indicating division

de·no·ta·tive \ˈdē-nō-ˌtā-tiv, di-ˈnō-tə-tiv\ *adj* **1** : denoting or tending to denote **2** : relating to denotation

de·note \di-'nōt\ vb 1 : to mark out plainly : INDICATE 2 : to make known 3 : MEAN, NAME — **de·no·ta·tion** \,dē-nō-'tā-shən\ n

de·noue·ment \,dā-,nü-'mäⁿ\ n [F *dé-nouement*, lit., untying] : the final outcome of the dramatic complications in a literary work

de·nounce \di-'nau̇ns\ vb **de·nounced**; **de·nounc·ing** 1 : to pronounce esp. publicly to be blameworthy or evil 2 : to inform against : ACCUSE 3 : to announce formally the termination of (as a treaty) — **de·nounce·ment** n

de no·vo \di-'nō-vō\ adv or adj [L] : over again : ANEW ⟨a case tried ∼⟩

dense \'dens\ adj **dens·er**; **dens·est** 1 : marked by compactness or crowding together of parts : THICK ⟨∼ forest⟩ ⟨a ∼ fog⟩ 2 : DULL, STUPID — **dense·ly** adv — **dense·ness** n

den·si·ty \'den-sə-tē\ n, pl **-ties** 1 : the quality or state of being dense 2 : the quantity of something per unit volume, unit area, or unit length

dent \'dent\ n 1 : a small depressed place made by a blow or by pressure 2 : an impression or weakening effect made usu. against resistance 3 : initial progress — **dent** vb

den·tal \'den-tᵊl\ adj : of or relating to teeth or dentistry — **den·tal·ly** adv

dental floss n : a thread used to clean between the teeth

dental hygienist n : a person licensed to clean and examine teeth

den·tate \'den-,tāt\ adj : having pointed projections : NOTCHED

den·ti·frice \'den-tə-frəs\ n [ME *dentifricie*, fr. L *dentifricium*, fr. *dent-, dens* tooth + *fricare* to rub] : a powder, paste, or liquid for cleaning the teeth

den·tin \'den-tᵊn\ or **den·tine** \'den-,tēn, den-'tēn\ n : a calcareous material like bone but harder and denser that composes the principal mass of a tooth

den·tist \'den-tist\ n : a person licensed in the care, treatment, and replacement of teeth — **den·tist·ry** n

den·ti·tion \den-'ti-shən\ n : the number, kind, and arrangement of teeth (as of a person or animal); also : TEETH

den·ture \'den-chər\ n : a set of teeth; esp : a partial or complete set of false teeth

de·nude \di-'nüd, -'nyüd\ vb **de·nud·ed**; **de·nud·ing** : to strip the covering from — **de·nu·da·tion** \,dē-nü-'dā-shən, -nyü-\ n

de·nun·ci·a·tion \di-,nən-sē-'ā-shən\ n : the act of denouncing; esp : a public condemnation — **de·nun·ci·a·to·ry** \-'nən-sē-ə-,tȯr-ē\ adj

de·ny \di-'nī\ vb **de·nied**; **de·ny·ing** 1 : to declare untrue 2 : to refuse to recognize or acknowledge : DISAVOW 3 : to refuse to grant ⟨∼ a request⟩ 4 : to reject as false ⟨∼ a theory⟩

de·o·dar \'dē-ə-,där\ n [Hindi & Urdu *devadār, deodār*, fr. Skt *devadāru*, fr. *deva* god + *dāru* wood] : a Himalayan cedar

de·odor·ant \dē-'ō-də-rənt\ n : a prepara-

tion that destroys or masks unpleasant odors

de·odor·ize \dē-'ō-də-,rīz\ vb : to eliminate the offensive odor of

de·ox·i·dize \dē-'äk-sə-,dīz\ vb : to remove esp. elemental oxygen from

de·oxy·ri·bo·nu·cle·ic acid \dē-'äk-si-,rī-bō-nü-,klē-ik-, -,nyü-\ n : DNA

de·oxy·ri·bose \dē-,äk-si-'rī-,bōs\ n : a sugar with five carbon and four oxygen atoms in each molecule that is part of DNA

dep abbr 1 depart; departure 2 deposit 3 deputy

de·part \di-'pärt\ vb 1 : to go away : go away from : LEAVE 2 : DIE 3 : to turn aside : DEVIATE

de·part·ee \di-pär-'tē\ n : a person who is departing or who has departed

de·part·ment \di-'pärt-mənt\ n 1 : a distinct sphere or category esp. of an activity or attribute 2 : a functional or territorial division (as of a government, business, or college) — **de·part·men·tal** \di-,pärt-'ment-ᵊl, ,dē-\ adj — **de·part·men·tal·ly** adv

department store n : a store having separate sections for a wide variety of goods

de·par·ture \di-'pär-chər\ n 1 : the act of going away 2 : a starting out (as on a journey) 3 : DIVERGENCE ⟨a ∼ from tradition⟩

de·pend \di-'pend\ vb 1 : to be determined, based, or contingent ⟨life ∼s on food⟩ 2 : TRUST, RELY ⟨you can ∼ on me⟩ 3 : to be dependent esp. for financial support 4 : to hang down ⟨a vine ∼ing from a tree⟩

de·pend·able \di-'pen-də-bəl\ adj : TRUSTWORTHY, RELIABLE — **de·pend·abil·i·ty** \-,pen-də-'bi-lə-tē\ n

de·pen·dence also **de·pen·dance** \di-'pen-dəns\ n 1 : the quality or state of being dependent; esp : the quality or state of being influenced by or subject to another 2 : RELIANCE, TRUST 3 : something on which one relies 4 : drug addiction; also : HABITUATION 2

de·pen·den·cy \-dən-sē\ n, pl **-cies** 1 : DEPENDENCE 2 : a territory under the jurisdiction of a nation but not formally annexed by it

¹**de·pen·dent** \-dənt\ adj 1 : hanging down 2 : determined or conditioned by another; also : affected with drug dependence 3 : relying on another for support 4 : subject to another's jurisdiction 5 : SUBORDINATE 4 ⟨∼ clauses⟩

²**dependent** also **de·pen·dant** \-dənt\ n : one that is dependent; esp : a person who relies on another for support

dependent variable n : a variable whose value is determined by that of one or more other variables in a function

de·pict \di-'pikt\ vb 1 : to represent by a picture 2 : to describe in words — **de·pic·tion** \-'pik-shən\ n

de·pil·a·to·ry \di-'pi-lə-,tȯr-ē\ n, pl **-ries** : a preparation for removing hair, wool, or bristles

de·plane \dē-'plān\ vb : to get out of an airplane

de·plete \di-'plēt\ vb **de·plet·ed; de·plet·ing** : to exhaust esp. of strength or resources — **de·ple·tion** \-'plē-shən\ n

de·plor·able \di-'plȯr-ə-bəl\ adj 1 : LAMENTABLE ⟨a ~ death⟩ 2 : WRETCHED — **de·plor·ably** adv

de·plore \-'plȯr\ vb **de·plored; de·plor·ing** 1 : to feel or express grief for 2 : to regret strongly 3 : to consider unfortunate or deserving of disapproval

de·ploy \di-'plȯi\ vb : to spread out (as troops or ships) in order for battle — **de·ploy·ment** \-mənt\ n

de·po·nent \di-'pō-nənt\ n : one who gives evidence

de·pop·u·late \dē-'pä-pyə-ˌlāt\ vb : to reduce greatly the population of — **de·pop·u·la·tion** \-ˌpä-pyə-'lā-shən\ n

de·port \di-'pȯrt\ vb 1 : CONDUCT, BEHAVE 2 : BANISH, EXILE — **de·por·ta·tion** \ˌdē-ˌpȯr-'tā-shən\ n

de·port·ment \di-'pȯrt-mənt\ n : BEHAVIOR, BEARING

de·pose \di-'pōz\ vb **de·posed; de·pos·ing** 1 : to remove from high office (as of king) 2 : to testify under oath or by affidavit

¹**de·pos·it** \di-'pä-zət\ vb **de·pos·it·ed** \-zə-təd\; **de·pos·it·ing** 1 : to place for safekeeping or as a pledge; esp : to put money in a bank 2 : to lay down : PLACE 3 : to let fall or sink ⟨silt ~ed by a flood⟩ — **de·pos·i·tor** \-zə-tər\ n

²**deposit** n 1 : the state of being deposited ⟨money on ~⟩ 2 : something placed for safekeeping; esp : money deposited in a bank 3 : money given as a pledge 4 : an act of depositing 5 : something laid down ⟨a ~ of silt⟩ 6 : a natural accumulation (as of a mineral)

de·po·si·tion \ˌde-pə-'zi-shən, ˌdē-\ n 1 : an act of removing from a position of authority 2 : TESTIMONY 3 : the process of depositing 4 : DEPOSIT

de·pos·i·to·ry \di-'pä-zə-ˌtȯr-ē\ n, pl **-ries** : a place where something is deposited esp. for safekeeping

de·pot \1, 2 usu 'dē-pō, 3 usu 'dē-\ n 1 : a place for storing goods or vehicles 2 : a place where military supplies or replacements are kept or assembled 3 : a building for railroad or bus passengers

depr abbr depreciation

de·prave \di-'prāv\ vb **de·praved; de·prav·ing** [ME, fr. AF depraver, fr. L depravare to pervert, fr. pravus crooked, bad] : CORRUPT, PERVERT — **de·praved** adj — **de·prav·i·ty** \-'pra-və-tē\ n

dep·re·cate \'de-pri-ˌkāt\ vb **-cat·ed; -cat·ing** [L deprecari to avert by prayer, fr. precari to pray] 1 : to express disapproval of 2 : BELITTLE — **dep·re·ca·tion** \ˌde-pri-'kā-shən\ n

dep·re·ca·to·ry \'de-pri-kə-ˌtȯr-ē\ adj 1 : APOLOGETIC 2 : serving to deprecate : DISAPPROVING

de·pre·ci·ate \di-'prē-shē-ˌāt\ vb **-at·ed; -at·ing** [ME, fr. LL depreciatus, pp. of depretiare, fr. L pretium price] 1 : BELITTLE, DISPARAGE 2 : to lessen in price or

value — **de·pre·cia·ble** \-shə-bəl\ adj — **de·pre·ci·a·tion** \-ˌprē-shē-'ā-shən\ n

dep·re·da·tion \ˌde-prə-'dā-shən\ n : a laying waste or plundering — **dep·re·date** \'de-prə-ˌdāt\ vb

de·press \di-'pres\ vb 1 : to press down : cause to sink to a lower position 2 : to lessen the activity or force of 3 : SADDEN, DISCOURAGE 4 : to lessen in price or value — **de·pres·sor** \-'pre-sər\ n

de·pres·sant \di-'pre-s°nt\ n : one that depresses; esp : a chemical substance (as a drug) that reduces bodily functional activity — **depressant** adj

de·pressed \-'prest\ adj 1 : low in spirits; also : affected with psychological depression 2 : suffering from economic depression

de·pres·sion \di-'pre-shən\ n 1 : an act of depressing : a state of being depressed 2 : a pressing down : LOWERING 3 : a state of feeling sad 4 : a psychological disorder marked esp. by sadness, inactivity, difficulty in thinking and concentration, and feelings of dejection 5 : a depressed area or part 6 : a period of low general economic activity with widespread unemployment

¹**de·pres·sive** \di-'pre-siv\ adj 1 : tending to depress 2 : characterized or affected by psychological depression

²**depressive** n : a person affected with or prone to psychological depression

de·pres·sur·ize \(ˌ)dē-'pre-shə-ˌrīz\ vb : to release pressure from

dep·ri·va·tion \ˌde-prə-'vā-shən\ n 1 : an act or instance of depriving : LOSS 2 : PRIVATION 2

de·prive \di-'prīv\ vb **de·prived; de·priv·ing** 1 : to take something away from 2 : to stop from having something

deprived adj : marked by deprivation esp. of the necessities of life

de·pro·gram \(ˌ)dē-'prō-ˌgram, -grəm\ vb : to dissuade from convictions usu. of a religious nature often by coercive means

dept abbr department

depth \'depth\ n, pl **depths** \'depths\ 1 : something that is deep; esp : the deep part of a body of water 2 : a part that is far from the outside or surface; also : the middle or innermost part 3 : ABYSS 4 : a profound or intense state ⟨the ~s of reflection⟩; also : the worst part ⟨during the ~s of the depression⟩ 5 : a reprehensibly low condition 6 : the distance from top to bottom or from front to back 7 : the quality of being deep 8 : the degree of intensity

depth charge n : an explosive device for use underwater esp. against submarines

dep·u·ta·tion \ˌde-pyə-'tā-shən\ n 1 : the act of appointing a deputy 2 : DELEGATION

de·pute \di-'pyüt\ vb **de·put·ed; de·put·ing** : DELEGATE

dep·u·tize \'de-pyə-ˌtīz\ vb **-tized; -tiz·ing** : to appoint or act as deputy

dep·u·ty \'de-pyə-tē\ n, pl **-ties** 1 : a person appointed to act for or in place of another 2 : an assistant empowered to act as a substitute in the absence of a superior **3** : a member of a lower house of a legislative assembly

der or **deriv** abbr derivation; derivative

de·rail \di-'rāl\ vb : to leave or cause to leave the rails — **de·rail·ment** n

de·rail·leur \di-'rā-lər\ n [F dérailleur] : a device for shifting gears on a bicycle by moving the chain from one set of exposed gears to another

de·range \di-'rānj\ vb **de·ranged**; **de·rang·ing** **1** : DISARRANGE, UPSET **2** : to make insane — **de·range·ment** n

der·by \'dər-bē, Brit 'där-\ n, pl **derbies** **1** : a horse race usu. for three-year-olds held annually **2** : a race or contest open to all **3** : a stiff felt hat with dome-shaped crown and narrow brim

de·reg·u·la·tion \(,)dē-,re-gyu̇-'lā-shən\ n : the act of removing restrictions or regulations — **de·reg·u·late** \-'re-gyu̇-,lāt\ vb

¹der·e·lict \'der-ə-,likt\ adj **1** : abandoned by the owner or occupant **2** : NEGLIGENT ⟨~ in his duty⟩

²derelict n **1** : something voluntarily abandoned; esp : a ship abandoned on the high seas **2** : a destitute homeless social misfit : VAGRANT, BUM

der·e·lic·tion \,der-ə-'lik-shən\ n **1** : the act of abandoning : the state of being abandoned **2** : intentional neglect ⟨~ of duty⟩

de·ride \di-'rīd\ vb **de·rid·ed**; **de·rid·ing** [L dērīdēre, fr. rīdēre to laugh] : to laugh at scornfully : RIDICULE

de ri·gueur \də-rē-'gər\ adj [F] : prescribed or required by fashion, etiquette, or custom : PROPER

de·ri·sion \də-'ri-zhən\ n : RIDICULE — **de·ri·sive** \-'rī-siv\ adj — **de·ri·sive·ly** adv — **de·ri·sive·ness** n — **de·ri·so·ry** \-'rī-sə-rē\ adj

der·i·va·tion \,der-ə-'vā-shən\ n **1** : the formation of a word from an earlier word or root; also : an act of ascertaining or stating the derivation of a word **2** : ETYMOLOGY **3** : SOURCE, ORIGIN; also : DESCENT **4** : an act or process of deriving

de·riv·a·tive \di-'ri-və-tiv\ n **1** : a word formed by derivation **2** : something derived **3** : the limit of the ratio of the change of a function's value to the change in its independent variable as the latter change approaches zero — **derivative** adj

de·rive \di-'rīv\ vb **de·rived**; **de·riv·ing** [ME, fr. AF deriver, fr. L derivare, lit., to draw off (water), fr. de- from + rivus stream] **1** : to receive or obtain from a source **2** : to obtain from a parent substance **3** : INFER, DEDUCE **4** : to trace the derivation of **5** : to come from a certain source

der·mal \'dər-məl\ adj : of or relating to the skin : CUTANEOUS

der·ma·ti·tis \,dər-mə-'tī-təs\ n, pl **-tit·i·des** \-'ti-tə-,dēz\ or **-ti·tis·es** : inflammation of the skin

der·ma·tol·o·gy \-'tä-lə-jē\ n : a branch of medical science dealing with the struc-

ture, functions, and diseases of the skin — **der·ma·tol·o·gist** \-jist\ n

der·mis \'dər-məs\ n : the sensitive vascular inner layer of the skin

de·ro·gate \'der-ə-,gāt\ vb **-gat·ed**; **-gat·ing** **1** : to cause to seem inferior : DISPARAGE **2** : DETRACT — **der·o·ga·tion** \,der-ə-'gā-shən\ n — **de·rog·a·tive** \di-'rä-gə-tiv\ adj

de·rog·a·to·ry \di-'rä-gə-,tȯr-ē\ adj : intended to lower the reputation of a person or thing : DISPARAGING — **de·rog·a·to·ri·ly** \-,rä-gə-'tȯr-ə-lē\ adv

der·rick \'der-ik\ n [obs. derrick hangman, gallows, fr. Derick, name of 17th cent. Eng. hangman] **1** : a hoisting apparatus : CRANE **2** : a framework over a drill hole (as for oil) for supporting machinery

der·ri·ere or **der·ri·ère** \,der-ē-'er\ n : BUTTOCKS

der·ring-do \,der-iŋ-'dü\ n : DARING

der·rin·ger \'der-ən-jər\ n : a short-barreled pocket pistol

der·vish \'dər-vish\ n [Turk derviş, lit., beggar, fr. Pers darvīsh] : a member of a Muslim religious order noted for devotional exercises (as bodily movements leading to a trance)

de·sal·i·nate \dē-'sa-lə-,nāt\ vb **-nat·ed**; **-nat·ing** : DESALT — **de·sal·i·na·tion** \-,sa-lə-'nā-shən\ n

de·sal·i·nize \dē-'sa-lə-,nīz\ vb **-nized**; **-niz·ing** : DESALT — **de·sal·i·ni·za·tion** \-,sa-lə-nə-'zā-shən\ n

de·salt \dē-'sȯlt\ vb : to remove salt from ⟨~ seawater⟩ — **de·salt·er** n

des·cant \'des-,kant\ vb **1** : to sing or play part music : SING **2** : to discourse or write at length

de·scend \di-'send\ vb **1** : to pass from a higher to a lower place or level : pass, move, or climb down or down along **2** : DERIVE ⟨~ed from royalty⟩ **3** : to pass by inheritance or transmission **4** : to incline, lead, or extend downward **5** : to swoop down or appear suddenly (as in an attack)

¹de·scen·dant also **de·scen·dent** \di-'sen-dənt\ adj **1** : DESCENDING **2** : proceeding from an ancestor or source

²descendant also **descendent** n **1** : one descended from another or from a common stock **2** : one deriving directly from a precursor or prototype

de·scent \di-'sent\ n **1** : ANCESTRY, BIRTH, LINEAGE **2** : the act or process of descending **3** : SLOPE **4** : a descending way (as a downgrade) **5** : a sudden hostile raid or assault **6** : a downward step (as in station or value) : DECLINE

de·scram·ble \dē-'skram-bəl\ vb : UNSCRAMBLE **2** — **de·scram·bler** \-b(ə-)lər\ n

de·scribe \di-'skrīb\ vb **de·scribed**; **de·scrib·ing** **1** : to represent or give an account of in words **2** : to trace the outline of — **de·scrib·able** adj

de·scrip·tion \di-'skrip-shən\ n **1** : an account of something; esp : an account that presents a picture to a person who reads or hears it **2** : KIND, SORT — **de-scrip-tive** \-'skrip-tiv\ adj

de-scry \di-'skrī\ vb **de-scried; de-scry-ing 1** : to catch sight of **2** : to discover by observation or investigation

des-e-crate \'de-si-ˌkrāt\ vb **-crat-ed; -crat-ing** : PROFANE — **des-e-cra-tion** \ˌde-si-'krā-shən\ n

de-seg-re-gate \dē-'se-gri-ˌgāt\ vb : to eliminate segregation in; esp : to free of any law or practice requiring isolation on the basis of race — **de-seg-re-ga-tion** \-ˌse-gri-'gā-shən\ n

de-sen-si-tize \dē-'sen-sə-ˌtīz\ vb : to make (a sensitized or hypersensitive individual) insensitive or nonreactive to a sensitizing agent — **de-sen-si-ti-za-tion** \-ˌsen-sə-tə-'zā-shən\ n

¹des-ert \'de-zərt\ n : dry land with few plants and little rainfall

²des-ert \'de-zərt\ adj : of, relating to, or resembling a desert; esp : being barren and without life ⟨a ~ island⟩

³de-sert \di-'zərt\ n : the quality or fact of deserving reward or punishment **2** : a just reward or punishment

⁴de-sert \di-'zərt\ vb **1** : to withdraw from **2** : ABANDON, FORSAKE — **de-sert-er** n — **de-ser-tion** \-'zər-shən\ n

de-serve \di-'zərv\ vb **de-served; de-serv-ing** : to be worthy of : MERIT — **de-serv-ing** adj

de-serv-ed-ly \-'zər-vəd-lē\ adv : according to merit : JUSTLY

deshabille var of DISHABILLE

des-ic-cate \'de-si-ˌkāt\ vb **-cat-ed; -cat-ing** : DRY, DEHYDRATE — **des-ic-ca-tion** \ˌde-si-'kā-shən\ n — **des-ic-ca-tor** \'de-si-ˌkā-tər\ n

de-sid-er-a-tum \di-ˌsi-də-'rä-təm, -ˌzi-, -'rä-\ n, pl **-ta** \-tə\ [L] : something desired as essential

¹de-sign \di-'zīn\ vb **1** : to conceive and plan out in the mind **2** : INTEND **3** : to devise for a specific function or end **4** : to make a pattern or sketch of **5** : to conceive and draw the plans for

²design n **1** : a particular purpose : deliberate planning **2** : a mental project or scheme : PLAN **3** : a secret project or scheme : PLOT **4** pl : aggressive or evil intent — used with on or against **5** : a preliminary sketch or plan **6** : an underlying scheme that governs functioning, developing, or unfolding : MOTIF ⟨the general ~ of the epic⟩ **7** : the arrangement of elements or details in a product or a work of art **8** : a decorative pattern ⟨a floral ~⟩ **9** : the art of executing designs

¹des-ig-nate \'de-zig-ˌnāt, -nət\ adj : chosen but not yet installed ⟨ambassador ~⟩

²des-ig-nate \-ˌnāt\ vb **-nat-ed; -nat-ing 1** : to appoint and set apart for a special purpose **2** : to mark or point out : INDICATE; also : SPECIFY, STIPULATE **3** : to call by a name or title — **des-ig-na-tion** \ˌde-zig-'nā-shən\ n

designated driver n : a person chosen to abstain from alcohol so as to transport others safely

designated hitter n : a baseball player designated at the start of the game to bat in place of the pitcher without causing the pitcher to be removed from the game

de-sign-er \di-'zī-nər\ n **1** : one who creates plans for a project or structure **2** : one who designs and manufactures high-fashion clothing — **designer** adj

designer drug n : a synthetic version of an illicit drug that has been chemically altered to avoid its prohibition

de-sign-ing \di-'zī-niŋ\ adj : CRAFTY, SCHEMING

de-sir-able \di-'zī-rə-bəl\ adj **1** : PLEASING, ATTRACTIVE **2** : ADVISABLE ⟨~ legislation⟩ — **de-sir-abil-i-ty** \-ˌzī-rə-'bi-lə-tē\ n — **de-sir-able-ness** n — **de-sir-ably** \-'zī-rə-blē\ adv

¹de-sire \di-'zī(-ə)r\ vb **de-sired; de-sir-ing** [ME, fr. AF desirer, fr. L desiderare, fr. sider-, sidus heavenly body] **1** : to long or hope for : exhibit or feel desire for **2** : REQUEST

²desire n **1** : a strong wish : LONGING, CRAVING **2** : sexual urge or appetite **3** : a usu. formal request for action **4** : something desired

de-sir-ous \di-'zī-(ə)r-əs\ adj : eagerly wishing : DESIRING ⟨~ of fame⟩

de-sist \di-'zist, -'sist\ vb : to cease to proceed or act

desk \'desk\ n [ME deske, fr. ML desca, fr. It desco table, fr. L discus dish, disc] **1** : a table, frame, or case esp. for writing and reading **2** : a counter, stand, or booth at which a person performs duties **3** : a specialized division of an organization (as a newspaper) ⟨city ~⟩

desk-top publishing \'desk-ˌtäp-\ n : the production of printed matter by means of a microcomputer

¹des-o-late \'de-sə-lət, -zə-\ adj **1** : DESERTED, ABANDONED **2** : FORSAKEN, LONELY **3** : DILAPIDATED **4** : BARREN, LIFELESS ⟨a ~ landscape⟩ **5** : CHEERLESS, GLOOMY ⟨~ memories⟩ — **des-o-late-ly** adv — **des-o-late-ness** n

²des-o-late \-ˌlāt\ vb **-lat-ed; -lat-ing** : to make desolate : lay waste : make wretched

des-o-la-tion \ˌde-sə-'lā-shən, -zə-\ n **1** : the action of desolating **2** : GRIEF, SADNESS **3** : LONELINESS **4** : DEVASTATION, RUIN **5** : barren wasteland

des-oxy-ri-bo-nu-cle-ic acid \(ˌ)de-ˌzäk-sē-'rī-bō-nú-ˌklē-ik-, -nyü-\ n : DNA

¹de-spair \di-'sper\ vb : to lose all hope or confidence — **de-spair-ing** \-iŋ\ adj — **de-spair-ing-ly** adv

²despair n **1** : utter loss of hope **2** : a cause of hopelessness

des-patch chiefly Brit var of DISPATCH

des-per-a-do \ˌdes-pə-'rä-dō, -'rä-\ n, pl **-does** or **-dos** : a bold or reckless criminal

des-per-ate \'des-pə-rət, -prət\ adj **1** : being beyond or almost beyond hope : causing despair **2** : RASH ⟨a ~ attempt⟩ **3** : extremely intense — **des-per-ate-ly** adv — **des-per-ate-ness** n

des-per-a-tion \ˌdes-pə-'rä-shən\ n **1** : a

loss of hope and surrender to despair **2** : a state of hopelessness leading to rashness

de·spi·ca·ble \di-'spi-kə-bəl, 'des-pi-\ *adj* : deserving to be despised — **de·spi·ca·bly** \-blē\ *adv*

de·spise \di-'spīz\ *vb* **de·spised; de·spis·ing 1** : to look down on with contempt or aversion : DISDAIN, DETEST **2** : to regard as negligible, worthless, or distasteful

de·spite \di-'spīt\ *prep* : in spite of

de·spoil \di-'spȯi(-ə)l\ *vb* : to strip of belongings, possessions, or value — **de·spoil·er** *n* — **de·spoil·ment** *n*

de·spo·li·a·tion \di-,spō-lē-'ā-shən\ *n* : the act of plundering : the state of being despoiled

¹de·spond \di-'spänd\ *vb* : to become discouraged or disheartened

²despond *n* : DESPONDENCY

de·spon·den·cy \-'spän-dən-sē\ *n* : DEJECTION, HOPELESSNESS — **de·spon·dent** \-dənt\ *adj* — **de·spon·dent·ly** *adv*

des·pot \'des-pət, -,pät\ *n* [MF *despote*, fr. Gk *despotēs* master, lord, autocrat] **1** : a ruler with absolute power and authority **2** : a person exercising power tyrannically — **des·pot·ic** \des-'pä-tik\ *adj* — **des·po·tism** \'des-pə-,ti-zəm\ *n*

des·sert \di-'zərt\ *n* : a course of sweet food, fruit, or cheese served at the close of a meal

de·stig·ma·tize \dē-'stig-mə-,tīz\ *vb* : to remove associations of shame or disgrace from

des·ti·na·tion \,des-tə-'nā-shən\ *n* **1** : a purpose for which something is destined **2** : an act of appointing, setting aside for a purpose, or predetermining **3** : a place to which one is journeying or to which something is sent

des·tine \'des-tən\ *vb* **des·tined; destin·ing 1** : to settle in advance **2** : to designate, assign, or dedicate in advance **3** : to direct or set apart for a specific purpose or place

des·ti·ny \'des-tə-nē\ *n, pl* **-nies 1** : something to which a person or thing is destined : FATE, FORTUNE **2** : a predetermined course of events

des·ti·tute \'des-tə-,tüt, -,tyüt\ *adj* **1** : lacking something needed or desirable **2** : suffering extreme poverty — **des·ti·tu·tion** \,des-tə-'tü-shən, -'tyü-\ *n*

de·stroy \di-'strȯi\ *vb* **1** : to put an end to : RUIN **2** : KILL

de·stroy·er \di-'strȯi-ər\ *n* **1** : one that destroys **2** : a small speedy warship

de·struc·ti·ble \di-'strək-tə-bəl\ *adj* : capable of being destroyed — **de·struc·ti·bil·i·ty** \-,strək-tə-'bi-lə-tē\ *n*

de·struc·tion \di-'strək-shən\ *n* **1** : RUIN **2** : the action or process of destroying something **3** : a destroying agency

de·struc·tive \di-'strək-tiv\ *adj* **1** : causing destruction : RUINOUS **2** : designed or tending to hurt or destroy — **de·struc·tive·ly** *adv* — **de·struc·tive·ness** *n*

de·sue·tude \'de-swi-,tüd, -,tyüd\ *n* : DISUSE

des·ul·to·ry \'de-səl-,tȯr-ē\ *adj* : passing aimlessly from one thing or subject to another : DISCONNECTED

det *abbr* **1** detached; detachment **2** detail

de·tach \di-'tach\ *vb* **1** : to separate esp. from a larger mass **2** : DISENGAGE, WITHDRAW — **de·tach·able** *adj*

de·tached \di-'tacht\ *adj* **1** : not joined or connected : SEPARATE **2** : ALOOF, IMPARTIAL ⟨a ~ attitude⟩

de·tach·ment \di-'tach-mənt\ *n* **1** : SEPARATION **2** : the dispatching of a body of troops or part of a fleet from the main body for special service; *also* : the portion so dispatched **3** : a small permanent military unit of special composition **4** : indifference to worldly concerns : ALOOFNESS **5** : IMPARTIALITY

¹de·tail \di-'tāl, 'dē-,tāl\ *n* [F *détail*, fr. OF *detail* slice, piece, fr. *detaillier* to cut in pieces, fr. *taillier* to cut] **1** : a dealing with something item by item ⟨go into ~⟩; *also* : ITEM, PARTICULAR ⟨the ~s of a story⟩ **2** : selection (as of soldiers) for special duty; *also* : the persons thus selected

²detail *vb* **1** : to report in particulars : SPECIFY **2** : to assign to a special duty

de·tailed \di-'tāld, 'dē-,tāld\ *adj* : marked by abundant detail

de·tail·ing \'dē-,tāl-iŋ\ *n* : the meticulous cleaning and refurbishing of an automobile

de·tain \di-'tān\ *vb* **1** : to hold in or as if in custody **2** : STOP, DELAY

de·tect \di-'tekt\ *vb* : to discover the nature, existence, presence, or fact of — **de·tect·able** *adj* — **de·tec·tion** \-'tek-shən\ *n* — **de·tec·tor** \-'tek-tər\ *n*

¹de·tec·tive \di-'tek-tiv\ *adj* **1** : fitted or used for detection **2** : of or relating to detectives

²detective *n* : a person employed or engaged in detecting lawbreakers or getting information that is not readily accessible

dé·tente *or* **de·tente** \dā-'tänt\ *n* [F] : a relaxation of strained relations or tensions (as between nations)

de·ten·tion \di-'ten-chən\ *n* **1** : the act or fact of detaining : CONFINEMENT; *esp* : a period of temporary custody prior to disposition by a court **2** : a forced delay

de·ter \di-'tər\ *vb* **de·terred; de·ter·ring** [L *deterrēre*, fr. *terrēre* to frighten] **1** : to turn aside, discourage, or prevent from acting (as by fear) **2** : INHIBIT

de·ter·gent \di-'tər-jənt\ *n* : a cleansing agent; *esp* : a chemical product similar to soap in its cleaning ability

de·te·ri·o·rate \di-'tir-ē-ə-,rāt\ *vb* **-rat·ed; -rat·ing** : to make or become worse in quality or condition — **de·te·ri·o·ra·tion** \-,tir-ē-ə-'rā-shən\ *n*

de·ter·min·able \-'tər-mə-nə-bəl\ *adj* : capable of being determined; *esp* : ASCERTAINABLE

de·ter·mi·nant \-mə-nənt\ *n* **1** : something that determines or conditions **2** : GENE

de·ter·mi·nate \di-'tər-mə-nət\ *adj* 1
: having fixed limits : DEFINITE ⟨a ∼ period of time⟩ 2 : definitely settled ⟨in ∼
order⟩ — **de·ter·mi·nate·ness** *n*

de·ter·mi·na·tion \di-,tər-mə-'nā-shən\
n 1 : the act of coming to a decision; *also*
: the decision or conclusion reached 2
: a fixing of the extent, position, or character of something 3 : accurate measurement (as of length or volume) 4
: firm or fixed purpose — **de·ter·mi·na·-
tive** \-'tər-mə-,nā-tiv, -'tər-mə-nə-\ *adj*

de·ter·mine \di-'tər-mən\ *vb* -mined;
-min·ing 1 : to fix conclusively or authoritatively 2 : to come to a decision
: SETTLE, RESOLVE 3 : to fix the form or
character of beforehand : ORDAIN; *also*
: REGULATE 4 : to find out the limits, nature, dimensions, or scope of ⟨∼ a position at sea⟩ 5 : to bring about as a result

de·ter·mined \-'tər-mənd\ *adj* 1 : firmly
resolved 2 : characterized by or showing determination — **de·ter·mined·ly**
\-mənd-lē, -mə-nəd-lē\ *adv* — **de·ter-
mined·ness** *n*

de·ter·min·ism \di-'tər-mə-,ni-zəm\ *n* : a
doctrine that acts of the will, natural
events, or social changes are determined
by preceding events or natural causes —
de·ter·min·ist \-nist\ *n* or *adj*

de·ter·rence \di-'tər-əns\ *n* : the inhibition of criminal behavior by fear esp. of
punishment

de·ter·rent \-ənt\ *adj* 1 : serving to
deter 2 : relating to deterrence — **de-
terrent** *n*

de·test \di-'test\ *vb* [L *detestari*, lit., to
curse while calling a deity to witness, fr.
de- from + *testari* to call to witness, fr.
testis witness] : LOATHE, HATE — **de-
test·able** *adj* — **de·tes·ta·tion** \,dē-,tes-
'tā-shən\ *n*

de·throne \di-'thrōn\ *vb* : to remove from
a throne : DEPOSE — **de·throne·ment** *n*

det·o·nate \'de-t²n-,āt\ *vb* -nat·ed; -nat·-
ing : to explode or cause to explode with
violence — **det·o·na·tion** \,de-t²n-'ā-
shən\ *n*

det·o·na·tor \'de-t²n-,ā-tər\ *n* : a device
for detonating an explosive

¹de·tour \'dē-,tùr\ *n* : an indirect way replacing part of a route

²detour *vb* : to go by detour

de·tox \'dē-,täks, di-'täks\ *n* : detoxifica-
tion from an intoxicating or addictive
substance — **detox** *vb*

de·tox·i·fy \dē-'täk-sə-,fī\ *vb* -fied; -fy·-
ing 1 : to remove a poison or toxin or
the effect of such from 2 : to free (as a
drug user) from an intoxicating or addictive substance or from dependence on it
— **de·tox·i·fi·ca·tion** \dē-,täk-sə-fə-'kā-
shən\ *n*

de·tract \di-'trakt\ *vb* 1 : to take away or
diminish the value or effect of
something 2 : DIVERT — **de·trac·tion**
\-'trak-shən\ *n* — **de·trac·tor** \-'trak-tər\
n

de·train \dē-'trān\ *vb* : to leave or cause to
leave a railroad train

det·ri·ment \'de-trə-mənt\ *n* : INJURY,
DAMAGE; *also* : a cause of injury or dam-

age — **det·ri·men·tal** \,de-trə-'ment-²l\
adj — **det·ri·men·tal·ly** *adv*

de·tri·tus \di-'trī-təs\ *n, pl* **de·tri·tus**
: fragments resulting from disintegration
(as of rocks) : DEBRIS

deuce \'düs, 'dyüs\ *n* 1 : a two in cards
or dice 2 : a tie in a tennis game with
both sides at 40 3 : DEVIL — used
chiefly as a mild oath

Deut *abbr* Deuteronomy

deu·te·ri·um \dü-'tir-ē-əm, dyü-\ *n* : an
isotope of hydrogen that has twice the
mass of ordinary hydrogen

Deu·ter·on·o·my \,dü-tə-'rä-nə-mē,
,dyü-\ *n* — see BIBLE table

deut·sche mark \'dòi-chə-,märk\ *n* : a
former basic monetary unit of Germany

dev *abbr* deviation

de·val·ue \dē-'val-yü\ *vb* : to reduce the
international exchange value of (a
currency) — **de·val·u·a·tion** \-,val-yə-
'wā-shən\ *n*

dev·as·tate \'de-və-,stāt\ *vb* -tat·ed; -tat·-
ing 1 : to bring to ruin 2 : to reduce to
chaos or helplessness — **dev·as·tat·ing·-
ly** *adv* — **dev·as·ta·tion** \,de-və-'stā-
shən\ *n*

de·vel·op \di-'ve-ləp\ *vb* 1 : to unfold
gradually or in detail 2 : to place (exposed photographic material) in chemicals to produce a visible image 3 : to
bring out the possibilities of 4 : to make
more available or usable ⟨∼ land⟩ 5 : to
acquire gradually ⟨∼ a taste for olives⟩
6 : to go through a natural process of
growth, differentiation, or evolution 7
: to come into being gradually — **de·vel-
op·er** *n* — **de·vel·op·ment** *n* — **de·vel-
op·men·tal** \-,ve-ləp-'men-t²l\ *adj* —
vel·op·men·tal·ly \-t²l-ē\ *adv*

de·vi·ant \'dē-vē-ənt\ *adj* : deviating esp.
from some accepted norm ⟨∼ behavior⟩
— **de·vi·ance** \-əns\ *n* — **de·vi·an·cy**
\-ən-sē\ *n* — **deviant** *n*

de·vi·ate \'dē-vē-,āt\ *vb* -at·ed; -at·ing
[LL *deviare*, fr. L *de-* from + *via* way] : to
turn aside from a course, standard, principle, or topic — **de·vi·ate** \-vē-ət, -vē-
,āt\ *n* — **de·vi·a·tion** \,dē-vē-'ā-shən\ *n*

de·vice \di-'vīs\ *n* 1 : SCHEME, STRATA-
GEM 2 : a piece of equipment or a mechanism for a special purpose 3 : DESIRE,
INCLINATION ⟨left to my own ∼s⟩ 4
: an emblematic design

¹dev·il \'de-vəl\ *n* [ME *devel*, fr. OE *dēofol*,
fr. LL *diabolus*, fr. Gk *diabolos*, lit., slan-
derer, fr. *diaballein* to throw across, slander, fr. *dia-* across + *ballein* to throw] 1
often cap : the personal supreme spirit of
evil 2 : DEMON 3 : a wicked person 4
: an energetic, reckless, or dashing person 5 : FELLOW ⟨poor ∼⟩ ⟨lucky ∼⟩

²devil *vb* -iled *or* -illed; -il·ing *or* -il·ling
1 : to season highly ⟨∼ed eggs⟩ 2
: TEASE, ANNOY

dev·il·ish \'de-və-lish\ *adj* 1 : befitting a
devil : EVIL; *also* : MISCHIEVOUS 2 : EX-
TREME ⟨in a ∼ hurry⟩ — **dev·il·ish·ly**
adv — **dev·il·ish·ness** *n*

dev·il·ment \'de-vəl-mənt, -,ment\ *n* : MIS-
CHIEF

dev·il·ry \-rē\ *or* **dev·il·try** \-trē\ *n, pl* **-il·ries** *or* **-il·tries** 1 : action performed with the help of the devil 2 : MISCHIEF

de·vi·ous \'dē-vē-əs\ *adj* 1 : deviating from a straight line : ROUNDABOUT 2 : ERRANT 3 3 : TRICKY, CUNNING

¹de·vise \di-'vīz\ *vb* **de·vised; de·vis·ing** [ME, fr. AF *deviser* to divide, distinguish, invent, fr. VL *divisare*, fr. L *dividere* to divide] 1 : INVENT 2 : PLOT 3 : to give (real estate) by will

²devise *n* 1 : a disposing of real property by will 2 : a will or clause of a will disposing of real property 3 : property given by will

de·vi·tal·ize \dē-'vī-tə-ˌlīz\ *vb* : to deprive of life or vitality

de·void \di-'vȯid\ *adj* : being without : VOID ⟨a book ~ of interest⟩

de·voir \də-'vwär\ *n* 1 : DUTY 2 : a formal act of civility or respect

de·volve \di-'välv\ *vb* **de·volved; de·volv·ing** : to pass (as rights or responsibility) from one to another usu. by succession or transmission — **dev·o·lu·tion** \ˌde-və-'lü-shən, ˌdē-\ *n*

De·vo·ni·an \di-'vō-nē-ən\ *adj* : of, relating to, or being the period of the Paleozoic era between the Silurian and the Mississippian — **Devonian** *n*

de·vote \di-'vōt\ *vb* **de·vot·ed; de·vot·ing** 1 : to commit to wholly or chiefly 2 : to set apart for a special purpose : DEDICATE

de·vot·ed \-'vō-təd\ *adj* : characterized by loyalty and devotion : FAITHFUL

dev·o·tee \ˌde-və-'tē, -'tā\ *n* : an ardent follower, supporter, or enthusiast

de·vo·tion \di-'vō-shən\ *n* 1 : religious fervor 2 : an act of prayer or private worship — usu. used in pl. 3 : a religious exercise for private use 4 : the fact or state of being dedicated and loyal ⟨~ to music⟩; *also* : the act of devoting — **de·vo·tion·al** \-shə-nəl\ *adj*

de·vour \di-'vau̇(-ə)r\ *vb* 1 : to eat up greedily or ravenously 2 : WASTE, ANNIHILATE 3 : to enjoy avidly ⟨~ a book⟩ — **de·vour·er** *n*

de·vout \di-'vau̇t\ *adj* 1 : devoted to religion : PIOUS 2 : expressing devotion or piety 3 : EARNEST, SERIOUS ⟨a ~ baseball fan⟩ — **de·vout·ly** *adv* — **de·vout·ness** *n*

dew \'dü, 'dyü\ *n* : moisture that condenses on the surfaces of cool bodies at night — **dewy** *adj*

dew·ber·ry \'dü-ˌber-ē, 'dyü-\ *n* : any of several sweet edible berries related to and resembling blackberries; *also* : a trailing bramble bearing these

dew·claw \-ˌklȯ\ *n* : a digit on the foot of a mammal that does not reach the ground; *also* : its claw or hoof

dew·lap \-ˌlap\ *n* : loose skin hanging under the neck of an animal

dew point *n* : the temperature at which the moisture in the air begins to condense

dex·ter·i·ty \dek-'ster-ə-tē\ *n, pl* **-ties** 1 : mental skill or quickness 2 : readiness and grace in physical activity; *esp* : skill and ease in using the hands

dex·ter·ous \'dek-strəs\ *adj* 1 : CLEVER 2 : done with skillfulness 3 : skillful and competent with the hands — **dex·ter·ous·ly** *adv*

dex·trose \'dek-ˌstrōs\ *n* : the naturally occurring form of glucose found in plants and blood

DFC *abbr* Distinguished Flying Cross

dg *abbr* decigram

DG *abbr* 1 [LL *Dei gratia*] by the grace of God 2 director general

DH \ˌdē-'āch\ *n* : DESIGNATED HITTER

dhow \'dau̇\ *n* : an Arab sailing ship usu. having a long overhang forward and a high poop

DI *abbr* drill instructor

dia *abbr* diameter

di·a·be·tes \ˌdī-ə-'bē-tēz, -təs\ *n* : an abnormal state marked by passage of excessive amounts of urine; *esp* : one (**diabetes mel·li·tus** \-'me-lə-təs\) characterized by deficient insulin, by excess sugar in the blood and urine, and by thirst, hunger, and loss of weight — **di·a·bet·ic** \-'be-tik\ *adj or n*

di·a·bol·i·cal \ˌdī-ə-'bä-li-kəl\ *or* **di·a·bol·ic** \-lik\ *adj* : DEVILISH ⟨a ~ plot⟩ — **di·a·bol·i·cal·ly** \-k(ə-)lē\ *adv*

di·a·crit·ic \ˌdī-ə-'kri-tik\ *n* : a mark accompanying a letter and indicating a sound value different from that of the same letter when unmarked — **di·a·crit·i·cal** \-ti-kəl\ *adj*

di·a·dem \'dī-ə-ˌdem\ *n* : CROWN; *esp* : a royal headband

di·aer·e·sis *or* **di·er·e·sis** \dī-'er-ə-səs\ *n, pl* **-e·ses** \-ˌsēz\ : a mark ¨ placed over a vowel to show that it is pronounced in a separate syllable (as in *naïve*)

diag *abbr* 1 diagonal 2 diagram

di·ag·no·sis \ˌdī-ig-'nō-səs\ *n, pl* **-no·ses** \-ˌsēz\ : the art or act of identifying a disease from its signs and symptoms; *also* : the decision reached by diagnosis — **di·ag·nose** \'dī-ig-ˌnōs\ *vb* — **di·ag·nos·tic** \ˌdī-ig-'näs-tik\ *adj* — **di·ag·nos·ti·cian** \-ˌnäs-'ti-shən\ *n*

¹di·ag·o·nal \dī-'a-gə-nəl\ *adj* 1 : extending from one corner to the opposite corner in a 4-sided figure 2 : running in a slanting direction ⟨~ stripes⟩ 3 : having slanting markings or parts ⟨a ~ weave⟩ — **di·ag·o·nal·ly** *adv*

²diagonal *n* 1 : a diagonal line 2 : a diagonal row, pattern, or direction 3 : SLASH 3

¹di·a·gram \'dī-ə-ˌgram\ *n* : a design and esp. a drawing that makes something easier to understand — **di·a·gram·ma·ble** \-ˌgra-mə-bəl\ *adj* — **di·a·gram·mat·ic** \ˌdī-ə-grə-'ma-tik\ *adj* — **di·a·gram·mat·i·cal·ly** \-ti-k(ə-)lē\ *adv*

²diagram *vb* **-grammed** *or* **-gramed** \-ˌgramd\; **-gram·ming** *or* **-gram·ing** : to represent by a diagram

¹di·al \'dī(-ə)l\ *n* [ME, fr. ML *dialis* clock wheel revolving daily, fr. L *dies* day] 1 : the face of a sundial 2 : the face of a timepiece 3 : a face with a pointer and numbers that indicate something ⟨the ~ of a gauge⟩ 4 : a device used for making electrical connections or for regulating operation (as of a radio)

²**dial** vb **di·aled** or **di·alled; di·al·ing** or **di·al·ling** 1 : to manipulate a dial so as to operate or select 2 : to make a telephone call or connection

³**dial** abbr dialect

di·a·lect \'dī-ə-ˌlekt\ n : a regional variety of a language

di·a·lec·tic \ˌdī-ə-'lek-tik\ n : the process or art of reasoning by discussion of conflicting ideas; also : the tension between opposing elements — **di·a·lec·ti·cal** \-ti-kəl\ adj

dialog box n : a window on a computer screen for choosing options or inputting information

di·a·logue \'dī-ə-ˌlòg\ n 1 : a conversation between two or more parties 2 : the parts of a literary or dramatic work that represent conversation

di·al·y·sis \dī-'a-lə-səs\ n, pl **-y·ses** \-ˌsēz\ 1 : the separation of substances from solution by means of their unequal diffusion through semipermeable membranes 2 : the medical procedure of removing blood from an artery, purifying it by dialysis, and returning it to a vein

diam abbr diameter

di·am·e·ter \dī-'a-mə-tər\ n [ME diametre, fr. MF, fr. L diametros, fr. Gk, fr. dia- through + metron measure] 1 : a straight line passing through the center of a figure or body; esp : one that divides a circle in half 2 : the length of a diameter

di·a·met·ric \ˌdī-ə-'me-trik\ or **di·a·met·ri·cal** \-tri-kəl\ adj 1 : of, relating to, or constituting a diameter 2 : completely opposed or opposite — **di·a·met·ri·cal·ly** \-k(ə-)lē\ adv

di·a·mond \'dī-mənd, 'dī-ə-\ n 1 : a hard brilliant mineral that consists of crystalline carbon and is used as a gem 2 : a flat figure having four equal sides, two acute angles, and two obtuse angles 3 : any of a suit of playing cards marked with a red diamond 4 : INFIELD; also : the entire playing field in baseball

di·a·mond·back rattlesnake \-ˌbak-\ n : either of two large and deadly rattlesnakes of the southern U.S.

di·an·thus \dī-'an-thəs\ n : ¹PINK 1

di·a·pa·son \ˌdī-ə-'pāz-ᵊn, -ˌsᵊn\ n 1 : the organ stop governing the flue pipes that form the primary basis of organ tone 2 : the entire range of musical tones

¹**di·a·per** \'dī-pər, 'dī-ə-\ n 1 : a cotton or linen fabric woven in a simple geometric pattern 2 : a garment for a baby drawn up between the legs and fastened about the waist

²**diaper** vb 1 : to ornament with diaper designs 2 : to put a diaper on

di·aph·a·nous \dī-'a-fə-nəs\ adj : of so fine a texture as to be transparent

di·a·pho·ret·ic \ˌdī-ə-fə-'re-tik\ adj : having the power to increase perspiration — **diaphoretic** n

di·a·phragm \'dī-ə-ˌfram\ n 1 : a sheet of muscle between the chest and abdominal cavities of a mammal 2 : a vibrating disk

(as in a microphone) 3 : a cup-shaped device usu. of thin rubber fitted over the uterine cervix to act as a mechanical contraceptive barrier — **di·a·phrag·mat·ic** \ˌdī-ə-frag-'ma-tik, -ˌfrag-\ adj

di·a·rist \'dī-ə-rist\ n : one who keeps a diary

di·a·ris·tic \ˌdī-ə-'ris-tik\ adj : of, relating to, or characteristic of a diary

di·ar·rhea \ˌdī-ə-'rē-ə\ n [ME diaria, fr. LL diarrhoea, fr. Gk diarrhoia, fr. diarhein to flow through, fr. dia- through + rhein to flow] : abnormally frequent and watery bowel movements — **di·ar·rhe·al** \-'rē-əl\ adj

di·ar·rhoea chiefly Brit var of DIARRHEA

di·a·ry \'dī-ə-rē\ n, pl **-ries** : a daily record esp. of personal experiences; also : a book used as a diary

di·as·po·ra \dī-'as-pə-rə\ n 1 cap : the settling of scattered colonies of Jews outside Palestine after the Babylonian exile 2 cap : the Jews living outside Palestine or modern Israel 3 : the migration or scattering of a people away from an ancestral homeland

di·as·to·le \dī-'as-tə-(ˌ)lē\ n : the stretching of the chambers of the heart during which they fill with blood — **di·a·stol·ic** \ˌdī-ə-'stä-lik\ adj

di·a·ther·my \'dī-ə-ˌthər-mē\ n : the generation of heat in tissue by electric currents for medical purposes

di·a·tom \'dī-ə-ˌtäm\ n : any of a class of planktonic one-celled or colonial algae with skeletons of silica

di·atom·ic \ˌdī-ə-'tä-mik\ adj : having two atoms in the molecule

di·a·tribe \'dī-ə-ˌtrīb\ n : biting or abusive speech or writing

di·az·e·pam \dī-'a-zə-ˌpam\ n : a tranquilizer used esp. to relieve anxiety, tension, and muscle spasms

dib·ble \'di-bəl\ n : a pointed hand tool for making holes (as for planting bulbs) in the ground — **dibble** vb

¹**dice** \'dīs\ n, pl **dice** : DIE 1

²**dice** vb **diced; dic·ing** 1 : to cut into small cubes ⟨~ carrots⟩ 2 : to play games with dice

di·chot·o·my \dī-'kä-tə-mē\ n, pl **-mies** : a division or the process of dividing into two esp. mutually exclusive or contradictory groups — **di·chot·o·mous** \-məs\ adj

dick·er \'di-kər\ vb : BARGAIN, HAGGLE

dick·ey or **dicky** \'di-kē\ n, pl **dickeys** or **dick·ies** : a small fabric insert worn to fill in the neckline

di·cot·y·le·don \ˌdī-ˌkä-tə-'lēd-ᵊn\ n : any of a group of seed plants having an embryo with two cotyledons — **di·cot·y·le·don·ous** adj

dict abbr dictionary

¹**dic·tate** \'dik-ˌtāt\ vb **dic·tat·ed; dic·tat·ing** 1 : to speak or read for a person to transcribe or for a machine to record 2 : COMMAND, ORDER — **dic·ta·tion** \dik-'tā-shən\ n

²**dic·tate** \'dik-ˌtāt\ n : an authoritative rule, prescription, or injunction : COMMAND ⟨the ~s of conscience⟩

dic·ta·tor \'dik-ˌtā-tər\ *n* **1** : a person ruling absolutely and often brutally and oppressively **2** : one that dictates

dic·ta·to·ri·al \ˌdik-tə-'tȯr-ē-əl\ *adj* : of, relating to, or characteristic of a dictator or a dictatorship

dic·ta·tor·ship \dik-'tā-tər-ˌship, 'dik-ˌtā-\ *n* **1** : the office of a dictator **2** : autocratic rule, control, or leadership **3** : a government or country in which absolute power is held by a dictator or a small clique

dic·tion \'dik-shən\ *n* **1** : choice of words esp. with regard to correctness, clearness, or effectiveness : WORDING **2** : ENUNCIATION

dic·tio·nary \'dik-shə-ˌner-ē\ *n, pl* **-nar·ies** : a reference book containing words usu. alphabetically arranged along with information about their forms, pronunciations, functions, etymologies, meanings, and syntactical and idiomatic uses

dic·tum \'dik-təm\ *n, pl* **dic·ta** \-tə\ *also* **dictums** : a noteworthy, formal, or authoritative statement or observation

did *past of* DO

di·dac·tic \dī-'dak-tik\ *adj* **1** : intended to instruct, inform, or teach a moral lesson **2** : making moral observations

di·do \'dī-dō\ *n, pl* **didoes** *or* **didos** : a mischievous act : PRANK

¹die \'dī\ *vb* **died; dy·ing** \'dī-iŋ\ [ME *dien,* fr. or akin to ON *deyja* to die] **1** : to stop living : EXPIRE **2** : to pass out of existence ⟨a *dying* race⟩ **3** : SUBSIDE **4** ⟨the wind *died* down⟩ **4** : to long keenly ⟨*dying* to go⟩ **5** : STOP ⟨the motor *died*⟩

²die \'dī\ *n* [ME *dee,* fr. AF *dé*] **1** *pl* **dice** \'dīs\ : a small cube marked on each face with one to six spots and used usu. in pairs in games and gambling **2** *pl* **dies** \'dīz\ : a device used to shape, finish, or impress an object

die·hard \'dī-ˌhärd\ *n* : one who is strongly devoted or determined — **die–hard** *adj*

dieresis *var of* DIAERESIS

die·sel \'dē-zəl, -səl\ *n* **1** : DIESEL ENGINE **2** : a vehicle driven by a diesel engine **3** : DIESEL FUEL

diesel engine *n* : an internal combustion engine in whose cylinders air is compressed to a temperature sufficiently high to ignite the fuel

diesel fuel *n* : a heavy mineral oil used as fuel in diesel engines

die·sel·ing \'dē-zə-liŋ\ *n* : the continued operation of an internal combustion engine after the ignition has been turned off

¹di·et \'dī-ət\ *n* [ME *diete,* fr. AF, fr. L *diaeta,* fr. Gk *diaita,* lit., manner of living, fr. *diaitasthai* to lead one's life] **1** : food and drink regularly consumed : FARE **2** : an allowance of food prescribed for a special reason (as to lose weight) — **di·e·tary** \-ə-ˌter-ē\ *adj or n*

²diet *vb* : to eat or cause to eat or drink less or according to a prescribed rule — **di·et·er** *n*

dietary supplement *n* : a product taken orally that contains ingredients (as vitamins or amino acids) intended to supplement one's diet

di·e·tet·ics \ˌdī-ə-'te-tiks\ *n sing or pl* : the science or art of applying the principles of nutrition to diet — **di·e·tet·ic** *adj*

di·e·ti·tian *or* **di·e·ti·cian** \ˌdī-ə-'ti-shən\ *n* : a specialist in dietetics

dif *or* **diff** *abbr* difference

dif·fer \'di-fər\ *vb* **dif·fered; dif·fer·ing** **1** : to be unlike **2** : VARY **3** : DISAGREE

dif·fer·ence \'di-frəns, 'di-fə-rəns\ *n* **1** : UNLIKENESS ⟨~ in their looks⟩ **2** : distinction or discrimination in preference **3** : DISAGREEMENT; *also* : an instance or cause of disagreement ⟨unable to settle their ~s⟩ **4** : the amount by which one number or quantity differs from another

dif·fer·ent \'di-frənt, 'di-fə-rənt\ *adj* **1** : unlike in nature or quality : DISTINCT ⟨~ age groups⟩; *also* : VARIOUS ⟨~ members of the club⟩ **3** : ANOTHER ⟨try a ~ channel⟩ **4** : UNUSUAL, SPECIAL — **dif·fer·ent·ly** *adv*

¹dif·fer·en·tial \ˌdi-fə-'ren-chəl\ *adj* : showing, creating, or relating to a difference

²differential *n* **1** : the amount or degree by which things differ **2** : an arrangement of gears in an automobile that allows one wheel to turn faster than another (as in rounding curves)

differential gear *n* : DIFFERENTIAL 2

dif·fer·en·ti·ate \ˌdi-fə-'ren-chē-ˌāt\ *vb* **-at·ed; -at·ing** **1** : to make or become different **2** : to attain a specialized adult form and function during development **3** : to recognize or state the difference ⟨~ between them⟩ — **dif·fer·en·ti·a·tion** \-ˌren-chē-'ā-shən\ *n*

dif·fi·cult \'di-fi-(ˌ)kəlt\ *adj* **1** : hard to do or make ⟨a ~ climb⟩ **2** : hard to understand or deal with ⟨~ reading⟩ ⟨a ~ child⟩

dif·fi·cul·ty \-(ˌ)kəl-tē\ *n, pl* **-ties** [ME *difficulte,* fr. AF *difficulté,* fr. L *difficilis* not easy, fr. *dis-* not + *facilis* easy] **1** : difficult nature ⟨the ~ of a task⟩ **2** : DISAGREEMENT ⟨settled their *difficulties*⟩ **3** : OBSTACLE ⟨overcome *difficulties*⟩ **4** : TROUBLE ⟨in financial *difficulties*⟩ **♦ Synonyms** HARDSHIP, RIGOR, VICISSITUDE

dif·fi·dent \'di-fə-dənt\ *adj* **1** : lacking confidence **2** : RESERVED 1 — **dif·fi·dence** \-dəns\ *n* — **dif·fi·dent·ly** *adv*

dif·frac·tion \di-'frak-shən\ *n* : the bending or spreading of waves (as of light) esp. when passing through narrow slits

¹dif·fuse \di-'fyüs\ *adj* **1** : VERBOSE, WORDY ⟨~ writing⟩ **2** : not concentrated or localized ⟨~ light⟩

²dif·fuse \di-'fyüz\ *vb* **dif·fused; dif·fus·ing** **1** : to pour out or spread widely **2** : to undergo or cause to undergo diffusion **3** : to break up light by diffusion

dif·fu·sion \di-'fyü-zhən\ *n* **1** : a diffusing or a being diffused **2** : movement of particles (as of a gas) from a region of high to one of lower concentration **3** : the reflection of light from a rough surface or the passage of light through a translucent material

¹dig \'dig\ *vb* **dug** \'dəg\; **dig·ging 1** : to turn up the soil (as with a spade) **2** : to hollow out or form by removing earth ⟨~ a hole⟩ **3** : to uncover or seek by turning up earth ⟨~ potatoes⟩ **4** : DISCOVER ⟨~ up information⟩ **5** : POKE, THRUST ⟨~ a person in the ribs⟩ **6** : to work hard **7** : UNDERSTAND, APPRECIATE; *also* : LIKE, ADMIRE

²dig *n* **1** : THRUST, POKE; *also* : a cutting remark : GIBE **2** *pl* : living or working accommodations

³dig *abbr* digest

¹di·gest \'dī-jest\ *n* : a summarized or shortened version esp. of a literary work

²di·gest \dī-'jest, də-\ *vb* **1** : to think over and arrange in the mind **2** : to convert (food) into simpler forms that can be absorbed by the body **3** : to compress into a short summary — **di·gest·ibil·i·ty** \-jes-tə-'bi-lə-tē\ *n* — **di·gest·ible** *adj* — **di·ges·tion** \-'jes-chən\ *n* — **di·ges·tive** \-'jes-tiv\ *adj*

di·ges·tif \dē-zhes-'tēf\ *n* : an alcoholic drink taken after a meal

dig in *vb* **1** : to take a defensive stand esp. by digging trenches **2** : to firmly set to work **3** : to begin eating

dig·it \'di-jət\ *n* [ME, fr. L *digitus* finger, toe] **1** : any of the Arabic numerals 1 to 9 and usu. the symbol 0 **2** : FINGER, TOE

dig·i·tal \'di-jə-tᵊl\ *adj* **1** : of, relating to, or done with a finger or toe **2** : of, relating to, or using calculation by numerical methods or by discrete units **3** : relating to or employing communications signals in the form of binary digits ⟨a ~ broadcast⟩ **4** : providing a readout in numerical digits ⟨a ~ watch⟩ **5** : ELECTRONIC; *also* : characterized by computerized technology ⟨the ~ age⟩ — **dig·i·tal·ly** *adv*

digital camera *n* : a camera that records images as digital data instead of on film

dig·i·tal·is \di-jə-'ta-ləs\ *n* : a drug from the common foxglove that is a powerful heart stimulant; *also* : FOXGLOVE

digital versatile disc *n* : DVD

digital video disc *n* : DVD

dig·ni·fied \'dig-nə-ˌfīd\ *adj* : showing or expressing dignity

dig·ni·fy \-ˌfī\ *vb* **-fied; -fy·ing** : to give dignity, distinction, or attention to

dig·ni·tary \'dig-nə-ˌter-ē\ *n, pl* **-tar·ies** : a person of high position or honor

dig·ni·ty \'dig-nə-tē\ *n, pl* **-ties 1** : the quality or state of being worthy, honored, or esteemed **2** : high rank, office, or position **3** : formal reserve of manner, language, or appearance

di·graph \'dī-ˌgraf\ *n* : a group of two successive letters whose phonetic value is a single sound (as *ea* in *bread*)

di·gress \dī-'gres, də-\ *vb* : to turn aside esp. from the main subject or argument — **di·gres·sion** \-'gre-shən\ *n* — **di·gres·sive** \-'gre-siv\ *adj*

Di·jon mustard \'dē-ˌzhän-, di-'zhän-\ *n* : a mustard made from dark mustard seeds, white wine, and spices

dike \'dīk\ *n* : a bank of earth constructed to control water : LEVEE

dil *abbr* dilute

di·lap·i·dat·ed \də-'la-pə-ˌdā-təd\ *adj* : fallen into partial ruin or decay — **di·lap·i·da·tion** \-ˌla-pə-'dā-shən\ *n*

di·late \dī-'lāt, 'dī-ˌlāt\ *vb* **di·lat·ed; di·lat·ing** : SWELL, DISTEND, EXPAND — **dil·a·ta·tion** \ˌdi-lə-'tā-shən\ *n* — **di·la·tion** \dī-'lā-shən\ *n*

dil·a·to·ry \'di-lə-ˌtȯr-ē\ *adj* **1** : DELAYING **2** : TARDY, SLOW

di·lem·ma \də-'le-mə\ *n* **1** : a usu. undesirable or unpleasant choice; *also* : a situation involving such a choice **2** : PREDICAMENT

dil·et·tante \ˌdi-lə-'tänt, -'tant\ *n, pl* **-tantes** *or* **-tan·ti** \-'tän-tē, -'tan-\ [It, fr. prp. of *dilettare* to delight, fr. L *dilectare*] : a person having a superficial interest in an art or a branch of knowledge

dil·i·gent \'di-lə-jənt\ *adj* : characterized by steady, earnest, and energetic effort : PAINSTAKING — **dil·i·gence** \-jəns\ *n* — **dil·i·gent·ly** *adv*

dill \'dil\ *n* : an herb related to the carrot with aromatic leaves and seeds used as a seasoning and in pickles

dil·ly \'di-lē\ *n, pl* **dil·lies** : one that is remarkable or outstanding

dil·ly·dal·ly \'di-lē-ˌda-lē\ *vb* : to waste time by loitering or delaying

¹di·lute \dī-'lüt, də-\ *vb* **di·lut·ed; di·lut·ing** : to lessen the consistency or strength of by mixing with something else — **di·lu·tion** \-'lü-shən\ *n*

²dilute *adj* : DILUTED, WEAK

¹dim \'dim\ *adj* **dim·mer; dim·mest 1** : LUSTERLESS, DULL ⟨~ colors⟩ **2** : not bright or distinct : OBSCURE, FAINT **3** : not seeing or understanding clearly — **dim·ly** *adv* — **dim·ness** *n*

²dim *vb* **dimmed; dim·ming 1** : to make or become dim or lusterless **2** : to reduce the light from

³dim *abbr* **1** dimension **2** diminished **3** diminutive

dime \'dīm\ *n* [ME, tenth part, tithe, fr. AF *disme, dime,* fr. L *decima,* fr. fem. of *decimus* tenth, fr. *decem* ten] : a U.S. coin worth ¹⁄₁₀ dollar

di·men·sion \də-'men-chən, dī-\ *n* **1** : the physical property of length, breadth, or thickness; *also* : a measure of this **2** : EXTENT, SCOPE, PROPORTIONS — usu. used in pl. — **di·men·sion·al** \-'men-chə-nəl\ *adj* — **di·men·sion·al·i·ty** \-ˌmen-chə-'na-lə-tē\ *n*

di·min·ish \də-'mi-nish\ *vb* **1** : to make less or cause to appear less **2** : BELITTLE **3** : DWINDLE **4** : TAPER — **dim·i·nu·tion** \ˌdi-mə-'nü-shən, -'nyü-\ *n*

di·min·u·en·do \də-ˌmin-yə-'wen-dō\ *adv or adj* : DECRESCENDO

¹di·min·u·tive \də-'min-yə-tiv\ *n* **1** : a diminutive word or affix **2** : a diminutive individual

²diminutive *adj* **1** : indicating small size and sometimes the state or quality of being lovable, pitiable, or contemptible ⟨the ~ suffixes *-ette* and *-ling*⟩ **2** : extremely small : TINY

dim·i·ty \'di-mə-tē\ *n, pl* **-ties** : a thin usu. corded cotton fabric

dim·mer \'di-mər\ *n* : a device for controlling the amount of light from an electric lighting unit

di·mor·phic \(ˌ)dī-'mȯr-fik\ *adj* : occurring in two distinct forms — **di·mor·phism** \-fi-zəm\ *n*

¹**dim·ple** \'dim-pəl\ *n* : a small depression esp. in the cheek or chin

²**dimple** *vb* **dim·pled; dim·pling** : to form dimples (as in smiling)

din \'din\ *n* : a loud confused mixture of noises

di·nar \di-'när\ *n* **1** — see MONEY table **2** — see *rial* at MONEY table

dine \'dīn\ *vb* **dined; din·ing** [ME, fr. AF *disner, diner* to eat, have a meal, fr. VL *disjejunare* to break one's fast, ultim. fr. L *jejunus* fasting] **1** : to eat dinner **2** : to give a dinner to

din·er \'dī-nər\ *n* **1** : one that dines **2** : a railroad dining car **3** : a restaurant usu. resembling a dining car

di·nette \dī-'net\ *n* : an alcove or small room used for dining

ding \'diŋ\ *vb* : to cause minor damage to a surface — **ding** *n*

din·ghy \'diŋ-ē\ *n, pl* **dinghies 1** : a small boat **2** : LIFE RAFT

din·gle \'diŋ-gəl\ *n* : a small wooded valley

din·go \'diŋ-gō\ *n, pl* **dingoes** : a reddish brown wild dog of Australia

din·gus \'diŋ-gəs, -əs\ *n* : DOODAD

din·gy \'din-jē\ *adj* **din·gi·er; -est** : DIRTY, UNCLEAN; *also* : SHABBY — **din·gi·ness** *n*

dink \'diŋk\ *n, often all cap* [*double income, no kids*] : a couple with two incomes and no children; *also* : a member of such a couple

din·ky \'diŋ-kē\ *adj* **din·ki·er; -est** : overly small \a ~ apartment\

din·ner \'di-nər\ *n* : the main meal of the day; *also* : a formal banquet

din·ner·ware \'di-nər-ˌwer\ *n* : tableware other than flatware

di·no \'dī-nō\ *n, pl* **dinos** : DINOSAUR

di·no·fla·gel·late \ˌdī-nō-'fla-jə-lət, -ˌlāt\ *n* : any of an order of planktonic plant-like unicellular flagellates of which some cause red tide

di·no·saur \'dī-nə-ˌsȯr\ *n* [ultim. fr. Gk *deinos* terrifying + *sauros* lizard] : any of a group of extinct long-tailed Mesozoic reptiles often of huge size

dint \'dint\ *n* **1** : FORCE \by ~ of sheer grit\ **2** : DENT

di·o·cese \'dī-ə-səs, -ˌsēz, -ˌsēs\ *n, pl* **-ces·es** \-sə-səz, -ˌsē-zəz, -ˌsē-səz\ : the territorial jurisdiction of a bishop — **di·oc·e·san** \dī-'ä-sə-sən, ˌdī-ə-'sē-z²n\ *adj or n*

di·ode \'dī-ˌōd\ *n* : an electronic device with two electrodes or terminals used esp. as a rectifier

di·ox·in \dī-'äk-sən\ *n* : a persistent toxic hydrocarbon that occurs esp. as a by-product of industrial processes and waste incineration

¹**dip** \'dip\ *vb* **dipped; dip·ping 1** : to plunge temporarily or partially under the surface (as of a liquid) **2** : to thrust in a way to suggest immersion **3** : to scoop up or out : LADLE **4** : to lower and then raise quickly \~ a flag in salute\ **5** : to drop or slope down esp. suddenly \the moon *dipped* below the crest\ **6** : to decrease moderately and usu. temporarily \prices *dipped*\ **7** : to reach inside or as if inside or below a surface *dipped* into their savings\ **8** : to delve casually into something; *esp* : to read superficially \~ into a book\

²**dip** *n* **1** : an act of dipping; *esp* : a short swim **2** : inclination downward : DROP **3** : something obtained by or used in dipping **4** : a sauce or soft mixture into which food may be dipped **5** : a liquid into which something may be dipped (as for cleansing or coloring)

diph·the·ria \dif-'thir-ē-ə\ *n* : an acute contagious bacterial disease marked by fever and by coating of the air passages with a membrane that interferes with breathing

diph·thong \'dif-ˌthȯŋ, 'dip-\ *n* : two vowel sounds joined in one syllable to form one speech sound (as *ou* in *out*)

dip·loid \'di-ˌplȯid\ *adj* : having two haploid sets of chromosomes \~ somatic cells\ — **diploid** *n*

di·plo·ma \də-'plō-mə\ *n* : an official record of graduation from or of a degree conferred by a school

di·plo·ma·cy \də-'plō-mə-sē\ *n* **1** : the art and practice of conducting negotiations between nations **2** : TACT

dip·lo·mat \'di-plə-ˌmat\ *n* : one employed or skilled in diplomacy — **dip·lo·mat·ic** \ˌdi-plə-'ma-tik\ *adj*

di·plo·ma·tist \də-'plō-mə-tist\ *n* : DIPLOMAT

dip·per \'di-pər\ *n* **1** : any of a genus of birds that are related to the thrushes and are skilled in diving **2** : something (as a ladle or scoop) that dips or is used for dipping **3** *cap* : BIG DIPPER **4** *cap* : LITTLE DIPPER

dip·so·ma·nia \ˌdip-sə-'mā-nē-ə\ *n* : an uncontrollable craving for alcoholic liquors — **dip·so·ma·ni·ac** \-nē-ˌak\ *n*

dip·stick \'dip-ˌstik\ *n* : a graduated rod for indicating depth

dip·ter·an \'dip-tə-rən\ *adj* : of, relating to, or being a fly (sense 2) — **dipteran** *n* — **dip·ter·ous** \-rəs\ *adj*

dir *abbr* **1** direction **2** director

di·ram \dē-'ram\ *n* — see *somoni* at MONEY table

dire \'dī(-ə)r\ *adj* **dir·er; dir·est 1** : very horrible : DREADFUL \~ suffering\ **2** : warning of disaster : OMINOUS \~ poverty\ **3** : EXTREME \~

¹**di·rect** \də-'rekt, dī-\ *vb* **1** : ADDRESS \~ a letter\; *also* : to impart orally : AIM \~ a remark to the gallery\ **2** : to regulate the activities or course of : guide the supervision, organizing, or performance of **3** : to cause to turn, move, or point or to follow a certain course **4** : to point, extend, or project in a specified line or course **5** : to request or instruct with authority **6** : to show or point out the way

²**direct** *adj* **1** : stemming immediately from a source ⟨∼ result⟩ **2** : being or passing in a straight line of descent : LINEAL ⟨∼ ancestor⟩ **3** : leading from one point to another in time or space without turn or stop : STRAIGHT **4** : NATURAL, STRAIGHTFORWARD ⟨a ∼ manner⟩ **5** : operating without an intervening agency or step ⟨∼ action⟩ **6** : effected by the action of the people or the electorate and not by representatives ⟨∼ democracy⟩ **7** : consisting of or reproducing the exact words of a speaker or writer — **direct** *adv* — **di·rect·ly** *adv* — **di·rect·ness** *n*

direct broadcast satellite *n* : a television broadcasting system in which satellite transmissions are received at the viewing location

direct current *n* : an electric current flowing in one direction only

direct deposit *n* : a method of payment in which money is transferred to the payee's account without the use of checks or cash

di·rec·tion \də-ˈrek-shən, dī-\ *n* **1** : MANAGEMENT, GUIDANCE **2** : COMMAND, ORDER, INSTRUCTION **3** : the course or line along which something moves, lies, or points **4** : TENDENCY, TREND — **di·rec·tion·al** \-shə-nəl\ *adj*

di·rec·tive \də-ˈrek-tiv, dī-\ *n* : something that directs and usu. implies toward an action or goal; *esp* : an order issued by a high-level body or official

direct mail *n* : printed matter used for soliciting business or contributions and mailed direct to individuals

di·rec·tor \də-ˈrek-tər, dī-\ *n* **1** : one that directs : MANAGER, SUPERVISOR, CONDUCTOR **2** : one of a group of persons who direct the affairs of an organized body — **di·rec·to·ri·al** \-ˌrek-ˈtōr-ē-əl\ *adj* — **di·rec·tor·ship** *n*

di·rec·tor·ate \-tə-rət\ *n* **1** : the office or position of director **2** : a board of directors; *also* : membership on such a board **3** : an executive staff

director's cut *n* : a version of a motion picture that is edited according to the director's wishes

di·rec·to·ry \-tə-rē\ *n, pl* **-ries** **1** : an alphabetical or classified list esp. of names and addresses **2** : FOLDER 4

dire·ful \ˈdī(-ə)r-fəl\ *adj* : DREADFUL; *also* : OMINOUS

dirge \ˈdərj\ *n* [ME *dirige* church service for the dead, fr. the first word of a LL anthem, fr. L, imper. of *dirigere* to direct] : a song of lamentation; *also* : a slow mournful piece of music

dir·ham \ˈdir-həm\ *n* **1** — see MONEY table **2** — see *dinar, riyal* at MONEY table

di·ri·gi·ble \ˈdir-ə-jə-bəl, də-ˈri-jə-\ *n* : AIRSHIP

dirk \ˈdərk\ *n* : DAGGER 1

dirndl \ˈdərn-dᵊl\ *n* [short for G *Dirndlkleid*, fr. G dial. *Dirndl* girl + G *Kleid* dress] : a full skirt with a tight waistband

dirt \ˈdərt\ *n* **1** : a filthy or soiling substance (as mud, dust, or grime) **2** : loose or packed earth : SOIL **3** : moral uncleanness **4** : scandalous gossip **5** : embarrassing or incriminating information

¹**dirty** \ˈdər-tē\ *adj* **dirt·i·er; -est** **1** : SOILED, FILTHY **2** : INDECENT, SMUTTY ⟨∼ jokes⟩ **3** : BASE, UNFAIR ⟨a ∼ trick⟩ **4** : STORMY, FOGGY ⟨∼ weather⟩ **5** : not clear in color : DULL ⟨a ∼ red⟩ — **dirt·i·ness** *n* — **dirty** *adv*

²**dirty** *vb* **dirt·ied; dirty·ing** : to make or become dirty

dis·able \di-ˈsā-bəl\ *vb* **dis·abled; disabling** **1** : to disqualify legally **2** : to make unable to perform by or as if by illness, injury, or malfunction — **dis·abil·i·ty** \ˌdi-sə-ˈbi-lə-tē\ *n*

dis·abled *adj* : incapacitated by illness or injury; *also* : physically or mentally impaired

dis·abuse \ˌdi-sə-ˈbyüz\ *vb* : to free from error, fallacy, or misconception

dis·ad·van·tage \ˌdi-səd-ˈvan-tij\ *n* **1** : loss or damage esp. to reputation or finances **2** : an unfavorable, inferior, or prejudicial condition, quality, or circumstance — **dis·ad·van·ta·geous** \di-ˌsad-ˌvan-ˈtā-jəs, -vən-\ *adj*

dis·ad·van·taged \-tijd\ *adj* : lacking in basic resources or conditions believed necessary for an equal position in society

dis·af·fect \ˌdi-sə-ˈfekt\ *vb* : to alienate the affection or loyalty of — **dis·af·fec·tion** \-ˈfek-shən\ *n*

dis·agree \ˌdi-sə-ˈgrē\ *vb* **1** : to fail to agree **2** : to differ in opinion **3** : to cause discomfort or distress ⟨fried foods ∼ with her⟩ — **dis·agree·ment** *n*

dis·agree·able \-ə-bəl\ *adj* **1** : causing discomfort : UNPLEASANT, OFFENSIVE ⟨a ∼ odor⟩ **2** : ILL-TEMPERED, PEEVISH — **dis·agree·able·ness** *n* — **dis·agree·ably** \-blē\ *adv*

dis·al·low \ˌdis-ə-ˈlau̇\ *vb* : to refuse to admit or recognize : REJECT ⟨∼ a claim⟩ — **dis·al·low·ance** *n*

dis·ap·pear \ˌdis-ə-ˈpir\ *vb* **1** : to pass out of sight **2** : to cease to be : become lost — **dis·ap·pear·ance** *n*

dis·ap·point \ˌdis-ə-ˈpȯint\ *vb* : to fail to fulfill the expectation or hope of — **dis·ap·point·ment** *n*

dis·ap·pro·ba·tion \dis-ˌa-prə-ˈbā-shən\ *n* : DISAPPROVAL

dis·ap·prov·al \ˌdis-ə-ˈprü-vəl\ *n* : adverse judgment : CENSURE

dis·ap·prove \-ˈprüv\ *vb* **1** : CONDEMN **2** : to feel or express disapproval ⟨∼s of smoking⟩ **3** : REJECT — **dis·ap·prov·ing·ly** \-ˈprü-viŋ-lē\ *adv*

dis·arm \dis-ˈärm\ *vb* **1** : to take arms or weapons from **2** : to reduce the size and strength of the armed forces of a country **3** : to make harmless, peaceable, or friendly : win over ⟨a ∼ing smile⟩ — **dis·ar·ma·ment** \-ˈär-mə-mənt\ *n*

dis·ar·range \ˌdis-ə-ˈrānj\ *vb* : to disturb the arrangement or order of — **dis·ar·range·ment** *n*

dis·ar·ray \-ˈrā\ *n* **1** : DISORDER, CONFUSION **2** : disorderly or careless dress

dis·as·sem·ble \ˌdis-ə-ˈsem-bəl\ *vb* : to take apart

dis·as·so·ci·ate \-'sō-shē-ˌāt, -sē-\ *vb* : to detach from association

di·sas·ter \di-'zas-tər, -'sas-\ *n* [MF *desastre,* fr. It *disastro,* fr. *astro* star, fr. L *astrum*] : a sudden or great misfortune — **di·sas·trous** \-'zas-trəs\ *adj* — **di·sas·trous·ly** *adv*

dis·avow \ˌdis-ə-'vau̇\ *vb* : to deny responsibility for : REPUDIATE — **dis·avow·al** \-'vau̇(-ə)l\ *n*

dis·band \dis-'band\ *vb* : to break up the organization of : DISPERSE

dis·bar \dis-'bär\ *vb* : to expel from the legal profession — **dis·bar·ment** *n*

dis·be·lieve \ˌdis-bə-'lēv\ *vb* 1 : to hold not worthy of belief : not believe 2 : to withhold or reject belief — **dis·be·lief** \-'lēf\ *n* — **dis·be·liev·er** *n*

dis·bur·den \dis-'bər-dⁿn\ *vb* : to rid of a burden

dis·burse \dis-'bərs\ *vb* **dis·bursed; dis·burs·ing** 1 : to pay out : EXPEND 2 : DISTRIBUTE — **dis·burse·ment** *n*

¹disc *var of* DISK

²disc *abbr* discount

dis·card \dis-'kärd, 'dis-ˌkärd\ *vb* 1 : to let go a playing card from one's hand; *also* : to play (a card) from a suit other than a trump but different from the one led 2 : to get rid of as unwanted — **discard** \'dis-ˌkärd\ *n*

disc brake *n* : a brake that operates by the friction of a pair of plates pressing against the sides of a rotating disc

dis·cern \di-'sərn, -'zərn\ *vb* 1 : to detect with the eyes : DISTINGUISH 2 : DISCRIMINATE 3 : to come to know or recognize mentally — **dis·cern·ible** *adj* — **dis·cern·ment** *n*

dis·cern·ing *adj* : revealing insight and understanding

¹dis·charge \dis-'chärj, 'dis-ˌchärj\ *vb* 1 : to relieve of a charge, load, or burden : UNLOAD; *esp* : to remove the electrical energy from ⟨~ a storage battery⟩ 2 : to let or put off ⟨~ passengers⟩ 3 : SHOOT ⟨~ an arrow⟩ 4 : to set free ⟨~ a prisoner⟩ 5 : to dismiss from service or employment ⟨~ a soldier⟩ 6 : to get rid of by paying or doing ⟨~ a debt⟩ 7 : to give forth fluid ⟨the river ~s into the ocean⟩

²dis·charge \'dis-ˌchärj, dis-'chärj\ *n* 1 : the act of discharging, unloading, or releasing 2 : something that discharges; *esp* : a certification of release or payment 3 : a firing off (as of a gun) 4 : a flowing out (as of blood from a wound); *also* : something that is emitted ⟨a purulent ~⟩ 5 : release or dismissal esp. from an office or employment; *also* : complete separation from military service 6 : a flow of electricity (as through a gas)

dis·ci·ple \di-'sī-pəl\ *n* [ultim. fr. LL *discipulus* follower of Jesus in his lifetime, fr. L, pupil] 1 : one who accepts and helps to spread the teachings of another; *also* : a convinced adherent 2 *cap* : a member of the Disciples of Christ

dis·ci·pli·nar·i·an \ˌdi-sə-plə-'ner-ē-ən\ *n* : one who enforces order

dis·ci·plin·ary \'di-sə-plə-ˌner-ē\ *adj* : of or relating to discipline; *also* : CORRECTIVE ⟨take ~ action⟩

¹dis·ci·pline \'di-sə-plən\ *n* 1 : PUNISHMENT 2 : a field of study : SUBJECT 3 : training that corrects, molds, or perfects 4 : control gained by obedience or training : orderly conduct 5 : a system of rules governing conduct

²discipline *vb* **-plined; -plin·ing** 1 : PUNISH 2 : to train or develop by instruction and exercise esp. in self-control 3 : to bring under control ⟨~ troops⟩; *also* : to impose order upon

disc jockey *or* **disk jockey** *n* : an announcer of a radio show of popular recorded music

dis·claim \dis-'klām\ *vb* : DENY, DISAVOW — **dis·claim·er** *n*

dis·close \dis-'klōz\ *vb* : to expose to view — **dis·clo·sure** \-'klō-zhər\ *n*

dis·co \'dis-kō\ *n, pl* **discos** 1 : a nightclub for dancing to live or recorded music 2 : popular dance music characterized by hypnotic rhythm, repetitive lyrics, and electronically produced sounds

dis·col·or \dis-'kə-lər\ *vb* : to alter or change in hue or color esp. for the worse — **dis·col·or·ation** \-ˌkə-lə-'rā-shən\ *n*

dis·com·bob·u·late \ˌdis-kəm-'bä-byù-ˌlāt\ *vb* **-lat·ed; -lat·ing** : UPSET, CONFUSE

dis·com·fit \dis-'kəm-fət, *esp Southern* ˌdis-kəm-'fit\ *vb* : UPSET, FRUSTRATE — **dis·com·fi·ture** \dis-'kəm-fə-ˌchùr\ *n*

¹dis·com·fort \dis-'kəm-fərt\ *vb* : to make uncomfortable or uneasy

²discomfort *n* : mental or physical uneasiness

dis·com·mode \ˌdis-kə-'mōd\ *vb* **-mod·ed; -mod·ing** : INCONVENIENCE, TROUBLE

dis·com·pose \-kəm-'pōz\ *vb* 1 : to destroy the calmness or peace of 2 : DISARRANGE — **dis·com·po·sure** \-'pō-zhər\ *n*

dis·con·cert \ˌdis-kən-'sərt\ *vb* : CONFUSE, UPSET

dis·con·nect \ˌdis-kə-'nekt\ *vb* : to undo the connection of — **dis·con·nec·tion** \-'nek-shən\ *n*

dis·con·nect·ed *adj* : not connected; *also* : INCOHERENT — **dis·con·nect·ed·ly** *adv* — **dis·con·nect·ed·ness** *n*

dis·con·so·late \dis-'kän-sə-lət\ *adj* 1 : CHEERLESS 2 : hopelessly sad — **dis·con·so·late·ly** *adv*

dis·con·tent \ˌdis-kən-'tent\ *n* : uneasiness of mind : DISSATISFACTION — **dis·con·tent·ed** *adj*

dis·con·tin·ue \ˌdis-kən-'tin-yü\ *vb* 1 : to break the continuity of : cease to operate, use, or take 2 : END — **dis·con·tin·u·ance** \-yə-wəns\ *n* — **dis·con·ti·nu·i·ty** \dis-ˌkän-tə-'nü-ə-tē, -ˌkän-\ *n* — **dis·con·tin·u·ous** \ˌdis-kən-'tin-yə-wəs\ *adj*

dis·cord \'dis-ˌkȯrd\ *n* 1 : lack of agreement or harmony : DISSENSION, CONFLICT 2 : a harsh combination of musical sounds 3 : a harsh or unpleasant sound — **dis·cor·dant** \dis-'kȯr-d°nt\ adj — **dis·cor·dant·ly** adv

dis·co·theque or discothèque \'dis-kə-ˌtek\ n : DISCO 1

¹dis·count \'dis-ˌkaùnt\ n 1 : a reduction made from a regular or list price 2 : a deduction of interest in advance when lending money

²dis·count \'dis-ˌkaùnt, dis-'kaùnt\ vb 1 : to deduct from the amount of a bill, debt, or charge usu. for cash or prompt payment; also : to sell or offer for sale at a discount 2 : to lend money after deducting the discount ⟨~ a note⟩ 3 : DISREGARD; also : MINIMIZE 4 : to make allowance for bias or exaggeration 5 : to take into account (as a future event) in present calculations — **dis·count·able** adj — **dis·count·er** n

³dis·count \'dis-ˌkaùnt\ adj : selling goods or services at a discount; also : sold at or reflecting a discount

dis·coun·te·nance \dis-'kaùn-tə-nənts\ vb 1 : EMBARRASS, DISCONCERT 2 : to look with disfavor on

dis·cour·age \dis-'kər-ij\ vb -aged; -ag·ing 1 : to deprive of courage or confidence : DISHEARTEN 2 : to hinder by disfavoring 3 : to attempt to dissuade — **dis·cour·age·ment** n — **dis·cour·ag·ing·ly** adv

¹dis·course \'dis-ˌkȯrs\ n [ME discours, fr. ML & LL discursus; ML, argument, fr. LL, conversation, fr. L, act of running about, fr. discurrere to run about, fr. currere to run] 1 : CONVERSATION 2 : formal and usu. extended expression of thought on a subject

²dis·course \'dis-ˌkȯrs\ vb dis·coursed; dis·cours·ing 1 : to express oneself in esp. oral discourse 2 : TALK, CONVERSE

dis·cour·te·ous \(ˌ)dis-'kər-tē-əs\ adj : lacking courtesy : UNCIVIL, RUDE — **dis·cour·te·ous·ly** adv

dis·cour·te·sy \-'kər-tə-sē\ n : RUDENESS; also : a rude act

dis·cov·er \dis-'kə-vər\ vb 1 : to make known or visible 2 : to obtain sight or knowledge of for the first time; also : FIND OUT — **dis·cov·er·er** n

dis·cov·ery \dis-'kə-və-rē\ n, pl -er·ies 1 : the act or process of discovering 2 : something discovered 3 : the disclosure usu. before a civil trial of pertinent facts or documents

¹dis·cred·it \(ˌ)dis-'kre-dət\ vb 1 : DISBELIEVE 2 : to cause disbelief in the accuracy or authority of 3 : DISGRACE — **dis·cred·it·able** adj

²discredit n 1 : loss of reputation 2 : lack or loss of belief or confidence

dis·creet \dis-'krēt\ adj : showing good judgment; esp : capable of observing prudent silence — **dis·creet·ly** adv

dis·crep·an·cy \dis-'kre-pən-sē\ n, pl -cies 1 : DIFFERENCE, DISAGREEMENT 2 : an instance of being discrepant

dis·crep·ant \-pənt\ adj [ME discrepaunt, fr. L discrepans, prp. of discrepare to sound discordantly, fr. discrepare to rattle, creak] : being at variance : DISAGREEING ⟨~ conclusions⟩

dis·crete \dis-'krēt, 'dis-ˌkrēt\ adj 1 : individually distinct ⟨several ~ sections⟩ 2 : NONCONTINUOUS

dis·cre·tion \dis-'kre-shən\ n 1 : the quality of being discreet : PRUDENCE 2 : individual choice or judgment ⟨left the decision to his ~⟩ 3 : power of free decision or latitude of choice — **dis·cre·tion·ary** adj

dis·crim·i·nate \dis-'kri-mə-ˌnāt\ vb -nat·ed; -nat·ing 1 : DISTINGUISH, DIFFERENTIATE 2 : to make a difference in treatment on a basis other than individual merit — **dis·crim·i·na·tion** \-ˌkri-mə-'nā-shən\ n

dis·crim·i·nat·ing adj : marked by discrimination; esp : DISCERNING, JUDICIOUS — **dis·crim·i·nat·ing·ly** adv

dis·crim·i·na·to·ry \dis-'kri-mə-nə-ˌtȯr-ē\ adj : marked by esp. unjust discrimination ⟨~ treatment⟩

dis·cur·sive \dis-'kər-siv\ adj : passing from one topic to another : RAMBLING — **dis·cur·sive·ly** adv — **dis·cur·sive·ness** n

dis·cus \'dis-kəs\ n, pl **dis·cus·es** : a heavy disk that is hurled for distance in a track-and-field contest

dis·cuss \di-'skəs\ vb [ME, fr. AF discusser, fr. L discussus, pp. of discutere to disperse, fr. dis- apart + quatere to shake] 1 : to argue or consider carefully by presenting the various sides 2 : to talk about — **dis·cus·sion** \-'skə-shən\ n

dis·cus·sant \di-'skə-s°nt\ n : one who takes part in a formal discussion

¹dis·dain \dis-'dān\ n : CONTEMPT, SCORN — **dis·dain·ful** \-fəl\ adj — **dis·dain·ful·ly** adv

²disdain vb 1 : to look on with scorn 2 : to reject or refrain from because of disdain

dis·ease \di-'zēz\ n : an abnormal bodily condition that impairs normal functioning and can usu. be recognized by signs and symptoms : SICKNESS — **dis·eased** \-'zēzd\ adj

dis·em·bark \ˌdi-səm-'bärk\ vb : to go or put ashore from a ship — **dis·em·bar·ka·tion** \di-ˌsem-ˌbär-'kā-shən\ n

dis·em·body \ˌdi-səm-'bä-dē\ vb : to deprive of bodily existence

dis·em·bow·el \-'baú-(ə)l\ vb : EVISCERATE 1 — **dis·em·bow·el·ment** n

dis·em·pow·er \ˌdis-im-'paú-(ə)r\ vb : to deprive of power, authority, or influence

dis·en·chant \ˌdis-in-'chant\ vb : DISILLUSION — **dis·en·chant·ment** \-mənt\ n

dis·en·chant·ed \-'chan-təd\ adj : DISAPPOINTED, DISSATISFIED

dis·en·cum·ber \ˌdis-°n-'kəm-bər\ vb : to free from something that burdens

dis·en·fran·chise \ˌdis-in-'fran-ˌchīz\ vb : to deprive of a franchise, a legal right, or a privilege; esp : to deprive of the right to vote — **dis·en·fran·chise·ment** n

dis·en·gage \ˌdis-°n-'gāj\ vb : RELEASE, EXTRICATE, DISENTANGLE — **dis·en·gage·ment** n

dis·en·gaged \-'gājd\ adj : IMPARTIAL, DETACHED ⟨a ~ observer⟩

dis·en·tan·gle \,dis-in-'taⁿ-gəl\ vb : to free from entanglement : UNRAVEL

dis·equi·lib·ri·um \dis-,ē-kwə-'li-brē-əm\ n : loss or lack of equilibrium

dis·es·tab·lish \dis-ə-'sta-blish\ vb : to end the establishment of; esp : to deprive of the status of an established church — **dis·es·tab·lish·ment** n

dis·es·teem \,dis-ə-'stēm\ n : lack of esteem : DISFAVOR, DISREPUTE

dis·fa·vor \(,)dis-'fā-vər\ n 1 : DISAPPROVAL, DISLIKE 2 : the state or fact of being no longer favored

dis·fig·ure \dis-'fi-gyər\ vb : to spoil the appearance of ⟨disfigured by a scar⟩ — **dis·fig·ure·ment** n

dis·fran·chise \dis-'fran-,chīz\ vb : DISENFRANCHISE — **dis·fran·chise·ment** n

disfunction var of DYSFUNCTION

dis·gorge \-'górj\ vb : VOMIT; also : to discharge forcefully or confusedly

¹**dis·grace** \di-'skrās, dis-'grās\ vb : to bring reproach or shame to

²**disgrace** n 1 : SHAME, DISHONOR; also : a cause of shame 2 : the condition of being out of favor : loss of respect — **dis·grace·ful** \-fəl\ adj — **dis·grace·ful·ly** adv

dis·grun·tle \dis-'grən-tᵊl\ vb **dis·gruntled**; **dis·grun·tling** : to put in bad humor

¹**dis·guise** \dis-'gīz\ vb **dis·guised**; **dis·guis·ing** 1 : to change the appearance of so as to conceal the identity or to resemble another 2 : HIDE, CONCEAL

²**disguise** n 1 : clothing put on to conceal one's identity or counterfeit another's 2 : an outward appearance that hides what something really is

¹**dis·gust** \dis-'gəst\ n : AVERSION, REPUGNANCE — **dis·gust·ful** \-fəl\ adj

²**disgust** vb : to provoke to loathing, repugnance, or aversion : be offensive to — **dis·gust·ed·ly** adv — **dis·gust·ing** \-'gəs-tiŋ\ adj — **dis·gust·ing·ly** adv

¹**dish** \'dish\ n [ME, fr. OE disc plate, fr. L discus quoit, disk, dish, fr. Gk diskos, fr. dikein to throw] 1 : a vessel used for serving food 2 : the food served in a dish ⟨a ~ of berries⟩ 3 : food prepared in a particular way 4 : something resembling a dish esp. in being shallow and concave 5 : SATELLITE DISH 6 : GOSSIP 2

²**dish** vb 1 : to put into a dish 2 : to make concave like a dish 3 : GOSSIP

dis·ha·bille \,di-sə-'bēl\ or **des·ha·bille** \,de-\ n [F déshabillé] : the state of being dressed in a casual or careless manner

dis·har·mo·ny \(,)dis-'här-mə-nē\ n : lack of harmony — **dis·har·mo·ni·ous** \,dis-(,)här-'mō-nē-əs\ adj

dish·cloth \'dish-,klóth\ n : a cloth for washing dishes

dis·heart·en \dis-'här-tᵊn\ vb : DISCOURAGE, DEJECT

dished \'disht\ adj : CONCAVE

di·shev·el \di-'she-vəl\ vb **-shev·eled** or **-shev·elled**; **-shev·el·ing** or **-shev·el·ling** [ME discheveled bareheaded, with disordered hair, fr. AF deschevelé, fr. des- apart + chevoil hair, fr. L capillus] : to

throw into disorder or disarray — **di·shev·eled** or **di·shev·elled** adj — **dishev·el·ment** \-mənt\ n

dis·hon·est \di-'sä-nəst\ adj : not honest : UNTRUSTWORTHY, DECEITFUL — **dis·hon·est·ly** adv — **dis·hon·es·ty** \-nə-stē\ n

¹**dis·hon·or** \dish-'ä-nər\ n 1 : lack or loss of honor 2 : SHAME, DISGRACE 3 : a cause of disgrace 4 : the act of dishonoring a negotiable instrument when presented for payment — **dis·hon·or·able** \dis-'ä-nə-rə-bəl\ adj — **dis·hon·or·ably** \-blē\ adv

²**dishonor** vb 1 : DISGRACE 2 : to refuse to accept or pay ⟨~ a check⟩

dish out vb : to give freely

dish·rag \'dish-,rag\ n : DISHCLOTH

dish·wash·er \-,wó-shər, -,wä-\ n : a person or machine that washes dishes

dish·wa·ter \-,wó-tər, -,wä-\ n : water used for washing dishes

dis·il·lu·sion \dis-ə-'lü-zhən\ vb : to free from illusion — **dis·il·lu·sion·ment** n

dis·il·lu·sioned adj : DISAPPOINTED, DISSATISFIED

dis·in·cli·na·tion \dis-,in-klə-'nā-shən\ n : a preference for avoiding something : slight aversion

dis·in·cline \,dis-in-'klīn\ vb : to make unwilling

dis·in·clined adj : unwilling because of dislike or disapproval

dis·in·fect \dis-in-'fekt\ vb : to cleanse of infection-causing germs — **dis·in·fec·tant** \-'fek-tənt\ n — **dis·in·fec·tion** \-'fek-shən\ n

dis·in·for·ma·tion \-,in-fər-'mā-shən\ n : false information deliberately and often covertly spread

dis·in·gen·u·ous \dis-in-'jen-yə-wəs\ adj : lacking in candor; also : giving a false appearance of simple frankness

dis·in·her·it \dis-in-'her-ət\ vb : to deprive of the right to inherit

dis·in·te·grate \dis-'in-tə-,grāt\ vb 1 : to break or decompose into constituent parts or small particles 2 : to destroy the unity or integrity of — **dis·in·te·gra·tion** \-,in-tə-'grā-shən\ n

dis·in·ter \dis-in-'tər\ vb 1 : to take from the grave or tomb 2 : UNEARTH

dis·in·ter·est·ed \(,)dis-'in-tə-rəs-təd, -,res-\ adj 1 : not interested 2 : free from selfish motive or interest : UNBIASED — **dis·in·ter·est·ed·ness** n

dis·join \(,)dis-'jóin\ vb : SEPARATE

dis·joint \(,)dis-'jóint\ vb : to disturb the orderly arrangement of; also : to separate at the joints

dis·joint·ed adj 1 : INCOHERENT ⟨~ conversation⟩ 2 : separated at or as if at the joint

disk or **disc** \'disk\ n 1 : something round and flat; esp : a flat rounded anatomical structure (as the central part of the flower head of a composite plant or a pad of cartilage between vertebrae) 2 usu disc : a phonograph record 3 : a round flat plate coated with a magnetic substance on which data for a computer is stored **4** *usu disc* : OPTICAL DISK

disk drive *n* : a device for accessing or storing data on a magnetic disk

dis·kette \dis-'ket\ *n* : FLOPPY DISK

disk jockey *var of* DISC JOCKEY

¹**dis·like** \(₁)dis-'līk\ *n* : a feeling of aversion or disapproval

²**dislike** *vb* : to regard with dislike : DISAPPROVE

dis·lo·cate \'dis-lō-₁kāt, dis-'lō-\ *vb* **1** : to put out of place; *esp* : to displace (a bone or joint) from normal connections ⟨~ a shoulder⟩ **2** : DISRUPT — **dis·lo·ca·tion** \₁dis-(₁)lō-'kā-shən\ *n*

dis·lodge \(₁)dis-'läj\ *vb* : to force out of a place esp. of rest, hiding, or defense

dis·loy·al \(₁)dis-'lȯi(-ə)l\ *adj* : lacking in loyalty — **dis·loy·al·ty** *n*

dis·mal \'diz-məl\ *adj* [ME, fr. *dismal*, n., days marked as unlucky in medieval calendars, fr. AF, fr. ML *dies mali*, lit., evil days] **1** : showing or causing gloom or depression **2** : lacking merit — **dis·mal·ly** *adv*

dis·man·tle \(₁)dis-'man-t²l\ *vb* **-tled**; **-tling 1** : to take apart **2** : to strip of furniture and equipment — **dis·man·tle·ment** *n*

dis·may \dis-'mā\ *vb* : to cause to lose courage or resolution from alarm or fear : DAUNT — **dismay** *n* — **dis·may·ing·ly** *adv*

dis·mem·ber \dis-'mem-bər\ *vb* **1** : to cut off or separate the limbs or parts of **2** : to break up or tear into pieces — **dis·mem·ber·ment** *n*

dis·miss \dis-'mis\ *vb* **1** : to send away **2** : DISCHARGE 5 **3** : to put aside or out of mind **4** : to put out of judicial consideration ⟨~ed all charges⟩ — **dis·miss·al** *n* — **dis·mis·sive** \-'mi-siv\ *adj* — **dis·mis·sive·ly** *adv*

dis·mount \dis-'maȯnt\ *vb* **1** : to get down from something (as a horse or bicycle) **2** : UNHORSE **3** : DISASSEMBLE

dis·obe·di·ence \₁dis-ə-'bē-dē-əns\ *n* : neglect or refusal to obey — **dis·obe·di·ent** \-ənt\ *adj*

dis·obey \₁dis-ə-'bā\ *vb* : to fail to obey : be disobedient

dis·oblige \₁dis-ə-'blīj\ *vb* **1** : to go counter to the wishes of **2** : INCONVENIENCE

¹**dis·or·der** \dis-'ȯr-dər\ *vb* **1** : to disturb the order of **2** : to disturb the regular or normal functions of

²**disorder** *n* **1** : lack of order : CONFUSION **2** : breach of the peace or public order : TUMULT **3** : an abnormal physical or mental condition : AILMENT

dis·or·der·ly \-lē\ *adj* **1** : offensive to public order **2** : marked by disorder ⟨a ~ desk⟩ — **dis·or·der·li·ness** *n*

dis·or·ga·nize \dis-'ȯr-gə-₁nīz\ *vb* : to break up the regular system of : throw into disorder — **dis·or·ga·ni·za·tion** \dis-₁ȯr-gə-nə-'zā-shən\ *n*

dis·ori·ent \dis-'ȯr-ē-₁ent\ *vb* : to cause to be confused or lost — **dis·ori·en·ta·tion** \₁dis-₁ȯr-ē-ən-'tā-shən\ *n*

dis·own \dis-'ōn\ *vb* : REPUDIATE, RENOUNCE, DISCLAIM

dis·par·age \di-'sper-ij\ *vb* **-aged; -aging** [ME to degrade by marriage below one's class, disparage, fr. AF *desparager* to marry below one's class, fr. *parage* equality, lineage, fr. *per* peer] **1** : to lower in rank or reputation : DEGRADE **2** : BELITTLE — **dis·par·age·ment** *n* — **dis·par·ag·ing·ly** *adv*

dis·pa·rate \'dis-pə-rət, di-'sper-ət\ *adj* : distinct in quality or character — **dis·par·i·ty** \di-'sper-ə-tē\ *n*

dis·pas·sion·ate \(₁)dis-'pa-shə-nət\ *adj* : not influenced by strong feeling : CALM, IMPARTIAL — **dis·pas·sion** \-'pa-shən\ *n* — **dis·pas·sion·ate·ly** *adv*

¹**dis·patch** \di-'spach\ *vb* **1** : to send off or away with promptness or speed esp. on official business **2** : to put to death **3** : to attend to rapidly or efficiently **4** : DEFEAT — **dis·patch·er** *n*

²**dis·patch** \di-'spach, 'dis-₁pach\ *n* **1** : MESSAGE **2** : a news item sent in by a correspondent to a newspaper **3** : the act of dispatching; *esp* : SHIPMENT **4** : the act of putting to death **5** : promptness and efficiency in performing a task

dis·pel \di-'spel\ *vb* **dis·pelled; dis·pelling** : to drive away by scattering : DISSIPATE

dis·pens·able \di-'spen-sə-bəl\ *adj* : capable of being dispensed with

dis·pen·sa·ry \di-'spen-sə-rē\ *n, pl* **-ries** : a place where medicine or medical or dental aid is dispensed

dis·pen·sa·tion \₁dis-pən-'sā-shən\ *n* **1** : a system of rules for ordering affairs **2** : a particular arrangement or provision esp. of nature **3** : an exemption from a rule or from a vow or oath **4** : the act of dispensing **5** : something dispensed or distributed

dis·pense \di-'spens\ *vb* **dis·pensed; dis·pens·ing 1** : to portion out **2** : ADMINISTER ⟨~ justice⟩ **3** : EXEMPT **4** : to make up and give out (remedies) — **dis·pens·er** *n* — **dispense with 1** : SUSPEND **2** : to do without

dis·perse \di-'spərs\ *vb* **dis·persed; dis·pers·ing** : to break up and scatter about : SPREAD — **dis·per·sal** \-'spər-səl\ *n* — **dis·per·sion** \-'spər-zhən\ *n*

dis·pir·it \dis-'pir-ət\ *vb* : DEPRESS, DISCOURAGE, DISHEARTEN

dis·place \dis-'plās\ *vb* **1** : to remove from the usual or proper place; *esp* : to expel or force to flee from home or native land ⟨*displaced* persons⟩ **2** : to move out of position ⟨water *displaced* by a floating object⟩ **3** : to take the place of : REPLACE

dis·place·ment \-mənt\ *n* **1** : the act of displacing : the state of being displaced **2** : the volume or weight of a fluid (as water) displaced by a floating body (as a ship) **3** : the difference between the initial position of an object and a later position

¹**dis·play** \di-'splā\ *vb* [ME, fr. AF *desplaier, desploier*, lit., to unfold, fr. *des-*

un- + *ploier, plier* to fold, fr. L *plicare*] : to present to view : make evident

²**display** *n* **1** : a displaying of something **2** : an electronic device (as a cathode-ray tube) that gives information in visual form; *also* : the visual information

dis·please \(͵)dis-'plēz\ *vb* **1** : to arouse the disapproval and dislike of **2** : to be offensive or : give displeasure

dis·plea·sure \-'ple-zhər\ *n* : a feeling of dislike and irritation

dis·port \di-'spȯrt\ *vb* **1** : DIVERT, AMUSE **2** : FROLIC **3** : DISPLAY

dis·pos·able \di-'spō-zə-bəl\ *adj* **1** : remaining after deduction of taxes 〈~ income〉 **2** : designed to be used once and then thrown away 〈~ diapers〉 — **dis·posable** *n*

dis·pos·al \di-'spō-zəl\ *n* **1** : CONTROL, COMMAND **2** : an orderly arrangement **3** : a getting rid of **4** : MANAGEMENT, ADMINISTRATION **5** : presenting or bestowing something 〈~ of favors〉 **6** : a device used to reduce waste matter (as by grinding)

dis·pose \di-'spōz\ *vb* **dis·posed; dis·pos·ing 1** : to give a tendency to : INCLINE 〈*disposed* to accept〉 **2** : to put in place : ARRANGE 〈troops *disposed* for withdrawal〉 **3** : SETTLE — **dis·pos·er** *n* — **dispose of 1** : to transfer to the control of another **2** : to get rid of **3** : to deal with conclusively

dis·po·si·tion \͵dis-pə-'zi-shən\ *n* **1** : the act or power of disposing : DISPOSAL **2** : RELINQUISHMENT **3** : ARRANGEMENT **4** : TENDENCY, INCLINATION **5** : natural attitude toward things 〈a cheerful ~〉

dis·pos·sess \͵dis-pə-'zes\ *vb* : to put out of possession or occupancy — **dis·posses·sion** \-'ze-shən\ *n*

dis·praise \(͵)dis-'prāz\ *vb* : DISPARAGE — **dispraise** *n* — **dis·prais·er** *n*

dis·pro·por·tion \͵dis-prə-'pȯr-shən\ *n* : lack of proportion, symmetry, or proper relation — **dis·pro·por·tion·ate** \-shə-nət\ *adj*

dis·prove \(͵)dis-'prüv\ *vb* : to prove to be false — **dis·proof** \-'prüf\ *n*

dis·pu·tant \di-'spyü-t⁰nt, 'dis-pyə-tənt\ *n* : one that is engaged in a dispute

dis·pu·ta·tion \͵dis-pyü-'tā-shən\ *n* **1** : DEBATE **2** : an oral defense of an academic thesis

dis·pu·ta·tious \-shəs\ *adj* : inclined to dispute : ARGUMENTATIVE

¹**dis·pute** \di-'spyüt\ *vb* **dis·put·ed; dis·put·ing 1** : ARGUE, DEBATE **2** : WRANGLE **3** : to deny the truth or rightness of **4** : to struggle against or over : OPPOSE — **dis·put·able** \di-'spyü-tə-bəl, 'dis-pyə-tə-bəl\ *adj* — **dis·put·er** *n*

²**dispute** *n* **1** : DEBATE **2** : QUARREL

dis·qual·i·fy \(͵)dis-'kwä-lə-͵fī\ *vb* : to make or declare unfit or not qualified — **dis·qual·i·fi·ca·tion** \-͵kwä-lə-fə-'kā-shən\ *n*

¹**dis·qui·et** \(͵)dis-'kwī-ət\ *vb* : to make uneasy or restless : DISTURB — **dis·qui·et·ing** *adj*

²**disquiet** *n* : lack of peace or tranquillity : ANXIETY

dis·qui·etude \(͵)dis-'kwī-ə-͵tüd, -͵tyüd\ *n* : AGITATION, ANXIETY

dis·qui·si·tion \͵dis-kwə-'zi-shən\ *n* : a formal inquiry or discussion

¹**dis·re·gard** \͵dis-ri-'gärd\ *vb* : to pay no attention to : treat as unworthy of notice or regard

²**disregard** *n* : the act of disregarding : the state of being disregarded : NEGLECT — **dis·re·gard·ful** *adj*

dis·re·pair \͵dis-ri-'per\ *n* : the state of being in need of repair

dis·rep·u·ta·ble \dis-'re·pyü-tə-bəl\ *adj* : having a bad reputation

dis·re·pute \͵dis-ri-'pyüt\ *n* : lack or decline of reputation : low esteem

dis·re·spect \͵dis-ri-'spekt\ *n* : DISCOURTESY — **dis·re·spect·ful** *adj*

dis·robe \dis-'rōb\ *vb* : UNDRESS

dis·rupt \dis-'rəpt\ *vb* **1** : to break apart **2** : to throw into disorder **3** : INTERRUPT — **dis·rup·tion** \-'rəp-shən\ *n* — **dis·rup·tive** \-'rəp-tiv\ *adj*

dis·sat·is·fac·tion \di-͵sa-təs-'fak-shən\ *n* : DISCONTENT

dis·sat·is·fy \di-'sa-təs-͵fī\ *vb* : to fail to satisfy : DISPLEASE

dis·sect \dī-'sekt, di-\ *vb* **1** : to divide into parts esp. for examination and study **2** : ANALYZE — **dis·sec·tion** \-'sek-shən\ *n* — **dis·sec·tor** \-'sek-tər\ *n*

dis·sect·ed *adj* : cut deeply into narrow lobes 〈a ~ leaf〉

dis·sem·ble \di-'sem-bəl\ *vb* **-bled; -bling 1** : to hide under or put on a false appearance : conceal facts, intentions, or feelings under some pretense **2** : SIMULATE — **dis·sem·bler** *n*

dis·sem·i·nate \di-'se-mə-͵nāt\ *vb* **-nated; -nat·ing** : to spread abroad as if sowing seed 〈~ ideas〉 — **dis·sem·i·na·tion** \-͵se-mə-'nā-shən\ *n*

dis·sen·sion \di-'sen-chən\ *n* : disagreement in opinion : DISCORD

¹**dis·sent** \di-'sent\ *vb* **1** : to withhold assent **2** : to differ in opinion

²**dissent** *n* **1** : difference of opinion; *esp* : religious nonconformity **2** : a written statement in which a justice disagrees with the opinion of the majority

dis·sent·er \di-'sen-tər\ *n* **1** : one that dissents **2** *cap* : an English Nonconformist

dis·ser·ta·tion \͵di-sər-'tā-shən\ *n* : an extended usu. written treatment of a subject; *esp* : one submitted for a doctorate

dis·ser·vice \di-'sər-vəs\ *n* : INJURY, HARM, MISCHIEF

dis·sev·er \di-'se-vər\ *vb* : SEPARATE, DISUNITE

dis·si·dent \'di-sə-dənt\ *adj* [L *dissidens*, prp. of *dissidēre* to sit apart, disagree, fr. *dis-* apart + *sedēre* to sit] : disagreeing esp. with an established religious or political system, organization, or belief — **dis·si·dence** \-dəns\ *n* — **dissident** *n*

dis·sim·i·lar \di-'si-mə-lər\ *adj* : UNLIKE — **dis·sim·i·lar·i·ty** \di-͵si-mə-'ler-ə-tē\ *n*

dis·sim·u·late \di-'si-myə-͵lāt\ *vb* : to hide under a false appearance : DISSEM-

BLE — **dis·sim·u·la·tion** \di-ˌsi-myə-ˈlā-shən\ n

dis·si·pate \ˈdi-sə-ˌpāt\ vb **-pat·ed; -pat·ing** **1** : to break up and drive off : DISPERSE, SCATTER ⟨the breeze *dissipated* the fog⟩ **2** : SQUANDER **3** : to break up and vanish **4** : to be dissolute; *esp* : to drink alcoholic beverages to excess — **dis·si·pat·ed** adj — **dis·si·pa·tion** \ˌdi-sə-ˈpā-shən\ n

dis·so·ci·ate \di-ˈsō-shē-ˌāt\ vb **-at·ed; -at·ing** : DISCONNECT, DISUNITE — **dis·so·ci·a·tion** \di-ˌsō-shē-ˈā-shən\ n — **dis·so·cia·tive** \di-ˈsō-shē-ˌā-tiv\ adj

dis·so·lute \ˈdi-sə-ˌlüt\ adj : loose in morals or conduct — **dis·so·lute·ly** adv — **dis·so·lute·ness** n

dis·so·lu·tion \ˌdi-sə-ˈlü-shən\ n **1** : the action or process of dissolving **2** : separation of a thing into its parts **3** : DECAY; *also* : DEATH **4** : the termination or breaking up of (as an assembly)

dis·solve \di-ˈzälv\ vb **1** : to separate into component parts **2** : to pass or cause to pass into solution ⟨sugar ∼s in water⟩ **3** : TERMINATE, DISPERSE ⟨∼ parliament⟩ **4** : to waste or fade away ⟨his courage *dissolved*⟩ **5** : to be overcome emotionally ⟨∼ in tears⟩ **6** : to resolve itself as if by dissolution

dis·so·nance \ˈdi-sə-nəns\ n : DISCORD — **dis·so·nant** \-nənt\ adj

dis·suade \di-ˈswād\ vb **dis·suad·ed; dis·suad·ing** : to advise against a course of action : persuade or try to persuade not to do something — **dis·sua·sion** \-ˈswā-zhən\ n — **dis·sua·sive** \-ˈswā-siv\ adj

dist abbr **1** distance **2** district

¹dis·taff \ˈdis-ˌtaf\ n, pl **distaffs** \-ˌtafs, -ˌtavz\ [ME *distaf*, fr. OE *distæf*, fr. *dis-* bunch of flax + *stæf* stick, staff] **1** : a staff for holding the flax, tow, or wool in spinning **2** : a woman's work or domain **3** : the female branch or side of a family

²distaff adj **1** : MATERNAL **2** ⟨the ∼ side of the family⟩ **2** : FEMALE **1** ⟨∼ executives⟩

dis·tal \ˈdis-tᵊl\ adj **1** : situated away from the point of attachment or origin esp. on the body **2** : of, relating to, or being the surface of a tooth that is farthest from the middle of the front of the jaw — **dis·tal·ly** adv

¹dis·tance \ˈdis-təns\ n **1** : measure of separation in space or time **2** : EXPANSE **3** : the full length ⟨go the ∼⟩ **4** : spatial remoteness **5** : COLDNESS, RESERVE **6** : DIFFERENCE, DISPARITY **7** : a distant point

²distance vb **dis·tanced; dis·tanc·ing** : to leave far behind : OUTSTRIP

³distance adj : taking place via electronic media linking instructors and students ⟨∼ learning⟩

dis·tant \ˈdis-tənt\ adj **1** : separate in space : AWAY **2** : FAR-OFF ⟨a ∼ galaxy⟩ **3** : far apart or behind **4** : not close in relationship ⟨a ∼ cousin⟩ **5** : different in kind **6** : RESERVED, ALOOF, COLD ⟨∼ politeness⟩ **7** : going a long

distance ⟨∼ voyages⟩ — **dis·tant·ly** adv — **dis·tant·ness** n

dis·taste \(ˌ)dis-ˈtāst\ n : DISINCLINATION, DISLIKE — **dis·taste·ful** adj

dis·tem·per \(ˌ)dis-ˈtem-pər\ n : a bodily disorder usu. of a domestic animal; *esp* : a contagious often fatal virus disease of dogs

dis·tend \di-ˈstend\ vb : EXPAND, SWELL — **dis·ten·si·ble** \-ˈsten-sə-bəl\ adj — **dis·ten·sion** or **dis·ten·tion** \-chən\ n

dis·tich \ˈdis-(ˌ)tik\ n : a unit of two lines of poetry

dis·till also **dis·til** \di-ˈstil\ vb **dis·tilled; dis·till·ing** **1** : to fall or let fall in drops **2** : to obtain or purify by distillation — **dis·till·er** n — **dis·till·ery** \-ˈsti-lə-rē\ n

dis·til·late \ˈdis-tə-ˌlāt, -lət\ n : a liquid product condensed from vapor during distillation

dis·til·la·tion \ˌdis-tə-ˈlā-shən\ n : the process of purifying a liquid by successive evaporation and condensation

dis·tinct \di-ˈstiŋkt\ adj **1** : SEPARATE, INDIVIDUAL ⟨a ∼ cultural group⟩ **2** : presenting a clear unmistakable impression — **dis·tinct·ly** adv — **dis·tinct·ness** n

dis·tinc·tion \di-ˈstiŋk-shən\ n **1** : the distinguishing of a difference; *also* : the difference distinguished **2** : something that distinguishes **3** : special honor or recognition

dis·tinc·tive \di-ˈstiŋk-tiv\ adj **1** : serving to distinguish ⟨the ∼ flight of the crane⟩ **2** : having or giving style or distinction — **dis·tinc·tive·ly** adv — **dis·tinc·tive·ness** n

dis·tin·guish \di-ˈstiŋ-gwish\ vb [alter. of ME *distinguen*, fr. AF *distinguer*, fr. L *distinguere*, lit., to separate by pricking] **1** : to recognize by some mark or characteristic **2** : to hear or see clearly : DISCERN **3** : to make distinctions ⟨∼ between right and wrong⟩ **4** : to give prominence or distinction to; *also* : to take special notice of — **dis·tin·guish·able** adj

dis·tin·guished \-gwisht\ adj **1** : marked by eminence or excellence **2** : befitting an eminent person

dis·tort \di-ˈstȯrt\ vb **1** : to twist out of the true meaning **2** : to twist out of a natural, normal, or original shape or condition **3** : to cause to be perceived unnaturally — **dis·tor·tion** \-ˈstȯr-shən\ n

distr abbr distribute; distribution

dis·tract \di-ˈstrakt\ vb **1** : to draw (the attention or mind) to a different object : DIVERT **2** : to stir up or confuse with conflicting emotions or motives — **dis·trac·tion** \-ˈstrak-shən\ n

dis·trait \di-ˈstrā\ adj : DISTRAUGHT **1**

dis·traught \di-ˈstrȯt\ adj **1** : agitated with doubt or mental conflict or pain **2** : INSANE

¹dis·tress \di-ˈstres\ n **1** : suffering of body or mind : PAIN, ANGUISH **2** : TROUBLE, MISFORTUNE **3** : a condition of danger or desperate need — **dis·tress·ful** adj

²**distress** vb 1 : to subject to great strain or difficulties 2 : UPSET

dis·tress·ed \-'strest\ adj : experiencing economic decline or difficulty

dis·trib·ute \di-'stri-byüt\ vb -**ut·ed; -ut·ing** 1 : to divide among several or many 2 : to spread out : SCATTER; also : DELIVER 3 : CLASSIFY — **dis·tri·bu·tion** \ˌdis-trə-'byü-shən\ n

dis·trib·u·tive \di-'stri-byù-tiv\ adj 1 : of or relating to distribution 2 : of, having, or being the property of producing the same value when an operation is carried out on a whole expression and when it is carried out on each part of an expression with the results then collected together $(a(b + c) = ab + ac$ because multiplication is ∼) — **dis·trib·u·tive·ly** adv

dis·trib·u·tor \di-'stri-byü-tər\ n 1 : one that distributes 2 : one that markets goods 3 : a device for directing current to the spark plugs of an engine

dis·trict \'dis-(ˌ)trikt\ n 1 : a fixed territorial division (as for administrative or electoral purposes) 2 : an area, region, or section with a distinguishing character

district attorney n : the prosecuting attorney of a judicial district

¹**dis·trust** \dis-'trəst\ n : a lack or absence of trust — **dis·trust·ful** \-fəl\ adj — **dis·trust·ful·ly** adv

²**distrust** vb : to have no trust or confidence in

dis·turb \di-'stərb\ vb 1 : to interfere with : INTERRUPT 2 : to alter the position or arrangement of; also : to upset the natural and esp. the ecological balance of 3 : to destroy the tranquillity or composure of : make uneasy 4 : to throw into disorder 5 : INCONVENIENCE — **dis·tur·bance** \-'stər-bəns\ n — **dis·turb·er** n — **dis·turb·ing·ly** \-'stər-biŋ-lē\ adv

dis·turbed \-'stərbd\ adj : showing symptoms of emotional illness

dis·unite \ˌdis-yü-'nīt\ vb : DIVIDE, SEPARATE

dis·uni·ty \dis-'yü-nə-tē\ n : lack of unity; esp : DISSENSION

dis·use \-'yüs\ n : a cessation of use or practice

dis·used \-'yüzd\ adj : no longer used or occupied

¹**ditch** \'dich\ n : a long narrow channel or trench dug in the earth

²**ditch** vb 1 : to enclose with a ditch; also : to dig a ditch in 2 : to get rid of : DISCARD 3 : to make a forced landing of an airplane on water

dith·er \'di_ith_ər\ n : a highly nervous, excited, or agitated state

dit·to \'di-tō\ n, pl **dittos** [It ditto, detto, pp. of dire to say, fr. L dicere] 1 : a thing mentioned previously or above — used to avoid repeating a word 2 : a mark " or " used as a symbol for the word ditto

dit·ty \'di-tē\ n, pl **ditties** : a short simple song

dit·zy or **dit·sy** \'dit-sē\ adj **ditz·i·er** or **dits·i·er; -est** : eccentrically silly, giddy, or inane

di·uret·ic \ˌdī-yə-'re-tik\ adj : tending to increase urine flow — **diuretic** n

di·ur·nal \dī-'ər-nᵊl\ adj 1 : DAILY ⟨a ∼ chore⟩ 2 : of, relating to, occurring, or active in the daytime ⟨∼ animals⟩

div abbr 1 divided 2 dividend 3 division 4 divorced

di·va \'dē-və\ n, pl **divas** or **di·ve** \-ˌvā\ [It, lit., goddess, fr. L, fem. of divus divine, god] 1 : PRIMA DONNA 2 : a usu. glamorous and successful female performer or personality

di·va·gate \'dī-və-ˌgāt\ vb -**gat·ed; -gat·ing** : to wander or stray from a course or subject : DIVERGE — **di·va·ga·tion** \ˌdī-və-'gā-shən\ n

di·van \'dī-ˌvan, di-'van\ n : COUCH, SOFA

¹**dive** \'dīv\ vb **dived** \'dīvd\ or **dove** \'dōv\; **dived; div·ing** 1 : to plunge into water headfirst 2 : SUBMERGE 3 : to come or drop down precipitously 4 : to descend in an airplane at a steep angle 5 : to plunge into some matter or activity 6 : DART, LUNGE — **div·er** n

²**dive** n 1 : the act or an instance of diving 2 : a sharp decline 3 : a disreputable bar or place of amusement

di·verge \də-'vərj, dī-\ vb **di·verged; di·verg·ing** 1 : to move or extend in different directions from a common point : draw apart 2 : to differ in character, form, or opinion 3 : DEVIATE 4 : DEFLECT — **di·ver·gence** \-'vər-jəns\ n — **di·ver·gent** \-jənt\ adj

di·vers \'dī-vərz\ adj : VARIOUS

di·verse \dī-'vərs, də-, 'dī-ˌvərs\ adj 1 : UNLIKE 2 : composed of distinct forms or qualities — **di·verse·ly** adv

di·ver·si·fy \də-'vər-sə-ˌfī, dī-\ vb -**fied; -fy·ing** : to make different or various in form or quality — **di·ver·si·fi·ca·tion** \-ˌvər-sə-fə-'kā-shən\ n

di·ver·sion \də-'vər-zhən, dī-\ n 1 : a turning aside from a course, activity, or use : DEVIATION 2 : something that diverts or amuses : PASTIME

di·ver·si·ty \də-'vər-sə-tē, dī-\ n, pl -**ties** 1 : the condition of being diverse : VARIETY 2 : an instance of being diverse

di·vert \də-'vərt, dī-\ vb 1 : to turn from a course or purpose : DEFLECT 2 : DISTRACT 3 : ENTERTAIN, AMUSE

di·vert·ing \-'vər-tiŋ\ adj : providing amusement or entertainment

di·vest \dī-'vest, də-\ vb 1 : to deprive or dispossess esp. of property, authority, or rights 2 : to strip esp. of clothing, ornament, or equipment

¹**di·vide** \də-'vīd\ vb **di·vid·ed; di·vid·ing** 1 : SEPARATE; also : CLASSIFY 2 : CLEAVE, PART ⟨a ship dividing the waves⟩ 3 : DISTRIBUTE, APPORTION 4 : to possess or make use of in common : share in 5 : to cause to be separate, distinct, or apart from one another 6 : to separate into opposing sides or parties 7 : to mark divisions on 8 : to subject to or use in mathematical division; also : to be used as a divisor with respect to 9 : to branch out

²**divide** n : WATERSHED 1

div·i·dend \'di-və-ˌdend\ *n* **1** : an individual share of something distributed **2** : BONUS **3** : a number to be divided **4** : a sum or fund to be divided or distributed

di·vid·er \də-'vī-dər\ *n* **1** : one that divides (as a partition) ⟨room ~⟩ **2** *pl* : COMPASS 5

div·i·na·tion \ˌdi-və-'nā-shən\ *n* **1** : the art or practice of using omens or magic powers to foretell the future **2** : unusual insight or intuitive perception

¹di·vine \də-'vīn\ *adj* **di·vin·er; -est 1** : of, relating to, or being God or a god **2** : supremely good : SUPERB; *also* : HEAVENLY — **di·vine·ly** *adv*

²divine *n* **1** : CLERGYMAN **2** : THEOLOGIAN

³divine *vb* **di·vined; di·vin·ing 1** : INFER, CONJECTURE **2** : PROPHESY **3** : DOWSE — **di·vin·er** *n*

divining rod *n* : a forked rod believed to reveal the presence of water or minerals by dipping downward when held over a vein

di·vin·i·ty \də-'vi-nə-tē\ *n, pl* **-ties 1** : THEOLOGY **2** : the quality or state of being divine **3** : a divine being; *esp* : GOD 1

di·vis·i·ble \də-'vi-zə-bəl\ *adj* : capable of being divided — **di·vis·i·bil·i·ty** \-ˌvi-zə-'bi-lə-tē\ *n*

di·vi·sion \də-'vi-zhən\ *n* **1** : DISTRIBUTION, SEPARATION **2** : one of the parts or groupings into which a whole is divided **3** : DISAGREEMENT, DISUNITY **4** : something that divides or separates **5** : the mathematical operation of finding how many times one number is contained in another **6** : a large self-contained military unit **7** : an administrative or operating unit of a governmental, business, or educational organization — **di·vi·sion·al** \-'vi-zhə-nəl\ *adj*

di·vi·sive \də-'vī-siv, -'vi-ziv\ *adj* : creating disunity or dissension — **di·vi·sive·ly** *adv* — **di·vi·sive·ness** *n*

di·vi·sor \də-'vī-zər\ *n* : the number by which a dividend is divided

di·vorce \də-'vȯrs\ *n* **1** : an act or instance of legally dissolving a marriage **2** : SEPARATION, SEVERANCE — **divorce** *vb* — **di·vorce·ment** *n*

di·vor·cé \də-ˌvȯr-'sā\ *n* [F] : a divorced man

di·vor·cée \də-ˌvȯr-'sā, -'sē\ *n* : a divorced woman

div·ot \'di-vət\ *n* : a piece of turf dug from a golf fairway in making a stroke

di·vulge \də-'vəlj, dī-\ *vb* **di·vulged; di·vulg·ing** : REVEAL, DISCLOSE

Dix·ie·land \'dik-sē-ˌland\ *n* : jazz music in duple time played in a style developed in New Orleans

diz·zy \'di-zē\ *adj* **diz·zi·er; -est** [ME *disy,* fr. OE *dysig* stupid] **1** : FOOLISH, SILLY **2** : having a sensation of whirling : GIDDY **3** : causing or caused by giddiness — **diz·zi·ly** \-zə-lē\ *adv* — **diz·zi·ness** \-zē-nəs\ *n*

DJ *n, often not cap* : DISC JOCKEY

dk *abbr* **1** dark **2** deck **3** dock

dl *abbr* deciliter

DLitt *or* **DLit** *abbr* [NL *doctor litterarum*] doctor of letters; doctor of literature

DLO *abbr* dead letter office

dm *abbr* decimeter

DMD *abbr* [NL *dentariae medicinae doctor*] doctor of dental medicine

DMZ *abbr* demilitarized zone

dn *abbr* down

DNA \ˌdē-(ˌ)en-'ā\ *n* : any of various nucleic acids that are usu. the molecular basis of heredity and are localized esp. in cell nuclei

DNR *abbr* do not resuscitate

¹do \'dü\ *vb* **did** \'did\; **done** \'dən\; **do·ing; does** \'dəz\ **1** : to bring to pass : ACCOMPLISH **2** : ACT, BEHAVE ⟨~ as I say⟩ **3** : to be active or busy ⟨up and ~ing⟩ **4** : HAPPEN ⟨what's ~ing?⟩ **5** : to be engaged in the study or practice of : work at ⟨he *does* tailoring⟩ **6** : COOK ⟨steak *done* rare⟩ **7** : to put in order (as by cleaning or arranging) ⟨~ the dishes⟩ **8** : DECORATE ⟨*did* the hall in blue⟩ **9** : GET ALONG ⟨~ well in school⟩ **10** : CARRY ON, MANAGE **11** : RENDER ⟨sleep will ~ you good⟩ **12** : FINISH ⟨when he had *done*⟩ **13** : EXERT ⟨*did* my best⟩ **14** : PRODUCE ⟨*did* a poem⟩ **15** : to play the part of **16** : CHEAT ⟨*did* him out of his share⟩ **17** : TRAVERSE, TOUR **18** : TRAVEL **19** : to spend or serve out a period of time ⟨*did* ten years in prison⟩ **20** : SUFFICE, SUIT **21** : to be fitting or proper **22** : USE ⟨doesn't ~ drugs⟩ **23** — used as an auxiliary verb (1) before the subject in an interrogative sentence ⟨*does* he work?⟩ and after some adverbs ⟨never *did* she say so⟩, (2) in a negative statement ⟨I *don't* know⟩, (3) for emphasis ⟨you ~ know⟩, and (4) as a substitute for a preceding predicate ⟨he works harder than I ~⟩ — **do·able** \'dü-ə-bəl\ *adj* — **do away with 1** : to put an end to **2** : DESTROY, KILL — **do by** : to deal with : TREAT ⟨*did* right *by* her⟩ — **do for** *chiefly Brit* : to bring about the death or ruin of — **do the trick** : to produce a desired result

²do *n* **1** : AFFAIR, PARTY **2** : a command or entreaty to do something ⟨list of ~s and don'ts⟩ **3** : HAIRSTYLE

³do *abbr* ditto

DOA *abbr* dead on arrival

DOB *abbr* date of birth

dob·bin \'dä-bən\ *n* [*Dobbin,* nickname for *Robert*] **1** : a farm horse **2** : a quiet plodding horse

Do·ber·man pin·scher \'dō-bər-mən-'pin-chər\ *n* : any of a German breed of short-haired medium-sized dogs

do·bra \'dō-brə\ *n* — see MONEY table

¹doc \'däk\ *n* : DOCTOR

²doc *abbr* document

do·cent \'dō-sᵊnt, dōt-'sent\ *n* [obs. G (now *Dozent*), fr. L *docens,* prp. of *docēre* to teach] : TEACHER, LECTURER; *also* : a person who leads a guided tour

doc·ile \'dä-səl\ *adj* [L *docilis,* fr. *docēre* to teach] : easily taught, led, or managed

: TRACTABLE — **do·cil·i·ty** \dä-'si-lə-tē\ *n*

¹dock \'däk\ *n* : any of a genus of coarse weedy herbs related to buckwheat

²dock *vb* **1** : to cut off the end of : cut short **2** : to take away a part of : deduct from ⟨~ a worker's wages⟩

³dock *n* **1** : an artificial basin to receive ships **2** : ²SLIP 2 **3** : a wharf or platform for loading or unloading materials or for mooring a boat

⁴dock *vb* **1** : to bring or come into dock **2** : to join (as two spacecraft) mechanically in space

⁵dock *n* : the place in a court where a prisoner stands or sits during trial

dock·age \'dä-kij\ *n* : docking facilities

dock·et \'dä-kət\ *n* **1** : a formal abridged record of the proceedings in a legal action; *also* : a register of such records **2** : a list of legal causes to be tried **3** : a calendar of matters to be acted on : AGENDA **4** : a label attached to a document containing identification or directions — **docket** *vb*

dock·hand \'däk-,hand\ *n* : LONGSHOREMAN

dock·work·er \-,wər-kər\ *n* : LONGSHOREMAN

dock·yard \-,yärd\ *n* : SHIPYARD

¹doc·tor \'däk-tər\ *n* [ME *doctour* teacher, doctor, fr. AF & ML; AF, fr. ML *doctor*, fr. L, teacher, fr. *docēre* to teach] **1** : a person holding one of the highest academic degrees (as a PhD) conferred by a university **2** : a person skilled in healing arts; *esp* : one (as a physician, dentist, or veterinarian) academically and legally qualified to practice **3** : a person who restores or repairs things — **doc·tor·al** \-tə-rəl\ *adj*

²doctor *vb* **1** : to give medical treatment to **2** : to practice medicine **3** : REPAIR **4** : to adapt or modify for a desired end **5** : to alter deceptively

doc·tor·ate \'däk-tə-rət\ *n* : the degree, title, or rank of a doctor

doc·tri·naire \,däk-trə-'ner\ *n* [F] : one who attempts to put an abstract theory into effect without regard to practical difficulties — **doctrinaire** *adj*

doc·trine \'däk-trən\ *n* **1** : something that is taught **2** : DOGMA, TENET — **doc·tri·nal** \-trə-nᵊl\ *adj*

docu·dra·ma \'dä-kyə-,drä-mə, -,dra-\ *n* : a drama made for television, motion pictures, or theater that deals freely with historical events

doc·u·ment \'dä-kyə-mənt\ *n* **1** : a paper that furnishes information, proof, or support of something else **2** : a computer file containing information input by a computer user usu. via a word processor — **doc·u·ment** \-,ment\ *vb* — **doc·u·men·ta·tion** \,dä-kyə-mən-'tä-shən\ *n* — **doc·u·ment·er** *n*

doc·u·men·ta·ry \,dä-kyə-'men-tə-rē\ *adj* **1** : consisting of documents; *also* : being in writing ⟨~ proof⟩ **2** : giving a factual presentation in artistic form ⟨a ~ movie⟩ — **documentary** *n*

DOD *abbr* Department of Defense

¹dod·der \'dä-dər\ *n* : any of a genus of leafless parasitic twining vines that are highly deficient in chlorophyll

²dodder *vb* **dod·dered; dod·der·ing 1** : to tremble or shake usu. from age **2** : to progress feebly and unsteadily

¹dodge \'däj\ *n* **1** : an act of evading by sudden bodily movement **2** : an artful device to evade, deceive, or trick **3** : EXPEDIENT

²dodge *vb* **dodged; dodg·ing 1** : to evade usu. by trickery **2** : to move suddenly aside; *also* : to avoid or evade by so doing — **dodg·er** *n*

do·do \'dō-dō\ *n, pl* **dodoes** *or* **dodos** [Pg *doudo*, fr. *doudo* silly, stupid] **1** : an extinct heavy flightless bird of the island of Mauritius related to the pigeons and larger than a turkey **2** : one hopelessly behind the times; *also* : a stupid person

doe \'dō\ *n, pl* **does** *or* **doe** : an adult female of various mammals (as a deer, rabbit, or kangaroo) of which the male is called **buck**

DOE *abbr* Department of Energy

do·er \'dü-ər\ *n* : one that does

does *pres 3d sing of* DO, *pl of* DOE

doff \'däf\ *vb* [ME, fr. *don* to do + *of* off] **1** : to take off (the hat) in greeting or as a sign of respect **2** : to rid oneself of

¹dog \'dȯg\ *n* **1** : a flesh-eating domestic mammal related to the wolves; *esp* : a male of this animal **2** : a worthless or contemptible person **3** : FELLOW, CHAP ⟨you lucky ~⟩ **4** : a mechanical device for holding something **5** : uncharacteristic or affected stylishness or dignity ⟨put on the ~⟩ **6** *pl* : RUIN ⟨gone to the ~s⟩

²dog *vb* **dogged; dog·ging 1** : to hunt or track like a hound **2** : to worry as if by pursuit with dogs : PLAGUE

dog·bane \'dȯg-,bān\ *n* : any of a genus of mostly poisonous herbs with milky juice and often showy flowers

dog·cart \-,kärt\ *n* : a light one-horse carriage with two seats back to back

dog·catch·er \-,ka-chər, -,ke-\ *n* : a community official assigned to catch and dispose of stray dogs

dog-ear \'dȯg-,ir\ *n* : the turned-down corner of a leaf of a book — **dog-ear** *vb* — **dog-eared** \-,ird\ *adj*

dog·fight \'dȯg-,fīt\ *n* : a fight between fighter planes at close range

dog·fish \-,fish\ *n* : any of various small usu. bottom-dwelling sharks

dog·ged \'dȯ-gəd\ *adj* : stubbornly determined : TENACIOUS — **dog·ged·ly** *adv* — **dog·ged·ness** *n*

dog·ger·el \'dȯ-gə-rəl\ *n* : verse that is loosely styled and irregular in measure esp. for comic effect

dog·gie bag *or* **doggy bag** \'dȯ-gē-\ *n* : a container for carrying home leftover food from a restaurant meal

¹dog·gy *or* **dog·gie** \'dȯ-gē\ *n, pl* **doggies** : a small dog

²dog·gy *adj* **dog·gi·er; -est** : of or resembling a dog ⟨a ~ odor⟩

dog·house \'dȯg-ˌhau̇s\ *n* : a shelter for a dog — **in the doghouse** : in a state of disfavor

do·gie \'dō-gē\ *n, chiefly West* : a motherless calf in a range herd

dog·leg \'dȯg-ˌleg\ *n* : a sharp bend or angle (as in a road or golf fairway) — **dogleg** *vb*

dog·ma \'dȯg-mə\ *n, pl* **dogmas** *also* **dog·ma·ta** \-mə-tə\ [L, fr. Gk, fr. *dokein* to think, have an opinion] **1** : a tenet or code of tenets **2** : a doctrine or body of doctrines formally proclaimed by a church

dog·ma·tism \'dȯg-mə-ˌti-zəm\ *n* : positiveness in stating matters of opinion esp. when unwarranted or arrogant — **dog·mat·ic** \dȯg-'ma-tik\ *adj* — **dog·mat·i·cal·ly** \-ti-k(ə-)lē\ *adv*

do·good·er \'dü-ˌgu̇-dər\ *n* : an earnest often naive humanitarian or reformer

dog·tooth violet \'dȯg-ˌtüth-\ *n* : any of a genus of small spring-flowering bulbous herbs related to the lilies

dog·trot \'dȯg-ˌträt\ *n* : a gentle trot — **dogtrot** *vb*

dog·wood \'dȯg-ˌwu̇d\ *n* : any of a genus of trees and shrubs having heads of small flowers often with showy white, pink, or red bracts

doi·ly \'dȯi-lē\ *n, pl* **doilies** : a small often decorative mat

do in *vb* **1** : RUIN **2** : KILL **3** : TIRE, EXHAUST ⟨the climb *did* him *in*⟩ **4** : CHEAT

do·ings \'dü-iŋz\ *n pl* : GOINGS-ON

do–it–yourself *n* : the activity of doing or making something without professional training or help — **do–it–your·self·er** *n*

dol *abbr* dollar

dol·drums \'dōl-drəmz, 'däl-\ *n pl* **1** : a spell of listlessness or despondency **2** *often cap* : a part of the ocean near the equator known for calms **3** : a state or period of inactivity, stagnation, or slump

¹dole \'dōl\ *n* **1** : a distribution esp. of food, money, or clothing to the needy; *also* : something so distributed **2** : a grant of government funds to the unemployed

²dole *vb* **doled; dol·ing** : to give or distribute as a charity — usu. used with *out*

dole·ful \'dōl-fəl\ *adj* : full of grief : SAD — **dole·ful·ly** *adv*

dole out *vb* **1** : to give or deliver in small portions **2** : DISH OUT

doll \'däl, 'dȯl\ *n* **1** : a small figure of a human being used esp. as a child's plaything **2** : a pretty woman **3** : an attractive person — **doll·ish** \'dä-lish, 'dȯ-\ *adj*

dol·lar \'dä-lər\ *n* [Dutch or LG *daler*, fr. G *Taler*, short for *Joachimstaler*, fr. Sankt *Joachimsthal*, Bohemia, where talers were first made] **1** : any of various basic monetary units (as in the U.S. and Canada) — see MONEY table **2** : a coin, note, or token representing one dollar **3** : RINGGIT

dol·lop \'dä-ləp\ *n* **1** : LUMP, GLOB **2** : PORTION 1 — **dollop** *vb*

doll up *vb* **1** : to dress elegantly or extravagantly **2** : to make more attractive **3** : to get dolled up

dol·ly \'dä-lē\ *n, pl* **dollies** : a small cart or wheeled platform (as for a television or movie camera)

dol·men \'dōl-mən, 'däl-\ *n* : a prehistoric monument consisting of two or more upright stones supporting a horizontal stone slab

do·lo·mite \'dō-lə-ˌmīt, 'dä-\ *n* : a mineral found in broad layers as a compact limestone

do·lor \'dō-lər, 'dä-\ *n* : mental suffering or anguish : SORROW — **do·lor·ous** *adj* — **do·lor·ous·ly** *adv*

do·lour *chiefly Brit var of* DOLOR

dol·phin \'däl-fən\ *n* **1** : any of various small whales with conical teeth and an elongated beaklike snout **2** : either of two active food fishes of tropical and temperate seas

dolt \'dōlt\ *n* : a stupid person — **dolt·ish** \'dōl-tish\ *adj* — **dolt·ish·ness** *n*

dom *abbr* **1** domestic **2** dominant **3** dominion

-dom *n suffix* **1** : dignity : office ⟨dukedom⟩ **2** : realm : jurisdiction ⟨kingdom⟩ **3** : state or fact of being ⟨freedom⟩ **4** : those having a (specified) office, occupation, interest, or character ⟨officialdom⟩

do·main \dō-'mān\ *n* **1** : complete and absolute ownership of land **2** : land completely owned **3** : a territory over which dominion is exercised **4** : a sphere of knowledge, influence, or activity ⟨the ~ of science⟩ **5** : a subdivision of the Internet made up of computers whose URLs share a characteristic abbreviation (as *com* or *gov*)

domain name *n* : a sequence of characters (as Merriam-Webster.com) that specifies a group of online resources and forms part of its URL

dome \'dōm\ *n* **1** : a large hemispherical roof or ceiling **2** : a structure or natural formation that resembles the dome of a building **3** : a roofed sports stadium — **dome** *vb*

¹do·mes·tic \də-'mes-tik\ *adj* **1** : living near or about human habitations **2** : TAME, DOMESTICATED **3** : relating and limited to one's own country or the country under consideration **4** : of or relating to the household or the family **5** : devoted to home duties and pleasures **6** : INDIGENOUS — **do·mes·ti·cal·ly** \-ti-k(ə-)lē\ *adv*

²domestic *n* : a household servant

do·mes·ti·cate \də-'mes-ti-ˌkāt\ *vb* **-cat·ed; -cat·ing** : to adapt to life in association with and to the use of humans — **do·mes·ti·ca·tion** \-ˌmes-ti-'kā-shən\ *n*

do·mes·tic·i·ty \ˌdō-ˌmes-'ti-sə-tē, də-\ *n, pl* **-ties** **1** : the quality or state of being domestic or domesticated **2** : domestic activities or life

domestic violence *n* : the inflicting of injury by one family or household member on another

do·mi·cile \'dä-mə-ˌsī(-ə)l, 'dō-; 'dä-mə-səl\ *n* : a dwelling place : HOME — **domicile** *vb* — **dom·i·cil·i·ary** \ˌdä-mə-ˈsi-lē-ˌer-ē, ˌdō-\ *adj*

dom·i·nance \'dä-mə-nəns\ *n* **1** : AUTHORITY, CONTROL **2** : the property of one of a pair of alleles or traits that suppresses expression of the other when both are present

¹dom·i·nant \-nənt\ *adj* **1** : controlling or prevailing over all others **2** : overlooking from a high position **3** : exhibiting genetic dominance

²dominant *n* : a dominant gene or trait

dom·i·nate \'dä-mə-ˌnāt\ *vb* **-nat·ed; -nat·ing 1** : RULE, CONTROL **2** : to have a commanding position or controlling power over **3** : to rise high above in a position suggesting power to dominate — **dom·i·na·tor** \-ˌnā-tər\ *n*

dom·i·na·tion \ˌdä-mə-ˈnā-shən\ *n* **1** : supremacy or preeminence over another **2** : exercise of mastery, ruling power, or preponderant influence

do·mi·na·trix \ˌdä-mə-ˈnā-triks\ *n, pl* **-tri·ces** \-ˈnā-trə-ˌsēz, -nə-ˈtrī-sēz\ : a woman who dominates her sexual partner; *also* : a dominating woman

dom·i·neer \ˌdä-mə-ˈnir\ *vb* **1** : to rule in an arrogant manner **2** : to be overbearing

do·mi·nie *1 usu* 'dä-mə-nē, *2 usu* 'dō-\ *n,* **1** *chiefly Scot* : SCHOOLMASTER **2** : CLERGYMAN

do·min·ion \də-ˈmin-yən\ *n* **1** : DOMAIN **2** : supreme authority : SOVEREIGNTY **3** *often cap* : a self-governing nation of the Commonwealth

dom·i·no \'dä-mə-ˌnō\ *n, pl* **-noes** *or* **-nos 1** : a long loose hooded cloak usu. worn with a half mask as a masquerade costume **2** : a flat rectangular block used as a piece in a game (dominoes)

¹don \'dän\ *vb* **donned; don·ning** [ME, fr. *don* to do + *on*] : to put on (as clothes)

²don *n* [Sp, fr. L *dominus* lord, master] **1** : a Spanish nobleman or gentleman — used as a title prefixed to the Christian name **2** : a head, tutor, or fellow in an English university

do·ña \'dō-nyə\ *n* : a Spanish woman of rank — used as a title prefixed to the Christian name

do·nate \'dō-ˌnāt\ *vb* **do·nat·ed; do·nat·ing 1** : to make a gift of : CONTRIBUTE **2** : to make a donation

do·na·tion \dō-ˈnā-shən\ *n* **1** : the making of a gift esp. to a charity **2** : a free contribution : GIFT

¹done \'dən\ *past part of* DO

²done *adj* **1** : doomed to failure, defeat, or death **2** : gone by : OVER ⟨when day is ~⟩ **3** : cooked sufficiently **4** : conformable to social convention

done deal *n* : FAIT ACCOMPLI

dong \'dȯŋ, 'däŋ\ *n* — see MONEY table

don·key \'däŋ-kē, 'dəŋ-\ *n, pl* **donkeys 1** : a sturdy and patient domestic mammal classified with the asses **2** : a stupid or obstinate person

don·ny·brook \'dä-nē-ˌbrùk\ *n, often cap* [*Donnybrook* Fair, annual Irish event

known for its brawls] : an uproarious brawl

do·nor \'dō-nər\ *n* : one that gives, donates, or presents

donut *var of* DOUGHNUT

doo·dad \'dü-ˌdad\ *n* : an often small article whose common name is unknown or forgotten

doo·dle \'dü-d³l\ *vb* **doo·dled; doo·dling** : to draw or scribble aimlessly while occupied with something else — **doodle** *n* — **doo·dler** *n*

doom \'düm\ *n* **1** : JUDGMENT; *esp* : a judicial condemnation or sentence **2** : DESTINY **3** : RUIN, DEATH — **doom** *vb*

dooms·day \'dümz-ˌdā\ *n* : JUDGMENT DAY

door \'dȯr\ *n* **1** : a barrier by which an entry is closed and opened; *also* : a similar part of a piece of furniture **2** : DOORWAY **3** : a means of access or participation : OPPORTUNITY

door·keep·er \-ˌkē-pər\ *n* : a person who tends a door

door·knob \-ˌnäb\ *n* : a knob that when turned releases a door latch

door·man \-ˌman, -mən\ *n* : a usu. uniformed attendant at the door of a building (as a hotel)

door·mat \-ˌmat\ *n* : a mat placed before or inside a door for wiping dirt from the shoes

door·plate \-ˌplāt\ *n* : a nameplate on a door

door·step \-ˌstep\ *n* : a step or series of steps before an outer door

door·way \-ˌwā\ *n* **1** : the opening that a door closes **2** : DOOR 3

do·pa \'dō-pə\ *n* : a form of an amino acid that is used esp. in the treatment of Parkinson's disease

do·pa·mine \'dō-pə-ˌmēn\ *n* : an organic compound that occurs esp. as a neurotransmitter in the brain

¹dope \'dōp\ *n* **1** : a preparation for giving a desired quality **2** : an illicit, habit-forming, or narcotic drug; *esp* : MARIJUANA **3** : a stupid person **4** : INFORMATION

²dope *vb* **doped; dop·ing 1** : to treat with dope; *esp* : to give a narcotic to **2** : FIGURE OUT — usu. used with *out* **3** : to take dope — **dop·er** *n*

dop·ey *also* **dopy** \'dō-pē\ *adj* **dop·i·er; -est 1** : dulled by alcohol or a narcotic **2** : SLUGGISH **3** : STUPID — **dop·i·ness** *n*

doping *n* : the use of a substance or technique to illegally improve athletic performance

Dopp·ler effect \'dä-plər-\ *n* : a change in the frequency at which waves (as of sound) reach an observer from a source in motion with respect to the observer

do–rag \'dü-ˌrag\ *n* : a kerchief worn esp. to cover the hair

dork \'dȯrk\ *n, slang* : NERD; *also* : JERK 2

dorm \'dȯrm\ *n* : DORMITORY

dor·mant \'dȯr-mənt\ *adj* : INACTIVE; *esp* : not actively growing or functioning ⟨~ buds⟩ — **dor·man·cy** \-mən-sē\ *n*

dor·mer \'dȯr-mər\ n [MF *dormeor* dormitory, fr. L *dormitorium*, fr. *dormire* to sleep] : a window built upright in a sloping roof; *also* : the roofed structure containing such a window

dor·mi·to·ry \'dȯr-mə-ˌtȯr-ē\ n, pl **-ries** 1 : a room for sleeping; *esp* : a large room containing a number of beds 2 : a residence hall providing sleeping rooms

dor·mouse \'dȯr-ˌmau̇s\ n : any of numerous Old World rodents that resemble small squirrels

dor·sal \'dȯr-səl\ adj : of, relating to, or located near or on the surface of the body that in humans is the back but in most other animals is the upper surface — **dor·sal·ly** adv

do·ry \'dȯr-ē\ n, pl **dories** : a flat-bottomed boat with high flaring sides and a sharp bow

DOS abbr disk operating system

¹**dose** \'dōs\ n [ME, fr. MF, fr. LL *dosis*, fr. Gk, lit., act of giving, fr. *didonai* to give] 1 : a measured quantity (as of medicine) to be taken or administered at one time 2 : the quantity of radiation administered or absorbed — **dos·age** \'dō-sij\ n

²**dose** vb **dosed; dos·ing** 1 : to give in doses 2 : to give medicine to

do·sim·e·ter \dō-'si-mə-tər\ n : a device for measuring doses of radiations (as X-rays) — **do·sim·e·try** \-mə-trē\ n

dos·sier \'dȯs-ˌyā, 'dȯ-sē-ˌā\ n [F, bundle of documents labeled on the back, dossier, fr. *dos* back, fr. OF, fr. L *dorsum*] : a file containing detailed records on a particular person or subject

¹**dot** \'dät\ n 1 : a small spot : SPECK 2 : a small round mark 3 : a precise point esp. in time ⟨be here on the ~⟩

²**dot** vb **dot·ted; dot·ting** 1 : to mark with a dot ⟨~ an *i*⟩ 2 : to cover with or as if with dots — **dot·ter** n

DOT abbr Department of Transportation

dot·age \'dō-tij\ n : feebleness of mind esp. in old age : SENILITY

dot·ard \-tərd\ n : a person in dotage

dot–com \'dät-ˌkäm\ n : a company that markets its products or services usu. exclusively via a Web site

dote \'dōt\ vb **dot·ed; dot·ing** 1 : to be feebleminded esp. from old age 2 : to be lavish or excessive in one's attention, affection, or fondness ⟨*doted* on her niece⟩

dot matrix n : a rectangular arrangement of dots from which alphanumeric characters can be formed (as by a computer printer)

Dou·ay Version \dü-'ā-\ n : an English translation of the Vulgate used by Roman Catholics

¹**dou·ble** \'də-bəl\ adj [ME, fr. AF, fr. L *duplus*, fr. *duo* two + *-plus* multiplied by] 1 : TWOFOLD, DUAL ⟨serving a ~ function⟩ 2 : consisting of two members or parts 3 : being twice as great or as many 4 : folded in two 5 : having more than one whorl of petals ⟨~ roses⟩

²**double** vb **dou·bled; dou·bling** 1 : to make, be, or become twice as great or as many 2 : to make a call in bridge that increases the trick values and penalties of

(an opponent's bid) 3 : FOLD 4 : CLENCH 5 : to be or cause to be bent over 6 : to take the place of another 7 : to hit a double 8 : to turn sharply and suddenly; *esp* : to turn back on one's course

³**double** adv 1 : DOUBLY 2 : two together ⟨sleep ~⟩

⁴**double** n 1 : something twice another in size, strength, speed, quantity, or value 2 : a base hit that enables the batter to reach second base 3 : COUNTERPART, DUPLICATE; *esp* : a person who closely resembles another 4 : UNDERSTUDY, SUBSTITUTE 5 : a sharp turn : REVERSAL 6 : FOLD 7 : a combined bet placed on two different contests 8 pl : a game between two pairs of players 9 : an act of doubling in a card game

double bond n : a chemical bond in which two atoms in a molecule share two pairs of electrons

double cross n : an act of betraying or cheating esp. an associate — **dou·ble-cross** \ˌdə-bəl-'krȯs\ vb — **dou·ble-cross·er** n

dou·ble-deal·ing \ˌdə-bəl-'dē-liŋ\ n : DUPLICITY — **dou·ble-deal·er** \-'dē-lər\ n — **double–dealing** adj

dou·ble-deck·er \-'de-kər\ n : something having two decks, levels, or layers — **dou·ble–deck** \-ˌdek\ or **dou·ble–decked** \-ˌdekt\ adj

dou·ble-dig·it \ˌdə-bəl-'di-jət\ adj : amounting to 10 percent or more

dou·ble en·ten·dre \ˌdüb-ᵊl-äⁿ-'täⁿd, ˌdə-bəl-, -'tänd-rᵊ\ n, pl **double entendres** \same or -'tän-drəz\ [obs. F, lit., double meaning] : a word or expression capable of two interpretations with one usu. risqué

dou·ble-head·er \ˌdə-bəl-'he-dər\ n : two games played consecutively on the same day

double helix n : a helix or spiral consisting of two strands (as of DNA) in the surface of a cylinder which coil around its axis

dou·ble–hung \ˌdə-bəl-'həŋ\ adj, of a window : having an upper and a lower sash that can slide past each other

dou·ble–joint·ed \-'jȯin-təd\ adj : having a joint that permits an exceptional degree of freedom of motion of the parts joined ⟨a ~ finger⟩

dou·ble–park \ˌdə-bəl-'pärk\ vb : to park a vehicle beside a row of vehicles already parked parallel to the curb

double play n : a play in baseball by which two players are put out

double pneumonia n : pneumonia affecting both lungs

double standard n : a set of principles that applies differently and usu. more rigorously to one group of people or circumstances than to another

dou·blet \'də-blət\ n 1 : a man's close-fitting jacket worn in Europe esp. in the 16th century 2 : one of two similar or identical things

dou·ble take \'də-bəl-ˌtāk\ n : a delayed reaction to a surprising or significant situation after an initial failure to notice anything unusual

dou·ble–talk \-ˌtȯk\ *n* : language that appears to be meaningful but in fact is a mixture of sense and nonsense

double up *vb* : to share accommodations designed for one

double whammy *n* : a combination of two usu. adverse forces, circumstances, or effects

dou·bloon \də-ˈblün\ *n* : a former gold coin of Spain and Spanish America

dou·bly \ˈdə-blē\ *adv* **1** : in a twofold manner **2** : to twice the degree ⟨~ glad⟩

¹**doubt** \ˈdau̇t\ *vb* **1** : to be uncertain about **2** : to lack confidence in : DISTRUST **3** : to consider unlikely — **doubt·able** *adj* — **doubt·er** *n*

²**doubt** *n* **1** : uncertainty of belief or opinion **2** : a condition causing uncertainty, hesitation, or suspense ⟨the outcome was in ~⟩ **3** : DISTRUST **4** : an inclination not to believe or accept

doubt·ful \ˈdau̇t-fəl\ *adj* **1** : QUESTIONABLE ⟨~ they knew what happened⟩ **2** : UNDECIDED ⟨the outcome of the election is ~⟩ — **doubt·ful·ly** *adv* — **doubt·ful·ness** *n*

¹**doubt·less** \ˈdau̇t-ləs\ *adv* **1** : without doubt **2** : PROBABLY

²**doubtless** *adj* : free from doubt : CERTAIN — **doubt·less·ly** *adv*

douche \ˈdüsh\ *n* [F] **1** : a jet of fluid (as water) directed against a part or into a cavity of the body; *also* : a cleansing with a douche **2** : a device for giving douches — **douche** *vb*

dough \ˈdō\ *n* **1** : a mixture that consists of flour or meal and a liquid (as milk or water) and is stiff enough to knead or roll **2** : something resembling dough esp. in consistency **3** : MONEY — **doughy** \ˈdō-ē\ *adj*

dough·boy \-ˌbȯi\ *n* : an American infantryman esp. in World War I

dough·nut *also* **do·nut** \-(ˌ)nət\ *n* : a small usu. ring-shaped cake fried in fat

dough·ty \ˈdau̇-tē\ *adj* **dough·ti·er; -est** : ABLE, VALIANT ⟨a ~ warrior⟩

Doug·las fir \ˈdə-gləs-\ *n* : a tall evergreen timber tree of the western U.S.

dou·la \ˈdü-lə\ *n* : a woman who provides assistance to a mother before, during, and just after childbirth

do up *vb* **1** : to prepare (as by cleaning) for use **2** : to wrap up **3** : CLOTHE, DECORATE **4** : FASTEN

dour \ˈdau̇(-ə)r, ˈdu̇r\ *adj* [ME, fr. L *durus* hard] **1** : STERN, HARSH **2** : OBSTINATE **3** : SULLEN — **dour·ly** *adv*

douse \ˈdau̇s, ˈdau̇z\ *vb* **doused; dous·ing** **1** : to plunge into water **2** : DRENCH **3** : EXTINGUISH ⟨~ a match⟩

¹**dove** \ˈdəv\ *n* **1** : any of numerous pigeons; *esp* : a small wild pigeon **2** : an advocate of peace or of a peaceful policy — **dov·ish** \ˈdə-vish\ *adj*

²**dove** \ˈdōv\ *past of* DIVE

¹**dove·tail** \ˈdəv-ˌtāl\ *n* : something that resembles a dove's tail; *esp* : a flaring tenon and a mortise into which it fits tightly

²**dovetail** *vb* **1** : to join by means of dovetails **2** : to fit skillfully together to form a whole ⟨our plans ~ nicely⟩

dow·a·ger \ˈdau̇-i-jər\ *n* **1** : a widow owning property or a title from her deceased husband **2** : a dignified elderly woman

dowdy \ˈdau̇-dē\ *adj* **dowd·i·er; -est** : lacking neatness and charm : SHABBY, UNTIDY; *also* : lacking smartness

dow·el \ˈdau̇(-ə)l\ *n* **1** : a pin used for fastening together two pieces of wood **2** : a round rod (as of wood) — **dowel** *vb*

¹**dow·er** \ˈdau̇(-ə)r\ *n* [ME *dowere*, fr. AF *dower, douaire*, fr. ML *dotarium*, fr. L *dot-, dos* gift, marriage portion] **1** : the part of a deceased husband's real estate which the law gives for life to his widow **2** : DOWRY

²**dower** *vb* : to supply with a dower or dowry : ENDOW

dow·itch·er \ˈdau̇-i-chər\ *n* : any of several long-billed wading birds related to the sandpipers

¹**down** \ˈdau̇n\ *adv* [ME *doun*, fr. OE *dūne*, short for *adūne*, of *dūne*, lit., from (the) hill] **1** : toward or in a lower physical position **2** : to a lying or sitting position **3** : toward or to the ground, floor, or bottom **4** : as a down payment ⟨paid $5 ~⟩ **5** : on paper ⟨put ~ what he says⟩ **6** : in a direction that is the opposite of up **7** : SOUTH **8** : to or in a lower or worse condition or status **9** : from a past time **10** : to or in a state of less activity **11** : into defeat ⟨voted the motion ~⟩

²**down** *prep* : down in, on, along, or through : toward the bottom of ⟨fell ~ a hole⟩ ⟨lives ~ the road⟩

³**down** *vb* **1** : to go or cause to go or come down ⟨~ed a warplane⟩ **2** : DEFEAT **3** : to cause (a football) to be out of play **4** : CONSUME **3** ⟨~ed two beers⟩

⁴**down** *adj* **1** : occupying a low position; *esp* : lying on the ground **2** : directed or going downward **3** : being in a state of reduced or low activity **4** : DEPRESSED, DEJECTED **5** : SICK ⟨~ with a cold⟩ **6** : FINISHED, DONE **7** : completely mastered ⟨got her lines ~⟩ **8** : being on record ⟨you're ~ for two tickets⟩

⁵**down** *n* **1** : a low or falling period (as in activity, emotional life, or fortunes) **2** : one of a series of attempts to advance a football **3** : a quark with a charge of -⅓ that is one of the constituents of the proton and neutron

⁶**down** *n* : a rolling usu. treeless upland with sparse soil — usu. used in pl.

⁷**down** *n* **1** : a covering of soft fluffy feathers; *also* : such feathers **2** : a downlike covering or material

down·beat \ˈdau̇n-ˌbēt\ *n* : the downward stroke of a conductor indicating the principally accented note of a measure of music

down·burst \-ˌbərst\ *n* : a powerful downdraft usu. associated with a thunderstorm that is a hazard for low-flying aircraft; *also* : MICROBURST

down·cast \-ˌkast\ *adj* **1** : DEJECTED **2** : directed down ⟨a ~ glance⟩

down·draft \-ˌdraft\ n : a downward current of gas (as air)

down·er \ˈdau̇-nər\ n 1 : a depressant drug; esp : BARBITURATE 2 : someone or something depressing

down·fall \ˈdau̇n-ˌfȯl\ n 1 : a sudden fall (as from high rank) 2 : something that causes a downfall — **down·fall·en** \-ˌfȯ-lən\ adj

¹**down·grade** \ˈdau̇n-ˌgrād\ n 1 : a downward slope (as of a road) 2 : a decline toward a worse condition

²**downgrade** vb : to lower in quality, value, extent, or status

down·heart·ed \-ˈhär-təd\ adj : DEJECTED

¹**down·hill** \ˈdau̇n-ˈhil\ adv : toward the bottom of a hill — **downhill** \-ˌhil\ adj

²**down·hill** \-ˌhil\ n : the sport of skiing downhill usu. in a race against time

¹**down·load** \ˈdau̇n-ˌlōd\ n : an act or instance of downloading something; also : the item downloaded

²**download** vb : to transfer (data) from a computer to another device — **down·load·able** \-ˌlō-də-bəl\ adj

down payment n : a part of the full price paid at the time of purchase or delivery with the balance to be paid later

down·play \ˈdau̇n-ˌplā\ vb : DE-EMPHASIZE ⟨~ed the allegations⟩

down·pour \ˈdau̇n-ˌpȯr\ n : a heavy rain

down·range \-ˈrānj\ adv : away from a launching site

¹**down·right** \-ˌrīt\ adv : THOROUGHLY

²**downright** adj 1 : ABSOLUTE, UTTER ⟨a ~ lie⟩ 2 : PLAIN, BLUNT ⟨a ~ man⟩

down·shift \-ˌshift\ vb : to shift an automotive vehicle into a lower gear

down·size \-ˌsīz\ vb : to reduce or undergo reduction in size or numbers

down·spout \-ˌspau̇t\ n : a vertical pipe used to drain rainwater from a roof

Down syndrome \ˈdau̇n-\ or **Down's syndrome** \ˈdau̇nz-\ n : a birth defect characterized by mental retardation, slanting eyes, a broad short skull, broad hands with short fingers, and the presence of an extra chromosome

down·stage \ˈdau̇n-ˈstāj\ adv or adj : toward or at the front of a theatrical stage — **down·stage** \-ˌstāj\ n

down·stairs \-ˈsterz\ adv : on or to a lower floor and esp. the main or ground floor — **down·stairs** \-ˌsterz\ adj or n

down·stream \-ˈstrēm\ adv or adj : in the direction of flow of a stream

down·stroke \-ˌstrōk\ n : a downward stroke

down·swing \-ˌswiŋ\ n 1 : a swing downward 2 : DOWNTURN

down–to–earth adj : PRACTICAL, REALISTIC

down·town \ˈdau̇n-ˌtau̇n\ n : the main business district of a town or city — **downtown** \ˈdau̇n-ˈtau̇n\ adj or adv

down·trod·den \ˈdau̇n-ˈträ-dᵊn\ adj : suffering oppression

down·turn \-ˌtərn\ n : a downward turn esp. in economic activity

¹**down·ward** \ˈdau̇n-wərd\ or **down·**

wards \-wərdz\ adv 1 : from a higher to a lower place or condition 2 : from an earlier time 3 : from an ancestor or predecessor

²**downward** adj : directed toward or situated in a lower place or condition

down·wind \ˈdau̇n-ˈwind\ adv or adj : in the direction that the wind is blowing

downy \ˈdau̇-nē\ adj **down·i·er; -est** : resembling or covered with down

downy mildew n : any of various parasitic fungi producing whitish masses esp. on the underside of plant leaves; also : a plant disease caused by downy mildew

downy woodpecker n : a small black-and-white woodpecker of No. America

dow·ry \ˈdau̇(-ə)r-ē\ n, pl **dowries** [ME dowarie, fr. AF, alter. of dower, douaire dower] : the property that a woman brings to her husband in marriage

dowse \ˈdau̇z\ vb **dowsed; dows·ing** : to use a divining rod esp. to find water — **dows·er** n

dox·ol·o·gy \däk-ˈsä-lə-jē\ n, pl **-gies** : a usu. short hymn of praise to God

doy·en \ˈdȯi-ən, ˈdwä-ˌyaⁿ\ n : the senior or most experienced person in a group

doy·enne \dȯi-ˈyen, dwä-ˈyen\ n : a woman who is a doyen

doy·ley chiefly Brit var of DOILY

doz abbr dozen

doze \ˈdōz\ vb **dozed; doz·ing** : to sleep lightly — **doze** n

doz·en \ˈdə-zᵊn\ n, pl **dozens** or **dozen** [ME dozeine, fr. AF duzeine, fr. duze twelve, fr. L duodecim, fr. duo two + decem ten] : a group of twelve — **doz·enth** \-zᵊnth\ adj

¹**DP** \ˈdē-ˈpē\ n, pl **DP's** or **DPs** 1 : a displaced person 2 : DOUBLE PLAY

²**DP** abbr data processing

dpt abbr department

DPT abbr diphtheria-pertussis-tetanus (vaccines)

dr abbr 1 debtor 2 dram 3 drive 4 drum

Dr abbr doctor

DR abbr 1 dead reckoning 2 dining room

drab \ˈdrab\ adj **drab·ber; drab·best** 1 : being of a light olive-brown color 2 : DULL, MONOTONOUS, CHEERLESS — **drab·ly** adv — **drab·ness** n

drach·ma \ˈdrak-mə\ n, pl **drach·mas** or **drach·mai** \-ˌmī\ or **drach·mae** \-ˌ(ˌ)mē\ : the former basic monetary unit of Greece

dra·co·ni·an \drā-ˈkō-nē-ən, drə-\ adj, often cap : CRUEL; also : SEVERE

¹**draft** \ˈdraft, ˈdraft\ n 1 : the act of drawing or hauling 2 : the act or an instance of drinking or inhaling; also : the portion drunk or inhaled in one such act 3 : DOSE, POTION 4 : DELINEATION, PLAN, DESIGN; also : a preliminary sketch, outline, or version ⟨a rough ~ of a speech⟩ 5 : the act of drawing (as from a cask); also : a portion of liquid so drawn 6 : the depth of water a ship draws esp. when loaded 7 : a system for or act of selecting persons (as for sports teams or compulsory military service); also : the persons so

selected **8** : an order for the payment of money drawn by one person or bank on another **9** : a heavy demand : STRAIN **10** : a current of air; *also* : a device to regulate air supply (as in a stove) — **on draft** : ready to be drawn from a receptacle ⟨beer *on draft*⟩

²**draft** *adj* **1** : used or adapted for drawing loads ⟨∼ horses⟩ **2** : being or having been on draft ⟨∼ beer⟩

³**draft** *vb* **1** : to select usu. on a compulsory basis; *esp* : to conscript for military service **2** : to draw the preliminary sketch, version, or plan of **3** : COMPOSE, PREPARE **4** : to draw off or away

draft·ee \draf-'tē, 'dräf-\ *n* : a person who is drafted

drafts·man \'draft-smən, 'dräft-\ *n* : a person who draws plans (as for buildings or machinery) — **drafts·man·ly** \-lē\ *adj*

drafty \'draf-tē, 'dräf-\ *adj* **draft·i·er; -est** : exposed to or abounding in drafts of air ⟨a ∼ room⟩

¹**drag** \'drag\ *n* **1** : a device pulled along under water for detecting or gathering **2** : something (as a harrow or sledge) that is dragged along over a surface **3** : the act or an instance of dragging **4** : something that hinders progress; *also* : something boring ⟨thinks school is a ∼⟩ **5** : STREET ⟨the main ∼⟩ **6** : clothing typical of one sex worn by a member of the opposite sex

²**drag** *vb* **dragged; drag·ging 1** : HAUL **2** : to move or proceed with slowness or difficulty ⟨*dragged* himself out of bed⟩ ⟨the lecture *dragged* on⟩ **3** : to force into or out of some situation, condition, or course of action **4** : PROTRACT ⟨∼ a story out⟩ **5** : to hang or lag behind **6** : to explore, search, or fish with a drag **7** : to trail along on the ground **8** : DRAW, PUFF ⟨∼ on a cigarette⟩ **9** : to move (items on a computer screen) esp. by using a mouse — **drag·ger** *n* — **drag one's feet** *also* **drag one's heels** : to act slowly or with hesitation

drag·net \-ₙnet\ *n* **1** : NET, TRAWL **2** : a network of planned actions for pursuing and catching ⟨a police ∼⟩

drag·o·man \'dra-gə-mən\ *n, pl* **-mans** *or* **-men** \-mən\ : an interpreter employed esp. in the Near East

drag·on \'dra-gən\ *n* [ME, fr. AF *dragun*, fr. L *dracon-, draco* serpent, dragon, fr. Gk *drakōn* serpent] : a fabulous animal usu. represented as a huge winged scaly serpent with a crested head and large claws

drag·on·fly \-ₙflī\ *n* : any of a group of large harmless 4-winged insects that hold the wings horizontal and unfolded in repose

¹**dra·goon** \drə-'gün, dra-\ *n* [F *dragon* dragon, dragoon, fr. MF] **1** : a heavily armed mounted soldier **2** : CAVALRYMAN

²**dragoon** *vb* : to force or attempt to force into submission : COERCE

drag race *n* : an acceleration contest between vehicles — **drag racer** *n*

drag·ster \'drag-stər\ *n* : a usu. high-powered vehicle used in a drag race

drag strip *n* : a site for drag races

¹**drain** \'drān\ *vb* **1** : to draw off or flow off gradually or completely **2** : to exhaust physically or emotionally ⟨∼ed by the work⟩ **3** : to make or become gradually dry or empty ⟨∼ a swamp⟩ **4** : to carry away the surface water of : discharge surface or surplus water **5** : EMPTY, EXHAUST ⟨∼ed our savings⟩ — **drain·er** *n*

²**drain** *n* **1** : a means (as a channel or sewer) of draining **2** : the act of draining **3** : a gradual outflow; *also* : something causing an outflow ⟨a ∼ on our savings⟩

drain·age \'drā-nij\ *n* **1** : the act or process of draining; *also* : something that is drained off **2** : a means for draining : DRAIN, SEWER **3** : an area drained

drain·pipe \'drān-ₙpīp\ *n* : a pipe for drainage

drake \'drāk\ *n* : a male duck

¹**dram** \'dram\ *n* **1** — see WEIGHT table **2** : FLUID DRAM **3** : a small drink

²**dram** \'dräm\ *n* — see MONEY table

dra·ma \'drä-mə, 'dra-\ *n* [LL, fr. Gk, deed, drama, fr. *dran* to do, act] **1** : a literary composition designed for theatrical presentation; *also* : a production (as a film) with a serious tone or subject **2** : dramatic art, literature, or affairs **3** : a series of events involving conflicting forces — **dra·mat·ic** \drə-'ma-tik\ *adj* — **dra·mat·i·cal·ly** \-ti-k(ə-)lē\ *adv* — **dra·ma·tist** \'dra-mə-tist, 'drä-\ *n*

dram·a·ti·sa·tion, dra·ma·tise *Brit var of* DRAMATIZATION, DRAMATIZE

dra·ma·tize \'dra-mə-ₙtīz, 'drä-\ *vb* **-tized; -tiz·ing 1** : to adapt for or be suitable for theatrical presentation **2** : to present or represent in a dramatic manner — **dram·a·ti·za·tion** \ₙdra-mə-tə-'zā-shən, ₙdrä-\ *n*

dra·me·dy \'drä-mə-ₙdē, 'dra-\ *n* : a comedy having dramatic moments

drank *past and past part of* DRINK

¹**drape** \'drāp\ *vb* **draped; drap·ing 1** : to cover or adorn with or as if with folds of cloth ⟨kings *draped* in robes⟩ **2** : to cause to hang or stretch out loosely or carelessly **3** : to arrange or become arranged in flowing lines or folds

²**drape** *n* **1** : CURTAIN **2** : arrangement in or of folds **3** : the cut or hang of clothing

drap·er \'drā-pər\ *n, chiefly Brit* : a dealer in cloth and sometimes in clothing and dry goods

drap·ery \'drā-pə-rē\ *n, pl* **-er·ies 1** *Brit* : DRY GOODS **2** : a decorative fabric esp. when hung loosely and in folds; *also* : hangings of heavy fabric used as a curtain

dras·tic \'dras-tik\ *adj* : HARSH, RIGOROUS, SEVERE ⟨∼ punishment⟩ — **dras·ti·cal·ly** \-ti-k(ə-)lē\ *adv*

draught \'dräft\, **draughty** \'dräf-tē\ *chiefly Brit var of* DRAFT, DRAFTY

draughts \'dráfts\ *n, Brit* : CHECKERS

draughts·man *chiefly Brit var of* DRAFTS-MAN

Dra·vid·i·an \drə-'vi-dē-ən\ *n* : a language family of south Asia that includes the major literary languages of southern India

¹**draw** \'dró\ *vb* **drew** \'drü\; **drawn** \'drón\; **draw·ing** **1** : to cause to move toward a force exerted **2** : to cause to go in a certain direction ⟨*drew* him aside⟩ **3** : to move or go steadily or gradually ⟨night ∼s near⟩ **4** : ATTRACT, ENTICE **5** : PROVOKE, ROUSE ⟨*drew* enemy fire⟩ **6** : INHALE ⟨∼ a deep breath⟩ **7** : to bring or pull out ⟨*drew* a gun⟩ **8** : to cause to come out of a container or source ⟨∼ blood⟩ ⟨∼ water for a bath⟩ **9** : EVISCERATE **10** : to require (a specified depth) to float in **11** : ACCUMULATE, GAIN ⟨∼ing interest⟩ **12** : to take money from a place of deposit : WITHDRAW **13** : to receive regularly ⟨∼ a salary⟩ **14** : to take (cards) from a stack or the dealer **15** : to receive or take at random ⟨∼ a winning number⟩ **16** : to bend (a bow) by pulling back the string **17** : WRINKLE, SHRINK **18** : to change shape by or as if by pulling or stretching ⟨a face *drawn* with sorrow⟩ **19** : to leave (a contest) undecided : TIE **20** : DELINEATE, SKETCH **21** : to write out in due form : DRAFT ⟨∼ up a will⟩ **22** : FORMULATE ⟨∼ comparisons⟩ **23** : INFER ⟨∼ a conclusion⟩ **24** : to spread or elongate (metal) by hammering or by pulling through dies **25** : to produce or allow a draft or current of air ⟨the chimney ∼s well⟩ **26** : to swell out in a wind ⟨all sails ∼ing⟩ — **draw a blank** : to be unable to think of something — **draw the line** *or* **draw a line** : to fix an arbitrary boundary usu. between two things

²**draw** *n* **1** : the act, process, or result of drawing **2** : a lot or chance drawn at random **3** : a contest left undecided or deadlocked : TIE **4** : one that draws attention or patronage : ATTRACTION

draw·back \'dró-,bak\ *n* : DISADVANTAGE 2

draw·bridge \-,brij\ *n* : a bridge made to be raised, lowered, or turned to permit or deny passage

draw·er \'dròr, 'dró-ər\ *n* **1** : one that draws **2** *pl* : an undergarment for the lower part of the body **3** : a sliding boxlike compartment (as in a table or desk)

draw·ing \'dró-iŋ\ *n* **1** : an act or instance of drawing; *esp* : an occasion when something is decided by drawing lots ⟨tonight's lottery ∼⟩ **2** : the act or art of making a figure, plan, or sketch by means of lines **3** : a representation made by drawing : SKETCH

drawing card *n* : DRAW 4

drawing room *n* : a formal reception room

drawl \'dról\ *vb* : to speak or utter slowly with vowels greatly prolonged — **drawl** *n*

draw on *vb* : APPROACH ⟨night *draws on*⟩

draw out *vb* **1** : PROLONG **2** : to cause to speak freely

draw·string \'dró-,striŋ\ *n* : a string, cord, or tape for use in closing a bag or controlling fullness in garments or curtains

draw up *vb* **1** : to prepare a draft or version of **2** : to pull oneself erect **3** : to bring or come to a stop

dray \'drā\ *n* : a strong low cart for carrying heavy loads

¹**dread** \'dred\ *vb* **1** : to fear greatly **2** : to feel extreme reluctance to meet or face

²**dread** *n* : great fear esp. of some harm to come

³**dread** *adj* **1** : causing great fear or anxiety **2** : inspiring awe

dread·ful \'dred-fəl\ *adj* **1** : inspiring dread or awe : FRIGHTENING **2** : extremely distasteful, unpleasant, or shocking — **dread·ful·ly** *adv*

dread·locks \'dred-,läks\ *n pl* : long braids of hair over the entire head

dread·nought \'dred-,nòt\ *n* : BATTLESHIP

¹**dream** \'drēm\ *n* [ME *dreem,* fr. OE *drēam* noise, joy, and ON *draumr* dream] **1** : a series of thoughts, images, or emotions occurring during sleep **2** : a dreamlike vision : DAYDREAM, REVERIE **3** : something notable for its beauty, excellence, or enjoyable quality **4** : IDEAL — **dream-like** \-,līk\ *adj* — **dreamy** *adj*

²**dream** \'drēm\ *vb* **dreamed** \'dremt, 'drēmd\ *or* **dreamt** \'dremt\; **dreaming** **1** : to have a dream of **2** : to indulge in daydreams or fantasies : pass (time) in reverie or inaction **3** : IMAGINE — **dream·er** *n*

dream·boat \'drēm-,bōt\ *n, slang* : something highly desirable; *esp* : a very attractive person

dream·land \'drēm-,land\ *n* : an unreal delightful country that exists in imagination or in dreams

dream up *vb* : INVENT, CONCOCT

dream·world \-,wərld\ *n* : a world of illusion or fantasy

drear \'drir\ *adj* : DREARY

drea·ry \'drir-ē\ *adj* **drea·ri·er; -est** [ME *drery,* fr. OE *drēorig* sad, bloody, fr. *drēor* gore] **1** : DOLEFUL, SAD **2** : DISMAL, GLOOMY — **drea·ri·ly** \-ə-lē\ *adv*

¹**dredge** \'drej\ *vb* **dredged; dredg·ing** : to gather or search with or as if with a dredge — **dredg·er** *n*

²**dredge** *n* : a machine or barge for removing earth or silt

³**dredge** *vb* **dredged; dredg·ing** : to coat (food) by sprinkling (as with flour)

dregs \'dregz\ *n pl* **1** : SEDIMENT 1 **2** : the most undesirable part ⟨the ∼ of humanity⟩

drench \'drench\ *vb* : to wet thoroughly

¹**dress** \'dres\ *vb* [ME, fr. AF *drescer* to direct, put right, fr. VL *directiare,* fr. L *directus* direct] **1** : to make or set straight : ALIGN **2** : to prepare for use; *esp* : BUTCHER **3** : TRIM, EMBELLISH ⟨∼ a store window⟩ **4** : to put clothes on : CLOTHE; *also* : to put on or wear formal or fancy clothes **5** : to apply dressings or

medicine to ⟨~ a wound⟩ 6 : to arrange (the hair) by combing, brushing, or curling 7 : to apply fertilizer to ⟨~ a field⟩ 8 : SMOOTH, FINISH ⟨~ leather⟩

²**dress** n 1 : APPAREL, CLOTHING ⟨casual ~⟩ 2 : a garment usu. consisting of a one-piece bodice and skirt — **dress-mak·er** \-ˌmā-kər\ n — **dress·mak·ing** \-ˌmā-kiŋ\ n

³**dress** adj : suitable for a formal occasion; also : requiring formal dress

dres·sage \drə-ˈsäzh\ n [F] : the execution by a trained horse of complex movements in response to barely perceptible signals from its rider

dress down vb : to scold severely

¹**dress·er** \ˈdre-sər\ n : a chest of drawers or bureau with a mirror

²**dresser** n : one that dresses

dress·ing \ˈdre-siŋ\ n 1 : the act or process of one who dresses 2 : a sauce for adding to a dish (as a salad) 3 : a seasoned mixture usu. used as stuffing 4 : material used to cover an injury (as a wound)

dressing gown n : a loose robe worn esp. while dressing or resting

dressy \ˈdre-sē\ adj **dress·i·er; -est** 1 : showy in dress 2 : STYLISH, SMART

drew past of DRAW

¹**drib·ble** \ˈdri-bəl\ vb **drib·bled; drib·bling** 1 : to fall or flow in drops : TRICKLE 2 : DROOL 3 : to propel by successive slight taps or bounces

²**dribble** n 1 : a small trickling stream or flow 2 : a drizzling shower 3 : the dribbling of a ball or puck

drib·let \ˈdri-blət\ n 1 : a trifling amount 2 : a drop of liquid

dri·er or **dry·er** \ˈdrī-ər\ n 1 : a substance that speeds drying (as of paint or ink) 2 usu **dryer** : a device for drying

¹**drift** \ˈdrift\ n 1 : the motion or course of something drifting; also : a gradual shift of position 2 : a mass of matter (as snow or sand) piled up esp. by wind 3 : earth, gravel, and rock deposited by a glacier 4 : a general underlying design or tendency : MEANING ⟨catch my ~⟩

²**drift** vb 1 : to float or be driven along by or as if by a current of water or air ⟨~ing logs⟩ 2 : to become piled up by wind or water ⟨~ing snow⟩

drift·er \ˈdrif-tər\ n : a person who moves about aimlessly

drift net n : a fishing net often miles in extent arranged to drift with the tide or current

drift·wood \ˈdrift-ˌwu̇d\ n : wood drifted or floated by water

¹**drill** \ˈdril\ n 1 : a tool for boring holes 2 : the training of soldiers in marching and the handling of arms 3 : a regularly practiced exercise ⟨a shooting ~⟩

²**drill** vb 1 : to instruct and exercise by repetition 2 : to train in or practice military drill 3 : to bore with a drill ⟨~ a hole⟩ — **drill·er** n

³**drill** n 1 : a shallow furrow or trench in which seed is sown 2 : an agricultural implement for making furrows and dropping seed into them

⁴**drill** n : a firm cotton twilled fabric

drill·mas·ter \ˈdril-ˌmas-tər\ n : an instructor in military drill

drill press n : an upright drilling machine in which the drill is pressed to the work usu. by a hand lever

drily var of DRYLY

¹**drink** \ˈdriŋk\ vb **drank** \ˈdraŋk\; **drunk** \ˈdrəŋk\ or **drank**; **drink·ing** 1 : to swallow liquid : IMBIBE 2 : ABSORB 3 : to take in through the senses ⟨~ in the beautiful scenery⟩ 4 : to give or join in a toast 5 : to drink alcoholic beverages esp. to excess — **drink·able** adj — **drink·er** n

²**drink** n 1 : BEVERAGE; also : an alcoholic beverage 2 : a draft or portion of liquid 3 : excessive consumption of alcoholic beverages

¹**drip** \ˈdrip\ vb **dripped; drip·ping** 1 : to fall or let fall in drops 2 : to let fall drops of moisture or liquid ⟨a dripping faucet⟩ 3 : to overflow with or as if with moisture ⟨clothes dripping with sweat⟩ ⟨stories dripping with irony⟩

²**drip** n 1 : a falling in drops 2 : liquid that falls, overflows, or is extruded in drops 3 : the sound made by or as if by falling drops

¹**drive** \ˈdrīv\ vb **drove** \ˈdrōv\; **driv·en** \ˈdri-vən\; **driv·ing** 1 : to urge, push, or force onward 2 : to carry through strongly ⟨~ a bargain⟩ 3 : to set or keep in motion or operation 4 : to direct the movement or course of 5 : to convey in a vehicle ⟨drove her to school⟩ 6 : to bring into a specified condition ⟨the noise ~s me crazy⟩ 7 : FORCE, COMPEL ⟨driven by hunger to steal⟩ 8 : to project, inject, or impress forcefully ⟨drove the lesson home⟩ 9 : to produce by opening a way ⟨~ a well⟩ 10 : to progress with strong momentum ⟨a driving rain⟩ 11 : to propel an object of play (as a golf ball) by a hard blow — **driv·er** n

²**drive** n 1 : a trip in a carriage or automobile 2 : a driving or collecting of animals ⟨a cattle ~⟩ 3 : the guiding of logs downstream to a mill 4 : the act of driving a ball; also : the flight of a ball 5 : DRIVEWAY 6 : a public road for driving ⟨as in a park⟩ 7 : the state of being hurried and under pressure 8 : an intensive campaign ⟨membership ~⟩ 9 : the apparatus by which motion is imparted to a machine 10 : an offensive or aggressive move : a military attack 11 : NEED, LONGING ⟨the ~ to succeed⟩ 12 : dynamic quality 13 : a device for reading and writing on magnetic media (as magnetic tape or disks)

drive-in \ˈdrī-ˌvin\ adj : accommodating patrons while they remain in their automobiles — **drive-in** n

¹**driv·el** \ˈdri-vəl\ vb **-eled** or **-elled; -el·ing** or **-el·ling** 1 : DROOL, SLAVER 2 : to talk or utter stupidly, carelessly, or in an infantile way — **driv·el·er** n

²**drivel** n : NONSENSE

drive·shaft \ˈdrīv-ˌshaft\ n : a shaft that transmits mechanical power

drive–through also **drive–thru** \'drīv-,thrü\ adj : designed for the service of patrons remaining in their automobiles — **drive–through** also **drive–thru** n

drive·way \-,wā\ n : a short private road leading from the street to a house, garage, or parking lot

¹**driz·zle** \'dri-zəl\ n : a fine misty rain

²**drizzle** vb **driz·zled**; **driz·zling** : to rain in very small drops

drogue \'drōg\ n : a small parachute for slowing down or stabilizing something (as a space capsule)

droll \'drōl\ adj [F drôle, fr. drôle scamp, fr. MF drolle, fr. MD, imp] : having a humorous, whimsical, or odd quality ⟨a ~ expression⟩ — **droll·ery** \'drō-lə-rē\ n — **drol·ly** adv

drom·e·dary \'drä-mə-,der-ē\ n, pl **-dar·ies** [ME dromedarie, fr. MF dromedaire, fr. LL dromedarius, fr. L dromad-, dromas, fr. Gk running] : CAMEL; esp : a domesticated one-humped camel of western Asia and northern Africa

¹**drone** \'drōn\ n 1 : a male honeybee 2 : one that lives on the labors of others : PARASITE 3 : an unmanned aircraft or ship guided by remote control 4 : DRUDGE

²**drone** vb **droned**; **dron·ing** : to sound with a low dull monotonous murmuring sound : speak monotonously

³**drone** n : a deep monotonous sound ⟨the ~ of engines⟩

drool \'drül\ vb 1 : to let liquid flow from the mouth 2 : to talk foolishly — **drool** n

droop \'drüp\ vb 1 : to hang or incline downward 2 : to sink gradually 3 : LANGUISH — **droop** n — **droopy** adj

¹**drop** \'dräp\ n 1 : the quantity of fluid that falls in one spherical mass 2 pl : a dose of medicine measured by drops 3 : a small quantity of drink 4 : the smallest practical unit of liquid measure 5 : something (as a pendant or a small round candy) that resembles a liquid drop 6 : FALL 7 : a decline in quantity or quality 8 : a descent by parachute 9 : the distance through which something drops 10 : a slot into which something is to be dropped 11 : something that drops or has dropped

²**drop** vb **dropped**; **drop·ping** 1 : to fall or let fall in drops 2 : to let fall : LOWER ⟨~ a glove⟩ ⟨dropped his voice⟩ 3 : SEND ⟨~ me a note⟩ 4 : to let go : DISMISS ⟨~ the subject⟩ 5 : MENTION ⟨~ a suggestion⟩ 6 : to knock down : cause to fall 7 : to go lower : become less ⟨prices dropped⟩ 8 : SPEND, LOSE ⟨~ $20⟩ ⟨dropped ten pounds⟩ 9 : to come or go unexpectedly or informally ⟨a friend dropped in⟩ 10 : to pass from one state into a less active one ⟨~ off to sleep⟩ 11 : to move downward or with a current 12 : QUIT ⟨dropped out of the race⟩ — **drop back** : to move toward the rear — **drop behind** : to fail to keep up

drop–down \'dräp-,daún\ adj : PULL-DOWN

drop–kick \-'kik\ n : a kick made by dropping a ball to the ground and kicking it at the moment it starts to rebound — **drop–kick** vb

drop·let \'drä-plət\ n : a tiny drop

drop–off \'dräp-,óf\ n 1 : a steep or perpendicular descent 2 : a marked decline ⟨a ~ in attendance⟩ 3 : an act or instance of delivering or depositing something ⟨~ points along the route⟩

drop off vb : to fall asleep

drop out vb : to withdraw from participation or membership; esp : to leave school before graduation — **drop·out** \'dräp-,aút\ n

drop·per \'drä-pər\ n 1 : one that drops 2 : a short glass tube with a rubber bulb used to measure out liquids by drops

drop·pings n pl : MANURE, DUNG

drop·sy \'dräp-sē\ n [ME dropesie, short for ydropesie, fr. AF, fr. L hydropisis, fr. Gk hydrōps, fr. hydōr water] : EDEMA — **drop·si·cal** \-si-kəl\ adj

drop–top \'dräp-,täp\ n : CONVERTIBLE

dross \'dräs\ n 1 : the scum that forms on the surface of a molten metal 2 : waste matter : REFUSE

drought \'draút\ also **drouth** \'draúth\ n : a long spell of dry weather

¹**drove** \'drōv\ n 1 : a group of animals driven or moving in a body 2 : a large number : CROWD — usu. used in pl. ⟨tourists arriving in ~s⟩

²**drove** past of DRIVE

drov·er \'drō-vər\ n : one who drives domestic animals usu. to market

drown \'draún\ vb **drowned** \'draúnd\; **drown·ing** 1 : to suffocate by submersion esp. in water 2 : to become drowned 3 : to cover with water 4 : to cause to be muted (as a sound) by a loud noise 5 : OVERPOWER, OVERWHELM

drowse \'draúz\ vb **drowsed**; **drows·ing** : DOZE — **drowse** n

drowsy \'draú-zē\ adj **drows·i·er**; **-est** 1 : ready to fall asleep 2 : making one sleepy ⟨~ music⟩ — **drows·i·ly** \-zə-lē\ adv — **drows·i·ness** \-zē-nəs\ n

drub \'drəb\ vb **drubbed**; **drub·bing** 1 : to beat severely 2 : to berate critically 3 : to defeat decisively

drudge \'drəj\ vb **drudged**; **drudg·ing** : to do hard, menial, or monotonous work — **drudge** n — **drudg·ery** \'drə-jə-rē\ n

¹**drug** \'drəg\ n 1 : a substance used as a medicine or in making medicine 2 : a substance (as heroin or marijuana) that can cause addiction, habituation, or a marked change in mental status

²**drug** vb **drugged**; **drug·ging** : to affect with or as if with drugs; esp : to stupefy with a narcotic

drug·gist \'drə-gist\ n : a dealer in drugs and medicines; also : PHARMACIST

drug·store \'drəg-,stór\ n : a retail shop where medicines and miscellaneous articles are sold

dru·id \'drü-əd\ n, often cap : one of an ancient Celtic priesthood appearing in Irish, Welsh, and Christian legends as magicians and wizards

¹**drum** \'drəm\ n 1 : a percussion instrument usu. consisting of a hollow cylinder with a skin or plastic head stretched over one or both ends that is beaten with the hands or with a stick 2 : the sound of a drum; also : a similar sound 3 : a drum-shaped object (as a structure or container)

²**drum** vb **drummed; drum·ming** 1 : to beat a drum 2 : to sound rhythmically : THROB, BEAT 3 : to summon or enlist by or as if by beating a drum ⟨*drummed* into service⟩ 5 : EXPEL — usu. used with *out* 5 : to drive or force by steady effort ⟨~ the facts into memory⟩ 6 : to strike or tap repeatedly so as to produce rhythmic sounds

drum·beat \'drəm-ˌbēt\ n : a stroke on a drum or its sound

drum major n : the leader of a marching band

drum ma·jor·ette \-ˌmā-jə-'ret\ n : a girl or woman who leads a marching band; also : a baton twirler who accompanies a marching band

drum·mer \'drə-mər\ n 1 : one that plays a drum 2 : a traveling salesman

drum·stick \'drəm-ˌstik\ n 1 : a stick for beating a drum 2 : the lower segment of a fowl's leg

drum up vb 1 : to bring about by persistent effort ⟨*drum up* business⟩ 2 : INVENT, ORIGINATE

¹**drunk** past part of DRINK

²**drunk** \'drəŋk\ adj 1 : having the faculties impaired by alcohol ⟨~ drivers⟩ 2 : dominated by an intense feeling ⟨~ with power⟩ 3 : of, relating to, caused by, or characterized by intoxication

³**drunk** n 1 : a period of excessive drinking 2 : a drunken person

drunk·ard \'drəŋ-kərd\ n : one who is habitually drunk

drunk·en \'drəŋ-kən\ adj 1 : DRUNK 2 : given to habitual excessive use of alcohol 3 : of, relating to, or resulting from intoxication ⟨a ~ brawl⟩ 4 : unsteady or lurching as if from intoxication ⟨walked with a ~ shuffle⟩ — **drunk·en·ly** adv — **drunk·en·ness** n

drupe \'drüp\ n : a partly fleshy fruit (as a plum or cherry) having one seed enclosed in a hard inner shell

¹**dry** \'drī\ adj **dri·er** \'drī-ər\; **dri·est** \-əst\ 1 : free or freed from water or liquid ⟨~ fruits⟩; also : not being in or under water 2 : characterized by lack of water or moisture ⟨~ climate⟩ 3 : lacking freshness : STALE 4 : devoid of natural moisture : THIRSTY 5 : no longer liquid or sticky ⟨the ink is ~⟩ 6 : not giving milk ⟨a ~ cow⟩ 7 : marked by the absence of alcoholic beverages ⟨a ~ dormitory⟩ 8 : prohibiting the making or distributing of alcoholic beverages 9 : not sweet ⟨~ wine⟩ 10 : solid as opposed to liquid ⟨~ groceries⟩ 11 : containing or employing no liquid 12 : SEVERE; also : UNINTERESTING, WEARISOME 13 : not productive ⟨a writer's ~ spell⟩ 14 : marked by a matter-of-fact, ironic, or terse manner of expression ⟨~

humor⟩ — **dri·ly** or **dry·ly** adv — **dry·ness** n

²**dry** vb **dried; dry·ing** : to make or become dry

³**dry** n, pl **drys** : PROHIBITIONIST

dry·ad \'drī-əd, -ˌad\ n : WOOD NYMPH

dry cell n : a battery whose contents are not spillable

dry–clean \'drī-ˌklēn\ vb : to clean (fabrics) chiefly with solvents other than water — **dry cleaning** n

dry dock \'drī-ˌdäk\ n : a dock that can be kept dry during ship construction or repair

dryer var of DRIER

dry farm·ing n : farming without irrigation in areas of limited rainfall — **dry–farm** vb — **dry farm·er** n

dry goods \'drī-ˌgudz\ n pl : cloth goods (as fabrics, ribbon, and ready-to-wear clothing)

dry ice n : solid carbon dioxide

dry measure n : a series of units of capacity for dry commodities — see METRIC SYSTEM table, WEIGHT table

dry rot n : decay of timber in which fungi consume the wood's cellulose

dry run n : REHEARSAL, TRIAL

dry·wall \'drī-ˌwol\ n : a wallboard consisting of fiberboard, paper, or felt over a plaster core

Ds symbol darmstadtium

DSC abbr 1 Distinguished Service Cross 2 doctor of surgical chiropody

DSM abbr Distinguished Service Medal

DST abbr daylight saving time

DTP abbr diphtheria, tetanus, pertussis (vaccines)

d.t.'s \ˌdē-'tēz\ n pl, often cap D&T : DELIRIUM TREMENS

du·al \'dü-əl, 'dyü-\ adj 1 : TWOFOLD, DOUBLE 2 : having a double character or nature — **du·al·ism** \-ə-ˌli-zəm\ n — **du·al·i·ty** \dü-'a-lə-tē, dyü-\ n

¹**dub** \'dəb\ vb **dubbed; dub·bing** 1 : to confer knighthood upon 2 : NAME, NICKNAME

²**dub** n : a clumsy person : DUFFER

³**dub** vb **dubbed; dub·bing** : to add (sound effects) to a motion picture or to a radio or television production

du·bi·e·ty \dü-'bī-ə-tē, dyü-\ n, pl **-eties** 1 : UNCERTAINTY 2 : a matter of doubt

du·bi·ous \'dü-bē-əs, 'dyü-\ adj 1 : UNCERTAIN 2 : QUESTIONABLE 3 : feeling doubt : UNDECIDED — **du·bi·ous·ly** adv — **du·bi·ous·ness** n

dub·ni·um \'düb-nē-əm, 'dəb-\ n : a short-lived radioactive chemical element produced artificially

du·cal \'dü-kəl, 'dyü-\ adj : of or relating to a duke or dukedom

duc·at \'də-kət\ n : a gold coin formerly used in various European countries

duch·ess \'də-chəs\ n 1 : the wife or widow of a duke 2 : a woman holding the rank of duke in her own right

duchy \'də-chē\ n, pl **duch·ies** : the territory of a duke or duchess : DUKEDOM

¹**duck** \'dək\ n, pl **ducks** : any of various swimming birds related to but smaller than geese and swans

²**duck** *vb* **1** : to thrust or plunge under water **2** : to lower the head or body suddenly : BOW; *also* : DODGE **3** : to evade a duty, question, or responsibility ⟨∼ the issue⟩

³**duck** *n* **1** : a durable closely woven usu. cotton fabric **2** *pl* : light clothes made of duck

duck-bill \'dək-ˌbil\ *n* : PLATYPUS

duck-ling \-liŋ\ *n* : a young duck

duck-pin \-ˌpin\ *n* **1** : a small bowling pin shorter and wider in the middle than a tenpin **2** *pl but sing in constr* : a bowling game using duckpins

duck sauce *n* : a thick sweet sauce made with fruits and seasonings and used in Chinese cuisine

duct \'dəkt\ *n* **1** : a tube or canal for conveying a bodily fluid **2** : a pipe or tube through which a fluid (as air) flows — **duct-less** *adj*

duc-tile \'dək-tᵊl\ *adj* **1** : capable of being drawn out into wire or thread **2** : easily led : DOCILE — **duc-til-i-ty** \ˌdək-'ti-lə-tē\ *n*

ductless gland *n* : an endocrine gland

duct tape *n* : a cloth adhesive tape orig. designed for sealing certain ducts and joints — **duct tape** *vb*

dud \'dəd\ *n* **1** *pl* : CLOTHING **2** : one that fails completely; *also* : a bomb or missile that fails to explode

dude \'düd, 'dyüd\ *n* **1** : DANDY 1 **2** : a city dweller; *esp* : an Easterner in the West **3** : FELLOW, GUY — sometimes used as an informal form of address

dude ranch *n* : a vacation resort offering activities (as horseback riding) typical of western ranches

dud-geon \'də-jən\ *n* : a fit or state of indignation ⟨in high ∼⟩

¹**due** \'dü, 'dyü\ *adj* [ME, fr. AF *deu*, pp. of *dever* to owe, fr. L *debēre*] **1** : owed or owing as a debt **2** : owed or owing as a right ⟨is ∼ a fair trial⟩ **3** : APPROPRIATE, FITTING ⟨with all ∼ respect⟩ **4** : SUFFICIENT, ADEQUATE **5** : REGULAR, LAWFUL ⟨∼ process of law⟩ **6** : ATTRIBUTABLE, ASCRIBABLE ⟨∼ to negligence⟩ **7** : PAYABLE ⟨a bill ∼ today⟩ **8** : SCHEDULED ⟨∼ to arrive soon⟩

²**due** *n* **1** : something that rightfully belongs to one ⟨give everyone their ∼⟩ **2** : DEBT **3** *pl* : FEES, CHARGES

³**due** *adv* : DIRECTLY, EXACTLY ⟨∼ north⟩

du-el \'dü-əl, 'dyü-\ *n* : a combat between two persons; *esp* : one fought with weapons in front of witnesses — **duel** *vb* — **du-el-ist** \-ə-list\ *n*

du-en-de \dü-'en-dā\ *n* [Sp dial., charm, fr. Sp, ghost, goblin, fr. *duen de casa*, prob. fr. *dueño de casa* owner of a house] : the power to attract through personal magnetism and charm

du-en-na \dü-'e-nə, dyü-\ *n* **1** : an elderly woman in charge of the younger ladies in a Spanish or Portuguese family **2** : CHAPERONE

du-et \dü-'et, dyü-\ *n* : a musical composition for two performers

due to *prep* : BECAUSE OF

duf-fel bag \'də-fəl-\ *n* : a soft oblong bag for personal belongings

duf-fer \'də-fər\ *n* : an incompetent or clumsy person

dug *past and past part of* DIG

dug-out \'dəg-ˌaut\ *n* **1** : a boat made by hollowing out a log **2** : a shelter dug in the ground **3** : a low shelter facing a baseball diamond that contains the players' bench

DUI *n* : the act or crime of driving while under the influence of alcohol

duke \'dük, 'dyük\ *n*, **1** : a sovereign ruler of a continental European duchy **2** : a nobleman of the highest rank; *esp* : a member of the highest grade of the British peerage **3** *slang* : FIST 1 ⟨put up your ∼s⟩ — **duke-dom** *n*

dul-cet \'dəl-sət\ *adj* **1** : pleasing to the ear **2** : AGREEABLE, SOOTHING

dul-ci-mer \'dəl-sə-mər\ *n* **1** : a stringed instrument of trapezoidal shape played with light hammers held in the hands **2** *or* **dul-ci-more** \-ˌmȯr\ : an American folk instrument with three or four strings that is held on the lap and played by plucking or strumming

¹**dull** \'dəl\ *adj* **1** : mentally slow : STUPID **2** : slow in perception or sensibility **3** : LISTLESS **4** : slow in action : SLUGGISH ⟨a ∼ market⟩ **5** : lacking intensity ⟨a ∼ pain⟩; *also* : not resonant or ringing **6** : BLUNT **7** : lacking brilliance or luster ⟨a ∼ finish⟩ **8** : low in saturation and lightness ⟨∼ color⟩ **9** : CLOUDY, OVERCAST ⟨∼ weather⟩ **10** : TEDIOUS, UNINTERESTING ⟨a ∼ lecture⟩ — **dull-ness** *also* **dul-ness** *n* — **dul-ly** *adv*

²**dull** *vb* : to make or become dull

dull-ard \'də-lərd\ *n* : a stupid person

du-ly \'dü-lē, 'dyü-\ *adv* : in a due manner or time

dumb \'dəm\ *adj* **1** *often offensive* : lacking the power of speech **2** : SILENT **3** : STUPID — **dumb-ly** *adv*

dumb-bell \'dəm-ˌbel\ *n* **1** : a bar with weights at the end used for exercise **2** : one who is stupid

dumb down *vb* : to lower the level of intelligence or intellectual content of

dumb-found *also* **dum-found** \ˌdəm-'faund\ *vb* : ASTONISH, AMAZE — **dumb-found-ing-ly** \-'faun-diŋ-lē\ *adv*

dumb-wait-er \'dəm-ˌwā-tər\ *n* : a small elevator for conveying food and dishes from one floor to another

dum-my \'də-mē\ *n, pl* **dummies 1** : a person who cannot speak; *also* : a stupid person **2** : the exposed hand in bridge played by the declarer in addition to that player's own hand; *also* : a bridge player whose hand is a dummy **3** : an imitative substitute for something; *also* : MANNEQUIN **4** : one seeming to act alone but really acting for another **5** : a mock-up of matter to be reproduced esp. by printing

¹**dump** \'dəmp\ *vb* : to let fall in a pile ⟨∼ laundry on the floor⟩; *also* : to get rid of carelessly ⟨∼ed her boyfriend⟩

²**dump** *n* **1** : a place for dumping some-

thing (as refuse) **2** : a reserve supply; *also* : a place where such supplies are kept ⟨an ammunition ∼⟩ **3** : a messy or objectionable place

dump·ing \'dəm-piŋ\ *n* : the selling of goods in quantity at below market price

dump·ling \'dəm-pliŋ\ *n* **1** : a small mass of boiled or steamed dough **2** : a dessert of fruit baked in biscuit dough

dumps \'dəmps\ *n pl* : a gloomy state of mind : low spirits ⟨in the ∼⟩

dump truck *n* : a truck for transporting and dumping bulk material

dumpy \'dəm-pē\ *adj* **dump·i·er; -est 1** : short and thick in build **2** : SHABBY

¹dun \'dən\ *n* : a brownish dark gray

²dun *vb* **dunned; dun·ning 1** : to make persistent demands for payment **2** : PLAGUE, PESTER — **dun** *n*

dunce \'dəns\ *n* [John *Duns* Scotus, whose once accepted writings were ridiculed in the 16th cent.] : a slow stupid person

dun·der·head \'dən-dər-,hed\ *n* : DUNCE, BLOCKHEAD

dune \'dün, 'dyün\ *n* : a hill or ridge of sand piled up by the wind

dune buggy *n* : a motor vehicle with oversize tires for use on sand

¹dung \'dəŋ\ *n* : MANURE

²dung *vb* : to dress (land) with dung

dun·ga·ree \,dəŋ-gə-'rē\ *n* **1** : a heavy coarse cotton twill; *esp* : blue denim **2** *pl* : clothes made of blue denim

dun·geon \'dən-jən\ *n* [ME *dongeoun* fortress, prison, fr. AF *donjun*, fr. VL **domnion-*, *domnio keep, mastery, fr. L *dominus* lord] : a dark prison commonly underground

dung·hill \'dəŋ-,hil\ *n* : a manure pile

dunk \'dəŋk\ *vb* **1** : to dip or submerge temporarily in liquid **2** : to submerge oneself in water **3** : to shoot a basketball into the basket from above the rim

duo \'dü-(,)ō, 'dyü-\ *n, pl* **du·os 1** : DUET **2** : PAIR **3**

duo·dec·i·mal \,dü-ə-'de-sə-məl, ,dyü-\ *adj* : of, relating to, or being a system of numbers with a base of 12

du·o·de·num \,dü-ə-'dē-nəm, ,dyü-, dü-'ä-də-nəm, dyü-\ *n, pl* **-de·na** \-'dē-nə, -də-nə\ *or* **-denums** : the first part of the small intestine extending from the stomach to the jejunum — **du·o·de·nal** \-'dē-nᵊl, -də-nəl\ *adj*

dup *abbr* **1** duplex **2** duplicate

¹dupe \'düp, 'dyüp\ *n* : one who is easily deceived or cheated : FOOL

²dupe *vb* **duped; dup·ing** : to make a dupe of : DECEIVE, FOOL

du·ple \'dü-pəl, 'dyü-\ *adj* : having two beats or a multiple of two beats to the measure ⟨∼ time⟩

¹du·plex \'dü-,pleks, 'dyü-\ *adj* : DOUBLE

²duplex *n* : something duplex; *esp* : a 2-family house

¹du·pli·cate \'dü-pli-kət, 'dyü-\ *adj* **1** : consisting of or existing in two corresponding or identical parts or examples **2** : being the same as another

²du·pli·cate \'dü-pli-,kāt, 'dyü-\ *vb* **-cat·ed; -cat·ing 1** : to make double or

twofold **2** : to make a copy of — **du·pli·ca·tion** \,dü-pli-'kā-shən, ,dyü-\ *n*

³du·pli·cate \-kət\ *n* : a thing that exactly resembles another in appearance, pattern, or content : COPY

du·pli·ca·tor \'dü-pli-,kā-tər, 'dyü-\ *n* : COPIER

du·plic·i·ty \dù-'pli-sə-tē, dyü-\ *n, pl* **-ties** : the disguising of true intentions by deceptive words or action — **du·plic·i·tous** \-təs\ *adj* — **du·plic·i·tous·ly** *adv*

du·ra·ble \'dur-ə-bəl, 'dyur-\ *adj* : able to exist for a long time without significant deterioration ⟨∼ goods⟩ — **du·ra·bil·i·ty** \,dur-ə-'bi-lə-tē, ,dyur-\ *n*

du·rance \'dur-əns, 'dyur-\ *n* : restraint by or as if by physical force ⟨held in ∼ vile⟩

du·ra·tion \dù-'rā-shən, dyü-\ *n* : the time during which something exists or lasts

du·ress \dù-'res, dyü-\ *n* : compulsion by threat ⟨confession made under ∼⟩

dur·ing \'dur-iŋ, 'dyur-\ *prep* **1** : THROUGHOUT ⟨swims every day ∼ the summer⟩ **2** : at some point in ⟨broke in ∼ the night⟩

dusk \'dəsk\ *n* **1** : the darker part of twilight esp. at night **2** : partial darkness

dusky \'dəs-kē\ *adj* **dusk·i·er; -est 1** : somewhat dark in color **2** : SHADOWY — **dusk·i·ly** \-kə-lē\ *adv* — **dusk·i·ness** *n*

¹dust \'dəst\ *n* **1** : fine particles of matter **2** : the particles into which something disintegrates **3** : something worthless **4** : the surface of the ground — **dust·less** *adj* — **dusty** *adj*

²dust *vb* **1** : to make free of or remove dust ⟨∼ the furniture⟩ **2** : to sprinkle with fine particles ⟨popcorn ∼ed with salt⟩ **3** : to sprinkle in the form of dust **4** : to defeat badly

dust bowl *n* : a region suffering from long droughts and dust storms

dust devil *n* : a small whirlwind containing sand or dust

dust·er \'dəs-tər\ *n* **1** : one that removes dust **2** : a dress-length housecoat **3** : one that scatters fine particles; *esp* : a device for applying insecticides to crops

dust·pan \'dəst-,pan\ *n* : a flat-ended pan for sweepings

dust storm *n* : a violent wind carrying dust across a dry region

dutch \'dəch\ *adv, often cap* : with each person paying his or her own way ⟨go ∼⟩

Dutch \'dəch\ *n* **1** **Dutch** *pl* : the people of the Netherlands **2** : the language of the Netherlands — **Dutch** *adj* — **Dutch·man** \-mən\ *n*

Dutch elm disease *n* : a fungus disease of elms characterized by yellowing of the foliage, defoliation, and death

dutch treat *n, often cap D* : an entertainment (as a meal) for which each person pays his or her own way — **dutch treat** *adv, often cap D*

du·te·ous \'dü-tē-əs, 'dyü-\ *adj* : DUTIFUL, OBEDIENT

du·ti·able \'dü-tē-ə-bəl, 'dyü-\ *adj* : subject to a duty ⟨∼ imports⟩

du·ti·ful \'dü-ti-fəl, 'dyü-\ *adj* **1** : motivated by a sense of duty ⟨a ∼ son⟩ **2** : coming from or showing a sense of duty ⟨∼ affection⟩ — **du·ti·ful·ly** *adv* — **du·ti·ful·ness** *n*

du·ty \'dü-tē, 'dyü-\ *n, pl* **duties 1** : conduct or action required by one's occupation or position **2** : assigned service or business; *esp* : active military service **3** : a moral or legal obligation **4** : TAX **5** : the service required (as of a machine) : USE ⟨a heavy-*duty* tire⟩

DV *abbr* **1** [L *Deo volente*] God willing **2** Douay Version

DVD \,dē-,vē-'dē\ *n* [*digital video disk*] : a high-capacity optical disk format; *also* : an optical disk using such a format

DVM *abbr* doctor of veterinary medicine

¹dwarf \'dwȯrf\ *n, pl* **dwarfs** \'dwȯrfs\ *also* **dwarves** \'dwȯrvz\ : one that is much below normal size — **dwarf·ish** *adj* — **dwarf·ism** \'dwȯr-,fi-zəm\ *n*

²dwarf *vb* **1** : to restrict the growth or development of : STUNT **2** : to cause to appear smaller ⟨*dwarfed* by comparison⟩

dwell \'dwel\ *vb* **dwelt** \'dwelt\ *or* **dwelled** \'dweld, 'dwelt\; **dwell·ing** [ME, fr. OE *dwellan* to go astray, hinder] **1** : ABIDE, REMAIN **2** : RESIDE, EXIST **3** : to keep the attention directed **4** : to write or speak insistently — used with *on* or *upon* — **dwell·er** *n*

dwell·ing \'dwe-liŋ\ *n* : RESIDENCE

DWI \,dē-,dəb-əl-(,)yü-'ī\ *n* [*driving while intoxicated*] : DUI

dwin·dle \'dwin-d°l\ *vb* **dwin·dled; dwin·dling** : to make or become steadily less : DIMINISH

dwt *abbr* pennyweight

Dy *symbol* dysprosium

dyb·buk \'di-bək\ *n, pl* **dyb·bu·kim** \,di-bú-'kēm\ *also* **dybbuks** : a wandering soul believed in Jewish folklore to enter and possess a person

¹dye \'dī\ *n* **1** : color produced by dyeing **2** : material used for coloring or staining

²dye *vb* **dyed; dye·ing 1** : to impart a new color to esp. by impregnating with a dye **2** : to take up or impart color in dyeing — **dy·er** \'dī-(ə)r\ *n*

dye·stuff \'dī-,stəf\ *n* : DYE 2

dying *pres part of* DIE

dyke *chiefly Brit var of* DIKE

dy·nam·ic \dī-'na-mik\ *also* **dy·nam·i·cal** \-mi-kəl\ *adj* : of or relating to physical force producing motion : ENERGETIC, FORCEFUL

¹dy·na·mite \'dī-nə-,mīt\ *n* : an explosive made of nitroglycerin absorbed in a porous material; *also* : an explosive made without nitroglycerin

²dynamite *vb* **-mit·ed; -mit·ing** : to blow up with dynamite

³dynamite *adj* : TERRIFIC, WONDERFUL

dy·na·mo \'dī-nə-,mō\ *n, pl* **-mos 1** : an electrical generator **2** : a forceful energetic individual

dy·na·mom·e·ter \,dī-nə-'mä-mə-tər\ *n* : an instrument for measuring mechanical power (as of an engine)

dy·nas·ty \'dī-nəs-tē, -,nas-\ *n, pl* **-ties 1** : a succession of rulers of the same family **2** : a powerful group or family that maintains its position for a long time — **dy·nas·tic** \dī-'nas-tik\ *adj*

dys·en·tery \'di-s°n-,ter-ē\ *n, pl* **-ter·ies** : a disease marked by diarrhea with blood and mucus in the feces; *also* : DIARRHEA

dys·func·tion *also* **dis·func·tion** \dis-'fəŋk-shən\ *n* **1** : impaired or abnormal functioning ⟨liver ∼⟩ **2** : abnormal or unhealthy behavior within a group ⟨family ∼⟩ — **dys·func·tion·al** \-shə-nəl\ *adj*

dys·lex·ia \dis-'lek-sē-ə\ *n* : a learning disability marked by difficulty in reading, writing, and spelling — **dys·lex·ic** \-sik\ *adj or n*

dys·pep·sia \dis-'pep-shə, -sē-ə\ *n* : INDIGESTION — **dys·pep·tic** \-'pep-tik\ *adj or n*

dys·pla·sia \dis-'plā-zh(ē-)ə\ *n* : abnormal growth or development

dys·pro·si·um \dis-'prō-zē-əm\ *n* : a metallic chemical element that forms highly magnetic compounds

dys·tro·phy \'dis-trə-fē\ *n, pl* **-phies** : a disorder involving atrophy of muscular tissue; *esp* : MUSCULAR DYSTROPHY

dz *abbr* dozen

¹e \'ē\ *n, pl* **e's** *or* **es** \'ēz\ *often cap* **1** : the 5th letter of the English alphabet **2** : the base of the system of natural logarithms having the approximate value 2.71828 **3** : a grade rating a student's work as poor or failing

²e *abbr, often cap* **1** east; eastern **2** error **3** excellent

e- *comb form* : electronic ⟨*e*-commerce⟩

ea *abbr* each

¹each \'ēch\ *adj* : being one of the class named ⟨∼ player⟩

²each *pron* : every individual one

³each *adv* : APIECE ⟨cost five cents ∼⟩

each other *pron* : each of two or more in reciprocal action or relation ⟨looked at *each other*⟩

ea·ger \'ē-gər\ *adj* : marked by urgent or enthusiastic desire or interest ⟨∼ to learn⟩ ♦ **Synonyms** AVID, ANXIOUS, ARDENT, KEEN — **ea·ger·ly** *adv* — **ea·ger·ness** *n*

¹ea·gle \'ē-gəl\ *n* **1** : a large bird of prey related to the hawks **2** : a score of two under par on a hole in golf

²eagle *vb* **ea·gled; ea·gling** : to score an eagle on a golf hole

ea·glet \'ē-glət\ *n* : a young eagle

-ean — see -AN

E and OE *abbr* errors and omissions excepted

¹**ear** \'ir\ *n* **1** : the organ of hearing; *also* : the outer part of this in a vertebrate **2** : something resembling a mammal's ear in shape, position, or function **3** : an ability to understand and appreciate something heard ⟨a good ~ for music⟩ **4** : sympathetic attention

²**ear** *n* : the fruiting spike of a cereal (as wheat or Indian corn)

ear·ache \-,āk\ *n* : an ache or pain in the ear

ear·drum \-,drəm\ *n* : a thin membrane that receives and transmits sound waves in the ear

eared \'ird\ *adj* : having ears esp. of a specified kind or number ⟨a long-*eared* dog⟩

ear·ful \'ir-,fùl\ *n* : a verbal outpouring (as of news, gossip, or complaint)

earl \'ərl\ *n* [ME *erl*, fr. OE *eorl* warrior, nobleman] : a member of the British peerage ranking below a marquess and above a viscount — **earl·dom** \-dəm\ *n*

ear·lobe \'ir-,lōb\ *n* : the pendent part of the ear

¹**ear·ly** \'ər-lē\ *adv* **ear·li·er; -est** : at an early time (as in a period or series)

²**early** *adj* **ear·li·er; -est 1** : of, relating to, or occurring near the beginning **2** : ANCIENT, PRIMITIVE ⟨~ tools⟩ **3** : occurring before the usual time ⟨an ~ breakfast⟩; *also* : occurring in the near future

¹**ear·mark** \'ir-,märk\ *n* : an identification mark (as on the ear of an animal); *also* : a distinguishing mark ⟨~*s* of poverty⟩

²**earmark** *vb* **1** : to mark with an earmark **2** : to designate for a specific purpose ⟨money ~*ed* for education⟩

ear·muff \-,məf\ *n* : one of a pair of ear coverings worn to protect against cold

earn \'ərn\ *vb* **1** : to receive as a return for service **2** : DESERVE, MERIT ✦ *Synonyms* GAIN, SECURE, GET, OBTAIN, ACQUIRE, WIN — **earn·er** *n*

earned run *n* : a run in baseball that scores without benefit of an error before the fielding team has had a chance to make the third putout of the inning

earned run average *n* : the average number of earned runs per game scored against a pitcher in baseball

¹**ear·nest** \'ər-nəst\ *n* : an intensely serious state of mind ⟨spoke in ~⟩

²**earnest** *adj* **1** : seriously intent and sober ⟨an ~ face⟩ ⟨an ~ attempt⟩ **2** : GRAVE, IMPORTANT ✦ *Synonyms* SOLEMN, SEDATE, STAID — **ear·nest·ly** *adv* — **ear·nest·ness** *n*

³**earnest** *n* **1** : something of value given by a buyer to a seller to bind a bargain **2** : PLEDGE

earn·ings \'ər-niŋz\ *n pl* **1** : something (as wages) earned **2** : the balance of revenue after deduction of costs and expenses

ear·phone \'ir-,fōn\ *n* : a device that reproduces sound and is worn over or in the ear

ear·piece \-,pēs\ *n* : a part of an instrument which is placed against or in the ear; *esp* : EARPHONE

ear·plug \-,pləg\ *n* : a protective device for insertion into the opening of the ear

ear·ring \-,riŋ\ *n* : an ornament for the earlobe

ear·shot \-,shät\ *n* : range of hearing

ear·split·ting \-,spli-tiŋ\ *adj* : intolerably loud or shrill

earth \'ərth\ *n* **1** : SOIL, DIRT **2** : LAND, GROUND **3** *often cap* : the planet on which we live that is 3d in order from the sun

earth·en \-thən\ *adj* : made of earth or baked clay

earth·en·ware \-,wer\ *n* : slightly porous opaque pottery fired at low heat

earth·ling \'ərth-liŋ\ *n* : an inhabitant of the earth

earth·ly \'ərth-lē\ *adj* : having to do with the earth esp. as distinguished from heaven — **earth·li·ness** *n*

earth·quake \-,kwāk\ *n* : a shaking or trembling of a portion of the earth

earth science *n* : any of the sciences (as geology or meteorology) that deal with the earth or one of its parts

earth·shak·ing \'ərth-,shā-kiŋ\ *adj* : of great importance : MOMENTOUS

earth·ward \-wərd\ *also* **earth·wards** \-wərdz\ *adv* : to or toward the earth

earth·work \'ərth-,wərk\ *n* : an embankment or fortification of earth

earth·worm \-,wərm\ *n* : a long segmented worm found in damp soil

earthy \'ər-thē\ *adj* **earth·i·er; -est 1** : of, relating to, or consisting of earth; *also* : suggesting earth ⟨~ flavors⟩ **2** : PRACTICAL **4 3** : COARSE, GROSS ⟨~ humor⟩ — **earth·i·ness** *n*

ear·wax \'ir-,waks\ *n* : the yellow waxy secretion from the ear

ear·wig \-,wig\ *n* : any of numerous insects with slender antennae and a pair of appendages resembling forceps at the end of the body

¹**ease** \'ēz\ *n* **1** : comfort of body or mind **2** : naturalness of manner **3** : freedom from difficulty or effort ✦ *Synonyms* RELAXATION, REST, REPOSE, LEISURE

²**ease** *vb* **eased; eas·ing 1** : to relieve from distress **2** : to lessen the pressure or tension of **3** : to make or become less difficult ⟨~ credit⟩

ea·sel \'ē-zəl\ *n* [Dutch *ezel*, lit., ass] : a frame for supporting something (as an artist's canvas)

¹**east** \'ēst\ *adv* : to or toward the east

²**east** *adj* **1** : situated toward or at the east ⟨an ~ window⟩ **2** : coming from the east ⟨an ~ wind⟩

³**east** *n* **1** : the general direction of sunrise **2** : the compass point directly opposite to west **3** *cap* : regions or countries east of a specified or implied point — **east·er·ly** \'ē-stər-lē\ *adv or adj* — **east·ward** *adv or adj* — **east·wards** *adv*

Eas·ter \'ē-stər\ *n* : a church feast observed on a Sunday in March or April in commemoration of Christ's resurrection

east·ern \'ē-stərn\ *adj* **1** *often cap* : of, relating to, or characteristic of a region designated East **2** *cap* : of, relating to, or being the Christian churches originating in the Church of the Eastern Roman Empire **3** : lying toward or coming from the east — **East·ern·er** *n*

easy \'ē-zē\ *adj* **eas·i·er; -est** **1** : marked by ease ⟨an ∼ life⟩; *esp* : not causing distress or difficulty ⟨∼ tasks⟩ **2** : MILD, LENIENT ⟨be ∼ on him⟩ **3** : GRADUAL ⟨an ∼ slope⟩ **4** : LEISURELY ⟨an ∼ pace⟩ **5** : free from pain, trouble, or worry **6** : COMFORTABLE ⟨an ∼ chair⟩ **7** : showing ease : NATURAL ⟨an ∼ manner⟩ — **eas·i·ly** \'ē-zə-lē\ *adv* — **eas·i·ness** \-zē-nəs\ *n*

easy·go·ing \ē-zē-'gō-iŋ\ *adj* : relaxed and casual in style or manner

eat \'ēt\ *vb* **ate** \'āt\; **eat·en** \'ēt-ᵊn\; **eat·ing** **1** : to take in as food : take food **2** : to use up : DEVOUR **3** : CORRODE — **eat·able** *adj or n* — **eat·er** *n*

eat·ery \'ē-tə-rē\ *n, pl* **-er·ies** : LUNCHEONETTE, RESTAURANT

eaves \'ēvz\ *n pl* : the overhanging lower edge of a roof

eaves·drop \'ēvz-ˌdräp\ *vb* : to listen secretly — **eaves·drop·per** *n*

¹ebb \'eb\ *n* **1** : the flowing back from shore of water brought in by the tide **2** : a point or state of decline

²ebb *vb* **1** : to recede from the flood : DECLINE ⟨his fortunes ∼*ed*⟩

EBCDIC \'eb-sə-ˌdik\ *n* [*extended binary coded decimal interchange code*] : a computer code for representing alphanumeric information

Ebo·la \ē-'bō-lə\ *n* : an often fatal hemorrhagic fever caused by a virus (**Ebola virus**) of African origin

¹eb·o·ny \'e-bə-nē\ *n, pl* **-nies** : a hard heavy blackish wood of various tropical trees related to the persimmon

²ebony *adj* **1** : made of or resembling ebony **2** : BLACK, DARK

ebul·lient \i-'bul-yənt, -'bəl-\ *adj* **1** : BOILING, AGITATED **2** : EXUBERANT — **ebul·lience** \-yəns\ *n*

EC *abbr* European Community

ec·cen·tric \ik-'sen-trik\ *adj* **1** : deviating from a usual or accepted pattern **2** : deviating from a circular path ⟨∼ orbits⟩ **3** : set with axis or support off center ⟨an ∼ cam⟩; *also* : being off center ✦ **Synonyms** ERRATIC, QUEER, SINGULAR, CURIOUS, ODD — **eccentric** *n* — **ec·cen·tri·cal·ly** \-tri-k(ə-)lē\ *adv* — **ec·cen·tric·i·ty** \ek-ˌsen-'tri-sə-tē\ *n*

Eccles *abbr* Ecclesiastes

Ec·cle·si·as·tes \i-ˌklē-zē-'as-tēz\ *n* — see BIBLE table

ec·cle·si·as·tic \i-ˌklē-zē-'as-tik\ *n* : CLERGYMAN

ec·cle·si·as·ti·cal \-ti-kəl\ *or* **ec·cle·si·as·tic** \-tik\ *adj* : of or relating to a church esp. as an institution ⟨∼ art⟩ — **ec·cle·si·as·ti·cal·ly** \-ti-k(ə-)lē\ *adv*

Ec·cle·si·as·ti·cus \i-ˌklē-zē-'as-ti-kəs\ *n* — see BIBLE table

Ecclus *abbr* Ecclesiasticus

ECG *abbr* electrocardiogram

ech·e·lon \'e-shə-ˌlän\ *n* [F *échelon*, lit., rung of a ladder] **1** : a steplike arrangement (as of troops or airplanes) **2** : a level (as of authority or responsibility) within an organization

ech·i·na·cea \ˌe-ki-'nā-sē-ə, -shə\ *n* : the dried root of three composite herbs that is used primarily in herbal remedies to boost the immune system; *also* : any of these herbs

echi·no·derm \i-'kī-nə-ˌdərm\ *n* : any of a phylum of marine animals (as starfishes and sea urchins) having similar body parts (as the arms of a starfish) arranged around a central axis and often having a calcium-containing outer skeleton

echo \'e-kō\ *n, pl* **ech·oes** *also* **ech·os** : repetition of a sound caused by a reflection of the sound waves; *also* : the reflection of a radar signal by an object — **echo** *vb* — **echo·ic** \e-'kō-ik\ *adj*

echo·lo·ca·tion \ˌe-kō-lō-'kā-shən\ *n* : a process for locating distant or invisible objects by sound waves reflected back to the sender (as a bat) from the objects

echt \'ekt\ *adj* [G] : TRUE, GENUINE ⟨an ∼ New Yorker⟩

éclair \ā-'kler\ *n* [F, lit., lightning] : an oblong shell of light pastry with whipped cream or custard filling

éclat \ā-'klä\ *n* [F] **1** : a dazzling effect or success **2** : ACCLAIM

eclec·tic \e-'klek-tik\ *adj* : selecting or made up of what seems best of varied sources — **eclectic** *n* — **eclec·ti·cism** \-'klek-tə-ˌsi-zəm\ *n*

¹eclipse \i-'klips\ *n* **1** : the total or partial obscuring of one heavenly body by another; *also* : a passing into the shadow of a heavenly body **2** : a falling into obscurity or decline

²eclipse *vb* **eclipsed; eclips·ing** : to cause an eclipse of; *also* : SURPASS

eclip·tic \i-'klip-tik\ *n* : the great circle of the celestial sphere that is the apparent path of the sun

ec·logue \'ek-ˌlog, -ˌläg\ *n* : a pastoral poem

ECM *abbr* European Common Market

ecol *abbr* ecological; ecology

E. coli \ˌē-'kō-ˌlī\ *n, pl* **E. coli** : a rod-shaped bacterium that sometimes causes intestinal illness

ecol·o·gy \i-'kä-lə-jē, e-\ *n, pl* **-gies** [G *Ökologie*, fr. Gk *oikos* house + *logos* word] **1** : a branch of science concerned with the relationships between organisms and their environment **2** : the pattern of relations between one or more organisms and the environment — **eco·log·i·cal** \ˌē-kə-'lä-ji-kəl, ˌe-\ *also* **eco·log·ic** \-jik\ *adj* — **eco·log·i·cal·ly** \-ji-k(ə-)lē\ *adv* — **ecol·o·gist** \i-'kä-lə-jist, e-\ *n*

e-com·merce \'ē-ˌkä-(ˌ)mərs\ *n* : commerce conducted via the Internet

econ *abbr* economics; economist; economy

eco·nom·ic \ˌe-kə-'nä-mik, ˌē-\ *adj* : of or relating to the production, distribution, and consumption of goods and services

eco·nom·i·cal \-'nä-mi-kəl\ adj 1 : THRIFTY 2 : operating with little waste or at a saving ✦ *Synonyms* FRUGAL, SPARING, PROVIDENT — **ec·o·nom·i·cal·ly** \-k(ə-)lē\ adv

eco·nom·ics \ˌe-kə-'nä-miks, ˌē-\ n sing or pl : a social science dealing with the production, distribution, and consumption of goods and services — **econ·o·mist** \i-'kä-nə-mist\ n

econ·o·mise Brit var of ECONOMIZE

econ·o·mize \i-'kä-nə-ˌmīz\ vb **-mized; -miz·ing** : to practice economy : be frugal — **econ·o·miz·er** n

¹**econ·o·my** \i-'kä-nə-mē\ n, pl **-mies** [MF yconomie, fr. ML oeconomia, fr. Gk oikonomia, fr. oikonomos household manager, fr. oikos house + nemein to manage] 1 : thrifty and efficient use of resources; also : an instance of this 2 : manner of arrangement or functioning : ORGANIZATION 3 : an economic system ⟨a money ∼⟩

²**economy** adj : ECONOMICAL ⟨∼ cars⟩

eco·sys·tem \'ē-kō-ˌsis-təm, 'e-\ n : the complex of an ecological community and its environment functioning as a unit in nature

eco·tour·ism \ˌe-kō-'tùr-ˌi-zəm, ˌe-\ n : the touring of natural habitats in a manner meant to minimize ecological impact — **eco·tour·ist** \-'tùr-ist\ n

ecru \'e-krü, 'ā-\ n [F écru, lit., unbleached] : BEIGE — **ecru** adj

ec·sta·sy \'ek-stə-sē\ n, pl **-sies** 1 : extreme and usu. rapturous emotional excitement 2 often cap : an illicit drug with hallucinogenic properties that is chemically related to amphetamine — **ec·stat·ic** \ek-'sta-tik, ik-\ adj — **ec·stat·i·cal·ly** \-ti-k(ə-)lē\ adv

Ecua abbr Ecuador

ec·u·men·i·cal \ˌe-kyù-'me-ni-kəl\ adj 1 : general in extent or influence 2 : promoting or tending toward worldwide Christian unity — **ec·u·men·i·cal·ly** \-k(ə-)lē\ adv

ec·ze·ma \ig-'zē-mə, 'eg-zə-mə, 'ek-sə-\ n : an itching skin inflammation with oozing and then crusted lesions — **ec·zem·a·tous** \ig-'ze-mə-təs\ adj

ed abbr 1 edited; edition; editor 2 education

¹**-ed** \d after a vowel or b, g, j, l, m, n, ŋ, r, th, v, z, zh; əd, id after d, t; t after other sounds\ vb suffix or adj suffix 1 — used to form the past participle of regular weak verbs ⟨ended⟩ ⟨faded⟩ ⟨tried⟩ ⟨patted⟩ 2 : having : characterized by ⟨cultured⟩ ⟨2-legged⟩; also : having the characteristics of ⟨bigoted⟩

²**-ed** vb suffix — used to form the past tense of regular weak verbs ⟨judged⟩ ⟨denied⟩ ⟨dropped⟩

Edam \'ē-dəm, -ˌdam\ n : a yellow Dutch pressed cheese made in balls

ed·dy \'e-dē\ n, pl **eddies** : WHIRLPOOL — **eddy** vb

edel·weiss \'ā-dəl-ˌwīs, -ˌvīs\ n [G, fr. edel noble + weiss white] : a small perennial woolly composite herb that grows high in the Alps

ede·ma \i-'dē-mə\ n : abnormal accumulation of watery fluid in connective tissue or in a serous cavity — **edem·a·tous** \-'de-mə-təs\ adj

Eden \'ē-dᵊn\ n : PARADISE 2

¹**edge** \'ej\ n 1 : the cutting side of a blade 2 : SHARPNESS; also : FORCE, EFFECTIVENESS 3 : the line where something begins or ends; also : the area adjoining such an edge 4 : ADVANTAGE ⟨has an ∼ on the competition⟩ — **edged** \'ejd\ adj

²**edge** vb **edged; edg·ing** 1 : to give or form an edge 2 : to move or force gradually ⟨∼ into a crowd⟩ 3 : to defeat by a small margin ⟨edged out her opponent⟩ — **edg·er** n

edge·wise \'ej-ˌwīz\ adv : SIDEWAYS

edg·ing \'e-jiŋ\ n : something that forms an edge or border ⟨a lace ∼⟩

edgy \'e-jē\ adj **edg·i·er; -est** 1 : SHARP ⟨an ∼ tone⟩ 2 : TENSE, NERVOUS 3 : having a bold, provocative, or unconventional quality — **edg·i·ness** n

ed·i·ble \'e-də-bəl\ adj : fit or safe to be eaten — **ed·i·bil·i·ty** \ˌe-də-'bi-lə-tē\ n — **edible** n

edict \'ē-ˌdikt\ n : ORDER, DECREE

ed·i·fi·ca·tion \ˌe-də-fə-'kā-shən\ n : instruction and improvement esp. in morality — **ed·i·fy** \'e-də-ˌfī\ vb

ed·i·fice \'e-də-fəs\ n : a usu. large building

ed·it \'e-dət\ vb 1 : to revise, assemble, or prepare for publication or release (as a motion picture) 2 : to direct the publication and policies of (as a newspaper) 3 : DELETE — **ed·i·tor** \'e-də-tər\ n — **ed·i·tor·ship** \-ˌship\ n — **ed·i·tress** \-trəs\ n

edi·tion \i-'di-shən\ n 1 : the form in which a text is published 2 : the total number of copies (as of a book) published at one time 3 : VERSION

¹**ed·i·to·ri·al** \ˌe-də-'tòr-ē-əl\ adj 1 : of or relating to an editor or editing 2 : being or resembling an editorial — **ed·i·to·ri·al·ly** adv

²**editorial** n : an article (as in a newspaper) giving the views of the editors or publishers; also : an expression of opinion resembling an editorial ⟨a television ∼⟩

ed·i·to·ri·al·ize \ˌe-də-'tòr-ē-ə-ˌlīz\ vb **-ized; -iz·ing** 1 : to express an opinion in an editorial 2 : to introduce opinions into factual reporting 3 : to express an opinion — **ed·i·to·ri·al·iza·tion** \-ˌtòr-ē-ə-lə-'zā-shən\ n — **ed·i·to·ri·al·iz·er** n

EDP abbr electronic data processing

EDT abbr Eastern daylight (saving) time

educ abbr education; educational

ed·u·ca·ble \'e-jə-kə-bəl\ adj : capable of being educated

ed·u·cate \'e-jə-ˌkāt\ vb **-cat·ed; -cat·ing** [ME, fr. L educatus, pp. of educare, fr. educere to lead forth, draw out] 1 : to provide with schooling 2 : to develop mentally and morally; also : to provide with information ✦ *Synonyms* TRAIN, DISCIPLINE, SCHOOL, INSTRUCT, TEACH — **ed·u·ca·tor** \-ˌkā-tər\ n

ed·u·ca·tion \ˌe-jə-'kā-shən\ n 1 : the action or process of educating or being educated **2** : a field of study dealing with methods of teaching and learning — **ed-u-ca-tion-al** \-shə-nəl\ *adj* — **ed-u-ca-tion-al-ly** *adv*

educational television *n* **1** : television that provides educational programming (as for students) **2** : television (as public television) that receives support from contributors

educe \i-ˈdüs, -ˈdyüs\ *vb* **educed; educ-ing** **1** : ELICIT, EVOKE **2** : DEDUCE ◆ **Synonyms** EXTRACT, EVINCE, EXTORT

ed-u-tain-ment \e-jə-ˈtān-mənt\ *n* : entertainment that is designed to be educational

¹**-ee** \ˈē, (ˌ)ē\ *n suffix* **1** : one that receives or benefits from (a specified action or thing) ⟨grant*ee*⟩ ⟨patent*ee*⟩ **2** : a person who does (a specified action) ⟨escap*ee*⟩

²**-ee** *n suffix* **1** : a particular esp. small kind of ⟨boot*ee*⟩ **2** : one resembling or suggestive of ⟨goat*ee*⟩

EE *abbr* electrical engineer

EEC *abbr* European Economic Community

EEG *abbr* **1** electroencephalogram **2** electroencephalograph

eel \ˈēl\ *n* : any of numerous snakelike bony fishes with a smooth slimy skin

EEO *abbr* equal employment opportunity

ee-rie *also* **ee-ry** \ˈir-ē\ *adj* **ee-ri-er; -est** : WEIRD, UNCANNY — **ee-ri-ly** \ˈir-ə-lē\ *adv*

eff *abbr* efficiency

ef-face \i-ˈfās, e-\ *vb* **ef-faced; ef-fac-ing** : to obliterate or obscure by or as if by rubbing out ◆ **Synonyms** ERASE, DELETE, ANNUL, CANCEL, EXPUNGE — **ef-face-able** *adj* — **ef-face-ment** *n*

¹**ef-fect** \i-ˈfekt\ *n* **1** : MEANING, INTENT **2** : RESULT **3** : APPEARANCE **4** : INFLU-ENCE **5** *pl* : GOODS, POSSESSIONS **6** : the quality or state of being operative : OPERATION ◆ **Synonyms** CONSE-QUENCE, OUTCOME, UPSHOT, AFTER-MATH, ISSUE

²**effect** *vb* : to cause to happen ⟨~ repairs⟩ ⟨~ changes⟩

ef-fec-tive \i-ˈfek-tiv\ *adj* **1** : producing a decisive or desired effect **2** : IMPRESSIVE, STRIKING **3** : ready for service or action ⟨~ manpower⟩ **4** : being in effect — **ef-fec-tive-ly** *adv* — **ef-fec-tive-ness** *n*

ef-fec-tu-al \i-ˈfek-chə-wəl\ *adj* : produc-ing an intended effect : ADEQUATE — **ef-fec-tu-al-ly** *adv*

ef-fec-tu-ate \i-ˈfek-chə-ˌwāt\ *vb* **-at-ed; -at-ing** : BRING ABOUT, EFFECT

ef-fem-i-nate \ə-ˈfe-mə-nət\ *adj* : marked by qualities more typical of women than men — **ef-fem-i-na-cy** \-nə-sē\ *n*

ef-fen-di \e-ˈfen-dē\ *n* [Turk *efendi* mas-ter, fr. ModGk *authentēs*] : a man of property, authority, or education in an eastern Mediterranean country

ef-fer-ent \ˈe-fə-rənt\ *adj* : bearing or con-ducting outward from a more central part ⟨~ nerves⟩

ef-fer-vesce \ˌe-fər-ˈves\ *vb* **-vesced; -vesc-ing** **1** : to bubble and hiss as gas escapes **2** : to show liveliness or exhila-ration — **ef-fer-ves-cence** \-ˈve-sᵊns\ *n*

— **ef-fer-ves-cent** \-sᵊnt\ *adj* — **ef-fer-ves-cent-ly** *adv*

ef-fete \e-ˈfēt\ *adj* **1** : having lost charac-ter, vitality, or strength; *also* : DECA-DENT **2** : EFFEMINATE

ef-fi-ca-cious \ˌe-fə-ˈkā-shəs\ *adj* : pro-ducing an intended effect ⟨~ remedies⟩ ◆ **Synonyms** EFFECTUAL, EFFECTIVE, EFFICIENT — **ef-fi-ca-cy** \ˈe-fi-kə-sē\ *n*

ef-fi-cient \i-ˈfi-shənt\ *adj* : productive of desired effects esp. without waste — **ef-fi-cien-cy** \-shən-sē\ *n* — **ef-fi-cient-ly** *adv*

ef-fi-gy \ˈe-fə-jē\ *n, pl* **-gies** : IMAGE; *esp* : a crude figure of a hated person

ef-flo-res-cence \ˌe-flə-ˈre-sᵊns\ *n* **1** : the period or state of flowering **2** : the ac-tion or process of developing **3** : fullness of development : FLOWERING

ef-flu-ence \ˈe-ˌflü-əns\ *n* : something that flows out

ef-flu-ent \ˈe-ˌflü-ənt\ *n* : something that flows out; *esp* : a fluid (as sewage) dis-charged as waste — **effluent** *adj*

ef-flu-vi-um \e-ˈflü-vē-əm\ *n, pl* **-via** \-vē-ə\ *also* **-vi-ums** [L, outflow] **1** : a usu. unpleasant emanation **2** : a by-product usu. in the form of waste

ef-fort \ˈe-fərt\ *n* **1** : EXERTION, ENDEAV-OR; *also* : a product of effort **2** : active or applied force — **ef-fort-less** *adj* — **ef-fort-less-ly** *adv*

ef-fron-tery \i-ˈfrən-tə-rē\ *n, pl* **-ter-ies** : shameless boldness : IMPUDENCE ◆ **Synonyms** TEMERITY, AUDACITY, BRASS, GALL, NERVE, CHUTZPAH

ef-ful-gence \i-ˈfu̇l-jəns, -ˈfəl-\ *n* : radiant splendor : BRILLIANCE — **ef-ful-gent** \-jənt\ *adj*

ef-fu-sion \i-ˈfyü-zhən, e-\ *n* : a gushing forth; *also* : unrestrained utterance — **ef-fuse** \-ˈfyüz, e-\ *vb* — **ef-fu-sive** \i-ˈfyü-siv, e-\ *adj* — **ef-fu-sive-ly** *adv*

eft \ˈeft\ *n* : NEWT

EFT *or* **EFTS** *abbr* electronic funds transfer (system)

e.g. *abbr* [L *exempli gratia*] for example

Eg *abbr* Egypt; Egyptian

egal-i-tar-i-an-ism \i-ˌga-lə-ˈter-ē-ə-ˌni-zəm\ *n* : a belief in human equality esp. in social, political, and economic affairs — **egal-i-tar-i-an** *adj or n*

¹**egg** \ˈeg\ *vb* [ME, fr. ON *eggja*; akin to OE *ecg* edge] : to urge to action — usu. used with *on*

²**egg** *n* [ME *egge*, fr. ON *egg*; akin to OE *ǣg* egg, L *ovum*] **1** : a rounded usu. hard-shelled reproductive body esp. of birds and reptiles from which the young hatch-es; *also* : the egg of the common domestic chicken as an article of food **2** : a germ cell produced by a female

egg-beat-er \ˈeg-ˌbē-tər\ *n* : a hand-oper-ated kitchen utensil for beating, stirring, or whipping

egg cell *n* : EGG 2

egg foo yong *or* **egg foo young** *or* **egg foo yung** \-ˈfü-ˈyəŋ\ *n* : a fried egg patty

egg-head \-ˌhed\ *n* : INTELLECTUAL, HIGHBROW

egg·nog \-ˌnäg\ *n* : a drink consisting of eggs beaten with sugar, milk or cream, and often alcoholic liquor

egg·plant \-ˌplant\ *n* : the edible usu. large and dark purplish fruit of a plant related to the potato; *also* : the plant

egg roll *n* : a thin egg-dough casing filled with minced vegetables and often bits of meat and usu. deep-fried

egg·shell \ˈeg-ˌshel\ *n* : the hard exterior covering of an egg

egis *var of* AEGIS

eg·lan·tine \ˈe-glən-ˌtīn, -ˌtēn\ *n* : SWEETBRIAR

ego \ˈē-gō\ *n, pl* **egos** [L, I] **1** : the self as distinguished from others **2** : the one of the three divisions of the psyche in psychoanalytic theory that is the organized conscious mediator between the person and reality

ego·cen·tric \ˌē-gō-ˈsen-trik\ *adj* : concerned or overly concerned with the self; *esp* : SELF-CENTERED

ego·ism \ˈē-gō-ˌi-zəm\ *n* **1** : a doctrine holding self-interest to be the motive or the valid end of action **2** : excessive concern for oneself with or without exaggerated feelings of self-importance — **ego·ist** \-ist\ *n* — **ego·is·tic** \ˌē-gō-ˈis-tik\ *adj* — **ego·is·ti·cal·ly** *adv*

ego·tism \ˈē-gə-ˌti-zəm\ *n* **1** : the practice of talking about oneself too much **2** : an exaggerated sense of self-importance : CONCEIT — **ego·tist** \-tist\ *n* — **ego·tis·tic** \ˌē-gə-ˈtis-tik\ *or* **ego·tis·ti·cal** \-ti-kəl\ *adj* — **ego·tis·ti·cal·ly** *adv*

ego trip *n* : an act that enhances and satisfies one's ego

egre·gious \i-ˈgrē-jəs\ *adj* [L *egregius* outstanding, fr. *ex, e* out of + *greg-, grex* flock, herd] : notably bad : FLAGRANT — **egre·gious·ly** *adv* — **egre·gious·ness** *n*

egress \ˈē-ˌgres\ *n* : a way out : EXIT

egret \ˈē-grət, i-ˈgret\ *n* : any of various herons that bear long plumes during the breeding season

Egyp·tian \i-ˈjip-shən\ *n* **1** : a native or inhabitant of Egypt **2** : the language of the ancient Egyptians from earliest times to about the 3d century A.D. — **Egyptian** *adj*

ei·der \ˈī-dər\ *n* : any of several northern sea ducks that yield a soft down

ei·der·down \-ˌdaůn\ *n* **1** : the down of the eider **2** : a comforter filled with eiderdown

ei·do·lon \ī-ˈdō-lən\ *n, pl* **-lons** *or* **-la** \-lə\ **1** : PHANTOM **2** : IDEAL

eight \ˈāt\ *n* **1** : one more than seven **2** : the 8th in a set or series **3** : something having eight units — **eight** *adj or pron* — **eighth** \ˈātth\ *adj or adv or n*

eight ball *n* : a black pool ball numbered 8 — **behind the eight ball** : in a highly disadvantageous position

eigh·teen \ˈāt-ˈtēn\ *n* : one more than 17 — **eighteen** *adj or pron* — **eigh·teenth** \-ˈtēnth\ *adj or n*

eighty \ˈā-tē\ *n, pl* **eight·ies** : eight times

10 — **eight·i·eth** \ˈā-tē-əth\ *adj or n* — **eighty** *adj or pron*

ein·stei·ni·um \īn-ˈstī-nē-əm\ *n* : an artificially produced radioactive element

ei·re·nic *chiefly Brit var of* IRENIC

¹ei·ther \ˈē-thər, ˈī-\ *adj* **1** : being the one and the other of two : EACH ⟨trees on ∼ side⟩ **2** : being the one or the other of two ⟨take ∼ road⟩

²either *pron* : the one or the other

³either *conj* — used as a function word before the first of two or more words or word groups of which the last is preceded by *or* to indicate that they represent alternatives ⟨a statement is ∼ true or false⟩

ejac·u·late \i-ˈja-kyə-ˌlāt\ *vb* **-lat·ed; -lat·ing** **1** : to eject a fluid (as semen) **2** : to utter suddenly : EXCLAIM — **ejac·u·la·tion** \-ˌja-kyə-ˈlā-shən\ *n* — **ejac·u·la·to·ry** \-ˈja-kyə-lə-ˌtōr-ē\ *adj*

eject \i-ˈjekt\ *vb* : to drive or throw out or off ♦ **Synonyms** EXPEL, OUST, EVICT, DISMISS — **ejec·tion** \-ˈjek-shən\ *n*

eke \ˈēk\ *vb* **eked; ek·ing** : to gain, supplement, or extend usu. with effort — usu. used with *out* ⟨∼ out a living⟩

EKG *abbr* [G *Elektrokardiogramm*] electrocardiogram; electrocardiograph

el *abbr* elevation

¹elab·o·rate \i-ˈla-bə-rət, -ˈla-brət\ *adj* **1** : planned or carried out with great care **2** : being complex and usu. ornate — **elab·o·rate·ly** *adv* — **elab·o·rate·ness** *n*

²elab·o·rate \i-ˈla-bə-ˌrāt\ *vb* **-rat·ed; -rat·ing** **1** : to build up from simpler ingredients **2** : to work out in detail : develop fully — **elab·o·ra·tion** \-ˌla-bə-ˈrā-shən\ *n*

élan \ā-ˈläⁿ\ *n* [F] : ARDOR, SPIRIT

eland \ˈē-lənd, -ˌland\ *n, pl* **eland** *also* **elands** [Afrikaans] : either of two large African antelopes with spirally twisted horns in both sexes

elapse \i-ˈlaps\ *vb* **elapsed; elaps·ing** : to slip by : PASS

¹elas·tic \i-ˈlas-tik\ *adj* **1** : SPRINGY **2** : FLEXIBLE, PLIABLE ⟨an ∼ bandage⟩ **3** : ADAPTABLE ⟨an ∼ plan⟩ ♦ **Synonyms** RESILIENT, SUPPLE, STRETCH — **elas·tic·i·ty** \-ˌlas-ˈti-sə-tē, ˌē-ˌlas-\ *n*

²elastic *n* **1** : elastic material **2** : a rubber band

elate \i-ˈlāt\ *vb* **elat·ed; elat·ing** : to fill with joy — **ela·tion** \-ˈlā-shən\ *n*

¹el·bow \ˈel-ˌbō\ *n* [ME *elbowe*, fr. OE *elboga*, fr. *el-* (akin to *eln* ell) + *boga* bow] **1** : the joint of the arm; *also* : the outer curve of the bent arm **2** : a bend or joint resembling an elbow in shape

²elbow *vb* : to push aside with the elbow; *also* : to make one's way by elbowing

el·bow room \ˈel-bō-ˌrüm, -ˌrùm\ *n* : enough space for work or operation

¹el·der \ˈel-dər\ *n* : ELDERBERRY 2

²elder *adj* **1** : OLDER **2** : EARLIER, FORMER **3** : of higher rank : SENIOR

³elder *n* **1** : an older individual : SENIOR **2** : one having authority by reason of age and experience **3** : a church officer

el·der·ber·ry \'el-dər-,ber-ē\ *n* **1** : the edible black or red fruit of a shrub or tree related to the honeysuckle and bearing flat clusters of small white or pink flowers **2** : a tree or shrub bearing elderberries

el·der·ly \'el-dər-lē\ *adj* **1** : rather old; *esp* : past middle age **2** : of, relating to, or characteristic of later life

el·dest \'el-dəst\ *adj* : of the greatest age

El Do·ra·do \,el-də-'rä-dō, -'rä-\ *n* [Sp, lit., the gilded one] : a place of vast riches, abundance, or opportunity

elec *abbr* electric; electrical; electricity

¹**elect** \i-'lekt\ *adj* **1** : CHOSEN, SELECT **2** : elected but not yet installed in office ⟨the president-*elect*⟩

²**elect** *n, pl* **elect** **1** : a selected person **2** *pl* : a select or exclusive group

³**elect** *vb* **1** : to select by vote (as for office or membership) **2** : CHOOSE, PICK

elec·tion \i-'lek-shən\ *n* **1** : an act or process of electing **2** : the fact of being elected

elec·tion·eer \i-,lek-shə-'nir\ *vb* : to work for the election of a candidate or party

¹**elec·tive** \i-'lek-tiv\ *adj* **1** : chosen or filled by election **2** : permitting a choice : OPTIONAL

²**elective** *n* : an elective course or subject of study

elec·tor \i-'lek-tər\ *n* **1** : one qualified to vote in an election **2** : one elected to an electoral college — **elec·tor·al** \i-'lek-tə-rəl\ *adj*

electoral college *n* : a body of electors who elect the president and vice president of the U.S.

elec·tor·ate \i-'lek-tə-rət\ *n* : a body of persons entitled to vote

elec·tric \i-'lek-trik\ *adj* [NL *electricus* produced from amber by friction, electric, fr. ML, of amber, fr. L *electrum* amber, fr. Gk *ēlektron*] **1** or **elec·tri·cal** \-tri-kəl\ : of, relating to, operated by, or produced by electricity **2** : ELECTRIFYING, THRILLING ⟨an ∼ performance⟩ — **elec·tri·cal·ly** *adv*

electrical storm *n* : THUNDERSTORM

electric chair *n* : a chair used to carry out the death penalty by electrocution

electric eye *n* : PHOTOELECTRIC CELL

elec·tri·cian \i-,lek-'tri-shən\ *n* : a person who installs, operates, or repairs electrical equipment

elec·tric·i·ty \i-,lek-'tri-sə-tē\ *n, pl* **-ties** **1** : a form of energy that occurs naturally (as in lightning) or is produced (as in a generator) and that is expressed in terms of the movement and interaction of electrons **2** : electric current

elec·tri·fy \i-'lek-trə-,fī\ *vb* **-fied; -fy·ing** **1** : to charge with electricity **2** : to equip for use of electric power **3** : THRILL — **elec·tri·fi·ca·tion** \i-,lek-trə-fə-'kā-shən\ *n*

elec·tro·car·dio·gram \i-,lek-trō-'kär-dē-ə-,gram\ *n* : the tracing made by an electrocardiograph

elec·tro·car·dio·graph \-,graf\ *n* : a device for recording the changes of electri-

cal potential occurring during the heartbeat — **elec·tro·car·dio·graph·ic** \-,kär-dē-ə-'gra-fik\ *adj* — **elec·tro·car·di·og·ra·phy** \-dē-'ä-grə-fē\ *n*

elec·tro·chem·is·try \-'ke-mə-strē\ *n* : a branch of chemistry that deals with the relation of electricity to chemical changes — **elec·tro·chem·i·cal** \-'ke-mi-kəl\ *adj*

elec·tro·cute \i-'lek-trə-,kyüt\ *vb* **-cut·ed; -cut·ing** **1** : to kill (a criminal) by electricity **2** : to kill by electric shock — **elec·tro·cu·tion** \-,lek-trə-'kyü-shən\ *n*

elec·trode \i-'lek-,trōd\ *n* : a conductor used to establish electrical contact with a nonmetallic part of a circuit

elec·tro·en·ceph·a·lo·gram \i-,lek-trō-in-'se-fə-lə-,gram\ *n* : the tracing made by an electroencephalograph

elec·tro·en·ceph·a·lo·graph \-,graf\ *n* : an apparatus for detecting and recording brain waves — **elec·tro·en·ceph·a·lo·graph·ic** \-,se-fə-lə-'gra-fik\ *adj* — **elec·tro·en·ceph·a·log·ra·phy** \-'lä-grə-fē\ *n*

elec·trol·o·gist \i-,lek-'trä-lə-jist\ *n* : one that uses electrical means to remove hair, warts, moles, and birthmarks from the body

elec·trol·y·sis \i-,lek-'trä-lə-səs\ *n* **1** : the production of chemical changes by passage of an electric current through an electrolyte **2** : the destruction of hair roots with an electric current — **elec·tro·lyt·ic** \-trə-'li-tik\ *adj*

elec·tro·lyte \i-'lek-trə-,līt\ *n* : a nonmetallic electric conductor in which current is carried by the movement of ions; *also* : a substance whose solution or molten form is such a conductor

elec·tro·mag·net \i-,lek-trō-'mag-nət\ *n* : a core of magnetic material (as iron) surrounded by a coil of wire through which an electric current is passed to magnetize the core

elec·tro·mag·net·ic \-mag-'ne-tik\ *adj* : of, relating to, or produced by electromagnetism — **elec·tro·mag·net·i·cal·ly** *adv*

electromagnetic radiation *n* : energy in the form of electromagnetic waves; *also* : a series of electromagnetic waves

electromagnetic wave *n* : a wave (as a radio wave, an X-ray, or a wave of visible light) that consists of associated electric and magnetic effects and that travels at the speed of light

elec·tro·mag·ne·tism \i-,lek-trō-'mag-nə-,ti-zəm\ *n* **1** : magnetism developed by a current of electricity **2** : a natural force responsible for interactions between charged particles which result from their charge

elec·tro·mo·tive force \i-,lek-trə-'mō-tiv-\ *n* : the potential difference derived from an electrical source per unit quantity of electricity passing through the source

elec·tron \i-'lek-,trän\ *n* : a negatively charged elementary particle

elec·tron·ic \i-ˌlek-ˈträ-nik\ adj **1** : of or relating to electrons or electronics **2** : involving a computer — **elec·tron·i·cal·ly** \-ni-k(ə-)lē\ adv

electronic mail n : E-MAIL

elec·tron·ics \i-ˌlek-ˈträ-niks\ n **1** : the physics of electrons and electronic devices **2** : electronic components, devices, or equipment

electron microscope n : an instrument in which a beam of electrons is used to produce an enlarged image of a minute object

electron tube n : a device in which electrical conduction by electrons takes place within a sealed container and which is used for the controlled flow of electrons

electron volt n : a unit of energy equal to 1.60×10^{-19} joule

elec·tro·pho·re·sis \i-ˌlek-trə-fə-ˈrē-səs\ n : the movement of suspended particles through a medium (as paper or gel) by an electromotive force — **elec·tro·pho·ret·ic** \-ˈre-tik\ adj

elec·tro·plate \i-ˈlek-trə-ˌplāt\ vb : to coat (as with metal) by electrolysis

elec·tro·shock therapy \i-ˈlek-trō-ˌshäk-\ n : the treatment of mental disorder by applying electric current to the head and inducing convulsions

elec·tro·stat·ics \i-ˌlek-trə-ˈsta-tiks\ n : physics dealing with the interactions of stationary electric charges

el·ee·mos·y·nary \ˌe-li-ˈmäs-sə-ˌner-ē\ adj : CHARITABLE

el·e·gance \ˈe-li-gəns\ n **1** : refined gracefulness; also : tasteful richness (as of design) **2** : something marked by elegance — **el·e·gant** \-gənt\ adj — **el·e·gant·ly** adv

ele·giac \ˌe-lə-ˈjī-ək, -ˌak\ adj : of or relating to an elegy

el·e·gy \ˈe-lə-jē\ n, pl **-gies** : a song, poem, or speech expressing grief for one who is dead; also : a reflective poem usu. melancholy in tone

elem abbr elementary

el·e·ment \ˈe-lə-mənt\ n **1** pl : weather conditions; esp : severe weather ⟨boards exposed to the ∼s⟩ **2** : natural environment ⟨in her ∼⟩ **3** : a constituent part **4** pl : the simplest principles (as of an art or science) : RUDIMENTS **5** : a member of a mathematical set **6** : any of the fundamental substances that consist of atoms of only one kind ✦ Synonyms COMPONENT, INGREDIENT, CONSTITUENT — **el·e·men·tal** \ˌe-lə-ˈmənt-ᵊl\ adj

el·e·men·ta·ry \ˌe-lə-ˈmen-trē, -tə-rē\ adj : SIMPLE, RUDIMENTARY; also : of, relating to, or teaching the basic subjects of education

elementary particle n : a subatomic particle of matter and energy that does not appear to be made up of other smaller particles

elementary school n : a school usu. including the first six or the first eight grades

el·e·phant \ˈe-lə-fənt\ n, pl **elephants** also **elephant** : any of a family of huge thickset nearly hairless mammals that have the snout lengthened into a trunk and two long curving pointed ivory tusks

el·e·phan·ti·a·sis \ˌe-lə-fən-ˈtī-ə-səs\ n, pl **-a·ses** \-ˌsēz\ : enlargement and thickening of tissues in response esp. to infection by minute parasitic worms

el·e·phan·tine \ˌe-lə-ˈfan-ˌtēn, -ˌtīn, ˈe-lə-fən-\ adj **1** : of great size or strength **2** : CLUMSY, PONDEROUS ⟨∼ verse⟩

elev abbr elevation

el·e·vate \ˈe-lə-ˌvāt\ vb **-vat·ed; -vat·ing 1** : to lift up : RAISE **2** : EXALT, ENNOBLE **3** : ELATE

el·e·va·tion \ˌe-lə-ˈvā-shən\ n **1** : the height to which something is raised (as above sea level) **2** : a lifting up **3** : something (as a hill or swelling) that is elevated

el·e·va·tor \ˈe-lə-ˌvā-tər\ n **1** : a cage or platform for conveying people or things from one level to another **2** : a building for storing and discharging grain **3** : a movable surface on an airplane to produce motion up or down

elev·en \i-ˈle-vən\ n **1** : one more than 10 **2** : the 11th in a set or series **3** : something having 11 units; esp : a football team — **eleven** adj or pron — **eleventh** \-vənth\ adj or n

elf \ˈelf\ n, pl **elves** \ˈelvz\ : a mischievous fairy — **elf·ish** \ˈel-fish\ adj

ELF abbr extremely low frequency

elf·in \ˈel-fən\ adj : of, relating to, or resembling an elf

elic·it \i-ˈli-sət\ vb : to draw out or forth ✦ Synonyms EVOKE, EDUCE, EXTRACT, EXTORT

elide \i-ˈlīd\ vb **elid·ed; elid·ing** : to suppress or alter by elision

el·i·gi·ble \ˈe-lə-jə-bəl\ adj : qualified to participate or to be chosen — **el·i·gi·bil·i·ty** \ˌe-lə-jə-ˈbi-lə-tē\ n — **eligible** n

elim·i·nate \i-ˈli-mə-ˌnāt\ vb **-nat·ed; -nat·ing** [L eliminatus, pp. of eliminare, fr. limen threshold] **1** : REMOVE, ERADICATE **2** : to pass (wastes) from the body **3** : to leave out : IGNORE — **elim·i·na·tion** \-ˌli-mə-ˈnā-shən\ n

eli·sion \i-ˈli-zhən\ n : the omission of a final or initial sound or a word; esp : the omission of an unstressed vowel or syllable in a verse to achieve a uniform rhythm

elite \ā-ˈlēt, ē-\ n [F élite] **1** : the choice part; also : a superior group **2** : a typewriter type providing 12 characters to the inch — **elite** adj

elit·ism \-ˈlē-ˌti-zəm\ n : leadership or rule by an elite; also : advocacy of such elitism — **elit·ist** \-tist\ n or adj

elix·ir \i-ˈlik-sər\ n [ME, fr. ML, fr. Ar al-iksīr the elixir, fr. al the + iksīr elixir] **1** : a substance held capable of prolonging life indefinitely; also : PANACEA **2** : a sweetened alcoholic medicinal solution

Eliz·a·be·than \i-ˌli-zə-ˈbē-thən\ adj : of, relating to, or characteristic of Elizabeth I of England or her times

elk \ˈelk\ n, pl **elk** or **elks 1** : MOOSE — used for one of the Old World **2** : a large gregarious deer of No. America, Europe,

233

CHEMICAL ELEMENTS

ELEMENT NAME	SYMBOL & ATOMIC NUMBER	ATOMIC WEIGHT[1]	ELEMENT NAME	SYMBOL & ATOMIC NUMBER	ATOMIC WEIGHT[1]
actinium	(Ac = 89)	227.0277	meitnerium	(Mt = 109)	(268)
aluminum	(Al = 13)	26.98154	mendelevium	(Md = 101)	(258)
americium	(Am = 95)	(243)	mercury	(Hg = 80)	200.59
antimony	(Sb = 51)	121.760	molybdenum	(Mo = 42)	95.94
argon	(Ar = 18)	39.948	neodymium	(Nd = 60)	144.24
arsenic	(As = 33)	74.92160	neon	(Ne = 10)	20.180
astatine	(At = 85)	(210)	neptunium	(Np = 93)	(237)
barium	(Ba = 56)	137.33	nickel	(Ni = 28)	58.6934
berkelium	(Bk = 97)	(247)	niobium	(Nb = 41)	92.90638
beryllium	(Be = 4)	9.012182	nitrogen	(N = 7)	14.0067
bismuth	(Bi = 83)	208.98038	nobelium	(No = 102)	(259)
bohrium	(Bh = 107)	(264)	osmium	(Os = 76)	190.23
boron	(B = 5)	10.81	oxygen	(O = 8)	15.9994
bromine	(Br = 35)	79.904	palladium	(Pd = 46)	106.42
cadmium	(Cd = 48)	112.41	phosphorus	(P = 15)	30.973761
calcium	(Ca = 20)	40.078	platinum	(Pt = 78)	195.078
californium	(Cf = 98)	(251)	plutonium	(Pu = 94)	(244)
carbon	(C = 6)	12.011	polonium	(Po = 84)	(209)
cerium	(Ce = 58)	140.116	potassium	(K = 19)	39.0983
cesium	(Cs = 55)	132.90545	praseodymium	(Pr = 59)	140.90765
chlorine	(Cl = 17)	35.453	promethium	(Pm = 61)	(145)
chromium	(Cr = 24)	51.996	protactinium	(Pa = 91)	(231)
cobalt	(Co = 27)	58.93320	radium	(Ra = 88)	(226)
copper	(Cu = 29)	63.546	radon	(Rn = 86)	(222)
curium	(Cm = 96)	(247)	rhenium	(Re = 75)	186.207
darmstadtium	(Ds = 110)	(269)	rhodium	(Rh = 45)	102.90550
dubnium	(Db = 105)	(262)	rubidium	(Rb = 37)	85.4678
dysprosium	(Dy = 66)	162.50	ruthenium	(Ru = 44)	101.07
einsteinium	(Es = 99)	(252)	rutherfordium	(Rf = 104)	(261)
erbium	(Er = 68)	167.259	samarium	(Sm = 62)	150.36
europium	(Eu = 63)	151.964	scandium	(Sc = 21)	44.95591
fermium	(Fm = 100)	(257)	seaborgium	(Sg = 106)	(266)
fluorine	(F = 9)	18.998403	selenium	(Se = 34)	78.96
francium	(Fr = 87)	(223)	silicon	(Si = 14)	28.0855
gadolinium	(Gd = 64)	157.25	silver	(Ag = 47)	107.8682
gallium	(Ga = 31)	69.723	sodium	(Na = 11)	22.989770
germanium	(Ge = 32)	72.64	strontium	(Sr = 38)	87.62
gold	(Au = 79)	196.96655	sulfur	(S = 16)	32.07
hafnium	(Hf = 72)	178.49	tantalum	(Ta = 73)	180.9479
hassium	(Hs = 108)	(277)	technetium	(Tc = 43)	(98)
helium	(He = 2)	4.002602	tellurium	(Te = 52)	127.60
holmium	(Ho = 67)	164.93032	terbium	(Tb = 65)	158.92534
hydrogen	(H = 1)	1.0079	thallium	(Tl = 81)	204.3833
indium	(In = 49)	114.818	thorium	(Th = 90)	232.0381
iodine	(I = 53)	126.90447	thulium	(Tm = 69)	168.93421
iridium	(Ir = 77)	192.217	tin	(Sn = 50)	118.71
iron	(Fe = 26)	55.845	titanium	(Ti = 22)	47.867
krypton	(Kr = 36)	83.80	tungsten	(W = 74)	183.84
lanthanum	(La = 57)	138.9055	uranium	(U = 92)	(238)
lawrencium	(Lr = 103)	(262)	vanadium	(V = 23)	50.9415
lead	(Pb = 82)	207.2	xenon	(Xe = 54)	131.29
lithium	(Li = 3)	6.941	ytterbium	(Yb = 70)	173.04
lutetium	(Lu = 71)	174.967	yttrium	(Y = 39)	88.90585
magnesium	(Mg = 12)	24.305	zinc	(Zn = 30)	65.39
manganese	(Mn = 25)	54.93805	zirconium	(Zr = 40)	91.224

[1]Weights are based on the naturally occurring isotope compositions and scaled to ^{12}C = 12. For elements lacking stable isotopes, the mass number of the most stable nuclide is shown in parentheses.

Asia, and northwestern Africa with curved antlers having many branches

¹ell \'el\ n [ME *eln*, fr. OE; akin to L *ulna* forearm, Gk *ōlenē* elbow] : a former English cloth measure of 45 inches

²ell n : an extension at right angles to a building

el·lipse \i-'lips, e-\ n : a closed curve of oval shape

el·lip·sis \i-'lip-səs, e-\ n, pl **el·lip·ses** \-,sēz\ **1** : omission from an expression of a word clearly implied **2** : marks (as . . .) to show omission

el·lip·soid \i-'lip-,sȯid, e-\ n : a surface all plane sections of which are circles or ellipses — **el·lip·soi·dal** \-,lip-'sȯi-d³l\ *also* **ellipsoid** *adj*

el·lip·ti·cal \i-'lip-ti-kəl, e-\ *or* **el·lip·tic** \-tik\ *adj* **1** : of, relating to, or shaped like an ellipse **2** : of, relating to, or marked by ellipsis — **el·lip·ti·cal·ly** \-ti-k(ə-)lē\ *adv*

elm \'elm\ n : any of a genus of large trees that have toothed leaves and nearly circular one-seeded winged fruits and are often grown as shade trees; *also* : the wood of an elm

El Ni·ño \el-'nē-nyō\ n : a flow of unusually warm Pacific Ocean water moving toward and along the west coast of So. America

el·o·cu·tion \,e-lə-'kyü-shən\ n : the art of effective public speaking — **el·o·cu·tion·ist** \-shə-nist\ n

elon·gate \i-'lȯn-,gāt\ vb **-gat·ed; -gat·ing** : to make or grow longer ♦ *Synonyms* EXTEND, LENGTHEN, PROLONG, PROTRACT — **elon·ga·tion** \(,)ē-,lȯn-'gā-shən\ n

elope \i-'lōp\ vb **eloped; elop·ing** : to run away esp. to be married — **elope·ment** n — **elop·er** n

el·o·quent \'e-lə-kwənt\ *adj* **1** : having or showing clear and forceful expression **2** : clearly showing some feeling or meaning — **el·o·quence** \-kwəns\ n — **el·o·quent·ly** *adv*

¹else \'els\ *adv* **1** : in a different or additional manner or place or at a different or additional time ⟨where ~ can we meet⟩ **2** : OTHERWISE ⟨obey or ~ you'll be sorry⟩

²else *adj* : OTHER; *esp* : being in addition ⟨what ~ do you want⟩

else·where \-,hwer\ *adv* : in or to another place ⟨took my business ~⟩

elu·ci·date \i-'lü-sə-,dāt\ vb **-dat·ed; -dat·ing** : to make clear usu. by explanation ♦ *Synonyms* CLARIFY, EXPLAIN, ILLUMINATE — **elu·ci·da·tion** \-,lü-sə-'dā-shən\ n

elude \ē-'lüd\ vb **elud·ed; elud·ing** **1** : EVADE **2** : to escape the notice of

elu·sive \ē-'lü-siv\ *adj* : tending to elude : EVASIVE — **elu·sive·ly** *adv* — **elu·sive·ness** n

el·ver \'el-vər\ n [alter. of *eelfare* migration of eels] : a young eel

elves *pl of* ELF

Ely·si·um \i-'li-zhē-əm, -zē-\ n, pl **-si·ums**

or **-sia** \-zhē-ə, -zē-\ : PARADISE 2 — **Elysian** \-'li-zhən\ *adj*

em \'em\ n : a length approximately the width of the letter *M*

EM *abbr* **1** electromagnetic **2** electron microscope **3** enlisted man

ema·ci·ate \i-'mā-shē-,āt\ vb **-at·ed; -at·ing** : to become or cause to become very thin — **ema·ci·a·tion** \-,mā-shē-'ā-shən, -sē-\ n

e-mail \'ē-,māl\ n **1** : a system for transmitting messages between computers on a network **2** : a message or messages sent and received through an e-mail system

emalangeni *pl of* LILANGENI

em·a·nate \'e-mə-,nāt\ vb **-nat·ed; -nat·ing** : to come out from a source ♦ *Synonyms* PROCEED, SPRING, RISE, ARISE, ORIGINATE — **em·a·na·tion** \,e-mə-'nā-shən\ n

eman·ci·pate \i-'man-sə-,pāt\ vb **-pat·ed; -pat·ing** : to set free ♦ *Synonyms* LIBERATE, RELEASE, DELIVER, DISCHARGE — **eman·ci·pa·tion** \-,man-sə-'pā-shən\ n — **eman·ci·pa·tor** \-'man-sə-,pā-tər\ n

emas·cu·late \i-'mas-kyù-,lāt\ vb **-lat·ed; -lat·ing** : to deprive of virility : CASTRATE; *also* : WEAKEN — **emas·cu·la·tion** \-,mas-kyù-'lā-shən\ n

em·balm \im-'bäm, -'bälm\ vb : to treat (a corpse) so as to protect from decay — **em·balm·er** n

em·bank·ment \im-'baŋk-mənt\ n : a raised structure (as of earth) to hold back water or carry a roadway

em·bar·go \im-'bär-gō\ n, pl **-goes** [Sp, fr. *embargar* to bar] : a prohibition on commerce — **embargo** vb

em·bark \im-'bärk\ vb **1** : to put or go on board a ship or airplane **2** : to make a start — **em·bar·ka·tion** \,em-,bär-'kā-shən\ n

em·bar·rass \im-'ber-əs\ vb **1** : CONFUSE, DISCONCERT **2** : to involve in financial difficulties **3** : to cause to experience self-conscious distress **4** : HINDER, IMPEDE — **em·bar·rass·ing·ly** *adv* — **em·bar·rass·ment** n

em·bas·sy \'em-bə-sē\ n, pl **-sies** **1** : a group of representatives headed by an ambassador **2** : the function, position, or mission of an ambassador **3** : the official residence and offices of an ambassador

em·bat·tle \im-'ba-t³l\ vb : to arrange in order for battle; *also* : FORTIFY

em·bat·tled *adj* **1** : engaged in battle, conflict, or controversy **2** : being a site of battle, conflict, or controversy **3** : characterized by conflict or controversy ⟨an ~ presidency⟩

em·bed \im-'bed\ vb **em·bed·ded; em·bed·ding** **1** : to enclose closely in a surrounding mass **2** : to make something an integral part of

em·bel·lish \im-'be-lish\ vb **1** : ADORN, DECORATE **2** : to add ornamental details to ♦ *Synonyms* BEAUTIFY, DECK, BEDECK, GARNISH, ORNAMENT, DRESS — **em·bel·lish·er** n — **em·bel·lish·ment** n

em·ber \'em-bər\ n **1** : a glowing or

smoldering fragment from a fire **2** *pl* : the smoldering remains of a fire

em·bez·zle \im-'be-zəl\ *vb* **-zled; -zling** : to steal (as money) by falsifying records — **em·bez·zle·ment** *n* — **em·bez·zler** *n*

em·bit·ter \im-'bi-tər\ *vb* **1** : to arouse bitter feelings in **2** : to make bitter

em·bla·zon \-'blā-zⁿn\ *vb* **1** : to adorn with heraldic devices **2** : to display conspicuously

em·blem \'em-bləm\ *n* : something (as an object or picture) suggesting another object or an idea : SYMBOL — **em·blem·at·ic** \,em-blə-'ma-tik\ *also* **em·blem·at·i·cal** \-ti-kəl\ *adj*

em·body \im-'bä-dē\ *vb* **em·bod·ied; em·body·ing 1** : INCARNATE **2** : to express in definite form **3** : to incorporate into a system or body **4** : PERSONIFY ✦ *Synonyms* COMBINE, INTEGRATE — **em·bodi·ment** \-di-mənt\ *n*

em·bold·en \im-'bōl-dən\ *vb* : to inspire with courage

em·bo·lism \'em-bə-,li-zəm\ *n* : the obstruction of a blood vessel by a foreign or abnormal particle

em·bon·point \äⁿ-bōⁿ-'pwaⁿ\ *n* [F] : plumpness of person : STOUTNESS

em·boss \im-'bäs, -'bós\ *vb* : to ornament with raised work

em·bou·chure \'äm-bu̇-,shu̇r, ,äm-bu̇-'shu̇r\ *n* [F, ultim. fr. *bouche* mouth] : the position and use of the lips, tongue, and teeth in playing a wind instrument

em·bow·er \im-'bau̇(-ə)r\ *vb* : to shelter or enclose in a bower

¹em·brace \im-'brās\ *vb* **em·braced; em·brac·ing 1** : to clasp in the arms; *also* : CHERISH, LOVE **2** : ENCIRCLE **3** : TAKE UP, ADOPT ⟨*embraced* the cause⟩; *also* : WELCOME ⟨*embraced* the opportunity⟩ **4** : INCLUDE **5** : to participate in an embrace ✦ *Synonyms* COMPREHEND, INVOLVE, ENCOMPASS, EMBODY

²embrace *n* : an encircling with the arms

em·bra·sure \im-'brā-zhər\ *n* **1** : an opening in a wall through which a weapon is fired **2** : a recess of a door or window

em·bro·ca·tion \,em-brə-'kā-shən\ *n* : LINIMENT

em·broi·der \im-'brȯi-dər\ *vb* **1** : to ornament with or do needlework **2** : to elaborate with exaggerated detail

em·broi·dery \im-'brȯi-də-rē\ *n, pl* **-der·ies 1** : the forming of decorative designs with needlework **2** : something embroidered

em·broil \im-'brȯi(-ə)l\ *vb* **1** : to throw into confusion or disorder **2** : to involve in conflict or difficulties — **em·broil·ment** *n*

em·bryo \'em-brē-,ō\ *n, pl* **embryos** : a living thing in its earliest stages of development — **em·bry·on·ic** \,em-brē-'ä-nik\ *adj*

em·bry·ol·o·gy \,em-brē-'ä-lə-jē\ *n* : a branch of biology dealing with embryos and their development — **em·bry·o·log·i·cal** \-brē-ə-'lä-ji-kəl\ *adj* — **em·bry·ol·o·gist** \-brē-'ä-lə-jist\ *n*

em·cee \'em-'sē\ *n* : MASTER OF CEREMONIES — **emcee** *vb*

emend \ē-'mend\ *vb* : to correct usu. by altering the text of ✦ *Synonyms* RECTIFY, REVISE, AMEND — **emen·da·tion** \,ē-,men-'dā-shən\ *n*

emer *abbr* emeritus

¹em·er·ald \'em-rəld, 'e-mə-\ *n* : a green beryl prized as a gem

²emerald *adj* : brightly or richly green

emerge \i-'mərj\ *vb* **emerged; emerg·ing** : to rise, come forth, or come into view — **emer·gence** \-'mər-jəns\ *n* — **emer·gent** \-jənt\ *adj*

emer·gen·cy \i-'mər-jən-sē\ *n, pl* **-cies** : an unforeseen event or condition requiring prompt action ✦ *Synonyms* EXIGENCY, CONTINGENCY, CRISIS, JUNCTURE

emergency room *n* : a hospital room for receiving and treating persons needing immediate medical care

emer·i·ta \i-'mer-ə-tə\ *adj* : EMERITUS — used of a woman

emer·i·tus \i-'mer-ə-təs\ *adj* [L] : retired from active duty ⟨professor ∼⟩

em·ery \'e-mə-rē\ *n, pl* **em·er·ies** : a dark granular mineral consisting primarily of corundum and used as an abrasive

emet·ic \i-'me-tik\ *n* : an agent that induces vomiting — **emetic** *adj*

emf *n* [*electromotive force*] : POTENTIAL DIFFERENCE

em·i·grate \'e-mə-,grāt\ *vb* **-grat·ed; -grat·ing** : to leave a place (as a country) to settle elsewhere — **em·i·grant** \-mi-grənt\ *n* — **em·i·gra·tion** \,e-mə-'grā-shən\ *n*

émi·gré *also* **emi·gré** \'e-mi-,grā, ,e-mi-'grā\ *n* [F] : a person who emigrates esp. because of political conditions

em·i·nence \'e-mə-nəns\ *n* **1** : high rank or position; *also* : a person of high rank or attainment **2** : a lofty place

em·i·nent \'e-mə-nənt\ *adj* **1** : CONSPICUOUS, EVIDENT **2** : DISTINGUISHED, PROMINENT ⟨an ∼ physician⟩ — **em·i·nent·ly** *adv*

eminent domain *n* : a right of a government to take private property for public use

emir *or* **amir** \ə-'mir, ā-\ *n* [Ar *amīr* commander] : a ruler, chief, or commander in Islamic countries — **emir·ate** \'e-mər-ət\ *n*

em·is·sary \'e-mə-,ser-ē\ *n, pl* **-sar·ies** : AGENT; *esp* : a secret agent

emis·sion \ē-'mi-shən\ *n* : something emitted; *esp* : substances discharged into the air

emit \ē-'mit\ *vb* **emit·ted; emit·ting 1** : to give off or out ⟨∼ light⟩; *also* : EJECT **2** : EXPRESS, UTTER — **emit·ter** *n*

emol·lient \i-'mäl-yənt\ *adj* : making soft or supple; *also* : soothing esp. to the skin or mucous membrane ⟨an ∼ hand lotion⟩ — **emol·lient** *n*

emol·u·ment \i-'mäl-yə-mənt\ *n* [ME, fr. L *emolumentum* advantage, fr. *emolere* to produce by grinding] : the product (as salary or fees) of an employment

emote \i-ˈmōt\ *vb* **emot·ed; emot·ing** : to give expression to emotion in or as if in a play

emo·ti·con \i-ˈmō-ti-ˌkän\ *n* : a group of keyboard characters (as :)) that represents a facial expression esp. in online communications

emo·tion \i-ˈmō-shən\ *n* : a usu. intense feeling (as of love, hate, or despair) — **emo·tion·al** \-shə-nəl\ *adj* — **emo·tion·al·ly** *adv*

emot·ive \i-ˈmō-tiv\ *adj* **1** : of or relating to the emotions **2** : appealing to or expressing emotion

emp *abbr* emperor; empress

empanel *var of* IMPANEL

em·pa·thy \ˈem-pə-thē\ *n* : the experiencing as one's own of the feelings of another; *also* : the capacity for this — **em·path·ic** \em-ˈpa-thik\ *adj*

em·pen·nage \ˌäm-pə-ˈnäzh, ˌem-\ *n* [F] : the tail assembly of an airplane

em·per·or \ˈem-pər-ər\ *n* : the sovereign male ruler of an empire

em·pha·sis \ˈem-fə-səs\ *n, pl* **-pha·ses** \-ˌsēz\ : particular prominence given (as to a syllable in speaking or to a phase of action)

em·pha·sise *Brit var of* EMPHASIZE

em·pha·size \-ˌsīz\ *vb* **-sized; -siz·ing** : to place emphasis on : STRESS

em·phat·ic \im-ˈfa-tik, em-\ *adj* : uttered with emphasis : STRESSED — **em·phat·i·cal·ly** \-ˈti-k(ə-)lē\ *adv*

em·phy·se·ma \ˌem-fə-ˈzē-mə, -ˈsē-\ *n* : a condition marked esp. by abnormal expansion of the air spaces of the lungs resulting in severe breathlessness

em·pire \ˈem-ˌpī(-ə)r\ *n* **1** : a large state or a group of states under a single sovereign who is usu. an emperor; *also* : something resembling a political empire **2** : imperial sovereignty or dominion

em·pir·i·cal \im-ˈpir-i-kəl\ *also* **em·pir·ic** \-ik\ *adj* : based on observation; *also* : subject to verification by observation or experiment ⟨~ laws⟩ — **em·pir·i·cal·ly** \-i-k(ə-)lē\ *adv*

em·pir·i·cism \im-ˈpir-ə-ˌsi-zəm, em-\ *n* : the practice of relying on observation and experiment esp. in the natural sciences — **em·pir·i·cist** \-sist\ *n*

em·place·ment \im-ˈplās-mənt\ *n* **1** : a prepared position for weapons or military equipment **2** : PLACEMENT

¹**em·ploy** \im-ˈplȯi\ *vb* **1** : to make use of **2** : to use the services of **3** : OCCUPY, DEVOTE — **em·ploy·er** *n*

²**em·ploy** \im-ˈplȯi; ˈim-ˌplȯi, ˈem-\ *n* : EMPLOYMENT

em·ploy·ee *also* **em·ploye** \im-ˌplȯi-ˈē, ˌem-; im-ˈplȯi-ˌē, em-\ *n* : a person who works for another

em·ploy·ment \im-ˈplȯi-mənt\ *n* **1** : OCCUPATION, ACTIVITY **2** : the act of employing : the condition of being employed

em·po·ri·um \im-ˈpȯr-ē-əm, em-\ *n, pl* **-ri·ums** *also* **-ria** \-ē-ə\ [L, fr. Gk *emporion*, fr. *emporos* traveler, trader] : a commercial center; *esp* : a store carrying varied articles

em·pow·er \im-ˈpaů(-ə)r\ *vb* : to give authority or power to; *also* : ENABLE — **em·pow·er·ment** \-mənt\ *n*

em·press \ˈem-prəs\ *n* **1** : the wife or widow of an emperor **2** : a sovereign female ruler of an empire

¹**emp·ty** \ˈemp-tē\ *adj* **emp·ti·er; -est** [ME, fr. OE *ǣmettig* unoccupied, fr. *ǣmetta* leisure] **1** : containing nothing ⟨~ shelves⟩ **2** : UNOCCUPIED, UNINHABITED ⟨an ~ building⟩ **3** : lacking value, force, sense, or purpose ♦ *Synonyms* VACANT, BLANK, VOID, STARK, VACUOUS — **emp·ti·ness** *n*

²**empty** *vb* **emp·tied; emp·ty·ing 1** : to make or become empty **2** : to discharge contents; *also* : to remove from what holds or encloses

³**empty** *n, pl* **empties** : an empty bottle or can

emp·ty–hand·ed \ˌemp-tē-ˈhan-dəd\ *adj* **1** : having or bringing nothing **2** : having acquired or gained nothing

em·py·re·an \ˌem-ˌpī-ˈrē-ən, -pə-\ *n* **1** : the highest heaven; *also* : FIRMAMENT **2** : an ideal place or state

EMT \ˌē-(ˌ)em-ˈtē\ *n* [*e*mergency *m*edical *t*echnician] : a specially trained medical technician certified to provide basic medical services before and during transport to a hospital

¹**emu** \ˈē-myü, -mü\ *n* : a swift-running flightless Australian bird smaller than the related ostrich

²**emu** *abbr* electromagnetic unit

em·u·late \ˈem-yù-ˌlāt\ *vb* **-lat·ed; -lat·ing** : to strive to equal or excel : IMITATE — **em·u·la·tion** \ˌem-yù-ˈlā-shən\ *n* — **em·u·lous** \ˈem-yù-ləs\ *adj*

emul·si·fi·er \i-ˈməl-sə-ˌfī(-ə)r\ *n* : a substance (as a soap) that helps to form and stabilize an emulsion

emul·si·fy \-ˌfī\ *vb* **-fied; -fy·ing** : to disperse (as an oil) in an emulsion — **emul·si·fi·ca·tion** \ˌi-ˌməl-sə-fə-ˈkā-shən\ *n*

emul·sion \i-ˈməl-shən\ *n* **1** : a mixture of mutually insoluble liquids in which one is dispersed in droplets throughout the other ⟨an ~ of oil in water⟩ **2** : a light-sensitive coating on photographic film or paper

en \ˈen\ *n* : a length approximately half the width of the letter *M*

¹**-en** *also* **-n** *adj suffix* : made of : consisting of ⟨earthen⟩

²**-en** *vb suffix* **1** : become or cause to be ⟨sharpen⟩ **2** : cause or come to have ⟨lengthen⟩

en·able \i-ˈnā-bəl\ *vb* **en·abled; en·abling 1** : to make able or feasible ⟨wings that ~ one to fly⟩ **2** : to give legal power, capacity, or sanction to

en·act \i-ˈnakt\ *vb* **1** : to make into law **2** : to act out — **en·act·ment** *n*

enam·el \i-ˈna-məl\ *n* **1** : a glasslike substance used to coat the surface of metal or pottery **2** : the hard outer layer of a tooth **3** : a usu. glossy paint that forms a hard coat — **enamel** *vb*

enam·el·ware \-ˌwer\ *n* : metal utensils coated with enamel

en·am·or \i-'na-mər\ *vb* : to inflame with love

en·am·our *chiefly Brit var of* ENAMOR

en bloc \äⁿ-'bläk\ *adv or adj* : as a whole : in a mass

enc *or* **encl** *abbr* enclosure

en·camp \in-'kamp\ *vb* : to make camp — **en·camp·ment** *n*

en·cap·su·late \in-'kap-sə-ˌlāt\ *vb* **-lat·ed; -lat·ing 1** : to encase or become encased in a capsule **2** : SUMMARIZE — **en·cap·su·la·tion** \-ˌkap-sə-'lā-shən\ *n*

en·case \in-'kās\ *vb* : to enclose in or as if in a case — **en·case·ment** \-'kā-smənt\ *n*

-ence *n suffix* **1** : action or process ⟨emerg*ence*⟩ : instance of an action or process ⟨refer*ence*⟩ **2** : quality or state ⟨depend*ence*⟩

en·ceinte \äⁿ-'sant\ *adj* : PREGNANT 1

en·ceph·a·li·tis \in-ˌse-fə-'lī-təs\ *n, pl* **-lit·i·des** \-'li-tə-ˌdēz\ : inflammation of the brain — **en·ceph·a·lit·ic** \-'li-tik\ *adj*

en·ceph·a·lop·a·thy \in-ˌse-fə-'lä-pə-thē\ *n, pl* **-thies** : a disease of the brain

en·chain \in-'chān\ *vb* : FETTER, CHAIN

en·chant \in-'chant\ *vb* **1** : BEWITCH **2** : ENRAPTURE, FASCINATE ⟨was ∼ed by his poetry⟩ — **en·chant·er** *n* — **en·chant·ing·ly** *adv* — **en·chant·ment** *n* — **en·chant·ress** \-'chan-trəs\ *n*

en·chi·la·da \ˌen-chə-'lä-də\ *n* : a tortilla rolled around a filling, covered with chili sauce, and usu. baked

en·ci·pher \in-'sī-fər, en-\ *vb* : ENCODE

en·cir·cle \in-'sər-kəl\ *vb* : to pass completely around : SURROUND — **en·cir·cle·ment** *n*

en·clave \'en-ˌklāv; 'än-ˌklāv\ *n* : a distinct territorial, cultural, or social unit enclosed within or as if within foreign territory

en·close \in-'klōz\ *vb* **1** : to shut up or in; *esp* : to surround with a fence **2** : to include along with something else in a parcel or envelope ⟨∼ a check⟩ — **en·clo·sure** \-'klō-zhər\ *n*

en·code \in-'kōd, en-\ *vb* : to convert (a message) into code

en·co·mi·um \en-'kō-mē-əm\ *n, pl* **-mi·ums** *also* **-mia** \-mē-ə\ : high or glowing praise

en·com·pass \in-'kəm-pəs\ *vb* **1** : ENCIRCLE **2** : ENVELOP, INCLUDE

en·core \'än-ˌkȯr\ *n* **1** : a demand for repetition or reappearance **2** : a further performance or appearance demanded by an audience **3** : a second achievement that usu. surpasses the first — **encore** *vb*

en·coun·ter \in-'kaůn-tər\ *vb* **1** : to meet as an enemy : FIGHT **2** : to meet usu. unexpectedly ⟨∼ problems⟩

²encounter *n* **1** : a hostile usu. violent meeting **2** : a chance meeting **3** : an experience shared with another ⟨a romantic ∼⟩

en·cour·age \in-'kər-ij\ *vb* **-aged; -ag·ing 1** : to inspire with courage and hope **2** : STIMULATE, INCITE ⟨tax cuts to ∼ spending⟩ **3** : FOSTER — **en·cour·age·ment** *n* — **en·cour·ag·ing·ly** *adv*

en·croach \in-'krōch\ *vb* [ME *encrochen* to seize, fr. AF *encrocher*, fr. *croche* hook] : to enter gradually or stealthily upon another's property or rights — **en·croach·er** *n* — **en·croach·ment** *n*

en·crust *also* **in·crust** \in-'krəst\ *vb* : to provide with or form a crust

en·crus·ta·tion \(ˌ)in-ˌkrəs-'tā-shən, ˌen-\ *var of* INCRUSTATION

en·cum·ber \in-'kəm-bər\ *vb* **1** : to weigh down : BURDEN **2** : to hinder the function or activity of ⟨relations ∼ed by mistrust⟩ — **en·cum·brance** \-brəns\ *n*

ency *or* **encyc** *abbr* encyclopedia

-en·cy *n suffix* : quality or state ⟨despondency⟩

¹en·cyc·li·cal \in-'si-kli-kəl, en-\ *adj* : addressed to all the individuals of a group

²encyclical *n* : an encyclical letter; *esp* : a papal letter to the bishops of the church

en·cy·clo·pae·dia, en·cy·clo·pae·dic *chiefly Brit var of* ENCYCLOPEDIA, ENCYCLOPEDIC

en·cy·clo·pe·dia \in-ˌsī-klə-'pē-dē-ə\ *n* [ML *encyclopaedia* course of general education, fr. Gk *enkyklios paideia* general education] : a work treating the various branches of learning — **en·cy·clo·pe·dic** \-'pē-dik\ *adj*

en·cyst \in-'sist, en-\ *vb* : to form or become enclosed in a cyst — **en·cyst·ment** *n*

¹end \'end\ *n* **1** : the part of an area that lies at the boundary; *also* : a point which marks the extent or limit of something or at which something ceases to exist **2** : a ceasing of a course (as of action or activity); *also* : DEATH **3** : the ultimate state; *also* : RESULT, ISSUE **4** : REMNANT **5** : PURPOSE, OBJECTIVE **6** : a player stationed at the extremity of a line (as in football) **7** : a share, operation, or aspect of an undertaking

²end *vb* **1** : to bring or come to an end **2** : DESTROY; *also* : DIE **3** : to form or be at the end of — **Synonyms** ✦ CLOSE, CONCLUDE, TERMINATE, FINISH, COMPLETE

en·dan·ger \in-'dān-jər\ *vb* : to bring into danger; *also* : to create danger

en·dan·gered *adj* : being or relating to an endangered species

endangered species *n* : a species threatened with extinction

en·dear \in-'dir\ *vb* : to cause to become beloved or admired

en·dear·ment \-mənt\ *n* : a sign of affection : CARESS

en·deav·or \in-'de-vər\ *vb* : TRY, ATTEMPT — **endeavor** *n*

en·deav·our *chiefly Brit var of* ENDEAVOR

en·dem·ic \en-'de-mik, in-\ *adj* : restricted to a particular place ⟨∼ plants⟩ ⟨an ∼ disease⟩ — **endemic** *n*

end·ing \'en-diŋ\ *n* : something that forms an end; *esp* : SUFFIX

en·dive \'en-ˌdīv\ *n* **1** : an herb related to chicory and grown as a salad plant **2** : the blanched shoot of chicory

end·less \'end-ləs\ *adj* **1** : having or seeming to have no end : ETERNAL ⟨∼ debates⟩ **2** : united at the ends : CON-

TINUOUS ⟨an ~ belt⟩ ✦ *Synonyms* INTERMINABLE, EVERLASTING, UNCEASING, CEASELESS, UNENDING — **end·less·ly** *adv*

end·most \-ˌmōst\ *adj* : situated at the very end

end·note \-ˌnōt\ *n* : a note placed at the end of a text

en·do·crine \ˈen-də-krən, -ˌkrīn, -ˌkrēn\ *adj* : producing secretions that are distributed by way of the bloodstream ⟨~ glands⟩ — **endocrine** *n* — **en·do·cri·nol·o·gist** \-kri-ˈnä-lə-jist\ *n* — **en·do·cri·nol·o·gy** \-jē\ *n*

en·dog·e·nous \en-ˈdä-jə-nəs\ *adj* : caused or produced by factors inside the organism or system ⟨~ depression⟩ — **en·dog·e·nous·ly** *adv*

en·do·me·tri·um \ˌen-dō-ˈmē-trē-əm\ *n, pl* **-tria** \-trē-ə\ : the mucous membrane lining the uterus — **en·do·me·tri·al** \-trē-əl\ *adj*

en·dor·phin \en-ˈdòr-fən\ *n* : any of a group of endogenous morphinelike proteins found esp. in the brain

en·dorse *also* **in·dorse** \in-ˈdòrs\ *vb* **en·dorsed; en·dors·ing** [ME *endosen*, fr. AF *endosser* to put on, don, write on the back of, fr. *dos* back, fr. L *dorsum*] **1** : to sign one's name on the back of (as a check) **2** : APPROVE, SANCTION **3** : to recommend (as a product) usu. for financial compensation — **en·dorse·ment** *also* **in·dorse·ment** *n*

en·do·scope \ˈen-də-ˌskōp\ *n* : an illuminated usu. fiber-optic instrument for visualizing the interior of a hollow organ or part (as the colon or esophagus) — **en·do·scop·ic** \ˌen-də-ˈskä-pik\ *adj* — **en·dos·co·py** \en-ˈdäs-kə-pē\ *n*

en·do·ther·mic \ˌen-də-ˈthər-mik\ *adj* : characterized by or formed with absorption of heat

en·dow \in-ˈdaú\ *vb* **1** : to furnish with funds for support ⟨~ a school⟩ **2** : to furnish with something freely or naturally — **en·dow·ment** *n*

en·due \in-ˈdü, -ˈdyü\ *vb* **en·dued; en·du·ing** : PROVIDE, ENDOW

en·dur·ance \in-ˈdúr-əns, -ˈdyùr-\ *n* **1** : DURATION **2** : the ability to withstand hardship or stress : FORTITUDE

en·dure \in-ˈdúr, -ˈdyúr\ *vb* **en·dured; en·dur·ing 1** : LAST, PERSIST **2** : to suffer firmly or patiently : BEAR **3** : TOLERATE — **en·dur·able** *adj*

end·ways \ˈend-ˌwāz\ *adv or adj* **1** : LENGTHWISE **2** : with the end forward **3** : on end

end·wise \-ˌwīz\ *adv or adj* : ENDWAYS

ENE *abbr* east-northeast

en·e·ma \ˈe-nə-mə\ *n, pl* **enemas** *also* **ene·ma·ta** \ˌe-nə-ˈmä-tə, ˈe-nə-mə-tə\ : injection of liquid into the rectum; *also* : material so injected

en·e·my \ˈe-nə-mē\ *n, pl* **-mies** [ME *enemi*, fr. AF, fr. L *inimicus*, fr. *in-* not + *amicus* friend] : one that attacks or tries to harm another : FOE; *esp* : a military opponent

en·er·get·ic \ˌe-nər-ˈje-tik\ *adj* : marked by energy : ACTIVE, VIGOROUS ✦ *Synonyms* STRENUOUS, LUSTY, DYNAMIC, VITAL — **en·er·get·i·cal·ly** \-ti-k(ə-)lē\ *adv*

en·er·gise *Brit var of* ENERGIZE

en·er·gize \ˈe-nər-ˌjīz\ *vb* **-gized; -giz·ing** : to give energy to

en·er·gy \ˈe-nər-jē\ *n, pl* **-gies 1** : vigorous action : EFFORT **2** : capacity for action **3** : a fundamental entity of nature usu. regarded as the capacity for performing work **4** : usable power (as heat or electricity); *also* : the resources for producing such power

energy level *n* : one of the stable states of constant energy that may be assumed by a physical system (as the electrons in an atom)

en·er·vate \ˈe-nər-ˌvāt\ *vb* **-vat·ed; -vat·ing** : to lessen the strength or vigor of : weaken in mind or body — **en·er·vat·ing·ly** \-ˌvā-tiŋ-lē\ *adv* — **en·er·va·tion** \ˌe-nər-ˈvā-shən\ *n*

en·fee·ble \in-ˈfē-bəl\ *vb* **-bled; -bling** : to make feeble ✦ *Synonyms* WEAKEN, DEBILITATE, SAP, UNDERMINE, CRIPPLE — **en·fee·ble·ment** *n*

en·fi·lade \ˈen-fə-ˌlād, -ˌläd\ *n* : gunfire directed along the length of an enemy battle line — **enfilade** *vb*

en·fold \in-ˈfōld\ *vb* **1** : ENVELOP **2** : EMBRACE

en·force \in-ˈfórs\ *vb* **1** : COMPEL ⟨~ obedience by threats⟩ **2** : to execute effectively ⟨~ the law⟩ — **en·force·able** *adj* — **en·force·ment** *n*

en·forc·er \in-ˈfòr-sər\ *n* : one that enforces; *esp* : a player (as in ice hockey) known for rough play

en·fran·chise \in-ˈfran-ˌchīz\ *vb* **-chised; -chis·ing 1** : to set free (as from slavery) **2** : to admit to citizenship; *also* : to grant the vote to — **en·fran·chise·ment** \-ˌchīz-mənt, -chəz-\ *n*

eng *abbr* engine; engineer; engineering

Eng *abbr* England; English

en·gage \in-ˈgāj\ *vb* **en·gaged; en·gag·ing 1** : PLEDGE; *esp* : to bind by a pledge to marry **2** : EMPLOY, HIRE **3** : to attract and hold esp. by interesting; *also* : to cause to participate **4** : to commence or take part in a venture ⟨*engaged* in shady deals⟩ **5** : to bring or enter into conflict ⟨~ the enemy⟩ **6** : to connect or interlock with : MESH; *also* : to cause to mesh

en·gage·ment \in-ˈgāj-mənt\ *n* **1** : APPOINTMENT **2** : EMPLOYMENT **3** : a mutual promise to marry : BETROTHAL **4** : a hostile encounter

en·gag·ing *adj* : ATTRACTIVE ⟨an ~ smile⟩ — **en·gag·ing·ly** *adv*

en·gen·der \in-ˈjen-dər\ *vb* **1** : BEGET **2** : BRING ABOUT, CREATE ⟨~ controversy⟩ ✦ *Synonyms* GENERATE, BREED, OCCASION, PRODUCE

en·gine \ˈen-jən\ *n* [ME *engin*, fr. AF, fr. L *ingenium* natural disposition, talent] **1** : a mechanical device **2** : a machine for converting energy into mechanical motion **3** : LOCOMOTIVE **4** : software that performs a fundamental function esp. of a larger program — **en·gine·less** *adj*

¹**en·gi·neer** \ₑen-jə-'nir\ *n* **1** : a member of a military unit specializing in engineering work **2** : a designer or builder of engines **3** : one trained in engineering **4** : one that operates an engine

²**engineer** *vb* **1** : to lay out or manage as an engineer **2** : to guide the course of ⟨∼ a rally⟩ ✦ *Synonyms* PILOT, LEAD, STEER

en·gi·neer·ing *n* : the practical applications of scientific and mathematical principles

En·glish \'iŋ-glish\ *n* **1** : the language of England, the U.S., and many areas now or formerly under British rule **2 English** *pl* : the people of England **3** : spin imparted to a ball that is driven or rolled — **English** *adj* — **En·glish·man** \-mən\ *n* — **En·glish·wom·an** \-ˌwu̇-mən\ *n*

English horn *n* : a woodwind instrument longer than and having a range lower than the oboe

English setter *n* : any of a breed of hunting dogs with a flat silky coat of white or white with color

English sparrow *n* : HOUSE SPARROW

English system *n* : a system of weights and measures in which the foot is the principal unit of length and the pound is the principal unit of weight

engr *abbr* **1** engineer **2** engraved

en·gram \'en-ˌgram\ *n* : a hypothetical change in neural tissue postulated in order to account for persistence of memory

en·grave \in-'grāv\ *vb* **en·graved**; **en·grav·ing** **1** : to produce (as letters or lines) by incising a surface **2** : to cut figures, letters, or designs on for printing; *also* : to print from an engraved plate ⟨∼ an invitation⟩ **3** : PHOTOENGRAVE — **en·grav·er** *n*

en·grav·ing \in-'grā-viŋ\ *n* **1** : the art of one who engraves **2** : an engraved plate; *also* : a print made from it

en·gross \in-'grōs\ *vb* : to take up the whole interest or attention of ✦ *Synonyms* MONOPOLIZE, ABSORB, CONSUME

en·gulf \in-'gəlf\ *vb* : to flow over and enclose : OVERWHELM ⟨∼ed in flames⟩

en·hance \in-'hans\ *vb* **en·hanced**; **en·hanc·ing** : to increase or improve (as in value or desirability) ✦ *Synonyms* HEIGHTEN, INTENSIFY, MAGNIFY — **en·hance·ment** *n*

enig·ma \i-'nig-mə\ *n* [L *aenigma*, fr. Gk *ainigma*, fr. *ainissesthai* to speak in riddles, fr. *ainos* fable] : something obscure or hard to understand

enig·mat·ic \ˌen-ig-'ma-tik\ *adj* : resembling an enigma ✦ *Synonyms* OBSCURE, CRYPTIC, MYSTIFYING — **en·ig·mat·i·cal·ly** \-ti-k(ə)lē\ *adv*

en·join \in-'jȯin\ *vb* **1** : COMMAND, ORDER ⟨∼ed us to desist⟩ **2** : FORBID ✦ *Synonyms* DIRECT, BID, CHARGE, COMMAND, INSTRUCT

en·joy \in-'jȯi\ *vb* **1** : to have for one's benefit or use ⟨∼ good health⟩ **2** : to take pleasure or satisfaction in ⟨∼ed the

concert⟩ — **en·joy·able** *adj* — **en·joy·ment** *n*

enl *abbr* **1** enlarged **2** enlisted

en·large \in-'lärj\ *vb* **en·larged**; **en·larg·ing** **1** : to make or grow larger **2** : ELABORATE ✦ *Synonyms* INCREASE, AUGMENT, MULTIPLY, EXPAND — **en·large·ment** *n*

en·light·en \in-'lī-t°n\ *vb* **1** : INSTRUCT, INFORM **2** : to give spiritual insight to — **en·light·en·ment** *n*

en·list \in-'list\ *vb* **1** : to secure the aid or support of **2** : to engage for service in the armed forces — **en·list·ee** \-ˌlis-'tē\ *n* — **en·list·ment** \-'list-mənt\ *n*

en·list·ed \in-'lis-təd\ *adj* : of, relating to, or forming the part of a military force below commissioned or warrant officers

enlisted man *n* : a man or woman in the armed forces ranking below a commissioned or warrant officer

en·liv·en \in-'lī-vən\ *vb* : to give life, action, or spirit to : ANIMATE

en masse \ä°n-'mas\ *adv* [F] : in a body : as a whole

en·mesh \in-'mesh\ *vb* : to catch or entangle in or as if in meshes

en·mi·ty \'en-mə-tē\ *n, pl* **-ties** : ILL WILL; *esp* : mutual hatred ✦ *Synonyms* HOSTILITY, ANTIPATHY, ANIMOSITY, RANCOR, ANTAGONISM

en·no·ble \i-'nō-bəl\ *vb* **-bled**; **-bling** : EXALT, ELEVATE; *esp* : to raise to noble rank — **en·no·ble·ment** *n*

en·nui \ˌän-'wē\ *n* [F] : BOREDOM

enor·mi·ty \i-'nȯr-mə-tē\ *n, pl* **-ties** **1** : an outrageous, vicious, or immoral act **2** : great wickedness **3** : IMMENSITY

enor·mous \i-'nȯr-məs\ *adj* [L *enormis*, fr. *e, ex* out of + *norma* rule] **1** : exceedingly wicked **2** : great in size, number, or degree : HUGE ✦ *Synonyms* IMMENSE, VAST, GIGANTIC, COLOSSAL, MAMMOTH, ELEPHANTINE — **enor·mous·ly** *adv*

¹**enough** \i-'nəf\ *adj* : SUFFICIENT

²**enough** *adv* **1** : SUFFICIENTLY **2** : FULLY, QUITE **3** : TOLERABLY

³**enough** *pron* : a sufficient number, quantity, or amount

en·quire \in-'kwī(-ə)r\, **en·qui·ry** \'in-ˌkwī(-ə)r-ē, in-'; 'in-kwə-rē, 'iŋ-\ *chiefly Brit var of* INQUIRE, INQUIRY

en·rage \in-'rāj\ *vb* : to fill with rage

en·rap·ture \in-'rap-chər\ *vb* **en·rap·tured**; **en·rap·tur·ing** : DELIGHT

en·rich \in-'rich\ *vb* **1** : to make rich or richer **2** : ORNAMENT, ADORN — **en·rich·ment** *n*

en·roll *also* **en·rol** \in-'rōl\ *vb* **en·rolled**; **en·roll·ing** **1** : to enter or register on a roll or list **2** : to offer (oneself) for enrolling — **en·roll·ment** *n*

en route \än-'rüt, en-\ *adv or adj* : on or along the way ⟨stalled while *en route* to work⟩

ENS *abbr* ensign

en·sconce \in-'skäns\ *vb* **en·sconced**; **en·sconc·ing** **1** : SHELTER, CONCEAL **2** : to settle snugly or securely ✦ *Synonyms* SECRETE, HIDE, CACHE, STASH

en·sem·ble \än-'säm-bəl\ *n* [F, fr. *ensemble* together, fr. L *insimul* at the same time] : a group (as of singers, dancers, or players) or a set (as of clothes) producing a single effect

en·sheathe \in-'shēth\ *vb* : to cover with or as if with a sheath

en·shrine \in-'shrīn\ *vb* 1 : to enclose in or as if in a shrine 2 : to cherish as sacred — **en·shrine·ment** \-mənt\ *n*

en·shroud \in-'shraud\ *vb* : SHROUD, OBSCURE

en·sign \'en-sən, *1 also* 'en-,sīn\ *n* 1 : FLAG; *also* : BADGE, EMBLEM 2 : a commissioned officer in the navy ranking next below a lieutenant junior grade

en·slave \in-'slāv\ *vb* : to make a slave of — **en·slave·ment** *n*

en·snare \in-'sner\ *vb* : SNARE, TRAP ♦ **Synonyms** ENTRAP, BAG, CATCH, CAPTURE

en·sue \in-'sü\ *vb* **en·sued; en·su·ing** : to follow in time or as a result ⟨the birds escaped and chaos *ensued*⟩

en·sure \in-'shur\ *vb* : INSURE, GUARANTEE

en·tail \in-'tāl\ *vb* 1 : to limit the inheritance of (property) to the owner's lineal descendants or to a class thereof 2 : to include or involve as a necessary step or result ⟨the sacrifices that parenting ∼*s*⟩ — **en·tail·ment** *n*

en·tan·gle \in-'taŋ-gəl\ *vb* : TANGLE, CONFUSE — **en·tan·gle·ment** *n*

en·tente \än-'tänt\ *n* [F] : an understanding providing for joint action; *also* : parties linked by such an entente

en·ter \'en-tər\ *vb* 1 : to go or come in or into 2 : to become a member of : JOIN ⟨∼ the ministry⟩ 3 : BEGIN 4 : to take part in : CONTRIBUTE 5 : to go into or upon and take possession 6 : to set down (as in a list) : REGISTER ⟨∼ the data⟩ 7 : to place (a complaint) before a court; *also* : to put on record ⟨∼ a complaint⟩

en·ter·i·tis \,en-tə-'rī-təs\ *n* : intestinal inflammation; *also* : a disease marked by this

en·ter·prise \'en-tər-,prīz\ *n* 1 : UNDERTAKING, PROJECT 2 : readiness for daring action : INITIATIVE 3 : a business organization

en·ter·pris·ing \-,prī-ziŋ\ *adj* : bold and vigorous in action : ENERGETIC

en·ter·tain \,en-tər-'tān\ *vb* 1 : to treat or receive as a guest 2 : AMUSE, DIVERT ⟨∼*ed* us with jokes⟩ 3 : to hold in mind ⟨∼*ed* thoughts of retirement⟩ ♦ **Synonyms** HARBOR, SHELTER, LODGE, HOUSE, BILLET — **en·ter·tain·er** *n* — **en·ter·tain·ment** *n*

en·thrall *or* **en·thral** \in-'thrȯl\ *vb* **en·thralled; en·thrall·ing** 1 : ENSLAVE 2 : to hold spellbound

en·throne \in-'thrōn\ *vb* 1 : to seat on or as if on a throne 2 : EXALT

en·thuse \in-'thüz, -'thyüz\ *vb* **en·thused; en·thus·ing** 1 : to make enthusiastic 2 : to show enthusiasm

en·thu·si·asm \in-'thü-zē-,a-zəm, -'thyü-\ *n* [Gk *enthousiasmos*, fr. *enthousiazein* to be inspired, irreg. fr. *entheos* inspired, fr. *theos* god] 1 : strong warmth of feeling

: keen interest : FERVOR 2 : a cause of fervor — **en·thu·si·ast** \-,ast, -əst\ *n* — **en·thu·si·as·tic** \in-,thü-zē-'as-tik, -,thyü-\ *adj* — **en·thu·si·as·ti·cal·ly** \-ti-k(ə-)lē\ *adv*

en·tice \in-'tīs\ *vb* **en·ticed; en·tic·ing** : ALLURE, TEMPT — **en·tice·ment** *n*

en·tire \in-'tī(-ə)r\ *adj* 1 : COMPLETE, WHOLE ♦ **Synonyms** SOUND, PERFECT, INTACT, UNDAMAGED — **en·tire·ly** *adv*

en·tire·ty \in-'tī-rə-tē, -'tī(-ə)r-tē\ *n, pl* **-ties** 1 : COMPLETENESS 2 : WHOLE, TOTALITY

en·ti·tle \in-'tī-t⁵l\ *vb* **en·ti·tled; en·ti·tling** 1 : NAME, DESIGNATE 2 : to give a right or claim to ⟨*entitled* to a fair trial⟩

en·ti·tle·ment \in-'tī-t⁵l-mənt\ *n* : a government program providing benefits to members of a specified group

en·ti·ty \'en-tə-tē\ *n, pl* **-ties** 1 : EXISTENCE, BEING 2 : something with separate and real existence

en·tomb \in-'tüm\ *vb* : to place in a tomb : BURY — **en·tomb·ment** *n*

en·to·mol·o·gy \,en-tə-'mä-lə-jē\ *n* : a branch of zoology that deals with insects — **en·to·mo·log·i·cal** \-mə-'lä-ji-kəl\ *adj* — **en·to·mol·o·gist** \-jist\ *n*

en·tou·rage \,än-tu̇-'räzh\ *n* [F] : RETINUE

en·tr'acte \'ä⁵n-,trakt\ *n* [F] 1 : something (as a dance) performed between two acts of a play 2 : the interval between two acts of a play

en·trails \'en-,trālz\ *n pl* : VISCERA; *esp* : INTESTINES

¹en·trance \'en-trəns\ *n* 1 : permission or right to enter 2 : the act of entering 3 : a means or place of entry

²en·trance \in-'trans\ *vb* **en·tranced; en·tranc·ing** : CHARM, DELIGHT

en·trant \in-'trənt\ *n* : one that enters esp. as a competitor

en·trap \in-'trap\ *vb* : ENSNARE, TRAP — **en·trap·ment** *n*

en·treat \in-'trēt\ *vb* : to ask urgently : BESEECH ♦ **Synonyms** BEG, IMPLORE, PLEAD, SUPPLICATE — **en·treaty** \-'trē-tē\ *n*

en·trée *or* **en·tree** \'än-,trā\ *n* [F *entrée*] 1 : freedom of entry or access 2 : the main course of a meal in the U.S. ♦ **Synonyms** ADMISSION, ADMITTANCE, ENTRANCE

en·trench \in-'trench\ *vb* 1 : to place within or surround with a trench esp. for defense; *also* : to establish solidly ⟨∼*ed* customs⟩ 2 : ENCROACH, TRESPASS — **en·trench·ment** *n*

en·tre·pre·neur \,än-trə-prə-'nər, -'nu̇r, -'nyu̇r\ *n* [F, fr. OF, fr. *entreprendre* to undertake] : one who organizes and assumes the risk of a business or enterprise — **en·tre·pre·neur·i·al** \-'nur-ē-əl, -'nyu̇r-, -'nər-\ *adj* — **en·tre·pre·neur·ship** \-,ship\ *n*

en·tro·py \'en-trə-pē\ *n, pl* **-pies** 1 : the degree of disorder in a system 2 : an ultimate state of inert uniformity

en·trust \in-'trəst\ *vb* 1 : to commit something to as a trust 2 : to commit to another with confidence ✦ *Synonyms* CONFIDE, CONSIGN, RELEGATE, COMMEND

en·try \'en-trē\ *n, pl* **entries 1** : ENTRANCE 2 **2** : ENTRANCE 3; *also* : VESTIBULE 1 **3** : an entering in a record; *also* : an item so entered **4** : a headword with its definition or identification; *also* : VOCABULARY ENTRY **5** : one entered in something (as a contest or market)

en·twine \in-'twīn\ *vb* : to twine together or around

enu·mer·ate \i-'nü-mə-,rāt, -'nyü-\ *vb* **-at·ed; -at·ing 1** : to determine the number of : COUNT **2** : LIST — **enu·mer·a·tion** \-,nü-mə-'rā-shən, -,nyü-\ *n*

enun·ci·ate \ē-'nən-sē-,āt\ *vb* **-at·ed; -at·ing 1** : to state definitely; *also* : ANNOUNCE, PROCLAIM **2** : PRONOUNCE, ARTICULATE — **enun·ci·a·tion** \-,nən-sē-'ā-shən\ *n*

en·ure·sis \,en-yù-'rē-səs\ *n* : involuntary discharge of urine : BED-WETTING

env *abbr* envelope

en·vel·op \in-'ve-ləp\ *vb* : to enclose completely with or as if with a covering — **en·vel·op·ment** *n*

en·ve·lope \'en-və-,lōp, 'än-\ *n* **1** : a usu. paper container for a letter **2** : WRAPPER, COVERING **3** : a conventionally accepted limit ⟨fashions that push the ∼⟩

en·ven·om \in-'ve-nəm\ *vb* **1** : to make poisonous **2** : EMBITTER

en·vi·able \'en-vē-ə-bəl\ *adj* : highly desirable — **en·vi·ably** \-blē\ *adv*

en·vi·ous \'en-vē-əs\ *adj* : feeling or showing envy — **en·vi·ous·ly** *adv* — **en·vi·ous·ness** *n*

en·vi·ron·ment \in-'vī-rən-mənt, -'vī(-ə)rn-\ *n* **1** : SURROUNDINGS **2** : the whole complex of factors (as soil, climate, and living things) that influence the form and the ability to survive of a plant or animal or ecological community — **en·vi·ron·men·tal** \-,vī-rən-'men-t°l, -,vī(-ə)rn-\ *adj* — **en·vi·ron·men·tal·ly** \-t°l-lē\ *adv*

en·vi·ron·men·tal·ist \-,vī-rən-'men-tə-list, -,vī(-ə)rn-\ *n* : a person concerned about environmental quality esp. with respect to control of pollution — **en·vi·ron·men·tal·ism** \-,vī-rən-'men-tə-,li-zəm, -,vī(-ə)rn-\ *n*

en·vi·rons \in-'vī-rənz\ *n pl* **1** : SUBURBS **2** : SURROUNDINGS; *also* : VICINITY

en·vis·age \in-'vi-zij\ *vb* **-aged; -ag·ing** : to have a mental picture of

en·vi·sion \in-'vi-zhən, en-\ *vb* : to picture to oneself ⟨∼s world peace⟩

en·voy \'en-,vòi, 'än-\ *n* **1** : a diplomatic agent **2** : REPRESENTATIVE, MESSENGER

¹en·vy \'en-vē\ *n, pl* **envies** [ME *envie,* fr. AF, fr. L *invidia,* fr. *invidus* envious, fr. *invidēre* to look askance at, envy, fr. *vidēre* to see] : painful or resentful awareness of another's advantages; *also* : an object of envy

²envy *vb* **en·vied; en·vy·ing** : to feel envy toward or on account of

en·zyme \'en-,zīm\ *n* : any of various complex proteins produced by living cells that catalyze specific biochemical reactions at body temperatures — **en·zy·mat·ic** \,en-zə-'ma-tik\ *adj*

Eo·cene \'ē-ə-,sēn\ *adj* : of, relating to, or being the epoch of the Tertiary between the Paleocene and the Oligocene — **Eocene** *n*

EOE *abbr* equal opportunity employer

eo·lian \ē-'ō-lē-ən\ *adj* : borne, deposited, or produced by the wind

EOM *abbr* end of month

eon *var of* AEON

EP *abbr* European plan

EPA *abbr* Environmental Protection Agency

ep·au·let *also* **ep·au·lette** \,e-pə-'let\ *n* [F *épaulette,* dim. of *épaule* shoulder] : a shoulder ornament esp. on a coat or military uniform

épée \'e-,pā, ā-'pā\ *n* [F] : a fencing or dueling sword

Eph *or* **Ephes** *abbr* Ephesians

ephed·rine \i-'fe-drən\ *n* : a stimulant drug used to treat asthma and nasal congestion

ephem·era \i-'fe-mər-ə\ *n pl* : paper items (as posters or tickets) of little original value collected usu. as a hobby

ephem·er·al \i-'fe-mə-rəl\ *adj* [Gk *ephēmeros* lasting a day, daily, fr. *epi* on + *hēmera* day] : SHORT-LIVED, TRANSITORY ✦ *Synonyms* PASSING, FLEETING, TRANSIENT, EVANESCENT — **ephem·er·al·i·ty** \i-,fe-mə-'ra-lə-tē\ *n*

Ephe·sians \i-'fē-zhənz\ *n* — see BIBLE table

ep·ic \'e-pik\ *n* : a long poem in elevated style narrating the deeds of a hero — **epic** *adj*

epi·cen·ter \'e-pi-,sen-tər\ *n* : the point on the earth's surface directly above the point of origin of an earthquake

ep·i·cure \'e-pi-,kyùr\ *n* : a person with sensitive and discriminating tastes esp. in food and wine

ep·i·cu·re·an \,e-pi-kyù-'rē-ən, -'kyùr-ē-\ *n* : EPICURE — **epicurean** *adj*

¹ep·i·dem·ic \,e-pə-'de-mik\ *adj* : affecting many persons at one time ⟨∼ disease⟩; *also* : excessively prevalent

²epidemic *n* : an epidemic outbreak esp. of disease

ep·i·de·mi·ol·o·gy \,ep-ə-,dē-mē-'ä-lə-jē\ *n* : the study of the incidence, distribution, and control of disease in a population — **ep·i·de·mi·o·log·i·cal** \,dē-mē-ə-'lä-ji-kəl\ *also* **ep·i·de·mi·o·log·ic** \-jik\ *adj* — **ep·i·de·mi·ol·o·gist** \'ä-lə-jist\ *n*

epi·der·mis \,e-pə-'dər-məs\ *n* : an outer layer esp. of skin — **epi·der·mal** \-məl\ *adj*

epi·du·ral \,e-pi-'d(y)ùr-əl\ *adj* : administered into the space outside the membrane that envelops the spinal cord ⟨∼ anesthesia⟩ — **epidural** *n*

epi·glot·tis \,e-pə-'glä-təs\ *n* : a thin plate of flexible tissue protecting the tracheal opening during swallowing

ep·i·gram \'e-pə-,gram\ *n* : a short witty poem or saying — **ep·i·gram·mat·ic** \,e-pə-grə-'ma-tik\ *adj*

ep·i·lep·sy \'e-pə-ˌlep-sē\ *n, pl* **-sies** [ultim. fr. Gk *epilēpsia,* fr. *epilambanein* to seize] : a disorder marked by abnormal electrical discharges in the brain and typically manifested by sudden periods of diminished consciousness or by convulsions — **ep·i·lep·tic** \ˌe-pə-ˈlep-tik\ *adj or n*

ep·i·logue *also* **ep·i·log** \'e-pə-ˌlóg, -ˌläg\ *n* **1** : a concluding section of a literary work **2** : a speech addressed to the spectators by an actor at the end of a play

epi·neph·rine \ˌe-pə-ˈne-frən\ *n* : an adrenal hormone used medicinally esp. as a heart stimulant, a muscle relaxant, and a vasoconstrictor

epiph·a·ny \i-ˈpi-fə-nē\ *n, pl* **-nies** **1** *cap* : January 6 observed as a church festival in commemoration of the coming of the Magi to Jesus at Bethlehem **2** : a sudden striking understanding of something

epis·co·pa·cy \i-ˈpis-kə-pə-sē\ *n, pl* **-cies** **1** : government of a church by bishops **2** : EPISCOPATE

epis·co·pal \i-ˈpis-kə-pəl\ *adj* **1** : of or relating to a bishop or episcopacy **2** *cap* : of or relating to the Protestant Episcopal Church

Epis·co·pa·lian \i-ˌpis-kə-ˈpāl-yən\ *n* : a member of the Protestant Episcopal Church

epis·co·pate \i-ˈpis-kə-pət, -ˌpāt\ *n* **1** : the rank, office, or term of a bishop **2** : a body of bishops

ep·i·sode \'e-pə-ˌsōd\ *n* [Gk *epeisodion,* fr. *epeisodios* coming in besides, fr. *eisodios* coming in, fr. *eis* into + *hodos* road, journey] **1** : a unit of action in a dramatic or literary work **2** : an incident in a course of events : OCCURRENCE ⟨a feverish ∼⟩ — **ep·i·sod·ic** \ˌe-pə-ˈsä-dik\ *adj*

epis·tle \i-ˈpi-səl\ *n* **1** *cap* : one of the letters of the New Testament **2** : LETTER — **epis·to·lary** \i-ˈpis-tə-ˌler-ē\ *adj*

ep·i·taph \'e-pə-ˌtaf\ *n* : an inscription in memory of a dead person

ep·i·tha·la·mi·um \ˌe-pə-thə-ˈlā-mē-əm\ *or* **ep·i·tha·la·mi·on** \-mē-ən\ *n, pl* **-mi·ums** *or* **-mia** \-mē-ə\ : a song or poem in honor of a bride and bridegroom

ep·i·the·li·um \ˌe-pə-ˈthē-lē-əm\ *n, pl* **-lia** \-lē-ə\ : a cellular membrane covering a bodily surface or lining a cavity — **ep·i·the·li·al** \-lē-əl\ *adj*

ep·i·thet \'e-pə-ˌthet, -thət\ *n* : a characterizing and often abusive word or phrase ⟨a racial ∼⟩

epit·o·me \i-ˈpi-tə-mē\ *n* **1** : ABSTRACT, SUMMARY **2** : EMBODIMENT — **epit·o·mize** \-ˌmīz\ *vb*

ep·och \'e-pək, -ˌpäk\ *n* : a usu. extended period : ERA, AGE — **ep·och·al** \'e-pə-kəl, -ˌpä-\ *adj*

ep·onym \'e-pə-ˌnim\ *n* **1** : one for whom something is or is believed to be named **2** : a name (as of a disease) based on or derived from an eponym — **epon·y·mous** \i-ˈpä-nə-məs\ *adj*

ep·oxy \i-ˈpäk-sē\ *vb* **ep·ox·ied** *or* **ep·oxyed; ep·oxy·ing** : to glue, fill, or coat with epoxy resin

epoxy resin *n* : a synthetic resin used in coatings and adhesives

ep·si·lon \'ep-sə-ˌlän, -lən\ *n* : the 5th letter of the Greek alphabet — E or ε

Ep·som salts \'ep-səm-\ *n* : a bitter colorless or white magnesium salt with cathartic properties

eq *abbr* **1** equal **2** equation

equa·ble \'e-kwə-bəl, 'ē-\ *adj* : UNIFORM, EVEN; *esp* : free from uncomfortable extremes — **eq·ua·bil·i·ty** \ˌe-kwə-ˈbi-lə-tē, ˌē-\ *n* — **eq·ua·bly** \'e-kwə-blē, 'ē-\ *adv*

¹equal \'ē-kwəl\ *adj* **1** : of the same measure, quantity, value, quality, number, degree, or status as another ⟨∼ opportunity⟩ **2** : IMPARTIAL **3** : free from extremes **4** : able to cope with a situation or task — **equal·i·ty** \i-ˈkwä-lə-tē\ *n* — **equal·ly** *adv*

²equal *vb* **equaled** *or* **equalled; equaling** *or* **equal·ling** : to be or become equal to; *also* : to be identical in value to

³equal *n* : one that is equal

equal·ise, equal·is·er *Brit var of* EQUALIZE, EQUALIZER

equal·ize \'ē-kwə-ˌlīz\ *vb* **-ized; -iz·ing** : to make equal, uniform, or constant — **equal·i·za·tion** \ˌē-kwə-lə-ˈzā-shən\ *n* — **equal·iz·er** *n*

equals sign *or* **equal sign** *n* : a sign = indicating equivalence

equa·nim·i·ty \ˌē-kwə-ˈni-mə-tē, ˌe-\ *n, pl* **-ties** : COMPOSURE

equate \i-ˈkwāt\ *vb* **equat·ed; equat·ing** : to make, treat, or regard as equal or comparable ⟨∼s liars with thieves⟩

equa·tion \i-ˈkwā-zhən\ *n* **1** : an act of equating : the state of being equated **2** : a usu. formal statement of equivalence esp. of mathematical expressions

equa·tor \i-ˈkwā-tər, 'ē-\ *n* : an imaginary circle around the earth that is everywhere equally distant from the two poles — **equa·to·ri·al** \ˌē-kwə-ˈtòr-ē-əl, ˌe-\ *adj*

equer·ry \'e-kwə-rē, i-ˈkwer-ē\ *n, pl* **-ries** **1** : an officer in charge of the horses of a prince or noble **2** : a personal attendant of a member of the British royal family

¹eques·tri·an \i-ˈkwes-trē-ən\ *adj* : of or relating to horseback riding ⟨∼ competition⟩; *also* : representing a person on horseback ⟨an ∼ statue⟩

²equestrian *n* : one who rides a horse

eques·tri·enne \i-ˌkwes-trē-ˈen\ *n* : a female rider on horseback

equi·dis·tant \ˌē-kwə-ˈdis-tənt\ *adj* : equally distant

equi·lat·er·al \ˌē-kwə-ˈla-tə-rəl\ *adj* : having all sides or faces equal ⟨∼ triangles⟩

equi·lib·ri·um \ˌē-kwə-ˈli-brē-əm, ˌe-\ *n, pl* **-ri·ums** *or* **-ria** \-brē-ə\ : a state of intellectual or emotional balance; *also* : a state of balance between opposing forces or actions ✦ **Synonyms** POISE, BALANCE, EQUIPOISE

equine \'ē-ˌkwīn, 'e-\ *adj* [L *equinus,* fr. *equus* horse] : of or relating to the horse — **equine** *n*

equi·noc·tial \ˌē-kwə-ˈnäk-shəl, ˌe-\ *adj* : relating to an equinox

equi·nox \'ē-kwə-ˌnäks, 'e-\ *n* : either of the two times each year when the sun appears directly overhead at the equator and day and night are everywhere on earth of equal length

equip \i-'kwip\ *vb* **equipped; equip-ping** [AF *eskiper* to load on board a ship, outfit, man, of Gmc origin] **1** : to supply with needed resources **2** : to make ready : PREPARE

eq·ui·page \'e-kwə-pij\ *n* : a horse-drawn carriage usu. with its servants

equip·ment \i-'kwip-mənt\ *n* **1** : things used in equipping : SUPPLIES, OUTFIT **2** : the equipping of a person or thing : the state of being equipped

equi·poise \'e-kwə-ˌpȯiz, 'ē-\ *n* **1** : BAL-ANCE, EQUILIBRIUM **2** : COUNTERBAL-ANCE

eq·ui·ta·ble \'e-kwə-tə-bəl\ *adj* : JUST, FAIR — **eq·ui·ta·bly** \-blē\ *adv*

eq·ui·ta·tion \ˌe-kwə-'tā-shən\ *n* : the act or art of riding on horseback

eq·ui·ty \'e-kwə-tē\ *n, pl* **-ties 1** : JUST-NESS, IMPARTIALITY **2** : value of a prop-erty or of an interest in it in excess of claims against it

equiv *abbr* equivalent

equiv·a·lent \i-'kwi-və-lənt\ *adj* : EQUAL; *also* : virtually identical — **equiv·a-lence** \-ləns\ *n* — **equivalent** *n*

equiv·o·cal \i-'kwi-və-kəl\ *adj* **1** : AM-BIGUOUS **2** : UNCERTAIN, UNDECIDED **3** : SUSPICIOUS, DUBIOUS 〈~ behavior〉 ◆ **Synonyms** OBSCURE, DARK, VAGUE, ENIGMATIC — **equiv·o·cal·ly** *adv*

equiv·o·cate \i-'kwi-və-ˌkāt\ *vb* **-cat·ed; -cat·ing 1** : to use misleading language **2** : to avoid giving a definite answer — **equiv·o·ca·tion** \-ˌkwi-və-'kā-shən\ *n*

¹**-er** \ər\ *adj suffix or adv suffix* — used to form the comparative degree of adjec-tives and adverbs of one or two syllables 〈*hotter*〉 〈*drier*〉 〈*sillier*〉 and sometimes of longer ones

²**-er** \ər\ *also* **-ier** \ē-ər, yər\ *or* **-yer** \yər\ *n suffix* **1** : a person occupationally con-nected with 〈*furrier*〉 〈*lawyer*〉 **2** : a per-son or thing belonging to or associated with 〈*old-timer*〉 **3** : a native of : resident of 〈*New Zealander*〉 **4** : one that has 〈*double-decker*〉 **5** : one that produces or yields 〈*porker*〉 **6** : one that does or performs (a specified action) 〈*batter*〉 **7** : one that is a suitable object of (a speci-fied action) 〈*broiler*〉 **8** : one that is 〈*for-eigner*〉

Er *symbol* erbium

ER *abbr* emergency room

era \'er-ə, 'e-rə, 'ir-ə\ *n* [LL *aera*, fr. L, counters, pl. of *aes* copper, money] **1** : a chronological order or system of notation reckoned from a given date as basis **2** : a period identified by some special feature 〈the ~ of industrialization〉 **3** : any of the four major divisions of geologic time ◆ **Synonyms** AGE, EPOCH, PERIOD, TIME

ERA *abbr* **1** earned run average **2** Equal Rights Amendment

erad·i·cate \i-'ra-də-ˌkāt\ *vb* **-cat·ed; -cat·ing** [L *eradicatus*, pp. of *eradicare*, fr. *e-* out + *radix* root] : UPROOT, ELIMI-NATE ◆ **Synonyms** EXTERMINATE, AN-NIHILATE, ABOLISH, EXTINGUISH — **erad·i·ca·ble** \-di-kə-bəl\ *adj* — **erad·i-ca·tion** \-ˌra-də-'kā-shən\ *n*

erase \i-'rās\ *vb* **erased; eras·ing** : to rub or scratch out (as written words); *also* : OBLITERATE ◆ **Synonyms** CANCEL, EF-FACE, DELETE, EXPUNGE — **eras·er** *n* — **era·sure** \i-'rā-shər\ *n*

er·bi·um \'ər-bē-əm\ *n* : a rare metallic el-ement found with yttrium

¹**ere** \'er\ *prep* : BEFORE

²**ere** *conj* : BEFORE

¹**erect** \i-'rekt\ *adj* **1** : not leaning or lying down : UPRIGHT **2** : being in a state of physiological erection

²**erect** *vb* **1** : BUILD **2** : to fix or set in an upright position 〈~ an antenna〉 **3** : SET UP; *also* : ESTABLISH, DEVELOP

erec·tile \i-'rek-tᵊl, -'rek-ˌtī(-ə)l\ *adj* : ca-pable of becoming erect 〈~ tissue〉 〈~ feathers of a bird〉

erec·tion \i-'rek-shən\ *n* **1** : the turgid state of a previously flaccid bodily part when it becomes dilated with blood **2** : CONSTRUCTION

ere·long \er-'lȯŋ\ *adv* : before long

er·e·mite \'er-ə-ˌmīt\ *n* : HERMIT

er·go \'er-gō, 'ər-\ *adv* [L] : THEREFORE

er·go·nom·ics \ˌər-gə-'nä-miks\ *n sing or pl* : an applied science concerned with de-signing and arranging things people use in order to improve efficiency and safety — **er·go·nom·ic** \-mik\ *adj*

er·got \'ər-gət, -ˌgät\ *n* **1** : a disease of rye and other cereals caused by a fungus; *also* : this fungus **2** : a medicinal compound or preparation derived from an ergot fun-gus

er·mine \'ər-mən\ *n, pl* **ermines 1** : any of several weasels with winter fur mostly white; *also* : this white fur **2** : a rank or office whose official robe is ornamented with ermine

erode \i-'rōd\ *vb* **erod·ed; erod·ing** : to diminish or destroy by degrees; *esp* : to gradually eat into or wear away 〈soil *eroded* by wind and water〉 — **erod·ible** *also* **erod·able** \-'rō-də-bəl\ *adj*

erog·e·nous \i-'rä-jə-nəs\ *adj* **1** : sexu-ally sensitive 〈~ zones〉 **2** : of, relating to, or arousing sexual feelings

ero·sion \i-'rō-zhən\ *n* : the process or state of being eroded — **ero·sion·al** \-'rō-zhə-nəl\ *adj* — **ero·sion·al·ly** *adv*

ero·sive \i-'rō-siv\ *adj* : tending to erode — **ero·sive·ness** *n*

erot·ic \i-'rä-tik\ *adj* : relating to or deal-ing with sexual love : AMATORY 〈~ art〉 — **erot·i·cal·ly** \-ti-k(ə-)lē\ *adv* — **erot·i-cism** \-tə-ˌsi-zəm\ *n*

err \'er, 'ər\ *vb* : to be or do wrong

er·rand \'er-ənd\ *n* : a short trip taken to do something; *also* : the object or purpose of such a trip

er·rant \'er-ənt\ *adj* **1** : WANDERING 〈an ~ knight〉 **2** : straying outside proper bounds 〈an ~ throw〉 **3** : behaving wrongly 〈an ~ child〉

er·ra·ta \e-'rä-tə\ *n* : a list of corrigenda

er·rat·ic \i-'ra-tik\ *adj* **1** : having no fixed course **2** : INCONSISTENT 〈~ dieting〉;

also : ECCENTRIC — **er·rat·i·cal·ly** \-ti-k(ə-)lē\ *adv*

er·ra·tum \e-ˈrä-təm\ *n, pl* **-ta** \-tə\ : CORRIGENDUM

er·ro·ne·ous \i-ˈrō-nē-əs, e-ˈrō-\ *adj* : INCORRECT — **er·ro·ne·ous·ly** *adv*

er·ror \ˈer-ər\ *n* **1** : a usu. ignorant or unintentional deviating from accuracy or truth ⟨made an ~ in adding⟩ **2** : a defensive misplay in baseball **3** : the state of one that errs ⟨to be in ~⟩ **4** : a product of mistake ⟨a typographical ~⟩ — **er·ror·less** *adj*

er·satz \ˈer-ˌzäts\ *adj* [G *ersatz-*, fr. *Ersatz*, n., substitute] : being usu. an artificial and inferior substitute

erst \ˈərst\ *adv, archaic* : ERSTWHILE

¹erst·while \-ˌhwīl(-ə)\ *adv* : in the past : FORMERLY

²erstwhile *adj* : FORMER, PREVIOUS

er·u·di·tion \ˌer-ə-ˈdi-shən, ˌer-yə-\ *n* : SCHOLARSHIP, LEARNING — **er·u·dite** \ˈer-ə-ˌdīt, ˈer-yə-\ *adj*

erupt \i-ˈrəpt\ *vb* **1** : to burst forth or cause to burst forth : EXPLODE **2** : to break through a surface ⟨teeth ~*ing* through the gum⟩ **3** : to break out with or as if with a skin rash — **erup·tion** \-ˈrəp-shən\ *n* — **erup·tive** \-tiv\ *adj*

-ery *n suffix* **1** : qualities collectively : character ⟨-NESS ⟨snobb*ery*⟩ **2** : art : practice ⟨cook*ery*⟩ **3** : place of doing, keeping, producing, or selling ⟨the thing specified⟩ ⟨fish*ery*⟩ ⟨bak*ery*⟩ **4** : collection : aggregate ⟨fin*ery*⟩ **5** : state or condition ⟨slav*ery*⟩

ery·sip·e·las \ˌer-ə-ˈsi-pə-ləs, ˌir-\ *n* : an acute bacterial disease marked by fever and severe skin inflammation

er·y·the·ma \ˌer-ə-ˈthē-mə\ *n* : abnormal redness of the skin due to capillary congestion (as in inflammation)

eryth·ro·cyte \i-ˈri-thrə-ˌsīt\ *n* : RED BLOOD CELL

Es *symbol* einsteinium

¹-es \əz, iz *after* s, z, sh, ch; z *after* v *or a vowel*\ *n pl suffix* — used to form the plural of most nouns that end in *s* ⟨glass*es*⟩, *z* ⟨fuzz*es*⟩, *sh* ⟨bush*es*⟩, *ch* ⟨peach*es*⟩, or a final *y* that changes to *i* ⟨lad*ies*⟩ and of some nouns ending in *f* that changes to *v* ⟨loav*es*⟩

²-es *vb suffix* — used to form the third person singular present of most verbs that end in *s* ⟨bless*es*⟩, *z* ⟨fizz*es*⟩, *sh* ⟨hush*es*⟩, *ch* ⟨catch*es*⟩, or a final *y* that changes to *i* ⟨defi*es*⟩

es·ca·late \ˈes-kə-ˌlāt\ *vb* **-lat·ed; -lat·ing** : to increase in extent, volume, number, intensity, or scope — **es·ca·la·tion** \ˌes-kə-ˈlā-shən\ *n*

es·ca·la·tor \ˈes-kə-ˌlā-tər\ *n* : a moving set of stairs

escallop *var of* SCALLOP

es·ca·pade \ˈes-kə-ˌpād\ *n* [F, action of escaping] : a mischievous adventure

¹es·cape \is-ˈkāp\ *vb* **es·caped; es·cap·ing** [ME, fr. AF *escaper, eschaper*, fr. VL **excappare*, fr. L *ex-* out + LL *cappa* head covering, cloak] **1** : to get free or away **2** : to avoid a threatening evil **3** : AVOID

2 ⟨~ injury⟩ **4** : ELUDE ⟨his name ~*s* me⟩ **5** : to be produced or uttered involuntarily by ⟨let a sob ~ him⟩

²escape *n* **1** : flight from or avoidance of something unpleasant **2** : LEAKAGE **3** : a means of escape

³escape *adj* : providing a means or way of escape

es·cap·ee \is-ˌkā-ˈpē, ˌes-(ˌ)kā-\ *n* : one that has escaped esp. from prison

escape velocity *n* : the minimum velocity needed by a body (as a rocket) to escape from the gravitational field of a celestial body (as the earth)

es·cap·ism \is-ˈkā-ˌpi-zəm\ *n* : diversion of the mind to imaginative activity as an escape from routine — **es·cap·ist** \-pist\ *adj or n*

es·car·got \ˌes-ˌkär-ˈgō\ *n, pl* **-gots** \-ˈgō(z)\ : a snail prepared for use as food

es·ca·role \ˈes-kə-ˌrōl\ *n* : ENDIVE 1

es·carp·ment \es-ˈkärp-mənt\ *n* **1** : a steep slope in front of a fortification **2** : a long cliff

es·chew \is-ˈchü\ *vb* : SHUN, AVOID

¹es·cort \ˈes-ˌkȯrt\ *n* : one (as a person or warship) accompanying another esp. as a protection or courtesy

²es·cort \is-ˈkȯrt, es-\ *vb* : to accompany as an escort

es·crow \ˈes-ˌkrō\ *n* [AF *escrowe* scroll, strip of parchment] : something (as a deed or a sum of money) delivered by one person to another to be delivered to a third party only upon the fulfillment of a condition; *also* : a fund or deposit serving as an escrow

es·cu·do \is-ˈkü-dō\ *n, pl* **-dos** **1** : the former basic monetary unit of Portugal **2** — see MONEY table

es·cutch·eon \is-ˈkə-chən\ *n* : the usu. shield-shaped surface on which a coat of arms is shown

Esd *abbr* Esdras

Es·dras \ˈez-drəs\ *n* — see BIBLE table

ESE *abbr* east-southeast

Es·ki·mo \ˈes-kə-ˌmō\ *n* **1** : a member of a group of peoples of northern Canada, Greenland, Alaska, and eastern Siberia **2** : any of the languages of the Eskimo peoples

Eskimo dog *n* : a sled dog of American origin

ESL *abbr* English as a second language

esoph·a·gus \i-ˈsä-fə-gəs\ *n, pl* **-gi** \-ˌgī, -ˌjī\ : a muscular tube that leads from the cavity behind the mouth to the stomach — **esoph·a·geal** \-ˌsä-fə-ˈjē-əl\ *adj*

es·o·ter·ic \ˌe-sə-ˈter-ik\ *adj* **1** : designed for or understood only by the specially initiated **2** : PRIVATE, SECRET

esp *abbr* especially

ESP \ˌē-(ˌ)es-ˈpē\ *n* : EXTRASENSORY PERCEPTION

es·pa·drille \ˈes-pə-ˌdril\ *n* [F] : a flat sandal usu. having a fabric upper and a flexible sole

es·pal·ier \is-ˈpal-yər, -ˌyā\ *n* : a plant (as a fruit tree) trained to grow flat against a support — **espalier** *vb*

es·pe·cial \is-'pe-shəl\ *adj* : SPECIAL, PARTICULAR — **es·pe·cial·ly** *adv*

Es·pe·ran·to \ˌes-pə-'ran-tō, -'rän-\ *n* : an artificial international language based esp. on words common to the chief European languages

es·pi·o·nage \'es-pē-ə-ˌnäzh, -nij\ *n* [F *espionnage*] : the practice of spying

es·pla·nade \'es-plə-ˌnäd\ *n* : a level open stretch or area; *esp* : one for walking or driving along a shore

es·pous·al \i-'spau̇-zəl\ *n* 1 : BETROTHAL; *also* : WEDDING 2 : a taking up (as of a cause) as a supporter ⟨~ of human rights⟩ — **es·pouse** \-'spau̇z\ *vb*

espres·so \e-'spre-sō\ *n, pl* **-sos** : coffee brewed by forcing steam or hot water through finely ground darkly roasted coffee beans

es·prit \i-'sprē\ *n* : sprightly wit

es·prit de corps \i-ˌsprē-də-'kȯr\ *n* [F] : the common spirit existing in the members of a group

es·py \i-'spī\ *vb* **es·pied; es·py·ing** : to catch sight of ♦ **Synonyms** BEHOLD, SEE, VIEW, DESCRY

Esq *or* **Esqr** *abbr* esquire

es·quire \'es-ˌkwī(-ə)r\ *n* [ME, fr. AF *esquier* squire, fr. LL *scutarius*, fr. L *scutum* shield] 1 : a man of the English gentry ranking next below a knight 2 : a candidate for knighthood serving as attendant to a knight 3 — used as a title of courtesy

-ess \əs, ˌes\ *n suffix* : female ⟨authoress⟩

¹**es·say** \e-'sā, 'e-ˌsā\ *vb* : ATTEMPT, TRY

²**es·say** \'e-ˌsā, e-'sā\ *n* 1 : ATTEMPT 2 \'e-ˌsā\ : a literary composition usu. dealing with a subject from a limited or personal point of view — **es·say·ist** \'e-ˌsā-ist\ *n*

es·sence \'e-sᵊns\ *n* 1 : fundamental nature or quality 2 : a substance distilled or extracted from another substance (as a plant or drug) and having the special qualities of the original substance 3 : PERFUME 4 : the most significant element or aspect of something ⟨the ~ of the issue⟩

¹**es·sen·tial** \i-'sen-chəl\ *adj* 1 : of, relating to, or constituting an essence ⟨voting is an ~ right of citizenship⟩ ⟨~ oils⟩ 2 : of the utmost importance : INDISPENSABLE 3 : being a substance that must be obtained from the diet because it is not sufficiently produced by the body ⟨~ amino acids⟩ ♦ **Synonyms** IMPERATIVE, NECESSARY, NECESSITOUS — **es·sen·tial·ly** *adv*

²**essential** *n* : something essential

est *abbr* 1 established 2 estimate; estimated

EST *abbr* eastern standard time

¹**-est** \əst, ist\ *adj suffix or adv suffix* — used to form the superlative degree of adjectives and adverbs of one or two syllables ⟨fattest⟩ ⟨latest⟩ ⟨luckiest⟩ ⟨oftenest⟩ and less often of longer ones

²**-est** \əst, ist\ *or* **-st** \st\ *vb suffix* — used to form the archaic second person singular of English verbs (with *thou*) ⟨didst⟩

es·tab·lish \i-'sta-blish\ *vb* 1 : to institute permanently ⟨~ a law⟩ 2 : FOUND ⟨~ a settlement⟩; *also* : EFFECT 3 : to make firm or stable 4 : to put on a firm basis : SET UP ⟨~ a son in business⟩ 5 : to gain acceptance or recognition of ⟨the movie ~ed her as a star⟩; *also* : PROVE

es·tab·lish·ment \-mənt\ *n* 1 : something established 2 : a place of residence or business with its furnishings and staff 3 : an established ruling or controlling group ⟨the literary ~⟩ 4 : the act or state of establishing or being established

es·tate \i-'stāt\ *n* 1 : STATE, CONDITION; *also* : social standing : STATUS 2 : a social or political class ⟨the three ~s of nobility, clergy, and commons⟩ 3 : a person's possessions : FORTUNE 4 : a landed property

¹**es·teem** \i-'stēm\ *n* : high regard

²**esteem** *vb* 1 : REGARD 2 : to set a high value on ♦ **Synonyms** RESPECT, ADMIRE, REVERE

es·ter \'es-tər\ *n* : an often fragrant organic compound formed by the reaction of an acid and an alcohol

Esth *abbr* Esther

Es·ther \'es-tər\ *n* — see BIBLE table

esthete, esthetic, esthetically, esthetics *var of* AESTHETE, AESTHETIC, AESTHETICALLY, AESTHETICS

es·ti·ma·ble \'es-tə-mə-bəl\ *adj* : worthy of esteem ⟨an ~ adversary⟩

¹**es·ti·mate** \'es-tə-ˌmāt\ *vb* **-mat·ed; -mat·ing** 1 : to give or form an approximation (as of value, size, or cost) 2 : JUDGE, CONCLUDE ♦ **Synonyms** EVALUATE, VALUE, RATE, APPRAISE, ASSAY, ASSESS — **es·ti·ma·tor** \-ˌmā-tər\ *n*

²**es·ti·mate** \'es-tə-mət\ *n* 1 : OPINION, JUDGMENT 2 : a rough or approximate calculation 3 : a statement of the cost of work to be done

es·ti·ma·tion \ˌes-tə-'mā-shən\ *n* 1 : JUDGMENT, OPINION 2 : ESTIMATE 3 : ESTEEM, HONOR

es·ti·vate \'es-tə-ˌvāt\ *vb* **-vat·ed; -vat·ing** : to pass the summer in an inactive or resting state — **es·ti·va·tion** \ˌes-tə-'vā-shən\ *n*

es·trange \i-'strānj\ *vb* **es·tranged; es·trang·ing** : to alienate the affections or confidence of — **es·trange·ment** *n*

es·tro·gen \'es-trə-jən\ *n* : a steroid (as a sex hormone) that tends to cause estrus and the development of female secondary sex characteristics — **es·tro·gen·ic** \ˌes-trə-'je-nik\ *adj*

estrous cycle *n* : the cycle of changes in the endocrine and reproductive systems of a female mammal from the beginning of one period of estrus to the beginning of the next

es·trus \'es-trəs\ *n* : a periodic state of sexual excitability during which the female of most mammals is willing to mate with the male and is capable of becoming pregnant : HEAT — **es·trous** \-trəs\ *adj*

es·tu·ary \'es-chə-ˌwer-ē\ *n, pl* **-ar·ies** : an

arm of the sea at the mouth of a river — **es·tu·a·rine** \-wə-ˌrīn, -ˌrēn, -rin\ *adj*

ET *abbr* eastern time

eta \ˈā-tə\ *n* : the 7th letter of the Greek alphabet — H or η

ETA *abbr* estimated time of arrival

et al \et-ˈal\ *abbr* [L *et alii* (masc.), *et aliae* (fem.), or *et alia* (neut.)] and others

etc *abbr* et cetera

et cet·era \et-ˈse-tə-rə, -ˈse-trə\ [L] and others esp. of the same kind

etch \ˈech\ *vb* [D *etsen*, fr. G *ätzen* to etch, corrode, fr. OHG *azzen* to feed] **1** : to produce (as a design) on a hard material by corroding its surface (as by acid) **2** : to delineate clearly — **etch·er** *n*

etch·ing *n* **1** : the action, process, or art of etching **2** : a design produced on or print made from an etched plate

ETD *abbr* estimated time of departure

eter·nal \i-ˈtər-nᵊl\ *adj* : EVERLASTING, PERPETUAL — **eter·nal·ly** *adv*

eter·ni·ty \i-ˈtər-nə-tē\ *n, pl* **-ties** **1** : infinite duration **2** : IMMORTALITY

¹-eth \əth, ith\ *or* **-th** \th\ *vb suffix* — used to form the archaic third person singular present of verbs ⟨do*th*⟩

²-eth — see **²-TH**

eth·ane \ˈe-ˌthān\ *n* : a colorless odorless gaseous hydrocarbon found in natural gas and used esp. as a fuel

eth·a·nol \ˈe-thə-ˌnȯl\ *n* : ALCOHOL 1

ether \ˈē-thər\ *n* **1** : the upper regions of space; *also* : the gaseous element formerly held to fill these regions **2** : a light flammable liquid used as an anesthetic and solvent

ethe·re·al \i-ˈthir-ē-əl\ *adj* **1** : CELESTIAL, HEAVENLY **2** : exceptionally delicate : AIRY, DAINTY — **ethe·re·al·ly** *adv* — **ethe·re·al·ness** *n*

Ether·net \ˈē-thər-ˌnet\ *n* : a computer network architecture for local area networks

eth·i·cal \ˈe-thi-kəl\ *adj* **1** : of or relating to ethics **2** : conforming to accepted and esp. professional standards of conduct ◆ *Synonyms* VIRTUOUS, MORAL, PRINCIPLED — **eth·i·cal·ly** *adv*

eth·ics \ˈe-thiks\ *n sing or pl* **1** : a discipline dealing with good and evil and with moral duty **2** : moral principles or practice

¹eth·nic \ˈeth-nik\ *adj* [ME, heathen, fr. LL *ethnicus*, fr. Gk *ethnikos* national, gentile, fr. *ethnos* nation, people] : of or relating to races or large groups of people classed according to common traits and customs — **eth·ni·cal·ly** *adv*

²ethnic *n* : a member of a minority ethnic group who retains its customs, language, or social views

eth·nol·o·gy \eth-ˈnä-lə-jē\ *n* : a science dealing with the races of human beings, their origin, distribution, characteristics, and relations — **eth·no·log·i·cal** \ˌeth-nə-ˈlä-ji-kəl\ *adj* — **eth·nol·o·gist** \eth-ˈnä-lə-jist\ *n*

ethol·o·gy \ē-ˈthä-lə-jē\ *n* : the scientific and objective study of animal behavior —

etho·log·i·cal \ˌē-thə-ˈlä-ji-kəl, ˌe-\ *adj* — **ethol·o·gist** \ē-ˈthä-lə-jist\ *n*

ethos \ˈē-ˌthäs\ *n* : the distinguishing character, sentiment, moral nature, or guiding beliefs of a person, group, or institution

ethyl alcohol *n* : ALCOHOL 1

eth·yl·ene \ˈe-thə-ˌlēn\ *n* : a colorless flammable gas found in coal gas or obtained from petroleum

eti·ol·o·gy \ˌē-tē-ˈä-lə-jē\ *n* : the causes of a disease or abnormal condition; *also* : a branch of medicine concerned with the causes and origins of diseases — **eti·o·log·ic** \ˌē-tē-ə-ˈlä-jik\ *or* **eti·o·log·i·cal** \-ji-kəl\ *adj*

et·i·quette \ˈe-ti-kət, -ˌket\ *n* [F *étiquette*, lit., label, list] : the forms prescribed by custom or authority to be observed in social, official, or professional life ◆ *Synonyms* PROPRIETY, DECORUM, DECENCY, DIGNITY

Etrus·can \i-ˈtrəs-kən\ *n* **1** : the language of the Etruscans **2** : an inhabitant of ancient Etruria — **Etruscan** *adj*

et seq *abbr* [L *et sequens*] and the following one; [L *et sequentes* (masc. & fem. pl.) or *et sequentia* (neut. pl.)] and the following ones

-ette \ˈet, ˌet, ət, it\ *n suffix* **1** : little one ⟨din*ette*⟩ **2** : female ⟨usher*ette*⟩

étude \ˈā-ˌtüd, -ˌtyüd\ *n* [F, lit., study] : a musical composition for practice to develop technical skill

et·y·mol·o·gy \ˌe-tə-ˈmä-lə-jē\ *n, pl* **-gies** **1** : the history of a linguistic form (as a word) shown by tracing its development and relationships **2** : a branch of linguistics dealing with etymologies — **et·y·mo·log·i·cal** \-mə-ˈlä-ji-kəl\ *adj* — **et·y·mol·o·gist** \-ˈmä-lə-jist\ *n*

Eu *symbol* europium

eu·ca·lyp·tus \ˌyü-kə-ˈlip-təs\ *n, pl* **-ti** \-ˌtī\ *or* **-tus·es** : any of a genus of mostly Australian evergreen trees widely grown for shade or their wood, oils, resins, and gums

Eu·cha·rist \ˈyü-kə-rəst\ *n* : COMMUNION 2 — **eu·cha·ris·tic** \ˌyü-kə-ˈris-tik\ *adj, often cap*

¹eu·chre \ˈyü-kər\ *n* : a card game in which the side naming the trump must take three of five tricks to win

²euchre *vb* **eu·chred; eu·chring** : CHEAT, TRICK

eu·clid·e·an *also* **eu·clid·i·an** \yü-ˈkli-dē-ən\ *adj, often cap* : of or relating to the geometry of Euclid or a geometry based on similar axioms

eu·gen·ics \yü-ˈje-niks\ *n* : a science dealing with the improvement of hereditary qualities esp. of human beings — **eu·gen·ic** \-nik\ *adj*

eu·lo·gy \ˈyü-lə-jē\ *n, pl* **-gies** **1** : a speech in praise of some person or thing esp. in honor of a deceased person **2** : high praise — **eu·lo·gis·tic** \ˌyü-lə-ˈjis-tik\ *adj* — **eu·lo·gize** \ˈyü-lə-ˌjīz\ *vb*

eu·nuch \ˈyü-nək\ *n* : a castrated man

eu·phe·mism \ˈyü-fə-ˌmi-zəm\ *n* [Gk *euphēmismos*, fr. *euphēmos* auspicious, sounding good, fr. *eu-* good + *phēmē* speech] : the substitution of a mild or pleasant expression for one offensive or unpleasant; *also* : the expression substituted — **eu·phe·mis·tic** \ˌyü-fə-'mis-tik\ *adj* — **eu·phe·mis·ti·cal·ly** \-ti-k(ə-)lē\ *adv*

eu·pho·ni·ous \yü-'fō-nē-əs\ *adj* : pleasing to the ear — **eu·pho·ni·ous·ly** *adv*

eu·pho·ny \'yü-fə-nē\ *n, pl* **-nies** : the effect produced by words so combined as to please the ear

eu·pho·ria \yü-'fōr-ē-ə\ *n* : a marked feeling of well-being or elation — **eu·phor·ic** \-'fōr-ik\ *adj*

Eur *abbr* Europe; European

Eur·asian \yu-'rā-zhən, -shən\ *adj* **1** : of mixed European and Asian origin **2** : of or relating to Europe and Asia — **Eurasian** *n*

eu·re·ka \yu-'rē-kə\ *interj* [Gk *heurēka* I have found, fr. *heuriskein* to find; fr. the exclamation attributed to Archimedes on discovering a method for determining the purity of gold] — used to express triumph on a discovery

eu·ro \'yür-ō\ *n, pl* **euros** : the common basic monetary unit of most countries of the European Union — see MONEY table

Eu·ro-Amer·i·can \ˌyür-ō-ə-'mer-ə-kən\ *n* **1** : a person of mixed European and American ancestry **2** : CAUCASIAN

Eu·ro·bond \'yür-ō-ˌbänd\ *n* : a bond of a U.S. corporation that is sold outside the U.S. but that is valued and paid for in dollars and yields interest in dollars

Eu·ro·cur·ren·cy \ˌyür-ō-'kər-ən-sē\ *n* : moneys (as of the U.S. and Japan) held outside their countries of origin and used in the money markets of Europe

Eu·ro·dol·lar \'yür-ō-ˌdä-lər\ *n* : a U.S. dollar held as Eurocurrency

Eu·ro·pe·an \ˌyür-ə-'pē-ən\ *n* **1** : a native or inhabitant of Europe **2** : a person of European descent — **European** *adj* — **Eu·ro·pe·an·ize** \-ə-ˌnīz\ *vb*

European–American *n* : EURO-AMERICAN

Eu·ro·pe·an·ism \ˌyür-ˌō-'pē-ə-ni-zəm\ *n* **1** : allegiance to the traditions, interests, or ideals of Europeans **2** : advocacy of political and economic integration of Europe — **eu·ro·pe·an·ist** \-nist\ *n*

European plan *n* : a hotel plan whereby the daily rates cover only the cost of the room

eu·ro·pi·um \yu-'rō-pē-əm\ *n* : a rare metallic chemical element

eu·sta·chian tube \yu-'stā-shən-\ *n, often cap E* : a tube connecting the inner cavity of the ear with the throat and equalizing air pressure on both sides of the eardrum

eu·tha·na·sia \ˌyü-thə-'nā-zhə\ *n* [Gk, easy death, fr. *eu-* good + *thanatos* death] : the act or practice of killing or permitting the death of hopelessly sick or injured persons or animals with as little pain as possible for reasons of mercy

EVA *abbr* extravehicular activity

evac·u·ate \i-'va-kyə-ˌwāt\ *vb* **-at·ed; -at·ing** **1** : EMPTY **2** : to discharge wastes from the body **3** : to remove or with-

draw from : VACATE — **evac·u·a·tion** \-ˌva-kyə-'wā-shən\ *n*

evac·u·ee \i-ˌva-kyə-'wē\ *n* : a person removed from a dangerous place

evade \i-'vād\ *vb* **evad·ed; evad·ing** : to manage to avoid esp. by dexterity or slyness : ELUDE, ESCAPE

eval·u·ate \i-'val-yə-ˌwāt\ *vb* **-at·ed; -at·ing** : APPRAISE, VALUE — **eval·u·a·tion** \-ˌval-yü-'wā-shən\ *n*

ev·a·nes·cent \ˌe-və-'ne-sᵊnt\ *adj* : tending to vanish like vapor ⟨~ pleasures⟩
◆ **Synonyms** PASSING, TRANSIENT, TRANSITORY, MOMENTARY — **ev·a·nes·cence** \-sᵊns\ *n*

evan·gel·i·cal \ˌē-ˌvan-'je-li-kəl, ˌe-vən-\ *adj* [LL *evangelium* gospel, fr. Gk *evangelion*, fr. *euangelos* bringing good news, fr. *eu-* good + *angelos* messenger] **1** : of or relating to the Christian gospel esp. as presented in the four Gospels **2** : of or relating to certain Protestant churches emphasizing the authority of Scripture and the importance of preaching as contrasted with ritual **3** : ZEALOUS ⟨~ fervor⟩ — **Evangelical** *n* — **Evan·gel·i·cal·ism** \-kə-ˌli-zəm\ *n* — **evan·gel·i·cal·ly** *adv*

evan·ge·lism \i-'van-jə-ˌli-zəm\ *n* **1** : the winning or revival of personal commitments to Christ **2** : militant or crusading zeal — **evan·ge·lis·tic** \-ˌvan-jə-'lis-tik\ *adj* — **evan·ge·lis·ti·cal·ly** *adv*

evan·ge·list \i-'van-jə-list\ *n* **1** *often cap* : the writer of any of the four Gospels **2** : a person who evangelizes; *esp* : a Protestant minister or layman who preaches at special services

evan·ge·lize \i-'van-jə-ˌlīz\ *vb* **-lized; -liz·ing** **1** : to preach the gospel **2** : to convert to Christianity

evap *abbr* evaporate

evap·o·rate \i-'va-pə-ˌrāt\ *vb* **-rat·ed; -rat·ing** **1** : to pass off or cause to pass off in vapor **2** : to disappear quickly **3** : to drive out the moisture from (as by heat) — **evap·o·ra·tion** \-ˌva-pə-'rā-shən\ *n* — **evap·o·ra·tor** \-ˌrā-tər\ *n*

evap·o·rite \i-'va-pə-ˌrīt\ *n* : a sedimentary rock that originates by the evaporation of seawater in an enclosed basin

eva·sion \i-'vā-zhən\ *n* **1** : a means of evading **2** : an act or instance of evading — **eva·sive** \i-'vā-siv\ *adj* — **eva·sive·ness** *n*

eve \'ēv\ *n* **1** : EVENING **2** : the period just before some important event

¹**even** \'ē-vən\ *adj* **1** : LEVEL, FLAT **2** : REGULAR, SMOOTH **3** : EQUAL, FAIR ⟨an ~ exchange⟩ **4** : BALANCED; *also* : fully revenged **5** : divisible by two **6** : EXACT ⟨an ~ dollar⟩ — **even·ly** *adv* — **even·ness** *n*

²**even** *adv* **1** : EXACTLY, PRECISELY **2** : FULLY, QUITE **3** : at the very time **4** — used as an intensive to stress identity ⟨~ I know that⟩ **5** — used as an intensive to emphasize something extreme or highly unlikely ⟨so simple ~ a child can do it⟩ **6** — used as an intensive to stress the comparative degree ⟨did ~ better⟩

7 — used as an intensive to indicate a small or minimum degree ⟨didn't ~ try⟩

³even *vb* : to make or become even

even·hand·ed \,ē-vən-'han-dəd\ *adj* : FAIR, IMPARTIAL — **even·hand·ed·ly** *adv*

eve·ning \'ēv-niŋ\ *n,* **1** : the end of the day and early part of the night **2** *chiefly Southern & Midland* : AFTERNOON

evening primrose *n* : a coarse biennial herb with yellow flowers that open in the evening

evening star *n* : a bright planet (as Venus) seen esp. in the western sky at or after sunset

even·song \'ē-vən-,soŋ\ *n, often cap* **1** : VESPERS **2** : evening prayer esp. when sung

event \i-'vent\ *n* [MF or L; MF, fr. L *eventus,* fr. *evenire* to happen, fr. *venire* to come] **1** : OCCURRENCE **2** : a noteworthy happening **3** : CONTINGENCY ⟨in the ~ of rain⟩ **4** : a contest in a program of sports — **event·ful** *adj*

even·tide \'ē-vən-,tīd\ *n* : EVENING

even·tu·al \i-'ven-chù-wəl\ *adj* : coming at some later time : ULTIMATE — **even·tu·al·ly** *adv*

even·tu·al·i·ty \i-,ven-chù-'wa-lə-tē\ *n, pl* **-ties** : a possible event or outcome

even·tu·ate \i-'ven-chù-,wāt\ *vb* **-at·ed; -at·ing** : to result finally

ev·er \'e-vər\ *adv* **1** : ALWAYS ⟨~ faithful⟩ **2** : at any time **3** : in any way : AT ALL

ev·er·glade \'e-vər-,glād\ *n* : a low-lying tract of swampy or marshy land

ev·er·green \-,grēn\ *adj* : having foliage that remains green ⟨most coniferous trees are ~⟩ — **evergreen** *n*

¹ev·er·last·ing \,e-vər-'las-tiŋ\ *adj* **1** : enduring forever : ETERNAL **2** : having or being flowers or foliage that retain form or color for a long time when dried — **ev·er·last·ing·ly** *adv*

²everlasting *n* **1** : ETERNITY ⟨from ~⟩ **2** : a plant with everlasting flowers; *also* : its flower

ev·er·more \,e-vər-'mòr\ *adv* : FOREVER

ev·ery \'ev-rē\ *adj* [ME *everich, every,* fr. OE *ǣfre ǣlc,* fr. *ǣfre* ever + *ǣlc* each] **1** : being each one of a group **2** : all possible ⟨given ~ chance⟩; *also* : COMPLETE ⟨have ~ confidence⟩

ev·ery·body \'ev-ri-,bä-dē, -bə-\ *pron* : every person

ev·ery·day \'ev-rē-,dā\ *adj* : encountered or used routinely : ORDINARY

ev·ery·one \-(,)wən\ *pron* : EVERYBODY

ev·ery·thing \'ev-rē-,thiŋ\ *pron* **1** : all that exists **2** : all that is relevant

ev·ery·where \'ev-rē-,hwer\ *adv* : in every place or part

evg *abbr* evening

evict \i-'vikt\ *vb* **1** : to put (a person) out from a property by legal process **2** : EXPEL ♦ **Synonyms** EJECT, OUST, DISMISS — **evic·tion** \-'vik-shən\ *n*

¹ev·i·dence \'e-və-dəns\ *n* **1** : an outward sign **2** : PROOF, TESTIMONY; *esp* : matter submitted in court to determine the truth of alleged facts

²evidence *vb* : PROVE, EVINCE

ev·i·dent \-dənt\ *adj* : clear to the vision and understanding ♦ **Synonyms** MANIFEST, DISTINCT, OBVIOUS, APPARENT, PLAIN

ev·i·dent·ly \'e-və-dənt-lē, ,e-və-'dent-\ *adv* **1** : in an evident manner **2** : on the basis of available evidence

¹evil \'ē-vəl\ *adj* **evil·er** *or* **evil·ler; evil·est** *or* **evil·lest** **1** : WICKED **2** : causing or threatening distress or harm : PERNICIOUS — **evil·ly** *adv*

²evil *n* **1** : the fact of suffering, misfortune, and wrongdoing **2** : a source of sorrow, distress, or calamity

evil·do·er \,ē-vəl-'dü-ər\ *n* : one who does evil

evil–mind·ed \-'mīn-dəd\ *adj* : having an evil disposition or evil thoughts — **evil–mind·ed·ly** *adv*

evince \i-'vins\ *vb* **evinced; evinc·ing** : SHOW, REVEAL

evis·cer·ate \i-'vi-sə-,rāt\ *vb* **-at·ed; -at·ing** **1** : to remove the entrails of **2** : to deprive of vital content or force — **evis·cer·a·tion** \-,vi-sə-'rā-shən\ *n*

evoke \i-'vōk\ *vb* **evoked; evok·ing** : to call forth or up — **evo·ca·tion** \,ē-vō-'kā-shən, ,e-və-\ *n* — **evoc·a·tive** \i-'vä-kə-tiv\ *adj*

evo·lu·tion \,e-və-'lü-shən\ *n* **1** : one of a set of prescribed movements (as in a dance) **2** : a process of change in a particular direction **3** : a theory that the various kinds of plants and animals are descended from other kinds that lived in earlier times and that the differences are due to inherited changes that occurred over many generations — **evo·lu·tion·ary** \-shə-,ner-ē\ *adj* — **evo·lu·tion·ist** \-shə-nist\ *n*

evolve \i-'välv\ *vb* **evolved; evolv·ing** [L *evolvere* to unroll] : to develop or change by or as if by evolution

EW *abbr* enlisted woman

ewe \'yü\ *n* : a female sheep

ew·er \'yü-ər\ *n* : a water pitcher

¹ex \'eks\ *prep* [L] : out of : FROM

²ex *n* : a former spouse

³ex *abbr* **1** example **2** express **3** extra

Ex *abbr* Exodus

ex- \e *also occurs in this prefix where only* i *is shown below (as in "express") and* ks *sometimes occurs where only* gz *is shown (as in "exact")\ prefix* **1** : out of : outside **2** : former ⟨ex-president⟩

ex·ac·er·bate \ig-'za-sər-,bāt\ *vb* **-bat·ed; -bat·ing** : to make more violent, bitter, or severe — **ex·ac·er·ba·tion** \-,za-sər-'bā-shən\ *n*

¹ex·act \ig-'zakt\ *vb* **1** : to compel to furnish **2** : to call for as suitable or necessary — **ex·ac·tion** \-'zak-shən\ *n*

²exact *adj* : precisely accurate or correct — **ex·act·ly** *adv* — **ex·act·ness** *n*

ex·act·ing \ig-'zak-tiŋ\ *adj* **1** : greatly demanding ⟨an ~ taskmaster⟩ **2** : requiring close attention and precision

ex·ac·ti·tude \ig-'zak-tə-,tüd, -,tyüd\ *n* : the quality or state of being exact

ex·ag·ger·ate \ig-'za-jə-,rāt\ *vb* **-at·ed;**

-at·ing [L *exaggeratus*, pp. of *exaggerare*, lit., to heap up, fr. *agger* heap] **:** to enlarge (as a statement) beyond normal **:** OVERSTATE — **ex·ag·ger·at·ed·ly** *adv* — **ex·ag·ger·a·tion** \-ˌza-jə-'rā-shən\ *n* — **ex·ag·ger·a·tor** \-'za-jə-ˌrā-tər\ *n*

ex·alt \ig-'zȯlt\ *vb* **1 :** to raise up esp. in rank, power, or dignity **2 :** GLORIFY — **ex·al·ta·tion** \ˌeg-ˌzȯl-'tā-shən, ˌek-ˌsȯl-\ *n*

ex·am \ig-'zam\ *n* **:** EXAMINATION

ex·am·ine \ig-'za-mən\ *vb* **ex·am·ined; ex·am·in·ing 1 :** to inspect closely **2 :** QUESTION; *esp* **:** to test by questioning ✦ *Synonyms* INTERROGATE, QUERY, QUIZ, CATECHIZE — **ex·am·i·na·tion** \-ˌza-mə-'nā-shən\ *n*

ex·am·ple \ig-'zam-pəl\ *n* **1 :** something forming a model to be followed or avoided **2 :** a representative sample **3 :** a problem to be solved in order to show the application of some rule

ex·as·per·ate \ig-'zas-pə-ˌrāt\ *vb* **-at·ed; -at·ing :** VEX, IRRITATE — **ex·as·per·a·tion** \-ˌzas-pə-'rā-shən\ *n*

exc *abbr* **1** excellent **2** except

ex·ca·vate \'ek-skə-ˌvāt\ *vb* **-vat·ed; -vat·ing 1 :** to hollow out; *also* **:** to form by hollowing out **2 :** to dig out and remove (as earth) **3 :** to reveal to view by digging away a covering — **ex·ca·va·tion** \ˌek-skə-'vā-shən\ *n* — **ex·ca·va·tor** \'ek-skə-ˌvā-tər\ *n*

ex·ceed \ik-'sēd\ *vb* **1 :** to go or be beyond the limit of **2 :** SURPASS — **ex·ceed·ance** \-'sē-dᵊns\ *n*

ex·ceed·ing·ly \-'sē-diŋ-lē\ *also* **ex·ceed·ing** *adv* **:** EXTREMELY, VERY

ex·cel \ik-'sel\ *vb* **ex·celled; ex·cel·ling :** SURPASS, OUTDO

ex·cel·lence \'ek-sə-ləns\ *n* **1 :** the quality of being excellent **2 :** an excellent or valuable quality **:** VIRTUE **3 :** EXCELLENCY 2

ex·cel·len·cy \-lən-sē\ *n, pl* **-cies 1 :** EXCELLENCE **2** — used as a title of honor

ex·cel·lent \-lənt\ *adj* **:** very good of its kind **:** FIRST-CLASS — **ex·cel·lent·ly** *adv*

ex·cel·si·or \ik-'sel-sē-ər\ *n* **:** fine curled wood shavings used esp. for packing fragile items

¹ex·cept \ik-'sept\ *also* **ex·cept·ing** *prep* **:** with the exclusion or exception of ⟨daily ∼ Sundays⟩

²except *vb* **1 :** to take or leave out **2 :** OBJECT

³except *also* **excepting** *conj* **1 :** UNLESS ⟨∼ you repent⟩ **2 :** ONLY ⟨I'd go, ∼ it's too far⟩

ex·cep·tion \ik-'sep-shən\ *n* **1 :** the act of excepting **2 :** something excepted **3 :** OBJECTION

ex·cep·tion·able \ik-'sep-shə-nə-bəl\ *adj* **:** OBJECTIONABLE

ex·cep·tion·al \ik-'sep-shə-nəl\ *adj* **1 :** UNUSUAL ⟨an ∼ number of rainy days⟩ **2 :** SUPERIOR ⟨∼ skill⟩ — **ex·cep·tion·al·ly** *adv*

ex·cerpt \'ek-ˌsərpt, 'eg-ˌzərpt\ *n* **:** a passage selected or copied **:** EXTRACT — **excerpt** \ek-'sərpt, eg-'zərpt; 'ek-ˌsərpt, 'eg-ˌzərpt\ *vb*

ex·cess \ik-'ses, 'ek-ˌses\ *n* **1 :** SUPERFLUITY, SURPLUS **2 :** the amount by which one quantity exceeds another **3 :** INTEMPERANCE; *also* **:** an instance of intemperance — **excess** *adj* — **ex·ces·sive** \ik-'se-siv\ *adj* — **ex·ces·sive·ly** *adv*

exch *abbr* exchange; exchanged

¹ex·change \iks-'chānj\ *n* **1 :** the giving or taking of one thing in return for another **:** TRADE **2 :** a substituting of one thing for another **3 :** interchange of valuables and esp. of bills of exchange or money of different countries **4 :** a place where things and services are exchanged; *esp* **:** a marketplace for securities **5 :** a central office in which telephone lines are connected for communication

²exchange *vb* **ex·changed; ex·chang·ing :** to transfer in return for some equivalent **:** BARTER, SWAP — **ex·change·able** \iks-'chān-jə-bəl\ *adj*

ex·che·quer \'eks-ˌche-kər\ *n* [ME *escheker*, fr. AF, chessboard, counting table, office charged with revenue collection, fr. *eschec* check (in chess), chess] **:** TREASURY; *esp* **:** a national treasury

ex·cise \'ek-ˌsīz\ *n* **:** a tax on the manufacture, sale, or consumption of a commodity

ex·ci·sion \ik-'si-zhən\ *n* **:** removal by or as if by cutting out esp. by surgical means — **ex·cise** \ik-'sīz\ *vb*

ex·cit·able \ik-'sī-tə-bəl\ *adj* **:** easily excited — **ex·cit·abil·i·ty** \-ˌsī-tə-'bi-lə-tē\ *n*

ex·cite \ik-'sīt\ *vb* **ex·cit·ed; ex·cit·ing 1 :** to stir up the emotions of **:** ROUSE **2 :** to increase the activity of **:** STIMULATE ✦ *Synonyms* PROVOKE, PIQUE, QUICKEN — **ex·ci·ta·tion** \ˌek-ˌsī-'tā-shən, ˌek-sə-\ *n* — **ex·cit·ed·ly** *adv* — **ex·cit·ing·ly** *adv*

ex·cite·ment \ik-'sīt-mənt\ *n* **:** AGITATION, STIR

ex·claim \iks-'klām\ *vb* **:** to cry out, speak, or utter sharply or vehemently — **ex·cla·ma·tion** \ˌeks-klə-'mā-shən\ *n* — **ex·clam·a·to·ry** \iks-'kla-mə-ˌtȯr-ē\ *adj*

exclamation point *n* **:** a punctuation mark ! used esp. after an interjection or exclamation

ex·clude \iks-'klüd\ *vb* **ex·clud·ed; exclud·ing 1 :** to prevent from using or participating **:** BAR **2 :** to put out **:** EXPEL — **ex·clu·sion** \-'klü-zhən\ *n* — **ex·clu·sion·ary** \-zhə-ˌner-ē\ *adj*

ex·clu·sive \iks-'klü-siv\ *adj* **1 :** reserved for particular persons **2 :** snobbishly aloof; *also* **:** STYLISH **3 :** SOLE ⟨∼ rights⟩; *also* **:** UNDIVIDED ⟨my ∼ attention⟩ ✦ *Synonyms* CHIC, MODISH, SMART, SWANK, FASHIONABLE — **exclusive** *n* — **ex·clu·sive·ly** *adv* — **ex·clu·sive·ness** *n* — **ex·clu·siv·i·ty** \ˌeks-ˌklü-si-və-tē, iks-, -zi-\ *n*

exclusive of *prep* **:** not taking into account

ex·cog·i·tate \ek-'skä-jə-ˌtāt\ *vb* **:** to think out **:** DEVISE

ex·com·mu·ni·cate \ˌek-skə-'myü-nə-ˌkāt\ *vb* **:** to cut off officially from the rites of the church — **ex·com·mu·ni·ca·tion** \-ˌmyü-nə-ˈkā-shən\ n

ex·co·ri·ate \ek-ˈskȯr-ē-ˌāt\ vb **-at·ed; -at·ing** : to criticize severely — **ex·co·ri·a·tion** \(ˌ)ek-ˌskȯr-ē-ˈā-shən\ n

ex·cre·ment \ˈek-skrə-mənt\ n : waste discharged from the body; esp : FECES — **ex·cre·men·tal** \ˌek-skrə-ˈmen-tᵊl\ adj

ex·cres·cence \ik-ˈskre-sᵊns\ n : OUT-GROWTH; esp : an abnormal outgrowth (as a wart)

ex·cre·ta \ik-ˈskrē-tə\ n pl : waste matter (as feces) separated or eliminated from the body

ex·crete \ik-ˈskrēt\ vb **ex·cret·ed; ex·cret·ing** : to separate and eliminate wastes from the body esp. in urine or sweat — **ex·cre·tion** \-ˈskrē-shən\ n — **ex·cre·to·ry** \ˈek-skrə-ˌtȯr-ē\ adj

ex·cru·ci·at·ing \ik-ˈskrü-shē-ˌā-tiŋ\ adj [L excruciare to torture, fr. cruciare to crucify, fr. crux cross] : intensely painful or distressing ◆ **Synonyms** AGONIZING, HARROWING, TORTUROUS — **ex·cru·ci·at·ing·ly** adv

ex·cul·pate \ˈek-(ˌ)skəl-ˌpāt\ vb **-pat·ed; -pat·ing** : to clear from alleged fault or guilt ◆ **Synonyms** ABSOLVE, EXONER-ATE, ACQUIT, VINDICATE, CLEAR

ex·cur·sion \ik-ˈskər-zhən\ n 1 : EXPE-DITION; esp : a pleasure trip 2 : DIGRES-SION — **ex·cur·sion·ist** \-zhə-nist\ n

ex·cur·sive \-ˈskər-siv\ adj : constituting or characterized by digression

¹**ex·cuse** \ik-ˈskyüz\ vb **ex·cused; ex·cus·ing** [ME, fr. AF excuser, fr. L excusare, fr. causa cause, explanation] 1 : to make apology for 2 : PARDON 3 : to release from an obligation 4 : JUSTIFY — **ex·cus·able** adj

²**excuse** \ik-ˈskyüs\ n 1 : an act of excus-ing 2 : something that excuses or is a reason for excusing : JUSTIFICATION

exec n : EXECUTIVE

ex·e·cra·ble \ˈek-si-krə-bəl\ adj 1 : DE-TESTABLE ⟨∼ crimes⟩ 2 : very bad ⟨∼ spelling⟩

ex·e·crate \ˈek-sə-ˌkrāt\ vb **-crat·ed; -crat·ing** [L exsecratus, pp. of exsecrari to put under a curse, fr. ex- out of + sacer sacred] : to denounce as evil or de-testable; also : DETEST — **ex·e·cra·tion** \ˌek-sə-ˈkrā-shən\ n

ex·e·cute \ˈek-si-ˌkyüt\ vb **-cut·ed; -cut·ing** 1 : to carry out fully : put com-pletely into effect 2 : to do what is called for (as by a law) 3 : to put to death in ac-cordance with a legal sentence 4 : to produce by carrying out a design 5 : to do what is needed to give validity to ⟨∼ a deed⟩ — **ex·e·cu·tion** \ˌek-si-ˈkyü-shən\ n — **ex·e·cu·tion·er** n

¹**ex·ec·u·tive** \ig-ˈze-kyə-tiv\ adj 1 : of or relating to the enforcement of laws and the conduct of affairs 2 : designed for or related to carrying out plans or purposes

²**executive** n 1 : the branch of govern-ment with executive duties 2 : one hav-ing administrative or managerial respon-sibility

ex·ec·u·tor \ig-ˈze-kyə-tər\ n : the person named in a will to execute it

ex·ec·u·trix \ig-ˈze-kyə-ˌtriks\ n, pl **ex·ec·u·tri·ces** \-ˌze-kyə-ˈtrī-ˌsēz\ or **ex·ec·u·trix·es** \-ˈze-kyə-ˌtrik-səz\ : a woman who is an executor

ex·e·ge·sis \ˌek-sə-ˈjē-səs\ n, pl **-ge·ses** \-ˈjē-ˌsēz\ : explanation or critical inter-pretation of a text

ex·e·gete \ˈek-sə-ˌjēt\ n : one who prac-tices exegesis — **ex·e·get·i·cal** \ˌek-sə-ˈje-ti-kəl\ adj

ex·em·plar \ig-ˈzem-ˌplär, -plər\ n 1 : one that serves as a model or example; esp : an ideal model 2 : a typical instance or example

ex·em·pla·ry \ig-ˈzem-plə-rē\ adj : serving as a pattern; also : COMMENDABLE ⟨∼ courage⟩

ex·em·pli·fy \ig-ˈzem-plə-ˌfī\ vb **-fied; -fy·ing** : to illustrate by example : serve as an example of — **ex·em·pli·fi·ca·tion** \-ˌzem-plə-fə-ˈkā-shən\ n

¹**ex·empt** \ig-ˈzempt\ adj : free from some liability to which others are subject ⟨∼ from taxation⟩

²**exempt** vb : to make exempt : EXCUSE — **ex·emp·tion** \ig-ˈzemp-shən\ n

¹**ex·er·cise** \ˈek-sər-ˌsīz\ n 1 : EMPLOY-MENT, USE ⟨∼ of authority⟩ 2 : exer-tion made for the sake of training or physical fitness 3 : a task or problem done to develop skill 4 pl : a public ex-hibition or ceremony

²**exercise** vb **-cised; -cis·ing** 1 : EXERT ⟨∼ control⟩ 2 : to train by or engage in exercise 3 : WORRY, DISTRESS — **ex·er·cis·er** n

ex·ert \ig-ˈzərt\ vb : to bring or put into action ⟨∼ influence⟩ ⟨∼ed himself⟩ — **ex·er·tion** \-ˈzər-shən\ n

ex·fo·li·ate \eks-ˈfō-lē-ˌāt\ vb **-at·ed; -at·ing** : to cast off in scales, layers, or splin-ters — **ex·fo·li·a·tion** \-ˌfō-lē-ˈā-shən\ n

ex·hale \eks-ˈhāl\ vb **ex·haled; ex·hal·ing** 1 : to breathe out 2 : to give or pass off in the form of vapor — **ex·ha·la·tion** \ˌeks-hə-ˈlā-shən\ n

¹**ex·haust** \ig-ˈzȯst\ vb 1 : to use up whol-ly 2 : to tire or wear out 3 : to draw off or let out completely; also : EMPTY 4 : to develop (a subject) completely

²**exhaust** n 1 : the escape of used vapor or gas from an engine; also : the gas that es-capes 2 : a system of pipes through which exhaust escapes

ex·haus·tion \ig-ˈzȯs-chən\ n : extreme weariness : FATIGUE

ex·haus·tive \ig-ˈzȯ-stiv\ adj : covering all possibilities : THOROUGH ⟨an ∼ inves-tigation⟩ — **ex·haus·tive·ly** adv

¹**ex·hib·it** \ig-ˈzi-bət\ vb 1 : to display esp. publicly 2 : to present to a court in legal form ◆ **Synonyms** DISPLAY, SHOW, PA-RADE, FLAUNT — **ex·hi·bi·tion** \ˌek-sə-ˈbi-shən\ n — **ex·hib·i·tor** \ig-ˈzi-bə-tər\ n

²**exhibit** n 1 : an act or instance of exhib-iting; also : something exhibited 2 : something produced and identified in court for use as evidence

ex·hi·bi·tion·ism \ˌek-sə-ˈbi-shə-ˌni-zəm\ n 1 : a perversion marked by a tendency to indecently expose one's genitals **2** : the act or practice of behaving so as to attract attention to oneself — **ex·hi·bi·tion·ist** \-nist\ *n or adj*

ex·hil·a·rate \ig-'zi-lə-ˌrāt\ *vb* **-rat·ed; -rat·ing** : ENLIVEN, STIMULATE — **ex·hil·a·ra·tion** \-ˌzi-lə-'rā-shən\ *n*

ex·hort \ig-'zȯrt\ *vb* : to urge, advise, or warn earnestly — **ex·hor·ta·tion** \ˌek-ˌsȯr-tā-shən, ˌeg-ˌzȯr-, -zər-\ *n*

ex·hume \ig-'züm, iks-'hyüm\ *vb* **ex·humed; ex·hum·ing** [ME fr. ML *exhumare,* fr. L *ex* out of + *humus* earth] : DISINTER — **ex·hu·ma·tion** \ˌeks-hyü-'mā-shən, ˌeg-zü-\ *n*

ex·i·gen·cy \'ek-sə-jən-sē, ig-'zi-jən-\ *n, pl* **-cies** **1** : REQUIREMENTS **2** : urgent need — **ex·i·gent** \'ek-sə-jənt\ *adj*

ex·ig·u·ous \ig-'zi-gyə-wəs\ *adj* : scanty in amount — **ex·i·gu·i·ty** \ˌeg-zi-'gyü-ə-tē\ *n*

¹ex·ile \'eg-ˌzī(-ə)l, 'ek-ˌsī(-ə)l\ *n* **1** : BANISHMENT; *also* : voluntary absence from one's country or home **2** : a person driven from his or her native place

²exile *vb* **ex·iled; ex·il·ing** : BANISH, EXPEL ✦ *Synonyms* EXPATRIATE, DEPORT, OSTRACIZE

ex·ist \ig-'zist\ *vb* **1** : to have being **2** : to continue to be

ex·is·tence \ig-'zis-təns\ *n* **1** : continuance in living **2** : actual or present occurrence ⟨~ of a state of war⟩ — **ex·is·tent** \-tənt\ *adj*

ex·is·ten·tial \ˌeg-zis-'ten-chəl, ˌek-sis-\ *adj* **1** : of or relating to existence **2** : EMPIRICAL **3** : having being in time and space **4** : of or relating to existentialism or existentialists

ex·is·ten·tial·ism \ˌeg-zis-'ten-chə-ˌli-zəm\ *n* : a philosophy centered on individual existence and personal responsibility for acts of free will in the absence of certain knowledge of what is right or wrong — **ex·is·ten·tial·ist** \-list\ *adj or n*

ex·it \'eg-zət, 'ek-sət\ *n* **1** : a departure from a stage **2** : a going out or away; *also* : DEATH **3** : a way out of an enclosed space **4** : a point of departure from an expressway — **exit** *vb*

exo·bi·ol·o·gy \ˌek-sō-bī-'ä-lə-jē\ *n* : biology concerned with life originating or existing outside the earth or its atmosphere — **exo·bi·ol·o·gist** \-jist\ *n*

exo·crine gland \'ek-sə-krən-, -ˌkrīn-, -ˌkrēn-\ *n* : a gland (as a salivary gland) that releases a secretion externally by means of a canal or duct

Exod *abbr* Exodus

ex·o·dus \'ek-sə-dəs\ *n* **1** *cap* — see BIBLE table **2** : a mass departure : EMIGRATION

ex of·fi·cio \ˌek-sə-'fi-shē-ˌō\ *adv or adj* : by virtue of or because of an office ⟨*ex officio* chairman⟩

ex·og·e·nous \ek-'sä-jə-nəs\ *adj* : caused or produced by factors outside the organism or system — **ex·og·e·nous·ly** *adv*

ex·on·er·ate \ig-'zä-nə-ˌrāt\ *vb* **-at·ed; -at·ing** [ME, fr. L *exoneratus,* pp. of *exonerare* to unburden, fr. *ex-* out + *onus*

load] : to free from blame ✦ *Synonyms* ACQUIT, ABSOLVE, EXCULPATE, VINDICATE — **ex·on·er·a·tion** \-ˌzä-nə-'rā-shən\ *n*

ex·or·bi·tant \ig-'zȯr-bə-tənt\ *adj* : exceeding what is usual or proper

ex·or·cise \'ek-ˌsȯr-ˌsīz, -sər-\ *vb* **-cised; -cis·ing** **1** : to get rid of by or as if by solemn command **2** : to free of an evil spirit — **ex·or·cism** \-ˌsi-zəm\ *n* — **ex·or·cist** \-ˌsist\ *n*

exo·sphere \'ek-sō-ˌsfir\ *n* : the outermost region of the atmosphere

exo·ther·mic \ˌek-sō-'thər-mik\ *adj* : characterized by or formed with evolution of heat

ex·ot·ic \ig-'zä-tik\ *adj* **1** : introduced from another country ⟨~ plants⟩ **2** : strikingly, excitingly, or mysteriously different or unusual ⟨~ flavors⟩ — **exotic** *n* — **ex·ot·i·cal·ly** \-ti-k(ə-)lē\ *adv* — **ex·ot·i·cism** \-tə-ˌsi-zəm\ *n*

exp *abbr* **1** expense **2** experiment **3** export **4** express

ex·pand \ik-'spand\ *vb* **1** : to open up : UNFOLD **2** : ENLARGE **3** : to develop in detail ✦ *Synonyms* AMPLIFY, SWELL, DISTEND, INFLATE, DILATE — **ex·pand·able** \-'span-də-bəl\ *adj* — **ex·pand·er** *n*

ex·panse \ik-'spans\ *n* : a broad extent (as of land or sea)

ex·pan·sion \ik-'span-chən\ *n* **1** : the act or process of expanding **2** : the quality or state of being expanded **3** : an expanded part or thing

expansion slot *n* : a socket on a motherboard for a circuit board (**expansion card**) offering additional capabilities

ex·pan·sive \ik-'span-siv\ *adj* **1** : tending to expand or to cause expansion **2** : warmly benevolent, generous, or ready to talk **3** : of large extent or scope — **ex·pan·sive·ly** *adv* — **ex·pan·sive·ness** *n*

ex par·te \eks-'pär-tē\ *adv or adj* [ML] : from a one-sided point of view

ex·pa·ti·ate \ek-'spā-shē-ˌāt\ *vb* **-at·ed; -at·ing** : to talk or write at length — **ex·pa·ti·a·tion** \ek-ˌspā-shē-'ā-shən\ *n*

¹ex·pa·tri·ate \ek-'spā-trē-ˌāt\ *vb* **-at·ed; -at·ing** : EXILE — **ex·pa·tri·a·tion** \ek-ˌspā-trē-'ā-shən\ *n*

²ex·pa·tri·ate \ek-'spā-trē-ˌāt, -trē-ət\ *adj* : living in a foreign country — **expatriate** *n*

ex·pect \ik-'spekt\ *vb* **1** : SUPPOSE, THINK **2** : to look forward to : ANTICIPATE **3** : to consider reasonable, due, or necessary **4** : to consider to be obliged

ex·pec·tan·cy \-'spek-tən-sē\ *n, pl* **-cies** **1** : EXPECTATION **2** : the expected amount (as of years of life)

ex·pec·tant \-tənt\ *adj* : marked by expectation; *esp* : expecting the birth of a child — **ex·pec·tant·ly** *adv*

ex·pec·ta·tion \ˌek-ˌspek-'tā-shən\ *n* **1** : the act or state of expecting **2** : prospect of inheritance — usu. used in pl. **3** : something expected

ex·pec·to·rant \ik-'spek-tə-rənt\ *n* : an agent that promotes the discharge or expulsion of mucus from the respiratory tract — **expectorant** *adj*

ex·pec·to·rate \-ˌrāt\ *vb* **-rat·ed; -rat·ing** : SPIT — **ex·pec·to·ra·tion** \-ˌspek-tə-ˈrā-shən\ *n*

ex·pe·di·ence \ik-ˈspē-dē-əns\ *n* : EXPEDIENCY

ex·pe·di·en·cy \-ən-sē\ *n, pl* **-cies** **1** : fitness to some end **2** : use of expedient means and methods; *also* : something expedient

¹ex·pe·di·ent \-ənt\ *adj* [ME, fr. AF or L; AF, fr. L *expediens*, prp. of *expedire* to extricate, prepare, be useful, fr. *ex-* out + *ped-, pes* foot] **1** : adapted for achieving a particular end **2** : marked by concern with what is advantageous; *esp* : governed by self-interest

²expedient *n* : something expedient; *esp* : a temporary means to an end

ex·pe·dite \ˈek-spə-ˌdīt\ *vb* **-dit·ed; -dit·ing** : to carry out promptly; *also* : to speed up

ex·pe·dit·er \-ˌdī-tər\ *n* : one that expedites; *esp* : one employed to ensure efficient movement of goods or supplies in a business

ex·pe·di·tion \ˌek-spə-ˈdi-shən\ *n* **1** : a journey for a particular purpose; *also* : the persons making it **2** : efficient promptness

ex·pe·di·tion·ary \-ˈdi-shə-ˌner-ē\ *adj* : of, relating to, or constituting an expedition; *also* : sent on military service abroad

ex·pe·di·tious \-ˈdi-shəs\ *adj* : marked by or acting with prompt efficiency ♦ *Synonyms* SWIFT, FAST, RAPID, SPEEDY

ex·pel \ik-ˈspel\ *vb* **ex·pelled; ex·pel·ling** : to drive or force out : EJECT

ex·pend \ik-ˈspend\ *vb* **1** : to pay out : SPEND **2** : UTILIZE; *also* : USE UP — **ex·pend·able** *adj*

ex·pen·di·ture \ik-ˈspen-di-chər, -ˌchùr\ *n* **1** : the act or process of expending **2** : something expended

ex·pense \ik-ˈspens\ *n* **1** : EXPENDITURE **2** : COST **3** : a cause of expenditure **4** : SACRIFICE ⟨had a laugh at my ∼⟩

ex·pen·sive \ik-ˈspen-siv\ *adj* : COSTLY, DEAR — **ex·pen·sive·ly** *adv*

¹ex·pe·ri·ence \ik-ˈspir-ē-əns\ *n* **1** : observation of or participation in events resulting in or tending toward knowledge **2** : knowledge, practice, or skill derived from observation or participation in events; *also* : the length of such participation **3** : something encountered, undergone, or lived through (as by a person or community)

²experience *vb* **-enced; -enc·ing** **1** : FIND OUT, DISCOVER **2** : to have experience of : UNDERGO

ex·pe·ri·enced *adj* : made capable through experience ⟨an ∼ pilot⟩

¹ex·per·i·ment \ik-ˈsper-ə-mənt\ *n* : a controlled procedure carried out to discover, test, or demonstrate something; *also* : the process of testing — **ex·per·i·men·tal** \-ˌsper-ə-ˈmen-t²l\ *adj* — **ex·per·i·men·tal·ly** \-ˈmen-t²l-ē\ *adv*

²ex·per·i·ment \-ˌment\ *vb* : to make experiments — **ex·per·i·men·ta·tion** \ik-ˌsper-ə-mən-ˈtā-shən\ *n* — **ex·per·i·ment·er** *n*

¹ex·pert \ˈek-ˌspərt\ *adj* : showing special skill or knowledge — **ex·pert·ly** *adv* — **ex·pert·ness** *n*

²ex·pert \ˈek-ˌspərt\ *n* : an expert person : SPECIALIST

ex·per·tise \ˌek-(ˌ)spər-ˈtēz\ *n* : the skill of an expert

expert system *n* : computer software that attempts to mimic the reasoning of a human specialist

ex·pi·ate \ˈek-spē-ˌāt\ *vb* **-at·ed; -at·ing** : to give satisfaction for : ATONE — **ex·pi·a·tion** \ˌek-spē-ˈā-shən\ *n*

ex·pi·a·to·ry \ˈek-spē-ə-ˌtȯr-ē\ *adj* : serving to expiate

expiration date *n* **1** : the date after which something is no longer in effect **2** : the date after which a product is expected to decline in quality or effectiveness

ex·pire \ik-ˈspī(-ə)r, ek-\ *vb* **ex·pired; ex·pir·ing** **1** : to breathe one's last breath : DIE **2** : to come to an end **3** : to breathe out from or as if from the lungs — **ex·pi·ra·tion** \ˌek-spə-ˈrā-shən\ *n*

ex·plain \ik-ˈsplān\ *vb* [ME *explanen*, fr. L *explanare*, lit., to make level, fr. *planus* level, flat] **1** : to make clear **2** : to give the reason for — **ex·pla·na·tion** \ˌek-splə-ˈnā-shən\ *n* — **ex·plan·a·to·ry** \ik-ˈspla-nə-ˌtȯr-ē\ *adj*

ex·ple·tive \ˈek-splə-tiv\ *n* : a usu. profane exclamation

ex·pli·ca·ble \ek-ˈspli-kə-bəl, ˈek-(ˌ)spli-\ *adj* : capable of being explained

ex·pli·cate \ˈek-splə-ˌkāt\ *vb* **-cat·ed; -cat·ing** : to give a detailed explanation of — **ex·pli·ca·tion** \ˌek-spli-ˈkā-shən\ *n*

ex·plic·it \ik-ˈspli-sət\ *adj* : clearly and precisely expressed — **ex·plic·it·ly** *adv* — **ex·plic·it·ness** *n*

ex·plode \ik-ˈsplōd\ *vb* **ex·plod·ed; ex·plod·ing** [L *explodere* to drive off the stage by clapping, fr. *ex-* out + *plaudere* to clap] **1** : DISCREDIT ⟨∼ a belief⟩ **2** : to burst or cause to burst violently and noisily ⟨∼ a bomb⟩ ⟨the boiler *exploded*⟩ **3** : to undergo a rapid chemical or nuclear reaction with production of heat and violent expansion of gas ⟨dynamite ∼s⟩ **4** : to give forth a sudden strong and noisy outburst of emotion **5** : to increase rapidly ⟨the city's population *exploded*⟩

exploded *adj* : showing the parts separated but in correct relationship to each other ⟨an ∼ view of a carburetor⟩

¹ex·ploit \ˈek-ˌsplȯit\ *n* : DEED; *esp* : a notable or heroic act

²ex·ploit \ik-ˈsplȯit\ *vb* **1** : to make productive use of : UTILIZE **2** : to use unfairly for one's own advantage — **ex·ploi·ta·tion** \ˌek-ˌsplȯi-ˈtā-shən\ *n*

ex·plore \ik-ˈsplȯr\ *vb* **ex·plored; ex·plor·ing** **1** : to look into or travel over thoroughly **2** : to examine carefully ⟨∼ a wound⟩ — **ex·plo·ra·tion** \ˌek-splə-ˈrā-shən\ *n* — **ex·plor·a·to·ry** \ik-ˈsplȯr-ə-ˌtȯr-ē\ *adj* — **ex·plor·er** *n*

ex·plo·sion \ik-ˈsplō-zhən\ *n* : the act or an instance of exploding

ex·plo·sive \ik-ˈsplō-siv\ *adj* 1 : relating to or able to cause explosion 2 : tending to explode — **explosive** *n* — **ex·plo·sive·ly** *adv*

ex·po \ˈek-ˌspō\ *n, pl* **expos** : EXPOSITION 2

ex·po·nent \ik-ˈspō-nənt, ˈek-ˌspō-\ *n* 1 : a symbol written above and to the right of a mathematical expression (as 3 in a^3) to signify how many times it is to be used as a factor 2 : INTERPRETER, EXPOUNDER 3 : ADVOCATE, CHAMPION — **ex·po·nen·tial** \ˌek-spə-ˈnen-chəl\ *adj* — **ex·po·nen·tial·ly** *adv*

ex·po·nen·ti·a·tion \ˌek-spə-ˌnen-chē-ˈā-shən\ *n* : the mathematical operation of raising a quantity to a power

¹**ex·port** \ek-ˈspȯrt, ˈek-ˌspȯrt\ *vb* : to send (as merchandise) to foreign countries — **ex·por·ta·tion** \ˌek-ˌspȯr-ˈtā-shən, -spər-\ *n* — **ex·port·er** *n*

²**ex·port** \ˈek-ˌspȯrt\ *n* 1 : something exported esp. for trade 2 : the act of exporting

ex·pose \ik-ˈspōz\ *vb* **ex·posed; ex·pos·ing** 1 : to deprive of shelter or protection 2 : to submit or subject to an action or influence; *esp* : to subject (as photographic film) to radiant energy (as light) 3 : to bring to light : DISCLOSE 4 : to cause to be open to view

ex·po·sé \ˌek-spō-ˈzā\ *n* : an exposure of something discreditable

ex·po·si·tion \ˌek-spə-ˈzi-shən\ *n* 1 : a setting forth of the meaning or purpose (as of a writing); *also* : discourse designed to convey information 2 : a public exhibition

ex·pos·i·tor \ik-ˈspä-zə-tər\ *n* : one who explains : COMMENTATOR

ex post fac·to \ˌeks-ˈpōst-ˌfak-tō\ *adv or adj* : after the fact

ex·pos·tu·late \ik-ˈspäs-chə-ˌlāt\ *vb* : to reason earnestly with a person esp. in dissuading : REMONSTRATE — **ex·pos·tu·la·tion** \-ˌspäs-chə-ˈlā-shən\ *n*

ex·po·sure \ik-ˈspō-zhər\ *n* 1 : the fact or condition of being exposed 2 : the act or an instance of exposing 3 : the length of time for which a film is exposed 4 : a section of a photographic film for one picture

ex·pound \ik-ˈspau̇nd\ *vb* 1 : STATE 2 : INTERPRET, EXPLAIN — **ex·pound·er** *n*

¹**ex·press** \ik-ˈspres\ *adj* 1 : EXPLICIT; *also* : EXACT, PRECISE 2 : SPECIFIC ⟨this ~ purpose⟩ 3 : traveling at high speed and esp. with few stops ⟨an ~ train⟩; *also* : adapted to high-speed use ⟨~ roads⟩ — **ex·press·ly** *adv*

²**express** *adv* : by express ⟨ship it ~⟩

³**express** *n* 1 : a system for the prompt transportation of goods; *also* : a company operating such a service or the shipments so transported 2 : an express vehicle

⁴**express** *vb* 1 : to make known : SHOW, STATE ⟨~ regret⟩; *also* : SYMBOLIZE 2

: to squeeze out : extract by pressing 3 : to send by express 4 : to manifest or produce by a genetic process

ex·pres·sion \ik-ˈspre-shən\ *n* 1 : UTTERANCE 2 : something that represents or symbolizes : SIGN; *esp* : a mathematical symbol or combination of signs and symbols representing a quantity or operation 3 : the detectable effect of a gene 4 : a significant word or phrase; *also* : manner of expressing (as in writing or music) 5 : facial aspect or vocal intonation indicative of feeling — **ex·pres·sion·less** *adj*

ex·pres·sion·ism \ik-ˈspre-shə-ˌni-zəm\ *n* : a theory or practice in art of seeking to depict the artist's subjective responses to objects and events — **ex·pres·sion·ist** \-nist\ *n or adj* — **ex·pres·sion·is·tic** \-ˌspre-shə-ˈnis-tik\ *adj*

ex·pres·sive \ik-ˈspre-siv\ *adj* 1 : of or relating to expression 2 : serving to express — **ex·pres·sive·ly** *adv* — **ex·pres·sive·ness** *n*

ex·press·way \ik-ˈspres-ˌwā\ *n* : a divided superhighway with limited access

ex·pro·pri·ate \ek-ˈsprō-prē-ˌāt\ *vb* **-at·ed; -at·ing** : to deprive of possession or the right to own — **ex·pro·pri·a·tion** \(ˌ)ek-ˌsprō-prē-ˈā-shən\ *n*

expt *abbr* experiment

ex·pul·sion \ik-ˈspəl-shən\ *n* : an expelling or being expelled : EJECTION

ex·punge \ik-ˈspənj\ *vb* **ex·punged; ex·pung·ing** [L *expungere* to mark for deletion by dots, fr. *ex-* out + *pungere* to prick] : OBLITERATE, ERASE

ex·pur·gate \ˈek-spər-ˌgāt\ *vb* **-gat·ed; -gat·ing** : to clear (as a book) of objectionable passages — **ex·pur·ga·tion** \ˌek-spər-ˈgā-shən\ *n*

ex·qui·site \ek-ˈskwi-zət, ˈek-(ˌ)skwi-\ *adj* [ME *exquisit*, fr. L *exquisitus*, pp. of *exquirere* to search out, fr. *ex* out + *quaerere* to seek] 1 : marked by flawless form or workmanship 2 : keenly appreciative or sensitive 3 : pleasingly beautiful or delicate 4 : INTENSE ⟨~ pain⟩

ext *abbr* 1 extension 2 exterior 3 external 4 extra 5 extract

ex·tant \ˈek-stənt; ek-ˈstant\ *adj* : EXISTENT; *esp* : not lost or destroyed

ex·tem·po·ra·ne·ous \ek-ˌstem-pə-ˈrā-nē-əs\ *adj* : not planned beforehand : IMPROMPTU — **ex·tem·po·ra·ne·ous·ly** *adv*

ex·tem·po·rary \ik-ˈstem-pə-ˌrer-ē\ *adj* : EXTEMPORANEOUS

ex·tem·po·re \ik-ˈstem-pə-(ˌ)rē\ *adv* : EXTEMPORANEOUSLY

ex·tem·po·rise *Brit var of* EXTEMPORIZE

ex·tem·po·rize \ik-ˈstem-pə-ˌrīz\ *vb* **-rized; -riz·ing** : to do something extemporaneously

ex·tend \ik-ˈstend\ *vb* 1 : to spread or stretch forth or out (as in reaching) 2 : to exert or cause to exert to full capacity 3 : PROFFER ⟨~ credit⟩ 4 : PROLONG ⟨~ a note⟩ 5 : to make greater or broader ⟨~ knowledge⟩ ⟨~ a business⟩ 6 : to stretch out or reach across a distance, space, or time **♦ Synonyms** LENGTHEN,

ELONGATE, PROTRACT — **ex·tend·able**
also **ex·tend·ible** \-'sten-də-bəl\ *adj*

ex·ten·sion \ik-'sten-chən\ *n* 1 : an extending or being extended 2 : a program that geographically extends the educational resources of an institution 3 : an additional part; *also* : an extra telephone connected to a line

ex·ten·sive \ik-'sten-siv\ *adj* : of considerable extent : FAR-REACHING, BROAD — **ex·ten·sive·ly** *adv*

ex·tent \ik-'stent\ *n* 1 : the range or space over which something extends ⟨a property of large ∼⟩ 2 : the point or degree to which something extends ⟨to the fullest ∼ of the law⟩

ex·ten·u·ate \ik-'sten-yù-ˌwāt\ *vb* **-at·ed; -at·ing** : to lessen the seriousness of — **ex·ten·u·a·tion** \-ˌsten-yù-'wā-shən\ *n*

¹**ex·te·ri·or** \ek-'stir-ē-ər\ *adj* 1 : EXTERNAL 2 : suitable for use on an outside surface ⟨∼ paint⟩

²**exterior** *n* : an exterior part or surface

ex·ter·mi·nate \ik-'stər-mə-ˌnāt\ *vb* **-nat·ed; -nat·ing** : to get rid of completely usu. by killing off ♦ *Synonyms* EXTIRPATE, ERADICATE, ABOLISH, ANNIHILATE — **ex·ter·mi·na·tion** \-ˌstər-mə-'nā-shən\ *n* — **ex·ter·mi·na·tor** \-'stər-mə-ˌnā-tər\ *n*

¹**ex·ter·nal** \ek-'stər-n°l\ *adj* 1 : outwardly perceivable; *also* : SUPERFICIAL 2 : of, relating to, or located on the outside or an outer part 3 : arising or acting from without; *also* : FOREIGN ⟨∼ affairs⟩ — **ex·ter·nal·ly** *adv*

²**external** *n* : an external feature

ex·tinct \ik-'stiŋkt\ *adj* 1 : EXTINGUISHED; *also* : no longer active ⟨an ∼ volcano⟩ 2 : no longer existing or in use ⟨dinosaurs are ∼⟩ ⟨∼ languages⟩ — **ex·tinc·tion** \ik-'stiŋk-shən\ *n*

ex·tin·guish \ik-'stiŋ-gwish\ *vb* : to cause to stop burning; *also* : to bring to an end (as by destroying) — **ex·tin·guish·able** *adj* — **ex·tin·guish·er** *n*

ex·tir·pate \'ek-stər-ˌpāt\ *vb* **-pat·ed; -pat·ing** [L *exstirpatus,* pp. of *exstirpare,* fr. *ex-* out + *stirps* trunk, root] 1 : to destroy completely 2 : UPROOT ♦ *Synonyms* EXTERMINATE, ERADICATE, ABOLISH, ANNIHILATE — **ex·tir·pa·tion** \ˌek-stər-'pā-shən\ *n*

ex·tol *also* **ex·toll** \ik-'stōl\ *vb* **ex·tolled; ex·tol·ling** : to praise highly : GLORIFY

ex·tort \ik-'stort\ *vb* [L *extortus,* pp. of *extorquēre* to wrench out, extort, fr. *ex-* out + *torquēre* to twist] : to obtain by force or improper pressure ⟨∼ a bribe⟩ — **ex·tor·tion** \-'stor-shən\ *n* — **ex·tor·tion·er** *n* — **ex·tor·tion·ist** *n*

ex·tor·tion·ate \ik-'stor-shə-nət\ *adj* : EXCESSIVE, EXORBITANT ⟨∼ prices⟩ — **ex·tor·tion·ate·ly** *adv*

¹**ex·tra** \'ek-strə\ *adj* 1 : ADDITIONAL ⟨∼ work⟩ 2 : SUPERIOR ⟨∼ quality⟩

²**extra** *n* 1 : a special edition of a newspaper 2 : an added charge 3 : an additional worker or performer (as in a motion picture)

³**extra** *adv* : beyond what is usual ⟨∼ large⟩

¹**ex·tract** \ik-'strakt, *esp for 3* 'ek-ˌstrakt\ *vb* 1 : to draw out; *esp* : to pull out forcibly ⟨∼ a tooth⟩ 2 : to withdraw (as a juice or a constituent) by a physical or chemical process 3 : to select for citation : QUOTE — **ex·tract·able** *adj* — **ex·trac·tion** \ik-'strak-shən\ *n* — **ex·trac·tor** \-tər\ *n*

²**ex·tract** \'ek-ˌstrakt\ *n* 1 : EXCERPT, CITATION 2 : a product (as a juice or concentrate) obtained by extracting

ex·tra·cur·ric·u·lar \ˌek-strə-kə-'ri-kyə-lər\ *adj* : lying outside the regular curriculum; *esp* : of or relating to school-connected activities (as sports) usu. carrying no academic credit

ex·tra·dite \'ek-strə-ˌdīt\ *vb* **-dit·ed; -dit·ing** : to obtain by or deliver up to extradition

ex·tra·di·tion \ˌek-strə-'di-shən\ *n* : the surrender of an alleged criminal to a different jurisdiction for trial

ex·tra·mar·i·tal \ˌek-strə-'ma-rə-t°l\ *adj* : of or relating to sexual intercourse by a married person with someone other than his or her spouse

ex·tra·mu·ral \-'myùr-əl\ *adj* : existing or functioning beyond the bounds of an organized unit

ex·tra·ne·ous \ek-'strā-nē-əs\ *adj* 1 : coming from without ⟨∼ light⟩ 2 : not forming a vital part; *also* : IRRELEVANT — **ex·tra·ne·ous·ly** *adv*

ex·tra·net \'ek-strə-ˌnet\ *n* : a network like an intranet but also allowing access by certain outside parties

ex·traor·di·nary \ik-'strȯr-də-ˌner-ē, ˌek-strə-'ȯr-\ *adj* 1 : notably unusual or exceptional 2 : employed on special service ⟨an ambassador ∼⟩ — **ex·traor·di·nari·ly** \-ˌstrȯr-də-'ner-ə-lē, ˌek-strə-ˌȯr-\ *adv*

ex·trap·o·late \ik-'stra-pə-ˌlāt\ *vb* **-lat·ed; -lat·ing** : to infer (unknown data) from known data — **ex·trap·o·la·tion** \-ˌstra-pə-'lā-shən\ *n*

ex·tra·sen·so·ry \ˌek-strə-'sen-sə-rē\ *adj* : not acting or occurring through the known senses

extrasensory perception *n* : perception (as in telepathy) of events external to the self not gained through the senses and not deducible from previous experience

ex·tra·so·lar \-'sō-lər\ *adj* : originating or existing outside the solar system

ex·tra·ter·res·tri·al \-tə-'res-trē-əl\ *adj* : originating or existing outside the earth or its atmosphere ⟨∼ life⟩ — **extraterrestrial** *n*

ex·tra·ter·ri·to·ri·al \-ˌter-ə-'tȯr-ē-əl\ *adj* : existing or taking place outside the territorial limits of a jurisdiction

ex·tra·ter·ri·to·ri·al·i·ty \-ˌtȯr-ē-'a-lə-tē\ *n* : exemption from the application or jurisdiction of local law or tribunals ⟨diplomats enjoy ∼⟩

ex·trav·a·gant \ik-'stra-vi-gənt\ *adj* 1 : EXCESSIVE ⟨∼ claims⟩ 2 : unduly lavish : WASTEFUL 3 : too costly ♦ *Synonyms* IMMODERATE, EXORBITANT, EXTREME, INORDINATE, UNDUE — **ex-**

trav·a·gance \-gəns\ n — **ex·trav·a·gant·ly** adv

ex·tra·van·za \ik-ˌstra-və-ˈgan-zə\ n 1 : a literary or musical work marked by extreme freedom of style and structure 2 : a spectacular show

ex·tra·ve·hic·u·lar \ˌek-strə-vē-ˈhi-kyə-lər\ adj : taking place outside a vehicle (as a spacecraft) ⟨∼ activity⟩

¹**ex·treme** \ik-ˈstrēm\ adj 1 : very great or intense ⟨∼ cold⟩ 2 : very severe or radical ⟨∼ measures⟩ 3 : going to great lengths or beyond normal limits ⟨politically ∼⟩ 4 : most remote ⟨the ∼ end⟩ 5 : UTMOST; also : MAXIMUM — **ex·treme·ly** adv

²**extreme** n 1 : something located at one end or the other of a range or series 2 : EXTREMITY 4

extremely low frequency n : a radio frequency in the lowest range of the radio spectrum

ex·trem·ism \ik-ˈstrē-ˌmi-zəm\ n : the quality or state of being extreme; esp : advocacy of extreme political measures — **ex·trem·ist** \-mist\ n or adj

ex·trem·i·ty \ik-ˈstre-mə-tē\ n, pl -ties 1 : the most remote part or point 2 : a limb of the body; esp : a human hand or foot 3 : the greatest need or danger 4 : the utmost degree 5 : a drastic or desperate measure

ex·tri·cate \ˈek-strə-ˌkāt\ vb -cat·ed; -cat·ing [L extricatus, pp. of extricare, fr. ex- out + tricae trifles, perplexities] : to free from an entanglement or difficulty
♦ **Synonyms** DISENTANGLE, UNTANGLE, DISENCUMBER — **ex·tri·ca·ble** \ik-ˈstri-kə-bəl, ek-; ˈek-(ˌ)stri-\ adj — **ex·tri·ca·tion** \ˌek-strə-ˈkā-shən\ n

ex·trin·sic \ek-ˈstrin-zik, -sik\ adj 1 : not forming part of or belonging to a thing 2 : EXTERNAL — **ex·trin·si·cal·ly** \-zi-k(ə-)lē, -si-\ adv

ex·tro·vert also **ex·tra·vert** \ˈek-strə-ˌvərt\ n : a gregarious and unreserved person — **ex·tro·ver·sion** or **ex·tra·ver·sion** \ˌek-strə-ˈvər-zhən\ n — **ex·tro·vert·ed** also **ex·tra·vert·ed** adj

ex·trude \ik-ˈstrüd\ vb **ex·trud·ed**; **ex·trud·ing** 1 : to force, press, or push out 2 : to shape (as plastic) by forcing through a die — **ex·tru·sion** \-ˈstrü-zhən\ n — **ex·trud·er** n

ex·u·ber·ant \ig-ˈzü-bə-rənt\ adj 1 : unrestrained in enthusiasm or style 2 : PROFUSE ⟨∼ vegetation⟩ — **ex·u·ber·ance** \-rəns\ n — **ex·u·ber·ant·ly** adv

ex·ude \ig-ˈzüd\ vb **ex·ud·ed**; **ex·ud·ing** [L exsudare, fr. ex- out + sudare to sweat] 1 : to discharge slowly through pores or cuts : OOZE 2 : to display conspicuously or abundantly ⟨∼s charm⟩ — **ex·u·date** \ˈek-sù-ˌdāt, -syù-\ n — **ex·u·da·tion** \ˌek-sù-ˈdā-shən, -syù-\ n

ex·ult \ig-ˈzəlt\ vb : REJOICE, GLORY — **ex·ul·tant** \-ˈzəl-tᵊnt\ adj — **ex·ul·tant·ly** adv — **ex·ul·ta·tion** \ˌek-(ˌ)səl-ˈtā-shən, ˌeg-(ˌ)zəl-\ n

ex·urb \ˈek-ˌsərb, ˈeg-ˌzərb\ n : a region outside a city and its suburbs inhabited

chiefly by well-to-do families — **ex·ur·ban** \ek-ˈsər-bən, eg-ˈzər-\ adj

ex·ur·ban·ite \ek-ˈsər-bə-ˌnīt; eg-ˈzər-\ n : one who lives in an exurb

ex·ur·bia \ek-ˈsər-bē-ə, eg-ˈzər-\ n : the generalized region of exurbs

-ey — see -Y

¹**eye** \ˈī\ n 1 : an organ of sight typically consisting in vertebrates of a globular structure that is located in a socket of the skull, is lined with a sensitive retina, and is normally paired 2 : VISION, PERCEPTION; also : faculty of discrimination ⟨an ∼ for bargains⟩ 3 : POINT OF VIEW, JUDGMENT — often used in pl. ⟨in the ∼s of the law⟩ 4 : something suggesting an eye (as the hole of a needle or the bud of a potato) 5 : the calm center of a cyclone — **eyed** \ˈīd\ adj

²**eye** vb **eyed**; **eye·ing** or **ey·ing** : to look at : WATCH

¹**eye·ball** \ˈī-ˌbȯl\ n : the globular capsule of the vertebrate eye

²**eyeball** vb : to look at intently

eye·brow \-ˌbraù\ n : the ridge over the eye or the hair growing on it

eye·drop·per \-ˌdrä-pər\ n : DROPPER 2

eye·glass \-ˌglas\ n : a lens worn to aid vision; also, pl : GLASSES

eye·lash \-ˌlash\ n 1 : the fringe of hair edging the eyelid — usu. used in pl. 2 : a single hair of the eyelashes

eye·let \-lət\ n 1 : a small hole intended for ornament or for passage of a cord or lace 2 : a typically metal ring for reinforcing an eyelet : GROMMET

eye·lid \-ˌlid\ n : either of the movable folds of skin and muscle that can be closed over the eyeball

eye·lin·er \-ˌlī-nər\ n : makeup used to emphasize the contour of the eyes

eye–open·er \-ˌō-pə-nər\ n : something startling or surprising — **eye–open·ing** adj

eye·piece \-ˌpēs\ n : the lens or combination of lenses at the eye end of an optical instrument

eye shadow n : a colored cosmetic applied to the eyelids to accent the eyes

eye·sight \-ˌsīt\ n : SIGHT, VISION

eye·sore \-ˌsȯr\ n : something offensive to view

eye·strain \-ˌstrān\ n : weariness or a strained state of the eye

eye·tooth \-ˈtüth\ n : a canine tooth of the upper jaw

eye·wash \-ˌwȯsh, -ˌwäsh\ n 1 : an eye lotion 2 : misleading or deceptive statements, actions, or procedures

eye·wit·ness \-ˈwit-nəs\ n : a person who actually sees something happen

ey·rie chiefly Brit var of AERIE

ey·rir \ˈā-ˌrir\ n, pl **au·rar** \ˈaù-ˌrär\ — see krona at MONEY table

Ez or **Ezr** abbr Ezra

Ezech abbr Ezechiel

Eze·chiel \i-ˈzē-kyəl\ n — see BIBLE table

Ezek abbr Ezekiel

Eze·kiel \i-ˈzē-kyəl\ n — see BIBLE table

e–zine \ˈē-ˌzēn\ n : an online magazine

Ez·ra \ˈez-rə\ n — see BIBLE table

¹f \'ef\ *n, pl* **f's** *or* **fs** \'efs\ *often cap* **1** : the 6th letter of the English alphabet **2** : a grade rating a student's work as failing

²f *abbr, often cap* **1** Fahrenheit **2** false **3** family **4** farad **5** female **6** feminine **7** forte **8** French **9** frequency **10** Friday

³f *symbol* focal length

F *symbol* fluorine

FAA *abbr* Federal Aviation Administration

fab \'fab\ *adj* : FABULOUS

Fa·bi·an \'fā-bē-ən\ *adj* : of, relating to, or being a society of socialists organized in England in 1884 to spread socialist principles gradually — **Fabian** *n* — **Fa·bi·an·ism** *n*

fa·ble \'fā-bəl\ *n* **1** : a legendary story of supernatural happenings **2** : a narration intended to teach a lesson; *esp* : one in which animals speak and act like people **3** : FALSEHOOD

fa·bled \'fā-bəld\ *adj* **1** : FICTITIOUS **2** : told or celebrated in fable

fab·ric \'fa-brik\ *n* [MF *fabrique,* fr. L *fabrica* workshop, structure] **1** : STRUCTURE, FRAMEWORK ⟨the ~ of society⟩ **2** : CLOTH; *also* : a material that resembles cloth

fab·ri·cate \'fa-bri-ˌkāt\ *vb* **-cat·ed; -cat·ing 1** : INVENT, CREATE ⟨to make up for the sake of deception ⟨reporters *fabricating* news stories⟩ **3** : CONSTRUCT, MANUFACTURE — **fab·ri·ca·tion** \ˌfa-bri-'kā-shən\ *n*

fab·u·lous \'fa-byə-ləs\ *adj* **1** : resembling a fable; *also* : INCREDIBLE, MARVELOUS ⟨had a ~ time⟩ **2** : told in or based on fable — **fab·u·lous·ly** *adv*

fac *abbr* **1** facsimile **2** faculty

fa·cade *also* **fa·çade** \fə-'säd\ *n* [F *façade,* fr. It *facciata,* fr. *faccia* face] **1** : the principal face or front of a building **2** : a false, superficial, or artificial appearance ✦ **Synonyms** MASK, DISGUISE, FRONT, GUISE, PRETENSE, VENEER

¹face \'fās\ *n* **1** : the front part of the head **2** : PRESENCE ⟨in the ~ of danger⟩ **3** : facial expression : LOOK ⟨put a sad ~ on⟩ **4** : GRIMACE ⟨made a ~⟩ **5** : outward appearance ⟨looks easy on the ~ of it⟩ **6** : CONFIDENCE; *also* : BOLDNESS **7** : DIGNITY, PRESTIGE ⟨afraid to lose ~⟩ **8** : SURFACE; *esp* : a front, principal, bounding, or contacting surface ⟨~ of a cliff⟩ ⟨the ~s of a cube⟩ ⟨the ~ of a golf club⟩ — **faced** \'fāst, 'fā-səd\ *adj*

²face *vb* **faced; fac·ing 1** : to confront brazenly **2** : to line near the edge esp. with a different material; *also* : to cover the front or surface of ⟨~ a building with marble⟩ **3** : to meet or bring in direct contact or confrontation ⟨*faced* the problem⟩ **4** : to stand or sit with the face toward ⟨~ the sun⟩ **5** : to have the front oriented toward ⟨a house *facing* the

park⟩ **6** : to have as or be a prospect ⟨~ a grim future⟩ **7** : to turn the face or body in a specified direction — **face the music** : to meet the unpleasant consequences of one's actions

face-down \ˌfās-'daun\ *adv* : with the face downward ⟨cards turned ~⟩

face·less \-ləs\ *n* **1** : lacking character or individuality **2** : lacking a face

face–lift \'fās-ˌlift\ *n* **1** : plastic surgery on the face and neck to remove defects (as wrinkles) typical of aging **2** : MODERNIZATION — **face–lift** *vb*

face–off \'fās-ˌȯf\ *n* **1** : a method of beginning play by dropping a puck or ball (as in hockey) between two opposing players each of whom attempts to control it **2** : CONFRONTATION — **face off** *vb*

fac·et \'fa-sət\ *n* [F *facette,* dim. of *face*] **1** : a small plane surface of a cut gem **2** : ASPECT, PHASE

fa·ce·tious \fə-'sē-shəs\ *adj* **1** : joking often inappropriately **2** : JOCULAR, JOCOSE ✦ **Synonyms** WITTY, HUMOROUS — **fa·ce·tious·ly** *adv* — **fa·ce·tious·ness** *n*

¹fa·cial \'fā-shəl\ *adj* **1** : of or relating to the face **2** : used to improve the appearance of the face

²facial *n* : a facial treatment

fac·ile \'fa-səl\ *adj* **1** : easily accomplished, handled, or attained **2** : SIMPLISTIC **3** : readily manifested and often insincere ⟨~ prose⟩ **4** : READY, FLUENT ⟨a ~ writer⟩

fa·cil·i·tate \fə-'si-lə-ˌtāt\ *vb* **-tat·ed; -tat·ing** : to make easier — **fa·cil·i·ta·tion** \-ˌsi-lə-'tā-shən\ *n* — **fa·cil·i·ta·tor** \-'si-lə-ˌtā-tər\ *n*

fa·cil·i·ty \fə-'si-lə-tē\ *n, pl* **-ties 1** : the quality of being easily performed **2** : ease in performance : APTITUDE **3** : PLIANCY **4** : something that makes easier an action, operation, or course of conduct; *also* : REST ROOM — often used in pl. **5** : something (as a hospital) built or installed for a particular purpose

fac·ing \'fā-siŋ\ *n* **1** : a lining at the edge esp. of a garment **2** *pl* : the collar, cuffs, and trimmings of a uniform coat **3** : an ornamental or protective layer **4** : material for facing

fac·sim·i·le \fak-'si-mə-lē\ *n* [L *fac simile* make similar] **1** : an exact copy **2** : a system of transmitting and reproducing printed matter or pictures by means of signals sent over telephone lines

fact \'fakt\ *n* **1** : DEED; *esp* : CRIME ⟨accessory after the ~⟩ **2** : the quality of being actual **3** : something that exists or occurs **4** : a piece of information — **in fact** : in truth

fac·tion \'fak-shən\ *n* : a group or combination (as in a government) acting together within and usu. against a larger body : CLIQUE — **fac·tion·al·ism** \-shə-nə-ˌli-zəm\ *n*

fac·tious \'fak-shəs\ *adj* **1** : of, relating to, or caused by faction **2** : inclined to faction or the formation of factions : causing dissension ✦ *Synonyms* INSUBORDINATE, CONTUMACIOUS, INSURGENT, SEDITIOUS, REBELLIOUS

fac·ti·tious \fak-'ti-shəs\ *adj* : ARTIFICIAL, SHAM ⟨a ~ display of grief⟩

fac·toid \'fak-ˌtȯid\ *n* **1** : an invented fact believed to be true because of its appearance in print **2** : a brief usu. trivial fact

¹**fac·tor** \'fak-tər\ *n* **1** : AGENT **2** : something that actively contributes to a result ⟨a ~ in her decision⟩ **3** : GENE **4** : any of the numbers or symbols in mathematics that when multiplied together form a product; *esp* : any of the integers that divide a given integer without a remainder

²**factor** *vb* **1** : to work as a factor **2** : to find the mathematical factors of and esp. the prime mathematical factors of

¹**fac·to·ri·al** \fak-'tȯr-ē-əl\ *adj* : of, relating to, or being a factor

²**factorial** *n* : the product of all the positive integers from 1 to a given integer *n*

fac·to·ry \'fak-trē, -tə-rē\ *n, pl* **-ries** **1** : a trading post where resident brokers trade **2** : a building or group of buildings used for manufacturing

fac·to·tum \fak-'tō-təm\ *n* [NL, lit., do everything, fr. L *fac* do + *totum* everything] : a person (as a servant) having numerous or varied duties

facts of life : the physiological processes and behavior involved in sex and reproduction

fac·tu·al \'fak-chə-wəl\ *adj* : of or relating to facts; *also* : based on fact — **fac·tu·al·ly** *adv*

fac·ul·ty \'fa-kəl-tē\ *n, pl* **-ties** **1** : ability to act or do : POWER; *also* : natural aptitude **2** : one of the powers of the mind or body ⟨the ~ of hearing⟩ **3** : the teachers in a school or college or one of its divisions

fad \'fad\ *n* : a practice or interest followed for a time with exaggerated zeal : CRAZE — **fad·dish** *adj* — **fad·dish·ly** *adv* — **fad·dist** *n*

¹**fade** \'fād\ *vb* **fad·ed; fad·ing** **1** : WITHER **2** : to lose or cause to lose freshness or brilliance of color **3** : VANISH ⟨a *fading* memory⟩ **4** : to grow dim or faint

²**fade** *n* : a short haircut in which hair on top of the head stands high

FADM *abbr* fleet admiral

fae·cal, fae·ces *chiefly Brit var of* FECAL, FECES

fae·er·ie *also* **fa·ery** \'fā-rē, 'fer-ē\ *n, pl* **fa·er·ies** **1** : FAIRYLAND **2** : FAIRY

¹**fag** \'fag\ *vb* **fagged; fag·ging** **1** : DRUDGE **2** : TIRE, EXHAUST ⟨*fagged* by the work⟩

²**fag** *n* : MENIAL, DRUDGE

³**fag** *n* : an English public-school boy who acts as servant to another

⁴**fag** *vb* : to act as a fag

⁵**fag** *n* : CIGARETTE

fag end *n* **1** : REMNANT **2** : the extreme end **3** : the last part or coarser end of a web of cloth **4** : the untwisted end of a rope

fag·ot *or* **fag·got** \'fa-gət\ *n* : a bundle of sticks or twigs

fag·ot·ing *or* **fag·got·ing** *n* : an embroidery produced by tying threads in hourglass-shaped clusters

Fah *or* **Fahr** *abbr* Fahrenheit

Fahr·en·heit \'fer-ən-ˌhīt\ *adj* : relating to, conforming to, or having a thermometer scale with the boiling point of water at 212 degrees and the freezing point at 32 degrees above zero

fa·ience *or* **fa·ïence** \fā-'äns\ *n* [F] : earthenware decorated with opaque colored glazes

¹**fail** \'fāl\ *vb* **1** : to become feeble; *esp* : to decline in health **2** : to die away **3** : to stop functioning **4** : to fall short ⟨~ed in his duty⟩ **5** : to be or become absent or inadequate **6** : to be unsuccessful esp. in achieving a passing grade **7** : to become bankrupt **8** : DISAPPOINT **9** : NEGLECT ⟨~ed to lock the door⟩

²**fail** *n* : FAILURE ⟨without ~⟩

¹**fail·ing** \'fā-liŋ\ *n* : WEAKNESS, SHORTCOMING

²**failing** *prep* : in the absence or lack of

faille \'fī(-ə)l\ *n* : a somewhat shiny closely woven ribbed fabric (as silk)

fail-safe \'fāl-ˌsāf\ *adj* **1** : incorporating a counteractive feature for a possible source of failure **2** : having no chance of failure — **fail-safe** *n*

fail·ure \'fāl-yər\ *n* **1** : a failing to do or perform **2** : a state of inability to perform a normal function adequately ⟨heart ~⟩; *also* : an abrupt cessation of functioning ⟨a power ~⟩ **3** : a fracturing or giving way under stress **4** : a lack of success **5** : BANKRUPTCY **6** : DEFICIENCY **7** : DETERIORATION, DECAY **8** : one that has failed

¹**fain** \'fān\ *adj* **1** *archaic* : GLAD; *also* : INCLINED **2** : being obliged or compelled

²**fain** *adv* **1** : with pleasure **2** : by preference

¹**faint** \'fānt\ *adj* [ME *faint, feint*, fr. AF, fr. *faindre, feindre* to feign, lose heart] **1** : COWARDLY, SPIRITLESS **2** : weak, dizzy, and likely to faint **3** : lacking vigor or strength : FEEBLE ⟨~ praise⟩ **4** : hardly perceptible ⟨~ handwriting⟩ — **faint·ly** *adv* — **faint·ness** *n*

²**faint** *vb* : to lose consciousness

³**faint** *n* : the action of fainting; *also* : the resulting condition

faint·heart·ed \'fānt-'här-təd\ *adj* : lacking courage : TIMID

¹**fair** \'fer\ *adj* **1** : pleasing in appearance : BEAUTIFUL **2** : superficially pleasing : SPECIOUS **3** : CLEAN, PURE **4** : CLEAR, LEGIBLE **5** : not stormy or cloudy **6** : JUST **7** : conforming with the rules : ALLOWED; *also* : being within the foul lines ⟨~ ball⟩ **8** : open to legitimate pursuit or attack ⟨~ game⟩ **9** : PROMISING, LIKELY ⟨a ~ chance of winning⟩ **10** : favorable to a ship's course ⟨a ~ wind⟩ **11** : light in complexion : BLOND **12** : ADEQUATE **13** : significant in size ⟨a ~ amount of traffic⟩ — **fair·ness** *n*

²**fair** *adv* **1** : in a fair manner ⟨play ~⟩ **2** *chiefly Brit* : FAIRLY 4

³**fair** n 1 : a gathering of buyers and sellers at a stated time and place for trade 2 : a competitive exhibition (as of farm products) 3 : a sale of assorted articles usu. for a charitable purpose ⟨a book ∼⟩ 4 : an exhibition that promotes available services ⟨a job ∼⟩

fair-ground \-ˌgrau̇nd\ n : an area where outdoor fairs, circuses, or exhibitions are held

fair-ing \ˈfer-iŋ\ n : a structure for producing a smooth outline and reducing drag (as on an airplane)

fair-ly \ˈfer-lē\ adv 1 : HANDSOMELY 2 : in a manner of speaking ⟨∼ bursting with pride⟩ 3 : without bias 4 : to a full degree or extent : PLAINLY, DISTINCTLY 5 : SOMEWHAT, RATHER ⟨a ∼ easy job⟩

fair-spo-ken \ˈfer-ˈspō-kən\ adj : pleasant and courteous in speech

fair-trade \-ˈtrād\ adj : of, relating to, or being an agreement between a producer and a seller that branded merchandise will be sold at or above a specified price — **fair-trade** vb

fair-way \-ˌwā\ n : the mowed part of a golf course between tee and green

fairy \ˈfer-ē\ n, pl **fair-ies** [ME fairie fairyland, enchantment, fr. AF faerie, fr. fee fairy, fr. L Fata, goddess of fate, fr. fatum fate] : an imaginary being of folklore and romance usu. having diminutive human form and magic powers — **fairy** adj

fairy-land \-ˌland\ n 1 : the land of fairies 2 : a beautiful or charming place

fairy tale n 1 : a children's story usu. about mythical beings (as fairies) 2 : FIB

fait ac-com-pli \ˈfāt-ˌa-kōⁿ-ˈplē\ n, pl **faits accomplis** \same or -ˈplēz\ [F, accomplished fact] : a thing accomplished and presumably irreversible

faith \ˈfāth\ n, pl **faiths** \ˈfāths, ˈfāthz\ [ME feith, fr. AF feid, fei, fr. L fides] 1 : allegiance to duty or a person : LOYALTY 2 : belief and trust in God 3 : complete trust 4 : a system of religious beliefs — **faith-ful** \-fəl\ adj — **faith-ful-ly** adv — **faith-ful-ness** n

faith-less \ˈfāth-ləs\ adj 1 : DISLOYAL 2 : not to be relied on ◆ **Synonyms** FALSE, TRAITOROUS, TREACHEROUS, UNFAITHFUL — **faith-less-ly** adv — **faith-less-ness** n

fa-ji-ta \fə-ˈhē-tə\ n : a marinated strip usu. of beef or chicken grilled or broiled and served usu. with a flour tortilla and savory fillings

¹**fake** \ˈfāk\ adj : COUNTERFEIT, SHAM

²**fake** n 1 : IMITATION, FRAUD; also : IMPOSTOR 2 : a simulated move in sports (as a pretended pass)

³**fake** vb **faked; fak-ing** 1 : to treat so as to falsify 2 : COUNTERFEIT 3 : to deceive (an opponent) in a sports contest by making a fake — **fak-er** n

fa-kir \fə-ˈkir\ n [Ar faqīr, lit., poor man] 1 : a Muslim mendicant : DERVISH 2 : a wandering Hindu ascetic

fal-con \ˈfal-kən, ˈfȯl-\ n 1 : a hawk trained for use in falconry 2 : any of various swift long-winged long-tailed hawks having a notched beak and usu. inhabiting open areas

fal-con-ry \ˈfal-kən-rē, ˈfȯl-\ n 1 : the art of training hawks to hunt in cooperation with a person 2 : the sport of hunting with hawks — **fal-con-er** n

¹**fall** \ˈfȯl\ vb **fell** \ˈfel\; **fall-en** \ˈfȯ-lən\; **fall-ing** 1 : to descend freely by the force of gravity 2 : to hang freely 3 : to come or go as if by falling ⟨darkness fell⟩ 4 : to become uttered 5 : to lower or become lowered : DROP ⟨her eyes fell⟩ 6 : to leave an erect position suddenly and involuntarily 7 : STUMBLE, STRAY 8 : to drop down wounded or dead esp. in battle 9 : to become captured ⟨the city fell to the enemy⟩ 10 : to suffer ruin, defeat, or failure 11 : to commit an immoral act 12 : to move or extend in a downward direction 13 : SUBSIDE, ABATE 14 : to decline in quality, activity, quantity, or value 15 : to assume a look of shame or dejection ⟨her face fell⟩ 16 : to occur at a certain time 17 : to come by chance 18 : DEVOLVE ⟨the duties fell to him⟩ 19 : to have the proper place or station ⟨the accent ∼s on the first syllable⟩ 20 : to come within the scope of something 21 : to pass from one condition to another ⟨fell ill⟩ 22 : to set about heartily or actively ⟨∼ to work⟩ — **fall all over oneself** or **fall over backward** : to display excessive eagerness — **fall flat** : to produce no response or result — **fall for** 1 : to fall in love with 2 : to become a victim of — **fall from grace** : BACKSLIDE — **fall into line** : to comply with a certain course of action — **fall short** 1 : to be deficient 2 : to fail to attain

²**fall** n 1 : the act of falling 2 : a falling out, off, or away : DROPPING 3 : AUTUMN 4 : a thing or quantity that falls ⟨a light ∼ of snow⟩ 5 : COLLAPSE, DOWNFALL 6 : the surrender or capture of a besieged place 7 : departure from virtue or goodness 8 : SLOPE 9 : WATERFALL — usu. used in pl. 10 : a decrease in size, quantity, degree, or value ⟨a ∼ in price⟩ 11 : the distance which something falls 12 : an act of forcing a wrestler's shoulders to the mat; also : a bout of wrestling

fal-la-cious \fə-ˈlā-shəs\ adj 1 : embodying a fallacy ⟨a ∼ argument⟩ 2 : MISLEADING, DECEPTIVE

fal-la-cy \ˈfa-lə-sē\ n, pl **-cies** 1 : a false or mistaken idea 2 : an often plausible argument using false or illogical reasoning

fall back vb : RETREAT, RECEDE

fall guy n : SCAPEGOAT

fal-li-ble \ˈfa-lə-bəl\ adj 1 : liable to be erroneous 2 : capable of making a mistake — **fal-li-bly** \-blē\ adv

fall-ing-out \ˌfȯl-iŋ-ˈau̇t\ n, pl **fallings-out** or **falling-outs** : QUARREL

falling star n : METEOR

fal-lo-pi-an tube \fə-ˈlō-pē-ən-\ n, often cap F : either of the pair of anatomical tubes that carry the eggs from the ovary to the uterus

fall·out \'fȯl-ˌaut\ *n* **1** : the often radioactive particles that result from a nuclear explosion and descend through the air **2** : a secondary and often lingering effect or result

fall out *vb* : QUARREL

¹fal·low \'fa-(ˌ)lō\ *n* : fallow land; *also* : the state or period of being fallow — **fallow** *vb*

²fallow *adj* **1** : left without tilling or sowing after plowing **2** : DORMANT, INACTIVE ⟨a writer's ∼ period⟩

false \'fȯls\ *adj* **fals·er; fals·est** **1** : not genuine : ARTIFICIAL ⟨∼ teeth⟩ **2** : intentionally untrue **3** : adjusted or made so as to deceive ⟨∼ scales⟩ **4** : tending to mislead : DECEPTIVE ⟨∼ promises⟩ **5** : not true ⟨∼ concepts⟩ **6** : not faithful or loyal : TREACHEROUS **7** : not essential or permanent ⟨∼ front⟩ **8** : inaccurate in pitch **9** : based on mistaken ideas — **false·ly** *adv* — **false·ness** *n* — **fal·si·ty** \'fȯl-sə-tē\ *n*

false·hood \'fȯls-ˌhu̇d\ *n* **1** : LIE **2** : absence of truth or accuracy **3** : the practice of lying

fal·set·to \fȯl-'se-tō\ *n, pl* **-tos** [It, fr. dim. of *falso* false] : an artificially high voice; *esp* : an artificial singing voice that overlaps and extends above the range of the full voice esp. of a tenor

fal·si·fy \'fȯl-sə-ˌfī\ *vb* **-fied; -fy·ing** **1** : to prove to be false **2** : to alter so as to deceive **3** : LIE; *also* : MISREPRESENT — **fal·si·fi·able** \ˌfȯl-sə-'fī-ə-bəl\ *adj* — **fal·si·fi·ca·tion** \ˌfȯl-sə-fə-'kā-shən\ *n*

fal·ter \'fȯl-tər\ *vb* **1** : to move unsteadily : STUMBLE, TOTTER **2** : to hesitate in speech : STAMMER **3** : to hesitate in purpose or action : WAVER, FLINCH **4** : to lose effectiveness ⟨a ∼ing business⟩ — **fal·ter·ing·ly** *adv*

fam *abbr* **1** familiar **2** family

fame \'fām\ *n* : public reputation : RENOWN — **famed** \'fāmd\ *adj*

fa·mil·ial \fə-'mil-yəl\ *adj* **1** : of, relating to, or suggestive of a family **2** : tending to occur in more members of a family than expected by chance alone ⟨a ∼ disorder⟩

¹fa·mil·iar \fə-'mil-yər\ *n* **1** : COMPANION **2** : a spirit held to attend and serve or guard a person **3** : one who frequents a place

²familiar *adj* **1** : closely acquainted : INTIMATE **2** : of or relating to a family **3** : INFORMAL **4** : FORWARD, PRESUMPTUOUS **5** : frequently seen or experienced **6** : of everyday occurrence — **fa·mil·iar·ly** *adv*

fa·mil·iar·ise *Brit var of* FAMILIARIZE

fa·mil·iar·i·ty \fə-ˌmil-'yar-ə-tē, -ˌmi-lē-'er-\ *n, pl* **-ties** **1** : close friendship : INTIMACY **2** : INFORMALITY **3** : an unduly bold or forward act or expression : IMPROPRIETY **4** : close acquaintance with something

fa·mil·iar·ize \fə-'mil-yə-ˌrīz\ *vb* **-ized; -iz·ing** **1** : to make known or familiar **2** : to make thoroughly acquainted

fam·i·ly \'fam-lē, 'fa-mə-\ *n, pl* **-lies** [ME *familie*, fr. L *familia* household, fr. *famu-lus* servant] **1** : a group of individuals living under one roof and under one head : HOUSEHOLD **2** : a group of persons of common ancestry : CLAN **3** : a group of things having common characteristics; *esp* : a group of related plants or animals ranking in biological classification above a genus and below an order **4** : a social unit usu. consisting of one or two parents and their children

family planning *n* : planning intended to determine the number and spacing of one's children by using birth control

family tree *n* : GENEALOGY; *also* : a genealogical diagram

fam·ine \'fa-mən\ *n* **1** : an extreme scarcity of food **2** : a great shortage

fam·ish \'fa-mish\ *vb* **1** : STARVE **2** : to suffer for lack of something necessary

fa·mous \'fā-məs\ *adj* **1** : widely known **2** : honored for achievement **3** : EXCELLENT, FIRST-RATE ♦ **Synonyms** RENOWNED, CELEBRATED, NOTED, NOTORIOUS, DISTINGUISHED, EMINENT, ILLUSTRIOUS

fa·mous·ly *adv* : SPLENDIDLY, EXCELLENTLY

¹fan \'fan\ *n* : a device (as a hand-waved triangular piece or a mechanism with blades) for producing a current of air

²fan *vb* **fanned; fan·ning** **1** : to drive away the chaff from grain by winnowing **2** : to move (air) with or as if with a fan **3** : to direct a current of air upon ⟨∼ a fire⟩ **4** : to stir up to activity : STIMULATE **5** : to spread like a fan **6** : to strike out in baseball

³fan *n* : an enthusiastic follower or admirer

fa·nat·ic \fə-'na-tik\ *or* **fa·nat·i·cal** \-ti-kəl\ *adj* [L *fanaticus* inspired by a deity, frenzied, fr. *fanum* temple] : marked by excessive enthusiasm and often intense uncritical devotion — **fanatic** *n* — **fa·nat·i·cism** \-tə-ˌsi-zəm\ *n*

fan·ci·er \'fan-sē-ər\ *n* **1** : one that has a special liking or interest **2** : a person who breeds or grows some kind of animal or plant for points of excellence

fan·ci·ful \'fan-si-fəl\ *adj* **1** : marked by, existing in, or given to unrestrained imagination or whim rather than reason **2** : curiously made or shaped ⟨a ∼ design⟩ — **fan·ci·ful·ly** *adv*

¹fan·cy \'fan-sē\ *vb* **fan·cied; fan·cy·ing** **1** : LIKE **2** : IMAGINE **3** : to believe without evidence or certainty **4** : to visualize or interpret as

²fancy *n, pl* **fancies** [ME *fantasie, fantsy* imagination, image, preference, fr. AF *fantasie* illusion, fr. L *phantasia*, fr. Gk *phantasia* appearance, imagination] **1** : LIKING, INCLINATION; *also* : LOVE **2** : WHIM, NOTION, IDEA ⟨a passing ∼⟩ **3** : IMAGINATION **4** : TASTE, JUDGMENT ♦ **Synonyms** CAPRICE, CROTCHET, VAGARY

³fancy *adj* **fan·ci·er; -est** **1** : WHIMSICAL **2** : not plain : ORNAMENTAL, POSH **3** : of particular excellence **4** : bred esp. for a showy appearance **5** : EXCESSIVE **6** : executed with technical skill and style — **fan·ci·ly** \'fan-sə-lē\ *adv*

fancy dress *n* : a costume (as for a masquerade) chosen to suit a fancy

fan·cy–free \,fan-sē-'frē\ *adj* : free from amorous attachment; *also* : free to imagine

fan·cy·work \'fan-sē-,wərk\ *n* : ornamental needlework (as embroidery)

fan·dan·go \fan-'daŋ-gō\ *n, pl* **-gos** 1 : a lively Spanish or Spanish-American dance 2 : TOMFOOLERY

fane \'fān\ *n* 1 : TEMPLE 2 : CHURCH

fan·fare \'fan-,fer\ *n* 1 : a flourish of trumpets 2 : a showy display

fang \'faŋ\ *n* : a long sharp tooth; *esp* : a grooved or hollow tooth of a venomous snake — **fanged** \'faŋd\ *adj*

fan·light \'fan-,līt\ *n* : a semicircular window with radiating bars like a fan that is set over a door or window

fan·ny \'fa-nē\ *n, pl* **fannies** : BUTTOCKS

fan·tail \'fan-,tāl\ *n* 1 : a fan-shaped tail or end 2 : an overhang at the stern of a ship

fan·ta·sia \fan-'tā-zhə, -zhē-ə, -zē-ə; ,fan-tə-'zē-ə\ *n* : a musical composition free and fanciful in form

fan·ta·sise *Brit var of* FANTASIZE

fan·ta·size \'fan-tə-,sīz\ *vb* **-sized; -siz·ing** : IMAGINE, DAYDREAM

fan·tas·tic \fan-'tas-tik\ *also* **fan·tas·ti·cal** \-ti-kəl\ *adj* 1 : IMAGINARY, UNREAL 2 : conceived by unrestrained fancy 3 : exceedingly or unbelievably great 4 : ECCENTRIC ✦ *Synonyms* CHIMERICAL, FANCIFUL, IMAGINARY — **fan·tas·ti·cal·ly** \-ti-k(ə-)lē\ *adv*

fan·ta·sy *also* **phan·ta·sy** \'fan-tə-sē\ *n, pl* **-sies** 1 : IMAGINATION, FANCY 2 : a product of the imagination : ILLUSION 3 : FANTASIA — **fantasy** *vb*

FAQ *abbr* frequently asked question

¹**far** \'fär\ *adv* **far·ther** \-thər\ *or* **fur·ther** \'fər-\; **far·thest** *or* **fur·thest** \-thəst\ *n* 1 : at or to a considerable distance in space or time ⟨~ from home⟩ 2 : by a broad interval ⟨~ better⟩ 3 : to or at a definite distance, point, or degree ⟨as ~ as I know⟩ 4 : to an advanced point or extent ⟨go ~ in his field⟩ — **by far** : by a considerable margin — **far and away** : DECIDEDLY — **so far** : until now

²**far** *adj* **farther** *or* **further; farthest** *or* **furthest** 1 : remote in space or time 2 : DIFFERENT 3 : LONG ⟨a ~ journey⟩ 4 : being the more distant of two ⟨on the ~ side of the lake⟩

far·ad \'fer-,ad, -əd\ *n* : a unit of capacitance equal to the capacitance of a capacitor having a potential difference of one volt between its plates when it is charged with one coulomb of electricity

far·away \'fär-ə-,wā\ *adj* 1 : DISTANT, REMOTE ⟨~ lands⟩ 2 : DREAMY

farce \'färs\ *n* 1 : a broadly satirical comedy with an improbable plot 2 : the humor characteristic of farce or pretense 3 : a ridiculous or empty display — **far·ci·cal** \'fär-si-kəl\ *adj*

far cry *n* 1 : a long distance 2 : something notably different ⟨a *far cry* from what we expected⟩

¹**fare** \'fer\ *vb* **fared; far·ing** 1 : GO, TRAVEL 2 : GET ALONG, SUCCEED ⟨*fared* well in math⟩ 3 : EAT, DINE

²**fare** *n* 1 : range of food : DIET; *also* : material provided for use, consumption, or enjoyment 2 : the price charged to transport a person 3 : a person paying a fare : PASSENGER

¹**fare·well** \fer-'wel\ *vb imper* : get along well — used interjectionally to or by one departing

²**farewell** *n* 1 : a wish of well-being at parting : GOOD-BYE 2 : LEAVE-TAKING

³**fare·well** \'fer-,wel\ *adj* : PARTING, FINAL ⟨a ~ concert⟩

far–fetched \'fär-'fecht\ *adj* : not easily or naturally deduced or introduced : IMPROBABLE ⟨a ~ story⟩

far–flung \-'fləŋ\ *adj* : widely spread or distributed ⟨a ~ empire⟩

fa·ri·na \fə-'rē-nə\ *n* [L, meal, flour] : a fine meal (as of wheat) used in puddings or as a breakfast cereal

far·i·na·ceous \,fer-ə-'nā-shəs\ *adj* 1 : having a mealy texture or surface 2 : containing or rich in starch

¹**farm** \'färm\ *n* [ME *ferme* rent, lease, fr. AF, fr. *fermer* to fix, rent, fr. L *firmare* to make firm, fr. *firmus* firm] 1 : a tract of land used for raising crops or livestock 2 : a minor-league subsidiary of a major-league team

²**farm** *vb* : to use (land) as a farm ⟨~ed 200 acres⟩; *also* : to raise crops or livestock — **farm·er** *n*

farm·hand \'färm-,hand\ *n* : a farm laborer

farm·house \-,haůs\ *n* : a dwelling on a farm

farm·ing \'fär-miŋ\ *n* : the occupation or business of a person who farms

farm·land \'färm-,land\ *n* : land used or suitable for farming

farm out *vb* : to turn over (as a task) to another

farm·stead \'färm-,sted\ *n* : a farm with its buildings

farm·yard \-,yärd\ *n* : land around or enclosed by farm buildings

far–off \'fär-'öf\ *adj* : remote in time or space : DISTANT

fa·rouche \fə-'rüsh\ *adj* [F] 1 : WILD 2 : marked by shyness and lack of polish

far–out \'fär-'aůt\ *adj* : very unconventional ⟨~ clothes⟩

far·ra·go \fə-'rä-gō, -'rā-\ *n, pl* **-goes** [L, mixed fodder, mixture] : a confused collection : MIXTURE

far–reach·ing \'fär-'rē-chiŋ\ *adj* : having a wide range or effect

far·ri·er \'fer-ē-ər\ *n* [alter. of ME *ferrour*, fr. AF, blacksmith, fr. *ferrer* to shoe (horses)] : a person who shoes horses

¹**far·row** \'fer-ō\ *vb* : to give birth to a litter of pigs

²**farrow** *n* : a litter of pigs

far·see·ing \'fär-,sē-iŋ\ *adj* 1 : FAR-SIGHTED 1 2 : FARSIGHTED 2

far·sight·ed \'fär-,sī-təd\ *adj* 1 : seeing or able to see to a great distance 2 : JUDICIOUS, WISE, SHREWD 3 : affected with an eye condition in which vision is

better for distant than near objects —
far·sight·ed·ness *n*

¹far·ther \'fär-thər\ *adv* **1** : at or to a greater distance or more advanced point **2** : to a greater degree or extent

²farther *adj* **1** : more distant **2** : ADDITIONAL

far·ther·most \-,mōst\ *adj* : FARTHEST

¹far·thest \'fär-thəst\ *adj* : most distant

²farthest *adv* **1** : to or at the greatest distance : REMOTEST **2** : to the most advanced point **3** : by the greatest degree or extent : MOST

far·thing \'fär-thiŋ\ *n* **1** : a former British monetary unit equal to ¼ of a penny; *also* : a coin representing this unit **2** : something of small value

fas·cia \ *is usu* 'fā-sh(ē-)ə, *2 is usu* 'fa-\ *n, pl* **-ci·ae** \-shē-,ē\ *or* **-cias** : a flat usu. horizontal part (as a band or board) of or on a building **2** : a sheet of connective tissue covering body structures (as muscles)

fas·ci·cle \'fa-si-kəl\ *n* **1** : a small or slender bundle (as of pine needles or nerve fibers) **2** : one of the divisions of a book published in parts — **fas·ci·cled** \-kəld\ *adj*

fas·ci·nate \'fa-sə-,nāt\ *vb* **-nat·ed; -nat·ing** [L *fascinare,* fr. *fascinum* evil spell] **1** : to transfix and hold spellbound by an irresistible power **2** : ALLURE **3** : to be irresistibly attractive — **fas·ci·na·tion** \,fa-sə-'nā-shən\ *n*

fas·cism \'fa-,shi-zəm\ *n, often cap* : a political philosophy, movement, or regime that exalts nation and often race and stands for a centralized autocratic often militaristic government — **fas·cist** \-shist\ *n or adj, often cap* — **fas·cis·tic** \fa-'shis-tik\ *adj, often cap*

¹fash·ion \'fa-shən\ *n* **1** : the make or form of something **2** : MANNER, WAY **3** : a prevailing custom, usage, or style **4** : the prevailing style (as in dress) ✦ *Synonyms* MODE, VOGUE, RAGE, TREND

²fashion *vb* **1** : MOLD, CONSTRUCT **2** : FIT, ADAPT

fash·ion·able \'fa-shə-nə-bəl\ *adj* **1** : dressing or behaving according to fashion : STYLISH **2** : of or relating to the world of fashion \~ resorts\ ✦ *Synonyms* CHIC, MODISH, SMART, SWANK — **fash·ion·ably** \-blē\ *adv*

¹fast \'fast\ *adj* **1** : firmly fixed **2** : tightly shut **3** : adhering firmly **4** : STUCK **5** : STAUNCH \~ friends\ **6** : characterized by quick motion, operation, or effect \a ~ trip\ \a ~ track\ **7** : indicating ahead of the correct time \the clock is ~\ **8** : not easily disturbed : SOUND \a ~ sleep\ **9** : permanently dyed; *also* : being proof against fading \colors ~ to sunlight\ **10** : DISSIPATED, WILD **11** : sexually promiscuous ✦ *Synonyms* RAPID, SWIFT, FLEET, QUICK, SPEEDY, HASTY

²fast *adv* **1** : in a firm or fixed manner \stuck ~ in the mud\ **2** : SOUNDLY, DEEPLY \~ asleep\ **3** : SWIFTLY **4** : RECKLESSLY

³fast *vb* **1** : to abstain from food **2** : to eat sparingly or abstain from some foods

⁴fast *n* **1** : the act or practice of fasting **2** : a time of fasting

fast·back \'fast-,bak\ *n* : an automobile having a roof with a long slope to the rear

fast·ball \-,bȯl\ *n* : a baseball pitch thrown at full speed

fas·ten \'fa-sᵊn\ *vb* **1** : to attach or join by or as if by pinning, tying, or nailing **2** : to make fast : fix securely **3** : to become fixed or joined **4** : to focus attention \~ed onto the newest trends\ — **fas·ten·er** *n*

fas·ten·ing *n* : something that fastens : FASTENER

fast–food \,fast-'füd\ *adj* : specializing in food that is prepared and served quickly \a ~ restaurant\

fast–for·ward \-'fȯr-wərd\ *n* **1** : a function of an electronic device that advances a recording rapidly **2** : a state of rapid advancement — **fast–forward** *vb*

fas·tid·i·ous \fa-'sti-dē-əs\ *adj* **1** : overly difficult to please **2** : showing a meticulous or demanding attitude \~ workmanship\ ✦ *Synonyms* NICE, FINICKY, FUSSY, PARTICULAR, PERSNICKETY, SQUEAMISH — **fas·tid·i·ous·ly** *adv* — **fas·tid·i·ous·ness** *n*

fast·ness \'fast-nəs\ *n* **1** : the quality or state of being fast **2** : a fortified or secure place : STRONGHOLD

fast–talk \'fast-,tȯk\ *vb* : to influence by persuasive and usu. deceptive talk

fast–track \'fast-,trak\ *vb* : to speed up the processing or production of

fast track *n* : a course leading to rapid advancement or success

¹fat \'fat\ *adj* **fat·ter; fat·test** **1** : PLUMP, OBESE **2** : OILY, GREASY **3** : well filled out : BIG **4** : well stocked : ABUNDANT **5** : richly rewarding — **fat·ness** *n*

²fat *n* **1** : animal tissue rich in greasy or oily matter **2** : any of various energy-rich esters that occur naturally in animal fats and in plants and are soluble in organic solvents (as ether) but not in water **3** : the best or richest portion \lived on the ~ of the land\ **4** : OBESITY **5** : excess matter

fa·tal \'fāt-ᵊl\ *adj* **1** : FATEFUL \that ~ day\ **2** : causing death or ruin \a ~ mistake\ — **fa·tal·ly** *adv*

fa·tal·ism \-,i-zəm\ *n* : the belief that events are determined by fate — **fa·tal·ist** \-ist\ *n* — **fa·tal·is·tic** \,fāt-ᵊl-'is-tik\ *adj* — **fa·tal·is·ti·cal·ly** \-ti-k(ə-)lē\ *adv*

fa·tal·i·ty \fā-'ta-lə-tē, fə-\ *n, pl* **-ties** **1** : DEADLINESS **2** : FATE **3** : death resulting from a disaster or accident; *also* : one who suffers such a death

fat·back \'fat-,bak\ *n* : a fatty strip from the back of the hog usu. cured by salting and drying

fat cat *n* **1** : a wealthy contributor to a political campaign **2** : a wealthy privileged person

fate \'fāt\ *n* [ME, fr. MF or L; MF, fr. L *fatum,* lit., what has been spoken, fr. *fari* to speak] **1** : the cause or will that is held to determine events : DESTINY 2 : LOT, FORTUNE 3 : DISASTER; *esp* : DEATH 4 : END, OUTCOME 5 *pl, cap* : the three goddesses of classical mythology who determine the course of human life

fat·ed \'fā-təd\ *adj* : decreed, controlled, or marked by fate

fate·ful \'fāt-fəl\ *adj* 1 : OMINOUS, PROPHETIC 2 : IMPORTANT, DECISIVE 3 : DEADLY, DESTRUCTIVE 4 : determined by fate — **fate·ful·ly** *adv*

fath *abbr* fathom

fat·head \'fat-,hed\ *n* : a stupid person — **fat·head·ed** \-'he-dəd\ *adj*

¹**fa·ther** \'fä-thər\ *n* 1 : a male parent 2 *cap* : God esp. as the first person of the Trinity 3 : FOREFATHER 4 : one deserving the respect and love given to a father 5 *often cap* : an early Christian writer accepted by the church as an authoritative witness to its teaching and practice 6 : ORIGINATOR ⟨the ~ of modern radio⟩; *also* : SOURCE 7 : PRIEST — used esp. as a title 8 : one of the leading men ⟨city ~s⟩ — **fa·ther·hood** \-,hud\ *n* — **fa·ther·less** *adj* — **fa·ther·ly** *adj*

²**father** *vb* 1 : BEGET 2 : to be the founder, producer, or author of 3 : to treat or care for as a father

father–in–law \'fä-thə-rən-,lo\ *n, pl* **fa·thers–in–law** \-thər-zən-\ : the father of one's husband or wife

fa·ther·land \'fä-thər-,land\ *n* 1 : the native land of one's ancestors 2 : one's native land

¹**fath·om** \'fa-thəm\ *n* [ME *fadme*, fr. OE *fæthm* length of the outstretched arms] : a unit of length equal to 6 feet (about 1.8 meters) used esp. for measuring the depth of water

²**fathom** *vb* 1 : to measure by a sounding line 2 : PROBE 3 : to penetrate and come to understand — **fath·om·able** \'fa-thə-mə-bəl\ *adj*

fath·om·less \'fa-thəm-ləs\ *adj* : incapable of being fathomed

¹**fa·tigue** \fə-'tēg\ *n* [F] 1 : manual or menial work performed by military personnel 2 *pl* : the uniform or work clothing worn on fatigue and in the field 3 : weariness from labor or stress 4 : the tendency of a material to break under repeated stress

²**fatigue** *vb* **fa·tigued; fa·tigu·ing** : WEARY, TIRE

fat·ten \'fa-t⁹n\ *vb* : to make or grow fat

Fat Tuesday *n* : MARDI GRAS

¹**fat·ty** \'fa-tē\ *adj* **fat·ti·er; -est** 1 : containing fat esp. in unusual amounts 2 : GREASY

²**fatty** *n, pl* **fat·ties** : a fat person

fatty acid *n* : any of numerous acids that contain only carbon, hydrogen, and oxygen and that occur naturally in fats and various oils

fa·tu·ity \fə-'tü-ə-tē, -'tyü-\ *n, pl* **-ities** : FOOLISHNESS, STUPIDITY

fat·u·ous \'fa-chü-wəs\ *adj* : FOOLISH, INANE, SILLY — **fat·u·ous·ly** *adv*

fau·bourg \fō-'bur\ *n* 1 : a suburb esp. of a French city 2 : a city quarter

fau·ces \'fo-,sēz\ *n pl* [L, throat] : the narrow passage located between the soft palate and the base of the tongue that joins the mouth to the pharynx

fau·cet \'fo-sət, 'fä-\ *n* : a fixture for drawing off a liquid (as from a pipe)

¹**fault** \'folt\ *n* 1 : a weakness in character : FAILING 2 : IMPERFECTION, IMPAIRMENT, DEFECT 3 : an error esp. in service in a net or racket game 4 : MISDEMEANOR; *also* : MISTAKE 5 : responsibility for something wrong 6 : a fracture in the earth's crust accompanied by a displacement of one side relative to the other — **fault·i·ly** \'fol-tə-lē\ *adv* — **fault·less** *adj* — **fault·less·ly** *adv* — **faulty** *adj*

²**fault** *vb* 1 : to commit a fault : ERR 2 : to fracture so as to produce a geologic fault 3 : to find a fault in

fault·find·er \'folt-,fīn-dər\ *n* : a person who tends to find fault or complain

♦ **Synonyms** CRITIC, CARPER, CAVILER, COMPLAINER — **fault·find·ing** *n or adj*

faun \'fon\ *n* : a Roman god similar to but gentler than a satyr

fau·na \'fo-nə\ *n, pl* **faunas** *also* **fau·nae** \-,nē, -,nī\ [NL, fr. L *Fauna*, sister of Faunus (the Roman god of animals)] : animals or animal life esp. of a region, period, or environment — **fau·nal** \-nəl\ *adj*

fau·vism \'fō-,vi-zəm\ *n, often cap* : a movement in painting characterized by vivid colors, free treatment of form, and a vibrant and decorative effect — **fau·vist** \-vist\ *n, often cap*

faux pas \'fō-,pä, fō-'\ *n, pl* **faux pas** *same or* -,päz, -'päz\ [F, lit., false step] : BLUNDER; *esp* : a social blunder

fa·va bean \'fä-və-\ *n* : the large flat edible seed of an Old World vetch; *also* : this plant

¹**fa·vor** \'fā-vər\ *n* 1 : friendly regard shown toward another esp. by a superior 2 : APPROVAL 3 : PARTIALITY 4 : POPULARITY 5 : gracious kindness; *also* : an act of such kindness 6 *pl* : effort in one's behalf 7 : ATTENTION 8 : a token of love (as a ribbon) usu. worn conspicuously 9 : a small gift or decorative item given out at a party 9 : a special privilege 10 : sexual privileges — usu. used in pl. 11 *archaic* : LETTER 12 : BEHALF, INTEREST

²**favor** *vb* 1 : to regard or treat with favor 2 : OBLIGE 3 : ENDOW ⟨~ed by nature⟩ 4 : to treat gently or carefully : SPARE ⟨~ a lame leg⟩ 5 : PREFER 6 : SUPPORT, SUSTAIN 7 : FACILITATE ⟨darkness ~s attack⟩ 8 : RESEMBLE ⟨he ~s his father⟩

fa·vor·able \'fā-və-rə-bəl\ *adj* 1 : APPROVING 2 : HELPFUL, PROMISING, ADVANTAGEOUS ⟨~ weather⟩ — **fa·vor·ably** \-blē\ *adv*

fa·vor·ite \'fā-və-rət, -vrət\ *n* 1 : a person or a thing that is favored above others 2 : a competitor regarded as most likely to win — **favorite** *adj*

favorite son *n* : a candidate supported by the delegates of his state at a presidential nominating convention

fa·vor·it·ism \ˈfā-və-rə-ˌti-zəm\ *n* : PARTIALITY, BIAS

fa·vour *chiefly Brit var of* FAVOR

¹**fawn** \ˈfȯn, ˈfän\ *vb* 1 : to show affection ⟨a dog ~*ing* on its master⟩ 2 : to court favor by a cringing or flattering manner ◆ *Synonyms* GROVEL, KOWTOW, TOADY, TRUCKLE

²**fawn** *n* 1 : a young deer 2 : a light grayish brown — **fawny** \ˈfȯ-nē, ˈfä-\ *adj*

fax \ˈfaks\ *n* 1 : FACSIMILE 2 2 : a device used to send or receive facsimile communications; *also* : such a communication — **fax** *vb*

fay \ˈfā\ *n* : FAIRY, ELF — **fay** *adj*

faze \ˈfāz\ *vb* **fazed; faz·ing** : to disturb the composure or courage of : DAUNT

FBI *abbr* Federal Bureau of Investigation

FCC *abbr* Federal Communications Commission

FD *abbr* fire department

FDA *abbr* Food and Drug Administration

FDIC *abbr* Federal Deposit Insurance Corporation

Fe *symbol* [L *ferrum*] iron

fe·al·ty \ˈfē-(ə)l-tē\ *n, pl* **-ties** : LOYALTY, ALLEGIANCE ◆ *Synonyms* FIDELITY, DEVOTION, FAITHFULNESS, PIETY

¹**fear** \ˈfir\ *vb* 1 : to have a reverent awe of ⟨~ God⟩ 2 : to be afraid of ⟨~s spiders⟩ 3 : to be apprehensive

²**fear** *n* 1 : an unpleasant often strong emotion caused by expectation or awareness of danger; *also* : an instance of or a state marked by this emotion 2 : anxious concern : SOLICITUDE 3 : profound reverence esp. toward God ◆ *Synonyms* DREAD, FRIGHT, ALARM, PANIC, TERROR, TREPIDATION

fear·ful \-fəl\ *adj* 1 : causing fear 2 : filled with fear 3 : showing or caused by fear 4 : extremely bad, intense, or large — **fear·ful·ly** *adv*

fear·less \-ləs\ *adj* : free from fear : BRAVE — **fear·less·ly** *adv* — **fear·less·ness** *n*

fear·some \-səm\ *adj* 1 : causing fear 2 : TIMID 3 : INTENSE ⟨~ determination⟩

fea·si·ble \ˈfē-zə-bəl\ *adj* [ME *faisible*, fr. AF *faisable*, fr. *fais-*, stem of *faire* to make, do] 1 : capable of being done or carried out ⟨a ~ plan⟩ 2 : SUITABLE 3 : REASONABLE, LIKELY ◆ *Synonyms* POSSIBLE, PRACTICABLE, VIABLE, WORKABLE — **fea·si·bil·i·ty** \ˌfē-zə-ˈbi-lə-tē\ *n* — **fea·si·bly** \ˈfē-zə-blē\ *adv*

¹**feast** \ˈfēst\ *n* 1 : an elaborate meal : BANQUET 2 : ABUNDANCE ⟨a ~ of good books⟩ 3 : FESTIVAL 1

²**feast** *vb* 1 : to take part in a feast; *also* : to give a feast for 2 : to enjoy some unusual pleasure or delight 3 : DELIGHT, GRATIFY

feat \ˈfēt\ *n* : DEED, EXPLOIT, ACHIEVEMENT; *esp* : an act notable for courage, skill, endurance, or ingenuity

¹**feath·er** \ˈfe-thər\ *n* 1 : any of the light horny outgrowths that form the external covering of the body of a bird 2 : the vane of an arrow 3 : PLUMAGE 4 : KIND, NATURE ⟨birds of a ~⟩ 5 : AT-

TIRE, DRESS ⟨in full ~⟩ 6 : CONDITION, MOOD ⟨in fine ~⟩ — **feath·ered** \-thərd\ *adj* — **feath·er·less** *adj* —

feath·ery *adj* — **a feather in one's cap** : a mark of distinction : HONOR

²**feather** *vb* 1 : to furnish with a feather ⟨~ an arrow⟩ 2 : to cover, clothe, line, or adorn with or as if with feathers —

feather one's nest : to provide for oneself financially esp. while exploiting a position of trust

feath·er·bed·ding \ˈfe-thər-ˌbe-diŋ\ *n* : the requiring of an employer usu. under a union rule or safety statute to employ more workers than are needed

feath·er·edge \-ˌej\ *n* : a very thin sharp edge

feath·er·weight \-ˌwāt\ *n* : one that is very light in weight; *esp* : a boxer weighing more than 118 but not over 126 pounds

¹**fea·ture** \ˈfē-chər\ *n* [ME *feture*, fr. AF, fr. L *factura* act of making, fr. *facere* to make] 1 : the shape or appearance of the face or its parts 2 : a part of the face : LINEAMENT 3 : a prominent part or characteristic 4 : a special attraction (as in a newspaper) 5 : something offered to the public or advertised as particularly attractive ⟨a new car's ~s⟩ — **fea·ture·less** *adj*

²**feature** *vb* 1 : to picture in the mind : IMAGINE 2 : to give special prominence to ⟨the show ~s new artists⟩ 3 : to play an important part

Feb *abbr* February

fe·brile \ˈfe-ˌbrī(-ə)l\ *adj* : FEVERISH

Feb·ru·ary \ˈfe-b(y)ə-ˌwer-ē, ˈfe-brə-\ *n* [ME *Februarie*, fr. L *Februarius*, fr. *Februa*, pl., feast of purification] : the 2d month of the year

fe·ces \ˈfē-ˌsēz\ *n pl* : bodily waste discharged from the intestine : EXCREMENT — **fe·cal** \-kəl\ *adj*

feck·less \ˈfek-ləs\ *adj* 1 : WEAK, INEFFECTIVE 2 : WORTHLESS, IRRESPONSIBLE

fe·cund \ˈfe-kənd, ˈfē-\ *adj* : FRUITFUL, PROLIFIC — **fe·cun·di·ty** \fi-ˈkən-də-tē, fe-\ *n*

fe·cun·date \ˈfe-kən-ˌdāt, ˈfē-\ *vb* **-dat·ed; -dat·ing** 1 : to make fecund 2 : IMPREGNATE — **fe·cun·da·tion** \ˌfe-kən-ˈdā-shən, ˌfē-\ *n*

fed *abbr* federal; federation

fed·er·al \ˈfe-də-rəl, -drəl\ *adj* 1 : formed by a compact between political units that surrender individual sovereignty to a central authority but retain certain limited powers 2 : of or constituting a form of government in which power is distributed between a central authority and constituent territorial units 3 : of or relating to the central government of a federation 4 *cap* : FEDERALIST 5 *often cap* : of, relating to, or loyal to the federal government or the Union armies of the U.S. in the American Civil War — **fed·er·al·ly** *adv*

Federal *n* : a supporter of the U.S. government in the Civil War; *esp* : a soldier in the federal armies

federal district *n* : a district (as the District of Columbia) set apart as the seat of the central government of a federation

fed·er·al·ism \'fe-də-rə-ˌli-zəm, -drə-\ *n* *often cap* : the distribution of power in an organization (as a government) between a central authority and the constituent units **2** : support or advocacy of federalism **3** *cap* : the principles of the Federalists

fed·er·al·ist \-list\ *n* **1** : an advocate of federalism **2** *often cap* : an advocate of a federal union between the American colonies after the Revolution and of adoption of the U.S. Constitution **3** *cap* : a member of a major political party in the early years of the U.S. favoring a strong centralized national government — **federalist** *adj, often cap*

fed·er·al·ize \'fe-də-rə-ˌlīz, -drə-\ *vb* **-ized; -iz·ing** **1** : to unite in or under a federal system **2** : to bring under the jurisdiction of a federal government

fed·er·ate \'fe-də-ˌrāt\ *vb* **-at·ed; -at·ing** : to join in a federation

fed·er·a·tion \ˌfe-də-'rā-shən\ *n* **1** : a political or societal entity formed by uniting smaller entities **2** : a federal government **3** : a union of organizations **4** : the forming of a federal union

fedn *abbr* federation

fe·do·ra \fi-'dȯr-ə\ *n* : a low soft felt hat with the crown creased lengthwise

fed up *adj* : utterly sated, tired, or disgusted

fee \'fē\ *n* [ME, fr. AF *fé, fief,* of Gmc origin; akin to OE *feoh* cattle, property] **1** : an estate in land held from a feudal lord **2** : an inherited or heritable estate in land **3** : a fixed charge; *also* : a charge for a service

fee·ble \'fē-bəl\ *adj* **fee·bler** \-bə-lər\; **fee·blest** \-bə-ləst\ [ME *feble,* fr. AF, fr. L *flebilis* lamentable, wretched, fr. *flēre* to weep] **1** : DECREPIT, FRAIL **2** : INEFFECTIVE, INADEQUATE ⟨a ~ protest⟩ — **fee·ble·ness** *n* — **fee·bly** \-blē\ *adv*

fee·ble·mind·ed \ˌfē-bəl-'mīn-dəd\ *adj* : lacking normal intelligence — **fee·ble·mind·ed·ness** *n*

¹**feed** \'fēd\ *vb* **fed** \'fed\; **feed·ing** **1** : to give food to; *also* : to give as food **2** : EAT 1; *also* : PREY **3** : to furnish what is necessary to the development or function of **4** : to supply for another to use ⟨~ a pass⟩ ⟨*fed* the actor his lines⟩ — **feed·er** *n*

²**feed** *n* **1** : a usu. large meal **2** : food for livestock **3** : a mechanism for feeding material to a machine

feed·back \'fēd-ˌbak\ *n* **1** : the return to the input of a part of the output of a machine, system, or process **2** : response esp. to one in authority about an activity or policy **3** : sound (as whistling) resulting from the retransmission of an amplified or broadcast signal

feed·lot \'fēd-ˌlät\ *n* : land on which cattle are fattened for market

feed·stuff \-ˌstəf\ *n* : FEED 2

¹**feel** \'fēl\ *vb* **felt** \'felt\; **feel·ing** **1** : to perceive or examine through physical contact : TOUCH, HANDLE **2** : EXPERIENCE; *also* : to suffer from **3** : to ascertain by cautious trial ⟨~ out public sentiment⟩ **4** : to be aware of **5** : to be conscious of an inward impression, state of mind, or physical condition **6** : BELIEVE, THINK ⟨say what you ~⟩ **7** : to search for something with the fingers : GROPE **8** : SEEM ⟨it ~s like spring⟩ **9** : to have sympathy or pity

²**feel** *n* **1** : the sense of touch **2** : SENSATION, FEELING **3** : the quality of a thing as imparted through touch

feel·er \'fē-lər\ *n* **1** : one that feels; *esp* : a tactile organ (as on the head of an insect) **2** : a proposal or remark made to find out the views of other people

¹**feel·ing** \'fē-liŋ\ *n* **1** : the sense of touch; *also* : a sensation perceived by this **2** : a state of mind ⟨a ~ of loneliness⟩ **3** *pl* : general emotional condition : SENSIBILITIES ⟨hurt their ~s⟩ **4** : OPINION, BELIEF **5** : capacity to respond emotionally

²**feeling** *adj* **1** : SENSITIVE; *esp* : easily moved emotionally **2** : expressing emotion or sensitivity — **feel·ing·ly** *adv*

feet *pl of* FOOT

feign \'fān\ *vb* **1** : to give a false appearance of : SHAM ⟨~ illness⟩ **2** : to assert as if true : PRETEND

feint \'fānt\ *n* : something feigned; *esp* : a mock blow or attack intended to distract attention from the real point of attack — **feint** *vb*

feisty \'fī-stē\ *adj* **feist·i·er; -est** : having or showing a lively aggressiveness ⟨a ~ heroine⟩

feld·spar \'feld-ˌspär\ *n* : any of a group of crystalline minerals consisting of silicates of aluminum with another element (as potassium or sodium)

fe·lic·i·tate \fi-'li-sə-ˌtāt\ *vb* **-tat·ed; -tat·ing** : CONGRATULATE — **fe·lic·i·ta·tion** \-ˌli-sə-'tā-shən\ *n*

fe·lic·i·tous \fi-'li-sə-təs\ *adj* **1** : well chosen : APT **2** : PLEASANT, DELIGHTFUL — **fe·lic·i·tous·ly** *adv*

fe·lic·i·ty \fi-'li-sə-tē\ *n, pl* **-ties** **1** : the quality or state of being happy; *esp* : great happiness **2** : something that causes happiness **3** : a pleasing manner or quality esp. in art or language **4** : an apt expression

fe·line \'fē-ˌlīn\ *adj* [L *felinus,* fr. *felis* cat] **1** : of or relating to cats or their kin **2** : SLY, TREACHEROUS **3** : STEALTHY — **feline** *n*

¹**fell** \'fel\ *n* : SKIN, HIDE, PELT

²**fell** *vb* **1** : to cut, beat, or knock down; *also* : KILL **2** : to sew (a seam) by folding one raw edge under the other

³**fell** *past of* FALL

⁴**fell** *adj* : CRUEL, FIERCE; *also* : DEADLY — **in one fell swoop** *also* **at one fell swoop** : all at once : with a single effort

fel·lah \'fe-lə, fə-'lä\ *n, pl* **fel·la·hin** *or* **fel·la·heen** \ˌfe-lə-'hēn\ : a peasant or agricultural laborer in Arab countries (as Egypt or Syria)

fel·la·tio \fə-'lä-shē-ˌō\ *also* **fel·la·tion** \-shən\ *n* : oral stimulation of the penis

fel·low \'fe-lō\ n [ME felawe, fr. OE fēolaga, fr. ON félagi, fr. félag partnership (fr. fē cattle, money) + lag act of laying] **1** : COMRADE, ASSOCIATE **2** : EQUAL, PEER **3** : one of a pair : MATE **4** : a member of an incorporated literary or scientific society **5** : MAN, BOY **6** : BOYFRIEND **7** : a person granted a stipend for advanced study

fellow man n : a kindred human being

fel·low·ship \'fe-lō-,ship\ n **1** : the condition of friendly relationship existing among persons : COMRADESHIP **2** : a community of interest or feeling **3** : a group with similar interests **4** : the position of a fellow (as of a university) **5** : the stipend granted a fellow

fellow traveler n : a sympathetic supporter of another's cause; esp : a person who sympathizes with and often furthers the ideals and program of an organized group (as the Communist party) without joining it

fel·on \'fe-lən\ n **1** : one who has committed a felony **2** : WHITLOW

fel·o·ny \'fe-lə-nē\ n, pl -nies : a serious crime punishable by a heavy sentence — **fe·lo·ni·ous** \fə-'lō-nē-əs\ adj

fel·spar chiefly Brit var of FELDSPAR

¹felt \'felt\ n **1** : a cloth made of wool and fur often mixed with natural or synthetic fibers **2** : a material resembling felt

²felt past and past part of FEEL

fem abbr **1** female **2** feminine

fe·male \'fē-,māl\ adj [ME, alter. of femel, fr. AF femele, fr. ML femella, fr. L, girl, dim. of femina woman] **1** : of, relating to, or being the sex that bears young; also : PISTILLATE **2** : characteristic of girls or women ⟨∼ voices⟩ ✦ Synonyms FEMININE, WOMANLY, WOMANLIKE, WOMANISH, EFFEMINATE — **female** n

¹fem·i·nine \'fe-mə-nən\ adj **1** : of the female sex; also : characteristic of or appropriate or peculiar to women **2** : of, relating to, or constituting the gender that includes most words or grammatical forms referring to females — **fem·i·nin·i·ty** \,fe-mə-'ni-nə-tē\ n

²feminine n : a noun, pronoun, adjective, or inflectional form or class of the feminine gender; also : the feminine gender

fem·i·nism \'fe-mə-,ni-zəm\ n **1** : the theory of the political, economic, and social equality of the sexes **2** : organized activity on behalf of women's rights and interests — **fem·i·nist** \-nist\ n or adj

femme fa·tale \,fem-fə-'tal\ n, pl **femmes fa·tales** \same or -'talz\ [F, lit., disastrous woman] : a seductive woman

fe·mur \'fē-mər\ n, pl **fe·murs** or **fem·o·ra** \'fe-mə-rə\ : the long leg bone extending from the hip to the knee — **fem·o·ral** \'fe-mə-rəl\ adj

¹fen \'fen\ n : low swampy land

²fen \'fən\ n, pl **fen** — see yuan at MONEY table

¹fence \'fens\ n [ME fens, short for defens defense] **1** : a barrier (as of wood or wire) to prevent escape or entry or to mark a boundary **2** : a person who receives stolen goods; also : a place where stolen goods are disposed of — **on the fence** : in a position of neutrality or indecision

²fence vb **fenced; fenc·ing 1** : to enclose with a fence **2** : to keep in or out with a fence **3** : to practice fencing **4** : to use tactics of attack and defense esp. in debate — **fenc·er** n

fenc·ing n **1** : the art or practice of attack and defense with the foil, épée, or saber **2** : the fences of a property or region **3** : material used for building fences

fend \'fend\ vb **1** : to keep or ward off : REPEL **2** : SHIFT ⟨∼ for yourself⟩

fend·er \'fen-dər\ n : a protective device (as a guard over the wheel of an automobile)

fen·es·tra·tion \,fe-nə-'strā-shən\ n : the arrangement and design of windows and doors in a building

Fe·ni·an \'fē-nē-ən\ n : a member of a secret 19th century Irish and Irish-American organization dedicated to overthrowing British rule in Ireland

fen·nel \'fe-n⁰l\ n : a garden plant related to the carrot and grown for its aromatic foliage and seeds

FEPC abbr Fair Employment Practices Commission

fe·ral \'fir-əl, 'fer-\ adj **1** : SAVAGE **2** : WILD **3** : having escaped from domestication and become wild

fer-de-lance \'fer-də-'lans\ n, pl **fer-de-lance** [F, lit., lance iron, spearhead] : a large venomous pit viper of Central and So. America

¹fer·ment \fər-'ment\ vb **1** : to cause or undergo fermentation **2** : to be or cause to be in a state of agitation or intense activity

²fer·ment \'fər-,ment\ n **1** : a living organism (as a yeast) causing fermentation by its enzymes; also : ENZYME **2** : AGITATION, TUMULT

fer·men·ta·tion \,fər-mən-'tā-shən, -,men-\ n **1** : chemical decomposition of an organic substance (as in the souring of milk or the formation of alcohol from sugar) by enzymatic action in the absence of oxygen often with formation of gas **2** : FERMENT 2

fer·mi·um \'fer-mē-əm, 'fər-\ n : an artificially produced radioactive metallic chemical element

fern \'fərn\ n : any of an order of vascular plants resembling seed plants in having roots, stems, and leaflike fronds but reproducing by spores instead of by flowers and seeds

fern·ery \'fər-nə-rē\ n, pl -er·ies **1** : a place for growing ferns **2** : a collection of growing ferns

fe·ro·cious \fə-'rō-shəs\ adj **1** : FIERCE, SAVAGE **2** : extremely intense — **fe·ro·cious·ly** adv — **fe·ro·cious·ness** n

fe·roc·i·ty \fə-'rä-sə-tē\ n : the quality or state of being ferocious

¹fer·ret \'fer-ət\ n : a partially domesticated usu. white European mammal related to the weasels

²ferret \\ *vb* **1** : to hunt game with ferrets **2** : to drive out of a hiding place **3** : to find and bring to light by searching ⟨~ out the truth⟩

fer·ric \'fer-ik\ *adj* : of, relating to, or containing iron

ferric oxide *n* : an oxide of iron found in nature as hematite and as rust and used esp. as a pigment, for polishing, and in magnetic materials

Fer·ris wheel \'fer-əs-\ *n* : an amusement device consisting of a large upright power-driven wheel with seats that remain horizontal around its rim

fer·ro·mag·net·ic \,fer-ō-mag-'ne-tik\ *adj* : of or relating to substances that are easily magnetized

fer·rous \'fer-əs\ *adj* : of, relating to, or containing iron

fer·rule \'fer-əl\ *n* : a metal ring or cap around a slender wooden shaft to prevent splitting

¹fer·ry \'fer-ē\ *vb* **fer·ried; fer·ry·ing** [ME *ferien*, fr. OE *ferian* to carry, convey] **1** : to carry by boat across a body of water **2** : to cross by a ferry **3** : to convey from one place to another

²ferry *n, pl* **ferries** **1** : a place where persons or things are ferried **2** : FERRYBOAT

fer·ry·boat \'fer-ē-,bōt\ *n* : a boat used in ferrying

fer·tile \'fər-t⁰l\ *adj* **1** : producing plentifully : PRODUCTIVE ⟨~ soils⟩ ⟨a ~ mind⟩ **2** : capable of developing or reproducing ⟨~ seed⟩ ⟨a ~ bull⟩ ♦ *Synonyms* FRUITFUL, PROLIFIC, FECUND, PRODUCTIVE — **fer·til·i·ty** \(,)fər-'ti-lə-tē\ *n*

fer·til·ize \'fər-tə-,līz\ *vb* **-ized; -iz·ing** **1** : to unite with in the process of fertilization ⟨a sperm ~s an egg⟩ **2** : to apply fertilizer to — **fer·til·i·za·tion** \,fər-tə-lə-'zā-shən\ *n*

fer·til·iz·er \'fər-tə-,lī-zər\ *n* : material (as manure or a chemical mixture) for enriching land

fer·ule \'fer-əl\ *n* : a rod or ruler used to punish children

fer·ven·cy \'fər-vən-sē\ *n, pl* **-cies** : FERVOR

fer·vent \'fər-vənt\ *adj* **1** : very hot : GLOWING **2** : marked by great intensity of feeling ♦ *Synonyms* IMPASSIONED, ARDENT, FERVID, FIERY, PASSIONATE — **fer·vent·ly** *adv*

fer·vid \-vəd\ *adj* **1** : very hot **2** : ARDENT, ZEALOUS — **fer·vid·ly** *adv*

fer·vor \'fər-vər\ *n* **1** : intense heat **2** : intensity of feeling or expression

fer·vour *chiefly Brit var of* FERVOR

fes·cue \'fes-kyü\ *n* : any of a genus of tufted perennial grasses

fes·tal \'fes-t⁰l\ *adj* : FESTIVE

fes·ter \'fes-tər\ *vb* **1** : to form pus **2** : PUTREFY, ROT **3** : RANKLE

fes·ti·val \'fes-tə-vəl\ *n* **1** : a time of celebration marked by special observances; *esp* : an occasion marked with religious ceremonies **2** : a periodic season or program of cultural events or entertainment ⟨a dance ~⟩

fes·tive \'fes-tiv\ *adj* **1** : of, relating to, or suitable for a feast or festival **2** : JOYFUL, GAY — **fes·tive·ly** *adv*

fes·tiv·i·ty \fes-'ti-və-tē\ *n, pl* **-ties** **1** : FESTIVAL **1** **2** : the quality or state of being festive **3** : festive activity

¹fes·toon \fes-'tün\ *n* [F *feston*, fr. It *festone*, fr. *festa* festival] **1** : a decorative chain or strip hanging between two points **2** : a carved, molded, or painted ornament representing a decorative chain

²festoon *vb* **1** : to hang or form festoons on **2** : to shape into festoons

fe·ta \'fe-tə\ *n* : a white crumbly Greek cheese made from sheep's or goat's milk

fe·tal \'fē-t⁰l\ *adj* : of, relating to, or being a fetus

fetch \'fech\ *vb* **1** : to go or come after and bring or take back ⟨teach a dog to ~ a stick⟩ **2** : to bring in (as a price) **3** : to cause to come : bring out ⟨~ed tears from the eyes⟩ **4** : to give by striking ⟨~ him a blow⟩

fetch·ing *adj* : ATTRACTIVE, PLEASING ⟨a ~ smile⟩ — **fetch·ing·ly** *adv*

¹fete *or* **fête** \'fāt, 'fet\ *n* [F *fête*, fr. OF *feste*] **1** : FESTIVAL **2** : a large elaborate entertainment or party

²fete *or* **fête** *vb* **fet·ed** *or* **fêt·ed; fet·ing** *or* **fêt·ing** **1** : to honor or commemorate with a fete **2** : to pay high honor to

fet·id \'fe-təd\ *adj* : having an offensive smell : STINKING

fe·tish *also* **fe·tich** \'fe-tish\ *n* [F & Pg; F *fétiche*, fr. Pg *feitiço*, fr. *feitiço* artificial, false, fr. L *facticius* factitious] **1** : an object (as an idol or image) believed to have magical powers (as in curing disease) **2** : an object of unreasoning devotion or concern **3** : an object whose real or fantasied presence is psychologically necessary for sexual gratification

fe·tish·ism \-ti-,shi-zəm\ *n* **1** : belief in or devotion to fetishes **2** : the pathological transfer of sexual interest and gratification to a fetish — **fe·tish·ist** \-shist\ *n* — **fe·tish·is·tic** \,fe-ti-'shis-tik\ *adj*

fe·tish·ize \-ti-,shīz\ *vb* **-ized -iz·ing** : to make a fetish of

fet·lock \'fet-,läk\ *n* : a projection on the back of a horse's leg above the hoof; *also* : a tuft of hair on this

fet·ter \'fe-tər\ *n* **1** : a chain or shackle for the feet **2** : something that confines : RESTRAINT — **fetter** *vb*

fet·tle \'fe-t⁰l\ *n* : a state of fitness or order : CONDITION ⟨in fine ~⟩

fe·tus \'fē-təs\ *n* : an unborn or unhatched vertebrate esp. after its basic structure is laid down; *esp* : a developing human in the uterus from usu. three months after conception to birth

feud \'fyüd\ *n* : a prolonged quarrel; *esp* : a lasting conflict between families or clans marked by violent attacks made for revenge — **feud** *vb*

feu·dal \'fyü-d⁰l\ *adj* **1** : of, relating to, or having the characteristics of a medieval fee **2** : of, relating to, or characteristic of feudalism

feu·dal·ism \'fyü-də-,li-zəm\ *n* : a system of political organization prevailing in medieval Europe in which a vassal renders service to a lord and receives protection and land in return; *also* : a similar political or social system — **feu·dal·is·tic** \ˌfyü-dᵊl-ˈis-tik\ *adj*

¹**feu·da·to·ry** \ˈfyü-də-ˌtȯr-ē\ *adj* : owing feudal allegiance

²**feudatory** *n, pl* **-ries** **1** : FIEF **2** : a person who holds lands by feudal law or usage

fe·ver \ˈfē-vər\ *n* **1** : a rise in body temperature above the normal; *also* : a disease of which this is a chief symptom **2** : a state of heightened emotion or activity **3** : CRAZE — **fe·ver·ish** *adj* — **fe·ver·ish·ly** *adv*

¹**few** \ˈfyü\ *pron* : not many : a small number

²**few** *adj* **1** : consisting of or amounting to a small number **2** : not many but some ⟨caught a ∼ fish⟩ — **few·ness** *n* — **few and far between** : RARE **3**

³**few** *n* **1** : a small number of units or individuals ⟨a ∼ of them⟩ **2** : a special limited number ⟨among the ∼⟩

few·er \ˈfyü-ər\ *pron* : a smaller number of persons or things

fey \ˈfā\ *adj,* **1** *chiefly Scot* : fated to die; *also* : marked by a foreboding of death or calamity **2** : able to see into the future : VISIONARY **3** : marked by an otherworldly air or attitude **4** : CRAZY, TOUCHED

fez \ˈfez\ *n, pl* **fez·zes** *also* **fez·es** : a round red felt hat that has a flat top and a tassel but no brim

ff *abbr* **1** folios **2** [following] and the following ones **3** fortissimo

FHA *abbr* Federal Housing Administration

fi·an·cé \ˌfē-ˌän-ˈsā\ *n* [F, fr. MF, fr. pp. of *fiancer* to promise, betroth, fr. OF *fiancier,* fr. *fiance* promise, trust, fr. *fier* to trust, ultim. fr. L *fidere*] : a man engaged to be married

fi·an·cée \ˌfē-ˌän-ˈsā\ *n* : a woman engaged to be married

fi·as·co \fē-ˈas-kō\ *n, pl* **-coes** [F] : a complete failure

fi·at \ˈfē-ət, -ˌat, -ˌät; ˈfī-ət, -ˌat\ *n* [L, let it be done] : an authoritative and often arbitrary order or decree

¹**fib** \ˈfib\ *n* : a trivial or childish lie

²**fib** *vb* **fibbed; fib·bing** : to tell a fib — **fib·ber** *n*

fi·ber \ˈfī-bər\ *n* **1** : a threadlike substance or structure (as a muscle cell or fine root); *esp* : a natural (as wool or flax) or artificial (as rayon) filament capable of being spun or woven **2** : indigestible material in food that stimulates the intestine to move its contents along **3** : an element that gives texture or substance **4** : basic toughness : STRENGTH — **fi·brous** \-brəs\ *adj*

fi·ber·board \ˈfī-bər-ˌbȯrd\ *n* : a material made by compressing fibers (as of wood) into stiff sheets

fi·ber·fill \-ˌfil\ *n* : synthetic fibers used as a filling material (as for cushions)

fi·ber·glass \-ˌglas\ *n* : glass in fibrous

form used in making various products (as insulation)

fiber optics *n* **1** *pl* : thin transparent fibers of glass or plastic that are enclosed by a less refractive material and that transmit light by internal reflection; *also* : a bundle of such fibers used in an instrument **2** : the technique of the use of fiber optics — **fiber–optic** *adj*

fibre *chiefly Brit var of* FIBER

fi·bril \ˈfī-brəl, ˈfi-\ *n* : a small fiber

fi·bril·la·tion \ˌfi-brə-ˈlā-shən, ˌfī-\ *n* : rapid irregular contractions of the heart muscle fibers resulting in a lack of synchronism between heartbeat and pulse — **fib·ril·late** \ˈfi-brə-ˌlāt, ˈfī-\ *vb*

fi·brin \ˈfī-brən\ *n* : a white insoluble fibrous protein formed in the clotting of blood

¹**fi·broid** \ˈfī-ˌbrȯid, ˈfi-\ *adj* : resembling, forming, or consisting of fibrous tissue ⟨∼ tumors⟩

²**fibroid** *n* : a benign tumor of the uterus

fi·bro·my·al·gia \ˌfī-ˌbrō-ˌmī-ˈal-jə\ *n* : any of a group of rheumatic disorders affecting soft tissues (as muscles or tendons)

fi·bro·sis \fī-ˈbrō-səs\ *n* : a condition marked by abnormal increase of fiber-containing tissue

fib·u·la \ˈfi-byə-lə\ *n, pl* **-lae** \-lē, -ˌlī\ *or* **-las** : the outer and usu. the smaller of the two bones between the knee and ankle — **fib·u·lar** \-lər\ *adj*

FICA *abbr* Federal Insurance Contributions Act

-fication *n comb form* : making : production ⟨simpli*fication*⟩

fiche \ˈfēsh\ *n, pl* **fiche** : MICROFICHE

fi·chu \ˈfi-shü\ *n* [F] : a woman's light triangular scarf draped over the shoulders and fastened in front

fick·le \ˈfi-kəl\ *adj* : not firm or steadfast in disposition or character : INCONSTANT — **fick·le·ness** *n*

fic·tion \ˈfik-shən\ *n* **1** : something (as a story) invented by the imagination **2** : fictitious literature (as novels) — **fic·tion·al** \-shə-nəl\ *adj* — **fic·tion·al·ly** *adv*

fic·ti·tious \fik-ˈti-shəs\ *adj* **1** : of, relating to, or characteristic of fiction : IMAGINARY **2** : FALSE, ASSUMED ⟨a ∼ name⟩ **3** : FEIGNED ♦ **Synonyms** CHIMERICAL, FANCIFUL, FANTASTIC, UNREAL

¹**fid·dle** \ˈfi-dᵊl\ *n* : VIOLIN

²**fiddle** *vb* **fid·dled; fid·dling** **1** : to play on a fiddle **2** : to move the hands or fingers restlessly **3** : PUTTER **4** : MEDDLE, TAMPER — **fid·dler** *n*

fid·dle·head \ˈfi-dᵊl-ˌhed\ *n* : one of the young unfurling fronds of some ferns that are often eaten as greens

fiddler crab *n* : any of a genus of burrowing crabs with one claw much enlarged in the male

fid·dle·stick \ˈfi-dᵊl-ˌstik\ *n* **1** : a violin bow **2** *pl* : NONSENSE — used as an interjection

fi·del·i·ty \fə-ˈde-lə-tē, fī-\ *n, pl* **-ties** **1** : the quality or state of being faithful **2** : ACCURACY ⟨∼ in sound reproduction⟩

♦ *Synonyms* ALLEGIANCE, LOYALTY, DEVOTION, FEALTY

¹fidg·et \'fi-jət\ *n* **1** : uneasiness or restlessness as shown by nervous movements — usu. used in pl. **2** : one that fidgets — **fidg·ety** *adj*

²fidget *vb* : to move or cause to move or act restlessly or nervously

fi·du·ci·ar·y \fə-'dü-shē-₁er-ē, -'dyü-, -shə-rē\ *adj* **1** : involving a confidence or trust **2** : held or holding in trust for another ⟨∼ accounts⟩ — **fiduciary** *n*

fie \'fī\ *interj* — used to express disgust or disapproval

fief \'fēf\ *n* [F, fr. OF] : a feudal estate : FEE

¹field \'fēld\ *n* **1** : open country **2** : a piece of cleared land for cultivation or pasture **3** : a piece of land yielding some special product **4** : the place where a battle is fought; *also* : BATTLE **5** : an area, division, or sphere of activity ⟨the ∼ of science⟩ ⟨salesmen in the ∼⟩ **6** : an area for military exercises **7** : an area for sports **8** : a background on which something is drawn or projected ⟨a flag with white stars on a ∼ of blue⟩ **9** : a region or space in which a given effect (as magnetism) exists — **field** *adj*

²field *vb* **1** : to handle a batted or thrown baseball while on defense **2** : to put into the field **3** : to answer satisfactorily ⟨∼ a tough question⟩ — **field·er** *n*

field day *n* **1** : a day devoted to outdoor sports and athletic competition **2** : a time of extraordinary pleasure or opportunity

field event *n* : a track-and-field event (as weight-throwing) other than a race

field glass *n* : a hand-held binocular telescope — usu. used in pl.

field guide *n* : a manual for identifying natural objects, plants, or animals

field hockey *n* : a field game played between two teams of 11 players each whose object is to knock a ball into the opponent's goal with a curved stick

field marshal *n* : an officer (as in the British army) of the highest rank

field–test \-₁test\ *vb* : to test (as a new product) in actual situations reflecting intended use — **field test** *n*

fiend \'fēnd\ *n* **1** : DEVIL 1 **2** : DEMON **3** : an extremely wicked or cruel person **4** : a person excessively devoted to a pursuit ⟨a golf ∼⟩ **5** : ADDICT ⟨a dope ∼⟩ — **fiend·ish** *adj* — **fiend·ish·ly** *adv*

fierce \'firs\ *adj* **fierc·er; fierc·est 1** : violently hostile or aggressive in temperament **2** : PUGNACIOUS **3** : INTENSE ⟨∼ pain⟩ **4** : furiously active or determined **5** : wild or menacing in appearance ♦ *Synonyms* FEROCIOUS, BARBAROUS, SAVAGE, CRUEL — **fierce·ly** *adv* — **fierce·ness** *n*

fi·ery \'fī-ə-rē\ *adj* **fi·er·i·er; -est 1** : consisting of fire **2** : BURNING, BLAZING **3** : FLAMMABLE **4** : hot like a fire : INFLAMED, FEVERISH **5** : RED ⟨a ∼ sunset⟩ **6** : full of emotion or spirit **7** : IRRITABLE — **fi·eri·ness** \-rē-nəs\ *n*

fi·es·ta \fē-'es-tə\ *n* [Sp] : FESTIVAL

fife \'fīf\ *n* [G *Pfeife* pipe, fife] : a small flute

FIFO *abbr* first in, first out

fif·teen \fif-'tēn\ *n* : one more than 14 — **fifteen** *adj or pron* — **fif·teenth** \-'tēnth\ *adj or n*

fifth \'fifth\ *n* **1** : one that is number five in a countable series **2** : one of five equal parts of something **3** : a unit of measure for liquor equal to ⅕ U.S. gallon (0.757 liter) — **fifth** *adj or adv*

fifth column *n* : a group of secret supporters of a nation's enemy that engage in espionage or sabotage within the country — **fifth columnist** *n*

fifth wheel *n* : one that is unnecessary and often burdensome

fif·ty \'fif-tē\ *n, pl* **fifties** : five times 10 — **fif·ti·eth** \-tē-əth\ *adj or n* — **fifty** *adj or pron*

fif·ty–fif·ty \₁fif-tē-'fif-tē\ *adj* **1** : shared equally ⟨a ∼ proposition⟩ **2** : half favorable and half unfavorable

¹fig \'fig\ *n* : a soft usu. pear-shaped edible fruit of a tree related to the mulberry; *also* : a tree bearing figs

²fig *abbr* **1** figurative; figuratively **2** figure

¹fight \'fīt\ *vb* **fought** \'fȯt\; **fight·ing 1** : to contend against another in battle or physical combat **2** : BOX **3** : to put forth a determined effort **4** : STRUGGLE, CONTEND **5** : to attempt to prevent the success or effectiveness of **6** : WAGE **7** : to gain by struggle

²fight *n* **1** : a hostile encounter : BATTLE **2** : a boxing match **3** : a verbal disagreement **4** : a struggle for a goal or an objective **5** : strength or disposition for fighting ⟨full of ∼⟩

fight·er \'fī-tər\ *n* **1** : one that fights; *esp* : WARRIOR **2** : BOXER 1 **3** : a fast maneuverable warplane for destroying enemy aircraft

fig·ment \'fig-mənt\ *n* : something imagined or made up

fig·u·ra·tion \₁fi-gyə-'rā-shən, -gə-\ *n* **1** : FORM, OUTLINE **2** : an act or instance of representation in figures and shapes

fig·u·ra·tive \'fi-gyə-rə-tiv, -gə-\ *adj* **1** : EMBLEMATIC **2** : SYMBOLIC, METAPHORICAL ⟨∼ language⟩ — **fig·u·ra·tive·ly** *adv*

¹fig·ure \'fi-gyər, -gər\ *n* [ME, fr. AF, fr. L *figura*, fr. *fingere* to shape] **1** : NUMERAL **2** *pl* : arithmetical calculations **3** : a written or printed character **4** : PRICE, SUM ⟨sold at a low ∼⟩ **5** : a combination of points, lines, or surfaces in geometry ⟨a circle is a closed plane ∼⟩ **6** : SHAPE, FORM, OUTLINE **7** : the graphic representation of a form esp. of a person **8** : a diagram or pictorial illustration of textual matter **9** : PATTERN, DESIGN **10** : appearance or impression produced ⟨they cut quite a ∼⟩ **11** : a series of movements (as in a dance) **12** : PERSONAGE

²figure *vb* **fig·ured; fig·ur·ing 1** : to represent by or as if by a figure or outline **2**

: to decorate with a pattern **3** : to indicate or represent by numerals **4** : REGARD, CONSIDER **5** : to be or appear important or conspicuous **6** : COMPUTE, CALCULATE

fig·ure·head \'fi-gyər-ˌhed, -gər-\ *n* **1** : a figure on the bow of a ship **2** : a head or chief in name only

figure of speech : a form of expression (as a simile or metaphor) that often compares or identifies one thing with another to convey meaning or heighten effect

figure out *vb* **1** : FIND OUT, DISCOVER **2** : SOLVE

figure skating *n* : skating that includes various jumps, spins, and dance movements

fig·u·rine \ˌfi-gyə-'rēn, -gə-\ *n* : a small carved or molded figure

fil·a·ment \'fi-lə-mənt\ *n* : a fine thread or threadlike object, part, or process — **fil·a·men·tous** \ˌfi-lə-'men-təs\ *adj*

fil·bert \'fil-bərt\ *n* : the sweet thick-shelled nut of either of two European hazels; *also* : a shrub or small tree bearing filberts

filch \'filch\ *vb* : to steal furtively

¹**file** \'fī(-ə)l\ *n* : a usu. steel tool with a ridged or toothed surface used esp. for smoothing a hard substance

²**file** *vb* **filed; fil·ing** : to rub, smooth, or cut away with a file

³**file** *vb* **filed; fil·ing** [ME, fr. ML *filare* to string documents on a string or wire, fr. *filum* file of documents, lit., thread, fr. L] **1** : to arrange in order **2** : to enter or record officially or as prescribed by law ⟨~ a lawsuit⟩ **3** : to send (copy) to a newspaper

⁴**file** *n* **1** : a device (as a folder or cabinet) by means of which papers may be kept in order **2** : a collection of papers or publications usu. arranged or classified **3** : a collection of data (as text) treated by a computer as a unit

⁵**file** *n* : a row of persons, animals, or things arranged one behind the other

⁶**file** *vb* **filed; fil·ing** : to march or proceed in file

fi·let mi·gnon \ˌfi-(ˌ)lā-mēn-'yōⁿ, fi-ˌlā-\ *n*, *pl* **filets mignons** \-(ˌ)lā-mēn-'yōⁿz, -ˌlā-\ [F, lit., dainty fillet] : a thick slice of beef cut from the narrow end of a beef tenderloin

fil·ial \'fi-lē-əl, 'fil-yəl\ *adj* : of, relating to, or befitting a son or daughter

fil·i·bus·ter \'fi-lə-ˌbəs-tər\ *n* [Sp *filibustero*, lit., freebooter] **1** : a military adventurer; *esp* : an American engaged in fomenting 19th century Latin American uprisings **2** : the use of delaying tactics (as extremely long speeches) esp. in a legislative assembly; *also* : an instance of this practice — **filibuster** *vb* — **fil·i·bus·ter·er** *n*

fil·i·cide \'fi-lə-ˌsīd\ *n* : the murder of one's own daughter or son

fil·i·gree \'fi-lə-ˌgrē\ *n* [F *filigrane*] : ornamental openwork (as of fine wire) — **fil·i·greed** \-ˌgrēd\ *adj*

fil·ing \'fī-liŋ\ *n* **1** : the act or instance of using a file **2** : a small piece scraped off by a file ⟨iron ~s⟩

Fil·i·pi·no \ˌfi-lə-'pē-nō\ *n, pl* **Filipinos** : a native or inhabitant of the Philippines — **Filipino** *adj*

¹**fill** \'fil\ *vb* **1** : to make or become full **2** : to stop up : PLUG ⟨~ a cavity⟩ **3** : FEED, SATIATE **4** : SATISFY, FULFILL ⟨~ all requirements⟩ **5** : to occupy fully **6** : to spread through ⟨laughter ~ed the room⟩ **7** : OCCUPY ⟨~ the office of president⟩ **8** : to put a person in ⟨~ a vacancy⟩ **9** : to supply as directed ⟨~ a prescription⟩

²**fill** *n* **1** : a full supply; *esp* : a quantity that satisfies or satiates **2** : material used for filling a low place

¹**fill·er** \'fi-lər\ *n* **1** : one that fills **2** : a substance added to another substance (as to increase bulk or weight) **3** : a material used for filling cracks and pores in wood before painting

²**fill·er** \'fi-ˌler\ *n, pl* **fillers** *or* **filler** — see *forint* at MONEY table

¹**fil·let** \'fi-lət, *in sense 2* fi-'lā, 'fi-(ˌ)lā\ *also* **fi·let** \fi-'lā, 'fi-(ˌ)lā\ *n* [ME *filet*, fr. AF, dim. of *fil* thread] **1** : a narrow band, strip, or ribbon **2** : a piece or slice of boneless meat or fish; *esp* : the tenderloin of beef

²**fil·let** \'fi-lət, *in sense 2 also* fi-'lā, 'fi-(ˌ)lā\ *vb* **1** : to bind or adorn with or as if with a fillet **2** : to cut into fillets

fill in *vb* **1** : to provide necessary or recent information **2** : to serve as a temporary substitute

fill·ing \'fi-liŋ\ *n* **1** : material used to fill something ⟨a ~ for a tooth⟩ **2** : the yarn interlacing the warp in a fabric **3** : a food mixture used to fill pastry or sandwiches

filling station *n* : GAS STATION

fil·lip \'fi-ləp\ *n* **1** : a blow or gesture made by a flick or snap of the finger across the thumb **2** : something that serves to arouse or excite — **fillip** *vb*

fill–up \'fil-ˌəp\ *n* : an act or instance of filling something

fil·ly \'fi-lē\ *n, pl* **fillies** : a young female horse usu. less than four years old

¹**film** \'film\ *n* **1** : a thin skin or membrane **2** : a thin coating or layer **3** : a flexible strip of chemically treated material used in taking pictures **4** : MOTION PICTURE — **filmy** *adj*

²**film** *vb* **1** : to cover with a film **2** : to make a motion picture of

film·dom \'film-dəm\ *n* : the motion-picture industry

film·og·ra·phy \film-'mä-grə-fē\ *n, pl* **-phies** : a list of motion pictures featuring the work of a film figure or a particular topic

film·strip \'film-ˌstrip\ *n* : a strip of film bearing a sequence of images for projection as still pictures

¹**fils** \'fēs\ *n* [F] : SON — used after a family name to distinguish a son from his father

²**fils** \'fils\ *n, pl* **fils** — see *dinar, dirham, rial* at MONEY table

¹**fil·ter** \'fil-tər\ *n* **1** : a porous material through which a fluid is passed to separate out matter in suspension; *also* : a device containing such material **2** : a device for suppressing waves of certain frequencies; *esp* : one (as for a camera) that absorbs light of certain colors **3** : software for sorting or blocking certain online material

²**filter** *vb* **1** : to remove by means of a filter **2** : to pass through a filter — **fil·ter·able** *also* **fil·tra·ble** \-tə-rə-bəl, -trə-\ *adj* — **fil·tra·tion** \fil-'trā-shən\ *n*

filth \'filth\ *n* [ME, fr. OE *fylth*, fr. *ful* foul] **1** : foul matter; *esp* : loathsome dirt or refuse **2** : moral corruption **3** : OBSCENITY — **filth·i·ness** *n* — **filthy** \'fil-thē\ *adj*

filthy *adv* : VERY, EXTREMELY ⟨∼ dirty⟩ ⟨∼ rich⟩

fil·trate \'fil-ˌtrāt\ *n* : fluid that has passed through a filter

¹**fin** \'fin\ *n* **1** : a thin external process by which an aquatic animal (as a fish) moves through water **2** : a fin-shaped part (as on an airplane) **3** : FLIPPER 2 — **finned** \'find\ *adj*

²**fin** *abbr* **1** finance; financial **2** finish

fi·na·gle \fə-'nā-gəl\ *vb* **-gled; -gling** **1** : to obtain by indirect or dishonest means : WANGLE **2** : to use devious dishonest methods to achieve one's ends — **fi·na·gler** *n*

¹**fi·nal** \'fī-nᵊl\ *adj* **1** : not to be altered or undone ⟨all sales are ∼⟩ **2** : ULTIMATE **3** : relating to or occurring at the end or conclusion — **fi·nal·i·ty** \fī-'na-lə-tē, fə-\ *n* — **fi·nal·ly** *adv*

²**final** *n* **1** : a deciding match or game — usu. used in pl. **2** : the last examination in a course — often used in pl.

fi·na·le \fə-'na-lē, fi-'nä-\ *n* : the close or end of something; *esp* : the last section of a musical composition

fi·nal·ise *Brit var of* FINALIZE

fi·nal·ist \'fī-nə-list\ *n* : a contestant in the finals of a competition

fi·nal·ize \'fī-nə-ˌlīz\ *vb* **-ized; -iz·ing** : to put in final or finished form

¹**fi·nance** \fə-'nans, 'fī-ˌnans\ *n* [ME, ending, payment, fr. AF, fr. *finer* to end, pay, fr. *fin* end, fr. L *finis* boundary, end] **1** *pl* : money resources available esp. to a government or business **2** : management of money affairs

²**finance** *vb* **fi·nanced; fi·nanc·ing** **1** : to raise or provide funds for **2** : to furnish with necessary funds **3** : to sell or supply on credit

finance company *n* : a company that makes usu. small short-term loans usu. to individuals

fi·nan·cial \fə-'nan-chəl, fī-\ *adj* : relating to finance or financiers — **fi·nan·cial·ly** *adv*

fi·nan·cials \-shəlz\ *n pl* : financial statistics

fi·nan·cier \ˌfi-nən-'sir, ˌfī-nan-\ *n* **1** : a person skilled in managing public moneys **2** : a person who deals with large-scale finance and investment

finch \'finch\ *n* : any of numerous songbirds with strong conical bills

¹**find** \'fīnd\ *vb* **found** \'faund\; **find·ing** **1** : to meet with either by chance or by searching or study : ENCOUNTER, DISCOVER **2** : to obtain by effort or management ⟨∼ time to read⟩ **3** : to arrive at : REACH ⟨the bullet *found* its mark⟩ **4** : EXPERIENCE, FEEL ⟨*found* happiness⟩ **5** : to gain or regain the use of ⟨*found* his voice again⟩ **6** : to determine and make a statement about ⟨∼ a verdict⟩

²**find** *n* **1** : an act or instance of finding **2** : something found; *esp* : a valuable item of discovery

find·er \'fīn-dər\ *n* : one that finds; *esp* : VIEWFINDER

fin de siè·cle \ˌfaⁿ-də-sē-'ekl⁾\ *adj* [F, end of century] **1** : of, relating to, or characteristic of the close of the 19th century **2** : of or relating to the end of a century

find·ing \'fīn-diŋ\ *n* **1** : the act of finding **2** : FIND 2 **3** : the result of a judicial proceeding or inquiry

find out *vb* : to learn by study, observation, or search : DISCOVER

¹**fine** \'fīn\ *n* : money exacted as a penalty for an offense

²**fine** *vb* **fined; fin·ing** : to impose a fine on : punish by a fine

³**fine** *adj* **fin·er; fin·est** **1** : free from impurity **2** : very thin in gauge or texture **3** : not coarse ⟨∼ sand⟩ **4** : SUBTLE, SENSITIVE ⟨a ∼ distinction⟩ **5** : superior in quality or appearance **6** : ELEGANT, REFINED ⟨∼ manners⟩ — **fine·ly** *adv* — **fine·ness** *n*

⁴**fine** *adv* **1** : very well **2** — used to express agreement

fine art *n* : art (as painting, sculpture, or music) concerned primarily with the creation of beautiful objects — usu. used in pl.

fin·ery \'fī-nə-rē\ *n, pl* **-er·ies** : ORNAMENT, DECORATION; *esp* : showy clothing and jewels

fine-spun \'fīn-'spən\ *adj* : developed with extremely or excessively fine delicacy or detail

fi·nesse \fə-'nes\ *n* **1** : refinement or delicacy of workmanship, structure, or texture **2** : CUNNING, SUBTLETY — **finesse** *vb*

fine-tune \'fīn-'tün\ *vb* : to adjust so as to bring to the highest level of performance or effectiveness

fin·fish \'fin-ˌfish\ *n* : FISH 2

¹**fin·ger** \'fiŋ-gər\ *n* **1** : any of the five divisions at the end of the hand; *esp* : one other than the thumb **2** : something that resembles or does the work of a finger **3** : a part of a glove into which a finger is inserted

²**finger** *vb* **fin·gered; fin·ger·ing** **1** : to touch or feel with the fingers : HANDLE **2** : to perform with the fingers or with a certain fingering **3** : to mark the notes of a piece of music as a guide in playing **4** : to point out

fin·ger·board \'fiŋ-gər-ˌbórd\ *n* : the part of a stringed instrument against which the fingers press the strings to vary the pitch

finger bowl *n* : a small water bowl for rinsing the fingers at the table

fin·ger·ing \'fiŋ-gə-riŋ\ *n* **1** : handling or touching with the fingers **2** : the act or method of using the fingers in playing an instrument **3** : the marking of the method of fingering

fin·ger·ling \'fiŋ-gər-liŋ\ *n* : a small fish

fin·ger·nail \'fiŋ-gər-,nāl\ *n* : the nail of a finger

fin·ger·print \-,print\ *n* : the pattern of marks made by pressing the tip of a finger or thumb on a surface; *esp* : an ink impression of such a pattern taken for the purpose of identification — **fingerprint** *vb*

fin·ger·tip \-,tip\ *n* : the tip of a finger

fin·i·al \'fi-nē-əl\ *n* : an ornamental projection or end (as on a spire)

fin·ick·ing \'fi-ni-kiŋ\ *adj* : FINICKY

fin·icky \'fi-ni-kē\ *adj* : excessively particular in taste or standards

fi·nis \'fi-nəs\ *n* : END, CONCLUSION

¹fin·ish \'fi-nish\ *vb* **1** : TERMINATE **2** : to use or dispose of entirely **3** : to bring to completion **4** : ACCOMPLISH **4** : to put a final coat or surface on **5** : to come to the end of a course or undertaking — **fin·ish·er** *n*

²finish *n* **1** : END, CONCLUSION **2** : something that completes or perfects **3** : the final treatment or coating of a surface

fi·nite \'fi-,nīt\ *adj* **1** : having definite or definable limits; *also* : having a limited nature or existence **2** : being less than some positive integer in number or measure and greater than its negative **3** : showing distinction of grammatical person and number ⟨a ~ verb⟩

fink \'fiŋk\ *n* **1** : a contemptible person **2** : STRIKEBREAKER **3** : INFORMER

Finn \'fin\ *n* : a native or inhabitant of Finland

fin·nan had·die \,fi-nən-'ha-dē\ *n* : smoked haddock

¹Finn·ish \'fi-nish\ *adj* : of or relating to Finland, the Finns, or Finnish

²Finnish *n* : the language of the Finns

fin·ny \'fi-nē\ *adj* **1** : having or characterized by fins **2** : relating to or being fish

fiord *var of* FJORD

fir \'fər\ *n* : any of a genus of usu. large evergreen trees related to the pines; *also* : the light soft wood of a fir

¹fire \'fī(-ə)r\ *n* **1** : the light or heat and esp. the flame of something burning **2** : ENTHUSIASM, ZEAL **3** : fuel that is burning (as in a stove or fireplace) **4** : destructive burning (as of a house) **5** : the firing of weapons — **fire·less** *adj*

²fire *vb* **fired; fir·ing** **1** : KINDLE, IGNITE ⟨~ a house⟩ **2** : STIR, ENLIVEN ⟨~ the imagination⟩ **3** : to dismiss from employment **4** : SHOOT ⟨~ a gun⟩ ⟨~ an arrow⟩ **5** : BAKE ⟨firing pottery in a kiln⟩ **6** : to apply fire or fuel to something ⟨~ a furnace⟩

fire ant *n* : either of two small fiercely stinging So. American ants introduced

into the southeastern U.S. where they are agricultural pests

fire·arm \'fī(-ə)r-,ärm\ *n* : a weapon (as a pistol) from which a shot is discharged by gunpowder

fire·ball \-,bȯl\ *n* **1** : a ball of fire **2** : a very bright meteor **3** : the highly luminous cloud of vapor and dust created by a nuclear explosion **4** : a highly energetic person

fire·boat \-,bōt\ *n* : a boat equipped for fighting fires

fire·bomb \-,bäm\ *n* : an incendiary bomb — **firebomb** *vb*

fire·box \-,bäks\ *n* **1** : a chamber (as of a furnace) that contains a fire **2** : a box containing a fire alarm

fire·brand \-,brand\ *n* **1** : a piece of burning wood **2** : a person who creates unrest or strife : AGITATOR

fire·break \-,brāk\ *n* : a barrier of cleared or plowed land intended to check a forest or grass fire

fire·bug \-,bəg\ *n* : a person who deliberately sets destructive fires

fire·crack·er \-,kra-kər\ *n* : a usu. paper tube containing an explosive and a fuse and set off to make a noise

fire department *n* : an organization for preventing or extinguishing fires; *also* : its members

fire engine *n* : a motor vehicle with equipment for extinguishing fires

fire escape *n* : a stairway or ladder for escape from a burning building

fire·fight·er \'fī(-ə)r-,fī-tər\ *n* : a person who fights fires; *esp* : a member of a fire department

fire·fly \-,flī\ *n* : any of various small night-flying beetles that produce flashes of light for courtship purposes

fire·house \-,haús\ *n* : FIRE STATION

fire irons *n pl* : tools for tending a fire esp. in a fireplace

fire·man \'fī(-ə)r-mən\ *n* **1** : STOKER **2** : FIREFIGHTER

fire off *vb* : to write and send

fire·place \-,plās\ *n* **1** : a framed opening made in a chimney to hold an open fire **2** : an outdoor structure of brick or stone for an open fire

fire·plug \-,pləg\ *n* : HYDRANT

fire·pow·er \-,paú(-ə)r\ *n* : the ability to deliver gunfire or warheads on a target

¹fire·proof \-'prüf\ *adj* : resistant to fire

²fireproof *vb* : to make fireproof

fire·sale \-,sāl\ *adj* : heavily discounted ⟨~ prices⟩

fire screen *n* : a protective screen before a fireplace

¹fire·side \'fī(-ə)r-,sīd\ *n* **1** : a place near the fire or hearth **2** : HOME

²fireside *adj* : having an informal or intimate quality

fire station *n* : a building housing fire engines and usu. firefighters

fire·storm \'fī(-ə)r-,stȯrm\ *n* **1** : a large destructive very hot fire **2** : a sudden or violent outburst ⟨~ of criticism⟩

fire tower *n* : a tower (as in a forest) from which a watch for fires is kept

fire·trap \\'fī(-ə)r-ˌtrap\\ *n* : a building or place apt to catch on fire or difficult to escape from in case of fire

fire truck *n* : FIRE ENGINE

fire·wall \\-ˌwȯl\\ *n* : computer hardware or software for preventing unauthorized access to data

fire·wa·ter \\'fī(-ə)r-ˌwȯ-tər, -ˌwä-\\ *n* : intoxicating liquor

fire·wood \\-ˌwu̇d\\ *n* : wood used for fuel

fire·work \\-ˌwərk\\ *n* : a device designed to produce a striking display by the burning of explosive or flammable materials

firing line *n* **1** : a line from which fire is delivered against a target **2** : the forefront of an activity

¹firm \\'fərm\\ *adj* **1** : securely fixed in place **2** : SOLID, VIGOROUS ⟨a ~ handshake⟩ **3** : having a solid or compact texture **4** : not subject to change or fluctuation : STEADY ⟨~ prices⟩ **5** : STEADFAST **6** : indicating firmness or resolution — **firm·ly** *adv* — **firm·ness** *n*

²firm *vb* : to make or become firm

³firm *n* [G *Firma*, fr. It, signature, ultim. fr. L *firmare* to make firm, confirm] **1** : the name under which a company transacts business **2** : a business partnership of two or more persons **3** : a business enterprise

fir·ma·ment \\'fər-mə-mənt\\ *n* : the arch of the sky : HEAVENS

firm·ware \\'firm-ˌwer\\ *n* : computer programs contained permanently in a hardware device

¹first \\'fərst\\ *adj* : preceding all others as in time, order, or importance

²first *adv* **1** : before any other **2** : for the first time **3** : in preference to something else

³first *n* **1** : number one in a countable series **2** : something that is first **3** : the lowest forward gear in an automotive vehicle **4** : the winning or highest place in a competition or examination

first aid *n* : emergency care or treatment given an injured or ill person

first·born \\'fərst-'bȯrn\\ *adj* : ELDEST — **firstborn** *n*

first class *n* : the best or highest group in a classification — **first–class** *adj or adv*

first·hand \\'fərst-'hand\\ *adj* : coming from direct personal observation or experience — **firsthand** *adv*

first lady *n, often cap F&L* : the wife or hostess of the chief executive of a political unit (as a country)

first lieutenant *n* : a commissioned officer (as in the army) ranking next below a captain

first·ling \\'fərst-liŋ\\ *n* : one that comes or is produced first

first·ly \\-lē\\ *adv* : in the first place : FIRST

¹first–rate \\-'rāt\\ *adj* : of the first order of size, importance, or quality

²first–rate *adv* : very well

first sergeant *n* **1** : a noncommissioned officer serving as the chief assistant to the commander of a military unit **2** : a rank in the army below a sergeant major and in the marine corps below a master gunnery sergeant

first strike *n* : a preemptive nuclear attack

first–string \\'fərst-'striŋ\\ *adj* : being a regular as distinguished from a substitute — **first–string·er** \\-ˌstriŋ-ər\\ *n*

firth \\'fərth\\ *n* [ME, fr. ON *fjǫrthr*] : ESTUARY

fis·cal \\'fis-kəl\\ *adj* [L *fiscalis*, fr. *fiscus* basket, treasury] **1** : of or relating to taxation, public revenues, or public debt **2** : of or relating to financial matters — **fis·cal·ly** *adv*

¹fish \\'fish\\ *n, pl* **fish** *or* **fish·es** **1** : a water-dwelling animal — usu. used in combination ⟨star*fish*⟩ ⟨shell*fish*⟩ **2** : any of numerous cold-blooded water-breathing vertebrates with fins, gills, and usu. scales that include the bony fishes and usu. the cartilaginous and jawless fishes **3** : the flesh of fish used as food

²fish *vb* **1** : to attempt to catch fish **2** : to seek something by roundabout means ⟨~ for praise⟩ **3** : to search for something underwater **4** : to engage in a search by groping **5** : to draw forth

fish–and–chips *n pl* : fried fish and french fried potatoes

fish·bowl \\'fish-ˌbōl\\ *n* **1** : a bowl for the keeping of live fish **2** : a place or condition that affords no privacy

fish·er \\'fi-shər\\ *n* **1** : one that fishes **2** : a dark brown No. American carnivorous mammal related to the weasels

fish·er·man \\-mən\\ *n* **1** : a person engaged in fishing **2** : a fishing boat

fish·ery \\'fi-shə-rē\\ *n, pl* **-er·ies** **1** : the business of catching fish **2** : a place for catching fish

fish·hook \\'fish-ˌhu̇k\\ *n* : a usu. barbed hook for catching fish

fish ladder *n* : an arrangement of pools in steps by which fish can pass over a dam in going upstream

fish·net \\'fish-ˌnet\\ *n* **1** : netting for catching fish **2** : a coarse open-mesh fabric

fish·tail \\-ˌtāl\\ *vb* : to have the rear end slide from side to side out of control while moving forward

fish·wife \\-ˌwīf\\ *n* **1** : a woman who sells fish **2** : a vulgar abusive woman

fishy \\'fi-shē\\ *adj* **fish·i·er; -est** **1** : of or resembling fish **2** : QUESTIONABLE ⟨the story sounds ~ to me⟩

fis·sion \\'fi-shən, -zhən\\ *n* [L *fissio*, fr. *findere* to split] **1** : a cleaving into parts **2** : a method of reproduction in which a living cell or body divides into two or more parts each of which grows into a whole new individual **3** : the splitting of an atomic nucleus resulting in the release of large amounts of energy — **fis·sion·able** \\'fi-shə-nə-bəl, -zhə-\\ *adj*

fis·sure \\'fi-shər\\ *n* : a narrow opening or crack

fist \\'fist\\ *n* **1** : the hand with fingers folded into the palm **2** : INDEX 6

fist·ful \\'fist-ˌfu̇l\\ *n* : HANDFUL

fist·i·cuffs \\'fis-ti-ˌkəfs\\ *n pl* : a fight with the fists

fis·tu·la \\'fis-chə-lə\\ *n, pl* **-las** *or* **-lae** : an abnormal passage leading from an ab-

scess or hollow organ — **fis·tu·lous**
\-ləs\ *adj*

¹fit \'fit\ *adj* **fit·ter; fit·test** **1** : adapted to
a purpose : APPROPRIATE **2** : PROPER,
RIGHT ⟨a movie ∼ for children⟩ **3**
: PREPARED, READY **4** : physically and
mentally sound — **fit·ly** *adv* — **fit·ness** *n*

²fit *n* **1** : a sudden violent attack (as in
epilepsy) **2** : a sudden outburst

³fit *vb* **fit·ted** *also* **fit; fit·ting** **1** : to be
suitable for or to **2** : to be correctly ad-
justed to or shaped for **3** : to insert or
adjust until correctly in place **4** : to
make a place or room for **5** : to be in
agreement or accord with **6** : PREPARE
7 : ADJUST **8** : SUPPLY, EQUIP ⟨*fitted* out
with gear⟩ **9** : BELONG — **fit·ter** *n*

⁴fit *n* : the fact, condition, or manner of fitting or being fitted

fit·ful \'fit-fəl\ *adj* : not regular : INTER-
MITTENT ⟨∼ sleep⟩ — **fit·ful·ly** *adv*

¹fit·ting \'fit-tiŋ\ *adj* : APPROPRIATE, SUIT-
ABLE — **fit·ting·ly** *adv*

²fitting *n* **1** : the action or act of one that
fits; *esp* : a trying on of clothes being
made or altered **2** : a small often standardized part ⟨a plumbing ∼⟩

five \'fīv\ *n* **1** : one more than four **2**
: the 5th in a set or series **3** : something
having five units; *esp* : a basketball team
4 : a 5-dollar bill — **five** *adj or pron*

¹fix \'fiks\ *vb* **1** : to make firm, stable, or
fast **2** : to give a permanent or final form
to **3** : AFFIX, ATTACH **4** : to hold or direct steadily ⟨∼*es* his eyes on the hori-
zon⟩ **5** : ESTABLISH, SET **6** : ASSIGN ⟨∼
the blame⟩ **7** : to set in order : ADJUST
8 : PREPARE **9** : to make whole or sound
again **10** : to get even with **11** : to influence by improper or illegal methods
⟨∼ a race⟩ — **fix·er** *n*

²fix *n* **1** : PREDICAMENT **2** : a determination of position (as of a ship) **3** : an accurate determination or understanding
4 : an act of improper influence **5** : a
supply or dose of something (as an addictive drug) strongly desired or craved **6**
: something that fixes or restores

fix·a·tion \fik-'sā-shən\ *n* : an obsessive or
unhealthy preoccupation or attachment
— **fix·ate** \'fik-ˌsāt\ *vb*

fix·a·tive \'fik-sə-tiv\ *n* : something that
stabilizes or sets

fixed \'fikst\ *adj* **1** : securely placed or
fastened : STATIONARY **2** : not volatile
3 : SETTLED, FINAL **4** : INTENT, CON-
CENTRATED ⟨a ∼ stare⟩ **5** : supplied
with a definite amount of something
needed (as money) — **fixed·ly** \'fik-
səd-lē\ *adv* — **fixed·ness** \'fik-səd-nəs\ *n*

fix·i·ty \'fik-sə-tē\ *n, pl* **-ties** : the quality
or state of being fixed or stable

fix·ture \'fiks-chər\ *n* **1** : something firmly attached as a permanent part of some
other thing **2** : a familiar feature in a
particular setting; *esp* : a person associated with a place or activity

¹fizz \'fiz\ *vb* : to make a hissing or sputter-
ing sound

²fizz *n* : an effervescent beverage

fiz·zle \'fi-zəl\ *vb* **fiz·zled; fiz·zling** **1**

: FIZZ **2** : to fail after a good start —
often used with *out*

²fizzle *n* : FAILURE

fjord \fē-'ȯrd\ *n* [Norw] : a narrow inlet of
the sea between cliffs or steep slopes

fl *abbr* **1** [L *floruit*] flourished **2** fluid

FL *or* **Fla** *abbr* Florida

flab \'flab\ *n* : soft flabby body tissue

flab·ber·gast \'fla-bər-ˌgast\ *vb* : AS-
TOUND

flab·by \'fla-bē\ *adj* **flab·bi·er; -est**
: lacking firmness : FLACCID ⟨∼ mus-
cles⟩ — **flab·bi·ness** \-bē-nəs\ *n*

flac·cid \'fla-səd\ *adj* : lacking firmness
⟨∼ muscles⟩

¹flag \'flag\ *n* : any of various irises; *esp* : a
wild iris

²flag *n* **1** : a usu. rectangular piece of fabric of distinctive design that is used as a
symbol (as of a nation) or as a signaling
device **2** : something used like a flag to
signal or attract attention **3** : one of the
cross strokes of a musical note less than a
quarter note in value

³flag *vb* **flagged; flag·ging** **1** : to signal
with or as if with a flag; *esp* : to signal to
stop ⟨∼ a taxi⟩ **2** : to mark or identify
with or as if with a flag **3** : to call a
penalty on

⁴flag *vb* **flagged; flag·ging** **1** : to hang
loose or limp **2** : to become unsteady,
feeble, or spiritless **3** : to decline in interest or attraction ⟨the topic *flagged*⟩

⁵flag *n* : a hard flat stone suitable for
paving

flag·el·late \'fla-jə-ˌlāt\ *vb* **-lat·ed; -lat·
ing** : to punish by whipping — **flag·el·la·
tion** \ˌfla-jə-'lā-shən\ *n*

fla·gel·lum \flə-'je-ləm\ *n, pl* **-la** \-lä\ *also*
-lums : a long whiplike process that is
the primary organ of motion of many microorganisms — **fla·gel·lar** \-lər\ *adj*

fla·geo·let \ˌfla-jə-'let, -'lä\ *n* [F] : a small
woodwind instrument belonging to the
flute class

fla·gi·tious \flə-'ji-shəs\ *adj* : grossly
wicked : VILLAINOUS

flag·on \'fla-gən\ *n* : a container for liquids usu. with a handle, spout, and lid

flag·pole \'flag-ˌpōl\ *n* : a pole on which
to raise a flag

fla·grant \'flā-grənt\ *adj* [L *flagrans*, prp.
of *flagrare* to burn] : conspicuously bad
⟨∼ abuse of power⟩ — **fla·grant·ly** *adv*

fla·gran·te de·lic·to \flə-ˌgran-tē-di-'lik-
tō\ *adv* : IN FLAGRANTE DELICTO

flag·ship \'flag-ˌship\ *n* **1** : the ship that
carries the commander of a fleet or subdivision thereof and flies his flag **2** : the
most important one of a group

flag·staff \-ˌstaf\ *n* : FLAGPOLE

flag·stone \-ˌstōn\ *n* : ⁵FLAG

¹flail \'flāl\ *n* : a tool for threshing grain by
hand

²flail *vb* : to strike or swing with or as if
with a flail

flair \'fler\ *n* [F, lit., sense of smell, fr. OF,
odor, fr. *flairier* to give off an odor, fr. VL
flagrare, alter. of L *fragrare*] **1** : ability
to appreciate or make good use of something : BENT, TALENT **2** : a unique style

flak \'flak\ *n, pl* **flak** [G, fr. *Fliegerabwehrkanonen*, fr. *Flieger* flyer + *Abwehr* defense + *Kanonen* cannons] **1** : antiaircraft guns or bursting shells fired from them : CRITICISM, OPPOSITION

¹flake \'flāk\ *n* **1** : a small loose mass or bit **2** : a thin flattened piece or layer : CHIP — **flaky** *adj*

²flake *vb* **flaked; flak·ing** : to form or separate into flakes

³flake *n* : a markedly eccentric person : ODDBALL — **flak·i·ness** \'flā-kē-nəs\ *n* — **flaky** *adj*

flam·beau \'flam-₁bō\ *n, pl* **flambeaux** \-₁bōz\ *or* **flambeaus** [F, fr. MF, fr. *flambe* flame] : a flaming torch

flam·boy·ant \flam-'bȯi-ənt\ *adj* : marked by or given to strikingly elaborate or colorful display or behavior — **flam·boy·ance** \-əns\ *n* — **flam·boy·an·cy** \-ən-sē\ *n* — **flam·boy·ant·ly** *adv*

flame \'flām\ *n* **1** : the glowing gaseous part of a fire **2** : a state of blazing combustion **3** : a flamelike condition **4** : burning zeal or passion **5** : BRILLIANCE **6** : SWEETHEART **7** : an angry, hostile, or abusive electronic message — **flame** *vb*

fla·men·co \flə-'meŋ-kō\ *n, pl* **-cos** [Sp, fr. *flamenco* of the Gypsies, lit., Flemish, fr. MD *Vlaminc* Fleming] : a vigorous rhythmic dance style of the Spanish Gypsies

flame·throw·er \'flām-₁thrō-ər\ *n* : a device that expels from a nozzle a burning stream of liquid or semiliquid fuel under pressure

fla·min·go \flə-'miŋ-gō\ *n, pl* **-gos** *also* **-goes** : any of several long-legged long-necked tropical water birds with scarlet wings and a broad bill bent downward

flam·ma·ble \'fla-mə-bəl\ *adj* : easily ignited and quick-burning — **flam·ma·bil·i·ty** \₁fla-mə-'bi-lə-tē\ *n* — **flammable** *n*

flan \'flan, 'flän\ *n* **1** : an open pie with a sweet or savory filling **2** : custard baked with a caramel glaze

flange \'flanj\ *n* : a rim used for strengthening or guiding something or for attachment to another object

¹flank \'flaŋk\ *n* **1** : the fleshy part of the side between the ribs and the hip; *also* : the side of a quadruped **2** : SIDE **3** : right or left of a formation

²flank *vb* **1** : to be situated on the side of : BORDER **2** : to attack or threaten the flank of

flank·er \'flaŋ-kər\ *n* : a football player stationed wide of the formation slightly behind the line of scrimmage as a pass receiver

flan·nel \'fla-nᵊl\ *n* **1** : a soft twilled wool or worsted fabric with a napped surface **2** : a stout cotton fabric napped on one side **3** *pl* : flannel underwear or pants

¹flap \'flap\ *n* **1** : a stroke with something broad : SLAP **2** : something broad, limber, or flat and usu. thin that hangs loose **3** : the motion or sound of something broad and limber as it swings to and fro **4** : a state of excitement or confusion

²flap *vb* **flapped; flap·ping 1** : to beat with something broad and flat **2** : FLING **3** : to move (as wings) with a beating motion **4** : to sway loosely usu. with a noise of striking

flap·jack \'flap-₁jak\ *n* : PANCAKE

flap·per \'fla-pər\ *n* **1** : one that flaps **2** : a young woman of the 1920s who showed freedom from conventions (as in conduct)

¹flare \'fler\ *n* **1** : a blaze of light used esp. to signal or illuminate; *also* : a device for producing such a blaze **2** : an unsteady glaring light

²flare *vb* **flared; flar·ing 1** : to flame with a sudden unsteady light **2** : to become suddenly excited or angry ⟨after his harangue, I *flared* up⟩ **3** : to spread outward

flare–up \-₁əp\ *n* : a sudden outburst or intensification

¹flash \'flash\ *vb* **1** : to break forth in or like a sudden flame **2** : to appear or pass suddenly or with great speed **3** : to send out in or as if in flashes ⟨~ a message⟩ **4** : to make a sudden display (as of brilliance or feeling) **5** : to gleam or glow intermittently **6** : to fill by a sudden rush of water **7** : to expose to view very briefly ⟨~ a badge⟩ ♦ **Synonyms** GLANCE, GLINT, SPARKLE, TWINKLE — **flash·er** *n*

²flash *n* **1** : a sudden burst of light **2** : a movement of a flag or light in signaling **3** : a sudden and brilliant burst (as of wit) **4** : a brief time **5** : SHOW, DISPLAY; *esp* : ostentatious display **6** : one that attracts notice; *esp* : an outstanding athlete **7** : GLIMPSE, LOOK **8** : a first brief news report **9** : FLASHLIGHT **10** : a device for producing a brief and very bright flash of light for taking photographs **11** : a quick-spreading flame or momentary intense outburst of radiant heat

³flash *adj* : of sudden origin and short duration ⟨a ~ fire⟩ ⟨a ~ flood⟩

⁴flash *adv* : by very brief exposure to an intense agent (as heat or cold) ⟨~ fry⟩ ⟨~ freeze⟩

flash·back \'flash-₁bak\ *n* **1** : interruption of the chronological sequence (as of a film or literary work) by an event of earlier occurrence **2** : a past event remembered vividly

flash back *vb* **1** : to vividly remember a past incident **2** : to employ a flashback

flash·bulb \-₁bəlb\ *n* : an electric bulb that can be used only once to produce a brief and very bright flash of light for taking photographs

flash card *n* : a card bearing words, numbers, or pictures briefly displayed usu. as a learning aid

flash·cube \'flash-₁kyüb\ *n* : a cubical device incorporating four flashbulbs

flash·gun \-₁gən\ *n* : a device for producing a bright flash of light for photography

flash·ing \'fla-shiŋ\ *n* : sheet metal used in waterproofing (as at the angle between a chimney and a roof)

flash·light \'flash-ˌlīt\ n : a battery-operated portable electric light

flash memory n : a computer memory chip not requiring connection to a power source to retain its data

flashy \'fla-shē\ adj **flash·i·er; -est** 1 : momentarily dazzling 2 : superficially attractive or impressive : SHOWY — **flash·i·ly** \-shə-lē\ adv — **flash·i·ness** \-shē-nəs\ n

flask \'flask\ n : a flattened bottle-shaped container ⟨a whiskey ∼⟩

¹flat \'flat\ adj **flat·ter; flat·test** 1 : spread out along a surface; also : being or characterized by a horizontal line 2 : having a smooth, level, or even surface 3 : having a broad smooth surface and little thickness 4 : DOWNRIGHT, POSITIVE ⟨a ∼ refusal⟩ 5 : FIXED, UNCHANGING ⟨charge a ∼ rate⟩ 6 : EXACT, PRECISE ⟨in four minutes ∼⟩ 7 : DULL, UNINTERESTING; also : INSIPID 8 : DEFLATED ⟨a ∼ tire⟩ 9 : lower than the true pitch; also : lower by a half step 10 : free from gloss ⟨a ∼ paint⟩ 11 : lacking depth of characterization — **flat·ly** adv — **flat·ness** n

²flat n 1 : a level surface of land : PLAIN 2 : a flat part or surface 3 : a character b that indicates that a specified note is to be lowered by a half step; also : the resulting note 4 : something flat 5 : an apartment on one floor 6 : a deflated tire

³flat adv 1 : FLATLY 2 : COMPLETELY ⟨∼ broke⟩ 3 : below the true musical pitch

⁴flat vb **flat·ted; flat·ting** 1 : FLATTEN 2 : to lower in pitch esp. by a half step

flat·bed \'flat-ˌbed\ n : a truck or trailer with a body in the form of a platform or shallow box

flat·boat \-ˌbōt\ n : a flat-bottomed boat used esp. for carrying bulky freight

flat·car \-ˌkär\ n : a railroad freight car without sides or roof

flat·fish \-ˌfish\ n : any of an order of flattened marine bony fishes with both eyes on the upper side

flat·foot \-ˌfut, -ˈfut\ n, pl **flat·feet** \-ˌfēt, -ˈfēt\ : a condition in which the arch of the foot is flattened so that the entire sole rests upon the ground — **flat–foot·ed** \-ˈfu̇-təd\ adj

Flat·head \-ˌhed\ n, pl **Flatheads** or **Flathead** : a member of an American Indian people of Montana

flat·iron \-ˌ(ī)(-ə)rn\ n : IRON 3

flat·land \-ˌland\ n : land lacking significant variation in elevation

flat–out \'flat-ˌaut\ adj 1 : being or going at maximum effort or speed 2 : OUT= AND-OUT, DOWNRIGHT ⟨it was a ∼ lie⟩

flat out adv 1 : BLUNTLY, DIRECTLY 2 : at top speed 3 usu **flat–out** : to the greatest degree : COMPLETELY ⟨is just flat-out confusing⟩

flat–pan·el \-ˈpa-nᵊl\ adj : relating to or being a thin flat video display

flat·ten \'fla-tᵊn\ vb : to make or become flat

flat·ter \'fla-tər\ vb [ME flateren, fr. AF flater to lap, flatter] 1 : to praise too

much or without sincerity 2 : to represent too favorably ⟨the portrait ∼s him⟩ 3 : to display to advantage 4 : to judge (oneself) favorably or too favorably — **flat·ter·er** n

flat·tery \'fla-tə-rē\ n, pl **-ter·ies** : flattering speech or attentions : insincere or excessive praise

flat·top \'flat-ˌtäp\ n 1 : AIRCRAFT CARRIER 2 : CREW CUT

flat·u·lent \'fla-chə-lənt\ adj 1 : full of gas ⟨a ∼ stomach⟩ 2 : INFLATED, POMPOUS — **flat·u·lence** \-ləns\ n

fla·tus \'flā-təs\ n : gas formed in the intestine or stomach

flat·ware \'flat-ˌwer\ n : eating and serving utensils

flat·worm \-ˌwərm\ n : any of a phylum of flattened mostly parasitic segmented worms (as trematodes and tapeworms)

flaunt \'flont\ vb 1 : to display oneself to public notice 2 : to wave or flutter showily 3 : to display ostentatiously or impudently : PARADE — **flaunt** n

flau·ta \'flaü-tə\ n : a tortilla rolled around a filling and deep-fried

flau·tist \'flo-tist, 'flaü-\ n [It flautista] : FLUTIST

¹fla·vor \'flā-vər\ n 1 : the quality of something that affects the sense of taste or of taste and smell 2 : a substance that adds flavor 3 : characteristic or predominant quality — **fla·vored** \-vərd\ adj — **fla·vor·ful** adj — **fla·vor·less** adj — **fla·vor·some** adj

²flavor vb : to give or add flavor to

fla·vor·ing n : FLAVOR 2

fla·vour chiefly Brit var of FLAVOR

flaw \'flo\ n : a small often hidden defect — **flaw·less** adj — **flaw·less·ly** adv — **flaw·less·ness** n

flax \'flaks\ n : a fiber that is the source of linen; also : a blue-flowered plant grown for this fiber and its oily seeds

flax·en \'flak-sən\ adj 1 : made of flax 2 : resembling flax esp. in pale soft straw color

flay \'flā\ vb 1 : to strip off the skin or surface of 2 : to criticize harshly

fl dr abbr fluid dram

flea \'flē\ n : any of an order of small wingless leaping bloodsucking insects

flea·bane \'flē-ˌbān\ n : any of various plants of the daisy family once believed to drive away fleas

flea–bit·ten \-ˌbi-tᵊn\ adj : bitten by or infested with fleas

flea market n : a usu. open-air market for secondhand articles and antiques

¹fleck \'flek\ vb : STREAK, SPOT

²fleck n 1 : SPOT, MARK 2 : FLAKE, PARTICLE

fledge \'flej\ vb **fledged; fledg·ing** : to develop the feathers necessary for flying or independent activity

fledg·ling \'flej-liŋ\ n 1 : a young bird just fledged 2 : an immature or inexperienced person

flee \'flē\ vb **fled** \'fled\; **flee·ing** 1 : to run away often from danger or evil 2 : VANISH 3 : to run away from : SHUN

¹**fleece** \'flēs\ *n* **1** : the woolly coat of an animal and esp. a sheep **2** : a soft or woolly covering — **fleecy** *adj*

²**fleece** *vb* **fleeced; fleec·ing 1** : to strip of money or property by fraud or extortion **2** : SHEAR

¹**fleet** \'flēt\ *vb* : to pass rapidly

²**fleet** *n* [ME *flete*, fr. OE *flēot* ship, fr. *flēotan* to float] **1** : a group of warships under one command **2** : a group (as of ships, planes, or trucks) under one management

³**fleet** *adj* **1** : SWIFT, NIMBLE **2** : not enduring : FLEETING — **fleet·ness** *n*

fleet admiral *n* : an admiral of the highest rank in the navy

fleet·ing \'flē-tiŋ\ *adj* : passing swiftly

Flem·ing \'fle-miŋ\ *n* : a member of a Germanic people inhabiting chiefly northern Belgium

Flem·ish \'fle-mish\ *n* **1** : the Dutch language as spoken by the Flemings **2 Flemish** *pl* : FLEMINGS — **Flemish** *adj*

¹**flesh** \'flesh\ *n* **1** : the soft parts of an animal's body; *esp* : muscular tissue **2** : MEAT **3** : the physical nature of humans as distinguished from the soul **4** : human beings; *also* : living beings **5** : STOCK, KINDRED **6** : fleshy plant tissue (as fruit pulp) — **fleshed** \'flesht\ *adj*

²**flesh** *vb* : to make fuller or more nearly complete — usu. used with *out* ⟨*flesh* out a schedule⟩

flesh fly *n* : a dipteran fly whose maggots feed on flesh

flesh·ly \'flesh-lē\ *adj* **1** : CORPOREAL, BODILY **2** : not spiritual : WORLDLY **3** : CARNAL, SENSUAL

flesh·pot \'flesh-,pät\ *n* **1** *pl* : bodily comfort : LUXURY **2** : a place of lascivious entertainment — usu. used in pl.

fleshy \'fle-shē\ *adj* **flesh·i·er; -est 1** : consisting of or resembling animal flesh **2** : PLUMP, FAT

flew *past of* ¹FLY

flex \'fleks\ *vb* : to bend esp. repeatedly — **flex** *n*

flex·i·ble \'flek-sə-bəl\ *adj* **1** : capable of being flexed : PLIANT **2** : yielding to influence : TRACTABLE **3** : readily changed or changing : ADAPTABLE ♦ *Synonyms* ELASTIC, SUPPLE, RESILIENT, SPRINGY — **flex·i·bil·i·ty** \,flek-sə-'bi-lə-tē\ *n*

flex·or \'flek-sər, -,sȯr\ *n* : a muscle serving to bend a body part

flex·ure \'flek-shər\ *n* : TURN, FOLD

flib·ber·ti·gib·bet \,fli-bər-tē-'ji-bət\ *n* : a silly flighty person

¹**flick** \'flik\ *n* **1** : a light sharp jerky stroke or movement **2** : a sound produced by a flick **3** : ²FLICKER

²**flick** *vb* **1** : to strike lightly with a quick sharp motion **2** : FLUTTER, FLIT

³**flick** *n* : MOVIE

¹**flick·er** \'fli-kər\ *vb* **1** : to move irregularly or unsteadily : FLUTTER **2** : to burn fitfully or with a fluctuating light — **flick·er·ing·ly** *adv*

²**flicker** *n* **1** : an act of flickering **2** : a sudden brief movement ⟨a ~ of an eyelid⟩ **3** : a momentary stirring ⟨a ~ of interest⟩ **4** : a slight indication : HINT **5** : a wavering light

³**flicker** *n* : a large barred and spotted No. American woodpecker with a brown back that occurs as an eastern form with yellow on the underside of the wings and tail and a western form with red in these areas

flied *past and past part of* ³FLY

fli·er \'flī(-ə)r\ *n* **1** : one that flies; *esp* : PILOT **2** : a reckless or speculative undertaking **3** *usu* **fly·er** : an advertising circular

¹**flight** \'flīt\ *n* **1** : an act or instance of flying **2** : the ability to fly **3** : a passing through air or space **4** : the distance covered in a flight **5** : swift movement **6** : a trip made by or in an airplane or spacecraft **7** : a group of similar individuals (as birds or airplanes) flying as a unit **8** : a passing (as of the imagination) beyond ordinary limits **9** : a series of stairs from one landing to another — **flight·less** *adj*

²**flight** *n* : an act or instance of running away

flight bag *n* **1** : a lightweight traveling bag with zippered outside pockets **2** : a small canvas satchel

flight line *n* : a parking and servicing area for airplanes

flighty \'flī-tē\ *adj* **flight·i·er; -est 1** : easily upset : VOLATILE **2** : easily excited : SKITTISH **3** : CAPRICIOUS, SILLY — **flight·i·ness** \-tē-nəs\ *n*

flim·flam \'flim-,flam\ *n* : DECEPTION, FRAUD — **flim·flam·mery** \-,fla-mə-re\ *n*

flim·sy \'flim-zē\ *adj* **flim·si·er; -est 1** : lacking strength or substance **2** : of inferior materials and workmanship **3** : having little worth or plausibility ⟨a ~ excuse⟩ — **flim·si·ly** \-zə-lē\ *adv* — **flim·si·ness** \-zē-nəs\ *n*

flinch \'flinch\ *vb* [MF *flenchir* to bend] : to shrink from or as if from pain : WINCE — **flinch** *n*

¹**fling** \'fliŋ\ *vb* **flung** \'fləŋ\; **fling·ing 1** : to move hastily, brusquely, or violently ⟨*flung* out of the room⟩ **2** : to kick or plunge vigorously **3** : to throw with force or recklessness; *also* : to cast as if by throwing **4** : to put suddenly into a state or condition

²**fling** *n* **1** : an act or instance of flinging **2** : a casual try : ATTEMPT **3** : a period of self-indulgence

flint \'flint\ *n* **1** : a hard dark quartz that produces a spark when struck by steel **2** : an alloy used for producing a spark in lighters — **flinty** *adj*

flint glass *n* : heavy glass containing an oxide of lead and used in lenses and prisms

flint·lock \'flint-,läk\ *n* **1** : a lock for a gun using a flint to ignite the charge **2** : a firearm fitted with a flintlock

¹**flip** \'flip\ *vb* **flipped; flip·ping 1** : to turn by tossing ⟨~ a coin⟩ **2** : to turn over; *also* : to leaf through **3** : FLICK, JERK ⟨~ a light switch⟩ **4** : to lose self-control — **flip** *n*

²**flip** *adj* : FLIPPANT, IMPERTINENT

flip·pant \'fli-pənt\ *adj* : lacking proper respect or seriousness — **flip·pan·cy** \'fli-pən-sē\ *n*

flip·per \'fli-pər\ *n* **1** : a broad flat limb (as of a seal) adapted for swimming **2** : a paddlelike shoe used in skin diving

flip side *n* : the reverse and usu. less popular side of a phonograph record

¹flirt \'flərt\ *vb* **1** : to move erratically : FLIT **2** : to behave amorously without serious intent **3** : to show casual interest ⟨~ed with the idea⟩; *also* : to come close to ⟨~ with danger⟩ — **flir·ta·tion** \,flər-'tā-shən\ *n* — **flir·ta·tious** \-shəs\ *adj*

²flirt *n* **1** : an act or instance of flirting **2** : a person who flirts

flit \'flit\ *vb* **flit·ted; flit·ting** : to pass or move quickly or abruptly from place to place : DART — **flit** *n*

flitch \'flich\ *n* : a side of cured meat; *esp* : a side of bacon

fliv·ver \'fli-vər\ *n* : a small cheap usu. old automobile

¹float \'flōt\ *n* **1** : something (as a raft) that floats **2** : a cork buoying up the baited end of a fishing line **3** : a hollow ball that floats at the end of a lever in a cistern or tank and regulates the liquid level **4** : a vehicle with a platform to carry an exhibit **5** : a soft drink with ice cream floating in it

²float *vb* **1** : to rest on the surface of or be suspended in a fluid **2** : to move gently on or through a fluid **3** : to cause to float **4** : WANDER **5** : to offer (securities) in order to finance an enterprise **6** : to finance by floating an issue of stocks or bonds **7** : to arrange for ⟨~ a loan⟩ — **float·er** *n*

floaty \'flō-tē\ *adj* **float·i·er; -est** **1** : tending to float : BUOYANT **2** : light and billowy

¹flock \'fläk\ *n* **1** : a group of animals (as birds or sheep) assembled or herded together **2** : a group of people under the guidance of a leader; *esp* : CONGREGATION **3** : a large number ⟨a ~ of tourists⟩

²flock *vb* : to gather or move in a flock ⟨people ~ed to the beach⟩

floe \'flō\ *n* : a flat mass of floating ice

flog \'fläg\ *vb* **flogged; flog·ging** **1** : to beat with or as if with a rod or whip **2** : SELL ⟨~ encyclopedias⟩ — **flog·ger** *n*

¹flood \'fləd\ *n* **1** : a great flow of water over the land **2** : the flowing in of the tide **3** : an overwhelming volume

²flood *vb* **1** : to cover or become filled with a flood **2** : to fill abundantly or excessively; *esp* : to supply an excess of fuel to **3** : to pour forth in a flood — **flood·er** *n*

flood·gate \'fləd-,gāt\ *n* : a gate for controlling a body of water : SLUICE

flood·light \-,līt\ *n* : a lamp that throws a broad beam of light; *also* : the beam itself — **floodlight** *vb*

flood·plain \-,plān\ *n* : a plain along a river or stream subject to periodic flooding

flood tide *n* **1** : a rising tide **2** : an overwhelming quantity **3** : a high point

flood·wa·ter \'fləd-,wȯ-tər, -,wä-\ *n* : the water of a flood

¹floor \'flȯr\ *n* **1** : the bottom of a room on which one stands **2** : a ground surface **3** : a story of a building **4** : a main level space (as in a legislative chamber) distinguished from a platform or gallery **5** : AUDIENCE **6** : the right to address an assembly **7** : a lower limit ⟨put a ~ under wheat prices⟩ — **floor·ing** *n*

²floor *vb* **1** : to furnish with a floor **2** : to knock down **3** : AMAZE, DUMBFOUND **4** : to press (a vehicle's accelerator) to the floorboard esp. rapidly

floor·board \-,bȯrd\ *n* **1** : a board in a floor **2** : the floor of an automobile

floor leader *n* : a member of a legislative body who has charge of a party's organization and strategy on the floor

floor show *n* : a series of acts presented in a nightclub

floor·walk·er \'flȯr-,wȯ-kər\ *n* : a person employed in a retail store to oversee the sales force and aid customers

floo·zy *or* **floo·zie** \'flü-zē\ *n, pl* **floozies** : a usu. young woman of loose morals

flop \'fläp\ *vb* **flopped; flop·ping** **1** : FLAP **2** : to throw oneself down heavily, clumsily, or in a relaxed manner ⟨*flopped* into a chair⟩ **3** : FAIL ⟨the show *flopped*⟩ — **flop** *n* — **flop** *adv* — **flop·per** *n*

flop·house \'fläp-,haůs\ *n* : a cheap hotel

¹flop·py \'flä-pē\ *adj* **flop·pi·er; -est** : tending to flop; *esp* : soft and flexible — **flop·pi·ly** \-pə-lē\ *adv*

²floppy *n, pl* **flop·pies** : FLOPPY DISK

floppy disk *n* : a thin plastic disk with a magnetic coating on which computer data can be stored

flop sweat *n* : sweat caused by the fear of failing

flo·ra \'flȯr-ə\ *n, pl* **floras** *also* **flo·rae** \-,ē, -,ī\ [L *Flora*, Roman goddess of flowers] : plants or plant life esp. of a region or period

flo·ral \'flȯr-əl\ *adj* : of, relating to, or depicting flowers ⟨a ~ design⟩

flo·res·cence \flȯ-'re-sᵊns, flə-\ *n* : a state or period of being in bloom or flourishing — **flo·res·cent** \-ᵊnt\ *adj*

flor·id \'flȯr-əd\ *adj* **1** : very flowery in style : ORNATE ⟨~ prose⟩ **2** : tinged with red : RUDDY **3** : marked by emotional or sexual fervor

flo·rin \'flȯr-ən\ *n* **1** : an old gold coin first struck at Florence, Italy, in 1252 **2** : a gold coin of a European country patterned after the florin of Florence **3** : any of several modern silver coins issued in Commonwealth countries **4** : GULDEN

flo·rist \'flȯr-ist\ *n* : a person who sells flowers or ornamental plants

¹floss \'fläs\ *n* **1** : soft thread of silk or mercerized cotton for embroidery **2** : DENTAL FLOSS **3** : fluffy fibrous material

²floss *vb* : to use dental floss on (one's teeth)

flossy \'flä-sē\ *adj* **floss·i·er; -est** **1** : of, relating to, or having the characteristics of floss **2** : STYLISH, GLAMOROUS ⟨∼ hotels⟩ — **floss·i·ly** \-sə-lē\ *adv*

flo·ta·tion \flō-'tā-shən\ *n* : the process or an instance of floating

flo·til·la \flō-'ti-lə\ *n* [Sp, dim. of *flota* fleet] : a fleet esp. of small ships

flot·sam \'flät-səm\ *n* : floating wreckage of a ship or its cargo

¹flounce \'flaůns\ *vb* **flounced; flounc·ing** **1** : to move with exaggerated jerky or bouncy motions **2** : to go with sudden determination

²flounce *n* : an act or instance of flouncing — **flouncy** \'flaůn-sē\ *adj*

³flounce *n* : a strip of fabric attached by one edge; *also* : a wide ruffle

¹floun·der \'flaůn-dər\ *n, pl* **flounder** *or* **flounders** : FLATFISH; *esp* : any of various important marine food fishes

²flounder *vb* **1** : to struggle to move or obtain footing **2** : to proceed clumsily ⟨∼ed through the speech⟩

¹flour \'flaů(-ə)r\ *n* [ME, flower, best of anything, flour, fr. AF *flur* flower] : finely ground and sifted meal of a grain (as wheat); *also* : a fine soft powder — **floury** *adj*

²flour *vb* : to coat with or as if with flour

¹flour·ish \'flər-ish\ *vb* **1** : THRIVE, PROSPER **2** : to be in a state of activity or production ⟨∼ed about 1850⟩ **3** : to reach a height of development or influence **4** : to make bold and sweeping gestures **5** : BRANDISH

²flourish *n* **1** : a florid bit of speech or writing; *also* : an ornamental touch or decorative detail **2** : FANFARE **3** : WAVE ⟨with a ∼ of his cane⟩ **4** : showiness in doing something

¹flout \'flaůt\ *vb* : to treat with contemptuous disregard ⟨∼ the law⟩ — **flout·er** *n*

²flout *n* : TAUNT

¹flow \'flō\ *vb* **1** : to issue or move in a stream **2** : RISE ⟨the tide ebbs and ∼s⟩ **3** : ABOUND **4** : to proceed smoothly and readily **5** : to have a smooth continuity **6** : to hang loose and billowing **7** : COME, ARISE **8** : MENSTRUATE

²flow *n* **1** : an act of flowing **2** : FLOOD 1, 2 **3** : a smooth uninterrupted movement **4** : STREAM; *also* : a mass of material that has flowed when molten **5** : the quantity that flows in a certain time **6** : MENSTRUATION **7** : a continuous transfer of energy — **flow·age** \'flō-ij\ *n*

flow·chart \'flō-,chärt\ *n* : a symbolic diagram showing step-by-step progression through a procedure

flow diagram *n* : FLOWCHART

¹flow·er \'flaů(-ə)r\ *n* [ME *flour, flour,* fr. AF *flur,* fr. L *flor-, flos*] **1** : a plant shoot modified for reproduction and bearing leaves specialized into floral organs; *esp* : one of a seed plant consisting of a calyx, corolla, stamens, and carpels **2** : a plant cultivated for its blossoms **3** : the best part or example **4** : the finest most vigorous period **5** : a state of blooming or flourishing — **flow·ered** \'flaů(-ə)rd\ *adj*

— **flow·er·less** *adj* — **flow·er·like** \-,līk\ *adj*

²flower *vb* **1** : DEVELOP; *also* : FLOURISH **2** : to produce flowers : BLOOM

flower girl *n* : a little girl who carries flowers at a wedding

flower head *n* : a compact cluster of small flowers without stems suggesting a single flower

flowering plant *n* : any of a major group of vascular plants (as magnolias, grasses, or roses) that produce flowers and fruit and have the seeds enclosed in an ovary

flow·er·pot \'flaů(-ə)r-,pät\ *n* : a pot in which to grow plants

flow·ery \'flaů(-ə)r-ē\ *adj* **1** : of, relating to, or resembling flowers **2** : full of fine words or phrases — **flow·er·i·ness** \-ē-nəs\ *n*

flown \'flōn\ *past part of* ¹FLY

fl oz *abbr* fluid ounce

flu \'flü\ *n* **1** : INFLUENZA **2** : any of several virus diseases marked esp. by respiratory or intestinal symptoms — **flu·like** \-,līk\ *adj*

flub \'fləb\ *vb* **flubbed; flub·bing** : BOTCH, BLUNDER — **flub** *n*

fluc·tu·ate \'flək-chə-,wāt\ *vb* **-at·ed; -at·ing** **1** : WAVER **2** : to move up and down or back and forth — **fluc·tu·a·tion** \,flək-chə-'wā-shən\ *n*

flue \'flü\ *n* : a passage (as in a chimney) for directing a current (as of smoke or gases)

flu·ent \'flü-ənt\ *adj* **1** : capable of flowing : FLUID **2** : ready or facile in speech ⟨∼ in French⟩; *also* : having or showing mastery in a subject or skill **3** : effortlessly smooth and rapid ⟨∼ speech⟩ — **flu·en·cy** \-ən-sē\ *n* — **flu·ent·ly** *adv*

flue pipe *n* : an organ pipe whose tone is produced by an air current striking the beveled opening of the pipe

¹fluff \'fləf\ *n* **1** : ⁷DOWN 1 ⟨∼ from a pillow⟩ **2** : something fluffy **3** : something inconsequential **4** : BLUNDER; *esp* : an actor's lapse of memory

²fluff *vb* **1** : to make or become fluffy ⟨∼ up a pillow⟩ **2** : to make a mistake

fluffy \'flə-fē\ *adj* **fluff·i·er; -est** **1** : covered with or resembling fluff **2** : being light and soft or airy ⟨a ∼ omelet⟩ **3** : lacking in meaning or substance — **fluff·i·ly** \-fə-lē\ *adv*

¹flu·id \'flü-əd\ *adj* **1** : capable of flowing **2** : subject to change or movement **3** : showing a smooth easy style ⟨∼ movements⟩ **4** : available for a different use; *esp* : LIQUID 5 ⟨∼ assets⟩ — **flu·id·i·ty** \flü-'i-də-tē\ *n* — **flu·id·ly** *adv*

²fluid *n* : a substance (as a liquid or gas) tending to flow or take the shape of its container

fluid dram *or* **flu·i·dram** \,flü-ə-'dram\ *n* — see WEIGHT table

fluid ounce *n* — see WEIGHT table

¹fluke \'flük\ *n* : any of various trematode flatworms

²fluke *n* **1** : the part of an anchor that fastens in the ground **2** : a lobe of a whale's tail

³**fluke** *n* : a stroke of luck — **fluky** *also* **fluk-ey** \'flü-kē\ *adj*

flume \'flüm\ *n* 1 : an inclined channel for carrying water 2 : a ravine or gorge with a stream running through it

flung *past and past part of* FLING

flunk \'fləŋk\ *vb* : to fail esp. in an examination or course — **flunk** *n*

flun-ky *also* **flun-key** *or* **flun-kie** \'fləŋ-kē\ *n, pl* **flunkies** *also* **flunkeys** 1 : a liveried servant; *also* : one performing menial or miscellaneous duties 2 : YES-MAN

fluo-res-cence \flȯ-'res-ᵊns\ *n* : luminescence caused by radiation absorption that ceases almost immediately after the incident radiation has stopped; *also* : the emitted radiation — **fluo-resce** \-'res\ *vb* — **fluo-res-cent** \-'res-ᵊnt\ *adj*

fluorescent lamp *n* : a tubular electric lamp in which light is produced by the action of ultraviolet light on a fluorescent material that coats the inner surface of the lamp

fluo-ri-date \'flȯr-ə-,dāt\ *vb* **-dat-ed; -dat-ing** : to add a fluoride to (as drinking water) to reduce tooth decay — **fluo-ri-da-tion** \,flȯr-ə-'dā-shən\ *n*

fluo-ride \'flȯr-,īd\ *n* : a compound of fluorine

fluo-ri-nate \'flȯr-ə-,nāt\ *vb* **-nat-ed; -nat-ing** : to treat or cause to combine with fluorine or a compound of fluorine — **fluo-ri-na-tion** \,flȯr-ə-'nā-shən\ *n*

fluo-rine \'flȯr-,ēn, -ən\ *n* : a pale yellowish flammable irritating toxic gaseous chemical element

fluo-rite \'flȯr-,īt\ *n* : a mineral that consists of the fluoride of calcium used as a flux and in making glass

fluo-ro-car-bon \,flȯr-ō-'kär-bən\ *n* : a compound containing fluorine and carbon used chiefly as a lubricant, refrigerant, or nonstick coating; *also* : CHLORO-FLUOROCARBON

fluo-ro-scope \'flȯr-ə-,skōp\ *n* : an instrument for observing the internal structure of an opaque object (as the living body) by means of X-rays — **fluo-ro-scop-ic** \,flȯr-ə-'skä-pik\ *adj* — **fluo-ros-co-py** \-'ä-skə-pē\ *n*

fluo-ro-sis \flü-'rō-səs, ,flȯ-\ *n* : an abnormal condition (as spotting of the teeth) caused by fluorine or its compounds

flu-ox-e-tine \flü-'äk-sə-,tēn\ *n* : an antidepressant drug that enhances serotonin activity

flur-ry \'flər-ē\ *n, pl* **flurries** 1 : a gust of wind 2 : a brief light snowfall 3 : COMMOTION, BUSTLE 4 : a brief outburst of activity ⟨a ~ of trading⟩ — **flurry** *vb*

¹**flush** \'fləsh\ *vb* : to cause (a bird) to fly away suddenly

²**flush** *n* : a hand of cards all of the same suit

³**flush** *n* 1 : a sudden flow (as of water) 2 : a surge esp. of emotion ⟨a ~ of triumph⟩ 3 : a tinge of red : BLUSH 4 : a fresh and vigorous state ⟨in the ~ of youth⟩ 5 : a passing sensation of extreme heat

⁴**flush** *vb* 1 : to flow and spread suddenly and freely 2 : to glow brightly 3 : BLUSH 4 : to wash out with a rush of fluid 5 : INFLAME, EXCITE 6 : to cause to blush

⁵**flush** *adj* 1 : of a ruddy healthy color 2 : full of life and vigor 3 : filled to overflowing 4 : AFFLUENT 5 : readily available : ABUNDANT 6 : having an unbroken or even surface 7 : directly abutting : immediately adjacent 8 : set even with an edge of a type page or column — **flush-ness** *n*

⁶**flush** *adv* 1 : in a flush manner 2 : SQUARELY ⟨a blow ~ on the chin⟩

⁷**flush** *vb* : to make flush

flus-ter \'fləs-tər\ *vb* : to put into a state of agitated confusion — **fluster** *n*

flute \'flüt\ *n* 1 : a hollow pipelike musical instrument 2 : a grooved pleat 3 : GROOVE — **flute** *vb* — **flut-ed** *adj*

flut-ing *n* : fluted decoration

flut-ist \'flü-tist\ *n* : a flute player

¹**flut-ter** \'flə-tər\ *vb* [ME *floteren* to float, flutter, fr. OE *floterian*, fr. *flotian* to float] 1 : to flap the wings rapidly 2 : to move with quick wavering or flapping motions 3 : to vibrate in irregular spasms 4 : to move about or behave in an agitated aimless manner — **flut-tery** \-tə-rē\ *adj*

²**flutter** *n* 1 : an act of fluttering 2 : a state of nervous confusion 3 : FLURRY

¹**flux** \'fləks\ *n* 1 : an act of flowing 2 : a state of continuous change 3 : a substance used to aid in fusing metals

²**flux** *vb* : ¹FUSE

¹**fly** \'flī\ *vb* **flew** \'flü\; **flown** \'flōn\; **fly-ing** 1 : to move in or pass through the air with wings 2 : to move through the air or before the wind 3 : to float or cause to float, wave, or soar in the air 4 : FLEE 5 : to fade and disappear : VANISH 6 : to move or pass swiftly ⟨time *flies*⟩ 7 : to become expended or dissipated rapidly 8 : to operate or travel in an aircraft or spacecraft 9 : to journey over by flying 10 : AVOID, SHUN 11 : to transport by flying

²**fly** *n, pl* **flies** 1 : the action or process of flying : FLIGHT 2 *pl* : the space over a theater stage 3 : a garment closing concealed by a fold of cloth 4 : the length of an extended flag from its staff or support 5 : a baseball hit high into the air 6 : the outer canvas of a tent with a double top — **on the fly** : while still in the air

³**fly** *vb* **flied; fly-ing** : to hit a fly in baseball

⁴**fly** *n, pl* **flies** 1 : a winged insect — usu. used in combination ⟨butter*fly*⟩ 2 : any of a large order of insects mostly with one pair of functional wings and another pair that if present are reduced to balancing organs and often with larvae without a head, eyes, or legs; *esp* : one (as a housefly) that is large and stout-bodied 3 : a fishhook dressed to suggest an insect

fly-able \'flī-ə-bəl\ *adj* : suitable for flying or being flown

fly ball *n* : ²FLY 5

fly·blown \'flī-ˌblōn\ *adj* : not pure : TAINTED, CORRUPT

fly-by \-ˌbī\ *n, pl* **flybys** 1 : a usu. low-altitude flight by an aircraft over a public gathering 2 : a flight of a spacecraft past a heavenly body (as Jupiter) close enough to obtain scientific data

fly-by-night \-bī-ˌnīt\ *adj* 1 : seeking a quick profit usu. by shady acts 2 : TRANSITORY, PASSING ⟨~ fashions⟩

fly casting *n* : the casting of artificial flies in fly-fishing or as a competitive sport

fly-catch·er \-ˌka-chər, -ˌke-\ *n* : any of various passerine birds that feed on insects caught in flight

flyer *var of* FLIER

fly-fish·ing \'flī-ˌfi-shiŋ\ *n* : a method of fishing in which an artificial fly is used for bait

flying boat *n* : a seaplane with a hull designed for floating

flying buttress *n* : a projecting arched structure to support a wall or building

flying fish *n* : any of numerous marine bony fishes capable of long gliding flights out of water by spreading their large fins like wings

flying saucer *n* : an unidentified flying object reported to be saucer-shaped or disk-shaped

flying squirrel *n* : either of two small nocturnal No. American squirrels with folds of skin connecting the forelegs and hind legs that enable them to make long gliding leaps

fly·leaf \'flī-ˌlēf\ *n, pl* **fly-leaves** \-ˌlēvz\ : a blank leaf at the beginning or end of a book

fly·pa·per \-ˌpā-pər\ *n* : paper poisoned or coated with a sticky substance for killing or catching flies

fly·speck \-ˌspek\ *n* 1 : a speck of fly dung 2 : something small and insignificant

fly·way \-ˌwā\ *n* : an established air route of migratory birds

fly·wheel \-ˌhwēl\ *n* : a heavy wheel for regulating the speed of machinery

fm *abbr* fathom

Fm *symbol* fermium

FM \'ef-ˌem\ *n* : a broadcasting system using frequency modulation; *also* : a radio receiver of such a system

fn *abbr* footnote

fo *or* **fol** *abbr* folio

FO *abbr* foreign office

¹foal \'fōl\ *n* : a young horse or related animal; *esp* : one under one year

²foal *vb* : to give birth to a foal

¹foam \'fōm\ *n* 1 : a mass of bubbles formed on the surface of a liquid : FROTH, SPUME 2 : material (as rubber) in a lightweight cellular form — **foamy** *adj*

²foam *vb* : to form foam : FROTH

fob \'fäb\ *n* 1 : a short strap, ribbon, or chain attached esp. to a pocket watch 2 : a small ornament worn on a fob

FOB *abbr* free on board

fob off *vb* 1 : to put off with a trick, ex-

cuse, or inferior substitute 2 : to pass or offer as genuine 3 : to put aside

FOC *abbr* free of charge

focal length *n* : the distance of a focus from a lens or curved mirror

fo'c'sle *var of* FORECASTLE

¹fo·cus \'fō-kəs\ *n, pl* **fo·ci** \-ˌsī\ *also* **fo·cus·es** [NL, fr. L, hearth] 1 : a point at which rays (as of light, heat, or sound) meet or diverge or appear to diverge; *esp* : the point at which an image is formed by a mirror, lens, or optical system 2 : FOCAL LENGTH 3 : adjustment (as of eyes or eyeglasses) that gives clear vision 4 : central point : CENTER — **fo·cal** \'fō-kəl\ *adj* — **fo·cal·ly** *adv*

²focus *vb* **-cused** *also* **-cussed; -cus·ing** *also* **-cus·sing** 1 : to bring or come to a focus ⟨~ rays of light⟩ 2 : CENTER ⟨~ attention on a problem⟩ 3 : to adjust the focus of

fod·der \'fä-dər\ *n* 1 : coarse dry food (as cornstalks) for livestock 2 : available material used to supply a heavy demand

foe \'fō\ *n* [ME *fo*, fr. OE *fāh*, fr. *fāh* hostile] : ENEMY

FOE *abbr* Fraternal Order of Eagles

foehn *or* **föhn** \'fərn, 'fœn, 'fān\ *n* [G *Föhn*] : a warm dry wind blowing down a mountainside

foe·man \'fō-mən\ *n* : FOE

foe·tal, foe·tus *chiefly Brit var of* FETAL, FETUS

¹fog \'fȯg, 'fäg\ *n* 1 : fine particles of water suspended in the lower atmosphere 2 : mental confusion — **fog·gy** *adj*

²fog *vb* **fogged; fog·ging** : to obscure or be obscured with or as if with fog

fog·horn \'fȯg-ˌhȯrn, 'fäg-\ *n* : a horn sounded in a fog to give warning

fo·gy *also* **fo·gey** \'fō-gē\ *n, pl* **fogies** *also* **fogeys** : a person with old-fashioned ideas ⟨an old ~⟩

foi·ble \'fȯi-bəl\ *n* : a minor failing or weakness in character or behavior

foie gras \ˌfwä-'grä\ *n* [F, lit., fat liver] : the fattened liver of an animal and esp. of a goose usu. served as a pâté

¹foil \'fȯi(-ə)l\ *vb* [ME, alter. of *fullen* to full cloth, fr. AF *foller*] 1 : to prevent from attaining an end : DEFEAT 2 : to bring to naught : THWART

²foil *n* [ME, leaf, fr. AF *fuille, foille*, fr. L *folia*, pl. of *folium* leaf] 1 : a very thin sheet of metal ⟨aluminum ~⟩ 2 : one that serves as a contrast to another ⟨acted as a ~ for a comedian⟩

³foil *n* : a light fencing sword with a flexible blade tapering to a blunt point

foist \'fȯist\ *vb* : to pass off (something false or worthless) as genuine

¹fold \'fōld\ *n* 1 : an enclosure for sheep 2 : a group of people with a common faith, belief, or interest

²fold *vb* : to house (sheep) in a fold

³fold *vb* 1 : to lay one part over or against another part 2 : to clasp together 3 : EMBRACE 4 : to bend (as a layer of rock) into folds 5 : to incorporate into a mixture by overturning repeatedly without stirring or beating **6** : to become doubled or pleated **7** : FAIL, COLLAPSE ⟨the business ~*ed*⟩

⁴fold *n* **1** : a doubling or folding over **2** : a part doubled or laid over another part

fold-away \'fōld-ə-,wā\ *adj* : designed to fold out of the way or out of sight

fold-er \'fōl-dər\ *n* **1** : one that folds **2** : a folded printed circular **3** : a folded cover or large envelope for loose papers **4** : an object in a computer operating system used to organize files or other folders

fol-de-rol \'fäl-də-,räl\ *n* **1** : a useless trifle **2** : NONSENSE

fold-out \'fōld-,aút\ *n* : a folded leaf (as in a magazine) larger in some dimension than the page

fo-liage \'fō-lē-ij\ *n* : a mass of leaves (as of a plant or forest)

fo-li-at-ed \'fō-lē-,ā-təd\ *adj* : composed of or separable into layers

fo-lic acid \,fō-lik-\ *n* : a vitamin of the vitamin B complex used esp. to treat nutritional anemias

fo-lio \'fō-lē-,ō\ *n, pl* **fo-li-os** **1** : a leaf of a book; *also* : a page number **2** : the size of a piece of paper cut two from a sheet **3** : a book printed on folio pages

¹folk \'fōk\ *n, pl* **folk** *or* **folks** **1** : the largest number or most characteristic part of a group of people forming a tribe or nation **2** *pl* : PEOPLE, PERSONS ⟨country ~⟩ ⟨old ~s⟩ **3** *folks pl* : the persons of one's own family

²folk *adj* : of, relating to, or originating among the common people ⟨~ music⟩

folk art *n* : the traditional anonymous art of usu. untrained people

folk-lore \'fōk-,lór\ *n* : customs, beliefs, stories, and sayings of a people handed down from generation to generation — **folk-lor-ic** \-,lór-ik\ *adj* — **folk-lor-ist** \-ist\ *n*

folk mass *n* : a mass in which traditional liturgical music is replaced by folk music

folk-sing-er \'fōk-,siņ-ər\ *n* : a singer of folk songs — **folk-sing-ing** *n*

folksy \'fōk-sē\ *adj* **folks-i-er; -est** **1** : SOCIABLE, FRIENDLY **2** : informal, casual, or familiar in manner or style ⟨~ humor⟩

folk-way \'fōk-,wā\ *n* : a way of thinking, feeling, or acting common to a given group of people; *esp* : a traditional social custom

fol-li-cle \'fä-li-kəl\ *n* **1** : a small anatomical cavity or gland ⟨a hair ~⟩ **2** : a small fluid-filled cavity in the ovary of a mammal enclosing a developing egg — **fol-lic-u-lar** \fə-'li-kyə-lər\ *adj*

fol-low \'fä-lō\ *vb* **1** : to go or come after **2** : to proceed along ⟨~ the path⟩ **3** : to engage in as a way of life ⟨~ the sea⟩ ⟨~ a profession⟩ **4** : OBEY ⟨~ instructions⟩ **5** : PURSUE **6** : to come after in order or rank or natural sequence **7** : to keep one's attention fixed on **8** : to result from ✦ *Synonyms* SUCCEED, ENSUE, SUPERVENE — **fol-low-er** *n* — **follow suit** **1** : to play a card of the same suit as the card led **2** : to follow an example set

¹fol-low-ing \'fä-lə-wiņ\ *adj* **1** : next after : SUCCEEDING ⟨the ~ day⟩ **2** : that immediately follows ⟨trains will leave at the ~ times⟩

²following *n* : a group of followers, adherents, or partisans

³following *prep* : subsequent to : AFTER ⟨~ the lecture tea was served⟩

follow-up \'fä-lō-,əp\ *n* : a system or instance of pursuing an initial effort by supplementary action

fol-ly \'fä-lē\ *n, pl* **follies** [ME *folie*, fr. AF, fr. *fol* fool] **1** : lack of good sense **2** : a foolish act or idea : FOOLISHNESS **3** : an excessively costly or unprofitable undertaking

fo-ment \fō-'ment\ *vb* : INCITE

fo-men-ta-tion \,fō-mən-'tā-shən, -,men-\ *n* **1** : a hot moist material (as a damp cloth) applied to the body to ease pain **2** : the act of fomenting : INSTIGATION

fond \'fänd\ *adj* [ME, fr. *fonne* fool] **1** : FOOLISH, SILLY ⟨~ pride⟩ **2** : prizing highly : DESIROUS ⟨~ of praise⟩ **3** : strongly attracted or predisposed ⟨~ of music⟩ **4** : foolishly tender : INDULGENT; *also* : LOVING, AFFECTIONATE **5** : CHERISHED, DEAR ⟨his ~*est* hopes⟩ — **fond-ly** *adv* — **fond-ness** *n*

fon-dant \'fän-dənt\ *n* : a creamy preparation of sugar used as a basis for candies or icings

fon-dle \'fän-d⁰l\ *vb* **fon-dled; fon-dling** : to touch or handle lovingly : CARESS

fon-due *also* **fon-du** \fän-'dü, -'dyü\ *n* [F] : a preparation of melted cheese often flavored with white wine

¹font \'fänt\ *n* **1** : a receptacle for baptismal or holy water **2** : FOUNTAIN, SOURCE ⟨a ~ of information⟩

²font *n* : an assortment of printing type of one style and sometimes one size

food \'füd\ *n* **1** : material taken into an organism and used for growth, repair, and vital processes and as a source of energy; *also* : organic material produced by green plants and used by them as food **2** : nourishment in solid form **3** : something that nourishes, sustains, or supplies ⟨~ for thought⟩

food chain *n* **1** : a hierarchical arrangement of organisms in an ecological community such that each uses the next usu. lower member as a food source **2** : a hierarchy based on power or importance

food court *n* : an area (as within a shopping mall) set apart for food concessions

food poisoning *n* : a digestive illness caused by bacteria or by chemicals in food

food-stuff \'füd-,stəf\ *n* : a substance with food value; *esp* : a specific nutrient (as fat or protein)

¹fool \'fül\ *n* [ME, fr. AF *fol*, fr. LL *follis*, fr. L, bellows, bag] **1** : a person who lacks sense or judgment **2** : JESTER **3** : DUPE **4** : IDIOT

²fool *vb* **1** : to spend time idly or aimlessly **2** : to meddle or tamper thoughtlessly or ignorantly **3** : JOKE **4** : DECEIVE **5** : FRITTER ⟨~*ed* away his time⟩

fool·ery \'fü-lə-rē\ n, pl **-er·ies** 1 : a foolish act, utterance, or belief 2 : foolish behavior

fool·har·dy \'fül-,här-dē\ adj : foolishly daring : RASH — **fool·har·di·ness** \-dē-nəs\ n

fool·ish \'fü-lish\ adj 1 : showing or arising from folly or lack of judgment 2 : ABSURD, RIDICULOUS 3 : ABASHED — **fool·ish·ly** adv — **fool·ish·ness** n

fool·proof \'fül-,prüf\ adj : so simple or reliable as to leave no opportunity for error, misuse, or failure ⟨a ~ plan⟩

fools·cap \'fül-,skap\ n [fr. the watermark of a fool's cap formerly applied to such paper] : a size of paper typically 16×13 inches

fool's gold n : PYRITE

¹foot \'fut\ n, pl **feet** \'fēt\ also **foot** 1 : the end part of a leg below the ankle of a vertebrate animal 2 — see WEIGHT table 3 : a group of syllables forming the basic unit of verse meter 4 : something resembling an animal's foot in position or use 5 : the lowest part : BOTTOM 6 : the part at the opposite end from the head 7 : the part (as of a stocking) that covers the foot

²foot vb 1 : DANCE 2 : to go on foot 3 : to add up 4 : to pay or provide for paying

foot·age \'fu-tij\ n 1 : length expressed in feet 2 : the length of film used for a scene; also : the material contained on such footage

foot–and–mouth disease n : an acute contagious viral disease esp. of cattle

foot·ball \'fut-,bol\ n 1 : any of several games played by two teams on a rectangular field with goalposts at each end in which the object is to get the ball over the goal line or between goalposts by running, passing, or kicking 2 : the ball used in football

foot·board \-,bord\ n 1 : a narrow platform on which to stand or brace the feet 2 : a board forming the foot of a bed

foot·bridge \-,brij\ n : a bridge for pedestrians

foot·ed \'fu-təd\ adj : having a foot or feet of a specified kind or number ⟨flat-footed⟩ ⟨four-footed⟩

-foot·er \'fu-tər\ comb form : one that is a specified number of feet in height, length, or breadth ⟨a six-footer⟩

foot·fall \'fut-,fol\ n : the sound of a footstep

foot·hill \-,hil\ n : a hill at the foot of higher hills or mountains

foot·hold \-,hōld\ n 1 : a hold for the feet : FOOTING 2 : a position usable as a base for further advance

foot·ing n 1 : the placing of one's feet in a stable position 2 : the act of moving on foot 3 : a place or space for standing : FOOTHOLD 4 : position with respect to one another : STATUS 5 : BASIS

foot·less \'fut-ləs\ adj 1 : having no feet ⟨~ tights⟩ 2 : INEPT, INEFFECTUAL

foot·lights \-,līts\ n pl 1 : a row of lights along the front of a stage floor 2 : the stage as a profession

foot·ling \'fut-liŋ\ adj 1 : INEPT ⟨~ amateurs⟩ 2 : TRIVIAL

foot·lock·er \'fut-,lä-kər\ n : a small trunk designed to be placed at the foot of a bed (as in a barracks)

foot·loose \-,lüs\ adj : having no ties : FREE, UNTRAMMELED

foot·man \-mən\ n : a male servant who attends a carriage or waits on table, admits visitors, and runs errands

foot·note \-,nōt\ n 1 : a note of reference, explanation, or comment placed usu. at the bottom of a page 2 : COMMENTARY

foot·pad \-,pad\ n : a round somewhat flat foot on the leg of a spacecraft for distributing weight to minimize sinking into a surface

foot·path \-,path, -,pȧth\ n : a narrow path for pedestrians

foot·print \-,print\ n 1 : an impression of the foot 2 : the area on a surface covered by something ⟨a tire with a wide ~⟩

foot·race \-,rās\ n : a race run on foot

foot·rest \-,rest\ n : a support for the feet

foot·sore \-,sȯr\ adj : having sore or tender feet (as from much walking)

foot·step \-,step\ n 1 : the mark of the foot : TRACK 2 : TREAD 3 : distance covered by a step : PACE 4 : a step on which to ascend or descend 5 : a way of life, conduct, or action

foot·stool \-,stül\ n : a low stool to support the feet

foot·wear \-,wer\ n : apparel (as shoes or boots) for the feet

foot·work \-,wərk\ n : the management of the feet (as in boxing)

fop \'fäp\ n : DANDY 1 — **fop·pery** \'fä-pə-rē\ n — **fop·pish** adj

¹for \fər, 'fȯr\ prep 1 : as a preparation toward ⟨dress ~ dinner⟩ 2 : toward the purpose or goal of ⟨need time ~ study⟩ ⟨money ~ a trip⟩ 3 : so as to reach or attain ⟨run ~ cover⟩ 4 : as being ⟨took him ~ a fool⟩ 5 : because of ⟨cry ~ joy⟩ 6 — used to indicate a recipient ⟨a letter ~ you⟩ 7 : in support of ⟨fought ~ his country⟩ 8 : directed at : AFFECTING ⟨a cure ~ what ails you⟩ 9 — used with a noun or pronoun followed by an infinitive to form the equivalent of a noun clause ⟨~ you to go would be silly⟩ 10 : in exchange as equal to : so as to return the value of ⟨a lot of trouble ~ nothing⟩ ⟨pay $10 ~ a hat⟩ 11 : CONCERNING ⟨a stickler ~ detail⟩ 12 : CONSIDERING ⟨tall ~ her age⟩ 13 : through the period of ⟨served ~ three years⟩ 14 : in honor of ⟨named ~ her grandmother⟩

²for conj : BECAUSE

³for abbr 1 foreign 2 forestry

fo·ra pl of FORUM

¹for·age \'fȯr-ij\ n [ME, fr. AF, fr. fuerre, foer fodder, straw, of Gmc origin] 1 : food for animals esp. when taken by browsing or grazing 2 : a search for food or supplies

²forage vb **for·aged; for·ag·ing** 1 : to collect forage from 2 : to search for food or supplies **3** : to get by foraging **4** : to make a search : RUMMAGE

for·ay \'for-ˌā, fo-'rā\ vb : to raid esp. in search of plunder : PILLAGE — **foray** n

¹**for·bear** \for-'ber\ vb **-bore** \-'bōr\; **-borne** \-'bōrn\; **-bear·ing 1** : to refrain from : ABSTAIN **2** : to be patient — **for·bear·ance** \-'ber-əns\ n

²**forbear** var of FOREBEAR

for·bid \fər-'bid\ vb **-bade** \-'bad, -'bād also **-bad** \-'bad\; **-bid·den** \-'bi-dᵊn\; **-bid·ding 1** : to command against : PROHIBIT **2** : HINDER, PREVENT ♦ *Synonyms* ENJOIN, INTERDICT, INHIBIT, BAN

forbidding adj : DISAGREEABLE, REPELLENT ⟨a ~ task⟩

¹**force** \'fōrs\ n **1** : strength or energy esp. of an exceptional degree : active power **2** : capacity to persuade or convince **3** : military strength; also, pl : the whole military strength (as of a nation) **4** : a body (as of persons or ships) available for a particular purpose **5** : VIOLENCE, COMPULSION **6** : an influence (as a push or pull) that causes motion or a change of motion — **force·ful** \-fəl\ adj — **force·ful·ly** adv — **in force 1** : in great numbers **2** : VALID, OPERATIVE ⟨the ban remains *in force*⟩

²**force** vb **forced; forc·ing 1** : COMPEL, COERCE **2** : to cause through necessity ⟨*forced* to admit defeat⟩ **3** : to press, attain to, or effect against resistance or inertia ⟨~ your way through⟩ **4** : to raise or accelerate to the utmost ⟨~ the pace⟩ **5** : to produce with unnatural or unwilling effort ⟨*forced* a smile⟩ **6** : to hasten (as in growth) by artificial means

for·ceps \'for-səps\ n, pl **forceps** [L] : a hand-held instrument for grasping, holding, or pulling objects esp. for delicate operations (as by a surgeon)

forc·ible \'for-sə-bəl\ adj **1** : obtained or done by force **2** : showing force or energy : POWERFUL — **forc·i·bly** \-blē\ adv

¹**ford** \'ford\ n : a place where a stream may be crossed by wading

²**ford** vb : to cross (a body of water) by wading

¹**fore** \'for\ adv : in, toward, or adjacent to the front : FORWARD

²**fore** adj : being or coming before in time, order, or space

³**fore** n : something that occupies a front position

⁴**fore** interj — used by a golfer to warn anyone within range of the probable line of flight of the ball

fore–and–aft \ˌfor-ə-'naft\ adj : lying, running, or acting along the length of a structure (as a ship)

¹**fore·arm** \(ˌ)for-'ärm\ vb : to arm in advance : PREPARE

²**fore·arm** \'for-ˌärm\ n : the part of the arm between the elbow and the wrist

fore·bear \-ˌber\ n : ANCESTOR, FOREFATHER

fore·bode also **for·bode** \for-'bōd\ vb **1** : to have a premonition esp. of misfortune **2** : FORETELL, PREDICT ♦ *Synonyms* AUGUR, BODE, FORESHADOW,

PORTEND, PROMISE — **fore·bod·ing** n or adj — **fore·bod·ing·ly** adv

fore·cast \'for-ˌkast\ vb **-cast** also **-casted; -cast·ing 1** : PREDICT, CALCULATE ⟨~ weather conditions⟩ **2** : to indicate as likely to occur — **forecast** n — **fore·cast·er** n

fore·cas·tle or **fo'c·sle** \'fōk-səl\ n **1** : the forward part of the upper deck of a ship **2** : the crew's quarters usu. in a ship's bow

fore·close \for-'klōz\ vb **1** : to shut out : PRECLUDE **2** : to take legal measures to terminate a mortgage and take possession of the mortgaged property

fore·clo·sure \-'klō-zhər\ n : the act of foreclosing; esp : the legal procedure of foreclosing a mortgage

fore·doom \for-'düm\ vb : to doom beforehand

fore·fa·ther \'for-ˌfä-thər\ n **1** : ANCESTOR **2** : a person of an earlier period and common heritage

forefend var of FORFEND

fore·fin·ger \-ˌfin-gər\ n : INDEX FINGER

fore·foot \-ˌfut\ n : either of the front feet of a quadruped; also : the front part of the human foot

fore·front \-ˌfrənt\ n : the foremost part or place

foregather var of FORGATHER

¹**fore·go** \for-'gō\ vb **-went** \-'went\; **-gone** \-'gon\; **-go·ing** : PRECEDE

²**forego** var of FORGO

fore·go·ing adj : PRECEDING ⟨the ~ statement can be proven⟩

fore·gone \'for-ˌgon\ adj : determined in advance ⟨a ~ conclusion⟩

fore·ground \-ˌgraund\ n **1** : the part of a scene or representation that appears nearest to and in front of the spectator **2** : a position of prominence

fore·hand \-ˌhand\ n : a stroke (as in tennis) made with the palm of the hand turned in the direction in which the hand is moving; also : the side on which such a stroke is made — **forehand** adj

fore·hand·ed \(ˌ)for-'han-dəd\ adj : mindful of the future : PRUDENT

fore·head \'for-əd, 'for-ˌhed\ n : the part of the face above the eyes

for·eign \'for-ən\ adj [ME forein, fr. AF, fr. LL foranus on the outside, fr. L foris outside] **1** : situated outside a place or country and esp. one's own country **2** : born in, belonging to, or characteristic of some place or country other than the one under consideration ⟨~ language⟩ **3** : not connected, pertinent, or characteristically present **4** : related to or dealing with other nations ⟨~ affairs⟩ **5** : occurring in an abnormal situation in the living body ⟨a ~ body in the eye⟩

for·eign·er \'for-ə-nər\ n : a person belonging to or owing allegiance to a foreign country

foreign minister n : a governmental minister for foreign affairs

fore·know \for-'nō\ vb **-knew** \-'nü, -'nyü\; **-known** \-'nōn\; **-know·ing** : to have previous knowledge of — **fore-knowl-edge** \'fȯr-ˌnä-lij, fȯr-'nä-\ *n*

fore-la-dy \'fȯr-ˌlā-dē\ *n* : FOREWOMAN

fore-leg \-ˌleg\ *n* : a front leg

fore-limb \-ˌlim\ *n* : a front or upper limb (as a wing, arm, fin, or leg)

fore-lock \-ˌläk\ *n* : a lock of hair growing from the front part of the head

fore-man \-mən\ *n* 1 : a spokesperson of a jury 2 : a person in charge of a group of workers

fore-mast \-ˌmast\ *n* : the mast nearest the bow of a ship

fore-most \-ˌmōst\ *adj* : first in time, place, or order : most important : PRE-EMINENT — **foremost** *adv*

fore-name \-ˌnām\ *n* : a first name

fore-named \-ˌnāmd\ *adj* : previously named : AFORESAID

fore-noon \-ˌnün\ *n* : MORNING

¹**fo-ren-sic** \fə-'ren-sik\ *adj* [L *forensis* public, forensic, fr. *forum* forum] 1 : belonging to, used in, or suitable to courts of law or to public speaking or debate 2 : relating to the application of scientific knowledge to legal problems ⟨∼ medicine⟩

²**forensic** *n* 1 : an argumentative exercise 2 *pl* : the art or study of argumentative discourse 3 *pl* : scientific analysis of physical evidence (as from a crime scene)

fore-or-dain \ˌfȯr-ȯr-'dān\ *vb* : to ordain or decree beforehand : PREDESTINE

fore-part \'fȯr-ˌpärt\ *n* 1 : the anterior part of something 2 : the earlier part of a period of time

fore-quar-ter \-ˌkwȯr-tər\ *n* : the front half of a lateral half of the body or carcass of a quadruped ⟨a ∼ of beef⟩

fore-run-ner \-ˌrə-nər\ *n* 1 : one that goes before to give notice of the approach of others : HARBINGER 2 : PREDECESSOR, ANCESTOR ♦ *Synonyms* PRECURSOR, HERALD

fore-sail \-ˌsāl, -səl\ *n* 1 : the lowest sail on the foremast of a square-rigged ship or schooner 2 : the principal sail forward of the foremast (as of a sloop)

fore-see \fȯr-'sē\ *vb* **-saw** \-'sȯ\; **-seen** \-'sēn\; **-see-ing** : to see or realize beforehand : EXPECT ♦ *Synonyms* FORE-KNOW, DIVINE, APPREHEND, ANTICIPATE — **fore-see-able** *adj*

fore-shad-ow \-'sha-dō\ *vb* : to give a hint or suggestion of beforehand

fore-short-en \fȯr-'shȯr-t⁸n\ *vb* : to shorten (a detail) in a drawing or painting so that it appears to have depth

fore-sight \'fȯr-ˌsīt\ *n* 1 : the act or power of foreseeing 2 : care or provision for the future : PRUDENCE 3 : an act of looking forward; *also* : a view forward — **fore-sight-ed** \-ˌsī-təd\ *adj* — **fore-sight-ed-ly** *adv* — **fore-sight-ed-ness** *n*

fore-skin \-ˌskin\ *n* : a fold of skin enclosing the end of the penis

for-est \'fȯr-əst\ *n* [ME, fr. AF, fr. LL *forestis* (*silva*) unenclosed (woodland), fr. L *foris* outside] : a large thick growth of

trees and underbrush — **for-est-ed** \'fȯr-ə-stəd\ *adj* — **for-est-land** \'fȯr-əst-ˌland\ *n*

fore-stall \fȯr-'stȯl, fȯr-\ *vb* 1 : to keep out, hinder, or prevent by measures taken in advance 2 : ANTICIPATE

forest ranger *n* : a person in charge of the management and protection of a portion of a forest

for-est-ry \'fȯr-ə-strē\ *n* : the science of growing and caring for forests — **for-est-er** \'fȯr-ə-stər\ *n*

foreswear *var of* FORSWEAR

¹**fore-taste** *n* : an advance indication, warning, or notion

²**fore-taste** \fȯr-'tāst\ *vb* : to taste beforehand : ANTICIPATE

fore-tell \fȯr-'tel\ *vb* **-told** \-'tōld\; **-tell-ing** : to tell of beforehand : PREDICT ♦ *Synonyms* FORECAST, PROPHESY, PROGNOSTICATE

fore-thought \'fȯr-ˌthȯt\ *n* 1 : PREMEDITATION 2 : consideration for the future

fore-to-ken \fȯr-'tō-kən\ *vb* : to indicate in advance

fore-top \'fȯr-ˌtäp\ *n* : a platform near the top of a ship's foremast

for-ev-er \fȯr-'e-vər\ *adv* 1 : for a limitless time 2 : at all times : ALWAYS

for-ev-er-more \-ˌe-vər-'mȯr\ *adv* : FOREVER

fore-warn \fȯr-'wȯrn\ *vb* : to warn beforehand — **fore-warn-ing** \'wȯr-niŋ\ *n*

forewent *past of* FOREGO

fore-wing \'fȯr-ˌwiŋ\ *n* : either of the anterior wings of a 4-winged insect

fore-wom-an \'fȯr-ˌwu̇-mən\ *n* : a woman having the responsibilities of a foreman

fore-word \-ˌwərd\ *n* : PREFACE

¹**for-feit** \'fȯr-fət\ *n* [ME *forfait*, fr. AF, pp. of *forfaire*, *forsfaire* to commit a crime, forfeit, fr. *fors* outside + *faire* to do] 1 : something forfeited : PENALTY, FINE 2 : FORFEITURE 3 : something deposited and then redeemed on payment of a fine 4 *pl* : a game in which forfeits are exacted

²**forfeit** *vb* : to lose or lose the right to esp. by some error, offense, or crime

for-fei-ture \'fȯr-fə-ˌchu̇r\ *n* 1 : the act of forfeiting 2 : something forfeited : PENALTY

for-fend \fȯr-'fend\ *vb* 1 : PREVENT 2 : PROTECT, PRESERVE

for-gath-er *or* **fore-gath-er** \fȯr-'ga-thər\ *vb* 1 : to come together : ASSEMBLE 2 : to meet someone usu. by chance

¹**forge** \'fȯrj\ *n* [ME, fr. AF, fr. L *fabrica*, fr. *faber* smith] : a furnace or shop with its furnace where metal is heated and worked

²**forge** *vb* **forged; forg-ing** 1 : to form (metal) by heating and hammering 2 : FASHION, SHAPE ⟨∼ an agreement⟩ 3 : to make or imitate falsely esp. with intent to defraud ⟨∼ a signature⟩ — **forg-er** *n* — **forg-ery** \'fȯr-jə-rē\ *n*

³**forge** *vb* **forged; forg-ing** : to move ahead steadily but gradually

for-get \fər-'get\ *vb* **-got** \-'gät\; **-got-ten** \-'gät-⁸n\ *or* **-got; -get-ting** 1 : to be unable to think of or recall **2** : to fail to become mindful of at the proper time **3** : NEGLECT, DISREGARD **4** : to give up hope for or expectation of — **for·get·ful** \-'get-fəl\ adj — **for·get·ful·ly** adv — **for·get·ful·ness** n

for·get–me–not \fər-'get-mē-ˌnät\ n : any of a genus of small herbs with bright blue or white flowers

forg·ing n : a piece of forged work

for·give \fər-'giv\ vb **-gave** \-'gāv\; **-giv·en** \-'gi-vən\; **-giv·ing 1** : to give up resentment of **2** : PARDON, ABSOLVE **3** : to grant relief from payment of — **for·giv·able** adj — **for·give·ness** n — **for·giv·er** n

forgiving adj **1** : willing or able to forgive **2** : allowing room for error or weakness

for·go \fȯr-'gō\ vb **-went** \-'went\; **-gone** \-'gȯn\; **-go·ing** : to give up the enjoyment or advantage of : do without

fo·rint \'fȯr-int\ n, pl **forints** also **forint** — see MONEY table

¹fork \'fȯrk\ n **1** : an implement with two or more prongs for taking up (as in eating), pitching, or digging **2** : a forked part, tool, or piece of equipment **3** : a dividing into branches or a place where something branches; also : a branch of such a fork

²fork vb **1** : to divide into two or more branches **2** : to give the form of a fork to ⟨~ing her fingers⟩ **3** : to raise or pitch with a fork ⟨~ hay⟩ **4** : PAY, CONTRIBUTE — used with over, out, or up

forked \'fȯrkt, 'fȯr-kəd\ adj : having a fork : shaped like a fork ⟨~ lightning⟩

fork·lift \'fȯrk-ˌlift\ n : a machine for lifting heavy objects by means of steel fingers inserted under the load

for·lorn \fər-'lȯrn, fȯr-\ adj **1** : sad and lonely because of isolation or desertion **2** : WRETCHED **3** : nearly hopeless — **for·lorn·ly** adv — **for·lorn·ness** n

¹form \'fȯrm\ n **1** : SHAPE, STRUCTURE **2** : a body esp. of a person : FIGURE **3** : the essential nature of a thing **4** : established manner of doing or saying something **5** : FORMULA **6** : a document with blank spaces for insertion of information ⟨tax ~⟩ **7** : CEREMONY **8** : manner of performing according to recognized standards **9** : a long seat : BENCH **10** : a model of the human figure used for displaying clothes **11** : MOLD ⟨a ~ for concrete⟩ **12** : type or plates in a frame ready for printing **13** : MODE, KIND, VARIETY ⟨coal is a ~ of carbon⟩ **14** : orderly method of arrangement; also : a particular kind or instance of such arrangement ⟨the sonnet ~ in poetry⟩ **15** : the structural element, plan, or design of a work of art **16** : a bounded surface or volume **17** : a grade in a British school or in some American private schools **18** : RACING FORM **19** : known ability to perform; also : condition (as of an athlete) suitable for performing **20** : one of the ways in which a word is

changed to show difference in use ⟨the plural ~ of a noun⟩ — **form·less** adj

²form vb **1** : to give form or shape to : FASHION, MAKE **2** : TRAIN, INSTRUCT **3** : CONSTITUTE, COMPOSE **4** : DEVELOP, ACQUIRE ⟨~ a habit⟩ **5** : to arrange in order ⟨~ a battle line⟩ **6** : to take form : ARISE ⟨clouds are ~ing⟩ **7** : to take a definite form, shape, or arrangement

¹for·mal \'fȯr-məl\ adj **1** : according with conventional forms and rules ⟨a ~ dinner party⟩ **2** : done in due or lawful form ⟨a ~ contract⟩ **3** : CEREMONIOUS, PRIM ⟨a ~ manner⟩ **4** : NOMINAL — **for·mal·ly** adv

²formal n : something (as a social event) formal in character

form·al·de·hyde \fȯr-'mal-də-ˌhīd\ n : a colorless pungent gas used in water solution as a preservative and disinfectant

for·mal·ise Brit var of FORMALIZE

for·mal·ism \'fȯr-mə-ˌli-zəm\ n : strict adherence to set forms

for·mal·i·ty \fȯr-'ma-lə-tē\ n, pl **-ties 1** : compliance with formal or conventional rules **2** : the quality or state of being formal **3** : an established form that is required or conventional

for·mal·ize \'fȯr-mə-ˌlīz\ vb **-ized; -iz·ing 1** : to give a certain or definite form to **2** : to make formal; also : to give formal status or approval to

¹for·mat \'fȯr-ˌmat\ n **1** : the general composition or style of a publication **2** : the general plan or arrangement of something **3** : a method of organizing data ⟨various file ~s⟩

²format vb **for·mat·ted; for·mat·ting** : to arrange (as material to be printed) in a particular format — **for·mat·ter** n

for·ma·tion \fȯr-'mā-shən\ n **1** : an act of giving form to something : DEVELOPMENT **2** : something that is formed **3** : STRUCTURE, SHAPE **4** : an arrangement of persons or things in a prescribed manner or for a certain purpose

for·ma·tive \'fȯr-mə-tiv\ adj **1** : giving or capable of giving form : CONSTRUCTIVE **2** : of, relating to, or characterized by important growth or formation ⟨a child's ~ years⟩

for·mer \'fȯr-mər\ adj **1** : PREVIOUS, EARLIER **2** : FOREGOING ⟨the ~ part of the chapter⟩ **3** : being first mentioned or in order of two or more things

for·mer·ly \-lē\ adv : in time past : PREVIOUSLY

form-fit·ting \'fȯrm-ˌfi-tiŋ\ adj : conforming to the outline of the body ⟨a ~ sweater⟩

for·mi·da·ble \'fȯr-mə-də-bəl, fȯr-'mi-\ adj **1** : exciting fear, dread, or awe ⟨a ~ foe⟩ **2** : imposing serious difficulties ⟨a ~ barrier⟩ — **for·mi·da·bly** \-blē\ adv

form letter n **1** : a letter on a frequently recurring topic that can be sent to different people at different times **2** : a letter for mass circulation sent out in many printed copies

for·mu·la \'fȯr-myə-lə\ n, pl **-las** or **-lae** \-ˌlē, -ˌlī\ **1** : a set form of words for ceremonial use **2** : RECIPE, PRESCRIPTION **3** : a milk mixture or substitute for a baby **4** : a group of symbols or figures joined to express information concisely **5** : a customary or set form or method

for·mu·late \-ˌlāt\ *vb* **-lat·ed; -lat·ing 1** : to express in a formula **2** : DESIGN, DEVISE ⟨∼ a policy⟩ **3** : to prepare according to a formula — **for·mu·la·tion** \ˌfȯr-myə-ˈlā-shən\ *n*

for·ni·ca·tion \ˌfȯr-nə-ˈkā-shən\ *n* : consensual sexual intercourse between two persons not married to each other — **for·ni·cate** \ˈfȯr-nə-ˌkāt\ *vb* — **for·ni·ca·tor** \-ˌkā-tər\ *n*

for·sake \fər-ˈsāk, fȯr-\ *vb* **for·sook** \-ˈsu̇k\; **for·sak·en** \-ˈsā-kən\; **for·sak·ing** [ME, fr. OE *forsacan*, fr. *sacan* to dispute] : to renounce or turn away from entirely

for·sooth \fər-ˈsüth\ *adv* : in truth : INDEED

for·swear \fȯr-ˈswer\ *vb* **-swore** \-ˈswȯr\; **-sworn** \-ˈswȯrn\; **-swear·ing 1** : to swear falsely : commit perjury **2** : to renounce earnestly or under oath **3** : to deny under oath

for·syth·ia \fər-ˈsi-thē-ə\ *n, pl* **-ias** *also* **-ia** : any of a genus of shrubs related to the olive and having yellow bell-shaped flowers appearing before the leaves in early spring

fort \ˈfȯrt\ *n* [ME *forte*, fr. AF *fort*, fr. *fort* strong, fr. L *fortis*] **1** : a fortified place **2** : a permanent army post

¹for·te \ˈfȯrt, ˈfȯr-ˌtā\ *n* [F *fort*, fr. *fort*, adj., strong] : one's strong point

²for·te \ˈfȯr-ˌtā\ *adv or adj* [It, fr. *forte* strong] : LOUD — used as a direction in music

forth \ˈfȯrth\ *adv* **1** : FORWARD, ONWARD ⟨from that day ∼⟩ **2** : out into view ⟨plants putting ∼ leaves⟩

forth·com·ing \ˈfȯrth-ˈkə-miŋ\ *adj* **1** : coming or available soon ⟨the ∼ holidays⟩ **2** : marked by openness and candor : OUTGOING

forth·right \ˈfȯrth-ˌrīt\ *adj* : free from ambiguity or evasiveness : going straight to the point ⟨a ∼ answer⟩ — **forth·right·ly** *adv* — **forth·right·ness** *n*

forth·with \ˌfȯrth-ˈwith\ *adv* : IMMEDIATELY

for·ti·fy \ˈfȯr-tə-ˌfī\ *vb* **-fied; -fy·ing 1** : to strengthen by military defenses **2** : to give physical strength or endurance to **3** : ENCOURAGE **4** : to strengthen or enrich with a material ⟨∼ bread with vitamins⟩ — **for·ti·fi·ca·tion** \ˌfȯr-tə-fə-ˈkā-shən\ *n*

for·tis·si·mo \fȯr-ˈti-sə-ˌmō\ *adv or adj* : very loud — used as a direction in music

for·ti·tude \ˈfȯr-tə-ˌtüd, -ˌtyüd\ *n* : strength of mind that enables one to meet danger or bear pain or adversity with courage ♦ **Synonyms** GRIT, BACKBONE, PLUCK, GUTS

fort·night \ˈfȯrt-ˌnīt\ *n* [ME *fourtenight*, alter. of *fourtene night* fourteen nights] : two weeks — **fort·night·ly** \-lē\ *adj or adv*

for·tress \ˈfȯr-trəs\ *n* : FORT 1

for·tu·itous \fȯr-ˈtü-ə-təs, -ˈtyü-\ *adj* **1** : happening by chance **2** : FORTUNATE — **for·tu·itous·ly** *adv*

for·tu·ity \-ə-tē\ *n, pl* **-ities 1** : the quality or state of being fortuitous **2** : a chance event or occurrence

for·tu·nate \ˈfȯr-chə-nət\ *adj* **1** : bringing some good thing not foreseen **2** : LUCKY

for·tu·nate·ly \-lē\ *adv* **1** : in a fortunate manner **2** : it is fortunate that

for·tune \ˈfȯr-chən\ *n* **1** : prosperity attained partly through luck; *also* : CHANCE, LUCK **2** : what happens to a person : good or bad luck **3** : FATE, DESTINY **4** : RICHES, WEALTH

fortune hunter *n* : a person who seeks wealth esp. by marriage

for·tune-tell·er \-ˌte-lər\ *n* : a person who professes to foretell future events — **fortune-tell·ing** *n or adj*

for·ty \ˈfȯr-tē\ *n, pl* **forties** : four times 10 — **for·ti·eth** \ˈfȯr-tē-əth\ *adj or n* — **forty** *adj or pron*

for·ty-five \ˌfȯr-tē-ˈfīv\ *n* **1** : a .45 caliber handgun — usu. written .45 **2** : a phonograph record designed to be played at 45 revolutions per minute — usu. written 45

for·ty-nin·er \-ˈnī-nər\ *n* : a person in the rush to California for gold in 1849

forty winks *n sing or pl* : a short sleep

fo·rum \ˈfȯr-əm\ *n, pl* **forums** *also* **fo·ra** \-ə\ [L] **1** : the marketplace or central meeting place of an ancient Roman city **2** : a medium (as a publication or online service) of open discussion **3** : COURT **4** : a public assembly, lecture, or program involving audience or panel discussion

¹for·ward \ˈfȯr-wərd\ *adj* **1** : being near or at or belonging to the front **2** : EAGER, READY **3** : BRASH, BOLD **4** : notably advanced or developed : PRECOCIOUS **5** : moving, tending, or leading toward a position in front **6** : EXTREME, RADICAL **7** : of, relating to, or getting ready for the future — **for·ward·ness** *n*

²forward *adv* : to or toward what is ahead or in front

³forward *vb* **1** : to help onward : ADVANCE **2** : to send forward : TRANSMIT **3** : to send or ship onward

⁴forward *n* : a player who plays at the front of a team's offensive formation near the opponent's goal

for·ward·er \-wər-dər\ *n* : one that forwards; *esp* : an agent who forwards goods

for·wards \ˈfȯr-wərdz\ *adv* : FORWARD

forwent *past of* FORGO

¹fos·sil \ˈfä-səl\ *adj* [L *fossilis* obtained by digging, fr. *fodere* to dig] **1** : preserved from a past geologic age ⟨∼ plants⟩ **2** : of or relating to fossil fuels

²fossil *n* **1** : a trace or impression or the remains of a plant or animal of a past geologic age preserved in the earth's crust **2** : a person whose ideas are out-of-date — **fos·sil·ize** \ˈfä-sə-ˌlīz\ *vb*

fossil fuel *n* : a fuel (as coal or oil) that is formed in the earth from plant or animal remains

¹fos·ter \ˈfȯs-tər\ *adj* [ME, fr. OE *fōstor-*, fr. *fōstor* food, feeding] : affording, receiving, or sharing nourishment or parental care though not related by blood or legal ties ⟨∼ parent⟩ ⟨∼ child⟩

²**foster** vb 1 : to give parental care to : NURTURE 2 : to promote the growth or development of : ENCOURAGE

foster home n : a household in which an orphaned, neglected, or delinquent child is placed for care

fos·ter·ling \-tər-liŋ\ n : a foster child

Fou·cault pendulum \ˌfü-ˈkō-\ n : a device that consists of a heavy weight hung by a long wire and that swings in a constant direction which appears to change showing that the earth rotates

fought past and past part of FIGHT

¹**foul** \ˈfaú-(ə)l\ adj 1 : offensive to the senses : LOATHSOME; also : clogged with dirt 2 : ODIOUS, DETESTABLE ⟨a ∼ crime⟩ 3 : OBSCENE, ABUSIVE ⟨∼ language⟩ 4 : DISAGREEABLE, STORMY ⟨∼ weather⟩ 5 : TREACHEROUS, DISHONORABLE, UNFAIR 6 : marking the bounds of a playing field ⟨∼ lines⟩; also : being outside the foul line ⟨∼ ball⟩ ⟨∼ territory⟩ 7 : containing marked-up corrections 8 : ENTANGLED — **foul·ly** adv — **foul·ness** n

²**foul** n 1 : an entanglement or collision in fishing or sailing 2 : an infraction of the rules in a game or sport; also : a baseball hit outside the foul line

³**foul** vb 1 : to make or become foul or filthy 2 : to entangle or become entangled 3 : OBSTRUCT, BLOCK 4 : to collide with 5 : to make or hit a foul

⁴**foul** adv : in a foul manner

fou·lard \fù-ˈlärd\ n : a lightweight silk of plain or twill weave usu. decorated with a printed pattern

foul·mouthed \ˈfaú(-ə)l-ˈmaút͟hd, -ˈmaútht\ adj : given to the use of obscene, profane, or abusive language

foul of prep : AFOUL OF

foul play n : VIOLENCE; esp : MURDER

foul–up \ˈfaú(-ə)l-ˌəp\ n 1 : a state of being fouled up 2 : a mechanical difficulty

foul up vb 1 : to spoil by mistakes or poor judgment 2 : to cause a foul-up : BUNGLE

¹**found** \ˈfaúnd\ past and past part of FIND

²**found** vb [ME, fr. AF funder, fonder, fr. L fundare, fr. fundus bottom] 1 : to take the first steps in building 2 : to set or ground on something solid : BASE 3 : to establish (as an institution) often with provision for future maintenance — **found·er** n

foun·da·tion \faún-ˈdā-shən\ n 1 : the act of founding 2 : a basis upon which something stands or is supported ⟨suspicions without ∼⟩ 3 : funds given for the permanent support of an institution : ENDOWMENT; also : an institution so endowed 4 : supporting structure : BASE 5 : CORSET — **foun·da·tion·al** \-shə-nəl\ adj

foun·der \ˈfaún-dər\ vb 1 : to make or become lame ⟨the horse ∼ed⟩ 2 : COLLAPSE 3 : SINK ⟨a ∼ing ship⟩ 4 : FAIL

found·ling \ˈfaúnd-liŋ\ n : an infant found after its unknown parents have abandoned it

found·ry \ˈfaún-drē\ n, pl **foundries** : a building or works where metal is cast

fount \ˈfaúnt\ n : SOURCE, FOUNTAIN

foun·tain \ˈfaún-t²n\ n 1 : a spring of water 2 : SOURCE 3 : an artificial jet of water 4 : a container for liquid that can be drawn off as needed

foun·tain·head \-ˌhed\ n : SOURCE

fountain pen n : a pen with a reservoir that feeds the writing point with ink

four \ˈfōr\ n 1 : one more than three 2 : the 4th in a set or series 3 : something having four units — **four** adj or pron

4x4 also **four–by–four** \ˈfōr-bī-ˌfōr\ n : a four-wheel automobile with four-wheel drive

four–flush \-ˌfləsh\ vb : to make a false claim : BLUFF — **four–flush·er** n

four·fold \-ˌfōld, -ˈfōld\ adj 1 : being four times as great or as many 2 : having four units or members — **four·fold** \-ˈfōld\ adv

4–H \ˈfōr-ˈāch\ adj [fr. the fourfold aim of improving the head, heart, hands, and health] : of or relating to a program set up by the U.S. Department of Agriculture to help young people become productive citizens — **4–H'·er** n

Four Hundred or **400** n : the exclusive social set of a community — used with the

four–in–hand \ˈfōr-ən-ˌhand\ n 1 : a team of four horses driven by one person; also : a vehicle drawn by such a team 2 : a necktie tied in a slipknot with long ends overlapping vertically in front

four–o'clock \ˈfōr-ə-ˌkläk\ n : a garden plant with fragrant yellow, red, or white flowers without petals that open late in the afternoon

four–post·er \ˌfōr-ˈpō-stər\ n : a bed with tall corner posts orig. designed to support curtains or a canopy

four·score \ˈfōr-ˌskōr\ adj : being four times twenty : EIGHTY

four·some \ˈfōr-səm\ n 1 : a group of four persons or things 2 : a golf match between two pairs of partners

four·square \-ˈskwer\ adj 1 : SQUARE 2 : marked by boldness and conviction : FORTHRIGHT — **foursquare** adv

four·teen \fōr-ˈtēn\ n : one more than 13 — **fourteen** adj or pron — **four·teenth** \-ˈtēnth\ adj or n

fourth \ˈfōrth\ n 1 : one that is number four in a countable series 2 : one of four equal parts of something — **fourth** adj or adv

fourth estate n, often cap F&E : the public press

fourth wall n : an imaginary wall that keeps performers from recognizing or directly addressing their audience

4WD abbr four-wheel drive

four–wheel \ˈfōr-ˌhwēl\ or **four–wheeled** \-ˌhwēld\ adj : acting on or by means of four wheels of a motor vehicle ⟨∼ disc brakes⟩

four–wheel drive *n* : an automotive drive mechanism that acts on all four wheels of the vehicle; *also* : a vehicle with such a drive

¹**fowl** \ˈfau̇(-ə)l\ *n, pl* **fowl** *or* **fowls** **1** : BIRD **2** : a cock or hen of the domestic chicken; *also* : the flesh of these used as food

²**fowl** *vb* : to hunt wildfowl

¹**fox** \ˈfäks\ *n, pl* **fox·es** *also* **fox** **1** : any of various flesh-eating mammals related to the wolves but smaller and with shorter legs and a more pointed muzzle; *also* : the fur of a fox **2** : a clever crafty person **3** *cap* : a member of an American Indian people formerly living in what is now Wisconsin

²**fox** *vb* : TRICK, OUTWIT

fox·glove \ˈfäks-ˌgləv\ *n* : a common plant related to the snapdragons that is grown for its showy spikes of dotted white or purple tubular flowers and as a source of digitalis

fox·hole \-ˌhōl\ *n* : a pit dug for protection against enemy fire

fox·hound \-ˌhau̇nd\ *n* : any of various large swift powerful hounds used in hunting foxes

fox·ing \ˈfäk-siŋ\ *n* : brownish spots on old paper

fox terrier *n* : a small lively terrier that occurs in varieties with smooth dense coats or with harsh wiry coats

fox–trot \ˈfäks-ˌträt\ *n* **1** : a short broken slow trotting gait **2** : a ballroom dance in duple time

foxy \ˈfäk-sē\ *adj* **fox·i·er; -est 1** : resembling or suggestive of a fox **2** : WILY **3** : physically attractive

foy·er \ˈfȯi(-ə)r, ˈfȯi-ˌyā\ *n* [F, lit., fireplace, fr. OF *foier*, fr. VL **focarium*, fr. L *focus* hearth] : LOBBY; *also* : an entrance hallway

fpm *abbr* feet per minute

FPO *abbr* fleet post office

fps *abbr* feet per second

fr *abbr* **1** father **2** franc **3** friar **4** from

¹**Fr** *abbr* **1** France; French **2** Friday

²**Fr** *symbol* francium

fra·cas \ˈfrā-kəs, ˈfra-\ *n, pl* **fra·cas·es** \-kə-səz\ [F, din, row, fr. It *fracasso*, fr. *fracassare* to shatter] : BRAWL

frac·tal \ˈfrak-tᵊl\ *n* : an irregular curve or shape that repeats itself at any scale on which it is examined — **fractal** *adj*

frac·tion \ˈfrak-shən\ *n* **1** : a numerical representation (as ¹/₂, ³/₄, or 3.323) indicating the quotient of two numbers **2** : FRAGMENT **3** : PORTION ⟨a small ∼ of voters⟩ — **frac·tion·al** \-shə-nəl\ *adj* — **frac·tion·al·ly** *adv*

frac·tious \ˈfrak-shəs\ *adj* **1** : tending to be troublesome : hard to handle or control **2** : QUARRELSOME, IRRITABLE

frac·ture \ˈfrak-chər\ *n* : a breaking of something and esp. a bone **2** : CRACK, CLEFT — **fracture** *vb*

frag·ile \ˈfra-jəl, -ˌjī(-ə)l\ *adj* : easily broken : DELICATE — **fra·gil·i·ty** \frə-ˈji-lə-tē\ *n*

¹**frag·ment** \ˈfrag-mənt\ *n* : a part broken off, detached, or incomplete

²**frag·ment** \-ˌment\ *vb* : to break into fragments — **frag·men·ta·tion** \ˌfrag-mən-ˈtā-shən, -ˌmən-\ *n*

frag·men·tary \ˈfrag-mən-ˌter-ē\ *adj* : made up of fragments : INCOMPLETE ⟨a ∼ account⟩

fra·grant \ˈfrā-grənt\ *adj* : sweet or agreeable in smell — **fra·grance** \-grəns\ *n* — **fra·grant·ly** *adv*

frail \ˈfrāl\ *adj* [ME, fr. AF *fraile*, fr. L *fragilis* fragile, fr. *frangere* to break] **1** : morally or physically weak **2** : FRAGILE, DELICATE

frail·ty \ˈfrāl-tē\ *n, pl* **frailties 1** : the quality or state of being frail **2** : a fault due to weakness

¹**frame** \ˈfrām\ *vb* **framed; fram·ing 1** : PLAN, CONTRIVE **2** : SHAPE, CONSTRUCT **3** : FORMULATE **4** : DRAW UP ⟨∼ a constitution⟩ **5** : to make appear guilty **6** : to fit or adjust for a purpose : ARRANGE **7** : to provide with or enclose in a frame — **fram·er** *n*

²**frame** *n* **1** : something made of parts fitted and joined together **2** : the physical makeup of the body **3** : an arrangement of structural parts that gives form or support **4** : a supporting or enclosing border or open case (as for a window or picture) **5** : one picture of a series (as on a length of film) **6** : FRAME-UP

³**frame** *adj* : having a wood frame ⟨∼ houses⟩

frame of mind *n* : mental attitude or outlook : MOOD

frame–up \ˈfrā-ˌməp\ *n* **1** : an act or series of actions in which someone is framed **2** : an action that is planned, contrived, or formulated

frame·work \ˈfrām-ˌwərk\ *n* : a basic supporting part or structure

franc \ˈfraŋk\ *n* **1** : any of various former basic monetary units (as of Belgium, France, and Luxembourg) **2** — see MONEY table

fran·chise \ˈfran-ˌchīz\ *n* [ME, fr. AF, fr. *franchir* to free, fr. *franc* free] **1** : a right or license granted to an individual or group ⟨a ∼ to operate a ferry⟩ **2** : a constitutional or statutory right or privilege; *esp* : the right to vote **3** : the right of membership in a professional sports league; *also* : a team having such membership

fran·chi·see \ˌfran-chī-ˈzē, -chə-\ *n* : one granted a franchise

fran·chis·er \ˈfran-ˌchī-zər\ *n* **1** : FRANCHISEE **2** : FRANCHISOR

fran·chi·sor \ˌfran-chī-ˈzȯr, -chə-\ *n* : one that grants a franchise

fran·ci·um \ˈfran-sē-əm\ *n* : a radioactive metallic chemical element

Fran·co–Amer·i·can \ˌfraŋ-kō-ə-ˈmer-ə-kən\ *n* : an American of French or esp. French-Canadian descent — **Franco-American** *adj*

fran·gi·ble \ˈfran-jə-bəl\ *adj* : BREAKABLE — **fran·gi·bil·i·ty** \ˌfran-jə-ˈbi-lə-tē\ *n*

¹**frank** \ˈfraŋk\ *adj* : marked by free, forth-

right, and sincere expression — **frank·ness** n

²**frank** vb : to mark (a piece of mail) with an official sign so that it can be mailed free; also : to mail free

³**frank** n 1 : the signature or mark on a piece of mail indicating free or paid postage 2 : the privilege of sending mail free

⁴**frank** n : FRANKFURTER

Fran·ken·stein \'fraŋ-kən-ˌstīn\ n 1 : a monstrous creation that usu. ruins its originator 2 : a monster in the shape of a man

frank·furt·er \'fraŋk-fər-tər, -ˌfər-\ or **frank·furt** \-fərt\ n : a seasoned sausage (as of beef or beef and pork)

frank·in·cense \'fraŋ-kən-ˌsens\ n : a fragrant resin burned as incense

frank·ly \'fraŋ-klē\ adv 1 : in a frank manner 2 : in truth : INDEED ⟨~, I don't know⟩

fran·tic \'fran-tik\ adj : marked by uncontrolled emotion or disordered anxious activity — **fran·ti·cal·ly** \-ti-k(ə-)lē\ adv

frap·pé \fra-'pā\ or **frappe** \same or 'frap\ n [F frappé, fr. pp. of frapper to strike, chill] 1 : an iced or frozen drink 2 : a thick milk shake — **frap·pé** \fra-'pā\ adj

fra·ter·nal \frə-'tər-n²l\ adj 1 : of, relating to, or involving brothers 2 : of, relating to, or being a fraternity or society 3 : derived from two ova ⟨~ twins⟩ 4 : FRIENDLY, BROTHERLY — **fra·ter·nal·ly** adv

fra·ter·ni·ty \frə-'tər-nə-tē\ n, pl **-ties** 1 : a social, honorary, or professional group; esp : a men's student organization 2 : BROTHERLINESS, BROTHERHOOD 3 : persons of the same class, profession, or tastes

frat·er·nize \'fra-tər-ˌnīz\ vb **-nized; -niz·ing** 1 : to mingle as friends 2 : to associate on close terms with members of a hostile group — **frat·er·ni·za·tion** \ˌfra-tər-nə-'zā-shən\ n

frat·ri·cide \'fra-trə-ˌsīd\ n 1 : one that kills a sibling or countryman 2 : the act of a fratricide — **frat·ri·cid·al** \ˌfra-trə-'sī-d²l\ adj

fraud \'frȯd\ n 1 : DECEIT, TRICKERY 2 : TRICK 3 : IMPOSTOR, CHEAT

fraud·ster \'frȯd-stər\ n, chiefly Brit : a person who engages in fraud

fraud·u·lent \'frȯ-jə-lənt\ adj : characterized by, based on, or done by fraud : DECEITFUL — **fraud·u·lence** \-ləns\ n — **fraud·u·lent·ly** adv

fraught \'frȯt\ adj : full of or accompanied by something specified ⟨~ with danger⟩

¹**fray** \'frā\ n : FIGHT, STRUGGLE; also : QUARREL, DISPUTE

²**fray** vb 1 : to wear (as an edge of cloth) by rubbing 2 : to separate the threads at the edge of 3 : STRAIN, IRRITATE ⟨~ed nerves⟩

fraz·zle \'fra-zəl\ vb **fraz·zled; frazzling** 1 : FRAY 2 : to put in a state of extreme physical or nervous fatigue — **frazzle** n

¹**freak** \'frēk\ n, 1 : WHIM, CAPRICE 2 : a strange, abnormal, or unusual person or thing 3 slang : a person who uses an illicit drug 4 : an ardent enthusiast — **freak·ish** adj — **freaky** \'frē-kē\ adj

²**freak** vb 1 : to experience the effects (as hallucinations) of taking illicit drugs — often used with out 2 : to distress or become distressed — often used with out — **freak–out** \'frē-ˌkau̇t\ n

freck·le \'fre-kəl\ n : a small brownish spot on the skin — **freckle** vb

¹**free** \'frē\ adj **fre·er; fre·est** 1 : having liberty 2 : enjoying political or personal independence; also : not subject to or allowing slavery 3 : made or done voluntarily : SPONTANEOUS 4 : relieved from or lacking something unpleasant 5 : not subject to a duty, tax, or charge 6 : not obstructed : CLEAR 7 : not being used or occupied ⟨waved with my ~ hand⟩ 8 : not fastened ⟨the ~ end of the rope⟩ 9 : LAVISH 10 : OPEN, FRANK 11 : given without charge 12 : not literal or exact ⟨~ translation⟩ 13 : not restricted to conventional forms ⟨~ skating⟩ — **free·ly** adv

²**free** vb **freed; free·ing** 1 : to set free 2 : RELIEVE, RID 3 : DISENTANGLE, CLEAR ✦ **Synonyms** RELEASE, LIBERATE, DISCHARGE, EMANCIPATE, LOOSE

³**free** adv 1 : FREELY 2 : without charge

free·base \'frē-ˌbās\ n : purified cocaine smoked as crack or heated to produce vapors for inhalation — **freebase** vb

free·bie or **free·bee** \'frē-bē\ n : something given without charge

free·board \'frē-ˌbȯrd\ n : the vertical distance between the waterline and the upper edge of the side of a boat

free·boot·er \-ˌbü-tər\ n [D vrijbuiter, fr. vrijbuit plunder, fr. vrij free + buit booty] : PLUNDERER, PIRATE

free·born \-'bȯrn\ adj 1 : not born in vassalage or slavery 2 : of, relating to, or befitting one that is freeborn

freed·man \'frēd-mən, -ˌman\ n : a person freed from slavery

free·dom \'frē-dəm\ n 1 : the quality or state of being free : INDEPENDENCE 2 : EXEMPTION, RELEASE 3 : EASE, FACILITY ⟨spoke the language with ~⟩ 4 : FRANKNESS 5 : unrestricted use 6 : a political right; also : FRANCHISE, PRIVILEGE

freedom fighter n : a person who takes part in a resistance movement against an oppressive political or social establishment

free enterprise n : freedom of private business to operate with little regulation by the government

free–for–all \'frē-fə-ˌrȯl\ n : a competition or fight open to all comers and usu. with no rules : BRAWL — **free–for–all** adj

free–hand \-ˌhand\ adj : done without mechanical aids or devices

free·hold \'frē-ˌhōld\ n : ownership of an estate for life usu. with the right to bequeath it to one's heirs; *also* : an estate thus owned — **free·hold·er** *n*

free·lance \-,lans\ *n* : one who pursues a profession (as writing) without a long-term commitment to any one employer — **free·lance** *adj or vb*

free–living \'frē-'li·viŋ\ *adj* 1 : unrestricted in pursuing personal pleasures 2 : being neither parasitic nor symbiotic ⟨∼ organisms⟩

free·load \'frē-,lōd\ *vb* : to impose upon another's hospitality — **free·load·er** *n*

free love *n* 1 : the practice of living openly with one of the opposite sex without marriage 2 : sexual relations without any commitments by either partner

free·man \'frē-mən, -,man\ *n* 1 : one who has civil or political liberty 2 : one having the full rights of a citizen

Free·ma·son \-,mā-s°n\ *n* : a member of a secret fraternal society called Free and Accepted Masons — **Free·ma·son·ry** \-rē\ *n*

free radical *n* : an esp. reactive atom or group of atoms with one or more unpaired electrons; *esp* : one that can cause bodily damage (as by altering the chemical structure of cells)

free–range \'frē-'rānj\ *adj* : allowed to range and forage with relative freedom ⟨∼ chickens⟩; *also* : produced by free-range animals ⟨∼ eggs⟩

free speech *n* : speech that is protected by the First Amendment to the U.S. Constitution

free spirit *n* : NONCONFORMIST

free·stand·ing \'frē-'stan-diŋ\ *adj* : standing alone or on its own foundation free of support

free·stone \'frē-,stōn\ *n* 1 : a stone that may be cut freely without splitting 2 : a fruit stone to which the flesh does not cling; *also* : a fruit (as a peach or cherry) having such a stone

free·think·er \-'thiŋ-kər\ *n* : one who forms opinions on the basis of reason independently of authority; *esp* : one who doubts or denies religious dogma — **free·think·ing** *n or adj*

free trade *n* : trade between nations without restrictions (as high taxes on imports)

free verse *n* : verse whose meter is irregular or whose rhythm is not metrical

free·ware \'frē-,wer\ *n* : software that is free or that has a small usu. optional cost

free·way \'frē-,wā\ *n* : an expressway without tolls

free·wheel \-'hwēl\ *vb* : to move, live, or play freely or irresponsibly

free·will \'frē-,wil\ *adj* : VOLUNTARY

free will *n* : voluntary choice or decision

¹**freeze** \'frēz\ *vb* **froze** \'frōz\; **fro·zen** \'frō-z°n\; **freez·ing** 1 : to harden or cause to harden into a solid (as ice) by loss of heat 2 : to withstand freezing 3 : to chill or become chilled with cold 4 : to damage by frost 5 : to adhere solidly by or as if by freezing 6 : to become fixed, motionless, or incapable of speech 7 : to cause to grip tightly 8 : to become clogged with ice 9 : to fix at a certain stage or level ⟨∼ wages⟩

²**freeze** *n* 1 : an act or instance of freezing 2 : the state of being frozen 3 : a state of weather marked by low temperature

freeze–dry \'frēz-'drī\ *vb* : to dry in a frozen state under vacuum esp. for preservation — **freeze–dried** *adj*

freez·er \'frē-zər\ *n* : a compartment, device, or room for freezing food or keeping it frozen

¹**freight** \'frāt\ *n* 1 : payment for carrying goods 2 : CARGO 3 : BURDEN 4 : the carrying of goods by a common carrier 5 : a train that carries freight

²**freight** *vb* 1 : to load with goods for transportation 2 : BURDEN, CHARGE 3 : to ship or transport by freight

freight·er \'frā-tər\ *n* : a ship or airplane used chiefly to carry freight

French \'french\ *n* 1 : the language of France 2 **French** *pl* : the people of France 3 : strong language — **French** *adj* — **French·man** \-mən\ *n* — **French·wom·an** \-,wù-mən\ *n*

French door *n* : a door with small panes of glass extending the full length

French dressing *n* 1 : a thin salad dressing usu. made of vinegar and oil with spices 2 : a creamy salad dressing flavored with tomatoes

french fry *n, often cap 1st F* : a strip of potato fried in deep fat until brown — **french fry** *vb, often cap 1st F*

French horn *n* : a curved brass instrument with a funnel-shaped mouthpiece and a flaring bell

French press *n* : a coffeepot in which ground beans are infused and then pressed by a plunger

French toast *n* : bread dipped in a mixture of eggs and milk and fried at a low heat

French twist *n* : a woman's hairstyle in which the hair is coiled at the rear and secured in place

fre·net·ic \fri-'ne-tik\ *adj* : FRANTIC — **fre·net·i·cal·ly** \-ti-k(ə-)lē\ *adv*

fren·zy \'fren-zē\ *n, pl* **frenzies** 1 : temporary madness or a violently agitated state 2 : intense often disordered activity — **fren·zied** \-zēd\ *adj*

freq *abbr* frequency; frequent; frequently

fre·quen·cy \'frē-kwən-sē\ *n, pl* **-cies** 1 : the fact or condition of occurring frequently 2 : rate of occurrence 3 : the number of cycles per second of an alternating current 4 : the number of waves (as of sound or electromagnetic energy) that pass a fixed point each second

frequency modulation *n* : variation of the frequency of a carrier wave according to another signal; *also* : FM

¹**fre·quent** \frē-'kwent, 'frē-kwənt\ *vb* : to associate with, be in, or resort to habitually — **fre·quent·er** *n*

²**fre·quent** \'frē-kwənt\ *adj* 1 : happening often or at short intervals ⟨making ∼ stops⟩ 2 : HABITUAL ⟨a ∼ visitor⟩ — **fre·quent·ly** *adv*

fre·quent–fli·er \'frē-kwənt-'flī-ər\ *adj* : of, relating to, or being an airline program offering awards for specified numbers of air miles traveled

fres·co \'fres-kō\ *n, pl* **frescoes** [It, fr. *fresco* fresh] : the art of painting on fresh plaster; *also* : a painting done by this method

fresh \'fresh\ *adj* **1** : VIGOROUS, REFRESHED **2** : not stale, sour, or decayed ⟨~ bread⟩ **3** : not faded **4** : not worn or rumpled **5** : not altered by processing (as freezing or canning) **6** : not containing salt **7** : free from taint : PURE ⟨~ air⟩ **8** : fairly strong : BRISK ⟨~ breeze⟩ **9** : experienced, made, or received newly or anew **10** : ADDITIONAL, ANOTHER ⟨made a ~ start⟩ **11** : ORIGINAL, VIVID ⟨a ~ portrayal⟩ **12** : INEXPERIENCED **13** : newly come or arrived ⟨~ from school⟩ **14** : IMPUDENT — **fresh·ly** *adv* — **fresh·ness** *n*

fresh·en \'fre-shən\ *vb* : to make, grow, or become fresh

fresh·et \'fre-shət\ *n* : an overflowing of a stream (as by heavy rains)

fresh·man \'fresh-mən\ *n* **1** : a 1st-year student **2** : BEGINNER, NEWCOMER

fresh·wa·ter \-,wȯ-tər, -,wä-\ *n* : water that is not salty — **freshwater** *adj*

¹**fret** \'fret\ *vb* **fret·ted**; **fret·ting** [ME, to devour, fret, fr. OE *fretan* to devour] **1** : WEAR, CORRODE; *also* : FRAY **2** : RUB, CHAFE **3** : to make by wearing away **4** : to become irritated : WORRY, VEX **5** : GRATE; *also* : AGITATE

²**fret** *n* : an irritated or worried state ⟨in a ~ about the interview⟩

³**fret** *n* : ornamental work esp. of straight lines in symmetrical patterns

⁴**fret** *n* : one of a series of ridges across the fingerboard of a stringed musical instrument — **fret·ted** *adj*

fret·ful \'fret-fəl\ *adj* : IRRITABLE — **fret·ful·ly** *adv* — **fret·ful·ness** *n*

fret·saw \-,sȯ\ *n* : a narrow-bladed handsaw used for cutting curved outlines

fret·work \-,wərk\ *n* **1** : decoration consisting of frets **2** : ornamental openwork or work in relief

Fri *abbr* Friday

fri·a·ble \'frī-ə-bəl\ *adj* : easily crumbled or pulverized ⟨~ soil⟩

fri·ar \'frī(-ə)r\ *n* [ME *frere, fryer,* fr. AF *frere, friere,* lit., brother, fr. L *frater*] : a member of a religious order that orig. lived by alms

fri·ary \'frī(-ə)r-ē\ *n, pl* **-ar·ies** : a monastery of friars

¹**fric·as·see** \'fri-kə-,sē, ,fri-kə-'sē\ *n* : a dish made of meat (as chicken) cut into pieces, stewed in stock, and served in sauce

²**fricassee** *vb* **-seed**; **-see·ing** : to cook as a fricassee

fric·tion \'frik-shən\ *n* **1** : the rubbing of one body against another **2** : the force that resists motion between bodies in contact **3** : clash in opinions between persons or groups : DISAGREEMENT — **fric·tion·al** *adj*

friction tape *n* : a usu. cloth adhesive tape impregnated with insulating material and used esp. to protect and insulate electrical conductors

Fri·day \'frī-dē, -(,)dā\ *n* : the sixth day of the week

fridge \'frij\ *n* : REFRIGERATOR

fried·cake \'frīd-,kāk\ *n* : DOUGHNUT, CRULLER

fried rice *n* : a dish of boiled or steamed rice that is stir-fried with soy sauce and typically includes egg, meat, and vegetables

friend \'frend\ *n* **1** : one attached to another by respect or affection **2** : ACQUAINTANCE **3** : one who is not hostile **4** : one who supports or favors something ⟨a ~ of art⟩ **5** *cap* : a member of the Society of Friends : QUAKER — **friend·less** *adj* — **friend·li·ness** \-lē-nəs\ *n* — **friend·ly** *adj* — **friend·ship** \-,ship\ *n*

frieze \'frēz\ *n* : an ornamental often sculptured band extending around something (as a building or room)

frig·ate \'fri-gət\ *n* **1** : a square-rigged warship **2** : a warship smaller than a destroyer

fright \'frīt\ *n* **1** : sudden terror : ALARM **2** : something that is ugly or shocking

fright·en \'frī-t³n\ *vb* **1** : to make afraid **2** : to drive away or out by frightening **3** : to become frightened — **fright·en·ing·ly** *adv*

fright·ful \'frīt-fəl\ *adj* **1** : TERRIFYING **2** : STARTLING **3** : EXTREME ⟨~ thirst⟩ — **fright·ful·ly** *adv* — **fright·ful·ness** *n*

frig·id \'fri-jəd\ *adj* **1** : intensely cold **2** : lacking warmth or ardor : INDIFFERENT **3** : abnormally averse to or unable to achieve orgasm during sexual intercourse — used esp. of women — **fri·gid·i·ty** \fri-'ji-də-tē\ *n*

frigid zone *n* : the area or region between the arctic circle and the north pole or between the antarctic circle and the south pole

frill \'fril\ *n* **1** : a gathered, pleated, or ruffled edging **2** : something unessential — **frilly** *adj*

fringe \'frinj\ *n* [ME *frenge,* fr. AF, fr. VL *frimbia,* alter. of L *fimbriae* (pl.)] **1** : an ornamental border consisting of short threads or strips hanging from an edge or band **2** : something that resembles a fringe : EDGE ⟨operated on the ~s of the law⟩ **3** : something that is additional or secondary to an activity, process, or subject — **fringe** *vb*

fringe benefit *n* **1** : an employment benefit paid for by an employer without affecting basic wage rates **2** : any additional benefit

frip·pery \'fri-pə-rē\ *n, pl* **-per·ies** [MF *friperie*] **1** : FINERY **2** : pretentious display

frisk \'frisk\ *vb* **1** : to leap, skip, or dance in a lively or playful way : GAMBOL **2** : to search (a person) esp. for concealed weapons by running the hand rapidly over the clothing

frisky \'fris-kē\ *adj* **frisk·i·er**; **-est** : PLAYFUL — **frisk·i·ly** \-kə-lē\ *adv* — **frisk·i·ness** \-kē-nəs\ *n*

¹**frit·ter** \'fri-tər\ n : a small lump of fried batter often containing fruit or meat

²**fritter** vb 1 : to reduce or waste piecemeal 2 : to break into small fragments

fritz \'frits\ n : a state of disorder or disrepair — used in the phrase *on the fritz*

friv·o·lous \'fri-və-ləs\ adj 1 : of little importance : TRIVIAL 2 : lacking in seriousness — **fri·vol·i·ty** \fri-'vä-lə-tē\ n — **friv·o·lous·ly** adv

frizz \'friz\ vb : to form into small tight curls — **frizz** n — **frizzy** adj

friz·zies \'fri-zēz\ n pl : hair which has become difficult to manage (as due to humidity)

¹**friz·zle** \'fri-zəl\ vb **friz·zled; friz·zling** : FRIZZ, CURL — **frizzle** n

²**frizzle** vb **friz·zled; friz·zling** 1 : to fry until crisp and curled 2 : to cook with a sizzling noise

fro \'frō\ adv : BACK, AWAY — used in the phrase *to and fro*

frock \'fräk\ n 1 : an outer garment worn by monks and friars 2 : an outer garment worn esp. by men 3 : a woman's or girl's dress

frock coat n : a man's knee-length usu. double-breasted coat

frog \'frög, 'fräg\ n 1 : any of various largely aquatic smooth-skinned tailless leaping amphibians 2 : an ornamental braiding for fastening the front of a garment by a loop through which a button passes 3 : a condition in the throat causing hoarseness 4 : a small holder (as of metal, glass, or plastic) with perforations or spikes that is placed in a bowl or vase to keep cut flowers in position

frog·man \'frög-,man, 'fräg-, -mən\ n : a swimmer equipped to work underwater for long periods of time

¹**frol·ic** \'frä-lik\ vb **frol·icked; frol·ick·ing** 1 : to make merry 2 : to play about happily : ROMP

²**frolic** n 1 : a playful or mischievous action 2 : FUN, MERRIMENT — **frol·ic·some** \-səm\ adj

from \'frəm, 'främ\ prep 1 — used to show a starting point ⟨a letter ∼ home⟩ 2 — used to show removal or separation ⟨subtract 3 ∼ 9⟩ 3 — used to show a material, source, or cause ⟨suffering ∼ a cold⟩

frond \'fränd\ n : a usu. large divided leaf esp. of a fern or palm tree

¹**front** \'frənt\ n 1 : FOREHEAD; *also* : the whole face 2 : external and often feigned appearance 3 : a region of active fighting; *also* : a sphere of activity 4 : a political coalition 5 : the side of a building containing the main entrance 6 : the forward part or surface 7 : FRONTAGE 8 : a boundary between two dissimilar air masses 9 : a position directly before or ahead of something else 10 : a person, group, or thing used to mask the identity of the actual controlling agent

²**front** vb 1 : to have the principal side adjacent to something 2 : to serve as a front 3 : CONFRONT

front·age \'frən-tij\ n 1 : a piece of land lying adjacent (as to a street or the ocean) 2 : the length of a frontage 3 : the front side of a building

front·al \'frən-t°l\ adj 1 : of, relating to, or next to the forehead 2 : of, relating to, or directed at the front ⟨a ∼ attack⟩ — **fron·tal·ly** adv

fron·tier \,frən-'tir\ n 1 : a border between two countries 2 : a region that forms the margin of settled territory 3 : the outer limits of knowledge or achievement ⟨the ∼s of science⟩ — **fron·tiers·man** \-'tirz-mən\ n

fron·tis·piece \'frən-tə-,spēs\ n : an illustration preceding and usu. facing the title page of a book

front man n : a person serving as a front or figurehead

front·ward \'frənt-wərd\ *or* **front·wards** \-wərdz\ adv or adj : toward the front

¹**frost** \'fröst\ n 1 : freezing temperature 2 : a covering of tiny ice crystals on a cold surface — **frosty** adj

²**frost** vb 1 : to cover with frost 2 : to put icing on (as a cake) 3 : to produce a slightly roughened surface on (as glass) 4 : to injure or kill by frost

¹**frost·bite** \'fröst-,bit\ vb **-bit** \-,bit\; **-bit·ten** \-,bi-t°n\; **-bit·ing** : to injure by frost or frostbite

²**frostbite** n : the freezing or the local effect of a partial freezing of some part of the body

frost heave n : an upthrust of pavement caused by freezing of moist soil

frost·ing \'frös-tiŋ\ n 1 : ICING 2 : dull finish on metal or glass

froth \'fröth\ n, pl **froths** \'frôths, 'fröthz\ [ME, fr. ON *frotha*] 1 : bubbles formed in or on a liquid 2 : something light or worthless — **frothy** adj

frou·frou \'frü-,frü\ n [F] 1 : a rustling esp. of a woman's skirts 2 : showy or frilly ornamentation

fro·ward \'frō-wərd\ adj : DISOBEDIENT, WILLFUL

frown \'fraun\ vb 1 : to wrinkle the forehead (as in displeasure or thought) 2 : to look with disapproval 3 : to express with a frown — **frown** n

frow·sy *or* **frow·zy** \'fraú-zē\ adj **frow·si·er** *or* **frow·zi·er; -est** : having a slovenly or uncared-for appearance

froze *past of* FREEZE

fro·zen \'frō-z°n\ adj 1 : treated, affected, or crusted over by freezing 2 : subject to long and severe cold 3 : incapable of being changed, moved, or undone : FIXED ⟨∼ wages⟩ 4 : not available for present use ⟨∼ capital⟩ 5 : expressing or characterized by cold unfriendliness

FRS *abbr* Federal Reserve System

frt *abbr* freight

fruc·ti·fy \'frək-tə-,fī, 'frúk-\ vb **-fied; -fy·ing** 1 : to bear fruit 2 : to make fruitful or productive

fruc·tose \'frək-,tōs, 'frúk-\ n : a very sweet soluble sugar that occurs esp. in fruit juices and honey

fru·gal \'frü-gəl\ adj : ECONOMICAL, THRIFTY — **fru·gal·i·ty** \frü-'ga-lə-tē\ n — **fru·gal·ly** adv

¹**fruit** \'früt\ *n* [ME, fr. AF *frut, fruit*, fr. L *fructus*, use, fr. *frui* to enjoy, have the use of] **1** : a product of plant growth; *esp* : a usu. edible and sweet reproductive body (as a strawberry or apple) of a seed plant **2** : a product of fertilization in a plant; *esp* : the ripe ovary of a seed plant with its contents and appendages **3** : CONSEQUENCE, RESULT — **fruit·ed** \'frü-təd\ *adj*

²**fruit** *vb* : to bear or cause to bear fruit

fruit·cake \'früt-ˌkāk\ *n* : a rich cake containing nuts, dried or candied fruits, and spices

fruit fly *n* : any of various small dipteran flies whose larvae feed on fruit or decaying vegetable matter

fruit·ful \'früt-fəl\ *adj* **1** : yielding or producing fruit **2** : very productive; *also* : bringing results ⟨a ~ idea⟩ — **fruit·ful·ly** *adv* — **fruit·ful·ness** *n*

fru·ition \frü-'i-shən\ *n* **1** : ENJOYMENT **2** : the state of bearing fruit **3** : REALIZATION, ACCOMPLISHMENT ⟨guided the project to ~⟩

fruit·less \'früt-ləs\ *adj* **1** : not bearing fruit **2** : UNSUCCESSFUL ⟨a ~ attempt⟩ — **fruit·less·ly** *adv*

fruity \'frü-tē\ *adj* **fruit·i·er; -est** : resembling a fruit esp. in flavor

frumpy \'frəm-pē\ *adj* **frump·i·er; -est** : DOWDY, DRAB

frus·trate \'frəs-ˌtrāt\ *vb* **frus·trat·ed; frus·trat·ing 1** : to balk or defeat in an endeavor **2** : to induce feelings of insecurity, discouragement, or dissatisfaction in **3** : to bring to nothing — **frus·trat·ing·ly** *adv* — **frus·tra·tion** \ˌfrəs-'trā-shən\ *n*

frus·tum \'frəs-təm\ *n, pl* **frustums** *or* **frus·ta** \-tə\ : the part of a cone or pyramid formed by cutting off the top by a plane parallel to the base

frwy *abbr* freeway

¹**fry** \'frī\ *vb* **fried; fry·ing** [ME *frien*, fr. AF *frire*, fr. L *frigere* to roast] **1** : to cook in a pan or on a griddle over heat esp. with the use of fat **2** : to undergo frying **3** : to damage or destroy by overheating esp. by high voltage

²**fry** *n, pl* **fries 1** : a social gathering where fried food is eaten **2** : a dish of something fried; *esp, pl* : FRENCH FRIES

³**fry** *n, pl* **fry** [ME, fr. AF *frie*, fr. *freier, frier* to rub, spawn, fr. L *fricare* to rub] **1** : recently hatched fishes; *also* : very small adult fishes **2** : members of a group or class ⟨small ~⟩

fry·er \'frī(-ə)r\ *n* **1** : something (as a young chicken) suitable for frying **2** : a deep utensil for frying foods

FSLIC *abbr* Federal Savings and Loan Insurance Corporation

ft *abbr* **1** feet; foot **2** fort

FTC *abbr* Federal Trade Commission

FTP \ˌef-ˌtē-'pē\ *n* [*file transfer protocol*] : a system for transferring computer files esp. via the Internet — **FTP** *vb*

fuch·sia \'fyü-shə\ *n* **1** : any of a genus of shrubs related to the evening primrose and grown for their showy nodding often red or purple flowers **2** : a vivid reddish purple color

fud·dle \'fə-d²l\ *vb* **fud·dled; fud·dling** : MUDDLE, CONFUSE

fud·dy–dud·dy \'fə-dē-ˌdə-dē\ *n, pl* **-dies** : one that is old-fashioned, unimaginative, or conservative

¹**fudge** \'fəj\ *vb* **fudged; fudg·ing 1** : to exceed the proper bounds of something **2** : CHEAT; *also* : FALSIFY **3** : to fail to come to grips with

²**fudge** *n* **1** : NONSENSE **2** : a soft candy of milk, sugar, butter, and flavoring

¹**fu·el** \'fyü-əl, 'fyül\ *n* : a material used to produce heat or power by burning; *also* : a material from which nuclear energy can be liberated

²**fuel** *vb* **-eled** *or* **-elled; -el·ing** *or* **-el·ling** : to provide with or take in fuel

fuel cell *n* : a device that continuously changes the chemical energy of a fuel directly into electrical energy

fuel injection *n* : a system for injecting a precise amount of atomized fuel into an internal combustion engine — **fuel-in·ject·ed** \'fyül-in-ˌjek-təd\ *adj*

¹**fu·gi·tive** \'fyü-jə-tiv\ *adj* **1** : running away or trying to escape **2** : likely to vanish suddenly : not fixed or lasting

²**fugitive** *n* **1** : one who flees or tries to escape **2** : something elusive or hard to find

fugue \'fyüg\ *n* **1** : a musical composition in which different parts successively repeat the theme **2** : a disturbed state of consciousness characterized by acts that are not recalled upon recovery

füh·rer *or* **fueh·rer** \'fyür-ər, 'fir-\ *n* [G] : LEADER; *esp* : TYRANT

¹**-ful** \fəl\ *adj suffix, sometimes* **-ful·ier;** *sometimes* **-ful·lest 1** : full of ⟨pride*ful*⟩ **2** : characterized by ⟨peace*ful*⟩ **3** : having the qualities of ⟨master*ful*⟩ **4** : tending, given, or liable to ⟨help*ful*⟩

²**-ful** \ˌfül\ *n suffix* : number or quantity that fills or would fill ⟨room*ful*⟩

ful·crum \'fül-krəm, 'fəl-\ *n, pl* **ful·crums** *or* **ful·cra** \-krə\ [LL, fr. L, bedpost] : the support on which a lever turns

ful·fill *or* **ful·fil** \fúl-'fil\ *vb* **ful·filled; ful·fill·ing 1** : to put into effect **2** : to bring to an end **3** : SATISFY — **ful·fill·ment** *or* **ful·fil·ment** *n*

¹**full** \'fúl\ *adj* **1** : FILLED **2** : complete esp. in detail, number, or duration **3** : having all the distinguishing characteristics ⟨a ~ member⟩ **4** : MAXIMUM ⟨~ strength⟩ **5** : rounded in outline ⟨a ~ figure⟩ **6** : possessing or containing an abundance ⟨~ of wrinkles⟩ **7** : having an abundance of material ⟨a ~ skirt⟩ **8** : satisfied esp. with food or drink **9** : having volume or depth of sound **10** : completely occupied with a thought or plan — **full·ness** *also* **ful·ness** *n*

²**full** *adv* **1** : VERY, EXTREMELY **2** : ENTIRELY ⟨fill a glass ~⟩ **3** : STRAIGHT, SQUARELY ⟨hit him ~ in the face⟩

³**full** *n* **1** : the highest or fullest state or degree **2** : the utmost extent — **in full** : to the requisite or complete amount

⁴**full** vb : to shrink and thicken (woolen cloth) by moistening, heating, and pressing — **full·er** n

full·back \ˈful-ˌbak\ n : a football back stationed between the halfbacks

full-blood·ed \ˈful-ˈbləd-dəd\ adj : of unmixed ancestry : PUREBRED

full-blown \-ˈblōn\ adj 1 : being at the height of bloom 2 : fully mature or developed

full-bod·ied \-ˈbä-dēd\ adj : marked by richness and fullness

full dress n : the style of dress worn for ceremonial or formal occasions

full-fledged \ˈful-ˈflejd\ adj 1 : fully developed 2 : having attained complete status ⟨a ~ lawyer⟩

full house n : a poker hand containing three of a kind and a pair

full moon n : the moon with its whole disk illuminated

full-on \-ˌȯn, -ˌän\ adj : COMPLETE, FULL-FLEDGED

full-scale \ˈful-ˈskāl\ adj 1 : identical to an original in proportion and size ⟨~ drawing⟩ 2 : involving full use of available resources ⟨a ~ revolt⟩

full-term \-ˌtərm\ adj : retained in the uterus for the normal period of gestation before birth ⟨a ~ baby⟩

full tilt adv : at high speed

full–time \ˈful-ˈtīm\ adj or adv : involving or working a normal or standard schedule

ful·ly \ˈful-lē\ adv 1 : in a full manner or degree : COMPLETELY 2 : at least ⟨~ nine tenths of us⟩

ful·mi·nate \ˈful-mə-ˌnāt, ˈfəl-\ vb -nat·ed; -nat·ing [ME, fr. ML fulminatus, pp. of fulminare, fr. L, to strike (of lightning), fr. fulmen lightning] : to utter or send out censure or invective : condemn severely — **ful·mi·na·tion** \ˌful-mə-ˈnā-shən, ˌfəl-\ n

ful·some \ˈful-səm\ adj 1 : COPIOUS, ABUNDANT ⟨~ detail⟩ 2 : generous in amount or extent ⟨a ~ victory⟩ 3 : excessively flattering ⟨~ praise⟩

fu·ma·role \ˈfyü-mə-ˌrōl\ n : a hole in a volcanic region from which hot gases issue

fum·ble \ˈfəm-bəl\ vb **fum·bled; fum·bling** 1 : to grope about clumsily 2 : to fail to hold, catch, or handle properly — **fumble** n

¹**fume** \ˈfyüm\ n : a usu. irritating smoke, vapor, or gas

²**fume** vb **fumed; fum·ing** 1 : to treat with fumes 2 : to give off fumes 3 : to express anger or annoyance

fu·mi·gant \ˈfyü-mi-gənt\ n : a substance used for fumigation

fu·mi·gate \ˈfyü-mə-ˌgāt\ vb **-gat·ed; -gat·ing** : to treat with fumes to disinfect or destroy pests — **fu·mi·ga·tion** \ˌfyü-mə-ˈgā-shən\ n — **fu·mi·ga·tor** \ˈfyü-mə-ˌgā-tər\ n

¹**fun** \ˈfən\ n [E dial. fun to hoax] 1 : something that provides amusement or enjoyment 2 : ENJOYMENT

²**fun** adj : full of fun ⟨a ~ person⟩ ⟨had a ~ time⟩

¹**func·tion** \ˈfəŋk-shən\ n 1 : OCCUPATION 2 : special purpose 3 : the particular purpose for which a person or thing is specially fitted or used or for which a thing exists ⟨the ~ of a hammer⟩; also : the natural or proper action of a bodily part in a living thing ⟨the ~ of the heart⟩ 4 : a formal ceremony or social affair 5 : a mathematical relationship that assigns to each element of a set one and only one element of the same or another set 6 : a variable (as a quality, trait, or measurement) that depends on and varies with another ⟨height is a ~ of age in children⟩ 7 : a computer subroutine that performs a calculation with variables provided by a program — **func·tion·al** \-shə-nəl\ adj — **func·tion·al·ly** adv

²**function** vb : to have or carry on a function

func·tion·ary \ˈfəŋk-shə-ˌner-ē\ n, pl **-ar·ies** : one who performs a certain function; esp : OFFICIAL

function word n : a word (as a preposition, auxiliary verb, or conjunction) expressing the grammatical relationship between other words

¹**fund** \ˈfənd\ n [L fundus bottom, country estate] 1 : a sum of money or resources intended for a special purpose 2 : STORE, SUPPLY 3 pl : available money 4 : an organization administering a special fund

²**fund** vb 1 : to provide funds for 2 : to convert (a short-term obligation) into a long-term interest-bearing debt — **fund·er** n

fun·da·men·tal \ˌfən-də-ˈmen-t³l\ adj 1 : serving as an origin : PRIMARY 2 : BASIC, ESSENTIAL 3 : RADICAL ⟨~ change⟩ 4 : of central importance : PRINCIPAL ⟨~ purpose⟩ — **fundamental** n — **fun·da·men·tal·ly** adv

fun·da·men·tal·ism \-tə-ˌli-zəm\ n 1 often cap : a Protestant religious movement emphasizing the literal infallibility of the Bible 2 : a movement or attitude stressing strict adherence to a set of basic principles — **fun·da·men·tal·ist** \-list\ adj or n

¹**fu·ner·al** \ˈfyü-nə-rəl\ adj 1 : of, relating to, or constituting a funeral 2 : FUNEREAL 2

²**funeral** n : the ceremonies held for a dead person usu. before burial

fu·ner·ary \ˈfyü-nə-ˌrer-ē\ adj : of, used for, or associated with burial

fu·ne·re·al \fyü-ˈnir-ē-əl\ adj 1 : of or relating to a funeral 2 : suggesting a funeral

fun·gi·cide \ˈfən-jə-ˌsīd, ˈfəŋ-gə-\ n : an agent that kills or checks the growth of fungi — **fun·gi·cid·al** \ˌfən-jə-ˈsī-d³l, ˌfəŋ-gə-\ adj

fun·gus \ˈfəŋ-gəs\ n, pl **fun·gi** \ˈfən-ˌjī, ˈfəŋ-ˌgī\ also **fun·gus·es** \ˈfəŋ-gə-səz\ : any of a kingdom of parasitic spore-producing organisms (as molds, mildews, and mushrooms) formerly classified as plants — **fun·gal** \-gəl\ adj — **fun·gous** \-gəs\ adj

fu·nic·u·lar \fyu̇-'ni-kyə-lər, fə-\ *n* : a cable railway ascending a mountain

¹funk \'fəŋk\ *n* : a strong offensive smell

²funk *n* : a depressed state of mind

funky \'fəŋ-kē\ *adj* **funk·i·er; -est** : having an earthy unsophisticated style and feeling; *esp* : having the style and feeling of older black American music **2** : odd or quaint in appearance or style — **funk·i·ness** *n*

¹fun·nel \'fə-nᵊl\ *n* **1** : a cone-shaped utensil with a tube used for catching and directing a downward flow (as of liquid) **2** : FLUE, SMOKESTACK

funnel *vb* **-neled** *also* **-nelled; -nel·ing** *also* **-nel·ling** **1** : to pass through or as if through a funnel **2** : to move to a central point or into a central channel

fun·nies \'fə-nēz\ *n pl* : a comic strip or a comic section (as of a newspaper) — used with *the*

fun·ny \'fə-nē\ *adj* **fun·ni·er; -est** **1** : AMUSING **2** : FACETIOUS **3** : PECULIAR **3 4** : UNDERHANDED — **funny** *adv*

funny bone *n* : a place at the back of the elbow where a blow easily compresses a nerve and causes a painful tingling sensation

fun·plex \'fən-ˌpleks\ *n* : a center containing various entertainment facilities

¹fur \'fər\ *n* **1** : an article of clothing made of or with fur **2** : the hairy coat of a mammal esp. when fine, soft, and thick; *also* : this coat dressed for use — **fur** *adj* — **furred** \'fərd\ *adj*

²fur *abbr* furlong

fur·be·low \'fər-bə-ˌlō\ *n* **1** : FLOUNCE, RUFFLE **2** : showy trimming

fur·bish \'fər-bish\ *vb* **1** : to make lustrous : POLISH **2** : to give a new look to : RENOVATE

fu·ri·ous \'fyu̇r-ē-əs\ *adj* **1** : FIERCE, ANGRY, VIOLENT **2** : BOISTEROUS **3** : INTENSE ⟨~ growth⟩ — **fu·ri·ous·ly** *adv*

furl \'fərl\ *vb* **1** : to wrap or roll (as a sail or a flag) close to or around something **2** : to curl in furls — **furl** *n*

fur·long \'fər-ˌlȯŋ\ *n* [ME, fr. OE *furlang*, fr. *furh* furrow + *lang* long] : a unit of distance equal to 220 yards (about 201 meters)

fur·lough \'fər-lō\ *n* [D *verlof*, lit., permission] : a leave of absence from duty granted esp. to a soldier — **furlough** *vb*

fur·nace \'fər-nəs\ *n* : an enclosed structure in which heat is produced

fur·nish \'fər-nish\ *vb* **1** : to provide with what is needed : EQUIP **2** : SUPPLY, GIVE ⟨~ed them with food⟩

fur·nish·ings \-ni-shiŋz\ *n pl* **1** : articles or accessories of dress **2** : FURNITURE

fur·ni·ture \'fər-ni-chər\ *n* : equipment that is necessary or desirable; *esp* : movable articles (as chairs or beds) for a room

fu·ror \'fyu̇r-ˌȯr\ *n* **1** : ANGER, RAGE **2** : a contagious excitement; *esp* : a fashionable craze **3** : UPROAR

fu·rore \-ˌȯr\ *n* [It] : FUROR 2, 3

fur·ri·er \'fər-ē-ər\ *n* : one who prepares or deals in fur

fur·ring \'fər-iŋ\ *n* : wood or metal strips applied to a wall or ceiling to form a level surface or an air space

fur·row \'fər-ō\ *n* **1** : a trench in the earth made by a plow **2** : a narrow groove or wrinkle — **furrow** *vb*

fur·ry \'fər-ē\ *adj* **fur·ri·er; -est** **1** : resembling or consisting of fur **2** : covered with fur

¹fur·ther \'fər-thər\ *adv* **1** : FARTHER 1 **2** : in addition : MOREOVER **3** : to a greater extent or degree

²further *vb* : to help forward — **fur·ther·ance** \'fər-thə-rəns\ *n*

³further *adj* **1** : FARTHER 1 **2** : ADDITIONAL ⟨~ education⟩

fur·ther·more \'fər-thər-ˌmȯr\ *adv* : in addition to what precedes : BESIDES

fur·ther·most \-ˌmōst\ *adj* : most distant : FARTHEST

fur·thest \'fər-thəst\ *adv or adj* : FARTHEST

fur·tive \'fər-tiv\ *adj* [F or L; F *furtif*, fr. L *furtivus*, fr. *furtum* theft, fr. *fur* thief] : done by stealth : SLY — **fur·tive·ly** *adv* — **fur·tive·ness** *n*

fu·ry \'fyu̇r-ē\ *n, pl* **furies** **1** : intense and often destructive rage **2** : extreme fierceness or violence **3** : FRENZY

furze \'fərz\ *n* : GORSE

¹fuse \'fyüz\ *vb* **fused; fus·ing** **1** : MELT **2** : to unite by or as if by melting together — **fus·ible** *adj*

²fuse *n* : an electrical safety device having a metal wire or strip that melts and interrupts the electric circuit when the current becomes too strong

³fuse *n* **1** : a cord or cable that is set afire to ignite an explosive charge **2** *usu* **fuze** : a mechanical or electrical device for setting off the explosive charge of a projectile, bomb, or torpedo

⁴fuse *also* **fuze** \'fyüz\ *vb* **fused** *also* **fuzed; fus·ing** *also* **fuz·ing** : to equip with a fuse

fu·se·lage \'fyü-sə-ˌläzh, -zə-\ *n* : the central body portion of an aircraft

fu·sil·lade \'fyü-sə-ˌläd, -ˌlād\ *n* : a number of shots fired simultaneously or in rapid succession

fu·sion \'fyü-zhən\ *n* **1** : the act or process of melting or making plastic by heat **2** : union by or as if by melting **3** : the union of light atomic nuclei to form heavier nuclei with the release of huge quantities of energy

¹fuss \'fəs\ *n* **1** : needless bustle or excitement : COMMOTION **2** : effusive praise **3** : a state of agitation **4** : OBJECTION, PROTEST **5** : DISPUTE

²fuss *vb* : to make a fuss

fuss·bud·get \'fəs-ˌbə-jət\ *n* : one who fusses or is fussy about trifles

fussy \'fə-sē\ *adj* **fuss·i·er; -est** **1** : IRRITABLE **2** : overly decorative ⟨a ~ wallpaper pattern⟩ **3** : requiring or giving close attention or concern to details or niceties — **fuss·i·ly** \-sə-lē\ *adv* — **fuss·i·ness** \-sē-nəs\ *n*

fus·tian \'fəs-chən\ *n* **1** : a strong usu.

cotton fabric **2** : pretentious writing or speech — **fustian** *adj*

fus·ty \'fəs-tē\ *adj* **fus·ti·er; -est** [prob. alter. of ME *foisted, foist* musty, fr. *foist* wine cask, fr. AF *fust, fuist* wood, tree trunk, cask] **1** : MUSTY **2** : OLD-FASH-IONED

fut *abbr* future

fu·tile \'fyü-t²l, 'fyü-₁tī(-ə)l\ *adj* **1** : USE-LESS, VAIN **2** : FRIVOLOUS, TRIVIAL — **fu·tile·ly** *adv* — **fu·til·i·ty** \fyü-'ti-lə-tē\ *n*

fu·ton \'fü-₁tän\ *n* [Jp] : a usu. cotton-filled mattress used on the floor or in a frame as a bed, couch, or chair

¹fu·ture \'fyü-chər\ *adj* **1** : of, relating to, or constituting a verb tense that expresses time yet to come **2** : coming after the present

²future *n* **1** : time that is to come **2** : what is going to happen **3** : an expectation of advancement or progressive development **4** : the future tense; *also* : a verb form in it

fu·tur·ism \'fyü-chə-₁ri-zəm\ *n* : a modern movement in art, music, and literature that tries esp. to express the energy and

activity of mechanical processes — **fu·tur·ist** \'fyü-chə-rist\ *n*

fu·tur·is·tic \₁fyü-chə-'ris-tik\ *adj* : of or relating to the future or to futurism; *also* : very modern

fu·tu·ri·ty \fyü-'tur-ə-tē, -'tyur-\ *n, pl* **-ties** **1** : FUTURE **2** : the quality or state of being future **3** *pl* : future events or prospects

fuze *var of* FUSE

fuzz \'fəz\ *n* : fine light particles or fibers (as of down or fluff)

fuzzy \'fə-zē\ *adj* **fuzz·i·er; -est** **1** : having or resembling fuzz **2** : INDISTINCT ⟨∼ photos⟩ **3** : being or relating to pleasant usu. sentimental emotions ⟨∼ feelings⟩ — **fuzz·i·ness** \-zē-nəs\ *n*

fuzzy logic *n* : a system of logic in which a statement can be true, false, or any of a continuum of values in between

fwd *abbr* forward

FWD *abbr* front-wheel drive

FY *abbr* fiscal year

-fy *vb suffix* : make : form into ⟨dandi*fy*⟩

FYI *abbr* for your information

¹g \'jē\ *n, pl* **g's** *or* **gs** \'jēz\ *often cap* **1** : the 7th letter of the English alphabet **2** : a unit of force equal to the force exerted by gravity on a body at rest and used to indicate the force to which a body is subjected when accelerated **3** *slang* : a sum of $1000

²g *abbr, often cap* **1** game **2** gauge **3** good **4** gram **5** gravity

ga *abbr* gauge

¹Ga *abbr* Georgia

²Ga *symbol* gallium

GA *abbr* **1** general assembly **2** general average **3** general of the army **4** Georgia

gab \'gab\ *vb* **gabbed; gab·bing** : to talk in a rapid or thoughtless manner — CHAT-TER — **gab** *n*

gab·ar·dine \'ga-bər-₁dēn\ *n* **1** : GABER-DINE 1 **2** : a firm durable twilled fabric having diagonal ribs and made of various fibers; *also* : a garment of gabardine

gab·ble \'ga-bəl\ *vb* **gab·bled; gab·bling** : JABBER, BABBLE

gab·by \'ga-bē\ *adj* **gab·bi·er; -est** : TALKATIVE, GARRULOUS

gab·er·dine \'ga-bər-₁dēn\ *n* **1** : a long loose outer garment worn in medieval times and associated esp. with Jews **2** : GABARDINE 2

gab·fest \'gab-₁fest\ *n* **1** : an informal gathering for general talk **2** : an extend-ed conversation

ga·ble \'gā-bəl\ *n* : the vertical triangular end of a building formed by the sides of the roof sloping from the ridge down to the eaves — **ga·bled** \-bəld\ *adj*

gad \'gad\ *vb* **gad·ded; gad·ding** : to be

constantly active without specific pur-pose — usu. used with *about* — **gad·der** *n*

gad·about \'ga-də-₁baut\ *n* : a person who flits about in social activity

gad·fly \'gad-₁flī\ *n* **1** : a fly that bites or harasses livestock **2** : a person who an-noys esp. by persistent criticism

gad·get \'ga-jət\ *n* : DEVICE, CONTRI-VANCE — **gad·get·ry** \'ga-jə-trē\ *n*

gad·o·lin·i·um \₁ga-də-'li-nē-əm\ *n* : a magnetic metallic chemical element

¹Gael \'gāl\ *n* : a Celtic inhabitant of Ire-land or Scotland

²Gael *abbr* Gaelic

Gael·ic \'gā-lik\ *adj* : of or relating to the Gaels or their languages — **Gaelic** *n*

gaff \'gaf\ *n* **1** : a spear used in taking fish or turtles; *also* : a metal hook for holding or lifting heavy fish **2** : the spar support-ing the top of a fore-and-aft sail **3** : rough treatment : ABUSE — **gaff** *vb*

gaffe \'gaf\ *n* : a usu. social blunder

gaf·fer \'ga-fər\ *n* **1** : an old man **2** : a lighting electrician on a motion-picture or television set

¹gag \'gag\ *vb* **gagged; gag·ging** **1** : to restrict use of the mouth with a gag **2** : to prevent from speaking freely **3** : to retch or cause to retch **4** : OBSTRUCT, CHOKE **5** : BALK **6** : to make quips — **gag·ger** *n*

²gag *n* **1** : something thrust into the mouth esp. to prevent speech or outcry **2** : an official check or restraint on free speech **3** : a laugh-provoking remark or act **4** : PRANK, TRICK

¹gage \'gāj\ *n* **1** : a token of defiance; *esp* : a glove or cap cast on the ground as a pledge of combat **2** : SECURITY

²gage *var of* GAUGE

gag·gle \'ga-gəl\ *n* [ME *gagyll,* fr. *gagelen* to cackle] **1** : a flock of geese **2** : an unorganized group

gai·ety *also* **gay·ety** \'gā-ə-tē\ *n, pl* **-eties** **1** : festive activity : MERRYMAKING **2** : MERRIMENT **3** : FINERY ✦ *Synonyms* MIRTH, FESTIVITY, GLEE, HILARITY, JOLLITY

gai·ly *also* **gay·ly** \'gā-lē\ *adv* : in a gay manner

¹gain \'gān\ *n* **1** : PROFIT **2** : ACQUISITION, ACCUMULATION **3** : INCREASE

²gain *vb* **1** : to get possession of : EARN **2** : WIN ⟨~ a victory⟩ **3** : to increase in ⟨~ momentum⟩ **4** : PERSUADE **5** : to arrive at **6** : ACHIEVE ⟨~ strength⟩ **7** : to run fast ⟨the watch ~s a minute a day⟩ **8** : PROFIT **9** : INCREASE **10** : to improve in health ✦ *Synonyms* ACCOMPLISH, ATTAIN, REALIZE — **gain·er** *n*

gain·ful \'gān-fəl\ *adj* : PROFITABLE ⟨~ employment⟩ — **gain·ful·ly** *adv*

gain·say \gān-'sā\ *vb* **-said** \-'sād, -'sed\; **-say·ing**; **-says** \-'sāz, -'sez\ [ME *gainsayen,* fr. *gain-* against + *sayen* to say] **1** : DENY, DISPUTE **2** : to speak against ✦ *Synonyms* CONTRADICT, CONTRAVENE, IMPUGN, NEGATE — **gain·say·er** *n*

gait \'gāt\ *n* : manner of moving on foot; *also* : a particular pattern or style of such moving — **gait·ed** *adj*

gai·ter \'gā-tər\ *n* **1** : a leg covering reaching from the instep to ankle, midcalf, or knee **2** : an overshoe with a fabric upper **3** : an ankle-high shoe with elastic gores in the sides

¹gal \'gal\ *n* : GIRL

²gal *abbr* gallon

Gal *abbr* Galatians

ga·la \'gā-lə, 'ga-, 'gä-\ *n* : a festive celebration : FESTIVITY — **gala** *adj*

ga·lac·tic \gə-'lak-tik\ *adj* : of or relating to a galaxy

Ga·la·tians \gə-'lā-shənz\ *n* — see BIBLE table

gal·axy \'ga-lək-sē\ *n, pl* **-ax·ies** [ME *galaxie, galaxias,* fr. LL *galaxias,* fr. Gk, fr. *galakt-, gala* milk] **1** *often cap* : MILKY WAY GALAXY — used with *the* **2** : a very large group of stars **3** : an assemblage of brilliant or famous persons or things

gale \'gāl\ *n* **1** : a strong wind **2** : an emotional outburst ⟨~s of laughter⟩

ga·le·na \gə-'lē-nə\ *n* : a lustrous bluish gray mineral that consists of the sulfide of lead and is the chief ore of lead

¹gall \'gȯl\ *n* **1** : BILE **2** : something bitter to endure **3** : RANCOR **4** : IMPUDENCE ✦ *Synonyms* EFFRONTERY, BRASS, CHEEK, CHUTZPAH, AUDACITY, PRESUMPTION

²gall *n* : a skin sore caused by chafing

³gall *vb* **1** : CHAFE; *esp* : to become sore or worn by rubbing **2** : VEX, HARASS

⁴gall *n* : an abnormal outgrowth of plant tissue usu. due to parasites

¹gal·lant \gə-'lant, -'länt; 'ga-lənt\ *n* **1** : a young man of fashion **2** : a man who shows a marked fondness for the company of women and who is esp. attentive to them **3** : SUITOR

²gal·lant \'ga-lənt *(usual for 2, 3, 4);* gə-'lant, -'länt *(usual for 5)*\ *adj* **1** : showy in dress or bearing : SMART **2** : SPLENDID, STATELY **3** : SPIRITED, BRAVE **4** : CHIVALROUS, NOBLE **5** : polite and attentive to women — **gal·lant·ly** *adv*

gal·lant·ry \'ga-lən-trē\ *n, pl* **-ries** **1** *archaic* : gallant appearance **2** : an act of marked courtesy **3** : courteous attention to a woman **4** : conspicuous bravery ✦ *Synonyms* HEROISM, VALOR, PROWESS

gall·blad·der \'gȯl-,bla-dər\ *n* : a membranous muscular sac attached to the liver and serving to store bile

gal·le·on \'ga-lē-ən\ *n* : a large square-rigged sailing ship formerly used esp. by the Spanish

gal·le·ria \,ga-lə-'rē-ə\ *n* [It] : a roofed and usu. glass-enclosed promenade or court

gal·lery \'ga-lə-rē\ *n, pl* **-ler·ies** **1** : an outdoor balcony; *also* : PORCH, VERANDA **2** : a long narrow passage, apartment, or hall **3** : a narrow passage (as one made underground by a miner or through wood by an insect) **4** : a room where works of art are exhibited; *also* : an organization dealing in works of art **5** : a balcony in a theater, auditorium, or church; *esp* : the highest one in a theater **6** : the spectators at a sporting event (as a tennis or golf match) **7** : a photographer's studio — **gal·ler·ied** \-rēd\ *adj*

gal·ley \'ga-lē\ *n, pl* **galleys** **1** : a long low ship propelled esp. by oars and formerly used esp. in the Mediterranean Sea **2** : the kitchen esp. of a ship or airplane **3** : a proof of typeset matter esp. in a single column

Gal·lic \'ga-lik\ *adj* : of or relating to Gaul or France

gal·li·mau·fry \,ga-lə-'mȯ-frē\ *n, pl* **-fries** [MF *galimafree* stew] : HODGEPODGE

gal·li·nule \'ga-lə-,nül, -,nyül\ *n* : any of several aquatic birds related to the rails

gal·li·um \'ga-lē-əm\ *n* : a bluish-white metallic chemical element used esp. in semiconductors

gal·li·vant \'ga-lə-,vant\ *vb* : to travel, roam, or move about for pleasure

gal·lon \'ga-lən\ *n* — see WEIGHT table

¹gal·lop \'ga-ləp\ *vb* **1** : to go or cause to go at a gallop **2** : to run fast — **gal·lop·er** *n*

²gallop *n* **1** : a bounding gait of a quadruped; *esp* : a fast 3-beat gait of a horse **2** : a ride or run at a gallop

gal·lows \'ga-lōz\ *n, pl* **gallows** *or* **gallows·es** : a frame usu. of two upright posts and a crosspiece from which criminals are hanged; *also* : the punishment of hanging

gall·stone \'gȯl-,stōn\ *n* : an abnormal concretion occurring in the gallbladder or bile passages

gal·lus·es \'ga-lə-səz\ *n pl* : SUSPENDERS

ga·lore \gə-'lȯr\ adj [Ir go leor enough] : ABUNDANT, PLENTIFUL

ga·losh \gə-'läsh\ n : a high overshoe

galv abbr galvanized

gal·va·nise Brit var of GALVANIZE

gal·va·nize \'gal-və-ˌnīz\ vb **-nized; -niz·ing** 1 : to stimulate as if by an electric shock ⟨∼ public opinion⟩ 2 : to coat (iron or steel) with zinc — **gal·va·ni·za·tion** \ˌgal-və-nə-'zā-shən\ n — **gal·va·niz·er** n

gal·va·nom·e·ter \ˌgal-və-'nä-mə-tər\ n : an instrument for detecting or measuring a small electric current

gam·bit \'gam-bət\ n [It gambetto, lit., act of tripping someone, fr. gamba leg] 1 : a chess opening in which a player risks one or more minor pieces to gain an advantage in position 2 : a calculated move : STRATAGEM ✦ Synonyms TRICK, ARTIFICE, GIMMICK, MANEUVER, PLAY, RUSE

¹**gam·ble** \'gam-bəl\ vb **gam·bled; gam·bling** 1 : to play a game for money or property 2 : BET, WAGER 3 : VENTURE, HAZARD — **gam·bler** n

²**gamble** n : a risky undertaking

gam·bol \'gam-bəl\ vb **-boled** or **-bolled; -bol·ing** or **-bol·ling** : to skip about in play : FRISK — **gambol** n

gam·brel roof \'gam-brəl-\ n : a roof with a lower steeper slope and an upper flatter one on each side

¹**game** \'gām\ n 1 : AMUSEMENT, DIVERSION 2 : SPORT, FUN ⟨made a ∼ of the strange boy⟩ 3 : SCHEME, PROJECT 4 : a line of work : PROFESSION 5 : CONTEST 6 : animals hunted for sport or food; also : the flesh of a game animal

²**game** vb **gamed; gam·ing** 1 : to play for a stake 2 : to take dishonest advantage of

³**game** adj : PLUCKY, RESOLUTE — **game·ly** adv — **game·ness** n

⁴**game** adj : LAME ⟨a ∼ leg⟩

game·cock \'gām-ˌkäk\ n : a rooster trained for fighting

game fish n : SPORT FISH

game·keep·er \'gām-ˌkē-pər\ n : a person in charge of the breeding and protection of game animals or birds on a private preserve

game show n : a television program on which contestants compete usu. for prizes in a game

game·some \'gām-səm\ adj : MERRY ✦ Synonyms PLAYFUL, FROLICSOME, SPORTIVE, ANTIC

game·ster \'gām-stər\ n : GAMBLER

gam·ete \'ga-ˌmēt\ n : a mature germ cell — **ga·met·ic** \gə-'me-tik\ adj

game theory n : the analysis of a situation involving conflicting interests (as in business) in terms of gains and losses among opposing players

gam·in \'ga-mən\ n [F] 1 : a boy who hangs around on the streets 2 : GAMINE 2

ga·mine \ga-'mēn\ n 1 : a girl who hangs around on the streets 2 : a small playfully mischievous girl

gam·ma \'ga-mə\ n : the 3d letter of the Greek alphabet — Γ or γ

gamma globulin n : a blood protein fraction rich in antibodies; also : a solution of this from human blood donors that is given to provide immunity against some infectious diseases (as measles)

gamma ray n : a photon emitted by a radioactive substance; also : a photon of higher energy than that of an X-ray — usu. used in pl.

gam·mon \'ga-mən\ n, chiefly Brit : a cured ham or side of bacon

gam·ut \'ga-mət\ n : an entire range or series ✦ Synonyms SCALE, SPECTRUM

gamy or **gam·ey** \'gā-mē\ adj **gam·i·er; -est** 1 : GAME, PLUCKY 2 : having the flavor of game esp. when near tainting 3 : SCANDALOUS; also : DISREPUTABLE — **gam·i·ness** \-mē-nəs\ n

¹**gan·der** \'gan-dər\ n : a male goose

²**gander** n : LOOK, GLANCE

¹**gang** \'gaŋ\ n 1 : a set of implements or devices arranged to operate together 2 : a group of persons working or associated together; esp : a group of criminals or young delinquents

²**gang** vb 1 : to attack in a gang — usu. used with up 2 : to form into or move or act as a gang

gang·land \'gaŋ-ˌland\ n : the world of organized crime

gan·gling \'gaŋ-gliŋ\ adj : loosely and awkwardly built : LANKY

gan·gli·on \'gaŋ-glē-ən\ n, pl **-glia** \-ə\ also **-gli·ons** : a mass of nerve tissue containing cell bodies of neurons outside the central nervous system; also : NUCLEUS 3 — **gan·gli·on·ic** \ˌgaŋ-glē-'ä-nik\ adj

gan·gly \'gaŋ-glē\ adj : GANGLING

gang·plank \'gaŋ-ˌplaŋk\ n : a movable bridge from a ship to the shore

gang·plow \-ˌplau̇\ n : a plow that turns two or more furrows at one time

gan·grene \'gaŋ-ˌgrēn, gaŋ-'grēn\ n : the death of soft tissues in a local area of the body due to loss of the blood supply — **gangrene** vb — **gan·gre·nous** \'gaŋ-grə-nəs\ adj

gang·sta \'gaŋ-stə\ n : a member of an urban street gang

gangsta rap n : rap music with usu. hostile lyrics portraying urban gang life

gang·ster \'gaŋ-stər\ n : a member of a gang of criminals : RACKETEER

gang·way \'gaŋ-ˌwā\ n 1 : PASSAGEWAY; also : GANGPLANK 2 : clear passage through a crowd

gan·net \'ga-nət\ n, pl **gannets** also **gannet** : any of several large fish-eating usu. white and black seabirds that breed chiefly on offshore islands

gantlet var of GAUNTLET

gan·try \'gan-trē\ n, pl **gantries** : a frame structure on side supports over or around something

GAO abbr General Accounting Office

gaol \'jāl\, **gaol·er** \'jā-lər\ chiefly Brit var of JAIL, JAILER

gap \'gap\ n 1 : BREACH, CLEFT 2 : a mountain pass 3 : a blank space; also : an incomplete or deficient area 4 : a wide difference in character or attitude

5 : a problem caused by a disparity ⟨credibility ∼⟩

gape \'gāp\ *vb* **gaped; gap·ing 1** : to open the mouth wide **2** : to open or part widely **3** : to stare with mouth open **4** : YAWN — **gape** *n*

¹**gar** \'gär\ *n* : any of several fishes that have a long body resembling that of a pike and long narrow jaws

²**gar** *abbr* garage

GAR *abbr* Grand Army of the Republic

¹**ga·rage** \gə-'räzh, -'räj\ *n* [F, act of docking, garage, fr. *garer* to dock, fr. MF *garer*, prob. ultim. fr. ON *vara* to beware, take care] : a shelter or repair shop for automobiles

²**garage** *vb* **ga·raged; ga·rag·ing** : to keep or put in a garage

garage sale *n* : a sale of used household or personal articles held on the seller's own premises

garb \'gärb\ *n* **1** : style of dress **2** : outward form : APPEARANCE — **garb** *vb*

gar·bage \'gär-bij\ *n* **1** : food waste **2** : unwanted or useless material — **garbage·man** \-ˌman\ *n*

gar·ble \'gär-bəl\ *vb* **gar·bled; gar·bling** : to distort the meaning of ⟨∼ a story⟩

gar·çon \gär-'sōⁿ\ *n, pl* **garçons** *same or* gär-'sōⁿz\ [F, boy, servant] : WAITER

¹**gar·den** \'gär-dᵊn\ *n* **1** : a plot for growing fruits, flowers, or vegetables **2** : a public recreation area; *esp* : one for displaying plants or animals

²**garden** *vb* : to lay out or work in a garden — **gar·den·er** *n*

gar·de·nia \gär-'dē-nyə\ *n* [NL, genus name, fr. Alexander *Garden* †1791 Scot. naturalist] : any of a genus of tropical trees or shrubs that are related to the madder and have fragrant white or yellow flowers

garden–variety *adj* : COMMONPLACE, ORDINARY

gar·fish \'gär-ˌfish\ *n* : GAR

gar·gan·tuan \gär-'gan-chə-wən\ *adj, often cap* : tremendous in size, volume, or degree ⟨∼ waterfalls⟩ ♦ **Synonyms** HUGE, COLOSSAL, GIGANTIC, MAMMOTH, MONSTROUS, TITANIC

gar·gle \'gär-gəl\ *vb* **gar·gled; gar·gling** : to rinse the throat with liquid agitated by air forced through it from the lungs — **gargle** *n*

gar·goyle \'gär-ˌgȯi(-ə)l\ *n* **1** : a waterspout in the form of a grotesque human or animal figure projecting from the roof or eaves of a building **2** : a grotesquely carved figure

gar·ish \'ger-ish\ *adj* : FLASHY, GLARING, SHOWY, GAUDY ⟨a ∼ wardrobe⟩

¹**gar·land** \'gär-lənd\ *n* : WREATH, CHAPLET

²**garland** *vb* : to form into or deck with a garland

gar·lic \'gär-lik\ *n* [ME *garlek*, fr. OE *gārlēac*, fr. *gār* spear + *lēac* leek] : an herb related to the lilies and grown for its pungent bulbs used in cooking; *also* : its bulb — **gar·licky** \-li-kē\ *adj*

gar·ment \'gär-mənt\ *n* : an article of clothing

gar·ner \'gär-nər\ *vb* **1** : to gather into storage **2** : to acquire by effort **3** : ACCUMULATE, COLLECT

gar·net \'gär-nət\ *n* [ME *gernet*, fr. AF *gernete*, fr. *gernet* dark red, fr. *pume gernete* pomegranate] : a transparent deep red mineral sometimes used as a gem

gar·nish \'gär-nish\ *vb* **1** : DECORATE, EMBELLISH **2** : to add decorative or savory touches to (food) **3** : GARNISHEE — **garnish** *n*

gar·nish·ee \ˌgär-nə-'shē\ *vb* **-eed; -ee·ing 1** : to serve with a garnishment **2** : to take (as a debtor's wages) by legal authority

gar·nish·ment \'gär-nish-mənt\ *n* **1** : GARNISH **2** : a legal warning concerning the attachment of property to satisfy a debt; *also* : the attachment of such property

gar·ret \'ger-ət\ *n* : the part of a house just under the roof : ATTIC

gar·ri·son \'ger-ə-sən\ *n* [ME *garisoun* protection, fr. AF *garisun* healing, protection, fr. *garir* to heal, protect, of Gmc origin] **1** : a military post; *esp* : a permanent military installation **2** : the troops stationed at a garrison — **garrison** *vb*

garrison state *n* : a state organized on a primarily military basis

gar·rote *or* **ga·rotte** \gə-'rät, -'rōt\ *n* [Sp *garrote*] **1** : a method of execution by strangulation; *also* : the apparatus used **2** : an implement (as a wire with handles) for strangulation — **garrote** *or* **garotte** *vb*

gar·ru·lous \'ger-ə-ləs\ *adj* : TALKATIVE, WORDY — **gar·ru·li·ty** \gə-'rü-lə-tē\ *n* — **gar·ru·lous·ly** *adv* — **gar·ru·lous·ness** *n*

gar·ter \'gär-tər\ *n* : a band or strap worn to hold up a stocking or sock

garter snake *n* : any of a genus of harmless American snakes with longitudinal stripes on the back

¹**gas** \'gas\ *n, pl* **gas·es** *also* **gas·ses** [NL, alter. of L *chaos* space, chaos] **1** : a fluid (as hydrogen or air) that tends to expand indefinitely **2** : a gas or mixture of gases used as a fuel or anesthetic **3** : a substance that can be used to produce a poisonous, asphyxiating, or irritant atmosphere **4** : GASOLINE — **gas·eous** \'ga-sē-əs, -shəs\ *adj*

²**gas** *vb* **gassed; gas·sing 1** : to treat with gas; *also* : to poison with gas **2** : to fill with gasoline ⟨∼ up the car⟩

gash \'gash\ *n* : a deep long cut — **gash** *vb*

gas·ket \'gas-kət\ *n* : material (as rubber) or a part used to seal a joint

gas·light \'gas-ˌlīt\ *n* **1** : light made by burning illuminating gas **2** : a gas flame; *also* : a gas lighting fixture

gas mask *n* : a mask with a chemical air filter used to protect the face and lungs against poison gas

gas·o·line \'ga-sə-ˌlēn, ˌga-sə-'lēn\ *n* : a flammable liquid mixture made from petroleum and used esp. as a motor fuel

gasp \'gasp\ vb **1** : to catch the breath audibly (as with shock) **2** : to breathe laboriously : PANT **3** : to utter in a gasping manner — **gasp** n

gas station n : a retail station for servicing and fueling motor vehicles

gas·tric \'gas-trik\ adj : of or relating to the stomach

gastric juice n : the acid digestive secretion of the stomach

gas·tri·tis \gas-'trī-təs\ n : inflammation of the lining of the stomach

gas·tro·en·ter·i·tis \ˌgas-trō-ˌen-tə-'rī-təs\ n : inflammation of the lining membrane of the stomach and intestines

gas·tro·en·ter·ol·o·gy \ˌgas-trō-ˌen-tə-'rä-lə-jē\ n : a branch of medicine concerned with the structure, functions, and diseases of the stomach and intestines — **gas·tro·en·ter·ol·o·gist** \-jist\ n

gas·tro·in·tes·ti·nal \ˌgas-trō-in-'tes-tə-nᵊl\ adj : of, relating to, affecting, or including both the stomach and intestine ⟨~ tract⟩ ⟨~ distress⟩

gas·tron·o·my \gas-'trä-nə-mē\ n [F gastronomie, fr. Gk Gastronomia, title of a 4th cent. B.C. poem, fr. gastēr belly + -nomia system of laws] : the art of good eating — **gas·tro·nom·ic** \ˌgas-trə-'nä-mik\ also **gas·tro·nom·i·cal** \-mi-kəl\ adj — **gas·tro·nom·i·cal·ly** \-k(ə-)lē\ adv

gas·tro·pod \'gas-trə-ˌpäd\ n : any of a large class of mollusks (as snails and slugs) with a muscular foot and a spiral shell or none — **gastropod** adj

gas·works \'gas-ˌwərks\ n sing or pl : a plant for manufacturing gas

gate \'gāt\ n **1** : an opening for passage in a wall or fence **2** : a city or castle entrance often with defensive structures **3** : the frame or door that closes a gate **4** : a device (as a valve) for controlling the passage of a fluid or signal **5** : the total admission receipts or the number of people at an event

-gate \ˌgāt\ n comb form [Watergate, scandal that resulted in the resignation of President Richard Nixon in 1974] : usu. political scandal often involving the concealment of wrongdoing

gate-crash·er \'gāt-ˌkra-shər\ n : a person who enters without paying admission or attends without invitation

gate·keep·er \-ˌkē-pər\ n : a person who tends or guards a gate

gate·post \-ˌpōst\ n : the post to which a gate is hung or the one against which it closes

gate·way \-ˌwā\ n **1** : an opening for a gate **2** : a means of entrance or exit

¹**gath·er** \'ga-thər\ vb **1** : to bring together : COLLECT **2** : PICK, HARVEST **3** : to pick up little by little ⟨~ed up the child⟩ **5** : to gain or win by gradual increase **6** : ATTRACT, ACCUMULATE ⟨~ dust⟩ **7** : to summon up ⟨~ courage to dive⟩ **8** : to gain control of ⟨~ed his wits⟩ **9** : to draw about or close to something **10** : to pull (fabric) along a line of stitching into puckers **11** : GUESS, DEDUCE, INFER **12** : ASSEMBLE **13** : to swell out and fill with pus **14** : GROW, INCREASE ✦ **Synonyms** CONGREGATE, FORGATHER — **gath·er·er** n

²**gather** n : a puckering in cloth made by gathering

GATT \'gat\ abbr General Agreement on Tariffs and Trade

gauche \'gōsh\ adj [F, lit., left] **1** : lacking social experience or grace; also : not tactful **2** : crudely made or done ✦ **Synonyms** CLUMSY, HEAVY-HANDED, INEPT, MALADROIT

gau·che·rie \ˌgō-shə-'rē\ n : a tactless or awkward action

gau·cho \'gau̇-chō\ n, pl **gauchos** : a cowboy of the So. American pampas

gaud \'gȯd\ n : ORNAMENT, TRINKET

gaudy \'gȯ-dē\ adj **gaud·i·er; -est 1** : ostentatiously or tastelessly ornamented **2** : marked by showiness or extravagance : OUTLANDISH **3** : EXCEPTIONAL ⟨a ~ batting average⟩ ✦ **Synonyms** GARISH, FLASHY, GLARING, TAWDRY — **gaud·i·ly** \-də-lē\ adv — **gaud·i·ness** \-dē-nəs\ n

¹**gauge** also **gage** \'gāj\ n **1** : measurement according to some standard or system **2** : DIMENSIONS, SIZE **3** usu **gage** : an instrument for measuring, testing, or registering

²**gauge** also **gage** vb **gauged** also **gaged; gaug·ing** also **gag·ing 1** : MEASURE **2** : to determine the capacity or contents of **3** : ESTIMATE, JUDGE

gaunt \'gȯnt\ adj **1** : excessively thin and angular ⟨a ~ face⟩ **2** : BARREN, DESOLATE ✦ **Synonyms** BONY, LANK, LANKY, LEAN, RAWBONED, SKINNY — **gaunt·ness** n

¹**gaunt·let** also **gant·let** \'gȯnt-lət\ n **1** : a protective glove **2** : an open challenge (as to combat) **3** : a dress glove extending above the wrist

²**gauntlet** also **gantlet** n **1** : a double file of men armed with weapons (as clubs) with which to strike at an individual who is made to run between them **2** : ORDEAL **3** : a line or series of something to be greeted or managed

gauss \'gaús\ n : the centimeter-gram-second unit of magnetic flux density that is equal to 1×10^{-4} tesla

gauze \'gȯz\ n : a very thin often transparent fabric used esp. for draperies and surgical dressings

gauzy \'gȯ-zē\ adj **gauz·i·er; -est 1** : made of or resembling gauze **2** : marked by vagueness or fuzziness ⟨a ~ memory⟩

gave past of GIVE

gav·el \'ga-vəl\ n : a mallet used by a presiding officer or auctioneer

ga·votte \gə-'vät\ n : a dance of French peasant origin marked by the raising rather than sliding of the feet

gawk \'gȯk\ vb : to gape or stare stupidly — **gawk·er** n

gawky \'gȯ-kē\ adj **gawk·i·er; -est** : AWKWARD, CLUMSY — **gawk·i·ly** \-kə-lē\ adv — **gawk·i·ness** n

gay \'gā\ adj **1** : MERRY **2** : BRIGHT, LIVELY **3** : brilliant in color **4** : given to social pleasures; also : LICENTIOUS **5** : HOMOSEXUAL; also : of, relating to, or used by homosexuals ⟨a ∼ bar⟩

gayety, gayly var of GAIETY, GAILY

gaz abbr gazette

gaze \'gāz\ vb gazed; gaz·ing : to fix the eyes in a steady intent look ✦ **Synonyms** GAPE, GAWK, GLARE, GOGGLE, PEER, STARE — gaze n — gaz·er n

ga·ze·bo \gə-'zē-bō\ n, pl **-bos** **1** : BELVEDERE **2** : a freestanding roofed structure usu. open on the sides

ga·zelle \gə-'zel\ n, pl **gazelles** also **gazelle** : any of numerous small swift graceful antelopes

ga·zette \gə-'zet\ n **1** : NEWSPAPER **2** : an official journal

gaz·et·teer \ˌga-zə-'tir\ n : a geographical dictionary

ga·zil·lion \gə-'zil-yən\ n : ZILLION — **gazillion** adj — **ga·zil·lionth** \-yənth\ adj

gaz·pa·cho \gəz-'pä-(ˌ)chō, gə-'spä-\ n, pl **-chos** [Sp] : a spicy soup usu. made from raw vegetables and served cold

GB abbr Great Britain

GCA abbr ground-controlled approach

gd abbr good

Gd symbol gadolinium

GDR abbr German Democratic Republic

Ge symbol germanium

gear \'gir\ n **1** : CLOTHING **2** : movable property : GOODS **3** : EQUIPMENT ⟨fishing ∼⟩ **4** : a mechanism that performs a specific function ⟨steering ∼⟩ **5** : a toothed wheel **6** : working order or adjustment ⟨got her career in ∼⟩ **7** : an adjustment of transmission gears (as of an automobile or bicycle) that determines speed and direction of travel — **gear** vb

gear·box \'gir-ˌbäks\ n : TRANSMISSION 3

gear·shift \-ˌshift\ n : a mechanism by which transmission gears are shifted

gear·wheel \-ˌhwēl\ n : GEAR 5

gecko \'ge-kō\ n, pl **geck·os** also **geck·oes** : any of numerous small chiefly tropical insect-eating lizards

GED abbr **1** General Educational Development (tests) **2** general equivalency diploma

geek \'gēk\ n : a person of an intellectual bent who is often disliked — **geek·i·ness** n — **geeky** adj

geese pl of GOOSE

gee·zer \'gē-zər\ n : an odd or eccentric person usu. of old age

Gei·ger counter \'gī-gər-\ n : an electronic instrument for detecting the presence of cosmic rays or radioactive substances

gei·sha \'gā-shə, 'gē-\ n, pl **geisha** or **geishas** [Jp, fr. gei art + -sha person] : a Japanese girl or woman who is trained to provide entertaining company for men

gel \'jel\ n : a solid jellylike colloid (as gelatin dessert) — **gel** vb

gel·a·tin also **gel·a·tine** \'je-lə-tən\ n : glutinous material and esp. protein obtained from animal tissues by boiling and used as a food, in dyeing, and in photography; also : an edible jelly formed with

gelatin — **ge·lat·i·nous** \jə-'la-tə-nəs\ adj

geld \'geld\ vb : CASTRATE

geld·ing n : a castrated male horse

gel·id \'je-ləd\ adj : extremely cold

gem \'jem\ n **1** : JEWEL **2** : a usu. valuable stone cut and polished for ornament **3** : something valued for beauty or perfection

Gem·i·ni \'je-mə-(ˌ)nē, -ˌnī; 'ge-mə-ˌnē\ n **1** : a zodiacal constellation between Taurus and Cancer usu. pictured as twins sitting together **2** : the 3d sign of the zodiac in astrology; also : one born under this sign

gem·ol·o·gy or **gem·mol·o·gy** \je-'mä-lə-jē, jə-\ n : the science of gems — **gem·olog·i·cal** \ˌje-mə-'lä-ji-kəl, jə-\ adj — **gem·ol·o·gist** also **gem·mol·o·gist** \-jist\ n

gem·stone \'jem-ˌstōn\ n : a mineral or petrified material that when cut and polished can be used in jewelry

gen abbr **1** general **2** genitive

Gen abbr Genesis

Gen AF abbr general of the air force

gen·darme \'zhän-ˌdärm, 'jän-\ n [F, intended as sing. of gensdarmes, pl. of gent d'armes, lit., armed people] : a member of a body of soldiers esp. in France serving as an armed police force

gen·der \'jen-dər\ n [ME gendre, fr. AF genre, gendre, fr. L gener-, genus birth, race, kind, gender] **1** : any of two or more divisions within a grammatical class that determine agreement with and selection of other words or grammatical forms **2** : SEX 1

gene \'jēn\ n : a part of DNA or RNA that contains chemical information needed to make a particular protein (as an enzyme) controlling or influencing an inherited bodily trait (as eye color) or activity (as metabolism) or that influences or controls the activity of another gene or genes — **gen·ic** \'jē-nik, 'je-\ adj

ge·ne·al·o·gy \ˌjē-nē-'ä-lə-jē, je-, -'a-\ n, pl **-gies** : PEDIGREE, LINEAGE; also : the study of family pedigrees — **ge·ne·a·log·i·cal** \ˌjē-nē-ə-'lä-ji-kəl, je-\ adj — **ge·ne·a·log·i·cal·ly** \-k(ə-)lē\ adv — **ge·ne·al·o·gist** \ˌjē-nē-'ä-lə-jist, je-; -'a-\ n

gene pool n : the total genetic information contained in a population of interbreeding organisms

genera pl of GENUS

¹gen·er·al \'je-nə-rəl, 'jen-rəl\ adj **1** : of or relating to the whole **2** : taken as a whole **3** : relating to or covering all instances **4** : not special or specialized **5** : common to many ⟨a ∼ custom⟩ **6** : not limited in meaning : not specific **7** : holding superior rank ⟨inspector ∼⟩ ✦ **Synonyms** GENERIC, UNIVERSAL

²general n **1** : something that involves or is applicable to the whole **2** : a commissioned officer ranking next below a general of the army or a general of the air force **3** : a commissioned officer of the highest rank in the marine corps — **in general** : for the most part

general assembly n **1** : a legislative

assembly; *esp* : a U.S. state legislature **2** *cap G&A* : the supreme deliberative body of the United Nations

gen·er·al·i·sa·tion, gen·er·al·ise, gen·er·al·ised *Brit var of* GENERALIZATION, GENERALIZE, GENERALIZED

gen·er·a·lis·si·mo \,je-nə-rə-'li-sə-,mō\ *n*, *pl* **-mos** [It, fr. *generale* general] : the chief commander of an army

gen·er·al·i·ty \,je-nə-'ra-lə-tē\ *n*, *pl* **-ties** **1** : the quality or state of being general **2** : GENERALIZATION 2 **3** : a vague or inadequate statement **4** : the greatest part : BULK

gen·er·al·i·za·tion \,je-nə-rə-lə-'zā-shən, ,jen-rə-\ *n* **1** : the act or process of generalizing **2** : a general statement, law, principle, or proposition

gen·er·al·ize \'je-nə-rə-,līz, 'jen-rə-\ *vb* **-ized; -iz·ing** **1** : to make general **2** : to draw general conclusions from **3** : to reach a general conclusion esp. on the basis of particular instances **4** : to extend throughout the body

gen·er·al·ly \'jen-rə-lē, 'jē-nə-\ *adv* **1** : in a general manner **2** : as a rule

general of the air force : a commissioned officer of the highest rank in the air force

general of the army : a commissioned officer of the highest rank in the army

general practitioner *n* : a physician or veterinarian whose practice is not limited to a specialty

gen·er·al·ship \'je-nə-rəl-,ship, 'jen-rəl-\ *n* **1** : office or tenure of office of a general **2** : LEADERSHIP **3** : military skill as a high commander

general store *n* : a retail store that carries a wide variety of goods but is not divided into departments

gen·er·ate \'je-nə-,rāt\ *vb* **-at·ed; -at·ing** : to bring into existence : PRODUCE 〈~ electricity〉 ◆ *Synonyms* CREATE, ORIGINATE, PROCREATE, SPAWN

gen·er·a·tion \,je-nə-'rā-shən\ *n* **1** : a body of living beings constituting a single step in the line of descent from an ancestor; *also* : the average period between generations **2** : PRODUCTION

Generation X *n* : the generation of Americans born in the 1960s and 1970s

gen·er·a·tive \'je-nə-rə-tiv, -,rā-tiv\ *adj* : having the power or function of generating, originating, producing, or reproducing 〈~ organs〉

gen·er·a·tor \'je-nə-,rā-tər\ *n* : one that generates; *esp* : a machine by which mechanical energy is changed into electrical energy

ge·ner·ic \jə-'ner-ik\ *adj* **1** : not specific : GENERAL **2** : not protected by a trademark 〈a ~ drug〉 **3** : of or relating to a biological genus **4** : having no particularly distinctive quality 〈~ towns〉 — **generic** *n* — **ge·ner·i·cal·ly** \-i-k(ə-)lē\ *adv*

gen·er·ous \'je-nə-rəs\ *adj* **1** : free in giving or sharing 〈~ donors〉 **2** : HIGHMINDED, NOBLE **3** : ABUNDANT, AMPLE, COPIOUS 〈a ~ salary〉 ◆ *Synonyms* LIBERAL, BOUNTIFUL, MUNIFICENT, OPEN-

HANDED — **gen·er·os·i·ty** \,je-nə-'rä-sə-tē\ *n* — **gen·er·ous·ly** \'je-nə-rəs-lē\ *adv* — **gen·er·ous·ness** *n*

gen·e·sis \'je-nə-səs\ *n*, *pl* **-e·ses** \-,sēz\ : the origin or coming into existence of something

Genesis *n* — see BIBLE table

gene-splic·ing \-,splī-siŋ\ *n* : the process of preparing recombinant DNA

gene therapy *n* : the insertion of normal or altered genes into cells esp. to replace defective genes in the treatment of genetic disorders or to provide a specialized disease-fighting function

ge·net·ic \jə-'ne-tik\ *adj* : of or relating to the origin, development, or causes of something; *also* : of, relating to, or caused by genes or genetics 〈~ research〉 — **ge·net·i·cal·ly** \-ti-k(ə-)lē\ *adv*

genetic code *n* : the chemical code that is the basis of genetic inheritance and consists of units of three linked chemical groups in DNA and RNA which specify particular amino acids used to make proteins or which start or stop the process of making proteins

genetic engineering *n* : the alteration of genetic material esp. by cutting up and joining together DNA from one or more species of organism and inserting the result into an organism — **genetically engineered** *adj*

ge·net·ics \jə-'ne-tiks\ *n* : a branch of biology dealing with heredity and variation — **ge·net·i·cist** \-tə-sist\ *n*

ge·nial \'jē-nyəl, 'jē-nē-əl\ *adj* **1** : favorable to growth or comfort 〈~ sunshine〉 **2** : CHEERFUL, KINDLY 〈a ~ host〉 ◆ *Synonyms* AFFABLE, CONGENIAL, CORDIAL, GRACIOUS, SOCIABLE — **ge·nial·i·ty** \,jē-nē-'a-lə-tē, jēn-'ya-\ *n* — **ge·nial·ly** *adv*

-gen·ic \'je-nik\ *adj comb form* **1** : producing : forming **2** : produced by : formed from **3** : suitable for production or reproduction by (such) a medium

ge·nie \'jē-nē\ *n*, *pl* **ge·nies** *also* **ge·nii** \-nē-,ī\ [F *génie*, fr. Ar *jinnī*] : a supernatural spirit that often takes human form usu. serving the person who calls on it

gen·i·tal \'je-nə-t²l\ *adj* **1** : concerned with reproduction 〈~ organs〉 **2** : of, relating to, or characterized by the stage of psychosexual development in psychoanalytic theory in which oral and anal impulses are subordinated to adaptive interpersonal mechanisms — **gen·i·tal·ly** *adv*

gen·i·ta·lia \,je-nə-'tāl-yə\ *n pl* : reproductive organs; *esp* : the external genital organs — **gen·i·ta·lic** \-'ta-lik, -'tā-\ *adj*

gen·i·tals \'je-nə-t²lz\ *n pl* : GENITALIA

gen·i·tive \'je-nə-tiv\ *adj* : of, relating to, or constituting a grammatical case marking typically a relationship of possessor or source — **genitive** *n*

gen·i·to·uri·nary \,je-nə-tō-'yùr-ə-,ner-ē\ *adj* : of or relating to the genital and urinary organs or functions

ge·nius \'jē-nyəs\ *n*, *pl* **ge·nius·es** *or* **ge·nii** \-nē-,ī\ [L, tutelary spirit, natural inclinations, fr. *gignere* to beget] **1** *pl genii* : an attendant spirit of a person or place;

also : a person who influences another for good or evil **2** : a strong leaning or inclination **3** : a peculiar or distinctive character or spirit (as of a nation or a language) **4** *pl usu* **genii** : SPIRIT, GENIE **5** *pl usu* **geniuses** : a single strongly marked capacity or aptitude **6** : extraordinary intellectual power; *also* : a person having such power ✦ *Synonyms* GIFT, FACULTY, FLAIR, KNACK, TALENT

genl *abbr* general

geno·cide \'je-nə-ˌsīd\ *n* : the deliberate and systematic destruction of a racial, political, or cultural group

ge·nome \'jē-ˌnōm\ *n* **1** : one haploid set of chromosomes **2** : the genetic material of an organism

ge·no·mics \jē-'nō-miks\ *n* : a branch of biotechnology concerned esp. with investigating and collecting data about the structure and function of all or part of an organism's genome

-genous \jə-nəs\ *adj comb form* **1** : producing; yielding ⟨erogenous⟩ **2** : having (such) an origin ⟨endogenous⟩

genre \'zhän-rə, 'zhäⁿ-; 'zhäⁿr; 'jän-rə\ *n* **1** : a distinctive type or category esp. of literary composition **2** : a style of painting in which everyday subjects are treated realistically

gens \'jenz, 'gens\ *n, pl* **gen·tes** \'jen-ˌtēz, 'gen-ˌtās\ [L] : a Roman clan embracing the families of the same stock in the male line

gent *n* : GENTLEMAN

gen·teel \jen-'tēl\ *adj* **1** : ARISTOCRATIC **2** : ELEGANT, STYLISH **3** : POLITE, REFINED **4** : maintaining the appearance of superior social status **5** : marked by false delicacy, prudery, or affectation — **gen·teel·ly** *adv* — **gen·teel·ness** *n*

gen·tian \'jen-chən\ *n* : any of numerous herbs with opposite leaves and showy usu. blue flowers in the fall

gen·tile \'jen-ˌtī(-ə)l\ *n* [ME, fr. LL *gentilis* heathen, pagan, fr. L *gent-, gens* clan, nation] **1** *often cap* : a person who is not Jewish; *esp* : a Christian as distinguished from a Jew **2** : HEATHEN, PAGAN — **gentile** *adj, often cap*

gen·til·i·ty \jen-'ti-lə-tē\ *n, pl* **-ties 1** : good birth and family **2** : the qualities characteristic of a well-bred person **3** : good manners **4** : superior social status shown in manners or mode of life

¹**gen·tle** \'jen-t^əl\ *adj* **gen·tler** \'jent-lər, -t^əl-ər\; **gen·tlest** \'jent-ləst, -t^əl-əst\ **1** : belonging to a family of high social station **2** : of, relating to, or characteristic of a gentleman **3** : KIND, AMIABLE ⟨a ~ pastor⟩ **4** : TRACTABLE, DOCILE ⟨a ~ dog⟩ **5** : not harsh, stern, or violent **6** : SOFT, DELICATE **7** : MODERATE — **gen·tle·ness** *n* — **gen·tly** *adv*

²**gentle** *vb* **gen·tled; gen·tling 1** : to make or become mild, docile, soft, or moderate **2** : MOLLIFY, PLACATE

gen·tle·folk \'jen-t^əl-ˌfōk\ *also* **gen·tle·folks** \-ˌfōks\ *n* : persons of good family and breeding

gen·tle·man \-mən\ *n* **1** : a man of good

family **2** : a well-bred man **3** : MAN — used in pl. as a form of address — **gen·tle·man·ly** *adj*

gen·tle·wom·an \-ˌwu̇-mən\ *n* **1** : a woman of good family **2** : a woman attending a lady of rank **3** : a woman with very good manners : LADY

gen·tri·fi·ca·tion \ˌjen-trə-fə-'kā-shən\ *n* : the process of renewal accompanying the influx of middle-class people into deteriorating areas that often displaces earlier usu. poorer residents — **gen·tri·fy** \'jen-trə-ˌfī\ *vb*

gen·try \'jen-trē\ *n, pl* **gentries 1** : people of good birth, breeding, and education : ARISTOCRACY **2** : the class of English people between the nobility and the yeomanry **3** : persons of a designated class

gen·u·flect \'jen-yù-ˌflekt\ *vb* : to bend the knee esp. in worship — **gen·u·flec·tion** \ˌjen-yù-'flek-shən\ *n*

gen·u·ine \'jen-yə-wən\ *adj* **1** : AUTHENTIC, REAL ⟨a ~ signature⟩ **2** : SINCERE, HONEST ⟨their love is ~⟩ ✦ *Synonyms* BONA FIDE, TRUE, VERITABLE — **gen·u·ine·ly** *adv* — **gen·u·ine·ness** *n*

ge·nus \'jē-nəs\ *n, pl* **gen·era** \'je-nə-rə\ [L, birth, race, kind] : a category of biological classification that ranks between the family and the species and contains related species

geo·cen·tric \ˌjē-ō-'sen-trik\ *adj* **1** : relating to or measured from the earth's center **2** : having or relating to the earth as a center

geo·chem·is·try \-'ke-mə-strē\ *n* : a branch of geology that deals with the chemical composition of and chemical changes in the earth — **geo·chem·i·cal** \-mi-kəl\ *adj* — **geo·chem·ist** \-mist\ *n*

ge·ode \'jē-ˌōd\ *n* : a nodule of stone having a cavity lined with mineral matter

¹**geo·de·sic** \ˌjē-ō-'de-sik\ *adj* : made of light straight structural elements ⟨a ~ dome⟩

²**geodesic** *n* : the shortest line between two points on a surface

geo·det·ic \ˌjē-ə-'de-tik\ *adj* : of, relating to, or being precise measurement of the earth and its features ⟨a ~ survey⟩

geog *abbr* geographic; geographical; geography

ge·og·ra·phy \jē-'ä-grə-fē\ *n, pl* **-phies 1** : a science that deals with the natural features of the earth and the climate, products, and inhabitants **2** : the natural features of a region — **ge·og·ra·pher** \-fər\ *n* — **geo·graph·ic** \ˌjē-ə-'gra-fik\ *or* **geo·graph·i·cal** \-fi-kəl\ *adj* — **geo·graph·i·cal·ly** \-fi-k(ə-)lē\ *adv*

geol *abbr* geologic; geological; geology

ge·ol·o·gy \jē-'ä-lə-jē\ *n, pl* **-gies 1** : a science that deals with the history of the earth and its life esp. as recorded in rocks; *also* : a study of the features of a celestial body (as the moon) **2** : the geologic features of an area — **geo·log·ic** \ˌjē-ə-'lä-jik\ *or* **geo·log·i·cal** \-ji-kəl\ *adj* — **geo·log·i·cal·ly** \-ji-k(ə-)lē\ *adv* — **ge·ol·o·gist** \jē-'ä-lə-jist\ *n*

geom *abbr* geometric; geometrical; geometry

geo·mag·net·ic \ˌjē-ō-mag-'ne-tik\ *adj* : of or relating to the magnetism of the earth — **geo·mag·ne·tism** \-'mag-nə-ˌti-zəm\ *n*

geometric mean *n* : the *n*th root of the product of *n* numbers; *esp* : a number that is the second term of three consecutive terms of a geometric progression ⟨the *geometric mean* of 9 and 4 is 6⟩

geometric progression *n* : a progression (as 1, ¹/₂, ¹/₄) in which the ratio of a term to its predecessor is always the same

ge·om·e·try \jē-'ä-mə-trē\ *n, pl* **-tries** [ultim. fr. Gk *geōmetria*, fr. *geōmetrein* to measure the earth, fr. *gē* earth + *metron* measure] **:** a branch of mathematics dealing with the relations, properties, and measurements of solids, surfaces, lines, points, and angles — **ge·om·e·ter** \-tər\ *n* — **geo·met·ric** \ˌjē-ə-'me-trik\ *or* **geo·met·ri·cal** \-tri-kəl\ *adj*

geo·phys·ics \ˌjē-ō-'fi-ziks\ *n* : the physics of the earth — **geo·phys·i·cal** \-zi-kəl\ *adj* — **geo·phys·i·cist** \-zə-sist\ *n*

geo·pol·i·tics \-'pä-lə-ˌtiks\ *n* : a combination of political and geographic factors relating to a state — **geo·po·lit·i·cal** \-pə-'li-ti-kəl\ *adj*

geo·ther·mal \ˌjē-ō-'thər-məl\ *adj* : of, relating to, or using the heat of the earth's interior

ger *abbr* gerund

Ger *abbr* German; Germany

ge·ra·ni·um \jə-'rā-nē-əm\ *n* [L, fr. Gk *geranion*, fr. *geranos* crane] **:** any of a genus of herbs with usu. deeply cut leaves and typically pink, purple, or white flowers; *also* : any of a related genus of herbs that are native to southern Africa and are widely grown for their clusters of showy usu. red, pink, or white flowers

ger·bil *also* **ger·bile** \'jər-bəl\ *n* : any of numerous Old World burrowing desert rodents with long hind legs

ge·ri·at·ric \ˌjer-ē-'a-trik\ *adj* **1** : of or relating to geriatrics or the process of aging **2** : of, relating to, or appropriate for elderly people **3** : OLD

ge·ri·at·rics \-triks\ *n* : a branch of medicine dealing with the problems and diseases of old age and aging

germ \'jərm\ *n* **1** : a bit of living matter capable of growth and development (as into an organism) **2** : SOURCE, RUDIMENTS **3** : MICROORGANISM; *esp* : one causing disease

Ger·man \'jər-mən\ *n* **1** : a native or inhabitant of Germany **2** : the language of Germany, Austria, and parts of Switzerland — **German** *adj* — **Ger·man·ic** \jər-'ma-nik\ *adj*

ger·mane \jər-'mān\ *adj* [ME *germain*, lit., having the same parents, fr. AF, fr. L *germanus*, fr. *germen* sprout, bud] **:** RELEVANT, APPROPRIATE ♦ **Synonyms** APPLICABLE, MATERIAL, PERTINENT

ger·ma·ni·um \jər-'mā-nē-əm\ *n* : a grayish white hard chemical element used esp. in semiconductor and optical materials and as a catalyst

German measles *n sing or pl* : an acute contagious virus disease milder than typical measles but damaging to the fetus when occurring early in pregnancy

German shepherd *n* : any of a breed of intelligent responsive working dogs of German origin often used in police work and as guide dogs for the blind

germ cell *n* : an egg or sperm or one of their antecedent cells

ger·mi·cide \'jər-mə-ˌsīd\ *n* : an agent that destroys germs — **ger·mi·cid·al** \ˌjər-mə-'sī-dᵊl\ *adj*

ger·mi·nal \'jər-mə-nəl\ *adj* : of or relating to a germ or germ cell; *also* : EMBRYONIC

ger·mi·nate \'jər-mə-ˌnāt\ *vb* **-nat·ed; -nat·ing 1** : to cause to develop : begin to develop : SPROUT **2** : to come into being : EVOLVE — **ger·mi·na·tion** \ˌjər-mə-'nā-shən\ *n*

ger·on·tol·o·gy \ˌjer-ən-'tä-lə-jē\ *n* : a scientific study of aging and the problems of the aged — **ge·ron·to·log·i·cal** \jə-ˌrän-tə-'lä-ji-kəl\ *adj* — **ger·on·tol·o·gist** \ˌjer-ən-'tä-lə-jist\ *n*

ger·ry·man·der \'jer-ē-ˌman-dər\ *vb* : to divide into election districts so as to give one political party an advantage — **gerrymander** *n*

ger·und \'jer-ənd\ *n* : a word having the characteristics of both verb and noun

ge·sta·po \gə-'stä-pō\ *n, pl* **-pos** [G, fr. *Geheime Staatspolizei*, lit., secret state police] **:** a usu. terrorist secret-police organization operating against persons suspected of disloyalty

ges·ta·tion \je-'stā-shən\ *n* : PREGNANCY, INCUBATION — **ges·tate** \'jes-ˌtāt\ *vb*

ges·tic·u·late \je-'sti-kyə-ˌlāt\ *vb* **-lat·ed; -lat·ing** : to make gestures esp. when speaking — **ges·tic·u·la·tion** \-ˌsti-kyə-'lā-shən\ *n*

ges·ture \'jes-chər\ *n* **1** : a movement usu. of the body or limbs that expresses or emphasizes an idea, sentiment, or attitude **2** : something said or done by way of formality or courtesy, as a symbol or token, or for its effect on the attitudes of others — **ges·tur·al** \-chə-rəl\ *adj* — **gesture** *vb*

ge·sund·heit \gə-'zunt-ˌhīt\ *interj* [G, lit., health] — used to wish good health esp. to one who has just sneezed

¹get \'get\ *vb* **got** \'gät\; **got** *or* **got·ten** \'gä-tᵊn\; **get·ting 1** : to gain possession of (as by receiving, acquiring, earning, buying, or winning) : PROCURE, OBTAIN, FETCH **2** : to succeed in coming or going ⟨*got* away to the lake⟩ **3** : to cause to come or go ⟨*got* the car to the station⟩ **4** : BEGET **5** : to cause to be in a certain condition or position ⟨don't ∼ wet⟩ **6** : BECOME ⟨∼ sick⟩ **7** : PREPARE **8** : SEIZE **9** : to move emotionally; *also* : IRRITATE **10** : BAFFLE, PUZZLE **11** : KILL **12** : HIT **13** : to be subjected to ⟨∼ the measles⟩ **14** : to receive as punishment **15** : to find out by calculation **16** : HEAR; *also* : UNDERSTAND ⟨*got* the joke⟩ **17** : PERSUADE,

INDUCE **18** : HAVE ⟨he's *got* no money⟩ **19** : to have as an obligation or necessity ⟨you have *got* to come⟩ **20** : to establish communication with **21** : to be able ⟨finally *got* to go to med school⟩ **22** : to come to be ⟨*got* talking about old times⟩ **23** : to leave at once — **get ahead** : to achieve success — **get a move on** : HURRY — **get away with** : to avoid punishment for (as a crime) — **get into** : to become strongly involved or interested in ⟨*got* into music⟩ — **get over** : to reconcile oneself to ⟨*got over* the breakup⟩

²**get** \'get\ *n* : OFFSPRING, PROGENY

get along *vb* **1** : GET BY **2** : to be on friendly terms

get·away \'ge-tə-ˌwā\ *n* **1** : ESCAPE **2** : START **3** : a usu. brief vacation

get by *vb* : to meet one's needs

get–to·geth·er \'get-tə-ˌge-thər\ *n* : an informal social gathering

get–up \'get-ˌəp\ *n* **1** : OUTFIT, COSTUME **2** : general composition or structure

gew·gaw \'gü-ˌgȯ, 'gyü-\ *n* : a showy trifle : BAUBLE, TRINKET

gey·ser \'gī-zər\ *n* [Icelandic *Geysir*, hot spring in Iceland] : a spring that intermittently shoots up hot water and steam

g–force \'jē-ˌfȯrs\ *n* : the force of gravity or acceleration on a body

ghast·ly \'gast-lē\ *adj* **ghast·li·er; -est 1** : HORRIBLE, SHOCKING **2** : resembling a ghost : DEATHLIKE, PALE ◆ *Synonyms* GRUESOME, GRIM, LURID, GRISLY, MACABRE

ghat \'gȯt\ *n* [Hindi & Urdu *ghāṭ*] : a broad flight of steps on an Indian riverbank that provides access to the water

gher·kin \'gər-kən\ *n* **1** : a small prickly fruit of a vine related to the cucumber used to make pickles **2** : an immature cucumber

ghet·to \'ge-tō\ *n, pl* **ghettos** *or* **ghettoes** : a quarter of a city in which members of a minority group live because of social, legal, or economic pressure

¹**ghost** \'gōst\ *n* **1** : the seat of life : SOUL **2** : a disembodied soul; *esp* : the soul of a dead person believed to be an inhabitant of the unseen world or to appear in bodily form to living people **3** : SPIRIT, DEMON **4** : a faint trace ⟨a ∼ of a smile⟩ **5** : a false image in a photographic negative or on a television screen — **ghost·ly** *adv*

²**ghost** *vb* : GHOSTWRITE

ghost·write \-ˌrīt\ *vb* **-wrote** \-ˌrōt\; **-writ·ten** \-ˌri-t³n\ : to write for and in the name of another — **ghost·writ·er** *n*

ghoul \'gül\ *n* [Ar *ghūl*] : a legendary evil being that robs graves and feeds on corpses — **ghoul·ish** *adj*

GHQ *abbr* general headquarters

gi *abbr* gill

¹**GI** \ˌjē-'ī\ *adj* [galvanized *i*ron; fr. abbr. used in listing such articles as garbage cans, but taken as abbr. for *government issue*] **1** : provided by an official U.S. military supply department ⟨∼ shoes⟩ **2** : of, relating to, or characteristic of U.S.

military personnel **3** : conforming to military regulations or customs ⟨a ∼ haircut⟩

²**GI** *n, pl* **GIs** *or* **GI's** \-'īz\ : a member or former member of the U.S. armed forces; *esp* : an enlisted man

³**GI** *abbr* **1** galvanized iron **2** gastrointestinal **3** general issue **4** government issue

gi·ant \'jī-ənt\ *n* **1** : a legendary humanlike being of great size and strength **2** : a living being or thing of extraordinary size or powers — **giant** *adj*

gi·ant·ess \'jī-ən-təs\ *n* : a female giant

giant panda *n* : PANDA 2

gib·ber \'ji-bər\ *vb* : to speak rapidly, inarticulately, and often foolishly

gib·ber·ish \'ji-bə-rish\ *n* : unintelligible or confused speech or language

¹**gib·bet** \'ji-bət\ *n* : GALLOWS

²**gibbet** *vb* **1** : to hang on a gibbet **2** : to expose to public scorn **3** : to execute by hanging

gib·bon \'gi-bən\ *n* : any of several tailless apes of southeastern Asia

gib·bous \'ji-bəs, 'gi-\ *adj* **1** : rounded like the exterior of a sphere or circle **2** : seen with more than half but not all of the apparent disk illuminated ⟨∼ moon⟩ **3** : having a hump : HUMP-BACKED

gibe *or* **jibe** \'jīb\ *vb* **gibed** *or* **jibed; gib·ing** *or* **jib·ing** : to utter taunting words : SNEER — **gibe** *or* **jibe** *n*

gib·lets \'jib-ləts\ *n pl* : the edible viscera of a fowl

Gib·son girl \'gib-sən-\ *adj* : of or relating to a style in women's clothing characterized by high necks, full sleeves, and slender waistlines

gid·dy \'gi-dē\ *adj* **gid·di·er; -est 1** : DIZZY **2** : causing dizziness ⟨a ∼ height⟩ **3** : not serious : FRIVOLOUS, SILLY — **gid·di·ness** \-dē-nəs\ *n*

gid·dy·ap \ˌgi-dē-'ap, -'āp\ *or* **gid·dy·up** \-'əp\ *vb imper* : a command (as to a horse) to go ahead or go faster

GIF \'gif, 'jif\ *n* [graphic interchange format] : a computer file format for digital images; *also* : the image itself

gift \'gift\ *n* **1** : a special ability : TALENT **2** : something given : PRESENT **3** : the act or power of giving

gift·ed \'gif-təd\ *adj* : TALENTED

¹**gig** \'gig\ *n* **1** : a long light ship's boat **2** : a light 2-wheeled one-horse carriage

²**gig** *n* : a pronged spear for catching fish — **gig** *vb*

³**gig** *n* : a job for a specified time; *esp* : an entertainer's engagement

⁴**gig** *n* : a military demerit — **gig** *vb*

giga·byte \'ji-gə-ˌbīt, 'gi-\ *n* : 1024 megabytes *or* 1,073,741,824 bytes; *also* : one billion bytes

gi·gan·tic \jī-'gan-tik\ *adj* : exceeding the usual (as in size or force)

gig·gle \'gi-gəl\ *vb* **gig·gled; gig·gling** : to laugh with repeated short catches of the breath — **giggle** *n* — **gig·gly** \-gə-lē\ *adj*

GIGO *abbr* garbage in, garbage out

gig·o·lo \ˈji-gə-ˌlō\ *n, pl* **-los** **1** : a man supported by a woman usu. in return for his attentions **2** : a professional dancing partner or male escort

Gi·la monster \ˈhē-lə-\ *n* : a large orange and black venomous lizard of the southwestern U.S.

¹**gild** \ˈgild\ *vb* **gild·ed** *or* **gilt** \ˈgilt\; **gild·ing** **1** : to overlay with or as if with a thin covering of gold **2** : to give an attractive but often deceptive appearance to

²**gild** *var of* GUILD

¹**gill** \ˈjil\ *n* — see WEIGHT table

²**gill** \ˈgil\ *n* : an organ (as of a fish) for obtaining oxygen from water

¹**gilt** \ˈgilt\ *adj* : of the color of gold

²**gilt** *n* : gold or a substance resembling gold laid on the surface of an object

³**gilt** *n* : a young female swine

gim·crack \ˈjim-ˌkrak\ *n* : a showy object of little use or value

²**gimcrack** *adj* : CHEAP, SHODDY

gim·let \ˈgim-lət\ *n* : a small tool with screw point and cross handle for boring holes

gim·me cap \ˈgi-mē-\ *n* : an adjustable visored cap featuring a corporate logo or slogan

gim·mick \ˈgi-mik\ *n* **1** : CONTRIVANCE, GADGET **2** : an important feature that is not immediately apparent : CATCH **3** : a new and ingenious scheme **4** : a device used to attract business or attention — **gim·micky** \-mi-kē\ *adj*

gim·mick·ry \ˈgi-mi-krē\ *n, pl* **-ries** : an array of or the use of gimmicks

gimpy \ˈgim-pē\ *adj* : LAME **1**

¹**gin** \ˈjin\ *n* [ME *gin*, fr. AF, short for *engin* engine] **1** : TRAP, SNARE **2** : a machine to separate seeds from cotton — **gin** *vb*

²**gin** *n* [by shortening & alter. fr. *geneva*, kind of gin] : a liquor distilled from a grain mash and flavored with juniper berries

gin·ger \ˈjin-jər\ *n* : the pungent aromatic rootstock of a tropical plant used esp. as a spice and in medicine; *also* : the spice or the plant

ginger ale *n* : a carbonated soft drink flavored with ginger

gin·ger·bread \ˈjin-jər-ˌbred\ *n* **1** : a cake made with molasses and flavored with ginger **2** : lavish or superfluous ornament esp. in architecture

gin·ger·ly \ˈjin-jər-lē\ *adj* : very cautious or careful — **gingerly** *adv*

gin·ger·snap \-ˌsnap\ *n* : a thin brittle molasses cookie flavored with ginger

ging·ham \ˈgiŋ-əm\ *n* : a clothing fabric usu. of yarn-dyed cotton in plain weave

gin·gi·vi·tis \ˌjin-jə-ˈvī-təs\ *n* : inflammation of the gums

gink·go *also* **ging·ko** \ˈgiŋ-(ˌ)kō\ *n, pl* **ginkgoes** *or* **ginkgos** *also* **gingkos** *or* **gingkoes** **1** : a tree of eastern China with fan-shaped leaves often grown as a shade tree **2** : GINKGO BILOBA

ginkgo bi·lo·ba \-ˌbī-ˈlō-bə\ *n* : an extract of the leaves of ginkgo that is held to enhance mental functioning

gin·seng \ˈjin-ˌseŋ\ *n* : an aromatic root of a Chinese or No. American herb used esp. in Chinese medicine; *also* : one of these herbs

Gip·sy *chiefly Brit var of* GYPSY

gi·raffe \jə-ˈraf\ *n, pl* **giraffes** [It *giraffa*, fr. Ar *zirāfa*] : an African ruminant mammal with a very long neck and a short coat with dark blotches

gird \ˈgərd\ *vb* **gird·ed** *or* **girt** \ˈgərt\; **gird·ing** **1** : to encircle or fasten (as a sword) with or as if with a belt **2** : to invest esp. with power or authority **3** : PREPARE, BRACE

gird·er \ˈgər-dər\ *n* : a horizontal main supporting beam

gir·dle \ˈgər-dᵊl\ *n* **1** : something (as a belt or sash) that encircles or confines **2** : a woman's supporting undergarment that extends from the waist to below the hips — **girdle** *vb*

girl \ˈgərl\ *n* **1** : a female child **2** : a young woman **3** : SWEETHEART — **girl·hood** \-ˌhu̇d\ *n* — **girl·ish** *adj*

girl Friday *n* : a female assistant (as in an office) entrusted with a wide variety of tasks

girl·friend \ˈgərl-ˌfrend\ *n* **1** : a female friend **2** : a regular female companion in a romantic or sexual relationship

Girl Scout *n* : a member of any of the scouting programs of the Girl Scouts of the United States of America

girth \ˈgərth\ *n* **1** : a band around an animal by which something (as a saddle) may be fastened on its back **2** : a measure around something

gist \ˈjist\ *n* [AF, it lies, fr. *gesir* to lie, ultim. fr. L *jacēre*] : the main point or part

git *dial var of* GET

¹**give** \ˈgiv\ *vb* **gave** \ˈgāv\; **giv·en** \ˈgi-vən\; **giv·ing** **1** : to make a present of **2** : to bestow by formal action **3** : to accord or yield to another **4** : to yield to force, strain, or pressure **5** : to put into the possession or keeping of another **6** : PROFFER ⟨*gave* her his hand⟩ **7** : DELIVER ⟨*gave* the bride away⟩ **8** : to present in public performance or to view **9** : PROVIDE ⟨~ a party⟩ **10** : ATTRIBUTE **11** : to make, form, or yield as a product or result ⟨cows ~ milk⟩ **12** : PAY **13** : to deliver by some bodily action ⟨*gave* me a push⟩ **14** : to offer as a pledge ⟨I ~ you my word⟩ **15** : DEVOTE **16** : to cause to have or receive

²**give** *n* **1** : capacity or tendency to yield to force or strain **2** : the quality or state of being springy

give–and–take \ˌgiv-ən-ˈtāk\ *n* **1** : COMPROMISE **2** : a usu. good-natured exchange (as of remarks or ideas)

give·away \ˈgi-və-ˌwā\ *n* **1** : an unintentional revelation or betrayal **2** : something given away free; *esp* : PREMIUM

give in *vb* : SUBMIT, SURRENDER

¹**giv·en** \ˈgi-vən\ *adj* **1** : DISPOSED; INCLINED ⟨~ to swearing⟩ **2** : SPECIFIED, PARTICULAR ⟨at a ~ time⟩

²**given** *n* : something taken for granted : a basic condition or assumption

³given *prep* : CONSIDERING
given name *n* : a name that precedes one's surname
give out *vb* 1 : EMIT 2 : BREAK DOWN 3 : to become exhausted : COLLAPSE
give up *vb* 1 : SURRENDER 2 : to abandon (oneself) to a feeling, influence, or activity 3 : QUIT
giz·mo *also* **gis·mo** \'giz-mō\ *n, pl* **gizmos** *also* **gismos** : GADGET
giz·zard \'gi-zərd\ *n* : the muscular usu. horny-lined enlargement of the alimentary canal of a bird used for churning and grinding up food
gla·cial \'glā-shəl\ *adj* 1 : extremely cold 2 : of or relating to glaciers 3 : being or relating to a past period of time when a large part of the earth was covered by glaciers 4 *cap* : PLEISTOCENE 5 : very slow ⟨a ~ pace⟩ — **gla·cial·ly** *adv*
gla·ci·ate \'glā-shē-,āt\ *vb* **-at·ed; -at·ing** 1 : to subject to glacial action 2 : to produce glacial effects in or on — **gla·ci·a·tion** \glā-shē-'ā-shən, -sē-\ *n*
gla·cier \'glā-shər\ *n* [F, fr. MF dial. (Savoy), fr. *glace* ice, fr. L *glacies*] : a large body of ice moving slowly down a slope or spreading outward on a land surface
¹glad \'glad\ *adj* **glad·der; glad·dest** 1 : experiencing pleasure, joy, or delight 2 : PLEASED 3 : very willing ⟨was ~ to help⟩ 4 : PLEASANT, JOYFUL 5 : CHEERFUL ⟨a ~ morning⟩ — **glad·ly** *adv* — **glad·ness** *n*
²glad *n* : GLADIOLUS
glad·den \'gla-d³n\ *vb* : to make glad
glade \'glād\ *n* : a grassy open space surrounded by woods
glad·i·a·tor \'gla-dē-,ā-tər\ *n* 1 : a person engaged in a fight to the death for public entertainment in ancient Rome 2 : a person engaging in a public fight or controversy; *also* : PRIZEFIGHTER — **glad·i·a·to·ri·al** \,gla-dē-ə-'tòr-ē-əl\ *adj*
glad·i·o·lus \,gla-dē-'ō-ləs\ *n, pl* **-li** \-'lō-(,)lē, -,lī\ *or* **-lus** *also* **-lus·es** [L, fr. dim. of *gladius* sword] : any of a genus of chiefly African plants related to the irises and having erect sword-shaped leaves and stalks of bright-colored flowers
glad·some \'glad-səm\ *adj* : giving or showing joy : CHEERFUL
glad·stone \'glad-,stōn\ *n, often cap* : a suitcase with flexible sides on a rigid frame that opens flat into two compartments
glam \'glam\ *n* : extravagantly showy glamour — **glam** *adj*
glam·or·ise *Brit var of* GLAMORIZE
glam·or·ize *also* **glam·our·ize** \'gla-mə-,rīz\ *vb* **-ized; -iz·ing** : to make or look upon as glamorous
glam·our *also* **glam·or** \'gla-mər\ *n* [Sc *glamour* magic spell, alter. of E *grammar;* fr. the popular association of erudition with occult practices] : an exciting and often illusory and romantic attractiveness; *esp* : alluring personal attractiveness — **glam·or·ous** *also* **glam·our·ous** \-mə-rəs\ *adj*

¹glance \'glans\ *vb* **glanced; glanc·ing** 1 : to strike and fly off to one side 2 : GLEAM 3 : to give a quick look
²glance *n* 1 : a quick intermittent flash or gleam 2 : a deflected impact or blow 3 : a quick look
gland \'gland\ *n* : a cell or group of cells that prepares and secretes a substance (as saliva or sweat) for further use in or discharge from the body
glan·du·lar \'glan-jə-lər\ *adj* : of, relating to, or involving glands
glans \'glanz\ *n, pl* **glan·des** \'glan-,dēz\ [L, lit., acorn] : a conical vascular body forming the extremity of the penis or clitoris
¹glare \'gler\ *vb* **glared; glar·ing** 1 : to shine with a harsh dazzling light 2 : to stare fiercely or angrily
²glare *n* 1 : a harsh dazzling light 2 : an angry or fierce stare
glar·ing *adj* : very conspicuous ⟨a ~ error⟩ — **glar·ing·ly** *adv*
glass \'glas\ *n* 1 : a hard brittle amorphous usu. transparent or translucent material consisting typically of silica 2 : something made of glass; *esp* : TUMBLER 2 3 *pl* : a pair of lenses used to correct defects of vision : SPECTACLES 4 : the quantity held by a glass container — **glass** *adj* — **glass·ful** \-,fùl\ *n* — **glassy** *adj*
glass-blow·ing \-,blō-iŋ\ *n* : the art of shaping a mass of glass that has been softened by heat by blowing air into it through a tube — **glass-blow·er** *n*
glass·ware \-,wer\ *n* : articles made of glass
glau·co·ma \glau-'kō-mə, glò-\ *n* : a disease of the eye marked by increased pressure within the eyeball resulting in damage to the retina and gradual loss of vision
¹glaze \'glāz\ *vb* **glazed; glaz·ing** 1 : to furnish (as a window frame) with glass 2 : to apply glaze to
²glaze *n* : a glassy coating or surface
gla·zier \'glā-zhər\ *n* : a person who sets glass in window frames
¹gleam \'glēm\ *n* 1 : a transient subdued or partly obscured light 2 : GLINT 3 : a faint trace ⟨a ~ of hope⟩
²gleam *vb* 1 : to shine with subdued light or moderate brightness 2 : to appear briefly or faintly ✦ *Synonyms* FLASH, GLIMMER, GLISTEN, GLITTER, SHIMMER, SPARKLE
glean \'glēn\ *vb* 1 : to gather grain left by reapers 2 : to collect little by little or with patient effort — **glean·able** *adj* — **glean·er** *n*
glean·ings \'glē-niŋz\ *n pl* : things acquired by gleaning
glee \'glē\ *n* [ME, fr. OE *glēo* entertainment, music] 1 : JOY, HILARITY 2 : a part-song for three usu. male voices — **glee·ful** *adj* — **glee·ful·ly** *adv*
glee club *n* : a chorus organized for singing usu. short choral pieces
glen \'glen\ *n* : a narrow hidden valley
glen·gar·ry \glen-'ga-rē\ *n, pl* **-ries** *often cap* : a woolen cap of Scottish origin

glib \'glib\ *adj* **glib·ber; glib·best** : speaking or spoken with careless ease — **glib·ly** *adv*

glide \'glīd\ *vb* **glid·ed; glid·ing 1** : to move smoothly and effortlessly **2** : to descend gradually without engine power ⟨∼ in an airplane⟩ — **glide** *n*

glid·er \'glī-dər\ *n* **1** : one that glides **2** : an aircraft resembling an airplane but having no engine **3** : a porch seat suspended from an upright frame

¹**glim·mer** \'gli-mər\ *vb* : to shine faintly or unsteadily

²**glimmer** *n* **1** : a faint unsteady light **2** : INKLING **3** : a small amount : HINT

¹**glimpse** \'glimps\ *vb* **glimpsed; glimps·ing** : to take a brief look : see momentarily or incompletely

²**glimpse** *n* **1** : a faint idea : GLIMMER **2** : a short hurried look

glint \'glint\ *vb* **1** : to shine by reflection : SPARKLE, GLITTER, GLEAM **2** : to appear briefly or faintly — **glint** *n*

glis·san·do \gli-'sän-(ˌ)dō\ *n, pl* **-di** \-(ˌ)dē\ *or* **-dos** : a rapid sliding up or down the musical scale

¹**glis·ten** \'gli-sᵊn\ *vb* : to shine by reflection with a soft luster or sparkle

²**glisten** *n* : GLITTER, SPARKLE

glis·ter \'glis-tər\ *vb* : GLITTER

glitch \'glich\ *n* : MALFUNCTION; *also* : SNAG **2**

¹**glit·ter** \'gli-tər\ *vb* **1** : to shine with brilliant or metallic luster : SPARKLE **2** : to shine with strong emotion : FLASH ⟨eyes ∼ing in anger⟩ **3** : to be brilliantly attractive esp. in a superficial way

²**glitter** *n* **1** : sparkling brilliancy, showiness, or attractiveness **2** : small glittering objects used for ornamentation — **glit·tery** \'gli-tə-rē\ *adj*

glitz \'glits\ *n* : extravagant showiness — **glitzy** \'glit-sē\ *adj*

²**glitz** *vb* : to make flashy or extravagant in appearance — often used with *up*

gloam·ing \'glō-miŋ\ *n* : TWILIGHT, DUSK

gloat \'glōt\ *vb* : to think about something with triumphant and often malicious delight

glob \'gläb\ *n* **1** : a small drop **2** : a large rounded mass

glob·al \'glō-bəl\ *adj* **1** : WORLDWIDE **2** : COMPREHENSIVE, GENERAL — **glob·al·ly** *adv*

glob·al·iza·tion \ˌglō-bə-lə-'zā-shən\ *n* : the development of an increasingly integrated global economy

Global Positioning System *n* : GPS

global warming *n* : an increase in the earth's atmospheric and oceanic temperatures due to an increase in the greenhouse effect

globe \'glōb\ *n* **1** : BALL, SPHERE **2** : EARTH; *also* : a spherical representation of the earth

globe–trot·ter \'glōb-ˌträ-tər\ *n* : a person who travels widely — **globe–trot·ting** *n or adj*

glob·u·lar \'glä-byə-lar\ *adj* : having the shape of a globe or globule

glob·ule \'glä-(ˌ)byül\ *n* : a tiny globe or ball esp. of a liquid

glob·u·lin \'glä-byə-lən\ *n* : any of a class of simple proteins insoluble in pure water but soluble in dilute salt solutions that occur widely in plant and animal tissues

glock·en·spiel \'glä-kən-ˌshpēl, -ˌspēl\ *n* [G, fr. *Glocke* bell + *Spiel* play] : a percussion musical instrument consisting of a series of metal bars played with two hammers

gloom \'glüm\ *n* **1** : partial or total darkness **2** : lowness of spirits : DEJECTION **3** : an atmosphere of despondency — **gloom·i·ly** \'glü-mə-lē\ *adv* — **gloom·i·ness** \-mē-nəs\ *n* — **gloomy** \'glü-mē\ *adj*

Gloomy Gus \-'gəs\ *n, pl* **Gloomy Gus·es** : a person who is habitually gloomy

glop \'gläp\ *n* : a messy mass or mixture

glo·ri·fy \'glōr-ə-ˌfī\ *vb* **-fied; -fy·ing 1** : to raise to heavenly glory **2** : to light up brilliantly **3** : EXTOL **4** : to give glory to (as in worship) — **glo·ri·fi·ca·tion** \ˌglōr-ə-fə-'kā-shən\ *n*

glo·ri·ous \'glōr-ē-əs\ *adj* **1** : possessing or deserving glory : PRAISEWORTHY **2** : conferring glory **3** : RESPLENDENT, MAGNIFICENT ⟨a ∼ sunset⟩ **4** : DELIGHTFUL, WONDERFUL ⟨had a ∼ weekend⟩ — **glo·ri·ous·ly** *adv*

¹**glo·ry** \'glōr-ē\ *n, pl* **glories 1** : RENOWN **2** : honor and praise rendered in worship **3** : something that secures praise or renown **4** : a distinguishing quality or asset **5** : RESPLENDENCE, MAGNIFICENCE **6** : heavenly bliss **7** : a height of prosperity or achievement

²**glory** *vb* **glo·ried; glo·ry·ing** : to rejoice proudly : EXULT

¹**gloss** \'gläs, 'glòs\ *n* **1** : LUSTER, SHEEN, BRIGHTNESS **2** : outward show

²**gloss** *vb* **1** : to give a false appearance of acceptableness to ⟨∼ over inadequacies⟩ **2** : to deal with too lightly or not at all

³**gloss** *n* [alter. of *gloze*, fr. ME *glose*, fr. AF, fr. ML *glosa, glossa*, fr. Gk *glōssa, glōtta* tongue, language, unusual word] **1** : an explanatory note (as in the margin of a text) **2** : GLOSSARY **3** : an interlinear translation **4** : a continuous commentary accompanying a text

⁴**gloss** *vb* : to furnish glosses for

glos·sa·ry \'glä-sə-rē, 'glò-\ *n, pl* **-ries** : a collection of difficult or specialized terms with their meanings — **glos·sar·i·al** \glä-'ser-ē-əl, glò-\ *adj*

glos·so·la·lia \ˌglä-sə-'lā-lē-ə, ˌglò-\ *n* [ultim. fr. Gk *glōssa* tongue, language + *lalia* chatter] : TONGUE 6

¹**glossy** \'glä-sē, 'glò-\ *adj* **gloss·i·er; -est** : having a surface luster or brightness — **gloss·i·ly** \-sə-lē\ *adv* — **gloss·i·ness** \-sē-nəs\ *n*

²**glossy** *n, pl* **gloss·ies** : a photograph printed on smooth shiny paper

glot·tis \'glä-təs\ *n, pl* **glot·tis·es** *or* **glot·ti·des** \-tə-ˌdēz\ : the slitlike opening between the vocal cords in the larynx — **glot·tal** \'glä-tᵊl\ *adj*

glove \'gləv\ *n* **1** : a covering for the hand having separate sections for each finger **2** : a padded leather covering for the hand for use in a sport

¹glow \'glō\ *vb* **1** : to shine with or as if with intense heat **2** : to have a rich warm usu. ruddy color : FLUSH, BLUSH **3** : to feel hot **4** : to show exuberance or elation ⟨~ with pride⟩

²glow *n* **1** : brightness or warmth of color; *esp* : REDNESS **2** : warmth of feeling or emotion **3** : a sensation of warmth **4** : light such as is emitted from a heated substance

glow-er \'glaủ(-ə)r\ *vb* : to stare angrily : SCOWL — **glower** *n*

glow-worm \'glō-,wərm\ *n* : any of various insect larvae or adults that give off light

glox-in-ia \gläk-'si-nē-ə\ *n* : any of a genus of tropical herbs related to the African violets; *esp* : one with showy bell-shaped or slipper-shaped flowers

gloze \'glōz\ *vb* **glozed; gloz-ing** : to make appear right or acceptable : GLOSS

glu-cose \'glü-,kōs\ *n* **1** : a form of crystalline sugar; *esp* : DEXTROSE **2** : a sweet light-colored syrup made from cornstarch

glue \'glü\ *n* : a jellylike protein substance made from animal materials and used for sticking things together; *also* : any of various other strong adhesives — **glue** *vb* — **glu-ey** \'glü-ē\ *adj*

glum \'gləm\ *adj* **glum-mer; glum-mest 1** : broodingly morose : SULLEN **2** : DREARY, GLOOMY ⟨a ~ countenance⟩ ♦ *Synonyms* CRABBED, DOUR, SATURNINE, SULLEN

¹glut \'glət\ *vb* **glut-ted; glut-ting 1** : OVERSUPPLY **2** : to fill esp. with food to satiety : SATIATE

²glut *n* : an excessive supply

glu-ten \'glü-t³n\ *n* : a gluey protein substance that causes dough to be sticky

glu-ti-nous \'glü-tə-nəs\ *adj* : STICKY

glut-ton \'glə-t³n\ *n* : one that eats to excess — **glut-ton-ous** \'glə-tə-nəs\ *adj* — **glut-tony** \'glə-tə-nē\ *n*

glyc-er-in *or* **glyc-er-ine** \'gli-sə-rən\ *n* : GLYCEROL

glyc-er-ol \'gli-sə-,ròl, -,rōl\ *n* : a sweet syrupy alcohol usu. obtained from fats and used esp. as a solvent

gly-co-gen \'glī-kə-jən\ *n* : a white tasteless carbohydrate that is the chief storage carbohydrate of animals

gm *abbr* gram

GM *abbr* **1** general manager **2** guided missile

G-man \'jē-,man\ *n* : a special agent of the Federal Bureau of Investigation

GMT *abbr* Greenwich mean time

gnarled \'närld\ *adj* **1** : KNOTTY ⟨~ hands⟩ **2** : GLOOMY, SULLEN

gnash \'nash\ *vb* : to grind (as teeth) together

gnat \'nat\ *n* : any of various usu. small biting dipteran flies

gnaw \'nò\ *vb* **1** : to consume, wear away, or make by persistent biting or nibbling **2** : to affect as if by gnawing — **gnaw-er** *n*

gneiss \'nīs\ *n* : a layered rock similar in composition to granite

gnome \'nōm\ *n* : a dwarf of folklore who lives inside the earth and guards precious ore or treasure — **gnome-like** \-,līk\ *adj* — **gnom-ish** *adj*

GNP *abbr* gross national product

gnu \'nü\ *n, pl* **gnu** *or* **gnus** : WILDEBEEST

¹go \'gō\ *vb* **went** \'went\; **gone** \'gòn, 'gän\; **go-ing; goes** \'gōz\ **1** : to move on a course : PROCEED ⟨~ slow⟩ **2** : LEAVE, DEPART **3** : to take a certain course or follow a certain procedure ⟨reports ~ through department channels⟩ **4** : EXTEND, RUN ⟨his land ~es to the river⟩; *also* : LEAD ⟨that door ~es to the cellar⟩ **5** : to be habitually in a certain state ⟨~es barefoot⟩ **6** : to become lost, consumed, or spent; *also* : DIE **7** : ELAPSE, PASS **8** : to pass by sale ⟨went for a good price⟩ **9** : to become impaired or weakened ⟨his hearing started to ~⟩ **10** : to give way under force or pressure : BREAK **11** : to move along in a specified manner ⟨it went well⟩ **12** : to be in general or on an average ⟨cheap, as yachts ~⟩ **13** : to become esp. as the result of a contest ⟨the decision went against him⟩ **14** : to put or subject oneself ⟨~ to great expense⟩ **15** : RESORT ⟨went to court to recover damages⟩ **16** : to begin or maintain an action or motion **17** : to function properly ⟨the clock doesn't ~⟩ **18** : to be known ⟨~es by an alias⟩ **19** : to be or act in accordance ⟨a good rule to ~ by⟩ **20** : to come to be applied **21** : to pass by award, assignment, or lot **22** : to contribute to a result ⟨qualities that ~ to make a hero⟩ **23** : to be about, intending, or expecting something ⟨is ~ing to leave town⟩ **24** : to arrive at a certain state or condition ⟨~ to sleep⟩ **25** : to come to be ⟨the tire went flat⟩ **26** : to be capable of being sung or played ⟨the tune ~es like this⟩ **27** : to be suitable or becoming : HARMONIZE **28** : to be capable of passing, extending, or being contained or inserted ⟨this coat will ~ in the trunk⟩ **29** : to have a usual or proper place or position : BELONG ⟨these books ~ on the top shelf⟩ **30** : to be capable of being divided ⟨3 ~es into 6 twice⟩ **31** : to have a tendency ⟨that ~es to show that he is honest⟩ **32** : to be acceptable, satisfactory, or adequate ⟨any color will ~ with black⟩ **33** : to empty the bladder or bowels **34** : to proceed along or according to : FOLLOW **35** : TRAVERSE **36** : BET, BID ⟨willing to ~ $50⟩ **37** : to assume the function or obligation of ⟨~ bail for a friend⟩ **38** : to participate to the extent of ⟨~ halves⟩ **39** : WEIGH **40** : ENDURE, TOLERATE **41** : AFFORD ⟨can't ~ the price⟩ **42** : SAY — used chiefly in oral narration of speech **43** : to engage in ⟨don't ~ telling everyone⟩ — **go at 1** : ATTACK, ATTEMPT **2** : UNDERTAKE — **go back on 1** : ABANDON **2** : BETRAY **3** : FAIL — **go by the board**

: to be discarded — **go for** 1 : to pass for or serve as 2 : to try to secure 3 : FAVOR — **go one better** : OUTDO, SURPASS — **go over** 1 : EXAMINE 2 : REPEAT 3 : STUDY, REVIEW — **go places** : to be on the way to success — **go steady** : to date one person exclusively — **go to bat for** : DEFEND, CHAMPION — **go to town** 1 : to work or act efficiently 2 : to be very successful

²**go** *n, pl* **goes** 1 : the act or manner of going 2 : the height of fashion ⟨boots are all the ~⟩ 3 : a turn of affairs : OCCURRENCE 4 : ENERGY, VIGOR 5 : ATTEMPT, TRY ⟨give it a ~⟩ 6 : a spell of activity ⟨finished the job at one ~⟩ — **no go** : USELESS, HOPELESS — **on the go** : constantly active

³**go** *adj* : functioning properly ⟨declared all systems ~⟩

goad \'gōd\ *n* [ME *gode*, fr. OE *gād* spear, goad] 1 : a pointed rod used to urge on an animal 2 : something that urges
♦ **Synonyms** STIMULUS, IMPETUS, INCENTIVE, SPUR, STIMULANT — **goad** *vb*

go–ahead \'gō-ə-,hed\ *n* : authority to proceed

goal \'gōl\ *n* 1 : the mark set as limit to a race; *also* : an area to be reached safely in children's games 2 : AIM, PURPOSE 3 : an area or object toward which play is directed to score; *also* : a successful attempt to score

goal·ie \'gō-lē\ *n* : GOALKEEPER

goal·keep·er \'gōl-,kē-pər\ *n* : a player who defends the goal in various games

goal·post \-,pōst\ *n* : one of the two vertical posts with a crossbar that constitute the goal in various games

goat \'gōt\ *n, pl* **goats** *or* **goat** : any of various hollow-horned ruminant mammals related to the sheep that have backward-curving horns, a short tail, and usu. straight hair

goa·tee \gō-'tē\ *n* : a small trim pointed or tufted beard on a man's chin

goat·herd \'gōt-,hərd\ *n* : a person who tends goats

goat·skin \-,skin\ *n* : the skin of a goat or a leather made from it

¹**gob** \'gäb\ *n* : LUMP, MASS

²**gob** *n* : SAILOR

gob·bet \'gä-bət\ *n* : LUMP, MASS

¹**gob·ble** \'gä-bəl\ *vb* **gob·bled; gob·bling** 1 : to swallow or eat greedily 2 : to take eagerly : GRAB

²**gobble** *vb* **gob·bled; gob·bling** : to make the natural guttural noise of a male turkey

gob·ble·dy·gook *also* **gob·ble·de·gook** \'gä-bəl-dē-,gúk, -,gük\ *n* : generally unintelligible jargon

gob·bler \'gä-blər\ *n* : a male turkey

go–be·tween \'gō-bə-,twēn\ *n* : an intermediate agent : BROKER

gob·let \'gä-blət\ *n* : a drinking glass with a foot and stem

gob·lin \'gä-blən\ *n* : an ugly or grotesque sprite that is mischievous and sometimes evil and malicious

go–by \'gō-bē\ *n, pl* **gobies** *also* **goby** : any of numerous spiny-finned fishes

usu. having the pelvic fins united to form a ventral sucking disk

god \'gäd, 'gòd\ *n* 1 *cap* : the supreme reality; *esp* : the Being worshiped as the creator and ruler of the universe 2 : a being or object believed to have supernatural attributes and powers and to require worship 3 : a thing of supreme value 4 : an extraordinarily attractive person

god·child \'gäd-,chī(-ə)ld, 'gòd-\ *n* : a person for whom another person stands as sponsor at baptism

god·daugh·ter \-,dò-tər\ *n* : a female godchild

god·dess \'gä-dəs, 'gò-\ *n* 1 : a female god 2 : a woman whose charm or beauty arouses adoration

god·fa·ther \'gäd-,fä-thər, 'gòd-\ *n* 1 : a man who sponsors a person at baptism 2 : the leader of an organized crime syndicate

god·head \-,hed\ *n* 1 : divine nature or essence 2 *cap* : GOD 1; *also* : the nature of God esp. as existing in three persons

god·hood \-,hùd\ *n* : DIVINITY

god·less \-ləs\ *adj* : not acknowledging a deity or divine law — **god·less·ness** *n*

god·like \-,līk\ *adj* : resembling or having the qualities of God or a god

god·ly \-lē\ *adj* **god·li·er; -est** 1 : DIVINE 2 : PIOUS, DEVOUT — **god·li·ness** *n*

god·moth·er \-,mə-thər\ *n* : a woman who sponsors a person at baptism

god·par·ent \-,per-ənt\ *n* : a sponsor at baptism

god·send \-,send\ *n* : a desirable or needed thing or event that comes unexpectedly

god·son \-,sən\ *n* : a male godchild

God·speed \-'spēd\ *n* : a prosperous journey : SUCCESS ⟨bade him ~⟩

go·fer *or* **go·pher** \'gō-fər\ *n* [alter. of *go for*] : an employee whose duties include running errands

go–get·ter \'gō-,ge-tər\ *n* : an aggressively enterprising person — **go–get·ting** *adj or n*

gog·gle \'gä-gəl\ *vb* **gog·gled; gog·gling** : to stare with wide or protuberant eyes

gog·gles \'gä-gəlz\ *n pl* : protective glasses set in a flexible frame that fits snugly against the face

go–go \'gō-,gō\ *adj* 1 : related to, being, or employed to entertain in a disco ⟨~ dancers⟩ 2 : aggressively enterprising and energetic

go·ings–on \,gō-iŋ-'zòn, -'zän\ *n pl* : ACTIONS, EVENTS

goi·ter \'gòi-tər\ *n* : an abnormally enlarged thyroid gland visible as a swelling at the base of the neck — **goi·trous** \-trəs, -tə-rəs\ *adj*

goi·tre *chiefly Brit var of* GOITER

go–kart \'gō-,kärt\ *n* : a small motorized vehicle used esp. for racing

gold \'gōld\ *n* 1 : a malleable yellow metallic chemical element used esp. for coins and jewelry 2 : gold coins; *also* : MONEY 3 : a yellow color

gold·brick \'gōld-ˌbrik\ n : a person who shirks assigned work — **goldbrick** vb

gold coast n, often cap G&C : an exclusive residential district

gold digger n : a person who uses charm to extract money or gifts from others

gold·en \'gōl-dən\ adj 1 : made of or relating to gold 2 : having the color of gold; also : BLOND 3 : SHINING, LUSTROUS 4 : SUPERB 5 : FLOURISHING, PROSPEROUS 6 : radiantly youthful and vigorous 7 : FAVORABLE, ADVANTAGEOUS ⟨a ~ opportunity⟩ 8 : MELLOW, RESONANT ⟨a ~ tenor⟩

gold·en·ag·er \'gōl-dən-ˌā-jər\ n : an elderly and often retired person usu. engaging in club activities

golden eagle n : a large dark brown eagle with gold-colored feathers on the back of the head and neck

golden hamster n : a small tawny hamster often kept as a pet

golden handcuffs n pl : special benefits offered to an employee as an inducement to continue service

golden handshake n : a generous severance agreement given esp. as an inducement to early retirement

golden retriever n : any of a breed of retrievers with a flat golden coat

gold·en·rod \'gōl-dən-ˌräd\ n : any of numerous herbs related to the daisies that have tall slender stalks with many tiny usu. yellow flower heads

golden years n pl : the advanced years in a lifetime

gold·finch \-ˌfinch\ n 1 : a small largely red, black, and yellow Old World finch often kept in a cage 2 : any of three small related American finches of which the males usu. become bright yellow and black in summer

gold·fish \-ˌfish\ n : a small usu. golden-orange carp often kept as an aquarium or pond fish

gold·smith \-ˌsmith\ n : a person who makes or deals in articles of gold

golf \'gälf, 'gȯlf\ n : a game played with a small ball and various clubs on a course having 9 or 18 holes — **golf** vb — **golf·er** n

-gon \ˌgän\ n comb form : figure having (so many) angles ⟨hexagon⟩

go·nad \'gō-ˌnad\ n : a sperm- or egg-producing gland : OVARY, TESTIS — **go·nad·al** \gō-'na-dᵊl\ adj

go·nad·o·trop·ic \gō-ˌna-də-'trä-pik\ also **go·nad·o·tro·phic** \-'trō-fik, -'trä-\ adj : acting on or stimulating the gonads

go·nad·o·tro·pin \-'trō-pən\ also **go·nad·o·tro·phin** \-fən\ n : a gonadotropic hormone

gon·do·la \'gän-də-lə (usual for 1), gän-'dō-\ n [It. dial. (Venice), prob. fr. MGk kontoura small vessel] 1 : a long narrow boat used on the canals of Venice 2 : a railroad car used for hauling loose freight (as coal) 3 : an enclosure beneath an airship or balloon 4 : an enclosed car usu. suspended from a cable and used esp. for transporting skiers

gon·do·lier \ˌgän-də-'lir\ n : a person who propels a gondola

¹gone \'gȯn\ past part of GO

²gone adj 1 : LOST, RUINED 2 : DEAD 3 : SINKING, WEAK 4 : INVOLVED, ABSORBED 5 : INFATUATED 6 : PREGNANT 7 : PAST

gon·er \'gȯ-nər\ n : one whose case is hopeless

gong \'gäŋ, 'gȯŋ\ n : a metallic disk that produces a resounding tone when struck

gono·coc·cus \ˌgä-nə-'kä-kəs\ n, pl **-coc·ci** \-'käk-ˌsī, -(ˌ)sē, -'kä-ˌkī, -(ˌ)kē\ : a pus-producing bacterium causing gonorrhea — **gono·coc·cal** \-'kä-kəl\ adj

gon·or·rhea \ˌgä-nə-'rē-ə\ n : a contagious sexually transmitted inflammation of the genital tract caused by the gonococcus — **gon·or·rhe·al** \-'rē-əl\ adj

goo \'gü\ n 1 : a viscid or sticky substance 2 : sentimental tripe — **goo·ey** \-ē\ adj

goo·ber \'gü-bər, 'gù-\ n, Southern & Midland : PEANUT

¹good \'gu̇d\ adj bet·ter \'be-tər\; best \'best\ 1 : of a favorable character or tendency 2 : BOUNTIFUL, FERTILE ⟨~ land⟩ 3 : COMELY, ATTRACTIVE 4 : SUITABLE, FIT 5 : SOUND, WHOLE ⟨only one ~ arm⟩ 6 : AGREEABLE, PLEASANT ⟨had a ~ time⟩ 7 : SALUTARY, WHOLESOME 8 : CONSIDERABLE, AMPLE ⟨a ~ bit of time⟩ 9 : FULL ⟨waited a ~ hour⟩ 10 : WELL-FOUNDED 11 : TRUE ⟨holds ~ for everybody⟩ 12 : legally valid or effectual 13 : ADEQUATE, SATISFACTORY 14 : conforming to a standard ⟨~ English⟩ 15 : DISCRIMINATING 16 : COMMENDABLE, VIRTUOUS 17 : KIND 18 : UPPER-CLASS 19 : COMPETENT 20 : LOYAL, CLOSE — **good·ish** adj

²good n 1 : something good 2 : GOODNESS 3 : BENEFIT, WELFARE ⟨for the ~ of mankind⟩ 4 : something that has economic utility 5 pl : personal property 6 pl : CLOTH 7 pl : WARES, MERCHANDISE ⟨canned ~s⟩ 8 : good persons ⟨the ~ die young⟩ 9 pl : proof of wrongdoing — **for good** : FOREVER, PERMANENTLY — **to the good** : in a position of net gain or profit ⟨$10 to the good⟩

³good adv : WELL

good–bye or **good–by** \gu̇d-'bī, gə-\ n : a concluding remark made at parting

good cholesterol n : HDL

good–for–noth·ing \'gu̇d-fər-ˌnə-thiŋ\ adj : of no use or value — **good–for–nothing** n

Good Friday n : the Friday before Easter observed as the anniversary of the crucifixion of Christ

good–heart·ed \'gu̇d-'här-təd\ adj : having a kindly generous disposition — **good–heart·ed·ly** adv — **good–heart·ed·ness** n

good–look·ing \'gu̇d-'lu̇-kiŋ\ adj : having an attractive appearance

good·ly \'gu̇d-lē\ adj **good·li·er; -est** 1 : of pleasing appearance 2 : LARGE, CONSIDERABLE

good·man \'gud-mən\ *n, archaic* : MR.

good–na·tured \'gud-'nā-chərd\ *adj* : of a cheerful disposition — **good–na·tured·ly** \-chərd-lē\ *adv*

good·ness \-nəs\ *n* : EXCELLENCE, VIRTUE

good·wife \-ˌwīf\ *n, archaic* : MRS.

good·will \-'wil\ *n* 1 : BENEVOLENCE 2 : the value of the trade a business has built up over time 3 : cheerful consent 4 : willing effort

goody *or* **good·ie** \'gu-dē\ *n, pl* **good·ies** : something that is good esp. to eat

goody–goody \ˌgu-dē-'gu-dē\ *adj* : affectedly good — **goody–goody** *n*

goof \'guf\ *vb* 1 : to spend time idly or foolishly 2 : BLUNDER — often used with *off* — **goof** *n*

goof–ball \'guf-ˌbȯl\ *n,* 1 *slang* : a barbiturate sleeping pill 2 : a goofy person

go off *vb* 1 : EXPLODE 2 : to follow a course ⟨the party *went off* well⟩

goof–off \'guf-ˌȯf\ *n* : one who evades work or responsibility

goofy \'gu-fē\ *adj* **goof·i·er; -est** : CRAZY, SILLY — **goof·i·ness** \-fē-nəs\ *n*

goon \'gun\ *n* : a man hired to terrorize or kill opponents

go on *vb* 1 : to continue in a course of action 2 : to take place : HAPPEN

goose \'gus\ *n, pl* **geese** \'gēs\ 1 : any of numerous long-necked web-footed birds related to the swans and ducks; *also* : a female goose as distinguished from a gander 2 : a foolish person 3 *pl* **goos·es** : a tailor's smoothing iron

goose·ber·ry \'gus-ˌber-ē, 'guz-, -bə-rē\ *n* : the acid berry of any of several shrubs related to the currant and used esp. in jams and pies

goose bumps *n pl* : roughening of the skin caused usu. by cold, fear, or a sudden feeling of excitement

goose·flesh \-ˌflesh\ *n* : GOOSE BUMPS

goose pimples *n pl* : GOOSE BUMPS

go out *vb* 1 : to become extinguished 2 : to become a candidate ⟨*went out* for the football team⟩

go over *vb* : SUCCEED

GOP *abbr* Grand Old Party (Republican)

¹go·pher \'gō-fər\ *n* 1 : a burrowing American land tortoise 2 : any of a family of No. American burrowing rodents with large cheek pouches opening beside the mouth 3 : any of several small ground squirrels of the prairie region of No. America

²gopher *var of* GOFER

go·pik \gȯ-'pēk, -'pik\ *n, pl* **gopik** — see *manat* at MONEY table

¹gore \'gȯr\ *n* : a tapering or triangular piece (as of cloth in a skirt)

²gore *vb* **gored; gor·ing** : to pierce or wound with something pointed

³gore *n* 1 : BLOOD 2 : gruesomeness depicted in vivid detail

¹gorge \'gȯrj\ *n* 1 : THROAT 2 : a narrow ravine 3 : a mass of matter that chokes up a passage

²gorge *vb* **gorged; gorg·ing** : to eat greedily : stuff to capacity : GLUT

gor·geous \'gȯr-jəs\ *adj* : resplendently beautiful

Gor·gon·zo·la \ˌgȯr-gən-'zō-lə\ *n* : a pungent blue cheese of Italian origin

go·ril·la \gə-'ri-lə\ *n* [NL, fr. Gk *Gorillai,* a tribe of hairy women in an account of a voyage around Africa] : an African anthropoid ape related to but much larger than the chimpanzee

gor·man·dise *chiefly Brit var of* GORMANDIZE

gor·man·dize \'gȯr-mən-ˌdīz\ *vb* **-dized; -diz·ing** : to eat ravenously — **gor·man·diz·er** *n*

gorp \'gȯrp\ *n* : a snack consisting of high-calorie food (as raisins and nuts)

gorse \'gȯrs\ *n* : a spiny yellow-flowered European evergreen shrub of the legume family

gory \'gȯr-ē\ *adj* **gor·i·er; -est** 1 : BLOODSTAINED 2 : HORRIBLE, SENSATIONAL

gos·hawk \'gäs-ˌhȯk\ *n* : any of several long-tailed hawks with short rounded wings

gos·ling \'gäz-liŋ, 'gȯz-\ *n* : a young goose

¹gos·pel \'gäs-pəl\ *n* [ME, fr. OE *gōdspel,* fr. *gōd* good + *spell* message, news] 1 : the teachings of Christ and the apostles 2 *cap* : any of the first four books of the New Testament 3 : something accepted or promoted as infallible truth

²gospel *adj* 1 : of, relating to, or emphasizing the gospel 2 : relating to or being American religious songs associated with evangelism

gos·sa·mer \'gä-sə-mər\ *n* [ME *gossomer,* fr. *gos* goose + *somer* summer] 1 : a film of cobwebs floating in the air 2 : something light, delicate, or tenuous

¹gos·sip \'gä-səp\ *n* 1 : a person who habitually reveals personal or sensational facts 2 : rumor or report of an intimate nature 3 : an informal conversation — **gos·sipy** *adj*

²gossip *vb* : to spread gossip

got *past and past part of* GET

Goth \'gäth\ *n* : a member of a Germanic people that early in the Christian era overran the Roman Empire

¹Goth·ic \'gä-thik\ *adj* 1 : of or relating to the Goths 2 : of or relating to a style of architecture prevalent in western Europe from the middle 12th to the early 16th century

²Gothic *n* 1 : the Germanic language of the Goths 2 : the Gothic architectural style or decoration

gotten *past part of* GET

Gou·da \'gu-də\ *n* : a mild Dutch milk cheese shaped in balls

¹gouge \'gauj\ *n* 1 : a rounded troughlike chisel 2 : a hole or groove made with or as if with a gouge

²gouge *vb* **gouged; goug·ing** : to cut holes or grooves in with or as if with a gouge 2 : DEFRAUD, CHEAT

gou·lash \'gu-ˌläsh, -ˌlash\ *n* [Hungarian *gulyás*] : a stew made with meat, assorted vegetables, and paprika

go under *vb* : to be overwhelmed, defeated, or destroyed : FAIL

gourd \'gȯrd, 'gu̇rd\ *n* **1** : any of a family of tendril-bearing vines including the cucumber, squash, and melon **2** : the fruit of a gourd; *esp* : any of various inedible hard-shelled fruits used esp. for ornament or implements

gourde \'gu̇rd\ *n* — see MONEY table

gour·mand \'gu̇r-ˌmänd\ *n* **1** : one who is excessively fond of eating and drinking **2** : GOURMET

gour·met \'gu̇r-ˌmā, gu̇r-'mā\ *n* [F, fr. MF, alter. of *gromet* boy servant, vintner's assistant] : a connoisseur of food and drink

gout \'gau̇t\ *n* : a metabolic disease marked by painful inflammation and swelling of the joints — **gouty** *adj*

gov *abbr* **1** government **2** governor **3** governmental institution — used in World Wide Web addresses

gov·ern \'gə-vərn\ *vb* [ME, fr. AF *governer*, fr. L *gubernare* to steer, govern, fr. Gk *kybernan*] **1** : to control and direct the making and administration of policy in : RULE **2** : CONTROL, DIRECT, INFLUENCE **3** : DETERMINE, REGULATE **4** : RESTRAIN — **gov·ern·able** \-vər-nə-bəl\ *adj* — **gov·er·nance** \-vər-nəns\ *n*

gov·ern·ess \'gə-vər-nəs\ *n* : a woman who teaches and trains a child esp. in a private home

gov·ern·ment \'gə-vərn-mənt\ *n* **1** : authoritative direction or control : RULE **2** : the making of policy **3** : the organization or agency through which a political unit exercises authority **4** : the complex of institutions, laws, and customs through which a political unit is governed **5** : the governing body — **gov·ern·men·tal** \ˌgə-vərn-'men-t^əl\ *adj* — **gov·ern·men·tal·ly** \-t^əl-ē\ *adv*

gov·er·nor \'gə-vər-nər\ *n* **1** : one that governs; *esp* : a ruler, chief executive, or head of a political unit (as a state) **2** : an attachment to a machine for automatic control of speed — **gov·er·nor·ship** *n*

govt *abbr* government

gown \'gau̇n\ *n* **1** : a loose flowing outer garment **2** : an official robe worn esp. by a judge, clergyman, or teacher **3** : a woman's dress ⟨evening ∼*s*⟩ **4** : a loose robe — **gown** *vb*

gp *abbr* group

GP *abbr* general practitioner

GPO *abbr* **1** general post office **2** Government Printing Office

GPS \ˌjē-ˌpē-'es\ *n* [Global Positioning System] : a navigation system that uses satellite signals to fix location; *also* : the signal receiver itself

GQ *abbr* general quarters

gr *abbr* **1** grade **2** grain **3** gram **4** gravity **5** gross

grab \'grab\ *vb* **grabbed; grab·bing** : to take hastily : SNATCH — **grab** *n*

¹grace \'grās\ *n* **1** : unmerited help given to people by God (as in overcoming temptation) **2** : freedom from sin through divine grace **3** : a virtue coming from God **4** — used as a title for a duke, a duchess, or an archbishop **5** : a short

prayer at a meal **6** : a temporary respite (as from the payment of a debt) **7** : APPROVAL, ACCEPTANCE ⟨in his good ∼*s*⟩ **8** : CHARM **9** : ATTRACTIVENESS, BEAUTY **10** : fitness or proportion of line or expression **11** : ease of movement **12** : a musical trill or ornament — **grace·ful** \-fəl\ *adj* — **grace·ful·ly** *adv* — **grace·ful·ness** *n* — **grace·less** *adj*

²grace *vb* **graced; grac·ing 1** : HONOR **2** : ADORN, EMBELLISH

gra·cious \'grā-shəs\ *adj* **1** : marked by kindness and courtesy ⟨a ∼ host⟩ **2** : GRACEFUL **3** : characterized by charm and good taste **4** : MERCIFUL — **gra·cious·ly** *adv* — **gra·cious·ness** *n*

grack·le \'gra-kəl\ *n* : any of several large American blackbirds with glossy iridescent plumage

grad *abbr* graduate; graduated

gra·da·tion \grā-'dā-shən, grə-\ *n* **1** : a series forming successive stages **2** : a step, degree, or stage in a series **3** : an advance by regular degrees **4** : the act or process of grading

¹grade \'grād\ *n* [L *gradus* step, degree, fr. *gradi* to step, go] **1** : a position in a scale of rank, quality, or order **2** : a stage in a process or ranking **3** : a division of the school course representing one year's work; *also* : the pupils in such a division **4** : a class of persons or things of the same rank or quality **5** : a mark or rating esp. of accomplishment in school **6** : the degree of slope (as of a road); *also* : SLOPE **7** *pl* : the elementary school system

²grade *vb* **grad·ed; grad·ing 1** : to arrange in grades : SORT **2** : to make level or evenly sloping ⟨∼ a highway⟩ **3** : to give a grade to ⟨∼ a pupil in history⟩ **4** : to assign to a grade

grade inflation *n* : the assigning of grades higher than previously assigned for given levels of achievement

grad·er \'grā-dər\ *n* **1** : a machine for leveling earth **2** : a pupil in a school grade

grade school *n* : ELEMENTARY SCHOOL

gra·di·ent \'grā-dē-ənt\ *n* : SLOPE, GRADE

grad·u·al \'gra-jə-wəl\ *adj* : proceeding or changing by steps or degrees — **grad·u·al·ly** *adv*

grad·u·al·ism \-wə-ˌli-zəm\ *n* : the policy of approaching a desired end gradually

¹grad·u·ate \'gra-jə-wət\ *n* **1** : a holder of an academic degree or diploma **2** : a graduated container for measuring contents

²graduate *adj* **1** : holding an academic degree or diploma **2** : of or relating to studies beyond the first or bachelor's degree ⟨∼ school⟩

³grad·u·ate \'gra-jə-ˌwāt\ *vb* **-at·ed; -at·ing 1** : to grant or receive an academic degree or diploma **2** : to divide into grades, classes, or intervals **3** : to admit to a particular standing or grade

grad·u·a·tion \ˌgra-jə-'wā-shən\ *n* **1** : a mark that graduates something **2** : an act or process of graduating **3** : COMMENCEMENT **2**

graf·fi·ti \grə-'fē-(ˌ)tē\ n : unauthorized writing or drawing on a public surface

graf·fi·to \grə-'fē-tō, grä-\ n, pl **-ti** \-(ˌ)tē\ : an inscription or drawing made on a public surface (as a wall)

¹graft \'graft\ n 1 : a grafted plant; also : the point of union in this 2 : material (as skin) used in grafting 3 : the getting of money or advantage dishonestly; also : the money or advantage so gained

²graft vb 1 : to insert a shoot from one plant into another so that they join and grow; also : to join one thing to another as in plant grafting ⟨∼ skin over a burn⟩ 2 : to get (as money) dishonestly — **graft·er** n

gra·ham cracker \'grā-əm-, 'gram-\ n : a slightly sweet cracker made chiefly of whole wheat flour

Grail \'grāl\ n 1 : the cup or platter used according to medieval legend by Christ at the Last Supper and thereafter the object of knightly quests 2 not cap : the object of an extended or difficult quest

grain \'grān\ n 1 : a seed or fruit of a cereal grass 2 : seeds or fruits of various food plants and esp. cereal grasses; also : a plant (as wheat) producing grain 3 : a small hard particle 4 : a unit of weight based on the weight of a grain of wheat — see WEIGHT table 5 : TEXTURE; also : the arrangement of fibers in wood 6 : natural disposition ⟨lying goes against my ∼⟩ — **grained** \'grānd\ adj

grain alcohol n : ALCOHOL 1

grainy \'grā-nē\ adj, **grain·i·er; -est** 1 : resembling or having some characteristic of grain : not smooth or fine 2 of a photograph : appearing to be composed of grain-like particles

¹gram \'gram\ n [F gramme, fr. LL gramma, a small weight, fr. Gk gramma letter, writing, a small weight, fr. graphein to write] : a metric unit of mass and weight equal to ¹/₁₀₀₀ kilogram — see METRIC SYSTEM table

²gram abbr grammar; grammatical

-gram \ˌgram\ n comb form : drawing : writing : record ⟨telegram⟩

gram·mar \'gra-mər\ n 1 : the study of the classes of words, their inflections, and their functions and relations in the sentence 2 : a study of what is to be preferred and what avoided in inflection and syntax 3 : speech or writing evaluated according to its conformity to grammatical rules — **gram·mar·i·an** \grə-'mer-ē-ən, -'mar-\ n — **gram·mat·i·cal** \-'ma-ti-kəl\ adj — **gram·mat·i·cal·ly** \-k(ə-)lē\ adv

grammar school n 1 : a secondary school emphasizing Latin and Greek in preparation for college; also : a British college preparatory school 2 : a school intermediate between the primary grades and high school 3 : ELEMENTARY SCHOOL

gramme \'gram\ chiefly Brit var of GRAM

gram·o·phone \'gra-mə-ˌfōn\ n : PHONOGRAPH

gra·na·ry \'grā-nə-rē, 'gra-\ n, pl **-ries** 1 : a storehouse for grain 2 : a region producing grain in abundance

¹grand \'grand\ adj 1 : higher in rank or importance : FOREMOST, CHIEF 2 : great in size 3 : INCLUSIVE, COMPLETE ⟨a ∼ total⟩ 4 : MAGNIFICENT, SPLENDID 5 : showing wealth or high social standing 6 : IMPRESSIVE, STATELY 7 : very good : FINE ⟨had a ∼ time⟩ — **grand·ly** adv — **grand·ness** n

²grand n, pl **grand** slang : a thousand dollars

gran·dam \'gran-ˌdam, -dəm\ or **gran·dame** \-ˌdām, -dəm\ n : an old woman

grand·child \'grand-ˌchī(-ə)ld\ n : a child of one's son or daughter

grand·daugh·ter \'gran-ˌdȯ-tər\ n : a daughter of one's son or daughter

grande dame \'grän-'däm\ n, pl **grandes dames** \same\ : a usu. elderly woman of great prestige or ability

gran·dee \gran-'dē\ n : a high-ranking Spanish or Portuguese nobleman

gran·deur \'gran-jər\ n 1 : the quality or state of being grand : MAGNIFICENCE 2 : something that is grand

grand·fa·ther \'grand-ˌfä-thər\ n : the father of one's father or mother; also : ANCESTOR

grandfather clock n : a tall clock that stands on the floor

gran·dil·o·quence \gran-'di-lə-kwəns\ n : pompous eloquence — **gran·dil·o·quent** \-kwənt\ adj

gran·di·ose \'gran-dē-ˌōs, ˌgran-dē-'ōs\ adj : IMPRESSIVE, IMPOSING; also : affectedly splendid — **gran·di·ose·ly** adv — **gran·di·os·i·ty** \ˌgran-dē-'ä-sə-tē\ n

grand jury n : a jury that examines accusations of crime against persons and makes formal charges on which the persons are later tried

grand mal \'grän-ˌmäl; 'grand-ˌmal\ n [F, lit., great illness] : severe epilepsy

grand·moth·er \'grand-ˌmə-thər\ n : the mother of one's father or mother; also : a female ancestor

grand·par·ent \-ˌper-ənt\ n : a parent of one's father or mother

grand piano n : a piano with horizontal frame and strings

grand prix \'grän-'prē\ n, pl **grand prix** \same or -'prēz\ often cap G&P : a long-distance auto race over a road course; also : a high-level competition in another sport (as sailing)

grand slam n 1 : a total victory or success 2 : a home run hit with three runners on base

grand·son \'grand-ˌsən\ n : a son of one's son or daughter

grand·stand \-ˌstand\ n : a usu. roofed stand for spectators at a racecourse or stadium

grange \'grānj\ n 1 : a farm or farmhouse with its various buildings 2 cap : one of the lodges of a national association originally made up of farmers; also : the association itself — **Grang·er** \'grān-jər\ n

gran·ite \'gra-nət\ n : a hard granular igneous rock used esp. for building — **gra-nit·ic** \gra-'ni-tik\ adj

gran·ite·ware \'gra-nət-,wer\ n : ironware with mottled enamel

gra·no·la \grə-'nō-lə\ n : a cereal made of rolled oats and usu. raisins and nuts

¹**grant** \'grant\ vb **1** : to consent to : ALLOW, PERMIT **2** : GIVE, BESTOW 〈~ed land to settlers〉 **3** : to admit as true — **grant·er** n — **grant·or** \'grant-ər, -,tȯr\ n

²**grant** n **1** : the act of granting **2** : something granted; esp : a gift for a particular purpose 〈a ~ for study abroad〉 **3** : a transfer of property by deed or writing; also : the instrument by which such a transfer is made **4** : the property transferred by grant — **grant·ee** \gran-'tē\ n

gran·u·lar \'gra-nyə-lər\ adj : consisting of or appearing to consist of granules — **gran·u·lar·i·ty** \,gra-nyə-'lar-ə-tē\ n

gran·u·late \'gra-nyə-,lāt\ vb **-lat·ed; -lat·ing** : to form into grains or crystals — **gran·u·la·tion** \,gra-nyə-'lā-shən\ n

gran·ule \'gra-nyül\ n : a small grain or particle

grape \'grāp\ n [ME, fr. AF, grape stalk, bunch of grapes, grape, of Gmc origin] **1** : a smooth-skinned juicy edible greenish white, deep red, or purple berry that is the chief source of wine **2** : any of numerous woody vines widely grown for their bunches of grapes

grape·fruit \'grāp-,früt\ n **1** pl **grape-fruit** or **grapefruits** : a large edible yellow-skinned citrus fruit **2** : a tree bearing grapefruit

grape hyacinth n : any of several small bulbous herbs related to the lilies that produce clusters of usu. blue flowers in the spring

grape·shot \'grāp-,shät\ n : a cluster of small iron balls formerly fired at people from short range by a cannon

grape·vine \-,vīn\ n **1** : GRAPE 2 **2** : RUMOR; also : an informal means of circulating information or gossip

graph \'graf\ n : a diagram that usu. by means of dots and lines shows change in one variable factor in comparison with one or more other factors — **graph** vb

-graph \,graf\ n comb form **1** : something written 〈autograph〉 **2** : instrument for making or transmitting records 〈seismograph〉

¹**graph·ic** \'gra-fik\ also **graph·i·cal** \-fi-kəl\ adj **1** : of or relating to the arts 〈graphic arts〉 of representation, decoration, and printing on flat surfaces **2** : being written, drawn, or engraved **3** : vividly described — **graph·i·cal·ly** \-fi-k(ə-)lē\ adv

²**graphic** n **1** : a picture, map, or graph used for illustration **2** : a pictorial image displayed on a computer screen

graphical user interface n : a computer program designed to allow easy user interaction esp. by having graphic menus or icons

graph·ics tablet \-fiks-\ n : a computer input device for entering pictorial information by drawing or tracing

graph·ite \'gra-,fīt\ n [G Graphit, fr. Gk graphein to write] : a soft black form of carbon used esp. for lead pencils and lubricants

grap·nel \'grap-nəl\ n : a small anchor used esp. to recover a sunken object or to anchor a small boat

¹**grap·ple** \'gra-pəl\ n : the act of grappling

²**grapple** vb **grap·pled; grap·pling** **1** : to seize or hold with or as if with a hooked implement **2** : to come to grips with : WRESTLE

¹**grasp** \'grasp\ vb **1** : to make the motion of seizing **2** : to take or seize firmly **3** : to enclose and hold with the fingers or arms **2** : COMPREHEND

²**grasp** n **1** : HANDLE **2** : EMBRACE **3** : HOLD, CONTROL **4** : the reach of the arms **5** : the power of seizing and holding or attaining **6** : COMPREHENSION

grasp·ing adj : GREEDY, AVARICIOUS

grass \'gras\ n **1** : herbage for grazing animals **2** : any of a large family of plants (as wheat, bamboo, or sugarcane) with jointed stems and narrow leaves **3** : grass-covered land **4** : MARIJUANA — **grass·like** \-,līk\ adj — **grassy** adj

grass·hop·per \-,hä-pər\ n : any of numerous leaping plant-eating insects

grass·land \-,land\ n : land covered naturally or under cultivation with grasses and low-growing herbs

grass roots n pl : society at the local level as distinguished from the centers of political leadership

¹**grate** \'grāt\ vb **grat·ed; grat·ing** **1** : to pulverize by rubbing against something rough **2** : to grind or rub against with a rasping noise **3** : IRRITATE — **grat·er** n — **grat·ing·ly** adv

²**grate** n **1** : GRATING **2** : a frame of iron bars for holding fuel while it burns

grate·ful \'grāt-fəl\ adj **1** : THANKFUL, APPRECIATIVE; also : expressing gratitude **2** : PLEASING — **grate·ful·ly** adv — **grate·ful·ness** n

grat·i·fy \'gra-tə-,fī\ vb **-fied; -fy·ing** : to afford pleasure to — **grat·i·fi·ca·tion** \,gra-tə-fə-'kā-shən\ n

grat·ing \'grā-tiŋ\ n : a framework with parallel bars or crossbars

gra·tis \'gra-təs, 'grä-\ adv or adj : without charge or recompense : FREE

grat·i·tude \'gra-tə-,tüd, -,tyüd\ n : THANKFULNESS

gra·tu·itous \grə-'tü-ə-təs, -'tyü-\ adj **1** : done or provided without recompense : FREE **2** : UNWARRANTED 〈a ~ assumption〉

gra·tu·ity \-ə-tē\ n, pl **-ities** : ¹⁰TIP

gra·va·men \grə-'vä-mən\ n, pl **-va·mens** or **-vam·i·na** \-'va-mə-nə\ [LL, burden] : the basic or significant part of a grievance or complaint

¹**grave** \'grāv\ vb **graved; grav·en** \'grā-vən\ or **graved; grav·ing** : SCULPTURE, ENGRAVE

²**grave** n : an excavation in the earth as a place of burial; also : TOMB

³**grave** \'grāv; 5 also 'gräv\ adj **1** : IMPORTANT **2** : threatening great harm or

danger **3** : DIGNIFIED, SOLEMN **4** : drab in color : SOMBER **5** : of, marked by, or being an accent mark having the form ` — **grave·ly** adv — **grave·ness** n

grav·el \'gra-vəl\ n : pebbles and small pieces of rock larger than grains of sand — **grav·el·ly** adj

Graves' disease \'grāvz-\ n : hyperthyroidism characterized by goiter and often protrusion of the eyeballs

grave·stone \'grāv-ˌstōn\ n : a burial monument

grave·yard \-ˌyärd\ n : CEMETERY

grav·id \'gra-vəd\ adj [L gravidus, fr. gravis heavy] : PREGNANT

gra·vi·me·ter \gra-'vi-mə-tər, 'gra-və-ˌmē-\ n : a device for measuring variations in a gravitational field

grav·i·tate \'gra-və-ˌtāt\ vb **-tat·ed; -tat·ing** : to move or tend to move toward something

grav·i·ta·tion \ˌgra-və-'tā-shən\ n **1** : a natural force of attraction that tends to draw bodies together and that occurs because of the mass of the bodies **2** : the action or process of gravitating — **grav·i·ta·tion·al** \-shə-nəl\ adj — **grav·i·ta·tion·al·ly** adv

grav·i·ty \'gra-və-tē\ n, pl **-ties** **1** : IMPORTANCE; esp : SERIOUSNESS **2** : ²MASS 5 **3** : the gravitational attraction of the mass of a celestial object (as earth) for bodies close to it; also : GRAVITATION 1

gra·vure \grə-'vyu̇r\ n [F] : PHOTOGRAVURE

gra·vy \'grā-vē\ n, pl **gravies** **1** : a sauce made from the thickened and seasoned juices of cooked meat **2** : unearned or illicit gain : GRAFT

¹gray also **grey** \'grā\ adj **1** : of the color gray; also : dull in color **2** : having gray hair **3** : CHEERLESS, DISMAL ⟨a ~ day⟩ **4** : intermediate in position or character ⟨an ethically ~ area⟩ — **gray·ish** adj — **gray·ness** n

²gray also **grey** n **1** : something of a gray color **2** : a neutral color ranging between black and white

³gray also **grey** vb : to make or become gray

gray·beard \'grā-ˌbird\ n : an old man

gray·ling \'grā-liŋ\ n, pl **grayling** also **graylings** : any of several slender freshwater food and sport fishes related to the trouts

gray matter n **1** : the grayish part of nervous tissue consisting mostly of the cell bodies of neurons **2** : INTELLIGENCE

gray wolf n : a large wolf of northern No. America and Asia that is usu. gray

¹graze \'grāz\ vb **grazed; graz·ing** [ME grasen, fr. OE grasian, fr. græs grass] **1** : to feed on herbage or pasture **2** : to feed (livestock) on grass or pasture — **graz·er** n

²graze vb **grazed; graz·ing** **1** : to touch lightly in passing **2** : SCRATCH, ABRADE

¹grease \'grēs\ n **1** : rendered animal fat **2** : oily material **3** : a thick lubricant — **greasy** \'grē-sē, -zē\ adj

²grease \'grēs, 'grēz\ vb **greased; greasing** : to smear or lubricate with grease

grease·paint \'grēs-ˌpānt\ n : theater makeup

great \'grāt\ adj **1** : large in size : BIG **2** : ELABORATE, AMPLE ⟨in ~ detail⟩ **3** : large in number : NUMEROUS **4** : being beyond the average : MIGHTY, INTENSE ⟨a ~ weight⟩ ⟨in ~ pain⟩ **5** : EMINENT, GRAND **6** : long continued ⟨a ~ while⟩ **7** : MAIN, PRINCIPAL ⟨a reception in the ~ hall⟩ **8** : more distant in a family relationship by one generation ⟨a great-grandfather⟩ **9** : markedly superior in character, quality, or skill ⟨~ at bridge⟩ **10** : EXCELLENT, FINE ⟨had a ~ time⟩ — **great·ly** adv — **great·ness** n

great ape n : any of a family of primates including the gorilla, orangutan, and chimpanzees

great blue heron n : a large crested grayish-blue American heron

great circle n : a circle on the surface of a sphere that has the same center as the sphere; esp : one on the surface of the earth an arc of which is the shortest travel distance between two points

great·coat \'grāt-ˌkōt\ n : a heavy overcoat

Great Dane n : any of a breed of very tall powerful smooth-coated dogs

great·heart·ed \'grāt-'här-təd\ adj **1** : COURAGEOUS **2** : MAGNANIMOUS

great power n, often cap G&P : one of the nations that figure most decisively in international affairs

great white shark n : a large and dangerous shark of warm seas that has large saw-edged teeth and is whitish below and bluish or brownish above

grebe \'grēb\ n : any of a family of lobe-toed diving birds related to the loons

Gre·cian \'grē-shən\ adj : GREEK

greed \'grēd\ n : acquisitive or selfish desire beyond reason — **greed·i·ly** \'grē-də-lē\ adv — **greed·i·ness** \-dē-nəs\ n — **greedy** \'grē-dē\ adj

¹Greek \'grēk\ n **1** : a native or inhabitant of Greece **2** : the ancient or modern language of Greece

²Greek adj **1** : of, relating to, or characteristic of Greece, the Greeks, or Greek **2** : ORTHODOX 3

¹green \'grēn\ adj **1** : of the color green **2** : covered with verdure; also : consisting of green plants or of the leafy parts of plants ⟨a ~ salad⟩ **3** : UNRIPE; also : IMMATURE **4** : having a sickly appearance **5** : not fully processed or treated ⟨~ liquor⟩ ⟨~ hides⟩ **6** : INEXPERIENCED; also : NAIVE **7** : concerned with or supporting environmentalism — **green·ish** adj — **green·ness** n

²green vb : to make or become green

³green n **1** : a color between blue and yellow in the spectrum : the color of growing fresh grass or of the emerald **2** : something of a green color **3** : green vegetation; esp, pl : leafy herbs or leafy parts of a vegetable ⟨collard ~s⟩ ⟨beet ~s⟩ **4** : a grassy plot; esp : a smooth grassy area around the hole into which the ball must be played in golf

green·back \'grēn-,bak\ *n* : a U.S. legal-tender note

green bean *n* : a kidney bean that is used as a snap bean when the pods are colored green

green·belt \'grēn-,belt\ *n* : a belt of parks or farmlands around a community

green card *n* : an identity card attesting the permanent resident status of an alien in the U.S.

green·ery \'grē-nə-rē\ *n, pl* **-er·ies** : green foliage or plants

green–eyed \'grē-'nīd\ *adj* : JEALOUS

green·gro·cer \'grēn-,grō-sər\ *n, chiefly Brit* : a retailer of fresh vegetables and fruit

green·horn \-,hȯrn\ *n* : an inexperienced person; *also* : NEWCOMER

green·house \-,haus\ *n* : a glass structure for the growing of tender plants

greenhouse effect *n* : warming of a planet's atmosphere that occurs when the sun's radiation passes through the atmosphere, is absorbed by the planet, and is reradiated as radiation of longer wavelength that can be absorbed by atmospheric gases

green manure *n* : an herbaceous crop (as clover) plowed under when green to enrich the soil

green onion *n* : a young onion pulled before the bulb has enlarged and used esp. in salads; *also* : SCALLION

green pepper *n* : a sweet pepper before it turns red at maturity

green·room \'grēn-,rüm, -,rum\ *n* : a room (as in a theater or studio) where performers can relax before, between, or after appearances

green·sward \-,sword\ *n* : turf that is green with growing grass

green thumb *n* : an unusual ability to make plants grow

green·wash·ing \'grēn-,wȯ-shiŋ, -,wä-\ *n* : expressions of environmentalist concerns as a cover for products, policies, or activities deleterious to the environment

Green·wich mean time \'gri-nij-, 'gre-, -nich-\ *n* [*Greenwich*, England] : the time of the meridian of Greenwich used historically as the basis of worldwide standard time

Greenwich time *n* : GREENWICH MEAN TIME

green·wood \'grēn-,wud\ *n* : a forest that is green with foliage

greet \'grēt\ *vb* **1** : to address with expressions of kind wishes **2** : to meet or react to in a specified manner **3** : to be perceived by — **greet·er** *n*

greet·ing *n* **1** : a salutation on meeting **2** *pl* : best wishes : REGARDS

greeting card *n* : a card that bears a message usu. sent on a special occasion

gre·gar·i·ous \gri-'ger-ē-əs\ *adj* [L *gregarius* of a flock or herd, fr. *greg-, grex* flock, herd] **1** : SOCIAL, COMPANIONABLE **2** : tending to flock together — **gre·gar·i·ous·ly** *adv* — **gre·gar·i·ous·ness** *n*

grem·lin \'grem-lən\ *n* : a cause of error or equipment malfunction conceived of as a small gnome

gre·nade \grə-'nād\ *n* [MF, lit., pomegranate, fr. LL *granata*, fr. L, fem. of *granatus* seedy, fr. *granum* grain] : a small bomb that is thrown by hand or launched (as by a rifle)

gren·a·dier \,gre-nə-'dir\ *n* : a member of a European regiment formerly armed with grenades

gren·a·dine \,gre-nə-'dēn, 'gre-nə-,dēn\ *n* : a syrup flavored with pomegranates and used in mixed drinks

grew *past of* GROW

grey *var of* GRAY

grey·hound \'grā-,haund\ *n* : any of a breed of tall slender dogs noted for speed and keen sight

grid \'grid\ *n* **1** : GRATING **2** : a network of conductors for distributing electric power **3** : a network of horizontal and perpendicular lines (as for locating points on a map) **4** : GRIDIRON 2; *also* : FOOTBALL

grid·dle \'gri-dᵊl\ *n* : a flat usu. metal surface for cooking food

griddle cake *n* : PANCAKE

grid·iron \'grid-,ī(-ə)rn\ *n* **1** : a grate for broiling food **2** : a football field

grid·lock \-,läk\ *n* : a traffic jam in which an intersection is so blocked that vehicles cannot move

grief \'grēf\ *n* **1** : emotional distress caused by or as if by bereavement; *also* : a cause of such distress **2** : DISASTER; *also* : MISHAP

griev·ance \'grē-vəns\ *n* **1** : a cause of distress affording reason for complaint or resistance **2** : COMPLAINT

grieve \'grēv\ *vb* **grieved; griev·ing** [ME *greven*, fr. AF *grever*, fr. L *gravare* to burden, fr. *gravis* heavy, grave] **1** : to cause grief or sorrow to : DISTRESS **2** : to feel grief : SORROW

griev·ous \'grē-vəs\ *adj* **1** : causing suffering, grief, or sorrow : SEVERE ⟨a ~ wound⟩ **2** : OPPRESSIVE, ONEROUS ⟨~ costs of war⟩ **3** : SERIOUS, GRAVE — **griev·ous·ly** *adv*

¹**grill** \'gril\ *vb* **1** : to broil on a grill; *also* : to fry or toast on a griddle **2** : to question intensely

²**grill** *n* **1** : a cooking utensil of parallel bars on which food is grilled **2** : a usu. informal restaurant

grille *or* **grill** \'gril\ *n* : a grating that forms a barrier or screen

grill·work \'gril-,wərk\ *n* : work constituting or resembling a grille

grim \'grim\ *adj* **grim·mer; grim·mest** **1** : CRUEL, FIERCE **2** : harsh and forbidding in appearance **3** : ghastly or repellent in character **4** : RELENTLESS — **grim·ly** *adv* — **grim·ness** *n*

gri·mace \'gri-məs, gri-'mās\ *n* : a facial expression usu. of disgust or disapproval — **grimace** *vb*

grime \'grīm\ *n* : soot, smut, or dirt adhering to or embedded in a surface; *also*

: accumulated dirtiness and disorder — **grimy** adj

grin \'grin\ vb **grinned; grin·ning** : to draw back the lips so as to show the teeth esp. in amusement — **grin** n

¹**grind** \'grīnd\ vb **ground** \'graund\; **grind·ing 1** : to reduce to small particles **2** : to wear down, polish, or sharpen by friction **3** : OPPRESS **4** : to press with a grating noise : GRIT ⟨~ the teeth⟩ **5** : to operate or produce by turning a crank **6** : DRUDGE; esp : to study hard **7** : to move with difficulty or friction ⟨gears ~ing⟩

²**grind** n **1** : dreary monotonous labor, routine, or study **2** : one who works or studies excessively

grind·er \'grīn-dər\ n **1** : MOLAR **2** pl : TEETH **3** : one that grinds **4** : SUBMARINE **2 5** : an athlete who succeeds through hard work and determination

grind·stone \'grīnd-,stōn\ n : a flat circular stone of natural sandstone that revolves on an axle and is used for grinding, shaping, or smoothing

¹**grip** \'grip\ vb **gripped; grip·ping 1** : to seize or hold firmly **2** : to hold the interest of strongly

²**grip** n **1** : GRASP; also : strength in gripping **2** : a firm tenacious hold **3** : UNDERSTANDING **4** : a device for gripping **5** : TRAVELING BAG

gripe \'grīp\ vb **griped; grip·ing 1** : IRRITATE, VEX **2** : to cause or experience spasmodic pains in the bowels **3** : COMPLAIN — **gripe** n

grippe \'grip\ n : INFLUENZA

gris-gris \'grē-,grē\ n, pl **gris-gris** \-,grēz\ [F] : an amulet or incantation used chiefly by people of black African ancestry

gris·ly \'griz-lē\ adj **gris·li·er; -est** : HORRIBLE, GRUESOME

grist \'grist\ n : grain to be ground or already ground

gris·tle \'gri-səl\ n : CARTILAGE — **gristly** \'gris-lē\ adj

grist·mill \'grist-,mil\ n : a mill for grinding grain

¹**grit** \'grit\ n **1** : a hard sharp granule (as of sand); also : material composed of such granules **2** : unyielding courage — **grit·ty** adj

²**grit** vb **grit·ted; grit·ting** : GRIND, GRATE

grits \'grits\ n pl : coarsely ground hulled grain ⟨hominy ~⟩

griz·zled \'gri-zəld\ adj : streaked or mixed with gray; also : having gray hair

griz·zly \'griz-lē\ adj **griz·zli·er; -est** : GRIZZLED

grizzly bear n : a large powerful brownish bear of western No. America

gro abbr gross

groan \'grōn\ vb **1** : MOAN **2** : to make a harsh sound under sudden or prolonged strain ⟨the chair ~ed under his weight⟩ — **groan** n

groat \'grōt\ n : an old British coin worth four pennies

gro·cer \'grō-sər\ n [ME, fr. AF groser wholesaler, fr. gros coarse, wholesale, fr. L grossus coarse] : a dealer esp. in staple foodstuffs — **gro·cery** \'grōs-rē, 'grōsh-, 'grō-sə-\ n

grog \'gräg\ n [Old Grog, nickname of Edward Vernon †1757 Eng. admiral responsible for diluting the sailors' rum] : alcoholic liquor; esp : liquor (as rum) mixed with water

grog·gy \'grä-gē\ adj **grog·gi·er; -est** : weak and unsteady on the feet or in action — **grog·gi·ly** \-gə-lē\ adv — **grog·gi·ness** \-gē-nəs\ n

groin \'groin\ n **1** : the juncture of the lower abdomen and inner part of the thigh; also : the region of this juncture **2** : the curved line or rib on a ceiling along which two vaults meet

grok \'gräk\ vb **grokked grok·king** : to understand profoundly and intuitively

grom·met \'grä-mət, 'grə-\ n **1** : a ring of rope **2** : an eyelet of firm material to strengthen or protect an opening

¹**groom** \'grüm, 'grum\ n **1** : a person responsible for the care of horses **2** : BRIDEGROOM

²**groom** vb **1** : to clean and care for (an animal) **2** : to make neat or attractive **3** : PREPARE

grooms·man \'grümz-mən, 'grumz-\ n : a male friend who attends a bridegroom at his wedding

groove \'grüv\ n **1** : a long narrow channel **2** : a fixed routine — **groove** vb

groovy \'grü-vē\ adj **groov·i·er; -est 1** : EXCELLENT **2** : HIP

grope \'grōp\ vb **groped; grop·ing 1** : to feel about or search for blindly or uncertainly ⟨~ for the right word⟩ **2** : to feel one's way by groping

gros·beak \'grōs-,bēk\ n : any of several finches of Europe or America with large stout conical bills

gros·chen \'grō-shən\ n, pl **groschen** : a former Austrian monetary unit equal to ¹/₁₀₀ schilling

gros·grain \'grō-,grān\ n [F gros grain coarse texture] : a silk or rayon fabric with crosswise cotton ribs

¹**gross** \'grōs\ adj **1** : glaringly noticeable **2** : OUT-AND-OUT, UTTER **3** : BIG, BULKY; esp : excessively fat **4** : GENERAL, BROAD **5** : consisting of an overall total exclusive of deductions ⟨~ earnings⟩ **6** : CARNAL, EARTHY ⟨~ pleasures⟩ **7** : UNREFINED; also : crudely vulgar **8** : lacking knowledge — **gross·ly** adv — **gross·ness** n

²**gross** n : an overall total exclusive of deductions — **gross** vb

³**gross** n, pl **gross** : a total of 12 dozen things ⟨a ~ of pencils⟩

gross domestic product n : the gross national product excluding the value of net income earned abroad

gross national product n : the total value of the goods and services produced in a nation during a year

gro·szy \'grō-shē\ n, pl **groszy** — see zloty at MONEY TABLE

grot \'grät\ n : GROTTO

gro·tesque \grō-'tesk\ adj **1** : FANCIFUL,

BIZARRE 2 : absurdly incongruous 3 : ECCENTRIC — **gro·tesque·ly** *adv*

grot·to \'grä-tō\ *n, pl* **grottoes** *also* **grottos** 1 : CAVE 2 : an artificial cavelike structure

grouch \'graùch\ *n* 1 : a fit of bad temper 2 : a habitually irritable or complaining person — **grouch** *vb* — **grouchy** *adj*

¹ground \'graùnd\ *n* 1 : the bottom of a body of water 2 *pl* : sediment at the bottom of a liquid 3 : a basis for belief, action, or argument 4 : BACKGROUND 5 : the surface of the earth; *also* : SOIL 6 : an area with a particular use ⟨fishing ∼s⟩ 7 *pl* : the area about and belonging to a building 8 : a conductor that makes electrical connection with the earth — **ground·less** *adj*

²ground *vb* 1 : to bring to or place on the ground 2 : to run or cause to run aground 3 : to provide a reason or justification for 4 : to furnish with a foundation of knowledge 5 : to connect electrically with a ground 6 : to restrict to the ground; *also* : prohibit from some activity

³ground *past and past part of* GRIND

ground ball *n* : a batted baseball that rolls or bounces along the ground

ground cover *n* : low plants that grow over and cover the soil; *also* : a plant suitable for use as ground cover

ground·ed \'graùn-dǝd\ *adj* : mentally and emotionally stable

ground·er \'graùn-dǝr\ *n* : GROUND BALL

ground·hog \'graùnd-,hòg, -,häg\ *n* : WOODCHUCK

ground·ling \'graùnd-liŋ\ *n* : a spectator in the pit of an Elizabethan theater

ground rule *n* 1 : a sports rule adopted to modify play on a particular field, court, or course 2 : a rule of procedure

ground squirrel *n* : any of various burrowing squirrels of No. America and Eurasia that often live in colonies in open areas

ground swell *n* 1 : a broad deep ocean swell caused by an often distant gale or earthquake 2 *usu* **ground-swell** : a rapid spontaneous growth (as of political opinion)

ground-wa·ter \'graùnd-,wò-tǝr, -,wä-\ *n* : water within the earth that supplies wells and springs

ground-work \-,wǝrk\ *n* : FOUNDATION, BASIS

ground zero *n* 1 : the point above, below, or at which a nuclear explosion occurs 2 : the center or origin of rapid, intense, or violent activity

¹group \'grüp\ *n* 1 : a number of individuals related by a common factor (as physical association, community of interests, or blood) 2 : a combination of atoms commonly found together in a molecule ⟨a methyl ∼⟩

²group *vb* : to associate in groups : CLUSTER, AGGREGATE

grou·per \'grü-pǝr\ *n, pl* **groupers** *also* **grouper** : any of numerous large solitary bottom fishes of warm seas

group home *n* : a residence for persons requiring care or supervision

group·ie \'grü-pē\ *n* : a fan of a rock group who usu. follows the group around on concert tours; *also* : ENTHUSIAST, FAN

group therapy *n* : therapy in the presence of a therapist in which several patients discuss their personal problems

groupware \'grüp-,wer\ *n* : software that enables users to work jointly via a network on projects or files

¹grouse \'graùs\ *n, pl* **grouse** *or* **grouses** : any of various chiefly ground-dwelling game birds that have feathered legs and are usu. of reddish brown or other protective color

²grouse *vb* **groused; grous·ing** : COMPLAIN, GRUMBLE

grout \'graùt\ *n* : material (as mortar) used for filling spaces — **grout** *vb*

grove \'grōv\ *n* : a small wood usu. without underbrush

grov·el \'grä-vǝl, 'grǝ-\ *vb* **-eled** *or* **-elled**; **-el·ing** *or* **-el·ling** 1 : to creep or lie with the body prostrate in fear or humility 2 : to abase oneself

grow \'grō\ *vb* **grew** \'grü\; **grown** \'grōn\; **grow·ing** 1 : to spring up and develop to maturity 2 : to be able to grow : THRIVE 3 : to take on some relation through or as if through growth ⟨tree limbs *grown* together⟩ 4 : INCREASE, EXPAND 5 : to develop from a parent source 6 : BECOME 7 : to have an increasing influence 8 : to cause to grow — **grow·er** *n*

growing pains *n pl* 1 : pains in the legs of growing children having no known relation to growth 2 : the stresses and strains attending a new project or development

growl \'graù(-ǝ)l\ *vb* 1 : RUMBLE 2 : to utter a deep throaty sound 3 : GRUMBLE — **growl** *n*

grown–up \'grō-,nǝp\ *adj* : not childish : ADULT — **grown–up** *n*

growth \'grōth\ *n* 1 : stage or condition attained in growing 2 : a process of growing esp. through progressive development or increase 3 : a result or product of growing ⟨a fine ∼ of hair⟩; *also* : an abnormal mass of tissue (as a tumor)

growth hormone *n* : a vertebrate hormone that is secreted by the pituitary gland and regulates growth

growth industry *n* : a business, interest, or activity that is increasingly popular, profitable, or trendy

¹grub \'grǝb\ *vb* **grubbed; grub·bing** 1 : to clear or root out by digging 2 : to dig in the ground usu. for a hidden object 3 : to search about

²grub *n* 1 : a soft thick wormlike insect larva ⟨beetle ∼s⟩ 2 : DRUDGE; *also* : a slovenly person 3 : FOOD

grub·by \'grǝ-bē\ *adj* **grub·bi·er; -est** : DIRTY, SLOVENLY — **grub·bi·ness** \-bē-nǝs\ *n*

grub·stake \'grǝb-,stāk\ *n* : supplies or funds furnished a mining prospector in return for a share in his finds

¹**grudge** \'grəj\ vb **grudged; grudg·ing** : to be reluctant to give : BEGRUDGE

²**grudge** n : a feeling of deep-seated resentment or ill will

gru·el \'grü-əl\ n : a thin porridge

gru·el·ing or **gru·el·ling** \'grü-liŋ, 'grü-ə-\ adj : requiring extreme effort : EXHAUSTING

grue·some \'grü-səm\ adj [fr. earlier growsome, fr. E dial. grow, grue to shiver] : inspiring horror or repulsion — **grue·some·ly** adv — **grue·some·ness** n

gruff \'grəf\ adj 1 : rough in speech or manner 2 : being deep and harsh : HOARSE — **gruff·ly** adv

grum·ble \'grəm-bəl\ vb **grum·bled; grum·bling** 1 : to mutter in discontent 2 : GROWL, RUMBLE — **grum·bler** n

grumpy \'grəm-pē\ adj **grump·i·er; -est** : moodily cross : SURLY — **grump·i·ly** \-pə-lē\ adv — **grump·i·ness** \-pē-nəs\ n

grunge \'grənj\ n 1 : one that is grungy 2 : heavy metal rock music expressing alienation and discontent 3 : untidy or tattered clothing typically worn by grunge fans

grun·gy \'grən-jē\ adj **grun·gi·er; -est** : shabby or dirty in character or condition

grun·ion \'grən-yən\ n : a fish of the California coast which comes inshore to spawn at nearly full moon

grunt \'grənt\ n : a deep throaty sound (as that of a hog) — **grunt** vb

GSA abbr 1 General Services Administration 2 Girl Scouts of America

G suit n [gravity] : a suit for a pilot or astronaut designed to counteract the physiological effects of acceleration

GSUSA abbr Girl Scouts of the United States of America

gt abbr great

Gt Brit abbr Great Britain

gtd abbr guaranteed

GU abbr Guam

gua·ca·mo·le \,gwä-kə-'mō-lē\ n [MexSp, fr. Nahuatl āhuacamōlli, fr. āhuacatl avocado + mōlli sauce] : mashed and seasoned avocado

gua·nine \'gwä-,nēn\ n : a purine base that codes genetic information in the molecular chain of DNA and RNA

gua·no \'gwä-nō\ n [Sp, fr. Quechua wanu fertilizer, dung] : excrement esp. of seabirds or bats; also : a fertilizer composed chiefly of this excrement

gua·ra·ni \,gwär-ə-'nē\ n, pl **guaranis** also **guaranis** — see MONEY table

¹**guar·an·tee** \,ger-ən-'tē\ n 1 : GUARANTOR 2 : GUARANTY 1 3 : an agreement by which one person undertakes to secure another in the possession or enjoyment of something 4 : an assurance of the quality of or of the length of use to be expected from a product offered for sale 5 : GUARANTY 4

²**guarantee** vb **-teed; -tee·ing** 1 : to undertake to answer for the debt, failure to perform, or faulty performance of (another) 2 : to undertake an obligation to establish, perform, or continue 3 : to give security to

guar·an·tor \,ger-ən-'tòr\ n : one who gives a guarantee

¹**guar·an·ty** \'ger-ən-tē\ n, pl **-ties** 1 : an undertaking to answer for another's failure to pay a debt or perform a duty 2 : GUARANTEE 3 3 : GUARANTOR 4 : PLEDGE, SECURITY

²**guaranty** vb **-tied; -ty·ing** : GUARANTEE

¹**guard** \'gärd\ n 1 : a person or a body of persons on sentinel duty 2 pl : troops assigned to protect a sovereign 3 : a defensive position (as in boxing) 4 : the act or duty of protecting or defending 5 : PROTECTION 6 : a protective or safety device 7 : a football lineman playing between center and tackle; also : a basketball player stationed farthest from the goal — **on guard** : WATCHFUL, ALERT

²**guard** vb 1 : PROTECT, DEFEND 2 : to watch over 3 : to be on guard

guard·house \'gärd-,haůs\ n 1 : a building occupied by a guard or used as a headquarters by soldiers on guard duty 2 : a military jail

guard·ian \'gär-dē-ən\ n 1 : CUSTODIAN 2 : one who has the care of the person or property of another — **guard·ian·ship** n

guard·room \'gärd-,rüm\ n 1 : a room used for guarding a military guard while on duty 2 : a room where military prisoners are confined

guards·man \'gärdz-mən\ n : a member of a military body called guard or guards

gua·va \'gwä-və\ n : the sweet yellow or pink acid fruit of a shrubby tropical American tree used esp. for making jam and jelly; also : the tree

gu·ber·na·to·ri·al \,gü-bər-nə-'tòr-ē-əl\ adj : of or relating to a governor

guer·don \'gər-d°n\ n : REWARD, RECOMPENSE

Guern·sey \'gərn-zē\ n, pl **Guernseys** : any of a breed of usu. reddish-brown and white dairy cattle that produce rich yellowish milk

guer·ril·la or **gue·ril·la** \gə-'ri-lə\ n [Sp guerrilla, fr. dim. of guerra war, of Gmc origin] : one who engages in irregular warfare esp. as a member of an independent unit

guess \'ges\ vb 1 : to form an opinion from little or no evidence 2 : BELIEVE, SUPPOSE 3 : to conjecture correctly about : DISCOVER — **guess** n

guest \'gest\ n 1 : a person to whom hospitality (as of a house or a club) is extended 2 : a patron of a commercial establishment (as a hotel) 3 : a person not a regular member of a cast who appears on a program

guest·house \'gest-,haůs\ n : a house run as a boarding house or bed-and-breakfast

guf·faw \(,)gə-'fò\ n : a loud burst of laughter — **guf·faw** vb

guid·ance \'gī-d°ns\ n 1 : the act or process of guiding 2 : ADVICE, DIRECTION

¹**guide** \'gīd\ n 1 : one who leads or directs another's course 2 : one who shows and explains points of interest 3 : something that provides guiding information;

also : SIGNPOST **4** : a device to direct the motion of something

²**guide** *vb* **guid·ed; guid·ing 1** : to act as a guide to **2** : MANAGE, DIRECT **3** : to superintend the training of — **guid·able** \\'gī-də-bəl\\ *adj*

guide·book \\'gīd-ˌbúk\\ *n* : a book of information for travelers

guided missile *n* : a missile whose course may be altered during flight

guide dog *n* : a dog trained to lead the blind

guide·line \\'gīd-ˌlīn\\ *n* : an indication or outline of policy or conduct

guide word *n* : a term at the head of a page of an alphabetical reference work that indicates the alphabetically first or last word on that page

gui·don \\'gī-ˌdän, 'gī-d°n\\ *n* : a small flag (as of a military unit)

guild \\'gild\\ *n* : an association of people with common aims and interests; *esp* : a medieval association of merchants or craftsmen — **guild·hall** \\-ˌhòl\\ *n*

guil·der \\'gil-\\ *n* : GULDEN

guile \\'gī(-ə)l\\ *n* : deceitful cunning : DUPLICITY — **guile·ful** *adj* — **guile·less** *adj* — **guile·less·ness** *n*

guil·lo·tine \\'gi-lə-ˌtēn, ˌgē-ə-'tēn\\ *n* [F, fr. Joseph *Guillotin* †1814 Fr. physician] : a machine for beheading persons — **guillotine** *vb*

guilt \\'gilt\\ *n* **1** : the fact of having committed an offense esp. against the law **2** : BLAMEWORTHINESS **3** : a feeling of responsibility for wrongdoing — **guilt·less** *adj*

guilt–trip \\'gilt-ˌtrip\\ *vb* : to cause feelings of guilt in

guilty \\'gil-tē\\ *adj* **guilt·i·er; -est 1** : having committed a breach of conduct or a crime **2** : suggesting or involving guilt **3** : aware of or suffering from guilt — **guilt·i·ly** \\-tə-lē\\ *adv* — **guilt·i·ness** \\-tē-nəs\\ *n*

guin·ea \\'gi-nē\\ *n* **1** : a British gold coin no longer issued worth 21 shillings **2** : a unit of value equal to 21 shillings

guinea fowl *n* : a gray and white spotted West African bird related to the pheasants and widely raised for food; *also* : any of several related birds

guinea hen *n* : a female guinea fowl; *also* : GUINEA FOWL

guinea pig *n* **1** : a small stocky short-eared and nearly tailless So. American rodent often kept as a pet or used in lab research **2** : a subject of research or testing

guise \\'gīz\\ *n* **1** : a form or style of dress : COSTUME **2** : external appearance : SEMBLANCE

gui·tar \\gi-'tär\\ *n* : a musical instrument with usu. six strings plucked with a pick or with the fingers

gulch \\'gəlch\\ *n* : RAVINE

gul·den \\'gúl-dən, 'gül-\\ *n, pl* **guldens** *or* **gulden 1** : the basic monetary unit of the Netherlands until 2002 **2** — see MONEY table

gulf \\'gəlf\\ *n* [ME *goulf*, fr. MF *golfe*, fr. It *golfo*, fr. LL *colpus*, fr. Gk *kolpos* bosom,

gulf] **1** : a part of an ocean or sea partly or mostly surrounded by land **2** : ABYSS, CHASM **3** : a wide separation ⟨the ~ between generations⟩

¹**gull** \\'gəl\\ *n* : any of numerous mostly white or gray long-winged web-footed seabirds

²**gull** *vb* : to make a dupe of : DECEIVE

³**gull** *n* : DUPE

gul·let \\'gə-lət\\ *n* : ESOPHAGUS; *also* : THROAT

gul·li·ble \\'gə-lə-bəl\\ *adj* : easily duped or cheated

gul·ly \\'gə-lē\\ *n, pl* **gullies** : a trench worn in the earth by and often filled with running water after rains

gulp \\'gəlp\\ *vb* **1** : to swallow hurriedly or greedily **2** : SUPPRESS ⟨~ down a sob⟩ **3** : to catch the breath as if in taking a long drink — **gulp** *n*

¹**gum** \\'gəm\\ *n* : the oral tissue that surrounds the necks of the teeth

²**gum** *n* [ME *gomme*, fr. MF, fr. L *cummi, gummi*, fr. Gk *kommi*, fr. Egyptian *qmy.t*] **1** : a sticky plant exudate; *esp* : one that hardens on drying **2** : a sticky substance **3** : a preparation usu. of a plant gum sweetened and flavored and used for chewing — **gum·my** *adj*

gum arabic *n* : a water-soluble gum obtained from several acacias and used esp. in making inks, adhesives, confections, and pharmaceuticals

gum·bo \\'gəm-bō\\ *n* [AmerF *gombo*, fr. Bantu origin] : a rich thick soup usu. thickened with okra

gum·drop \\'gəm-ˌdräp\\ *n* : a candy made usu. from corn syrup with gelatin and coated with sugar crystals

gump·tion \\'gəmp-shən\\ *n* **1** *chiefly dial* : shrewd common sense **2** : ENTERPRISE, INITIATIVE ⟨lacked the ~ to try⟩

gum·shoe \\'gəm-ˌshü\\ *n* : DETECTIVE — **gumshoe** *vb*

¹**gun** \\'gən\\ *n* **1** : CANNON **2** : a portable firearm **3** : a discharge of a gun **4** : something suggesting a gun in shape or function **5** : THROTTLE — **gunned** \\'gənd\\ *adj*

²**gun** *vb* **gunned; gun·ning 1** : to hunt with a gun **2** : SHOOT **3** : to open up the throttle of so as to increase speed

gun·boat \\'gən-ˌbōt\\ *n* : a small lightly armed ship for use in shallow waters

gun·fight \\-ˌfīt\\ *n* : a duel with guns — **gun·fight·er** *n*

gun·fire \\-ˌfī(-ə)r\\ *n* : the firing of guns

gung ho \\'gəŋ-'hō\\ *adj* : extremely zealous or enthusiastic

gun·man \\-mən\\ *n* : a man armed with a gun; *esp* : a professional killer

gun·ner \\'gə-nər\\ *n* **1** : a soldier or airman who operates or aims a gun **2** : one who hunts with a gun

gun·nery \\'gə-nə-rē\\ *n* : the use of guns; *esp* : the science of the flight of projectiles and effective use of guns

gunnery sergeant *n* : a noncommissioned officer in the marine corps ranking next below a master sergeant

gun·ny·sack \\'gə-nē-ˌsak\\ *n* : a sack made of a coarse heavy fabric (as burlap)

gun·point \'gən-ˌpȯint\ *n* : the muzzle of a gun — **at gunpoint** : under a threat of death by being shot

gun·pow·der \-ˌpau̇-dər\ *n* : an explosive powder used in guns and blasting

gun·shot \-ˌshät\ *n* **1** : shot fired from a gun **2** : the range of a gun ⟨within ∼⟩

gun–shy \-ˌshī\ *adj* **1** : afraid of a loud noise **2** : markedly distrustful

gun·sling·er \-ˌsliŋ-ər\ *n* : a skilled gunman esp. in the American West

gun·smith \-ˌsmith\ *n* : one who designs, makes, or repairs firearms

gun·wale *also* **gun·nel** \'gə-n°l\ *n* : the upper edge of a ship's or boat's side

gup·py \'gə-pē\ *n, pl* **guppies** [R.J.L. *Guppy* †1916 Trinidadian naturalist] : a small brightly colored tropical fish

gur·gle \'gər-gəl\ *vb* **gur·gled; gur·gling** : to make a sound like that of an irregularly flowing or gently splashing liquid — **gurgle** *n*

Gur·kha \'gu̇r-kə, 'gər-\ *n* : a soldier from Nepal in the British or Indian army

gur·ney \'gər-nē\ *n, pl* **gurneys** : a wheeled cot or stretcher

gu·ru \'gu̇r-ü\ *n, pl* **gurus** [ultim. fr. Sanskrit *guru*, fr. *guru*, adj., heavy, venerable] **1** : a personal religious and spiritual teacher in Hinduism **2** : a teacher in matters of fundamental concern **3** : EXPERT ⟨a fitness ∼⟩

gush \'gəsh\ *vb* **1** : to issue or pour forth copiously or violently : SPOUT **2** : to make an effusive display of affection or enthusiasm

gush·er \'gə-shər\ *n* : one that gushes; *esp* : an oil well with a large natural flow

gushy \'gə-shē\ *adj* **gush·i·er; -est** : marked by effusive sentimentality

gus·set \'gə-sət\ *n* : a triangular insert (as in a seam of a sleeve) to give width or strength — **gusset** *vb*

gus·sy up \'gə-sē-\ *vb* **gus·sied up; gus·sy·ing up** **1** : to dress in best or formal clothes **2** : to make more attractive, glamorous, or fancy

¹**gust** \'gəst\ *n* **1** : a sudden brief rush of wind **2** : a sudden outburst : SURGE — **gusty** *adj*

²**gust** *vb* : to blow in gusts

gus·ta·to·ry \'gəs-tə-ˌtȯr-ē\ *adj* : relating to or associated with the sense of taste

gus·to \'gəs-tō\ *n, pl* **gustoes** : enthusiastic enjoyment; *also* : VITALITY 4

¹**gut** \'gət\ *n* **1** *pl* : BOWELS, ENTRAILS **2** : the alimentary canal or a part of it (as the intestine); *also* : BELLY, ABDOMEN **3** *pl* : the inner essential parts ⟨a car's ∼s⟩ **4** *pl* : COURAGE, PLUCK

²**gut** *vb* **gut·ted; gut·ting** **1** : EVISCERATE **2** : to destroy the inside of ⟨fire *gutted* the building⟩

gut check *n* : a test of courage, character, or determination

gutsy \'gət-sē\ *adj* **guts·i·er; -est** : marked by courage and determination

gut·ter \'gə-tər\ *n* : a groove or channel for carrying off esp. rainwater

gut·ter·snipe \-ˌsnīp\ *n* : a street urchin

gut·tur·al \'gə-tə-rəl\ *adj* **1** : sounded in the throat **2** : being or marked by an utterance that is strange, unpleasant, or disagreeable — **guttural** *n*

gut·ty \'gə-tē\ *adj* **gut·ti·er; -est** **1** : GUTSY **2** : having a vigorous challenging quality

gut–wrench·ing \'gət-ˌren-chin\ *adj* : causing emotional anguish

¹**guy** \'gī\ *n* : a rope, chain, or rod attached to something as a brace or guide

²**guy** *vb* : to steady or reinforce with a guy

³**guy** *n* : MAN, FELLOW; *also, pl* : PERSONS

⁴**guy** *vb* : to make fun of : RIDICULE

guz·zle \'gə-zəl\ *vb* **guz·zled; guz·zling** : to drink greedily

gym \'jim\ *n* : GYMNASIUM

gym·kha·na \jim-'kä-nə\ *n* : a meet featuring sports contests; *esp* : a contest of automobile-driving skill

gym·na·si·um *for 1* jim-'nä-zē-əm, -zhəm, *for 2* gim-'nä-zē-əm\ *n, pl* **-na·si·ums** *or* **-na·sia** \-'nä-zē-ə, -'nä-zhə; -'nä-zē-ə\ [L, exercise ground, school, fr. Gk *gymnasion*, fr. *gymnazein* to exercise naked, fr. *gymnos* naked] **1** : a room or building for indoor sports **2** : a European secondary school that prepares students for the university

gym·nas·tics \jim-'nas-tiks\ *n* : a competitive sport developed from physical exercises designed to demonstrate strength, balance, and body control — **gym·nast** \'jim-ˌnast\ *n* — **gym·nas·tic** *adj*

gym·no·sperm \'jim-nə-ˌspərm\ *n* : any of a group of woody vascular seed plants (as conifers) that produce naked seeds not enclosed in an ovary

gyn *or* **gynecol** *abbr* gynecology

gy·nae·col·o·gy *chiefly Brit var of* GYNECOLOGY

gy·ne·col·o·gy \ˌgī-nə-'kä-lə-jē\ *n* : a branch of medicine dealing with the diseases and hygiene of women — **gy·ne·co·log·ic** \-ni-kə-'lä-jik\ *or* **gy·ne·co·log·i·cal** \-ji-kəl\ *adj* — **gy·ne·col·o·gist** \-nə-'kä-lə-jist\ *n*

gy·no·cen·tric \ˌgī-nə-'sen-trik\ *adj* : emphasizing feminine interests or a feminine point of view

gyp \'jip\ *n* **1** : CHEAT, SWINDLER **2** : FRAUD, SWINDLE — **gyp** *vb*

gyp·sum \'jip-səm\ *n* : a calcium-containing mineral used in making plaster of paris

Gyp·sy \'jip-sē\ *n, pl* **Gypsies** [by shortening & alter. fr. *Egyptian*] : a member of a traditionally traveling people coming orig. from India and living chiefly in Europe, Asia, and No. America; *also* : the language of the Gypsies

gypsy moth *n* : an Old World moth that was introduced into the U.S. where its caterpillar is a destructive defoliator of many trees

gy·rate \'jī-ˌrāt\ *vb* **gy·rat·ed; gy·rat·ing** **1** : to revolve around a point or axis **2** : to oscillate with or as if with a circular or spiral motion — **gy·ra·tion** \jī-'rā-shən\ *n*

gyr·fal·con \'jər-ˌfal-kən, -ˌfȯl-\ *n* : an arctic falcon with several color forms that is the largest of all falcons

¹gy·ro \ˈjī-rō\ *n, pl* **gyros** : GYROSCOPE

²gy·ro \ˈyē-ˌrō, ˈzhir-ō\ *n, pl* **gyros** : a sandwich eps. of lamb and beef, tomato, onion, and yogurt sauce on pita bread

gy·ro·scope \ˈjī-rō-ˌskōp\ *n* : a wheel or disk mounted to spin rapidly about an axis that is free to turn in various directions

Gy Sgt *abbr* gunnery sergeant

gyve \ˈjīv, ˈgīv\ *n* : FETTER — **gyve** *vb*

¹h \ˈāch\ *n, pl* **h's** *or* **hs** \ˈā-chəz\ *often cap* : the 8th letter of the English alphabet

²h *abbr, often cap* **1** hard; hardness **2** heroin **3** hit **4** husband

H *symbol* hydrogen

¹ha \ˈhä\ *interj* — used esp. to express surprise or joy

²ha *abbr* hectare

Hab *abbr* Habacuc; Habakkuk

Ha·ba·cuc \ˈha-bə-ˌkək, hə-ˈba-kək\ *n* : HABAKKUK

Ha·bak·kuk \ˈha-bə-ˌkək, hə-ˈba-kək\ *n* — see BIBLE table

ha·ba·ne·ra \ˌhä-bə-ˈner-ə\ *n* [Sp (*danza*) *habanera*, lit., dance of Havana] : a Cuban dance in slow time; *also* : the music for this dance

ha·ba·ne·ro *also* **ha·ba·ñe·ro** \ˌ(h)ä-bə-ˈn(y)er-ō\ *n* : a very hot chili pepper that is usu. orange when mature

ha·be·as cor·pus \ˈhä-bē-əs-ˈkȯr-pəs\ *n* [ME, fr. ML, lit., you should have the body (the opening words of the writ)] : a writ issued to bring a party before a court

hab·er·dash·er \ˈha-bər-ˌda-shər\ *n* : a dealer in men's clothing and accessories

hab·er·dash·ery \-ˌda-shə-rē\ *n, pl* **-er·ies** **1** : goods sold by a haberdasher **2** : a haberdasher's shop

ha·bil·i·ment \hə-ˈbi-lə-mənt\ *n* **1** *pl* : TRAPPINGS, EQUIPMENT **2** : DRESS; *esp* : the dress characteristic of an occupation or occasion — usu. used in pl.

hab·it \ˈha-bət\ *n* **1** : DRESS, GARB **2** : BEARING, CONDUCT **3** : PHYSIQUE **4** : mental makeup **5** : a usual manner of behavior : CUSTOM **6** : a behavior pattern acquired by frequent repetition ⟨has a ~ of swearing⟩ **7** : ADDICTION ⟨a drug ~⟩ **8** : mode of growth or occurrence ⟨trees with a spreading ~⟩

hab·it·able \ˈha-bə-tə-bəl\ *adj* : capable of being lived in — **hab·it·abil·i·ty** \ˌha-bə-tə-ˈbi-lə-tē\ *n*

hab·i·tat \ˈha-bə-ˌtat\ *n* [L, it inhabits] : the place or environment where a plant or animal naturally occurs

hab·i·ta·tion \ˌha-bə-ˈtā-shən\ *n* **1** : OCCUPANCY **2** : a dwelling place : RESIDENCE **3** : SETTLEMENT

hab·it—form·ing \ˈha-bət-ˌfȯr-miŋ\ *adj* : causing addiction : ADDICTIVE

ha·bit·u·al \hə-ˈbi-chə-wəl\ *adj* **1** : CUSTOMARY **2** : doing, practicing, or acting by force of habit **3** : inherent in an individual ⟨~ grace⟩ — **ha·bit·u·al·ly** *adv* — **ha·bit·u·al·ness** *n*

ha·bit·u·ate \hə-ˈbi-chə-ˌwāt\ *vb* **-at·ed;** **-at·ing** **1** : ACCUSTOM **2** : to cause or undergo habituation

ha·bit·u·a·tion \hə-ˌbi-chə-ˈwā-shən\ *n* **1** : the process of making habitual **2** : psychological dependence on a drug after a period of use

ha·bi·tué *also* **ha·bi·tue** \hə-ˈbi-chə-ˌwā\ *n* [F] **1** : one who may be regularly found in or at (as a place of entertainment) **2** : DEVOTEE

ha·ci·en·da \ˌhä-sē-ˈen-də\ *n* **1** : a large estate in a Spanish-speaking country **2** : the main building of a farm or ranch

¹hack \ˈhak\ *vb* **1** : to cut or sever with repeated irregular blows **2** : to cough in a short dry manner **3** : to manage successfully; *also* : TOLERATE ⟨can't ~ the pressure⟩ **4** : to gain access to a computer illegally

²hack *n* **1** : an implement for hacking **2** : a short dry cough **3** : a hacking blow

³hack *n* **1** : a horse hired or used for varied work **2** : a horse worn out in service **3** : a light easy often 3-gaited saddle horse **4** : HACKNEY, TAXICAB **5** : a person who works solely for mercenary reasons; *esp* : a writer working solely for commercial success — **hack** *adj*

⁴hack *vb* : to operate a taxicab

hack·er \ˈha-kər\ *n* **1** : one that hacks; *also* : a person unskilled at something **2** : an expert at using a computer **3** : a person who illegally gains access to and sometimes tampers with information in a computer system

hack·ie \ˈha-kē\ *n* : a taxicab driver

hack·le \ˈha-kəl\ *n* **1** : one of the long feathers on the neck or back of a bird **2** *pl* : hairs (as on a dog's neck) that can be erected **3** *pl* : TEMPER, DANDER

hack·man \ˈhak-mən\ *n* : HACKIE

¹hack·ney \ˈhak-nē\ *n, pl* **hackneys** **1** : a horse for riding or driving **2** : a carriage or automobile kept for hire

²hackney *vb* : to make trite

hack·neyed \ˈhak-nēd\ *adj* : lacking in freshness or originality ⟨~ slogans⟩

hack·saw \ˈhak-ˌsȯ\ *n* : a fine-tooth saw in a frame for cutting metal

hack·work \-ˌwərk\ *n* : work done on order usu. according to a formula

had *past and past part of* HAVE

had·dock \ˈha-dək\ *n, pl* **haddock** *also* **haddocks** : an Atlantic food fish usu. smaller than the related cod

Ha·des \ˈhā-(ˌ)dēz\ *n* **1** : the abode of the dead in Greek mythology **2** *often not cap* : HELL

haem *chiefly Brit var of* HEME

hae·ma·tite *Brit var of* HEMATITE

haf·ni·um \'haf-nē-əm\ *n* : a gray metallic chemical element

haft \'haft\ *n* : the handle of a weapon or tool

hag \'hag\ *n* **1** : an ugly or evil-looking old woman **2** : WITCH 1

Hag *abbr* Haggai

Hag·gai \'ha-gē-ˌī, 'ha-ˌgī\ *n* — see BIBLE table

hag·gard \'ha-gərd\ *adj* : having a worn or emaciated appearance ⟨∼ faces⟩ ♦ **Synonyms** CAREWORN, WASTED, DRAWN — **hag·gard·ly** *adv* — **hag·gard·ness** *n*

hag·gis \'ha-gəs\ *n* : a traditionally Scottish dish made of the heart, liver, and lungs of a sheep or a calf minced with suet, onions, oatmeal, and seasonings

hag·gle \'ha-gəl\ *vb* **hag·gled; hag·gling** : to argue in bargaining — **hag·gler** *n*

Ha·gi·og·ra·pha \ˌha-gē-'ä-grə-fə, ˌhä-jē-\ *n pl* — see WRITINGS

ha·gio·graph·ic \ˌha-gē-ə-'gra-fik, ˌhä-, -jē-\ *adj* : of or relating to hagiography; *esp* : excessively flattering

ha·gi·og·ra·phy \ˌha-gē-'ä-grə-fē, ˌhä-jē-\ *n* **1** : biography of saints or venerated persons **2** : idealizing or idolizing biography — **ha·gi·og·ra·pher** \-fər\ *n*

hai·ku \'hī-(ˌ)kü\ *n, pl* **haiku** [Jp] : an unrhymed Japanese verse form of three lines containing usu. five, seven, and five syllables respectively; *also* : a poem in this form

¹hail \'hāl\ *n* **1** : precipitation in the form of small lumps of ice **2** : something that gives the effect of falling hail

²hail *vb* **1** : to precipitate hail **2** : to pour down and strike like hail

³hail *interj* [ME, fr. ON *heill*, fr. *heill* healthy] — used to express acclamation

⁴hail *vb* **1** : SALUTE, GREET **2** : SUMMON

⁵hail *n* **1** : an expression of greeting, approval, or praise **2** : hearing distance

Hail Mary *n* : a salutation and prayer to the Virgin Mary

hail·stone \'hāl-ˌstōn\ *n* : a pellet of hail

hail·storm \-ˌstorm\ *n* : a storm accompanied by hail

hair \'her\ *n* : a threadlike outgrowth esp. from the skin of a mammal; *also* : a covering or growth of hairs of an animal or a body part — **haired** \'herd\ *adj* — **hairless** *adj*

hair·breadth \'her-ˌbredth\ *or* **hairsbreadth** \'herz-\ *n* : a very small distance or margin

hair·brush \-ˌbrəsh\ *n* : a brush for the hair

hair·cloth \-ˌkloth\ *n* : a stiff wiry fabric used esp. for upholstery

hair·cut \-ˌkət\ *n* : the act, process, or style of cutting and shaping the hair

hair·do \-ˌdü\ *n, pl* **hairdos** : HAIRSTYLE

hair·dress·er \-ˌdre-sər\ *n* : a person who dresses or cuts hair — **hair·dress·ing** *n*

hair·line \-ˌlīn\ *n* **1** : a very thin line **2** : the outline of the hair on the head

hair·piece \-ˌpēs\ *n* **1** : supplementary hair (as a switch) used in some women's hairdos **2** : TOUPEE

hair·pin \-ˌpin\ *n* **1** : a U-shaped pin to hold the hair in place **2** : a sharp U-shaped turn in a road — **hairpin** *adj*

hair–rais·ing \'her-ˌrā-ziŋ\ *adj* : causing terror or astonishment

hair·split·ter \-ˌspli-tər\ *n* : a person who makes excessively fine distinctions in reasoning — **hair·split·ting** \-ˌspli-tiŋ\ *adj or n*

hair·spray \'her-ˌsprā\ *n* : a liquid sprayed onto the hair to hold it in place

hair·style \-ˌstī(-ə)l\ *n* : a way of wearing the hair — **hair·styl·ing** *n*

hair·styl·ist \-ˌstī-list\ *n* : HAIRDRESSER

hair–trigger *adj* : immediately responsive to the slightest stimulus

hairy \'her-ē\ *adj* **hair·i·er; -est 1** : covered with or as if with hair **2** : tending to cause nervous tension ⟨a few ∼ moments⟩ **3** : difficult to deal with — **hair·i·ness** \-ē-nəs\ *n*

hairy woodpecker *n* : a common No. American woodpecker with a white back that is larger than the similarly marked downy woodpecker

hajj \'haj\ *n* : a pilgrimage to Mecca prescribed as a religious duty for Muslims

hajji \'ha-jē\ *n* : one who has made a pilgrimage to Mecca — often used as a title

hake \'hāk\ *n* : any of several marine food fishes related to the cod

ha·la·la \hə-'lä-lə\ *n, pl* **halala** *or* **halalas** — see *riyal* at MONEY table

hal·berd \'hal-bərd, 'hol-\ *also* **hal·bert** \-bərt\ *n* : a weapon esp. of the 15th and 16th centuries consisting of a battle-ax and pike on a long handle

hal·cy·on \'hal-sē-ən\ *adj* [Gk *halkyōn, alkyōn*, a mythical bird believed to nest at sea and to calm the waves] **1** : CALM, PEACEFUL ⟨a ∼ lake⟩ **2** : being a time of happiness, success, or prosperity

¹hale \'hāl\ *adj* : free from defect, disease, or infirmity ♦ **Synonyms** HEALTHY, SOUND, ROBUST, WELL

²hale *vb* **haled; hal·ing 1** : HAUL, PULL **2** : to compel to go

ha·ler \'hä-lər\ *n, pl* **ha·le·ru** \'hä-lə-ˌrü\ — see *koruna* at MONEY table

¹half \'haf, 'häf\ *n, pl* **halves** \'havz, 'hävz\ **1** : either of two equal parts into which something is divisible **2** : one of a pair

²half *adj* **1** : being one of two equal parts **2** : amounting to nearly half **3** : PARTIAL, INCOMPLETE — **half** *adv*

half–and–half \ˌhaf-ᵊn-'haf, ˌhäf-ᵊn-'häf\ *n* : something that is half one thing and half another

half·back \'haf-ˌbak, 'häf-\ *n* **1** : a football back stationed on or near the flank **2** : a player stationed immediately behind the forward line

half–baked \-'bākt\ *adj* **1** : poorly planned **2** : lacking common sense **3** : not thoroughly baked

half–breed \-ˌbrēd\ *n, often disparaging* : one of mixed racial descent — **half–breed** *adj*

half·brother *n* : a brother related through one parent only

half–caste \'haf-ˌkast, 'häf-\ *n* : HALF-
BREED — **half–caste** *adj*

half–cocked \'haf-'käkt, 'häf-\ *adj* : lacking adequate preparation

half–dol·lar \-'dä-lər\ *n* **1** : a coin representing one half of a dollar **2** : the sum
of fifty cents

half–heart·ed \-'här-təd\ *adj* : lacking
spirit or interest — **half–heart·ed·ly** *adv*
— **half–heart·ed·ness** *n*

half–life \-ˌlīf\ *n* : the time required for
half of something (as atoms or a drug) to
undergo a process

half–mast \-'mast\ *n* : a point about halfway down from the top of a mast or staff

half note *n* : a musical note equal in time
to one half that of a whole note

half–pen·ny \'häp-nē\ *n, pl* **half·pence**
\'hā-pəns\ *or* **halfpennies** : a former
British coin representing one half of a
penny

half–pint \'haf-ˌpīnt, 'häf-\ *adj* : of less
than average size — **half–pint** *n*

half sister *n* : a sister related through one
parent only

half sole *n* : a shoe sole extending from
the shank forward — **half–sole** *vb*

half–staff \'haf-'staf, 'häf-\ *n* : HALF-MAST

half step *n* : a musical interval equivalent
to one twelfth of an octave

half–time \'haf-ˌtīm, 'häf-\ *n* : an intermission between halves of a game

half–track \-ˌtrak\ *n* : a motor vehicle
propelled by an endless chain-track drive
system; *esp* : such a vehicle lightly armored for military use

half–truth \-ˌtrüth\ *n* : a statement that is
only partially true; *esp* : one that deliberately mixes truth and falsehood

half·way \-'wā\ *adj* **1** : midway between
two points **2** : PARTIAL 1 — **halfway** *adv*

half–wit \-ˌwit\ *n* : a foolish or imbecilic
person — **half–wit·ted** \-'wi-təd\ *adj* —
half–wit·ted·ness *n*

hal·i·but \'ha-lə-bət\ *n, pl* **halibut** *also*
halibuts [ME *halybutte*, fr. *haly*, *holy*
holy + *butte* flatfish; fr. its being eaten on
holy days] : any of several large edible
marine flatfishes

ha·lite \'ha-ˌlīt, 'hā-\ *n* : ROCK SALT

hal·i·to·sis \ˌha-lə-'tō-səs\ *n* : the condition of having fetid breath

hall \'hól\ *n* **1** : the residence of a medieval king or noble; *also* : the house of a
landed proprietor **2** : a large public
building **3** : a college or university building; *also* : DORMITORY **4** : LOBBY; *also*
: CORRIDOR **5** : AUDITORIUM

hal·le·lu·jah \ˌha-lə-'lü-yə\ *interj* [Heb
hallĕlūyāh praise (ye) the Lord] — used
to express praise, joy, or thanks

hall·mark \'hól-ˌmärk\ *n* **1** : a mark put
on an article to indicate origin, purity, or
genuineness **2** : a distinguishing characteristic

hal·low \'ha-lō\ *vb* **1** : CONSECRATE **2**
: REVERE, VENERATE 〈our ∼*ed* leader〉
— **hal·lowed** \-lōd, -lə-wəd\ *adj*

Hal·low·een \ˌha-lə-'wēn, ˌhä-\ *n* : the evening of October 31
observed esp. by children in merrymak-
ing and masquerading

hal·lu·ci·nate \hə-'lü-sə-ˌnāt\ *vb* **-nat·ed;**
-nat·ing : to have hallucinations or experience as a hallucination

hal·lu·ci·na·tion \hə-ˌlü-sə-'nā-shən\ *n*
: perception of objects with no reality
due usu. to use of drugs (as LSD) or to
disorder of the nervous system; *also*
: something so perceived ♦ **Synonyms**
DELUSION, ILLUSION, MIRAGE — **hal·lu-**
ci·na·to·ry \-'lü-sə-nə-ˌtòr-ē\ *adj*

hal·lu·ci·no·gen \hə-'lü-sə-nə-jən\ *n* : a
substance that induces hallucinations —
hal·lu·ci·no·gen·ic \-ˌlü-sə-nə-'je-nik\
adj or n

hall·way \'hòl-ˌwā\ *n* **1** : an entrance
hall **2** : CORRIDOR

ha·lo \'hā-lo\ *n, pl* **halos** *or* **haloes** [L *ha-*
los, fr. Gk *halōs* threshing floor, disk,
halo] **1** : a circle of light appearing to
surround a shining body (as the sun) **2**
: the aura of glory surrounding an idealized person or thing

¹**hal·o·gen** \'ha-lə-jən\ *n* : any of the five
elements fluorine, chlorine, bromine, iodine, and astatine

²**hal·o·gen** *adj* : containing, using, or being
a halogen 〈a ∼ lamp〉

¹**halt** \'hòlt\ *adj* : LAME 1

²**halt** *n* : STOP

³**halt** *vb* **1** : to stop marching or traveling
2 : DISCONTINUE, END 〈∼ protests〉

¹**hal·ter** \'hòl-tər\ *n* **1** : a rope or strap for
leading or tying an animal; *also* : HEAD-
STALL **2** : NOOSE **3** : a brief blouse held
in place by straps around the neck and
across the back

²**halter** *vb* **hal·tered; hal·ter·ing 1** : to
catch with or as if with a halter; *also* : to
put a halter on (as a horse) **2** : HANG **3**
: IMPEDE, RESTRAIN

halt·ing \'hòl-tiŋ\ *adj* : UNCERTAIN, FAL-
TERING — **halt·ing·ly** *adv*

halve \'hav, 'häv\ *vb* **halved; halv·ing 1**
: to divide into two equal parts **2** : to reduce to one half

halv·ers \'ha-vərz, 'hä-\ *n pl* : half shares
: HALVES

halves *pl of* HALF

hal·yard \'hal-yərd\ *n* : a rope or tackle
for hoisting and lowering (as sails)

¹**ham** \'ham\ *n* **1** : a buttock with its associated thigh — usu. used in pl. **2** : a cut
of meat and esp. pork from the thigh **3**
: a showy performer **4** : an operator of
an amateur radio station — **ham** *adj*

²**ham** *vb* **hammed; ham·ming** : to over-
play a part — **OVERACT**

ham·burg·er \'ham-ˌbər-gər\ *or* **ham-**
burg \-ˌbərg\ *n* [G *Hamburger* of Ham-
burg, Germany] **1** : ground beef **2** : a
sandwich consisting of a ground-beef
patty in a round roll

ham·let \'ham-lət\ *n* : a small village

¹**ham·mer** \'ha-mər\ *n* **1** : a hand tool
used for pounding; *also* : something resembling a hammer in form or function
2 : the part of a gun whose striking action
causes explosion of the charge **3** : a
metal sphere hurled by a flexible handle
for distance in a track-and-field event
(**hammer throw**) **4** : ACCELERATOR 2

²**hammer** *vb* **1** : to beat, drive, or shape with repeated blows of a hammer : POUND **2** : to produce or bring about as if by repeated blows — usu. used with *out* **3** : to criticize severely

ham·mer·head \'ha-mər-,hed\ *n* **1** : the striking part of a hammer **2** : any of a family of medium-sized sharks with eyes at the ends of lateral extensions of the flattened head

ham·mer·lock \-,läk\ *n* : a wrestling hold in which an opponent's arm is held bent behind the back

ham·mer·toe \-,tō\ *n* : a toe deformed by having one or more joints permanently flexed

¹**ham·mock** \'ha-mək\ *n* [Sp *hamaca*, of AmerInd origin] : a swinging couch hung by cords at each end

²**hammock** *n* : a fertile elevated area of the southern U.S. and esp. Florida with hardwood vegetation and soil rich in humus

¹**ham·per** \'ham-pər\ *vb* : IMPEDE; *also* : RESTRAIN ♦ **Synonyms** TRAMMEL, CLOG, FETTER, SHACKLE

²**hamper** *n* : a large usu. lidded basket

ham·ster \'ham-stər\ *n* [G, fr. OHG *hamustro*, of Slavic origin] : any of a subfamily of small Old World rodents with large cheek pouches

¹**ham·string** \'ham-,striŋ\ *n* : any of several muscles at the back of the thigh or tendons at the back of the knee

²**hamstring** *vb* **-strung** \-,strəŋ\; **-stringing 1** : to make ineffective or powerless ⟨*hamstrung* by guilt⟩ **2** : to cripple by cutting the leg tendons

¹**hand** \'hand\ *n* **1** : the end of a front limb when modified (as in humans) for grasping **2** : an indicator or pointer on a dial **3** : personal possession — usu. used in pl.; *also* : CONTROL **4** : SIDE **5** : a pledge esp. of betrothal **6** : HANDWRITING **7** : SKILL, ABILITY; *also* : a significant part ⟨had a ~ in the victory⟩ **8** : ASSISTANCE; *also* : PARTICIPATION ⟨had no ~ in the affair⟩ **9** : an outburst of applause **10** : a single round in a card game; *also* : the cards held by a player after a deal **11** : WORKER, EMPLOYEE; *also* : a member of a ship's crew — **hand-less** *adj* — **at hand** : near in time or place — **on hand** : in present possession or readily available — **out of hand** : out of control

²**hand** *vb* **1** : to lead, guide, or assist with the hand **2** : to give, pass, or transmit with the hand

hand·bag \'hand-,bag\ *n* : a bag for carrying small personal articles and money

hand·ball \-,bȯl\ *n* : a game played by striking a small rubber ball against a wall with the hand

hand·bill \-,bil\ *n* : a small printed sheet for distribution by hand

hand·book \-,bu̇k\ *n* : a concise reference book : MANUAL

hand·car \-,kär\ *n* : a small 4-wheeled railroad car propelled by hand or by a small motor

hand·clasp \-,klasp\ *n* : HANDSHAKE

hand·craft \-,kraft\ *vb* : to fashion by manual skill

¹**hand·cuff** \-,kəf\ *n* : a metal fastening that can be locked around a wrist and is usu. connected with another such fastening — usu. used in pl.

²**handcuff** *vb* : MANACLE

hand·ed \'han-dəd\ *adj* : having or using such or so many hands ⟨a left-*handed* person⟩ — **hand·ed·ness** *n*

hand·ful \'hand-,fu̇l\ *n*, *pl* **hand·fuls** \-,fu̇lz\ *also* **hands·ful** \'handz-,fu̇l\ **1** : as much or as many as the hand will grasp **2** : a small number **3** : as much as one can manage

hand·gun \-,gən\ *n* : a firearm held and fired with one hand

hand·held \-,held\ *adj* : designed for use while being held in the hand — **handheld** *n*

¹**hand·i·cap** \'han-di-,kap\ *n* [obs. E *handicap*, a game in which forfeit money was held in a cap, fr. *hand in cap*] **1** : a contest in which an artificial advantage is given or disadvantage imposed on a contestant to equalize chances of winning; *also* : the advantage given or disadvantage imposed **2** : a disadvantage that makes achievement difficult

²**handicap** *vb* **-capped; -cap·ping 1** : to give a handicap to **2** : to put at a disadvantage

hand·i·capped *adj, sometimes offensive* : having a physical or mental disability

hand·i·cap·per \-,ka-pər\ *n* : a person who predicts the winners in a contest

hand·i·craft \-di-,kraft\ *n* **1** : manual skill **2** : an occupation requiring manual skill **3** : the articles fashioned by those engaged in handicraft — **hand·i·craft·er** \-,kraf-tər\ *n* — **hand·i·crafts·man** \-,krafts-mən\ *n*

hand in glove *or* **hand and glove** *adv* : in an extremely close relationship

hand·i·work \'han-di-,wərk\ *n* : work done personally or by the hands

hand·ker·chief \'haŋ-kər-chəf, -,chēf\ *n*, *pl* **-chiefs** \-chəfs, -,chēfs\ *also* **-chieves** \-,chēvz\ : a small piece of cloth used for various personal purposes (as the wiping of the face)

¹**han·dle** \'han-dᵊl\ *n* **1** : a part (as of a tool) designed to be grasped by the hand **2** : NAME; *also* : NICKNAME — **han·dled** \-dᵊld\ *adj* — **off the handle** : into a state of sudden and violent anger — usu. used with *fly*

²**handle** *vb* **han·dled; han·dling 1** : to touch, hold, or manage with the hands **2** : to have responsibility for **3** : to deal or trade in **4** : to behave in a certain way when managed or directed ⟨a car that ~s well⟩ — **han·dler** *n*

han·dle·bar \'han-dᵊl-bär\ *n* : a usu. bent bar with a grip at each end (as for steering a bicycle) — usu. used in pl.

hand·made \'hand-'mād\ *adj* : made by hand or by a hand process

hand·maid·en \-,mā-dᵊn\ *also* **hand·maid** \-,mād\ *n* : a female attendant

hand—me—down \-me-,dau̇n\ *adj* : used

by one person after having been used by another — **hand-me-down** *n*

hand-out \'hand-ˌaut\ *n* **1** : a portion (as of food) given to a beggar **2** : a piece of printed information for free distribution; *also* : a prepared statement released to the press

hand over *vb* : to yield control of

hand-pick \'hand-'pik\ *vb* : to select personally ⟨a ~ed candidate⟩

hand-rail \-ˌrāl\ *n* : a narrow rail for grasping as a support

hand-saw \-ˌsȯ\ *n* : a saw designed to be used with one hand

hands down *adv* **1** : with little effort **2** : without question

hand-sel \'han-səl\ *n* **1** : a gift made as a token of good luck **2** : a first installment : earnest money

hand-set \'hand-ˌset\ *n* : a combined telephone transmitter and receiver mounted on a handheld device

hand-shake \-ˌshāk\ *n* : a clasping usu. of right hands by two people

hands-off \'handz-'ȯf\ *adj* : characterized by noninterference

hand-some \'han-səm\ *adj* **hand-som-er; -est** [ME *handsom* easy to manipulate] **1** : SIZABLE, AMPLE **2** : GENEROUS, LIBERAL **3** : pleasing and usu. impressive in appearance ◆ *Synonyms* BEAUTIFUL, LOVELY, PRETTY, COMELY, FAIR — **hand-some-ly** *adv* — **hand-some-ness** *n*

hands-on \'handz-'ȯn, -'än\ *adj* **1** : being or providing direct practical experience in the operation of something **2** : characterized by active personal involvement ⟨~ management⟩

hand-spring \'hand-ˌspriŋ\ *n* : an acrobatic feat in which the body turns in a full circle from a standing position and lands first on the hands and then on the feet

hand-stand \-ˌstand\ *n* : an act of supporting the body on the hands with the trunk and legs balanced in the air

hand-to-hand *adj* : involving physical contact or very close range ⟨~ fighting⟩ — **hand to hand** *adv*

hand-to-mouth *adj* : having or providing nothing to spare — **hand to mouth** *adv*

hand-wo-ven \'hand-ˌwō-vən\ *adj* : produced on a hand-operated loom

hand-writ-ing \-ˌrī-tiŋ\ *n* : writing done by hand; *also* : the form of writing peculiar to a person — **hand-writ-ten** \-ˌri-tᵊn\ *adj*

handy \'han-dē\ *adj* **hand-i-er; -est** **1** : conveniently near **2** : easily used **3** : DEXTEROUS — **hand-i-ly** \-də-lē\ *adv* — **hand-i-ness** \-dē-nəs\ *n*

handy-man \-ˌman\ *n* **1** : one who does odd jobs **2** : one competent in a variety of small skills or repair work

¹hang \'haŋ\ *vb* **hung** \'həŋ\ *also* **hanged; hang-ing 1** : to fasten or remain fastened to an elevated point without support from below; *also* : to fasten or be fastened so as to allow free motion on the point of suspension ⟨~ a door⟩ **2** : to suspend by the neck until dead; *also* : to

die by hanging **3** : DROOP ⟨*hung* his head in shame⟩ **4** : to fasten to a wall ⟨~ wallpaper⟩ **5** : to prevent (a jury) from coming to a decision **6** : to display (pictures) in a gallery **7** : to remain stationary in the air **8** : to be imminent **9** : DEPEND **10** : to take hold for support **11** : to be burdensome **12** : to undergo delay **13** : to incline downward; *also* : to fit or fall from the figure in easy lines **14** : to be raptly attentive **15** : to pass time idly by relaxing or socializing ⟨~ing at the mall⟩ — often used with *around* or *out* — **hang out to dry** : to subject to ruin by abandonment

²hang *n* **1** : the manner in which a thing hangs **2** : an understanding of something ⟨got the ~ of skiing⟩

han-gar \'haŋ-ər\ *n* [F] : a covered and usu. enclosed area for housing and repairing aircraft

hang-dog \'haŋ-ˌdȯg\ *adj* **1** : SAD, DEJECTED **2** : SHEEPISH

hang-er \'haŋ-ər\ *n* **1** : one that hangs **2** : a device that fits inside or around a garment for hanging from a hook or rod

hang-er-on \'haŋ-ər-'ȯn, -'än\ *n, pl* **hangers-on** : one who hangs around a person or place esp. for personal gain

hang in *vb* : to persist tenaciously

hang-ing *n* **1** : an execution by strangling or snapping the neck by a suspended noose **2** : something hung

hang-man \'haŋ-mən\ *n* **1** : a public executioner **2** : a game in which players must identify an unknown word by guessing the letters that comprise it within a designated number of chances

hang-nail \-ˌnāl\ *n* : a bit of skin hanging loose at the edge of a fingernail

hang on *vb* **1** : to keep hold onto something **2** : HANG IN **3** : to await something desired

hang-out \'haŋ-ˌaut\ *n* : a favorite place for spending time

hang-over \-ˌō-vər\ *n* **1** : something that remains from what is past **2** : disagreeable physical effects following heavy drinking or the use of drugs

hang-up \'haŋ-ˌəp\ *n* : a source of mental or emotional difficulty

hang up *vb* **1** : to place on a hook or hanger **2** : to end a telephone conversation by breaking the connection **3** : to keep delayed or suspended

hank \'haŋk\ *n* : COIL, LOOP

han-ker \'haŋ-kər\ *vb* : to desire strongly or persistently — **han-ker-ing** *n*

han-kie *or* **han-ky** \'haŋ-kē\ *n, pl* **hankies** : HANDKERCHIEF

han-ky-pan-ky \ˌhaŋ-kē-'paŋ-kē\ *n* **1** : questionable or underhanded activity **2** : sexual dalliance

hansel *var of* HANDSEL

han-som \'han-səm\ *n* : a 2-wheeled covered carriage with the driver's seat elevated at the rear

han-ta-virus \'hän-tə-ˌvī-rəs, 'hən-, 'han-\ *n* : any of a genus of viruses including some transmitted by rodents that cause pneumonia or hemorrhagic fevers

Ha·nuk·kah also **Cha·nu·kah** \'kä-nə-kə, 'hä-\ n [Heb ḥănukkāh dedication] : an 8-day Jewish holiday commemorating the rededication of the Temple of Jerusalem after its defilement by Antiochus of Syria

hap \'hap\ n 1 : HAPPENING 2 : CHANCE, FORTUNE

¹hap·haz·ard \hap-'ha-zərd\ n : CHANCE

²haphazard adj : marked by lack of plan or order — **hap·haz·ard·ly** adv — **hap·haz·ard·ness** n

hap·less \'hap-ləs\ adj : UNFORTUNATE — **hap·less·ly** adv — **hap·less·ness** n

hap·loid \'hap-ˌlȯid\ adj : having the number of chromosomes characteristic of gametic cells — **haploid** n

hap·ly \'hap-lē\ adv : by chance

hap·pen \'ha-pən\ vb 1 : to occur by chance 2 : to take place 3 : CHANCE 2

¹hap·pen·ing n 1 : OCCURRENCE 2 : an event that is especially interesting, entertaining, or important

²happening adj 1 : very fashionable 2 : offering much stimulating activity ⟨a ~ nightclub⟩

hap·pi·ly \'ha-pə-lē\ adv 1 : LUCKILY 2 : in a happy manner or state ⟨lived ~ ever after⟩ 3 : APTLY, SUCCESSFULLY

hap·pi·ness \'ha-pē-nəs\ n 1 : a state of well-being and contentment; also : a pleasurable satisfaction 2 : APTNESS

hap·py \'ha-pē\ adj **hap·pi·er; -est** 1 : FORTUNATE 2 : APT, FELICITOUS 3 : enjoying well-being and contentment ⟨a ~ childhood⟩ 4 : PLEASANT ⟨a ~ ending⟩; also : PLEASED, GRATIFIED ⟨~ to meet you⟩ 5 : quick or enthusiastic to use or do something ⟨trigger-happy⟩ ⟨a cliché-happy writer⟩ ♦ **Synonyms** GLAD, CHEERFUL, LIGHTHEARTED, JOYFUL, JOYOUS

hap·py-go-lucky \ˌha-pē-gō-'lə-kē\ adj : CAREFREE

happy hour n : a period of time when the price of drinks at a bar is reduced

hara-kiri \ˌha-ri-'kir-ē, -'ka-rē\ n [Jp harakiri, fr. hara belly + kiri cutting] : ritual suicide by disembowelment

ha·rangue \hə-'raŋ\ n 1 : a ranting speech or writing 2 : LECTURE — **harangue** vb — **ha·rangu·er** n

ha·rass \hə-'ras, 'ha-rəs\ vb [F harasser, fr. MF, fr. harer to set a dog on, fr. OF hare, interj. used to incite dogs, of Gmc origin] 1 : EXHAUST, FATIGUE 2 : to worry and impede by repeated raids 3 : to annoy continually 4 : to create an unpleasant or hostile situation for esp. by one's verbal or physical conduct ♦ **Synonyms** HARRY, PLAGUE, PESTER, TEASE, BEDEVIL — **ha·rass·ment** n

har·bin·ger \'här-bən-jər\ n : one that announces or foreshadows what is coming : PRECURSOR; also : PORTENT

¹har·bor \'här-bər\ n 1 : a place of security and comfort 2 : a part of a body of water protected and deep enough to furnish anchorage • PORT

²harbor vb 1 : to give or take refuge : SHELTER ⟨~ a fugitive⟩ ⟨~ed in the barn⟩ 2 : to be the home or habitat of; also : LIVE 3 : to hold a thought or feeling ⟨~ a grudge⟩

har·bor·age \'här-bə-rij\ n : HARBOR

har·bour chiefly Brit var of HARBOR

hard \'härd\ adj 1 : not easily penetrated : not easily yielding to pressure 2 : high in alcoholic content 3 : containing salts that prevent lathering with soap ⟨~ water⟩ 4 : stable in value ⟨~ currency⟩ 5 : physically fit 6 : FIRM, DEFINITE ⟨~ agreement⟩; also : based on clear fact ⟨~ evidence⟩ 7 : CLOSE, SEARCHING ⟨a ~ look⟩ 8 : REALISTIC ⟨good ~ sense⟩ 9 : OBDURATE, UNFEELING ⟨a ~ heart⟩ 10 : difficult to bear ⟨~ times⟩; also : HARSH, SEVERE 11 : RESENTFUL ⟨~ feelings⟩ 12 : STRICT, UNRELENTING ⟨a ~ bargain⟩ 13 : INCLEMENT ⟨a ~ winter⟩ 14 : intense in force or manner ⟨a ~ gust of wind⟩ 15 : ARDUOUS, STRENUOUS ⟨~ work⟩ 16 : sounding as in arcing and geese respectively — used of c and g 17 : TROUBLESOME ⟨a ~ problem⟩ 18 : having difficulty in doing something ⟨~ of hearing⟩ 19 : addictive and gravely detrimental to health ⟨~ drugs⟩ 20 : of or relating to the natural sciences and esp. the physical sciences — **hard** adv — **hard·ness** n

hard-and-fast adj : rigidly binding : STRICT ⟨a ~ rule⟩

hard·back \'härd-ˌbak\ n : a hardcover book

hard·ball \-ˌbȯl\ n 1 : BASEBALL 2 : forceful uncompromising methods

hard-bit·ten \-'bi-tᵊn\ adj : SEASONED, TOUGH ⟨~ campaigners⟩

hard·board \-ˌbȯrd\ n : a very dense fiberboard

hard-boiled \-'bȯi(-ə)ld\ adj, 1 of an egg : boiled until both white and yolk have solidified 2 : lacking sentiment : TOUGH; also : HARDHEADED 2

hard·bound \-ˌbau̇nd\ adj : HARDCOVER

hard copy n : copy of textual or graphic information (as from computer storage) produced on paper

hard-core \'härd-'kȯr\ adj 1 : extremely resistant to solution or improvement 2 : being the most determined or dedicated members of a specified group 3 : containing explicit depictions of sex acts — **hard core** n

hard·cov·er \-'kə-vər\ adj : having rigid boards on the sides covered in cloth or paper ⟨~ books⟩

hard disk n : a sealed rigid metal disk used as a computer storage device; also : HARD DRIVE

hard drive n : a data-storage device consisting of a drive and one or more hard disks

hard·en \'här-dᵊn\ vb 1 : to make or become hard or harder 2 : to confirm or become confirmed in disposition or action — **hard·en·er** n

hard·hack \'härd-ˌhak\ n : an American spirea with dense clusters of pink or white flowers and leaves having a hairy rusty yellow underside

hard hat n 1 : a protective hat worn esp.

by construction workers **2** : a construction worker

hard·head·ed \'härd-'he-dəd\ adj **1** : STUBBORN, WILLFUL **2** : SOBER, REALISTIC ⟨some ~ advice⟩ — **hard·head·ed·ly** adv — **hard·head·ed·ness** n

hard–heart·ed \-'här-təd\ adj : PITILESS, CRUEL — **hard–heart·ed·ly** adv — **hard–heart·ed·ness** n

har·di·hood \'här-dē-,hŭd\ n **1** : resolute courage and fortitude **2** : VIGOR, ROBUSTNESS

hard–line \'härd-'līn\ adj : advocating or involving a rigidly uncompromising course of action — **hard–lin·er** \-'lī-nər\ n

hard–luck \-,lək\ adj : marked by or relating to bad luck ⟨~ losing teams⟩

hard·ly \'härd-lē\ adv **1** : with force **2** : SEVERELY **3** : with difficulty **4** : only just : BARELY ⟨can ~ tell the difference⟩ **5** : certainly not ⟨is ~ a friend of mine⟩

hard–nosed \'härd-'nōzd\ adj : TOUGH, UNCOMPROMISING; also : HARDHEADED 2

hard palate n : the bony anterior part of the palate forming the roof of the mouth

hard·pan \'härd-,pan\ n : a compact layer in soil that is impenetrable by roots

hard–pressed \-'prest\ adj : HARD PUT; esp : being under financial strain

hard put adj **1** : barely able **2** : faced with difficulty or perplexity

hard rock n : rock music marked by a heavy beat, high amplification, and usu. frenzied performances

hard–shell \'härd-,shel\ or **hard–shelled** \-,sheld\ adj **1** : having a hard shell **2** : HIDEBOUND, UNCOMPROMISING ⟨a ~ conservative⟩

hard·ship \-,ship\ n **1** : SUFFERING, PRIVATION **2** : something that causes suffering or privation

hard·tack \-,tak\ n : a saltless hard biscuit, bread, or cracker

hard·top \-,täp\ n : an automobile having a permanent rigid top

hard·ware \-,wer\ n **1** : ware (as cutlery or tools) made of metal **2** : the physical components (as electronic devices) of a vehicle (as a spacecraft) or an apparatus (as a computer)

hard–wired \-,wī(-ə)rd\ adj **1** : connected or incorporated by or as if by permanent electrical connections **2** : genetically or innately determined or predisposed ⟨~ reactions⟩ ⟨is ~ to avoid change⟩

hard·wood \-,wŭd\ n : the wood of a broad-leaved usu. deciduous tree as distinguished from that of a conifer; also : such a tree — **hardwood** adj

hard·work·ing \-'wər-kiŋ\ adj : INDUSTRIOUS, DILIGENT

har·dy \'här-dē\ adj **har·di·er; -est 1** : BOLD, BRAVE **2** : AUDACIOUS, BRAZEN **3** : ROBUST; also : able to withstand adverse conditions (as of weather) ⟨~ shrubs⟩ — **har·di·ly** \-də-lē\ adv — **har·di·ness** \-dē-nəs\ n

hare \'her\ n, pl **hare** or **hares** : any of various swift timid long-eared mammals like the related rabbits but born with open eyes and fur

hare·bell \'her-,bel\ n : a slender herb with bright blue bell-shaped flowers

hare·brained \-'brānd\ adj : FOOLISH, ABSURD

hare·lip \-'lip\ n, sometimes offensive : CLEFT LIP

ha·rem \'her-əm\ n [Ar ḥarīm, lit., something forbidden & ḥaram, lit., sanctuary] **1** : a house or part of a house allotted to women in a Muslim household **2** : the women and servants occupying a harem **3** : a group of females associated with one male

hark \'härk\ vb : LISTEN

harken var of HEARKEN

har·le·quin \'här-li-kən, -kwən\ n **1** cap : a character (as in comedy) with a shaved head, masked face, variegated tights, and wooden sword **2** : CLOWN 2

har·lot \'här-lət\ n : PROSTITUTE

¹harm \'härm\ n **1** : physical or mental damage : INJURY **2** : MISCHIEF, HURT — **harm·ful** \-fəl\ adj — **harm·ful·ly** adv — **harm·ful·ness** n — **harm·less** adj — **harm·less·ly** adv — **harm·less·ness** n

²harm vb : to cause harm to : INJURE

¹har·mon·ic \här-'mä-nik\ adj **1** : of or relating to musical harmony or harmonics **2** : pleasing to the ear — **har·mon·i·cal·ly** \-ni-k(ə-)lē\ adv

²harmonic n : a musical overtone

har·mon·i·ca \här-'mä-ni-kə\ n : a small wind instrument in which the sound is produced by metal reeds

har·mo·ni·ous \här-'mō-nē-əs\ adj **1** : musically concordant **2** : CONGRUOUS **3** : marked by accord in sentiment or action — **har·mo·ni·ous·ly** adv — **har·mo·ni·ous·ness** n

har·mo·nise Brit var of HARMONIZE

har·mo·ni·um \här-'mō-nē-əm\ n : a keyboard wind instrument in which the wind acts on a set of metal reeds

har·mo·nize \'här-mə-,nīz\ vb **-nized; -niz·ing 1** : to play or sing in harmony **2** : to be in harmony **3** : to bring into consonance or accord — **har·mo·ni·za·tion** \,här-mə-nə-'zā-shən\ n

har·mo·ny \'här-mə-nē\ n, pl **-nies** [ME armony, fr. AF armonie, fr. L harmonia, fr. Gk. joint, harmony, fr. harmos joint] **1** : musical agreement of sounds; esp : the combination of tones into chords and progressions of chords **2** : a pleasing arrangement of parts; also : ACCORD **3** : internal calm

¹har·ness \'här-nəs\ n **1** : the gear other than a yoke of a draft animal **2** : something that resembles a harness

²harness vb **1** : to put a harness on; also : YOKE **2** : UTILIZE ⟨~ one's potential⟩

¹harp \'härp\ n : a musical instrument consisting of a triangular frame set with strings plucked by the fingers — **harp·ist** \'här-pist\ n

²harp vb **1** : to play on a harp **2** : to dwell on a subject tiresomely — **harp·er** n

har·poon \här-'pün\ n : a barbed spear

used esp. in hunting whales — **harpoon**
vb — **har·poon·er** *n*

harp·si·chord \'härp-si-ˌkȯrd\ *n* : a key-board instrument producing tones by the plucking of its strings with quills or with leather or plastic points

har·py \'här-pē\ *n, pl* **harpies** [L *Harpyia*, a malign creature of myth having a woman's head and a bird's body, fr. Gk] **1** : a predatory person : LEECH **2** : a shrewish woman

har·ri·dan \'her-ə-dən\ *n* : SHREW 2

¹har·ri·er \'her-ē-ər\ *n* **1** : any of a breed of medium-sized foxhounds **2** : a runner on a cross-country team

²harrier *n* : a slender long-legged hawk

¹har·row \'her-ō\ *n* : a cultivating tool that has spikes, spring teeth, or disks and is used esp. to pulverize and smooth the soil

²harrow *vb* **1** : to cultivate with a harrow **2** : TORMENT, VEX

har·rumph \hə-'rəmf\ *vb* : to comment disapprovingly as though clearing the throat

har·ry \'her-ē\ *vb* **har·ried; har·ry·ing 1** : RAID, PILLAGE **2** : to torment by or as if by constant attack ♦ **Synonyms** WORRY, ANNOY, PLAGUE, PESTER

harsh \'härsh\ *adj* **1** : disagreeably rough **2** : causing discomfort or pain **3** : unduly exacting : SEVERE — **harsh·ly** *adv* — **harsh·ness** *n*

harsh·en \'här-shən\ *vb* : to make or become harsh ⟨~ed his voice⟩

hart \'härt\ *n, chiefly Brit* : STAG

har·um-scar·um \ˌhar-əm-'skar-əm\ *adj* : RECKLESS, IRRESPONSIBLE

¹har·vest \'här-vəst\ *n* **1** : the season for gathering in crops; *also* : the act of gathering in a crop **2** : a mature crop **3** : the product or reward of effort

²harvest *vb* **1** : to gather in a crop : REAP **2** : to gather, hunt, or kill (as deer) for human use or population control **3** : to remove cells, tissues, or organs from a living or recently deceased body esp. for transplanting — **har·vest·er** *n*

has *pres 3d sing of* HAVE

has-been \'haz-ˌbin\ *n* : one that has passed the peak of ability, power, effectiveness, or popularity

¹hash \'hash\ *vb* [F *hacher*, fr. OF *hachier*, fr. *hache* battle-ax, of Gmc origin] **1** : to chop into small pieces **2** : to talk about — often used with *over* or *out*

²hash *n* **1** : chopped meat mixed with potatoes and browned **2** : HODGEPODGE, JUMBLE

³hash *n* : HASHISH

hash browns *n pl* : boiled potatoes that have been diced, mixed with chopped onions and shortening, and fried

hash·ish \'ha-ˌshēsh; ha-'shēsh\ *n* [Ar *ḥashīsh*] : the intoxicating concentrated resin from the flowering tops of the female hemp plant

hasp \'hasp\ *n* : a fastener (as for a door) consisting of a hinged metal strap that fits over a staple and is secured by a pin or padlock

has·si·um \'ha-sē-əm\ *n* : an artificially

produced radioactive metallic chemical element

has·sle \'ha-səl\ *n* **1** : WRANGLE; *also* : FIGHT **2** : an annoying or troublesome concern — **hassle** *vb*

has·sock \'ha-sək\ *n* : a cushion that serves as a seat or leg rest; *also* : a cushion to kneel on in prayer

haste \'hāst\ *n* **1** : rapidity of motion or action : SPEED **2** : rash or headlong action **3** : excessive eagerness — **hast·i·ly** \'hā-stə-lē\ *adv* — **hast·i·ness** \-stē-nəs\ *n* — **hasty** \'hā-stē\ *adj*

has·ten \'hā-sᵊn\ *vb* **1** : to urge on **2** : to move or act quickly : HURRY ♦ **Synonyms** SPEED, ACCELERATE, QUICKEN

hat \'hat\ *n* : a covering for the head usu. having a shaped crown and brim — **under one's hat** : SECRET ⟨kept the plans *under his hat*⟩

hat·box \'hat-ˌbäks\ *n* : a round piece of luggage esp. for carrying hats

¹hatch \'hach\ *n* **1** : a small door or opening **2** : a door or cover for access down into a compartment of a ship

²hatch *vb* **1** : to produce by incubation; *also* : INCUBATE **2** : to emerge from an egg or pupa; *also* : to give forth young **3** : ORIGINATE ⟨~ a scheme⟩ — **hatch·ery** \'ha-chə-rē\ *n*

hatch·back \'hach-ˌbak\ *n* : an automobile with a rear hatch that opens upward

hatch·et \'ha-chət\ *n* **1** : a short-handled ax with a hammerlike part opposite the blade **2** : TOMAHAWK

hatchet man *n* : a person hired for murder, coercion, or unscrupulous attack

hatch·ing \'ha-chiŋ\ *n* : the engraving or drawing of closely spaced fine lines chiefly to give an effect of shading; *also* : the pattern so created

hatch·way \'hach-ˌwā\ *n* : a hatch giving access usu. by a ladder or stairs

¹hate \'hāt\ *n* **1** : intense hostility and aversion **2** : an object of hatred — **hate·ful** \-fəl\ *adj* — **hate·ful·ly** *adv* — **hate·ful·ness** *n*

²hate *vb* **hat·ed; hat·ing 1** : to express or feel extreme enmity **2** : to find distasteful ♦ **Synonyms** DETEST, ABHOR, ABOMINATE, LOATHE — **hat·er** *n*

ha·tred \'hā-trəd\ *n* : HATE; *also* : prejudiced hostility or animosity

hat·ter \'ha-tər\ *n* : one that makes, sells, or cleans and repairs hats

hau·berk \'hȯ-bərk\ *n* : a coat of mail

haugh·ty \'hȯ-tē\ *adj* **haugh·ti·er; -est** [obs. *haught*, fr. ME *haute*, fr. AF *halt, haut*, lit., high, fr. L *altus*] : disdainfully proud ♦ **Synonyms** INSOLENT, LORDLY, OVERBEARING, ARROGANT — **haugh·ti·ly** \-tə-lē\ *adv* — **haugh·ti·ness** \-tē-nəs\ *n*

¹haul \'hȯl\ *vb* **1** : to exert traction on : DRAW, PULL **2** : to furnish transportation : CART — **haul·er** *n*

²haul *n* **1** : PULL, TUG **2** : the result of an effort to obtain, collect, or win **3** : the length or course of a transportation route; *also* : LOAD

haul·age \'hȯ-lij\ *n* **1** : the act or process of hauling **2** : a charge for hauling

haunch \'hȯnch\ *n* **1** : ²HIP 1 **2** : HIND-QUARTER 2 — usu. used in pl. **3** : HIND-QUARTER 1

¹haunt \'hȯnt\ *vb* **1** : to visit often : FREQUENT **2** : to have a disquieting effect on ⟨was ~*ed* by his past⟩; *also* : to reappear continually in **3** : to visit or inhabit as a ghost — **haunt·er** *n* — **haunt·ing·ly** *adv*

²haunt \'hȯnt, *2 is usu* 'hant\ *n,* **1** : a place habitually frequented **2** *chiefly dial* : GHOST

haute cou·ture \,ōt-kü-'tür\ *n* [F] : the establishments or designers that create exclusive and often trend-setting fashions for women; *also* : the fashions created

haute cui·sine \-kwi-'zēn\ *n* : artful or elaborate cuisine

hau·teur \hȯ-'tər, ō-, hō-\ *n* : ARROGANCE, HAUGHTINESS

¹have \'hav, həv, v; *in sense 2 before "to" usu* 'haf\ *vb* **had** \'had, həd\; **hav·ing** \'ha-viŋ\; **has** \'haz, həz, *in sense 2 before "to" usu* 'has\ **1** : to hold in possession; *also* : to hold in one's use, service, or regard ⟨*has* a good job⟩ **2** : to be compelled or forced ⟨~ to go now⟩ **3** : to stand in relationship to ⟨*has* many enemies⟩ **4** : OBTAIN; *also* : RECEIVE, ACCEPT **5** : to be marked by ⟨*has* red hair⟩ **6** : SHOW; *also* : USE, EXERCISE ⟨~ mercy⟩ **7** : EXPERIENCE; *also* : TAKE ⟨~ a look⟩ **8** : to entertain in the mind ⟨~ an idea⟩ **9** : to cause to **10** : ALLOW **11** : to be competent in **12** : to hold in a disadvantageous position; *also* : TRICK **13** : BEGET **14** : to partake of **15** — used as an auxiliary with the past participle to form the present perfect, past perfect, or future perfect — **have at** : ATTACK — **have coming** : DESERVE — **have done with** : to be finished with — **have had it** : to have endured all one will permit or can stand — **have to do with** : to have in the way of relation with or effect on

²have \'hav\ *n* : one that has material wealth

ha·ven \'hā-vən\ *n* **1** : HARBOR, PORT **2** : a place of safety **3** : a place offering favorable conditions ⟨an artist's ~⟩

have–not \'hav-,nät, -'nät\ *n* : one that is poor in material wealth

hav·er·sack \'ha-vər-,sak\ *n* [F *havresac,* fr. G *Habersack* bag for oats] : a bag similar to a knapsack but worn over one shoulder

hav·oc \'ha-vək\ *n* **1** : wide and general destruction **2** : great confusion and disorder

haw \'hȯ\ *n* : a hawthorn berry; *also* : HAWTHORN

Ha·wai·ian \hə-'wä-yən\ *n* **1** : a native or resident of Hawaii; *esp* : one of Polynesisan ancestry **2** : the Polynesian language of Hawaii

¹hawk \'hȯk\ *n* **1** : any of numerous mostly small or medium-sized day-flying birds of prey (as a falcon or kite) **2** : a supporter of a war or a warlike policy — **hawk·ish** *adj*

²hawk *vb* : to make a harsh coughing sound in or as if in clearing the throat; *also* : to raise by hawking

³hawk *vb* : to offer goods for sale by calling out in the street — **hawk·er** *n*

hawk·weed \'hȯk-,wēd\ *n* : any of several plants related to the daisies usu. having yellow flowers

haw·ser \'hȯ-zər\ *n* : a large rope for towing, mooring, or securing a ship

haw·thorn \'hȯ-,thȯrn\ *n* : any of a genus of spiny spring-flowering shrubs or small trees related to the apple

¹hay \'hā\ *n,* **1** : herbage (as grass) mowed and cured for fodder **2** : REWARD **3** *slang* : BED ⟨hit the ~⟩ **4** : a small amount of money

²hay *vb* : to cut, cure, and store for hay

hay·cock \'hā-,käk\ *n* : a small conical pile of hay

hay fever *n* : an acute allergic reaction esp. to plant pollen that resembles a cold

hay·loft \'hā-,lȯft\ *n* : a loft for hay

hay·mow \-,maú\ *n* : a mow of or for hay

hay·rick \-,rik\ *n* : a large sometimes thatched outdoor stack of hay

hay·seed \-,sēd\ *n, pl* **hayseed** *or* **hayseeds** **1** : clinging bits of straw or chaff from hay **2** : BUMPKIN, YOKEL

hay·stack \-,stak\ *n* : a stack of hay

hay·wire \-,wī(-ə)r\ *adj* : being out of order or control : CRAZY ⟨things went ~⟩

¹haz·ard \'ha-zərd\ *n* [ME, a dice game, fr. AF *hasard,* fr. Sp *azar,* Ar *al-zahr* the die] **1** : a source of danger **2** : CHANCE; *also* : ACCIDENT **3** : an obstacle on a golf course — **haz·ard·ous** *adj*

²hazard *vb* : VENTURE, RISK ⟨~ a guess⟩

¹haze \'hāz\ *n* **1** : fine dust, smoke, or light vapor causing lack of transparency in the air **2** : vagueness of mind or perception

²haze *vb* **hazed**; **haz·ing** : to harass by abusive and humiliating tricks usu. by way of initiation

ha·zel \'hā-zəl\ *n* **1** : any of a genus of shrubs or small trees related to the birches and bearing edible brown nuts (**ha·zel·nuts** \-,nəts\) **2** : a light brown color

hazy \'hā-zē\ *adj* **haz·i·er; -est** **1** : obscured or darkened by haze **2** : VAGUE, INDEFINITE ⟨a ~ memory⟩; *also* : UNCERTAIN — **haz·i·ly** \-zə-lē\ *adv* — **haz·i·ness** \-zē-nəs\ *n*

Hb *abbr* hemoglobin

HBM *abbr* Her Britannic Majesty; His Britannic Majesty

H–bomb \'āch-,bäm\ *n* : HYDROGEN BOMB

HC *abbr* **1** Holy Communion **2** House of Commons

hd *abbr* head

HD *abbr* heavy-duty

hdbk *abbr* handbook

hdkf *abbr* handkerchief

HDL \,āch-(,)dē-'el\ *n* [*h*igh-*d*ensity *l*ipoprotein] : a cholesterol-poor protein-rich lipoprotein of blood plasma correlated with reduced risk of atherosclerosis

hdwe *abbr* hardware

he \ˈhē\ *pron* **1** : that male one **2** : a person : the person ⟨∼ who hesitates is lost⟩

He *symbol* helium

HE *abbr* **1** Her Excellency **2** His Eminence **3** His Excellency

¹head \ˈhed\ *n* **1** : the front or upper part of the body containing the brain, the chief sense organs, and the mouth **2** : MIND; *also* : natural aptitude ⟨has a ∼ for math⟩ **3** : POISE ⟨a level ∼⟩ **4** : the obverse of a coin **5** : INDIVIDUAL; *also*, *pl* **head** : one of a number (as of cattle) **6** : the end that is upper or higher or opposite the foot; *also* : either end of something (as a drum) whose two ends need not be distinguished **7** : a compact mass of plant parts (as leaves or flowers) **8** : the source of a stream **9** : DIRECTOR, LEADER; *also* : a leading element (as of a procession) **10** : a projecting part; *also* : the striking part of a weapon **11** : the place of leadership or honor **12** : a separate part or topic **13** : the foam on a fermenting or effervescing liquid **14** : a critical point ⟨events came to a ∼⟩ — **head·ed** \ˈhe-dəd\ *adj* — **head·less** *adj* — **over one's head** : beyond one's comprehension or competence

²head *adj* : PRINCIPAL, CHIEF ⟨∼ chef⟩

³head *vb* **1** : to provide with or form a head; *also* : to form the head of **2** : LEAD, CONDUCT ⟨∼ed the search⟩ **3** : to get in front of esp. so as to stop; *also* : SURPASS **4** : to put or stand at the head **5** : to point or proceed in a certain direction ⟨∼ed west⟩

head·ache \ˈhe-ˌdāk\ *n* **1** : pain in the head **2** : a baffling situation or problem — **head·achy** *also* **head·achey** \-ˌā-kē\ *adj*

head·band \ˈhed-ˌband\ *n* : a band worn on or around the head

head·bang·er \-ˌbaŋ-ər\ *n* : one who performs or enjoys hard rock

head·board \-ˌbórd\ *n* : a board forming the head (as of a bed)

head cold *n* : a common cold centered in the nasal passages and adjacent mucous tissues

head·dress \ˈhed-ˌdres\ *n* : an often elaborate covering for the head

head·first \-ˈfərst\ *adv* : HEADLONG 1 ⟨dove ∼ into the water⟩ — **headfirst** *adj*

head·gear \-ˌgir\ *n* : a covering or protective device for the head

head·hunt·er \-ˌhən-tər\ *n* **1** : one that engages in head-hunting **2** : a recruiter of esp. executive personnel

head·hunt·ing \-ˌhən-tiŋ\ *n* : the practice of seeking out and decapitating enemies and preserving their heads as trophies

head·ing \ˈhe-diŋ\ *n* **1** : the compass direction in which the longitudinal axis of a ship or airplane points **2** : something that appears at the top or beginning of something else (as a document)

head·land \ˈhed-lənd, -ˌland\ *n* : PROMONTORY

head·light \-ˌlīt\ *n* : a light mounted on the front of a vehicle to illuminate the road ahead

¹head·line \-ˌlīn\ *n* : a head of a newspaper story or article usu. printed in large type

²headline *vb* **1** : to provide with a headline **2** : to publicize highly **3** : to be a leading performer in

head·lock \-ˌläk\ *n* : a wrestling hold in which one encircles the opponent's head with one arm

¹head·long \-ˈlóŋ\ *adv* **1** : with the head foremost **2** : RECKLESSLY **3** : without delay

²head·long \-ˌlóŋ\ *adj* **1** : PRECIPITATE, RASH ⟨∼ flight⟩ **2** : plunging with the head foremost

head·man \ˈhed-ˈman, -ˌman\ *n* : one who is a leader : CHIEF

head·mas·ter \-ˌmas-tər\ *n* : a man who is head of a private school

head·mis·tress \-ˌmis-trəs\ *n* : a woman who is head of a private school

head of stream : strong driving force : MOMENTUM

head–on \ˈhed-ˈòn, -ˈän\ *adj* : having the front facing in the direction of initial contact or line of sight ⟨∼ collision⟩ — **head–on** *adv*

head·phone \-ˌfōn\ *n* : an earphone held on by a band over the head

head·piece \-ˌpēs\ *n* : a covering for the head

head·pin \-ˌpin\ *n* : a bowling pin that stands foremost in the arrangement of pins

head·quar·ters \-ˌkwòr-tərz\ *n sing or pl* **1** : a place from which a commander exercises command **2** : the administrative center of an enterprise

head·rest \-ˌrest\ *n* **1** : a support for the head **2** : a pad at the top of the back of an automobile seat

head·room \-ˌrüm, -ˌrùm\ *n* : vertical space in which to stand, sit, or move

head–scratcher \-ˌskra-chər\ *n* : PUZZLE, MYSTERY

head·set \-ˌset\ *n* : a pair of headphones

head·ship \-ˌship\ *n* : the position, office, or dignity of a head

heads·man \ˈhedz-mən\ *n* : EXECUTIONER

head·stall \ˈhed-ˌstól\ *n* : a part of a bridle or halter that encircles the head

head·stone \-ˌstōn\ *n* : a memorial stone at the head of a grave

head·strong \ˈhed-ˌstróŋ\ *adj* **1** : not easily restrained **2** : directed by ungovernable will ♦ *Synonyms* UNRULY, INTRACTABLE, WILLFUL, PERTINACIOUS, REFRACTORY, STUBBORN

heads–up \ˈhedz-ˈəp\ *n* : WARNING

head·wait·er \-ˈwā-tər\ *n* : the head of the dining-room staff of a restaurant or hotel

head·wa·ter \-ˌwò-tər, -ˌwä-\ *n* : the source of a stream — usu. used in pl.

head·way \-ˌwā\ *n* : forward motion; *also* : PROGRESS

head·wind \-ˌwind\ *n* : a wind blowing in a direction opposite to a course esp. of a ship or aircraft

head·word \ˈhed-ˌwərd\ *n* **1** : a word or term placed at the beginning **2** : a word qualified by a modifier

head·work \-,wərk\ *n* : mental work or effort : THINKING

heady \'he-dē\ *adj* **head·i·er; -est** **1** : WILLFUL, RASH; *also* : IMPETUOUS **2** : INTOXICATING **3** : SHREWD

heal \'hēl\ *vb* **1** : to make or become healthy, sound, or whole **2** : CURE, REMEDY — **heal·er** *n*

health \'helth\ *n* **1** : sound physical or mental condition; *also* : overall condition of the body ⟨in poor ∼⟩ **2** : WELL-BEING **3** : a toast to someone's health or prosperity

health care *n* : efforts made to maintain or restore health — usu. hyphenated when used attributively

health club *n* : a commercial establishment providing health and fitness facilities and equipment for members

health·ful \'helth-fəl\ *adj* **1** : beneficial to health **2** : HEALTHY — **health·ful·ly** *adv* — **health·ful·ness** *n*

health maintenance organization *n* : HMO

healthy \'hel-thē\ *adj* **health·i·er; -est** **1** : enjoying or typical of good health : WELL **2** : evincing or conducive to health **3** : PROSPEROUS ⟨a ∼ economy⟩; *also* : CONSIDERABLE **2** ⟨a ∼ savings⟩ — **health·i·ly** \-thə-lē\ *adv* — **health·i·ness** \-thē-nəs\ *n*

¹**heap** \'hēp\ *n* **1** : PILE ⟨rubbish ∼⟩; *also* : LOT **5** ⟨a ∼ of fun⟩

²**heap** *vb* **1** : to throw or lay in a heap **2** : to give in large quantities; *also* : to load heavily

hear \'hir\ *vb* **heard** \'hərd\; **hear·ing** **1** : to perceive by the ear **2** : to gain knowledge of by hearing : LEARN **3** : HEED; *also* : ATTEND **4** : to give a legal hearing to or take testimony from — **hear·er** *n*

hear·ing *n* **1** : the process, function, or power of perceiving sound; *esp* : the special sense by which noises and tones are received as stimuli **2** : EARSHOT **3** : opportunity to be heard **4** : a listening to arguments (as in a court); *also* : a session of (as of a legislative committee) in which testimony is taken from witnesses

hear·ken \'här-kən\ *vb* : to give attention : LISTEN ♦ **Synonyms** HEAR, HARK, HEED

hear·say \'hir-,sā\ *n* : RUMOR

hearse \'hərs\ *n* : a vehicle for carrying the dead to the grave

heart \'härt\ *n* **1** : a hollow muscular organ that by rhythmic contraction keeps up the circulation of the blood in the body; *also* : something resembling a heart in shape **2** : any of a suit of playing cards marked with a red figure of a heart; *also*, *pl* : a card game in which the object is to avoid taking tricks containing hearts **3** : the whole personality; *also* : the emotional or moral as distinguished from the intellectual nature **4** : COURAGE **5** : one's innermost being ⟨knew it in his ∼⟩ **6** : CENTER; *also* : the essential part **7** : the younger central part of a compact leafy cluster (as of lettuce) — **heart·ed** \'här-təd\ *adj* — **by heart** : by rote or from memory

heart·ache \-,āk\ *n* : anguish of mind

heart attack *n* : an acute episode of heart disease due to insufficient blood supply to the heart muscle

heart·beat \'härt-,bēt\ *n* : one complete pulsation of the heart

heart·break \-,brāk\ *n* : crushing grief

heart·break·ing \-,brā-kiŋ\ *adj* : causing extreme sorrow or distress — **heart·break·er** \-,brā-kər\ *n* — **heart·break·ing·ly** *adv*

heart·bro·ken \-,brō-kən\ *adj* : overcome by sorrow

heart·burn \-,bərn\ *n* : a burning distress behind the sternum due esp. to the backward flow of acid from the stomach to the esophagus

heart disease *n* : an abnormal organic condition of the heart or of the heart and circulation

heart·en \'här-t⁰n\ *vb* : ENCOURAGE, CHEER

heart·felt \'härt-,felt\ *adj* : deeply felt : SINCERE

hearth \'härth\ *n* **1** : an area (as of brick) in front of a fireplace; *also* : the floor of a fireplace **2** : HOME

hearth·stone \'härth-,stōn\ *n* **1** : stone forming a hearth **2** : HOME

heart·less \'härt-ləs\ *adj* : CRUEL

heart·rend·ing \-,ren-diŋ\ *adj* : HEART-BREAKING

heart·sick \-,sik\ *adj* : very despondent — **heart·sick·ness** *n*

heart–stop·ping \-,stä-piŋ\ *adj* : extremely shocking or exciting

heart·strings \-,striŋz\ *n pl* : the deepest emotions or affections

heart·throb \-,thräb\ *n* **1** : the throb of a heart **2** : sentimental emotion **3** : SWEETHEART **4** : an entertainer noted for his sex appeal

heart–to–heart *adj* : SINCERE, FRANK

heart·warm·ing \'härt-,wòr-miŋ\ *adj* : inspiring sympathetic feeling

heart·wood \-,wùd\ *n* : the older harder nonliving and usu. darker wood of the central part of a tree trunk

¹**hearty** \'här-tē\ *adj* **heart·i·er; -est** **1** : giving full support; *also* : JOVIAL **2** : vigorously healthy **3** : ABUNDANT; *also* : NOURISHING ♦ **Synonyms** SINCERE, WHOLEHEARTED, UNFEIGNED, HEARTFELT — **heart·i·ly** \-tə-lē\ *adv* — **heart·i·ness** \-tē-nəs\ *n*

²**hearty** *n, pl* **heart·ies** : an enthusiastic jovial fellow; *also* : SAILOR

¹**heat** \'hēt\ *vb* **1** : to make or become warm or hot **2** : EXCITE — **heat·ed·ly** *adv* — **heat·er** *n*

²**heat** *n* **1** : a condition of being hot : WARMTH **2** : a form of energy that when added to a body causes the body to rise in temperature, to fuse, to evaporate, or to expand **3** : high temperature **4** : intensity of feeling; *also* : sexual excitement esp. in a female mammal **5** : a preliminary race for narrowing the competition **6** : pungency of flavor **7** *slang* : POLICE **8** : PRESSURE, COERCION; *also* : ABUSE, CRITICISM ⟨took ∼ for my mistakes⟩

heat exchanger *n* : a device (as an automobile radiator) for transferring heat from one fluid to another without allowing them to mix

heat exhaustion *n* : a condition marked by weakness, nausea, dizziness, and profuse sweating resulting from physical exertion in a hot environment

heath \'hēth\ *n* **1** : a tract of wasteland **2** : any of a family of often evergreen shrubby plants (as a blueberry or heather) of wet acid soils — **heathy** *adj*

hea·then \'hē-thən\ *n, pl* **heathens** *or* **heathen** **1** : an unconverted member of a people or nation that does not acknowledge the God of the Bible **2** : an uncivilized or irreligious person — **heathen** *adj* — **hea·then·dom** *n* — **hea·then·ish** *adj* — **hea·then·ism** *n*

heath·er \'he-thər\ *n* : a northern and alpine evergreen heath with usu. lavender flowers — **heath·ery** *adj*

heat lightning *n* : flashes of light without thunder ascribed to distant lightning reflected by high clouds

heat·stroke \'hēt-ˌstrōk\ *n* : a disorder marked esp. by high body temperature without sweating and by collapse that follows prolonged exposure to excessive heat

¹heave \'hēv\ *vb* **heaved** *or* **hove** \'hōv\; **heav·ing** **1** : to rise or lift upward **2** : THROW **3** : to rise and fall rhythmically; *also* : PANT **4** : RETCH **5** : PULL, PUSH — **heav·er** *n*

²heave *n* **1** : an effort to lift or raise **2** : THROW, CAST **3** : an upward motion **4** *pl* : a chronic lung disease of horses marked by difficult breathing and persistent cough

heav·en \'he-vən\ *n* **1** : FIRMAMENT — usu. used in pl. **2** *often cap* : the abode of the Deity and of the blessed dead; *also* : a spiritual state of everlasting communion with God **3** *cap* : GOD 1 **4** : a place of supreme happiness — **heav·en·ly** *adj* — **heav·en·ward** *adv or adj*

¹heavy \'he-vē\ *adj* **heavi·er; -est** **1** : having great weight **2** : hard to bear **3** : SERIOUS **4** : DEEP, PROFOUND ⟨a ~ silence⟩ **5** : burdened with something oppressive; *also* : PREGNANT **6** : SLUGGISH **7** : DRAB; *also* : DOLEFUL **8** : DROWSY **9** : greater than the average of its kind or class **10** : very rich and hard to digest; *also* : not properly raised or leavened **11** : producing goods (as steel) used in the production of other goods — **heavi·ly** \-və-lē\ *adv* — **heavi·ness** \-vē-nəs\ *n*

²heavy *n, pl* **heav·ies** : a theatrical role representing a dignified or imposing person; *also* : a villain esp. in a story

heavy–du·ty \ˌhe-vē-'dü-tē, -'dyü-\ *adj* : able to withstand unusual strain

heavy–hand·ed \-'han-dəd\ *adj* **1** : CLUMSY **2** : OPPRESSIVE, HARSH

heavy–heart·ed \-'här-təd\ *adj* : SADDENED, DESPONDENT

heavy lifting *n* : a burdensome or laborious duty

heavy metal *n* : energetic and highly amplified electronic rock music

heavy–set \ˌhe-vē-'set\ *adj* : stocky and compact in build

heavy water *n* : water enriched in deuterium

heavy·weight \'he-vē-ˌwāt\ *n* : one above average in weight; *esp* : a boxer in an unlimited weight division

Heb *abbr* Hebrews

He·bra·ism \'hē-brā-ˌi-zəm\ *n* : the thought, spirit, or practice characteristic of the Hebrews — **He·bra·ic** \hi-'brā-ik\ *adj*

He·bra·ist \'hē-ˌbrā-ist\ *n* : a specialist in Hebrew and Hebraic studies

He·brew \'hē-brü\ *n* **1** : the language of the Hebrews **2** : a member of or descendant from a group of Semitic peoples; *esp* : ISRAELITE — **Hebrew** *adj*

He·brews \'hē-(ˌ)brüz\ *n* — see BIBLE table

hec·a·tomb \'he-kə-ˌtōm\ *n* : an ancient Greek and Roman sacrifice of 100 oxen or cattle

heck·le \'he-kəl\ *vb* **heck·led; heck·ling** : to harass with questions or gibes : BADGER — **heck·ler** *n*

hect·are \'hek-ˌter\ *n* — see METRIC SYSTEM table

hec·tic \'hek-tik\ *adj* **1** : being hot and flushed **2** : filled with excitement, activity, or confusion — **hec·ti·cal·ly** \-ti-k(ə-)lē\ *adv*

hec·to·gram \'hek-tə-ˌgram\ *n* — see METRIC SYSTEM table

hec·to·li·ter \'hek-tə-ˌlē-tər\ *n* — see METRIC SYSTEM table

hec·to·me·ter \'hek-tə-ˌmē-tər, hek-'tä-mə-tər\ *n* — see METRIC SYSTEM table

hec·tor \'hek-tər\ *vb* [*Hector* bully, fr. *Hector*, champion of Troy in Greek legend] **1** : SWAGGER **2** : to intimidate by bluster or personal pressure

¹hedge \'hej\ *n* **1** : a fence or boundary formed of shrubs or small trees **2** : BARRIER **3** : a means of protection (as against financial loss)

²hedge *vb* **hedged; hedg·ing** **1** : ENCIRCLE **2** : HINDER **3** : to protect oneself financially by a counterbalancing action **4** : to evade the risk of commitment — **hedg·er** *n*

hedge·hog \'hej-ˌhȯg, -ˌhäg\ *n* : a small Old World insect-eating mammal covered with spines; *also* : PORCUPINE

hedge·hop \-ˌhäp\ *vb* : to fly an airplane very close to the ground

hedge·row \-ˌrō\ *n* : a row of shrubs or trees bounding or separating fields

he·do·nism \'hē-də-ˌni-zəm\ *n* [Gk *hēdonē* pleasure] : the doctrine that pleasure is the chief good in life; *also* : a way of life based on this — **he·do·nist** \-nist\ *n* — **he·do·nis·tic** \ˌhēdə-'ni-stik\ *adj*

¹heed \'hēd\ *vb* : to pay attention

²heed *n* : ATTENTION, NOTICE — **heed·ful** \-fəl\ *adj* — **heed·ful·ly** *adv* — **heed·fulness** *n* — **heed·less** *adj* — **heed·less·ly** *adv* — **heed·less·ness** *n*

¹heel \'hēl\ *n* **1** : the hind part of the foot

2 : one of the crusty ends of a loaf of bread **3** : a solid attachment forming the back of the sole of a shoe **4** : a rear, low, or bottom part **5** : a contemptible person

²**heel** vb : to tilt to one side : LIST

¹**heft** \'heft\ n : WEIGHT, HEAVINESS

²**heft** vb : to test the weight of by lifting

hefty \'hef-tē\ adj **heft·i·er; -est 1** : marked by bigness, bulk, and usu. strength **2** : impressively large ⟨got a ~ raise⟩

he·ge·mo·ny \hi-'je-mə-nē\ n : preponderant influence or authority over others : DOMINATION

he·gi·ra \hi-'jī-rə\ n [the Hegira, flight of Muhammad from Mecca in A.D. 622, fr. ML, fr. Ar hijra, lit., departure] : a journey esp. when undertaken to escape a dangerous or undesirable environment

heif·er \'he-fər\ n : a young cow; esp : one that has not had a calf

height \'hīt\ n **1** : the highest part or point **2** : the distance from the bottom to the top of something standing upright **3** : ALTITUDE

height·en \'hī-t²n\ vb **1** : to increase in amount or degree **2** : to make or become high or higher ✦ Synonyms ENHANCE, INTENSIFY, AGGRAVATE, MAGNIFY

Heim·lich maneuver \'hīm-lik-\ n [Henry J. Heimlich b1920 Am. surgeon] : the manual application of sudden upward pressure on the upper abdomen of a choking victim to force a foreign object from the trachea

hei·nous \'hā-nəs\ adj [ME, fr. AF hainus, heinous, fr. haine hate, fr. hair to hate] : hatefully or shockingly evil — **hei·nous·ly** adv — **hei·nous·ness** n

heir \'er\ n : one who inherits or is entitled to inherit property, rank, title, or office — **heir·ship** n

heir apparent n, pl **heirs apparent** : an heir whose right to succeed (as to a title) cannot be taken away if he or she survives the present holder

heir·ess \'er-əs\ n : a female heir esp. to great wealth

heir·loom \'er-ˌlüm\ n **1** : a piece of personal property that descends by inheritance **2** : something handed on from one generation to another

heir presumptive n, pl **heirs presumptive** : an heir whose present right to inherit could be lost through the birth of a nearer relative

heist \'hīst\ vb : to commit armed robbery on; also : STEAL — **heist** n

held past and past part of HOLD

he·li·cal \'he-li-kəl, 'hē-\ adj : SPIRAL

he·li·cop·ter \'he-lə-ˌkäp-tər, 'hē-\ n [F hélicoptère, fr. Gk helik-, helix spiral + pteron wing] : an aircraft that is supported in the air by one or more rotors revolving on substantially vertical axes

he·lio·cen·tric \ˌhē-lē-ō-'sen-trik\ adj : having or relating to the sun as center

he·lio·sphere \'hē-lē-ə-ˌsfir, -ō-\ n : the region in space influenced by the sun or solar wind

he·lio·trope \'hē-lē-ə-ˌtrōp\ n [L heliotropium, fr. Gk hēliotropion, fr. hēlios sun + tropos turn; fr. its flowers' turning toward the sun] : any of a genus of herbs or shrubs related to the forget-me-nots that have small white or purple flowers

he·li·port \'he-lə-ˌpȯrt\ n : a landing and takeoff place for a helicopter

he·li·um \'hē-lē-əm\ n [NL, fr. Gk hēlios sun] : a very light inert gaseous chemical element occurring in various natural gases

he·lix \'hē-liks\ n, pl **he·li·ces** \'he-lə-ˌsēz, 'hē-\ also **he·lix·es** \'hē-lik-səz\ : something spiral in form

hell \'hel\ n **1** : a nether world in which the dead continue to exist **2** : the realm of the devil where the damned suffer everlasting punishment **3** : a place or state of torment or destruction — **hell·ish** adj

hel·la·cious \he-'lā-shəs\ adj **1** : exceptionally powerful or violent **2** : remarkably good **3** : extremely difficult **4** : extraordinarily large

hell-bent \'hel-ˌbent\ adj : stubbornly determined

hell·cat \-ˌkat\ n **1** : WITCH 2 **2** : a violently temperamental person; esp : an ill-tempered woman

hel·le·bore \'he-lə-ˌbȯr\ n **1** : any of a genus of poisonous herbs related to the buttercups; also : the dried root of a hellebore **2** : a poisonous plant related to the lilies; also : its dried roots used in medicine and insecticides

Hel·lene \'he-ˌlēn\ n : GREEK

Hel·le·nism \'he-lə-ˌni-zəm\ n : a body of humanistic and classical ideals associated with ancient Greece — **Hel·len·ic** \he-'le-nik\ adj — **Hel·le·nist** \'he-lə-nist\ n

Hel·le·nis·tic \ˌhe-lə-'nis-tik\ adj : of or relating to Greek history, culture, or art after Alexander the Great

hell–for–leather adv : at full speed

hell·gram·mite \'hel-grə-ˌmīt\ n : an aquatic insect larva that is used as bait in fishing

hell·hole \'hel-ˌhōl\ n : a place of extreme misery or squalor

hel·lion \'hel-yən\ n : a troublesome or mischievous person

hel·lo \hə-'lō, he-\ n, pl **hellos** : an expression of greeting — used interjectionally

helm \'helm\ n **1** : a lever or wheel for steering a ship **2** : a position of control

hel·met \'hel-mət\ n : a protective covering for the head

helms·man \'helmz-mən\ n : the person at the helm : STEERSMAN

helms·per·son \-ˌpər-s²n\ n : HELMSMAN

hel·ot \'he-lət\ n : SLAVE, SERF

¹**help** \'help\ vb **1** : AID, ASSIST **2** : IMPROVE, RELIEVE **3** : to be of use; also : PROMOTE **4** : to change for the better **5** : to refrain from; also : PREVENT **6** : to serve with food or drink ⟨~ yourself⟩ — **help·er** n

²**help** n **1** : AID, ASSISTANCE; also : a source of aid **2** : REMEDY, RELIEF **3**

: one who assists another **4** : EMPLOYEE — **help·ful** \-fəl\ adj — **help·ful·ly** adv — **help·ful·ness** n — **help·less** — **help·less·ly** adv — **help·less·ness** n

helper T cell n : a T cell that participates in the immune response by recognizing foreign antigens and has a protein on its surface to which HIV attaches

help·ing n : a portion of food

help·mate \'help-ˌmāt\ n **1** : HELPER **2** : WIFE

help·meet \-ˌmēt\ n : HELPMATE

hel·ter–skel·ter \ˌhel-tər-'skel-tər\ adv **1** : in undue haste or disorder **2** : HAPHAZARDLY

helve \'helv\ n : a handle of a tool or weapon

Hel·ve·tian \hel-'vē-shən\ adj : SWISS — **Helvetian** n

¹**hem** \'hem\ n **1** : a border of an article (as of cloth) doubled back and stitched down **2** : RIM, MARGIN

²**hem** vb **hemmed**; **hem·ming 1** : to make a hem in sewing; also : BORDER, EDGE **2** : to surround restrictively

he–man \'hē-ˌman\ n : a strong virile man

he·ma·tite \'hē-mə-ˌtīt\ n : a mineral that consists of an oxide of iron and that constitutes an important iron ore

he·ma·tol·o·gy \ˌhē-mə-'tä-lə-jē\ n : a branch of biology that deals with the blood and blood-forming organs — **he·ma·to·log·ic** \-tə-'lä-jik\ also **he·ma·to·log·i·cal** \-ji-kəl\ adj — **he·ma·tol·o·gist** \-'tä-lə-jist\ n

he·ma·to·ma \-'tō-mə\ n, pl **-mas** also **-ma·ta** \-mə-tə\ : a usu. clotted mass of blood forming as a result of a broken blood vessel

heme \'hēm\ n : the deep red iron-containing part of hemoglobin

hemi·sphere \'he-mə-ˌsfir\ n **1** : one of the halves of the earth as divided by the equator into northern and southern parts or by a meridian into eastern and western parts **2** : either of two half spheres formed by a plane through the sphere's center — **hemi·spher·ic** \ˌhe-mə-'sfir-ik, -'sfer-\ or **hemi·spher·i·cal** \-'sfir-i-kəl, -'sfer-\ adj

hem·line \'hem-ˌlīn\ n : the line formed by the lower edge of a garment

hem·lock \'hem-ˌläk\ n **1** : any of several poisonous herbs related to the carrot **2** : an evergreen tree related to the pines; also : its soft light wood

he·mo·glo·bin \'hē-mə-ˌglō-bən\ n : an iron-containing compound found in red blood cells that carries oxygen from the lungs to the body tissues

he·mo·phil·ia \ˌhē-mə-'fi-lē-ə\ n : a hereditary blood defect usu. of males that slows blood clotting with resulting difficulty in stopping bleeding — **he·mo·phil·i·ac** \-lē-ˌak\ adj or n

hem·or·rhage \'hem-rij, -mə-\ n : a large discharge of blood from the blood vessels — **hemorrhage** vb — **hem·or·rhag·ic** \ˌhe-mə-'ra-jik\ adj

hemorrhagic fever n : any of a group of virus diseases characterized chiefly by sudden onset, fever, aching, and bleeding in the internal organs

hem·or·rhoid \'hem-ˌroid, 'he-mə-\ n : a swollen mass of dilated veins at or just within the anus — usu. used in pl.

hemp \'hemp\ n : a tall widely grown Asian herb that is the source of a tough fiber used in rope and of marijuana and hashish from its flowers and leaves; also : the fiber — **hemp·en** \'hem-pən\ adj

hem·stitch \'hem-ˌstich\ vb : to embroider (fabric) by drawing out parallel threads and stitching the exposed threads in groups to form designs

hen \'hen\ n : a female chicken esp. over a year old; also : a female bird

hence \'hens\ adv **1** : AWAY **2** : from this time ⟨four years ∼⟩ **3** : CONSEQUENTLY **4** : from this source or origin

hence·forth \hens-ˌfȯrth\ adv : from this point on

hence·for·ward \-ˈfȯr-wərd\ adv : HENCEFORTH

hench·man \'hench-mən\ n [ME hengestman groom, fr. hengest stallion] : a trusted follower or supporter

hen·na \'he-nə\ n **1** : an Old World tropical shrub with fragrant white flowers; also : a reddish brown dye obtained from its leaves and used esp. on hair **2** : the color of henna dye

hen·peck \'hen-ˌpek\ vb : to nag and boss one's husband

hep \'hep\ adj : HIP

hep·a·rin \'he-pə-rən\ n : a compound found esp. in liver that slows the clotting of blood and is used medically

he·pat·ic \hi-'pa-tik\ adj : of, relating to, or associated with the liver

he·pat·i·ca \hi-'pa-ti-kə\ n : any of a genus of herbs related to the buttercups that have lobed leaves and delicate white, pink, or bluish flowers

hep·a·ti·tis \ˌhe-pə-'tī-təs\ n, pl **-tit·i·des** \-'ti-tə-ˌdēz\ : inflammation of the liver; also : a virus disease of which this is a feature

hep·tam·e·ter \hep-'ta-mə-tər\ n : a line of verse containing seven metrical feet

hep·tath·lon \hep-'tath-lən, -ˌlän\ n : a 7-event athletic contest for women

¹**her** \'hər\ adj : of or relating to her or herself

²**her** pron objective case of SHE

¹**her·ald** \'her-əld\ n **1** : an official crier or messenger **2** : HARBINGER **3** : ANNOUNCER **4** : ADVOCATE

²**herald** vb **1** : to give notice of **2** : HAIL, GREET; also : PUBLICIZE

he·ral·dic \he-'ral-dik, hə-\ adj : of or relating to heralds or heraldry

her·ald·ry \'her-əl-drē\ n, pl **-ries 1** : the practice of devising and granting armorial insignia and of tracing genealogies **2** : INSIGNIA **3** : PAGEANTRY

herb \'ərb, 'hərb\ n **1** : a seed plant that lacks woody tissue and dies to the ground at the end of a growing season **2** : a plant or plant part valued for medicinal or savory qualities — **her·ba·ceous** \ˌər-'bā-shəs, ˌhər-\ adj

herb·age \'ər-bij, 'hər-\ *n* : green plants esp. when used or fit for grazing

her·bal \'ər-bəl, 'hər-\ *adj* : of, relating to, utilizing, or made of herbs

herb·al·ist \'ər-bə-list, 'hər-\ *n* **1** : a person who practices healing by the use of herbs **2** : a person who collects or grows herbs

her·bar·i·um \ˌər-'ber-ē-əm, ˌhər-\ *n, pl* **-ia** \-ē-ə\ **1** : a collection of dried plant specimens **2** : a place that houses an herbarium

her·bi·cide \'ər-bə-ˌsīd, 'hər-\ *n* : an agent used to destroy or inhibit plant growth — **her·bi·cid·al** \ˌər-bə-'sī-dᵊl, ˌhər-\ *adj*

her·biv·o·rous \ˌər-'bi-və-rəs, ˌhər-\ *adj* : feeding on plants — **her·bi·vore** \'ər-bə-ˌvȯr, 'hər-\ *n*

her·cu·le·an \ˌhər-kyə-'lē-ən, ˌhər-'kyü-lē-\ *adj, often cap* [*Hercules*, hero of Greek myth renowned for his strength] : of extraordinary power, size, or difficulty

¹herd \'hərd\ *n* **1** : a group of animals of one kind kept or living together **2** : a group of people with a common bond ⟨a ~ of tourists⟩ **3** : MOB

²herd *vb* : to assemble or move in a herd — **herd·er** *n*

herds·man \'hərdz-mən\ *n* : one who manages, breeds, or tends livestock

¹here \'hir\ *adv* **1** : in or at this place; *also* : NOW **2** : at or in this point, particular, or case **3** : in the present life or state **4** : to this place ⟨come ~⟩

²here *n* : this place ⟨get away from ~⟩

here·abouts \'hir-ə-ˌbaùts\ *or* **here·about** \-ˌbaùt\ *adv* : in this vicinity

¹here·af·ter \hir-'af-tər\ *adv* **1** : after this in sequence or in time **2** : in some future time or state

²hereafter *n, often cap* **1** : FUTURE **2** : an existence beyond earthly life

here·by \hir-'bī\ *adv* : by means of this

he·red·i·tary \hə-'re-də-ˌter-ē\ *adj* **1** : genetically passed or passable from parent to offspring **2** : passing by inheritance; *also* : having title or possession through inheritance **3** : of a kind established by tradition

he·red·i·ty \-də-tē\ *n* : the characteristics and potentialities genetically derived from one's ancestors; *also* : the passing of these from ancestor to descendant

Her·e·ford \'hər-fərd\ *n* : any of a breed of red-coated beef cattle with white faces and markings

here·in \hir-'in\ *adv* : in this

here·of \-'ȯv, -'äv\ *adv* : of this

here·on \-'ȯn, -'än\ *adv* : on this

here·sy \'her-ə-sē\ *n, pl* **-sies** [ME *heresie*, fr. AF, fr. LL *haeresis*, fr. LGk *hairesis*, fr. Gk, action of taking, choice, sect, fr. *hairein* to take] **1** : adherence to a religious opinion contrary to church dogma **2** : an opinion or doctrine contrary to church dogma **3** : dissent from a dominant theory, opinion, or practice — **her·e·tic** \-ˌtik\ *n* — **he·ret·i·cal** \hə-'re-ti-kəl\ *adj*

here·to \hir-'tü\ *adv* : to this document

here·to·fore \'hir-tə-ˌfȯr\ *adv* : up to this time

here·un·der \hir-'ən-dər\ *adv* : under this or according to this writing

here·un·to \hir-'ən-tü\ *adv* : to this

here·upon \'hir-ə-ˌpȯn, -ˌpän\ *adv* : on this or immediately after this

here·with \'hir-'with, -'with\ *adv* **1** : with this **2** : HEREBY

her·i·ta·ble \'her-ə-tə-bəl\ *adj* : capable of being inherited

her·i·tage \'her-ə-tij\ *n* **1** : property that descends to an heir **2** : LEGACY **3** : BIRTHRIGHT

her·maph·ro·dite \(ˌ)hər-'ma-frə-ˌdīt\ *n* : an animal or plant having both male and female reproductive organs — **hermaphrodite** *adj* — **her·maph·ro·dit·ic** \(ˌ)hər-ˌma-frə-'di-tik\ *adj*

her·met·ic \hər-'me-tik\ *also* **her·met·i·cal** \-ti-kəl\ *adj* : AIRTIGHT — **her·met·i·cal·ly** \-ti-k(ə-)lē\ *adv*

her·mit \'hər-mət\ *n* [ME *heremite*, *eremite*, fr. AF, fr. LL *eremita*, fr. LGk *erēmitēs*, fr. Gk, adj., living in the desert, fr. *erēmia* desert, fr. *erēmos* desolate] : one who lives in solitude esp. for religious reasons

her·mit·age \-mə-tij\ *n* **1** : the dwelling of a hermit **2** : a secluded dwelling

hermit crab *n* : any of numerous crabs that occupy empty mollusk shells

her·nia \'hər-nē-ə\ *n, pl* **-nias** *or* **-ni·ae** \-nē-ˌē, -nē-ˌī\ : a protrusion of a bodily part (as a loop of intestine) into a pouch of the weakened wall of a cavity in which it is normally enclosed — **her·ni·ate** \-nē-ˌāt\ *vb* — **her·ni·a·tion** \ˌhər-nē-'ā-shən\ *n*

he·ro \'hē-rō\ *n, pl* **heroes** **1** : a mythological or legendary figure of great strength or ability **2** : a man admired for his achievements and qualities **3** : the chief male character in a literary or dramatic work **4** *pl usu* **heros** : SUBMARINE **2** — **he·ro·ic** \hi-'rō-ik\ *adj* — **he·ro·i·cal·ly** \-i-k(ə-)lē\ *adv*

heroic couplet *n* : a rhyming couplet in iambic pentameter

he·ro·ics \hi-'rō-iks\ *n pl* : heroic or showy behavior

her·o·in \'her-ə-wən\ *n* : an illicit addictive narcotic drug made from morphine

her·o·ine \'her-ə-wən\ *n* **1** : a woman admired for her achievements and qualities **2** : the chief female character in a literary or dramatic work

her·o·ism \'her-ə-ˌwi-zəm\ *n* **1** : heroic conduct **2** : the qualities of a hero ♦ *Synonyms* VALOR, PROWESS, GALLANTRY

her·on \'her-ən\ *n, pl* **herons** *also* **heron** : any of various long-legged long-billed wading birds with soft plumage

her·pes \'hər-pēz\ *n* : any of several virus diseases characterized by the formation of blisters on the skin or mucous membranes

herpes sim·plex \-'sim-ˌpleks\ *n* : either of two virus diseases marked in one by watery blisters above the waist (as on the mouth and lips) and in the other on the sex organs

herpes zos·ter \-'zäs-tər\ *n* : SHINGLES

her·pe·tol·o·gy \,hər-pə-'tä-lə-jē\ *n* : a branch of zoology dealing with reptiles and amphibians — **her·pe·tol·o·gist** \,hər-pə-'tä-lə-jist\ *n*

her·ring \'her-iŋ\ *n, pl* **herring** *or* **her·rings** : a valuable narrow-bodied food fish of the No. Atlantic; *also* : a related fish of the No. Pacific harvested esp. for its roe

her·ring·bone \'her-iŋ-,bōn\ *n* : a pattern made up of rows of parallel lines with adjacent rows slanting in reverse directions; *also* : a twilled fabric with this pattern

hers \'hərz\ *pron* : one or the ones belonging to her

her·self \hər-'self\ *pron* : SHE, HER — used reflexively, for emphasis, or in absolute constructions

hertz \'hərts, 'herts\ *n, pl* **hertz** : a unit of frequency equal to one cycle per second

hes·i·tant \'he-zə-tənt\ *adj* : tending to hesitate — **hes·i·tance** \-təns\ *n* — **hes·i·tan·cy** \-tən-sē\ *n* — **hes·i·tant·ly** *adv*

hes·i·tate \'he-zə-,tāt\ *vb* **-tat·ed; -tat·ing** 1 : to hold back (as in doubt) 2 : PAUSE ◆ *Synonyms* WAVER, VACILLATE, FALTER, SHILLY-SHALLY — **hes·i·ta·tion** \,he-zə-'tā-shən\ *n*

het·ero·dox \'he-tə-rə-,däks\ *adj* 1 : differing from an acknowledged standard 2 : holding unorthodox opinions — **het·er·o·doxy** \-,däk-sē\ *n*

het·er·o·ge·neous \,he-tə-rə-'jē-nē-əs, -nyəs\ *adj* : consisting of dissimilar ingredients or constituents : MIXED — **het·er·o·ge·ne·ity** \-jə-'nē-ə-tē\ *n* — **het·er·o·ge·neous·ly** *adv*

het·ero·glos·sia \,he-tə-rō-'glä-sē-ə, -'glö-\ *n* : a diversity of voices, styles of discourse, or points of view in a literary work

het·ero·sex·ism \,he-tə-rō-'sek-si-zəm\ *n* : discrimination or prejudice by heterosexuals against homosexuals

het·ero·sex·u·al \,he-tə-rō-,sek-shə-wəl\ *adj* 1 : of, relating to, or marked by sexual interest in the opposite sex; *also* : of, relating to, or involving sexual intercourse between members of opposite sex 2 : of or relating to different sexes — **heterosexual** *n* — **het·ero·sex·u·al·i·ty** \-,sek-shə-'wa-lə-tē\ *n*

hew \'hyü\ *vb* **hewed; hewed** *or* **hewn** \'hyün\; **hew·ing** 1 : to cut or fell with blows (as of an ax) 2 : to give shape to with or as if with an ax 3 : to conform strictly — **hew·er** *n*

HEW *abbr* Department of Health, Education, and Welfare

¹**hex** \'heks\ *vb* 1 : to practice witchcraft 2 : JINX

²**hex** *n* : SPELL, JINX

³**hex** *adj* : HEXAGONAL

⁴**hex** *abbr* hexagon

hexa·gon \'hek-sə-,gän\ *n* [ultim. fr. Gk *hex* six + *gōnia* angle] : a polygon having six angles and six sides — **hex·ag·o·nal** \hek-'sa-gən-ᵊl\ *adj*

hex·am·e·ter \hek-'sa-mə-tər\ *n* : a line of verse containing six metrical feet

hey \'hā\ *interj* — used esp. to call attention or to express doubt, surprise, or joy

hey·day \'hā-,dā\ *n* : a period of greatest strength, vigor, or prosperity

hf *abbr* half

Hf *symbol* hafnium

HF *abbr* high frequency

hg *abbr* hectogram

Hg *symbol* [NL *hydrargyrum,* lit., water silver] mercury

hgt *abbr* height

hgwy *abbr* highway

HH *abbr* 1 Her Highness 2 His Highness 3 His Holiness

HHS *abbr* Department of Health and Human Services

HI *abbr* 1 Hawaii 2 humidity index

hi·a·tus \hī-'ā-təs\ *n* [L, fr. *hiare* to yawn] 1 : a break in an object : GAP 2 : a period when something is suspended or interrupted

hi·ba·chi \hi-'bä-chē\ *n* [Jp] : a charcoal brazier

hi·ber·nate \'hī-bər-,nāt\ *vb* **-nat·ed; -nat·ing** : to pass the winter in a torpid or resting state — **hi·ber·na·tion** \,hī-bər-'nā-shən\ *n* — **hi·ber·na·tor** \'hī-bər-,nā-tər\ *n*

hi·bis·cus \hī-'bis-kəs, hə-\ *n* : any of a genus of herbs, shrubs, and trees related to the mallows and noted for large showy flowers

hic·cup *also* **hic·cough** \'hi-(,)kəp\ *n* 1 : a spasmodic breathing movement checked by sudden closing of the glottis accompanied by a peculiar sound; *also, pl* : an attack of hiccuping 2 : a slight irregularity, error, or malfunction 3 : a brief minor interruption or change — **hiccup** *vb*

hick \'hik\ *n* [*Hick,* nickname for *Richard*] : an unsophisticated provincial person — **hick** *adj*

hick·o·ry \'hi-kə-rē\ *n, pl* **-ries** : any of a genus of No. American hardwood trees related to the walnuts; *also* : the wood of a hickory — **hickory** *adj*

hi·dal·go \hi-'dal-gō\ *n, pl* **-gos** *often cap* [Sp, fr. earlier *fijo dalgo,* lit., son of something] : a member of the lower nobility of Spain

hidden tax *n* 1 : a tax ultimately paid by someone other than the person on whom it is formally levied 2 : an economic injustice that reduces one's income or buying power

¹**hide** \'hīd\ *vb* **hid** \'hid\; **hid·den** \'hid-ᵊn\ *or* **hid; hid·ing** 1 : to put or remain out of sight 2 : to conceal for shelter or protection; *also* : to seek protection 3 : to keep secret 4 : to turn away in shame or anger — **hid·er** *n*

²**hide** *n* : the skin of an animal

hide-and-seek \,hīd-ᵊn-'sēk\ *n* : a children's game in which everyone hides from one player who tries to find them

hide·away \'hī-də-,wā\ *n* : HIDEOUT

hide·bound \'hīd-,baund\ *adj* : being inflexible or conservative

hid·eous \'hi-dē-əs\ adj [ME hidous, fr. AF hidus, hisdos, fr. hisde, hide terror] **1** : offensive to one of the senses : UGLY **2** : morally offensive : SHOCKING ♦ Synonyms GHASTLY, GRISLY, GRUESOME, HORRIBLE, LURID, MACABRE — hid·eous·ly adv — hid·eous·ness n

hide-out \'hīd-ˌaut\ n : a place of refuge or concealment

hie \'hī\ vb hied; hy·ing or hie·ing : HASTEN

hi·er·ar·chy \'hī-ə-ˌrär-kē\ n, pl -chies **1** : a ruling body of clergy organized into ranks **2** : persons or things arranged in a graded series — hi·er·ar·chi·cal \ˌhī-ə-'rär-ki-kəl\ adj — hi·er·ar·chi·cal·ly \-k(ə-)lē\ adv

hi·er·o·glyph·ic \ˌhī-ə-rə-'gli-fik\ n [MF hieroglyphique, adj., ultim. fr. Gk hieroglyphikos, fr. hieros sacred + glyphein to carve] **1** : a character in a system of picture writing (as of the ancient Egyptians) **2** : a symbol or sign difficult to decipher

hi–fi \'hī-'fī\ n **1** : HIGH FIDELITY **2** : equipment for reproduction of sound with high fidelity

hig·gle·dy–pig·gle·dy \ˌhi-gəl-dē-'pi-gəl-dē\ adv : in confusion

¹high \'hī\ adj **1** : ELEVATED; also : TALL **2** : advanced toward fullness or culmination; also : slightly tainted **3** : advanced esp. in complexity ⟨∼er mathematics⟩ **4** : long past **5** : SHRILL, SHARP **6** : far from the equator ⟨∼ latitudes⟩ **7** : exalted in character **8** : of greater degree, size, or amount than average ⟨∼ in cholesterol⟩ **9** : of relatively great importance **10** : FORCIBLE, STRONG ⟨∼ winds⟩ **11** : showing elation or excitement **12** : INTOXICATED; also : excited or stupefied by or as if by a drug — high·ly adv

²high adv **1** : at or to a high place or degree **2** : LUXURIOUSLY ⟨living ∼⟩

³high n **1** : an elevated place **2** : a region of high barometric pressure **3** : a high point or level **4** : the gear of a vehicle giving the highest speed **5** : an excited or stupefied state produced by or as if by a drug

high·ball \'hī-ˌbȯl\ n : a usu. tall drink of liquor mixed with water or a carbonated beverage

high beam n : a vehicle headlight with a long-range focus

high·born \'hī-'bȯrn\ adj : of noble birth

high·boy \-ˌbȯi\ n : a high chest of drawers mounted on a base with legs

high·bred \-'bred\ adj : coming from superior stock

high·brow \-ˌbraú\ n : a person of superior learning or culture — highbrow adj — high·brow·ism \-ˌbraú-ˌi-zəm\ n

high–definition adj : being or relating to a television system with twice as many scan lines per frame as a conventional system

high–density li·po·pro·tein \-ˌlī-pō-'prō-tēn, -ˌli-\ n : HDL

high·er–up \ˌhī-ər-'əp\ n : a superior officer or official

high·fa·lu·tin \ˌhī-fə-'lü-t³n\ adj : PRETENTIOUS, POMPOUS

high fashion n **1** : HIGH STYLE **2** : HAUTE COUTURE

high fidelity n : the reproduction of sound or image with a high degree of faithfulness to the original

high five n : a slapping of upraised right hands by two people (as in celebration) — high–five vb

high–flown \'hī-'flōn\ adj **1** : EXALTED **2** : BOMBASTIC

high frequency n : a radio frequency between 3 and 30 megahertz

high gear n **1** : HIGH **4 2** : a state of intense or maximum activity

high–hand·ed \'hī-'han-dəd\ adj : OVERBEARING — high–hand·ed·ly adv — high–hand·ed·ness n

high–hat \-'hat\ adj : SUPERCILIOUS, SNOBBISH — high–hat vb

high·land \'hī-lənd\ n : elevated or mountainous land

high·land·er \-lən-dər\ n **1** : an inhabitant of a highland **2** cap : an inhabitant of the Scottish Highlands

high–lev·el \'hī-'le-vəl\ adj **1** : being of high importance or rank **2** : being or relating to highly concentrated and environmentally hazardous nuclear waste

¹high·light \-ˌlīt\ n : an event or detail of major importance

²highlight vb **1** : EMPHASIZE **2** : to constitute a highlight of **3** : to mark (text) with a highlighter **4** : to cause to be displayed in a way that stands out on a computer screen

high·light·er \-ˌlīt-ər\ n : a pen with transparent ink used for marking text passages

high–mind·ed \-'mīn-dəd\ adj : marked by elevated principles and feelings — high–mind·ed·ness n

high·ness \'hī-nəs\ n **1** : the quality or state of being high **2** — used as a title (as for kings)

high–pres·sure \-'pre-shər\ adj : using or involving aggressive and insistent sales techniques

high–rise \-'rīz\ adj **1** : having several stories and being equipped with elevators ⟨∼ apartments⟩ **2** : of or relating to high-rise buildings

high road n : HIGHWAY

high school n : a school usu. including grades 9 to 12 or 10 to 12

high sea n : the open sea outside territorial waters — usu. used in pl.

high–sound·ing \'hī-'saún-diŋ\ adj : POMPOUS, IMPOSING

high–spir·it·ed \-'spir-ə-təd\ adj : characterized by a bold or energetic spirit

high–strung \-'strəŋ\ adj : having an extremely nervous or sensitive temperament

high style n : the newest in fashion or design

high·tail \'hī-ˌtāl\ vb : to retreat at full speed

high tech \-'tek\ n : HIGH TECHNOLOGY

high technology n : technology involving the use of advanced devices

high–ten·sion \'hī-'ten-chən\ *adj* : having or using a high voltage

high–test \-'test\ *adj* : having a high octane number

high–tick·et \-'ti-kət\ *adj* : EXPENSIVE

high–toned \-'tōnd\ *adj* **1** : high in social, moral, or intellectual quality **2** : PRETENTIOUS, POMPOUS

high·way \'hī-,wā\ *n* : a main direct road

high·way·man \'hī-,wā-mən\ *n* : a thief who robs travelers on a road

hi·jack *also* **high·jack** \'hī-,jak\ *vb* : to steal esp. by stopping a vehicle on the highway; *also* : to commandeer a flying airplane — **hijack** *n* — **hi·jack·er** *n*

¹**hike** \'hīk\ *vb* **hiked**; **hik·ing 1** : to move or raise with a sudden motion **2** : to take a long walk — **hik·er** *n*

²**hike** *n* **1** : a long walk **2** : RISE, INCREASE ⟨price ∼⟩

hi·lar·i·ous \hi-'ler-ē-əs, hī-\ *adj* : marked by or providing boisterous merriment — **hi·lar·i·ous·ly** *adv* — **hi·lar·i·ty** \-ə-tē\ *n*

hill \'hil\ *n* **1** : a usu. rounded elevation of land **2** : a little heap or mound (as of earth) — **hilly** *adj*

hill·bil·ly \'hil-,bi-lē\ *n, pl* **-lies** : a person from a backwoods area

hill·ock \'hi-lək\ *n* : a small hill

hill·side \'hil-,sīd\ *n* : the part of a hill between the summit and the foot

hill·top \-,täp\ *n* : the top of a hill

hilt \'hilt\ *n* : a handle esp. of a sword or dagger

him \'him\ *pron, objective case of* HE

him·self \him-'self\ *pron* : HE, HIM — used reflexively, for emphasis, or in absolute constructions

hind \'hīnd\ *n, pl* **hinds** *also* **hind** : a female of a common Eurasian deer

²**hind** *adj* : REAR ⟨the dog's ∼ legs⟩

¹**hin·der** \'hin-dər\ *vb* **1** : to impede the progress of **2** : to hold back ✦ *Synonyms* OBSTRUCT, BLOCK, BAR, IMPEDE

²**hin·der** \'hin-dər\ *adj* : HIND

Hin·di \'hin-dē\ *n* : a literary and official language of northern India

hind·most \'hīnd-,mōst\ *adj* : farthest to the rear

hind·quar·ter \-,kwȯr-tər\ *n* **1** : one side of the back half of the carcass of a quadruped **2** *pl* : the part of the body of a quadruped behind the junction of hind limbs and trunk

hin·drance \'hin-drəns\ *n* **1** : the state of being hindered **2** : IMPEDIMENT 1 **3** : the action of hindering

hind·sight \'hīnd-,sīt\ *n* : understanding of an event after it has happened

Hindu–Arabic *adj* : relating to, being, or composed of Arabic numerals

Hin·du·ism \'hin-dü-,i-zəm\ *n* : a body of religious beliefs and practices native to India — **Hin·du** *n or adj*

hind wing *n* : either of the posterior wings of a 4-winged insect

¹**hinge** \'hinj\ *n* : a jointed device on which a swinging part (as a door, gate, or lid) turns

²**hinge** *vb* **hinged**; **hing·ing 1** : to attach by or furnish with hinges **2** : to be contingent on a single consideration

hint \'hint\ *n* **1** : an indirect or summary suggestion **2** : CLUE **3** : a very small amount ✦ *Synonyms* DASH, SOUPÇON, SUSPICION, TINCTURE, TOUCH — **hint** *vb*

hin·ter·land \'hin-tər-,land\ *n* **1** : a region behind a coast **2** : a region remote from cities

¹**hip** \'hip\ *n* : the fruit of a rose

²**hip** *n* **1** : the part of the body on either side below the waist consisting of the side of the pelvis and the upper thigh **2** : HIP JOINT

³**hip** *adj* **hip·per**; **hip·pest** : keenly aware of or interested in the newest developments or styles — **hip·ness** *n*

⁴**hip** *vb* **hipped**; **hip·ping** : TELL, INFORM

hip·bone \'hip-'bōn, -,bōn\ *n* : the large flaring bone that makes a lateral half of the pelvis in mammals

hip–hop \'hip-,häp\ *n* **1** : a subculture esp. of inner-city youths who are devotees of rap music **2** : the stylized rhythmic music that accompanies rap — **hip–hop** *adj*

hip–hug·gers \'hip-,hə-gərz\ *n pl* : low-slung close-fitting pants that rest on the hips

hip joint *n* : the articulation between the femur and the hipbone

hipped \'hipt\ *adj* : having hips esp. of a specified kind ⟨broad-*hipped*⟩

hip·pie *or* **hip·py** \'hi-pē\ *n, pl* **hippies** : a usu. young person who rejects established mores and advocates nonviolence; *also* : a long-haired unconventionally dressed young person

hip·po \'hi-pō\ *n, pl* **hippos** : HIPPOPOTAMUS

hip·po·drome \'hi-pə-,drōm\ *n* : an arena for equestrian performances

hip·po·pot·a·mus \,hi-pə-'pä-tə-məs\ *n, pl* **-mus·es** *or* **-mi** \-,mī\ [L, fr. Gk *hippopotamos*, alter. of *hippos potamios*, lit., river horse] : a large thick-skinned aquatic mammal of sub-Saharan Africa that is related to the swine

¹**hire** \'hī-(ə)r\ *n* **1** : payment for labor or personal services : WAGES **2** : EMPLOYMENT **3** : one who is hired

²**hire** *vb* **hired**; **hir·ing 1** : to employ for pay **2** : to engage the temporary use of for pay **3** : to take employment

hire·ling \'hī-(ə)r-liŋ\ *n* : a hired person; *esp* : one with mercenary motives

hir·sute \'hər-,süt, 'hir-\ *adj* : HAIRY

¹**his** \'hiz\ *adj* : of or relating to him or himself

²**his** *pron* : one or the ones belonging to him

His·pan·ic \hi-'spa-nik\ *adj* : of, relating to, or being a person of Latin-American descent living in the U.S. — **Hispanic** *n*

hiss \'his\ *vb* : to make a sharp sibilant sound; *also* : to express disapproval of by hissing — **hiss** *n*

hissy fit \'hi-sē-\ *n* : TANTRUM

hist *abbr* historian; historical; history

his·ta·mine \'his-tə-,mēn, -mən\ *n* : a compound widespread in animal tissues that plays a major role in allergic reactions (as hay fever)

his·to·gram \'his-tə-ˌgram\ *n* : a representation of statistical data by rectangles whose widths represent class intervals and whose heights usu. represent corresponding frequencies

his·tol·o·gy \his-'tä-lə-jē\ *n, pl* **-gies 1** : a branch of anatomy dealing with tissue structure **2** : tissue structure or organization — **his·to·log·i·cal** \ˌhis-tə-'lä-ji-kəl\ *or* **his·to·log·ic** \-'lä-jik\ *adj* — **his·tol·o·gist** \-'tä-lə-jist\ *n*

his·to·ri·an \hi-'stȯr-ē-ən\ *n* : a student or writer of history

his·to·ric·i·ty \ˌhis-tə-'ri-sə-tē\ *n* : historical actuality

his·to·ri·og·ra·pher \hi-ˌstȯr-ē-'ä-grə-fər\ *n* : HISTORIAN

his·to·ry \'his-tə-rē\ *n, pl* **-ries** [ultim. fr. L *historia*, fr. Gk, inquiry, history, fr. *histōr, istōr* knowing, learned] **1** : a chronological record of significant events often with an explanation of their causes **2** : a branch of knowledge that records and explains past events **3** : events that form the subject matter of history **4** : an established record ⟨a convict's ~ of violence⟩ — **his·tor·ic** \hi-'stȯr-ik\ *adj* — **his·tor·i·cal** \-i-kəl\ *adj* — **his·tor·i·cal·ly** \-k(ə-)lē\ *adv*

his·tri·on·ic \ˌhis-trē-'ä-nik\ *adj* [LL *histrionicus*, fr. L *histrio* actor] **1** : deliberately affected **2** : of or relating to actors, acting, or the theater — **his·tri·on·i·cal·ly** \-ni-k(ə-)lē\ *adv*

his·tri·on·ics \-niks\ *n pl* **1** : theatrical performances **2** : deliberate display of emotion for effect

¹hit \'hit\ *vb* **hit; hit·ting 1** : to reach with a blow : STRIKE; *also* : to arrive with a force like a blow ⟨the storm ~⟩ **2** : to make or bring into contact : COLLIDE **3** : to affect detrimentally ⟨was ~ by the flu⟩ **4** : to make a request of **5** : to come upon **6** : to accord with : SUIT **7** : REACH, ATTAIN **8** : to indulge in often to excess — **hit·ter** *n*

²hit *n* **1** : an act or instance of hitting or being hit **2** : a great success **3** : BASE HIT **4** : a dose of a drug **5** : a murder committed by a gangster **6** : an instance of connecting to a particular Web site **7** : a successful match in a search (as of the Internet)

¹hitch \'hich\ *vb* **1** : to move by jerks **2** : to catch or fasten esp. by a hook or knot **3** : HITCHHIKE

²hitch *n* **1** : JERK, PULL **2** : a sudden halt **3** : a connection between something towed and its mover **4** : KNOT

hitch·hike \'hich-ˌhīk\ *vb* : to travel by securing free rides from passing vehicles — **hitch·hik·er** *n*

¹hith·er \'hi-thər\ *adv* : to this place

²hither *adj* : being on the near or adjacent side

hith·er·to \-ˌtü\ *adv* : up to this time

HIV \ˌāch-(ˌ)ī-'vē\ *n* [*h*uman *i*mmunodeficiency *v*irus] : any of several retroviruses that infect and destroy helper T cells causing the great reduction in their numbers that is diagnostic of AIDS

hive \'hīv\ *n* **1** : a container for housing honeybees **2** : a colony of bees **3** : a place swarming with busy occupants — **hive** *vb*

hives \'hīvz\ *n sing or pl* : an allergic disorder marked by raised itching patches on the skin or mucous membranes

hl *abbr* hectoliter

HL *abbr* House of Lords

hm *abbr* hectometer

HM *abbr* **1** Her Majesty; Her Majesty's **2** His Majesty; His Majesty's

HMO \ˌāch-(ˌ)em-'ō\ *n* [*h*ealth *m*aintenance *o*rganization] : a comprehensive health-care organization financed by periodic fixed payments by voluntarily enrolled individuals and families

HMS *abbr* **1** Her Majesty's ship **2** His Majesty's ship

Ho *symbol* holmium

hoa·gie *also* **hoa·gy** \'hō-gē\ *n, pl* **hoa·gies** : SUBMARINE 2

hoard \'hȯrd\ *n* : a hidden accumulation — **hoard** *vb* — **hoard·er** *n*

hoar·frost \'hȯr-ˌfrȯst\ *n* : FROST 2

hoarse \'hȯrs\ *adj* **hoars·er; hoars·est 1** : rough and harsh in sound **2** : having a grating voice — **hoarse·ly** *adv* — **hoarse·ness** *n*

hoary \'hȯr-ē\ *adj* **hoar·i·er; -est 1** : gray or white with or as if with age **2** : ANCIENT — **hoar·i·ness** \'hȯr-ē-nəs\ *n*

hoax \'hōks\ *n* : an act intended to trick or dupe; *also* : something accepted or established by fraud — **hoax** *vb* — **hoax·er** *n*

hob \'häb\ *n* : MISCHIEF, TROUBLE ⟨raising ~⟩

¹hob·ble \'hä-bəl\ *vb* **hob·bled; hob·bling 1** : to limp along; *also* : to make lame **2** : FETTER

²hobble *n* **1** : a hobbling movement **2** : something used to hobble an animal

hob·by \'hä-bē\ *n, pl* **hobbies** : a pursuit or interest engaged in for relaxation — **hob·by·ist** \-ist\ *n*

hob·by·horse \'hä-bē-ˌhȯrs\ *n* **1** : a stick with a horse's head on which children pretend to ride **2** : a toy horse mounted on rockers **3** : a topic to which one constantly reverts

hob·gob·lin \'häb-ˌgäb-lən\ *n* **1** : a mischievous goblin **2** : BOGEY 1

hob·nail \-ˌnāl\ *n* : a short large-headed nail for studding shoe soles — **hob·nailed** \-ˌnāld\ *adj*

hob·nob \-ˌnäb\ *vb* **hob·nobbed; hob·nob·bing** : to associate familiarly

ho·bo \'hō-bō\ *n, pl* **hoboes** *also* **hobos** : TRAMP 2

¹hock \'häk\ *n* : a joint or region in the hind limb of a quadruped just above the foot and corresponding to the human ankle

²hock *n* [D *hok* pen, prison] : ²PAWN 2 ⟨got his watch out of ~⟩; *also* : DEBT 3 — **hock** *vb*

hock·ey \'hä-kē\ *n* **1** : FIELD HOCKEY **2** : ICE HOCKEY

ho·cus–po·cus \ˌhō-kəs-'pō-kəs\ *n* **1** : SLEIGHT OF HAND **2** : nonsense or sham used to conceal deception

hod \\'häd\\ *n* : a long-handled carrier for mortar or bricks

hodge-podge \\'häj-ˌpäj\\ *n* : a heterogeneous mixture : JUMBLE

Hodgkin's disease \\'häj-kinz-\\ *n* : a neoplastic disease of lymphoid tissue characterized esp. by enlargement of lymph ·nodes, spleen, and liver

hoe \\'hō\\ *n* : a long-handled implement with a thin flat blade used esp. for cultivating, weeding, or loosening the earth around plants — **hoe** *vb*

hoe-cake \\'hō-ˌkāk\\ *n* : a small cornmeal cake

hoe-down \\-ˌdaůn\\ *n* **1** : SQUARE DANCE **2** : a gathering featuring hoedowns

¹**hog** \\'hóg, 'häg\\ *n*, *pl* **hogs** *also* **hog** **1** : a domestic swine esp. when grown **2** : a selfish, gluttonous, or filthy person — **hog-gish** *adj*

²**hog** *vb* **hogged; hog-ging** : to take or hold selfishly

ho-gan \\'hō-ˌgän\\ *n* : a Navajo Indian dwelling usu. made of logs and mud

hog-back \\'hóg-ˌbak, 'häg-\\ *n* : a ridge with a sharp summit and steep sides

hog-nose snake \\'hóg-ˌnōz-, 'häg-\\ *or* **hog-nosed snake** \\-ˌnōzd-\\ *n* : any of a genus of rather small harmless short-bodied No. American snakes that seldom bite but hiss wildly and often play dead when disturbed

hogs-head \\'hógz-ˌhed, 'hägz-\\ *n* **1** : a large cask or barrel **2** : a liquid measure equal to 63 U.S. gallons

hog-tie \\'hóg-ˌtī, 'häg-\\ *vb* **1** : to tie together the feet of ⟨∼ a calf⟩ **2** : to make helpless

hog-wash \\-ˌwȯsh, -ˌwäsh\\ *n* **1** : SWILL, SLOP **2** : NONSENSE, BALONEY

hog wild *adj* : lacking in restraint

hoi pol-loi \\ˌhȯi-pə-'lȯi\\ *n pl* [Gk, the many] : the general populace

hoi-sin sauce \\'hȯi-ˌsin-\\ *n* : a thick reddish sauce of soybeans, spices, and garlic used in Asian cookery

¹**hoist** \\'hȯist\\ *vb* : RAISE, LIFT

²**hoist** *n* **1** : LIFT **2** : an apparatus for hoisting

hoke \\'hōk\\ *vb* **hoked; hok-ing** : FAKE — usu. used with *up*

hok-ey \\'hō-kē\\ *adj* **hok-i-er; -est** **1** : CORNY **2** : PHONY

ho-kum \\'hō-kəm\\ *n* : NONSENSE

¹**hold** \\'hōld\\ *vb* **held** \\'held\\; **hold-ing** **1** : POSSESS; *also* : KEEP **2** : RESTRAIN **3** : to have a grasp on **4** : to support, remain, or keep in a particular situation or position **5** : SUSTAIN; *also* : RESERVE **6** : BEAR, COMPORT **7** : to maintain in being or action : PERSIST **8** : CONTAIN, ACCOMMODATE **9** : HARBOR, ENTERTAIN; *also* : CONSIDER, REGARD **10** : to carry on by concerted action; *also* : CONVOKE **11** : to occupy esp. by appointment or election **12** : to be valid **13** : HALT, PAUSE — **hold-er** *n* — **hold forth** : to speak at length — **hold to** : to adhere to : MAINTAIN — **hold with** : to agree with or approve of

²**hold** *n* **1** : STRONGHOLD **2** : CONFINE-MENT; *also* : PRISON **3** : the act or manner of holding : GRIP **4** : a restraining, dominating, or controlling influence **5** : something that may be grasped as a support **6** : an order or indication that something is to be reserved or delayed — **on hold** : in a temporary state of waiting (as during a phone call); *also* : in a state of postponement ⟨plans *on hold*⟩

³**hold** *n* **1** : the interior of a ship below decks; *esp* : a ship's cargo deck **2** : an airplane's cargo compartment

hold-ing *n* **1** : land or other property owned **2** : a ruling of a court esp. on an issue of law

holding pattern *n* : a course flown by an aircraft waiting to land

hold out *vb* **1** : to continue to fight or work **2** : to refuse to come to an agreement — **hold-out** \\'hōl-ˌdaůt\\ *n*

hold-over \\'hōl-ˌdō-vər\\ *n* : one that is held over

hold-up \\'hōl-ˌdəp\\ *n* **1** : DELAY **2** : robbery at the point of a gun

hole \\'hōl\\ *n* **1** : an opening into or through something **2** : a hollow place (as a pit or cave) **3** : DEN, BURROW **4** : a wretched or dingy place **5** : a unit of play from tee to cup in golf **6** : an awkward position — **hole** *vb*

hol-i-day \\'hä-lə-ˌdā\\ *n* [ME, fr. OE *hāligdæg*, fr. *hālig* holy + *dæg* day] **1** : a day set aside for special religious observance **2** : a day of freedom from work; *esp* : one in commemoration of an event **3** : VACATION — **holiday** *vb*

ho-li-ness \\'hō-lē-nəs\\ *n* : the quality or state of being holy — used as a title for various high religious officials

ho-lis-tic \\hō-'lis-tik\\ *adj* : relating to or concerned with integrated wholes or complete systems rather than with the analysis or treatment of separate parts ⟨∼ medicine⟩ ⟨∼ ecology⟩

hol-lan-daise \\ˌhä-lən-'dāz\\ *n* : a rich sauce made basically of butter, egg yolks, and lemon juice or vinegar

hol-ler \\'hä-lər\\ *vb* : to cry out : SHOUT — **holler** *n*

¹**hol-low** \\'hä-lō\\ *n* **1** : CAVITY, HOLE **2** : a surface depression

²**hollow** *adj* **hol-low-er** \\'hä-lə-wər\\; **hol-low-est** \\-lə-wəst\\ **1** : CONCAVE, SUNKEN **2** : having a cavity within **3** : lacking in real value, sincerity, or substance; *also* : FALSE **4** : MUFFLED ⟨a ∼ sound⟩ — **hol-low-ness** *n*

³**hollow** *vb* : to make or become hollow

hol-low-ware *or* **hol-o-ware** \\'hä-lō-ˌwar\\ *n* : vessels (as bowls or cups) with a significant depth and volume

hol-ly \\'hä-lē\\ *n*, *pl* **hollies** : either of two trees or shrubs with branches of usu. evergreen glossy spiny-margined leaves and red berries

hol-ly-hock \\'hä-lē-ˌhäk, -ˌhȯk\\ *n* [ME *holihoc*, fr. *holi* holy + *hoc* mallow] : a biennial or perennial herb related to the mallows that is widely grown for its tall stalks of showy flowers

hol-mi-um \\'hōl-mē-əm\\ *n* : a metallic chemical element

ho·lo·caust \'hä-lə-ˌkȯst, 'hō-\ n 1 : a thorough destruction esp. by fire 2 *often cap* : the killing of European Jews by the Nazis during World War II; *also* : GENOCIDE

Ho·lo·cene \'hō-lə-ˌsēn\ adj : of, relating to, or being the present geologic epoch — **Holocene** n

ho·lo·gram \'hō-lə-ˌgram, 'hä-\ n : a three-dimensional image produced by an interference pattern of light (as laser light)

ho·lo·graph \'hō-lə-ˌgraf, 'hä-\ n : a document wholly in the handwriting of its author

ho·log·ra·phy \hō-'lä-grə-fē\ n : the process of making a hologram — **ho·lo·graph·ic** \ˌhō-lə-'gra-fik, ˌhä-\ adj

Hol·stein \'hōl-ˌstēn, -ˌstīn\ n : any of a breed of large black-and-white dairy cattle that produce large quantities of comparatively low-fat milk

Hol·stein–Frie·sian \-'frē-zhən\ n : HOLSTEIN

hol·ster \'hōl-stər\ n [D] : a usu. leather case for a firearm

ho·ly \'hō-lē\ adj ho·li·er; -est 1 : worthy of absolute devotion 2 : SACRED 3 : having a divine quality ◆ *Synonyms* HALLOWED, BLESSED, SANCTIFIED, CONSECRATED — **ho·li·ly** \-lə-lē\ adv

Holy Spirit n : the third person of the Christian Trinity

ho·ly·stone \'hō-lē-ˌstōn\ n : a soft sandstone used to scrub a ship's wooden decks — **holystone** vb

hom·age \'ä-mij, 'hä-\ n [ME, fr. AF *homage, omage*, fr. *home* man, vassal, fr. L *homo* human being] : expression of high regard; *also* : TRIBUTE 3

hom·bre \'äm-ˌbrā, 'əm-, -brē\ n : GUY, FELLOW

hom·burg \'häm-ˌbərg\ n [*Homburg*, Germany] : a man's felt hat with a stiff curled brim and a high crown creased lengthwise

¹**home** \'hōm\ n 1 : one's residence; *also* : HOUSE 2 : the social unit formed by a family living together 3 : a congenial environment; *also* : HABITAT 4 : a place of origin 5 : the objective in various games

²**home** vb homed; hom·ing 1 : to go or return home 2 : to proceed to or toward a source of radiated energy used as a guide

home·body \'hōm-ˌbä-dē\ n : one whose life centers on home

home·boy \-ˌbȯi\ n 1 : a boy or man from one's neighborhood, hometown, or region 2 : a fellow member of a youth gang 3 : an inner-city youth

home·bred \-'bred\ adj : produced at home : INDIGENOUS

home·com·ing \-ˌkə-miŋ\ n 1 : a return home 2 : an annual celebration for alumni at a college or university

home computer n : a small inexpensive microcomputer

home economics n : the theory and practice of homemaking

home·girl \'hōm-ˌgərl\ n 1 : a girl or woman from one's neighborhood, hometown, or region 2 : a girl or woman who is a member of one's peer group 3 : an inner-city girl or woman

home·grown \'hōm-'grōn\ adj 1 : grown domestically (~ peaches) 2 : LOCAL, INDIGENOUS (a ~ artist)

home·land \-ˌland\ n 1 : native land 2 : an area set aside to be a state for a people of a particular national, cultural, or racial origin

home·less \-ləs\ adj : having no home or permanent residence — **home·less·ness** n

home·ly \'hōm-lē\ adj home·li·er; -est 1 : FAMILIAR 2 : unaffectedly natural 3 : lacking beauty or proportion — **home·li·ness** \-lē-nəs\ n

home·made \'hōm-'mād\ adj : made in the home, on the premises, or by one's own efforts

home·mak·er \-ˌmā-kər\ n : one who manages a household esp. as a wife and mother — **home·mak·ing** \-kiŋ\ n

ho·me·op·a·thy \ˌhō-mē-'ä-pə-thē\ n : a system of medical practice that treats disease esp. with minute doses of a remedy that would in healthy persons produce symptoms similar to those of the disease treated — **ho·meo·path** \'hō-mē-ə-ˌpath\ n — **ho·meo·path·ic** \ˌhō-mē-ə-'pa-thik\ adj

ho·meo·sta·sis \ˌhō-mē-ō-'stā-səs\ n : the maintenance of a relatively stable state of equilibrium between interrelated physiological, psychological, or social factors characteristic of an individual or group — **ho·meo·stat·ic** \-'sta-tik\ adj

home page n : the page usu. encountered first at a Web site that usu. contains hyperlinks to the other pages of the site

home plate n : a slab at the apex of a baseball diamond that a base runner must touch in order to score

hom·er \'hō-mər\ n : HOME RUN — **homer** vb

home·room \'hōm-ˌrüm, -ˌru̇m\ n : a classroom where pupils report at the beginning of each school year

home run n : a hit in baseball that enables the batter to go around all the bases and score a run

home·school \'hōm-ˌskül\ vb : to teach school subjects to one's children at home — **home·school·er** \-ˌskü-lər\ n

home·sick \'hōm-ˌsik\ adj : longing for home and family while absent from them — **home·sick·ness** n

home·spun \-ˌspən\ adj 1 : spun or made at home; *also* : made of a loosely woven usu. woolen or linen fabric 2 : SIMPLE, HOMELY

¹**home·stead** \-ˌsted\ n : the home and land occupied by a family

²**homestead** vb : to acquire or settle on public land — **home·stead·er** n

home·stretch \-'strech\ n 1 : the part of a racecourse between the last curve and the winning post 2 : a final stage (as of a project)

home theater n : an entertainment system (as a television with surround sound and a DVD player) for the home

home video *n* : prerecorded videocassettes or videodiscs for home viewing

¹**home·ward** \-wərd\ *or* **home·wards** \-wərdz\ *adv* : toward home

²**homeward** *adj* : being or going toward home

home·work \-ˌwərk\ *n* **1** : an assignment given a student to be completed outside the classroom **2** : preparatory reading or research

¹**hom·ey** \'hō-mē\ *adj* **hom·i·er; -est** : characteristic of home

²**homey** *or* **hom·ie** \'hō-mē\ *n, pl* **homeys** *or* **homies** : HOMEBOY

ho·mi·cide \'hä-mə-ˌsīd, 'hō-\ *n* [L *homicida* murderer & *homicidium* manslaughter; both fr. *homo* human being + *caedere* to cut, kill] **1** : a person who kills another **2** : a killing of one human being by another — **hom·i·cid·al** \ˌhä-mə-'sī-dᵊl\ *adj*

hom·i·ly \'hä-mə-lē\ *n, pl* **-lies** : SERMON — **hom·i·let·ic** \ˌhä-mə-'le-tik\ *adj*

homing pigeon *n* : a racing pigeon trained to return home

hom·i·nid \'hä-mə-nəd, -ˌnid\ *n* : any of a family of primate mammals that comprise all living humans and extinct ancestral and related forms — **hominid** *adj*

hom·i·ny \'hä-mə-nē\ *n* : hulled corn with the germ removed

ho·mo·cys·te·ine \ˌhō-mō-'sis-tə-ˌēn\ *n* : an amino acid associated with an increased risk of heart disease when occurring at high levels in the blood

ho·mo·erot·ic \ˌhō-mō-i-'rä-tik\ *adj* : marked by or portraying homosexual desire — **ho·mo·erot·i·cism** \-'re-tə-ˌsi-zəm\ *n*

ho·mo·ge·neous \ˌhō-mə-'jē-nē-əs, -nyəs\ *adj* : of the same or a similar kind; *also* : of uniform structure — **ho·mo·ge·ne·i·ty** \-jə-'nē-ə-tē\ *n* — **ho·mo·ge·neous·ly** *adv*

ho·mog·e·ni·sa·tion, ho·mog·e·nise *Brit var of* HOMOGENIZATION, HOMOGENIZE

ho·mog·e·nize \hō-'mä-jə-ˌnīz, hə-\ *vb* **-nized; -niz·ing** **1** : to make homogeneous **2** : to reduce the particles in (as milk) to uniform size and distribute them evenly throughout the liquid — **ho·mog·e·ni·za·tion** \-ˌmä-jə-nə-'zā-shən\ *n* — **ho·mog·e·niz·er** *n*

ho·mo·graph \'hä-mə-ˌgraf, 'hō-\ *n* : one of two or more words spelled alike but different in origin, meaning, or pronunciation (as the *bow* of a ship, a *bow* and arrow)

ho·mol·o·gy \hō-'mä-lə-jē, hə-\ *n, pl* **-gies** **1** : structural likeness between corresponding parts of different plants or animals due to evolution from a common ancestor **2** : structural likeness between different parts of the same individual — **ho·mol·o·gous** \-'mä-lə-gəs\ *adj*

hom·onym \'hä-mə-ˌnim, 'hō-\ *n* **1** : HOMOPHONE, HOMOGRAPH **2** : one of two or more words spelled and pronounced alike but different in meaning (as *pool* of water and *pool* the game)

ho·mo·pho·bia \ˌhō-mə-'fō-bē-ə\ *n* : irrational fear of, aversion to, or discrimination against homosexuality or homosexuals — **ho·mo·phobe** \'hō-mə-ˌfōb\ *n* — **ho·mo·pho·bic** \-'fō-bik\ *adj*

ho·mo·phone \'hä-mə-ˌfōn, 'hō-\ *n* : one of two or more words (as *to, too, two*) pronounced alike but different in meaning or derivation or spelling

Ho·mo sa·pi·ens \ˌhō-mō-'sä-pē-ənz, -'sa-\ *n* : HUMANKIND

ho·mo·sex·u·al \ˌhō-mō-'sek-shə-wəl\ *adj* : of, relating to, or marked by sexual interest in the same sex as oneself; *also* : of, relating to, or involving sexual intercourse between members of the same sex — **homosexual** *n* — **ho·mo·sex·u·al·i·ty** \-ˌsek-shə-'wa-lə-tē\ *n*

hon *abbr* honor; honorable; honorary

hone \'hōn\ *n* : WHETSTONE — **hone** *vb* — **hon·er** *n*

hone in *vb* : to move toward or direct attention to an objective

¹**hon·est** \'ä-nəst\ *adj* [ME, fr. AF, fr. L *honestus* honorable, fr. *honos, honor* honor] **1** : free from deception : TRUTHFUL; *also* : GENUINE, REAL **2** : REPUTABLE **3** : CREDITABLE ⟨an ∼ day's work⟩ **4** : marked by integrity **5** : FRANK ♦ **Synonyms** UPRIGHT, JUST, CONSCIENTIOUS, HONORABLE — **hon·est·ly** *adv* — **hon·es·ty** \-nə-stē\ *n*

²**honest** *adv* : HONESTLY; *also* : with all sincerity ⟨I didn't do it, ∼⟩

hon·ey \'hə-nē\ *n, pl* **honeys** : a sweet sticky substance made by honeybees from the nectar of flowers — **hon·eyed** \-nēd\ *adj*

hon·ey·bee \'hə-nē-ˌbē\ *n* : a honey-producing bee often kept in hives

¹**hon·ey·comb** \-ˌkōm\ *n* : a mass of 6-sided wax cells built by honeybees; *also* : something of similar structure or appearance

²**honeycomb** *vb* : to make or become full of cavities like a honeycomb

hon·ey·dew \-ˌdü, -ˌdyü\ *n* : a sweetish deposit secreted on plants by aphids, scale insects, or fungi

honeydew melon *n* : a smooth-skinned muskmelon with sweet green flesh

honey locust *n* : a tall usu. spiny No. American leguminous tree with hard durable wood and long twisted pods

hon·ey·moon \'hə-nē-ˌmün\ *n* **1** : a period of harmony esp. just after marriage **2** : a holiday taken by a newly married couple — **honeymoon** *vb* — **hon·ey·moon·er** *n*

hon·ey·suck·le \'hə-nē-ˌsə-kəl\ *n* : any of a genus of shrubs with fragrant tube-shaped flowers rich in nectar

honk \'häŋk, 'hȯŋk\ *n* : the cry of a goose; *also* : a similar sound (as of a horn) — **honk** *vb* — **honk·er** *n*

hon·ky-tonk \'häŋ-kē-ˌtäŋk, 'hȯŋ-kē-ˌtȯŋk\ *n* : a tawdry nightclub or dance hall — **honky-tonk** *adj*

¹**hon·or** \'ä-nər\ *n* **1** : good name : REPUTATION; *also* : outward respect **2** : PRIVILEGE **3** : a person of superior standing — used esp. as a title **4** : one who brings respect or fame ⟨an ∼ to the class⟩ **5**

: an evidence or symbol of distinction **6**
: CHASTITY, PURITY **7** : INTEGRITY
♦ Synonyms HOMAGE, REVERENCE,
DEFERENCE, OBEISANCE

²**honor** *vb* **1** : to regard or treat with
honor **2** : to confer honor on **3** : to fulfill the terms of; *also* : to accept as
payment — **hon·or·ee** \ˌä-nə-ˈrē\ *n* —
hon·or·er *n*

hon·or·able \ˈä-nə-rə-bəl\ *adj* **1** : deserving of honor **2** : of great renown **3** : accompanied with marks of honor **4**
: doing credit to the possessor **5** : characterized by integrity — **hon·or·able-
ness** *n* — **hon·or·ably** \-blē\ *adv*

hon·o·rar·i·um \ˌä-nə-ˈrer-ē-əm\ *n, pl* **-ia**
\-ē-ə\ *also* **-iums** : a reward usu. for services on which custom or propriety for-
bids a price to be set

hon·or·ary \ˈä-nə-ˌrer-ē\ *adj* **1** : having
or conferring distinction **2** : conferred in
recognition of achievement without the
usual prerequisites ⟨~ degree⟩ **3** : UN-
PAID, VOLUNTARY ⟨an ~ chairman⟩ —
hon·or·ari·ly \ˌä-nə-ˈrer-ə-lē\ *adv*

hon·or·if·ic \ˌä-nə-ˈri-fik\ *adj* : conferring
or conveying honor ⟨~ titles⟩

hon·our, hon·our·able *chiefly Brit var of*
HONOR, HONORABLE

¹**hood** \ˈhu̇d\ *n* **1** : a covering for the head
and neck and sometimes the face **2** : an
ornamental fold (as at the back of an ecclesiastical vestment) **3** : a cover for
parts of mechanisms; *esp* : the covering
over an automobile engine — **hood·ed**
\ˈhu̇d-əd\ *adj*

²**hood** \ˈhu̇d, ˈhüd\ *n* : HOODLUM

³**hood** \ˈhu̇d\ *n* : an inner-city neighborhood; *also* : INNER CITY

-hood \ˌhu̇d\ *n suffix* **1** : state : condition
: quality : character ⟨boyhood⟩ ⟨hardi-
hood⟩ **2** : instance of a (specified) state
or quality ⟨falsehood⟩ **3** : individuals
sharing a (specified) state or character
⟨brotherhood⟩

hood·ie \ˈhu̇-dē\ *n* : a hooded sweatshirt

hood·lum \ˈhüd-ləm, ˈhu̇d-\ *n* **1** : THUG
2 : a young ruffian

hoo·doo \ˈhü-dü\ *n, pl* **hoodoos 1** : a
body of magical practices traditional esp.
among blacks in the southern U.S. **2**
: something that brings bad luck —
hoodoo *vb*

hood·wink \ˈhu̇d-ˌwiŋk\ *vb* : to deceive by
false appearance

hoo·ey \ˈhü-ē\ *n* : NONSENSE

hoof \ˈhu̇f, ˈhüf\ *n, pl* **hooves** \ˈhu̇vz,
ˈhüvz\ *also* **hoofs** : a horny covering that
protects the ends of the toes of ungulate
mammals (as horses or cattle); *also* : a
hoofed foot — **hoofed** \ˈhu̇ft, ˈhüft\ *adj*

¹**hook** \ˈhu̇k\ *n* **1** : a curved or bent device
for catching, holding, or pulling **2**
: something curved or bent like a hook **3**
: a flight of a ball (as in golf) that curves
in a direction opposite to the dominant
hand of the player propelling it **4** : a
short punch delivered with a circular motion and with the elbow bent and rigid

²**hook** *vb* **1** : CURVE, CROOK **2** : to seize
or make fast with a hook **3** : STEAL **4**
: to work as a prostitute

hoo·kah \ˈhu̇-kə, ˈhü-\ *n* [Ar *ḥuqqa* bottle
of a water pipe] : WATER PIPE

hook·er \ˈhu̇-kər\ *n* **1** : one that hooks
2 : PROSTITUTE

hook·up \ˈhu̇-ˌkəp\ *n* : an assemblage (as
of apparatus or circuits) used for a specific purpose (as in radio)

hook·worm \ˈhu̇k-ˌwərm\ *n* : any of several parasitic intestinal nematode worms
having hooks or plates around the mouth;
also : infestation with or disease caused
by hookworms

hoo·li·gan \ˈhü-li-gən\ *n* : RUFFIAN,
HOODLUM — **hoo·li·gan·ism** \-gə-ˌni-
zəm\ *n*

hoop \ˈhu̇p, ˈhüp\ *n* **1** : a circular strip
used esp. for holding together the staves
of a barrel **2** : a circular figure or object
: RING **3** : a circle of flexible material for
expanding a woman's skirt **4** : BASKET-
BALL — usu. used in pl.

hoop·la \ˈhüp-ˌlä, ˈhu̇p-\ *n* [F *houp-là*, interj.] : TO-DO; *also* : BALLYHOO

hoop·ster \ˈhüp-stər\ *n* : a basketball
player

hoo·ray \hu̇-ˈrā\ *interj* — used to express
joy, approval, or encouragement

hoose·gow \ˈhüs-ˌgau̇\ *n* [Sp *juzgado*
panel of judges, courtroom] : JAIL

¹**hoot** \ˈhüt\ *vb* **1** : to shout or laugh usu.
in contempt **2** : to make the natural
throat noise of an owl — **hoot·er** *n*

²**hoot** *n* **1** : a sound of hooting **2** : the
least bit ⟨don't give a ~⟩ **3** : something
or someone amusing ⟨the play is a real
~⟩

hoo·te·nan·ny \ˈhü-tə-ˌna-nē\ *n, pl* **-nies**
: a gathering at which folksingers entertain often with the audience joining in

¹**hop** \ˈhäp\ *vb* **hopped; hop·ping 1** : to
move by short springy leaps **2** : to make
a quick trip **3** : to ride on esp. surrepti-
tiously and without authorization

²**hop** *n* **1** : a short brisk leap esp. on one
leg **2** : DANCE **3** : a short trip by air

³**hop** *n* : a vine related to the hemp plant
whose ripe dried pistillate catkins are
used esp. in flavoring malt liquors; *also, pl*
: its pistillate catkins

¹**hope** \ˈhōp\ *vb* **hoped; hop·ing** : to desire with expectation of fulfillment

²**hope** *n* **1** : TRUST, RELIANCE **2** : desire
accompanied by expectation of fulfill-
ment; *also* : something hoped for **3** : one
that gives promise for the future —
hope·ful \-fəl\ *adj* — **hope·ful·ness** *n*
— **hope·less** *adj* — **hope·less·ly** *adv*
— **hope·less·ness** *n*

HOPE *abbr* Health Opportunity for People Everywhere

hope·ful·ly \ˈhōp-fə-lē\ *adv* **1** : in a hopeful manner **2** : it is hoped

Ho·pi \ˈhō-pē\ *n, pl* **Hopi** *or* **Hopis** : a
member of an American Indian people of
Arizona; *also* : the language of the Hopi
people

hopped–up \ˈhäpt-ˈəp\ *adj* **1** : being
under the influence of a narcotic; *also*
: full of enthusiasm or excitement **2**
: having more than usual power ⟨a ~ en-
gine⟩

hop·per \'hä-pər\ n 1 : a usu. immature hopping insect (as a grasshopper) 2 : a usu. funnel-shaped container for delivering material (as grain) 3 : a freight car with hinged doors in a sloping bottom 4 : a box into which a bill to be considered by a legislative body is dropped 5 : a tank holding a liquid and having a device for releasing its contents through a pipe

hop·scotch \'häp-ˌskäch\ n : a child's game in which a player tosses an object (as a stone) into areas of a figure drawn on the ground and hops through the figure to pick up the object

hor abbr horizontal

horde \'hȯrd\ n : THRONG, SWARM

ho·ri·zon \hə-'rī-z²n\ n [ME, fr. LL, fr. Gk horizont-, horizōn, fr. prp. of horizein to bound, fr. horos limit, boundary] 1 : the apparent junction of earth and sky 2 : range of outlook or experience

hor·i·zon·tal \ˌhȯr-ə-'zän-t²l\ adj : parallel to the horizon : LEVEL — horizontal n — hor·i·zon·tal·ly adv

hor·mon·al \hȯr-'mō-n²l\ adj : of, relating to, or effected by hormones — hor·mon·al·ly \-n²l-ē\ adv

hor·mone \'hȯr-ˌmōn\ n [Gk hormōn, prp. of horman to stir up, fr. hormē impulse, assault] : a product of living cells that circulates in body fluids and has a specific effect on the activity of cells remote from its point of origin

horn \'hȯrn\ n 1 : one of the hard projections of bone or keratin on the head of many hoofed mammals 2 : something resembling or suggesting a horn 3 : a brass wind instrument 4 : a usu. electrical device that makes a noise ⟨an automobile ∼⟩ — horned \'hȯrnd\ adj — horn·less adj

horn·book \'hȯrn-ˌbu̇k\ n 1 : a child's primer consisting of a sheet of parchment or paper protected by a sheet of transparent horn 2 : a rudimentary treatise

horned toad n : any of several small harmless insect-eating lizards with spines on the head resembling horns and scales on the body

hor·net \'hȯr-nət\ n : any of the larger social wasps

horn in vb : to participate without invitation : INTRUDE

horn·pipe \'hȯrn-ˌpīp\ n : a lively folk dance of the British Isles

horny \'hȯr-nē\ adj horn·i·er; -est 1 : of or made of horn; also : HARD, CALLOUS 2 : having horns 3 : desiring sexual gratification; also : excited sexually

ho·rol·o·gy \hə-'rä-lə-jē\ n : the science of measuring time or constructing time-indicating instruments — hor·o·log·i·cal \ˌhȯr-ə-'lä-ji-kəl\ adj — ho·rol·o·gist \hə-'rä-lə-jist\ n

horo·scope \'hȯr-ə-ˌskōp\ n [ME horoscopum, fr. L horoscopus, fr. Gk hōroskopos, fr. hōra hour + skopos watcher] 1 : a diagram of the relative positions of planets and signs of the zodiac at a particular time for use by astrologers to foretell events of a person's life 2 : an astrological forecast

hor·ren·dous \hȯ-'ren-dəs\ adj : DREADFUL, HORRIBLE

hor·ri·ble \'hȯr-ə-bəl\ adj 1 : marked by or conducive to horror 2 : highly disagreeable — hor·ri·ble·ness n — hor·ri·bly \-blē\ adv

hor·rid \'hȯr-əd\ adj 1 : HIDEOUS 2 : REPULSIVE — hor·rid·ly adv

hor·rif·ic \hȯ-'ri-fik\ adj : having the power to horrify — hor·rif·i·cal·ly \-fi-k(ə-)lē\ adv

hor·ri·fy \'hȯr-ə-ˌfī\ vb -fied; -fy·ing : to cause to feel horror ♦ Synonyms APPALL, DAUNT, DISMAY

hor·ror \'hȯr-ər\ n 1 : painful and intense fear, dread, or dismay 2 : intense repugnance 3 : something that horrifies

horror story n : an account of an unsettling or unfortunate occurrence

hors de com·bat \ˌȯr-də-kōⁿ-'bä\ adv or adj : in a disabled condition

hors d'oeuvre \ȯr-'dərv\ n, pl hors d'oeuvres \same or -'dərvz\ also hors d'oeuvre [F hors-d'oeuvre, lit., outside of the work] : any of various savory foods usu. served as appetizers

horse \'hȯrs\ n, pl hors·es also horse 1 : a large solid-hoofed herbivorous mammal domesticated as a draft and saddle animal 2 : a supporting framework usu. with legs — horse·less adj

¹horse·back \'hȯrs-ˌbak\ n : the back of a horse

²horseback adv : on horseback

horse chestnut n : a large tree with palmate leaves, erect conical clusters of showy flowers, and large glossy brown seeds enclosed in a prickly bur; also : its seed

horse·flesh \'hȯrs-ˌflesh\ n : horses for riding, driving, or racing

horse·fly \-ˌflī\ n : any of a family of large dipteran flies with bloodsucking females

horse·hair \-ˌher\ n 1 : the hair of a horse esp. from the mane or tail 2 : cloth made from horsehair

horse·hide \-ˌhīd\ n 1 : the dressed or raw hide of a horse 2 : the ball used in baseball

horse latitudes n pl : either of two calm regions near 30°N and 30°S latitude

horse·laugh \'hȯrs-ˌlaf, -ˌläf\ n : a loud boisterous laugh

horse·man \-mən\ n 1 : one who rides horseback; also : one skilled in managing horses 2 : a breeder or raiser of horses — horse·man·ship n

horse·play \-ˌplā\ n : rough boisterous play

horse·play·er \-ər\ n : a bettor on horse races

horse·pow·er \'hȯrs-ˌpau̇(-ə)r\ n : a unit of power equal in the U.S. to 746 watts

horse·rad·ish \-ˌra-dish\ n : a tall white-flowered herb related to the mustards whose pungent root is used as a condiment; also : the pungent condiment

horse·shoe \'hȯrs-ˌshü\ n 1 : a usu. U-shaped protective metal plate fitted to the rim of a horse's hoof 2 pl : a game in which horseshoes are pitched at a fixed object — **horse·shoe** vb — **horse·sho·er** n

horseshoe crab n : any of several marine arthropods with a broad crescent-shaped combined head and thorax

horse·tail \'hȯrs-ˌtāl\ n : any of a genus of primitive spore-producing plants with hollow jointed stems and leaves reduced to sheaths about the joints

horse·whip \-ˌhwip\ vb : to flog with a whip made to be used on a horse

horse·wom·an \-ˌwu̇-mən\ n 1 : a woman skilled in riding horseback or in caring for or managing horses 2 : a woman who breeds or raises horses

hors·ey also **horsy** \'hȯr-sē\ adj **hors·i·er; -est** 1 : of, relating to, or suggesting a horse 2 : having to do with horses or horse racing

hort abbr horticultural; horticulture

hor·ta·tive \'hȯr-tə-tiv\ adj : giving exhortation

hor·ta·to·ry \'hȯr-tə-ˌtȯr-ē\ adj : HORTATIVE

hor·ti·cul·ture \'hȯr-tə-ˌkəl-chər\ n : the science and art of growing fruits, vegetables, flowers, and ornamental plants — **hor·ti·cul·tur·al** \ˌhȯr-tə-ˈkəl-chə-rəl\ adj — **hor·ti·cul·tur·ist** \-rist\ n

Hos abbr Hosea

ho·san·na \hō-ˈza-nə, -ˈzä-\ interj [Gk hōsanna, fr. Heb hōshī'āh-nnā pray, save (us)!] — used as a cry of acclamation and adoration — **hosanna** n

¹**hose** \'hōz\ n, pl **hose** or **hos·es** 1 pl **hose** : STOCKING, SOCK; also : a close-fitting garment covering the legs and waist 2 : a flexible tube for conveying fluids (as from a faucet)

²**hose** vb **hosed; hos·ing** : to spray, water, or wash with a hose

Ho·sea \hō-ˈzā-ə, -ˈzē-\ n — see BIBLE table

ho·siery \'hō-zhə-rē, -zə-\ n : STOCKINGS, SOCKS

hosp abbr hospital

hos·pice \'häs-pəs\ n 1 : a lodging for travelers or for young persons or the underprivileged 2 : a facility or program for caring for dying persons

hos·pi·ta·ble \hä-ˈspi-tə-bəl, ˈhäs-(ˌ)pi-\ adj 1 : given to generous and cordial reception of guests 2 : readily receptive — **hos·pi·ta·bly** \-blē\ adv

hos·pi·tal \'häs-ˌpi-tᵊl\ n [ME, fr. AF, fr. ML hospitale hospice, guest house, fr. neut. of L hospitalis of a guest, fr. hospit-, hospes guest, host] : an institution where the sick or injured receive medical or surgical care

hos·pi·tal·ise Brit var of HOSPITALIZE

hos·pi·tal·i·ty \ˌhäs-pə-ˈta-lə-tē\ n, pl **-ties** : hospitable treatment, reception, or disposition

hos·pi·tal·ize \'häs-ˌpi-tə-ˌlīz\ vb **-ized; -iz·ing** : to place in a hospital as a patient — **hos·pi·tal·i·za·tion** \ˌhäs-ˌpi-tᵊl-ə-ˈzā-shən\ n

¹**host** \'hōst\ n [ME, fr. AF ost, fr. LL hostis, fr. L, stranger, enemy] 1 : ARMY 2 : MULTITUDE

²**host** n [ME hoste host, guest, fr. AF, fr. L hospit-, hospes] 1 : one who receives or entertains guests 2 : an animal or plant on or in which a parasite lives 3 : one into which something (as an organ) is transplanted 4 : SERVER 2 — **host** vb

³**host** n, often cap [ultim. fr. L hostia sacrifice] : the eucharistic bread

hos·tage \'häs-tij\ n 1 : a person kept as a pledge pending the fulfillment of an agreement 2 : a person taken by force to secure the taker's demands

hos·tel \'häs-tᵊl\ n [ME, fr. AF, fr. ML hospitale hospice] 1 : INN 2 : a supervised lodging for youth — **hos·tel·er** or **hos·tel·ler** n

hos·tel·ry \-rē\ n, pl **-ries** : INN, HOTEL

host·ess \'hō-stəs\ n : a woman who acts as host

hos·tile \'häs-tᵊl, -ˌtī(-ə)l\ adj : marked by usu. overt antagonism : UNFRIENDLY — **hostile** n — **hos·tile·ly** adv

hos·til·i·ty \hä-ˈsti-lə-tē\ n, pl **-ties** 1 : an unfriendly state or action 2 pl : overt acts of war

hos·tler \'häs-lər, 'äs-\ n : one who takes care of horses or mules

hot \'hät\ adj **hot·ter; hot·test** 1 : marked by a high temperature or an uncomfortable degree of body heat 2 : giving a sensation of heat or of burning 3 : ARDENT, FIERY 4 : sexually excited 5 : EAGER 6 : newly made or received 7 : PUNGENT 8 : unusually lucky or favorable ⟨∼ dice⟩ 9 : recently and illegally obtained ⟨∼ jewels⟩ — **hot** adv — **hot·ly** adv — **hot·ness** n

hot·bed \-ˌbed\ n 1 : a glass-covered bed of soil heated (as by fermenting manure) and used esp. for raising seedlings 2 : an environment that favors rapid growth or development

hot–blood·ed \-ˈblə-dəd\ adj : easily roused or excited

hot·box \-ˌbäks\ n : a bearing (as of a railroad car) overheated by friction

hot button n : an emotional issue or concern that triggers immediate intense reaction

hot·cake \-ˌkāk\ n : PANCAKE

hot dog n : a cooked frankfurter usu. served in a long split roll

ho·tel \hō-ˈtel\ n [F hôtel, fr. OF hostel, fr. ML hospitale hospice] : a building where lodging and usu. meals, entertainment, and various personal services are provided for the public

hot flash n : a sudden brief flushing and sensation of heat usu. associated with menopausal endocrine imbalance

hot·head·ed \'hät-ˈhe-dəd\ adj : FIERY, IMPETUOUS — **hot·head** \-ˌhed\ n — **hot·head·ed·ly** adv — **hot·head·ed·ness** n

hot·house \-ˌhau̇s\ n : a heated greenhouse esp. for raising tropical plants

hotline n : a telephone line for emergency use (as between governments or to a counseling service)

hot pants n pl : very short shorts

hot pepper n : a small usu. thin-walled

pepper with a pungent taste; *also* : a plant bearing hot peppers

hot plate *n* : a simple portable appliance for heating or for cooking

hot potato *n* : an embarrassing or controversial issue

hot rod *n* : an automobile modified for high speed and fast acceleration — **hot-rod-der** \'-'rä-dər\ *n*

hots \'häts\ *n pl* : strong sexual desire — usu. used with *the*

hot seat *n* : a position of anxiety or embarrassment

hot-shot \'hät-,shät\ *n* : a showily skillful person

hot tub *n* : a large tub of hot water for one or more bathers

hot water *n* : TROUBLE, DIFFICULTY

hot-wire \'hät-,wī(-ə)r\ *vb* : to start (an automobile) by short-circuiting the ignition system

¹**hound** \'haùnd\ *n* **1** : : any of various hunting dogs that track prey by scent or sight **2** : FAN, ADDICT

²**hound** *vb* : to pursue relentlessly

hour \'aù(-ə)r\ *n* **1** : the 24th part of a day : 60 minutes **2** : the time of day **3** : a particular or customary time **4** : a class session — **hour-ly** *adv or adj*

hour-glass \'aù(-ə)r-,glas\ *n* : a glass vessel for measuring time in which sand runs from an upper compartment to a lower compartment in an hour

hou-ri \'hur-ē\ *n* [F, fr. Pers *hūri*, fr. Ar *hūrīya*] : one of the beautiful maidens of the Muslim paradise

¹**house** \'haùs\ *n, pl* **hous-es** \'haù-zəz\ **1** : a building for human habitation **2** : an animal shelter (as a den or nest) **3** : a building in which something is stored **4** : HOUSEHOLD; *also* : FAMILY **5** : a residence for a religious community or for students; *also* : those in residence **6** : a legislative body **7** : a place of business or entertainment **8** : a business organization **9** : the audience in a theater or concert hall — **house-ful** *n*

²**house** \'haùz\ *vb* **housed; hous-ing 1** : to provide with or take shelter : LODGE **2** : STORE

house-boat \'haùs-,bōt\ *n* : a pleasure boat fitted for use as a dwelling or for leisurely cruising

house-boy \-,bòi\ *n* : a boy or man hired to act as a household servant

house-break \-,brāk\ *vb* **-broke; -broken; -break-ing** : to train (a pet) in excretory habits acceptable in indoor living

house-break-ing \-,brā-kiŋ\ *n* : the act of breaking into a dwelling with the intent of committing a felony

house-clean \-,klēn\ *vb* : to clean a house and its furniture — **house-clean-ing** *n*

house-coat \-,kōt\ *n* : a woman's often long-skirted informal garment for wear around the house

house-fly \-,flī\ *n* : a dipteran fly that is common about human habitations

¹**house-hold** \-,hōld\ *n* : those who dwell as a family under the same roof — **house-hold-er** *n*

²**household** *adj* **1** : DOMESTIC **2** : FAMILIAR, COMMON ⟨a ~ name⟩

house-keep-er \-,kē-pər\ *n* : a woman employed to take care of a house

house-keep-ing \-,kē-piŋ\ *n* : the care and management of a house or institutional property

house-lights \-,līts\ *n pl* : the lights that illuminate the auditorium of a theater

house-maid \-,mād\ *n* : a girl or woman who is a servant employed to do housework

house-moth-er \-,mə-thər\ *n* : a woman acting as hostess, chaperone, and often housekeeper in a group residence

house-plant \-,plant\ *n* : a plant grown or kept indoors

house sparrow *n* : a Eurasian sparrow widely introduced in urban and agricultural areas

house-top \'haùs-,täp\ *n* : ROOF

house-wares \-,werz\ *n pl* : small articles of household equipment

house-warm-ing \-,wòr-miŋ\ *n* : a party to celebrate the taking possession of a house or premises

house-wife \-,wīf\ *n* : a married woman in charge of a household — **house-wife-ly** *adj* — **house-wif-ery** \-,wī-fə-rē\ *n*

house-work \-,wərk\ *n* : the work of housekeeping

¹**hous-ing** \'haù-ziŋ\ *n* **1** : SHELTER; *also* : dwellings provided for people **2** : something that covers or protects

²**housing** *n* : CAPARISON 1

HOV *abbr* high-occupancy vehicle

hove *past and past part of* HEAVE

hov-el \'hə-vəl, 'hä-\ *n* : a small, wretched, and often dirty house : HUT

hov-er \'hə-vər, 'hä-\ *vb* **hov-ered; hover-ing 1** : FLUTTER; *also* : to move to and fro **2** : to be in an uncertain state

hov-er-craft \-,kraft\ *n* : a vehicle that rides on a cushion of air over a surface

¹**how** \'haù\ *adv* **1** : in what way or manner ⟨~ was it done⟩ **2** : with what meaning ⟨~ do we interpret such behavior⟩ **3** : for what reason ⟨~ could you have done such a thing⟩ **4** : to what extent or degree ⟨~ deep is it⟩ **5** : in what state or condition ⟨~ are you⟩ — **how about** : what do you say to or think of ⟨how about coming with me⟩ — **how come** : why is it that

²**how** *conj* **1** : the way or manner in which ⟨remember ~ they fought⟩ **2** : HOWEVER ⟨do it ~ you like⟩

¹**how-be-it** \haù-'bē-ət\ *conj* : ALTHOUGH

²**howbeit** *adv* : NEVERTHELESS

how-dah \'haù-də\ *n* [Hindi & Urdu *hauda*, fr. Ar *haudaj*] : a seat or covered pavilion on the back of an elephant or camel

¹**how-ev-er** \haù-'e-vər\ *conj* : in whatever manner that

²**however** *adv* **1** : in whatever manner; *also* : to whatever degree **2** : in spite of that

how-it-zer \'haù-ət-sər\ *n* : a short cannon that shoots shells at a high angle

howl \'haù(-ə)l\ *vb* **1** : to emit a loud long

doleful sound characteristic of dogs **2** : to cry loudly — **howl** n

howl·er \'haù-lər\ n **1** : one that howls **2** : a humorous and ridiculous blunder

howl·ing adj **1** : DESOLATE, WILD **2** : very great ⟨a ~ success⟩

how·so·ev·er \ˌhaù-sə-'we-vər\ adv : HOWEVER **1**

hoy·den \'hói-d²n\ n : a girl or woman of saucy, boisterous, or carefree behavior — **hoy·den·ish** adj

hp abbr horsepower

HP abbr high pressure

HPF abbr highest possible frequency

HQ abbr headquarters

hr abbr **1** here **2** hour

HR abbr House of Representatives

HRH abbr **1** Her Royal Highness **2** His Royal Highness

hryv·nia \'(h)riv-nē-ə\ n, pl **hryvnia** or **hryvnias** — see MONEY table

hrzn abbr horizon

Hs symbol hassium

HS abbr high school

HST abbr Hawaiian standard time

ht abbr height

HT abbr **1** Hawaii time **2** high-tension

HTML \ˌāch-ˌtē-ˌem-'el\ n [hypertext markup language] : a computer language used to create World Wide Web documents

http abbr hypertext transfer protocol

hua·ra·che \wə-'rä-chē\ n [MexSp] : a sandal with an upper made of interwoven leather strips

hub \'həb\ n **1** : the central part of a circular object (as a wheel) **2** : a center of activity; esp : an airport or city through which an airline routes most of its traffic

hub·bub \'hə-bəb\ n : UPROAR; also : TURMOIL

hub·cap \'həb-ˌkap\ n : a removable metal cap over the end of an axle

hu·bris \'hyü-brəs\ n : exaggerated pride or self-confidence

huck·le·ber·ry \'hə-kəl-ˌber-ē\ n **1** : any of a genus of American shrubs of the heath family; also : its edible dark blue berry **2** : BLUEBERRY

huck·ster \'hək-stər\ n : PEDDLER, HAWKER — **huck·ster·ism** \-stə-ˌri-zəm\ n

HUD abbr Department of Housing and Urban Development

¹hud·dle \'hə-d²l\ vb **hud·dled**; **hud·dling** **1** : to crowd together **2** : CONFER

²huddle n **1** : a closely packed group **2** : MEETING, CONFERENCE

hue \'hyü\ n **1** : COLOR; also : gradation of color **2** : the attribute of colors that permits them to be classed as red, yellow, green, blue, or an intermediate color — **hued** \'hyüd\ adj

hue and cry n : a clamor of pursuit or protest

huff \'həf\ n : a fit of anger or pique — **huff** vb — **huff·i·ly** \'hə-fə-lē\ adv — **huffy** \'hə-fē\ adj

hug \'həg\ vb **hugged**; **hug·ging** **1** : EMBRACE **2** : to stay close to — **hug** n

huge \'hyüj\ adj **hug·er**; **hug·est** : very

large or extensive — **huge·ly** adv — **huge·ness** n

hug·ger–mug·ger \'hə-gər-ˌmə-gər\ n **1** : SECRECY **2** : CONFUSION, MUDDLE

Hu·gue·not \'hyü-gə-ˌnät\ n : a French Protestant of the 16th and 17th centuries

hu·la \'hü-lə\ n : a sinuous Polynesian dance usu. accompanied by chants

hulk \'həlk\ n **1** : a heavy clumsy ship **2** : an old ship unfit for service **3** : a bulky or unwieldy person or thing

hulk·ing \'həl-kin\ adj : BURLY, MASSIVE

¹hull \'həl\ n **1** : the outer covering of a fruit or seed **2** : the frame or body esp. of a ship or boat

²hull vb : to remove the hulls of — **hull·er** n

hul·la·ba·loo \'hə-lə-bə-ˌlü\ n, pl **-loos** : a confused noise : UPROAR

hul·lo \ˌhə-'lō\ chiefly Brit var of HELLO

hum \'həm\ vb **hummed**; **hum·ming** **1** : to utter a sound like that of the speech sound \m\ prolonged **2** : DRONE **3** : to be busily active **4** : to run smoothly **5** : to sing with closed lips — **hum** n — **hum·mer** n

¹hu·man \'hyü-mən, 'yü-\ adj **1** : of, relating to, being, or characteristic of humans **2** : having human form or attributes — **hu·man·ly** adv — **hu·man·ness** n

²human n : any of a species of bipedal primate mammals comprising all living persons and their recent ancestors; also : HOMINID — **hu·man·like** \-ˌlīk\ adj

hu·mane \hyü-'mān, yü-\ adj : marked by compassion, sympathy, or consideration for others **2** : HUMANISTIC — **hu·mane·ly** adv — **hu·mane·ness** n

human immunodeficiency virus n : HIV

hu·man·ism \'hyü-mə-ˌni-zəm, 'yü-\ n **1** : devotion to the humanities; also : the revival of classical letters characteristic of the Renaissance **2** : a doctrine or way of life centered on human interests or values — **hu·man·ist** \-nist\ n or adj — **hu·man·is·tic** \ˌhyü-mə-'nis-tik, ˌyü-\ adj

hu·man·i·tar·i·an \hyü-ˌma-nə-'ter-ē-ən, yü-\ n : one who practices philanthropy — **humanitarian** adj — **hu·man·i·tar·i·an·ism** n

hu·man·i·ty \hyü-'ma-nə-tē, yü-\ n, pl **-ties** **1** : the quality or state of being human or humane **2** pl : the branches of learning dealing with human concerns (as philosophy) as opposed to natural processes (as physics) **3** : the human race

hu·man·ize \'hyü-mə-ˌnīz, 'yü-\ vb **-ized**; **-iz·ing** : to make human or humane — **hu·man·i·za·tion** \ˌhyü-mə-nə-'zā-shən, ˌyü-\ n — **hu·man·iz·er** n

hu·man·kind \'hyü-mən-ˌkīnd, 'yü-\ n : the human race

hu·man·oid \'hyü-mə-ˌnóid, 'yü-\ adj : having human form or characteristics — **humanoid** n

human pap·il·lo·ma·virus \-ˌpa-pə-'lō-mə-ˌvī-rəs\ n : any of numerous DNA=containing viruses that cause various human warts

¹hum·ble \'həm-bəl\ adj **hum·bler** \-bə-lər\; **hum·blest** \-bə-ləst\ [ME, fr. AF, fr. L humilis low, humble, fr. humus earth] **1** : not proud or haughty **2** : not pretentious : UNASSUMING **3** : INSIGNIFICANT ✦ **Synonyms** MEEK, MODEST, LOWLY — **hum·ble·ness** n — **hum·bly** adv

²humble vb **hum·bled; hum·bling 1** : to make humble **2** : to destroy the power or prestige of — **hum·bler** n

¹hum·bug \'həm-,bəg\ n **1** : HOAX, FRAUD **2** : NONSENSE

²humbug vb **hum·bugged; hum·bug·ging** : DECEIVE

hum·ding·er \'həm-'diŋ-ər\ n : a person or thing of striking excellence

hum·drum \'həm-,drəm\ adj : MONOTONOUS, DULL — **humdrum** n

hu·mer·us \'hyü-mə-rəs\ n, pl **hu·meri** \'hyü-mə-,rī, -,rē\ : the long bone extending from shoulder to elbow

hu·mid \'hyü-məd, 'yü-\ adj : containing or characterized by perceptible moisture : DAMP — **hu·mid·ly** adv

hu·mid·i·fy \hyü-'mi-də-,fī\ vb **-fied; -fy·ing** : to make humid — **hu·mid·i·fi·ca·tion** \-,mi-də-fə-'kā-shən\ n — **hu·mid·i·fi·er** \-'mi-də-,fī-ər\ n

hu·mid·i·ty \hyü-'mi-də-tē, yü-\ n, pl **-ties** : the amount of atmospheric moisture

hu·mi·dor \'hyü-mə-,dòr, 'yü-\ n : a case (as for storing cigars) in which the air is kept properly humidified

hu·mil·i·ate \hyü-'mi-lē-,āt, yü-\ vb **-at·ed; -at·ing** : to injure the self-respect of : MORTIFY — **hu·mil·i·at·ing·ly** adv — **hu·mil·i·a·tion** \-,mi-lē-'ā-shən\ n

hu·mil·i·ty \hyü-'mi-lə-tē, yü-\ n : the quality or state of being humble

hum·ming·bird \'hə-miŋ-,bərd\ n : any of a family of tiny brightly colored American birds related to the swifts

hum·mock \'hə-mək\ n : a rounded mound : KNOLL — **hum·mocky** \-mə-kē\ adj

hum·mus \'hə-məs, 'hù-\ n [Ar ḥummuṣ chickpeas] : a paste of pureed chickpeas usu. mixed with sesame oil or paste

hu·mon·gous \hyü-'məŋ-gəs, -'mäŋ-\ adj [perh. alter. of huge + monstrous] : extremely large

¹hu·mor \'hyü-mər, 'yü-\ n **1** : TEMPERAMENT **2** : MOOD **3** : WHIM **4** : a quality that appeals to a sense of the ludicrous or incongruous; also : a keen perception of the ludicrous or incongruous **5** : comical or amusing entertainment — **hu·mor·ist** \'hyü-mə-rist, 'yü-\ n — **hu·mor·less** \'hyü-mər-ləs, 'yü-\ adj — **hu·mor·less·ly** adv — **hu·mor·less·ness** n — **hu·mor·ous** \'hyü-mə-rəs, 'yü-\ adj — **hu·mor·ous·ly** adv — **hu·mor·ous·ness** n

²humor vb : to comply with the wishes or mood of

hu·mour chiefly Brit var of HUMOR

hump \'həmp\ n **1** : a rounded protuberance (as on the back of a camel) **2** : a difficult phase or obstacle ⟨over the ∼⟩ — **humped** adj

hump·back \'həmp-,bak; 1 also -'bak\ n **1** : HUNCHBACK **2** : HUMPBACK WHALE — **hump·backed** adj

humpback whale n : a large baleen whale having very long flippers

hu·mus \'hyü-məs, 'yü-\ n : the dark organic part of soil formed from decaying matter

Hun \'hən\ n : a member of an Asian people that invaded Europe about A.D. 450

¹hunch \'hənch\ vb **1** : to thrust oneself forward **2** : to assume or cause to assume a bent or crooked posture

²hunch n **1** : PUSH **2** : a strong intuitive feeling about what will happen

hunch·back \'hənch-,bak\ n : a person with a crooked back; also : a back with a hump — **hunch·backed** adj

hun·dred \'hən-drəd\ n, pl **hundreds** or **hundred** : 10 times 10 — **hundred** adj — **hun·dredth** \-drədth\ adj or n

hun·dred·weight \-,wāt\ n, pl **hundredweight** or **hundredweights** — see WEIGHT table

¹hung past and past part of HANG

²hung adj : unable to reach a decision or verdict ⟨a ∼ jury⟩

Hung abbr Hungarian; Hungary

Hun·gar·i·an \,həŋ-'ger-ē-ən\ n **1** : a native or inhabitant of Hungary **2** : the language of the Hungarians — **Hungarian** adj

hun·ger \'həŋ-gər\ n **1** : a craving or urgent need for food **2** : a strong desire — **hunger** vb — **hun·gri·ly** adv — **hun·gry** adj

hung·over \'həŋ-'ō-vər\ adj : having a hangover

hung up adj **1** : DELAYED **2** : ENTHUSIASTIC; also : PREOCCUPIED — usu. used with on ⟨hung up on winning⟩

hunk \'həŋk\ n **1** : a large piece **2** : an attractive well-built man — **hunky** adj

hun·ker \'həŋ-kər\ vb **1** : CROUCH, SQUAT — usu. used with down **2** : to settle in for a sustained period — used with down

hun·ky-do·ry \,həŋ-kē-'dòr-ē\ adj : quite satisfactory : FINE

¹hunt \'hənt\ vb **1** : to pursue for food or in sport; also : to take part in a hunt **2** : to try to find : SEEK **3** : to drive or chase esp. by harrying **4** : to traverse in search of prey — **hunt·er** n

²hunt n : an act, practice, or instance of hunting

Hun·ting·ton's disease \'hən-tiŋ-tənz-\ n : a chorea that usu. begins in middle age and leads to dementia

hunt·ress \'hən-trəs\ n : a woman who hunts game

hunts·man \'hənts-mən\ n **1** : HUNTER **2** : a person who manages a hunt and looks after the hounds

hur·dle \'hər-d⁹l\ n **1** : a barrier to leap over in a race **2** : OBSTACLE — **hurdle** vb — **hur·dler** n

hur·dy-gur·dy \,hər-dē-'gər-dē, 'hər-dē-,gər-dē\ n, pl **-gur·dies** : a musical instrument in which the sound is produced by turning a crank

hurl \'hərl\ vb **1** : to move or cause to

move vigorously **2** : to throw down with violence **3** : FLING; *also* : PITCH — **hurl** *n* — **hurl·er** *n*

hur·ly–bur·ly \ˌhər-lē-ˈbər-lē\ *n* : UPROAR, TUMULT

Hu·ron \ˈhyùr-ən, ˈhyùr-ˌän\ *n*, *pl* **Hurons** *or* **Huron** : a member of a confederacy of American Indian peoples formerly living between Georgian Bay and Lake Ontario

hur·rah \hù-ˈrö, -ˈrä\ *also* **hur·ray** \hù-ˈrä\ *interj* — used to express joy, approval, or encouragement

hur·ri·cane \ˈhər-ə-ˌkän\ *n* [Sp *huracán*, of AmerInd origin] : a tropical cyclone with winds of 74 miles (118 kilometers) per hour or greater that is usu. accompanied by rain, thunder, and lightning

¹**hur·ry** \ˈhər-ē\ *vb* **hur·ried; hur·ry·ing 1** : to carry or cause to go with haste **2** : to impel to a greater speed **3** : to move or act with haste — **hurried** *adj* — **hur·ried·ly** *adv*

²**hurry** *n* : extreme haste or eagerness

¹**hurt** \ˈhərt\ *vb* **hurt; hurt·ing 1** : to feel or cause to feel physical or emotional pain **2** : to do harm to : DAMAGE **3** : OFFEND **4** : HAMPER **5** : to be in need — usu. used with *for* — **hurt** *adj*

²**hurt** *n* **1** : a bodily injury or wound **2** : SUFFERING **3** : HARM, WRONG — **hurtful** *adj* — **hurt·ful·ness** *n*

hur·tle \ˈhər-t°l\ *vb* **hur·tled; hur·tling 1** : to move rapidly or forcefully — **2** : HURL, FLING

¹**hus·band** \ˈhəz-bənd\ *n* [ME *husbonde*, fr. OE *hūsbonda* master of a house, fr. ON *hūsbōndi*, fr. *hūs* house + *bōndi* householder] : a male partner in a marriage

²**husband** *vb* : to manage prudently

hus·band·man \ˈhəz-bənd-mən\ *n* : FARMER

hus·band·ry \ˈhəz-bən-drē\ *n* **1** : the control or judicious use of resources **2** : AGRICULTURE **3** : the production and care of domestic animals

¹**hush** \ˈhəsh\ *vb* **1** : to make or become quiet or calm **2** : SUPPRESS

²**hush** *n* : SILENCE, QUIET

hush–hush \ˈhəsh-ˌhəsh\ *adj* : SECRET, CONFIDENTIAL

¹**husk** \ˈhəsk\ *n* **1** : a usu. thin dry outer covering of a seed or fruit **2** : an outer layer : SHELL

²**husk** *vb* : to strip the husk from — **husk·er** *n*

¹**hus·ky** \ˈhəs-kē\ *adj* **hus·ki·er; -est** : HOARSE — **hus·ki·ly** \-kə-lē\ *adv* — **hus·ki·ness** \-kē-nəs\ *n*

²**husky** *n*, *pl* **huskies 1** : a heavy-coated working dog of the New World Arctic **2** : SIBERIAN HUSKY

³**husky** *adj* **1** : BURLY, ROBUST **2** : LARGE

hus·sar \(ˌ)hə-ˈzär\ *n* [Hung *huszár*] : a member of any of various European cavalry units

hus·sy \ˈhə-zē, -sē\ *n*, *pl* **hussies** [alter. of *housewife*] **1** : a lewd or brazen woman **2** : a pert or mischievous girl

hus·tings \ˈhəs-tiŋz\ *n pl* : a place where political campaign speeches are made;

also : the proceedings in an election campaign

hus·tle \ˈhə-səl\ *vb* **hus·tled; hus·tling 1** : JOSTLE, SHOVE **2** : HASTEN, HURRY **3** : to work energetically — **hustle** *n* — **hus·tler** \ˈhəs-lər\ *n*

hut \ˈhət\ *n* : a small and often temporary dwelling : SHACK

hutch \ˈhəch\ *n* **1** : a chest or compartment for storage **2** : a cupboard usu. surmounted with open shelves **3** : a pen or coop for an animal **4** : HUT

huz·zah *or* **huz·za** \(ˌ)hə-ˈzä\ *n* : a shout of acclaim — often used interjectionally to express joy or approbation

HV *abbr* **1** high velocity **2** high voltage

HVAC *abbr* heating, ventilating and air-conditioning

hvy *abbr* heavy

HW *abbr* hot water

hwy *abbr* highway

hy·a·cinth \ˈhī-ə-(ˌ)sinth\ *n* : a bulbous Mediterranean herb related to the lilies that is widely grown for its spikes of fragrant bell-shaped flowers

hy·brid \ˈhī-brəd\ *n* **1** : an offspring of genetically differing parents (as members of different breeds or species) **2** : one of mixed origin or composition — **hybrid** *adj* — **hy·brid·i·za·tion** \ˌhī-brə-də-ˈzā-shən\ *n* — **hy·brid·ize** \ˈhī-brə-ˌdīz\ *vb* — **hy·brid·iz·er** *n*

hy·dra \ˈhī-drə\ *n* : any of numerous small tubular freshwater coelenterates that are polyps having at one end a mouth surrounded by tentacles

hy·dran·gea \hī-ˈdrän-jə\ *n* : any of a genus of shrubs related to the currants and grown for their showy clusters of white, pink, or bluish flowers

hy·drant \ˈhī-drənt\ *n* : a pipe with a valve and spout at which water may be drawn from a main pipe

hy·drate \ˈhī-ˌdrāt\ *n* : a compound formed by union of water with some other substance — **hydrate** *vb*

hy·drau·lic \hī-ˈdrö-lik\ *adj* [ultim. fr. Gk *hydraulis* pipe organ using water pressure, fr. *hydōr* water + *aulos* reed instrument] **1** : operated, moved, or effected by means of water **2** : of or relating to hydraulics **3** : operated by the resistance offered or the pressure transmitted when a quantity of liquid is forced through a small orifice or through a tube **4** : hardening or setting under water

hy·drau·lics \-liks\ *n* : a science that deals with practical applications of liquid (as water) in motion

hydro \ˈhī-drō\ *n* : HYDROPOWER

hy·dro·car·bon \ˈhī-drō-ˌkär-bən\ *n* : an organic compound containing only carbon and hydrogen

hy·dro·ceph·a·lus \ˌhī-drō-ˈse-fə-ləs\ *n* : abnormal increase in the amount of fluid in the cranial cavity accompanied by enlargement of the skull and atrophy of the brain

hy·dro·chlo·ric acid \ˌhī-drə-ˈklör-ik-\ *n* : a sharp-smelling corrosive acid used in the laboratory and in industry and present in dilute form in gastric juice

hy·dro·dy·nam·ics \ˌhī-drō-dī-ˈna-miks\ *n* : a science that deals with the motion of fluids and the forces acting on moving bodies immersed in fluids — **hy·dro·dy·nam·ic** *adj*

hy·dro·elec·tric \ˌhī-drō-i-ˈlek-trik\ : of or relating to production of electricity by waterpower — **hy·dro·elec·tric·i·ty** \-ˌlek-ˈtri-sə-tē\ *n*

hy·dro·foil \ˈhī-drə-ˌfȯi(-ə)l\ *n* : a boat that has fins attached to the bottom by struts for lifting the hull clear of the water to allow faster speeds

hy·dro·gen \ˈhī-drə-jən\ *n* [F *hydrogène*, fr. Gk *hydōr* water + *-genēs* born; fr. the fact that water is generated by its combustion] : a gaseous colorless odorless highly flammable chemical element that is the lightest of the elements — **hy·drog·e·nous** \hī-ˈdrä-jə-nəs\ *adj*

hy·dro·ge·nate \hī-ˈdrä-jə-ˌnāt, ˈhī-drə-\ *vb* **-nat·ed; -nat·ing** : to combine or treat with hydrogen; *esp* : to add hydrogen to the molecule of — **hy·dro·ge·na·tion** \hī-ˌdrä-jə-ˈnā-shən, ˌhī-drə-\ *n*

hydrogen bomb *n* : a bomb whose violent explosive power is due to the sudden release of atomic energy resulting from the fusion of light nuclei (as of hydrogen atoms)

hydrogen peroxide *n* : an unstable compound of hydrogen and oxygen used esp. as an oxidizing and bleaching agent, an antiseptic, and a propellant

hy·dro·graph·ic \ˌhī-drə-ˈgra-fik\ *adj* : of or relating to the description and study of bodies of water — **hy·drog·ra·pher** *n* — **hy·drog·ra·phy** \hī-ˈdrä-grə-fē\ *n*

hy·drol·o·gy \hī-ˈdrä-lə-jē\ *n* : a science dealing with the properties, distribution, and circulation of water — **hy·dro·log·ic** \ˌhī-drə-ˈlä-jik\ *or* **hy·dro·log·i·cal** \-ji-kəl\ *adj* — **hy·drol·o·gist** \hī-ˈdrä-lə-jist\ *n*

hy·dro·ly·sis \hī-ˈdrä-lə-səs\ *n* : a chemical decomposition involving the addition of the elements of water

hy·drom·e·ter \hī-ˈdrä-mə-tər\ *n* : a floating instrument for determining specific gravities of liquids and hence the strength (as of alcoholic liquors)

hy·dro·pho·bia \ˌhī-drə-ˈfō-bē-ə\ *n* [LL, fr. Gk, fr. *hydōr* water + *phobos* fear] : RABIES

hy·dro·phone \ˈhī-drə-ˌfōn\ *n* : an underwater listening device

¹hy·dro·plane \ˈhī-drə-ˌplān\ *n* **1** : a powerboat designed for racing that skims the surface of the water **2** : SEAPLANE

²hydroplane *vb* : to skid on a wet road due to loss of contact between the tires and road

hy·dro·pon·ics \ˌhī-drə-ˈpä-niks\ *n* : the growing of plants in nutrient solutions — **hy·dro·pon·ic** *adj*

hy·dro·pow·er \ˈhī-drə-ˌpau̇(-ə)r\ *n* : hydroelectric power

hy·dro·sphere \ˈhī-drə-ˌsfir\ *n* : the water (as vapor or lakes) of the earth

hy·dro·stat·ic \ˌhī-drə-ˈsta-tik\ *adj* : of or relating to fluids at rest or to the pressures they exert or transmit

hy·dro·ther·a·py \ˌhī-drə-ˈther-ə-pē\ *n* : the use of water esp. externally in the treatment of disease or disability

hy·dro·ther·mal \ˌhī-drə-ˈthər-məl\ *adj* : of or relating to hot water

hy·drous \ˈhī-drəs\ *adj* : containing water

hy·drox·ide \hī-ˈdräk-ˌsīd\ *n* **1** : a negatively charged ion consisting of one atom of oxygen and one atom of hydrogen **2** : a compound of hydroxide with an element or group

hy·e·na \hī-ˈē-nə\ *n* [ME *hyene*, fr. L *hyaena*, fr. Gk *hyaina*, fr. *hys* hog] : any of several large doglike carnivorous mammals of Asia and Africa

hy·giene \ˈhī-ˌjēn\ *n* **1** : a science concerned with establishing and maintaining good health **2** : conditions or practices conducive to health — **hy·gien·ic** \hī-ˈje-nik, -ˈjē-\ *adj* — **hy·gien·i·cal·ly** \-ni-k(ə-)lē\ *adv* — **hy·gien·ist** \hī-ˈjē-nist, ˈhī-ˌjē-, hī-ˈje-\ *n*

hy·grom·e·ter \hī-ˈgrä-mə-tər\ *n* : any of several instruments for measuring the humidity of the atmosphere

hy·gro·scop·ic \ˌhī-grə-ˈskä-pik\ *adj* : readily taking up and retaining moisture

hying *pres part of* HIE

hy·men \ˈhī-mən\ *n* : a fold of mucous membrane partly closing the opening of the vagina

hy·me·ne·al \ˌhī-mə-ˈnē-əl\ *adj* : NUPTIAL

hymn \ˈhim\ *n* : a song of praise esp. to God — **hymn** *vb*

hym·nal \ˈhim-nəl\ *n* : a book of hymns

hyp *abbr* hypothesis; hypothetical

¹hype \ˈhīp\ *vb* **hyped; hyp·ing** **1** : STIMULATE — usu. used with *up* **2** : INCREASE — **hyped–up** *adj*

²hype *vb* **hyped; hyping** **1** : DECEIVE **2** : PUBLICIZE

³hype *n* **1** : DECEPTION, PUT-ON **2** : PUBLICITY

hy·per \ˈhī-pər\ *adj* **1** : HIGH-STRUNG, EXCITABLE **2** : extremely active

hy·per·acid·i·ty \ˌhī-pər-ə-ˈsi-də-tē\ *n* : the condition of containing excessive acid esp. in the stomach — **hy·per·ac·id** \-ˈa-səd\ *adj*

hy·per·ac·tive \-ˈak-tiv\ *adj* : excessively or pathologically active — **hy·per·ac·tiv·i·ty** \-ˌak-ˈti-və-tē\ *n*

hy·per·bar·ic \ˌhī-pər-ˈber-ik\ *adj* : of, relating to, or utilizing greater than normal pressure (as of oxygen)

hy·per·bo·la \hī-ˈpər-bə-lə\ *n, pl* **-las** *or* **-lae** \-(ˌ)lē\ : a curve formed by the intersection of a double right circular cone with a plane that cuts both halves of the cone — **hy·per·bol·ic** \ˌhī-pər-ˈbä-lik\ *adj*

hy·per·bo·le \hī-ˈpər-bə-(ˌ)lē\ *n* : extravagant exaggeration used as a figure of speech

hy·per·crit·i·cal \ˌhī-pər-ˈkri-ti-kəl\ *adj* : excessively critical — **hy·per·crit·i·cal·ly** \-k(ə-)lē\ *adv*

hy·per·drive \ˈhī-pər-ˌdrīv\ *n* : a state of extremely heightened activity

hy·per·ex·tend \ˌhī-pər-ik-ˈstend\ *vb* : to extend beyond the normal range of motion — **hy·per·ex·ten·sion** \-'sten-shən\ n

hy·per·gly·ce·mia \ˌhī-pər-glī-'sē-mē-ə\ n : excess of sugar in the blood — **hy·per·gly·ce·mic** \-mik\ adj

hy·per·ki·net·ic \-kə-'ne-tik\ adj : characterized by fast-paced or frenetic activity

hy·per·link \'hī-pər-ˌliŋk\ n : a connecting element (as highlighted text) between one place in a hypertext or hypermedia document and another

hy·per·me·dia \'hī-pər-ˌmē-dē-ə\ n : a database format offering direct access to text, sound, or images related to that on display

hy·per·opia \ˌhī-pə-'rō-pē-ə\ n : a condition in which visual images come to focus behind the retina resulting esp. in defective vision for near objects — **hy·per·opic** \-'rō-pik, -'rä-\ adj

hy·per·sen·si·tive \-'sen-sə-tiv\ adj 1 : excessively or abnormally sensitive 2 : abnormally susceptible physiologically to a specific agent (as a drug) — **hy·per·sen·si·tive·ness** n — **hy·per·sen·si·tiv·i·ty** \-ˌsen-sə-'ti-və-tē\ n

hy·per·ten·sion \'hī-pər-ˌten-chən\ n : high blood pressure — **hy·per·ten·sive** \ˌhī-pər-'ten-siv\ adj or n

hy·per·text \'hī-pər-ˌtekst\ n : a database format in which information related to that on display can be accessed directly from the display

hy·per·thy·roid·ism \ˌhī-pər-'thī-ˌrȯi-ˌdi-zəm\ n : excessive activity of the thyroid gland; also : the resulting bodily condition — **hy·per·thy·roid** \-'thī-ˌrȯid\ adj

hy·per·tro·phy \hī-'pər-trə-fē\ n, pl -phies : excessive development of a body part — **hy·per·tro·phic** \ˌhī-pər-'trō-fik\ adj — **hypertrophy** vb

hy·per·ven·ti·late \ˌhī-pər-'ven-tə-ˌlāt\ vb : to breathe rapidly and deeply esp. to the point of losing an abnormal amount of carbon dioxide from the blood — **hy·per·ven·ti·la·tion** \-ˌven-tə-'lā-shən\ n

hy·phen \'hī-fən\ n : a punctuation mark - used esp. to divide or to compound words or word parts — **hyphen** vb

hy·phen·ate \'hī-fə-ˌnāt\ vb -at·ed; -at·ing : to connect or divide with a hyphen — **hy·phen·ation** \ˌhī-fə-'nā-shən\ n

hyp·no·sis \hip-'nō-səs\ n, pl -no·ses \-ˌsēz\ : an induced state that resembles sleep and in which the subject is responsive to suggestions of the inducer (**hyp·no·tist** \'hip-nə-tist\) — **hyp·no·tism** \'hip-nə-ˌti-zəm\ n — **hyp·no·tiz·able** \'hip-nə-ˌtī-zə-bəl\ adj — **hyp·no·tize** \-ˌtīz\ vb

¹**hyp·not·ic** \hip-'nä-tik\ adj 1 : inducing sleep : SOPORIFIC 2 : of or relating to hypnosis or hypnotism 3 : readily holding the attention — **hyp·not·i·cal·ly** \-ti-k(ə-)lē\ adv

²**hypnotic** n : a sleep-inducing drug

hy·po \'hī-pō\ n, pl **hypos** : SODIUM THIOSULFATE; also : a solution of sodium thiosulfate

hy·po·al·ler·gen·ic \ˌhī-pō-ˌa-lər-'je-nik\ adj : having little likelihood of causing an allergic response

hy·po·cen·ter \'hī-pə-ˌsen-tər\ n : the point of origin of an earthquake

hy·po·chon·dria \ˌhī-pə-'kän-drē-ə\ n [NL, fr. LL, pl., upper abdomen (formerly regarded as the seat of hypochondria), fr. Gk, lit., the parts under the cartilage (of the breastbone), fr. hypo- under + chondros cartilage] : depression of mind often centered on imaginary physical ailments — **hy·po·chon·dri·ac** \-drē-ˌak\ adj or n

hy·poc·ri·sy \hi-'pä-krə-sē\ n, pl -sies : a feigning to be what one is not or to believe what one does not; esp : the false assumption of an appearance of virtue or religion — **hyp·o·crite** \'hi-pə-ˌkrit\ n — **hyp·o·crit·i·cal** \ˌhi-pə-'kri-ti-kəl\ adj — **hyp·o·crit·i·cal·ly** \-k(ə-)lē\ adv

¹**hy·po·der·mic** \ˌhī-pə-'dər-mik\ adj : administered by or used in making an injection beneath the skin

²**hypodermic** n : HYPODERMIC SYRINGE; also : an injection made with this

hypodermic needle n : NEEDLE 3; also : HYPODERMIC SYRINGE

hypodermic syringe n : a small syringe with a hollow needle for injecting material into or through the skin

hy·po·gly·ce·mia \ˌhī-pō-glī-'sē-mē-ə\ n : abnormal decrease of sugar in the blood — **hy·po·gly·ce·mic** \-mik\ adj

hy·pot·e·nuse \hī-'pä-tə-ˌnüs, -ˌnyüs, -ˌnüz, -ˌnyüz\ n : the side of a right triangle that is opposite the right angle; also : its length

hy·po·thal·a·mus \ˌhī-pō-'tha-lə-məs\ n : a part of the brain that lies beneath the thalamus and is a control center for the autonomic nervous system

hy·poth·e·sis \hī-'pä-thə-səs\ n, pl -e·ses \-ˌsēz\ : an assumption made esp. in order to test its logical or empirical consequences — **hy·po·thet·i·cal** \ˌhī-pə-'the-ti-kəl\ adj — **hy·po·thet·i·cal·ly** \-k(ə-)lē\ adv

hy·poth·e·size \-ˌsīz\ vb -sized; -siz·ing : to adopt as a hypothesis

hy·po·thy·roid·ism \ˌhī-pō-'thī-ˌrȯi-ˌdi-zəm\ n : deficient activity of the thyroid gland; also : a resultant lowered metabolic rate and general loss of vigor — **hy·po·thy·roid** adj

hys·sop \'hi-səp\ n : a European mint sometimes used as a potherb

hys·ter·ec·to·my \ˌhis-tə-'rek-tə-mē\ n, pl -mies : surgical removal of the uterus

hys·te·ria \hi-'ster-ē-ə, -'stir-\ n [NL, fr. E hysteric, adj., fr. L hystericus, fr. Gk hysterikos, fr. hystera womb; fr. the Greek notion that hysteria was peculiar to women and caused by disturbances in the uterus] 1 : a nervous disorder marked esp. by defective emotional control 2 : unmanageable fear or outburst of emotion — **hys·ter·ic** \-'ster-ik\ n — **hys·ter·i·cal** \-'ster-i-kəl\ also **hysteric** adj — **hys·ter·i·cal·ly** \-k(ə-)lē\ adv

hys·ter·ics \-'ster-iks\ n pl : a fit of uncontrollable laughter or crying

Hz abbr hertz

I

¹**i** \'ī\ *n, pl* **i's** *or* **is** \'īz\ *often cap* : the 9th letter of the English alphabet

²**i** *abbr, often cap* island; isle

³**i** *symbol* imaginary unit

¹**I** \'ī, ə\ *pron* : the one speaking or writing

²**I** *abbr* interstate

³**I** *symbol* iodine

Ia *or* **IA** *abbr* Iowa

-ial *adj suffix* : ¹-AL ⟨manor*ial*⟩

iamb \'ī-ˌam\ *or* **iam·bus** \ī-'am-bəs\ *n, pl* **iambs** \'ī-ˌamz\ *or* **iam·bus·es** : a metrical foot of one unaccented syllable followed by one accented syllable — **iam·bic** \ī-'am-bik\ *adj or n*

-ian — see -AN

-iatric *also* **-iatrical** *adj comb form* : of or relating to (such) medical treatment or healing ⟨pediatric⟩

-iatrics *n pl comb form* : medical treatment ⟨pediatrics⟩

ib *or* **ibid** *abbr* ibidem

ibex \'ī-ˌbeks\ *n, pl* **ibex** *or* **ibex·es** [L] : any of several Old World wild goats with large curved horns

ibi·dem \'i-bə-ˌdem, i-'bī-dəm\ *adv* [L] : in the same place

-ibility — see -ABILITY

ibis \'ī-bəs\ *n, pl* **ibis** *or* **ibis·es** [L, fr. Gk, fr. Egypt *hbw*] : any of various wading birds related to the herons but having a downwardly curved bill

-ible — see -ABLE

ibu·pro·fen \ˌī-byü-'prō-fən\ *n* : a nonsteroidal anti-inflammatory drug used to relieve pain and fever

IC \ˌī-'sē\ *n* : INTEGRATED CIRCUIT

¹**-ic** *adj suffix* **1** : of, relating to, or having the form of : being ⟨panoramic⟩ **2** : related to, derived from, or containing ⟨alcoholic⟩ **3** : in the manner of : like that of : characteristic of **4** : associated or dealing with : utilizing ⟨electronic⟩ **5** : characterized by : exhibiting ⟨nostalgic⟩ : affected with ⟨allergic⟩ **6** : caused by **7** : tending to produce ⟨analgesic⟩

²**-ic** *n suffix* : one having the character or nature of : one belonging to or associated with : one exhibiting or affected by : one that produces

-ical *adj suffix* : -IC ⟨symmetrical⟩ ⟨geological⟩ — **-ically** *adv suffix*

ICBM \ˌī-ˌsē-(ˌ)bē-'em\ *n, pl* **ICBM's** *or* **ICBMs** \-'emz\ : an intercontinental ballistic missile

ICC *abbr* Interstate Commerce Commission

¹**ice** \'īs\ *n* **1** : frozen water **2** : a substance resembling ice **3** : a state of coldness (as from formality or reserve) **4** : a flavored frozen dessert; *esp* : one containing no milk or cream

²**ice** *vb* **iced; ic·ing 1** : FREEZE **2** : CHILL **3** : to cover with or as if with icing

ice age *n* : a time of widespread glaciation

ice bag *n* : a waterproof bag to hold ice for local application of cold to the body

ice·berg \'īs-ˌbərg\ *n* : a large floating mass of ice broken off from a glacier

iceberg lettuce *n* : any of various crisp light green lettuces that form a compact head like a cabbage

ice·boat \'īs-ˌbōt\ *n* : a boatlike frame on runners propelled on ice by sails

ice·bound \-ˌbau̇nd\ *adj* : surrounded, obstructed, or covered by ice

ice·box \-ˌbäks\ *n* : REFRIGERATOR

ice·break·er \-ˌbrā-kər\ *n* : a ship equipped (as with a reinforced bow) to make a channel through ice

ice cap *n* : a glacier forming on relatively level land and flowing outward from its center

ice cream *n* : a frozen food containing sweetened or flavored cream or butterfat

ice hockey *n* : a game in which two teams of ice-skating players try to shoot a puck into the opponent's goal

ice·house \'īs-ˌhau̇s\ *n* : a building in which ice is made or stored

¹**Ice·lan·dic** \īs-'lan-dik\ *adj* : of, relating to, or characteristic of Iceland, the Icelanders, or their language

²**Icelandic** *n* : the language of Iceland

ice·man \'īs-ˌman\ *n* : one who sells or delivers ice

ice milk *n* : a sweetened frozen food made of skim milk

ice pick *n* : a hand tool ending in a spike for chipping ice

ice-skate \'īs-ˌskāt\ *vb* : to skate on ice — **ice–skater** *n*

ice storm *n* : a storm in which falling rain freezes on contact

ice water *n* : chilled or iced water esp. for drinking

ich·thy·ol·o·gy \ˌik-thē-'ä-lə-jē\ *n* : a branch of zoology dealing with fishes — **ich·thy·ol·o·gist** \-jist\ *n*

ici·cle \'ī-ˌsi-kəl\ *n* [ME *isikel*, fr. *is* ice + *ikel* icicle, fr. OE *gicel*] : a hanging mass of ice formed by the freezing of dripping water

ic·ing \'ī-siŋ\ *n* : a sweet usu. creamy mixture used to coat baked goods

ICJ *abbr* International Court of Justice

icky \'i-kē\ *adj* **ick·i·er; -est** : OFFENSIVE, DISTASTEFUL — **ick·i·ness** *n*

icon *also* **ikon** \'ī-ˌkän\ *n* **1** : IMAGE; *esp* : a religious image painted on a wood panel **2** : a small picture on a computer display that suggests the purpose of an available function — **icon·ic** \ī-'kä-nik\ *adj*

icon·o·clasm \ī-'kä-nə-ˌkla-zəm\ *n* : the doctrine, practice, or attitude of an iconoclast

icon·o·clast \-ˌklast\ *n* [ML *iconoclastes*, fr. MGk *eikonoklastēs*, lit., image destroyer, fr. Gk *eikōn* image + *klan* to break] **1** : one who destroys religious images or opposes their veneration **2** : one who attacks cherished beliefs or institutions

-ics \iks\ *n sing or pl suffix* **1** : study : knowledge : skill : practice ⟨linguist*ics*⟩ ⟨electron*ics*⟩ **2** : characteristic actions or activities ⟨acrobat*ics*⟩ **3** : characteristic qualities, operations, or phenomena ⟨mechan*ics*⟩

ic·tus \'ik-təs\ *n* : the recurring stress or beat in a rhythmic or metrical series of sounds

ICU *abbr* intensive care unit

icy \'ī-sē\ *adj* **ic·i·er; -est 1** : covered with, abounding in, or consisting of ice **2** : intensely cold **3** : being cold and unfriendly — **ic·i·ly** \'ī-sə-lē\ *adv* — **ic·i·ness** \-sē-nəs\ *n*

1id \'id\ *n* [L, it] : the part of the psyche in psychoanalytic theory that is completely unconscious and concerned with instinctual needs and drives

2id *abbr* idem

1ID \'ī-'dē\ *vb* **ID'd** *or* **IDed; ID'ing** *or* **IDing** : IDENTIFY

2ID *abbr* **1** Idaho **2** identification

idea \ī-'dē-ə\ *n* **1** : a plan for action : DESIGN **2** : something imagined or pictured in the mind **3** : a central meaning or purpose ◆ **Synonyms** CONCEPT, CONCEPTION, NOTION, IMPRESSION

1ide·al \ī-'dēl\ *adj* **1** : existing only in the mind : IMAGINARY; *also* : lacking practicality **2** : of or relating to an ideal or to perfection : PERFECT

2ideal *n* **1** : a standard of excellence **2** : one regarded as a model worthy of imitation **3** : GOAL ◆ **Synonyms** ARCHETYPE, EXAMPLE, EXEMPLAR, PARADIGM, PATTERN

ide·al·ise *Brit var of* IDEALIZE

ide·al·ism \ī-'dē-ə-ˌli-zəm\ *n* : the practice of forming ideals or living under their influence; *also* : an idealized representation — **ide·al·ist** \-list\ *n* — **ide·al·is·tic** \ī-ˌdē-ə-'lis-tik\ *adj* — **ide·al·is·ti·cal·ly** \-ti-k(ə-)lē\ *adv*

ide·al·ize \ī-'dē-ə-ˌlīz\ *vb* **-ized; -iz·ing** : to think of or represent as ideal — **ide·al·i·za·tion** \ī-ˌdē-ə-lə-'zā-shən\ *n*

ide·al·ly \ī-'dē-lē, -'dē-ə-lē\ *adv* **1** : in idea or imagination : MENTALLY **2** : in agreement with an ideal : PERFECTLY

ide·a·tion \ˌī-dē-'ā-shən\ *n* : the forming or entertaining of ideas — **ide·ate** \'ī-dē-ˌāt\ *vb* — **ide·a·tion·al** \ˌī-dē-'ā-shə-nəl\ *adj*

idem \'ī-ˌdem, 'ē-, 'i-\ *pron* [L, same] : the same as something previously mentioned

iden·ti·cal \ī-'den-ti-kəl\ *adj* **1** : being the same **2** : essentially alike ◆ **Synonyms** EQUIVALENT, EQUAL, TANTAMOUNT

iden·ti·fi·ca·tion \ī-ˌden-tə-fə-'kā-shən\ *n* **1** : an act of identifying : the state of being identified **2** : evidence of identity **3** : an unconscious psychological process by which an individual models thoughts, feelings, and actions after another person or an object

iden·ti·fy \ī-'den-tə-ˌfī\ *vb* **-fied; -fy·ing 1** : to regard as identical **2** : ASSOCIATE **3** : to establish the identity of **4** : to practice psychological identification — **iden·ti·fi·able** \-ˌden-tə-'fī-ə-bəl\ *adj* —

iden·ti·fi·ably \-blē\ *adv* — **iden·ti·fi·er** \-ˌfī(-ə)r\ *n*

iden·ti·ty \ī-'den-tə-tē\ *n, pl* **-ties 1** : sameness of essential character **2** : INDIVIDUALITY **3** : the fact of being the same person or thing as claimed

identity crisis *n* : psychological conflict esp. in adolescence involving confusion about one's social role and one's personality

identity theft *n* : the illegal use of someone else's personal information to obtain money or credit

ideo·gram \'ī-dē-ə-ˌgram, 'i-\ *n* **1** : a picture or symbol used in a system of writing to represent a thing or an idea **2** : a character or symbol used in a system of writing to represent an entire word

ideo·logue *also* **idea·logue** \'ī-dē-ə-ˌlóg\ *n* : a partisan advocate or adherent of a particular ideology

ide·ol·o·gy \ˌī-dē-'ä-lə-jē, ˌi-\ *also* **ide·al·o·gy** \-'ä-lə-jē, -'a-\ *n, pl* **-gies 1** : the body of ideas characteristic of a particular individual, group, or culture **2** : the assertions, theories, and aims that constitute a political, social, and economic program — **ide·o·log·i·cal** \ˌī-dē-ə-'lä-ji-kəl, ˌi-\ *adj* — **ideo·log·i·cal·ly** \-'lä-ji-k(ə-)lē\ *adv* — **ide·ol·o·gist** \-dē-'ä-lə-jist\ *n*

ides \'īdz\ *n sing or pl* : the 15th day of March, May, July, or October or the 13th day of any other month in the ancient Roman calendar

id·i·o·cy \'i-dē-ə-sē\ *n, pl* **-cies 1** *usu offensive* : extreme mental retardation **2** : something notably stupid or foolish

id·i·om \'i-dē-əm\ *n* **1** : the language peculiar to a person or group **2** : the characteristic form or structure of a language **3** : an expression that cannot be understood from the meanings of its separate words (as *give way*) — **id·i·o·mat·ic** \ˌi-dē-ə-'ma-tik\ *adj* — **id·i·o·mat·i·cal·ly** \-ti-k(ə-)lē\ *adv*

id·i·o·path·ic \ˌi-dē-ə-'pa-thik\ *adj* : arising spontaneously or from an obscure or unknown cause ⟨an ~ disease⟩

id·i·o·syn·cra·sy \ˌi-dē-ə-'sin-krə-sē\ *n, pl* **-sies** : personal peculiarity — **id·i·o·syn·crat·ic** \ˌi-dē-ō-sin-'kra-tik\ *adj* — **id·i·o·syn·crat·i·cal·ly** \-'kra-ti-k(ə-)lē\ *adv*

id·i·ot \'i-dē-ət\ *n,* [ME, fr. AF *ydiote,* fr. L *idiota* ignorant person, fr. Gk *idiōtēs* one in a private station, layman, ignorant person, fr. *idios* one's own, private] **1** *usu offensive* : a person affected with idiocy **2** : a foolish or stupid person — **id·i·ot·ic** \ˌi-dē-'ä-tik\ *adj* — **id·i·ot·i·cal·ly** \-ti-k(ə-)lē\ *adv*

id·i·ot-proof \'i-dē-ət-ˌprüf\ *adj* : extremely easy to operate or maintain

1idle \'ī-d°l\ *adj* **idler** \'ī-də-lər\; **idlest** \'ī-də-ləst\ **1** : GROUNDLESS, WORTHLESS, USELESS ⟨~ talk⟩ **2** : not occupied or employed : INACTIVE **3** : LAZY — **idle·ness** \-nəs\ *n* — **idly** \'īd-lē\ *adv*

2idle *vb* **idled; idling 1** : to spend time doing nothing **2** : to make idle **3** : to run without being connected so that

power is not used for useful work —
idler n

idol \'ī-d°l\ n 1 : an image worshipped as a god; *also* : a false god 2 : an object of passionate devotion

idol·a·ter or **idol·a·tor** \ī-'dä-lə-tər\ n : a worshiper of idols

idol·a·try \-trē\ n, pl **-tries** 1 : the worship of a physical object as a god 2 : excessive devotion — **idol·a·trous** \-trəs\ adj

idol·ize \'ī-də-‚līz\ vb **-ized; -iz·ing** : to make an idol of — **idol·i·za·tion** \‚ī-də-lə-'zā-shən\ n

ikon var of ICON

idyll \'ī-d°l\ n 1 : a simple work of writing or poetry that describes country life or suggests a peaceful setting 2 : a fit subject for an idyll — **idyl·lic** \ī-'di-lik\ adj

i.e. \'ī-'ē\ abbr [L id est] that is

IE abbr industrial engineer

-ier — see -ER

if \'if\ conj 1 : in the event that ⟨∼ he stays, I leave⟩ 2 : WHETHER ⟨ask ∼ he left⟩ 3 — used as a function word to introduce an exclamation expressing a wish ⟨∼ it would only rain⟩ 4 : even though ⟨an interesting ∼ untenable argument⟩ 5 : and perhaps not even ⟨few ∼ any changes are expected⟩

IF abbr intermediate frequency

if·fy \'i-fē\ adj : full of contingencies or unknown conditions

-i·fy \ə-‚fī\ vb suffix : -FY

IG abbr inspector general

ig·loo \'i-glü\ n, pl **igloos** [Inuit (an Eskimo language) iglu house] : an Eskimo house or hut often made of snow blocks and in the shape of a dome

ig·ne·ous \'ig-nē-əs\ adj 1 : FIERY 2 : formed by solidification of molten rock

ig·nite \ig-'nīt\ vb **ig·nit·ed; ig·nit·ing** : to set afire or catch fire — **ig·nit·able** \-'nī-tə-bəl\ adj

ig·ni·tion \ig-'ni-shən\ n 1 : a setting on fire 2 : the process or means (as an electric spark) of igniting the fuel mixture in an engine 3 : a device that activates an ignition system

ig·no·ble \ig-'nō-bəl\ adj 1 : of common birth 2 : not honorable : BASE, MEAN ✦ *Synonyms* DESPICABLE, SCURVY, SORDID, VILE, WRETCHED — **ig·no·bly** adv

ig·no·min·i·ous \‚ig-nə-'mi-nē-əs\ adj 1 : DISHONORABLE 2 : DESPICABLE 3 : HUMILIATING, DEGRADING ✦ *Synonyms* DISREPUTABLE, DISCREDITABLE, DISGRACEFUL, INGLORIOUS — **ig·no·min·i·ous·ly** adv — **ig·no·mi·ny** \'ig-nə-‚mi-nē, ig-'nä-mə-nē\ n

ig·no·ra·mus \‚ig-nə-'rā-məs\ n, pl **-mus·es** also **-mi** \-mē\ [Ignoramus, ignorant lawyer in Ignoramus (1615), play by George Ruggle] : an utterly ignorant person

ig·no·rance \'ig-nə-rəns\ n : the state of being ignorant

ig·no·rant \'ig-nə-rənt\ adj 1 : lacking knowledge 2 : resulting from or showing lack of knowledge or intelligence 3 : UNAWARE, UNINFORMED ✦ *Synonyms* BENIGHTED, ILLITERATE, UNEDUCATED,

UNLETTERED, UNTUTORED — **ig·no·rant·ly** adv

ig·nore \ig-'nȯr\ vb **ig·nored; ig·nor·ing** : to refuse to take notice of ✦ *Synonyms* OVERLOOK, SLIGHT, NEGLECT

igua·na \i-'gwä-nə\ n : any of various large tropical American lizards

ihp abbr indicated horsepower

IHS \‚ī-‚äch-'es\ [LL, part transliteration of Gk IHΣ, abbr. for IHΣΟΥΣ Iēsous Jesus] — used as a Christian symbol and monogram for Jesus

IL abbr Illinois

il·e·itis \‚i-lē-'ī-təs\ n : inflammation of the ileum

il·e·um \'i-lē-əm\ n, pl **il·ea** \-lē-ə\ : the part of the small intestine between the jejunum and the large intestine

il·i·ac \'i-lē-‚ak\ adj : of, relating to, or located near the ilium

il·i·um \'i-lē-əm\ n, pl **il·ia** \-lē-ə\ : the uppermost and largest of the three bones making up either side of the pelvis

ilk \'ilk\ n : SORT, KIND

¹**ill** \'il\ adj **worse** \'wərs\; **worst** \'wərst\ 1 : attended or caused by an evil intent ⟨∼ deeds⟩ 2 : not normal or sound ⟨∼ health⟩; also : not in good health : SICK 3 : BAD, UNLUCKY ⟨an ∼ omen⟩ 4 : not right or proper ⟨∼ manners⟩ 5 : UNFRIENDLY, HOSTILE ⟨∼ feeling⟩

²**ill** adv **worse; worst** 1 : with displeasure 2 : in a harsh manner 3 : HARDLY, SCARCELY ⟨can ∼ afford it⟩ 4 : BADLY, UNLUCKILY 5 : in a faulty way

³**ill** n 1 : EVIL 2 : MISFORTUNE, DISTRESS 3 : AILMENT, SICKNESS; also : TROUBLE

⁴**ill** abbr illustrated; illustration; illustrator

Ill abbr Illinois

ill–ad·vised \'il-əd-'vīzd\ adj : not well counseled ⟨∼ efforts⟩ — **ill–ad·vis·ed·ly** \-'vī-zəd-lē\ adv

ill–bred \-'bred\ adj : badly brought up : IMPOLITE

il·le·gal \il-'lē-gəl\ adj : not lawful; also : not sanctioned by official rules ✦ *Synonyms* UNLAWFUL, CRIMINAL, ILLEGITIMATE, ILLICIT, WRONGFUL — **il·le·gal·i·ty** \‚i-li-'ga-lə-tē\ n — **il·le·gal·ly** adv

il·leg·i·ble \il-'le-jə-bəl\ adj : not legible — **il·leg·i·bil·i·ty** \il-‚le-jə-'bi-lə-tē\ n — **il·leg·i·bly** \il-'le-jə-blē\ adv

il·le·git·i·mate \‚i-li-'ji-tə-mət\ adj 1 : born of unmarried parents 2 : ILLOGICAL 3 : ILLEGAL — **il·le·git·i·ma·cy** \-'ji-tə-mə-sē\ n — **il·le·git·i·mate·ly** adv

ill–fat·ed \'il-'fā-təd\ adj : UNFORTUNATE ⟨an ∼ expedition⟩

ill–fa·vored \-'fā-vərd\ adj : UGLY, UNATTRACTIVE

ill–got·ten \-'gä-t°n\ adj : acquired by improper means ⟨∼ gains⟩

ill–hu·mored \-'hyü-mərd, -'yü-\ adj : SURLY, IRRITABLE

il·lib·er·al \il-'li-bə-rəl\ adj : not liberal : NARROW, BIGOTED

il·lic·it \il-'li-sət\ adj : not permitted : UNLAWFUL — **il·lic·it·ly** adv

il·lim·it·able \il-'li-mə-tə-bəl\ adj : BOUNDLESS, MEASURELESS — **il·lim·it·ably** \-blē\ adv

Il·li·nois \ˌi-lə-ˈnȯi *also* -ˈnȯiz\ *n, pl* **Illi·nois** : a member of an American Indian people of Illinois, Iowa, and Wisconsin

il·lit·er·ate \il-ˈli-tə-rət\ *adj* **1** : having little or no education; *esp* : unable to read or write **2** : showing a lack of familiarity with the fundamentals of a particular field of knowledge — **il·lit·er·a·cy** \-ˈli-tə-rə-sē\ *n* — **illiterate** *n*

ill-man·nered \ˈil-ˈma-nərd\ *adj* : marked by bad manners : RUDE

ill-na·tured \-ˈnā-chərd\ *adj* : CROSS, SURLY — **ill-na·tured·ly** *adv*

ill·ness \ˈil-nəs\ *n* : SICKNESS

il·log·i·cal \il-ˈlä-ji-kəl\ *adj* : lacking sound reasoning; *also* : SENSELESS — **il·log·i·cal·ly** \-ji-k(ə-)lē\ *adv*

ill-starred \ˈil-ˈstärd\ *adj* : UNLUCKY 1 ⟨an ~ venture⟩

ill-tem·pered \-ˈtem-pərd\ *adj* : CROSS

ill-treat \-ˈtrēt\ *vb* : to treat cruelly or improperly : MALTREAT — **ill-treat·ment** *n*

il·lu·mi·nate \i-ˈlü-mə-ˌnāt\ *vb* **-nat·ed; -nat·ing** **1** : to supply or brighten with light : light up **2** : to make clear : ELUCIDATE; *also* : to bring to the fore **3** : to decorate (as a manuscript) with designs or pictures in gold or colors — **il·lu·mi·nat·ing·ly** *adv* — **il·lu·mi·na·tion** \-ˌlü-mə-ˈnā-shən\ *n* — **il·lu·mi·na·tor** \-ˈlü-mə-ˌnā-tər\ *n*

il·lu·mine \i-ˈlü-mən\ *vb* **-mined; -min·ing** : ILLUMINATE

ill-us·age \ˈil-ˈyü-sij\ *n* : harsh, unkind, or abusive treatment

ill-use \-ˈyüz\ *vb* : MALTREAT, ABUSE

il·lu·sion \i-ˈlü-zhən\ *n* [ME, fr. AF, fr. LL *illusio*, fr. L, action of mocking, fr. *illudere* to mock at, fr. *ludere* to play, mock] **1** : a mistaken idea : MISCONCEPTION **2** : a misleading visual image; *also* : HALLUCINATION

il·lu·sion·ist \i-ˈlü-zhə-nist\ *n* : one that produces illusions; *esp* : a sleight-of-hand performer

il·lu·sive \i-ˈlü-siv\ *adj* : DECEPTIVE

il·lu·so·ry \i-ˈlü-sə-rē, -zə-\ *adj* : DECEPTIVE ⟨~ hopes⟩

illust *or* **illus** *abbr* illustrated; illustration

il·lus·trate \ˈi-ləs-ˌtrāt\ *vb* **-trat·ed; -trat·ing** [L *illustrare*, fr. *lustrare* to purify, make bright] **1** : to explain by use of examples : CLARIFY; *also* : DEMONSTRATE **2** : to provide with pictures or figures that explain or decorate **3** : to serve to explain or decorate — **il·lus·tra·tor** \ˈi-ləs-ˌtrā-tər\ *n*

il·lus·tra·tion \ˌi-ləs-ˈtrā-shən\ *n* **1** : the act of illustrating : the condition of being illustrated **2** : an example or instance that helps make something clear **3** : a picture or diagram that explains or decorates

il·lus·tra·tive \i-ˈləs-trə-tiv, ˈi-lə-ˌstrā-\ *adj* : serving, tending, or designed to illustrate — **il·lus·tra·tive·ly** *adv*

il·lus·tri·ous \i-ˈləs-trē-əs\ *adj* : notably outstanding because of rank or achievement ♦ *Synonyms* DISTINGUISHED, EMINENT, FAMOUS, GREAT, NOTABLE, PROMINENT — **il·lus·tri·ous·ness** *n*

ill will *n* : unfriendly feeling

ILS *abbr* instrument landing system

¹im·age \ˈi-mij\ *n* **1** : a likeness or imitation of a person or thing; *esp* : STATUE **2** : a picture of an object formed by a device (as a mirror or lens) **3** : a visual representation of something ⟨a computer ~⟩ **4** a person strikingly like another person ⟨he is the ~ of his father⟩ **5** : a mental picture or conception : IMPRESSION, IDEA, CONCEPT **6** : a vivid representation or description

²image *vb* **im·aged; im·ag·ing** **1** : to call up a mental picture of **2** : to describe or portray in words **3** : to create a representation of **4** : REFLECT, MIRROR **5** : to make appear : PROJECT

im·ag·ery \ˈi-mij-rē\ *n, pl* **-er·ies** **1** : IMAGES; *also* : the art of making images **2** : figurative language **3** : mental images; *esp* : the products of imagination

imag·in·able \i-ˈma-jə-nə-bəl\ *adj* : capable of being imagined : CONCEIVABLE — **imag·in·ably** *adv*

imag·i·nary \i-ˈma-jə-ˌner-ē\ *adj* **1** : existing only in the imagination **2** : containing or relating to a quantity **(imaginary unit)** that is the positive square root of minus 1 (√-1)

imaginary number : a complex number (as 2 + 3*i*) with a nonzero term **(imaginary part)** containing the imaginary unit as a factor

imag·i·na·tion \i-ˌma-jə-ˈnā-shən\ *n* **1** : the act or power of forming a mental image of something not present to the senses or not previously known or experienced **2** : creative ability **3** : RESOURCEFULNESS **4** : a mental image : a creation of the mind — **imag·i·na·tive** \i-ˈma-jə-nə-tiv, -ˌnā-\ *adj* — **imag·i·na·tive·ly** *adv*

imag·ine \i-ˈma-jən\ *vb* **imag·ined; imag·in·ing** **1** : to form a mental picture of something not present **2** : THINK, GUESS ⟨I ~ it will rain⟩

imag·in·ings \-ˈmaj-niŋz, -ˈma-jə-\ *n pl* : products of the imagination

im·ag·ism \ˈi-mi-ˌji-zəm\ *n, often cap* : a movement in poetry advocating free verse and the expression of ideas and emotions through clear precise images — **im·ag·ist** \-jist\ *n*

ima·go \i-ˈmā-gō, -ˈmä-\ *n, pl* **imagoes** *or* **ima·gi·nes** \-ˈmā-gə-ˌnēz, -ˈmä-\ [NL, fr. L, image] : an insect in its final adult stage — **ima·gi·nal** \i-ˈmā-gə-nᵊl, -ˈmä-\ *adj*

im·bal·ance \ˈim-ˈba-ləns\ *n* : lack of balance : the state of being out of equilibrium or out of proportion

im·be·cile \ˈim-bə-səl, -ˌsil\ *n,* **1** *usu offensive* : a person affected with moderate mental retardation **2** : FOOL, IDIOT — **imbecile** *or* **im·be·cil·ic** \ˌim-bə-ˈsi-lik\ *adj* — **im·be·cil·i·ty** \ˌim-bə-ˈsi-lə-tē\ *n*

imbed *var of* EMBED

im·bibe \im-ˈbīb\ *vb* **im·bibed; im·bib·ing** **1** : to receive and retain in the mind **2** : to drink alcoholic beverages **3** : to take in or up : ABSORB — **im·bib·er** *n*

im·bri·ca·tion \,im-brə-'kā-shən\ n   1
: an overlapping of edges (as of tiles)   2
: a pattern showing imbrication — **im·bri·cate** \'im-bri-kət\ adj

im·bro·glio \im-'brōl-yō\ n, pl **-glios** [It,
fr. *imbrogliare* to entangle]   1 : a confused mass   2 : a complicated situation;
also : a serious or embarrassing misunderstanding

im·brue \im-'brü\ vb **im·brued; im·bru·ing** : STAIN ⟨hands imbrued with blood⟩

im·bue \-'byü\ vb **im·bued; im·bu·ing**   1
: to permeate or influence as if by dyeing   2 : to tinge or color deeply

IMF abbr International Monetary Fund

imit abbr imitative

im·i·ta·ble \'i-mə-tə-bəl\ adj : capable or
worthy of being imitated or copied

im·i·tate \'i-mə-,tāt\ vb **-tat·ed; -tat·ing**
1 : to follow as a model : COPY   2 : RE-
SEMBLE   3 : REPRODUCE   4 : MIMIC,
COUNTERFEIT — **im·i·ta·tor** \-,tā-tər\ n

im·i·ta·tion \,i-mə-'tā-shən\ n   1 : an act
of imitating   2 : COPY, COUNTERFEIT
: a literary work that reproduces the style
of another author — **imitation** adj

im·i·ta·tive \'i-mə-,tā-tiv\ adj   1 : marked
by imitation   2 : inclined to imitate   3
: COUNTERFEIT

im·mac·u·late \i-'ma-kyə-lət\ adj   1
: being without stain or blemish : PURE
2 : spotlessly clean ⟨∼ linen⟩ — **im·mac·u·late·ly** adv

im·ma·nent \'i-mə-nənt\ adj   1 INHER-
ENT   2 : being within the limits of experience or knowledge — **im·ma·nence**
\-nəns\ n — **im·ma·nen·cy** \-nən-sē\ n

im·ma·te·ri·al \,i-mə-'tir-ē-əl\ adj   1 : not
consisting of matter : SPIRITUAL   2 : UN-
IMPORTANT, TRIFLING   ♦ **Synonyms**
BODILESS, DISEMBODIED, INCORPOREAL,
INSUBSTANTIAL, NONPHYSICAL — **im·ma·te·ri·al·i·ty** \-,tir-ē-'a-lə-tē\ n

im·ma·ture \,i-mə-'tur, -'tyur\ adj : lacking complete development : not yet mature — **im·ma·tu·ri·ty** \-'tur-ə-tē, -'tyur-\
n

im·mea·sur·able \(,)i-'me-zhə-rə-bəl\ adj
: not capable of being measured : indefi-
nitely extensive : ILLIMITABLE — **im·mea·sur·ably** \-blē\ adv

im·me·di·a·cy \i-'mē-dē-ə-sē\ n, pl **-cies**
1 : the quality or state of being immediate   2 : something that is of immediate
importance

im·me·di·ate \i-'mē-dē-ət\ adj   1 : acting
directly and alone : DIRECT ⟨the ∼ cause
of death⟩   2 : being next in line or relation ⟨members of the ∼ family⟩   3 : not
distant : CLOSE   4 : made or done at once
⟨an ∼ response⟩   5 : near to or related
to the present time ⟨the ∼ future⟩ — **im·me·di·ate·ly** adv

im·me·mo·ri·al \,i-mə-'mòr-ē-əl\ adj : extending beyond the reach of memory,
record, or tradition

im·mense \i-'mens\ adj [ME, fr. MF, fr. L
immensus immeasurable, fr. *mensus*, pp.
of *metiri* to measure]   1 : very great in
size or degree : VAST, HUGE   2 : EXCEL-

LENT — **im·mense·ly** adv — **im·men·si·ty** \-'men-sə-tē\ n

im·merse \i-'mərs\ vb **im·mersed; im·mers·ing**   1 : to plunge or dip esp. into a
fluid   2 : ENGROSS, ABSORB   3 : to bap-
tize by immersing — **im·mer·sion**
\-'mər-zhən\ n

im·mi·grant \'i-mi-grənt\ n   1 : a person
who immigrates   2 : a plant or animal
that becomes established where it did not
previously occur

im·mi·grate \'i-mə-,grāt\ vb **-grat·ed;
-grat·ing** : to come into a foreign coun-
try and take up residence — **im·mi·gra·tion** \,i-mə-'grā-shən\ n

im·mi·nent \'i-mə-nənt\ adj : ready to
take place; esp : hanging threateningly
over one's head — **im·mi·nence** \-nəns\
n — **im·mi·nent·ly** adv

im·mis·ci·ble \(,)i-'mi-sə-bəl\ adj : inca-
pable of mixing — **im·mis·ci·bil·i·ty**
\-,mi-sə-'bi-lə-tē\ n

im·mis·er·a·tion \(,)i-,mi-zə-'rā-shən\ n
: IMPOVERISHMENT

im·mo·bile \(,)i-'mō-bəl\ adj : incapable
of being moved : FIXED — **im·mo·bil·i·ty** \,i-mō-'bi-lə-tē\ n

im·mo·bi·lize \i-'mō-bə-,līz\ vb : to make
immobile — **im·mo·bi·li·za·tion** \i-,mō-bə-lə-'zā-shən\ n

im·mod·er·ate \(,)i-'mä-də-rət\ adj : lack-
ing in moderation : EXCESSIVE — **im·mod·er·a·cy** \-rə-sē\ n — **im·mod·er·ate·ly** adv

im·mod·est \(,)i-'mä-dəst\ adj : not mod-
est : BRAZEN, INDECENT ⟨an ∼ dress⟩
⟨∼ conduct⟩ — **im·mod·est·ly** adv —
im·mod·es·ty \-də-stē\ n

im·mo·late \'i-mə-,lāt\ vb **-lat·ed; -lat·ing**
[L *immolare*, to sprinkle with meal before
sacrificing, sacrifice, fr. *mola* sacrificial
barley cake, lit., millstone] : to offer in
sacrifice; esp : to kill as a sacrificial victim
— **im·mo·la·tion** \,i-mə-'lā-shən\ n

im·mor·al \(,)i-'mòr-əl\ adj : not moral —
im·mor·al·ly adv

im·mo·ral·i·ty \,i-mò-'ra-lə-tē, ,i-mə-\ n   1
: WICKEDNESS; esp : UNCHASTITY   2 : an
immoral act or practice

¹**im·mor·tal** \(,)i-'mòr-t°l\ adj   1 : not mor-
tal : exempt from death ⟨∼ gods⟩   2
: destined to be remembered forever
⟨those ∼ words⟩ — **im·mor·tal·ly** adv

²**immortal** n   1 : one exempt from death
2 pl, often cap : the gods in Greek and
Roman mythology   3 : a person whose
fame is lasting ⟨an ∼ of baseball⟩

im·mor·tal·ise Brit var of IMMORTALIZE

im·mor·tal·i·ty \,i-,mòr-'ta-lə-tē\ n : the
quality or state of being immortal; esp
: unending existence

im·mor·tal·ize \i-'mòr-tə-,līz\ vb **-ized;
-iz·ing** : to make immortal

im·mov·able \(,)i-'mü-və-bəl\ adj   1
: firmly fixed, settled, or fastened : FAST,
STATIONARY ⟨∼ mountains⟩   2 : STEAD-
FAST, UNYIELDING — **im·mov·abil·i·ty**
\-,mü-və-'bi-lə-tē\ n — **im·mov·ably** \-blē\ adv

im·mune \i-'myün\ adj   1 : EXEMPT   2
: having a special capacity for resistance
(as to a disease)   3 : containing or pro-

ducing antibodies — **im·mu·ni·ty** \-'myü-nə-tē\ n

immune response n : a response of the body to an antigen resulting in the formation of antibodies and cells designed to react with the antigen and render it harmless

immune system n : the bodily system that protects the body from foreign substances, cells, and tissues by producing the immune response and that includes esp. the thymus, spleen, lymph nodes, and lymphocytes

im·mu·nize \'i-myə-ˌnīz\ vb **-nized; -niz·ing** : to make immune — **im·mu·ni·za·tion** \ˌi-myə-nə-'zā-shən\ n

im·mu·no·de·fi·cien·cy \ˌi-myə-nō-di-'fi-shən-sē\ n : inability to produce the normal number of antibodies or immunologically sensitized cells esp. in response to specific antigens — **im·mu·no·de·fi·cient** \-'fi-shənt\ adj

im·mu·no·glob·u·lin \ˌi-myə-nō-'glä-byə-lən\ n : ANTIBODY

im·mu·nol·o·gy \ˌi-myə-'nä-lə-jē\ n : a science that deals with the immune system, immunity, and the immune response — **im·mu·no·log·ic** \-nə-'lä-jik\ or **im·mu·no·log·i·cal** \-ji-kəl\ adj — **im·mu·no·log·i·cal·ly** \-ji-k(ə-)lē\ adv — **im·mu·nol·o·gist** \-'nä-lə-jist\ n

im·mu·no·sup·pres·sion \ˌi-myə-nō-sə-'pre-shən\ n : suppression (as by drugs) of natural immune responses — **im·mu·no·sup·press** \-'pres\ vb — **im·mu·no·sup·pres·sant** \-'pre-sᵊnt\ n or adj — **im·mu·no·sup·pres·sive** \-'pre-siv\ adj

im·mu·no·ther·a·py \-'ther-ə-pē\ n : the treatment or prevention of disease by attempting to induce immunity

im·mure \i-'myu̇r\ vb **im·mured; mur·ing 1** : to enclose within or as if within walls **2** : to build into a wall; esp : to entomb in a wall

im·mu·ta·ble \(ˌ)i-'myü-tə-bəl\ adj : UNCHANGEABLE, UNCHANGING — **im·mu·ta·bil·i·ty** \-ˌmyü-tə-'bi-lə-tē\ n — **im·mu·ta·bly** \-'myü-tə-blē\ adv

¹**imp** \'imp\ n **1** : a small demon : FIEND **2** : a mischievous child

²**imp** abbr **1** imperative **2** imperfect **3** imperial **4** import; imported

¹**im·pact** \im-'pakt\ vb **1** : to press together **2** : to have an impact on

²**im·pact** \'im-ˌpakt\ n **1** : a forceful contact, collision, or onset; also : the impetus communicated in or as if in a collision **2** : EFFECT

im·pact·ed \im-'pak-təd\ adj **1** : packed or wedged in **2** : wedged between the jawbone and another tooth

im·pair \im-'per\ vb : to diminish in quantity, value, excellence, or strength : DAMAGE, LESSEN — **im·pair·ment** n

im·paired \-'pard\ adj : being in a less than perfect or whole condition; esp : disabled or functionally defective — often used in combination ⟨hearing-impaired⟩

im·pa·la \im-'pa-lə\ n, pl **impalas** or **impala** : a large brownish African antelope that in the male has slender curved horns with ridges

im·pale \im-'pāl\ vb **im·paled; im·pal·ing** : to pierce with or as if with something pointed — **im·pale·ment** n

im·pal·pa·ble \(ˌ)im-'pal-pə-bəl\ adj **1** : unable to be felt by touch : INTANGIBLE **2** : not easily seen or understood — **im·pal·pa·bly** \-blē\ adv

im·pan·el or **em·pan·el** \im-'pan-ᵊl\ vb : to enter in or on a panel : ENROLL ⟨~ a jury⟩

im·part \im-'pärt\ vb **1** : to give from one's store or abundance ⟨the sun ~s warmth⟩ **2** : to make known

im·par·tial \(ˌ)im-'pär-shəl\ adj : not partial : UNBIASED, JUST — **im·par·tial·i·ty** \-ˌpär-shē-'a-lə-tē\ n — **im·par·tial·ly** adv

im·pass·able \(ˌ)im-'pa-sə-bəl\ adj : incapable of being passed, traversed, or crossed ⟨~ roads⟩ — **im·pass·ably** \-blē\ adv

im·passe \'im-ˌpas\ n **1** : a predicament from which there is no obvious escape **2** : an impassable road or way

im·pas·si·ble \(ˌ)im-'pa-sə-bəl\ adj : incapable of feeling : IMPASSIVE

im·pas·sioned \im-'pa-shənd\ adj : filled with passion or zeal : showing great warmth or intensity of feeling ◆ **Syn·onyms** PASSIONATE, ARDENT, FERVENT, FERVID

im·pas·sive \(ˌ)im-'pa-siv\ adj : showing no signs of feeling, emotion, or interest : EXPRESSIONLESS, INDIFFERENT ◆ **Syn·onyms** STOIC, PHLEGMATIC, APATHETIC, STOLID — **im·pas·sive·ly** adv — **im·pas·siv·i·ty** \ˌim-ˌpa-'si-və-tē\ n

im·pas·to \im-'pas-tō, -'päs-\ n : the thick application of a pigment to a canvas or panel in painting; also : the body of pigment so applied

im·pa·tiens \im-'pā-shənz, -shəns\ n : any of a genus of herbs with usu. spurred flowers and seed capsules that readily split open

im·pa·tient \(ˌ)im-'pā-shənt\ adj **1** : not patient : restless or short of temper esp. under irritation, delay, or opposition **2** : INTOLERANT ⟨~ of poverty⟩ **3** : prompted or marked by impatience ⟨an ~ reply⟩ **4** : ANXIOUS — **im·pa·tience** \-shəns\ n — **im·pa·tient·ly** adv

im·peach \im-'pēch\ vb [ME empechen to accuse, fr. AF empecher, enpechier to ensnare, impede, prosecute, fr. LL impedicare to fetter, fr. L pedica fetter, fr. ped-, pes foot] **1** : to charge (a public official) before an authorized tribunal with misconduct in office **2** : to challenge the credibility or validity of **3** : to remove from public office for misconduct — **im·peach·ment** n

im·pec·ca·ble \(ˌ)im-'pe-kə-bəl\ adj **1** : not capable of sinning or wrongdoing **2** : FAULTLESS, IRREPROACHABLE ⟨a man of ~ character⟩ — **im·pec·ca·bil·i·ty** \-ˌpe-kə-'bi-lə-tē\ n — **im·pec·ca·bly** \-'pe-kə-blē\ adv

im·pe·cu·nious \ˌim-pi-'kyü-nyəs, -nē-əs\ adj : having little or no money — **im·pe·cu·nious·ness** n

im·ped·ance \im-ˈpē-dᵊns\ *n* : the opposition in an electrical circuit to the flow of an alternating current

im·pede \im-ˈpēd\ *vb* **im·ped·ed; im·ped·ing** [L *impedire*, fr. *ped-, pes* foot] : to interfere with the progress of

im·ped·i·ment \im-ˈpe-də-mənt\ *n* **1** : something that impedes, hinders, or obstructs **2** : a speech defect

im·ped·i·men·ta \im-ˌpe-də-ˈmen-tə\ *n pl* : things that impede

im·pel \im-ˈpel\ *vb* **im·pelled; im·pel·ling** : to urge or drive forward or on : FORCE; *also* : PROPEL

im·pel·ler *also* **im·pel·lor** \im-ˈpe-lər\ *n* : a rotor esp. in a pump

im·pend \im-ˈpend\ *vb* **1** : to hover or hang over threateningly : MENACE **2** : to be about to occur

im·pen·e·tra·ble \(ˌ)im-ˈpe-nə-trə-bəl\ *adj* **1** : incapable of being penetrated or pierced ⟨an ∼ jungle⟩ **2** : incapable of being comprehended : INSCRUTABLE ⟨an ∼ mystery⟩ — **im·pen·e·tra·bil·i·ty** \-ˌpe-nə-trə-ˈbi-lə-tē\ *n* — **im·pen·e·tra·bly** \-ˈpe-nə-trə-blē\ *adv*

im·pen·i·tent \(ˌ)im-ˈpe-nə-tənt\ *adj* : not penitent : not repenting of sin — **im·pen·i·tence** \-təns\ *n*

im·per·a·tive \im-ˈper-ə-tiv\ *adj* **1** : expressing a command, request, or encouragement ⟨∼ sentence⟩ **2** : having power to restrain, control, or direct **3** : NECESSARY ⟨an ∼ duty⟩ — **imperative** *n* — **im·per·a·tive·ly** *adv*

im·per·cep·ti·ble \ˌim-pər-ˈsep-tə-bəl\ *adj* : not perceptible; *esp* : too slight to be perceived ⟨∼ changes⟩ — **im·per·cep·ti·bly** \-blē\ *adv*

im·per·cep·tive \ˌim-pər-ˈsep-tiv\ *adj* : not perceptive ⟨an ∼ reader⟩

imperf *abbr* imperfect

¹im·per·fect \(ˌ)im-ˈpər-fikt\ *adj* **1** : not perfect : DEFECTIVE, INCOMPLETE **2** : of, relating to, or being a verb tense used to designate a continuing state or an incomplete action esp. in the past — **im·per·fect·ly** *adv*

²imperfect *n* : the imperfect tense; *also* : a verb form in it

im·per·fec·tion \ˌim-pər-ˈfek-shən\ *n* : the quality or state of being imperfect; *also* : FAULT, BLEMISH

im·pe·ri·al \im-ˈpir-ē-əl\ *adj* **1** : of, relating to, or befitting an empire or an emperor; *also* : of or relating to the United Kingdom or to the Commonwealth or British Empire **2** : ROYAL, SOVEREIGN; *also* : REGAL, IMPERIOUS **3** : of unusual size or excellence

im·pe·ri·al·ism \im-ˈpir-ē-ə-ˌli-zəm\ *n* : the policy of seeking to extend the power, dominion, or territories of a nation — **im·pe·ri·al·ist** \-list\ *n or adj* — **im·pe·ri·al·is·tic** \-ˌpir-ē-ə-ˈlis-tik\ *adj* — **im·pe·ri·al·is·ti·cal·ly** \-ti-k(ə-)lē\ *adv*

im·per·il \im-ˈper-əl\ *vb* **-iled** *or* **-illed; -il·ing** *or* **-il·ling** : ENDANGER

im·pe·ri·ous \im-ˈpir-ē-əs\ *adj* **1** : COMMANDING, LORDLY **2** : ARROGANT,

DOMINEERING **3** : IMPERATIVE, URGENT ⟨∼ problems⟩ — **im·pe·ri·ous·ly** *adv*

im·per·ish·able \(ˌ)im-ˈper-i-shə-bəl\ *adj* : not perishable or subject to decay

im·per·ma·nent \(ˌ)im-ˈpər-mə-nənt\ *adj* : not permanent : TRANSIENT — **im·per·ma·nent·ly** *adv*

im·per·me·able \(ˌ)im-ˈpər-mē-ə-bəl\ *adj* : not permitting passage (as of a fluid) through its substance

im·per·mis·si·ble \ˌim-pər-ˈmi-sə-bəl\ *adj* : not permissible

im·per·son·al \(ˌ)im-ˈpər-sə-nəl\ *adj* **1** : not referring to any particular person or thing **2** : not involving human emotions — **im·per·son·al·i·ty** \-ˌpər-sə-ˈna-lə-tē\ *n* — **im·per·son·al·ly** *adv*

im·per·son·ate \im-ˈpər-sə-ˌnāt\ *vb* **-at·ed; -at·ing** : to assume or act the character of — **im·per·son·a·tion** \-ˌpər-sə-ˈnā-shən\ *n* — **im·per·son·a·tor** \-ˈpər-sə-ˌnā-tər\ *n*

im·per·ti·nent \(ˌ)im-ˈpər-tə-nənt\ *adj* **1** : IRRELEVANT **2** : not restrained within due or proper bounds : RUDE, INSOLENT, SAUCY — **im·per·ti·nence** \-nəns\ *n* — **im·per·ti·nent·ly** *adv*

im·per·turb·able \ˌim-pər-ˈtər-bə-bəl\ *adj* : marked by extreme calm, impassivity, and steadiness : SERENE

im·per·vi·ous \(ˌ)im-ˈpər-vē-əs\ *adj* **1** : incapable of being penetrated (as by moisture) **2** : not capable of being affected or disturbed ⟨∼ to criticism⟩

im·pe·ti·go \ˌim-pə-ˈtē-gō, -ˈtī-\ *n* : a contagious skin disease characterized by vesicles, pustules, and yellowish crusts

im·pet·u·ous \im-ˈpe-chə-wəs\ *adj* **1** : marked by impulsive vehemence ⟨∼ temper⟩ **2** : marked by force and violence ⟨with ∼ speed⟩ — **im·pet·u·os·i·ty** \-ˌpe-chə-ˈwä-sə-tē\ *n* — **im·pet·u·ous·ly** *adv*

im·pe·tus \ˈim-pə-təs\ *n* [L, assault, impetus, fr. *impetere* to attack, fr. *petere* to go to, seek] **1** : a driving force : IMPULSE; *also* : INCENTIVE **2** : MOMENTUM

im·pi·e·ty \(ˌ)im-ˈpī-ə-tē\ *n, pl* **-ties** **1** : the quality or state of being impious **2** : an impious act

im·pinge \im-ˈpinj\ *vb* **im·pinged; im·ping·ing** **1** : to strike or dash esp. with a sharp collision **2** : ENCROACH, INFRINGE — **im·pinge·ment** *n*

im·pi·ous \ˈim-pē-əs, (ˌ)im-ˈpī-\ *adj* : not pious : IRREVERENT, PROFANE

imp·ish \ˈim-pish\ *adj* : of, relating to, or befitting an imp; *esp* : MISCHIEVOUS — **imp·ish·ly** *adv* — **imp·ish·ness** *n*

im·pla·ca·ble \(ˌ)im-ˈpla-kə-bəl, -ˈplā-\ *adj* : not capable of being appeased, pacified, mitigated, or changed ⟨an ∼ enemy⟩ — **im·pla·ca·bil·i·ty** \-ˌpla-kə-ˈbi-lə-tē, -ˌplā-\ *n* — **im·pla·ca·bly** \-ˈpla-kə-blē\ *adv*

im·plant \im-ˈplant\ *vb* **1** : to set firmly or deeply **2** : to fix in the mind or spirit **3** : to insert in living tissue (as for growth or absorption) — **im·plant** \ˈim-ˌplant\ *n* — **im·plan·ta·tion** \ˌim-ˌplan-ˈtā-shən\ *n*

im·plau·si·ble \(ˌ)im-ˈplȯ-zə-bəl\ *adj* : not

plausible — **im·plau·si·bil·i·ty** \-ˌplȯ-zə-ˈbi-lə-tē\ n — **im·plau·si·bly** \-ˈplȯ-zə-blē\ adv

¹**im·ple·ment** \ˈim-plə-mənt\ n [ME, fr. AF, fr. ML *implementum* item making a full complement, appurtenance, tool, fr. LL, act of filling up, fr. L *implēre* to fill up] : TOOL, UTENSIL, INSTRUMENT

²**im·ple·ment** \-ˌment\ vb 1 : CARRY OUT; *esp* : to put into practice 2 : to provide implements for — **im·ple·men·ta·tion** \ˌim-plə-mən-ˈtā-shən\ n

im·pli·cate \ˈim-plə-ˌkāt\ vb **-cat·ed; -cat·ing** 1 : IMPLY 2 : INVOLVE — **im·pli·ca·tion** \ˌim-plə-ˈkā-shən\ n

im·plic·it \im-ˈpli-sət\ adj 1 : understood though not directly stated or expressed : IMPLIED; *also* : POTENTIAL 2 : COMPLETE, UNQUESTIONING, ABSOLUTE ⟨~ faith⟩ — **im·plic·it·ly** adv

im·plode \im-ˈplōd\ vb **im·plod·ed; im·plod·ing** 1 : to burst or collapse inward 2 : SELF-DESTRUCT — **im·plo·sion** \-ˈplō-zhən\ n — **im·plo·sive** \-siv\ adj

im·plore \im-ˈplȯr\ vb **im·plored; im·plor·ing** : BESEECH, ENTREAT ◆ *Synonyms* SUPPLICATE, BEG, IMPORTUNE, PLEAD

im·ply \im-ˈplī\ vb **im·plied; im·ply·ing** 1 : to involve or indicate by inference, association, or necessary consequence rather than by direct statement ⟨war *implies* fighting⟩ 2 : to express indirectly : hint at : SUGGEST

im·po·lite \ˌim-pə-ˈlīt\ adj : not polite : RUDE, DISCOURTEOUS

im·pol·i·tic \(ˌ)im-ˈpä-lə-ˌtik\ adj : not politic : UNWISE

im·pon·der·a·ble \(ˌ)im-ˈpän-də-rə-bəl\ adj : incapable of being weighed or evaluated with exactness — **imponderable** n

¹**im·port** \im-ˈpȯrt\ vb 1 : MEAN, SIGNIFY 2 : to bring (as merchandise) into a place or country from a foreign or external source — **im·port·er** n

²**im·port** \ˈim-ˌpȯrt\ n 1 : IMPORTANCE, SIGNIFICANCE 2 : MEANING, SIGNIFICATION 3 : something (as merchandise) brought in from another country

im·por·tance \im-ˈpȯr-t³ns\ n : the quality or state of being important : MOMENT, SIGNIFICANCE ◆ *Synonyms* CONSEQUENCE, IMPORT, WEIGHT

im·por·tant \im-ˈpȯr-t³nt\ adj 1 : marked by importance : SIGNIFICANT 2 : giving an impression of importance — **im·por·tant·ly** adv

im·por·ta·tion \ˌim-ˌpȯr-ˈtā-shən, -pər-\ n 1 : the act or practice of importing 2 : something imported

im·por·tu·nate \im-ˈpȯr-chə-nət\ adj 1 : troublesomely urgent or persistent 2 : BURDENSOME, TROUBLESOME

im·por·tune \ˌim-pər-ˈtün, -ˈtyün; im-ˈpȯr-chən\ vb **-tuned; -tun·ing** : to urge or beg with troublesome persistence — **im·por·tu·ni·ty** \ˌim-pər-ˈtü-nə-tē, -ˈtyü-\ n

im·pose \im-ˈpōz\ vb **im·posed; im·pos·ing** 1 : to establish or apply by authority ⟨~ a tax⟩; *also* : to establish by force ⟨*imposed* a government⟩ 2 : OBTRUDE ⟨*imposed* herself on others⟩ 3 : to take unwarranted advantage of something ⟨~ on her good nature⟩ — **im·po·si·tion** \ˌim-pə-ˈzi-shən\ n

im·pos·ing adj : impressive because of size, bearing, dignity, or grandeur — **im·pos·ing·ly** adv

im·pos·si·ble \(ˌ)im-ˈpä-sə-bəl\ adj 1 : incapable of being or of occurring 2 : enormously difficult 3 : extremely undesirable : UNACCEPTABLE — **im·pos·si·bil·i·ty** \-ˌpä-sə-ˈbi-lə-tē\ n — **im·pos·si·bly** \-ˈpä-sə-blē\ adv

¹**im·post** \ˈim-ˌpōst\ n : TAX, DUTY

²**impost** n : a block, capital, or molding from which an arch springs

im·pos·tor or **im·pos·ter** \im-ˈpäs-tər\ n : one that assumes an identity or title not one's own in order to deceive

im·pos·ture \im-ˈpäs-chər\ n : DECEPTION; *esp* : fraudulent impersonation

im·po·tent \ˈim-pə-tənt\ adj 1 : lacking in power or strength : HELPLESS 2 : unable to copulate; *also* : STERILE — **im·po·tence** \-təns\ n — **im·po·ten·cy** \-tən-sē\ n — **im·po·tent·ly** adv

im·pound \im-ˈpau̇nd\ vb 1 : CONFINE, ENCLOSE ⟨~ stray dogs⟩ 2 : to seize and hold in legal custody 3 : to collect in a reservoir ⟨~ water⟩ — **im·pound·ment** n

im·pov·er·ish \im-ˈpä-və-rish\ vb : to make poor; *also* : to deprive of strength, richness, or fertility — **im·pov·er·ish·ment** n

im·prac·ti·ca·ble \(ˌ)im-ˈprak-ti-kə-bəl\ adj : not practicable : incapable of being put into practice or use

im·prac·ti·cal \(ˌ)im-ˈprak-ti-kəl\ adj 1 : not practical 2 : IMPRACTICABLE

im·pre·cate \ˈim-pri-ˌkāt\ vb **-cat·ed; -cat·ing** : CURSE — **im·pre·ca·tion** \ˌim-pri-ˈkā-shən\ n

im·pre·cise \ˌim-pri-ˈsīs\ adj : not precise — **im·pre·cise·ly** adv — **im·pre·cise·ness** n — **im·pre·ci·sion** \-ˈsi-zhən\ n

im·preg·na·ble \im-ˈpreg-nə-bəl\ adj : incapable of being taken by assault : UNCONQUERABLE, UNASSAILABLE — **im·preg·na·bil·i·ty** \(ˌ)im-ˌpreg-nə-ˈbi-lə-tē\ n

im·preg·nate \im-ˈpreg-ˌnāt\ vb **-nat·ed; -nat·ing** 1 : to fertilize or make pregnant 2 : to cause to be filled, permeated, or saturated — **im·preg·na·tion** \ˌim-ˌpreg-ˈnā-shən\ n

im·pre·sa·rio \ˌim-prə-ˈsär-ē-ˌō\ n, pl **-ri·os** [It, fr. *impresa* undertaking, fr. *imprendere* to undertake] 1 : the manager or conductor of an opera or concert company 2 : one who puts on an entertainment 3 : MANAGER, PRODUCER

¹**im·press** \im-ˈpres\ vb 1 : to apply with or produce (as a mark) by pressure : IMPRINT 2 : to press, stamp, or print in or upon 3 : to produce a vivid impression of 4 : to affect esp. forcibly or deeply — **im·press·ible** adj

²**im·press** \ˈim-ˌpres\ n 1 : a characteristic or distinctive mark 2 : IMPRESSION,

EFFECT **3** : an impression or image of something formed by or as if by pressure; *also* : a product of pressure or influence

³**im·press** \im-'pres\ *vb* **1** : to force into naval service **2** : to get the aid or services of by forcible argument or persuasion — **im·press·ment** \-mənt\ *n*

im·pres·sion \im-'pre-shən\ *n* **1** : a characteristic trait or feature resulting from influence : IMPRESS **2** : a stamp, form, or figure made by impressing : IMPRINT **3** : an esp. marked influence or effect on feeling, sense, or mind **4** : a single print or copy (as from type or from an engraved plate or book) **5** : all the copies of a publication (as a book) printed for one issue : PRINTING **6** : a usu. vague notion or remembrance **7** : an imitation in caricature of a noted personality as a form of entertainment

im·pres·sion·able \im-'pre-shə-nə-bəl\ *adj* : capable of being easily impressed : easily molded or influenced

im·pres·sion·ism \im-'pre-shə-,ni-zəm\ *n, often cap* : a theory or practice in modern art of depicting the natural appearances of objects by dabs or strokes of primary unmixed colors in order to simulate actual reflected light — **im·pres·sion·is·tic** \-,pre-shə-'nis-tik\ *adj*

im·pres·sion·ist \im-'pre-shə-nist\ *n* **1** *often cap* : a painter who practices impressionism **2** : an entertainer who does impressions

im·pres·sive \im-'pre-siv\ *adj* : making or tending to make a marked impression ⟨an ~ speech⟩ — **im·pres·sive·ly** *adv* — **im·pres·sive·ness** *n*

im·pri·ma·tur \,im-prə-'mä-,tùr\ *n* [NL, let it be printed] **1** : a license to print or publish; *also* : official approval of a publication by a censor : SANCTION, APPROVAL

¹**im·print** \im-'print, 'im-,print\ *vb* **1** : to stamp or mark by or as if by pressure : IMPRESS **2** : to fix firmly (as on the memory)

²**im·print** \'im-,print\ *n* **1** : something imprinted or printed : a publisher's name printed at the foot of a title page **3** : an indelible distinguishing effect or influence

im·pris·on \im-'pri-z³n\ *vb* : to put in or as if in prison : CONFINE — **im·pris·on·ment** *n*

im·prob·a·ble \(,)im-'prä-bə-bəl\ *adj* : unlikely to be true or to occur — **im·prob·a·bil·i·ty** \-,prä-bə-'bi-lə-tē\ *n* — **im·prob·a·bly** \-'prä-bə-blē\ *adv*

im·promp·tu \im-'prämp-tü, -tyü\ *adj* [F, fr. *impromptu* extemporaneously, fr. L *in promptu* in readiness] **1** : made or done on or as if on the spur of the moment **2** : EXTEMPORANEOUS, UNREHEARSED ⟨an ~ speech⟩ — **impromptu** *adv or n*

im·prop·er \(,)im-'prä-pər\ *adj* **1** : not proper, fit, or suitable **2** : INCORRECT, INACCURATE **3** : not in accord with propriety, modesty, or good manners — **im·prop·er·ly** *adv*

improper fraction *n* : a fraction whose numerator is equal to or larger than the denominator

im·pro·pri·e·ty \,im-prə-'prī-ə-tē\ *n, pl* **-ties** **1** : an improper act or remark; *esp* : an unacceptable use of a word or of language **2** : the quality or state of being improper

im·prov \'im-,präv\ *adj* : of, relating to, or being an improvised comedy routine — **improv** *n*

im·prove \im-'prüv\ *vb* **im·proved; im·prov·ing** **1** : to enhance or increase in value or quality **2** : to grow or become better ⟨your work is *improving*⟩ **3** : to make good use of ⟨~ the time by reading⟩ — **im·prov·able** \-'prü-və-bəl\ *adj*

im·prove·ment \im-'prüv-mənt\ *n* **1** : the act or process of improving **2** : increased value or excellence of something **3** : something that adds to the value or appearance of a thing

im·prov·i·dent \(,)im-'prä-və-dənt\ *adj* : not providing for the future — **im·prov·i·dence** \-dəns\ *n*

im·pro·vise \'im-prə-,vīz\ *vb* **-vised; -vis·ing** [F *improviser*, fr. It *improvvisare*, fr. *improvviso* sudden, fr. L *improvisus*, lit., unforeseen] **1** : to compose, recite, play, or sing on the spur of the moment : EXTEMPORIZE ⟨~ on the piano⟩ **2** : to make, invent, or arrange offhand ⟨~ a sail out of shirts⟩ — **im·pro·vi·sa·tion** \im-,prä-və-'zā-shən, ,im-prə-və-\ *n* — **im·pro·vis·er** *or* **im·pro·vi·sor** \,im-prə-'vī-zər, 'im-prə-,\ *n*

im·pru·dent \(,)im-'prü-d³nt\ *adj* : not prudent : lacking discretion, wisdom, or good judgement — **im·pru·dence** \-d³ns\ *n* — **im·pru·dent·ly** *adv*

im·pu·dent \'im-pyü-dənt\ *adj* : marked by contemptuous boldness or disregard of others — **im·pu·dence** \-dəns\ *n* — **im·pu·dent·ly** *adv*

im·pugn \im-'pyün\ *vb* [ME, to assail, fr. AF *empugner*, fr. L *inpugnare*, fr. *pugnare* to fight] : to attack by words or arguments : oppose or attack as false or as lacking integrity

im·puis·sance \im-'pwi-s³ns, -'pyü-ə-s³ns\ *n* [ME, fr. MF] : the quality or state of being powerless : WEAKNESS

im·pulse \'im-,pəls\ *n* **1** : a force that starts a body into motion; *also* : the motion produced by such a force **2** : an arousing of the mind and spirit to some usu. unpremeditated action **3** : NERVE IMPULSE

im·pul·sion \im-'pəl-shən\ *n* **1** : the act of impelling : the state of being impelled **2** : a force that impels **3** : IMPULSE 2; *also* : COMPULSION 3

im·pul·sive \im-'pəl-siv\ *adj* **1** : having the power of or actually driving or impelling **2** : arising from or prone to act on impulse — **im·pul·sive·ly** *adv* — **im·pul·sive·ness** *n*

im·pu·ni·ty \im-'pyü-nə-tē\ *n* [MF or L; MF *impunité*, fr. L *impunitas*, fr. *impune* without punishment, fr. *poena* penalty, punishment] : exemption from punishment, harm, or loss

im·pure \(ˌ)im-ˈpyu̇r\ *adj* **1** : not pure : UNCHASTE, OBSCENE **2** : DIRTY, FOUL ⟨~ water⟩ **3** : ADULTERATED, MIXED — **im·pu·ri·ty** \-ˈpyu̇r-ə-tē\ *n*

im·pute \im-ˈpyüt\ *vb* **im·put·ed; im·put·ing 1** : to lay the responsibility or blame for often falsely or unjustly **2** : to credit to a person or a cause : ATTRIBUTE — **im·put·able** \-ˈpyü-tə-bəl\ *adj* — **im·pu·ta·tion** \ˌim-pyü-ˈtā-shən\ *n*

¹**in** \ˈin\ *prep* **1** — used to indicate physical surroundings ⟨swim ~ the lake⟩ **2** : INTO ⟨ran ~ the house⟩ **3** : DURING ⟨~ the summer⟩ **4** : WITH ⟨written ~ pencil⟩ **5** — used to indicate one's situation or state of being ⟨~ luck⟩ ⟨~ love⟩ **6** — used to indicate manner or purpose ⟨~ a hurry⟩ ⟨said ~ reply⟩ **7** : INTO 2 ⟨broke ~ pieces⟩

²**in** *adv* **1** : to or toward the inside ⟨come ~⟩; *also* : to or toward some destination or place ⟨flew ~ from the South⟩ **2** : at close quarters : NEAR ⟨the enemy closed ~⟩ **3** : into the midst of something ⟨mix ~ the flour⟩ **4** : to or at its proper place ⟨fit a piece ~⟩ **5** : WITHIN ⟨locked ~⟩ **6** : in vogue or season **7** : in one's presence, possession, or control ⟨the results are ~⟩

³**in** *adj* **1** : located inside or within **2** : that is in position, operation, or power ⟨the ~ party⟩ **3** : directed inward : IN-COMING ⟨the ~ train⟩ **4** : keenly aware of and responsive to what is new and fashionable ⟨the ~ crowd⟩; *also* : extremely fashionable ⟨the ~ thing to do⟩

⁴**in** *n* **1** : one who is in office or power or on the inside **2** : INFLUENCE, PULL ⟨he has an ~ with the owner⟩

⁵**in** *abbr* **1** inch **2** inlet

In *symbol* indium

IN *abbr* Indiana

in- \(ˌ)in\ *prefix* : not : absence of : NON-, UN-

in·abil·i·ty \ˌi-nə-ˈbi-lə-tē\ *n* : the quality or state of being unable

in ab·sen·tia \ˌin-ab-ˈsen-chə, -chē-ə\ *adv* : in one's absence

in·ac·ti·vate \(ˌ)i-ˈnak-tə-ˌvāt\ *vb* : to make inactive — **in·ac·ti·va·tion** \(ˌ)i-ˌnak-tə-ˈvā-shən\ *n*

in·ad·e·quate \(ˌ)i-ˈna-di-kwət\ *adj* : not adequate : INSUFFICIENT — **in·ad·e·qua·cy** \-kwə-sē\ *n* — **in·ad·e·quate·ly** *adv* — **in·ad·e·quate·ness** *n*

in·ad·ver·tent \ˌi-nəd-ˈvər-t²nt\ *adj* **1** : HEEDLESS, INATTENTIVE **2** : UNINTENTIONAL ⟨an ~ omission⟩ — **in·ad·ver·tence** \-t²ns\ *n* — **in·ad·ver·ten·cy** \-t²n-sē\ *n* — **in·ad·ver·tent·ly** *adv*

in·alien·able \(ˌ)i-ˈnāl-yə-nə-bəl, -ˈnā-lē-ə-\ *adj* : incapable of being alienated, surrendered, or transferred ⟨~ rights⟩ — **in·alien·abil·i·ty** \(ˌ)i-ˌnāl-yə-nə-ˈbi-lə-tē, -ˌnā-lē-ə-\ *n* — **in·alien·ably** *adv*

in·amo·ra·ta \i-ˌnä-mə-ˈrä-tə\ *n* : a woman with whom one is in love

inane \i-ˈnān\ *adj* **inan·er; -est** : EMPTY, INSUBSTANTIAL; *also* : SHALLOW, SILLY ⟨~ comments⟩ — **inane·ly** *adv* — **inan·i·ty** \i-ˈna-nə-tē\ *n*

in·an·i·mate \(ˌ)i-ˈna-nə-mət\ *adj* : not inimate or animated : lacking the qualities of living things — **in·an·i·mate·ly** *adv* — **in·an·i·mate·ness** *n*

in·ap·pre·cia·ble \ˌi-nə-ˈprē-shə-bəl\ *adj* : too small to be perceived — **in·ap·pre·cia·bly** \-blē\ *adv*

in·apt \(ˌ)i-ˈnapt\ *adj* **1** : not suitable **2** : INEPT — **in·apt·ly** *adv* — **in·apt·ness** *n*

in·ar·tic·u·late \ˌi-när-ˈti-kyə-lət\ *adj* **1** : not understandable as spoken words **2** : MUTE **3** : incapable of being expressed by speech ⟨~ fear⟩; *also* : UNSPOKEN **4** : not having the power of distinct utterance or effective expression — **in·ar·tic·u·late·ly** *adv*

in·as·much as \ˌi-nəz-ˈməch-\ *conj* : seeing that : SINCE

¹**in·au·gu·ral** \i-ˈnȯ-gyə-rəl, -gə-\ *adj* **1** : of or relating to an inauguration **2** : marking a beginning

²**inaugural** *n* **1** : an inaugural address **2** : INAUGURATION

in·au·gu·rate \i-ˈnȯ-gyə-ˌrāt, -gə-\ *vb* **-rat·ed; -rat·ing 1** : to introduce into an office with suitable ceremonies : INSTALL **2** : to dedicate ceremoniously **3** : BEGIN, INITIATE — **in·au·gu·ra·tion** \-ˌnȯ-gyə-ˈrā-shən, -gə-\ *n*

in·board \ˈin-ˌbȯrd\ *adv* **1** : inside the hull of a ship **2** : close or closest to the center line of a vehicle or craft — **inboard** *adj*

in·born \ˈin-ˈbȯrn\ *adj* **1** : present from or as if from birth **2** : HEREDITARY, INHERITED ◆ **Synonyms** INNATE, CONGENITAL, NATIVE

in·bound \ˈin-ˌbau̇nd\ *adj* : inward bound ⟨~ traffic⟩

in–box \ˈin-ˌbäks\ *n* : a receptacle for incoming interoffice letters; *also* : a computer folder for incoming e-mail

in·bred \ˈin-ˈbred\ *adj* **1** : ingrained in one's nature as deeply as if by heredity **2** : subjected to or produced by inbreeding

in·breed·ing \ˈin-ˌbrē-diŋ\ *n* **1** : the interbreeding of closely related individuals esp. to preserve and fix desirable characters of and to eliminate unfavorable characters from a stock **2** : confinement to a narrow range or a local or limited field of choice — **in·breed** \ˈin-ˈbrēd\ *vb*

inc *abbr* **1** incomplete **2** incorporated **3** increase

In·ca \ˈiŋ-kə\ *n* [Sp, fr. Quechua *inka* ruler

of the Inca empire] **1** : a noble or a member of the ruling family of an Indian empire of Peru, Bolivia, and Ecuador until the Spanish conquest **2** : a member of any people under Inca influence

in·cal·cu·la·ble \(ˌ)in-ˈkal-kyə-lə-bəl\ *adj* **1** : not capable of being calculated; *esp* : very great **2** : not predictable — **in·cal·cu·la·bly** \-blē\ *adv*

in·can·des·cent \ˌin-kən-ˈde-sᵊnt\ *adj* **1** : glowing with heat **2** : SHINING, BRILLIANT — **in·can·des·cence** \-sᵊns\ *n*

incandescent lamp *n* : LIGHT BULB 1

in·can·ta·tion \ˌin-ˌkan-ˈtā-shən\ *n* : a use of spells or verbal charms spoken or sung as a part of a ritual of magic; *also* : a formula of words used in or as if in such a ritual

in·ca·pa·ble \(ˌ)in-ˈkā-pə-bəl\ *adj* : lacking ability or qualification for a particular purpose; *also* : UNQUALIFIED — **in·ca·pa·bil·i·ty** \-ˌkā-pə-ˈbi-lə-tē\ *n*

in·ca·pac·i·tate \ˌin-kə-ˈpa-sə-ˌtāt\ *vb* **-tat·ed; -tat·ing** : to make incapable or unfit

in·ca·pac·i·ty \ˌin-kə-ˈpa-sə-tē\ *n, pl* **-ties** : the quality or state of being incapable

in·car·cer·ate \in-ˈkär-sə-ˌrāt\ *vb* **-at·ed; -at·ing** : IMPRISON, CONFINE — **in·car·cer·a·tion** \(ˌ)in-ˌkär-sə-ˈrā-shən\ *n*

in·car·na·dine \in-ˈkär-nə-ˌdīn, -ˌdēn\ *vb* **-dined; -din·ing** : REDDEN

in·car·nate \in-ˈkär-nət, -ˌnāt\ *adj* **1** : having bodily and esp. human form and substance **2** : PERSONIFIED — **in·car·nate** \-ˌnāt\ *vb*

in·car·na·tion \ˌin-ˌkär-ˈnā-shən\ *n* **1** : the embodiment of a deity or spirit in an earthly form **2** *cap* : the union of divine and human natures in Jesus Christ **3** : a person showing a trait or typical character to a marked degree **4** : the act of incarnating : the state of being incarnate

in·cen·di·ary \in-ˈsen-dē-ˌer-ē\ *adj* **1** : of or relating to a deliberate burning of property **2** : tending to excite or inflame **3** : designed to start fires ⟨an ∼ bomb⟩ — **incendiary** *n*

¹in·cense \ˈin-ˌsens\ *n* **1** : material used to produce a fragrant odor when burned **2** : the perfume or smoke from some spices and gums when burned

²in·cense \in-ˈsens\ *vb* **in·censed; in·cens·ing** : to make extremely angry

in·cen·tive \in-ˈsen-tiv\ *n* [ME, fr. LL *incentivum*, fr. *incentivus* stimulating, fr. L, setting the tune, fr. *incinere* to play (a tune), fr. *canere* to sing] : something that incites or is likely to incite to determination or action

in·cep·tion \in-ˈsep-shən\ *n* : BEGINNING, COMMENCEMENT

in·cer·ti·tude \(ˌ)in-ˈsər-tə-ˌtüd, -ˌtyüd\ *n* **1** : UNCERTAINTY, DOUBT, INDECISION **2** : INSECURITY, INSTABILITY

in·ces·sant \(ˌ)in-ˈse-sᵊnt\ *adj* : continuing or flowing without interruption ⟨∼ rains⟩ — **in·ces·sant·ly** *adv*

in·cest \ˈin-ˌsest\ *n* [ME, fr. L *incestus* sexual impurity, fr. *incestus* impure, fr. *castus* pure] : sexual intercourse between persons so closely related that marriage is

illegal — **in·ces·tu·ous** \in-ˈses-chù-wəs\ *adj*

¹inch \ˈinch\ *n* [ME, fr. OE *ynce*, fr. L *uncia* twelfth part, inch, ounce] — see WEIGHT table

²inch *vb* : to move by small degrees

in·cho·ate \in-ˈkō-ət, ˈin-kə-ˌwāt\ *adj* : being only partly in existence or operation : INCOMPLETE, INCIPIENT

inch·worm \ˈinch-ˌwərm\ *n* : LOOPER

in·ci·dence \ˈin-sə-dəns\ *n* : rate of occurrence or effect

¹in·ci·dent \-dənt\ *n* **1** : OCCURRENCE, HAPPENING **2** : an action likely to lead to grave consequences esp. in diplomatic matters

²incident *adj* **1** : occurring or likely to occur esp. in connection with some other happening **2** : falling or striking on something ⟨∼ light rays⟩

¹in·ci·den·tal \ˌin-sə-ˈden-tᵊl\ *adj* **1** : subordinate, nonessential, or attendant in position or significance ⟨∼ expenses⟩ **2** : CASUAL, CHANCE

²incidental *n* **1** *pl* : minor items (as of expense) that are not individually accounted for **2** : something incidental

in·ci·den·tal·ly \ˌin-sə-ˈden-tə-lē, -ˈdent-lē\ *adv* **1** : in an incidental manner **2** : by the way

in·cin·er·ate \in-ˈsi-nə-ˌrāt\ *vb* **-at·ed; -at·ing** : to burn to ashes — **in·cin·er·a·tion** \-ˌsi-nə-ˈrā-shən\ *n*

in·cin·er·a·tor \in-ˈsi-nə-ˌrā-tər\ *n* : a furnace for burning waste

in·cip·i·ent \in-ˈsi-pē-ənt\ *adj* : beginning to be or become apparent

in·cise \in-ˈsīz\ *vb* **in·cised; in·cis·ing** **1** : to cut into **2** : CARVE, ENGRAVE

in·ci·sion \in-ˈsi-zhən\ *n* : CUT, GASH; *esp* : a surgical cut

in·ci·sive \in-ˈsī-siv\ *adj* : impressively direct and decisive — **in·ci·sive·ly** *adv*

in·ci·sor \in-ˈsī-zər\ *n* : a front tooth typically adapted for cutting

in·cite \in-ˈsīt\ *vb* **in·cit·ed; in·cit·ing** : to arouse to action : stir up — **in·cite·ment** *n* — **in·cit·er** *n*

in·ci·vil·i·ty \ˌin-sə-ˈvi-lə-tē\ *n* **1** : RUDENESS, DISCOURTESY **2** : a rude or discourteous act

incl *abbr* include; included; including; inclusive

in·clem·ent \(ˌ)in-ˈkle-mənt\ *adj* : SEVERE, STORMY ⟨∼ weather⟩ — **in·clem·en·cy** \-mən-sē\ *n*

in·cli·na·tion \ˌin-klə-ˈnā-shən\ *n* **1** : PROPENSITY, BENT; *esp* : LIKING **2** : BOW, NOD ⟨an ∼ of the head⟩ : a tilting of something **4** : SLANT, SLOPE

¹in·cline \in-ˈklīn\ *vb* **in·clined; in·clin·ing** **1** : BOW, BEND **2** : to be drawn toward an opinion or course of action **3** : to deviate from the vertical or horizontal : SLOPE **4** : INFLUENCE, PERSUADE — **in·clin·er** *n*

²in·cline \ˈin-ˌklīn\ *n* : SLOPE

inclose, inclosure *var of* ENCLOSE, ENCLOSURE

in·clude \in-ˈklüd\ *vb* **in·clud·ed; in·clud·ing** : to take in or comprise as a part of a whole ⟨the price ∼s tax⟩ — **in·clu·sion** \in-'klü-zhən\ n

in·clu·sive \in-'klü-siv\ adj **1** : including stated limits or extremes ⟨from Monday to Friday ∼⟩ **2** : broad in scope; esp : covering all items, costs, or services — **in·clu·sive·ly** adj — **in·clu·sive·ness** n

incog abbr incognito

¹**in·cog·ni·to** \,in-,käg-'nē-to, in-'käg-nə-,tō\ adv or adj [It, fr. L incognitus unknown, fr. cognoscere to know] : with one's identity concealed

²**incognito** n, pl **-tos 1** : one appearing or living incognito **2** : the state or disguise of an incognito

in·co·her·ent \,in-kō-'hir-ənt, -'her-\ adj **1** : not sticking closely or compactly together : LOOSE **2** : lacking normal clarity or intelligibility in speech or thought — **in·co·her·ence** \-əns\ n — **in·co·her·ent·ly** adv

in·come \'in-,kəm\ n : a gain usu. measured in money that derives from labor, business, or property

income tax n : a tax on the net income of an individual or business concern

in·com·ing \'in-,kə-min\ adj : coming in ⟨the ∼ tide⟩ ⟨∼ freshmen⟩

in·com·men·su·rate \,in-kə-'men-sə-rət, -'men-chə-\ adj : not commensurate; esp : INADEQUATE

in·com·mode \,in-kə-'mōd\ vb **-mod·ed; -mod·ing** : INCONVENIENCE, DISTURB

in·com·mu·ni·ca·ble \,in-kə-'myü-ni-kə-bəl\ adj : not communicable : not capable of being communicated or imparted; also : UNCOMMUNICATIVE

in·com·mu·ni·ca·do \,in-kə-,myü-nə-'kä-dō\ adv or adj : without means of communication; also : in solitary confinement ⟨a prisoner held ∼⟩

in·com·pa·ra·ble \(,)in-'käm-pə-rə-bəl, -prə-\ adj **1** : eminent beyond comparison : MATCHLESS **2** : not suitable for comparison — **in·com·pa·ra·bly** \-blē\ adv

in·com·pat·i·ble \,in-kəm-'pa-tə-bəl\ adj : incapable of or unsuitable for association or use together ⟨∼ colors⟩ ⟨temperamentally ∼⟩ — **in·com·pat·i·bil·i·ty** \,in-kəm-,pa-tə-'bi-lə-tē\ n

in·com·pe·tent \(,)in-'käm-pə-tənt\ adj **1** : not legally qualified **2** : not competent : lacking sufficient knowledge, skill, or ability — **in·com·pe·tence** \-təns\ n — **in·com·pe·ten·cy** \-tən-sē\ n — **incompetent** n

in·com·plete \,in-kəm-'plēt\ adj : lacking a part or parts : UNFINISHED, IMPERFECT — **in·com·plete·ly** adv — **in·com·plete·ness** n

in·com·pre·hen·si·ble \,in-,käm-prē-'hen-sə-bəl\ adj : impossible to comprehend : UNINTELLIGIBLE

in·con·ceiv·able \,in-kən-'sē-və-bəl\ adj **1** : impossible to comprehend **2** : UNBELIEVABLE

in·con·gru·ous \(,)in-'kän-grü-wəs\ adj : not consistent with or suitable to the surroundings or associations — **in·con·gru·i·ty** \,in-kən-'grü-ə-tē, -,kän-\ n — **in·con·gru·ous·ly** adv

in·con·se·quen·tial \,in-,kän-sə-'kwen-chəl\ adj **1** : ILLOGICAL; also : IRRELEVANT **2** : of no significance : UNIMPORTANT — **in·con·se·quence** \(,)in-'kän-sə-,kwens\ n — **in·con·se·quen·tial·ly** adv

in·con·sid·er·able \,in-kən-'si-də-rə-bəl\ adj : SLIGHT, TRIVIAL ⟨the cost was not ∼⟩

in·con·sid·er·ate \,in-kən-'si-də-rət\ adj : HEEDLESS, THOUGHTLESS; esp : not respecting the rights or feelings of others — **in·con·sid·er·ate·ly** adv — **in·con·sid·er·ate·ness** n

in·con·sol·able \,in-kən-'sō-lə-bəl\ adj : incapable of being consoled — **in·con·sol·ably** \-blē\ adv

in·con·spic·u·ous \,in-kən-'spi-kyə-wəs\ adj : not readily noticeable — **in·con·spic·u·ous·ly** adv

in·con·stant \(,)in-'kän-stənt\ adj : not constant : CHANGEABLE ♦ **Synonyms** FICKLE, CAPRICIOUS, MERCURIAL, UNSTABLE, VOLATILE — **in·con·stan·cy** \-stən-sē\ n — **in·con·stant·ly** adv

in·con·test·able \,in-kən-'tes-tə-bəl\ adj : not contestable : INDISPUTABLE — **in·con·test·ably** \-'tes-tə-blē\ adv

in·con·ti·nent \(,)in-'känt-ᵊn-ənt\ adj **1** : lacking self-restraint **2** : unable to retain urine or feces voluntarily — **in·con·ti·nence** \-əns\ n

in·con·tro·vert·ible \,in-,kän-trə-'vər-tə-bəl\ adj : not open to question : INDISPUTABLE ⟨∼ evidence⟩ — **in·con·tro·vert·ibly** \-blē\ adv

¹**in·con·ve·nience** \,in-kən-'vē-nyəns\ n **1** : something that is inconvenient **2** : the quality or state of being inconvenient

²**inconvenience** vb **-nienced; -nienc·ing** : to subject to inconvenience

in·con·ve·nient \,in-kən-'vē-nyənt\ adj : not convenient : causing trouble or annoyance : INOPPORTUNE — **in·con·ve·nient·ly** adv

in·cor·po·rate \in-'kȯr-pə-,rāt\ vb **-rat·ed; -rat·ing 1** : to unite closely or so as to form one body : BLEND **2** : to form, form into, or become a corporation **3** : to give material form to : EMBODY — **in·cor·po·ra·tion** \-,kȯr-pə-'rā-shən\ n

in·cor·po·re·al \,in-kȯr-'pȯr-ē-əl\ adj : having no material body or form

in·cor·rect \,in-kə-'rekt\ adj **1** : INACCURATE, FAULTY ⟨an ∼ transcription⟩ **2** : not true : WRONG **3** : UNBECOMING, IMPROPER — **in·cor·rect·ly** adv — **in·cor·rect·ness** n

in·cor·ri·gi·ble \(,)in-'kȯr-ə-jə-bəl\ adj : incapable of being corrected, amended, or reformed — **in·cor·ri·gi·bil·i·ty** \(,)in-,kȯr-ə-jə-'bi-lə-tē\ n — **in·cor·ri·gi·bly** \-'kȯr-ə-jə-blē\ adv

in·cor·rupt·ible \,in-kə-'rəp-tə-bəl\ adj **1** : not subject to decay or dissolution **2** : incapable of being bribed or morally corrupted — **in·cor·rupt·ibil·i·ty** \-,rəp-tə-'bi-lə-tē\ *n* — **in·cor·rupt·ibly** \-'rəp-tə-blē\ *adv*

incr *abbr* increase; increased

¹**in·crease** \in-'krēs, 'in-,krēs\ *vb* **increased; in·creas·ing** [ME *encresen,* fr. AF *encreistre,* fr. L. *increscere,* fr. *crescere* to grow] **1** : to become greater : GROW **2** : to multiply by the production of young ⟨rabbits ~ rapidly⟩ **3** : to make greater — **increased** *adj* — **in·creas·ing·ly** \-'krē-siŋ-lē\ *adv*

²**in·crease** \'in-,krēs, in-'krēs\ *n* **1** : addition or enlargement in size, extent, or quantity : GROWTH **2** : something that is added to an original stock or amount (as by growth)

in·cred·i·ble \(,)in-'kre-də-bəl\ *adj* : too extraordinary and improbable to be believed; *also* : hard to believe — **in·cred·i·bil·i·ty** \(,)in-,kre-də-'bi-lə-tē\ *n* — **in·cred·i·bly** \-'kre-də-blē\ *adv*

in·cred·u·lous \-'kre-jə-ləs\ *adj* **1** : SKEPTICAL **2** : expressing disbelief — **in·cre·du·li·ty** \in-kri-'dü-lə-tē, -'dyü-\ *n* — **in·cred·u·lous·ly** *adv*

in·cre·ment \'in-krə-mənt, 'in-\ *n* **1** : the action or process of increasing esp. in quantity or value : ENLARGEMENT **2** : something gained or added; *esp* : one of a series of regular consecutive additions — **in·cre·men·tal** \,in-krə-'men-t³l, ,in-\ *adj* — **in·cre·men·tal·ly** *adv*

in·crim·i·nate \in-'kri-mə-,nāt\ *vb* **-nated; -nat·ing** : to charge with or prove involvement in a crime or fault : ACCUSE — **in·crim·i·na·tion** \-,kri-mə-'nā-shən\ *n* — **in·crim·i·na·to·ry** \-'kri-mə-nə-,tòr-ē\ *adj*

incrust *var of* ENCRUST

in·crus·ta·tion \,in-,krəs-'tā-shən\ *n* **1** : CRUST; *also* : an accumulation (as of habits, opinions, or customs) resembling a crust **2** : the act of encrusting : the state of being encrusted

in·cu·bate \'in-kyù-,bāt, 'in-\ *vb* **-bat·ed; -bat·ing** : to sit on (eggs) to hatch by the warmth of the body; *also* : to keep (as an embryo) under conditions favorable for development — **in·cu·ba·tion** \,in-kyù-'bā-shən, ,in-\ *n*

in·cu·ba·tor \'in-kyù-,bāt-ər, 'in-\ *n* : one that incubates; *esp* : an apparatus providing suitable conditions (as of warmth and moisture) for incubating something (as a premature baby)

in·cu·bus \'in-kyə-bəs, 'in-\ *n, pl* **-bi** \-,bī, -,bē\ *also* **-bus·es** [ME, fr. LL, fr. L *incubare* to lie on] **1** : a spirit supposed to work evil on persons in their sleep **2** : NIGHTMARE 1 **3** : one that oppresses like a nightmare

in·cul·cate \in-'kəl-,kāt, 'in-(,)kəl-\ *vb* **-cat·ed; -cat·ing** [L *inculcare,* lit., to tread on, fr. *calcare* to trample, fr. *calx* heel] : to teach and impress by frequent repetitions or admonitions — **in·cul·ca·tion** \,in-(,)kəl-'kā-shən\ *n*

in·cul·pa·ble \(,)in-'kəl-pə-bəl\ *adj* : free from guilt : INNOCENT

in·cul·pate \in-'kəl-,pāt, 'in-(,)kəl-\ *vb* **-pat·ed; -pat·ing** : INCRIMINATE

in·cum·ben·cy \in-'kəm-bən-sē\ *n, pl* **-cies** **1** : something that is incumbent **2** : the quality or state of being incumbent **3** : the office or period of office of an incumbent

¹**in·cum·bent** \in-'kəm-bənt\ *n* : the holder of an office or position

²**incumbent** *adj* **1** : imposed as a duty **2** : occupying a specified office **3** : lying or resting on something else

in·cu·nab·u·lum \in-kyə-'na-byə-ləm, iŋ-\ *n, pl* **-la** \-lə\ [NL, fr. L *incunabula,* pl., bands holding the baby in a cradle, fr. *cunae* cradle] : a book printed before 1501

in·cur \in-'kər\ *vb* **in·curred; in·cur·ring** : to become liable or subject to : bring down upon oneself

in·cur·able \(,)in-'kyùr-ə-bəl\ *adj* **1** : not curable **2** : not likely to be changed — **incurable** *n* — **in·cur·ably** \(,)in-'kyùr-ə-blē\ *adv*

in·cur·sion \in-'kər-zhən\ *n* **1** : a sudden hostile invasion : RAID **2** : an entering in or into (as an activity)

in·cus \'iŋ-kəs\ *n, pl* **in·cu·des** \iŋ-'kyü-(,)dēz\ [NL, fr. L, anvil] : the middle bone of a chain of three small bones in the middle ear of a mammal

ind *abbr* **1** independent **2** index **3** industrial; industry

Ind *abbr* **1** Indian **2** Indiana

in·debt·ed \in-'de-təd\ *adj* **1** : owing gratitude or recognition to another **2** : owing money — **in·debt·ed·ness** *n*

in·de·cent \(,)in-'dē-s³nt\ *adj* : not decent; *esp* : grossly improper or offensive — **in·de·cen·cy** \-s³n-sē\ *n* — **in·de·cent·ly** *adv*

in·de·ci·sion \,in-di-'si-zhən\ *n* : a wavering between two or more possible courses of action : IRRESOLUTION

in·de·ci·sive \,in-di-'sī-siv\ *adj* **1** : INCONCLUSIVE ⟨an ~ battle⟩ **2** : marked by or prone to indecision **3** : INDEFINITE — **in·de·ci·sive·ly** *adv* — **in·de·ci·sive·ness** *n*

in·de·co·rous \(,)in-'de-kə-rəs; ,in-di-'kòr-əs\ *adj* : conflicting with accepted standards of good conduct or good taste **✦ Synonyms** IMPROPER, UNSEEMLY, INDECENT, UNBECOMING, INDELICATE — **in·de·co·rous·ly** *adv* — **in·de·co·rous·ness** *n*

in·deed \in-'dēd\ *adv* **1** : without any question : TRULY — often used interjectionally to express irony, disbelief, or surprise **2** : in reality **3** : all things considered

in·de·fat·i·ga·ble \,in-di-'fa-ti-gə-bəl\ *adj* : UNTIRING ⟨an ~ worker⟩ — **in·de·fat·i·ga·bly** \-blē\ *adv*

in·de·fea·si·ble \-'fē-zə-bəl\ *adj* : not capable of being annulled or voided — **in·de·fea·si·bly** \-blē\ *adv*

in·de·fen·si·ble \-'fen-sə-bəl\ *adj* **1** : incapable of being maintained as right or valid **2** : INEXCUSABLE ⟨~ comments⟩

3 : incapable of being protected against physical attack

in·de·fin·able \-'fī-nə-bəl\ *adj* : incapable of being precisely described or analyzed — **in·de·fin·ably** \-blē\ *adv*

in·def·i·nite \(ˌ)in-'def-ə-nət\ *adj* 1 : not defining or identifying ⟨*an* is an ~ article⟩ 2 : not precise : VAGUE 3 : having no fixed limits — **in·def·i·nite·ly** *adv* — **in·def·i·nite·ness** *n*

in·del·i·ble \in-'del-ə-bəl\ *adj* [ME, fr. ML *indelibilis*, alter. of L *indelebilis*, fr. *delēre* to delete, destroy] 1 : not capable of being removed or erased 2 : making marks that cannot be erased 3 : LASTING, UNFORGETTABLE — **in·del·i·bly** \in-'del-ə-blē\ *adv*

in·del·i·cate \(ˌ)in-'del-i-kət\ *adj* : not delicate; *esp* : IMPROPER, COARSE, TACTLESS ♦ **Synonyms** INDECENT, UNSEEMLY, INDECOROUS, UNBECOMING — **in·del·i·ca·cy** \in-'del-ə-kə-sē\ *n*

in·dem·ni·fy \in-'dem-nə-ˌfī\ *vb* **-fied; -fy·ing** [L *indemnis* unharmed, fr. *in-* not + *damnum* damage] 1 : to secure against hurt, loss, or damage 2 : to make compensation to for hurt, loss, or damage — **in·dem·ni·fi·ca·tion** \-ˌdem-nə-fə-'kā-shən\ *n*

in·dem·ni·ty \in-'dem-nə-tē\ *n, pl* **-ties** 1 : security against hurt, loss, or damage; *also* : exemption from incurred penalties or liabilities 2 : something that indemnifies

¹in·dent \in-'dent\ *vb* [ME, fr. AF *endenter*, fr. *dent* tooth, fr. L *dent-, dens*] 1 : to notch the edge of 2 : INDENTURE 3 : to set (as a line of a paragraph) in from the margin

²indent *vb* 1 : to force inward so as to form a depression 2 : to form a dent in

in·den·ta·tion \ˌin-ˌden-'tā-shən\ *n* 1 : NOTCH; *also* : a recess in a surface 2 : the action of indenting : the condition of being indented 3 : DENT 4 : INDENTION 2

in·den·tion \in-'den-chən\ *n* 1 : INDENTATION 2 2 : the blank space produced by indenting

¹in·den·ture \in-'den-chər\ *n* 1 : a written certificate or agreement; *esp* : a contract binding one person (as an apprentice) to work for another for a given period of time — often used in pl. 2 : INDENTATION 3 : DENT

²indenture *vb* **in·den·tured; in·den·tur·ing** : to bind (as an apprentice) by indentures

in·de·pen·dence \ˌin-də-'pen-dəns\ *n* : the quality or state of being independent : FREEDOM

Independence Day *n* : July 4 observed as a legal holiday in the U.S. in commemoration of the adoption of the Declaration of Independence in 1776

in·de·pen·dent \ˌin-də-'pen-dənt\ *adj* 1 : SELF-GOVERNING; *also* : not affiliated with a larger controlling unit 2 : not requiring or relying on something else or somebody else ⟨an ~ conclusion⟩ ⟨~ of

her parents⟩ 3 : not easily influenced : showing self-reliance and personal freedom ⟨an ~ mind⟩ 4 : not committed to a political party ⟨an ~ voter⟩ 5 : MAIN ⟨an ~ clause⟩ — **independent** *n* — **in·de·pen·dent·ly** *adv*

independent variable *n* : a variable whose value is not determined by that of any other variable in a function

in·de·scrib·able \ˌin-di-'skrī-bə-bəl\ *adj* 1 : that cannot be described 2 : being too intense or great for description — **in·de·scrib·ably** \-blē\ *adv*

in·de·ter·mi·nate \ˌin-di-'tər-mə-nət\ *adj* 1 : VAGUE; *also* : not known in advance 2 : not limited in advance; *also* : not leading to a definite end or result — **in·de·ter·mi·na·cy** \-nə-sē\ *n* — **in·de·ter·mi·nate·ly** *adv*

¹in·dex \'in-ˌdeks\ *n, pl* **in·dex·es** or **in·di·ces** \-də-ˌsēz\ 1 : POINTER 2 : SIGN, INDICATION ⟨an ~ of character⟩ 3 : a guide for facilitating references; *esp* : an alphabetical list of items treated in a printed work with the page number where each item may be found 4 : a list of restricted or prohibited material 5 *pl usu* **indices** : a number or symbol or expression (as an exponent) associated with another to indicate a mathematical operation or use or position in an arrangement or expansion 6 : a character ☞ used to direct attention (as to a note) 7 : INDEX NUMBER

²index *vb* 1 : to provide with or put into an index 2 : to serve as an index of 3 : to regulate by indexation

in·dex·ation \ˌin-ˌdek-'sā-shən\ *n* : a system of economic control in which a body of variables (as wages and interest) rise or fall at the same rate as an index of the cost of living

index finger *n* : the finger next to the thumb

in·dex·ing *n* : INDEXATION

index number *n* : a number used to indicate change in magnitude (as of cost) as compared with the magnitude at some specified time

index of refraction : REFRACTIVE INDEX

in·dia ink \'in-dē-ə-\ *n, often cap 1st I* 1 : a solid black pigment used in drawing 2 : a fluid made from india ink

In·di·an \'in-dē-ən\ *n* 1 : a native or inhabitant of India or of the East Indies; *also* : a person of Indian descent 2 : AMERICAN INDIAN — **Indian** *adj*

Indian corn *n* : a tall widely grown American cereal grass bearing seeds on long ears; *also* : its ears or seeds

Indian meal *n* : CORNMEAL

Indian paintbrush *n* : any of a genus of herbaceous plants related to the snapdragons that have brightly colored bracts

Indian pipe *n* : a waxy white leafless saprophytic herb of Asia and the U.S.

Indian summer *n* : a period of mild weather in late autumn or early winter

In·dia paper \'in-dē-ə-\ *n*, 1 : a thin absorbent paper used esp. for taking im-

---

indemonstrable　　　indestructible　　　indeterminable

pressions (as of steel engravings) **2** : a thin tough opaque printing paper

in·di·cate \'in-də-ˌkāt\ *vb* **-cat·ed; -cat·ing** **1** : to point out or to **2** : to show indirectly **3** : to state briefly — **in·di·ca·tion** \ˌin-də-ˌkā-tər\ *n* — **in·di·ca·tor** \'in-də-ˌkā-tər\ *n*

¹in·dic·a·tive \in-'di-kə-tiv\ *adj* **1** : of, relating to, or being a verb form that represents an act or state as a fact ⟨~ mood⟩ **2** : serving to indicate ⟨actions ~ of fear⟩

²indicative *n* **1** : the indicative mood of a language **2** : a form in the indicative mood

in·di·cia \in-'di-shə, -shē-ə\ *n pl* **1** : distinctive marks **2** : postal markings often imprinted on mail or mailing labels

in·dict \in-'dīt\ *vb* [alter. of earlier *indite*, fr. ME, fr. AF *enditer* to write, point out, indict, ultim. fr. L *indicere* to make known formally, fr. *dicere* to say] **1** : to charge with a fault or offense **2** : to charge with a crime by the finding of a jury — **in·dict·able** *adj* — **in·dict·ment** *n*

in·die \'in-dē\ *n* **1** : one that is independent; *esp* : an unaffiliated record or motion-picture production company **2** something produced by an indie — **indie** *adj*

in·dif·fer·ent \in-'di-frənt, -fə-rənt\ *adj* **1** : UNBIASED, UNPREJUDICED **2** : of no importance one way or the other **3** : marked by no special liking for or dislike of something **4** : being neither excessive nor inadequate **5** : PASSABLE, MEDIOCRE : being neither right nor wrong — **in·dif·fer·ence** \-frəns, -fə-rəns\ *n* — **in·dif·fer·ent·ly** *adv*

in·dig·e·nous \in-'di-jə-nəs\ *adj* : produced, growing, or living naturally in a particular region

in·di·gent \'in-di-jənt\ *adj* : IMPOVERISHED, NEEDY — **in·di·gence** \-jəns\ *n*

in·di·gest·ible \ˌin-dī-'jes-tə-bəl, -də-\ *adj* : not readily digested

in·di·ges·tion \-'jes-chən\ *n* : inadequate or difficult digestion : DYSPEPSIA

in·dig·nant \in-'dig-nənt\ *adj* : filled with or marked by indignation — **in·dig·nant·ly** *adv*

in·dig·na·tion \ˌin-dig-'nā-shən\ *n* : anger aroused by something unjust, unworthy, or mean

in·dig·ni·ty \in-'dig-nə-tē\ *n, pl* **-ties** : an offense against personal dignity or self-respect; *also* : humiliating treatment

in·di·go \'in-di-ˌgō\ *n, pl* **-gos** *or* **-goes** [It dial., fr. L *indicum*, fr. Gk *indikon*, fr. *indikos* Indic, fr. *Indos* India] **1** : a blue dye obtained from plants or synthesized **2** : a deep reddish blue color

in·di·rect \ˌin-də-'rekt, -dī-\ *adj* **1** : not straight ⟨an ~ route⟩ **2** : not straightforward and open ⟨~ methods⟩ **3** : not having a plainly seen connection ⟨an ~ cause⟩ **4** : not directly to the point ⟨an ~ answer⟩ — **in·di·rec·tion** \-'rek-shən\ *n* — **in·di·rect·ly** *adv* — **in·di·rect·ness** *n*

in·dis·creet \ˌin-di-'skrēt\ *adj* : not discreet : IMPRUDENT — **in·dis·creet·ly** *adv*

in·dis·cre·tion \ˌin-di-'skre-shən\ *n* **1** : IMPRUDENCE ⟨dietary ~⟩ **2** : something marked by lack of discretion; *esp* : an act deviating from accepted morality

in·dis·crim·i·nate \ˌin-di-'skri-mə-nət\ *adj* **1** : not marked by discrimination or careful distinction **2** : HAPHAZARD, RANDOM ⟨an ~ application of a law⟩ **3** : UNRESTRAINED **4** : MOTLEY — **in·dis·crim·i·nate·ly** *adv*

in·dis·pens·able \ˌin-di-'spen-sə-bəl\ *adj* : absolutely essential : REQUISITE — **in·dis·pens·abil·i·ty** \-ˌspen-sə-bi-lə-tē\ *n* — **indispensable** *n* — **in·dis·pens·ably** \-'spen-sə-blē\ *adv*

in·dis·posed \-'spōzd\ *adj* **1** : slightly ill **2** : AVERSE — **in·dis·po·si·tion** \(ˌ)in-ˌdis-pə-'zi-shən\ *n*

in·dis·put·able \ˌin-di-'spyü-tə-bəl, (ˌ)in-'dis-pyə-\ *adj* : not disputable : UNQUESTIONABLE ⟨~ proof⟩ — **in·dis·put·ably** \-blē\ *adv*

in·dis·sol·u·ble \ˌin-di-'säl-yə-bəl\ *adj* : not capable of being dissolved, undone, or broken : PERMANENT ⟨an ~ contract⟩

in·dis·tinct \ˌin-di-'stiŋkt\ *adj* **1** : not sharply outlined or separable : BLURRED, FAINT, DIM **2** : not readily distinguishable : UNCERTAIN — **in·dis·tinct·ly** *adv* — **in·dis·tinct·ness** *n*

in·dite \in-'dīt\ *vb* **in·dit·ed; in·dit·ing** : COMPOSE ⟨~ a poem⟩; *also* : to put in writing ⟨~ a letter⟩

in·di·um \'in-dē-əm\ *n* : a malleable silvery metallic chemical element

indiv *abbr* individual

¹in·di·vid·u·al \ˌin-də-'vi-jə-wəl\ *adj* **1** : of, relating to, or associated with an individual ⟨~ traits⟩ **2** : being an individual : existing as an indivisible whole **3** : intended for one person **4** : SEPARATE ⟨~ copies⟩ **5** : having marked individuality ⟨an ~ style⟩ — **in·di·vid·u·al·ly** *adv*

²individual *n* **1** : a single member of a category : a particular person, animal, or thing **2** : PERSON ⟨a disagreeable ~⟩

in·di·vid·u·al·ise *Brit var of* INDIVIDUALIZE

in·di·vid·u·al·ism \ˌin-də-'vi-jə-wə-ˌli-zəm\ *n* **1** : a doctrine that the interests of the individual are primary **2** : a doctrine holding that the individual has political or economic rights with which the state must not interfere **3** : INDIVIDUALITY

in·di·vid·u·al·ist \-list\ *n* **1** : one that pursues a markedly independent course in thought or action **2** : one that advocates or practices individualism — **individualist** *or* **in·di·vid·u·al·is·tic** \-ˌvi-jə-wə-'lis-tik\ *adj*

in·di·vid·u·al·i·ty \-ˌvi-jə-'wa-lə-tē\ *n, pl* **-ties** **1** : the sum of qualities that characterize and distinguish an individual from all others; *also* : PERSONALITY **2** : separate or distinct existence **3** : INDIVIDUAL, PERSON

indiscernible   **indistinguishable**

in·di·vid·u·al·ize \-'vi-jə-wə-ˌlīz\ *vb* **-ized; -iz·ing 1** : to make individual in character **2** : to treat or notice individually : PARTICULARIZE **3** : to adapt to the needs of an individual

individual retirement account *n* : IRA

in·di·vid·u·ate \ˌin-də-'vi-jə-ˌwāt\ *vb* **-at·ed; -at·ing** : to give individuality to : form into an individual — **in·di·vid·u·a·tion** \-ˌvi-jə-'wā-shən\ *n*

in·di·vis·i·ble \ˌin-də-'vi-zə-bəl\ *adj* : impossible to divide or separate — **in·di·vis·i·bil·i·ty** \-ˌvi-zə-'bi-lə-tē\ *n* — **in·di·vis·i·bly** *adv*

In·do-Ar·y·an \ˌin-dō-'er-ē-ən\ *n* : a branch of the Indo-European language family that includes Hindi and other languages of south Asia

in·doc·tri·nate \in-'däk-trə-ˌnāt\ *vb* **-nat·ed; -nat·ing 1** : to instruct in fundamentals or rudiments : TEACH **2** : to teach the beliefs and doctrines of a particular group — **in·doc·tri·na·tion** \ˌ(ˌ)in-ˌdäk-trə-'nā-shən\ *n* — **in·doc·tri·na·tor** *n*

In·do-Eu·ro·pe·an \ˌin-dō-ˌyùr-ə-'pē-ən\ *adj* : of, relating to, or constituting a family of languages comprising those spoken in most of Europe and in the parts of the world colonized by Europeans since 1500 and also in Persia, the subcontinent of India, and some other parts of Asia

in·do·lent \'in-də-lənt\ *adj* [LL *indolens* insensitive to pain, fr. L *dolēre* to feel pain] **1** : slow to develop or heal ⟨~ ulcers⟩ **2** : LAZY — **in·do·lence** \-ləns\ *n* — **in·do·lent·ly** *adv*

in·dom·i·ta·ble \in-'dä-mə-tə-bəl\ *adj* : UNCONQUERABLE ⟨~ courage⟩ — **in·dom·i·ta·bly** \-blē\ *adv*

in·door \'in-ˌdòr\ *adj* **1** : of or relating to the inside of a building **2** : living, located, or carried on within a building

in·doors \in-'dòrz\ *adv* : in or into a building

indorse, indorsement *var of* ENDORSE, ENDORSEMENT

in·du·bi·ta·ble \ˌ(ˌ)in-'dü-bə-tə-bəl, -'dyü-\ *adj* : UNQUESTIONABLE — **in·du·bi·ta·bly** \-blē\ *adv*

in·duce \in-'düs, -'dyüs\ *vb* **in·duced; in·duc·ing 1** : PERSUADE, INFLUENCE **2** : BRING ABOUT **3** : to produce (as an electric current) by induction **4** : to determine by induction; *esp* : to infer from particulars — **in·duc·er** *n*

in·duce·ment \-mənt\ *n* **1** : something that induces : MOTIVE **2** : the act or process of inducing

in·duct \in-'dəkt\ *vb* **1** : to place in office **2** : to admit as a member **3** : to enroll for military training or service — **in·duct·ee** \ˌdək-'tē\ *n*

in·duc·tance \in-'dək-təns\ *n* : a property of an electric circuit by which a varying current produces an electromotive force in that circuit or in a nearby circuit; *also* : the measure of this property

in·duc·tion \in-'dək-shən\ *n* **1** : the act or process of inducting; *also* : INITIATION **2**
: the formality by which a civilian is inducted into military service **3** : inference of a generalized conclusion from particular instances; *also* : a conclusion so reached **4** : the act of causing or bringing on or about **5** : the process by which an electric current, an electric charge, or magnetism is produced in a body by the proximity of an electric or magnetic field

in·duc·tive \in-'dək-tiv\ *adj* : of, relating to, or employing induction

in·duc·tor \in-'dək-tər\ *n* : an electrical component that acts upon another or is itself acted upon by induction

in·dulge \in-'dəlj\ *vb* **in·dulged; in·dulg·ing 1** : to give free rein to : GRATIFY **2** : HUMOR **3** : to gratify one's taste or desire for ⟨~ in alcohol⟩

in·dul·gence \in-'dəl-jəns\ *n* **1** : remission of temporal punishment due in Roman Catholic doctrine for sins whose eternal punishment has been remitted by reception of the sacrifice of penance **2** : the act of indulging : the state of being indulgent **3** : an indulgent act **4** : the thing indulged in **5** : SELF-INDULGENCE — **in·dul·gent** \-jənt\ *adj* — **in·dul·gent·ly** *adv*

in·du·rat·ed \'in-dyù-ˌrā-təd, -dü-\ *adj* : physically or emotionally hardened — **in·du·ra·tion** \ˌin-dyù-'rā-shən, -dü-\ *n*

in·dus·tri·al \in-'dəs-trē-əl\ *adj* **1** : of or relating to industry **2** : HEAVY-DUTY ⟨an ~ zipper⟩ **3** : characterized by highly developed industries — **in·dus·tri·al·ly** *adv*

in·dus·tri·al·ise *Brit var of* INDUSTRIALIZE

in·dus·tri·al·ist \-ə-list\ *n* : a person owning or engaged in the management of an industry

in·dus·tri·al·ize \in-'dəs-trē-ə-ˌlīz\ *vb* **-ized; -iz·ing** : to make or become industrial — **in·dus·tri·al·i·za·tion** \-ˌdəs-trē-ə-lə-'zā-shən\ *n*

in·dus·tri·ous \in-'dəs-trē-əs\ *adj* : DILIGENT, BUSY — **in·dus·tri·ous·ly** *adv* — **in·dus·tri·ous·ness** *n*

in·dus·try \'in-(ˌ)dəs-trē\ *n, pl* **-tries 1** : DILIGENCE **2** : a department or branch of a craft, art, business, or manufacture; *esp* : one that employs a large personnel and capital **3** : a distinct group of productive enterprises **4** : manufacturing activity as a whole

in·dwell \ˌ(ˌ)in-'dwel\ *vb* : to exist within an as an activating spirit or force

In·dy car \'in-dē-\ *n* : a single-seat, open cockpit racing car with the engine in the rear

¹in·ebri·ate \i-'nē-brē-ˌāt\ *vb* **-at·ed; -at·ing** : to make drunk : INTOXICATE — **in·ebri·a·tion** \-ˌnē-brē-'ā-shən\ *n*

²in·ebri·ate \-ət\ *n* : one that is drunk; *esp* : DRUNKARD

in·ef·fa·ble \ˌ(ˌ)in-'e-fə-bəl\ *adj* : incapable of being expressed in words : INDESCRIBABLE ⟨~ joy⟩ **2** : UNSPEAKABLE ⟨~ disgust⟩ **3** : not to be uttered : TABOO — **in·ef·fa·bly** \-blē\ *adv*

in·ef·fec·tive \ˌi-nə-'fek-tiv\ *adj* **1** : INEF-

FECTUAL 2 : not able to perform efficiently or as expected : INCAPABLE — **in·ef·fec·tive·ly** *adv* — **in·ef·fec·tive·ness** *n*

in·ef·fec·tu·al \-'fek-chə-wəl\ *adj* 1 : not producing the proper or usual effect 2 : INEFFECTIVE 2 — **in·ef·fec·tu·al·ly** *adv*

in·ef·fi·cient \ˌi-nə-'fi-shənt\ *adj* 1 : not producing the desired effect 2 : wasteful of time or energy 3 : INCAPABLE, INCOMPETENT — **in·ef·fi·cien·cy** \-'fi-shən-sē\ *n* — **in·ef·fi·cient·ly** *adv*

in·el·e·gant \(ˌ)i-'ne-li-gənt\ *adj* : lacking in refinement, grace, or good taste — **in·el·e·gance** \-gəns\ *n* — **in·el·e·gant·ly** *adv*

in·el·i·gi·ble \(ˌ)i-'ne-lə-jə-bəl\ *adj* : not qualified for an office or position — **in·el·i·gi·bil·i·ty** \(ˌ)i-ˌne-lə-jə-'bi-lə-tē\ *n*

in·eluc·ta·ble \ˌi-ni-'lək-tə-bəl\ *adj* : not to be avoided, changed, or resisted — **in·eluc·ta·bly** \-blē\ *adv*

in·ept \i-'nept\ *adj* 1 : lacking in fitness or aptitude : UNFIT 2 : FOOLISH 3 : being out of place : INAPPROPRIATE 4 : generally incompetent : BUNGLING — **in·ept·ly** *adv* — **in·ept·ness** *n*

in·ep·ti·tude \(ˌ)i-'nep-ti-ˌtüd, -ˌtyüd\ *n* : the quality or state of being inept; *esp* : INCOMPETENCE

in·equal·i·ty \ˌi-ni-'kwä-lə-tē\ *n* 1 : the quality of being unequal or uneven; *esp* : UNEVENNESS, DISPARITY 2 : an instance of being unequal

in·ert \i-'nərt\ *adj* [L *inert-, iners* unskilled, idle, fr. *art-, ars* skill] 1 : powerless to move 2 : SLUGGISH 3 : lacking in active properties ⟨chemically ∼⟩ — **in·ert·ly** *adv* — **in·ert·ness** *n*

in·er·tia \i-'nər-shə, -shē-ə\ *n* 1 : a property of matter whereby it remains at rest or continues in uniform motion unless acted upon by some outside force 2 : INERTNESS, SLUGGISHNESS — **in·er·tial** \-shəl\ *adj*

in·es·cap·able \ˌi-nə-'skä-pə-bəl\ *adj* : incapable of being escaped : INEVITABLE — **in·es·cap·ably** \-blē\ *adv*

in·es·ti·ma·ble \(ˌ)i-'nes-tə-mə-bəl\ *adj* 1 : incapable of being estimated or computed ⟨∼ errors⟩ 2 : too valuable or excellent to be fully appreciated — **in·es·ti·ma·bly** \-blē\ *adv*

in·ev·i·ta·ble \i-'ne-və-tə-bəl\ *adj* : incapable of being avoided or evaded : bound to happen — **in·ev·i·ta·bil·i·ty** \(ˌ)i-ˌne-və-tə-'bi-lə-tē\ *n*

in·ev·i·ta·bly \-blē\ *adv* 1 : in an inevitable way 2 : as is to be expected

in·ex·act \ˌi-nig-'zakt\ *adj* 1 : not precisely correct or true : INACCURATE 2 : not rigorous and careful — **in·ex·act·ly** *adv* — **in·ex·act·ness** *n*

in·ex·cus·able \ˌi-nik-'skyü-zə-bəl\ *adj* : impossible to excuse or justify — **in·ex·cus·ably** \-blē\ *adv*

in·ex·haust·ible \ˌi-nig-'zȯ-stə-bəl\ *adj* 1

: incapable of being used up ⟨an ∼ supply⟩ 2 : UNTIRING ⟨an ∼ hiker⟩ — **in·ex·haust·ibly** \-blē\ *adv*

in·ex·o·ra·ble \(ˌ)i-'nek-sə-rə-bəl\ *adj* : not to be persuaded, moved, or stopped : RELENTLESS — **in·ex·o·ra·bly** *adv*

in·ex·pe·ri·ence \ˌi-nik-'spir-ē-əns\ *n* : lack of experience or of knowledge gained by experience — **in·ex·pe·ri·enced** \-ənst\ *adj*

in·ex·pert \(ˌ)i-'nek-ˌspərt\ *adj* : not expert : UNSKILLED — **in·ex·pert·ly** *adv*

in·ex·pi·a·ble \(ˌ)i-'nek-spē-ə-bəl\ *adj* : not capable of being atoned for

in·ex·pli·ca·ble \ˌi-nik-'spli-kə-bəl, (ˌ)i-'nek-(ˌ)spli-\ *adj* : incapable of being explained or accounted for — **in·ex·pli·ca·bly** \-blē\ *adv*

in·ex·press·ible \-'spre-sə-bəl\ *adj* : not capable of being expressed — **in·ex·press·ibly** \-blē\ *adv*

in ex·tre·mis \ˌin-ik-'strā-məs, -'strē-\ *adv* : in extreme circumstances; *esp* : at the point of death

in·ex·tri·ca·ble \ˌi-nik-'stri-kə-bəl, (ˌ)i-'nek-(ˌ)stri-\ *adj* 1 : forming a maze or tangle from which it is impossible to get free 2 : incapable of being disentangled or untied — **in·ex·tri·ca·bly** \-blē\ *adv*

inf *abbr* 1 infantry 2 infinitive

in·fal·li·ble \(ˌ)in-'fa-lə-bəl\ *adj* 1 : incapable of error : UNERRING 2 : SURE, CERTAIN ⟨an ∼ remedy⟩ — **in·fal·li·bil·i·ty** \(ˌ)in-ˌfa-lə-'bi-lə-tē\ *n* — **in·fal·li·bly** \(ˌ)in-'fa-lə-blē\ *adv*

in·fa·mous \'in-fə-məs\ *adj* 1 : having a reputation of the worst kind 2 : DISGRACEFUL — **in·fa·mous·ly** *adv*

in·fa·my \-mē\ *n, pl* **-mies** 1 : evil reputation brought about by something grossly criminal, shocking, or brutal 2 : an extreme and publicly known criminal or evil act 3 : the state of being infamous

in·fan·cy \'in-fən-sē\ *n, pl* **-cies** 1 : early childhood 2 : a beginning or early period of existence

in·fant \'in-fənt\ *n* [ME *enfaunt*, fr. AF *enfant*, fr. L *infant-, infans*, adj., incapable of speech, young, fr. *fant-, fans*, prp. of *fari* to speak] : BABY; *also* : a person who is a legal minor

in·fan·ti·cide \in-'fan-tə-ˌsīd\ *n* : the killing of an infant

in·fan·tile \'in-fən-ˌtī(-ə)l, -t°l, -ˌtēl\ *adj* : of or relating to infants; *also* : CHILDISH

infantile paralysis *n* : POLIOMYELITIS

in·fan·try \'in-fən-trē\ *n, pl* **-tries** [MF & It; MF *infanterie*, fr. It *infanteria*, fr. *infante* boy, foot soldier] : soldiers trained, armed, and equipped to fight on foot — **in·fan·try·man** \-mən\ *n*

in·farct \'in-ˌfärkt\ *n* [L *infarctus*, pp. of *infarcire* to stuff] : an area of dead tissue (as of the heart wall) caused by blocking of local blood circulation — **in·farc·tion** \in-'färk-shən\ *n*

in·fat·u·ate \in-'fa-chə-ˌwāt\ *vb* **-at·ed;**

---

inefficacious	inequitable	inerrant	inexpressive
inefficacy	inequity	inexpedient	inextinguishable
inelastic	ineradicable	inexpensive	infeasible
inelasticity			

-at·ing : to inspire with a foolish or extravagant love or admiration — **in·fat·u·a·tion** \-ˌfa-chə-ˈwā-shən\ *n*

in·fect \in-ˈfekt\ *vb* **1** : to contaminate with disease-producing matter **2** : to communicate a pathogen or disease to **3** : to cause to share one's feelings ⟨~ed us with his enthusiasm⟩

in·fec·tion \in-ˈfek-shən\ *n* **1** : a disease or condition caused by a germ or parasite; *also* : such a germ or parasite **2** : an act or process of infecting — **in·fec·tious** \-shəs\ *adj* — **in·fec·tive** \-ˈfek-tiv\ *adj*

infectious mononucleosis *n* : an acute infectious disease characterized by fever, swelling of lymph glands, and increased numbers of lymph cells in the blood

in·fe·lic·i·tous \ˌin-fi-ˈli-sə-təs\ *adj* : not appropriate in application or expression — **in·fe·lic·i·ty** \-sə-tē\ *n*

in·fer \in-ˈfər\ *vb* **-ferred; -fer·ring 1** : to derive as a conclusion from facts or premises **2** : GUESS, SURMISE **3** : to lead to as a conclusion or consequence **4** : HINT, SUGGEST ◆ *Synonyms* DEDUCE, CONCLUDE, JUDGE, GATHER — **in·fer·ence** \ˈin-frəns, -fə-rəns\ *n* — **in·fer·en·tial** \ˌin-fə-ˈren-chəl\ *adj*

in·fe·ri·or \in-ˈfir-ē-ər\ *adj* **1** : situated lower down **2** : of low or lower degree or rank **3** : of lesser quality **4** : of little or less importance, value, or merit — **inferior** *n* — **in·fe·ri·or·i·ty** \(ˌ)in-ˌfir-ē-ˈȯr-ə-tē\ *n*

in·fer·nal \in-ˈfər-nᵊl\ *adj* **1** : of or relating to hell **2** : HELLISH, FIENDISH ⟨~ schemes⟩ **3** : DAMNABLE ⟨an ~ pest⟩ — **in·fer·nal·ly** *adv*

in·fer·no \in-ˈfər-nō\ *n, pl* **-nos** [It, hell, fr. LL *infernus,* fr. L, lower] : a place or a state that resembles or suggests hell; *also* : intense heat

in·fer·tile \(ˌ)in-ˈfər-tᵊl\ *adj* : not fertile or productive : BARREN — **in·fer·til·i·ty** \ˌin-fər-ˈti-lə-tē\ *n*

in·fest \in-ˈfest\ *vb* : to trouble by spreading or swarming in or over; *also* : to live in or on as a parasite — **in·fes·ta·tion** \ˌin-ˌfes-ˈtā-shən\ *n*

in·fi·del \ˈin-fə-dᵊl, -fə-ˌdel\ *n* **1** : one who is not a Christian or opposes Christianity **2** : an unbeliever esp. with respect to a particular religion

in·fi·del·i·ty \ˌin-fə-ˈde-lə-tē, -fī-\ *n, pl* **-ties 1** : lack of belief in a religion **2** : unfaithfulness or an instance of it esp. in marriage

in·field \ˈin-ˌfēld\ *n* : the part of a baseball field inside the baselines — **in·field·er** *n*

in·fight·ing \ˈin-ˌfī-tin\ *n* **1** : fighting at close quarters **2** : dissension or rivalry among members of a group

in·fil·trate \in-ˈfil-ˌtrāt, ˈin-(ˌ)fil-\ *vb* **-trat·ed; -trat·ing 1** : to enter or filter into or through something **2** : to pass into or through by or as if by filtering or permeating — **in·fil·tra·tion** \ˌin-(ˌ)fil-ˈtrā-shən\ *n* — **in·fil·tra·tor** *n*

in·fi·nite \ˈin-fə-nət\ *adj* **1** : LIMITLESS, BOUNDLESS, ENDLESS ⟨~ space⟩ ⟨~ patience⟩ **2** : VAST, IMMENSE; *also* : INEX-

HAUSTIBLE ⟨~ wealth⟩ **3** : greater than any preassigned finite value however large ⟨~ number of positive integers⟩; *also* : extending to infinity ⟨~ plane surface⟩ — **infinite** *n* — **in·fi·nite·ly** *adv*

in·fin·i·tes·i·mal \(ˌ)in-ˌfi-nə-ˈte-sə-məl\ *adj* : immeasurably or incalculably small — **in·fin·i·tes·i·mal·ly** *adv*

in·fin·i·tive \in-ˈfi-nə-tiv\ *n* : a verb form having the characteristics of both verb and noun and in English usu. being used with *to*

in·fin·i·tude \in-ˈfi-nə-ˌtüd, -ˌtyüd\ *n* **1** : the quality or state of being infinite **2** : something that is infinite esp. in extent

in·fin·i·ty \in-ˈfi-nə-tē\ *n, pl* **-ties 1** : the quality or state of being infinite **2** : unlimited extent of time, space, or quantity : BOUNDLESSNESS **3** : an indefinitely great number or amount

in·firm \in-ˈfərm\ *adj* **1** : deficient in vitality; *esp* : feeble from age **2** : weak of mind, will, or character : IRRESOLUTE **3** : not solid or stable : INSECURE

in·fir·ma·ry \in-ˈfər-mə-rē\ *n, pl* **-ries** : a place for the care of the infirm or sick

in·fir·mi·ty \in-ˈfər-mə-tē\ *n, pl* **-ties 1** : FEEBLENESS **2** : DISEASE, AILMENT **3** : a personal failing : FOIBLE

infl *abbr* influenced

in fla·gran·te de·lic·to \ˌin-flə-ˈgrän-tē-di-ˈlik-tō, -ˈgran-\ *adv* **1** : in the very act of committing a misdeed **2** : in the midst of sexual activity

in·flame \in-ˈflām\ *vb* **in·flamed; in·flam·ing 1** : KINDLE **2** : to excite to excessive or uncontrollable action or feeling; *also* : INTENSIFY **3** : to affect or become affected with inflammation

in·flam·ma·ble \in-ˈfla-mə-bəl\ *adj* **1** : FLAMMABLE **2** : easily inflamed, excited, or angered : IRASCIBLE

in·flam·ma·tion \ˌin-flə-ˈmā-shən\ *n* : a bodily response to injury in which an affected area becomes red, hot, and painful and congested with blood

in·flam·ma·to·ry \in-ˈfla-mə-ˌtȯr-ē\ *adj* **1** : tending to excite the senses or to arouse anger, disorder, or tumult : SEDITIOUS **2** : causing or accompanied by inflammation ⟨an ~ disease⟩

in·flate \in-ˈflāt\ *vb* **in·flat·ed; in·flat·ing 1** : to swell with air or gas ⟨~ a balloon⟩ **2** : to puff up : ELATE ⟨~ one's ego⟩ **3** : to expand or increase abnormally ⟨~ prices⟩ — **in·flat·able** *adj*

in·fla·tion \in-ˈflā-shən\ *n* **1** : an act of inflating **2** : the state of being inflated **2** : empty pretentiousness : POMPOSITY **3** : a continuing rise in the general price level usu. attributed to an increase in the volume of money and credit

in·fla·tion·ary \-shə-ˌner-ē\ *adj* : of, characterized by, or productive of inflation

in·flect \in-ˈflekt\ *vb* **1** : to turn from a direct line or course : CURVE **2** : to vary a word by inflection **3** : to change or vary the pitch of the voice

in·flec·tion \in-ˈflek-shən\ *n* **1** : the act or result of curving or bending **2** : a change in pitch or loudness of the voice **3** : the change of form that words undergo to mark case, gender, number, tense, person, mood, or voice — **in·flec·tion·al** \-shə-nəl\ adj

in·flex·i·ble \(ˌ)in-ˈflek-sə-bəl\ adj 1 : UNYIELDING 2 : RIGID 3 : incapable of change — **in·flex·i·bil·i·ty** \-ˌflek-sə-ˈbi-lə-tē\ n — **in·flex·i·bly** \-ˈflek-sə-blē\ adv

in·flex·ion \in-ˈflek-shən\ chiefly Brit var of INFLECTION

in·flict \in-ˈflikt\ vb : AFFLICT; also : to give by or as if by striking — **in·flic·tion** \-ˈflik-shən\ n

in·flo·res·cence \ˌin-flə-ˈre-sᵊn(t)s\ n : the manner of development and arrangement of flowers on a stem; also : a flowering stem with its appendages : a flower cluster

in·flow \ˈin-ˌflō\ n : a flowing in

¹**in·flu·ence** \ˈin-ˌflü-əns\ n 1 : the act or power of producing an effect without apparent force or direct authority 2 : the power or capacity of causing an effect in indirect or intangible ways 3 : one that exerts influence — **in·flu·en·tial** \ˌin-flü-ˈen-chəl\ adj — **under the influence** : affected by alcohol

²**influence** vb **-enced; -enc·ing** 1 : to affect or alter by influence : SWAY 2 : to have an effect on the condition or development of : MODIFY

in·flu·en·za \ˌin-flü-ˈen-zə\ n [It, lit., influence, fr. ML influentia; fr. the belief that epidemics were due to the influence of the stars] : an acute and highly contagious virus disease marked by fever, prostration, aches and pains, and respiratory inflammation; also : any of various feverish usu. virus diseases typically with respiratory symptoms

in·flux \ˈin-ˌfləks\ n : a coming in

in·fo \ˈin-(ˌ)fō\ n : INFORMATION

in·fold \in-ˈfōld\ vb 1 : ENFOLD 2 : to fold inward or toward one another

in·fo·mer·cial \ˈin-fō-ˌmər-shəl\ n : a television program that is an extended advertisement often including a discussion or demonstration

in·form \in-ˈfȯrm\ vb 1 : to communicate knowledge to : TELL 2 : to give information or knowledge 3 : to act as an informer ✦ **Synonyms** ACQUAINT, APPRISE, ADVISE, NOTIFY

in·for·mal \(ˌ)in-ˈfȯr-məl\ adj 1 : conducted or carried out without formality or ceremony ⟨an ∼ party⟩ 2 : characteristic of or appropriate to ordinary, casual, or familiar use ⟨∼ clothes⟩ — **in·for·mal·i·ty** \ˌin-fȯr-ˈma-lə-tē, -fər-\ n — **in·for·mal·ly** \(ˌ)in-ˈfȯr-mə-lē\ adv

in·for·mant \in-ˈfȯr-mənt\ n : a person who gives information : INFORMER

in·for·ma·tion \ˌin-fər-ˈmā-shən\ n 1 : the communication or reception of knowledge or intelligence 2 : knowledge obtained from investigation, study, or instruction : FACTS, DATA 3 : the attribute communicated by one of two or more alternative sequences of something (as nucleotides in DNA or binary digits in a computer program) — **in·for·ma·tion·al** \-shə-nəl\ adj

information superhighway n : INTERNET

in·for·ma·tive \in-ˈfȯr-mə-tiv\ adj : imparting knowledge : INSTRUCTIVE

in·formed \in-ˈfȯrmd\ adj 1 : having or based on information ⟨an ∼ decision⟩ 2 : EDUCATED, KNOWLEDGEABLE

informed consent n : consent to a medical procedure by someone who understands what is involved

in·form·er \-ˈfȯr-mər\ n : one that informs; esp : a person who informs against others for illegalities esp. for financial gain

in·fo·tain·ment \ˌin-fō-ˈtān-mənt\ n : a television program that presents information (as news) in a manner intended to be entertaining

in·frac·tion \in-ˈfrak-shən\ n [ME, fr. ML infractio, fr. L, subduing, fr. infringere to break, crush] : the act of infringing : VIOLATION

in·fra dig \ˌin-frə-ˈdig\ adj [short for L infra dignitatem] : being beneath one's dignity

in·fra·red \ˌin-frə-ˈred\ adj : being, relating to, or using radiation having wavelengths longer than those of red light — **infrared** n

in·fra·struc·ture \ˈin-frə-ˌstrək-chər\ n 1 : the underlying foundation or basic framework (as of a system or organization) 2 : the system of public works of a country, state, or region; also : the resources (as buildings or equipment) required for an activity

in·fre·quent \(ˌ)in-ˈfrē-kwənt\ adj 1 : seldom happening : RARE 2 : placed or occurring at wide intervals in space or time ✦ **Synonyms** UNCOMMON, SCARCE, SPORADIC — **in·fre·quent·ly** adv

in·fringe \in-ˈfrinj\ vb **in·fringed; in·fring·ing** 1 : VIOLATE, TRANSGRESS ⟨∼ a patent⟩ 2 : ENCROACH, TRESPASS ⟨∼ on our rights⟩ — **in·fringe·ment** n

in·fu·ri·ate \in-ˈfyu̇r-ē-ˌāt\ vb **-at·ed; -at·ing** : to make furious : ENRAGE — **in·fu·ri·at·ing·ly** adv

in·fuse \in-ˈfyüz\ vb **in·fused; in·fus·ing** 1 : to instill a principle or quality in ⟨infused the team with confidence⟩ 2 : INSPIRE, ANIMATE 3 : to steep (as tea) without boiling — **in·fu·sion** \-ˈfyü-zhən\ n

¹**-ing** \iŋ\ n suffix 1 : action or process ⟨sleeping⟩ : instance of an action or process ⟨a meeting⟩ 2 : product or result of an action or process ⟨an engraving⟩ ⟨earnings⟩ 3 : something used in an action or process ⟨a bed covering⟩ 4 : something connected with, consisting of, or used in making (a specified thing) ⟨scaffolding⟩ 5 : something related to (a specified concept) ⟨offing⟩

²**-ing** n suffix : one of a (specified) kind

³**-ing** vb suffix or adj suffix — used to form the present participle ⟨sailing⟩ and sometimes to form an adjective resembling a present participle but not derived from a verb ⟨swashbuckling⟩

in·ga·ther \ˈin-ˌga-thər\ vb : to gather in : ASSEMBLE

in·ge·nious \in-'jēn-yəs\ *adj* **1** : marked by special aptitude at discovering, inventing, or contriving **2** : marked by originality, resourcefulness, and cleverness in conception or execution — **in·ge·nious·ly** *adv* — **in·ge·nious·ness** *n*

in·ge·nue *or* **in·gé·nue** \'an-jə-ˌnü, 'än-; 'aⁿ-zhə-, 'äⁿ-\ *n* : a naive girl or young woman; *esp* : an actress portraying such a person

in·ge·nu·i·ty \ˌin-jə-'nü-ə-tē, -'nyü-\ *n, pl* **-ties** : skill or cleverness in planning or inventing : INVENTIVENESS

in·gen·u·ous \in-'jen-yə-wəs\ *adj* [L *ingenuus* native, freeborn, fr. *gignere* to beget] **1** : innocently straightforward ⟨her ∼ curiosity⟩ **2** : lacking craft or subtlety ⟨∼ comments⟩ — **in·gen·u·ous·ly** *adv* — **in·gen·u·ous·ness** *n*

in·gest \in-'jest\ *vb* : to take in for or as if for digestion — **in·ges·tion** \-'jes-chən\ *n*

in·gle·nook \'iŋ-gəl-ˌnùk\ *n* : a nook by a large open fireplace; *also* : a bench occupying this nook

in·glo·ri·ous \ˌ(ˌ)in-'glôr-ē-əs\ *adj* **1** : SHAMEFUL **2** : not glorious : lacking fame or honor — **in·glo·ri·ous·ly** *adv*

in·got \'iŋ-gət\ *n* : a mass of metal cast in a form convenient for storage or transportation

¹in·grain \ˌ(ˌ)in-'grān\ *vb* : to work indelibly into the natural texture or mental or moral constitution — **in·grained** *adj*

²in·grain \'in-ˌgrān\ *adj* **1** : made of fiber that is dyed before being spun into yarn **2** : made of yarn that is dyed before being woven or knitted **3** : INNATE — **in·grain** *n*

in·grate \'in-ˌgrāt\ *n* : an ungrateful person

in·gra·ti·ate \in-'grā-shē-ˌāt\ *vb* **-at·ed; -at·ing** : to gain favor by deliberate effort

in·gra·ti·at·ing *adj* **1** : capable of winning favor : PLEASING ⟨an ∼ smile⟩ **2** : FLATTERING ⟨an ∼ manner⟩

in·grat·i·tude \ˌ(ˌ)in-'gra-tə-ˌtüd, -ˌtyüd\ *n* : lack of gratitude : UNGRATEFULNESS

in·gre·di·ent \in-'grēd-ē-ənt\ *n* : one of the substances that make up a mixture or compound : CONSTITUENT

in·gress \'in-ˌgres\ *n* : ENTRANCE, ACCESS — **in·gres·sion** \in-'gre-shən\ *n*

in·grow·ing \'in-ˌgrō-iŋ\ *adj* : growing or tending inward

in·grown \-ˌgrōn\ *adj* : grown in; *esp* : having the free tip or edge embedded in the flesh ⟨an ∼ toenail⟩

in·gui·nal \'iŋ-gwə-nᵊl\ *adj* : of, relating to, or situated in or near the region of the groin ⟨an ∼ hernia⟩

in·hab·it \in-'ha-bət\ *vb* : to live or dwell in ⟨spiders that ∼ caves⟩ — **in·hab·it·able** *adj* — **in·hab·i·ta·tion** \in-ˌha-bə-'tā-shən\ *n*

in·hab·i·tant \in-'ha-bə-tənt\ *n* : a permanent resident in a place

in·hal·ant \in-'hā-lənt\ *n* : something (as a medicine) that is inhaled

in·ha·la·tor \'in-hə-ˌlā-tər\ *n* : a device that provides a mixture of carbon dioxide and oxygen for breathing

in·hale \in-'hāl\ *vb* **in·haled; in·hal·ing** : to breathe in — **in·ha·la·tion** \ˌin-hə-'lā-shən\ *n*

in·hal·er \in-'hā-lər\ *n* : a device by means of which medicinal material is inhaled

in·here \in-'hir\ *vb* **in·hered; in·her·ing** : to be inherent

in·her·ent \in-'hir-ənt, -'her-\ *adj* : established as an essential part of something : INTRINSIC ⟨risks ∼ in the venture⟩ — **in·her·ent·ly** *adv*

in·her·it \in-'her-ət\ *vb* **1** : to receive esp. from one's ancestors **2** : to receive by genetic transmission — **in·her·it·able** \-ə-tə-bəl\ *adj* — **in·her·i·tance** \-ə-təns\ *n* — **in·her·i·tor** \-ə-tər\ *n*

in·hib·it \in-'hi-bət\ *vb* **1** : PROHIBIT, FORBID **2** : to hold in check : RESTRAIN — **in·hib·i·tor** \-bə-tər\ *n* — **in·hib·i·to·ry** \-bə-ˌtôr-ē\ *adj*

in·hi·bi·tion \ˌin-hə-'bi-shən\ *n* **1** : PROHIBITION, RESTRAINT **2** : a usu. inner check on free activity, expression, or functioning

in–house \'in-ˌhaús, -'haús\ *adj* : existing, originating, or carried on within a group or organization

in·hu·man \ˌ(ˌ)in-'hyü-mən, -'yü-\ *adj* **1** : lacking pity, kindness, or mercy : SAVAGE ⟨an ∼ tyrant⟩ **2** : COLD, IMPERSONAL **3** : not worthy of or conforming to the needs of human beings ⟨∼ living conditions⟩ **4** : of or suggesting a nonhuman class of beings — **in·hu·man·ly** *adv* — **in·hu·man·ness** *n*

in·hu·mane \ˌin-hyü-'mān, -yü-\ *adj* : not humane : INHUMAN 1

in·hu·man·i·ty \-'ma-nə-tē\ *n, pl* **-ties** **1** : the quality or state of being cruel or barbarous **2** : a cruel or barbarous act

in·im·i·cal \i-'ni-mi-kəl\ *adj* **1** : being adverse often by reason of hostility ⟨forces ∼ to change⟩ **2** : HOSTILE, UNFRIENDLY ⟨∼ factions⟩ — **in·im·i·cal·ly** *adv*

in·im·i·ta·ble \ˌ(ˌ)i-'ni-mə-tə-bəl\ *adj* : not capable of being imitated

in·iq·ui·ty \i-'ni-kwə-tē\ *n, pl* **-ties** [ME *iniquite*, fr. AF *iniquité*, fr. L *iniquitas*, fr. *iniquus* uneven, fr. *aequus* equal] **1** : WICKEDNESS **2** : a wicked act — **in·iq·ui·tous** \-təs\ *adj*

¹ini·tial \i-'ni-shəl\ *adj* **1** : of or relating to the beginning : INCIPIENT ⟨my ∼ reaction⟩ **2** : being at the beginning — **ini·tial·ly** *adv*

²initial *n* : the first letter of a word or name

³initial *vb* **-tialed** *or* **-tialled; -tial·ing** *or* **-tial·ling** : to affix an initial to

¹ini·ti·ate \i-'ni-shē-ˌāt\ *vb* **-at·ed; -at·ing** **1** : START, BEGIN **2** : to induct into membership by or as if by special ceremonies **3** : to instruct in the rudiments or principles of something — **ini·ti·a·tion** \-ˌni-shē-'ā-shən\ *n*

²ini·ti·ate \i-'ni-shē-ət\ *n* **1** : a person who is undergoing or has passed an initiation **2** : a person who is instructed or adept in some special field

---

inharmonious   inhospitable

ini·tia·tive \i-'ni-shə-tiv\ n **1** : an introductory step **2** : self-reliant enterprise ⟨showed great ∼⟩ **3** : a process by which laws may be introduced or enacted directly by vote of the people

ini·tia·to·ry \i-'ni-shē-ə-,tȯr-ē\ adj **1** : INTRODUCTORY **2** : tending or serving to initiate ⟨∼ rites⟩

in·ject \in-'jekt\ vb **1** : to force into something ⟨∼ serum with a needle⟩ **2** : to introduce as an element into some situation or subject ⟨∼ a note of suspicion⟩ — **in·jec·tion** \-'jek-shən\ n

in·junc·tion \in-'jəŋk-shən\ n **1** : ORDER, ADMONITION **2** : a court writ whereby one is required to do or to refrain from doing a specified act

in·jure \'in-jər\ vb **in·jured; in·jur·ing 1** : WRONG **2** : to damage or hurt esp. physically ♦ **Synonyms** HARM, IMPAIR, MAR, SPOIL

in·ju·ry \'in-jə-rē\ n, pl **-ries 1** : an act that damages or hurts : WRONG **2** : hurt, damage, or loss sustained — **in·ju·ri·ous** \in-'jùr-ē-əs\ adj

in·jus·tice \(,)in-'jəs-təs\ n **1** : violation of a person's rights : UNFAIRNESS **2** : an unjust act or deed : WRONG

¹ink \'iŋk\ n [ME enke, fr. AF encre, enke, fr. LL encaustum, fr. L encaustus burned in, fr. Gk enkaustos, fr. enkaiein to burn in] : a usu. liquid and colored material for writing and printing — **inky** adj

²ink vb : to put ink on; esp : SIGN

ink·blot test \'iŋk-,blät-\ n : any of several psychological tests based on the interpretation of irregular figures

ink·horn \-,hȯrn\ n : a small bottle (as of horn) for holding ink

in–kind \'in-'kīnd\ adj : consisting of something (as goods) other than money

ink–jet n : a computer printer that sprays electrically charged droplets of ink onto paper — **ink–jet** adj

in·kling \'iŋ-kliŋ\ n **1** : HINT, INTIMATION **2** : a vague idea

ink·stand \'iŋk-,stand\ n : INKWELL; also : a pen and ink stand

ink·well \-,wel\ n : a container for ink

in·laid \'in-'lād\ adj : decorated with material set into a surface

¹in·land \'in-,land, -lənd\ adj **1** chiefly Brit : not foreign : DOMESTIC ⟨∼ revenue⟩ **2** : of or relating to the interior of a country ⟨the ∼ states⟩

²inland n : the interior of a country

³inland adv : into or toward the interior

in–law \'in-,lȯ\ n : a relative by marriage

¹in·lay \(,)in-'lā, 'in-,lā\ vb **in·laid** \-'lād\; **in·lay·ing** : to set (a material) into a surface or ground material esp. for decoration

²in·lay \'in-,lā\ n **1** : inlaid work **2** : a shaped filling cemented into a tooth

in·let \'in-,let, -lət\ n **1** : a small or narrow bay **2** : an opening for intake esp. of a fluid

in–line skate n : a roller skate whose four wheels are set in a straight line — **in–line skater** n — **in–line skating** n

in·mate \'in-,māt\ n : any of a group occupying a single place of residence; esp : a person confined (as in a hospital or prison)

in me·di·as res \in-,mā-dē-əs-'rās\ adv [L, lit., into the midst of things] : in or into the middle of a narrative or plot

in me·mo·ri·am \,in-mə-'mȯr-ē-əm\ prep [L] : in memory of

in·most \'in-,mōst\ adj : deepest within : INNERMOST

inn \'in\ n : HOTEL, TAVERN

in·nards \'i-nərdz\ n pl [alter. of inwards] **1** : the internal organs of a human being or animal; esp : VISCERA **2** : the internal parts of a structure or mechanism

in·nate \i-'nāt\ adj **1** : existing in, belonging to, or determined by factors present in an individual from birth : NATIVE **2** : INHERENT, INTRINSIC — **in·nate·ly** adv

in·ner \'i-nər\ adj **1** : situated farther in ⟨the ∼ bark⟩ **2** : near a center esp. of influence ⟨the ∼ circle⟩ **3** : of or relating to the mind or spirit ⟨an ∼ voice⟩ **4** : being a usu. repressed part of one's psychological makeup ⟨the ∼ child⟩

inner city n : the usu. older, poorer, and more densely populated section of a city — **inner–city** adj

in·ner–di·rect·ed \,i-nər-də-'rek-təd, -(,)dī-\ adj : directed in thought and action by one's own scale of values as opposed to external norms

inner ear n : the part of the ear that is most important for hearing, is located in a cavity in the temporal bone, and contains sense organs of hearing and of awareness of position in space

in·ner·most \'i-nər-,mōst\ adj : farthest inward : INMOST

in·ner·sole \,i-nər-'sōl\ n : INSOLE

in·ner·spring \'i-nər-'spriŋ\ adj : having coil springs inside a padded casing ⟨an ∼ mattress⟩

inner tube n : an airtight rubber tube inside a tire to hold air under pressure

in·ning \'i-niŋ\ n **1** sing or pl : a division of a cricket match **2** : a baseball team's turn at bat; also : a division of a baseball game consisting of a turn at bat for each team

inn·keep·er \'in-,kē-pər\ n **1** : a proprietor of an inn **2** : a hotel manager

in·no·cence \'i-nə-səns\ n **1** : BLAMELESSNESS; also : freedom from legal guilt **2** : GUILELESSNESS, SIMPLICITY; also : IGNORANCE

in·no·cent \-sənt\ adj [ME, fr. AF, fr. L innocens, fr. nocens wicked, fr. nocēre to harm] **1** : free from guilt or sin : BLAMELESS **2** : harmless in effect or intention; also : CANDID ⟨an ∼ remark⟩ **3** : free from legal guilt or fault : LAWFUL **4** : INGENUOUS **5** : UNAWARE — **innocent** n — **in·no·cent·ly** adv

in·noc·u·ous \i-'nä-kyə-wəs\ adj **1** : HARMLESS **2** : not offensive; also : INSIPID ⟨∼ jokes⟩

in·nom·i·nate \i-'nä-mə-nət\ adj : having no name; also : ANONYMOUS

in·no·vate \'i-nə-,vāt\ vb **-vat·ed; -vat·ing** : to introduce as or as if new : make changes — **in·no·va·tive** \-,vā-tiv\ *adj* — **in·no·va·tor** \-,vā-tər\ *n*

in·no·va·tion \,i-nə-'vā-shən\ *n* **1** : the introduction of something new **2** : a new idea, method, or device

in·nu·en·do \,in-yə-'wen-dō\ *n, pl* **-dos** *or* **-does** [L, by nodding, fr. *innuere* to nod to, make a sign to, fr. *nuere* to nod] : HINT, INSINUATION; *esp* : a veiled reflection on character or reputation

in·nu·mer·a·ble \i-'nü-mə-rə-bəl, -'nyü-\ *adj* : too many to be numbered

in·oc·u·late \i-'nä-kyə-lāt\ *vb* **-lat·ed; -lat·ing** [ME, to insert a bud in a plant, fr. L *inoculare*, fr. *oculus* eye, bud] : to introduce something into; *esp* : to introduce a serum or antibody into (an organism) to treat or prevent a disease — **in·oc·u·la·tion** \-,nä-kyə-'lā-shən\ *n*

in·op·er·a·ble \(,)in-'ä-pə-rə-bəl\ *adj* **1** : not suitable for surgery ⟨an ∼ tumor⟩ **2** : not operable ⟨∼ vehicles⟩

in·op·er·a·tive \-'ä-pə-rə-tiv, -'ä-pə-,rä-\ *adj* : not functioning

in·op·por·tune \(,)in-,ä-pər-'tün, -'tyün\ *adj* : INCONVENIENT, INAPPROPRIATE — **in·op·por·tune·ly** *adv*

in·or·di·nate \in-'ör-d⁹n-ət\ *adj* : exceeding reasonable limits : IMMODERATE ⟨drank an ∼ amount of water⟩ — **in·or·di·nate·ly** *adv*

in·or·gan·ic \,in-,ör-'ga-nik\ *adj* : being or composed of matter of other than plant or animal origin : MINERAL

in·pa·tient \'in-,pā-shənt\ *n* : a hospital patient who receives lodging and food as well as treatment

in·put \'in-,put\ *n* **1** : something put in **2** : power or energy put into a machine or system **3** : information fed into a computer or data processing system **4** : ADVICE, OPINION — **input** *vb*

in·quest \'in-,kwest\ *n* **1** : an official inquiry or examination esp. before a jury **2** : INQUIRY, INVESTIGATION

in·qui·etude \(,)in-'kwī-ə-,tüd, -,tyüd\ *n* : UNEASINESS, RESTLESSNESS

in·quire \in-'kwī(-ə)r\ *vb* **in·quired; in·quir·ing 1** : to ask about : ASK **2** : to INVESTIGATE, EXAMINE — **in·quir·er** *n* — **in·quir·ing·ly** *adv*

in·qui·ry \'in-,kwī(-ə)r-ē, in-'kwī(-ə)r-ē; 'in-kwə-rē, 'iŋ-\ *n, pl* **-ries** : a request for information; *also* : RESEARCH **2** : a systematic investigation of a matter of public interest

in·qui·si·tion \,in-kwə-'zi-shən, ,iŋ-\ *n* **1** : a judicial or official inquiry usu. before a jury **2** *cap* : a former Roman Catholic tribunal for the discovery and punishment of heresy **3** : a severe questioning — **in·quis·i·tor** \in-'kwi-zə-tər\ *n* — **in·quis·i·to·ri·al** \-,kwi-zə-'tór-ē-əl\ *adj*

in·quis·i·tive \in-'kwi-zə-tiv\ *adj* **1** : given to examination or investigation **2** : unduly curious — **in·quis·i·tive·ly** *adv* — **in·quis·i·tive·ness** *n*

in re \in-'rā, -'rē\ *prep* : in the matter of

INRI *abbr* [L *Iesus Nazarenus Rex Iudaeorum*] Jesus of Nazareth, King of the Jews

in·road \'in-,rōd\ *n* **1** : INVASION, RAID **2** : an advance made usu. at the expense of another ⟨made ∼s toward getting the job⟩

in·rush \'in-,rəsh\ *n* : a crowding or flooding in

ins *abbr* **1** inches **2** insurance

INS *abbr* Immigration and Naturalization Service

in·sa·lu·bri·ous \,in-sə-'lü-brē-əs\ *adj* : UNWHOLESOME, NOXIOUS

ins and outs *n pl* **1** : characteristic peculiarities **2** : RAMIFICATIONS

in·sane \(,)in-'sān\ *adj* **1** : exhibiting serious and debilitating mental disorder; *also* : used by or for the insane **2** : ABSURD **3** : greatly exceeding the ordinary, usual, or expected — **in·sane·ly** *adv* — **in·san·i·ty** \in-'sa-nə-tē\ *n*

in·sa·tia·ble \(,)in-'sā-shə-bəl\ *adj* : incapable of being satisfied ⟨an ∼ thirst⟩ — **in·sa·tia·bil·i·ty** \(,)in-,sā-shə-'bi-lə-tē\ *n* — **in·sa·tia·bly** *adv*

in·sa·tiate \(,)in-'sā-shē-ət, -shət\ *adj* : INSATIABLE — **in·sa·tiate·ly** *adv*

in·scribe \in-'skrīb\ *vb* **1** : to write, engrave, or print as a lasting record **2** : ENROLL **3** : to write, engrave, or print characters upon **4** : to dedicate to someone **5** : to draw within a figure so as to touch in as many places as possible — **in·scrip·tion** \-'skrip-shən\ *n*

in·scru·ta·ble \in-'skrü-tə-bəl\ *adj* : not readily comprehensible : MYSTERIOUS — **in·scru·ta·bly** \-blē\ *adv*

in·seam \'in-,sēm\ *n* : the seam on the inside of the leg of a pair of pants; *also* : the length of this seam

in·sect \'in-,sekt\ *n* [L *insectum*, fr. *insectus*, pp. of *insecare* to cut into, fr. *secare* to cut] : any of a class of small usu. winged arthropod animals (as flies, bees, beetles, and moths) with usu. three pairs of legs as adults

in·sec·ti·cide \in-'sek-tə-,sīd\ *n* : an agent for destroying insects — **in·sec·ti·cid·al** \(,)in-,sek-tə-'sī-d⁹l\ *adj*

in·sec·tiv·o·rous \,in-,sek-'ti-və-rəs\ *adj* : feeding on insects

in·se·cure \,in-si-'kyúr\ *adj* **1** : UNCERTAIN **2** : not protected : UNSAFE ⟨an ∼ investment⟩ **3** : LOOSE, SHAKY ⟨an ∼ hinge⟩ **4** : not highly stable ⟨an ∼ marriage⟩; *also* : lacking assurance : ANXIOUS, FEARFUL — **in·se·cure·ly** *adv* — **in·se·cu·ri·ty** \-'kyúr-ə-tē\ *n*

in·sem·i·nate \in-'se-mə-,nāt\ *vb* **-nat·ed; -nat·ing** : to introduce semen into the genital tract of (a female) — **in·sem·i·na·tion** \-,se-mə-'nā-shən\ *n*

in·sen·sate \(,)in-'sen-,sāt, -sət\ *adj* **1** : lacking sense or understanding; *also* : FOOLISH **2** : INANIMATE **3** : BRUTAL, INHUMAN ⟨∼ rage⟩

in·sen·si·ble \(,)in-'sen-sə-bəl\ *adj* **1** : IMPERCEPTIBLE; *also* : SLIGHT, GRADUAL **2** : INANIMATE **3** : UNCONSCIOUS **4** : lacking sensory perception or ability to react ⟨∼ to pain⟩ **5** : APATHETIC, INDIFFERENT; *also* : UNAWARE ⟨∼ of their danger⟩ 6 : MEANINGLESS 7 : lacking delicacy or refinement — **in·sen·si·bil·i·ty** \-ˌsen-sə-ˈbi-lə-tē\ n — **in·sen·si·bly** \-ˈsen-sə-blē\ adv

in·sen·tient \(ˌ)in-ˈsen-chē-ənt\ adj : lacking perception, consciousness, or animation — **in·sen·tience** \-chē-əns\ n

in·sep·a·ra·ble \(ˌ)in-ˈse-prə-bəl, -pə-rə-\ adj 1 : incapable of being separated or disjoined 2 : very close or intimate ⟨~ friends⟩ — **in·sep·a·ra·bil·i·ty** \-ˌse-prə-ˈbi-lə-tē, -pə-rə-\ n — **inseparable** n — **in·sep·a·ra·bly** \-ˈse-prə-blē, -pə-rə-\ adv

¹**in·sert** \in-ˈsərt\ vb 1 : to put or thrust in ⟨~ a key in a lock⟩ ⟨~ a comma⟩ 2 : INTERPOLATE 3 : to set in (as a piece of fabric) and make fast

²**in·sert** \ˈin-ˌsərt\ n : something that is inserted or is for insertion; esp : written or printed material inserted (as between the leaves of a book)

in·ser·tion \in-ˈsər-shən\ n 1 : something that is inserted 2 : the act or process of inserting

in·set \ˈin-ˌset\ vb inset or in·set·ted; in·set·ting : to set in : INSERT — **inset** n

¹**in·shore** \ˈin-ˈshȯr\ adj 1 : situated, living, or carried on near shore 2 : moving toward shore ⟨an ~ current⟩

²**inshore** adv : to or toward shore

¹**in·side** \in-ˈsīd, ˈin-ˌsīd\ n 1 : an inner side or surface : INTERIOR 2 : inward nature, thoughts, or feeling 3 pl : VISCERA, ENTRAILS 4 : a position of power, trust, or familiarity — **inside** adj

²**inside** adv 1 : on the inner side 2 : in or into the interior

³**inside** prep 1 : in or into the inside of ⟨~ the house⟩ 2 : WITHIN ⟨~ an hour⟩

inside of prep : INSIDE

inside out adv 1 : in such a manner that the inner surface becomes the outer ⟨turned the shirt inside out⟩ 2 : in a state of disarray or reorganization ⟨turned her life inside out⟩

in·sid·er \in-ˈsī-dər\ n : a person who is in a position of power or has access to confidential information

in·sid·i·ous \in-ˈsi-dē-əs\ adj [L insidiosus, fr. insidiae ambush, fr. insidēre to sit in, sit on, fr. sedēre to sit] 1 : SLY, TREACHEROUS 2 : SEDUCTIVE 3 : having a gradual and cumulative effect : SUBTLE — **in·sid·i·ous·ly** adv — **in·sid·i·ous·ness** n

in·sight \ˈin-ˌsīt\ n : the power, act, or result of seeing into a situation : UNDERSTANDING, PENETRATION — **in·sight·ful** \ˈin-ˌsīt-fəl, in-ˈsīt-\ adj

in·sig·nia \in-ˈsig-nē-ə\ also **in·sig·ne** \-(ˌ)nē\ n, pl -nia or -ni·as : a distinguishing mark esp. of authority or honor : BADGE

in·sin·cere \ˌin-sin-ˈsir\ adj : not sincere : HYPOCRITICAL — **in·sin·cere·ly** adv — **in·sin·cer·i·ty** \-ˈser-ə-tē\ n

in·sin·u·ate \in-ˈsin-yə-ˌwāt\ vb -at·ed; -at·ing [L insinuare, fr. sinuare to bend, curve, fr. sinus curve] 1 : to introduce gradually or in a subtle, indirect, or artful way 2 : to imply in a subtle or devious way — **in·sin·u·a·tion** \-(ˌ)in-ˌsin-yə-ˈwā-shən\ n

in·sin·u·at·ing adj 1 : winning favor and confidence by imperceptible degrees 2 : tending gradually to cause doubt, distrust, or change of outlook

in·sip·id \in-ˈsi-pəd\ adj 1 : lacking taste or savor 2 : DULL, FLAT — **in·si·pid·i·ty** \ˌin-sə-ˈpi-də-tē\ n

in·sist \in-ˈsist\ vb [MF or L; MF insister, fr. L insistere to stand upon, persist, fr. sistere to take a stand] : to take a resolute stand ⟨~ed on paying⟩

in·sis·tence \in-ˈsis-təns\ n : the act of insisting; also : an insistent attitude or quality : URGENCY

in·sis·tent \in-ˈsis-tənt\ adj : disposed to insist — **in·sis·tent·ly** adv

in si·tu \in-ˈsī-tü, -ˈsē-\ adv or adj [L, in position] : in the natural or original position ⟨an in situ cancer⟩

in·sol abbr insoluble

in·so·la·tion \ˌin-(ˌ)sō-ˈlā-shən\ n : solar radiation that has been received

in·sole \ˈin-ˌsōl\ n 1 : an inside sole of a shoe 2 : a loose thin strip placed inside a shoe for warmth or comfort

in·so·lent \ˈin-sə-lənt\ adj : contemptuous, rude, disrespectful, or bold in behavior or language — **in·so·lence** \-ləns\ n

in·sol·u·ble \(ˌ)in-ˈsäl-yə-bəl\ adj 1 : having or admitting of no solution or explanation 2 : difficult or impossible to dissolve — **in·sol·u·bil·i·ty** \-ˌsäl-yə-ˈbi-lə-tē\ n

in·sol·vent \(ˌ)in-ˈsäl-vənt\ adj 1 : unable or insufficient to pay all debts ⟨an ~ estate⟩ 2 : IMPOVERISHED, DEFICIENT — **in·sol·ven·cy** \-vən-sē\ n

in·som·nia \in-ˈsäm-nē-ə\ n : prolonged and usu. abnormal sleeplessness — **in·som·ni·ac** \-nē-ˌak\ n

in·so·much as \ˌin-sə-ˈməch-\ conj : INASMUCH AS

insomuch that conj : to such a degree that : SO

in·sou·ci·ance \in-ˈsü-sē-əns, aⁿ-süs-ˈyäⁿs\ n [F] : lighthearted unconcern — **in·sou·ci·ant** \in-ˈsü-sē-ənt, aⁿ-süs-ˈyäⁿ\ adj

insp abbr inspector

in·spect \in-ˈspekt\ vb : to view closely and critically : EXAMINE ⟨~ the gem for flaws⟩ — **in·spec·tion** \-ˈspek-shən\ n — **in·spec·tor** \-tər\ n

inspector general n : the head of a system of inspection (as of an army)

in·spi·ra·tion \ˌin-spə-ˈrā-shən\ n 1 : the act or power of moving the intellect or emotions 2 : INHALATION 3 : the quality or state of being inspired; also : something that is inspired 4 : an inspiring agent or influence — **in·spi·ra·tion·al** \-shə-nəl\ adj

in·spire \in-ˈspīr\ vb **in·spired; in·spir-**

---

insensitive   insensitivity   insignificance   insignificant
insolvable   insusceptible

ing **1** : to influence, move, or guide by divine or supernatural inspiration **2** : to exert an animating, enlivening, or exalting influence upon ⟨a painter *inspired* by cubism⟩; *also* : AFFECT **3** : to communicate to an agent supernaturally; *also* : bring out or about **4** : INHALE **5** : INCITE **6** : to spread by indirect means — **in·spir·er** *n*

in·spir·it \in-'spir-ət\ *vb* : ENCOURAGE, HEARTEN

inst *abbr* **1** instant **2** institute; institution; institutional

in·sta·bil·i·ty \ˌin-stə-'bi-lə-tē\ *n* : lack of steadiness; *esp* : lack of emotional or mental stability

in·stal *chiefly Brit var of* INSTALL

in·stall \in-'stȯl\ *vb* **1** : to place formally in office : induct into an office, rank, or order **2** : to establish in an indicated place, condition, or status **3** : to set up for use or service — **in·stal·la·tion** \ˌin-stə-'lā-shən\ *n*

¹in·stall·ment *also* **in·stal·ment** \in-'stȯl-mənt\ *n* : INSTALLATION

²installment *also* **instalment** *n* **1** : one of the parts into which a debt or sum is divided for payment **2** : one of several parts presented at intervals

¹in·stance \'in-stəns\ *n* **1** : INSTIGATION, REQUEST **2** : EXAMPLE ⟨for ∼⟩ **3** : an event or step that is part of a process or series ◆ **Synonyms** CASE, ILLUSTRATION, SAMPLE, SPECIMEN

²instance *vb* **in·stanced; in·stanc·ing** : to mention as a case or example

¹in·stant \'in-stənt\ *n* **1** : MOMENT ⟨the ∼ we met⟩ **2** : the present or current month

²instant *adj* **1** : URGENT **2** : PRESENT, CURRENT **3** : IMMEDIATE ⟨∼ relief⟩ **4** : premixed or precooked for easy final preparation ⟨∼ cake mix⟩; *also* : immediately soluble in water ⟨∼ coffee⟩

in·stan·ta·neous \ˌin-stən-'tā-nē-əs\ *adj* : done or occurring in an instant or without delay ⟨an ∼ chemical reaction⟩ — **in·stan·ta·neous·ly** *adv*

in·stan·ter \in-'stan-tər\ *adv* : at once

in·stan·ti·ate \in-'stan-chē-ˌāt\ *vb* **-at·ed; -at·ing** : to represent (an abstraction) by a concrete example — **in·stan·ti·a·tion** \-ˌstan-chē-'ā-shən\ *n*

in·stant·ly \'in-stənt-lē\ *adv* : at once : IMMEDIATELY

in·state \in-'stāt\ *vb* : to establish in a rank or office : INSTALL

in·stead \in-'sted\ *adv* **1** : as a substitute or equivalent **2** : as an alternative : RATHER

instead of *prep* : as a substitute for or alternative to ⟨use glue *instead of* paste⟩

in·step \'in-ˌstep\ *n* : the arched part of the human foot in front of the ankle joint; *esp* : its upper surface

in·sti·gate \'in-stə-ˌgāt\ *vb* **-gat·ed; -gat·ing** : to goad or urge forward : PROVOKE, INCITE ⟨∼ a revolt⟩ — **in·sti·ga·tion** \ˌin-stə-'gā-shən\ *n* — **in·sti·ga·tor** \'in-stə-ˌgā-tər\ *n*

in·stil *chiefly Brit var of* INSTILL

in·still \in-'stil\ *vb* **1** : to cause to enter drop by drop **2** : to impart gradually

¹in·stinct \'in-ˌstiŋkt\ *n* **1** : a natural aptitude **2** : a largely inheritable and unalterable tendency of an organism to make a complex and specific response to environmental stimuli without involving reason; *also* : behavior originating below the conscious level — **in·stinc·tive** \in-'stiŋk-tiv\ *adj* — **in·stinc·tive·ly** *adv*

²in·stinct \in-'stiŋkt, 'in-ˌstiŋkt\ *adj* : IMBUED, INFUSED

in·stinc·tu·al \in-'stiŋk-chə-wəl\ *adj* : of, relating to, or based on instinct

¹in·sti·tute \'in-stə-ˌtüt, -ˌtyüt\ *vb* **-tut·ed; -tut·ing** **1** : to establish in a position or office **2** : ORGANIZE **3** : INAUGURATE, INITIATE

²institute *n* **1** : an elementary principle recognized as authoritative; *also, pl* : a collection of such principles and precepts **2** : an organization for the promotion of a cause : ASSOCIATION **3** : an educational institution **4** : a brief course of instruction on a particular field

in·sti·tu·tion \ˌin-stə-'tü-shən, -'tyü-\ *n* **1** : an act of originating, setting up, or founding **2** : an established practice, law, or custom **3** : a society or corporation esp. of a public character ⟨a charitable ∼⟩; *also* : ASYLUM **3** — **in·sti·tu·tion·al** \-'tü-shə-nəl, -'tyü-\ *adj* — **in·sti·tu·tion·al·ize** \-nə-ˌlīz\ *vb* — **in·sti·tu·tion·al·ly** *adv*

instr *abbr* **1** instructor **2** instrument; instrumental

in·struct \in-'strəkt\ *vb* [ME, fr. L *instructus,* pp. of *instruere,* fr. *struere* to build] **1** : TEACH **2** : INFORM **3** : to give an order or a command to

in·struc·tion \in-'strək-shən\ *n* **1** : LESSON, PRECEPT **2** : COMMAND, ORDER **3** *pl* : DIRECTIONS **4** : the action, practice, or profession of a teacher — **in·struc·tion·al** \-shə-nəl\ *adj*

in·struc·tive \in-'strək-tiv\ *adj* : carrying a lesson : ENLIGHTENING

in·struc·tor \in-'strək-tər\ *n* : one that instructs; *esp* : a college teacher below professorial rank — **in·struc·tor·ship** *n*

in·stru·ment \'in-strə-mənt\ *n* **1** : a device used to produce music **2** : a means by which something is done **3** : a device for doing work and esp. precision work ⟨a drafting ∼⟩ **4** : a legal document (as a deed) **5** : a device used in navigating an airplane — **in·stru·ment** \-ˌment\ *vb*

in·stru·men·tal \ˌin-strə-'men-t°l\ *adj* **1** : acting as a crucial agent or means ⟨was ∼ in arranging the deal⟩ **2** : of, relating to, or done with an instrument **3** : relating to, composed for, or performed on a musical instrument

in·stru·men·tal·ist \-'men-tə-list\ *n* : a player on a musical instrument

in·stru·men·tal·i·ty \ˌin-strə-mən-'ta-lə-tē, -ˌmen-\ *n, pl* **-ties** **1** : the quality or state of being instrumental **2** : MEANS, AGENCY

in·stru·men·ta·tion \ˌin-strə-mən-'tā-shən, -ˌmen-\ *n* **1** : ORCHESTRATION **2** : instruments for a particular purpose

instrument panel *n* : DASHBOARD

in·sub·or·di·nate \ˌin-sə-'bȯr-də-nət\ *adj* : disobedient to authority — **in·sub·or·di·na·tion** \-ˌbȯr-də-'nā-shən\ *n*

in·sub·stan·tial \ˌin-səb-'stan-chəl\ *adj* 1 : lacking substance or reality 2 : lacking firmness or solidity

in·suf·fer·able \(ˌ)in-'sə-fə-rə-bəl\ *adj* : not to be endured : INTOLERABLE ⟨an ∼ bore⟩ — **in·suf·fer·ably** \-blē\ *adv*

in·suf·fi·cient \ˌin-sə-'fi-shənt\ *adj* : not sufficient ⟨∼ funds⟩; *also* : lacking capacity — **in·suf·fi·cien·cy** \-shən-sē\ *n* — **in·suf·fi·cient·ly** *adv*

in·su·lar \'in-sə-lər, -syə-\ *adj* 1 : of, relating to, or forming an island 2 : dwelling or situated on an island 3 : NARROW-MINDED — **in·su·lar·i·ty** \ˌin-sə-'lar-ə-tē, -syə-\ *n*

in·su·late \'in-sə-ˌlāt\ *vb* -**lat·ed**; -**lat·ing** [L *insula* island] : ISOLATE; *esp* : to separate a conductor of electricity, heat, or sound from other conducting bodies by means of a nonconductor — **in·su·la·tion** \ˌin-sə-'lā-shən\ *n* — **in·su·la·tor** \'in-sə-ˌlā-tər\ *n*

in·su·lin \'in-sə-lən\ *n* : a pancreatic hormone essential esp. for the metabolism of carbohydrates and the regulation of glucose levels in the blood

¹**in·sult** \in-'səlt\ *vb* [MF or L; MF *insulter,* fr. L *insultare,* lit., to spring upon, fr. *saltare* to leap] : to treat with insolence or contempt : AFFRONT — **in·sult·ing·ly** *adv*

²**in·sult** \'in-ˌsəlt\ *n* : gross indignity

in·su·per·a·ble \(ˌ)in-'sü-pə-rə-bəl\ *adj* : incapable of being surmounted, overcome, passed over, or solved — **in·su·per·a·bly** \-blē\ *adv*

in·sup·port·able \ˌin-sə-'pȯr-tə-bəl\ *adj* 1 : UNENDURABLE 2 : UNJUSTIFIABLE

in·sur·able \in-'shu̇r-ə-bəl\ *adj* : capable of being or proper to be insured

in·sur·ance \in-'shu̇r-əns\ *n* 1 : the business of insuring persons or property 2 : coverage by contract whereby one party agrees to guarantee another against a specified loss 3 : the sum for which something is insured 4 : a means of guaranteeing protection or safety

in·sure \in-'shu̇r\ *vb* **in·sured**; **in·sur·ing** 1 : to provide or obtain insurance on or for : UNDERWRITE 2 : to make certain : ENSURE

in·sured \in-'shu̇rd\ *n* : a person whose life or property is insured

in·sur·er \in-'shu̇r-ər\ *n* : one that insures; *esp* : an insurance company

in·sur·gent \in-'sər-jənt\ *n* 1 : a person who revolts against civil authority or an established government : REBEL 2 : a member of a political party who rebels against it — **in·sur·gence** \-jəns\ *n* — **in·sur·gen·cy** \-jən-sē\ *n* — **in·sur·gent** *adj*

in·sur·mount·able \ˌin-sər-maủn-tə-bəl\ *adj* : INSUPERABLE ⟨∼ problems⟩ — **in·sur·mount·ably** \-blē\ *adv*

in·sur·rec·tion \ˌin-sə-'rek-shən\ *n* : an act or instance of revolting against civil authority or an established government — **in·sur·rec·tion·ist** \-shə-nist\ *n*

int *abbr* 1 interest 2 interior 3 intermediate 4 internal 5 international 6 intransitive

in·tact \in-'takt\ *adj* : untouched esp. by anything that harms or diminishes

in·ta·glio \in-'tal-yō\ *n, pl* -**glios** [It] : an engraving cut deeply into the surface of a hard material (as stone)

in·take \'in-ˌtāk\ *n* 1 : an opening through which fluid enters 2 : the act of taking in 3 : something taken in

¹**in·tan·gi·ble** \(ˌ)in-'tan-jə-bəl\ *adj* : incapable of being touched : IMPALPABLE — **in·tan·gi·bly** \-blē\ *adv*

²**intangible** *n* 1 : an incorporeal asset 2 : an abstract quality or attribute

in·te·ger \'in-ti-jər\ *n* [L, adj., whole, entire] : a number (as 1, 2, 3, 12, 432) that is not a fraction and does not include a fraction, is the negative of such a number, or is 0

¹**in·te·gral** \'in-ti-grəl\ *adj* 1 : essential to completeness ⟨∼ to the company⟩ 2 : formed as a unit with another part 3 : composed of parts that make up a whole 4 : ENTIRE

²**integral** *n* : the result of a mathematical integration

in·te·grate \'in-tə-ˌgrāt\ *vb* -**grat·ed**; -**grat·ing** 1 : to find a function that has a given derivative 2 : to form, coordinate, or blend into a functioning whole : UNITE 3 : to incorporate into a larger unit 4 : to end the segregation of and bring into equal membership in society or an organization; *also* : DESEGREGATE — **in·te·gra·tion** \ˌin-tə-'grā-shən\ *n*

integrated circuit *n* : a group of tiny electronic components and their connections that is produced in or on a small slice of material (as silicon)

in·teg·ri·ty \in-'te-grə-tē\ *n* 1 : adherence to a code of values : INCORRUPTIBILITY 2 : SOUNDNESS 3 : COMPLETENESS

in·teg·u·ment \in-'te-gyə-mənt\ *n* : a covering layer (as a skin or cuticle) of an organism or one of its parts

in·tel·lect \'in-tə-ˌlekt\ *n* 1 : the power of knowing : the capacity for knowledge 2 : the capacity for rational or intelligent thought esp. when highly developed 3 : a person with great intellectual powers

in·tel·lec·tu·al \ˌin-tə-'lek-chə-wəl\ *adj* 1 : of, relating to, or performed by the intellect : RATIONAL 2 : given to study, reflection, and speculation ⟨∼ games⟩ 3 : engaged in activity requiring the creative use of the intellect — **intellectual** *n* — **in·tel·lec·tu·al·ly** *adv*

in·tel·lec·tu·al·ism \-chə-wə-ˌli-zəm\ *n* : devotion to the exercise of intellect or to intellectual pursuits

in·tel·li·gence \in-'te-lə-jəns\ *n* 1 : ability to learn and understand or to deal with new or trying situations 2 : mental acuteness 3 : INFORMATION, NEWS 4 : an agency engaged in obtaining information esp. concerning an enemy or possible enemy; *also* : the information so gained

intelligence quotient *n* : IQ

in·tel·li·gent \in-'te-lə-jənt\ *adj* [L *intelligens*, fr. *intelligere* to understand, fr. *inter* between + *legere* to select] : having or showing intelligence or intellect — **in·tel·li·gent·ly** *adv*

in·tel·li·gen·tsia \in-,te-lə-'jent-sē-ə, -'gent-\ *n* [Russ *intelligentsiya*, fr. L *intelligentia* intelligence] : intellectuals forming a vanguard or elite

in·tel·li·gi·ble \in-'te-lə-jə-bəl\ *adj* : capable of being understood or comprehended — **in·tel·li·gi·bil·i·ty** \-,te-lə-jə-'bi-lə-tē\ *n* — **in·tel·li·gi·bly** \-'te-lə-jə-blē\ *adv*

in·tem·per·ance \(,)in-'tem-pə-rəns\ *n* : lack of moderation; *esp* : habitual or excessive drinking of intoxicants — **in·tem·per·ate** \-pə-rət\ *adj* — **in·tem·per·ate·ness** *n*

in·tend \in-'tend\ *vb* [ME *entenden, intenden*, fr. AF *entendre*, fr. L *intendere* to stretch out, direct, aim at, fr. *tendere* to stretch] **1** : to have in mind as a purpose or aim ⟨~s to retire⟩ **2** : to design for a specified use or future ⟨programs ~ed to help students⟩

in·ten·dant \in-'ten-dənt\ *n* : an official (as a governor) esp. under the French, Spanish, or Portuguese monarchies

¹in·tend·ed *adj* **1** : expected to be such in the future; *esp* : BETROTHED **2** : INTENTIONAL ⟨an ~ pun⟩

²intended *n* : an engaged person

in·tense \in-'tens\ *adj* **1** : existing in an extreme degree ⟨~ pain⟩ **2** : marked by great zeal, energy, or eagerness ⟨~ effort⟩ **3** : showing strong feeling; *also* : deeply felt — **in·tense·ly** *adv*

in·ten·si·fy \in-'ten-sə-,fī\ *vb* **-fied; -fy·ing 1** : to make or become intense or more intensive **2** : to make more acute : SHARPEN ♦ *Synonyms* AGGRAVATE, HEIGHTEN, ENHANCE, MAGNIFY — **in·ten·si·fi·ca·tion** \-,ten-sə-fə-'kā-shən\ *n*

in·ten·si·ty \in-'ten-sə-tē\ *n, pl* **-ties 1** : the quality or state of being intense; *esp* : degree of strength, energy, or force

¹in·ten·sive \in-'ten-siv\ *adj* **1** : highly concentrated **2** : serving to give emphasis — **in·ten·sive·ly** *adv*

²intensive *n* : an intensive word, particle, or prefix

intensive care *n* : continuous monitoring and treatment of seriously ill patients; *also* : an area of a hospital providing this treatment

¹in·tent \in-'tent\ *n* **1** : the state of mind with which an act is done : VOLITION **2** : PURPOSE, AIM ⟨the artist's ~⟩ **3** : MEANING, SIGNIFICANCE

²intent *adj* **1** : directed with keen attention ⟨an ~ gaze⟩ **2** : ENGROSSED; *also* : DETERMINED ⟨~ on winning⟩ — **in·tent·ly** *adv* — **in·tent·ness** *n*

in·ten·tion \in-'ten-chən\ *n* **1** : a determination to act in a certain way **2** : PURPOSE, AIM, END ♦ *Synonyms* INTENT, DESIGN, OBJECT, OBJECTIVE, GOAL

in·ten·tion·al \in-'ten-chə-nəl\ *adj* : done by intention or design : INTENDED — **in·ten·tion·al·ly** *adv*

in·ter \in-'tər\ *vb* **in·terred; in·ter·ring** : BURY

in·ter·ac·tion \,in-tər-'ak-shən\ *n* : mutual or reciprocal action or influence — **in·ter·act** \-'akt\ *vb*

in·ter·ac·tive \-'ak-tiv\ *adj* **1** : mutually or reciprocally active **2** : involving the actions or input of a user ⟨~ exhibits⟩ **3** : allowing two-way electronic communications (as between a person and a computer) — **in·ter·ac·tive·ly** *adv* — **in·ter·ac·tiv·i·ty** \-ak-'ti-və-tē\ *n*

in·ter alia \,in-tər-'ā-lē-ə, -'ä-\ *adv* : among other things

in·ter·atom·ic \,in-tər-ə-'tä-mik\ *adj* : existing or acting between atoms

in·ter·breed \-'brēd\ *vb* **-bred** \-'bred\; **-breed·ing** : to breed together

in·ter·ca·la·ry \in-'tər-kə-,ler-ē\ *adj* **1** : INTERCALATED ⟨February 29 is an ~ day⟩ **2** : INTERPOLATED

in·ter·ca·late \-,lāt\ *vb* **-lat·ed; -lat·ing 1** : to insert (as a day) in a calendar **2** : to insert between or among existing elements or layers — **in·ter·ca·la·tion** \-,tər-kə-'lā-shən\ *n*

in·ter·cede \,in-tər-'sēd\ *vb* **-ced·ed; -ced·ing** : to act between parties with a view to reconciling differences

¹in·ter·cept \,in-tər-'sept\ *vb* **1** : to stop or interrupt the progress or course of **2** : to include (as part of a curve or solid) between two points, curves, or surfaces **3** : to gain possession of (an opponent's pass) — **in·ter·cep·tion** \-'sep-shən\ *n*

²in·ter·cept \'in-tər-,sept\ *n* : INTERCEPTION; *esp* : the interception of a target by an interceptor or missile

in·ter·cep·tor \,in-tər-'sep-tər\ *n* : a fighter plane designed for defense against attacking bombers

in·ter·ces·sion \,in-tər-'se-shən\ *n* **1** : MEDIATION **2** : prayer or petition in favor of another — **in·ter·ces·sor** \-'se-sər\ *n* — **in·ter·ces·so·ry** \-'se-sə-rē\ *adj*

¹in·ter·change \,in-tər-'chānj\ *vb* **1** : to put each in the place of the other **2** : EXCHANGE **3** : to change places mutually — **in·ter·change·able** \-'chān-jə-bəl\ *adj* — **in·ter·change·ably** \-blē\ *adv*

²in·ter·change \'in-tər-,chānj\ *n* **1** : EXCHANGE **2** : a highway junction that by separated levels permits passage between highways without crossing traffic streams

in·ter·col·le·giate \,in-tər-kə-'lē-jət\ *adj* : existing or carried on between colleges ⟨~ sports⟩

in·ter·com \'in-tər-,käm\ *n* : a two-way system for localized communication

in·ter·con·nect \,in-tər-kə-'nekt\ *vb* : to connect with one another — **in·ter·con·nec·tion** \-'nek-shən\ *n*

in·ter·con·ti·nen·tal \-,kän-tə-'nen-t°l\ *adj* **1** : extending among or carried on between continents ⟨~ trade⟩ **2** : capable of traveling between continents ⟨~ ballistic missiles⟩

in·ter·course \'in-tər-,kòrs\ *n* **1** : connection or dealings between persons or nations   2 : physical sexual contact between individuals that involves the genitalia of at least one person ⟨anal ∼⟩; *esp* : SEXUAL INTERCOURSE

in·ter·de·nom·i·na·tion·al \ˌin-tər-di-ˌnä-mə-ˈnā-shə-nəl\ *adj* : involving different denominations

in·ter·de·part·men·tal \ˌin-tər-di-ˈpärt-ˈmen-t°l, -ˌdē-\ *adj* : carried on between or involving different departments (as of a college)

in·ter·de·pen·dent \ˌin-tər-di-ˈpen-dənt\ *adj* : dependent upon one another — **in·ter·de·pen·dence** \-dəns\ *n*

in·ter·dict \ˌin-tər-ˈdikt\ *vb*   1 : to prohibit by decree   2 : to destroy, cut off, or damage (as an enemy line of supply) : INTERCEPT ⟨∼ed drug shipments⟩ — **in·ter·dic·tion** \-ˈdik-shən\ *n*

in·ter·dis·ci·plin·ary \-ˈdi-sə-plə-ˌner-ē\ *adj* : involving two or more academic, scientific, or artistic disciplines

¹in·ter·est \ˈin-trəst; ˈin-tə-rəst, -ˌrest\ *n*   1 : right, title, or legal share in something   2 : a charge for borrowed money that is generally a percentage of the amount borrowed; *also* : the return received by capital on its investment   3 : WELFARE, BENEFIT; *also* : SELF-INTEREST   4 : CURIOSITY, CONCERN   5 : readiness to be concerned with or moved by an object or class of objects   6 : a quality in a thing that arouses interest

²interest *vb*   1 : to persuade to participate or engage   2 : to engage the attention of

in·ter·est·ing *adj* : holding the attention — **in·ter·est·ing·ly** *adv*

¹in·ter·face \ˈin-tər-ˌfās\ *n*   1 : a surface forming a common boundary of two bodies, spaces, or phases ⟨an oil-water ∼⟩   2 : the place at which two independent systems meet and act on or communicate with each other ⟨the man-machine ∼⟩   3 : the means by which interaction or communication is achieved at an interface — **in·ter·fa·cial** \ˌin-tər-ˈfā-shəl\ *adj*

²interface *vb* **-faced; -fac·ing**   1 : to connect by means of an interface   2 : to serve as an interface

in·ter·faith \ˌin-tər-ˈfāth\ *adj* : involving persons of different religious faiths

in·ter·fere \ˌin-tər-ˈfir\ *vb* **-fered; -fer·ing** [ME *enterferen*, fr. AF *(s')entreferir* to strike one another, fr. *entre* between, among + *ferir* to strike, fr. L *ferire*]   1 : to come in collision or be in opposition : CLASH   2 : to enter into the affairs of others   3 : to affect one another

in·ter·fer·ence \-ˈfir-əns\ *n*   1 : the act or process of interfering   2 : something that interferes : OBSTRUCTION   3 : the mutual effect on meeting of two waves resulting in areas of increased and decreased amplitude   4 : the blocking of an opponent in football to make way for the ballcarrier   5 : the illegal hindering of an opponent in sports

in·ter·fer·om·e·ter \ˌin-tər-fə-ˈrä-mə-tər\ *n* : an apparatus that uses the interference of waves (as of light) for making precise measurements — **in·ter·fer·om·e·try** \-fə-ˈrä-mə-trē\ *n*

in·ter·fer·on \ˌin-tər-ˈfir-ˌän\ *n* : any of a group of antiviral proteins of low molecular weight produced usu. by animal cells in response to a virus, a parasite in the cell, or a chemical

in·ter·ga·lac·tic \ˌin-tər-gə-ˈlak-tik\ *adj* : relating to or situated in the spaces between galaxies

in·ter·gen·er·a·tion·al \-ˈje-nə-ˈrā-shə-nəl\ *adj* : existing or occurring between generations

in·ter·gla·cial \-ˈglā-shəl\ *n* : a warm period between successive glaciations

in·ter·gov·ern·men·tal \-ˌgə-vərn-ˈmen-t°l\ *adj* : existing or occurring between two governments or levels of government

in·ter·im \ˈin-tə-rəm\ *n* [L, adv., meanwhile, fr. *inter* between] : a time intervening : INTERVAL — **interim** *adj*

¹in·te·ri·or \in-ˈtir-ē-ər\ *adj*   1 : lying, occurring, or functioning within the limiting boundaries : INSIDE, INNER   2 : remote from the surface, border, or shore : INLAND

²interior *n*   1 : the inland part (as of a country)   2 : INSIDE   3 : the internal affairs of a state or nation   4 : a scene or view of the interior of a building

interior decoration *n* : INTERIOR DESIGN — **interior decorator** *n*

interior design *n* : the art or practice of planning and supervising the design and execution of architectural interiors and their furnishings — **interior designer** *n*

interj *abbr* interjection

in·ter·ject \ˌin-tər-ˈjekt\ *vb* : to throw in between or among other things

in·ter·jec·tion \ˌin-tər-ˈjek-shən\ *n* : an exclamatory word (as *ouch*) — **in·ter·jec·tion·al·ly** \-shə-nə-lē\ *adv*

in·ter·lace \ˌin-tər-ˈlās\ *vb*   1 : to unite by or as if by lacing together : INTERWEAVE   2 : INTERSPERSE

in·ter·lard \ˌin-tər-ˈlärd\ *vb* : to vary by inserting or interjecting something

in·ter·leave \ˌin-tər-ˈlēv\ *vb* **-leaved; -leav·ing** : to arrange in alternate layers

in·ter·leu·kin \ˌin-tər-ˈlü-kən\ *n* : any of several proteins of low molecular weight that are produced by cells of the body and regulate the immune system and immune responses

¹in·ter·line \ˌin-tər-ˈlin\ *vb* : to insert between lines already written or printed

²interline *vb* : to provide (as a coat) with an interlining

in·ter·lin·ear \ˌin-tər-ˈli-nē-ər\ *adj* : inserted between lines already written or printed ⟨an ∼ translation of a text⟩

in·ter·lin·gual \ˌin-tər-ˈliŋ-gwəl\ *adj* : of, relating to, or existing between two or more languages

in·ter·lin·ing \ˈin-tər-ˌli-niŋ\ *n* : a lining (as of a coat) between the ordinary lining and the outside fabric

in·ter·link \ˌin-tər-ˈliŋk\ *vb* : to link together

in·ter·lock \ˌin-tər-ˈläk\ *vb*   1 : to engage or interlace together : lock together : UNITE   2 : to connect so that action of one part affects action of another part — **in·ter·lock** \'in-tər-,läk\ *n*

in·ter·loc·u·tor \,in-tər-'lä-kyə-tər\ *n* : one who takes part in dialogue or conversation

in·ter·loc·u·to·ry \-,tȯr-ē\ *adj* : made during the progress of a legal action and not final or definite ⟨an ∼ decree⟩

in·ter·lope \,in-tər-'lōp\ *vb* -**loped; -lop·ing** **1** : to encroach on the rights (as in trade) of others **2** : INTRUDE, INTERFERE — **in·ter·lop·er** *n*

in·ter·lude \'in-tər-,lüd\ *n* **1** : a usu. short simple play or dramatic entertainment **2** : an intervening period, space, or event **3** : a piece of music inserted between the parts of a longer composition or a religious service

in·ter·mar·riage \,in-tər-'mer-ij\ *n* **1** : marriage within one's own group as required by custom **2** : marriage between members of different groups

in·ter·mar·ry \-'mer-ē\ *vb* **1** : to marry each other **2** : to marry within a group **3** : to become connected by intermarriage

¹in·ter·me·di·ary \,in-tər-'mē-dē-,er-ē\ *adj* **1** : INTERMEDIATE **2** : acting as a mediator

²intermediary *n, pl* -**ar·ies** : MEDIATOR, GO-BETWEEN

¹in·ter·me·di·ate \,in-tər-'mē-dē-ət\ *adj* : being or occurring at the middle place or degree or between extremes

²intermediate *n* **1** : one that is intermediate **2** : INTERMEDIARY

intermediate school *n* **1** : JUNIOR HIGH SCHOOL **2** : a school usu. comprising grades 4–6

in·ter·ment \in-'tər-mənt\ *n* : BURIAL

in·ter·mez·zo \,in-tər-'met-sō, -'med-zō\ *n, pl* -**zi** \-sē, -zē\ *or* -**zos** [It, ultim. fr. L *intermedius* intermediate] : a short movement connecting major sections of an extended musical work (as a symphony); *also* : a short independent instrumental composition

in·ter·mi·na·ble \(,)in-'tər-mə-nə-bəl\ *adj* : ENDLESS; *esp* : wearisomely protracted — **in·ter·mi·na·bly** \-blē\ *adv*

in·ter·min·gle \,in-tər-'miŋ-gəl\ *vb* : to mingle or mix together

in·ter·mis·sion \,in-tər-'mi-shən\ *n* **1** : INTERRUPTION, BREAK **2** : a temporary halt esp. in a public performance

in·ter·mit \-'mit\ *vb* -**mit·ted; -mit·ting** : DISCONTINUE; *also* : to be intermittent

in·ter·mit·tent \-'mi-t³nt\ *adj* : coming and going at intervals ♦ *Synonyms* RECURRENT, PERIODIC, ALTERNATE — **in·ter·mit·tent·ly** *adv*

in·ter·mix \,in-tər-'miks\ *vb* : to mix together : INTERMINGLE — **in·ter·mix·ture** \-'miks-chər\ *n*

in·ter·mo·lec·u·lar \-mə-'le-kyə-lər\ *adj* : existing or acting between molecules

in·ter·mon·tane \,in-tər-'män-,tān\ *adj* : situated between mountains

¹in·tern \'in-,tərn, in-'tərn\ *vb* : to confine or impound esp. during a war — **in·tern·ee** \(,)in-,tər-'nē\ *n* — **in·tern·ment** \in-'tərn-mənt\ *n*

²in·tern *also* **in·terne** \'in-,tərn\ *n* : an advanced student or recent graduate (as in medicine) gaining supervised practical experience — **in·tern·ship** *n*

³in·tern \'in-,tərn\ *vb* : to work as an intern

in·ter·nal \in-'tər-n³l\ *adj* **1** : INWARD, INTERIOR **2** : relating to or located in the inside of the body ⟨∼ pain⟩ **3** : of, relating to, or occurring within the confines of an organized structure ⟨∼ affairs⟩ **4** : of, relating to, or existing within the mind **5** : INTRINSIC, INHERENT ⟨∼ evidence⟩ — **in·ter·nal·ly** *adv*

internal combustion engine *n* : an engine in which the fuel is ignited within the engine cylinder

in·ter·nal·ise *Brit var of* INTERNALIZE

in·ter·nal·ize \in-'tər-nə-,līz\ *vb* -**ized; -iz·ing** : to incorporate (as values) within the self through learning or socialization — **in·ter·nal·i·za·tion** \-,tər-nə-lə-'zā-shən\ *n*

internal medicine *n* : a branch of medicine that deals with the diagnosis and treatment of diseases not requiring surgery

¹in·ter·na·tion·al \,in-tər-'na-shə-nəl\ *adj* **1** : common to or affecting two or more nations ⟨∼ trade⟩ **2** : of, relating to, or constituting a group having members in two or more nations — **in·ter·na·tion·al·ly** *adv*

²international *n* : one that is international; *esp* : an organization of international scope

in·ter·na·tion·al·ise *Brit var of* INTERNATIONALIZE

in·ter·na·tion·al·ism \-'na-shə-nə-,li-zəm\ *n* : a policy of cooperation among nations; *also* : an attitude favoring such a policy — **in·ter·na·tion·al·ist** \-,list\ *n or adj*

in·ter·na·tion·al·ize \-'na-shə-nə-,līz\ *vb* : to make international; *esp* : to place under international control

International System of Units *n* : a system of units based on the metric system and used by international convention esp. for scientific work

in·ter·ne·cine \,in-tər-'ne-,sēn, -'nē-,sīn\ *adj* [L *internecinus*, fr. *internecare* to destroy, kill, fr. *necare* to kill, fr. *nec-, nex* violent death] **1** : DEADLY; *esp* : mutually destructive **2** : of, relating to, or involving conflict within a group ⟨∼ feuds⟩

In·ter·net \'in-tər-,net\ *n* : an electronic communications network that connects computer networks worldwide

in·ter·nist \'in-,tər-nist\ *n* : a physician who specializes in internal medicine

in·ter·nun·cio \,in-tər-'nən-sē-,ō, -'nún-\ *n* [It *internunzio*] : a papal legate of lower rank than a nuncio

in·ter·of·fice \-'ȯ-fəs\ *adj* : functioning or communicating between the offices of an organization

in·ter·per·son·al \-'pər-sə-nəl\ *adj* : being, relating to, or involving relations between persons — **in·ter·per·son·al·ly** *adv*

in·ter·plan·e·tary \ˌin-tər-ˈpla-nə-ˌter-ē\ *adj* : existing, carried on, or operating between planets ⟨~ space⟩

in·ter·play \ˈin-tər-ˌplā\ *n* : INTERACTION

in·ter·po·late \in-ˈtər-pə-ˌlāt\ *vb* **-lat·ed; -lat·ing** **1** : to change (a text) by inserting new or foreign matter **2** : to insert (as words) into a text or into a conversation **3** : to estimate values of (data or a function) between two known values — **in·ter·po·la·tion** \-ˌtər-pə-ˈlā-shən\ *n*

in·ter·pose \ˌin-tər-ˈpōz\ *vb* **-posed; -pos·ing** **1** : to place between **2** : to thrust in : INTRUDE, INTERRUPT **3** : to inject between parts of a conversation or argument **4** : to come or be between ◆ *Synonyms* INTERFERE, INTERCEDE, INTERMEDIATE, INTERVENE — **in·ter·po·si·tion** \-pə-ˈzi-shən\ *n*

in·ter·pret \in-ˈtər-prət\ *vb* **1** : to explain the meaning of; *also* : to act as an interpreter : TRANSLATE **2** : to understand according to individual belief, judgment, or interest **3** : to represent artistically — **in·ter·pret·er** *n* — **in·ter·pre·tive** \-ˈtər-prə-tiv\ *adj*

in·ter·pre·ta·tion \in-ˌtər-prə-ˈtā-shən\ *n* **1** : EXPLANATION **2** : an instance of artistic interpretation in performance or adaptation — **in·ter·pre·ta·tive** \-ˈtər-prə-ˌtā-tiv\ *adj*

in·ter·ra·cial \-ˈrā-shəl\ *adj* : of, involving, or designed for members of different races

in·ter·reg·num \ˌin-tə-ˈreg-nəm\ *n, pl* **-nums** *or* **-na** \-nə\ **1** : the time during which a throne is vacant between two successive reigns or regimes **2** : a pause in a continuous series

in·ter·re·late \ˌin-tər-ri-ˈlāt\ *vb* : to bring into or have a mutual relationship — **in·ter·re·lat·ed·ness** \-ˈlā-təd-nəs\ *n* — **in·ter·re·la·tion** \-ˈlā-shən\ *n* — **in·ter·re·la·tion·ship** *n*

interrog *abbr* interrogative

in·ter·ro·gate \in-ˈter-ə-ˌgāt\ *vb* **-gat·ed; -gat·ing** : to question esp. formally and systematically — **in·ter·ro·ga·tion** \-ˌter-ə-ˈgā-shən\ *n* — **in·ter·ro·ga·tor** \-ˈter-ə-ˌgā-tər\ *n*

in·ter·rog·a·tive \ˌin-tə-ˈrä-gə-tiv\ *adj* : asking a question ⟨~ sentence⟩ — **interrogative** *n* — **in·ter·rog·a·tive·ly** *adv*

in·ter·rog·a·to·ry \ˌin-tə-ˈrä-gə-ˌtòr-ē\ *adj* : INTERROGATIVE

in·ter·rupt \ˌin-tə-ˈrəpt\ *vb* **1** : to stop or hinder by breaking in **2** : to break the uniformity or continuity of **3** : to break in by speaking while another is speaking — **in·ter·rupt·er** *n* — **in·ter·rup·tion** \-ˈrəp-shən\ *n* — **in·ter·rup·tive** \-ˈrəp-tiv\ *adv*

in·ter·scho·las·tic \ˌin-tər-skə-ˈlas-tik\ *adj* : existing or carried on between schools

in·ter·sect \ˌin-tər-ˈsekt\ *vb* **1** : to divide by passing through or across **2** : to meet and cross (as at a point); *also* : OVERLAP — **in·ter·sec·tion** \-ˈsek-shən\ *n*

in·ter·sperse \ˌin-tər-ˈspərs\ *vb* **-spersed; -spers·ing** **1** : to place something at in-

tervals in or among **2** : to insert at intervals among other things — **in·ter·sper·sion** \-ˈspər-zhən\ *n*

¹in·ter·state \ˌin-tər-ˈstāt\ *adj* : relating to, including, or connecting two or more states esp. of the U.S.

²in·ter·state \ˈin-tər-ˌstāt\ *n* : an interstate highway

in·ter·stel·lar \ˌin-tər-ˈste-lər\ *adj* : located or taking place among the stars

in·ter·stice \in-ˈtər-stəs\ *n, pl* **-stic·es** \-stə-ˌsēz, -stə-səz\ : a space that intervenes between things : CHINK — **in·ter·sti·tial** \ˌin-tər-ˈsti-shəl\ *adj*

in·ter·tid·al \ˌin-tər-ˈtī-dᵊl\ *adj* : of, relating to, or being the area that is above low tide mark but exposed to tidal flooding ⟨life in the ~ mud⟩

in·ter·twine \-ˈtwīn\ *vb* : to twine or cause to twine about one another : INTERLACE — **in·ter·twine·ment** *n*

in·ter·twist \-ˈtwist\ *vb* : INTERTWINE

in·ter·ur·ban \-ˈər-bən\ *adj* : connecting cities or towns

in·ter·val \ˈin-tər-vəl\ *n* [ME *intervalle*, fr. AF & L; AF *entreval*, fr. L *intervallum* space between ramparts, interval, fr. *inter-* between + *vallum* rampart] **1** : a space of time between events or states : PAUSE **2** : a space between objects, units, or states **3** : the difference in pitch between two tones

in·ter·vene \ˌin-tər-ˈvēn\ *vb* **-vened; -ven·ing** **1** : to occur, fall, or come between points of time or between events **2** : to enter or appear as an unrelated feature or circumstance ⟨rain *intervened* and we postponed the trip⟩ **3** : to come in or between in order to stop, settle, or modify ⟨~ in a quarrel⟩ **4** : to occur or lie between two things — **in·ter·ven·tion** \-ˈven-chən\ *n*

in·ter·ven·tion·ism \-ˈven-chə-ˌni-zəm\ *n* : interference by one country in the political affairs of another — **in·ter·ven·tion·ist** \ˈven-chə-nist\ *n or adj*

in·ter·view \ˈin-tər-ˌvyü\ *n* **1** : a formal consultation usu. to evaluate qualifications **2** : a meeting at which a writer or reporter obtains information from a person; *also* : the recorded or written account of such a meeting — **interview** *vb* — **in·ter·view·ee** \ˌin-tər-(ˌ)vyü-ˈē\ *n* — **in·ter·view·er** *n*

in·ter·vo·cal·ic \ˌin-tər-vō-ˈka-lik\ *adj* : immediately preceded and immediately followed by a vowel

in·ter·weave \ˌin-tər-ˈwēv\ *vb* **-wove** \-ˈwōv\ *also* **-weaved; -wo·ven** \-ˈwō-vən\ *also* **-weaved; -weav·ing** : to weave or blend together : INTERTWINE, INTERMINGLE — **interwoven** *adj*

in·tes·tate \in-ˈtes-ˌtāt, -tət\ *adj* **1** : having made no valid will ⟨died ~⟩ **2** : not disposed of by will ⟨~ estate⟩

in·tes·tine \in-ˈtes-tən\ *n* : the tubular part of the alimentary canal that extends from stomach to anus and consists of a long narrow upper part (**small intestine**) followed by a broader shorter lower part (**large intestine**) — **in·tes·ti·nal** \-tə-nᵊl\ *adj*

in·ti·fa·da \ˌin-tə-ˈfä-də\ *n* : an armed uprising of Palestinians against Israeli occupation of the West Bank and Gaza Strip

¹in·ti·mate \ˈin-tə-ˌmāt\ *vb* **-mat·ed; -mat·ing** [LL *intimare* to put in, announce, fr. L *intimus* innermost] **1** : ANNOUNCE, NOTIFY **2** : to communicate indirectly : HINT — **in·ti·ma·tion** \ˌin-tə-mā-shən\ *n*

²in·ti·mate \ˈin-tə-mət\ *adj* **1** : INTRINSIC; *also* : INNERMOST **2** : marked by very close association, contact, or familiarity **3** : marked by a warm friendship **4** : suggesting informal warmth or privacy **5** : of a very personal or private nature — **in·ti·ma·cy** \ˈin-tə-mə-sē\ *n* — **in·ti·mate·ly** *adv*

³in·ti·mate \ˈin-tə-mət\ *n* : an intimate friend, associate, or confidant

in·tim·i·date \in-ˈti-mə-ˌdāt\ *vb* **-dat·ed; -dat·ing** : to make timid or fearful : FRIGHTEN; *esp* : to compel or deter by or as if by threats ♦ *Synonyms* COW, BULLDOZE, BULLY, BROWBEAT — **in·tim·i·dat·ing·ly** *adv* — **in·tim·i·da·tion** \-ˌti-mə-ˈdā-shən\ *n*

intl *or* **intnl** *abbr* international

in·to \ˈin-tü\ *prep* **1** : to the inside of ⟨ran ~ the house⟩ **2** : to the state, condition, or form of ⟨got ~ trouble⟩ **3** : AGAINST ⟨ran ~ a wall⟩

in·tol·er·a·ble \(ˌ)in-ˈtä-lə-rə-bəl\ *adj* **1** : UNBEARABLE ⟨~ pain⟩ **2** : EXCESSIVE — **in·tol·er·a·bly** \-blē\ *adv*

in·tol·er·ant \(ˌ)in-ˈtä-lə-rənt\ *adj* **1** : unable or unwilling to endure **2** : unwilling to grant equality, freedom, or other social rights : BIGOTED — **in·tol·er·ance** \-rəns\ *n*

in·to·na·tion \ˌin-tō-ˈnā-shən\ *n* **1** : something that is intoned **2** : the act of intoning and esp. of chanting **3** : the manner of singing, playing, or uttering tones; *esp* : the rise and fall in pitch of the voice in speech

in·tone \in-ˈtōn\ *vb* **in·toned; in·ton·ing** : to utter in musical or prolonged tones : CHANT

in to·to \in-ˈtō-tō\ *adv* [L, on the whole] : TOTALLY, ENTIRELY

in·tox·i·cant \in-ˈtäk-si-kənt\ *n* : something that intoxicates; *esp* : an alcoholic drink — **intoxicant** *adj*

in·tox·i·cate \-sə-ˌkāt\ *vb* **-cat·ed; -cat·ing** **1** : to affect by a drug (as alcohol or cocaine) esp. to the point of physical or mental impairment **2** : to excite to enthusiasm or frenzy — **in·tox·i·ca·tion** \-ˌtäk-sə-ˈkā-shən\ *n*

in·trac·ta·ble \(ˌ)in-ˈtrak-tə-bəl\ *adj* : not easily controlled

in·tra·mu·ral \-ˈmyur-əl\ *adj* : being or occurring within the walls or limits (as of a city or college) ⟨~ sports⟩

in·tra·mus·cu·lar \-ˈməs-kyə-lər\ *adj* : situated within, occurring in, or administered by entering a muscle — **in·tra·mus·cu·lar·ly** *adv*

in·tra·net \ˈin-trə-ˌnet\ *n* : a network similar to the World Wide Web but having access limited to certain authorized users

intrans *abbr* intransitive

in·tran·si·gent \-jənt\ *adj* : UNCOMPROMISING ⟨an ~ attitude⟩ — **in·tran·si·gence** \-jəns\ *n* — **intransigent** *n*

in·tran·si·tive \(ˌ)in-ˈtran-sə-tiv, -zə-\ *adj* : not transitive; *esp* : not having or containing an object ⟨an ~ verb⟩ — **in·tran·si·tive·ly** *adv* — **in·tran·si·tive·ness** *n*

in·tra·state \ˌin-trə-ˈstāt\ *adj* : existing or occurring within a state

in·tra·uter·ine device \-ˈyü-tə-rən-, -ˌrīn-\ *n* : a device inserted into and left in the uterus to prevent pregnancy

in·tra·ve·nous \ˌin-trə-ˈvē-nəs\ *adj* : being within or entering by way of the veins ⟨~ feeding⟩; *also* : used in or using intravenous procedures ⟨~ needles⟩ — **in·tra·ve·nous·ly** *adv*

intrench *var of* ENTRENCH

in·trep·id \in-ˈtre-pəd\ *adj* : characterized by resolute fearlessness, fortitude, and endurance — **in·tre·pid·i·ty** \ˌin-trə-ˈpi-də-tē\ *n*

in·tri·cate \ˈin-tri-kət\ *adj* [ME, fr. L *intricatus*, pp. of *intricare* to entangle, fr. *tricae* trifles, complications] **1** : having many complexly interrelated parts : COMPLICATED **2** : difficult to follow, understand, or solve — **in·tri·ca·cy** \-tri-kə-sē\ *n* — **in·tri·cate·ly** *adv*

¹in·trigue \ˈin-ˌtrēg, in-ˈtrēg\ *n* **1** : a secret scheme : MACHINATION **2** : a clandestine love affair

²in·trigue \in-ˈtrēg\ *vb* **in·trigued; in·tri·gu·ing** **1** : to accomplish by intrigue **2** : to carry on an intrigue; *esp* : PLOT, SCHEME **3** : to arouse the interest, desire, or curiosity of — **in·tri·gu·ing·ly** *adv*

in·trin·sic \in-ˈtrin-zik, -sik\ *adj* : belonging to the essential nature or constitution of a thing — **in·trin·si·cal·ly** \-zi-k(ə-)lē, -si-\ *adv*

introd *abbr* introduction

in·tro·duce \ˌin-trə-ˈdüs, -ˈdyüs\ *vb* **-duced; -duc·ing** **1** : to lead or bring in esp. for the first time **2** : to bring into practice or use **3** : to cause to be acquainted **4** : to present for discussion **5** : PLACE, INSERT ♦ *Synonyms* INSINUATE, INTERPOLATE, INTERPOSE, INTERJECT — **in·tro·duc·tion** \-ˈdək-shən\ *n* — **in·tro·duc·to·ry** \-ˈdək-tə-rē\ *adj*

in·troit \ˈin-ˌtroit, -ˌtrō-ət\ *n* **1** *often cap* : the first part of the traditional proper of the Mass **2** : a piece of music sung or played at the beginning of a worship service

in·tro·spec·tion \-ˈspek-shən\ *n* : a reflective looking inward : an examination of one's own thoughts or feelings — **in·tro·spect** \ˌin-trə-ˈspekt\ *vb* — **in·tro·spec·tive** \-ˈspek-tiv\ *adj* — **in·tro·spec·tive·ly** *adv*

in·tro·vert \ˈin-trə-ˌvərt\ *n* : a reserved or shy person — **in·tro·ver·sion** \ˌin-trə-ˈvər-zhən\ *n* — **introvert** *adj* — **in·tro·vert·ed** \ˈin-trə-ˌvər-təd\ *adj*

in·trude \in-ˈtrüd\ *vb* **in·trud·ed; in·trud·ing** **1** : to thrust, enter, or force in or upon **2** : ENCROACH, TRESPASS — **in·trud·er** *n* — **in·tru·sion** \-ˈtrü-zhən\ *n* —

in·tru·sive \-'trü-siv\ adj — **in·tru·sive·ness** n

intrust var of ENTRUST

in·tu·it \in-'tü-ət, -'tyü-\ vb : to know, sense, or understand by intuition

in·tu·ition \,in-tù-'wi-shən, -tyù-\ n 1 : quick and ready insight 2 : the power or faculty of knowing things without conscious reasoning — **in·tu·i·tive** \in-'tü-ə-tiv, -'tyü-\ adj — **in·tu·i·tive·ly** adv

In·u·it \'i-nü-wət, 'in-yü-\ n [Inuit inuit, pl. of inuk person] 1 pl Inuit or Inuits : a member of the Eskimo people of No. America and Greenland 2 : the language of the Inuit people

in·un·date \'i-nən-,dāt\ vb **-dat·ed; -dat·ing** : to cover with or as if with a flood : OVERFLOW — **in·un·da·tion** \,i-nən-'dā-shən\ n

in·ure \i-'nùr, -'nyùr\ vb **in·ured; in·ur·ing** [ME enuren, fr. in ure customary, fr. putten in ure to use, put into practice, part trans. of AF mettre en ovre, en uevre] 1 : to accustom to accept something undesirable 2 : to become of advantage

in utero \in-'yü-tə-,rō\ adv or adj [L] : in the uterus : before birth

inv abbr 1 inventor 2 invoice

in vac·uo \in-'va-kyù-,wō\ adv [L] : in a vacuum

in·vade \in-'vād\ vb **in·vad·ed; in·vad·ing** 1 : to enter for conquest or plunder 2 : to encroach upon 3 : to spread through and usu. harm ⟨germs ~ the tissues⟩ — **in·vad·er** n

¹**in·val·id** \(,)in-'va-ləd\ adj : being without foundation or force in fact, reason, or law — **in·va·lid·i·ty** \in-və-'li-də-tē\ n — **in·val·id·ly** adv

²**in·va·lid** \'in-və-ləd\ adj : being in ill health : SICKLY

³**invalid** \'in-və-ləd\ n : a person in usu. chronic ill health — **in·va·lid·ism** \-lə-,di-zəm\ n

⁴**in·va·lid** \'in-və-ləd, -,lid\ vb 1 : to remove from active duty by reason of sickness or disability 2 : to make sickly or disabled

in·val·i·date \(,)in-'va-lə-,dāt\ vb : to make invalid; esp : to weaken or make valueless — **in·val·i·da·tion** \in-,va-lə-'dā-shən\ n

in·valu·able \'val-yə-bəl, -yə-wə-bəl\ adj : valuable beyond estimation

in·vari·able \-'ver-ē-ə-bəl\ adj : not changing or capable of change : CONSTANT — **in·vari·ably** \-blē\ adv

in·va·sion \in-'vā-zhən\ n : an act or instance of invading; esp : entry of an army into a country for conquest

in·va·sive \in-'vā-siv, -ziv\ adj 1 : tending to spread ⟨~ cancer cells⟩ 2 : involving entry into the living body (as by surgery) ⟨~ therapy⟩

in·vec·tive \in-'vek-tiv\ n 1 : an abusive expression or speech 2 : abusive language — **invective** adj

in·veigh \in-'vā\ vb : to protest or complain bitterly or vehemently : RAIL

in·vei·gle \in-'vā-gəl, -'vē-\ vb **in·vei·gled; in·vei·gling** [AF enveegler, aveogler to blind, hoodwink, fr. avogle,

enveugle blind, fr. ML ab oculis, lit., lacking eyes] 1 : to win over by flattery : ENTICE 2 : to acquire by ingenuity or flattery

in·vent \in-'vent\ vb 1 : to think up 2 : to create or produce for the first time — **in·ven·tor** \-'ven-tər\ n

in·ven·tion \in-'ven-chən\ n 1 : INVENTIVENESS 2 : a creation of the imagination; esp : a false conception 3 : a device, contrivance, or process originated after study and experiment 4 : the act or process of inventing

in·ven·tive \in-'ven-tiv\ adj 1 : CREATIVE, INGENIOUS ⟨an ~ composer⟩ 2 : characterized by invention ⟨an ~ turn of mind⟩ — **in·ven·tive·ness** n

in·ven·to·ry \'in-vən-,tòr-ē\ n, pl **-ries** 1 : an itemized list of current goods or assets 2 : SURVEY, SUMMARY 3 : STOCK, SUPPLY 4 : the act or process of taking an inventory — **inventory** vb

¹**in·verse** \(,)in-'vərs, 'in-,vərs\ adj : opposite in order, nature, or effect : REVERSED — **in·verse·ly** adv

²**inverse** n : something inverse or resulting in or from inversion : OPPOSITE

in·ver·sion \in-'vər-zhən\ n 1 : a reversal of position, order, or relationship; esp : an increase of temperature with altitude through a layer of air 2 : the act or process of inverting

in·vert \in-'vərt\ vb 1 : to reverse in position, order, or relationship 2 : to turn upside down or inside out 3 : to turn inward

in·ver·te·brate \(,)in-'vər-tə-brət, -,brāt\ adj : lacking a backbone; also : of or relating to invertebrate animals — **invertebrate** n

¹**in·vest** \in-'vest\ vb 1 : to install formally in an office or honor 2 : to furnish with power or authority : VEST 3 : to cover completely : ENVELOP 4 : CLOTHE, ADORN 5 : BESIEGE 6 : to endow with a quality or characteristic

²**invest** vb 1 : to commit (money) in order to earn a financial return 2 : to expend for future benefits or advantages 3 : to make an investment — **in·ves·tor** \-'ves-tər\ n

in·ves·ti·gate \in-'ves-tə-,gāt\ vb **-gat·ed; -gat·ing** [L investigare to track, investigate, fr. vestigium footprint, track] : to study by close examination and systematic inquiry — **in·ves·ti·ga·tion** \-,ves-tə-'gā-shən\ n — **in·ves·ti·ga·tive** \-'ves-tə-,gā-tiv\ adj — **in·ves·ti·ga·tor** \-,gā-tər\ n

in·ves·ti·ture \in-'ves-tə-,chùr, -chər\ n 1 : the act of ratifying or establishing in office 2 : something that covers or adorns

¹**in·vest·ment** \in-'vest-mənt\ n 1 : an outer layer : ENVELOPE 2 : INVESTITURE 1 3 : BLOCKADE, SIEGE

²**investment** n : the outlay of money for income or profit; also : the sum invested or the property purchased

in·vet·er·ate \in-'ve-tə-rət\ adj 1 : firmly established by age or long persistence 2 : confirmed in a habit

in·vi·a·ble \(ˌ)in-ˈvī-ə-bəl\ *adj* : incapable of surviving

in·vid·i·ous \in-ˈvi-dē-əs\ *adj* **1** : tending to cause discontent, animosity, or envy **2** : ENVIOUS **3** : OBNOXIOUS ⟨∼ remarks⟩ — **in·vid·i·ous·ly** *adv*

in·vig·o·rate \in-ˈvi-gə-ˌrāt\ *vb* **-rat·ed; -rat·ing** : to give life and energy to : ANIMATE — **in·vig·o·ra·tion** \-ˌvi-gə-ˈrā-shən\ *n*

in·vin·ci·ble \(ˌ)in-ˈvin-sə-bəl\ *adj* : incapable of being conquered, overcome, or subdued — **in·vin·ci·bil·i·ty** \-ˌvin-sə-ˈbi-lə-tē\ *n* — **in·vin·ci·bly** \ˈvin-sə-blē\ *adv*

in·vi·o·la·ble \-ˈvī-ə-lə-bəl\ *adj* **1** : safe from violation or profanation **2** : UNASSAILABLE ⟨∼ borders⟩ — **in·vi·o·la·bil·i·ty** \-ˌvī-ə-lə-ˈbi-lə-tē\ *n*

in·vi·o·late \-ˈvī-ə-lət\ *adj* : not violated or profaned : PURE

in·vis·i·ble \-ˈvi-zə-bəl\ *adj* **1** : incapable of being seen ⟨∼ to the naked eye⟩ **2** : HIDDEN **3** : IMPERCEPTIBLE, INCONSPICUOUS — **in·vis·i·bil·i·ty** \-ˌvi-zə-ˈbi-lə-tē\ *n* — **in·vis·i·bly** \-ˈvi-zə-blē\ *adv*

invisible hand *n* : a hypothetical economic force that works for the benefit of all

in·vi·ta·tion·al \ˌin-və-ˈtā-shə-nəl\ *adj* : limited to invited participants ⟨an ∼ tournament⟩ — **invitational** *n*

in·vite \in-ˈvīt\ *vb* **in·vit·ed; in·vit·ing 1** : ENTICE, TEMPT **2** : to increase the likelihood of ⟨∼ trouble⟩ **3** : to request the presence or participation of : ASK **4** : to request formally **5** : ENCOURAGE ⟨∼ suggestions⟩ — **in·vi·ta·tion** \ˌin-və-ˈtā-shən\ *n*

in·vit·ing *adj* : ATTRACTIVE, TEMPTING

in vi·tro \in-ˈvē-trō, -ˈvī-, -ˈvi-\ *adv or adj* [NL, lit., in glass] : outside the living body and in an artificial environment ⟨*in vitro* fertilization⟩

in·vo·ca·tion \ˌin-və-ˈkā-shən\ *n* **1** : SUPPLICATION; *esp* : a prayer at the beginning of a service **2** : a formula for conjuring : INCANTATION

¹in·voice \ˈin-ˌvȯis\ *n* [modif. of MF *envois*, pl. of *envoi* message] : an itemized list of goods shipped usu. specifying the price and the terms of sale : BILL

²invoice *vb* **in·voiced; in·voic·ing** : to send an invoice to or for : BILL

in·voke \in-ˈvōk\ *vb* **in·voked; in·vok·ing 1** : to petition for help or support **2** : to appeal to or cite as authority ⟨∼ a law⟩ **3** : to call forth by incantation : CONJURE ⟨∼ spirits⟩ **4** : to make an earnest request for : SOLICIT **5** : to put into effect or operation **6** : to bring about : CAUSE

in·vol·un·tary \(ˌ)in-ˈvä-lən-ˌter-ē\ *adj* **1** : done contrary to or without choice **2** : COMPULSORY ⟨∼ servitude⟩ **3** : not controlled by the will : REFLEX ⟨∼ contractions⟩ — **in·vol·un·tari·ly** \-ˌvä-lən-ˈter-ə-lē\ *adv*

in·vo·lute \ˈin-və-ˌlüt\ *adj* : INVOLVED, INTRICATE

in·vo·lu·tion \ˌin-və-ˈlü-shən\ *n* **1** : the act or an instance of enfolding or entangling **2** : COMPLEXITY, INTRICACY

in·volve \in-ˈvälv\ *vb* **in·volved; in·volv·ing 1** : to draw in as a participant **2** : ENVELOP **3** : to occupy (as oneself) absorbingly; *esp* : to commit oneself emotionally **4** : to relate closely : CONNECT **5** : to have as part of itself : INCLUDE **6** : ENTAIL, IMPLY **7** : ²AFFECT — **in·volve·ment** *n*

in·volved \-ˈvälvd\ *adj* : INTRICATE, COMPLEX ⟨an ∼ plot⟩

in·vul·ner·a·ble \(ˌ)in-ˈvəl-nə-rə-bəl\ *adj* **1** : incapable of being wounded, injured, or damaged **2** : immune to or proof against attack — **in·vul·ner·a·bil·i·ty** \-ˌvəl-nə-rə-ˈbi-lə-tē\ *n* — **in·vul·ner·a·bly** \-ˈvəl-nə-rə-blē\ *adv*

¹in·ward \ˈin-wərd\ *adj* **1** : situated on the inside **2** : MENTAL; *also* : SPIRITUAL **3** : directed toward the interior

²inward *or* **in·wards** \-wərdz\ *adv* **1** : toward the inside, center, or interior **2** : toward the inner being ⟨turned his thoughts ∼⟩

in·ward·ly \ˈin-wərd-lē\ *adv* **1** : MENTALLY, SPIRITUALLY **2** : INTERNALLY ⟨bled ∼⟩ **3** : to oneself ⟨cursed ∼⟩

IOC *abbr* International Olympic Committee

io·dide \ˈī-ə-ˌdīd\ *n* : a compound of iodine with another element or group

io·dine \ˈī-ə-ˌdīn, -dʰn\ *n* **1** : a nonmetallic chemical element used esp. in medicine and photography **2** : a solution of iodine used as a local antiseptic

io·dise *Brit var of* IODIZE

io·dize \ˈī-ə-ˌdīz\ *vb* **io·dized; io·diz·ing** : to treat with iodine or an iodide

ion \ˈī-ən, ˈī-ˌän\ *n* [Gk, neut. of *iōn*, prp. of *ienai* to go; so called because in electrolysis it goes to one of the two poles] : an electrically charged particle, atom, or group of atoms — **ion·ic** \ī-ˈä-nik\ *adj*

-ion *n suffix* : act, process, state, or condition ⟨validat*ion*⟩

ion·ise *Brit var of* IONIZE

ion·ize \ˈī-ə-ˌnīz\ *vb* **ion·ized; ion·iz·ing 1** : to convert wholly or partly into ions **2** : to become ionized — **ion·iz·able** \ˌī-ə-ˈnī-zə-bəl\ *adj* — **ion·i·za·tion** \ˌī-ə-nə-ˈzā-shən\ *n* — **ion·iz·er** \ˈī-ə-ˌnī-zər\ *n*

ion·o·sphere \ī-ˈä-nə-ˌsfir\ *n* : the part of the earth's atmosphere extending from about 30 miles (50 kilometers) to the exosphere that contains ionized atmospheric gases — **ion·o·spher·ic** \ī-ˌä-nə-ˈsfir-ik, -ˈsfer-\ *adj*

IOOF *abbr* Independent Order of Odd Fellows

io·ta \ī-ˈō-tə\ *n* [L, fr. Gk *iōta*] **1** : the 9th letter of the Greek alphabet — I or ι **2** : a very small quantity : JOT

IOU \ˌī-(ˌ)ō-ˈyü\ *n* : an acknowledgement of a debt

IP *abbr* innings pitched

IP address \ˈī-ˈpē\ *n* [*I*nternet *p*rotocol] : the numeric address of a computer on the Internet

ip·e·cac \ˈi-pi-ˌkak\ *n* [Pg *ipecacuanha*] : an emetic and expectorant drug used esp. as a syrup in treating accidental poisoning; *also* : either of two tropical American plants or their rhizomes and roots used to make ipecac

IPO \ˌī-ˌpē-ˈō\ *n, pl* **IPOs** : an initial public offering of a company's stock

ip·so fac·to \ˌip-sō-ˈfak-tō\ *adv* [NL, lit., by the fact itself] : by the very nature of the case

iq *abbr* [L *idem quod*] the same as

IQ \ˈī-ˈkyü\ *n* : a number used to express a person's relative intelligence as determined by a standardized test

¹**Ir** *abbr* Irish

²**Ir** *symbol* iridium

IR *abbr* infrared

¹**IRA** \ˌī-(ˌ)är-ˈā; ˈī-rə\ *n* [*individual retirement account*] : a retirement savings account in which income taxes are deferred until withdrawals are made

²**IRA** *abbr* Irish Republican Army

iras·ci·ble \i-ˈra-sə-bəl\ *adj* : marked by hot temper and easily provoked anger
✦ *Synonyms* CHOLERIC, TESTY, TOUCHY, CRANKY, CROSS — **iras·ci·bil·i·ty** \ˌra-sə-ˈbi-lə-tē\ *n*

irate \ī-ˈrāt\ *adj* **1** : roused to ire **2** : arising from anger — **irate·ly** *adv*

ire \ˈī(-ə)r\ *n* : ANGER, WRATH — **ire·ful** *adj*

Ire *abbr* Ireland

ire·nic \ī-ˈre-nik\ *adj* : favoring, conducive to, or operating toward peace or conciliation

ir·i·des·cence \ˌir-ə-ˈde-sᵊns\ *n* : a rainbowlike play of colors — **ir·i·des·cent** \-sᵊnt\ *adj*

irid·i·um \ir-ˈi-dē-əm\ *n* : a hard brittle heavy metallic chemical element

iris \ˈī-rəs\ *n, pl* **iris·es** *also* **iri·des** \ˈī-rə-ˌdēz, ˈir-ə-\ [ME, fr. L *iris* rainbow, iris plant, fr. Gk, rainbow, iris plant, iris of the eye] **1** : the colored part around the pupil of the eye **2** : any of a large genus of plants with linear basal leaves and large showy flowers

Irish \ˈī-rish\ *n* **1** *Irish pl* : the people of Ireland **2** : the Celtic language of Ireland — **Irish** *adj* — **Irish·man** \-mən\ *n* — **Irish·wom·an** \-ˌwu̇-mən\ *n*

Irish bull *n* : an incongruous statement (as "it was hereditary in his family to have no children")

Irish coffee *n* : hot sugared coffee with Irish whiskey and whipped cream

Irish moss *n* : the dried and bleached plants of a red alga that is a source of carrageenan; *also* : this red alga

Irish setter *n* : any of a breed of hunting dogs with a mahogany-red coat

irk \ˈərk\ *vb* : to make weary, irritated, or bored : ANNOY

irk·some \ˈərk-səm\ *adj* : tending to irk : ANNOYING — **irk·some·ly** *adv*

¹**iron** \ˈī(-ə)rn\ *n* [ME, fr. OE *īsern, īren*] **1** : a heavy malleable magnetic metallic chemical element that rusts easily and is vital to biological processes **2** : something made of metal and esp. iron; *also* : something (as handcuffs) used to bind or restrain ⟨put them in ∼s⟩ **3** : a household device with a flat base that is heated and used for pressing cloth **4** : STRENGTH, HARDNESS

²**iron** *vb* **1** : to press or smooth with or as if with a heated iron **2** : to remove (as wrinkles) by ironing — **iron·er** *n*

¹**iron·clad** \-ˈklad\ *adj* **1** : sheathed in iron armor **2** : so firm or secure as to be unbreakable

²**iron·clad** \-ˌklad\ *n* : an armored naval vessel esp. of the 19th century

iron curtain *n* : a political, military, and ideological barrier that isolates an area; *esp, often cap* : one formerly isolating an area under Soviet control

iron·ic \ī-ˈrä-nik\ *also* **iron·i·cal** \-ni-kəl\ *adj* **1** : of, relating to, or marked by irony **2** : given to irony

iron·i·cal·ly \-ni-k(ə-)lē\ *adv* **1** : in an ironic manner **2** : it is ironic

iron·ing *n* : clothes ironed or to be ironed

iron lung *n* : a device for artificial respiration that encloses the chest in a chamber in which changes of pressure force air into and out of the lungs

iron out *vb* : to remove or lessen difficulties in or extremes of

iron oxide *n* : FERRIC OXIDE

iron·stone \ˈī(-ə)rn-ˌstōn\ *n* **1** : a hard iron-rich sedimentary rock **2** : a hard heavy durable pottery developed in England in the 19th century

iron·ware \-ˌwer\ *n* : articles made of iron

iron·weed \-ˌwēd\ *n* : any of a genus of mostly weedy plants related to the asters that have terminal heads of red, purple, or white flowers

iron·wood \-ˌwu̇d\ *n* : any of numerous trees or shrubs with exceptionally hard wood; *also* : the wood

iron·work \-ˌwərk\ *n* **1** : work in iron **2** *pl* : a mill or building where iron or steel is smelted or heavy iron or steel products are made — **iron·work·er** *n*

iro·ny \ˈī-rə-nē\ *n, pl* **-nies** [L *ironia*, fr. Gk *eirōnia*, fr. *eirōn* dissembler] **1** : the use of words to express the opposite of what one really means **2** : incongruity between the actual result of a sequence of events and the expected result

Ir·o·quois \ˈir-ə-ˌkwȯi, -ˌkwȯiz\ *n, pl* **Iroquois** *same or* -ˌkwȯiz\ **1** *pl* : an American Indian confederacy orig. of New York that consisted of the Cayuga, Mohawk, Oneida, Onondaga, and Seneca and later included the Tuscarora **2** : a member of any of the Iroquois peoples

ir·ra·di·ate \i-ˈrā-dē-ˌāt\ *vb* **-at·ed; -at·ing** **1** : ILLUMINATE **2** : ENLIGHTEN **3** : to treat by exposure to radiation **4** : RADIATE — **ir·ra·di·a·tion** \-ˌrā-dē-ˈā-shən\ *n*

¹**ir·ra·tio·nal** \(ˌ)i-ˈra-shə-nəl\ *adj* **1** : incapable of reasoning ⟨∼ beasts⟩; *also* : defective in mental power ⟨∼ with fever⟩ **2** : not based on reason ⟨∼ fears⟩ **3** : being or numerically equal to an irrational number — **ir·ra·tio·nal·i·ty** \(ˌ)i-ˌra-shə-ˈna-lə-tē\ *n* — **ir·ra·tio·nal·ly** *adv*

²**irrational** *n* : IRRATIONAL NUMBER

irrational number *n* : a real number that cannot be expressed as the quotient of two integers

ir·rec·on·cil·able \\(ˌ)i-ˌre-kən-ˈsī-lə-bəl, -ˈre-kən-ˌsī-\\ *adj* : impossible to reconcile, adjust, or harmonize — **ir·rec·on·cil·abil·i·ty** \\(ˌ)i-ˌre-kən-ˌsī-lə-ˈbi-lə-tē\\ *n*

ir·re·cov·er·able \\ˌir-i-ˈkə-və-rə-bəl\\ *adj* : not capable of being recovered or rectified : IRREPARABLE ⟨an ∼ loss⟩ — **ir·re·cov·er·ably** \\-blē\\ *adv*

ir·re·deem·able \\ir-i-ˈdē-mə-bəl\\ *adj* **1** : not redeemable; *esp* : not terminable by payment of the principal ⟨an ∼ bond⟩ **2** : not convertible into gold or silver at the will of the holder **3** : being beyond remedy : HOPELESS

ir·re·den·tism \\-ˈden-ˌti-zəm\\ *n* : a principle or policy directed toward the incorporation of a territory historically or ethnically part of another into that other — **ir·re·den·tist** \\-tist\\ *n or adj*

ir·re·duc·ible \\ˌir-i-ˈdü-sə-bəl, -ˈdyü-\\ *adj* : not reducible — **ir·re·duc·ibly** \\-blē\\ *adv*

ir·re·fut·able \\ˌir-i-ˈfyü-tə-bəl, (ˌ)i-ˈre-fyət-\\ *adj* : impossible to refute

irreg *abbr* irregular

ir·reg·u·lar \\(ˌ)i-ˈre-gyə-lər\\ *adj* **1** : not regular : not natural or uniform **2** : not conforming to the normal or usual manner of inflection ⟨∼ verbs⟩ **3** : not belonging to a regular or organized army ⟨∼ troops⟩ — **irregular** *n* — **ir·reg·u·lar·ly** *adv*

ir·reg·u·lar·i·ty \\i-ˌre-gyə-ˈla-rə-tē\\ *n, pl* **-ties 1** : something that is irregular **2** : the quality or state of being irregular **3** : occasional constipation

ir·rel·e·vant \\(ˌ)i-ˈre-lə-vənt\\ *adj* : not relevant — **ir·rel·e·vance** \\-vəns\\ *n*

ir·re·li·gious \\ˌir-i-ˈli-jəs\\ *adj* : lacking religious emotions, doctrines, or practices

ir·re·me·di·a·ble \\ˌir-i-ˈmē-dē-ə-bəl\\ *adj* : impossible to remedy or correct

ir·re·mov·able \\-ˈmü-və-bəl\\ *adj* : not removable

ir·rep·a·ra·ble \\(ˌ)i-ˈre-pə-rə-bəl\\ *adj* : impossible to make good, undo, repair, or remedy ⟨∼ damage⟩

ir·re·place·able \\ˌir-i-ˈplā-sə-bəl\\ *adj* : not replaceable ⟨∼ antiques⟩

ir·re·press·ible \\-ˈpre-sə-bəl\\ *adj* : impossible to repress or control

ir·re·proach·able \\-ˈprō-chə-bəl\\ *adj* : not reproachable : BLAMELESS

ir·re·sist·ible \\ˌir-i-ˈzis-tə-bəl\\ *adj* : impossible to successfully resist — **ir·re·sist·ibly** \\-blē\\ *adv*

ir·res·o·lute \\(ˌ)i-ˈre-zə-ˌlüt\\ *adj* : uncertain how to act or proceed : VACILLATING — **ir·res·o·lute·ly** \\-ˌlüt-lē; (ˌ)i-ˌre-zə-ˈlüt-\\ *adv* — **ir·res·o·lu·tion** \\(ˌ)i-ˌre-zə-ˈlü-shən\\ *n*

ir·re·spec·tive of \\ˌir-i-ˈspek-tiv-\\ *prep* : without regard to

ir·re·spon·si·ble \\-ˈspän-sə-bəl\\ *adj* : not responsible — **ir·re·spon·si·bil·i·ty** \\-ˌspän-sə-ˈbi-lə-tē\\ *n* — **ir·re·spon·si·bly** \\-ˈspän-sə-blē\\ *adv*

ir·re·triev·able \\ˌir-i-ˈtrē-və-bəl\\ *adj* : not retrievable : IRRECOVERABLE

ir·rev·er·ence \\(ˌ)i-ˈre-və-rəns\\ *n* **1** : lack of reverence **2** : an irreverent act or utterance — **ir·rev·er·ent** \\-rənt\\ *adj* — **ir·rev·er·ent·ly** *adv*

ir·re·vers·ible \\ˌir-i-ˈvər-sə-bəl\\ *adj* : incapable of being reversed

ir·rev·o·ca·ble \\(ˌ)i-ˈre-və-kə-bəl\\ *adj* : incapable of being revoked or recalled — **ir·rev·o·ca·bly** \\-blē\\ *adv*

ir·ri·gate \\ˈir-ə-ˌgāt\\ *vb* **-gat·ed; -gat·ing** : to supply (as land) with water by artificial means; *also* : to flush with liquid — **ir·ri·ga·tion** \\ˌir-ə-ˈgā-shən\\ *n*

ir·ri·ta·bil·i·ty \\ˌir-ə-tə-ˈbi-lə-tē\\ *n* **1** : the property of living things and of protoplasm that enables reaction to stimuli **2** : the quality or state of being irritable; *esp* : readiness to become annoyed or angry

ir·ri·ta·ble \\ˈir-ə-tə-bəl\\ *adj* : capable of being irritated; *esp* : readily or easily irritated — **ir·ri·ta·bly** \\-blē\\ *adv*

ir·ri·tate \\ˈir-ə-ˌtāt\\ *vb* **-tat·ed; -tat·ing 1** : to excite to anger : EXASPERATE **2** : to make sore or inflamed — **ir·ri·tant** \\ˈir-ə-tənt\\ *adj or n* — **ir·ri·tat·ing·ly** *adv* — **ir·ri·ta·tion** \\ˌir-ə-ˈtā-shən\\ *n*

ir·rupt \\(ˌ)i-ˈrəpt\\ *vb* **1** : to rush in forcibly or violently **2** : to increase suddenly in numbers ⟨rabbits ∼ in cycles⟩ — **ir·rup·tion** \\-ˈrəp-shən\\ *n*

IRS *abbr* Internal Revenue Service

is *pres 3d sing of* BE

Isa *or* **Is** *abbr* Isaiah

Isa·iah \\ī-ˈzā-ə\\ *n* — see BIBLE table

Isa·ias \\ī-ˈzā-əs\\ *n* : ISAIAH

ISBN *abbr* International Standard Book Number

is·che·mia \\is-ˈkē-mē-ə\\ *n* : deficient supply of blood to a body part (as the brain) — **is·che·mic** \\-mik\\ *adj*

-ish *adj suffix* **1** : of, relating to, or being ⟨Finnish⟩ **2** : characteristic of ⟨boyish⟩ ⟨mulish⟩ **3** : inclined or liable to ⟨bookish⟩ **4** : having a touch or trace of : somewhat ⟨purplish⟩ **5** : having the approximate age of ⟨fortyish⟩

isin·glass \\ˈī-zᵊn-ˌglas, ˈī-ziŋ-\\ *n* **1** : a gelatin obtained from various fish **2** : mica esp. in thin sheets

isl *abbr* island

Is·lam \\is-ˈläm, iz-, -ˈlam, ˈis-ˌ, ˈiz-ˌ\\ *n* [Ar *islām* submission (to the will of God)] : the religious faith of Muslims including belief in Allah as the sole deity and in Muhammad as his prophet; *also* : the civilization built on this faith — **Is·lam·ic** \\is-ˈlä-mik, iz-, -ˈla-\\ *adj*

is·land \\ˈī-lənd\\ *n* [ME *iland*, fr. OE *īgland*, fr. *īg* island + *land* land] **1** : a body of land smaller than a continent surrounded by water **2** : something resembling an island in its isolation

is·land·er \\ˈī-lən-dər\\ *n* : a native or inhabitant of an island

isle \\ˈī(-ə)l\\ *n* : ISLAND; *esp* : a small island

is·let \\ˈī-lət\\ *n* : a small island

ism \\ˈi-zəm\\ *n* : a distinctive doctrine, cause, or theory

-ism *n suffix* **1** : act : practice : process ⟨criticism⟩ **2** : manner of action or behavior characteristic of a (specified) person or thing ⟨fanaticism⟩ **3** : state : condition : property ⟨dualism⟩ **4** : abnormal state or condition ⟨alcohol*ism*⟩ 5 : doctrine : theory : cult ⟨Buddh*ism*⟩ 6 : adherence to a set of principles ⟨stoic*ism*⟩ 7 : prejudice or discrimination on the basis of a (specified) attribute ⟨rac*ism*⟩ ⟨sex*ism*⟩ 8 : characteristic or peculiar feature or trait ⟨colloquial*ism*⟩

iso·bar \ˈī-sə-ˌbär\ *n* : a line on a map connecting places of equal barometric pressure — **iso·bar·ic** \ˌī-sə-ˈbär-ik, -ˈber-\ *adj*

iso·late \ˈī-sə-ˌlāt\ *vb* **-lat·ed; -lat·ing** [fr. *isolated* set apart, fr. F *isolé*, fr. *isolato*, fr. *isola* island, fr. L *insula*] : to place or keep by itself : separate from others — **iso·la·tion** \ˌī-sə-ˈlā-shən\ *n*

isolated *adj* **1** : occurring alone or once : UNIQUE **2** : SPORADIC

iso·la·tion·ism \ˌī-sə-ˈlā-shə-ˌni-zəm\ *n* : a policy of national isolation by abstention from international political and economic relations — **iso·la·tion·ist** \-shə-nist\ *n or adj*

iso·mer \ˈī-sə-mər\ *n* : any of two or more chemical compounds that contain the same numbers of atoms of the same elements but differ in structural arrangement and properties — **iso·mer·ic** \ˌī-sə-ˈmer-ik\ *adj* — **isom·er·ism** \ī-ˈsä-mə-ˌri-zəm\ *n*

iso·met·rics \ˌī-sə-ˈme-triks\ *n sing or pl* : exercise involving a series of brief and intense contractions of muscles against each other or against an immovable resistance — **iso·met·ric** *adj*

iso·prene \ˈī-sə-ˌprēn\ *n* : a hydrocarbon used esp. in making synthetic rubber

isos·ce·les \ī-ˈsä-sə-ˌlēz\ *adj* : having two equal sides ⟨an ∼ triangle⟩

iso·therm \ˈī-sə-ˌthərm\ *n* : a line on a map connecting points having the same temperature

iso·ther·mal \ˌī-sə-ˈthər-məl\ *adj* : of, relating to, or marked by equality of temperature

iso·tope \ˈī-sə-ˌtōp\ *n* [Gk *isos* equal + *topos* place] : any of the forms of a chemical element that differ chiefly in the number of neutrons in an atom — **iso·to·pic** \ˌī-sə-ˈtä-pik, -ˈtō-\ *adj* — **iso·to·pi·cal·ly** \-ˈtä-pi-k(ə-)lē, -ˈtō-\ *adv*

Isr *abbr* Israel; Israeli

Is·ra·el·ite \ˈiz-rē-ə-ˌlīt\ *n* : a member of the Hebrew people descended from Jacob

is·su·ance \ˈi-shü-wəns\ *n* : the act of issuing or giving out esp. officially

¹is·sue \ˈi-shü\ *n* [ME, exit, proceeds, fr. AF, fr. *issir* to come out, go out, fr. L. *exire*, fr. *ire* to go] **1** : the action of going, coming, or flowing out : EGRESS, EMERGENCE **2** : EXIT, OUTLET, VENT **3** : OFFSPRING, PROGENY **4** : OUTCOME, RESULT **5** : a point of debate or controversy; *also* : the point at which an unsettled matter is ready for a decision **6** : a discharge (as of blood) from the body **7** : something coming forth from a specified source **8** : the act of officially giving out or printing : PUBLICATION; *also* : the quantity of things given out at one time

²issue *vb* **is·sued; is·su·ing 1** : to go,

come, or flow out **2** : to come forth or cause to come forth : EMERGE, DISCHARGE, EMIT **3** : ACCRUE **4** : to descend from a specified parent or ancestor **5** : to result in **6** : to put forth or distribute officially **7** : PUBLISH **8** : EMANATE, RESULT — **is·su·er** *n*

¹-ist *n suffix* **1** : one that performs a (specified) action ⟨cycl*ist*⟩ : one that makes or produces ⟨novel*ist*⟩ **2** : one that plays a (specified) musical instrument ⟨harp*ist*⟩ **3** : one that operates a (specified) mechanical instrument or contrivance ⟨machin*ist*⟩ **4** : one that specializes in a (specified) art or science or skill ⟨geolog*ist*⟩ **5** : one that adheres to or advocates a (specified) doctrine or system or code of behavior ⟨social*ist*⟩ or that of a (specified) individual ⟨Darwin*ist*⟩

²-ist *adj suffix* : -ISTIC

isth·mi·an \ˈis-mē-ən\ *adj* : of, relating to, or situated in or near an isthmus

isth·mus \ˈis-məs\ *n* : a narrow strip of land connecting two larger portions of land

¹it \ˈit, ət\ *pron* **1** : that one — used of a lifeless thing, a plant, a person or animal, or an abstract entity ⟨∼'s a big building⟩ ⟨∼'s a shade tree⟩ ⟨who is ∼⟩ ⟨beauty is everywhere and ∼ is a source of joy⟩ **2** — used as a subject of an impersonal verb that expresses a condition or action without reference to an agent ⟨∼ is raining⟩ **3** — used as an anticipatory subject or object ⟨∼'s good to see you⟩

²it \ˈit\ *n* : the player in a game who performs the principal action of the game (as trying to find others in hide-and-seek)

It *abbr* Italian; Italy

ital *abbr* italic; italicized

Ital *abbr* Italian

Ital·ian \i-ˈtal-yən\ *n* **1** : a native or inhabitant of Italy **2** : the language of Italy — **Italian** *adj*

ital·ic \i-ˈta-lik, ī-\ *adj* : relating to type in which the letters slope upward toward the right (as in *"italic"*) — **italic** *n*

ital·i·cise *Brit var of* ITALICIZE

ital·i·cize \i-ˈta-lə-ˌsīz, ī-\ *vb* **-cized; -ciz·ing** : to print in italics — **ital·i·ci·za·tion** \-ˌta-lə-sə-ˈzā-shən\ *n*

itch \ˈich\ *n* **1** : an uneasy irritating skin sensation that evokes a desire to scratch the affected area **2** : a skin disorder accompanied by an itch **3** : a persistent desire — **itch** *vb* — **itchy** *adj*

-ite *n suffix* **1** : native : resident ⟨suburban*ite*⟩ **2** : adherent : follower ⟨Lenin*ite*⟩ **3** : product ⟨metabol*ite*⟩ **4** : mineral : rock ⟨quartz*ite*⟩

item \ˈī-təm\ *n* [L, likewise, also] **1** : a separate particular in a list, account, or series : ARTICLE **2** : a separate piece of news (as in a newspaper)

item·ise *Brit var of* ITEMIZE

item·ize \ˈī-tə-ˌmīz\ *vb* **-ized; -iz·ing** : to set down in detail : LIST — **item·i·za·tion** \ˌī-tə-mə-ˈzā-shən\ *n*

it·er·ate \ˈi-tə-ˌrāt\ *vb* **-at·ed; -at·ing** : REITERATE, REPEAT

it·er·a·tion \ˌi-tə-ˈrā-shən\ *n* **1** : REPETITION; *esp* : a computational process in which a series of operations is repeated until a condition is met **2** : one repetition of the series of operations in iteration **3** : VERSION

itin·er·ant \ī-'ti-nə-rənt, ə-\ *adj* : traveling from place to place; *esp* : covering a circuit ⟨an ~ preacher⟩

itin·er·ary \ī-'ti-nə-ˌrer-ē, ə-\ *n, pl* **-ar·ies 1** : the route of a journey or the proposed outline of one **2** : a travel diary **3** : GUIDEBOOK

its \'its\ *adj* : of or relating to it or itself

it·self \it-'self\ *pron* : that identical one — used reflexively, for emphasis, or in absolute constructions

-ity *n suffix* : quality : state : degree ⟨alkalin*ity*⟩

IUD \ˌī-(ˌ)yü-'dē\ *n* : INTRAUTERINE DEVICE

IV \ˌī-'vē\ *n, pl* **IVs** [intravenous] : an apparatus used to administer a fluid (as of nutrients) intravenously; *also* : a fluid administered by IV

-ive *adj suffix* : that performs or tends toward an (indicated) action ⟨correct*ive*⟩

ivo·ry \'ī-vrē, -və-rē\ *n, pl* **-ries** [ME *ivorie*, fr. AF *ivoire, ivurie*, fr. L *eboreus* of ivory, fr. *ebur* ivory] **1** : the hard creamy-white material composing the tusks of an elephant or walrus **2** : a pale yellow color **3** : something made of ivory or of a similar substance

ivory tower *n* **1** : an impractical lack of concern with urgent problems **2** : a place of learning

ivy \'ī-vē\ *n, pl* **ivies** : a trailing woody evergreen vine with small black berries that is related to ginseng

IWW *abbr* Industrial Workers of the World

-ize *vb suffix* **1** : cause to be or conform to or resemble ⟨American*ize*⟩ : cause to be formed into ⟨union*ize*⟩ **2** : subject to a (specified) action ⟨satir*ize*⟩ **3** : saturate, treat, or combine with ⟨macadam*ize*⟩ **4** : treat like ⟨idol*ize*⟩ **5** : become : become like ⟨crystall*ize*⟩ **6** : be productive in or of : engage in a (specified) activity ⟨philosoph*ize*⟩ **7** : adopt or spread the manner of activity or the teaching of ⟨Christian*ize*⟩

¹j \'jā\ *n, pl* **j's** or **js** \'jāz\ *often cap* : the 10th letter of the English alphabet

²j *abbr, often cap* **1** jack **2** journal **3** judge **4** justice

¹jab \'jab\ *vb* **jabbed; jab·bing** : to thrust quickly or abruptly : POKE

²jab *n* : a usu. short straight punch

jab·ber \'ja-bər\ *vb* : to talk rapidly, indistinctly, or unintelligibly : CHATTER — **jabber** *n* — **jab·ber·er** *n*

jab·ber·wocky \'ja-bər-ˌwä-kē\ *n* : meaningless speech or writing

ja·bot \zha-'bō, 'ja-ˌbō\ *n* : a ruffle worn down the front of a dress or shirt

jac·a·ran·da \ˌja-kə-'ran-də\ *n* : any of a genus of pinnate-leaved tropical American trees with clusters of showy blue flowers

¹jack \'jak\ *n* **1** : a mechanical device; *esp* : one used to raise a heavy body a short distance **2** : a male donkey **3** : a small target ball in lawn bowling **4** : a small national flag flown by a ship **5** : a small 6-pointed metal object used in a game (**jacks**) **6** : a playing card bearing the figure of a soldier or servant **7** : a socket into which a plug is inserted for connecting electric circuits

²jack *vb* **1** : to raise by means of a jack **2** : INCREASE ⟨~ up prices⟩

jack·al \'ja-kəl\ *n* [Turk *çakal*, fr. Pers *shaqāl*] : any of several mammals of Asia and Africa related to the wolves

jack·a·napes \'ja-kə-ˌnāps\ *n* **1** : MONKEY, APE **2** : an impudent or conceited person

jack·ass \'jak-ˌas\ *n* **1** : DONKEY; *esp* : a male donkey **2** : a stupid person : FOOL

jack·boot \-ˌbüt\ *n* **1** : a heavy military boot of glossy black leather extending above the knee **2** : a laceless military boot reaching to the calf

jack·daw \'jak-ˌdȯ\ *n* : a black and gray Old World crowlike bird

jack·et \'ja-kət\ *n* [ME *jaket*, fr. AF *jackés*, pl., dim. of MF *jaque* short jacket, fr. *jacques* peasant, fr. the name *Jacques* James] **1** : a garment for the upper body usu. having a front opening, collar, and sleeves **2** : an outer covering or casing ⟨a book ~⟩

Jack Frost *n* : frost or frosty weather personified

jack·ham·mer \'jak-ˌha-mər\ *n* : a pneumatic percussion tool for drilling rock or breaking pavement

jack–in–the–box *n, pl* **jack–in–the–boxes** or **jacks–in–the–box** : a toy consisting of a small box out of which a figure springs when the lid is raised

jack–in–the–pulpit *n, pl* **jack–in–the–pulpits** *also* **jacks–in–the–pulpit** : a No. American spring-flowering woodland herb having an upright club-shaped spadix arched over by a green and purple spathe

¹jack·knife \'jak-ˌnīf\ *n* **1** : a large pocketknife **2** : a dive in which the diver bends from the waist and touches the ankles before straightening out

²jackknife *vb* : to fold like a jackknife ⟨the trailer truck *jackknifed*⟩

jack·leg \'jak-ˌleg\ *adj* **1** : lacking skill or training **2** : MAKESHIFT

jack–of–all–trades *n, pl* **jacks–of–all–**

trades : one who is able to do passable work at various tasks

jack-o'-lan-tern \'jä-kə-ˌlan-tərn\ *n* : a lantern made of a pumpkin cut to look like a human face

jack-pot \'jak-ˌpät\ *n* **1** : a large sum of money formed by the accumulation of stakes from previous play (as in poker) **2** : an impressive and often unexpected success or reward

jack-rab-bit \-ˌra-bət\ *n* : any of several large hares of western No. America with very long ears and hind legs

Jack Russell terrier \'jak-'rə-səl-\ *n* : any of a breed of small terriers having a white coat with dark markings

jack-straw \-ˌstrô\ *n* **1** *pl* : a game in which straws or thin sticks are let fall in a heap and each player in turn tries to remove them one at a time without disturbing the rest **2** : one of the pieces used in jackstraws

jack-tar \-'tär\ *n, often cap* : SAILOR

Ja-cob's ladder \'jā-kəbz-\ *n* : any of several perennial herbs related to phlox that have pinnate leaves and blue or white bell-shaped flowers

jac-quard \'ja-ˌkärd\ *n, often cap* : a fabric of intricate variegated weave or pattern

¹**jade** \'jād\ *n* **1** : a broken-down, vicious, or worthless horse **2** : a disreputable woman

²**jade** *vb* **jad-ed; jad-ing** **1** : to wear out by overwork or abuse **2** : to become weary ♦ *Synonyms* EXHAUST, FATIGUE, TIRE

³**jade** *n* [F, prob. Sp (*piedra de la*) *ijada,* lit., loin stone; fr. the belief that jade cures renal colic] : a usu. green gemstone that takes a high polish

jad-ed *adj* : made dull, apathetic, or cynical by experience or by surfeit

¹**jag** \'jag\ *n* : a sharp projecting part

²**jag** *n* : SPREE ⟨a crying ∼⟩

jag-ged \'ja-gəd\ *adj* : sharply notched

jag-uar \'ja-ˌgwär\ *n* : a black-spotted tropical American cat that is larger and stockier than the Old World leopard

jai alai \'hī-ˌlī\ *n* [Sp, fr. Basque, fr. *jai* festival + *alai* merry] : a court game played by usu. two or four players with a ball and a curved wicker basket strapped to the wrist

jail \'jāl\ *n* [ME *jaiole,* fr. AF *gaiole, jaiole,* fr. LL *caveola,* dim. of L *cavea* cage] : PRISON; *esp* : one for persons held in lawful custody — **jail** *vb*

jail-bird \-ˌbərd\ *n* : a habitual criminal

jail-break \-ˌbrāk\ *n* : a forcible escape from jail

jail-er *also* **jail-or** \'jā-lər\ *n* : a keeper of a jail

jal-ap \'ja-ləp, 'jä-\ *n* : a powdered purgative drug from the root of a Mexican plant related to the morning glory; *also* : this root or plant

ja-la-pe-ño \ˌhä-lə-'pān-(ˌ)yō\ *n* : a small plump dark green chili pepper

ja-lopy \jə-'lä-pē\ *n, pl* **ja-lop-ies** : a dilapidated vehicle (as an automobile)

jal-ou-sie \'ja-lə-sē\ *n* [F, lit., jealousy] : a blind, window, or door with adjustable horizontal slats or louvers

¹**jam** \'jam\ *vb* **jammed; jam-ming** **1** : to press into a close or tight position **2** : to cause to become wedged so as to be unworkable; *also* : to make or become unworkable through the jamming of a movable part **3** : to push forcibly ⟨∼ on the brakes⟩ **4** : CRUSH, BRUISE ⟨*jammed* a finger in the door⟩ **5** : to make unintelligible by sending out interfering signals or messages **6** : to take part in a jam session — **jam-mer** *n*

²**jam** *n* **1** : a crowded mass that impedes or blocks ⟨traffic ∼⟩ **2** : a difficult state of affairs

³**jam** *n* : a food made by boiling fruit and sugar to a thick consistency

Jam *abbr* Jamaica

jamb \'jam\ *n* [ME *jambe,* fr. AF *jambe, gambe,* lit., leg] : an upright piece forming the side of an opening (as of a door)

jam-ba-laya \ˌjəm-bə-'lī-ə\ *n* [LaF] : rice cooked with ham, sausage, chicken, shrimp, or oysters and seasoned with herbs

jam-bo-ree \ˌjam-bə-'rē\ *n* : a large festive gathering

James \'jāmz\ *n* — see BIBLE table

jam-pack \'jam-'pak\ *vb* : to pack tightly or to excess

jam session *n* : an impromptu performance esp. by jazz musicians

Jan *abbr* January

jan-gle \'jaŋ-gəl\ *vb* **jan-gled; jan-gling** : to make a harsh or discordant sound — **jangle** *n*

jan-i-tor \'ja-nə-tər\ *n* [L, doorkeeper, fr. *janus* arch, gate] : a person who has the care of a building — **jan-i-to-ri-al** \ˌja-nə-'tôr-ē-əl\ *adj*

Jan-u-ary \'ja-nyə-ˌwer-ē\ *n* [ME *Januarie,* fr. L *Januarius,* first month of the ancient Roman year, fr. *Janus,* two-faced god of gates and beginnings] : the 1st month of the year

¹**ja-pan** \jə-'pan\ *n* : a varnish giving a hard brilliant finish

²**japan** *vb* **ja-panned; ja-pan-ning** : to cover with a coat of japan

Jap-a-nese \ˌja-pə-'nēz, -'nēs\ *n, pl* **Japanese** **1** : a native or inhabitant of Japan **2** : the language of Japan — **Japanese** *adj*

Japanese beetle *n* : a small metallic green and brown scarab beetle introduced from Japan that is a pest on the roots of grasses as a grub and on foliage and fruits as an adult

¹**jape** \'jāp\ *vb* **japed; jap-ing** **1** : JOKE **2** : MOCK

²**jape** *n* : JEST, GIBE

¹**jar** \'jär\ *vb* **jarred; jar-ring** **1** : to make a harsh or discordant sound **2** : to have a harsh or disagreeable effect **3** : VIBRATE, SHAKE

²**jar** *n* **1** : a state of conflict **2** : a harsh discordant sound **3** : JOLT **4** : a painful effect : SHOCK

³**jar** *n* : a widemouthed container usu. of glass or earthenware

jar·di·niere \,jär-də-'nir\ *n* : an ornamental stand for plants or flowers

jar·gon \'jär-gən\ *n* **1** : confused unintelligible language **2** : the special vocabulary of a particular group or activity **3** : obscure and often pretentious language

Jas *abbr* James

jas·mine \'jaz-mən\ *also* **jes·sa·mine** \'jes-mən, 'je-sə-\ *n* [MF *jasmin,* fr. Ar *yāsamīn,* fr. Pers] : any of various climbing shrubs with fragrant flowers

jas·per \'jas-pər\ *n* : a usu. red, yellow, or brown opaque quartz

jaun·dice \'jón-dəs\ *n* : yellowish discoloration of skin, tissues, and body fluids by bile pigments; *also* : an abnormal condition marked by jaundice

jaun·diced \-dəst\ *adj* **1** : affected with or as if with jaundice **2** : exhibiting envy, distaste, or hostility

jaunt \'jónt\ *n* : a short trip usu. for pleasure

jaun·ty \'jón-tē\ *adj* **jaun·ti·er; -est** : sprightly in manner or appearance : LIVELY — **jaun·ti·ly** \-tə-lē\ *adv* — **jaun·ti·ness** \-tē-nəs\ *n*

jav·e·lin \'ja-və-lən\ *n* **1** : a light spear **2** : a slender shaft thrown for distance in a track-and-field contest

¹jaw \'jó\ *n* **1** : either of the bony or cartilaginous structures that support the soft tissues enclosing the mouth and that usu. bear teeth **2** : the parts forming the walls of the mouth and serving to open and close it — usu. used in pl. **3** : one of a pair of movable parts for holding or crushing something — **jawed** \'jód\ *adj*

²jaw *vb* : to talk abusively, indignantly, or at length

¹jaw·bone \-,bōn\ *n* : JAW 1

²jawbone *vb* : to talk forcefully and persuasively

jaw·break·er \-,brā-kər\ *n* **1** : a word difficult to pronounce **2** : a round hard candy

jaw–drop·ping \'jó-,dra-piŋ\ *adj* : causing great surprise or astonishment

jaw·less fish \'jó-ləs-\ *n* : any of a group of primitive vertebrates (as lampreys) without jaws

jay \'jā\ *n* : any of various noisy brightly colored often largely blue birds smaller than the related crows

jay·bird \'jā-,bərd\ *n* : JAY

jay·vee \jā-'vē\ *n* **1** : JUNIOR VARSITY **2** : a member of a junior varsity team

jay·walk \'jā-,wók\ *vb* : to cross a street carelessly without regard for traffic regulations — **jay·walk·er** *n*

¹jazz \'jaz\ *n* **1** : American music characterized by improvisation, syncopated rhythms, and contrapuntal ensemble playing **2** : empty talk **3** : similar but unspecified things : STUFF

²jazz *vb* : ENLIVEN ⟨~ things up⟩

jazzy \'ja-zē\ *adj* **jazz·i·er; -est** **1** : having the characteristics of jazz **2** : marked by unrestraint, animation, or flashiness

JCS *abbr* joint chiefs of staff

jct *abbr* junction

JD *abbr* **1** [L *juris doctor*] doctor of jurisprudence; doctor of law **2** [L *jurum doctor*] doctor of laws **3** justice department **4** juvenile delinquent

jeal·ous \'je-ləs\ *adj* **1** : demanding complete devotion **2** : suspicious of a rival or of one believed to enjoy an advantage **3** : VIGILANT — **jeal·ous·ly** *adv* — **jeal·ou·sy** \-lə-sē\ *n*

jeans \'jēnz\ *n pl* [pl. of *jean* twilled cloth, short for *jean fustian,* fr. ME *Gene* Genoa, Italy] : pants made of durable twilled cotton cloth

jeep \'jēp\ *n* : a small four-wheel drive general-purpose motor vehicle used in World War II

¹jeer \'jir\ *vb* : to speak or cry out in derision : MOCK

²jeer *n* : TAUNT

Je·ho·vah \ji-'hō-və\ *n* : GOD 1

je·hu \'jē-hü, -hyü\ *n* : a driver of a coach or cab

je·june \ji-'jün\ *adj* [L *jejunus* empty of food, hungry, meager] : lacking interest or significance : DULL

je·ju·num \ji-'jü-nəm\ *n* [L] : the section of the small intestine between the duodenum and the ileum — **je·ju·nal** \-'jü-nᵊl\ *adj*

jell \'jel\ *vb* **1** : to come to the consistency of jelly **2** : to take shape ⟨my idea began to ~⟩

jel·ly \'je-lē\ *n, pl* **jellies** **1** : a food with a soft elastic consistency due usu. to the presence of gelatin or pectin; *esp* : a fruit product made by boiling sugar and the juice of a fruit **2** : a substance resembling jelly — **jelly** *vb* — **jel·ly·like** *adj*

jelly bean *n* : a bean-shaped candy

jel·ly·fish \'je-lē-,fish\ *n* : a marine coelenterate with a nearly transparent jellylike body and stinging tentacles

jen·net \'je-nət\ *n* **1** : a small Spanish horse **2** : a female donkey

jen·ny \'je-nē\ *n, pl* **jennies** : a female bird or donkey

jeop·ar·dy \'je-pər-dē\ *n* [ME *jeopardie,* fr. AF *juparti, jeuparti* alternative, lit., divided game] : exposure to death, loss, or injury ◆ *Synonyms* PERIL, HAZARD, RISK, DANGER — **jeop·ar·dize** \-,dīz\ *vb*

Jer *abbr* Jeremiah; Jeremias

jer·e·mi·ad \,jer-ə-'mī-əd, -,ad\ *n* : a prolonged lamentation or complaint; *also* : a cautionary or angry harangue

Jer·e·mi·ah \,jer-ə-'mī-ə\ *n* — see BIBLE table

Jer·e·mi·as \,jer-ə-'mī-əs\ *n* : JEREMIAH

¹jerk \'jərk\ *n* **1** : a short quick pull or twist : TWITCH **2** : an annoyingly stupid or foolish person — **jerk·i·ly** \'jər-kə-lē\ *adv* — **jerky** \'jər-kē\ *adj*

²jerk *vb* **1** : to give a sharp quick push, pull, or twist **2** : to move in short abrupt motions

jer·kin \'jər-kən\ *n* : a close-fitting usu. sleeveless jacket

jerk·wa·ter \'jərk-,wò-tər, -,wä-\ *adj* [fr. *jerkwater* rural train] : of minor importance : INSIGNIFICANT ⟨~ towns⟩

jer·ry–built \'jer-ē-,bilt\ *adj* : built cheaply and flimsily

jer·ry–rigged \-ˌrigd\ *adj* : organized or constructed in a crude or improvised manner

jer·sey \ˈjər-zē\ *n, pl* **jerseys** [*Jersey*, one of the Channel islands] **1** : a plain weft-knitted fabric **2** : a close-fitting knitted shirt **3** *often cap* : any of a breed of small usu. fawn-colored dairy cattle

Jersey barrier *n* : a concrete slab that is used with others to block or reroute traffic or to divide a highway

Je·ru·sa·lem artichoke \jə-ˈrü-sə-ləm-\ *n* : a No. American sunflower widely grown for its edible tubers that are used as a vegetable; *also* : its tubers

jess \ˈjes\ *n* : a leg strap by which a captive bird of prey may be controlled

jessamine *var of* JASMINE

jest \ˈjest\ *n* **1** : an act intended to provoke laughter **2** : a witty remark **3** : a frivolous mood ⟨said in ~⟩ — **jest** *vb*

jest·er \ˈjes-tər\ *n* : a retainer formerly kept to provide casual entertainment

¹jet \ˈjet\ *n* : a velvet-black coal that takes a good polish and is often used for jewelry

²jet *vb* **jet·ted; jet·ting** : to spout or emit in a stream

³jet *n* **1** : a forceful rush (as of liquid or gas) through a narrow opening; *also* : a nozzle for a jet of fluid **2** : a jet-propelled airplane

⁴jet *vb* **jet·ted; jet·ting** : to travel by jet

jet lag *n* : a condition that is marked esp. by fatigue and irritability and occurs following a long flight through several time zones — **jet–lagged** *adj*

jet·lin·er \ˈjet-ˌlī-nər\ *n* : a jet-propelled airliner

jet·port \-ˌpȯrt\ *n* : an airport designed to handle jets

jet–pro·pelled \ˌjet-prə-ˈpeld\ *adj* : driven by an engine (**jet engine**) that produces propulsion (**jet propulsion**) by the rearward discharge of a jet of fluid (as heated air and exhaust gases)

jet·sam \ˈjet-səm\ *n* : jettisoned goods; *esp* : such goods washed ashore

jet set *n* : an international group of wealthy people who frequent fashionable resorts

jet stream *n* : a long narrow high-altitude current of high-speed winds blowing generally from the west

jet·ti·son \ˈje-tə-sən\ *vb* **1** : to throw (goods) overboard to lighten a ship or aircraft in distress **2** : DISCARD — **jettison** *n*

jet·ty \ˈje-tē\ *n, pl* **jetties** **1** : a pier built to influence the current or to protect a harbor **2** : a landing wharf

jeu d'es·prit \zhœ-des-ˈprē\ *n, pl* **jeux d'esprit** *same*\ [F, lit., play of the mind] : a witty comment or composition

Jew \ˈjü\ *n* **1** : ISRAELITE **2** : one whose religion is Judaism — **Jew·ish** *adj*

¹jew·el \ˈjü-əl\ *n* [ME *juel*, fr. AF, dim. of *ju, jeu* game, play, fr. L *jocus* game, joke] **1** : an ornament of precious metal **2** : GEMSTONE, GEM

²jewel *vb* **-eled** *or* **-elled; -el·ing** *or* **-el·ling** : to adorn or equip with jewels

jewel box *n* : a thin plastic case for a CD or DVD

jew·el·er *or* **jew·el·ler** \ˈjü-ə-lər\ *n* : a person who makes or deals in jewelry and related articles

jew·el·lery *chiefly Brit var of* JEWELRY

jew·el·ry \ˈjü-əl-rē\ *n* : JEWELS; *esp* : objects of precious metal set with gems and worn for personal adornment

Jew·ry \ˈju̇r-ē, ˈju̇-ər-ē, ˈjü-rē\ *n* : the Jewish people

jg *abbr* junior grade

¹jib \ˈjib\ *n* : a triangular sail set on a line running from the bow to the mast

²jib *vb* **jibbed; jib·bing** : to refuse to proceed further

¹jibe *var of* GIBE

²jibe \ˈjīb\ *vb* **jibed; jib·ing** : to be in accord : AGREE

ji·ca·ma \ˈhē-kə-mə\ *n* : an edible starchy tuber of a tropical American vine of the legume family

jif·fy \ˈji-fē\ *n, pl* **jiffies** : MOMENT, INSTANT ⟨I'll be ready in a ~⟩

¹jig \ˈjig\ *n* **1** : a lively dance in triple rhythm **2** : TRICK, GAME ⟨the ~ is up⟩ **3** : a device used to hold work during manufacture or assembly

²jig *vb* **jigged; jig·ging** : to dance a jig

jig·ger \ˈji-gər\ *n* : a measure usu. holding 1 to 2 ounces (30 to 60 milliliters) used in mixing drinks

jig·gle \ˈji-gəl\ *vb* **jig·gled; jig·gling** : to move with quick little jerks — **jiggle** *n*

jig·saw \ˈjig-ˌsȯ\ *n* : SCROLL SAW 2

jigsaw puzzle *n* : a puzzle consisting of small irregularly cut pieces that are to be fitted together to form a picture

ji·had \ji-ˈhäd, -ˈhad\ *n* **1** : a Muslim holy war **2** : CRUSADE 2

¹jilt \ˈjilt\ *vb* : to drop (as a lover) capriciously or unfeelingly

²jilt *n* : one who jilts a lover

jim crow \ˈjim-ˈkrō\ *n, often cap J&C* : discrimination against blacks esp. by legal enforcement or traditional sanctions — **jim crow** *adj, often cap J&C* — **jim crow·ism** \-ˈkrō-ˌi-zəm\ *n, often cap J&C*

jim–dan·dy \ˈjim-ˈdan-dē\ *n* : something excellent of its kind — **jim–dandy** *adj*

jim·mies \ˈji-mēz\ *n pl* : tiny rod-shaped bits of usu. chocolate-flavored candy often sprinkled on ice cream

¹jim·my \ˈji-mē\ *n, pl* **jimmies** : a small crowbar

²jimmy *vb* **jim·mied; jim·my·ing** : to force open with a jimmy

jim·son·weed \ˈjim-sən-ˌwēd\ *n, often cap* : a coarse poisonous weed related to the tomato that has large trumpet-shaped white or violet flowers

¹jin·gle \ˈjiŋ-gəl\ *vb* **jin·gled; jin·gling** : to make a light clinking or tinkling sound

²jingle *n* **1** : a light clinking or tinkling sound **2** : a short verse or song with catchy repetition

jin·go·ism \ˈjiŋ-gō-ˌi-zəm\ *n* : extreme chauvinism or nationalism marked esp. by a belligerent foreign policy — **jin·go·ist** \-ist\ *n* — **jin·go·is·tic** \ˌjiŋ-gō-ˈis-tik\ *adj*

jin·rik·sha \jin-ˈrik-ˌshȯ\ *n* : RICKSHAW
¹jinx \ˈjiŋks\ *n* : one that brings bad luck
²jinx *vb* : to foredoom to failure or misfortune
jit·ney \ˈjit-nē\ *n, pl* **jitneys** : a small bus that serves a regular route on a flexible schedule
jit·ter·bug \ˈji-tər-ˌbəg\ *n* : a dance in which couples two-step, balance, and twirl vigorously in standardized patterns — **jitterbug** *vb*
jit·ters \ˈji-tərz\ *n pl* : extreme nervousness — **jit·tery** \-tə-rē\ *adj*
¹jive \ˈjiv\ *n* **1** : swing music or dancing performed to it **2** : glib, deceptive, or foolish talk **3** : the jargon of jazz enthusiasts
²jive *vb* **jived; jiv·ing 1** : KID, TEASE **2** : to dance to or play jive
Jn *or* **Jno** *abbr* John
Jo *abbr* Joel
¹job \ˈjäb\ *n* **1** : a piece of work **2** : something that has to be done : TASK **3** : a regular remunerative position — **job·less** *adj*
²job *vb* **jobbed; job·bing 1** : to do occasional pieces of work for hire **2** : to hire or let by the job
Job \ˈjōb\ *n* — see BIBLE table
job action *n* : a protest action by workers to force compliance with demands
job·ber \ˈjä-bər\ *n* **1** : a person who buys goods and then sells them to other dealers : MIDDLEMAN **2** : a person who does work by the job
job·hold·er \ˈjäb-ˌhōl-dər\ *n* : one having a regular job
jock \ˈjäk\ *n* [*jockstrap*] : ATHLETE; *esp* : a school or college athlete
¹jock·ey \ˈjä-kē\ *n, pl* **jockeys** : one who rides a horse esp. as a professional in a race
²jockey *vb* **jock·eyed; jock·ey·ing** : to maneuver or manipulate by adroit or devious means
jock·strap \ˈjäk-ˌstrap\ *n* [E slang *jock* penis] : ATHLETIC SUPPORTER
jo·cose \jō-ˈkōs\ *adj* **1** : MERRY **2** : HUMOROUS ◆ *Synonyms* JOCULAR, FACETIOUS, WITTY
joc·u·lar \ˈjä-kyə-lər\ *adj* : marked by jesting : PLAYFUL — **joc·u·lar·i·ty** \ˌjäk-yə-ˈlar-ə-tē\ *n* — **joc·u·lar·ly** *adv*
jo·cund \ˈjä-kənd\ *adj* : marked by mirth or cheerfulness
jodh·pur \ˈjäd-pər\ *n* **1** *pl* : riding breeches loose above the knee and tight-fitting below **2** : an ankle-high boot fastened with a strap
Joe Blow \ˈjō-\ *n* : an average or ordinary man
Jo·el \ˈjō-əl\ *n* — see BIBLE table
Joe Six–Pack \ˈjō-\ *n* : a blue-collar worker
¹jog \ˈjäg\ *vb* **jogged; jog·ging 1** : to give a slight shake or push to **2** : to go at a slow monotonous pace **3** : to run or ride at a slow trot — **jog·ger** *n*
²jog *n* **1** : a slight shake **2** : a jogging movement or pace
³jog *n* **1** : a projecting or retreating part of

a line or surface **2** : a brief abrupt change in direction
jog·gle \ˈjä-gəl\ *vb* **jog·gled; jog·gling** : to shake slightly — **joggle** *n*
john \ˈjän\ *n* **1** : TOILET **2** : a prostitute's client
John \ˈjän\ *n* — see BIBLE table
john·ny \ˈjä-nē\ *n, pl* **johnnies** : a short-sleeved gown opening in the back that is worn by hospital patients
John·ny–jump–up \ˌjä-nē-ˈjəmp-ˌəp\ *n* : any of various small-flowered cultivated pansies
joie de vi·vre \ˌzhwä-də-ˈvēvrᵊ\ *n* [F] : keen enjoyment of life
join \ˈjȯin\ *vb* **1** : to come or bring together so as to form a unit **2** : to come or bring into close association **3** : to become a member of **4** : ADJOIN **5** : to take part in a collective activity
join·er \ˈjȯi-nər\ *n* **1** : a worker who constructs articles by joining pieces of wood **2** : a gregarious person who joins many organizations
¹joint \ˈjȯint\ *n* **1** : the point of contact between bones of an animal skeleton with the parts that surround and support it **2** : a cut of meat suitable for roasting **3** : a place where two things or parts are connected **4** : ESTABLISHMENT; *esp* : a shabby or disreputable establishment **5** : a marijuana cigarette — **joint·ed** *adj*
²joint *adj* **1** : UNITED **2** : common to two or more — **joint·ly** *adv*
³joint *vb* **1** : to unite by or provide with a joint **2** : to separate the joints of
joist \ˈjȯist\ *n* : any of the small beams ranged parallel from wall to wall in a building to support a floor or ceiling
¹joke \ˈjōk\ *n* : something said or done to provoke laughter; *esp* : a brief narrative with a humorous climax
²joke *vb* **joked; jok·ing** : to make jokes — **jok·ing·ly** *adv*
jok·er \ˈjō-kər\ *n* **1** : a person who jokes **2** : an extra card used in some card games **3** : a misleading part of an agreement that works to one party's disadvantage
jol·li·fi·ca·tion \ˌjä-li-fə-ˈkā-shən\ *n* : a festive celebration
jol·li·ty \ˈjä-lə-tē\ *n, pl* **-ties** : GAIETY, MERRIMENT
jol·ly \ˈjä-lē\ *adj* **jol·li·er; -est** : full of high spirits : MERRY
¹jolt \ˈjōlt\ *vb* **1** : to give a quick hard knock or blow to **2** : to move with a sudden jerky motion — **jolt·er** *n*
²jolt *n* **1** : an abrupt jerky blow or movement **2** : a sudden shock
Jon *abbr* Jonah; Jonas
Jo·nah \ˈjō-nə\ *n* — see BIBLE table
Jo·nas \ˈjō-nəs\ *n* : JONAH
¹jones \ˈjōnz\ *n* **1** *slang* : addiction to heroin **2** *slang* : HEROIN **3** *slang* : a craving for something
²jones *vb, slang* : to have a craving for something
jon·gleur \zhōⁿ-ˈglər\ *n* : an itinerant medieval minstrel
jon·quil \ˈjän-kwəl\ *n* [F *jonquille*, fr. Sp *junquillo*, dim. of *junco* reed, fr. L *juncus*]

: a narcissus with fragrant clustered white or yellow flowers

josh \ˈjäsh\ vb : TEASE, JOKE

Josh abbr Joshua

Josh•ua \ˈjä-shə-wə\ n — see BIBLE table

Joshua tree n : a tall branched yucca of the southwestern U.S.

jos•tle \ˈjä-səl\ vb jos•tled; jos•tling 1 : to come in contact or into collision 2 : to make one's way by pushing and shoving

Jos•ue \ˈjä-shü-ē\ n : JOSHUA

¹**jot** \ˈjät\ n : the least bit : IOTA

²**jot** vb jot•ted; jot•ting : to write briefly and hurriedly

jot•ting \ˈjä-tiŋ\ n : a brief note

joule \ˈjül\ n : a unit of work or energy equal to the work done by a force of one newton acting through a distance of one meter

jounce \ˈjaůns\ vb jounced; jounc•ing : JOLT — jounce n

jour abbr 1 journal 2 journeyman

jour•nal \ˈjər-nᵊl\ n [ME, service book containing the day hours, fr. AF jurnal, fr. jurnal daily, fr. L diurnalis, fr. dies day] 1 : a brief account of daily events 2 : a record of proceedings (as of a legislative body) 3 : a periodical (as a newspaper) dealing esp. with current events 4 : the part of a rotating axle or spindle that turns in a bearing

jour•nal•ese \ˌjər-nə-ˈlēz, -ˈlēs\ n : a style of writing held to be characteristic of newspapers

jour•nal•ism \ˈjər-nə-ˌli-zəm\ n 1 : the business of writing for, editing, or publishing periodicals (as newspapers) 2 : writing designed for or characteristic of newspapers — **jour•nal•ist** \-list\ n — **jour•nal•is•tic** \ˌjər-nə-ˈlis-tik\ adj

¹**jour•ney** \ˈjər-nē\ n, pl journeys [ME, fr. OF journee day's journey, fr. jour day] : a traveling from one place to another

²**journey** vb jour•neyed; jour•ney•ing : to go on a journey : TRAVEL

jour•ney•man \-mən\ n 1 : a worker who has learned a trade and works for another person 2 : an experienced reliable worker

¹**joust** \ˈjaůst\ vb : to engage in a joust

²**joust** n : a combat on horseback between two knights with lances esp. as part of a tournament

jo•vial \ˈjō-vē-əl\ adj : marked by good humor — **jo•vi•al•i•ty** \ˌjō-vē-ˈa-lə-tē\ n — **jo•vi•al•ly** adv

¹**jowl** \ˈjaů(-ə)l\ n : loose flesh about the lower jaw or throat

²**jowl** n 1 : the lower jaw 2 : CHEEK

¹**joy** \ˈjói\ n [ME, fr. AF joie, fr. L gaudia] 1 : a feeling of happiness that comes from success, good fortune, or a sense of well-being 2 : a source of happiness ✦ Synonyms BLISS, DELIGHT, ENJOYMENT, PLEASURE — **joy•less** adj

²**joy** vb : REJOICE

joy•ful \-fəl\ adj : experiencing, causing, or showing joy — **joy•ful•ly** adv

joy•ous \ˈjói-əs\ adj : JOYFUL — **joy•ous•ly** adv — **joy•ous•ness** n

joy•ride \ˈjói-ˌrīd\ n : a ride for pleasure often marked by reckless driving — **joyride** vb — **joy•rid•er** n — **joy•rid•ing** n

joy•stick \-ˌstik\ n : a control device (as for a computer) consisting of a lever capable of motion in two or more directions

JP abbr 1 jet propulsion 2 justice of the peace

JPEG \ˈjā-ˌpeg\ n [Joint Photographic Experts Group] : a computer file format for usu. high-quality digital images

Jr abbr junior

Jt or **jnt** abbr joint

ju•bi•lant \ˈjü-bə-lənt\ adj [L jubilans, prp. of jubilare to rejoice] : EXULTANT — **ju•bi•lant•ly** adv

ju•bi•la•tion \ˌjü-bə-ˈlā-shən\ n : EXULTATION

ju•bi•lee \ˈjü-bə-ˌlē, ˌjü-bə-ˈlē\ n [ME, fr. AF & LL; AF jubilé, fr. LL jubilaeus, fr. LGk iōbēlaios, fr. Heb yōbhēl ram's horn, trumpet, jubilee] 1 : a 50th anniversary 2 : a season or occasion of celebration

ju•co \ˈjü-ˌkō\ n, pl jucos : JUNIOR COLLEGE; also : an athlete at a junior college

Jud abbr Judith

Ju•da•ic \jü-ˈdā-ik\ also **Ju•da•ical** \-ˈdā-ə-kəl\ adj : of, relating to, or characteristic of Jews or Judaism

Ju•da•ism \ˈjü-də-ˌi-zəm, -dā-, -dē-\ n : a religion developed among the ancient Hebrews and marked by belief in one God and by the moral and ceremonial laws of the Old Testament and the rabbinic tradition

Jude \ˈjüd\ n — see BIBLE table

Judg abbr Judges

¹**judge** \ˈjəj\ vb judged; judg•ing 1 : to form an authoritative opinion 2 : to decide as a judge : TRY 3 : to form an estimate or evaluation about something : THINK ✦ Synonyms CONCLUDE, DEDUCE, GATHER, INFER

²**judge** n 1 : a public official authorized to decide questions brought before a court 2 : UMPIRE 3 : one who gives an authoritative opinion : CRITIC — **judge•ship** n

Judges n — see BIBLE table

judg•ment or **judge•ment** \ˈjəj-mənt\ n 1 : a decision or opinion given after judging; esp : a formal decision given by a court 2 cap : the final judging of mankind by God 3 : the process of forming an opinion by discerning and comparing 4 : the capacity for judging : DISCERNMENT

judg•men•tal \ˌjəj-ˈmen-təl\ adj 1 : of, relating to, or involving judgment 2 : characterized by a tendency to judge harshly — **judg•men•tal•ly** adv

judgment call n : a subjective decision, ruling, or opinion

Judgment Day n : the day of the final judging of all human beings by God

ju•di•ca•ture \ˈjü-di-kə-ˌchúr\ n 1 : the administration of justice : JUDICIARY 1

ju•di•cial \jü-ˈdi-shəl\ adj 1 : of or relating to the administration of justice or the judiciary 2 : ordered or enforced by a court 3 : CRITICAL — **ju•di•cial•ly** adv

ju·di·cia·ry \ju̇-'di-shē-,er-ē, -shə-rē\ n 1 : a system of courts of law; also : the judges of these courts 2 : a branch of government in which judicial power is vested — **judiciary** adj

ju·di·cious \ju̇-'di-shəs\ adj : having, exercising, or characterized by sound judgment ◆ **Synonyms** PRUDENT, SAGE, SANE, SENSIBLE, WISE — **ju·di·cious·ly** adv

Ju·dith \'jü-dəth\ n — see BIBLE table

ju·do \'jü-dō\ n [Jp, fr. jū weakness, gentleness + dō art] : a sport derived from jujitsu that emphasizes the use of quick movement and leverage to throw an opponent — **ju·do·ist** \-ist\ n

ju·do·ka \'jü-dō-,kä\ n, pl **judoka** or **ju·dokas** : one who participates in judo

¹**jug** \'jəg\ n 1 : a large deep container with a narrow mouth and a handle 2 : JAIL, PRISON

²**jug** vb **jugged; jug·ging** : JAIL, IMPRISON

jug–eared \'jəg-,ird\ adj : having protuberant ears

jug·ger·naut \'jə-gər-,nȯt\ n [Hindi Jagannāth, title of Vishnu (a Hindu god), lit., lord of the world] : a massive inexorable force or object that crushes everything in its path

jug·gle \'jə-gəl\ vb **jug·gled; jug·gling** 1 : to keep several objects in motion in the air at the same time 2 : to manipulate esp. in order to achieve a desired and often fraudulent end — **jug·gler** \'jə-glər\ n

jug·u·lar \'jə-gyə-lər\ adj : of, relating to, or situated in or on the throat or neck ⟨the ~ veins⟩

juice \'jüs\ n 1 : the extractable fluid contents of cells or tissues 2 pl : the natural fluids of an animal body 3 : something that supplies power; esp : ELECTRICITY 2

juic·er \'jü-sər\ n : an appliance for extracting juice (as from fruit)

juice up vb : to give life, energy, or spirit to

juicy \'jü-sē\ adj **juic·i·er; -est** 1 : SUCCULENT 2 : rich in interest; also : RACY — **juic·i·ly** \-sə-lē\ adv — **juic·i·ness** \-sē-nəs\ n

ju·jit·su also **ju·jut·su** or **jiu·jit·su** \jü-'jit-sü\ n : an art of fighting employing holds, throws, and paralyzing blows

ju·ju \'jü-jü\ n : a style of African music characterized by a rapid beat, use of percussion instruments, and vocal harmonies

ju·jube \'jü-jüb, 'jü-jü-,bē\ n : a fruit-flavored gumdrop or lozenge

juke·box \'jük-,bäks\ n : a coin-operated machine that automatically plays selected recordings

Jul abbr July

ju·lep \'jü-ləp\ n [ME, sweetened water, fr. MF, fr. Ar julāb, fr. Pers gulāb, fr. gul rose + āb water] : a drink made of bourbon, sugar, and mint served over crushed ice

Ju·ly \ju̇-'lī\ n [ME Julie, fr. OE Julius, fr. L, fr. Gaius Julius Caesar] : the 7th month of the year

¹**jum·ble** \'jəm-bəl\ vb **jum·bled; jum·bling** : to mix in a confused mass

²**jumble** n : a disorderly mass or pile

jum·bo \'jəm-bō\ n, pl **jumbos** [Jumbo, a huge elephant exhibited by P.T. Barnum] : a very large specimen of its kind — **jumbo** adj

¹**jump** \'jəmp\ vb 1 : to spring into the air : leap over 2 : to give a start 3 : to rise or increase suddenly or sharply 4 : to make a sudden attack 5 : to leave hurriedly and often furtively ⟨~ town⟩ 6 : to act or move before (as a signal) — **jump bail** : to abscond after being released from custody on bail — **jump ship** 1 : to leave the company of a ship without authority 2 : to desert a cause — **jump the gun** : to begin something before the proper time

²**jump** n 1 : a spring into the air; esp : one made for height or distance in a track meet 2 : a sharp sudden increase 3 : an initial advantage

¹**jump·er** \'jəm-pər\ n : one that jumps

²**jumper** n 1 : a loose blouse 2 : a sleeveless one-piece dress worn usu. with a blouse 3 pl : a child's sleeveless coverall

jumping bean n : a seed of any of several Mexican shrubs that tumbles about because of the movements of a small moth larva inside it

jumping–off place n 1 : a remote or isolated place 2 : a place from which an enterprise is launched

jump·mas·ter \'jəmp-,mas-tər\ n : a person who supervises parachutists

jump–start \'jəmp-,stärt\ vb : to start (an engine or vehicle) by connection to an external power source

jump·suit \'jəmp-,süt\ n 1 : a coverall worn by parachutists in jumping 2 : a one-piece garment consisting of a blouse or shirt with attached pants or shorts

jumpy \'jəm-pē\ adj **jump·i·er; -est** : NERVOUS, JITTERY

jun abbr junior

Jun abbr June

junc abbr junction

jun·co \'jəŋ-kō\ n, pl **juncos** or **juncoes** : any of a genus of small common pink-billed No. American finches that are largely gray with conspicuous white tail feathers

junc·tion \'jəŋk-shən\ n 1 : an act of joining 2 : a place or point of meeting

junc·ture \'jəŋk-chər\ n 1 : JOINT, CONNECTION 2 : UNION 3 : a critical time or state of affairs

June \'jün\ n [ME, fr. L Junius] : the 6th month of the year

jun·gle \'jəŋ-gəl\ n [Hindi & Urdu jangal forest] 1 : a thick tangled mass of tropical vegetation; also : a tract overgrown with vegetation 2 : a place of ruthless struggle for survival

¹**ju·nior** \'jü-nyər\ adj 1 : YOUNGER 2 : lower in rank ⟨a ~ partner⟩ 3 : of or relating to juniors

²**junior** n 1 : a person who is younger or of lower rank than another 2 : a student in the next-to-last year before graduating

junior college n : a school that offers studies corresponding to those of the 1st two years of college

junior high school n : a school usu. including grades 7–9

junior varsity n : a team whose members lack the experience or qualifications required for the varsity

ju·ni·per \'jü-nə-pər\ n : any of numerous coniferous shrubs or trees with leaves like needles or scales and female cones like berries

¹**junk** \'jəŋk\ n, **1** : old iron, glass, paper, or waste; also : discarded articles **2** : a shoddy product **3** : something of little meaning, worth, or significance **4** slang : NARCOTICS; esp : HEROIN — **junky** adj

²**junk** vb : DISCARD, SCRAP

³**junk** n : a ship of eastern Asia with a high stern and 4-cornered sails

junk·er \'jəŋ-kər\ n : something (as an old automobile) ready for scrapping

Jun·ker \'yun̄-kər\ n [G] : a member of the Prussian landed aristocracy

jun·ket \'jəŋ-kət\ n **1** : a pudding of sweetened flavored milk set by rennet **2** : a trip made by an official at public expense

junk food n : food that is high in calories but low in nutritional content

junk·ie also **junky** \'jəŋ-kē\ n, pl **junkies** **1** : a narcotics peddler or addict **2** : one that derives inordinate pleasure from or is dependent on something ⟨a sugar ∼⟩

jun·ta \'hun̄-tə, 'jən-, 'hən-\ n [Sp, fr. junto joined, fr. L junctus, pp. of jungere to join] : a group of persons controlling a government esp. after a revolutionary seizure of power

Ju·pi·ter \'jü-pə-tər\ n : the largest of the planets and the one 5th in order of distance from the sun

Ju·ras·sic \ju-'ra-sik\ adj : of, relating to, or being the period of the Mesozoic era between the Triassic and the Cretaceous that is marked esp. by the presence of dinosaurs — **Jurassic** n

ju·rid·i·cal \ju-'ri-di-kəl\ also **ju·rid·ic** \-dik\ adj **1** : of or relating to the administration of justice **2** : LEGAL — **ju·rid·i·cal·ly** \-di-k(ə-)lē\ adv

ju·ris·dic·tion \jur-əs-'dik-shən\ n **1** : the power, right, or authority to interpret and apply the law **2** : the authority of a sovereign power **3** : the limits or territory within which authority may be exercised — **ju·ris·dic·tion·al** \-shə-nəl\ adj

ju·ris·pru·dence \-'prü-dⁿns\ n **1** : the science or philosophy of law **2** : a system of laws

ju·rist \'jur-ist\ n : one having a thorough knowledge of law; esp : JUDGE

ju·ris·tic \ju-'ris-tik\ adj **1** : of or relating to a jurist or jurisprudence **2** : of, relating to, or recognized in law

ju·ror \'jur-ər, -ȯr\ n : a member of a jury

¹**ju·ry** \'jur-ē\ n, pl **juries** **1** : a body of persons sworn to inquire into a matter submitted to them and to give their verdict **2** : a committee for judging and awarding prizes

²**jury** adj : improvised for temporary use esp. in an emergency ⟨a ∼ mast⟩

jury nullification n : the acquitting of a defendant by a jury in disregard of the judge's instructions and contrary to the jury's findings of fact

jury–rig \'jur-ē-ˌrig\ vb : to construct or arrange in a makeshift fashion

¹**just** \'jəst\ adj **1** : having a basis in or conforming to fact or reason : REASONABLE ⟨∼ comment⟩ **2** : CORRECT, PROPER ⟨∼ proportions⟩ **3** : morally or legally right ⟨a ∼ title⟩ **4** : DESERVED, MERITED ⟨∼ punishment⟩ ♦ **Synonyms** UPRIGHT, HONORABLE, CONSCIENTIOUS, HONEST — **just·ly** adv — **just·ness** n

²**just** \'jəst, 'jist\ adv **1** : EXACTLY ⟨∼ right⟩ **2** : very recently ⟨has ∼ left⟩ **3** : BARELY ⟨∼ too late⟩ **4** : DIRECTLY ⟨∼ west of here⟩ **5** : ONLY ⟨∼ last year⟩ **6** : QUITE ⟨∼ wonderful⟩ **7** : POSSIBLY ⟨it ∼ might work⟩

jus·tice \'jəs-təs\ n **1** : the administration of what is just (as by assigning merited rewards or punishments) **2** : JUDGE **3** : the administration of law **4** : FAIRNESS; also : RIGHTEOUSNESS

justice of the peace n : a local magistrate empowered chiefly to try minor cases, to administer oaths, and to perform marriages

jus·ti·fy \'jəs-tə-ˌfī\ vb **-fied; -fy·ing** **1** : to prove to be just, right, or reasonable **2** : to pronounce free from guilt or blame **3** : to adjust spaces in a line of printed text so the margins are even — **jus·ti·fi·able** adj — **jus·ti·fi·ca·tion** \ˌjəs-tə-fə-'kā-shən\ n

jut \'jət\ vb **jut·ted; jut·ting** : PROJECT, PROTRUDE

jute \'jüt\ n : a strong glossy fiber from either of two tropical plants used esp. for making sacks and twine

juv abbr juvenile

¹**ju·ve·nile** \'jü-və-ˌnī(-ə)l, -nəl\ adj **1** : showing incomplete development **2** : of, relating to, or characteristic of children or young people

²**juvenile** n **1** : a young person; esp : one below the legally established age of adulthood **2** : a young animal (as a fish or a bird) or plant **3** : an actor or actress who plays youthful parts

juvenile delinquency n : violation of the law or antisocial behavior by a juvenile — **juvenile delinquent** n

jux·ta·pose \'jək-stə-ˌpōz\ vb **-posed; -pos·ing** : to place side by side — **jux·ta·po·si·tion** \ˌjək-stə-pə-'zi-shən\ n

JV abbr junior varsity

K

¹k \'kā\ *n, pl* **k's** *or* **ks** \'kāz\ **1** *often cap* : the 11th letter of the English alphabet **2** *cap* : STRIKEOUT

²k *abbr* **1** karat **2** kitchen **3** knit **4** kosher — often enclosed in a circle

¹K *abbr* **1** Kelvin **2** kindergarten

²K *symbol* [NL *kalium*] potassium

kab·ba·lah *also* **kab·ba·la** *or* **ka·ba·la** *or* **ca·ba·la** \kə-'bä-lə, 'ka-bə-lə\ *n, often cap* **1** : a medieval Jewish mysticism marked by belief in creation through emanation and a cipher method of interpreting Scripture **2** : esoteric or mysterious doctrine

kabob *var of* KEBAB

Ka·bu·ki \kə-'bü-kē\ *n* : traditional Japanese popular drama with highly stylized singing and dancing

kad·dish \'kä-dish\ *n, often cap* : a Jewish prayer recited in the daily synagogue ritual and by mourners at public services after the death of a close relative

kaf·fee·klatsch \'kó-fē-ˌklach, 'kä-\ *n, often cap* [G] : an informal social gathering for coffee and conversation

kai·ser \'kī-zər\ *n* : EMPEROR; *esp* : the ruler of Germany from 1871 to 1918

Ka·lash·ni·kov \kə-'lash-nə-ˌkóf\ *n* [M. T. *Kalashnikov* b1919 Soviet weapons designer] : a Soviet-designed assault rifle

kale \'kāl\ *n* : a hardy cabbage with curled leaves that do not form a head

ka·lei·do·scope \kə-'lī-də-ˌskōp\ *n* : a tube containing loose bits of colored material (as glass) and two mirrors at one end that shows many different patterns as it is turned — **ka·lei·do·scop·ic** \-ˌlī-də-'skä-pik\ *adj* — **ka·lei·do·scop·i·cal·ly** \-pi-k(ə-)lē\ *adv*

ka·ma·ai·na \ˌkä-mə-'ī-nə\ *n* [Hawaiian *kama'āina*, fr. *kama* child + *'āina* land] : one who has lived in Hawaii for a long time

kame \'kām\ *n* [Sc, lit., comb] : a short ridge or mound of material deposited by water from a melting glacier

ka·mi·ka·ze \ˌkä-mi-'kä-zē\ *n* [Jp, lit., divine wind] : a member of a corps of Japanese pilots assigned to make a suicidal crash on a target; *also* : an airplane flown in such an attack

Kan *or* **Kans** *abbr* Kansas

kan·ga·roo \ˌkaŋ-gə-'rü\ *n, pl* **-roos** : any of various large leaping marsupial mammals of Australia and adjacent islands with powerful hind legs and a long thick tail used as a support

kangaroo court *n* : a court or an illegal self-appointed tribunal characterized by irresponsible, perverted, or irregular procedures

ka·o·lin \'kā-ə-lən\ *n* : a fine usu. white clay used in ceramics and refractories and for the treatment of diarrhea

ka·pok \'kā-ˌpäk\ *n* : silky fiber from the seeds of a tropical tree used esp. as a filling (as for life preservers)

Kap·o·si's sar·co·ma \'ka-pə-sēz-sär-'kō-mə\ *n* : a neoplastic disease associated esp. with AIDS that affects esp. the skin and mucous membranes and is characterized usu. by the formation of pink to reddish-brown or bluish plaques

kap·pa \'ka-pə\ *n* : the 10th letter of the Greek alphabet — K or κ

ka·put *also* **ka·putt** \kä-'pút, kə-, -'püt\ *adj* [G, fr. F *capot* not having made a trick at piquet] **1** : utterly defeated or destroyed **2** : unable to function : USELESS

kar·a·kul \'ker-ə-kəl\ *n* : the usu. curly glossy black coat of a very young lamb of a hardy Asian breed of sheep

kar·a·o·ke \ˌker-ē-'ō-kē\ *n* [Jp] : a device that plays instrumental accompaniments for songs to which the user sings along

kar·at \'ker-ət\ *n* : a unit for expressing proportion of gold in an alloy equal to ¹/₂₄ part of pure gold

ka·ra·te \kə-'rä-tē\ *n* [Jp, lit., empty hand] : an art of self-defense in which an attacker is disabled by crippling kicks and punches

kar·ma \'kär-mə\ *n, often cap* [Skt] : the force generated by a person's actions held in Hinduism and Buddhism to perpetuate reincarnation and to determine the nature of the person's next existence — **kar·mic** \-mik\ *adj*

karst \'kärst\ *n* [G] : an irregular limestone region with sinks, underground streams, and caverns

ka·ty·did \'kā-tē-ˌdid\ *n* : any of several large green tree-dwelling American grasshoppers with long antennae

kay·ak \'kī-ˌak\ *n* : an Eskimo canoe made of a skin-covered frame with a small opening and propelled by a double-bladed paddle; *also* : a similar portable boat — **kay·ak·er** *n*

kayo \(ˌ)kā-'ō, 'kā-ō\ *n* : KNOCKOUT — **kayo** *vb*

ka·zoo \kə-'zü\ *n, pl* **kazoos** : a toy musical instrument consisting of a tube with a membrane sealing one end and a side hole to sing or hum into

KB *abbr* kilobyte

kc *abbr* kilocycle

KC *abbr* **1** Kansas City **2** King's Counsel **3** Knights of Columbus

kc/s *abbr* kilocycles per second

KD *abbr* knocked down

ke·bab *or* **ke·bob** *also* **ka·bob** \kə-'bäb\ *n* : cubes of meat cooked with vegetables usu. on a skewer

kedge \'kej\ *n* : a small anchor

¹keel \'kēl\ *n* **1** : the chief structural member of a ship running lengthwise along the center of its bottom **2** : something (as a bird's breastbone) like a ship's keel in form or use — **keeled** \'kēld\ *adj*

²keel *vb* : FAINT, SWOON — usu. used with *over*

keel·boat \'kēl-ˌbōt\ *n* : a shallow covered

keeled riverboat for freight that is usu. rowed, poled, or towed

keel·haul \-,hȯl\ *vb* : to haul under the keel of a ship as punishment

¹**keen** \'kēn\ *adj* **1** : SHARP ⟨a ~ knife⟩ **2** : SEVERE ⟨a ~ wind⟩ **3** : ENTHUSIASTIC ⟨~ about swimming⟩ **4** : mentally alert ⟨a ~ mind⟩ **5** : STRONG, ACUTE ⟨~ eyesight⟩ **6** : WONDERFUL, EXCELLENT — **keen·ly** *adv* — **keen·ness** *n*

²**keen** *n* : a lamentation for the dead uttered in a loud wailing voice or in a wordless cry — **keen** *vb*

¹**keep** \'kēp\ *vb* **kept** \'kept\; **keep·ing** **1** : FULFILL, OBSERVE ⟨~ a promise⟩ ⟨~ a holiday⟩ **2** : GUARD ⟨~ us from harm⟩; *also* : to take care of ⟨~ a neighbor's children⟩ **3** : MAINTAIN ⟨~ silence⟩ **4** : to have in one's service or at one's disposal ⟨~ a horse⟩ **5** : to preserve a record in ⟨~ a diary⟩ **6** : to have in stock for sale **7** : to retain in one's possession ⟨~ what you find⟩ **8** : to carry on (as a business) : CONDUCT **9** : HOLD, DETAIN ⟨~ him in jail⟩ **10** : to refrain from revealing ⟨~ a secret⟩ **11** : to continue in good condition ⟨meat will ~ in a freezer⟩ **12** : ABSTAIN, REFRAIN — **keep·er** *n*

²**keep** *n* **1** : FORTRESS **2** : the means or provisions by which one is kept — **for keeps 1** : with the provision that one keep what one has won ⟨play marbles *for keeps*⟩ **2** : PERMANENTLY ⟨came home *for keeps*⟩

keep·away \'kēp-ə-,wā\ *n* : a game in which players try to keep an object from one or more other players

keeping *n* : CONFORMITY ⟨in ~ with good taste⟩

keeping room *n* : a common room used for multiple purposes

keep·sake \'kēp-,sāk\ *n* : MEMENTO

keep up *vb* **1** : to persevere in **2** : MAINTAIN, SUSTAIN **3** : to keep informed **4** : to continue without interruption

keg \'keg\ *n* : a small cask or barrel

keg·ger \'ke-gər\ *n* : a party featuring one or more kegs of beer

keg·ler \'ke-glər\ *n* : ¹BOWLER

kelp \'kelp\ *n* : any of various coarse brown seaweeds; *also* : a mass of these or their ashes often used as fertilizer

kel·vin \'kel-vən\ *n* : a unit of temperature equal to ¹⁄₂₇₃.₁₆ of the Kelvin scale temperature of the triple point of water and equal to the Celsius degree

Kelvin *adj* : relating to, conforming to, or being a temperature scale according to which absolute zero is 0 K, the equivalent of −273.15°C

ken \'ken\ *n* **1** : range of vision : SIGHT **2** : range of understanding

ken·nel \'ke-nᵊl\ *n* : a shelter for a dog or cat; *also* : an establishment for the breeding or boarding of dogs or cats — **kennel** *vb*

ke·no \'kē-nō\ *n* : a game resembling bingo

ke·no·sis \kə-'nō-səs\ *n* : the relinquishment of divine attributes by Jesus Christ in becoming human — **ke·not·ic** \-'nä-tik\ *adj*

ken·te cloth \'ken-,tā-\ *n* : colorfully patterned cloth traditionally woven by hand in Ghana

Ken·tucky bluegrass \kən-'tə-kē-\ *n* : a valuable pasture and meadow grass of both Europe and America

Ke·ogh plan \'kē-(,)ō-\ *n* [Eugene James *Keogh* †1989 Am. politician] : an individual retirement account for the self-employed

ke·pi \'kā-pē, 'ke-\ *n* [F] : a military cap with a round flat top and a visor

ker·a·tin \'ker-ə-tən\ *n* : any of various sulfur-containing proteins that make up hair and horny tissues

kerb \'kərb\, *Brit* : CURB 3

ker·chief \'kər-chəf, -,chēf\ *n*, *pl* **kerchiefs** \-chəfs, -,chēfs\ *also* **kerchieves** \-,chēvz\ [ME *courchef*, fr. AF *coverchef*, *cuerchief*, fr. *coverir* to cover + *chef* head] **1** : a square of cloth worn esp. as a head covering **2** : HANDKERCHIEF

kerf \'kərf\ *n* : a slit or notch made by a saw or cutting torch

ker·nel \'kər-nᵊl\ *n* **1** : the inner softer part of a seed, fruit stone, or nut **2** : a whole seed of a cereal ⟨a ~ of corn⟩ **3** : a central or essential part : CORE

ker·o·sene *also* **ker·o·sine** \'ker-ə-,sēn, ,ker-ə-'sēn\ *n* : a flammable oil produced from petroleum and used for a fuel and as a solvent

kes·trel \'kes-trəl\ *n* : any of various small falcons that usu. hover in the air while searching for prey

ketch \'kech\ *n* : a large fore-and-aft rigged boat with two masts

ketch·up *also* **catch·up** \'ke-chəp, 'ka-\ *or* **cat·sup** \'ke-chəp, 'ka-; 'kat-səp\ *n* : a seasoned tomato puree

ket·tle \'ke-tᵊl\ *n* : a metallic vessel for boiling liquids

ket·tle·drum \-,drəm\ *n* : a brass, copper, or fiberglass drum with calfskin or plastic stretched across the top

¹**key** \'kē\ *n* **1** : a usu. metal instrument by which the bolt of a lock is turned; *also* : a device having the form or function of a key **2** : a means of gaining or preventing entrance, possession, or control **3** : EXPLANATION, SOLUTION **4** : one of the levers pressed by a finger in operating or playing an instrument **5** : a leading individual or principle **6** : a system of seven tones based on their relationship to a tonic; *also* : the tone or pitch of a voice **7** : a small switch for opening or closing an electric circuit ⟨a telegraph ~⟩

²**key** *vb* **1** : SECURE, FASTEN **2** : to regulate the musical pitch of **3** : to bring into harmony or conformity **4** : to make nervous — usu. used with *up*

³**key** *adj* : BASIC, CENTRAL ⟨~ issues⟩

⁴**key** *n* : a low island or reef (as off the southern coast of Florida)

⁵**key** *n*, *slang* : a kilogram esp. of marijuana or heroin

key·board \-,bȯrd\ *n* **1** : a row of keys (as on a piano) **2** : an assemblage of keys for operating a machine

key club *n* : a private club serving liquor and providing entertainment

key·hole \'kē-₂hōl\ *n* : a hole for receiving a key

¹**key·note** \-₂nōt\ *n* **1** : the first and harmonically fundamental tone of a scale **2** : the central fact, idea, or mood

²**keynote** *vb* **1** : to set the keynote of **2** : to deliver the major address (as at a convention) — **key·not·er** *n*

key·punch \'kē-₂pənch\ *n* : a machine with a keyboard used to cut holes or notches in punch cards — **keypunch** *vb* — **key·punch·er** *n*

key·stone \-₂stōn\ *n* : the wedge-shaped piece at the crown of an arch that locks the other pieces in place

key·stroke \-₂strōk\ *n* : an act or instance of depressing a key on a keyboard

key word *n* : a word that is a key; *esp, usu* **key·word** : a significant word from a title or document used esp. as an indication of the content

kg *abbr* kilogram

KGB *abbr* [Russ *Komitet gosudarstvennoĭ bezopasnosti*] (Soviet) State Security Committee

kha·ki \'ka-kē, 'kä-\ *n* [Hindi & Urdu *khākī* dust-colored, fr. *khāk* dust, fr. Pers] **1** : a light yellowish brown color **2** : a khaki-colored cloth; *also* : a military uniform of this cloth

khan \'kän, 'kan\ *n* : a Mongol leader; *esp* : a successor of Genghis Khan

khe·dive \kə-'dēv\ *n* : a ruler of Egypt from 1867 to 1914 governing as a viceroy of the sultan of Turkey

khoum \'küm\ *n* — see *ouguiya* at MONEY table

kHz *abbr* kilohertz

KIA *abbr* killed in action

kib·ble \'ki-bəl\ *vb* **kib·bled; kib·bling** : to grind coarsely — **kibble** *n*

kib·butz \ki-'bùts, -'büts\ *n, pl* **kib·but·zim** \-₂bùt-'sēm, -₂büt-\ [ModHeb *qibbūṣ*] : a communal farm or settlement in Israel

ki·bitz·er \'ki-bət-sər, kə-'bit-\ *n* : one who looks on and usu. offers unwanted advice — **ki·bitz** \'ki-bəts\ *vb*

ki·bosh \'kī-₂bäsh\ *n* : something that serves as a check or stop ⟨put the ∼ on his plan⟩

¹**kick** \'kik\ *vb* **1** : to strike out or hit with the foot; *also* : to score by kicking a ball **2** : to object strongly **3** : to recoil when fired — **kick·er** *n*

²**kick** *n* **1** : a blow or thrust with the foot; *esp* : a propelling of a ball with the foot **2** : the recoil of a gun **3** : a feeling or expression of objection **4** : stimulating effect esp. of pleasure

kick·back \'kik-₂bak\ *n* **1** : a sharp violent reaction **2** : a secret return of a part of a sum received

kick back *vb* : to assume a relaxed position or attitude

kick·box·ing \'kik-₂bäk-siŋ\ *n* : boxing in which boxers are permitted to kick with bare feet — **kick·box·er** \-sər\ *n*

kick in *vb* **1** : CONTRIBUTE **2** *slang* : DIE **3** : to begin operating or having an effect

kick·off \'kik-₂óf\ *n* **1** : a kick that puts

the ball in play (as in football) **2** : COMMENCEMENT ⟨campaign ∼⟩

kick off *vb* **1** : to start or resume play with a placekick **2** : to begin proceedings **3** *slang* : DIE

kick over *vb* : to begin or cause to begin to fire — used of an internal combustion engine

kick·shaw \'kik-₂shó\ *n* [modif. of F *quelque chose* something] **1** : DELICACY **2** : TRINKET

kick·stand \'kik-₂stand\ *n* : a swiveling metal bar attached to a 2-wheeled vehicle for holding it up when not in use

kick–start \'kik-₂stärt\ *vb* : JUMP-START

kicky \'ki-kē\ *adj* : providing a kick or thrill : EXCITING

¹**kid** \'kid\ *n* **1** : a young goat **2** : the flesh, fur, or skin of a young goat; *also* : something made of kid **3** : CHILD, YOUNGSTER — **kid·dish** *adj*

²**kid** *vb* **kid·ded; kid·ding** **1** : FOOL **2** : TEASE — **kid·der** *n* — **kid·ding·ly** *adv*

kid·do \'ki-dō\ *n, pl* **kiddos** — used as a familiar form of address ⟨you're okay, ∼⟩ **2** : CHILD, KID

kid·nap \'kid-₂nap\ *vb* **kid·napped** *also* **kid·naped** \-₂napt\; **kid·nap·ping** *also* **kid·nap·ing** \-₂na-piŋ\ : to hold or carry a person away by unlawful force or by fraud and against one's will — **kid·nap·per** *also* **kid·nap·er** \-₂na-pər\ *n*

kid·ney \'kid-nē\ *n, pl* **kidneys** : either of a pair of organs lying near the backbone that excrete waste products of the body in the form of urine

kidney bean *n* **1** : an edible seed of the common cultivated bean; *esp* : one that is large and dark red **2** : a plant bearing kidney beans

kid·skin \'kid-₂skin\ *n* : the skin of a young goat used for leather

kiel·ba·sa \kēl-'bä-sə, kil-\ *n, pl* **-basas** *also* **-ba·sy** \-'bä-sē\ [Pol *kiełbasa*] : a smoked sausage of Polish origin

¹**kill** \'kil\ *vb* **1** : to deprive of life **2** : to put an end to ⟨∼ competition⟩; *also* : DEFEAT ⟨∼ a proposed amendment⟩ **3** : USE UP ⟨∼ time⟩ **4** : to mark for omission • **Synonyms** SLAY, MURDER, ASSASSINATE, EXECUTE — **kill·er** *n*

²**kill** *n* **1** : an act of killing **2** : an animal or animals killed (as in a hunt); *also* : an aircraft, ship, or vehicle destroyed by military action

kill·deer \'kil-₂dir\ *n, pl* **killdeers** *or* **killdeer** [imit.] : an American plover with a plaintive penetrating cry

killer app \-'ap\ *n* : a component (as a computer application) that in itself makes something worth having or using

killer bee *n* : AFRICANIZED BEE

killer whale *n* : a small gregarious black and white flesh-eating whale with a white oval patch behind each eye

kill·ing *n* : a sudden notable gain or profit

killing field *n* : a scene of mass killing

kill·joy \'kil-₂jói\ *n* : one who spoils the pleasures of others

kiln \'kil, 'kiln\ *n* [ME *kilne*, fr. OE *cyln*, fr. L *culina* kitchen] : a heated enclosure (as an oven) for processing a substance by burning, firing, or drying — **kiln** vb

ki·lo \'kē-lō\ n, pl **kilos** : KILOGRAM

ki·lo·byte \'ki-lə-,bīt, 'kē-\ n : 1024 bytes

kilo·cy·cle \'ki-lə-,sī-kəl\ n : KILOHERTZ

ki·lo·gram \'kē-lə-,gram, 'ki-\ n 1 : the basic metric unit of mass that is nearly equal to the mass of 1000 cubic centimeters of water at its maximum density — see METRIC SYSTEM table 2 : the weight of a kilogram mass under earth's gravity

ki·lo·hertz \'ki-lə-,hərts, 'kē-, -,herts\ n : 1000 hertz

kilo·li·ter \'ki-lə-,lē-tər\ n — see METRIC SYSTEM table

ki·lo·me·ter \ki-'lä-mə-tər, 'ki-lə-,mē-\ n : a metric unit of length equal to 1000 meters — see METRIC SYSTEM table

ki·lo·ton \'ki-lə-,tən, 'kē-lō-\ n 1 : 1000 tons 2 : an explosive force equivalent to that of 1000 tons of TNT

ki·lo·volt \-,vōlt\ n : 1000 volts

kilo·watt \'ki-lə-,wät\ n : 1000 watts

kilowatt–hour n : a unit of energy equal to that expended by one kilowatt in one hour

kilt \'kilt\ n : a knee-length pleated skirt usu. of tartan worn by men in Scotland

kil·ter \'kil-tər\ n : proper condition ⟨out of ∼⟩

ki·mo·no \kə-'mō-nə\ n, pl **-nos** 1 : a loose robe with wide sleeves traditionally worn with a wide sash as an outer garment by the Japanese 2 : a loose dressing gown or jacket

kin \'kin\ n 1 : an individual's relatives 2 : KINSMAN

ki·na \'kē-nə\ n, pl **kina** — see MONEY table

ki·na·ra \kē-'nä-rə\ n : a candelabra with seven candlesticks used during Kwanzaa

¹**kind** \'kīnd\ n 1 : essential quality or character 2 : a group united by common traits or interests : CATEGORY; also : VARIETY 3 : goods or commodities as distinguished from money

²**kind** adj 1 : of a sympathetic, forbearing, or pleasant nature 2 : arising from sympathy or forbearance ⟨∼ deeds⟩ ♦ **Synonyms** BENEVOLENT, BENIGN, BENIGNANT, KINDLY — **kind·ness** n

kin·der·gar·ten \'kin-dər-,gär-t²n\ n [G, lit., children's garden] : a school or class for children usu. from four to six years old

kin·der·gart·ner \-,gärt-nər\ n 1 : a kindergarten teacher 2 : a kindergarten pupil

kind·heart·ed \,kīnd-'här-təd\ adj : marked by a sympathetic nature

kin·dle \'kin-d²l\ vb **kin·dled; kin·dling** 1 : to set on fire : start burning 2 : to stir up : AROUSE 3 : ILLUMINATE, GLOW

kin·dling \'kind-liŋ, 'kin-lən\ n : easily combustible material for starting a fire

¹**kind·ly** \'kīnd-lē\ adj **kind·li·er; -est** 1 : of an agreeable or beneficial nature 2 : of a sympathetic or generous nature — **kind·li·ness** n

²**kindly** adv 1 : READILY ⟨does not take

∼ to criticism⟩ 2 : SYMPATHETICALLY 3 : COURTEOUSLY, OBLIGINGLY

kind of adv : to a moderate degree ⟨it's kind of late to begin⟩

¹**kin·dred** \'kin-drəd\ n 1 : a group of related individuals 2 : one's relatives

²**kindred** adj : of a like nature or character

kine \'kīn\ archaic pl of COW

kin·e·ma \'ki-nə-mə\ Brit var of CINEMA

ki·ne·mat·ics \,ki-nə-'ma-tiks\ n : a science that deals with motion apart from considerations of mass and force — **ki·ne·mat·ic** \-tik\ or **ki·ne·mat·i·cal** \-ti-kəl\ adj

kin·es·the·sia \,ki-nəs-'thē-zhə, -zhē-ə\ or **kin·es·the·sis** \-'thē-səs\ n, pl **-the·sias** or **-the·ses** \-,sēz\ : a sense that perceives bodily movement, position, and weight and is mediated by nervous receptors in tendons, muscles, and joints; also : sensory experience derived from this sense — **kin·es·thet·ic** \-'the-tik\ adj

ki·net·ic \kə-'ne-tik\ adj : of or relating to the motion of material bodies or the forces and energy (**kinetic energy**) associated with them

ki·net·ics \-tiks\ n sing or pl : a science that deals with the effects of forces upon the motions of material bodies or with changes in a physical or chemical system

kin·folk \'kin-,fōk\ or **kinfolks** n pl : RELATIVES

king \'kiŋ\ n 1 : a male sovereign 2 : a chief among competitors ⟨home-run ∼⟩ 3 : the principal piece in the game of chess 4 : a playing card bearing the figure of a king 5 : a checker that has been crowned — **king·less** adj — **king·ly** adj — **king·ship** n

king crab n 1 : HORSESHOE CRAB 2 : a large crab of the No. Pacific caught commercially for food

king·dom \'kiŋ-dəm\ n 1 : a country whose head is a king or queen 2 : a realm or region in which something or someone is dominant ⟨a cattle ∼⟩ 3 : one of the three primary divisions of lifeless material, plants, and animals into which natural objects are grouped; also : a biological category that ranks above the phylum

king·fish·er \-,fi-shər\ n : any of numerous usu. bright-colored crested birds that feed chiefly on fish

king·pin \'kiŋ-,pin\ n 1 : HEADPIN 2 : the leader in a group or undertaking

Kings n — see BIBLE table

king–size \'kiŋ-,sīz\ or **king–sized** \-,sīzd\ adj 1 : longer than the regular or standard size 2 : unusually large 3 : having dimensions of about 76 by 80 inches (1.9 by 2.0 meters) ⟨a ∼ bed⟩; also : of a size that fits a king-size bed

kink \'kiŋk\ n 1 : a short tight twist or curl 2 : a mental peculiarity : QUIRK 3 : CRAMP ⟨a ∼ in the back⟩ 4 : an imperfection likely to cause difficulties in operation — **kinky** adj

kin·ship \'kin-,ship\ n : RELATIONSHIP

kins·man \'kinz-mən\ n : RELATIVE; esp : a male relative

kins·wom·an \-ˌwu̇-mən\ *n* : a female relative

ki·osk \ˈkē-ˌäsk\ *n* **1** : a small structure with one or more open sides **2** : a stand-alone device providing information and services on a computer screen ⟨interactive ∼*s* at the museum⟩

Ki·o·wa \ˈkī-ə-ˌwȯ, -ˌwä, -ˌwä\ *n, pl* **Kiowa** *or* **Kiowas** : a member of an American Indian people of Colorado, Kansas, New Mexico, Oklahoma, and Texas

kip \ˈkip, ˈgip\ *n, pl* **kip** *or* **kips** — see MONEY table

kip·per \ˈki-pər\ *n* : a fish (as a herring) preserved by salting and drying or smoking — **kipper** *vb*

kirk \ˈkərk, ˈkirk\ *n, chiefly Scot* : CHURCH

kir·tle \ˈkər-tᵊl\ *n* : a long gown or dress worn by women

kis·met \ˈkiz-ˌmet, -mət\ *n, often cap* [Turk., fr. *ar qisma* portion, lot] : FATE

¹kiss \ˈkis\ *vb* **1** : to touch or caress with the lips as a mark of affection or greeting **2** : to touch gently or lightly

²kiss *n* **1** : a caress with the lips **2** : a gentle touch or contact **3** : a bite-size candy

kiss·er \ˈki-sər\ *n* **1** : one that kisses **2** *slang* : MOUTH **3** *slang* : FACE

kit \ˈkit\ *n* **1** : a set of articles for personal use; *also* : a set of tools or implements or of parts to be assembled **2** : a container (as a case) for a kit

kitch·en \ˈki-chən\ *n* **1** : a room with cooking facilities **2** : the personnel that prepares, cooks, and serves food

kitch·en·ette \ˌki-chə-ˈnet\ *n* : a small kitchen or an alcove containing cooking facilities

kitchen police *n* **1** : KP **2** : the work of KPs

kitch·en·ware \ˈki-chən-ˌwer\ *n* : utensils and appliances for kitchen use

kite \ˈkīt\ *n* **1** : any of various long-winged hawks often with deeply forked tails **2** : a light frame covered with paper or cloth and designed to be flown in the air at the end of a long string

kith \ˈkith\ *n* [ME, fr. OE *cȳthth*, fr. *cūth* known] : familiar friends, neighbors, or relatives ⟨∼ and kin⟩

kitsch \ˈkich\ *n* [G] : something often of poor quality that appeals to popular or lowbrow taste — **kitschy** \ˈki-chē\ *adj*

kit·ten \ˈki-tᵊn\ *n* : a young cat — **kit·ten·ish** *adj*

¹kit·ty \ˈki-tē\ *n, pl* **kitties** : CAT; *esp* : KITTEN

²kitty *n, pl* **kitties** : a fund in a poker game made up of contributions from each pot; *also* : POOL

kit·ty–cor·ner *also* **cat·ty–cor·ner** *or* **cat·er–cor·ner** \ˈki-tē-ˌkȯr-nər, ˈka-; ˈka-tə-\ *or* **kit·ty–cor·nered** *or* **cat·ty–cor·nered** *or* **cat·er–cornered** \-nərd\ *adv or adj* : in a diagonal or oblique position

ki·wi \ˈkē-(ˌ)wē\ *n* **1** : any of a small genus of flightless New Zealand birds **2** : KIWIFRUIT

ki·wi·fruit \-ˌfrüt\ *n* : a brownish hairy egg-shaped fruit of a subtropical vine that has sweet bright green flesh and small edible black seeds

KJV *abbr* King James Version

KKK *abbr* Ku Klux Klan

kl *abbr* kiloliter

klatch *also* **klatsch** \ˈklach\ *n* [G *Klatsch* gossip] : a gathering marked by informal conversation

klep·toc·ra·cy \klep-ˈtä-krə-sē\ *n, pl* **-cies** : government by those who seek chiefly status and personal gain at the expense of the governed

klep·to·ma·nia \ˌklep-tə-ˈmā-nē-ə\ *n* : a persistent neurotic impulse to steal esp. without economic motive — **klep·to·ma·ni·ac** \-nē-ˌak\ *n*

klieg light *or* **kleig light** \ˈklēg-\ *n* : a very bright lamp used in making motion pictures

klutz \ˈkləts\ *n* [Yiddish *klots*, lit., wooden beam] : a clumsy person — **klutzy** *adj*

km *abbr* kilometer

kn *abbr* knot

knack \ˈnak\ *n* **1** : a clever way of doing something **2** : natural aptitude

knap·sack \ˈnap-ˌsak\ *n* : a bag (as of canvas) strapped on the back and used esp. for carrying supplies

knave \ˈnāv\ *n* **1** : ROGUE **2** : JACK 6 — **knav·ery** \ˈnā-və-rē\ *n* — **knav·ish** \ˈnā-vish\ *adj*

knead \ˈnēd\ *vb* : to work and press into a mass with the hands; *also* : MASSAGE — **knead·er** *n*

knee \ˈnē\ *n* : the joint in the middle part of the leg — **kneed** \ˈnēd\ *adj*

knee·cap \ˈnē-ˌkap\ *n* : a thick flat triangular movable bone forming the front of the knee

knee·hole \-ˌhōl\ *n* : a space (as under a desk) for the knees

knee–jerk \ˈnē-ˌjərk\ *adj* : readily predictable ⟨a ∼ reaction⟩

kneel \ˈnēl\ *vb* **knelt** \ˈnelt\ *or* **kneeled**; **kneel·ing** : to bend the knee : fall or rest on the knees

¹knell \ˈnel\ *vb* **1** : to ring esp. for a death or disaster **2** : to summon, announce, or proclaim by a knell

²knell *n* **1** : a stroke of a bell esp. when tolled (as for a funeral) **2** : an indication of the end or failure of something

knew *past of* KNOW

knick·ers \ˈni-kərz\ *n pl* : loose-fitting short pants gathered at the knee

knick·knack \ˈnik-ˌnak\ *n* : a small trivial article intended for ornament

¹knife \ˈnīf\ *n, pl* **knives** \ˈnīvz\ **1** : a cutting instrument consisting of a sharp blade fastened to a handle **2** : a sharp cutting tool in a machine

²knife *vb* **knifed**; **knif·ing** : to stab, slash, or wound with a knife

¹knight \ˈnīt\ *n* **1** : a mounted warrior of feudal times serving a king **2** : a man honored by a sovereign for merit and in Great Britain ranking below a baronet **3** : a man devoted to the service of a lady **4** : a member of an order or society **5** : a chess piece having an L-shaped move — **knight·ly** *adj*

²knight *vb* : to make a knight of

knight·hood \ˈnīt-ˌhu̇d\ *n* **1** : the rank,

dignity, or profession of a knight **2** : CHIVALRY **3** : knights as a class or body

knish \kə-'nish\ *n* [Yiddish] : a small round or square of dough stuffed with a filling (as of meat or fruit) and baked or fried

¹knit \'nit\ *vb* **knit** *or* **knit·ted; knit·ting 1** : to link firmly or closely **2** : WRINKLE ⟨∼ her brows⟩ **3** : to form a fabric by interlacing yarn or thread in connected loops with needles **4** : to grow together — **knit·ter** *n*

²knit *n* **1** : a basic knitting stitch **2** : a knitted garment or fabric

knit·wear \-ˌwer\ *n* : knitted clothing

knob \'näb\ *n* **1** : a rounded protuberance; *also* : a small rounded ornament or handle **2** : a rounded usu. isolated hill — **knobbed** \'näbd\ *adj* — **knob·by** \'nä-bē\ *adj*

¹knock \'näk\ *vb* **1** : to strike with a sharp blow **2** : BUMP, COLLIDE **3** : to make a pounding noise; *esp* : to have engine knock **4** : to find fault with

²knock *n* **1** : a sharp blow **2** : a pounding noise; *esp* : one caused by abnormal ignition in an automobile engine

knock–down \'näk-ˌdaùn\ *n* **1** : the action of knocking down **2** : something (as a blow) that knocks down **3** : something that can be easily assembled or disassembled

knock down *vb* **1** : to strike to the ground with or as if with a sharp blow **2** : to take apart : DISASSEMBLE **3** : to receive as income or salary : EARN **4** : to make a reduction in

knock·er \'nä-kər\ *n* : one that knocks; *esp* : a device hinged to a door for use in knocking

knock–knee \'näk-ˌnē\ *n* : a condition in which the legs curve inward at the knees — **knock–kneed** \-ˌnēd\ *adj*

knock–off \'näk-ˌȯf\ *n* : a copy or imitation of someone or something popular

knock off *vb* **1** : to stop doing something **2** : to do quickly, carelessly, or routinely **3** : to deduct from a price **4** : KILL **5** : ROB **6** : COPY, IMITATE

knock·out \'näk-ˌaùt\ *n* **1** : a blow that fells and immobilizes an opponent (as in boxing) **2** : something sensationally striking or attractive

knock out *vb* **1** : to defeat by a knockout **2** : to make unconscious or inoperative **3** : to tire out : EXHAUST

knock·wurst *also* **knack·wurst** \'näk-ˌwərst, -ˌvùrst\ *n* : a short thick heavily seasoned sausage

knoll \'nōl\ *n* : a small round hill

¹knot \'nät\ *n* **1** : an interlacing (as of string) forming a lump or knob and often used for fastening or tying together **2** : PROBLEM **3** : a bond of union; *esp* : the marriage bond **4** : a protuberant lump or swelling in tissue **5** : a rounded cross-grained area in lumber that is a section through the junction of a tree branch with the trunk; *also* : the woody tissue forming this junction in a tree **6** : GROUP, CLUSTER **7** : an ornamental

bow of ribbon **8** : one nautical mile per hour; *also* : one nautical mile — **knot·ty** *adj*

²knot *vb* **knot·ted; knot·ting 1** : to tie in or with a knot **2** : ENTANGLE

knot–hole \-ˌhōl\ *n* : a hole in a board or tree trunk where a knot has come out

knout \'naùt, 'nüt\ *n* : a whip used for flogging

know \'nō\ *vb* **knew** \'nü, 'nyü\; **known** \'nōn\; **know·ing 1** : to perceive directly : have understanding or direct cognition of; *also* : to recognize the nature of **2** : to be acquainted or familiar with **3** : to be aware of the truth of **4** : to have a practical understanding of — **know·able** *adj* — **know·er** *n* — **in the know** : possessing confidential information

know–how \'nō-ˌhaù\ *n* : knowledge of how to do something smoothly and efficiently

knowing *adj* **1** : having or reflecting knowledge, intelligence, or information **2** : shrewdly and keenly alert **3** : DELIBERATE ⟨∼ interference⟩ ♦ **Synonyms** CLEVER, BRIGHT, SMART — **know·ing·ly** *adv*

knowl·edge \'nä-lij\ *n* **1** : understanding gained by actual experience ⟨a ∼ of carpentry⟩ **2** : range of information ⟨to the best of my ∼⟩ **3** : clear perception of truth **4** : something learned and kept in the mind

knowl·edge·able \'nä-li-jə-bəl\ *adj* : having or showing knowledge or intelligence

knuck·le \'nə-kəl\ *n* : the rounded knob at a joint and esp. at a finger joint

knuckle down *vb* : to apply oneself earnestly

knuckle under *vb* : SUBMIT, SURRENDER

knurl \'nərl\ *n* **1** : KNOB **2** : one of a series of small ridges on a metal surface to aid in gripping — **knurled** \'nərld\ *adj* — **knurly** *adj*

¹KO \(ˌ)kā-'ō, 'kā-ˌō\ *n* : KNOCKOUT

²KO *vb* **KO'd; KO'·ing** : to knock out in boxing

ko·ala \kō-'ä-lə\ *n* : a gray furry Australian marsupial that has large hairy ears and feeds on eucalyptus leaves

ko·bo \'kō-(ˌ)bō\ *n, pl* **kobo** — see *naira* at MONEY table

K of C *abbr* Knights of Columbus

kohl·ra·bi \kōl-'rä-bē\ *n, pl* **-bies** [G, fr. It *cavolo rapa*, lit., cabbage turnip] : a cabbage that forms no head but has a swollen fleshy edible stem

koi \'kȯi\ *n, pl* **koi** [Jp] : a carp bred for large size and a variety of colors and often stocked in ornamental ponds

ko·lin·sky \kə-'lin-skē\ *n, pl* **-skies** : the fur of various Asian minks

Ko·mo·do dragon \kə-'mō-dō-\ *n* [*Komodo* Island, Indonesia] : a carnivorous lizard of Indonesia that is the largest of all known lizards

kook \'kük\ *n* : SCREWBALL 2

kooky *also* **kook·ie** \'kü-kē\ *adj* **kook·i·er; -est** : having the characteristics of a kook : CRAZY, ECCENTRIC — **kook·i·ness** *n*

Koo·te·nai or **Ku·te·nai** \'kü-tə-,nä\ n, pl **-nai** or **-nais** : a member of an American Indian people of the Rocky Mountains in both the U.S. and Canada; also : their language

ko·peck or **ko·pek** \'kō-,pek\ n [Russ kopeĭka] — see **ruble** at MONEY table

ko·piy·ka \,kō-'pē-kə\ n — see **hryvnia** at MONEY table

ko·ra \'kòr-ə\ n : a 21-stringed African musical instrument

Ko·ran \kə-'ran, -'rän\ n [Ar qur'ān] : a sacred book of Islam that contains revelations made to Muhammad by Allah

ko·ru·na \'kòr-ə-,nä\ n, pl **ko·ru·ny** \-ə-nē\ or **korunas** or **ko·run** \-ən\ — see MONEY table

ko·sher \'kō-shər\ adj [Yiddish, fr. Heb kāshēr fit, proper] 1 : ritually fit for use according to Jewish law 2 : selling or serving kosher food

kow·tow \kaù-'taù, 'kaù-,taù\ vb [Chin kòutóu, fr. kòu to knock + tóu head] 1 : to show obsequious deference 2 : to kneel and touch the forehead to the ground as a sign of homage or deep respect

KP \,kā-'pē\ n 1 : an enlisted man detailed to help the cooks in a military mess 2 : the work of KPs

kph abbr kilometers per hour

Kr symbol krypton

kraal \'kräl, 'kròl\ n 1 : a native village in southern Africa 2 : an enclosure for domestic animals in southern Africa

kraut \'kraùt\ n : SAUERKRAUT

Krem·lin \'krem-lən\ n : the Russian government

Krem·lin·ol·o·gist \,krem-lə-'nä-lə-jist\ n : a specialist in the policies and practices of the government of the Soviet Union

¹**kro·na** \'krō-nə\ n, pl **kro·nor** \-,nór\ [Sw] — see MONEY table

²**kro·na** \'krō-nə\ n, pl **kro·nur** \-nər\ [Icel] — see MONEY table

kro·ne \'krō-nə\ n, pl **kro·ner** \-nər\ — see MONEY table

kroon \'krōn\ n, pl **kroo·ni** \'krō-nē\ or **kroons** — see MONEY table

Kru·ger·rand \'krü-gər-,rand, -,ränd\ n : a 1-ounce gold coin of the Republic of South Africa

kryp·ton \'krip-,tän\ n : a gaseous chemical element used esp. in electric lamps

KS abbr Kansas

kt abbr 1 karat 2 knight

ku·do \'kü-dō, 'kyü-\ n, pl **kudos** [fr. kudos (taken as pl.)] 1 : AWARD, HONOR 2 : COMPLIMENT, PRAISE

ku·dos \'kü-,däs, 'kyü-\ n : fame and renown resulting from achievement

kud·zu \'kùd-zü, 'kəd-\ n [Jp kuzu] : a fast-growing weedy leguminous vine used for forage and erosion control

ku·lak \kü-'lak, kyü-, -'läk\ n [Russ, lit., fist] 1 : a wealthy peasant farmer in 19th century Russia 2 : a farmer characterized by Communists as too wealthy

kum·quat \'kəm-,kwät\ n : any of several small citrus fruits with sweet spongy rind and acid pulp

ku·na \'kü-,nä\ n, pl **kuna** or **ku·ne** \-nä\ — see MONEY table

kung fu \,kəŋ-'fü, ,kùŋ-\ n : a Chinese art of self-defense resembling karate

kung pao \'kəŋ-'paù, 'kùŋ-, 'kùŋ-\ adj : being stir-fried or deep-fried and served in a spicy hot sauce usu. with peanuts

kur·ta \'kər-tə\ n : a long loose-fitting collarless shirt

ku·rus \kə-'rüsh\ n, pl **kurus** — see **lira** at MONEY table

kV abbr kilovolt

kvell \'kvel\ vb : to be extraordinarily proud

kvetch \'kvech, 'kfech\ vb : to complain habitually — **kvetch** n

kW abbr kilowatt

kwa·cha \'kwä-chə\ n, pl **kwacha** — see MONEY table

kwan·za \'kwän-zə\ n, pl **kwanzas** or **kwanza** — see MONEY table

Kwan·zaa also **Kwan·za** \'kwän-zə\ n [Swahili kwanza first] : an African-American cultural festival held from December 26 to January 1

kwash·i·or·kor \,kwä-shē-'òr-kòr, -òr-'kòr\ n : a disease of young children caused by deficient intake of protein

kWh abbr kilowatt-hour

Ky or **KY** abbr Kentucky

kyat \'chät\ n, pl **kyats** or **kyat** — see MONEY table

ky·bosh chiefly Brit var of KIBOSH

¹**l** \'el\ n, pl **l's** or **ls** \'elz\ often cap : the 12th letter of the English alphabet

²**l** abbr, often cap 1 lake 2 large 3 left 4 [L libra] pound 5 line 6 liter

¹**La** abbr Louisiana

²**La** symbol lanthanum

LA abbr 1 law agent 2 Los Angeles 3 Louisiana

laa·ri \'lä-rē\ n, pl **laari** — see **rufiyaa** at MONEY table

lab \'lab\ n : LABORATORY

Lab n : LABRADOR RETRIEVER

¹**la·bel** \'lā-bəl\ n 1 : a slip attached to something for identification or description 2 : a descriptive or identifying word or phrase 3 : BRAND 3

²**label** vb **-beled** or **-belled; -bel·ing** or **-bel·ling** 1 : to affix a label to 2 : to describe or name with a label

la·bi·al \'lā-bē-əl\ adj : of, relating to, or situated near the lips or labia

la·bia ma·jo·ra \'lā-bē-ə-mə-'jór-ə\ n pl : the outer fatty folds of the vulva

labia mi·no·ra \-mə-ˈnȯr-ə\ *n pl* : the inner highly vascular folds of the vulva

la·bile \ˈlā-ˌbī(-ə)l, -bəl\ *adj* 1 : UNSTABLE 2 : ADAPTABLE

la·bi·um \ˈlā-bē-əm\ *n, pl* **la·bia** \-ə\ [NL, fr. L, lip] : any of the folds at the margin of the vulva

¹**la·bor** \ˈlā-bər\ *n* 1 : physical or mental effort; *also* : human activity that provides the goods or services in an economy 2 : the physical efforts of giving birth; *also* : the period of such labor 3 : TASK 4 : those who do manual labor or work for wages; *also* : labor unions or their officials

²**labor** *vb* 1 : WORK 2 : to move with great effort 3 : to be in the labor of giving birth 4 : to suffer from some disadvantage or distress ⟨∼ under a delusion⟩ 5 : to treat or work out laboriously — **la·bor·er** *n*

lab·o·ra·to·ry \ˈla-brə-ˌtȯr-ē, -brə-rə-\ *n, pl* **-ries** : a place equipped for making scientific experiments or tests

Labor Day *n* : the 1st Monday in September observed as a legal holiday in recognition of the working people

la·bored \ˈlā-bərd\ *adj* : not freely or easily done ⟨∼ breathing⟩

la·bo·ri·ous \lə-ˈbȯr-ē-əs\ *adj* 1 : INDUSTRIOUS 2 : requiring great effort — **la·bo·ri·ous·ly** *adv*

la·bor-sav·ing \ˈlā-bər-ˌsā-viŋ\ *adj* : designed to replace or decrease labor

labor union *n* : an organization of workers formed to advance its members' interest in respect to wages and working conditions

la·bour *chiefly Brit var of* LABOR

lab·ra·dor·ite \ˈla-brə-ˌdȯr-ˌīt\ *n* : an iridescent feldspar used in jewelry

Lab·ra·dor retriever \ˈla-brə-ˌdȯr-\ *n* : any of a breed of strongly built retrievers having a short dense black, yellow, or chocolate coat

la·bur·num \lə-ˈbər-nəm\ *n* : any of a genus of leguminous shrubs or trees with hanging clusters of yellow flowers

lab·y·rinth \ˈla-bə-ˌrinth\ *n* : a place constructed of or filled with confusing intricate passageways : MAZE

lab·y·rin·thine \ˌla-bə-ˈrin-thən, -ˌthīn, -ˌthēn\ *adj* : INTRICATE, INVOLVED

lac \ˈlak\ *n* : a resinous substance secreted by a scale insect and used chiefly in the form of shellac

¹**lace** \ˈlās\ *vb* **laced; lac·ing** 1 : TIE 2 : to adorn with lace 3 : INTERTWINE 4 : BEAT, LASH 5 : to add something that taints (as a drug) or enhances flavor (as a spice) 6 : to criticize sharply — used with *into*

²**lace** *n* [ME, fr. AF *lace, laz,* fr. L *laqueus* snare] 1 : a cord or string used for drawing together two edges 2 : an ornamental braid 3 : a fine openwork usu. figured fabric made of thread — **lacy** \ˈlā-sē\ *adj*

lac·er·ate \ˈla-sə-ˌrāt\ *vb* **-at·ed; -at·ing** : to tear roughly — **lac·er·a·tion** \ˌla-sə-ˈrā-shən\ *n*

lace·wing \ˈlās-ˌwiŋ\ *n* : any of various insects with delicate wing veins, long antennae, and often brilliant eyes

lach·ry·mal *or* **lac·ri·mal** \ˈla-krə-məl\ *adj* 1 *usu* lacrimal : of, relating to, or being glands that produce tears 2 : of, relating to, or marked by tears

lach·ry·mose \ˈla-krə-ˌmōs\ *adj* 1 : TEARFUL 2 : MOURNFUL

¹**lack** \ˈlak\ *vb* 1 : to be wanting or missing 2 : to be deficient in

²**lack** *n* : the fact or state of being wanting or deficient : NEED

lack·a·dai·si·cal \ˌla-kə-ˈdā-zi-kəl\ *adj* : lacking life, spirit, or zest — **lack·a·dai·si·cal·ly** \-k(ə-)lē\ *adv*

lack·ey \ˈla-kē\ *n, pl* **lackeys** 1 : FOOTMAN, SERVANT 2 : TOADY

lack·lus·ter \ˈlak-ˌləs-tər\ *adj* : DULL

la·con·ic \lə-ˈkä-nik\ *adj* [L *laconicus* Spartan, fr. Gk *lakōnikos;* fr. the Spartan reputation for terseness of speech] : sparing of words : TERSE ✦ **Synonyms** CONCISE, CURT, SHORT, SUCCINCT, BRUSQUE — **la·con·i·cal·ly** \-ni-k(ə-)lē\ *adv*

lac·quer \ˈla-kər\ *n* : a clear or colored usu. glossy and quick-drying surface coating — **lacquer** *vb*

lac·ri·ma·tion \ˌla-krə-ˈmā-shən\ *n* : secretion of tears

la·crosse \lə-ˈkrȯs\ *n* [CanF *la crosse,* lit., the crooked stick] : a goal game in which players use a long-handled triangular-headed stick having a mesh pouch for catching, carrying, and throwing the ball

lac·tate \ˈlak-ˌtāt\ *vb* **lac·tat·ed; lac·tat·ing** : to secrete milk — **lac·ta·tion** \lak-ˈtā-shən\ *n*

lac·tic \ˈlak-tik\ *adj* 1 : of or relating to milk 2 : obtained from sour milk or whey

lactic acid *n* : a syrupy acid present in blood and muscle tissue and used esp. in food and medicine

lac·tose \ˈlak-ˌtōs\ *n* : a sugar present in milk

la·cu·na \lə-ˈkü-nə, -ˈkyü-\ *n, pl* **la·cu·nae** \-nē\ *also* **la·cu·nas** [L, pool, pit, gap, fr. *lacus* lake] : a blank space or missing part : GAP, DEFICIENCY

lad \ˈlad\ *n* : YOUTH; *also* : FELLOW

lad·der \ˈla-dər\ *n* 1 : a structure for climbing that consists of two parallel sidepieces joined at intervals by crosspieces 2 : something resembling a ladder in having ascending steps or stages ⟨a tournament ∼⟩

lad·die \ˈla-dē\ *n* : a young lad

lad·en \ˈlā-dᵊn\ *adj* : LOADED, BURDENED

lad·ing \ˈlā-diŋ\ *n* : CARGO, FREIGHT

la·dle \ˈlā-dᵊl\ *n* : a deep-bowled long-handled spoon used in taking up and conveying liquids — **ladle** *vb*

la·dy \ˈlā-dē\ *n, pl* **ladies** [ME, fr. OE *hlǣfdīge,* fr. *hlāf* bread + *-dīge* (akin to *dǣge* kneader of bread)] 1 : a woman of property, rank, or authority; *also* : a woman of superior social position or of refinement 2 : WOMAN 3 : WIFE

lady beetle *n* : LADYBUG

la·dy·bird \ˈlā-dē-ˌbərd\ *n* : LADYBUG

la·dy·bug \-ˌbəg\ *n* : any of various small nearly hemispherical and usu. brightly colored beetles that feed mostly on other insects

la·dy·fin·ger \-ˌfiŋ-gər\ n : a small finger-shaped sponge cake

lady–in–waiting n, pl **ladies–in–waiting** : a lady appointed to attend or wait on a queen or princess

la·dy·like \ˈlā-dē-ˌlīk\ adj : WELL-BRED

la·dy·ship \-ˌship\ n : the condition of being a lady : rank of lady

lady's slipper also **lady slipper** n : any of several No. American orchids with slipper-shaped flowers

¹lag \ˈlag\ n 1 : a slowing up or falling behind; also : the amount by which one lags 2 : INTERVAL

²lag vb **lagged; lag·ging** 1 : to fail to keep up : stay behind 2 : to slacken gradually ◆ **Synonyms** DAWDLE, DALLY, TARRY, LOITER

la·ger \ˈlä-gər\ n : a usu. dry beer slowly brewed and matured under refrigeration

lag·gard \ˈla-gərd\ adj : tending to lag ⟨~ workers⟩ — **laggard** n — **lag·gard·ly** adv or adj — **lag·gard·ness** n

la·gniappe \ˈlan-ˌyap\ n : something given free esp. with a purchase

la·goon \lə-ˈgün\ n : a shallow sound, channel, or pond near or connected to a larger body of water

laid past and past part of LAY

laid–back \ˈlād-ˈbak\ adj : having a relaxed style or character ⟨~ music⟩

lain past part of ¹LIE

lair \ˈler\ n 1 : the resting or living place of a wild animal : DEN 2 : a usu. hidden refuge

laird \ˈlerd\ n, chiefly Scot : a landed proprietor

lais·ser–faire chiefly Brit var of LAISSEZ-FAIRE

lais·sez–faire \ˌle-ˌsā-ˈfer, ˌlā-, -ˌzā-\ n [F laissez faire let do] : a doctrine opposing governmental control of economic affairs beyond that necessary to maintain peace and property rights

la·ity \ˈlā-ə-tē\ n 1 : the people of a religious faith as distinct from its clergy 2 : the mass of people as distinct from those of a particular field

lake \ˈlāk\ n : an inland body of standing water of considerable size; also : a pool of liquid (as lava or pitch)

La·ko·ta \lə-ˈkō-tə\ n, pl Lakota also Lakotas : a member of a western division of the Dakota peoples; also : their language

¹lam \ˈlam\ vb **lammed; lam·ming** : to flee hastily — **lam** n

²lam abbr laminated

Lam abbr Lamentations

la·ma \ˈlä-mə\ n : a Buddhist monk of Tibet or Mongolia

la·ma·sery \ˈlä-mə-ˌser-ē\ n, pl -ser·ies : a monastery for lamas

¹lamb \ˈlam\ n 1 : a young sheep; also : its flesh used as food 2 : an innocent or gentle person

²lamb vb : to bring forth a lamb

lam·baste or **lam·bast** \lam-ˈbāst, -ˈbast\ vb 1 : BEAT 2 : EXCORIATE ◆ **Synonyms** CASTIGATE, FLAY, LASH

lamb·da \ˈlam-də\ n : the 11th letter of the Greek alphabet — Λ or λ

lam·bent \ˈlam-bənt\ adj [L lambens, prp. of lambere to lick] 1 : FLICKERING ⟨a ~ flame⟩ 2 : softly radiant ⟨~ eyes⟩ 3 : marked by lightness or brilliance ⟨~ humor⟩ ◆ **Synonyms** EFFULGENT, IN-CANDESCENT, LUCENT, LUMINOUS — **lam·ben·cy** \-bən-sē\ n — **lam·bent·ly** adv

lamb·skin \ˈlam-ˌskin\ n : a lamb's skin or a small fine-grade sheepskin or the leather made from either

¹lame \ˈlām\ adj **lam·er; lam·est** 1 : having a body part and esp. a limb so disabled as to impair freedom of movement; also : marked by stiffness and soreness 2 : lacking substance : WEAK ⟨~ excuses⟩ 3 : INFERIOR, PITIFUL — **lame·ly** adv — **lame·ness** n

²lame vb **lamed; lam·ing** : to make lame : DISABLE

la·mé \lä-ˈmā, la-\ n [F] : a brocaded clothing fabric with tinsel filling threads (as of gold or silver)

lame·brain \ˈlām-ˌbrān\ n : DOLT

lame duck n : an elected official continuing to hold office between an election and the inauguration of a successor — **lame–duck** adj

la·ment \lə-ˈment\ vb 1 : to mourn aloud : WAIL 2 : to express sorrow or regret for : BEWAIL — **lam·en·ta·ble** \ˈla-mən-tə-bəl, lə-ˈmen-tə-\ adj — **lam·en·ta·bly** \-blē\ adv — **lam·en·ta·tion** \ˌla-mən-ˈtā-shən\ n

²lament n 1 : a crying out in grief : WAIL 2 : DIRGE, ELEGY 3 : COMPLAINT

Lamentations n — see BIBLE table

la·mia \ˈlā-mē-ə\ n : a female demon

lam·i·na \ˈla-mə-nə\ n, pl **-nae** \-ˌnē\ or **-nas** : a thin plate or scale

¹lam·i·nate \ˈla-mə-ˌnāt\ vb **-nat·ed; -nat·ing** : to make by uniting layers of one or more materials — **lam·i·na·tion** \ˌla-mə-ˈnā-shən\ n

²lam·i·nate \-nət\ n : a product manufactured by laminating

lamp \ˈlamp\ n 1 : a vessel with a wick for burning a flammable liquid (as oil) to produce light 2 : a device for producing light or heat

lamp·black \-ˌblak\ n : black soot used esp. as a pigment

lamp·light·er \-ˌlī-tər\ n : one that lights a lamp

lam·poon \lam-ˈpün\ n : SATIRE; esp : a harsh satire directed against an individual — **lampoon** vb

lam·prey \ˈlam-prē\ n, pl **lampreys** : any of a family of eel-shaped jawless fishes that have well-developed eyes and a large disk-shaped sucking mouth armed with horny teeth

LAN \ˈlan, ˌel-ˌā-ˈen\ n : LOCAL AREA NETWORK

la·nai \lə-ˈnī\ n [Hawaiian lānai] : PORCH, VERANDA

lance \ˈlans\ n 1 : a spear carried by mounted soldiers 2 : any of various sharp-pointed implements; esp : LANCET

²**lance** *vb* **lanced; lanc·ing** : to pierce or open with a lance ⟨~ a boil⟩

lance corporal *n* : an enlisted man in the marine corps ranking above a private first class and below a corporal

lanc·er \'lan-sər\ *n* : a cavalryman of a unit formerly armed with lances

lan·cet \'lan-sət\ *n* : a sharp-pointed and usu. 2-edged surgical instrument

¹**land** \'land\ *n* **1** : the solid part of the surface of the earth; *also* : a part of the earth's surface ⟨fenced ~⟩ ⟨marshy ~⟩ **2** : NATION **3** : REALM, DOMAIN — **land·less** *adj*

²**land** *vb* **1** : DISEMBARK; *also* : to touch at a place on shore **2** : to alight or cause to alight on a surface ⟨~ a punch⟩ **3** : to bring to or arrive at a destination **4** : to catch and bring in ⟨~ a fish⟩; *also* : GAIN, SECURE ⟨~ a job⟩

lan·dau \'lan-,dau\ *n* : a 4-wheeled carriage with a top divided into two sections that can be lowered, thrown back, or removed

land·ed *adj* : having an estate in land ⟨~ gentry⟩

land·er \'lan-dər\ *n* : a space vehicle designed to land on a celestial body

land·fall \'land-,föl\ *n* : a sighting or making of land (as after a voyage); *also* : the land first sighted

land·fill \-,fil\ *n* : a low-lying area on which refuse is buried between layers of earth — **landfill** *vb*

land·form \-,förm\ *n* : a natural feature of a land surface

land·hold·er \-,hōl-dər\ *n* : a holder or owner of land — **land·hold·ing** \-diŋ\ *adj or n*

land·ing \'lan-diŋ\ *n* **1** : the action of one that lands **2** : a place for discharging or taking on passengers and cargo **3** : a level part of a staircase

landing gear *n* : the part that supports the weight of an aircraft when it is on the ground

land·la·dy \'land-,lā-dē\ *n* : a woman who is a landlord

land·locked \-,läkt\ *adj* **1** : enclosed or nearly enclosed by land ⟨a ~ country⟩ **2** : confined to fresh water by some barrier ⟨~ salmon⟩

land·lord \-,lórd\ *n* **1** : the owner of property leased or rented to another **2** : a person who rents lodgings : INNKEEPER

land·lub·ber \-,lə-bər\ *n* : one who knows little of the sea or seamanship

land·mark \-,märk\ *n* **1** : an object that marks a course or boundary or serves as a guide **2** : an event that marks a turning point **3** : a structure of unusual historical and usu. aesthetic interest

land·mass \-,mas\ *n* : a large area of land

land mine *n* **1** : a mine placed on or just below the surface of the ground and designed to be exploded by the weight of someone or something passing over it **2** : a trap for the unwary

land·own·er \-,ō-nər\ *n* : an owner of land

¹**land·scape** \-,skāp\ *n* **1** : a picture of natural inland scenery **2** : a portion of land that can be seen in one glance

²**landscape** *vb* **land·scaped; land·scap·ing** : to modify (a natural landscape) by grading, clearing, or decorative planting

land·slide \-,slīd\ *n* **1** : the slipping down of a mass of rocks or earth on a steep slope; *also* : the mass of material that slides **2** : an overwhelming victory esp. in a political contest

lands·man \'landz-mən\ *n* : a person who lives on land; *esp* : LANDLUBBER

land·ward \'land-wərd\ *adv or adj* : to or toward the land

lane \'lān\ *n* **1** : a narrow passageway (as between fences) **2** : a relatively narrow way or track ⟨traffic ~⟩

lang *abbr* language

lan·guage \'laŋ-gwij\ *n* [ME, fr. AF *langage*, fr. *langue* tongue, language, fr. L *lingua*] **1** : the words, their pronunciation, and the methods of combining them used and understood by a community **2** : form or style of verbal expression ⟨legal ~⟩ **3** : a system of signs and symbols and rules for using them that is used to carry information

lan·guid \'laŋ-gwəd\ *adj* **1** : WEAK **2** : sluggish in character or disposition : LISTLESS **3** : SLOW — **lan·guid·ly** *adv* — **lan·guid·ness** *n*

lan·guish \'laŋ-gwish\ *vb* **1** : to become languid **2** : to become dispirited : PINE **3** : to appeal for sympathy by assuming an expression of grief

lan·guor \'laŋ-gər\ *n* **1** : a languid feeling **2** : listless indolence or inertia ♦ *Synonyms* LETHARGY, LASSITUDE, TORPIDITY, TORPOR — **lan·guor·ous** *adj* — **lan·guor·ous·ly** *adv*

La Ni·ña \lä-'nē-nya\ *n* : an upwelling of unusually cold ocean water along the west coast of So. America that often follows an El Niño

lank \'laŋk\ *adj* **1** : not well filled out **2** : hanging straight and limp

lanky \'laŋ-kē\ *adj* **lank·i·er; -est** : ungracefully tall and thin

lan·o·lin \'lan-ᵊl-ən\ *n* : the fatty coating of sheep's wool esp. when refined for use in ointments and cosmetics

lan·ta·na \lan-'tä-nə\ *n* : any of a genus of tropical shrubs related to the vervains with showy heads of small bright flowers

lan·tern \'lan-tərn\ *n* [ME *lanterne*, fr. AF, fr. L *lanterna*, fr. Gk *lamptēr*, fr. *lampein* to shine] **1** : a usu. portable light with a protective covering **2** : the chamber in a lighthouse containing the light **3** : a projector for slides

lan·tha·num \'lan-thə-nəm\ *n* : a soft malleable metallic chemical element

lan·yard \'lan-yərd\ *n* : a piece of rope for fastening something in ships; *also* : any of various cords

¹**lap** \'lap\ *n* **1** : a loose panel of a garment **2** : the clothing that lies on the knees, thighs, and lower part of the trunk when one sits; *also* : the front part of the lower trunk and thighs of a seated per-

son **3** : an environment of nurture ⟨the ∼ of luxury⟩ **4** : CHARGE, CONTROL ⟨in the ∼ of the gods⟩

²**lap** *vb* **lapped; lap•ping 1** : FOLD **2** : WRAP **3** : to lay over or near so as to partly cover

³**lap** *n* **1** : the amount by which an object overlaps another; *also* : the part of an object that overlaps another **2** : an act or instance of going over a course (as a track or swimming pool)

⁴**lap** *vb* **lapped; lap•ping 1** : to scoop up food or drink with the tip of the tongue; *also* : DEVOUR — usu. used with *up* **2** : to splash gently ⟨*lapping* waves⟩

⁵**lap** *n* **1** : an act or instance of lapping **2** : a gentle splashing sound

lap•a•ros•co•py \ˌla-pə-ˈräs-kə-pē\ *n, pl* **-pies** : visual examination of the abdomen by means of an endoscope; *also* : surgery using laparoscopy — **lap•a•ro•scope** \ˈla-pə-rə-ˌskōp\ *n* — **lap•a•ro•scop•ic** \ˌla-pə-rə-ˈskä-pik\ *adj*

lap•dog \ˈlap-ˌdȯg\ *n* : a small dog that may be held in the lap

la•pel \lə-ˈpel\ *n* : the fold of the front of a coat that is usu. a continuation of the collar

¹**lap•i•dary** \ˈla-pə-ˌder-ē\ *n, pl* **-dar•ies** : a person who cuts, polishes, or engraves precious stones

²**lapidary** *adj* **1** : of, relating to, or suitable for engraved inscriptions **2** : of, relating to, or suggestive of precious stones or the art of cutting them

lap•in \ˈla-pən\ *n* : rabbit fur usu. sheared and dyed

la•pis la•zu•li \ˌla-pəs-ˈla-zə-lē, -zhə-\ *n* : a usu. blue semiprecious stone often having sparkling bits of pyrite

lap•pet \ˈla-pət\ *n* : a fold or flap on a garment

¹**lapse** \ˈlaps\ *n* [L *lapsus*, fr. *labi* to slip] **1** : a slight error ⟨a mental ∼⟩ **2** : a fall from a higher to a lower state **3** : the termination of a right or privilege through failure to meet requirements **4** : INTERRUPTION **5** : APOSTASY **6** : a passage of time; *also* : INTERVAL ✦ *Synonyms* BLOOPER, BLUNDER, BONER, GOOF, MISTAKE, SLIP

²**lapse** *vb* **lapsed; laps•ing 1** : to commit apostasy **2** : SINK, SLIP **3** : CEASE

lap•top \ˈlap-ˌtäp\ *adj* : of a size that can be used conveniently on one's lap ⟨a ∼ computer⟩ — **laptop** *n*

lap•wing \ˈlap-ˌwiŋ\ *n* : an Old World crested plover

lar•board \ˈlär-bərd\ *n* : ⁵PORT

lar•ce•ny \ˈlär-sə-nē\ *n, pl* **-nies** [ME, fr. AF *larcecin* theft, fr. L *latrocinium* robbery, fr. *latro* mercenary soldier] : THEFT — **lar•ce•nous** \-nəs\ *adj*

larch \ˈlärch\ *n* : any of a genus of trees related to the pines that shed their needles in the fall

¹**lard** \ˈlärd\ *vb*, **1** : to insert strips of usu. pork fat into (meat) before cooking; *also* : GREASE **2** *obs* : ENRICH

²**lard** *n* : a soft white fat obtained by rendering fatty tissue of the hog

lar•der \ˈlär-dər\ *n* : a place where foods (as meat) are kept

large \ˈlärj\ *adj* **larg•er; larg•est 1** : having more than usual power, capacity, or scope **2** : exceeding most other things of like kind in quantity or size ✦ *Synonyms* BIG, GREAT, OVERSIZE — **large** *adv* — **large•ness** *n* — **at large 1** : UNCONFINED **2** : as a whole

large•ly \ˈlärj-lē\ *adv* : to a large extent

lar•gesse *or* **lar•gess** \lär-ˈzhes, -ˈjes\ *n* **1** : liberal giving **2** : a generous gift

¹**lar•go** \ˈlär-gō\ *adv or adj* [It, slow, broad, fr. L *largus* abundant] : at a very slow tempo — used as a direction in music

²**largo** *n, pl* **largos** : a largo movement

lari \ˈlä-rē\ *n, pl* **lari** — see MONEY table

lar•i•at \ˈlar-ē-ət\ *n* [AmerSp *la reata* the lasso, fr. Sp *la* the + AmerSp *reata* lasso, fr. Sp *reatar* to tie again] : a long rope used to catch or tether livestock : LASSO

¹**lark** \ˈlärk\ *n* : any of a family of small songbirds; *esp* : SKYLARK

²**lark** *n* : a source of or quest for fun or adventure

³**lark** *vb* : to engage in harmless fun or mischief — often used with *about*

lark•spur \ˈlärk-ˌspər\ *n* : DELPHINIUM; *esp* : any of the widely cultivated annual delphiniums

lar•va \ˈlär-və\ *n, pl* **lar•vae** \-(ˌ)vē\ *also* **larvas** [NL, fr. L, specter, mask] : the wingless often wormlike form in which insects hatch from the egg; *also* : any young animal (as a tadpole) that is fundamentally unlike its parent — **lar•val** \-vəl\ *adj*

lar•yn•gi•tis \ˌlar-ən-ˈjī-təs\ *n* : inflammation of the larynx

lar•ynx \ˈlar-iŋks\ *n, pl* **la•ryn•ges** \lə-ˈrin-ˌjēz\ *or* **lar•ynx•es** : the upper part of the trachea containing the vocal cords — **la•ryn•ge•al** \lə-ˈrin-jəl\ *adj*

la•sa•gna \lə-ˈzän-yə\ *n* [It] : boiled broad flat noodles baked with a sauce usu. of tomatoes, cheese, and meat

las•car \ˈlas-kər\ *n* : an Indian sailor

las•civ•i•ous \lə-ˈsi-vē-əs\ *adj* : LUSTFUL, LEWD ✦ *Synonyms* LICENTIOUS, LECHEROUS, LIBIDINOUS, SALACIOUS — **las•civ•i•ous•ness** *n*

la•ser \ˈlā-zər\ *n* [*light amplification by stimulated emission of radiation*] **1** : a device that produces an intense monochromatic beam of light **2** : something thrown or directed straight with high speed or intensity

laser disc *n* : OPTICAL DISK; *esp* : one containing a video recording

¹**lash** \ˈlash\ *vb* **1** : to move violently or suddenly **2** : WHIP **3** : to attack verbally

²**lash** *n* **1** : a stroke esp. with a whip; *also* : WHIP **2** : a stinging rebuke **3** : EYELASH

³**lash** *vb* : to bind with or as if with a line

lass \ˈlas\ *n* : GIRL

lass•ie \ˈla-sē\ *n* : LASS

las•si•tude \ˈla-sə-ˌtüd, -ˌtyüd\ *n* **1** : WEARINESS, FATIGUE **2** : LANGUOR

las•so \ˈla-sō, la-ˈsü\ *n, pl* **lassos** *or* **lassoes** [Sp *lazo*] : a rope or long leather thong with a noose used for catching live-stock — **lasso** *vb*

¹**last** \'last\ *vb* **1** : to continue in existence or operation **2** : to remain fresh or unimpaired : ENDURE **3** : to manage to continue **4** : to be enough for the needs of

²**last** *n* : a foot-shaped form on which a shoe is shaped or repaired

³**last** *vb* : to shape with a last

⁴**last** *adv* **1** : at the end **2** : most recently **3** : in conclusion

⁵**last** *adj* **1** : following all the rest : FINAL **2** : next before the present ⟨~ week⟩ **3** : most up-to-date **4** : farthest from a specified quality, attitude, or likelihood ⟨the ~ thing we want⟩ **5** : CONCLUSIVE; *also* : SUPREME — **last·ly** *adv*

⁶**last** *n* : something that is last — **at last** : FINALLY

last–ditch \'last-‚dich\ *adj* : made as a final effort esp. to avert disaster

last laugh *n* : an ultimate satisfaction or triumph despite previous doubt or criticism

Last Supper *n* : the supper eaten by Jesus and his disciples on the night of his betrayal

lat *abbr* latitude

Lat *abbr* Latin

¹**latch** \'lach\ *vb* : to catch or get hold

²**latch** *n* : a catch that holds a door or gate closed

³**latch** *vb* : to make fast with a latch

latch·et \'la-chət\ *n* : a strap, thong, or lace for fastening a shoe or sandal

latch·key \'lach-‚kē\ *n* : a key for opening a door latch esp. from the outside

latch·string \-‚striŋ\ *n* : a string on a latch that may be left hanging outside the door for raising the latch

¹**late** \'lāt\ *adj* **lat·er; lat·est 1** : coming or remaining after the due, usual, or proper time **2** : far advanced toward the close or end **3** : recently deceased **4** : made, appearing, or happening just previous to the present : RECENT — **late·ly** *adv* — **late·ness** *n*

²**late** *adv* **lat·er; lat·est 1** : after the usual or proper time; *also* : at or to an advanced point in time **2** : RECENTLY

late·com·er \'lāt-‚kə-mər\ *n* : one who arrives late

la·teen \la-'tēn\ *adj* : relating to or being a triangular sail extended by a long spar slung to a low mast

la·tent \'lāt-ᵊnt\ *adj* : present but not visible or active ✦ *Synonyms* DORMANT, QUIESCENT, POTENTIAL — **la·ten·cy** \-ᵊn-sē\ *n*

¹**lat·er·al** \'la-tə-rəl\ *adj* : situated on, directed toward, or coming from the side — **lat·er·al·ly** *adv*

²**lateral** *n* **1** : a branch from the main part **2** : a football pass thrown parallel to the line of scrimmage or away from the opponent's goal

la·tex \'lā-‚teks\ *n, pl* **la·ti·ces** \'lā-tə-‚sēz, 'la-\ *or* **la·tex·es 1** : a milky juice produced by various plant cells (as of milkweeds, poppies, and the rubber tree) **2** : a water emulsion of a synthetic rubber or plastic used esp. in paint

lath \'lath, 'lath\ *n, pl* **laths** *or* **lath** : a thin narrow strip of wood used esp. as a base for plaster; *also* : a building material in sheets used for the same purpose — **lath** *vb*

lathe \'lāth\ *n* : a machine in which a piece of material is held and turned while being shaped by a tool

¹**lath·er** \'la-thər\ *n* **1** : a foam or froth formed when a detergent is agitated in water; *also* : foam from profuse sweating (as by a horse) **2** : DITHER

²**lather** *vb* : to spread lather over; *also* : to form a lather

Lat·in \'lat-ᵊn\ *n* **1** : the language of ancient Rome **2** : a member of any of the peoples whose languages derive from Latin — **Latin** *adj*

La·ti·na \lə-'tē-nə\ *n* : a woman or girl who is a native or inhabitant of Latin America; *also* : a woman or girl of Latin-American origin living in the U.S.

Latin American *n* : a native or inhabitant of any of the countries of No., Central, or So. America whose official language is Spanish or Portuguese — **Latin–American** *adj*

La·ti·no \lə-'tē-nō\ *n, pl* **-nos** : a native or inhabitant of Latin America; *also* : a person of Latin-American origin living in the U.S. — **Latino** *adj*

lat·i·tude \'la-tə-‚tüd, -‚tyüd\ *n* **1** : angular distance north or south from the earth's equator measured in degrees **2** : a region marked by its latitude **3** : freedom of action or choice

lat·i·tu·di·nar·i·an \‚la-tə-‚tü-də-'ner-ē-ən, -‚tyü-\ *n* : a person who is liberal in religious belief and conduct

la·trine \lə-'trēn\ *n* : TOILET

lats \'läts\ *n, pl* **la·ti** \'lä-tē\ *or* **la·tu** \'lä-tü\ — see MONEY table

lat·ter \'la-tər\ *adj* **1** : more recent; *also* : FINAL **2** : of, relating to, or being the second of two things referred to

lat·ter–day *adj* **1** : of present or recent times **2** : of a later or subsequent time

Latter–day Saint *n* : a member of a religious body founded by Joseph Smith in 1830 and accepting the Book of Mormon as divine revelation : MORMON

lat·ter·ly \'la-tər-lē\ *adv* **1** : LATER **2** : of late : RECENTLY

lat·tice \'la-təs\ *n* **1** : a framework of crossed wood or metal strips; *also* : a window, door, or gate having a lattice **2** : a regular geometrical arrangement

lat·tice·work \-‚wərk\ *n* : LATTICE; *also* : work made of lattices

Lat·vi·an \'lat-vē-ən\ *n* **1** : a native or inhabitant of Latvia **2** : the language of the Latvians — **Latvian** *adj*

¹**laud** \'lȯd\ *n* : PRAISE, ACCLAIM

²**laud** *vb* : PRAISE, EXTOL ✦ *Synonyms* CELEBRATE, EULOGIZE, GLORIFY, MAGNIFY — **laud·able** *adj* — **laud·ably** *adv*

lau·da·num \'lȯd-ᵊn-əm\ *n* : a tincture of opium

lau·da·to·ry \'lȯ-də-‚tȯr-ē\ *adj* : of, relating to, or expressive of praise

laugh \'laf, 'laf\ *vb* [ME, fr. OE *hliehhan*] : to show mirth, joy, or scorn with a chuckle or explosive vocal sound; *also* : to become amused or derisive — **laugh-able** *adj* — **laugh-ing-ly** *adv*

²**laugh** \'lȯnch\ *n* **1** : the act of laughing **2** : JOKE; *also* : JEER **3** *pl* : SPORT 1

laughing gas *n* : NITROUS OXIDE

laugh-ing-stock \'la-fiŋ-ˌstäk, 'lȧ-\ *n* : an object of ridicule

laugh-ter \'laf-tər, 'lȧf-\ *n* : the action or sound of laughing

¹**launch** \'lȯnch\ *vb* **1** : THROW, HURL; *also* : to send off ⟨~ a rocket⟩ **2** : to set afloat **3** : to set in operation : START — **launch-er** *n*

²**launch** *n* : an act or instance of launching

³**launch** *n* : a small open or half-decked motorboat

launch-pad \'lȯnch-ˌpad\ *n* : a platform from which a rocket is launched

laun-der \'lȯn-dər\ *vb* **1** : to wash or wash and iron clothing and household linens **2** : to transfer (as money of an illegal origin) through an outside party to conceal the true source — **laun-der-er** *n*

laun-dress \'lȯn-drəs\ *n* : a woman who is a laundry worker

laun-dry \'lȯn-drē\ *n, pl* **laundries** [fr. obs. *launder* launderer, fr. AF *lavandere*, fr. ML *lavandarius*, fr. L *lavandus* needing to be washed, fr. *lavare* to wash] **1** : a place where laundering is done **2** : clothes or linens that have been or are to be laundered — **laun-dry-man** \-mən\ *n*

lau-re-ate \'lȯr-ē-ət\ *n* : the recipient of honor for achievement in an art or science — **lau-re-ate-ship** *n*

lau-rel \'lȯ-rəl\ *n* **1** : an evergreen tree or shrub of southern Europe that is related to the sassafras and cinnamon and has glossy aromatic leaves **2** : MOUNTAIN LAUREL **3** : a crown of laurel awarded as an honor — usu. used in pl.

lav *abbr* lavatory

la-va \'lä-və, 'la-\ *n* [It] : melted rock coming from a volcano; *also* : such rock that has cooled and hardened

la-vage \lə-'väzh\ *n* [F] : WASHING; *esp* : the washing out (as of an organ) esp. for medicinal reasons

lav-a-to-ry \'la-və-ˌtȯr-ē\ *n, pl* **-ries** **1** : a fixed washbowl with running water and drainpipe **2** : BATHROOM

lave \'lāv\ *vb* **laved**; **lav-ing** : WASH

lav-en-der \'la-vən-dər\ *n* **1** : a Mediterranean mint or its dried leaves and flowers used to perfume clothing and bed linen **2** : a pale purple color

¹**lav-ish** \'la-vish\ *adj* [ME *laves, lavage*, prob. fr. MF *lavasse, lavache* downpour, fr. *laver* to wash] **1** : expending or bestowing profusely **2** : expended or produced in abundance ⟨~ gifts⟩ **3** : marked by excess ⟨~ decor⟩ — **lav-ish-ly** *adv* — **lav-ish-ness** *n*

²**lavish** *vb* : to expend or give freely

law \'lȯ\ *n* **1** : a rule of conduct or action established by custom or laid down and enforced by a governing authority; *also* : the whole body of such rules **2** : the control brought about by enforcing rules **3** *cap* : the revelation of the divine will set forth in the Old Testament; *also*

: the first part of the Jewish scriptures — see BIBLE table **4** : a rule or principle of construction or procedure **5** : the science that deals with laws and their interpretation and application **6** : the profession of a lawyer **7** : a rule or principle stating something that always works in the same way under the same conditions

law-break-er \'lȯ-ˌbrā-kər\ *n* : a person who violates the law

law-ful \'lȯ-fəl\ *adj* **1** : permitted by law **2** : RIGHTFUL — **law-ful-ly** *adv*

law-giv-er \-ˌgi-vər\ *n* : LEGISLATOR

law-less \'lȯ-ləs\ *adj* **1** : having no laws **2** : UNRULY, DISORDERLY ⟨a ~ mob⟩ — **law-less-ly** *adv* — **law-less-ness** *n*

law-mak-er \-ˌmā-kər\ *n* : LEGISLATOR

law-man \'lȯ-mən\ *n* : a law enforcement official (as a sheriff or marshal)

¹**lawn** \'lȯn\ *n* : ground (as around a house) covered with mowed grass

²**lawn** *n* : a fine sheer linen or cotton fabric

lawn bowling *n* : a bowling game played on a green with wooden balls which are rolled at a jack

law-ren-ci-um \lȯ-'ren-sē-əm\ *n* : a short-lived radioactive element

law-suit \'lȯ-ˌsüt\ *n* : a suit in law

law-yer \'lȯ-yər\ *n* : one who conducts lawsuits for clients or advises as to legal rights and obligations in other matters — **law-yer-ly** *adj*

lax \'laks\ *adj* **1** : not strict ⟨~ discipline⟩ **2** : not tense or rigid ♦ *Synonyms* REMISS, NEGLIGENT, NEGLECTFUL, DELINQUENT, DERELICT — **lax-i-ty** \'lak-sə-tē\ *n* — **lax-ly** *adv* — **lax-ness** *n*

¹**lax-a-tive** \'lak-sə-tiv\ *adj* : relieving constipation

²**laxative** *n* : a usu. mild laxative drug

¹**lay** \'lā\ *vb* **laid** \'lād\; **lay-ing** **1** : to beat or strike down **2** : to put on or set down : PLACE **3** : to produce and deposit eggs **4** : SETTLE; *also* : ALLAY **5** : SPREAD **6** : PREPARE, CONTRIVE **7** : WAGER **8** : to impose esp. as a duty or burden **9** : to set in order or position **10** : to bring to a specified condition **11** : to put forward : SUBMIT

²**lay** *n* : the way in which something lies or is laid in relation to something else

³**lay** *past of* ¹LIE

⁴**lay** *n* **1** : a simple narrative poem **2** : SONG

⁵**lay** *adj* **1** : of or relating to the laity **2** : not of a particular profession; *also* : lacking extensive knowledge of a particular subject

lay-away \'lā-ə-ˌwā\ *n* : a purchasing agreement by which a retailer agrees to hold merchandise secured by a deposit until the price is paid in full

lay-er \'lā-ər\ *n* **1** : one that lays **2** : one thickness, course, or fold laid or lying over or under another

lay-ette \lā-'et\ *n* [F, fr. MF, dim. of *laye* box] : an outfit of clothing and equipment for a newborn infant

lay-man \'lā-mən\ *n* : a person who is a member of the laity

lay·off \'lā-ˌȯf\ n 1 : a period of inactivity 2 : the act of laying off an employee

lay off vb 1 : to cease to employ (a worker) often temporarily 2 : to leave undisturbed 3 : to stop doing something

lay·out \'lā-ˌaůt\ n : the final arrangement, plan, or design of something

lay·over \-ˌō-vər\ n : STOPOVER

lay·per·son \-ˌpər-sən\ n : a member of the laity

lay·wom·an \'lā-ˌwů-mən\ n : a woman who is a member of the laity

la·zar \'la-zər, 'lā-\ n : LEPER

laze \'lāz\ vb **lazed; laz·ing** : to pass time in idleness or relaxation

la·zy \'lā-zē\ adj **la·zi·er; -est** 1 : disliking activity or exertion 2 : encouraging idleness ⟨a ~ day⟩ 3 : SLUGGISH 4 : DROOPY, LAX 5 : not rigorous or strict ⟨~ work habits⟩ — **la·zi·ly** \-zə-lē\ adv — **la·zi·ness** \-zē-nəs\ n

la·zy·bones \-ˌbōnz\ n sing or pl : a lazy person

lazy Su·san \ˌlā-zē-'süz-ᵊn\ n : a revolving tray used for serving food

lb abbr [L libra] pound

lc abbr lowercase

LC abbr Library of Congress

¹**LCD** \ˌel-(ˌ)sē-'dē\ n [liquid crystal display] : a display (as of the time in a digital watch) that consists of segments of a liquid crystal whose reflectivity varies with the voltage applied to them

²**LCD** abbr least common denominator; lowest common denominator

LCDR abbr lieutenant commander

LCM abbr least common multiple; lowest common multiple

LCpl abbr lance corporal

LCS abbr League Championship Series

ld abbr 1 load 2 lord

LD abbr learning disabled; learning disability

LDC abbr less developed country

ldg abbr 1 landing 2 loading

LDL \ˌel-(ˌ)dē-'el\ n [low-density lipoprotein] : a cholesterol-rich protein-poor lipoprotein of blood plasma correlated with increased probability of developing atherosclerosis

L–do·pa \'el-'dō-pə\ n : an isomer of dopa used esp. in the treatment of Parkinson's disease

LDS abbr Latter-day Saints

lea \'lē, 'lā\ n : PASTURE, MEADOW

leach \'lēch\ vb : to pass a liquid (as water) through to carry off the soluble components; also : to dissolve out by such means ⟨~ alkali from ashes⟩

¹**lead** \'lēd\ vb **led** \'led\; **lead·ing** 1 : to guide on a way 2 : LIVE ⟨~ a quiet life⟩ 3 : to direct the operations, activity, or performance of ⟨~ an orchestra⟩ 4 : to go at the head of : be first ⟨~ a parade⟩ 5 : to begin play with; also : BEGIN, OPEN 6 : to tend toward a definite result ⟨study ~ing to a degree⟩ — **lead·er** n — **lead·er·less** adj — **lead·er·ship** n

²**lead** \'lēd\ n 1 : a position at the front; also : a margin by which one leads 2 : the privilege of leading in cards; also

: the card or suit led 3 : EXAMPLE 4 : one that leads 5 : a principal role (as in a play); also : one who plays such a role 6 : INDICATION, CLUE 7 : an insulated electrical conductor

³**lead** \'led\ n 1 : a heavy malleable bluish white chemical element 2 : an article made of lead; esp : a weight for sounding at sea 3 : a thin strip of metal used to separate lines of type in printing 4 : a thin stick of marking substance in or for a pencil

⁴**lead** \'led\ vb 1 : to cover, line, or weight with lead 2 : to fix (glass) in position with lead 3 : to treat or mix with lead or a lead compound

lead·en \'led-ᵊn\ adj 1 : made of lead; also : of the color of lead 2 : SLUGGISH, DULL

lead off vb : OPEN, BEGIN; esp : to bat first in an inning — **lead-off** \'lēd-ˌȯf\ n or adj

¹**leaf** \'lēf\ n, pl **leaves** \'lēvz\ 1 : a usu. flat and green outgrowth of a plant stem that is a unit of foliage and functions esp. in photosynthesis; also : FOLIAGE 2 : something (as a page or a flat moving part) that is suggestive of a leaf — **leaf·less** adj — **leafy** adj

²**leaf** vb 1 : to produce leaves 2 : to turn the pages of a book

leaf·age \'lē-fij\ n : FOLIAGE

leafed \'lēft\ adj : LEAVED

leaf·hop·per \'lēf-ˌhä-pər\ n : any of a family of small leaping insects related to the cicadas that suck the juices of plants

leaf·let \'lē-flət\ n 1 : a division of a compound leaf 2 : PAMPHLET, FOLDER

leaf mold n : a compost or layer composed chiefly of decayed leaves

leaf·stalk \'lēf-ˌstȯk\ n : PETIOLE

¹**league** \'lēg\ n : a unit of distance equal to about three miles (five kilometers)

²**league** n 1 : an association or alliance (as of nations or sports teams) for a common purpose 2 : CLASS, CATEGORY — **league** vb — **leagu·er** \'lē-gər\ n

¹**leak** \'lēk\ vb 1 : to enter or escape through a leak 2 : to let a substance in or out through an opening 3 : to become or make known ⟨~ed the news⟩

²**leak** n 1 : a crack or hole that accidentally admits a fluid or light or lets it escape; also : something that secretly or accidentally permits the admission or escape of something else 2 : LEAKAGE — **leaky** adj

leak·age \'lē-kij\ n 1 : the act of leaking 2 : the thing or amount that leaks

¹**lean** \'lēn\ vb 1 : to bend from a vertical position : INCLINE 2 : to cast one's weight to one side for support 3 : to rely on for support 4 : to incline in opinion, taste, or desire — **lean** n

²**lean** adj 1 : lacking or deficient in flesh and esp. in fat ⟨~ meat⟩ 2 : lacking richness or productiveness ⟨~ profits⟩ 3 : low in fuel content — **lean·ness** n

leant \'lent\ chiefly Brit past of LEAN

lean–to \'lēn-ˌtü\ n, pl **lean–tos** \-ˌtüz\ : a wing or extension of a building having a roof of only one slope; also : a rough shed or shelter with a similar roof

¹**leap** \ˈlēp\ vb **leapt** \ˈlēpt, ˈlept\ or **leaped; leap·ing** : to spring free from a surface or over an obstacle : JUMP

²**leap** n : JUMP

leap·frog \ˈlep-ˌfrog, -ˌfräg\ n : a game in which a player bends down and is vaulted over by another — **leapfrog** vb

leap year n : a year containing 366 days with February 29 as the extra day

learn \ˈlərn\ vb **learned** \ˈlərnd, ˈlərnt\; **learn·ing** 1 : to gain knowledge, understanding, or skill by study or experience; also : MEMORIZE 2 : to find out : ASCERTAIN — **learn·er** n

learn·ed \ˈlər-nəd\ adj : SCHOLARLY, ERUDITE — **learn·ed·ly** adv — **learn·ed·ness** n

learn·ing \ˈlər-niŋ\ n : KNOWLEDGE, ERUDITION

learning disability n : any of various conditions (as dyslexia) that interfere with a person's ability to learn and so result in impaired functioning (as in language) — **learning disabled** adj

learnt \ˈlərnt\ chiefly Brit past and past part of LEARN

¹**lease** \ˈlēs\ n : a contract transferring real estate for a term of years or at will usu. for a specified rent

²**lease** vb **leased; leas·ing** [AF lesser, lescher to leave, hand over, lease, fr. L laxare to loosen, fr. laxus slack] 1 : to grant by lease 2 : to hold under a lease ✦ **Synonyms** LET, CHARTER, HIRE, RENT

lease·hold \ˈlēs-ˌhōld\ n 1 : a tenure by lease 2 : land held by lease — **lease·hold·er** n

leash \ˈlēsh\ n [ME lees, leshe, fr. AF *lesche, lesse fr. lesser to leave, let go] 1 : a line for leading or restraining an animal 2 : a state of restraint ⟨kept spending on a tight ∼⟩ — **leash** vb

¹**least** \ˈlēst\ adj 1 : lowest in importance or position 2 : smallest in size or degree 3 : SLIGHTEST

²**least** n : one that is least

³**least** adv : in the smallest or lowest degree

least common denominator n : the least common multiple of two or more denominators

least common multiple n : the smallest common multiple of two or more numbers

least·wise \ˈlēst-ˌwīz\ adv : at least

leath·er \ˈle-thər\ n : animal skin dressed for use — **leath·ern** \-thərn\ adj — **leath·ery** adj

leath·er·back \-ˌbak\ n : the largest existing sea turtle with a flexible leathery carapace

leath·er·neck \-ˌnek\ n : MARINE

¹**leave** \ˈlēv\ vb **left** \ˈleft\; **leav·ing** 1 : to allow or cause to remain behind 2 : to have as a remainder 3 : BEQUEATH 4 : to let stay without interference 5 : to go away : depart from 6 : GIVE UP, ABANDON

²**leave** n 1 : PERMISSION; also : authorized absence from duty 2 : DEPARTURE

³**leave** vb **leaved; leav·ing** : LEAF

leaved \ˈlēvd\ adj : having leaves

¹**leav·en** \ˈle-vən\ n 1 : a substance (as yeast) used to produce fermentation (as in dough) 2 : something that modifies or lightens

²**leaven** vb : to raise (dough) with a leaven; also : to permeate with a modifying or vivifying element ⟨lectures ∼ed with humor⟩

leav·en·ing n : LEAVEN

leaves pl of LEAF

leave–tak·ing \ˈlēv-ˌtā-kiŋ\ n : DEPARTURE, FAREWELL

leav·ings \ˈlē-viŋz\ n pl : REMNANT, RESIDUE

lech·ery \ˈle-chə-rē\ n : inordinate indulgence in sexual activity — **lech·er** \ˈle-chər\ n — **lech·er·ous** \ˈle-chə-rəs\ adj — **lech·er·ous·ly** adv — **lech·er·ous·ness** n

lec·i·thin \ˈle-sə-thən\ n : any of several waxy phosphorus-containing substances that are common in animals and plants, form colloidal solutions in water, and have emulsifying and wetting properties

lect abbr lecture; lecturer

lec·tern \ˈlek-tərn\ n : a stand to support a book for a standing reader

lec·tor \-tər\ n : one whose chief duty is to read the lessons in a church service

lec·ture \ˈlek-chər\ n 1 : a discourse given before an audience esp. for instruction 2 : REPRIMAND — **lec·ture** vb — **lec·tur·er** n — **lec·ture·ship** n

led past and past part of LEAD

LED \ˌel-(ˌ)ē-ˈdē\ n [light-emitting diode] : a semiconductor diode that emits light when a voltage is applied to it and is used esp. for electronic displays

le·der·ho·sen \ˈlā-dər-ˌhōz-ᵊn\ n pl : leather shorts often with suspenders worn esp. in Bavaria

ledge \ˈlej\ n [ME legge bar of a gate] 1 : a shelflike projection from a top or an edge 2 : REEF

led·ger \ˈle-jər\ n : a book containing accounts to which debits and credits are transferred in final form

lee \ˈlē\ n 1 : a protecting shelter 2 : the side (as of a ship) that is sheltered from the wind — **lee** adj

leech \ˈlēch\ n 1 : any of various bloodsucking segmented usu. freshwater worms that are related to the earthworms and have a sucker at each end 2 : a hanger-on who seeks gain

leek \ˈlēk\ n : an onionlike herb grown for its mildly pungent leaves and stalk

leer \ˈlir\ n : a suggestive, knowing, or malicious look — **leer** vb

leery \ˈlir-ē\ adj : SUSPICIOUS, WARY

lees \ˈlēz\ n pl : DREGS

¹**lee·ward** \ˈlē-wərd, ˈlü-ərd\ n : the lee side

²**leeward** adj : situated away from the wind

lee·way \ˈlē-ˌwā\ n 1 : lateral movement of a ship when under way 2 : an allowable margin of freedom or variation

¹**left** \ˈleft\ adj [ME, fr. OE, weak; fr. the left hand's being the weaker in most individuals] 1 : of, relating to, or being the side of the body in which the heart is mostly located; also : located nearer to

this side than to the right **2** *often cap* : of, adhering to, or constituted by the political left — **left** *adv*

²**left** *n* **1** : the left hand; *also* : the side or part that is on or toward the left side **2** *often cap* : those professing political views marked by desire to reform the established order and usu. to give greater freedom to the common people — **left·ward** \-wərd\ *adv or adj*

³**left** *past and past part of* LEAVE

left-hand *adj* **1** : situated on the left **2** : LEFT-HANDED

left-hand·ed \'left-'han-dəd\ *adj* **1** : using the left hand habitually or more easily than the right **2** : designed for or done with the left hand **3** : INSINCERE, BACK-HANDED ⟨a ~ compliment⟩ **4** : COUNTERCLOCKWISE — **left-handed** *adv* — **left-hand·ed·ness** *n* — **left-hand·er** \-dər\ *n*

left·ism \'lef-ˌti-zəm\ *n* **1** : the principles and views of the left **2** : advocacy of the doctrines of the left — **left·ist** \-tist\ *n or adj*

left·over \'left-ˌō-vər\ *n* : something that remains unused or unconsumed

lefty \'lef-tē\ *n, pl* **left·ies 1** : a left-handed person **2** : an advocate of leftism

¹**leg** \'leg\ *n* **1** : a limb of an animal used esp. for supporting the body and in walking; *also* : the part of the vertebrate leg between knee and foot **2** : something resembling or analogous to an animal leg ⟨table ~⟩ **3** : the part of an article of clothing that covers the leg **4** : a portion of a trip **5** *pl* : long-term appeal or interest ⟨a musical that has ~s⟩ — **leg·ged** \'le-gəd\ *adj* — **leg·less** *adj*

²**leg** *vb* **legged; leg·ging** : to use the legs in walking or esp. in running

³**leg** *abbr* **1** legal **2** legislative; legislature

leg·a·cy \'le-gə-sē\ *n, pl* **-cies** : INHERITANCE; *also* : something that has come from a predecessor or the past

le·gal \'lē-gəl\ *adj* **1** : of or relating to law or lawyers **2** : LAWFUL; *also* : STATUTORY **3** : enforced in courts of law — **le·gal·i·ty** \li-'ga-lə-tē\ *n* — **le·gal·ize** \'lē-gə-ˌlīz\ *vb* — **le·gal·ly** *adv*

le·gal·ese \ˌlē-gə-'lēz\ *n* : the specialized language of the legal profession

le·gal·ism \'lē-gə-ˌli-zəm\ *n* **1** : strict, literal, or excessive conformity to the law or to a religious or moral code **2** : a legal term — **le·gal·is·tic** \ˌlē-gə-'lis-tik\ *adj*

leg·ate \'le-gət\ *n* : an official representative

leg·a·tee \ˌle-gə-'tē\ *n* : a person to whom a legacy is bequeathed

le·ga·tion \li-'gā-shən\ *n* **1** : a diplomatic mission headed by a minister **2** : the official residence and office of a minister in a foreign country

le·ga·to \li-'gä-tō\ *adv or adj* [It, lit., tied] : in a smooth and connected manner (as of music)

leg·end \'le-jənd\ *n* [ME *legende*, fr. AF & ML; AF *legende*, fr. ML *legenda*, fr. L *legere* to read] **1** : a story coming down from the past; *esp* : one popularly accept-

ed as historical though not verifiable **2** : an inscription on an object; *also* : CAPTION **3** : an explanatory list of the symbols on a map or chart

leg·end·ary \'le-jən-ˌder-ē\ *adj* **1** : of, relating to, or characteristic of a legend **2** : FAMOUS — **leg·en·dari·ly** \-ˌder-ə-lē\ *adv*

leg·er·de·main \ˌle-jər-də-'mān\ *n* [ME, fr. MF *leger de main* light of hand] : SLEIGHT OF HAND

leg·ging *or* **leg·gin** \'le-gən, -gin\ *n* : a covering for the leg; *also* : TIGHTS

leg·gy \'le-gē\ *adj* **leg·gi·er; -est 1** : having unusually long legs **2** : having long and attractive legs **3** : SPINDLY — used of a plant

leg·horn \'leg-ˌhȯrn, 'le-gərn\ *n* **1** : a fine plaited straw; *also* : a hat made of this straw **2** : any of a Mediterranean breed of small hardy chickens

leg·i·ble \'le-jə-bəl\ *adj* : capable of being read : CLEAR — **leg·i·bil·i·ty** \ˌle-jə-'bi-lə-tē\ *n* — **leg·i·bly** \'le-jə-blē\ *adv*

¹**le·gion** \'lē-jən\ *n* **1** : a unit of the Roman army comprising 3000 to 6000 soldiers **2** : MULTITUDE **3** : an association of ex-servicemen — **le·gion·ary** \-jə-ˌner-ē\ *n* — **le·gion·naire** \ˌlē-jə-'nar\ *n*

²**legion** *adj* : MANY, NUMEROUS

Legionnaires' disease *also* **Legionnaire's disease** \-'nerz-\ *n* : a lobar pneumonia caused by a bacterium

legis *abbr* legislation; legislative; legislature

leg·is·late \'le-jəs-ˌlāt\ *vb* **-lat·ed; -lat·ing** : to make or enact laws; *also* : to bring about by legislation — **leg·is·la·tor** \-ˌlā-tər\ *n*

leg·is·la·tion \ˌle-jəs-'lā-shən\ *n* **1** : the action of legislating **2** : laws made by a legislative body

leg·is·la·tive \'le-jəs-ˌlā-tiv\ *adj* **1** : having the power of legislating **2** : of or relating to a legislature or legislation

leg·is·la·ture \'le-jəs-ˌlā-chər\ *n* : an organized body of persons having the authority to make laws

le·git \li-'jit\ *adj, slang* : LEGITIMATE

¹**le·git·i·mate** \li-'ji-tə-mət\ *adj* **1** : lawfully begotten **2** : GENUINE **3** : LAWFUL **4** : conforming to recognized principles or accepted rules or standards — **le·git·i·ma·cy** \-mə-sē\ *n* — **le·git·i·mate·ly** *adv*

²**le·git·i·mate** \-ˌmāt\ *vb* : to make legitimate

le·git·i·mise *Brit var of* LEGITIMIZE

le·git·i·mize \li-'ji-tə-ˌmīz\ *vb* **-mized; -miz·ing** : LEGITIMATE

leg·man \'leg-ˌman\ *n* **1** : a reporter assigned usu. to gather information **2** : an assistant who gathers information and runs errands

le·gume \'le-ˌgyüm, li-'gyüm\ *n* [F] **1** : any of a large family of plants having fruits that are dry pods and split when ripe and including important food and forage plants (as beans and clover); *also* : the part (as seeds or pods) of a legume used as food **2** : the pod of a legume — **le·gu·mi·nous** \li-'gyü-mə-nəs\ *adj*

¹**lei** \'lā, 'lā-ͺē\ *n* : a wreath or necklace usu. of flowers

²**lei** \'lā\ *pl of* LEU

lei·sure \'lē-zhər, 'le-, 'lā-\ *n* **1** : time free from work or duties **2** : EASE; *also* : CONVENIENCE ♦ *Synonyms* RELAXATION, REST, REPOSE — **lei·sure·ly** *adj or adv*

leit·mo·tif *also* **leit·mo·tiv** \'līt-mō-ͺtēf\ *n* [G *Leitmotiv*, fr. *leiten* to lead + *Motiv* motive] : a dominant recurring theme

lek \'lek\ *n, pl* **leks** *or* **le·ke** *or* **lekë** \'le-kə\ — see MONEY table

lem·ming \'le-miŋ\ *n* [Norw] : any of various short-tailed rodents found mostly in northern regions and noted for recurrent mass migrations

lem·on \'le-mən\ *n* **1** : an acid yellow usu. nearly oblong citrus fruit; *also* : a citrus tree that bears lemons **2** : something (as an automobile) unsatisfactory or defective — **lem·ony** *adj*

lem·on·ade \ͺle-mə-'nād\ *n* : a beverage of lemon juice, sugar, and water

lemon curd *n* : a custard made with lemon juice, butter, sugar, and eggs

lem·on·grass \'le-mən-ͺgras\ *n* : a tropical Asian grass grown for its lemon-scented foliage used as a seasoning

lem·pi·ra \lem-'pir-ə\ *n* — see MONEY table

le·mur \'lē-mər\ *n* : any of various arboreal primates largely of Madagascar that have large eyes, very soft woolly fur, and a long furry tail

Len·ape \'le-nə-pē, lə-'nä-pē\ *n, pl* **Lenape** *or* **Lenapes** : DELAWARE

lend \'lend\ *vb* **lent** \'lent\; **lend·ing 1** : to give for temporary use on condition that the same or its equivalent be returned **2** : AFFORD, FURNISH **3** : ACCOMMODATE — **lend·er** *n*

lend–lease \-'lēs\ *n* : the transfer of goods and services to an ally to aid in a common cause with payment made by a return of the items or their use in the cause or by a similar transfer of other goods and services

length \'leŋth\ *n* **1** : the longer or longest dimension of an object; *also* : a measured distance **2** : duration or extent in time or space **3** : the length of something taken as a unit of measure **4** : a single piece of a series of pieces that may be joined together ⟨a ~ of pipe⟩ — **at length 1** : in full **2** : FINALLY

length·en \'leŋ-thən\ *vb* : to make or become longer ♦ *Synonyms* EXTEND, ELONGATE, PROLONG, PROTRACT

length·wise \'leŋth-ͺwīz\ *adv* : in the direction of the length — **lengthwise** *adj*

lengthy \'leŋ-thē\ *adj* **length·i·er; -est 1** : protracted excessively **2** : EXTENDED, LONG ⟨a ~ journey⟩

le·nient \'lē-nē-ənt, -nyənt\ *adj* : of mild and tolerant disposition or effect ♦ *Synonyms* INDULGENT, FORBEARING, MERCIFUL, TOLERANT — **le·ni·en·cy** \'lē-nē-ən-sē, -nyən-sē\ *n* — **le·ni·ent·ly** *adv*

len·i·tive \'le-nə-tiv\ *adj* : alleviating pain or harshness

len·i·ty \'le-nə-tē\ *n* : LENIENCY

lens \'lenz\ *n* [L *lent-, lens* lentil; so called fr. the shape of a convex lens] **1** : a curved piece of glass or plastic used singly or combined in an optical instrument for forming an image; *also* : a device for focusing radiation other than light **2** : a transparent body in the eye that focuses light rays on receptors at the back of the eye

Lent \'lent\ *n* : a 40-day period of penitence and fasting observed from Ash Wednesday to Easter by many churches — **Lent·en** \'len-tᵊn\ *adj*

len·til \'len-tᵊl\ *n* : a Eurasian annual legume grown for its flat edible seeds and for fodder; *also* : its seed

Leo \'lē-ō\ *n* [L, lit., lion] **1** : a zodiacal constellation between Cancer and Virgo usu. pictured as a lion **2** : the 5th sign of the zodiac in astrology; *also* : one born under this sign

le·one \lē-'ōn\ *n, pl* **leones** *or* **leone** — see MONEY table

le·o·nine \'lē-ə-ͺnīn\ *adj* : of, relating to, or resembling a lion

leop·ard \'le-pərd\ *n* : a large usu. tawny and black-spotted cat of southern Asia and Africa

le·o·tard \'lē-ə-ͺtärd\ *n* : a close-fitting garment worn esp. by dancers and for exercise

lep·er \'le-pər\ *n* **1** : a person affected with leprosy **2** : OUTCAST

lep·re·chaun \'le-prə-ͺkän\ *n* : a mischievous elf of Irish folklore

lep·ro·sy \'le-prə-sē\ *n* : a chronic bacterial disease marked esp. if not treated by slow-growing swellings with deformity and loss of sensation of affected parts — **lep·rous** \-prəs\ *adj*

lep·tin \'lep-tin\ *n* : a hormone that is produced by fat-containing cells and plays a role in body weight regulation

lep·ton \lep-'tän\ *n, pl* **lep·ta** \-'tä\ : a former monetary unit equal to ¹/₁₀₀ drachma

les·bi·an \'lez-bē-ən\ *n* [fr. the reputed homosexual group associated with the poet Sappho of Lesbos] : a woman who is a homosexual — **lesbian** *adj* — **les·bi·an·ism** \-ə-ͺni-zəm\ *n*

lèse ma·jes·té *or* **lese maj·es·ty** \'läz-ͺma-jə-stē, 'lez-, 'lēz-\ *n* [MF *lese majesté*, fr. L *laesa majestas*, lit., injured majesty] : an offense violating the dignity of a sovereign

le·sion \'lē-zhən\ *n* : an abnormal structural change in the body due to injury or disease; *esp* : one clearly marked off from healthy tissue around it

¹**less** \'les\ *adj comparative of* ¹LITTLE **1** : FEWER ⟨~ than six⟩ **2** : of lower rank, degree, or importance **3** : SMALLER; *also* : more limited in quantity

²**less** *adv comparative of* ²LITTLE : to a lesser extent or degree

³**less** *n, pl* **less 1** : a smaller portion **2** : something of less importance

⁴**less** *prep* : diminished by : MINUS ⟨list price ~ the discount⟩

-less \ləs\ *adj suffix* **1** : destitute of : not having ⟨child*less*⟩ **2** : unable to be acted on or to act (in a specified way) ⟨daunt*less*⟩

les·see \le-'sē\ *n* : a tenant under a lease

less·en \'le-s°n\ *vb* : to make or become less **♦ Synonyms** DECREASE, DIMINISH, DWINDLE, ABATE

less·er \'le-sər\ *adj comparative of* ¹LIT-TLE : of less size, quality, or significance

les·son \'le-s°n\ *n* **1** : a passage from sacred writings read in a service of worship **2** : a reading or exercise to be studied by a pupil; *also* : something learned **3** : a period of instruction **4** : an instructive example

les·sor \'le-sȯr, le-'sȯr\ *n* : one who conveys property by a lease

lest \'lest\ *conj* : for fear that

¹**let** \'let\ *n* [ME *lette*, fr. *letten* to delay, hinder, fr. OE *lettan*] **1** : HINDRANCE, OBSTACLE **2** : a shot or point in racket games that does not count

²**let** *vb* **let; let·ting** [ME *leten*, fr. OE *lǣtan*] **1** : to cause to : MAKE ⟨∼ it be known⟩ **2** : RENT, LEASE; *also* : to assign esp. after bids **3** : ALLOW, PERMIT ⟨∼ me go⟩

-let *n suffix* **1** : small one ⟨book*let*⟩ **2** : article worn on ⟨wrist*let*⟩

let·down \'let-,daůn\ *n* **1** : DISAPPOINTMENT **2** : a slackening of effort

le·thal \'lē-thəl\ *adj* : DEADLY, FATAL — **le·thal·ly** *adv*

leth·ar·gy \'le-thər-jē\ *n* **1** : abnormal drowsiness **2** : the quality or state of being lazy or indifferent **♦ Synonyms** LANGUOR, LASSITUDE, TORPOR — **le·thar·gic** \li-'thär-jik\ *adj*

let on *vb* **1** : REVEAL 1 **2** : PRETEND

¹**let·ter** \'le-tər\ *n* **1** : a symbol that stands for a speech sound and constitutes a unit of an alphabet **2** : a written or printed communication **3** *pl* : LITERATURE; *also* : LEARNING **4** : the literal meaning ⟨the ∼ of the law⟩ **5** : a single piece of type

²**letter** *vb* : to mark with letters : INSCRIBE — **let·ter·er** *n*

letter bomb *n* : an explosive device concealed in an envelope and mailed to the intended victim

let·ter·boxed \'le-tər-,bäkst\ *adj* : being a video recording formatted to display a frame size proportional to a standard theater screen

let·ter·head \'le-tər-,hed\ *n* : stationery with a printed or engraved heading; *also* : the heading itself

let·ter–per·fect \,le-tər-'pər-fikt\ *adj* : correct to the smallest detail

let·ter·press \'le-tər-,pres\ *n* : printing done directly by impressing the paper on an inked raised surface

letters of marque \-'märk\ : a license granted to a private person by a government to fit out an armed ship to capture enemy shipping

letters patent *n pl* : a written grant from a government to a person in a form readily open for inspection by all

let·tuce \'le-təs\ *n* [ME *letuse*, fr. AF, prob. fr. pl. of *letue* lettuce plant, fr. L

lactuca, fr. *lac* milk; fr. its milky juice] : a garden composite plant with crisp leaves used esp. in salads

let-up \'let-,əp\ *n* : a lessening of effort

leu \'leů\ *n, pl* **lei** \'lā\ — see MONEY table

leu·kae·mia *chiefly Brit var of* LEUKEMIA

leu·ke·mia \lü-'kē-mē-ə\ *n* : a malignant disease characterized by an abnormal increase in the number of white blood cells in the blood-forming tissues — **leu·ke·mic** \-mik\ *adj or n*

leu·ko·cyte \'lü-kə-,sīt\ *n* : WHITE BLOOD CELL

lev \'lef\ *n, pl* **le·va** \'le-və\ — see MONEY table

Lev *or* **Levit** *abbr* Leviticus

¹**le·vee** \'le-vē, lə-'vē, -'vā\ *n* [F *lever* act of arising] : a reception held by or for a person of distinction

²**lev·ee** \'le-vē\ *n* : an embankment to prevent or confine flooding; *also* : a river landing place

¹**lev·el** \'le-vəl\ *n* **1** : a device for establishing a horizontal line or plane **2** : horizontal condition **3** : a horizontal position, line, or surface often taken as an index of altitude; *also* : a flat area of ground **4** : height, position, rank, or size in a scale

²**level** *vb* **-eled** *or* **-elled; -el·ing** *or* **-el·ling 1** : to make flat or level; *also* : to come to a level **2** : AIM, DIRECT **3** : EQUALIZE **4** : RAZE — **lev·el·er** *n*

³**level** *adj* **1** : having a flat even surface **2** : HORIZONTAL **3** : of the same height or rank; *also* : UNIFORM **4** : steady and cool in judgment — **lev·el·ly** *adv* — **lev·el·ness** *n*

lev·el·head·ed \,le-vəl-'he-dəd\ *adj* : having or showing sound judgment : SENSIBLE

le·ver \'le-vər, 'lē-\ *n* **1** : a bar used for prying or dislodging something; *also* : a means for achieving one's purpose **2** : a rigid piece turning about an axis and used for transmitting and changing force and motion

le·ver·age \'le-vrij, 'lē-, -və-rij\ *n* : the action or mechanical effect of a lever

le·vi·a·than \li-'vī-ə-thən\ *n* **1** : a large sea animal **2** : something large or formidable

lev·i·tate \'le-və-,tāt\ *vb* **-tat·ed; -tat·ing** : to rise or cause to rise in the air in seeming defiance of gravitation — **lev·i·ta·tion** \,le-və-'tā-shən\ *n*

Le·vit·i·cus \li-'vi-tə-kəs\ *n* — see BIBLE table

lev·i·ty \'le-və-tē\ *n* : lack of seriousness **♦ Synonyms** LIGHTNESS, FLIPPANCY, FRIVOLITY

levo·do·pa \,le-və-'dō-pə\ *n* : L-DOPA

¹**levy** \'le-vē\ *n, pl* **lev·ies 1** : the imposition or collection of an assessment; *also* : an amount levied **2** : the enlistment or conscription of men for military service; *also* : troops raised by levy

²**levy** *vb* **lev·ied; levy·ing 1** : to impose or collect by legal authority **2** : to enlist for military service : WAGE ⟨∼ war⟩ **4** : to seize property

lewd \'lüd\ *adj* [ME *lewed* vulgar, fr. OE *lǣwede* lay, ignorant] : sexually unchaste; *also* : OBSCENE, VULGAR — **lewd·ly** *adv* — **lewd·ness** *n*

lex·i·cog·ra·phy \ˌlek-sə-'kä-grə-fē\ *n* **1** : the editing or making of a dictionary **2** : the principles and practices of dictionary making — **lex·i·cog·ra·pher** \-fər\ *n* — **lex·i·co·graph·i·cal** \-kō-'gra-fi-kəl\ *or* **lex·i·co·graph·ic** \-fik\ *adj*

lex·i·con \'lek-sə-ˌkän\ *n, pl* **lex·i·ca** \-si-kə\ *or* **lexicons** **1** : DICTIONARY **2** : the vocabulary of a language, speaker, or subject

lg *abbr* **1** large **2** long

LH *abbr* **1** left hand **2** lower half

li *abbr* link

Li *symbol* lithium

LI *abbr* Long Island

li·a·bil·i·ty \ˌlī-ə-'bi-lə-tē\ *n, pl* **-ties 1** : the quality or state of being liable **2** *pl* : DEBTS **3** : DISADVANTAGE

li·a·ble \'lī-ə-bəl\ *adj* **1** : legally obligated : RESPONSIBLE **2** : LIKELY, APT ⟨~ to fall⟩ **3** : SUSCEPTIBLE ⟨~ to disease⟩

li·ai·son \'lē-ə-ˌzän, lē-'ā-\ *n* [F] **1** : a close bond : INTERRELATIONSHIP **2** : an illicit sexual relationship **3** : communication for mutual understanding (as between parts of an armed force); *also* : one that carries on a liaison

li·ar \'lī(-ə)r\ *n* : a person who lies

¹lib \'lib\ *n* : LIBERATION

²lib *abbr* **1** liberal **2** librarian; library

li·ba·tion \lī-'bā-shən\ *n* **1** : an act of pouring a liquid as a sacrifice (as to a god); *also* : the liquid poured **2** : DRINK

¹li·bel \'lī-bəl\ *n* [ME, written declaration, fr. AF, fr. L *libellus*, dim. of *liber* book] **1** : a spoken or written statement or a representation that gives an unjustly unfavorable impression of a person or thing **2** : the action or crime of publishing a libel — **li·bel·ous** *or* **li·bel·lous** \-bə-ləs\ *adj*

²libel *vb* **-beled** *or* **-belled; -bel·ing** *or* **-bel·ling** : to make or publish a libel — **li·bel·er** *n* — **li·bel·ist** *n*

¹lib·er·al \'li-brəl, -bə-rəl\ *adj* [ME, fr. AF, fr. L *liberalis* suitable for a freeman, generous, fr. *liber* free] **1** : of, relating to, or based on the liberal arts **2** : GENEROUS, BOUNTIFUL ⟨a ~ serving⟩ **3** : not literal **4** : not narrow in opinion or judgment : TOLERANT; *also* : not orthodox **5** : not conservative — **lib·er·al·i·ty** \ˌli-bə-'ra-lə-tē\ *n* — **lib·er·al·i·za·tion** \ˌli-brə-lə-'zā-shən, -bə-rə-\ *n* — **lib·er·al·ize** \'li-brə-ˌlīz, -bə-rə-\ *vb* — **lib·er·al·ly** *adv*

²liberal *n* : a person who holds liberal views

liberal arts *n pl* : the studies (as language, philosophy, history, literature, or abstract science) in a college or university intended to provide chiefly general knowledge and to develop the general intellectual capacities

lib·er·al·ism \'li-brə-ˌli-zəm, -bə-rə-\ *n* : liberal principles and theories

lib·er·ate \'li-bə-ˌrāt\ *vb* **-at·ed; -at·ing 1** : to free from bondage or restraint; *also* : to raise to equal rights and status **2** : to free (as a gas) from combination — **lib·er·a·tion** \ˌli-bə-'rā-shən\ *n* — **lib·er·a·tor** \'li-bə-ˌrā-tər\ *n*

liberated *adj* : freed from or opposed to traditional social and sexual attitudes or roles ⟨a ~ marriage⟩

lib·er·tar·i·an \ˌli-bər-'ter-ē-ən\ *n* **1** : an advocate of the doctrine of free will **2** : one who upholds the principles of unrestricted liberty

lib·er·tine \'li-bər-ˌtēn\ *n* : a person who leads a dissolute life

lib·er·ty \'li-bər-tē\ *n, pl* **-ties 1** : FREEDOM **2** : an action going beyond normal limits; *esp* : FAMILIARITY **3** : a short leave from naval duty

li·bid·i·nous \lə-'bi-də-nəs\ *adj* **1** : LASCIVIOUS **2** : LIBIDINAL

li·bi·do \lə-'bē-dō\ *n, pl* **-dos** [NL, fr. L desire, lust] **1** : psychic energy derived from basic biological urges **2** : sexual drive — **li·bid·i·nal** \lə-'bi-də-nəl\ *adj*

Li·bra \'lē-brə\ *n* [L, lit., scales] **1** : a zodiacal constellation between Virgo and Scorpio usu. pictured as a balance scale **2** : the 7th sign of the zodiac in astrology; *also* : one born under this sign

li·brar·i·an \lī-'brer-ē-ən\ *n* : a specialist in the management of a library

li·brary \'lī-ˌbrer-ē\ *n, pl* **-brar·ies 1** : a place in which books and related materials are kept for use but not for sale **2** : a collection of books

li·bret·to \lə-'bre-tō\ *n, pl* **-tos** *or* **-ti** \-tē\ [It, dim. of *libro* book, fr. L *liber*] : the text esp. of an opera — **li·bret·tist** \-tist\ *n*

lice *pl of* LOUSE

li·cense *or* **li·cence** \'lī-sᵊns\ *n* **1** : permission to act **2** : a permission granted by authority to engage in an activity **3** : a document, plate, or tag providing proof of a license **4** : freedom used irresponsibly — **license** *vb*

licensed practical nurse *n* : a specially trained person who is licensed (as by a state) to provide routine care for the sick

li·cens·ee \ˌlī-sᵊn-'sē\ *n* : a licensed person

licente *pl of* SENTE

li·cen·ti·ate \lī-'sen-chē-ət\ *n* : one licensed to practice a profession

li·cen·tious \lī-'sen-chəs\ *adj* : LEWD, LASCIVIOUS — **li·cen·tious·ly** *adv* — **li·cen·tious·ness** *n*

lichee *var of* LITCHI

li·chen \'lī-kən\ *n* : any of various complex plantlike organisms made up of an alga and a fungus growing as a unit on a solid surface — **li·chen·ous** *adj*

lic·it \'li-sət\ *adj* : LAWFUL

¹lick \'lik\ *vb* **1** : to draw the tongue over; *also* : to flicker over like a tongue **2** : THRASH; *also* : DEFEAT

²lick *n* **1** : a stroke of the tongue **2** : a small amount **3** : a hasty careless effort **4** : BLOW **5** : a natural deposit of salt that animals lick

lick·e·ty–split \ˌli-kə-tē-'split\ *adv* : at great speed

lick·spit·tle \'lik-ˌspi-t°l\ *n* : a fawning subordinate : TOADY

lic·o·rice \'li-kə-rish, -rəs\ *n* [ME, fr. AF *licoris*, fr. LL *liquiritia*, alter. of L *glycyrrhiza*, fr. Gk *glykyrrhiza*, fr. *glykys* sweet + *rhiza* root] **1** : the dried root of a European leguminous plant; *also* : an extract from it used esp. as a flavoring and in medicine **2** : a candy flavored with licorice **3** : a plant yielding licorice

lid \'lid\ *n* **1** : a movable cover **2** : EYELID **3** : something that confines or suppresses — **lid·ded** \'li-dəd\ *adj*

li·do \'lē-dō\ *n*, *pl* **lidos** : a fashionable beach resort

¹lie \'lī\ *vb* **lay** \'lā\; **lain** \'lān\; **ly·ing** \'lī-iŋ\ **1** : to be in, stay at rest in, or assume a horizontal position; *also* : to be in a helpless or defenseless state **2** : EXTEND ⟨our route *lay* to the west⟩ **3** : to occupy a certain relative position **4** : to have an effect esp. through mere presence

²lie *n* : the position in which something lies

³lie *vb* **lied**; **ly·ing** \'lī-iŋ\ : to tell a lie

⁴lie *n* : an untrue statement made with intent to deceive

lied \'lēt\ *n*, *pl* **lie·der** \'lē-dər\ [G] : a German song esp. of the 19th century

lie detector *n* : a polygraph for detecting physiological evidence of the tension that accompanies lying

lief \'lēv, 'lēf\ *adv* : GLADLY, WILLINGLY

¹liege \'lēj\ *adj* : LOYAL, FAITHFUL

²liege *n* **1** : VASSAL **2** : a feudal superior

lien \'lēn, 'lē-ən\ *n* : a legal claim on the property of another for the satisfaction of a debt or duty

lieu \'lü\ *n*, *archaic* : PLACE, STEAD — **in lieu of** : in the place of

lieut *abbr* lieutenant

lieu·ten·ant \lü-'te-nənt\ *n* [ME, fr. AF *lieu tenant*, fr. *liu, lieu* place + *tenant* holding, fr. *tenir* to hold, fr. L *tenēre*] **1** : a representative of another in the performance of duty **2** : FIRST LIEUTENANT; *also* : SECOND LIEUTENANT **3** : a commissioned officer in the navy ranking next below a lieutenant commander — **lieu·ten·an·cy** \-nən-sē\ *n*

lieutenant colonel *n* : a commissioned officer (as in the army) ranking next below a colonel

lieutenant commander *n* : a commissioned officer in the navy ranking next below a commander

lieutenant general *n* : a commissioned officer (as in the army) ranking next below a general

lieutenant governor *n* : a deputy or subordinate governor

lieutenant junior grade *n*, *pl* **lieutenants junior grade** : a commissioned officer in the navy ranking next below a lieutenant

life \'līf\ *n*, *pl* **lives** \'līvz\ **1** : the quality that distinguishes a vital and functional being from a dead body or inanimate matter; *also* : a state of an organism characterized esp. by capacity for metabolism, growth, reaction to stimuli, and reproduction **2** : the physical and mental experiences of an individual **3** : BIOGRAPHY **4** : a specific phase or period ⟨adult ∼⟩ **5** : the period from birth to death; *also* : a sentence of imprisonment for the remainder of a person's life **6** : a way of living **7** : PERSON ⟨many *lives* were lost in the fire⟩ **8** : ANIMATION, SPIRIT ⟨danced without ∼⟩ **9** : living beings ⟨forest ∼⟩ **10** : animate activity ⟨signs of ∼⟩ **11** : one providing interest and vigor ⟨∼ of the party⟩ — **life·less** *adj* — **life·like** *adj*

life·blood \'līf-ˌbləd\ *n* : a basic source of strength and vitality

life·boat \-ˌbōt\ *n* : a sturdy boat designed for use in saving lives at sea

life·guard \-ˌgärd\ *n* : a usu. expert swimmer employed to safeguard bathers

life·line \-ˌlīn\ *n* **1** : a line to which persons may cling for safety **2** : something considered vital for survival

life·long \-ˌlȯŋ\ *adj* : continuing through life

life preserver *n* : a buoyant device designed to save a person from drowning

lif·er \'lī-fər\ *n* **1** : a person sentenced to life imprisonment **2** : a person who makes a career in the armed forces

life raft *n* : a raft for use by people forced into the water

life·sav·ing \'līf-ˌsā-viŋ\ *n* : the skill or practice of saving or protecting lives esp. of drowning persons — **life·sav·er** \-ˌsā-vər\ *n*

life science *n* : a branch of science (as biology, medicine, and sometimes anthropology or sociology) that deals with living organisms and life processes — usu. used in pl. — **life scientist** *n*

¹life·style \'līf-ˌstī(-ə)l\ *n* : a way of living

²lifestyle *adj* : associated with, reflecting, or promoting an enhanced or more desirable lifestyle

life·time \-ˌtīm\ *n* : the duration of an individual's existence

life·work \-'wərk\ *n* : the entire or principal work of one's lifetime; *also* : a work extending over a lifetime

life·world \-ˌwər(-ə)ld\ *n* : the total of an individual's physical surroundings and everyday experiences

LIFO *abbr* last in, first out

¹lift \'lift\ *vb* **1** : RAISE, ELEVATE; *also* : RISE, ASCEND **2** : to put an end to : STOP **3** : to pay off ⟨∼ a mortgage⟩ — **lift·er** *n*

²lift *n* **1** : LOAD **2** : the action or an instance of lifting **3** : HELP; *also* : a ride along one's way **4** : RISE, ADVANCE **5** *chiefly Brit* : ELEVATOR **6** : an elevation of the spirits **7** : the upward force that is developed by a moving airfoil and that opposes the pull of gravity

lift·off \-ˌȯf\ *n* : a vertical takeoff (as by a rocket)

lift truck *n* : a small truck for lifting and transporting loads

lig·a·ment \'li-gə-mənt\ *n* : a band of tough fibrous tissue that holds bones together or supports an organ in place

li·gate \'lī-ˌgāt\ *vb* **li·gat·ed**; **li·gat·ing**

: to tie with a ligature — **li·ga·tion** \lī-'gā-shən\ n

lig·a·ture \'li-gə-ˌchùr, -chər\ n 1 : something that binds or ties; also : a thread used in surgery esp. for tying blood vessels 2 : a printed or written character consisting of two or more letters or characters (as æ) united

¹light \'līt\ n 1 : something that makes vision possible : electromagnetic radiation visible to the human eye; also : the sensation aroused by stimulation of the visual sense organs 2 : DAYLIGHT 3 : a source of light (as a candle) 4 : ENLIGHTENMENT; also : TRUTH 5 : public knowledge ⟨facts brought to ∼⟩ 6 : a particular aspect presented to view ⟨saw the matter in a different ∼⟩ 7 : WINDOW 8 pl : STANDARDS ⟨according to his ∼s⟩ 9 : CELEBRITY 10 : LIGHTHOUSE, BEACON; also : TRAFFIC LIGHT 11 : a flame for lighting something

²light adj 1 : having light : BRIGHT 2 : PALE 2 ⟨∼ blue⟩ — **light·ness** n

³light vb **lit** \'lit\ or **light·ed; light·ing** 1 : to make or become light 2 : to cause to burn : BURN 3 : to conduct with a light 4 : ILLUMINATE

⁴light adj 1 : not heavy 2 : not serious ⟨∼ reading⟩ 3 : SCANTY ⟨∼ rain⟩ 4 : easily disturbed ⟨a ∼ sleeper⟩ 5 : GENTLE ⟨a ∼ blow⟩ 6 : easily endurable ⟨a ∼ cold⟩; also : requiring little effort ⟨∼ exercise⟩ 7 : SWIFT, NIMBLE 8 : FRIVOLOUS 9 : DIZZY 10 : made with lower calorie content or less of some ingredient than usual ⟨∼ salad dressing⟩ 11 : producing goods for direct consumption by the consumer ⟨∼ industry⟩ — **light·ly** adv — **light·ness** n

⁵light adv 1 : LIGHTLY 2 : with little baggage ⟨travel ∼⟩

⁶light vb **lit** \'lit\ or **light·ed; light·ing** 1 : SETTLE, ALIGHT 2 : to fall unexpectedly 3 : HAPPEN

light bulb n 1 : a lamp in which an electrically heated filament emits light 2 : FLUORESCENT LAMP

light–emitting diode n : LED

¹light·en \'līt-ᵊn\ vb 1 : ILLUMINATE, BRIGHTEN 2 : to give out flashes of lightning

²lighten vb 1 : to relieve of a burden 2 : GLADDEN 3 : to become lighter

lighten up vb : to take things less seriously

¹light·er \'lī-tər\ n : a barge used esp. in loading or unloading ships

²light·er \'lī-tər\ n : one that lights; esp : a device for lighting (as a fire or cigarette)

light·face \'līt-ˌfās\ n : a type having light thin lines — **light·faced** \-ˌfāst\ adj

light–head·ed \'līt-ˌhe-dəd\ adj 1 : feeling confused or dizzy 2 : lacking maturity or seriousness

light–heart·ed \-ˌhär-təd\ adj : free from worry — **light–heart·ed·ly** adv — **light–heart·ed·ness** n

light·house \-ˌhaùs\ n : a structure with a powerful light for guiding sailors

light meter n : a usu. handheld device for indicating correct photographic exposure

¹light·ning \'līt-niŋ\ n : the flashing of light produced by a discharge of atmospheric electricity; also : the discharge itself

²lightning adj : extremely fast

lightning bug n : FIREFLY

lightning rod n : a grounded metallic rod set up on a structure to protect it from lightning

light out vb : to leave in a hurry

light·proof \'līt-ˌprüf\ adj : impenetrable by light

lights \'līts\ n pl : the lungs esp. of a slaughtered animal

light·ship \'līt-ˌship\ n : a ship with a powerful light moored at a place dangerous to navigation

light show n : a kaleidoscopic display (as of colored lights)

light·some \'līt-səm\ adj 1 : free from care 2 : NIMBLE

¹light·weight \'līt-ˌwāt\ n : one of less than average weight; esp : a boxer weighing not over 135 pounds

²lightweight adj 1 : INCONSEQUENTIAL 2 : of less than average weight

light–year \'līt-ˌyir\ n 1 : an astronomical unit of distance equal to the distance that light travels in one year in a vacuum or about 5.88 trillion miles (9.46 trillion kilometers) 2 : an extremely large measure of comparison ⟨saw it ∼s ago⟩

lig·nin \'lig-nən\ n : a substance related to cellulose that occurs in the woody cell walls of plants and in the cementing material between them

lig·nite \'lig-ˌnīt\ n : brownish black soft coal

¹like \'līk\ vb **liked; lik·ing** 1 : ENJOY ⟨∼s baseball⟩ 2 : WANT ⟨would ∼ a drink⟩ 3 : CHOOSE ⟨does as she ∼s⟩ — **lik·able** or **like·able** \'lī-kə-bəl\ adj

²like n : PREFERENCE

³like adj : SIMILAR ✦ *Synonyms* ALIKE, ANALOGOUS, COMPARABLE, PARALLEL, UNIFORM

⁴like prep 1 : similar or similarly to ⟨seems ∼ a dream⟩ 2 : typical of 3 : comparable to 4 : as though there would be ⟨looks ∼ rain⟩ 5 : such as ⟨a subject ∼ physics⟩

⁵like n 1 : COUNTERPART 2 : one that is similar to another — **and the like** : ET CETERA

⁶like conj 1 : AS IF ⟨acted — they were scared⟩ 2 : in the same way that ⟨do it ∼ mom said⟩

-like adj comb form : resembling or characteristic of ⟨ladylike⟩ ⟨lifelike⟩

like·li·hood \'lī-klē-ˌhúd\ n : PROBABILITY

¹like·ly \'lī-klē\ adj **like·li·er; -est** 1 : very probable 2 : BELIEVABLE 3 : PROMISING ⟨a ∼ place to fish⟩

²likely adv : in all probability

lik·en \'lī-kən\ vb : COMPARE

like·ness \'līk-nəs\ n 1 : COPY, PORTRAIT 2 : SEMBLANCE 3 : RESEMBLANCE

like·wise \-ˌwīz\ adv 1 : in like manner 2 : in addition : ALSO

lik·ing \'lī-kiŋ\ n : favorable regard ⟨took a ∼ to the newcomer⟩; also : TASTE

li·lac \'lī-lək, -ˌlak, -ˌläk\ n [obs. F (now lilas), fr. Ar līlak, fr. Pers nīlak bluish, fr. nīl blue, fr. Skt nīla dark blue] **1** : a shrub related to the olive that produces large clusters of fragrant grayish pink, purple, or white flowers **2** : a moderate purple color

lil·an·ge·ni \ˌli-lən-'ge-nē\ n, pl em·a·lan·ge·ni \ˌe-mə-lən-'ge-nē\ — see MONEY table

lil·li·pu·tian \ˌli-lə-'pyü-shən\ adj, often cap **1** : SMALL, MINIATURE **2** : PETTY

lilt \'lilt\ n **1** : a cheerful lively song or tune **2** : a rhythmical swing or flow

lily \'li-lē\ n, pl **lil·ies** : any of a genus of tall bulbous herbs with leafy stems and usu. funnel-shaped flowers; also : any of various related plants

lily of the valley : a low perennial herb related to the lilies that produces a raceme of fragrant nodding bell-shaped white flowers

li·ma bean \'lī-mə-\ n : a bushy or tall-growing bean widely cultivated for its flat edible usu. pale green or whitish seeds; also : the seed

limb \'lim\ n **1** : one of the projecting paired appendages (as legs, arms, or wings) used by an animal esp. in moving or grasping **2** : a large branch of a tree : BOUGH — **limb·less** adj

¹lim·ber \'lim-bər\ adj **1** : FLEXIBLE, SUPPLE **2** : LITHE, NIMBLE

²limber vb : to make or become limber

lim·bic \'lim-bik\ adj : of, relating to, or being a group of structures of the brain (**limbic system**) concerned esp. with emotion and motivation

¹lim·bo \'lim-bō\ n, pl **limbos** [ME, fr. ML, abl. of limbus limbo, fr. L, border] **1** often cap : an abode of souls barred from heaven through no fault of their own **2** : a place or state of confinement, oblivion, or uncertainty

²limbo n, pl **limbos** : an acrobatic dance or contest that involves passing under a horizontal pole

Lim·burg·er \'lim-ˌbər-gər\ n : a pungent semisoft surface-ripened cheese

¹lime \'līm\ n : a caustic powdery white solid that consists of calcium and oxygen, is obtained from limestone or shells, and is used in making cement and in fertilizer — **lime** vb — **limy** \'lī-mē\ adj

²lime n : a small yellowish green citrus fruit with juicy acid pulp

lime·ade \ˌlīm-'ād, 'lī-ˌmād\ n : a beverage of lime juice, sugar, and water

lime·light \'līm-ˌlīt\ n **1** : a device in which flame is directed against a cylinder of lime formerly used in the theater to cast a strong white light on the stage **2** : the center of public attention

lim·er·ick \'li-mə-rik\ n : a light or humorous poem of 5 lines

lime·stone \'līm-ˌstōn\ n : a rock that is formed by accumulation of organic remains (as shells), is used in building, and yields lime when burned

¹lim·it \'li-mət\ n **1** : something that restrains or confines; also : the utmost extent **2** : BOUNDARY; also, pl : BOUNDS **3** : a prescribed maximum or minimum **4** : a number whose value becomes arbitrarily close to that of a function as its independent variable approaches a given value — **lim·it·less** adj — **lim·it·less·ness** n

²limit vb **1** : to set limits to **2** : to reduce in quantity or extent — **lim·i·ta·tion** \ˌli-mə-'tā-shən\ n

lim·it·ed adj **1** : confined within limits **2** : offering faster service esp. by making fewer stops

limn \'lim\ vb **limned; limn·ing** \'li-miŋ, 'lim-niŋ\ **1** : DRAW; also : PAINT **2** : DELINEATE **3** : DESCRIBE

limo \'li-(ˌ)mō\ n, pl **limos** : LIMOUSINE

li·mo·nite \'lī-mə-ˌnīt\ n : a ferric oxide that is a major ore of iron — **li·mo·nit·ic** \ˌlī-mə-'ni-tik\ adj

lim·ou·sine \'li-mə-ˌzēn, ˌli-mə-'zēn\ n [F] **1** : a large luxurious often chauffeur-driven sedan **2** : a large vehicle for transporting passengers to and from an airport

¹limp \'limp\ vb : to walk lamely; also : to proceed with difficulty

²limp n : a limping movement or gait

³limp adj : having no defined shape; also : not stiff or rigid **2** : lacking in strength or firmness — **limp·ly** adv — **limp·ness** n

lim·pet \'lim-pət\ n : any of numerous gastropod sea mollusks with a conical shell that clings to rocks or timbers

lim·pid \'lim-pəd\ adj : CLEAR, TRANSPARENT

lin abbr **1** lineal **2** linear

lin·age \'lī-nij\ n : the number of lines of written or printed matter

linch·pin \'linch-ˌpin\ n : a locking pin inserted crosswise (as through the end of an axle)

lin·den \'lin-dən\ n : any of a genus of trees with large heart-shaped leaves and clustered yellowish flowers; also : the light white wood of a linden

¹line \'līn\ n **1** : CORD, ROPE, WIRE; also : a length of material used in measuring and leveling **2** : pipes for conveying a fluid ⟨a gas ∼⟩ **3** : a horizontal row of written or printed characters; also : VERSE **4** : NOTE **5** : the words making up a part in a drama — usu. used in pl. **6** : something distinct, long, and narrow; also : ROUTE **7** : a state of agreement **8** : a course of conduct, action, or thought; also : OCCUPATION **9** : LIMIT **10** : an arrangement of persons or objects of one kind in an orderly series ⟨waiting in ∼⟩ **11** : a transportation system **12 a** : the football players who are stationed on the line of scrimmage **b** : a group of three players who play together as a unit in hockey **13** : a long narrow mark; also : EQUATOR **14** : a geometric element that is the path of a moving point **15** : CONTOUR **16** : a general plan ⟨thinking along these ∼s⟩ **17** : an indication based on insight or investigation

²line vb **lined; lin·ing** **1** : to mark with a line **2** : to place or form a line along **3** : ALIGN

³**line** \'*vb* **lined; lin·ing** : to cover the inner surface of

lin·eage \'li-nē-ij\ *n* : lineal descent from a common progenitor; *also* : FAMILY

lin·eal \'li-nē-əl\ *adj* **1** : LINEAR **2** : consisting of or being in a direct line of ancestry; *also* : HEREDITARY

lin·ea·ment \'li-nē-ə-mənt\ *n* : an outline, feature, or contour of a body and esp. of a face — usu. used in pl.

lin·ear \'li-nē-ər\ *adj* **1** : of, relating to, resembling, or having a graph that is a line and esp. a straight line : STRAIGHT **2** : composed of simply drawn lines with little attempt at pictorial representation ⟨~ script⟩ **3** : being long and uniformly narrow

line·back·er \'līn-ˌba-kər\ *n* : a defensive football player who lines up just behind the line of scrimmage

line drive *n* : a batted baseball hit in a flatter path than a fly ball

line–item veto *n* : the power of a government executive to veto specific items in an appropriations bill

line·man \'līn-mən\ *n* **1** : a person who sets up or repairs communication or power lines **2** : a player in the line in football

lin·en \'li-nən\ *n* **1** : cloth made of flax; *also* : thread or yarn spun from flax **2** : clothing or household articles made of linen cloth or similar fabric

line of scrimmage : an imaginary line in football parallel to the goal lines and tangent to the nose of the ball laid on the ground before a play

¹**lin·er** \'lī-nər\ *n* : a ship or airplane of a regular transportation line

²**liner** *n* : one that lines or is used as a lining — **lin·er·less** *adj*

line score *n* : a score of a baseball game giving the runs, hits, and errors made by each team

lines·man \'līnz-mən\ *n* **1** : LINEMAN 1 **2** : an official who assists a referee

line·up \'lī-ˌnəp\ *n* **1** : a list of players taking part in a game (as of baseball) **2** : a line of persons arranged esp. for identification by police

ling \'liŋ\ *n* : any of various fishes related to the cod

-ling *n suffix* **1** : one associated with ⟨nest*ling*⟩ **2** : young, small, or minor one ⟨duck*ling*⟩

lin·ger \'liŋ-gər\ *vb* : TARRY; *also* : PROCRASTINATE — **lin·ger·er** *n*

lin·ge·rie \ˌlän-jə-'rā, ˌlaⁿ-zhə-, -'rē\ *n* [F, fr. MF, fr. *linge* linen, fr. L *lineus* made of linen, fr. *linum* flax, linen] : women's intimate apparel

lin·go \'liŋ-gō\ *n, pl* **lingoes** : a usu. strange or incomprehensible language

lin·gua fran·ca \ˌliŋ-gwə-'fraŋ-kə\ *n, pl* **lingua francas** *or* **lin·guae fran·cae** \-gwē-'fraŋ-ˌkē\ [It] **1** *often cap* : a common language consisting of Italian mixed with French, Spanish, Greek, and Arabic that was formerly spoken in Mediterranean ports **2** : a common or commercial tongue among speakers of different languages

lin·gual \'liŋ-gwəl\ *adj* : of, relating to, or produced by the tongue

lin·gui·ca \liŋ-'gwē-sə\ *n* : a spicy Portuguese sausage

lin·guist \'liŋ-gwist\ *n* **1** : a person skilled in languages **2** : a person who specializes in linguistics

lin·guis·tics \liŋ-'gwis-tiks\ *n* : the study of human speech including the units, nature, structure, and modification of language — **lin·guis·tic** \-tik\ *adj*

lin·i·ment \'li-nə-mənt\ *n* : a liquid preparation rubbed on the skin esp. to relieve pain

lin·ing \'lī-niŋ\ *n* : material used to line esp. an inner surface

link \'liŋk\ *n* **1** : a connecting structure; *esp* : a single ring of a chain **2** : BOND, TIE **3** : HYPERLINK — **link** *vb* — **link·er** *n*

link·age \'liŋ-kij\ *n* **1** : the manner or style of being united **2** : the quality or state of being linked **3** : a system of links

linking verb *n* : a word or expression (as a form of *be, become, feel,* or *seem*) that links a subject with its predicate

links \'liŋks\ *n pl* : a golf course

link·up \'liŋk-ˌkəp\ *n* **1** : MEETING **2** : something that serves as a linking device or factor

lin·net \'li-nət\ *n* : an Old World finch

li·no·leum \lə-'nō-lē-əm\ *n* [L *linum* flax + *oleum* oil] : a floor covering with a canvas back and a surface of hardened linseed oil and a filler

lin·seed \'lin-ˌsēd\ *n* : the seeds of flax yielding a yellowish oil (**linseed oil**) used esp. in paints and linoleum

lin·sey–wool·sey \ˌlin-zē-'wùl-zē\ *n* : a coarse sturdy fabric of wool and linen or cotton

lint \'lint\ *n* **1** : linen made into a soft fleecy substance **2** : fine ravels and short fibers of yarn or fabric **3** : the fibers that surround cotton seeds and form the cotton staple

lin·tel \'lin-tᵊl\ *n* : a horizontal piece across the top of an opening (as of a door) that carries the weight of the structure above it

linz·er torte \'lin-sər-, -zər-\ *n, often cap L* : a baked buttery torte made with chopped almonds, sugar, and spices and filled with jam or preserves

li·on \'lī-ən\ *n, pl* **lions** : a large heavily built cat of Africa and southern Asia with a shaggy mane in the male

li·on·ess \'lī-ə-nəs\ *n* : a female lion

li·on·heart·ed \ˌlī-ən-'här-təd\ *adj* : COURAGEOUS, BRAVE

li·on·ise *Brit var of* LIONIZE

li·on·ize \'lī-ə-ˌnīz\ *vb* **-ized; -iz·ing** : to treat as an object of great interest or importance — **li·on·i·za·tion** \ˌlī-ə-nə-'zā-shən\ *n*

lion's den *n* : a place or state of extreme disadvantage, antagonism, or hostility

lip \'lip\ *n* **1** : either of the two fleshy folds that surround the mouth; *also* : the margin of the human lip **2** : a part or projection suggesting a lip **3** : the edge of a hollow vessel or cavity — **lipped** \'lipt\ *adj*

li·pa \'lē-ˌpä, -pə\ *n, pl* **lipa** — see **kuna** at MONEY table

lip·id \'li-pəd\ *n* : any of various substances (as fats and waxes) that with proteins and carbohydrates make up the principal structural parts of living cells

lip·lock \'lip-ˌläk\ *n* : a long amorous kiss

li·po·pro·tein \ˌlī-pō-'prō-ˌtēn, ˌli-\ *n* : a protein that is a complex of protein and lipid

li·po·suc·tion \'li-pə-ˌsək-shən, 'lī-\ *n* : surgical removal of local fat deposits (as in the thighs) esp. for cosmetic purposes

lip·read·ing \'lip-ˌrē-diŋ\ *n* : the interpreting of a speaker's words by watching lip and facial movements without hearing the voice

lip service *n* : an avowal of allegiance that is not matched by action

lip·stick \'lip-ˌstik\ *n* : a waxy solid colored cosmetic in stick form for the lips — **lip·sticked** \-ˌstikt\ *adj*

liq *abbr* **1** liquid **2** liquor

liq·ue·fy *also* **liq·ui·fy** \'li-kwə-ˌfī\ *vb* **-fied; -fy·ing** : to make or become liquid — **liq·ue·fi·er** \-ˌfī(-ə)r\ *n*

li·queur \li-'kər\ *n* [F] : a distilled alcoholic liquor flavored with aromatic substances and usu. sweetened

¹**liq·uid** \'li-kwəd\ *adj* **1** : flowing freely like water **2** : neither solid nor gaseous **3** : shining and clear ⟨large ∼ eyes⟩ **4** : smooth and musical in tone; *also* : smooth and unconstrained in movement **5** : consisting of or capable of ready conversion into cash ⟨∼ assets⟩ — **li·quid·i·ty** \li-'kwi-də-tē\ *n*

²**liquid** *n* : a liquid substance

liq·ui·date \'li-kwə-ˌdāt\ *vb* **-dat·ed; -dat·ing** **1** : to settle the accounts and distribute the assets of (as a business) **2** : to pay off ⟨∼ a debt⟩ **3** : to get rid of; *esp* : KILL — **liq·ui·da·tion** \ˌli-kwə-'dā-shən\ *n*

liquid crystal *n* : an organic liquid that resembles a crystal in having ordered molecular arrays

liquid crystal display *n* : LCD

liquid measure *n* : a unit or series of units for measuring liquid capacity — see METRIC SYSTEM table, WEIGHT table

li·quor \'li-kər\ *n* [ME *licour*, fr. AF, fr. L *liquor*, fr. *liquēre* to be fluid] : a liquid substance; *esp* : a distilled alcoholic beverage

li·quo·rice *chiefly Brit var of* LICORICE

li·ra \'lir-ə, 'lē-rə\ *n* **1** *pl* **li·re** \'lē-rā\ : the former basic monetary unit of Italy **2** : the basic monetary unit of Turkey — see MONEY table **3** *pl* **li·ri** \'lē-rē\ : the basic monetary unit of Malta — see MONEY table

lisente *pl of* SENTE

lisle \'līl-(ə)l\ *n* : a smooth tightly twisted thread usu. made of long-staple cotton

lisp \'lisp\ *vb* : to pronounce \s\ and \z\ imperfectly esp. by turning them into \th\ and \th\; *also* : to speak childishly — **lisp** *n* — **lisp·er** *n*

lis·some *also* **lis·som** \'li-səm\ *adj* **1** : easily flexed **2** : LITHE 2 **3** : NIMBLE — **lis·some·ly** *adv*

¹**list** \'list\ *vb, archaic* : PLEASE; *also* : WISH

²**list** *vb, archaic* : LISTEN

³**list** *n* : a leaning to one side : TILT

⁴**list** *vb* : TILT

⁵**list** *n* **1** : a simple series of words or numerals; *also* : an official roster **2** : CATALOG, CHECKLIST

⁶**list** *vb* : to make a list of; *also* : to include on a list — **list·ee** \li-'stē\ *n*

lis·ten \'li-sᵊn\ *vb* **1** : to pay attention in order to hear **2** : HEED — **lis·ten·er** *n*

lis·ten·er·ship \'li-sᵊn-ər-ˌship\ *n* : the audience for a radio program or recording

list·ing \'lis-tiŋ\ *n* **1** : an act or instance of making or including in a list **2** : something that is listed

list·less \'list-ləs\ *adj* : SPIRITLESS, LANGUID ⟨a ∼ performance⟩ — **list·less·ly** *adv* — **list·less·ness** *n*

list price *n* : the price of an item as published in a catalog, price list, or advertisement before being discounted

lists \'lists\ *n pl* : an arena for combat (as jousting)

¹**lit** \'lit\ *past and past part of* LIGHT

²**lit** *abbr* **1** liter **2** literal; literally **3** literary **4** literature

lit·a·ny \'li-tᵊn-nē\ *n, pl* **-nies** [ME *letanie*, fr. AF & LL; AF, fr. LL *litania*, fr. LGk *litaneia*, fr. Gk, entreaty, fr. *litanos* suppliant] **1** : a prayer consisting of a series of supplications and responses said alternately by a leader and a group **2** : a lengthy recitation ⟨a ∼ of complaints⟩

li·tas \'lē-ˌtäs\ *n, pl* **li·tai** \-ˌtī\ *or* **li·tu** \-ˌtü\ — see MONEY table

litchi *var of* LYCHEE

lite \'līt\ *adj* **1** : ⁴LIGHT 10 ⟨∼ beer⟩ **2** : lacking in substance or seriousness ⟨∼ news⟩

li·ter \'lē-tər\ *n* — see METRIC SYSTEM table

lit·er·al \'li-tə-rəl\ *adj* **1** : adhering to fact or to the ordinary or usual meaning (as of a word) **2** : UNADORNED; *also* : PROSAIC **3** : VERBATIM

lit·er·al·ism \-rə-ˌli-zəm\ *n* **1** : adherence to the explicit substance (as of an idea) **2** : fidelity to observable fact — **lit·er·al·ist** \-list\ *n* — **lit·er·al·is·tic** \ˌli-tə-rə-'lis-tik\ *adj*

lit·er·al·ly \'li-tə-rə-lē, 'li-trə-\ *adv* **1** : ACTUALLY ⟨was ∼ insane⟩ **2** : VIRTUALLY ⟨∼ poured out new ideas⟩

lit·er·ary \'li-tə-ˌrer-ē\ *adj* **1** : of or relating to literature **2** : WELL-READ

lit·er·ate \'li-trət, -tə-rət\ *adj* **1** : EDUCATED; *also* : able to read and write **2** : LITERARY; *also* : POLISHED, LUCID — **lit·er·a·cy** \'li-trə-sē, -tə-rə-\ *n* — **literate** *n*

li·te·ra·ti \ˌli-tə-'rä-tē\ *n pl* **1** : the educated class **2** : persons interested in literature or the arts

lit·er·a·ture \'li-trə-ˌchu̇r, -tə-rə-, -chər\ *n* **1** : the production of written works having excellence of form or expression and dealing with ideas of permanent interest **2** : the written works produced in a particular language, country, or age

lithe \\'līth, 'lĭth\ *adj* 1 : SUPPLE 2 : characterized by effortless grace; *also* : athletically slim

lithe·some \\'līth-səm, 'lĭth-\ *adj* : LISSOME

lith·i·um \\'li-thē-əm\ *n* : a light silver-white metallic chemical element

li·thog·ra·phy \li-'thä-grə-fē\ *n* : the process of printing from a plane surface (as a smooth stone or metal plate) on which the image to be printed is ink-receptive and the blank area ink-repellent — **lith·o·graph** \\'li-thə-ˌgraf\ *vb* — **lithograph** *n* — **li·thog·ra·pher** \li-'thä-grə-fər, 'li-thə-ˌgra-fər\ *n* — **lith·o·graph·ic** \ˌli-thə-'gra-fik\ *adj* — **lith·o·graph·i·cal·ly** \-fi-k(ə-)lē\ *adv*

li·thol·o·gy \li-'thä-lə-jē\ *n, pl* -**gies** : the study of rocks — **lith·o·log·ic** \ˌli-thə-'lä-jik\ *or* **lith·o·log·i·cal** \-ji-kəl\ *adj*

lith·o·sphere \\'li-thə-ˌsfir\ *n* : the outer part of the solid earth

Lith·u·a·nian \ˌli-thə-'wā-nē-ən, -thyü-\ *n* 1 : a native or inhabitant of Lithuania 2 : the language of the Lithuanians — **Lithuanian** *adj*

lit·i·gant \\'li-ti-gənt\ *n* : a party to a lawsuit — **litigant** *adj*

lit·i·gate \\-ˌgāt\ *vb* -**gat·ed**; -**gat·ing** : to carry on a legal contest by judicial process; *also* : to contest at law — **lit·i·ga·tion** \ˌli-tə-'gā-shən\ *n*

li·ti·gious \lə-'ti-jəs\ *adj* 1 : CONTENTIOUS 2 : prone to engage in lawsuits 3 : of or relating to litigation — **li·ti·gious·ly** *adv* — **li·ti·gious·ness** *n*

lit·mus \\'lit-məs\ *n* : a coloring matter from lichens that turns red in acid solutions and blue in alkaline

litmus test *n* : a test in which a single factor (as an attitude) is decisive

Litt D *or* **Lit D** *abbr* [ML *litterarum doctor*] : doctor of letters; doctor of literature

¹**lit·ter** \\'li-tər\ *n* [ME, fr. AF *litere*, fr. *lit* bed, fr. L *lectus*] 1 : a covered and curtained couch with shafts that is used to carry a single passenger; *also* : a device (as a stretcher) for carrying a sick or injured person 2 : material used as bedding for animals; *also* : material used to absorb the urine and feces of animals 3 : the offspring of an animal at one birth 4 : RUBBISH

²**litter** *vb* 1 : to give birth to young 2 : to strew or mark with scattered objects

lit·ter·bug \\'li-tər-ˌbəg\ *n* : one who litters a public area

¹**lit·tle** \\'li-t³l\ *adj* **lit·tler** \\'li-t³l-ər\ *or* **less** \\'les\ *or* **less·er** \\'le-sər\; **lit·tlest** \\'li-t³l-əst\ *or* **least** \\'lēst\ 1 : not big; *also* : YOUNG 2 : not important 3 : PETTY 3 4 : not much — **lit·tle·ness** *n*

²**little** *adv* **less** \\'les\; **least** \\'lēst\ 1 : SLIGHTLY; *also* : not at all 2 : INFREQUENTLY

³**little** *n* 1 : a small amount or quantity 2 : a short time or distance

Little Dipper *n* : the seven bright stars of Ursa Minor arranged in a form resembling a dipper

little finger *n* : PINKIE

little theater *n* : a small theater for low-cost dramatic productions designed for a limited audience

lit·to·ral \\'li-tə-rəl; ˌli-tə-'ral\ *adj* : of, relating to, or growing on or near a shore esp. of the sea — **littoral** *n*

lit·ur·gy \\'li-tər-jē\ *n, pl* -**gies** : a rite or body of rites prescribed for public worship — **li·tur·gi·cal** \lə-'tər-ji-kəl\ *adj* — **li·tur·gi·cal·ly** \-k(ə-)lē\ *adv* — **lit·ur·gist** \\'li-tər-jist\ *n*

liv·able *also* **live·able** \\'li-və-bəl\ *adj* 1 : suitable for living in or with ⟨a ~ house⟩ ⟨~ wages⟩ 2 : ENDURABLE — **liv·a·bil·i·ty** \ˌli-və-'bi-lə-tē\ *n*

¹**live** \\'liv\ *vb* **lived**; **liv·ing** 1 : to be or continue alive ⟨*lived* 80 years⟩ 2 : SUBSIST 3 : RESIDE ⟨~s next door⟩ 4 : to conduct one's life 5 : to remain in human memory or record ⟨his legacy ~s⟩

²**live** \\'līv\ *adj* 1 : having life ⟨~ worms⟩ 2 : ACTUAL ⟨a real ~ celebrity⟩ 3 : BURNING, GLOWING ⟨a ~ cigar⟩ 4 : connected to electric power ⟨a ~ wire⟩ 5 : UNEXPLODED ⟨a ~ bomb⟩ 6 : of continuing interest ⟨a ~ issue⟩ 7 : of or involving the actual presence of real people ⟨~ audience⟩; *also* : broadcast directly at the time of production 8 : being in play ⟨a ~ ball⟩

lived-in \\'livd-ˌin\ *adj* : of or suggesting long-term human habitation or use

live down *vb* : to live so as to wipe out the memory or effects of

live in *vb* : to live in one's place of employment — used of a servant — **live-in** \\'liv-ˌin\ *adj*

live·li·hood \\'līv-lē-ˌhud\ *n* : means of support or subsistence

live·long \\'liv-ˌlȯŋ\ *adj* [ME *lef long*, fr. *lef* dear + *long* long] : WHOLE, ENTIRE ⟨the ~ day⟩

live·ly \\'līv-lē\ *adj* **live·li·er**; -**est** 1 : ANIMATED ⟨~ debate⟩ 2 : KEEN, VIVID ⟨~ interest⟩ 3 : showing activity or vigor ⟨a ~ manner⟩ 4 : quick to rebound ⟨a ~ ball⟩ 5 : full of life ♦ *Synonyms* VIVACIOUS, SPRIGHTLY, GAY, SPIRITED — **live·li·ness** *n* — **live·ly** *adv*

liv·en \\'lī-vən\ *vb* : ENLIVEN

live oak *n* : any of several American evergreen oaks; *esp* : one of the southeastern U.S. that is often planted as a shade tree

¹**liv·er** \\'li-vər\ *n* 1 : a large glandular organ of vertebrates that secretes bile and is a center of metabolic activity 2 : the liver of an animal (as a calf or chicken) eaten as food

²**liver** *n* : one that lives esp. in a specified way ⟨a fast ~⟩

liv·er·ish \\'li-və-rish\ *adj* 1 : resembling liver esp. in color 2 : BILIOUS 3 : PEEVISH — **liv·er·ish·ness** *adj*

liver spots *n pl* : AGE SPOTS

liv·er·wort \\'li-vər-ˌwərt\ *n* : any of a class of flowerless plants resembling the related mosses

liv·er·wurst \-ˌwərst, -ˌwu̇rst\ *n* [part trans. of G *Leberwurst*, fr. *Leber* liver + *Wurst* sausage] : a sausage consisting chiefly of liver

liv·ery \'li-və-rē\ *n, pl* **-er·ies** 1 : a servant's uniform; *also* : distinctive dress 2 : the feeding, care, and stabling of horses for pay; *also* : an establishment (as a stable or business) keeping horses or vehicles for hire — **liv·er·ied** \-rēd\ *adj* — **liv·ery·man** \'li-və-rē-mən\ *n*

lives *pl of* LIFE

live·stock \'liv-,stäk\ *n* : farm animals kept for use and profit

live wire *n* : an alert, active, or aggressive person — **live–wire** *adj*

liv·id \'li-vəd\ *adj* [F *livide*, fr. L *lividus*, fr. *livēre* to be blue] 1 : discolored by bruising 2 : ASHEN, PALLID 3 : REDDISH 4 : ENRAGED — **li·vid·i·ty** \li-'vi-də-tē\ *n*

¹**liv·ing** \'li-viŋ\ *adj* 1 : having life 2 : NATURAL 3 : full of life and vigor; *also* : VIVID ⟨in ∼ color⟩

²**living** *n* 1 : the condition of being alive 2 : LIVELIHOOD 3 : manner of life

living room *n* : a room in a residence used for the common social activities of the occupants

living wage *n* : a wage sufficient to provide an acceptable standard of living

living will *n* : a document requesting that the signer not be kept alive by artificial means unless there is a reasonable expectation of recovery

livre \'lēvrᵃ\ *n* : the pound of Lebanon

liz·ard \'li-zərd\ *n* : any of a group of 4-legged reptiles with long tapering tails

Lk *abbr* Luke

ll *abbr* lines

lla·ma \'lä-mə\ *n* [Sp, fr. Quechua] : any of a genus of wild or domesticated So. American mammals related to the camels but smaller and without a hump

lla·no \'lä-nō\ *n, pl* **llanos** : an open grassy plain esp. of Latin America

LLD *abbr* [NL *legum doctor*] doctor of laws

LNG *abbr* liquefied natural gas

¹**load** \'lōd\ *n* 1 : PACK; *also* : CARGO 2 : a mass of weight supported by something 3 : something that burdens the mind or spirits 4 : a large quantity — usu. used in pl. 5 : a standard, expected, or authorized burden

²**load** *vb* 1 : to put a load in or on; *also* : to receive a load 2 : to encumber with an obligation or something heavy or disheartening 3 : to increase the weight of by adding something 4 : to supply abundantly 5 : to put a charge in (as a firearm) 6 : to copy or transfer into a computer's memory esp. from an external source

load·ed *adj,* 1 *slang* : HIGH 12 2 : having a large amount of money 3 : equipped with an abundance of options ⟨a ∼ car⟩

load·stone *var of* LODESTONE

¹**loaf** \'lōf\ *n, pl* **loaves** \'lōvz\ : a shaped or molded mass esp. of bread

²**loaf** *vb* : to spend time in idleness : LOUNGE

loaf·er \'lō-fər\ *n* 1 : one that loafs : IDLER 2 : a low step-in shoe

loam \'lōm, 'lüm\ *n* : SOIL; *esp* : a loose soil of mixed clay, sand, and silt — **loamy** *adj*

¹**loan** \'lōn\ *n* 1 : money lent at interest; *also* : something lent for the borrower's temporary use 2 : the grant of temporary use

²**loan** *vb* : LEND

loan shark *n* : a person who lends money at excessive rates of interest — **loan-shark·ing** \'lōn-,shär-kiŋ\ *n*

loan·word \'lōn-,wərd\ *n* : a word taken from another language and at least partly naturalized

loath *also* **loth** \'lōth, 'lōth\ *or* **loathe** \'lōth, 'lōth\ *adj* : RELUCTANT

loathe \'lōth\ *vb* **loathed; loath·ing** : to dislike greatly ♦ **Synonyms** ABOMINATE, ABHOR, DETEST, HATE

loath·ing \'lō-thiŋ\ *n* : extreme disgust

loath·some \'lōth-səm, 'lōth-\ *adj* : exciting loathing : REPULSIVE

lob \'läb\ *vb* **lobbed; lob·bing** 1 : to throw, hit, or propel something in a high arc 2 : to direct (as a question) so as to elicit a response — **lob** *n*

¹**lob·by** \'lä-bē\ *n, pl* **lobbies** 1 : a corridor used esp. as a passageway or waiting room 2 : a group of persons engaged in lobbying

²**lobby** *vb* **lob·bied; lob·by·ing** : to try to influence public officials and esp. legislators — **lob·by·ist** *n*

lobe \'lōb\ *n* : a curved or rounded part esp. of a bodily organ — **lo·bar** \'lō-bər\ *adj* — **lobed** \'lōbd\ *adj*

lo·be·lia \lō-'bēl-yə\ *n* : any of a genus of plants often grown for their clusters of showy flowers

lo·bot·o·my \lō-'bä-tə-mē\ *n, pl* **-mies** : surgical severance of certain nerve fibers in the brain used esp. formerly to relieve some mental disorders

lob·ster \'läb-stər\ *n* [ME, fr. OE *loppestre*, fr. *loppe* spider] : any of a family of edible marine crustaceans with two large pincerlike claws and four other pairs of legs; *also* : SPINY LOBSTER

¹**lo·cal** \'lō-kəl\ *adj* 1 : of, relating to, or occupying a particular place 2 : serving a particular limited district; *also* : making all stops ⟨a ∼ train⟩ 3 : affecting a small part of the body ⟨a ∼ infection⟩ — **lo·cal·ly** *adv*

²**local** *n* : one that is local

local area network *n* : a network of personal computers in a small area (as an office)

lo·cale \lō-'kal\ *n* : a place that is the setting for a particular event

lo·cal·ise *Brit var of* LOCALIZE

lo·cal·i·ty \lō-'ka-lə-tē\ *n, pl* **-ties** : a particular spot, situation, or location

lo·cal·ize \'lō-kə-,līz\ *vb* **-ized; -iz·ing** : to fix in or confine to a definite place or locality — **lo·cal·i·za·tion** \,lō-kə-lə-'zā-shən\ *n*

lo·cate \'lō-,kāt, lō-'kāt\ *vb* **lo·cat·ed; lo·cat·ing** 1 : STATION, SETTLE 2 : to determine the site of 3 : to find or fix the place of in a sequence

lo·ca·tion \lō-'kā-shən\ *n* 1 : SITUATION,

PLACE **2** : the process of locating **3** : a place outside a studio where a motion picture is filmed

loc cit *abbr* [L *loco citato*] in the place cited

loch \'läk, 'läk\ *n, Scot* : LAKE; *also* : a bay or arm of the sea esp. when nearly land-locked

¹**lock** \'läk\ *n* : a tuft, strand, or ringlet of hair; *also* : a cohering bunch (as of wool or flax)

²**lock** *n* **1** : a fastening in which a bolt is operated **2** : the mechanism of a firearm by which the charge is exploded **3** : an enclosure (as in a canal) used in raising or lowering boats from level to level **4** : AIR LOCK **5** : a wrestling hold

³**lock** *vb* **1** : to fasten the lock of; *also* : to make fast with a lock **2** : to confine or exclude by means of a lock **3** : INTER-LOCK **4** : to make or become motionless by the interlocking of parts

lock·er \'lä-kər\ *n* **1** : a drawer, cup-board, or compartment for individual storage use **2** : an insulated compart-ment for storing frozen food

lock·et \'lä-kət\ *n* : a small usu. metal case for a memento worn suspended from a chain or necklace

lock·jaw \'läk-jȯ\ *n* : a symptom of tetanus marked by spasms of the jaw muscles and inability to open the jaws; *also* : TETANUS

lock·nut \-ˌnət\ *n* **1** : a nut screwed tight on another to prevent it from slacking back **2** : a nut designed to lock itself when screwed tight

lock·out \-ˌau̇t\ *n* : the suspension of work by an employer during a labor dispute in order to make employees accept the terms being offered

lock·smith \-ˌsmith\ *n* : one who makes or repairs locks

lock·step \-ˌstep\ *n* : a mode of marching in step by a body of men moving in a very close single file

lock·up \-ˌəp\ *n* : JAIL

lo·co \'lō-kō\ *adj,* [Sp] *slang* : CRAZY, FRENZIED

lo·co·mo·tion \ˌlō-kə-'mō-shən\ *n* **1** : the act or power of moving from place to place **2** : TRAVEL

¹**lo·co·mo·tive** \ˌlō-kə-'mō-tiv\ *adj* : of or relating to locomotion or a locomotive

²**locomotive** *n* : a self-propelled vehicle used to move railroad cars

lo·co·mo·tor \ˌlō-kə-'mō-tər\ *adj* : of or relating to locomotion or organs used in locomotion

lo·co·weed \'lō-kō-ˌwēd\ *n* : any of several leguminous plants of western No. America that are poisonous to livestock

lo·cus \'lō-kəs\ *n, pl* **lo·ci** \'lō-ˌsī\ [L] **1** : PLACE, LOCALITY **2** : the set of all points whose location is determined by stated conditions

lo·cust \'lō-kəst\ *n* **1** : a usu. destructive migratory grasshopper **2** : CICADA **3** : any of various leguminous trees; *also* : the wood of a locust

lo·cu·tion \lō-'kyü-shən\ *n* : a particular form of expression; *also* : PHRASEOLOGY

lode \'lōd\ *n* : an ore deposit

lode·stone \-ˌstōn\ *n* : an iron-containing rock with magnetic properties

¹**lodge** \'läj\ *vb* **lodged; lodg·ing 1** : to provide quarters for; *also* : to settle in a place **2** : CONTAIN **3** : to come to a rest and remain ⟨*lodged* in his throat⟩ **4** : to deposit for safekeeping **5** : to vest (as au-thority) in an agent **6** : FILE ⟨~ a com-plaint⟩

²**lodge** *n* **1** : a house set apart for resi-dence in a special season or by an em-ployee on an estate; *also* : INN **2** : a den or lair esp. of gregarious animals **3** : the meeting place of a branch of a fraternal organization; *also* : the members of such a branch

lodg·er \'lä-jər\ *n* : a person who occupies a rented room in another's house

lodg·ing \'lä-jiŋ\ *n* **1** : DWELLING **2** : a room or suite of rooms in another's house rented as a dwelling place — usu. used in pl.

lodg·ment *or* **lodge·ment** \'läj-mənt\ *n* **1** : a lodging place **2** : the act or manner of lodging **3** : DEPOSIT

loess \'les, 'ləs\ *n* : a usu. yellowish brown loamy deposit believed to be chiefly de-posited by the wind

lo–fi \'lō-ˌfī\ *n* : audio production of rough or unpolished sound quality — **lo-fi** *adj*

¹**loft** \'lȯft\ *n* [ME, fr. OE, air, sky, fr. ON *lopt*] **1** : ATTIC **2** : GALLERY ⟨organ ~⟩ **3** : an upper floor (as in a warehouse or barn) esp. when not partitioned **4** : the thickness of a fabric or insulated material (as of a sleeping bag)

²**loft** *vb* : to strike or throw a ball so that it rises high in the air

lofty \'lȯf-tē\ *adj* **loft·i·er; -est 1** : NOBLE; *also* : SUPERIOR ⟨~ ideals⟩ **2** : extremely proud **3** : HIGH, TALL — **loft·i·ly** \'lȯf-tə-lē\ *adv* — **loft·i·ness** \-tē-nəs\ *n*

¹**log** \'lȯg, 'läg\ *n* **1** : a bulky piece of a cut or fallen tree **2** : an apparatus for mea-suring a ship's speed **3** : the daily record of a ship's progress; *also* : a regularly kept record of performance or events ⟨a pilot's ~⟩ ⟨a runner's ~⟩

²**log** *vb* **logged; log·ging 1** : to cut (trees) for lumber; *also* : to clear (land) of trees in lumbering **2** : to enter in a log **3** : to sail a ship or fly an airplane for (an in-dicated distance or period of time) **4** : to have (an indicated record) to one's credit : ACHIEVE — **log·ger** \'lȯ-gər, 'lä-\ *n*

³**log** *n* : LOGARITHM

lo·gan·ber·ry \'lō-gən-ˌber-ē\ *n* : a red-fruited upright-growing dewberry; *also* : its berry

log·a·rithm \'lȯ-gə-ˌri-t͟həm, 'lä-\ *n* : the exponent that indicates the power to which a base is raised to produce a given number ⟨the ~ of 100 to base 10 is 2 since $10^2 = 100$⟩ — **log·a·rith·mic** \ˌlȯ-gə-'ri-t͟h-mik, ˌlä-\ *adj*

loge \'lōzh\ *n* **1** : a small compartment; *also* : a box in a theater **2** : a small parti-tioned area; *also* : the forward section of a theater mezzanine **3** : a raised level of seats in a stadium

log·ger·head \'lȯ-gər-,hed, 'lä-\ n : a large sea turtle of subtropical and temperate waters — **at loggerheads** : in a state of quarrelsome disagreement

log·gia \'lȯ-jē-ə, 'lȯ-jä\ n, pl **loggias** \'lȯ-jē-əz, 'lȯ-jäz\ : a roofed open gallery

log·ic \'lä-jik\ n 1 : a science that deals with the rules and tests of sound thinking and proof by reasoning 2 : sound reasoning 3 : the arrangement of circuit elements for arithmetical computation in a computer — **log·i·cal** \-ji-kəl\ adj — **log·i·cal·ly** \-jik(ə-)lē\ adv — **lo·gi·cian** \lō-'ji-shən\ n

lo·gis·tics \lō-'jis-tiks\ n sing or pl : the procurement, maintenance, and transportation of matériel, facilities, and personnel — **lo·gis·tic** \-tik\ or **lo·gis·ti·cal** \-ti-kəl\ adj

log·jam \'lȯg-,jam, 'läg-\ n 1 : a deadlocked jumble of logs in a watercourse 2 : DEADLOCK — **logjam** vt

logo \'lȯ-gō\ n, pl **log·os** \-gōz\ : an identifying symbol (as for advertising)

logo·type \'lȯ-gə-,tīp, 'lä-\ n : LOGO

log·roll·ing \-,rō-liŋ\ n : the trading of votes by legislators to secure favorable action on projects of individual interest

lo·gy \'lō-gē\ also **log·gy** \'lȯ-gē, 'lä-\ adj **lo·gi·er; -est** : deficient in vitality : SLUGGISH

loin \'lȯin\ n [ME loyne, fr. AF loigne, fr. VL *lumbea, fr. L lumbus] 1 : the part of the body on each side of the spinal column and between the hip and the lower ribs; also : a cut of meat from this part of an animal 2 pl : the pubic region; also : the organs of reproduction

loin·cloth \-,klȯth\ n : a cloth worn about the loins often as the sole article of clothing in warm climates

loi·ter \'lȯi-tər\ vb 1 : LINGER 2 : to hang around idly ♦ Synonyms DAWDLE, DALLY, PROCRASTINATE, LAG, TARRY — **loi·ter·er** n

loll \'läl\ vb 1 : DROOP, DANGLE 2 : LOUNGE

lol·la·pa·loo·za \,lä-lə-pə-'lü-zə\ n : something extraordinarily impressive or outstanding

lol·li·pop or **lol·ly·pop** \'lä-li-,päp\ n : a lump of hard candy on a stick

lol·ly·gag \'lä-lē-,gag\ vb **-gagged; -gagging** : DAWDLE

Lond abbr London

lone \'lōn\ adj 1 : SOLITARY ⟨a ~ sentinel⟩ 2 : SOLE, ONLY ⟨the ~ theater in town⟩ 3 : ISOLATED ⟨a ~ tree⟩

lone·ly \'lōn-lē\ adj **lone·li·er; -est** 1 : being without company 2 : UNFREQUENTED ⟨a ~ spot⟩ 3 : LONESOME — **lone·li·ness** n

lon·er \'lō-nər\ n : one that avoids others

lone·some \'lōn-səm\ adj 1 : sad from lack of companionship 2 : REMOTE; also : SOLITARY ⟨a ~ road⟩ — **lone·some·ly** adv — **lone·some·ness** n

¹long \'lȯŋ\ adj **lon·ger** \'lȯŋ-gər\; **longest** \'lȯŋ-gəst\ -1 : extending for a considerable distance ⟨a ~ corridor⟩; also : TALL, ELONGATED ⟨~ legs⟩ 2 : having

a specified length 3 : extending over a considerable time; also : TEDIOUS ⟨~ lectures⟩ 4 : containing many items in a series ⟨a ~ list⟩ 5 : being a syllable or speech sound of relatively great duration 6 : extending far into the future 7 : well furnished with something — used with on

²long adv : for or during a long time

³long n : a long period of time

⁴long vb **longed; long·ing** \'lȯŋ-iŋ\ : to feel a strong desire or wish ♦ Synonyms YEARN, HANKER, PINE, HUNGER, THIRST

⁵long abbr longitude

long·boat \'lȯŋ-,bōt\ n : a large boat usu. carried by a merchant sailing ship

long·bow \-,bō\ n : a wooden bow drawn by hand and used esp. by medieval English archers

lon·gev·i·ty \län-'je-və-tē\ n [LL longaevitas, fr. L longaevus long-lived, fr. longus long + aevum age] : a long duration of individual life; also : length of life

long·hair \'lȯŋ-,her\ n 1 : a lover of classical music 2 : HIPPIE 3 : a domestic cat having long outer fur — **long-haired** \-,herd\ or **long·hair** adj

long·hand \-,hand\ n : HANDWRITING

long·horn \-,hȯrn\ n : any of the cattle with long horns formerly common in the southwestern U.S.

long hundredweight n, Brit — see WEIGHT table

long·ing \'lȯŋ-iŋ\ n : a strong desire esp. for something unattainable — **long·ing·ly** adv

lon·gi·tude \'län-jə-,tüd, -,tyüd\ n : angular distance expressed usu. in degrees east or west from the prime meridian through Greenwich, England

lon·gi·tu·di·nal \,län-jə-'tü-dᵊn-əl, -'tyüd-\ adj 1 : extending lengthwise 2 : of or relating to length — **lon·gi·tu·di·nal·ly** adv

long-range \'lȯŋ-'rānj\ adj 1 : relating to or fit for long distances 2 : involving a long period of time

long·shore·man \'lȯŋ-,shȯr-mən\ n : a laborer at a wharf who loads and unloads cargo

long-suf·fer·ing \-'sə-friŋ, -fə-riŋ\ adj : patiently enduring lasting offense or hardship

long-term \'lȯŋ-'tərm\ adj 1 : extending over or involving a long period of time 2 : constituting a financial obligation based on a term usu. of more than 10 years ⟨~ bonds⟩

long·time \'lȯŋ-'tīm\ adj : of long duration ⟨~ friends⟩

long ton n — see WEIGHT table

lon·gueur \lōⁿ-'gœr\ n, pl **longueurs** \same or -'gœrz\ [F, lit., length] : a dull tedious portion (as of a book)

long-wind·ed \,lȯŋ-'win-dəd\ adj : tediously long in speaking or writing

loo·fah \'lü-fə\ n : a sponge consisting of the fibrous skeleton of a gourd

¹look \'lu̇k\ vb 1 : to exercise the power of vision : SEE ⟨~ what I won⟩ 2 : EXPECT 3 : to have an appearance that befits ⟨~s the part⟩ 4 : SEEM ⟨~s thin⟩

5 : to direct one's attention : HEED ⟨∼ at the sign⟩ 6 : POINT, FACE ⟨∼s east⟩ 7 : to show a tendency — **look after** : to take care of — **look at** 1 : CONSIDER ⟨*looking at* all possibilities⟩ 2 : CONFRONT, FACE ⟨*looking at* stiff fines⟩ — **look for** : EXPECT — **look forward** : to anticipate with pleasure ⟨*look forward* to summer⟩

²**look** n 1 : the action of looking : GLANCE 2 : EXPRESSION; *also* : physical appearance 3 : ASPECT

look down vb : to regard with contempt — used with *on* or *upon*

looking glass n : MIRROR

look·out \'lùk-ˌaùt\ n 1 : a person assigned to watch (as on a ship) 2 : a careful watch 3 : VIEW 4 : a matter of concern

look up vb 1 : IMPROVE ⟨business is *looking up*⟩ 2 : to search for in or as if in a reference work 3 : to seek out esp. for a brief visit

¹**loom** \'lüm\ n : a frame or machine for weaving together threads or yarns into cloth

²**loom** vb 1 : to come into sight in an unnaturally large, indistinct, or distorted form 2 : to appear in an impressively exaggerated form

loon \'lün\ n : any of several web-footed black-and-white fish-eating diving birds

loo·ny or **loo·ney** \'lü-nē\ adj **loo·ni·er; -est** : CRAZY, FOOLISH

loony bin n : a psychiatric hospital

¹**loop** \'lüp\ n 1 : a fold or doubling of a line through which another line or hook can be passed; *also* : a loop-shaped figure or course ⟨a ∼ in a river⟩ 2 : a circular airplane maneuver executed in the vertical plane 3 : a continuously repeated segment of film, music, or sound — **loop** vb

loop·er \'lü-pər\ n : any of numerous rather small hairless moth caterpillars that move with a looping motion

loop·hole \'lüp-ˌhōl\ n 1 : a small opening in a wall through which firearms may be discharged 2 : a means of escape; *esp* : an ambiguity or omission that allows one to evade the intent of a law or contract

loopy \'lü-pē\ adj **loop·i·er; -est** : having loops 2 : CRAZY, BIZARRE — **loop·i·ly** \-pə-lē\ adv — **loop·i·ness** \-pē-nəs\ n

loose \'lüs\ adj **loos·er; loos·est** 1 : not rigidly fastened 2 : free from restraint or obligation 3 : not dense or compact in structure 4 : not chaste : LEWD 5 : SLACK 6 : not precise or exact — **loose·ly** adv — **loose·ness** n

²**loose** vb **loosed; loos·ing** 1 : RELEASE 2 : UNTIE 3 : DETACH 4 : DISCHARGE 5 : RELAX, SLACKEN

³**loose** adv : LOOSELY

loos·en \'lü-sᵊn\ vb 1 : FREE 2 : to make or become loose 3 : to relax the severity of ⟨∼ rules⟩

¹**loot** \'lüt\ n [Hindi & Urdu *lūṭ*; akin to Skt *luṇṭati* he plunders] : goods taken in war

or by robbery : PLUNDER — **loot** vb — **loot·er** n

¹**lop** \'läp\ vb **lopped; lop·ping** : to cut branches or twigs from : TRIM; *also* : to cut off

²**lop** vb **lopped; lop·ping** : to hang downward; *also* : to flop or sway loosely

lope \'lōp\ n : an easy bounding gait — **lope** vb

lop·sid·ed \'läp-'sī-dəd\ adj 1 : leaning to one side 2 : UNSYMMETRICAL — **lop·sid·ed·ly** adv — **lop·sid·ed·ness** n

lo·qua·cious \lō-'kwā-shəs\ adj : excessively talkative — **lo·quac·i·ty** \-'kwa-sə-tē\ n

¹**lord** \'lòrd\ n [ME *loverd, lord*, fr. OE *hlāford*, fr. *hlāf* loaf + *weard* keeper] 1 : one having power and authority over others; *esp* : a person from whom a feudal fee or estate is held 2 *cap* : GOD 1 3 : a man of rank or high position; *esp* : a British nobleman 4 *pl, cap* : the upper house of the British parliament 5 : a person of great power in some field

²**lord** vb : to act like a lord; *esp* : to put on airs — usu. used with *it*

lord chancellor n, pl **lords chancellor** : a British officer of state who presides over the House of Lords, serves as head of the British judiciary, and is usu. a leading member of the cabinet

lord·ly \-lē\ adj **lord·li·er; -est** 1 : DIGNIFIED; *also* : NOBLE 2 : HAUGHTY

lord·ship \-ˌship\ n 1 : the rank or dignity of a lord — used as a title 2 : the authority or territory of a lord

Lord's Supper n : COMMUNION

lore \'lōr\ n : KNOWLEDGE; *esp* : traditional knowledge or belief

lor·gnette \lòrn-'yet\ n [F, fr. *lorgner* to take a sidelong look at, fr. MF, fr. *lorgne* squinting] : a pair of eyeglasses or opera glasses with a handle

lorn \'lòrn\ adj : FORSAKEN, DESOLATE

lor·ry \'lòr-ē\ n, pl **lorries** chiefly Brit : MOTORTRUCK

lose \'lüz\ vb **lost** \'lòst\; **los·ing** \'lü-ziŋ\ 1 : DESTROY 2 : to miss from a customary place : MISLAY 3 : to suffer deprivation of 4 : to fail to use : WASTE ⟨no time to ∼⟩ 5 : to fail to win or obtain ⟨∼ the game⟩ 6 : to fail to keep or maintain ⟨∼ his balance⟩ 7 : to wander from ⟨∼ her way⟩ 8 : to get rid of ⟨should ∼ the beard⟩ — **los·er** n — **lose it** 1 : to go crazy 2 : to fail to keep one's composure

loss \'lòs\ n 1 : RUIN 2 : the harm resulting from losing 3 : something that is lost 4 *pl* : killed, wounded, or captured soldiers 5 : failure to win 6 : an amount by which the cost exceeds the selling price 7 : decrease in amount or degree

loss leader n : an article sold at a loss in order to draw customers

lost \'lòst\ adj 1 : not used, won, or claimed 2 : no longer possessed or known 3 : ruined or destroyed physically or morally 4 : DENIED; *also* : HARDENED 5 : unable to find the way; *also* : HELPLESS 6 : ABSORBED, RAPT 7 : not appreciated or understood ⟨his jokes were ~ on me⟩ **8** : made obscure : OVERLOOKED ⟨~ in translation⟩ **9** : FUTILE ⟨a ~ cause⟩

lot \'lät\ *n* **1** : an object used in deciding something by chance; *also* : the use of lots to decide something **2** : SHARE, PORTION; *also* : FORTUNE, FATE **3** : a plot of land **4** : a group of individuals : SET **5** : a considerable quantity

loth *var of* LOATH

lo·ti \'lō-tē\ *n, pl* **ma·lo·ti** \mə-'lō-tē\ — see MONEY table

lo·tion \'lō-shən\ *n* : a liquid preparation for cosmetic and external medicinal use

lot·tery \'lä-tə-rē\ *n, pl* **-ter·ies** **1** : a drawing of lots in which prizes are given to the winning names or numbers **2** : a matter determined by chance

lo·tus \'lō-təs\ *n* **1** : a fruit held in Greek legend to cause dreamy contentment and forgetfulness **2** : any of various water lilies represented esp. in ancient Egyptian and Hindu art **3** : any of several leguminous forage plants

loud \'laůd\ *adj* **1** : marked by intensity or volume of sound **2** : CLAMOROUS, NOISY **3** : obtrusive or offensive in color or pattern ⟨a ~ tie⟩ — **loud** *adv* — **loud·ly** *adv* — **loud·ness** *n*

loud–mouthed \-₁maůtht, -₁maůthd\ *adj* : given to loud offensive talk

loud·speak·er \-₁spē-kər\ *n* : a device that changes electrical signals into sound

¹**lounge** \'laůnj\ *vb* **lounged; loung·ing** : to act or move lazily or listlessly

²**lounge** *n* **1** : a room with comfortable furniture; *also* : a room (as in a theater) with lounging, smoking, and toilet facilities **2** : a long couch

lour, loury *var of* LOWER, LOWERY

louse \'laůs\ *n, pl* **lice** \'līs\ **1** : any of various small wingless usu. flattened insects parasitic on warm-blooded animals **2** : a plant pest (as an aphid) **3** *pl* **lous·es** \'laů-səz\ : a contemptible person

lousy \'laů-zē\ *adj* **lous·i·er; -est** **1** : infested with lice **2** : POOR, INFERIOR **3** : somewhat ill **4** : amply supplied ⟨~ with money⟩ — **lous·i·ly** \-zə-lē\ *adv* — **lous·i·ness** \-zē-nəs\ *n*

lout \'laůt\ *n* : a stupid awkward fellow — **lout·ish** *adj* — **lout·ish·ly** *adv*

lou·ver *or* **lou·vre** \'lü-vər\ *n* **1** : an opening having parallel slanted slats to allow flow of air but to exclude rain or sun or to provide privacy; *also* : a slat in such an opening **2** : a device with movable slats for controlling the flow of air or light

¹**love** \'ləv\ *n* **1** : strong affection **2** : warm attachment ⟨~ of the sea⟩ **3** : attraction based on sexual desire **4** : a beloved person **5** : unselfish loyal and benevolent concern for others **6** : a score of zero in tennis — **love·less** *adj*

²**love** *vb* **loved; lov·ing** **1** : CHERISH **2** : to feel a passion, devotion, or tenderness for **3** : CARESS **4** : to take pleasure in ⟨~s to play bridge⟩ — **lov·able** *also* **love·able** \'lə-və-bəl\ *adj* — **lov·er** *n*

love·bird \'ləv-₁bərd\ *n* : any of various small usu. gray or green parrots that

seem to show caring behavior for their mates

love·lorn \-₁lȯrn\ *adj* : deprived of love or of a lover

love·ly \'ləv-lē\ *adj* **love·li·er; -est** : BEAUTIFUL — **love·li·ly** \'ləv-lə-lē\ *adv* — **love·li·ness** *n* — **lovely** *adv*

love·mak·ing \-₁mā-kiŋ\ *n* **1** : COURTSHIP **2** : sexual activity; *esp* : COPULATION

love·sick \-₁sik\ *adj* **1** : YEARNING **2** : expressing a lover's longing — **love·sick·ness** *n*

lov·ing \'lə-viŋ\ *adj* **1** : AFFECTIONATE **2** : PAINSTAKING — **lov·ing·ly** *adv*

¹**low** \'lō\ *vb* : MOO

²**low** *n* : MOO

³**low** *adj* **low·er** \'lō-ər\; **low·est** \'lō-əst\ **1** : not high or tall ⟨~ wall⟩; *also* : DÉCOLLETÉ **2** : situated or passing below the normal level or surface ⟨~ ground⟩; *also* : marking a nadir **3** : not loud ⟨~ voice⟩ **4** : being near the equator **5** : humble in status **6** : WEAK; *also* : DEPRESSED **7** : STRICKEN, PROSTRATE **8** : less than usual in number, amount, or value; *also* : of lesser degree than average **9** : falling short of a standard **10** : UNFAVORABLE — **low** *adv* — **low·ness** *n*

⁴**low** *n* **1** : something that is low **2** : a region of low barometric pressure **3** : the arrangement of gears in an automobile transmission that gives the slowest speed and greatest power

low–ball \'lō-₁bȯl\ *vb* : to give a deceptively low price, cost estimate, or offer to

low beam *n* : a vehicle headlight beam with short-range focus

low blow *n* : an unprincipled attack

low·brow \'lō-₁braů\ *adj* : having little taste or intellectual interest ⟨~ humor⟩ — **lowbrow** *n*

low–density lipoprotein *n* : LDL

low·down \-₁daůn\ *n* : pertinent and esp. guarded information

low–down \-₁daůn\ *adj* **1** : MEAN, CONTEMPTIBLE **2** : deeply emotional

low–end \-₁end\ *adj* : of, relating to, or being the lowest-priced merchandise in a manufacturer's line

¹**low·er** *also* **lour** \'laů(-ə)r\ *vb* **1** : FROWN **2** : to become dark, gloomy, and threatening — **lower** *also* **lour** *n*

²**low·er** \'lō-ər\ *adj* **1** : relatively low (as in rank) **2** : SOUTHERN ⟨the ~ states⟩ **3** : less advanced in the scale of evolutionary development ⟨~ animals⟩ **4** : situated beneath the earth's surface **5** : constituting the popular and more representative branch of a bicameral legislative body

³**low·er** \'lō-ər\ *vb* **1** : DROP; *also* : DIMINISH **2** : to let descend by its own weight; *also* : to reduce the height of **3** : to reduce in value, number, or amount **4** : DEGRADE; *also* : HUMBLE

low·er·case \₁lō-ər-'kās\ *adj* : being a letter that belongs to or conforms to the series a, b, c, etc., rather than A, B, C, etc. — **lowercase** *n*

lower class *n* : a social class occupying a position below the middle class and having the lowest status in a society — **lower-class** \-'klas\ *adj*

low·er·most \'lō-ər-ˌmōst\ *adj* : LOWEST

low·ery *also* **loury** \'laú-(ə-)rē\ *adj* : GLOOMY, LOWERING

lowest common denominator *n* **1** : LEAST COMMON DENOMINATOR **2** : something designed to appeal to a low-brow audience; *also* : such an audience

lowest common multiple *n* : LEAST COMMON MULTIPLE

low–key \'lō-'kē\ *also* **low–keyed** \-'kēd\ *adj* : of low intensity : RESTRAINED

low·land \'lō-lənd, -ˌland\ *n* : low and usu. level country

low–lev·el \'lō-'le-vəl\ *adj* **1** : being of low importance or rank **2** : being or relating to nuclear waste of low concentration

low–life \'lō-ˌlīf\ *n*, *pl* **low–lifes** \-ˌlīfs\ *also* **low–lives** \-ˌlīvz\ : a person of low social status or moral character

low·ly \'lō-lē\ *adj* **low·li·er**; **-est** **1** : HUMBLE, MEEK **2** : ranking low in some hierarchy — **low·li·ness** *n*

low–rise \'lō-ˌrīz\ *adj* **1** : having few stories and not equipped with elevators ⟨a ~ building⟩ **2** : of, relating to, or characterized by low-rise buildings

low–slung \'lō-ˌsləŋ\ *adj* : relatively low to the ground or floor ⟨a ~ building⟩ ⟨~ pants⟩

low–tech \'lō-ˈtek\ *adj* : technologically simple or unsophisticated

lox \'läks\ *n* : liquid oxygen

lox *n*, *pl* **lox** *or* **lox·es** : salmon cured in brine and sometimes smoked

loy·al \'lói-(ə)l\ *adj* [MF, fr. OF *leial*, *leel*, fr. L *legalis* legal] **1** : faithful in allegiance to one's government **2** : faithful esp. to a cause or ideal : CONSTANT — **loy·al·ly** \'lói-ə-lē\ *adv* — **loy·al·ty** \'lói-(ə)l-tē\ *n*

loy·al·ist \'lói-ə-list\ *n* : one who is or remains loyal to a political party, government, or sovereign

loz·enge \'lä-zənj\ *n* **1** : a diamond-shaped figure **2** : a small flat often medicated candy

LP *abbr* low pressure

LPG *abbr* liquefied petroleum gas

LPGA *abbr* Ladies Professional Golf Association

LPN \'el-ˌpē-'en\ *n* : LICENSED PRACTICAL NURSE

Lr *symbol* Lawrencium

LSD \ˌel-(ˌ)es-'dē\ *n* [G *Lysergsäure-Diäthylamid* lysergic acid diethylamide] : an illicit and highly potent hallucinogenic drug derived from ergot or produced synthetically

lt *abbr* light

Lt *abbr* lieutenant

LT *abbr* long ton

LTC *or* **Lt Col** *abbr* lieutenant colonel

Lt Comdr *abbr* lieutenant commander

ltd *abbr* limited

LTG *or* **Lt Gen** *abbr* lieutenant general

LTJG *abbr* lieutenant, junior grade

ltr *abbr* letter

Lu *symbol* lutetium

lu·au \'lü-ˌaú\ *n* : a Hawaiian feast

lub *abbr* lubricant; lubricating

lub·ber \'lə-bər\ *n* **1** : LOUT **2** : an unskilled seaman — **lub·ber·ly** *adj*

lube \'lüb\ *n* : LUBRICANT; *also* : an application of a lubricant

lu·bri·cant \'lü-bri-kənt\ *n* : a material capable of reducing friction when applied between moving parts

lu·bri·cate \'lü-brə-ˌkāt\ *vb* **-cat·ed**; **-cat·ing** : to apply a lubricant to — **lu·bri·ca·tion** \ˌlü-brə-'kā-shən\ *n* — **lu·bri·ca·tor** \'lü-brə-ˌkā-tər\ *n*

lu·bri·cious \lü-'bri-shəs\ *or* **lu·bri·cous** \'lü-bri-kəs\ *adj* **1** : SMOOTH, SLIPPERY **2** : LECHEROUS; *also* : SALACIOUS — **lu·bric·i·ty** \lü-'bri-sə-tē\ *n*

lu·cent \'lü-s°nt\ *adj* **1** : LUMINOUS **2** : CLEAR, LUCID — **lu·cent·ly** *adv*

lu·cerne \lü-'sərn\ *n*, *chiefly Brit* : ALFALFA

lu·cid \'lü-səd\ *adj* **1** : SHINING **2** : mentally sound **3** : easily understood — **lu·cid·i·ty** \lü-'si-də-tē\ *n* — **lu·cid·ly** *adv* — **lu·cid·ness** *n*

Lu·ci·fer \'lü-sə-fər\ *n* [ME, the morning star, a fallen rebel archangel, the Devil, fr. OE, fr. L, the morning star, fr. *lucifer* light-bearing] : DEVIL, SATAN

luck \'lək\ *n* **1** : CHANCE, FORTUNE **2** : good fortune — **luck·less** *adj*

luck *vb* **1** : to prosper or succeed esp. through chance or good fortune — usu. used with *out* **2** : to come upon something desirable by chance — usu. used with *out*, *on*, *onto*, or *into*

luck·i·ly \'lə-kə-lē\ *adv* **1** : in a lucky manner **2** : FORTUNATELY

lucky \'lə-kē\ *adj* **luck·i·er**; **-est** **1** : favored by luck : FORTUNATE **2** : FORTUITOUS **3** : seeming to bring good luck ⟨a ~ penny⟩ — **luck·i·ness** *n*

lu·cra·tive \'lü-krə-tiv\ *adj* : PROFITABLE ⟨~ business deals⟩ — **lu·cra·tive·ly** *adv* — **lu·cra·tive·ness** *n*

lu·cre \'lü-kər\ *n* [ME, fr. AF, fr. L *lucrum*] : PROFIT; *also* : MONEY

lu·cu·bra·tion \ˌlü-kyə-'brā-shən, -kə-\ *n* : laborious study : MEDITATION

Lud·dite \'lə-ˌdīt\ *n* [perh. fr. Ned *Ludd*, 18th cent. Eng. workman who destroyed a knitting frame] : one who is opposed to technological change

lu·di·crous \'lü-də-krəs\ *adj* : LAUGHABLE, RIDICULOUS — **lu·di·crous·ly** *adv* — **lu·di·crous·ness** *n*

luff \'ləf\ *vb* : to turn the head of a ship toward the wind

lug \'ləg\ *vb* **lugged**; **lug·ging** **1** : DRAG, PULL **2** : to carry laboriously

lug *n* **1** : a projecting piece (as for fastening, support, or traction) **2** : a nut securing a wheel on an automobile

lug·gage \'lə-gij\ *n* : containers (as suitcases) for carrying personal belongings : BAGGAGE

lu·gu·bri·ous \lú-'gü-brē-əs\ *adj* : mournful often to an exaggerated degree — **lu·gu·bri·ous·ly** *adv* — **lu·gu·bri·ous·ness** *n*

Luke \'lük\ *n* — see BIBLE table

luke·warm \'lük-'wȯrm\ adj 1 : moderately warm : TEPID 2 : not enthusiastic ⟨∼ praise⟩ — **luke·warm·ly** adv

¹**lull** \'ləl\ vb 1 : SOOTHE, CALM 2 : to cause to relax vigilance

²**lull** n 1 : a temporary calm (as during a storm) 2 : a temporary drop in activity ⟨a ∼ in sales⟩

lul·la·by \'lə-lə-ˌbī\ n, pl **-bies** : a song to lull children to sleep

lu·ma \ˌlü-'mä\ n — see *dram* at MONEY table

lum·ba·go \ˌləm-'bā-gō\ n : acute or chronic pain in the lower back

lum·bar \'ləm-bər, -ˌbär\ adj : of, relating to, or constituting the loins or the vertebrae between the thoracic vertebrae and sacrum ⟨∼ region⟩

¹**lum·ber** \'ləm-bər\ vb : to move heavily or clumsily

²**lumber** n 1 : surplus or disused articles that are stored away 2 : timber or logs esp. when dressed for use

³**lumber** vb : to cut logs; also : to saw logs into lumber — **lum·ber·man** \-mən\ n

lum·ber·jack \-ˌjak\ n : LOGGER

lum·ber·yard \-ˌyärd\ n : a place where lumber is kept for sale

lu·mi·nary \'lü-mə-ˌner-ē\ n, pl **-nar·ies** 1 : a very famous person 2 : a source of light; esp : a celestial body

lu·mi·nes·cence \ˌlü-mə-'ne-sᵊns\ n : the low-temperature emission of light (as by a chemical or physiological process); also : such light — **lu·mi·nes·cent** \-sᵊnt\ adj

lu·mi·nous \'lü-mə-nəs\ adj 1 : emitting light; also : LIGHTED 2 : CLEAR, INTELLIGIBLE 3 : ILLUSTRIOUS — **lu·mi·nance** \-nəns\ n — **lu·mi·nos·i·ty** \ˌlü-mə-'nä-sə-tē\ n — **lu·mi·nous·ly** adv

lum·mox \'lə-məks\ n : a clumsy person

¹**lump** \'ləmp\ n 1 : a piece or mass of indefinite size and shape 2 : AGGREGATE, TOTALITY 3 : a usu. abnormal swelling — **lump·ish** adj — **lumpy** adj

²**lump** vb 1 : to heap together in a lump 2 : to form into lumps

³**lump** adj : not divided into parts ⟨a ∼ sum⟩

lump·ec·to·my \ˌləm-'pek-tə-mē\ n, pl **-mies** : excision of a breast tumor

lu·na·cy \'lü-nə-sē\ n, pl **-cies** 1 : INSANITY 2 : extreme folly

lu·nar \'lü-nər\ adj : of or relating to the moon

lu·nate \'lü-ˌnät\ adj : shaped like a crescent

lu·na·tic \'lü-nə-ˌtik\ adj [ME lunatik, fr. AF & LL; AF lunatik, fr. LL lunaticus, fr. L luna moon; fr. the belief that lunacy fluctuated with the phases of the moon] 1 : INSANE; also : used for insane persons 2 : extremely foolish — **lunatic** n

¹**lunch** \'lənch\ n 1 : a light meal usu. eaten in the middle of the day 2 : the food prepared for a lunch

²**lunch** vb : to eat lunch

lun·cheon \'lən-chən\ n : a usu. formal lunch

lun·cheon·ette \ˌlən-chə-'net\ n : a small restaurant serving light lunches

lunch·room \'lənch-ˌrüm, -ˌru̇m\ n 1 : LUNCHEONETTE 2 : a room (as in a school) where lunches are sold and eaten or lunches brought from home may be eaten

lu·nette \lü-'net\ n : something shaped like a crescent

lung \'ləŋ\ n 1 : one of the usu. paired baglike breathing organs in the chest of an air-breathing vertebrate 2 : a mechanical device to promote breathing and make it easier — **lunged** \'ləŋd\ adj

lunge \'lənj\ n 1 : a sudden thrust or pass (as with a sword) 2 : a sudden forward stride or leap — **lunge** vb

lu·pine \'lü-pən\ n : any of a genus of leguminous plants with long upright clusters of pealike flowers

lu·pus \'lü-pəs\ n [ML, fr. L, wolf] : any of several diseases characterized by skin lesions; esp : SYSTEMIC LUPUS ERYTHEMATOSUS

lurch \'lərch\ n : a sudden swaying or tipping movement — **lurch** vb

¹**lure** \'lu̇r\ n 1 : ENTICEMENT; also : APPEAL 2 : an artificial bait for catching fish

²**lure** vb **lured; lur·ing** : to draw on with a promise of pleasure or gain

lu·rid \'lu̇r-əd\ adj 1 : GRUESOME; also : SENSATIONAL 2 : wan and ghostly pale in appearance 3 : shining with the red glow of fire seen through smoke or cloud
♦ **Synonyms** GHASTLY, GRISLY, GRIM, HORRIBLE, MACABRE — **lu·rid·ly** adv

lurk \'lərk\ vb 1 : to move furtively : SNEAK 2 : to lie concealed

lus·cious \'lə-shəs\ adj 1 : having a pleasingly sweet taste or smell 2 : sensually appealing — **lus·cious·ly** adv — **lus·cious·ness** n

¹**lush** \'ləsh\ adj : having or covered with abundant growth ⟨∼ pastures⟩

²**lush** n : a habitual heavy drinker

lust \'ləst\ n 1 : usu. intense or unbridled sexual desire : LASCIVIOUSNESS 2 : an intense longing ⟨a ∼ to succeed⟩ — **lust** vb — **lust·ful** adj

lus·ter or **lus·tre** \'ləs-tər\ n 1 : a shine or sheen esp. from reflected light 2 : BRIGHTNESS, GLITTER 3 : GLORY, SPLENDOR — **lus·ter·less** adj — **lustrous** \-trəs\ adj

lus·tral \'ləs-trəl\ adj : serving or intended to purify ⟨∼ water⟩

lusty \'ləs-tē\ adj **lust·i·er; -est** : full of vitality : ROBUST — **lust·i·ly** \'ləs-tə-lē\ adv — **lust·i·ness** \-tē-nəs\ n

lute \'lüt\ n : a stringed musical instrument with a large pear-shaped body and a fretted fingerboard — **lu·te·nist** or **lu·ta·nist** \'lü-tə-nist\ n

lu·te·tium also **lu·te·cium** \lü-'tē-shē-əm, -shəm\ n : a metallic chemical element

Lu·ther·an \'lü-thə-rən\ n : a member of a Protestant denomination adhering to the doctrines of Martin Luther — **Lu·ther·an·ism** \-rə-ˌni-zəm\ n

lux·u·ri·ant \ˌləg-'zhu̇r-ē-ənt, ˌlək-'shu̇r-\ adj 1 : yielding or growing abundantly : LUSH, PRODUCTIVE ⟨∼ vegetation⟩ 2 : abundantly rich and varied; also

: FLORID ⟨a ~ fabric⟩ ✦ *Synonyms* EX-UBERANT, LAVISH, OPULENT, PRODIGAL, PROFUSE, RIOTOUS — **lux·u·ri·ance** \-ē-əns\ *n* — **lux·u·ri·ant·ly** *adv*

lux·u·ri·ate \-ē-,āt\ *vb* **-at·ed; -at·ing** **1** : to grow profusely **2** : REVEL

lux·u·ry \'lək-shə-rē, 'ləg-zhə-\ *n, pl* **-ries** **1** : great ease and comfort **2** : something adding to pleasure or comfort but not absolutely necessary — **lux·u·ri·ous** \,ləg-'zhùr-ē-əs, ,lək-'shùr-\ *adj* — **lux·u·ri·ous·ly** *adv*

lv *abbr* leave

lwei \lə-'wā\ *n, pl* **lwei** — see *kwanza* at MONEY table

LWV *abbr* League of Women Voters

¹-ly \lē\ *adj suffix* **1** : like in appearance, manner, or nature ⟨queen*ly*⟩ **2** : characterized by regular recurrence in (specified) units of time : every ⟨hour*ly*⟩ ⟨week*ly*⟩

²-ly *adv suffix* **1** : in a (specified) manner ⟨slow*ly*⟩ **2** : from a (specified) point of view ⟨grammatical*ly*⟩

ly·ce·um \lī-'sē-əm, 'lī-sē-\ *n* **1** : a hall for public lectures **2** : an association providing public lectures, concerts, and entertainments

ly·chee *or* **li·tchi** \'lē-chē, 'lī-\ *n* [Ch(Beijing) *lìzhī*] **1** : an oval fruit with a hard scaly outer covering, a small hard seed, and edible flesh **2** : an Asian tree bearing lychees

lye \'lī\ *n* : a corrosive alkaline substance used esp. in making soap

ly·ing \'lī-iŋ\ *adj* : UNTRUTHFUL, FALSE

ly·ing-in \,lī-iŋ-'in\ *n, pl* **lyings-in** *or* **lying-ins** : the state during and consequent to childbirth : CONFINEMENT

Lyme disease \'līm-\ *n* [*Lyme*, Connecticut, where it was first reported] : an acute inflammatory disease that is caused by a spirochete transmitted by ticks, is characterized usu. by chills and fever, and if left untreated may result in joint pain, arthritis, and cardiac and neurological disorders

lymph \'limf\ *n* : a usu. clear fluid consisting chiefly of blood plasma and white blood cells, circulating in thin-walled tubes (**lymphatic vessels**), and bathing the body tissues — **lym·phat·ic** \lim-'fa-tik\ *adj*

lymph·ade·nop·a·thy \lim-,fa-də-'nä-pə-thē\ *n, pl* **-thies** : abnormal enlargement of the lymph nodes

lymph node *n* : any of the rounded masses of lymphoid tissue surrounded by a capsule of connective tissue

lym·pho·cyte \'lim-fə-,sīt\ *n* : any of the white blood cells arising from lymphoid tissue that are typically found in lymph and blood and that include the cellular mediators (as a B cell or a T cell) of immunity — **lym·pho·cyt·ic** \,lim-fə-'si-tik\ *adj*

lym·phoid \'lim-,fóid\ *adj* **1** : of, relating to, or being tissue (as of the lymph nodes) containing lymphocytes **2** : of, relating to, or resembling lymph

lym·pho·ma \lim-'fō-mə\ *n, pl* **-mas** *also* **-ma·ta** \-mə-tə\ : a usu. malignant tumor of lymphoid tissue

lynch \'linch\ *vb* : to put to death by mob action without legal sanction or due process of law

lynx \'liŋks\ *n, pl* **lynx** *or* **lynx·es** : any of several wildcats with a short tail, long legs, and usu. tufted ears

lyre \'lī(-ə)r\ *n* : a stringed musical instrument of the harp class having a U-shaped frame and used by the ancient Greeks

¹lyr·ic \'lir-ik\ *n* **1** : a lyric poem **2** *pl* : the words of a popular song — **lyr·i·cal** \-i-kəl\ *adj*

²lyric *adj* **1** : suitable for singing : MELODIC **2** : expressing direct and usu. intense personal emotion

ly·ser·gic acid di·eth·yl·am·ide \lə-'sər-jik . . . ,dī-,e-thə-'la-,mīd, lī-, -'la-məd\ *n* : LSD

LZ *abbr* landing zone

Ⓜ

¹m \'em\ *n, pl* **m's** *or* **ms** \'emz\ *often cap* : the 13th letter of the English alphabet

²m *abbr, often cap* **1** Mach **2** male **3** married **4** masculine **5** medium **6** [L *meridies*] noon **7** meter **8** mile **9** [L *mille*] thousand **10** minute **11** month **12** moon

ma \'mä, 'mó\ *n* : MOTHER

MA *abbr* **1** [ML *magister artium*] master of arts **2** Massachusetts **3** mental age

ma'am \'mam, *after* "yes" *often* əm\ *n* : MADAM

Mac *abbr* Machabees

Mac *or* **Macc** *abbr* Maccabees

ma·ca·bre \mə-'käb; -'kä-brə, -bər\ *adj* [F] **1** : having death as a subject **2** : GRUESOME **3** : HORRIBLE

mac·ad·am \mə-'ka-dəm\ *n* [John L. *McAdam* †1836 Brit. engineer] : a roadway or pavement of small closely packed broken stone — **mac·ad·am·ize** \-də-,mīz\ *vb*

mac·a·da·mia nut \,ma-kə-'dā-mē-ə-\ *n* : a hard-shelled richly-flavored nut of any of several Australian trees

ma·caque \mə-'kak, -'käk\ *n* : any of a genus of short-tailed chiefly Asian monkeys; *esp* : RHESUS MONKEY

mac·a·ro·ni \,ma-kə-'rō-nē\ *n* **1** : pasta made chiefly of wheat flour and shaped in the form of slender tubes **2** *pl* **-nis** *or* **-nies** : FOP, DANDY

mac·a·roon \,ma-kə-'rün\ *n* : a small cookie made chiefly of egg whites, sugar, and ground almonds or coconut

ma·caw \mə-ˈkò\ n : any of numerous parrots of Central and So. America

Mac·ca·bees \ˈma-kə-ˌbēz\ n — see BIBLE table

¹**mace** \ˈmās\ n : a spice made from the fibrous coating of the nutmeg

²**mace** n 1 : a heavy often spiked club used as a weapon esp. in the Middle Ages 2 : an ornamental staff carried as a symbol of authority

mac·er·ate \ˈma-sə-ˌrāt\ vb **-at·ed; -at·ing** 1 : to cause to waste away 2 : to soften by steeping or soaking so as to separate the parts — **mac·er·a·tion** \ˌma-sə-ˈrā-shən\ n

Mac·Guf·fin or **Mc·Guf·fin** \mə-ˈgə-fən\ n : an object, event, or character whose main purpose is to advance the plot of a motion picture

mach abbr machine; machinery; machinist

Mach \ˈmäk\ n : a speed expressed by a Mach number

Mach·a·bees \ˈma-kə-ˌbēz\ n : MACCABEES

ma·chete \mə-ˈshe-tē\ n : a large heavy knife used for cutting sugarcane and underbrush and as a weapon

Ma·chi·a·vel·lian \ˌma-kē-ə-ˈve-lē-ən\ adj [Niccolò *Machiavelli*, †1527 Ital. political philosopher] : characterized by cunning, duplicity, and bad faith — **Ma·chi·a·vel·lian·ism** n

mach·i·na·tion \ˌma-kə-ˈnā-shən, ˌma-shə-\ n : an act of planning esp. to do harm; esp : PLOT — **mach·i·nate** \ˈma-kə-ˌnāt, ˈma-shə-\ vb

¹**ma·chine** \mə-ˈshēn\ n 1 : CONVEYANCE, VEHICLE; esp : AUTOMOBILE 2 : a combination of mechanical parts that transmit forces, motion, and energy one to another 3 : an instrument (as a lever) for transmitting or modifying force or motion 4 : an electrical, electronic, or mechanical device for performing a task ⟨a sewing ∼⟩ 5 : a highly organized political group under the leadership of a boss or small clique

²**machine** vb **ma·chined; ma·chin·ing** : to shape or finish by machine-operated tools — **ma·chin·able** \-ˈshē-nə-bəl\ adj

machine gun n : an automatic gun capable of rapid continuous firing — **machine–gun** vb — **machine gunner** n

machine language n : the set of symbolic instruction codes used to represent operations and data in a machine (as a computer)

machine–readable adj : directly usable by a computer

ma·chin·ery \mə-ˈshē-nə-rē\ n, pl **-er·ies** 1 : MACHINES; also : the working parts of a machine 2 : the means by which something is done

ma·chin·ist \mə-ˈshē-nist\ n : a person who makes or works on machines

ma·chis·mo \mä-ˈchēz-(ˌ)mō, -ˈchiz-\ n : a strong or exaggerated pride in one's masculinity

Mach number \ˈmäk-\ n : a number representing the ratio of the speed of a body

(as an aircraft) to the speed of sound in the surrounding atmosphere

ma·cho \ˈmä-chō\ adj [Sp, lit., male, fr. L *masculus*] : characterized by machismo

mack·er·el \ˈma-kə-rəl\ n, pl **mackerel** or **mackerels** : a No. Atlantic food fish greenish above and silvery below

mack·i·naw \ˈma-kə-ˌnò\ n : a short heavy plaid coat

mack·in·tosh also **mac·in·tosh** \ˈma-kən-ˌtäsh\ n, 1 chiefly Brit : RAINCOAT 2 : a lightweight waterproof fabric

mac·ra·mé also **mac·ra·me** \ˈma-krə-ˌmā\ n [ultim. fr. Ar *miqrama* coverlet] : a coarse lace or fringe made by knotting threads or cords in a geometrical pattern

¹**mac·ro** \ˈma-(ˌ)krō\ adj : very large; also : involving large quantities or being on a large scale

²**macro** n, pl **macros** : a single computer instruction that stands for a sequence of operations

mac·ro·bi·ot·ic \ˌma-krō-bī-ˈä-tik, -bē-\ adj : relating to or being a very restricted diet (as one containing chiefly whole cereals or grains)

mac·ro·cosm \ˈma-krə-ˌkä-zəm\ n : the great world : UNIVERSE

ma·cron \ˈmā-ˌkrän, ˈma-\ n : a mark placed over a vowel (as in \ˈmāk\) to show that the vowel is long

mac·ro·scop·ic \ˌma-krə-ˈskä-pik\ adj : visible to the naked eye — **mac·ro·scop·i·cal·ly** \-pi-k(ə-)lē\ adv

mac·u·la \ˈma-kyə-lə\ n, pl **-lae** \-ˌlē, -ˌlī\ also **-las** : an anatomical spot distinguishable from surrounding tissues — **mac·u·lar** \-lər\ adj

mad \ˈmad\ adj **mad·der; mad·dest** 1 : disordered in mind : INSANE 2 : being rash and foolish 3 : FURIOUS, ENRAGED 4 : carried away by enthusiasm 5 : RABID 6 : marked by wild gaiety and merriment 7 : FRANTIC — **mad·ly** adv — **mad·ness** n

mad·am \ˈma-dəm\ n 1 pl **mes·dames** \mā-ˈdäm\ — used as a form of polite address to a woman 2 pl **madams** : the female head of a house of prostitution

ma·dame \mə-ˈdam, before a surname also \ˈma-dəm\ n, pl **mes·dames** \mā-ˈdäm\ : MISTRESS — used as a title equivalent to Mrs. for a married woman not of English-speaking nationality

mad·cap \ˈmad-ˌkap\ adj : WILD, RECKLESS ⟨a ∼ scheme⟩ — **madcap** n

mad cow disease n : a fatal encephalopathy of cattle that affects the nervous system causing the brain tissue to resemble a porous sponge

mad·den \ˈma-dᵊn\ vb : to make mad — **mad·den·ing·ly** adv

mad·der \ˈma-dər\ n : a Eurasian herb with yellow flowers and fleshy red roots; also : its root or a dye prepared from it

made past and past part of MAKE

Ma·dei·ra \mə-ˈdir-ə\ n : an amber-colored dessert wine

ma·de·moi·selle \ˌma-də-mə-ˈzel, -mwə-, mam-ˈzel\ n, pl **ma·de·moi·selles** \-ˈzelz\ or **mes·de·moi·selles** \ˌmā-də-me-ˈzel, -mwə-\ : an unmarried girl or woman — used as a title for an unmarried woman not of English-speaking nationality

made-to-measure adj : CUSTOM-MADE

made-up \'mād-'əp\ adj 1 : fancifully conceived or falsely devised 2 : marked by the use of makeup

mad-man \'mad-ˌman, -mən\ n : LUNATIC

Ma-don-na \mə-'dä-nə\ n : a representation (as a picture or statue) of the Virgin Mary

ma-dras \'ma-drəs; ˌmə-'dras, -'dräs\ n [Madras, India] : a fine usu. cotton fabric with various designs (as plaid)

ma-dras-sa or **ma-dra-sa** \mə-'dra-sə, -'drä-\ n : a Muslim school, college, or university that is often part of a mosque

mad-ri-gal \'ma-dri-gəl\ n [It madrigale] 1 : a short lyrical poem in a strict poetic form 2 : an elaborate part-song esp. of the 16th and 17th centuries

mad-wom-an \'mad-ˌwù-mən\ n : a woman who is insane

mael-strom \'māl-strəm\ n 1 : a violent whirlpool 2 : TUMULT

mae-stro \'mī-strō\ n, pl **maestros** or **mae-stri** \-ˌstrē\ [It] : a master in an art; esp : an eminent composer, conductor, or teacher of music

Ma-fia \'mä-fē-ə\ n [It] : a secret criminal society of Sicily or Italy; also : a similar organization elsewhere

ma-fi-o-so \ˌmä-fē-'ō-(ˌ)sō\ n, pl **-si** \-(ˌ)sē\ : a member of the Mafia

¹mag \'mag\ n : MAGAZINE

²mag abbr 1 magnetism 2 magneto 3 magnitude

mag-a-zine \'ma-gə-ˌzēn\ n [MF, fr. Old Occitan, fr. Ar makhāzin, pl. of makhzan storehouse] 1 : a storehouse esp. for military supplies 2 : a place for keeping gunpowder in a fort or ship 3 : a publication usu. containing stories, articles, or poems and issued periodically 4 : a container in a gun for holding cartridges; also : a chamber (as on a camera) for film

ma-gen-ta \mə-'jen-tə\ n : a deep purplish red color

mag-got \'ma-gət\ n : the legless wormlike larva of a dipteran fly — **mag-goty** adj

ma-gi \'mā-jī\ n pl, often cap : the three wise men from the East who paid homage to the infant Jesus

mag-ic \'ma-jik\ n 1 : the use of means (as charms or spells) believed to have supernatural power over natural forces 2 : an extraordinary power or influence seemingly from a supernatural source 3 : SLEIGHT OF HAND — **magic** adj — **mag-i-cal** \-ji-kəl\ adj — **mag-i-cal-ly** \-ji-k(ə-)lē\ adv

ma-gi-cian \mə-'ji-shən\ n : a person skilled in magic

mag-is-te-ri-al \ˌma-jə-'stir-ē-əl\ adj 1 : AUTHORITATIVE 2 : of or relating to a magistrate or a magistrate's office or duties

ma-gis-tral \'ma-jə-strəl\ adj : AUTHORITATIVE

mag-is-trate \'ma-jə-ˌstrāt\ n : an official entrusted with administration of the laws — **mag-is-tra-cy** \-strə-sē\ n

mag-lev \'mag-lev\ n 1 : the use of magnetic fields to float an object above a solid surface 2 : a train using maglev technology

mag-ma \'mag-mə\ n : molten rock material within the earth — **mag-mat-ic** \mag-'ma-tik\ adj

mag-nan-i-mous \mag-'na-nə-məs\ adj 1 : showing or suggesting a lofty and courageous spirit 2 : NOBLE, GENEROUS — **mag-na-nim-i-ty** \ˌmag-nə-'ni-mə-tē\ n — **mag-nan-i-mous-ly** adv — **mag-nan-i-mous-ness** n

mag-nate \'mag-ˌnāt\ n : a person of rank, influence, or distinction

mag-ne-sia \mag-'nē-shə, -zhə\ n [NL, fr. magnes carneus, a white earth, lit., flesh magnet] : a light white oxide of magnesium used as a laxative

mag-ne-sium \mag-'nē-zē-əm, -zhəm\ n : a silver-white light malleable metallic chemical element

mag-net \'mag-nət\ n 1 : LODESTONE 2 : a body that is able to attract iron 3 : something that attracts

mag-net-ic \mag-'ne-tik\ adj 1 : having an unusual ability to attract ⟨a ~ leader⟩ 2 : of or relating to a magnet or magnetism 3 : magnetized or capable of being magnetized — **mag-net-i-cal-ly** \-ti-k(ə-)lē\ adv

magnetic disk n : DISK 3

magnetic levitation n : MAGLEV 1

magnetic north n : the northerly direction in the earth's magnetic field indicated by the north-seeking pole of a compass needle

magnetic resonance imaging n : a noninvasive diagnostic technique that produces computerized images of internal body tissues based on electromagnetically induced activity of atoms within the body

magnetic tape n : a ribbon coated with a magnetic material on which information (as sound) may be stored

mag-ne-tise Brit var of MAGNETIZE

mag-ne-tism \'mag-nə-ˌti-zəm\ n 1 : the power (as of a magnet) to attract iron 2 : the science that deals with magnetic phenomena 3 : an ability to attract or charm

mag-ne-tite \'mag-nə-ˌtīt\ n : a black mineral that is an important iron ore

mag-ne-tize \'mag-nə-ˌtīz\ vb **-tized; -tizing** 1 : to induce magnetic properties in 2 : to attract like a magnet : CHARM — **mag-ne-tiz-able** adj — **mag-ne-ti-za-tion** \ˌmag-nə-tə-'zā-shən\ n — **mag-ne-tiz-er** n

mag-ne-to \mag-'nē-tō\ n, pl **-tos** : a generator used to produce sparks in an internal combustion engine

mag-ne-tom-e-ter \ˌmag-nə-'tä-mə-tər\ n : an instrument for measuring the strength of a magnetic field

mag-ne-to-sphere \mag-'nē-tə-ˌsfir, -'ne-\ n : a region around a celestial object (as the earth) in which charged particles are trapped by its magnetic field — **mag·ne·to·spher·ic** \-ˌne-tə-ˈsfir-ik, -ˈsfer-\ adj

mag·ni·fi·ca·tion \ˌmag-nə-fə-ˈkā-shən\ n   **1** : the act of magnifying   **2** : the amount by which an optical lens or instrument magnifies

mag·nif·i·cent \mag-ˈni-fə-sənt\ adj   **1** : characterized by grandeur or beauty : SPLENDID   **2** : EXALTED, NOBLE ♦ **Synonyms** IMPOSING, STATELY, GRAND, MAJESTIC — **mag·nif·i·cence** \-səns\ n — **mag·nif·i·cent·ly** adv

mag·nif·i·co \mag-ˈni-fi-ˌkō\ n, pl **-coes** or **-cos**   **1** : a nobleman of Venice   **2** : a person of high position

mag·ni·fy \ˈmag-nə-ˌfī\ vb **-fied; -fy·ing**   **1** : EXTOL, LAUD; also : to cause to be held in greater esteem   **2** : INTENSIFY; also : EXAGGERATE   **3** : to enlarge in fact or in appearance ⟨a microscope magnifies an object⟩ — **mag·ni·fi·er** \ˈmag-nə-ˌfī-(ə)r\ n

mag·nil·o·quent \mag-ˈni-lə-kwənt\ adj : characterized by an exalted and often bombastic style or manner — **mag·nil·o·quence** \-kwəns\ n

mag·ni·tude \ˈmag-nə-ˌtüd, -ˌtyüd\ n   **1** : greatness of size or extent   **2** : SIZE   **3** : QUANTITY   **4** : a number representing the brightness of a celestial body   **5** : a number representing the intensity of an earthquake

mag·no·lia \mag-ˈnōl-yə\ n : any of a genus of usu. spring-flowering shrubs and trees with large often fragrant flowers

mag·num opus \ˈmag-nəm-ˈō-pəs\ n [L] : the greatest achievement of an artist or writer

mag·pie \ˈmag-ˌpī\ n : any of various long-tailed often black-and-white birds related to the jays

Mag·yar \ˈmag-ˌyär, ˈmäg-; ˈmä-ˌjär\ n : a member of the dominant people of Hungary — **Magyar** adj

ma·ha·ra·ja or **ma·ha·ra·jah** \ˌmä-hə-ˈrä-jə\ n : a Hindu prince ranking above a raja

ma·ha·ra·ni or **ma·ha·ra·nee** \-ˈrä-nē\ n   **1** : the wife of a maharaja   **2** : a Hindu princess ranking above a rani

ma·ha·ri·shi \ˌmä-hə-ˈrē-shē\ n : a Hindu teacher of mystical knowledge

ma·hat·ma \mə-ˈhät-mə, -ˈhat-\ n [Skt mahātman, fr. mahātman great-souled, fr. mahat great + ātman soul] : a person revered for high-mindedness, wisdom, and selflessness

Ma·hi·can \mə-ˈhē-kən\ or **Mo·hi·can** \mō-, mə-\ n, pl **-can** or **-cans** : a member of an American Indian people of the upper Hudson River valley

ma·hog·a·ny \mə-ˈhä-gə-nē\ n, pl **-nies** : the reddish wood of any of various chiefly tropical trees that is used in furniture; also : a tree yielding this wood

ma·hout \mə-ˈhaut\ n [Hindi & Urdu mahāwat, mahāut] : a keeper and driver of an elephant

maid \ˈmād\ n   **1** : an unmarried girl or

young woman   **2** : MAIDSERVANT; also : a woman or girl employed to do domestic work

¹**maid·en** \ˈmā-dᵊn\ n : MAID 1 — **maid·en·ly** adj

²**maiden** adj   **1** : UNMARRIED; also : VIRGIN   **2** : of, relating to, or befitting a maiden   **3** : FIRST ⟨a ship's ∼ voyage⟩

maid·en·hair fern \-ˌher-\ n : any of a genus of ferns with delicate feathery fronds

maid·en·head \ˈmā-dᵊn-ˌhed\ n   **1** : VIRGINITY   **2** : HYMEN

maid·en·hood \-ˌhud\ n : the condition or time of being a maiden

maid–in–waiting n, pl **maids–in–waiting** : a young woman appointed to attend a queen or princess

maid of honor : a bride's principal unmarried wedding attendant

maid·ser·vant \ˈmād-ˌsər-vənt\ n : a girl or woman who is a servant

¹**mail** \ˈmāl\ n [ME male bag, fr. AF, of Gmc origin]   **1** : material sent or carried in the postal system   **2** : a nation's postal system — often used in pl.   **3** : E-MAIL

²**mail** vb : to send by mail

³**mail** n [ME maille metal link, mail, fr. AF, fr. L macula spot, mesh] : armor made of metal links or plates

mail·box \ˈmāl-ˌbäks\ n   **1** : a public box for the collection of mail   **2** : a private box for the delivery of mail

mail·man \-ˌman\ n : a man who delivers mail

maim \ˈmām\ vb : to mutilate, disfigure, or wound seriously

¹**main** \ˈmān\ n   **1** : FORCE ⟨with might and ∼⟩   **2** : MAINLAND; also : HIGH SEA   **3** : the chief part   **4** : a principal pipe, duct, or circuit of a utility system

²**main** adj   **1** : CHIEF, PRINCIPAL ⟨the ∼ idea⟩   **2** : fully exerted ⟨∼ force⟩   **3** : expressing the chief predication in a complex sentence ⟨the ∼ clause⟩ — **main·ly** adv

main·frame \ˈmān-ˌfrām\ n : a large fast computer

main·land \-ˌland, -lənd\ n : a continuous body of land constituting the chief part of a country or continent

main·line \-ˌlīn\ vb, slang : to inject a narcotic drug into a vein

main line n : a principal highway or railroad line

main·mast \ˈmān-ˌmast, -məst\ n : the principal mast on a sailing ship

main·sail \-ˌsāl, -səl\ n : the largest sail on the mainmast

main·spring \-ˌspriŋ\ n   **1** : the chief spring in a mechanism (as of a watch)   **2** : the chief motive, agent, or cause

main·stay \-ˌstā\ n   **1** : a stay running from the head of the mainmast to the foot of the foremast   **2** : a chief support

main·stream \-ˌstrēm\ n : a prevailing current or direction of activity or influence — **mainstream** adj

main·tain \mān-ˈtān\ vb [ME mainteinen, fr. AF maintenir, maynteiner, fr. ML manutenēre, fr. L manu tenēre to hold in the hand] **1** : to keep in an existing state (as of repair) **2** : to sustain against opposition or danger **3** : to continue in : CARRY ON **4** : to provide for : SUPPORT **5** : ASSERT ⟨*~ed* his innocence⟩ — **main·tain·abil·i·ty** \-ˌtā-nə-ˈbi-lə-tē\ *n* — **main·tain·able** \-ˈtā-nə-bəl\ *adj* — **main·te·nance** \ˈmān-tə-nəns\ *n*

main·top \ˈmän-ˌtäp\ *n* : a platform at the head of the mainmast of a square-rigged ship

mai·son·ette \ˌmā-zə-ˈnet\ *n* **1** : a small house **2** : an apartment often on two floors

mai tai \ˈmī-ˌtī\ *n* : a cocktail made with liquors and fruit juices

maî·tre d' *or* **mai·tre d'** \ˌmā-trə-ˈdē, ˌme-\ *n, pl* **maî·tre d's** *or* **maitre d's** \-ˈdēz\ : MAÎTRE D'HÔTEL

maî·tre d'hô·tel \ˌmā-trə-dō-ˈtel, ˌme-\ *n, pl* **maîtres d'hôtel** *same*\ [F, lit., master of house] **1** : MAJORDOMO **2** : HEADWAITER

maize \ˈmāz\ *n* : INDIAN CORN

Maj *abbr* major

maj·es·ty \ˈma-jə-stē\ *n, pl* **-ties 1** : sovereign power, authority, or dignity; *also* : the person of a sovereign — used as a title **2** : GRANDEUR, SPLENDOR — **majes·tic** \mə-ˈjes-tik\ *adj* — **ma·jes·ti·cal·ly** \-ti-k(ə-)lē\ *adv*

Maj Gen *abbr* Major General

ma·jol·i·ca \mə-ˈjä-li-kə\ *also* **ma·iol·i·ca** \-ˈyä-\ *n* : any of several faiences; *esp* : an Italian tin-glazed pottery

¹ma·jor \ˈmā-jər\ *adj* **1** : greater in number, extent, or importance ⟨a *~* poet⟩ **2** : notable or conspicuous in effect or scope ⟨a *~* improvement⟩ **3** : SERIOUS ⟨a *~* illness⟩ **4** : having half steps between the 3d and 4th and the 7th and 8th degrees ⟨*~* scale⟩; *also* : based on a major scale ⟨*~* key⟩ ⟨*~* chord⟩

²major *n* **1** : a commissioned officer (as in the army) ranking next below a lieutenant colonel **2** : an academic subject chosen as a field of specialization; *also* : a student specializing in such a field ⟨a history *~*⟩

³major *vb* : to pursue an academic major

ma·jor·do·mo \ˌmā-jər-ˈdō-mō\ *n, pl* **-mos** [Sp *mayordomo* or obs. It *maiordomo,* fr. ML *major domus,* lit., chief of the house] **1** : a head steward **2** : BUTLER

ma·jor·ette \ˌmā-jə-ˈret\ *n* : DRUM MAJORETTE

major general *n* : a commissioned officer (as in the army) ranking next below a lieutenant general

ma·jor·i·ty \mə-ˈjȯr-ə-tē\ *n, pl* **-ties 1** : the age at which full civil rights are accorded; *also* : the status of one who has attained this age **2** : a number greater than half of a total; *also* : the excess of this greater number over the remainder **3** : the rank of a major

ma·jus·cule \ˈma-jəs-ˌkyül, mə-ˈjəs-\ *n* : a large letter (as a capital)

Ma·kah \ˈmä-kä\ *n, pl* **Makah** *or* **Makahs** : a member of an American Indian people of the northwest coast of No. America

¹make \ˈmāk\ *vb* **made** \ˈmād\; **mak·ing 1** : to cause to exist, occur, or appear; *also* : DESTINE ⟨was *made* to be an actor⟩ **2** : FASHION ⟨*~* a dress⟩; *also* : COMPOSE **3** : to formulate in the mind ⟨*~* plans⟩ **4** : CONSTITUTE ⟨house *made* of stone⟩ **5** : to compute to be **6** : to set in order : PREPARE ⟨*~* a bed⟩ **7** : to cause to be or become; *also* : APPOINT **8** : ENACT; *also* : EXECUTE ⟨*~* a will⟩ **9** : CONCLUDE ⟨didn't know what to *~* of it⟩ **10** : CARRY OUT, PERFORM ⟨*~* a gesture⟩ **11** : COMPEL **12** : to assure the success of ⟨will *~* us or break us⟩ **13** : to amount to in significance ⟨*~s* no difference⟩ **14** : to be capable of developing or being fashioned into **15** : REACH, ATTAIN; *also* : GAIN **16** : to start out : GO **17** : to have weight or effect ⟨courtesy *~s* for safer driving⟩ ◆ *Synonyms* FORM, SHAPE, FABRICATE, MANUFACTURE — **mak·er** *n* — **make believe** : PRETEND — **make do** : to manage with the means at hand — **make fun of** : RIDICULE, MOCK — **make good 1** : INDEMNIFY ⟨*make good* the loss⟩; *also* : to carry out successfully ⟨*make good* his promise⟩ **2** : SUCCEED — **make way 1** : to give room for passing, entering, or occupying **2** : to make progress

²make *n* **1** : the manner or style of construction; *also* : BRAND **2** : MAKEUP **3** : the action of manufacturing — **on the make** : in search of wealth, social status, or sexual advantage

¹make–be·lieve \ˈmāk-bə-ˌlēv\ *n* : a pretending that what is not real is real

²make–believe *adj* : IMAGINED, PRETENDED

make–do \-ˌdü\ *adj* : MAKESHIFT

make out *vb* **1** : to draw up in writing ⟨*make out* a list⟩ **2** : to find or grasp the meaning of ⟨can you *make* that *out*⟩ **3** : to represent as being **4** : to pretend to be true **5** : DISCERN ⟨*make out* a ship in the fog⟩ **6** : GET ALONG, FARE ⟨*make out* well in life⟩ **7** : to engage in amorous kissing and caressing

make over *vb* : REMAKE, REMODEL — **make·over** \ˈmā-ˌkō-vər\ *n*

make·shift \ˈmāk-ˌshift\ *n* : a temporary expedient — **makeshift** *adj*

make·up \ˈmā-ˌkəp\ *n* **1** : the way in which something is put together; *also* : physical, mental, and moral constitution **2** : cosmetics esp. for the face; *also* : materials (as wigs and cosmetics) used in making up

make up *vb* **1** : FORM, COMPOSE **2** : to compensate for a deficiency **3** : SETTLE ⟨*made* up my mind⟩ **4** : INVENT, IMPROVISE **5** : to become reconciled **6** : to put on makeup (as for a play)

make–work \ˈmāk-ˌwərk\ *n* : BUSYWORK

mak·ings \ˈmā-kiŋz\ *n pl* : the material from which something is made

Mal *abbr* Malachi

Mal·a·chi \ˈma-lə-ˌkī\ *n* — see BIBLE table

Mal·a·chi·as \ˌma-lə-ˈkī-əs\ *n* : MALACHI

mal·a·chite \ˈma-lə-ˌkīt\ *n* : a green mineral that is a carbonate of copper used for making ornamental objects

mal·adapt·ed \,ma-lə-'dap-təd\ *adj*
: poorly suited to a particular use, purpose, or situation

mal·ad·just·ed \,ma-lə-'jəs-təd\ *adj*
: poorly or inadequately adjusted (as to one's environment) — **mal·ad·just·ment** \-'jəst-mənt\ *n*

mal·adroit \,ma-lə-'dròit\ *adj* : not adroit
: INEPT

mal·a·dy \'ma-lə-dē\ *n, pl* **-dies** : a disease or disorder of body or mind

mal·aise \mə-'lāz, ma-\ *n* [F] : a hazy feeling of not being well

mal·a·mute \'ma-lə-,myüt\ *n* : a dog often used to draw sleds esp. in northern No. America

mal·a·prop·ism \'ma-lə-,prä-,pi-zəm\ *n*
: a usu. humorous misuse of a word

mal·ap·ro·pos \,ma-,la-prə-'pō, ,ma-'la-prə-,pō\ *adv* : in an inappropriate or inopportune way — **malapropos** *adj*

ma·lar·ia \mə-'ler-ē-ə\ *n* [It, fr. *mala aria* bad air] : a disease marked by recurring chills and fever and caused by a protozoan parasite of the blood that is transmitted by anopheles mosquitoes — **ma·lar·i·al** \-əl\ *adj*

ma·lar·key \mə-'lär-kē\ *n* : insincere or foolish talk

mal·a·thi·on \,ma-lə-'thī-ən, -,än\ *n* : an insecticide with a relatively low toxicity for mammals

Ma·lay \mə-'lā, 'mā-,lā\ *n* 1 : a member of a people of the Malay Peninsula and Archipelago 2 : the language of the Malays — **Malay** *adj* — **Ma·lay·an** \mə-'lā-ən, 'mā-,lā-\ *n or adj*

mal·con·tent \,mal-kən-'tent\ *adj*
: marked by a dissatisfaction with the existing state of affairs : DISCONTENTED — **malcontent** *n*

mal de mer \,mal-də-'mer\ *n* [F] : SEASICKNESS

¹**male** \'māl\ *n* : a male individual

²**male** *adj* 1 : of, relating to, or being the sex that produces germ cells which fertilize the eggs of a female; *also* : STAMINATE 2 : MASCULINE — **male·ness** *n*

male·dic·tion \,ma-lə-'dik-shən\ *n*
: CURSE, EXECRATION

male·fac·tor \'ma-lə-,fak-tər\ *n* : EVILDOER; *esp* : one who commits an offense against the law — **male·fac·tion** \,ma-lə-'fak-shən\ *n*

ma·lef·ic \mə-'le-fik\ *adj* 1 : BALEFUL 2
: MALICIOUS

ma·lef·i·cent \-fə-sənt\ *adj* : working or productive of harm or evil

ma·lev·o·lent \mə-'le-və-lənt\ *adj* : having, showing, or arising from ill will, spite, or hatred ✦ *Synonyms* MALIGNANT, MALIGN, MALICIOUS, SPITEFUL — **ma·lev·o·lence** \-ləns\ *n*

mal·fea·sance \mal-'fē-z°ns\ *n* : wrongful conduct esp. by a public official

mal·for·ma·tion \,mal-fór-'mā-shən\ *n*
: irregular or faulty formation or structure; *also* : an instance of this — **malformed** \-'fórmd\ *adj*

mal·func·tion \mal-'fəŋk-shən\ *vb* : to fail to operate normally — **malfunction** *n*

mal·ice \'ma-ləs\ *n* : desire to cause injury or distress to another — **ma·li·cious** \mə-'li-shəs\ *adj* — **ma·li·cious·ly** *adv*

¹**ma·lign** \mə-'līn\ *adj* 1 : evil in nature, influence, or effect; *also* : MALIGNANT 2
2 : moved by ill will

²**malign** *vb* : to speak evil of : DEFAME

ma·lig·nant \mə-'lig-nənt\ *adj* 1 : INJURIOUS, MALIGN 2 : tending to produce death or deterioration ⟨a ~ tumor⟩ —
ma·lig·nan·cy \-nən-sē\ *n* — **ma·lig·nant·ly** *adv* — **ma·lig·ni·ty** \-nə-tē\ *n*

ma·lin·ger \mə-'liŋ-gər\ *vb* [F *malingre* sickly] : to pretend illness so as to avoid duty — **ma·lin·ger·er** *n*

mal·i·son \'ma-lə-sən, -zən\ *n* : CURSE

mall \'mól, 'mal\ *n* 1 : a shaded walk
: PROMENADE 2 : an urban shopping area featuring a variety of shops surrounding a concourse 3 : a usu. large enclosed suburban shopping area containing various shops

mal·lard \'ma-lərd\ *n, pl* **mallard** *or* **mallards** : a common wild duck that is the source of domestic ducks

mal·lea·ble \'ma-lē-ə-bəl\ *adj* 1 : capable of being extended or shaped by beating with a hammer or by the pressure of rollers 2 : ADAPTABLE, PLIABLE ✦ *Synonyms* PLASTIC, PLIANT, DUCTILE, SUPPLE — **mal·lea·bil·i·ty** \,ma-lē-ə-'bi-lə-tē\ *n*

mal·let \'ma-lət\ *n* 1 : a tool with a large head for driving another tool or for striking a surface without marring it 2 : a long-handled hammerlike implement for striking a ball (as in croquet)

mal·le·us \'ma-lē-əs\ *n, pl* **mal·lei** \-lē-,ī, -lē-,ē\ [NL, fr. L, hammer] : the outermost of the three small bones of the mammalian middle ear

mal·low \'ma-lō\ *n* : any of a genus of herbs with lobed leaves, usu. showy flowers, and a disk-shaped fruit

malm·sey \'mälm-zē\ *n, often cap* : the sweetest variety of Madeira

mal·nour·ished \mal-'nər-isht\ *adj* : UNDERNOURISHED

mal·nu·tri·tion \,mal-nü-'tri-shən, -nyü-\ *n* : faulty and esp. inadequate nutrition

mal·oc·clu·sion \,ma-lə-'klü-zhən\ *n*
: faulty coming together of teeth in biting

mal·odor·ous \ma-'lō-də-rəs\ *adj* : ill-smelling — **mal·odor·ous·ly** *adv* — **mal·odor·ous·ness** *n*

maloti *pl of* LOTI

mal·prac·tice \mal-'prak-təs\ *n* : a dereliction of professional duty or a failure of professional skill that results in injury, loss, or damage

malt \'mólt\ *n* 1 : grain and esp. barley steeped in water until it has sprouted and used in brewing and distilling 2 : liquor made with malt — **malty** *adj*

malted milk \'mól-təd-\ *n* : a powder prepared from dried milk and an extract from malt; *also* : a beverage of this powder in milk or other liquid

Mal·thu·sian \mal-'thü-zhən, -'thyü-\ *adj*
: of or relating to a theory that population unless checked (as by war) tends to increase faster than its means of subsis-

tence — **Malthusian** n — **Mal·thu·sian·ism** \-zhə-ˌni-zəm\ n

malt·ose \ˈmȯl-ˌtōs\ n : a sugar formed esp. from starch by the action of enzymes

mal·treat \mal-ˈtrēt\ vb : to treat cruelly or roughly : ABUSE — **mal·treat·ment** n

ma·ma or **mam·ma** \ˈmä-mə\ n : MOTHER

mam·bo \ˈmäm-bō\ n, pl **mambos** : a dance of Cuban origin related to the rumba — **mambo** vb

mam·mal \ˈma-məl\ n [NL Mammalia, fr. LL, neut. pl. of mammalis of the breast, fr. L mamma breast] : any of a class of warm-blooded vertebrates that includes humans and all other animals which nourish their young with milk and have the skin more or less covered with hair — **mam·ma·li·an** \mə-ˈma-lē-ən, ma-\ adj or n

mam·ma·ry \ˈma-mə-rē\ adj : of, relating to, or being the glands (**mammary glands**) that in female mammals secrete milk

mam·mo·gram \ˈma-mə-ˌgram\ n : an X-ray photograph of the breasts

mam·mog·ra·phy \ma-ˈmä-grə-fē\ n : X-ray examination of the breasts (as for early detection of cancer)

mam·mon \ˈma-mən\ n, often cap : material wealth having a debasing influence

¹**mam·moth** \ˈma-məth\ n : any of a genus of large hairy extinct elephants

²**mammoth** adj : of very great size : GIGANTIC ♦ **Synonyms** COLOSSAL, ENORMOUS, IMMENSE, VAST, ELEPHANTINE

¹**man** \ˈman\ n, pl **men** \ˈmen\ 1 : a human being; esp : an adult male 2 : the human race : MANKIND 3 : one possessing in high degree the qualities considered distinctive of manhood 4 : an adult male servant or employee 5 : the individual who can fulfill one's requirements ⟨he's your ∼⟩ 6 a : one of the pieces with which various games (as chess) are played b : one of the players on a team 7 often cap : white society or people

²**man** vb **manned**; **man·ning** 1 : to supply with men ⟨∼ a fleet⟩ 2 : FORTIFY, BRACE

³**man** abbr manual

Man abbr Manitoba

man–about–town n, pl **men–about–town** : a worldly and socially active man

man·a·cle \ˈma-ni-kəl\ n 1 : a shackle for the hand or wrist 2 : something used as a restraint

man·age \ˈma-nij\ vb **man·aged**; **man·ag·ing** 1 : HANDLE, CONTROL ⟨∼s her skis well⟩; also : to direct or carry on business or affairs 2 : to make and keep compliant 3 : to treat with care : HUSBAND 4 : to achieve one's purpose : CONTRIVE — **man·age·abil·i·ty** \ˌma-ni-jə-ˈbi-lə-tē\ n — **man·age·able** \ˈma-ni-jə-bəl\ adj — **man·age·able·ness** n — **man·age·ably** \-blē\ adv

managed care n : a health-care system that controls costs by limiting doctor's fees and by restricting the patient's choice of doctors

man·age·ment \ˈma-nij-mənt\ n 1 : the act or art of managing : CONTROL 2 : judicious use of means to accomplish an end 3 : the group of those who manage or direct an enterprise

man·ag·er \ˈma-ni-jər\ n : one that manages — **man·a·ge·ri·al** \ˌma-nə-ˈjir-ē-əl\ adj

ma·ña·na \mən-ˈyä-nə\ n [Sp, lit., tomorrow] : an indefinite time in the future

ma·nat \ˈmä-ˌnät\ n, pl **manat** or **manats** — see MONEY table

man–at–arms n, pl **men–at–arms** : SOLDIER; esp : one who is heavily armed and mounted

man·a·tee \ˈma-nə-ˌtē\ n : any of a genus of chiefly tropical plant-eating aquatic mammals having a broad rounded tail

man·ci·ple \ˈman-sə-pəl\ n : a steward or purveyor esp. for a college or monastery

man·da·mus \man-ˈdā-məs\ n [L, we enjoin] : a writ issued by a superior court commanding that an official act or duty be performed

man·da·rin \ˈman-də-rən\ n 1 : a public official of high rank under the Chinese Empire 2 cap : the chief dialect group of China 3 : a yellow to reddish orange loose-skinned citrus fruit; also : a tree that bears mandarins

man·date \ˈman-ˌdāt\ n 1 : an authoritative command 2 : an authorization to act given to a representative 3 : a commission granted by the League of Nations to a member nation for governing conquered territory; also : a territory so governed

man·da·to·ry \ˈman-də-ˌtȯr-ē\ adj 1 : containing or constituting a command : OBLIGATORY 2 : of or relating to a League of Nations mandate

man·di·ble \ˈman-də-bəl\ n 1 : JAW; esp : a lower jaw 2 : either segment of a bird's bill — **man·dib·u·lar** \man-ˈdi-byə-lər\ adj

man·do·lin \ˌman-də-ˈlin, ˈman-də-lən\ n : a stringed musical instrument with a pear-shaped body and a fretted neck

man·drake \ˈman-ˌdrāk\ n 1 : an Old World herb related to the nightshades or its large forked root formerly credited with magical properties 2 : MAYAPPLE

man·drel also **man·dril** \ˈman-drəl\ n 1 : an axle or spindle inserted into a hole in a piece of work to support it during machining 2 : a metal bar used as a core around which material may be cast, shaped, or molded

man·drill \ˈman-drəl\ n : a large baboon of western central Africa

mane \ˈmān\ n : long heavy hair growing about the neck of some mammals (as horses) — **maned** \ˈmānd\ adj

man–eat·er \ˈman-ˌē-tər\ n : one (as a shark or cannibal) that has or is thought to have an appetite for human flesh — **man–eat·ing** adj

ma·nège \ma-ˈnezh, mə-\ n : the art of horsemanship or of training horses

ma·nes \ˈmä-ˌnäs, ˈmä-ˌnēz\ n pl, often cap : the spirits of the dead and gods of the lower world in ancient Roman belief

ma·neu·ver \mə-'nü-vər, -'nyü-\ n [F manœuvre, fr. OF maneuvre work done by hand, fr. ML manuopera, fr. manu operare to work by hand] 1 : a military or naval movement; also : an armed forces training exercise — often used in pl. 2 : a procedure involving expert physical movement 3 : an evasive movement or shift of tactics; also : an action taken to gain a tactical end — **maneuver** vb — **ma·neu·ver·abil·i·ty** \-,nü-və-rə-'bi-lə-tē, -,nyü-\ n — **ma·neu·ver·able** \-'nü-və-rə-bəl, -'nyü-\ adj

man Friday n : an efficient and devoted aide or employee

man·ful \'man-fəl\ adj : having or showing courage and resolution — **man·ful·ly** adv

man·ga·nese \'maŋ-gə-,nēz, -,nēs\ n : a metallic chemical element resembling iron but not magnetic

mange \'mānj\ n : any of several contagious itchy skin diseases esp. of domestic animals — **mangy** \'mān-jē\ adj

man·ger \'mān-jər\ n : a trough or open box for livestock feed or fodder

¹**man·gle** \'maŋ-gəl\ vb **man·gled; mangling** 1 : to cut, bruise, or hack with repeated blows 2 : to spoil or injure esp. through ineptitude — **man·gler** n

²**mangle** n : a machine with heated rollers for ironing laundry

man·go \'maŋ-gō\ n, pl **mangoes** also **mangos** [Pg manga, prob. fr. Malayalam (Dravidian language of India) māñña] : an edible juicy yellowish-red fruit borne by a tropical evergreen tree related to the sumacs; also : this tree

man·grove \'man-,grōv\ n : any of a genus of tropical maritime trees that send out many prop roots and form dense thickets important in coastal land building

man·han·dle \'man-,han-dᵊl\ vb : to handle roughly

man·hat·tan \man-'ha-tᵊn\ n, often cap : a cocktail made of whiskey and vermouth

man·hole \'man-,hōl\ n : a hole through which a person may go esp. to gain access to an underground or enclosed structure

man·hood \-,hüd\ n 1 : the condition of being an adult male 2 : qualities associated with men : MANLINESS 3 : MEN ⟨the nation's ∼⟩

man-hour \-'au̇(-ə)r\ n : a unit of one hour's work by one person

man·hunt \-,hənt\ n : an organized hunt for a person and esp. for one charged with a crime

ma·nia \'mā-nē-ə, -nyə\ n 1 : excitement manifested by mental and physical hyperactivity, disorganized behavior, and elevated mood 2 : excessive enthusiasm

ma·ni·ac \'mā-nē-,ak\ n : LUNATIC, MADMAN

ma·ni·a·cal \mə-'nī-ə-kəl\ also **ma·ni·ac** \'mā-nē-ak\ adj 1 : affected with or suggestive of madness 2 : FRANTIC ⟨a ∼ mob⟩

man·ic \'ma-nik\ adj : affected with, relating to, characterized by, or resulting from

mania — **manic** n — **man·i·cal·ly** \-ni-k(ə-)lē\ adv

manic depression n : BIPOLAR DISORDER

man·ic–de·pres·sive \,ma-nik-di-'pre-siv\ adj : characterized by or affected with either mania or depression or alternating episodes of mania and depression — **manic–depressive** n

¹**man·i·cure** \'ma-nə-,kyu̇r\ n 1 : MANICURIST 2 : a treatment for the care of the hands and nails

²**manicure** vb **-cured; -cur·ing** 1 : to do manicure work on 2 : to trim closely and evenly

man·i·cur·ist \-,kyu̇r-ist\ n : a person who gives manicure treatments

¹**man·i·fest** \'ma-nə-,fest\ adj [ME, fr. AF or L; AF manifeste, fr. L manifestus, caught in the act, flagrant, obvious, perh. fr. manus hand + -festus (akin to L infestus hostile)] 1 : readily perceived by the senses and esp. by the sight 2 : easily understood : OBVIOUS — **man·i·fest·ly** adv

²**manifest** vb : to make evident or certain by showing or displaying ✦ **Synonyms** EVINCE, DEMONSTRATE, EXHIBIT

³**manifest** n : a list of passengers or an invoice of cargo for a ship or plane

man·i·fes·ta·tion \,ma-nə-fə-'stä-shən\ n : DISPLAY, DEMONSTRATION

man·i·fes·to \,ma-nə-'fes-tō\ n, pl **-tos** or **-toes** : a public declaration of intentions, motives, or views

¹**man·i·fold** \'ma-nə-,fōld\ adj 1 : marked by diversity or variety 2 : consisting of or operating many of one kind combined

²**manifold** n : a pipe fitting with several lateral outlets for connecting it with other pipes

³**manifold** vb 1 : MULTIPLY 2 : to make a number of copies of (as a letter)

man·i·kin also **man·ni·kin** \'ma-ni-kən\ n 1 : MANNEQUIN 2 : a little man : DWARF

Ma·ni·la hemp \mə-'ni-lə-\ n : a tough fiber from a Philippine plant related to the banana that is used for cordage

manila paper n, often cap M : a tough brownish paper made orig. from Manila hemp

man·i·oc \'ma-nē-,äk\ n : CASSAVA

ma·nip·u·late \mə-'ni-pyə-,lāt\ vb **-lat·ed; -lat·ing** 1 : to treat or operate manually or mechanically esp. with skill 2 : to manage or use skillfully 3 : to influence esp. with intent to deceive — **ma·nip·u·la·tion** \mə-,ni-pyə-'lā-shən\ n — **ma·nip·u·la·tive** \-'ni-pyə-,lā-tiv\ adj — **ma·nip·u·la·tor** \-,lā-tər\ n

ma·nip·u·la·tives \mə-'ni-pyə-,lā-tivz\ n pl : objects that a student is instructed to use in a way that teaches or reinforces a lesson

man·kind n 1 \'man-'kīnd\ : the human race 2 \-,kīnd\ : men as distinguished from women

¹**man·ly** \'man-lē\ adv : in a manly manner

²**manly** adj **man·li·er; -est** : having qualities appropriate to or generally associated

with a man : BOLD, RESOLUTE — **man·li·ness** *n*

man–made \'man-ˈmād\ *adj* : made by humans rather than nature ⟨∼ systems⟩; *esp* : SYNTHETIC ⟨∼ fibers⟩

man·na \'ma-nə\ *n* **1** : food miraculously supplied to the Israelites in the wilderness **2** : something of value that comes unexpectedly : WINDFALL

manned \'mand\ *adj* : carrying or performed by a person ⟨∼ spaceflight⟩

man·ne·quin \'ma-ni-kən\ *n* **1** : a form representing the human figure used esp. for displaying clothes **2** : a person employed to model clothing

man·ner \'ma-nər\ *n* **1** : KIND, SORT ⟨what ∼ of man is he⟩ **2** : a way of acting or proceeding ⟨worked in a brisk ∼⟩; *also* : normal behavior ⟨spoke bluntly as was his ∼⟩ **3** : a method of artistic execution **4** *pl* : social conduct; *also* : BEARING **5** *pl* : BEHAVIOR ⟨taught the child good ∼s⟩

man·nered \'ma-nərd\ *adj* **1** : having manners of a specified kind ⟨well-*mannered*⟩ **2** : having an artificial character ⟨a highly ∼ style⟩

man·ner·ism \'ma-nə-ˌri-zəm\ *n* **1** : ARTIFICIALITY, PRECIOSITY **2** : a peculiarity of action, bearing, or treatment ✦ *Synonyms* POSE, AIR, AFFECTATION

man·ner·ly \'ma-nər-lē\ *adj* : showing good manners : POLITE — **man·ner·li·ness** *n* — **mannerly** *adv*

man·nish \'ma-nish\ *adj* : resembling or suggesting a man rather than a woman **2** : generally associated with or characteristic of a man — **man·nish·ly** *adv* — **man·nish·ness** *n*

ma·no a ma·no \ˌmä-nō-ä-ˈmä-nō\ *adv or adj* : in direct competition or conflict

ma·noeu·vre \mə-ˈnü-vər, -ˈnyü-\ *chiefly Brit var of* MANEUVER

man–of–war \ˌman-əv-ˈwȯr\ *n, pl* **men–of–war** \ˌmen-\ : WARSHIP

ma·nom·e·ter \mə-ˈnä-mə-tər\ *n* : an instrument for measuring the pressure of gases and vapors — **mano·met·ric** \ˌma-nə-ˈme-trik\ *adj*

man·or \'ma-nər\ *n* **1** : the house or hall of an estate; *also* : a landed estate **2** : an English estate of a feudal lord — **ma·no·ri·al** \mə-ˈnȯr-ē-əl\ *adj* — **ma·no·ri·al·ism** \-ə-ˌli-zəm\ *n*

man power *n* **1** : power available from or supplied by the physical effort of human beings **2** *usu* **man·pow·er** : the total supply of persons available and fitted for service

man·qué \mäⁿ-ˈkā\ *adj* [F, fr. pp. of *manquer* to lack, fail] : short of or frustrated in the fulfillment of one's aspirations or talents ⟨a poet ∼⟩

man·sard \'man-ˌsärd, -sərd\ *n* : a roof having two slopes on all sides with the lower slope steeper than the upper one

manse \'mans\ *n* : the residence esp. of a Presbyterian minister

man·ser·vant \'man-ˌsər-vənt\ *n, pl* **men·ser·vants** \'men-ˌsər-vənts\ : a male servant

man·sion \'man-chən\ *n* : a large imposing residence; *also* : a separate apartment in a large structure

man–size \'man-ˌsīz\ *or* **man–sized** \-ˌsīzd\ *adj* : suitable for or requiring a man

man·slaugh·ter \-ˌslȯ-tər\ *n* : the unlawful killing of a human being without express or implied malice

man·ta \'man-tə\ *n* : a square piece of cloth or blanket used in southwestern U.S. and Latin America as a cloak or shawl

man·teau \man-ˈtō\ *n* : a loose cloak, coat, or robe

man·tel \'man-tᵊl\ *n* : a beam, stone, or arch serving as a lintel to support the masonry above a fireplace; *also* : a shelf above a fireplace

man·tel·piece \'man-tᵊl-ˌpēs\ *n* : the shelf of a mantel

man·til·la \man-ˈtē-yə, -ˈti-lə\ *n* : a light scarf worn over the head and shoulders esp. by Spanish and Latin-American women

man·tis \'man-təs\ *n, pl* **man·tis·es** *also* **man·tes** \-ˌtēz\ [NL, fr. Gk, lit., diviner, prophet] : any of a group of large usu. green insect-eating insects that hold their prey in forelimbs folded as if in prayer

man·tis·sa \man-ˈti-sə\ *n* : the part of a logarithm to the right of the decimal point

¹man·tle \'man-tᵊl\ *n* **1** : a loose sleeveless garment worn over other clothes **2** : something that covers, enfolds, or envelops **3** : a lacy sheath that gives light by incandescence when placed over a flame **4** : the portion of the earth lying between the crust and the core **5** : MANTEL

²mantle *vb* **man·tled; man·tling 1** : to cover with a mantle **2** : BLUSH

man·tra \'man-trə\ *n* : a mystical formula of invocation or incantation (as in Hinduism)

¹man·u·al \'man-yə-wəl\ *adj* **1** : of, relating to, or involving the hands; *also* : worked by hand ⟨a ∼ pump⟩ **2** : requiring or using physical skill and energy — **man·u·al·ly** *adv*

²manual *n* **1** : a small book; *esp* : HANDBOOK **2** : the prescribed movements in the handling of a military item and esp. a weapon during a drill or ceremony ⟨the ∼ of arms⟩ **3** : a keyboard esp. of an organ

man·u·fac·to·ry \ˌman-yə-ˈfak-tə-rē\ *n* : FACTORY

¹man·u·fac·ture \ˌman-yə-ˈfak-chər\ *n* [MF, fr. ML *manufactura*, L *manu factus* made by hand] **1** : something made from raw materials **2** : the process of making wares by hand or by machinery; *also* : a productive industry using machinery

²manufacture *vb* **-tured; -tur·ing 1** : to make from raw materials by hand or by machinery; *also* : to engage in manufacture **2** : INVENT, FABRICATE; *also* : CREATE — **man·u·fac·tur·er** *n*

man·u·mit \ˌman-yə-ˈmit\ *vb* **-mit·ted;**

-mit·ting : to free from slavery — **man·u·mis·sion** \-'mi-shən\ n

¹**ma·nure** \mə-'nūr, -'nyūr\ vb **ma·nured; ma·nur·ing** : to fertilize land with manure

²**manure** n : FERTILIZER; esp : refuse from stables and barnyards — **ma·nu·ri·al** \-'nūr-ē-əl, -'nyūr-\ adj

man·u·script \'man-yə-ˌskript\ n [L manu scriptus written by hand] **1** : a written or typewritten composition or document; also : a document submitted for publication **2** : writing as opposed to print

Manx \'maŋks\ n pl : the people of the Isle of Man — **Manx** adj

¹**many** \'me-nē\ adj **more** \'mȯr\; **most** \'mōst\ : consisting of or amounting to a large but indefinite number ⟨~ years ago⟩

²**many** pron : a large number ⟨~ are called⟩

³**many** n : a large but indefinite number ⟨a good ~ of them⟩

many·fold \ˌme-nē-'fōld\ adv : by many times

many–sid·ed \-'sī-dəd\ adj **1** : having many sides or aspects **2** : VERSATILE

Mao·ism \'maù-ˌi-zəm\ n : the theory and practice of Communism developed in China chiefly by Mao Zedong — **Mao·ist** \'maù-ist\ n or adj

Mao·ri \'maù(-ə)r-ē\ n, pl **Maori** or **Mao·ris** : a member of a Polynesian people native to New Zealand

¹**map** \'map\ n [ML mappa, fr. L, napkin, towel] **1** : a representation usu. on a flat surface of the whole or part of an area **2** : a representation of the celestial sphere or part of it

²**map** vb **mapped; map·ping 1** : to make a map of **2** : to plan in detail ⟨~ out a program⟩ — **map·pa·ble** \'ma-pə-bəl\ adj — **map·per** n

MAP abbr modified American plan

ma·ple \'mā-pəl\ n : any of a genus of trees or shrubs with 2-winged dry fruit and opposite leaves; also : the hard light-colored wood of a maple used esp. for floors and furniture

maple sugar n : sugar made by boiling maple syrup

maple syrup n : syrup made by concentrating the sap of maple trees and esp. the sugar maple

mar \'mär\ vb **marred; mar·ring** : to detract from the wholeness or perfection of : SPOIL ◆ **Synonyms** INJURE, HURT, HARM, DAMAGE, IMPAIR, BLEMISH

Mar abbr March

ma·ra·ca \mə-'rä-kə, -'ra-\ n [Pg maracá] : a rattle usu. made from a gourd and used as a percussion instrument

mar·a·schi·no \ˌmer-ə-'skē-nō-, -'shē-\ n, often cap : a cherry preserved in a sweet liqueur made from the juice of a bitter wild cherry

mar·a·thon \'mer-ə-ˌthän\ n [Marathon, Greece, site of a victory of Greeks over Persians in 490 B.C. the news of which was carried to Athens by a long-distance

runner] **1** : a long-distance race esp. on foot **2** : an endurance contest

mar·a·thon·er \'mer-ə-ˌthä-nər\ n : a person who takes part in a marathon — **mar·a·thon·ing** n

ma·raud \mə-'rȯd\ vb : to roam about and raid in search of plunder : PILLAGE — **ma·raud·er** n

mar·ble \'mär-bəl\ n **1** : a limestone that can be polished and used in fine building work **2** : something resembling marble (as in coldness) **3** : a small ball (as of glass) used in various games; also, pl : a children's game played with these small balls — **marble** adj

mar·bling \-bə-liŋ, -bliŋ\ n : an intermixture of fat through the lean of a cut of meat

mar·cel \mär-'sel\ n : a deep soft wave made in the hair by the use of a heated curling iron — **marcel** vb

¹**march** \'märch\ n : a border region : FRONTIER

²**march** vb **1** : to move along in or as if in military formation **2** : to walk in a direct purposeful manner; also : PROGRESS, ADVANCE **3** : TRAVERSE ⟨~ed 10 miles⟩ — **march·er** n

³**march** n **1** : the action of marching; also : the distance covered (as by a military unit) in a march **2** : a regular measured stride or rhythmic step used in marching **3** : forward movement **4** : a piece of music with marked rhythm suitable for marching to

March n [ME, fr. AF, fr. L martius, fr. martius of Mars, fr. Mart-, Mars, Roman god of war] : the 3d month of the year

mar·chio·ness \'mär-shə-nəs\ n **1** : the wife or widow of a marquess **2** : a woman holding the rank of a marquess in her own right

Mar·di Gras \'mär-dē-ˌgrä\ n [F, lit., fat Tuesday] : the Tuesday before Ash Wednesday often observed with parades and merrymaking

¹**mare** \'mer\ n : an adult female of the horse or a related mammal

²**ma·re** \'mär-(ˌ)ā\ n, pl **ma·ria** \'mär-ē-ə\ : any of several large dark areas on the surface of the moon or Mars

mar·ga·rine \'mär-jə-rən\ n : a food product made usu. from vegetable oils churned with skimmed milk and used as a substitute for butter

mar·ga·ri·ta \ˌmär-gə-'rē-tə\ n : a cocktail consisting of tequila, lime or lemon juice, and an orange-flavored liqueur

mar·gin \'mär-jən\ n **1** : the part of a page outside the main body of printed or written matter **2** : EDGE ⟨continental ~⟩ **3** : a spare amount, measure, or degree allowed for use if needed **4** : measure or degree of difference ⟨a one-vote ~⟩

mar·gin·al \-jə-nəl\ adj **1** : written or printed in the margin **2** : of, relating to, or situated at a margin or border **3** : close to the lower limit of quality or acceptability **4** : excluded from or existing outside the mainstream of society or a group — **mar·gin·al·ly** adv

mar·gi·na·lia \ˌmär-jə-ˈnā-lē-ə\ n pl : marginal notes or embellishments

mar·gin·al·ize \ˈmär-jə-nᵊl-ˌīz\ vb **-ized; -iz·ing** : to relegate to an unimportant position within a society or group

mar·grave \ˈmär-ˌgräv\ n : the military governor esp. of a medieval German border province

ma·ri·a·chi \ˌmär-ē-ˈä-chē, ˌmer-\ n : a Mexican street band; also : a member of or the music of such a band

mari·gold \ˈmer-ə-ˌgōld\ n : any of a genus of tropical American herbs related to the daisies that are grown for their showy usu. yellow, orange, or maroon flower heads

mar·i·jua·na also **mar·i·hua·na** \ˌmer-ə-ˈwä-nə, -ˈhwä-\ n [MexSp marihuana] : the dried leaves and flowering tops of the female hemp plant smoked usu. illegally for their intoxicating effect; also : HEMP

ma·rim·ba \mə-ˈrim-bə\ n : a xylophone of southern Africa and Central America; also : a modern version of it

ma·ri·na \mə-ˈrē-nə\ n : a dock or basin providing secure moorings for pleasure boats

mar·i·na·ra \ˌmer-ə-ˈner-ə\ adj [It (alla) marinara, lit., in sailor style] : made with tomatoes, onions, garlic, and spices; also : served with marinara sauce

mar·i·nade \ˌmer-ə-ˈnäd\ n : a savory usu. acidic sauce in which meat, fish, or a vegetable is soaked to enrich its flavor or to tenderize it

mar·i·nate \ˈmer-ə-ˌnāt\ vb **-nat·ed; -nat·ing** : to steep (as meat or fish) in a marinade

¹**ma·rine** \mə-ˈrēn\ adj **1** : of or relating to the sea or its navigation or commerce **2** : of or relating to marines

²**marine** n **1** : the mercantile and naval shipping of a country **2** : any of a class of soldiers serving on shipboard or with a naval force

mar·i·ner \ˈmer-ə-nər\ n : SAILOR

mar·i·o·nette \ˌmer-ē-ə-ˈnet\ n : a puppet moved by strings or by hand

mar·i·tal \ˈmer-ə-ᵊtᵊl\ adj : of or relating to marriage : CONJUGAL ♦ **Synonyms** MATRIMONIAL, CONNUBIAL, NUPTIAL

mar·i·time \ˈmer-ə-ˌtīm\ adj **1** : of, relating to, or bordering on the sea **2** : of or relating to navigation or commerce of the sea

mar·jo·ram \ˈmär-jə-rəm\ n : any of various fragrant mints often used as seasoning

¹**mark** \ˈmärk\ n **1** : something (as a line or fixed object) designed to record position; also : the starting line or position in a track event **2** : TARGET; also : GOAL, OBJECT **3** : an object of abuse or ridicule **4** : the question under discussion **5** : NORM ⟨not up to the ~⟩ **6** : a visible sign : INDICATION; also : CHARACTERISTIC **7** : a written or printed symbol **8** : GRADE 5 ⟨a ~ of B+⟩ **9** : IM-

PORTANCE, DISTINCTION **10** : a lasting impression ⟨made his ~ in the world⟩; also : a damaging impression left on a surface

²**mark** vb **1** : to set apart by a line or boundary **2** : to designate by a mark or make a mark on **3** : CHARACTERIZE ⟨the vehemence that ~s his speeches⟩; also : SIGNALIZE ⟨this year ~s our 50th anniversary⟩ **4** : to take notice of : OBSERVE — **mark·er** n

³**mark** n : DEUTSCHE MARK

Mark \ˈmärk\ n — see BIBLE table

mark·down \ˈmärk-ˌdau̇n\ n **1** : a lowering of price **2** : the amount by which an original price is reduced

mark down vb : to put a lower price on

marked \ˈmärkt\ adj : NOTICEABLE — **mark·ed·ly** \ˈmär-kəd-lē\ adv

¹**mar·ket** \ˈmär-kət\ n **1** : a meeting together of people for trade by purchase and sale; also : a public place where such a meeting is held **2** : the rate or price offered for a commodity or security **3** : the course of commercial activity by which the exchange of commodities is effected **4** : a geographical area of demand for commodities; also : extent of demand **5** : a retail establishment usu. of a specific kind

²**market** vb : to go to a market to buy or sell; also : SELL — **mar·ket·able** adj

mar·ket·place \ˈmär-kət-ˌplās\ n **1** : an open square in a town where markets are held **2** : the world of trade or economic activity

mark·ka \ˈmär-ˌkä\ n, pl **mark·kaa** \ˈmär-ˌkä\ or **markkas** \-ˌkäz\ : the basic monetary unit of Finland from 1917 to 2001

marks·man \ˈmärks-mən\ n : a person skillful at hitting a target — **marks·man·ship** n

mark·up \ˈmär-ˌkəp\ n **1** : a raising of price **2** : an amount added to the cost price of an article to determine the selling price

mark up vb : to put a higher price on

markup language n : a system for marking the components and layout of a computer document

marl \ˈmärl\ n : an earthy deposit rich in lime used esp. as fertilizer — **marly** \ˈmär-lē\ adj

mar·lin \ˈmär-lən\ n : any of several large oceanic sport fishes related to sailfishes

mar·line·spike also **mar·lin·spike** \ˈmär-lən-ˌspīk\ n : a pointed iron tool used to separate strands of rope or wire (as in splicing)

mar·ma·lade \ˈmär-mə-ˌlād\ n : a clear jelly holding in suspension pieces of fruit and fruit rind

mar·mo·re·al \mär-ˈmȯr-ē-əl\ adj : of, relating to, or suggestive of marble

mar·mo·set \ˈmär-mə-ˌset\ n : any of numerous small bushy-tailed monkeys of Central and So. America

mar·mot \ˈmär-mət\ n : any of a genus of stout short-legged burrowing No. American rodents

¹**ma·roon** \mə-ˈrün\ vb **1** : to put ashore (as on a desolate island) and leave to one's

fate **2** : to leave in isolation and without hope of escape

²**maroon** *n* : a dark red color

¹**mar·quee** \mär-ˈkē\ *n* [modif. of F *marquise*, lit., marchioness] **1** : a large tent set up (as for an outdoor party) **2** : a usu. metal and glass canopy over an entrance (as of a theater) **3** : a sign over the entrance of a theater or arena advertising a performance

²**marquee** *adj* : having or being a great attraction : PREEMINENT ⟨∼ athletes⟩

mar·quess \ˈmär-kwəs\ *or* **mar·quis** \ˈmär-kwəs, mär-ˈkē\ *n* **1** : a nobleman of hereditary rank in Europe and Japan **2** : a member of the British peerage ranking below a duke and above an earl

mar·que·try \ˈmär-kə-trē\ *n* : inlaid work of wood, shell, or ivory (as on a table or cabinet)

mar·quise \mär-ˈkēz\ *n, pl* **mar·quises** *same or* -ˈkē-zəz\ : MARCHIONESS

mar·riage \ˈmer-ij\ *n* **1** : the state of being united to another person as a usu. contractual relationship according to law or custom **2** : a wedding ceremony and attendant festivities **3** : a close union ⟨a ∼ of light and shadow⟩ — **mar·riage·able** *adj*

married name *n* : a woman's surname acquired through marriage

mar·row \ˈmer-ō\ *n* : a soft vascular tissue that fills the cavities of most bones

mar·row·bone \ˈmer-ə-ˌbōn, ˈmer-ō-\ *n* : a bone (as a shinbone) rich in marrow

mar·ry \ˈmer-ē\ *vb* **mar·ried; mar·ry·ing** **1** : to join in marriage **2** : to take as a spouse : WED **3** : to enter into a close union **4** : COMBINE, UNITE — **mar·ried** *adj or n*

Mars \ˈmärz\ *n* : the planet 4th from the sun and conspicuous for its red color

marsh \ˈmärsh\ *n* : a tract of soft wet land — **marshy** *adj*

¹**mar·shal** \ˈmär-shəl\ *n* [ME, fr. AF *mareschal*, of Gmc origin; akin to OHG *marahscalc* marshal, fr. *marah* horse + *scalc* servant] **1** : a high official in a medieval household; *also* : a person in charge of the ceremonial aspects of a gathering **2** : a general officer of the highest military rank **3** : an administrative officer (as of a U.S. judicial district) having duties similar to a sheriff's **4** : the administrative head of a city police or fire department

²**marshal** *vb* **mar·shaled** *or* **mar·shalled; mar·shal·ing** *or* **mar·shal·ling** **1** : to arrange in order, rank, or position **2** : to bring together **3** : to lead with ceremony : USHER

marsh gas *n* : METHANE

marsh·mal·low \ˈmärsh-ˌme-lō, -ˌma-\ *n* : a light spongy confection made from corn syrup, sugar, albumen, and gelatin

marsh marigold *n* : a swamp herb related to the buttercups that has bright yellow flowers

mar·su·pi·al \mär-ˈsü-pē-əl\ *n* : any of an order of primitive mammals (as opossums, kangaroos, or wombats) that bear very immature young which are nourished in a pouch on the abdomen of the female — **marsupial** *adj*

mart \ˈmärt\ *n* : MARKET

mar·ten \ˈmär-tᵊn\ *n, pl* **marten** *or* **martens** : a slender mammal that is larger than the related weasels and has soft gray or brown fur; *also* : this fur

mar·tial \ˈmär-shəl\ *adj* [L *martialis* of Mars, fr. *Mart-, Mars* Mars, Roman god of war] **1** : of, relating to, or suited for war or a warrior ⟨∼ music⟩ **2** : of or relating to an army or military life **3** : WARLIKE

martial law *n* **1** : the law applied in occupied territory by the occupying military forces **2** : the established law of a country administered by military forces in an emergency when civilian law enforcement agencies are unable to maintain public order and safety

mar·tian \ˈmär-shən\ *adj, often cap* : of or relating to the planet Mars or its hypothetical inhabitants — **martian** *n, often cap*

mar·tin \ˈmär-tᵊn\ *n* : any of several swallows and esp. one of No. America with purplish blue plumage

mar·ti·net \ˌmär-tə-ˈnet\ *n* : a strict disciplinarian

mar·tin·gale \ˈmär-tᵊn-ˌgāl\ *n* : a strap connecting a horse's girth to the bit or reins so as to hold down its head

mar·ti·ni \mär-ˈtē-nē\ *n* : a cocktail made of gin or vodka and dry vermouth

¹**mar·tyr** \ˈmär-tər\ *n* [ME, fr. OE, fr. LL, fr. Gk *martyr-, martys* witness] **1** : a person who dies rather than renounce a religion; *also* : a person who makes a great sacrifice for the sake of principle **2** : a great or constant sufferer

²**martyr** *vb* **1** : to put to death for adhering to a belief **2** : TORTURE

mar·tyr·dom \ˈmär-tər-dəm\ *n* **1** : the suffering and death of a martyr **2** : TORTURE

¹**mar·vel** \ˈmär-vəl\ *n* **1** : one that causes wonder or astonishment **2** : intense surprise or interest

²**marvel** *vb* **mar·veled** *or* **mar·velled; mar·vel·ing** *or* **mar·vel·ling** : to feel surprise, wonder, or amazed curiosity ⟨∼ed at the circus act⟩

mar·vel·ous *or* **mar·vel·lous** \ˈmär-və-ləs\ *adj* **1** : causing wonder **2** : of the highest kind or quality — **mar·vel·ous·ly** *adv* — **mar·vel·ous·ness** *n*

Marx·ism \ˈmärk-ˌsi-zəm\ *n* : the political, economic, and social principles and policies advocated by Karl Marx — **Marx·ist** \-sist\ *n or adj*

mar·zi·pan \ˈmärt-sə-ˌpän, -ˌpan; ˈmär-zə-ˌpan\ *n* [G, fr. It *marzapane*] : a confection of almond paste, sugar, and egg whites

masc *abbr* masculine

mas·cara \ma-ˈsker-ə\ *n* : a cosmetic esp. for darkening the eyelashes

mas·car·po·ne \ˌmas-kär-ˈpō-nā\ *n* : an Italian cream cheese

mas·cot \ˈmas-ˌkät, -kət\ *n* [F *mascotte*, fr. Occitan *mascoto*, fr. *masco* witch, fr. ML *masca*] : a person, animal, or object adopted usu. by a group to bring good luck

¹mas·cu·line \'mas-kyə-lən\ *adj* **1** : MALE; *also* : MANLY **2** : of, relating to, or constituting the gender that includes most words or grammatical forms referring to males — **mas·cu·lin·i·ty** \,mas-kyə-'li-nə-tē\ *n*

²masculine *n* : a noun, pronoun, adjective, or inflectional form or class of the masculine gender; *also* : the masculine gender

¹mash \'mash\ *n* **1** : a mixture of ground feeds for livestock **2** : crushed malt or grain steeped in hot water to make wort **3** : a soft pulpy mass

²mash *vb* **1** : to reduce to a soft pulpy state **2** : CRUSH, SMASH ⟨∼ a finger⟩ — **mash·er** *n*

MASH *abbr* mobile army surgical hospital

¹mask \'mask\ *n* **1** : a cover for the face usu. for disguise or protection **2** : MASQUE **3** : a figure of a head worn on the stage in antiquity **4** : a copy of a face made by means of a mold ⟨death ∼⟩ **5** : something that conceals or disguises **6** : the face of an animal

²mask *vb* **1** : to conceal from view : DISGUISE **2** : to cover for protection

mask·er \'mas-kər\ *n* : a participant in a masquerade

mas·och·ism \'ma-sə-,ki-zəm, 'ma-zə-\ *n* **1** : a sexual perversion characterized by pleasure in being subjected to pain or humiliation **2** : pleasure in being abused or dominated — **mas·och·ist** \-kist\ *n* — **mas·och·is·tic** \,ma-sə-'kis-tik, ,ma-zə-\ *adj*

ma·son \'mā-s³n\ *n* : a skilled worker who builds with stone, brick, or concrete **2** *cap* : FREEMASON

Ma·son·ic \mə-'sä-nik\ *adj* : of or relating to Freemasons or Freemasonry

ma·son·ry \'mā-s³n-rē\ *n, pl* **-ries 1** : something constructed of materials used by masons **2** : the art, trade, or work of a mason **3** *cap* : FREEMASONRY

masque \'mask\ *n* **1** : MASQUERADE **2** : a short allegorical dramatic performance (as of the 17th century)

¹mas·quer·ade \,mas-kə-'rād\ *n* **1** : a social gathering of persons wearing masks; *also* : a costume for wear at such a gathering **2** : DISGUISE

²masquerade *vb* **-ad·ed; -ad·ing 1** : to disguise oneself : POSE **2** : to take part in a masquerade — **mas·quer·ad·er** *n*

¹mass \'mas\ *n* **1** *cap* : a sequence of prayers and ceremonies forming the eucharistic service of the Roman Catholic Church **2** *often cap* : a celebration of the Eucharist **3** : a musical setting for parts of the Mass

²mass *n* **1** : a quantity or aggregate of matter usu. of considerable size **2** : EXPANSE, BULK; *also* : MASSIVENESS **3** : the principal part **4** : AGGREGATE, WHOLE **5** : the quantity of matter that a body possesses as measured by its inertia **6** : a large quantity, amount, or number **7**

: the great body of people — usu. used in pl. — **massy** *adj*

³mass *vb* : to form or collect into a mass

Mass *abbr* Massachusetts

mas·sa·cre \'ma-si-kər\ *n* **1** : the killing of many persons under cruel or atrocious circumstances **2** : a wholesale slaughter — **massacre** *vb*

¹mas·sage \mə-'säzh, -'säj\ *n* : manipulation of tissues (as by rubbing and kneading) for therapeutic purposes

²massage *vb* **mas·saged; mas·sag·ing 1** : to subject to massage **2** : to treat flatteringly; *also* : MANIPULATE, DOCTOR ⟨∼ data⟩

mas·seur \ma-'sər\ *n* : a man who practices massage

mas·seuse \-'sərz, -'süz\ *n* : a woman who practices massage

mas·sif \ma-'sēf\ *n* : a principal mountain mass

mas·sive \'ma-siv\ *adj* **1** : forming or consisting of a large mass **2** : large in structure, scope, or degree — **mas·sive·ly** *adv* — **mas·sive·ness** *n*

mass·less \'mas-ləs\ *adj* : having no mass ⟨∼ particles⟩

mass medium *n, pl* **mass media** : a medium of communication (as the newspapers or television) that is designed to reach the mass of the people

mass–pro·duce \,mas-prə-'düs, -'dyüs\ *vb* : to produce in quantity usu. by machinery — **mass production** *n*

¹mast \'mast\ *n* **1** : a long pole or spar rising from the keel or deck of a ship and supporting the yards, booms, and rigging **2** : a slender vertical structure — **mast·ed** \'mas-təd\ *adj*

²mast *n* : nuts (as acorns) accumulated on the forest floor and often serving as food for animals (as hogs)

mas·tec·to·my \ma-'stek-tə-mē\ *n, pl* **-mies** : surgical removal of the breast

¹mas·ter \'mas-tər\ *n* **1** : a male teacher; *also* : a person holding an academic degree higher than a bachelor's but lower than a doctor's **2** : one highly skilled (as in an art or profession) **3** : one having authority or control **4** : VICTOR, SUPERIOR **5** : the commander of a merchant ship **6** : a youth or boy too young to be called *mister* — used as a title **7** : an original from which copies are made

²master *vb* **1** : to become master of : OVERCOME **2** : to become skilled or proficient in **3** : to produce a master recording of (as a musical performance)

master chief petty officer *n* : a petty officer of the highest rank in the navy

mas·ter·ful \'mas-tər-fəl\ *adj* **1** : inclined and usu. competent to act as master **2** : having or reflecting the skill of a master ⟨∼ verse⟩ — **mas·ter·ful·ly** *adv* — **mas·ter·ful·ness** *n*

master gunnery sergeant *n* : a noncommissioned officer in the marine corps ranking above a master sergeant

master key *n* : a key designed to open several different locks

mas·ter·ly \'mas-tər-lē\ *adj* **1** : indicating thorough knowledge or superior skill ⟨∼

performance⟩ 2 : having the skill of a master ⟨a ∼ writer⟩ — **mas·ter·ly** *adv*

mas·ter·mind \-ˌmīnd\ *n* : a person who directs or provides creative intelligence for a project — **mastermind** *vb*

master of ceremonies : a person who acts as host at a formal event or a program of entertainment

mas·ter·piece \ˈmas-tər-ˌpēs\ *n* : a work done with extraordinary skill

master plan *n* : an overall plan

mas·ter's \ˈmas-tərz\ *n* : a master's degree

master sergeant *n* 1 : a noncommissioned officer in the army ranking next below a sergeant major 2 : a noncommissioned officer in the air force ranking next below a senior master sergeant 3 : a noncommissioned officer in the marine corps ranking next below a master gunnery sergeant

mas·ter·stroke \ˈmas-tər-ˌstrōk\ *n* : a masterly performance or move

mas·ter·work \-ˌwərk\ *n* : MASTERPIECE

mas·tery \ˈmas-tə-rē\ *n* 1 : DOMINION; *also* : SUPERIORITY 2 : possession or display of great skill or knowledge

mast·head \ˈmast-ˌhed\ *n* 1 : the top of a mast 2 : the printed matter in a newspaper or periodical giving the title and details of ownership and rates of subscription or advertising

mas·tic \ˈmas-tik\ *n* : a pasty material used as a coating or cement

mas·ti·cate \ˈmas-tə-ˌkāt\ *vb* -cat·ed; -cat·ing — CHEW — **mas·ti·ca·tion** \ˌmas-tə-ˈkā-shən\

mas·tiff \ˈmas-təf\ *n* : any of a breed of large smooth-coated dogs used esp. as guard dogs

mast·odon \ˈmas-tə-ˌdän\ *n* [NL, fr. Gk *mastos* breast + *odōn, odous* tooth] : any of numerous huge extinct mammals related to the mammoths

mas·toid \ˈmas-ˌtȯid\ *n* : a bony prominence behind the ear — **mastoid** *adj*

mas·tur·ba·tion \ˌmas-tər-ˈbā-shən\ *n* : stimulation of the genital organs apart from sexual intercourse, usu. to orgasm, and esp. by use of one's own hand — **mas·tur·bate** \ˈmas-tər-ˌbāt\ *vb* — **mas·tur·ba·to·ry** \ˈmas-tər-bə-ˌtȯr-ē\ *adj*

¹**mat** \ˈmat\ *n* 1 : a piece of coarse woven or plaited fabric 2 : something made up of many intertwined strands 3 : a large thick pad used as a surface for wrestling and gymnastics

²**mat** *vb* **mat·ted; mat·ting** 1 : to provide with a mat 2 : to form into a tangled mass ⟨dirt *matted* her hair⟩

³**mat** *vb* **mat·ted; mat·ting** 1 *also* **matte** *or* **matt** : to make (as a color) matte 2 : to provide (a picture) with a mat

⁴**mat** *var of* ²MATTE

⁵**mat** *or* **matt** *or* **matte** *n* : a border going around a picture between picture and frame or serving as the frame

mat·a·dor \ˈma-tə-ˌdȯr\ *n* [Sp, fr. *matar* to kill] : a bullfighter whose role is to kill the bull in a bullfight

¹**match** \ˈmach\ *n* 1 : a person or thing equal or similar to another; *also* : one

able to cope with another : RIVAL 2 : a suitable pairing of persons or objects 3 : a contest or game between two or more individuals 4 : a marriage union; *also* : a prospective marriage partner — **match·less** *adj*

²**match** *vb* 1 : to meet as an antagonist; *also* : PIT ⟨∼ wits⟩ 2 : to provide with a worthy competitor; *also* : to set in comparison with 3 : MARRY 4 : to combine suitably or congenially ⟨∼ed the drapes with the rug⟩; *also* : ADAPT, SUIT 5 : to act in harmony ⟨his shoes and belt ∼⟩ 6 : to provide with a counterpart

³**match** *n* : a short slender piece of flammable material (as wood) tipped with a combustible mixture that ignites through friction

match·book \ˈmach-ˌbu̇k\ *n* : a small folder containing rows of paper matches

match·lock \-ˌläk\ *n* : a musket with a slow-burning cord lowered over a hole in the breech to ignite the charge

match·mak·er \-ˌmā-kər\ *n* : one who arranges a match and esp. a marriage

match·wood \-ˌwu̇d\ *n* : small pieces of wood

¹**mate** \ˈmāt\ *vb* **mat·ed; mat·ing** : CHECKMATE — **mate** *n*

²**mate** *n* 1 : ASSOCIATE, COMPANION; *also* : HELPER 2 : a deck officer on a merchant ship ranking below the captain 3 : one of a pair; *esp* : either member of a married couple or a breeding pair of animals

³**mate** *vb* **mat·ed; mat·ing** 1 : to join or fit together 2 : to come or bring together as mates 3 : COPULATE

¹**ma·te·ri·al** \mə-ˈtir-ē-əl\ *adj* 1 : PHYSICAL ⟨∼ world⟩; *also* : BODILY ⟨∼ needs⟩ 2 : of or relating to matter rather than form ⟨∼ cause⟩; *also* : EMPIRICAL ⟨∼ knowledge⟩ 3 : highly important : SIGNIFICANT 4 : of a physical or worldly nature ⟨∼ progress⟩ — **ma·te·ri·al·ly** *adv*

²**material** *n* 1 : the elements or substance of which something is composed or made 2 : apparatus necessary for doing or making something

ma·te·ri·al·ise *Brit var of* MATERIALIZE

ma·te·ri·al·ism \mə-ˈtir-ē-ə-ˌli-zəm\ *n* 1 : a theory that everything can be explained as being or coming from matter 2 : a preoccupation with material rather than intellectual or spiritual things — **ma·te·ri·al·ist** \-list\ *n or adj* — **ma·te·ri·al·is·tic** \-ˌtir-ē-ə-ˈlis-tik\ *adj* — **ma·te·ri·al·is·ti·cal·ly** \-ti-k(ə-)lē\ *adv*

ma·te·ri·al·ize \mə-ˈtir-ē-ə-ˌlīz\ *vb* -ized; -iz·ing 1 : to give material form to; *also* : to assume bodily form 2 : to make an often unexpected appearance — **ma·te·ri·al·i·za·tion** \mə-ˌtir-ē-ə-lə-ˈzā-shən\ *n*

ma·té·ri·el *or* **ma·te·ri·el** \mə-ˌtir-ē-ˈel\ *n* [F *matériel*] : equipment, apparatus, and supplies used by an organization

ma·ter·nal \mə-ˈtər-nᵊl\ *adj* 1 : MOTHERLY 2 : related through or inherited or derived from a female parent — **ma·ter·nal·ly** *adv*

¹ma·ter·ni·ty \mə-'tər-nə-tē\ *n, pl* **-ties 1** : the quality or state of being a mother; *also* : MOTHERLINESS **2** : a hospital facility for the care of women before and during childbirth and for newborn babies

²maternity *adj* **1** : designed for wear during pregnancy ⟨a ~ dress⟩ **2** : effective for the period close to and including childbirth ⟨~ leave⟩

¹math \'math\ *n* : MATHEMATICS

²math *abbr* mathematical; mathematician

math·e·mat·ics \ˌma-thə-'ma-tiks\ *n* : the science of numbers and their properties, operations, and relations and with shapes in space and their structure and measurement — **math·e·mat·i·cal** \-'ma-ti-kəl\ *adj* — **math·e·mat·i·cal·ly** \-ti-k(ə-)lē\ *adv* — **math·e·ma·ti·cian** \ˌma-thə-mə-'ti-shən\ *n*

mat·i·nee *or* **mat·i·née** \ˌma-tə-'nā\ *n* [F *matinée*, lit., morning, fr. OF, fr. *matin* morning, fr. L *matutinum*, fr. neut. of *matutinus* of the morning, fr. *Matuta*, goddess of morning] : a musical or dramatic performance in the daytime and esp. the afternoon

mat·ins \'ma-tⁿnz\ *n pl, often cap* **1** : special prayers said between midnight and 4 a.m. **2** : a morning service of liturgical prayer in Anglican churches

ma·tri·arch \'mā-trē-ˌärk\ *n* : a woman who rules or dominates a family, group, or state — **ma·tri·ar·chal** \ˌmā-trē-'är-kəl\ *adj* — **ma·tri·ar·chy** \'mā-trē-ˌär-kē\ *n*

ma·tri·cide \'ma-trə-ˌsīd, 'mā-\ *n* : the murder of a mother by her child — **ma·tri·cid·al** \ˌma-trə-'sī-dᵊl, ˌmā-\ *adj*

ma·tric·u·late \mə-'tri-kyə-ˌlāt\ *vb* **-lat·ed; -lat·ing** : to enroll as a member of a body and esp. of a college or university — **ma·tric·u·la·tion** \-ˌtri-kyə-'lā-shən\ *n*

mat·ri·mo·ny \'ma-trə-ˌmō-nē\ *n* [ME, fr. AF *matrimoignie*, fr. L *matrimonium*, fr. *mater* mother, matron] : MARRIAGE — **mat·ri·mo·nial** \ˌma-trə-'mō-nē-əl\ *adj* — **mat·ri·mo·nial·ly** *adv*

ma·trix \'mā-triks\ *n, pl* **ma·tri·ces** \'mā-trə-ˌsēz, 'ma-\ *or* **ma·trix·es** \'mā-trik-səz\ **1** : something within or from which something else originates, develops, or takes form **2** : a mold from which a relief surface (as a piece of type) is made

ma·tron \'mā-trən\ *n* **1** : a married woman usu. of dignified maturity or social distinction **2** : a woman supervisor (as in a school or police station) — **ma·tron·ly** *adj*

Matt *abbr* Matthew

¹matte *or* **matt** *var of* ³MAT

²matte *also* **matt** \'mat\ *adj* : not shiny : DULL

¹mat·ter \'ma-tər\ *n* **1** : a subject of interest or concern **2** *pl* : events or circumstances of a particular situation **3** : the subject of a discourse or writing **4** : TROUBLE, DIFFICULTY ⟨what's the ~⟩ **5** : the substance of which a physical object is composed **6** : PUS **7** : an indefinite amount or quantity ⟨a ~ of a few days⟩ **8** : something written or printed

9 : MAIL — **as a matter of fact** : ACTUALLY — **no matter** : without regard to ⟨will follow *no matter* where you go⟩ — **no matter what** : regardless of the consequences ⟨must win, *no matter what*⟩

²matter *vb* : to be of importance

mat·ter–of–fact \ˌma-tə-rəv-'fakt\ *adj* : adhering to fact; *also* : being plain, straightforward, or unemotional — **matter–of–fact·ly** *adv* — **mat·ter–of–fact·ness** *n*

Mat·thew \'ma-thyü\ *n* — see BIBLE table

mat·tins *often cap chiefly Brit var of* MATINS

mat·tock \'ma-tək\ *n* : a digging and grubbing tool with features of an adze and an ax or pick

mat·tress \'ma-trəs\ *n* **1** : a fabric case filled with resilient material used as or for a bed **2** : an inflatable airtight sack for use as a mattress

mat·u·rate \'ma-chə-ˌrāt\ *vb* **-rat·ed; -rat·ing** : MATURE

mat·u·ra·tion \ˌma-chə-'rā-shən\ *n* **1** : the process of becoming mature **2** : the emergence of personal and behavioral characteristics through growth processes — **mat·u·ra·tion·al** \-shə-nəl\ *adj*

¹ma·ture \mə-'túr, -'tyúr\ *adj* **ma·tur·er; -est 1** : based on slow careful consideration **2** : having attained a final or desired state **3** : of or relating to a condition of full development **4** : suitable only for adults ⟨~ content⟩ **5** : due for payment — **ma·ture·ly** *adv*

²mature *vb* **ma·tured; ma·tur·ing** : to reach or bring to maturity or completion

ma·tu·ri·ty \mə-'túr-ə-tē, -'tyúr-\ *n* **1** : the quality or state of being mature; *esp* : full development **2** : the date when a note becomes due for payment

ma·tu·ti·nal \ˌma-chù-'tī-nᵊl; mə-'tü-tə-nᵊl, -'tyü-\ *adj* : of, relating to, or occurring in the morning : EARLY

mat·zo *or* **mat·zoh** \'mät-sə\ *n, pl* **mat·zoth** \-ˌsōt, -ˌsōth, -ˌsōs\ *or* **mat·zos** *or* **mat·zohs** [Yiddish *matse*, fr. Heb *maṣṣāh*] : unleavened bread eaten esp. at the Passover

maud·lin \'mȯd-lən\ *adj* [alter. of Mary *Magdalene*; fr. her depiction as a weeping, penitent sinner] **1** : drunk enough to be silly **2** : weakly and effusively sentimental

¹maul \'mȯl\ *n* : a heavy hammer often with a wooden head used esp. for driving wedges

²maul *vb* **1** : BEAT, BRUISE; *also* : MANGLE **2** : to handle roughly

maun·der \'mȯn-dər\ *vb* **1** : to wander slowly and idly **2** : to speak indistinctly or disconnectedly

mau·so·le·um \ˌmȯ-sə-'lē-əm, ˌmȯ-zə-\ *n, pl* **-leums** *or* **-lea** \-'lē-ə\ [L, fr. Gk *mausōleion*, fr. *Mausōlos* Mausolus † *ab* 353 B.C. ruler of Caria whose tomb was one of the seven wonders of the ancient world] : a large tomb; *esp* : a usu. stone building for entombment of the dead above ground

mauve \'mōv, 'mȯv\ *n* : a moderate purple, violet, or lilac color

ma·ven *also* **ma·vin** \'mā-vən\ *n* [Yiddish *meyvn,* fr. LHeb *mēbhīn*] : EXPERT

mav·er·ick \'ma-vrik, -və-rik\ *n* [Samuel A. *Maverick* † 1870 Am. pioneer who did not brand his calves] **1** : an unbranded range animal **2** : NONCONFORMIST

maw \'mò\ *n* **1** : STOMACH; *also* : the crop of a bird **2** : the throat, gullet, or jaws esp. of a voracious animal

mawk·ish \'mò-kish\ *adj* : sickly sentimental — **mawk·ish·ly** *adv* — **mawk·ish·ness** *n*

max *abbr* maximum

maxi \'mak-sē\ *n, pl* **max·is** : a long skirt, dress, or coat

maxi- *comb form* **1** : extra long ⟨*maxi*-kilt⟩ **2** : extra large ⟨*maxi*-problems⟩

max·il·la \mak-'si-lə\ *n, pl* **max·il·lae** \-'si-(,)lē\ *or* **maxillas** : JAW 1; *esp* : an upper jaw — **max·il·lary** \'mak-sə-,ler-ē\ *adj*

max·im \'mak-səm\ *n* : a proverbial saying

max·i·mal \'mak-sə-məl\ *adj* : MAXIMUM — **max·i·mal·ly** *adv*

max·i·mise *Brit var of* MAXIMIZE

max·i·mize \'mak-sə-,mīz\ *vb* **-mized; -miz·ing** **1** : to increase to a maximum **2** : to make the most of — **max·i·mi·za·tion** \,mak-sə-mə-'zā-shən\ *n*

max·i·mum \'mak-sə-məm\ *n, pl* **-ma** \-mə\ *or* **-mums** **1** : the greatest quantity, value, or degree **2** : an upper limit allowed by authority **3** : the largest of a set of numbers — **maximum** *adj*

max out *vb* **1** : to push to or reach a limit or an extreme **2** : to use up all available credit on (a credit card)

may \'mā\ *verbal auxiliary, past* **might** \'mīt\ *pres sing & pl* **may** **1** : have permission or liberty to ⟨you ~ go now⟩ **2** : be in some degree likely to ⟨you ~ be right⟩ **3** — used as an auxiliary to express a wish, purpose, contingency, or concession ⟨~ the best man win⟩

May \'mā\ *n* [ME, fr. OF *mai,* fr. L *Maius,* fr. *Maia,* Roman goddess] : the 5th month of the year

Ma·ya \'mī-ə\ *n, pl* **Maya** *or* **Mayas** : a member of a group of American Indian peoples of Yucatán, Guatemala, and adjacent areas — **Ma·yan** \'mī-ən\ *n or adj*

may·ap·ple \'mā-,a-pəl\ *n* : a No. American woodland herb related to the barberry that has a poisonous root, one or two large leaves, and an edible egg-shaped yellow fruit

may·be \'mā-bē, 'me-\ *adv* : PERHAPS

May Day \'mā-,dā\ *n* : May 1 celebrated as a springtime festival and in some countries as Labor Day

may·flow·er \'mā-,flaù(-ə)r\ *n* : any of several spring blooming herbs (as the trailing arbutus or an anemone)

may·fly \'mā-flī\ *n* : any of an order of insects with an aquatic nymph and a short-lived fragile adult having membranous wings

may·hem \'mā-,hem, 'mā-əm\ *n* **1** : willful and permanent crippling, mutilation,

or disfigurement of a person **2** : needless or willful damage

may·on·naise \'mā-ə-,nāz\ *n* [F] : a dressing made of egg yolks, vegetable oil, and vinegar or lemon juice

may·or \'mā-ər\ *n* : an official elected to act as chief executive or nominal head of a city or borough — **may·or·al** \-əl\ *adj* — **may·or·al·ty** \-əl-tē\ *n*

may·pole \'mā-,pōl\ *n, often cap* : a tall flower-wreathed pole forming a center for May Day sports and dances

maze \'māz\ *n* : a confusing intricate network of passages — **mazy** *adj*

ma·zur·ka \mə-'zər-kə\ *n* : a Polish dance in moderate triple measure

MB *abbr* Manitoba

MBA *abbr* master of business administration

mc *abbr* megacycle

¹MC *n* : MASTER OF CEREMONIES

²MC *abbr* member of Congress

Mc- \mak\ *prefix* **; m**ə *before forms beginning with* **k** *or* **g**\ *prefix* : used to indicate a convenient, low-quality version of a specified thing ⟨*Mc*Book⟩

Mc·Coy \mə-'kòi\ *n* : something that is neither imitation nor substitute ⟨the real ~⟩

McGuffin *var of* MACGUFFIN

MCPO *abbr* master chief petty officer

¹Md *abbr* Maryland

²Md *symbol* mendelevium

MD *abbr* **1** [NL *medicinae doctor*] doctor of medicine **2** Maryland **3** muscular dystrophy

MDMA \,em-,dē-,em-'ā\ *n* : ECSTASY 2

mdnt *abbr* midnight

mdse *abbr* merchandise

MDT *abbr* mountain daylight (saving) time

me \'mē\ *pron objective case of* I

Me *abbr* Maine

ME *abbr* **1** Maine **2** mechanical engineer **3** medical examiner

¹mead \'mēd\ *n* : an alcoholic beverage brewed from water and honey, malt, and yeast

²mead *n, archaic* : MEADOW

mead·ow \'me-dō\ *n* : land in or mainly in grass; *esp* : a tract of moist low-lying usu. level grassland — **mead·ow·land** \-,land\ *n* — **mead·owy** \'me-də-wē\ *adj*

mead·ow·lark \'me-dō-,lärk\ *n* : any of several American songbirds related to the orioles that are streaked brown above and in northernmost forms have a yellow breast marked with a black crescent

mead·ow·sweet \-,swēt\ *n* : a No. American native or naturalized spirea

mea·ger *or* **mea·gre** \'mē-gər\ *adj* **1** : THIN **2** : lacking richness, fertility, or strength; *also* : POOR ⟨a ~ income⟩ ✦ *Synonyms* SCANTY, SCANT, SPARE, SPARSE — **mea·ger·ly** *adv* — **mea·ger·ness** *n*

¹meal \'mēl\ *n* **1** : an act or the time of eating a portion of food **2** : the portion of food eaten at a meal

²meal *n* **1** : usu. coarsely ground seeds of

a cereal **2** : a product resembling seed meal — **mealy** *adj*

meal·time \'mēl-ˌtīm\ *n* : the usual time at which a meal is served

mealy·bug \'mē-lē-ˌbəg\ *n* : any of a family of scale insects with a white cottony or waxy covering that are destructive pests esp. of fruit trees

mealy-mouthed \ˌmē-lē-ˌmau̇thd, -ˌmau̇tht\ *adj* : not plain and straightforward : DEVIOUS

¹mean \'mēn\ *vb* **meant** \'ment\; **meaning** **1** : to have in the mind as a purpose **2** : to serve to convey, show, or indicate : SIGNIFY ⟨red ~s stop⟩ **3** : to have importance to the degree of ⟨~s the world to me⟩ **4** : to direct to a particular individual ⟨a gift *meant* for me⟩

²mean *adj* **1** : HUMBLE **2** : lacking acumen : DULL **3** : SHABBY, CONTEMPTIBLE ⟨no ~ feat⟩ **4** : IGNOBLE, BASE **5** : STINGY **6** : pettily selfish or malicious **7** : VEXATIOUS **8** : EXCELLENT ⟨throws a ~ slider⟩ — **mean·ly** *adv* — **mean·ness** *n*

³mean *adj* **1** : occupying a middle position (as in space, order, or time) **2** : being a mean : AVERAGE ⟨a ~ value⟩

⁴mean *n* **1** : a middle point between extremes **2** *pl* : something helpful in achieving a desired end **3** *pl* : material resources affording a secure life **4** : ARITHMETIC MEAN

¹me·an·der \mē-'an-dər\ *n* [L *maeander*, fr. Gk *maiandros*, fr. *Maiandros* (now *Menderes*), river in Asia Minor] **1** : a winding course **2** : a winding of a stream — **me·an·drous** \-drəs\ *adj*

²meander *vb* **1** : to follow a winding course **2** : to wander aimlessly or casually

mean·ing *n* **1** : the thing one intends to convey esp. by language; *also* : the thing that is thus conveyed **2** : AIM **3** : SIGNIFICANCE; *esp* : implication of a hidden significance **4** : CONNOTATION; *also* : DENOTATION — **mean·ing·ful** \-fəl\ *adj* — **mean·ing·ful·ly** *adv* — **mean·ing·less** *adj*

¹mean·time \'mēn-ˌtīm\ *n* : the intervening time

²meantime *adv* : MEANWHILE

¹mean·while \-ˌhwī(-ə)l\ *n* : MEANTIME

²meanwhile *adv* **1** : during the intervening time **2** : at the same time

meas *abbr* measure

mea·sles \'mē-zəlz\ *n sing or pl* : an acute virus disease marked by fever and an eruption of distinct circular red spots

mea·sly \'mēz-lē, -zə-lē\ *adj* **mea·sli·er; -est** : contemptibly small or insignificant

¹mea·sure \'me-zhər, 'mā-\ *n* **1** : an adequate or moderate portion; *also* : a suitable limit **2** : the dimensions, capacity, or amount of something ascertained by measuring; *also* : an instrument for measuring **3** : a unit of measurement; *also* : a system of such units **4** : the act or process of measuring **5** : rhythmic structure or movement **6** : the part of a musical staff between two bars **7** : CRITERI-

ON **8** : a means to an end **9** : a legislative bill — **mea·sure·less** *adj*

²measure *vb* **mea·sured; mea·sur·ing** **1** : to mark or fix in multiples of a specific unit ⟨~ off five centimeters⟩ **2** : to find out the size, extent, or amount of **3** : to bring into comparison or competition **4** : to serve as a means of measuring **5** : to have a specified measurement — **mea·sur·able** \'me-zhə-rə-bəl, 'mā-\ *adj* — **mea·sur·ably** \-blē\ *adv* — **mea·sur·er** *n*

mea·sure·ment \'me-zhər-mənt, 'mā-\ *n* **1** : the act or process of measuring **2** : a figure, extent, or amount obtained by measuring

measure up *vb* **1** : to have necessary or fitting qualifications **2** : to equal esp. in ability

meat \'mēt\ *n* **1** : FOOD; *esp* : solid food as distinguished from drink **2** : animal and esp. mammal flesh considered as food **3** : the edible part inside a covering (as a shell or rind) — **meaty** *adj*

meat·ball \-ˌbȯl\ *n* : a small ball of chopped or ground meat

meat loaf *n* : a dish of ground meat seasoned and baked in the form of a loaf

mec·ca \'me-kə\ *n, often cap* [*Mecca*, Saudi Arabia, a destination of pilgrims in the Islamic world] : a center of a specified activity or interest ⟨a shopping ~⟩

mech *abbr* mechanical; mechanics

¹me·chan·ic \mi-'ka-nik\ *adj* : of or relating to manual work or skill

²mechanic *n* **1** : a manual worker **2** : MACHINIST; *esp* : one who repairs cars

me·chan·i·cal \mi-'ka-ni-kəl\ *adj* **1** : of or relating to machinery, to manual operations, or to mechanics **2** : done as if by a machine : AUTOMATIC ⟨a ~ response⟩
♦ Synonyms INSTINCTIVE, IMPULSIVE, SPONTANEOUS — **me·chan·i·cal·ly** \-k(ə-)lē\ *adv*

mechanical drawing *n* : drawing done with the aid of instruments

me·chan·ics \mi-'ka-niks\ *n sing or pl* **1** : a branch of physics that deals with energy and forces and their effect on bodies **2** : the practical application of mechanics (as to the operation of machines) **3** : mechanical or functional details ⟨the ~ of the brain⟩

mech·a·nism \'me-kə-ˌni-zəm\ *n* **1** : a piece of machinery; *also* : a process or technique for achieving a result **2** : mechanical operation or action **3** : the fundamental processes involved in or responsible for a natural phenomenon ⟨the visual ~⟩

mech·a·nis·tic \ˌme-kə-'nis-tik\ *adj* **1** : mechanically determined ⟨~ universe⟩ **2** : MECHANICAL — **mech·a·nis·ti·cal·ly** \-ti-k(ə-)lē\ *adv*

mech·a·nize \'me-kə-ˌnīz\ *vb* **-nized; -niz·ing** **1** : to make mechanical **2** : to equip with machinery esp. in order to replace human or animal labor **3** : to equip with armed and armored motor vehicles — **mech·a·ni·za·tion** \ˌme-kə-nə-'zā-shən\ *n* — **mech·a·niz·er** *n*

¹med \'med\ *adj* : MEDICAL ⟨∼ school⟩

²med *n* : MEDICINE 1 — usu. used in pl.

³med *abbr* **1** medical; medicine **2** medieval **3** medium

MEd *abbr* master of education

med·al \'me-d³l\ *n* [MF *medaille*, fr. OIt *medaglia* coin worth half a denarius, medal, fr. VL **medalis* half, alter. of LL *medialis* middle, fr. L *medius*] **1** : a small usu. metal object bearing a religious emblem or picture **2** : a piece of metal issued to commemorate a person or event or to award excellence or achievement

med·al·ist *or* **med·al·list** \'me-d³l-ist\ *n* **1** : a designer or maker of medals **2** : a recipient of a medal as an award

me·dal·lion \mə-'dal-yən\ *n* **1** : a large medal **2** : a tablet or panel bearing a portrait or an ornament

med·dle \'me-d³l\ *vb* **med·dled**; **med·dling** : to interfere without right or propriety — **med·dler** \'me-d³l-ər\ *n*

med·dle·some \'me-d³l-səm\ *adj* : inclined to meddle

med·e·vac *also* **med·i·vac** \'me-də-ˌvak\ *n* **1** : emergency evacuation of the sick or wounded **2** : a helicopter used for medevac

me·dia \'mē-dē-ə\ *n, pl* **me·di·as 1** : MEDIUM 4 **2** *sing or pl in constr* : MASS MEDIA

me·di·al \'mē-dē-əl\ *adj* : occurring in or extending toward the middle

¹me·di·an \'mē-dē-ən\ *n* **1** : a value in an ordered set of values below and above which there are an equal number of values **2** : MEDIAN STRIP

²median *adj* **1** : being in the middle or in an intermediate position **2** : relating to or constituting a statistical median

median strip *n* : a strip dividing a highway into lanes according to the direction of travel

me·di·ate \'mē-dē-ˌāt\ *vb* **-at·ed**; **-at·ing 1** : to act as an intermediary; *esp* : to work with opposing sides in order to resolve (as a dispute) or bring about (as a settlement) **2** : to bring about, influence, or transmit (as a physical process or effect) by acting as an intermediate or controlling agent or mechanism ♦ *Synonyms* INTERCEDE, INTERVENE, INTERPOSE, INTERFERE — **me·di·a·tion** \ˌmē-dē-'ā-shən\ *n* — **me·di·a·tor** \'mē-dē-ˌā-tər\ *n*

med·ic \'me-dik\ *n* : one engaged in medical work; *esp* : CORPSMAN

med·i·ca·ble \'me-di-kə-bəl\ *adj* : CURABLE

Med·ic·aid \'me-di-ˌkād\ *n* : a program of financial assistance for medical care designed for those unable to afford regular medical service and financed jointly by the state and federal governments

med·i·cal \'me-di-kəl\ *adj* : of or relating to the science or practice of medicine or the treatment of disease — **med·i·cal·ly** \-k(ə-)lē\ *adv*

medical examiner *n* : a public officer who performs autopsies on bodies to find the cause of death

me·di·ca·ment \mi-'di-kə-mənt, 'me-di-kə-\ *n* : a substance used in therapy

Medi·care \'me-di-ˌker\ *n* : a government program of financial assistance for medical care esp. for the aged

med·i·cate \'me-də-ˌkāt\ *vb* **-cat·ed**; **-cat·ing** : to treat with medicine

med·i·ca·tion \ˌme-də-'kā-shən\ *n* **1** : the act or process of medicating **2** : MEDICINE 1

me·dic·i·nal \mə-'di-s³n-əl\ *adj* : tending or used to cure disease or relieve pain — **me·dic·i·nal·ly** *adv*

med·i·cine \'me-də-sən\ *n* **1** : a substance or preparation used in treating disease **2** : a science and art dealing with the prevention, alleviation, and cure of disease

medicine ball *n* : a heavy stuffed leather ball used for conditioning exercises

medicine man *n* : a priestly healer or sorcerer esp. among the American Indians : SHAMAN

med·i·co \'me-di-ˌkō\ *n, pl* **-cos** : a medical practitioner or student

me·di·e·val *also* **me·di·ae·val** \ˌme-dē-'ē-vəl, ˌmē-, mē-'dē-vəl\ *adj* **1** : of, relating to, or characteristic of the Middle Ages **2** : having a quality (as cruelty) associated with the Middle Ages **3** : extremely outmoded or antiquated — **me·di·e·val·ism** \-və-ˌli-zəm\ *n* — **me·di·e·val·ist** \-list\ *n*

me·di·o·cre \ˌmē-dē-'ō-kər\ *adj* [MF, fr. L *mediocris*, fr. *medius* middle + *ocris* stony mountain] : of moderate or low quality : ORDINARY — **me·di·oc·ri·ty** \-'ä-krə-tē\ *n*

med·i·tate \'me-də-ˌtāt\ *vb* **-tat·ed**; **-tat·ing 1** : to muse over : CONTEMPLATE, PONDER **2** : to engage in deep mental exercise directed toward a heightened level of spiritual awareness **3** : INTEND, PLAN — **med·i·ta·tion** \ˌme-də-'tā-shən\ *n* — **med·i·ta·tive** \'me-də-ˌtā-tiv\ *adj* — **med·i·ta·tive·ly** *adv*

Med·i·ter·ra·nean \ˌme-də-tə-'rā-nē-ən, -'rā-nyən\ *adj* : of or relating to the Mediterranean Sea or to the lands or people around it

¹me·di·um \'mē-dē-əm\ *n, pl* **mediums** *or* **me·dia** \-dē-ə\ [L] **1** : something in a middle position; *also* : a middle position or degree **2** : a means of effecting or conveying something **3** : a surrounding or enveloping substance **4** : a channel or system of communication, information, or entertainment **5** : a mode of artistic expression **6** : an individual held to be a channel of communication between the earthly world and a world of spirits **7** : a condition or environment in which something may function or flourish

²medium *adj* : intermediate in amount, quality, position, or degree

me·di·um·is·tic \ˌmē-dē-ə-'mis-tik\ *adj* : of, relating to, or being a spiritualistic medium

medivac *var of* MEDEVAC

med·ley \'med-lē\ *n, pl* **medleys 1** : HODGEPODGE **2** : a musical composition made up esp. of a series of songs

me·dul·la \mə-ˈdə-lə\ *n, pl* **-las** *or* **-lae** \-ˌlē, -ˌlī\ : an inner or deep anatomical part; *also* : the posterior part (**medulla ob·lon·ga·ta** \-ˌä-ˌblŏŋ-ˈgä-tə\) of the vertebrate brain that is continuous with the spinal cord

meed \ˈmēd\ *n* : a fitting return

meek \ˈmēk\ *adj* **1** : enduring injury with patience and without resentment **2** : deficient in spirit and courage **3** : MODERATE — **meek·ly** *adv* — **meek·ness** *n*

meer·schaum \ˈmir-shəm, -ˌshŏm\ *n* [G, fr. *Meer* sea + *Schaum* foam] : a tobacco pipe made of a light white clayey mineral

¹meet \ˈmēt\ *vb* **met** \ˈmet\; **meet·ing 1** : to come upon : FIND **2** : JOIN, INTERSECT **3** : to appear to the perception of **4** : OPPOSE, FIGHT **5** : to join in conversation or discussion; *also* : ASSEMBLE **6** : to conform to **7** : to pay fully **8** : to cope with **9** : to provide for **10** : to be introduced to

²meet *n* : an assembling esp. for a hunt or for competitive sports

³meet *adj* : SUITABLE, PROPER

meet·ing \ˈmē-tiŋ\ *n* **1** : an act of coming together : ASSEMBLY **2** : JUNCTION, INTERSECTION

meet·ing·house \-ˌhaûs\ *n* : a building for public assembly and esp. for Protestant worship

meg \ˈmeg\ *n* : MEGABYTE

mega- *or* **meg-** *comb form* **1** : great : large ⟨*mega*hit⟩ **2** : million ⟨*mega*hertz⟩

mega·byte \ˈme-gə-ˌbīt\ *n* : 1024 kilobytes or 1,048,576 bytes; *also* : one million bytes

mega·cy·cle \-ˌsī-kəl\ *n* : MEGAHERTZ

mega·death \-ˌdeth\ *n* : one million deaths — used as a unit in reference to nuclear warfare

mega·hertz \ˈme-gə-ˌhərts, -ˌherts\ *n* : a unit of frequency equal to one million hertz

mega·lith \ˈme-gə-ˌlith\ *n* : a large stone used in prehistoric monuments — **mega·lith·ic** \ˌme-gə-ˈli-thik\ *adj*

meg·a·lo·ma·nia \ˌme-gə-lō-ˈmā-nē-ə, -nyə\ *n* : a mental disorder marked by feelings of personal omnipotence and grandeur — **meg·a·lo·ma·ni·ac** \-ˈmā-nē-ˌak\ *adj or n* — **meg·a·lo·ma·ni·a·cal** \-mə-ˈnī-ə-kəl\ *adj*

meg·a·lop·o·lis \ˌme-gə-ˈlä-pə-ləs\ *n* : a very large urban unit

mega·phone \ˈme-gə-ˌfōn\ *n* : a cone-shaped device used to intensify or direct the voice — **megaphone** *vb*

mega·pix·el \ˈme-gə-ˌpik-səl\ *n* : one million pixels

mega·plex \-ˌpleks\ *n* : a cineplex having usu. at least 16 movie theaters

mega·ton \-ˌtən\ *n* : an explosive force equivalent to that of one million tons of TNT

mega·vi·ta·min \-ˌvī-tə-mən\ *adj* : relating to or consisting of very large doses of vitamins — **mega·vi·ta·mins** *n pl*

mei·o·sis \mī-ˈō-səs\ *n* : a process of cell division in gamete-producing cells in which the number of chromosomes is reduced to one half — **mei·ot·ic** \mī-ˈä-tik\ *adj*

meit·ner·i·um \mīt-ˈnir-ē-əm, -ˈner-\ *n* : an artificially produced radioactive chemical element

mel·an·cho·lia \ˌme-lən-ˈkō-lē-ə\ *n* : a mental condition marked by extreme depression often with delusions

mel·an·chol·ic \ˌme-lən-ˈkä-lik\ *adj* **1** : DEPRESSED **2** : of or relating to melancholia

mel·an·choly \ˈme-lən-ˌkä-lē\ *n, pl* **-chol·ies** [ME *malencolie*, fr. AF, fr. LL *melancholia*, fr. Gk, fr. *melan-, melas* black + *cholē* bile; so called fr. the former belief that it was caused by an excess of black bile] : depression of spirits : DEJECTION — **melancholy** *adj*

Mel·a·ne·sian \ˌme-lə-ˈnē-zhən\ *n* : a member of the dominant native group of the Pacific island grouping of Melanesia — **Melanesian** *adj*

mé·lange \mā-ˈlä⁼zh, -ˈlänj\ *n* : a mixture esp. of incongruous elements

mel·a·nin \ˈme-lə-nən\ *n* : any of various dark brown pigments of animal or plant structures (as skin or hair)

mel·a·nism \ˈme-lə-ˌni-zəm\ *n* : an increased amount of black or nearly black pigmentation

mel·a·no·ma \ˌme-lə-ˈnō-mə\ *n, pl* **-mas** *also* **-ma·ta** \-mə-tə\ : a usu. malignant tumor containing dark pigment

¹meld \ˈmeld\ *vb* : to show or announce for a score in a card game

²meld *n* : a card or combination of cards that is or can be melded

me·lee \ˈmā-ˌlā, mā-ˈlā\ *n* [F *mêlée*] : a confused struggle ◆ **Synonyms** FRACAS, ROW, BRAWL, DONNYBROOK

me·lio·rate \ˈmēl-yə-ˌrāt, ˈmē-lē-ə-\ *vb* **-rat·ed; -rat·ing** : AMELIORATE — **me·lio·ra·tion** \ˌmēl-yə-ˈrā-shən, ˌmē-lē-ə-\ *n* — **me·lio·ra·tive** \ˈmēl-yə-ˌrā-tiv, ˈmē-lē-ə-\ *adj*

mel·lif·lu·ous \me-ˈli-flə-wəs, mə-\ *adj* [ME *mellyfluous*, fr. LL *mellifluus*, fr. L *mel* honey + *fluere* to flow] : sweetly flowing — **mel·lif·lu·ous·ly** *adv* — **mel·lif·lu·ous·ness** *n*

¹mel·low \ˈme-lō\ *adj* **1** : soft and sweet because of ripeness; *also* : well aged and pleasingly mild ⟨∼ wine⟩ **2** : made gentle by age or experience **3** : being rich and full but not garish or strident ⟨∼ colors⟩ **4** : of soft loamy consistency ⟨∼ soil⟩ — **mel·low·ness** *n*

²mellow *vb* : to make or become mellow — often used with *out*

me·lo·di·ous \mə-ˈlō-dē-əs\ *adj* : pleasing to the ear — **me·lo·di·ous·ly** *adv* — **me·lo·di·ous·ness** *n*

melo·dra·ma \ˈme-lə-ˌdrä-mə, -ˌdra-\ *n* **1** : an extravagantly theatrical play in which action and plot predominate over characterization **2** : something having a sensational or theatrical quality — **melo·dra·mat·ic** \ˌme-lə-drə-ˈma-tik\ *adj* — **melo·dra·mat·i·cal·ly** \-ti-k(ə-)lē\ *adv* — **melo·dra·ma·tist** \ˌme-lə-ˈdra-mə-tist, -ˈdrä-\ *n*

mel·o·dy \'me-lə-dē\ n, pl **-dies 1** : sweet or agreeable sound **2** : a particular succession of notes : TUNE, AIR — **me·lod·ic** \mə-'lä-dik\ adj — **me·lod·i·cal·ly** \-di-k(ə-)lē\ adv

mel·on \'me-lən\ n : any of various typically sweet fruits (as a muskmelon or watermelon) of the gourd family usu. eaten raw

¹**melt** \'melt\ vb **1** : to change from a solid to a liquid state usu. by heat **2** : DISSOLVE, DISINTEGRATE; also : to cause to disperse or disappear **3** : to make or become tender or gentle

²**melt** n : a melted substance

melt·down \'melt-,daủn\ n **1** : the melting of the core of a nuclear reactor **2** : a collapse of something (as one's self-control)

melting pot n : a place where different races, cultures, or individuals assimilate into a cohesive whole

melt·wa·ter \-,wỏ-tər, -,wä-\ n : water derived from the melting of ice and snow

mem abbr **1** member **2** memoir **3** memorial

mem·ber \'mem-bər\ n **1** : a part (as an arm, leg, leaf, or branch) of an animal or plant **2** : one of the individuals composing a group **3** : a part of a whole ⟨~s of a set⟩

mem·ber·ship \-,ship\ n **1** : the state or status of being a member **2** : the body of members

mem·brane \'mem-,brān\ n : a thin pliable layer esp. of animal or plant origin — **mem·bra·nous** \-brə-nəs\ adj

me·men·to \mə-'men-tō\ n, pl **-tos** or **-toes** [ME, fr. L, remember, imper. of meminisse to remember] : something that serves to warn or remind; also : SOUVENIR

memo \'me-mō\ n, pl **mem·os** : MEMORANDUM

mem·oir \'mem-,wär\ n **1** : MEMORANDUM **2** : AUTOBIOGRAPHY — usu. used in pl. **3** : an account of something noteworthy; also, pl : the record of the proceedings of a learned society

mem·o·ra·bil·ia \,me-mə-rə-'bi-lē-ə, -'bil-yə\ n pl [L] **1** : things worthy of remembrance **2** : things associated with a particular interest and that are usu. collected : MEMENTOS

mem·o·ra·ble \'me-mə-rə-bəl\ adj : worth remembering : NOTABLE — **mem·o·ra·bil·i·ty** \,me-mə-rə-'bi-lə-tē\ n — **mem·o·ra·ble·ness** n — **mem·o·ra·bly** \-blē\ adv

mem·o·ran·dum \,me-mə-'ran-dəm\ n, pl **-dums** or **-da** \-də\ **1** : an informal record; also : a written reminder **2** : an informal written note

¹**me·mo·ri·al** \mə-'mȯr-ē-əl\ adj : serving to preserve remembrance

²**memorial** n **1** : something designed to keep remembrance alive; esp : MONUMENT **2** : a statement of facts often accompanied with a petition — **me·mo·ri·al·ize** vb

Memorial Day n : the last Monday in May or formerly May 30 observed as a legal holiday in honor of those who died in war

mem·o·rise Brit var of MEMORIZE

mem·o·rize \'me-mə-,rīz\ vb **-rized; -riz·ing** : to learn by heart — **mem·o·ri·za·tion** \,me-mə-rə-'zā-shən\ n — **mem·o·riz·er** n

mem·o·ry \'me-mə-rē\ n, pl **-ries 1** : the power or process of remembering **2** : the store of things remembered **3** : COMMEMORATION **4** : something remembered **5** : the time within which past events are remembered **6** : a device (as in a computer) in which information can be stored; esp : RAM **7** : capacity for storing information ⟨512 megabytes of ~⟩
♦ Synonyms REMEMBRANCE, RECOLLECTION, REMINISCENCE

men pl of MAN

¹**men·ace** \'me-nəs\ n **1** : THREAT **2** : DANGER; also : NUISANCE

²**menace** vb **men·aced; men·ac·ing 1** : THREATEN **2** : ENDANGER — **men·ac·ing·ly** adv

mé·nage \mā-'näzh\ n [F] : HOUSEHOLD

ménage à trois \-ä-'trwä\ n : an arrangement in which three persons share sexual relations esp. while living together

me·nag·er·ie \mə-'na-jə-rē\ n : a collection of wild animals esp. for exhibition

¹**mend** \'mend\ vb **1** : to improve in manners or morals **2** : to put into good shape : REPAIR **3** : to improve in or restore to health : HEAL — **mend·er** n

²**mend** n **1** : an act of mending **2** : a mended place

men·da·cious \men-'dā-shəs\ adj : given to deception or falsehood : UNTRUTHFUL
♦ Synonyms DISHONEST, DECEITFUL — **men·da·cious·ly** adv — **men·dac·i·ty** \-'da-sə-tē\ n

men·de·le·vi·um \,men-də-'lē-vē-əm, -'lā-\ n : a radioactive metallic chemical element artificially produced

men·di·cant \'men-di-kənt\ n **1** : BEGGAR **2** often cap : FRIAR — **men·di·can·cy** \-kən-sē\ n — **mendicant** adj

men·folk \'men-,fōk\ or **men·folks** \-,fōks\ n pl **1** : men in general **2** : the men of a family or community

men·ha·den \men-'hā-dᵊn, mən-\ n, pl **-den** also **-dens** : a marine fish related to the herring that is abundant along the Atlantic coast of the U.S.

¹**me·nial** \'mē-nē-əl, -nyəl\ n : a domestic servant

²**menial** adj **1** : of or relating to servants **2** : HUMBLE, SERVILE ⟨answered in ~ tones⟩ — **me·ni·al·ly** adv

men·in·gi·tis \,me-nən-'jī-təs\ n, pl **-git·i·des** \-'ji-tə-,dēz\ : inflammation of the membranes enclosing the brain and spinal cord; also : a usu. bacterial disease marked by this

me·ninx \'mē-niŋks, 'me-\ n, pl **me·nin·ges** \mə-'nin-(,)jēz\ : any of the three membranes that envelop the brain and spinal cord — **men·in·ge·al** \,me-nən-'jē-əl\ adj

me·nis·cus \mə-'nis-kəs\ n, pl **me·nis·ci** \-'nis-,kī, -,kē\ also **me·nis·cus·es 1**

: CRESCENT 2 : the curved upper surface of a column of liquid

men·o·pause \'me-nə-ˌpóz\ n : the period of life when menstruation stops naturally — **men·o·paus·al** \ˌme-nə-'pó-zəl\ adj

me·no·rah \mə-'nór-ə\ n [Heb měnōrāh candlestick] : a candelabrum that is used in Jewish worship

men·ses \'men-ˌsēz\ n sing or pl : the menstrual flow

menstrual cycle n : the complete cycle of physiological changes from the beginning of one menstrual period to the beginning of the next

men·stru·a·tion \ˌmen-strə-'wā-shən, men-'strā-\ n : a discharging of bloody matter at approximately monthly intervals from the uterus of breeding-age nonpregnant primate females; also : PERIOD 6 — **men·stru·al** \'men-strə-wəl\ adj — **men·stru·ate** \'men-strə-ˌwāt, -ˌstrāt\ vb

men·su·ra·ble \'men-sə-rə-bəl, '-chə-\ adj : MEASURABLE

men·su·ra·tion \ˌmen-sə-'rā-shən, ˌmen-chə-\ n : MEASUREMENT

-ment n suffix 1 : concrete result, object, or agent of a (specified) action ⟨embankment⟩ ⟨entanglement⟩ 2 : concrete means or instrument of a (specified) action ⟨entertainment⟩ 3 : action : process ⟨encirclement⟩ ⟨development⟩ 4 : place of a (specified) action ⟨encampment⟩ 5 : state : condition ⟨amazement⟩

men·tal \'ment-ᵊl\ adj 1 : of or relating to the mind 2 : of, relating to, or affected with a disorder of the mind ⟨∼ illness⟩ — **men·tal·ly** adv

mental age n : a measure of a child's mental development in terms of the number of years it takes an average child to reach the same level

mental deficiency n : MENTAL RETARDATION

men·tal·i·ty \men-'ta-lə-tē\ n, pl -ties 1 : mental power or capacity 2 : mode or way of thought

mental retardation n : subaverage intellectual ability present from infancy that is characterized by an IQ of 70 or less and problems in development, learning, and social adjustment — **mentally retarded** adj

men·tee \men-'tē\ n : PROTÉGÉ

men·thol \'men-ˌthól, -ˌthôl\ n : an alcohol occurring esp. in mint oils that has the odor and cooling properties of peppermint — **men·tho·lat·ed** \-thə-ˌlā-təd\ adj

¹men·tion \'men-chən\ n 1 : a brief or casual reference 2 : a formal citation for outstanding achievement

²mention vb 1 : to refer to : CITE 2 : to cite for superior achievement — **not to mention** : not even yet counting or considering

men·tor \'men-ˌtòr, -tər\ n : a trusted counselor or guide; also : TUTOR, COACH — **mentor** vb

menu \'men-yü, 'mān-\ n, pl menus [F, fr. menu small, detailed, fr. OF, fr. L minutus minute (adj.)] 1 : a list of the dishes available (as in a restaurant) for a meal;

also : the dishes served 2 : a list of offerings or options

me·ow \mē-'aú\ vb : to make the characteristic cry of a cat — **meow** n

mer abbr meridian

mer·can·tile \'mər-kən-ˌtēl, -ˌtī(-ə)l\ adj : of or relating to merchants or trading

¹mer·ce·nary \'mər-sə-ˌner-ē\ n, pl -nar·ies : a person who serves merely for wages; esp : a soldier hired into foreign service

²mercenary adj 1 : serving merely for pay or gain 2 : hired for service in a foreign army

mer·cer \'mər-sər\ n, Brit : a dealer in usu. expensive fabrics

mer·cer·ise Brit var of MERCERIZE

mer·cer·ize \'mər-sə-ˌrīz\ vb -ized; -iz·ing : to treat cotton yarn or cloth with alkali so that it looks silky or takes a better dye

¹mer·chan·dise \'mər-chən-ˌdīz, -ˌdīs\ n : the commodities or goods that are bought and sold in business

²mer·chan·dise \-ˌdīz\ vb -dised; -dis·ing : to buy and sell in business : TRADE — **mer·chan·dis·er** n

mer·chant \'mər-chənt\ n 1 : a buyer and seller of commodities for profit 2 : STOREKEEPER

mer·chant·able \'mər-chən-tə-bəl\ adj : acceptable to buyers : MARKETABLE

mer·chant·man \'mər-chənt-mən\ n : a ship used in commerce

merchant marine n : the commercial ships of a nation

merchant ship n : MERCHANTMAN

mer·ci·ful·ly \'mər-si-fə-lē\ adv 1 : in a merciful manner 2 : FORTUNATELY 2 ⟨∼ we didn't have to attend⟩

mer·cu·ri·al \ˌmər-'kyúr-ē-əl\ adj 1 : unpredictably changeable 2 : MERCURIC — **mer·cu·ri·al·ly** adv — **mer·cu·ri·al·ness** n

mer·cu·ric \ˌmər-'kyúr-ik\ adj : of, relating to, or containing mercury

mercuric chloride n : a poisonous compound of mercury and chlorine used as an antiseptic and fungicide

mer·cu·ry \'mər-kyə-rē\ n, pl -ries 1 : a heavy silver-white liquid metallic chemical element used esp. in scientific instruments 2 cap : the planet nearest the sun

mer·cy \'mər-sē\ n, pl mercies [ME, fr. AF merci, fr. ML merced-, merces, fr. L, price paid, wages, fr. merc-, merx merchandise] 1 : compassion shown to an offender; also : imprisonment rather than death for first-degree murder 2 : a blessing resulting from divine favor or compassion; also : a fortunate circumstance 3 : compassion shown to victims of misfortune — **mer·ci·ful** \-si-fəl\ adj — **mer·ci·less** \-si-ləs\ adj — **mer·ci·less·ly** adv — **mer·ci·less·ness** n

mercy killing n : EUTHANASIA

¹mere \'mir\ n : LAKE, POOL

²mere adj, superlative mer·est 1 : not diluted : PURE 2 : being nothing more than ⟨a ∼ child⟩ — **mere·ly** adv

mer·e·tri·cious \ˌmer-ə-'tri-shəs\ *adj* [L *meretricius*, fr. *meretrix* prostitute, fr. *merēre* to earn] : tawdrily attractive ⟨~ trinkets⟩; *also* : SPECIOUS — **mer·e·tri·cious·ly** *adv* — **mer·e·tri·cious·ness** *n*

mer·gan·ser \(ˌ)mər-'gan-sər\ *n* : any of various fish-eating wild ducks with a usu. crested head and a slender bill hooked at the end and serrated along the margins

merge \'mərj\ *vb* **merged; merg·ing** **1** : to blend gradually **2** : to combine, unite, or coalesce into one ♦ **Synonyms** MINGLE, AMALGAMATE, FUSE, INTERFUSE, INTERMINGLE

merg·er \'mər-jər\ *n* **1** : the act or process of merging **2** : absorption by a corporation of one or more others

me·rid·i·an \mə-'ri-dē-ən\ *n* [ME, fr. AF *meridien*, fr. *meridien* of noon, fr. L *meridianus*, fr. *meridies* noon, south, irreg. fr. *medius* mid + *dies* day] **1** : the highest point : CULMINATION **2** : any of the imaginary circles on the earth's surface passing through the north and south poles **3** : any of the pathways along which the body's vital energy flows according to the theory behind acupuncture — **meridian** *adj*

me·ringue \mə-'raŋ\ *n* [F] : a baked dessert topping of stiffly beaten egg whites and powdered sugar

me·ri·no \mə-'rē-nō\ *n, pl* **-nos** [Sp] **1** : any of a breed of sheep noted for fine soft wool **2** : a fine soft fabric or yarn of wool or wool and cotton

¹mer·it \'mer-ət\ *n* **1** : laudable or blameworthy traits or actions **2** : a praiseworthy quality; *also* : character or conduct deserving reward or honor **3** *pl* : the intrinsic nature of a legal case; *also* : legal significance

²merit *vb* : EARN, DESERVE

mer·i·toc·ra·cy \ˌmer-ə-'tä-krə-sē\ *n, pl* **-cies** : a system in which the talented are chosen and moved ahead based on their achievement; *also* : leadership by the talented

mer·i·to·ri·ous \ˌmer-ə-'tòr-ē-əs\ *adj* : deserving honor or esteem — **mer·i·to·ri·ous·ly** *adv* — **mer·i·to·ri·ous·ness** *n*

mer·lin \'mər-lən\ *n* : a small compact falcon of the northern hemisphere

mer·lot \mer-'lō, mər-\ *n* : a dry red wine made from a widely grown grape; *also* : the grape itself

mer·maid \'mər-ˌmād\ *n* : a legendary sea creature with a woman's upper body and a fish's tail

mer·man \-ˌman, -mən\ *n* : a legendary sea creature with a man's upper body and a fish's tail

mer·ri·ment \'mer-i-mənt\ *n* **1** : HILARITY **2** : FESTIVITY

mer·ry \'mer-ē\ *adj* **mer·ri·er; -est** **1** : full of gaiety or high spirits **2** : marked by festivity **3** : BRISK ⟨a ~pace⟩ ♦ **Synonyms** BLITHE, JOCUND, JOVIAL, JOLLY, MIRTHFUL — **mer·ri·ly** \'mer-ə-lē\ *adv*

merry–go–round \'mer-ē-gō-ˌraùnd\ *n* **1** : a circular revolving platform with benches and figures of animals on which

people sit for a ride **2** : a busy round of activities

mer·ry·mak·ing \'mer-ē-ˌmā-kiŋ\ *n* **1** : jovial or festive activity **2** : a festive occasion — **mer·ry·mak·er** \-ˌmā-kər\ *n*

me·sa \'mā-sə\ *n* [Sp, lit., table, fr. L *mensa*] : a flat-topped hill with steep sides

mes·cal \me-'skal, mə-\ *n* **1** : PEYOTE 2 **2** : a usu. colorless liquor distilled from the leaves of an agave; *also* : this agave

mes·ca·line \'mes-kə-lən, -ˌlēn\ *n* : a hallucinatory alkaloid from the peyote cactus

mes·clun \'mes-klən\ *n* : a mixture of young tender greens; *also* : a salad made with mesclun

mesdames *pl of* MADAM, *or of* MADAME, *or of* MRS.

mesdemoiselles *pl of* MADEMOISELLE

¹mesh \'mesh\ *n* **1** : one of the openings between the threads or cords of a net; *also* : one of the similar spaces in a network **2** : the fabric of a net **3** : NETWORK **4** : working contact (as of the teeth of gears) ⟨in ~⟩ — **meshed** \'mesht\ *adj*

²mesh *vb* **1** : to catch in or as if in a mesh **2** : to be in or come into mesh : ENGAGE **3** : to fit together properly

mesh·work \'mesh-ˌwərk\ *n* : NETWORK

me·si·al \'mē-zē-əl, -sē-\ *adj* : of, relating to, or being the surface of a tooth that is closest to the middle of the front of the jaw

mes·mer·ise *Brit var of* MESMERIZE

mes·mer·ize \'mez-mə-ˌrīz\ *vb* **-ized; -iz·ing** : HYPNOTIZE — **mes·mer·ic** \mez-'mer-ik\ *adj* — **mes·mer·ism** \'mez-mə-ˌri-zəm\ *n*

Me·so·lith·ic \ˌme-zə-'li-thik\ *adj* : of, relating to, or being a transitional period of the Stone Age between the Paleolithic and the Neolithic periods

me·so·sphere \'me-zə-ˌsfir\ *n* : a layer of the atmosphere between the stratosphere and the thermosphere

Me·so·zo·ic \ˌme-zə-'zō-ik, ˌmē-\ *adj* : of, relating to, or being the era of geologic history between the Paleozoic and the Cenozoic and extending from about 245 million years ago to about 65 million years ago — **Mesozoic** *n*

mes·quite \mə-'skēt, me-\ *n* : any of several spiny leguminous trees and shrubs chiefly of the southwestern U.S. with sugar-rich pods important as fodder; *also* : mesquite wood used esp. in grilling food

¹mess \'mes\ *n* [ME *mes*, fr. AF, fr. LL *missus* course at a meal, fr. *missus*, pp. of *mittere* to put, fr. L, to send] **1** : a quantity of food; *also* : enough food of a specified kind for a dish or meal ⟨a ~ of beans⟩ **2** : a group of persons who regularly eat together; *also* : a meal eaten by such a group **3** : a place where meals are regularly served to a group **4** : a confused, dirty, or offensive state — **messy** *adj*

²mess *vb* **1** : to supply with meals; *also* : to take meals with a mess **2** : to make dirty or untidy; *also* : BUNGLE **3** : IN-

TERFERE, MEDDLE ⟨don't ∼ with me⟩　4 : PUTTER, TRIFLE

mes·sage \'me-sij\ n : a communication sent by one person to another

message board n : BULLETIN BOARD 2

messeigneurs pl of MONSEIGNEUR

mes·sen·ger \'me-sᵊn-jər\ n : one who carries a message or does an errand

messenger RNA n : an RNA that carries the code for a particular protein from DNA in the nucleus to a ribosome in the cytoplasm and acts as a template for the formation of that protein

Mes·si·ah \mə-'sī-ə\ n 1 : the expected king and deliverer of the Jews 2 : Jesus 3 not cap : a professed or accepted leader of a cause — **mes·si·an·ic** \ˌme-sē-'a-nik\ adj

messieurs pl of MONSIEUR

mess·mate \'mes-ˌmāt\ n : a member of a group who eat regularly together

Messrs. \'me-sərz\ pl of MR.

mes·ti·zo \me-'stē-zō\ n, pl -zos [Sp] : a person of mixed blood

¹**met** past and past part of MEET

²**met** abbr metropolitan

me·tab·o·lism \mə-'ta-bə-ˌli-zəm\ n : the processes by which the substance of plants and animals incidental to life is built up and broken down; also : the processes by which a substance is handled in the living body ⟨the ∼ of sugar⟩ — **met·a·bol·ic** \ˌme-tə-'bä-lik\ adj — **me·tab·o·lize** \mə-'ta-bə-ˌlīz\ vb

me·tab·o·lite \-ˌlīt\ n 1 : a product of metabolism 2 : a substance essential to the metabolism of a particular organism or to a metabolic process

meta·car·pal \ˌme-tə-'kär-pəl\ n : any of usu. five more or less elongated bones of the part of the hand or forefoot between the wrist and the bones of the digits — **metacarpal** adj

meta·car·pus \-'kär-pəs\ n : the part of the hand or forefoot that contains the metacarpals

met·al \'me-tᵊl\ n 1 : any of various opaque, fusible, ductile, and typically lustrous substances that are good conductors of electricity and heat 2 : METTLE; also : the material out of which a person or thing is made — **me·tal·lic** \mə-'ta-lik\ adj

met·al·lur·gy \'me-tᵊl-ˌər-jē\ n : the science and technology of metals — **met·al·lur·gi·cal** \ˌme-tᵊl-'ər-ji-kəl\ adj — **met·al·lur·gist** \'me-tᵊl-ˌər-jist\ n

met·al·ware \'me-tᵊl-ˌwer\ n : metal utensils for household use

met·al·work \-ˌwərk\ n : work and esp. artistic work made of metal — **met·al·work·er** \-ˌwər-kər\ n — **met·al·work·ing** n

meta·mor·phism \ˌme-tə-'mȯr-ˌfi-zəm\ n : a change in the structure of rock; esp : a change to a more compact and more highly crystalline form produced by pressure, heat, and water — **meta·mor·phic** \-'mȯr-fik\ adj

meta·mor·pho·sis \ˌme-tə-'mȯr-fə-səs\ n, pl -pho·ses \-ˌsēz\ 1 : a change of physical form, structure, or substance esp. by

supernatural means; also : a striking alteration (as in appearance or character) 2 : a fundamental change in form and often habits of an animal accompanying the transformation of a larva into an adult — **meta·mor·phose** \-ˌfōz, -ˌfōs\ vb

met·a·phor \'me-tə-ˌfȯr\ n : a figure of speech in which a word for one idea or thing is used in place of another to suggest a likeness between them (as in "the ship plows the sea") — **met·a·phor·ic** \ˌme-tə-'fȯr-ik\ or **met·a·phor·i·cal** \-'fȯr-i-kəl\ adj — **met·a·phor·i·cal·ly** \-i-k(ə-)lē\ adv

meta·phys·ics \ˌme-tə-'fi-ziks\ n [ML Metaphysica, title of Aristotle's treatise on the physics, fr. Gk (ta) meta (ta) physika, lit., the (works) after the physical (works); fr. its position in his collected works] : the philosophical study of the ultimate causes and underlying nature of things — **meta·phys·i·cal** \-'fi-zi-kəl\ adj — **meta·phy·si·cian** \-fə-'zi-shən\ n

me·tas·ta·sis \mə-'tas-tə-səs\ n, pl -ses \-ˌsēz\ : the spread of a health-impairing agency (as cancer cells) from the initial or primary site of disease to another part of the body; also : a secondary growth of a malignant tumor — **me·tas·ta·size** \-tə-ˌsīz\ vb — **met·a·stat·ic** \ˌme-tə-'sta-tik\ adj

meta·tar·sal \ˌme-tə-'tär-səl\ n : any of the bones of the foot between the tarsus and the bones of the digits that in humans include five elongated bones — **metatarsal** adj

meta·tar·sus \-'tär-səs\ n : the part of the human foot or the hind foot in quadrupeds that contains the metatarsals

¹**mete** \'mēt\ vb, met·ed; met·ing 1 archaic : MEASURE 2 : ALLOT — usu. used with out ⟨∼ out punishment⟩

²**mete** n : BOUNDARY ⟨∼s and bounds⟩

me·te·or \'mē-tē-ər, -ˌȯr\ n 1 : a small particle of matter in the solar system directly observable only by its glow from frictional heating on falling into the earth's atmosphere 2 : the streak of light produced by a meteor

me·te·or·ic \ˌmē-tē-'ȯr-ik\ adj 1 : of, relating to, or resembling a meteor 2 : transiently brilliant ⟨a ∼ career⟩ — **me·te·or·i·cal·ly** \-i-k(ə-)lē\ adv

me·te·or·ite \'mē-tē-ə-ˌrīt\ n : a meteor that reaches the surface of the earth

me·te·or·oid \'mē-tē-ə-ˌrȯid\ n : a small particle of matter in the solar system

me·te·o·rol·o·gy \ˌmē-tē-ə-'rä-lə-jē\ n : a science that deals with the atmosphere and its phenomena and esp. with weather forecasting — **me·te·o·ro·log·ic** \ˌmē-tē-ˌȯr-ə-'lä-jik\ or **me·te·o·ro·log·i·cal** \-'lä-ji-kəl\ adj — **me·te·o·rol·o·gist** \ˌmē-tē-ə-'rä-lə-jist\ n

¹**me·ter** \'mē-tər\ n : rhythm in verse or music

²**meter** n : the basic metric unit of length — see METRIC SYSTEM table

³**meter** n : a measuring and sometimes recording instrument

⁴meter *vb* **1** : to measure by means of a meter **2** : to print postal indicia on by means of a postage meter ⟨~*ed* mail⟩

meter–kilogram–second *adj* : of, relating to, or being a system of units based on the meter, the kilogram, and the second

meter maid *n* : a woman assigned to write tickets for parking violations

meth·a·done \'me-thə-ˌdōn\ *also* **meth·a·don** \-ˌdän\ *n* : a synthetic addictive narcotic drug used esp. as a substitute narcotic in the treatment of heroin addiction

meth·am·phet·amine \ˌme-tham-'fe-tə-ˌmēn, -thəm-, -mən\ *n* : a drug used medically in the form of its hydrochloride in the treatment of obesity and often illicitly as a stimulant

meth·ane \'me-ˌthān\ *n* : a colorless odorless flammable gas produced by decomposition of organic matter or from coal and used esp. as a fuel

meth·a·nol \'me-thə-ˌnȯl, -ˌnōl\ *n* : a volatile flammable poisonous liquid alcohol used esp. as a solvent and as an antifreeze

meth·aqua·lone \me-'tha-kwə-ˌlōn\ *n* : a sedative and hypnotic habit-forming drug that is not a barbiturate

meth·od \'me-thəd\ *n* [ME, prescribed treatment, fr. L *methodus*, fr. Gk *methodos*, fr. *meta* with + *hodos* way] **1** : a procedure or process for achieving an end **2** : orderly arrangement : PLAN ✦ *Synonyms* MODE, MANNER, WAY, FASHION, SYSTEM — **me·thod·i·cal** \mə-'thä-di-kəl\ *adj* — **me·thod·i·cal·ly** \-k(ə-)lē\ *adv* — **me·thod·i·cal·ness** *n*

meth·od·ise *Brit var of* METHODIZE

Meth·od·ist \'me-thə-dist\ *n* : a member of a Protestant denomination adhering to the doctrines of John Wesley — **Meth·od·ism** \-ˌdi-zəm\ *n*

meth·od·ize \'me-thə-ˌdīz\ *vb* -**ized**; -**iz·ing** : SYSTEMATIZE

meth·od·ol·o·gy \ˌme-thə-'dä-lə-jē\ *n, pl* -**gies** **1** : a body of methods and rules followed in a science or discipline **2** : the study of the principles or procedures of inquiry in a particular field

meth·yl \'me-thəl\ *n* : a chemical radical consisting of carbon and hydrogen

methyl alcohol *n* : METHANOL

meth·yl·mer·cu·ry \ˌme-thəl-'mər-kyə-rē\ *n* : any of various toxic compounds of mercury that often occur as pollutants which accumulate in animals esp. at the top of a food chain

met·i·cal \'me-ti-kəl\ *n, pl* **met·i·cais** \-kī\ *also* **meticals** — see MONEY table

me·tic·u·lous \mə-'ti-kyə-ləs\ *adj* [L *meticulosus* fearful, fr. *metus* fear] : extremely careful in attending to details — **me·tic·u·lous·ly** *adv* — **me·tic·u·lous·ness** *n*

mé·tier \'me-ˌtyā, me-'tyā\ *n* : an area of activity in which one is expert or successful

me·tre \'mē-tər\ *chiefly Brit var of* METER

met·ric \'me-trik\ *adj* **1** : of or relating to measurement; *esp* : of or relating to the metric system **2** : METRICAL 1

met·ri·cal \'me-tri-kəl\ *adj* **1** : of, relating to, or composed in meter **2** : METRIC 1 — **met·ri·cal·ly** \-k(ə-)lē\ *adv*

met·ri·ca·tion \ˌme-tri-'kā-shən\ *n* : the act or process of converting into or expressing in the metric system

met·ri·cize \'me-trə-ˌsīz\ *vb* -**cized**; -**ciz·ing** : to change into or express in the metric system

metric system *n* : a decimal system of weights and measures based on the meter and on the kilogram

metric ton *n* — see METRIC SYSTEM table

¹met·ro \'me-trō\ *n, pl* **metros** : SUBWAY

²metro *adj* : of, relating to, or characteristic of a metropolis and sometimes including its suburbs

met·ro·nome \'me-trə-ˌnōm\ *n* : an instrument for marking exact time by a regularly repeated tick

me·trop·o·lis \mə-'trä-pə-ləs\ *n* [ME, fr. LL, fr. Gk *mētropolis*, fr. *mētēr* mother + *polis* city] : the chief or capital city of a country, state, or region — **met·ro·pol·i·tan** \ˌme-trə-'pä-lə-tən\ *adj*

met·tle \'me-tᵊl\ *n* **1** : SPIRIT, COURAGE **2** : quality of temperament

met·tle·some \'me-tᵊl-səm\ *adj* : full of mettle : COURAGEOUS

MeV *abbr* million electron volts

¹mew \'myü\ *vb* : MEOW — **mew** *n*

²mew *vb* : CONFINE

mews \'myüz\ *n sing or pl, chiefly Brit* : stables usu. with living quarters built around a court; *also* : a narrow street with dwellings converted from stables

Mex *abbr* Mexican; Mexico

mez·za·nine \'me-zə-ˌnēn, ˌme-zə-'\ *n* **1** : a low-ceilinged story between two main stories of a building **2** : the lowest balcony in a theater; *also* : the first few rows of such a balcony

mez·zo for·te \ˌmet-(ˌ)sō-'fȯr-ˌtā, ˌmed-(ˌ)zō-, -tē\ *adj or adv* [It] : moderately loud — used as a direction in music

mez·zo pia·no \-pē-'ä-(ˌ)nō\ *adj or adv* [It] : moderately soft — used as a direction in music

mez·zo-so·pra·no \-sə-'pra-nō, -'prä-\ *n* : a woman's voice having a range between that of the soprano and contralto; *also* : a singer having such a voice

MFA *abbr* master of fine arts

mfr *abbr* manufacture; manufacturer

mg *abbr* milligram

Mg *symbol* magnesium

MG *abbr* **1** machine gun **2** major general **3** military government

mgr *abbr* **1** manager **2** monseigneur **3** monsignor

mgt *or* **mgmt** *abbr* management

MGy Sgt *abbr* master gunnery sergeant

MHz *abbr* megahertz

mi *abbr* **1** mile; mileage **2** mill

MI *abbr* **1** Michigan **2** military intelligence

MIA \ˌem-(ˌ)ī-'ā\ *n* [missing in action] : a member of the armed forces whose whereabouts following a combat mission are unknown

METRIC SYSTEM

LENGTH

UNIT	SYMBOL	METRIC EQUIVALENT	U.S. EQUIVALENT
kilometer	km	1,000 meters	0.62 mile
hectometer	hm	100 meters	328.08 feet
dekameter	dam	10 meters	32.81 feet
meter	m		39.37 inches
decimeter	dm	0.1 meter	3.94 inches
centimeter	cm	0.01 meter	0.39 inch
millimeter	mm	0.001 meter	0.039 inch
micrometer	μm	0.000001 meter	0.000039 inch

AREA

UNIT	SYMBOL	METRIC EQUIVALENT	U.S. EQUIVALENT
square kilometer	sq km *or* km^2	1,000,000 square meters	0.39 square miles
hectare	ha	10,000 square meters	2.47 acres
are	a	100 square meters	119.60 square yards
square centimeter	sq cm *or* cm^2	0.0001 square meter	0.16 square inch

VOLUME

UNIT	SYMBOL	METRIC EQUIVALENT	U.S. EQUIVALENT
cubic meter	m^3		1.31 cubic yards
cubic decimeter	dm^3	0.001 cubic meter	61.02 cubic inches
cubic centimeter	cu cm *or* cm^3 *also* cc	0.000001 cubic meter	0.061 cubic inch

MASS AND WEIGHT

UNIT	SYMBOL	METRIC EQUIVALENT	U.S. EQUIVALENT
metric ton	t	1,000,000 grams	1.10 short tons
kilogram	kg	1,000 grams	2.20 pounds
hectogram	hg	100 grams	3.53 ounces
dekagram	dag	10 grams	0.35 ounce
gram	g		0.035 ounce
decigram	dg	0.1 gram	1.54 grains
centigram	cg	0.01 gram	0.15 grain
milligram	mg	0.001 gram	0.015 grain
microgram	μg *or* mcg	0.000001 gram	0.000015 grain

CAPACITY

UNIT	METRIC EQUIVALENT	U.S. EQUIVALENT UNITS		
		CUBIC	DRY	LIQUID
kiloliter (kl)	1,000 liters	1.31 cubic yards	28.38 bushels	264.17 gallons
hectoliter (hl)	100 liters	3.53 cubic feet	2.84 bushels	26.42 gallons
dekaliter (dal)	10 liters	0.35 cubic foot	1.14 pecks	2.64 gallons
liter (l)		61.02 cubic inches	0.91 quart	1.06 quarts
deciliter (dl)	0.1 liter	6.10 cubic inches	0.18 pint	0.21 pint
centiliter (cl)	0.01 liter	0.61 cubic inch		0.34 fluid ounce
milliliter (ml)	0.001 liter	0.061 cubic inch		0.27 fluid dram
microliter (μl)	0.000001 liter	0.000061 cubic inch		0.00027 fluid dram

For metric system equivalents of U.S. system units, see WEIGHTS AND MEASURES table.

Mi·ami \mī-ʹa-mē, -mə\ n, pl **Mi·ami** or **Mi·am·is** : a member of an American Indian people orig. of Wisconsin and Indiana

mi·as·ma \mī-ʹaz-mə, mē-\ n, pl **-mas** also **-ma·ta** \-mə-tə\ 1 : a vapor from a swamp formerly believed to cause disease 2 : a harmful influence or atmosphere — **mi·as·mal** \-məl\ adj — **mi·as·mic** \-mik\ adj

mic \ʹmīk\ n : MICROPHONE

Mic abbr Micah

mi·ca \ʹmī-kə\ n [NL, fr. L, grain, crumb] : any of various mineral silicates readily separable into thin transparent sheets

Mi·cah \ʹmī-kə\ n — see BIBLE table

mice pl of MOUSE

Mich abbr Michigan

Mi·che·as \ʹmī-kē-əs, mī-ʹkē-əs\ n : MICAH

Mic·mac \ʹmik-,mak\ n, pl **Micmac** or **Micmacs** : a member of an American Indian people of eastern Canada

micr- or **micro-** comb form 1 : small : minute ⟨microcapsule⟩ 2 : one millionth part of a specified unit ⟨microsecond⟩

¹**mi·cro** \ʹmī-krō\ adj 1 : very small; esp : MICROSCOPIC 2 : involving minute quantities or variations

²**micro** n : MICROCOMPUTER

mi·crobe \ʹmī-,krōb\ n : MICROORGANISM; esp : one causing disease — **mi·cro·bi·al** \mī-ʹkrō-bē-əl\ adj

mi·cro·bi·ol·o·gy \,mī-krō-bī-ʹä-lə-jē\ n : a branch of biology dealing esp. with microscopic forms of life — **mi·cro·bi·o·log·i·cal** \-,bī-ə-ʹläji-kəl\ adj — **mi·cro·bi·ol·o·gist** \-bī-ʹä-lə-jist\ n

mi·cro·brew·ery \ʹmī-krō-,brü-ə-rē\ n : a small brewery making specialty beer in limited quantities

mi·cro·burst \-,bərst\ n : a violent short-lived localized downdraft that creates extreme wind shears at low altitudes

mi·cro·cap·sule \ʹmī-krō-,kap-səl, -sül\ n : a tiny capsule containing material (as a medicine) released when the capsule is broken, melted, or dissolved

mi·cro·chip \-,chip\ n : INTEGRATED CIRCUIT

mi·cro·cir·cuit \-,sər-kət\ n : a compact electronic circuit

mi·cro·com·put·er \-kəm-,pyü-tər\ n : a small computer that uses a microprocessor; esp : PERSONAL COMPUTER

mi·cro·cosm \ʹmī-krō-,käz-əm\ n : an individual or community thought of as a miniature world or universe

mi·cro·elec·tron·ics \ʹmī-krō-i-,lek-ʹträ-niks\ n : a branch of electronics that deals with the miniaturization of electronic circuits and components — **mi·cro·elec·tron·ic** \-nik\ adj

mi·cro·en·cap·su·late \,mī-krō-in-ʹkap-sə-,lāt\ vb : to enclose (as a drug) in a microcapsule — **mi·cro·en·cap·su·la·tion** \-in-,kap-sə-ʹlā-shən\ n

mi·cro·fi·ber \ʹmī-krō-,fī-bər\ n : a fine usu. soft polyester fiber; also : fabric made from such fibers

mi·cro·fiche \ʹmī-krō-,fēsh, -,fish\ n, pl **-fiche** or **-fiches** \same or -,fē-shəz, -,fi-\ : a sheet of microfilm containing rows of images of pages of printed matter

mi·cro·film \-,film\ n : a film bearing a photographic record (as of print) on a reduced scale — **microfilm** vb

mi·cro·graph \ʹmī-krə-,graf\ n : a graphic reproduction of the image of an object formed by a microscope

mi·cro·man·age \,mī-krō-ʹma-nij\ vb : to manage esp. with excessive control or attention to details — **mi·cro·man·age·ment** \-mənt\ n — **mi·cro·man·ag·er** \-ni-jər\ n

mi·cro·me·te·or·ite \,mī-krō-ʹmē-tē-ə-,rīt\ n : a very small particle in interplanetary space

mi·crom·e·ter \mī-ʹkrä-mə-tər\ n : an instrument used with a telescope or microscope for measuring minute distances

mi·cro·min·ia·tur·i·za·tion \,mī-krō-,mi-nē-ə-,chùr-ə-ʹzā-shən, -,mi-ni-,chùr-, -chər-\ n : the process of producing things in a very small size and esp. in a size smaller than one considered miniature — **mi·cro·min·ia·tur·ized** \-ʹmi-nē-ə-chə-,rīzd, -ʹmi-ni-chə-\ adj

mi·cron \ʹmī-,krän\ n : one millionth of a meter

mi·cro·or·gan·ism \,mī-krō-ʹòr-gə-,ni-zəm\ n : an organism (as a bacterium) too tiny to be seen by the unaided eye

mi·cro·phone \ʹmī-krə-,fōn\ n : an instrument for converting sound waves into variations of an electric current for transmitting or recording sound

mi·cro·pho·to·graph \,mī-krō-ʹfō-tə-,graf\ n : PHOTOMICROGRAPH

mi·cro·pro·ces·sor \,mī-krō-ʹprä-,se-sər\ n : a computer processor contained on a microchip

mi·cro·scope \ʹmī-krə-,skōp\ n : an instrument for making magnified images of minute objects usu. using light — **mi·cros·co·py** \mī-ʹkräs-kə-pē\ n

mi·cro·scop·ic \,mī-krə-ʹskä-pik\ also **mi·cro·scop·i·cal** \-pi-kəl\ adj 1 : of, relating to, or involving the use of the microscope 2 : too tiny to be seen without the use of a microscope : very small — **mi·cro·scop·i·cal·ly** \-pi-k(ə-)lē\ adv

mi·cro·sec·ond \ʹmī-krō-,se-kənd\ n : one millionth of a second

mi·cro·sur·gery \,mī-krō-ʹsər-jə-rē\ n : minute dissection or manipulation (as by a laser beam) of living structures or tissue — **mi·cro·sur·gi·cal** \-ʹsər-ji-kəl\ adj

mi·cro·tech·nol·o·gy \-tek-ʹnä-lə-jē\ n : technology on a small or microscopic scale

¹**mi·cro·wave** \ʹmī-krə-,wāv\ n 1 : a radio wave between one millimeter and one meter in wavelength 2 : MICROWAVE OVEN

²**microwave** vb : to heat or cook in a microwave oven — **mi·cro·wav·able** or **mi·cro·wave·able** \,mī-krə-ʹwā-və-bəl\ adj

microwave oven n : an oven in which food is cooked by the absorption of microwave energy by water molecules in the food

¹mid \'mid\ *adj* : MIDDLE

²mid *abbr* middle

mid-air \'mid-'er\ *n* : a point or region in the air well above the ground

mid-day \'mid-,dā, -'dā\ *n* : NOON

mid-den \'mi-d°n\ *n* : a refuse heap

¹mid-dle \'mi-d°l\ *adj* 1 : equally distant from the extremes : MEDIAL, CENTRAL 2 : being at neither extreme : INTERMEDIATE 3 *cap* : constituting an intermediate period

²middle *n* 1 : a middle part, point, or position 2 : WAIST

middle age *n* : the period of life from about 45 to about 64 — **mid-dle-aged** \,mi-d°l-'ājd\ *adj*

Middle Ages *n pl* : the period of European history from about A.D. 500 to about 1500

mid-dle-brow \'mi-d°l-,braü\ *n* : a person who is moderately but not highly cultivated — **middlebrow** *adj*

middle class *n* : a social class holding a position between the upper class and the lower class — **middle-class** *adj*

middle ear *n* : a small membrane-lined cavity of the ear through which sound waves are transmitted by a chain of tiny bones

middle finger *n* : the midmost of the five digits of the hand

mid-dle-man \'mi-d°l-,man\ *n* : INTERMEDIARY; *esp* : one intermediate between the producer of goods and the retailer or consumer

middle-of-the-road *adj* : standing for or following a course of action midway between extremes; *esp* : being neither liberal nor conservative in politics — **middle-of-the-road-er** \-'rō-dər\ *n* — **middle-of-the-road-ism** \-'rō-,di-zəm\ *n*

middle school *n* : a school usu. including grades 5 to 8 or 6 to 8

mid-dle-weight \'mi-d°l-,wāt\ *n* : one of average weight; *esp* : a boxer weighing not over 160 pounds

mid-dling \'mid-liŋ, -lən\ *adj* 1 : of middle, medium, or moderate size, degree, or quality 2 : MEDIOCRE

mid-dy \'mi-dē\ *n, pl* middies : MIDSHIPMAN

midge \'mij\ *n* : a very small fly : GNAT

midg-et \'mi-jət\ *n* 1 : something (as an animal) very small for its kind 2 *sometimes offensive* : a very small person

midi \'mi-dē\ *n* : a calf-length dress, coat, or skirt

MIDI \'mi-dē\ *n* [*musical instrument digital interface*] : a protocol for the transmission of digitally encoded music

mid-land \'mid-lənd, -,land\ *n* : the interior or central region of a country

mid-life \'mid-'līf\ *n* : MIDDLE AGE

midlife crisis *n* : a period of emotional turmoil in middle age characterized esp. by a strong desire for change

mid-most \-,mōst\ *adj* : being in or near the exact middle — **midmost** *adv*

mid-night \-,nīt\ *n* : 12 o'clock at night

mid-ocean ridge \'mid-'ō-shən-\ *n* : an elevation on an ocean floor at the boundary of diverging tectonic plates

mid-point \'mid-,point, -'point\ *n* : a point at or near the center or middle

mid-riff \'mi-,drif\ *n* [ME *midrif*, fr. OE *midhrif*, fr. *midde* mid + *hrif* belly] 1 : DIAPHRAGM 1 2 : the mid-region of the human torso

mid-sec-tion \-,sek-shən\ *n* : a section midway between the extremes; *esp* : MIDRIFF 2

mid-ship-man \'mid-,ship-mən, (,)mid-'ship-\ *n* : a student in a naval academy

mid-ships \-,ships\ *adv* : AMIDSHIPS

midst \'midst\ *n* 1 : the interior or central part or point 2 : a position of proximity to the members of a group ⟨in our ~⟩ 3 : the condition of being surrounded or beset — **midst** *prep*

mid-stream \'mid-'strēm, -,strēm\ *n* : the middle of a stream

mid-sum-mer \-'sə-mər, -,sə-\ *n* 1 : the middle of summer 2 : the summer solstice

mid-town \'mid-,taün, -'taün\ *n* : a central section of a city; *esp* : one situated between sections called *downtown* and *uptown* — **midtown** *adj*

¹mid-way \'mid-,wā, -'wā\ *adv* : in the middle of the way or distance

²mid-way \-,wā\ *n* : an avenue (as at a carnival) for concessions and amusements

mid-week \-,wēk\ *n* : the middle of the week — **mid-week-ly** \-,wē-klē, -'wē-\ *adj or adv*

mid-wife \'mid-,wīf\ *n* : a person who helps women in childbirth — **mid-wife-ry** \-,wi-fə-rē\ *n*

mid-win-ter \'mid-'win-tər, -,win-\ *n* 1 : the winter solstice 2 : the middle of winter

mid-year \-,yir\ *n* 1 : the middle of a year 2 : a midyear examination — **midyear** *adj*

mien \'mēn\ *n* 1 : air or bearing esp. as expressive of mood or personality : DEMEANOR 2 : APPEARANCE, ASPECT ⟨dresses of formal ~⟩

miff \'mif\ *vb* : to put into an ill humor

¹might \'mīt\ *verbal auxiliary past of* MAY — used as an auxiliary to express permission or possibility in the past, a present condition contrary to fact, less probability or possibility than *may*, or as a polite alternative to *may, ought,* or *should*

²might *n* : the power, authority, or resources of an individual or a group

mighty \'mī-tē\ *adj* **might-i-er; -est** 1 : very strong : POWERFUL 2 : GREAT, NOTABLE — **might-i-ly** \'mī-tə-lē\ *adv* — **might-i-ness** \-tē-nəs\ *n* — **mighty** *adv*

mi-gnon-ette \,min-yə-'net\ *n* : an annual garden herb with spikes of tiny fragrant flowers

mi-graine \'mī-,grān\ *n* [ME *mygreyn*, fr. MF *migraine*, fr. LL *hemicrania* pain in one side of the head, fr. Gk *hēmikrania*, fr. *hēmi-* half + *kranion* cranium] : a condition marked by recurrent severe headache and often nausea; *also* : an attack of migraine

mi·grant \'mī-grənt\ *n* : one that migrates; *esp* : a person who moves in order to find work (as picking crops) — **migrant** *adj*

mi·grate \'mī-ˌgrāt\ *vb* **mi·grat·ed; mi·grat·ing** **1** : to move from one country or place to another **2** : to pass usu. periodically from one region or climate to another for feeding or breeding — **mi·gra·tion** \mī-'grā-shən\ *n* — **mi·gra·to·ry** \'mī-grə-ˌtȯr-ē\ *adj*

mi·ka·do \mə-'kä-dō\ *n, pl* **-dos** : an emperor of Japan

mike \'mīk\ *n* : MICROPHONE

¹mil \'mil\ *n* : a unit of length equal to ¹/₁₀₀₀ inch

²mil *abbr* military

milch \'milk, 'milch\ *adj* : giving milk ⟨~ cow⟩

mild \'mī(-ə)ld\ *adj* **1** : gentle in nature or behavior **2** : moderate in action or effect **3** : TEMPERATE ⟨~ weather⟩
◆ **Synonyms** EASY, COMPLAISANT, AMIABLE, LENIENT — **mild·ly** *adv* — **mild·ness** *n*

mil·dew \'mil-ˌdü, -ˌdyü\ *n* : a superficial usu. whitish growth produced on organic matter and on plants by a fungus; *also* : a fungus producing this growth — **mildew** *vb*

mile \'mī(-ə)l\ *n* [ME, fr. OE *mīl*, fr. L *milia* miles, fr. *milia passuum*, lit., thousands of paces] **1** — see WEIGHT table **2** : NAUTICAL MILE

mile·age \'mī-lij\ *n* **1** : an allowance for traveling expenses at a certain rate per mile **2** : distance in miles traveled (as in a day) **3** : the amount of service yielded (as by a tire) expressed in terms of miles of travel **4** : the average number of miles a motor vehicle will travel on a gallon of gasoline

mile·post \'mī(-ə)l-ˌpōst\ *n* : a post indicating the distance in miles from a given point

mile·stone \-ˌstōn\ *n* **1** : a stone serving as a milepost **2** : a significant point in development

mi·lieu \mēl-'yər, -'yü, -'yœ\ *n, pl* **milieus** *or* **mi·lieux** *same or* -'yərz, -'yüz, -'yœz\ [F] : ENVIRONMENT, SETTING

mil·i·tant \'mi-lə-tənt\ *adj* **1** : engaged in warfare **2** : aggressively active esp. in a cause — **mil·i·tance** \-təns\ *n* — **mil·i·tan·cy** \-tən-sē\ *n* — **militant** *n* — **mil·i·tant·ly** *adv*

mil·i·ta·rise *Brit var of* MILITARIZE

mil·i·ta·rism \'mi-lə-tə-ˌri-zəm\ *n* **1** : predominance of the military class or its ideals **2** : a policy of aggressive military preparedness — **mil·i·ta·rist** \-rist\ *n* — **mil·i·ta·ris·tic** \ˌmi-lə-tə-'ris-tik\ *adj*

mil·i·ta·rize \'mi-lə-tə-ˌrīz\ *vb* **-rized; -riz·ing** **1** : to equip with military forces and defenses **2** : to give a military character to

¹mil·i·tary \'mi-lə-ˌter-ē\ *adj* **1** : of or relating to soldiers, arms, war, or the army **2** : performed by armed forces; *also* : supported by armed force ◆ **Synonyms** MARTIAL, WARLIKE — **mil·i·tar·i·ly** \ˌmi-lə-'ter-ə-lē\ *adv*

²military *n, pl* **military** *also* **mil·i·tar·ies** **1** : the military, naval, and air forces of a nation **2** : military persons

military police *n* : a branch of an army that exercises guard and police functions

mil·i·tate \'mi-lə-ˌtāt\ *vb* **-tat·ed; -tat·ing** : to have weight or effect ⟨disagreements ~ against an alliance⟩

mi·li·tia \mə-'li-shə\ *n* : a part of the organized armed forces of a country liable to call only in emergency — **mi·li·tia·man** \-mən\ *n*

¹milk \'milk\ *n* **1** : a nutritive usu. whitish fluid secreted by female mammals for feeding their young **2** : a milklike liquid (as a plant juice) — **milk·i·ness** \'mil-kē-nəs\ *n* — **milky** *adj*

²milk *vb* **1** : to draw off the milk of ⟨~ a cow⟩ **2** : to draw something from as if by milking

milk·maid \'milk-ˌmād\ *n* : DAIRYMAID

milk·man \-ˌman, -mən\ *n* : a person who sells or delivers milk

milk of magnesia : a milk-white mixture of hydroxide of magnesium and water used as an antacid and laxative

milk shake *n* : a thoroughly blended drink made of milk, a flavoring syrup, and often ice cream

milk·sop \'milk-ˌsäp\ *n* : an unmanly man

milk·weed \-ˌwēd\ *n* : any of a genus of herbs with milky juice and clustered flowers

Milky Way *n* **1** : a broad irregular band of light that stretches across the sky and is caused by the light of a very great number of faint stars **2** : MILKY WAY GALAXY

Milky Way galaxy *n* : the galaxy of which the sun is a member and which includes the stars that create the light of the Milky Way

¹mill \'mil\ *n* **1** : a building with machinery for grinding grain into flour **2** : a machine used in processing (as by grinding, stamping, cutting, or finishing) raw material **3** : FACTORY

²mill *vb* **1** : to process in a mill **2** : to move in a circle or in an eddying mass

³mill *n* : one tenth of a cent

mill·age \'mi-lij\ *n* : a rate (as of taxation) expressed in mills

mil·len·ni·um \mə-'le-nē-əm\ *n, pl* **-nia** \-nē-ə\ *or* **-niums** **1** : a period of 1000 years; *also* : a 1000th anniversary or its celebration **2** : the 1000 years mentioned in Revelation 20 when holiness is to prevail and Christ is to reign on earth **3** : a period of great happiness or human perfection

mill·er \'mi-lər\ *n* **1** : one that operates a mill and esp. a flour mill **2** : any of various moths having powdery wings

mil·let \'mi-lət\ *n* : any of several small-seeded cereal and forage grasses cultivated for grain or hay; *also* : the grain of a millet

milli- *comb form* : one thousandth part of

mil·li·am·pere \ˌmi-lē-'am-ˌpir\ *n* : one thousandth of an ampere

mil·liard \'mil-ˌyärd, 'mi-lē-ˌärd\ *n, Brit* : a thousand millions

mil·li·bar \'mi-lə-ˌbär\ *n* : a unit of atmospheric pressure

mil·li·gram \-ˌgram\ *n* — see METRIC SYSTEM table

mil·li·li·ter \-ˌlē-tər\ *n* — see METRIC SYSTEM table

mil·lime \mə-'lēm\ *n* — see *dinar* at MONEY table

mil·li·me·ter \'mi-lə-ˌmē-tər\ *n* — see METRIC SYSTEM table

mil·li·ner \'mi-lə-nər\ *n* [irreg. fr. *Milan*, Italy; fr. the importation of women's finery from Italy in the 16th century] : a person who designs, makes, trims, or sells women's hats

mil·li·nery \'mi-lə-ˌner-ē\ *n* 1 : women's apparel for the head 2 : the business or work of a milliner

mill·ing \'mi-liŋ\ *n* : a corrugated edge on a coin

mil·lion \'mil-yən\ *n, pl* **millions** *or* **million** : a thousand thousands — **million** *adj* — **mil·lionth** \-yənth\ *adj or n*

mil·lion·aire \ˌmil-yə-'ner, 'mil-yə-ˌner\ *n* : one whose wealth is estimated at a million or more (as of dollars or pounds)

mil·li·pede \'mi-lə-ˌpēd\ *n* : any of a class of arthropods related to the centipedes and having a long segmented body with a hard covering, two pairs of legs on most segments, and no poison fangs

mil·li·sec·ond \-ˌse-kənd\ *n* : one thousandth of a second

mil·li·volt \-ˌvōlt\ *n* : one thousandth of a volt

mill·pond \'mil-ˌpänd\ *n* : a pond made by damming a stream to produce a fall of water for operating a mill

mill·race \-ˌrās\ *n* : a canal in which water flows to and from a mill wheel

mill·stone \-ˌstōn\ *n* : either of two round flat stones used for grinding grain

mill·stream \-ˌstrēm\ *n* : a stream whose flow is used to run a mill; *also* : the stream in a millrace

mill wheel *n* : a waterwheel that drives a mill

mill·wright \'mil-ˌrīt\ *n* : a person who builds mills or sets up or maintains their machinery

milt \'milt\ *n* : the sperm-containing fluid of a male fish

mime \'mīm\ *n* 1 : MIMIC 2 : PANTOMIME — **mime** *vb*

mim·eo·graph \'mi-mē-ə-ˌgraf\ *n* : a machine for making many copies by means of a stencil through which ink is pressed — **mimeograph** *vb*

mi·me·sis \mə-'mē-səs, mī-\ *n* : IMITATION, MIMICRY

mi·met·ic \-'me-tik\ *adj* 1 : IMITATIVE 2 : relating to, characterized by, or exhibiting mimicry

¹mim·ic \'mi-mik\ *n* : one that mimics

²mimic *vb* **mim·icked** \-mikt\; **mim·ick·ing** 1 : to imitate closely 2 : to ridicule by imitation 3 : to resemble by biological mimicry

mim·ic·ry \'mi-mi-krē\ *n, pl* -ries 1 : an instance of mimicking 2 : a superficial resemblance of one organism to another or to natural objects among which it lives

that gives it an advantage (as protection from predation)

mi·mo·sa \mə-'mō-sə, mī-, -zə\ *n* : any of a genus of trees, shrubs, and herbs of the legume family that occur in warm regions and have ball-shaped heads of small white or pink flowers

min *abbr* 1 minim 2 minimum 3 mining 4 minister 5 minor 6 minute

min·a·ret \ˌmi-nə-'ret\ *n* [F, fr. Turk *minare*, fr. Ar *manāra* lighthouse] : a tall slender tower of a mosque from which a muezzin calls the faithful to prayer

mi·na·to·ry \'mi-nə-ˌtȯr-ē, 'mī-\ *adj* : THREATENING, MENACING

mince \'mins\ *vb* **minced; minc·ing** [ME, fr. AF *mincer*, fr. VL *minutiare, fr.* L *minutia* smallness, fr. *minutus* small, fr. pp. of *minuere* to lessen] 1 : to cut into very small pieces 2 : to restrain (words) within the bounds of decorum 3 : to walk in a prim affected manner

mince·meat \'mins-ˌmēt\ *n* : a finely chopped mixture esp. of raisins, apples, spices, and often meat used as a filling for a pie

¹mind \'mīnd\ *n* 1 : MEMORY 2 : the part of an individual that feels, perceives, thinks, wills, and esp. reasons 3 : INTENTION, DESIRE 4 : normal mental condition 5 : OPINION, VIEW 6 : MOOD 7 : mental qualities of a person or group 8 : intellectual ability 9 : ATTENTION ⟨pay him no ~⟩

²mind *vb* 1 *chiefly dial* : REMEMBER 2 : to attend to closely 3 : HEED, OBEY 4 : to be concerned about; *also* : DISLIKE 5 : to be careful or cautious 6 : to take charge of 7 : to regard with attention

mind–bend·ing \'mīnd-ˌben-diŋ\ *adj* : MIND-BLOWING — **mind–bend·ing·ly** *adv*

mind–blow·ing \-ˌblō-iŋ\ *adj* : PSYCHEDELIC 1; *also* : MIND-BOGGLING — **mind-blow·er** \-ˌblō-ər\ *n* — **mind–blow·ing·ly** *adv*

mind–bog·gling \-ˌbä-gə-liŋ\ *adj* : mentally or emotionally exciting or overwhelming

mind·ed \'mīn-dəd\ *adj* 1 : INCLINED, DISPOSED 2 : having a mind of a specified kind or concerned with a specific thing — usu. used in combination ⟨narrow-*minded*⟩ ⟨health-*minded*⟩

mind·ful \'mīnd-fəl\ *adj* : bearing in mind : AWARE — **mind·ful·ly** *adv* — **mind·ful·ness** *n*

mind·less \-ləs\ *adj* 1 : marked by a lack of mind or consciousness; *esp* : marked by no use of the intellect 2 : not mindful : HEEDLESS — **mind·less·ly** *adv* — **mind·less·ness** *n*

¹mine \'mīn\ *pron* : that which belongs to me

²mine *n* 1 : an excavation in the earth from which minerals are taken; *also* : an ore deposit 2 : an underground passage beneath an enemy position 3 : an explosive device for destroying enemy personnel, vehicles, or ships 4 : a rich source of supply

³**mine** *vb* **mined; min·ing 1 :** to dig a mine **2 :** UNDERMINE **3 :** to get ore from the earth **4 :** to place military mines in — **min·er** *n*

mine·field \'mīn-ˌfēld\ *n* **1 :** an area set with mines **2 :** something resembling a minefield esp. in having many dangers ⟨a political ∼⟩

mine-lay·er \-ˌlā-ər\ *n* : a naval vessel for laying underwater mines

min·er·al \'mi-nə-rəl\ *n* **1 :** a crystalline substance (as diamond or quartz) of inorganic origin **2 :** a naturally occurring substance (as coal, salt, or water) obtained usu. from the ground — **mineral** *adj*

min·er·al·ise *Brit var of* MINERALIZE

min·er·al·ize \'mi-nə-rə-ˌlīz\ *vb* **-ized; -iz·ing 1 :** to impregnate or supply with minerals **2 :** to change into mineral form — **min·er·al·i·za·tion** \-rə-lə-'zā-shən\ *n*

min·er·al·o·gy \ˌmi-nə-'rä-lə-jē, -'ra-\ *n* : a science dealing with minerals — **min·er·al·og·i·cal** \ˌmi-nə-rə-'lä-ji-kəl\ *adj* — **min·er·al·o·gist** \ˌmi-nə-'rä-lə-jist, -'ra-\ *n*

mineral oil *n* : an oil of mineral origin; *esp* : a refined petroleum oil used as a laxative

mineral water *n* : water infused with mineral salts or gases

min·e·stro·ne \ˌmi-nə-'strō-nē, -'strön\ *n* [It, fr. *minestra*, fr. *minestrare* to serve, dish up, fr. L *ministrare*, fr. *minister* servant] : a rich thick vegetable soup

mine·sweep·er \'mīn-ˌswē-pər\ *n* : a warship for removing or neutralizing underwater mines

min·gle \'miŋ-gəl\ *vb* **min·gled; min·gling 1 :** to bring or combine together : MIX ⟨*mingling* odors⟩ **2 :** ASSOCIATE; *also* : to move about socially ⟨*mingled* with the guests⟩

ming tree \'miŋ-\ *n* : a dwarfed usu. evergreen tree grown as bonsai; *also* : an artificial plant resembling this

mini \'mi-nē\ *n, pl* **min·is** : something small of its kind — **mini** *adj*

mini- *comb form* : smaller or briefer than usual, normal, or standard

min·ia·ture \'mi-nē-ə-ˌchu̇r, 'mi-ni-ˌchu̇r, -chər\ *n* [It *miniatura* art of illuminating a manuscript, fr. ML, fr. L *miniare* to color with red lead, fr. *minium* red lead] **1 :** a copy on a much reduced scale; *also* : something small of its kind **2 :** a small painting (as on ivory or metal) — **miniature** *adj* — **min·ia·tur·ist** \-chu̇r-ist, -chər-\ *n*

min·ia·tur·ize \'mi-nē-ə-ˌchə-ˌrīz, 'mi-ni-\ *vb* **-ized; -iz·ing :** to design or construct in small size — **min·ia·tur·i·za·tion** \ˌmi-nē-ə-ˌchu̇r-ə-'zā-shən, ˌmi-ni-, -chər-\ *n*

mini-bar \'mi-nē-ˌbär\ *n* : a small refrigerator in a hotel room that is stocked with beverages and snacks

mini-bike \'mi-nē-ˌbīk\ *n* : a small one-passenger motorcycle

mini-bus \-ˌbəs\ *n* : a small bus or van

mini-com·put·er \-kəm-ˌpyü-tər\ *n* : a computer between a mainframe and a microcomputer in size and speed

mini-disc \'mi-nē-ˌdisk\ *n* : a miniature optical disk

min·im \'mi-nəm\ *n* — see WEIGHT table

min·i·mal \'mi-nə-məl\ *adj* **1 :** relating to or being a minimum : LEAST **2 :** of or relating to minimalism or minimal art — **min·i·mal·ly** *adv*

minimal art *n* : abstract art consisting primarily of simple geometric forms executed in an impersonal style — **minimal artist** *n*

min·i·mal·ism \'mi-nə-mə-ˌli-zəm\ *n* : MINIMAL ART; *also* : a style (as in music or literature) marked by extreme spareness or simplicity — **min·i·mal·ist** \-list\ *n*

mini-mart \'mi-nē-ˌmärt\ *n* : CONVENIENCE STORE

min·i·mise *Brit var of* MINIMIZE

min·i·mize \'mi-nə-ˌmīz\ *vb* **-mized; -miz·ing 1 :** to reduce or keep to a minimum **2 :** to underestimate intentionally ⟨∼ the defects⟩ ♦ **Synonyms** DEPRECIATE, DECRY, DISPARAGE

min·i·mum \'mi-nə-məm\ *n, pl* **-ma** \-mə\ *or* **-mums 1 :** the least quantity assignable, admissible, or possible **2 :** the least of a set of numbers **3 :** the lowest degree or amount of variation (as of temperature) reached or recorded — **minimum** *adj*

min·ion \'min-yən\ *n* [MF *mignon* darling] **1 :** a servile dependent, follower, or underling **2 :** one highly favored **3 :** a subordinate official

min·is·cule \'mi-nəs-ˌkyül\ *var of* MINUSCULE

mini-se·ries \'mi-nē-ˌsir-ēz\ *n* : a television story presented in sequential episodes

mini-skirt \-ˌskərt\ *n* : a skirt with the hemline several inches above the knee

¹**min·is·ter** \'mi-nə-stər\ *n* **1 :** AGENT **2 :** a member of the clergy esp. of a Protestant communion **3 :** a high officer of state who heads a division of governmental activities **4 :** a diplomatic representative to a foreign state — **min·is·te·ri·al** \ˌmi-nə-'stir-ē-əl\ *adj*

²**minister** *vb* **1 :** to perform the functions of a minister of religion **2 :** to give aid or service — **min·is·tra·tion** \ˌmi-nə-'strā-shən\ *n*

¹**min·is·trant** \'mi-nə-strənt\ *adj, archaic* : performing service as a minister

²**ministrant** *n* : one that ministers

min·is·try \'mi-nə-strē\ *n, pl* **-tries 1 :** MINISTRATION **2 :** the office, duties, or functions of a minister; *also* : the period of service or office **3 :** CLERGY **4 :** AGENCY **5** *often cap* : the body of ministers governing a nation or state; *also* : a government department headed by a minister

mini-tower \'mi-nē-ˌtau̇(-ə)r\ *n* : a computer tower of intermediate size

mini-van \'mi-nē-ˌvan\ *n* : a small van

mink \'miŋk\ *n, pl* **mink** *or* **minks :** either of two slender flesh-eating mammals resembling the related weasels; *also* : the soft lustrous typically dark brown fur of a mink

min·ke whale \'miŋ-kə-\ *n* : a small gray-ish baleen whale with a whitish underside

Minn *abbr* Minnesota

min·ne·sing·er \'mi-ni-ˌsiŋ-ər, -ˌziŋ-\ *n* [G, fr. Middle High German, fr. *minne* love + *singer* singer] : any of a class of German lyric poets and musicians of the 12th to the 14th centuries

min·now \'mi-nō\ *n, pl* **minnows** *also* **minnow** : any of numerous small fresh-water fishes

¹mi·nor \'mī-nər\ *adj* **1** : inferior in importance, size, or degree **2** : not having reached majority **3** : having the third, sixth, and sometimes the seventh degrees lowered by a half step ⟨∼ scale⟩; *also* : based on a minor scale ⟨∼ key⟩ **4** : not serious ⟨∼ illness⟩

²minor *n* **1** : a person who has not attained majority **2** : a subject of academic study chosen as a secondary field of specialization

³minor *vb* : to pursue an academic minor ⟨∼ed in philosophy⟩

mi·nor·i·ty \mə-'nȯr-ə-tē, mī-\ *n, pl* **-ties** **1** : the period or state of being a minor **2** : the smaller in number of two groups; *esp* : a group having less than the number of votes necessary for control **3** : a part of a population differing from others (as in race); *also* : a member of a minority

mi·nox·i·dil \mə-'näk-sə-ˌdil\ *n* : a drug used orally to treat hypertension and topically in solution to promote hair regrowth in some forms of baldness

min·ster \'min-stər\ *n* : a large or important church

min·strel \'min-strəl\ *n* **1** : a medieval singer of verses; *also* : MUSICIAN, POET **2** : any of a group of performers usu. with blackened faces in a program of black American songs, jokes, and impersonations ⟨a ∼ show⟩

min·strel·sy \-sē\ *n* : the singing and playing of a minstrel; *also* : a body of minstrels

¹mint \'mint\ *n* **1** : any of a large family of aromatic square-stemmed herbs and shrubs; *esp* : one (as spearmint) that is fragrant and is the source of a flavoring oil **2** : a mint-flavored piece of candy — **minty** *adj*

²mint *n* **1** : a place where coins are made **2** : a vast sum ⟨worth a ∼⟩

³mint *vb* **1** : to make (as coins) out of metal **2** : CREATE; *also* : to give a certain status to ⟨newly ∼ed lawyers⟩ — **mint·age** \-ij\ *n* — **mint·er** *n*

⁴mint *adj* : unmarred as if fresh from a mint ⟨in ∼ condition⟩

min·u·end \'min-yə-ˌwend\ *n* : a number from which another is to be subtracted

min·u·et \ˌmin-yə-'wet\ *n* : a slow graceful dance

¹mi·nus \'mī-nəs\ *prep* **1** : diminished by : LESS ⟨seven ∼ three equals four⟩ **2** : LACKING, WITHOUT ⟨∼ his hat⟩

²minus *n* : a negative quantity or quality

³minus *adj* **1** : algebraically negative ⟨∼ quantity⟩ **2** : having a negative quality

¹mi·nus·cule \'mi-nəs-ˌkyül\ *n* : a lower-case letter

²minuscule *also* **min·is·cule** *adj* : very small

minus sign *n* : a sign — used in mathematics to indicate subtraction or a negative quantity

¹min·ute \'mi-nət\ *n* **1** : the 60th part of an hour or of a degree : 60 seconds **2** : a short space of time **3** *pl* : the official record of the proceedings of a meeting

²mi·nute \mī-'nüt, mə-, -'nyüt\ *adj* **mi·nut·er; -est 1** : very small **2** : of little importance : TRIFLING **3** : marked by close attention to details ♦ **Synonyms** DIMINUTIVE, TINY, MINIATURE, WEE — **mi·nute·ly** *adv* — **mi·nute·ness** *n*

min·ute·man \'mi-nət-ˌman\ *n* : a member of a group of armed men pledged to take the field at a minute's notice during and immediately before the American Revolution

mi·nu·tia \mə-'nü-shə, -'nyü-, -shē-ə\ *n, pl* **-ti·ae** \-shē-ˌē\ [L] : a minute or minor detail — usu. used in pl.

minx \'miŋks\ *n* : a pert girl

Mio·cene \'mī-ə-ˌsēn\ *adj* : of, relating to, or being the epoch of the Tertiary between the Oligocene and the Pliocene — **Miocene** *n*

mir·a·cle \'mir-i-kəl\ *n* **1** : an extraordinary event manifesting divine intervention in human affairs **2** : an unusual event, thing, or accomplishment : WONDER, MARVEL — **mi·rac·u·lous** \mə-'ra-kyə-ləs\ *adj* — **mi·rac·u·lous·ly** *adv*

miracle drug *n* : a usu. newly discovered drug that elicits a dramatic response in a patient's condition

mi·rage \mə-'räzh\ *n* **1** : an illusion that often appears as a pool of water or a mirror in which distant objects are seen inverted, is sometimes seen at sea, in the desert, or over a hot pavement, and results from atmospheric conditions **2** : something illusory and unattainable

¹mire \'mī(-ə)r\ *n* : heavy and often deep mud or slush — **miry** *adj*

²mire *vb* **mired; mir·ing** : to stick or sink in or as if in mire

mire·poix \mir-'pwä\ *n, pl* **mirepoix** : a mixture of diced vegetables and sometimes meats used in soups, stews, and sauces

¹mir·ror \'mir-ər\ *n* **1** : a polished or smooth surface (as of glass) that forms images by reflection **2** : a true representation

²mirror *vb* **1** : to reflect in or as if in a mirror **2** : RESEMBLE

mirth \'mərth\ *n* : gladness or gaiety accompanied with laughter ♦ **Synonyms** GLEE, JOLLITY, HILARITY, MERRIMENT — **mirth·ful** \-fəl\ *adj* — **mirth·ful·ly** *adv* — **mirth·ful·ness** *n* — **mirth·less** *adj*

MIRV \'mərv\ *n* [*m*ultiple *i*ndependently targeted *r*eentry *v*ehicle] : an ICBM with multiple warheads that have different targets — **MIRV** *vb*

mis·ad·ven·ture \ˌmi-səd-'ven-chər\ *n* : MISFORTUNE, MISHAP

mis·aligned \ˌmi-sə-'līnd\ *adj* : not prop·

erly aligned — **mis·align·ment** \-'līn-mənt\ n

mis·al·li·ance \ˌmi-sə-'lī-əns\ n : an improper or unsuitable marriage

mis·al·lo·ca·tion \ˌmi-ˌsa-lə-'kā-shən\ n : faulty or improper allocation

mis·an·dry \'mi-ˌsan-drē\ n : a hatred of men — **mis·an·drist** \-drist\ n or adj

mis·an·thrope \'mi-sⁿn-ˌthrōp\ n : one who hates humankind — **mis·an·throp·ic** \ˌmi-sⁿn-'thrä-pik\ adj — **mis·an·throp·i·cal·ly** \-pi-k(ə-)lē\ adv — **mis·an·thro·py** \mi-'san-thrə-pē\ n

mis·ap·ply \ˌmi-sə-'plī\ vb : to apply wrongly — **mis·ap·pli·ca·tion** \ˌmi-ˌsa-plə-'kā-shən\ n

mis·ap·pre·hend \ˌmi-ˌsa-pri-'hend\ vb : MISUNDERSTAND — **mis·ap·pre·hen·sion** \-'hen-chən\ n

mis·ap·pro·pri·ate \ˌmi-sə-'prō-prē-ˌāt\ vb : to appropriate wrongly (as by embezzlement) — **mis·ap·pro·pri·a·tion** \-ˌprō-prē-'ā-shən\ n

mis·be·got·ten \-bi-'gä-tⁿn\ adj : ILLEGITIMATE; also : ill-conceived

mis·be·have \ˌmis-bi-'hāv\ vb : to behave improperly — **mis·be·hav·er** n — **mis·be·hav·ior** \-'hā-vyər\ n

mis·be·liev·er \-bə-'lē-vər\ n : one who holds a false or unorthodox belief

mis·brand \mis-'brand\ vb : to brand falsely or in a misleading manner

misc abbr miscellaneous

mis·cal·cu·late \mis-'kal-kyə-ˌlāt\ vb : to calculate wrongly — **mis·cal·cu·la·tion** \ˌmis-ˌkal-kyə-'lā-shən\ n

mis·call \mis-'kȯl\ vb : MISNAME

mis·car·riage \-'ker-ij\ n 1 : failure in the administration of justice 2 : spontaneous expulsion of a fetus before it is capable of independent life

mis·car·ry \-'ker-ē\ vb 1 : to have a miscarriage of a fetus 2 : to go wrong; also : to be unsuccessful

mis·ce·ge·na·tion \ˌmi-si-jə-'nā-shən, ˌmi-si-jə-'nā-\ n [L miscēre to mix + genus race] : marriage, cohabitation, or sexual intercourse between persons of different races

mis·cel·la·neous \ˌmi-sə-'lā-nē-əs\ adj 1 : consisting of diverse things or members 2 : having various traits; also : dealing with or interested in diverse subjects — **mis·cel·la·neous·ly** adv — **mis·cel·la·neous·ness** n

mis·cel·la·ny \'mi-sə-ˌlā-nē\ n, pl -nies 1 : a collection of writings on various subjects 2 : HODGEPODGE

mis·chance \mis-'chans\ n : bad luck; also : MISHAP

mis·chief \'mis-chəf\ n [ME meschief, fr. AF, misfortune, hardship, fr. OF meschever to come out badly, fr. mes- badly + chief head, end] 1 : injury caused by a particular agent 2 : a source of harm or irritation 3 : action that annoys; also : MISCHIEVOUSNESS

mis·chie·vous \'mis-chə-vəs\ adj 1 : HARMFUL, INJURIOUS 2 : causing annoyance or minor injury 3 : irresponsi-

bly playful — **mis·chie·vous·ly** adv — **mis·chie·vous·ness** n

mis·ci·ble \'mi-sə-bəl\ adj : capable of being mixed

mis·com·mu·ni·ca·tion \ˌmis-kə-ˌmyü-nə-'kā-shən\ n : failure to communicate clearly

mis·con·ceive \ˌmis-kən-'sēv\ vb : to interpret incorrectly — **mis·con·cep·tion** \-'sep-shən\ n

mis·con·duct \mis-'kän-(ˌ)dəkt\ n 1 : MISMANAGEMENT 2 : intentional wrongdoing 3 : improper behavior; also : a penalty in a sport for improper behavior

mis·con·strue \ˌmis-kən-'strü\ vb : MISINTERPRET — **mis·con·struc·tion** \-'strək-shən\ n

mis·count \mis-'kaunt\ vb : to count incorrectly : MISCALCULATE

mis·cre·ant \'mis-krē-ənt\ n : one who behaves criminally or viciously — **miscreant** adj

mis·cue \mis-'kyü\ n : MISTAKE, ERROR — **miscue** vb

mis·deed \mis-'dēd\ n : a wrong deed

mis·de·mean·or \ˌmis-di-'mē-nər\ n 1 : a crime less serious than a felony 2 : MISDEED

mis·di·rect \ˌmis-də-'rekt, -dī-\ vb : to give a wrong direction to — **mis·di·rec·tion** \-'rek-shən\ n

mis·do·ing \mis-'dü-iŋ\ n : WRONGDOING — **misdo** \-'dü\ vb — **mis·do·er** \-'dü-ər\ n

mise—en—scène \ˌmē-ˌzän-'sen, -'sän\ n, pl **mise—en—scènes** \same or -'senz, -'sänz\ [F] 1 : the arrangement of the scenery, property, and actors on a stage 2 : SETTING; also : ENVIRONMENT

mi·ser \'mī-zər\ n [L miser miserable] : a person who hoards and is stingy with money — **mi·ser·li·ness** \-lē-nəs\ n — **mi·ser·ly** adj

mis·er·a·ble \'mi-zə-rə-bəl, 'miz-rə-\ adj 1 : wretchedly deficient; also : causing extreme discomfort 2 : being in a state of distress 3 : SHAMEFUL — **mis·er·a·ble·ness** n — **mis·er·a·bly** \-blē\ adv

mis·ery \'mi-zə-rē\ n, pl -er·ies 1 : suffering and want caused by poverty or affliction 2 : a cause of suffering or discomfort 3 : emotional distress

mis·fea·sance \mis-'fē-zⁿns\ n : the performance of a lawful action in an illegal or improper manner

mis·file \-'fī(-ə)l\ vb : to file in the wrong place

mis·fire \-'fī(-ə)r\ vb 1 : to fail to fire 2 : to miss an intended effect — **misfire** n

mis·fit \'mis-ˌfit, sense 1 also mis-'fit\ n 1 : something that fits badly 2 : a person who is poorly adjusted to a situation or environment

mis·for·tune \mis-'fȯr-chən\ n 1 : bad luck 2 : an unfortunate condition or event

mis·giv·ing \-'gi-viŋ\ n : a feeling of doubt or suspicion esp. concerning a future event

mis·gov·ern \-'gə-vərn\ *vb* : to govern badly — **mis·gov·ern·ment** *n*

mis·guid·ance \mis-'gī-dᵊns\ *n* : faulty guidance — **mis·guide** \-'gīd\ *vb*

mis·guid·ed \-'gī-dəd\ *adj* : led or prompted by wrong or inappropriate motives or ideals — **mis·guid·ed·ly** *adv*

mis·han·dle \-'han-dᵊl\ *vb* 1 : MALTREAT 2 : to manage wrongly

mis·hap \'mis-ˌhap\ *n* : an unfortunate accident

mish·mash \'mish-ˌmash, -ˌmäsh\ *n* : HODGEPODGE, JUMBLE

mis·in·form \ˌmi-sᵊn-'fȯrm\ *vb* : to give false or misleading information to — **mis·in·for·ma·tion** \ˌmi-ˌsin-fər-'mā-shən\ *n*

mis·in·ter·pret \ˌmi-sᵊn-'tər-prət\ *vb* : to understand or explain wrongly — **mis·in·ter·pre·ta·tion** \-ˌtər-prə-'tā-shən\ *n*

mis·judge \-'jəj\ *vb* 1 : to estimate wrongly 2 : to have an unjust opinion of — **mis·judg·ment** \mis-'jəj-mənt\ *n*

mis·la·bel \-'lā-bəl\ *vb* : to label incorrectly or falsely ⟨was ∼ed a liar⟩

mis·lay \mis-'lā\ *vb* **-laid** \-'lād\; **-lay·ing** : MISPLACE, LOSE ⟨mislaid his keys⟩

mis·lead \mis-'lēd\ *vb* **-led** \-'led\; **-lead·ing** : to lead in a wrong direction or into a mistaken action or belief — **mis·lead·ing·ly** *adv*

mis·like \-'līk\ *vb* : DISLIKE — **mis·like** *n*

mis·man·age \-'ma-nij\ *vb* : to manage badly — **mis·man·age·ment** *n*

mis·match \-'mach\ *vb* : to match unsuitably or badly — **mis·match** \mis-'mach, 'mis-ˌmach\ *n*

mis·name \-'nām\ *vb* : to name incorrectly : MISCALL

mis·no·mer \mis-'nō-mər\ *n* : a wrong or inappropriate name or designation

mi·so \'mē-sō\ *n* : a high-protein fermented food paste consisting chiefly of soybeans, salt, and usu. grain

mi·sog·y·ny \mə-'sä-jə-nē\ *n* [Gk *misogynia*, fr. *misein* to hate + *gynē* woman] : a hatred of women — **mi·sog·y·nist** \-nist\ *n or adj* — **mi·sog·y·nis·tic** \mə-ˌsä-jə-'nis-tik\ *adj*

mis·ori·ent \mi-'sȯr-ē-ˌent\ *vb* : to orient improperly or incorrectly — **mis·ori·en·ta·tion** \mi-ˌsȯr-ē-ən-'tā-shən\ *n*

mis·place \mis-'plās\ *vb* 1 : to put in a wrong or unremembered place 2 : to set on a wrong object ⟨∼ trust⟩

mis·play \-'plā\ *n* : a wrong or unskillful play — **mis·play** \mis-'plā, 'mis-ˌplā\ *vb*

mis·print \'mis-ˌprint\ *n* : a mistake in printed matter — **mis·print** \mis-'print\ *vb*

mis·pro·nounce \ˌmis-prə-'naůns\ *vb* : to pronounce incorrectly — **mis·pro·nun·ci·a·tion** \-prə-ˌnən-sē-'ā-shən\ *n*

mis·quote \mis-'kwōt\ *vb* : to quote incorrectly — **mis·quo·ta·tion** \ˌmis-kwō-'tā-shən\ *n*

mis·read \-'rēd\ *vb* **-read** \-'red\; **-read·ing** \-'rē-diŋ\ : to read or interpret incorrectly ⟨∼ her expression⟩

mis·rep·re·sent \ˌmis-ˌre-pri-'zent\ *vb* : to represent falsely or unfairly ⟨∼the facts⟩ — **mis·rep·re·sen·ta·tion** \-ˌzen-'tā-shən\ *n*

¹**mis·rule** \mis-'rül\ *vb* : MISGOVERN

²**misrule** *n* 1 : MISGOVERNMENT 2 : DISORDER

¹**miss** \'mis\ *vb* 1 : to fail to hit, reach, or contact 2 : to feel the absence of 3 : to fail to obtain 4 : AVOID ⟨just ∼ed hitting the other car⟩ 5 : OMIT 6 : to fail to understand ⟨∼ the point⟩ 7 : to fail to perform or attend; *also* : MISFIRE

²**miss** *n* 1 : a failure to hit or to attain a result 2 : MISFIRE

³**miss** *n* 1 *cap* — used as a title prefixed to the name of an unmarried woman or girl 2 : a young unmarried woman or girl

Miss *abbr* Mississippi

mis·sal \'mi-səl\ *n* : a book containing all that is said or sung at mass during the entire year

mis·send \mis-'send\ *vb* : to send incorrectly (as to a wrong destination)

mis·shap·en \-'shā-pən\ *adj* : badly shaped : having an ugly shape

mis·sile \'mi-səl\ *n* [L, fr. neut. of *missilis* capable of being thrown, fr. *mittere* to let go, send] : an object (as a stone, bullet, or rocket) thrown or projected usu. so as to strike a target

miss·ing \'mi-siŋ\ *adj* : ABSENT; *also* : LOST ⟨∼ in action⟩

mis·sion \'mi-shən\ *n* 1 : a group of missionaries; *also* : a place where missionaries work 2 : a group of envoys to a foreign country; *also* : a team of specialists or cultural leaders sent to a foreign country 3 : TASK, OBJECTIVE

¹**mis·sion·ary** \'mi-shə-ˌner-ē\ *adj* : of, relating to, or engaged in missions

²**missionary** *n, pl* **-ar·ies** : a person commissioned by a church to spread its faith or carry on humanitarian work

mis·sion·er \'mi-shə-nər\ *n* : MISSIONARY

Mis·sis·sip·pi·an \ˌmi-sə-'si-pē-ən\ *adj* 1 : of or relating to Mississippi, its people, or the Mississippi River 2 : of, relating to, or being the period of the Paleozoic era between the Devonian and the Pennsylvanian — **Mississippian** *n*

mis·sive \'mi-siv\ *n* : LETTER

mis·speak \mis-'spēk\ *vb* : to say imperfectly or incorrectly

mis·spell \-'spel\ *vb* : to spell incorrectly — **mis·spell·ing** *n*

mis·spend \-'spend\ *vb* **-spent** \-'spent\; **-spend·ing** : WASTE, SQUANDER ⟨my misspent youth⟩

mis·state \mis-'stāt\ *vb* : to state incorrectly — **mis·state·ment** *n*

mis·step \-'step\ *n* 1 : a wrong step 2 : MISTAKE, BLUNDER

mist \'mist\ *n* 1 : water in the form of particles suspended or falling in the air 2 : something that obscures understanding — **mist** *vb*

mis·tak·able \mə-'stā-kə-bəl\ *adj* : capable of being misunderstood or mistaken

¹**mis·take** \mə-'stāk\ *vb* **-took** \-'stůk\; **-tak·en** \-'stā-kən\; **-tak·ing** 1 : to blunder in the choice of 2 : MISINTERPRET

3 : to make a wrong judgment of the character or ability of **4** : to confuse with another — **mis·tak·en·ly** adv — **mis·tak·er** n

²**mistake** n **1** : a wrong judgment : MISUNDERSTANDING **2** : a wrong action or statement : ERROR

¹**mis·ter** \'mis-tər\ n **1** cap — used sometimes instead of Mr. **2** : SIR — used without a name in addressing a man

²**mist·er** \'mis-tər\ n : a device for spraying mist

mis·tle·toe \'mi-səl-ˌtō\ n : a European parasitic green shrub that grows on trees and has yellowish flowers and waxy white berries

mis·tral \'mis-trəl, mi-'sträl\ n [F, fr. Occitan, fr. mistral masterful, fr. LL magistralis of a teacher, fr. L magister master] : a strong cold dry northerly wind of southern France

mis·treat \mis-'trēt\ vb : to treat badly : ABUSE — **mis·treat·ment** n

mis·tress \'mis-trəs\ n **1** : a woman who has power, authority, or ownership ⟨∼ of the house⟩ **2** : something personified as female that rules or dominates ⟨when Rome was ∼ of the world⟩ **3** : a woman other than his wife with whom a married man has sexual relations; also, archaic : SWEETHEART **4** — used archaically as a title prefixed to the name of a married or unmarried woman

mis·tri·al \'mis-ˌtrī(-ə)l\ n : a trial that has no legal effect

¹**mis·trust** \mis-'trəst\ n : a lack of confidence : DISTRUST — **mis·trust·ful** \-fəl\ adj — **mis·trust·ful·ly** adv — **mis·trust·ful·ness** n

²**mistrust** vb : to have no trust or confidence in : SUSPECT

misty \'mis-tē\ adj **mist·i·er; -est 1** : obscured by or as if by mist : INDISTINCT **2** : TEARFUL — **mist·i·ly** \-tə-lē\ adv — **mist·i·ness** \-tē-nəs\ n

mis·un·der·stand \ˌmi-ˌsən-dər-'stand\ vb **-stood** \-'stud\; **-stand·ing 1** : to fail to understand **2** : to interpret incorrectly

mis·un·der·stand·ing \-'stan-diŋ\ n **1** : MISINTERPRETATION **2** : DISAGREEMENT, QUARREL

mis·us·age \mis-'yü-sij\ n **1** : bad treatment : ABUSE **2** : wrong or improper use

mis·use \mis-'yüz\ vb **1** : to use incorrectly **2** : ABUSE, MISTREAT — **mis·use** \-'yüs\ n

¹**mite** \'mīt\ n : any of numerous tiny arthropod animals related to the spiders that often live and feed on animals or plants

²**mite** n **1** : a small coin or sum of money **2** : a small amount : BIT

¹**mi·ter** or **mi·tre** \'mī-tər\ n [ME mitre, fr. AF, fr. L mitra headband, turban, fr. Gk] **1** : a headdress worn by bishops and abbots **2** : MITER JOINT

²**miter** or **mitre** vb **mi·tered** or **mi·tred**; **mi·ter·ing** or **mi·tring** \'mī-tə-riŋ\ **1** : to match or fit together in a miter joint **2** : to bevel the ends of for making a miter joint

miter joint n : a usu. perpendicular joint made by fitting together two parts with the ends cut at an angle

mit·i·gate \'mi-tə-ˌgāt\ vb **-gat·ed; -gat·ing 1** : to make less harsh or hostile **2** : to make less severe or painful — **mit·i·ga·tion** \ˌmi-tə-'gā-shən\ n — **mit·i·ga·tive** \'mi-tə-ˌgā-tiv\ adj

mi·to·chon·dri·on \ˌmī-tə-'kän-drē-ən\ n, pl **-dria** \-drē-ə\ : any of various round or long cellular organelles that produce energy for the cell — **mi·to·chon·dri·al** \-drē-əl\ adj

mi·to·sis \mī-'tō-səs\ n, pl **-to·ses** \-ˌsēz\ : a process that takes place in the nucleus of a dividing cell and results in the formation of two new nuclei each of which has the same number of chromosomes as the parent nucleus; also : cell division in which mitosis occurs — **mi·tot·ic** \-'tä-tik\ adj

mitt \'mit\ n, **1** : a baseball catcher's or first baseman's glove **2** slang : HAND

mit·ten \'mi-tᵊn\ n : a covering for the hand having a separate section for the thumb only — **mit·tened** \-tᵊnd\ adj

¹**mix** \'miks\ vb **1** : to combine into one mass **2** : ASSOCIATE **3** : to form by mingling components **4** : to produce (a recording) by electronically combining sounds from different sources **5** : HYBRIDIZE **6** : CONFUSE ⟨∼es up the facts⟩ **7** : to become involved ◆ Synonyms BLEND, MERGE, COALESCE, AMALGAMATE, FUSE — **mix·able** adj — **mix it up** : to engage in a fight, contest, or dispute

²**mix** n : a product of mixing; esp : a commercially prepared mixture of food ingredients

mixed \'mikst\ adj **1** : combining features of more than one kind **2** : made up of or involving individuals or items of more than one kind **3** : including or accompanied by different or opposing elements ⟨a ∼ blessing⟩ **4** : resulting from the crossing or breeding of individuals of different races or breeds ⟨a stallion of ∼ blood⟩

mixed number n : a number (as $5^2/_3$) composed of an integer and a fraction

mixed-up \'mikst-'əp\ adj : CONFUSED

mix·er \'mik-sər\ n **1** : one that mixes; esp : a machine or device for mixing **2** : an event (as a dance) that encourages meeting and socializing **3** : a nonalcoholic beverage used in a cocktail

mixt abbr mixture

mix·ture \'miks-chər\ n **1** : the act or process of mixing; also : the state of being mixed **2** : a product of mixing

mix-up \'miks-ˌəp\ n **1** : an instance of confusion **2** : CONFLICT, FIGHT

miz·zen also **miz·en** \'mi-zᵊn\ n **1** : a fore-and-aft sail set on the mizzenmast **2** : MIZZENMAST — **mizzen** also **mizen** adj

miz·zen·mast \-ˌmast, -məst\ n : the mast aft or next aft of the mainmast

mk abbr **1** mark **2** markka

Mk abbr Mark

mks abbr meter-kilogram-second

mkt *abbr* market
mktg *abbr* marketing
ml *abbr* milliliter
Mlle *abbr* [F] mademoiselle
Mlles *abbr* [F] mesdemoiselles
mm *abbr* millimeter
MM *abbr* [F] messieurs
Mme *abbr* [F] madame
Mmes *abbr* [F] mesdames
Mn *symbol* manganese
MN *abbr* Minnesota
mne·mon·ic \nə-ˈmä-nik\ *adj* : assisting or designed to assist memory; *also* : of or relating to memory
mo *abbr* month
¹**Mo** *abbr* **1** Missouri **2** Monday
²**Mo** *symbol* molybdenum
MO *abbr* **1** mail order **2** medical officer **3** Missouri **4** modus operandi **5** money order
moan \ˈmōn\ *n* : a low prolonged sound indicative of pain or grief — **moan** *vb*
moat \ˈmōt\ *n* : a deep wide usu. water-filled trench around a castle
¹**mob** \ˈmäb\ *n* [L *mobile vulgus* vacillating crowd] **1** : MASSES, RABBLE **2** : a disorderly crowd **3** : a criminal gang
²**mob** *vb* **mobbed; mob·bing 1** : to crowd about and attack or annoy ⟨*mobbed* by fans⟩ **2** : to crowd into or around ⟨shoppers *mobbed* the stores⟩
¹**mo·bile** \ˈmō-bəl, -ˌbī(-ə)l, -ˌbēl\ *adj* **1** : capable of moving or being moved **2** : changeable in appearance, mood, or purpose; *also* : ADAPTABLE **3** : having the opportunity for or undergoing a shift in social status **4** : using vehicles for transportation ⟨~ warfare⟩ **5** : CELLULAR **2** — **mo·bil·i·ty** \mō-ˈbi-lə-tē\ *n*
²**mo·bile** \ˈmō-ˌbēl\ *n* : a construction or sculpture (as of wire and sheet metal) with parts that can be set in motion by air currents; *also* : a similar structure suspended so that it is moved by a current of air
mobile home *n* : a trailer used as a permanent dwelling
mo·bi·lise *chiefly Brit var of* MOBILIZE
mo·bi·lize \ˈmō-bə-ˌlīz\ *vb* **-lized; -liz·ing 1** : to put into movement or circulation **2** : to assemble and make ready for action ⟨~ army reserves⟩ — **mo·bi·li·za·tion** \ˌmō-bə-lə-ˈzā-shən\ *n* — **mo·bi·liz·er** \ˈmō-bə-ˌlī-zər\ *n*
mob·ster \ˈmäb-stər\ *n* : a member of a criminal gang
moc·ca·sin \ˈmä-kə-sən\ *n* **1** : a soft leather heelless shoe **2** : WATER MOCCASIN
mo·cha \ˈmō-kə\ *n* [*Mocha,* port in Yemen] **1** : choice coffee grown in Arabia **2** : a mixture of coffee and chocolate or cocoa **3** : a dark chocolate-brown color
¹**mock** \ˈmäk, ˈmȯk\ *vb* **1** : to treat with contempt or ridicule **2** : DELUDE **3** : DEFY **4** : to mimic in sport or derision — **mock·er** *n* — **mock·ery** \ˈmä-kə-rē, ˈmȯ-\ *n* — **mock·ing·ly** *adv*
²**mock** *adj* : SIMULATED ⟨a ~ trial⟩
mock–he·ro·ic \ˌmäk-hi-ˈrō-ik, ˌmȯk-\

adj : ridiculing or burlesquing heroic style, character, or action ⟨a ~ poem⟩
mock·ing·bird \ˈmä-kiŋ-ˌbərd, ˈmȯ-\ *n* : a grayish No. American songbird related to the catbirds and thrashers that mimics the calls of other birds
mock–up \ˈmä-ˌkəp, ˈmȯ-\ *n* **1** : a full-sized structural model built for study, testing, or display ⟨a ~ of a car⟩ **2** : a working sample (as of a magazine) for review
¹**mod** \ˈmäd\ *adj* **1** : of, relating to, or being the style of the 1960s British youth culture **2** : HIP, TRENDY
²**mod** *abbr* **1** moderate **2** modern **3** modification; modified
mode \ˈmōd\ *n* **1** : a particular form or variety of something; *also* : STYLE **2** : a manner of doing something **3** : the most frequent value of a set of data — **mod·al** \ˈmō-dᵊl\ *adj*
¹**mod·el** \ˈmä-dᵊl\ *n* **1** : structural design **2** : a miniature representation; *also* : a pattern of something to be made **3** : an example for imitation or emulation **4** : one who poses (as for an artist or to display clothes) **5** : TYPE, DESIGN ⟨a new car ~⟩
²**model** *vb* **mod·eled** *or* **mod·elled; mod·el·ing** *or* **mod·el·ling 1** : SHAPE, FASHION, CONSTRUCT ⟨~ed in clay⟩ **2** : to work as a fashion model
³**model** *adj* **1** : serving as or worthy of being a pattern ⟨a ~ student⟩ **2** : being a miniature representation of something ⟨a ~ airplane⟩
mo·dem \ˈmō-dəm, -ˌdem\ *n* : a device that converts signals from one device (as a computer) to a form compatible with another (as a telephone)
¹**mod·er·ate** \ˈmä-də-rət\ *adj* **1** : avoiding extremes; *also* : TEMPERATE **2** : AVERAGE; *also* : MEDIOCRE **3** : limited in scope or effect **4** : not expensive — **moderate** *n* — **mod·er·ate·ly** *adv* — **mod·er·ate·ness** *n*
²**mod·er·ate** \ˈmä-də-ˌrāt\ *vb* **-at·ed; -at·ing 1** : to lessen the intensity of : TEMPER **2** : to act as a moderator — **mod·er·a·tion** \ˌmä-də-ˈrā-shən\ *n*
mod·er·a·tor \ˈmä-də-ˌrā-tər\ *n* **1** : MEDIATOR **2** : one who presides over an assembly, meeting, or discussion
mod·ern \ˈmä-dərn\ *adj* [LL *modernus,* fr. L *modo* just now, fr. *modus* measure] : of, relating to, or characteristic of the present or the immediate past : CONTEMPORARY — **modern** *n* — **mo·der·ni·ty** \mə-ˈdər-nə-tē\ *n* — **mod·ern·ly** *adv* — **mod·ern·ness** *n*
mod·ern·ise, mod·ern·i·sa·tion *Brit var of* MODERNIZE, MODERNIZATION
mod·ern·ism \ˈmä-dər-ˌni-zəm\ *n* : a practice, movement, or belief peculiar to modern times
mod·ern·ize \ˈmä-dər-ˌnīz\ *vb* **-ized; -iz·ing** : to make or become modern — **mod·ern·i·za·tion** \ˌmä-dər-nə-ˈzā-shən\ *n* — **mod·ern·iz·er** *n*
mod·est \ˈmä-dəst\ *adj* **1** : having a moderate estimate of oneself; *also* : DIFFI-

DENT **2** : observing the proprieties of dress and behavior **3** : limited in size, amount, or scope ⟨a ~ income⟩ — **mod-est-ly** *adv* — **mod-es-ty** \-də-stē\ *n*

mod-i-cum \'mä-di-kəm\ *n* : a small amount

modif *abbr* modification

mod-i-fy \'mä-də-ˌfī\ *vb* **-fied; -fy-ing 1** : MODERATE **2** : to limit the meaning of esp. in a grammatical construction **3** : CHANGE, ALTER — **mod-i-fi-ca-tion** \ˌmä-də-fə-ˈkā-shən\ *n* — **mod-i-fi-er** \'mä-də-ˌfī-ər\ *n*

mod-ish \'mō-dish\ *adj* : FASHIONABLE, STYLISH — **mod-ish-ly** *adv* — **mod-ish-ness** *n*

mo-diste \mō-'dēst\ *n* : a maker of fashionable dresses and hats

mod-u-lar \'mä-jə-lər\ *adj* : constructed with standardized units

mod-u-lar-ized \'mä-jə-lə-ˌrīzd\ *adj* : containing or consisting of modules

mod-u-late \'mä-jə-ˌlāt\ *vb* **-lat-ed; -lat-ing 1** : to tune to a key or pitch **2** : to keep in proper measure or proportion : TEMPER **3** : to vary the amplitude or frequency of a carrier wave for the transmission of information (as in radio or television) — **mod-u-la-tion** \ˌmä-jə-ˈlā-shən\ *n* — **mod-u-la-tor** \'mä-jə-ˌlā-tər\ *n* — **mod-u-la-to-ry** \-lə-ˌtór-ē\ *adj*

mod-ule \'mä-jül\ *n* **1** : any in a series of standardized units for use together **2** : an assembly of wired electronic parts for use with other such assemblies **3** : an independent unit that constitutes a part of the total structure of a space vehicle ⟨a propulsion ~⟩

mo-dus ope-ran-di \ˌmō-dəs-ˌä-pə-'ran-dē, -ˌdī\ *n, pl* **mo-di operandi** \ˌmō-dē-, ˌmō-ˌdī-\ [NL] : a method of procedure

¹mo-gul \'mō-gəl, mō-'gəl\ *n* [fr. *Mogul*, member of a Muslim dynasty ruling northern India] : an important person : MAGNATE ⟨a media ~⟩

²mogul \'mō-gəl\ *n* : a bump in a ski run

mo-hair \'mō-ˌher\ *n* [modif. of obs. It *mocaiarro*, fr. Ar *mukhayyar*, lit., choice] : a fabric or yarn made wholly or in part from the long silky hair of the Angora goat; *also* : this goat hair

Mo-ham-med-an *also* **Mu-ham-mad-an** \mō-'ha-mə-dən, -'hä-, mü-\ *n* : MUSLIM — **Mo-ham-med-an-ism** *also* **Mu-ham-mad-an-ism** \-də-ˌni-zəm\ *n*

Mo-hawk \'mō-ˌhók\ *n, pl* **Mohawk** *or* **Mohawks 1** : a member of an American Indian people of the Mohawk River valley, New York; *also* : the language of the Mohawk people **2** : a hairstyle with a narrow strip of upright hair down the center and the sides shaved

Mo-he-gan \mō-'hē-gən, mə-\ *or* **Mo-hi-can** \-'hē-kən\ *n, pl* **Mohegan** *or* **Mohegans** *or* **Mohican** *or* **Mohicans** : a member of an American Indian people of southeastern Connecticut

mo-hel \'mō-(h)el, 'mói-(ə)l\ *n, pl* **mohels** *also* **mo-hal-im** \mō-hä-'lēm\ *also* **mo-hel-im** \-(h)e-'lēm\ : a person who performs Jewish circumcisions

Mohican *var of* MAHICAN

moi-e-ty \'mói-ə-tē\ *n, pl* **-ties** : one of two equal or approximately equal parts

moil \'mói(-ə)l\ *vb* : to work hard : DRUDGE — **moil** *n* — **moil-er** *n*

moi-ré \mó-'rā, mwä-\ *or* **moire** *same or* 'mói r, 'mwär\ *n* : a fabric (as silk) having a watered appearance

moist \'móist\ *adj* : slightly or moderately wet — **moist-ly** *adv* — **moist-ness** *n*

moist-en \'mói-sᵊn\ *vb* : to make or become moist — **moist-en-er** *n*

mois-ture \'móis-chər\ *n* : the small amount of liquid that causes dampness

mois-tur-ise *Brit var of* MOISTURIZE

mois-tur-ize \'móis-chə-ˌrīz\ *vb* **-ized; -iz-ing** : to add moisture to ⟨~ the skin⟩ — **mois-tur-iz-er** *n*

mol *abbr* molecular; molecule

mo-lar \'mō-lər\ *n* [ME *molares*, pl., fr. L *molaris*, fr. *molaris* of a mill, fr. *mola* millstone] : any of the broad teeth adapted to grinding food and located in the back of the jaw — **molar** *adj*

mo-las-ses \mə-'la-səz\ *n* : the thick brown syrup that is separated from raw sugar in sugar manufacture

¹mold \'mōld\ *n* : crumbly soil rich in organic matter

²mold *n* **1** : distinctive nature or character **2** : the frame on or around which something is constructed **3** : a cavity in which something is shaped; *also* : an object so shaped **4** : MOLDING

³mold *vb* **1** : to shape in or as if in a mold **2** : to ornament with molding — **mold-er** *n*

⁴mold *n* : a surface growth of fungus esp. on damp or decaying matter; *also* : a fungus that produces mold — **mold-i-ness** \'mōl-dē-nəs\ *n* — **moldy** *adj*

⁵mold *vb* : to become moldy

mold-board \'mōld-ˌbórd\ *n* : a curved iron plate attached above the plowshare to lift and turn the soil

mold-er \'mōl-dər\ *vb* : to crumble into small pieces

mold-ing \'mōl-diŋ\ *n* **1** : an act or process of shaping in a mold; *also* : an object so shaped **2** : a decorative surface, plane, or curved strip

¹mole \'mōl\ *n* : a small often pigmented spot or protuberance on the skin

²mole *n* **1** : any of numerous small burrowing insect-eating mammals related to the shrews and hedgehogs **2** : a spy embedded within an organization

³mole *n* : a massive breakwater or jetty

molecular biology *n* : a branch of biology dealing with the ultimate physical and chemical organization of living matter and esp. with the molecular basis of inheritance and protein synthesis — **molecular biologist** *n*

molecular weight *n* : the mass of a molecule that is equal to the sum of the masses of all atoms contained in the molecule's formula

mol-e-cule \'mä-li-ˌkyül\ *n* : the smallest particle of matter that is the same chemically as the whole mass — **mo-lec-u-lar** \mə-'le-kyə-lər\ *adj*

mole·hill \'mōl-ˌhil\ *n* : a little ridge of earth thrown up by a mole

mole·skin \-ˌskin\ *n* **1** : the skin of the mole used as fur **2** : a heavy durable cotton fabric

mo·lest \mə-'lest\ *vb* **1** : ANNOY, DISTURB **2** : to make annoying sexual advances to; *esp* : to force physical and usu. sexual contact on — **mo·les·ta·tion** \ˌmō-ˌles-'tā-shən\ *n* — **mo·lest·er** *n*

moll \'mäl\ *n* : a gangster's girlfriend

mol·li·fy \'mä-lə-ˌfī\ *vb* **-fied; -fy·ing** **1** : to soothe in temper : APPEASE **2** : SOFTEN **3** : to reduce in intensity : ASSUAGE — **mol·li·fi·ca·tion** \ˌmä-lə-fə-'kā-shən\ *n*

mol·lusk *or* **mol·lusc** \'mä-ləsk\ *n* : any of a large phylum of usu. shelled and aquatic invertebrate animals (as snails, clams, and squids) — **mol·lus·can** *also* **mol·lus·kan** \mə-'ləs-kən\ *adj*

1mol·ly·cod·dle \'mä-lē-ˌkä-d²l\ *n* : a pampered man or boy

2mollycoddle *vb* **mol·ly·cod·dled; mol·ly·cod·dling** : PAMPER

Mo·lo·tov cocktail \'mä-lə-ˌtȯf-, 'mō-\ *n* [Vyacheslav M. *Molotov* †1986 Soviet foreign minister] : a crude bomb made of a bottle filled usu. with gasoline and fitted with a wick (as a saturated rag) that is ignited just prior to hurling

1molt \'mōlt\ *vb* : to shed hair, feathers, outer skin, or horns periodically with the cast-off parts being replaced by new growth — **molt·er** *n*

2molt *n* : the act or process of molting

mol·ten \'mōl-t²n\ *adj* **1** : fused or liquefied by heat **2** : GLOWING

mo·ly \'mō-lē\ *n* : a mythical herb with black root, white flowers, and magic powers

mo·lyb·de·num \mə-'lib-də-nəm\ *n* : a metallic chemical element used in strengthening and hardening steel

mom \'mäm, 'məm\ *n* : MOTHER

mom–and–pop *adj* : being a small owner-operated business

mo·ment \'mō-mənt\ *n* **1** : a minute portion of time : INSTANT **2** : a time of excellence ⟨he has his ∼s⟩ **3** : IMPORTANCE ♦ *Synonyms* CONSEQUENCE, SIGNIFICANCE, WEIGHT, IMPORT

mo·men·tar·i·ly \ˌmō-mən-'ter-ə-lē\ *adv* **1** : for a moment **2** *archaic* : INSTANTLY **3** : at any moment : SOON

mo·men·tary \'mō-mən-ˌter-ē\ *adj* **1** : continuing only a moment; *also* : EPHEMERAL **2** : recurring at every moment — **mo·men·tar·i·ness** \-ˌter-ē-nəs\ *n*

mo·men·tous \mō-'men-təs\ *adj* : very important — **mo·men·tous·ly** *adv* — **mo·men·tous·ness** *n*

mo·men·tum \mō-'men-təm\ *n, pl* **mo·men·ta** \-'men-tə\ *or* **momentums** : a property that a moving body has due to its mass and motion; *also* : IMPETUS

mom·my \'mä-mē, 'mə-\ *n, pl* **mom·mies** : MOTHER

Mon *abbr* Monday

mon·arch \'mä-nərk, -ˌnärk\ *n* **1** : a person who reigns over a kingdom or an empire **2** : one holding preeminent position or power **3** : MONARCH BUTTERFLY —**mo·nar·chi·cal** \mə-'när-ki-kəl\ *also* **mo·nar·chic** \-'när-kik\ *adj*

monarch butterfly *n* : a large orange and black migratory American butterfly whose larva feeds on milkweed

mon·ar·chist \'mä-nər-kist\ *n* : a believer in monarchical government — **mon·ar·chism** \-ˌki-zəm\ *n*

mon·ar·chy \'mä-nər-kē\ *n, pl* **-chies** : a nation or state governed by a monarch

mon·as·tery \'mä-nə-ˌster-ē\ *n, pl* **-ter·ies** : a house for persons under religious vows (as monks)

mo·nas·tic \mə-'nas-tik\ *adj* : of or relating to monasteries or to monks or nuns — **monastic** *n* — **mo·nas·ti·cal·ly** \-ti-k(ə-)lē\ *adv* — **mo·nas·ti·cism** \-tə-ˌsi-zəm\ *n*

mon·au·ral \mä-'nȯr-əl\ *adj* : MONOPHONIC — **mon·au·ral·ly** *adv*

Mon·day \'mən-dē, -ˌdā\ *n* : the second day of the week

mon·e·tary \'mä-nə-ˌter-ē, 'mə-\ *adj* : of or relating to money or to the mechanisms by which it is supplied and circulated in the economy

mon·ey \'mə-nē\ *n, pl* **moneys** *or* **monies** \'mə-nēz\ **1** : something (as metal currency) accepted as a medium of exchange **2** : wealth reckoned in monetary terms **3** : the 1st, 2d, and 3d places in a horse or dog race
☞ the MONEY table is on page 466

mon·eyed \'mə-nēd\ *adj* **1** : having money : WEALTHY **2** : consisting in or derived from money

mon·ey·lend·er \'mə-nē-ˌlen-dər\ *n* : one (as a bank or pawnbroker) whose business is lending money

money market *n* : the trade in short-term negotiable financial instruments

money of account *n* : a denominator of value or basis of exchange used in keeping accounts

money order *n* : an order purchased at a post office, bank, or telegraph office directing another office to pay a sum of money to a party named on it

mon·ger \'mən-gər, 'mäŋ-\ *n* **1** : DEALER **2** : one who tries to stir up or spread something — usu. used in combination ⟨warmonger⟩

mon·go \'mäŋ-(ˌ)gō\ *n, pl* **mongo** — see *tugrik* at MONEY table

Mon·gol \'mäŋ-gəl, 'män-ˌgōl\ *n* : a member of any of several traditionally pastoral peoples of Mongolia — **Mongol** *adj*

Mon·go·lian \män-'gōl-yən, mäŋ-, -'gō-lē-ən\ *n* **1** : a native or inhabitant of Mongolia **2** : a member of the Mongoloid racial stock — **Mongolian** *adj*

Mon·gol·oid \'mäŋ-gə-ˌlȯid\ *adj* : of or relating to a major racial stock native to Asia that includes peoples of northern and eastern Asia, Malaysians, Eskimos, and often American Indians — **Mongoloid** *n*

mon·goose \'män-ˌgüs, 'mäŋ-\ *n, pl* **mon·goos·es** *also* **mon·geese** \-ˌgēs\ : any of a group of small agile Old World

MONEY — WORLD CURRENCIES

NAME	SUBDIVISION	COUNTRY
afghani	100 puls	Afghanistan
baht *or* tical	100 satang	Thailand
balboa[1]	100 centesimos	Panama
birr	100 cents	Ethiopia
bolivar	100 centimos	Venezuela
boliviano	100 centavos	Bolivia
cedi	100 pesewas	Ghana
colón	100 centimos	Costa Rica
colón[1]	100 centavos	El Salvador
córdoba	100 centavos	Nicaragua
dalasi	100 bututs	Gambia
denar	100 deni[2]	Republic of Macedonia
dinar	100 centimes	Algeria
dinar	1000 fils	Bahrain
dinar	1000 fils	Iraq
dinar	1000 fils	Jordan
dinar	1000 fils	Kuwait
dinar	1000 dirhams	Libya
dinar		Sudan
dinar	1000 millimes	Tunisia
dirham	100 centimes	Morocco
dirham	100 fils	United Arab Emirates
dobra	100 centimos	São Tomé and Príncipe
dollar[3]	100 cents	Antigua and Barbuda, Dominica, Grenada, Guinea-Bissau, St. Kitts-Nevis, St. Lucia, St. Vincent and the Grenadines
dollar	100 cents	Australia
dollar	100 cents	Bahamas
dollar	100 cents	Barbados
dollar	100 cents	Belize
dollar	100 cents	Bermuda
dollar	100 sen *or* cents	Brunei
dollar	100 cents	Canada
dollar	100 cents	Fiji
dollar	100 cents	Guyana
dollar	100 cents	Hong Kong
dollar	100 cents	Jamaica
dollar	100 cents	Liberia
dollar	100 cents	Namibia
dollar	100 cents	New Zealand
dollar	100 cents	Singapore
dollar	100 cents	Solomon Islands
dollar *or* yuan	100 cents	Taiwan
dollar	100 cents	Trinidad and Tobago
dollar	100 cents	United States
dollar	100 cents	Zimbabwe
dollar — see RINGGIT, below		

NAME	SUBDIVISION	COUNTRY
dong	100 xu	Vietnam
dram	100 luma	Armenia
escudo	100 centavos	Cape Verde
euro[4]	100 cents	Austria, Belgium, Finland, France, Germany, Greece, Ireland, Italy, Luxembourg, Netherlands, Portugal, Spain
florin — see GULDEN, below		
forint	100 fillers	Hungary
franc[5]	100 centimes	Benin, Burkina Faso, Cameroon, Central African Republic, Chad, Republic of the Congo, Equatorial Guinea, Gabon, Ivory Coast, Mali, Niger, Senegal, Togo
franc	100 centimes	Burundi
franc	100 centimes	Comoros
franc	100 centimes	Democratic Republic of the Congo
franc	100 centimes	Djibouti
franc	100 centimes	Guinea
franc	100 centimes	Madagascar
franc	100 centimes[2]	Rwanda
franc	100 centimes *or* rappen	Switzerland
gourde	100 centimes	Haiti
guarani	100 centimos	Paraguay
gulden *or* florin	100 cents	Suriname
hryvnia	100 kopiykas	Ukraine
kina	100 toea	Papua New Guinea
kip	100 at	Laos
koruna	100 haleru	Czech Republic
koruna	100 haleru	Slovakia
krona	100 aurar (*sing* eyrir)	Iceland
krona	100 ore	Sweden
krone	100 ore	Denmark
krone	100 ore	Norway
kroon	100 senti (*sing* sent)	Estonia
kuna	100 lipa	Croatia
kwacha	100 tambala	Malawi
kwacha	100 ngwee	Zambia
kwanza	100 lwei	Angola
kyat	100 pyas	Myanmar
lari	100 tetri	Republic of Georgia
lats	100 santimi (*sing* santims)	Latvia
lek	100 qindarka (*sing* qintar)	Albania
lempira	100 centavos	Honduras
leone	100 cents	Sierra Leone

MONEY — WORLD CURRENCIES

NAME	SUBDIVISION	COUNTRY	NAME	SUBDIVISION	COUNTRY
leu	100 bani (*sing* ban)	Moldova	rial	1000 baiza	Oman
leu	100 bani (*sing* ban)	Romania	rial	100 fils	Yemen
lev	100 stotinki	Bulgaria	*also* riyal		
lilangeni (*pl* emalangeni)	100 cents	Swaziland	rial — see RIYAL, below		
lira	100 cents	Malta	riel	100 sen	Cambodia
or pound			ringgit	100 sen	Malaysia
lira	100 kurus	Turkey	*or* dollar		
litas	100 centai (*sing* centas)	Lithuania	riyal	100 dirhams	Qatar
livre — see POUND, below			riyal	100 halala	Saudi Arabia
loti	100 licente (*sing* sente)	Lesotho	*also* rial		
manat	100 gopik	Azerbaijan	riyal — see RIAL, above		
metical	100 centavos	Mozambique	ruble	100 kopecks	Russia
naira	100 kobo	Nigeria	rufiyaa	100 laari	Maldives
nakfa	100 cents	Eritrea	rupee	100 paisa	India
ngultrum	100 chetrums	Bhutan	rupee	100 cents	Mauritius
ouguiya	5 khoums	Mauritania	rupee	100 paisa	Nepal
pa'anga	100 seniti	Tonga	rupee	100 paisa	Pakistan
pataca	100 avos	Macao	rupee	100 cents	Seychelles
peso	100 centavos	Argentina	rupee	100 cents	Sri Lanka
peso	100 centavos	Chile	rupiah	100 sen	Indonesia
peso	100 centavos	Colombia	shekel	100 agorot	Israel
peso	100 centavos	Cuba	shilling	100 cents	Kenya
peso	100 centavos	Dominican Republic	shilling	100 cents	Somalia
peso	100 centavos	Mexico	shilling	100 cents	Tanzania
peso	100 sentimos *or* centavos	Philippines	shilling	100 cents	Uganda
or piso			sol	100 centimos	Peru
peso	100 centesimos	Uruguay	som	100 tyiyn	Kyrgyzstan
pound	100 cents	Cyprus	somoni	100 dirams	Tajikistan
pound	100 piastres	Egypt	sucre[1]	100 centavos	Ecuador
pound	100 piastres	Lebanon	taka	100 paisa *or* poisha	Bangladesh
or livre					
pound	100 piastres	Syria	tala	100 sene	Samoa
pound	100 pence (*sing* penny)	United Kingdom	tenge	100 tyin	Kazakhstan
			tical — see BAHT, above		
pound — see LIRA, above			tolar	100 stotinov (*sing* stotin)	Slovenia
pula	100 thebe	Botswana	tugrik	100 mongo	Mongolia
quetzal	100 centavos	Guatemala	vatu		Vanuatu
rand	100 cents	South Africa	won	100 chon	North Korea
real	100 centavos	Brazil	won	100 chon	South Korea
rial	100 dinars	Iran	yen	100 sen[2]	Japan
			yuan	100 fen	China
			yuan — see DOLLAR, above		
			zloty	100 groszy	Poland

[1] A monetary unit in name only; replaced by the U.S. dollar.

[2] Now a subdivision in name only.

[3] Dollars issued by the Eastern Caribbean Central Bank, established to promote economic cooperation among the member nations.

[4] Replaced the individual monetary units of participating European Union countries Jan. 1, 2002.

[5] Francs issued by the African Financial Community, established to promote economic cooperation among member nations.

mammals that are related to the civet cats and feed chiefly on small animals and fruits

mon·grel \'mäŋ-grəl, 'məŋ-\ n : an offspring of parents of different breeds; esp : one of uncertain ancestry

mon·i·ker \'mä-ni-kər\ n : NAME, NICKNAME

mo·nism \'mō-,ni-zəm, 'mä-\ n : a view that reality is basically one unitary organic whole — **mo·nist** \'mō-nist, 'mä-\ n

mo·ni·tion \mō-'ni-shən, mə-\ n : WARNING, CAUTION

¹**mon·i·tor** \'mä-nə-tər\ n 1 : a student appointed to assist a teacher 2 : one that monitors; esp : a video display screen (as for a computer)

²**monitor** vb : to watch, check, or observe for a special purpose

mon·i·to·ry \'mä-nə-,tór-ē\ adj : giving admonition : WARNING

¹**monk** \'məŋk\ n [ME, fr. OE munuc, fr. LL monachus, fr. LGk monachos, fr. Gk, adj., single, fr. monos single, alone] : a man belonging to a religious order and living in a monastery — **monk·ish** adj

²**monk** n : MONKEY

¹**mon·key** \'məŋ-kē\ n, pl **monkeys** : a nonhuman primate mammal; esp : one of the smaller, longer-tailed, and usu. more arboreal primates as contrasted with the apes

²**monkey** vb **mon·keyed; mon·key·ing** 1 : FOOL, TRIFLE — often used with around 2 : TAMPER — usu. used with with

monkey bars n pl : a framework of bars on which children can play

mon·key·shine \'məŋ-kē-,shīn\ n : PRANK — usu. used in pl.

monkey wrench n : a wrench with one fixed and one adjustable jaw at right angles to a handle

monk·fish \'məŋk-,fish\ n : either of two marine bony fishes that have a large flattened head and are used for food

monks·hood \'məŋks-,hùd\ n : any of a genus of poisonous plants related to the buttercups; esp : a tall Eurasian herb with white or purplish flowers

¹**mono** \'mä-nō\ adj : MONOPHONIC

²**mono** n : INFECTIOUS MONONUCLEOSIS

mono·chro·mat·ic \,mä-nə-krō-'ma-tik\ adj 1 : having or consisting of one color 2 : consisting of radiation (as light) of a single wavelength

mono·chrome \'mä-nə-,krōm\ adj : involving or producing visual images in a single colour or in varying tones of a single color ⟨~ television⟩

mon·o·cle \'mä-ni-kəl\ n : an eyeglass for one eye

mono·clo·nal \,mä-nə-'klō-nəl\ adj : produced by, being, or composed of cells derived from a single cell ⟨~ antibodies⟩

mono·cot·y·le·don \,mä-nə-,kät-tə-'lēdᵊn\ n : any of a class or subclass of chiefly herbaceous seed plants having an embryo with a single cotyledon and usu. parallel-veined leaves

mon·o·dy \'mä-nə-dē\ n, pl **-dies**

: ELEGY, DIRGE — **mo·nod·ic** \mə-'nädik\ or **mo·nod·i·cal** \-di-kəl\ adj — **mon·o·dist** \'mä-nə-dist\ n

mo·nog·a·my \mə-'nä-gə-mē\ n 1 : marriage with but one person at a time 2 : the practice of having a single mate during a period of time — **mo·nog·a·mist** \-mist\ n — **mo·nog·a·mous** \-məs\ adj

mono·gram \'mä-nə-,gram\ n : a sign of identity composed of the combined initials of a name — **monogram** vb

mono·graph \'mä-nə-,graf\ n : a learned treatise on a small area of learning

mono·lin·gual \,mä-nə-'liŋ-gwəl\ adj : knowing or using only one language

mono·lith \'mä-nə-,lith\ n 1 : a single great stone often in the form of a monument or column 2 : something large and powerful that acts as a single unified force — **mono·lith·ic** \,mä-nə-'li-thik\ adj

mono·logue also **mono·log** \'mä-nə-,lóg\ n 1 : a dramatic soliloquy; also : a long speech monopolizing conversation 2 : the routine of a stand-up comic — **mono·logu·ist** \-,lóg-ist\ or **mo·nol·o·gist** \mə-'nä-lə-jist; 'mä-nə-,lò-gist\ n

mono·ma·nia \,mä-nə-'mā-nē-ə, -nyə\ n 1 : mental disorder limited in expression to one area of thought 2 : excessive concentration on a single object or idea — **mono·ma·ni·ac** \-nē-,ak\ n or adj

mono·mer \'mä-nə-mər\ n : a simple chemical compound that can be polymerized

mono·nu·cle·o·sis \,mä-nō-,nü-klē-'ō-səs, -,nyü-\ n : INFECTIOUS MONONUCLEOSIS

mono·phon·ic \,mä-nə-'fä-nik\ adj : of or relating to sound recording or reproduction involving a single transmission path

mono·plane \'mä-nə-,plān\ n : an airplane with only one set of wings

mo·nop·o·ly \mə-'nä-pə-lē\ n, pl **-lies** [L monopolium, fr. Gk monopōlion, fr. monos alone, single + pōlein to sell] 1 : exclusive ownership (as through command of supply) 2 : a commodity controlled by one party 3 : one that has a monopoly — **mo·nop·o·list** \-list\ n — **mo·nop·o·lis·tic** \mə-,nä-pə-'lis-tik\ adj — **mo·nop·o·li·za·tion** \-lə-'zā-shən\ n — **mo·nop·o·lize** \mə-'nä-pə-,līz\ vb

mono·rail \'mä-nə-,rāl\ n : a single rail serving as a track for a vehicle; also : a vehicle traveling on such a track

mono·so·di·um glu·ta·mate \,mä-nə-,sō-dē-əm-'glü-tə-,māt\ n : a crystalline salt used to enhance the flavor of food

mono·syl·la·ble \'mä-nə-,si-lə-bəl\ n : a word of one syllable — **mono·syl·lab·ic** \,mä-nə-sə-'la-bik\ adj — **mono·syl·lab·i·cal·ly** \-bi-k(ə-)lē\ adv

mono·the·ism \'mä-nə-(,)thē-,i-zəm\ n : a doctrine or belief that there is only one deity — **mono·the·ist** \-,thē-ist\ n — **mono·the·is·tic** \-thē-'is-tik\ adj

mono·tone \'mä-nə-,tōn\ n : a succession of syllables, words, or sentences in one unvaried key or pitch

mo·not·o·nous \mə-'nä-tə-nəs\ adj 1 : uttered or sounded in one unvarying tone 2 : tediously uniform — **mo·not·o·nous·ly** adv — **mo·not·o·nous·ness** n

mo·not·o·ny \mə-ˈnä-tə-nē\ n : tedious sameness or uniformity

mono·un·sat·u·rat·ed \ˌmä-nō-ˌən-ˈsa-chə-ˌrā-təd\ adj : containing one double or triple bond per molecule — used esp. of an oil, fat, or fatty acid

mon·ox·ide \mə-ˈnäk-ˌsīd\ n : an oxide containing one atom of oxygen in a molecule

mon·sei·gneur \ˌmōⁿ-ˌsän-ˈyər\ n, pl **mes·sei·gneurs** \ˌmā-ˌsän-ˈyər, -ˈyərz\ : a French dignitary — used as a title

mon·sieur \məs-ˈyər\ n, pl **mes·sieurs** \same or -ˈyərz\ : a Frenchman of high rank or station — used as a title equivalent to Mister

mon·si·gnor \män-ˈsē-nyər\ n, pl **monsignors** or **mon·si·gno·ri** \ˌmän-ˌsēn-ˈyōr-ē\ [It monsignore] : a Roman Catholic prelate — used as a title

mon·soon \män-ˈsün\ n [obs. Dutch monssoen, fr. Pg monção, fr. Ar mawsim time, season] 1 : a periodic wind esp. in the Indian Ocean and southern Asia 2 : the season of the southwest monsoon esp. in India 3 : rainfall associated with the monsoon

¹**mon·ster** \ˈmän-stər\ n 1 : an abnormally developed plant or animal 2 : an animal of strange or terrifying shape; also : one unusually large of its kind 3 : an extremely ugly, wicked, or cruel person — **mon·stros·i·ty** \män-ˈsträ-sə-tē\ n — **mon·strous** \ˈmän-strəs\ adj — **mon·strous·ly** adv

²**monster** adj : very large : ENORMOUS

mon·strance \ˈmän-strəns\ n : a vessel in which the consecrated Host is exposed for the adoration of the faithful

Mont abbr Montana

mon·tage \män-ˈtäzh\ n [F] 1 : a composite photograph made by combining several separate pictures 2 : an artistic composition made up of several different kinds of elements 3 : a varied mixture : JUMBLE

month \ˈmənth\ n, pl **months** \ˈməns, ˈmənths\ : one of the 12 parts into which the year is divided — **month·ly** adv or adj or n

month·long \ˈmənth-ˈlȯŋ\ adj : lasting a month

mon·u·ment \ˈmän-yə-mənt\ n 1 : a lasting reminder; esp : a structure erected in remembrance of a person or event 2 : NATIONAL MONUMENT

mon·u·men·tal \ˌmän-yə-ˈmen-tᵊl\ adj 1 : of or relating to a monument 2 : MASSIVE; also : OUTSTANDING ⟨a ∼ achievement⟩ 3 : very great — **mon·u·men·tal·ly** adv

moo \ˈmü\ vb : to make the natural throat noise of a cow — **moo** n

¹**mood** \ˈmüd\ n 1 : a conscious state of mind or predominant emotion : FEELING 2 : a prevailing attitude : DISPOSITION 3 : a distinctive atmosphere

²**mood** n : distinction of form of a verb to express whether its action or state is conceived as fact or in some other manner (as wish)

moody \ˈmü-dē\ adj **mood·i·er; -est** 1 : GLOOMY 2 : subject to moods : TEMPERAMENTAL — **mood·i·ly** \-də-lē\ adv — **mood·i·ness** \-dē-nəs\ n

¹**moon** \ˈmün\ n 1 : the earth's natural satellite 2 : SATELLITE 2

²**moon** vb : to engage in idle reverie

moon·beam \ˈmün-ˌbēm\ n : a ray of light from the moon

¹**moon·light** \-ˌlīt\ n : the light of the moon — **moon·lit** \-ˌlit\ adj

²**moonlight** vb **moon·light·ed; moon·light·ing** : to hold a second job in addition to a regular one — **moon·light·er** n

moon·roof \-ˌrüf, -ˌrȯf\ n : a glass sunroof

moon·scape \-ˌskāp\ n : the surface of the moon as seen or as pictured

moon·shine \-ˌshīn\ n 1 : MOONLIGHT 2 : empty talk 3 : intoxicating liquor usu. illegally distilled

moon·stone \-ˌstōn\ n : a transparent or translucent feldspar of pearly luster used as a gem

moon·struck \-ˌstrək\ adj 1 : mentally unbalanced 2 : romantically sentimental 3 : lost in fantasy

¹**moor** \ˈmur\ n, 1 chiefly Brit : an expanse of open rolling infertile land 2 : a boggy area; esp : one that is peaty and dominated by grasses and sedges

²**moor** vb : to make fast with or as if with cables, lines, or anchors

Moor \ˈmur\ n : one of the Arab and Berber conquerors of Spain — **Moor·ish** adj

moor·ing \ˈmur-iŋ\ n 1 : a place where or an object to which a craft can be made fast 2 : an established practice or stabilizing influence — usu. used in pl.

moor·land \-lənd, -ˌland\ n : land consisting of moors

moose \ˈmüs\ n, pl **moose** : a large heavy-antlered ruminant mammal related to the deer that has humped shoulders and long legs and inhabits northern forested areas

¹**moot** \ˈmüt\ vb : to bring up for discussion; also : DEBATE

²**moot** adj 1 : open to question; also : DISPUTED 2 : having no practical significance

¹**mop** \ˈmäp\ n : an implement made of absorbent material fastened to a handle and used esp. for cleaning floors

²**mop** vb **mopped; mop·ping** : to use a mop on : clean with a mop

mope \ˈmōp\ vb **moped; mop·ing** 1 : to become dull, dejected, or listless 2 : DAWDLE

mo·ped \ˈmō-ˌped\ n : a light low-powered motorbike that can be pedaled

mop·pet \ˈmä-pət\ n [obs. E mop fool, child] : CHILD

mo·raine \mə-ˈrān\ n : an accumulation of earth and stones left by a glacier

¹**mor·al** \ˈmȯr-əl\ adj 1 : of or relating to principles of right and wrong 2 : conforming to a standard of right behavior; also : capable of right and wrong action

3 : probable but not proved ⟨a ~ certainty⟩ 4 : perceptual or psychological rather than tangible or practical in nature or effect ⟨a ~ victory⟩ ◆ **Synonyms** VIRTUOUS, RIGHTEOUS, NOBLE, ETHICAL, PRINCIPLED — **mor·al·ly** adv

²**moral** n 1 : the practical meaning (as of a story) 2 pl : moral practices or teachings

mo·rale \mə-ˈral\ n 1 : MORALITY 2 : the mental and emotional attitudes of an individual to the tasks at hand; also : ESPRIT DE CORPS

mor·al·ise Brit var of MORALIZE

mor·al·ist \ˈmȯr-ə-list\ n 1 : one who leads a moral life 2 : a thinker or writer concerned with morals 3 : one concerned with regulating the morals of others — **mor·al·is·tic** \ˌmȯr-ə-ˈlis-tik\ adj — **mor·al·is·ti·cal·ly** \-ti-k(ə-)lē\ adv

mo·ral·i·ty \mə-ˈra-lə-tē\ n, pl **-ties** : moral conduct : VIRTUE

mor·al·ize \ˈmȯr-ə-ˌlīz\ vb **-ized; -iz·ing** : to make moral reflections — **mor·al·i·za·tion** \ˌmȯr-ə-lə-ˈzā-shən\ n — **mor·al·iz·er** \ˈmȯr-ə-ˌlī-zər\ n

mo·rass \mə-ˈras\ n [D moeras, fr. OF maresc, fr. of Gmc origin; akin to OE mersc marsh] : SWAMP; also : something that entangles, impedes, or confuses

mor·a·to·ri·um \ˌmȯr-ə-ˈtȯr-ē-əm\ n, pl **-ri·ums** or **-ria** \-ē-ə\ [ultim. fr. L mora delay] : a suspension of activity

mo·ray eel \mə-ˈrā-, ˈmȯr-ˌā-\ n : any of numerous often brightly colored biting eels of warm seas

mor·bid \ˈmȯr-bəd\ adj 1 : of, relating to, or typical of disease; also : DISEASED, SICKLY 2 : characterized by gloomy or unwholesome ideas or feelings 3 : GRISLY, GRUESOME ⟨~ details⟩ — **mor·bid·i·ty** \mȯr-ˈbi-də-tē\ n — **mor·bid·ly** adv — **mor·bid·ness** n

mor·dant \ˈmȯr-dᵊnt\ adj 1 : biting or caustic in manner or style 2 : BURNING, PUNGENT — **mor·dant·ly** adv

¹**more** \ˈmȯr\ adj 1 : GREATER ⟨something ~ than I expected⟩ 2 : ADDITIONAL

²**more** adv 1 : in addition 2 : to a greater or higher degree ⟨~ evenly matched⟩

³**more** n 1 : a greater quantity, number, or amount ⟨the ~ the merrier⟩ 2 : an additional amount ⟨costs a little ~⟩

⁴**more** pron : additional persons or things or a greater amount

mo·rel \mə-ˈrel\ n : any of several pitted edible fungi

more·over \mȯr-ˈō-vər\ adv : in addition : FURTHER

mo·res \ˈmȯr-ˌāz\ n pl [L, pl. of mor-, mos custom] 1 : the fixed morally binding customs of a group 2 : HABITS, MANNERS

Mor·gan \ˈmȯr-gən\ n : any of an American breed of lightly built horses

morgue \ˈmȯrg\ n : a place where the bodies of dead persons are kept until released for burial or autopsy

mor·i·bund \ˈmȯr-ə-(ˌ)bənd\ adj : being in a dying condition

Mor·mon \ˈmȯr-mən\ n : a member of the Church of Jesus Christ of Latter-day Saints — **Mor·mon·ism** \-mə-ˌni-zəm\ n

morn \ˈmȯrn\ n : MORNING

morn·ing \ˈmȯr-niŋ\ n 1 : the early part of the day; esp : the time from the sunrise to noon 2 : BEGINNING

morn·ing–after pill \ˌmȯr-niŋ-ˈaf-tər-\ n : a contraceptive drug taken up to usu. three days after sexual intercourse

morning glory n : any of various twining plants related to the sweet potato that have often showy bell-shaped or funnel-shaped flowers

morning sickness n : nausea and vomiting that typically occur in the morning esp. during early pregnancy

morning star n : a bright planet (as Venus) seen in the eastern sky before or at sunrise

mo·roc·co \mə-ˈrä-kō\ n : a fine leather made of goatskins tanned with sumac

mo·ron \ˈmȯr-ˌän\ n 1 usu. offensive : a mildly mentally retarded person 2 : a very stupid person — **mo·ron·ic** \mə-ˈrä-nik\ adj — **mo·ron·i·cal·ly** \-ni-k(ə-)lē\ adv

mo·rose \mə-ˈrōs\ adj [L morosus hard to please, exacting, fr. mor-, mos custom, disposition] : having a sullen disposition; also : GLOOMY — **mo·rose·ly** adv — **mo·rose·ness** n

morph \ˈmȯrf\ vb : to change the form or character of : TRANSFORM

mor·pheme \ˈmȯr-ˌfēm\ n : a meaningful linguistic unit that contains no smaller meaningful parts — **mor·phe·mic** \mȯr-ˈfē-mik\ adj

mor·phia \ˈmȯr-fē-ə\ n : MORPHINE

mor·phine \ˈmȯr-ˌfēn\ n [F, fr. Gk Morpheus, Greek god of dreams] : an addictive drug obtained from opium and used to ease pain or induce sleep

mor·phol·o·gy \mȯr-ˈfä-lə-jē\ n 1 : a branch of biology dealing with the form and structure of organisms 2 : a study and description of word formation in a language — **mor·pho·log·i·cal** \ˌmȯr-fə-ˈlä-ji-kəl\ adj — **mor·phol·o·gist** \mȯr-ˈfä-lə-jist\ n

mor·ris \ˈmȯr-əs\ n : a vigorous English dance traditionally performed by men wearing costumes and bells

mor·row \ˈmär-ō\ n : the next day

Morse code \ˈmȯrs-\ n : either of two codes consisting of dots and dashes or long and short sounds used for transmitting messages

mor·sel \ˈmȯr-səl\ n [ME, fr. AF, dim. of mors bite, fr. L morsus, fr. mordēre to bite] 1 : a small piece or quantity 2 : a tasty dish

mor·tal \ˈmȯr-tᵊl\ adj 1 : causing death : FATAL; also : leading to eternal punishment ⟨~ sin⟩ 2 : subject to death ⟨~ man⟩ 3 : implacably hostile ⟨~ foe⟩ 4 : very great : EXTREME ⟨~ fear⟩ 5 : HUMAN ⟨~ limitations⟩ — **mortal** n — **mor·tal·i·ty** \mȯr-ˈta-lə-tē\ n — **mor·tal·ly** \ˈmȯr-tᵊl-ē\ adv

¹**mor·tar** \ˈmȯr-tər\ n 1 : a strong bowl in which substances are pounded or crushed

with a pestle **2** : a short-barreled cannon used to fire shells at high angles

²mortar *n* : a building material (as a mixture of lime and cement with sand and water) that is spread between bricks or stones to bind them together as it hardens — **mortar** *vb*

mor·tar·board \'mȯr-tər-ˌbȯrd\ *n* **1** : a square board for holding mortar **2** : an academic cap with a flat square top

mort·gage \'mȯr-gij\ *n* [ME *morgage*, fr. AF *mortgage*, fr. *mort* dead + *gage* pledge] : a transfer of rights to a piece of property usu. as security for the payment of a loan or debt that becomes void when the debt is paid — **mortgage** *vb* — **mort·gag·ee** \ˌmȯr-gi-'jē\ *n* — **mort·gag·or** \ˌmȯr-gi-'jȯr\ *n*

mor·ti·cian \mȯr-'ti-shən\ *n* [L *mort-, mors* death + E *-ician* (as in *physician*)] : UNDERTAKER

mor·ti·fy \'mȯr-tə-ˌfī\ *vb* **-fied; -fy·ing 1** : to subdue (as the body) esp. by abstinence or self-inflicted pain **2** : HUMILIATE **3** : to become necrotic or gangrenous — **mor·ti·fi·ca·tion** \ˌmȯr-tə-fə-'kā-shən\ *n*

mor·tise *also* **mor·tice** \'mȯr-təs\ *n* : a hole cut in a piece of wood into which another piece fits to form a joint

mor·tu·ary \'mȯr-chə-ˌwer-ē\ *n, pl* **-ar·ies** : a place in which dead bodies are kept until burial

mos *abbr* months

mo·sa·ic \mō-'zā-ik\ *n* : a surface decoration made by inlaying small pieces (as of colored glass or stone) to form figures or patterns; *also* : a design made in mosaic — **mosaic** *adj*

mo·sey \'mō-zē\ *vb* **mo·seyed; mo·sey·ing** : SAUNTER

mosh \'mäsh\ *vb* : to engage in rough uninhibited dancing near the stage at a rock concert

mosh pit *n* : an area in front of a stage where rough dancing takes place at a rock concert

Mos·lem \'mäz-ləm\ *var of* MUSLIM

mosque \'mäsk\ *n* : a building used for public worship by Muslims

mos·qui·to \mə-'skē-tō\ *n, pl* **-toes** *also* **-tos** : any of a family of dipteran flies the female of which sucks the blood of animals

mosquito net *n* : a net or screen for keeping out mosquitoes

moss \'mȯs\ *n* : any of a class of green plants that lack flowers but have small leafy stems and often grow in clumps — **mossy** *adj*

moss·back \'mȯs-ˌbak\ *n* : an extremely conservative person : FOGY

¹most \'mōst\ *adj* **1** : GREATEST ⟨the ~ ability⟩ **2** : the majority of ⟨~ people⟩

²most *adv* **1** : to the greatest or highest degree ⟨~ beautiful⟩ **2** : to a very great degree ⟨a ~ careful driver⟩

³most *n* : the greatest amount ⟨the ~ I can do⟩

⁴most *pron* : the greatest number or part ⟨~ became discouraged⟩

-most *adj suffix* : most ⟨inner*most*⟩ : most toward ⟨end*most*⟩

most·ly \'mōst-lē\ *adv* : MAINLY

mot \'mō\ *n, pl* **mots** *same or* 'mōz\ [F, word, saying, fr. LL *muttum* grunt] : a witty saying

mote \'mōt\ *n* : a small particle

mo·tel \mō-'tel\ *n* [blend of *motor* and *hotel*] : a hotel in which the rooms are accessible from the parking area

mo·tet \mō-'tet\ *n* : a choral work on a sacred text for several voices usu. without instrumental accompaniment

moth \'mȯth\ *n, pl* **moths** \'mȯthz, 'mȯths\ : any of various insects belonging to the same order as the butterflies but usu. night-flying and with a stouter body and smaller wings

moth·ball \'mȯth-ˌbȯl\ *n* **1** : a ball (as of naphthalene) used to keep moths out of clothing **2** *pl* : protective storage

¹moth·er \'mə-thər\ *n* **1** : a female parent **2** : the superior of a religious community of women **3** : SOURCE, ORIGIN ⟨necessity is the ~ of invention⟩ — **moth·er·hood** \-ˌhu̇d\ *n* — **moth·er·less** *adj* — **moth·er·li·ness** \-lē-nəs\ *n* — **moth·er·ly** *adj*

²mother *vb* **1** : to give birth to; *also* : PRODUCE **2** : to care for or protect like a mother

moth·er·board \'mə-thər-ˌbȯrd\ *n* : the main circuit board esp. of a microcomputer

moth·er–in–law \'mə-thər-ən-ˌlȯ\ *n, pl* **mothers–in–law** \'mə-thərz-\ : the mother of one's spouse

moth·er·land \'mə-thər-ˌland\ *n* **1** : the land of origin of something **2** : the native land of one's ancestors

moth·er–of–pearl \ˌmə-thər-əv-'pərl\ *n* : the hard pearly matter forming the inner layer of a mollusk shell

mother ship *n* : a ship serving smaller craft

mo·tif \mō-'tēf\ *n* [F, motive, motif] : a dominant idea or central theme (as in a work of art)

mo·tile \'mō-t°l, 'mō-ˌtī(-ə)l\ *adj* : capable of spontaneous movement — **mo·til·i·ty** \mō-'ti-lə-tē\ *n*

¹mo·tion \'mō-shən\ *n* **1** : an act, process, or instance of moving **2** : a proposal for action (as by a deliberative body) **3** *pl* : ACTIVITIES, MOVEMENTS — **mo·tion·less** *adj* — **mo·tion·less·ly** *adv* — **mo·tion·less·ness** *n*

²motion *vb* : to direct or signal by a movement

motion picture *n* : a series of pictures projected on a screen so rapidly that they produce a continuous picture in which persons and objects seem to move

motion sickness *n* : sickness induced by motion and characterized by nausea

mo·ti·vate \'mō-tə-ˌvāt\ *vb* **-vat·ed; -vat·ing** : to provide with a motive : IMPEL — **mo·ti·va·tion** \ˌmō-tə-'vā-shən\ *n* — **mo·ti·va·tion·al** \-shə-nəl\ *adj* — **mo·ti·va·tor** \'mō-tə-ˌvā-tər\ *n*

¹mo·tive \'mō-tiv, *2 also* mō-'tēv\ *n* **1** : something (as a need or desire) that causes a person to act **2** : a recurrent theme in a musical composition **3** : MOTIF — **mo·tive·less** adj

²**motive** \'mō-tiv\ adj **1** : moving to action **2** : of or relating to motion

mot·ley \'mät-lē\ adj **1** : variegated in color **2** : made up of diverse often incongruous elements ✦ **Synonyms** HETEROGENEOUS, MISCELLANEOUS, ASSORTED, MIXED, VARIED

¹**mo·tor** \'mō-tər\ n [L, fr. *movēre* to move] **1** : one that imparts motion **2** : a machine that produces motion or power for doing work **3** : AUTOMOBILE

²**motor** vb : to travel or transport by automobile : DRIVE — **mo·tor·ist** n

mo·tor·bike \'mō-tər-ˌbīk\ n : a small lightweight motorcycle

mo·tor·boat \-ˌbōt\ n : a boat propelled by a motor

mo·tor·cade \-ˌkād\ n : a procession of motor vehicles

mo·tor·car \-ˌkär\ n : AUTOMOBILE

mo·tor·cy·cle \'mō-tər-ˌsī-kəl\ n : a 2-wheeled automotive vehicle — **mo·tor·cy·clist** \-k(ə-)list\ n

motor home n : a large motor vehicle equipped as living quarters

motor inn n : MOTEL

mo·tor·ise Brit var of MOTORIZE

mo·tor·ize \'mō-tə-ˌrīz\ vb **-ized; -iz·ing** **1** : to equip with a motor **2** : to equip with automobiles

mo·tor·man \'mō-tər-mən\ n : an operator of a motor-driven vehicle (as a streetcar or subway train)

motor scooter n : a low 2- or 3-wheeled automotive vehicle resembling a child's scooter but having a seat

mo·tor·truck \'mō-tər-ˌtrək\ n : an automotive truck

motor vehicle n : an automotive vehicle (as an automobile) not operated on rails

mot·tle \'mä-tᵊl\ vb **mot·tled; mot·tling** : to mark with spots of different color : BLOTCH

mot·to \'mä-tō\ n, pl **mottoes** also **mottos** [It, fr. LL *muttum* grunt, fr. L *muttire* to mutter] **1** : a sentence, phrase, or word inscribed on something to indicate its character or use **2** : a short expression of a guiding rule of conduct

moue \'mü\ n : a little grimace

mould chiefly Brit var of MOLD

moult chiefly Brit var of MOLT

mound \'maund\ n **1** : an artificial bank or hill of earth or stones **2** : KNOLL **3** : HEAP, PILE ⟨a ~ of work⟩

¹**mount** \'maunt\ n : a high hill

²**mount** vb **1** : to increase in amount or extent; also : RISE, ASCEND **2** : to get up on something; esp : to seat oneself on (as a horse) for riding **3** : to put in position ⟨~ artillery⟩ **4** : to set on something that elevates **5** : to attach to a support **6** : to prepare esp. for examination or display — **mount·able** adj — **mount·er** n

³**mount** n **1** : FRAME, SUPPORT **2** : a means of conveyance; esp : SADDLE HORSE

moun·tain \'maun-tᵊn\ n : a landmass higher than a hill — **moun·tain·ous** \-tə-nəs\ adj — **moun·tainy** \-tᵊn-ē\ adj

mountain ash n : any of various trees related to the roses that have pinnate leaves and red or orange-red fruits

mountain bike n : a bicycle with wide knobby tires, straight handlebars, and 18 or 21 gears that is designed to operate esp. over unpaved terrain

moun·tain·eer \ˌmaun-tə-'nir\ n **1** : a native or inhabitant of a mountainous region **2** : one who climbs mountains for sport

mountain goat n : a ruminant mammal of mountainous northwestern No. America that resembles a goat

mountain laurel n : a No. American evergreen shrub or small tree of the heath family with glossy leaves and clusters of rose-colored or white flowers

mountain lion n : COUGAR

moun·tain·side \'maun-tᵊn-ˌsīd\ n : the side of a mountain

moun·tain·top \-ˌtäp\ n : the summit of a mountain

moun·te·bank \'maun-ti-ˌbaŋk\ n [It *montimbanco*, fr. *montare* to mount + *in* in, on + *banco, banca* bench] : QUACK, CHARLATAN

Mount·ie \'maun-tē\ n : a member of the Royal Canadian Mounted Police

mount·ing \'maun-tiŋ\ n : something that serves as a frame or support

mourn \'mōrn\ vb : to feel or express grief or sorrow — **mourn·er** n

mourn·ful \-fəl\ adj : expressing, feeling, or causing sorrow — **mourn·ful·ly** adv — **mourn·ful·ness** n

mourn·ing \'mōr-niŋ\ n **1** : an outward sign (as black clothes) of grief for a person's death **2** : a period of time during which signs of grief are shown

mouse \'maus\ n, pl **mice** \'mīs\ **1** : any of numerous small rodents with pointed snout, long body, and slender tail **2** : a small manual device that controls cursor movement on a computer display

mouse pad n : a thin flat pad on which a computer mouse is used

mous·er \'mau-sər\ n : a cat proficient at catching mice

mouse·trap \'maus-ˌtrap\ n **1** : a trap for catching mice **2** : a stratagem that lures one to defeat or destruction — **mousetrap** vb

mousse \'müs\ n [F, lit., froth, moss] **1** : a molded chilled dessert made with sweetened and flavored whipped cream or egg whites and gelatin **2** : a foamy preparation used in styling hair — **mousse** vb

moustache var of MUSTACHE

mousy or **mous·ey** \'mau-sē, -zē\ adj **mous·i·er; -est** **1** : QUIET, STEALTHY **2** : TIMID **3** : grayish brown — **mous·i·ness** \'mau-sē-nəs, -zē-\ n

¹**mouth** \'mauth\ n, pl **mouths** \'mauthz, 'mauths\ **1** : the opening through which an animal takes in food; also : the cavity that encloses the tongue, lips, and teeth in the typical vertebrate **2** : something resembling a mouth (as in affording en-

trance) — **mouthed** \'mau̇thd, 'mau̇tht\ *adj* — **mouth·ful** *n*

²mouth \'mau̇th\ *vb* **1** : SPEAK; *also* : DECLAIM **2** : to repeat without comprehension or sincerity **3** : to form soundlessly with the lips

mouth harp *n* : HARMONICA

mouth·part \'mau̇th-ˌpärt\ *n* : a structure or appendage near the mouth (as of an insect) esp. when adapted for eating

mouth·piece \-ˌpēs\ *n* **1** : a part (as of a musical instrument) that goes in the mouth or to which the mouth is applied **2** : SPOKESMAN

mouth–to–mouth *adj* : of, relating to, or being a method of artificial respiration in which air from a rescuer's mouth is forced into a victim's lungs

mouth·wash \-ˌwȯsh, -ˌwäsh\ *n* : a usu. antiseptic liquid preparation for cleaning the mouth and teeth

mou·ton \'mü-ˌtän\ *n* : processed sheepskin that has been sheared or dyed to resemble beaver or seal

¹move \'müv\ *vb* **moved; mov·ing 1** : to change or cause to change position or posture **2** : to go or cause to go from one point to another; *also* : DEPART **3** : to take or cause to take action **4** : to show marked activity **5** : to stir the emotions **6** : to make a formal request, application, or appeal **7** : to change one's residence **8** : EVACUATE **2** — **mov·able** *or* **move·able** \'mü-və-bəl\ *adj*

²move *n* **1** : an act of moving **2** : a calculated step taken to gain an objective **3** : a change of location **4** : an agile action esp. in sports

move·ment \'müv-mənt\ *n* **1** : the act or process of moving : MOVE **2** : a series of organized activities working toward an objective **3** : the moving parts of a mechanism (as of a watch) **4** : RHYTHM **5** : a section of an extended musical composition **6** : an act of voiding the bowels; *also* : STOOL **4**

mov·er \'mü-vər\ *n* : one that moves; *esp* : one that moves the belongings of others from one location to another

mov·ie \'mü-vē\ *n* **1** : MOTION PICTURE **2** *pl* : a showing of a motion picture **3** *pl* : the motion-picture industry

¹mow \'mau̇\ *n* : the part of a barn where hay or straw is stored

²mow \'mō\ *vb* **mowed; mowed** *or* **mown** \'mōn\; **mow·ing 1** : to cut (as grass) with a scythe or machine **2** : to cut the standing herbage of ⟨∼ the lawn⟩ — **mow·er** *n*

mox·ie \'mäk-sē\ *n* **1** : ENERGY, PEP **2** : COURAGE, DETERMINATION

moz·za·rel·la \ˌmät-sə-'re-lə\ *n* [It] : a moist white unsalted unripened mild cheese of a smooth rubbery texture

¹MP \'em-'pē\ *n* **1** : a member of the military police **2** : an elected member of a parliament

²MP *abbr* **1** melting point **2** metropolitan police

mpg *abbr* miles per gallon

mph *abbr* miles per hour

Mr. \'mis-tər\ *n, pl* **Messrs.** \'me-sərz\ — used as a conventional title of courtesy before a man's surname or his title of office

MRI *n* MAGNETIC RESONANCE IMAGING; *also* : the procedure in which magnetic resonance imaging is used

Mr. Right *n* : a man who would make the perfect husband

Mrs. \'mi-səz, -səs, *esp Southern* 'mi-zəz, -zəs\ *n, pl* **Mes·dames** \mā-'däm, -'dam\ — used as a conventional title of courtesy before a married woman's surname

Ms. \'miz\ *n, pl* **Mss.** *or* **Mses.** \'mi-zez\ — used instead of *Miss* or *Mrs.*

MS *abbr* **1** manuscript **2** master of science **3** military science **4** Mississippi **5** motor ship **6** multiple sclerosis

msec *abbr* millisecond

msg *abbr* message

MSG *abbr* **1** master sergeant **2** monosodium glutamate

msgr *abbr* **1** monseigneur **2** monsignor

MSgt *abbr* master sergeant

MSS *abbr* manuscripts

MST *abbr* mountain standard time

mt *abbr* mount; mountain

¹Mt *abbr* Matthew

²Mt *symbol* meitnerium

MT *abbr* **1** metric ton **2** Montana **3** mountain time

mtg *abbr* **1** meeting **2** mortgage

mtge *abbr* mortgage

mu \'myü, 'mü\ *n* : the 12th letter of the Greek alphabet — M or μ

¹much \'məch\ *adj* **more** \'mȯr\; **most** \'mōst\ : great in quantity, amount, extent, or degree ⟨∼ money⟩

²much *adv* **more; most 1** : to a great degree or extent ⟨∼ happier⟩ **2** : ALMOST, NEARLY ⟨looks ∼ as he did before⟩

³much *n* **1** : a great quantity, amount, extent, or degree **2** : something considerable or impressive

mu·ci·lage \'myü-sə-lij\ *n* : a watery sticky solution (as of a gum) used esp. as an adhesive — **mu·ci·lag·i·nous** \ˌmyü-sə-'la-jə-nəs\ *adj*

muck \'mək\ *n* **1** : soft moist barnyard manure **2** : FILTH, DIRT **3** : a dark richly organic soil; *also* : MUD, MIRE — **mucky** *adj*

muck·rake \-ˌrāk\ *vb* : to expose publicly real or apparent misconduct of a prominent individual or business — **muck·rak·er** *n*

mu·cus \'myü-kəs\ *n* : a slimy slippery protective secretion of membranes (**mucous membranes**) lining some body cavities — **mu·cous** \-kəs\ *adj*

mud \'məd\ *n* : soft wet earth : MIRE

mud·dle \'mə-dᵊl\ *vb* **mud·dled; mud·dling 1** : to make muddy **2** : to confuse esp. with liquor **3** : to mix up or make a mess of **4** : to think or act in a confused way

mud·dle·head·ed \ˌmə-dᵊl-'he-dəd\ *adj* **1** : mentally confused **2** : INEPT

¹mud·dy \'mə-dē\ *adj* **mud·di·er; -est 1**

: full of or covered with mud **2** : suggestive of mud **3** : CLOUDY, OBSCURE — **mud·di·ness** *n*

²**muddy** *vb* **mud·died; mud·dy·ing 1** : to soil or stain with or as if with mud **2** : to make cloudy or obscure **3** : CONFUSE

mud·flat \'məd-ˌflat\ *n* : a level tract alternately covered and left bare by the tide

mud·guard \'məd-ˌgärd\ *n* : a guard over or a flap behind a wheel of a vehicle to catch or deflect mud

mud·room \-ˌrüm, -ˌrüm\ *n* : a room in a house for removing dirty or wet footwear and clothing

mud·sling·er \-ˌsliŋ-ər\ *n* : one who uses invective esp. against a political opponent — **mud·sling·ing** \-ˌsliŋ-iŋ\ *n*

Muen·ster \'mən-stər, 'mün-, 'mün-\ *n* : a semisoft bland cheese

mu·ez·zin \mü-'e-zᵊn, myü-\ *n* : a Muslim crier who calls the hour of daily prayer

¹**muff** \'məf\ *n* : a warm tubular covering for the hands

²**muff** *n* : a bungling performance; *esp* : a failure to hold a ball in attempting a catch — **muff** *vb*

muf·fin \'mə-fən\ *n* : a small soft cake baked in a cup-shaped container

muf·fle \'mə-fəl\ *vb* **muf·fled; muf·fling 1** : to wrap up so as to conceal or protect **2** : to wrap or pad with something to dull the sound of **3** : to keep down : SUPPRESS

muf·fler \'mə-flər\ *n* **1** : a scarf worn around the neck **2** : a device (as on a car's exhaust) to deaden noise

muf·ti \'məf-tē\ *n* : civilian clothes

¹**mug** \'məg\ *n* : a usu. metal or earthenware cylindrical drinking cup

²**mug** *vb* **mugged; mug·ging 1** : to pose or make faces esp. to attract attention or for a camera **2** : PHOTOGRAPH

³**mug** *vb* **mugged; mug·ging** : to assault usu. with intent to rob — **mug·ger** *n*

mug·gy \'mə-gē\ *adj* **mug·gi·er; -est** : being warm and humid — **mug·gi·ness** \-gē-nəs\ *n*

mug·wump \'məg-ˌwəmp\ *n* [obs. slang *mugwump* kingpin, fr. Massachusett (Algonquian language of New England) *mugquomp* war leader] : an independent in politics

Muhammadan, Muhammadanism *var of* MOHAMMEDAN, MOHAMMEDANISM

mu·ja·hed·een *or* **mu·ja·hed·in** \ˌmü-jə-hi-'dēn, -jä-\ *n, pl* [Ar *mujāhidīn*, pl. of *mujāhid*, lit., person who wages jihad] : Islamic guerrilla fighters esp. in the Middle East

muk·luk \'mək-ˌlək\ *n* **1** : an Eskimo boot of sealskin or reindeer skin **2** : a boot with a soft leather sole worn over several pairs of socks

mu·lat·to \mü-'la-tō, myü-, -'lä-\ *n, pl* **-toes** *or* **-tos** [Sp *mulato*, fr. *mulo* mule, fr. L *mulus*] : a first-generation offspring of a black person and a white person; *also* : a person of mixed white and black ancestry

mul·ber·ry \'məl-ˌber-ē\ *n* : any of a genus of trees with edible berrylike fruit and leaves used as food for silkworms; *also* : the fruit

mulch \'məlch\ *n* : a protective covering (as of straw or leaves) spread on the ground esp. to reduce evaporation or control weeds — **mulch** *vb*

¹**mulct** \'məlkt\ *n* : FINE, PENALTY

²**mulct** *vb* **1** : FINE **2** : CHEAT, DEFRAUD

¹**mule** \'myül\ *n* **1** : a hybrid offspring of a male donkey and a female horse **2** : a very stubborn person — **mul·ish** \'myü-lish\ *adj* — **mul·ish·ly** *adv* — **mu·lish·ness** *n*

²**mule** *n* : a slipper whose upper does not extend around the heel of the foot

mule deer *n* : a long-eared deer of western No. America

mu·le·teer \ˌmyü-lə-'tir\ *n* : one who drives mules

¹**mull** \'məl\ *vb* : PONDER, MEDITATE

²**mull** *vb* : to heat, sweeten, and flavor (as wine) with spices

mul·lein \'mə-lən\ *n* : a tall herb related to the snapdragons that has coarse woolly leaves and flowers in spikes

mul·let \'mə-lət\ *n, pl* **mullet** *or* **mullets** : any of a family of largely gray chiefly marine bony fishes including valuable food fishes

mul·li·gan stew \ˈmə-li-gən-\ *n* : a stew made from whatever ingredients are available

mul·li·ga·taw·ny \ˌmə-li-gə-'tȯ-nē\ *n* : a soup usu. of chicken stock seasoned with curry

mul·lion \'məl-yən\ *n* : a vertical strip separating windowpanes

multi- *comb form* **1** : many : multiple ⟨*multi*unit⟩ **2** : many times over ⟨*multi*millionaire⟩

mul·ti·col·ored \ˌməl-ti-'kə-lərd\ *adj* : having many colors

mul·ti·cul·tur·al \ˌməl-tē-'kəl-chə-rəl, -tī-\ *adj* : of, relating to, reflecting, or adapted to diverse cultures ⟨a ∼ society⟩ — **mul·ti·cul·tur·al·ism** \-rə-ˌli-zəm\ *n* — **mul·ti·cul·tur·al·ist** \-rə-list\ *n or adj*

mul·ti·di·men·sion·al \-ti-də-'men-chə-nəl, -ˌdī-\ *adj* : of, relating to, or having many facets or dimensions ⟨a ∼ problem⟩ ⟨∼ space⟩

mul·ti·eth·nic \-'eth-nik\ *adj* : including, involving, or made up of people of various ethnic groups

mul·ti·fac·et·ed \-'fa-sə-təd\ *adj* : having many facets or aspects

mul·ti·fam·i·ly \-'fam-lē, -'fa-mə-\ *adj* : designed for use by several families

mul·ti·far·i·ous \ˌməl-tə-'fer-ē-əs\ *adj* : having great variety : DIVERSE — **mul·ti·far·i·ous·ness** *n*

mul·ti·form \'məl-ti-ˌfȯrm\ *adj* : having many forms or appearances — **mul·ti·for·mi·ty** \ˌməl-ti-'fȯr-mə-tē\ *n*

mul·ti·lat·er·al \ˌməl-ti-'la-tə-rəl, -ˌtī-, -'la-trəl\ *adj* : having many sides or participants ⟨∼ treaty⟩ — **mul·ti·lat·er·al·ism** \-'la-tə-rə-ˌli-zəm\ *n* — **mul·ti·lat·er·al·ly** *adv*

multilayered \-'lā-ərd, -'lerd\ *or* **multilayer** \-'lā-ər, 'ler\ *adj* : having or involving several distinct layers or levels

mul·ti·lev·el \-'le-vəl\ *adj* : having several levels

mul·ti·lin·gual \-'liŋ-gwəl\ *adj* : knowing or using several languages — **mul·ti·lin·gual·ism** \-gwə,li-zəm\ *n*

¹mul·ti·me·dia \-'mē-dē-ə\ *adj* : using, involving, or encompassing several media ⟨a ∼ advertising campaign⟩

²multimedia *n sing or pl* : the technique of using several media (as in art); *also* : something (as software) that uses or facilitates it

mul·ti·mil·lion·aire \,məl-ti-,mil-yə-'nar, -,tī-, -'mil-yə-,nar\ *n* : a person worth several million dollars

mul·ti·na·tion·al \-'na-shə-nəl\ *adj* **1** : of or relating to several nationalities **2** : relating to or involving several nations **3** : having divisions in several countries ⟨a ∼ corporation⟩ — **multinational** *n*

mul·ti·pack \'məl-tē-,pak\ *n* : a package of several individually packed items sold as a unit

¹mul·ti·ple \'məl-tə-pəl\ *adj* **1** : more than one; *also* : MANY ⟨∼ achievements⟩ **2** : VARIOUS

²multiple *n* : the product of a quantity by an integer ⟨35 is a ∼ of 7⟩

multiple–choice *adj* : having several answers given from which the correct one is to be chosen ⟨a ∼ question⟩

multiple personality disorder *n* : a neurosis in which the personality becomes separated into two or more parts each of which controls behavior part of the time

multiple sclerosis *n* : a disease marked by patches of hardened tissue in the brain or spinal cord and associated esp. with partial or complete paralysis and muscular tremor

mul·ti·plex \'məl-tə-,pleks\ *n* : CINEPLEX

mul·ti·pli·cand \,məl-tə-pli-'kand\ *n* : the number that is to be multiplied by another

mul·ti·pli·ca·tion \,məl-tə-plə-'kā-shən\ *n* **1** : INCREASE **2** : a short method of finding the result of adding a figure the number of times indicated by another figure

multiplication sign *n* **1** : TIMES SIGN **2** : a centered dot indicating multiplication

mul·ti·plic·i·ty \,məl-tə-pli'-sə-tē\ *n, pl* **-ties** : a great number or variety

mul·ti·pli·er \'məl-tə-,pli-(ə)r\ *n* : one that multiplies; *esp* : a number by which another number is multiplied

mul·ti·ply \'məl-tə-,plī\ *vb* **-plied; -ply·ing 1** : to increase in number (as by breeding) **2** : to find the product of by multiplication; *also* : to perform multiplication

mul·ti·pur·pose \,məl-ti-'pər-pəs, -,tī-\ *adj* : having or serving several purposes

mul·ti·ra·cial \-'rā-shəl\ *adj* : composed of, involving, or representing various races

mul·ti·sense \-,sens\ *adj* : having several meanings ⟨∼ words⟩

mul·ti·sto·ry \-,stȯr-ē\ *adj* : having several stories ⟨∼ buildings⟩

mul·ti·task·ing \'məl-tē-,tas-kiŋ, -,tī-\ *n* **1** : the concurrent performance of several jobs by a computer **2** : the performance of multiple tasks at one time — **mul·ti·task** \-,task\ *vb* — **mul·ti·task·er** \-,taskər\ *n*

mul·ti·tude \'məl-tə-,tüd, -,tyüd\ *n* : a great number — **mul·ti·tu·di·nous** \,məl-tə-'tü-d°n-əs, -'tyüd-\ *adj*

mul·ti·unit \,məl-ti-'yü-nət, -,tī-\ *adj* : having several units

mul·ti·vi·ta·min \-'vī-tə-mən\ *adj* : containing several vitamins and esp. all known to be essential to health — **multivitamin** *n*

¹mum \'məm\ *adj* : SILENT

²mum *chiefly Brit var of* MOM

³mum *n* : CHRYSANTHEMUM

mum·ble \'məm-bəl\ *vb* **mum·bled; mum·bling** : to speak in a low indistinct manner — **mumble** *n* — **mum·bler** *n* — **mum·bly** *adj*

mum·ble·ty–peg \'məm-bəl-tē-,peg\ *also* **mum·ble–the–peg** \'məm-bəl-thə-\ *n* : a game in which the players try to flip a knife from various positions so that the blade will stick into the ground

mum·bo jum·bo \,məm-bō-'jəm-bō\ *n* **1** : a complicated ritual with elaborate trappings **2** : GIBBERISH, NONSENSE

mum·mer \'mə-mər\ *n* **1** : an actor esp. in a pantomime **2** : a person who goes merrymaking in disguise during festivals — **mum·mery** *n*

mum·my \'mə-mē\ *n, pl* **mummies** [ME *mummie* powdered parts of a mummified body used as a drug, fr. AF *mumie*, fr. ML *mumia*, fr. Ar *mūmiya* bitumen, mummy, fr. Per *mūm* wax] : a body embalmed for burial in the manner of the ancient Egyptians — **mum·mi·fi·ca·tion** \,mə-mi-fə-'kā-shən\ *n* — **mum·mi·fy** \'mə-mi-,fī\ *vb*

mumps \'məmps\ *n sing or pl* [fr. pl. of obs. *mump* grimace] : a virus disease marked by fever and swelling esp. of the salivary glands

mun *or* **munic** *abbr* municipal

munch \'mənch\ *vb* : to eat with a chewing action; *also* : to snack on

munch·ies \'mən-chēz\ *n pl* **1** : hunger pangs **2** : light snack foods

mun·dane \,mən-'dān, 'mən-,dān\ *adj* **1** : of or relating to the world **2** : concerned with the practical details of everyday life — **mun·dane·ly** *adv*

mung bean \'məŋ-\ *n* : an erect bushy bean widely grown in warm regions for its edible seeds and as the chief source of bean sprouts; *also* : its seed

mu·nic·i·pal \myù-'ni-sə-pəl\ *adj* **1** : of, relating to, or characteristic of a municipality **2** : restricted to one locality — **mu·nic·i·pal·ly** *adv*

mu·nic·i·pal·i·ty \myù-,ni-sə-'pa-lə-tē\ *n, pl* **-ties** : an urban political unit with corporate status and usu. powers of self-government

mu·nif·i·cent \myù-'ni-fə-sənt\ *adj* : liberal in giving : GENEROUS — **mu·nif·i·cence** \-səns\ *n*

mu·ni·tion \myù-'ni-shən\ *n* : ARMAMENT, AMMUNITION

¹mu·ral \'myùr-əl\ adj 1 : of or relating to a wall 2 : applied to and made part of a wall or ceiling surface

²mural n : a mural painting — mu·ral·ist n

¹mur·der \'mər-dər\ n 1 : the crime of unlawfully killing a person esp. with malice aforethought 2 : something unusually difficult or dangerous

²murder vb 1 : to commit a murder; also : to kill brutally 2 : to put an end to 3 : to spoil by performing poorly ⟨~ a song⟩ — mur·der·er n

mur·der·ess \'mər-də-rəs\ n : a woman who murders

mur·der·ous \'mər-də-rəs\ adj 1 : having or appearing to have the purpose of murder 2 : marked by or causing murder or bloodshed ⟨~ gunfire⟩ — mur·der·ous·ly adv

murk \'mərk\ n : DARKNESS, GLOOM — murk·i·ly \'mər-kə-lē\ adv — murk·i·ness \-kē-nəs\ n — murky adj

mur·mur \'mər-mər\ n 1 : a muttered complaint 2 : a low indistinct often continuous sound — murmur vb — mur·mur·er n — mur·mur·ous adj

mus abbr 1 museum 2 music; musical; musician

mus·ca·tel \,məs-kə-'tel\ n : a sweet fortified wine

¹mus·cle \'mə-səl\ n [ME, fr. L musculus, fr. dim. of mus mouse] 1 : a body tissue consisting of long cells that contract when stimulated and produce motion; also : an organ consisting of this tissue and functioning in moving a body part 2 : STRENGTH, BRAWN — mus·cled \'mə-səld\ adj — mus·cu·lar \'məs-kyə-lər\ adj — mus·cu·lar·i·ty \,məs-kyə-'lar-ə-tē\ n

²muscle vb mus·cled; mus·cling : to force one's way

mus·cle–bound \'mə-səl-,baúnd\ adj : having some of the muscles abnormally enlarged and lacking in elasticity (as from excessive exercise)

mus·cle·man \-,man\ n : a man with a muscular physique

muscular dystrophy n : any of a group of diseases characterized by progressive wasting of muscles

mus·cu·la·ture \'məs-kyə-lə-,chùr\ n : the muscles of the body or its parts

mus·cu·lo·skel·e·tal \,məs-kyə-lō-'ske-lə-tᵊl\ adj : of, relating to, or involving both musculature and skeleton

¹muse \'myüz\ vb mused; mus·ing [ME, fr. AF muser to gape, idle, muse, fr. OF *mus mouth of an animal, fr. ML musus] : to become absorbed in thought — mus·ing·ly adv

²muse n [fr. Muse any of the nine sister goddesses of learning and the arts in Greek myth, fr. ME, fr. MF, fr. L Musa, fr. Gk Mousa] : a source of inspiration

mu·se·um \myù-'zē-əm\ n : an institution devoted to the procurement, care, and display of objects of lasting interest or value

¹mush \'məsh\ n 1 : cornmeal boiled in water 2 : sentimental drivel

²mush vb : to travel esp. over snow with a sled drawn by dogs

¹mush·room \'məsh-,rüm, -,rùm\ n : the fleshy usu.caplike spore-bearing organ of various fungi esp.when edible; also : such a fungus

²mushroom vb 1 : to spread out : EXPAND 2 : to collect wild mushrooms 3 : to grow rapidly

mushy \'mə-shē\ adj mush·i·er; -est 1 : soft like mush 2 : excessively sentimental

mu·sic \'myü-zik\ n 1 : the science or art of combining tones into a composition having structure and continuity; also : vocal or instrumental sounds having rhythm, melody, or harmony 2 : an agreeable sound

¹mu·si·cal \'myü-zi-kəl\ adj 1 : of or relating to music or musicians 2 : having the pleasing tonal qualities of music 3 : fond of or gifted in music — mu·si·cal·ly \-k(ə-)lē\ adv

²musical n : a film or theatrical production consisting of musical numbers and dialogue based on a unifying plot

mu·si·cale \,myü-zi-'kal\ n : a usu. private social gathering featuring music

mu·si·cian \myù-'zi-shən\ n : a composer, conductor, or performer of music — mu·si·cian·ly adj — mu·si·cian·ship n

mu·si·col·o·gy \,myü-zi-'kä-lə-jē\ n : the study of music as a field of knowledge or research — mu·si·co·log·i·cal \-kə-'lä-ji-kəl\ adj — mu·si·col·o·gist \-'kä-lə-jist\ n

musk \'məsk\ n : a substance obtained esp. from a small Asian deer (musk deer) and used as a perfume fixative — musk·i·ness \'məs-kē-nəs\ n — musky adj

mus·keg \'məs-,keg\ n : BOG; esp : a mossy bog in northern No. America

mus·kel·lunge \'məs-kə-,lənj\ n, pl muskellunge : a large No. American pike that is a valuable sport fish

mus·ket \'məs-kət\ n [MF mousquet, fr. It moschetto small artillery piece, kind of small hawk, fr. dim. of mosca fly, fr. L musca] : a heavy large-caliber muzzle-loading shoulder firearm — mus·ke·teer \,məs-kə-'tir\ n

mus·ket·ry \'məs-kə-trē\ n 1 : MUSKETS 2 : MUSKETEERS 3 : musket fire

musk·mel·on \'məsk-,me-lən\ n : a small round to oval melon that has usu. a sweet edible green or orange flesh and a musky odor

musk ox n : a heavyset shaggy-coated wild ox of Greenland and the arctic tundra of northern No. America

musk·rat \'məs-,krat\ n, pl muskrat or muskrats : a large No. American aquatic rodent with webbed feet and dark brown fur; also : its fur

Mus·lim \'məz-ləm\ n : an adherent of Islam — Muslim adj

mus·lin \'məz-lən\ n : a plain-woven sheer to coarse cotton fabric

¹muss \'məs\ n : a state of disorder —

muss·i·ly \'mə-sə-lē\ adv — muss·i·ness \-sē-nəs\ n — mussy adj

²muss vb : to make untidy : DISARRANGE

mus·sel \'mə-səl\ n 1 : a dark edible salt-water bivalve mollusk 2 : any of various freshwater bivalve mollusks of the central U.S. having shells with a pearly lining

¹must \'məst\ vb — used as an auxiliary esp. to express a command, requirement, obligation, or necessity

²must n 1 : an imperative duty 2 : an indispensable item

mus·tache also mous·tache \'məs-,tash, (,)məs-'tash\ n : the hair growing on the human upper lip — mous·tached also mous·tached \-,tasht, -'tasht\ adj

mus·tang \'məs-,taŋ\ n [MexSp mestengo, fr. Sp, stray, fr. mesteño strayed, fr. mesta annual roundup of cattle that disposed of strays, fr. ML (animalia) mixta mixed animals] : a small hardy naturalized horse of the western plains of America; also : BRONC

mus·tard \'məs-tərd\ n 1 : a pungent yellow powder of the seeds of an herb related to the cabbage and used as a condiment or in medicine 2 : a plant that yields mustard; also : a closely related plant — mustardy adj

mustard gas n : a poison gas used in warfare that has violent irritating and blistering effects

¹mus·ter \'məs-tər\ n 1 : an act of assembling (as for military inspection); also : critical examination 2 : an assembled group

²muster vb [ME mustren to show, muster, fr. AF mustrer, monstrer, fr. L monstrare to show, fr. monstrum evil omen, monster] 1 : CONVENE, ASSEMBLE; also : to call the roll of 2 : ACCUMULATE 3 : to call forth : ROUSE 4 : to amount to : COMPRISE

muster out vb : to discharge from military service

musty \'məs-tē\ adj mus·ti·er; -est : MOLDY, STALE; also : tasting or smelling of damp or decay — mus·ti·ly \-tə-lē\ adv — must·i·ness \-tē-nəs\ n

mu·ta·ble \'myü-tə-bəl\ adj 1 : prone to change : FICKLE 2 : capable of or liable to mutation : VARIABLE — mu·ta·bil·i·ty \,myü-tə-'bi-lə-tē\ n

mu·tant \'myü-t²nt\ adj : of, relating to, or produced by mutation — mutant n

mu·tate \'myü-,tāt\ vb mu·tat·ed; mu·tat·ing : to undergo or cause to undergo mutation — mu·ta·tive \'myü-,tā-tiv, -tə-tiv\ adj

mu·ta·tion \myü-'tā-shən\ n 1 : CHANGE 2 : an inherited physical or biochemical change in genetic material; also : the process of producing a mutation 3 : an individual, strain, or trait resulting from mutation — mu·ta·tion·al adj

¹mute \'myüt\ adj mut·er; mut·est 1 : unable to speak 2 : SILENT — mute·ly adv — mute·ness n

²mute n 1 : a person who cannot or does not speak 2 : a device on a musical instrument that reduces, softens, or muffles the tone

³mute vb mut·ed; mut·ing : to muffle, reduce, or eliminate the sound of

mu·ti·late \'myü-tə-,lāt\ vb -lat·ed; -lat·ing 1 : to cut up or alter radically so as to make imperfect 2 : MAIM, CRIPPLE — mu·ti·la·tion \,myü-tə-'lā-shən\ n — mu·ti·la·tor \'myü-tə-,lā-tər\ n

mu·ti·ny \'myü-tə-nē\ n, pl -nies : willful refusal to obey constituted authority; esp : revolt against a superior officer — mu·ti·neer \,myü-tə-'nir\ n — mu·ti·nous \'myü-tə-nəs\ adj — mu·ti·nous·ly adv — mutiny vb

mutt \'mət\ n : MONGREL, CUR

mut·ter \'mə-tər\ vb 1 : to speak indistinctly or with a low voice and lips partly closed 2 : GRUMBLE — mutter n

mut·ton \'mə-t²n\ n [ME motoun mutton, sheep, fr. AF mutun ram, sheep, mutton] : the flesh of a mature sheep used for food — mut·tony adj

mut·ton·chops \'mə-t²n-,chäps\ n pl : whiskers on the side of the face that are narrow at the temple and broad and round by the lower jaws

mu·tu·al \'myü-chə-wəl\ adj 1 : given and received in equal amount ⟨∼ trust⟩ 2 : having the same feelings one for the other ⟨∼ enemies⟩ 3 : COMMON, JOINT ⟨a ∼ friend⟩ — mu·tu·al·ly adv

mutual fund n : an investment company that invests money of its shareholders in a usu. diversified group of securities of other corporations

muu-muu \'mü-,mü\ n : a loose dress of Hawaiian origin

¹muz·zle \'mə-zəl\ n 1 : the nose and jaws of an animal; also : a covering for the muzzle to prevent biting or eating 2 : the mouth of a gun

²muzzle vb muz·zled; muz·zling 1 : to put a muzzle on 2 : to restrain from expression : GAG

mV abbr millivolt

MV abbr motor vessel

MVP abbr most valuable player

MW abbr megawatt

my \'mī\ adj 1 : of or relating to me or myself 2 — used interjectionally esp. to express surprise

my·col·o·gy \mī-'kä-lə-jē\ n : a branch of biology dealing with fungi — my·co·log·i·cal \,mī-kə-'lä-ji-kəl\ adj — my·col·o·gist \mī-'kä-lə-jist\ n

my·elo·ma \,mī-ə-'lō-mə\ n, pl -mas or -ma·ta \-mə-tə\ : a primary tumor of the bone marrow

my·nah or my·na \'mī-nə\ n : any of several Asian starlings; esp : a dark brown slightly crested bird sometimes taught to mimic speech

my·o·pia \mī-'ō-pē-ə\ n : a condition in which visual images come to a focus in front of the retina resulting esp. in defective vision of distant objects — my·o·pic \-'ō-pik, -'ä-\ adj — my·o·pi·cal·ly \-pi-k(ə-)lē\ adv

¹myr·i·ad \'mir-ē-əd\ n [Gk myriad-, myrias, fr. myrioi countless, ten thousand] : an indefinitely large number

²myriad adj : consisting of a very great but indefinite number

myr·mi·don \'mər-mə-,dän\ *n* : a loyal follower; *esp* : one who executes orders without protest or pity

myrrh \'mər\ *n* : a fragrant aromatic plant gum used in perfumes and formerly for incense

myr·tle \'mər-t³l\ *n* : an evergreen shrub of southern Europe with shiny leaves, fragrant flowers, and black berries; *also* : PERIWINKLE

my·self \mī-'self, mə-\ *pron* : I, ME — used reflexively, for emphasis, or in absolute constructions ⟨I hurt ∼⟩ ⟨I ∼ did it⟩ ⟨∼ busy, I sent him instead⟩

mys·tery \'mis-tə-rē\ *n, pl* **-ter·ies** 1 : a religious truth known by revelation alone 2 : something not understood or beyond understanding 3 : enigmatic quality or character 4 : a work of fiction dealing with the solution of a mysterious crime — **mys·te·ri·ous** \mis-'tir-ē-əs\ *adj* — **mys·te·ri·ous·ly** *adv* — **mys·te·ri·ous·ness** *n*

¹**mys·tic** \'mis-tik\ *adj* 1 : of or relating to mystics or mysticism 2 : MYSTERIOUS; *also* : MYSTIFYING

²**mystic** *n* : a person who follows, advocates, or experiences mysticism

mys·ti·cal \'mis-ti-kəl\ *adj* 1 : SPIRITUAL, SYMBOLIC 2 : of or relating to an intimate knowledge of or direct communion with God (as through contemplation or visions)

mys·ti·cism \'mis-tə-,si-zəm\ *n* : the belief that direct knowledge of God or ultimate reality is attainable through immediate intuition or insight

mys·ti·fy \'mis-tə-,fī\ *vb* **-fied; -fy·ing** 1 : to perplex the mind of 2 : to make mysterious — **mys·ti·fi·ca·tion** \,mis-tə-fə-'kā-shən\ *n*

mys·tique \mi-'stēk\ *n* [F] 1 : an air or attitude of mystery and reverence developing around something or someone 2 : the special esoteric skill essential in a calling or activity

myth \'mith\ *n* 1 : a usu. legendary narrative that presents part of the beliefs of a people or explains a practice or natural phenomenon 2 : an imaginary or unverifiable person or thing — **myth·i·cal** \'mi-thi-kəl\ *or* **myth·ic** \-thik\ *adj*

my·thol·o·gy \mi-'thä-lə-jē\ *n, pl* **-gies** : a body of myths and esp. of those dealing with the gods and heroes of a people — **myth·o·log·i·cal** \,mi-thə-'lä-ji-kəl\ *adj* — **my·thol·o·gist** \mi-'thä-lə-jist\ *n* — **my·thol·o·gize** \-,jīz\ *vb*

¹**n** \'en\ *n, pl* **n's** *or* **ns** \'enz\ *often cap* 1 : the 14th letter of the English alphabet 2 : an unspecified quantity

²**n** *abbr, often cap* 1 **net** 2 **neuter** 3 **noon** 4 **normal** 5 **north; northern** 6 **note** 7 **noun** 8 **number**

N *symbol* nitrogen

Na *symbol* [NL *natrium*] sodium

-n — see -EN

NA *abbr* 1 **no account** 2 **North America** 3 **not applicable** 4 **not available**

NAACP \,en-,də-bəl-,ā-,sē-'pē, ,en-,ā-,ā-,sē-\ *abbr* National Association for the Advancement of Colored People

nab \'nab\ *vb* **nabbed; nab·bing** : SEIZE; *esp* : ARREST

NAB *abbr* New American Bible

na·bob \'nā-,bäb\ *n* [Hindi *navāb* & Urdu *nawāb*, provincial governor (in the Mogul empire), fr. Ar *nuwwāb*, pl. of *nā'ib* governor] : a person of great wealth or prominence

na·celle \nə-'sel\ *n* : an enclosure (as for an engine) on an aircraft

na·cho \'nä-chō\ *n, pl* **nachos** [AmerSp] : a tortilla chip topped with melted cheese and often additional savory toppings

na·cre \'nā-kər\ *n* : MOTHER-OF-PEARL — **na·cre·ous** \'nā-krē-əs\ *adj*

na·dir \'nā-,dir, -dər\ *n* [ME, fr. MF, fr. Ar *naḍhīr* opposite] 1 : the point of the celestial sphere that is directly opposite the zenith and directly beneath the observer 2 : the lowest point

¹**nag** \'nag\ *n* : HORSE; *esp* : an old or decrepit horse

²**nag** *vb* **nagged; nag·ging** 1 : to find fault incessantly : COMPLAIN 2 : to irritate by constant scolding or urging 3 : to be a continuing source of annoyance ⟨a *nagging* backache⟩

³**nag** *n* : one who nags habitually

Nah *abbr* Nahum

Na·huatl \'nä-,wä-t³l\ *n* : a group of American Indian languages of central and southern Mexico

Na·hum \'nā-həm, -əm\ *n* — see BIBLE table

NAIA *abbr* National Association of Intercollegiate Athletes

na·iad \'nā-əd, 'nī-, -,ad\ *n, pl* **naiads** *or* **na·ia·des** \-ə-,dēz\ 1 : one of the nymphs in ancient mythology living in lakes, rivers, springs, and fountains 2 : an aquatic young of some insects (as a dragonfly)

¹**na·if** *or* **na·if** \nä-'ēf\ *adj* : NAIVE

²**naïf** *or* **naif** *n* : a naive person

¹**nail** \'nāl\ *n* 1 : a horny sheath protecting the end of each finger and toe in humans and related primates 2 : a slender pointed fastener with a head designed to be pounded in

²**nail** *vb* : to fasten with or as if with a nail — **nail·er** *n*

nail down *vb* : to settle or establish clearly and unmistakably

nain·sook \'nān-,sůk\ *n* : a soft lightweight muslin

nai·ra \'nī-rə\ *n* — see MONEY table

na·ive *or* **na·ïve** \nä-'ēv\ *adj* **na·iv·er**; **-est** [F *naïve*, fem. of *naïf*, fr. OF, inborn, natural, fr. L *nativus* native] **1** : marked by unaffected simplicity : ARTLESS, INGENUOUS **2** : CREDULOUS ♦ *Synonyms* NATURAL, INNOCENT, SIMPLE, UNAFFECTED, UNSOPHISTICATED, UNSTUDIED — **na·ive·ly** *adv* — **na·ive·ness** *n*

na·ïve·té *also* **na·ive·te** *or* **na·ive·té** \nä-,ē-və-'tā, nä-'ē-və-,tā\ *n* **1** : a naive remark or action **2** : the quality or state of being naive

na·ive·ty *also* **na·ive·ty** \nä-'ē-və-tē\ *n, pl* **-ties** : NAÏVETÉ

na·ked \'nā-kəd\ *adj* **1** : having no clothes on : NUDE **2** : UNSHEATHED ⟨a ∼ sword⟩ **3** : lacking a usual or natural covering (as of foliage or feathers) **4** : PLAIN, UNADORNED ⟨the ∼ truth⟩ **5** : not aided by artificial means ⟨seen by the ∼ eye⟩ — **na·ked·ly** *adv* — **na·ked·ness** *n*

nak·fa \'näk-,fä\ *n, pl* **nakfa** — see MONEY table

nam·by–pam·by \,nam-bē-'pam-bē\ *adj* **1** : INSIPID **2** : WEAK, INDECISIVE ♦ *Synonyms* BLAND, FLAT, INANE, JEJUNE, VAPID, WISHY-WASHY

¹name \'nām\ *n* **1** : a word or words by which a person or thing is known **2** : a disparaging epithet ⟨call him ∼*s*⟩ **3** : REPUTATION; *esp* : distinguished reputation ⟨made a ∼ for herself⟩ **4** : FAMILY, CLAN ⟨was a disgrace to their ∼⟩ **5** : appearance as opposed to reality ⟨a friend in ∼ only⟩

²name *vb* **named**; **nam·ing** **1** : to give a name to : CALL **2** : to mention or identify by name **3** : NOMINATE, APPOINT **4** : to decide on : CHOOSE **5** : to mention explicitly : SPECIFY ⟨∼ a price⟩ — **name·able** *adj*

³name *adj* **1** : of, relating to, or bearing a name ⟨∼ tag⟩ **2** : having an established reputation ⟨∼ brands⟩

name day *n* : the church feast day of the saint after whom one is named

name·less \'nām-ləs\ *adj* **1** : having no name **2** : not marked with a name ⟨a ∼ grave⟩ **3** : not known by name ⟨a ∼ hero⟩ **4** : too distressing to be described ⟨∼ fears⟩ — **name·less·ly** *adv*

name·ly \-lē\ *adv* : that is to say : AS ⟨the cat family, ∼, lions, tigers, and similar animals⟩

name·plate \-,plāt\ *n* : a plate or plaque bearing a name (as of a resident)

name·sake \-,sāk\ *n* : one that has the same name as another; *esp* : one named after another

nan·keen \nan-'kēn\ *n* : a durable brownish yellow cotton fabric orig. woven by hand in China

nan·ny goat \'na-nē-\ *n* : a female domestic goat

nano·me·ter \'na-nə-,mē-tər\ *n* : one billionth of a meter

nano·scale \-,skāl\ *adj* : having dimensions measured in nanometers

nano·sec·ond \-,se-kənd\ *n* : one billionth of a second

nano·tech·nol·o·gy \,na-nō-tek-'nä-lə-jē\ *n* : the manipulation of materials on an atomic or molecular scale

nano·tube \'na-nō-,tüb\ *n* : a microscope tube (as of carbon) whose diameter is measured in nanometers

¹nap \'nap\ *vb* **napped**; **nap·ping** **1** : to sleep briefly esp. during the day : DOZE **2** : to be off guard ⟨was caught *napping*⟩

²nap *n* : a short sleep esp. during the day

³nap *n* : a soft downy fibrous surface (as on yarn and cloth) — **nap·less** *adj* — **napped** \'napt\ *adj*

na·palm \'nā-,pälm, -,päm\ *n* [*naphthalene* + *palmitate*, salt of a fatty acid] **1** : a thickener used in jelling gasoline (as for incendiary bombs) **2** : fuel jelled with napalm

nape \'nāp, 'nap\ *n* : the back of the neck

na·pery \'nā-pə-rē\ *n* : household linen esp. for the table

naph·tha \'naf-thə, 'nap-\ *n* : any of various liquid hydrocarbon mixtures used chiefly as solvents

naph·tha·lene \-,lēn\ *n* : a crystalline substance used esp. in organic synthesis and as a moth repellent

nap·kin \'nap-kən\ *n* **1** : a piece of material (as cloth) used at table to wipe the lips or fingers and protect the clothes **2** : a small cloth or towel

na·po·leon \nə-'pōl-yən, -'pō-lē-ən\ *n* : an oblong pastry with a filling of cream, custard, or jelly

Na·po·le·on·ic \nə-,pō-lē-'ä-nik\ *adj* : of, relating to, or characteristic of Napoleon I or his family

narc *also* **nark** \'närk\ *n, slang* : a person (as a government agent) who investigates narcotics violations

nar·cis·sism \'när-sə-,si-zəm\ *n* [G *Narzissismus*, fr. *Narziss* Narcissus, beautiful youth of Greek mythology who fell in love with his own image] **1** : undue dwelling on one's own self or attainments **2** : love of or sexual desire for one's own body — **nar·cis·sist** \-sist\ *n or adj* — **nar·cis·sis·tic** \,när-sə-'sis-tik\ *adj*

nar·cis·sus \när-'si-səs\ *n, pl* **nar·cis·si** \-,sī, -,sē\ *or* **nar·cis·sus·es** *or* **narcissus** : DAFFODIL; *esp* : one with short-tubed flowers usu. borne separately

nar·co·lep·sy \'när-kə-,lep-sē\ *n, pl* **-sies** : a condition characterized by brief attacks of deep sleep — **nar·co·lep·tic** \,när-kə-'lep-tik\ *adj or n*

nar·co·sis \när-'kō-səs\ *n, pl* **-co·ses** \-,sēz\ : a state of stupor, unconsciousness, or arrested activity produced by the influence of chemicals (as narcotics)

nar·co·ter·ror·ism \'när-kō-'ter-ər-,i-zəm\ *n* : terrorism financed by profits from illegal drug trafficking

nar·cot·ic \när-'kä-tik\ *n* [ME *narkotik*, fr. MF *narcotique*, fr. *narcotique*, adj., fr. ML *narcoticus*, fr. Gk *narkōtikos*, fr. *narkoun* to benumb, fr. *narkē* numbness] **1** : a drug (as opium) that dulls the senses, relieves pain, and induces sleep **2** : an illegal drug (as marijuana or LSD) — **narcotic** *adj*

nar·co·tize \'när-kə-ˌtīz\ *vb* **-tized; -tiz·ing** **1** : to treat with or subject to a narcotic; *also* : to put into a state of narcosis **2** : to soothe to unconsciousness or unawareness

nard \'närd\ *n* : a fragrant ointment of the ancients

na·res \'ner-(ˌ)ēz\ *n pl* [L] : the pair of openings of the nose

Nar·ra·gan·sett \ˌna-rə-'gan-sət\ *n, pl* **-sett** *or* **-setts** **1** : a member of an American Indian people of Rhode Island **2** : the Algonquian language of the Narragansett people

nar·rate \'ner-ˌāt\ *vb* **nar·rat·ed; nar·rat·ing** : to recite the details of (as a story) : RELATE, TELL — **nar·ra·tion** \na-'rā-shən\ *n* — **nar·ra·tor** \'ner-ˌā-tər\ *n*

nar·ra·tive \'ner-ə-tiv\ *n* **1** : something that is narrated : STORY **2** : the art or practice of narrating

¹nar·row \'ner-ō\ *adj* **1** : of slender or less than standard width **2** : limited in size or scope : RESTRICTED **3** : not liberal in views : PREJUDICED **4** : interpreted or interpreting strictly **5** : CLOSE ⟨won by a ∼ margin⟩; *also* : barely successful ⟨a ∼ escape⟩ — **nar·row·ly** *adv* — **nar·row·ness** *n*

²narrow *vb* : to lessen in width or extent

³narrow *n* : a narrow passage : STRAIT — usu. used in pl.

nar·row–mind·ed \ˌner-ō-'mīn-dəd\ *adj* : not liberal or broad-minded ♦ *Synonyms* ILLIBERAL, BIGOTED, HIDEBOUND, INTOLERANT

nar·whal \'när-ˌhwäl, 'när-wəl\ *n* : an arctic sea mammal about 20 feet (6 meters) long that is related to the dolphins and in the male has a long twisted ivory tusk

NAS *abbr* naval air station

NASA \'na-sə\ *abbr* National Aeronautics and Space Administration

¹na·sal \'nā-zəl\ *n* **1** : a nasal part **2** : a nasal consonant or vowel

²nasal *adj* **1** : of or relating to the nose **2** : uttered through the nose — **na·sal·ly** *adv*

na·sal·ize \'nā-zə-ˌlīz\ *vb* **-ized; -iz·ing** : to make nasal or pronounce as a nasal sound — **na·sal·i·za·tion** \ˌnā-zə-lə-'zā-shən\ *n*

na·scent \'na-sᵊnt, 'nā-\ *adj* : coming into existence : beginning to grow or develop — **na·scence** \-ᵊns\ *n*

nas·tur·tium \nə-'stər-shəm, na-\ *n* : either of two widely cultivated watery-stemmed herbs with showy spurred flowers and pungent edible seeds

nas·ty \'nas-tē\ *adj* **nas·ti·er; -est** **1** : FILTHY **2** : INDECENT, OBSCENE **3** : HARMFUL, DANGEROUS ⟨took a ∼ fall⟩ **4** : DISAGREEABLE ⟨∼ weather⟩ **5** : MEAN, ILL-NATURED ⟨a ∼ temper⟩ **6** : DIFFICULT, VEXATIOUS ⟨a ∼ problem⟩ **7** : UNFAIR, DIRTY ⟨a ∼ trick⟩ — **nas·ti·ly** \'nas-tə-lē\ *adv* — **nas·ti·ness** \-tē-nəs\ *n*

nat *abbr* **1** national **2** native **3** natural

na·tal \'nā-tᵊl\ *adj* **1** : NATIVE **2** : of, relating to, or present at birth

na·ta·to·ri·um \ˌnā-tə-'tȯr-ē-əm, ˌna-\ *n* : a swimming pool esp. indoors

na·tion \'nā-shən\ *n* [ME *nacioun*, fr. AF *naciun* fr. L *nation-, natio* birth, race, nation, fr. *nasci* to be born] **1** : NATIONALITY 5; *also* : a politically organized nationality **2** : a community of people composed of one or more nationalities with its own territory and government **3** : the territory of a nation **4** : a federation of tribes (as of American Indians) — **na·tion·hood** *n*

¹na·tion·al \'na-shə-nəl\ *adj* **1** : of or relating to a nation **2** : comprising or characteristic of a nationality **3** : FEDERAL 3 — **na·tion·al·ly** *adv*

²national *n* **1** : one who owes allegiance to a nation **2** : a competition that is national in scope — usu. used in pl.

national guard *n* **1** : a military force serving as a national constabulary and defense force **2** *cap N & G* : a militia force recruited by each state of the U.S., equipped by the federal government, and jointly maintained subject to the call of either — **national guardsman** *n, often cap*

na·tion·al·ise *chiefly Brit var of* NATIONALIZE

na·tion·al·ism \'na-shə-nə-ˌli-zəm\ *n* : devotion to national interests, unity, and independence

na·tion·al·ist \-list\ *n* **1** : an advocate of or believer in nationalism **2** : a member of a political party or group advocating national independence or strong national government — **nationalist** *adj* — **na·tion·al·is·tic** \ˌna-shə-nə-'lis-tik\ *adj*

na·tion·al·i·ty \ˌna-shə-nə-'na-lə-tē\ *n, pl* **-ties** **1** : national character **2** : a legal relationship involving allegiance of an individual and protection on the part of the state **3** : membership in a particular nation **4** : political independence or existence as a separate nation **5** : a people having a common origin, tradition, and language and capable of forming a state **6** : an ethnic group within a larger unit (as a nation)

na·tion·al·ize \'na-shə-nə-ˌlīz\ *vb* **-ized; -iz·ing** **1** : to make national : make a nation of **2** : to remove from private ownership and place under government control — **na·tion·al·i·za·tion** \ˌna-shə-nə-lə-'zā-shən\ *n*

national monument *n* : a place of historic, scenic, or scientific interest set aside for preservation usu. by presidential proclamation

national park *n* : an area of special scenic, historical, or scientific importance set aside and maintained by a national government esp. for recreation or study

national seashore *n* : a recreational area adjacent to a seacoast and maintained by the federal government

na·tion·wide \ˌnā-shən-'wīd\ *adj* : extending throughout a nation

¹na·tive \'nā-tiv\ *adj* **1** : INBORN, NATURAL ⟨∼ talents⟩ **2** : born in a particular place or country **3** : belonging to a person because of the place or circumstances of birth ⟨her ~ language⟩ 4 : grown, produced, or originating in a particular place : INDIGENOUS 5 cap : NATIVE AMERICAN ♦ Synonyms ABORIGINAL, AUTOCHTHONOUS, ENDEMIC

²native n : one that is native; esp : a person who belongs to a particular country by birth

Native American n : a member of any of the aboriginal peoples of No. America and esp. the U.S.

na·tiv·ism \'nā-ti-ˌvi-zəm\ n 1 : a policy of favoring native inhabitants over immigrants 2 : the revival or perpetuation of a native culture esp. in opposition to acculturation

na·tiv·i·ty \nə-'ti-və-tē, nā-\ n, pl -ties 1 : the process or circumstances of being born : BIRTH 2 cap : the birth of Christ

natl abbr national

NATO \'nā-ˌ)tō\ abbr North Atlantic Treaty Organization

nat·ty \'na-tē\ adj nat·ti·er; -est : trimly neat and tidy : SMART — nat·ti·ly \-tə-lē\ adv — nat·ti·ness \-tē-nəs\ n

¹nat·u·ral \'na-chə-rəl\ adj 1 : determined by nature : INBORN, INNATE ⟨~ ability⟩ 2 : BORN ⟨a ~ fool⟩ 3 : ILLEGITIMATE ⟨a ~ child⟩ 4 : HUMAN 5 : of or relating to nature 6 : not artificial 7 : being simple and sincere : not affected 8 : LIFELIKE 9 : being neither sharp nor flat ♦ Synonyms INGENUOUS, NAIVE, UNSOPHISTICATED, ARTLESS, GUILELESS — nat·u·ral·ness n

²natural n 1 : IDIOT 2 : a character ♭ placed on a line or space of the musical staff to nullify the effect of a preceding sharp or flat 3 : one obviously suitable for a purpose ⟨a ~ for the job⟩

natural childbirth n : a system of managing childbirth in which the mother prepares to remain conscious and assist in delivery with little or no use of drugs

natural gas n : a combustible gaseous mixture of hydrocarbons coming from the earth's crust and used chiefly as a fuel and raw material

natural history n 1 : a treatise on some aspect of nature 2 : the study of natural objects esp. from an amateur or popular point of view

nat·u·ral·ise Brit var of NATURALIZE

nat·u·ral·ism \'na-chə-rə-ˌli-zəm\ n 1 : action or thought based only on natural desires and instincts 2 : a doctrine that denies a supernatural explanation of the origin or development of the universe and holds that scientific laws account for all of nature 3 : realism in art and literature — nat·u·ral·is·tic \ˌna-chə-rə-'lis-tik\ adj

nat·u·ral·ist \-list\ n 1 : one that advocates or practices naturalism 2 : a student of animals or plants esp. in the field

nat·u·ral·ize \-ˌlīz\ vb -ized; -iz·ing 1 : to confer the rights of a citizen on 2 : to become or cause to become established as if native ⟨~ new forage crops⟩ — nat·u·ral·i·za·tion \ˌna-chə-rə-lə-'zā-shən\ n

nat·u·ral·ly \'na-chə-rə-lē, 'nach-rə-\ adv 1 : by nature : by natural character or ability 2 : as might be expected 3 : without artificial aid; also : without affectation 4 : REALISTICALLY

natural science n : a science (as physics, chemistry, or biology) that deals with matter, energy, and their interrelations and transformations or with objectively measurable phenomena — natural scientist n

natural selection n : the natural process that results in the survival of individuals or groups best adjusted to their environment

na·ture \'nā-chər\ n [ME, fr. MF, fr. L natura, fr. natus, pp. of nasci to be born] 1 : the inherent quality or basic constitution of a person or thing; also : DISPOSITION, TEMPERAMENT 2 : KIND, SORT 3 : the physical universe 4 : one's natural instincts or way of life ⟨quirks of human ~⟩; also : primitive state ⟨a return to ~⟩ 5 : natural scenery or environment ⟨beauties of ~⟩

¹naught also nought \'nòt, 'nät\ pron : NOTHING ⟨efforts came to ~⟩

²naught also nought n 1 : NOTHINGNESS, NONEXISTENCE 2 : the arithmetical symbol 0 : ZERO

naugh·ty \'nò-tē, 'nä-\ adj naugh·ti·er; -est 1 : guilty of disobedience or misbehavior 2 : lacking in taste or propriety — naugh·ti·ly \-tə-lē\ adv — naugh·ti·ness \-tē-nəs\ n

nau·sea \'nò-zē-ə, -sē-; 'nò-zhə, -shə\ n [L, seasickness, nausea, fr. Gk nautia, nausia, fr. nautēs sailor] 1 : sickness of the stomach with a desire to vomit 2 : extreme disgust

nau·se·ate \'nò-zē-ˌāt, -sē-, -zhē-, -shē-\ vb -at·ed; -at·ing : to affect or become affected with nausea — nau·se·at·ing·ly adv

nau·seous \'nò-shəs, -zē-əs\ adj 1 : causing nausea or disgust 2 : affected with nausea or disgust

naut abbr nautical

nau·ti·cal \'nò-ti-kəl\ adj : of or relating to sailors, navigation, or ships — nau·ti·cal·ly \-k(ə-)lē\ adv

nautical mile n : a unit of distance equal to about 6080 feet (1852 meters)

nau·ti·lus \'nò-tə-ləs\ n, pl -lus·es or -li \ˌlī, -ˌlē\ : any of a genus of sea mollusks related to the octopuses but having a spiral chambered shell

nav abbr 1 naval 2 navigable; navigation

Na·va·jo also Na·va·ho \'na-və-ˌhō, 'nä-\ n, pl -jo or -jos also -ho or -hos : a member of an American Indian people of northern New Mexico and Arizona; also : their language

na·val \'nā-vəl\ adj : of, relating to, or possessing a navy

naval stores n pl : products (as pitch, turpentine, or rosin) obtained from resinous conifers (as pines)

nave \'nāv\ n [ML navis, fr. L, ship] : the central part of a church running lengthwise

na·vel \\'nā-vəl\\ *n* : a depression in the middle of the abdomen that marks the point of attachment of fetus and mother

navel–gaz·ing \\'nā-vəl-ˌgā-ziŋ\\ *n* : useless or excessive self-contemplation

navel orange *n* : a seedless orange having a pit at the blossom end where the fruit encloses a small secondary fruit

nav·i·ga·ble \\'na-vi-gə-bəl\\ *adj* 1 : capable of being navigated ⟨a ~ river⟩ 2 : capable of being steered — **nav·i·ga·bil·i·ty** \\ˌna-vi-gə-'bi-lə-tē\\ *n*

nav·i·gate \\'na-və-ˌgāt\\ *vb* **-gat·ed; -gat·ing** 1 : to sail on or through ⟨~ the Atlantic Ocean⟩ 2 : to steer or direct the course of a ship or aircraft 3 : MOVE; *esp* : WALK ⟨could hardly ~⟩ — **nav·i·ga·tion** \\ˌna-və-'gā-shən\\ *n* — **nav·i·ga·tor** \\'na-və-ˌgā-tər\\ *n*

na·vy \\'nā-vē\\ *n, pl* **navies** 1 : FLEET; *also* : the warships belonging to a nation 2 *often cap* : a nation's organization for naval warfare

navy yard *n* : a yard where naval vessels are built or repaired

¹nay \\'nā\\ *adv* : NO

²nay *n* : a negative vote; *also* : a person casting such a vote

³nay *conj* : not merely this but also : not only so but ⟨he was happy, ~, ecstatic⟩

nay·say·er \\'nā-ˌsā-ər\\ *n* : one who denies, refuses, or opposes something

Na·zi \\'nät-sē, 'nat-\\ *n* [G, fr. *Nationalsozialist*, lit., national socialist] : a member of a German fascist party controlling Germany from 1933 to 1945 under Adolf Hitler — **Nazi** *adj* — **Na·zism** \\'nät-ˌsi-zəm, 'nat-\\ *also* **Na·zi·ism** \\-sē-ˌi-zəm\\ *n*

Nb *symbol* niobium

NB *abbr* 1 New Brunswick 2 nota bene

NBA *abbr* 1 National Basketball Association 2 National Boxing Association

NBC *abbr* National Broadcasting Company

NBS *abbr* National Bureau of Standards

NC *abbr* 1 no charge 2 North Carolina

NCAA *abbr* National Collegiate Athletic Association

NCO \\ˌen-ˌsē-'ō\\ *n* : NONCOMMISSIONED OFFICER

nd *abbr* no date

Nd *symbol* neodymium

ND *abbr* North Dakota

N Dak *abbr* North Dakota

Ne *symbol* neon

NE *abbr* 1 Nebraska 2 New England 3 northeast

Ne·an·der·thal \\nē-'an-dər-ˌthȯl, nā-'än-dər-ˌtäl\\ *n* 1 *or* **Ne·an·der·tal** \\-ˌtäl\\ : an extinct Old World hominid that lived from about 30,000 to 200,000 years ago 2 : a person who resembles or suggests a caveman — **Neanderthal** *or* **Neandertal** *adj*

neap tide \\'nēp-\\ *n* : a tide of minimum range occurring at the first and third quarters of the moon

¹near \\'nir\\ *adv* 1 : at, within, or to a short distance or time 2 : ALMOST ⟨was ~ dead⟩

²near *prep* : close to

³near *adj* 1 : closely related or associated; *also* : INTIMATE 2 : not far away; *also* : being the closer or left-hand member of a pair 3 : barely avoided ⟨a ~ accident⟩ 4 : DIRECT, SHORT ⟨by the ~est route⟩ 5 : STINGY 6 : not real but very like ⟨~ silk⟩ — **near·ly** *adv* — **near·ness** *n*

⁴near *vb* : APPROACH

near beer *n* : any of various malt liquors low in alcohol

near·by \\nir-'bī, 'nir-ˌbī\\ *adv or adj* : close at hand

near·sight·ed \\'nir-'sī-təd\\ *adj* : able to see near things more clearly than distant ones : MYOPIC — **near·sight·ed·ly** *adv* — **near·sight·ed·ness** *n*

neat \\'nēt\\ *adj* [MF *net*, fr. L *nitidus* bright, neat, fr. *nitēre* to shine] 1 : being orderly and clean 2 : not mixed or diluted ⟨~ brandy⟩ 3 : marked by tasteful simplicity 4 : PRECISE, SYSTEMATIC 5 : SKILLFUL, ADROIT 6 : FINE, ADMIRABLE ♦ **Synonyms** SHIPSHAPE, TIDY, TRIG, TRIM — **neat** *adv* — **neat·ly** *adv* — **neat·ness** *n*

neath \\'nēth\\ *prep, dial* : BENEATH

neat·nik \\'nēt-nik\\ *n* : a person who is compulsively neat

neb \\'neb\\ *n* 1 : the beak of a bird or tortoise; *also* : NOSE, SNOUT 2 : NIB

Neb *or* **Nebr** *abbr* Nebraska

NEB *abbr* New English Bible

neb·u·la \\'ne-byə-lə\\ *n, pl* **-lae** \\-ˌlē, -ˌlī\\ *also* **-las** [NL, fr. L, mist, cloud] 1 : any of numerous clouds of gas or dust in interstellar space 2 : GALAXY — **neb·u·lar** \\-lər\\ *adj*

neb·u·liz·er \\'ne-byə-ˌlī-zər\\ *n* : ATOMIZER

neb·u·lous \\'ne-byə-ləs\\ *adj* 1 : of or relating to a nebula 2 : HAZY, INDISTINCT

¹nec·es·sary \\'ne-sə-ˌser-ē\\ *adj* 1 : INEVITABLE, INESCAPABLE; *also* : CERTAIN 2 : PREDETERMINED 3 : COMPULSORY 4 : positively needed : INDISPENSABLE ♦ **Synonyms** IMPERATIVE, NECESSITOUS, ESSENTIAL — **nec·es·sar·i·ly** \\ˌne-sə-'ser-ə-lē\\ *adv*

²necessary *n, pl* **-sar·ies** : an indispensable item

ne·ces·si·tate \\ni-'se-sə-ˌtāt\\ *vb* **-tat·ed; -tat·ing** : to make necessary

ne·ces·si·tous \\ni-'se-sə-təs\\ *adj* 1 : NEEDY, IMPOVERISHED 2 : URGENT 3 : NECESSARY ⟨~ bargaining⟩

ne·ces·si·ty \\ni-'se-sə-tē\\ *n, pl* **-ties** 1 : conditions that cannot be changed 2 : WANT, POVERTY 3 : something that is necessary 4 : very great need

¹neck \\'nek\\ *n* 1 : the part of the body connecting the head and the trunk 2 : the part of a garment covering or near to the neck 3 : a relatively narrow part suggestive of a neck ⟨~ of a bottle⟩ ⟨~ of land⟩ 4 : a narrow margin esp. of victory ⟨won by a ~⟩ — **necked** \\'nekt\\ *adj*

²neck *vb* : to kiss and caress amorously

neck and neck *adv or adj* : very close (as in a race)

neck·er·chief \\'ne-kər-chəf, -ˌchēf\\ *n, pl*

-chiefs \-chəfs, -ˌchēfs\ *also* **-chieves** \-ˌchēvz\ : a square of cloth worn folded about the neck like a scarf

neck·lace \'ne-kləs\ *n* : an ornament worn around the neck

neck·line \'nek-ˌlīn\ *n* : the outline of the neck opening of a garment

neck·tie \-ˌtī\ *n* : a strip of cloth worn around the neck and tied in front

ne·crol·o·gy \nə-'krä-lə-jē\ *n, pl* **-gies** 1 : OBITUARY 2 : a list of the recently dead

nec·ro·man·cy \'ne-krə-ˌman-sē\ *n* 1 : the art or practice of conjuring up the spirits of the dead for purposes of magically revealing the future 2 : MAGIC, SORCERY — **nec·ro·man·cer** \-sər\ *n*

ne·crop·o·lis \nə-'krä-pə-ləs, ne-\ *n, pl* **-lis·es** *or* **-les** \-ˌlēz\ *or* **-leis** \-ˌlās\ *or* **-li** \-ˌlī, -ˌlē\ [LL, fr. Gk *nekropolis*, fr. *nekros* dead body + *polis* city] : CEMETERY; *esp* : a large elaborate cemetery of an ancient city

nec·rop·sy \'ne-ˌkräp-sē\ *n, pl* **-sies** : AUTOPSY; *esp* : an autopsy performed on an animal

ne·cro·sis \nə-'krō-səs, ne-\ *n, pl* **ne·cro·ses** \-ˌsēz\ : usu. local death of body tissue — **ne·crot·ic** \-'krä-tik\ *adj*

nec·tar \'nek-tər\ *n* 1 : the drink of the Greek and Roman gods; *also* : any delicious drink 2 : a sweet plant secretion that is the raw material of honey

nec·tar·ine \ˌnek-tə-'rēn\ *n* : a smooth-skinned peach

née *or* **nee** \'nā\ *adj* [F, lit., born] — used to identify a woman by her maiden family name

¹**need** \'nēd\ *n* 1 : OBLIGATION ⟨no ~ to hurry⟩ 2 : a lack of something requisite, desirable, or useful 3 : a condition requiring supply or relief ⟨when the ~ arises⟩ 4 : POVERTY ◆ **Synonyms** NECESSITY, EXIGENCY

²**need** *vb* 1 : to be in want 2 : to have cause or occasion for : REQUIRE ⟨he ~s advice⟩ 3 : to be under obligation or necessity ⟨we ~ to know the truth⟩

need·ful \'nēd-fəl\ *adj* : NECESSARY, REQUISITE

¹**nee·dle** \'nē-dəl\ *n* 1 : a slender pointed usu. steel implement used in sewing 2 : a slender rod (as for knitting, controlling a small opening, or transmitting vibrations to or from a recording) ⟨a phonograph ~⟩ 3 : a slender hollow instrument by which material is introduced into or withdrawn from the body 4 : a slender indicator on a dial 5 : a needle-shaped leaf (as of a pine)

²**needle** *vb* **nee·dled; nee·dling** : PROD, GOAD; *esp* : to incite to action by repeated gibes

nee·dle-nose pliers \'nē-dəl-ˌnōz-\ *n pl* : pliers with long slender jaws for grasping small or thin objects

nee·dle·point \'nē-dəl-ˌpóint\ *n* 1 : lace worked with a needle over a paper pattern 2 : embroidery done on canvas across counted threads — **needlepoint** *adj*

need·less \'nēd-ləs\ *adj* : UNNECESSARY ⟨~ waste⟩ — **need·less·ly** *adv* — **need·less·ness** *n*

nee·dle·wom·an \'nē-dəl-ˌwu̇-mən\ *n* : a woman who does needlework; *esp* : SEAMSTRESS

nee·dle·work \-ˌwərk\ *n* : work done with a needle; *esp* : work (as embroidery) other than plain sewing

needs \'nēdz\ *adv* : of necessity : NECESSARILY ⟨must ~ be recognized⟩

needy \'nē-dē\ *adj* **need·i·er; -est** : being in want : POVERTY-STRICKEN

ne'er \'ner\ *adv* : NEVER

ne'er–do–well \'ner-dù-ˌwel\ *n* : an idle worthless person — **ne'er–do–well** *adj*

ne·far·i·ous \ni-'fer-ē-əs\ *adj* [L *nefarius*, fr. *nefas* crime, fr. *ne-* not + *fas* right, divine law] : very wicked : EVIL ◆ **Synonyms** BAD, IMMORAL, INIQUITOUS, SINFUL, VICIOUS — **ne·far·i·ous·ly** *adv*

neg *abbr* negative

ne·gate \ni-'gāt\ *vb* **ne·gat·ed; ne·gat·ing** 1 : to deny the existence or truth of 2 : to cause to be ineffective or invalid : NULLIFY

ne·ga·tion \ni-'gā-shən\ *n* 1 : the action or operation of negating or making negative 2 : a negative doctrine or statement

¹**neg·a·tive** \'ne-gə-tiv\ *adj* 1 : marked by denial, prohibition, or refusal ⟨a ~ reply⟩ 2 : not positive or constructive; *esp* : not affirming the presence of what is sought or suspected to be present ⟨test results were ~⟩ 3 : less than zero ⟨a ~ number⟩ 4 : being, relating to, or charged with electricity of which the electron is the elementary unit 5 : having the light and dark parts opposite to what they were in the original photographic subject — **neg·a·tive·ly** *adv* — **neg·a·tive·ness** *n* — **neg·a·tiv·i·ty** \ˌne-gə-'ti-və-tē\ *n*

²**negative** *n* 1 : a negative word or statement 2 : a negative vote or reply; *also* : REFUSAL 3 : something that is the opposite or negation of something else 4 : a negative number 5 : the side that votes or argues for the opposition (as in a debate) 6 : a negative photographic image on transparent material

³**negative** *vb* **-tived; -tiv·ing** 1 : to refuse to accept or approve 2 : to vote against 3 : DISPROVE

negative income tax *n* : a system of federal subsidy payments to families with incomes below a stipulated level

neg·a·tiv·ism \'ne-gə-ti-ˌvi-zəm\ *n* : an attitude of skepticism and denial of nearly everything affirmed or suggested by others

¹**ne·glect** \ni-'glekt\ *vb* [L *neglectus*, pp. of *neglegere, neclegere*, fr. *nec-* not + *legere* to gather] 1 : DISREGARD 2 : to leave undone or unattended to esp. through carelessness ◆ **Synonyms** OMIT, IGNORE, OVERLOOK, SLIGHT, FORGET, MISS

²**neglect** *n* 1 : an act or instance of neglecting something 2 : the condition of being neglected — **ne·glect·ful** *adj*

neg·li·gee *also* **neg·li·gé** \ˌne-glə-'zhā\ *n* : a woman's long flowing dressing gown

neg·li·gent \'ne-gli-jənt\ *adj* : marked by

neglect ✦ *Synonyms* NEGLECTFUL, RE-MISS, DELINQUENT, DERELICT — **neg·li·gence** \-jəns\ *n* — **neg·li·gent·ly** *adv*

neg·li·gi·ble \'ne-gli-jə-bəl\ *adj* : so small as to be neglected or disregarded

ne·go·tiant \ni-'gō-shē-ənt\ *n* : NEGOTIATOR

ne·go·ti·ate \ni-'gō-shē-ˌāt\ *vb* **-at·ed; -at·ing** [L *negotiari* to carry on business, fr. *negotium* business, fr. *neg-* not + *otium* leisure] **1** : to confer with another so as to arrive at the settlement of some matter; *also* : to arrange for or bring about by such conferences ⟨∼ a treaty⟩ **2** : to transfer to another by delivery or endorsement in return for equivalent value ⟨∼ a check⟩ **3** : to get through, around, or over successfully ⟨∼ a turn⟩ — **ne·go·tia·ble** \-shə-bəl, -shē-ə-\ *adj* — **ne·go·ti·a·tion** \ni-ˌgō-sē-'ā-shən, -shē-\ *n* — **ne·go·ti·a·tor** \-'gō-shē-ˌā-tər\ *n*

ne·gri·tude \'ne-grə-ˌtüd, -ˌtyüd, 'nē-\ *n* : a consciousness of and pride in one's African heritage

Ne·gro \'nē-grō\ *n, pl* **Negroes** [Sp or Pg, fr. *negro* black] *sometimes offensive* : a member of the human race native to Africa and classified according to physical features (as dark skin pigmentation) — **Negro** *adj, sometimes offensive* — **Negroid** \'nē-ˌgròid\ *n or adj, often not cap, sometimes offensive*

Neh *abbr* Nehemiah

Ne·he·mi·ah \ˌnē-ə-'mī-ə\ *n* — see BIBLE table

neigh \'nā\ *n* : a loud prolonged cry of a horse — **neigh** *vb*

¹neigh·bor \'nā-bər\ *n* **1** : one living or located near another **2** : FELLOW MAN

²neighbor *vb* : to be next to or near to : border on

neigh·bor·hood \'nā-bər-ˌhùd\ *n* **1** : NEARNESS **2** : a place or region near : VICINITY; *also* : a number or amount near ⟨costs in the ∼ of $10⟩ **3** : the people living near one another **4** : a section lived in by neighbors and usu. having distinguishing characteristics

neigh·bor·ly \-lē\ *adj* : befitting congenial neighbors; *esp* : FRIENDLY ⟨a ∼ welcome⟩ — **neigh·bor·li·ness** *n*

neigh·bour *chiefly Brit var of* NEIGHBOR

¹nei·ther \'nē-thər, 'nī-\ *conj* **1** : not either ⟨∼ good nor bad⟩ **2** : NOR ⟨∼ did I⟩

²neither *pron* : neither one : not the one and not the other ⟨∼ of the two⟩

³neither *adj* : not either ⟨∼ hand⟩

nel·son \'nel-sən\ *n* : a wrestling hold in which one applies leverage against an opponent's arm, neck, and head

nem·a·tode \'ne-mə-ˌtōd\ *n* : any of a phylum of elongated cylindrical worms parasitic in animals or plants or free-living in soil or water

nem·e·sis \'ne-mə-səs\ *n, pl* **-e·ses** \-ˌsēz\ [L *Nemesis*, goddess of divine retribution, fr. Gk] **1** : one that inflicts retribution or vengeance **2** : a formidable and usu. victorious rival **3** : an act or effect of retribution; *also* : CURSE

neo·clas·sic \ˌnē-ō-'kla-sik\ *or* **neo·clas-**

si·cal \-si-kəl\ *adj* : of or relating to a revival or adaptation of the classical style esp. in literature, art, or music

neo·co·lo·nial·ism \ˌnē-ō-kə-'lō-nē-ə-ˌli-zəm\ *n* : the economic and political policies by which a nation indirectly maintains or extends its influence over other areas or peoples — **neo·co·lo·nial** *adj* — **neo·co·lo·nial·ist** \-list\ *n or adj*

neo·con \'nē-ō-ˌkän\ *n* : NEOCONSERVATIVE

neo·con·ser·va·tive \-kən-'sər-və-tiv\ *n* : a former liberal espousing political conservatism — **neo·con·ser·va·tism** \-və-ˌti-zəm\ *n* — **neoconservative** *adj*

neo·dym·i·um \ˌnē-ō-'di-mē-əm\ *n* : a silver-white to yellow metallic chemical element

neo·im·pres·sion·ism \ˌnē-ō-im-'presh-ə-ˌni-zəm\ *n, often cap N&I* : a late 19th century French art movement that attempted to make impressionism more precise and to use a pointillist painting technique

Neo·lith·ic \ˌnē-ə-'li-thik\ *adj* : of or relating to the latest period of the Stone Age characterized by polished stone implements

ne·ol·o·gism \nē-'ä-lə-ˌji-zəm\ *n* : a new word or expression

ne·on \'nē-ˌän\ *n* [Gk, neut. of *neos* new] **1** : a gaseous colorless chemical element used in electric lamps **2** : a lamp in which a discharge through neon gives a reddish glow — **neon** *adj*

neo·na·tal \ˌnē-ō-'nāt-ᵊl\ *adj* : of, relating to, or affecting the newborn ⟨a ∼ infection⟩ — **neo·na·tal·ly** *adv*

ne·o·nate \'nē-ə-ˌnāt\ *n* : a newborn child

neo·pa·gan \ˌnē-ō-'pā-gən\ *n* : a person who practices a contemporary form of paganism

neo·phyte \'nē-ə-ˌfīt\ *n* **1** : a new convert : PROSELYTE **2** : NOVICE **3** : BEGINNER ✦ *Synonyms* APPRENTICE, FRESHMAN, NEWCOMER, ROOKIE, TENDERFOOT, TYRO

neo·plasm \'nē-ə-ˌpla-zəm\ *n* : a new growth of tissue serving no useful purpose in the body : TUMOR — **neo·plas·tic** \ˌnē-ə-'plas-tik\ *adj*

neo·prene \'nē-ə-ˌprēn\ *n* : a synthetic rubber used esp. for special-purpose clothing (as wet suits)

neo·trop·i·cal \ˌnē-ō-'trä-pi-kəl\ *adj, often cap* : of or relating to a zoogeographic region of America that extends south from the central plateau of Mexico

ne·pen·the \nə-'pen-thē\ *n* **1** : a potion used by the ancients to dull pain and sorrow **2** : something capable of making one forget grief or suffering

neph·ew \'ne-fyü, *chiefly Brit* -vyü\ *n* [ME *nevew*, fr. AF *neveu*, fr. LL *nepot-*, *nepos*, fr. L, grandson, descendant] : a son of one's brother, sister, brother-in-law, or sister-in-law

ne·phrit·ic \ni-'fri-tik\ *adj* **1** : RENAL **2** : of, relating to, or affected with nephritis

ne·phri·tis \ni-'frī-təs\ *n, pl* **ne·phrit·i·des** \-'fri-tə-ˌdēz\ : kidney inflammation

ne plus ul·tra \ˌnē-ˌpləs-ˈəl-trə\ n [NL, (go) no more beyond] : the highest point capable of being attained

nep·o·tism \ˈne-pə-ˌti-zəm\ n [F *népotisme*, fr. It *nepotismo*, fr. *nepote* nephew, fr. LL *nepot-, nepos*] : favoritism shown to a relative (as in the granting of jobs)

Nep·tune \ˈnep-ˌtün, -ˌtyün\ n : the planet 8th in order from the sun — **Nep·tu·ni·an** \nep-ˈtü-nē-ən, -ˈtyü-\ adj

nep·tu·ni·um \nep-ˈtü-nē-əm, -ˈtyü-\ n : a short-lived radioactive element

nerd \ˈnərd\ n : an unstylish or socially inept person; *esp* : one slavishly devoted to intellectual pursuits — **nerdy** adj

Ne·re·id \ˈnir-ē-əd\ n : a sea nymph in Greek mythology

¹**nerve** \ˈnərv\ n 1 : SINEW, TENDON ⟨strain every ∼⟩ 2 : any of the strands of nervous tissue that carry nerve impulses between the brain and spinal cord and every part of the body 3 : power of endurance or control : FORTITUDE; *also* : BOLDNESS, DARING 4 *pl* : NERVOUSNESS 5 : a vein of a leaf or insect wing — **nerved** \ˈnərvd\ adj — **nerve·less** adj

²**nerve** vb **nerved; nerv·ing** : to give strength or courage to

nerve cell n : NEURON; *also* : CELL BODY

nerve gas n : a chemical weapon damaging esp. to the nervous and respiratory systems

nerve impulse n : a physical and chemical change that moves along a process of a neuron after stimulation and carries a record of sensation or an instruction to act

nerve–rack·ing *or* **nerve–wrack·ing** \ˈnərv-ˌra-kiŋ\ adj : extremely trying on the nerves

ner·vous \ˈnər-vəs\ adj 1 : FORCIBLE, SPIRITED 2 : of, relating to, or made up of neurons or nerves 3 : easily excited or annoyed : JUMPY 4 : TIMID, APPREHENSIVE ⟨a ∼ smile⟩ 5 : UNEASY, UNSTEADY — **ner·vous·ly** adv — **ner·vous·ness** n

nervous breakdown n : an attack of mental or emotional disorder of sufficient severity to be incapacitating esp. when requiring hospitalization

nervous system n : a bodily system that in vertebrates is made up of the brain and spinal cord, nerves, ganglia, and parts of the sense organs and that receives and interprets stimuli and transmits nerve impulses

nervy \ˈnər-vē\ adj **nerv·i·er; -est** 1 : showing calm courage 2 : marked by impudence or presumption ⟨a ∼ salesperson⟩ 3 : EXCITABLE, NERVOUS
✦ *Synonyms* BOLD, CHEEKY, FORWARD, FRESH, IMPUDENT, SAUCY

-ness \nəs\ n *suffix* : state : condition : quality : degree ⟨good*ness*⟩

¹**nest** \ˈnest\ n 1 : the shelter prepared by a bird for its eggs and young 2 : a place where eggs (as of insects or fish) are laid and hatched 3 : a place of rest, retreat, or lodging 4 : DEN, HANGOUT ⟨a ∼ of

thieves⟩ 5 : the occupants of a nest 6 : a series of objects (as bowls or tables) fitting inside or under one another

²**nest** vb 1 : to build or occupy a nest 2 : to fit compactly together or within one another

nest egg n : a fund of money accumulated as a reserve

nes·tle \ˈne-səl\ vb **nes·tled; nes·tling** 1 : to settle snugly or comfortably 2 : to press closely and affectionately : CUDDLE 3 : to settle, shelter, or house as if in a nest

nest·ling \ˈnest-liŋ\ n : a bird too young to leave its nest

¹**net** \ˈnet\ n 1 : a meshed fabric twisted, knotted, or woven together at regular intervals 2 : a device made all or partly of net and used esp. to catch birds, fish, or insects 3 : something made of net used esp. for protecting, confining, carrying, or dividing ⟨a tennis ∼⟩ 4 : SNARE, TRAP 5 *often cap* : INTERNET

²**net** vb **net·ted; net·ting** 1 : to cover or enclose with or as if with a net 2 : to catch in or as if in a net

³**net** adj : free from all charges or deductions ⟨∼ profit⟩ ⟨∼ weight⟩

⁴**net** vb **net·ted; net·ting** : to gain or produce as profit : CLEAR, YIELD ⟨his business *netted* $50,000 a year⟩

⁵**net** n : a net amount, profit, weight, or price

Neth *abbr* Netherlands

neth·er \ˈne-thər\ adj : situated down or below ⟨the ∼ regions of the earth⟩

neth·er·most \-ˌmōst\ adj : LOWEST

neth·er·world \-ˌwərld\ n 1 : the world of the dead 2 : UNDERWORLD

net·i·quette \ˈne-ti-kət, -ˌket\ n : etiquette governing communication on the Internet

nett *Brit var of* NET

net·ting n 1 : NETWORK 2 : the act or process of making a net or network

¹**net·tle** \ˈne-tᵊl\ n : any of a genus of coarse herbs with stinging hairs

²**nettle** vb **net·tled; net·tling** : PROVOKE, VEX, IRRITATE

net·tle·some \ˈne-tᵊl-səm\ adj : causing vexation : IRRITATING

net·work \ˈnet-ˌwərk\ n 1 : NET 2 : a system of elements (as lines or channels) that cross in the manner of the threads in a net 3 : a group or system of related or connected parts; *esp* : a chain of radio or television stations 4 : a system of computers that are connected (as by telephone wires)

net·work·ing \ˈnet-ˌwər-kiŋ\ n 1 : the exchange of information or services among individuals, groups, or institutions 2 : the cultivation of productive business relationships

neu·ral \ˈnùr-əl, ˈnyùr-\ adj : of, relating to, or involving a nerve or the nervous system ⟨∼ pathways⟩

neu·ral·gia \nù-ˈral-jə, nyù-\ n : acute pain that follows the course of a nerve — **neu·ral·gic** \-jik\ adj

neur·as·the·nia \ˌnùr-əs-ˈthē-nē-ə, ˌnyùr-\ n [NL, fr. Gk *neuron* nerve + *asthenia* weakness, fr. *asthenēs* weak, fr. *a-* not + *sthenos* strength] : a psychological disorder marked esp. by fatiguing easily, lack of motivation, feelings of inadequacy, and psychosomatic symptoms — **neur·as·then·ic** \-the-nik, -ˈthē-\ *adj or n*

neu·ri·tis \nu̇-ˈrī-təs, nyu̇-\ *n, pl* **-rit·i·des** \-ˈri-tə-ˌdēz\ *or* **-ri·tis·es** : inflammation of a nerve — **neu·rit·ic** \-ˈri-tik\ *adj or n*

neu·ro·bi·ol·o·gy \ˌnu̇r-ō-bī-ˈä-lə-jē\ *n* : a branch of biology that deals with the nervous system — **neu·ro·bi·o·log·i·cal** \-ˌbī-ə-ˈlä-ji-kəl\ *adj* — **neu·ro·bi·ol·o·gist** \-bī-ˈä-lə-jist\ *n*

neu·rol·o·gy \nu̇-ˈrä-lə-jē, nyu̇-\ *n* : the scientific study of the nervous system — **neu·ro·log·i·cal** \ˌnu̇r-ə-ˈlä-ji-kəl, ˌnyu̇r-\ *or* **neu·ro·log·ic** \-jik\ *adj* — **neu·ro·log·i·cal·ly** \-ji-k(ə-)lē\ *adv* — **neu·rol·o·gist** \nu̇-ˈrä-lə-jist, nyu̇-\ *n*

neu·ro·mus·cu·lar \ˌnu̇r-ō-ˈməs-kyə-lər, ˌnyu̇r-\ *adj* : of, relating to, or affecting nerves and muscles ⟨a ∼ disease⟩

neu·ron \ˈnu̇-ˌrän, ˈnyu̇-\ *n* : a cell with specialized processes that is the fundamental functional unit of nervous tissue — **neu·ro·nal** \ˈnu̇r-ə-nᵊl, ˈnyu̇r-\ *adj*

neu·rone \-ˌrōn\ *chiefly Brit var of* NEURON

neu·ro·sci·ence \ˌnu̇r-ō-ˈsī-əns, ˌnyu̇r-\ *n* : a branch of the life sciences that deals with the anatomy, physiology, biochemistry, or molecular biology of nerves and nervous tissue and esp. with their relation to behavior and learning — **neu·ro·sci·en·tist** \-ən-tist\ *n*

neu·ro·sis \nu̇-ˈrō-səs, nyu̇-\ *n, pl* **-ro·ses** \-ˌsēz\ : a mental and emotional disorder that is less serious than a psychosis, is not characterized by disturbance of the use of language, and is accompanied by various bodily and mental disturbances (as visceral symptoms, anxieties, or phobias)

neu·ro·sur·gery \ˌnu̇r-ō-ˈsər-jə-rē, ˌnyu̇r-\ *n* : surgery of nervous structures (as nerves, the brain, or the spinal cord) — **neu·ro·sur·geon** \-ˈsər-jən\ *n*

¹**neu·rot·ic** \nu̇-ˈrä-tik, nyu̇-\ *adj* : of, relating to, being, or affected with a neurosis — **neu·rot·i·cal·ly** \-ti-k(ə-)lē\ *adv*

²**neurotic** *n* : an emotionally unstable or neurotic person

neu·ro·trans·mit·ter \ˌnu̇r-ō-trans-ˈmi-tər, ˌnyu̇r-, -tranz-\ *n* : a substance (as acetylcholine) that transmits nerve impulses across a synapse

neut *abbr* neuter

¹**neu·ter** \ˈnü-tər, ˈnyu̇-\ *adj* [ME *neutre*, fr. MF & L; MF *neutre*, fr. L *neuter*, lit., neither, fr. *ne-* not + *uter* which of two] **1** : of, relating to, or constituting the gender that includes most words or grammatical forms referring to things classed as neither masculine nor feminine **2** : lacking or having imperfectly developed sex organs

²**neuter** *n* **1** : a noun, pronoun, adjective, or inflectional form or class of the neuter gender; *also* : the neuter gender **2** : WORKER 2; *also* : a spayed or castrated animal

³**neuter** *vb* **1** : CASTRATE, SPAY **2** : to remove the force or effectiveness of

¹**neu·tral** \ˈnü-trəl, ˈnyu̇-\ *n* **1** : one that is neutral **2** : a neutral color **3** : a position of disengagement (as of gears)

²**neutral** *adj* **1** : not favoring either side in a quarrel, contest, or war **2** : of or relating to a neutral state or power **3** : MIDDLING, INDIFFERENT **4** : having no hue : GRAY; *also* : not decided in color **5** : neither acid nor basic ⟨a ∼ solution⟩ **6** : not electrically charged

neu·tral·ise *Brit var of* NEUTRALIZE

neu·tral·ism \ˈnü-trə-ˌli-zəm, ˈnyu̇-\ *n* : a policy or the advocacy of neutrality esp. in international affairs

neu·tral·i·ty \nü-ˈtra-lə-tē, nyu̇-\ *n* : the quality or state of being neutral; *esp* : refusal to take part in a war between other powers

neu·tral·ize \ˈnü-trə-ˌlīz, ˈnyu̇-\ *vb* **-ized**; **-iz·ing** : to make neutral; *esp* : COUNTERACT — **neu·tral·i·za·tion** \ˌnü-trə-lə-ˈzā-shən, ˌnyu̇-\ *n*

neu·tri·no \nü-ˈtrē-nō, nyu̇-\ *n, pl* **-nos** : an uncharged elementary particle held to be massless or very light

neu·tron \ˈnü-ˌträn, ˈnyu̇-\ *n* : an uncharged atomic particle that is nearly equal in mass to the proton

neutron bomb *n* : a nuclear bomb designed to produce lethal neutrons but less blast and fire damage than other nuclear bombs

neutron star *n* : a dense celestial object that results from the collapse of a large star

Nev *abbr* Nevada

nev·er \ˈne-vər\ *adv* **1** : not ever **2** : not in any degree, way, or condition

nev·er·more \ˌne-vər-ˈmȯr\ *adv* : never again

nev·er–nev·er land \ˌne-vər-ˈne-vər-\ *n* : an ideal or imaginary place

nev·er·the·less \ˌne-vər-thə-ˈles\ *adv* : in spite of that : HOWEVER

ne·vus \ˈnē-vəs\ *n, pl* **ne·vi** \-ˌvī\ : a usu. pigmented area on the skin : MOLE

¹**new** \ˈnü, ˈnyu̇\ *adj* **1** : not old : RECENT, MODERN **2** : recently discovered, recognized, or learned about ⟨∼ drugs⟩ **3** : UNFAMILIAR ⟨visit ∼ places⟩ **4** : different from the former **5** : not accustomed ⟨∼ to the work⟩ **6** : beginning as a repetition of a previous act or thing ⟨a ∼ year⟩ **7** : REFRESHED, REGENERATED ⟨rest made a ∼ man of him⟩ **8** : being in a position or place for the first time ⟨a ∼ member⟩ **9** *cap* : having been in use after medieval times : MODERN ⟨*New* Latin⟩ • **Synonyms** NOVEL, NEWFANGLED, FRESH — **new·ish** *adj* — **new·ness** *n*

²**new** *adv* : NEWLY ⟨*new*-mown hay⟩

¹**new age** *adj, often cap* N&A **1** : of, relating to, or being New Age **2** : CONTEMPORARY, MODERN

²**new age** *n* **1** *cap* : a group of late 20th century social attitudes adapted from a variety of ancient and modern beliefs relating to spirituality, right living, and

health **2** : a soft soothing form of instrumental music

new·bie \'nü-bē, 'nyü-\ *n* : a newcomer esp. to cyberspace

new blood *n* : persons accepted into a group or organization and expected to provide fresh ideas and vitality

¹new·born \-'bórn\ *adj* **1** : recently born **2** : born anew ⟨~ hope⟩

²newborn *n, pl* **newborn** *or* **newborns** : a newborn individual

new·com·er \'-,kə-mər\ *n* **1** : one recently arrived **2** : BEGINNER

New Deal *n* : the legislative and administrative program of President F. D. Roosevelt to promote economic recovery and social reform during the 1930s — **New Dealer** *n*

new·el \'nü-əl, 'nyü-\ *n* : a post about which the steps of a circular staircase wind; *also* : a post at the foot of a stairway or one at a landing

new·fan·gled \'nü-'faŋ-gəld, 'nyü-\ *adj* **1** : attracted to novelty **2** : of the newest style : NOVEL

new–fash·ioned \-'fa-shənd\ *adj* **1** : made in a new fashion or form **2** : UP-TO-DATE

new·found \-'faùnd\ *adj* : newly found

New Left *n* : a radical political movement originating in the 1960s

new·ly \'nü-lē, 'nyü-\ *adv* **1** : LATELY, RECENTLY ⟨a ~ married couple⟩ **2** : ANEW, AFRESH ⟨~ painted⟩

new·ly·wed \-,wed\ *n* : a person recently married

new moon *n* : the phase of the moon with its dark side toward the earth; *also* : the thin crescent moon seen for a few days after the new moon phase

news \'nüz, 'nyüz\ *n* **1** : a report of recent events : TIDINGS **2** : material reported in a newspaper or news periodical or on a newscast

news·boy \'nüz-,bói, 'nyüz-\ *n* : one who delivers or sells newspapers

news·cast \-,kast\ *n* : a radio or television broadcast of news — **news·cast·er** \-,kas-tər\ *n*

news·group \-,grüp\ : an Internet bulletin devoted to a certain topic

news·let·ter \'nüz-,le-tər, 'nyüz-\ *n* : a small newspaper containing news or information of interest chiefly to a special group

news·mag·a·zine \-,ma-gə-,zēn\ *n* : a usu. weekly magazine devoted chiefly to summarizing and analyzing news

news·man \-mən, -,man\ *n* : a person who gathers, reports, or comments on the news : REPORTER

news·pa·per \-,pā-pər\ *n* : a paper that is published at regular intervals and contains news, articles of opinion, features, and advertising

news·pa·per·man \-,pā-pər-,man\ *n* : a person who owns or is employed by a newspaper

news·print \-,print\ *n* : paper made chiefly from wood pulp and used mostly for newspapers

news·reel \-,rēl\ *n* : a short motion picture portraying current events

news·stand \-,stand\ *n* : a place where newspapers and periodicals are sold

news·week·ly \-,wēk-lē\ *n* : a weekly newspaper or newsmagazine

news·wire \-,wī(-ə)r\ *n* : WIRE SERVICE

news·wom·an \-,wù-mən\ *n* : a woman who is a reporter

news·wor·thy \-,wər-thē\ *adj* : sufficiently interesting to the general public to warrant reporting

newsy \'nü-zē, 'nyü-\ *adj* **news·i·er; -est** : filled with news; *esp* : TALKATIVE

newt \'nüt, 'nyüt\ *n* [ME, alter. (from misdivision of *an ewte*) of *ewt, evete*, fr. OE *efete*] : any of various small chiefly aquatic salamanders

New Testament *n* : the second of the two chief divisions of the Christian Bible — see BIBLE table

new·ton \'nü-t³n, 'nyü-\ *n* : the unit of force in the metric system equal to the force required to impart an acceleration of one meter per second per second to a mass of one kilogram

new wave *n, often cap N&W* : the latest and esp. the most outrageous style — **new–wave** *adj*

New Year *n* **1** : NEW YEAR'S DAY; *also* : the first days of the year **2** : ROSH HASHANAH

New Year's Day *n* : January 1 observed as a legal holiday

¹next \'nekst\ *adj* : immediately preceding or following : NEAREST

²next *prep* : nearest or adjacent to

³next *adv* **1** : in the time, place, or order nearest or immediately succeeding **2** : on the first occasion to come

⁴next *n* : one that is next

nex·us \'nek-səs\ *n, pl* **nex·us·es** \-sə-səz\ *or* **nex·us** \-səs, -,süs\ : CONNECTION, LINK

Nez Percé \'nez-'pərs\ *n* : a member of an American Indian people of Idaho, Washington, and Oregon; *also* : the language of the Nez Percé

NF *abbr* Newfoundland

NFC *abbr* National Football Conference

NFL *abbr* National Football League

Nfld *abbr* Newfoundland

NG *abbr* **1** National Guard **2** no good

ngul·trum \eŋ-'gúl-trəm\ *n* — see MONEY table

ngwee \eŋ-'gwē\ *n, pl* **ngwee** — see *kwacha* at MONEY table

NH *abbr* New Hampshire

NHL *abbr* National Hockey League

Ni *symbol* nickel

ni·a·cin \'nī-ə-sən\ *n* : an organic acid of the vitamin B complex found widely in plants and animals and used esp. against pellagra

nib \'nib\ *n* : POINT; *esp* : a pen point

¹nib·ble \'ni-bəl\ *vb* **nib·bled; nib·bling** : to bite gently or bit by bit

²nibble *n* : a small or cautious bite

ni·cad \'nī-,kad\ *n* : a rechargeable dry cell that has a nickel cathode and a cadmium anode

nice \'nīs\ *adj* **nic·er; nic·est** [ME, foolish, wanton, fr. AF, silly, simple, fr. L *nescius* ignorant, fr. *nescire* to not know] **1** : FASTIDIOUS, DISCRIMINATING **2** : marked by delicate discrimination or treatment **3** : PLEASING, AGREEABLE ⟨had a ~ time⟩; *also* : well-executed ⟨a ~ shot⟩ **4** : WELL-BRED ⟨~ people⟩ **5** : VIRTUOUS, RESPECTABLE ◆ **Synonyms** CHOOSY, FINICKY, PARTICULAR, PERSNICKETY, PICKY — **nice·ly** *adv* — **nice·ness** *n*

nice·nel·ly \'nīs-'ne-lē\ *adj, often cap 2d N* **1** : marked by euphemism **2** : PRUDISH — **nice nelly** *n, often cap 2d N* — **nice·nel·ly·ism** \-,i-zəm\ *n, often cap 2d N*

nice·ty \'nī-sə-tē\ *n, pl* **-ties** **1** : a dainty, delicate, or elegant thing ⟨enjoy the *niceties* of life⟩ **2** : a fine point or distinction ⟨*niceties* of workmanship⟩ **3** : EXACTNESS, PRECISION, ACCURACY

niche \'nich\ *n* [F] **1** : a recess in a wall esp. for a statue **2** : a place, employment, or activity for which a person or thing is best fitted **3** : the living space or role of an organism in an ecological community esp. with regard to food consumption

¹nick \'nik\ *n* **1** : a small notch, groove, or chip **2** : the final critical moment ⟨in the ~ of time⟩

²nick *vb* : NOTCH, CHIP

nick·el \'ni-kəl\ *n* **1** : a hard silver-white metallic chemical element capable of a high polish and used in alloys **2** : the U.S. 5-cent piece made of copper and nickel; *also* : the Canadian 5-cent piece

nick·el·ode·on \,ni-kə-'lō-dē-ən\ *n* **1** : an early movie theater to which admission cost five cents **2** : JUKEBOX

nick·er \'ni-kər\ *vb* : NEIGH, WHINNY — **nicker** *n*

nick·name \'nik-,nām\ *n* [ME *nekename* additional name, alter. (from misdivision of *an ekename*) of *ekename*, fr. *eke* also + *name*] **1** : a usu. descriptive name given instead of or in addition to the one belonging to a person, place, or thing **2** : a familiar form of a proper name — **nickname** *vb*

nic·o·tine \'ni-kə-,tēn\ *n* : a poisonous and addictive substance in tobacco that is used as an insecticide

nic·o·tin·ic acid \,ni-kə-'tē-nik-, -'ti-\ *n* : NIACIN

niece \'nēs\ *n* : a daughter of one's brother, sister, brother-in-law, or sister-in-law

nif·ty \'nif-tē\ *adj* **nif·ti·er; -est** : very good : very attractive

nig·gard \'ni-gərd\ *n* : a stingy person : MISER — **nig·gard·li·ness** \-lē-nəs\ *n* — **nig·gard·ly** *adj or adv*

nig·gling \'ni-gə-liŋ\ *adj* **1** : PETTY **2** : bothersome in a petty way ◆ **Synonyms** INCONSEQUENTIAL, MEASLY, PICAYUNE, PIDDLING, TRIFLING, TRIVIAL

¹nigh \'nī\ *adv* **1** : near in place, time, or relationship **2** : NEARLY, ALMOST

²nigh *adj* : CLOSE, NEAR

³nigh *prep* : NEAR

night \'nīt\ *n* **1** : the period between dusk and dawn **2** : the darkness of night **3** : a period of misery or unhappiness **4** : NIGHTFALL — **night** *adj*

night blindness *n* : reduced visual capacity in faint light (as at night)

night·cap \'nīt-,kap\ *n* **1** : a cloth cap worn with nightclothes **2** : a usu. alcoholic drink taken at bedtime

night·clothes \-,klōthz, -,klōz\ *n pl* : garments worn in bed

night·club \-,kləb\ *n* : a place of entertainment open at night usu. serving food and liquor and providing music for dancing

night crawl·er \-,krò-lər\ *n* : EARTHWORM; *esp* : a large earthworm found on the soil surface at night

night·dress \'nīt-,dres\ *n* : NIGHTGOWN

night·fall \-,fòl\ *n* : the coming of night

night·gown \-,gaùn\ *n* : a loose garment for wear in bed

night·hawk \-,hòk\ *n* : any of a genus of American birds related to and resembling the whip-poor-will

night·in·gale \'nī-tᵊn-,gāl, 'nī-tin-\ *n* [ME, fr. OE *nihtegale*, fr. *niht* night + *galan* to sing] : any of several Old World thrushes noted for the sweet usu. nocturnal song of the male

night·life \'nīt-,līf\ *n* : the activity of pleasure-seekers at night

night·ly \'nīt-lē\ *adj* **1** : happening, done, or produced by night or every night **2** : of or relating to the night or every night — **nightly** *adv*

night·mare \'nīt-,mer\ *n* **1** : a frightening dream **2** : a frightening or horrible experience — **nightmare** *adj* — **night·mar·ish** *adj*

night rider *n* : a member of a secret band who ride masked at night doing violence to punish or terrorize

night·shade \'nīt-,shād\ *n* : any of a large genus of herbs, shrubs, and trees that includes poisonous forms (as the belladonna), ornamentals (as the petunias), and important food plants (as the potato and eggplant)

night·shirt \-,shərt\ *n* : a nightgown resembling a shirt

night soil *n* : human feces used esp. for fertilizing the soil

night·stick \'nīt-,stik\ *n* : a police officer's club

night·time \-,tīm\ *n* : the time from dusk to dawn

night·walk·er \-,wò-kər\ *n* : a person who roves about at night esp. with criminal or immoral intent

ni·hil·ism \'nī-ə-,li-zəm, 'nē-hə-\ *n* **1** : a viewpoint that traditional values and beliefs are unfounded and that existence is senseless and useless **2** : ANARCHISM — **ni·hil·ist** \-list\ *n or adj* — **ni·hil·is·tic** \,nī-ə-'lis-tik, ,nē-hə-\ *adj*

nil \'nil\ *n* : ZERO, NOTHING

nim·ble \'nim-bəl\ *adj* **nim·bler; nimblest** [ME *nimel*, fr. OE *numol* holding much, fr. *niman* to take] **1** : quick and light in motion : AGILE ⟨a ~ dancer⟩ **2** : quick in understanding and learning

: CLEVER ⟨a ∼ mind⟩ ♦ **Synonyms** AC-
TIVE, BRISK, SPRIGHTLY, SPRY, ZIPPY —
nim·ble·ness *n* — **nim·bly** \-blē\ *adv*

nim·bus \'nim-bəs\ *n, pl* **nim·bi** \-ˌbī, -bē\
or **nim·bus·es** 1 : a figure (as a disk) in
an art work suggesting radiant light about
the head of a divinity, saint, or sovereign
2 : a rain cloud; *also* : THUNDERHEAD

NIMBY \'nim-bē\ *n* [*not in my backyard*]
: opposition to the placement of something undesirable (as a prison) in one's
neighborhood

nim·rod \'nim-ˌräd\ *n* 1 : HUNTER 2
: IDIOT, JERK

nin·com·poop \'nin-kəm-ˌpüp\ *n* : FOOL,
SIMPLETON

nine \'nīn\ *n* 1 : one more than eight 2
: the 9th in a set or series 3 : something
having nine units; *esp* : a baseball team —
nine *adj or pron* — **ninth** \'nīnth\ *adj or
adv or n* — **to the nines** 1 : to perfection 2 : in an elaborate manner ⟨dressed
to the nines⟩

nine days' wonder *n* : something that
creates a short-lived sensation

nine·pins \'nīn-ˌpinz\ *n* : a bowling game
using nine pins arranged usu. in a diamond-shaped configuration

nine·teen \'nīn-'tēn\ *n* : one more than 18
— **nineteen** *adj or pron* — **nine·teenth**
\-'tēnth\ *adj or n*

nine·ty \'nīn-tē\ *n, pl* **nineties** : nine
times 10 — **nine·ti·eth** \-tē-əth\ *adj or n*
— **ninety** *adj or pron*

nin·ja \'nin-jə, -(ˌ)jä\ *n, pl* **ninja** *or* **ninjas**
[Jp] : a person trained in ancient Japanese
martial arts and employed esp. for espionage and assassinations

nin·ny \'ni-nē\ *n, pl* **ninnies** : FOOL

ni·o·bi·um \nī-'ō-bē-əm\ *n* : a gray metallic chemical element used in alloys

¹**nip** \'nip\ *vb* **nipped; nip·ping** 1 : to
catch hold of and squeeze tightly between
two surfaces, edges, or points 2 : ³CLIP
3 : to destroy the growth, progress, or fulfillment of ⟨*nipped* in the bud⟩ 4 : to injure or make numb with cold : CHILL 5
: SNATCH, STEAL

²**nip** *n* 1 : a sharp stinging cold 2 : a biting or pungent flavor 3 : PINCH, BITE 4
: a small portion : BIT

³**nip** *n* : a small quantity of liquor : SIP

⁴**nip** *vb* **nipped; nip·ping** : to take liquor
in nips : TIPPLE

nip and tuck *adj or adv* : so close that the
lead shifts rapidly from one contestant to
another

nip·per \'ni-pər\ *n* 1 : one that nips 2 *pl*
: PINCERS 3 : CHILD; *esp* : a small boy

nip·ple \'ni-pəl\ *n* : the protuberance of a
mammary gland through which milk is
drawn off : TEAT; *also* : something resembling a nipple

nip·py \'ni-pē\ *adj* **nip·pi·er; -est** 1
: PUNGENT, SHARP 2 : CHILLY

nir·va·na \nər-'vä-nə\ *n, often cap* [Skt
nirvāṇa, lit., act of extinguishing, fr. *nis*-
out + *vāti* it blows] 1 : the final freeing of
a soul from all that enslaves it; *esp* : the
supreme happiness that according to
Buddhism comes when all passion, hatred, and delusion die out and the soul is

released from the necessity of further purification 2 : OBLIVION; *also* : PARADISE

ni·sei \nē-'sā, 'nē-ˌsā\ *n, pl* **nisei** *often cap*
: a son or daughter of immigrant Japan-
ese parents who is born and educated in
America

ni·si \'nī-ˌsī\ *adj* [L, unless, fr. *ne*- not + *si*
if] : taking effect at a specified time un-
less previously modified or voided ⟨a divorce decree ∼⟩

nit \'nit\ *n* 1 : the egg of a parasitic insect
(as a louse); *also* : the young insect 2 : a
minor shortcoming

nite *var of* NIGHT

ni·ter \'nī-tər\ *n* : POTASSIUM NITRATE

nit-pick·ing \'nit-ˌpi-kiŋ\ *n* : minute and
usu. unjustified criticism — **nit-pick·er** *n*

¹**ni·trate** \'nī-ˌtrāt, -trət\ *n* 1 : a salt or
ester of nitric acid 2 : sodium nitrate or
potassium nitrate used as a fertilizer

²**ni·trate** \-ˌtrāt\ *vb* **ni·trat·ed; ni·trat·ing**
: to treat or combine with nitric acid or a
nitrate — **ni·tra·tion** \nī-'trā-shən\ *n*

ni·tre *chiefly Brit var of* NITER

ni·tric acid \'nī-trik-\ *n* : a corrosive liquid acid used esp. in making dyes, explosives, and fertilizers

ni·tri·fi·ca·tion \ˌnī-trə-fə-'kā-shən\ *n*
: the oxidation (as by bacteria) of ammonium salts to nitrites and then to nitrates
— **ni·tri·fy·ing** \'nī-trə-fī-iŋ\ *adj*

ni·trite \'nī-ˌtrīt\ *n* : a salt of nitrous acid

ni·tro \'nī-trō\ *n, pl* **nitros** : any of various
nitrated products; *esp* : NITROGLYCERIN

ni·tro·gen \'nī-trə-jən\ *n* : a tasteless odorless gaseous chemical element constituting 78 percent of the atmosphere by
volume — **ni·trog·e·nous** \nī-'trä-jə-
nəs\ *adj*

nitrogen narcosis *n* : a state of euphoria
and confusion caused by nitrogen forced
into a diver's bloodstream from atmospheric air under pressure

ni·tro·glyc·er·in *or* **ni·tro·glyc·er·ine**
\ˌnī-trə-'gli-sə-rən\ *n* : an oily explosive
liquid used to make dynamite and in
medicine to dilate blood vessels

ni·trous acid \'nī-trəs-\ *n* : an unstable nitrogen-containing acid known only in solution or in the form of its salts

nitrous oxide *n* : a colorless gas used esp.
as an anesthetic in dentistry

nit·ty-grit·ty \'ni-tē-ˌgri-tē, ˌni-tē-'gri-tē\ *n*
: what is essential and basic : specific
practical details

nit·wit \'nit-ˌwit\ *n* : a scatterbrained or
stupid person

¹**nix** \'niks\ *n* : NOTHING

²**nix** *vb* : VETO, REJECT

³**nix** *adv* : NO

NJ *abbr* New Jersey

NL *abbr* National League

NLRB *abbr* National Labor Relations
Board

NM *abbr* 1 nautical mile 2 New Mexico

N Mex *abbr* New Mexico

NMI *abbr* no middle initial

NNE *abbr* north-northeast

NNW *abbr* north-northwest

¹**no** \'nō\ *adv* 1 — used to express the
negative of an alternative ⟨shall we con-

tinue or ~〉 **2** : in no respect or degree 〈he is ~ better than the others〉 **3** : not so 〈~, I'm not ready〉 **4** — used with an adjective to imply a meaning opposite to the positive statement 〈in ~ uncertain terms〉 **5** — used to introduce a more emphatic or explicit statement 〈has the right, ~, the duty to continue〉 **6** — used as an interjection to express surprise or doubt 〈~—you don't say〉 **7** — used in combination with a verb to form a compound adjective 〈*no*-bake pie〉 **8** : in negation 〈shook his head ~〉

²**no** *adj* **1** : not any; *also* : hardly any **2** : not a 〈she's ~ expert〉

³**no** \'nō\ *n, pl* **noes** *or* **nos** \'nōz\ **1** : RE-FUSAL, DENIAL 〈got a ~ in reply〉 **2** : a negative vote or decision; *also, pl* : persons voting in the negative

⁴**no** *abbr* **1** north; northern **2** [L *nu-mero,* abl. of *numerus*] number

¹**No** *var of* NOH

²**No** *symbol* nobelium

No·bel·ist \nō-'be-list\ *n* : a winner of a Nobel prize

no·bel·i·um \nō-'be-lē-əm\ *n* : a radioactive metallic chemical element produced artificially

Nobel prize \nō-'bel-, 'nō-ˌbel-\ *n* : any of various annual prizes (as in peace, literature, or medicine) established by the will of Alfred Nobel for the encouragement of persons who work for the interests of humanity

no·bil·i·ty \nō-'bi-lə-tē\ *n* **1** : the quality or state of being noble **2** : nobles considered as forming a class

¹**no·ble** \'nō-bəl\ *adj* **no·bler; no·blest** [ME, fr. AF, fr. L *nobilis* well known, noble, fr. *noscere* to come to know] **1** : ILLUSTRIOUS; *also* : FAMOUS, NOTABLE **2** : of high birth, rank, or station : ARIS-TOCRATIC **3** : EXCELLENT **4** : STATELY, IMPOSING 〈a ~ edifice〉 **5** : of a superior nature ✦ **Synonyms** AUGUST, BARO-NIAL, GRAND, GRANDIOSE, MAGNIFI-CENT, MAJESTIC — **no·ble·ness** *n* — **no·bly** \-blē\ *adv*

²**noble** *n* : a person of noble rank or birth

noble gas *n* : any of a group of rare gases that exhibit great stability and extremely low reaction rates

no·ble·man \'nō-bəl-mən\ *n* : a member of the nobility : PEER

no·blesse oblige \nō-ˌbles-ə-'blēzh\ *n* [F, lit., nobility obligates] : the obligation of honorable, generous, and responsible behavior associated with high rank or birth

no·ble·wom·an \'nō-bəl-ˌwu̇-mən\ *n* : a woman of noble rank : PEERESS

¹**no·body** \'nō-ˌbä-dē, -bə-\ *pron* : no person

²**nobody** *n, pl* **no·bod·ies** : a person of no influence or importance

no–brain·er \'nō-'brā-nər\ *n* : something that requires a minimum of thought

noc·tur·nal \näk-'tər-n³l\ *adj* **1** : of, relating to, or occurring in the night **2** : active at night 〈a ~ bird〉

noc·turne \'näk-ˌtərn\ *n* : a work of art dealing with night; *esp* : a dreamy pensive composition for the piano

noc·u·ous \'nä-kyə-wəs\ *adj* : HARMFUL — **noc·u·ous·ly** *adv*

nod \'näd\ *vb* **nod·ded; nod·ding** **1** : to bend the head downward or forward (as in bowing, going to sleep, or giving assent) **2** : to move up and down 〈tulips *nodding* in the breeze〉 **3** : to show by a nod of the head 〈~ agreement〉 **4** : to make a slip or error in a moment of abstraction — **nod** *n*

nod·dle \'nä-d³l\ *n* : HEAD

nod·dy \'nä-dē\ *n, pl* **noddies** **1** : FOOL **2** : a stout-bodied tropical tern

node \'nōd\ *n* : a thickened, swollen, or differentiated area (as of tissue); *esp* : the part of a stem from which a leaf arises — **nod·al** \-³l\ *adj*

nod·ule \'nä-jül\ *n* : a small lump or swelling — **nod·u·lar** \'nä-jə-lər\ *adj*

no·el \nō-'el\ *n* [F *noël* Christmas, carol, fr. OF *Nael* (Deu), *Noel* Christmas, fr. L *natalis* birthday] **1** : a Christmas carol **2** *cap* : the Christmas season

noes *pl of* NO

no–fault \'nō-'fȯlt\ *adj* **1** : of, relating to, or being a motor vehicle insurance plan under which someone involved in an accident is compensated usu. up to a stipulated limit for actual losses by that person's own insurance company regardless of who is responsible **2** : of, relating to, or being a divorce law under which neither party is held responsible for the breakup of the marriage

nog·gin \'nä-gən\ *n* **1** : a small mug or cup; *also* : a small quantity of drink **2** : a person's head

no–good \'nō-'gu̇d\ *adj* : having no worth, virtue, use, or chance of success — **no–good** \-'gu̇d\ *n*

Noh *also* **No** \'nō\ *n, pl* **Noh** *also* **No** : classic Japanese dance-drama having a heroic theme, a chorus, and highly stylized action, costuming, and scenery

no–hit·ter \(ˌ)nō-'hi-tər\ *n* : a baseball game or part of a game in which a pitcher allows no base hits

no–how \'nō-ˌhau̇\ *adv* : in no manner

¹**noise** \'nȯiz\ *n* [ME, fr. AF, disturbance, noise, fr. L *nausea* nausea] **1** : loud, confused, or senseless shouting or outcry **2** : SOUND; *esp* : one that lacks agreeable musical quality or is noticeably unpleasant **3** : unwanted electronic signal or disturbance — **noise·less** *adj* — **noise·less·ly** *adv*

²**noise** *vb* **noised; nois·ing** : to spread by rumor or report 〈the story was *noised* abroad〉

noise·mak·er \'nȯiz-ˌmā-kər\ *n* : one that makes noise; *esp* : a device used to make noise at parties

noise pollution *n* : annoying or harmful noise in an environment

noi·some \'nȯi-səm\ *adj* **1** : HARMFUL, UNWHOLESOME **2** : offensive to the senses (as smell) : DISGUSTING ✦ **Syno-nyms** INSALUBRIOUS, NOXIOUS, SICKLY, UNHEALTHFUL, UNHEALTHY

noisy \'nȯi-zē\ *adj* **nois·i·er; -est** **1** : making loud noises **2** : full of noises

: LOUD — **nois·i·ly** \-zə-lē\ *adv* — **noisi·ness** \-zē-nəs\ *n*

nol·le pro·se·qui \ˌnä-lē-ˈprä-sə-ˌkwī\ *n* [L, to be unwilling to pursue] : an entry on the record of a legal action that the prosecutor or plaintiff will proceed no further in an action or suit or in some aspect of it

no·lo con·ten·de·re \ˌnō-lō-kən-ˈten-də-rē\ *n* [L, I do not wish to contend] : a plea in a criminal prosecution that subjects the defendant to conviction but does not admit guilt or preclude denying the charges in another proceeding

nol–pros \ˈnäl-ˈpräs\ *vb* **nol–prossed**; **nol–pros·sing** : to discontinue by entering a nolle prosequi

nom *abbr* nominative

no·mad \ˈnō-ˌmad\ *n* **1** : a member of a people who have no fixed residence but move from place to place **2** : an individual who roams about aimlessly — **nomad** *adj* — **no·mad·ic** \nō-ˈma-dik\ *adj*

no–man's–land \ˈnō-ˌmanz-ˌland\ *n* **1** : an area of unowned, unclaimed, or uninhabited land **2** : an unoccupied area between opposing troops

nom de guerre \ˌnäm-di-ˈger\ *n, pl* **noms de guerre** *same or* ˌnämz-\ [F, lit., war name] : PSEUDONYM

nom de plume \-ˈplüm\ *n, pl* **noms de plume** *same or* ˌnämz-\ [F, pen name; prob. coined in E] : PEN NAME

no·men·cla·ture \ˈnō-mən-ˌklā-chər\ *n* **1** : NAME, DESIGNATION **2** : a system of terms used in a science or art

nom·i·nal \ˈnä-mə-nᵊl\ *adj* **1** : being something in name or form only ⟨∼ head of a party⟩ **2** : TRIFLING ⟨a ∼ price⟩ — **nom·i·nal·ly** *adv*

nom·i·nate \ˈnä-mə-ˌnāt\ *vb* **-nat·ed**; **-nat·ing** : to choose as a candidate for election, appointment, or honor ♦ *Synonyms* APPOINT, DESIGNATE, NAME, TAP — **nom·i·na·tion** \ˌnä-mə-ˈnā-shən\ *n*

nom·i·na·tive \ˈnä-mə-nə-tiv\ *adj* : of, relating to, or constituting a grammatical case marking typically the subject of a verb — **nominative** *n*

nom·i·nee \ˌnä-mə-ˈnē\ *n* : a person nominated for an office, duty, or position

non- \ˈ(ˌ)nän *or* ˌnän *before stressed syllables;* ˌnän *elsewhere*\ *prefix* **1** : not : reverse of : absence of **2** : having no importance

non·age \ˈnä-nij, ˈnō-\ *n* **1** : legal minority **2** : a period of youth **3** : IMMATURITY

no·na·ge·nar·i·an \ˌnō-nə-jə-ˈner-ē-ən, ˌnä-\ *n* : a person whose age is in the nineties

non–aligned \ˌnän-ə-ˈlīnd\ *adj* : not allied with other nations

no–name \ˈnō-ˌnām\ *adj* : not having a readily recognizable name ⟨∼ brands⟩

non–book \ˈnän-ˌbu̇k\ *n* : a book of little literary merit that is often a compilation (as of pictures or speeches)

¹nonce \ˈnäns\ *n* : the one, particular, or present occasion or purpose ⟨for the ∼⟩

²nonce *adj* : occurring, used, or made only once or for a special occasion ⟨a ∼ word⟩

non·cha·lant \ˌnän-shə-ˈlänt\ *adj* [F, fr. OF, fr. prp. of *nonchaloir* to disregard, fr. *non-* not + *chaloir* to concern, fr. L *calēre* to be warm] : giving an effect of unconcern or indifference ♦ *Synonyms* COLLECTED, COMPOSED, COOL, IMPERTURBABLE, UNFLAPPABLE, UNRUFFLED — **non·cha·lance** \-ˈläns\ *n* — **non·cha·lant·ly** *adv*

non–com \ˈnän-ˌkäm\ *n* : NONCOMMISSIONED OFFICER

non·com·ba·tant \ˌnän-kəm-ˈba-tᵊnt, nän-ˈkäm-bə-tənt\ *n* : a member (as a chaplain) of the armed forces whose duties do not include fighting; *also* : CIVILIAN — **noncombatant** *adj*

non·com·mis·sioned officer \ˌnän-kə-ˈmi-shənd\ *n* : a subordinate officer in the armed forces appointed from enlisted personnel

non·com·mit·tal \ˌnän-kə-ˈmi-tᵊl\ *adj* : indicating neither consent nor dissent ⟨a ∼ reply⟩

non com·pos men·tis \ˌnän-ˌkäm-pəs-ˈmen-təs\ *adj* : not of sound mind

non·con·duc·tor \ˌnän-kən-ˈdək-tər\ *n* : a substance that is a very poor conductor of heat, electricity, or sound

non·con·form·ist \-kən-ˈfȯr-mist\ *n* **1** *often cap* : a person who does not conform to an established church and esp. the Church of England **2** : a person who does not conform to a generally accepted pattern of thought or action ♦ *Synonyms* DISSENTER, DISSIDENT, HERETIC, SCHISMATIC, SECTARY, SEPARATIST — **non·con·for·mi·ty** \-ˈfȯr-mə-tē\ *n*

non·co·op·er·a·tion \ˌnän-kō-ˌä-pə-ˈrā-shən\ *n* : failure or refusal to cooperate; *esp* : refusal through civil disobedience of a people to cooperate with the government of a country

non·cred·it \(ˌ)nän-ˈkre-dət\ *adj* : not offering credit toward a degree

---

nonabrasive
nonabsorbent
nonacademic
nonacceptance
nonacid
nonactivated
nonadaptive
nonaddictive
nonadhesive
nonadjacent
nonadjustable

nonaggression
nonalcoholic
nonappearance
nonaromatic
nonathletic
nonattendance
nonbeliever
nonbelligerent
nonbreakable
noncancerous
noncandidate

noncellular
nonclerical
noncoital
noncombat
noncombative
noncombustible
noncommercial
noncommunist
noncompeting
noncompetitive
noncompliance

noncomplying
nonconducting
nonconflicting
nonconformance
nonconforming
nonconstructive
noncontagious
noncontinuous
noncorroding
noncorrosive

non·cus·to·di·al \,nän-kə-'stō-dē-əl\ *adj*
: of or being a parent who does not have
legal custody of a child

non-dairy \'nän-'der-ē\ *adj* : containing
no milk or milk products

non-de-script \,nän-di-'skript\ *adj* 1
: not belonging to any particular class or
kind 2 : lacking distinctive qualities ⟨a
∼ building⟩

non-drink-er \-'driŋ-kər\ *n* : a person who
abstains from alcohol

¹**none** \'nən\ *pron* 1 : not any ⟨∼ of them
went⟩ 2 : not one ⟨∼ of the family⟩ 3
: not any such thing or person ⟨half a loaf
is better than ∼⟩

²**none** *adj, archaic* : not any : NO

³**none** *adv* : by no means : not at all ⟨he got
there ∼ too soon⟩

non-en-ti-ty \,nän-'en-tə-tē\ *n* 1 : something that does not exist or exists only in
the imagination 2 : one of no consequence or significance ✦ *Synonyms* NO-
BODY, NOTHING, WHIPPERSNAPPER

nones \'nōnz\ *n sing or pl* : the 7th day of
March, May, July, or October or the 5th
day of any other month in the ancient
Roman calendar

non-es-sen-tial \,nän-i-'sen-shəl\ *adj* 1
: not essential 2 : being a substance synthesized by the body in sufficient quantity to satisfy dietary needs

none-such \'nən-,səch\ *n* : one without
an equal — **nonesuch** *adj*

none-the-less \,nən-thə-'les\ *adv* : NEV-
ERTHELESS

non-event \'nän-i-,vent\ *n* 1 : an event
that fails to take place or to satisfy expectations 2 : a highly promoted event of
little intrinsic interest

non-fat \-'fat\ *adj* : lacking fat solids
: having fat solids removed ⟨∼ milk⟩

non-gono-coc-cal \,nän-,gä-nə-'kä-kəl\
adj : not caused by a gonococcus

non-he-ro \'nän-,hē-rō\ *n* : ANTIHERO

non–Hodg-kin's lymphoma \'nän-'häj-
kənz-\ *n* : any of numerous malignant
lymphomas not classified as Hodgkin's
disease

non-in-ter-ven-tion \,nän-,in-tər-'ven-
chən\ *n* : refusal or failure to intervene
(as in the affairs of other countries)

non-is-sue \'nän-'i-shü\ *n* : an issue of little importance or concern

non-met-al \'nän-'me-t⁹l\ *n* : a chemical
element (as carbon) that lacks the characteristics of a metal — **non·me·tal·lic**
\,nän-mə-'ta-lik\ *adj*

non-neg-a-tive \-'ne-gə-tiv\ *adj* : not negative : being either positive or zero

non-nu-cle-ar \'nän-'nü-klē-ər\ *adj* 1
: not nuclear 2 : not having, using, or involving nuclear weapons

non-ob-jec-tive \,nän-əb-'jek-tiv\ *adj* 1
: not objective 2 : representing no natural or actual object, figure, or scene ⟨∼
art⟩

¹**non-pa-reil** \,nän-pə-'rel\ *adj* : having no
equal : PEERLESS

²**nonpareil** *n* 1 : an individual of unequaled excellence : PARAGON 2 : a
small flat disk of chocolate covered with
white sugar pellets

non-par-ti-san \'nän-'pär-tə-zən\ *adj*
: not partisan ; *esp* : not influenced by political party spirit or interests

non-per-son \-'pər-sⁿn\ *n* 1 : UNPER-
SON 2 : a person having no social or
legal status

non-plus \'nän-'pləs\ *vb* -**plussed** *also*
-**plused** \-'pləst\; -**plus·sing** *also* -**plus-
ing** : PUZZLE, PERPLEX

non-pre-scrip-tion \,nän-pri-'skrip-shən\
adj : available for sale legally without a
doctor's prescription

non-prof-it \'nän-'prä-fət\ *adj* : not conducted or maintained for the purpose of
making a profit ⟨a ∼ organization⟩

non-pro-lif-er-a-tion \,nän-prə-,li-fə-'rā-

noncritical	nonexempt	nonindustrial	nonmotile
noncrystalline	nonexistence	noninfectious	nonmoving
nondeductible	nonexistent	noninflammable	nonnegotiable
nondelivery	nonexplosive	nonintellectual	nonobservance
nondemocratic	nonfarm	nonintercourse	nonoccurrence
nondenomination-al	nonfatal	noninterference	nonofficial
nondepartmental	nonfattening	nonintoxicant	nonoily
nondestructive	nonfederated	nonintoxicating	nonorthodox
nondevelopment	nonferrous	noninvasive	nonparallel
nondiscrimination	nonfiction	nonionizing	nonparasitic
nondiscriminatory	nonfictional	nonirritating	nonparticipant
nondistinctive	nonfilamentous	nonlegal	nonparticipating
nondurable	nonfilterable	nonlethal	nonpathogenic
noneconomic	nonflammable	nonlife	nonpaying
noneducational	nonflowering	nonlinear	nonpayment
nonelastic	nonfood	nonliterary	nonperformance
nonelection	nonfreezing	nonliving	nonperishable
nonelective	nonfulfillment	nonlogical	nonphysical
nonelectric	nonfunctional	nonmagnetic	nonpoisonous
nonelectrical	nongraded	nonmalignant	nonpolar
nonemotional	nonhereditary	nonmaterial	nonpolitical
nonenforcement	nonhomogeneous	nonmember	nonporous
nonethical	nonhomologous	nonmembership	nonpregnant
non-euclidean	nonhuman	nonmigratory	nonproductive
nonexclusive	nonidentical	nonmilitary	nonprofessional
	nonimportation	nonmoral	

shən\ *adj* : providing for the stoppage of proliferation (as of nuclear arms) ⟨a ~ treaty⟩

non·read·er \'nän-ˌrē-dər\ *n* : one who does not read or has difficulty reading

non·rep·re·sen·ta·tion·al \ˌnän-ˌre-pri-ˌzen-ˈtā-shə-nəl\ *adj* : NONOBJECTIVE 2

non·res·i·dent \ˈnän-ˈre-zə-dənt\ *adj* : not living in a particular place — **non·res·i·dence** \-dəns\ *n* — **nonresident** *n*

non·re·sis·tance \ˌnän-ri-ˈzis-təns\ *n* : the principles or practice of passive submission to authority even when unjust or oppressive

non·re·stric·tive \-ri-ˈstrik-tiv\ *adj* **1** : not serving or tending to restrict **2** : not limiting the reference of the word or phrase modified ⟨a ~ clause⟩

non·sched·uled \ˈnän-ˈske-jüld\ *adj* : licensed to carry passengers or freight by air without a regular schedule

non·sense \ˈnän-ˌsens, -səns\ *n* **1** : foolish or meaningless words or actions **2** : things of no importance or value — **non·sen·si·cal** \nän-ˈsen-si-kəl\ *adj* — **non·sen·si·cal·ly** \-k(ə-)lē\ *adv*

non se·qui·tur \nän-ˈse-kwə-tər\ *n* [L, it does not follow] : an inference that does not follow from the premises

non·skid \ˈnän-ˈskid\ *adj* : designed to prevent skidding

non·slip \-ˈslip\ *adj* : designed to prevent slipping

non·stan·dard \ˌnän-ˈstan-dərd\ *adj* **1** : not standard **2** : not conforming to the usage characteristic of educated native speakers of a language

non·start·er \ˈnän-ˈstär-tər\ *n* **1** : one that does not start **2** : one that is not productive or effective

non·stick \-ˈstik\ *adj* : allowing easy removal of cooked food particles

¹non·stop \-ˈstäp\ *adj* : done or made without a stop — **nonstop** *adv*

²nonstop *n* : a nonstop airplane flight

non·sup·port \ˌnän-sə-ˈpȯrt\ *n* : failure to support; *esp* : failure on the part of one under obligation to provide maintenance

non·threat·en·ing \-ˈthret-niŋ, -ˈthret-ᵊn-iŋ\ *adj* : not likely to cause danger or anxiety ⟨a ~ illness⟩ ⟨a ~ environment⟩

non–U \ˈnän-ˈyü\ *adj* : not characteristic of the upper classes

non·union \-ˈyü-nyən\ *adj* **1** : not belonging to a trade union ⟨~ carpenters⟩ **2** : not recognizing or favoring trade unions or their members ⟨~ employers⟩

non·us·er \-ˈyü-zər\ *n* : one who does not make use of something (as drugs)

non·vi·o·lence \ˈnän-ˈvī-ə-ləns\ *n* **1** : abstention from violence as a matter of principle **2** : avoidance of violence **3** : nonviolent political demonstrations — **non·vi·o·lent** \-lənt\ *adj*

non·white \ˌnän-ˈhwīt, -ˈwīt\ *n* : a person whose features and esp. skin color are different from those of peoples of northwestern Europe — **nonwhite** *adj*

non·wo·ven \ˈnän-ˈwō-vən\ *adj* : made of fibers held together by interlocking or bonding (as by chemical or thermal means) — **nonwoven** *n*

noo·dle \ˈnü-dᵊl\ *n* [G *Nudel*] : a food paste made usu. with egg and shaped typically in ribbon form

nook \ˈnu̇k\ *n* **1** : an interior angle or corner formed usu. by two walls ⟨a chimney ~⟩ **2** : a sheltered or hidden place ⟨searched every ~ and cranny⟩ **3** : a usu. recessed section of a larger room ⟨a breakfast ~⟩

noon \ˈnün\ *n* : the middle of the day : 12 o'clock in the daytime — **noon** *adj*

noon·day \ˈnün-ˌdā\ *n* : NOON, MIDDAY

no one *pron* : NOBODY

noon·tide \ˈnün-ˌtīd\ *n* : NOON

noon·time \-ˌtīm\ *n* : NOON

noose \ˈnüs\ *n* : a loop with a slipknot that binds closer the more it is drawn

nope \ˈnōp\ *adv* : NO

nor \ˈnȯr\ *conj* : and not ⟨not for you ~ for me⟩ — used esp. to introduce and negate the second member and each later member of a series of items preceded by *neither* ⟨neither here ~ there⟩

Nor·dic \ˈnȯr-dik\ *adj* **1** : of or relating to the Germanic peoples of northern Europe and esp. of Scandinavia **2** : of or relating to competitive ski events involving cross-country racing, ski jumping, or biathlon — **Nordic** *n*

nor·epi·neph·rine \ˌnȯr-ˌe-pə-ˈne-frən\ *n* : a nitrogen-containing neurotransmitter in parts of the sympathetic and central nervous systems

norm \ˈnȯrm\ *n* [L *norma*, lit., carpenter's square] **1** : an authoritative standard or model; *esp* : a set standard of develop-

nonprotein	nonruminant	nonsocial	nontransferable
nonradioactive	nonsalable	nonspeaking	nontypical
nonrandom	nonscientific	nonspecialist	nonuniform
nonreactive	nonscientist	nonspecific	nonvascular
nonreciprocal	nonseasonal	nonsteroidal	nonvenomous
nonrecognition	nonsectarian	nonsuccess	nonverbal
nonrecurrent	nonsegregated	nonsurgical	nonviable
nonrecurring	nonselective	nontaxable	nonvisual
nonrefillable	non-self-govern-	nonteaching	nonvocal
nonreligious	ing	nontechnical	nonvolatile
nonrenewable	nonsexist	nontemporal	nonvoter
nonresidential	nonsexual	nontenured	nonvoting
nonrestricted	nonshrinkable	nontheistic	nonworker
nonreturnable	nonsinkable	nonthreatening	nonworking
nonreversible	nonsmoker	nontoxic	nonzero
nonrigid	nonsmoking	nontraditional	

ment or achievement usu. derived from the average or median achievement of a large group **2** : a typical or widespread practice, procedure, or custom ♦ *Synonyms* AVERAGE, MEAN, MEDIAN, PAR

¹nor·mal \'nȯr-məl\ *adj* **1** : REGULAR, STANDARD, NATURAL **2** : of average intelligence; *also* : sound in mind and body — **nor·mal·cy** \-sē\ *n* — **nor·mal·i·ty** \nȯr-'ma-lə-tē\ *n* — **nor·mal·ly** *adv*

²normal *n* **1** : one that is normal **2** : the usual condition, level, or quantity

nor·mal·ise *Brit var of* NORMALIZE

nor·mal·ize \'nȯr-mə-ˌlīz\ *vb* **-ized; -iz·ing** : to make or restore to normal — **nor·mal·i·za·tion** \ˌnȯr-mə-lə-'zā-shən\ *n*

Nor·man \'nȯr-mən\ *n* **1** : a native or inhabitant of Normandy **2** : one of the 10th century Scandinavian conquerors of Normandy **3** : one of the Norman-French conquerors of England in 1066 — **Norman** *adj*

nor·ma·tive \'nȯr-mə-tiv\ *adj* : of, relating to, or determining norms — **nor·ma·tive·ly** *adv* — **nor·ma·tive·ness** *n*

Norse \'nȯrs\ *n, pl* **Norse 1** : NORWEGIAN; *also* : any of the western Scandinavian dialects or languages **2** *pl* : SCANDINAVIANS; *also* : NORWEGIANS

Norse·man \-mən\ *n* : any of the ancient Scandinavians

¹north \'nȯrth\ *adv* : to, toward, or in the north

²north *adj* **1** : situated toward or at the north **2** : coming from the north

³north *n* **1** : the direction to the left of one facing east **2** : the compass point directly opposite to south **3** *cap* : regions or countries north of a specified or implied point — **north·er·ly** \'nȯr-thər-lē\ *adv or adj* — **north·ern** \-thərn\ *adj* — **North·ern·er** \-thər-nər\ *n* — **north·ern·most** \-thərn-ˌmōst\ *adj* — **north·ward** \'nȯrth-wərd\ *adv or adj* — **north·wards** \-wərdz\ *adv*

north·east \nȯrth-'ēst\ *n* **1** : the general direction between north and east **2** : the compass point midway between north and east **3** *cap* : regions or countries northeast of a specified or implied point — **northeast** *adj or adv* — **north·east·er·ly** \-'thē-stər-lē\ *adv or adj* — **north·east·ern** \-stərn\ *adj*

north·east·er \-'ē-stər\ *n* **1** : a strong northeast wind **2** : a storm with northeast winds

north·er \'nȯr-thər\ *n* **1** : a strong north wind **2** : a storm with north winds

northern lights *n pl* : AURORA BOREALIS

north pole *n, often cap N&P* : the northernmost point of the earth

North Star *n* : the star toward which the northern end of the earth's axis points

north·west \nȯrth-'west\ *n* **1** : the general direction between north and west **2** : the compass point midway between north and west **3** *cap* : regions or countries northwest of a specified or implied point — **northwest** *adj or adv* — **north-**

west·er·ly \-'we-stər-lē\ *adv or adj* — **north·west·ern** \-'we-stərn\ *adj*

Norw *abbr* Norway; Norwegian

Nor·we·gian \nȯr-'wē-jən\ *n* **1** : a native or inhabitant of Norway **2** : the language of Norway — **Norwegian** *adj*

nos *abbr* numbers

¹nose \'nōz\ *n* **1** : the part of the face or head containing the nostrils and covering the front of the nasal cavity **2** : the sense of smell **3** : something (as a point, edge, or projecting front part) that resembles a nose ⟨the ~ of a plane⟩ — **nosed** \'nōzd\ *adj* — **on the nose** : on target : ACCURATE — **under one's nose** : extremely near : in one's presence

²nose *vb* **nosed; nos·ing 1** : to detect by or as if by smell : SCENT **2** : to push or move with the nose **3** : to touch or rub with the nose : NUZZLE **4** : PRY **5** : to move ahead slowly ⟨the ship *nosed* into her berth⟩

nose·bleed \'nōz-ˌblēd\ *n* : a bleeding from the nose

nose cone *n* : a protective cone constituting the forward end of an aerospace vehicle

nose·dive \'nōz-ˌdīv\ *n* **1** : a downward nose-first plunge (as of an airplane) **2** : a sudden extreme drop (as in prices)

nose·gay \'nōz-ˌgā\ *n* : a small bunch of flowers : POSY

nose out *vb* **1** : to discover often by prying **2** : to defeat by a narrow margin

nose·piece \-ˌpēs\ *n* **1** : a fitting at the lower end of a microscope tube to which the objectives are attached **2** : the bridge of a pair of eyeglasses

no–show \'nō-'shō\ *n* : a person who does not show up for an event as expected

nos·tal·gia \nä-'stal-jə\ *n* [NL, fr. Gk *nostos* return home + *algos* pain, grief] **1** : HOMESICKNESS **2** : a wistful yearning for something past or irrecoverable — **nos·tal·gic** \-jik\ *adj* — **nos·tal·gist** \-jist\ *n*

nos·tril \'näs-trəl\ *n* [ME *nosethirl*, fr. OE *nosthyrl*, fr. *nosu* nose + *thyrel* hole] **1** : either of the nares usu. with the adjoining nasal wall and passage **2** : either fleshy lateral wall of the nose

nos·trum \'näs-trəm\ *n* [L, neut. of *noster* our, ours, fr. *nos* we] : a questionable medicine or remedy

nosy *or* **nos·ey** \'nō-zē\ *adj* **nos·i·er; -est** : INQUISITIVE, PRYING

not \'nät\ *adv* **1** — used to make negative a group of words or a word ⟨the boys are ~ here⟩ **2** — used to stand for the negative of a preceding group of words ⟨sometimes hard to see and sometimes ~⟩

no·ta be·ne \ˌnō-tə-'bē-nē, -'be-\ [L, mark well] — used to call attention to something important

no·ta·bil·i·ty \ˌnō-tə-'bi-lə-tē\ *n, pl* **-ties 1** : the quality or state of being notable **2** : NOTABLE

¹no·ta·ble \'nō-tə-bəl\ *adj* **1** : NOTEWORTHY, REMARKABLE ⟨a ~ achievement⟩ **2** : DISTINGUISHED, PROMINENT ⟨two ~ politicians made speeches⟩

²**notable** *n* : a person of note ✦ *Synonyms* BIGWIG, EMINENCE, NABOB, PERSONAGE, SOMEBODY, VIP

no·ta·bly \'nō-tə-blē\ *adv* **1** : in a notable manner **2** : ESPECIALLY, PARTICULARLY

no·tar·i·al \nō-'ter-ē-əl\ *adj* : of, relating to, or done by a notary public

no·ta·rize \'nō-tə-ˌrīz\ *vb* **-rized; -riz·ing** : to acknowledge or make legally authentic as a notary public

no·ta·ry public \'nō-tə-rē-\ *n, pl* **notaries public** *or* **notary publics** : a public official who attests or certifies writings (as deeds) to make them legally authentic

no·ta·tion \nō-'tā-shən\ *n* **1** : ANNOTATION, NOTE **2** : the act, process, or method of representing data by marks, signs, figures, or characters; *also* : a system of symbols (as letters, numerals, or musical notes) used in such notation

¹**notch** \'näch\ *n* **1** : a V-shaped hollow in an edge or surface **2** : a narrow pass between two mountains

²**notch** *vb* **1** : to cut or make notches in **2** : to score or record by or as if by cutting a series of notches ⟨*~ed* 20 points for the team⟩

notch·back \'näch-ˌbak\ *n* : an automobile with a trunk whose lid forms a distinct deck

¹**note** \'nōt\ *vb* **not·ed; not·ing 1** : to notice or observe with care; *also* : to record or preserve in writing **2** : to make special mention of : REMARK

²**note** *n* **1** : a musical sound **2** : a cry, call, or sound esp. of a bird **3** : a special tone in a person's words or voice ⟨a ~ of fear⟩ **4** : a character in music used to indicate duration of a tone by its shape and pitch by its position on the staff **5** : a characteristic feature : MOOD, QUALITY ⟨a ~ of optimism⟩ **6** : MEMORANDUM **7** : a brief and informal record; *also* : a written or printed comment or explanation **8** : a written promise to pay a debt **9** : a piece of paper money **10** : a short informal letter **11** : a formal diplomatic or official communication **12** : DISTINCTION, REPUTATION ⟨an artist of ~⟩ **13** : OBSERVATION, NOTICE, HEED ⟨take ~ of the time⟩

note·book \'nōt-ˌbuk\ *n* **1** : a book for notes or memoranda **2** : a portable microcomputer smaller than a laptop computer

not·ed \'nō-təd\ *adj* : well known by reputation : EMINENT, CELEBRATED

note·wor·thy \'nōt-ˌwər-thē\ *adj* : worthy of note : REMARKABLE

¹**noth·ing** \'nə-thiŋ\ *pron* **1** : no thing ⟨*leaves ~* to the imagination⟩ **2** : no part **3** : one of no interest, value, or importance ⟨she's ~ to me⟩ **4** : a light playful remark ⟨sweet ~s⟩

²**nothing** *adv* : not at all : in no degree

³**nothing** *n* **1** : something that does not exist **2** : ZERO **3** : a person or thing of little or no value or importance

⁴**nothing** *adj* : of no account : WORTHLESS

noth·ing·ness \'nə-thiŋ-nəs\ *n* **1** : the quality or state of being nothing **2** : NONEXISTENCE; *also* : utter insignificance **3** : something insignificant or valueless

¹**no·tice** \'nō-təs\ *n* **1** : WARNING, ANNOUNCEMENT **2** : notification of the termination of an agreement or contract at a specified time **3** : ATTENTION, HEED ⟨bring the matter to my ~⟩ **4** : a written or printed announcement **5** : a short critical account or examination (as of a play) : REVIEW

²**notice** *vb* **no·ticed; no·tic·ing 1** : to make mention of : remark on : NOTE **2** : to take notice of : OBSERVE, MARK

no·tice·able \'nō-tə-sə-bəl\ *adj* **1** : worthy of notice **2** : likely to be noticed — **no·tice·ably** \-blē\ *adv*

no·ti·fy \'nō-tə-ˌfī\ *vb* **-fied; -fy·ing 1** : to give notice of : report the occurrence of **2** : to give notice to — **no·ti·fi·ca·tion** \ˌnō-tə-fə-'kā-shən\ *n*

no·tion \'nō-shən\ *n* **1** : IDEA, CONCEPTION ⟨have a ~ of what he means⟩ **2** : a belief held : OPINION, VIEW **3** : WHIM, FANCY ⟨a sudden ~ to go⟩ **4** *pl* : small useful articles (as pins, needles, or thread)

no·tion·al \'nō-shə-nəl\ *adj* **1** : existing in the mind only : IMAGINARY, UNREAL **2** : given to foolish or fanciful moods or ideas : WHIMSICAL

no·to·ri·ous \nō-'tōr-ē-əs\ *adj* : generally known and talked of; *esp* : widely and unfavorably known — **no·to·ri·ety** \ˌnō-tə-'rī-ə-tē\ *n* — **no·to·ri·ous·ly** \nō-'tōr-ē-əs-lē\ *adv*

¹**not·with·stand·ing** \ˌnät-with-'stan-diŋ, -with-\ *prep* : in spite of

²**notwithstanding** *adv* : NEVERTHELESS

³**notwithstanding** *conj* : ALTHOUGH

nou·gat \'nü-gət\ *n* [F, fr. Occitan, fr. Old Occitan, *nogat*, fr. *noga* nut, ultim. fr. L *nuc-, nux*] : a confection of nuts or fruit pieces in a sugar paste

nought *var of* NAUGHT

noun \'naun\ *n* : a word that is the name of a subject of discourse (as a person or place)

nour·ish \'nər-ish\ *vb* : to promote the growth or development of

nour·ish·ing *adj* : giving nourishment

nour·ish·ment \'nər-ish-mənt\ *n* **1** : FOOD, NUTRIENT **2** : the action or process of nourishing

nou·veau riche \ˌnü-ˌvō-'rēsh\ *n, pl* **nouveaux riches** *same*\ [F] : a person newly rich : PARVENU

Nov *abbr* November

no·va \'nō-və\ *n, pl* **novas** *or* **no·vae** \-(ˌ)vē, -ˌvī\ [NL, fem. of L *novus* new] : a star that suddenly increases greatly in brightness and then within a few months or years grows dim again

¹**nov·el** \'nä-vəl\ *adj* **1** : having no precedent : NEW **2** : STRANGE, UNUSUAL

²**novel** *n* : a long invented prose narrative dealing with human experience through a connected sequence of events — **nov·el·ist** \-və-list\ *n*

nov·el·ette \ˌnä-və-'let\ *n* : a brief novel or long short story

nov·el·ize \'nä-və-ˌlīz\ *vb* **-ized; -iz·ing**

: to convert into the form of a novel — **nov·el·i·za·tion** \ˌnä-və-lə-ˈzā-shən\ n

no·vel·la \nō-ˈve-lə\ n, pl **novellas** or **no·vel·le** \-ˈve-lē\ : NOVELETTE

nov·el·ty \ˈnä-vəl-tē\ n, pl **-ties** 1 : something new or unusual 2 : NEWNESS 3 : a small manufactured article intended mainly for personal or household adornment — usu. used in pl.

No·vem·ber \nō-ˈvem-bər\ n [ME Novembre, fr. AF, fr. L November ninth month of the early Roman calendar, fr. novem nine] : the 11th month of the year

no·ve·na \nō-ˈvē-nə\ n : a Roman Catholic nine-day period of prayer

nov·ice \ˈnä-vəs\ n 1 : a new member of a religious order who is preparing to take the vows of religion 2 : one who is inexperienced or untrained

no·vi·tiate \nō-ˈvi-shət\ n 1 : the period or state of being a novice 2 : a house where novices are trained 3 : NOVICE

¹**now** \ˈnaü\ adv 1 : at the present time or moment 2 : in the time immediately before the present 3 : IMMEDIATELY, FORTHWITH 4 — used with the sense of present time weakened or lost (as to express command, introduce an important point, or indicate a transition) ⟨~ hear this⟩ 5 : SOMETIMES ⟨~ one and ~ another⟩ 6 : under the present circumstances 7 : at the time referred to 8 : by this time

²**now** conj : in view of the fact ⟨~ that you're here, we'll start⟩

³**now** n : the present time or moment : PRESENT

⁴**now** adj 1 : of or relating to the present time ⟨the ~ president⟩ 2 : excitingly new ⟨~ clothes⟩; also : constantly aware of what is new ⟨~ people⟩

NOW abbr 1 National Organization for Women 2 negotiable order of withdrawal

now·a·days \ˈnaü-ə-ˌdāz\ adv : at the present time

no·way \ˈnō-ˌwā\ or **no·ways** \-ˌwāz\ adv : NOWISE

no·where \-ˌhwer\ adv 1 : not anywhere : not at all — usu. used with near ⟨~ near enough⟩ — **nowhere** n

no·wise \ˈnō-ˌwīz\ adv : in no way

nox·ious \ˈnäk-shəs\ adj : harmful esp. to health or morals

noz·zle \ˈnä-zəl\ n : a short tube constricted in the middle or at one end and used (as on a hose) to speed up or direct a flow of fluid

np abbr 1 no pagination 2 no place (of publication)

Np symbol neptunium

NP abbr notary public

NR abbr not rated

NRA abbr National Rifle Association

NS abbr 1 not specified 2 Nova Scotia

NSA abbr National Security Agency

NSC abbr National Security Council

NSF abbr 1 National Science Foundation 2 not sufficient funds

NSW abbr New South Wales

NT abbr 1 New Testament 2 Northern Territory 3 Northwest Territories

nth \ˈenth\ adj 1 : numbered with an unspecified or indefinitely large ordinal number ⟨for the ~ time⟩ 2 : EXTREME, UTMOST ⟨to the ~ degree⟩

NTP abbr normal temperature and pressure

nt wt or **n wt** abbr net weight

nu \ˈnü, ˈnyü\ n : the 13th letter of the Greek alphabet — N or ν

NU abbr name unknown

nu·ance \ˈnü-ˌäns, ˈnyü-, nü-ˈäns, nyü-\ n [F] : a shade of difference : a delicate variation (as in tone or meaning)

nub \ˈnəb\ n 1 : KNOB, LUMP 2 : GIST, POINT ⟨the ~ of the story⟩

nub·bin \ˈnə-bən\ n 1 : something (as an ear of Indian corn) that is small for its kind, stunted, undeveloped, or imperfect 2 : a small projecting bit

nu·bile \ˈnü-ˌbī(-ə)l, ˈnyü-, -bəl\ adj 1 : of marriageable condition or age 2 : sexually attractive ⟨~ young women⟩

nu·cle·ar \ˈnü-klē-ər, ˈnyü-\ adj 1 : of, relating to, or constituting a nucleus 2 : of, relating to, or using the atomic nucleus or energy derived from it 3 : of, relating to, or being a weapon whose destructive power results from an uncontrolled nuclear reaction

nu·cle·ate \ˈnü-klē-ˌāt, ˈnyü-\ vb **-at·ed**; **-at·ing** : to form, act as, or have a nucleus — **nu·cle·ation** \ˌnü-klē-ˈā-shən, ˌnyü-\ n

nu·cle·ic acid \nü-ˈklē-ik-, nyü-, -ˈklā-\ n : any of various complex organic acids (as DNA or RNA) found esp. in cell nuclei

nu·cle·o·tide \ˈnü-klē-ə-ˌtīd, ˈnyü-\ n : any of several compounds that are the basic structural units of nucleic acids

nu·cle·us \ˈnü-klē-əs, ˈnyü-\ n, pl **nu·clei** \-klē-ˌī\ also **nu·cle·us·es** [NL, fr. L, kernel, dim. of nuc-, nux nut] 1 : a central mass or part about which matter gathers or is collected : CORE 2 : a cell part that is characteristic of all living things except viruses, bacteria, and certain algae, that is necessary for heredity and for making proteins, that contains the chromosomes with their genes, and that is enclosed in a membrane 3 : a mass of gray matter or group of cell bodies of neurons in the central nervous system 4 : the central part of an atom that comprises nearly all of the atomic mass 5 : a basic or essential part

¹**nude** \ˈnüd, ˈnyüd\ adj **nud·er**; **nud·est** 1 : BARE, NAKED, UNCLOTHED 2 : featuring or catering to naked people ⟨a ~ beach⟩ — **nu·di·ty** \ˈnü-də-tē, ˈnyü-\ n

²**nude** n 1 : a nude human figure esp. as depicted in art 2 : the condition of being nude ⟨in the ~⟩

nudge \ˈnəj\ vb **nudged**; **nudg·ing** : to touch or push gently (as with the elbow) usu. in order to seek attention — **nudge** n

nud·ism \ˈnü-ˌdi-zəm, ˈnyü-\ n : the practice of going nude esp. in mixed groups at specially secluded places — **nud·ist** \-dist\ n

nu·ga·to·ry \'nü-gə⸳ˌtȯr-ē\ adj **1** : IN-CONSEQUENTIAL, WORTHLESS **2** : having no force : INEFFECTUAL

nug·get \'nə-gət\ n **1** : a lump of precious metal (as gold) **2** : TIDBIT

nui·sance \'nü-sᵊns, 'nyü-\ n : an annoying or troublesome person or thing

nuisance tax n : an excise tax collected in small amounts directly from the consumer

¹**nuke** \'nük, 'nyük\ n **1** : a nuclear weapon **2** : a nuclear power plant

²**nuke** vb **nuked; nuk·ing 1** : to attack with nuclear weapons **2** : MICROWAVE

null \'nəl\ adj **1** : having no legal or binding force : INVALID, VOID **2** : amounting to nothing **3** : INSIGNIFICANT — **nul·li·ty** \'nə-lə-tē\ n

null and void adj : having no force, binding power, or validity

nul·li·fy \'nə-lə-ˌfī\ vb **-fied; -fy·ing** : to make null or valueless; also : ANNUL — **nul·li·fi·ca·tion** \ˌnə-lə-fə-'kā-shən\ n

num abbr numeral

Num or **Numb** abbr Numbers

numb \'nəm\ adj : lacking sensation or emotion : BENUMBED — **numb** vb — **numb·ly** adv — **numb·ness** n

¹**num·ber** \'nəm-bər\ n **1** : the total of individuals or units taken together **2** : an indefinite total ⟨a small ∼ of tickets remain unsold⟩ **3** : an ascertainable total ⟨the sands of the desert are without ∼⟩ **4** : a distinction of word form to denote reference to one or more than one **5** : a unit belonging to a mathematical system and subject to its laws; also, pl : ARITHMETIC **6** : a symbol used to represent a mathematical number; also : such a number used to identify or designate ⟨a phone ∼⟩ **7** : one in a series of musical or theatrical performances **8** : an act of transforming or impairing ⟨tripped and did a ∼ on her knee⟩

²**number** vb **1** : COUNT, ENUMERATE **2** : to include with or be one of a group **3** : to restrict to a small or definite number **4** : to assign a number to **5** : to comprise in number : TOTAL

num·ber·less \-ləs\ adj : INNUMERABLE, COUNTLESS

Numbers n — see BIBLE table

numb·ing \'nə-miŋ\ adj : tending to make numb ⟨a ∼ lecture⟩ ⟨a ∼ realization⟩

numbskull var of NUMSKULL

nu·mer·a·cy \'nü-mə-rə-sē, 'nyü-\ n : the capacity for quantitative thought or expression

nu·mer·al \'nü-mə-rəl, 'nyü-\ n : a conventional symbol representing a number — **numeral** adj

nu·mer·ate \'nü-mə-ˌrāt, 'nyü-\ vb **-at·ed; -at·ing** : ENUMERATE

nu·mer·a·tor \-ˌrā-tər\ n : the part of a fraction above the line

nu·mer·ic \nü-'mer-ik, nyü-\ adj : NUMERICAL; esp : denoting a number or a system of numbers

nu·mer·i·cal \-'mer-i-kəl\ adj **1** : of or relating to numbers **2** : expressed in or involving numbers — **nu·mer·i·cal·ly** \-k(ə-)lē\ adv

nu·mer·ol·o·gy \ˌnü-mə-'rä-lə-jē, ˌnyü-\ n : the study of the occult significance of numbers — **nu·mer·ol·o·gist** \-jist\ n

nu·mer·ous \'nü-mə-rəs, 'nyü-\ adj : consisting of, including, or relating to a great number : MANY

nu·mis·mat·ics \ˌnü-məz-'ma-tiks, ˌnyü-\ n : the study or collection of monetary objects — **nu·mis·mat·ic** \-tik\ adj — **nu·mis·ma·tist** \nü-'miz-mə-tist, nyü-\ n

num·skull also **numb·skull** \'nəm-ˌskəl\ n : a stupid person : DUNCE

nun \'nən\ n : a woman belonging to a religious order; esp : one under solemn vows of poverty, chastity, and obedience

nun·cio \'nən-sē-ˌō, 'nùn-\ n, pl **-ci·os** [It, fr. L nuntius messenger] : a permanent high-ranking papal representative to a civil government

nun·nery \'nə-nə-rē\ n, pl **-ner·ies** : a convent of nuns

¹**nup·tial** \'nəp-shəl\ adj : of or relating to marriage or a wedding

²**nuptial** n : MARRIAGE, WEDDING — usu. used in pl.

¹**nurse** \'nərs\ n [ME norice, nurse, fr. AF nurice, fr. LL nutricia, fr. L, fem. of nutricius nourishing] **1** : a girl or woman employed to take care of children **2** : a person trained to care for sick people

²**nurse** vb **nursed; nurs·ing 1** : SUCKLE **2** : to take charge of and watch over **3** : TEND ⟨∼ an invalid⟩ **4** : to treat with special care ⟨∼ a headache⟩ **5** : to hold in one's mind or consideration ⟨∼ a grudge⟩ **6** : to act or serve as a nurse

nurse·maid \'nərs-ˌmād\ n : NURSE 1

nurse–prac·ti·tion·er \-prak-'ti-shə-nər\ n : a registered nurse who is qualified to assume some of the duties formerly assumed only by a physician

nurs·ery \'nər-sə-rē\ n, pl **-er·ies 1** : a room for children **2** : a place where children are temporarily cared for in their parents' absence **3** : a place where young plants are grown usu. for transplanting

nurs·ery·man \-mən\ n : a man who keeps or works in a plant nursery

nursery school n : a school for children under kindergarten age

nursing home n : a private establishment providing care for persons (as the aged or the chronically ill) who are unable to care for themselves

nurs·ling \'nərs-liŋ\ n **1** : one that is solicitously cared for **2** : a nursing child

¹**nur·ture** \'nər-chər\ n **1** : TRAINING, UPBRINGING; also : the influences that modify the expression of an individual's heredity **2** : FOOD, NOURISHMENT

²**nurture** vb **nur·tured; nur·tur·ing 1** : to care for : FEED, NOURISH **2** : EDUCATE, TRAIN **3** : FOSTER

nut \'nət\ n **1** : a dry fruit or seed with a hard shell and a firm inner kernel; also : its kernel **2** : a metal block with a hole through it that is fastened to a bolt or screw by means of a screw thread within the hole **3** : the ridge on the upper end of the fingerboard in a stringed musical instrument over which the strings pass **4**

: a foolish, eccentric, or crazy person **5**
: ENTHUSIAST
nut·crack·er \'nət-,kra-kər\ *n* : an instrument for cracking nuts
nut·hatch \-,hach\ *n* : any of various small tree-climbing chiefly insect-eating birds
nut·meg \-,meg, -,māg\ *n* [ME *notemuge*, ultim. fr. Old Occitan *noz muscada*, lit., musky nut] : a spice made by grinding the nutlike aromatic seed of a tropical tree; *also* : the seed or tree
nu·tria \'nü-trē-ə, 'nyü-\ *n* [Sp] **1** : the durable usu. light brown fur of a nutria **2** : a large So. American aquatic rodent with webbed hind feet
¹nu·tri·ent \'nü-trē-ənt, 'nyü-\ *adj* : NOURISHING
²nutrient *n* : a nutritive substance or ingredient
nu·tri·ment \-trə-mənt\ *n* : NUTRIENT
nu·tri·tion \nü-'tri-shən, nyü-\ *n* : the act or process of nourishing; *esp* : the processes by which an individual takes in and utilizes food material — **nu·tri·tion·al** \-shə-nəl\ *adj* — **nu·tri·tion·al·ly** *adv* — **nu·tri·tion·ist** \-shə-nist\ *n* — **nu·tri·tive** \'nü-trə-tiv, 'nyü-\ *adj*
nu·tri·tious \-shəs\ *adj* : NOURISHING — **nu·tri·tious·ly** *adv*

nuts \'nəts\ *adj* **1** : ENTHUSIASTIC, KEEN **2** : CRAZY, DEMENTED
nut·shell \'nət-,shel\ *n* : the shell of a nut — **in a nutshell** : in a few words ⟨that's the story *in a nutshell*⟩
nut·ty \'nə-tē\ *adj* **nut·ti·er; -est** **1** : containing or suggesting nuts ⟨a ~ flavor⟩ **2** : mentally unbalanced
nuz·zle \'nə-zəl\ *vb* **nuz·zled; nuz·zling** **1** : to root around, push, or touch with or as if with the nose **2** : NESTLE, SNUGGLE
NV *abbr* Nevada
NW *abbr* northwest
NWT *abbr* Northwest Territories
NY *abbr* New York
NYC *abbr* New York City
ny·lon \'nī-,län\ *n* **1** : any of numerous strong tough elastic synthetic materials used esp. in textiles and plastics **2** *pl* : stockings made of nylon
nymph \'nimf\ *n* **1** : any of the lesser goddesses in ancient mythology represented as maidens living in the mountains, forests, meadows, and waters **2** : GIRL **3** : an immature insect resembling the adult but smaller, less differentiated, and usu. lacking developed wings
nym·pho·ma·nia \,nim-fə-'mā-nē-ə, -nyə\ *n* : excessive sexual desire by a female — **nym·pho·ma·ni·ac** \-nē-,ak\ *n or adj*
NZ *abbr* New Zealand

¹o \'ō\ *n, pl* **o's** *or* **os** \'ōz\ *often cap* **1** : the 15th letter of the English alphabet **2** : ZERO
²o *abbr, often cap* **1** ocean **2** Ohio **3** ohm
¹O *var of* OH
²O *symbol* oxygen
o/a *abbr* on or about
oaf \'ōf\ *n* : a stupid or awkward person — **oaf·ish** *adj*
oak \'ōk\ *n, pl* **oaks** *or* **oak** : any of a genus of trees or shrubs related to the beech and chestnut and bearing a rounded thin-shelled nut surrounded at the base by a hardened cup; *also* : the usu. tough hard durable wood of an oak — **oak·en** \'ō-kən\ *adj*
oa·kum \'ō-kəm\ *n* [ME *okum*, fr. OE *ācumba* flax fiber, fr. *a-* out + *-cumba* (akin to OE *camb* comb)] : loosely twisted hemp or jute fiber impregnated with tar and used esp. in caulking ships
oar \'ōr\ *n* : a long pole with a broad blade at one end used for propelling or steering a boat
oar·lock \'ōr-,läk\ *n* : a U-shaped device for holding an oar in place
oars·man \'ōrz-mən\ *n* : one who rows esp. in a racing crew
OAS *abbr* Organization of American States
oa·sis \ō-'ā-səs\ *n, pl* **oa·ses** \-,sēz\ : a fertile or green area in an arid region

oat \'ōt\ *n* : a cereal grass widely grown for its edible seed; *also* : this seed — **oat·en** \'ō-t°n\ *adj*
oat·cake \'ōt-,kāk\ *n* : a thin flat oatmeal cake
oath \'ōth\ *n, pl* **oaths** \'ōthz, 'ōths\ **1** : a solemn appeal to God to witness to the truth of a statement or the sacredness of a promise **2** : an irreverent or careless use of a sacred name
oat·meal \'ōt-,mēl\ *n* **1** : ground or rolled oats **2** : porridge made from ground or rolled oats
Ob *or* **Obad** Obadiah
Oba·di·ah \,ō-bə-'dī-ə\ *n* — see BIBLE table
ob·bli·ga·to \,ä-blə-'gä-tō\ *n, pl* **-tos** *also* **-ti** \-'gä-tē\ [It] : an accompanying part usu. played by a solo instrument
ob·du·rate \'äb-də-rət, -dyə-\ *adj* : stubbornly resistant : UNYIELDING ♦ *Synonyms* INFLEXIBLE, ADAMANT, RIGID, UNCOMPROMISING — **ob·du·ra·cy** \-rə-sē\ *n*
obe·di·ent \ō-'bē-dē-ənt\ *adj* : submissive to the restraint or command of authority ♦ *Synonyms* DOCILE, TRACTABLE, AMENABLE, BIDDABLE — **obe·di·ence** \-əns\ *n* — **obe·di·ent·ly** *adv*
obei·sance \ō-'bē-səns, -'bā-\ *n* **1** : a bow made to show respect or submission **2** : DEFERENCE, HOMAGE ⟨makes ~ to her mentors⟩

obe·lisk \'ä-bə-ˌlisk\ n [MF obelisque, fr. L obeliscus, fr. Gk obeliskos, fr. dim. of obelos spit, pointed pillar] : a 4-sided pillar that tapers toward the top and ends in a pyramid

obese \ō-'bēs\ adj [L obesus, fr. ob- against + esus, pp. of edere to eat] : having excessive body fat ✦ Synonyms CORPULENT, FLESHY, GROSS, OVERWEIGHT, PORTLY, STOUT — **obe·si·ty** \-'bē-sə-tē\ n

obey \ō-'bā\ vb **obeyed; obey·ing** 1 : to follow the commands or guidance of : behave obediently 2 : to comply with ⟨~ orders⟩ ✦ Synonyms CONFORM, KEEP, MIND, OBSERVE

ob·fus·cate \'äb-fə-ˌskāt\ vb **-cat·ed; -cat·ing** 1 : to make dark or obscure 2 : CONFUSE — **ob·fus·ca·tion** \ˌäb-fəs-'kā-shən\ n

OB–GYN abbr obstetrician gynecologist; obstetrics gynecology

obi \'ō-bē\ n [Jp] : a broad sash worn esp. with a Japanese kimono

obit \ō-'bit, 'ō-bət\ n : OBITUARY

obi·ter dic·tum \ˌō-bə-tər-'dik-təm\ n, pl **obiter dic·ta** \-tə\ [LL, lit., something said in passing] : an incidental remark or observation

obit·u·ary \ə-'bi-chə-ˌwer-ē\ n, pl **-ar·ies** : a notice of a person's death usu. with a short biographical account

obj abbr object; objective

¹ob·ject \'äb-jikt\ n 1 : something that may be seen or felt; also : something that may be perceived or examined mentally 2 : something that arouses an emotional response (as of affection or pity) 3 : AIM, PURPOSE ⟨the ~ is to raise money⟩ 4 : a word or word group denoting that on or toward which the action of a verb is directed; also : a noun or noun equivalent in a prepositional phrase

²ob·ject \əb-'jekt\ vb 1 : to offer in opposition 2 : to oppose something; also : DISAPPROVE ✦ Synonyms PROTEST, REMONSTRATE, EXPOSTULATE — **ob·jec·tor** \-'jek-tər\ n

object code n : a computer program after translation from source code

ob·jec·ti·fy \əb-'jek-tə-ˌfī\ vb **-fied; -fy·ing** : to make objective

ob·jec·tion \əb-'jek-shən\ n 1 : the act of objecting 2 : a reason for or a feeling of disapproval

ob·jec·tion·able \əb-'jek-shə-nə-bəl\ adj : UNDESIRABLE, OFFENSIVE — **ob·jec·tion·ably** \-blē\ adv

¹ob·jec·tive \əb-'jek-tiv\ adj 1 : of or relating to an object or end 2 : existing outside and independent of the mind 3 : of, relating to, or constituting a grammatical case marking typically the object of a verb or preposition 4 : treating or dealing with facts without distortion by personal feelings or prejudices — **ob·jec·tive·ly** adv — **ob·jec·tive·ness** n — **ob·jec·tiv·i·ty** \ˌäb-jek-'ti-və-tē\ n

²objective n 1 : the lens (as in a microscope) nearest the object and forming an image of it 2 : an aim, goal, or end of action

ob·jet d'art \ˌōb-ˌzhā-'där\ n, pl **ob·jets d'art** \same\ [F] 1 : an article of artistic worth 2 : CURIO ✦ Synonyms KNICK-KNACK, BAUBLE, BIBELOT, GEWGAW, NOVELTY, TRINKET

ob·jet trou·vé \'ōb-ˌzhā-trü-'vā\ n, pl **objets trouvés** \same\ [F, lit., found object] : a found natural or discarded object (as a piece of driftwood or an old bathtub) held to have aesthetic value

ob·jur·ga·tion \ˌäb-jər-'gā-shən\ n : a harsh rebuke — **ob·jur·gate** \'äb-jər-ˌgāt\ vb

obl abbr 1 oblique 2 oblong

ob·late \ä-'blāt\ adj : flattened or depressed at the poles ⟨an ~ spheroid⟩

ob·la·tion \ə-'blā-shən\ n : a religious offering

ob·li·gate \'ä-blə-ˌgāt\ vb **-gat·ed; -gat·ing** : to bind legally or morally

ob·li·ga·tion \ˌä-blə-'gā-shən\ n 1 : an act of obligating oneself to a course of action 2 : something (as a promise or a contract) that binds one to a course of action 3 : INDEBTEDNESS; also : LIABILITY 4 : DUTY — **oblig·a·to·ry** \ə-'bli-gə-ˌtȯr-ē\ adj

oblige \ə-'blīj\ vb **obliged; oblig·ing** [ME, fr. AF obliger, fr. L obligare, lit., to bind to, fr. ob- toward + ligare to bind] 1 : FORCE, COMPEL ⟨the soldiers were obliged to retreat⟩ 2 : to bind by a favor; also : to do a favor for or do something as a favor

oblig·ing adj : willing to do favors — **oblig·ing·ly** adv

oblique \ō-'blēk\ adj 1 : neither perpendicular nor parallel : SLANTING 2 : not straightforward : INDIRECT — **oblique·ly** adv — **oblique·ness** n — **obliq·ui·ty** \-'bli-kwə-tē\ n

oblique case n : a grammatical case other than the nominative or vocative

oblit·er·ate \ə-'bli-tə-ˌrāt\ vb **-at·ed; -at·ing** [L oblitterare, fr. ob in the way of + littera letter] 1 : to remove from recognition or memory 2 : to make undecipherable by wiping out or covering over 3 : CANCEL — **oblit·er·a·tion** \-ˌbli-tə-'rā-shən\ n

obliv·i·on \ə-'bli-vē-ən\ n 1 : the condition of being oblivious 2 : the condition or state of being forgotten

obliv·i·ous \ə-'bli-vē-əs\ adj 1 : lacking memory or mindful attention 2 : UNAWARE ⟨~ of the risks⟩ — **obliv·i·ous·ly** adv — **obliv·i·ous·ness** n

ob·long \'ä-ˌblȯŋ\ adj : deviating from a square, circular, or spherical form by elongation in one dimension — **oblong** n

ob·lo·quy \'ä-blə-kwē\ n, pl **-quies** 1 : strongly condemnatory utterance or language 2 : bad repute : DISGRACE ✦ Synonyms DISHONOR, SHAME, INFAMY, DISREPUTE, IGNOMINY

ob·nox·ious \äb-'näk-shəs\ adj : REPUGNANT, OFFENSIVE — **ob·nox·ious·ly** adv — **ob·nox·ious·ness** n

oboe \'ō-bō\ n [It, fr. F hautbois, fr. haut high + bois wood] : a woodwind instrument with a slender conical tube and a double reed mouthpiece — **obo·ist** \'ō-ˌbō-ist\ *n*

ob·scene \äb-'sēn\ *adj* **1** : REPULSIVE **2** : deeply offensive to morality or decency; *esp* : designed to incite to lust or depravity ◆ **Synonyms** GROSS, VULGAR, COARSE, CRUDE, INDECENT — **ob·scene·ly** *adv* — **ob·scen·i·ty** \-'se-nə-tē\ *n*

ob·scu·ran·tism \äb-'skyür-ən-ˌti-zəm, ˌäb-skyü-'ran-\ *n* **1** : opposition to the spread of knowledge **2** : deliberate vagueness or abstruseness — **ob·scu·ran·tist** \-tist\ *n or adj*

¹**ob·scure** \äb-'skyür\ *adj* **1** : DIM, GLOOMY **2** : not readily understood : VAGUE **3** : REMOTE; *also* : HUMBLE ◆ **Synonyms** DARK, DUSKY, MURKY, TENEBROUS — **ob·scure·ly** *adv* — **ob·scu·ri·ty** \-'skyür-ə-tē\ *n*

²**obscure** *vb* **ob·scured; ob·scur·ing 1** : to make dark, dim, or indistinct **2** : to conceal or hide by or as if by covering

ob·se·qui·ous \əb-'sē-kwē-əs\ *adj* : humbly or excessively attentive (as to a person in authority) : FAWNING, SYCOPHANTIC ◆ **Synonyms** MENIAL, SERVILE, SLAVISH, SUBSERVIENT — **ob·se·qui·ous·ly** *adv* — **ob·se·qui·ous·ness** *n*

ob·se·quy \'äb-sə-kwē\ *n, pl* **-quies** : a funeral or burial rite — usu. used in pl.

ob·serv·able \əb-'zər-və-bəl\ *adj* **1** : NOTEWORTHY **2** : capable of being observed — **ob·serv·abil·i·ty** \-'bi-lə-tē\ *n*

ob·ser·vance \əb-'zər-vəns\ *n* **1** : a customary practice or ceremony **2** : an act or instance of following a custom, rule, or law **3** : OBSERVATION

ob·ser·vant \-vənt\ *adj* **1** : WATCHFUL ⟨∼ spectators⟩ **2** : KEEN, PERCEPTIVE **3** : MINDFUL ⟨∼ of the amenities⟩

¹**ob·ser·va·tion** \ˌäb-sər-'vā-shən, -zər-\ *n* **1** : an act or instance of observing : the gathering of information (as for scientific studies) by noting facts or occurrences **3** : a conclusion drawn from observing; *also* : REMARK, STATEMENT **4** : the fact of being observed — **ob·ser·va·tion·al** \-shə-nəl\ *adj*

²**observation** *adj* : designed for use in viewing or in making observations

ob·ser·va·to·ry \əb-'zər-və-ˌtōr-ē\ *n, pl* **-ries** : a place or institution equipped for observation of natural phenomena (as in astronomy)

ob·serve \əb-'zərv\ *vb* **ob·served; ob·serv·ing 1** : to conform one's action or practice to **2** : CELEBRATE **3** : to make a scientific observation of **4** : to see or sense esp. through careful attention **5** : to come to realize esp. through consideration of noted facts **6** : REMARK — **ob·serv·er** *n*

ob·sess \əb-'ses\ *vb* : to preoccupy intensely or abnormally

ob·ses·sion \äb-'se-shən\ *n* : a persistent disturbing preoccupation with an idea or feeling; *also* : an emotion or idea causing such a preoccupation — **ob·ses·sive** \-'se-siv\ *adj or n* — **ob·ses·sive·ly** *adv*

obsessive–compulsive *adj* : relating to, characterized by, or affected with recurring obsessions and compulsions esp. as symptoms of a neurotic state

ob·sid·i·an \əb-'si-dē-ən\ *n* : a dark natural glass formed by the cooling of molten lava

ob·so·les·cent \ˌäb-sə-'le-sᵊnt\ *adj* : going out of use : becoming obsolete — **ob·so·les·cence** \-sᵊns\ *n*

ob·so·lete \ˌäb-sə-'lēt, 'äb-sə-ˌlēt\ *adj* : no longer in use; *also* : OLD-FASHIONED ⟨an ∼ technology⟩ ◆ **Synonyms** EXTINCT, OUTWORN, PASSÉ, SUPERSEDED

ob·sta·cle \'äb-sti-kəl\ *n* : something that stands in the way or opposes

ob·stet·rics \əb-'ste-triks\ *n sing or pl* : a branch of medicine that deals with birth and with its antecedents and sequels — **ob·stet·ric** \-trik\ *or* **ob·stet·ri·cal** \-tri-kəl\ *adj* — **ob·ste·tri·cian** \ˌäb-stə-'tri-shən\ *n*

ob·sti·nate \'äb-stə-nət\ *adj* : fixed and unyielding (as in an opinion or course) despite reason or persuasion : STUBBORN — **ob·sti·na·cy** \-nə-sē\ *n* — **ob·sti·nate·ly** *adv*

ob·strep·er·ous \əb-'stre-pə-rəs\ *adj* **1** : uncontrollably noisy **2** : stubbornly resistant to control : UNRULY — **ob·strep·er·ous·ness** *n*

ob·struct \əb-'strəkt\ *vb* **1** : to block by an obstacle **2** : to impede the passage, action, or operation of **3** : to cut off from sight — **ob·struc·tive** \-'strək-tiv\ *adj* — **ob·struc·tor** \-tər\ *n*

ob·struc·tion \əb-'strək-shən\ *n* **1** : an act of obstructing : the state of being obstructed **2** : something that obstructs : HINDRANCE

ob·struc·tion·ist \-shə-nist\ *n* : a person who hinders progress or business esp. in a legislative body — **ob·struc·tion·ism** \-shə-ˌni-zəm\ *n*

ob·tain \əb-'tān\ *vb* **1** : to gain or attain usu. by planning or effort **2** : to be generally recognized or established ◆ **Synonyms** PROCURE, SECURE, WIN, EARN, ACQUIRE — **ob·tain·able** *adj*

ob·trude \əb-'trüd\ *vb* **ob·trud·ed; ob·trud·ing 1** : to thrust out **2** : to thrust forward without warrant or request **3** : INTRUDE — **ob·tru·sion** \-'trü-zhən\ *n* — **ob·tru·sive** \-'trü-siv\ *adj* — **ob·tru·sive·ly** *adv* — **ob·tru·sive·ness** *n*

ob·tuse \äb-'tüs, -'tyüs\ *adj* **ob·tus·er; -est 1** : exceeding 90 degrees but less than 180 degrees ⟨∼ angle⟩ **2** : not pointed or acute : BLUNT **3** : not sharp or quick of wit — **ob·tuse·ly** *adv* — **ob·tuse·ness** *n*

obv *abbr* obverse

¹**ob·verse** \äb-'vərs, 'äb-ˌvərs\ *adj* **1** : facing the observer or opponent **2** : being a counterpart or complement — **ob·verse·ly** *adv*

²**ob·verse** \'äb-ˌvərs, äb-'vərs\ *n* **1** : the side (as of a coin) bearing the principal design and lettering **2** : a front or principal surface **3** : a counterpart having the opposite orientation or force

ob·vi·ate \'äb-vē-ˌāt\ *vb* **-at·ed; -at·ing** : to anticipate and prevent (as a situation) or make unnecessary (as an action) ♦ **Synonyms** PREVENT, AVERT, FORE-STALL, FORFEND, PRECLUDE — **ob·vi·a·tion** \ˌäb-vē-'ā-shən\ n

ob·vi·ous \'äb-vē-əs\ adj [L obvius, fr. obviam in the way, fr. ob in the way of + viam, acc. of via way] : easily found, seen, or understood : PLAIN ♦ **Synonyms** EVI-DENT, MANIFEST, PATENT, CLEAR — **ob·vi·ous·ly** adv — **ob·vi·ous·ness** n

OC abbr officer candidate

oc·a·ri·na \ˌä-kə-'rē-nə\ n [It] : a wind in-strument typically having an oval body with finger holes and a projecting mouth-piece

occas abbr occasionally

¹oc·ca·sion \ə-'kā-zhən\ n 1 : a favorable opportunity 2 : a direct or indirect cause 3 : the time of an event 4 : EXI-GENCY 5 pl : AFFAIRS, BUSINESS 6 : a special event : CELEBRATION

²occasion vb : BRING ABOUT, CAUSE

oc·ca·sion·al \ə-'kāzh-nəl\ adj 1 : hap-pening or met with now and then ⟨~ vis-its⟩ 2 : used or designed for a special occasion ⟨~ verse⟩ ♦ **Synonyms** IN-FREQUENT, RARE, SPORADIC — **oc·ca·sion·al·ly** adv

oc·ci·den·tal \ˌäk-sə-'den-tᵊl\ adj, often cap [fr. Occident West, fr. ME, fr. AF, fr. L occident-, occidens, fr. prp. of occidere to fall, set (of the sun)] : WESTERN — **Oc·ci·den·tal** n

Oc·ci·tan \'äk-sə-ˌtan\ n [F, fr. ML occi-tanus, fr. Old Occitan oc yes (contrasted with OF oïl yes)] : a Romance language spoken in southern France

oc·clude \ə-'klüd\ vb **oc·clud·ed; oc·clud·ing** 1 : OBSTRUCT ⟨an occluded ar-tery⟩ 2 : to come together with opposing surfaces in contact — used of teeth — **oc·clu·sion** \-'klü-zhən\ n — **oc·clu·sive** \-'klü-siv\ adj

¹oc·cult \ə-'kəlt\ adj 1 : not revealed : SE-CRET 2 : ABSTRUSE, MYSTERIOUS 3 : of or relating to supernatural agencies, their effects, or knowledge of them — **oc·cult·ism** \-'kəl-ˌti-zəm\ n — **oc·cult·ist** \-'tist\ n

²occult n : occult matters — used with the

oc·cu·pan·cy \'ä-kyə-pən-sē\ n, pl **-cies** 1 : the act of occupying : the state of being occupied 2 : an occupied building or part of a building

oc·cu·pant \-pənt\ n : one who occupies something; esp : RESIDENT

oc·cu·pa·tion \ˌä-kyə-'pā-shən\ n 1 : an activity in which one engages; esp : VOCA-TION 2 : the taking possession of proper-ty; also : the taking possession of an area by a foreign military force — **oc·cu·pa·tion·al** \-shə nəl\ adj — **oc·cu·pa·tion·al·ly** adv

occupational therapy n : therapy by means of activity; esp : creative activity prescribed for its effect in promoting re-covery or rehabilitation — **occupa-tional therapist** n

oc·cu·py \'ä-kyə-ˌpī\ vb **-pied; -py·ing** 1 : to engage the attention or energies of 2 : to fill up (an extent in space or time) 3

: to take or hold possession of 4 : to re-side in as owner or tenant — **oc·cu·pi·er** n

oc·cur \ə-'kər\ vb **oc·curred; oc·cur·ring** [L occurrere, fr. ob- in the way + cur-rere to run] 1 : to be found or met with : APPEAR 2 : HAPPEN 3 : to come to mind

oc·cur·rence \ə-'kər-əns\ n 1 : some-thing that takes place 2 : the action or process of occurring

ocean \'ō-shən\ n 1 : the whole body of salt water that covers nearly three fourths of the surface of the earth 2 : any of the large bodies of water into which the great ocean is divided — **ocean·ic** \ˌō-shē-'a-nik\ adj

ocean·ar·i·um \ˌō-shə-'nar-ē-əm\ n, pl **-iums** or **-ia** \-ē-ə\ : a large marine aquar-ium

ocean·front \'ō-shən-ˌfrənt\ n : a shore area on the ocean

ocean·go·ing \-ˌgō-iŋ\ adj : of, relating to, or suitable for travel on the ocean

ocean·og·ra·phy \ˌō-shə-'nä-grə-fē\ n : a science dealing with the ocean and its phenomena — **ocean·og·ra·pher** \-fər\ n — **ocean·o·graph·ic** \-nə-'gra-fik\ adj

oce·lot \'ä-sə-ˌlät, 'ō-\ n : a medium-sized American wildcat ranging southward from Texas to northern Argentina and having a tawny yellow or gray coat with black markings

ocher or **ochre** \'ō-kər\ n : an earthy usu. red or yellow iron ore used as a pigment; also : the color esp. of yellow ocher

o'clock \ə-'kläk\ adv : according to the clock

OCR abbr optical character reader; opti-cal character recognition

OCS abbr officer candidate school

oct abbr octavo

Oct abbr October

oc·ta·gon \'äk-tə-ˌgän\ n : a polygon of eight angles and eight sides — **oc·tag·o·nal** \äk-'ta-gə-nᵊl\ adj

oc·tane \'äk-ˌtān\ n : OCTANE NUMBER

octane number n : a number used to measure the antiknock properties of gasoline that increases as the likelihood of knocking decreases

oc·tave \'äk-tiv\ n 1 : a musical interval embracing eight degrees; also : a tone or note at this interval or the whole series of notes, tones, or keys within this interval 2 : a group of eight

oc·ta·vo \äk-'tā-vō, -'tä-\ n, pl **-vos** 1 : the size of a piece of paper cut eight from a sheet 2 : a book printed on octa-vo pages

oc·tet \äk-'tet\ n 1 : a musical composi-tion for eight voices or eight instruments; also : the performers of such a composi-tion 2 : a group or set of eight

Oc·to·ber \äk-'tō-bər\ n [ME Octobre, fr. OE October, fr. L, eighth month of the early Roman calendar, fr. octo eight] : the 10th month of the year

oc·to·ge·nar·i·an \ˌäk-tə-jə-'ner-ē-ən\ n : a person whose age is in the eighties

oc·to·pus \'äk-tə-pəs\ n, pl **-pus·es** or **-pi** \-ˌpī\ : any of various sea mollusks with eight long muscular arms furnished with suckers

oc·to·syl·lab·ic \ˌäk-tə-sə-ˈla-bik\ *adj* : composed òf verses having eight syllables — **octosyllabic** *n*

¹**oc·u·lar** \ˈä-kyə-lər\ *adj* 1 : VISUAL 2 : of or relating to the eye or the eyesight

²**ocular** *n* : EYEPIECE

oc·u·list \ˈä-kyə-ləst\ *n* 1 : OPHTHALMOLOGIST 2 : OPTOMETRIST

¹**OD** \ˌō-ˈdē\ *n* : an overdose of a drug and esp. a narcotic

²**OD** *vb* **OD'd** *or* **ODed; OD'ing; OD's** : to become ill or die from an OD

³**OD** *abbr* 1 doctor of optometry 2 [L *oculus dexter*] right eye 3 officer of the day 4 olive drab 5 overdraft 6 overdrawn

odd \ˈäd\ *adj* [ME *odde*, fr. ON *oddi* point of land, triangle, odd number] 1 : being only one of a pair or set ⟨an ~ shoe⟩ 2 : somewhat more than the number mentioned ⟨forty ~ years ago⟩ 3 : being an integer (as 1, 3, or 5) not divisible by two without leaving a remainder 4 : additional to what is usual ⟨~ jobs⟩ 5 : STRANGE ⟨an ~ way of behaving⟩ — **odd·ness** *n*

odd·ball \ˈäd-ˌbȯl\ *n* : one that is eccentric — **oddball** *adj*

odd·i·ty \ˈä-də-tē\ *n, pl* **-ties** 1 : one that is odd 2 : the quality or state of being odd

odd·ly \ˈäd-lē\ *adv* 1 : in an odd manner 2 : as is odd

odd·ment \ˈäd-mənt\ *n* : something left over : REMNANT

odds \ˈädz\ *n pl* 1 : a difference by which one thing is favored over another 2 : DISAGREEMENT — usu. used with *at* 3 : the ratio between the amount to be paid for a winning bet and the amount of the bet ⟨the horse went off at ~ of 6–1⟩

odds and ends *n pl* : miscellaneous things or matters

odds-on \ˈädz-ˈȯn, -ˈän\ *adj* : having a better than even chance to win

ode \ˈōd\ *n* : a lyric poem that expresses a noble feeling with dignity

odi·ous \ˈō-dē-əs\ *adj* : arousing or deserving hatred or repugnance — **odi·ous·ly** *adv* — **odi·ous·ness** *n*

odi·um \ˈō-dē-əm\ *n* 1 : merited loathing : HATRED 2 : DISGRACE

odom·e·ter \ō-ˈdä-mə-tər\ *n* [F *odomètre*, fr. Gk *hodometron*, fr. *hodos* way, road + *metron* measure] : an instrument for measuring distance traveled (as by a vehicle)

odor \ˈō-dər\ *n* 1 : the quality of something that stimulates the sense of smell; *also* : a sensation resulting from such stimulation 2 : REPUTE, ESTIMATION — **odored** \ˈō-dərd\ *adj* — **odor·less** *adj* — **odor·ous** *adj*

odor·if·er·ous \ˌō-də-ˈri-fə-rəs\ *adj* : having or yielding an odor

odour *chiefly Brit var of* ODOR

od·ys·sey \ˈä-də-sē\ *n, pl* **-seys** [the *Odyssey*, epic poem attributed to Homer recounting the long wanderings of Odysseus] : a long wandering marked usu. by many changes of fortune

oe·cu·men·i·cal \esp *Brit* ˌē-\ *chiefly Brit var of* ECUMENICAL

OED *abbr* Oxford English Dictionary

oe·de·ma *chiefly Brit var of* EDEMA

oe·di·pal \ˈe-də-pəl, ˈē-\ *adj, often cap* : of, relating to, or resulting from the Oedipus complex

Oe·di·pus complex \-pəs-\ *n* : the positive sexual feelings of a child toward the parent of the opposite sex and hostile or jealous feelings toward the parent of the same sex that may be a source of adult personality disorder when unresolved

OEO *abbr* Office of Economic Opportunity

o'er \ˈȯr\ *adv or prep* : OVER

OES *abbr* Order of the Eastern Star

oe·soph·a·gus *chiefly Brit var of* ESOPHAGUS

oeu·vre \ˈœr-vrə, ˈœvrᵊ\ *n, pl* **oeuvres** *same*\ : a substantial body of work constituting the lifework of a writer, an artist, or a composer

of \ˈəv, ˈäv\ *prep* 1 : FROM ⟨a man ~ the West⟩ 2 : having as a significant background or character element ⟨a man ~ noble birth⟩ ⟨a woman ~ ability⟩ 3 : owing to ⟨died ~ flu⟩ 4 : BY ⟨the plays ~ Shakespeare⟩ 5 : having as component parts or material, contents, or members ⟨a house ~ brick⟩ ⟨a glass ~ water⟩ ⟨a pack ~ fools⟩ 6 : belonging to or included by ⟨the front ~ the house⟩ ⟨a time ~ life⟩ ⟨one ~ you⟩ ⟨the best ~ its kind⟩ ⟨the son ~ a doctor⟩ 7 : ABOUT ⟨tales ~ the West⟩ 8 : connected with : OVER ⟨the queen ~ England⟩ 9 : that is : signified as ⟨the city ~ Rome⟩ 10 — used to indicate apposition of the words it joins ⟨that fool ~ a husband⟩ 11 : as concerns : FOR ⟨love ~ nature⟩ 12 — used to indicate the application of an adjective ⟨fond ~ candy⟩ 13 : BEFORE ⟨quarter ~ ten⟩

OF *abbr* outfield

¹**off** \ˈȯf\ *adv* 1 : from a place or position ⟨drove ~ in a new car⟩; *also* : ASIDE ⟨turned ~ into a side road⟩ 2 : at a distance in time or space ⟨stood ~ a few yards⟩ ⟨several years ~⟩ 3 : so as to be unattached or removed ⟨the lid blew ~⟩ 4 : to a state of discontinuance, exhaustion, or completion ⟨shut the radio ~⟩ 5 : away from regular work ⟨took time ~ for lunch⟩

²**off** *prep* 1 : away from ⟨just ~ the highway⟩ ⟨take it ~ the table⟩ 2 : to seaward of ⟨two miles ~ the coast⟩ 3 : FROM ⟨borrowed a dollar ~ me⟩ 4 : at the expense of ⟨lives ~ his parents⟩ 5 : not now engaged in ⟨~ duty⟩ 6 : abstaining from ⟨~ liquor⟩ 7 : below the usual level of ⟨~ his game⟩

³**off** *adj* 1 : more removed or distant 2 : started on the way 3 : not operating 4 : not correct 5 : REMOTE, SLIGHT ⟨an ~ chance⟩ 6 : INFERIOR ⟨~ grade of oil⟩ 7 : provided for ⟨well ~⟩

⁴**off** *abbr* office; officer; official

⁴**of·fal** \ˈȯ-fəl\ *n* [ME, fr. *of* off + *fall* fall] : the waste or by-product of a process; *esp*

: the viscera and trimmings of a butchered animal removed in dressing

off and on *adv* : INTERMITTENTLY ⟨rained *off and on*⟩

¹off·beat \'óf-,bēt\ *n* : the unaccented part of a musical measure

²offbeat *adj* : ECCENTRIC, UNCONVENTIONAL ⟨an ~ style⟩

off–col·or \'óf-'kə-lər\ *or* **off–col·ored** \-lərd\ *adj* **1** : not having the right or standard color **2** : of doubtful propriety : verging on indecency ⟨~ stories⟩

of·fend \ə-'fend\ *vb* **1** : SIN, TRANSGRESS **2** : to cause discomfort or pain : HURT **3** : to cause dislike or vexation : ANNOY ◆ **Synonyms** AFFRONT, INSULT, OUTRAGE — **of·fend·er** *n*

of·fense *or* **of·fence** \ə-'fens, esp for 2 & 3 'ä-,fens\ *n* **1** : something that outrages the senses **2** : ATTACK, ASSAULT **3** : the offensive team or members of a team playing offensive positions **4** : DISPLEASURE **5** : SIN, MISDEED **6** : an infraction of law : CRIME

¹of·fen·sive \ə-'fen-siv esp for 1 & 2 'ä-,fen-\ *adj* **1** : AGGRESSIVE **2** : of or relating to an attempt to score in a game; *also* : of or relating to a team in possession of the ball or puck **3** : OBNOXIOUS ⟨an ~ odor⟩ **4** : INSULTING ⟨~ remarks⟩ — **of·fen·sive·ly** *adv* — **of·fen·sive·ness** *n*

²offensive *n* : ATTACK

¹of·fer \'ó-fər\ *vb* **of·fered; of·fer·ing 1** : SACRIFICE **2** : to present for acceptance : TENDER; *also* : to propose as payment **3** : PROPOSE, SUGGEST; *also* : to declare one's readiness **4** : to try or begin to exert ⟨~ resistance⟩ **5** : to place on sale — **of·fer·ing** *n*

²offer *n* **1** : PROPOSAL **2** : BID **3** : TRY

of·fer·to·ry \'ó-fər-,tór-ē\ *n, pl* **-ries** : the presentation of offerings at a church service; *also* : the musical accompaniment during it

off–gas·sing \'óf-,ga-siŋ\ *n* : the emission of esp. noxious gases (as from a building material)

off·hand \'óf-'hand\ *adv or adj* : without previous thought or preparation

off–hour \-,aú(-ə)r\ *n* : a period of time other than a rush hour; *also* : a period of time other than business hours

of·fice \'ó-fəs\ *n* **1** : a special duty or position; *esp* : a position of authority in government ⟨run for ~⟩ **2** : a prescribed form or service of worship; *also* : RITE **3** : an assigned or assumed duty or role **4** : a place where a business is transacted or a service is supplied

of·fice·hold·er \'ó-fəs-,hōl-dər\ *n* : one holding a public office

of·fi·cer \'ó-fə-sər\ *n* **1** : one charged with the enforcement of law **2** : one who holds an office of trust or authority **3** : a person who holds a position of authority or command in the armed forces; *esp* : COMMISSIONED OFFICER

¹of·fi·cial \ə-'fi-shəl\ *n* : OFFICER 2

²official *adj* **1** : of or relating to an office or to officers **2** : AUTHORIZED, AUTHOR-

ITATIVE ⟨~ statement⟩ **3** : befitting or characteristic of a person in office — **of·fi·cial·ly** *adv*

of·fi·cial·dom \ə-'fi-shəl-dəm\ *n* : officials as a class

of·fi·cial·ism \ə-'fi-shə-,li-zəm\ *n* : lack of flexibility and initiative combined with excessive adherence to regulations

of·fi·ci·ant \ə-'fi-shē-ənt\ *n* : one (as a priest) who officiates at a religious rite

of·fi·ci·ate \ə-'fi-shē-,āt\ *vb* **-at·ed; -at·ing 1** : to perform a ceremony, function, or duty **2** : to act in an official capacity

of·fi·cious \ə-'fi-shəs\ *adj* : volunteering one's services where they are neither asked for nor needed — **of·fi·cious·ly** *adv* — **of·fi·cious·ness** *n*

off·ing \'ó-fiŋ\ *n* : the near or foreseeable future

off–line \'óf-'līn\ *adj or adv* : not connected to or controlled directly by a computer

off of *prep* : OFF

off·print \'óf-,print\ *n* : a separately printed excerpt (as from a magazine)

off–road \-'rōd\ *adj* : of, relating to, or being a vehicle designed for use away from public roads — **off–road·er** \-'rō-dər\ *n*

off–sea·son \-,sē-z³n\ *n* : a time of suspended or reduced activity

¹off·set \-,set\ *n* **1** : a sharp bend (as in a pipe) by which one part is turned aside out of line **2** : a printing process in which an inked impression is first made on a rubber-blanketed cylinder and then transferred to the paper

²off·set *vb* **off·set; off·set·ting 1** : to place over against : BALANCE **2** : to compensate for **3** : to form an offset in ⟨~ a wall⟩

off·shoot \'óf-,shüt\ *n* **1** : a collateral or derived branch, descendant, or member **2** : a branch of a main stem (as of a plant)

¹off·shore \'óf-'shór\ *adv* **1** : at a distance from the shore **2** : outside the country : ABROAD

²off·shore \'óf-,shór\ *adj* **1** : moving away from the shore **2** : situated off the shore but within waters under a country's control

off·side \-'sīd\ *adv or adj* : illegally in advance of the ball or puck

off·spring \-,spriŋ\ *n, pl* **offspring** *also* **offsprings** : PROGENY, YOUNG

off·stage \'óf-'stāj, -,stāj\ *adv or adj* **1** : off or away from the stage **2** : out of the public view ⟨deals made ~⟩

off–the–record *adj* : given or made in confidence and not for publication

off–the–shelf *adj* : available as a stock item : not specially designed or made

off–the–wall *adj* : highly unusual : BIZARRE

off·track \'óf-'trak\ *adv or adj* : away from a racetrack

off–white \'óf-'hwīt\ *n* : a yellowish or grayish white color

off year *n* **1** : a year in which no major election is held **2** : a year of diminished activity or production

oft \ˈȯft\ *adv* : OFTEN

of·ten \ˈȯ-fən\ *adv* : many times : FREQUENTLY

of·ten·times \-ˌtīmz\ *or* **oft·times** \ˈȯf-ˌtīmz, ˈȯft-\ *adv* : OFTEN

ogle \ˈō-gəl\ *vb* **ogled; ogling** : to look at in a flirtatious way — **ogle** *n* — **ogler** *n*

ogre \ˈō-gər\ *n* **1** : a monster of fairy tales and folklore that eats people **2** : a dreaded person or object

ogress \ˈō-grəs\ *n* : a female ogre

oh *also* **O** \ˈō\ *interj* **1** — used to express an emotion or in response to physical stimuli **2** — used in direct address

OH *abbr* Ohio

ohm \ˈōm\ *n* : a unit of electrical resistance equal to the resistance of a circuit in which a potential difference of one volt produces a current of one ampere — **ohm·ic** \ˈō-mik\ *adj*

ohm·me·ter \ˈōm-ˌmē-tər\ *n* : an instrument for indicating resistance in ohms directly

¹oil \ˈȯi(-ə)l\ *n* [ME *oile,* fr. AF, fr. L *oleum* olive oil, fr. Gk *elaion,* fr. *elaia* olive] **1** : any of numerous fatty or greasy liquid substances obtained from plants, animals, or minerals and used for fuel, food, medicines, and manufacturing **2** : PETROLEUM **3** : artists' colors made with oil; *also* : a painting in such colors — **oil·i·ness** \ˈȯi-lē-nəs\ *n* — **oily** \ˈȯi-lē\ *adj*

²oil *vb* : to put oil in or on — **oil·er** *n*

oil·cloth \ˈȯi(-ə)l-ˌklȯth\ *n* : cloth treated with oil or paint and used for table and shelf coverings

oil pan *n* : the lower section of a crankcase used as an oil reservoir

oil shale *n* : a rock (as shale) from which oil can be recovered

oil·skin \ˈȯi(-ə)l-ˌskin\ *n* **1** : an oiled waterproof cloth **2** : an oilskin raincoat **3** *pl* : an oilskin coat and pants

oink \ˈȯiŋk\ *n* : the natural noise of a hog — **oink** *vb*

oint·ment \ˈȯint-mənt\ *n* : a salve for use on the skin

OJ *abbr* orange juice

Ojib·wa *or* **Ojib·way** *or* **Ojibwe** \ō-ˈjib-ˌwä\ *n, pl* **Ojibwa** *or* **Ojibwas** *or* **Ojibway** *or* **Ojibways** *or* **Ojibwe** *or* **Ojibwes 1** : a member of an American Indian people of the region around Lake Superior and westward **2** : the Algonquian language of the Ojibwa people

OJT *abbr* on-the-job training

¹OK *or* **okay** \ō-ˈkā\ *adv or adj* : all right

²OK *or* **okay** *vb* **OK'd** *or* **okayed; OK'·ing** *or* **okay·ing** : APPROVE, AUTHORIZE — **OK** *or* **okay** *n*

³OK *abbr* Oklahoma

Okla *abbr* Oklahoma

okra \ˈō-krə\ *n* : a tall annual plant related to the mallows that has edible green pods; *also* : these pods

¹old \ˈōld\ *adj* **1** : ANCIENT; *also* : of long standing **2** *cap* : belonging to an early period ⟨*Old* Irish⟩ **3** : having existed for a specified period of time **4** : of or relating to a past era **5** : advanced in years **6** : showing the effects of age or use **7** : no longer in use — **old·ish** \ˈōl-dish\ *adj*

²old *n* : old or earlier time ⟨days of ∼⟩

old·en \ˈōl-dən\ *adj* : of or relating to a bygone era

¹old–fash·ioned \ˈōld-ˈfa-shənd\ *adj* **1** : OUT-OF-DATE, ANTIQUATED **2** : CONSERVATIVE

²old–fashioned *n* : a cocktail usu. made with whiskey, bitters, sugar, a twist of lemon peel, and water for soda water

old–growth \ˈōld-ˈgrōth\ *adj* : of, relating to, or being a forest with large old trees, numerous snags and woody debris, and a multilayered canopy

old guard *n, often cap O&G* : the conservative members of an organization

old hat *adj* **1** : OLD-FASHIONED **2** : STALE, TRITE

old·ie \ˈōl-dē\ *n* : something old; *esp* : a popular song from the past

old–line \ˈōld-ˈlīn\ *adj* **1** : ORIGINAL, ESTABLISHED ⟨an ∼ business⟩ **2** : adhering to old policies or practices

old maid *n* **1** : SPINSTER **2** : a prim fussy person — **old–maid·ish** \ˈōld-ˈmā-dish\ *adj*

old man *n* **1** : HUSBAND **2** : FATHER

old–school *adj* : adhering to traditional policies or practices

old·ster \ˈōld-stər\ *n* : an old or elderly person

Old Testament *n* : the first of the two chief divisions of the Christian Bible — see BIBLE table

old–time \ˈōld-ˈtīm\ *adj* **1** : of, relating to, or characteristic of an earlier period **2** : of long standing

old–tim·er \-ˈtī-mər\ *n* : VETERAN; *also* : OLDSTER

old–world \-ˈwərld\ *adj* : having old-fashioned charm

ole·ag·i·nous \ˌō-lē-ˈa-jə-nəs\ *adj* : OILY

ole·an·der \ˈō-lē-ˌan-dər\ *n* : a poisonous evergreen shrub often grown for its fragrant white to red flowers

oleo \ˈō-lē-ˌō\ *n, pl* **ole·os** : MARGARINE

oleo·mar·ga·rine \ˌō-lē-ō-ˈmär-jə-rən\ *n* : MARGARINE

ol·fac·to·ry \äl-ˈfak-tə-rē, ōl-\ *adj* : of or relating to the sense of smell

oli·gar·chy \ˈä-lə-ˌgär-kē, ˈō-\ *n, pl* **-chies 1** : a government in which power is in the hands of a few **2** : a state having an oligarchy; *also* : the group holding power in such a state — **oli·garch** \-ˌgärk\ *n* — **oli·gar·chic** \ˌä-lə-ˈgär-kik, ˌō-\ *or* **oli·gar·chi·cal** \-ki-kəl\ *adj*

Oli·go·cene \ˈä-li-gō-ˌsēn, ə-ˈli-gə-ˌsēn\ *adj* : of, relating to, or being the epoch of the Tertiary between the Eocene and the Miocene — **Oligocene** *n*

olio \ˈō-lē-ˌō\ *n, pl* **oli·os** : HODGEPODGE, MEDLEY

ol·ive \ˈä-liv\ *n* **1** : an Old World evergreen tree grown in warm regions for its fruit that is a food and the source of an edible oil (**olive oil**) **2** : a dull yellowish green color

olive drab *n* **1** : a grayish olive color **2** : an olive drab wool or cotton fabric; *also* : a uniform of this fabric

ol·iv·ine \'ä-lə-ˌvēn\ *n* : a usu. greenish mineral that is a complex silicate of magnesium and iron

Olym·pic Games \ō-'lim-pik-\ *n pl* : a modified revival of an ancient Greek festival consisting of international athletic contests that are held at separate winter and summer gatherings at four-year intervals

om \'ōm\ *n* : a mantra consisting of the sound "om" used in contemplating ultimate reality

Oma·ha \'ō-mə-ˌhä, -ˌhȯ\ *n, pl* **Omaha** or **Omahas** : a member of an American Indian people of northeastern Nebraska

om·buds·man \'äm-ˌbu̇dz-mən, äm-'bu̇dz-\ *n, pl* **-men** \-mən\ **1** : a government official appointed to investigate complaints made by individuals against abuses or capricious acts of public officials **2** : one that investigates reported complaints (as from students or consumers)

ome·ga \ō-'mā-gə\ *n* : the 24th and last letter of the Greek alphabet — Ω or ω

om·elet or **om·elette** \'äm-lət, 'ä-mə-\ *n* [F *omelette*, alter. of MF *amelette*, *alemette*, alter. of *alemelle* thin plate, ultim. fr. L *lamella*, dim. of *lamina*] : eggs beaten with milk or water, cooked without stirring until set, and folded over

omen \'ō-mən\ *n* : an event or phenomenon believed to be a sign or warning of a future occurrence

om·i·cron \'ä-mə-ˌkrän, 'ō-\ *n* : the 15th letter of the Greek alphabet — O or ο

om·i·nous \'ä-mə-nəs\ *adj* : foretelling evil : THREATENING — **om·i·nous·ly** *adv* — **om·i·nous·ness** *n*

omis·si·ble \ō-'mi-sə-bəl\ *adj* : that may be omitted

omis·sion \ō-'mi-shən\ *n* **1** : something neglected or left undone **2** : the act of omitting : the state of being omitted

omit \ō-'mit\ *vb* **omit·ted; omit·ting** **1** : to leave out or leave unmentioned **2** : to leave undone : FAIL

¹om·ni·bus \'äm-ni-(ˌ)bəs\ *n* : BUS

²omnibus *adj* : of, relating to, or providing for many things at once ⟨an ~ bill⟩

om·nip·o·tent \äm-'ni-pə-tənt\ *adj* **1** *often cap* : ALMIGHTY 1 **2** : having unlimited authority or influence — **om·nip·o·tence** \-əns\ *n* — **om·nip·o·tent·ly** *adv*

om·ni·pres·ent \ˌäm-ni-'pre-zᵊnt\ *adj* : present in all places at all times — **om·ni·pres·ence** \-zᵊns\ *n*

om·ni·scient \äm-'ni-shənt\ *adj* : having infinite awareness, understanding, and insight — **om·ni·science** \-shəns\ *n* — **om·ni·scient·ly** *adv*

om·ni·um-gath·er·um \ˌäm-nē-əm-'ga-thə-rəm\ *n, pl* **omnium-gatherums** : a miscellaneous collection

om·niv·o·rous \äm-'ni-və-rəs\ *adj* **1** : feeding on both animal and vegetable substances **2** : AVID ⟨an ~ reader⟩ — **om·ni·vore** \'äm-ni-ˌvȯr\ *n* — **om·niv·o·rous·ly** *adv*

¹on \'ȯn, 'än\ *prep* **1** : in or to a position over and in contact with ⟨jumped ~ his horse⟩ **2** : touching the surface of ⟨shadows ~ the wall⟩ **3** : AT, TO ⟨~ the right were the mountains⟩ **4** : IN, ABOARD ⟨went ~ the train⟩ **5** : during or at the time of ⟨came ~ Monday⟩ ⟨every hour ~ the hour⟩ **6** : through the agency of ⟨was cut ~ a tin can⟩ **7** : in a state or process of ⟨~ fire⟩ ⟨~ the wane⟩ **8** : connected with as a member or participant ⟨~ a committee⟩ ⟨~ tour⟩ **9** — used to indicate a basis, source, or standard of computation ⟨has it ~ good authority⟩ ⟨10 cents ~ the dollar⟩ **10** : with regard to ⟨a monopoly ~ wheat⟩ **11** : at or toward as an object ⟨crept up ~ her⟩ **12** : ABOUT, CONCERNING ⟨a book ~ minerals⟩

²on *adv* **1** : in or into a position of contact with or attachment to a surface **2** : FORWARD **3** : into operation

³on *adj* : being in operation or in progress

ON *abbr* Ontario

¹once \'wəns\ *adv* [ME *ones*, fr. genitive of *on* one] **1** : one time only **2** : at any one time ⟨didn't ~ thank me⟩ **3** : FORMERLY ⟨was ~ young⟩ **4** : by one degree of relationship ⟨first cousin ~ removed⟩

²once *n* : one single time — **at once 1** : at the same time **2** : IMMEDIATELY

³once *adj* : FORMER ⟨a ~ successful actor⟩

⁴once *conj* : AS SOON AS ⟨~ we're finished, we can leave⟩

once–over \'wəns-ˌō-vər\ *n* : a swift examination or survey

on·co·gene \'äŋ-kō-ˌjēn\ *n* : a gene having the potential to cause a normal cell to become cancerous

on·col·o·gy \än-'kä-lə-jē\ *n* : the study of tumors — **on·co·log·i·cal** \ˌäŋ-kə-'lä-ji-kəl\ *also* **on·co·log·ic** \-jik\ *adj* — **on·col·o·gist** \än-'kä-lə-jist\ *n*

on·com·ing \'ȯn-ˌkə-miŋ, 'än-\ *adj* : APPROACHING ⟨~ traffic⟩

¹one \'wən\ *adj* **1** : being a single unit or thing ⟨~ person went⟩ **2** : being one in particular ⟨early ~ morning⟩ **3** : being the same in kind or quality ⟨members of ~ race⟩; *also* : UNITED **4** : being not specified or fixed ⟨~ day soon⟩

²one *n* **1** : the number denoting unity **2** : the 1st in a set or series **3** : a single person or thing — **one·ness** \'wən-nəs\ *n*

³one *pron* **1** : a certain indefinitely indicated person or thing ⟨saw ~ of his friends⟩ **2** : a person in general ⟨~ never knows⟩ **3** — used in place of a first-person pronoun

Onei·da \ō-'nī-də\ *n, pl* **Oneida** or **Onei·das** : a member of an American Indian people orig. of New York

one–man band *n* **1** : a musician who plays several instruments during a solo performance **2** : a person who alone undertakes or is responsible for several tasks

oner·ous \'ä-nə-rəs, 'ō-\ *adj* : imposing or constituting a burden : TROUBLESOME ✦ **Synonyms** OPPRESSIVE, EXACTING, BURDENSOME, WEIGHTY

one·self \(ˌ)wən-'self\ *also* **one's self**

pron : one's own self — usu. used reflexively or for emphasis

one–sid·ed \'wən-'sī-dəd\ *adj* 1 : having or occurring on one side only; *also* : having one side prominent or more developed 2 : PARTIAL ⟨a ~ interpretation⟩

one–time \-,tīm\ *adj* : FORMER ⟨a ~ actor⟩

one–to–one \,wən-tə-'wən\ *adj* : pairing each element of a set uniquely with an element of another set

one up *adj* : being in a position of advantage ⟨was *one up* on the others⟩

one–way *adj* : moving, allowing movement, or functioning in only one direction ⟨~ streets⟩

on·go·ing \'on-,gō-in, 'än-\ *adj* : continuously moving forward

on·ion \'ən-yən\ *n* : the pungent edible bulb of a widely cultivated plant related to the lilies; *also* : this plant

on·ion·skin \-,skin\ *n* : a thin strong translucent paper of very light weight

on-line \'ȯn-'līn, 'än-\ *adj or adv* : connected to, served by, or available through a computer network (as the Internet); *also* done while online ⟨~shopping⟩ — **online** *adv*

on·look·er \'ȯn-,lu̇-kər, 'än-\ *n* : SPECTATOR

¹**on·ly** \'ōn-lē\ *adj* 1 : unquestionably the best 2 : SOLE ⟨the ~ one left⟩

²**only** *adv* 1 : MERELY, JUST ⟨~ $2⟩ 2 : SOLELY ⟨known ~ to me⟩ 3 : at the very least ⟨was ~ too true⟩ 4 : as a final result ⟨will ~ make you sick⟩

³**only** *conj* : except that

on·o·mato·poe·ia \,ä-nə-,mä-tə-'pē-ə\ *n* [LL, fr. Gk *onomatopoiia*, fr. *onoma* name + *poiein* to make] 1 : formation of words in imitation of natural sounds (as *buzz* or *hiss*) 2 : the use of words whose sound suggests the sense — **on·o·mato·poe·ic** \-'pē-ik\ *or* **on·o·mato·po·et·ic** \-pō-'e-tik\ *adj* — **on·o·mato·poe·i·cal·ly** \-'pē-ə-k(ə-)lē\ *or* **on·o·mato·po·et·i·cal·ly** \-pō-'e-ti-k(ə-)lē\ *adv*

On·on·da·ga \,ä-nən-'dȯ-gə, -'dä-, -'dä-\ *n, pl* **-ga** *or* **-gas** : a member of an American Indian people of New York and Canada

on·rush \'ȯn-,rəsh, 'än-\ *n* : a rushing onward — **on·rush·ing** *adj*

on–screen \'ȯn-'skrēn, 'än-\ *adv or adj* : on a computer or television screen

on·set \-,set\ *n* 1 : ATTACK 2 : BEGINNING ⟨the ~ of winter⟩

on·shore \-,shȯr\ *adj* 1 : moving toward the shore 2 : situated on or near the shore — **on·shore** \-'shȯr\ *adv*

on·slaught \'ȯn-,slȯt, 'än-\ *n* : a fierce attack; *also* : something resembling such an attack ⟨an ~ of questions⟩

Ont *abbr* Ontario

on·to \'ȯn-tü, 'än-\ *prep* : to a position or point on

onus \'ō-nəs\ *n* 1 : BURDEN 2 : OBLIGATION 3 : BLAME

¹**on·ward** \'ȯn-wərd, 'än-\ *also* **on·wards** \-wərdz\ *adv* : FORWARD ⟨kept moving ~⟩

²**onward** *adj* : directed or moving onward : FORWARD

on·yx \'ä-niks\ *n* [ME *oniche, onyx*, fr. AF & L; AF, fr. L *onyx*, fr. Gk, lit., claw, nail] : a translucent chalcedony in parallel layers of different colors

oo·dles \'ü-d³lz\ *n pl* : a great quantity

oo·lite \'ō-ə-,līt\ *n* : a rock consisting of small round grains cemented together — **oo·lit·ic** \,ō-ə-'li-tik\ *adj*

¹**ooze** \'üz\ *n* [ME *wose*, fr. OE *wāse* mire] 1 : a soft deposit (as of mud) on the bottom of a body of water 2 : soft wet ground : MUD — **oozy** \'ü-zē\ *adj*

²**ooze** *vb* **oozed; ooz·ing** 1 : to flow or leak out slowly or imperceptibly 2 : EXUDE ⟨~ confidence⟩

³**ooze** *n* : something that oozes

op *abbr* 1 operation; operative; operator 2 opportunity 3 opus

OP *abbr* 1 observation post 2 out of print

opac·i·ty \ō-'pa-sə-tē\ *n, pl* **-ties** 1 : obscurity of meaning 2 : mental dullness 3 : the quality or state of being opaque 4 : an opaque spot in a normally transparent structure

opal \'ō-pəl\ *n* : a mineral with iridescent colors that is used as a gem

opal·es·cent \,ō-pə-'le-s³nt\ *adj* : IRIDESCENT — **opal·es·cence** \-s³ns\ *n*

opaque \ō-'pāk\ *adj* 1 : blocking the passage of radiant energy and esp. light 2 : not easily understood; *also* : OBTUSE — **opaque·ly** *adv* — **opaque·ness** *n*

op art \'äp-\ *n* : OPTICAL ART — **op artist** *n*

op cit *abbr* [L *opere citato*] in the work cited

ope \'ōp\ *vb*, **oped; op·ing** *archaic* : OPEN

OPEC *abbr* Organization of Petroleum Exporting Countries

op–ed \'äp-'ed\ *n, often cap O&E* : a page of special features usu. opposite the editorial page of a newspaper

¹**open** \'ō-pən\ *adj* **open·er; open·est** 1 : not shut or shut up ⟨an ~ door⟩ 2 : not secret or hidden; *also* : FRANK 3 : not enclosed or covered ⟨an ~ fire⟩; *also* : not protected 4 : free to be entered or used ⟨an ~ tournament⟩ 5 : easy to get through or see ⟨~ country⟩ 6 : spread out : EXTENDED 7 : not decided ⟨an ~ question⟩ 8 : readily accessible and cooperative; *also* : GENEROUS 9 : having openings, interruptions, or spaces ⟨an ~ mesh⟩; *also* : having components separated by a space in writing and printing ⟨the name *Spanish moss* is an ~ compound⟩ 10 : ready to operate ⟨stores are ~⟩ 11 : free from restraints or controls ⟨~ season⟩ — **open·ly** *adv* — **open·ness** *n*

²**open** \'ō-pən\ *vb* **opened; open·ing** 1 : to change or move from a shut position; *also* : to make open by clearing away obstacles 2 : to make accessible 3 : to make openings in 4 : to make or become functional ⟨~ a store⟩ 5 : REVEAL; *also*

: ENLIGHTEN **6** : BEGIN ⟨~ talks⟩ — **open·er** n

³**open** n **1** : OUTDOORS **2** : a contest or tournament open to all

open–air adj : OUTDOOR ⟨~ theaters⟩

open arms n pl : an eager or warm welcome

open–faced \-'fāst\ also **open–face** \-'fās\ adj : served without a covering layer of bread ⟨an ~ sandwich⟩

open–hand·ed \₁ō-pən-'han-dəd\ adj : GENEROUS — **open·hand·ed·ly** adv

open–heart adj : of, relating to, or performed on a heart temporarily relieved of circulatory function and laid open for repair of defects or damage

open–hearth adj : of, relating to, or being a process of making steel in a furnace that reflects the heat from the roof onto the material

opening n **1** : an act or instance of making or becoming open **2** : BEGINNING **3** : something that is open **4** : OCCASION; also : an opportunity for employment

open mike n : an event in which amateurs may perform

open–mind·ed \₁ō-pən-'mīn-dəd\ adj : free from rigidly fixed preconceptions — **open–mind·ed·ness** n

open sentence n : a statement (as in mathematics) containing at least one blank or unknown so that when the blank is filled or a quantity substituted for the unknown the statement becomes a complete statement that is either true or false

open shop n : an establishment having members and nonmembers of a labor union on the payroll

open·work \'ō-pən-₁wərk\ n : work so made as to show openings through its substance ⟨a railing of wrought-iron ~⟩ — **open–worked** \-₁wərkt\ adj

¹**opera** pl of OPUS

²**op·era** \'ä-prə, -pə-rə\ n : a drama set to music — **op·er·at·ic** \₁ä-pə-'ra-tik\ adj

op·er·a·ble \'ä-pə-rə-bəl\ adj **1** : fit, possible, or desirable to use **2** : likely to result in a favorable outcome upon surgical treatment

opera glasses n pl : small binoculars for use in a theater

op·er·ate \'ä-pə-₁rāt\ vb **-at·ed; -at·ing** **1** : to perform work : FUNCTION **2** : to produce an effect **3** : to put or keep in operation **4** : to perform or subject to an operation — **op·er·a·tor** \-₁rā-tər\ n

operating system n : software that controls the operation of a computer

op·er·a·tion \₁ä-pə-'rā-shən\ n **1** : a doing or performing of a practical work **2** : an exertion of power or influence; also : method or manner of functioning **3** : a surgical procedure **4** : a process of deriving one mathematical expression from others according to a rule **5** : a military action or mission **6** : a usu. small business — **op·er·a·tion·al** \-shə-nəl\ adj

¹**op·er·a·tive** \'ä-pə-rə-tiv, -₁rā-\ adj **1** : producing an appropriate effect; also : most significant or essential **2** : OPERATING ⟨an ~ force⟩ **3** : having to do with physical operations; also : WORKING

⟨an ~ craftsman⟩ **4** : based on or consisting of an operation ⟨~ dentistry⟩

²**operative** n **1** : OPERATOR; esp : a secret agent **2** : a person who works toward achieving the objectives of a larger interest

op·er·et·ta \₁ä-pə-'re-tə\ n [It, dim. of opera opera] : a light musical-dramatic work with a romantic plot, spoken dialogue, and dancing scenes

oph·thal·mic \äf-'thal-mik, äp-\ adj [Gk ophthalmikos, fr. ophthalmos eye] : of, relating to, or located near the eye

oph·thal·mol·o·gy \₁äf-₁thal-'mä-lə-jē, ₁äp-\ n : a branch of medicine dealing with the structure, functions, and diseases of the eye — **oph·thal·mol·o·gist** \-jist\ n

oph·thal·mo·scope \äf-'thal-mə-₁skōp, äp-\ n : an instrument for use in viewing the interior of the eye and esp. the retina

opi·ate \'ō-pē-ət, -pē-₁āt\ n : a preparation or derivative of opium; also : a narcotic or a substance with similar activity — **opiate** adj

opine \ō-'pīn\ vb **opined; opin·ing** : to express an opinion : STATE

opin·ion \ə-'pin-yən\ n **1** : JUDGMENT **2** : a belief stronger than impression and less strong than positive knowledge **3** : a formal statement by an expert after careful study

opin·ion·at·ed \ə-'pin-yə-₁nā-təd\ adj : obstinately adhering to personal opinions

opi·um \'ō-pē-əm\ n [ME, fr. L, fr. Gk opion, fr. dim. of opos sap] : an addictive narcotic drug that is the dried latex of a Eurasian poppy

opos·sum \ə-'pä-səm\ n, pl **opossums** also **opossum** : an omnivorous tree-dwelling No. American marsupial that is active chiefly at night and has a pointed snout and a prehensile tail

opp abbr opposite

op·po·nent \ə-'pō-nənt\ n : one that opposes : ADVERSARY

op·por·tune \₁ä-pər-'tün, -'tyün\ adj [ME, fr. MF opportun, fr. L opportunus, fr. ob- toward + portus port, harbor] : SUITABLE ⟨an ~ moment⟩ — **op·por·tune·ly** adv

op·por·tun·ism \₁ä-pər-'tü-₁ni-zəm, -'tyü-\ n : a taking advantage of opportunities or circumstances esp. with little regard for principles or ultimate consequences — **op·por·tun·ist** \-nist\ n — **op·por·tu·nis·tic** \-tü-'nis-tik, -tyü-\ adj

op·por·tu·ni·ty \₁ä-pər-'tü-nə-tē, -'tyü-\ n, pl **-ties** **1** : a favorable combination of circumstances, time, and place **2** : a chance for advancement

op·pose \ə-'pōz\ vb **op·posed; op·pos·ing** **1** : to place opposite or against something (as to provide resistance or contrast) **2** : to strive against : RESIST — **op·po·si·tion** \₁ä-pə-'zi-shən\ n

¹**op·po·site** \'ä-pə-zət\ adj **1** : set over against something that is at the other end or side **2** : OPPOSED, HOSTILE; also : CONTRARY **3** : contrarily turned or moving **4** : being the other of a matching

or contrasting pair ⟨the ~ sex⟩ — **op·po·site·ly** *adv* — **op·po·site·ness** *n*

²opposite *n* : one that is opposed or contrary

³opposite *adv* : on or to an opposite side

⁴opposite *prep* : across from and usu. facing ⟨the house ~ ours⟩

op·press \ə-'pres\ *vb* **1** : to crush by abuse of power or authority **2** : to weigh down • BURDEN ✦ *Synonyms* AGGRIEVE, WRONG, PERSECUTE — **op·pres·sive** \-'pre-siv\ *adj* — **op·pres·sive·ly** *adv* — **op·pres·sor** \-'pre-sər\ *n*

op·pres·sion \ə-'pre-shən\ *n* **1** : unjust or cruel exercise of power or authority **2** : DEPRESSION

op·pro·bri·ous \ə-'prō-brē-əs\ *adj* : expressing or deserving opprobrium — **op·pro·bri·ous·ly** *adv*

op·pro·bri·um \-brē-əm\ *n* **1** : something that brings disgrace **2** : public disgrace or ill fame

¹opt \'äpt\ *vb* : to make a choice; *esp* : to decide in favor of something

²opt *abbr* **1** optical; optician; optics **2** option; optional

op·tic \'äp-tik\ *adj* : of or relating to vision or the eye

op·ti·cal \'äp-ti-kəl\ *adj* **1** : relating to optics **2** : OPTIC **3** : of, relating to, or using light

optical art *n* : nonobjective art characterized by the use of geometric patterns often for an illusory effect

optical disk *n* : a disk on which information has been recorded digitally and which is read using a laser

optical fiber *n* : a single fiber-optic strand

op·ti·cian \äp-'ti-shən\ *n* **1** : a maker of or dealer in optical items and instruments **2** : a person who makes or orders eyeglasses and contact lenses to prescription and sells them

op·tics \'äp-tiks\ *n* : a science that deals with the nature and properties of light

op·ti·mal \'äp-tə-məl\ *adj* : most desirable or satisfactory — **op·ti·mal·ly** *adv*

op·ti·mism \'äp-tə-ˌmi-zəm\ *n* [F *optimisme*, fr. L *optimum*, n., best, fr. neut. of *optimus* best] **1** : a doctrine that this world is the best possible world **2** : an inclination to anticipate the best possible outcome of actions or events — **op·ti·mist** \-mist\ *n* — **op·ti·mis·tic** \ˌäp-tə-mis-tik\ *adj* — **op·ti·mis·ti·cal·ly** \-ti-k(ə-)lē\ *adv*

op·ti·mize \'äp-tə-ˌmīz\ *vb* **-mized; -miz·ing** : to make as perfect, effective, or functional as possible — **op·ti·mi·za·tion** \ˌäp-tə-mə-'zā-shən\ *n*

op·ti·mum \'äp-tə-məm\ *n, pl* **-ma** \-mə\ *also* **-mums** [L] : the amount or degree of something most favorable to an end; *also* : greatest degree attained under implied or specified conditions

op·tion \'äp-shən\ *n* **1** : the power or right to choose **2** : a right to buy or sell something at a specified price during a specified period **3** : something offered for choice — **op·tion·al** \-shə-nəl\ *adj*

op·tom·e·try \äp-'tä-mə-trē\ *n* : the health-care profession concerned esp.

with examining the eyes for defects of vision and with prescribing corrective lenses or eye exercises — **op·to·met·ric** \ˌäp-tə-'me-trik\ *adj* — **op·tom·e·trist** \äp-'tä-mə-trist\ *n*

opt out *vb* : to choose not to participate

op·u·lence \'ä-pyə-ləns\ *n* **1** : WEALTH **2** : ABUNDANCE

op·u·lent \'ä-pyə-lənt\ *adj* **1** : WEALTHY **2** : richly abundant — **op·u·lent·ly** *adv*

opus \'ō-pəs\ *n, pl* **opera** \'ō-pə-rə, 'ä-\ *also* **opus·es** \'ō-pə-səz\ : WORK; *esp* : a musical composition

or \'ȯr\ *conj* — used as a function word to indicate an alternative ⟨sink ~ swim⟩

OR *abbr* **1** operating room **2** Oregon

-or *n suffix* : one that does a (specified) thing ⟨calculator⟩

or·a·cle \'ȯr-ə-kəl\ *n* **1** : one held to give divinely inspired answers or revelations **2** : an authoritative or wise utterance; *also* : a person of great authority or wisdom — **orac·u·lar** \ȯ-'ra-kyə-lər\ *adj*

¹oral \'ȯr-əl\ *adj* **1** : SPOKEN ⟨an ~ report⟩ **2** : of, given through, or involving the mouth ⟨an ~ vaccine⟩ **3** : of, relating to, or characterized by the first stage of psychosexual development in psychoanalytic theory in which libidinal gratification is derived from intake (as of food), by sucking, and later by biting **4** : relating to or characterized by personality traits of passive dependency and aggressiveness — **oral·ly** *adv*

²oral *n* : an oral examination — usu. used in pl.

oral sex *n* : oral stimulation of the genitals : CUNNILINGUS, FELLATIO

orang \ə-'raŋ\ *n* : ORANGUTAN

or·ange \'är-inj, 'ȯr-\ *n* **1** : a juicy citrus fruit with reddish yellow rind; *also* : an evergreen tree with fragrant white flowers that bears this fruit **2** : a color between red and yellow — **or·ange·y** *or* **or·angy** \'är-in-jē, 'ȯr-\ *adj*

or·ange·ade \ˌär-in-'jād, ˌȯr-\ *n* : a beverage of orange juice, sugar, and water

orange hawkweed *n* : a weedy herb related to the daisies with bright orange-red flower heads

or·ange·ry \'är-inj-rē, 'ȯr-\ *n, pl* **-ries** : a protected place (as a greenhouse) for raising oranges in cool climates

orang·utan \ə-'raŋ-ə-ˌtaŋ, -ˌtan\ *n* [Bazaar Malay (Malay-based pidgin), fr. Malay *orang* man + *hutan* forest] : a large reddish brown tree-living anthropoid ape of Borneo and Sumatra

orate \ȯ-'rāt\ *vb* **orat·ed; orat·ing** : to speak in a declamatory manner

ora·tion \ə-'rā-shən\ *n* : an elaborate discourse delivered in a formal and dignified manner

or·a·tor \'ȯr-ə-tər\ *n* : one noted for skill and power as a public speaker

or·a·tor·i·cal \ˌȯr-ə-'tȯr-i-kəl\ *adj* : of, relating to, or characteristic of an orator or oratory — **or·a·tor·i·cal·ly** \-'tȯr-i-k(ə-)lē\ *adv*

or·a·to·rio \ˌȯr-ə-'tȯr-ē-ˌō\ *n, pl* **-rios** : a lengthy choral work usu. on a scriptural subject

¹**or·a·to·ry** \'ȯr-ə-ˌtȯr-ē\ *n, pl* **-ries** : a private or institutional chapel

²**oratory** *n* : the art of speaking eloquently and effectively in public ✦ *Synonyms* RHETORIC, ELOCUTION

orb \'ȯrb\ *n* : a spherical body; *also* : EYE

¹**or·bit** \'ȯr-bət\ *n* [L *orbita*, lit., path, rut] **1** : a path described by one body in its revolution about another **2** : range or sphere of activity — **or·bit·al** \-bə-t³l\ *adj*

²**orbit** *vb* **1** : CIRCLE **2** : to send up and make revolve in an orbit ⟨∼ a satellite⟩ — **or·bit·er** *n*

or·ca \'ȯr-kə\ *n* : KILLER WHALE

orch *abbr* orchestra

or·chard \'ȯr-chərd\ *n* [ME, fr. OE *ortgeard*, fr. *ort-* (fr. L *hortus* garden) + *geard* yard] : a place where fruit trees, sugar maples, or nut trees are grown; *also* : the trees of such a place — **or·chard·ist** \-chər-dist\ *n*

or·ches·tra \'ȯr-kə-strə\ *n* **1** : the front section of seats on the main floor of a theater **2** : a group of instrumentalists organized to perform ensemble music — **or·ches·tral** \ȯr-'kes-trəl\ *adj* — **or·ches·tral·ly** *adv*

or·ches·trate \'ȯr-kə-ˌstrāt\ *vb* **-trat·ed;** **-trat·ing** **1** : to compose or arrange for an orchestra **2** : to arrange so as to achieve a desired effect — **or·ches·tra·tion** \ˌȯr-kə-'strā-shən\ *n*

or·chid \'ȯr-kəd\ *n* : any of a large family of plants having often showy flowers with three petals of which the middle one is enlarged into a lip; *also* : a flower of an orchid

ord *abbr* **1** order **2** ordnance

or·dain \ȯr-'dān\ *vb* **1** : to admit to the ministry or priesthood by the ritual of a church **2** : DECREE, ENACT; *also* : DESTINE — **or·dain·ment** *n*

or·deal \ȯr-'dēl, 'ȯr-ˌdēl\ *n* : a severe trial or experience

¹**or·der** \'ȯr-dər\ *vb* **1** : ARRANGE, REGULATE **2** : COMMAND **3** : to place an order

²**order** *n* **1** : a group of people formally united; *also* : a badge or medal of such a group **2** : any of the several grades of the Christian ministry; *also, pl* : ORDINATION **3** : a rank, class, or special group of persons or things **4** : a category of biological classification ranking above the family and below the class **5** : ARRANGEMENT, SEQUENCE; *also* : the prevailing state of things **6** : a customary mode of procedure; *also* : the rule of law or proper authority **7** : a specific rule, regulation, or authoritative direction **8** : a style of building; *also* : an architectural column forming the unit of a style **9** : condition esp. with regard to repair **10** : a direction to pay money or to buy or sell goods; *also* : goods bought or sold — **in order** : APPROPRIATE, DESIRABLE ⟨apologies are *in order*⟩ — **in order to** : for the purpose of

¹**or·der·ly** \'ȯr-dər-lē\ *adj* **1** : arranged according to some order; *also* : NEAT, TIDY **2** : well behaved ⟨an ∼ crowd⟩ ✦ *Synonyms* METHODICAL, SYSTEMATIC, REGULAR — **or·der·li·ness** *n*

²**orderly** *n, pl* **-lies** **1** : a soldier who attends a superior officer **2** : a hospital attendant who does general work

or·di·nal \'ȯr-də-nəl\ *adj* : indicating order or rank (as sixth) in a series

ordinal number *n* : a number (as first, second, or third) that designates the place of an item in an ordered sequence — compare CARDINAL NUMBER

or·di·nance \'ȯr-də-nəns\ *n* : an authoritative decree or law; *esp* : a municipal regulation

or·di·nary \'ȯr-də-ˌner-ē\ *adj* **1** : to be expected : USUAL **2** : of common quality, rank, or ability ⟨∼ kids⟩; *also* : POOR, INFERIOR ⟨∼ wine⟩ ✦ *Synonyms* CUSTOMARY, ROUTINE, NORMAL, EVERYDAY — **or·di·nar·i·ly** \ˌȯr-də-'ner-ə-lē\ *adv* — **or·di·nar·i·ness** \'ȯr-də-ˌner-ē-nəs\ *n*

or·di·nate \'ȯr-də-nət, -ˌnāt\ *n* : the vertical coordinate of a point in a plane coordinate system obtained by measuring parallel to the y-axis

or·di·na·tion \ˌȯr-də-'nā-shən\ *n* : the act or ceremony by which a person is ordained

ord·nance \'ȯrd-nəns\ *n* **1** : military supplies **2** : CANNON, ARTILLERY

Or·do·vi·cian \ˌȯr-də-'vi-shən\ *adj* : of, relating to, or being the period of the Paleozoic era between the Cambrian and the Silurian — **Ordovician** *n*

or·dure \'ȯr-jər\ *n* : EXCREMENT

¹**ore** \'ȯr\ *n* : a naturally occurring mineral mined to obtain a substance that it contains

²**ore** \'ər-ə\ *n, pl* **ore** — see *krona, krone* at MONEY table

Ore *or* **Oreg** *abbr* Oregon

oreg·a·no \ə-'re-gə-ˌnō\ *n* : a bushy perennial mint used as a seasoning and a source of oil

org *abbr* organization; organized

or·gan \'ȯr-gən\ *n* **1** : a musical instrument having sets of pipes sounded by compressed air and controlled by keyboards; *also* : an electronic keyboard instrument that approximates the sounds of the pipe organ **2** : a differentiated animal or plant structure (as a heart or a leaf) made up of cells and tissues and performing some bodily function **3** : a group that performs a specialized function ⟨the various ∼s of government⟩ **4** : PERIODICAL

or·gan·dy *also* **or·gan·die** \'ȯr-gən-dē\ *n, pl* **-dies** [F *organdi*] : a fine transparent muslin with a stiff finish

or·gan·elle \ˌȯr-gə-'nel\ *n* : a specialized cell part that resembles an organ in having a special function

or·gan·ic \ȯr-'ga-nik\ *adj* **1** : of, relating to, or arising in a bodily organ **2** : of, relating to, or derived from living things **3** : of, relating to, or containing carbon compounds **4** : of or relating to a branch of chemistry dealing with carbon compounds **5** : involving, producing, or dealing in foods produced without the use of laboratory-made fertilizers, growth substances, antibiotics, or pesticides ⟨∼

farming⟩ **6** : ORGANIZED ⟨an ∼ whole⟩ — **or·gan·i·cal·ly** \-ni-k(ə-)lē\ *adv*

or·ga·ni·sa·tion, or·ga·nise *Brit var of* ORGANIZATION, ORGANIZE

or·gan·ism \'ȯr-gə-ˌni-zəm\ *n* : an individual living thing (as a person, animal, or plant) — **or·gan·is·mic** \ˌȯr-gə-'niz-mik\ *adj*

or·gan·ist \'ȯr-gə-nist\ *n* : a person who plays an organ

or·ga·ni·za·tion \ˌȯr-gə-nə-'zā-shən\ *n* **1** : the act or process of organizing or of being organized; *also* : the condition or manner of being organized **2** : ASSOCIATION, SOCIETY **3** : an administrative structure (as a business or a political party) — **or·ga·ni·za·tion·al** \-shə-nəl\ *adj*

or·ga·nize \'ȯr-gə-ˌnīz\ *vb* **-nized; -niz·ing 1** : to develop an organic structure **2** : to form into a complete and functioning whole **3** : to set up an administrative structure for **4** : to arrange by systematic planning and united effort **5** : to join in a union; *also* : UNIONIZE ♦ *Synonyms* INSTITUTE, FOUND, ESTABLISH, CONSTITUTE — **or·ga·niz·er** *n*

or·gano·chlo·rine \ȯr-ˌga-nə-'klȯr-ˌēn\ *adj* : of, relating to, or being a chlorinated hydrocarbon pesticide (as DDT) — **organochlorine** *n*

or·gano·phos·phate \-'fäs-ˌfāt\ *n* : an organophosphorus pesticide — **organophosphate** *adj*

or·gano·phos·pho·rus \-'fäs-fə-rəs\ *also* **or·gano·phos·pho·rous** \-fäs-'fȯr-əs\ *adj* : of, relating to, or being a phosphorus-containing organic pesticide (as malathion)

or·gan·za \ȯr-'gan-zə\ *n* : a sheer dress fabric resembling organdy and usu. made of silk, rayon, or nylon

or·gasm \'ȯr-ˌga-zəm\ *n* : the climax of sexual excitement — **or·gas·mic** \ȯr-'gaz-mik\ *adj*

or·gi·as·tic \ˌȯr-jē-'as-tik\ *adj* : of, relating to, or marked by orgies

or·gu·lous \'ȯr-gyə-ləs, -gə-\ *adj* : PROUD

or·gy \'ȯr-jē\ *n, pl* **orgies** : a gathering marked by unrestrained indulgence (as in sexual activity, alcohol, or drugs)

ori·el \'ȯr-ē-əl\ *n* : a window built out from a wall and usu. supported by a bracket

ori·ent \'ȯr-ē-ˌent\ *vb* **1** : to set in a definite position esp. in relation to the points of the compass **2** : to acquaint with an existing situation or environment **3** : to direct toward the interests of a particular group

Orient *n* : EAST **3**; *esp* : the countries of eastern Asia

ori·en·tal \ˌȯr-ē-'en-tᵊl\ *adj, often cap* [fr. *Orient* East, fr. ME, fr. AF, fr. L *orient-, oriens*, fr. prp. of *oriri* to rise] : of or situated in Asia

ori·en·tate \'ȯr-ē-ən-ˌtāt\ *vb* **-tat·ed; -tat·ing 1** : ORIENT **2** : to face east

ori·en·ta·tion \ˌȯr-ē-ən-tā-shən\ *n* **1** : the act or state of being oriented **2** : a person's identity based on sexual tendencies

or·i·fice \'ȯr-ə-fəs\ *n* : OPENING, MOUTH

ori·flamme \'ȯr-ə-ˌflam\ *n* : a brightly colored banner used as a standard or ensign in battle

orig *abbr* original; originally

ori·ga·mi \ˌȯr-ə-'gä-mē\ *n* : the Japanese art or process of paper folding

or·i·gin \'ȯr-ə-jən\ *n* **1** : ANCESTRY **2** : rise, beginning, or derivation from a source; *also* : CAUSE **3** : the intersection of coordinate axes

¹orig·i·nal \ə-'ri-jə-nəl\ *n* : something from which a copy, reproduction, or translation is made : PROTOTYPE

²original *adj* **1** : FIRST, INITIAL **2** : not copied from something else : FRESH **3** : INVENTIVE — **orig·i·nal·i·ty** \ˌri-jə-'na-lə-tē\ *n* — **orig·i·nal·ly** \'ri-jə-nᵊl-ē\ *adv*

orig·i·nate \ə-'ri-jə-ˌnāt\ *vb* **-nat·ed; -nat·ing 1** : to give rise to : INITIATE **2** : to come into existence : BEGIN — **orig·i·na·tor** \-ˌnā-tər\ *n*

ori·ole \'ȯr-ē-ˌōl\ *n* : any of various New World birds of which the males are usu. black and yellow or black and orange

or·i·son \'ȯr-ə-sən\ *n* : PRAYER

or·mo·lu \'ȯr-mə-ˌlü\ *n* : a golden or gilded brass used for decorative purposes

¹or·na·ment \'ȯr-nə-mənt\ *n* : something that lends grace or beauty — **or·na·men·tal** \ˌȯr-nə-'men-tᵊl\ *adj*

²or·na·ment \-ˌment\ *vb* : to provide with ornament : ADORN — **or·na·men·ta·tion** \ˌȯr-nə-mən-'tā-shən\ *n*

or·nate \ȯr-'nāt\ *adj* : elaborately decorated ⟨an ∼ mantel⟩ — **or·nate·ly** *adv* — **or·nate·ness** *n*

or·nery \'ȯr-nə-rē, 'ä-nə-\ *adj* : having an irritable disposition

or·ni·thol·o·gy \ˌȯr-nə-'thä-lə-jē\ *n, pl* **-gies** : a branch of zoology dealing with birds — **or·ni·tho·log·i·cal** \-thə-'lä-ji-kəl\ *adj* — **or·ni·thol·o·gist** \-'thä-lə-jist\ *n*

oro·tund \'ȯr-ə-ˌtənd\ *adj* **1** : SONOROUS ⟨an ∼ voice⟩ **2** : POMPOUS ⟨an ∼ speech⟩ — **oro·tun·di·ty** \ȯr-ə-'tən-di-tē\ *n*

or·phan \'ȯr-fən\ *n* : a child deprived by death of one or usu. both parents — **orphan** *vb*

or·phan·age \'ȯr-fə-nij\ *n* : an institution for the care of orphans

or·tho·don·tia \ˌȯr-thə-'dän-chə, -chē-ə\ *n* : ORTHODONTICS

or·tho·don·tics \ˌȯr-thə-'dän-tiks\ *n* : a branch of dentistry concerned with the correction of faults in the arrangement and placing of the teeth — **or·tho·don·tic** \-tik\ *adj* — **or·tho·don·tist** \-'dän-tist\ *n*

or·tho·dox \'ȯr-thə-ˌdäks\ *adj* [ME *orthodoxe*, fr. MF or LL; MF *orthodoxe*, fr. LL *orthodoxus*, fr. LGk *orthodoxos*, fr. Gk *orthos* right + *doxa* opinion] **1** : conforming to established doctrine esp. in religion **2** : CONVENTIONAL **3** *cap* : of or relating to a Christian church originating in the church of the Eastern Roman Empire — **or·tho·doxy** \-ˌdäk-sē\ *n*

or·thog·ra·phy \ȯr-'thä-grə-fē\ *n* : SPELL-

ING — **or·tho·graph·ic** \ˌȯr-thə-ˈgra-fik\ adj

or·tho·pe·dics also **or·tho·pae·dics** \ˌȯr-thə-ˈpē-diks\ n sing or pl : a branch of medicine concerned with the correction or prevention of skeletal injuries or disorders — **or·tho·pe·dic** also **or·tho·pae·dic** \-dik\ adj — **or·tho·pe·dist** \-dist\ n

-ory adj suffix 1 : of, relating to, or characterized by ⟨anticipatory⟩ 2 : serving for, producing, or maintaining ⟨illusory⟩

Os symbol osmium

OS abbr 1 [L oculus sinister] left eye 2 ordinary seaman 3 out of stock

Osage \ō-ˈsāj\ n, pl **Osag·es** or **Osage** : a member of an American Indian people orig. of Missouri

os·cil·late \ˈä-sə-ˌlāt\ vb **-lat·ed; -lat·ing** 1 : to swing backward and forward like a pendulum 2 : to move or travel back and forth between two points 3 : VARY, FLUCTUATE — **os·cil·la·tion** \ˌä-sə-ˈlā-shən\ n — **os·cil·la·tor** \ˈä-sə-ˌlā-tər\ n — **os·cil·la·to·ry** \ˈä-sə-lə-ˌtȯr-ē\ adj

os·cil·lo·scope \ä-ˈsi-lə-ˌskōp\ n : an instrument in which variations in current or voltage appear as a visible wave form on a fluorescent screen

os·cu·late \ˈäs-kyə-ˌlāt\ vb **-lat·ed; -lat·ing** : KISS — **os·cu·la·tion** \ˌäs-kyə-ˈlā-shən\ n — **os·cu·la·to·ry** \ˈäs-kyə-lə-ˌtȯr-ē\ adj

Osee \ˈō-ˌzē, ō-ˈzā-ə\ n : HOSEA

OSHA \ˈō-shə\ abbr Occupational Safety and Health Administration

osier \ˈō-zhər\ n : any of various willows with pliable twigs used esp. in making baskets and furniture; also : a twig from an osier

os·mi·um \ˈäz-mē-əm\ n : a very heavy hard brittle metallic chemical element used esp. as a catalyst and in alloys

os·mo·sis \äz-ˈmō-səs, äs-\ n : movement of a solvent through a semipermeable membrane into a solution of higher concentration that tends to equalize the concentrations of the solutions on either side of the membrane — **os·mot·ic** \-ˈmä-tik\ adj

os·prey \ˈäs-prē, -ˌprā\ n, pl **ospreys** : a large dark brown and white fish-eating hawk

os·si·fy \ˈä-sə-ˌfī\ vb **-fied; -fy·ing** : to make or become hardened or set in one's ways — **os·si·fi·ca·tion** \ˌä-sə-fə-ˈkā-shən\ n

os·su·ary \ˈä-shə-ˌwer-ē, -syə-\ n, pl **-ar·ies** : a depository for the bones of the dead

os·ten·si·ble \ä-ˈsten-sə-bəl\ adj : shown outwardly : PROFESSED, APPARENT — **os·ten·si·bly** \-blē\ adv

os·ten·ta·tion \ˌäs-tən-ˈtā-shən\ n : pretentious or excessive display — **os·ten·ta·tious** \-shəs\ adj — **os·ten·ta·tious·ly** adv

os·te·o·ar·thri·tis \ˌäs-tē-ō-är-ˈthrī-təs\ n : arthritis marked by degeneration of the cartilage and bone of joints

os·teo·path \ˈäs-tē-ə-ˌpath\ n : a practitioner of osteopathy

os·te·op·a·thy \ˌäs-tē-ˈä-pə-thē\ n : a system of treating diseases emphasizing manipulation (as of joints) but not excluding other agencies (as the use of medicine and surgery) — **os·teo·path·ic** \ˌäs-tē-ə-ˈpa-thik\ adj

os·teo·po·ro·sis \ˌäs-tē-ō-pə-ˈrō-səs\ n, pl **-ro·ses** \-ˌsēz\ : a condition affecting esp. older women and characterized by fragile and porous bones

os·tra·cise Brit var of OSTRACIZE

os·tra·cize \ˈäs-trə-ˌsīz\ vb **-cized; -ciz·ing** [Gk ostrakizein to banish by voting with potsherds, fr. ostrakon shell, potsherd] : to exclude from a group by common consent — **os·tra·cism** \-ˌsi-zəm\ n

os·trich \ˈäs-trich, ˈȯs-\ n : a very large swift-footed flightless bird of Africa

Os·we·go tea \ä-ˈswē-gō-\ n : a No. American mint with showy scarlet flowers

OT abbr 1 occupational therapy 2 Old Testament 3 overtime

¹**oth·er** \ˈə-thər\ adj 1 : being the one left; also : being the ones distinct from those first mentioned 2 : ALTERNATE ⟨every ~ day⟩ 3 : DIFFERENT 4 : ADDITIONAL 5 : recently past ⟨the ~ night⟩

²**other** pron 1 : remaining one or ones 2 : a different or additional one ⟨something or ~⟩

oth·er·wise \ˈə-thər-ˌwīz\ adv 1 : in a different way 2 : in different circumstances 3 : in other respects 4 : if not 5 : NOT — **otherwise** adj

oth·er·world \-ˌwərld\ n : a world beyond death or beyond present reality

oth·er·world·ly \ˌə-thər-ˈwərld-lē\ adj : not worldly : concerned with spiritual, intellectual, or imaginative matters

oti·ose \ˈō-shē-ˌōs, ˈō-tē-\ adj 1 : FUTILE 2 : IDLE 3 : USELESS ⟨~ details⟩

oto·lar·yn·gol·o·gy \ˌō-tō-ˌla-rən-ˈgä-lə-jē\ n : a medical specialty concerned esp. with the ear, nose, and throat — **oto·lar·yn·gol·o·gist** \-jist\ n

oto·rhi·no·lar·yn·gol·o·gy \ˌō-tō-ˌrī-nō-ˌla-rən-ˈgä-lə-jē\ n : OTOLARYNGOLOGY — **oto·rhi·no·lar·yn·gol·o·gist** \-jist\ n

OTS abbr officers' training school

Ot·ta·wa \ˈä-tə-wə, -ˌwä, -ˌwȯ\ n, pl **Ottawas** or **Ottawa** : a member of an American Indian people of Michigan and southern Ontario

ot·ter \ˈä-tər\ n, pl **otters** also **otter** : any of various web-footed fish-eating mammals with dark brown fur that are related to the weasels; also : the fur

ot·to·man \ˈä-tə-mən\ n : an upholstered seat or couch usu. without a back; also : an overstuffed footstool

ou·bli·ette \ˌü-blē-ˈet\ n [F, fr. MF, fr. oublier to forget, ultim. fr. L oblivisci] : a dungeon with an opening at the top

ought \ˈȯt\ verbal auxiliary — used to express moral obligation, advisability, natural expectation, or logical consequence

ou·gui·ya \ü-ˈgwē-ə, -ˈgē-\ n, pl **ouguiya** — see MONEY table

ounce \ˈau̇ns\ n [ME, fr. AF unce, fr. L uncia twelfth part, ounce, fr. unus one]

1 : a unit of avoirdupois, troy, and apothecaries' weight — see WEIGHT table **2** : FLUID OUNCE

our \är, 'aù(-ə)r\ *adj* : of or relating to us or ourselves

ours \'aúrz, 'ärz\ *pron* : that which belongs to us

our·selves \är-'selvz, aú(-ə)r-\ *pron* : our own selves — used reflexively, for emphasis, or in absolute constructions ⟨we pleased ∼⟩ ⟨we'll do it ∼⟩ ⟨we were tourists ∼⟩

-ous *adj suffix* : full of : abounding in : having : possessing the qualities of ⟨clamorous⟩ ⟨poisonous⟩

oust \'aùst\ *vb* : to eject from or deprive of property or position : EXPEL ✦ *Synonyms* EVICT, DISMISS, BANISH, DEPORT

oust·er \'aús-tər\ *n* : EXPULSION

¹out \'aút\ *adv* **1** : in a direction away from the inside or center **2** : beyond control **3** : to extinction, exhaustion, or completion **4** : in or into the open **5** : so as to retire a batter or base runner; *also* : so as to be retired

²out *vb* : to become known ⟨the truth will ∼⟩

³out *prep* **1** : out through ⟨looked ∼ the window⟩ **2** : outward on or along ⟨drive ∼ the river road⟩

⁴out *adj* **1** : situated outside or at a distance **2** : not in : ABSENT; *also* : not being in power **3** : removed from play as a batter or base runner **4** : not being in vogue or fashion : not up-to-date **5** : attempting a particular activity ⟨won his first time ∼⟩

⁵out *n* **1** : one who is out of office **2** : the retiring of a batter or base runner

out·age \'aú-tij\ *n* : a period or instance of interruption esp. of electricity

out-and-out *adj* : COMPLETE, THOROUGHGOING ⟨an ∼ fraud⟩

out·bid \aút-'bid\ *vb* : to make a higher bid than

¹out·board \'aút-,bórd\ *adj* **1** : situated outboard **2** : having or using an outboard motor

²outboard *adv* **1** : outside a ship's hull : away from the long axis of a ship **2** : in a position closer to the wing tip of an airplane

outboard motor *n* : a small internal combustion engine with propeller attached for mounting at the stern of a small boat

out·bound \'aút-,baúnd\ *adj* : outward bound ⟨∼ traffic⟩

out·break \-,brāk\ *n* **1** : a sudden increase in activity, incidence, or numbers **2** : INSURRECTION, REVOLT

out·build·ing \-,bil-diŋ\ *n* : a building separate from but accessory to a main house

out·burst \-,bərst\ *n* : ERUPTION; *esp* : a violent expression of feeling

out·cast \-,kast\ *n* : one that is cast out by society

out·class \aút-'klas\ *vb* : SURPASS

out·come \'aút-,kəm\ *n* : a final consequence : RESULT

out·crop \-,kräp\ *n* : a coming out of bedrock to the surface of the ground; *also*

: the part of a rock formation that thus appears — **outcrop** *vb*

out·cry \-,krī\ *n* : a loud cry : CLAMOR

out·dat·ed \aút-'dā-təd\ *adj* : OUTMODED

out·dis·tance \-'dis-təns\ *vb* : to go far ahead of (as in a race) : OUTSTRIP

out·do \-'dü\ *vb* **-did** \-'did\; **-done** \-'dən\; **-do·ing**; **-does** \-'dəz\ : to go beyond in action or performance

out·door \'aút-,dór, -'dór\ *also* **out·doors** \-,dórz, -'dórz\ *adj* **1** : of or relating to the outdoors **2** : performed outdoors **3** : not enclosed (as by a roof)

¹out·doors \'aút-,dórz, -'dórz\ *adv* : in or into the open air

²outdoors *n* **1** : the open air **2** : the world away from human habitation — **out·doorsy** \aút-'dór-zē\ *adj*

out·draw \aút-'dró\ *vb* **-drew** \-'drü\; **-drawn** \-'drón\; **-draw·ing** **1** : to attract a larger audience than **2** : to draw a handgun more quickly than

out·er \'aú-tər\ *adj* **1** : EXTERNAL **2** : situated farther out; *also* : being away from a center

outer ear *n* : the outer visible portion of the ear that collects and directs sound waves toward the eardrum

out·er·most \-,mōst\ *adj* : farthest out

outer space *n* : SPACE 5

out·er·wear \'aú-tər-,wer\ *n* **1** : clothing for outdoor wear **2** : outer clothing as opposed to underwear

out·face \aút-'fās\ *vb* **1** : to cause to waver or submit **2** : DEFY

out·field \'aút-,fēld\ *n* : the part of a baseball field beyond the infield and within the foul lines; *also* : players in the outfield — **out·field·er** \-,fēl-dər\ *n*

out·fight \aút-'fīt\ *vb* : to surpass in fighting : DEFEAT

¹out·fit \'aút-,fit\ *n* **1** : the equipment or apparel for a special purpose or occasion **2** : GROUP

²outfit *vb* **out·fit·ted**; **out·fit·ting** : EQUIP — **out·fit·ter** *n*

out·flank \aút-'flaŋk\ *vb* : to get around the flank of (an opposing force)

out·flow \'aút-,flō\ *n* **1** : a flowing out **2** : something that flows out

out·fox \aút-'fäks\ *vb* : OUTWIT

out·go \'aút-,gō\ *n, pl* **outgoes** : EXPENDITURES, OUTLAY

out·go·ing \-,gō-iŋ\ *adj* **1** : going out ⟨∼ tide⟩ **2** : retiring from a place or position **3** : FRIENDLY

out·grow \aút-'grō\ *vb* **-grew** \-'grü\; **-grown** \-'grōn\; **-grow·ing** **1** : to grow faster than **2** : to grow too large for

out·growth \'aút-,grōth\ *n* : a product of growing out : OFFSHOOT; *also* : CONSEQUENCE, RESULT

out·guess \aút-'ges\ *vb* : OUTWIT

out·gun \-'gən\ *vb* : to surpass in firepower

out·house \'aút-,haús\ *n* : OUTBUILDING; *esp* : an outdoor toilet

out·ing \'aú-tiŋ\ *n* : a brief stay or trip in the open

out·land·ish \aút-'lan-dish\ *adj* **1** : of foreign appearance or manner; *also*

: BIZARRE   **2** : remote from civilization — **out·land·ish·ly** adv

out·last \-'last\ vb : to last longer than

¹out·law \'aut-ˌlȯ\ n   **1** : a person excluded from the protection of the law   **2** : a lawless person

²outlaw vb   **1** : to deprive of the protection of the law   **2** : to make illegal — **out·law·ry** \'aut-ˌlȯr-ē\ n

out·lay \'aut-ˌlā\ n : the act of spending   **2** : EXPENDITURE

out·let \'aut-ˌlet, -lət\ n   **1** : EXIT, VENT   **2** : a means of release (as for an emotion)   **3** : a medium for usu. public expression : a media organization   **4** : a market for a commodity   **5** : a receptacle for the plug of an electrical device

¹out·line \'aut-ˌlīn\ n   **1** : a line marking the outer limits of an object or figure   **2** : a drawing in which only contours are marked   **3** : SUMMARY, SYNOPSIS   **4** : PLAN

²outline vb   **1** : to draw the outline of   **2** : to indicate the chief features or parts of

out·live \aut-'liv\ vb : to live longer than
  ♦ Synonyms OUTLAST, SURVIVE

out·look \'aut-ˌlùk\ n   **1** : a place offering a view; also : VIEW   **2** : STANDPOINT   **3** : the prospect for the future

out·ly·ing \-ˌlī-iŋ\ adj : distant from a center or main body

out·ma·neu·ver \ˌaut-mə-'nü-vər, -'nyü-\ vb : to defeat by more skillful maneuvering

out·mod·ed \aut-'mō-dəd\ adj   **1** : no longer in style   **2** : no longer acceptable or current

out·num·ber \-'nəm-bər\ vb : to exceed in number

out of prep   **1** : out from within or behind ⟨walk out of the room⟩ ⟨look out of the window⟩   **2** : from a state of ⟨wake up out of a deep sleep⟩   **3** : beyond the limits of ⟨out of sight⟩   **4** : BECAUSE OF ⟨asked out of curiosity⟩   **5** : FROM, WITH ⟨built it out of scrap⟩   **6** : in or into a state of loss or not having ⟨cheated him out of $5000⟩ ⟨we're out of matches⟩   **7** : from among ⟨one out of four⟩ — **out of it** : SQUARE, OLD-FASHIONED

out–of–bounds adv or adj : outside the prescribed boundaries or limits

out–of–date adj : no longer in fashion or in use : OUTMODED

out–of–door or **out–of–doors** adj : OUTDOOR

out–of–the–way adj   **1** : UNUSUAL   **2** : being off the beaten track

out·pa·tient \'aut-ˌpā-shənt\ n : a patient who visits a hospital or clinic for diagnosis or treatment without staying overnight

out·per·form \ˌaut-pər-'fȯrm\ vb : to perform better than

out·play \aut-'plā\ vb : to play more skillfully than

out·point \-'pȯint\ vb : to win more points than

out·post \'aut-ˌpōst\ n   **1** : a security detachment dispatched by a main body of troops to protect it from enemy surprise; also : a military base established (as by

treaty) in a foreign country   **2** : an outlying or frontier settlement

out·pour·ing \-ˌpȯr-iŋ\ n : something that pours out or is poured out

out·pull \aut-'pul\ vb : OUTDRAW 1

¹out·put \'aut-ˌput\ n   **1** : the amount produced (as by a machine or factory) : PRODUCTION   **2** : the information produced by a computer

²output vb **out·put·ted** or **output**; **out·put·ting** : to produce as output

¹out·rage \'aut-ˌrāj\ n [ME, fr. AF utrage, outrage insult, excess, fr. utre, outre beyond, fr. L ultra]   **1** : a violent or shameful act   **2** : INJURY, INSULT   **3** : the anger or resentment aroused by injury or insult

²outrage vb **out·raged**; **out·rag·ing**   **1** : RAPE   **2** : to subject to violent injury or gross insult   **3** : to arouse to extreme resentment

out·ra·geous \aut-'rā-jəs\ adj : extremely offensive, insulting, or shameful : SHOCKING — **out·ra·geous·ly** adv

out·rank \-'raŋk\ vb : to rank higher than

ou·tré \ü-'trā\ adj [F] : violating convention or propriety : BIZARRE

¹out·reach \aut-'rēch\ vb   **1** : to surpass in reach   **2** : to get the better of by trickery

²out·reach \'aut-ˌrēch\ n   **1** : the act of reaching out   **2** : the extent of reach   **3** : the extending of services beyond usual limits

out·rid·er \-ˌrī-dər\ n : a mounted attendant

out·rig·ger \-ˌri-gər\ n   **1** : a frame attached to the side of a boat to prevent capsizing   **2** : a craft equipped with an outrigger

¹out·right \aut-'rīt\ adv   **1** : COMPLETELY   **2** : INSTANTANEOUSLY

²out·right \'aut-ˌrīt\ adj   **1** : being exactly what is stated ⟨an ~ lie⟩   **2** : given or made without reservation or encumbrance ⟨an ~ sale⟩

out·run \aut-'rən\ vb **-ran** \-'ran\; **-run**; **-run·ning** : to run faster than; also : EXCEED

out·sell \-'sel\ vb **-sold** \-'sōld\; **-sell·ing** : to exceed in sales

out·set \'aut-ˌset\ n : BEGINNING, START

out·shine \aut-'shīn\ vb **-shone** \-'shōn\ or **-shined**; **-shin·ing**   **1** : to shine brighter than   **2** : SURPASS

¹out·side \aut-'sīd, 'aut-ˌsīd\ n   **1** : a place or region beyond an enclosure or boundary   **2** : EXTERIOR   **3** : the utmost limit or extent

²outside adj   **1** : OUTER   **2** : coming from without ⟨~ influences⟩   **3** : being apart from one's regular duties ⟨~ activities⟩   **4** : REMOTE ⟨an ~ chance⟩

³outside adv : on or to the outside

⁴outside prep   **1** : on or to the outside of   **2** : beyond the limits of   **3** : EXCEPT

outside of prep   **1** : OUTSIDE   **2** : BESIDES

out·sid·er \aut-'sī-dər\ n : a person who does not belong to a group

out·size \'aut-ˌsīz\ also **out·sized** \-ˌsīzd\ adj : unusually large : extravagant in size or degree

out·skirts \-ˌskərts\ *n pl* : the outlying parts (as of a city) : BORDERS

out·smart \aut-ˈsmärt\ *vb* : OUTWIT

out·source \ˈaut-ˌsȯrs\ *vb* **-sourced**; **-sourcing** : to obtain (goods or services) from an outside supplier

out·spend \-ˈspend\ *vb* **1** : to exceed the limits of in spending ⟨∼s his income⟩ **2** : to spend more than

out·spo·ken \aut-ˈspō-kən\ *adj* : direct and open in speech or expression — **out·spo·ken·ly** *adv* — **out·spo·ken·ness** *n*

out·spread \-ˈspred\ *vb* **-spread**; **-spread·ing** : to spread out

out·stand·ing \-ˈstan-diŋ\ *adj* **1** : PROJECTING **2** : UNPAID; *also* : UNRESOLVED ⟨∼ warrants⟩ **3** : publicly issued and sold **4** : CONSPICUOUS; *also* : DISTINGUISHED — **out·stand·ing·ly** *adv*

out·stay \-ˈstā\ *vb* **1** : OVERSTAY **2** : to surpass in endurance

out·stretch \ˌaut-ˈstrech\ *vb* : to stretch out : EXTEND

out·strip \-ˈstrip\ *vb* **1** : to go faster than **2** : EXCEL, SURPASS

out·take \ˈaut-ˌtāk\ *n* : something taken out; *esp* : a take that is not used in an edited version of a film or videotape

out·vote \-ˈvōt\ *vb* : to defeat by a majority of votes

¹**out·ward** \ˈaut-wərd\ *adj* **1** : moving or directed toward the outside **2** : showing outwardly

²**outward** *or* **out·wards** \-wərdz\ *adv* : toward the outside

out·ward·ly \-wərd-lē\ *adv* : on the outside : EXTERNALLY

out·wear \aut-ˈwer\ *vb* **-wore** \-ˈwȯr\; **-worn** \-ˈwȯrn\; **-wear·ing** : to wear longer than : OUTLAST

out·weigh \-ˈwā\ *vb* : to exceed in weight, value, or importance

out·wit \-ˈwit\ *vb* : to get the better of by superior cleverness

¹**out·work** \-ˈwərk\ *vb* : to outdo in working

²**out·work** \ˈaut-ˌwərk\ *n* : a minor defensive position outside a fortified area

out·worn \aut-ˈwȯrn\ *adj* : OUTMODED

ou·zo \ˈü-(ˌ)zō\ *n* : a colorless anise-flavored unsweetened Greek liqueur

ova *pl of* OVUM

oval \ˈō-vəl\ *adj* [ML *ovalis*, fr. LL, of an egg, fr. L *ovum* egg] : egg-shaped; *also* : broadly elliptical — **oval** *n*

ova·ry \ˈō-və-rē\ *n, pl* **-ries** **1** : one of the usu. paired female reproductive organs producing eggs and in vertebrates sex hormones **2** : the part of a flower in which seeds are produced — **ovar·i·an** \ō-ˈver-ē-ən\ *adj*

ovate \ˈō-ˌvāt\ *adj* : egg-shaped

ova·tion \ō-ˈvā-shən\ *n* [L *ovation-, ovatio*, fr. *ovare* to exult] : an enthusiastic popular tribute

ov·en \ˈə-vən\ *n* : a chamber (as in a stove) for baking, heating, or drying

oven·bird \-ˌbərd\ *n* : a large olive-green American warbler that builds its dome-shaped nest on the ground

¹**over** \ˈō-vər\ *adv* **1** : across a barrier or intervening space **2** : across the brim ⟨boil ∼⟩ **3** : so as to bring the underside up **4** : out of a vertical position **5** : beyond some quantity, limit, or norm **6** : ABOVE **7** : at an end **8** : THROUGH ⟨read it ∼⟩; *also* : THOROUGHLY **9** : AGAIN ⟨do it ∼⟩

²**over** *prep* **1** : above in position, authority, or scope ⟨towered ∼ her⟩ ⟨obeyed those ∼ him⟩ **2** : more than ⟨cost ∼ $100⟩ **3** : ON, UPON ⟨a cape ∼ her shoulders⟩ **4** : along the length of ⟨∼ the road⟩ **5** : through the medium of : ON ⟨spoke ∼ TV⟩ **6** : all through ⟨showed me ∼ the house⟩ **7** : on or to the other side or beyond ⟨jump ∼ a ditch⟩ **8** : DURING ⟨∼ the past 25 years⟩ **9** : on account of ⟨trouble ∼ money⟩

³**over** *adj* **1** : UPPER, HIGHER **2** : REMAINING **3** : ENDED

over- *prefix* **1** : so as to exceed or surpass **2** : excessive; excessively

over·act \ˌō-vər-ˈakt\ *vb* : to exaggerate in acting

¹**over·age** \ˌō-vər-ˈāj\ *adj* **1** : too old to be useful **2** : older than is normal for one's position, function, or grade

²**over·age** \ˈō-və-rij\ *n* : SURPLUS

over·all \ˌō-vər-ˈȯl\ *adj* : including everything ⟨∼ expenses⟩

over·alls \ˈō-vər-ˌȯlz\ *n pl* : pants of strong material usu. with a piece extending up to cover the chest

over·arm \-ˌärm\ *adj* : done with the arm raised above the shoulder

over·awe \ˌō-vər-ˈȯ\ *vb* : to restrain or subdue by awe

over·bal·ance \-ˈba-ləns\ *vb* **1** : OUTWEIGH **2** : to cause to lose balance

over·bear·ing \-ˈber-iŋ\ *adj* : ARROGANT, DOMINEERING

over·bite \ˈō-vər-ˌbīt\ *n* : the projection of the upper front teeth over the lower

over·blown \-ˈblōn\ *adj* **1** : PORTLY **2** : INFLATED, PRETENTIOUS

over·board \ˈō-vər-ˌbȯrd\ *adv* **1** : over the side of a ship into the water **2** : to extremes of enthusiasm

¹**over·cast** \ˈō-vər-ˌkast\ *adj* : clouded over : GLOOMY

²**overcast** *n* : COVERING; *esp* : a covering of clouds

over·charge \ˌō-vər-ˈchärj\ *vb* **1** : to charge too much **2** : to fill or load too full — **over·charge** \ˈō-vər-ˌchärj\ *n*

over·coat \ˈō-vər-ˌkōt\ *n* : a warm coat worn over indoor clothing

over·come \ˌō-vər-ˈkəm\ *vb* **-came**

overabundance	overambitious	overburden	overcautious
overabundant	overanxious	overbuy	overcompensation
overachiever	overbid	overcapacity	overconfidence
overactive	overbold	overcapitalize	overconfident
overaggressive	overbuild	overcareful	overconscientious

\-'käm\; **-come; -com-ing 1 :** CON-
QUER **2 :** to make helpless or exhausted
over-do \ˌō-vər-'dü\ *vb* **-did** \-'did\;
-done \-'dən\; **-do-ing; -does** \-'dəz\ **1
:** to do too much; *also :* to tire oneself **2
:** EXAGGERATE **3 :** to cook too long
over-dose \ˌō-vər-ˌdōs\ *n :* too great a
dose (as of medicine); *also :* a lethal or
toxic amount (as of a drug) — **over-
dose** \ˌō-vər-'dōs\ *vb*
over-draft \'ō-vər-ˌdraft\ *n :* an overdraw-
ing of a bank account; *also :* the sum
overdrawn
over-draw \ˌō-vər-'drȯ\ *vb* **-drew** \-'drü\;
-drawn \-'drȯn\; **-draw-ing 1 :** to draw
checks on a bank account for more than
the balance **2 :** EXAGGERATE
over-drive \'ō-vər-ˌdrīv\ *n :* an automotive transmission gear that transmits to
the driveshaft a speed greater than the engine speed
over-dub \ˌō-vər-'dəb\ *vb :* to transfer (recorded sound) onto an earlier recording
for a combined effect — **over-dub** \'ō-
vər-ˌdəb\ *n*
over-due \-'dü, -'dyü\ *adj* **1 :** unpaid
when due ⟨an ~ bill⟩; *also :* not appearing or presented on time ⟨an ~ train⟩ **2
:** more than ready
over-ex-pose \ˌō-vər-ik-'spōz\ *vb :* to expose (as film) for more time than is needed — **over-ex-po-sure** \-'spō-zhər\ *n*
¹over-flow \-'flō\ *vb* **1 :** INUNDATE; *also
:* to pour forth in a flood **2 :** to flow over
the brim or top of
²over-flow \'ō-vər-ˌflō\ *n* **1 :** FLOOD; *also
:* SURPLUS **2 :** an outlet for surplus liquid
over-fly \ˌō-vər-'flī\ *vb* **-flew** \-'flü\;
-flown \-'flōn\; **-fly-ing :** to fly over in an
aircraft or spacecraft — **over-flight** \'ō-
vər-ˌflīt\ *n*
over-grow \ˌō-vər-'grō\ *vb* **-grew** \-'grü\;
-grown \-'grōn\; **-grow-ing 1 :** to grow
over so as to cover **2 :** OUTGROW **3 :** to
grow excessively — **over-growth** \-'ō-vər-
ˌgrōth\ *n*
over-hand \'ō-vər-ˌhand\ *adj :* made with
the hand brought down from above —
overhand *adv* — **over-hand-ed** \-ˌhan-
dəd\ *adv or adj*
¹over-hang \'ō-vər-ˌhaŋ, ˌō-vər-'haŋ\ *vb*
-hung \-ˌhəŋ, -'həŋ\; **-hang-ing 1 :** to
project over : jut out **2 :** to hang over
threateningly
²over-hang \'ō-vər-ˌhaŋ\ *n :* a part (as of a
roof) that overhangs
over-haul \ˌō-vər-'hȯl\ *vb* **1 :** to examine
thoroughly and make necessary repairs
and adjustments **2 :** OVERTAKE
¹over-head \ˌō-vər-'hed\ *adv :* ALOFT

²over-head \'ō-vər-ˌhed\ *adj :* operating or
lying above ⟨~ door⟩
³over-head \'ō-vər-ˌhed\ *n :* business expenses not chargeable to a particular part
of the work
over-hear \ˌō-vər-'hir\ *vb* **-heard** \-'hərd\;
-hear-ing : to hear without the speaker's
knowledge or intention
over-joyed \ˌō-vər-'jȯid\ *adj :* filled with
great joy
over-kill \'ō-vər-ˌkil\ *n* **1 :** destructive capacity greatly exceeding that required for
a target **2 :** a large excess
over-land \'ō-vər-ˌland, -lənd\ *adv or adj
:* by, on, or across land
over-lap \ˌō-vər-'lap\ *vb* **1 :** to lap over
2 : to have something in common —
over-lap \'ō-vər-ˌlap\ *n*
over-lay \ˌō-vər-'lā\ *vb* **-laid** \-'lād\; **-lay-
ing :** to lay or spread over or across —
over-lay \'ō-vər-ˌlā\ *n*
over-leap \ˌō-vər-'lēp\ *vb* **-leaped** *or*
-leapt \-'lēpt, -'lept\; **-leap-ing 1 :** to
leap over or across **2 :** to defeat (oneself)
by going too far
over-lie \ˌō-vər-'lī\ *vb* **-lay** \-'lā\; **-lain**
\-'lān\; **-ly-ing :** to lie over or upon
¹over-look \ˌō-vər-'lük\ *vb* **1 :** INSPECT **2
:** to look down on from above **3 :** to fail
to see **4 :** IGNORE; *also :* EXCUSE **5 :** SU-
PERINTEND
²over-look \'ō-vər-ˌlük\ *n :* a place from
which to look upon a scene below
over-lord \-ˌlȯrd\ *n :* a lord who has supremacy over other lords
over-ly \'ō-vər-lē\ *adv :* EXCESSIVELY
over-match \ˌō-vər-'mach\ *vb :* to be
more than a match for : DEFEAT
over-much \-'məch\ *adj or adv :* too much
¹over-night \-'nīt\ *adv* **1 :** on or during
the night **2 :** SUDDENLY ⟨became famous ~⟩
overnight *adj :* of, lasting, or staying the
night ⟨~ guests⟩
over-pass \ˌō-vər-ˌpas\ *n* **1 :** a crossing
(as of two highways) at different levels by
means of a bridge **2 :** the upper level of
an overpass
over-play \ˌō-vər-'plā\ *vb* **1 :** EXAGGER-
ATE; *also :* OVEREMPHASIZE **2 :** to rely
too much on the strength of
over-pop-u-la-tion \ˌō-vər-ˌpä-pyə-'lā-
shən\ *n :* the condition of having a population so dense as to cause a decline in
population or in living conditions —
over-pop-u-lat-ed \-'pä-pyə-ˌlā-təd\ *adj*
over-pow-er \-'pau̇(-ə)r\ *vb :* to overcome
by superior force
over-price \ˌō-vər-'prīs\ *vb :* to price too
high

overcook	overemphasis	overfill	overlearn
overcritical	overemphasize	overgeneralization	overload
overcrowd	overenthusiastic	overgeneralize	overlong
overdecorated	overestimate	overgenerous	overmodest
overdependence	overexcite	overgraze	overnice
overdetermined	overexcited	overhasty	overoptimism
overdevelop	overexert	overheat	overoptimistic
overdress	overexertion	overindulge	overpay
overeager	overextend	overindulgence	overpraise
overeat	overfatigued	overindulgent	
overeducated	overfeed	overlarge	

over·print \-'print\ vb : to print over with something additional — **over·print** \'ō-vər-,print\ n

over·qual·i·fied \-'kwä-lə-,fīd\ adj : having more education, training, or experience than a job calls for

over·reach \,ō-vər-'rēch\ vb : to defeat (oneself) by too great an effort

over·ride \-'rīd\ vb **-rode** \-'rōd\; **-ridden** \-'ri-d³n\; **-rid·ing 1** : to ride over or across **2** : to prevail over; also : to set aside ⟨~ a veto⟩

over·rule \-'rül\ vb **1** : to prevail over **2** : to rule against **3** : to set aside

¹**over·run** \-'rən\ vb **-ran** \-'ran\; **-run; -run·ning 1** : to defeat and occupy the positions of **2** : OVERSPREAD; also : INFEST **3** : to go beyond **4** : to flow over

²**over·run** \'ō-vər-,rən\ n **1** : an act or instance of overrunning; esp : an exceeding of estimated costs **2** : the amount by which something overruns

over·sea \,ō-vər-'sē, 'ō-vər-,sē\ adj or adv : OVERSEAS

over·seas \,ō-vər-'sēz, -,sēz\ adv or adj : beyond or across the sea : ABROAD

over·see \,ō-vər-'sē\ vb **-saw** \-'sȯ\; **-seen** \-'sēn\; **-see·ing 1** : OVERLOOK **2** : INSPECT; also : SUPERVISE — **over·seer** \'ō-vər-,sir\ n

over·sell \,ō-vər-'sel\ vb **-sold; -sel·ling** : to sell too much to or too much of

over·sexed \,ō-vər-'sekst\ adj : exhibiting excessive sexual drive or interest

over·shad·ow \-'sha-dō\ vb **1** : to cast a shadow over **2** : to exceed in importance

over·shoe \'ō-vər-,shü\ n : a protective outer shoe; esp : GALOSH

over·shoot \,ō-vər-'shüt\ vb **-shot** \-'shät\; **-shoot·ing 1** : to pass swiftly beyond **2** : to shoot over or beyond

over·sight \'ō-vər-,sīt\ n **1** : SUPERVISION **2** : an inadvertent omission or error

over·size \,ō-vər-'sīz\ or **over·sized** \-'sīzd\ adj : of more than ordinary size

over·sleep \,ō-vər-'slēp\ vb **-slept** \-'slept\; **-sleep·ing** : to sleep beyond the time for waking

over·spread \-'spred\ vb **-spread; -spread·ing** : to spread over or above

over·state \-'stāt\ vb : EXAGGERATE — **over·state·ment** n

over·stay \-'stā\ vb : to stay beyond the time or limits of

over·step \-'step\ vb : EXCEED

over·sub·scribe \-səb-'skrīb\ vb : to subscribe for more of than is available, asked for, or offered for sale

overt \ō-'vərt, 'ō-,vərt\ adj [ME, fr. AF, fr. pp. of ovrir to open] : not secret — **overt·ly** adv

over·take \,ō-vər-'tāk\ vb **-took** \-'tuk\; **-tak·en** \-'tā-kən\; **-tak·ing** : to catch up with; also : to catch up with and pass by ⟨~ the lead runner⟩

over-the-counter adj : sold lawfully without a prescription ⟨~ drugs⟩

over-the-hill adj **1** : past one's prime **2** : advanced in age

over-the-top adj **1** : extremely flamboyant or outrageous ⟨an ~ performance⟩

over·throw \,ō-vər-'thrō\ vb **-threw** \-'thrü\; **-thrown** \-'thrōn\; **-throw·ing 1** : UPSET **2** : to bring down : DEFEAT ⟨~ a government⟩ **3** : to throw over or past — **over·throw** \'ō-vər-,thrō\ n

over·time \'ō-vər-,tīm\ n : time beyond a set limit; esp : working time in excess of a standard day or week — **overtime** adv

over·tone \-,tōn\ n **1** : one of the higher tones in a complex musical tone **2** : IMPLICATION, SUGGESTION

over·trick \'ō-vər-,trik\ n : a card trick won in excess of the number bid

over·ture \'ō-vər-,chur, -chər\ n [ME, lit., opening, fr. AF, fr. VL *opertura, alter. of L apertura] **1** : an opening offer **2** : an orchestral introduction to a musical dramatic work

over·turn \,ō-vər-'tərn\ vb **1** : to turn over : UPSET ⟨~ a vase⟩ **2** : INVALIDATE ⟨~ a court ruling⟩

over·view \'ō-vər-,vyü\ n : a general survey : SUMMARY

over·ween·ing \,ō-vər-'wē-niŋ\ adj **1** : ARROGANT **2** : IMMODERATE

over·weight \'ō-vər-,wāt\ n **1** : weight above what is required or allowed **2** : bodily weight greater than normal — **overweight** adj

over·whelm \,ō-vər-'hwelm\ vb **1** : OVERTHROW **2** : SUBMERGE **3** : to overcome completely

over·whelm·ing adj : EXTREME, GREAT ⟨~ joy⟩ — **over·whelm·ing·ly** adv

over·win·ter \-'win-tər\ vb : to survive or pass the winter

over·work \-'wərk\ vb **1** : to work or cause to work too hard or long **2** : to use too much — **overwork** n

over·wrought \,ō-vər-'rȯt\ adj **1** : extremely excited **2** : elaborated to excess

ovi·duct \'ō-və-,dəkt\ n : a tube that serves for the passage of eggs from an ovary

ovip·a·rous \ō-'vi-pə-rəs\ adj : reproducing by eggs that hatch outside the parent's body

ovoid \'ō-,vȯid\ or **ovoi·dal** \ō-'vȯi-d³l\ adj : egg-shaped : OVAL

ovu·la·tion \,äv-yə-'lā-shən, ,ōv-\ n : the discharge of a mature egg from the ovary — **ovu·late** \'äv-yə-,lāt, 'ōv-\ vb

ovule \'äv-yül, 'ōv-\ n : any of the bodies in a plant ovary that after fertilization become seeds

overproduce	overrefinement	oversimplify	oversupply
overproduction	overrepresented	overspecialization	overtax
overprotect	overripe	overspecialize	overtired
overprotective	oversensitive	overspend	overtrain
overrate	oversensitiveness	overstimulation	overuse
overreact	oversimple	overstock	overvalue
overreaction	oversimplification	oversubtle	overzealous

ovum \'ō-vəm\ *n, pl* **ova** \-və\ : EGG 2

ow \'aù\ *interj* — used esp. to express sudden pain

owe \'ō\ *vb* **owed; ow·ing 1** : to be under obligation to pay or render **2** : to be indebted to or for; *also* : to be in debt

owing to *prep* : BECAUSE OF

owl \'aù(-ə)l\ *n* : any of an order of chiefly nocturnal birds of prey with a large head and eyes and strong talons — **owl·ish** *adj* — **owl·ish·ly** *adv*

owl·et \'aù-lət\ *n* : a young or small owl

¹own \'ōn\ *adj* : belonging to oneself — used as an intensive after a possessive adjective ⟨her ~ car⟩

²own *vb* **1** : to have or hold as property **2** : to have power or mastery over **3** : ACKNOWLEDGE; *also* : CONFESS — **own·er** *n* — **own·er·ship** *n*

³own *pron* : one or ones belonging to oneself — **on one's own 1** : for or by oneself : left to one's own resources

ox \'äks\ *n, pl* **ox·en** \'äk-sən\ *also* **ox** : any of the large domestic bovine mammals kept for milk, draft, and meat; *esp* : an adult castrated male ox

ox·blood \'äks-ˌbləd\ *n* : a moderate reddish brown

ox·bow \-ˌbō\ *n* **1** : a U-shaped collar worn by a draft ox **2** : a U-shaped bend in a river — **oxbow** *adj*

ox·ford \'äks-fərd\ *n* : a low shoe laced or tied over the instep

ox·i·dant \'äk-sə-dənt\ *n* : OXIDIZING AGENT — **oxidant** *adj*

ox·i·da·tion \ˌäk-sə-'dā-shən\ *n* : the act or process of oxidizing; *also* : the condition of being oxidized — **ox·i·da·tive** \'äk-sə-ˌdā-tiv\ *adj*

ox·ide \'äk-ˌsīd\ *n* : a compound of oxygen with another element or group

ox·i·dize \'äk-sə-ˌdīz\ *vb* **-dized; -diz·ing** : to combine with oxygen ⟨iron rusts because it is *oxidized* by exposure to the air⟩ — **ox·i·diz·er** *n*

oxidizing agent *n* : a substance (as oxygen or nitric acid) that oxidizes by taking up electrons

ox·y·gen \'äk-si-jən\ *n* [F *oxygène*, fr. Gk *oxys* acidic, lit., sharp + *-genēs* giving rise to; so called because it was once thought to be an essential element of all acids] : a colorless odorless gaseous chemical element that is found in the air, is essential to life, and is involved in combustion

ox·y·gen·ate \'äk-si-jə-ˌnāt\ *vb* **-at·ed; -at·ing** : to impregnate, combine, or supply with oxygen — **ox·y·gen·a·tion** \ˌäk-si-jə-'nā-shən\ *n*

oxygen mask *n* : a device worn over the nose and mouth through which oxygen is supplied

oxygen tent *n* : a canopy which can be placed over a bedridden person and within which a flow of oxygen can be maintained

ox·y·mo·ron \ˌäk-sē-'mȯr-ˌän\ *n* : a combination of contradictory words (as *cruel kindness*) — **ox·y·mo·ron·ic** \-mə-'rä-nik\ *adj*

oys·ter \'ȯis-tər\ *n* : any of various marine mollusks with an irregular 2-valved shell that include commercially important edible shellfish and pearl producers — **oys·ter·ing** *n* — **oys·ter·man** \-mən\ *n*

oz *abbr* [obs. It *onza* (now *oncia*)] ounce; ounces

ozone \'ō-ˌzōn\ *n* **1** : a bluish gaseous reactive form of oxygen that is formed naturally in the atmosphere and is used for disinfecting, deodorizing, and bleaching **2** : pure and refreshing air

ozone layer *n* : an atmospheric layer at heights of about 25 miles (40 kilometers) with high ozone content which blocks most solar ultraviolet radiation

¹p \'pē\ *n, pl* **p's** *or* **ps** \'pēz\ *often cap* : the 16th letter of the English alphabet

²p *abbr, often cap* **1** page **2** participle **3** past **4** pawn **5** pence; penny **6** per **7** petite **8** pint **9** pressure **10** purl

P *symbol* phosphorus

pa \'pä, 'pȯ\ *n* : FATHER

¹Pa *abbr* **1** pascal **2** Pennsylvania

²Pa *symbol* protactinium

¹PA \ˌ(ˌ)pē-'ā\ *n* : PHYSICIAN'S ASSISTANT

²PA *abbr* **1** Pennsylvania **2** per annum **3** power of attorney **4** press agent **5** private account **6** professional association **7** public address **8** purchasing agent

pa·'an·ga \pä-'äŋ-gə\ *n* — see MONEY table

pab·u·lum \'pa-byə-ləm\ *n* [L, food, fodder] : usu. soft digestible food

Pac *abbr* Pacific

PAC *abbr* political action committee

¹pace \'pās\ *n* **1** : rate of movement or progress (as in walking or working) **2** : a step in walking; *also* : a measure of length based on such a step **3** : GAIT; *esp* : a horse's gait in which the legs on the same side move together

²pace *vb* **paced; pac·ing 1** : to go or cover at a pace or with slow steps **2** : to measure off by paces **3** : to set or regulate the pace of

³pace \'pä-sē; 'pä-ˌkā, -ˌchä\ *prep* : contrary to the opinion of

pace·mak·er \'pās-ˌmā-kər\ *n* **1** : one that sets the pace for another **2** : a body part (as of the heart) that serves to establish and maintain a rhythmic activity **3** : an electrical device for stimulating or steadying the heartbeat

pac·er \'pā-sər\ *n* **1** : a horse that paces **2** : PACEMAKER

pachy·derm \'pa-ki-ˌdərm\ *n* [F *pachy-*

derme, fr. Gk *pachydermos* thick-skinned, fr. *pachys* thick + *derma* skin] : any of various thick-skinned hoofed mammals (as an elephant)

pach·ys·an·dra \,pa-ki-'san-drǝ\ *n* : any of a genus of low perennial evergreen plants used as a ground cover

pa·cif·ic \pǝ-'si-fik\ *adj* **1** : tending to lessen conflict **2** : CALM, PEACEFUL

pac·i·fi·er \'pa-sǝ-,fī(-ǝ)r\ *n* : one that pacifies; *esp* : a device for a baby to chew or suck on

pac·i·fism \'pa-sǝ-,fi-zǝm\ *n* : opposition to war or violence as a means of settling disputes — **pac·i·fist** \-fist\ *n or adj* — **pac·i·fis·tic** \,pa-sǝ-'fis-tik\ *adj*

pac·i·fy \'pa-sǝ-,fī\ *vb* **-fied; -fy·ing 1** : to allay anger or agitation in : SOOTHE **2** : SETTLE; *also* : SUBDUE — **pac·i·fi·ca·tion** \,pa-sǝ-fǝ-'kā-shǝn\ *n*

¹pack \'pak\ *n* **1** : a compact bundle; *also* : a flexible container for carrying a bundle esp. on the back **2** : a large amount : HEAP **3** : a set of playing cards **4** : a group or band of people or animals **5** : wet absorbent material for application to the body

²pack *vb* **1** : to stow goods in for transportation **2** : to fill in or surround so as to prevent passage of air, steam, or water **3** : to put into a protective container **4** : to load with a pack ⟨∼ a mule⟩ **5** : to crowd in **6** : to make into a pack **7** : to cause to go without ceremony ⟨∼ them off to school⟩ **8** : WEAR, CARRY ⟨∼ a gun⟩

³pack *vb* : to make up fraudulently so as to secure a desired result ⟨∼ a jury⟩

¹pack·age \'pa-kij\ *n* **1** : BUNDLE, PARCEL **2** : a group of related things offered as a whole

²package *vb* **pack·aged; pack·ag·ing** : to make into or enclose in a package

package deal *n* : an offer containing several items all or none of which must be accepted

package store *n* : a store that sells alcoholic beverages in sealed containers for consumption off the premises

pack·er \'pa-kǝr\ *n* : one that packs; *esp* : a wholesale food dealer

pack·et \'pa-kǝt\ *n* **1** : a small bundle or package **2** : a passenger boat carrying mail and cargo on a regular schedule

pack·horse \'pak-,hȯrs\ *n* : a horse used to carry goods or supplies

pack·ing \'pa-kiŋ\ *n* : material used to pack something

pack·ing·house \-,haủs\ *n* : an establishment for processing and packing food and esp. meat and its by-products

pack rat *n* **1** : a bushy-tailed rodent of western No. America that hoards food and miscellaneous objects; *also* : any of several rodents of similar habit **2** : a person who collects or saves many esp. unneeded items

pack·sad·dle \'pak-,sa-dᵊl\ *n* : a saddle for supporting loads on the back of an animal

pack·thread \-,thred\ *n* : strong thread for tying

pact \'pakt\ *n* : AGREEMENT, TREATY

¹pad \'pad\ *n* **1** : a cushioning part or thing : CUSHION **2** : the cushioned underside of the foot or toes of some mammals **3** : the floating leaf of a water plant **4** : a writing tablet **5** : LAUNCH-PAD **6** : living quarters; *also* : BED

²pad *vb* **pad·ded; pad·ding 1** : to furnish with a pad or padding **2** : to expand with needless or fraudulent matter

pad·ding *n* : the material with which something is padded

¹pad·dle \'pa-dᵊl\ *vb* **pad·dled; pad·dling** : to move the hands and feet about in shallow water

²paddle *n* **1** : an implement with a flat blade used in propelling and steering a small craft (as a canoe) **2** : an implement used for stirring, mixing, or beating **3** : a broad board on the outer rim of a waterwheel or a paddle wheel

³paddle *vb* **pad·dled; pad·dling 1** : to move on or through water by or as if by using a paddle **2** : to beat or stir with a paddle

paddle wheel *n* : a wheel with paddles around its outer edge used to move a boat

paddle wheeler *n* : a steam-driven vessel propelled by a paddle wheel

pad·dock \'pa-dǝk\ *n* **1** : a usu. enclosed area for pasturing or exercising animals; *esp* : one where racehorses are saddled and paraded before a race **2** : an area at a racecourse where racing cars are parked

pad·dy \'pa-dē\ *n, pl* **paddies** : wet land where rice is grown

paddy wagon *n* : an enclosed motortruck for carrying prisoners

pad·lock \'pad-,läk\ *n* : a removable lock with a curved piece that snaps into a catch — **padlock** *vb*

pa·dre \'pä-drā\ *n* [Sp or It or Pg, lit., father, fr. L *pater*] **1** : PRIEST **2** : a military chaplain

pad thai \'päd-'tī\ *n, often cap T* : a Thai dish of rice noodles stir-fried with additional ingredients

pae·an \'pē-ǝn\ *n* : an exultant song of praise or thanksgiving

pae·di·at·ric, pae·di·a·tri·cian, pae·di·at·rics *chiefly Brit var of* PEDIATRIC, PEDIATRICIAN, PEDIATRICS

pa·el·la \pä-'e-lǝ; -'äl-yǝ, -'ā-yǝ\ *n* : a saffron-flavored dish of rice, meat, seafood, and vegetables

pa·gan \'pā-gǝn\ *n* [ME, fr. LL *paganus,* fr. L, civilian, country dweller, fr. *pagus* country district] : HEATHEN — **pagan** *adj* — **pa·gan·ism** \-gǝ-,ni-zǝm\ *n*

¹page \'pāj\ *n* : ATTENDANT; *esp* : one employed to deliver messages

²page *vb* **paged; pag·ing 1** : to summon by repeatedly calling out the name of **2** : to send a message to via a pager

³page *n* **1** : a single leaf (as of a book); *also* : a single side of such a leaf **2** : the information at a single World Wide Web address

⁴page *vb* **paged; pag·ing** : to mark or number the pages of

pag·eant \'pa-jənt\ n [ME *pagyn, pad-geant,* lit., scene of a play, fr. AF *pagine, pagent,* fr. ML *pagina,* perh. fr. L, page] : an elaborate spectacle, show, or procession esp. with tableaux or floats — **pag·eant·ry** \-jən-trē\ n

page·boy \'pāj-,bȯi\ n [¹*page*] : an often shoulder-length hairdo with the ends of the hair turned smoothly under

pag·er \'pā-jər\ n : one that pages; *esp* : a small radio receiver that alerts its user to incoming messages

pag·i·nate \'pa-jə-,nāt\ vb **-nat·ed; -nat·ing** : ⁴PAGE

pag·i·na·tion \,pa-jə-'nā-shən\ n 1 : the paging of written or printed matter 2 : the number and arrangement of pages (as of a book)

pa·go·da \pə-'gō-də\ n : a tower with roofs curving upward at the division of each of several stories

paid *past and past part of* PAY

pail \'pāl\ n : a usu. cylindrical vessel with a handle — **pail·ful** \-,fȯl\ n

¹**pain** \'pān\ n 1 : PUNISHMENT, PENALTY 2 : suffering or distress of body or mind; *also* : a basic bodily sensation marked by discomfort (as throbbing or aching) 3 *pl* : great care 4 : one that irks or annoys — **pain·ful** \-fəl\ adj — **pain·ful·ly** adv — **pain·less** adj — **pain·less·ly** adv

²**pain** vb : to cause or experience pain

pain·kill·er \'pān-,ki-lər\ n : something (as a drug) that relieves pain — **pain·kill·ing** adj

pains·tak·ing \-,stā-kiŋ\ adj : taking pains : showing care — **pains·taking** n — **pains·tak·ing·ly** adv

¹**paint** \'pānt\ vb 1 : to apply color, pigment, or paint to 2 : to produce or portray in lines or colors on a surface; *also* : to practice the art of painting 3 : to decorate with colors 4 : to use cosmetics 5 : to describe vividly 6 : SWAB — **paint·er** n

²**paint** n 1 : something produced by painting 2 : MAKEUP 3 : a mixture of a pigment and a liquid that forms a thin adherent coating when spread on a surface; *also* : the dry pigment used in making this mixture 4 : an applied coating of paint

paint·ball \'pānt-,bȯl\ n : a game in which two teams try to capture each other's flag using guns that shoot paint-filled pellets

paint·brush \'pānt-,brəsh\ n : a brush for applying paint

painted lady n : a migratory butterfly with wings mottled in brown, orange, black, and white

painting n 1 : a work (as a picture) produced by painting 2 : the art or occupation of painting

¹**pair** \'per\ n, *pl* **pairs** *also* **pair** [ME *paire,* fr. AF, fr. L *paria* equal things, fr. neut. pl. of *par* equal] 1 : two things of a kind designed for use together 2 : something made up of two corresponding pieces ⟨a ~ of pants⟩ 3 : a set of two people or animals

²**pair** vb 1 : to arrange in pairs 2 : to form

a pair : MATCH 3 : to become associated with another

pai·sa \pī-'sä\ n, *pl* **paisa** *or* **pai·se** \-'sä\ — see *rupee, taka* at MONEY table

pais·ley \'pāz-lē\ adj, *often cap* : decorated with colorful curved abstract figures ⟨a ~ shawl⟩

Pai·ute \'pī-,üt, -,yüt\ n : a member of an American Indian people orig. of Utah, Arizona, Nevada, and California

pa·ja·mas \pə-'jä-məz, -'ja-\ n pl : a loose suit for sleeping or lounging

pal \'pal\ n : a close friend

pal·ace \'pa-ləs\ n [ME *palais,* fr. AF, fr. L *palatium,* fr. *Palatium,* the Palatine Hill in Rome where the emperors' residences were built] 1 : the official residence of a chief of state 2 : MANSION

pal·a·din \'pa-lə-dən\ n 1 : a trusted military leader (as for a medieval prince) 2 : a leading champion of a cause

pa·laes·tra \pə-'les-trə\ n, *pl* **-trae** \-(,)trē\ : a school in ancient Greece or Rome for sports (as wrestling)

pa·lan·quin \,pa-lən-'kēn\ n : an enclosed couch for one person borne on the shoulders of men by means of poles

pal·at·able \'pa-lə-tə-bəl\ adj : agreeable to the taste + Synonyms APPETIZING, SAVORY, TASTY, TOOTHSOME

pal·a·tal \'pa-lə-tᵊl\ adj 1 : of or relating to the palate 2 : pronounced with some part of the tongue near or touching the hard palate ⟨the \y\ in *yeast* and the \sh\ in *she* are ~ sounds⟩

pal·a·tal·ize \'pa-lə-tə-,līz\ vb **-ized; -iz·ing** : to pronounce as or change into a palatal sound — **pal·a·tal·i·za·tion** \,pa-lə-tə-lə-'zā-shən\ n

pal·ate \'pa-lət\ n 1 : the roof of the mouth separating the mouth from the nasal cavity 2 : TASTE

pa·la·tial \pə-'lā-shəl\ adj 1 : of, relating to, or being a palace 2 : MAGNIFICENT

pa·lat·i·nate \pə-'la-tə-nət\ n : the territory of a palatine

¹**pal·a·tine** \'pa-lə-,tīn\ adj 1 : possessing royal privileges; *also* : of or relating to a palatine or a palatinate 2 : of or relating to a palace : PALATIAL

²**palatine** n 1 : a feudal lord having sovereign power within his domains 2 : a high officer of an imperial palace

pa·la·ver \pə-'la-vər, -'lä-\ n [Pg *palavra* word, speech, fr. LL *parabola* parable, speech] 1 : a long parley 2 : idle talk — **palaver** vb

¹**pale** \'pāl\ n 1 : a stake or picket of a fence 2 : an enclosed place; *also* : a district or territory within certain bounds or under a particular jurisdiction 3 : LIMITS, BOUNDS ⟨conduct beyond the ~⟩

²**pale** vb **paled; pal·ing** : to enclose with or as if with pales : FENCE

³**pale** adj **pal·er; pal·est** 1 : deficient in color or intensity : WAN ⟨a ~ face⟩ 2 : lacking in brightness : DIM ⟨a ~ star⟩ 3 : not dark or intense in hue ⟨a ~ blue⟩ — **pale·ness** n

⁴**pale** vb **paled; pal·ing** : to make or become pale

pale ale *n* : a medium-colored very dry ale

pale-face \'pāl-ˌfās\ *n* : a white person

Pa·leo·cene \'pā-lē-ə-ˌsēn\ *adj* : of, relating to, or being the earliest epoch of the Tertiary — **Paleocene** *n*

pa·leo·con·ser·va·tive \ˌpā-lē-ō-kən-ˈsər-və-tiv\ *n* : a conservative espousing traditional principles and policies

pa·le·og·ra·phy \ˌpā-lē-ˈä-grə-fē\ *n* [NL *palaeographia*, fr. Gk *palaios* ancient + *graphein* to write] : the study of ancient writings and inscriptions — **pa·le·og·ra·pher** *n*

Pa·leo·lith·ic \ˌpā-lē-ə-ˈli-thik\ *adj* : of or relating to the earliest period of the Stone Age characterized by rough or chipped stone implements

pa·le·on·tol·o·gy \ˌpā-lē-ˌän-ˈtä-lə-jē\ *n* : a science dealing with the life of past geologic periods as known from fossil remains — **pa·le·on·to·log·i·cal** \-ˌän-tə-ˈlä-ji-kəl\ *adj* — **pa·le·on·tol·o·gist** \-ˌän-ˈtä-lə-jist, -ən-\ *n*

Pa·leo·zo·ic \ˌpā-lē-ə-ˈzō-ik\ *adj* : of, relating to, or being the era of geologic history extending from about 570 million years ago to about 245 million years ago — **Paleozoic** *n*

pal·ette \'pa-lət\ *n* : a thin often oval board that a painter holds and mixes colors on; *also* : the colors on a palette

pal·frey \'pȯl-frē\ *n, pl* **palfreys** *archaic* : a saddle horse that is not a warhorse; *esp* : one suitable for a woman

pa·limp·sest \'pa-ləmp-ˌsest\ *n* [L *palimpsestus*, fr. Gk *palimpsēstos* scraped again] : writing material (as a parchment) used after the erasure of earlier writing

pal·in·drome \'pa-lən-ˌdrōm\ *n* : a word, verse, or sentence (as "Able was I ere I saw Elba") or a number (as 1881) that reads the same backward or forward

pal·ing \'pā-liŋ\ *n* **1** : a fence of pales **2** : material for pales **3** : PALE, PICKET

pal·i·sade \ˌpa-lə-ˈsād\ *n* **1** : a high fence of stakes esp. for defense **2** : a line of steep cliffs

¹pall \'pȯl\ *vb* **1** : to lose in interest or attraction **2** : SATIATE, CLOY

²pall *n* **1** : a heavy cloth draped over a coffin **2** : something that produces a gloomy atmosphere

pal·la·di·um \pə-ˈlā-dē-əm\ *n* : a silver-white metallic chemical element used esp. as a catalyst and in alloys

pall-bear·er \'pȯl-ˌber-ər\ *n* : a person who attends the coffin at a funeral

¹pal·let \'pa-lət\ *n* : a small, hard, or makeshift bed

²pallet *n* : a portable platform for transporting and storing materials

pal·li·ate \'pa-lē-ˌāt\ *vb* **-at·ed; -at·ing** **1** : to ease (as a disease) without curing **2** : to cover by excuses and apologies — **pal·li·a·tion** \ˌpa-lē-ˈā-shən\ *n* — **pal·li·a·tive** \'pa-lē-ˌā-tiv\ *adj or n*

pal·lid \'pa-ləd\ *adj* : PALE, WAN

pal·lor \'pa-lər\ *n* : PALENESS

¹palm \'päm, 'pälm\ *n* [ME, fr. OE, fr. L *palma* palm of the hand, palm tree; fr. the resemblance of the tree's leaves to the outstretched hand] **1** : any of a family of mostly tropical trees, shrubs, or vines usu. with a tall unbranched stem topped by a crown of large leaves **2** : a symbol of victory; *also* : VICTORY

²palm *n* : the underpart of the hand between the fingers and the wrist

³palm *vb* **1** : to conceal in or with the hand **2** : to impose by fraud

pal·mate \'pal-ˌmāt, 'päl-\ *also* **pal·mat·ed** \-ˌmā-təd\ *adj* : resembling a hand with the fingers spread

pal·met·to \pal-ˈme-tō\ *n, pl* **-tos** *or* **-toes** : any of several usu. small palms with fan-shaped leaves

palm·ist·ry \'pä-mə-strē, 'päl-\ *n* : the practice of reading a person's character or future from the markings on the palms — **palm·ist** \'pä-mist, 'päl-\ *n*

Palm Sunday *n* : the Sunday preceding Easter and commemorating Christ's triumphal entry into Jerusalem

palm·top \'päm-ˌtäp, 'pälm-\ *n* : a portable computer small enough to hold in the hand

palmy \'pä-mē, 'päl-\ *adj* **palm·i·er; -est** **1** : abounding in or bearing palms **2** : FLOURISHING, PROSPEROUS

pal·o·mi·no \ˌpa-lə-ˈmē-nō\ *n, pl* **-nos** [AmerSp, fr. Sp, like a dove, fr. L *palumbinus*, fr. *palumbes*, a species of dove] : a horse with a pale cream to golden coat and cream or white mane and tail

pal·pa·ble \'pal-pə-bəl\ *adj* **1** : capable of being touched or felt : TANGIBLE **2** : OBVIOUS, PLAIN ♦ **Synonyms** PERCEPTIBLE, SENSIBLE, APPRECIABLE, TANGIBLE, DETECTABLE — **pal·pa·bly** \-blē\ *adv*

pal·pate \'pal-ˌpāt\ *vb* **pal·pat·ed; pal·pat·ing** : to examine by touch esp. medically — **pal·pa·tion** \pal-ˈpā-shən\ *n*

pal·pi·tate \'pal-pə-ˌtāt\ *vb* **-tat·ed; -tat·ing** : to beat rapidly and strongly : THROB — **pal·pi·ta·tion** \ˌpal-pə-ˈtā-shən\ *n*

pal·sy \'pȯl-zē\ *n, pl* **palsies** **1** : PARALYSIS **2** : a condition marked by tremor — **pal·sied** \-zēd\ *adj*

pal·ter \'pȯl-tər\ *vb* **pal·tered; pal·ter·ing** **1** : to act insincerely : EQUIVOCATE **2** : HAGGLE

pal·try \'pȯl-trē\ *adj* **pal·tri·er; -est** **1** : TRASHY ⟨a ~ pamphlet⟩ **2** : MEAN, DESPICABLE ⟨a ~ trick⟩ **3** : TRIVIAL ⟨~ excuses⟩ **4** : MEAGER, MEASLY ⟨a ~ sum⟩

pam *abbr* pamphlet

pam·pas \'pam-pəz, 'päm-, -pəs\ *n pl* : wide grassy So. American plains

pam·per \'pam-pər\ *vb* : to treat with excessive attention : INDULGE ♦ **Synonyms** CODDLE, HUMOR, BABY, SPOIL

pam·phlet \'pam-flət\ *n* [ME *pamflet* unbound booklet, fr. *Pamphilus seu De Amore* Pamphilus or On Love, popular Latin love poem of the 12th cent.] : an unbound printed publication

pam·phle·teer \ˌpam-flə-ˈtir\ *n* : a writer of pamphlets attacking something or urging a cause

¹pan \'pan\ *n* **1** : a usu. broad, shallow, and open container for domestic use; *also* : something resembling such a container

2 : a basin or depression in land **3** : HARDPAN

²pan *vb* **panned; pan·ning 1** : to wash earth or gravel in a pan in searching for gold **2** : to criticize severely

Pan *abbr* Panama

pan·a·cea \,pa-nə-'sē-ə\ *n* : a remedy for all ills or difficulties : CURE-ALL

pa·nache \pə-'nash, -'näsh\ *n* [MF *pennache*, ultim. fr. LL *pinnaculum* small wing] **1** : an ornamental tuft (as of feathers) esp. on a helmet **2** : dash or flamboyance in style and action

pan·a·ma \'pa-nə-,mä, -,mò\ *n, often cap* : a handmade hat braided from strips of the leaves from a tropical American tree

pan·a·tela \,pa-nə-'te-lə\ *n* : a long slender cigar with straight sides

pan·cake \'pan-,kāk\ *n* : a flat cake of thin batter and fried on both sides

pan·chro·mat·ic \,pan-krō-'ma-tik\ *adj* : sensitive to all colors of visible light ⟨∼ film⟩

pan·cre·as \'paŋ-krē-əs, 'pan-\ *n* : a large compound gland of vertebrates that produces insulin and discharges enzymes into the intestine — **pan·cre·at·ic** \,paŋ-krē-'a-tik, ,pan-\ *adj*

pan·da \'pan-də\ *n* **1** : a long-tailed reddish brown Himalayan mammal related to and resembling the racoon **2** : a large black-and-white mammal of China usu. classified with the bears

pan·dem·ic \pan-'de-mik\ *n* : a widespread outbreak of disease — **pandemic** *adj*

pan·de·mo·ni·um \,pan-də-'mō-nē-əm\ *n* : a wild uproar : TUMULT

¹pan·der \'pan-dər\ *vb* : to act as a pander

²pander *n* **1** : a go-between in love intrigues; *also* : PIMP **2** : a person who caters to or exploits others' desires or weaknesses

P & I *abbr* principal and interest

P & L *abbr* profit and loss

Pan·do·ra's box \pan-'dòr-əz-\ *n* : a prolific source of troubles

pan·dow·dy \pan-'daů-dē\ *n, pl* **-dies** : a deep-dish apple dessert spiced, sweetened, and covered with a crust

pane \'pān\ *n* : a sheet of glass (as in a door or window)

pan·e·gyr·ic \,pa-nə-'jir-ik\ *n* : a eulogistic oration or writing — **pan·e·gyr·ist** \-'jir-ist\ *n*

¹pan·el \'pa-nᵊl\ *n* [ME, piece of cloth, jury list on a piece of parchment, fr. AF, fr. VL **pannellus*, dim. of L *pannus* cloth, rag] **1** : a list of persons appointed for special duty ⟨a jury ∼⟩; *also* : a group of people taking part in a discussion or quiz program **2** : a section of something (as a wall or door) often sunk below the level of the frame; *also* : a flat piece of construction material **3** : a flat piece of wood on which a picture is painted **4** : a mount for controls or dials

²panel *vb* **-eled** *or* **-elled; -el·ing** *or* **-el·ling** : to decorate with panels

paneling *n* : decorative panels

pan·el·ist \'pa-nᵊl-ist\ *n* : a member of a discussion or quiz panel

panel truck *n* : a small motortruck with a fully enclosed body

pang \'paŋ\ *n* : a sudden sharp spasm (as of pain) or attack (as of remorse)

¹pan·han·dle \'pan-,han-dᵊl\ *n* : a narrow projection of a larger territory (as a state) ⟨the Texas ∼⟩

²panhandle *vb* **-dled; -dling** : to ask for money on the street — **pan·han·dler** *n*

¹pan·ic \'pa-nik\ *n* : a sudden overpowering fright; *also* : extreme anxiety ⟨a ∼ disorder⟩ ⟨∼ attacks⟩ ♦ **Synonyms** TERROR, CONSTERNATION, DISMAY, ALARM, DREAD, FEAR — **pan·icky** \-ni-kē\ *adj*

²panic *vb* **pan·icked** \-nikt\; **pan·ick·ing** : to affect or be affected with panic

pan·i·cle \'pa-ni-kəl\ *n* : a branched flower cluster (as of a lilac) in which each branch from the main stem has one or more flowers

pan·jan·drum \pan-'jan-drəm\ *n, pl* **-drums** *also* **-dra** \-drə\ : a powerful personage or pretentious official

pan·nier *also* **pan·ier** \'pan-yər\ *n* : a large basket esp. for bearing on the back

pan·o·ply \'pa-nə-plē\ *n, pl* **-plies 1** : a full suit of armor **2** : a protective covering **3** : an impressive array

pan·o·ra·ma \,pa-nə-'ra-mə, -'rä-\ *n* **1** : a picture unrolled before one's eyes **2** : a complete view in every direction — **pan·oram·ic** \-'ra-mik\ *adj*

pan out *vb* : TURN OUT; *esp* : SUCCEED

pan·sy \'pan-zē\ *n, pl* **pansies** [ME *pancy, pensee*, fr. MF *pensée*, fr. *pensée* thought, fr. *penser* to think, fr. L *pensare* to ponder] : a low-growing garden herb related to the violet; *also* : its showy flower

¹pant \'pant\ *vb* [ME, fr. AF *panteiser*, fr. VL **phantasiare* to have hallucinations, fr. Gk *phantasioun*, fr. *phantasia* appearance, imagination] **1** : to breathe in a labored manner **2** : YEARN **3** : THROB

²pant *n* : a panting breath or sound

³pant *n* **1** : an outer garment covering each leg separately and usu. extending from the waist to the ankle — usu. used in pl. **2** *pl* : PANTIE

pan·ta·loons \,pan-tə-'lünz\ *n pl* **1** : close-fitting pants of the 19th century usu. having straps passing under the instep **2** : loose-fitting usu. shorter than ankle-length trousers

pan·the·ism \'pan-thē-,i-zəm\ *n* : a doctrine that equates God with the forces and laws of the universe — **pan·the·ist** \-ist\ *n* — **pan·the·is·tic** \,pan-thē-'is-tik\ *adj*

pan·the·on \'pan-thē-,än, -ən\ *n* **1** : a temple dedicated to all the gods; *also* : the gods of a people **2** : a group of illustrious people

pan·ther \'pan-thər\ *n, pl* **panthers** *also* **panther 1** : LEOPARD; *esp* : a black one **2** : COUGAR **3** : JAGUAR

pant·ie *or* **panty** \'pan-tē\ *n, pl* **pant·ies** : a woman's or child's short underpants — usu. used in pl.

pan·to·mime \'pan-tə-,mīm\ *n* **1** : a play

in which the actors use no words **2** : expression of something by bodily or facial movements only — **pantomime** *vb* — **pan·to·mim·ic** \ˌpan-tə-ˈmi-mik\ *adj*

pan·try \ˈpan-trē\ *n, pl* **pantries** : a storage room for food or dishes

pant·suit \ˈpant-ˌsüt\ *n* : a woman's outfit consisting usu. of a long jacket and pants of the same material

panty hose *n pl* : a one-piece undergarment for women consisting of hosiery combined with a pantie

panty·waist \ˈpan-tē-ˌwāst\ *n* : SISSY

pap \ˈpap\ *n* : soft food for infants or invalids

pa·pa \ˈpä-pə\ *n* : FATHER

pa·pa·cy \ˈpä-pə-sē\ *n, pl* **-cies 1** : the office of pope **2** : a succession of popes **3** : the term of a pope's reign **4** *cap* : the system of government of the Roman Catholic Church

pa·pa·in \pə-ˈpā-ən, -ˈpī-ən\ *n* : an enzyme in papaya juice used esp. as a meat tenderizer and in medicine

pa·pal \ˈpä-pəl\ *adj* : of or relating to the pope or to the Roman Catholic Church

papaw *var of* PAWPAW

pa·pa·ya \pə-ˈpī-ə\ *n* : a tropical American tree with large yellow black-seeded edible fruit; *also* : its fruit

pa·per \ˈpä-pər\ *n* [ME *papir*, fr. AF, fr. L *papyrus* papyrus, paper, fr. Gk *papyros*] **1** : a pliable substance made usu. of vegetable matter and used to write or print on, to wrap things in, or to cover walls; *also* : a single sheet of this substance **2** : a printed or written document **3** : NEWSPAPER **4** : WALLPAPER — **paper** *adj or vb* — **pa·pery** \ˈpä-pə-rē\ *adj*

pa·per·back \-ˌbak\ *n* : a paper-covered book

pa·per·board \-ˌbȯrd\ *n* : CARDBOARD

pa·per·hang·er \ˈpä-pər-ˌhaŋ-ər\ *n* : one that applies wallpaper — **pa·per·hang·ing** *n*

pa·per·weight \-ˌwāt\ *n* : an object used to hold down loose papers by its weight

pa·pier-mâ·ché \ˌpā-pər-mə-ˈshā, ˌpa-ˌpyä-mə-, -ma-\ *n* [F, lit., chewed paper] : a molding material of wastepaper and additives (as glue) — **papier-mâché** *adj*

pa·pil·la \pə-ˈpi-lə\ *n, pl* **-lae** \-(ˌ)lē, -ˌlī\ [L, nipple] : a small projecting bodily part (as one of the nubs on the surface of the tongue) that resembles a tiny nipple in form — **pap·il·lary** \ˈpa-pə-ˌler-ē, pə-ˈpi-lə-rē\ *adj*

pa·poose \pa-ˈpüs, pə-\ *n* [Narragansett *papoòs*] : a young child of No. American Indian parents

pa·pri·ka \pə-ˈprē-kə, pa-\ *n* [Hung] : a mild red spice made from the fruit of various cultivated sweet peppers

Pap smear \ˈpap-\ *n* : a method for the early detection of cancer esp. of the uterine cervix

Pap test *n* : PAP SMEAR

pap·ule \ˈpa-pyül\ *n* : a small solid usu. conical elevation of the skin — **pap·u·lar** \-pyə-lər\ *adj*

pa·py·rus \pə-ˈpī-rəs\ *n, pl* **-ri** \-(ˌ)rē, -ˌrī\ *or* **-rus·es 1** : a tall grassy sedge of the Nile valley **2** : paper made from papyrus pith

¹par \ˈpär\ *n* **1** : a stated value (as of a security) **2** : a common level : EQUALITY **3** : an accepted standard or normal condition **4** : the score standard set for each hole of a golf course — **par** *adj*

²par *abbr* **1** paragraph **2** parallel **3** parish

par·a·ble \ˈpa-rə-bəl\ *n* : a simple story told to illustrate a moral truth

pa·rab·o·la \pə-ˈra-bə-lə\ *n* : a plane curve formed by a point moving so that its distance from a fixed point is equal to its distance from a fixed line — **par·a·bol·ic** \ˌpa-rə-ˈbä-lik\ *adj*

para·chute \ˈpa-rə-ˌshüt\ *n* [F, fr. *para-* (as in *parasol*) + *chute* fall] : a device for slowing the descent of a person or object through the air that consists of a usu. hemispherical canopy beneath which the person or object is suspended — **parachute** *vb* — **para·chut·ist** \-ˈshü-tist\ *n*

parachute pants *n pl* : baggy casual pants of lightweight fabric

¹pa·rade \pə-ˈrād\ *n* **1** : a pompous display : EXHIBITION **2** : MARCH, PROCESSION; *esp* : a ceremonial formation and march **3** : a place for strolling

²parade *vb* **pa·rad·ed; pa·rad·ing 1** : to march in a parade **2** : PROMENADE **3** : SHOW OFF ⟨*paraded* her knowledge⟩ **4** : MASQUERADE

par·a·digm \ˈpa-rə-ˌdīm, -ˌdim\ *n* **1** : MODEL, PATTERN **2** : a systematic inflection of a verb or noun showing a complete conjugation or declension — **par·a·dig·mat·ic** \ˌpa-rə-dig-ˈma-tik\ *adj*

par·a·dise \ˈpa-rə-ˌdīs, -ˌdīz\ *n* [ME *paradis*, fr. AF, fr. LL *paradisus*, fr. Gk *paradeisos*, lit., enclosed park, of Iranian origin] **1** : HEAVEN **2** : a place or state of bliss

par·a·di·si·a·cal \ˌpa-rə-də-ˈsī-ə-kəl\ *or* **par·a·dis·i·ac** \-ˈdi-zē-ˌak, -sē-\ *adj* : of, relating to, or resembling paradise

par·a·dox \ˈpa-rə-ˌdäks\ *n* : a statement that seems contrary to common sense and yet is perhaps true — **par·a·dox·i·cal** \ˌpa-rə-ˈdäk-si-kəl\ *adj* — **par·a·dox·i·cal·ly** \-k(ə-)lē\ *adv*

par·af·fin \ˈpa-rə-fən\ *n* : a waxy substance used esp. for making candles and sealing foods

para·glid·ing \ˈpa-rə-ˌglī-diŋ\ *n* : the sport of soaring from a slope or cliff using a modified parachute

par·a·gon \ˈpa-rə-ˌgän, -gən\ *n* : a model of perfection : PATTERN

¹para·graph \ˈpa-rə-ˌgraf\ *n* : a subdivision of a written composition that deals with one point or gives the words of one speaker; *also* : a character (as ¶) marking the beginning of a paragraph

²paragraph *vb* : to divide into paragraphs

par·a·keet \ˈpa-rə-ˌkēt\ *n* : any of numerous usu. small slender parrots with a long graduated tail

para·le·gal \ˌpa-rə-ˈlē-gəl\ *adj* : of, relating to, or being a paraprofessional who assists a lawyer — **paralegal** *n*

Par·a·li·pom·e·non \ˌpa-rə-lə-ˈpä-mə-ˌnän\ *n* : CHRONICLES

par·al·lax \ˈpa-rə-ˌlaks\ *n* : the difference in apparent direction of an object as seen from two different points

¹**par·al·lel** \ˈpa-rə-ˌlel\ *adj* [L *parallelus*, fr. Gk *parallēlos*, fr. *para* beside + *allēlōn* of one another, fr. *allos . . . allos* one . . . another, fr. *allos* other] **1** : lying or moving in the same direction but always the same distance apart **2** : similar in essential parts — **par·al·lel·ism** \ˌ-le-ˌli-zəm\ *n*

²**parallel** *n* **1** : a parallel line, curve, or surface **2** : one of the imaginary circles on the earth's surface that parallel the equator and mark the latitude **3** : something essentially similar to another **4** : SIMILARITY, LIKENESS

³**parallel** *vb* **1** : COMPARE **2** : to correspond to **3** : to extend in a parallel direction with

par·al·lel·o·gram \ˌpa-rə-ˈle-lə-ˌgram\ *n* : a 4-sided geometric figure with opposite sides equal and parallel

par·a·lyse *Brit var of* PARALYZE

pa·ral·y·sis \pə-ˈra-lə-səs\ *n, pl* **-y·ses** \-ˌsēz\ : complete or partial loss of function esp. when involving the motion or sensation in a part of the body — **par·a·lyt·ic** \ˌpa-rə-ˈli-tik\ *adj or n*

par·a·lyze \ˈpa-rə-ˌlīz\ *vb* **-lyzed; -lyzing 1** : to affect with paralysis **2** : to make powerless or inactive — **par·a·lyz·ing·ly** *adv*

par·a·me·cium \ˌpa-rə-ˈmē-shəm, -shē-əm, -sē-əm\ *n, pl* **-cia** \-shə, -shē-ə, -sē-ə\ *also* **-ci·ums** : any of a genus of slipper-shaped protozoans that move by cilia

para·med·ic \ˌpa-rə-ˈme-dik\ *also* **para·med·i·cal** \-di-kəl\ *n* **1** : a person who assists a physician in a paramedical capacity **2** : a specially trained medical technician licensed to provide a wide range of emergency services before or during transportation to a hospital

para·med·i·cal \ˌpa-rə-ˈme-di-kəl\ *also* **para·med·ic** \-ˈme-dik\ *adj* : concerned with supplementing the work of trained medical professionals

pa·ram·e·ter \pə-ˈra-mə-tər\ *n* **1** : a quantity whose value characterizes a statistical population or a member of a system (as a family of curves) **2** : a physical property whose value determines the characteristics or behavior of a system **3** : a characteristic element — FACTOR — **para·met·ric** \ˌpa-rə-ˈme-trik\ *adj*

para·mil·i·tary \ˌpa-rə-ˈmi-lə-ˌter-ē\ *adj* : formed on a military pattern esp. as an auxiliary military force

par·a·mount \ˈpa-rə-ˌmaunt\ *adj* : superior to all others : SUPREME ♦ *Synonyms* PREPONDERANT, PREDOMINANT, DOMINANT, CHIEF, SOVEREIGN

par·amour \ˈpa-rə-ˌmúr\ *n* : an illicit lover

para·noia \ˌpa-rə-ˈnói-ə\ *n* : a psychosis marked by delusions and irrational suspi-

cion usu. without hallucinations — **para·noid** \ˈpa-rə-ˌnóid\ *adj or n*

para·nor·mal \ˌpa-rə-ˈnór-məl\ *adj* : not scientifically explainable : SUPERNATURAL

par·a·pet \ˈpa-rə-pət, -ˌpet\ *n* **1** : a protecting rampart **2** : a low wall or railing (as at the edge of a bridge)

par·a·pher·na·lia \ˌpa-rə-fə-ˈnāl-yə, -fər-\ *n sing or pl* **1** : personal belongings **2** : EQUIPMENT, APPARATUS

para·phrase \ˈpa-rə-ˌfrāz\ *n* : a restatement of a text giving the meaning in different words — **paraphrase** *vb*

para·ple·gia \ˌpa-rə-ˈplē-jə, -jē-ə\ *n* : paralysis of the lower trunk and legs — **para·ple·gic** \-jik\ *adj or n*

para·pro·fes·sion·al \-prə-ˈfe-shə-nəl\ *n* : a trained aide who assists a professional — **paraprofessional** *adj*

para·psy·chol·o·gy \ˌpa-rə-sī-ˈkä-lə-jē\ *n* : a field of study concerned with investigating paranormal psychological phenomena (as extrasensory perception) — **para·psy·chol·o·gist** \-jist\ *n*

par·a·site \ˈpa-rə-ˌsīt\ *n* [MF, fr. L *parasitus*, fr. Gk *parasitos*, fr. *para-* beside + *sitos* grain, food] **1** : a plant or animal living in, with, or on another organism usu. to its harm **2** : one depending on another and not making adequate return — **par·a·sit·ic** \ˌpa-rə-ˈsi-tik\ *adj* — **par·a·sit·ism** \ˈpa-rə-sə-ˌti-zəm, -ˌsī-, -ˌsi-ti-\ *n* — **par·a·sit·ize** \-sə-ˌtīz\ *vb*

par·a·si·tol·o·gy \ˌpa-rə-sə-ˈtä-lə-jē\ *n* : a branch of biology dealing with parasites and parasitism esp. among animals — **par·a·si·tol·o·gist** \-jist\ *n*

para·sol \ˈpa-rə-ˌsòl\ *n* [F, fr. It *parasole*, fr. *parare* to shield + *sole* sun, fr. L *sol*] : a lightweight umbrella used as a shield against the sun

para·sym·pa·thet·ic nervous system \ˌpa-rə-ˌsim-pə-ˈthe-tik-\ *n* : the part of the autonomic nervous system that tends to induce secretion, to increase the tone and contractility of smooth muscle, and to slow heart rate

para·thi·on \ˌpa-rə-ˈthī-ən, -ˌän\ *n* : an extremely toxic insecticide

para·thy·roid \-ˈthī-ˌróid\ *n* : PARATHYROID GLAND — **parathyroid** *adj*

parathyroid gland *n* : any of usu. four small endocrine glands adjacent to or embedded in the thyroid gland that produce a hormone (**parathyroid hormone**) concerned with calcium and phosphorus metabolism

para·tran·sit \ˌpa-rə-ˈtran-sət, -zət\ *n* : transportation service that provides individualized rules without fixed routes or timetables

para·troop·er \ˈpa-rə-ˌtrü-pər\ *n* : a member of the paratroops

para·troops \-ˌtrüps\ *n pl* : troops trained to parachute from an airplane

para·ty·phoid \ˌpa-rə-ˈtī-ˌfóid\ *n* : a bacterial food poisoning resembling typhoid fever

par·boil \ˈpär-ˌbói(-ə)l\ *vb* : to boil briefly

¹**par·cel** \ˈpär-səl\ *n* **1** : a tract or plot of

land **2** : COLLECTION, LOT ⟨the story
was a ~ of lies⟩ **3** : a wrapped bundle
: PACKAGE

²par·cel vb **-celed** or **-celled; -cel·ing** or
-cel·ling : to divide into portions

parcel post n **1** : a mail service handling
parcels **2** : packages handled by parcel
post

parch \'pärch\ vb **1** : to toast under dry
heat **2** : to shrivel with heat

parch·ment \'pärch-mənt\ n : the skin of
an animal prepared for writing on; also
: a writing on such material

pard \'pärd\ n : LEOPARD

¹par·don \'pär-d³n\ n : excuse of an offense without penalty; esp : an official
release from legal punishment

²pardon vb : to free from penalty : EX-
CUSE, FORGIVE — **par·don·able** \'pär-
d³n-ə-bəl\ adj

par·don·er \'pär-d³n-ər\ n **1** : a medieval
preacher delegated to raise money for religious works by soliciting offerings and
granting indulgences **2** : one that par-
dons

pare \'per\ vb **pared; par·ing** **1** : to trim
off an outside part (as the skin or rind)
of **2** : to reduce as if by paring ⟨~ ex-
penses⟩ — **par·er** n

par·e·gor·ic \,per-ə-'gòr-ik\ n : an alcoholic preparation of opium and camphor
used esp. to relieve pain

par·ent \'per-ənt\ n **1** : one that begets or
brings forth offspring : FATHER, MOTH-
ER **2** : one who brings up and cares for
another **3** : SOURCE, ORIGIN — **par·ent·
age** \-ən-tij\ n — **pa·ren·tal** \pə-'rent-³l\
adj — **par·ent·hood** n

pa·ren·the·sis \pə-'ren-thə-səs\ n, pl
-the·ses \-,sēz\ **1** : a word, phrase, or
sentence inserted in a passage to explain
or modify the thought **2** : one of a pair
of punctuation marks ( ) used esp. to enclose parenthetic matter — **par·en·thet·
ic** \,per-ən-'the-tik\ or **par·en·thet·i·cal**
\-ti-kəl\ adj — **par·en·thet·i·cal·ly**
\-k(ə-)lē\ adv

pa·ren·the·size \pə-'ren-thə-,sīz\ vb
-sized; -siz·ing : to make a parenthesis
of

par·ent·ing \'per-ən-tiŋ\ n : the raising of
a child by its parents

pa·re·sis \pə-'rē-səs, 'par-ə-\ n, pl **pa·re·
ses** \-,sēz\ **1** : a usu. incomplete paralysis;
also : insanity caused by syphilitic alteration of the brain that leads to dementia
and paralysis

par ex·cel·lence \,pär-,ek-sə-'läⁿs\ adj [F,
lit., by excellence] : being the best of a
kind : PREEMINENT

par·fait \pär-'fā\ n [F, lit., something per-
fect] : a cold dessert made of layers of
fruit, syrup, ice cream, and whipped
cream

pa·ri·ah \pə-'rī-ə\ n : OUTCAST

pa·ri·etal \pə-'rī-ə-t³l\ adj **1** : of, relating
to, or forming the walls of an anatomical
structure **2** : of or relating to college living or its regulation

pari–mu·tu·el \,per-i-'myü-chə-wəl\ n : a
betting system in which winners share the

total stakes minus a percentage for the
management

paring n : a pared-off piece

pa·ri pas·su \'pa-ri-'pa-sü\ adv or adj [L,
with equal step] : at an equal rate or pace

par·ish \'per-ish\ n **1** : a church district
in the care of one pastor; also : the residents of such an area **2** : a local church
community **3** : a civil division of the
state of Louisiana : COUNTY

pa·rish·io·ner \pə-'ri-shə-nər\ n : a member or resident of a parish

par·i·ty \'per-ə-tē\ n, pl **-ties** : EQUALITY,
EQUIVALENCE

¹park \'pärk\ n **1** : a tract of ground kept
as a game preserve or recreation area **2**
: a place where vehicles (as automobiles)
are parked **3** : an enclosed stadium used
esp. for ball games

²park vb **1** : to leave a vehicle temporarily
(as in a parking lot or garage) **2** : to set
and leave temporarily

par·ka \'pär-kə\ n : a very warm jacket
with a hood

Par·kin·son's disease \'pär-kən-sənz-\ n
: a chronic progressive neurological disease chiefly of later life marked esp. by
tremor and weakness of resting muscles
and by a shuffling gait

Parkinson's Law n : an observation in office organization: work expands so as to
fill the time available for its completion

park·way \'pärk-,wā\ n : a broad landscaped thoroughfare

par·lance \'pär-ləns\ n **1** : SPEECH **2**
: manner of speaking ⟨military ~⟩

¹par·lay \'pär-,lā, -lē\ vb : to increase or
change into something of much greater
value

²parlay n : a series of bets in which the
original stake plus its winnings are risked
on successive wagers

par·ley \'pär-lē\ n, pl **parleys** : a conference usu. over matters in dispute : DIS-
CUSSION — **parley** vb

par·lia·ment \'pär-lə-mənt\ n [ME, fr. AF
parlement, fr. parler to speak, fr. ML
parabolāre, fr. LL parabola speech, para-
ble] **1** : a formal governmental conference **2** cap : an assembly that constitutes the supreme legislative body of a
country (as the United Kingdom) — **par·
lia·men·ta·ry** \,pär-lə-'men-tə-rē\ adj

par·lia·men·tar·i·an \,pär-lə-,men-'ter-ē-
ən\ n **1** often cap : an adherent of the
parliament during the English Civil War
2 : an expert in parliamentary procedure

par·lor \'pär-lər\ n **1** : a room for conversation or the reception of guests **2** : a
place of business ⟨beauty ~⟩

par·lour \'pär-lər\ chiefly Brit var of PAR-
LOR

par·lous \'pär-ləs\ adj : full of danger or
risk : PRECARIOUS — **par·lous·ly** adv

Par·me·san \'pär-mə-,zän, -,zhän, -,zan\
n : a hard dry cheese with a sharp flavor

par·mi·gia·na \,pär-mi-'jä-nə, ,pär-mi-
'zhän\ or **par·mi·gia·no** \-'jä-(,)nō\ adj
: made or covered with Parmesan cheese
⟨veal ~⟩

pa·ro·chi·al \pə-'rō-kē-əl\ adj **1** : of or

relating to a church parish **2** : limited in scope : NARROW, PROVINCIAL — **pa·ro·chi·al·ism** \-ə-ˌli-zəm\ n

parochial school n : a school maintained by a religious body

par·o·dy \ˈper-ə-dē\ n, pl **-dies** [L parodia, fr. Gk parōidia, fr. para- beside + aidein to sing] : a humorous or satirical imitation — **parody** vb

pa·role \pə-ˈrōl\ n : a conditional release of a prisoner whose sentence has not expired — **parole** vb — **pa·rol·ee** \-ˌrō-ˈlē, -ˈrō-ˌlē\ n

par·ox·ysm \ˈpa-rək-ˌsi-zəm, pə-ˈräk-\ n : a sudden sharp attack (as of pain or coughing) : CONVULSION — **par·ox·ys·mal** \ˌpa-rək-ˈsiz-məl, pə-ˌräk-\ adj

par·quet \ˈpär-ˌkā, pär-ˈkā\ n [F] **1** : a flooring of parquetry **2** : the lower floor of a theater; esp : the forward part of the orchestra

par·que·try \ˈpär-kə-trē\ n, pl **-tries** : fine woodwork inlaid in patterns

par·ri·cide \ˈpa-rə-ˌsīd\ n **1** : one that murders a parent or a close relative **2** : the act of a parricide

par·rot \ˈper-ət\ n : any of numerous bright-colored tropical birds that have a stout hooked bill

parrot fever n : PSITTACOSIS

par·ry \ˈper-ē\ vb **par·ried; par·ry·ing 1** : to ward off a weapon or blow **2** : to evade esp. by an adroit answer — **parry** n

parse \ˈpärs also ˈpärz\ vb **parsed; parsing** : to give a grammatical description of a word or a group of words

par·sec \ˈpär-ˌsek\ n : a unit of measure for interstellar space equal to 3.26 light-years

par·si·mo·ny \ˈpär-sə-ˌmō-nē\ n : extreme or excessive frugality — **par·si·mo·ni·ous** \ˌpär-sə-ˈmō-nē-əs\ adj — **par·si·mo·ni·ous·ly** adv

pars·ley \ˈpär-slē\ n : a garden plant related to the carrot that has finely divided leaves used as a seasoning or garnish; also : the leaves

pars·nip \ˈpär-snəp\ n : a garden plant related to the carrot that has a long edible usu. whitish root which is cooked as a vegetable; also : the root

par·son \ˈpär-sⁿn\ n [ME persone, fr. AF, fr. ML persona, lit., person, fr. L] : MINISTER 2, PASTOR

par·son·age \ˈpär-sə-nij\ n : a house provided by a church for its pastor

¹part \ˈpärt\ n **1** : a division or portion of a whole **2** : the melody or score for a particular voice or instrument **3** : a spare piece for a machine **4** : DUTY, FUNCTION **5** : one of the sides in a dispute **6** : ROLE; also : an actor's lines in a play **7** pl : TALENTS, ABILITY ⟨a man of many ~s⟩ **8** : the line where one's hair divides (as in combing)

²part vb **1** : to take leave of someone **2** : to divide or break into parts : SEPARATE **3** : to go away : DEPART; also : DIE **4** : to give up possession ⟨~ed with her jewels⟩ **5** : APPORTION, SHARE

³part abbr **1** participial; participle **2** particular

par·take \pär-ˈtāk\ vb **-took** \-ˈtůk\; **-taken** \-ˈtā-kən\; **-tak·ing 1** : to have a share or part **2** : to take a portion (as of food) — **par·tak·er** n

par·terre \pär-ˈter\ n [F, fr. MF, fr. par terre on the ground] **1** : an ornamental garden with paths between the flower beds **2** : the part of a theater floor behind the orchestra

par·the·no·gen·e·sis \ˌpär-thə-nō-ˈje-nə-səs\ n [NL, fr. Gk parthenos virgin + L genesis genesis] : development of a new individual from an unfertilized usu. female sex cell — **par·the·no·ge·net·ic** \-jə-ˈne-tik\ adj

par·tial \ˈpär-shəl\ adj **1** : not total or general : affecting a part only **2** : favoring one party over the other : BIASED **3** : markedly fond — used with to — **par·tial·i·ty** \ˌpär-shē-ˈa-lə-tē\ n — **par·tial·ly** adv

par·tic·i·pate \pär-ˈti-sə-ˌpāt\ vb **-pat·ed; -pat·ing 1** : to take part in something ⟨~ in a game⟩ **2** : SHARE — **par·tic·i·pant** \-pənt\ adj or n — **par·tic·i·pa·tion** \-ˌti-sə-ˈpā-shən\ n — **par·tic·i·pa·tor** \-ˈti-sə-ˌpā-tər\ n — **par·tic·i·pa·to·ry** \-ˈti-sə-pə-ˌtȯr-ē\ adj

par·ti·ci·ple \ˈpär-tə-ˌsi-pəl\ n : a word having the characteristics of both verb and adjective — **par·ti·cip·i·al** \ˌpär-tə-ˈsi-pē-əl\ adj

par·ti·cle \ˈpär-ti-kəl\ n **1** : a very small bit of matter **2** : a unit of speech (as an article, preposition, or conjunction) expressing some general aspect of meaning or some connective or limiting relation

par·ti·cle·board \-ˌbȯrd\ n : a board made of very small pieces of wood bonded together

par·ti–col·or \ˌpär-tē-ˈkə-lər\ or **par·ti–col·ored** \-lərd\ adj : showing different colors or tints; esp : having one main color broken by patches of one or more other colors

¹par·tic·u·lar \pər-ˈti-kyə-lər\ adj **1** : of or relating to a specific person or thing ⟨the laws of a ~ state⟩ **2** : DISTINCTIVE, SPECIAL ⟨the ~ point of his talk⟩ **3** : SEPARATE, INDIVIDUAL ⟨each ~ hair⟩ **4** : attentive to details : PRECISE **5** : hard to please : EXACTING — **par·tic·u·lar·i·ty** \-ˌti-kyə-ˈlar-ə-tē\ n — **par·tic·u·lar·ly** adv

²particular n : an individual fact or detail

par·tic·u·lar·ise Brit var of PARTICULARIZE

par·tic·u·lar·ize \pər-ˈti-kyə-lə-ˌrīz\ vb **-ized; -iz·ing 1** : to state in detail : SPECIFY **2** : to go into details

par·tic·u·late \pər-ˈti-kyə-lət, pär-, -ˌlāt\ adj : relating to or existing as minute separate particles — **particulate** n

¹part·ing n : a place or point of separation or divergence

²parting adj : given, taken, or done at parting ⟨a ~ kiss⟩

par·ti·san also **par·ti·zan** \ˈpär-tə-zən, -sən\ n **1** : one that takes the part of another : ADHERENT **2** : GUERRILLA — **partisan** adj — **par·ti·san·ship** n

par·tite \'pär-ˌtīt\ *adj* : divided into a usu. specified number of parts

par·ti·tion \pär-'ti-shən\ *n* **1** : DIVISION **2** : something that divides or separates; *esp* : an interior dividing wall — **parti·tion** *vb*

par·ti·tive \'pär-tə-tiv\ *adj* : of, relating to, or denoting a part

part·ly \'pärt-lē\ *adv* : in part : in some measure or degree

part·ner \'pärt-nər\ *n* **1** : ASSOCIATE, COLLEAGUE **2** : either of two persons who dance together **3** : one who plays on the same team with another **4** : SPOUSE **5** : one of two or more persons contractually associated as joint principals in a business — **part·ner·ship** *n*

part of speech : a class of words (as nouns or verbs) distinguished according to the kind of idea denoted and the function performed in a sentence

par·tridge \'pär-trij\ *n, pl* **partridge** *or* **par·tridg·es** : any of various stout-bodied Old World game birds

part—song \'pärt-ˌsóŋ\ *n* : a song with two or more voice parts

part—time \-'tīm\ *adj or adv* : involving or working less than a full or regular schedule — **part—tim·er** \-ˌtī-mər\ *n*

par·tu·ri·tion \ˌpär-tə-'ri-shən, ˌpär-chə-, ˌpär-tyü-\ *n* : CHILDBIRTH

part·way \'pärt-'wā\ *adv* : to some extent : PARTLY

par·ty \'pär-tē\ *n, pl* **parties** **1** : a person or group taking one side of a question; *esp* : a group of persons organized for the purpose of directing the policies of a government **2** : a person or group concerned in an action or affair : PARTICIPANT **3** : a group of persons detailed for a common task **4** : a social gathering

party animal *n* : a person known for frequent attendance at parties

par·ty-go·er \'pär-tē-ˌgō-ər\ *n* : a person who attends a party or who attends parties frequently

par·ve·nu \'pär-və-ˌnü, -ˌnyü\ *n* [F, fr. pp. of *parvenir* to arrive, fr. L *pervenire*, fr. *per* through + *venire* to come] : one who has recently or suddenly risen to wealth or power but has not yet secured the social position associated with it

pas \'pä\ *n, pl* **pas** *same or* \'päz\ : a dance step or combination of steps

pas·cal \pas-'kal\ *n* : a unit of pressure in the metric system equal to one newton per square meter

pas·chal \'pas-kəl\ *adj* : of, relating to, appropriate for, or used during Passover or Easter ceremonies

pa·sha \'pä-shə, 'pa-; pə-'shä\ *n* : a man (as formerly a governor in Turkey) of high rank

pash·mi·na \ˌpəsh-'mē-nə\ *n* : a fine wool from the undercoat of domestic Himalayan goats; *also* : a shawl made from this wool

¹pass \'pas\ *vb* **1** : MOVE, PROCEED **2** : to go away; *also* : DIE **3** : to move past, beyond, or over **4** : to allow to elapse : SPEND **5** : to go or make way through **6** : to go or allow to go unchallenged **7** : to undergo transfer **8** : to render a legal judgment **9** : OCCUR **10** : to secure the approval of (as a legislature) **11** : to go or cause to go through an inspection, test, or course of study successfully **12** : to be regarded **13** : CIRCULATE ⟨∼ a note⟩ **14** : VOID **2** **15** : to transfer the ball or puck to another player **16** : to decline to bid or bet on one's hand in a card game **17** : to give a base on balls to **18** : to let something go by without accepting ⟨∼ed on his offer⟩ — **pass·er** *n*

²pass *n* : a gap in a mountain range

³pass *n* **1** : the act or an instance of passing **2** : REALIZATION, ACCOMPLISHMENT **3** : a state of affairs **4** : a written authorization to leave, enter, or move about freely **5** : a transfer of a ball or puck from one player to another **6** : BASE ON BALLS **7** : EFFORT, TRY **8** : a sexually inviting gesture or approach

⁴pass *abbr* **1** passenger **2** passive

pass·able \'pa-sə-bəl\ *adj* **1** : capable of being passed or traveled on **2** : just good enough : TOLERABLE — **pass·ably** \-blē\ *adv*

pas·sage \'pa-sij\ *n* **1** : a means (as a road or corridor) of passing **2** : the action or process of passing **3** : a voyage esp. by sea or air **4** : a right or permission to pass **5** : ENACTMENT **6** : a usu. brief portion or section (as of a book)

pas·sage·way \-ˌwā\ *n* : a way that allows passage

pass·book \'pas-ˌbúk\ *n* : BANKBOOK

pas·sé \pa-'sā\ *adj* **1** : past one's prime **2** : not up-to-date : OUTMODED

pas·sel \'pa-səl\ *n* : a large number

pas·sen·ger \'pa-sᵊn-jər\ *n* : a traveler in a public or private conveyance

pass·er·by \'pa-sər-ˌbī\ *n, pl* **pass·ers·by** : one who passes by

pas·ser·ine \'pa-sə-ˌrīn\ *adj* : of or relating to the large order of birds comprising singing birds that perch

pas·sim \'pa-səm\ *adv* [L, fr. *passus* scattered, fr. pp. of *pandere* to spread] : here and there : THROUGHOUT

pass·ing *n* : the act of one that passes or causes to pass; *esp* : DEATH

pas·sion \'pa-shən\ *n* **1** *often cap* : the sufferings of Christ between the night of the Last Supper and his death **2** : strong feeling; *also, pl* : the emotions as distinguished from reason **3** : RAGE, ANGER **4** : LOVE; *also* : an object of affection or enthusiasm **5** : sexual desire — **pas·sion·ate** \'pa-shə-nət\ *adj* — **pas·sion·ate·ly** *adv* — **pas·sion·less** *adj*

pas·sion·flow·er \'pa-shən-ˌflaú-(ə)r\ *n* [fr. the fancied resemblance of parts of the flower to the instruments of Christ's crucifixion] : any of a genus of chiefly tropical woody climbing vines or erect herbs with showy flowers and pulpy often edible berries (**passion fruit**)

pas·sive \'pa-siv\ *adj* **1** : not active : acted upon **2** : asserting that the grammatical subject is subjected to or affected by the action represented by the verb ⟨∼

voice⟩ **3** : making use of the sun's heat usu. without the aid of mechanical devices **4** : SUBMISSIVE, PATIENT — **passive** n — **pas·sive·ly** adv — **pas·siv·i·ty** \pa-ˈsi-və-tē\ n

pas·sive-ma·trix \-ˈmā-triks\ adj : of, relating to, or being on LCD in which pixels are controlled in groups

pass-key \ˈpas-ˌkē\ n : a key for opening two or more locks

pass out vb : to lose consciousness

Pass-over \ˈpas-ˌō-vər\ n [fr. the exemption of the Israelites from the slaughter of the firstborn in Egypt (Exod 12:23–27)] : a Jewish holiday celebrated in March or April in commemoration of the Hebrews' liberation from slavery in Egypt

pass-port \ˈpas-ˌpȯrt\ n : an official document issued by a country upon request to a citizen requesting protection during travel abroad

pass up vb : DECLINE, REJECT

pass-word \ˈpas-ˌwərd\ n **1** : a word or phrase that must be spoken by a person before being allowed to pass a guard **2** : a sequence of characters required for access to a computer system

¹past \ˈpast\ adj : AGO ⟨10 years ∼⟩ **2** : just gone or elapsed ⟨the ∼ month⟩ **3** : having existed or taken place in a period before the present : BYGONE **4** : of, relating to, or constituting a verb tense that expresses time gone by

²past prep or adv : BEYOND

³past n **1** : time gone by **2** : something that happened or was done in a former time : the past tense; also : a verb form in it **3** : a secret past life

pas·ta \ˈpäs-tə\ n [It] **1** : a paste in processed form (as macaroni) or in the form of fresh dough (as ravioli) **2** : a dish of cooked pasta

¹paste \ˈpāst\ n [ME, fr. AF, fr. LL pasta dough, paste] **1** : DOUGH **2** : a smooth food product made by evaporation or grinding ⟨tomato ∼⟩ **3** : a shaped dough (as spaghetti or ravioli) **4** : a preparation (as of flour and water) for sticking things together **5** : a brilliant glass used for artificial gems

²paste vb past·ed; past·ing : to cause to adhere by paste : STICK

paste-board \ˈpāst-ˌbȯrd\ n : CARD-BOARD

¹pas·tel \pas-ˈtel\ n **1** : a paste made of powdered pigment; also : a crayon of such paste **2** : a drawing in pastel **3** : a pale or light color

²pastel adj **1** : of or relating to a pastel **2** : pale in color

pas·tern \ˈpas-tərn\ n : the part of a horse's foot extending from the fetlock to the top of the hoof

pas·teur·i·za·tion \ˌpas-chə-rə-ˈzā-shən, ˌpas-tə-\ n : partial sterilization of a substance (as milk) by heat or radiation — **pas·teur·ize** \ˈpas-chə-ˌrīz, ˈpas-tə-\ vb — **pas·teur·iz·er** n

pas·tiche \pas-ˈtēsh\ n : a composition (as in literature or music) made up of selections from different works

pas·tille \pas-ˈtēl\ n : LOZENGE 2

pas·time \ˈpas-ˌtīm\ n : DIVERSION; esp : something that serves to make time pass agreeably

pas·tor \ˈpas-tər\ n [ME pastour, fr. AF, fr. L pastor, herdsman, fr. pāscere to feed, pasture, nurture] : a minister or priest serving a local church or parish — **pas·tor·ate** \-tə-rət\ n

¹pas·to·ral \ˈpas-tə-rəl\ adj **1** : of or relating to shepherds or to rural life **2** : of or relating to spiritual guidance esp. of a congregation **3** : of or relating to the pastor of a church

²pastoral n : a literary work dealing with shepherds or rural life

pas·to·rale \ˌpas-tə-ˈräl, -ˈral\ n [It] : a musical composition having a pastoral theme

past participle n : a participle that typically expresses completed action, that is one of the principal parts of the verb, and that is used in the formation of perfect tenses in the active voice and of all tenses in the passive voice

pas·tra·mi \pə-ˈsträ-mē\ n [Yiddish pastrame] : a highly seasoned smoked beef prepared esp. from shoulder cuts

pas·try \ˈpā-strē\ n, pl pastries : sweet baked goods made of dough or with a crust made of enriched dough

pas·tur·age \ˈpas-chə-rij\ n : PASTURE

¹pas·ture \ˈpas-chər\ n **1** : plants (as grass) for the feeding esp. of grazing livestock **2** : land or a plot of land used for grazing

²pasture vb pas·tured; pas·tur·ing **1** : GRAZE **2** : to use as pasture

pasty \ˈpā-stē\ adj past·i·er; -est : resembling paste; esp : pallid and unhealthy in appearance

¹pat \ˈpat\ n **1** : a light tap esp. with the hand or a flat instrument; also : the sound made by it **2** : something (as butter) shaped into a small flat usu. square individual portion

²pat adv : in a pat manner : PERFECTLY

³pat vb pat·ted; pat·ting **1** : to strike lightly with a flat instrument **2** : to flatten, smooth, or put into place or shape with a pat **3** : to tap gently or lovingly with the hand

⁴pat adj **1** : exactly suited to the occasion : APT **2** : memorized exactly **3** : UN-YIELDING ⟨stood ∼ on the issue⟩

PAT abbr point after touchdown

pa·ta·ca \pə-ˈtä-kə\ n — see MONEY table

¹patch \ˈpach\ n **1** : a piece used to cover a torn or worn place; also : one worn on a garment as an ornament or insignia **2** : a small area distinct from that about it **3** : a shield worn over the socket of an injured or missing eye

²patch vb **1** : to mend or cover with a patch **2** : to make of fragments **3** : to repair usu. in hasty fashion

patch·ou·li \ˈpa-chə-lē, pə-ˈchü-lē\ n : a heavy perfume made from the fragrant essential oil of an Asian mint; also : the plant itself

patch test n : a test for allergic sensitivity made by applying to the unbroken skin small pads soaked with the allergen to be tested

patch·work \'pach-ˌwərk\ *n* : something made of pieces of different materials, shapes, or colors

patchy \'pa-chē\ *adj* **patch·i·er; -est** : marked by or consisting of patches; *also* : irregular in appearance or quality — **patch·i·ness** \-chē-nəs\ *n*

pate \'pāt\ *n* : HEAD; *esp* : the crown of the head

pâ·té *also* **pate** \pä-ˈtā\ *n* [F] **1** : a meat or fish pie or patty **2** : a spread of finely chopped or pureed seasoned meat

pa·tel·la \pə-ˈte-lə\ *n, pl* **-lae** \-ˈte-(ˌ)lē, -ˌlī\ *or* **-las** [L] : KNEECAP — **pa·tel·lar** \-ˈte-lər\ *adj*

pat·en \'pa-tᵊn\ *n* **1** : PLATE; *esp* : one of precious metal for the eucharistic bread **2** : a thin disk

¹pa·tent *1 & 4 are* 'pa-tᵊnt, *Brit also* 'pā-, 2 & 3 are* 'pa-tᵊnt, 'pā-\ *adj* **1** : open to public inspection — used chiefly in the phrase *letters patent* **2** : free from obstruction **3** : EVIDENT, OBVIOUS **4** : protected by a patent ✦ *Synonyms* MANIFEST, DISTINCT, APPARENT, PALPABLE, PLAIN, CLEAR — **pat·ent·ly** *adv*

²pat·ent \'pa-tᵊnt, *Brit also* 'pā-\ *n* **1** : an official document conferring a right or privilege **2** : a document securing to an inventor for a term of years exclusive right to his or her invention **3** : something patented

³pat·ent *vb* : to secure by patent

pat·en·tee \ˌpa-tᵊn-ˈtē, *Brit also* ˌpā-\ *n* : one to whom a grant is made or a privilege secured by patent

pat·ent medicine \'pa-tᵊnt-\ *n* : a packaged nonprescription drug protected by a trademark; *also* : any proprietary drug

pa·ter·fa·mil·i·as \ˌpā-tər-fə-ˈmi-lē-əs\ *n, pl* **pa·tres·fa·mil·i·as** \ˌpā-ˌtrēz-\ [L] : the father of a family : the male head of a household

pa·ter·nal \pə-ˈtər-nᵊl\ *adj* **1** : FATHERLY **2** : related through or inherited or derived from a father — **pa·ter·nal·ly** *adv*

pa·ter·nal·ism \-nə-ˌli-zəm\ *n* : a system under which an authority treats those under its control paternally (as by regulating their conduct and supplying their needs)

¹pa·ter·ni·ty \pə-ˈtər-nə-tē\ *n* **1** : FATHERHOOD **2** : descent from a father

²paternity *adj* **1** : granted to a father ⟨~ leave⟩ **2** : of or relating to the determination of paternity ⟨a ~ suit⟩

¹path \'path, 'päth\ *n, pl* **paths** \'pathz, 'paths, 'päthz, 'päths\ **1** : a trodden way **2** : ROUTE, COURSE — **path·less** *adj*

²path *or* **pathol** *abbr* pathology

path·break·ing \'path-ˌbrā-kiŋ\ *adj* : TRAILBLAZING

pa·thet·ic \pə-ˈthe-tik\ *adj* **1** : evoking tenderness, pity, or sorrow **2** : pitifully inadequate ⟨a ~ performance⟩ ✦ *Synonyms* PITIFUL, PITEOUS, PITIABLE, POOR — **pa·thet·i·cal·ly** \-ti-k(ə-)lē\ *adv*

path·find·er \'path-ˌfīn-dər, 'päth-\ *n* : one that discovers a way; *esp* : one that

explores untraveled regions to mark out a new route

patho·gen \'pa-thə-jən\ *n* : a specific agent (as a bacterium) causing disease — **patho·gen·ic** \ˌpa-thə-ˈje-nik\ *adj* — **patho·ge·nic·i·ty** \-jə-ˈni-sə-tē\ *n*

pa·thog·ra·phy \pə-ˈthä-grə-fē\ *n* : biography focusing on a person's flaws and misfortunes

pa·thol·o·gy \pə-ˈthä-lə-jē\ *n, pl* **-gies** **1** : the study of the essential nature of disease **2** : the abnormality of structure and function characteristic of a disease **3** : deviation giving rise to social ills — **path·o·log·i·cal** \ˌpa-thə-ˈlä-ji-kəl\ *adj* — **pa·thol·o·gist** \pə-ˈthä-lə-jist\ *n*

pa·thos \'pā-ˌthäs, -ˌthȯs\ *n* : an element in experience or artistic representation evoking pity or compassion

path·way \'path-ˌwā, 'päth-\ *n* : PATH

pa·tience \'pā-shəns\ *n,* **1** : the capacity, habit, or fact of being patient **2** *chiefly Brit* : SOLITAIRE 2

¹pa·tient \'pā-shənt\ *adj* **1** : bearing pain or trials without complaint **2** : showing self-control : CALM **3** : STEADFAST, PERSEVERING — **pa·tient·ly** *adv*

²patient *n* : one under medical care

pa·ti·na \'pa-tə-nə, pə-ˈtē-\ *n, pl* **pa·ti·nas** \-nəz\ *or* **pa·ti·nae** \'pa-tə-ˌnē, -ˌnī\ **1** : a green film formed on copper and bronze by exposure to moist air **2** : a superficial covering or exterior

pa·tio \'pa-tē-ˌō, 'pä-\ *n, pl* **pa·ti·os** **1** : COURTYARD **2** : an often paved area near a dwelling used esp. for outdoor dining

pa·tois \'pa-ˌtwä\ *n, pl* **pa·tois** \-ˌtwäz\ [F] **1** : a dialect other than the standard dialect; *esp* : uneducated or provincial speech **2** : JARGON 2

pa·tri·arch \'pā-trē-ˌärk\ *n* **1** : a man revered as father or founder (as of a tribe) **2** : a venerable old man **3** : an ecclesiastical dignitary (as the bishop of an Eastern Orthodox see) — **pa·tri·ar·chal** \ˌpā-trē-ˈär-kəl\ *adj* — **pa·tri·arch·ate** \'pā-trē-ˌär-kət, -ˌkät\ *n* — **pa·tri·ar·chy** \-ˌär-kē\ *n*

pa·tri·cian \pə-ˈtri-shən\ *n* : a person of high birth : ARISTOCRAT — **patrician** *adj*

pat·ri·cide \'pa-trə-ˌsīd\ *n* **1** : one who murders his or her own father **2** : the murder of one's own father

pat·ri·mo·ny \'pa-trə-ˌmō-nē\ *n* : something (as an estate) inherited or derived esp. from one's father : HERITAGE — **pat·ri·mo·ni·al** \ˌpa-trə-ˈmō-nē-əl\ *adj*

pa·tri·ot \'pā-trē-ət, -ˌät\ *n* [MF *patriote* compatriot, fr. LL *patriota,* fr. Gk *patriōtēs,* fr. *patria* lineage, fr. *patr-, patēr* father] : one who loves his or her country — **pa·tri·ot·ic** \ˌpā-trē-ˈä-tik\ *adj* — **pa·tri·ot·i·cal·ly** \-ti-k(ə-)lē\ *adv* — **pa·tri·o·tism** \'pā-trē-ə-ˌti-zəm\ *n*

pa·tris·tic \pə-ˈtris-tik\ *adj* : of or relating to the church fathers or their writings

¹pa·trol \pə-ˈtrōl\ *n* : the action of going the rounds (as of an area) for observation or the maintenance of security; *also* : a person or group performing such an action

²**patrol** *vb* **pa·trolled; pa·trol·ling** : to carry out a patrol

pa·trol·man \pə-'trōl-mən\ *n* : a police officer assigned to a beat

patrol wagon *n* : PADDY WAGON

pa·tron \'pā-trən\ *n* [ME, fr. AF, fr. ML & L; ML *patronus* patron saint, patron of a benefice, pattern, fr. L, defender, fr. *patr-, pater* father] **1** : a person chosen or named as special protector **2** : a wealthy or influential supporter ⟨∼ of poets⟩; *also* : BENEFACTOR **3** : a regular client or customer ⟨diner ∼s⟩

pa·tron·age \'pa-trə-nij, 'pā-\ *n* **1** : the support or influence of a patron **2** : the trade of customers **3** : control of appointment to government jobs

pa·tron·ess \'pā-trə-nəs\ *n* : a woman who is a patron

pa·tron·ise *Brit var of* PATRONIZE

pa·tron·ize \'pā-trə-ˌnīz, 'pa-\ *vb* **-ized; -iz·ing 1** : to be a customer of **2** : to treat condescendingly, haughtily, or coolly

pat·ro·nym·ic \ˌpa-trə-'ni-mik\ *n* : a name derived from the name of one's father or a paternal ancestor usu. by the addition of an affix

pa·troon \pə-'trün\ *n* : the proprietor of a manorial estate esp. in New York under Dutch rule

pat·sy \'pat-sē\ *n, pl* **pat·sies** : a person who is easily duped or victimized

¹**pat·ter** \'pa-tər\ *vb* : to talk glibly or mechanically ◆ **Synonyms** CHATTER, PRATE, CHAT, PRATTLE, BABBLE

²**patter** *n* **1** : a specialized lingo **2** : extremely rapid talk ⟨a comedian's ∼⟩

³**patter** *vb* : to strike, pat, or tap rapidly

⁴**patter** *n* : a quick succession of taps or pats ⟨the ∼ of rain⟩

¹**pat·tern** \'pa-tərn\ *n* [ME *patron*, fr. AF, fr. ML *patronus*, fr. L, defender, fr. *patr-, pater* father] **1** : an ideal model **2** : something used as a model for making things ⟨a dressmaker's ∼⟩ **3** : SAMPLE **4** : an artistic design **5** : CONFIGURATION **6** : a sample of a person's behavior or characteristics ⟨a ∼ of violence⟩

²**pattern** *vb* : to form according to a pattern

pat·ty *also* **pat·tie** \'pa-tē\ *n, pl* **patties 1** : a little pie **2** : a small flat cake esp. of chopped food

pau·ci·ty \'pȯ-sə-tē\ *n* : smallness of number or quantity

paunch \'pȯnch\ *n* : a usu. large belly : POTBELLY — **paunchy** *adj*

pau·per \'pȯ-pər\ *n* : a person without means of support except from charity — **pau·per·ism** \-pə-ˌri-zəm\ *n* — **pau·per·ize** \-pə-ˌrīz\ *vb*

¹**pause** \'pȯz\ *n* **1** : a temporary stop; *also* : a period of inaction **2** : a brief suspension of the voice **3** : a sign ⌒ or ⌣ above or below a musical note or rest to show it is to be prolonged **4** : a reason for pausing **5** : a function of an electronic device that pauses a recording

²**pause** *vb* **paused; paus·ing** : to stop, rest, or linger for a time

pave \'pāv\ *vb* **paved; pav·ing** : to cover (as a road) with hard material in order to smooth or firm the surface

pave·ment \'pāv-mənt\ *n* **1** : a paved surface **2** : the material with which something is paved

pa·vil·ion \pə-'vil-yən\ *n* [ME *pavilloun, pavillioun,* fr. AF, fr. L *papilion-, papilio* butterfly] **1** : a large tent **2** : a usu. open structure (as in a park) used for entertainment or shelter

pav·ing \'pā-viŋ\ *n* : PAVEMENT

¹**paw** \'pȯ\ *n* : the foot of a quadruped (as a dog or lion) having claws

²**paw** *vb* **1** : to touch or strike with a paw; *also* : to scrape with a hoof **2** : to feel or handle clumsily or rudely **3** : to flail about or grab for with the hands

pawl \'pȯl\ *n* : a pivoted tongue or sliding bolt designed to fall into notches on another machine part to permit motion in one direction only

¹**pawn** \'pȯn\ *n* [ME *pown*, fr. AF *peoun, paun,* fr. ML *pedon-, pedo* foot soldier, fr. LL, one with broad feet, fr. L *ped-, pes* foot] **1** : a chess piece of the least value **2** : one used for the purposes of another

²**pawn** *n* **1** : something deposited as security for a loan; *also* : HOSTAGE **2** : the state of being pledged

³**pawn** *vb* : to deposit as a pledge

pawn·bro·ker \'pȯn-ˌbrō-kər\ *n* : one who lends money on goods pledged

Paw·nee \pȯ-'nē\ *n, pl* **Pawnee** *or* **Pawnees** : a member of an American Indian people orig. of Kansas and Nebraska

pawn·shop \'pȯn-ˌshäp\ *n* : a pawnbroker's place of business

paw·paw *also* **pa·paw 1** \pə-'pȯ\; PA·PAYA **2** \'pä-ˌpȯ, 'pȯ-\ : a No. American tree with green-skinned edible fruit; *also* : its fruit

¹**pay** \'pā\ *vb* **paid** \'pād\ *also in sense 7* **payed; pay·ing** [ME, fr. AF *paier,* fr. L *pacare* to pacify, fr. *pac-, pax* peace] **1** : to make due return to for goods or services **2** : to discharge indebtedness for : SETTLE ⟨∼ a bill⟩ **3** : to give in forfeit ⟨∼ the penalty⟩ **4** : REQUITE **5** : to give, offer, or make freely or as fitting ⟨∼ attention⟩ **6** : to be profitable to : RETURN **7** : to make slack and allow to run out ⟨∼ out a rope⟩ — **pay·able** *adj* — **pay·ee** \pā-'ē\ *n* — **pay·er** *n*

²**pay** *n* **1** : something paid; *esp* : WAGES **2** : the status of being paid by an employer : EMPLOY

³**pay** *adj* **1** : containing something valuable (as gold) ⟨∼ dirt⟩ **2** : equipped to receive a fee for use ⟨∼ telephone⟩ **3** : requiring payment

pay·back \'pā-ˌbak\ *n* **1** : a return on an investment equal to the original capital outlay **2** : something given in return, compensation, or retaliation

pay·check \'pā-ˌchek\ *n* **1** : a check in payment of wages or salary **2** : WAGES, SALARY

pay·load \-ˌlōd\ *n* : the load carried by a vehicle in addition to what is necessary for its operation; *also* : the weight of such a load

pay·mas·ter \-ˌmas-tər\ n : one who distributes the payroll

pay·ment \ˈpā-mənt\ n 1 : the act of paying 2 : something paid

pay·off \-ˌȯf\ n 1 : PROFIT, REWARD; also : RETRIBUTION 2 : the climax of an incident or enterprise ⟨the ~ of a story⟩

pay–per–view n : a cable television service by which customers can order access to a single airing of a TV feature

pay·roll \-ˌrōl\ n : a list of persons entitled to receive pay; also : the money to pay those on such a list

payt abbr payment

pay up vb : to pay what is due; also : to pay in full

Pb symbol [L plumbum] lead

PBS abbr Public Broadcasting Service

PBX \ˌpē-(ˌ)bē-ˈeks\ n [private branch exchange] : a private telephone switchboard

1PC \ˌpē-ˈsē\ n, pl **PCs** or **PC's** [personal computer] : MICROCOMPUTER

2PC abbr 1 Peace Corps 2 percent; percentage 3 politically correct 4 postcard 5 [L post cibum] after meals 6 professional corporation

PCB \ˌpē-ˌsē-ˈbē\ n : POLYCHLORINATED BIPHENYL

PCP \ˌpē-ˌsē-ˈpē\ n : PHENCYCLIDINE

pct abbr percent; percentage

pd abbr paid

Pd symbol palladium

PD abbr 1 per diem 2 police department 3 potential difference

PDA \ˌpē-ˌdē-ˈā\ n [personal digital assistant] : a small microprocessor device for storing and organizing personal information

PDQ \ˌpē-ˌdē-ˈkyü\ adv, often not cap [abbr. of pretty damned quick] : IMMEDIATELY

PDT abbr Pacific daylight (saving) time

PE abbr 1 physical education 2 printer's error 3 professional engineer

pea \ˈpē\ n, pl **peas** also **pease** \ˈpēz\ 1 : the round edible protein-rich seed borne in the pod of a widely grown leguminous vine; also : this vine 2 : any of various plants resembling or related to the pea

peace \ˈpēs\ n 1 : a state of calm and quiet; esp : public security under law 2 : freedom from disturbing thoughts or emotions 3 : a state of concord (as between persons or governments); also : an agreement to end hostilities — **peace·able** \ˈpē-sə-bəl\ adj — **peace·ably** \-blē\ adv — **peace·ful** adj — **peace·ful·ly** adv

peace·keep·ing \ˈpēs-ˌkē-piŋ\ n : the preserving of peace; esp : international enforcement and supervision of a truce — **peace·keep·er** n

peace·mak·er \-ˌmā-kər\ n : one who settles an argument or stops a fight

peace·time \-ˌtīm\ n : a time when a nation is not at war

peach \ˈpēch\ n [ME peche, fr. AF pesche, peche, fr. LL persica, fr. L (malum) Persicum, lit., Persian fruit] : a sweet juicy fuzzy-skinned fruit of a small usu. pink-flowered tree related to the cherry and plums; also : this tree — **peachy** adj

pea·cock \ˈpē-ˌkäk\ n [ME pecok, fr. pe- (fr. OE pēa peafowl, fr. L pavo peacock) + cok cock] : the male peafowl that can spread its long tail feathers to make a colorful display

pea·fowl \-ˌfau̇(-ə)l\ n : either of two large domesticated Asian pheasants

pea·hen \-ˌhen\ n : the female peafowl

1peak \ˈpēk\ n 1 : a pointed or projecting part 2 : the top of a hill or mountain; also : MOUNTAIN 3 : the front projecting part of a cap 4 : the narrow part of a ship's bow or stern 5 : the highest level or greatest degree — **peak** adj

2peak vb : to bring to or reach a maximum

peak·ed \ˈpē-kəd\ adj : THIN, SICKLY

1peal \ˈpēl\ n 1 : the loud ringing of bells 2 : a set of tuned bells 3 : a loud sound or succession of sounds

2peal vb : to give out peals : RESOUND

pea·nut \ˈpē-(ˌ)nət\ n 1 : an annual herb related to the pea but having pods that ripen underground; also : this pod or one of the edible seeds it bears 2 pl : a very small amount 3 : a pellet of polystyrene foam

pear \ˈper\ n : the fleshy fruit of a tree related to the apple; also : this tree

pearl \ˈpərl\ n 1 : a small hard often lustrous body formed within the shell of some mollusks and used as a gem 2 : one that is choice or precious ⟨~s of wisdom⟩ 3 : a slightly bluish medium gray color — **pearly** \ˈpər-lē\ adj

peas·ant \ˈpe-zᵊnt\ n 1 : any of a class of small landowners or laborers tilling the soil 2 : a usu. uneducated person of low social status — **peas·ant·ry** \-zᵊn-trē\ n

pea·shoot·er \ˈpē-ˌshü-tər\ n : a toy blowgun for shooting peas

peat \ˈpēt\ n : a dark substance formed by partial decay of plants (as mosses) in water — **peaty** adj

peat moss n : SPHAGNUM

1peb·ble \ˈpe-bəl\ n : a small usu. round stone — **peb·bly** \-b(ə-)lē\ adj

2pebble vb **peb·bled**; **peb·bling** : to produce a rough surface texture in ⟨~ leather⟩

pec \ˈpek\ n : PECTORAL MUSCLE

pe·can \pi-ˈkän, -ˈkan; ˈpē-ˌkan\ n : the smooth thin-shelled edible nut of a large American hickory; also : this tree

pec·ca·dil·lo \ˌpe-kə-ˈdi-lō\ n, pl **-loes** or **-los** : a slight offense

pec·ca·ry \ˈpe-kə-rē\ n, pl **-ries** : any of several American chiefly tropical mammals resembling but smaller than the related pigs

pec·ca·vi \pe-ˈkä-ˌvē\ n [L, I have sinned, fr. peccare to sin] : an acknowledgment of sin

1peck \ˈpek\ n — see WEIGHT table

2peck vb 1 : to strike or pierce with or as if with the bill 2 : to make (as a hole) by pecking 3 : to pick up with or as if with the bill

3peck n 1 : an impression made by pecking 2 : a quick sharp stroke

pecking order also **peck order** n : a basic pattern of social organization within a flock of poultry in which each bird pecks another lower in the scale without being pecked in return and submits to pecking by one of higher rank; also : a social hierarchy

pec·tin \'pek-tən\ n : any of various water-soluble plant substances that cause fruit jellies to set — **pec·tic** \-tik\ adj

pec·to·ral \'pek-tə-rəl\ adj : of or relating to the breast or chest

pectoral muscle n : either of two muscles on each side of the body which connect the front walls of the chest with the bones of the upper arm and shoulder

pe·cu·liar \pi-'kyül-yər\ adj [ME peculier, fr. L peculiaris of private property, special, fr. peculium private property, fr. pecus cattle] **1** : belonging exclusively to one person or group **2** : CHARACTERISTIC, DISTINCTIVE **3** : QUEER, ODD ♦ Synonyms IDIOSYNCRATIC, ECCENTRIC, SINGULAR, STRANGE, WEIRD — **pe·cu·liar·i·ty** \-ˌkyül-'ya-rə-tē, -ˌkyü-lē-'a-\ n — **pe·cu·liar·ly** adv

pe·cu·ni·ary \pi-'kyü-nē-ˌer-ē\ adj : of or relating to money : MONETARY

ped·a·gogue also **ped·a·gog** \'pe-də-ˌgäg\ n : TEACHER, SCHOOLMASTER

ped·a·go·gy \'pe-də-ˌgō-jē, -ˌgä-\ n : the art or profession of teaching; esp : EDUCATION **2** — **ped·a·gog·ic** \ˌpe-də-'gä-jik, -'gō-\ or **ped·a·gog·i·cal** \-ji-kəl\ adj

¹ped·al \'pe-dᵊl\ n : a lever worked by the foot

²pedal adj : of or relating to the foot

³pedal vb **ped·aled** also **ped·alled; ped·al·ing** also **ped·al·ling** **1** : to use or work a pedal (as of a piano or bicycle) **2** : to ride a bicycle

ped·ant \'pe-dᵊnt\ n **1** : a person who makes a show of knowledge **2** : a formal uninspired teacher — **pe·dan·tic** \pi-'dan-tik\ adj — **ped·ant·ry** \'pe-dᵊn-trē\ n

ped·dle \'pe-dᵊl\ vb **ped·dled; ped·dling** : to sell or offer for sale from place to place — **ped·dler** also **ped·lar** \'ped-lər\ n

ped·er·ast \'pe-də-ˌrast\ n [Gk paiderastēs, lit., lover of boys] : one who practices anal intercourse esp. with a boy — **ped·er·as·ty** \'pe-də-ˌras-tē\ n

ped·es·tal \'pe-dəs-tᵊl\ n **1** : the support or foot of something (as a column, statue, or vase) that is upright **2** : a position of high regard

¹pe·des·tri·an \pə-'des-trē-ən\ adj **1** : ORDINARY **2** : going on foot

²pedestrian n : WALKER

pe·di·at·rics \ˌpē-dē-'a-triks\ n : a branch of medicine dealing with the development, care, and diseases of children — **pe·di·at·ric** \-trik\ adj — **pe·di·a·tri·cian** \ˌpē-dē-ə-'tri-shən\ n

pedi·cab \'pe-di-ˌkab\ n : a pedal-driven tricycle with seats for a driver and two passengers

ped·i·cure \'pe-di-ˌkyur\ n : care of the feet, toes, and nails; also : a single treatment of these parts — **ped·i·cur·ist** \-ˌkyur-ist\ n

ped·i·gree \'pe-də-ˌgrē\ n [ME pedegru, fr. AF pé de grue, lit., crane's foot; fr. the shape made by the lines of a genealogical chart] **1** : a record of a line of ancestors **2** : an ancestral line — **ped·i·greed** \-ˌgrēd\ adj

ped·i·ment \'pe-də-mənt\ n : a low triangular gablelike decoration (as over a door or window) on a building

pe·dom·e·ter \pi-'dä-mə-tər\ n : an instrument that measures the distance one walks

pe·do·phile \'pe-də-ˌfī(-ə)l, 'pē-\ n : one affected with pedophilia

pe·do·phil·ia \ˌpe-də-'fi-lē-ə, ˌpē-\ n : sexual perversion in which children are the preferred sexual object

pe·dun·cle \'pi-ˌdəŋ-kəl\ n : a narrow supporting stalk

peek \'pēk\ vb **1** : to look furtively **2** : to peer from a place of concealment **3** : GLANCE — **peek** n

¹peel \'pēl\ vb [ME pelen, fr. AF peler, fr. L pilare to remove the hair from, fr. pilus hair] **1** : to strip the skin, bark, or rind from **2** : to strip off (as a coat); also : to come off **3** : to lose the skin, bark, or rind

²peel n : a skin or rind esp. of a fruit

peel·ing \'pē-liŋ\ n : a peeled-off piece or strip (as of skin or rind)

peen \'pēn\ n : the usu. hemispherical or wedge-shaped end of the head of a hammer opposite the face

¹peep \'pēp\ vb : to utter a feeble shrill sound or the slightest sound

²peep n : a feeble shrill sound

³peep vb **1** : to look slyly esp. through an aperture : PEEK **2** : to begin to emerge **3** : to look at : WATCH — **peep·er** n

⁴peep n **1** : a first faint appearance **2** : a brief or furtive look

peep·hole \'pēp-ˌhōl\ n : a hole to peep through

¹peer \'pir\ n **1** : one of equal standing with another : EQUAL **2** : NOBLE — **peer·age** \-ij\ n

²peer vb **1** : to look intently or curiously **2** : to come slightly into view

peer·ess \'pir-əs\ n : a woman who is a peer

peer·less \'pir-ləs\ adj : having no equal : MATCHLESS ♦ Synonyms SUPREME, UNEQUALED, UNPARALLELED, INCOMPARABLE

¹peeve \'pēv\ vb **peeved; peev·ing** : to make resentful : ANNOY

²peeve n **1** : a feeling or mood of resentment **2** : a particular grievance

pee·vish \'pē-vish\ adj : querulous in temperament : FRETFUL ♦ Synonyms IRRITABLE, PETULANT, HUFFY — **peevish·ly** adv — **pee·vish·ness** n

pee·wee \'pē-(ˌ)wē\ n **1** : one that is diminutive or tiny **2** : a level of sports usu. for young children — **peewee** adj

¹peg \'peg\ n **1** : a small pointed piece (as of wood) used to pin down or fasten things or to fit into holes **2** : a projecting piece used as a support or boundary marker **3** : SUPPORT, PRETEXT **4** : STEP, DEGREE **5** : THROW

²**peg** *vb* **pegged; peg·ging 1** : to put a peg into : fasten, pin down, or attach with or as if with pegs **2** : to work hard and steadily : PLUG **3** : HUSTLE **4** : to mark by pegs **5** : to hold (as prices) at a set level or rate **6** : IDENTIFY ⟨was *pegged* as an intellectual⟩ **7** : THROW

PEI *abbr* Prince Edward Island

pei·gnoir \pān-ˈwär, pen-\ *n* [F, lit., garment worn while combing the hair, fr. MF, fr. *peigner* to comb the hair, fr. L *pectinare*, fr. *pectin-, pecten* comb] : NEGLIGEE

¹**pe·jo·ra·tive** \pi-ˈjor-ə-tiv\ *n* : a pejorative word or phrase

²**pejorative** *adj* : having negative connotations : DISPARAGING — **pe·jo·ra·tive·ly** *adv*

peke \ˈpēk\ *n, often cap* : PEKINGESE

Pe·king·ese *or* **Pe·kin·ese** \ˌpē-kə-ˈnēz, -ˈnēs; -kiŋ-ˈēz, -ˈēs\ *n, pl* **Pekingese** *or* **Pekinese** : any of a breed of Chinese origin of small short-legged long-haired dogs

pe·koe \ˈpē-(ˌ)kō\ *n* : a black tea made from young tea leaves

pel·age \ˈpe-lij\ *n* : the hairy covering of a mammal

pe·lag·ic \pə-ˈla-jik\ *adj* : OCEANIC

pelf \ˈpelf\ *n* : MONEY, RICHES

pel·i·can \ˈpe-li-kən\ *n* : any of a genus of large web-footed birds having a pouched lower bill used to scoop in fish

pel·la·gra \pə-ˈla-grə, -ˈlä-\ *n* : a disease caused by a diet with too little niacin and protein and marked by a skin rash, disease of the digestive system, and mental disturbances

pel·let \ˈpe-lət\ *n* **1** : a little ball (as of medicine) **2** : BULLET — **pel·let·al** \-lə-təl\ *adj* — **pel·let·ize** \-ˌtīz\ *vb*

pell-mell \ˈpel-ˈmel\ *adv* **1** : in mingled confusion ⟨papers strewn ∼ on the desk⟩ **2** : HEADLONG ⟨ran ∼ for the door⟩

pel·lu·cid \pe-ˈlü-səd\ *adj* : extremely clear : LIMPID, TRANSPARENT ⟨a ∼ stream⟩ ✦ *Synonyms* TRANSLUCENT, LUCID, LUCENT

pe·lo·ton \ˌpe-lə-ˈtän\ *n* : the main body of riders in a bicycle race

¹**pelt** \ˈpelt\ *n* : a skin esp. of a fur-bearing animal

²**pelt** *vb* : to strike with a succession of blows or missiles

pel·vis \ˈpel-vəs\ *n, pl* **pel·vis·es** \-və-səz\ *or* **pel·ves** \-ˌvēz\ : a basin-shaped part of the vertebrate skeleton consisting of the large bone of each hip and the nearby bones of the spine — **pel·vic** \-vik\ *adj*

pem·mi·can *also* **pem·i·can** \ˈpe-mi-kən\ *n* : dried meat pounded fine and mixed with melted fat

¹**pen** \ˈpen\ *vb* **penned; pen·ning** : to shut in or as if in a pen

²**pen** *n* **1** : a small enclosure for animals **2** : a small place of confinement or storage

³**pen** *n* **1** : an implement for writing or drawing with ink or a similar fluid **2** : a

writing instrument regarded as a means of expression **3** : STYLUS 3

⁴**pen** *vb* **penned; pen·ning** : WRITE

⁵**pen** *n* : PENITENTIARY

⁶**pen** *abbr* peninsula

PEN *abbr* International Association of Poets, Playwrights, Editors, Essayists and Novelists

pe·nal \ˈpē-nᵊl\ *adj* : of or relating to punishment

pe·nal·ise *Brit var of* PENALIZE

pe·nal·ize \ˈpē-nə-ˌlīz, ˈpe-\ *vb* **-ized; -iz·ing** : to put a penalty on

pen·al·ty \ˈpe-nᵊl-tē\ *n, pl* **-ties 1** : punishment for crime or offense **2** : something forfeited when a person fails to do something agreed to **3** : disadvantage, loss, or hardship (as to a competitor) due to some action

pen·ance \ˈpe-nəns\ *n* **1** : an act performed to show sorrow or repentance for sin **2** : a sacrament (as in the Roman Catholic Church) consisting of confession, absolution, and a penance directed by the confessor

pence \ˈpens\ *pl of* PENNY

pen·chant \ˈpen-chənt\ *n* [F, fr. prp. of *pencher* to incline, fr. VL *pendicare, fr. L *pendere* to weigh] : a strong inclination : LIKING ✦ *Synonyms* LEANING, PROPENSITY, PREDILECTION, PREDISPOSITION

¹**pen·cil** \ˈpen-səl\ *n* : a writing or drawing tool consisting of or containing a slender cylinder of a solid marking substance

²**pencil** *vb* **-ciled** *or* **-cilled; -cil·ing** *or* **-cil·ling 1** : to draw or write with a pencil **2** : to plan or designate tentatively ⟨∼ed in the appointment⟩

pen·dant *also* **pen·dent** \ˈpen-dənt\ *n* : a hanging ornament (as on a necklace)

pen·dent *or* **pen·dant** \ˈpen-dənt\ *adj* : SUSPENDED, OVERHANGING

¹**pend·ing** \ˈpen-diŋ\ *prep* **1** : DURING **2** : while awaiting ⟨∼ approval⟩

²**pending** *adj* **1** : not yet decided ⟨a ∼ application⟩ **2** : IMMINENT

pen·du·lous \ˈpen-jə-ləs, -də-\ *adj* : hanging loosely : DROOPING

pen·du·lum \-ləm\ *n* : a body that swings freely from a fixed point

pe·ne·plain *also* **pe·ne·plane** \ˈpē-ni-ˌplān\ *n* : a large almost flat land surface shaped by erosion

pen·e·trate \ˈpe-nə-ˌtrāt\ *vb* **-trat·ed; -trat·ing 1** : to enter into : PIERCE **2** : PERMEATE **3** : to see into : UNDERSTAND **4** : to affect deeply — **pen·e·tra·ble** \-trə-bəl\ *adj* — **pen·e·tra·tion** \ˌpe-nə-ˈtrā-shən\ *n* — **pen·e·tra·tive** \ˈpe-nə-ˌtrā-tiv\ *adj*

penetrating *adj* **1** : having the power of entering, piercing, or pervading ⟨a ∼ shriek⟩ ⟨a ∼ odor⟩ **2** : ACUTE, DISCERNING ⟨a ∼ look⟩

pen·guin \ˈpen-gwən, ˈpeŋ-\ *n* : any of various erect short-legged flightless seabirds of the southern hemisphere

pen·i·cil·lin \ˌpe-nə-ˈsi-lən\ *n* : any of several antibiotics produced by molds or synthetically and used against various bacteria

pen·in·su·la \pə-'nin-sə-lə\ n [L *paeninsula*, fr. *paene* almost + *insula* island] : a long narrow portion of land extending out into the water — **pen·in·su·lar** \-lər\ adj

pe·nis \'pē-nəs\ n, pl **pe·nis·es** also **pe·nes** \-,nēz\ : a male organ of copulation that in the human male also functions as the channel by which urine leaves the body

¹pen·i·tent \'pe-nə-tənt\ adj : feeling sorrow for sins or offenses : REPENTANT — **pen·i·tence** \-təns\ n — **pen·i·ten·tial** \,pe-nə-'ten-chəl\ adj

²penitent n : a penitent person

¹pen·i·ten·tia·ry \,pe-nə-'ten-chə-rē\ n, pl **-ries** : a state or federal prison

²penitentiary adj : of, relating to, or incurring confinement in a penitentiary

pen·knife \'pen-,nīf\ n : a small pocketknife

pen·light also **pen·lite** \-,līt\ n : a small flashlight resembling a fountain pen in size or shape

pen·man \'pen-mən\ n 1 : COPYIST 2 : one skilled in penmanship 3 : AUTHOR

pen·man·ship \-,ship\ n : the art or practice of writing with the pen

Penn or **Penna** abbr Pennsylvania

pen name n : an author's pseudonym

pen·nant \'pe-nont\ n 1 : a tapering flag used esp. for signaling 2 : a flag symbolic of championship

pen·ne \'pe-nā\ n : short diagonally cut tubular pasta

pen·ni \'pe-nē\ n, pl **pen·nia** \-nē-ə\ or **pen·nis** \-nēz\ : a former monetary unit equal to ¹⁄₁₀₀ markka

pen·non \'pe-nən\ n 1 : a long narrow ribbonlike flag borne on a lance 2 : WING

Penn·syl·va·nian \,pen-səl-'vā-nyən\ adj 1 : of or relating to Pennsylvania or its people 2 : of, relating to, or being the period of the Paleozoic era between the Mississippian and the Permian — **Pennsylvanian** n

pen·ny \'pe-nē\ n, pl **pennies** \-nēz\ or **pence** \'pens\ 1 pl usu **pence** : a British monetary unit formerly equal to ¹⁄₁₂ shilling but now equal to ¹⁄₁₀₀ pound; also : a coin of this value — see *pound* at MONEY table 2 pl **pennies** : a cent of the U.S. or Canada 3 pl usu **pence** : a former monetary unit equal to ¹⁄₁₀₀ Irish pound — **pen·ni·less** \'pe-ni-ləs\ adj

pen·ny-pinch·ing \'pe-nē-,pin-chiŋ\ : PARSIMONY — **pen·ny-pinch·er** n — **penny-pinching** adj

pen·ny·weight \-,wāt\ n — see WEIGHT table

pen·ny-wise \-,wīz\ adj : wise or prudent only in small matters

pe·nol·o·gy \pi-'nä-lə-jē\ n : a branch of criminology dealing with prisons and the treatment of offenders

¹pen·sion \'pen-chən\ n : a fixed sum paid regularly esp. to a person retired from service

²pension vb : to pay a pension to — **pen·sion·er** n

pen·sive \'pen-siv\ adj : musingly, dreamily, or sadly thoughtful **♦ Synonyms** REFLECTIVE, SPECULATIVE, CONTEMPLATIVE, MEDITATIVE — **pen·sive·ly** adv

pen·stock \'pen-,stäk\ n 1 : a sluice or gate for regulating a flow 2 : a pipe for carrying water

pent \'pent\ adj : shut up : CONFINED

pen·ta·gon \'pen-tə-,gän\ n : a polygon of five angles and five sides — **pen·tag·o·nal** \pen-'ta-gə-nᵊl\ adj

pen·tam·e·ter \pen-'ta-mə-tər\ n : a line of verse containing five metrical feet

pen·tath·lon \pen-'tath-lən\ n : a composite athletic contest consisting of five events

Pen·te·cost \'pen-ti-,kòst\ n : the 7th Sunday after Easter observed as a church festival commemorating the descent of the Holy Spirit on the apostles — **Pen·te·cos·tal** \,pen-ti-'käs-tᵊl\ adj

Pentecostal n : a member of a Christian religious body that stresses expressive worship, evangelism, and spiritual gifts — **Pen·te·cos·tal·ism** \,pen-ti-'käs-tə-,li-zəm\

pent·house \'pent-,haùs\ n [alter. of ME *pentis*, fr. AF *apentiz*, fr. *apent*, pp. of *apendre* to attach, hang against] 1 : a shed or sloping roof attached to a wall or building 2 : an apartment built on the roof of a building

pen·ul·ti·mate \pi-'nəl-tə-mət\ adj : next to the last ⟨— syllable⟩

pen·um·bra \pə-'nəm-brə\ n, pl **-brae** \-(,)brē\ or **-bras** 1 : the partial shadow surrounding a complete shadow (as in an eclipse) 2 : something that covers or obscures ⟨a — of secrecy⟩

pe·nu·ri·ous \pə-'nùr-ē-əs, -'nyùr-\ adj 1 : marked by penury 2 : MISERLY **♦ Synonyms** STINGY, CLOSE, TIGHTFISTED, PARSIMONIOUS

pen·u·ry \'pe-nyə-rē\ n 1 : extreme poverty 2 : extreme frugality

pe·on \'pē-,än, -ən\ n, pl **peons** or **pe·o·nes** \pā-'ō-nēz\ 1 : a member of the landless laboring class in Spanish America 2 : one bound to service for payment of a debt — **pe·on·age** \-ə-nij\ n

pe·o·ny \'pē-ə-nē\ n, pl **-nies** : any of a genus of chiefly Eurasian plants with large often double red, pink, or white flowers; also : the flower

¹peo·ple \'pē-pəl\ n, pl **people** [ME *peple*, fr. AF *peple, peuple*, fr. L *populus*] 1 pl : human beings making up a group or linked by a common characteristic or interest 2 pl : human beings — often used in compounds instead of *persons* ⟨salespeople⟩ or attributively ⟨— skills⟩ 3 pl : the mass of persons in a community : POPULACE; also : ELECTORATE ⟨the —'s choice⟩ 4 pl **peoples** : a body of persons (as a tribe, nation, or race) united by a common culture, sense of kinship, or political organization

²people vb **peo·pled; peo·pling** : to supply or fill with or as if with people

¹pep \'pep\ n : brisk energy or initiative — **pep·py** adj

²**pep** *vb* **pepped; pep·ping** : to put pep into : STIMULATE

¹**pep·per** \'pe-pər\ *n* 1 : either of two pungent condiments from the berry (**pep·per·corn** \-ˌkȯrn\) of an Indian climbing plant : BLACK PEPPER, WHITE PEPPER; *also* : this plant 2 : a plant related to the tomato and widely grown for its hot or mild sweet fruit; *also* : this fruit

²**pepper** *vb* **pep·pered; pep·per·ing** 1 : to shower with missiles or rapid blows 2 : to sprinkle or season with or as if with pepper 3 : to deliver something in rapid succession ⟨~ed him with questions⟩

pep·per·mint \-ˌmint, -mənt\ *n* : a pungent aromatic mint; *also* : candy flavored with its oil

pep·per·o·ni \ˌpe-pə-'rō-nē\ *n* : a highly seasoned beef and pork sausage

pepper spray *n* : a temporarily disabling aerosol that causes irritation and blinding of the eyes and inflammation of the nose, throat, and skin

pep·pery \'pe-pə-rē\ *adj* 1 : having the qualities of pepper : PUNGENT, HOT 2 : having a hot temper 3 : FIERY

pep·sin \'pep-sən\ *n* : an enzyme of the stomach that promotes digestion by breaking down proteins; *also* : a preparation of this used medicinally

pep·tic \'pep-tik\ *adj* [L *pepticus*, fr. Gk *peptikos*, fr. *peptos* cooked, *peptein* to cook, digest] 1 : relating to or promoting digestion 2 : caused by digestive juices ⟨a ~ ulcer⟩

pep·tide \'pep-ˌtīd\ *n* : any of various organic compounds composed of two or more amino acids bonded together

Pe·quot \'pē-ˌkwät\ *n* : a member of an American Indian people of eastern Connecticut

¹**per** \'pər\ *prep* 1 : by means of 2 : to or for each 3 : ACCORDING TO

²**per** *adv* : for each : APIECE

³**per** *abbr* 1 period 2 person

¹**per·ad·ven·ture** \'pər-əd-ˌven-chər\ *adv*, *archaic* : PERHAPS

²**peradventure** *n* 1 : DOUBT 2 : CHANCE 4

per·am·bu·late \pə-'ram-byə-ˌlāt\ *vb* **-lat·ed; -lat·ing** : to travel over esp. on foot — **per·am·bu·la·tion** \-ˌram-byə-'lā-shən\ *n*

per·am·bu·la·tor \pə-'ram-byə-ˌlā-tər\ *n*, *chiefly Brit* : a baby carriage

per an·num \(ˌ)pər-'a-nəm\ *adv* [ML] : in or for each year : ANNUALLY

per·cale \(ˌ)pər-'kāl, 'pər-ˌ; (ˌ)pər-'kal\ *n* : a fine woven cotton cloth

per cap·i·ta \(ˌ)pər-'ka-pə-tə\ *adv or adj* [ML, by heads] : by or for each person

per·ceive \pər-'sēv\ *vb* **per·ceived; per·ceiv·ing** 1 : to attain awareness : REALIZE 2 : to become aware of through the senses — **per·ceiv·able** *adj*

¹**per·cent** \pər-'sent\ *adv* [*per* + L *centum* hundred] : in each hundred

²**percent** *n, pl* **percent** *or* **percents** 1 : one part in a hundred : HUNDREDTH 2 : PERCENTAGE

per·cent·age \pər-'sen-tij\ *n* 1 : a part of a whole expressed in hundredths 2 : the result obtained by multiplying a number

by a percent 3 : ADVANTAGE, PROFIT 4 : PROBABILITY; *also* : favorable odds

percentage point *n* : one hundredth of a whole ⟨rates rose one *percentage point* from 6.5 to 7.5 percent⟩

per·cen·tile \pər-'sen-ˌtī(-ə)l\ *n* : a value on a scale of one hundred indicating the standing of a score or grade in terms of the percentage of scores or grades falling with or below it

per·cept \'pər-ˌsept\ *n* : an impression of an object obtained by use of the senses

per·cep·ti·ble \pər-'sep-tə-bəl\ *adj* : capable of being perceived ⟨a barely ~ light⟩ — **per·cep·ti·bly** \-blē\ *adv*

per·cep·tion \pər-'sep-shən\ *n* 1 : an act or result of perceiving 2 : awareness of one's environment through physical sensation 3 : ability to understand : INSIGHT, COMPREHENSION ✦ *Synonyms* PENETRATION, DISCERNMENT, DISCRIMINATION

per·cep·tive \pər-'sep-tiv\ *adj* : capable of or exhibiting keen perception : OBSERVANT — **per·cep·tive·ly** *adv*

per·cep·tu·al \pər-'sep-chə-wəl\ *adj* : of, relating to, or involving sensory stimulus as opposed to abstract concept — **per·cep·tu·al·ly** *adv*

¹**perch** \'pərch\ *n* 1 : a roost for a bird 2 : a high station or vantage point

²**perch** *vb* : ROOST

³**perch** *n, pl* **perch** *or* **perch·es** : either of two small freshwater bony fishes used for food; *also* : any of various fishes resembling or related to these

per·chance \pər-'chans\ *adv* : PERHAPS

per·cip·i·ent \pər-'si-pē-ənt\ *adj* : capable of or characterized by perception — **per·cip·i·ence** \-əns\ *n*

per·co·late \'pər-kə-ˌlāt\ *vb* **-lat·ed; -lat·ing** 1 : to trickle or filter through a permeable substance 2 : to filter hot water through to extract the essence ⟨~ coffee⟩ — **per·co·la·tor** \-ˌlā-tər\ *n*

per con·tra \(ˌ)pər-'kän-trə\ *adv* [It, by the opposite side (of the ledger)] 1 : on the contrary 2 : by way of contrast

per·cus·sion \pər-'kə-shən\ *n* 1 : a sharp blow : IMPACT; *esp* : a blow upon a cap (**percussion cap**) designed to explode the charge in a firearm 2 : the beating or striking of a musical instrument; *also* : instruments sounded by striking, shaking, or scraping

per di·em \pər-'dē-əm, -'dī-\ *adv* [ML] : by the day — **per diem** *adj or n*

per·di·tion \pər-'di-shən\ *n* 1 : eternal damnation 2 : HELL

per·du·ra·ble \(ˌ)pər-'dur-ə-bəl, -'dyur-\ *adj* : very durable — **per·du·ra·bil·i·ty** \-ˌdur-ə-'bi-lə-tē, -ˌdyur-\ *n*

père \'per\ *n* [F, fr. OF *paire, perre*, fr. L *pater*] : FATHER — used after a name to distinguish a father from a son

per·e·gri·na·tion \ˌper-ə-grə-'nā-shən\ *n* : a traveling about esp. on foot

per·e·grine falcon \'per-ə-grən, -ˌgrēn\ *n* : a swift nearly cosmopolitan falcon that often nests in cities and is often used in falconry

pe·remp·to·ry \pə-'remp-tə-rē\ *adj* **1** : barring a right of action or delay **2** : expressive of urgency or command : IMPERATIVE **3** : marked by arrogant self-assurance ✦ *Synonyms* IMPERIOUS, MASTERFUL, DOMINEERING, MAGISTERIAL — **pe·remp·to·ri·ly** \-tə-rə-lē\ *adv*

¹**pe·ren·ni·al** \pə-'re-nē-əl\ *adj* **1** : present at all seasons of the year ⟨~ streams⟩ **2** : continuing to live from year to year ⟨~ plants⟩ **3** : recurring regularly : PERMANENT ⟨~ problems⟩ ✦ *Synonyms* LASTING, PERPETUAL, ENDURING, EVERLASTING — **pe·ren·ni·al·ly** *adv*

²**perennial** *n* : a perennial plant

perf *abbr* **1** perfect **2** perforated

¹**per·fect** \'pər-fikt\ *adj* **1** : being without fault or defect **2** : EXACT, PRECISE **3** : COMPLETE **4** : relating to or being a verb tense that expresses an action or state completed at the time of speaking or at a time spoken of — **per·fect·ly** *adv* — **per·fect·ness** *n*

²**per·fect** \pər-'fekt\ *vb* : to make perfect

³**per·fect** \'pər-fikt\ *n* : the perfect tense; *also* : a verb form in it

per·fect·ible \pər-'fek-tə-bəl, 'pər-fik-\ *adj* : capable of improvement or perfection — **per·fect·ibil·i·ty** \pər-,fek-tə-'bi-lə-tē, ,pər-fik-\ *n*

per·fec·tion \pər-'fek-shən\ *n* **1** : the quality or state of being perfect **2** : the highest degree of excellence **3** : the act or process of perfecting

per·fec·tion·ist \-shə-nist\ *n* : a person who will not accept or be content with anything less than perfection

per·fec·to \pər-'fek-tō\ *n, pl* **-tos** : a cigar that is thick in the middle and tapers almost to a point at each end

per·fi·dy \'pər-fə-dē\ *n, pl* **-dies** [L *perfidia,* fr. *perfidus* faithless, fr. *per-* detrimental to + *fides* faith] : violation of faith or loyalty : TREACHERY — **per·fid·i·ous** \pər-'fi-dē-əs\ *adj* — **per·fid·i·ous·ly** *adv*

per·fo·rate \'pər-fə-,rāt\ *vb* **-rat·ed; -rat·ing** : to bore through : PIERCE; *esp* : to make a line of holes in to facilitate separation — **per·fo·ra·tion** \,pər-fə-'rā-shən\ *n*

per·force \pər-'fòrs\ *adv* : of necessity ⟨we attended ~⟩

per·form \pər-'fòrm\ *vb* **1** : FULFILL **2** : CARRY OUT, DO **3** : FUNCTION **4** : to do in a set manner **5** : to give a performance — **per·form·er** *n*

per·for·mance \pər-'fòr-,məns\ *n* **1** : the act or process of performing **2** : DEED, FEAT **3** : a public presentation

¹**per·fume** \pər-'fyüm, 'pər-,fyüm\ *n* **1** : a usu. pleasant odor : FRAGRANCE **2** : a preparation used for scenting

²**per·fume** \pər-'fyüm, 'pər-,fyüm\ *vb* **per·fumed; per·fum·ing** : SCENT

per·fum·ery \pər-'fyü-mə-rē\ *n, pl* **-er·ies 1** : the art or process of making perfume **2** : PERFUMES **3** : an establishment where perfumes are made

per·func·to·ry \pər-'fəŋk-tə-rē\ *adj* : done merely as a duty — **per·func·to·ri·ly** *adv*

per·go·la \'pər-gə-lə\ *n* [It] : a structure consisting of posts supporting an open roof in the form of a trellis

perh *abbr* perhaps

per·haps \pər-'haps\ *adv* : possibly but not certainly

per·i·gee \'per-ə-,jē\ *n* [MF, fr. NL *perigeum,* fr. Gk *perigeion,* fr. *peri* around, near + *gē* earth] : the point at which an orbiting object is nearest the body (as the earth) being orbited

peri·he·lion \,per-ə-'hēl-yən\ *n, pl* **-he·lia** \-'hēl-yə\ : the point in the path of a celestial body (as a planet) that is nearest to the sun

per·il \'per-əl\ *n* : DANGER; *also* : a source of danger : RISK — **per·il·ous** *adj* — **per·il·ous·ly** *adv*

pe·rim·e·ter \pə-'ri-mə-tər\ *n* **1** : the boundary of a closed plane figure; *also* : its length **2** : a line bounding or protecting an area

peri·na·tal \,per-ə-'nā-t°l\ *adj* : occurring in, concerned with, or being in the period around the time of birth ⟨~ care⟩

¹**pe·ri·od** \'pir-ē-əd\ *n* [ultim. fr. Gk *periodos* circuit, period of time; rhetorical period, fr. *peri* around + *hodos* way] **1** : SENTENCE; *also* : the full pause closing the utterance of a sentence **2** : END, STOP **3** : a punctuation mark . used esp. to mark the end of a declarative sentence or an abbreviation **4** : an extent of time; *esp* : one regarded as a stage or division in a process or development **5** : a portion of time in which a recurring phenomenon completes one cycle and is ready to begin again **6** : a single cyclic occurrence of menstruation

²**period** *adj* : of or relating to a particular historical period ⟨~ furniture⟩

pe·ri·od·ic \,pir-ē-'ä-dik\ *adj* **1** : occurring at regular intervals of time **2** : happening repeatedly **3** : of or relating to a sentence that has no trailing elements following full grammatical statement of the essential idea

¹**pe·ri·od·i·cal** \,pir-ē-'ä-di-kəl\ *adj* **1** : PERIODIC **2** : published at regular intervals **3** : of or relating to a periodical — **pe·ri·od·i·cal·ly** \-k(ə-)lē\ *adv*

²**periodical** *n* : a periodical publication

periodic table *n* : an arrangement of chemical elements based on their atomic structure and on their properties

peri·odon·tal \,per-ē-ō-'dän-t°l\ *adj* **1** : surrounding a tooth **2** : of or affecting periodontal tissues or regions

peri·pa·tet·ic \,per-ə-pə-'te-tik\ *adj* : performed or performing while moving about : ITINERANT

pe·riph·er·al \pə-'ri-fər-əl\ *n* : a device connected to a computer to provide communication or auxiliary functions

peripheral nervous system *n* : the part of the nervous system that is outside the central nervous system and comprises the spinal nerves, the cranial nerves except the one supplying the retina, and the autonomic nervous system

pe·riph·ery \pə-'ri-fə-rē\ *n, pl* **-er·ies 1** : the boundary of a rounded figure **2** : outward bounds : border area — **pe·riph·er·al** \-fə-rəl\ *adj*

PERIODIC TABLE

This is the common long form of the table, with atomic numbers given along with the symbols. Roman numerals and letters heading the vertical columns indicate the groups. (There are differences of opinion regarding the letter designations, but those given here are probably the most generally used. International standards favor numbering the groups 1-18 from left to right using Arabic numerals, but the designations shown below remain quite common.) Horizontal rows represent the periods, with two very long periods and represented below the main table.

IA[1]	IIA[2]	IIIB	IVB	VB	VIB	VIIB		VIII		IB	IIB	IIIA	IVA	VA	VIA	VIIA[3]	VIIIA[4]
1 H																1 H	2 He
3 Li	4 Be											5 B	6 C	7 N	8 O	9 F	10 Ne
11 Na	12 Mg											13 Al	14 Si	15 P	16 S	17 Cl	18 Ar
19 K	20 Ca	21 Sc	22 Ti	23 V	24 Cr	25 Mn	26 Fe	27 Co	28 Ni	29 Cu	30 Zn	31 Ga	32 Ge	33 As	34 Se	35 Br	36 Kr
37 Rb	38 Sr	39 Y	40 Zr	41 Nb	42 Mo	43 Tc	44 Ru	45 Rh	46 Pd	47 Ag	48 Cd	49 In	50 Sn	51 Sb	52 Te	53 I	54 Xe
55 Cs	56 Ba	57 *La	72 Hf	73 Ta	74 W	75 Re	76 Os	77 Ir	78 Pt	79 Au	80 Hg	81 Tl	82 Pb	83 Bi	84 Po	85 At	86 Rn
87 Fr	88 Ra	89 #Ac	104 Rf	105 Db	106 Sg	107 Bh	108 Hs	109 Mt	110 Ds								

*LANTHANIDE SERIES	58 Ce	59 Pr	60 Nd	61 Pm	62 Sm	63 Eu	64 Gd	65 Tb	66 Dy	67 Ho	68 Er	69 Tm	70 Yb	71 Lu
#ACTINIDE SERIES	90 Th	91 Pa	92 U	93 Np	94 Pu	95 Am	96 Cm	97 Bk	98 Cf	99 Es	100 Fm	101 Md	102 No	103 Lr

[1] Group IA (excluding hydrogen) comprises the alkali metals.
[2] Group IIA comprises the alkaline earth metals.
[3] Group VIIA (excluding hydrogen) comprises the halogens.
[4] Group VIIIA (also called group Zero) comprises the noble gases.

pe·riph·ra·sis \pə-'ri-frə-səs\ *n, pl* **-ra·ses** \-ˌsēz\ : CIRCUMLOCUTION

peri·scope \'per-ə-ˌskōp\ *n* : a tubular optical instrument enabling an observer to see an otherwise blocked field of view

per·ish \'per-ish\ *vb* : to become destroyed or ruined : cease to exist

per·ish·able \'per-i-shə-bəl\ *adj* : easily spoiled (~ foods) — **perishable** *n*

peri·stal·sis \ˌper-ə-'stȯl-səs, -'stal-\ *n, pl* **-stal·ses** : waves of contraction passing along the walls of a hollow muscular organ (as the intestine) and forcing its contents onward — **per·i·stal·tic** \-'stȯl-tik, -'stal-\ *adj*

peri·style \'per-ə-ˌstīl\ *n* : a row of columns surrounding a building or court

peri·to·ne·um \ˌper-ə-tə-'nē-əm\ *n, pl* **-ne·ums** *or* **-nea** : the smooth transparent serous membrane that lines the cavity of the abdomen — **peri·to·ne·al** \-'nē-əl\ *adj*

peri·to·ni·tis \ˌper-ə-tə-'nī-təs\ *n* : inflammation of the peritoneum

peri·wig \'per-i-ˌwig\ *n* : WIG

¹**peri·win·kle** \'per-i-ˌwiŋ-kəl\ *n* : a usu. blue-flowered creeping plant cultivated as a ground cover

²**periwinkle** *n* : any of various small edible seashore snails

per·ju·ry \'pər-jə-rē\ *n* : the voluntary violation of an oath to tell the truth : lying under oath — **per·jure** \'pər-jər\ *vb* — **per·jur·er** *n*

¹**perk** \'pərk\ *vb* **1** : to thrust (as the head) up impudently or jauntily **2** : to regain vigor or spirit **3** : to make trim or brisk : FRESHEN — **perky** *adj*

²**perk** *vb* : PERCOLATE

³**perk** *n* : PERQUISITE — usu. used in pl.

per·lite \'pər-ˌlīt\ *n* : volcanic glass that when expanded by heat forms a lightweight material used esp. in concrete and plaster and for potting plants

¹**perm** \'pərm\ *n* : PERMANENT

²**perm** *vb* : to give (hair) a permanent

³**perm** *abbr* permanent

per·ma·frost \'pər-mə-ˌfrȯst\ *n* : a permanently frozen layer below the surface in frigid regions of a planet

¹**per·ma·nent** \'pər-mə-nənt\ *adj* : LASTING, STABLE — **per·ma·nence** \-nəns\ *n* — **per·ma·nen·cy** \-nən-sē\ *n* — **per·ma·nent·ly** *adv*

²**permanent** *n* : a long-lasting hair wave or straightening

permanent press *n* : the process of treating fabrics with chemicals (as resin) and heat for setting the shape and for aiding wrinkle resistance

per·me·able \'pər-mē-ə-bəl\ *adj* : having small openings that permit liquids or gases to seep through — **per·me·a·bil·i·ty** \ˌpər-mē-ə-'bi-lə-tē\ *n*

per·me·ate \'pər-mē-ˌāt\ *vb* **-at·ed; -at·ing** **1** : PERVADE **2** : to seep through the pores of : PENETRATE — **per·me·ation** \ˌpər-mē-'ā-shən\ *n*

Perm·ian \'pər-mē-ən\ *adj* : of, relating to, or being the latest period of the Paleozoic era — **Permian** *n*

per·mis·si·ble \pər-'mi-sə-bəl\ *adj* : that may be permitted : ALLOWABLE

per·mis·sion \pər-'mi-shən\ *n* : formal consent : AUTHORIZATION

per·mis·sive \pər-'mi-siv\ *adj* : granting permission; *esp* : INDULGENT — **per·mis·sive·ly** *adv* — **per·mis·sive·ness** *n*

¹**per·mit** \pər-'mit\ *vb* **per·mit·ted; per·mit·ting** **1** : to consent to : ALLOW **2** : to make possible

²**per·mit** \'pər-ˌmit, pər-'mit\ *n* : a written permission : LICENSE

per·mu·ta·tion \ˌpər-myü-'tā-shən\ *n* **1** : a major or fundamental change **2** : the act or process of changing the order of an ordered set of objects ♦ *Synonyms* INNOVATION, MUTATION, VICISSITUDE

per·ni·cious \pər-'ni-shəs\ *adj* [ME, fr. AF, fr. L *perniciosus*, fr. *pernicies* destruction, fr. *per-* through + *nec-, nex* violent death] : very destructive or injurious — **per·ni·cious·ly** *adv*

per·ora·tion \'per-ə-ˌrā-shən, 'pər-\ *n* : the concluding part of a speech

¹**per·ox·ide** \pə-'räk-ˌsīd\ *n* : an oxide containing a large proportion of oxygen; *esp* : HYDROGEN PEROXIDE

²**peroxide** *vb* **-id·ed; -id·ing** : to bleach with hydrogen peroxide

perp *abbr* **1** perpendicular **2** perpetrator

per·pen·dic·u·lar \ˌpər-pən-'di-kyə-lər\ *adj* **1** : standing at right angles to the plane of the horizon **2** : forming a right angle with each other or with a given line or plane — **perpendicular** *n* — **per·pen·dic·u·lar·i·ty** \-ˌdi-kyə-'la-rə-tē\ *n* — **per·pen·dic·u·lar·ly** *adv*

per·pe·trate \'pər-pə-ˌtrāt\ *vb* **-trat·ed; -trat·ing** : to carry out (as a crime) : COMMIT — **per·pe·tra·tion** \ˌpər-pə-'trā-shən\ *n* — **per·pe·tra·tor** \'pər-pə-ˌtrā-tər\ *n*

per·pet·u·al \pər-'pe-chə-wəl\ *adj* **1** : continuing forever : EVERLASTING **2** : occurring continually : CONSTANT (~ annoyance) ♦ *Synonyms* CEASELESS, UNCEASING, CONTINUAL, CONTINUOUS, INCESSANT, UNREMITTING — **per·pet·u·al·ly** *adv*

per·pet·u·ate \pər-'pe-chə-ˌwāt\ *vb* **-at·ed; -at·ing** : to make perpetual : cause to last indefinitely — **per·pet·u·a·tion** \-ˌpe-chə-'wā-shən\ *n*

per·pe·tu·i·ty \ˌpər-pə-'tü-ə-tē, -'tyü-\ *n, pl* **-ties** **1** : ETERNITY 1 **2** : the quality or state of being perpetual

per·plex \pər-'pleks\ *vb* : to disturb mentally; *esp* : CONFUSE — **per·plex·i·ty** \-'plek-sə-tē\ *n*

per·plexed \-'plekst\ *adj* **1** : filled with uncertainty : PUZZLED **2** : full of difficulty : COMPLICATED — **per·plexed·ly** \-'plek-səd-lē\ *adv*

per·qui·site \'pər-kwə-zət\ *n* : a privilege or profit beyond regular pay

pers *abbr* person; personal

¹**per se** \(ˌ)pər-'sā\ *adv* [L] : by, of, or in itself : as such

²**per se** *adj* : being such inherently, clearly, or as a matter of law

per·se·cute \'pər-si-ˌkyüt\ vb **-cut·ed; -cut·ing** : to pursue in such a way as to injure or afflict : HARASS; esp : to cause to suffer because of belief — **per·se·cu·tion** \ˌpər-si-'kyü-shən\ n — **per·se·cu·tor** \'pər-si-ˌkyü-tər\ n

per·se·vere \ˌpər-sə-'vir\ vb **-vered; -ver·ing** : to persist (as in an undertaking) in spite of difficulties — **per·se·ver·ance** \-'vir-əns\ n

Per·sian \'pər-zhən\ n 1 : a native or inhabitant of ancient Persia 2 : a member of one of the peoples of modern Iran 3 : the language of the Persians

Persian cat n : any of a breed of stocky round-headed domestic cats that have a long silky coat

Persian lamb n : a pelt with very silky tightly curled fur that is obtained from newborn lambs which are older than those yielding broadtail

per·si·flage \'pər-si-ˌfläzh, 'per-\ n [F, fr. persifler to banter, fr. per- thoroughly + siffler to whistle, hiss, boo, ultim. fr. L sibilare] : lightly jesting or mocking talk

per·sim·mon \pər-'si-mən\ n : either of two trees related to the ebony; also : the edible usu. orange or red plumlike fruit of a persimmon

per·sist \pər-'sist, -'zist\ vb 1 : to go on resolutely or stubbornly in spite of difficulties 2 : to continue to exist — **per·sis·tence** \-'sis-təns, -'zis-\ n — **per·sis·ten·cy** \-tən-sē\ n — **per·sis·tent** \-tənt\ adj — **per·sis·tent·ly** adv

per·snick·e·ty \pər-'sni-kə-tē\ adj : fussy about small details

per·son \'pər-sən\ n [ME, fr. AF persone, fr. L persona actor's mask, character in a play, person, prob. fr. Etruscan phersu mask, fr. Gk prosōpa, pl. of prosōpon face, mask] 1 : a human being : INDIVIDUAL — used in combination esp. by those who prefer to avoid man in compounds applicable to both sexes ⟨chairperson⟩ 2 : one of the three modes of being in the Godhead as understood by Trinitarians 3 : the body of a human being 4 : the individual personality of a human being : SELF 5 : reference of a segment of discourse to the speaker, to one spoken to, or to one spoken of esp. as indicated by certain pronouns

per·so·na \pər-'sō-nə\ n, pl **-nae** \-nē\ or **-nas** : the personality that a person projects in public

per·son·able \'pər-sə-nə-bəl\ adj : pleasant in person : ATTRACTIVE

per·son·age \'pər-sə-nij\ n : a person of rank, note, or distinction

¹**per·son·al** \'pər-sə-nəl\ adj 1 : of, relating to, or affecting a person : PRIVATE ⟨~ correspondence⟩ 2 : done in person ⟨a ~ inquiry⟩ 3 : relating to the person or body ⟨~ injuries⟩ 4 : relating to an individual esp. in an offensive way ⟨resented such ~ remarks⟩ 5 : of or relating to temporary or movable property as distinguished from real estate 6 : denoting grammatical person 7 : intended for use by one person

²**personal** n 1 : a short newspaper paragraph relating to a person or group or to personal matters 2 : a short personal or private communication in the classified ads section of a newspaper

personal computer n : a computer with a microprocessor designed for an individual user to run esp. commercial software

personal digital assistant n : PDA

per·son·al·ise Brit var of PERSONALIZE

per·son·al·i·ty \ˌpər-sə-'na-lə-tē\ n, pl **-ties** 1 : an offensively personal remark ⟨indulges in personalities⟩ 2 : the collection of emotional and behavioral traits that characterize a person 3 : distinction of personal and social traits 4 : a well-known person ⟨a TV ~⟩ ♦ Synonyms INDIVIDUALITY, TEMPERAMENT, DISPOSITION, MAKEUP

per·son·al·ize \'pər-sə-nə-ˌlīz\ vb **-ized; -iz·ing** : to make personal or individual; esp : to mark as belonging to a particular person

per·son·al·ly \-nə-lē\ adv 1 : in person 2 : as a person 3 : as far as oneself is concerned ⟨~, I don't want to go⟩

per·son·al·ty \'pər-sə-nəl-tē\ n, pl **-ties** : personal property

per·so·na non gra·ta \pər-ˌsō-nə-ˌnän-'grä-tə, -ˈgrä-\ adj [L] : being personally unacceptable or unwelcome

per·son·ate \'pər-sə-ˌnāt\ vb **-at·ed; -at·ing** : IMPERSONATE, REPRESENT

per·son·i·fy \pər-'sä-nə-ˌfī\ vb **-fied; -fy·ing** 1 : to think of or represent as a person 2 : to be the embodiment of : INCARNATE ⟨~ the law⟩ — **per·son·i·fi·ca·tion** \-ˌsä-nə-fə-'kā-shən\ n

per·son·nel \ˌpər-sə-'nel\ n : a body of persons employed

per·spec·tive \pər-'spek-tiv\ n 1 : the science of painting and drawing so that objects represented have apparent depth and distance 2 : the aspect in which a subject or its parts are mentally viewed; esp : a view of things (as objects or events) in their true relationship or relative importance

per·spi·ca·cious \ˌpər-spə-'kā-shəs\ adj : having or showing keen understanding or discernment — **per·spi·cac·i·ty** \-'ka-sə-tē\ n

per·spic·u·ous \pər-'spi-kyə-wəs\ adj : plain to the understanding — **per·spi·cu·i·ty** \ˌpər-spə-'kyü-ə-tē\ n

per·spire \pər-'spī(-ə)r\ vb **per·spired; per·spir·ing** : SWEAT — **per·spi·ra·tion** \ˌpər-spə-'rā-shən\ n

per·suade \pər-'swād\ vb **per·suad·ed; per·suad·ing** : to win over to a belief or course of action by argument or entreaty — **per·sua·sive** \-'swā-siv, -ziv\ adj — **per·sua·sive·ly** adv — **per·sua·sive·ness** n

per·sua·sion \pər-'swā-zhən\ n 1 : the act or process of persuading 2 : a system of religious beliefs; also : a group holding such beliefs

pert \'pərt\ adj [ME, evident, attractive, saucy, short for apert evident, fr. AF, fr. L apertus open, fr. pp. of aperire to open] 1

: saucily free and forward : IMPUDENT **2**
: stylishly trim : JAUNTY **3** : LIVELY

per·tain \pər-'tān\ vb **1** : to belong to as
a part, quality, or function ⟨duties ~ing
to the office⟩ **2** : to have reference : RE-
LATE ⟨books ~ing to birds⟩

per·ti·na·cious \ˌpər-tə-'nā-shəs\ adj **1**
: holding resolutely to an opinion or purpose **2** : obstinately persistent ⟨a ~ bill
collector⟩ ✦ **Synonyms** DOGGED, MUL-
ISH, HEADSTRONG, PERVERSE — **per·ti-
nac·i·ty** \-'na-sə-tē\ n

per·ti·nent \'pər-tə-nənt\ adj : relating to
the matter under consideration ✦ **Synonyms** RELEVANT, GERMANE, APPLICA-
BLE, APROPOS — **per·ti·nence** \-əns\ n

per·turb \pər-'tərb\ vb : to disturb greatly
esp. in mind : UPSET — **per·tur·ba·tion**
\ˌpər-tər-'bā-shən\ n

per·tus·sis \pər-'tə-səs\ n : WHOOPING
COUGH

pe·ruke \pə-'rük\ n : WIG

pe·ruse \pə-'rüz\ vb **pe·rused; pe·rus-
ing** : READ; esp : to read over attentively
or leisurely — **pe·rus·al** \-'rü-zəl\ n

per·vade \pər-'vād\ vb **per·vad·ed; per-
vad·ing** : to spread through every part of
: PERMEATE, PENETRATE — **per·va·sive**
\-'vā-siv, -ziv\ adj

per·verse \pər-'vərs\ adj **1** : turned away
from what is right or good : CORRUPT **2**
: obstinate in opposing what is reasonable
or accepted **3** : marked by perversion —
per·verse·ly adv — **per·verse·ness** n
— **per·ver·si·ty** \-'vər-sə-tē\ n

per·ver·sion \pər-'vər-zhən\ n **1** : the action of perverting : the condition of being
perverted **2** : a perverted form of something; esp : aberrant sexual behavior

¹per·vert \pər-'vərt\ vb **1** : to lead astray
: CORRUPT ⟨~ the young⟩ **2** : to divert
to a wrong purpose : MISAPPLY ⟨~ evi-
dence⟩ ✦ **Synonyms** DEPRAVE, DEBASE,
DEBAUCH, DEMORALIZE — **per·ver·ter** n

²per·vert \'pər-ˌvərt\ n : one that is perverted; esp : one given to sexual perversion

pe·se·ta \pə-'sā-tə\ n : the former basic
monetary unit of Spain

pe·se·wa \pə-'sā-wə\ n — see cedi at
MONEY table

pes·ky \'pes-kē\ adj **pes·ki·er; -est**
: causing annoyance : TROUBLESOME

pe·so \'pā-sō\ n, pl **pesos** — see MONEY
table

pes·si·mism \'pe-sə-ˌmi-zəm\ n [F pes-
simisme, fr. L pessimus worst] : an inclination to take the least favorable view (as
of events) or to expect the worst — **pes-
si·mist** \-mist\ n — **pes·si·mis·tic** \ˌpe-
sə-'mis-tik\ adj

pest \'pest\ n **1** : a destructive epidemic
disease : PLAGUE **2** : a plant or animal
detrimental to humans **3** : one that pes-
ters : NUISANCE — **pesty** adj

pes·ter \'pes-tər\ vb : to harass with petty
irritations : ANNOY

pes·ti·cide \'pes-tə-ˌsīd\ n : an agent used
to destroy pests

pes·tif·er·ous \pes-'ti-fə-rəs\ adj **1** : PES-
TILENT **2** : ANNOYING

pes·ti·lence \'pes-tə-ləns\ n : a destructive infectious swiftly spreading disease;
esp : BUBONIC PLAGUE

pes·ti·lent \-lənt\ adj **1** : dangerous to
life : DEADLY **2** : PERNICIOUS, HARM-
FUL **3** : TROUBLESOME **4** : INFECTIOUS,
CONTAGIOUS

pes·ti·len·tial \ˌpes-tə-'len-chəl\ adj **1**
: causing or tending to cause pestilence
: DEADLY **2** : morally harmful

pes·tle \'pes-əl, 'pes-t⁵l\ n : an implement
for grinding substances in a mortar —
pestle vb

¹pet \'pet\ n **1** : FAVORITE, DARLING **2** : a
domesticated animal kept for pleasure
rather than utility

²pet adj **1** : kept or treated as a pet ⟨~
dog⟩ **2** : expressing fondness ⟨~ name⟩
3 : particularly liked or favored

³pet vb **pet·ted; pet·ting 1** : to stroke
gently or lovingly **2** : to make a pet of
: PAMPER **3** : to engage in amorous kissing and caressing

⁴pet n : a fit of peevishness, sulkiness, or
anger — **pet·tish** adj

Pet abbr Peter

pet·al \'pe-t⁵l\ n : one of the modified
leaves of a flower's corolla

pe·tard \pə-'tärd, -'tär\ n : a case containing an explosive to break down a door or
gate or breach a wall

pe·ter \'pē-tər\ vb : to diminish gradually
and come to an end ⟨his energy ~ed out⟩

Pe·ter \'pē-tər\ n — see BIBLE table

pet·i·ole \'pe-tē-ˌōl\ n : a slender stem that
supports a leaf

pe·tite \pə-'tēt\ adj [F] : small and trim of
figure ⟨a ~ woman⟩ — **petite** n

pe·tit four \pe-tē-'fȯr\ n, pl **petits fours**
or **petit fours** \-'fȯrz\ [F, lit., small oven]
: a small cake cut from pound or sponge
cake and frosted

¹pe·ti·tion \pə-'ti-shən\ n : an earnest request : ENTREATY; esp : a formal written
request made to an authority

²petition vb : to make a request to or for
— **pe·ti·tion·er** n

pe·trel \'pe-trəl\ n : any of numerous seabirds that fly far from land

pe·tri dish \'pē-trē-\ n **1** : a small shallow
dish used esp. for growing bacteria **2**
: something fostering development or innovation

pet·ri·fy \'pe-trə-ˌfī\ vb **-fied; -fy·ing 1**
: to convert (organic matter) into stone or
stony material **2** : to make rigid or inactive (as from fear or awe) — **pet·ri·fac-
tion** \ˌpe-trə-'fak-shən\ n

pet·ro·chem·i·cal \ˌpe-trō-'ke-mi-kəl\ n
: a chemical isolated or derived from petroleum or natural gas — **pet·ro·chem-
is·try** \-'ke-mə-strē\ n

pet·rol \'pe-trəl\ n, chiefly Brit : GASOLINE

pet·ro·la·tum \ˌpe-trə-'lā-təm\ n : PETRO-
LEUM JELLY

pe·tro·leum \pə-'trō-lē-əm\ n [ML, fr. Gk
petra rock + L oleum oil] : an oily flammable liquid obtained from wells drilled
in the ground and refined into gasoline,
fuel oils, and other products

petroleum jelly n : a tasteless, odorless,
and oily or greasy substance from petro-

leum that is used esp. in ointments and dressings

¹pet·ti·coat \'pe-tē-ˌkōt\ *n* **1** : a skirt worn under a dress **2** : an outer skirt

²petticoat *adj* : of, relating to, or exercised by women : FEMALE

pet·ti·fog·ger \'pe-tē-ˌfȯ-gər, -ˌfä-\ *n* **1** : a lawyer whose methods are petty, underhanded, or disreputable **2** : one given to quibbling over trifles — **pet·ti·fog·ging** \-ˌgiŋ\ *adj or n*

pet·ty \'pe-tē\ *adj* **pet·ti·er; -est** [ME *pety* small, minor, alter. of *petit*, fr. AF, small] **1** : having secondary rank : MINOR ⟨∼ prince⟩ **2** : of little importance : TRIFLING ⟨∼ faults⟩ **3** : marked by narrowness or meanness — **pet·ti·ly** \'pe-tə-lē\ *adv* — **pet·ti·ness** \-tē-nəs\ *n*

petty officer *n* : a subordinate officer in the navy or coast guard appointed from among the enlisted men

petty officer first class *n* : a petty officer ranking below a chief petty officer

petty officer second class *n* : a petty officer ranking below a petty officer first class

petty officer third class *n* : a petty officer ranking below a petty officer second class

pet·u·lant \'pe-chə-lənt\ *adj* : marked by capricious ill humor ♦ *Synonyms* IRRITABLE, PEEVISH, FRETFUL, FRACTIOUS, QUERULOUS — **pet·u·lance** \-ləns\ *n* — **pet·u·lant·ly** *adv*

pe·tu·nia \pi-'tün-yə, -'tyün-\ *n* : any of a genus of tropical So. American herbs related to the potato and having bright funnel-shaped flowers

pew \'pyü\ *n* [ME *pewe*, fr. MF *puie* balustrade, fr. L *podia*, pl. of *podium* parapet, podium, fr. Gk *podion* base, dim. of *pod-, pous* foot] : any of the benches with backs fixed in rows in a church

pe·wee \'pē-(ˌ)wē\ *n* : any of various small American flycatchers

pew·ter \'pyü-tər\ *n* **1** : an alloy of tin used esp. for household utensils **2** : a bluish gray color — **pewter** *adj* — **pew·ter·er** *n*

pey·o·te \pā-'ō-tē\ *also* **pey·otl** \-'ō-t²l\ *n* **1** : a hallucinogenic drug derived from the peyote cactus and containing mescaline **2** : a small cactus of the southwestern U.S. and Mexico

pf *abbr* **1** pfennig **2** preferred

PFC *or* **Pfc** *abbr* private first class

pfd *abbr* preferred

pfen·nig \'fe-nig\ *n, pl* **pfennig** *also* **pfennigs** *or* **pfen·ni·ge** \'fe-ni-gə\ : a former monetary unit equal to ¹/₁₀₀ deutsche mark

pg *abbr* page

PG *abbr* postgraduate

PGA *abbr* Professional Golfers' Association

pH \(ˌ)pē-'āch\ *n* : a value used to express acidity and alkalinity; *also* : the condition represented by such a value

PH *abbr* **1** pinch hit **2** public health

pha·eton \'fā-ə-t²n\ *n* [F *phaéton*, fr. Gk *Phaethōn*, son of the sun god who persuaded his father to let him drive the chariot of the sun but who lost control of the horses with disastrous consequences] **1** : a light 4-wheeled horse-drawn vehicle **2** : an open automobile with two cross seats

phage \'fāj\ *n* : BACTERIOPHAGE

pha·lanx \'fā-ˌlaŋks\ *n, pl* **pha·lanx·es** *or* **pha·lan·ges** \fə-'lan-ˌjēz\ **1** : a group or body (as of troops) in compact formation **2** *pl phalanges* : one of the digital bones of the hand or foot of a vertebrate

phal·a·rope \'fa-lə-ˌrōp\ *n, pl* **-ropes** *also* **-rope** : any of a genus of small shorebirds related to sandpipers

phal·lic \'fa-lik\ *adj* **1** : of, relating to, or resembling a phallus **2** : relating to or being the stage of psychosexual development in psychoanalytic theory during which children become interested in their own sexual organs

phal·lus \'fa-ləs\ *n, pl* **phal·li** \'fa-ˌlī\ *or* **phal·lus·es** : PENIS; *also* : a symbolic representation of the penis

Phan·er·o·zo·ic \ˌfa-nə-rə-'zō-ik\ *adj* : of, relating to, or being an eon of geologic history comprising the Paleozoic, Mesozoic, and Cenozoic

phan·tasm \'fan-ˌta-zəm\ *n* : a product of the imagination : ILLUSION — **phan·tas·mal** \fan-'taz-məl\ *adj*

phan·tas·ma·go·ria \fan-ˌtaz-mə-'gȯr-ē-ə\ *n* : a constantly shifting complex succession of things seen or imagined; *also* : a scene that constantly changes or fluctuates

phantasy *var of* FANTASY

phan·tom \'fan-təm\ *n* **1** : something (as a specter) that is apparent to sense but has no substantial existence **2** : a mere show : SHADOW — **phantom** *adj*

pha·raoh \'fer-ō, 'fā-rō\ *n, often cap* : a ruler of ancient Egypt

phar·i·sa·ical \ˌfa-rə-'sā-ə-kəl\ *adj* : hypocritically self-righteous

phar·i·see \'fa-rə-ˌsē\ *n* **1** *cap* : a member of an ancient Jewish sect noted for strict observance of rites and ceremonies of the traditional law **2** : a self-righteous or hypocritical person — **phar·i·sa·ic** \ˌfa-rə-'sā-ik\ *adj*

pharm *abbr* pharmaceutical; pharmacist; pharmacy

phar·ma·ceu·ti·cal \ˌfär-mə-'sü-ti-kəl\ *adj* : of, relating to, or engaged in pharmacy or the manufacture and sale of medicinal drugs — **pharmaceutical** *n*

phar·ma·col·o·gy \ˌfär-mə-'kä-lə-jē\ *n* : the science of drugs esp. as related to medicinal uses **2** : the reactions and properties of one or more drugs — **phar·ma·co·log·i·cal** \-kə-'lä-ji-kəl\ *also* **phar·ma·co·log·ic** \-kə-'lä-jik\ *adj* — **phar·ma·col·o·gist** \-'kä-lə-jist\ *n*

phar·ma·co·poe·ia \ˌfär-mə-kə-'pē-ə\ *also* **phar·ma·co·pe·ia** \-kə-'pē-ə\ *n* **1** : a book describing drugs and medicinal preparations **2** : a stock of drugs

phar·ma·cy \'fär-mə-sē\ *n, pl* **-cies** **1** : the art, practice, or profession of preparing and dispensing medical drugs **2** : DRUGSTORE — **phar·ma·cist** \-sist\ *n*

phar·ynx \'fa-riŋks\ *n, pl* **pha·ryn·ges** \fə-'rin-jēz\ *also* **phar·ynx·es** : the muscular tubular passage extending from the back of the nasal cavity and mouth to the esophagus — **pha·ryn·ge·al** \fə-'rin-jəl, ˌfa-rən-'jē-əl\ *adj*

phase \'fāz\ *n* **1** : a particular appearance in a recurring series of changes ⟨∼s of the moon⟩ **2** : a stage or interval in a process or cycle ⟨first ∼ of an experiment⟩ **3** : an aspect or part under consideration — **pha·sic** \'fā-zik\ *adj*

phase down *vb* : to reduce the size or amount of by phases

phase in *vb* : to introduce in stages

phase-out \'fāz-ˌaüt\ *n* : a gradual stopping of operations or production

phase out *vb* : to stop production or use of in stages

PhD *abbr* [L *philosophiae doctor*] doctor of philosophy

pheas·ant \'fe-zᵊnt\ *n, pl* **pheasant** *or* **pheasants** : any of numerous longtailed brilliantly colored game birds related to the domestic chicken

phen·cy·cli·dine \ˌfen-'sī-klə-ˌdēn\ *n* : a drug used esp. as a veterinary anesthetic and sometimes illicitly as a hallucinogenic drug

phe·no·bar·bi·tal \ˌfē-nō-'bär-bə-ˌtól\ *n* : a crystalline drug used as a hypnotic and sedative

phe·nol \'fē-ˌnól\ *n* : a corrosive poisonous acidic compound present in coal and wood tars and used in solution as a disinfectant

phe·nom·e·non \fi-'nä-mə-ˌnän, -nən\ *n, pl* **-na** \-nə\ *or* **-nons** [LL *phaenomenon,* fr. Gk *phainomenon,* fr. neut. of *phainomenos,* prp. of *phainesthai* to appear] **1** *pl* **-na** : an observable fact or event **2** : an outward sign of the working of a law of nature **3** *pl* **-nons** : an extraordinary person or thing : PRODIGY — **phe·nom·e·nal** \-'nä-mə-nᵊl\ *adj* — **phe·nom·e·non·al·ly** *adv*

pher·o·mone \'fer-ə-ˌmōn\ *n* : a chemical substance that is usu. produced by an animal and serves to stimulate a behavioral response in other individuals of the same species — **pher·o·mon·al** \ˌfer-ə-'mō-nᵊl\ *adj*

phi \'fī\ *n* : the 21st letter of the Greek alphabet — Φ or φ

phi·al \'fī(-ə)l\ *n* : VIAL

Phil *abbr* Philippians

phi·lan·der \fə-'lan-dər\ *vb* : to have casual or illicit sexual relations with many women — **phi·lan·der·er** *n*

phi·lan·thro·py \fə-'lan-thrə-pē\ *n, pl* **-pies** **1** : goodwill toward all people; *esp* : effort to promote human welfare **2** : a charitable act or gift; *also* : an organization that distributes or is supported by donated funds — **phil·an·throp·ic** \ˌfi-lən-'thrä-pik\ *adj* — **phil·an·throp·i·cal·ly** \-pi-k(ə-)lē\ *adv* — **phi·lan·thro·pist** \fə-'lan-thrə-pist\ *n*

phi·lat·e·ly \fə-'la-tə-lē\ *n* : the collection and study of postage and imprinted

stamps — **phil·a·tel·ic** \ˌfi-lə-'te-lik\ *adj* — **phi·lat·e·list** \fə-'la-tə-list\ *n*

Phi·le·mon \fə-'lē-mən, fī-\ *n* — see BIBLE table

Phi·lip·pi·ans \fə-'li-pē-ənz\ *n* — see BIBLE table

phi·lip·pic \fə-'li-pik\ *n* : TIRADE

phi·lis·tine \'fi-lə-ˌstēn; fə-'lis-tən\ *n, often cap* [*Philistine,* inhabitant of ancient Philistia (Palestine)] : a person who is smugly insensitive or indifferent to intellectual or artistic values — **philistine** *adj, often cap*

Phil·lips \'fi-ləps\ *adj* : of, relating to, or being a screw having a head with a cross slot or its corresponding screwdriver

philo·den·dron \ˌfi-lə-'den-drən\ *n, pl* **-drons** *also* **-dra** \-drə\ [NL, fr. Gk, neut. of *philodendros* loving trees, fr. *philos* dear, friendly + *dendron* tree] : any of various plants of the arum family grown for their showy foliage

phi·lol·o·gy \fə-'lä-lə-jē\ *n* **1** : the study of literature and relevant fields **2** : LINGUISTICS; *esp* : historical and comparative linguistics — **phil·o·log·i·cal** \ˌfi-lə-'lä-ji-kəl\ *adj* — **phi·lol·o·gist** \fə-'lä-lə-jist\ *n*

philos *abbr* philosopher; philosophy

phi·los·o·pher \fə-'lä-sə-fər\ *n* **1** : a reflective thinker : SCHOLAR **2** : a student of or specialist in philosophy **3** : a person whose philosophical perspective makes it possible to meet trouble calmly

phi·los·o·phise *Brit var of* PHILOSOPHIZE

phi·los·o·phize \fə-'lä-sə-ˌfīz\ *vb* **-phized; -phiz·ing** **1** : to reason like a philosopher : THEORIZE **2** : to expound a philosophy esp. superficially

phi·los·o·phy \fə-'lä-sə-fē\ *n, pl* **-phies** **1** : sciences and liberal arts exclusive of medicine, law, and theology ⟨doctor of ∼⟩ **2** : a critical study of fundamental beliefs and the grounds for them **3** : a system of philosophical concepts ⟨Aristotelian ∼⟩ **4** : a basic theory concerning a particular subject or sphere of activity **5** : the sum of the ideas and convictions of an individual or group ⟨her ∼ of life⟩ **6** : calmness of temper and judgment — **phil·o·soph·i·cal** \ˌfi-lə-'sä-fi-kəl\ *also* **phil·o·soph·ic** \-'sä-fik\ *adj* — **phil·o·soph·i·cal·ly** \-k(ə-)lē\ *adv*

phil·ter \'fil-tər\ *n* **1** : a magic potion **2** : a potion, drug, or charm held to arouse sexual passion

phil·tre *chiefly Brit var of* PHILTER

phle·bi·tis \fli-'bī-təs\ *n* : inflammation of a vein

phle·bot·o·my \fli-'bä-tə-mē\ *n, pl* **-mies** : the opening of a vein esp. for removing or releasing blood

phlegm \'flem\ *n* [ME *fleume,* fr. AF, fr. LL *phlegma,* fr. Gk, flame, inflammation, phlegm, fr. *phlegein* to burn] : thick mucus secreted in abnormal quantity esp. in the nose and throat

phleg·mat·ic \fleg-'ma-tik\ *adj* : having or showing a slow and stolid temperament ♦ **Synonyms** IMPASSIVE, APATHETIC, STOIC

phlo·em \'flō-,em\ n : a vascular plant tissue external to the xylem that carries dissolved food material and functions in support and storage

phlox \'fläks\ n, pl **phlox** or **phlox·es** : any of a genus of American herbs that have tall stalks with showy spreading terminal clusters of flowers

pho·bia \'fō-bē-ə\ n : an irrational persistent fear or dread — **pho·bic** \'fō-bik\ adj

phoe·be \'fē-(,)bē\ n : a flycatcher of the eastern U.S. that has a slight crest and is grayish brown above and yellowish white below

phoe·nix \'fē-niks\ n : a legendary bird held to live for centuries and then to burn itself to death and rise fresh and young from its ashes

¹**phone** \'fōn\ n 1 : TELEPHONE 2 : EARPHONE

²**phone** vb **phoned; phon·ing** : TELEPHONE

phone card n : a prepaid card used in paying for telephone calls

pho·neme \'fō-,nēm\ n : one of the elementary units of speech that distinguish one utterance from another — **pho·ne·mic** \fō-'nē-mik\ adj

pho·net·ics \fə-'ne-tiks\ n : the study and systematic classification of the sounds made in spoken utterance — **pho·net·ic** \-tik\ adj — **pho·ne·ti·cian** \,fō-nə-'tishən\ n

pho·nic \'fä-nik\ adj 1 : of, relating to, or producing sound 2 : of or relating to the sounds of speech or to phonics — **pho·ni·cal·ly** \-ni-k(ə-)lē\ adv

pho·nics \'fä-niks\ n : a method of teaching people to read and pronounce words by learning the phonetic value of letters, letter groups, and syllables

pho·no·graph \'fō-nə-,graf\ n : an instrument for reproducing sounds by means of the vibration of a needle following a spiral groove on a revolving disc

pho·nol·o·gy \fə-'nä-lə-jē\ n : a study and description of the sound changes in a language — **pho·no·log·i·cal** \,fōn-ə-'lä-ji-kəl\ adj — **pho·nol·o·gist** \fə-'nä-lə-jist\ n

pho·ny also **pho·ney** \'fō-nē\ adj **pho·ni·er; -est** : marked by empty pretension : FAKE — **phony** n

phos·phate \'fäs-,fāt\ n : a salt of a phosphoric acid — **phos·phat·ic** \fäs-'fa-tik\ adj

phos·phor \'fäs-fər\ n : a phosphorescent substance

phos·pho·res·cence \,fäs-fə-'re-s°ns\ n 1 : luminescence caused by the absorption of radiations (as light or electrons) and continuing after these radiations stop 2 : an enduring luminescence without sensible heat — **phos·pho·res·cent** \-s°nt\ adj — **phos·pho·res·cent·ly** adv

phosphoric acid \,fäs-'for-ik-, -'fär-\ : any of several oxygen-containing acids of phosphorus

phos·pho·rus also **phos·pho·rous** \'fäs-fə-rəs\ n [NL, fr. Gk phōsphoros light-bearing, fr. phōs light + pherein to carry, bring] : a nonmetallic chemical element that has characteristics similar to nitrogen and occurs widely esp. as phosphates — **phos·pho·ric** \fäs-'for-ik, -'fär-\ adj — **phos·pho·rous** \'fäs-fə-rəs; fäs-'for-əs\ adj

phot- or **photo-** comb form 1 : light ⟨photography⟩ 2 : photograph : photographic ⟨photoengraving⟩ 3 : photoelectric ⟨photocell⟩

pho·to \'fō-tō\ n, pl **photos** : PHOTOGRAPH — **photo** vb or adj

pho·to·cell \'fō-tə-,sel\ n : PHOTOELECTRIC CELL

pho·to·chem·i·cal \,fō-tō-'ke-mi-kəl\ : of, relating to, or resulting from the chemical action of radiant energy

pho·to·com·pose \-kəm-'pōz\ vb : to compose reading matter for reproduction by means of characters photographed on film — **pho·to·com·po·si·tion** \-,käm-pə-'zi-shən\ n

pho·to·copy \'fō-tə-,kä-pē\ n : a photographic reproduction of graphic matter — **photocopy** vb

pho·to·elec·tric \,fō-tō-i-'lek-trik\ adj : relating to an electrical effect due to the interaction of light with matter — **pho·to·elec·tri·cal·ly** \-tri-k(ə-)lē\ adv

photoelectric cell n : a device whose electrical properties are modified by the action of light

pho·to·en·grave \,fō-tō-in-'grāv\ vb : to make a photoengraving of

pho·to·en·grav·ing n : a process by which an etched printing plate is made from a photograph or drawing; also : a print made from such a plate

photo finish n : a race finish so close that a photograph of the finish is used to determine the winner

pho·tog \fə-'täg\ n : PHOTOGRAPHER

pho·to·gen·ic \,fō-tə-'je-nik\ adj : eminently suitable esp. aesthetically for being photographed

pho·to·graph \'fō-tə-,graf\ n : a picture taken by photography — **photograph** vb — **pho·tog·ra·pher** \fə-'tä-grə-fər\ n

pho·tog·ra·phy \fə-'tä-grə-fē\ n : the art or process of producing images on a sensitive surface (as film or a CCD chip) by the action of light — **pho·to·graph·ic** \,fō-tə-'gra-fik\ adj — **pho·to·graph·i·cal·ly** \-fi-k(ə-)lē\ adv

pho·to·gra·vure \,fō-tə-grə-'vyúr\ n : a process for making prints from an intaglio plate prepared by photographic methods

pho·to·li·thog·ra·phy \,fō-tō-li-'thä-grə-fē\ n : the process of photographically transferring a pattern to a surface for etching (as in making an integrated circuit)

pho·tom·e·ter \fō-'tä-mə-tər\ n : an instrument for measuring the intensity of light — **pho·to·met·ric** \,fō-tə-'me-trik\ adj — **pho·tom·e·try** \fō-'tä-mə-trē\ n

pho·to·mi·cro·graph \,fō-tō-'mī-krə-,graf\ n : a photograph of a microscope image — **pho·to·mi·crog·ra·phy** \-,mī-'krä-grə-fē\ n

pho·ton \'fō-,tän\ n : a quantum of electromagnetic radiation

photo op *n* : a situation or event that lends itself to the taking of pictures which favor the individuals photographed

pho·to·play \'fō-tō-ˌplā\ *n* : MOTION PICTURE

pho·to·sen·si·tive \ˌfō-tə-'sen-sə-tiv\ *adj* : sensitive or sensitized to the action of radiant energy

pho·to·sphere \'fō-tə-ˌsfir\ *n* : the luminous surface of a star — **pho·to·spher·ic** \ˌfō-tə-'sfir-ik, -'sfer-\ *adj*

pho·to·syn·the·sis \ˌfō-tō-'sin-thə-səs\ *n* : the process by which chlorophyll-containing plants make carbohydrates from water and from carbon dioxide in the air in the presence of light — **pho·to·syn·the·size** \-ˌsīz\ *vb* — **pho·to·syn·thet·ic** \-sin-'the-tik\ *adj*

phr *abbr* phrase

¹phrase \'frāz\ *n* **1** : a brief expression **2** : a group of two or more grammatically related words that form a sense unit expressing a thought

²phrase *vb* **phrased; phras·ing** : to express in words

phrase·ol·o·gy \ˌfrā-zē-'ä-lə-jē\ *n, pl* **-gies** : a manner of phrasing : STYLE

phras·ing *n* : style of expression

phre·net·ic *archaic var of* FRENETIC

phren·ic \'fre-nik\ *adj* : of or relating to the diaphragm ⟨~ nerves⟩

phre·nol·o·gy \fri-'nä-lə-jē\ *n* : the study of the conformation of the skull based on the belief that it indicates mental faculties and character traits

phy·lac·tery \fə-'lak-tə-rē\ *n, pl* **-ter·ies** **1** : one of two small square leather boxes containing slips inscribed with scripture passages and traditionally worn on the left arm and forehead by Jewish men during morning weekday prayers **2** : AMULET

phy·lum \'fī-ləm\ *n, pl* **phy·la** \-lə\ [NL, fr. Gk *phylon* tribe, race] : a major category in biological classification esp. of animals that ranks above the class and below the kingdom; *also* : a group (as of people) apparently of common origin

phys *abbr* **1** physical **2** physics

¹phys·ic \'fi-zik\ *n* **1** : the profession of medicine **2** : MEDICINE; *esp* : PURGATIVE

²physic *vb* **phys·icked; phys·ick·ing** : PURGE **2**

¹phys·i·cal \'fi-zi-kəl\ *adj* **1** : of or relating to nature or the laws of nature **2** : material as opposed to mental or spiritual **3** : of, relating to, or produced by the forces and operations of physics **4** : of or relating to the body — **phys·i·cal·ly** \-k(ə-)lē\ *adv*

²physical *n* : PHYSICAL EXAMINATION

physical education *n* : instruction in the development and care of the body ranging from simple calisthenics to training in hygiene, gymnastics, and the performance and management of athletic games

physical examination *n* : an examination of the bodily functions and condition of an individual

phys·i·cal·ize \'fi-zə-kə-ˌlīz\ *vb* **-ized; -iz-** ing : to give physical form or expression to

physical science *n* : any of the sciences (as physics and astronomy) that deal primarily with nonliving materials — **physical scientist** *n*

physical therapy *n* : the treatment of disease by physical and mechanical means (as massage, exercise, water, or heat) — **physical therapist** *n*

phy·si·cian \fə-'zi-shən\ *n* : a doctor of medicine

physician's assistant *n* : a person certified to provide basic medical care usu. under a licensed physician's supervision

phys·i·cist \'fi-zə-sist\ *n* : a scientist who specializes in physics

phys·ics \'fi-ziks\ *n* [L *physica*, pl., natural sciences, fr. Gk *physika*, fr. *physis* growth, nature, fr. *phyein* to bring forth] **1** : the science of matter and energy and their interactions **2** : the physical properties and composition of something

phys·i·og·no·my \ˌfi-zē-'äg-nə-mē\ *n, pl* **-mies** : facial appearance esp. as a reflection of inner character

phys·i·og·ra·phy \ˌfi-zē-'ä-grə-fē\ *n* : geography dealing with physical features of the earth — **phys·io·graph·ic** \ˌfi-zē-ō-'gra-fik\ *adj*

phys·i·ol·o·gy \ˌfi-zē-'ä-lə-jē\ *n* **1** : a branch of biology dealing with the functions and functioning of living matter and organisms **2** : functional processes in an organism or any of its parts — **phys·i·o·log·i·cal** \-zē-ə-'lä-ji-kəl\ *or* **phys·i·o·log·ic** \-jik\ *adj* — **phys·i·o·log·i·cal·ly** \-ji-k(ə-)lē\ *adv* — **phys·i·ol·o·gist** \-zē-'ä-lə-jist\ *n*

phys·io·ther·a·py \ˌfi-zē-ō-'ther-ə-pē\ *n* : PHYSICAL THERAPY — **phys·io·ther·a·pist** \-pist\ *n*

phy·sique \fə-'zēk\ *n* : the build of a person's body : bodily constitution

phy·to·chem·i·cal \ˌfi-tō-'ke-mi-kəl\ *n* : a chemical compound occurring naturally in plants

phy·to·plank·ton \'fī-tō-ˌplaŋk-tən\ *n* : plant life of the plankton

pi \'pī\ *n, pl* **pis** \'pīz\ **1** : the 16th letter of the Greek alphabet — Π or π **2** : the symbol π denoting the ratio of the circumference of a circle to its diameter; *also* : the ratio itself equal to approximately 3.1416

PI *abbr* private investigator

pi·a·nis·si·mo \ˌpē-ə-'ni-sə-ˌmō\ *adv or adj* : very softly — used as a direction in music

pi·a·nist \pē-'a-nist, 'pē-ə-\ *n* : a person who plays the piano

¹pi·a·no \pē-'ä-nō\ *adv or adj* : SOFTLY — used as a direction in music

²piano \pē-'a-nō\ *n, pl* **pianos** [It, short for *pianoforte*, fr. *gravicembalo col piano e forte*, lit., harpsichord with soft and loud; fr. the fact that its tones could be varied in loudness] : a musical instrument having steel strings sounded by felt-covered hammers operated from a keyboard

pi·ano·forte \pē-ˌa-nō-'fòr-ˌtā, -ˌtē; pē-'a-nə-ˌfòrt\ *n* : PIANO

pi·as·tre *also* **pi·as·ter** \pē-ˈas-tər\ *n* — see *pound* at MONEY table

pi·az·za \pē-ˈa-zə, *esp for 1* -ˈat-sə\ *n, pl* **pi·azzas** *or* **pi·az·ze** \-ˈat-(ˌ)sā, -ˈät-\ [It, fr. L *platea* broad street] **1** : an open square esp. in an Italian town **2** : a long hall with an arched roof **3** *dial* : VERANDA, PORCH

pi·broch \ˈpē-ˌbräk\ *n* : a set of variations for the bagpipe

pic \ˈpik\ *n, pl* **pics** *or* **pix** \ˈpiks\ **1** : PHOTOGRAPH **2** : MOTION PICTURE

pi·ca \ˈpī-kə\ *n* : a typewriter type with 10 characters to the inch

pic·a·resque \ˌpik-ə-ˈresk, ˌpē-\ *adj* : of or relating to rogues ⟨~ fiction⟩

pic·a·yune \ˌpik-ē-ˈyün\ *adj* : of little value : TRIVIAL; *also* : PETTY

pic·ca·lil·li \ˌpik-ə-ˈli-lē\ *n* : a relish of chopped vegetables and spices

pic·co·lo \ˈpi-kə-ˌlō\ *n, pl* **-los** [It, short for *piccolo flauto* small flute] : a small shrill flute pitched an octave higher than the ordinary flute

pice \ˈpīs\ *n, pl* **pice** : PAISA

¹pick \ˈpik\ *vb* **1** : to pierce or break up with a pointed instrument **2** : to remove bit by bit; *also* : to remove covering matter from **3** : to gather by plucking ⟨~ apples⟩ **4** : CULL, SELECT ⟨~ a pocket⟩ **5** : ROB ⟨~ a pocket⟩ : PROVOKE ⟨~ a quarrel⟩ **7** : to dig into or pull lightly at **8** : to pluck with fingers or a pick ⟨~ wool⟩ **10** : to unlock with a wire **11** : to eat sparingly — **pick·er** *n* — **pick on** : to single out for criticism, teasing, or bullying

²pick *n* **1** : the act or privilege of choosing **2** : the best or choicest one **3** : the part of a crop gathered at one time

³pick *n* **1** : a heavy wooden-handled tool pointed at one or both ends **2** : a pointed implement used for picking **3** : a small thin piece (as of plastic) used to pluck the strings of a stringed instrument

pick·a·back \ˈpi-gē-ˌbak, ˈpi-kə-\ *var of* PIGGYBACK

pick·ax \ˈpik-ˌaks\ *n* : ³PICK 1

pick·er·el \ˈpi-kə-rəl\ *n, pl* **pickerel** *or* **pickerels** : either of two bony fishes related to the pikes; *also* : WALLEYE 2

pick·er·el·weed \-ˌwēd\ *n* : a No. American shallow-water herb that bears spikes of purplish blue flowers

¹pick·et \ˈpi-kət\ *n* **1** : a pointed stake (as for a fence) **2** : a detached body of soldiers on outpost duty; *also* : SENTINEL **3** : a person posted by a labor union where workers are on strike; *also* : a person posted for a protest

²picket *vb* **1** : to guard with pickets **2** : TETHER ⟨~ a horse⟩ **3** : to post pickets at ⟨~ a factory⟩ **4** : to serve as a picket

pick·ings \ˈpi-kiŋz, -kənz\ *n pl* **1** : gleanable or eatable fragments : SCRAPS **2** : yield for effort expended : RETURN

pick·le \ˈpi-kəl\ *n* **1** : a brine or vinegar solution for preserving foods; *also* : a food (as a cucumber) preserved in a pick-

le **2** : a difficult situation : PLIGHT — **pickle** *vb*

pick·lock \ˈpik-ˌläk\ *n* **1** : BURGLAR, THIEF **2** : a tool for picking locks

pick·pock·et \ˈpik-ˌpä-kət\ *n* : one who steals from pockets

¹pick·up \ˈpik-ˌəp\ *n* **1** : a hitchhiker who is given a ride **2** : a temporary chance acquaintance **3** : a picking up **4** : revival of business activity **5** : ACCELERATION **6** : the conversion of mechanical movements into electrical impulses in the reproduction of sound; *also* : a device for making such conversion **7** : a light truck having an enclosed cab and an open body with low sides and a tailgate **8** : a pickup game **9** : a player acquired from another team

²pickup *adj* : using or comprising local or available personnel ⟨a ~ game⟩

pick up *vb* **1** : to take hold of and lift **2** : IMPROVE **3** : to put in order

picky \ˈpi-kē\ *adj* **pick·i·er; -est** : FUSSY, FINICKY ⟨a ~ eater⟩

¹pic·nic \ˈpik-ˌnik\ *n* : an outing with food usu. provided by members of the group and eaten in the open

²picnic *vb* **pic·nicked; pic·nick·ing** : to go on a picnic : eat in picnic fashion

pi·cot \ˈpē-ˌkō\ *n* : one of a series of small loops forming an edging on ribbon or lace

pic·to·ri·al \pik-ˈtōr-ē-əl\ *adj* : of, relating to, or consisting of pictures

¹pic·ture \ˈpik-chər\ *n* **1** : a representation made by painting, drawing, or photography **2** : a vivid description in words **3** : IMAGE, COPY ⟨was the ~ of his father⟩ **4** : a transitory visual image (as on a TV screen) **5** : MOTION PICTURE **6** : SITUATION ⟨a bleak economic ~⟩

²picture *vb* **pic·tured; pic·tur·ing** **1** : to paint or draw a picture of **2** : to describe vividly in words **3** : to form a mental image of

pic·tur·esque \ˌpik-chə-ˈresk\ *adj* **1** : resembling a picture ⟨a ~ landscape⟩ **2** : CHARMING, QUAINT ⟨a ~ character⟩ **3** : GRAPHIC, VIVID ⟨a ~ account⟩ — **pic·tur·esque·ness** *n*

picture tube *n* : a cathode-ray tube on which the picture appears in a television

pid·dle \ˈpi-dᵊl\ *vb* **pid·dled; pid·dling** : to act or work idly : DAWDLE

pid·dling \ˈpi-dᵊl-ən, -iŋ\ *adj* : TRIVIAL, PALTRY ⟨spent a ~ sum⟩

pid·dly \ˈpid-lē\ *adj* : TRIVIAL, PIDDLING

pid·gin \ˈpi-jən\ *n* [fr. *pidgin English*, fr. Chinese Pidgin English *pidgin* business] : a simplified speech used for communication between people with different languages

pie \ˈpī\ *n* : a dish consisting of a pastry crust and a filling (as of fruit or meat)

¹pie·bald \ˈpī-ˌbȯld\ *adj* : of different colors; *esp* : blotched with white and black ⟨a ~ horse⟩

²piebald *n* : a piebald animal

¹piece \ˈpēs\ *n* **1** : a part of a whole : FRAGMENT, PORTION **2** : one of a group, set, or mass ⟨~s of flatware⟩; *also* : a single item or instance ⟨a ~ of nonsense⟩ ⟨a ~ of news⟩ **3** : a movable object used in a board game **4** : a length, weight, or size in which something is made or sold **5** : a product (as an essay) of creative work **6** : FIREARM **7** : COIN

²**piece** vb **pieced; piec·ing 1** : to repair or complete by adding pieces : PATCH **2** : to join into a whole

pièce de ré·sis·tance \pē-ˌes-də-rā-ˌzē-'stäns\ n, pl **pièces de ré·sis·tance** \same\ [F] **1** : the chief dish of a meal **2** : an outstanding item

piece·meal \'pēs-ˌmēl\ adv or adj : one piece at a time : GRADUALLY

piece·work \-ˌwərk\ n : work done and paid for by the piece — **piece·work·er** n

pie chart n : a circular chart that shows quantities or frequencies by parts of a circle shaped like pieces of pie

pied \'pīd\ adj : of two or more colors in blotches : VARIEGATED

pied–à–terre \pē-ˌā-də-'ter\ n, pl **pieds–à–terre** \same\ [F, lit., foot to the ground] : a temporary or second lodging

pier \'pir\ n **1** : a support for a bridge span **2** : a structure built out into the water for use as a landing place or a promenade or to protect or form a harbor **3** : an upright supporting part (as a pillar) of a building or structure

pierce \'pirs\ vb **pierced; pierc·ing 1** : to enter or thrust into sharply or painfully : STAB **2** : to make a hole in or through : PERFORATE ⟨pierced ears⟩ **3** : to force or make a way into or through : PENETRATE **4** : to see through : DISCERN — **pierc·er** n

piercing n : a piece of jewelry attached to pierced flesh

pies pl of PI, or of PIE

pi·ety \'pī-ə-tē\ n, pl **pi·et·ies 1** : fidelity to natural obligations (as to parents) **2** : dutifulness in religion : DEVOUTNESS **3** : a pious act

pif·fle \'pi-fəl\ n : trifling talk or action

pig \'pig\ n **1** : SWINE; esp : a young domesticated swine **2** : PORK **3** : a dirty, gluttonous, or repulsive person **4** : a crude casting of metal (as iron)

pi·geon \'pi-jən\ n : any of numerous stout-bodied short-legged birds with smooth thick plumage

¹**pi·geon·hole** \'pi-jən-ˌhōl\ n : a small open compartment (as in a desk) for keeping letters or documents

²**pigeonhole** vb **1** : to place in or as if in a pigeonhole : FILE **2** : to lay aside **3** : to assign to a usu. restrictive category

pi·geon–toed \-ˌtōd\ adj : having the toes and forefoot turned inward

pig·gish \'pi-gish\ adj **1** : GREEDY **2** : STUBBORN

pig·gy·back \'pi-gē-ˌbak\ also **pick·a·back** \'pi-kə-, 'pi-kə-\ adv or adj **1** : up on the back and shoulders **2** : on a railroad flatcar

pig·head·ed \'pig-'he-dəd\ adj : OBSTINATE, STUBBORN

pig latin n, often cap L : a jargon that is made by systematic alteration of English

pig·let \'pi-glət\ n : a small usu. young swine

pig·ment \'pig-mənt\ n **1** : coloring matter **2** : a powder mixed with a liquid to give color (as in paints) — **pig·ment·ed** \-mən-təd\ adj

pig·men·ta·tion \ˌpig-mən-'tā-shən\ n : coloration with or deposition of pigment; esp : an excessive deposition of bodily pigment

pigmy var of PYGMY

pig·nut \'pig-ˌnət\ n : the bitter nut of any of several hickory trees; also : any of these trees

pig·pen \-ˌpen\ n **1** : a pen for pigs **2** : a dirty place

pig·skin \-ˌskin\ n **1** : the skin of a swine or leather made of it **2** : FOOTBALL 2

pig·sty \-ˌstī\ n : PIGPEN

pig·tail \-ˌtāl\ n : a tight braid of hair

pi·ka \'pē-kə, 'pī-\ n : any of various small short-eared mammals related to the rabbits and occurring in rocky uplands of Asia and western No. America

¹**pike** \'pīk\ n : a sharp point or spike

²**pike** n, pl **pike** or **pikes** : a large slender long-snouted freshwater bony fish valued for food; also : any of various related fishes

³**pike** n : a long wooden shaft with a pointed steel head formerly used as a foot soldier's weapon

⁴**pike** n : TURNPIKE

pik·er \'pī-kər\ n **1** : one who does things in a small way or on a small scale **2** : TIGHTWAD, CHEAPSKATE

pike·staff \'pīk-ˌstaf\ n : the staff of a foot soldier's pike

pi·laf also **pi·laff** \pi-'läf, 'pē-ˌläf\ or **pi·lau** \pi-'lȯ, -'lȯ, 'pē-lȯ, -lȯ\ n : a dish made of seasoned rice often with meat

pi·las·ter \pi-'las-tər, 'pī-ˌlas-tər\ n : an architectural support that looks like a rectangular column and projects slightly from a wall

pil·chard \'pil-chərd\ n : a small European marine fish related to the herrings and often packed as a sardine

¹**pile** \'pī(-ə)l\ n : a long slender column (as of wood or steel) driven into the ground to support a vertical load

²**pile** n **1** : a quantity of things heaped together **2** : PYRE **3** : a great number or quantity : LOT

³**pile** vb **piled; pil·ing 1** : to lay in a pile : STACK **2** : to heap up : ACCUMULATE **3** : to press forward in a mass : CROWD

⁴**pile** n : a velvety surface of fine short hairs or threads (as on cloth) — **piled** \'pī(-ə)ld\ adj — **pile·less** adj

piles \'pī(-ə)lz\ n pl : HEMORRHOIDS

pil·fer \'pil-fər\ vb : to steal in small quantities

pil·grim \'pil-grəm\ n [ME, fr. AF pelerin, pilegrin, fr. LL pelegrinus, alter. of L peregrinus foreigner, fr. peregrinus foreign, fr. peregri abroad, fr. per through + ager land] **1** : one who journeys in foreign lands : WAYFARER **2** : one who travels to a shrine or holy place as an act of devotion **3** cap : one of the English settlers founding Plymouth colony in 1620

pil·grim·age \-grə-mij\ *n* : a journey of a pilgrim esp. to a shrine or holy place

pil·ing \'pī-liŋ\ *n* : a structure of piles

¹**pill** \'pil\ *n* **1** : a small rounded mass usu. of medicine that is swallowed whole **2** : a disagreeable or tiresome person **3** *often cap* : an oral contraceptive — usu. used with *the*

pil·lage \'pi-lij\ *vb* **pil·laged; pil·lag·ing** : to take booty : LOOT, PLUNDER — **pillage** *n* — **pil·lag·er** *n*

pil·lar \'pi-lər\ *n* **1** : a strong upright support (as for a roof) **2** : a column or shaft standing alone esp. as a monument **3** : an integral or upstanding member or part **4** : a fundamental tenet ⟨the five ~s of Islam⟩ — **pil·lared** \-lərd\ *adj*

pill·box \'pil-,bäks\ *n* **1** : a shallow round box for pills **2** : a low concrete emplacement esp. for machine guns

pil·lion \'pil-yən\ *n*, **1** : a pad or cushion placed behind a saddle for an extra rider **2** *chiefly Brit* : a motorcycle or bicycle saddle for a passenger

¹**pil·lo·ry** \'pi-lə-rē\ *n*, *pl* **-ries** : a wooden frame for public punishment having holes in which the head and hands can be locked

²**pillory** *vb* **-ried; -ry·ing** **1** : to set in a pillory **2** : to expose to public scorn

¹**pil·low** \'pi-lō\ *n* : a case filled with springy material (as feathers) and used to support the head of a resting person

²**pillow** *vb* : to rest or place on or as if on a pillow; *also* : to serve as a pillow for

pil·low·case \-,kās\ *n* : a removable covering for a pillow

¹**pi·lot** \'pī-lət\ *n* **1** : HELMSMAN, STEERSMAN **2** : a person qualified and licensed to take ships into and out of a port **3** : GUIDE, LEADER **4** : one that flies an aircraft or spacecraft **5** : a television show filmed or taped as a sample of a proposed series — **pi·lot·less** *adj*

²**pilot** *vb* : CONDUCT, GUIDE; *esp* : to act as pilot of

³**pilot** *adj* : serving as a guiding or activating device or as a testing or trial unit ⟨a ~ light⟩ ⟨a ~ factory⟩

pi·lot·house \'pī-lət-,haus\ *n* : a shelter on the upper deck of a ship for the steering gear and the helmsman

pilot whale *n* : either of two mostly black medium-sized whales

pil·sner *also* **pil·sen·er** \'pilz-nər, 'pil-zə-\ *n* [G, lit., of Pilsen (Plzeň), city in the Czech Republic] **1** : a light beer with a strong flavor of hops **2** : a tall slender footed glass for beer

pi·men·to \pə-'men-tō\ *n*, *pl* **pimentos** *or* **pimento** [Sp *pimienta* allspice, pepper, fr. LL *pigmenta*, pl. of *pigmentum* plant juice, fr. L, pigment] **1** : ALLSPICE **2** : PIMIENTO

pi·mien·to \pə-'men-tō\ *n*, *pl* **-tos** : any of various mild red sweet pepper fruits used esp. to stuff olives and to make paprika

pimp \'pimp\ *n* : a man who solicits clients for a prostitute — **pimp** *vb*

pim·per·nel \'pim-pər-,nel, -nəl\ *n* : any of a genus of herbs related to the primroses

pim·ple \'pim-pəl\ *n* : a small inflamed swelling on the skin often containing pus — **pim·ply** \-p(ə-)lē\ *adj*

¹**pin** \'pin\ *n* **1** : a piece of wood or metal used esp. for fastening things together or as a support by which one thing may be suspended from another; *esp* : a small pointed piece of wire with a head used for fastening clothes or attaching papers **2** : an ornament or emblem fastened to clothing with a pin **3** : one of the pieces constituting the target (as in bowling); *also* : the staff of the flag marking a hole on a golf course **4** : LEG

²**pin** *vb* **pinned; pin·ning** **1** : to fasten, join, or secure with a pin **2** : to hold fast or immobile **3** : ATTACH, HANG ⟨*pinned* their hopes on one man⟩ **4** : to assign the blame for ⟨~ a crime on someone⟩ **5** : to define clearly : ESTABLISH ⟨~ down an idea⟩

PIN *abbr* personal identification number

pi·ña co·la·da \,pēn-yə-kō-'lä-də, ,pē-nə-\ *n* [Sp, lit., strained pineapple] : a tall drink made of rum, cream of coconut, and pineapple juice mixed with ice

pin·afore \'pi-nə-,fōr\ *n* : a sleeveless dress or apron fastened at the back

pin·ball machine \'pin-,bȯl-\ *n* : an amusement device in which a ball is maneuvered along a slanted surface among a series of targets for points

pince-nez \pa⁰s-'nā\ *n*, *pl* **pince-nez** *same or* -'nāz\ [F, fr. *pincer* to pinch + *nez* nose] : eyeglasses clipped to the nose by a spring

pin·cer \'pin-sər\ *n* **1** *pl* : a gripping instrument with two handles and two grasping jaws **2** : a claw (as of a lobster) resembling pincers

¹**pinch** \'pinch\ *vb* [ME, fr. AF *pincher, *pincer*, fr. VL *pinctiare, *punctiare, fr. L *punctum* puncture] **1** : to squeeze between the finger and thumb or between the jaws of an instrument **2** : to compress painfully **3** : CONTRACT, SHRIVEL **4** : to be miserly; *also* : to subject to strict economy **5** : to confine or limit narrowly **6** : STEAL **7** : ARREST

²**pinch** *n* **1** : a critical point : EMERGENCY **2** : painful effect **3** : an act of pinching **4** : a very small quantity **5** : ARREST

³**pinch** *adj* : SUBSTITUTE ⟨a ~ runner⟩

pinch–hit \,pinch-'hit\ *vb* **1** : to bat in the place of another player esp. when a hit is particularly needed **2** : to act or serve in place of another — **pinch hit** *n* — **pinch hitter** *n*

pin curl *n* : a curl made usu. by dampening a strand of hair, coiling it, and securing it by a hairpin or clip

pin·cush·ion \'pin-,kú-shən\ *n* : a cushion for pins not in use

¹**pine** \'pīn\ *n* : any of a genus of evergreen cone-bearing trees; *also* : the light durable resinous wood of a pine

²**pine** *vb* **pined; pin·ing** **1** : to lose vigor or health through distress **2** : to long for something intensely

pi·ne·al \'pī-nē-əl, pī-'nē-əl\ *n* : PINEAL GLAND — **pineal** *adj*

pineal gland *n* : a small usu. conical appendage of the brain of all vertebrates with a cranium that functions primarily as an endocrine organ

pine·ap·ple \'pīn-ˌa-pəl\ *n* : a tropical plant bearing a large edible juicy fruit; *also* : its fruit

pin·feath·er \'pin-ˌfe-thər\ *n* : a new feather just coming through the skin

ping \'piŋ\ *n* **1** : a sharp sound like that of a bullet striking **2** : engine knock

pin·hole \'pin-ˌhōl\ *n* : a small hole made by, for, or as if by a pin

¹pin·ion \'pin-yən\ *n* : the end section of a bird's wing; *also* : WING

²pinion *vb* : to restrain by binding the arms; *also* : SHACKLE

³pinion *n* : a gear with a small number of teeth designed to mesh with a larger wheel or rack

¹pink \'piŋk\ *n* **1** : any of a genus of plants with narrow leaves often grown for their showy flowers **2** : the highest degree : HEIGHT ⟨the ~ of condition⟩

²pink *n* : a light tint of red

³pink *adj* **1** : of the color pink **2** : holding socialistic views — **pink·ish** *adj*

⁴pink *vb* **1** : to perforate in an ornamental pattern **2** : PIERCE, STAB **3** : to cut a saw-toothed edge on

pink·eye \'piŋk-ˌī\ *n* : an acute contagious eye inflammation

pin·kie or **pin·ky** \'piŋ-kē\ *n, pl* **pinkies** : the smallest finger of the hand

pin·nace \'pi-nəs\ *n* **1** : a light sailing ship **2** : a ship's boat

pin·na·cle \'pi-ni-kəl\ *n* [ME *pinacle*, fr. AF, fr. LL *pinnaculum* small wing, gable, fr. L *pinna* wing, battlement] **1** : a turret ending in a small spire **2** : a lofty peak **3** : ACME

pin·nate \'pi-ˌnāt\ *adj* : resembling a feather esp. in having similar parts arranged on each side of an axis ⟨a ~ leaf⟩ — **pin·nate·ly** *adv*

pi·noch·le \'pē-ˌnə-kəl\ *n* : a card game played with a 48-card deck

pi·ñon or **pin·yon** \'pin-ˌyon, -ˌyän\ *n, pl* **pi·ñons** or **pin·yons** or **pi·ño·nes** \pin-'yō-nēz\ [AmerSp *piñón*] : any of various small pines of western No. America with edible seeds; *also* : the edible seed of a piñon

pin·point \'pin-ˌpȯint\ *vb* : to locate, hit, or aim with great precision

pin·prick \-ˌprik\ *n* **1** : a small puncture made by or as if by a pin **2** : a petty irritation or annoyance

pins and needles *n pl* : a pricking tingling sensation in a limb growing numb or recovering from numbness — **on pins and needles** : in a nervous or jumpy state of anticipation

pin·stripe \'pin-ˌstrīp\ *n* : a narrow stripe on a fabric; *also* : a suit with such stripes — **pin–striped** \-ˌstrīpt\ *adj*

pint \'pīnt\ *n* — see WEIGHT table

pin·to \'pin-ˌtō\ *n, pl* **pintos** *also* **pintoes** : a spotted horse or pony

pinto bean *n* : a spotted seed produced by a kind of kidney bean and used for food

pin·up \'pin-ˌəp\ *adj* : suitable for or designed for hanging on a wall; *also* : suited (as by beauty) to be the subject of a pinup photograph

pin·wheel \-ˌhwēl, -ˌwēl\ *n* **1** : a fireworks device in the form of a revolving wheel of colored fire **2** : a toy consisting of lightweight vanes that revolve at the end of a stick

pin·worm \-ˌwərm\ *n* : a nematode worm parasitic in the human intestine

pin·yin \'pin-'yin\ *n, often cap* : a system for writing Chinese ideograms by using Roman letters to represent the sounds

¹pi·o·neer \ˌpī-ə-'nir\ *n* **1** : one that originates or helps open up a new line of thought or activity **2** : an early settler in a territory

²pioneer *vb* **1** : to act as a pioneer **2** : to open or prepare for others to follow; *also* : SETTLE

pi·ous \'pī-əs\ *adj* **1** : marked by reverence for deity : DEVOUT **2** : excessively or affectedly religious **3** : SACRED, DEVOTIONAL **4** : showing loyal reverence for a person or thing : DUTIFUL **5** : marked by sham or hypocrisy — **pi·ous·ly** *adv*

¹pip \'pip\ *n* : one of the dots used on dice and dominoes to indicate numerical value

²pip *n* : a small fruit seed (as of an apple)

¹pipe \'pīp\ *n* **1** : a tubular musical instrument played by forcing air through it **2** : BAGPIPE **3** : a tube designed to conduct something (as water, steam, or oil) **4** : a device for smoking having a tube with a bowl at one end and a mouthpiece at the other **5** : a means of transmission (as of computer data)

²pipe *vb* **piped; pip·ing** **1** : to play on a pipe **2** : to speak in a high or shrill voice **3** : to convey by or as if by pipes — **pip·er** *n*

pipe down *vb* : to stop talking or making noise

pipe dream *n* : an illusory or fantastic hope

pipe·line \'pīp-ˌlīn\ *n* **1** : a line of pipe with pumps, valves, and control devices for conveying fluids **2** : a channel for information **3** : PIPE 5

pi·pette or **pi·pet** \pī-'pet\ *n* : a device for measuring and transferring small volumes of liquid

pipe up *vb* : to speak loudly and distinctly; *also* : to express an opinion freely

pip·ing \'pī-piŋ\ *n* **1** : the music of pipes **2** : a narrow fold of material used to decorate edges or seams

piping hot *adj* : very hot

pip·pin \'pi-pən\ *n* : a crisp tart usu. yellowish apple

pip–squeak \'pip-ˌskwēk\ *n* : one that is small or insignificant

pi·quant \'pē-kənt\ *adj* **1** : pleasantly savory : PUNGENT **2** : engagingly provocative; *also* : having a lively charm — **pi·quan·cy** \-kən-sē\ *n*

¹pique \'pēk\ *n* [F] : a passing feeling of wounded vanity : RESENTMENT

²**pique** *vb* **piqued; piqu·ing 1** : IRRITATE 1 **2** : to arouse by a provocation or challenge : GOAD

pi·qué *or* **pi·que** \pi-'kā\ *n* : a durable ribbed clothing fabric

pi·quet \pi-'kā\ *n* : a 2-handed card game played with 32 cards

pi·ra·cy \'pī-rə-sē\ *n, pl* **-cies. 1** : robbery on the high seas; *also* : an act resembling such robbery **2** : the unauthorized use of another's production or invention

pi·ra·nha \pə-'rä-nə, -'rän-yə\ *n* [Pg., fr. Tupi (So. American Indian language) *piráña*, fr. *pirá* fish + *áña* tooth] : any of various usu. small So. American fishes with sharp teeth that include some known to attack humans and large animals

pi·rate \'pī-rət\ *n* [ME, fr. MF or L; MF, fr. L *pirata*, fr. Gk *peiratēs*, fr. *peiran* to attempt, test] : one who commits piracy — **pirate** *vb* — **pi·rat·i·cal** \pə-'ra-ti-kəl, pī-\ *adj*

pir·ou·ette \pir-ə-'wet\ *n* [F] : a rapid whirling about of the body; *esp* : a full turn on the toe or ball of one foot in ballet — **pirouette** *vb*

pis *pl of* PI

pis·ca·to·ri·al \pis-kə-'tȯr-ē-əl\ *adj* : of or relating to fishing

Pi·sces \'pī-sēz\ *n* [ME, fr. L, lit., fishes] **1** : a zodiacal constellation between Aquarius and Aries usu. pictured as a fish **2** : the 12th sign of the zodiac in astrology; *also* : one born under this sign

pis·mire \'pis-‚mī(-ə)r\ *n* : ANT

pi·so \'pē-(‚)sō\ *n* : the peso of the Philippines

pis·ta·chio \pə-'sta-shē-‚ō, -'stä-\ *n, pl* **-chios** : the greenish edible seed of a small Asian tree related to the sumacs; *also* : the tree

pis·til \'pis-t³l\ *n* : the female reproductive organ in a flower — **pis·til·late** \'pis-tə-‚lāt\ *adj*

pis·tol \'pis-t³l\ *n* : a handgun whose chamber is integral with the barrel

pis·tol–whip \-‚hwip\ *vb* : to beat with a pistol

pis·ton \'pis-tən\ *n* : a sliding piece that receives and transmits motion and that usu. consists of a short cylinder inside a large cylinder

¹**pit** \'pit\ *n* **1** : a hole, shaft, or cavity in the ground **2** : an often sunken area designed for a particular use; *also* : an enclosed place (as for cockfights) **3** : HELL; *also, pl* : WORST ⟨it's the ~s⟩ **4** : a natural hollow or indentation in a surface **5** : a small indented mark or scar (as from disease or corrosion) **6** : an area beside a racecourse where cars are fueled and repaired during a race

²**pit** *vb* **pit·ted; pit·ting 1** : to form pits in or become marred with pits **2** : to match for fighting

³**pit** *n* : the stony seed of some fruits (as the cherry, peach, and date)

⁴**pit** *vb* **pit·ted; pit·ting** : to remove the pit from

pi·ta \'pē-tə\ *n* [ModGk] : a thin flat bread

pit–a–pat \‚pi-ti-'pat\ *n* : PITTER-PATTER — **pit–a–pat** *adv or adj*

pit bull *n* : a powerful compact short-haired dog developed for fighting

¹**pitch** \'pich\ *n* **1** : a dark sticky substance left over esp. from distilling tar or petroleum **2** : resin from various conifers — **pitchy** *adj*

²**pitch** *vb* **1** : to erect and fix firmly in place ⟨~ a tent⟩ **2** : THROW, FLING **3** : to deliver a baseball to a batter **4** : to toss (as coins) toward a mark **5** : to set at a particular level ⟨~ the voice low⟩ **6** : to fall headlong **7** : to have the front end (as of a ship) alternately plunge and rise **8** : to incline downward : SLOPE

³**pitch** *n* **1** : the action or a manner of pitching **2** : degree of slope ⟨~ of a roof⟩ **3** : the relative level of some quality or state ⟨a high ~ of excitement⟩ **4** : highness or lowness of sound; *also* : a standard frequency for tuning instruments **5** : a presentation delivered to sell or promote something **6** : the delivery of a baseball to a batter; *also* : the baseball delivered

pitch·blende \'pich-‚blend\ *n* : a dark mineral that is the chief source of uranium

¹**pitch·er** \'pi-chər\ *n* : a container for liquids that usu. has a lip and a handle

²**pitcher** *n* : one that pitches esp. in a baseball game

pitcher plant *n* : any of various plants with leaves modified to resemble pitchers in which insects are trapped and digested

pitch·fork \'pich-‚fȯrk\ *n* : a long-handled fork used esp. in pitching hay

pitch in *vb* **1** : to begin to work **2** : to contribute to a common effort

pitch·man \'pich-mən\ *n* : SALESMAN; *esp* : one who sells merchandise on the streets or from a concession

pitch–per·fect \'pich-'pər-fikt\ *adj* : having just the right tone or style ⟨a ~ translation⟩

pit·e·ous \'pi-tē-əs\ *adj* : arousing pity : PITIFUL — **pit·e·ous·ly** *adv*

pit·fall \'pit-‚fȯl\ *n* **1** : TRAP, SNARE; *esp* : a covered pit used for capturing animals **2** : a hidden danger or difficulty

pith \'pith\ *n* **1** : loose spongy tissue esp. in the center of the stem of vascular plants **2** : the essential part : CORE

pithy \'pi-thē\ *adj* **pith·i·er, -est 1** : consisting of or filled with pith **2** : having substance and point : CONCISE

piti·able \'pi-tē-ə-bəl\ *adj* : PITIFUL

piti·ful \'pi-ti-fəl\ *adj* **1** : arousing or deserving pity ⟨a ~ sight⟩ **2** : lamentably inadequate : MEAGER — **piti·ful·ly** *adv*

piti·less \'pi-ti-ləs\ *adj* : devoid of pity : HARSH, CRUEL — **piti·less·ly** *adv*

pi·ton \'pē-‚tän\ *n* [F] : a spike, wedge, or peg that can be driven into a rock or ice surface as a support

pit·tance \'pi-t³ns\ *n* : a small portion, amount, or allowance

pit·ted \'pi-təd\ *adj* : marked with pits

pit·ter–pat·ter \'pi-tər-‚pa-tər, 'pi-tē-\ *n* : a rapid succession of light taps or sounds — **pitter–patter** \,pi-tər-'pa-tər, ,pi-tē-\ *adv or adj* — **pitter–patter** *same as adv*\ *vb*

pi·tu·i·tary \pə-'tü-ə-,ter-ē, -'tyü-\ *n, pl* **-itar·ies** : PITUITARY GLAND — **pituitary** *adj*

pituitary gland *n* : a small oval endocrine gland located at the base of the brain that produces various hormones that affect most basic bodily functions (as growth and reproduction)

pit viper *n* : any of various mostly New World venomous snakes with a heat-sensing pit on each side of the head and hollow perforated fangs

¹**pity** \'pi-tē\ *n, pl* **pit·ies** [ME *pite*, fr. AF *pité*, fr. L *pietas* piety, pity, fr. *pius* pious] **1** : sympathetic sorrow : COMPASSION **2** : something to be regretted

²**pity** *vb* **pit·ied**; **pity·ing** : to feel pity for

¹**piv·ot** \'pi-vət\ *n* : a fixed pin on which something turns — **pivot** *adj*

²**pivot** *vb* : to turn on or as if on a pivot

piv·ot·al \'pi-və-t°l\ *adj* **1** : of or relating to a pivot **2** : vitally important : CRITICAL

pix *pl of* PIC

pix·el \'pik-səl, -,sel\ *n* **1** : any of the small elements that together make up an image (as on a television screen) **2** : any of the detecting elements of a charge-coupled device used as an optical sensor

pix·ie *also* **pixy** \'pik-sē\ *n, pl* **pix·ies** : FAIRY; *esp* : a mischievous sprite

piz·za \'pēt-sə\ *n* [It] : an open pie made of rolled bread dough spread with a spiced mixture (as of tomatoes, cheese, and ground meat) and baked

piz·zazz *or* **pi·zazz** \pə-'zaz\ *n* **1** : GLAMOUR **2** : VITALITY

piz·ze·ria \,pēt-sə-'rē-ə\ *n* : an establishment where pizzas are made and sold

piz·zi·ca·to \,pit-si-'kä-tō\ *adv or adj* [It] : by means of plucking instead of bowing — used as a direction in music

pj's \'pē-,jāz\ *n pl* : PAJAMAS

pk *abbr* **1** park **2** peak **3** peck **4** pike

pkg *abbr* package

pkt *abbr* **1** packet **2** pocket

pkwy *abbr* parkway

pl *abbr* **1** place **2** plate **3** plural

¹**plac·ard** \'pla-kərd, -,kärd\ *n* : a notice posted in a public place : POSTER

²**plac·ard** \-,kärd, -kərd\ *vb* **1** : to cover with or as if with placards **2** : to announce by or as if by posting

pla·cate \'plā-,kāt, 'pla-\ *vb* **pla·cat·ed**; **pla·cat·ing** : to soothe esp. by concessions : APPEASE — **pla·ca·ble** \'pla-kə-bəl, 'plā-\ *adj*

¹**place** \'plās\ *n* [ME, fr. AF, open space, fr. L *platea* broad street, fr. Gk *plateia* (*hodos*), fr. fem. of *platys* broad, flat] **1** : SPACE, ROOM **2** : an indefinite region : AREA **3** : a building or locality used for a special purpose **4** : a center of population **5** : a particular part of a surface : SPOT **6** : relative position in a scale or sequence; *also* : position at the end of a competition ⟨last ∼⟩ **7** : ACCOMMODA-

TION; *esp* : SEAT **8** : the position of a figure within a numeral ⟨12 is a two ∼ number⟩ **9** : JOB; *esp* : public office **10** : a public square **11** : 2d place at the finish (as of a horse race) — **in place of** : INSTEAD OF — **out of place** : not in the proper location : INAPPROPRIATE

²**place** *vb* **placed**; **plac·ing** **1** : to put in a particular place : SET **2** : to distribute in an orderly manner : ARRANGE **3** : IDENTIFY **4** : to give an order for ⟨∼ a bet⟩ **5** : to earn a given spot in a competition; *esp* : to come in 2d

pla·ce·bo \plə-'sē-bō\ *n, pl* **-bos** [L, I shall please] : an inert medication used for its psychological effect or for purposes of comparison in an experiment

place·hold·er \'plās-,hōl-dər\ *n* : a symbol in a mathematical or logical expression that may be replaced by the name of any element of a set

place·kick \-,kik\ *n* : the kicking of a ball placed or held on the ground — **place·kick** *vb* — **place·kick·er** *n*

place·ment \'plās-mənt\ *n* : an act or instance of placing

place–name \-,nām\ *n* : the name of a geographical locality

pla·cen·ta \plə-'sen-tə\ *n, pl* **-tas** *or* **-tae** \-(,)tē\ [NL, fr. L, flat cake] : the organ in most mammals by which the fetus is joined to the maternal uterus and is nourished — **pla·cen·tal** \-'sen-t°l\ *adj or n*

plac·er \'pla-sər\ *n* : a deposit of sand or gravel containing particles of valuable mineral (as gold)

plac·id \'pla-səd\ *adj* : UNDISTURBED, PEACEFUL ♦ *Synonyms* TRANQUIL, SERENE, CALM — **pla·cid·i·ty** \pla-'si-də-tē\ *n* — **plac·id·ly** *adv*

plack·et \'pla-kət\ *n* : a slit in a garment

pla·gia·rise *Brit var of* PLAGIARIZE

pla·gia·rize \'plā-jə-,rīz\ *vb* **-rized**; **-rizing** : to present the ideas or words of another as one's own — **pla·gia·rism** \-,ri-zəm\ *n* — **pla·gia·rist** \-rist\ *n*

¹**plague** \'plāg\ *n* **1** : a disastrous evil or influx; *also* : NUISANCE **2** : PESTILENCE; *esp* : a destructive contagious bacterial disease (as bubonic plague)

²**plague** *vb* **plagued**; **plagu·ing** **1** : to afflict with or as if with disease or disaster **2** : TEASE, TORMENT, HARASS

plaid \'plad\ *n* [ScGael *plaide*] **1** : a rectangular length of tartan worn esp. over the left shoulder as part of the Scottish national costume **2** : a twilled woolen fabric with a tartan pattern **3** : a pattern of unevenly spaced repeated stripes crossing at right angles — **plaid** *adj*

¹**plain** \'plān\ *n* : an extensive area of level or rolling treeless country

²**plain** *adj* **1** : lacking ornament ⟨a ∼ dress⟩ **2** : free of extraneous matter **3** : OPEN, UNOBSTRUCTED ⟨∼ view⟩ **4** : EVIDENT, OBVIOUS **5** : easily understood : CLEAR **6** : CANDID, BLUNT **7** : SIMPLE, UNCOMPLICATED ⟨∼ cooking⟩ **8** : lacking beauty or ugliness — **plain·ly** *adv* — **plain·ness** *n*

plain·clothes·man \'plān-'klōthz-mən, -'klōz-, -,man\ *n* : a police officer who wears civilian clothes instead of a uniform while on duty : DETECTIVE

plain·spo·ken \-'spō-kən\ *adj* : FRANK

plaint \'plānt\ *n* **1** : LAMENTATION, WAIL **2** : PROTEST, COMPLAINT

plain·tiff \'plān-təf\ *n* : the complaining party in a lawsuit

plain·tive \'plān-tiv\ *adj* : expressive of suffering or woe : MELANCHOLY ⟨a ~ sigh⟩ — **plain·tive·ly** *adv*

plait \'plāt, 'plat\ *n* **1** : PLEAT **2** : a braid esp. of hair or straw — **plait** *vb*

¹**plan** \'plan\ *n* **1** : a drawing or diagram showing the parts or details of something **2** : a method for accomplishing an objective; *also* : GOAL, AIM

²**plan** *vb* **planned; plan·ning 1** : to form a plan of ⟨~ a new city⟩ **2** : INTEND ⟨planned to go⟩ — **plan·ner** *n*

¹**plane** \'plān\ *vb* **planed; plan·ing** : to smooth or level off with or as if with a plane — **plan·er** *n*

²**plane** *n* : PLANE TREE

³**plane** *n* : a tool for smoothing or shaping a wood surface

⁴**plane** *n* **1** : a level or flat surface **2** : a level of existence, consciousness, or development **3** : AIRPLANE

⁵**plane** *adj* **1** : FLAT, LEVEL **2** : dealing with flat surfaces or figures ⟨~ geometry⟩

plane·load \'plān-,lōd\ *n* : a load that fills an airplane

plan·et \'pla-nət\ *n* [ME *planete*, fr. AF, fr. LL *planeta*, fr. Gk *planēt-, planēs*, lit., wanderer, fr. *planasthai* to wander] : any of the large bodies in the solar system that revolve around the sun — **plan·e·tary** \-nə-,ter-ē\ *adj*

plan·e·tar·i·um \,pla-nə-'ter-ē-əm\ *n, pl* **-i·ums** *or* **-ia** \-ē-ə\ : a building or room housing a device to project images of celestial bodies

plan·e·tes·i·mal \,pla-nə-'tes-ə-məl\ *n* : any of numerous small solid celestial bodies which may have existed during the formation of the solar system

plan·e·toid \'pla-nə-,tȯid\ *n* : a body resembling a planet; *esp* : ASTEROID

plane tree *n* : any of a genus of trees (as a sycamore) with large lobed leaves and globe-shaped fruit

plan·gent \'plan-jənt\ *adj* **1** : having a loud reverberating sound ⟨a ~ roar⟩ **2** : having an expressive esp. plaintive quality ⟨~ lyrics⟩ — **plan·gen·cy** \-jən-sē\ *n*

¹**plank** \'plaŋk\ *n* **1** : a heavy thick board **2** : an article in the platform of a political party

²**plank** *vb* **1** : to cover with planks **2** : to set or lay down forcibly **3** : to cook and serve on a board

plank·ing \'plaŋ-kiŋ\ *n* : a quantity or covering of planks

plank·ton \'plaŋk-tən\ *n* [G, fr. Gk, neut. of *planktos* drifting] : the passively floating or weakly swimming animal and plant life of a body of water — **plank·ton·ic** \plaŋk-'tä-nik\ *adj*

¹**plant** \'plant\ *vb* **1** : to set in the ground to grow **2** : ESTABLISH, SETTLE **3** : to

stock or provide with something **4** : to place firmly or forcibly **5** : to hide or arrange with intent to deceive

²**plant** *n* **1** : any of a kingdom of living things that usu. have no locomotor ability or obvious sense organs and have cellulose cell walls and usu. capacity for indefinite growth **2** : the land, buildings, and machinery used in carrying on a trade or business

¹**plan·tain** \'plan-t³n\ *n* [ME, fr. AF, fr. L *plantagin-, plantago*, fr. *planta* sole of the foot; fr. its broad leaves] : any of a genus of weedy herbs with spikes of tiny greenish flowers

²**plantain** *n* [Sp *plántano, plátano* plane tree, banana tree, fr. ML *plantanus* plane tree, alter. of L *platanus*] : a banana plant with starchy greenish fruit that is eaten cooked; *also* : its fruit

plan·tar \'plan-tər, -,tär\ *adj* : of or relating to the sole of the foot

plan·ta·tion \plan-'tä-shən\ *n* **1** : a large group of plants and esp. trees under cultivation **2** : an agricultural estate usu. worked by resident laborers

plant·er \'plan-tər\ *n* **1** : one that plants or sows; *esp* : an owner or operator of a plantation **2** : a container for plants

plant louse *n* : APHID

plaque \'plak\ *n* [F] **1** : an ornamental brooch **2** : a flat thin piece (as of metal) used for decoration; *also* : a commemorative tablet **3** : a bacteria-containing film on a tooth

plash \'plash\ *n* : SPLASH — **plash** *vb*

plas·ma \'plaz-mə\ *n* **1** : the fluid part of blood, lymph, or milk **2** : a gas composed of ionized particles **3** : a display (as a television screen) in which cells of plasma emit light upon receiving an electric current — **plas·mat·ic** \plaz-'ma-tik\ *adj*

¹**plas·ter** \'plas-tər\ *n* **1** : a dressing consisting of a backing spread with an often medicated substance that clings to the skin ⟨adhesive ~⟩ **2** : a paste that hardens as it dries and is used for coating walls and ceilings

²**plaster** *vb* : to cover with or as if with plaster — **plas·ter·er** *n*

plas·ter·board \'plas-tər-,bȯrd\ *n* : DRYWALL

plaster of par·is \-'pa-rəs\ *often cap 2d P* : a white powder made from gypsum and used as a quick-setting paste with water for casts and molds

¹**plas·tic** \'plas-tik\ *adj* [L *plasticus* of molding, fr. Gk *plastikos*, fr. *plassein* to mold, form] **1** : capable of being molded ⟨~ clay⟩ **2** : characterized by or using modeling ⟨~ arts⟩ **3** : made or consisting of a plastic ✦ *Synonyms* PLIABLE, PLIANT, DUCTILE, MALLEABLE, ADAPTABLE — **plas·tic·i·ty** \plas-'ti-sə-tē\ *n*

²**plastic** *n* : a plastic substance; *esp* : a synthetic or processed material that can be formed into rigid objects or into films or filaments

plastic surgery *n* : surgery to repair, restore, or improve lost, injured, defective, or misshapen body parts — **plastic sur‐geon** n

¹**plat** \'plat\ n 1 : a small plot of ground 2 : a plan of a piece of land with actual or proposed features (as lots)

²**plat** vb **plat‐ted; plat‐ting** : to make a plat of

¹**plate** \'plāt\ n 1 : a flat thin piece of material 2 : domestic hollowware made of or plated with gold, silver, or base metals 3 : DISH 4 : HOME PLATE 5 : the molded metal or plastic cast of a page of type to be printed from 6 : a sheet of glass or plastic coated with a chemical sensitive to light and used in photography 7 : the part of a denture that fits to the mouth; also : DENTURE 8 : something printed from an engraving 9 : a huge mobile segment of the earth's crust

²**plate** vb **plat‐ed; plat‐ing** 1 : to overlay with metal (as gold or silver) 2 : to make a printing plate of

pla‐teau \pla‐'tō\ n, pl **plateaus** or **plateaux** \-'tōz\ [F] : a large level area of high land

plate glass n : rolled, ground, and polished sheet glass

plate‐let \'plāt‐lət\ n : a minute flattened body; esp. : a minute colorless disklike body of mammalian blood that assists in blood clotting

plat‐en \'pla‐tᵊn\ n 1 : a flat plate; esp : one that exerts or receives pressure (as in a printing press) 2 : the roller of a typewriter or printer

plate tectonics n 1 : a theory in geology that the lithosphere is divided into plates at the boundaries of which much of earth's seismic activity occurs 2 : the process and dynamics of tectonic plate movement — **plate–tectonic** adj

plat‐form \'plat‐ˌfȯrm\ n 1 : a raised flooring or stage for speakers, performers, or workers 2 : a declaration of the principles on which a group of persons (as a political party) stands 3 : OPERATING SYSTEM

plat‐ing \'plā‐tiŋ\ n : a coating of metal plates or plate (the ～ of a ship)

plat‐i‐num \'pla‐tə‐nəm\ n : a heavy grayish white metallic chemical element

plat‐i‐tude \'pla‐tə‐ˌtüd, ‐ˌtyüd\ n : a flat or trite remark — **plat‐i‐tu‐di‐nous** \‐'tü‐də‐nəs, ‐'tyü‐\ adj

pla‐ton‐ic love \plə‐'tä‐nik‐, plā‐\ n, often cap P : a close relationship between two persons without sexual desire

pla‐toon \plə‐'tün\ n [F peloton small detachment, lit., ball, fr. pelote little ball] 1 : a subdivision of a company‐size military unit usu. consisting of two or more squads or sections 2 : a group of football players trained either for offense or for defense and sent into the game as a body

platoon sergeant n : a noncommissioned officer in the army ranking below a first sergeant

plat‐ter \'pla‐tər\ n 1 : a large serving plate 2 : a phonograph record

platy \'pla‐tē\ n, pl **platy** or **plat‐ys** or **plat‐ies** : either of two small stocky usu.

brilliantly colored bony fishes often kept in tropical aquariums

platy‐pus \'pla‐ti‐pəs\ n, pl **platy‐pus‐es** also **platy‐pi** \‐ˌpī\ [NL, fr. Gk platypous flat‐footed, fr. platys broad, flat + pous foot] : a small aquatic egg‐laying marsupial mammal of Australia with webbed feet and a fleshy bill like a duck's

plau‐dit \'plȯ‐dət\ n : an act of applause

plau‐si‐ble \'plȯ‐zə‐bəl\ adj [L plausibilis worthy of applause, fr. plausus, pp. of plaudere to applaud] : seemingly worthy of belief — **plau‐si‐bil‐i‐ty** \ˌplȯ‐zə‐'bi‐lə‐tē\ n — **plau‐si‐bly** \'plȯ‐zə‐blē\ adv

¹**play** \'plā\ n 1 : brisk handling of something (as a weapon) 2 : the course of a game; also : a particular act or maneuver in a game 3 : recreational activity; esp : the spontaneous activity of children 4 : JEST ⟨said in ～⟩ 5 : the act or an instance of punning 6 : GAMBLING 7 : OPERATION ⟨bring extra force into ～⟩ 8 : a brisk or light movement 9 : free motion (as of part of a machine) 10 : scope for action 11 : PUBLICITY 12 : an effort to arouse liking ⟨made a ～ for her⟩ 13 : a stage representation of a drama; also : a dramatic composition 14 : a function of an electronic device that causes a recording to play — **play‐ful** \‐fəl\ adj — **play‐ful‐ly** adv — **play‐ful‐ness** n — **in play** : in condition or position to be played

²**play** vb 1 : to engage in recreation : FROLIC 2 : to handle or behave lightly or absentmindedly 3 : to make a pun ⟨～ on words⟩ 4 : to take advantage ⟨～ on fears⟩ 5 : to move or operate in a brisk or irregular manner ⟨a flashlight ～ed over the wall⟩ 6 : to perform music ⟨～ on a violin⟩; also : to perform (music) on an instrument ⟨～ a waltz⟩ 7 : to perform music upon ⟨～ the piano⟩; also : to sound in performance ⟨the organ is ～ing⟩ 8 : to cause to emit sounds ⟨～ a radio⟩; also : to cause to reproduce recorded material ⟨～ a DVD⟩ 9 : to act in a dramatic medium; also : to act in the character of ⟨～ the hero⟩ 10 : GAMBLE 11 : to produce a specified impression in performance ⟨～s like a comedy⟩ 12 : to behave in a specified way ⟨～ safe⟩; also : COOPERATE ⟨～ along with him⟩ 13 : to deal with; also : EMPHASIZE ⟨～ up her good qualities⟩ 14 : to perform for amusement ⟨～ a trick⟩ 15 : WREAK 16 : to use as an esp. political strategy 17 : to contend with in a game; also : to fill (a certain position) on a team 18 : to make wagers on ⟨～ the races⟩ 19 : WIELD, PLY 20 : to keep in action — **play‐er** n

play‐act‐ing \'plā‐ˌak‐tiŋ\ n 1 : performance in theatrical productions 2 : insincere or artificial behavior

play‐back \‐ˌbak\ n : an act of reproducing recorded sound or pictures — **play back** vb

play‐bill \‐ˌbil\ n : a poster advertising the performance of a play

play‐book \‐ˌbu̇k\ n 1 : a notebook containing diagrammed football plays 2 : a stock of usual tactics or methods

play·boy \-ˌbȯi\ n : a man whose chief interest is the pursuit of pleasure

play·date \-ˌdāt\ n : a usu. prearranged play session for small children

play·go·er \-ˌgō-ər\ n : a person who frequently attends plays

play·ground \-ˌgrau̇nd\ n : an area used for games and play esp. by children

play·house \-ˌhau̇s\ n 1 : THEATER 2 : a small house for children to play in

playing card n : any of a set of 24 to 78 cards marked to show its rank and suit and used to play a game of cards

play·let \'plā-lət\ n : a short play

play·mate \-ˌmāt\ n : a companion in play

play·off \-ˌȯf\ n : a contest or series of contests to break a tie or determine a championship

play out vb : DEVELOP, UNFOLD ⟨see how things *play out*⟩

play·pen \-ˌpen\ n : a portable enclosure in which a young child may play

play·suit \-ˌsüt\ n : a sports and play outfit for women and children

play·thing \-ˌthiŋ\ n : TOY

play·wright \-ˌrīt\ n : a writer of plays

pla·za \'pla-zə, 'plä-\ n [Sp, fr. L *platea* broad street] 1 : a public square in a city or town 2 : a shopping center

PLC abbr, Brit public limited company

plea \'plē\ n 1 : a defendant's answer in law to a charge or indictment 2 : something alleged as an excuse 3 : ENTREATY, APPEAL

plead \'plēd\ vb **plead·ed** or **pled** \'pled\; **plead·ing** 1 : to argue before a court or authority ⟨~ a case⟩ 2 : to answer to a charge or indictment ⟨~ guilty⟩ 3 : to argue for or against something ⟨~ for acquittal⟩ 4 : to appeal earnestly ⟨~s for help⟩ 5 : to offer as a plea (as in defense) ⟨~ed illness⟩ — **plead·er** n

pleas·ant \'ple-zᵊnt\ adj 1 : giving pleasure : AGREEABLE ⟨a ~ experience⟩ 2 : marked by pleasing behavior or appearance ⟨a ~ person⟩ — **pleas·ant·ly** adv — **pleas·ant·ness** n

pleas·ant·ry \-zᵊn-trē\ n, pl **-ries** : a pleasant and casual act or speech

¹**please** \'plēz\ vb **pleased; pleas·ing** 1 : to give pleasure or satisfaction to 2 : LIKE ⟨do as you ~⟩ 3 : to be the will or pleasure of ⟨may it ~ his Majesty⟩

²**please** adv — used as a function word to express politeness or emphasis in a request ⟨~ come in⟩

pleas·ing adj : giving pleasure — **pleas·ing·ly** adv

plea·sur·able \'ple-zhə-rə-bəl\ adj : PLEASANT, GRATIFYING — **plea·sur·ably** \-blē\ adv

plea·sure \'ple-zhər\ n 1 : DESIRE, INCLINATION ⟨await your ~⟩ 2 : a state of gratification : ENJOYMENT 3 : a source of delight or joy

¹**pleat** \'plēt\ vb 1 : FOLD; esp : to arrange in pleats 2 : BRAID

²**pleat** n : a fold (as in cloth) made by doubling material over on itself

plebe \'plēb\ n : a freshman at a military or naval academy

¹**ple·be·ian** \pli-'bē-ən\ n 1 : a member of the Roman plebs 2 : one of the common people

²**plebeian** adj 1 : of or relating to plebeians 2 : COMMON, VULGAR

pleb·i·scite \'ple-bə-ˌsīt, -sət\ n : a vote of the people (as of a country) on a proposal submitted to them

plebs \'plebz\ n, pl **ple·bes** \'plē-ˌbēz\ 1 : the general populace 2 : the common people of ancient Rome

plec·trum \'plek-trəm\ n, pl **plec·tra** \-trə\ or **plec·trums** [L] : ³PICK 3

¹**pledge** \'plej\ n [ME *plegge* security, fr. AF *plege*, fr. LL *plebium*, fr. *plebere* to pledge, prob. fr. Gmc origin] 1 : something given as security for the performance of an act 2 : the state of being held as a security or guaranty 3 : TOAST 3 4 : PROMISE, VOW

²**pledge** vb **pledged; pledg·ing** 1 : to deposit as a pledge 2 : TOAST 3 3 : to bind by a pledge : PLIGHT 4 : PROMISE

Pleis·to·cene \'plī-stə-ˌsēn\ adj : of, relating to, or being the earlier epoch of the Quaternary — **Pleistocene** n

ple·na·ry \'plē-nə-rē, 'ple-\ adj 1 : FULL ⟨~ power⟩ 2 : including all entitled to attend ⟨~ session⟩

pleni·po·ten·tia·ry \ˌple-nə-pə-'ten-chə-rē, -'ten-chē-ˌer-ē\ n, pl **-ries** : a diplomatic agent having full authority — **plenipotentiary** adj

plen·i·tude \'ple-nə-ˌtüd, -ˌtyüd\ n 1 : COMPLETENESS 2 : ABUNDANCE

plen·te·ous \'plen-tē-əs\ adj 1 : FRUITFUL 2 : existing in plenty

plen·ti·ful \'plen-ti-fəl\ adj 1 : containing or yielding plenty 2 : ABUNDANT — **plen·ti·ful·ly** adv

plen·ty \'plen-tē\ n : a more than adequate number or amount

ple·num \'ple-nəm, 'plē-\ n, pl **-nums** or **-na** \-nə\ : a general assembly of all members esp. of a legislative body

pleth·o·ra \'ple-thə-rə\ n : an excessive quantity or fullness; also : PROFUSION

pleu·ri·sy \'plu̇r-ə-sē\ n : inflammation of the membrane that lines the chest and covers the lungs

plex·us \'plek-səs\ n, pl **plex·us·es** \-sə-səz\ : an interlacing network esp. of blood vessels or nerves

pli·able \'plī-ə-bəl\ adj 1 : FLEXIBLE 2 : yielding easily to others ♦ *Synonyms* PLASTIC, PLIANT, DUCTILE, MALLEABLE, ADAPTABLE — **pli·abil·i·ty** \ˌplī-ə-'bi-lə-tē\ n

pli·ant \'plī-ənt\ adj 1 : FLEXIBLE 2 : easily influenced : PLIABLE — **pli·an·cy** \-ən-sē\ n

pli·ers \'plī-ərz\ n pl : small pincers for bending or cutting wire or handling small objects

¹**plight** \'plīt\ vb : to put or give in pledge : ENGAGE

²**plight** n : an unfortunate, difficult, or precarious situation

plinth \'plinth\ n : the lowest part of the base of an architectural column

Plio·cene \'plī-ə-ˌsēn\ *adj* : of, relating to, or being the latest epoch of the Tertiary — **Pliocene** *n*

PLO *abbr* Palestine Liberation Organization

plod \'pläd\ *vb* **plod·ded; plod·ding** **1** : to walk heavily or slowly : TRUDGE **2** : to work laboriously and monotonously : DRUDGE — **plod·der** *n* — **plod·ding·ly** *adv*

plonk *var of* PLUNK

plop \'pläp\ *vb* **plopped; plop·ping** **1** : to fall or move with a sound like that of something dropping into water **2** : to set, drop, or throw heavily or hastily ⟨*plopped* down on the couch⟩ ⟨∼ down $20⟩ — **plop** *n*

¹plot \'plät\ *n* **1** : a small area of ground **2** : a ground plan (as of an area) **3** : the main story (as of a book or movie) **4** : a secret scheme : INTRIGUE

²plot *vb* **plot·ted; plot·ting** **1** : to make a plot or plan of **2** : to mark on or as if on a chart **3** : to plan or contrive esp. secretly — **plot·ter** *n*

plo·ver \'plə-vər, 'plō-\ *n, pl* **plover** or **plovers** [ME, fr. AF, fr. VL *pluviarius,* fr. L *pluvia* rain] : any of a family of shorebirds that differ from the sandpipers in having shorter stouter bills

¹plow or **plough** \'plau̇\ *n* **1** : an implement used to cut, lift, turn over, and partly break up soil **2** : a device (as a snow-plow) operating like a plow

²plow or **plough** *vb* **1** : to open, break up, or work with a plow **2** : to move through like a plow ⟨a ship ∼*ing* the waves⟩ **3** : to proceed laboriously — **plow·able** *adj* — **plow·er** *n*

plow·boy \'plau̇-ˌbȯi\ *n* : a boy who leads the horse drawing a plow

plow·man \-mən, -ˌman\ *n* **1** : a man who guides a plow **2** : a farm laborer

plow·share \-ˌsher\ *n* : a part of a plow that cuts the earth

ploy \'plȯi\ *n* : a tactic intended to embarrass or frustrate an opponent

¹pluck \'plək\ *vb* **1** : to pull off or out : PICK; *also* : to pull something from **2** : to play (an instrument) by pulling the strings — **plot·ter** *n*

²pluck *n* **1** : an act or instance of plucking **2** : SPIRIT, COURAGE

plucky \'plə-kē\ *adj* **pluck·i·er; -est** : COURAGEOUS, SPIRITED

¹plug \'pləg\ *n* **1** : STOPPER; *also* : an obstructing mass **2** : a cake of tobacco **3** : a poor or worn-out horse **4** : SPARK PLUG **5** : a lure with several hooks used in fishing **6** : a device on the end of a cord for making an electrical connection **7** : a piece of favorable publicity

²plug *vb* **plugged; plug·ging** **1** : to stop, make tight, or secure by inserting a plug **2** : HIT, SHOOT **3** : to publicize insistently **4** : PLOD, DRUDGE

plug and play *n* : a computer feature enabling the operating system to automatically detect and configure peripherals — **plug-and-play** *adj*

plugged–in \'pləgd-'in\ *adj* : technologically or socially informed and connected

plug–in \'pləg-ˌin\ *n* : a small piece of software that supplements a larger program

plum \'pləm\ *n* [ME, fr. OE *plūme,* modif. of L *prunum* plum, fr. Gk *proumnon*] **1** : a smooth-skinned juicy fruit borne by trees related to the peach and cherry; *also* : a tree bearing plums **2** : a raisin when used in desserts (as puddings) **3** : something excellent; *esp* : something desirable given in return for a favor

plum·age \'plü-mij\ *n* : the feathers of a bird — **plum·aged** \-mijd\ *adj*

¹plumb \'pləm\ *n* : a weight on the end of a line (**plumb line**) used esp. by builders to show vertical direction

²plumb *adv* **1** : VERTICALLY **2** : COMPLETELY **3** : EXACTLY; *also* : IMMEDIATELY

³plumb *vb* : to sound, adjust, or test with a plumb ⟨∼ the depth of a well⟩

⁴plumb *adj* **1** : VERTICAL **2** : COMPLETE

plumb·er \'plə-mər\ *n* : a worker who fits or repairs pipes and fixtures

plumb·ing \'plə-miŋ\ *n* : a system of pipes in a building for supplying and carrying off water

¹plume \'plüm\ *n* : FEATHER; *esp* : a large, conspicuous, or showy feather — **plumed** \'plümd\ *adj* — **plumy** \'plü-mē\ *adj*

²plume *vb* **plumed; plum·ing** **1** : to provide or deck with feathers **2** : to indulge (oneself) in pride

¹plum·met \'plə-mət\ *n* : PLUMB; *also* : PLUMB LINE

²plummet *vb* : to drop or plunge straight down

¹plump \'pləmp\ *vb* **1** : to drop or fall suddenly or heavily **2** : to favor something strongly ⟨∼*ing* for change⟩

²plump *n* : a sudden heavy fall or blow; *also* : the sound made by it

³plump *adv* **1** : straight down; *also* : straight ahead **2** : UNQUALIFIEDLY ⟨came out ∼ for free trade⟩

⁴plump *adj* : having a full rounded usu. pleasing form ♦ *Synonyms* FLESHY, STOUT, ROLY-POLY, ROTUND — **plump·ness** *n*

¹plun·der \'plən-dər\ *vb* : to take the goods of by force or wrongfully : PILLAGE — **plun·der·er** *n*

²plunder *n* : something taken by force or theft : LOOT

¹plunge \'plənj\ *vb* **plunged; plung·ing** **1** : IMMERSE, SUBMERGE **2** : to enter or cause to enter a state or course of action suddenly or violently ⟨∼ into war⟩ **3** : to cast oneself into or as if into water **4** : to gamble heavily and recklessly **5** : to descend suddenly

²plunge *n* : a sudden dive, leap, or rush

plung·er \'plən-jər\ *n* **1** : one that plunges **2** : a sliding piece driven by or against fluid pressure : PISTON **3** : a rubber cup on a handle pushed against an opening to free a waste outlet of an obstruction

plunk \'pləŋk\ *or* **plonk** \'pläŋk, 'plȯŋk\ *vb* **1** : to make or cause to make a hollow metallic sound **2** : to drop heavily or suddenly — **plunk** n

plu·per·fect \(ˌ)plü-ˈpər-fikt\ adj [ME pluperfyth, modif. of LL plusquamperfectus, lit., more than perfect] : of, relating to, or constituting a verb tense that denotes an action or state as completed at or before a past time spoken of — **pluperfect** n

plu·ral \ˈplu̇r-əl\ adj [ME, fr. AF & L; AF plurel, fr. L pluralis, fr. plur-, plus more] : of, relating to, or constituting a word form used to denote more than one — **plural** n

plu·ral·i·ty \plu̇-ˈra-lə-tē\ n, pl **-ties** **1** : the state of being plural **2** : an excess of votes over those cast for an opposing candidate **3** : the greatest number of votes cast when not a majority

plu·ral·ize \ˈplu̇r-ə-ˌlīz\ vb **-ized; -iz·ing** : to make plural or express in the plural form — **plu·ral·i·za·tion** \ˌplu̇r-ə-lə-ˈzā-shən\ n

¹plus \ˈpləs\ adj [L, more] **1** : mathematically positive **2** : having or being in addition to what is anticipated **3** : falling high in a specified range ⟨a grade of B ∼⟩

²plus n, pl **plus·es** \ˈplə-səz\ also **plus·ses** **1** : a sign + (plus sign) used in mathematics to indicate addition or a positive quantity **2** : an added quantity; also : a positive quality **3** : SURPLUS

³plus prep **1** : increased by : with the addition of ⟨3 ∼ 4⟩ **2** : BESIDES

⁴plus conj : AND ⟨soup ∼ salad and bread⟩

¹plush \ˈpləsh\ n : a fabric with a pile longer and less dense than velvet pile — **plushy** adj

²plush adj : notably luxurious — **plush·ly** adv — **plush·ness** n

plus/minus sign n : the sign ± used to indicate a quantity taking on both a positive value and its negative or to indicate a plus or minus quantity

plus or minus adj : indicating a quantity whose positive and negative values bracket a range of values ⟨plus or minus 3 inches⟩

Plu·to \ˈplü-tō\ n : the planet farthest from the sun

plu·toc·ra·cy \plü-ˈtä-krə-sē\ n, pl **-cies** **1** : government by the wealthy **2** : a controlling class of the wealthy — **plu·to·crat** \ˈplü-tə-ˌkrat\ n — **plu·to·crat·ic** \ˌplü-tə-ˈkra-tik\ adj

plu·to·ni·um \plü-ˈtō-nē-əm\ n : a radioactive chemical element formed by the decay of neptunium

plu·vi·al \ˈplü-vē-əl\ adj **1** : of or relating to rain **2** : characterized by abundant rain

¹ply \ˈplī\ vb **plied; ply·ing** **1** : to use, practice, or work diligently ⟨∼ a trade⟩ **2** : to keep supplying something to ⟨plied them with liquor⟩ **3** : to go or travel regularly esp. by sea

²ply n, pl **plies** : one of the folds, thicknesses, or strands of which something (as plywood or yarn) is made

³ply vb **plied; ply·ing** : to twist together ⟨∼ yarns⟩

ply·wood \ˈplī-ˌwu̇d\ n : material made of thin sheets of wood glued and pressed together

pm abbr premium

Pm symbol promethium

PM abbr **1** paymaster **2** police magistrate **3** postmaster **4** post meridiem — often not cap. and often punctuated **5** postmortem **6** prime minister **7** provost marshal

pmk abbr postmark

PMS \ˌpē-ˌem-ˈes\ n : PREMENSTRUAL SYNDROME

pmt abbr payment

pneu·mat·ic \nu̇-ˈma-tik, nyu̇-\ adj **1** : of, relating to, or using air or wind **2** : moved by air pressure **3** : filled with compressed air — **pneu·mat·i·cal·ly** \-ti-k(ə-)lē\ adv

pneu·mo·coc·cus \ˌnü-mə-ˈkä-kəs, ˌnyü-\ n, pl **-coc·ci** \-ˈkäk-ˌsī, -ˌsē; -ˈkä-ˌkī, -ˌkē\ : a bacterium that causes pneumonia — **pneu·mo·coc·cal** \-ˈkä-kəl\ adj

pneu·mo·co·ni·o·sis \ˌnü-mō-ˌkō-nē-ˈō-səs, ˌnyü-\ n : a disease of the lungs caused by habitual inhalation of irritant mineral or metallic particles

pneu·mo·nia \nu̇-ˈmō-nyə, nyu̇-\ n : an inflammatory disease of the lungs

Po symbol polonium

PO abbr **1** petty officer **2** post office

¹poach \ˈpōch\ vb [ME pocchen, fr. MF pocher, fr. OF poché poached, lit., bagged, fr. poche bag, pouch, of Gmc origin] : to cook (as an egg or fish) in simmering liquid

²poach vb : to hunt or fish unlawfully — **poach·er** n

POB abbr post office box

po·bla·no \pō-ˈblä-nō\ n, pl **-nos** : a heart-shaped usu. mild chili pepper esp. when fresh and dark green

po'·boy \ˈpō-ˌbȯi\ also **poor boy** n : SUBMARINE 2

pock \ˈpäk\ n : a small swelling on the skin (as in smallpox); also : a spot suggesting this

¹pock·et \ˈpä-kət\ n **1** : a small bag open at the top or side inserted in a garment **2** : supply of money : MEANS **3** : RECEPTACLE, CONTAINER **4** : a small isolated area or group **5** : a small body of ore — **pock·et·ful** n

²pocket vb **1** : to put in or as if in a pocket **2** : STEAL ⟨∼ed the profits⟩

³pocket adj **1** : small enough to fit in a pocket; also : SMALL, MINIATURE ⟨a ∼ park⟩ **2** : carried in or paid from one's own pocket

¹pock·et·book \-ˌbu̇k\ n **1** : PURSE; also : HANDBAG **2** : financial resources

²pocketbook adj : relating to money

pocket gopher n : GOPHER 2

pock·et·knife \ˈpä-kət-ˌnīf\ n : a knife with a folding blade to be carried in the pocket

pocket veto n : an indirect veto of a legislative bill by an executive through retention of the bill unsigned until after adjournment of the legislature

pock·mark \ˈpäk-ˌmärk\ n : a pit or scar

caused by smallpox or acne — **pock-marked** \-ˌmärkt\ *adj*

po·co \ˈpō-kō, ˈpȯ-\ *adv* [It, little, fr. L *paucus*] : SOMEWHAT — used to qualify a direction in music ⟨~ allegro⟩

po·co a po·co \ˌpō-kō-ä-ˈpō-kō, ˌpȯ-kō-ä-ˈpȯ-\ *adv* : little by little : GRADUALLY — used as a direction in music

pod \ˈpäd\ *n* **1** : a dry fruit (as of a pea) that splits open when ripe **2** : an external streamlined compartment (as for a jet engine) on an airplane **3** : a compartment (as for personnel, a power unit, or an instrument) on a ship or craft

POD *abbr* pay on delivery

po·di·a·try \pə-ˈdī-ə-trē, pō-\ *n* : the medical care and treatment of the human foot — **po·di·at·ric** \ˌpō-dē-ˈa-trik\ *adj* — **po·di·a·trist** \pə-ˈdī-ə-trist, pō-\ *n*

po·di·um \ˈpō-dē-əm\ *n, pl* **podiums** or **po·dia** \-dē-ə\ **1** : a dais esp. for an orchestral conductor **2** : LECTERN

POE *abbr* port of entry

po·em \ˈpō-əm\ *n* : a composition in verse

po·esy \ˈpō-ə-zē\ *n* : POETRY

po·et \ˈpō-ət\ *n* [ME, fr. AF *poete*, fr. L *poeta*, fr. Gk *poiētēs* maker, poet, fr. *poiein* to make] : a writer of poetry; *also* : a creative artist of great sensitivity

po·et·as·ter \ˈpō-ə-ˌtas-tər\ *n* : an inferior poet

po·et·ess \ˈpō-ə-təs\ *n* : a girl or woman who is a poet

poetic justice *n* : an outcome in which vice is punished and virtue rewarded usu. in a manner peculiarly or ironically appropriate

po·et·ry \ˈpō-ə-trē\ *n* **1** : metrical writing **2** : POEMS — **po·et·ic** \pō-ˈe-tik\ *or* **po·et·i·cal** \-ti-kəl\ *adj*

po·grom \ˈpō-grəm, pō-ˈgräm\ *n* [Yiddish, fr. Russ, lit., devastation] : an organized massacre of helpless people and esp. of Jews

poi \ˈpȯi\ *n, pl* **poi** *or* **pois** : a Hawaiian food of taro root cooked, pounded, and kneaded to a paste and often allowed to ferment

poi·gnant \ˈpȯi-nyənt\ *adj* **1** : painfully affecting the feelings ⟨~ grief⟩ **2** : deeply moving ⟨~ scene⟩ — **poi·gnan·cy** \-nyən-sē\ *n*

poin·ci·ana \ˌpȯin-sē-ˈa-nə\ *n* : any of several ornamental tropical leguminous trees or shrubs with bright orange or red flowers

poin·set·tia \pȯin-ˈse-tē-ə\ *n* : a showy tropical American spurge with usu. scarlet bracts that suggest petals and surround small yellow flowers

¹point \ˈpȯint\ *n* **1** : an individual detail; *also* : the most important essential **2** : PURPOSE ⟨no ~ in continuing⟩ **3** : a geometric element that has position but no size **4** : a particular place : LOCALITY **5** : a particular stage or degree **6** : a sharp end **7** : a projecting piece of land **8** : a punctuation mark; *esp* : PERIOD **9** : DECIMAL POINT **10** : one of the divisions of the compass **11** : a unit of counting (as in a game score) — **point-**

less *adj* — **pointy** \ˈpȯin-tē\ *adj* — **beside the point** : IRRELEVANT — **to the point** : RELEVANT, PERTINENT ⟨her remark was *to the point*⟩

²point *vb* **1** : to furnish with a point : SHARPEN **2** : PUNCTUATE **3** : to separate (a decimal fraction) from an integer by a decimal point — usu. used with *off* **4** : to indicate the position of esp. by extending a finger **5** : to direct attention to ⟨~ out an error⟩ **6** : AIM, DIRECT **7** : to lie extended, aimed, or turned in a particular direction : FACE, LOOK

point–and–click *adj* : relating to or being a computer interface that allows the activation of a file by selection with a pointing device (as a mouse)

point–and–shoot *adj* : having or using preset or automatically adjusted controls ⟨a ~ camera⟩

point–blank \ˈpȯint-ˈblaŋk\ *adj* **1** : so close to the target that a missile fired will travel in a straight line to the mark **2** : DIRECT, BLUNT ⟨a ~ refusal⟩ — **point–blank** *adv*

point·ed \ˈpȯin-təd\ *adj* **1** : having a point **2** : being to the point : DIRECT **3** : aimed at a particular person or group; *also* : CONSPICUOUS, MARKED ⟨~ indifference⟩ — **point·ed·ly** *adv*

point·er \ˈpȯin-tər\ *n* **1** : one that points out : INDICATOR **2** : a large short-haired hunting dog **3** : HINT, TIP ⟨gave me some ~s on how to play⟩

poin·til·lism \ˈpwan-tē-ˌyi-zəm, ˈpȯin-tə-ˌli-zəm\ *n* [F *pointillisme*, fr. *pointiller* to stipple, fr. *point* spot, point] : the theory or practice in painting of applying small strokes or dots of color to a surface so that from a distance they blend together — **poin·til·list** \ˌpwan-tē-ˈyēst, ˈpȯin-tə-list\ *n or adj*

point man *n* : a principal spokesman or advocate

point of no return : a critical point at which turning back or reversal is not possible

point of view : a position from which something is considered or evaluated

point spread *n* : the number of points by which a favorite is expected to defeat an underdog

¹poise \ˈpȯiz\ *vb* **poised; pois·ing** : BALANCE

²poise *n* **1** : BALANCE **2** : self-possessed calmness; *also* : a particular way of carrying oneself

poi·sha \ˈpȯi-shə\ *n, pl* **poisha** : the paisa of Bangladesh

¹poi·son \ˈpȯi-zᵊn\ *n* [ME, fr. AF *poisun* drink, potion, poison, fr. L *potion-, potio* drink] : a substance that through its chemical action can injure or kill — **poi·son·ous** \-zᵊn-əs\ *adj*

²poison *vb* **1** : to injure or kill with poison **2** : to treat or taint with poison **3** : to affect destructively : CORRUPT ⟨~ed her mind⟩ — **poi·son·er** *n*

poison hemlock *n* : a large branching poisonous herb with finely divided leaves and white flowers that is related to the carrot

poison ivy *n* **1** : a usu. climbing plant related to the sumacs that has leaves composed of three shiny leaflets and produces an irritating oil causing a usu. intensely itching skin rash; *also* : any of several related plants **2** : a skin rash caused by poison ivy

poison oak *n* : any of several shrubby plants closely related to poison ivy and having similar properties

poison sumac *n* : a No. American swamp shrub with pinnate leaves, greenish flowers, greenish white berries, and irritating properties

¹**poke** \'pōk\ *n, chiefly Southern & Midland* : BAG, SACK

²**poke** *vb* **poked; pok·ing 1** : PROD; *also* : to stir up by prodding **2** : to make a prodding or jabbing movement esp. repeatedly **3** : HIT, PUNCH **4** : to thrust forward obtrusively **5** : RUMMAGE ⟨*poking* around the attic⟩ **6** : MEDDLE, PRY **7** : DAWDLE — **poke fun at** : RIDICULE, MOCK

³**poke** *n* : a quick thrust; *also* : PUNCH

¹**pok·er** \'pō-kər\ *n* : a metal rod for stirring a fire

²**pok·er** \'pō-kər\ *n* : any of several card games in which the player with the highest hand at the end of the betting wins

poke·weed \'pōk-ˌwēd\ *n* : a coarse American perennial herb with clusters of white flowers and dark purple juicy berries

poky *or* **pok·ey** \'pō-kē\ *adj* **pok·i·er; -est 1** : small and cramped **2** : SHABBY, DULL **3** : annoyingly slow

pol \'päl\ *n* : POLITICIAN

po·lar \'pō-lər\ *adj* **1** : of or relating to a geographical pole **2** : of or relating to a pole (as of a magnet)

polar bear *n* : a large creamy-white bear that inhabits arctic regions

Po·lar·is \pə-'ler-əs\ *n* : NORTH STAR

po·lar·ise *Brit var of* POLARIZE

po·lar·i·ty \pō-'ler-ə-tē\ *n, pl* **-ties** : the condition of having poles and esp. magnetic or electrical poles

po·lar·i·za·tion \ˌpō-lə-rə-'zā-shən\ *n* **1** : the action of polarizing : the state of being polarized **2** : concentration about opposing extremes

po·lar·ize \'pō-lə-ˌrīz\ *vb* **-ized; -iz·ing 1** : to cause (light waves) to vibrate in a definite way **2** : to give physical polarity to **3** : to break up into opposing groups

pol·der \'pōl-dər, 'päl-\ *n* [D] : a tract of low land reclaimed from the sea

¹**pole** \'pōl\ *n* : a long slender piece of wood or metal ⟨telephone ∼⟩

²**pole** *vb* **poled; pol·ing** : to impel or push with a pole

³**pole** *n* **1** : either end of an axis esp. of the earth **2** : either of the terminals of an electric device (as a battery or generator) **3** : one of two or more regions in a magnetized body at which the magnetism is concentrated — **pole·ward** \'pōl-wərd\ *adj or adv*

¹**pole·ax** \'pōl-ˌaks\ *n* : a battle-ax with a short handle

²**poleax** *vb* : to attack or fell with or as if with a poleax

pole·cat \'pōl-ˌkat\ *n, pl* **polecats** *or* **polecat 1** : a European carnivorous mammal of which the ferret is considered a domesticated variety **2** : SKUNK

po·lem·ic \pə-'le-mik\ *n* ; the art or practice of disputation — usu. used in pl. — **po·lem·i·cal** \-mi-kəl\ *also* **po·lem·ic** \-mik\ *adj* — **po·lem·i·cist** \-sist\ *n*

pole·star \'pōl-ˌstär\ *n* **1** : NORTH STAR **2** : a directing principle : GUIDE

pole vault *n* : a field contest in which each contestant uses a pole to vault for height over a crossbar — **pole–vault** *vb* — **pole–vault·er** *n*

¹**po·lice** \pə-'lēs\ *vb* **po·liced; po·lic·ing 1** : to control, regulate, or keep in order esp. by use of police ⟨∼ a highway⟩ **2** : to make clean and put in order

²**police** *n, pl* **police** [F, government, fr. OF, fr. LL *politia*, fr. Gk *politeia*, fr. *politēs* citizen, fr. *polis* city, state] **1** : the department of government that keeps public order and safety and enforces the laws; *also* : the members of this department **2** : a private organization resembling a police force; *also* : its members **3** : military personnel detailed to clean and put in order

po·lice·man \-mən\ *n* : POLICE OFFICER

police officer *n* : a member of a police force

police state *n* : a state characterized by repressive, arbitrary, totalitarian rule by means of secret police

po·lice·wom·an \pə-'lēs-ˌwu̇-mən\ *n* : a woman who is a police officer

¹**pol·i·cy** \'pä-lə-sē\ *n, pl* **-cies** : a definite course or method of action selected to guide and determine present and future decisions

²**policy** *n, pl* **-cies** : a writing whereby a contract of insurance is made

pol·i·cy·hold·er \'pä-lə-sē-ˌhōl-dər\ *n* : one granted an insurance policy

po·lio \'pō-lē-ˌō\ *n* : POLIOMYELITIS — **polio** *adj*

po·lio·my·eli·tis \-ˌmī-ə-'lī-təs\ *n* : an acute virus disease marked by inflammation of the gray matter of the spinal cord leading usu. to paralysis

¹**pol·ish** \'pä-lish\ *vb* **1** : to make smooth and glossy usu. by rubbing **2** : to refine or improve in manners, condition, or style

²**polish** *n* **1** : a smooth glossy surface : LUSTER **2** : REFINEMENT, CULTURE **3** : the action or process of polishing **4** : a preparation used to produce a gloss

Pol·ish \'pō-lish\ *n* : the Slavic language of the Poles — **Polish** *adj*

polit *abbr* political; politician

po·lit·bu·ro \'pä-lət-ˌbyu̇r-ō, 'pō-, pə-'lit-\ *n* [Russ *politbyuro*] : the principal policy-making committee of a Communist party

po·lite \pə-'līt\ *adj* **po·lit·er; -est 1** : REFINED, CULTIVATED ⟨∼ society⟩ **2** : marked by correct social conduct : COURTEOUS; *also* : CONSIDERATE, TACTFUL — **po·lite·ly** *adv* — **po·lite·ness** *n*

po·li·tesse \ˌpä-li-ˈtes\ n [F] : formal politeness

pol·i·tic \ˈpä-lə-ˌtik\ adj **1** : wise in promoting a policy ⟨a ~ statesman⟩ **2** : shrewdly tactful ⟨a ~ move⟩

po·lit·i·cal \pə-ˈli-ti-kəl\ adj **1** : of or relating to government or politics **2** : involving or charged or concerned with acts against a government or a political system ⟨~ prisoners⟩ — **po·lit·i·cal·ly** \-k(ə-)lē\ adv

politically correct adj : conforming to a belief that language and practices which could offend sensibilities (as in matters of sex or race) should be eliminated — **political correctness** n

pol·i·ti·cian \ˌpä-lə-ˈti-shən\ n : a person actively engaged in government or politics

pol·i·tick \ˈpä-lə-ˌtik\ vb : to engage in political discussion or activity

po·lit·i·co \pə-ˈli-ti-ˌkō\ n, pl **-cos** also **-coes** : POLITICIAN

pol·i·tics \ˈpä-lə-ˌtiks\ n sing or pl **1** : the art or science of government, of guiding or influencing governmental policy, or of winning and holding control over a government **2** : political affairs or business; esp : competition between groups or individuals for power and leadership **3** : political opinions

pol·i·ty \ˈpä-lə-tē\ n, pl **-ties** : a politically organized unit; also : the form or constitution of such a unit

pol·ka \ˈpōl-kə, ˈpō-kə\ n [Czech, fr. Polka Polish woman, fem. of Polák Pole] : a lively couple dance of Bohemian origin; also : music for this dance — **polka** vb

pol·ka dot \ˈpō-kə-ˌdät\ n : a dot in a pattern of regularly distributed dots — **polka–dot** or **polka–dot·ted** \-ˌdä-təd\ adj

¹poll \ˈpōl\ n **1** : HEAD **2** : the casting and recording of votes; also : the total vote cast **3** : the place where votes are cast — usu. used in pl. **4** : a questioning of persons to obtain information or opinions to be analyzed

²poll vb **1** : to cut off or shorten a growth or part of : CLIP, SHEAR **2** : to receive and record the votes of **3** : to receive (as votes) in an election **4** : to question in a poll

pol·lack or **pol·lock** \ˈpä-lək\ n, pl **pollack** or **pollock** : an important No. Atlantic food fish that is related to the cods; also : a related food fish of the No. Pacific

pol·len \ˈpä-lən\ n [NL, fr. L, fine flour] : a mass of male spores of a seed plant usu. appearing as a yellow dust

pol·li·na·tion \ˌpä-lə-ˈnā-shən\ n : the carrying of pollen to the female part of a plant to fertilize the seed — **pol·li·nate** \ˈpä-lə-ˌnāt\ vb — **pol·li·na·tor** \-ˌnā-tər\ n

poll·ster \ˈpōl-stər\ n : one that conducts a poll or compiles data obtained by a poll

poll tax n : a tax of a fixed amount per person levied on adults and often linked to the right to vote

pol·lute \pə-ˈlüt\ vb **pol·lut·ed; pol·lut·ing** : to make impure; esp : to contaminate (an environment) esp. with manmade waste — **pol·lut·ant** \-ˈlüt-ᵊnt\ n — **pol·lut·er** n — **pol·lu·tion** \-ˈlü-shən\ n

pol·ly·wog or **pol·li·wog** \ˈpä-lē-ˌwäg\ n : TADPOLE

po·lo \ˈpō-lō\ n [Balti (Tibetan language of northern Kashmir), ball] : a game played by two teams on horseback using long-handled mallets to drive a wooden ball

po·lo·ni·um \pə-ˈlō-nē-əm\ n : a radioactive metallic chemical element

pol·ter·geist \ˈpōl-tər-ˌgīst\ n [G, fr. poltern to knock + Geist spirit] : a noisy usu. mischievous ghost held to be responsible for unexplained noises

pol·troon \päl-ˈtrün\ n : COWARD

poly- comb form [Gk, fr. polys many] **1** : many : several ⟨polysyllabic⟩ **2** : polymeric ⟨polyester⟩

poly·chlo·ri·nat·ed bi·phe·nyl \ˌpä-li-ˈklōr-ə-ˌnā-təd-ˌbī-ˈfen-ᵊl, -ˈfēn-\ n : any of several industrial compounds that are toxic environmental pollutants

poly·clin·ic \ˌpä-li-ˈkli-nik\ n : a clinic or hospital treating diseases of many sorts

poly·es·ter \ˈpä-lē-ˌes-tər\ n : a polymer composed of ester groups used esp. in making fibers or plastics; also : a product (as fabric) composed of polyester

poly·eth·yl·ene \ˌpä-li-ˈe-thə-ˌlēn\ n : a lightweight plastic resistant to chemicals and moisture and used chiefly in packaging

po·lyg·a·my \pə-ˈli-gə-mē\ n : the practice of having more than one wife or husband at one time — **po·lyg·a·mist** \-mist\ n — **po·lyg·a·mous** \-məs\ adj

poly·glot \ˈpä-li-ˌglät\ adj **1** : speaking or writing several languages **2** : containing or made up of several languages — **polyglot** n

poly·gon \ˈpä-li-ˌgän\ n : a closed plane figure bounded by straight lines — **po·lyg·o·nal** \pə-ˈli-gə-nᵊl\ adj

poly·graph \ˈpä-li-ˌgraf\ n : an instrument (as a lie detector) for recording variations of several bodily functions (as blood pressure) simultaneously — **po·lyg·ra·pher** \pə-ˈli-grə-fər, ˈpä-li-ˌgra-fər\ n

poly·he·dron \ˌpä-li-ˈhē-drən\ n : a solid formed by plane faces that are polygons — **poly·he·dral** \-drəl\ adj

poly·math \ˈpä-li-ˌmath\ n : a person of encyclopedic learning

poly·mer \ˈpä-lə-mər\ n : a chemical compound formed by union of small molecules and usu. consisting of repeating structural units — **poly·mer·ic** \ˌpä-lə-ˈmer-ik\ adj

po·lym·er·i·za·tion \pə-ˌli-mə-rə-ˈzā-shən\ n : a chemical reaction in which two or more small molecules combine to form polymers — **po·lym·er·ize** \pə-ˈli-mə-ˌrīz\ vb

Poly·ne·sian \ˌpä-lə-ˈnē-zhən\ n **1** : a member of any of the indigenous peoples of Polynesia **2** : a group of Austronesian languages spoken in Polynesia — **Poly-nesian** *adj*

poly·no·mi·al \ˌpä-lə-ˈnō-mē-əl\ *n* : an algebraic expression having one or more terms each of which consists of a constant multiplied by one or more variables raised to a nonnegative integral power — **polynomial** *adj*

pol·yp \ˈpä-ləp\ *n* **1** : an invertebrate animal (as a coral) that is a coelenterate having a hollow cylindrical body closed at one end **2** : a growth projecting from a mucous membrane (as of the colon or vocal cords)

po·lyph·o·ny \pə-ˈli-fə-nē\ *n* : music consisting of two or more melodically independent but harmonizing voice parts — **poly·phon·ic** \ˌpä-li-ˈfä-nik\ *adj*

poly·pro·pyl·ene \ˌpä-lē-ˈprō-pə-ˌlēn\ *n* : any of various polymer plastics or fibers

poly·sty·rene \ˌpä-li-ˈstī-ˌrēn\ *n* : a rigid transparent nonconducting thermoplastic used esp. in molded products and foams

poly·syl·lab·ic \-sə-ˈla-bik\ *adj* **1** : having more than three syllables **2** : characterized by polysyllabic words

poly·syl·la·ble \ˈpä-li-ˌsi-lə-bəl\ *n* : a polysyllabic word

poly·tech·nic \ˌpä-li-ˈtek-nik\ *adj* : of, relating to, or instructing in many technical arts or applied sciences

poly·the·ism \ˈpä-li-thē-ˌi-zəm\ *n* : belief in or worship of many gods — **poly·the·ist** \-ˌthē-ist\ *adj or n* — **poly·the·is·tic** \ˌpä-li-thē-ˈis-tik\ *adj*

poly·un·sat·u·rat·ed \ˌpä-lē-ˌən-ˈsa-chə-ˌrā-təd\ *adj* : having many double or triple bonds in a molecule — used esp. of an oil or fatty acid

poly·ure·thane \ˌpä-lē-ˈyu̇r-ə-ˌthān\ *n* : any of various polymers used esp. in foams and in resins (as for coatings)

poly·vi·nyl \ˌpä-li-ˈvī-nᵊl\ *adj* : of, relating to, or being a polymerized vinyl compound, resin, or plastic — often used in combination

pome·gran·ate \ˈpä-mə-ˌgra-nət\ *n* [ME *poumgrenet*, fr. AF *pome garnette*, lit., seedy fruit] : a many-seeded reddish fruit that has an edible crimson pulp and is borne by a tropical Asian tree; *also* : the tree

¹pom·mel \ˈpə-məl, ˈpä-\ *n* **1** : the knob on the hilt of a sword **2** : the knoblike bulge at the front and top of a saddlebow

²pom·mel \ˈpə-məl, ˈpä-\ *vb* **-meled** *or* **-melled**; **-mel·ing** *or* **-mel·ling** : PUMMEL

pomp \ˈpämp\ *n* **1** : brilliant display : SPLENDOR **2** : OSTENTATION

pom·pa·dour \ˈpäm-pə-ˌdȯr\ *n* : a style of dressing the hair high over the forehead

pom·pa·no \ˈpäm-pə-ˌnō, ˈpəm-\ *n, pl* **-no** *or* **-nos** : a narrow silvery fish of coastal waters of the western Atlantic

pom–pom \ˈpäm-ˌpäm\ *n* **1** : an ornamental ball or tuft used on a cap or costume **2** : a fluffy ball flourished by cheerleaders

pom–pon \ˈpäm-ˌpän\ *n* **1** : POM-POM **2** : a chrysanthemum or dahlia with small rounded flower heads

pomp·ous \ˈpäm-pəs\ *adj* **1** : suggestive of pomp; *esp* : OSTENTATIOUS **2** : pretentiously dignified **3** : excessively elevated or ornate ♦ *Synonyms* ARROGANT, MAGISTERIAL, SELF-IMPORTANT — **pom·pos·i·ty** \päm-ˈpä-sə-tē\ *n* — **pomp·ous·ly** *adv*

pon·cho \ˈpän-chō\ *n, pl* **ponchos** [AmerSp, fr. Mapuche (American Indian language of Chile)] **1** : a blanket with a slit in the middle for the head so that it can be worn as a garment **2** : a waterproof garment resembling a poncho

pond \ˈpänd\ *n* : a small body of water

pon·der \ˈpän-dər\ *vb* **pon·dered**; **pon·der·ing 1** : to weigh in the mind **2** : to consider carefully

pon·der·o·sa pine \ˈpän-də-ˌrō-sə-, -zə-\ *n* : a tall pine of western No. America with long needles; *also* : its strong reddish wood

pon·der·ous \ˈpän-də-rəs\ *adj* **1** : of very great weight **2** : UNWIELDY, CLUMSY ⟨a ∼ weapon⟩ **3** : oppressively dull ⟨a ∼ speech⟩ ♦ *Synonyms* CUMBROUS, CUMBERSOME, WEIGHTY

pone \ˈpōn\ *n, Southern & Midland* : an oval-shaped cornmeal cake; *also* : corn bread in the form of pones

pon·iard \ˈpän-yərd\ *n* : DAGGER

pon·tiff \ˈpän-təf\ *n* : POPE — **pon·tif·i·cal** \pän-ˈti-fi-kəl\ *adj*

¹pon·tif·i·cate \pän-ˈti-fi-kət, -fə-ˌkāt\ *n* : the state, office, or term of office of a pontiff

²pon·tif·i·cate \pän-ˈti-fə-ˌkāt\ *vb* **-cat·ed**; **-cat·ing** : to deliver dogmatic opinions

pon·toon \pän-ˈtün\ *n* **1** : a flat-bottomed boat **2** : a boat or float used in building a floating temporary bridge **3** : a float of a seaplane

po·ny \ˈpō-nē\ *n, pl* **ponies** : a small horse

po·ny·tail \-ˌtāl\ *n* : a style of arranging hair to resemble the tail of a pony

pooch \ˈpüch\ *n* : DOG

poo·dle \ˈpü-dᵊl\ *n* [G *Pudel*, short for *Pudelhund*, fr. *pudeln* to splash + *Hund* dog] : any of a breed of active intelligent dogs with a dense curly solid-colored coat

pooh–pooh \ˈpü-ˈpü\ *also* **pooh** \ˈpü\ *vb* **1** : to express contempt or impatience **2** : DERIDE, SCORN ⟨∼ed my idea⟩

¹pool \ˈpül\ *n* **1** : a small deep body of usu. fresh water **2** : a small body of standing liquid **3** : SWIMMING POOL

²pool *vb* : to form a pool

³pool *n* **1** : all the money bet on the result of a particular event **2** : any of several games of billiards played on a table having six pockets **3** : the amount contributed by the participants in a joint venture **4** : a combination between competing firms for mutual profit **5** : a readily available supply

⁴pool *vb* : to combine (as resources) in a common fund or effort

¹poop \ˈpüp\ *n* : an enclosed superstructure at the stern of a ship

²poop *n, slang* : INFORMATION

poop deck *n* : a partial deck above a ship's main afterdeck

poor \'pùr\ *adj* **1** : lacking material possessions ⟨∼ people⟩ **2** : less than adequate : MEAGER ⟨a ∼ crop⟩ **3** : arousing pity ⟨you ∼ thing⟩ **4** : inferior in quality or value **5** : UNPRODUCTIVE, BARREN ⟨∼ soil⟩ **6** : fairly unsatisfactory ⟨∼ prospects⟩; *also* : UNFAVORABLE ⟨∼ opinion⟩ — **poor·ly** *adv*

poor boy *var of* PO'BOY

poor·house \'pùr-,haùs\ *n* : a publicly supported home for needy or dependent persons

poor–mouth \-,maùth, -,maùth\ *vb* : to plead poverty as a defense or excuse

¹**pop** \'päp\ *vb* **popped; pop·ping 1** : to go, come, enter, or issue forth suddenly or quickly ⟨∼ into bed⟩ **2** : to put or thrust suddenly ⟨∼ questions⟩ **3** : to burst or cause to burst with a sharp sound; *also* : to make a sharp sound **4** : to protrude from the sockets **5** : SHOOT **6** : to hit a pop-up

²**pop** *n* **1** : a sharp explosive sound **2** : SHOT **3** : SODA POP

³**pop** *n* : FATHER

⁴**pop** *adj* **1** : POPULAR ⟨∼ music⟩ **2** : of or relating to pop music ⟨∼ singer⟩ **3** : of or relating to the popular culture disseminated through the mass media ⟨∼ psychology⟩ **4** : of, relating to, or imitating pop art ⟨∼ painter⟩

⁵**pop** *n* : pop music or culture; *also* : POP ART

⁶**pop** *abbr* population

pop art *n, often cap P&A* : art in which commonplace objects (as comic strips or soup cans) are used as subject matter — **pop artist** *n*

¹**pop·corn** \'päp-,kòrn\ *n* : an Indian corn whose kernels burst open into a white starchy mass when heated; *also* : the burst kernels

²**popcorn** *adj* : having widespread appeal but little artistic merit

pope \'pōp\ *n, often cap* : the head of the Roman Catholic Church

pop–eyed \'päp-,īd\ *adj* : having eyes that bulge (as from disease)

pop fly *n* : POP-UP

pop·gun \'päp-,gən\ *n* : a toy gun for shooting pellets with compressed air

pop·in·jay \'pä-pən-,jā\ *n* [ME *papejay* parrot, fr. MF *papegai, papejai*, fr. Ar *babghā*'] : a strutting supercilious person

pop·lar \'pä-plər\ *n* **1** : any of a genus of slender quick-growing trees (as a cottonwood) related to the willows **2** : the wood of a poplar

pop·lin \'pä-plən\ *n* : a strong plain-woven fabric with crosswise ribs

pop·over \'päp-,ō-vər\ *n* : a hollow muffin made from a thin batter rich in egg

pop·per \'pä-pər\ *n* : a utensil for popping corn

pop·py \'pä-pē\ *n, pl* **poppies** : any of a genus of herbs with showy flowers including one that yields opium

pop·py·cock \-,käk\ *n* : empty talk or writing : NONSENSE

pop·u·lace \'pä-pyə-ləs\ *n* **1** : the common people **2** : POPULATION

pop·u·lar \'pä-pyə-lər\ *adj* **1** : of or relating to the general public ⟨∼ government⟩ **2** : suited to the tastes of the general public ⟨∼ style⟩ **3** : INEXPENSIVE ⟨∼ rates⟩ **4** : frequently encountered or widely accepted ⟨∼ notion⟩ **5** : commonly liked or approved ⟨a ∼ teacher⟩ — **pop·u·lar·i·ty** \,pä-pyə-'la-rə-tē\ *n* — **pop·u·lar·ize** \'pä-pyə-lə-,rīz\ *vb* — **pop·u·lar·ly** *adv*

pop·u·late \'pä-pyə-,lāt\ *vb* **-lat·ed; -lat·ing 1** : to have a place in : INHABIT **2** : PEOPLE

pop·u·la·tion \,pä-pyə-'lā-shən\ *n* **1** : the people or number of people in an area **2** : the organisms inhabiting a particular locality **3** : a group of individuals or items from which samples are taken for statistical measurement

population explosion *n* : a pyramiding of numbers of a biological population; *esp* : the recent great increase in human numbers resulting from increased survival and exponential population growth

pop·u·list \'pä-pyə-list\ *n* : a believer in or advocate of the rights, wisdom, or virtues of the common people — **pop·u·lism** \-,li-zəm\ *n*

pop·u·lous \'pä-pyə-ləs\ *adj* **1** : densely populated; *also* : having a large population **2** : CROWDED — **pop·u·lous·ness** *n*

¹**pop–up** \'päp-,əp\ *n* : a short high fly in baseball

²**pop–up** *adj* : of, relating to, or having a component or device that pops up

por·ce·lain \'pòr-sə-lən\ *n* : a fine-grained translucent ceramic ware

porch \'pòrch\ *n* : a covered entrance usu. with a separate roof

por·cine \'pòr-,sīn\ *adj* : of, relating to, or suggesting swine

por·ci·ni \pòr-'chē-nē\ *n, pl* **porcini** [It] : a large edible brown mushroom

por·ci·no \pòr-'chē-nō\ *n, pl* **-ni** : PORCINI

por·cu·pine \'pòr-kyə-,pīn\ *n* [ME *porke despyne*, fr. MF *porc espin*, fr. It *porcospino*, fr. L *porcus* pig + *spina* spine, prickle] : any of various mammals having stiff sharp spines mingled with their hair

¹**pore** \'pòr\ *vb* **pored; por·ing 1** : to read studiously or attentively ⟨∼ over a book⟩ **2** : PONDER, REFLECT

²**pore** *n* : a tiny hole or space (as in the skin or soil) — **pored** \'pòrd\ *adj*

pork \'pòrk\ *n* : the flesh of swine dressed for use as food

pork barrel *n* : government projects or appropriations yielding rich patronage benefits

pork·er \'pòr-kər\ *n* : HOG; *esp* : a young pig suitable for use as fresh pork

por·nog·ra·phy \pòr-'nä-grə-fē\ *n* : the depiction of erotic behavior intended to cause sexual excitement — **por·no·graph·ic** \,pòr-nə-'gra-fik\ *adj*

po·rous \'pòr-əs\ *adj* **1** : full of pores **2** : permeable to fluids : ABSORPTIVE — **po·ros·i·ty** \pə-'rä-sə-tē\ *n*

por·phy·ry \'pòr-fə-rē\ *n, pl* **-ries** : a rock consisting of feldspar crystals embedded in a compact fine-grained base material — **por·phy·rit·ic** \,pòr-fə-'ri-tik\ adj

por·poise \'pòr-pəs\ n [ME porpoys, fr. AF porpeis, fr. ML porcopiscis, fr. L porcus pig + piscis fish] : any of a family of small gregarious blunt-snouted whales with spadelike teeth; also : DOLPHIN 1

por·ridge \'pòr-ij\ n : a soft food made by boiling meal of grains or legumes in milk or water

por·rin·ger \'pòr-ən-jər\ n : a low one-handled metal bowl or cup

¹**port** \'pòrt\ n 1 : HARBOR 2 : a city with a harbor 3 : AIRPORT

²**port** n 1 : an inlet or outlet (as in an engine) for a fluid 2 : PORTHOLE 3 : JACK 7

³**port** vb : to turn or put a helm to the left

⁴**port** n : the left side of a ship or airplane looking forward — **port** adj

⁵**port** n : a sweet fortified wine

portabella or **portabello** var of PORTOBELLO

por·ta·bil·i·ty \,pòr-tə-'bil-ə-tē\ n, pl -ties 1 : the quality or state of being portable 2 : the ability to transfer benefits from one pension fund to another when a worker changes jobs

por·ta·ble \'pòr-tə-bəl\ adj : capable of being carried — **portable** n

¹**por·tage** \'pòr-tij, pòr-'täzh\ n [ME, fr. AF, fr. porter to carry] : the carrying of boats and goods overland between navigable bodies of water; also : a route for such carrying

²**portage** vb **por·taged**; **por·tag·ing** : to carry gear over a portage

por·tal \'pòr-t³l\ n : DOOR, ENTRANCE; esp : a grand or imposing one

portal-to-portal adj : of or relating to the time spent by a worker in traveling from the entrance to an employer's property to the worker's actual job site (as in a mine)

port·cul·lis \pòrt-'kə-ləs\ n : a grating at the gateway of a castle or fortress that can be let down to stop entrance

porte co·chere \,pòrt-kō-'sher\ n [F porte cochère, lit., coach door] : a roofed structure extending from the entrance of a building over an adjacent driveway and sheltering those getting in or out of vehicles

por·tend \pòr-'tend\ vb 1 : to give a sign or warning of beforehand 2 : INDICATE, SIGNIFY ♦ **Synonyms** AUGUR, PROGNOSTICATE, FORETELL, PREDICT, FORECAST, PROPHESY

por·tent \'pòr-,tent\ n 1 : something that foreshadows a coming event : OMEN 2 : MARVEL, PRODIGY

por·ten·tous \pòr-'ten-təs\ adj 1 : of, relating to, or constituting a portent 2 : PRODIGIOUS 3 : self-consciously solemn : POMPOUS

¹**por·ter** \'pòr-tər\ n, chiefly Brit : DOORKEEPER

²**porter** n 1 : a person who carries burdens; esp : one employed (as at a terminal) to carry baggage 2 : an attendant in a railroad car 3 : a dark heavy ale

por·ter·house \'pòr-tər-,haùs\ n : a choice beefsteak with a large tenderloin

port·fo·lio \pòrt-'fō-lē-,ō\ n, pl -li·os 1 : a portable case for papers or drawings 2 : the office and functions of a minister of state 3 : the securities held by an investor

port·hole \'pòrt-,hōl\ n : an opening (as a window) in the side of a ship or aircraft

por·ti·co \'pòr-ti-,kō\ n, pl -coes or -cos [It] : a row of columns supporting a roof around or at the entrance of a building

¹**por·tion** \'pòr-shən\ n 1 : one's part or share ⟨a ~ of food⟩ 2 : DOWRY 3 : an individual's lot 4 : a part of a whole ⟨a ~ of the sky⟩

²**portion** vb 1 : to divide into portions 2 : to allot to as a portion

port·land cement \'pòrt-lənd-\ n : a cement made by calcining and grinding a mixture of clay and limestone

port·ly \'pòrt-lē\ adj **port·li·er**; **-est** : somewhat stout

port·man·teau \pòrt-'man-,tō\ n, pl -teaus or -teaux \-,tōz\ [MF portemanteau, fr. porter to carry + manteau mantle, fr. L mantellum] : a large traveling bag

por·to·bel·lo \,pòr-tə-'be-lō\ also **por·ta·bel·la** \-lə\ or **por·ta·bel·lo** \-lō\ n, pl -los also -las : a large dark mature mushroom noted for its meaty texture

port of call : an intermediate port where ships customarily stop for supplies, repairs, or transshipment of cargo

port of entry 1 : a place where foreign goods may be cleared through a customhouse 2 : a place where an alien may enter a country

por·trait \'pòr-trət, -,trāt\ n : a picture (as a painting or photograph) of a person usu. showing the face — **por·trait·ist** \-trə-tist\ n

por·trai·ture \'pòr-trə-,chùr\ n : the practice or art of making portraits

por·tray \pòr-'trā\ vb 1 : to make a picture of : DEPICT 2 : to describe in words 3 : to play the role of — **por·tray·al** n

Por·tu·guese \'pòr-chə-,gēz, -,gēs; ,pòr-chə-'gēz, -'gēs\ n, pl **Portuguese** 1 : a native or inhabitant of Portugal 2 : the language of Portugal and Brazil — **Portuguese** adj

Portuguese man-of-war n : any of several large colonial marine invertebrate animals related to the jellyfishes and having a large sac by which the colony floats at the surface

por·tu·laca \,pòr-chə-'la-kə\ n : any of a genus of succulent herbs cultivated for their showy flowers

pos abbr 1 position 2 positive

¹**pose** \'pōz\ vb **posed**; **pos·ing** 1 : to assume or cause to assume a posture usu. for artistic purposes 2 : to set forth : PROPOSE ⟨~ a question⟩ 3 : to affect an attitude or character

²**pose** n 1 : a sustained posture; esp : one assumed by a model 2 : an attitude assumed for effect : PRETENSE

¹**pos·er** \'pō-zər\ n : a puzzling question

²**poser** *n* : a person who poses

po·seur \pō-'zər\ *n* [F, lit., poser] : an affected or insincere person

posh \'päsh\ *adj* : FASHIONABLE ⟨a ~ restaurant⟩

pos·it \'pä-zət\ *vb* : to assume the existence of : POSTULATE

po·si·tion \pə-'zi-shən\ *n* **1** : an arranging in order **2** : the stand taken on a question **3** : the point or area occupied by something : SITUATION **4** : a certain arrangement of bodily parts ⟨exercise in a sitting ~⟩ **5** : RANK, STATUS **6** : EMPLOYMENT, JOB — **position** *vb* — **po·si·tion·al** \-shə-nəl\ *adj*

¹**pos·i·tive** \'pä-zə-tiv\ *adj* **1** : expressed definitely ⟨her answer was a ~ no⟩ **2** : CONFIDENT, CERTAIN ⟨~ it was my book⟩ **3** : of, relating to, or constituting the degree of grammatical comparison that denotes no increase in quality, quantity, or relation **4** : not fictitious : REAL **5** : active and effective in function ⟨~ leadership⟩ **6** : having the light and shade as existing in the original subject ⟨a ~ photograph⟩ **7** : numerically greater than zero ⟨a ~ number⟩ **8** : being, relating to, or charged with electricity of which the proton is the elementary unit **9** : AFFIRMATIVE ⟨a ~ response⟩ **10** : FAVORABLE; *also* : marked by optimism — **pos·i·tive·ly** *adv* — **pos·i·tive·ness** *n*

²**positive** *n* **1** : the positive degree or a positive form in a language **2** : a positive photograph

pos·i·tron \'pä-zə-ˌträn\ *n* : a positively charged particle having the same mass and magnitude of charge as the electron

po·so·le *or* **po·zo·le** \pō-'sō-lā\ *n* : a thick Mexican soup made with pork, hominy, garlic, and chili

poss *abbr* possessive

pos·se \'pä-sē\ *n* [ML *posse comitatus*, lit., power or authority of the county] **1** : a body of persons organized to assist a sheriff in an emergency **2** : a body of attendants or followers

pos·sess \pə-'zes\ *vb* **1** : to have as property : OWN **2** : to have as an attribute, knowledge, or skill **3** : to enter into and control firmly ⟨~ed by a devil⟩ — **pos·ses·sor** \-'ze-sər\ *n*

pos·ses·sion \-'ze-shən\ *n* **1** : control or occupancy of property **2** : OWNERSHIP **3** : something owned : PROPERTY **4** : domination by something (as an evil spirit, a passion, or an idea) **5** : SELF-CONTROL

pos·ses·sive \pə-'ze-siv\ *adj* **1** : of, relating to, or constituting a grammatical case denoting ownership **2** : showing the desire to possess ⟨a ~ nature⟩ — **possessive** *n* — **pos·ses·sive·ness** *n*

pos·si·ble \'pä-sə-bəl\ *adj* **1** : being within the limits of ability, capacity, or realization **2** : being something that may or may not occur ⟨~ dangers⟩ **3** : able or fitted to become ⟨a ~ site for a bridge⟩ — **pos·si·bil·i·ty** \ˌpä-sə-'bi-lə-tē\ *n* — **pos·si·bly** \'pä-sə-blē\ *adv*

pos·sum \'pä-səm\ *n* : OPOSSUM

¹**post** \'pōst\ *n* **1** : an upright piece of timber or metal serving esp. as a support : PILLAR **2** : a pole or stake set up as a mark or indicator

²**post** *vb* **1** : to affix to a usual place (as a wall) for public notices **2** : to publish or announce by or as if by a public notice ⟨~ grades⟩ **3** : to forbid (property) to trespassers by putting up a notice **4** : SCORE **5** : to publish in an online forum

³**post** *n* **1** *obs* : COURIER **2** *chiefly Brit* : ¹MAIL; *also* : POST OFFICE **3** : something published online

⁴**post** *vb* **1** : to ride or travel with haste : HURRY **2** : MAIL ⟨~ a letter⟩ **3** : to enter in a ledger **4** : INFORM ⟨kept him ~ed on new developments⟩

⁵**post** *n* **1** : the place at which a soldier is stationed; *esp* : a sentry's beat or station **2** : a station or task to which a person is assigned **3** : the place at which a body of troops is stationed : CAMP **4** : OFFICE, POSITION **5** : a trading settlement or station

⁶**post** *vb* **1** : to station in a given place **2** : to put up (as bond)

post·age \'pōs-tij\ *n* : the fee for postal service; *also* : stamps representing this fee

post·al \'pōs-t⁰l\ *adj* : of or relating to the mails or the post office

postal card *n* : POSTCARD

postal service *n* : a government agency or department handling the transmission of mail

¹**post·card** \'pōst-ˌkärd\ *n* : a card on which a message may be written for mailing without an envelope

²**postcard** *adj* : PICTURESQUE

post chaise *n* : a 4-wheeled closed carriage for two to four persons

post·con·sum·er \ˌpōst-kən-'sü-mər\ *adj* **1** : discarded by a consumer **2** : having been used and recycled for reuse in another product

post·date \ˌpōst-'dāt\ *vb* : to date with a date later than that of execution ⟨~ a check⟩

post·doc·tor·al \-'däk-tə-rəl\ *also* **post·doc·tor·ate** \-tə-rət\ *adj* : of, relating to, or engaged in advanced academic or professional work beyond a doctor's degree

post·er \'pō-stər\ *n* : a bill or placard for posting often in a public place

¹**pos·te·ri·or** \pō-'stir-ē-ər, pä-\ *adj* **1** : later in time **2** : situated behind

²**pos·te·ri·or** \pä-'stir-ē-ər, pō-\ *n* : the hinder bodily parts; *esp* : BUTTOCKS

pos·ter·i·ty \pä-'ster-ə-tē\ *n* **1** : the descendants from one ancestor **2** : all future generations

pos·tern \'pōs-tərn, 'päs-\ *n* **1** : a back door or gate **2** : a private or side entrance

post exchange *n* : a store at a military post that sells to military personnel and authorized civilians

post·grad \'pōst-ˌgrad\ *adj* : POSTGRADUATE

post·grad·u·ate \(ˌ)pōst-'gra-jə-wət\ *adj*

: of or relating to studies beyond the bachelor's degree — **postgraduate** *n*

post·haste \'pōst-'hāst\ *adv* : with all possible speed

post·hole \-ˌhōl\ *n* : a hole for a post and esp. a fence post

post·hu·mous \'päs-chə-məs\ *adj* [L *posthumus*, alter. of *postumus* last-born, posthumous, fr. superl. of *posterus* coming after] **1** : born after the death of the father **2** : published after the death of the author — **post·hu·mous·ly** *adv*

post·hyp·not·ic \ˌpōst-hip-'nä-tik\ *adj* : of, relating to, or characteristic of the period following a hypnotic trance

pos·til·ion *or* **pos·til·lion** \pō-'stil-yən\ *n* : a rider on the left-hand horse of a pair drawing a coach

Post·im·pres·sion·ism \ˌpōst-im-'presh·ə-ˌni-zəm\ *n* : a late 19th century French theory or practice of art that stresses variously volume, picture structure, or expressionism

post·lude \'pōst-ˌlüd\ *n* : an organ solo played at the end of a church service

post·man \-mən, -ˌman\ *n* : MAILMAN

post·mark \-ˌmärk\ *n* : an official postal marking on a piece of mail; *esp* : the mark canceling the postage stamp — **postmark** *vb*

post·mas·ter \-ˌmas-tər\ *n* : a person who has charge of a post office

postmaster general *n, pl* **postmasters general** : an official in charge of a national postal service

post·men·o·paus·al \ˌpōst-ˌme-nə-'pȯ-zəl\ *adj* **1** : having undergone menopause **2** : occurring or administered after menopause

post me·ri·di·em \ˌpōst-mə-'ri-dē-əm\ *adj* [L] : being after noon

post·mis·tress \'pōst-ˌmis-trəs\ *n* : a woman in charge of a post office

post·mod·ern \ˌpōst-'mä-dərn\ *adj* : of, relating to, or being any of various movements in reaction to modernism

¹post·mor·tem \ˌpōst-'mȯr-təm\ *adj* [L *post mortem* after death] **1** : done, occurring, or collected after death **2** : following the event

²postmortem *n* **1** : AUTOPSY **2** : an analysis or discussion of an event after it is over

post·na·sal drip \ˌpōst-ˌnā-zəl-\ *n* : flow of mucous secretion from the posterior part of the nasal cavity onto the wall of the pharynx

post·na·tal \(ˌ)pōst-'nā-tᵊl\ *adj* : occurring or being after birth; *esp* : of or relating to a newborn infant

post office *n* **1** : POSTAL SERVICE **2** : a local branch of a post office department

post·op·er·a·tive \(ˌ)pōst-'ä-prə-tiv, -pə-ˌrä-\ *adj* : following or having undergone a surgical operation ⟨~ care⟩

post·paid \'pōst-'pād\ *adj* : having the postage paid by the sender and not chargeable to the receiver

post·par·tum \(ˌ)pōst-'pär-təm\ *adj* [NL *post partum* after birth] : following parturition — **postpartum** *adv*

post·pone \pōst-'pōn\ *vb* **post·poned**; **post·pon·ing** : to put off to a later time — **post·pone·ment** *n*

post road *n* : a road over which mail is carried

post·script \'pōst-ˌskript\ *n* : a note added esp. to a completed letter

post time *n* : the designated time for the start of a horse race

post–traumatic *adj* : occurring after or as a result of trauma ⟨~ stress⟩

pos·tu·lant \'päs-chə-lənt\ *n* : a probationary candidate for membership in a religious order

¹pos·tu·late \'päs-chə-ˌlāt\ *vb* **-lat·ed**; **-lat·ing** : to assume as true

²pos·tu·late \'päs-chə-lət, -ˌlāt\ *n* : a proposition taken for granted as true esp. as a basis for a chain of reasoning

¹pos·ture \'päs-chər\ *n* **1** : the position or bearing of the body or one of its parts **2** : STATE, CONDITION **3** : ATTITUDE ⟨a ~ of arrogance⟩

²posture *vb* **pos·tured**; **pos·tur·ing** : to strike a pose esp. for effect

post·war \'pōst-'wȯr\ *adj* : occurring or existing after a war

po·sy \'pō-zē\ *n, pl* **posies** **1** : a brief sentiment; MOTTO **2** : a bunch of flowers; *also* : FLOWER

¹pot \'pät\ *n* **1** : a rounded container used chiefly for domestic purposes **2** : the total of the bets at stake at one time **3** : RUIN ⟨go to ~⟩ — **pot·ful** *n*

²pot *vb* **pot·ted**; **pot·ting** **1** : to preserve or place in a pot **2** : SHOOT

³pot *n* : MARIJUANA

po·ta·ble \'pō-tə-bəl\ *adj* : suitable for drinking — **po·ta·bil·i·ty** \ˌpō-tə-'bi-lə-tē\ *n*

po·tage \pȯ-'täzh\ *n* : a thick soup

pot·ash \'pät-ˌash\ *n* [sing. of *pot ashes*] : potassium or any of its various compounds esp. as used in agriculture

po·tas·si·um \pə-'ta-sē-əm\ *n* : a silver-white soft metallic chemical element that occurs abundantly in nature

potassium bromide *n* : a crystalline salt used as a sedative and in photography

potassium carbonate *n* : a white salt used in making glass and soap

potassium nitrate *n* : a soluble salt used in making gunpowder, as a fertilizer, and in medicine

po·ta·tion \pō-'tā-shən\ *n* : a usu. alcoholic drink; *also* : the act of drinking

po·ta·to \pə-'tā-tō\ *n, pl* **-toes** : the edible starchy tuber of a plant related to the tomato; *also* : this plant

potato beetle *n* : COLORADO POTATO BEETLE

potato bug *n* : COLORADO POTATO BEETLE

potbellied pig *n* : any of an Asian breed of small pigs having a straight tail, potbelly, and black, white, or black and white coat

pot·bel·ly \'pät-ˌbe-lē\ *n* : a protruding abdomen — **pot·bel·lied** \-ˌlēd\ *adj*

pot·boil·er \-ˌbȯi-lər\ *n* : a usu. inferior work of art or literature produced chiefly for profit

po·tent \'pō-t⁸nt\ *adj* **1** : having authority or influence : POWERFUL **2** : chemically or medicinally effective **3** : able to copulate — used esp. of the male ♦ *Synonyms* FORCEFUL, FORCIBLE, MIGHTY, PUISSANT — **po·ten·cy** \-t⁸n-sē\ *n*

po·ten·tate \'pō-t⁸n-ˌtāt\ *n* ; one who wields controlling power : RULER

¹po·ten·tial \pə-'ten-chəl\ *adj* : existing in possibility : capable of becoming actual ⟨a ~ champion⟩ ♦ *Synonyms* DORMANT, LATENT, QUIESCENT — **po·ten·ti·al·i·ty** \pə-ˌten-chē-'a-lə-tē\ *n* — **po·ten·tial·ly** \-'ten-chə-lē\ *adv*

²potential *n* **1** : something that can develop or become actual ⟨a ~ for violence⟩ **2** : the work required to move a unit positive charge from infinity to a point in question; *also* : POTENTIAL DIFFERENCE

potential difference *n* : the difference in potential between two points that represents the work involved in the transfer of a unit quantity of electricity from one point to the other

potential energy *n* : the energy an object has because of its position or nature or the arrangement of its parts

po·ten·ti·ate \pə-'ten-chē-ˌāt\ *vb* **-at·ed; -at·ing** : to make potent; *esp* : to augment the activity of (as a drug) synergistically — **po·ten·ti·a·tion** \-ˌten-chē-'ā-shən\ *n*

pot·head \'pät-ˌhed\ *n* : a person who frequently smokes marijuana

poth·er \'pä-thər\ *n* : a noisy disturbance; *also* : FUSS

pot·herb \'pät-ˌərb, -ˌhərb\ *n* : an herb whose leaves or stems are boiled for greens or used to season food

pot·hole \'pät-ˌhōl\ *n* : a large pit or hole (as in a road surface)

pot·hook \-ˌhu̇k\ *n* : an S-shaped hook for hanging pots and kettles over an open fire

po·tion \'pō-shən\ *n* : a mixture of liquids (as liquor or medicine)

pot·luck \'pät-'lək\ *n* : the regular meal available to a guest for whom no special preparations have been made

pot·pie \-'pī\ *n* : pastry-covered meat and vegetables cooked in a deep dish

pot·pour·ri \ˌpō-pu̇-'rē\ *n* [F *pot pourri*, lit., rotten pot] **1** : a mixture of flowers, herbs, and spices used for scent **2** : a miscellaneous collection

pot·sherd \'pät-ˌshərd\ *n* : a pottery fragment

pot·shot \-ˌshät\ *n* **1** : a shot taken from ambush or at a random or easy target **2** : a critical remark made in a random or sporadic manner

pot sticker *n* : a crescent-shaped dumpling that is steamed and fried

pot·tage \'pä-tij\ *n* : a thick soup of vegetables and often meat

¹pot·ter \'pä-tər\ *n* : one that makes pottery

²potter *vb* : PUTTER

pot·tery \'pä-tə-rē\ *n, pl* **-ter·ies 1** : a place where earthen pots and dishes are made **2** : the art of the potter **3** : dishes, pots, and vases made from clay

pot·ty–mouthed \'pä-tē-ˌmau̇thd, -ˌmau̇tht\ *adj* : given to the use of vulgar language

¹pouch \'pau̇ch\ *n* [ME *pouche*, fr. AF, of Gmc origin; akin to OE *pocca* bag] **1** : a small bag (as for tobacco) carried on the person **2** : a bag for storing or transporting goods ⟨mail ~⟩ ⟨diplomatic ~⟩ **3** : an anatomical sac; *esp* : one for carrying the young on the abdomen of a female marsupial (as a kangaroo)

²pouch *vb* : to put or form into or as if into a pouch

poult \'pōlt\ *n* : a young fowl; *esp* : a young turkey

poul·ter·er \'pōl-tər-ər\ *n* : one that deals in poultry

poul·tice \'pōl-təs\ *n* : a soft usu. heated and medicated mass spread on cloth and applied to a sore or injury — **poultice** *vb*

poul·try \'pōl-trē\ *n* : domesticated birds kept for eggs or meat — **poul·try·man** \-mən\ *n*

pounce \'pau̇ns\ *vb* **pounced; pounc·ing** : to spring or swoop upon and seize something

¹pound \'pau̇nd\ *n, pl* **pounds** *also* **pound 1** : a unit of avoirdupois, troy, and apothecaries' weight — see WEIGHT table **2** — see MONEY table **3** : the former basic monetary unit of Ireland

²pound *n* : a public enclosure where stray animals are kept

³pound *vb* **1** : to crush to a powder or pulp by beating **2** : to strike or beat heavily or repeatedly **3** : DRILL 1 **4** : to move or move along heavily

pound·age \'pau̇n-dij\ *n* : POUNDS; *also* : weight in pounds

pound cake *n* : a rich cake made with a large proportion of eggs and shortening

pound–fool·ish \'pau̇nd-'fü-lish\ *adj* : imprudent in dealing with large sums or large matters

pour \'pȯr\ *vb* **1** : to flow or cause to flow in a stream or flood **2** : to rain hard **3** : to supply freely and copiously

pour·boire \pu̇r-'bwär\ *n* [F, fr. *pour boire* for drinking] : TIP, GRATUITY

pout \'pau̇t\ *vb* : to show displeasure by thrusting out the lips; *also* : to look sullen — **pout** *n*

pov·er·ty \'pä-vər-tē\ *n* [ME *poverte*, fr. AF *poverté*, fr. L *paupertat-, paupertas*, fr. *pauper* poor] **1** : lack of money or material possessions : WANT **2** : poor quality (as of soil)

poverty line *n* : a level of personal or family income below which one is classified as poor according to government standards

pov·er·ty–strick·en \'pä-vər-tē-ˌstri-kən\ *adj* : very poor : DESTITUTE

POW \ˌpē-(ˌ)ō-'də-bəl-(ˌ)yü\ *n* : PRISONER OF WAR

¹pow·der \'pau̇-dər\ *vb* **1** : to sprinkle or cover with or as if with powder **2** : to reduce to powder

²powder *n* [ME *poudre*, fr. AF *pudre, podre*, fr. L *pulver-, pulvis* dust] **1** : dry material made up of fine particles; *also* : a usu. medicinal or cosmetic preparation in this form **2** : a solid explosive (as gunpowder) — **pow·dery** *adj*

powder room *n* : a rest room for women

¹**pow·er** \'paù(-ə)r\ *n* **1** : the ability to act or produce an effect **2** : a position of ascendancy over others : AUTHORITY **3** : one that has control or authority; *esp* : a sovereign state **4** : physical might; *also* : mental or moral vigor **5** : the number of times as indicated by an exponent a number is to be multiplied by itself ⟨5 to the third ∼ is 125⟩; *also* : the product itself ⟨8 is a ∼ of 2⟩ **6** : force or energy used to do work; *also* : the time rate at which work is done or energy transferred **7** : MAGNIFICATION — **pow·er·ful** \-fəl\ *adj* — **pow·er·ful·ly** *adv* — **pow·er·less** *adj*

²**power** *vb* : to supply with power and esp. motive power

³**power** *adj* **1** : operated mechanically or electrically rather than manually **2** : of, relating to, or utilizing strength

pow·er·boat \-ˌbōt\ *n* = MOTORBOAT

pow·er·house \'paù(-ə)r-ˌhaùs\ *n* **1** : POWER PLANT **2** : one having great drive, energy, or ability

power plant *n* **1** : a building in which electric power is generated **2** : an engine and related parts supplying the motive power of a self-propelled vehicle

pow·wow \'paù-ˌwaù\ *n* **1** : a No. American Indian ceremony (as for victory in war) **2** : a meeting for discussion : CONFERENCE

pox \'päks\ *n, pl* **pox** *or* **pox·es** : any of various diseases (as smallpox or syphilis) marked by a rash on the skin

pozole *var of* POSOLE

pp *abbr* **1** pages **2** pianissimo

PP *abbr* **1** parcel post **2** past participle **3** postpaid **4** prepaid

ppd *abbr* **1** postpaid **2** prepaid

PPO \ˌpē-ˌpē-'ō\ *n, pl* **PPOs** [preferred provider organization] : a health-care organization that gives economic incentives to enrolled individuals who use certain health-care providers

PPS *abbr* [L *post postscriptum*] an additional postscript

ppt *abbr* precipitate

PQ *abbr* Province of Quebec

pr *abbr* **1** pair **2** price

Pr *symbol* praseodymium

¹**PR** *or* **p.r.** \'pē-'är\ *n* : PUBLIC RELATIONS

²**PR** *abbr* **1** payroll **2** public relations **3** Puerto Rico

prac·ti·ca·ble \'prak-ti-kə-bəl\ *adj* : capable of being put into practice, done, or accomplished — **prac·ti·ca·bil·i·ty** \ˌprak-ti-kə-'bi-lə-tē\ *n*

prac·ti·cal \'prak-ti-kəl\ *adj* **1** : of, relating to, or shown in practice ⟨∼ questions⟩ **2** : VIRTUAL ⟨∼ control⟩ **3** : capable of being put to use ⟨a ∼ knowledge of French⟩ **4** : inclined to action as opposed to speculation ⟨a ∼ person⟩ **5** : qualified by practice ⟨a good ∼ mechanic⟩ — **prac·ti·cal·i·ty** \ˌprak-ti-'ka-lə-tē\ *n* — **prac·ti·cal·ly** \-k(ə-)lē\ *adv*

practical joke *n* : a prank intended to trick or embarrass someone or cause physical discomfort

practical nurse *n* : a professional nurse without all the qualifications of a registered nurse; *esp* : LICENSED PRACTICAL NURSE

¹**prac·tice** *also* **prac·tise** \'prak-təs\ *vb* **prac·ticed** *also* **prac·tised; prac·tic·ing** *also* **prac·tis·ing** **1** : CARRY OUT, APPLY ⟨∼ what you preach⟩ **2** : to perform or work at repeatedly so as to become proficient ⟨∼ tennis strokes⟩ **3** : to do or perform customarily ⟨∼ politeness⟩ **4** : to be professionally engaged in ⟨∼ law⟩

²**practice** *also* **practise** *n* **1** : actual performance or application **2** : customary action : HABIT **3** : systematic exercise for proficiency **4** : the exercise of a profession; *also* : a professional business

prac·ti·tion·er \prak-'ti-shə-nər\ *n* : one who practices a profession

prae·tor \'prē-tər\ *n* : an ancient Roman magistrate ranking below a consul — **prae·to·ri·an** \prē-'tȯr-ē-ən\ *adj*

prag·mat·ic \prag-'ma-tik\ *also* **prag·mat·i·cal** \-ti-kəl\ *adj* **1** : of or relating to practical affairs **2** : concerned with the practical consequences of actions or beliefs — **pragmatic** *n* — **prag·mat·i·cal·ly** \-ti-k(ə-)lē\ *adv*

prag·ma·tism \'prag-mə-ˌti-zəm\ *n* : a practical approach to problems and affairs

prai·rie \'prer-ē\ *n* [F, fr. OF *prairie,* fr. VL **prataria,* fr. L *pratum* meadow] : a broad tract of level or rolling grassland

prairie dog *n* : an American burrowing black-tailed rodent related to the squirrels and living in colonies

prairie schooner *n* : a covered wagon used by pioneers in cross-country travel

praise \'prāz\ *vb* **praised; prais·ing** **1** : to express approval of : COMMEND **2** : to glorify (a divinity or a saint) esp. in song — **praise** *n*

praise·wor·thy \-ˌwər-thē\ *adj* : LAUDABLE ⟨a ∼ effort⟩

pra·line \'prä-ˌlēn, 'prā-\ *n* [F] : a confection of nuts and sugar

pram \'pram\ *n, chiefly Brit* : PERAMBULATOR

prance \'prans\ *vb* **pranced; pranc·ing** **1** : to spring from the hind legs ⟨a *prancing* horse⟩ **2** : SWAGGER; *also* : CAPER — **prance** *n* — **pranc·er** *n*

prank \'praŋk\ *n* : a playful or mildly mischievous act : TRICK

prank·ster \'praŋk-stər\ *n* : a person who plays pranks

pra·seo·dym·i·um \ˌprā-zē-ō-'di-mē-əm\ *n* : a yellowish white metallic chemical element

prate \'prāt\ *vb* **prat·ed; prat·ing** : to talk long and idly : chatter foolishly

prat·fall \'prat-ˌfȯl\ *n* **1** : a fall on the buttocks **2** : a humiliating blunder

¹**prat·tle** \'pra-tᵊl\ *vb* **prat·tled; prat·tling** : PRATE, BABBLE

²**prattle** *n* : trifling or childish talk

prawn \'prȯn\ *n* : any of various edible shrimplike crustaceans; *also* : SHRIMP 1

pray \'prā\ *vb* 1 : ENTREAT, IMPLORE 2 : to ask earnestly for something 3 : to address God or a god esp. with supplication

prayer \'prer\ *n* 1 : a supplication or expression addressed to God or a god; *also* : a set order of words used in praying 2 : an earnest request or wish 3 : the act or practice of praying to God or a god 4 : a religious service consisting chiefly of prayers — often used in pl. 5 : something prayed for 6 : a slight chance

prayer book *n* : a book containing prayers and often directions for worship

prayer·ful \'prer-fəl\ *adj* 1 : DEVOUT 2 : EARNEST — **prayer·ful·ly** *adv*

praying mantis *n* : MANTIS

PRC *abbr* People's Republic of China

preach \'prēch\ *vb* 1 : to deliver a sermon 2 : to set forth in a sermon 3 : to advocate earnestly — **preach·er** *n* — **preach·ment** *n*

pre·ad·o·les·cence \'prē-ˌa-də-'le-sᵊns\ *n* : the period of human development just preceding adolescence — **pre·ad·o·les·cent** \-sᵊnt\ *adj or n*

pre·am·ble \'prē-ˌam-bəl\ *n* [ME, fr. MF *preambule*, fr. ML *preambulum*, fr. LL, neut. of *praeambulus* walking in front of, fr. L *prae* in front of + *ambulare* to walk] : an introductory part ⟨the ∼ to a constitution⟩

pre·ar·range \ˌprē-ə-'rānj\ *vb* : to arrange beforehand — **pre·ar·range·ment** *n*

pre·as·sign \ˌprē-ə-'sīn\ *vb* : to assign beforehand

Pre·cam·bri·an \ˌprē-'kam-brē-ən, -'kām-\ *adj* : of, relating to, or being the era that is earliest in geologic history and is characterized esp. by the appearance of single=celled organisms — **Precambrian** *n*

pre·can·cel \(ˌ)prē-'kan-səl\ *vb* : to cancel (a postage stamp) in advance of use — **precancel** *n* — **pre·can·cel·la·tion** \ˌprē-ˌkan-sə-'lā-shən\ *n*

pre·can·cer·ous \(ˌ)prē-'kan-sə-rəs\ *adj* : likely to become cancerous

pre·car·i·ous \pri-'ker-ē-əs\ *adj* : dependent on uncertain conditions : dangerously insecure : UNSTABLE ⟨a ∼ foothold⟩ ⟨∼ prosperity⟩ ✦ *Synonyms* DELICATE, SENSITIVE, TICKLISH, TOUCHY, TRICKY — **pre·car·i·ous·ly** *adv* — **pre·car·i·ous·ness** *n*

pre·cau·tion \pri-'kȯ-shən\ *n* : a measure taken beforehand to prevent harm or secure good — **pre·cau·tion·ary** \-shə-ˌner-ē\ *adj*

pre·cede \pri-'sēd\ *vb* **pre·ced·ed**; **pre·ced·ing** : to be, go, or come ahead or in front of (as in rank or time)

pre·ce·dence \'pre-sə-dəns, pri-'sēd-ᵊns\ *n* 1 : the act or fact of preceding 2 : consideration based on order of importance : PRIORITY

¹prec·e·dent \pri-'sē-dᵊnt, 'pre-sə-dənt\ *adj* : prior in time, order, or significance

²prec·e·dent \'pre-sə-dənt\ *n* : something said or done that may serve to authorize or justify further words or acts of the same or a similar kind

pre·ced·ing \pri-'sē-diŋ\ *adj* : that precedes ✦ *Synonyms* ANTECEDENT, FOREGOING, PRIOR, FORMER, ANTERIOR

pre·cen·tor \pri-'sen-tər\ *n* : a leader of the singing of a choir or congregation

pre·cept \'prē-ˌsept\ *n* : a command or principle intended as a general rule of action or conduct

pre·cep·tor \pri-'sep-tər, 'prē-ˌsep-\ *n* : TUTOR

pre·ces·sion \prē-'se-shən\ *n* : a slow gyration of the rotation axis of a spinning body (as the earth) — **pre·cess** \prē-'ses\ *vb* — **pre·ces·sion·al** \-'se-shə-nəl\ *adj*

pre·cinct \'prē-ˌsiŋkt\ *n* 1 : an administrative subdivision (as of a city) : DISTRICT ⟨police ∼⟩ ⟨electoral ∼⟩ 2 : an enclosure bounded by the limits of a building or place — often used in pl. 3 *pl* : ENVIRONS

pre·ci·os·i·ty \ˌpre-shē-'ä-sə-tē\ *n, pl* **-ties** : fastidious refinement

pre·cious \'pre-shəs\ *adj* 1 : of great value ⟨∼ jewels⟩ 2 : greatly cherished : DEAR ⟨∼ memories⟩ 3 : AFFECTED ⟨∼ language⟩

prec·i·pice \'pre-sə-pəs\ *n* : a steep cliff

pre·cip·i·tan·cy \pri-'si-pə-tən-sē\ *n* : undue hastiness or suddenness

¹pre·cip·i·tate \pri-'si-pə-ˌtāt\ *vb* **-tat·ed**; **-tat·ing** [L *praecipitare*, fr. *praecipit-*, *praeceps* headlong, fr. *prae* in front of + *caput* head] 1 : to throw violently 2 : to throw down 3 : to cause to happen quickly or abruptly ⟨∼ a quarrel⟩ 4 : to cause to separate from solution or suspension 5 : to fall as rain, snow, or hail ✦ *Synonyms* SPEED, ACCELERATE, QUICKEN, HASTEN, HURRY

²pre·cip·i·tate \pri-'si-pə-tət, -ˌtāt\ *n* : the solid matter that separates from a solution or suspension

³pre·cip·i·tate \pri-'si-pə-tət\ *adj* 1 : showing extreme or unwise haste : RASH 2 : falling with steep descent; *also* : PRECIPITOUS — **pre·cip·i·tate·ly** *adv* — **pre·cip·i·tate·ness** *n*

pre·cip·i·ta·tion \pri-ˌsi-pə-'tā-shən\ *n* 1 : rash haste 2 : the process of precipitating or forming a precipitate 3 : water that falls to earth esp. as rain or snow; *also* : the quantity of this water

pre·cip·i·tous \pri-'si-pə-təs\ *adj* 1 : PRECIPITATE 2 : having the character of a precipice : very steep ⟨a ∼ slope⟩; *also* : containing precipices ⟨∼ trails⟩ — **pre·cip·i·tous·ly** *adv*

pré·cis \prā-'sē\ *n, pl* **pré·cis** \-'sēz\ [F] : a concise summary of essentials

pre·cise \pri-'sīs\ *adj* 1 : exactly defined or stated : DEFINITE 2 : highly accurate : EXACT 3 : conforming strictly to a standard : SCRUPULOUS — **pre·cise·ly** *adv* — **pre·cise·ness** *n*

pre·ci·sion \pri-'si-zhən\ *n* : the quality or state of being precise

pre·clude \pri-'klüd\ *vb* **pre·clud·ed**; **pre·clud·ing** : to make impossible : BAR, PREVENT

pre·co·cious \pri-'kō-shəs\ *adj* [L *praecoc-*, *praecox*, lit., ripening early, fr. *prae-* ahead + *coquere* to cook] : early in development and esp. in mental development — **pre·co·cious·ly** *adv* — **pre·coc·i·ty** \pri-'kä-sə-tē\ *n*

pre·con·ceive \ˌprē-kən-'sēv\ *vb* : to form an opinion of beforehand — **pre·con·cep·tion** \-'sep-shən\ *n*

pre·con·di·tion \-'di-shən\ *vb* : to put in proper or desired condition or frame of mind in advance

pre·cook \ˌprē-'kük\ *vb* : to cook partially or entirely before final cooking or reheating

pre·cur·sor \pri-'kər-sər\ *n* : one that precedes and indicates the approach of another : FORERUNNER

pred *abbr* predicate

pre·da·ceous *or* **pre·da·cious** \pri-'dā-shəs\ *adj* : living by preying on others : PREDATORY

pre·date \ˈprē-ˈdāt\ *vb* : ANTEDATE

pre·da·tion \pri-'dā-shən\ *n* **1** : the act of preying or plundering **2** : a mode of life in which food is primarily obtained by killing and consuming animals

pred·a·tor \ˈpre-də-tər\ *n* : an animal that lives by predation

pred·a·to·ry \ˈpre-də-ˌtȯr-ē\ *adj* **1** : of or relating to plunder ⟨∼ warfare⟩ **2** : disposed to exploit others **3** : preying upon other animals

pre·dawn \(ˈ)prē-ˈdȯn\ *adj* : of or relating to the time just before dawn

pre·de·cease \ˌprē-di-'sēs\ *vb* **-ceased**; **-ceas·ing** : to die before another person

pre·de·ces·sor \ˈpre-də-ˌse-sər, ˈprē-\ *n* : a previous holder of a position to which another has succeeded

pre·des·ig·nate \(ˌ)prē-'de-zig-ˌnāt\ *vb* : to designate beforehand

pre·des·ti·na·tion \ˌprē-ˌdes-tə-'nā-shən\ *n* : the act of foreordaining to an earthly lot or eternal destiny by divine decree; *also* : the state of being so foreordained — **pre·des·ti·nate** \ˈprē-ˈdes-tə-ˌnāt\ *vb*

pre·des·tine \ˈprē-ˈdes-tən\ *vb* : to settle beforehand : FOREORDAIN

pre·de·ter·mine \ˌprē-di-'tər-mən\ *vb* : to determine beforehand

pred·i·ca·ble \ˈpre-di-kə-bəl\ *adj* : capable of being predicated or affirmed

pre·dic·a·ment \pri-'di-kə-mənt\ *n* : a difficult or trying situation ✦ *Synonyms* DILEMMA, PICKLE, QUAGMIRE, JAM

¹pred·i·cate \ˈpre-di-kət\ *n* : the part of a sentence or clause that expresses what is said of the subject

²pred·i·cate \ˈpre-də-ˌkāt\ *vb* **-cat·ed**; **-cat·ing 1** : AFFIRM **2** : to assert to be a quality or attribute **3** : FOUND, BASE — usu. used with *on* — **pred·i·ca·tion** \ˌpre-də-'kā-shən\ *n*

pre·dict \pri-'dikt\ *vb* : to declare in advance — **pre·dict·abil·i·ty** \-ˌdik-tə-'bi-lə-tē\ *n* — **pre·dict·able** \-'dik-tə-bəl\ *adj* — **pre·dict·ably** \-blē\ *adv* — **pre·dic·tion** \-'dik-shən\ *n*

pre·di·gest \ˌprē-dī-'jest\ *vb* : to simplify for easy use; *also* : to subject to artificial or natural partial digestion

pre·di·lec·tion \ˌpre-də-'lek-shən, ˌprē-\ *n* : an established preference for something

pre·dis·pose \ˌprē-di-'spōz\ *vb* : to incline in advance : make susceptible — **pre·dis·po·si·tion** \ˌprē-ˌdis-pə-'zi-shən\ *n*

pre·dom·i·nant \pri-'dä-mə-nənt\ *adj* : greater in importance, strength, influence, or authority — **pre·dom·i·nance** \-nəns\ *n*

pre·dom·i·nant·ly \-nənt-lē\ *adv* : for the most part : MAINLY

pre·dom·i·nate \pri-'dä-mə-ˌnāt\ *vb* : to be superior esp. in power or numbers : PREVAIL

pre·dom·i·nate·ly \pri-'dä-mə-nət-lē\ *adv* : PREDOMINANTLY

pree·mie \ˈprē-mē\ *n* : a premature baby

pre·em·i·nent \prē-'e-mə-nənt\ *adj* : having highest rank : OUTSTANDING — **pre·em·i·nence** \-nəns\ *n* — **pre·em·i·nent·ly** *adv*

pre·empt \prē-'empt\ *vb* **1** : to settle upon (public land) with the right to purchase before others; *also* : to take by such right **2** : to seize upon before someone else can **3** : to take the place of ✦ *Synonyms* USURP, CONFISCATE, APPROPRIATE, EXPROPRIATE — **pre·emp·tion** \-'emp-shən\ *n*

pre·emp·tive \prē-'emp-tiv\ *adj* : marked by the seizing of the initiative : initiated by oneself ⟨∼ attack⟩

preen \ˈprēn\ *vb* [ME *prenen*, alter. of *proynen, prunen*, fr. AF *puroindre, proindre*, fr. *pur-* thoroughly + *oindre* to anoint, rub, fr. L *unguere*] **1** : to groom with the bill — used of a bird **2** : to dress or smooth up : PRIMP **3** : to pride (oneself) for achievement

pre·ex·ist \ˌprē-ig-'zist\ *vb* : to exist before — **pre·ex·is·tence** \-'zis-fəns\ *n* — **pre·ex·is·tent** \-tənt\ *adj*

pref *abbr* **1** preface **2** preference **3** preferred **4** prefix

¹pre·fab \(ˌ)prē-'fab, 'prē-ˌfab\ *adj* : produced by prefabrication

²prefab *n* : a prefabricated structure

pre·fab·ri·cate \(ˌ)prē-'fa-brə-ˌkāt\ *vb* : to manufacture the parts of (a structure) beforehand for later assembly — **pre·fab·ri·ca·tion** \ˌprē-ˌfa-bri-'kā-shən\ *n*

¹pref·ace \ˈpre-fəs\ *n* : the introductory remarks of a speaker or writer — **pref·a·to·ry** \ˈpre-fə-ˌtȯr-ē\ *adj*

²preface *vb* **pref·aced**; **pref·ac·ing** : to introduce with a preface

pre·fect \ˈprē-ˌfekt\ *n* **1** : a high official; *esp* : a chief officer or magistrate **2** : a student monitor

pre·fec·ture \ˈprē-ˌfek-chər\ *n* : the office, term, or residence of a prefect

pre·fer \pri-'fər\ *vb* **pre·ferred**; **pre·fer·ring 1** : PROMOTE **2** : to like better **3** : to bring (as a charge) against a person — **pref·er·a·ble** \ˈpre-fə-rə-bəl\ *adj* — **pref·er·a·bly** \-blē\ *adv*

pref·er·ence \ˈpre-frəns, -fə-rəns\ *n* **1** : a special liking for one thing over another **2** : CHOICE, SELECTION — **pref·er·en·tial** \ˌpre-fə-'ren-chəl\ *adj*

pre·fer·ment \pri-'fər-mənt\ *n* : PROMOTION, ADVANCEMENT

preferred provider organization *n* : PPO

pre·fig·ure \prē-'fi-gyər\ *vb* 1 : FORESHADOW 2 : to imagine beforehand

¹**pre·fix** \'prē-ˌfiks, prē-'fiks\ *vb* : to place before ⟨~ a title to a name⟩

²**pre·fix** \'prē-ˌfiks\ *n* : an affix occurring at the beginning of a word

pre·flight \prē-'flīt\ *adj* : preparing for or preliminary to flight

pre·form \(ˌ)prē-'form, 'prē-ˌform\ *vb* : to form or shape beforehand

preg·na·ble \'preg-nə-bəl\ *adj* : vulnerable to capture ⟨a ~ fort⟩

preg·nant \'preg-nənt\ *adj* 1 : containing unborn offspring within the body 2 : rich in significance : MEANINGFUL — **preg·nan·cy** \-nən-sē\ *n*

pre·heat \prē-'hēt\ *vb* : to heat beforehand; *esp* : to heat (an oven) to a designated temperature before using

pre·hen·sile \prē-'hen-səl, -ˌsī(-ə)l\ *adj* : adapted for grasping esp. by wrapping around ⟨a monkey with a ~ tail⟩

pre·his·tor·ic \ˌprē-his-'tor-ik\ *also* **pre·his·tor·i·cal** \-i-kəl\ *adj* : of, relating to, or existing in the period before written history began

pre·judge \(ˌ)prē-'jəj\ *vb* : to judge before full hearing or examination

¹**prej·u·dice** \'pre-jə-dəs\ *n* 1 : DAMAGE; *esp* : detriment to one's rights or claims 2 : an opinion made without adequate basis — **prej·u·di·cial** \ˌpre-jə-'di-shəl\ *adj*

²**prejudice** *vb* **-diced; -dic·ing** 1 : to damage by a judgment or action esp. at law 2 : to cause to have prejudice

pre·kin·der·gar·ten \(ˌ)prē-'kin-dər-ˌgär-t³n\ *n* 1 : NURSERY SCHOOL 2 : a class or program preceding kindergarten

prel·ate \'pre-lət\ *n* : an ecclesiastic (as a bishop) of high rank — **prel·a·cy** \-lə-sē\ *n*

pre·launch \'prē-ˌlonch\ *adj* : preparing for or preliminary to launch

pre·lim \'prē-ˌlim, pri-'lim\ *n or adj* : PRELIMINARY

¹**pre·lim·i·nary** \pri-'li-mə-ˌner-ē\ *n, pl* **-nar·ies** : something that precedes or introduces the main business or event

²**preliminary** *adj* : preceding the main discourse or business

pre·lude \'prel-ˌyüd; 'pre-ˌlüd, 'prā-\ *n* 1 : an introductory performance or event 2 : a musical section or movement introducing the main theme; *also* : an organ solo played at the beginning of a church service

pre·mar·i·tal \(ˌ)prē-'mer-ə-t³l\ *adj* : existing or occurring before marriage

pre·ma·ture \ˌprē-mə-'tùr, -'tyùr, -'chùr\ *adj* : happening, coming, born, or done before the usual or proper time — **pre·ma·ture·ly** *adv*

¹**pre·med** \'prē-'med\ *n* : a premedical student or course of study

²**premed** *adj* : PREMEDICAL

pre·med·i·cal \(ˌ)prē-'me-di-kəl\ *adj* : preceding and preparing for the professional study of medicine

pre·med·i·tate \pri-'me-də-ˌtāt\ *vb* : to consider and plan beforehand — **pre·med·i·ta·tion** \-ˌme-də-'tā-shən\ *n*

pre·men·o·paus·al \(ˌ)prē-ˌme-nə-'po-zəl\ *adj* : of, relating to, or being in the period preceding menopause

pre·men·stru·al \(ˌ)prē-'men-strə-wəl\ *adj* : of, relating to, or occurring in the period just before menstruation

premenstrual syndrome *n* : a varying group of symptoms manifested by some women prior to menstruation

premie *var of* PREEMIE

¹**pre·mier** \pri-'mir, -'myir, 'prē-mē-ər\ *adj* [ME *primer, primier,* fr. AF, first, chief, fr. L *primarius* of the first rank] : first in rank or importance : CHIEF; *also* : first in time : EARLIEST

²**premier** *n* : PRIME MINISTER — **pre·mier·ship** *n*

¹**pre·miere** \pri-'myer, -'mir\ *n* : a first performance

²**premiere** *also* **pre·mier** *same as* ¹PREMIERE\ *vb* **pre·miered; pre·mier·ing** : to give or receive a first public performance

prem·ise \'pre-məs\ *n* 1 : a statement of fact or a supposition made or implied as a basis of argument 2 *pl* : a piece of land with the structures on it; *also* : the place of business of an enterprise

premise *vb* **prem·ised; prem·is·ing** : to base on certain assumptions

pre·mi·um \'prē-mē-əm\ *n* [L *praemium* booty, profit, reward, fr. *prae* before + *emere* to take, buy] 1 : REWARD, PRIZE 2 : a sum over and above the stated value 3 : something paid over and above a fixed wage or price 4 : something given with a purchase 5 : the sum paid for a contract of insurance 6 : an unusually high value

pre·mix \prē-'miks\ *vb* : to mix before use

pre·mo·lar \(ˌ)prē-'mō-lər\ *adj* : situated in front of or preceding the molar teeth; *esp* : being or relating to those teeth of a mammal in front of the true molars and behind the canines — **premolar** *n*

pre·mo·ni·tion \ˌprē-mə-'ni-shən, ˌpre-\ *n* 1 : previous warning 2 : PRESENTIMENT — **pre·mon·i·to·ry** \pri-'mä-nə-ˌtor-ē\ *adj*

pre·na·tal \'prē-'nā-t³l\ *adj* : occurring, existing, or taking place before birth

pre·nup·tial \prē-'nəp-shəl\ *adj* : made or occurring before marriage

prenuptial agreement *n* : an agreement between a man and woman before marrying in which they give up future rights to each other's property in the event of divorce or death

pre·oc·cu·pa·tion \prē-ˌä-kyə-'pā-shən\ *n* : complete absorption of the mind or interests; *also* : something that causes such absorption

pre·oc·cu·pied \prē-'ä-kyə-ˌpīd\ *adj* 1 : lost in thought; *also* : absorbed in some preoccupation 2 : already occupied ♦ *Synonyms* ABSTRACTED, ABSENT, ABSENTMINDED

pre·oc·cu·py \-ˌpī\ *vb* 1 : to occupy the

attention of beforehand **2** : to take possession of before another

pre·op·er·a·tive \(,)prē-'ä-prə-tiv, -pə-,rā-\ *adj* : occurring before a surgical operation

pre·or·dain \,prē-òr-'dān\ *vb* : FOREORDAIN

pre–owned \(,)prē-'ōnd\ *adj* : SECONDHAND ⟨~ vehicles⟩

prep *abbr* **1** preparatory **2** preposition

pre·pack·age \(,)prē-'pa-kij\ *vb* : to package (as food) before offering for sale to the customer

preparatory school *n*, **1** : a usu. private school preparing students primarily for college **2** *Brit* : a private elementary school preparing students primarily for British public schools

pre·pare \pri-'per\ *vb* **pre·pared; pre·par·ing 1** : to make or get ready ⟨~ dinner⟩ ⟨~ a student for college⟩ **2** : to get ready beforehand **3** : to put together : COMPOUND ⟨~ a prescription⟩ — **prep·a·ra·tion** \,pre-pə-'rā-shən\ *n* — **pre·pa·ra·to·ry** \pri-'per-ə-,tòr-ē\ *adj*

pre·pared·ness \pri-'per-əd-nəs\ *n* : a state of adequate preparation

pre·pay \(,)prē-'pā\ *vb* **-paid** \-'pād\; **-pay·ing** : to pay or pay the charge on in advance

pre·pon·der·ant \pri-'pän-d-rənt\ *adj* : having greater weight, force, influence, or frequency — **pre·pon·der·ance** \-rəns\ *n* — **pre·pon·der·ant·ly** *adv*

pre·pon·der·ate \pri-'pän-də-,rāt\ *vb* **-at·ed; -at·ing** [L *praeponderare,* fr. *prae-* ahead + *ponder-, pondus* weight] : to exceed in weight, force, influence, or frequency : PREDOMINATE

prep·o·si·tion \,pre-pə-'zi-shən\ *n* : a word that combines with a noun or pronoun to form a phrase — **prep·o·si·tion·al** \-'zi-shə-nəl\ *adj*

pre·pos·sess \,prē-pə-'zes\ *vb* **1** : to cause to be preoccupied **2** : to influence beforehand esp. favorably

pre·pos·sess·ing *adj* : tending to create a favorable impression ⟨a ~ manner⟩

pre·pos·ses·sion \-'ze-shən\ *n* **1** : PREJUDICE **2** : an exclusive concern with one idea or object

pre·pos·ter·ous \pri-'päs-tə-rəs\ *adj* : contrary to nature or reason : ABSURD

prep·py *or* **prep·pie** \'pre-pē\ *n, pl* **prep·pies 1** : a student at or a graduate of a preparatory school **2** : a person deemed to dress or behave like a preppy

pre·puce \'prē-,pyüs\ *n* : FORESKIN

pre·quel \'prē-kwəl\ *n* : a literary or dramatic work whose story precedes that of an earlier work

pre·re·cord·ed \(,)prē-ri-'kòr-dəd\ *adj* : recorded for later broadcast or play

pre·req·ui·site \prē-'re-kwə-zət\ *n* : something required beforehand or for the end in view — **prerequisite** *adj*

pre·rog·a·tive \pri-'rä-gə-tiv\ *n* : an exclusive or special right, power, or privilege

pres *abbr* **1** present **2** president

[1]**pres·age** \'pre-sij\ *n* [ME, fr. L *praesagium,* fr. *praesagus* having a foreboding, fr.

prae before + *sagus* prophetic] **1** : something that foreshadows a future event : OMEN **2** : FOREBODING

[2]**pres·age** \'pre-sij, pri-'sāj\ *vb* **pre·saged; pre·sag·ing 1** : to give an omen or warning of : FORESHADOW **2** : FORETELL, PREDICT

pres·by·o·pia \,prez-bē-'ō-pē-ə\ *n* : a visual condition in which loss of elasticity of the lens of the eye causes defective accommodation and inability to focus sharply for near vision — **pres·by·o·pic** \-'ō-pik, -'ä-\ *adj or n*

pres·by·ter \'prez-bə-tər\ *n* [LL, elder, priest, fr. Gk *presbyteros,* compar. of *presbys* elder, old man] **1** : PRIEST, MINISTER **2** : an elder in a Presbyterian church

[1]**Pres·by·te·ri·an** \,prez-bə-'tir-ē-ən\ *n* : a member of a Presbyterian church

[2]**Presbyterian** *adj* **1** *often not cap* : characterized by a graded system of representative ecclesiastical bodies (as presbyteries) exercising legislative and judicial powers **2** : of or relating to a group of Protestant Christian bodies that are presbyterian in government — **Pres·by·te·ri·an·ism** \-ə-,ni-zəm\ *n*

pres·by·tery \'prez-bə-,ter-ē\ *n, pl* **-ter·ies 1** : the part of a church reserved for the officiating clergy **2** : a ruling body in Presbyterian churches consisting of the ministers and representative elders of a district

[1]**pre·school** \'prē-,skül\ *adj* : of or relating to the period in a child's life from infancy to the age of five or six — **pre·school·er** \-,skü-lər\ *n*

[2]**preschool** *n* : NURSERY SCHOOL

pre·science \'pre-shəns, 'prē-\ *n* : foreknowledge of events; *also* : FORESIGHT — **pre·scient** \-shənt, -shē-ənt\ *adj*

pre·scribe \pri-'skrīb\ *vb* **pre·scribed; pre·scrib·ing 1** : to lay down as a guide or rule of action **2** : to direct the use of (as a medicine) as a remedy

pre·scrip·tion \pri-'skrip-shən\ *n* **1** : the action of prescribing rules or directions **2** : a written direction for the preparation and use of a medicine; *also* : a medicine prescribed

pre·scrip·tive \pri-'skrip-tiv\ *adj* **1** : serving to prescribe ⟨~ rules⟩ **2** : acquired by, based on, or determined by prescription or by custom

pres·ence \'pre-z²ns\ *n* **1** : the fact or condition of being present **2** : the space immediately around a person **3** : one that is present **4** : the bearing of a person; *esp* : stately bearing

[1]**pres·ent** \'pre-z²nt\ *n* : something presented : GIFT

[2]**pre·sent** \pri-'zent\ *vb* **1** : to bring into the presence or acquaintance of : INTRODUCE **2** : to bring before the public ⟨~ a play⟩ **3** : to make a gift to **4** : to give formally **5** : to lay (as a charge) before a court for inquiry **6** : to aim or direct (as a weapon) so as to face in a particular direction — **pre·sent·able** *adj* — **pre·**

sen·ta·tion \ˌprē-ˌzen-'tā-shən, ˌpres-z°n-\ n — pre·sent·ment \pri-'zent-mənt\ n

³pres·ent \'pre-z°nt\ adj 1 : now existing or in progress ⟨∼ conditions⟩ 2 : being in view or at hand ⟨∼ at the meeting⟩ 3 : under consideration ⟨the ∼ problem⟩ 4 : of, relating to, or constituting a verb tense that expresses present time or the time of speaking

⁴pres·ent \'pre-z°nt\ n 1 pl : the present legal document 2 : the present tense; also : a verb form in it 3 : the present time

pres·ent–day \'pre-z°nt-'dā\ adj : now existing or occurring : CURRENT

pre·sen·ti·ment \pri-'zen-tə-mənt\ n : a feeling that something is about to happen : PREMONITION

pres·ent·ly \'pre-z°nt-lē\ adv 1 : SOON ⟨∼ they arrived⟩ 2 : NOW ⟨∼ busy⟩

present participle n : a participle that typically expresses present action and that in English is formed with the suffix -ing and is used in the formation of the progressive tenses

¹pre·serve \pri-'zərv\ vb pre·served; pre·serv·ing 1 : to keep safe : GUARD, PROTECT 2 : to keep from decaying; esp : to process food (as by canning or pickling) to prevent spoilage 3 : MAINTAIN ⟨∼ silence⟩ — pres·er·va·tion \ˌpre-zər-'vā-shən\ n — pre·ser·va·tive \pri-'zər-və-tiv\ adj or n — pre·serv·er n

²preserve n 1 : preserved fruit — often used in pl. 2 : an area for the protection of natural resources (as animals)

pre·set \'prē-ˌset\ vb -set; -set·ting : to set beforehand — preset n

pre·shrink \prē-'shriŋk\ vb -shrank \-'shraŋk\; -shrunk \-'shrəŋk\ : to shrink (as a fabric) before making into a garment

pre·side \pri-'zīd\ vb pre·sid·ed; pre·sid·ing [L praesidēre to guard, preside over, fr. prae in front of + sedēre to sit] 1 : to exercise guidance or control 2 : to occupy the place of authority; esp : to act as chairman

pres·i·dent \'pre-zə-dənt\ n 1 : one chosen to preside ⟨∼ of the assembly⟩ 2 : the chief officer of an organization (as a corporation or society) 3 : an elected official serving as both chief of state and chief political executive; also : a chief of state often with only minimal political powers — pres·i·den·cy \-dən-sē\ n — pres·i·den·tial \ˌpre-zə-'den-chəl\ adj

pre·si·dio \pri-'sē-dē-ˌō, -'si-\ n, pl -di·os [Sp] : a military post or fortified settlement in an area currently or orig. under Spanish control

pre·sid·i·um \pri-'si-dē-əm\ n, pl -ia \-ē-ə\ or -iums [Russ prezidium, fr. L praesidium garrison] : a permanent executive committee that acts for a larger body in a Communist country

¹pre·soak \(ˌ)prē-'sōk\ vb : to soak beforehand

²pre·soak \'prē-ˌsōk\ n 1 : an instance of presoaking 2 : a preparation used in presoaking clothes

pre·sort \(ˌ)prē-'sòrt\ vb : to sort (mail) by zip code usu. before delivery to a post office

¹press \'pres\ n 1 : a crowded condition 2 : THRONG 2 : a machine for exerting pressure 3 : CLOSET, CUPBOARD 4 : PRESSURE 5 : the properly creased condition of a freshly pressed garment 6 : PRINTING PRESS; also : the act or the process of printing 7 : a printing or publishing establishment 8 : the media (as newspapers and magazines) of public news and comment; also : persons (as reporters) employed in these media 9 : comment in newspapers and periodicals

²press vb 1 : to bear down upon : push steadily against 2 : ASSAIL, COMPEL 3 : to squeeze out the juice or contents of ⟨∼ grapes⟩ 4 : to squeeze to a desired density, shape, or smoothness; esp : IRON 5 : to try hard to persuade : URGE 6 : to follow through : PROSECUTE 7 : CROWD 8 : to force one's way 9 : to require haste or speed in action — press·er n

press agent n : an agent employed to establish and maintain good public relations through publicity

press·ing adj : URGENT ⟨a ∼ need⟩

press·man \'pres-mən, -ˌman\ n : the operator of a press and esp. a printing press

press·room \-ˌrüm, -ˌrum\ n 1 : a room in a printing plant containing the printing presses 2 : a room for the use of reporters

¹pres·sure \'pre-shər\ n 1 : the burden of physical or mental distress 2 : the action of pressing; esp : the application of force to something by something else in direct contact with it 3 : the force exerted over a surface divided by its area 4 : the stress or urgency of matters demanding attention

²pressure vb pres·sured; pres·sur·ing : to apply pressure to

pressure group n : a group that seeks to influence governmental policy but not to elect candidates to office

pressure suit n : an inflatable suit for high-altitude flight or spaceflight to protect the body from low pressure

pres·sur·ise Brit var of PRESSURIZE

pres·sur·ize \'pre-shə-ˌrīz\ vb -ized; -iz·ing 1 : to maintain higher pressure within than without; esp : to maintain normal atmospheric pressure within (as an airplane cabin) during high-altitude flight or spaceflight 2 : to apply pressure to 3 : to design to withstand pressure — pres·sur·i·za·tion \ˌpre-shə-rə-'zā-shən\ n

pres·ti·dig·i·ta·tion \ˌpres-tə-ˌdi-jə-'tā-shən\ n : SLEIGHT OF HAND

pres·tige \pres-'tēzh, -'tēj\ n [F, fr. MF, conjuror's trick, illusion, fr. L prae- tigium, fr. LL praestigium, fr. L praestigiae pl., conjuror's tricks, fr. praestringere to graze, blunt, constrict, fr. prae- in front of + stringere to bind tight] : standing or estimation in the eyes of people : REPUTATION ♦ Synonyms INFLUENCE, AUTHORITY, WEIGHT, CACHET — pres·ti·gious \-'ti-jəs, -'tē-\ adj

¹**pres·to** \'pres-tō\ *interj* [It, quick, quickly] — used to indicate the sudden appearance or occurrence of something

²**presto** *adv or adj* 1 : suddenly as if by magic : IMMEDIATELY 2 : at a rapid tempo — used as a direction in music

pre·stress \(ˌ)prē-'stres\ *vb* : to introduce internal stresses into (as a structural beam) to counteract later load stresses

pre·sum·ably \pri-'zü-mə-blē\ *adv* : by reasonable assumption

pre·sume \pri-'züm\ *vb* **pre·sumed**; **pre·sum·ing** 1 : to take upon oneself without leave or warrant : DARE 2 : to take for granted : ASSUME 3 : to act or behave with undue boldness — **pre·sum·able** \-'zü-mə-bəl\ *adj*

pre·sump·tion \pri-'zəmp-shən\ *n* 1 : presumptuous attitude or conduct : AUDACITY 2 : an attitude or belief dictated by probability; *also* : the grounds lending probability to a belief — **pre·sump·tive** \-tiv\ *adj*

pre·sump·tu·ous \pri-'zəmp-chə-wəs\ *adj* : overstepping due bounds : taking liberties — **pre·sump·tu·ous·ly** *adv*

pre·sup·pose \ˌprē-sə-'pōz\ *vb* 1 : to suppose beforehand 2 : to require beforehand as a necessary condition — **pre·sup·po·si·tion** \(ˌ)prē-ˌsə-pə-'zi-shən\ *n*

pre·teen \'prē-'tēn\ *n* : a boy or girl not yet 13 years old — **preteen** *adj*

pre·tend \pri-'tend\ *vb* 1 : PROFESS ⟨doesn't ～ to be scientific⟩ 2 : FEIGN ⟨～ to be angry⟩ 3 : to lay claim ⟨～ to a throne⟩ — **pre·tend·er** *n*

pre·tense *or* **pre·tence** \'prē-ˌtens, pri-'tens\ *n* 1 : CLAIM; *esp* : one not supported by fact 2 : mere display : SHOW 3 : an attempt to attain a certain condition ⟨made a ～ at discipline⟩ 4 : false show : PRETEXT — **pre·ten·sion** \pri-'ten-chən\ *n*

pre·ten·tious \pri-'ten-chəs\ *adj* 1 : making or possessing usu. unjustified claims (as to excellence) ⟨a ～ literary style⟩ 2 : making demands on one's ability or means : AMBITIOUS ⟨too ～ an undertaking⟩ — **pre·ten·tious·ly** *adv* — **pre·ten·tious·ness** *n*

pret·er·it *or* **pret·er·ite** \'pre-tə-rət\ *n* : a verb form expressing action in the past

pre·term \(ˌ)prē-'tərm, 'prē-ˌ\ *adj* : of, relating to, being, or brought forth by premature birth ⟨a ～ infant⟩

pre·ter·nat·u·ral \ˌprē-tər-'na-chə-rəl\ *adj* 1 : exceeding what is natural 2 : inexplicable by ordinary means — **pre·ter·nat·u·ral·ly** *adv*

pre·text \'prē-ˌtekst\ *n* : a purpose stated or assumed to cloak the real intention or state of affairs

pret·ti·fy \'pri-ti-ˌfī\ *vb* **-fied**; **-fy·ing** : to make pretty — **pret·ti·fi·ca·tion** \ˌpri-ti-fə-'kā-shən\ *n*

¹**pret·ty** \'pri-tē\ *adj* **pret·ti·er**; **-est** [ME *praty, prety,* fr. OE *prættig* tricky, fr. *prætt* trick] 1 : pleasing by delicacy or grace : having conventionally accepted elements of beauty ⟨～ flowers⟩ 2 : MISERABLE, TERRIBLE ⟨a ～ state of affairs⟩ 3 : moderately large ⟨a ～ profit⟩ 4 : PLEASANT — usu. used in negative constructions ⟨the truth was not so ～⟩ ♦ **Synonyms** COMELY, FAIR, BEAUTIFUL, ATTRACTIVE, LOVELY — **pret·ti·ly** \-tə-lē\ *adv* — **pret·ti·ness** \-tē-nəs\ *n*

²**pretty** *adv* : in some degree : MODERATELY; *also* : QUITE, MAINLY

³**pretty** *vb* **pret·tied**; **pret·ty·ing** : to make pretty — usu. used with *up*

pretty boy *n* : a man who is notably good-looking

pret·zel \'pret-səl\ *n* [G *Brezel*, ultim. fr. L *brachiatus* having branches like arms, fr. *brachium* arm] : a brittle or chewy glazed usu. salted slender bread often shaped like a loose knot

prev *abbr* previous; previously

pre·vail \pri-'vāl\ *vb* 1 : to win mastery : TRIUMPH 2 : to be or become effective : SUCCEED 3 : to urge successfully ⟨～ed upon her to sing⟩ 4 : to be frequent : PREDOMINATE — **pre·vail·ing·ly** *adv*

prev·a·lent \'pre-və-lənt\ *adj* : generally or widely existent : WIDESPREAD — **prev·a·lence** \-ləns\ *n*

pre·var·i·cate \pri-'ver-ə-ˌkāt\ *vb* **-cat·ed**; **-cat·ing** [L *praevaricari* to act in collusion, lit., to straddle, fr. *prae* in front of + *varicare* to straddle, fr. *varus* bowlegged] : to deviate from the truth : EQUIVOCATE — **pre·var·i·ca·tion** \-ˌver-ə-'kā-shən\ *n* — **pre·var·i·ca·tor** \-'ver-ə-ˌkā-tər\ *n*

pre·vent \pri-'vent\ *vb* 1 : to keep from happening or existing ⟨steps to ～ war⟩ 2 : to hold back : HINDER, STOP ⟨～ us from going⟩ — **pre·vent·able** *also* **pre·vent·ible** \-'ven-tə-bəl\ *adj* — **pre·ven·tion** \-'ven-chən\ *n* — **pre·ven·tive** \-'ven-tiv\ *adj or n* — **pre·ven·ta·tive** \-'ven-tə-tiv\ *adj or n*

pre·ver·bal \ˌprē-'vər-bəl\ *adj* : having not yet acquired the faculty of speech

¹**pre·view** \'prē-ˌvyü\ *vb* : to see or discuss beforehand; *esp* : to view or show in advance of public presentation

²**preview** *n* 1 : FORETASTE 2 : an advance showing or viewing 3 *also* **pre·vue** \-ˌvyü\ : a showing of snatches from a motion picture advertised for future appearance

pre·vi·ous \'prē-vē-əs\ *adj* : going before : EARLIER, FORMER ♦ **Synonyms** FOREGOING, PRIOR, PRECEDING, ANTECEDENT — **pre·vi·ous·ly** *adv*

pre·vi·sion \prē-'vi-zhən\ *n* 1 : FORESIGHT, PRESCIENCE 2 : FORECAST, PREDICTION

pre·war \'prē-'wȯr\ *adj* : occurring or existing before a war

¹**prey** \'prā\ *n, pl* **prey** *also* **preys** 1 : an animal taken for food by a predator; *also* : VICTIM 2 : the act or habit of preying

²**prey** *vb* 1 : to raid for booty 2 : to seize and devour prey 3 : to have a harmful or wearing effect

prf *abbr* proof

¹**price** \'prīs\ *n* 1 *archaic* : VALUE 2 : the amount of money paid or asked for the sale of a specified thing; *also* : the cost at which something is obtained

²**price** vb **priced; pric·ing 1 :** to set a price on **2 :** to ask the price of **3 :** to drive by raising prices ⟨*priced* themselves out of the market⟩

price–fix·ing \'prīs-,fik-siŋ\ n **:** the setting of prices artificially (as by producers or government)

price·less \-ləs\ adj **:** having a value beyond any price **:** INVALUABLE ◆ *Synonyms* PRECIOUS, COSTLY, EXPENSIVE

price support n **:** artificial maintenance of prices of a commodity at a level usu. fixed through government action

price war n **:** a period of commercial competition in which prices are repeatedly cut by the competitors

pric·ey also **pricy** \'prī-sē\ adj **pric·i·er; -est :** EXPENSIVE

¹**prick** \'prik\ n **1 :** a mark or small wound made by a pointed instrument **2 :** something sharp or pointed **3 :** an instance of pricking; also **:** a sensation of being pricked

²**prick** vb **1 :** to pierce slightly with a sharp point; also **:** to have or cause a pricking sensation **2 :** to affect with anguish or remorse ⟨∼s his conscience⟩ **3 :** to outline with punctures ⟨∼ out a pattern⟩ **4 :** to stand or cause to stand erect ⟨the dog's ears ∼ed up at the sound⟩ ◆ *Synonyms* PUNCH, PUNCTURE, PERFORATE, BORE, DRILL

prick·er \'pri-kər\ n **:** BRIAR; also **:** THORN

¹**prick·le** \'pri-kəl\ n **1 :** a small sharp process (as on a plant) **2 :** a slight stinging pain — **prick·ly** \'pri-klē\ adj

²**prickle** vb **prick·led; prick·ling 1 :** to prick lightly **2 :** TINGLE

prickly heat n **:** a red cutaneous eruption with intense itching and tingling caused by inflammation around the ducts of the sweat glands

prickly pear n **:** any of numerous cacti with usu. yellow flowers and prickly flat or rounded joints; also **:** the sweet pulpy pear-shaped edible fruit of various prickly pears

¹**pride** \'prīd\ n **1 :** CONCEIT **2 :** justifiable self-respect **3 :** elation over an act or possession **4 :** haughty behavior **:** DISDAIN **5 :** ostentatious display — **pride·ful** adj

²**pride** vb **prid·ed; prid·ing :** to indulge (oneself) in pride

priest \'prēst\ n [ME *preist*, fr. OE *prēost*, ultim. fr. LL *presbyter* elder, priest, fr. Gk *presbyteros*, fr. compar. of *presbys* old man, elder] **:** a person having authority to perform the sacred rites of a religion; esp **:** a member of the Anglican, Eastern, or Roman Catholic clergy ranking below a bishop and above a deacon — **priest·hood** n — **priest·li·ness** n — **priest·ly** adj

priest·ess \'prēs-təs\ n **:** a woman authorized to perform the sacred rites of a religion

prig \'prig\ n **:** one who irritates by rigid or pointed observance of proprieties — **prig·gish** \'pri-gish\ adj — **prig·gish·ly** adv

¹**prim** \'prim\ adj **prim·mer; prim·mest : :** stiffly formal and precise — **prim·ly** adv — **prim·ness** n

²**prim** abbr **1** primary **2** primitive

pri·ma·cy \'prī-mə-sē\ n **1 :** the state of being first (as in rank) **2 :** the office, rank, or character of an ecclesiastical primate

pri·ma don·na \,prī-mə-'dä-nə\ n, pl **prima donnas** [It, lit., first lady] **1 :** a principal female singer (as in an opera company) **2 :** a vain undisciplined usu. uncooperative person

pri·ma fa·cie \'prī-mə-'fā-shə, -sē, -shē\ adj or adv [L, at first view] **1 :** based on immediate impression **:** APPARENT **2 :** SELF-EVIDENT

pri·mal \'prī-məl\ adj **1 :** ORIGINAL, PRIMITIVE **2 :** first in importance

pri·mar·i·ly \prī-'mer-ə-lē\ adv **1 :** FUNDAMENTALLY **2 :** ORIGINALLY

¹**pri·ma·ry** \'prī-,mer-ē, -mə-rē\ adj **1 :** first in order of time or development; also **:** PREPARATORY **2 :** of first rank or importance; also **:** FUNDAMENTAL **3 :** not derived from or dependent on something else ⟨∼ sources⟩

²**primary** n, pl **-ries :** a preliminary election in which voters nominate or express a preference among candidates usu. of their own party

primary care n **:** health care provided by a medical professional with whom a patient has initial contact

primary color n **:** any of a set of colors from which all other colors may be derived

primary school n **1 :** a school usu. including grades 1-3 and sometimes kindergarten **2 :** ELEMENTARY SCHOOL

pri·mate \'prī-,māt or esp for 1 -mət\ n **1** often cap **:** the highest-ranking bishop of a province or nation **2 :** any of an order of mammals including humans, apes, and monkeys

¹**prime** \'prīm\ n **1 :** the earliest stage of something; esp **:** SPRINGTIME **2 :** the most active, thriving, or successful stage or period (as of one's life) **3 :** the best individual; also **:** the best part of something **4 :** any integer other than 0, +1, or –1 that is not divisible without remainder by any integer except +1, –1, and plus or minus itself; esp **:** any such integer that is positive

²**prime** adj **1 :** standing first (as in time, rank, significance, or quality) ⟨∼ requisite⟩ **2 :** of, relating to, or being a number that is prime

³**prime** vb **primed; prim·ing 1 :** FILL, LOAD **2 :** to lay a preparatory coating upon (as in painting) **3 :** to put in working condition **4 :** to instruct beforehand **:** COACH

prime meridian n **:** the meridian of 0° longitude which runs through Greenwich, England, and from which other longitudes are reckoned east and west

prime minister n **1 :** the chief minister of a ruler or state **2 :** the chief executive of a parliamentary government

¹prim·er \'pri-mər\ *n* [ME, layperson's prayer book, fr. AF, fr. ML *primarium*, fr. LL, neut. of *primarius* primary] **1** : a small book for teaching children to read **2** : a small introductory book on a subject **3** : a short informative piece of writing

²prim·er \'prī-mər\ *n* **1** : one that primes **2** : a device for igniting an explosive **3** : material for priming a surface

prime rate *n* : an interest rate announced by a bank to be the lowest available to its most credit-worthy customers

prime time *n* **1** : the time period when the television or radio audience is largest; *also* : television shows aired in prime time **2** : the choicest or busiest time

pri·me·val \prī-'mē-vəl\ *adj* : of or relating to the earliest ages : PRIMITIVE

¹prim·i·tive \'pri-mə-tiv\ *adj* **1** : ORIGINAL, PRIMARY **2** : of, relating to, or characteristic of an early stage of development or evolution **3** : ELEMENTAL, NATURAL **4** : of, relating to, or produced by a tribal people or culture **5** : SELF-TAUGHT; *also* : produced by a self-taught artist — **prim·i·tive·ly** *adv* — **prim·i·tive·ness** *n* — **prim·i·tiv·i·ty** \,pri-mə-'ti-və-tē\ *n*

²primitive *n* **1** : something primitive **2** : a primitive artist **3** : a member of a primitive people

prim·i·tiv·ism \'pri-mə-ti-,vi-zəm\ *n* **1** : primitive practices or procedures; *also* : a primitive quality or state **2** : belief in the superiority of a simple way of life close to nature **3** : the style of art of primitive peoples or primitive artists

pri·mo·gen·i·tor \,prī-mō-'je-nə-tər\ *n* : ANCESTOR, FOREFATHER

pri·mo·gen·i·ture \-'je-nə-,chùr\ *n* **1** : the state of being the firstborn of a family **2** : an exclusive right of inheritance belonging to the eldest son

pri·mor·di·al \prī-'mȯr-dē-əl\ *adj* : first created or developed : existing in its original state : PRIMEVAL

primp \'primp\ *vb* : to dress in a careful or finicky manner

prim·rose \'prim-,rōz\ *n* : any of a genus of perennial herbs with large leaves arranged at the base of the stem and clusters of showy flowers

prin *abbr* **1** principal **2** principle

prince \'prins\ *n* [ME, fr. AF, fr. L *princeps* leader, initiator, fr. *primus* first + *capere* to take] **1** : MONARCH, KING **2** : a male member of a royal family; *esp* : a son of the monarch **3** : a person of high standing (as in a class) — **prince·dom** \-dəm\ *n* — **prince·ly** *adj*

prince·ling \-liŋ\ *n* : a petty prince

prin·cess \'prin-səs, -,ses\ *n* **1** : a female member of a royal family **2** : the consort of a prince

¹prin·ci·pal \'prin-sə-pəl\ *adj* : most important — **prin·ci·pal·ly** *adv*

²principal *n* **1** : a leading person (as in a play) **2** : the chief officer of an educational institution **3** : the person from whom an agent's authority derives **4** : a

capital sum earning interest or used as a fund

prin·ci·pal·i·ty \,prin-sə-'pa-lə-tē\ *n, pl* **-ties** : the position, territory, or jurisdiction of a prince

principal parts *n pl* : the inflected forms of a verb

prin·ci·ple \'prin-sə-pəl\ *n* **1** : a general or fundamental law, doctrine, or assumption **2** : a rule or code of conduct; *also* : devotion to such a code **3** : the laws or facts of nature underlying the working of an artificial device **4** : a primary source : ORIGIN; *also* : an underlying faculty or endowment **5** : the active part (as of a drug)

prin·ci·pled \-pəld\ *adj* : exhibiting, based on, or characterized by principle ⟨high-*principled*⟩

prink \'priŋk\ *vb* : PRIMP

¹print \'print\ *n* [ME *prente*, fr. AF, fr. *preint, prient*, pp. of *priendre* to press, fr. L. *premere*] **1** : a mark made by pressure **2** : something stamped with an impression **3** : printed state or form **4** : printed matter **5** : a copy made by printing **6** : cloth with a pattern applied by printing

²print *vb* **1** : to stamp (as a mark) in or on something **2** : to produce impressions of (as from type) **3** : to write in letters like those of printer's type **4** : to make (a positive picture) from a photographic negative

print·able \'prin-tə-bəl\ *adj* **1** : capable of being printed or of being printed from **2** : worthy or fit to be published

print·er \'prin-tər\ *n* : one that prints; *esp* : a device that produces printout

print·ing *n* **1** : reproduction in printed form **2** : the art, practice, or business of a printer **3** : IMPRESSION 5

printing press *n* : a machine that produces printed copies

print·out \'print-,aůt\ *n* : a printed output produced by a computer — **print out** *vb*

¹pri·or \'prī-(ə)r\ *n* : the superior ranking next to the abbot or abbess of a religious house

²prior *adj* **1** : earlier in time or order **2** : taking precedence logically or in importance — **pri·or·i·ty** \prī-'ȯr-ə-tē\ *n*

pri·or·ess \'prī-ə-rəs\ *n* : a nun corresponding in rank to a prior

pri·or·i·tize \prī-'ȯr-ə-,tīz, 'prī-ə-rə-,tīz\ *vb* **-tized; -tiz·ing** : to list or rate in order of priority

prior to *prep* : in advance of : BEFORE

pri·o·ry \'prī-ə-rē\ *n, pl* **-ries** : a religious house under a prior or prioress

prise *chiefly Brit var of* ⁵PRIZE

prism \'pri-zəm\ *n* [LL *prisma*, fr. Gk. lit., something sawed, fr. *priein* to saw] **1** : a solid whose sides are parallelograms and whose ends are parallel and alike in shape and size **2** : a usu. 3-sided transparent object that refracts light so that it breaks up into rainbow colors — **pris·mat·ic** \priz-'ma-tik\ *adj*

pris·on \'pri-z⁹n\ *n* : a place or state of confinement esp. for criminals

pris·on·er \'pri-z°n-ər\ *n* : a person deprived of liberty; *esp* : one on trial or in prison

prisoner of war : a person captured in war

pris·sy \'pri-sē\ *adj* **pris·si·er; -est** : being overly prim and precise : PRIGGISH — **pris·si·ness** \-sē-nəs\ *n*

pris·tine \'pris-ˌtēn, pri-'stēn\ *adj* **1** : PRIMITIVE **2** : having the purity of its original state : UNSPOILED

prith·ee \'pri-thē\ *interj, archaic* — used to express a wish or request

pri·va·cy \'prī-və-sē\ *n, pl* **-cies 1** : the quality or state of being apart from others **2** : SECRECY

¹pri·vate \'prī-vət\ *adj* **1** : belonging to or intended for a particular individual or group ⟨∼ property⟩ **2** : restricted to the individual ⟨∼ opinion⟩ **3** : carried on by the individual independently ⟨∼ study⟩ **4** : not holding public office ⟨∼ citizen⟩ **5** : withdrawn from company or observation ⟨a ∼ place⟩ **6** : not known publicly ⟨∼ dealings⟩ — **pri·vate·ly** *adv*

²private *n* : an enlisted man of the lowest rank in the marine corps or of one of the two lowest ranks in the army — **in private** : not openly or in public

pri·va·teer \ˌprī-və-'tir\ *n* : an armed private ship licensed to attack enemy shipping; *also* : a sailor on such a ship

private first class *n* : an enlisted man ranking next below a corporal in the army and next below a lance corporal in the marine corps

pri·va·tion \prī-'vā-shən\ *n* **1** : DEPRIVATION **1 2** : the state of being deprived; *esp* : lack of what is needed for existence

priv·et \'pri-vət\ *n* : a nearly evergreen shrub related to the olive and widely used for hedges

¹priv·i·lege \'priv-lij, 'pri-və-\ *n* [ME, fr. AF, fr. L *privilegium* law for or against a private person, fr. *privus* private + *leg-, lex* law] : a right or immunity granted as an advantage or favor esp. to some and not others

²privilege *vb* **-leged; -leg·ing 1** : to grant a privilege to **2** : to accord a higher value to : FAVOR

privileged *adj* **1** : having or enjoying one or more privileges ⟨∼ classes⟩ **2** : not subject to disclosure in a court of law ⟨a ∼ communication⟩

¹privy \'pri-vē\ *adj* **1** : PERSONAL, PRIVATE **2** : SECRET **3** : admitted as one sharing in a secret ⟨∼ to the conspiracy⟩ — **priv·i·ly** \'pri-və-lē\ *adv*

²privy *n, pl* **priv·ies** : TOILET; *esp* : OUTHOUSE

¹prize \'prīz\ *n* **1** : something offered or striven for in competition or in contests of chance **2** : something exceptionally desirable

²prize *adj* **1** : awarded or worthy of a prize ⟨a ∼ essay⟩; *also* : awarded as a prize ⟨a ∼ medal⟩ **2** : OUTSTANDING

³prize *vb* **prized; priz·ing** : to value highly : ESTEEM ⟨a *prized* possession⟩

⁴prize *n* : property (as a ship) lawfully captured in time of war

⁵prize *vb* **prized; priz·ing** : PRY

prize·fight \'prīz-ˌfīt\ *n* : a professional boxing match — **prize·fight·er** *n* — **prize·fight·ing** *n*

prize·win·ner \-ˌwi-nər\ *n* : a winner of a prize — **prize·win·ning** *adj*

¹pro \'prō\ *n, pl* **pros** : a favorable argument, person, or position

²pro *adv* : in favor of : FOR

³pro *n or adj* : PROFESSIONAL

PRO *abbr* public relations officer

pro·ac·tive \prō-'ak-tiv\ *adj* : acting in anticipation of future problems or needs — **pro·ac·tive·ly** *adv*

pro–am \'prō-'am\ *adj* : involving professionals competing alongside or against amateurs ⟨a ∼ tournament⟩ — **pro–am** *n*

prob *abbr* **1** probable; probably **2** problem

prob·a·bil·i·ty \ˌprä-bə-'bi-lə-tē\ *n, pl* **-ties 1** : the quality or state of being probable **2** : something probable **3** : a measure of how often a particular event will occur if something (as tossing a coin) is done repeatedly which results in any of a number of possible events

prob·a·ble \'prä-bə-bəl\ *adj* **1** : apparently or presumably true ⟨a ∼ hypothesis⟩ **2** : likely to be or become true or real ⟨a ∼ result⟩ — **prob·a·bly** \-bə-blē\ *adv*

¹pro·bate \'prō-ˌbāt\ *n* : the judicial determination of the validity of a will

²pro·bate *vb* **pro·bat·ed; pro·bat·ing** : to establish (a will) by probate as genuine and valid

pro·ba·tion \prō-'bā-shən\ *n* **1** : subjection of an individual to a period of testing and trial to ascertain fitness (as for a job) **2** : the action of giving a convicted offender freedom during good behavior under the supervision of a probation officer — **pro·ba·tion·ary** \-shə-ˌner-ē\ *adj*

pro·ba·tion·er \-shə-nər\ *n* **1** : a person (as a newly admitted student nurse) whose fitness is being tested during a trial period **2** : a convicted offender on probation

pro·ba·tive \'prō-bə-tiv\ *adj* **1** : serving to test or try **2** : serving to prove

¹probe \'prōb\ *n* **1** : a slender instrument for examining a cavity (as a wound) **2** : an information-gathering device sent into outer space **3** : a penetrating investigation ◆ **Synonyms** INQUIRY, INQUEST, RESEARCH, INQUISITION

²probe *vb* **probed; prob·ing 1** : to examine with a probe **2** : to investigate thoroughly

pro·bi·ty \'prō-bə-tē\ *n* : UPRIGHTNESS, HONESTY

prob·lem \'prä-bləm\ *n* **1** : a question raised for consideration or solution **2** : an intricate unsettled question **3** : a source of perplexity or vexation — **problem** *adj*

prob·lem·at·ic \ˌprä-blə-'ma-tik\ *also* **prob·lem·at·i·cal** \-ti-kəl\ *adj* **1** : diffi-

cult to solve or decide : PUZZLING **2**
: DUBIOUS, QUESTIONABLE

pro·bos·cis \prə-'bä-səs, -'bäs-kəs\ *n, pl*
-bos·cis·es *also* **-bos·ci·des** \-'bä-sə-
ˌdēz\ [L, fr. Gk *proboskis*, fr. *pro-* before +
boskein to feed] : a long flexible snout (as
the trunk of an elephant)

proc *abbr* proceedings

pro·caine \'prō-ˌkān\ *n* : a drug used esp.
as a local anesthetic

pro·ce·dure \prə-'sē-jər\ *n* **1** : a particular way of doing something ⟨democratic
∼⟩ **2** : a series of steps followed in a regular order ⟨a surgical ∼⟩ — **pro·ce·dur-
al** \-'sē-jə-rəl\ *adj*

pro·ceed \prō-'sēd\ *vb* **1** : to come forth
: ISSUE **2** : to go on in an orderly way;
also : CONTINUE **3** : to begin and carry
on an action **4** : to take legal action **5**
: to go forward : ADVANCE

pro·ceed·ing *n* **1** : PROCEDURE **2** *pl*
: DOINGS **3** *pl* : legal action **4** : TRANS-
ACTION **5** *pl* : an official record of
things said or done

pro·ceeds \'prō-ˌsēdz\ *n pl* : the total
amount or the profit arising from a business deal : RETURN

¹pro·cess \'prä-ˌses, 'prō-\ *n, pl* **pro·cess-
es** \-ˌse-səz, -sə-səz, -sə-ˌsēz\ **1** : PROG-
RESS, ADVANCE **2** : something going on
: PROCEEDING **3** : a natural phenomenon marked by gradual changes that lead
toward a particular result ⟨the ∼ of
growth⟩ **4** : a series of actions or operations directed toward a particular result
⟨a manufacturing ∼⟩ **5** : legal action **6**
: a mandate issued by a court; *esp* : SUM-
MONS **7** : a projecting part of an organism or organic structure

²process *vb* : to subject to a special
process

pro·ces·sion \prə-'se-shən\ *n* : a group of
individuals moving along in an orderly
often ceremonial way

pro·ces·sion·al \-'se-shə-nəl\ *n* **1** : music
for a procession **2** : a ceremonial procession

pro·ces·sor \'prä-ˌse-sər, 'prō-\ *n* **1** : one
that processes **2** : CPU

pro–choice \(ˌ)prō-'chȯis\ *adj* : favoring
the legalization of abortion

pro·claim \prō-'klām\ *vb* : to make known
publicly : DECLARE

proc·la·ma·tion \ˌprä-klə-'mā-shən\ *n*
: an official public announcement

pro·cliv·i·ty \prō-'kli-və-tē\ *n, pl* **-ties** : an
inherent inclination esp. toward some-
thing objectionable

pro·con·sul \-'kän-səl\ *n* **1** : a governor
or military commander of an ancient
Roman province **2** : an administrator in
a modern colony or occupied area —
pro·con·su·lar \-sə-lər\ *adj*

pro·cras·ti·nate \prə-'kras-tə-ˌnāt, prō-\
vb **-nat·ed; -nat·ing** [L *procrastinare*, fr.
pro- forward + *crastinus* of tomorrow, fr.
cras tomorrow] : to put off usu. habitually doing something that should be done
♦ *Synonyms* DAWDLE, DELAY — **pro-
cras·ti·na·tion** \-ˌkras-tə-'nā-shən\ *n* —
pro·cras·ti·na·tor \-'kras-tə-ˌnā-tər\ *n*

pro·cre·ate \'prō-krē-ˌāt\ *vb* **-at·ed; -at-
ing** : to beget or bring forth offspring
♦ *Synonyms* REPRODUCE, BREED, GEN-
ERATE, PROPAGATE — **pro·cre·ation**
\ˌprō-krē-'ā-shən\ *n* — **pro·cre·ative**
\'prō-krē-ˌā-tiv\ *adj* — **pro·cre·ator** \-ˌā-
tər\ *n*

pro·crus·te·an \prə-'krəs-tē-ən\ *adj, often
cap* [fr. *Procrustes*, villain of Greek
mythology who made victims fit his bed
by stretching them or cutting off their
legs] : marked by arbitrary often ruthless
disregard of individual differences or special circumstances

proc·tor \'präk-tər\ *n* : one appointed to
supervise students (as at an examination)
— **proctor** *vb* — **proc·to·ri·al** \präk-
'tȯr-ē-əl\ *adj*

proc·u·ra·tor \'prä-kyə-ˌrā-tər\ *n* : a
Roman provincial administrator

pro·cure \prə-'kyu̇r\ *vb* **pro·cured; pro-
cur·ing** **1** : to get possession of : OB-
TAIN **2** : to make women available for
promiscuous sexual intercourse **3**
: ACHIEVE ♦ *Synonyms* SECURE, AC-
QUIRE, GAIN, WIN, EARN — **pro·cur-
able** \-'kyu̇r-ə-bəl\ *adj* — **pro·cure-
ment** *n* — **pro·cur·er** *n*

¹prod \'präd\ *vb* **prod·ded; prod·ding** **1**
: to thrust a pointed instrument into
: GOAD **2** : INCITE, STIR — **prod** *n*

²prod *abbr* product; production

prod·i·gal \'prä-di-gəl\ *adj* **1** : recklessly
extravagant; *also* : LUXURIANT **2**
: WASTEFUL, LAVISH ♦ *Synonyms* PRO-
FUSE, LUSH, OPULENT — **prodigal** *n* —
prod·i·gal·i·ty \ˌprä-də-'ga-lə-tē\ *n*

pro·di·gious \prə-'di-jəs\ *adj* **1** : exciting
wonder **2** : extraordinary in size or degree : ENORMOUS ♦ *Synonyms* MON-
STROUS, TREMENDOUS, STUPENDOUS,
MONUMENTAL — **pro·di·gious·ly** *adv*

prod·i·gy \'prä-də-jē\ *n, pl* **-gies** **1**
: something extraordinary : WONDER **2**
: a highly talented child

¹pro·duce \prə-'düs, -'dyüs\ *vb* **produced; pro·duc·ing** **1** : to present to
view : EXHIBIT **2** : to give birth or rise
to : YIELD **3** : EXTEND, PROLONG **4** : to
give being or form to : BRING ABOUT,
MAKE; *esp* : MANUFACTURE **5** : to sponsor or oversee the making of **6** : to cause
to accrue ⟨∼ a profit⟩ — **pro·duc·er** *n*

²pro·duce \'prä-(ˌ)düs, 'prō- *also* -(ˌ)dyüs\
n : PRODUCT **2**; *also* : agricultural products and esp. fresh fruits and vegetables

prod·uct \'prä-(ˌ)dəkt\ *n* **1** : the number
resulting from multiplication **2** : something produced

pro·duc·tion \prə-'dək-shən\ *n* **1** : something produced : PRODUCT **2** : the act or
process of producing — **pro·duc·tive**
\-'dək-tiv\ *adj* — **pro·duc·tive·ness** *n*
— **pro·duc·tiv·i·ty** \(ˌ)prō-ˌdək-'ti-və-tē,
ˌprä-(ˌ)dək-\ *n*

product placement *n* : the inclusion of a
product in a television program or film as
a means of advertising

pro·em \'prō-ˌem\ *n* **1** : preliminary
comment : PREFACE **2** : PRELUDE

¹prof \'präf\ *n* : PROFESSOR

²**prof** abbr professional

¹**pro·fane** \prō-'fān\ vb **pro·faned; pro·fan·ing 1** : to treat (something sacred) with irreverence or contempt **2** : to debase by an unworthy use — **prof·a·na·tion** \,prä-fə-'nā-shən\ n

²**profane** adj [ME prophane, fr. MF, fr. L profanus, fr. pro- before + fanum temple] **1** : not concerned with religion : SECULAR **2** : not holy because unconsecrated, impure, or defiled **3** : serving to debase what is holy : IRREVERENT **4** : OBSCENE, VULGAR — **pro·fane·ly** adv — **pro·fane·ness** n

pro·fan·i·ty \prō-'fa-nə-tē\ n, pl **-ties 1** : the quality or state of being profane **2** : the use of profane language **3** : profane language

pro·fess \prə-'fes\ vb **1** : to declare or admit openly : AFFIRM **2** : to declare in words only : PRETEND **3** : to confess one's faith in **4** : to practice or claim to be versed in (a calling or occupation) — **pro·fess·ed·ly** \-'fe-səd-lē\ adv

pro·fes·sion \prə-'fe-shən\ n **1** : an open declaration or avowal of a belief or opinion **2** : a calling requiring specialized knowledge and often long academic preparation **3** : the whole body of persons engaged in a calling

¹**pro·fes·sion·al** \prə-'fe-shə-nəl\ adj **1** : of, relating to, or characteristic of a profession **2** : engaged in one of the professions **3** : participating for gain in an activity often engaged in by amateurs — **pro·fes·sion·al·ly** adv

²**professional** n : one that engages in an activity professionally

pro·fes·sion·al·ism \-nə-,li-zəm\ n **1** : the conduct, aims, or qualities that characterize or mark a profession or a professional person **2** : the following of a profession (as athletics) for gain or livelihood

pro·fes·sion·al·ize \-nə-,līz\ vb **-ized; -iz·ing** : to give a professional nature to

pro·fes·sor \prə-'fe-sər\ n : a teacher at a university or college; esp : a faculty member of the highest academic rank — **pro·fes·so·ri·al** \,prō-fə-'sȯr-ē-əl, ,prä-\ adj — **pro·fes·sor·ship** n

prof·fer \'prä-fər\ vb **prof·fered; prof·fer·ing** : to present for acceptance : OFFER — **proffer** n

pro·fi·cient \prə-'fi-shənt\ adj : well advanced in an art, occupation, or branch of knowledge ◆ Synonyms ADEPT, SKILLFUL, EXPERT, MASTERFUL, MASTERLY — **pro·fi·cien·cy** \-shən-sē\ n — **proficient** n — **pro·fi·cient·ly** adv

¹**pro·file** \'prō-,fī(-ə)l\ n [It profilo, fr. profilare to draw in outline, fr. pro- forward (fr. L) + filare to spin, fr. LL, fr. L filum thread] **1** : a representation of something in outline; esp : a human head seen in side view **2** : a concise biographical sketch **3** : degree or level of public exposure ⟨keep a low ~⟩

²**profile** vb **pro·filed; pro·fil·ing** : to write or draw a profile of

profiling n : the act of suspecting or targeting a person solely on the basis of observed characteristics or behavior ⟨racial ~⟩

¹**prof·it** \'prä-fət\ n **1** : a valuable return : GAIN **2** : the excess of the selling price of goods over their cost — **prof·it·less** adj

²**profit** vb **1** : to be of use : BENEFIT **2** : to derive benefit : GAIN — **prof·it·able** \'prä-fə-tə-bəl\ adj — **prof·it·ably** \-blē\ adv

prof·i·teer \,prä-fə-'tir\ n : one who makes what is considered an unreasonable profit — **profiteer** vb

prof·li·gate \'prä-fli-gət, -flə-,gāt\ adj **1** : completely given up to dissipation and licentiousness **2** : wildly extravagant — **prof·li·ga·cy** \-gə-sē\ n — **profligate** n — **prof·li·gate·ly** adv

pro for·ma \(,)prō-'fȯr-mə\ adj : done or existing as a matter of form

pro·found \prə-'faůnd, prō-\ adj **1** : marked by intellectual depth or insight ⟨a ~ thought⟩ **2** : coming from or reaching to a depth ⟨a ~ sigh⟩ **3** : deeply felt : INTENSE ⟨~ sympathy⟩ — **pro·found·ly** adv — **pro·fun·di·ty** \-'fən-də-tē\ n

pro·fuse \prə-'fyüs, prō-\ adj : pouring forth liberally : ABUNDANT ⟨~ bleeding⟩ ◆ Synonyms LAVISH, PRODIGAL, LUXURIANT, EXUBERANT — **pro·fuse·ly** adv — **pro·fu·sion** \-'fyü-zhən\ n

prog abbr program

pro·gen·i·tor \prō-'je-nə-tər\ n **1** : a direct ancestor : FOREFATHER **2** : ORIGINATOR, PRECURSOR

prog·e·ny \'prä-jə-nē\ n, pl **-nies** : OFFSPRING, CHILDREN, DESCENDANTS

pro·ges·ter·one \prō-'jes-tə-,rōn\ n : a female hormone that causes the uterus to undergo changes so as to provide a suitable environment for a fertilized egg

prog·na·thous \'präg-nə-thəs\ adj : having the lower jaw projecting beyond the upper part of the face

prog·no·sis \präg-'nō-səs\ n, pl **-no·ses** \-,sēz\ **1** : the prospect of recovery from disease **2** : FORECAST

¹**prog·nos·tic** \präg-'näs-tik\ n **1** : PORTENT **2** : PROPHECY

²**prognostic** adj : of, relating to, or serving as ground for prognostication or a prognosis

prog·nos·ti·cate \präg-'näs-tə-,kāt\ vb **-cat·ed; -cat·ing** : to foretell from signs or symptoms — **prog·nos·ti·ca·tion** \-,näs-tə-'kā-shən\ n — **prog·nos·ti·ca·tor** \-'näs-tə-,kā-tər\ n

¹**pro·gram** \'prō-,gram, -grəm\ n [F programme agenda, public notice, fr. Gk programma, fr. prographein to write in advance, fr. pro- before + graphein to write] **1** : a brief outline of the order to be pursued or the subjects included (as in a public entertainment); also : PERFORMANCE **2** : a plan of procedure esp. toward a goal : coded instructions for a computer — **pro·gram·mat·ic** \,prō-grə-'ma-tik\ adj

²**program** also **programme** vb **-grammed** or **-gramed; -gram·ming** or **-gram·ing**

1 : to arrange or furnish a program of or for 2 : to enter in a program 3 : to provide (as a computer) with a program — **pro·gram·ma·bil·i·ty** \(,)prō-,gra-mə-'bi-lə-tē\ n — **pro·gram·ma·ble** \'prō-,gra-mə-bəl\ adj — **pro·gram·mer** also **pro·gram·er** \'prō-,gra-mər, -grə-\ n

programme chiefly Brit var of PROGRAM

programmed instruction n : instruction through information given in small steps with each requiring a correct response by the learner before going on to the next step

pro·gram·ming also **pro·gram·ing** n 1 : the planning, scheduling, or performing of a program 2 : the process of instructing or learning by means of an instruction program 3 : the process of preparing an instruction program

¹**prog·ress** \'prä-grəs, -,gres\ n 1 : a forward movement : ADVANCE 2 : a gradual betterment

²**pro·gress** \prə-'gres\ vb 1 : to move forward : PROCEED 2 : to develop to a more advanced stage : IMPROVE

pro·gres·sion \prə-'gre-shən\ n 1 : an act of progressing : ADVANCE 2 : a continuous and connected series

¹**pro·gres·sive** \prə-'gre-siv\ adj 1 : of, relating to, or characterized by progress ⟨a ~ city⟩ 2 : moving forward or onward : ADVANCING 3 : increasing in extent or severity ⟨a ~ disease⟩ 4 often cap : of or relating to political Progressives 5 : of, relating to, or constituting a verb form that expresses action in progress at the time of speaking or a time spoken of — **pro·gres·sive·ly** adv

²**progressive** n 1 : one that is progressive 2 : a person believing in moderate political change and social improvement by government action; esp, cap : a member of a Progressive Party in the U.S.

pro·hib·it \prō-'hi-bət\ vb 1 : to forbid by authority 2 : to prevent from doing something

pro·hi·bi·tion \,prō-ə-'bi-shən\ n 1 : the act of prohibiting 2 : the forbidding by law of the sale or manufacture of alcoholic beverages — **pro·hi·bi·tion·ist** \-'bi-shə-nist\ n — **pro·hib·i·tive** \prō-'hi-bə-tiv\ adj — **pro·hib·i·tive·ly** adv — **pro·hib·i·to·ry** \-'hi-bə-,tōr-ē\ adj

¹**proj·ect** \'prä-,jekt, -jikt\ n 1 : a specific plan or design : SCHEME 2 : a planned undertaking ⟨a research ~⟩

²**pro·ject** \prə-'jekt\ vb 1 : to devise in the mind : DESIGN 2 : to throw forward 3 : PROTRUDE 4 : to cause (light or shadow) to fall into space or (an image) to fall on a surface ⟨a ~ beam of light⟩ 5 : to attribute (a thought, feeling, or personal characteristic) to a person, group, or object 6 : to display outwardly — **pro·jec·tion** \-'jek-shən\ n

pro·jec·tile \prə-'jek-t°l, -'jek-tī(-ə)l\ n 1 : a body hurled or projected by external force; esp : a missile for a firearm 2 : a self-propelling weapon

pro·jec·tion·ist \prə-'jek-shə-nist\ n : one that operates a motion-picture projector or television equipment

pro·jec·tor \-'jek-tər\ n : one that projects; esp : a device for projecting pictures on a screen

pro·lapse \prō-'laps, 'prō-,\ n : the falling down or slipping of a body part from its usual position

pro·le·gom·e·non \,prō-li-'gä-mə-,nän, -nən\ n, pl **-e·na** \-nə\ : prefatory remarks

pro·le·tar·i·an \,prō-lə-'ter-ē-ən\ n [L proletarius belonging to the lowest class of citizens, fr. proles progeny, fr. pro- forth + -oles (akin to alere to nourish)] : a member of the proletariat — **proletarian** adj

pro·le·tar·i·at \-ē-ət\ n : the laboring class; esp : industrial workers who sell their labor to live

pro—life \(,)prō-'līf\ n : ANTIABORTION

pro·lif·er·ate \prə-'li-fə-,rāt\ vb **-at·ed; -at·ing** : to grow or increase by rapid production of new units (as cells, offspring, or nuclear weapons) — **pro·lif·er·a·tion** \-,li-fə-'rā-shən\ n

pro·lif·ic \prə-'li-fik\ adj 1 : producing young or fruit abundantly 2 : marked by abundant inventiveness or productivity ⟨a ~ writer⟩ — **pro·lif·i·cal·ly** \-fi-k(ə-)lē\ adv

pro·lix \prō-'liks, 'prō-,liks\ adj : VERBOSE ♦ Synonyms WORDY, DIFFUSE, REDUNDANT — **pro·lix·i·ty** \prō-'lik-sə-tē\ n

pro·logue also **pro·log** \'prō-,lȯg, -,läg\ n : PREFACE ⟨~ of a play⟩

pro·long \prə-'lȯŋ\ vb 1 : to lengthen in time : CONTINUE ⟨~ a meeting⟩ 2 : to lengthen in extent or range ♦ Synonyms PROTRACT, EXTEND, ELONGATE, STRETCH — **pro·lon·ga·tion** \,prō-,lȯŋ-'gā-shən\ n

prom \'präm\ n : a formal dance given by a high school or college class

¹**prom·e·nade** \,prä-mə-'nād, -'näd\ vb **-nad·ed; -nad·ing** 1 : to take a promenade 2 : to walk about in or on

²**promenade** n [F, fr. promener to take for a walk, fr. MF, alter. of OF pourmener, fr. pour- completely (fr. L pro-) + mener to lead, fr. LL minare to drive, fr. L minari to threaten] 1 : a place for strolling 2 : a leisurely walk for pleasure or display 3 : an opening grand march at a formal ball

pro·me·thi·um \prə-'mē-thē-əm\ n : a metallic chemical element obtained from uranium or neodymium

prom·i·nence \'prä-mə-nəns\ n 1 : something prominent 2 : the quality, state, or fact of being prominent or conspicuous 3 : a mass of cloudlike gas that arises from the sun's chromosphere

prom·i·nent \-nənt\ adj 1 : jutting out : PROJECTING 2 : readily noticeable : CONSPICUOUS 3 : DISTINGUISHED, EMINENT ♦ Synonyms REMARKABLE, OUTSTANDING, STRIKING, SALIENT — **prom·i·nent·ly** adv

pro·mis·cu·ous \prə-'mis-kyə-wəs\ adj 1 : consisting of various sorts and kinds : MIXED 2 : not restricted to one class or person 3 : having a number of sexual partners ♦ Synonyms MISCELLANEOUS, ASSORTED, HETEROGENEOUS, MOTLEY,

VARIED — pro·mis·cu·i·ty \,prä-mis-'kyü-ə-tē, ,prō-,mis-\ n — pro·mis·cu·ous·ly adv — pro·mis·cu·ous·ness n

¹prom·ise \'prä-məs\ n 1 : a pledge to do or not to do something specified 2 : ground for expectation of success or improvement 3 : something promised

²promise vb prom·ised; prom·is·ing 1 : to engage to do, bring about, or provide ⟨~ help⟩ 2 : to suggest beforehand ⟨dark clouds ~ rain⟩ 3 : to give ground for expectation ⟨it ~s to be a good game⟩

promising adj : likely to succeed or yield good results ⟨a ~ new medicine⟩ — prom·is·ing·ly adv

prom·is·so·ry \'prä-mə-,sòr-ē\ adj : containing a promise

prom·on·to·ry \'prä-mən-,tòr-ē\ n, pl -ries : a point of land jutting into the sea : HEADLAND

pro·mote \prə-'mōt\ vb pro·mot·ed; pro·mot·ing 1 : to advance in station, rank, or honor 2 : to contribute to the growth or prosperity of : FURTHER 3 : LAUNCH — pro·mo·tion \-'mō-shən\ n — pro·mo·tion·al \-shə-nəl\ adj

pro·mot·er \-'mō-tər\ n : one that promotes; esp : one that assumes the financial responsibilities of a sports event ⟨a boxing ~⟩

¹prompt \'prämpt\ vb 1 : INCITE 2 : to assist (one acting or reciting) by suggesting the next words 3 : INSPIRE, URGE — prompt·er n

²prompt adj 1 : being ready and quick to act; also : PUNCTUAL 2 : performed readily or immediately ⟨~ service⟩ — prompt·ly adv — prompt·ness n

prompt·book \-,bùk\ n : a copy of a play with directions for performance used by a theater prompter

promp·ti·tude \'prämp-tə-,tüd, -,tyüd\ n : the quality or habit of being prompt : PROMPTNESS

pro·mul·gate \'prä-məl-,gāt; prō-'məl-\ vb -gat·ed; -gat·ing : to make known or put into force by open declaration — prom·ul·ga·tion \,prä-məl-'gā-shən, ,prō-(,)məl-\ n

pron abbr 1 pronoun 2 pronounced 3 pronunciation

prone \'prōn\ adj 1 : having a tendency or inclination : DISPOSED 2 : lying face downward; also : lying flat or prostrate ♦ Synonyms SUBJECT, EXPOSED, OPEN, LIABLE, SUSCEPTIBLE — prone·ness n

prong \'pròŋ\ n : one of the sharp points of a fork : TINE; also : a slender projecting part (as of an antler) — pronged \'pròŋd\ adj

prong·horn \'pròŋ-,hòrn\ n, pl prong·horn or pronghorns : a swift horned ruminant mammal chiefly of grasslands of western No. America that resembles an antelope

pro·noun \'prō-,naùn\ n : a word used as a substitute for a noun

pro·nounce \prə-'naùns\ vb pro·nounced; pro·nounc·ing 1 : to utter officially or as an opinion ⟨~ sentence⟩ 2 : to employ the organs of speech in order to produce ⟨~ a word⟩; esp : to say or speak correctly ⟨she can't ~ his name⟩ — pro·nounce·able adj — pro·nun·ci·a·tion \-,nən-sē-'ā-shən\ n

pro·nounced adj : strongly marked : DECIDED ⟨a ~ dislike⟩

pro·nounce·ment \prə-'naùns-mənt\ n : a formal declaration of opinion; also : ANNOUNCEMENT

pron·to \'prän-,tō\ adv [Sp, fr. L promptus prompt] : QUICKLY

pro·nu·clear \'prō-'nü-klē-ər, -'nyü-\ adj : supporting the use of nuclear-powered electric generating stations

pro·nun·ci·a·men·to \prō-,nən-sē-ə-'men-tō\ n, pl -tos or -toes : PROCLAMATION, MANIFESTO

¹proof \'prüf\ n [ME prof, prove, alter. of preve, fr. AF preove, fr. LL proba, fr. L probare to test, prove, fr. probus good, honest] 1 : the evidence that compels acceptance by the mind of a truth or fact 2 : a process or operation that establishes validity or truth : TEST 3 : a trial impression (as from type) 4 : a trial print from a photographic negative 5 : alcoholic content (as of a beverage) indicated by a number that is twice the percent by volume of alcohol present ⟨whiskey of 90 ~ is 45% alcohol⟩

²proof adj 1 : successful in resisting or repelling ⟨~ against tampering⟩ ⟨waterproof⟩ 2 : of standard strength or quality or alcoholic content

proof·read \-,rēd\ vb : to read and mark corrections in — proof·read·er n

¹prop \'präp\ n : something that props

²prop vb propped; prop·ping 1 : to support by placing something under or against 2 : SUSTAIN, STRENGTHEN

³prop n : PROPERTY 4

⁴prop n : PROPELLER

⁵prop abbr 1 property 2 proposition 3 proprietor

prop·a·gan·da \,prä-pə-'gan-də, ,prō-\ n [NL, fr. Congregatio de propaganda fide Congregation for propagating the faith, organization established by Pope Gregory XV] : the spreading of ideas or information to further or damage a cause; also : ideas or allegations spread for such a purpose — prop·a·gan·dist \-dist\ n

pro·pa·gan·dize \-,dīz\ vb -dized; -dizing : to subject to or carry on propaganda

prop·a·gate \'prä-pə-,gāt\ vb -gat·ed; -gat·ing 1 : to reproduce or cause to reproduce biologically : MULTIPLY 2 : to cause to spread — prop·a·ga·tion \,prä-pə-'gā-shən\ n

pro·pane \'prō-,pān\ n : a heavy flammable gas found in petroleum and natural gas and used esp. as a fuel

pro·pel \prə-'pel\ vb pro·pelled; pro·pelling : to drive forward or onward ♦ Synonyms PUSH, SHOVE, THRUST

pro·pel·lant also pro·pel·lent \-'pe-lənt\ n : something (as a fuel) that propels — propellant also propellent adj

pro·pel·ler \prə-'pe-lər\ n : a device consisting of a hub fitted with blades that is used to propel a vehicle (as a motorboat or an airplane)

pro·pen·si·ty \prə-ˈpen-sə-tē\ *n, pl* **-ties** : an often intense natural inclination or preference

¹**prop·er** \ˈprä-pər\ *adj* **1** : referring to one individual only ⟨~ noun⟩ **2** : belonging characteristically to a species or individual : PECULIAR **3** : very satisfactory : EXCELLENT **4** : strictly limited to a specified thing ⟨the city ~⟩ **5** : CORRECT ⟨the ~ way to proceed⟩ **6** : strictly decorous : GENTEEL **7** : marked by suitability or rightness ⟨~ punishment⟩
♦ *Synonyms* MEET, APPROPRIATE, FITTING, SEEMLY — **prop·er·ly** *adv*

²**proper** *n* : the parts of the Mass that vary according to the liturgical calendar

prop·er·tied \ˈprä-pər-tēd\ *adj* : owning property and esp. much property

prop·er·ty \ˈprä-pər-tē\ *n, pl* **-ties 1** : a quality peculiar to an individual or thing **2** : something owned; *esp* : a piece of real estate **3** : OWNERSHIP **4** : an article or object used in a play or motion picture other than painted scenery and actor's costumes

proph·e·cy *also* **proph·e·sy** \ˈprä-fə-sē\ *n, pl* **-cies** *also* **-sies 1** : an inspired utterance of a prophet **2** : PREDICTION

proph·e·sy \-ˌsī\ *vb* **-sied; -sy·ing 1** : to speak or utter by divine inspiration **2** : PREDICT — **proph·e·si·er** *n*

proph·et \ˈprä-fət\ *n* [ME *prophete*, fr. AF, fr. L *propheta*, fr. Gk *prophētēs*, fr. *pro* for + *phanai* to speak] **1** : one who utters divinely inspired revelations **2** : one who foretells future events

proph·et·ess \ˈprä-fə-təs\ *n* : a woman who is a prophet

pro·phet·ic \prə-ˈfe-tik\ *or* **pro·phet·i·cal** \-ti-kəl\ *adj* : of, relating to, or characteristic of a prophet or prophecy — **pro·phet·i·cal·ly** \-ti-k(ə-)lē\ *adv*

Proph·ets \ˈprä-fəts\ *n pl* — see BIBLE table

¹**pro·phy·lac·tic** \ˌprō-fə-ˈlak-tik, ˌprä-\ *adj* **1** : preventing or guarding from the spread or occurrence of disease or infection **2** : PREVENTIVE

²**prophylactic** *n* : something prophylactic; *esp* : a device (as a condom) for preventing venereal infection or conception

pro·phy·lax·is \-ˈlak-səs\ *n, pl* **-lax·es** \-ˈlak-ˌsēz\ : measures designed to preserve health and prevent the spread of disease

pro·pin·qui·ty \prə-ˈpiŋ-kwə-tē\ *n* **1** : KINSHIP **2** : nearness in place or time : PROXIMITY

pro·pi·ti·ate \prō-ˈpi-shē-ˌāt\ *vb* **-at·ed; -at·ing** : to gain or regain the favor of : APPEASE — **pro·pi·ti·a·tion** \-ˌpi-shē-ˈā-shən\ *n* — **pro·pi·ti·a·to·ry** \-ˈpi-shē-ə-ˌtȯr-ē\ *adj*

pro·pi·tious \prə-ˈpi-shəs\ *adj* **1** : favorably disposed ⟨~ deities⟩ **2** : being of good omen ⟨~ circumstances⟩

prop·man \ˈpräp-ˌman\ *n* : one who is in charge of stage properties

pro·po·nent \prə-ˈpō-nənt\ *n* : one who argues in favor of something

¹**pro·por·tion** \prə-ˈpȯr-shən\ *n* **1** : BALANCE, SYMMETRY **2** : SHARE, QUOTA **3** : the relation of one part to another or to the whole with respect to magnitude, quantity, or degree : RATIO **4** : SIZE, DEGREE — **in proportion** : PROPORTIONAL

²**proportion** *vb* **-tioned; -tion·ing 1** : to adjust (a part or thing) in size relative to other parts or things **2** : to make the parts of harmonious

pro·por·tion·al \prə-ˈpȯr-shə-nəl\ *adj* : corresponding in size, degree, or intensity; *also* : having the same or a constant ratio — **pro·por·tion·al·ly** *adv*

pro·por·tion·ate \prə-ˈpȯr-shə-nət\ *adj* : PROPORTIONAL — **pro·por·tion·ate·ly** *adv*

pro·pose \prə-ˈpōz\ *vb* **pro·posed; pro·pos·ing 1** : PLAN, INTEND ⟨~s to buy a house⟩ **2** : to make an offer of marriage **3** : to offer for consideration : SUGGEST ⟨~ a policy⟩ — **pro·pos·al** \-ˈpō-zəl\ *n* — **pro·pos·er** *n*

¹**prop·o·si·tion** \ˌprä-pə-ˈzi-shən\ *n* **1** : something proposed for consideration : PROPOSAL **2** : a request for sexual intercourse **3** : a statement of something to be discussed, proved, or explained **4** : SITUATION, AFFAIR ⟨a tough ~⟩ — **prop·o·si·tion·al** \-ˈzi-shə-nəl\ *adj*

²**proposition** *vb* **-tioned; -tion·ing** : to make a proposal to; *esp* : to suggest sexual intercourse to

pro·pound \prə-ˈpaůnd\ *vb* : to set forth for consideration ⟨~ a doctrine⟩

pro·pri·e·tary \prə-ˈprī-ə-ˌter-ē\ *adj* **1** : of, relating to, or characteristic of a proprietor ⟨~ rights⟩ **2** : made and sold by one with the sole right to do so ⟨~ medicines⟩ ⟨~ software⟩

pro·pri·e·tor \prə-ˈprī-ə-tər\ *n* : OWNER — **pro·pri·e·tor·ship** *n*

pro·pri·e·tress \-ˈprī-ə-trəs\ *n* : a woman who is a proprietor

pro·pri·e·ty \prə-ˈprī-ə-tē\ *n, pl* **-ties 1** : the standard of what is socially acceptable in conduct or speech **2** *pl* : the customs of polite society

props \ˈpräps\ *n sing or pl* **1** *slang* : DUE **1** ⟨gave him his ~⟩ **2** *slang* : RESPECT **2** ⟨earned the ~ of his peers⟩ **3** *slang* : ACKNOWLEDGMENT ⟨deserves ~ for the effort⟩

pro·pul·sion \prə-ˈpəl-shən\ *n* **1** : the action or process of propelling **2** : something that propels — **pro·pul·sive** \-siv\ *adj*

pro ra·ta \(ˌ)prō-ˈrä-tə, -ˈrä-\ *adv* : in proportion to the share of each : PROPORTIONATELY

pro·rate \(ˌ)prō-ˈrāt\ *vb* **pro·rat·ed; pro·rat·ing** : to divide, distribute, or assess proportionately

pro·rogue \prə-ˈrōg\ *vb* **pro·rogued; pro·rogu·ing** : to suspend or end a session of (a legislative body) — **pro·ro·ga·tion** \ˌprō-rō-ˈgā-shən\ *n*

pros *pl of* PRO

pro·sa·ic \prō-ˈzā-ik\ *adj* : lacking imagination or excitement : DULL

pro·sce·ni·um \prō-ˈsē-nē-əm\ *n* **1** : the

part of a stage in front of the curtain 2 : the wall containing the arch that frames the stage

pro·scribe \prō-'skrīb\ *vb* **pro·scribed; pro·scrib·ing** 1 : OUTLAW 2 : to condemn or forbid as harmful — **pro·scrip·tion** \-'skrip-shən\ *n*

prose \'prōz\ *n* [ME, fr. AF, fr. L *prosa*, fr. fem. of *prorsus, prosus*, straightforward, being in prose, alter. of *proversus*, pp. of *provertere* to turn forward] : the ordinary language people use in speaking or writing

pros·e·cute \'prä-si-ˌkyüt\ *vb* **-cut·ed; -cut·ing** 1 : to follow to the end ⟨∼ an investigation⟩ 2 : to seek legal punishment of ⟨∼ a forger⟩ — **pros·e·cu·tion** \ˌprä-si-ˈkyü-shən\ *n* — **pros·e·cu·tor** \'prä-si-ˌkyü-tər\ *n* — **pros·e·cu·to·ri·al** \ˌprä-si-kyü-ˈtȯr-ē-əl\ *adj*

¹**pros·e·lyte** \'prä-sə-ˌlīt\ *n* : a new convert to a religion, belief, or party — **pros·e·ly·tism** \-ˌlī-ˌti-zəm\ *n*

²**proselyte** *vb* **-lyt·ed; -lyt·ing** : PROSELYTIZE

pros·e·ly·tise *Brit var of* PROSELYTIZE

pros·e·ly·tize \'prä-sə-lə-ˌtīz\ *vb* **-tized; -tiz·ing** 1 : to induce someone to convert to one's faith 2 : to recruit someone to join one's party, institution, or cause

pros·o·dy \'prä-sə-dē\ *n, pl* **-dies** : the study of versification and esp. of metrical structure — **pro·sod·ic** \prə-ˈsä-dik\ *adj*

¹**pros·pect** \'prä-ˌspekt\ *n* 1 : an extensive view; *also* : OUTLOOK 2 : the act of looking forward 3 : a mental vision of something to come 4 : something that is awaited or expected : POSSIBILITY 5 : a potential buyer or customer; *also* : a likely candidate (as for a job) — **pro·spec·tive** \prə-ˈspek-tiv, ˈprä-ˌspek-\ *adj* — **pro·spec·tive·ly** *adv*

²**pros·pect** \'prä-ˌspekt\ *vb* : to explore esp. for mineral deposits — **pros·pec·tor** \-ˌspek-tər, prä-ˈspek-\ *n*

pro·spec·tus \prə-ˈspek-təs\ *n* : a preliminary statement that describes an enterprise and is distributed to prospective buyers or participants

pros·per \'präs-pər\ *vb* **pros·pered; pros·per·ing** : SUCCEED; *esp* : to achieve economic success

pros·per·i·ty \präs-ˈper-ə-tē\ *n* : thriving condition : SUCCESS; *esp* : economic well-being

pros·per·ous \'präs-pə-rəs\ *adj* 1 : FAVORABLE ⟨∼ winds⟩ 2 : marked by success or economic well-being ⟨a ∼ business⟩

pros·ta·glan·din \ˌpräs-tə-ˈglan-dən\ *n* : any of various oxygenated unsaturated fatty acids of animals that perform a variety of hormonelike actions

pros·tate \'präs-ˌtāt\ *n* [NL *prostata*, fr. Gk *prostatēs*, fr. *proïstanai* to put in front] : PROSTATE GLAND — **pros·tat·ic** \prä-ˈsta-tik\ *adj*

prostate gland *n* : a glandular body about the base of the male urethra that produces a secretion which is a major

---

part of the fluid ejaculated during an orgasm

pros·ta·ti·tis \ˌpräs-tə-ˈtī-təs\ *n* : inflammation of the prostate gland

pros·the·sis \präs-ˈthē-səs, ˈpräs-thə-\ *n, pl* **-the·ses** \-ˌsēz\ : an artificial replacement for a missing body part — **pros·thet·ic** \präs-ˈthe-tik\ *adj*

pros·thet·ics \-ˈthe-tiks\ *n pl* : the surgical or dental specialty concerned with the design, construction, and fitting of prostheses

¹**pros·ti·tute** \'präs-tə-ˌtüt, -ˌtyüt\ *vb* **-tut·ed; -tut·ing** 1 : to offer indiscriminately for sexual activity esp. for money 2 : to devote to corrupt or unworthy purposes — **pros·ti·tu·tion** \ˌpräs-tə-ˈtü-shən, -ˈtyü-\ *n*

²**prostitute** *n* : one who engages in sexual activities for money

¹**pros·trate** \'prä-ˌstrāt\ *adj* 1 : stretched out with face on the ground in adoration or submission 2 : lying flat 3 : completely overcome ⟨∼ with a cold⟩

²**prostrate** *vb* **pros·trat·ed; pros·trat·ing** 1 : to throw or put into a prostrate position 2 : to reduce to a weak or powerless condition — **pros·tra·tion** \prä-ˈstrā-shən\ *n*

prosy \'prō-zē\ *adj* **pros·i·er; -est** 1 : PROSAIC, ORDINARY 2 : TEDIOUS

Prot *abbr* Protestant

prot·ac·tin·i·um \ˌprō-ˌtak-ˈti-nē-əm\ *n* : a metallic radioactive chemical element of relatively short life

pro·tag·o·nist \prō-ˈta-gə-nist\ *n* 1 : the principal character in a drama or story 2 : a leader or supporter of a cause

pro·te·an \'prō-tē-ən\ *adj* : able to assume different shapes or roles

pro·tect \prə-ˈtekt\ *vb* : to shield from injury : GUARD

pro·tec·tion \prə-ˈtek-shən\ *n* 1 : the act of protecting : the state of being protected 2 : one that protects ⟨wear a helmet as a ∼⟩ 3 : the supervision or support of one that is smaller and weaker 4 : the freeing of producers from foreign competition in their home market by high duties on foreign competitive goods — **pro·tec·tive** \-ˈtek-tiv\ *adj*

pro·tec·tion·ist \-shə-nist\ *n* : an advocate of government economic protection for domestic producers through restrictions on foreign competitors — **pro·tec·tion·ism** \-shə-ˌni-zəm\ *n*

pro·tec·tor \prə-ˈtek-tər\ *n* 1 : one that protects : GUARDIAN 2 : a device used to prevent injury : GUARD 3 : REGENT 1

pro·tec·tor·ate \-tə-rət\ *n* 1 : government by a protector 2 : the relationship of superior authority assumed by one state over a dependent one; *also* : the dependent political unit in such a relationship

pro·té·gé \'prō-tə-ˌzhā\ *n* [F] : one who is protected, trained, or guided by an influential person

pro·tein \'prō-ˌtēn\ *n* [F *protéine*, fr. LGk *prōteios* primary, fr. Gk *prōtos* first] : any of various complex nitrogen-containing substances that consist of chains of amino acids, are present in all living cells, and are an essential part of the human diet

pro tem \prō-'tem\ adv : PRO TEMPORE

pro tem·po·re \prō-'tem-pə-rē\ adv [L] : for the time being

Pro·te·ro·zo·ic \ˌprä-tə-rə-'zō-ik, ˌprō-\ adj : of, relating to, or being the eon of geologic history between the Archean and the Phanerozoic — **Proterozoic** n

¹**pro·test** \'prō-ˌtest\ n 1 : the act of protesting; esp : an organized public demonstration of disapproval 2 : a complaint or objection against an idea, an act, or a course of action

²**pro·test** \prō-'test\ vb 1 : to assert positively : make solemn declaration of ⟨~s his innocence⟩ 2 : to object strongly : make a protest against ⟨~ a ruling⟩ — **pro·tes·ta·tion** \ˌprä-təs-'tā-shən\ n — **pro·test·er** or **pro·tes·tor** \-tər\ n

Prot·es·tant \'prä-təs-tənt, 3 also prə-'tes-\ n 1 : a member or adherent of one of the Christian churches deriving from the Reformation 2 : a Christian not of a Catholic or Orthodox church 3 not cap : one who makes a protest — **Prot·es·tant·ism** \'prä-təs-tən-ˌti-zəm\ n

pro·tha·la·mi·on \ˌprō-thə-'lā-mē-ən\ or **pro·tha·la·mi·um** \-mē-əm\ n, pl -mia \-mē-ə\ : a song in celebration of a marriage

pro·to·col \'prō-tə-ˌkȯl\ n [MF prothocole, fr. ML protocollum, fr. LGk prōtokollon first sheet of a papyrus roll bearing data of manufacture, fr. Gk prōtos first + kollan to glue together, fr. kolla glue] 1 : an original draft or record 2 : a preliminary memorandum of diplomatic negotiation 3 : a code of diplomatic or military etiquette 4 : a set of conventions for formatting data in an electronic communications system

pro·ton \'prō-ˌtän\ n [Gk prōton, neut. of prōtos first] : a positively charged atomic particle present in all atomic nuclei — **pro·ton·ic** \-'tä-nik\ adj

pro·to·plasm \'prō-tə-ˌpla-zəm\ n : the complex colloidal largely protein substance of living plant and animal cells — **pro·to·plas·mic** \ˌprō-tə-'plaz-mik\ adj

pro·to·type \'prō-tə-ˌtīp\ n : an original model : ARCHETYPE

pro·to·zo·an \ˌprō-tə-'zō-ən\ n : any of a phylum or subkingdom of unicellular lower invertebrate animals that include some pathogenic parasites of humans and domestic animals — **protozoan** adj

pro·tract \prō-'trakt\ vb : to prolong in time or space ✦ Synonyms EXTEND, LENGTHEN, ELONGATE, STRETCH

pro·trac·tor \-'trak-tər\ n : an instrument for drawing and measuring angles

pro·trude \prō-'trüd\ vb **pro·trud·ed; pro·trud·ing** : to stick out or cause to stick out : jut out — **pro·tru·sion** \-'trü-zhən\ n

pro·tu·ber·ance \prō-'tü-bə-rəns, -'tyü-\ n : something that protrudes

pro·tu·ber·ant \-rənt\ adj : extending beyond the surrounding surface in a bulge

proud \'praud\ adj 1 : having or showing excessive self-esteem : HAUGHTY 2 : highly pleased : EXULTANT 3 : having proper self-respect ⟨too ~ to beg⟩ 4 : GLORIOUS ⟨a ~ occasion⟩ 5 : SPIRITED ⟨a ~ steed⟩ ✦ Synonyms ARROGANT, INSOLENT, OVERBEARING, DISDAINFUL — **proud·ly** adv

prov abbr 1 province; provincial 2 provisional

Prov abbr Proverbs

prove \'prüv\ vb **proved; proved** or **prov·en** \'prü-vən\; **prov·ing** 1 : to test by experiment or trial 2 : to establish the truth of by argument or evidence 3 : to show to be correct, valid, or genuine 4 : to turn out esp. after trial or test ⟨the car proved to be a good choice⟩ — **prov·able** \'prü-və-bəl\ adj

prov·e·nance \'prä-və-nəns\ n : ORIGIN, SOURCE

Pro·ven·çal \ˌprō-ˌvän-'säl, ˌprä-vən-\ n 1 : a native or inhabitant of Provence 2 : OCCITAN — **Provençal** adj

prov·en·der \'prä-vən-dər\ n 1 : dry food for domestic animals : FEED 2 : FOOD, VICTUALS

pro·ve·nience \prə-'vē-nyəns\ n : ORIGIN, SOURCE

prov·erb \'prä-ˌvərb\ n : a pithy popular saying : ADAGE

pro·ver·bi·al \prə-'vər-bē-əl\ adj 1 : of, relating to, or resembling a proverb 2 : commonly spoken of

Proverbs n — see BIBLE table

pro·vide \prə-'vīd\ vb **pro·vid·ed; pro·vid·ing** [ME, fr. L providēre, lit., to see ahead, fr. pro- forward + vidēre to see] 1 : to take measures beforehand ⟨~ against inflation⟩ 2 : to make a proviso or stipulation 3 : to supply what is needed ⟨~ for a family⟩ 4 : EQUIP 5 : to supply for use : YIELD — **pro·vid·er** n

pro·vid·ed conj : on condition that : IF

prov·i·dence \'prä-və-dəns\ n 1 often cap : divine guidance or care 2 cap : GOD 1 3 : the quality or state of being provident

prov·i·dent \-dənt\ adj 1 : making provision for the future : PRUDENT 2 : FRUGAL — **prov·i·dent·ly** adv

prov·i·den·tial \ˌprä-və-'den-chəl\ adj 1 : of, relating to, or determined by Providence 2 : OPPORTUNE, LUCKY

providing conj : PROVIDED

prov·ince \'prä-vəns\ n 1 : an administrative district or division of a country 2 pl : all of a country except the metropolises 3 : proper business or scope : SPHERE

pro·vin·cial \prə-'vin-chəl\ adj 1 : of or relating to a province 2 : limited in outlook : NARROW ⟨~ ideas⟩ — **pro·vin·cial·ism** \-chə-ˌli-zəm\ n

proving ground n : a place for scientific experimentation or testing

¹**pro·vi·sion** \prə-'vi-zhən\ n 1 : the act or process of providing; also : a measure taken beforehand 2 : a stock of needed supplies; esp : a stock of food — usu. used in pl. 3 : PROVISO

²**provision** *vb* : to supply with provisions

pro·vi·sion·al \-'vi-zhə-nəl\ *adj* : provided for a temporary need : CONDITIONAL — **pro·vi·sion·al·ly** *adv*

pro·vi·so \prə-'vī-zō\ *n, pl* **-sos** *also* **-soes** [ME, fr. ML *proviso quod* provided that] : an article or clause that introduces a condition : STIPULATION

pro·vo·ca·teur \prō-ˌvä-kə-'tər\ *n* : one who provokes

prov·o·ca·tion \ˌprä-və-'kā-shən\ *n* 1 : the act of provoking 2 : something that provokes

pro·voc·a·tive \prə-'vä-kə-tiv\ *adj* : serving to provoke or excite

pro·voke \prə-'vōk\ *vb* **pro·voked**; **pro·vok·ing** 1 : to incite to anger : INCENSE 2 : to call forth : EVOKE ⟨a remark that *provoked* laughter⟩ 3 : to stir up on purpose ⟨~ an argument⟩ ♦ *Synonyms* IRRITATE, EXASPERATE, AGGRAVATE, INFLAME, RILE, PIQUE — **pro·vok·er** *n*

pro·vo·lo·ne \ˌprō-və-'lō-nē\ *n* : a usu. firm pliant often smoked Italian cheese

pro·vost \'prō-ˌvōst, 'prä-vəst\ *n* : a high official : DIGNITARY; *esp* : a high-ranking university administrative officer

pro·vost mar·shal \'prō-ˌvō-'mär-shəl\ *n* : an officer who supervises the military police of a command

prow \'praù\ *n* : the bow of a ship

prow·ess \'praù-əs\ *n* 1 : military valor and skill 2 : extraordinary ability

prowl \'praùl\ *vb* : to roam about stealthily — **prowl** *n* — **prowl·er** *n*

prox·i·mal \'präk-sə-məl\ *adj* 1 : next to or nearest the point of attachment or origin; *esp* : located toward the center of the body 2 : of, relating to, or being the mesial and distal surfaces of a tooth — **prox·i·mal·ly** *adv*

prox·i·mate \'präk-sə-mət\ *adj* 1 : DIRECT ⟨the ~ cause⟩ 2 : very near

prox·im·i·ty \präk-'si-mə-tē\ *n* : NEARNESS

prox·i·mo \'präk-sə-ˌmō\ *adj* [L *proximo mense* in the next month] : of or occurring in the next month after the present

proxy \'präk-sē\ *n, pl* **prox·ies** [ME *proxi, procucie*, alter. of *procuracie*, fr. AF, fr. ML *procuratia*, alter. of L *procuratio* appointment of another as an agent, fr. *procurare* to take care of] : the authority or power to act for another; *also* : a document giving such authorization — **proxy** *adj*

prude \'prüd\ *n* : a person who shows or affects extreme modesty — **prud·ery** \'prü-də-rē\ *n* — **prud·ish** *adj* — **prud·ish·ly** *adv*

pru·dent \'prü-dᵊnt\ *adj* 1 : shrewd in the management of practical affairs 2 : CAUTIOUS, DISCREET 3 : PROVIDENT, FRUGAL ♦ *Synonyms* JUDICIOUS, FORESIGHTED, SENSIBLE, SANE — **pru·dence** \-dᵊns\ *n* — **pru·den·tial** \prü-'den-chəl\ *adj* — **pru·dent·ly** *adv*

¹**prune** \'prün\ *n* : a dried plum

²**prune** *vb* **pruned**; **prun·ing** : to cut off unwanted parts (as of a tree)

pru·ri·ent \'prùr-ē-ənt\ *adj* : LASCIVIOUS; *also* : exciting to lasciviousness — **pru·ri·ence** \-ē-əns\ *n*

¹**pry** \'prī\ *vb* **pried**; **pry·ing** : to look closely or inquisitively; *esp* : SNOOP

²**pry** *vb* **pried**; **pry·ing** 1 : to raise, move, or pull apart with a pry or lever 2 : to detach or open with difficulty

³**pry** *n* : a tool for prying

Ps *or* **Psa** *abbr* Psalms

PS *abbr* 1 [L *postscriptum*] postscript 2 public school

PSA *abbr* public service announcement

psalm \'säm, 'sälm\ *n, often cap* [ME, fr. OE *psealm*, fr. LL *psalmus*, fr. Gk *psalmos*, lit., twanging of a harp, fr. *psallein* to pluck, play a stringed instrument] : a sacred song or poem; *esp* : one of the hymns collected in the Book of Psalms — **psalm·ist** *n*

psalm·o·dy \'sä-mə-dē, 'säl-\ *n* : the singing of psalms in worship

Psalms *n* — see BIBLE table

Psal·ter \'sòl-tər\ *n* : the Book of Psalms; *also* : a collection of the Psalms arranged for devotional use

pseud *abbr* pseudonym; pseudonymous

pseu·do \'sü-dō\ *adj* : SPURIOUS, SHAM

pseu·do·nym \'sü-də-ˌnim\ *n* : a fictitious name — **pseu·don·y·mous** \sü-'dä-nə-məs\ *adj*

pseu·do·sci·ence \ˌsü-dō-'sī-əns\ *n* : a system of theories, assumptions, and methods erroneously regarded as scientific — **pseu·do·sci·en·tif·ic** \-ˌsī-ən-'ti-fik\ *adj*

PSG *abbr* platoon sergeant

¹**psi** \'sī, 'psī\ *n* : the 23d letter of the Greek alphabet — Ψ or ψ

²**psi** *abbr* pounds per square inch

psit·ta·co·sis \ˌsi-tə-'kō-səs\ *n* : an infectious disease of birds marked by diarrhea and wasting and transmissible to humans

pso·ri·a·sis \sə-'rī-ə-səs\ *n* : a chronic skin disease characterized by red patches covered with white scales

PST *abbr* Pacific standard time

¹**psych** *or* **psyche** \'sīk\ *vb* **psyched**; **psych·ing** 1 : OUTWIT, OUTGUESS; *also* : to analyze beforehand 2 : INTIMIDATE; *also* : to prepare oneself psychologically ⟨get *psyched* up for the game⟩

²**psych** *abbr* psychology

psy·che \'sī-kē\ *n* : SOUL, PERSONALITY; *also* : MIND

psy·che·del·ic \ˌsī-kə-'de-lik\ *adj* 1 : of, relating to, or causing abnormal psychic effects ⟨~ drugs⟩ 2 : relating to the taking of psychedelic drugs ⟨~ experience⟩ 3 : imitating, suggestive of, or reproducing the effects of psychedelic drugs ⟨~ art⟩ ⟨~ colors⟩ — **psyche·delic** *n* — **psy·che·del·i·cal·ly** \-li-k(ə-)lē\ *adv*

psy·chi·a·try \sə-'kī-ə-trē, sī-\ *n* [prob. fr. F *psychiatrie*, fr. *psychiatre* psychiatrist, fr. Gk *psychē* breath, soul + *iatros* physician] : a branch of medicine dealing with mental, emotional, and behavioral disorders — **psy·chi·at·ric** \ˌsī-kē-'a-trik\ *adj* — **psy·chi·a·trist** \sə-'kī-ə-trist, sī-\ *n*

¹psy·chic \'sī-kik\ *also* psy·chi·cal \-ki-kəl\ *adj* 1 : of or relating to the psyche 2 : lying outside the sphere of physical science 3 : sensitive to nonphysical or supernatural forces — psy·chi·cal·ly \-k(ə-)lē\ *adv*

²psychic *n* : a person apparently sensitive to nonphysical forces; *also* : MEDIUM 6

psy·cho \'sī-kō\ *n, pl* psychos : a mentally disturbed person — psycho *adj*

psy·cho·ac·tive \,sī-kō-'ak-tiv\ *adj* : affecting the mind or behavior

psy·cho·anal·y·sis \,sī-kō-ə-'na-lə-səs\ *n* : a method of dealing with psychic disorders by having the patient talk freely about early childhood and dreams — psy·cho·an·a·lyst \-'a-nə-list\ *n* — psy·cho·an·a·lyt·ic \-,a-nə-'li-tik\ *adj* — psy·cho·an·a·lyze \-'a-nə-,līz\ *vb*

psy·cho·bab·ble \'sī-kō-,ba-bəl\ *n* : psychological jargon esp. when used in a trite or simplistic manner

psy·cho·dra·ma \,sī-kə-'drä-mə, -'dra-\ *n* 1 : an extemporized dramatization designed to afford catharsis for one or more of the participants from whose life the plot is taken 2 : a dramatic event or story with psychological overtones

psy·cho·gen·ic \-'je-nik\ *adj* : originating in the mind or in mental or emotional conflict

psy·cho·graph·ics \,sī-kə-'gra-fiks\ *n sing or pl* : market research or statistics classifying population groups according to psychological variables

psychol *abbr* psychologist; psychology

psy·chol·o·gy \sī-'kä-lə-jē\ *n, pl* -gies 1 : the science of mind and behavior 2 : the mental and behavioral characteristics of an individual or group — psy·cho·log·i·cal \,sī-kə-'lä-ji-kəl\ *adj* — psy·cho·log·i·cal·ly \-ji-k(ə-)lē\ *adv* — psy·chol·o·gist \sī-'kä-lə-jist\ *n*

psy·cho·path \'sī-kō-,path\ *n* : a mentally ill or unstable person; *esp* : a person who engages in antisocial behavior and exhibits a pervasive disregard for the rights, feelings, and safety of others — psy·cho·path·ic \,sī-kə-'pa-thik\ *adj*

psy·cho·sex·u·al \,sī-kō-'sek-shə-wəl\ *adj* 1 : of or relating to the mental, emotional, and behavioral aspects of sexual development 2 : of or relating to the physiological psychology of sex

psy·cho·sis \sī-'kō-səs\ *n, pl* -cho·ses \-,sēz\ : a serious mental illness (as schizophrenia) marked by loss of or greatly lessened ability to test whether what one is thinking and feeling about the real world is really true

psy·cho·so·cial \,sī-kō-'sō-shəl\ *adj* 1 : involving both psychological and social aspects 2 : relating social conditions to mental health

psy·cho·so·mat·ic \,sī-kō-sə-'ma-tik\ *adj* : of, relating to, involving, or concerned with bodily symptoms caused by mental or emotional disturbance

psy·cho·ther·a·py \,sī-kō-'ther-ə-pē\ *n* : treatment of mental or emotional disorder or of related bodily ills by psychologi-

cal means — psy·cho·ther·a·pist \-pist\ *n*

psy·chot·ic \sī-'kä-tik\ *adj* : of or relating to psychosis 〈~ behavior〉 〈a ~ patient〉 — psychotic *n*

psy·cho·tro·pic \,sī-kə-'trō-pik\ *adj* : acting on the mind 〈~ drugs〉

pt *abbr* 1 part 2 payment 3 pint 4 point 5 port

Pt *symbol* platinum

PT *abbr* 1 Pacific time 2 part-time 3 physical therapy 4 physical training

PTA *abbr* Parent-Teacher Association

ptar·mi·gan \'tär-mi-gən\ *n, pl* -gan *or* -gans : any of various grouses of northern regions with completely feathered feet

PT boat \(,)pē-'tē-\ *n* [*patrol torpedo*] : a small fast patrol craft usu. armed with torpedos

pte *abbr, Brit* private

ptg *abbr* printing

PTO *abbr* 1 Parent-Teacher Organization 2 please turn over

pto·maine \'tō-,mān\ *n* : any of various chemical substances formed by bacteria in decaying matter (as meat) and including a few poisonous ones

Pu *symbol* plutonium

¹pub \'pəb\ *n* 1 *chiefly Brit* : PUBLIC HOUSE 2 : TAVERN

²pub *abbr* 1 public 2 publication 3 published; publisher; publishing

pu·ber·ty \'pyü-bər-tē\ *n* : the condition of being or period of becoming first capable of reproducing sexually — pu·ber·tal \-bər-t°l\ *adj*

pu·bes \'pyü-bēz\ *n, pl* pubes [NL, fr. L, manhood, body hair, pubic region] 1 : the hair that appears upon the lower middle region of the abdomen at puberty 2 : the pubic region

pu·bes·cence \pyü-'be-s°ns\ *n* 1 : the quality or state of being pubescent 2 : a pubescent covering or surface

pu·bes·cent \-s°nt\ *adj* 1 : arriving at or having reached puberty 2 : covered with fine soft short hairs

pu·bic \'pyü-bik\ *adj* : of, relating to, or situated near the pubes or the pubis

pu·bis \'pyü-bəs\ *n, pl* pu·bes \-bēz\ : the ventral and anterior of the three principal bones composing either half of the pelvis

publ *abbr* 1 publication 2 published; publisher

¹pub·lic \'pə-blik\ *adj* 1 : exposed to general view 〈the story became ~〉 2 : of, relating to, or affecting the people as a whole 〈~ opinion〉 3 : CIVIC, GOVERNMENTAL 〈~ expenditures〉 4 : of, relating to, or serving the community 〈~ officials〉 5 : not private : SOCIAL 〈~ morality〉 6 : open to all 〈~ library〉 7 : well known : PROMINENT 〈~ figures〉 8 : supported by public funds and public contributions rather than by income from commercials — pub·lic·ly *adv*

²public *n* 1 : the people as a whole : POPULACE 2 : a group of people having common interests

pub·li·can \'pə-bli-kən\ *n,* 1 : a Jewish

tax collector for the ancient Romans **2** *chiefly Brit* : the licensee of a pub

pub·li·ca·tion \ˌpə-blə-'kā-shən\ *n* **1** : the act or process of publishing **2** : a published work

public house *n*, **1** : INN **2** *chiefly Brit* : a licensed saloon or bar

pub·li·cise *Brit var of* PUBLICIZE

pub·li·cist \'pə-blə-sist\ *n* : one that publicizes; *esp* : PRESS AGENT

pub·lic·i·ty \(ˌ)pə-'bli-sə-tē\ *n* **1** : information with news value issued to gain public attention or support **2** : public attention or acclaim

pub·li·cize \'pə-blə-ˌsīz\ *vb* **-cized; -ciz·ing** : to bring to public attention : ADVERTISE

pub·lic–key \'pə-blik-'kē\ *n* : the publicly shared element of a code usable only to encode messages

public relations *n sing or pl* : the business of fostering public goodwill toward a person, firm, or institution; *also* : the degree of goodwill and understanding achieved

public school *n* **1** : an endowed secondary boarding school in Great Britain offering a classical curriculum and preparation for the universities or public service **2** : a free tax-supported school controlled by a local governmental authority

public–spirited *adj* : motivated by devotion to the general or national welfare

public works *n pl* : works (as schools or highways) constructed with public funds for public use

pub·lish \'pə-blish\ *vb* **1** : to make generally known : announce publicly **2** : to produce or release literature, information, musical scores or sometimes recordings, or art for sale to the public — **pub·lish·er** *n*

¹**puck** \'pək\ *n* : a mischievous sprite — **puck·ish** *adj* — **puck·ish·ly** *adv*

²**puck** *n* : a disk used in ice hockey

¹**puck·er** \'pə-kər\ *vb* : to contract into folds or wrinkles

²**pucker** *n* : FOLD, WRINKLE

pud·ding \'pu̇-diŋ\ *n* : a soft, spongy, or thick creamy dessert

pud·dle \'pə-dᵊl\ *n* : a very small pool of usu. dirty or muddy water

pu·den·dum \pyu̇-'den-dəm\ *n, pl* **-da** \-də\ [NL, fr. L *pudēre* to be ashamed] : the human external genital organs esp. of a woman

pudgy \'pə-jē\ *adj* **pudg·i·er; -est** : being short and plump : CHUBBY

pueb·lo \'pwe-blō, pü-'e-\ *n, pl* **-los** [Sp, village, lit., people, fr. L *populus*] **1** : an American Indian village of Arizona or New Mexico that consists of flat-roofed stone or adobe houses joined in groups sometimes several stories high **2** *cap* : a member of a group of American Indian peoples of the southwestern U.S.

pu·er·ile \'pyu̇-ə-rəl\ *adj* : CHILDISH, SILLY ⟨∼ remarks⟩ — **pu·er·il·i·ty** \ˌpyu̇-ə-'ri-lə-tē\ *n*

pu·er·per·al \pyu̇-'ər-pə-rəl\ *adj* : of, relating to, or occurring during childbirth or the period immediately following ⟨∼ infection⟩ ⟨∼ depression⟩

puerperal fever *n* : an abnormal condition that results from infection of the placental site following childbirth or abortion

¹**puff** \'pəf\ *vb* **1** : to blow in short gusts **2** : PANT **3** : to emit small whiffs or clouds **4** : BLUSTER, BRAG **5** : INFLATE, SWELL **6** : to make proud or conceited **7** : to praise extravagantly

²**puff** *n* **1** : a short discharge (as of air or smoke); *also* : a slight explosive sound accompanying it **2** : a light fluffy pastry **3** : a slight swelling **4** : a fluffy mass; *also* : a small pad for applying cosmetic powder **5** : a laudatory notice or review — **puffy** *adj*

³**puff** *adj* : of, relating to, or designed for promotion or flattery ⟨∼ articles on the new TV series⟩

puff·ball \'pəf-ˌbȯl\ *n* : any of various globe-shaped and often edible fungi

puf·fin \'pə-fən\ *n* : any of several seabirds having a short neck and a deep grooved parti-colored bill

¹**pug** \'pəg\ *n* **1** : any of a breed of small stocky short-haired dogs with a wrinkled face **2** : a close coil of hair

²**pug** *n* : ¹BOXER

pu·gi·lism \'pyü-jə-ˌli-zəm\ *n* : BOXING — **pu·gi·list** \-list\ *n* — **pu·gi·lis·tic** \ˌpyü-jə-'lis-tik\ *adj*

pug·na·cious \ˌpəg-'nā-shəs\ *adj* : having a quarrelsome or combative nature
◆ *Synonyms* BELLIGERENT, BELLICOSE, CONTENTIOUS, TRUCULENT — **pug·nac·i·ty** \-'na-sə-tē\ *n*

puis·sance \'pwi-səns, 'pyü-ə-\ *n* : POWER, STRENGTH — **puis·sant** \-sənt\ *adj*

puke \'pyük\ *vb* **puked; puk·ing** : VOMIT — **puke** *n*

puk·ka \'pə-kə\ *adj* [Hindi *pakkā* cooked, ripe, solid, fr. Skt *pakva*] : GENUINE, AUTHENTIC; *also* : FIRST-CLASS, COMPLETE

pul \'pül\ *n, pl* **puls** \'pülz\ *or* **pul** — see *afghani* at MONEY table

pu·la \'pü-lə, 'pyü-\ *n, pl* **pula** — see MONEY table

pul·chri·tude \'pəl-krə-ˌtüd, -ˌtyüd\ *n* : BEAUTY — **pul·chri·tu·di·nous** \ˌpəl-krə-'tü-dᵊn-əs, -'tyü-\ *adj*

pule \'pyül\ *vb* **puled; pul·ing** : WHINE, WHIMPER

¹**pull** \'pu̇l\ *vb* **1** : to exert force so as to draw (something) toward the force; *also* : MOVE ⟨∼ out of a driveway⟩ **2** : PLUCK; *also* : EXTRACT ⟨∼ a tooth⟩ **3** : STRETCH, STRAIN ⟨∼ a tendon⟩ **4** : to draw apart : TEAR **5** : to make (as a proof) by printing **6** : REMOVE ⟨∼ed the pitcher in the third inning⟩ **7** : DRAW ⟨∼ a gun⟩ **8** : to carry out esp. with daring ⟨∼ a robbery⟩ **9** : PERPETRATE, COMMIT **10** : ATTRACT **11** : to express strong sympathy — **pull·er** *n*

²**pull** *n* **1** : the act or an instance of pulling **2** : the effort expended in moving **3** : ADVANTAGE ⟨had the ∼ of a respected family name⟩; *esp* : special influence **4** : a device for pulling something or for operating by pulling **5** : a force that at-

tracts or compels **6** : an injury from abnormal straining or stretching ⟨a muscle ∼⟩

pull·back \'pủl-,bak\ n : an orderly withdrawal of troops

pull–down adj : appearing below a selected item (as a menu title) on a computer display ⟨a ∼ menu⟩

pul·let \'pủl-lət\ n : a young hen esp. of the domestic chicken when less than a year old

pul·ley \'pủl-lē\ n, pl **pulleys** : a wheel used to transmit power by means of a belt, rope, or chain; esp : one with a grooved rim that forms part of a tackle for hoisting or for changing the direction of a force

Pull·man \'pủl-mən\ n : a railroad passenger car with comfortable furnishings esp. for night travel

pull off vb : to accomplish successfully

pull·out \'pủl-,aủt\ n : PULLBACK

pull·over \'pủl-,ō-vər\ adj : put on by being pulled over the head ⟨∼ sweater⟩ — **pull·over** n

pull–up \'pủl-,əp\ n : CHIN-UP

pull up vb : to bring or come to an often abrupt halt : STOP

pul·mo·nary \'pủl-mə-,ner-ē, 'pəl-\ adj : of, relating to, or carried on by the lungs ⟨the ∼ circulation⟩

pulp \'pəlp\ n **1** : the soft juicy or fleshy part of a fruit or vegetable **2** : a soft moist mass **3** : the soft sensitive tissue that fills the central cavity of a tooth **4** : a material (as from wood) used in making paper **5** : a magazine using cheap paper and often dealing with sensational material — **pulpy** adj

pul·pit \'pủl-,pit\ n : a raised platform or high reading desk used in preaching or conducting a worship service

pulp·wood \'pəlp-,wủd\ n : wood used in making pulp for paper

pul·sar \'pəl-,sär\ n : a celestial source of pulsating electromagnetic radiation (as radio waves)

pul·sate \'pəl-,sāt\ vb **pul·sat·ed; pul·sat·ing** : to expand and contract rhythmically : BEAT — **pul·sa·tion** \,pəl-'sā-shən\ n

pulse \'pəls\ n **1** : the regular throbbing in the arteries caused by the contractions of the heart **2** : rhythmical beating, vibrating, or sounding **3** : a brief change in electrical current or voltage — **pulse** vb

pul·ver·ise Brit var of PULVERIZE

pul·ver·ize \'pəl-və-,rīz\ vb **-ized; -iz·ing** **1** : to reduce (as by crushing or grinding) or be reduced to very small particles **2** : DEMOLISH

pu·ma \'pü-mə, 'pyü-\ n, pl **pumas** also **puma** [Sp, fr. Quechua] : COUGAR

pum·ice \'pə-məs\ n : a light porous volcanic glass used esp. for smoothing and polishing

pum·mel \'pə-məl\ vb **-meled** also **-melled; -mel·ing** also **-mel·ling** : POUND, BEAT

¹pump \'pəmp\ n : a device for raising, transferring, or compressing fluids esp. by suction or pressure

²pump vb **1** : to raise (as water) with a pump **2** : to draw fluid from with a pump; also : to fill by means of a pump ⟨∼ up a tire⟩ **3** : to force or propel in the manner of a pump — **pump·er** n

³pump n : a low shoe that grips the foot chiefly at the toe and heel

pumped \'pəmpt\ adj : filled with energetic excitement and enthusiasm

pum·per·nick·el \'pəm-pər-,ni-kəl\ n : a dark rye bread

pump·kin \'pəmp-kən, 'pəŋ-kən\ n : the large usu. orange fruit of a vine of the gourd family that is widely used as food; also : this vine

pun \'pən\ n : the humorous use of a word in a way that suggests two or more interpretations — **pun** vb

¹punch \'pənch\ n : a tool for piercing, stamping, cutting, or forming

²punch vb **1** : PROD, POKE; also : DRIVE, HERD ⟨∼ing cattle⟩ **2** : to strike with the fist **3** : to emboss, perforate, or make with a punch **4** : to operate, produce, or enter (as data) by or as if by punching — **punch·er** n

³punch n **1** : a quick blow with or as if with the fist **2** : effective energy or forcefulness

⁴punch n [perh. fr. Hindi pāc five, fr. Skt pañca; fr. the number of ingredients] : a drink usu. composed of wine or alcoholic liquor and nonalcoholic beverages; also : a drink composed of nonalcoholic beverages

punch card n : a card with holes punched in particular positions to represent data

punch–drunk \'pənch-,drəŋk\ adj **1** : suffering from brain injury resulting from repeated head blows received in boxing **2** : DAZED, CONFUSED

pun·cheon \'pən-chən\ n : a large cask

punch line n : the sentence or phrase in a joke that makes the point

punch list n : a list of tasks to be completed at the end of a project

punchy \'pən-chē\ adj **punch·i·er; -est** **1** : having punch : FORCEFUL **2** : DAZED, CONFUSED **3** : VIVID, VIBRANT ⟨∼ graphics⟩

punc·til·io \,pəŋk-'ti-lē-,ō\ n, pl **-i·os** **1** : a nice detail of conduct in a ceremony or in observance of a code **2** : careful observance of forms (as in social conduct)

punc·til·i·ous \,pəŋk-'ti-lē-əs\ adj : marked by precise accordance with codes or conventions ♦ **Synonyms** METICULOUS, SCRUPULOUS, CAREFUL, PUNCTUAL

punc·tu·al \'pəŋk-chə-wəl\ adj : being on time : PROMPT — **punc·tu·al·i·ty** \,pəŋk-chə-'wa-lə-tē\ n — **punc·tu·al·ly** adv

punc·tu·ate \'pəŋk-chə-,wāt\ vb **-at·ed; -at·ing** **1** : to mark or divide (written matter) with punctuation marks **2** : to break into at intervals **3** : EMPHASIZE

punc·tu·a·tion \,pəŋk-chə-'wā-shən\ n : the act, practice, or system of inserting standardized marks in written matter to clarify the meaning and separate structural units

¹punc·ture \'pəŋk-chər\ n　**1** : an act of puncturing　**2** : a small hole or wound made by puncturing

²puncture vb **punc·tured**; **punc·tur·ing**　**1** : to make a hole in : PIERCE　**2** : to make useless as if by a puncture

pun·dit \'pən-dət\ n [Hindi paṇḍit, fr. Skt paṇḍita, fr. paṇḍita learned]　**1** : a learned person : TEACHER　**2** : AUTHORITY, CRITIC

pun·dit·oc·ra·cy \,pən-dət-'ä-krə-sē\ n, pl **-cies** : a group of powerful and influential political commentators

pun·gent \'pən-jənt\ adj　**1** : having a sharp incisive quality : CAUSTIC ⟨a ~ editorial⟩　**2** : causing a sharp, intense, or irritating sensation (as of taste or smell); esp : ACRID ⟨a ~ odor⟩ — **pun·gen·cy** \-jən-sē\ n — **pun·gent·ly** adv

pun·ish \'pə-nish\ vb　**1** : to impose a penalty on for a fault or crime ⟨~ an offender⟩　**2** : to inflict a penalty for ⟨~ treason with death⟩　**3** : to inflict injury on : HURT ♦ **Synonyms** CHASTISE, CASTIGATE, CHASTEN, DISCIPLINE, CORRECT — **pun·ish·able** adj

pun·ish·ment n　**1** : retributive suffering, pain, or loss : PENALTY　**2** : rough treatment

pu·ni·tive \'pyü-nə-tiv\ adj : inflicting, involving, or aiming at punishment

¹punk \'pəŋk\ n　**1** : a young inexperienced person　**2** : a petty hoodlum

²punk adj : very poor : INFERIOR

³punk n : dry crumbly wood useful for tinder; also : a substance made from fungi for use as tinder

pun·ster \'pən-stər\ n : one who is given to punning

¹punt \'pənt\ n : a long narrow flat-bottomed boat with square ends

²punt vb : to propel (as a punt) with a pole

³punt vb : to kick a football or soccer ball dropped from the hands before it touches the ground

⁴punt n : the act or an instance of punting a ball

pu·ny \'pyü-nē\ adj **pu·ni·er**; **-est** [AF puisné younger, weakly, lit., born afterward, fr. puis afterward (fr. L post) + né born, fr. L natus] : slight in power, size, or importance : WEAK

pup \'pəp\ n : a young dog; also : one of the young of some other animals

pu·pa \'pyü-pə\ n, pl **pu·pae** \-(,)pē\ or **pupas** [NL, fr. L pupa doll] : a form of some insects (as a bee, moth, or beetle) between the larva and the adult that usu. has a protective covering (as a cocoon) — **pu·pal** \-pəl\ adj

¹pu·pil \'pyü-pəl\ n　**1** : a child or young person in school or in the charge of a tutor　**2** : DISCIPLE

²pupil n : the dark central opening of the iris of the eye

pup·pet \'pə-pət\ n [ME popet youth, doll, fr. MF poupette, ultim. fr. L pupa doll]　**1** : a small figure of a person or animal moved by hand or by strings or wires　**2**

: DOLL　**3** : one whose acts are controlled by an outside force or influence

pup·pe·teer \,pə-pə-'tir\ n : one who manipulates puppets

pup·py \'pə-pē\ n, pl **puppies** : a young domestic dog

pu·pu \'pü-,pü\ n : an Asian dish consisting of a variety of foods

pur·blind \'pər-,blīnd\ adj　**1** : partly blind　**2** : lacking in insight : OBTUSE

¹pur·chase \'pər-chəs\ vb **pur·chased**; **pur·chas·ing** : to obtain by paying money or its equivalent : BUY — **pur·chas·able** \-chə-sə-bəl\ adj — **pur·chas·er** n

²purchase n　**1** : an act or instance of purchasing　**2** : something purchased　**3** : a secure hold or grasp; also : advantageous leverage

pur·dah \'pər-də\ n : seclusion of women from public observation among Muslims and some Hindus esp. in India; also : a state of seclusion

pure \'pyur\ adj **pur·er**; **pur·est**　**1** : unmixed with any other matter : free from taint ⟨~ gold⟩ ⟨~ water⟩　**2** : SHEER, ABSOLUTE ⟨~ nonsense⟩　**3** : ABSTRACT, THEORETICAL ⟨~ mathematics⟩　**4** : free from what vitiates, weakens, or pollutes ⟨speaks a ~ French⟩　**5** : free from moral fault : INNOCENT　**6** : CHASTE, CONTINENT — **pure·ly** adv

pure–blood·ed \-,bləd-əd\ or **pure–blood** \-,bləd\ adj : FULL-BLOODED — **pure·blood** n

pure·bred \-'bred\ adj : bred from members of a recognized breed, strain, or kind without crossbreeding over many generations — **pure·bred** \-,bred\ n

¹pu·ree \pyu̇-'rā, -'rē\ n [F purée, fr. MF, fr. fem. of puré, pp. of purer to purify, strain, fr. L purare to purify] : a paste or thick liquid suspension usu. made from finely ground cooked food; also : a thick soup made of pureed vegetables

²puree vb **pu·reed**; **pu·ree·ing** : to make a puree of

pur·ga·tion \,pər-'gā-shən\ n : the act or result of purging

¹pur·ga·tive \'pər-gə-tiv\ adj : purging or tending to purge

²purgative n : a strong laxative : CATHARTIC

pur·ga·to·ry \'pər-gə-,tȯr-ē\ n, pl **-ries**　**1** : an intermediate state after death for expiatory purification　**2** : a place or state of temporary punishment — **pur·ga·tor·i·al** \,pər-gə-'tȯr-ē-əl\ adj

¹purge \'pərj\ vb **purged**; **purg·ing**　**1** : to cleanse or purify esp. from sin　**2** : to have or cause strong and usu. repeated emptying of the bowels　**3** : to get rid of ⟨the leaders had been purged⟩

²purge n　**1** : something that purges; esp : PURGATIVE　**2** : an act or result of purging; esp : a ridding of persons regarded as treacherous or disloyal

pu·ri·fy \'pyur-ə-,fī\ vb **-fied**; **-fy·ing** : to make or become pure — **pu·ri·fi·ca·tion** \,pyur-ə-fə-'kā-shən\ n — **pu·ri·fi·ca·to·ry** \pyur-'i-fi-kə-,tȯr-ē\ adj — **pu·ri·fi·er** n

Pu·rim \'pur-(,)im\ *n* : a Jewish holiday celebrated in February or March in commemoration of the deliverance of the Jews from the massacre plotted by Haman

pu·rine \'pyur-,ēn\ *n* : any of a group of bases including several (as adenine or guanine) that are constituents of DNA or RNA

pur·ism \'pyur-,i-zəm\ *n* : rigid adherence to or insistence on purity or nicety esp. in use of words — **pur·ist** \-ist\ *n* — **pu·ris·tic** \pyu-'ris-tik\ *adj*

pu·ri·tan \'pyur-ə-tən\ *n* **1** *cap* : a member of a 16th and 17th century Protestant group in England and New England opposing the ceremonies and government of the Church of England **2** : one who practices or preaches a stricter or professedly purer moral code than that which prevails — **pu·ri·tan·i·cal** \,pyur-ə-'ta-ni-kəl\ *adj* — **pu·ri·tan·i·cal·ly** *adv*

pu·ri·ty \'pyur-ə-tē\ *n* : the quality or state of being pure

¹**purl** \'pərl\ *n* : a stitch in knitting

²**purl** *vb* : to knit in purl stitch

³**purl** *n* : a gentle murmur or movement (as of purling water)

⁴**purl** *vb* **1** : EDDY, SWIRL **2** : to make a soft murmuring sound

pur·lieu \'pər-lü, 'pərl-yü\ *n* **1** : an outlying district : SUBURB **2** *pl* : ENVIRONS

pur·loin \(,)pər-'loin, 'pər-,loin\ *vb* : STEAL, FILCH

¹**pur·ple** \'pər-pəl\ *adj* **pur·pler; pur·plest 1** : of the color purple **2** : highly rhetorical ⟨a ~ passage⟩ **3** : PROFANE ⟨~ language⟩ — **pur·plish** *adj*

²**purple** *n* **1** : a bluish red color **2** : a purple robe emblematic esp. of regal rank or authority

¹**pur·port** \'pər-,pōrt, -,port\ *n* [ME, fr. AF, content, tenor, fr. *purporter* to carry, mean, purport, fr. *pur-* thoroughly + *porter* to carry] : meaning conveyed or implied; *also* : GIST

²**pur·port** \(,)pər-'pōrt\ *vb* : to convey or profess outwardly as the meaning or intention : CLAIM — **pur·port·ed·ly** \-'pōr-təd-lē\ *adv*

¹**pur·pose** \'pər-pəs\ *n* **1** : an object or result aimed at : INTENTION **2** : RESOLUTION, DETERMINATION — **pur·pose·ful** \-fəl\ *adj* — **pur·pose·ful·ly** *adv* — **pur·pose·less** *adj* — **pur·pose·ly** *adv*

²**purpose** *vb* **pur·posed; pur·pos·ing** : to propose as an aim to oneself

purr \'pər\ *n* : a low murmur typical of a contented cat — **purr** *vb*

¹**purse** \'pərs\ *n* **1** : a receptacle (as a pouch) to carry money and often other small objects in **2** : RESOURCES **3** : a sum of money offered as a prize or present

²**purse** *vb* **pursed; purs·ing** : PUCKER

purs·er \'pər-sər\ *n* : an official on a ship who keeps accounts and attends to the comfort of passengers

purs·lane \'pər-slən, -,slān\ *n* : a fleshy-leaved weedy trailing plant with tiny yellow flowers that is sometimes used in salads

pur·su·ance \pər-'sü-əns\ *n* : the act of carrying out or into effect

pur·su·ant to \-'sü-ənt-\ *prep* : in carrying out : ACCORDING TO

pur·sue \pər-'sü\ *vb* **pur·sued; pur·su·ing 1** : to follow in order to overtake or overcome : CHASE **2** : to seek to accomplish ⟨~ a goal⟩ **3** : to proceed along ⟨~ a course⟩ **4** : to engage in ⟨~ a career⟩ — **pur·su·er** *n*

pur·suit \pər-'süt\ *n* **1** : the act of pursuing **2** : OCCUPATION, BUSINESS

pu·ru·lent \'pyur-ə-lənt, -yə-\ *adj* : containing or accompanied by pus ⟨a ~ discharge⟩ — **pu·ru·lence** \-ləns\ *n*

pur·vey \(,)pər-'vā\ *vb* **pur·veyed; pur·vey·ing** : to supply (as provisions) usu. as a business — **pur·vey·ance** \-əns\ *n* — **pur·vey·or** \-ər\ *n*

pur·view \'pər-,vyü\ *n* **1** : the range or limit esp. of authority, responsibility, or intention **2** : range of vision, understanding, or cognizance

pus \'pəs\ *n* : thick yellowish white fluid matter (as in a boil) formed at a place of inflammation and infection (as an abscess) and containing germs, white blood cells, and tissue debris

¹**push** \'push\ *vb* [ME *possen, pusshen,* prob. fr. OF *pousser* to exert pressure, fr. L *pulsare,* fr. *pellere* to drive, strike] **1** : to press against with force in order to drive or impel **2** : to thrust forward, downward, or outward **3** : to urge on : press forward **4** : to cause to increase ⟨~ prices to record levels⟩ **5** : to urge or press the advancement, adoption, or practice of; *esp* : to make aggressive efforts to sell **6** : to engage in the illicit sale of narcotics

²**push** *n* **1** : a vigorous effort : DRIVE **2** : an act of pushing : SHOVE **3** : vigorous enterprise : ENERGY

push-button *adj* **1** : operated or done by means of push buttons **2** : using or dependent on complex and more or less automatic mechanisms ⟨~ warfare⟩

push button *n* : a small button or knob that when pushed operates something esp. by closing an electric circuit

push·cart \'push-,kärt\ *n* : a cart or barrow pushed by hand

push·er \'pu-shər\ *n* : one that pushes; *esp* : one that pushes illegal drugs

push·over \-,ō-vər\ *n* : something easily accomplished **2** : an opponent easy to defeat **3** : SUCKER

push-up \-,əp\ *n* : a conditioning exercise performed in a prone position by raising and lowering the body with the straightening and bending of the arms while keeping the back straight and supporting the body on the hands and toes

pushy \'pu-shē\ *adj* **push·i·er; -est** : aggressive often to an objectionable degree

pu·sil·lan·i·mous \,pyü-sə-'la-nə-məs\ *adj* [LL *pusillanimis,* fr. L *pusillus* very small (dim. of *pusus* boy) + *animus* spirit] : contemptibly timid : COWARDLY — **pu·sil·la·nim·i·ty** \,pyü-sə-lə-'ni-mə-tē\ *n*

¹**puss** \'pus\ *n* : CAT

²**puss** n, slang : FACE

¹**pussy** \'pu̇-sē\ n, pl **puss·ies** : CAT

²**pus·sy** \'pə-sē\ adj **pus·si·er; -est** : full of or resembling pus

pussy·cat \'pu̇-sē-ˌkat\ n : CAT

pussy·foot \-ˌfu̇t\ vb 1 : to tread or move warily or stealthily 2 : to refrain from committing oneself

pussy willow \'pu̇-sē-\ n : a willow having large silky catkins

pus·tule \'pəs-chül\ n : a pus-filled pimple

put \'pu̇t\ vb **put; put·ting** 1 : to bring into a specified position : PLACE ⟨~ the book on the table⟩ 2 : SEND, THRUST 3 : to throw with an upward pushing motion ⟨~ the shot⟩ 4 : to bring into a specified state ⟨~ the plan into effect⟩ 5 : SUBJECT ⟨~ traitors to death⟩ 6 : IMPOSE 7 : to set before one for decision ⟨~ the question⟩ 8 : EXPRESS, STATE ⟨~ my feelings into words⟩ 9 : TRANSLATE, ADAPT 10 : APPLY, ASSIGN ⟨~ them to work⟩ 11 : ESTIMATE ⟨~ the number at 20⟩ 12 : ATTACH, ATTRIBUTE ⟨~ a high value on it⟩ 13 : to take a specified course ⟨the ship ~ out to sea⟩

pu·ta·tive \'pyü-tə-tiv\ adj 1 : commonly accepted 2 : assumed to exist or to have existed

put–down \'pu̇t-ˌdau̇n\ n : a belittling remark

put in vb 1 : to come in with : INTERPOSE ⟨put in a good word for me⟩ 2 : to spend time at some occupation or job ⟨put in eight hours at the office⟩

put off vb : POSTPONE, DELAY ⟨put off my visit⟩

¹**put–on** \'pu̇t-ˌȯn, -ˌän\ adj : PRETENDED, ASSUMED

²**put–on** n 1 : a deliberate act of misleading someone 2 : PARODY, SPOOF

put·out \'pu̇t-ˌau̇t\ n : the retiring of a base runner or batter in baseball

put out vb 1 : EXTINGUISH 2 : ANNOY; also : INCONVENIENCE 3 : to cause to be out (as in baseball)

pu·tre·fy \'pyü-trə-ˌfī\ vb **-fied; -fy·ing** : to make or become putrid : ROT — **pu·tre·fac·tion** \ˌpyü-trə-'fak-shən\ n — **pu·tre·fac·tive** \-tiv\ adj

pu·tres·cent \pyü-'tre-sᵊnt\ adj : becoming putrid : ROTTING — **pu·tres·cence** \-sᵊns\ n

pu·trid \'pyü-trəd\ adj 1 : ROTTEN, DECAYED ⟨~ meat⟩ 2 : VILE, CORRUPT — **pu·trid·i·ty** \pyü-'tri-də-tē\ n

putsch \'pu̇ch\ n [G] : a secretly plotted and suddenly executed attempt to overthrow a government

putt \'pət\ n : a golf stroke made on the green to cause the ball to roll into the hole — **putt** vb

put·ta·nes·ca \ˌpü-tä-'nes-kä\ adj : served with or being a pungent tomato sauce

put·tee \ˌpə-'tē, 'pə-tē\ n [Hindi paṭṭī strip of cloth] 1 : a cloth strip wrapped around the lower leg 2 : a leather legging

¹**put·ter** \'pu̇-tər\ n : one that puts

²**putt·er** \'pə-tər\ n 1 : a golf club used in putting 2 : one that putts

³**put·ter** \'pə-tər\ vb 1 : to move or act aimlessly or idly 2 : TINKER

put·ty \'pə-tē\ n, pl **putties** [F potée potter's glaze, lit., potful, fr. OF, fr. pot pot] 1 : a doughlike cement used esp. to fasten glass in sashes 2 : one who is easily manipulated — **putty** vb

put up vb 1 : SHEATHE 2 : to prepare so as to preserve for later use 3 : to offer for public sale ⟨put the house up for auction⟩ 4 : ACCOMMODATE, LODGE ⟨put us up for the night⟩ 5 : BUILD 6 : to engage in ⟨put up a struggle⟩ 7 : CONTRIBUTE, PAY — **put up with** : TOLERATE 2

¹**puz·zle** \'pə-zəl\ vb **puz·zled; puz·zling** 1 : to bewilder mentally : PERPLEX 2 : to solve with difficulty or ingenuity ⟨~ out a riddle⟩ 3 : to be in a quandary ⟨~ over what to do⟩ 4 : to attempt a solution of a puzzle ⟨~ over a person's words⟩ ♦ *Synonyms* MYSTIFY, BEWILDER, NONPLUS, CONFOUND — **puz·zle·ment** n — **puz·zler** n

²**puzzle** n 1 : something that puzzles 2 : a question, problem, or contrivance designed for testing ingenuity

PVC abbr polyvinyl chloride

pvt abbr private

PW abbr prisoner of war

pwt abbr pennyweight

PX abbr post exchange

pya \pē-'ä\ n — see kyat at MONEY table

pyg·my also **pig·my** \'pig-mē\ n, pl **pygmies** also **pigmies** [ME pigmei, fr. L pygmaeus of a pygmy, dwarfish, fr. Gk pygmaios, fr. pygmē fist, measure of length] 1 cap : any of a small people of equatorial Africa 2 : an unusually small person; also : an insignificant or unimpressive person — **pygmy** adj

py·ja·mas \pə-'jä-məz\ chiefly Brit var of PAJAMAS

py·lon \'pī-ˌlän, -lən\ n 1 : a usu. massive gateway; esp : an Egyptian one flanked by flat-topped pyramids 2 : a tower that supports wires over a long span 3 : a post or tower marking the course in an airplane race

py·or·rhea \ˌpī-ə-'rē-ə\ n : an inflammation with pus of the sockets of the teeth

¹**pyr·a·mid** \'pir-ə-ˌmid\ n 1 : a massive structure with a square base and four triangular faces meeting at a point 2 : a geometrical solid having a polygon for its base and three or more triangles that meet at a point to form the top — **py·ra·mi·dal** \pə-'ra-mə-dᵊl, ˌpir-ə-'mid-\ adj

²**pyramid** vb 1 : to build up in the form of a pyramid : heap up 2 : to increase rapidly on a broadening base

pyramid scheme n : a usu. illegal operation in which participants pay to join and profit from payments made by subsequent participants

pyre \'pī(-ə)r\ n : a combustible heap for burning a dead body as a funeral rite

py·re·thrum \pī-'rē-thrəm\ n : an insecticide made from the dried heads of any of several Old World chrysanthemums

py·rim·i·dine \pī-'ri-mə-ˌdēn\ n : any of a group of bases including several (as cytosine, thymine, or uracil) that are constituents of DNA or RNA

py·rite \'pī-,rīt\ *n* : a mineral containing sulfur and iron that is brass-yellow in color

py·rol·y·sis \pī-'rä-lə-səs\ *n* : chemical change caused by the action of heat

py·ro·ma·nia \,pī-rō-'mā-nē-ə\ *n* : an irresistible impulse to start fires — **py·ro·ma·ni·ac** \-nē-,ak\ *n*

py·ro·tech·nics \,pī-rə-'tek-niks\ *n pl* 1 : a display of fireworks 2 : a spectacular display (as of extreme virtuosity) — **py·ro·tech·nic** \-nik\ *also* **py·ro·tech·ni·cal** \-ni-kəl\ *adj*

Pyr·rhic \'pir-ik\ *adj* : achieved at excessive cost ⟨a ∼ victory⟩; *also* : costly to the point of outweighing expected benefits

Py·thag·o·re·an theorem \pī-,tha-gə-'rē-ən-\ *n* : a theorem in geometry: the square of the length of the hypotenuse of a right triangle equals the sum of the squares of the lengths of the other two sides

py·thon \'pī-,thän, -thən\ *n* [L, monstrous serpent killed by the god Apollo, fr. Gk *Pythōn*] : a large snake (as a boa) that squeezes and suffocates its prey; *esp* : any of the large Old World snakes that include the largest snakes living at the present time

pyx \'piks\ *n* : a small case used to carry the Eucharist to the sick

¹**q** \'kyü\ *n, pl* **q's** *or* **qs** \'kyüz\ *often cap* : the 17th letter of the English alphabet

²**q** *abbr, often cap* 1 **quart** 2 **quarto** 3 **queen** 4 **query** 5 **question**

QB *abbr* quarterback

QED *abbr* [L *quod erat demonstrandum*] which was to be demonstrated

qin·tar \kin-'tär\ *n, pl* **qin·dar·ka** \kin-'där-kə\ — see *lek* at MONEY table

qi·vi·ut \'kē-vē-,üt\ *n* [Inuit] : the wool of the undercoat of the musk ox

Qld *abbr* Queensland

QM *abbr* quartermaster

QMC *abbr* quartermaster corps

QMG *abbr* quartermaster general

qq v *abbr* [L *quae vide*] which (*pl*) see

qr *abbr* quarter

Q rating *n* [quotient] : a scale measuring popularity based on dividing an assessment of familiarity or recognition by an assessment of favorable opinion; *also* : position on such a scale

qt *abbr* 1 **quantity** 2 **quart**

q.t. \,kyü-'tē\ *n, often cap Q&T* : QUIET — usu. used in the phrase *on the q.t.*

qto *abbr* quarto

qty *abbr* quantity

qu *or* **ques** *abbr* question

¹**quack** \'kwak\ *vb* : to make the characteristic cry of a duck

²**quack** *n* : a sound made by quacking

³**quack** *n* 1 : CHARLATAN 2 : a pretender to medical skill ◆ **Synonyms** FAKER, IMPOSTOR, MOUNTEBANK — **quack** *adj* — **quack·ery** \'kwa-kə-rē\ *n* — **quack·ish** *adj*

¹**quad** \'kwäd\ *n* : QUADRANGLE

²**quad** *n* 1 : QUADRUPLET 2 : a ski lift that accommodates four people

³**quad** *abbr* quadrant

quad·ran·gle \'kwä-,draŋ-gəl\ *n* 1 : QUADRILATERAL 2 : a 4-sided courtyard or enclosure — **quad·ran·gu·lar** \kwä-'draŋ-gyə-lər\ *adj*

quad·rant \'kwä-drənt\ *n* 1 : one quarter of a circle : an arc of 90° 2 : any of the four quarters into which something is divided by two lines intersecting each other at right angles

qua·drat·ic \kwä-'dra-tik\ *adj* : having or being a term in which the variable (as *x*) is squared but containing no term in which the variable is raised to a higher power than a square ⟨a ∼ equation⟩ — **quadratic** *n*

qua·dren·ni·al \kwä-'dre-nē-əl\ *adj* 1 : consisting of or lasting for four years 2 : occurring every four years

qua·dren·ni·um \-nē-əm\ *n, pl* **-ni·ums** *or* **-nia** \-nē-ə\ : a period of four years

quad·ri·ceps \'kwä-drə-,seps\ *n* : a muscle of the front of the thigh that is divided into four parts

¹**quad·ri·lat·er·al** \,kwä-drə-'la-tə-rəl\ *n* : a polygon of four sides

²**quadrilateral** *adj* : having four sides

qua·drille \kwä-'dril, kə-\ *n* : a square dance made up of five or six figures in various rhythms

quad·ri·par·tite \,kwä-drə-'pär-,tīt\ *adj* 1 : consisting of four parts 2 : shared by four parties or persons

quad·ri·ple·gia \,kwä-drə-'plē-jə, -jē-ə\ *n* : paralysis of both arms and both legs — **quad·ri·ple·gic** \-jik\ *adj or n*

qua·driv·i·um \kwä-'dri-vē-əm\ *n* : the four liberal arts of arithmetic, music, geometry, and astronomy in a medieval university

quad·ru·ped \'kwä-drə-,ped\ *n* : an animal having four feet — **qua·dru·pe·dal** \kwä-'drü-pə-d²l, ,kwä-drə-'pe-\ *adj*

¹**qua·dru·ple** \kwä-'drü-pəl, -'drə-; 'kwä-drə-\ *vb* **qua·dru·pled; qua·dru·pling** : to make or become four times as great or as many

²**quadruple** *adj* : FOURFOLD

qua·dru·plet \kwä-'drə-plət, -'drü-; 'kwä-drə-\ *n* 1 : a combination of four of a kind 2 : one of four offspring born at one birth

¹**qua·dru·pli·cate** \kwä-'drü-pli-kət\ *adj* 1 : repeated four times 2 : FOURTH

²**qua·dru·pli·cate** \-plə-,kāt\ *vb* **-cat·ed; -cat·ing** 1 : QUADRUPLE 2 : to prepare

in quadruplicate — **qua·dru·pli·ca·tion** \-ˌdrü-plə-ˈkā-shən\ n

³**qua·dru·pli·cate** \-ˈdrü-pli-kət\ n 1 : four copies all alike ⟨typed in ⁓⟩ 2 : one of four like things

quaff \ˈkwäf, ˈkwaf\ vb : to drink deeply or repeatedly — **quaff** n

quag·mire \ˈkwag-ˌmī(-ə)r, ˈkwäg-\ n 1 : soft miry land that yields under the foot 2 : PREDICAMENT

qua·hog \ˈkō-ˌhȯg, ˈkwo-, ˈkwō-, -ˌhäg\ n [modif. of Narragansett *poquaûhock*] : a round thick-shelled edible clam of the U.S.

quai \ˈkā\ n : QUAY

¹**quail** \ˈkwāl\ n, pl **quail** or **quails** [ME *quaile*, fr. AF, fr. ML *quaccula*, of imit. origin] : any of numerous small short-winged plump game birds (as a bobwhite) related to the domestic chicken

²**quail** vb [ME, to grow feeble, fr. MD *quelen*] : to lose heart : COWER ◆ *Synonyms* RECOIL, SHRINK, FLINCH, WINCE, BLANCH

quaint \ˈkwānt\ adj : unusual or different in character or appearance; esp : pleasingly old-fashioned or unfamiliar ◆ *Synonyms* ODD, QUEER, CURIOUS, STRANGE — **quaint·ly** adv — **quaint·ness** n

¹**quake** \ˈkwāk\ vb **quaked; quak·ing** 1 : to shake usu. from shock or instability 2 : to tremble usu. from cold or fear

²**quake** n : a shaking or trembling; esp : EARTHQUAKE

Quak·er \ˈkwā-kər\ n : FRIEND 5

qual abbr quality

qual·i·fi·ca·tion \ˌkwä-lə-fə-ˈkā-shən\ n 1 : LIMITATION, MODIFICATION ⟨her statement stands without ⁓⟩ 2 : a special skill that fits a person for some work or position 3 : REQUIREMENT ⟨a ⁓ for membership⟩

qual·i·fied \ˈkwä-lə-ˌfīd\ adj 1 : fitted for a given purpose or job 2 : limited in some way ⟨⁓ approval⟩

qual·i·fi·er \ˈkwä-lə-ˌfī(-ə)r\ n 1 : one that satisfies requirements 2 : a word or word group that limits the meaning of another word or word group

qual·i·fy \ˈkwä-lə-ˌfī\ vb **-fied; -fy·ing** 1 : to reduce from a general to a particular form : MODIFY 2 : to make less harsh 3 : to limit the meaning of (as a noun) 4 : to fit by skill or training for some purpose 5 : to give or have a legal right to do something 6 : to demonstrate the necessary ability ⟨⁓ for the finals⟩ ◆ *Synonyms* MODERATE, TEMPER

qual·i·ta·tive \ˈkwä-lə-ˌtā-tiv\ adj : of, relating to, or involving quality — **qual·i·ta·tive·ly** adv

¹**qual·i·ty** \ˈkwä-lə-tē\ n, pl **-ties** 1 : peculiar and essential character : NATURE 2 : degree of excellence 3 : high social status 4 : a distinguishing attribute

²**quality** adj : being of high quality

qualm \ˈkwäm, ˈkwälm\ n 1 : a sudden attack (as of nausea) 2 : a sudden feeling of doubt, fear, or uneasiness esp. in not following one's conscience or better judgment

qualm·ish \ˈkwä-mish, ˈkwäl-\ adj 1 : feeling qualms : NAUSEATED 2 : overly scrupulous : SQUEAMISH 3 : of, relating to, or producing qualms

quan·da·ry \ˈkwän-drē\ n, pl **-ries** : a state of perplexity or doubt

quan·ti·fy \ˈkwän-tə-ˌfī\ vb **-fied; -fy·ing** : to determine, express, or measure the quantity of — **quan·ti·fi·able** \ˌkwän-tə-ˈfī-ə-bəl\ adj

quan·ti·ta·tive \ˈkwän-tə-ˌtā-tiv\ adj : of, relating to, or involving quantity — **quan·ti·ta·tive·ly** adv

quan·ti·ty \ˈkwän-tə-tē\ n, pl **-ties** 1 : AMOUNT, NUMBER 2 : a considerable amount

quan·tize \ˈkwän-ˌtīz\ vb **quan·tized; quan·tiz·ing** : to subdivide (as energy) into small units

¹**quan·tum** \ˈkwän-təm\ n, pl **quan·ta** \-tə\ [L, neut. of *quantus* how much] 1 : QUANTITY, AMOUNT 2 : an elemental unit of energy

²**quantum** adj 1 : LARGE, SIGNIFICANT 2 : relating to or employing the principles of quantum mechanics

quantum mechanics n sing or pl : a theory of matter based on the concept of possession of wave properties by elementary particles — **quantum mechanical** adj — **quantum mechanically** adv

quantum theory n 1 : a theory in physics based on the idea that radiant energy (as light) is composed of small separate packets of energy 2 : QUANTUM MECHANICS

quar abbr quarterly

quar·an·tine \ˈkwȯr-ən-ˌtēn\ n [modif. of It *quarantena*, lit., period of forty days, fr. *quaranta* forty, fr. L *quadraginta*] 1 : a period during which a ship suspected of carrying contagious disease is forbidden contact with the shore 2 : a restraint on the movements of persons or goods to prevent the spread of pests or disease 3 : a place or period of quarantine 4 : a state of enforced isolation — **quarantine** vb

quark \ˈkwȯrk, ˈkwärk\ n : a hypothetical elementary particle that carries a fractional charge and is held to be a constituent of heavier particles (as protons and neutrons)

¹**quar·rel** \ˈkwȯr-əl\ n 1 : a ground of dispute 2 : a verbal clash : CONFLICT — **quar·rel·some** \-səm\ adj

²**quarrel** vb **-reled** or **-relled; -rel·ing** or **-rel·ling** 1 : to find fault 2 : to dispute angrily : WRANGLE

¹**quar·ry** \ˈkwȯr-ē\ n, pl **quarries** [ME *querre* entrails of game given to the hounds, fr. AF *cureie, quereie*, fr. *quir, cuir* skin, hide (on which the entrails were placed), fr. L *corium*] 1 : game hunted with hawks 2 : PREY

²**quarry** n, pl **quarries** [ME *quarey*, alter. of *quarrere*, fr. AF, fr. VL *quadraria, fr. LL *quadrus* hewn (lit., squared) stone, fr. L *quadrum* square] : an open excavation usu. for obtaining building stone or limestone — **quarry** vb

quart \'kwȯrt\ *n* — see WEIGHT table

¹**quar·ter** \'kwȯr-tər\ *n* 1 : one of four equal parts 2 : a fourth of a dollar; *also* : a coin of this value 3 : a district of a city 4 *pl* : LODGINGS ⟨moved into new ∼s⟩ 5 : MERCY, CLEMENCY ⟨gave no ∼⟩ 6 : a fourth part of the moon's period

²**quarter** *vb* 1 : to divide into four equal parts 2 : to provide with shelter

¹**quar·ter·back** \-ˌbak\ *n* : a football player who calls the signals and directs the offensive play for the team

²**quarterback** *vb* 1 : to direct the offensive play of a football team 2 : LEAD, BOSS

quar·ter·deck \-ˌdek\ *n* : the stern area of a ship's upper deck

quarter horse *n* : any of a breed of compact muscular saddle horses characterized by great endurance and by high speed for short distances

¹**quar·ter·ly** \'kwȯr-tər-lē\ *adv* : at 3-month intervals

²**quarterly** *adj* : occurring, issued, or payable at 3-month intervals

³**quarterly** *n, pl* **-lies** : a periodical published four times a year

quar·ter·mas·ter \-ˌmas-tər\ *n* 1 : a petty officer who attends to a ship's helm, binnacle, and signals 2 : an army officer who provides clothing and subsistence for troops

quar·ter·staff \-ˌstaf\ *n, pl* **-staves** \-ˌstavz, -ˌstāvz\ : a long stout staff formerly used as a weapon

quar·tet *also* **quar·tette** \kwȯr-'tet\ *n* 1 : a musical composition for four instruments or voices 2 : a group of four and esp. of four musicians

quar·to \'kwȯr-tō\ *n, pl* **quartos** 1 : the size of a piece of paper cut four from a sheet 2 : a book printed on quarto pages

quartz \'kwȯrts\ *n* : a common often transparent crystalline mineral that is a form of silica

quartz·ite \'kwȯrts-ˌsīt\ *n* : a compact granular rock composed of quartz and derived from sandstone

qua·sar \'kwā-ˌzär, -ˌsär\ *n* : any of a class of extremely distant starlike celestial objects

¹**quash** \'kwäsh, 'kwȯsh\ *vb* : to suppress or extinguish summarily and completely : QUELL

²**quash** *vb* : to nullify by judicial action

qua·si \'kwā-ˌzī, -ˌsī; 'kwä-zē, -sē\ *adj* : being in some sense or degree ⟨a ∼ corporation⟩

quasi- *comb form* [L, as if, as it were, approximately, fr. *quam* as + *si* if] : in some sense or degree ⟨*quasi*-historical⟩

qua·si-gov·ern·men·tal \-ˌgə-vərn-'men-tᵊl\ *adj* : supported by the government but managed privately

Qua·ter·na·ry \'kwä-tər-ˌner-ē, kwə-'tər-nə-rē\ *adj* : of, relating to, or being the geologic period from the end of the Tertiary to the present — **Quaternary** *n*

qua·train \'kwä-ˌträn\ *n* : a unit of four lines of verse

qua·tre·foil \'ka-tər-ˌfȯi(-ə)l, 'ka-trə-\ *n* : a stylized figure often of a flower with four petals

qua·ver \'kwā-vər\ *vb* 1 : TREMBLE, SHAKE 2 : TRILL 3 : to speak in tremulous tones ♦ *Synonyms* SHUDDER, QUAKE, TWITTER, QUIVER, SHIVER — **quaver** *n*

quay \'kē, 'kwā, 'kā\ *n* : WHARF

Que *abbr* Quebec

quean \'kwēn\ *n* : PROSTITUTE

quea·sy \'kwē-zē\ *adj* **quea·si·er; -est** : NAUSEATED — **quea·si·ly** \-zə-lē\ *adv* — **quea·si·ness** \-zē-nəs\ *n*

Que·chua \'ke-chə-wə, 'kech-wə\ *n* : a family of languages spoken in Peru and adjacent countries of the So. American Andes

queen \'kwēn\ *n* [ME *quene*, fr. OE *cwēn* woman, wife, queen] 1 : the wife or widow of a king 2 : a female monarch 3 : a woman notable for rank, power, or attractiveness 4 : the most powerful piece in the game of chess 5 : a playing card bearing the figure of a queen 6 : a fertile female of a social insect (as a bee or termite) — **queen·ly** *adj*

Queen Anne's lace \-'anz-\ *n* : a widely naturalized Eurasian herb from which the cultivated carrot originated

queen consort *n, pl* **queens consort** : the wife of a reigning king

queen mother *n* : a dowager queen who is mother of the reigning sovereign

queen–size *adj* : having dimensions of approximately 60 inches by 80 inches ⟨a ∼ bed⟩; *also* : of a size that fits a queen-size bed

¹**queer** \'kwir\ *adj* 1 : COUNTERFEIT ⟨∼ money⟩ 2 : differing from the usual or normal : PECULIAR, STRANGE 3 *often disparaging* : HOMOSEXUAL; *also, sometimes offensive* : of, relating to, or used by homosexuals ♦ *Synonyms* WEIRD, BIZARRE, ECCENTRIC, CURIOUS — **queer** *n* — **queer·ly** *adv* — **queer·ness** *n*

²**queer** *vb* : to spoil the effect of : DISRUPT ⟨∼ed our plans⟩

queer theory *n* : an approach to literary and cultural study that rejects traditional categories of gender and sexuality

quell \'kwel\ *vb* 1 : to put an end to by force ⟨∼ a riot⟩ 2 : CALM, PACIFY ⟨∼ fears⟩

quench \'kwench\ *vb* 1 : PUT OUT, EXTINGUISH 2 : SUBDUE 3 : SLAKE, SATISFY ⟨∼ed his thirst⟩ — **quench·able** *adj* — **quench·er** *n* — **quench·less** *adj*

quer·u·lous \'kwer-ə-ləs, -yə-\ *adj* 1 : constantly complaining 2 : FRETFUL, WHINING ⟨a ∼ voice⟩ ♦ *Synonyms* PETULANT, PETTISH, IRRITABLE, PEEVISH, HUFFY — **quer·u·lous·ly** *adv* — **quer·u·lous·ness** *n*

que·ry \'kwir-ē, 'kwer-\ *n, pl* **queries** : QUESTION — **query** *vb*

que·sa·dil·la \ˌkā-sə-'dē-ə\ *n* : a tortilla filled with a savory mixture, folded, and usu. fried

quest \'kwest\ *n* : SEARCH ⟨in ∼ of game⟩ — **quest** *vb*

¹**ques·tion** \'kwes-chən\ *n* **1** : an interrogative expression **2** : a subject for debate; *also* : a proposition to be voted on **3** : INQUIRY **4** : DISPUTE ⟨true beyond ∼⟩

²**question** *vb* **1** : to ask questions **2** : DOUBT, DISPUTE ⟨∼ed the verdict⟩ **3** : to subject to analysis : EXAMINE ✦ *Synonyms* INTERROGATE, QUIZ, QUERY — **ques·tion·er** *n*

ques·tion·able \'kwes-chə-nə-bəl\ *adj* **1** : not certain or exact : DOUBTFUL **2** : not believed to be true, sound, or moral ✦ *Synonyms* DUBIOUS, PROBLEMATICAL, MOOT, DEBATABLE — **ques·tion·ably** \-blē\ *adv*

question mark *n* : a punctuation mark ? used esp. at the end of a sentence to indicate a direct question

ques·tion·naire \ˌkwes-chə-'ner\ *n* : a set of questions for obtaining information

quet·zal \ket-'säl, -'sal\ *n, pl* **quetzals** *or* **quet·za·les** \-'sä-läs, -'sa-\ **1** : a Central American bird with brilliant plumage **2** *pl* **quetzales** — see MONEY table

¹**queue** \'kyü\ *n* [F, lit., tail, fr. OF *cue, coe,* fr. L *cauda, coda*] **1** : a braid of hair usu. worn hanging at the back of the head **2** : a waiting line (as of persons)

²**queue** *vb* **queued; queu·ing** *or* **queue·ing** : to line up in a queue

quib·ble \'kwi-bəl\ *n* **1** : an evasion of or shifting from the point at issue **2** : a minor objection or criticism — **quibble** *vb* — **quib·bler** *n*

¹**quick** \'kwik\ *adj* **1** : LIVING **2** : RAPID, SPEEDY ⟨∼ steps⟩ **3** : prompt to understand, think, or perceive : ALERT **4** : easily aroused ⟨a ∼ temper⟩ **5** : turning or bending sharply ⟨a ∼ turn in the road⟩ ✦ *Synonyms* FLEET, FAST, HASTY, EXPEDITIOUS — **quick** *adv* — **quick·ly** *adv* — **quick·ness** *n*

²**quick** *n* **1** : a sensitive area of living flesh **2** : a vital part : HEART

quick bread *n* : a bread made with a leavening agent that permits immediate baking of the dough or batter

quick·en \'kwi-kən\ *vb* **1** : to come to life : REVIVE **2** : AROUSE, STIMULATE ⟨curiosity ∼ed my interest⟩ **3** : to increase in speed : HASTEN **4** : to show vitality (as by growing or moving) ✦ *Synonyms* ANIMATE, ENLIVEN, LIVEN, VIVIFY

quick-freeze \'kwik-'frēz\ *vb* **-froze** \-'frōz\; **-fro·zen** \-'frō-zᵊn\; **-freez·ing** : to freeze (food) for preservation so rapidly that the natural juices and flavor are not lost

quick·ie \'kwi-kē\ *n* : something hurriedly done or made

quick·lime \'kwik-ˌlīm\ *n* : ¹LIME

quick·sand \-ˌsand\ *n* : a deep mass of loose sand mixed with water

quick·sil·ver \-ˌsil-vər\ *n* : MERCURY 1

quick·step \-ˌstep\ *n* : a spirited march tune or dance

quick-wit·ted \'kwik-'wi-təd\ *adj* : mentally alert ✦ *Synonyms* CLEVER, BRIGHT, SMART, INTELLIGENT

quid \'kwid\ *n* : a lump of something chewable ⟨a ∼ of tobacco⟩

quid pro quo \ˌkwid-ˌprō-'kwō\ *n* [NL, something for something] : something given or received for something else

qui·es·cent \kwī-'e-sᵊnt\ *adj* : being at rest : QUIET ✦ *Synonyms* LATENT, DORMANT, POTENTIAL — **qui·es·cence** \-sᵊns\ *n*

¹**qui·et** \'kwī-ət\ *n* : REPOSE

²**quiet** *adj* **1** : marked by little motion or activity : CALM **2** : GENTLE, MILD ⟨a ∼ disposition⟩ **3** : enjoyed in peace and relaxation ⟨a ∼ cup of tea⟩ **4** : free from noise or uproar **5** : not showy : MODEST ⟨∼ clothes⟩ **6** : SECLUDED ⟨a ∼ nook⟩ — **quiet** *adv* — **qui·et·ly** *adv* — **qui·et·ness** *n*

³**quiet** *vb* **1** : CALM, PACIFY **2** : to become quiet — usu. used with *down*

qui·etude \'kwī-ə-ˌtüd, -ˌtyüd\ *n* : QUIETNESS, REPOSE

qui·etus \kwī-'ē-təs\ *n* [ME *quietus est*, fr. ML, he is quit, formula of discharge from obligation] **1** : final settlement (as of a debt) **2** : DEATH

quill \'kwil\ *n* **1** : a large stiff feather; *also* : the hollow tubular part of a feather **2** : one of the hollow sharp spines of a hedgehog or porcupine **3** : a pen made from a feather

¹**quilt** \'kwilt\ *n* : a padded bed coverlet

²**quilt** *vb* **1** : to fill, pad, or line like a quilt **2** : to stitch or sew in layers with padding in between **3** : to make quilts

quince \'kwins\ *n* : a hard yellow apple-like fruit; *also* : a tree related to the roses that bears this fruit

qui·nine \'kwī-ˌnīn\ *n* : a bitter white drug obtained from cinchona bark and used esp. in treating malaria

qui·noa \'kēn-ə-ˌwä, kē-'nō-ə\ *n* [Sp, fr. Quechua *kinua*] : the starchy seeds of an annual herb related to spinach which are used as food and ground into flour; *also* : this herb

quint \'kwint\ *n* : QUINTUPLET

quin·tal \'kwin-tᵊl, 'kan-\ *n* : HUNDREDWEIGHT

quin·tes·sence \kwin-'te-sᵊns\ *n* **1** : the purest essence of something **2** : the most typical example — **quin·tes·sen·tial** \ˌkwin-tə-'sen-chəl\ *adj* — **quin·tes·sen·tial·ly** *adv*

quin·tet \kwin-'tet\ *n* **1** : a musical composition for five instruments or voices **2** : a group of five and esp. of five musicians

¹**quin·tu·ple** \kwin-'tü-pəl, -'tyü-, -'tə-\ *adj* **1** : having five units or members **2** : being five times as great or as many — **quintuple** *n*

²**quintuple** *vb* **quin·tu·pled; quin·tu·pling** : to make or become five times as great or as many

quin·tu·plet \kwin-'tə-plət, -'tü-, -'tyü-\ *n* **1** : a group of five of a kind **2** : one of five offspring born at one birth

¹**quin·tu·pli·cate** \kwin-'tü-pli-kət, -'tyü-\ *adj* **1** : repeated five times **2** : FIFTH ⟨file the ∼ copy⟩

²**quintuplicate** *n* **1** : one of five like things **2** : five copies all alike ⟨typed in ∼⟩

³**quin·tu·pli·cate** \-plə-ˌkāt\ vb **-cat·ed; -cat·ing** 1 : QUINTUPLE 2 : to provide in quintuplicate

¹**quip** \'kwip\ n : a clever remark : GIBE

²**quip** vb **quipped; quip·ping** 1 : to make quips : GIBE 2 : to jest or gibe at

quire \'kwī(-ə)r\ n : a set of 24 or sometimes 25 sheets of paper of the same size and quality

quirk \'kwərk\ n : a peculiarity of action or behavior — **quirky** adj

quirt \'kwərt\ n : a riding whip with a short handle and a rawhide lash

quis·ling \'kwiz-liŋ\ n [Vidkun *Quisling* †1945 Norw. politician who collaborated with the Nazis] : one who helps the invaders of one's own country

quit \'kwit\ vb **quit** also **quit·ted; quit·ting** 1 : CONDUCT, BEHAVE ⟨~ themselves well⟩ 2 : to depart from : LEAVE; also : to bring to an end 3 : to give up for good ⟨~ smoking⟩ ⟨~ my job⟩ ✦ *Synonyms* ACQUIT, COMPORT, DEPORT, DEMEAN — **quit·ter** n

quite \'kwīt\ adv 1 : COMPLETELY, WHOLLY ⟨not ~ finished⟩ 2 : to an extreme : POSITIVELY 3 : to a considerable extent : RATHER

quits \'kwits\ adj : even or equal with another

quit·tance \'kwi-t³ns\ n : REQUITAL

¹**quiv·er** \'kwi-vər\ n : a case for carrying arrows

²**quiver** vb **quiv·ered; quiv·er·ing** : to shake with a slight trembling motion ✦ *Synonyms* SHIVER, SHUDDER, QUAVER, QUAKE, TREMBLE — **quiv·er·ing·ly** adv

³**quiver** n : the act or action of quivering : TREMOR

qui vive \kē-'vēv\ n [F *qui-vive*, fr. *qui vive?* long live who?, challenge of a French sentry] : ALERT ⟨on the *qui vive* for prowlers⟩

quix·ot·ic \kwik-'sä-tik\ adj [fr. Don *Quixote*, hero of the novel *Don Quixote de la Mancha* by Cervantes] : foolishly impractical esp. in the pursuit of ideals — **quix·ot·i·cal·ly** \-ti-kə-lē\ adv

¹**quiz** \'kwiz\ n, pl **quiz·zes** 1 : an eccentric person 2 : PRACTICAL JOKE 3 : a short oral or written test

²**quiz** vb **quizzed; quiz·zing** 1 : MOCK 2 : to look at inquisitively 3 : to question

closely ✦ *Synonyms* ASK, INTERROGATE, QUERY

quiz·zi·cal \'kwi-zi-kəl\ adj 1 : comically quaint 2 : mildly teasing or mocking 3 : expressive of puzzlement, curiosity, or disbelief

quoit \'kwāt, 'kwȯit, 'kȯit\ n 1 : a flattened ring of iron or circle of rope used in a throwing game 2 pl : a game in which quoits are thrown at an upright pin in an attempt to ring the pin

quon·dam \'kwän-dəm, -ˌdam\ adj [L, at one time, formerly, fr. *quom, cum* when] : FORMER ⟨a ~ friend⟩

quo·rum \'kwȯr-əm\ n : the number of members required to be present for business to be legally transacted

quot abbr quotation

quo·ta \'kwō-tə\ n : a proportional part esp. when assigned : SHARE

quot·able \'kwō-tə-bəl\ adj : fit for or worth quoting — **quot·abil·i·ty** \-'bi-lə-tē\ n

quo·ta·tion \kwō-'tā-shən\ n 1 : the act or process of quoting 2 : the price currently bid or offered for something 3 : something that is quoted

quotation mark n : one of a pair of punctuation marks " " or ' ' used esp. to indicate the beginning and end of a quotation in which exact phraseology is directly cited

quote \'kwōt\ vb **quot·ed; quot·ing** [ML *quotare* to mark the number of, number references, fr. L *quotus* of what number or quantity, fr. *quot* how many, (as) many as] 1 : to speak or write a passage from another usu. with acknowledgment; also : to repeat a passage in substantiation or illustration 2 : to state the market price of a commodity, stock, or bond 3 : to inform a hearer or reader that matter following is quoted — **quote** n

quoth \'kwōth\ vb past, [ME, past of *quethen* to say, fr. OE *cwethan*] archaic : SAID — usu. used in the 1st and 3d persons with the subject following

quo·tid·i·an \kwō-'ti-dē-ən\ adj 1 : DAILY 2 : COMMONPLACE, ORDINARY ⟨~ concerns⟩

quo·tient \'kwō-shənt\ n : the number obtained by dividing one number by another

qv abbr [L *quod vide*] which see

qy abbr query

¹**r** \'är\ n, pl **r's** or **rs** \'ärz\ often cap : the 18th letter of the English alphabet

²**r** abbr, often cap 1 rabbi 2 radius 3 rare 4 Republican 5 rerun 6 resistance 7 right 8 river 9 roentgen 10 rook 11 run

Ra symbol radium

RA abbr 1 regular army 2 Royal Academy

¹**rab·bet** \'ra-bət\ n : a groove in the edge or face of a surface (as a board) esp. to receive another piece

²**rabbet** vb : to cut a rabbet in; also : to join by means of a rabbet

rab·bi \'ra-ˌbī\ n [ME, fr. OE, fr. LL, fr. Gk *rhabbi*, fr. Heb *rabbī* my master, fr. *rabh* master + *-ī* my] 1 : MASTER, TEACHER — used by Jews as a term of address **2** : a Jew trained and ordained for professional religious leadership — **rab·bin·ic** \rə-'bi-nik\ *or* **rab·bin·i·cal** \-ni-kəl\ *adj*

rab·bin·ate \'ra-bə-nət, -ˌnāt\ *n* **1** : the office of a rabbi **2** : the whole body of rabbis

rab·bit \'ra-bət\ *n, pl* **rabbit** *or* **rabbits** : any of various long-eared short-tailed burrowing mammals distinguished from the related hares by being blind, furless, and helpless at birth; *also* : the pelt of a rabbit

rabbit ears *n pl* : an indoor V-shaped television antenna

rab·ble \'ra-bəl\ *n* **1** : MOB **2** : the lowest class of people

rab·ble–rous·er \'ra-bəl-ˌrau̇-zər\ *n* : one that stirs up (as to hatred or violence) the masses of the people

ra·bid \'ra-bəd\ *adj* **1** : VIOLENT, FURIOUS **2** : being fanatical or extreme **3** : affected with rabies — **ra·bid·ly** *adv*

ra·bies \'rā-bēz\ *n, pl* **rabies** [NL, fr. L, madness] : an acute deadly virus disease of the nervous system transmitted by the bite of an affected animal

rac·coon \ra-'kün\ *n, pl* **raccoon** *or* **raccoons** : a gray No. American chiefly tree-dwelling mammal with a black mask, a bushy ringed tail, and nocturnal habits; *also* : its pelt

¹**race** \'rās\ *n* **1** : a strong current of running water; *also* : its channel **2** : an onward course (as of time or life) **3** : a contest of speed **4** : a contest for a desired end (as election to office)

²**race** *vb* **raced; rac·ing** **1** : to run in a race **2** : to run swiftly : RUSH **3** : to engage in a race with **4** : to drive or ride at high speed — **rac·er** *n*

³**race** *n* **1** : a family, tribe, people, or nation of the same stock **2** : a group of individuals within a biological species able to breed together **3** : a category of humankind that shares certain distinctive physical traits — **ra·cial** \'rā-shəl\ *adj* — **ra·cial·ly** *adv*

race·course \'rās-ˌkȯrs\ *n* : a course for racing

race·horse \-ˌhȯrs\ *n* : a horse bred or kept for racing

ra·ceme \rā-'sēm\ *n* [L *racemus* bunch of grapes] : a flower cluster with flowers borne along a stem and blooming from the base toward the tip — **rac·e·mose** \'ra-sə-ˌmōs\ *adj*

race·track \'rās-ˌtrak\ *n* : a usu. oval course on which races are run

race·way \-ˌwā\ *n* **1** : a channel for a current of water **2** : RACECOURSE

ra·cial·ism \'rā-shə-ˌli-zəm\ *n* : a theory that race determines human traits and capacities; *also* : RACISM — **ra·cial·ist** \-list\ *n* — **ra·cial·is·tic** \ˌrā-shə-'lis-tik\ *adj*

ra·cial·ize \'rā-shə-ˌlīz\ *vb* **-ized; -iz·ing** : to give a racial character to

racing form *n* : a paper giving data about racehorses for use by bettors

rac·ism \'rā-ˌsi-zəm\ *n* : a belief that some races are by nature superior to others;

also : discrimination based on such belief — **rac·ist** \-sist\ *n*

¹**rack** \'rak\ *n* **1** : an instrument of torture on which a body is stretched **2** : a framework on or in which something may be placed (as for display or storage) **3** : a bar with teeth on one side to mesh with a pinion or worm gear

²**rack** *vb* **1** : to torture on or as if on a rack **2** : to stretch or strain by force **3** : TORMENT **4** : to place on or in a rack

¹**rack·et** *or* **rac·quet** \'ra-kət\ *n* [MF *raquette*, ultim. fr. ML *rasceta* wrist, carpus, fr. Ar *rusgh* wrist] : a light bat made of netting stretched in an oval open frame having a handle and used for striking a ball or shuttlecock

²**racket** *n* **1** : confused noise : DIN **2** : a fraudulent or dishonest scheme or activity

³**racket** *vb* : to make a racket

rack·e·teer \ˌra-kə-'tir\ *n* : a person who obtains money by an illegal enterprise usu. involving intimidation — **rack·e·teer·ing** *n*

rack up *vb* : ACHIEVE, GAIN ⟨*racked up* their 10th victory⟩

ra·con·teur \ˌra-ˌkän-'tər\ *n* : one good at telling anecdotes

rac·quet·ball \'ra-kət-ˌbȯl\ *n* : a game similar to handball that is played on a 4-walled court with a short-handled racket

racy \'rā-sē\ *adj* **rac·i·er; -est** **1** : full of zest **2** : PUNGENT, SPICY **3** : RISQUÉ, SUGGESTIVE ⟨~ jokes⟩ — **rac·i·ly** \'rā-sə-lē\ *adv* — **rac·i·ness** \-sē-nəs\ *n*

rad *abbr* **1** radical **2** radio **3** radius

ra·dar \'rā-ˌdär\ *n* [*radio detecting and ranging*] : a device that emits radio waves for detecting and locating an object by the reflection of the radio waves and that may use this reflection to determine the object's direction and speed

radar gun *n* : a handheld device that uses radar to measure the speed of a moving object

ra·dar·scope \'rā-ˌdär-ˌskōp\ *n* : a visual display for a radar receiver

¹**ra·di·al** \'rā-dē-əl\ *adj* : arranged or having parts arranged like rays around a common center ⟨the ~ form of a starfish⟩ — **ra·di·al·ly** *adv*

²**radial** *n* : a pneumatic tire with cords laid perpendicular to the center line

radial engine *n* : an internal combustion engine with cylinders arranged radially like the spokes of a wheel

ra·di·an \'rā-dē-ən\ *n* : a unit of measure for angles that is equal to approximately 57.3 degrees

ra·di·ant \'rā-dē-ənt\ *adj* **1** : SHINING, GLOWING **2** : beaming with happiness **3** : transmitted by radiation ✦ **Synonyms** BRILLIANT, BRIGHT, LUMINOUS, LUSTROUS — **ra·di·ance** \-əns\ *n* — **ra·di·ant·ly** *adv*

radiant energy *n* : energy traveling as electromagnetic waves

ra·di·ate \'rā-dē-ˌāt\ *vb* **-at·ed; -at·ing** **1** : to send out rays : SHINE, GLOW **2** : to issue in or as if in rays ⟨light ~*s*⟩ **3** : to spread around as from a center

ra·di·a·tion \ˌrā-dē-'ā-shən\ *n* **1** : the action or process of radiating **2** : the process of emitting radiant energy in the form of waves or particles; *also* : something (as an X-ray beam) that is radiated

radiation sickness *n* : sickness that results from exposure to radiation and is commonly marked by fatigue, nausea, vomiting, loss of teeth and hair, and in more severe cases by damage to blood-forming tissue

radiation therapy *n* : RADIOTHERAPY

ra·di·a·tor \'rā-dē-ˌā-tər\ *n* : any of various devices (as a set of pipes or tubes) for transferring heat from a fluid within to an area or object outside

¹**rad·i·cal** \'ra-di-kəl\ *adj* [ME, fr. LL *radicalis*, fr. L *radic-*, *radix* root] **1** : FUNDAMENTAL, EXTREME, THOROUGHGOING **2** : of or relating to radicals in politics — **rad·i·cal·ism** \-kə-ˌli-zəm\ *n* — **rad·i·cal·ly** *adv*

²**radical** *n* **1** : a person who favors rapid and sweeping changes in laws and methods of government **2** FREE RADICAL; *also* : a group of atoms considered as a unit in certain reactions or as a subunit of a larger molecule **3** : a mathematical expression indicating a root by means of a radical sign; *also* : RADICAL SIGN

rad·i·cal·ise *Brit var of* RADICALIZE

rad·i·cal·ize \-kə-ˌlīz\ *vb* **-ized; -iz·ing** : to make radical esp. in politics — **rad·i·cal·i·za·tion** \ˌra-di-kə-lə-'zā-shən\ *n*

radical sign *n* : the sign √ placed before a mathematical expression to indicate that its root is to be taken

ra·dic·chio \rä-'di-kē-ō\ *n, pl* **–chios** : a chicory with reddish variegated leaves

radii *pl of* RADIUS

¹**ra·dio** \'rā-dē-ˌō\ *n, pl* **ra·di·os 1** : the wireless transmission or reception of signals using electromagnetic waves **2** : a radio receiving set **3** : the radio broadcasting industry — **radio** *adj*

²**radio** *vb* : to communicate or send a message to by radio

ra·dio·ac·tiv·i·ty \ˌrā-dē-ō-ˌak-'ti-və-tē\ *n* : the property that some elements or isotopes have of spontaneously emitting energetic particles by the disintegration of their atomic nuclei — **ra·dio·ac·tive** \-'ak-tiv\ *adj*

radio astronomy *n* : astronomy dealing with radio waves received from outside the earth's atmosphere

ra·dio·car·bon \ˌrā-dē-ō-'kär-bən\ *n* : CARBON 14

radio frequency *n* : an electromagnetic wave frequency intermediate between audio frequencies and infrared frequencies used esp. for communication and radar signals

ra·dio·gram \'rā-dē-ō-ˌgram\ *n* : a message transmitted by radio

ra·dio·graph \-ˌgraf\ *n* : a photograph made by some form of radiation other than light; *esp* : an X-ray photograph — **radiograph** *vb* — **ra·dio·graph·ic** \ˌrā-

dē-ō-'gra-fik\ *adj* — **ra·dio·graph·i·cal·ly** \-fi-k(ə-)lē\ *adv* — **ra·di·og·ra·phy** \ˌrā-dē-'ä-grə-fē\ *n*

ra·dio·iso·tope \ˌrā-dē-ō-'ī-sə-ˌtōp\ *n* : a radioactive isotope

ra·di·ol·o·gy \ˌrā-dē-'ä-lə-jē\ *n* : the use of radiant energy (as X-rays and radium radiations) in medicine — **ra·di·ol·o·gist** \-jist\ *n*

ra·dio·man \'rā-dē-ō-ˌman\ *n* : a radio operator or technician

ra·di·om·e·ter \ˌrā-dē-'ä-mə-tər\ *n* : an instrument for measuring the intensity of radiant energy — **ra·dio·met·ric** \ˌrā-dē-ō-'me-trik\ *adj* — **ra·di·om·e·try** \-mə-trē\ *n*

ra·dio·phone \'rā-dē-ə-ˌfōn\ *n* : RADIO-TELEPHONE

ra·dio·sonde \'rā-dē-ō-ˌsänd\ *n* : a small radio transmitter carried aloft (as by balloon) and used to transmit meteorological data

ra·dio·tele·phone \ˌrā-dē-ō-'te-lə-ˌfōn\ *n* : a telephone that uses radio waves wholly or partly instead of connecting wires — **ra·dio·te·le·pho·ny** \-tə-'le-fə-nē, -'te-lə-ˌfō-nē\ *n*

radio telescope *n* : a radio receiver-antenna combination used for observation in radio astronomy

ra·dio·ther·a·py \ˌrā-dē-ō-'ther-ə-pē\ *n* : the treatment of disease by means of radiation (as X-rays) — **ra·dio·ther·a·pist** \-pist\ *n*

rad·ish \'ra-dish\ *n* [ME, alter. of OE *rædic*, fr. L *radic-*, *radix* root, radish] : a pungent fleshy root usu. eaten raw; *also* : a plant related to the mustards that produces this root

ra·di·um \'rā-dē-əm\ *n* [NL, fr. L *radius* ray] : a very radioactive metallic chemical element that is used in the treatment of cancer

ra·di·us \'rā-dē-əs\ *n, pl* **ra·dii** \-ē-ˌī\ *also* **ra·di·us·es 1** : a straight line extending from the center of a circle or a sphere to the circumference or surface; *also* : the length of a radius **2** : the bone on the thumb side of the human forearm **3** : a circular area defined by the length of its radius ♦ *Synonyms* RANGE, REACH, SCOPE, COMPASS

RADM *abbr* rear admiral

ra·don \'rā-ˌdän\ *n* : a heavy radioactive gaseous chemical element

RAF *abbr* Royal Air Force

raf·fia \'ra-fē-ə\ *n* : fiber used esp. for making baskets and hats that is obtained from the stalks of the leaves of a tropical African palm (**raffia palm**)

raff·ish \'ra-fish\ *adj* : jaunty or sporty esp. in a flashy or vulgar manner — **raff·ish·ly** *adv* — **raff·ish·ness** *n*

¹**raf·fle** \'ra-fəl\ *vb* **raf·fled; raf·fling** : to dispose of by a raffle

²**raffle** *n* : a lottery in which the prize is won by one of a number of persons buying chances

¹**raft** \'raft\ *n* **1** : a number of logs or timbers fastened together to form a float **2** : a flat structure for support or transportation on water

²raft vb **1** : to travel or transport by raft **2** : to make into a raft

³raft n : a large amount or number

raf·ter \'raf-tər\ n : any of the parallel beams that support a roof

¹rag \'rag\ n **1** : a waste piece of cloth **2** : a sleazy newspaper

²rag n : a composition in ragtime

ra·ga \'rä-gə\ n **1** : a traditional melodic pattern or mode in Indian music **2** : an improvisation based on a raga

rag·a·muf·fin \'ra-gə-ˌmə-fən\ n [ME *Ragamuffyn*, name for a ragged, oafish person] : a ragged dirty person; *esp* : a poorly clothed often dirty child

¹rage \'rāj\ n **1** : violent and uncontrolled anger **2** : VOGUE, FASHION

²rage vb **raged**; **rag·ing 1** : to be furiously angry : RAVE **2** : to continue out of control ⟨the fire *raged*⟩

rag·ged \'ra-gəd\ adj **1** : TORN, TATTERED ⟨a ~ dress⟩; *also* : wearing tattered clothes **2** : done in an uneven way ⟨a ~ performance⟩ — **rag·ged·ly** adv — **rag·ged·ness** n

rag·lan \'ra-glən\ n : an overcoat with sleeves (**raglan sleeves**) sewn in with seams slanting from neck to underarm

ra·gout \ra-ˈgü\ n [F *ragoût*, fr. MF *ragouster* to revive the taste, fr. MF *re-* + *a-* to (fr. L *ad-*) + *goust* taste, fr. L *gustus*] : a highly seasoned meat stew with vegetables

rag·pick·er \'rag-ˌpi-kər\ n : one who collects rags and refuse for a living

rag·time \-ˌtīm\ n : music in which there is more or less continuous syncopation in the melody

rag·top \'rag-ˌtäp\ n : CONVERTIBLE

rag·weed \-ˌwēd\ n : any of several chiefly No. American weedy composite herbs with allergenic pollen

¹raid \'rād\ n : a sudden usu. surprise attack or invasion : FORAY

²raid vb : to make a raid on — **raid·er** n

¹rail \'rāl\ n [ME *raile*, fr. AF *raille, reille* bar, rule, fr. L *regula* straightedge, rule, fr. *regere* to keep straight, direct] **1** : a bar extending from one support to another as a guard or barrier **2** : a bar of steel forming a track for wheeled vehicles **3** : RAILROAD

²rail vb : to provide with a railing

³rail n, pl **rail** or **rails** : any of numerous small wading birds often hunted as game birds

⁴rail vb [ME, fr. MF *railler* to mock, prob. fr. OF *reillier* to growl, mutter, fr. VL **ragulare* to bray, fr. LL *ragere* to neigh] : to complain angrily : SCOLD, REVILE — **rail·er** n

rail·ing \'rā-liŋ\ n : a barrier of rails

rail·lery \'rā-lə-rē\ n, pl **-ler·ies** : good-natured ridicule : BANTER

¹rail·road \'rāl-ˌrōd\ n : a permanent road with rails fixed to ties providing a track for cars; *also* : such a road and its assets constituting a property

²railroad vb **1** : to put through (as a law) too hastily **2** : to convict hastily or with insufficient or improper evidence **3** : to

send by rail **4** : to work on a railroad — **rail·road·er** n — **rail·road·ing** n

rail·way \-ˌwā\ n : RAILROAD

rai·ment \'rā-mənt\ n : CLOTHING

¹rain \'rān\ n **1** : water falling in drops from the clouds **2** : a shower of objects ⟨a ~ of bullets⟩ — **rainy** adj

²rain vb **1** : to send down rain **2** : to fall as or like rain **3** : to pour down

¹rain·bow \-ˌbō\ n : an arc or circle of colors formed by the refraction and reflection of the sun's rays in rain, spray, or mist

²rainbow adj **1** : having many colors **2** : of, relating to, or made up of people of different races or cultural backgrounds

rainbow trout n : a large stout-bodied fish of western No. America closely related to the salmons of the Pacific and usu. having red or pink stripes with black dots along its sides

rain check n **1** : a ticket stub good for a later performance when the scheduled one is rained out **2** : an assurance of a deferred extension of an offer

rain·coat \'rān-ˌkōt\ n : a waterproof or water-repellent coat

rain date n : an alternative date for an event postponed due to rain

rain·drop \-ˌdräp\ n : a drop of rain

rain·fall \-ˌfȯl\ n **1** : amount of precipitation measured by depth **2** : a fall of rain

rain forest n : a tropical woodland having an annual rainfall of at least 100 inches (254 centimeters) and marked by lofty broad-leaved evergreen trees forming a continuous canopy

rain·mak·ing \'rān-ˌmā-kiŋ\ n : the action or process of producing or attempting to produce rain by artificial means — **rain·mak·er** n

rain out vb : to interrupt or prevent by rain

rain·storm \'rān-ˌstȯrm\ n : a storm of or with rain

rain·wa·ter \-ˌwȯ-tər, -ˌwä-\ n : water fallen as rain

¹raise \'rāz\ vb **raised**; **rais·ing 1** : to cause or help to rise : LIFT ⟨~ a window⟩ **2** : AWAKEN, AROUSE ⟨enough to ~ the dead⟩ **3** : BUILD, ERECT ⟨~ a monument⟩ **4** : PROMOTE ⟨was *raised* to captain⟩ **5** : END ⟨~ a siege⟩ **6** : COLLECT ⟨~ money⟩ **7** : BREED, GROW ⟨~ cattle⟩; *also* : BRING UP ⟨~ a family⟩ **8** : PROVOKE ⟨~ a laugh⟩ **9** : to bring to notice ⟨~ an objection⟩ **10** : INCREASE ⟨~ prices⟩; *also* : to bet more than **11** : to make light and spongy ⟨~ dough⟩ **12** : to multiply a quantity by itself a specified number of times ⟨~ 2 to the third power⟩ **13** : to cause to form ⟨~ a blister⟩ ♦ **Synonyms** LIFT, HOIST, BOOST, ELEVATE — **rais·er** n — **raise the bar** : to set a higher standard

²raise n : an increase in amount (as of a bid or bet); *also* : an increase in pay

rai·sin \'rā-zᵊn\ n [ME, fr. AF, grape, raisin, fr. L *racemus* cluster of grapes or berries] : a grape dried for food

rai·son d'être \ˌrā-ˌzōⁿ-ˈdetrᵊ\ n, pl **rai-**

sons d'être \-ˌzōⁿz-\ : reason or justification for existence

ra·ja or **ra·jah** \ˈrä-jə\ n [Hindi rājā, fr. Skt rājan king] : an Indian prince

¹**rake** \ˈrāk\ n : a long-handled garden tool having a crossbar with prongs

²**rake** vb **raked; rak·ing** 1 : to gather, loosen, or smooth with or as if with a rake 2 : to sweep the length of (as a trench or ship) with gunfire

³**rake** n : inclination from either perpendicular or horizontal : SLANT

⁴**rake** n : a dissolute man : LIBERTINE

rake–off \ˈrāk-ˌȯf\ n : a percentage or cut taken

¹**rak·ish** \ˈrā-kish\ adj : DISSOLUTE — **rak·ish·ly** adv — **rak·ish·ness** n

²**rakish** adj 1 : having a trim appearance indicative of speed ⟨a ~ sloop⟩ 2 : JAUNTY, SPORTY ⟨~ clothes⟩ — **rak·ish·ly** adv — **rak·ish·ness** n

ral·ly \ˈra-lē\ vb **ral·lied; ral·ly·ing** 1 : to bring together for a common purpose; also : to bring back to order ⟨a leader ~ing his forces⟩ 2 : to arouse to activity or from depression or weakness 3 : to make a comeback ♦ **Synonyms** STIR, ROUSE, AWAKEN, WAKEN, KINDLE

rally n, pl **rallies** 1 : an act of rallying 2 : a mass meeting to arouse enthusiasm 3 : a competitive automobile event run over public roads

³**rally** vb **ral·lied; ral·ly·ing** : BANTER

rallying cry n : WAR CRY 2

¹**ram** \ˈram\ n 1 : a male sheep 2 : BATTERING RAM

²**ram** vb **rammed; ram·ming** 1 : to force or drive in or through 2 : CRAM, CROWD 3 : to strike against violently

RAM \ˈram\ n : a computer memory that provides the main internal storage for programs and data

¹**ram·ble** \ˈram-bəl\ vb **ram·bled; ram·bling** : to go about aimlessly : ROAM, WANDER

²**ramble** n : a leisurely excursion; esp : an aimless walk

ram·bler \ˈram-blər\ n 1 : a person who rambles 2 : any of various climbing roses with large clusters of small often double flowers

ram·bunc·tious \ram-ˈbəŋk-shəs\ adj : UNRULY

ra·mie \ˈrā-mē, ˈra-\ n : a strong lustrous bast fiber from an Asian nettle

ram·i·fi·ca·tion \ˌra-mə-fə-ˈkā-shən\ n 1 : the act or process of branching 2 : CONSEQUENCE, OUTGROWTH ⟨the ~s of the decision⟩

ram·i·fy \ˈra-mə-ˌfī\ vb **-fied; -fy·ing** : to branch out

ramp \ˈramp\ n : a sloping passage or roadway connecting different levels

¹**ram·page** \ˈram-ˌpāj, (ˌ)ram-ˈpāj\ vb **rampaged; ram·pag·ing** : to rush about wildly

²**ram·page** \ˈram-ˌpāj\ n : a course of violent or riotous action or behavior — **ram·pa·geous** \ram-ˈpā-jəs\ adj

ram·pant \ˈram-pənt\ adj : unchecked in growth or spread : RIFE ⟨fear was ~ in

the town⟩ — **ram·pan·cy** \-pən-sē\ n — **ram·pant·ly** adv

ram·part \ˈram-ˌpärt\ n 1 : a protective barrier 2 : a broad embankment raised as a fortification

¹**ram·rod** \ˈram-ˌräd\ n 1 : a rod used to ram a charge into a muzzle-loading gun 2 : a cleaning rod for small arms 3 : BOSS, OVERSEER

²**ramrod** adj : marked by rigidity or severity

³**ramrod** vb : to direct, supervise, and control

ram·shack·le \ˈram-ˌsha-kəl\ adj : RICKETY, TUMBLEDOWN

ran past of RUN

¹**ranch** \ˈranch\ n [MexSp rancho small ranch, fr. Sp, camp, hut & Sp dial., small farm, fr. Old Spanish ranchear (se) to take up quarters, fr. MF (se) ranger to take up a position, fr. ranger to set in a row] 1 : an establishment for the raising and grazing of livestock (as cattle, sheep, or horses) 2 : a large farm devoted to a specialty 3 : RANCH HOUSE 2

²**ranch** vb : to live or work on a ranch — **ranch·er** n

ranch house n 1 : the main house on a ranch 2 : a one-story house typically with a low-pitched roof

ran·cho \ˈran-chō, ˈrän-\ n, pl **ranchos** : RANCH 1

ran·cid \ˈran-səd\ adj 1 : having a rank smell or taste 2 : OFFENSIVE 3 — **ran·cid·i·ty** \ran-ˈsi-də-tē\ n

ran·cor \ˈraŋ-kər\ n : bitter deep-seated ill will ♦ **Synonyms** ANTAGONISM, ANIMOSITY, ANTIPATHY, ENMITY, HOSTILITY — **ran·cor·ous** adj

ran·cour Brit var of RANCOR

rand \ˈrand, ˈränd, ˈränt\ n, pl **rand** — see MONEY table

R & B abbr rhythm and blues

R & D abbr research and development

ran·dom \ˈran-dəm\ adj : CHANCE, HAPHAZARD — **ran·dom·ly** adv — **ran·dom·ness** n

random–access adj : allowing access to stored data in any order the user desires

random–access memory n : RAM

ran·dom·ize \ˈran-də-ˌmīz\ vb **-ized; -izing** : to select, assign, or arrange in a random way — **ran·dom·i·za·tion** \ˌran-də-mə-ˈzā-shən\ n

R & R abbr rest and recreation; rest and recuperation

rang past of RING

¹**range** \ˈrānj\ n 1 : a series of things in a row 2 : a cooking stove having an oven and a flat top with burners 3 : open land where animals (as livestock) may roam and graze 4 : the region throughout which an organism occurs 5 : the act of ranging 6 : the distance a weapon will shoot or is to be shot 7 : a place where shooting is practiced 8 : the space or extent included, covered, or used : SCOPE 9 : a variation within limits ♦ **Synonyms** REACH, COMPASS, RADIUS, CIRCLE

²**range** vb **ranged; rang·ing** [ME, fr. AF renger, fr. renc, reng line, place, row, of

Gmc origin] **1** : to set in a row or in proper order **2** : to set in place among others of the same kind **3** : to roam over or through : EXPLORE **4** : to roam at large or freely **5** : to correspond in direction or line **6** : to vary within limits **7** : to find the range of an object by instrument (as radar)

rang·er \ˈrān-jər\ n **1** : FOREST RANGER **2** : a member of a body of troops who range over a region **3** : an expert in close-range fighting and raiding tactics

rangy \ˈrān-jē\ adj **rang·i·er**; **-est** : being long-limbed and slender — **rang·i·ness** \ˈrān-jē-nəs\ n

ra·ni or **ra·nee** \rä-ˈnē, ˈrä-ˌnē\ n : a raja's wife

¹rank \ˈraŋk\ adj **1** : strong and vigorous and usu. coarse in growth **2** : unpleasantly strong-smelling — **rank·ly** adv — **rank·ness** n

²rank n **1** : ROW ⟨~s of houses⟩ **2** : a line of soldiers ranged side by side **3** pl : the body of enlisted personnel ⟨rose from the ~s⟩ **4** : position in a group **5** : superior or position **6** : a grade of official standing (as in an army) **7** : an orderly arrangement **8** : CLASS, DIVISION — usu. used in pl.

³rank vb **1** : to arrange in lines or in regular formation **2** : RATE **3** : to rate above (as in official standing) **4** : to take or have a relative position

rank and file n : the general membership of a body as contrasted with its leaders

rank·ing \ˈraŋ-kiŋ\ adj **1** : having a high position : of the highest rank **2** : being next to the chairman in seniority

ran·kle \ˈraŋ-kəl\ vb **ran·kled**; **ran·kling** [ME ranclen to fester, fr. AF rancler, fr. OF draoncler, raoncler, fr. draoncle, raoncle festering sore, fr. ML dracunculus, fr. L, dim. of draco serpent] : to cause anger, irritation, or bitterness

ran·sack \ˈran-ˌsak\ vb : to search thoroughly; esp : to search through and rob

¹ran·som \ˈran-səm\ n [ME ransoun, fr. OF rançun, fr. L redemption-, redemptio act of buying back, fr. redimere to buy back, redeem] **1** : something paid or demanded for the freedom of a captive **2** : the act of ransoming

²ransom vb : to free from captivity or punishment by paying a price — **ran·som·er** n

rant \ˈrant\ vb **1** : to talk loudly and wildly **2** : to scold violently — **rant·er** n — **rant·ing·ly** adv

¹rap \ˈrap\ n **1** : a sharp blow **2** : a sharp rebuke **3** : a negative often undeserved reputation ⟨a bum ~⟩ **4** : responsibility for or consequences of an action ⟨take the ~⟩

²rap vb **rapped**; **rap·ping** **1** : to strike sharply : KNOCK **2** : to utter sharply **3** : to criticize sharply

³rap vb **rapped**; **rap·ping** **1** : to talk freely and frankly **2** : to perform rap music — **rap·per** n

⁴rap n **1** : TALK, CONVERSATION **2** : a rhythmic chanting of usu. rhymed couplets to a musical accompaniment; also : a piece so performed

ra·pa·cious \rə-ˈpā-shəs\ adj **1** : excessively greedy or covetous **2** : living on prey **3** : RAVENOUS 2 ⟨a ~ appetite⟩ — **ra·pa·cious·ly** adv — **ra·pa·cious·ness** n — **ra·pac·i·ty** \-ˈpa-sə-tē\ n

¹rape \ˈrāp\ n : an Old World herb related to the mustards that is grown as a forage crop and for its seeds (**rapeseed** \-ˌsēd\)

²rape vb **raped**; **rap·ing** : to commit rape on — **rap·er** n — **rap·ist** \ˈrā-pist\ n

³rape n **1** : a carrying away by force **2** : unlawful sexual activity and usu. sexual intercourse carried out forcibly or under threat of injury

¹rap·id \ˈra-pəd\ adj [L rapidus strong-flowing, rapid, fr. rapere to seize, carry away] : very fast : SWIFT ♦ Synonyms FLEET, QUICK, SPEEDY — **ra·pid·i·ty** \rə-ˈpi-də-tē\ n — **rap·id·ly** adv

²rapid n : a place in a stream where the current flows very fast usu. over obstructions — usu. used in pl.

rapid eye movement n : rapid conjugate movement of the eyes associated with REM sleep

rapid transit n : fast passenger transportation (as by subway) in cities

¹ra·pi·er \ˈrā-pē-ər\ n : a straight 2-edged sword with a narrow pointed blade

²rapier adj : extremely sharp or keen ⟨~ wit⟩

rap·ine \ˈra-pən, -ˌpīn\ n : PILLAGE, PLUNDER

rap·pel \ra-ˈpel, ra-\ vb **-pelled**; **-pel·ling** : to descend (as from a cliff) by sliding down a rope

rap·pen \ˈrä-pən\ n, pl **rappen** : the centime of Switzerland

rap·port \ra-ˈpór\ n : RELATION; esp : relation characterized by harmony

rap·proche·ment \ˌra-ˌprōsh-ˈmäⁿ, ra-ˈprōsh-ˌmäⁿ\ n : the establishment of or a state of having cordial relations

rapt \ˈrapt\ adj **1** : carried away with emotion **2** : ABSORBED, ENGROSSED ⟨listened with ~ attention⟩ — **rapt·ly** \ˈrapt-lē\ adv — **rapt·ness** n

rap·tor \ˈrap-tər, -ˌtór\ n **1** : BIRD OF PREY **2** : a usu. small-to-medium-sized predatory dinosaur

rap·ture \ˈrap-chər\ n : spiritual or emotional ecstasy — **rap·tur·ous** \-chə-rəs\ adj — **rap·tur·ous·ly** adv

rapture of the deep : NITROGEN NARCOSIS

ra·ra avis \ˌrer-ə-ˈā-vəs, ˌrär-ə-ˈā-wəs\ n, pl **ra·ra avis·es** \-ˈā-və-səz\ or **ra·rae aves** \ˌrär-ˌī-ˈā-ˌwās\ [L, rare bird] : a rare person or thing : RARITY

¹rare \ˈrer\ adj **rar·er**; **rar·est** **1** : not thick or dense : THIN ⟨~ air⟩ **2** : unusually fine : EXCELLENT, SPLENDID **3** : seldom met with — **rare·ly** adv — **rare·ness** n — **rar·i·ty** \ˈrar-ə-tē\ n

²rare adj **rar·er**; **rar·est** : cooked so that the inside is still red ⟨~ beef⟩

rare·bit \ˈrer-bət\ n : WELSH RABBIT

rar·efac·tion \\,rer-ə-'fak-shən\ n 1 : the action or process of rarefying 2 : the state of being rarefied

rar·e·fy also **rar·i·fy** \\'rer-ə-,fī\ vb **-fied; -fy·ing** : to make or become rare, thin, or less dense

rar·ing \\'rer-əṇ, -iŋ\ adj : full of enthusiasm or eagerness ⟨~ to go⟩

ras·cal \\'ras-kəl\ n [ME rascaille foot soldiers, commoners, worthless person, fr. AF rascaille, fr. OF dial. *rasquer to scrape, clean off, ultim. fr. L radere to scrape, shave] 1 : a mean or dishonest person 2 : a mischievous person — **ras·cal·i·ty** \\ra-'ska-lə-tē\ n — **ras·cal·ly** \\'ras-kə-lē\ adj

¹rash \\'rash\ adj : having or showing little regard for consequences : too hasty in decision, action, or speech : RECKLESS ♦ **Synonyms** DARING, FOOLHARDY, ADVENTUROUS, VENTURESOME — **rash·ly** adv — **rash·ness** n

²rash n : an eruption on the body

rash·er \\'ra-shər\ n : a thin slice of bacon or ham broiled or fried; also : a portion consisting of several such slices

¹rasp \\'rasp\ vb 1 : to rub with or as if with a rough file 2 : to grate harshly on (as one's nerves) 3 : to speak in a grating tone

²rasp n : a coarse file with cutting points instead of ridges

rasp·ber·ry \\'raz-,ber-ē, -bə-rē\ n 1 : any of various edible usu. black or red berries produced by some brambles; also : such a bramble 2 : a sound of contempt made by protruding the tongue through the lips and expelling air forcibly

¹rat \\'rat\ n 1 : any of numerous rodents larger than the related mice 2 : a contemptible person; esp : one that betrays friends or associates

²rat vb **rat·ted; rat·ting** 1 : to betray or inform on one's associates 2 : to hunt or catch rats

rat cheese n : CHEDDAR

ratch·et \\'ra-chət\ n : a device that consists of a bar or wheel having slanted teeth into which a pawl drops so as to allow motion in only one direction

¹rate \\'rāt\ vb **rat·ed; rat·ing** : to scold violently

²rate n 1 : quantity, amount, or degree measured by some standard 2 : an amount (as of payment) measured by its relation to some other amount (as of time) 3 : a charge, payment, or price fixed according to a ratio, scale, or standard ⟨tax ~⟩ 4 : RANK, CLASS

³rate vb **rat·ed; rat·ing** 1 : ESTIMATE 2 : CONSIDER, REGARD ⟨rated as a good pianist⟩ 3 : to settle the relative rank or class of 4 : to be classed : RANK 5 : to have a right to : DESERVE 6 : to be of consequence — **rat·er** n

rath·er \\'ra-thər, 'rä-, 'ra-\ adv [ME, fr. OE hrathor, compar. of hrathe quickly] 1 : more properly 2 : PREFERABLY ⟨I'd ~ not go⟩ 3 : more correctly speaking 4 : to the contrary : INSTEAD 5 : SOMEWHAT ⟨~ warm⟩

rather than prep : INSTEAD OF

raths·kel·ler \\'rät-,ske-lər, 'rat-\ n [obs. G (now Ratskeller), city-hall basement restaurant, fr. Rat council + Keller cellar] : a usu. basement tavern or restaurant

rat·i·fy \\'ra-tə-,fī\ vb **-fied; -fy·ing** : to approve and accept formally — **rat·i·fi·ca·tion** \\,ra-tə-fə-'kā-shən\ n

rat·ing \\'rā-tiŋ\ n 1 : a classification according to grade : RANK 2 Brit : a naval enlisted man 3 : an estimate of the credit standing and business responsibility of a person or firm

ra·tio \\'rā-shō, -shē-ō\ n, pl **ra·tios** 1 : the indicated quotient of two numbers or mathematical expressions 2 : the relationship in number, quantity, or degree between two or more things

ra·ti·o·ci·na·tion \\,ra-tē-,ō-sə-'nā-shən, -,ä-\ n : exact thinking : REASONING — **ra·ti·o·ci·nate** \\-'ō-sə-,nāt, -'ä-\ vb — **ra·ti·o·ci·na·tive** \\-'ō-sə-,nā-tiv, -'ä-\ adj — **ra·ti·o·ci·na·tor** \\-'ō-sə-,nā-tər, -'ä-sə-\ n

¹ra·tion \\'ra-shən, 'rä-\ n 1 : a food allowance for one day 2 : FOOD, PROVISIONS, DIET — usu. used in pl. 3 : SHARE, ALLOTMENT

²ration vb 1 : to supply with or allot as rations 2 : to use or allot sparingly ♦ **Synonyms** APPORTION, PORTION, PRORATE, PARCEL

¹ra·tio·nal \\'ra-shə-nəl\ adj 1 : having reason or understanding 2 : of or relating to reason 3 : relating to, consisting of, or being one or more rational numbers — **ra·tio·nal·ly** adv

²rational n : RATIONAL NUMBER

ra·tio·nale \\,ra-shə-'nal\ n 1 : an explanation of principles controlling belief or practice 2 : an underlying reason

ra·tio·nal·ise Brit var of RATIONALIZE

ra·tio·nal·ism \\'ra-shə-nə-,li-zəm\ n : the practice of guiding one's actions and opinions solely by what seems reasonable — **ra·tio·nal·ist** \\-list\ n — **rationalist** or **ra·tio·nal·is·tic** \\,ra-shə-nə-'lis-tik\ adj — **ra·tio·nal·is·ti·cal·ly** \\-ti-k(ə-)lē\ adv

ra·tio·nal·i·ty \\,ra-shə-'na-lə-tē\ n, pl **-ties** : the quality or state of being rational

ra·tio·nal·ize \\'ra-shə-nə-,līz\ vb **-ized; -iz·ing** 1 : to make (something irrational) appear rational or reasonable 2 : to provide a natural explanation of (as a myth) 3 : to justify (as one's behavior or weaknesses) esp. to oneself 4 : to find plausible but untrue reasons for conduct — **ra·tio·nal·i·za·tion** \\,ra-shə-nə-lə-'zā-shən\ n

rational number n : a number that can be expressed as an integer or the quotient of an integer divided by a nonzero integer

rat race n : strenuous, tiresome, and usu. competitive activity or rush

rat·tan \\ra-'tan, rə-\ n : a cane or switch made from one of the long stems of an Asian climbing palm; also : this palm

rat·ter \\'ra-tər\ n : a rat-catching dog or cat

¹rat·tle \\'ra-t°l\ vb **rat·tled; rat·tling** 1 : to make or cause to make a series of clattering sounds **2** : to move with a clattering sound **3** : to say or do in a brisk lively fashion ⟨~ off the answers⟩ **4** : CONFUSE, UPSET ⟨~ a witness⟩

²rattle *n* **1** : a toy that produces a rattle when shaken **2** : a series of clattering and knocking sounds : a rattling organ at the end of a rattlesnake's tail

rat·tler \'rat-lər\ *n* : RATTLESNAKE

rat·tle·snake \'ra-t⁰l-ˌsnāk\ *n* : any of various American pit vipers with a rattle at the end of the tail

rat·tle·trap \'ra-t⁰l-ˌtrap\ *n* : something (as an old car) rickety and full of rattles

rat·tling \'rat-liŋ\ *adj* **1** : LIVELY, BRISK ⟨moved at a ~ pace⟩ **2** : FIRST-RATE, SPLENDID

rat·trap \'rat-ˌtrap\ *n* **1** : a trap for rats **2** : a dilapidated building

rat·ty \'ra-tē\ *adj* **rat·ti·er; -est 1** : infested with rats **2** : of, relating to, or suggestive of rats **3** : SHABBY ⟨a ~ old coat⟩

rau·cous \'ró-kəs\ *adj* **1** : HARSH, HOARSE, STRIDENT ⟨~ voices⟩ **2** : boisterously disorderly — **rau·cous·ly** *adv* — **rau·cous·ness** *n*

raun·chy \'rón-chē, 'rän-\ *adj* **raun·chi·er; -est 1** : SLOVENLY, DIRTY **2** : OBSCENE, SMUTTY ⟨~ jokes⟩ — **raun·chi·ness** \-chē-nəs\ *n*

¹rav·age \'ra-vij\ *n* [F] : an act or result of ravaging : DEVASTATION

²ravage *vb* **rav·aged; rav·ag·ing** : to lay waste : DEVASTATE — **rav·ag·er** *n*

¹rave \'rāv\ *vb* **raved; rav·ing 1** : to talk wildly in or as if in delirium : STORM, RAGE **2** : to talk with extreme enthusiasm — **rav·er** *n*

²rave *n* **1** : an act or instance of raving **2** : an extravagant favorable criticism

¹rav·el \'ra-vəl\ *vb* **-eled** *or* **-elled; -el·ing** *or* **-el·ling 1** : UNRAVEL, UNTWIST **2** : TANGLE, CONFUSE

²ravel *n* **1** : something tangled **2** : something raveled out; *esp* : a loose thread

¹ra·ven \'rā-vən\ *n* : a large black bird related to the crow

²raven *adj* : black and glossy like a raven's feathers

³rav·en \'ra-vən\ *vb* **1** : to devour greedily **2** : DESPOIL, PLUNDER **3** : PREY

rav·en·ous \'ra-və-nəs\ *adj* **1** : RAPACIOUS, VORACIOUS ⟨~ wolves⟩ **2** : eager for food : very hungry — **rav·en·ous·ly** *adv* — **rav·en·ous·ness** *n*

ra·vine \rə-'vēn\ *n* : a small narrow steepsided valley larger than a gully

rav·i·o·li \ˌra-vē-'ō-lē\ *n, pl* **ravioli** *also* **raviolis** [It, fr. It dial., pl. of *raviolo*, lit., little turnip, dim. of *rava* turnip, fr. L *rapa*] : small cases of dough with a savory filling (as of meat or cheese)

rav·ish \'ra-vish\ *vb* **1** : to seize and take away by violence **2** : to overcome with emotion and esp. with joy or delight **3** : RAPE — **rav·ish·er** *n* — **rav·ish·ment** *n*

¹raw \'ró\ *adj* **raw·er** \'ró-ər\; **raw·est** \'ró-əst\ **1** : not cooked **2** : changed little from the original form : not processed

⟨~ materials⟩ **3** : having the surface abraded or irritated ⟨a ~ sore⟩ **4** : not trained or experienced ⟨~ recruits⟩ **5** : VULGAR, COARSE ⟨~ language⟩ **6** : disagreeably cold and damp ⟨a ~ day⟩ **7** : UNFAIR ⟨~ deal⟩ — **raw·ness** *n*

²raw *n* : a raw place or state — **in the raw** : NAKED

raw-boned \'ró-ˌbónd\ *adj* : LEAN, GAUNT; *also* : having a heavy frame that seems to have little flesh

raw·hide \'ró-ˌhīd\ *n* : the untanned skin of cattle; *also* : a whip made of this

¹ray \'rā\ *n* : any of an order of large flat cartilaginous fishes that have the eyes on the upper surface and the hind end of the body slender and taillike

²ray *n* [ME, fr. AF *rai*, fr. L *radius* rod, ray] **1** : any of the lines of light that appear to radiate from a bright object **2** : a thin beam of radiant energy (as light) **3** : light from a beam **4** : a thin line like a beam of light **5** : an animal or plant structure resembling a ray **6** : a tiny bit : PARTICLE ⟨a ~ of hope⟩

ray·on \'rā-ˌän\ *n* : a fiber made from cellulose; *also* : a yarn, thread, or fabric made from such fibers

raze \'rāz\ *vb* **razed; raz·ing 1** : to scrape, cut, or shave off **2** : to destroy to the ground : DEMOLISH

ra·zor \'rā-zər\ *n* : a sharp cutting instrument used to shave off hair

ra·zor-backed \'rā-zər-ˌbakt\ *or* **ra·zor-back** \-ˌbak\ *adj* : having a sharp narrow back ⟨a ~ horse⟩

razor clam *n* : any of a family of marine bivalve mollusks having a long narrow curved thin shell

razor wire *n* : coiled wire fitted with sharp edges and used as an obstacle or barrier

¹razz \'raz\ *n* : RASPBERRY 2

²razz *vb* : RIDICULE, TEASE ⟨fans ~ed visiting players⟩

Rb *symbol* rubidium

RBC *abbr* red blood cells

RBI \ˌär-(ˌ)bē-'ī, 'ri-bē\ *n, pl* **RBIs** *or* **RBI** [*run batted in*] : a run in baseball that is driven in by a batter

RC *abbr* **1** Red Cross **2** Roman Catholic

RCAF *abbr* Royal Canadian Air Force

RCMP *abbr* Royal Canadian Mounted Police

RCN *abbr* Royal Canadian Navy

rct *abbr* recruit

rd *abbr* **1** road **2** rod **3** round

RD *abbr* rural delivery

RDA *abbr* recommended daily allowance; recommended dietary allowance

re \'rā, 'rē\ *prep* : with regard to

Re *symbol* rhenium

re- \rē, ˌrē, 'rē\ *prefix* **1** : again : for a second time **2** : anew : in a new or different form **3** : back : backward

¹reach \'rēch\ *vb* **1** : to stretch out **2** : to touch or attempt to touch or seize **3** : to extend to **4** : to communicate with **5** : to arrive at ♦ *Synonyms* GAIN, REALIZE, ACHIEVE, ATTAIN — **reach·able** *adj* — **reach·er** *n*

²**reach** *n* **1** : an unbroken stretch of a river **2** : the act of reaching **3** : a reachable distance; *also* : ability to reach **4** : a range of knowledge or comprehension

re·act \rē-'akt\ *vb* **1** : to exert a return or counteracting influence **2** : to have or show a reaction **3** : to act in opposition to a force or influence **4** : to move or tend in a reverse direction **5** : to undergo chemical reaction

re·ac·tant \-'ak-tənt\ *n* : a chemically reacting substance

re·ac·tion \rē-'ak-shən\ *n* **1** : the act or process of reacting **2** : a counter tendency; *esp* : a tendency toward a former esp. outmoded political or social order or policy **3** : bodily, mental, or emotional response to a stimulus **4** : chemical change **5** : a process involving change in atomic nuclei

re·ac·tion·ary \rē-'ak-shə-ner-ē\ *adj* : relating to, marked by, or favoring esp. political reaction — **reactionary** *n*

re·ac·tive \rē-'ak-tiv\ *adj* : reacting or tending to react

re·ac·tor \rē-'ak-tər\ *n* **1** : one that reacts **2** : a device for the controlled release of nuclear energy

¹**read** \'rēd\ *vb* **read** \'red\; **read·ing** [ME *reden* to advise, interpret, read, fr. OE *rǣdan*] **1** : to understand language by interpreting written symbols for speech sounds **2** : to utter aloud written or printed words **3** : to learn by observing ⟨~ nature's signs⟩ **4** : to study by a course of reading ⟨~*s* law⟩ **5** : to discover the meaning of ⟨~ the clues⟩ **6** : to recognize or interpret as if by reading **7** : to attribute (a meaning) to something ⟨~ guilt in his manner⟩ **8** : INDICATE ⟨thermometer ~*s* 10°⟩ **9** : to consist in phrasing or meaning ⟨the two versions ~ differently⟩ — **read·abil·i·ty** \rē-də-'bi-lə-tē\ *n* — **read·able** \'rē-də-bəl\ *adj* — **read·ably** \-blē\ *adv* — **read·er** *n*

²**read** \'red\ *adj* : informed by reading ⟨widely ~⟩

read·er·ship \'rē-dər-ˌship\ *n* : the mass or a particular group of readers

read·ing *n* **1** : something read or for reading **2** : a particular version **3** : data indicated by an instrument ⟨thermometer ~⟩ **4** : a particular interpretation (as of a law) **5** : a particular performance (as of a musical work) **6** : an indication of a certain state of affairs

read–only memory *n* : ROM

read·out \'rēd-ˌau̇t\ *n* **1** : the process of removing information from an automatic device (as a computer) and displaying it in an understandable form; *also* : the information removed from such a device **2** : an electronic device that presents information in visual form

read out *vb* **1** : to read aloud **2** : to expel from an organization

¹**ready** \'re-dē\ *adj* **read·i·er; -est 1** : pre-

pared for use or action **2** : likely to do something indicated; *also* : willingly disposed : INCLINED **3** : spontaneously prompt ⟨her ~ wit⟩ **4** : immediately available ⟨~ cash⟩ — **read·i·ly** \'re-də-lē\ *adv* — **read·i·ness** \-dē-nəs\ *n* — **at the ready** : ready for immediate use

²**ready** *vb* **read·ied; ready·ing** : to make ready : PREPARE

ready–made \ˌre-dē-'mād\ *adj* : already made up for general sale : not specially made — **ready–made** *n*

ready room *n* : a room in which pilots are briefed and await orders

re·agent \rē-'ā-jənt\ *n* : a substance that takes part in or brings about a particular chemical reaction

¹**re·al** \'rēl\ *adj* [ME, real, relating to things (in law), fr. AF, fr. ML & LL; ML *realis* relating to things (in law), fr. LL, real, fr. L *res* thing, fact] **1** : of or relating to fixed or immovable things (as land) ⟨~ property⟩ **2** : not artificial : GENUINE; *also* : not imaginary — **re·al·ness** *n* — **for real 1** : in earnest **2** : GENUINE ⟨the threat was *for real*⟩

²**real** *adv* : VERY ⟨had a ~ good time⟩

³**re·al** \rā-'äl\ *n* — see MONEY table

real estate *n* : property in buildings and land

re·al·ism \'rē-ə-ˌli-zəm\ *n* **1** : the disposition to face facts and to deal with them practically **2** : true and faithful portrayal of nature and of people in art or literature — **re·al·ist** \-list\ *adj or n* — **re·al·is·tic** \ˌrē-ə-'lis-tik\ *adj* — **re·al·is·ti·cal·ly** \-ti-k(ə-)lē\ *adv*

re·al·i·ty \rē-'a-lə-tē\ *n, pl* **-ties 1** : the quality or state of being real **2** : something real **3** : the totality of real things and events

re·al·ize \'rē-ə-ˌlīz\ *vb* **-ized; -iz·ing 1** : to make actual : ACCOMPLISH **2** : to convert into money ⟨~ assets⟩ **3** : OBTAIN, GAIN ⟨~ a profit⟩ **4** : to be aware of : UNDERSTAND — **re·al·iz·able** *adj* — **re·al·i·za·tion** \ˌrē-ə-lə-'zā-shən\ *n*

re·al·ly \'rē-lē, 'ri-\ *adv* : in truth : in fact : ACTUALLY

realm \'relm\ *n* **1** : KINGDOM **2** : SPHERE, DOMAIN ⟨within the ~ of possibility⟩

real number *n* : a number that has no imaginary part ⟨the set of all *real numbers* comprises the rationals and the irrationals⟩

re·al·po·li·tik \rā-'äl-ˌpō-li-ˌtēk\ *n, often cap* [G] : politics based on practical and material factors rather than on theoretical or ethical objectives

real time *n* : the actual time during which something takes place — **real–time** *adj*

re·al·ty \'rēl-tē\ *n* : REAL ESTATE

¹**ream** \'rēm\ *n* [ME *reme*, fr. AF, ultim. fr. Ar *rizma*, lit., bundle] : a quantity of paper that is variously 480, 500, or 516 sheets

reabsorb	readdress	readmit	realignment
reacquire	readjust	reaffirm	reallocate
reactivate	readjustment	reaffirmation	reallocation
reactivation	readmission	realign	

²**ream** *vb* : to enlarge, shape, or clear with a reamer

ream·er \'rē-mər\ *n* : a tool with cutting edges that is used to enlarge or shape a hole

reap \'rēp\ *vb* **1** : to cut or clear with a scythe, sickle, or machine **2** : to gather by or as if by cutting : HARVEST ⟨∼ a reward⟩ — **reap·er** *n*

¹**rear** \'rir\ *vb* **1** : to erect by building **2** : to set or raise upright **3** : to breed and raise for use or market ⟨∼ livestock⟩ **4** : BRING UP, FOSTER **5** : to lift or rise up; *esp* : to rise on the hind legs

²**rear** *n* **1** : the unit (as of an army) or area farthest from the enemy **2** : BACK; *also* : the position at the back of something

³**rear** *adj* : being at the back

rear admiral *n* : a commissioned officer in the navy or coast guard ranking next below a vice admiral

¹**rear·ward** \'rir-wərd\ *adj* **1** : being at or toward the rear **2** : directed toward the rear ⟨a ∼ glance⟩

²**rear·ward** *also* **rear·wards** \-wərdz\ *adv* : at or toward the rear ⟨looking ∼⟩

reas *abbr* reasonable

¹**rea·son** \'rē-z⁰n\ *n* [ME *resoun,* fr. AF *raisun,* fr. L *ration-, ratio* reason, computation] **1** : a statement offered in explanation or justification **2** : GROUND, CAUSE **3** : the power to think : INTELLECT **4** : a sane or sound mind **5** : due exercise of the faculty of logical thought

²**reason** *vb* **1** : to talk with another to cause a change of mind **2** : to use the faculty of reason : THINK **3** : to discover or formulate by the use of reason — **rea·son·er** *n* — **rea·son·ing** *n*

rea·son·able \'rē-z⁰n-ə-bəl\ *adj* **1** : being within the bounds of reason : not extreme **2** : INEXPENSIVE **3** : able to reason : RATIONAL — **rea·son·able·ness** *n* — **rea·son·ably** \-blē\ *adv*

re·as·sure \,rē-ə-'shùr\ *vb* **1** : to assure again **2** : to restore confidence to ; free from fear — **re·as·sur·ance** \-'shùr-əns\ *n* — **re·as·sur·ing·ly** *adv*

¹**re·bate** \'rē-,bāt\ *vb* **re·bat·ed; re·bat·ing** : to make or give a rebate

²**rebate** *n* : a return of part of a payment ✦ *Synonyms* DEDUCTION, ABATEMENT, DISCOUNT

¹**reb·el** \'re-bəl\ *adj* [ME, fr. AF fr. L *rebellis,* fr. *re-* + *bellum* war] : of or relating to rebels

²**rebel** *n* : one that rebels against authority

³**re·bel** \ri-'bel\ *vb* **re·belled; re·bel·ling 1** : to resist the authority of one's govern-

ment **2** : to act in or show disobedience **3** : to feel or exhibit anger or revulsion

re·bel·lion \ri-'bel-yən\ *n* : resistance to authority; *esp* : defiance against a government through uprising or revolt

re·bel·lious \-yəs\ *adj* **1** : given to or engaged in rebellion **2** : inclined to resist authority — **re·bel·lious·ly** *adv* — **re·bel·lious·ness** *n*

re·birth \,rē-'bərth\ *n* **1** : a new or second birth **2** : RENAISSANCE, REVIVAL

re·born \-'bòrn\ *adj* : born again : REGENERATED, REVIVED

¹**re·bound** \,rē-'baùnd, 'rē-,baùnd\ *vb* **1** : to spring back on or as if on striking another body **2** : to recover from a setback or frustration

²**re·bound** \'rē-,baùnd\ *n* **1** : the action of rebounding **2** : a rebounding ball **3** : a reaction to setback or frustration

re·buff \ri-'bəf\ *vb* : to reject or criticize sharply : SNUB — **rebuff** *n*

re·build \(,)rē-'bild\ *vb* **-built** \-'bilt\; **-build·ing 1** : REPAIR, RECONSTRUCT; *also* : REMODEL **2** : to build again

re·buke \ri-'byük\ *vb* **re·buked; re·buk·ing** : to reprimand sharply : REPROVE

²**rebuke** *n* : a sharp reprimand

re·bus \'rē-bəs\ *n* [L, by things, abl. pl. of *res* thing] : a representation of syllables or words by means of pictures; *also* : a riddle composed of such pictures

re·but \ri-'bət\ *vb* **re·but·ted; re·but·ting** : to refute esp. formally (as in debate) by evidence and arguments ✦ *Synonyms* DISPROVE, CONTROVERT, CONFUTE — **re·but·ter** *n*

re·but·tal \ri-'bə-t⁰l\ *n* : the act of rebutting

rec *abbr* **1** receipt **2** record; recording **3** recreation

re·cal·ci·trant \ri-'kal-sə-trənt\ *adj* [LL *recalcitrant-, recalcitrans,* prp. of *recalcitrare* to be stubbornly disobedient, fr. L, to kick back, fr. *re-* back, again + *calcitrare* to kick, fr. *calc-, calx* heel] **1** : stubbornly resisting authority **2** : resistant to handling or treatment ✦ *Synonyms* REFRACTORY, HEADSTRONG, WILLFUL, UNRULY, UNGOVERNABLE — **re·cal·ci·trance** \-trəns\ *n*

¹**re·call** \ri-'kòl\ *vb* **1** : REVOKE, CANCEL **2** : to call back **3** : REMEMBER, RECOLLECT ⟨∼ed their last meeting⟩

²**re·call** \ri-'kòl, 'rē-,kòl\ *n* **1** : a summons to return **2** : the procedure of removing an official by popular vote **3** : remembrance of things learned or experienced **4** : the act of revoking **5** : a call by a

---

manufacturer for the return of a product that may be defective or contaminated

re·cant \ri-'kant\ vb : to take back (something one has said) publicly : make an open confession of error — **re·can·ta·tion** \ˌrē-ˌkan-'tā-shən\ n

¹**re·cap** \'rē-ˌkap, rē-'kap\ vb **re·capped**; **re·cap·ping** : RECAPITULATE — **re·cap** \'rē-ˌkap\ n

²**recap** vb **re·capped**; **re·cap·ping** : RETREAD — **re·cap** \'rē-ˌkap\ n

re·ca·pit·u·late \ˌrē-kə-'pi-chə-ˌlāt\ vb **-lat·ed**; **-lat·ing** : to restate briefly : SUMMARIZE — **re·ca·pit·u·la·tion** \-ˌpi-chə-'lā-shən\ n

re·cap·ture \(ˌ)rē-'kap-chər\ vb 1 : to capture again 2 : to experience again ⟨~ happy times⟩

re·cast \(ˌ)rē-'kast\ vb 1 : to cast again 2 : REVISE, REMODEL ⟨~ a sentence⟩

recd abbr received

re·cede \ri-'sēd\ vb **re·ced·ed**; **re·ced·ing** 1 : to move back or away ⟨a receding hairline⟩ 2 : to slant backward 3 : DIMINISH, CONTRACT ⟨a receding deficit⟩

¹**re·ceipt** \ri-'sēt\ n 1 : RECIPE 2 : the act of receiving 3 : something received — usu. used in pl. 4 : a written acknowledgment of something received

²**receipt** vb 1 : to give a receipt for 2 : to mark as paid

re·ceiv·able \ri-'sē-və-bəl\ adj 1 : capable of being received; esp : acceptable as legal ⟨~ certificates⟩ 2 : subject to call for payment ⟨notes ~⟩

re·ceive \ri-'sēv\ vb **re·ceived**; **re·ceiv·ing** 1 : to take in or accept (as something sent or paid) : come into possession of : GET 2 : CONTAIN, HOLD 3 : to permit to enter : GREET, WELCOME 4 : to be at home to visitors 5 : to accept as true or authoritative 6 : to be the subject of : UNDERGO, EXPERIENCE ⟨~ a shock⟩ 7 : to change incoming radio waves into sounds or pictures

re·ceiv·er \ri-'sē-vər\ n 1 : one that receives 2 : a person legally appointed to receive and have charge of property or money involved in a lawsuit 3 : a device for converting electromagnetic waves or signals into audio or visual form ⟨telephone ~⟩

re·ceiv·er·ship \-ˌship\ n 1 : the office or function of a receiver 2 : the condition of being in the hands of a receiver

re·cen·cy \'rē-sⁿn-sē\ n : RECENTNESS

re·cent \'rē-sⁿnt\ adj 1 : of the present time or time just past ⟨~ history⟩ 2 : having lately come into existence : NEW, FRESH 3 cap : HOLOCENE — **re·cent·ly** adv — **re·cent·ness** n

re·cep·ta·cle \ri-'sep-ti-kəl\ n 1 : something used to receive and hold something else : CONTAINER 2 : the enlarged end of a flower stalk upon which the parts of the flower grow 3 : an electrical fitting containing the live parts of a circuit

re·cep·tion \ri-'sep-shən\ n 1 : the act of

receiving 2 : a social gathering at which guests are formally welcomed

re·cep·tion·ist \ri-'sep-shə-nist\ n : a person employed to greet callers

re·cep·tive \ri-'sep-tiv\ adj : able or inclined to receive; esp : open and responsive to ideas, impressions, or suggestions — **re·cep·tive·ly** adv — **re·cep·tive·ness** n — **re·cep·tiv·i·ty** \ˌrē-ˌsep-'ti-və-tē\ n

re·cep·tor \ri-'sep-tər\ n 1 : one that receives stimuli : SENSE ORGAN 2 : a chemical group or molecule in the outer cell membrane or in the cell interior that has an affinity for a specific chemical group, molecule, or virus

¹**re·cess** \'rē-ˌses, ri-'ses\ n 1 : a secret or secluded place 2 : an indentation in a line or surface (as an alcove in a room) 3 : a suspension of business or procedure for rest or relaxation

²**recess** vb 1 : to put into a recess 2 : to make a recess in 3 : to interrupt for a recess 4 : to take a recess

re·ces·sion \ri-'se-shən\ n 1 : the act of receding : WITHDRAWAL 2 : a departing procession (as at the end of a church service) 3 : a period of reduced economic activity

re·ces·sion·al \ri-'se-shə-nəl\ n 1 : a hymn or musical piece at the conclusion of a service or program 2 : RECESSION 2

¹**re·ces·sive** \ri-'se-siv\ adj 1 : tending to recede 2 : producing or being a bodily characteristic that is masked or not expressed when a contrasting dominant gene or trait is present ⟨~ genes⟩ ⟨~ traits⟩

²**recessive** n : a recessive characteristic or gene; also : an individual that has one or more recessive characteristics

re·cher·ché \rə-ˌsher-'shā, -'sher-ˌshā\ adj [F] 1 : CHOICE, RARE 2 : excessively refined

re·cid·i·vism \ri-'si-də-ˌvi-zəm\ n : a tendency to relapse into a previous condition; esp : relapse into criminal behavior — **re·cid·i·vist** \-vist\ n

rec·i·pe \'re-sə-(ˌ)pē\ n [L, take, imperative of recipere to take, receive, fr. re- back + capere to take] 1 : a set of instructions for making something from various ingredients 2 : a method of procedure : FORMULA

re·cip·i·ent \ri-'si-pē-ənt\ n : one that receives

¹**re·cip·ro·cal** \ri-'si-prə-kəl\ adj 1 : inversely related 2 : MUTUAL, SHARED 3 : serving to reciprocate 4 : mutually corresponding — **re·cip·ro·cal·ly** adv

²**reciprocal** n 1 : something in a reciprocal relationship to another 2 : one of a pair of numbers (as ⅔ and 3/2) whose product is one

re·cip·ro·cate \-ˌkāt\ vb **-cat·ed**; **-cat·ing** 1 : to move backward and forward alternately 2 : to give and take mutually 3 : to make a return for something

---

rechannel	rechargeable	recheck	rechristen
recharge	recharter		

done or given — **re·cip·ro·ca·tion** \-ˌsi-prə-ˈkā-shən\ *n*

rec·i·proc·i·ty \ˌre-sə-ˈprä-sə-tē\ *n, pl* **-ties** 1 : the quality or state of being reciprocal 2 : mutual exchange of privileges (as trade advantages between countries)

re·cit·al \ri-ˈsī-t°l\ *n* 1 : an act or instance of reciting : ACCOUNT 2 : a public reading or recitation ⟨a poetry ∼⟩ 3 : a concert given by a musician, dancer, or dance troupe 4 : a public exhibition of skill given by music or dance pupils — **re·cit·al·ist** \-t°l-ist\ *n*

rec·i·ta·tion \ˌre-sə-ˈtā-shən\ *n* 1 : RECITING, RECITAL 2 : delivery before an audience usu. of something memorized 3 : a classroom exercise in which pupils answer questions on a lesson they have studied

re·cite \ri-ˈsīt\ *vb* **re·cit·ed; re·cit·ing** 1 : to repeat verbatim (as something memorized) 2 : to recount in some detail : RELATE 3 : to reply to a teacher's questions on a lesson — **re·cit·er** *n*

reck·less \ˈre-kləs\ *adj* : lacking caution ⟨a ∼ driver⟩ ◆ *Synonyms* HASTY, BRASH, HOTHEADED, THOUGHTLESS — **reck·less·ly** *adv* — **reck·less·ness** *n*

reck·on \ˈre-kən\ *vb,* 1 : COUNT, CALCULATE, COMPUTE 2 : CONSIDER, REGARD 3 *.chiefly dial* : THINK, SUPPOSE, GUESS

reck·on·ing *n* 1 : an act or instance of reckoning : a settling of accounts ⟨day of ∼⟩

re·claim \ri-ˈklām\ *vb* 1 : to recall from wrong conduct : REFORM 2 : to change from an undesirable to a desired condition ⟨∼ marshy land⟩ 3 : to obtain from a waste product or by-product ⟨∼ed plastic⟩ 4 : to demand or obtain the return of — **re·claim·able** *adj* — **rec·la·ma·tion** \ˌre-klə-ˈmā-shən\ *n*

re·cline \ri-ˈklīn\ *vb* **re·clined; re·clin·ing** 1 : to lean or incline backward 2 : to lie down : REST

re·clin·er \ri-ˈklī-nər\ *n* : a chair with an adjustable back and footrest

re·cluse \ˈre-ˌklüs, ri-ˈklüs\ *n* : a person who leads a secluded or solitary life : HERMIT — **re·clu·sive** \ri-ˈklü-siv\ *adj*

rec·og·nise *chiefly Brit var of* RECOGNIZE

rec·og·ni·tion \ˌre-kəg-ˈni-shən\ *n* 1 : the act of recognizing : the state of being recognized : ACKNOWLEDGMENT 2 : special notice or attention

re·cog·ni·zance \ri-ˈkäg-nə-zəns\ *n* : a promise recorded before a court or magistrate to do something (as to appear in court or to keep the peace) usu. under penalty of a money forfeiture

rec·og·nize \ˈre-kəg-ˌnīz\ *vb* **-nized; -niz·ing** 1 : to acknowledge (as a speaker in a meeting) as one entitled to be heard at the time 2 : to acknowledge the existence or

the independence of (a country or government) 3 : to take notice of 4 : to acknowledge with appreciation 5 : to acknowledge acquaintance with 6 : to identify as previously known 7 : to perceive clearly : REALIZE — **rec·og·niz·able** \ˈre-kəg-ˌnī-zə-bəl\ *adj* — **rec·og·niz·ably** \-blē\ *adv*

¹**re·coil** \ri-ˈkȯi(-ə)l\ *vb* [ME *reculen, recoilen,* fr. AF *reculer, recuiler,* fr. *re-* back + *cul* backside, fr. L *culus*] 1 : to draw back : RETREAT 2 : to spring back to or as if to a starting point ◆ *Synonyms* SHRINK, FLINCH, WINCE, QUAIL, BLENCH

²**re·coil** \ˈrē-ˌkȯi(-ə)l, ri-ˈkȯil\ *n* : the action of recoiling (as by a gun or spring)

re·coil·less \-ˌkȯi(-ə)l-ləs, -ˈkȯi(-ə)l-\ *adj* : venting expanding propellant gas before recoil is produced ⟨∼ gun⟩

rec·ol·lect \ˌre-kə-ˈlekt\ *vb* : to recall to mind : REMEMBER ◆ *Synonyms* RECALL, REMIND, REMINISCE, BETHINK

rec·ol·lec·tion \ˌre-kə-ˈlek-shən\ *n* 1 : the act or power of recollecting 2 : something recollected

re·com·bi·nant \(ˌ)rē-ˈkäm-bə-nənt\ *adj* 1 : relating to genetic recombination 2 : containing or produced by recombinant DNA ⟨∼ vaccines⟩

recombinant DNA *n* : genetically engineered DNA prepared in vitro by joining together DNA usu. from more than one species of organism

re·com·bi·na·tion \ˌrē-ˌkäm-bə-ˈnā-shən\ *n* : the formation of new combinations of genes

rec·om·mend \ˌre-kə-ˈmend\ *vb* 1 : to present as deserving of acceptance or trial 2 : to give in charge : COMMIT 3 : to make acceptable 4 : ADVISE, COUNSEL — **rec·om·mend·able** \-ˈmen-də-bəl\ *adj*

rec·om·men·da·tion \ˌre-kə-mən-ˈdā-shən\ *n* 1 : the act of recommending 2 : something recommended 3 : something that recommends

¹**rec·om·pense** \ˈre-kəm-ˌpens\ *vb* **-pensed; -pens·ing** 1 : to give compensation to : pay for 2 : to return in kind : REQUITE ◆ *Synonyms* REIMBURSE, INDEMNIFY, REPAY, COMPENSATE

²**recompense** *n* : COMPENSATION

rec·on·cile \ˈre-kən-ˌsī(-ə)l\ *vb* **-ciled; -cil·ing** 1 : to cause to be friendly or harmonious again 2 : ADJUST, SETTLE ⟨∼ differences⟩ 3 : to bring to submission or acceptance ◆ *Synonyms* CONFORM, ACCOMMODATE, HARMONIZE, COORDINATE — **rec·on·cil·able** *adj* — **rec·on·cile·ment** *n* — **rec·on·cil·er** *n*

rec·on·cil·i·a·tion \ˌre-kən-ˌsi-lē-ˈā-shən\ *n* 1 : the action of reconciling 2 : the Roman Catholic sacrament of penance

re·con·dite \ˈre-kən-ˌdīt\ *adj* 1 : hard to understand : PROFOUND, ABSTRUSE 2 : little known : OBSCURE

reclassification	recolor	recompile	reconcentrate
reclassify	recombine	recompose	reconception
recoin	recommence	recomputation	recondensation
recolonization	recommission	recompute	recondense
recolonize	recommit	reconceive	

re·con·di·tion \ˌrē-kən-'di-shən\ *vb* 1 : to restore to good condition (as by replacing parts) 2 : to condition anew

re·con·nais·sance \ri-'kä-nə-zəns, -səns\ *n* [F, lit., recognition] : a preliminary survey of an area; *esp* : an exploratory military survey of enemy territory

re·con·noi·ter *or* **re·con·noi·tre** \ˌrē-kə-'nȯi-tər, ˌre-\ *vb* **-noi·tered** *or* **-noi·tred; -noi·ter·ing** *or* **-noi·tring** : to make a reconnaissance of : engage in reconnaissance

re·con·sid·er \ˌrē-kən-'si-dər\ *vb* : to consider again with a view to changing or reversing — **re·con·sid·er·a·tion** \-ˌsi-də-'rā-shən\ *n*

re·con·sti·tute \ˌrē-'kän-stə-ˌtüt, -ˌtyüt\ *vb* : to restore to a former condition by adding water ⟨~ powdered milk⟩

re·con·struct \ˌrē-kən-'strəkt\ *vb* : to construct again : REBUILD

re·con·struc·tion \ˌrē-kən-'strək-shən\ *n* 1 : the action of reconstructing : the state of being reconstructed 2 *often cap* : the reorganization and reestablishment of the seceded states in the Union after the American Civil War 3 : something reconstructed

¹**re·cord** \ri-'kȯrd\ *vb* [ME, lit., to recall, fr. AF *recorder*, fr. L *recordari*, fr. *re-* back, again + *cord-, cors* heart] 1 : to set down in writing 2 : to register permanently 3 : INDICATE, READ 4 : to give evidence of 5 : to cause (as sound or visual images) to be registered (as on a disc or a magnetic tape) in a form that permits reproduction

²**rec·ord** \'re-kərd\ *n* 1 : the act of being recorded 2 : a written account of proceedings 3 : known facts about a person; *also* : a collection of items of information (as in a database) treated as a unit 4 : an attested top performance 5 : something on which sound or visual images have been recorded

³**re·cord** \ri-'kȯrd\ *n* : a function of an electronic device that causes it to record

re·cord·er \ri-'kȯr-dər\ *n* 1 : a judge in some city courts 2 : one who records transactions officially 3 : a recording device 4 : a wind instrument with a whistle mouthpiece and eight fingerholes

re·cord·ing *n* : RECORD 5

re·cord·ist \ri-'kȯr-dist\ *n* : one who records sound esp. on film

¹**re·count** \ri-'kau̇nt\ *vb* : to relate in detail : TELL ♦ *Synonyms* RECITE, REHEARSE, NARRATE, DESCRIBE, STATE, REPORT

²**re·count** \'rē-ˌkau̇nt, (ˌ)rē-'kau̇nt\ *vb* : to count again

³**re·count** \'rē-ˌkau̇nt, (ˌ)rē-'kau̇nt\ *n* : a second or fresh count

re·coup \ri-'küp\ *vb* : to get an equivalent or compensation for : make up for something lost

re·course \'rē-ˌkȯrs, ri-'kȯrs\ *n* 1 : a turning to someone or something for assistance or protection 2 : a source of aid : RESORT

re·cov·er \ri-'kə-vər\ *vb* 1 : to get back again : REGAIN, RETRIEVE 2 : to regain normal health, poise, or status 3 : to make up for : RECOUP ⟨~ed all his losses⟩ 4 : RECLAIM ⟨~ land from the sea⟩ 5 : to obtain a legal judgment in one's favor — **re·cov·er·able** *adj*

re-cov·er \ˌrē-'kə-vər\ *vb* : to cover again

recovering *adj* : being in the process of overcoming a shortcoming or problem ⟨a ~ alcoholic⟩

re·cov·ery \ri-'kə-və-rē\ *n* 1 : an act or instance of recovering; *esp* : an economic upturn 2 : the process of combating a disorder or problem

¹**rec·re·ant** \'re-krē-ənt\ *adj* [ME, fr. AF, fr. prp. of *(se) recreire* to give up, yield, fr. ML *(se) recredere* to resign oneself (to a judgment), fr. L *re-* back +*credere* to believe] 1 : COWARDLY 2 : UNFAITHFUL

²**recreant** *n* 1 : COWARD 2 : DESERTER

rec·re·ate \'re-krē-ˌāt\ *vb* **-at·ed; -at·ing** 1 : to give new life or freshness to 2 : to take recreation — **rec·re·ative** \-ˌā-tiv\ *adj*

re-cre·ate \ˌrē-krē-'āt\ *vb* : to create again — **re-cre·ation** \-'ā-shən\ *n* — **re-cre·ative** \-'ā-tiv\ *adj*

rec·re·ation \ˌre-krē-'ā-shən\ *n* : a refreshing of strength or spirits after work; *also* : a means of refreshment ♦ *Synonyms* DIVERSION, ENTERTAINMENT, AMUSEMENT — **rec·re·ation·al** \-shə-nəl\ *adj*

recreational vehicle *n* : a vehicle designed for recreational use (as camping)

re·crim·i·na·tion \ri-ˌkri-mə-'nā-shən\ *n* : a retaliatory accusation — **re·crim·i·nate** \-'kri-mə-ˌnāt\ *vb* — **re·crim·i·na·tory** \-'kri-mə-nə-ˌtȯr-ē\ *adj*

re·cru·des·cence \ˌrē-krü-'de-sᵊns\ *n* : a renewal or breaking out again esp. of something unhealthful or dangerous

¹**re·cruit** \ri-'krüt\ *vb* 1 : to form or strengthen with new members ⟨~ an army⟩ 2 : to enlist as a member of an armed service 3 : to secure the services of 4 : to seek to enroll 5 : to restore or increase in health or vigor ⟨resting to ~ his strength⟩ — **re·cruit·er** *n* — **re·cruit·ment** *n*

²**recruit** *n* [F *recrute, recrue* fresh growth, new levy of soldiers, fr. MF, fr. *recroistre* to grow up again, fr. L *recrescere*] : a newcomer to an activity or field; *esp* : a newly enlisted member of the armed forces

rec·tal \'rek-tᵊl\ *adj* : of or relating to the rectum — **rec·tal·ly** *adv*

rect·an·gle \'rek-ˌtaŋ-gəl\ *n* : a 4-sided figure with four right angles; *esp* : one with adjacent sides of unequal length — **rect·an·gu·lar** \rek-'taŋ-gyə-lər\ *adj*

rec·ti·fi·er \'rek-tə-ˌfī-(ə)r\ *n* : one that rectifies; *esp* : a device for converting alternating current into direct current

reconfirm	reconquest	recontaminate	recook
reconfirmation	reconsecrate	recontamination	recopy
reconnect	reconsecration	reconvene	recross
reconquer	recontact	reconvert	recrystallize

rec·ti·fy \'rek-tə-ˌfī\ *vb* **-fied; -fy·ing** : to make or set right : CORRECT ◆ *Synonyms* EMEND, AMEND, MEND, RIGHT — **rec·ti·fi·ca·tion** \ˌrek-tə-fə-'kā-shən\ *n*

rec·ti·lin·ear \ˌrek-tə-'li-nē-ər\ *adj* **1** : moving in a straight line ⟨∼ motion⟩ **2** : characterized by straight lines

rec·ti·tude \'rek-tə-ˌtüd, -ˌtyüd\ *n* **1** : moral integrity **2** : correctness of procedure ◆ *Synonyms* VIRTUE, GOODNESS, MORALITY, PROBITY

rec·to \'rek-tō\ *n, pl* **rectos** : a right-hand page

rec·tor \'rek-tər\ *n* **1** : a priest or minister in charge of a parish **2** : the head of a university or school — **rec·to·ri·al** \rek-'tōr-ē-əl\ *adj*

rec·to·ry \'rek-tə-rē\ *n, pl* **-ries** : the residence of a rector or a parish priest

rec·tum \'rek-təm\ *n, pl* **rectums** *or* **rec·ta** \-tə\ [ME, fr. ML, fr. *rectum intestinum*, lit., straight intestine] : the last part of the intestine joining the colon and anus

re·cum·bent \ri-'kəm-bənt\ *adj* : lying down : RECLINING

re·cu·per·ate \ri-'kü-pə-ˌrāt-, -'kyü-\ *vb* **-at·ed; -at·ing** : to get back (as health or strength) : RECOVER — **re·cu·per·a·tion** \-ˌkü-pə-'rā-shən, -ˌkyü-\ *n* — **re·cu·per·a·tive** \-'kü-pə-ˌrā-tiv, -ˌkyü-\ *adj*

re·cur \ri-'kər\ *vb* **re·curred; re·cur·ring** **1** : to go or come back in thought or discussion **2** : to occur or appear again esp. after an interval : occur time after time ⟨recurring headaches⟩ — **re·cur·rence** \-'kər-əns\ *n* — **re·cur·rent** \-ənt\ *adj*

re·cy·cle \rē-'sī-kəl\ *vb* **1** : to pass again through a cycle of changes or treatment **2** : to process (as liquid body waste, glass, or cans) in order to regain materials for human use — **re·cy·cla·bil·i·ty** \-ˌsī-klə-'bil-ə-tē\ *n* — **re·cy·cla·ble** \-k(ə)lə-bəl\ *adj* — **recycle** *vb*

¹red \'red\ *adj* **red·der; red·dest** **1** : of the color red **2** : endorsing radical social or political change esp. by force **3** *often cap* : of or relating to the former U.S.S.R. or its allies — **red·ly** *adv* — **red·ness** *n*

²red *n* **1** : the color of blood or of the ruby **2** : a revolutionary in politics **3** *cap* : COMMUNIST **4** : the condition of showing a loss ⟨in the ∼⟩

re·dact \ri-'dakt\ *vb* **1** : to put in writing : FRAME **2** : EDIT — **re·dac·tor** \-'dak-tər\ *n*

re·dac·tion \-'dak-shən\ *n* **1** : an act or instance of redacting **2** : EDITION

red alga *n* : any of a group of reddish usu. marine algae

red blood cell *n* : any of the hemoglobin-containing cells that carry oxygen from the lungs to the tissues and are responsible for the red color of vertebrate blood

red·breast \'red-ˌbrest\ *n* : ROBIN

red–carpet *adj* : marked by ceremonial courtesy

red cedar *n* : an American juniper with scalelike leaves and fragrant close-grained red wood; *also* : its wood

red clover *n* : a European clover that has globe-shaped heads of reddish flowers and is widely cultivated for hay and forage

red-coat \'red-ˌkōt\ *n* : a British soldier esp. during the Revolutionary War

red·den \'re-dᵊn\ *vb* : to make or become red or reddish : FLUSH, BLUSH

red·dish \'re-dish\ *adj* : tinged with red — **red·dish·ness** *n*

red dwarf *n* : a star with lower temperature and less mass than the sun

re·deem \ri-'dēm\ *vb* [ME *redemen*, fr. AF *redemer*, modif. of L *redimere*, fr. *re-*, *red-* back, again + *emere* to take, buy] **1** : to recover (property) by discharging an obligation **2** : to ransom, free, or rescue by paying a price **3** : to free from the consequences of sin **4** : to remove the obligation of by payment ⟨the government ∼s savings bonds⟩; *also* : to convert into something of value **5** : to make good (a promise) by performing : FULFILL **6** : to atone for — **re·deem·able** *adj* — **re·deem·er** *n*

re·demp·tion \ri-'demp-shən\ *n* : the act of redeeming : the state of being redeemed — **re·demp·tive** \-tiv\ *adj* — **re·demp·to·ry** \-tə-rē\ *adj*

re·de·ploy \ˌrē-di-'ploi\ *vb* **1** : to transfer from one area or activity to another **2** : to relocate men or equipment — **re·deploy·ment** *n*

red–eye \'red-ˌī\ *n* **1** : cheap whiskey **2** : a late night or overnight flight

red·fish \'red-ˌfish\ *n* : any of various reddish marine fishes of the Atlantic including some used for food

red fox *n* : a fox with orange-red to reddish brown fur

red giant *n* : a very large star with a relatively low surface temperature

red–hand·ed \'red-'han-dəd\ *adv or adj* : in the act of committing a misdeed

red·head \-ˌhed\ *n* : a person having red hair — **red·head·ed** \-'he-dəd\ *adj*

red herring *n* : a diversion intended to distract attention from the real issue

red–hot \'red-'hät\ *adj* **1** : extremely hot; *esp* : glowing with heat **2** : EXCITED, FURIOUS **3** : very new ⟨∼ news⟩

re·dial \'rē-ˌdī(-ə)l\ *n* : a telephone function that automatically repeats the dialing of the last number called — **redial** *vb*

re·dis·trib·ute \ˌrē-də-'stri-byüt\ *vb* **1** : to alter the distribution of **2** : to spread to other areas — **re·dis·tri·bu·tion** \(ˌ)rē-ˌdis-trə-'byü-shən\ *n*

re·dis·trict \ˌrē-'dis-(ˌ)trikt\ *vb* : to organize into new territorial and esp. political divisions

red–let·ter \'red-₁le-tər\ *adj* : of special significance : MEMORABLE

red–light *adj* : having many houses of prostitution ⟨a ∼district⟩

re·do \(₁)rē-'dü\ *vb* : to do over or again; *esp* : REDECORATE

red oak *n* : any of various No. American oaks with leaves usu. having spiny-tipped lobes and acorns that take two years to mature; *also* : the wood of a red oak

red·o·lent \'re-də-lənt\ *adj* **1** : FRAGRANT, AROMATIC **2** : having a specified fragrance ⟨a room ∼ of cooked cabbage⟩ **3** : REMINISCENT, SUGGESTIVE — **red·o·lence** \-ləns\ *n* — **red·o·lent·ly** *adv*

re·dou·ble \(₁)rē-'də-bəl\ *vb* : to make twice as great in size or amount; *also* : INTENSIFY

re·doubt \ri-'daút\ *n* [F *redoute*, fr. It *ridotto*, fr. ML *reductus* secret place, fr. L, withdrawn, fr. *reducere* to lead back, fr. *re-* back + *ducere* to lead] : a small usu. temporary fortification

re·doubt·able \ri-'daú-tə-bəl\ *adj* [ME *redoutable*, fr. AF, fr. *reduter* to dread, fr. *re-* back, again + *duter* to doubt] : arousing dread or fear : FORMIDABLE

re·dound \ri-'daúnd\ *vb* **1** : to have an effect **2** : to become added or transferred : ACCRUE

red pepper *n* **1** : CAYENNE PEPPER **2** : a mature red hot pepper or sweet pepper

¹re·dress \ri-'dres\ *vb* **1** : to set right : REMEDY **2** : COMPENSATE **3** : to remove the cause of (a grievance) **4** : AVENGE

²re·dress *n* **1** : relief from distress **2** : means or possibility of seeking a remedy **3** : compensation for loss or injury **4** : an act or instance of redressing

red·shift \'red-¸shift\ *n* : displacement of the spectrum of a heavenly body toward longer wavelength; *also* : a measure of this displacement

red snapper *n* : any of various reddish fishes including several food fishes

red spider *n* : SPIDER MITE

red squirrel *n* : a common No. American squirrel with the upper parts chiefly red

red–tailed hawk \'red-¸tāld-\ *n* : a rodent-eating No. American hawk with a rather short tyically reddish tail

red tape *n* [fr. the red tape formerly used to bind legal documents in England] : official routine or procedure marked by excessive complexity which results in delay or inaction

red tide *n* : seawater discolored by the presence of large numbers of dinoflagellates which produce a toxin that renders infected shellfish poisonous

re·duce \ri-'düs, -'dyüs\ *vb* **re·duced; re·duc·ing 1** : LESSEN **2** : to bring to a specified state or condition ⟨*reduced* them to tears⟩ **3** : to put in a lower rank or grade **4** : CONQUER ⟨∼ a fort⟩ **5** : to bring into a certain order or classification **6** : to correct (as a fracture) by

restoration of displaced parts **7** : to lessen one's weight **♦ Synonyms** DECREASE, DIMINISH, ABATE, DWINDLE, RECEDE — **re·duc·er** *n* — **re·duc·ible** \-'dü-sə-bəl, -'dyü-\ *adj*

re·duc·tion \ri-'dək-shən\ *n* **1** : the act of reducing : the state of being reduced **2** : something made by reducing **3** : the amount taken off in reducing something

re·dun·dan·cy \ri-'dən-dən-sē\ *n, pl* **-cies 1** : the quality or state of being redundant : SUPERFLUITY **2** : something redundant or in excess **3** : the use of surplus words

re·dun·dant \-dənt\ *adj* **1** : exceeding what is needed or normal : SUPERFLUOUS; *esp* : using more words than necessary **2** : marked by repetition — **re·dun·dant·ly** *adv*

red–winged blackbird \'red-¸wind-\ *n* : a No. American blackbird of which the adult male is black with a patch of bright scarlet on the wings

red·wood \'red-¸wúd\ *n* : a tall coniferous timber tree esp. of coastal California; *also* : its durable wood

reed \'rēd\ *n* **1** : any of various tall slender grasses of wet areas; *also* : a stem or growth of reed **2** : a musical instrument made from the hollow stem of a reed **3** : an elastic tongue of cane, wood, or metal by which tones are produced in organ pipes and certain other wind instruments — **reedy** *adj*

re·ed·u·cate \(₁)rē-'e-jə-¸kāt\ *vb* : to train again; *esp* : to rehabilitate through education — **re·ed·u·ca·tion** *n*

¹reef \'rēf\ *n* **1** : a part of a sail taken in or let out in regulating the sail's size **2** : reduction in sail area by reefing

²reef *vb* : to reduce the area of a sail by rolling or folding part of it

³reef *n* : a ridge of rocks, sand or coral at or near the surface of the water

reef·er \'rē-fər\ *n* : a marijuana cigarette

¹reek \'rēk\ *n* : a strong or disagreeable fume or odor

²reek *vb* **1** : to give off or become permeated with a strong or offensive odor **2** : to give a strong impression of some constituent quality ⟨an excuse that ∼*ed* of falsehood⟩ — **reek·er** *n* — **reeky** \'rē-kē\ *adj*

¹reel \'rēl\ *n* : a revolvable device on which something flexible (as film or tape) is wound; *also* : a quantity of something wound on such a device

²reel *vb* **1** : to wind on or as if on a reel **2** : to pull or draw (as a fish) by reeling a line — **reel·able** *adj* — **reel·er** *n*

³reel *vb* **1** : WHIRL; *also* : to be giddy **2** : to waver or fall back (as from a blow) **3** : to walk or move unsteadily

⁴reel *n* : a reeling motion

⁵reel *n* : a lively Scottish dance or its music

reel off *vb* **1** : to tell or recite rapidly and easily ⟨*reeled off* the right answers⟩ **2** : to achieve usu. consecutively ⟨*reeled off* six straight wins⟩

---

redraft	reecho	reelect	reelection
redraw	reedit		

re·en·try \ˌrē-ˈen-trē\ n **1** : a second or new entry **2** : the action of reentering the earth's atmosphere from space

reeve \ˈrēv\ vb **rove** \ˈrōv\ or **reeved**; **reev·ing** : to pass (as a rope) through a hole in a block or cleat

¹ref \ˈref\ n : REFEREE 2

²ref abbr **1** reference **2** referred **3** reformed **4** refunding

re·fec·tion \ri-ˈfek-shən\ n **1** : refreshment esp. after hunger or fatigue **2** : food and drink together : REPAST

re·fec·to·ry \ri-ˈfek-tə-rē\ n, pl **-ries** : a dining hall (as in a monastery or college)

re·fer \ri-ˈfər\ vb **re·ferred**; **re·fer·ring** [ME referren, fr. AF referer, referir, fr. L referre to bring back, report, refer, fr. re- back + ferre to carry] **1** : to assign to a certain source, cause, or relationship **2** : to direct or send to some person or place (as for information or help) **3** : to submit to someone else for consideration or action **4** : to have recourse (as for information or aid) **5** : to have connection : RELATE **6** : to direct attention : speak of : MENTION, ALLUDE ◆ **Synonyms** RECUR, REPAIR, RESORT, APPLY, GO, TURN — **re·fer·able** \ˈre-fə-rə-bəl, ri-ˈfər-ə-\ adj

¹ref·er·ee \ˌre-fə-ˈrē\ n **1** : a person to whom an issue esp. in law is referred for investigation or settlement **2** : an umpire in certain games

²referee vb **-eed**; **-ee·ing** : to act as referee

ref·er·ence \ˈre-frəns, -fə-rəns\ n **1** : the act of referring **2** : RELATION, RESPECT **3** : ALLUSION, MENTION **4** : something that refers a reader to another passage or book **5** : consultation esp. for obtaining information ⟨books for ∼⟩ **6** : a person of whom inquiries as to character or ability can be made **7** : a written recommendation of a person for employment

ref·er·en·dum \ˌre-fə-ˈren-dəm\ n, pl **-da** \-də\ or **-dums** : the submitting of legislative measures to the voters for approval or rejection; also : a vote on a measure so submitted

ref·er·ent \ˈre-frənt, -fə-rənt\ n : one that refers or is referred to; esp : the thing a word stands for — **referent** adj

re·fer·ral \ri-ˈfər-əl\ n **1** : the act or an instance of referring **2** : one that is referred

¹re·fill \ˌrē-ˈfil\ vb : to fill again : REPLENISH — **re·fill·able** adj

²re·fill \ˈrē-ˌfil\ n : a new or fresh supply of something

re·fi·nance \ˌrē-fə-ˈnans, (ˌ)rē-ˈfī-nans\ vb : to renew or reorganize the financing of

re·fine \ri-ˈfīn\ vb **re·fined**; **re·fin·ing** **1** : to free from impurities or waste matter **2** : IMPROVE, PERFECT **3** : to free or become free of what is coarse or uncouth **4** : to make improvements by introducing subtle changes — **re·fin·er** n

re·fined \ri-ˈfīnd\ adj **1** : freed from impurities **2** : CULTURED, CULTIVATED **3** : SUBTLE

re·fine·ment \ri-ˈfīn-mənt\ n **1** : the action of refining **2** : the quality or state of being refined **3** : a refined feature or method; also : something intended to improve or perfect

re·fin·ery \ri-ˈfī-nə-rē\ n, pl **-er·ies** : a building and equipment for refining metals, oil, or sugar

re·flect \ri-ˈflekt\ vb [ME, fr. L reflectere to bend back, fr. re- back + flectere to bend] **1** : to bend or cast back (as light, heat, or sound) **2** : to give back a likeness or image of as a mirror does **3** : to bring as a result ⟨∼ed credit on him⟩ **4** : to make apparent : SHOW ⟨figures that ∼ economic growth⟩ **5** : to cast reproach or blame ⟨their bad conduct ∼ed on their training⟩ **6** : PONDER, MEDITATE — **re·flec·tion** \-ˈflek-shən\ n — **re·flec·tive** \-tiv\ adj — **re·flec·tiv·i·ty** \(ˌ)rē-ˌflek-ˈti-və-tē\ n

re·flec·tor \ri-ˈflek-tər\ n : one that reflects; esp : a polished surface for reflecting radiation (as light)

¹re·flex \ˈrē-ˌfleks\ n **1** : an automatic and usu. inborn response to a stimulus not involving higher mental centers **2** pl : the power of acting or responding with enough speed ⟨an athlete with great ∼es⟩

²reflex adj **1** : bent or directed back **2** : of, relating to, or produced by a reflex ⟨a ∼ action⟩ — **re·flex·ly** adv

¹re·flex·ive \ri-ˈflek-siv\ adj : of or relating to an action directed back upon the doer or the grammatical subject ⟨a ∼ verb⟩ ⟨the ∼ pronoun himself⟩ — **re·flex·ive·ly** adv — **re·flex·ive·ness** n

²reflexive n : a reflexive verb or pronoun

re·flex·ol·o·gy \ˌrē-ˌflek-ˈsä-lə-jē\ n : massage in which pressure is applied to specific points on the hands or feet

re·flux \ˈrē-ˌfləks\ n : a flowing back

re·fo·cus \(ˌ)rē-ˈfō-kəs\ vb **1** : to focus again **2** : to change the emphasis or direction of ⟨∼ed her life⟩

re·for·es·ta·tion \ˌrē-ˌfór-ə-ˈstā-shən\ n : the action of renewing forest cover by planting seeds or young trees — **re·for·est** \rē-ˈfór-əst\ vb

¹re·form \ri-ˈfórm\ vb **1** : to make better or improve by removal of faults **2** : to correct or improve one's own character or habits ◆ **Synonyms** CORRECT, RECTIFY, EMEND, REMEDY, REDRESS, REVISE — **re·form·able** adj — **re·for·ma·tive** \-ˈfór-mə-tiv\ adj

reemerge	reenergize	reevaluate	refigure
reemergence	reenlist	reevaluation	refinish
reemphasis	reenlistment	reexamination	refit
reemphasize	reenter	reexamine	refix
reemploy	reequip	reexport	refloat
reemployment	reestablish	refashion	refold
reenact	reestablishment	refight	reforge
reenactment			

²**reform** n : improvement or correction of what is corrupt or defective

re—form \ˌrē-ˈfȯrm\ vb : to form again

ref·or·ma·tion \ˌre-fər-ˈmā-shən\ n 1 : the act of reforming : the state of being reformed 2 cap : a 16th century religious movement marked by the establishment of the Protestant churches

¹**re·for·ma·to·ry** \ri-ˈfȯr-mə-ˌtȯr-ē\ adj : aiming at or tending toward reformation : REFORMATIVE

²**reformatory** n, pl **-ries** : a penal institution for reforming esp. young or first offenders

re·form·er \ri-ˈfȯr-mər\ n 1 : one that works for or urges reform 2 cap : a leader of the Protestant Reformation

refr abbr refraction

re·fract \ri-ˈfrakt\ vb [L refractus, pp. of refringere to break open, break up, fr. re- back + frangere to break] : to subject to refraction

re·frac·tion \ri-ˈfrak-shən\ n : the bending of a ray (as of light) when it passes obliquely from one medium into another in which its speed is different — **re·frac·tive** \-tiv\ adj

refractive index n : the ratio of the speed of radiation in one medium to that in another medium

re·frac·to·ry \ri-ˈfrak-tə-rē\ adj 1 : OBSTINATE, STUBBORN, UNMANAGEABLE 2 : capable of enduring high temperature ⟨∼ bricks⟩ ♦ Synonyms RECALCITRANT, INTRACTABLE, UNGOVERNABLE, UNRULY, HEADSTRONG, WILLFUL — **re·frac·to·ri·ness** \ri-ˈfrak-tə-rē-nəs\ n — **refractory** n

¹**re·frain** \ri-ˈfrān\ vb : to hold oneself back : FORBEAR — **re·frain·ment** n

²**refrain** n : a phrase or verse recurring regularly in a poem or song

re·fresh \ri-ˈfresh\ vb 1 : to make or become fresh or fresher 2 : to revive by or as if by renewal of supplies ⟨∼ one's memory⟩ 3 : to freshen up 4 : to supply or take refreshment 5 : to update or renew esp. by sending a new signal ⟨∼ the Web page⟩ ♦ Synonyms RESTORE, REJUVENATE, RENOVATE, REFURBISH — **re·fresh·er** n — **re·fresh·ing·ly** adv

re·fresh·ment \-mənt\ n 1 : the act of refreshing : the state of being refreshed 2 : something that refreshes 3 pl : a light meal; also : assorted light foods

re·fried beans \ˈrē-ˌfrīd-\ n pl : beans cooked with seasonings, fried, then mashed and fried again

refrig abbr refrigerating; refrigeration

re·frig·er·ate \ri-ˈfri-jə-ˌrāt\ vb **-at·ed; -at·ing** : to make cool; esp : to chill or freeze (food) for preservation — **re·frig·er·ant** \-jə-rənt\ adj or n — **re·frig·er·a·tion** \-ˌfri-jə-ˈrā-shən\ n — **re·frig·er·a·tor** \-ˈfri-jə-ˌrā-tər\ n

ref·uge \ˈre-ˌfyüj\ n 1 : shelter or protection from danger or distress 2 : a place that provides protection

ref·u·gee \ˌre-fyù-ˈjē\ n : one who flees for safety esp. to a foreign country

re·ful·gence \ri-ˈful-jəns, -ˈfəl-\ n : a radiant or resplendent quality or state — **re·ful·gent** \-jənt\ adj

¹**re·fund** \ri-ˈfənd, ˈrē-ˌfənd\ vb : to give or put back (money) : REPAY — **re·fund·able** adj

²**re·fund** \ˈrē-ˌfənd\ n 1 : the act of refunding 2 : a sum refunded

re·fur·bish \ri-ˈfər-bish\ vb : to brighten or freshen up : RENOVATE

¹**re·fuse** \ri-ˈfyüz\ vb **re·fused; re·fus·ing** 1 : to decline to accept : REJECT 2 : to decline to do, give, or grant : DENY — **re·fus·al** \-ˈfyü-zəl\ n

²**ref·use** \ˈre-ˌfyüs, -ˌfyüz\ n : rejected or worthless matter : RUBBISH, TRASH

re·fute \ri-ˈfyüt\ vb **re·fut·ed; re·fut·ing** [L refutare to check, suppress, refute] : to prove to be false by argument or evidence — **ref·u·ta·tion** \ˌre-fyù-ˈtā-shən\ n — **re·fut·er** n

¹**reg** \ˈreg\ n : REGULATION

²**reg** abbr 1 region 2 register; registered; registration 3 regular

re·gal \ˈrē-gəl\ adj 1 : of, relating to, or befitting a king : ROYAL 2 : STATELY, SPLENDID — **re·gal·ly** adv

re·gale \ri-ˈgāl\ vb **re·galed; re·gal·ing** 1 : to entertain richly or agreeably 2 : to give pleasure or amusement to ⟨regaled us with stories⟩ ♦ Synonyms GRATIFY, DELIGHT, PLEASE, REJOICE, GLADDEN

re·ga·lia \ri-ˈgāl-yə\ n pl 1 : the emblems, symbols, or paraphernalia of royalty (as the crown and scepter) 2 : the insignia of an office or order 3 : special costume : FINERY

¹**re·gard** \ri-ˈgärd\ n 1 : CONSIDERATION, HEED; also : CARE, CONCERN 2 : GAZE, GLANCE, LOOK 3 : RESPECT, ESTEEM ⟨held in high ∼⟩ 4 pl : friendly greetings implying respect and esteem 5 : an aspect to be considered : PARTICULAR — **re·gard·ful** adj — **re·gard·less** adj

²**regard** vb, 1 : to think of : CONSIDER 2 : to pay attention to 3 : to show respect for : HEED ⟨∼s his elders⟩ 4 : to hold in high esteem : care for 5 : to look at : gaze upon ⟨∼ed the landscape⟩ 6 archaic : to relate to

re·gard·ing prep : CONCERNING

re·gard·less of \ri-ˈgärd-ləs-\ prep : in spite of

re·gat·ta \ri-ˈgä-tə, -ˈga-\ n : a boat race or a series of boat races

re·gen·cy \ˈrē-jən-sē\ n, pl **-cies** 1 : the office or government of a regent or body of regents 2 : a body of regents 3 : the period during which a regent governs

re·gen·er·a·cy \ri-ˈje-nə-rə-sē\ n : the state of being regenerated

¹**re·gen·er·ate** \ri-ˈje-nə-rət\ adj 1 : formed or created again 2 : spiritually reborn or converted

²**re·gen·er·ate** \ri-ˈje-nə-ˌrāt\ vb 1 : to subject to spiritual renewal 2 : to reform

reformulate	refound	refuel	regain
reformulation	refreeze	refurnish	regather
refortify			

completely **3** : to replace (a body part) by a new growth of tissue **4** : to give new life to : REVIVE — **re·gen·er·a·tion** \-je-nə-ˈrā-shən\ *n* — **re·gen·er·a·tive** \-ˈje-nə-ˌrā-tiv\ *adj* — **ˈre·gen·er·a·tor** \-ˌrā-tər\ *n*

re·gent \ˈrē-jənt\ *n* **1** : a person who rules during the childhood, absence, or incapacity of the sovereign **2** : a member of a governing board (as of a state university) — **regent** *adj*

reg·gae \ˈre-ˌgā\ *n* : popular music of Jamaican origin that combines native styles with elements of rock and soul music

reg·i·cide \ˈre-jə-ˌsīd\ *n* **1** : one who murders a king **2** : murder of a king

re·gime *also* **ré·gime** \rā-ˈzhēm, ri-\ *n* **1** : REGIMEN **2** : a form or system of government **3** : a government in power; *also* : a period of rule

reg·i·men \ˈre-jə-mən\ *n* [ME, fr. ML, position of authority, direction, set of rules, fr. L, steering, control, fr. *regere* to direct] **1** : a systematic course of treatment or training ⟨a strict dietary ∼⟩ **2** : GOVERNMENT

ˈreg·i·ment \ˈre-jə-mənt\ *n* : a military unit consisting usu. of a number of battalions — **reg·i·men·tal** \ˌre-jə-ˈment-əl\ *adj*

²reg·i·ment \ˈre-jə-ˌment\ *vb* : to organize rigidly esp. for regulation or central control; *also* : to subject to order or uniformity — **reg·i·men·ta·tion** \ˌre-jə-mən-ˈtā-shən\ *n*

reg·i·men·tals \ˌre-jə-ˈmen-təlz\ *n pl* **1** : a regimental uniform **2** : military dress

re·gion \ˈrē-jən\ *n* [ME, fr. AF *regiun*, fr. L *region-, regio*, line, direction, area, fr. *regere* to rule] : an often indefinitely defined part or area

re·gion·al \ˈrē-jə-nəl\ *adj* **1** : affecting a particular region : LOCALIZED **2** : of, relating to, characteristic of, or serving a region — **re·gion·al·ly** *adv*

ˈreg·is·ter \ˈre-jə-stər\ *n* **1** : a record of items or details; *also* : a book or system for keeping such a record **2** : the range of a voice or instrument **3** : a device to regulate ventilation or heating **4** : an automatic device recording a number or quantity **5** : CASH REGISTER

²register *vb* **-tered; -ter·ing** **1** : to enter in a register (as in a list of guests) **2** : to record automatically **3** : to secure special care for (mail matter) by paying additional postage **4** : to convey an impression of : EXPRESS **5** : to make or adjust so as to correspond exactly

registered nurse *n* : a graduate trained nurse who has been licensed to practice by a state authority after passing qualifying examinations

reg·is·trant \ˈre-jə-strənt\ *n* : one that registers or is registered

reg·is·trar \-ˌsträr\ *n* : an official recorder or keeper of records (as at an educational institution)

reg·is·tra·tion \ˌre-jə-ˈstrā-shən\ *n* **1** : the act of registering **2** : an entry in a register **3** : the number of persons registered : ENROLLMENT **4** : a document certifying an act of registering

reg·is·try \ˈre-jə-strē\ *n, pl* **-tries** **1** : ENROLLMENT, REGISTRATION **2** : a place of registration **3** : an official record book or an entry in one

reg·nant \ˈreg-nənt\ *adj* **1** : REIGNING **2** : DOMINANT **3** : of common or widespread occurrence

ˈre·gress \ˈrē-ˌgres\ *n* **1** : an act or the privilege of going or coming back **2** : RETROGRESSION

²re·gress \ri-ˈgres\ *vb* : to go or cause to go back or to a lower level — **re·gres·sive** *adj* — **re·gres·sor** \-ˈgre-sər\ *n*

re·gres·sion \ri-ˈgre-shən\ *n* : the act or an instance of regressing; *esp* : reversion to an earlier mental or behavioral level

ˈre·gret \ri-ˈgret\ *vb* **re·gret·ted; re·gret·ting** **1** : to mourn the loss or death of **2** : to be very sorry for **3** : to experience regret — **re·gret·ta·ble** \-ˈgre-tə-bəl\ *adj* — **re·gret·ter** *n*

²regret *n* **1** : sorrow caused by something beyond one's power to remedy **2** : an expression of sorrow **3** *pl* : a note politely declining an invitation — **re·gret·ful** \-fəl\ *adj* — **re·gret·ful·ly** *adv*

re·gret·ta·bly \-ˈgre-tə-blē\ *adv* **1** : to a regrettable extent **2** : it is to be regretted

re·group \(ˌ)rē-ˈgrüp\ *vb* : to form into a new grouping

regt *abbr* regiment

ˈreg·u·lar \ˈre-gyə-lər\ *adj* [ME *reguler*, fr. AF, fr. LL *regularis* regular, fr. L, of a bar, fr. *regula* rule, straightedge, fr. *regere* to keep straight, direct] **1** : belonging to a religious order **2** : made, built, or arranged according to a rule, standard, or type; *also* : even or symmetrical in form or structure **3** : ORDERLY, METHODICAL ⟨∼ habits⟩; *also* : not varying : STEADY ⟨a ∼ pace⟩ **4** : made, selected, or conducted according to rule or custom **5** : properly qualified ⟨not a ∼ lawyer⟩ **6** : conforming to the normal or usual manner or inflection **7** : of, relating to, or constituting the permanent standing military force of a state — **reg·u·lar·i·ty** \ˌre-gyə-ˈla-rə-tē\ *n* — **reg·u·lar·ize** \ˈre-gyə-lə-ˌrīz\ *vb* — **reg·u·lar·ly** *adv*

²regular *n* **1** : one that is regular (as in attendance) **2** : a member of the regular clergy **3** : a soldier in a regular army **4** : a player on an athletic team who is usu. in the starting lineup

reg·u·late \ˈre-gyə-ˌlāt\ *vb* **-lat·ed; -lat·ing** **1** : to govern or direct according to rule : CONTROL **2** : to bring under the control of law or authority **3** : to put in good order **4** : to fix or adjust the time, amount, degree, or rate of — **reg·u·la·tive** \-ˌlā-tiv\ *adj* — **reg·u·la·tor** \-ˌlā-tər\ *n* — **reg·u·la·to·ry** \-lə-ˌtōr-ē\ *adj*

reg·u·la·tion \ˌre-gyə-ˈlā-shən\ *n* **1** : the act of regulating : the state of being regulated **2** : a rule dealing with details of procedure **3** : an order issued by an ex-

---

regild   regrade   regrow   regrowth
regive   regrind

ecutive authority of a government and having the force of law

re·gur·gi·tate \rē-ˈgər-jə-ˌtāt\ vb **-tat·ed; -tat·ing** [ML regurgitare, fr. L re- re- + LL gurgitare to engulf, fr. L gurgit-, gurges whirlpool] : to throw or be thrown back, up, or out ⟨∼ food⟩ — **re·gur·gi·ta·tion** \-ˌgər-jə-ˈtā-shən\ n

re·hab \ˈrē-ˌhab\ n **1** : REHABILITATION **2** : a rehabilitated building — **rehab** vb

re·ha·bil·i·tate \ˌrē-hə-ˈbi-lə-ˌtāt, ˌrē-ə-\ vb **-tat·ed; -tat·ing 1** : to restore to a former capacity, rank, or right : REINSTATE **2** : to restore to good condition or health — **re·ha·bil·i·ta·tion** \-ˌbi-lə-ˈtā-shən\ n — **re·ha·bil·i·ta·tive** \-ˌtā-tiv\ adj

re·hash \ˌrē-ˈhash\ vb : to present again in another form without real change or improvement — **rehash** n

re·hear·ing \ˌrē-ˈhir-iŋ\ n : a second or new hearing by the same tribunal

re·hears·al \ri-ˈhər-səl\ n **1** : something told again : RECITAL **2** : a private performance or practice session preparatory to a public appearance

re·hearse \ri-ˈhərs\ vb **re·hearsed; re·hears·ing 1** : to say again : REPEAT **2** : to recount in order : ENUMERATE; also : RELATE **1 3** : to give a rehearsal of **4** : to train by rehearsal **5** : to engage in a rehearsal — **re·hears·er** n

¹reign \ˈrān\ n **1** : the authority or rule of a sovereign **2** : the time during which a sovereign rules

²reign vb **1** : to rule as a sovereign **2** : to be predominant or prevalent

re·im·burse \ˌrē-əm-ˈbərs\ vb **-bursed; -burs·ing** [re- re- + obs. E imburse to put in the pocket, pay, fr. ML imbursare to put into a purse, fr. L in- in + ML bursa purse, fr. LL, hide of an ox, fr. Gk byrsa] : to pay back : make restitution : REPAY ♦ **Synonyms** INDEMNIFY, RECOMPENSE, REQUITE, COMPENSATE — **re·im·burs·able** adj — **re·im·burse·ment** n

¹rein \ˈrān\ n **1** : a strap fastened to a bit by which a rider or driver controls an animal **2** : a restraining influence : CHECK **3** : controlling or guiding power **4** : complete freedom — usu. used in the phrase give rein to

²rein vb : to check or direct by reins

re·in·car·na·tion \ˌrē-(ˌ)in-(ˌ)kär-ˈnā-shən\ n : rebirth of the soul in a new body — **re·in·car·nate** \ˌrē-in-ˈkär-ˌnāt\ vb

rein·deer \ˈrān-ˌdir\ n [ME reindere, fr. ON hreinn reindeer + ME deer animal, deer] : CARIBOU — used esp. for one of the Old World

reindeer moss n : a gray, erect, tufted, and much-branched edible lichen of northern regions that is an important food of reindeer

re·in·fec·tion \ˌrē-in-ˈfek-shən\ n : infec-

tion following another infection of the same type

re·in·force \ˌrē-ən-ˈfōrs\ vb **1** : to strengthen with additional forces ⟨∼ our troops⟩ **2** : to strengthen with new force, aid, material, or support — **re·in·force·ment** n — **re·in·forc·er** n

re·in·scribe \ˌrē-ən-ˈskrīb\ vb : to reestablish or rename in a new and esp. stronger form or context

re·in·state \ˌrē-in-ˈstāt\ vb **-stat·ed; -stat·ing** : to restore to a former position, condition, or capacity — **re·in·state·ment** n

re·in·vent \ˌrē-in-ˈvent\ vb **1** : to make as if for the first time something already invented ⟨∼ the wheel⟩ **2** : to remake completely

re·it·er·ate \rē-ˈi-tə-ˌrāt\ vb **-at·ed; -at·ing** : to state or do over again or repeatedly — **re·it·er·a·tion** \-ˌi-tə-ˈrā-shən\ n

¹re·ject \ri-ˈjekt\ vb **1** : to refuse to accept, consider, use, or submit to **2** : to refuse to hear, receive, or admit : REPEL **3** : to rebuff or withhold love from **4** : to throw out esp. as useless or unsatisfactory **5** : to subject (a transplanted tissue) to an attack by immune system components of the recipient organism — **re·jec·tion** \-ˈjek-shən\ n

²re·ject \ˈrē-ˌjekt\ n : a rejected person or thing

re·joice \ri-ˈjȯis\ vb **re·joiced; re·joic·ing 1** : to give joy to : GLADDEN **2** : to feel joy or great delight — **re·joic·er** n

re·join \(ˌ)rē-ˈjȯin for 1, ri- for 2\ vb **1** : to join again **2** : to say in answer (as to a plaintiff's plea in court) : REPLY

re·join·der \ri-ˈjȯin-dər\ n : REPLY; esp : an answer to a reply

re·ju·ve·nate \ri-ˈjü-və-ˌnāt\ vb **-nat·ed; -nat·ing** : to make young or youthful again : give new vigor to ♦ **Synonyms** RENEW, REFRESH, RENOVATE, RESTORE — **re·ju·ve·na·tion** \-ˌjü-və-ˈnā-shən\ n

rel abbr **1** relating; relative **2** religion; religious

¹re·lapse \ri-ˈlaps, ˈrē-ˌlaps\ n [ME, fr. ML relapsus, fr. L relabi to slide back] **1** : the act or process of backsliding or worsening **2** : a recurrence of illness after a period of improvement

²re·lapse \ri-ˈlaps\ vb **re·lapsed; re·laps·ing** : to slip or fall back into a former, worse state (as of illness)

re·late \ri-ˈlāt\ vb **re·lat·ed; re·lat·ing 1** : to give an account of : TELL, NARRATE **2** : to show or establish logical or causal connection between **3** : to have relationship or connection **4** : to have or establish relationship (the way a child ∼s to a teacher) **5** : to respond favorably — **re·lat·able** adj — **re·lat·er** or **re·la·tor** \-ˈlā-tər\ n

re·lat·ed adj **1** : connected by some understood relationship **2** : connected through membership in the same family — **re·lat·ed·ness** n

re·la·tion \ri-'lā-shən\ n 1 : NARRATION, ACCOUNT 2 : CONNECTION, RELATIONSHIP 3 : connection by blood or marriage : KINSHIP; also : RELATIVE 4 : REFERENCE, RESPECT ⟨in ~ to⟩ 5 : the state of being mutually interested or involved (as in social or commercial matters) 6 pl : DEALINGS, AFFAIRS ⟨foreign ~s⟩ 7 pl : SEXUAL INTERCOURSE — **re·la·tion·al** \-shə-nəl\ adj

re·la·tion·ship \-,ship\ n : the state of being related or interrelated

¹**rel·a·tive** \'re-lə-tiv\ n 1 : a word referring grammatically to an antecedent 2 : a thing having a relation to or a dependence upon another thing 3 : a person connected with another by blood or marriage

²**relative** adj 1 : introducing a subordinate clause qualifying an expressed or implied antecedent ⟨~ pronoun⟩; also : introduced by such a connective ⟨~ clause⟩ 2 : PERTINENT, RELEVANT ⟨matters ~ to world peace⟩ 3 : not absolute or independent : COMPARATIVE 4 : expressed as the ratio of the specified quantity to the total magnitude or to the mean of all quantities involved ✦ **Synonyms** DEPENDENT, CONTINGENT, CONDITIONAL — **rel·a·tive·ly** adv — **rel·a·tive·ness** n

relative humidity n : the ratio of the amount of water vapor actually present in the air to the greatest amount possible at the same temperature

rel·a·tiv·is·tic \,re-lə-ti-'vis-tik\ adj 1 : of, relating to, or characterized by relativity 2 : moving at a velocity that is a significant fraction of the speed of light so that effects predicted by the theory of relativity become evident ⟨a ~ electron⟩ — **rel·a·tiv·is·ti·cal·ly** \-ti-k(ə-)lē\ adv

rel·a·tiv·i·ty \,re-lə-'ti-və-tē\ n, pl **-ties** 1 : the quality or state of being relative 2 : a theory in physics that considers mass and energy to be equivalent and that predicts changes in mass, dimension, and time which are related to speed but are noticeable esp. at speeds approaching that of light; also : an extension of the theory to include gravitation and related acceleration phenomena

re·lax \ri-'laks\ vb 1 : to make or become less firm, tense, or rigid 2 : to make less severe or strict 3 : to seek rest or recreation — **re·lax·er** n

¹**re·lax·ant** \ri-'lak-sənt\ adj : of, relating to, or producing relaxation

²**relaxant** n : a relaxing agent; esp : a drug that induces muscular relaxation

re·lax·ation \,rē-,lak-'sā-shən\ n 1 : the act of relaxing or state of being relaxed : a lessening of tension 2 : DIVERSION, RECREATION

¹**re·lay** \'rē-,lā\ n [ME, set of fresh hounds, fr. relayen to release fresh hounds, take a fresh horse, fr. MF relaier, fr. re- again + laier to let go, leave] 1 : a fresh supply

(as of horses or men) arranged beforehand to relieve others 2 : a race between teams in which each team member covers a specified part of a course 3 : an electromagnetic device in which the opening or closing of one circuit activates another device (as a switch in another circuit) 4 : the act of passing along by stages

²**re·lay** \'rē-,lā, ri-'lā\ vb **re·layed; re·lay·ing** 1 : to place in or provide with relays 2 : to pass along by relays 3 : to control or operate by a relay

³**re·lay** \(,)rē-'lā\ vb **-laid** \-'lād\; **-lay·ing** : to lay again

¹**re·lease** \ri-'lēs\ vb **re·leased; re·leas·ing** 1 : to set free from confinement or restraint; also : DISMISS ⟨released from her job⟩ 2 : to relieve from something that oppresses, confines, or burdens 3 : RELINQUISH ⟨~ a claim⟩ 4 : to permit publication, performance, exhibition, or sale of; also : to make available to the public ✦ **Synonyms** EMANCIPATE, DISCHARGE, FREE, LIBERATE

²**release** n 1 : relief or deliverance from sorrow, suffering, or trouble 2 : discharge from an obligation or responsibility 3 : an act of setting free : the state of being freed 4 : a document effecting a legal release 5 : a releasing for performance or publication; also : the matter released (as to the press) 6 : a device for holding or releasing a mechanism as required

rel·e·gate \'re-lə-,gāt\ vb **-gat·ed; -gat·ing** 1 : to send into exile : BANISH 2 : to remove or dismiss to some less prominent position 3 : to assign to a particular class or sphere 4 : to submit to someone or something for appropriate action : DELEGATE ✦ **Synonyms** COMMIT, ENTRUST, CONSIGN, COMMEND — **rel·e·ga·tion** \,re-lə-'gā-shən\ n

re·lent \ri-'lent\ vb 1 : to become less stern, severe, or harsh 2 : SLACKEN

re·lent·less \-ləs\ adj : showing or promising no abatement of severity, intensity, or pace ⟨~ pressure⟩ — **re·lent·less·ly** adv — **re·lent·less·ness** n

rel·e·vance \'re-lə-vəns\ n : relation to the matter at hand; also : practical and esp. social applicability

rel·e·van·cy \-vən-sē\ n : RELEVANCE

rel·e·vant \'re-lə-vənt\ adj : bearing on the matter at hand : PERTINENT ✦ **Synonyms** GERMANE, MATERIAL, APPLICABLE, APROPOS — **rel·e·vant·ly** adv

re·li·able \ri-'lī-ə-bəl\ adj : fit to be trusted or relied on : DEPENDABLE, TRUSTWORTHY — **re·li·abil·i·ty** \-,lī-ə-'bi-lə-tē\ n — **re·li·able·ness** n — **re·li·ably** \-'lī-ə-blē\ adv

re·li·ance \ri-'lī-əns\ n 1 : the act of relying 2 : the state of being reliant 3 : one relied on

re·li·ant \ri-'lī-ənt\ adj : having reliance on someone or something : DEPENDENT

rel·ic \'re-lik\ n 1 : an object venerated because of its association with a saint or martyr 2 : SOUVENIR, MEMENTO 3 pl

: REMAINS, RUINS 4 : a remaining trace : VESTIGE

rel·ict \'re-likt\ n : WIDOW

re·lief \ri-'lēf\ n 1 : removal or lightening of something oppressive, painful, or distressing 2 : WELFARE 2 3 : military assistance to an endangered post or force 4 : release from a post or from performance of a duty; *also* : one that takes the place of another on duty 5 : legal remedy or redress 6 : projection of figures or ornaments from the background (as in sculpture) 7 : the state of being distinguished by contrast 8 : the elevations of a land surface

relief pitcher n : a baseball pitcher who takes over for another during a game

re·lieve \ri-'lēv\ vb **re·lieved; re·liev·ing 1** : to free partly or wholly from a burden or from distress 2 : to bring about the removal or alleviation of : MITIGATE 3 : to release from a post or duty; *also* : to take the place of 4 : to break the monotony of 5 : to discharge the bladder or bowels of (oneself) ♦ *Synonyms* ALLEVIATE, LIGHTEN, ASSUAGE, ALLAY — **re·liev·er** n

relig abbr religion

re·li·gion \ri-'li-jən\ n 1 : the service and worship of God or the supernatural 2 : devotion to a religious faith 3 : a personal set or institutionalized system of religious beliefs, attitudes, and practices 4 : a cause, principle, or belief held to with faith and ardor — **re·li·gion·ist** n

¹**re·li·gious** \ri-'li-jəs\ adj 1 : relating or devoted to an acknowledged ultimate reality or deity 2 : of or relating to religious beliefs or observances 3 : scrupulously and conscientiously faithful 4 : FERVENT, ZEALOUS — **re·li·gious·ly** adv

²**religious** n, pl **religious** : a member of a religious order under monastic vows

re·lin·quish \ri-'liŋ-kwish, -'lin-\ vb 1 : to withdraw or retreat from : ABANDON, QUIT 2 : GIVE UP ⟨~ a title⟩ 3 : to let go of : RELEASE ♦ *Synonyms* YIELD, LEAVE, RESIGN, SURRENDER, CEDE, WAIVE — **re·lin·quish·ment** n

rel·i·quary \'re-lə-,kwer-ē\ n, pl **-quar·ies** : a container for religious relics

¹**rel·ish** \'re-lish\ n [ME *reles* taste, fr. OF, something left behind, release, fr. *relessier* to relax, release, fr. L *relaxare*] 1 : characteristic flavor : SAVOR 2 : keen enjoyment or delight in something : GUSTO 3 : APPETITE, INCLINATION ⟨has no ~ for sports⟩ 4 : a highly seasoned sauce (as of pickles) eaten with other food to add flavor

²**relish** vb 1 : to add relish to 2 : to take pleasure in : ENJOY 3 : to eat with pleasure — **rel·ish·able** adj

re·live \(,)rē-'liv\ vb : to live again or over again; *esp* : to experience again in the imagination

re·lo·cate \(,)rē-'lō-,kāt, ,rē-lō-'kāt\ vb 1

: to locate again 2 : to move to a new location — **re·lo·ca·tion** \,rē-lō-'kā-shən\ n

re·luc·tant \ri-'lək-tənt\ adj : feeling or showing aversion, hesitation or unwillingness ⟨~ to get involved⟩ ♦ *Synonyms* DISINCLINED, INDISPOSED, HESITANT, LOATH, AVERSE — **re·luc·tance** \-təns\ n — **re·luc·tant·ly** adv

re·ly \ri-'lī\ vb **re·lied; re·ly·ing** [ME *relien* to rally, fr. AF *relier* to retie, gather, rally, fr. L *religare* to tie out of the way, fr. *re-* back + *ligare* to tie] : to place faith or confidence : DEPEND

REM \'rem\ n : RAPID EYE MOVEMENT

re·main \ri-'mān\ vb 1 : to be left after others have been removed, subtracted, or destroyed 2 : to be something yet to be shown, done, or treated ⟨it ~s to be seen⟩ 3 : to stay after others have gone 4 : to continue unchanged

re·main·der \ri-'mān-dər\ n 1 : that which is left over : a remaining group, part, or trace 2 : the number left after a subtraction 3 : the number that is left over from the dividend after division and that is less than the divisor 4 : a book sold at a reduced price by the publisher after sales have slowed ♦ *Synonyms* LEAVINGS, REST, BALANCE, REMNANT, RESIDUE

re·mains \-'mānz\ n pl 1 : a remaining part or trace ⟨the ~ of a meal⟩ 2 : a dead body

¹**re·make** \(,)rē-'māk\ vb **-made** \-'mād\; **-mak·ing** : to make anew or in a different form

²**re·make** \'rē-,māk\ n : one that is remade; *esp* : a new version of a motion picture

re·mand \ri-'mand\ vb : to order back; *esp* : to return to custody pending trial or for further detention

¹**re·mark** \ri-'märk\ n 1 : the act of remarking : OBSERVATION, NOTICE 2 : a passing observation or comment

²**remark** vb 1 : to take notice of : OBSERVE 2 : to express as an observation or comment : SAY

re·mark·able \ri-'mär-kə-bəl\ adj : worthy of being or likely to be noticed : UNUSUAL, EXTRAORDINARY, NOTEWORTHY — **re·mark·able·ness** n

re·mark·ably \ri-'mär-kə-blē\ adv 1 : in a remarkable manner 2 : as is remarkable ⟨~, no one was hurt⟩

re·me·di·a·ble \ri-'mē-dē-ə-bəl\ adj : capable of being remedied

re·me·di·al \ri-'mē-dē-əl\ adj : intended to remedy or improve

¹**rem·e·dy** \'re-mə-dē\ n, pl **-dies** [ME *remedie*, fr. AF, fr. L *remedium*, fr. *re-* back, again + *mederi* to heal] 1 : a medicine or treatment that cures or relieves a disease or condition 2 : something that corrects or counteracts an evil or compensates for a loss

²**remedy** vb **-died; -dy·ing** : to provide or serve as a remedy for

---

relight	remanufacture	remarriage	rematch
reline	remap	remarry	remelt
reload			

re·mem·ber \ri-'mem-bər\ *vb* **-bered; -ber·ing** **1** : to bring to mind or think of again : RECOLLECT **2** : to keep from forgetting : keep in mind **3** : to convey greetings from **4** : COMMEMORATE

re·mem·brance \-brəns\ *n* **1** : an act of remembering : RECOLLECTION **2** : the ability to remember : MEMORY **3** : the period over which one's memory extends **4** : a memory of a person, thing, or event **5** : something that serves to bring to mind : REMINDER **6** : a greeting or gift recalling or expressing friendship or affection

re·mind \ri-'mīnd\ *vb* : to put in mind of something : cause to remember — **re·mind·er** *n*

rem·i·nisce \ˌre-mə-'nis\ *vb* **-nisced; -nisc·ing** : to indulge in reminiscence

rem·i·nis·cence \-'ni-sᵊns\ *n* **1** : a recalling or telling of a past experience **2** : an account of a memorable experience

rem·i·nis·cent \-sᵊnt\ *adj* **1** : of or relating to reminiscence **2** : marked by or given to reminiscence **3** : serving to remind : SUGGESTIVE — **rem·i·nis·cent·ly** *adv*

re·miss \ri-'mis\ *adj* **1** : negligent or careless in the performance of work or duty **2** : showing neglect or inattention ◆ *Synonyms* LAX, NEGLECTFUL, DELINQUENT, DERELICT — **re·miss·ness** *n*

re·mis·sion \ri-'mi-shən\ *n* **1** : the act or process of remitting **2** : a state or period during which something is remitted

re·mit \ri-'mit\ *vb* **re·mit·ted; re·mit·ting** **1** : FORGIVE, PARDON ⟨~ sins⟩ **2** : to give or gain relief from (as pain) **3** : to refer for consideration, report, or decision **4** : to refrain from exacting or enforcing (as a penalty) **5** : to send (money) in payment of a bill

re·mit·tal \ri-'mi-tᵊl\ *n* : REMISSION

re·mit·tance \ri-'mi-tᵊns\ *n* **1** : a sum of money remitted **2** : transmittal of money (as to a distant place)

rem·nant \'rem-nənt\ *n* **1** : a usu. small part or trace remaining **2** : an unsold or unused end of a fabric that is sold by the yard

re·mod·el \ˌrē-'mä-dᵊl\ *vb* : to alter the structure of : MAKE OVER

re·mon·strance \ri-'män-strəns\ *n* : an act or instance of remonstrating

re·mon·strant \-strənt\ *adj* : vigorously objecting or opposing — **remonstrant** *n* — **re·mon·strant·ly** *adv*

re·mon·strate \ri-'män-ˌstrāt\ *vb* **-strat·ed; -strat·ing** : to plead in opposition to something : speak in protest or reproof ◆ *Synonyms* EXPOSTULATE, OBJECT, PROTEST — **re·mon·stra·tion** \ri-ˌmän-'strā-shən, ˌre-mən-\ *n* — **re·mon·stra·tor** \ri-'män-ˌstrā-tər\ *n*

rem·o·ra \'re-mə-rə\ *n* : any of a family of marine bony fishes with sucking organs on the head by which they cling esp. to other fishes

re·morse \ri-'mȯrs\ *n* [ME, fr. AF *remors*, fr. ML *remorsus*, fr. LL, act of biting again, fr. L *remordēre* to bite again, fr. *re-* again + *mordēre* to bite] : a gnawing distress arising from a sense of guilt for past wrongs ◆ *Synonyms* PENITENCE, REPENTANCE, CONTRITION — **re·morse·ful** *adj*

re·morse·less \-ləs\ *adj* **1** : MERCILESS **2** : PERSISTENT, RELENTLESS

¹**re·mote** \ri-'mōt\ *adj* **re·mot·er; -est** **1** : far off in place or time : not near **2** : not closely related : DISTANT **3** : located out of the way : SECLUDED **4** : acting, acted on, or controlled indirectly or from a distance **5** : small in degree : SLIGHT ⟨a ~ chance⟩ **6** : distant in manner — **re·mote·ly** *adv* — **re·mote·ness** *n*

²**remote** *n* **1** : a radio or television program or a portion of a program originating outside the studio **2** : REMOTE CONTROL 2

remote control *n* **1** : control (as by radio signal) of operation from a point at some distance removed **2** : a device or mechanism for controlling something from a distance

¹**re·mount** \(ˌ)rē-'maunt\ *vb* **1** : to mount again **2** : to furnish remounts to

²**re·mount** \'rē-ˌmaunt\ *n* : a fresh horse to replace one now mounted or available

¹**re·move** \ri-'müv\ *vb* **re·moved; re·mov·ing** **1** : to move from one place to another : TRANSFER **2** : to move by lifting or taking off or away **3** : DISMISS, DISCHARGE **4** : to get rid of : ELIMINATE ⟨~ a fire hazard⟩ **5** : to change one's residence or location **6** : to go away : DEPART **7** : to be capable of being removed — **re·mov·able** *adj* — **re·mov·al** \-'mü-vəl\ *n* — **re·mov·er** *n*

²**remove** *n* **1** : a transfer from one location to another : MOVE **2** : a degree or stage of separation

REM sleep *n* : a state of sleep that recurs cyclically several times during normal sleep and is associated with rapid eye movements and dreaming

re·mu·ner·ate \ri-'myü-nə-ˌrāt\ *vb* **-at·ed; -at·ing** : to pay an equivalent for or to : RECOMPENSE — **re·mu·ner·a·tor** \-ˌrā-tər\ *n*

re·mu·ner·a·tion \ri-ˌmyü-nə-'rā-shən\ *n* : COMPENSATION, PAYMENT

re·mu·ner·a·tive \ri-'myü-nə-rə-tiv, -ˌrā-\ *adj* : serving to remunerate : GAINFUL

re·nais·sance \ˌre-nə-'säns, -'zäns\ *n* **1** *cap* : the cultural revival and beginnings of modern science in Europe in the 14th–17th centuries; *also* : the period of the Renaissance **2** *often cap* : a movement or period of vigorous artistic and intellectual activity **3** : REBIRTH, REVIVAL

re·nal \'rē-nᵊl\ *adj* : of, relating to, or located in or near the kidneys

re·na·scence \ri-'na-sᵊns, -'nā-\ *n, often cap* : RENAISSANCE

rend \'rend\ *vb* **rent** \'rent\; **rend·ing** **1** : to remove by violence : WREST **2** : to tear forcibly apart : SPLIT

ren·der \'ren-dər\ *vb* **1** : to extract (as

lard) by heating **2** : to give to another; *also* : YIELD **3** : to give in return **4** : to do (a service) for another ⟨∼ aid⟩ **5** : to cause to be or become : MAKE **6** : to reproduce or represent by artistic or verbal means **7** : TRANSLATE ⟨∼ into English⟩

¹ren·dez·vous \'rän-di-ˌvü, -dā-\ *n, pl* **ren·dez·vous** \-ˌvüz\ [MF, fr. *rendez vous* present yourselves] **1** : a place appointed for a meeting; *also* : a meeting at an appointed place **2** : a place of popular resort **3** : the process of bringing two spacecraft together

²rendezvous *vb* **-voused** \-ˌvüd\; **-vous·ing** \-ˌvü-iŋ\; **-vouses** \-ˌvüz\ : to come or bring together at a rendezvous

ren·di·tion \ren-'di-shən\ *n* : an act or a result of rendering ⟨first ∼ of the work into English⟩

ren·e·gade \'re-ni-ˌgäd\ *n* [Sp *renegado*, fr. ML *renegatus*, fr. pp. of *renegare* to deny, fr. L *re-* + *negare* to deny] : a deserter from one faith, cause, principle, or party for another

re·nege \ri-'neg\ *vb* **re·neged; re·neg·ing** **1** : to go back on a promise or commitment **2** : to fail to follow suit when able in a card game in violation of the rules — **re·neg·er** *n*

re·new \ri-'nü, -'nyü\ *vb* **1** : to make or become new, fresh, or strong again **2** : to restore to existence : RECREATE, REVIVE **3** : to make or do again : REPEAT ⟨∼ a complaint⟩ **4** : to begin again : RESUME ⟨∼ed his efforts⟩ **5** : REPLACE ⟨∼ the lining of a coat⟩ **6** : to grant or obtain an extension of or on ⟨∼ a lease⟩ ⟨∼ a subscription⟩ — **re·new·er** *n*

re·new·able \ri-'nü-ə-bəl, -'nyü-\ *adj* **1** : capable of being renewed **2** : capable of being replaced by natural ecological cycles or sound management procedures ⟨∼ resources⟩

re·new·al \ri-'nü-əl, -'nyü-\ *n* **1** : the act of renewing : the state of being renewed **2** : something renewed

ren·net \'re-nət\ *n* **1** : the contents of the stomach of an unweaned animal (as a calf) or the lining membrane of the stomach used for curdling milk **2** : rennin or a substitute used to curdle milk

ren·nin \'re-nən\ *n* : a stomach enzyme that coagulates casein and is used commercially to curdle milk in the making of cheese

re·nounce \ri-'naùns\ *vb* **re·nounced; re·nounc·ing** **1** : to give up, refuse, or resign usu. by formal declaration **2** : to refuse further to follow, obey, or recognize : REPUDIATE — **re·nounce·ment** *n*

ren·o·vate \'re-nə-ˌvät\ *vb* **-vat·ed; -vat·ing** **1** : to make like new again : put in good condition : REPAIR **2** : to restore to vigor or activity — **ren·o·va·tion** \ˌre-nə-'vä-shən\ *n* — **ren·o·va·tor** \'re-nə-ˌvä-tər\ *n*

re·nown \ri-'naùn\ *n* : a state of being widely acclaimed and honored : FAME, CELEBRITY ♦ *Synonyms* HONOR, GLORY, REPUTATION, REPUTE — **re·nowned** \-'naùnd\ *adj*

¹rent \'rent\ *n* **1** : money or the amount of money paid or due at intervals for the use of another's property **2** : property rented or for rent

²rent *vb* **1** : to give possession and use of in return for rent **2** : to take and hold under an agreement to pay rent **3** : to be for rent ⟨∼*s* for $100 a month⟩ — **rent·er** *n*

³rent *n* **1** : a tear made by or as if by rending **2** : a split in a party or organized group : SCHISM

¹rent·al \'ren-təl\ *n* **1** : an amount paid or collected as rent **2** : something that is rented **3** : an act of renting

²rental *adj* : of or relating to rent

re·nun·ci·a·tion \ri-ˌnən-sē-'ā-shən\ *n* : the act of renouncing : REPUDIATION

¹rep \'rep\ *n* : REPRESENTATIVE ⟨sales ∼*s*⟩

²rep *abbr* **1** repair **2** repeat **3** report; reporter **4** republic

Rep *abbr* Republican

re·pack·age \ˌ)rē-'pa-kij\ *vb* : to package again or anew; *esp* : to put into a more attractive form

¹re·pair \ri-'per\ *vb* [ME, fr. AF *repairer* to go back, return, fr. LL *repatriare* to go home again, fr. L *re-* back + *patria* native country] : to make one's way : GO ⟨∼ed to the drawing room⟩

²repair *vb* [ME, fr. AF *reparer*, fr. L *reparare*, fr. *re-* back + *parare* to prepare] **1** : to restore to good condition : FIX **2** : to restore to a healthy state **3** : REMEDY ⟨∼ a wrong⟩ — **re·pair·er** *n* — **re·pair·man** \-ˌman\ *n*

³repair *n* **1** : a result of repairing **2** : an act of repairing **3** : condition with respect to need of repairing ⟨in bad ∼⟩

rep·a·ra·tion \ˌre-pə-'rä-shən\ *n* **1** : the act of making amends for a wrong **2** : amends made for a wrong; *esp* : money paid by a defeated nation in compensation for damages caused during hostilities — usu. used in pl. ♦ *Synonyms* REDRESS, RESTITUTION, INDEMNITY

re·par·a·tive \ri-'pa-rə-tiv\ *adj* **1** : of, relating to, or effecting repairs **2** : serving to make amends

rep·ar·tee \ˌre-pər-'tē\ *n* **1** : a witty reply **2** : a succession of clever replies; *also* : skill in making such replies

re·past \ri-'past, 'rē-ˌpast\ *n* : a supply of food and drink served as a meal

re·pa·tri·ate \rē-'pā-trē-ˌāt\ *vb* **-at·ed; -at·ing** : to send or bring back to the country of origin or citizenship ⟨∼ prisoners of war⟩ — **re·pa·tri·ate** \-trē-ət, -trē-ˌāt\ *n* — **re·pa·tri·a·tion** \-ˌpā-trē-'ā-shən\ *n*

re·pay \rē-'pā\ *vb* **-paid** \-'pād\; **-pay·ing** **1** : to pay back : REFUND **2** : to give or do in return or requital **3** : to make a return payment to : RECOM-

renegotiate	renumber	reorder	reorientation
renegotiation	reoccupy	reorganization	repack
renominate	reoccur	reorganize	repaint
renomination	reopen	reorient	repass

PENSE, REQUITE ✦ *Synonyms* REMUNERATE, COMPENSATE, REIMBURSE, INDEMNIFY — **re·pay·able** *adj* — **re·pay·ment** *n*

re·peal \ri-'pēl\ *vb* [ME *repelen*, fr. AF *repeler*, lit., to call back, fr. *re-* back + *apeler* to appeal, call] : to annul by authoritative and esp. legislative action — **repeal** *n* — **re·peal·er** *n*

¹**re·peat** \ri-'pēt\ *vb* **1** : to say again **2** : to do again **3** : to say over from memory — **re·peat·able** *adj* — **re·peat·er** *n*

²**re·peat** \ri-'pēt, 'rē-,pēt\ *n* **1** : the act of repeating **2** : something repeated or to be repeated (as a radio or television program)

³**re·peat** \ri-'pēt\ *adj* : of, relating to, or being one that repeats an offense, achievement, or action

re·peat·ed \ri-'pē-təd\ *adj* : done or recurring again and again : FREQUENT — **re·peat·ed·ly** *adv*

re·pel \ri-'pel\ *vb* **re·pelled; re·pel·ling** **1** : to drive away : REPULSE **2** : to fight against : RESIST **3** : to turn away : REJECT **4** : to cause aversion in : DISGUST

¹**re·pel·lent** *also* **re·pel·lant** \ri-'pe-lənt\ *adj* **1** : tending to drive away ⟨a mosquito-*repellent* spray⟩ **2** : causing disgust

²**repellent** *also* **repellant** *n* : something that repels; *esp* : a substance that repels insects

re·pent \ri-'pent\ *vb* **1** : to turn from sin and resolve to reform one's life **2** : to feel sorry for (something done) : REGRET — **re·pen·tance** \-'pen-t²ns\ *n* — **re·pen·tant** \-t²nt\ *adj*

re·per·cus·sion \,rē-pər-'kə-shən, ,re-\ *n* **1** : REVERBERATION **2** : a reciprocal action or effect **3** : a widespread, indirect, or unforeseen effect of something done or said

rep·er·toire \'re-pər-,twär\ *n* [F] **1** : a list of plays, operas, pieces, or parts which a company or performer is prepared to present **2** : a list of the skills or devices possessed by a person or needed in a person's occupation

rep·er·to·ry \'re-pər-,tòr-ē\ *n, pl* **-ries** **1** : REPOSITORY **2** : REPERTOIRE **3** : a company that presents its repertoire in the course of one season at one theater

rep·e·ti·tion \,re-pə-'ti-shən\ *n* **1** : the act or an instance of repeating **2** : the fact of being repeated

rep·e·ti·tious \-'ti-shəs\ *adj* : marked by repetition; *esp* : tediously repeating — **rep·e·ti·tious·ly** *adv* — **rep·e·ti·tious·ness** *n*

re·pet·i·tive \ri-'pe-tə-tiv\ *adj* : REPETITIOUS — **re·pet·i·tive·ly** *adv* — **re·pet·i·tive·ness** *n*

re·pine \ri-'pīn\ *vb* **re·pined; re·pin·ing** **1** : to feel or express discontent or dejection **2** : to long for something

repl *abbr* replace; replacement

re·place \ri-'plās\ *vb* **1** : to restore to a former place or position **2** : to take the place of : SUPPLANT **3** : to put something

new in the place of — **re·place·able** *adj* — **re·plac·er** *n*

re·place·ment \ri-'plās-mənt\ *n* **1** : the act of replacing : the state of being replaced **2** : one that replaces another esp. in a job or function

¹**re·play** \(,)rē-'plā\ *vb* : to play again or over

²**re·play** \'rē-,plā\ *n* **1** : an act or instance of replaying **2** : the playing of a tape (as a videotape)

re·plen·ish \ri-'ple-nish\ *vb* : to fill or build up again : stock or supply anew — **re·plen·ish·ment** *n*

re·plete \ri-'plēt\ *adj* **1** : fully provided ⟨a kit ∼ with instructions⟩ **2** : FULL; *esp* : full of food — **re·plete·ness** *n* — **re·ple·tion** \ri-'plē-shən\ *n*

rep·li·ca \'re-pli-kə\ *n* [It, repetition, fr. *replicare* to repeat, fr. LL, fr. L, to fold back, fr. *re-* back + *plicare* to fold] **1** : an exact reproduction (as of a painting) executed by the original artist **2** : a copy exact in all details : DUPLICATE

¹**rep·li·cate** \'re-plə-,kāt\ *vb* **-cat·ed; -cat·ing** : DUPLICATE, REPEAT

²**rep·li·cate** \-pli-kət\ *n* : one of several identical experiments or procedures

rep·li·ca·tion \,re-plə-'kā-shən\ *n* **1** : ANSWER, REPLY **2** : precise copying or reproduction; *also* : an act or process of this ⟨∼ of DNA⟩

¹**re·ply** \ri-'plī\ *vb* **re·plied; re·ply·ing** : to say or do in answer : RESPOND

²**reply** *n, pl* **replies** : ANSWER, RESPONSE

repo \'rē,pō\ *adj* : of, relating to, or being in the business of repossessing property (as a car)

¹**re·port** \ri-'pòrt\ *n* [ME, fr. AF, fr. *reporter* to bring back, report, fr. L *reportare*, fr. *re-* back + *portare* to carry] **1** : common talk : RUMOR **2** : FAME, REPUTATION ⟨a person of good ∼⟩ **3** : a usu. detailed account or statement **4** : an explosive noise

²**report** *vb* **1** : to give an account of : RELATE, TELL **2** : to serve as carrier of (a message) **3** : to prepare or present (as an account of an event) for a newspaper or a broadcast **4** : to make a charge of misconduct against **5** : to present oneself (as for work) **6** : to make known to the authorities ⟨∼ a fire⟩ **7** : to return or present (as a matter referred to a committee) with conclusions and recommendations **8** : to work as a subordinate ⟨∼s to the vice president⟩ — **re·port·able** *adj*

re·port·age \ri-'pòr-tij, *esp for 2* ,re-pər-'täzh, ,re-,pòr-'\ *n* [F] **1** : the act or process of reporting news **2** : writing intended to give an account of observed or documented events

report card *n* : a periodic report on a student's grades

re·port·ed·ly \ri-'pòr-təd-lē\ *adv* : according to report

re·port·er \ri-'pòr-tər\ *n* : one that reports; *esp* : a person who gathers and re-

repeople   **rephrase**   **replant**   **repopulate**
rephotograph

ports news for a news medium — **re·por·to·ri·al** \ˌre-pər-ˈtȯr-ē-əl\ *adj*

¹re·pose \ri-ˈpōz\ *vb* **re·posed; re·pos·ing** **1** : to lay at rest **2** : to lie at rest **3** : to lie dead **4** : to take a rest **5** : to rest for support : LIE

²repose *n* **1** : a state of resting (as after exertion); *esp* : SLEEP **2** : eternal or heavenly rest **3** : CALM, PEACE ⟨the ~ of the bayous⟩ **4** : cessation or absence of activity, movement, or animation **5** : composure of manner : POISE — **re·pose·ful** *adj*

³repose *vb* **re·posed; re·pos·ing** **1** : to place (as trust) in someone or something **2** : to place for control, management, or use

re·pos·i·to·ry \ri-ˈpä-zə-ˌtȯr-ē\ *n, pl* **-ries** **1** : a place where something is deposited or stored **2** : a person to whom something is entrusted

re·pos·sess \ˌrē-pə-ˈzes\ *vb* **1** : to regain possession of **2** : to take possession of in default of the payment of installments due — **re·pos·ses·sion** \-ˈze-shən\ *n*

rep·re·hend \ˌre-pri-ˈhend\ *vb* : to express disapproval of : CENSURE ✦ *Synonyms* CRITICIZE, CONDEMN, DENOUNCE, BLAME, PAN — **rep·re·hen·sion** \-ˈhen-chən\ *n*

rep·re·hen·si·ble \-ˈhen-sə-bəl\ *adj* : deserving blame or censure : CULPABLE — **rep·re·hen·si·bly** \-blē\ *adv*

rep·re·sent \ˌre-pri-ˈzent\ *vb* **1** : to present a picture or a likeness of : PORTRAY, DEPICT **2** : to serve as a sign or symbol of **3** : to act the role of **4** : to stand in the place of : act or speak for; *also* : to manage the legal and business affairs of **5** : to be a member or example of : TYPIFY **6** : to serve as an elected representative of **7** : to describe as having a specified quality or character **8** : to state with the purpose of affecting judgment or action

rep·re·sen·ta·tion \ˌre-pri-ˌzen-ˈtā-shən\ *n* **1** : the act of representing **2** : one (as a picture or image) that represents something else **3** : the state of being represented in a legislative body; *also* : the body of persons representing a constituency **4** : a usu. formal statement made to effect a change

¹rep·re·sen·ta·tive \ˌre-pri-ˈzen-tə-tiv\ *adj* **1** : serving to represent **2** : standing or acting for another **3** : founded on the principle of representation : carried on by elected representatives ⟨~ government⟩ — **rep·re·sen·ta·tive·ly** *adv* — **rep·re·sen·ta·tive·ness** *n*

²representative *n* **1** : one that represents another; *esp* : one representing a district in a legislative body usu. as a member of a lower house **2** : a typical example of a group, class, or quality

re·press \ri-ˈpres\ *vb* **1** : CURB, SUBDUE **2** : RESTRAIN, SUPPRESS **3** : to exclude from consciousness — **re·pres·sion** \-ˈpre-shən\ *n* — **re·pres·sive** \-ˈpre-siv\ *adj*

¹re·prieve \ri-ˈprēv\ *vb* **re·prieved; re·priev·ing** **1** : to delay the punishment or execution of **2** : to give temporary relief to

²reprieve *n* **1** : the act of reprieving : the state of being reprieved **2** : a formal temporary suspension of a sentence esp. of death **3** : a temporary respite

¹rep·ri·mand \ˈre-prə-ˌmand\ *n* : a severe or formal reproof

²reprimand *vb* : to reprove severely or formally

¹re·print \ˌ(ˌ)rē-ˈprint\ *vb* : to print again

²re·print \ˈrē-ˌprint\ *n* : a reproduction of printed matter

re·pri·sal \ri-ˈprī-zəl\ *n* : an act in retaliation for something done by another

re·prise \ri-ˈprēz\ *n* : a recurrence, renewal, or resumption of an action; *also* : a musical repetition

¹re·proach \ri-ˈprōch\ *n* **1** : an expression of disapproval **2** : DISGRACE, DISCREDIT **3** : the act of reproaching : REBUKE **4** : a cause or occasion of blame or disgrace — **re·proach·ful** \-fəl\ *adj* — **re·proach·ful·ly** *adv* — **re·proach·ful·ness** *n*

²reproach *vb* **1** : CENSURE, REBUKE **2** : to cast discredit on ✦ *Synonyms* CHIDE, ADMONISH, REPROVE, REPRIMAND — **re·proach·able** *adj*

rep·ro·bate \ˈre-prə-ˌbāt\ *n* **1** : a person foreordained to damnation **2** : a thoroughly bad person : SCOUNDREL — **reprobate** *adj*

rep·ro·ba·tion \ˌre-prə-ˈbā-shən\ *n* : strong disapproval : CONDEMNATION

re·pro·duce \ˌrē-prə-ˈdüs, -ˈdyüs\ *vb* **1** : to produce again or anew **2** : to produce offspring — **re·pro·duc·ible** \-ˈdü-sə-bəl, -ˈdyü-\ *adj* — **re·pro·duc·tion** \-ˈdək-shən\ *n* — **re·pro·duc·tive** \-ˈdək-tiv\ *adj*

re·proof \ri-ˈprüf\ *n* : blame or censure for a fault

re·prove \ri-ˈprüv\ *vb* **re·proved; re·prov·ing** **1** : to administer a rebuke to **2** : to express disapproval of ✦ *Synonyms* REPRIMAND, ADMONISH, REPROACH, CHIDE — **re·prov·er** *n*

rept *abbr* report

rep·tile \ˈrep-tī(-ə)l, -ˌtᵊl\ *n* [ME *reptil*, fr. MF or LL; MF *reptile*, fr. LL *reptile*, fr. L *repere* to crawl] : any of a large class of air-breathing scaly vertebrates including snakes, lizards, alligators, turtles, and extinct related forms (as dinosaurs) — **rep·til·i·an** \rep-ˈti-lē-ən\ *adj or n*

re·pub·lic \ri-ˈpə-blik\ *n* [F *république*, fr. MF *republique*, fr. L *respublica*, fr. *res* thing, wealth + *publica*, fem. of *publicus* public] **1** : a government having a chief of state who is not a monarch and is usu. a president; *also* : a nation or other political unit having such a government **2** : a government in which supreme power is held by the citizens entitled to vote and is exercised by elected officers and representatives governing according to law; *also* : a nation or other political unit hav-

---

reprice   reprocess   reprogram

ing such a form of government **3** : a constituent political and territorial unit of the former nations of Czechoslovakia, the U.S.S.R., or Yugoslavia

¹**re·pub·li·can** \-bli-kən\ n **1** : one that favors or supports a republican form of government **2** cap : a member of a republican party and esp. of the Republican party of the U.S.

²**republican** adj **1** : of, relating to, or resembling a republic **2** : favoring or supporting a republic **3** cap : of, relating to, or constituting one of the two major political parties in the U.S. evolving in the mid-19th century — **re·pub·li·can·ism** n, often cap

re·pu·di·ate \ri-'pyü-dē-,āt\ vb **-at·ed; -at·ing** [L repudiare to cast off, divorce, fr. repudium rejection of a prospective spouse, divorce] **1** : to cast off : DIS-OWN **2** : to refuse to have anything to do with : refuse to acknowledge, accept, or pay ⟨∼ a charge⟩ ⟨∼ a debt⟩ ♦ **Synonyms** SPURN, REJECT, DECLINE — **re·pu·di·a·tion** \-,pyü-dē-'ā-shən\ n — **re·pu·di·a·tor** \-'pyü-dē-,ā-tər\ n

re·pug·nance \ri-'pəg-nəns\ n **1** : the quality or fact of being contradictory or inconsistent **2** : strong dislike, distaste, or antagonism

re·pug·nant \-nənt\ adj **1** : marked by repugnance **2** : contrary to a person's tastes or principles : exciting distaste or aversion ♦ **Synonyms** REPELLENT, ABHORRENT, DISTASTEFUL, OBNOXIOUS, REVOLTING, LOATHSOME — **re·pug·nant·ly** adv

¹**re·pulse** \ri-'pəls\ vb **re·pulsed; re·puls·ing** **1** : to drive or beat back : REPEL **2** : to repel by discourtesy or denial : REBUFF **3** : to cause a feeling of repulsion in : DISGUST

²**repulse** n **1** : REBUFF, REJECTION **2** : the action of repelling an attacker : the fact of being repelled

re·pul·sion \ri-'pəl-shən\ n **1** : the action of repulsing : the state of being repulsed **2** : the force with which bodies, particles, or like forces repel one another **3** : a feeling of aversion

re·pul·sive \-siv\ adj **1** : serving or tending to repel or reject **2** : arousing aversion or disgust ♦ **Synonyms** REPUGNANT, REVOLTING, LOATHSOME, NOISOME — **re·pul·sive·ly** adv — **re·pul·sive·ness** n

re·pur·pose \(,)rē-'pər-pəs\ vb : to give a new purpose or use to

rep·u·ta·ble \'re-pyə-tə-bəl\ adj : having a good reputation : ESTIMABLE — **rep·u·ta·bly** \-blē\ adv

rep·u·ta·tion \,re-pyù-'tā-shən\ n **1** : overall quality or character as seen or judged by people in general **2** : place in public esteem or regard

¹**re·pute** \ri-'pyüt\ vb **re·put·ed; re·put·ing** : BELIEVE, CONSIDER ⟨reputed to be a millionaire⟩

²**repute** n **1** : REPUTATION ⟨knew her by

∼⟩ **2** : the state of being favorably known or spoken of

re·put·ed \ri-'pyü-təd\ adj **1** : REPUTABLE **2** : according to reputation : SUPPOSED — **re·put·ed·ly** adv

req abbr **1** request **2** require; required **3** requisition

¹**re·quest** \ri-'kwest\ n **1** : an act or instance of asking for something **2** : a thing asked for **3** : the condition of being asked for ⟨available on ∼⟩

²**request** vb **1** : to make a request to or of **2** : to ask for — **re·quest·er** or **re·quest·or** n

re·qui·em \'re-kwē-əm, 'rā-\ n [ME, fr. L (first word of the requiem mass), acc. of requies rest, fr. quies quiet, rest] **1** : a mass for a dead person; also : a musical setting for this **2** : a musical service or hymn in honor of the dead

re·quire \ri-'kwī(-ə)r\ vb **re·quired; re·quir·ing** **1** : to demand as necessary or essential **2** : COMMAND, ORDER ⟨the law ∼s that everyone pay the tax⟩

re·quire·ment \-mənt\ n **1** : something (as a condition or quality) required ⟨entrance ∼s⟩ **2** : NECESSITY ⟨production was sufficient to satisfy military ∼s⟩

req·ui·site \'re-kwə-zət\ adj : REQUIRED, NECESSARY — **requisite** n

req·ui·si·tion \,re-kwə-'zi-shən\ n **1** : formal application or demand (as for supplies) **2** : the state of being in demand or use — **requisition** vb

re·quite \ri-'kwīt\ vb **re·quit·ed; re·quit·ing** **1** : to make return for : REPAY **2** : to make retaliation for : AVENGE **3** : to make return to — **re·quit·al** \-'kwī-t°l\ n

rere·dos \'rer-ə-,däs\ n : a usu. ornamental wood or stone screen or partition wall behind an altar

re·run \'rē-,rən, (,)rē-'rən\ n : the act or an instance of running again or anew; esp : a showing of a motion picture or television program after its first run — **re·run** \(,)rē-'rən\ vb

res abbr **1** research **2** reservation; reserve **3** reservoir **4** residence; resident **5** resolution

re·sale \'rē-,sāl, (,)rē-'sāl\ n : the act of selling again usu. to a new party — **re·sal·able** \(,)rē-'sā-lə-bəl\ adj

re·scind \ri-'sind\ vb : REPEAL, CANCEL, ANNUL — **re·scis·sion** \-'si-zhən\ n

re·script \'rē-,skript\ n : an official or authoritative order or decree

res·cue \'res-kyü\ vb **res·cued; res·cu·ing** [ME rescouen, rescuen, fr. AF rescure, fr. re- back, again + escure to shake off, fr. L excutere] : to free from danger, harm, or confinement — **rescue** n — **res·cu·er** n

re·search \ri-'sərch, 'rē-,sərch\ n **1** : careful or diligent search **2** : studious inquiry or examination aimed at the discovery and interpretation of new knowledge **3** : the collecting of information about a particular subject — **research** vb — **re·search·er** n

---

republication	repurchase	reread	rerecord
republish	reradiate	rereading	reroute

re·sec·tion \ri-'sek-shən\ n : the surgical removal of part of an organ or structure

re·sem·blance \ri-'zem-bləns\ n : the quality or state of resembling

re·sem·ble \ri-'zem-bəl\ vb **-bled; -bling** : to be like or similar to

re·sent \ri-'zent\ vb : to feel or exhibit annoyance or indignation at — **re·sent·ful** \-fəl\ adj — **re·sent·ful·ly** adv — **re·sent·ment** n

re·ser·pine \ri-'sər-ˌpēn, -pən\ n : a drug used in treating high blood pressure and nervous tension

res·er·va·tion \ˌre-zər-'vā-shən\ n 1 : an act of reserving 2 : something (as a room in a hotel) arranged for in advance 3 : something reserved; esp : a tract of public land set aside for special use 4 : a limiting condition

¹re·serve \ri-'zərv\ vb **re·served; re·serv·ing** 1 : to store for future or special use 2 : to hold back for oneself 3 : to set aside or arrange to have set aside or held for special use

²reserve n 1 : something reserved : STOCK, STORE 2 : a military force withheld from action for later use — usu. used in pl. 3 : the military forces of a country not part of the regular services; also : RESERVIST 4 : a tract set apart : RESERVATION 5 : an act of reserving 6 : restraint or caution in one's words or bearing 7 : money or its equivalent kept in hand or set apart to meet liabilities

re·served \ri-'zərvd\ adj 1 : restrained in words and actions 2 : set aside for future or special use — **re·serv·ed·ly** \-'zər-vəd-lē\ adv — **re·serv·ed·ness** \-vəd-nəs\ n

re·serv·ist \ri-'zər-vist\ n : a member of a military reserve

res·er·voir \'re-zə-ˌvwär, -zər-, -ˌvwȯr\ n [F] : a place where something is kept in store; esp : an artificial lake where water is collected and kept for use

re·shuf·fle \rē-'shə-fəl\ vb 1 : to shuffle again 2 : to reorganize usu. by redistribution of existing elements — **reshuffle** n

re·side \ri-'zīd\ vb **re·sid·ed; re·sid·ing** 1 : to make one's home : DWELL 2 : to be present as a quality or vested as a right

res·i·dence \'re-zə-dəns\ n 1 : the act or fact of residing in a place as a dweller or in discharge of a duty or an obligation 2 : the place where one actually lives 3 : a building used as a home : DWELLING 4 : the period of living in a place

res·i·den·cy \'re-zə-dən-sē\ n, pl **-cies** 1 : the residence of or the territory under a diplomatic resident 2 : a period of advanced training in a medical specialty

¹res·i·dent \-dənt\ adj 1 : RESIDING 2 : being in residence 3 : not migratory

²resident n 1 : one who resides in a place 2 : a diplomatic representative with governing powers (as in a protec-

torate) 3 : a physician serving a residency

res·i·den·tial \ˌre-zə-'den-chəl\ adj 1 : used as a residence or by residents 2 : occupied by or restricted to residences — **res·i·den·tial·ly** adv

¹re·sid·u·al \ri-'zi-jə-wəl\ n 1 : a residual product or substance 2 : a payment (as to an actor or writer) for each rerun after an initial showing (as of a taped TV show)

²residual adj : being a residue or remainder

re·sid·u·ary \ri-'zi-jə-ˌwer-ē\ adj : of, relating to, or constituting a residue esp. of an estate

res·i·due \'re-zə-ˌdü, -ˌdyü\ n : a part remaining after another part has been taken away : REMAINDER

re·sid·u·um \ri-'zi-jə-wəm\ n, pl **re·sid·ua** \-jə-wə\ [L] 1 : something remaining or residual after certain deductions are made 2 : a residual product

re·sign \ri-'zīn\ vb [ME, fr. AF resigner, fr. L resignare, lit., to unseal, cancel, fr. signare to sign, seal] 1 : to give up deliberately (as one's position) esp. by a formal act 2 : to give (oneself) over (as to grief or despair) without resistance — **re·sign·ed·ly** \-'zī-nəd-lē\ adv

re·sign \(ˌ)rē-'sīn\ vb : to sign again

res·ig·na·tion \ˌre-zig-'nā-shən\ n 1 : an act or instance of resigning; also : a formal notification of such an act 2 : the quality or state of being resigned

re·sil·ience \ri-'zil-yəns\ n 1 : the ability of a body to regain its original size and shape after being compressed, bent, or stretched 2 : an ability to recover from or adjust easily to change or misfortune

re·sil·ien·cy \-yən-sē\ n : RESILIENCE

re·sil·ient \-yənt\ adj : marked by resilience

res·in \'re-zᵊn\ n : any of various substances obtained from the gum or sap of some trees and used esp. in varnishes, plastics, and medicine; also : a comparable synthetic product — **res·in·ous** adj

¹re·sist \ri-'zist\ vb 1 : to fight against : OPPOSE ⟨~ aggression⟩ 2 : to withstand the force or effect of ⟨~ed temptation⟩ ⟨~ disease⟩ : COMBAT, REPEL — **re·sist·ible** \-'zis-tə-bəl\ adj — **re·sist·less** adj

²resist n : something (as a coating) that resists or prevents a particular action

re·sis·tance \ri-'zis-təns\ n 1 : the act or an instance of resisting : OPPOSITION 2 : the power or capacity to resist; esp : the inherent ability of an organism to resist harmful influences (as disease or infection) 3 : the opposition offered by a body to the passage through it of a steady electric current

re·sis·tant \-tənt\ adj : giving, capable of, or exhibiting resistance

re·sis·tor \ri-'zis-tər\ n : a device used to provide resistance to the flow of an electric current in a circuit

---

reschedule	reseal	reset	resew
rescore	reseed	resettle	reshow
rescreen	resell	resettlement	resocialization

res·o·lute \'re-zə-ˌlüt\ *adj* : firmly determined in purpose : RESOLVED ⟨a ~ leader⟩ ◆ **Synonyms** STEADFAST, STAUNCH, FAITHFUL, TRUE, LOYAL — **res·o·lute·ly** *adv* — **res·o·lute·ness** *n*

res·o·lu·tion \ˌre-zə-'lü-shən\ *n* 1 : the act or process of resolving 2 : the action of solving; *also* : SOLUTION 3 : the quality of being resolute : FIRMNESS, DETERMINATION 4 : a formal statement expressing the opinion, will, or intent of a body of persons 5 : a measure of the sharpness of an image or of the fineness with which a device can produce or record such an image

¹re·solve \ri-'zälv\ *vb* **re·solved; re·solv·ing** 1 : to break up into constituent parts : ANALYZE 2 : to distinguish between or make visible adjacent parts of 3 : to find an answer to : SOLVE ⟨~ a dispute⟩ 4 : DETERMINE, DECIDE 5 : to make or pass a formal resolution — **re·solv·able** *adj*

²resolve *n* 1 : fixity of purpose 2 : something resolved

res·o·nance \'re-zə-nəns\ *n* 1 : the quality or state of being resonant 2 : a reinforcement of sound in a vibrating body caused by waves from another body vibrating at nearly the same rate

res·o·nant \-nənt\ *adj* 1 : continuing to sound : RESOUNDING 2 : relating to or exhibiting resonance 3 : intensified and enriched by or as if by resonance — **res·o·nant·ly** *adv*

res·o·nate \-ˌnāt\ *vb* **-nat·ed; -nat·ing** 1 : to produce or exhibit resonance 2 : REVERBERATE, RESOUND 3 : to relate harmoniously ⟨~ with voters⟩

res·o·na·tor \-ˌnā-tər\ *n* : something that resounds or exhibits resonance

re·sorp·tion \rē-'sȯrp-shən, -'zȯrp-\ *n* : the action or process of breaking down and assimilating something (as a tooth or an embryo)

¹re·sort \ri-'zȯrt\ *n* [ME, fr. AF, fr. *resortir* to rebound, resort, fr. *sortir* to go out, leave] 1 : one looked to for help : REFUGE 2 : RECOURSE 3 : frequent or general visiting ⟨place of ~⟩ 4 : a frequently visited place : HAUNT 5 : a place providing recreation esp. to vacationers

²resort *vb* 1 : to go often or habitually 2 : to have recourse ⟨~ed to violence⟩

re·sound \ri-'zau̇nd\ *vb* 1 : to become filled with sound : REVERBERATE, RING 2 : to sound loudly

re·sound·ing *adj* 1 : RESONATING, RESONANT 2 : impressively sonorous ⟨~ name⟩ : EMPHATIC, UNEQUIVOCAL ⟨a ~ success⟩ — **re·sound·ing·ly** *adv*

re·source \'rē-ˌsȯrs, ri-'sȯrs\ *n* [F *ressource*, fr. OF *ressourse* relief, resource, fr. *resourdre* to relieve, lit., to rise again, fr. L *resurgere*, fr. *re-* again + *surgere* to rise] 1 : a source of supply or support — usu. used in pl. 2 : a natural feature or phenomenon that enhances the quality of human life 3 *pl* : available

funds 4 : a possibility of relief or recovery 5 : a means of spending leisure time 6 : ability to meet and handle situations — **re·source·ful** \ri-'sȯrs-fəl\ *adj* — **re·source·ful·ness** *n*

¹re·spect \ri-'spekt\ *n* 1 : relation to something usu. specified : REGARD ⟨in ~ to⟩ 2 : high or special regard : ESTEEM 3 *pl* : an expression of respect or deference 4 : DETAIL, PARTICULAR — **re·spect·ful** \-fəl\ *adj* — **re·spect·ful·ly** *adv* — **re·spect·ful·ness** *n*

²respect *vb* 1 : to consider deserving of high regard : ESTEEM 2 : to refrain from interfering with ⟨~ another's privacy⟩ 3 : to have reference to : CONCERN — **re·spect·er** *n*

re·spect·able \ri-'spek-tə-bəl\ *adj* 1 : worthy of respect : ESTIMABLE 2 : decent or correct in conduct : PROPER 3 : fair in size, quantity, or quality ⟨a ~ score⟩ : MODERATE, TOLERABLE 4 : fit to be seen : PRESENTABLE — **re·spect·a·bil·i·ty** \-ˌspek-tə-'bi-lə-tē\ *n* — **re·spect·ably** \-'spek-tə-blē\ *adv*

re·spect·ing *prep* : with regard to

re·spec·tive \-tiv\ *adj* : PARTICULAR, SEPARATE ⟨returned to their ~ homes⟩

re·spec·tive·ly \-lē\ *adv* 1 : as relating to each 2 : each in the order given

res·pi·ra·tion \ˌres-pə-'rā-shən\ *n* 1 : an act or the process of breathing 2 : the physical and chemical processes (as breathing and oxidation) by which a living thing obtains oxygen and eliminates waste gases (as carbon dioxide) — **re·spi·ra·to·ry** \'res-pə-rə-ˌtȯr-ē, ri-'spī-rə-\ *adj* — **re·spire** \ri-'spī(-ə)r\ *vb*

res·pi·ra·tor \'res-pə-ˌrā-tər\ *n* 1 : a device covering the mouth and nose esp. to prevent inhaling harmful vapors 2 : a device for artificial respiration

re·spite \'res-pət\ *n* [ME *respit*, fr. AF, fr. ML *respectus*, fr. L, act of looking back] 1 : a temporary delay 2 : an interval of rest or relief

re·splen·dent \ri-'splen-dənt\ *adj* : shining brilliantly : gloriously bright : SPLENDID — **re·splen·dence** \-dəns\ *n* — **re·splen·dent·ly** *adv*

re·spond \ri-'spänd\ *vb* 1 : ANSWER, REPLY 2 : REACT ⟨~ed to a call for help⟩ 3 : to show favorable reaction ⟨~ to medication⟩ — **re·spond·er** *n*

re·spon·dent \ri-'spän-dənt\ *n* : one who responds; *esp* : one who answers in various legal proceedings — **respondent** *adj*

re·sponse \ri-'späns\ *n* 1 : an act of responding 2 : something constituting a reply or a reaction

re·spon·si·bil·i·ty \ri-ˌspän-sə-'bi-lə-tē\ *n*, *pl* **-ties** 1 : the quality or state of being responsible 2 : something for which one is responsible

re·spon·si·ble \ri-'spän-sə-bəl\ *adj* 1 : liable to be called upon to answer for one's acts or decisions : ANSWERABLE 2 : able to fulfill one's obligations : RELIABLE, TRUSTWORTHY 3 : able to choose for oneself between right and wrong 4 : involving accountability or important duties ⟨~ position⟩ — **re·spon·si·ble·ness** n — **re·spon·si·bly** \-blē\ adv

re·spon·sive \-siv\ adj 1 : RESPONDING 2 : quick to respond : SENSITIVE 3 : using responses ⟨~ readings⟩ — **re·spon·sive·ly** adv — **re·spon·sive·ness** n

¹**rest** \'rest\ n 1 : REPOSE, SLEEP 2 : freedom from work or activity 3 : a state of motionlessness or inactivity 4 : a place of shelter or lodging 5 : a silence in music equivalent in duration to a note of the same value; also : a character indicating this 6 : something used as a support — **rest·ful** \-fəl\ adj — **rest·ful·ly** adv

²**rest** vb 1 : to get rest by lying down; esp : SLEEP 2 : to cease from action or motion 3 : to give rest to : set at rest 4 : to sit or lie fixed or supported 5 : to place on or against a support 6 : to remain based or founded 7 : to cause to be firmly fixed : GROUND 8 : to remain for action : DEPEND

³**rest** n : something left over

res·tau·rant \'res-trənt, -tə-ˌränt\ n [F, fr. prp. of restaurer to restore, fr. L restaurare] : a public eating place

res·tau·ra·teur \ˌres-tə-rə-'tər\ also **res·tau·ran·teur** \-ˌrän-\ n : the operator or proprietor of a restaurant

rest home n : an establishment that gives care for the aged or convalescent

res·ti·tu·tion \ˌres-tə-'tü-shən, -'tyü-\ n : the act of restoring : the state of being restored; esp : restoration of something to its rightful owner ♦ **Synonyms** AMENDS, REDRESS, REPARATION, INDEMNITY, COMPENSATION

res·tive \'res-tiv\ adj [ME restyf, fr. AF restif, fr. rester to stop, resist, remain, fr. L restare, fr. re- back + stare to stand] 1 : BALKY 2 : UNEASY, FIDGETY ♦ **Synonyms** RESTLESS, IMPATIENT, NERVOUS — **res·tive·ly** adv — **res·tive·ness** n

rest·less \'rest-ləs\ adj 1 : lacking or denying rest ⟨a ~ night⟩ 2 : never resting or settled : always moving ⟨the ~ sea⟩ 3 : marked by or showing unrest esp. of mind ⟨~ pacing back and forth⟩ ♦ **Synonyms** RESTIVE, IMPATIENT, NERVOUS, FIDGETY — **rest·less·ly** adv — **rest·less·ness** n

re·stor·able \ri-'stȯr-ə-bəl\ adj : fit for restoring or reclaiming

res·to·ra·tion \ˌres-tə-'rā-shən\ n 1 : an act of restoring : the state of being restored 2 : something (as a building) that has been restored

re·stor·ative \ri-'stȯr-ə-tiv\ n : something that restores esp. to consciousness or health — **restorative** adj

re·store \ri-'stȯr\ vb **re·stored; re·stor·ing** 1 : to give back : RETURN 2 : to put back into use or service 3 : to put or bring back into a former or original state 4 : to put again in possession of something — **re·stor·er** n

re·strain \ri-'strān\ vb 1 : to prevent from doing something 2 : to limit, restrict, or keep under control : CURB 3 : to place under restraint or arrest — **re·strain·able** adj — **re·strain·er** n

re·strained \ri-'strānd\ adj : marked by restraint : DISCIPLINED — **re·strain·ed·ly** \-'strā-nəd-lē\ adv

restraining order n : a legal order directing one person to stay away from another

re·straint \ri-'strānt\ n 1 : an act of restraining : the state of being restrained 2 : a restraining force, agency, or device 3 : deprivation or limitation of liberty : CONFINEMENT 4 : control over one's feelings : RESERVE

re·strict \ri-'strikt\ vb 1 : to confine within bounds : LIMIT 2 : to place under restriction as to use — **re·stric·tive** adj — **re·stric·tive·ly** adv

re·stric·tion \ri-'strik-shən\ n 1 : something (as a law or rule) that restricts 2 : an act of restricting : the state of being restricted

rest room n : a room or suite of rooms that includes sinks and toilets

¹**re·sult** \ri-'zəlt\ vb [ME, fr. ML resultare, fr. L, to rebound, fr. re- re- + saltare to leap] : to come about as an effect or consequence ⟨an injury ~ing from a fall⟩ — **re·sul·tant** \-'zəl-tᵊnt\ adj or n

²**result** n 1 : something that results : EFFECT, CONSEQUENCE 2 : beneficial or discernible effect 3 : something obtained by calculation or investigation

re·sume \ri-'züm\ vb **re·sumed; re·sum·ing** 1 : to take or assume again 2 : to return to or begin again after interruption 3 : to take back to oneself — **re·sump·tion** \-'zəmp-shən\ n

ré·su·mé or **re·su·me** or **re·su·mé** \'re-zə-ˌmā, ˌre-zə-'mā\ n [F résumé] 1 : SUMMARY; esp : a short account of one's career and qualifications usu. prepared by a job applicant 2 : a set of accomplishments ⟨a musical ~⟩

re·sur·gence \ri-'sər-jəns\ n : a rising again into life, activity, or prominence — **re·sur·gent** \-jənt\ adj

res·ur·rect \ˌre-zə-'rekt\ vb 1 : to raise from the dead 2 : to bring to attention or use again

res·ur·rec·tion \ˌre-zə-'rek-shən\ n 1 cap : the rising of Christ from the dead 2 often cap : the rising to life of all human dead before the final judgment 3 : REVIVAL

re·sus·ci·tate \ri-'sə-sə-ˌtāt\ vb **-tat·ed; -tat·ing** : to revive from apparent death or unconsciousness; also : REVITALIZE — **re·sus·ci·ta·tion** \ri-ˌsə-sə-'tā-shən, ˌrē-\ n — **re·sus·ci·ta·tor** \ri-'sə-sə-ˌtā-tər\ n

ret abbr retired

¹**re·tail** \'rē-ˌtāl, esp for 2 also ri-'tāl\ vb 1

: to sell in small quantities directly to the ultimate consumer **2** : to tell in detail or to one person after another — **re·tail·er** n

²**re·tail** \'rē-,tāl\ n : the sale of goods in small amounts to ultimate consumers — **retail** adj or adv

re·tain \ri-'tān\ vb **1** : to hold in possession or use **2** : to engage (as a lawyer) by paying a fee in advance **3** : to keep in a fixed place or position ◆ **Synonyms** DETAIN, WITHHOLD, RESERVE

¹**re·tain·er** \ri-'tā-nər\ n **1** : one that retains **2** : a servant in a wealthy household; also : EMPLOYEE **3** : a device that holds something (as teeth) in place

²**retainer** n : a fee paid to secure services (as of a lawyer)

¹**re·take** \(,)rē-'tāk\ vb **-took** \-'tu̇k\; **-tak·en** \-'tā-kən\; **-tak·ing 1** : to take or seize again **2** : to photograph again

²**re·take** \'rē-,tāk\ n : a second photographing of a motion-picture scene

re·tal·i·ate \ri-'ta-lē-,āt\ vb **-at·ed; -at·ing** : to return like for like; esp : to get revenge — **re·tal·i·a·tion** \-,ta-lē-'ā-shən\ n — **re·tal·ia·to·ry** \-'tal-yə-,tȯr-ē\ adj

re·tard \ri-'tärd\ vb : to hold back : delay the progress of ◆ **Synonyms** SLOW, SLACKEN, DETAIN — **re·tar·da·tion** \,rē-,tär-'dā-shən, ri-\ n — **re·tard·er** n

re·tar·dant \ri-'tär-dᵊnt\ adj : serving or tending to retard — **retardant** n

re·tard·ed adj, sometimes offensive : slow or limited in intellectual, emotional, or academic progress

retch \'rech\ vb : to try to vomit; also : VOMIT

re·ten·tion \ri-'ten-chən\ n **1** : the act of retaining : the state of being retained **2** : the power of retaining esp. in the mind : RETENTIVENESS

re·ten·tive \-'ten-tiv\ adj : having the power of retaining; esp : retaining knowledge easily — **re·ten·tive·ness** n

re·think \(,)rē-'think\ vb **-thought** \-'thȯt\; **-think·ing** : to think about again : RECONSIDER

ret·i·cent \'re-tə-sənt\ adj **1** : tending not to talk or give out information **2** : RELUCTANT ◆ **Synonyms** RESERVED, TACITURN, CLOSEMOUTHED — **ret·i·cence** \-səns\ n — **ret·i·cent·ly** adv

ret·i·na \'re-tə-nə\ n, pl **retinas** or **ret·i·nae** \-,nē\ : the sensory membrane lining the eye that receives the image formed by the lens — **ret·i·nal** \'re-tə-nəl\ adj

ret·i·nue \'re-tə-,nü, -,nyü\ n : the body of attendants or followers of a distinguished person

re·tire \ri-'tī(-ə)r\ vb **re·tired; re·tir·ing 1** : RETREAT **2** : to withdraw esp. for privacy **3** : to withdraw from one's occupation or position : conclude one's career **4** : to withdraw from use or service **5** : to go to bed **6** : to cause to be out in baseball — **re·tire·ment** n

re·tired \ri-'tī(-ə)rd\ adj **1** : SECLUDED, QUIET **2** : withdrawn from active duty or from one's career

re·tir·ee \ri-,tī-'rē\ n : a person who has retired from a career

re·tir·ing adj : SHY, RESERVED

re·tool \(,)rē-'tül\ vb **1** : to reequip with tools **2** : to modify with usu. minor improvements ⟨∼ed the team for next year⟩

¹**re·tort** \ri-'tȯrt\ vb [L retortus, pp. of retorquēre, lit., to twist back, hurl back, fr. re- back + torquēre to twist] **1** : to say in reply : answer back usu. sharply **2** : to answer (an argument) by a counter argument **3** : RETALIATE

²**retort** n : a quick, witty, or cutting reply

³**re·tort** \ri-'tȯrt, 'rē-,tȯrt\ n [MF retorte, fr. ML retorta, fr. L, fem. of retortus, pp. of retorquēre to twist back; fr. its shape] : a vessel in which substances are distilled or broken up by heat

re·touch \(,)rē-'təch\ vb : TOUCH UP; esp : to change (as a photographic negative) in order to produce a more desirable appearance

re·trace \(,)rē-'trās\ vb : to go over again or in a reverse direction ⟨retraced his steps⟩

re·tract \ri-'trakt\ vb **1** : to draw back or in **2** : to withdraw (as a charge or promise) : DISAVOW — **re·tract·able** adj — **re·trac·tion** \-'trak-shən\ n

re·trac·tile \ri-'trak-tᵊl, -'trak-,tī(-ə)l\ adj : capable of being drawn back or in ⟨∼ claws⟩

¹**re·tread** \(,)rē-'tred\ vb **re·tread·ed; re·tread·ing** : to put a new tread on (a worn tire)

²**re·tread** \'rē-,tred\ n **1** : a retreaded tire **2** : one pressed into service again; also : REMAKE

¹**re·treat** \ri-'trēt\ n **1** : an act of withdrawing esp. from something dangerous, difficult, or disagreeable **2** : a military signal for withdrawal; also : a military flag-lowering ceremony **3** : a place of privacy or safety : REFUGE **4** : a group withdrawal for prayer, meditation, or study

²**retreat** vb **1** : to make a retreat : WITHDRAW **2** : to slope backward

re·trench \ri-'trench\ vb [obs. F retrencher (now retrancher), fr. MF retrenchier, fr. re- + trenchier to cut] **1** : to cut down or pare away : REDUCE, CURTAIL **2** : to cut down expenses : ECONOMIZE — **re·trench·ment** n

ret·ri·bu·tion \,re-trə-'byü-shən\ n : something administered or exacted in recompense; esp : PUNISHMENT ◆ **Synonyms** REPRISAL, VENGEANCE, REVENGE, RETALIATION — **re·trib·u·tive** \ri-'tri-byə-tiv\ adj — **re·trib·u·to·ry** \-byə-,tȯr-ē\ adj

re·trieve \ri-'trēv\ vb **re·trieved; re·triev·ing 1** : to search about for and bring in (killed or wounded game) **2** : RECOVER, RESTORE — **re·triev·able** adj — **re·triev·al** \-'trē-vəl\ n

re·triev·er \ri-'trē-vər\ n : one that retrieves; esp : a dog of any of several breeds used esp. for retrieving game

---

retaste   retest   retransmission   retrial
retell   retrain   retransmit

ret·ro \'re-trō\ *adj* : relating to or being the styles and fashions of the past ⟨∼ clothing⟩

ret·ro·ac·tive \ˌre-trō-'ak-tiv\ *adj* : made effective as of a date prior to enactment ⟨a ∼ pay raise⟩ — **ret·ro·ac·tive·ly** *adv*

ret·ro·fit \'re-tro-ˌfit, ˌre-trō-'fit\ *vb* **1** : to furnish (as an aircraft) with newly available equipment **2** : to adapt to a new purpose or need : MODIFY — **ret·ro·fit** \'re-trō-ˌfit\ *n*

¹ret·ro·grade \'re-trə-ˌgrād\ *adj* **1** : moving or tending backward **2** : tending toward or resulting in a worse condition

²retrograde *vb* **1** : RETREAT **2** : DETERIORATE, DEGENERATE

ret·ro·gres·sion \ˌre-trə-'gre-shən\ *n* : return to a former and less complex level of development or organization — **ret·ro·gress** \ˌre-trə-'gres\ *vb* — **ret·ro·gres·sive** \ˌre-trə-'gre-siv\ *adj*

ret·ro–rock·et \'re-trō-ˌrä-kət\ *n* : an auxiliary rocket engine (as on a spacecraft) used to slow forward motion

ret·ro·spect \'re-tra-ˌspekt\ *n* : a review of past events — **ret·ro·spec·tion** \ˌre-trə-'spek-shən\ *n*

ret·ro·spec·tive \ˌre-trə-'spek-tiv\ *n* **1** : a comprehensive examination of an artist's work over many years **2** : REVIEW **4** ⟨a war ∼⟩ — **retrospective** *adj* — **ret·ro·spec·tive·ly** *adv*

ret·ro·vi·rus \'re-trō-ˌvī-rəs\ *n* : any of a group of RNA-containing viruses (as HIV) that make DNA using RNA instead of the reverse — **re·tro·vi·ral** \-rəl\ *adj*

¹re·turn \ri-'tərn\ *vb* **1** : to go or come back **2** : to pass, give, or send back to an earlier possessor **3** : to put back to or in a former place or state **4** : REPLY, ANSWER **5** : to report esp. officially **6** : to elect to office **7** : to bring in (as profit) : YIELD **8** : to give or perform in return ⟨∼ a favor⟩ — **re·turn·er** *n*

²return *n* **1** : an act of coming or going back to or from a former place or state **2** : RECURRENCE **3** : a report of the results of balloting **4** : a formal statement of taxable income **5** : the profit from labor, investment, or business : YIELD **6** : the act of returning something **7** : something that returns or is returned; *also* : a means for conveying something (as water) back to its starting point **8** : something given in repayment or reciprocation; *also* : ANSWER, RETORT **9** : an answering play — **return** *adj*

¹re·turn·able \ri-'tər-nə-bəl\ *adj* : capable of being returned (as for reuse); *also* : permitted to be returned

²returnable *n* : a returnable beverage container

re·turn·ee \ri-ˌtər-'nē\ *n* : one who returns

re·union \rē-'yün-yən\ *n* **1** : an act of reuniting : the state of being reunited **2** : a meeting of persons after separation

¹rev \'rev\ *n* : a revolution of a motor

²rev *vb* **revved; rev·ving** **1** : to increase the revolutions per minute of (a motor) **2** : STIMULATE, EXCITE

³rev *abbr* **1** revenue **2** reverse **3** review; reviewed **4** revised; revision **5** revolution

Rev *abbr* **1** Revelation **2** Reverend

re·vamp \(ˌ)rē-'vamp\ *vb* : RECONSTRUCT, REVISE; *also* : RENOVATE

re·vanche \rə-'väⁿsh\ *n* [F] : REVENGE; *esp* : a usu. political policy designed to recover lost territory or status

re·veal \ri-'vēl\ *vb* **1** : to make known **2** : to show plainly : open up to view

rev·eil·le \'re-və-lē\ *n* [modif. of F *réveillez*, imper. pl. of *réveiller* to awaken, fr. MF *eveiller* to awaken, fr. VL *exvigilare*, fr. L *vigilare* to keep watch, stay awake] : a military signal sounded at about sunrise

¹rev·el \'re-vəl\ *vb* **-eled** *or* **-elled; -el·ing** *or* **-el·ling** **1** : to take part in a revel **2** : to take great pleasure or satisfaction ⟨∼ed in the quiet⟩ — **rev·el·er** *or* **rev·el·ler** *n* — **rev·el·ry** \-vəl-rē\ *n*

²revel *n* : a usu. wild party or celebration

rev·e·la·tion \ˌre-və-'lā-shən\ *n* **1** : an act of revealing **2** : something revealed; *esp* : an enlightening or astonishing disclosure

Revelation *n* — see BIBLE table

¹re·venge \ri-'venj\ *vb* **re·venged; re·veng·ing** : to inflict harm or injury in return for (a wrong) : AVENGE — **re·veng·er** *n*

²revenge *n* **1** : a desire for revenge **2** : an act or instance of retaliation to get even **3** : an opportunity for getting satisfaction ✦ *Synonyms* VENGEANCE, RETRIBUTION, REPRISAL — **re·venge·ful** *adj*

rev·e·nue \'re-və-ˌnü, -ˌnyü\ *n* [ME, return, revenue, fr. AF, fr. *revenir* to return, fr. L *revenire*, fr. *re-* back + *venire* to come] **1** : investment income **2** : money collected by a government (as through taxes)

rev·e·nu·er \'re-və-ˌnü-ər, -ˌnyü-\ *n* : a revenue officer or boat

re·verb \ri-'vərb, 'rē-ˌvərb\ *n* : an electronically produced echo effect in recorded music; *also* : a device for producing reverb

re·ver·ber·ate \ri-'vər-bə-ˌrāt\ *vb* **-at·ed; -at·ing** **1** : REFLECT ⟨∼ light or heat⟩ **2** : to resound in or as if in a series of echoes — **re·ver·ber·a·tion** \-ˌvər-bə-'rā-shən\ *n*

re·vere \ri-'vir\ *vb* **re·vered; re·ver·ing** : to show honor and devotion to : VENERATE ⟨a teacher *revered* by students⟩ ✦ *Synonyms* REVERENCE, WORSHIP, ADORE

¹rev·er·ence \'re-vrəns, -və-rəns\ *n* **1** : honor or respect felt or shown **2** : a gesture (as a bow or curtsy) of respect

²reverence *vb* **-enced; -enc·ing** : to regard or treat with reverence

reunification	reusable	revaluation
reunify	reuse	revalue
reunite	revaluate	revisit

¹**rev·er·end** \ˈre-vrənd, -və-rənd\ *adj* **1** : worthy of reverence : REVERED **2** : being a member of the clergy — used as a title

²**reverend** *n* : a member of the clergy

rev·er·ent \ˈre-vrənt, -və-rənt\ *adj* : expressing reverence — **rev·er·ent·ly** *adv*

rev·er·en·tial \ˌre-və-ˈren-chəl\ *adj* : REVERENT

rev·er·ie *also* **rev·ery** \ˈre-və-rē\ *n, pl* **-er·ies** [F *rêverie*, fr. MF, delirium, fr. *resver, rever* to wander, be delirious] **1** : DAYDREAM **2** : the state of being lost in thought

re·ver·sal \ri-ˈvər-səl\ *n* : an act or process of reversing

¹**re·verse** \ri-ˈvərs\ *adj* **1** : opposite to a previous or normal condition ⟨in ∼ order⟩ **2** : acting or working in a manner opposite the usual **3** : bringing about reverse movement ⟨∼ gear⟩ — **re·verse·ly** *adv*

²**reverse** *vb* **re·versed; re·vers·ing 1** : to turn upside down or completely about in position or direction **2** : to set aside or change (as a legal decision) **3** : to change to the contrary ⟨∼ a policy⟩ **4** : to go or cause to go in the opposite direction **5** : to put (as a car) in reverse — **re·vers·ible** \-ˈvər-sə-bəl\ *adj*

³**reverse** *n* **1** : something contrary to something else : OPPOSITE **2** : an act or instance of reversing; *esp* : a change for the worse **3** : the back side of something (as a coin or card) **4** : a gear that reverses something

reverse engineer *vb* : to disassemble or analyze in detail in order to discover concepts involved in manufacture — **reverse engineering** *n*

re·ver·sion \ri-ˈvər-zhən\ *n* **1** : the right of succession or future possession (as to a title or property) **2** : return toward some former or ancestral condition; *also* : a product of this — **re·ver·sion·ary** \-zhə-ˌner-ē\ *adj*

re·vert \ri-ˈvərt\ *vb* **1** : to come or go back ⟨∼ed to savagery⟩ **2** : to return to a proprietor or his or her heirs **3** : to return to an ancestral type

¹**re·view** \ri-ˈvyü\ *n* **1** : an act of revising **2** : a formal military inspection **3** : a general survey **4** : INSPECTION, EXAMINATION; *esp* : REEXAMINATION **5** : a critical evaluation (as of a book) **6** : a magazine devoted to reviews and essays **7** : a renewed study of previously studied material **8** : REVUE

²**re·view** \ri-ˈvyü, *1 also* ˈrē-\ *vb* **1** : to examine or study again; *esp* : to reexamine judicially **2** : to hold a review of ⟨∼ troops⟩ **3** : to write a critical examination of ⟨∼ a novel⟩ **4** : to look back over ⟨∼ed her accomplishments⟩ **5** : to study material again

re·view·er \ri-ˈvyü-ər\ *n* : one that reviews; *esp* : a writer of critical reviews

re·vile \ri-ˈvī(-ə)l\ *vb* **re·viled; re·vil·ing** : to abuse verbally : rail at ♦ **Synonyms** VITUPERATE, BERATE, RATE, UPBRAID, SCOLD — **re·vile·ment** *n* — **re·vil·er** *n*

re·vise \ri-ˈvīz\ *vb* **re·vised; re·vis·ing 1** : to look over something written in order to correct or improve ⟨∼ an essay⟩ **2** : to make a new version of ⟨∼ an almanac⟩ — **re·vis·able** *adj* — **re·vise** *n* — **re·vis·er** *or* **re·vi·sor** \-ˈvī-zər\ *n* — **re·vi·sion** \-ˈvi-zhən\ *n*

re·vi·tal·ise *Brit var of* REVITALIZE

re·vi·tal·ize \ˌrē-ˈvīt-tə-ˌlīz\ *vb* **-ized; -izing** : to give new life or vigor to ⟨∼ the shopping district⟩ — **re·vi·tal·i·za·tion** \ˌ(ˌ)rē-ˌvīt-tə-lə-ˈzā-shən\ *n*

re·viv·al \ri-ˈvī-vəl\ *n* **1** : an act of reviving : the state of being revived **2** : a new publication or presentation (as of a book or play) **3** : an evangelistic meeting or series of meetings

re·vive \ri-ˈvīv\ *vb* **re·vived; re·viv·ing 1** : to bring back to life, consciousness, or activity : make or become fresh or strong again **2** : to bring back into use — **re·viv·er** *n*

re·viv·i·fy \rē-ˈvi-və-ˌfī\ *vb* : REVIVE — **re·viv·i·fi·ca·tion** \-ˌvi-və-fə-ˈkā-shən\ *n*

re·vo·ca·ble \ˈre-və-kə-bəl *also* ri-ˈvō-kə-bəl\ *adj* : capable of being revoked

re·vo·ca·tion \ˌre-və-ˈkā-shən\ *n* : an act or instance of revoking

re·voke \ri-ˈvōk\ *vb* **re·voked; re·vok·ing 1** : to annul by recalling or taking back : REPEAL, RESCIND ⟨∼ a license⟩ **2** : RENEGE **2** — **re·vok·er** *n*

¹**re·volt** \ri-ˈvōlt\ *vb* [MF *revolter*, fr. It *rivoltare* to overthrow, fr. VL **revolvitare*, fr. L *revolvere* to revolve, roll back] **1** : to throw off allegiance to a ruler or government : REBEL **2** : to experience disgust or shock **3** : to turn or cause to turn away with disgust or abhorrence — **re·volt·er** *n*

²**revolt** *n* : REBELLION, INSURRECTION

re·volt·ing *adj* : extremely offensive ⟨a ∼ odor⟩ — **re·volt·ing·ly** *adv*

rev·o·lu·tion \ˌre-və-ˈlü-shən\ *n* **1** : the action by a heavenly body of going round in an orbit **2** : ROTATION **3** : a sudden, radical, or complete change; *esp* : the overthrow or renunciation of one ruler or government and substitution of another by the governed

¹**rev·o·lu·tion·ary** \-shə-ˌner-ē\ *adj* **1** : of or relating to revolution **2** : tending to or promoting revolution **3** : constituting or bringing about a major change

²**revolutionary** *n, pl* **-ar·ies** : one who takes part in a revolution or who advocates revolutionary doctrines

rev·o·lu·tion·ise *Brit var of* REVOLUTIONIZE

rev·o·lu·tion·ist \ˌre-və-ˈlü-shə-nist\ *n* : REVOLUTIONARY — **revolutionist** *adj*

rev·o·lu·tion·ize \-ˌnīz\ *vb* **-ized; -iz·ing** : to change fundamentally or completely ⟨∼ an industry⟩ — **rev·o·lu·tion·iz·er** *n*

re·volve \ri-ˈvälv\ *vb* **re·volved; re·volv·ing 1** : to turn over in the mind : reflect upon : PONDER **2** : to move in an orbit; *also* : ROTATE **3** : to have a specified focus ⟨the debate *revolved* around taxes⟩ — **re·volv·able** *adj*

re·volv·er \ri-'väl-vər\ *n* : a pistol with a revolving cylinder of several chambers

re·vue \ri-'vyü\ *n* : a theatrical production consisting typically of brief often satirical sketches and songs

re·vul·sion \ri-'vəl-shən\ *n* **1** : a strong sudden reaction or change of feeling **2** : a feeling of complete distaste or repugnance

revved *past and past part of* REV

revving *pres part of* REV

¹re·ward \ri-'word\ *vb* **1** : to give a reward to or for **2** : RECOMPENSE

²reward *n* **1** : something given in return for good or evil done or received or for some service or attainment **2** : a stimulus that is administered to an organism after a response and that increases the probability of occurrence of the response
◆ *Synonyms* PREMIUM, PRIZE, AWARD

¹re·wind \(,)rē-'wīnd\ *vb* **-wound; -winding 1** : to wind again **2** : to reverse the winding of (as film)

²re·wind \'rē-,wīnd\ *n* **1** : something that rewinds **2** : an act of rewinding **3** : a function of an electronic device that reverses a recording to a previous portion

re·work \(,)rē-'wərk\ *vb* **1** : REVISE **2** : to reprocess for further use

¹re·write \(,)rē-'rīt\ *vb* **-wrote; -writ·ten; -writ·ing** : to make a revision of : REVISE

²re·write \'rē-,rīt\ *n* : an instance or a piece of rewriting

RF *abbr* radio frequency

RFD *abbr* rural free delivery

Rh *symbol* rhodium

RH *abbr* right hand

rhap·so·dy \'rap-sə-dē\ *n, pl* **-dies** [L *rhapsodia* portion of an epic poem adapted for recitation, fr. Gk *rhapsōidia* recitation of selections from epic poetry, ultim. fr. *rhaptein* to sew, stitch together + *aidein* to sing] **1** : an expression of extravagant praise or ecstasy **2** : a musical composition of irregular form — **rhap·sod·ic** \rap-'sä-dik\ *adj* — **rhap·sod·i·cal·ly** \-di-k(ə-)lē\ *adv* — **rhap·so·dize** \'rap-sə-,dīz\ *vb*

rhea \'rē-ə\ *n* : either of two large flightless 3-toed So. American birds that resemble but are smaller than the African ostrich

rhe·ni·um \'rē-nē-əm\ *n* : a rare heavy metallic chemical element

rheo·stat \'rē-ə-,stat\ *n* : a resistor for regulating an electric current by means of variable resistances — **rheo·stat·ic** \,rē-ə-'sta-tik\ *adj*

rhe·sus monkey \'rē-səs-\ *n* : a pale brown Asian monkey often used in medical research

rhet·o·ric \'re-tə-rik\ *n* [ME *rethorik*, fr. AF *rethorique*, fr. L *rhetorica*, fr. Gk *rhētorikē*, lit., art of oratory, fr. *rhētōr* public speaker, fr. *eirein* to speak] : the art of speaking or writing effectively — **rhet·o·ri·cian** \,re-tə-'ri-shən\ *n*

rhe·tor·i·cal \ri-'tȯr-i-kəl\ *adj* **1** : of or relating to rhetoric **2** : asked merely for

effect with no answer expected ⟨a ~ question⟩

rheum \'rüm\ *n* : a watery discharge from the mucous membranes esp. of the eyes or nose — **rheumy** *adj*

rheu·mat·ic fever \rü-'ma-tik-\ *n* : an acute disease chiefly of children and young adults that is characterized by fever, by inflammation and pain in and around the joints, and by inflammation of the membranes surrounding the heart and the heart valves

rheu·ma·tism \'rü-mə-,ti-zəm, 'rù-\ *n* **1** : any of various conditions marked by stiffness, pain, or swelling in muscles or joints **2** : RHEUMATOID ARTHRITIS — **rheu·mat·ic** \rù-'ma-tik\ *adj*

rheu·ma·toid arthritis \,tȯid-\ *n* : a usu. chronic progressive autoimmune disease characterized by inflammation and swelling of joint structures

rheu·ma·tol·o·gy \,rü-mə-'tä-lə-jē, ,rù-\ *n* : a medical science dealing with rheumatic diseases — **rheu·ma·tol·o·gist** \-jist\ *n*

Rh factor \,är-'āch-\ *n* [*rh*esus monkey (in which it was first detected)] : any of one or more inherited substances in red blood cells that may cause dangerous reactions in some infants or in transfusions

rhine·stone \'rīn-,stōn\ *n* : a colorless imitation stone of high luster made of glass, paste, or gem quartz

rhi·no \'rī-nō\ *n, pl* **rhinos** *also* **rhino** : RHINOCEROS

rhi·noc·er·os \rī-'nä-sə-rəs\ *n, pl* **-noc·er·os·es** *also* **-noc·er·os** *or* **-noc·eri** \-'nä-sə-,rī\ [ME *rinoceros*, fr. AF, fr. L *rhinoceros*, fr. Gk *rhinokerōs*, fr. *rhin-, rhis* nose + *keras* horn] : any of a family of large thick-skinned mammals of Africa and Asia with one or two upright horns of keratin on the snout and three toes on each foot

rhi·zome \'rī-,zōm\ *n* : a fleshy, rootlike, and usu. horizontal underground plant stem that forms shoots above and roots below — **rhi·zom·a·tous** \rī-'zä-mə-təs\ *adj*

Rh–neg·a·tive \,är-,āch-'ne-gə-tiv\ *adj* : lacking Rh factors in the red blood cells

rho \'rō\ *n* : the 17th letter of the Greek alphabet — P or ρ

rho·di·um \'rō-dē-əm\ *n* : a rare hard ductile metallic chemical element

rho·do·den·dron \,rō-də-'den-drən\ *n* : any of a genus of shrubs or trees of the heath family with clusters of large bright flowers

rhom·boid \'räm-,bȯid\ *n* : a parallelogram with unequal adjacent sides and angles that are not right angles — **rhomboid** *or* **rhom·boi·dal** \räm-'bȯi-dᵊl\ *adj*

rhom·bus \'räm-bəs\ *n, pl* **rhom·bus·es** *or* **rhom·bi** \-,bī\ : a parallelogram having all four sides equal

Rh–pos·i·tive \,är-,āch-'pä-zə-tiv\ *adj* : containing one or more Rh factors in the red blood cells

---

rewarm	reweave	reweigh	rezone
rewash	rewed	rewire	

rhu·barb \'rü-ˌbärb\ *n* [ME *rubarbe,* fr. AF *reubarbe,* fr. ML *reubarbarum,* alter. of *rha barbarum,* lit., barbarian rhubarb] : a garden plant related to the buckwheat having leaves with thick juicy edible pink and red stems

¹**rhyme** *also* **rime** \'rīm\ *n* **1** : a composition in verse that rhymes; *also* : POETRY **2** : correspondence in terminal sounds (as of two lines of verse)

²**rhyme** *also* **rime** *vb* **rhymed** *also* **rimed; rhym·ing** *also* **rim·ing 1** : to make rhymes; *also* : to write poetry **2** : to have rhymes : be in rhyme

rhythm \'ri-thəm\ *n* **1** : regular rise and fall in the flow of sound in speech **2** : a movement or activity in which some action or element recurs regularly — **rhyth·mic** \'rith-mik\ *or* **rhyth·mi·cal** \-mi-kəl\ *adj* — **rhyth·mi·cal·ly** \-k(ə-)lē\ *adv*

rhythm and blues *n* : popular music based on blues and black folk music

rhythm method *n* : birth control by refraining from sexual intercourse during the time when ovulation is most likely to occur

RI *abbr* Rhode Island

ri·al \rē-'ȯl, -'äl\ *n* — see MONEY table

¹**rib** \'rib\ *n* **1** : any of the series of curved bones of the chest of most vertebrates that are joined to the backbone in pairs and help to support the body wall and protect the organs inside **2** : something resembling a rib in shape or function **3** : an elongated ridge (as in fabric)

²**rib** *vb* **ribbed; rib·bing 1** : to furnish or strengthen with ribs **2** : to knit so as to form ridges

³**rib** *vb* **ribbed; rib·bing** : to poke fun at : TEASE — **rib·ber** *n*

rib·ald \'ri-bəld\ *adj* : coarse or indecent esp. in language ⟨~ jokes⟩ — **rib·ald·ry** \-bəl-drē\ *n*

rib·and \'ri-bənd\ *n* : RIBBON

rib·bon \'ri-bən\ *n* **1** : a narrow fabric typically of silk or velvet used for trimming and for badges **2** : a strip of inked cloth (as in a typewriter) **3** : TATTER, SHRED ⟨torn to ~s⟩

ri·bo·fla·vin \ˌrī-bə-'flā-vən, 'rī-bə-ˌflā-vən\ *n* : a growth-promoting vitamin of the vitamin B complex occurring esp. in milk and liver

ri·bo·nu·cle·ic acid \ˌrī-bō-nü-ˌklē-ik-, -nyü-, -ˌklā-\ *n* : RNA

ri·bose \'rī-ˌbōs\ *n* : a sugar with five carbon atoms and five oxygen atoms in each molecule that is part of RNA

ri·bo·some \'rī-bə-ˌsōm\ *n* : any of the RNA-rich cytoplasmic granules in a cell that are sites of protein synthesis — **ri·bo·som·al** \ˌrī-bə-'sō-məl\ *adj*

rice \'rīs\ *n* : the starchy seeds of an annual grass that are cooked and used for food; *also* : this widely cultivated grass of warm wet areas

rich \'rich\ *adj* **1** : possessing or controlling great wealth : WEALTHY **2** : COSTLY, VALUABLE **3** : deep and pleasing in color or tone **4** : ABUNDANT **5** : containing much sugar, fat, or seasoning; *also* : high in combustible content **6** : FRUITFUL, FERTILE — **rich·ly** *adv* — **rich·ness** *n*

rich·es \'ri-chəz\ *n pl* [ME, sing. or pl., fr. *richesse* wealth, fr. AF *richesce,* fr. *riche* rich] : things that make one rich : WEALTH

Rich·ter scale \'rik-tər-\ *n* : a scale for expressing the magnitude of a seismic disturbance (as an earthquake) in terms of the energy dissipated in it

rick \'rik\ *n* : a large stack (as of hay) in the open air

rick·ets \'ri-kəts\ *n* : a childhood deficiency disease marked esp. by soft deformed bones and caused by lack of vitamin D

rick·ett·sia \ri-'ket-sē-ə\ *n, pl* **-si·as** *or* **-si·ae** \-sē-ˌē\ : any of a group of usu. rod-shaped bacteria that cause various diseases (as typhus)

rick·ety \'ri-kə-tē\ *adj* **1** : affected with rickets **2** : SHAKY; *also* : in unsound physical condition ⟨~ stairs⟩

rick·shaw *also* **rick·sha** \'rik-ˌshȯ\ *n* : a small covered 2-wheeled carriage pulled by one person and used orig. in Japan

¹**ric·o·chet** \'ri-kə-ˌshā, *Brit also* -ˌshet\ *n* [F] : a bouncing off at an angle (as of a bullet off a wall); *also* : an object that ricochets

²**ricochet** *vb* **-cheted** \-ˌshād\ *also* **-chetted** \-ˌshe-təd\; **-chet·ing** \-ˌshā-iŋ\ *or* **-chet·ting** \-ˌshe-tiŋ\ : to bounce or skip with or as if with a glancing rebound

ri·cot·ta \ri-'kä-tə, -'kȯ-\ *n* : a white unripened whey cheese of Italy that resembles cottage cheese

rid \'rid\ *vb* **rid** *also* **rid·ded; rid·ding** : to make free : CLEAR, RELIEVE — **rid·dance** \'ri-dᵊns\ *n*

rid·den \'ri-dᵊn\ *adj* : harassed, oppressed, or obsessed by ⟨debt-*ridden*⟩ **2** : excessively full of or supplied with ⟨slum-*ridden*⟩

¹**rid·dle** \'ri-dᵊl\ *n* : a puzzling question to be solved or answered by guessing

²**riddle** *vb* **rid·dled; rid·dling 1** : EXPLAIN, SOLVE **2** : to speak in riddles

³**riddle** *n* : a coarse sieve

⁴**riddle** *vb* **rid·dled; rid·dling 1** : to sift with a riddle **2** : to pierce with many holes **3** : PERMEATE

¹**ride** \'rīd\ *vb* **rode** \'rōd\; **rid·den** \'ri-dᵊn\; **rid·ing 1** : to go on an animal's back or in a conveyance (as a boat, car, or airplane); *also* : to sit on and control so as to be carried along ⟨~ a bicycle⟩ **2** : to float or move on water ⟨~ at anchor⟩; *also* : to move like a floating object **3** : to bear along : CARRY ⟨rode her on their shoulders⟩ **4** : to travel over a surface ⟨the car ~s well⟩ **5** : to proceed over on horseback **6** : to torment by nagging or teasing

²**ride** *n* **1** : an act of riding; *esp* : a trip on horseback or by vehicle **2** : a way (as a road or path) suitable for riding **3** : a mechanical device (as a merry-go-round) for riding on **4** : a means of transportation

rid·er \'rī-dər\ *n* **1** : one that rides **2** : an addition to a document often attached on a separate piece of paper **3** : a clause dealing with an unrelated matter attached to a legislative bill during passage — **rid-er-less** *adj*

¹ridge \'rij\ *n* [ME *rigge*, fr. OE *hrycg*] **1** : an elevated body part or structure **2** : a range of hills **3** : a raised line or strip **4** : the line made where two sloping surfaces (as of a roof) meet — **ridgy** *adj*

²ridge *vb* **ridged; ridg-ing 1** : to form into a ridge **2** : to extend in ridges

¹rid-i-cule \'ri-də-ˌkyül\ *n* : the act of ridiculing : DERISION, MOCKERY

²ridicule *vb* **-culed; -cul-ing** : to laugh at or make fun of mockingly or contemptuously ⟨was *ridiculed* by his peers⟩ ♦ *Synonyms* DERIDE, TAUNT, TWIT, MOCK

ri-dic-u-lous \rə-'di-kyə-ləs\ *adj* : arousing or deserving ridicule : ABSURD, PREPOSTEROUS ♦ *Synonyms* LAUGHABLE, LUDICROUS, FARCICAL, RISIBLE — **ri-dic-u-lous-ly** *adv* — **ri-dic-u-lous-ness** *n*

rid-ley \'rid-lē\ *n* : either of two relatively small sea turtles

ri-el \rē-'el\ *n* — see MONEY table

Ries-ling \'rēz-liŋ, 'rēs-\ *n* : a sweet to very dry white wine made from a single variety of grape orig. grown in Germany

RIF *abbr* reduction in force

rife \'rīf\ *adj* : WIDESPREAD, PREVALENT, ABOUNDING — **rife** *adv* — **rife-ly** *adv*

¹riff \'rif\ *n* **1** : a repeated phrase in jazz typically supporting a solo improvisation; *also* : a piece based on such a phrase **2** : a usu. witty or improvised remark or outpouring **3** : a distinct variation : TAKE — **riff** *vb*

riff-raff \'rif-ˌraf\ *n* [ME *riffe raffe*, fr. *rif and raf* every single one, fr. AF *rif et raf* altogether] **1** : RABBLE **2** : REFUSE, RUBBISH

¹ri-fle \'rī-fəl\ *vb* **ri-fled; ri-fling** : to ransack esp. with the intent to steal — **ri-fler** *n*

²rifle *vb* **ri-fled; ri-fling** : to cut spiral grooves into the bore of ⟨*rifled* pipe⟩ — **rifling** *n*

³rifle *n* **1** : a shoulder weapon with a rifled bore **2** *pl* : soldiers armed with rifles — **ri-fle-man** \-fəl-mən\ *n*

rift \'rift\ *n* **1** : CLEFT, FISSURE **2** : FAULT 6 **3** : ESTRANGEMENT, SEPARATION ⟨a ~ between spouses⟩ — **rift** *vb*

¹rig \'rig\ *vb* **rigged; rig-ging 1** : to fit out (as a ship) with rigging **2** : CLOTHE, DRESS **3** : EQUIP **4** : to set up esp. as a makeshift ⟨~ up a shelter⟩

²rig *n* **1** : the distinctive shape, number, and arrangement of sails and masts of a ship **2** : a carriage with its horse **3** : CLOTHING, DRESS **4** : EQUIPMENT

³rig *vb* **rigged; rig-ging 1** : to manipulate or control esp. by deceptive or dishonest means **2** : to fix in advance for a desired result — **rig-ger** *n*

rig-ging \'ri-giŋ, -gən\ *n* **1** : the ropes and chains that hold and move masts, sails, and spars of a ship **2** : a network (as in theater scenery) used for support and manipulation

¹right \'rīt\ *adj* **1** : RIGHTEOUS, UPRIGHT

2 : JUST, PROPER **3** : conforming to truth or fact : CORRECT **4** : APPROPRIATE, SUITABLE **5** : STRAIGHT ⟨a ~ line⟩ **6** : GENUINE, REAL **7** : of, relating to, or being the side of the body which is away from the side on which the heart is mostly located **8** : located nearer to the right hand; *esp* : being on the right when facing in the same direction as the observer **9** : made to be placed or worn outward ⟨~ side of a rug⟩ **10** : NORMAL, SOUND ⟨not in her ~ mind⟩ ♦ *Synonyms* CORRECT, ACCURATE, EXACT, PRECISE, NICE — **right-ness** *n*

²right *n* **1** : qualities that constitute what is correct, just, proper, or honorable **2** : something (as a power or privilege) to which one has a just or lawful claim **3** : just action or decision : the cause of justice **4** : the side or part that is on or toward the right side **5** *cap* : political conservatives **6** *often cap* : a conservative position — **right-ward** \-wərd\ *adj or adv*

³right *adv* **1** : according to what is right ⟨live ~⟩ **2** : EXACTLY, PRECISELY ⟨~ here and now⟩ **3** : DIRECTLY ⟨went ~ home⟩ **4** : according to fact or truth ⟨guess ~⟩ **5** : all the way : COMPLETELY ⟨~ to the end⟩ **6** : IMMEDIATELY ⟨~ after lunch⟩ **7** : QUITE, VERY ⟨~ nice weather⟩ **8** : on or to the right ⟨looked ~ and left⟩

⁴right *vb* **1** : to relieve from wrong **2** : to adjust or restore to a proper state or position **3** : to bring or restore to an upright position **4** : to become upright — **right-er** *n*

right angle *n* : an angle whose measure is 90° : an angle whose sides are perpendicular to each other — **right-an-gled** \'rīt-ˌaŋ-gəld\ *or* **right-an-gle** \-gəl\ *adj*

right circular cone *n* : CONE 2

righ-teous \'rī-chəs\ *adj* : acting or being in accordance with what is just, honorable, and free from guilt or wrong : UPRIGHT ♦ *Synonyms* VIRTUOUS, NOBLE, MORAL, ETHICAL — **righ-teous-ly** *adv* — **righ-teous-ness** *n*

right-ful \'rīt-fəl\ *adj* **1** : JUST; *also* : FITTING **2** : having or held by a legally just claim — **right-ful-ly** *adv* — **right-ful-ness** *n*

right–hand \'rīt-ˌhand\ *adj* **1** : situated on the right **2** : RIGHT-HANDED **3** : chiefly relied on ⟨his ~ man⟩

right–hand-ed \-'han-dəd\ *adj* **1** : using the right hand habitually or better than the left **2** : designed for or done with the right hand **3** : CLOCKWISE ⟨a ~ twist⟩ — **right–handed** *adv* — **right–hand-ed-ly** *adv* — **right–hand-ed-ness** *n*

right-ly \'rīt-lē\ *adv* **1** : FAIRLY, JUSTLY **2** : PROPERLY **3** : CORRECTLY, EXACTLY

right–of–way *n, pl* **rights–of–way 1** : a legal right of passage over another person's ground **2** : the area over which a right-of-way exists **3** : the land on which a public road is built **4** : the land occupied by a railroad **5** : the land used by a public utility **6** : the right of traffic to take precedence over other traffic

right on *interj* — used to express agreement or give encouragement

right–to–life *adj* : ANTIABORTION — **right–to–lifer** *n*

right triangle *n* : a triangle having one right angle

right whale *n* : any of a family of large baleen whales having a very large head on a stocky body

rig·id \'ri-jəd\ *adj* **1** : lacking flexibility **2** : strictly observed **♦ Synonyms** SEVERE, STERN, RIGOROUS, STRINGENT — **ri·gid·i·ty** \rə-'ji-də-tē\ *n* — **rig·id·ly** *adv*

rig·ma·role \'ri-gə-mə-ˌrōl\ *n* [alter. of obs. *ragman roll* long list, catalog] **1** : confused or senseless talk **2** : a complex and ritualistic procedure

rig·or \'ri-gər\ *n* **1** : the quality of being inflexible or unyielding : STRICTNESS **2** : HARSHNESS, SEVERITY **3** : a tremor caused by a chill **4** : strict precision : EXACTNESS — **rig·or·ous** *adj* — **rig·or·ous·ly** *adv*

rig·or mor·tis \ˌri-gər-'mȯr-təs\ *n* [NL, stiffness of death] : temporary rigidity of muscles occurring after death

rig·our *chiefly Brit var of* RIGOR

rile \'rī(-ə)l\ *vb* **riled; ril·ing 1** : to make angry **2** : ROIL 1

rill \'ril\ *n* : a very small brook

¹rim \'rim\ *n* **1** : the outer part of a wheel **2** : an outer edge esp. of something curved : BORDER, MARGIN

²rim *vb* **rimmed; rim·ming 1** : to serve as a rim for : BORDER **2** : to run around the rim of

¹rime \'rīm\ *n* : FROST 2 — **rimy** \'rī-mē\ *adj*

²rime *var of* RHYME

rind \'rīnd\ *n* : a usu. hard or tough outer layer 〈lemon ~〉

¹ring \'riŋ\ *n* **1** : a circular band worn as an ornament or token or used for holding or fastening 〈wedding ~〉 〈key ~〉 **2** : something circular in shape 〈smoke ~〉 **3** : a place for contest or display 〈boxing ~〉; *also* : PRIZEFIGHTING **4** : ANNUAL RING **5** : a group of people who work together for selfish or dishonest purposes — **ringed** *adj* — **ring·like** \'riŋ-ˌlīk\ *adj*

²ring *vb* **ringed; ring·ing** \'riŋ-iŋ\ **1** : ENCIRCLE **2** : to throw a ring over (a mark) in a game (as quoits) **3** : to move in a ring or spirally

³ring *vb* **rang** \'raŋ\; **rung** \'rəŋ\; **ring·ing** \'riŋ-iŋ\ **1** : to sound resonantly when struck; *also* : to feel as if filled with such sound **2** : to cause to make a clear metallic sound by striking **3** : to announce or call by or as if by striking a bell 〈~ an alarm〉 **4** : to repeat loudly and persistently **5** : to summon esp. by a bell 〈~ for the butler〉 — **ring a bell** : to arouse a response 〈that name *rings a bell*〉

⁴ring *n* **1** : a set of bells **2** : the clear resonant sound of vibrating metal **3** : resonant tone : SONORITY **4** : a sound or character expressive of a particular quality **5** : an act or instance of ringing; *esp* : a telephone call

¹ring·er \'riŋ-ər\ *n* **1** : one that sounds by ringing **2** : one that enters a competition under false representations **3** : one that closely resembles another

²ringer *n* : one that encircles or puts a ring around

ring finger *n* : the third finger of the left hand counting the index finger as the first

ring·git \'riŋ-git\ *n* — see MONEY table

ring·lead·er \'riŋ-ˌlē-dər\ *n* : a leader esp. of a group of troublemakers

ring·let \-lət\ *n* : a long curl

ring·mas·ter \-ˌmas-tər\ *n* : one in charge of performances in a circus ring

ring up *vb* **1** : to total and record esp. by means of a cash register **2** : ACHIEVE 〈*rang up* many triumphs〉

ring·worm \'riŋ-ˌwərm\ *n* : any of several contagious skin diseases caused by fungi and marked by ring-shaped discolored patches

rink \'riŋk\ *n* : a level extent of ice marked off for skating or various games; *also* : a similar surface (as of wood) marked off or enclosed for a sport or game 〈roller-skating ~〉

¹rinse \'rins\ *vb* **rinsed; rins·ing** [ME *rincen*, AF *rincer*, alter. of OF *recincier*, fr. VL **recentiare*, fr. L *recent-, recens* fresh, recent] **1** : to wash lightly or in water only **2** : to cleanse (as of soap) with clear water **3** : to treat (hair) with a rinse — **rins·er** *n*

²rinse *n* **1** : an act of rinsing **2** : a liquid used for rinsing **3** : a solution that temporarily tints hair

ri·ot \'rī-ət\ *n,* **1** *archaic* : disorderly behavior **2** : disturbance of the public peace; *esp* : a violent public disorder **3** : random or disorderly profusion 〈a ~ of color〉 **4** : one that is wildly amusing 〈the comedy is a ~〉 — **riot** *vb* — **ri·ot·er** *n* — **ri·ot·ous** *adj*

¹rip \'rip\ *vb* **ripped; rip·ping 1** : to cut or tear open **2** : to saw or split (wood) with the grain **3** : CRITICIZE, DISPARAGE — **rip·per** *n*

²rip *n* : a rent made by ripping

RIP *abbr* [L *requiescat in pace*] may he rest in peace, may she rest in peace; [L *requiescant in pace*] may they rest in peace

ri·par·i·an \rə-'per-ē-ən\ *adj* : of or relating to the bank of a stream, river, or lake 〈~ trees〉

rip cord *n* : a cord that is pulled to release a parachute out of its container

ripe \'rīp\ *adj* **rip·er; rip·est 1** : fully grown and developed : MATURE 〈~ fruit〉 **2** : fully prepared : READY 〈slaves ~ for a revolt〉 — **ripe·ly** *adv* — **ripe·ness** *n*

rip·en \'rī-pən\ *vb* **rip·ened; rip·en·ing 1** : to grow or make ripe **2** : to bring to completeness or perfection; *also* : to age or cure (cheese) to develop characteristic flavor, odor, body, texture, and color

rip-off \'rip-ˌȯf\ *n* **1** : an act of stealing : THEFT **2** : a cheap imitation — **rip off** *vb*

ri·poste \ri-'pōst\ *n* [F, modif. of It *riposta*, lit., answer] **1** : a fencer's return thrust after a parry **2** : a retaliatory maneuver or response; *esp* : a quick retort — **riposte** *vb*

ripped \'ript\ *adj* : having high muscle definition

rip·ple \'ri-pəl\ *vb* **rip·pled; rip·pling 1** : to become lightly ruffled on the surface **2** : to make a sound like that of rippling water — **ripple** *n*

rip·saw \'rip-ˌsȯ\ *n* : a coarse-toothed saw used to cut wood in the direction of the grain

rip-stop \-ˌstäp\ *adj* : being a fabric woven in such a way that small tears do not spread ⟨~ nylon⟩ — **ripstop** *n*

¹rise \'rīz\ *vb* **rose** \'rōz\; **ris·en** \'riz-²n\; **ris·ing 1** : to get up from sitting, kneeling, or lying **2** : to get up from sleep or from one's bed **3** : to return from death **4** : to take up arms **5** : to end a session : ADJOURN **6** : to appear above the horizon **7** : to move upward : ASCEND **8** : to extend above other objects **9** : to attain a higher level or rank **10** : to increase in quantity, intensity, or pitch **11** : to come into being : HAPPEN, BEGIN, ORIGINATE

²rise *n* **1** : a spot higher than surrounding ground **2** : an upward slope **3** : an act of rising **4** : a state of being risen **4** : BEGINNING, ORIGIN **5** : the elevation of one point above another **6** : an increase in amount, number, or volume **7** : an angry reaction

ris·er \'rī-zər\ *n* **1** : one that rises **2** : the upright part between stair treads

ris·i·bil·i·ty \ˌri-zə-'bi-lə-tē\ *n, pl* **-ties** : the ability or inclination to laugh — often used in pl.

ris·i·ble \'ri-zə-bəl\ *adj* **1** : able or inclined to laugh **2** : arousing laughter; *esp* : amusingly ridiculous

¹risk \'risk\ *n* **1** : exposure to possible loss or injury : DANGER, PERIL **2** : the chance that an investment will lose value — **risk·i·ness** \'ris-kē-nəs\ *n* — **risky** *adj*

²risk *vb* **1** : to expose to danger ⟨~ed his life⟩ **2** : to incur the danger of

ri·sot·to \ri-'sȯ-tō, -'zȯ-\ *n, pl* **-tos** : rice cooked usu. in meat or seafood stock and seasoned

ris·qué \ris-'kā\ *adj* [F] : verging on impropriety or indecency ⟨~ jokes⟩

ri·tard \ri-'tärd\ *adv or adj* : with a gradual slackening in tempo — used as a direction in music

rite \'rīt\ *n* **1** : a set form for conducting a ceremony **2** : the liturgy of a church **3** : a ceremonial act or action

rit·u·al \'ri-chə-wəl\ *n* **1** : the established form esp. for a religious ceremony **2** : a system of rites **3** : a ceremonial act or action **4** : an act or series of acts regularly repeated in a precise manner — **rit·ual** *adj* — **rit·u·al·ism** \-wə-ˌli-zəm\ *n* — **rit·u·al·is·tic** \ˌri-chə-wə-'lis-tik\ *adj* — **rit·u·al·is·ti·cal·ly** \-ti-k(ə-)lē\ *adv* — **rit·u·al·ly** *adv*

ritzy \'rit-sē\ *adj* **ritz·i·er; -est** : showily elegant : POSH

riv *abbr* river

¹ri·val \'rī-vəl\ *n* [MF or L; MF, fr. L *rivalis* one using the same stream as another, rival in love, fr. *rivalis* of a stream, fr. *rivus* stream] **1** : one of two or more trying to get what only one can have **2** : one striving for competitive advantage **3** : one that equals another esp. in desired qualities : MATCH, PEER

²rival *adj* : COMPETING

rival *vb* **-valed** *or* **-valled; -val·ing** *or* **-val·ling 1** : to be in competition with **2** : to try to equal or excel **3** : to have qualities that approach or equal another's

ri·val·ry \'rī-vəl-rē\ *n, pl* **-ries** : COMPETITION

rive \'rīv\ *vb* **rived** \'rīvd\; **riv·en** \'ri-vən\ *also* **rived; riv·ing 1** : SPLIT, REND **2** : SHATTER ⟨nations *riven* by war⟩

riv·er \'ri-vər\ *n* **1** : a natural stream larger than a brook **2** : a large stream or flow

riv·er·bank \-ˌbaŋk\ *n* : the bank of a river

riv·er·bed \-ˌbed\ *n* : the channel occupied by a river

riv·er·boat \-ˌbōt\ *n* : a boat for use on a river

riv·er·front \-ˌfrənt\ *n* : the land or area along a river

riv·er·side \-ˌsīd\ *n* : the side or bank of a river

¹riv·et \'ri-vət\ *n* : a metal bolt with a head at one end used to join parts by being put through holes in them and then being flattened on the plain end to make another head

²rivet *vb* : to fasten with or as if with a rivet — **riv·et·er** *n*

riv·u·let \'ri-vyə-lət, -və-\ *n* : a small stream

ri·yal *also* **ri·al** \rē-'äl, -'al\ *n* — see MONEY table

rm *abbr* room

Rn *symbol* radon

¹RN \ˌär-'en\ *n* : REGISTERED NURSE

²RN *abbr* Royal Navy

RNA \ˌär-(ˌ)en-'ā\ *n* : any of various nucleic acids (as messenger RNA) that are found esp. in the cytoplasm of cells, have ribose as the 5-carbon sugar, and are associated with the control of cellular chemical activities

rnd *abbr* round

¹roach \'rōch\ *n, pl* **roach** *also* **roach·es** : any of various bony fishes related to the carp; *also* : any of several sunfishes

²roach *n* **1** : COCKROACH **2** : the butt of a marijuana cigarette

road \'rōd\ *n* [ME *rode*, fr. OE *rād* ride, journey] **1** : ROADSTEAD — often used in pl. **2** : an open way for vehicles, persons, and animals : HIGHWAY **3** : a way to a conclusion or end ⟨the ~ to success⟩ **4** : a series of scheduled visits (as games or performances) in several locations or the travel necessary to make these visits ⟨the team is on the ~⟩

road·bed \'rōd-ˌbed\ *n* **1** : the foundation of a road or railroad **2** : the part of the surface of a road on which vehicles travel

road·block \-ˌbläk\ *n* **1** : a barricade on

the road ⟨a police ∼⟩ **2** : an obstruction to progress

road·ie \'rō-dē\ *n* : a person who works for traveling entertainers

road·kill \'rōd-ˌkil\ *n* **1** : the remains of an animal that has been killed on a road by a motor vehicle **2** : one that falls victim to intense competition ⟨political ∼⟩

road·run·ner \-ˌrə-nər\ *n* : a largely terrestrial bird of the southwestern U.S. and Mexico that is a speedy runner

road·side \'rōd-ˌsīd\ *n* : the strip of land along a road — **roadside** *adj*

road·stead \-ˌsted\ *n* : an anchorage for ships usu. less sheltered than a harbor

road·ster \'rōd-stər\ *n* **1** : a driving horse **2** : an open automobile that seats two often with a storage compartment or rumble seat in the rear

road·way \-ˌwā\ *n* : ROAD; *esp* : ROADBED

road·work \-ˌwərk\ *n* **1** : work done in constructing or repairing roads **2** : conditioning for an athletic contest (as a boxing match) consisting mainly of long runs

roam \'rōm\ *vb* **1** : WANDER, ROVE **2** : to range or wander over or about **3** : to use a cell phone outside one's local calling area

¹roan \'rōn\ *adj* : of dark color (as black, red, or brown) sprinkled with white ⟨a ∼ horse⟩

²roan *n* : an animal (as a horse) with a roan coat; *also* : its color

¹roar \'rȯr\ *vb* **1** : to utter a full loud prolonged sound **2** : to make a loud confused sound (as of wind or waves) — **roar·er** *n*

²roar *n* : a sound of roaring

¹roast \'rōst\ *vb* **1** : to cook by exposure to dry heat or an open flame **2** : to criticize severely or kiddingly

²roast *n* **1** : a piece of meat suitable for roasting **2** : an outing at which food is roasted ⟨corn ∼⟩ **3** : severe criticism or kidding

³roast *adj* : ROASTED

roast·er \'rō-stər\ *n* **1** : one that roasts **2** : a device for roasting **3** : something (as a young chicken) fit for roasting

rob \'räb\ *vb* **robbed**; **rob·bing** **1** : to steal from **2** : to deprive of something due or expected **3** : to commit robbery — **rob·ber** *n*

robber fly *n* : any of a family of predaceous flies resembling bumblebees

rob·bery \'rä-bə-rē\ *n, pl* **-ber·ies** : the act or practice of robbing; *esp* : theft of something from a person by use of violence or threat

¹robe \'rōb\ *n* **1** : a long flowing outer garment; *esp* : one used for ceremonial occasions **2** : a wrap or covering for the lower body (as for sitting outdoors)

²robe *vb* **robed**; **rob·ing** **1** : to clothe with or as if with a robe **2** : DRESS

rob·in \'rä-bən\ *n* **1** : a small chiefly European thrush with a somewhat orange face and breast **2** : a large No. American thrush with a grayish back, a streaked throat, and a chiefly dull reddish breast

ro·bot \'rō-ˌbät, -bət\ *n* [Czech, fr. *robota*

compulsory labor] **1** : a machine that looks and acts like a human being **2** : an efficient but insensitive person **3** : a device that automatically performs esp. repetitive tasks **4** : something guided by automatic controls — **ro·bot·ic** \rō-'bä-tik\ *adj*

ro·bot·ics \rō-'bä-tiks\ *n* : technology dealing with the design, construction, and operation of robots

ro·bust \rō-'bəst, 'rō-(ˌ)bəst\ *adj* [L *robustus* oaken, strong, fr. *robur* oak, strength] **1** : strong and vigorously healthy **2** : capable of performing without failure under a wide range of conditions ⟨∼ software⟩ — **ro·bust·ly** *adv* — **ro·bust·ness** *n*

ROC *abbr* Republic of China (Taiwan)

¹rock \'räk\ *vb* **1** : to move back and forth in or as if in a cradle **2** : to sway or cause to sway back and forth **3** : to arouse to excitement (as with rock music) ⟨∼ed the crowd⟩ **4** *slang* : to be extremely enjoyable or effective ⟨this car ∼s⟩

²rock *n* **1** : a rocking movement **2** : popular music usu. played on electric instruments and characterized by a strong beat and much repetition

³rock *n* **1** : a mass of stony material; *also* : broken pieces of stone **2** : solid mineral deposits **3** : something like a rock in firmness **4** : GEM; *esp* : DIAMOND — **rock** *adj* — **rock·like** *adj* — **rocky** *adj* — **on the rocks** **1** : in a state of ruin ⟨a marriage *on the rocks*⟩ **2** : on ice cubes ⟨bourbon *on the rocks*⟩

rock and roll *n* : ²ROCK 2

rock·bound \'räk-ˌbau̇nd\ *adj* : fringed or covered with rocks

rock·er \'rä-kər\ *n* **1** : one of the curved pieces on which something (as a chair or cradle) rocks **2** : a chair that rocks on rockers **3** : a device that works with a rocking motion **4** : a rock performer, song, or enthusiast

¹rock·et \'rä-kət\ *n* [It *rocchetta*, lit., small distaff] **1** : a firework that is propelled through the air by the discharge of gases produced by a burning substance **2** : a jet engine that operates on the same principle as a firework rocket but carries the oxygen needed for burning its fuel **3** : a rocket-propelled bomb or missile

²rocket *vb* **1** : to convey by means of a rocket **2** : to rise abruptly and rapidly

rock·et·ry \'rä-kə-trē\ *n* : the study or use of rockets

rocket ship *n* : a rocket-propelled spacecraft

rock·fall \'räk-ˌfȯl\ *n* : a mass of falling or fallen rocks

rock·fish \-ˌfish\ *n* : any of various bony fishes that live among rocks or on rocky bottoms

rock salt *n* : common salt in rocklike masses or large crystals

Rocky Mountain sheep *n* : BIGHORN

ro·co·co \rə-'kō-kō\ *adj* [F, irreg. fr. *rocaille* style of ornament, lit., stone debris] : of or relating to an artistic style esp. of the 18th century marked by fanciful curved forms and elaborate ornamentation — **rococo** n

rod \'räd\ n, 1 : a straight slender stick 2 : a stick or bundle of twigs used in punishing a person; also : PUNISHMENT 3 : a staff borne to show rank 4 — see WEIGHT table 5 : any of the rod-shaped receptor cells of the retina that are sensitive to faint light 6 slang : HANDGUN

rode past of RIDE

ro·dent \'rō-dᵊnt\ n [ultim. fr. L rodent-, rodens, prp. of rodere to gnaw] : any of an order of relatively small mammals (as mice, squirrels, and beavers) with sharp front teeth used for gnawing

ro·deo \'rō-dē-ō, rə-'dā-ō\ n, pl **ro·de·os** [Sp, fr. rodear to surround, fr. rueda wheel, fr. L rota] 1 : ROUNDUP 1 2 : a public performance featuring cowboy skills (as riding and roping)

¹**roe** \'rō\ n, pl **roe** or **roes** : DOE

²**roe** n : the eggs of a fish esp. while bound together in a mass

roe·buck \'rō-ˌbək\ n, pl **roebuck** or **roebucks** : a male roe deer

roe deer n : either of two small nimble European or Asian deers

roent·gen \'rent-gən, 'rənt-, -jən\ n : the international unit of measurement for X-rays and gamma rays

rog·er \'rä-jər\ interj — used esp. in radio and signaling to indicate that a message has been received and understood

¹**rogue** \'rōg\ n 1 : a dishonest person : SCOUNDREL 2 : a mischievous person : SCAMP — **rogu·ery** \'rō-gə-rē\ n — **rogu·ish** adj — **rogu·ish·ly** adv — **rogu·ish·ness** n

²**rogue** adj 1 : CORRUPT, DISHONEST 〈~ cops〉 2 : of or being a nation whose leaders defy international law or norms

roil \'rȯi(-ə)l, for 2 also 'rī(-ə)l\ vb 1 : to make cloudy or muddy by stirring up 2 : RILE 1 — **roily** \'rȯi-lē\ adj

rois·ter \'rȯi-stər\ vb **rois·tered**; **rois·ter·ing** : to engage in noisy revelry : CAROUSE — **rois·ter·er** n — **rois·ter·ous** \-stə-rəs\ adj

ROK abbr Republic of Korea (South Korea)

role also **rôle** \'rōl\ n 1 : an assigned or assumed character; also : a part played (as by an actor) 2 : FUNCTION

role model n : a person whose behavior in a particular role is imitated by others

¹**roll** \'rōl\ n [ME rolle scroll, fr. AF, fr. ML rolla, alter. of rotula, fr. L, dim. of rota wheel] 1 : a document containing an official record 2 : an official list of names 3 : something (as a bun) that is rolled up or rounded as if rolled 4 : something that rolls : ROLLER

²**roll** vb 1 : to move by turning over and over 〈~ dice〉 〈~ed her eyes〉 2 : to press with a roller 〈~ dough〉 3 : to move on wheels 4 : to sound with a full reverberating tone 5 : to make a continuous beating sound (as on a drum) 6 : to utter with a trill 7 : to move onward as if by completing a revolution 〈years ~ed by〉 8 : to flow or seem to flow in a continuous stream or with a rising and falling

motion 〈the river ~ed on〉 9 : to swing or sway from side to side 10 : to shape or become shaped in rounded form 〈~ up the paper〉 11 : to move by or as if by turning a crank 〈~down the window〉

³**roll** n 1 : a sound produced by rapid strokes on a drum 2 : a heavy reverberating sound 3 : a rolling movement or action 4 : a swaying movement (as of a ship) 5 : a somersault made in contact with the ground

roll·back \'rōl-ˌbak\ n : the act or an instance of rolling back

roll back vb 1 : to reduce (as a commodity price) on a national scale 2 : to cause to withdraw : push back

roll bar n : an overhead metal bar on an automobile designed to protect riders in case the automobile overturns

roll call n : the act or an instance of calling off a list of names (as of soldiers); also : a time for a roll call

roll·er \'rō-lər\ n 1 : a revolving cylinder used for moving, pressing, shaping, applying, or smoothing something 2 : a rod on which something is rolled up 3 : a long heavy ocean wave

roll·er coast·er \'rō-lər-ˌkō-stər\ n : an amusement ride consisting of an elevated railway having sharp curves and steep slopes

roller skate n : a skate with wheels instead of a runner — **roller–skate** vb — **roller skater** n

rol·lick \'rä-lik\ vb : ROMP, FROLIC

rol·lick·ing adj : full of fun and good spirits 〈a ~ good time〉

roly–poly \ˌrō-lē-'pō-lē\ adj : ROTUND

Rom abbr 1 Roman 2 Romance 3 Romania; Romanian 4 Romans

ROM \'räm\ n : a computer memory that contains special-purpose information (as a program) which cannot be altered

ro·maine \rō-'mān\ n [F, lit., Roman] : a garden lettuce with a tall loose head of long crisp leaves

¹**Ro·man** \'rō-mən\ n 1 : a native or resident of Rome 2 not cap : roman letters or type

²**Roman** adj 1 : of or relating to Rome or the Romans and esp. the ancient Romans 2 not cap : relating to type in which the letters are upright 3 : of or relating to the Roman Catholic Church

Roman candle n : a cylindrical firework that discharges balls of fire

Roman Catholic adj : of, relating to, or being a Christian church led by the pope and having a liturgy centered in the Mass — **Roman Catholicism** n

¹**ro·mance** \rō-'mans, 'rō-ˌmans\ n [ME romauns, fr. AF romanz French, something written in French, tale in verse, fr. ML Romanice in a vernacular language, ultim. fr. L Romanus Roman] 1 : a medieval tale of knightly adventure 2 : a prose narrative dealing with heroic or mysterious events set in a remote time or place 3 : a love story 4 : a romantic attachment or episode between lovers — **ro·manc·er** n

²**romance** *vb* **ro·manced; ro·manc·ing 1** : to exaggerate or invent detail or incident **2** : to have romantic fancies **3** : to carry on a romantic episode with

Ro·mance \rō-'mans, 'rō-ˌmans\ *adj* : of or relating to any of several languages developed from Latin

Ro·ma·nian \rù-'mä-nē-ən, rō-, -nyən\ *also* **Ru·ma·nian** \rù-\ **1** : a native or inhabitant of Romania **2** : the language of the Romanians

Roman numeral *n* : a numeral in a system of notation that is based on the ancient Roman system

Ro·ma·no \rō-'mä-nō\ *n* : a hard Italian cheese that is sharper than Parmesan

Ro·mans \'rō-mənz\ *n* — see BIBLE table

¹**ro·man·tic** \rō-'man-tik\ *adj* **1** : IMAGINARY **2** : VISIONARY **3** : having an imaginative or emotional appeal **4** : of, relating to, or having the characteristics of romanticism — **ro·man·ti·cal·ly** \-ti-k(ə-)lē\ *adv*

²**romantic** *n* : a romantic person; *esp* : a romantic writer, composer, or artist

ro·man·ti·cism \rō-'man-tə-ˌsi-zəm\ *n, often cap* : a literary movement (as in early 19th century England) marked esp. by emphasis on the imagination and the emotions and by the use of autobiographical material — **ro·man·ti·cist** \-sist\ *n, often cap*

ro·man·ti·cize \-'man-tə-ˌsīz\ *vb* **-cized; -ciz·ing 1** : to make romantic **2** : to have romantic ideas

romp \'rämp\ *vb* **1** : to play actively and noisily **2** : to win a contest easily — **romp** *n*

romp·er \'räm-pər\ *n* **1** : one that romps **2** : a jumpsuit usu. for infants — usu. used in pl.

rood \'rüd\ *n* : CROSS, CRUCIFIX

¹**roof** \'rüf, 'rùf\ *n, pl* **roofs** \'rüfs, 'rùfs; 'rüvz, 'rùvz\ **1** : the upper covering part of a building **2** : something suggesting a roof of a building — **roofed** \'rüft, 'rùft\ *adj* — **roof·ing** *n* — **roof·less** *adj* — **through the roof** : to an extremely high level ⟨prices went *through the roof*⟩

²**roof** *vb* : to cover with a roof

roof·top \-ˌtäp\ *n* : a roof esp. of a house

¹**rook** \'rùk\ *n* : a common Old World bird resembling the related crow

²**rook** *vb* : CHEAT, SWINDLE

³**rook** *n* : a chess piece that can move parallel to the sides of the board across any number of unoccupied squares

rook·ery \'rù-kə-rē\ *n, pl* **-er·ies** : a breeding ground or haunt of gregarious birds or mammals; *also* : a colony of such birds or mammals

rook·ie \'rù-kē\ *n* : BEGINNER, RECRUIT; *esp* : a first-year player in a professional sport

¹**room** \'rüm, 'rùm\ *n* **1** : an extent of space occupied by or sufficient or available for something **2** : a partitioned part of a building : CHAMBER; *also* : the people in a room **3** : OPPORTUNITY, CHANCE ⟨∼ to develop his talents⟩ — **room·ful** *n* — **roomy** *adj*

²**room** *vb* : to occupy or share lodgings : LODGE — **room·er** *n*

room·ette \rü-'met, rù-\ *n* : a small private room on a railroad sleeping car

room·mate \'rüm-ˌmāt, 'rùm-\ *n* : one of two or more persons sharing the same room or dwelling

¹**roost** \'rüst\ *n* : a support on which or a place where birds perch

²**roost** *vb* : to settle on or as if on a roost

roost·er \'rüs-tər, 'rùs-\ *n* : an adult male domestic chicken : COCK

¹**root** \'rüt, 'rùt\ *n* **1** : the leafless usu. underground part of a seed plant that functions in absorption, aeration, and storage or as a means of anchorage; *also* : an underground plant part esp. when fleshy and edible **2** : something (as the basal part of a tooth or hair) resembling a root **3** : SOURCE, ORIGIN; *esp* : ANCESTRY — usu. used in pl. **4** : the essential core : HEART ⟨get to the ∼ of the matter⟩ **5** : a number that when taken as a factor an indicated number of times gives a specified number **6** : the lower part — **root·less** *adj* — **root·like** *adj*

²**root** *vb* **1** : to form roots **2** : to fix or become fixed by or as if by roots : ESTABLISH **3** : UPROOT

³**root** *vb* **1** : to turn up or dig with the snout ⟨pigs ∼*ing*⟩ **2** : to poke or dig around (as in search of something)

⁴**root** \'rüt\ *vb* **1** : to applaud or encourage noisily : CHEER **2** : to wish success or lend support to — **root·er** *n*

root beer *n* : a sweetened carbonated beverage flavored with extracts of roots and herbs

root canal *n* : a dental operation to save a tooth by removing the pulp in the root of the tooth and filling the cavity with a protective substance

root·let \'rüt-lət, 'rùt-\ *n* : a small root

root·stock \-ˌstäk\ *n* : an underground part of a plant that resembles a rhizome

¹**rope** \'rōp\ *n* **1** : a large strong cord made of strands of fiber **2** : a hangman's noose **3** : a thick string (as of pearls) made by twisting or braiding

²**rope** *vb* **roped; rop·ing 1** : to bind, tie, or fasten together with a rope **2** : to separate or divide by means of a rope **3** : LASSO

Ror·schach test \'ror-ˌshäk-\ *n* : a psychological test in which a subject interprets ink-blot designs in terms that reveal intellectual and emotional factors

ro·sa·ry \'rō-zə-rē\ *n, pl* **-ries 1** *often cap* : a Roman Catholic devotion consisting of meditation on sacred mysteries during recitation of Hail Marys **2** : a string of beads used in praying

¹**rose** *past of* RISE

²**rose** \'rōz\ *n* **1** : any of a genus of usu. prickly often climbing shrubs with divided leaves and bright often fragrant flowers; *also* : one of these flowers **2** : something resembling a rose in form **3** : a moderate purplish red color — **rose** *adj*

ro·sé \rō-'zā\ *n* [F] : a light pink wine

ro·se·ate \'rō-zē-ət, -zē-ˌāt\ *adj* **1** : re-

rose·bud \'rōz-ˌbəd\ *n* : the flower of a rose when it is at most partly open

rose·bush \-ˌbu̇sh\ *n* : a shrubby rose

rose·mary \'rōz-ˌmer-ē\ *n, pl* **-mar·ies** [ME *rosmarine*, fr. AF *rosmarin*, fr. L *rosmarinus*, fr. *ros* dew + *marinus* of the sea, fr. *mare* sea] : a fragrant shrubby Mediterranean mint; *also* : its leaves used as a seasoning

ro·sette \rō-'zet\ *n* [F] **1** : a usu. small badge or ornament of ribbon gathered in the shape of a rose **2** : a circular ornament filled with representations of leaves

rose wa·ter \'rōz-ˌwȯ-tər, -ˌwä-\ *n* : a watery solution of the fragrant constituents of the rose used as a perfume

rose·wood \-ˌwu̇d\ *n* : any of various tropical trees with dark red wood streaked with black; *also* : this wood

Rosh Ha·sha·nah \ˌräsh-hə-'shä-nə, ˌrōsh-, -'shō-\ *n* [Heb *rōsh hashshānāh*, lit., beginning of the year] : the Jewish New Year observed as a religious holiday in September or October

ros·in \'rä-z²n\ *n* : a brittle resin obtained esp. from pine trees and used esp. in varnishes and on violin bows

ros·ter \'räs-tər\ *n* **1** : a list of personnel; *also* : the persons listed on a roster **2** : an itemized list

ros·trum \'räs-trəm\ *n, pl* **rostrums** or **ros·tra** \-trə\ [L *Rostra*, pl., a platform for speakers in the Roman Forum decorated with the beaks of captured ships, fr. pl. of *rostrum* beak, ship's beak, fr. *rodere* to gnaw] : a stage or platform for public speaking

rosy \'rō-zē\ *adj* **ros·i·er; -est** **1** : of the color rose **2** : HOPEFUL, PROMISING ⟨a ~ outlook⟩ — **ros·i·ly** \'rō-zə-lē\ *adv* — **ros·i·ness** \-zē-nəs\ *n*

¹rot \'rät\ *vb* **rot·ted; rot·ting** : to undergo decomposition : DECAY

²rot *n* **1** : DECAY **2** : any of various diseases of plants or animals in which tissue breaks down **3** : NONSENSE

¹ro·ta·ry \'rō-tə-rē\ *adj* **1** : turning on an axis like a wheel **2** : having a rotating part ⟨a ~ telephone⟩

²rotary *n, pl* **-ries** **1** : a rotary machine **2** : a one-way circular road junction

ro·tate \'rō-ˌtāt\ *vb* **ro·tat·ed; ro·tat·ing** **1** : to turn or cause to turn about an axis or a center : REVOLVE **2** : to alternate in a series ♦ **Synonyms** TURN, CIRCLE, SPIN, WHIRL, TWIRL — **ro·ta·tion** \rō-'tā-shən\ *n* — **ro·ta·tor** \'rō-ˌtā-tər\ *n* — **ro·ta·to·ry** \'rō-tə-ˌtȯr-ē\ *adj*

ROTC *abbr* Reserve Officers' Training Corps

rote \'rōt\ *n* **1** : repetition from memory often without attention to meaning ⟨learn by ~⟩ **2** : mechanical or unthinking routine or repetition — **rote** *adj*

ro·tis·ser·ie \rō-'ti-sə-rē\ *n* [F] **1** : a restaurant specializing in broiled and barbecued meats **2** : an appliance fitted with a spit on which food is rotated before or over a source of heat

ro·to·gra·vure \ˌrō-tə-grə-'vyu̇r\ *n* : PHOTOGRAVURE

ro·tor \'rō-tər\ *n* **1** : a part that rotates; *esp* : the rotating part of an electrical machine **2** : a system of rotating horizontal blades for supporting a helicopter

ro·to·till·er \'rō-tō-ˌti-lər\ *n* : an engine-powered machine with rotating blades used to lift and turn over soil

rot·ten \'rä-t²n\ *adj* **1** : having rotted **2** : CORRUPT **3** : extremely unpleasant or inferior — **rot·ten·ness** *n*

rot·ten·stone \'rä-t²n-ˌstōn\ *n* : a decomposed siliceous limestone used for polishing

rott·wei·ler \'rät-ˌwī-lər\ *n, often cap* : any of a breed of tall powerful black-and-tan short-haired dogs

ro·tund \rō-'tənd\ *adj* : rounded out ♦ **Synonyms** PLUMP, CHUBBY, PORTLY, STOUT — **ro·tun·di·ty** \-'tən-də-tē\ *n*

ro·tun·da \rō-'tən-də\ *n* **1** : a round building; *esp* : one covered by a dome **2** : a large round room

rouble *var of* RUBLE

roué \rü-'ā\ *n* [F, lit., broken on the wheel, fr. pp. of *rouer* to break on the wheel, fr. ML *rotare*, fr. L, to rotate; fr. the feeling that such a person deserves this punishment] : a man devoted to a life of sensual pleasure : RAKE

rouge \'rüzh, 'rüj\ *n* [F, lit., red] : a cosmetic used to give a red color to cheeks and lips — **rouge** *vb*

¹rough \'rəf\ *adj* **rough·er; rough·est** **1** : uneven in surface : not smooth **2** : SHAGGY **3** : not calm : TURBULENT, TEMPESTUOUS **4** : marked by harshness or violence **5** : DIFFICULT, TRYING **6** : coarse or rugged in character or appearance **7** : marked by lack of refinement **8** : CRUDE, UNFINISHED **9** : done or made hastily or tentatively — **rough·ly** *adv* — **rough·ness** *n*

²rough *n* **1** : uneven ground covered with high grass esp. along a golf fairway **2** : a crude, unfinished, or preliminary state; *also* : something in such a state **3** : ROWDY, TOUGH

³rough *vb* **1** : ROUGHEN **2** : MANHANDLE **3** : to make or shape roughly esp. in a preliminary way — **rough·er** *n*

rough·age \'rə-fij\ *n* : FIBER 2; *also* : food containing much indigestible material acting as fiber

rough–and–ready \ˌrə-fən-'re-dē\ *adj* : rude or unpolished in nature, method, or manner but effective in action or use ⟨a ~ solution⟩

rough–and–tum·ble \-'təm-bəl\ *n* : rough unrestrained fighting or struggling — **rough–and–tumble** *adj*

rough·en \'rə-fən\ *vb* **rough·ened; rough·en·ing** : to make or become rough

rough–hewn \'rəf-'hyün\ *adj* **1** : being rough and unfinished ⟨~ beams⟩ **2** : lacking smooth manners or social grace — **rough–hew** \-'hyü\ *vb*

rough·house \'rəf-ˌhau̇s\ *vb* **rough·housed; rough·hous·ing** : to participate in rough noisy behavior — **rough-house** *n*

rough·neck \'rəf-ˌnek\ *n* **1** : ROWDY, TOUGH **2** : a worker on a crew drilling oil wells

rough·shod \'rəf-ˌshäd\ *adv* : in a roughly forceful manner ⟨rode ∼ over the opposition⟩

rou·lette \rü-'let\ *n* [F, lit., small wheel] **1** : a gambling game in which a whirling wheel is used **2** : a wheel or disk with teeth around the outside

¹round \'rau̇nd\ *adj* **1** : having every part of the surface or circumference the same distance from the center **2** : CYLINDRI-CAL **3** : COMPLETE, FULL **4** : approximately correct; *esp* : exact only to a specific decimal or place ⟨∼ numbers⟩ **5** : liberal or ample in size or amount **6** : BLUNT, OUTSPOKEN **7** : moving in or forming a circle **8** : having curves rather than angles — **round·ish** *adj* — **round·ness** *n*

²round *prep or adv* : AROUND

³round *n* **1** : something round (as a circle, globe, or ring) **2** : a curved or rounded part (as a rung of a ladder) **3** : an indirect path or course; *also* : a regularly covered route (as of a security guard) **4** : a series or cycle of recurring actions or events **5** : one shot fired by a soldier or a gun; *also* : ammunition for one shot **6** : a period of time or a unit of play in a game or contest **7** : a cut of meat (as beef) esp. between the rump and the lower leg — **in the round 1** : FREESTANDING **2** : with a center stage surrounded by an audience ⟨theater *in the round*⟩

⁴round *vb* **1** : to make or become round **2** : to go or pass around or part way around **3** : COMPLETE, FINISH **4** : to become plump or shapely **5** : to express as a round number — often used with *off* **6** : to follow a winding course : BEND

¹round·about \'rau̇n-də-ˌbau̇t\ *adj* : INDI-RECT, CIRCUITOUS

²roundabout *n, Brit* : MERRY-GO-ROUND

roun·de·lay \'rau̇n-də-ˌlā\ *n* **1** : a simple song with a refrain **2** : a poem with a recurring refrain

round·house \'rau̇nd-ˌhau̇s\ *n* **1** : a circular building for housing and repairing locomotives **2** : a blow with the hand made with a wide swing — **roundhouse** *adj*

round·ly \'rau̇nd-lē\ *adv* **1** : in a complete manner; *also* : WIDELY **2** : in a blunt way **3** : with vigor

round–rob·in \'rau̇nd-ˌrä-bən\ *n* : a tournament in which each contestant meets every other contestant in turn

round–shoul·dered \-ˌshōl-dərd\ *adj* : having the shoulders stooping or rounded

round–trip *n* : a trip to a place and back

round·up \'rau̇nd-ˌəp\ *n* **1** : the gathering together of cattle on the range by riding around them and driving them in; *also* : the ranch hands and horses engaged in a roundup **2** : a gathering in of scattered persons or things **3** : SUMMARY ⟨news ∼⟩ — **round up** *vb*

round·worm \-ˌwərm\ *n* : NEMATODE

rouse \'rau̇z\ *vb* **roused; rous·ing 1** : to excite to activity : stir up **2** : to wake from sleep — **rous·er** *n*

roust·about \'rau̇s-tə-ˌbau̇t\ *n* **1** : one who does heavy unskilled labor (as on a dock or in an oil field) **2** : a laborer at a circus **3** : a person with no established home or occupation

¹rout \'rau̇t\ *n* **1** : MOB 1, 2 **2** : DISTUR-BANCE **3** : a fashionable gathering

²rout *vb* **1** : RUMMAGE **2** : to gouge out **3** : to expel by force

³rout *n* **1** : a state of wild confusion or disorderly retreat **2** : a disastrous defeat

⁴rout *vb* **1** : to put to flight **2** : to defeat decisively

¹route \'rüt, 'rau̇t\ *n* [ME, fr. AF *rute*, fr. VL **rupta (via)*, lit., broken way] **1** : a traveled way **2** : CHANNEL **3** : a line of travel

²route *vb* **rout·ed; rout·ing** : to send by a selected route : DIRECT

route·man \-mən, -ˌman\ *n* : a person who sells and makes deliveries on an assigned route

rout·er \'rau̇-tər\ *n* : a machine with a revolving spindle and cutter for shaping a surface (as of wood)

rou·tine \rü-'tēn\ *n* [F, fr. MF, fr. *route* traveled way] **1** : a regular course of procedure **2** : an often repeated speech or formula **3** : a part fully worked out ⟨a comedy ∼⟩ **4** : a set of computer instructions that will perform a certain task — **routine** *adj* — **rou·tine·ly** *adv* — **rou·tin·ize** \-'tē-ˌnīz\ *vb*

¹rove \'rōv\ *vb* **roved; rov·ing** : to wander over or through — **rov·er** *n*

²rove *past and past part of* REEVE

¹row \'rō\ *vb* **1** : to propel a boat with oars **2** : to transport in a rowboat **3** : to pull an oar in a crew — **row·er** \'rō-ər\ *n*

²row *n* : an act or instance of rowing

³row *n* **1** : a number of objects in an orderly sequence **2** : WAY, STREET

⁴row \'rau̇\ *n* : a noisy quarrel

⁵row \'rau̇\ *vb* : to engage in a row

row·boat \'rō-ˌbōt\ *n* : a small boat designed to be rowed

row·dy \'rau̇-dē\ *adj* **row·di·er; -est** : coarse or boisterous in behavior : ROUGH — **row·di·ness** \'rau̇-dē-nəs\ *n* — **rowdy** *n* — **row·dy·ish** *adj* — **row·dy·ism** *n*

row·el \'rau̇-(ə)l\ *n* : a small pointed wheel on a rider's spur — **rowel** *vb*

¹roy·al \'rȯi-(ə)l\ *adj* [ME *roial*, fr. AF *real, roial*, fr. L *regalis*, fr. *reg-, rex* king] **1** : of or relating to a sovereign : REGAL **2** : fit for a king or queen ⟨a ∼ welcome⟩ — **roy·al·ly** *adv*

²royal *n* : a person of royal blood

royal flush *n* : a straight flush having an ace as the highest card

roy·al·ist \'rȯi-ə-list\ *n* : an adherent of a king or of monarchical government

roy·al·ty \'rȯi-əl-tē\ *n, pl* **-ties 1** : the state of being royal **2** : royal persons **3** : a share of a product or profit (as of a mine or oil well) claimed by the owner for allowing another person to use the property **4** : a payment made to an author or composer for each copy of a work sold or to an inventor for each article sold under a patent

RP *abbr* **1** relief pitcher **2** Republic of the Philippines

rpm *abbr* revolutions per minute

rps *abbr* revolutions per second

rpt *abbr* **1** repeat **2** report

RR *abbr* **1** railroad **2** rural route

RS *abbr* **1** recording secretary **2** revised statutes **3** Royal Society

RSV *abbr* Revised Standard Version

RSVP *abbr* [F *répondez s'il vous plaît*] please reply

rt *abbr* **1** right **2** route

RT *abbr* round-trip

rte *abbr* route

Ru *symbol* ruthenium

¹**rub** \'rəb\ *vb* **rubbed; rub·bing 1** : to use pressure and friction on a body or object **2** : to fret or chafe with friction **3** : to scour, polish, erase, or smear by pressure and friction

²**rub** *n* **1** : DIFFICULTY, OBSTRUCTION **2** : something grating to the feelings

¹**rub·ber** \'rə-bər\ *n* **1** : one that rubs **2** : ERASER **3** : a flexible waterproof elastic substance made from the milky juice of various tropical plants or made synthetically; *also* : something made of this material **4** : CONDOM — **rubber** *adj* — **rub·ber·ize** \-rə-bə-ˌrīz\ *vb* — **rub·bery** *adj*

²**rubber** *n* **1** : a contest that consists of an odd number of games and is won by the side that takes a majority **2** : an extra game played to decide a tie

¹**rub·ber·neck** \-ˌnek\ *n* **1** : an idly or overly inquisitive person **2** : a person on a guided tour

²**rubberneck** *vb* : to look around, stare, or listen with excessive curiosity ⟨*~ing* drivers⟩ — **rub·ber·neck·er** *n*

rub·bish \'rə-bish\ *n* **1** : useless waste or rejected matter : TRASH **2** : something worthless or nonsensical

rub·ble \'rə-bəl\ *n* : broken fragments esp. of a destroyed building

ru·bel·la \rü-'be-lə\ *n* : GERMAN MEASLES

ru·bi·cund \'rü-bi-(ˌ)kənd\ *adj* : RED, RUDDY

ru·bid·i·um \rü-'bi-dē-əm\ *n* : a soft silvery metallic chemical element

ru·ble *also* **rou·ble** \'rü-bəl\ *n* — see MONEY table

ru·bric \'rü-brik\ *n* [ME *rubrike* red ocher, heading in red letters of part of a book, fr. AF, fr. L *rubrica*, fr. *ruber* red] **1** : HEADING, TITLE; *also* : CLASS, CATEGORY **2** : a rule esp. for the conduct of a religious service

ru·by \'rü-bē\ *n, pl* **rubies** : a clear red precious stone — **ruby** *adj*

ru·by–throat·ed hummingbird \'rü-bē-ˌthrō-təd-\ *n* : a bright green and small hummingbird of eastern No. America with a red throat in the male

ruck·us \'rə-kəs\ *n* : ROW, DISTURBANCE

rud·der \'rə-dər\ *n* : a movable flat piece

attached at the rear of a ship or aircraft for steering

rud·dy \'rə-dē\ *adj* **rud·di·er; -est** : REDDISH; *esp* : of a healthy reddish complexion — **rud·di·ness** \'rə-dē-nəs\ *n*

rude \'rüd\ *adj* **rud·er; rud·est 1** : roughly made : CRUDE **2** : UNDEVELOPED, PRIMITIVE **3** : IMPOLITE **4** : UNSKILLED — **rude·ly** *adv* — **rude·ness** *n*

ru·di·ment \'rü-də-mənt\ *n* **1** : an elementary principle or basic skill — usu. used in pl. ⟨the *~s* of mathematics⟩ **2** : something not fully developed — usu. used in pl. ⟨the *~s* of a plan⟩ — **ru·di·men·ta·ry** \ˌrü-də-'men-tə-rē\ *adj*

¹**rue** \'rü\ *n* : REGRET, SORROW — **rue·ful** \-fəl\ *adj* — **rue·ful·ly** *adv* — **rue·ful·ness** *n*

²**rue** *vb* **rued; ru·ing** : to feel regret, remorse, or penitence for

³**rue** *n* : a European strong-scented woody herb with bitter-tasting leaves

ruff \'rəf\ *n* **1** : a large round pleated collar worn about 1600 **2** : a fringe of long hair or feathers around the neck of an animal — **ruffed** \'rəft\ *adj*

ruf·fi·an \'rə-fē-ən\ *n* : a brutal person — **ruf·fi·an·ly** *adj*

¹**ruf·fle** \'rə-fəl\ *vb* **ruf·fled; ruf·fling 1** : to roughen the surface of **2** : IRRITATE, VEX **3** : to erect (as hair or feathers) in or like a ruff **4** : to flip through (as pages) **5** : to draw into or provide with plaits or folds

²**ruffle** *n* **1** : a strip of fabric gathered or pleated on one edge **2** : RUFF **2 3** : RIPPLE — **ruf·fly** \'rə-fə-lē, -flē\ *adj*

ru·fi·yaa \'rü-fē-ˌyä\ *n, pl* **rufiyaa** — see MONEY table

RU–486 \'är-ˌyü-ˌfȯr-ˌā-tē-'siks\ *n* : a drug taken orally to induce abortion esp. early in pregnancy

rug \'rəg\ *n* **1** : a covering for the legs, lap, and feet **2** : a piece of heavy fabric usu. with a nap or pile used as a floor covering

rug·by \'rəg-bē\ *n, often cap* [*Rugby* School, Rugby, England, where it was first played] : a football game in which play is continuous and interference and forward passing are not permitted

rug·ged \'rə-gəd\ *adj* **1** : having a rough uneven surface **2** : TURBULENT, STORMY **3** : HARSH, STERN **4** : ROBUST, STURDY — **rug·ged·ize** \'rə-gə-ˌdīz\ *vb* — **rug·ged·ly** *adv* — **rug·ged·ness** *n*

¹**ru·in** \'rü-ən\ *n* **1** : complete collapse or destruction **2** : the remains of something destroyed — usu. used in pl. **3** : a cause of destruction **4** : the action of destroying

²**ruin** *vb* **1** : DESTROY **2** : to damage beyond repair **3** : BANKRUPT

ru·in·ation \ˌrü-ə-'nā-shən\ *n* : RUIN, DESTRUCTION

ru·in·ous \'rü-ə-nəs\ *adj* **1** : RUINED, DILAPIDATED **2** : causing ruin — **ru·in·ous·ly** *adv*

¹**rule** \'rül\ *n* [ME *reule*, fr. AF, fr. L *regula* straightedge, rule, fr. *regere* to keep straight, direct] **1** : a guide or principle

for governing action : REGULATION 2 : the usual way of doing something 3 : the exercise of authority or control : GOVERNMENT 4 : RULER 2

²**rule** vb, **ruled; rul·ing 1** : CONTROL; also : GOVERN **2** : to be supreme or outstanding in **3** : to give or state as a considered decision **4** : to mark on paper with or as if with a ruler **5** slang : to be extremely cool or popular

rul·er \'rü-lər\ n **1** : SOVEREIGN **2** : a straight strip of material (as wood or metal) marked off in units and used for measuring or as a straightedge

rum \'rəm\ n **1** : an alcoholic liquor made from sugarcane products (as molasses) **2** : alcoholic liquor

Ru·ma·nian var of ROMANIAN

rum·ba \'rəm-bə, 'rùm-\ n : a dance of Cuban origin marked by strong rhythmic movements

¹**rum·ble** \'rəm-bəl\ vb **rum·bled; rumbling** : to make a low heavy rolling sound; also : to move along with such a sound — **rum·bler** n

²**rumble** n **1** : a low heavy rolling sound **2** : a street fight esp. among gangs

rumble seat n : a folding seat in the back of an automobile that is not covered by the top

rum·bling \'rəm-bliŋ\ n **1** : RUMBLE **2** : widespread talk or complaints — usu. used in pl.

ru·men \'rü-mən\ n, pl **ru·mi·na** \-mə-nə\ or **rumens** : the large first compartment of the stomach of a ruminant (as a cow)

¹**ru·mi·nant** \'rü-mə-nənt\ n : a ruminant mammal

²**ruminant** adj **1** : chewing the cud; also : of or relating to a group of hoofed mammals (as cattle, deer, and camels) that chew the cud and have a complex 3- or 4-chambered stomach **2** : MEDITATIVE

ru·mi·nate \'rü-mə-ˌnāt\ vb **-nat·ed; -nating** [L ruminari to chew the cud, muse upon, fr. rumin-, rumen first stomach chamber of a ruminant] **1** : MEDITATE, MUSE **2** : to chew the cud — **ru·mi·nation** \ˌrü-mə-'nā-shən\ n

¹**rum·mage** \'rə-mij\ vb **rum·maged; rum·mag·ing** : to search thoroughly — **rum·mag·er** n

²**rummage** n **1** : a miscellaneous collection **2** : an act of rummaging

rum·my \'rə-mē\ n : any of several card games for two or more players

ru·mor \'rü-mər\ n **1** : common talk **2** : a statement or report current but not authenticated — **rumor** vb

ru·mour chiefly Brit var of RUMOR

rump \'rəmp\ n **1** : the rear part of an animal; also : a cut of meat (as beef) behind the upper sirloin **2** : a small or inferior remnant (as of a group)

rum·ple \'rəm-pəl\ vb **rum·pled; rumpling** : TOUSLE, MUSS, WRINKLE — **rumple** n — **rum·ply** \'rəm-pə-lē\ adj

rum·pus \'rəm-pəs\ n : DISTURBANCE, RUCKUS

rumpus room n : a room usu. in the basement of a home that is used for games, parties, and recreation

¹**run** \'rən\ vb **ran** \'ran\; **run; run·ning 1** : to go faster than a walk **2** : to take to flight : FLEE **3** : to go without restraint ⟨let chickens ~ loose⟩ **4** : to go rapidly or hurriedly : HASTEN, RUSH **5** : to make a quick or casual trip or visit **6** : to contend in a race; esp : to enter an election ⟨~ for mayor⟩ **7** : to put forward as a candidate for office **8** : to move on or as if on wheels : pass or slide freely **9** : to go back and forth : PLY **10** : to move in large numbers esp. to a spawning ground ⟨shad are running⟩ **11** : FUNCTION, OPERATE ⟨~s on gasoline⟩ ⟨software that ~s on her computer⟩ **12** : to continue in force ⟨two years to ~⟩ **13** : to flow rapidly or under pressure : MELT, FUSE, DISSOLVE; also : DISCHARGE 7 ⟨my nose is running⟩ **14** : to tend to produce or to recur ⟨family ~s to blonds⟩ ⟨stubbornness ~s in the family⟩ **15** : to take a certain direction **16** : to be worded or written **17** : to be current ⟨rumors running wild⟩ **18** : to cause to produce a flow ⟨ran the faucet⟩ **19** : TRACE ⟨~ down a rumor⟩ **20** : to perform or bring about by running **21** : to cause to pass ⟨~ a wire from the antenna⟩ **22** : to cause to collide **23** : SMUGGLE **24** : MANAGE, CONDUCT, OPERATE ⟨~ a business⟩ **25** : INCUR ⟨~ a risk⟩ **26** : to permit to accumulate before settling ⟨~ up a bill⟩ **27** : PRINT, PUBLISH ⟨~ a news story⟩

²**run** n **1** : an act or the action of running **2** : a migration of fish; also : the migrating fish **3** : a score in baseball **4** : BROOK, CREEK **5** : a continuous series esp. of similar things **6** : persistent heavy demands from depositors, creditors, or customers **7** : the quantity of work turned out in a continuous operation; also : a period of operation (as of a machine or plant) **8** : the usual or normal kind ⟨the ordinary ~ of students⟩ **9** : the distance covered in continuous travel or sailing **10** : a regular course or trip **11** : freedom of movement in a place or area ⟨has the ~ of the house⟩ **12** : an enclosure for animals **13** : an inclined course (as for skiing) **14** : a lengthwise ravel (as in a stocking) — **run·less** adj

run·about \'rə-nə-ˌbaùt\ n : a light wagon, automobile, or motorboat

run·a·gate \'rə-nə-ˌgāt\ n **1** : VAGABOND **2** : FUGITIVE

run·around \'rə-nə-ˌraùnd\ n : evasive or delaying action esp. in response to a request

¹**run·away** \'rə-nə-ˌwā\ n **1** : one that runs away : FUGITIVE **2** : the act of running away out of control; also : something (as a horse) that is running out of control

²**runaway** adj **1** : FUGITIVE **2** : won by a long lead; also : extremely successful **3** : subject to uncontrolled changes ⟨~ inflation⟩ **4** : operating out of control ⟨a ~ locomotive⟩

run-down \'rən-ˌdaùn\ n : an item-by-item report or review : SUMMARY

run—down \'rən-'daùn\ adj **1** : EX-

HAUSTED, WORN-OUT ⟨that ~ feeling⟩
2 : being in poor repair ⟨a ~ farm⟩

run down *vb* **1** : to collide with and knock down **2** : to chase until exhausted or captured **3** : to find by search **4** : DISPARAGE **5** : to cease to operate for lack of motive power **6** : to decline in physical condition

rune \ˈrün\ *n* **1** : any of the characters of any of several alphabets formerly used by the Germanic peoples **2** : MYSTERY, MAGIC **3** : a poem esp. in Finnish or Old Norse — **ru·nic** \ˈrü-nik\ *adj*

¹**rung** *past part of* RING

²**rung** \ˈrəŋ\ *n* **1** : a rounded crosspiece between the legs of a chair **2** : one of the crosspieces of a ladder

run–in \ˈrən-ˌin\ *n* **1** : ALTERCATION, QUARREL **2** : something run in

run in *vb* **1** : to insert as additional matter **2** : to arrest esp. for a minor offense **3** : to pay a casual visit

run·nel \ˈrə-nᵊl\ *n* : BROOK, STREAMLET

run·ner \ˈrə-nər\ *n* **1** : one that runs **2** : BASE RUNNER **3** : BALLCARRIER **4** : a thin piece or part on which something (as a sled or an ice skate) slides **5** : the support of a drawer or a sliding door **6** : a horizontal branch from the base of a plant that produces new plants **7** : a plant producing runners **8** : a long narrow carpet **9** : a narrow decorative cloth cover for a table or dresser top

run·ner–up \ˈrə-nər-ˌəp\ *n, pl* **runners–up** *also* **runner–ups** : the competitor in a contest who finishes second

¹**run·ning** \ˈrə-niŋ\ *adj* **1** : FLOWING **2** : FLUID, RUNNY **3** : CONTINUOUS, INCESSANT **4** : measured in a straight line ⟨cost per ~ foot⟩ **5** : of or relating to an act of running **6** : made or trained for running ⟨~ horse⟩ ⟨~ shoes⟩

²**running** *adv* : in succession

running light *n* : any of the lights carried by a vehicle (as a ship) at night

run·ny \ˈrə-nē\ *adj* : having a tendency to run ⟨a ~ dough⟩ ⟨a ~ nose⟩

run·off \ˈrən-ˌof\ *n* : a final contest (as an election) to decide a previous indecisive contest

run–of–the–mill *adj* : not outstanding : AVERAGE

run on *vb* **1** : to talk at length **2** : to continue (matter in type) without a break or a new paragraph **3** : to place or add (as an entry in a dictionary) at the end of a paragraphed item — **run–on** \ˈrən-ˌon, -ˌän\ *n*

run out *vb* : to use up or exhaust a supply ⟨ran out of gas⟩

runt \ˈrənt\ *n* : an unusually small person or animal : DWARF — **runty** *adj*

run·way \ˈrən-ˌwā\ *n* **1** : a beaten path made by animals; *also* : a passage for animals **2** : a paved strip of ground for the landing and takeoff of aircraft **3** : a narrow platform from a stage into an auditorium **4** : a support (as a track) on which something runs

ru·pee \rü-ˈpē, ˈrü-ˌpē\ *n* — see MONEY table

ru·pi·ah \rü-ˈpē-ə\ *n, pl* **rupiah** *or* **rupiahs** — see MONEY table

¹**rup·ture** \ˈrəp-chər\ *n* : a breaking or tearing apart; *also* : HERNIA

²**rupture** *vb* **rup·tured; rup·tur·ing** : to cause or undergo rupture

ru·ral \ˈrùr-əl\ *adj* : of or relating to the country, country people, or agriculture

ruse \ˈrüs, ˈrüz\ *n* : a wily subterfuge : TRICK, ARTIFICE

¹**rush** \ˈrəsh\ *n* : any of various often tufted and hollow-stemmed grasslike marsh plants — **rushy** *adj*

²**rush** *vb* [ME *russhen*, fr. AF *reuser, ruser, russher* to drive back, repulse, fr. L *recusare* to oppose] **1** : to move forward or act with too great haste or eagerness or without preparation **2** : to perform in a short time or at high speed **3** : ATTACK, CHARGE **4** : to advance a football by running — **rush·er** *n*

³**rush** *n* **1** : a violent forward motion **2** : unusual demand or activity **3** : a crowding of people to one place **4** : a running play in football **5** : a sudden feeling of pleasure

⁴**rush** *adj* : requiring or marked by special speed or urgency ⟨~ orders⟩

rush hour *n* : a time when the amount of traffic or business is at a peak

rusk \ˈrəsk\ *n* : a sweet or plain bread baked, sliced, and baked again until dry and crisp

rus·set \ˈrə-sət\ *n* **1** : a coarse reddish brown cloth **2** : a reddish brown **3** : a baking potato — **russet** *adj*

Rus·sian \ˈrə-shən\ *n* **1** : a native or inhabitant of Russia **2** : a Slavic language of the Russian people — **Russian** *adj*

rust \ˈrəst\ *n* **1** : a reddish coating formed on iron when it is exposed to esp. moist air **2** : any of numerous plant diseases characterized by usu. reddish spots; *also* : a fungus causing rust **3** : a strong reddish brown — **rust** *vb* — **rusty** *adj*

¹**rus·tic** \ˈrəs-tik\ *adj* : of, relating to, or suitable for the country or country people — **rus·ti·cal·ly** \-ti-k(ə-)lē\ *adv* — **rus·tic·i·ty** \ˌrəs-ˈti-sə-tē\ *n*

²**rustic** *n* : a rustic person

rus·ti·cate \ˈrəs-ti-ˌkāt\ *vb* **-cat·ed; -cat·ing** : to go into or reside in the country — **rus·ti·ca·tion** \ˌrəs-ti-ˈkā-shən\ *n*

¹**rus·tle** \ˈrə-səl\ *vb* **rus·tled; rus·tling** **1** : to make or cause a rustle **2** : to cause to rustle ⟨~ a newspaper⟩ **3** : to act or move with energy or speed; *also* : to procure in this way **4** : to forage food **5** : to steal cattle from the range — **rus·tler** *n*

²**rustle** *n* : a quick series of small sounds ⟨~ of leaves⟩

¹**rut** \ˈrət\ *n* : state or period of sexual excitement esp. in male deer — **rut** *vb*

²**rut** *n* **1** : a track worn by wheels or by habitual passage of something **2** : a usual or fixed routine

ru·ta·ba·ga \ˌrü-tə-ˈbā-gə, ˌrü-\ *n* : a turnip with a large yellowish root

Ruth \ˈrüth\ *n* — see BIBLE table

ru·the·ni·um \rü-ˈthē-nē-əm\ *n* : a rare hard metallic chemical element

ruth·er·ford·ium \ˌrə-thər-ˈfȯr-dē-əm\ n : an artifically produced radioactive chemical element

ruth·less \ˈrüth-ləs\ adj [fr. ruth compassion, pity, fr. ME ruthe, fr. ruen to rue, fr. OE hrēowan] : having no pity : MERCILESS, CRUEL ⟨a ~ tyrant⟩ — **ruth·less·ly** adv — **ruth·less·ness** n

¹**RV** \ˌär-ˈvē\ n : RECREATIONAL VEHICLE

²**RV** abbr Revised Version

R–value \ˈär-ˌval-yü\ n : a measure of resistance to the flow of heat through a substance (as insulation)

RW abbr   1 right worshipful   2 right worthy

rwy or **ry** abbr   railway

-ry n suffix : -ERY ⟨bigotry⟩

rye \ˈrī\ n   1 : a hardy annual grass grown for grain or as a cover crop; also : its seed   2 : a whiskey distilled from a rye mash

¹**s** \ˈes\ n, pl **s's** or **ss** \ˈe-səz\ often cap : the 19th letter of the English alphabet

²**s** abbr, often cap   1 saint   2 second   3 senate   4 series   5 shilling   6 singular   7 small   8 son   9 south; southern

¹**-s** \s after sounds f, k, ḵ, p, t, th; əz after sounds ch, j, s, sh, z, zh; z after other sounds\ n pl suffix — used to form the plural of most nouns that do not end in s, z, sh, or ch or y following a consonant ⟨heads⟩ ⟨books⟩ ⟨boys⟩ ⟨beliefs⟩, to form the plural of proper nouns that end in y following a consonant ⟨Marys⟩, and with or without a preceding apostrophe to form the plural of abbreviations, numbers, letters, and symbols used as nouns ⟨MCs⟩ ⟨4s⟩ ⟨#s⟩ ⟨B's⟩

²**-s** adv suffix — used to form adverbs denoting usual or repeated action or state ⟨works nights⟩

³**-s** vb suffix — used to form the third person singular present of most verbs that do not end in s, z, sh, or ch or y following a consonant ⟨falls⟩ ⟨takes⟩ ⟨plays⟩

S symbol   sulfur

SA abbr   1 Salvation Army   2 seaman apprentice   3 sex appeal   4 [L sine anno without year] without date   5 South Africa   6 South America   7 subject to approval

Saami var of SAMI

Sab·bath \ˈsa-bəth\ n [ME sabat, fr. AF & OE, fr. L sabbatum, fr. Gk sabbaton, fr. Heb shabbāth, lit., rest]   1 : the 7th day of the week observed as a day of worship by Jews and some Christians   2 : Sunday observed among Christians as a day of worship

sab·bat·i·cal \sə-ˈba-ti-kəl\ n : a leave often with pay granted (as to a college professor) usu. every 7th year for rest, travel, or research

sa·ber or **sa·bre** \ˈsā-bər\ n [F sabre] : a cavalry sword with a curved blade and thick back

saber saw n : a portable electric saw with a pointed reciprocating blade; esp : JIGSAW

sa·ble \ˈsā-bəl\ n, pl **sables**   1 : the color black   2 pl : mourning garments   3 : a dark brown mammal chiefly of northern Asia related to the weasels; also : its fur or pelt

¹**sab·o·tage** \ˈsa-bə-ˌtäzh\ n [F]   1 : deliberate destruction of an employer's property or hindering of production by workers   2 : destructive or hampering action by enemy agents or sympathizers in time of war

²**sabotage** vb **-taged; -tag·ing** : to practice sabotage on : WRECK

sab·o·teur \ˌsa-bə-ˈtər\ n : a person who practices sabotage

sac \ˈsak\ n : a pouch in an animal or plant often containing a fluid

SAC abbr   Strategic Air Command

sac·cha·rin \ˈsa-kə-rən\ n : a white crystalline compound used as an artificial calorie-free sweetener

sac·cha·rine \ˈsa-kə-rən\ adj : nauseatingly sweet ⟨~ poetry⟩

sac·er·do·tal \ˌsa-sər-ˈdōt-ᵊl, -kər-\ adj : PRIESTLY

sac·er·do·tal·ism \-tə-ˌli-zəm\ n : a religious belief emphasizing the powers of priests as essential mediators between God and man

sa·chem \ˈsā-chəm\ n [Narragansett sâchim] : a No. American Indian chief

sa·chet \sa-ˈshā\ n [MF, fr. OF, dim. of sac bag] : a small bag filled with perfumed powder for scenting clothes

¹**sack** \ˈsak\ n   1 : a usu. rectangular-shaped bag (as of paper or burlap)   2 : a loose jacket or short coat

²**sack** vb : DISMISS, FIRE

³**sack** n [modif. of MF sec dry, fr. L siccus] : a white wine popular in England in the 16th and 17th centuries

⁴**sack** vb : to plunder a captured town

sack·cloth \-ˌklȯth\ n : a rough garment worn as a sign of penitence

sac·ra·ment \ˈsa-krə-mənt\ n   1 : a formal religious act or rite; esp : one (as baptism or the Eucharist) held to have been instituted by Christ   2 : the elements of the Eucharist — **sac·ra·men·tal** \ˌsa-krə-ˈmen-tᵊl\ adj

sa·cred \ˈsā-krəd\ adj   1 : set apart for the service or worship of deity   2 : devoted exclusively to one service or use   3 : worthy of veneration or reverence   4 : of or relating to religion : RELIGIOUS ♦ Synonyms BLESSED, DIVINE, HALLOWED, HOLY, SANCTIFIED — **sa·cred·ly** adv — **sa·cred·ness** n

sacred cow n : one that is often unreasonably immune from criticism

¹sac·ri·fice \'sa-krə-ˌfīs\ n 1 : the offering of something precious to deity 2 : something offered in sacrifice 3 : LOSS, DEPRIVATION 4 : a bunt allowing a base runner to advance while the batter is put out; also : a fly ball allowing a runner to score after the catch — **sac·ri·fi·cial** \ˌsa-krə-'fi-shəl\ adj — **sac·ri·fi·cial·ly** adv

²sacrifice vb **-ficed; -fic·ing** 1 : to offer up or kill as a sacrifice 2 : to accept the loss or destruction of for an end, cause, or ideal 3 : to make a sacrifice in baseball

sac·ri·lege \'sa-krə-lij\ n [ME, fr. AF, fr. L sacrilegium, fr. sacrilegus one who robs sacred property fr. sacr-, sacer sacred + legere to gather, steal] 1 : violation of something consecrated to God 2 : gross irreverence toward a hallowed person, place, or thing — **sac·ri·le·gious** \ˌsa-krə-'li-jəs, -'lē-\ adj — **sac·ri·le·gious·ly** adv

sac·ris·tan \'sa-krə-stən\ n 1 : a church officer in charge of the sacristy 2 : SEXTON

sac·ris·ty \'sa-krə-stē\ n, pl **-ties** : VESTRY

sac·ro·il·i·ac \ˌsa-krō-'i-lē-ˌak\ n : the joint between the upper part of the hipbone and the sacrum

sac·ro·sanct \'sa-krō-ˌsaŋkt\ adj : SACRED, INVIOLABLE

sa·crum \'sa-krəm, 'sā-\ n, pl **sa·cra** \'sa-krə, 'sā-\ : the part of the vertebral column that is directly connected with or forms a part of the pelvis and in humans consists of five fused vertebrae

sad \'sad\ adj **sad·der; sad·dest** 1 : GRIEVING, MOURNFUL, DOWNCAST 2 : causing sorrow 3 : DULL, SOMBER — **sad·ly** adv — **sad·ness** n

sad·den \'sa-dᵊn\ vb : to make sad

¹sad·dle \'sa-dᵊl\ n : a usu. padded leather-covered seat (as for a rider on horseback)

²saddle vb **sad·dled; sad·dling** 1 : to put a saddle on 2 : OPPRESS, BURDEN

sad·dle·bow \'sa-dᵊl-ˌbō\ n : the arch in the front of a saddle

saddle horse n : a horse suited for or trained for riding

Sad·du·cee \'sa-jə-ˌsē, 'sa-dyə-\ n : a member of an ancient Jewish sect consisting of a ruling class of priests and rejecting certain doctrines — **Sad·du·ce·an** \ˌsa-jə-'sē-ən, ˌsa-dyə-\ adj

sad·iron \'sa-ˌdī-ərn\ n : a flatiron with a removable handle

sa·dism \'sā-ˌdi-zəm, 'sa-\ n : a sexual perversion in which gratification is obtained by inflicting physical or mental pain on others — **sa·dist** \'sā-dist, 'sa-\ n — **sa·dis·tic** \sə-'dis-tik\ adj — **sa·dis·ti·cal·ly** \-ti-k(ə-)lē\ adv

sa·do·mas·och·ism \ˌsā-(ˌ)dō-'ma-sə-ˌki-zəm, ˌsa-, -'ma-zə-\ n : the derivation of pleasure from the infliction of physical or mental pain either on others or on oneself — **sa·do·mas·och·is·tic** \-ˌma-sə-'kis-tik, -ˌma-zə-\ adj

SAE abbr 1 self-addressed envelope 2 Society of Automotive Engineers 3 stamped addressed envelope

sa·fa·ri \sə-'fär-ē\ n [Swahili, trip, fr. Ar safari of a trip] 1 : a hunting expedition esp. in eastern Africa 2 : JOURNEY, TRIP

¹safe \'sāf\ adj **saf·er; saf·est** 1 : free from harm or risk 2 : affording safety; also : secure from danger or loss 3 : RELIABLE — **safe·ly** adv

²safe n : a container for keeping articles (as valuables) safe

safe–con·duct \-'kän-(ˌ)dəkt\ n : a pass permitting a person to go through enemy lines

¹safe·guard \-ˌgärd\ n : a measure or device for preventing accident

²safeguard vb : to provide a safeguard for : PROTECT

safe·keep·ing \'sāf-'kē-piŋ\ n : a keeping or being kept in safety

safer sex n : SAFE SEX

safe sex n : sexual activity and esp. sexual intercourse in which various measures (as the use of latex condoms) are taken to avoid disease (as AIDS) transmitted by sexual contact

safe·ty \'sāf-tē\ n, pl **safeties** 1 : freedom from danger : SECURITY 2 : a protective device 3 : a football play in which the ball is downed by the offensive team behind its own goal line 4 : a defensive football back in the deepest position — **safety** adj

safety glass n : shatter-resistant material formed of two sheets of glass with a sheet of clear plastic between them

safety match n : a match that ignites only when struck on a special surface

saf·flow·er \'sa-ˌflau̇(-ə)r\ n : a widely grown Old World herb related to the daisies that has large orange or red flower heads yielding a dyestuff and seeds rich in edible oil

saf·fron \'sa-frən\ n : a deep orange powder from the flower of a crocus used to color and flavor foods

sag \'sag\ vb **sagged; sag·ging** 1 : to droop or settle from or as if from pressure 2 : to lose firmness or vigor — **sag** n

sa·ga \'sä-gə\ n [ON] : a narrative of heroic deeds; esp : one recorded in Iceland in the 12th and 13th centuries

sa·ga·cious \sə-'gā-shəs\ adj : of keen mind : SHREWD — **sa·gac·i·ty** \-'ga-sə-tē\ n

sag·a·more \'sa-gə-ˌmȯr\ n : a subordinate No. American Indian chief

¹sage \'sāj\ adj [ME, fr. AF, fr. VL *sapius, fr. L sapere to taste, have good taste, be wise] 1 : WISE, PRUDENT — **sage·ly** adv

²sage n : one who is distinguished for wisdom

³sage n [ME, fr. AF sage, salge, fr. L salvia, fr. salvus healthy; fr. its use as a medicinal herb] 1 : a perennial mint with aromatic leaves used in flavoring; also : its leaves 2 : SAGEBRUSH 3 : a light grayish green

sage·brush \'sāj-ˌbrəsh\ n : any of several low shrubby No. American composite plants; esp : one of the western U.S. with a sagelike odor

Sag·it·tar·i·us \ˌsa-jə-'ter-ē-əs\ n [L, lit.,

archer] **1** : a zodiacal constellation between Scorpio and Capricorn usu. pictured as a centaur archer **2** : the 9th sign of the zodiac in astrology; *also* : one born under this sign

sa·go \'sā-gō\ *n, pl* **sagos** : a dry granulated starch esp. from the pith of various tropical palms (**sago palm**)

sa·gua·ro \sə-'wär-ə, -'gwär-ə, -ō\ *n, pl* **-ros** [MexSp] : a tall columnar usu. sparsely-branched cactus of dry areas of the southwestern U.S. and Mexico that may attain a height of up to 50 feet (16 meters)

said *past and past part of* SAY

¹**sail** \'sāl\ *n* **1** : a piece of fabric by means of which the wind is used to propel a ship **2** : a sailing ship **3** : something resembling a sail **4** : a trip on a sailboat

²**sail** *vb* **1** : to travel on a sailing ship **2** : to pass over in a ship **3** : to manage or direct the course of a ship **4** : to move with ease, grace, or nonchalance

sail·board \'sāl-,bórd\ *n* : a modified surfboard having a mast and sailed by a standing person

sail·boat \-,bōt\ *n* : a boat propelled primarily by sail

sail·cloth \-,klóth\ *n* : a heavy canvas used for sails, tents, or upholstery

sail·fish \-,fish\ *n* : any of a genus of large marine bony fishes with a large dorsal fin that are related to marlins

sail·ing *n* : the sport of handling or riding in a sailboat

sail·or \'sā-lər\ *n* : one that sails; *esp* : a member of a ship's crew

sail·plane \'sāl-,plān\ *n* : a glider designed to rise in an upward air current

saint \'sānt, *before a name* (,)sānt *or* sənt\ *n* **1** : one officially recognized as preeminent for holiness **2** : one of the spirits of the departed in heaven **3** : a holy or godly person — **saint·ed** \'sān-təd\ *adj* — **saint·hood** \-,hüd\ *n*

Saint Ber·nard \-bər-'närd\ *n* : any of a Swiss alpine breed of tall powerful working dogs used esp. formerly in aiding lost travelers

Saint-John's-wort \'sānt-'jänz-,wərt, -,wórt\ *n* **1** : any of a genus of herbs and shrubs with showy yellow flowers **2** : the dried aerial parts of a Saint-John's-wort used esp. in herbal remedies

saint·ly \'sānt-lē\ *adj* : relating to, resembling, or befitting a saint — **saint·li·ness** \-lē-nəs\ *n*

Saint Val·en·tine's Day \-'va-lən-,tīnz-\ *n* : VALENTINE'S DAY

¹**sake** \'sāk\ *n* **1** : END, PURPOSE **2** : personal or social welfare, safety, or well-being

²**sa·ke** *or* **sa·ki** \'sä-kē\ *n* : a Japanese alcoholic beverage of fermented rice

sa·laam \sə-'läm\ *n* [Ar *salām*, lit., peace] **1** : a salutation or ceremonial greeting in the East **2** : an obeisance performed by bowing very low and placing the right palm on the forehead — **salaam** *vb*

sa·la·cious \sə-'lā-shəs\ *adj* **1** : arousing

sexual desire or imagination **2** : LUSTFUL — **sa·la·cious·ly** *adv* — **sa·la·cious·ness** *n*

sal·ad \'sa-ləd\ *n* : a cold dish (as of lettuce, vegetables, fish, eggs, or fruit) served with dressing

sal·a·man·der \'sa-lə-,man-dər\ *n* : any of numerous amphibians that look like lizards but have scaleless usu. smooth moist skin

sa·la·mi \sə-'lä-mē\ *n* [It] : a highly seasoned sausage of pork and beef

sal·a·ry \'sa-lə-rē\ *n, pl* **-ries** [ME *salarie*, fr. AF, fr. L *salarium* pension, salary, fr. neut. of *salarius* of salt, fr. *sal* salt] : payment made at regular intervals for services

sale \'sāl\ *n* **1** : transfer of ownership of property from one person to another in return for money **2** : ready market : DEMAND **3** : AUCTION **4** : a selling of goods at bargain prices — **sal·able** *or* **sale·able** \'sā-lə-bəl\ *adj*

sales·girl \'sālz-,gərl\ *n* : SALESWOMAN

sales·man \-mən\ *n* : a person who sells in a store or to outside customers — **sales·man·ship** *n*

sales·per·son \-,pər-sən\ *n* : a salesman or saleswoman

sales·wom·an \-,wù-mən\ *n* : a woman who sells merchandise

sal·i·cyl·ic acid \,sa-lə-'si-lik-\ *n* : a crystalline organic acid used in making aspirin and other medicinal preparations (as skin lotions)

¹**sa·lient** \'sāl-yənt, 'sā-lē-ənt\ *adj* : jutting forward beyond a line; *also* : PROMINENT
♦ Synonyms CONSPICUOUS, STRIKING, NOTICEABLE

²**salient** *n* : a projecting part in a line of defense

¹**sa·line** \'sā-,lēn, -,līn\ *adj* : consisting of or containing salt : SALTY — **sa·lin·i·ty** \sā-'li-nə-tē, sə-\ *n*

²**saline** *n* **1** : a metallic salt esp. with a purgative action **2** : a saline solution

sa·li·va \sə-'lī-və\ *n* : a liquid secreted into the mouth that helps digestion — **sal·i·vary** \'sa-lə-,ver-ē\ *adj*

sal·i·vate \'sa-lə-,vāt\ *vb* **-vat·ed; -vat·ing** : to produce saliva esp. in excess — **sal·i·va·tion** \,sa-lə-'vā-shən\ *n*

sal·low \'sa-lō\ *adj* : of a yellowish sickly color ⟨a ∼ face⟩

sal·ly \'sa-lē\ *n, pl* **sallies** **1** : a rushing attack on besiegers by troops of a besieged place **2** : a witty remark or retort **3** : a brief excursion — **sally** *vb*

salm·on \'sa-mən\ *n, pl* **salmon** *also* **salmons** **1** : any of several bony fishes with pinkish flesh that are used for food and are related to the trouts **2** : a strong yellowish pink color

sal·mo·nel·la \,sal-mə-'ne-lə\ *n, pl* **-nellae** \-'ne-(,)lē, -,lī\ *or* **-nellas** *or* **-nella** : any of a genus of rod-shaped bacteria that cause various illnesses (as food poisoning)

sa·lon \sə-'län, 'sa-,län, sa-'lōⁿ\ *n* [F] : an elegant drawing room; *also* : a fashionable shop ⟨beauty ∼⟩

sa·loon \sə-'lün\ n, **1** : a large public cabin on a ship **2** : a place where liquors are sold and drunk : BARROOM **3** Brit : SEDAN 2

sal·sa \'sól-sə, 'säl-\ n : a spicy sauce of tomatoes, onions, and hot peppers

¹**salt** \'sólt\ n **1** : a white crystalline substance that consists of sodium and chlorine and is used in seasoning foods **2** : a saltlike cathartic substance (as Epsom salts) **3** : a compound formed usu. by action of an acid on metal **4** : SAILOR — **salt·i·ness** \'sól-tē-nəs\ n — **salty** \'sól-tē\ adj

²**salt** vb : to preserve, season, or feed with salt

³**salt** adj : preserved or treated with salt; also : SALTY

SALT abbr Strategic Arms Limitation Talks

salt away vb : to lay away safely : SAVE

salt·box \'sólt-ˌbäks\ n : a frame dwelling with two stories in front and one behind and a long sloping roof

salt·cel·lar \-ˌse-lər\ n : a small container for holding salt at the table

sal·tine \sól-'tēn\ n : a thin crisp cracker sprinkled with salt

salt lick n : LICK 5

salt·pe·ter \'sólt-'pē-tər\ n [ME salt petre, alter. of salpetre, fr. ML sal petrae, lit., salt of the rock] **1** : POTASSIUM NITRATE **2** : SODIUM NITRATE

salt·wa·ter \-ˌwó-tər, -ˌwä-\ adj : of, relating to, or living in salt water

sa·lu·bri·ous \sə-'lü-brē-əs\ adj : favorable to health ⟨a ~ climate⟩

sal·u·tary \'sal-yə-ˌter-ē\ adj : health-giving; also : BENEFICIAL ⟨~ effects⟩

sal·u·ta·tion \ˌsal-yə-'tā-shən\ n : an expression of greeting, goodwill, or courtesy usu. by word or gesture

sa·lu·ta·to·ri·an \sə-ˌlü-tə-'tór-ē-ən\ n : the student having the 2d highest rank in a graduating class who delivers the salutatory address

sa·lu·ta·to·ry \sə-'lü-tə-ˌtór-ē\ adj : relating to or being the welcoming oration delivered at an academic commencement

¹**sa·lute** \sə-'lüt\ vb **sa·lut·ed; sa·lut·ing** **1** : GREET **2** : to honor by special ceremonies **3** : to show respect to (a superior or officer) by a formal position of hand, rifle, or sword

²**salute** n **1** : GREETING **2** : the formal position assumed in saluting a superior

¹**sal·vage** \'sal-vij\ n **1** : money paid for saving a ship, its cargo, or passengers when the ship is wrecked or in danger **2** : the saving of a ship **3** : the saving of possessions in danger of being lost **4** : things saved from loss or destruction (as by a wreck or fire)

²**salvage** vb **sal·vaged; sal·vag·ing** : to rescue from destruction

sal·va·tion \sal-'vā-shən\ n **1** : the saving of a person from sin or its consequences esp. in the life after death **2** : the saving from danger, difficulty, or evil **3** : something that saves

¹**salve** \'sav, 'säv\ n **1** : a medicinal substance applied to the skin **2** : a soothing influence

²**salve** vb **salved; salv·ing** : EASE, SOOTHE

sal·ver \'sal-vər\ n [F salve, fr. Sp salva sampling of food to detect poison, tray, fr. salvar to save, sample food to detect poison, fr. LL salvare to save, fr. L salvus safe] : a small serving tray

sal·vo \'sal-vō\ n, pl salvos or salvoes : a simultaneous discharge of guns

Sam or **Saml** abbr Samuel

SAM \'sam, ˌes-ˌā-'em\ n [surface-to-air missile] : a guided missile for use against aircraft by ground units

Sa·mar·i·tan \sə-'mer-ə-tən\ n **1** : a native or inhabitant of Samaria **2** : a person who is generous in helping those in distress

sa·mar·i·um \sə-'mer-ē-əm\ n : a silvery-white lustrous rare metallic chemical element

¹**same** \'sām\ adj **1** : being the one referred to : not different **2** : SIMILAR — **same·ness** n

²**same** pron : the same one or ones

³**same** adv : in the same manner

Sa·mi also **Saa·mi** \'sä-mē\ n, pl Sami or Samis also Saami or Saamis : a member of a people of northern Scandinavia, Finland, and the Kola Peninsula of Russia

Sa·mo·an \sə-'mō-ən\ n : a native or inhabitant of Samoa — **Samoan** adj

sa·mo·sa \sə-'mō-sə\ n : a small triangular pastry filled with spiced meat or vegetables and fried

sam·o·var \'sa-mə-ˌvär\ n [Russ, fr. samo-self + varit' to boil] : an urn with a spigot at the base used esp. in Russia to boil water for tea

sam·pan \'sam-ˌpan\ n : a flat-bottomed skiff of eastern Asia usu. propelled by two short oars

¹**sam·ple** \'sam-pəl\ n : a representative piece, item, or set of individuals that shows the quality or nature of the whole from which it was taken : EXAMPLE, SPECIMEN

²**sample** vb **sam·pled; sam·pling** : to judge the quality of by a sample

sam·pler \'sam-plər\ n : a piece of needlework; esp : one testing skill in embroidering

Sam·u·el \'sam-yə-wəl\ n — see BIBLE table

sam·u·rai \'sa-mə-ˌrī, 'sam-yə-\ n, pl samurai : a military retainer of a Japanese feudal lord who adhered to strict principles of honor and duty

san·a·to·ri·um \ˌsa-nə-'tór-ē-əm\ n, pl -ri·ums or -ria \-ē-ə\ **1** : a health resort **2** : an establishment for the care esp. of convalescents or the chronically ill

sanc·ti·fy \'saŋk-tə-ˌfī\ vb -fied; -fy·ing **1** : to make holy : CONSECRATE **2** : to free from sin — **sanc·ti·fi·ca·tion** \ˌsaŋk-tə-fə-'kā-shən\ n

sanc·ti·mo·nious \ˌsaŋk-tə-'mō-nē-əs\ adj : hypocritically pious — **sanc·ti·mo·nious·ly** adv

¹**sanc·tion** \'saŋk-shən\ n **1** : authoritative approval **2** : a measure (as a threat

or fine) designed to enforce a law or standard ⟨economic ∼s⟩

²**sanction** vb : to give approval to : RATIFY
♦ **Synonyms** ENDORSE, ACCREDIT, CERTIFY, APPROVE

sanc·ti·ty \'saŋk-tə-tē\ n, pl **-ties** 1 : GODLINESS 2 : SACREDNESS

sanc·tu·ary \'saŋk-chə‚wer-ē\ n, pl **-ar·ies** 1 : a consecrated place (as the part of a church in which the altar is placed) 2 : a place of refuge ⟨bird ∼⟩

sanc·tum \'saŋk-təm\ n, pl **sanctums** also **sanc·ta** \-tə\ : a private office or study : DEN ⟨an editor's ∼⟩

¹**sand** \'sand\ n : loose particles of hard broken rock — **sandy** adj

²**sand** vb 1 : to cover or fill with sand 2 : to scour, smooth, or polish with an abrasive (as sandpaper) — **sand·er** n

san·dal \'san-dᵊl\ n : a shoe consisting of a sole strapped to the foot; also : a low or open slipper or rubber overshoe

san·dal·wood \-‚wu̇d\ n : the fragrant yellowish heartwood of a parasitic tree of southern Asia that is much used in ornamental carving and cabinetwork; also : the tree

sand·bag \'sand-‚bag\ n : a bag filled with sand and used in fortifications, as ballast, or as a weapon

sand·bank \-‚baŋk\ n : a deposit of sand (as in a bar or shoal)

sand·bar \-‚bär\ n : a ridge of sand formed in water by tides or currents

sand·blast \-‚blast\ vb : to treat with a stream of sand blown (as for cleaning stone) by compressed air — **sand·blast·er** n

sand dollar n : any of numerous flat circular sea urchins living chiefly on sandy bottoms in shallow water

S & H abbr shipping and handling

sand·hog \'sand-‚hȯg, -‚häg\ n : a laborer who builds underwater tunnels

sand·lot \-‚lät\ n : a vacant lot esp. when used for the unorganized sports of children — **sand·lot** adj — **sand·lot·ter** n

sand·man \-‚man\ n : the genie of folklore who makes children sleepy

sand·pa·per \-‚pā-pər\ n : paper with abrasive (as sand) glued on one side used in smoothing and polishing surfaces — **sandpaper** vb

sand·pip·er \-‚pī-pər\ n : any of various shorebirds with a soft-tipped bill longer than that of the related plovers

sand·stone \-‚stōn\ n : rock made of sand united by a natural cement

sand·storm \-‚stȯrm\ n : a windstorm that drives clouds of sand

sand trap n : a hazard on a golf course consisting of a hollow containing sand

¹**sand·wich** \'sand-(‚)wich\ n [after John Montagu, 4th Earl of Sandwich †1792 Eng. diplomat] 1 : two or more slices of bread with a layer (as of meat or cheese) spread between them 2 : something resembling a sandwich

²**sandwich** vb : to squeeze or crowd in

sane \'sān\ adj **san·er**; **san·est** : men-

tally sound and healthy; also : SENSIBLE, RATIONAL — **sane·ly** adv

sang past of SING

sang-froid \sä⁼-'frwä\ n [F sang-froid, lit., cold blood] : self-possession or an imperturbable state esp. under strain

san·gui·nary \'saŋ-gwə-‚ner-ē\ adj : BLOODY ⟨∼ battle⟩

san·guine \'saŋ-gwən\ adj 1 : RUDDY 2 : CHEERFUL, HOPEFUL

sanit abbr sanitary; sanitation

san·i·tar·i·an \‚sa-nə-'ter-ē-ən\ n : a specialist in sanitation and public health

san·i·tar·i·um \‚sa-nə-'ter-ē-əm\ n, pl **-i·ums** or **-ia** \-ē-ə\ : SANATORIUM

san·i·tary \'sa-nə-‚ter-ē\ adj 1 : of or relating to health : HYGIENIC 2 : free from filth or infective matter

sanitary napkin n : a disposable absorbent pad used to absorb uterine flow (as during menstruation)

san·i·ta·tion \‚sa-nə-'tā-shən\ n : the act or process of making sanitary; also : protection of health by maintenance of sanitary conditions

san·i·tize \'sa-nə-‚tīz\ vb **-tized**; **-tiz·ing** 1 : to make sanitary 2 : to make more acceptable by removing unpleasant features

san·i·ty \'sa-nə-tē\ n : soundness of mind

sank past of SINK

sans \'sanz\ prep : WITHOUT

San·skrit \'san-‚skrit\ n : an ancient language that is the classical language of India and of Hinduism — **Sanskrit** adj

San·ta Ana \‚san-tə-'a-nə\ n [Santa Ana Mountains in southern Calif.] : a hot dry wind from the north, northeast, or east in southern California

san·tims \'sän-‚tims\ n, pl **san·ti·mi** \-ti-mē\ — see lats at MONEY table

¹**sap** \'sap\ n 1 : a vital fluid; esp : a watery fluid that circulates through a vascular plant 2 : a foolish gullible person — **sap·less** adj

²**sap** vb **sapped**; **sap·ping** 1 : UNDERMINE 2 : to weaken gradually

sap·id \'sa-pəd\ adj : FLAVORFUL

sa·pi·ent \'sā-pē-ənt, 'sa-\ adj : WISE, DISCERNING — **sa·pi·ence** \-əns\ n

sap·ling \'sa-pliŋ\ n : a young tree

sap·phire \'sa-‚fī(-ə)r\ n : a hard transparent usu. rich blue gem

sap·py \'sa-pē\ adj **sap·pi·er**; **-est** 1 : full of sap 2 : overly sentimental 3 : SILLY, FOOLISH

sap·ro·phyte \'sa-prə-‚fīt\ n : a living thing and esp. a plant living on dead or decaying organic matter — **sap·ro·phyt·ic** \‚sa-prə-'fi-tik\ adj

sap·suck·er \'sap-‚sə-kər\ n : any of a genus of No. American woodpeckers

sap·wood \-‚wu̇d\ n : the younger active and usu. lighter and softer outer layer of wood (as of a tree trunk)

sar·casm \'sär-‚ka-zəm\ n 1 : a cutting or contemptuous remark 2 : ironic criticism or reproach — **sar·cas·tic** \sär-'kas-tik\ adj — **sar·cas·ti·cal·ly** \-ti-k(ə-)lē\ adv

sar·co·ma \sär-'kō-mə\ n, pl **-mas** also

-ma·ta \-mə-tə\ : a malignant tumor esp. of connective tissue, bone, cartilage, or striated muscle

sar·coph·a·gus \sär-'kä-fə-gəs\ n, pl **-gi** \-ˌgī, -ˌjī\ also **-gus·es** [L sarcophagus (lapis) limestone used for coffins, fr. Gk (lithos) sarkophagos, lit., flesh-eating stone, fr. sark-, sarx flesh + phagein to eat] : a large stone coffin

sar·dine \sär-'dēn\ n, pl **sardines** also **sardine** : a young or small fish preserved for use as food

sar·don·ic \sär-'dä-nik\ adj : disdainfully or skeptically humorous : derisively mocking ♦ Synonyms IRONIC, SATIRIC, SARCASTIC — **sar·don·i·cal·ly** \-ni-k(ə-)lē\ adv

sa·ri also **sa·ree** \'sär-ē\ n [Hindi sāṛī] : a garment worn by women in southern Asia that consists of a long cloth draped around the body and head or shoulder

sa·rin \'sär-ən, zä-'rēn\ n : an extremely toxic chemical weapon used as a lethal nerve gas

sa·rong \sə-'rȯŋ, -'räŋ\ n : a loose garment wrapped around the body and worn by men and women of the Malay Archipelago and the Pacific islands

sar·sa·pa·ril·la \ˌsas-pə-'ri-lə, ˌsärs-\ n 1 : the dried roots of a tropical American smilax used esp. for flavoring; also : the plant 2 : a sweetened carbonated beverage flavored with sassafras and an oil from a birch

sar·to·ri·al \sär-'tȯr-ē-əl\ adj : of or relating to a tailor or tailored clothes — **sar·to·ri·al·ly** adv

SASE abbr self-addressed stamped envelope

¹sash \'sash\ n : a broad band worn around the waist or over the shoulder

²sash n, pl **sash** also **sash·es** : a frame for panes of glass in a door or window; also : the movable part of a window

sa·shay \sa-'shā\ vb 1 : WALK, GLIDE, GO 2 : to strut or move about in an ostentatious manner 3 : to proceed in a diagonal or sideways manner

Sask abbr Saskatchewan

Sas·quatch \'sas-ˌkwach, -ˌkwäch\ n [Halkomelem (American Indian language of British Columbia) sésqəc] : a large hairy humanlike creature reported to exist in the northwestern U.S. and western Canada

sas·sa·fras \'sa-sə-ˌfras\ n [Sp sasafrás] : an aromatic No. American tree related to the laurel; also : its carcinogenic dried root bark

sassy \'sa-sē\ adj **sass·i·er; -est** : SAUCY

¹sat past and past part of SIT

²sat abbr 1 satellite 2 saturated

Sat abbr Saturday

Sa·tan \'sā-tᵊn\ n : DEVIL

sa·tang \sə-'täŋ\ n, pl **satang** or **satangs** — see baht at MONEY TABLE

sa·tan·ic \sə-'ta-nik, sā-\ adj 1 : of or characteristic of Satan 2 : extremely malicious or wicked — **sa·tan·i·cal·ly** \-ni-k(ə-)lē\ adv

satch·el \'sa-chəl\ n : SUITCASE

sate \'sāt\ vb **sat·ed; sat·ing** : to satisfy to the full; also : SURFEIT, GLUT

sa·teen \sa-'tēn, sə-\ n : a cotton cloth finished to resemble satin

sat·el·lite \'sa-tə-ˌlīt\ n [MF, fr. L satelles attendant] 1 : an obsequious follower of a distinguished person : TOADY 2 : a celestial body that orbits a larger body 3 : a manufactured object that orbits a celestial body

satellite dish n : a microwave dish for receiving usu. television transmissions from an orbiting satellite

sa·ti·ate \'sā-shē-ˌāt\ vb **-at·ed; -at·ing** : to satisfy fully or to excess

sa·ti·ety \sə-'tī-ə-tē\ n : fullness to the point of excess

sat·in \'sa-tᵊn\ n : a fabric (as of silk) with a glossy surface — **sat·iny** adj

sat·in·wood \'sa-tᵊn-ˌwu̇d\ n : a hard yellowish brown wood of satiny luster; also : a tree yielding this wood

sat·ire \'sa-ˌtī(-ə)r\ n : biting wit, irony, or sarcasm used to expose vice or folly; also : a literary work having these qualities — **sa·tir·ic** \sə-'tir-ik\ or **sa·tir·i·cal** \-i-kəl\ adj — **sa·tir·i·cal·ly** adv — **sat·i·rist** \'sa-tə-rist\ n — **sat·i·rize** \-tə-ˌrīz\ vb

sat·is·fac·tion \ˌsa-təs-'fak-shən\ n 1 : payment through penance of punishment incurred by sin 2 : CONTENTMENT, GRATIFICATION 3 : reparation for an insult 4 : settlement of a claim

sat·is·fac·to·ry \-'fak-tə-rē\ adj : giving satisfaction : ADEQUATE — **sat·is·fac·to·ri·ly** \-'fak-tə-rə-lē\ adv

sat·is·fy \'sa-təs-ˌfī\ vb **-fied; -fy·ing** 1 : to answer or discharge (a claim) in full 2 : to make happy : GRATIFY 3 : to pay what is due to 4 : CONVINCE 5 : to meet the requirements of — **sat·is·fy·ing·ly** adv

sa·trap \'sā-ˌtrap, 'sa-\ n [ME, fr. L satrapes, fr. Gk satrapēs, fr. OPers khshathrapāvan, lit., protector of the dominion] : a petty prince : a subordinate ruler

sat·u·rate \'sa-chə-ˌrāt\ vb **-rat·ed; -rat·ing** 1 : to soak thoroughly 2 : to treat or charge with something to the point where no more can be absorbed, dissolved, or retained — **sat·u·ra·ble** \'sa-chə-rə-bəl\ adj — **sat·u·ra·tion** \ˌsa-chə-'rā-shən\ n

saturated adj 1 : full of moisture 2 : having no double or triple bonds between carbon atoms ⟨~ fats⟩

Sat·ur·day \'sa-tər-dē, -ˌdā\ n : the 7th day of the week

Saturday night special n : a cheap easily concealed handgun

Sat·urn \'sa-tərn\ n : the planet 6th in order from the sun

sat·ur·nine \'sa-tər-ˌnīn\ adj : SULLEN, SARDONIC

sa·tyr \'sā-tər\ n 1 often cap : a woodland deity in Greek mythology having certain characteristics of a horse or goat 2 : a lecherous man

¹sauce \'sȯs, 3 usu 'sas\ n 1 : a fluid dressing or topping for food   **2** : stewed fruit   **3** : IMPUDENCE

²**sauce** \'sȯs, *2 usu* 'sas\ *vb* **sauced; sauc·ing** **1** : to put sauce on; *also* : to add zest to   **2** : to be impudent to

sauce·pan \'sȯs-ˌpan\ *n* : a small deep cooking pan with a handle

sau·cer \'sȯ-sər\ *n* : a rounded shallow dish for use under a cup

saucy \'sa-sē, 'sȯ-\ *adj* **sauc·i·er; -est** : IMPUDENT, PERT — **sauc·i·ly** \-sə-lē\ *adv* — **sauc·i·ness** \-sē-nəs\ *n*

Sau·di \'saů-dē, 'sȯ-; sä-'ü-dē\ *n* : SAUDI ARABIAN — **Saudi** *adj*

Saudi Arabian *n* : a native or inhabitant of Saudi Arabia — **Saudi Arabian** *adj*

sau·er·kraut \'saů-(ə)r-ˌkraůt\ *n* [G, fr. *sauer* sour + *Kraut* greens] : finely cut cabbage fermented in brine

Sauk \'sȯk\ *or* **Sac** \'sak, 'sȯk\ *n, pl* **Sauk** *or* **Sauks** *or* **Sac** *or* **Sacs** : a member of an American Indian people formerly living in what is now Wisconsin

sau·na \'sȯ-nə, 'saů-nə\ *n* **1** : a Finnish steam bath in which the steam is provided by water thrown on hot stones   **2** : a dry heat bath; *also* : a room or cabinet used for such a bath

saun·ter \'sȯn-tər, 'sän-\ *vb* : STROLL

sau·ro·pod \'sȯr-ə-ˌpäd\ *n* : any of a suborder of plant-eating dinosaurs (as a brontosaurus) with a long neck and tail and a small head — **sauropod** *adj*

sau·sage \'sȯ-sij\ *n* [ME *sausige*, fr. AF *sauseche*, fr. LL *salsicia*, fr. L *salsus* salted] : minced and highly seasoned meat (as pork) usu. enclosed in a tubular casing

S Aust *abbr* South Australia

sau·té \sȯ-'tā, sō-\ *vb* **sau·téed** *or* **sau·téd; sau·té·ing** [F] : to fry lightly in a little fat — **sauté** *n*

sau·terne \sō-'tərn, sȯ-\ *n, often cap* : a usu. semisweet American white wine

¹**sav·age** \'sa-vij\ *adj* [ME, fr. AF *salvage*, *savage*, LL *salvaticus*, alter. of L *silvaticus* of the woods, wild, fr. *silva* forest] **1** : WILD, UNTAMED   **2** : UNCIVILIZED, BARBAROUS   **3** : CRUEL, FIERCE — **sav·age·ly** *adv* — **sav·age·ness** *n* — **sav·age·ry** \-rē\ *n*

²**savage** *n* **1** : a member of a primitive human society   **2** : a rude, unmannerly, or brutal person

sa·van·na *or* **sa·van·nah** \sə-'va-nə\ *n* [Sp *zavana*] : grassland containing scattered trees

sa·vant \sa-'vänt, sə-, 'sa-vənt\ *n* : a learned person : SCHOLAR

¹**save** \'sāv\ *vb* **saved; sav·ing** **1** : to redeem from sin   **2** : to rescue from danger   **3** : to preserve or guard from destruction or loss; *also* : to store (data) in a computer or on a storage device   **4** : to put aside as a store or reserve — **sav·er** *n*

²**save** *n* : a play that prevents an opponent from scoring or winning

³**save** *prep* : EXCEPT

⁴**save** *conj* : BUT

savings and loan association *n* : a cooperative association that holds savings of members in the form of dividend-bear-

ing shares and that invests chiefly in mortgage loans

savings bank *n* : a bank that holds funds of individual depositors in interest-bearing accounts and makes long-term investments (as mortgage loans)

savings bond *n* : a registered U.S. bond issued in denominations of $50 to $10,000

sav·ior *or* **sav·iour** \'sāv-yər\ *n* **1** : one who saves   **2** *cap* : Jesus Christ

sa·voir faire \ˌsav-ˌwär-'fer\ *n* [F *savoir-faire*, lit., knowing how to do] : sureness in social behavior

¹**sa·vor** *also* **sa·vour** \'sā-vər\ *n* **1** : the taste and odor of something   **2** : a special flavor or quality — **sa·vory** *adj*

²**savor** *also* **savour** *vb* **1** : to have a specified taste, smell, or quality   **2** : to taste with pleasure

sa·vo·ry \'sā-və-rē\ *n, pl* **-ries** : either of two aromatic mints used in cooking

¹**sav·vy** \'sa-vē\ *vb* **sav·vied; sav·vy·ing** : UNDERSTAND, COMPREHEND

²**savvy** *n* : practical know-how ⟨political ∼⟩ — **savvy** *adj*

¹**saw** *past of* SEE

²**saw** \'sȯ\ *n* : a cutting tool with a blade having a line of teeth along its edge

³**saw** *vb* **sawed** \'sȯd\; **sawed** *or* **sawn** \'sȯn\; **saw·ing** : to cut or shape with or as if with a saw

⁴**saw** *n* : a common saying : MAXIM

saw·dust \'sȯ-(ˌ)dəst\ *n* : fine particles made by a saw in cutting

saw·fly \-ˌflī\ *n* : any of numerous insects belonging to the same order as bees and wasps and including many whose larvae are plant-feeding pests

saw·horse \-ˌhȯrs\ *n* : a rack on which wood is rested while being sawed by hand

saw·mill \-ˌmil\ *n* : a mill for sawing logs

saw palmetto *n* **1** : any of several shrubby palms with spiny-toothed petioles   **2** : the fruit of a saw palmetto used esp. in herbal remedies

saw·yer \'sȯ-yər\ *n* : a person who saws timber

sax \'saks\ *n* : SAXOPHONE

sax·i·frage \'sak-sə-frij, -ˌfräj\ *n* [ME, fr. AF, fr. LL *saxifraga*, fr. L, fem. of *saxifragus*, breaking rocks] : any of a genus of plants with showy flowers and usu. with leaves growing in tufts close to the ground

sax·o·phone \'sak-sə-ˌfōn\ *n* : a musical instrument having a conical metal tube with a reed mouthpiece and finger keys — **sax·o·phon·ist** \-ˌfō-nist\ *n*

¹**say** \'sā\ *vb* **said** \'sed\; **say·ing; says** \'sez\ **1** : to express in words ⟨∼ what you mean⟩   **2** : to state as opinion or belief   **3** : PRONOUNCE; *also* : RECITE, REPEAT ⟨∼ your prayers⟩   **4** : INDICATE ⟨the clock ∼s noon⟩

²**say** *n, pl* **says** \'sāz\ **1** : an expression of opinion   **2** : power of decision

say·ing *n* : a commonly repeated statement

say-so \'sā-(ˌ)sō\ *n* : an esp. authoritative assertion or decision; *also* : the right to decide

sb *abbr* substantive

Sb *symbol* [L *stibium*] antimony

SB *abbr* [NL *scientiae baccalaureus*] bachelor of science

SBA *abbr* Small Business Administration

sc *abbr* **1** scene **2** science

Sc *symbol* scandium

SC *abbr* **1** South Carolina **2** supreme court

¹**scab** \'skab\ *n* **1** : scabies of domestic animals **2** : a crust of hardened blood forming over a wound **3** : a worker who replaces a striker or works under conditions not authorized by a union **4** : any of various bacterial or fungus plant diseases marked by crusted spots on stems or leaves — **scab·by** *adj*

²**scab** *vb* **scabbed; scab·bing 1** : to become covered with a scab **2** : to work as a scab

scab·bard \'ska-bərd\ *n* : a sheath for the blade of a weapon (as a sword)

sca·bies \'skā-bēz\ *n* [L] : contagious itch or mange caused by mites living as parasites under the skin

sca·brous \'ska-brəs, 'skā-\ *adj* **1** : DIFFICULT, KNOTTY **2** : rough to the touch : SCALY, SCURFY ⟨a ~ leaf⟩ **3** : dealing with suggestive, indecent, or scandalous themes; *also* : SQUALID

scad \'skad\ *n* : a large number or quantity — usu. used in pl.

scaf·fold \'ska-fəld, -,fōld\ *n* **1** : a raised platform for workers to sit or stand on **2** : a platform on which a criminal is executed (as by hanging)

scaf·fold·ing *n* : a system of scaffolds; *also* : materials for scaffolds

scal·a·wag *or* **scal·ly·wag** \'ska-li-,wag\ *n* : RASCAL

¹**scald** \'skȯld\ *vb* **1** : to burn with or as if with hot liquid or steam **2** : to heat to just below the boiling point

²**scald** *n* : a burn caused by scalding

¹**scale** \'skāl\ *n* **1** : either pan of a balance **2** : BALANCE — usu. used in pl. **3** : a weighing instrument

²**scale** *vb* **scaled; scal·ing** : WEIGH

³**scale** *n* **1** : one of the small thin plates that cover the body esp. of a fish or reptile **2** : a thin plate or flake **3** : a thin coating, layer, or incrustation **4** : SCALE INSECT — **scaled** \'skāld\ *adj* — **scale·less** \'skāl-ləs\ *adj* — **scaly** *adj*

⁴**scale** *vb* **scaled; scal·ing** : to strip of scales

⁵**scale** *n* [ME, fr. LL *scala* ladder, staircase, fr. L *scalae*, pl., stairs, rungs, ladder] **1** : something divided into regular spaces as a help in drawing or measuring **2** : a graduated series **3** : the size of a sample (as a model) in proportion to the size of the actual thing **4** : a standard of estimation or judgment **5** : a series of musical tones going up or down in pitch according to a specified scheme

⁶**scale** *vb* **scaled; scal·ing 1** : to climb by or as if by a ladder **2** : to arrange in a graded series

scale insect *n* : any of numerous small insects with wingless scale-covered females that are related to aphids and feed on and are often pests of plants

scale-pan \'skāl-,pan\ *n* : ¹SCALE 1

scal·lion \'skal-yən\ *n* [ultim. fr. L *ascalonia (caepa)* onion of Ascalon (seaport in Palestine)] : an onion without an enlarged bulb

¹**scal·lop** \'skä-ləp, 'ska-\ *n* **1** : any of numerous marine bivalve mollusks with radially ridged shells; *also* : a large edible muscle of this mollusk **2** : one of a continuous series of rounded projections forming an edge

²**scallop** *vb* **1** : to bake in a casserole ⟨~ed potatoes⟩ **2** : to shape, cut, or finish in scallops ⟨~ed edges⟩

¹**scalp** \'skalp\ *n* : the part of the skin and flesh of the head usu. covered with hair

²**scalp** *vb* **1** : to remove the scalp from **2** : to resell at greatly increased prices ⟨~ tickets⟩ — **scalp·er** *n*

scal·pel \'skal-pəl\ *n* : a small straight knife with a thin blade used esp. in surgery

scam \'skam\ *n* : a fraudulent or deceptive act or operation

scamp \'skamp\ *n* : RASCAL

scam·per \'skam-pər\ *vb* : to run nimbly and playfully — **scamper** *n*

scam·pi \'skam-pē\ *n, pl* **scampi** [It] : a usu. large shrimp; *also* : large shrimp prepared with a garlic-flavored sauce

¹**scan** \'skan\ *vb* **scanned; scan·ning 1** : to read (verses) so as to show metrical structure **2** : to examine closely **3** : to input or examine systematically in order to obtain data esp. for display or storage **4** : to make a scan of (as the human body) — **scan·ner** *n*

²**scan** *n* **1** : the act or process of scanning **2** : a picture of the distribution of radioactive material in something; *also* : an image of a bodily part produced (as by computer) by combining radiographic data obtained from several angles or sections

Scand *abbr* Scandinavia

scan·dal \'skan-dᵊl\ *n* [ME, fr. LL *scandalum* stumbling block, offense, fr. Gk *skandalon*] **1** : DISGRACE, DISHONOR **2** : malicious gossip : SLANDER — **scandal·ize** *vb* — **scan·dal·ous** *adj* — **scandal·ous·ly** *adv*

scan·dal·mon·ger \-,mən-gər, -,mäŋ-\ *n* : a person who circulates scandal

Scan·di·na·vian \,skan-də-'nā-vē-ən\ *n* : a native or inhabitant of Scandinavia — **Scandinavian** *adj*

scan·di·um \'skan-dē-əm\ *n* : a silvery-white metallic chemical element

scan·ner \'ska-nər\ *n* **1** : a radio receiver that sequentially scans a range of frequencies for a signal **2** : a device that scans an image or document esp. for use or storage on a computer

¹**scant** \'skant\ *adj* **1** : barely sufficient **2** : having scarcely enough ✦ *Synonyms* SCANTY, SKIMPY, MEAGER, SPARSE, EXIGUOUS

²**scant** *vb* **1** : SKIMP **2** : STINT

scant·ling \'skant-liŋ\ *n* : a small piece of lumber (as an upright in a house)

scanty \'skan-tē\ *adj* **scant·i·er; -est** : barely sufficient : SCANT — **scant·i·ly** \'skan-tə-lē\ *adv* — **scant·i·ness** \-tē-nəs\ *n*

scape·goat \'skāp-ˌgōt\ *n* : one that bears the blame for others

scape·grace \-ˌgrās\ *n* [*scape* (escape)] : an incorrigible rascal

scap·u·la \'ska-pyə-lə\ *n, pl* **-lae** \-ˌlē\ *or* **-las** [L] : SHOULDER BLADE

scap·u·lar \-lər\ *n* : a pair of small cloth squares worn on the breast and back under the clothing esp. for religious purposes

scar \'skär\ *n* : a mark left after injured tissue has healed — **scar** *vb*

scar·ab \'ska-rəb\ *n* [MF *scarabee*, fr. L *scarabaeus*] : any of a family of large stout beetles; *also* : an ornament (as a gem) representing such a beetle

scarce \'skers\ *adj* **scarc·er; scarc·est** **1** : deficient in quantity or number : not plentiful **2** : intentionally absent ⟨made himself ∼ at inspection time⟩ — **scar·ci·ty** \'sker-sə-tē\ *n*

scarce·ly \-lē\ *adv* **1** : BARELY **2** : almost not **3** : very probably not

¹scare \'sker\ *vb* **scared; scar·ing** : FRIGHTEN, STARTLE

²scare *n* : FRIGHT — **scary** *adj*

scare·crow \'sker-ˌkrō\ *n* : a crude figure set up to scare birds away from crops

¹scarf \'skärf\ *n, pl* **scarves** \'skärvz\ *or* **scarfs** **1** : a broad band (as of cloth) worn about the shoulders, around the neck, over the head, or about the waist **2** : a long narrow cloth cover for a table or dresser top

²scarf *vb* [alter. of earlier *scoff* eat greedily] : to eat greedily

scar·i·fy \'sker-ə-ˌfī\ *vb* **-fied; -fy·ing** **1** : to make scratches or small cuts in ⟨∼ skin for vaccination⟩ ⟨∼ seeds to help them germinate⟩ **2** : to lacerate the feelings of **3** : to break up and loosen the surface of (as a road) — **scar·i·fi·ca·tion** \ˌskar-ə-fə-ˈkā-shən\ *n*

scar·let \'skär-lət\ *n* : a bright red color — **scarlet** *adj*

scarlet fever *n* : an acute contagious disease marked by fever, sore throat, and red rash and caused by certain streptococci

scarp \'skärp\ *n* : a line of cliffs produced by faulting or erosion

scath·ing \'skā-thiŋ\ *adj* : bitterly severe ⟨a ∼ condemnation⟩

scat·o·log·i·cal \ˌska-tə-ˈlä-ji-kəl\ *adj* : concerned with obscene matters

scat·ter \'ska-tər\ *vb* **1** : to distribute or strew about irregularly **2** : DISPERSE

scat·ter·brain \'ska-tər-ˌbrān\ *n* : a silly careless person — **scat·ter·brained** \-ˌbrānd\ *adj*

scav·enge \'ska-vənj\ *vb* **scav·enged; scav·eng·ing** : to work or function as a scavenger

scav·en·ger \'ska-vən-jər\ *n* [alter. of earlier *scavager*, fr. AF *scawageour* collector of scavage (duty imposed on nonresident street merchants), fr. *skawage* scavage, fr. MF dial. (Flanders) *escauver* to inspect,

fr. MD *scouwen*] : a person or animal that collects, eats, or disposes of refuse or waste

sce·nar·io \sə-ˈner-ē-ˌō\ *n, pl* **-i·os** : the plot or outline of a dramatic work; *also* : an account of a possible action

scene \'sēn\ *n* [MF, stage, fr. L *scena*, *scaena* stage, scene, prob. fr. Etruscan, fr. Gk *skēnē* temporary shelter, tent, building forming the background for a dramatic performance, stage] **1** : a division of one act of a play **2** : a single situation or sequence in a play or motion picture **3** : a stage setting **4** : VIEW, PROSPECT **5** : the place of an occurrence or action **6** : a display of strong feeling and esp. anger **7** : a sphere of activity ⟨the fashion ∼⟩ — **sce·nic** \'sē-nik\ *adj*

scen·ery \'sē-nə-rē\ *n, pl* **-er·ies** **1** : the painted scenes or hangings and accessories used on a theater stage **2** : a picturesque view or landscape

¹scent \'sent\ *n* **1** : ODOR, SMELL **2** : sense of smell **3** : course of pursuit : TRACK **4** : PERFUME **2** — **scent·ed** \'sen-təd\ *adj* — **scent·less** *adj*

²scent *vb* **1** : SMELL **2** : to imbue or fill with odor

scep·ter \'sep-tər\ *n* : a staff borne by a sovereign as an emblem of authority

sceptic *var of* SKEPTIC

scep·tre *Brit var of* SCEPTER

sch *abbr* school

¹sched·ule \'ske-jül, *esp Brit* 'she-dyül\ *n* **1** : a list of items or details **2** : TIMETABLE

²schedule *vb* **sched·uled; sched·ul·ing** **1** : to appoint, assign, or designate for a fixed time **2** : to make a schedule of; *also* : to enter on a schedule

sche·ma \'skē-mə\ *n, pl* **sche·ma·ta** \-mə-tə\ *also* **schemas** : a diagrammatic presentation or plan : OUTLINE

sche·mat·ic \ski-ˈma-tik\ *adj* : of or relating to a scheme or diagram : DIAGRAMMATIC — **schematic** *n* — **sche·mat·i·cal·ly** \-ti-k(ə-)lē\ *adv*

¹scheme \'skēm\ *n* **1** : a plan for doing something; *esp* : a crafty plot **2** : a systematic design ⟨a color ∼⟩

²scheme *vb* **schemed; schem·ing** : to form a plot : INTRIGUE — **schem·er** *n*

schil·ling \'shi-liŋ\ *n* : a former basic monetary unit of Austria

schism \'si-zəm, 'ski-\ *n* **1** : DIVISION, SPLIT; *also* : DISCORD, DISSENSION **2** : a formal division in or separation from a religious body

schis·mat·ic \siz-ˈma-tik, ski-\ *n* : one who creates or takes part in schism — **schismatic** *adj*

schist \'shist\ *n* : a metamorphic crystalline rock

schizo·phre·nia \ˌskit-sə-ˈfrē-nē-ə\ *n* [NL, fr. Gk *schizein* to split + *phrēn* diaphragm, mind] : a psychotic mental illness that is characterized by a distorted view of the real world, by a greatly reduced ability to carry out one's daily tasks, and by abnormal ways of thinking, feeling, perceiving, and behaving — **schizoid** \'skit-ˌsóid\ *adj or n* — **schizo·phren·ic** \ˌskit-sə-ˈfre-nik\ *adj or n*

schle·miel *also* **shle·miel** \shlə-'mēl\ *n* : an unlucky bungler : CHUMP

schlep *or* **schlepp** \'shlep\ *vb* [Yiddish *shlepn*] **1** : DRAG, HAUL **2** : to move slowly or awkwardly

schlock \'shläk\ *or* **schlocky** \'shlä-kē\ *adj* : of low quality or value — **schlock** *n*

schlub *also* **shlub** \'shləb\ *n* [Yiddish *zhlob, zhlub* yokel, boor] *slang* : a stupid, ineffectual, or unattractive person

schmaltz *also* **schmalz** \'shmölts, 'shmälts\ *n* [Yiddish *shmalts*, lit., rendered fat] : sentimental or florid music or art — **schmaltzy** *adj*

schmooze *or* **shmooze** \'shmüz\ *vb* : to chat informally esp. to gain favor — **schmooze** *n*

schnapps \'shnäps\ *n, pl* **schnapps** : a liquor (as gin) of high alcoholic content

schnau·zer \'shnaủ-zər, 'shnaủt-sər\ *n* [G, fr. *Schnauze* snout] : a dog of any of three breeds that are characterized by a wiry coat, long head, pointed ears, heavy eyebrows, and long hair on the muzzle

schol·ar \'skä-lər\ *n* **1** : STUDENT, PUPIL **2** : a learned person : SAVANT — **schol·ar·ly** *adj*

schol·ar·ship \-,ship\ *n* **1** : the qualities or learning of a scholar **2** : money awarded to a student to help pay for further education

scho·las·tic \skə-'las-tik\ *adj* : of or relating to schools, scholars, or scholarship

¹school \'skül\ *n* **1** : an institution for teaching and learning; *also* : the pupils in attendance **2** : a body of persons of like opinions or beliefs ⟨the radical ∼⟩

²school *vb* : TEACH, TRAIN, DRILL

³school *n* : a large number of one kind of water animal swimming and feeding together

school·boy \-,bȯi\ *n* : a boy attending school

school·fel·low \-,fe-lō\ *n* : SCHOOLMATE

school·girl \-,gərl\ *n* : a girl attending school

school·house \-,haủs\ *n* : a building used as a school

school·marm \-,märm\ *or* **school·ma'am** \-,mäm, -,mam\ *n* **1** : a woman who is a schoolteacher **2** : a person who exhibits characteristics popularly attributed to schoolteachers

school·mas·ter \-,mas-tər\ *n* : a man who is a schoolteacher

school·mate \-,māt\ *n* : a school companion

school·mis·tress \-,mis-trəs\ *n* : a woman who is a schoolteacher

school·room \-,rüm, -,rủm\ *n* : CLASSROOM

school·teach·er \-,tē-chər\ *n* : one who teaches in a school

schoo·ner \'skü-nər\ *n* : a fore-and-aft rigged sailing ship

schtick *var of* SHTICK

schuss \'shủs, 'shüs\ *vb* [G *Schuss*, n., lit., shot] : to ski down a slope at high speed — **schuss** *n*

sci *abbr* science; scientific

sci·at·i·ca \sī-'a-ti-kə\ *n* : pain in the region of the hips or along the course of the nerve at the back of the thigh

sci·ence \'sī-əns\ *n* [ME, fr. AF, fr. L *scientia*, fr. *scient-, sciens* having knowledge, fr. prp. of *scire* to know] **1** : an area of knowledge that is an object of study; *esp* : NATURAL SCIENCE **2** : knowledge covering general truths or the operation of general laws especially as obtained and tested through the scientific method — **sci·en·tif·ic** \sī-ən-'ti-fik\ *adj* — **sci·en·tif·i·cal·ly** \-fi-k(ə-)lē\ *adv* — **sci·en·tist** \'sī-ən-tist\ *n*

science fiction *n* : fiction dealing principally with the impact of actual or imagined science on society or individuals

scientific method *n* : the rules and methods for the pursuit of knowledge involving the finding and stating of a problem, the collection of facts through observation and experiment, and the making and testing of ideas that need to be proven right or wrong

scim·i·tar \'si-mə-tər\ *n* : a curved sword used chiefly by Arabs and Turks

scin·til·la \sin-'ti-lə\ *n* : SPARK, TRACE

scin·til·late \'sin-tə-,lāt\ *vb* **-lat·ed; -lat·ing** : SPARKLE, GLEAM — **scin·til·la·tion** \,sin-tə-'lā-shən\ *n*

sci·on \'sī-ən\ *n* **1** : a shoot of a plant joined to a stock in grafting **2** : DESCENDANT

scis·sors \'si-zərz\ *n pl* : a cutting instrument like shears but usu. smaller

scissors kick *n* : a swimming kick in which the legs move like scissors

scle·ro·der·ma \,skler-ə-'dər-mə\ *n* : a chronic disease characterized by the usu. progressive hardening and thickening of the skin

scle·ro·sis \sklə-'rō-səs\ *n* : abnormal hardening of tissue (as of an artery); *also* : a disease characterized by this — **scle·rot·ic** \-'rä-tik\ *adj*

scoff \'skäf\ *vb* : MOCK, JEER — **scoff·er** *n*

scoff·law \-,lȯ\ *n* : a contemptuous law violator

¹scold \'skōld\ *n* : a person who scolds

²scold *vb* : to censure severely or angrily

sconce \'skäns\ *n* : a candlestick or an electric light fixture fastened to a wall

scone \'skōn, 'skän\ *n* : a biscuit (as of oatmeal) baked on a griddle

¹scoop \'sküp\ *n* **1** : a large shovel; *also* : a utensil with a shovellike or rounded end **2** : the amount contained by a scoop **3** : an act of scooping **4** : information of immediate interest

²scoop *vb* **1** : to take out or up or empty with or as if with a scoop **2** : to make hollow **3** : to report a news item in advance of

scoot \'sküt\ *vb* : to move swiftly

scoot·er \'skü-tər\ *n* **1** : a child's vehicle consisting of a narrow board mounted between two wheels tandem with an upright steering handle attached to the front wheel **2** : MOTOR SCOOTER

¹scope \'skōp\ *n* [It *scopo* purpose, goal,

fr. Gk *skopos*] **1** : space or opportunity for action or thought **2** : extent covered : RANGE

²scope *n* : an instrument (as a microscope or telescope) for viewing

scorch \'skȯrch\ *vb* : to burn the surface of; *also* : to dry or shrivel with heat ⟨~ed lawns⟩

¹score \'skȯr\ *n, pl* **scores** **1** *or pl* **score** : TWENTY **2** : CUT, SCRATCH, SLASH **3** : a record of points made (as in a game) **4** : DEBT **5** : REASON, GROUND **6** : the music of a composition or arrangement with different parts indicated **7** : success in obtaining something (as drugs) esp. illegally

²score *vb* **scored; scor·ing** **1** : RECORD **2** : to keep score in a game **3** : to mark with lines, grooves, scratches, or notches **4** : to gain or tally in or as if in a game ⟨*scored* a point⟩ **5** : to assign a grade or score to ⟨~ the tests⟩ **6** : to compose a score for **7** : SUCCEED **8** : ACQUIRE ⟨*scored* tickets to the game⟩ — **score·less** *adj* — **scor·er** *n*

¹scorn \'skȯrn\ *n* : an emotion involving both anger and disgust : CONTEMPT — **scorn·ful** \-fəl\ *adj* — **scorn·ful·ly** *adv*

²scorn *vb* : to hold in contempt : DISDAIN — **scorn·er** *n*

Scor·pio \'skȯr-pē-ˌō\ *n* [L, lit., scorpion] **1** : a zodiacal constellation between Libra and Sagittarius usu. pictured as a scorpion **2** : the 8th sign of the zodiac in astrology; *also* : one born under this sign

scor·pi·on \'skȯr-pē-ən\ *n* : any of an order of arthropods related to the spiders that have a poisonous stinger at the tip of a long jointed tail

¹Scot \'skät\ *n* : a native or inhabitant of Scotland

²Scot *abbr* Scotland; Scottish

Scotch \'skäch\ *n* **1** : SCOTS **2** Scotch *pl* : the people of Scotland **3** : a whiskey distilled in Scotland esp. from malted barley — **Scotch** *adj* — **Scotch·man** \-mən\ *n* — **Scotch·wom·an** \-ˌwu̇-mən\ *n*

Scotch bonnet *n* : a small roundish very hot chili pepper esp. of the Caribbean

Scotch pine *n* : a pine that is naturalized in the U.S. from northern Europe and Asia and is a valuable timber tree

Scotch terrier *n* : SCOTTISH TERRIER

scot–free \'skät-'frē\ *adj* : free from obligation, harm, or penalty

Scots \'skäts\ *n* : the English language of Scotland

Scots·man \'skäts-mən\ *n* : SCOT

Scots·wom·an \-ˌwu̇-mən\ *n* : a woman who is a Scot

Scot·tie \'skä-tē\ *n* : SCOTTISH TERRIER

Scot·tish \'skä-tish\ *adj* : of, relating to, or characteristic of Scotland, Scots, or the Scots

Scottish terrier *n* : any of an old Scottish breed of terrier with short legs, a long head with small erect ears, a broad deep chest, and a thick rough coat

scoun·drel \'skau̇n-drəl\ *n* : a disreputable person : VILLAIN

¹scour \'skau̇(-ə)r\ *vb* **1** : to rub (as with a gritty substance) in order to clean **2** : to cleanse by or as if by rubbing

²scour *vb* **1** : to move rapidly through : RUSH **2** : to examine thoroughly

¹scourge \'skərj\ *n* **1** : LASH, WHIP **2** : PUNISHMENT; *also* : a cause of affliction (as a plague)

²scourge *vb* **scourged; scourg·ing** **1** : LASH, FLOG **2** : to punish severely

¹scout \'skau̇t\ *vb* [ME, fr. AF *escuter* to listen, fr. L *auscultare*] **1** : to look around : RECONNOITER **2** : to inspect or observe to get information

²scout *n* **1** : a person sent out to get information; *also* : a soldier, airplane, or ship sent out to reconnoiter **2** : BOY SCOUT **3** : GIRL SCOUT — **scout·mas·ter** \-ˌmas-tər\ *n*

³scout *vb* : SCORN, SCOFF

scow \'skau̇\ *n* : a large flat-bottomed boat with square ends

scowl \'skau̇(-ə)l\ *vb* : to make a frowning expression of displeasure — **scowl** *n*

SCPO *abbr* senior chief petty officer

scrab·ble \'skra-bəl\ *vb* **scrab·bled; scrab·bling** **1** : SCRAPE, SCRATCH **2** : CLAMBER, SCRAMBLE **3** : to work hard and long **4** : SCRIBBLE — **scrabble** *n* — **scrab·bler** *n*

scrag·gly \'skra-glē\ *adj* : IRREGULAR; *also* : RAGGED, UNKEMPT ⟨a ~ beard⟩

scram \'skram\ *vb* **scrammed; scram·ming** : to go away at once

scram·ble \'skram-bəl\ *vb* **scram·bled; scram·bling** **1** : to clamber clumsily around **2** : to struggle for or as if for possession of something **3** : to spread irregularly **4** : to mix together **5** : to cook (eggs) by stirring during frying — **scramble** *n*

¹scrap \'skrap\ *n* **1** : FRAGMENT, PIECE **2** : discarded material : REFUSE

²scrap *vb* **scrapped; scrap·ping** **1** : to make into scrap ⟨~ a battleship⟩ **2** : to get rid of as useless ⟨*scrapped* the plans⟩

³scrap *n* : FIGHT

⁴scrap *vb* **scrapped; scrap·ping** : FIGHT, QUARREL — **scrap·per** *n*

scrap·book \'skrap-ˌbu̇k\ *n* : a blank book in which mementos are kept

¹scrape \'skrāp\ *vb* **scraped; scrap·ing** **1** : to remove by drawing a knife over; *also* : to clean or smooth by rubbing off the covering **2** : to damage or injure the surface of by contact with something rough **3** : to draw across a surface with a grating sound **4** : to get together (money) by strict economy **5** : to get along with difficulty ⟨barely *scraping* by on her income⟩ — **scrap·er** *n*

²scrape *n* **1** : the act or the effect of scraping **2** : a bow accompanied by a drawing back of the foot **3** : an unpleasant predicament

scra·pie \'skrā-pē\ *n* : a usu. fatal degenerative disease of the brain esp. of sheep that is related to mad cow disease

¹scrap·py \'skra-pē\ *adj* **scrap·pi·er; -est** : DISCONNECTED, FRAGMENTARY

²scrappy *adj* **scrap·pi·er; -est** **1** : QUAR-

RELSOME 2 : having an aggressive and determined spirit ⟨a ~ competitor⟩

¹**scratch** \'skrach\ vb 1 : to scrape, dig, or rub with or as if with claws or nails ⟨a dog ~ing at the door⟩ ⟨~ed my arm⟩ 2 : SCRAPE 3 ⟨~ed his nails across the blackboard⟩ 3 : SCRAPE 4 4 : to cancel or erase by or as if by drawing a line through 5 : to withdraw from a contest — **scratchy** adj — **scratch one's head** : to become confused or perplexed

²**scratch** n 1 : a mark or injury made by or as if by scratching; also : a sound so made 2 : the starting line in a race — **from scratch** : with no steps completed or ingredients prepared ahead of time ⟨built from ~⟩

³**scratch** adj 1 : made or done by chance ⟨a ~ hit⟩ 2 : made as or used for a trial attempt ⟨~ paper⟩

scrawl \'skról\ vb : to write hastily and carelessly — **scrawl** n

scraw·ny \'skró-nē\ adj **scraw·ni·er; -est** : very thin : SKINNY

¹**scream** \'skrēm\ vb : to cry out loudly and shrilly

²**scream** n : a loud shrill cry

scream·ing \'skrē-miŋ\ adj : so striking as to attract notice as if by screaming ⟨~ headlines⟩

screech \'skrēch\ vb : SHRIEK — **screech** n — **screechy** \'skrē-chē\ adj

screech·ing \'skrē-chiŋ\ adj : ABRUPT ⟨came to a ~ halt⟩

¹**screen** \'skrēn\ n 1 : a device or partition used to hide, restrain, protect, or decorate ⟨a window ~⟩; also : something that shelters, protects, or conceals 2 : a sieve or perforated material for separating finer from coarser parts (as of sand) 3 : a surface on which an image is made to appear (as in television); also : the information displayed on a computer screen at one time 4 : the motion-picture industry

²**screen** vb 1 : to shield with or as if with a screen 2 : to separate with a screen; also : to select or categorize methodically ⟨~ contestants⟩ 3 : to present (as a motion picture) on the screen

screen·ing \'skrē-niŋ\ n 1 : metal or plastic mesh (as for window screens) 2 : a showing of a motion picture

screen saver n : a computer program that displays something (as images) on the screen of a computer that is on but not in use

¹**screw** \'skrü\ n [ME, fr. MF escroe female screw, nut, fr. ML scrofa, fr. L, sow] 1 : a machine consisting of a solid cylinder with a spiral groove around it and a corresponding hollow cylinder into which it fits 2 : a naillike metal piece with a spiral groove and a head with a slot that is inserted into material by rotating and is used to fasten pieces of solid material together 3 : PROPELLER

²**screw** vb 1 : to fasten or close by means of a screw 2 : to operate or adjust by means of a screw 3 : to move or cause to move spirally; also : to close or set in position by such an action

screw·ball \'skrü-,ból\ n 1 : a baseball pitch breaking in a direction opposite to a curve 2 : a whimsical, eccentric, or crazy person

screw·driv·er \-,drī-vər\ n 1 : a tool for turning screws 2 : a drink made of vodka and orange juice

screw·worm \'skrü-,wərm\ n : an American blowfly of warm regions whose larva matures in wounds or sores of mammals and may cause disease or death; esp : its larva

screwy \'skrü-ē\ adj **screw·i·er; -est** 1 : crazily absurd, eccentric, or unusual 2 : CRAZY, INSANE

scrib·ble \'skri-bəl\ vb **scrib·bled; scrib·bling** : to write hastily or carelessly — **scribble** n — **scrib·bler** n

scribe \'skrīb\ n 1 : a scholar of Jewish law in New Testament times 2 : a person whose business is the copying of writing 3 : JOURNALIST

scrim \'skrim\ n : a light loosely woven cotton or linen cloth

scrim·mage \'skri-mij\ n : the play between two football teams beginning with the snap of the ball; also : practice play between two teams — **scrimmage** vb

scrimp \'skrimp\ vb : to economize greatly ⟨~ and save⟩

scrim·shaw \'skrim-,shó\ n : carved or engraved articles made orig. by American whalers usu. from baleen or whale ivory — **scrimshaw** vb

scrip \'skrip\ n 1 : a certificate showing its holder is entitled to something (as stock or land) 2 : paper money issued for temporary use in an emergency

¹**script** \'skript\ n 1 : written matter (as lines for a play or broadcast) 2 : HANDWRITING

²**script** abbr scripture

scrip·ture \'skrip-chər\ n 1 cap : the books of the Bible — often used in pl. 2 : the sacred writings of a religion — **scrip·tur·al** \'skrip-chə-rəl\ adj — **scrip·tur·al·ly** adv

scriv·en·er \'skri-və-nər\ n : SCRIBE, COPYIST, WRITER

scrod \'skräd\ n [prob. fr. Brit. dial. (Cornwall) scrawed, pp. of scraw, scrawl to split, salt, and dry (young fish)] : a young fish (as a cod or haddock); esp : one split and boned for cooking

scrof·u·la \'skró-fyə-lə\ n : tuberculosis of lymph nodes esp. in the neck

¹**scroll** \'skrōl\ n : a roll of paper or parchment for writing a document; also : a spiral or coiled ornamental form suggesting a loosely or partly rolled scroll

²**scroll** vb : to move or cause to move text or graphics up, down, or across a display screen

scroll saw n 1 : FRETSAW 2 : a machine saw with a narrow vertically reciprocating blade for cutting curved lines or openwork

scro·tum \'skrō-təm\ n, pl **scro·ta** \-tə\ or **scrotums** [L] : a pouch that in most male mammals contains the testes

scrounge \'skraúnj\ vb **scrounged;**

scroung·ing : to collect by or as if by foraging

¹scrub \'skrəb\ n 1 : a thick growth of stunted trees or shrubs; also : an area of land covered with scrub 2 : an inferior domestic animal 3 : a person of insignificant size or standing 4 : a player not on the first team — **scrub** adj — **scrub·by** adj

²scrub vb **scrubbed; scrub·bing** 1 : to clean or wash by rubbing ⟨∼ clothes⟩ ⟨∼ out a spot⟩ 2 : CANCEL

³scrub n 1 : an act or instance of scrubbing ⟨gave the clothes a good ∼⟩ 2 pl : loose-fitting clothing worn by hospital staff ⟨surgical ∼s⟩

scrub·ber \'skrə-bər\ n : one that scrubs; esp : an apparatus for removing impurities esp. from gases

scruff \'skrəf\ n : the loose skin of the back of the neck : NAPE

scruffy \'skrə-fē\ adj **scruff·i·er; -est** : UNKEMPT, SLOVENLY

scrump·tious \'skrəmp-shəs\ adj : DELIGHTFUL, EXCELLENT; esp : DELICIOUS — **scrump·tious·ly** adv

scrunch·ie or **scrunchy** \'skrən-chē, 'skrün-\ n : a fabric-covered elastic for the hair

¹scru·ple \'skrü-pəl\ n [ME scrupil, scriple, fr. AF scruble, fr. L scrupulus, dim. of scrupus source of uneasiness, lit., sharp stone] 1 : a point of conscience or honor 2 : hesitation due to ethical considerations

²scruple vb **scru·pled; scru·pling** : to be reluctant on grounds of conscience : HESITATE

scru·pu·lous \'skrü-pyə-ləs\ adj 1 : having moral integrity 2 : PAINSTAKING — **scru·pu·lous·ly** adv — **scru·pu·lous·ness** n

scru·ti·nise Brit var of SCRUTINIZE

scru·ti·nize \'skrü-tə-ˌnīz\ vb **-nized; -niz·ing** : to examine closely

scru·ti·ny \'skrü-tə-nē\ n, pl **-nies** [L scrutinium, fr. scrutari to search, examine, prob. fr. scruta trash] : a careful looking over ✦ **Synonyms** INSPECTION, EXAMINATION, ANALYSIS

scu·ba \'skü-bə\ n [self-contained underwater breathing apparatus] : an apparatus for breathing while swimming underwater

scuba diver n : one who swims underwater with the aid of scuba gear

¹scud \'skəd\ vb **scud·ded; scud·ding** : to move speedily

²scud n : light clouds driven by the wind

¹scuff \'skəf\ vb 1 : to scrape the feet while walking : SHUFFLE 2 : to scratch or become scratched or worn away

²scuff n 1 : a mark or injury caused by scuffing 2 : a flat-soled slipper without heel strap

scuf·fle \'skə-fəl\ vb **scuf·fled; scuf·fling** 1 : to struggle confusedly at close quarters 2 : to shuffle one's feet — **scuffle** n

¹scull \'skəl\ n 1 : an oar for use in sculling; also : one of a pair of short oars for a single oarsman 2 : a racing shell propelled by one or two persons using sculls

²scull vb : to propel (a boat) by an oar over the stern

scul·lery \'skə-lə-rē\ n, pl **-ler·ies** [ME squilerie, sculerie department of household in charge of dishes, fr. AF esquilerie, fr. escuele bowl, fr. L scutella drinking bowl] : a small room near the kitchen used for cleaning dishes, cooking utensils, and vegetables

scul·lion \'skəl-yən\ n : a kitchen helper

sculpt \'skəlpt\ vb : CARVE, SCULPTURE

sculp·tor \'skəlp-tər\ n : a person who produces works of sculpture

¹sculp·ture \'skəlp-chər\ n : the act, process, or art of carving or molding material (as stone, wood, or plastic); also : work produced this way — **sculp·tur·al** \'skəlp-chə-rəl\ adj

²sculpture vb **sculp·tured; sculp·tur·ing** : to form or alter as or as if a work of sculpture

scum \'skəm\ n 1 : a slimy or filmy covering on the surface of a liquid 2 : waste matter 3 : RABBLE

scup·per \'skə-pər\ n [ME skopper-, perh. fr. AF *escopir, fr. escopir to spit out] : an opening in the side of a ship through which water on deck is drained overboard

scurf \'skərf\ n : thin dry scales of skin (as dandruff); also : a scaly deposit or covering — **scurfy** \'skər-fē\ adj

scur·ri·lous \'skər-ə-ləs\ adj : coarsely jesting : OBSCENE, VULGAR

scur·ry \'skər-ē\ vb **scur·ried; scur·ry·ing** : SCAMPER

¹scur·vy \'skər-vē\ n : a disease caused by a lack of vitamin C and characterized by spongy gums, loosened teeth, and bleeding under the skin

²scurvy adj : MEAN, CONTEMPTIBLE — **scur·vi·ly** \'skər-və-lē\ adv

scutch·eon \'skə-chən\ n : ESCUTCHEON

¹scut·tle \'skə-tᵊl\ n : a pail for carrying coal

²scuttle n : a small opening with a lid esp. in the deck, side, or bottom of a ship

³scuttle vb **scut·tled; scut·tling** : to cut a hole in the deck, side, or bottom of (a ship) in order to sink

⁴scuttle vb **scut·tled; scut·tling** : SCURRY, SCAMPER

scut·tle·butt \'skə-tᵊl-ˌbət\ n : GOSSIP

scythe \'sīth\ n : an implement for mowing (as grass or grain) by hand — **scythe** vb

SD abbr 1 South Dakota 2 special delivery

S Dak abbr South Dakota

SDI abbr Strategic Defense Initiative

Se symbol selenium

SE abbr southeast

sea \'sē\ n 1 : a large body of salt water 2 : OCEAN 3 : rough water; also : a large wave 4 : something likened to the sea esp. in vastness — **sea** adj — **at sea** : LOST, BEWILDERED

sea anemone n : any of numerous coelenterate polyps whose form, bright and varied colors, and cluster of tentacles superficially resemble a flower

sea-bird \'sē-ˌbərd\ *n* : a bird (as a gull) frequenting the open ocean

sea-board \-ˌbȯrd\ *n* : SEACOAST; *also* : the land bordering a coast

sea-borg-i-um \sē-ˈbȯr-gē-əm\ *n* : a short-lived radioactive chemical element produced artificially

sea-coast \-ˌkōst\ *n* : the shore of the sea

sea-far-er \-ˌfer-ər\ *n* : SEAMAN 1

sea-far-ing \-ˌfer-iŋ\ *n* : the use of the sea for travel or transportation — **seafaring** *adj*

sea-food \-ˌfüd\ *n* : edible marine fish and shellfish

sea-go-ing \-ˌgō-iŋ\ *adj* : OCEANGOING

sea-gull \'sē-ˌgəl\ : GULL

sea horse *n* : any of a genus of small marine fishes with the head and forepart of the body sharply flexed like the head and neck of a horse

¹**seal** \'sēl\ *n, pl* **seals** *also* **seal** [ME *sele*, fr. OE *seolh*] **1** : any of numerous large carnivorous sea mammals occurring chiefly in cold regions and having limbs adapted for swimming **2** : the pelt of a seal

²**seal** *vb* : to hunt seals

³**seal** *n* [ME *sele*, *seel*, fr. AF *seal*, *sel*, fr. L *sigillum*, fr. dim. of *signum* sign, seal] **1** : GUARANTEE, PLEDGE **2** : a device having a raised design that can be stamped on clay or wax; *also* : the impression made by stamping with such a device **3** : something that seals or closes up ⟨safety ~⟩

⁴**seal** *vb* **1** : to affix a seal to; *also* : AUTHENTICATE **2** : to fasten with or as if with a seal to prevent tampering **3** : to close or make secure against access, leakage, or passage **4** : to determine irrevocably ⟨*~ed* his fate⟩

sea–lane \'sē-ˌlān\ *n* : an established sea route

seal-ant \'sē-lənt\ *n* : a sealing agent

seal-er \'sē-lər\ *n* : a coat applied to prevent subsequent coats of paint or varnish from sinking in

sea level *n* : the level of the surface of the sea esp. at its mean midway between mean high and low water

sea-lift \'sē-ˌlift\ *n* : transport of military personnel and equipment by ship

sea lion *n* : any of several large Pacific seals with small external ears

seal-skin \'sēl-ˌskin\ *n* **1** : ¹SEAL 2 **2** : a garment of sealskin

¹**seam** \'sēm\ *n* **1** : the line of junction of two edges and esp. of edges of fabric sewn together **2** : a layer of mineral matter **3** : WRINKLE

²**seam** *vb* **1** : to join by or as if by sewing **2** : WRINKLE, FURROW

sea-man \'sē-mən\ *n* **1** : one who assists in the handling of ships : MARINER **2** : an enlisted man in the navy ranking next below a petty officer third class

seaman apprentice *n* : an enlisted man in the navy ranking next below a seaman

seaman recruit *n* : an enlisted man of the lowest rank in the navy

sea-man-ship \'sē-mən-ˌship\ *n* : the art or skill of handling a ship

seam-less \'sēm-ləs\ *adj* : having no flaws or interruptions ⟨a ~ transition⟩ — **seam-less-ly** *adv*

sea-mount \'sē-ˌmau̇nt\ *n* : an underwater mountain

seam-stress \'sēm-strəs\ *n* : a woman who does sewing

seamy \'sē-mē\ *adj* **seam-i-er; -est 1** : UNPLEASANT **2** : DEGRADED, SORDID ⟨the ~ part of town⟩

sé-ance \'sā-ˌäns\ *n* [F] : a meeting to receive communications from spirits

sea-plane \'sē-ˌplān\ *n* : an airplane that can take off from and land on water

sea-port \-ˌpȯrt\ *n* : a port for oceangoing ships

sear \'sir\ *vb* **1** : WITHER **2** : to cook, burn, or scorch esp. on the surface; *also* : BRAND — **sear** *n*

¹**search** \'sərch\ *vb* [ME *cerchen*, fr. AF *cercher* to travel about, investigate, search, fr. LL *circare* to go about, fr. L *circum* round about] **1** : to look through in trying to find something **2** : SEEK **3** : PROBE — **search-er** *n*

²**search** *n* : the act of searching

search engine *n* : computer software or a Web site used to search data (as text or other Web sites) for specified information

search-light \-ˌlīt\ *n* : an apparatus for projecting a powerful beam of light; *also* : the light projected

sear-ing \'sir-iŋ\ *adj* : very sharp, harsh or intense ⟨~ pain⟩ ⟨a ~ review⟩

sea scallop *n* : a large scallop of the Atlantic coast of No. America that is harvested for food

sea-scape \'sē-ˌskāp\ *n* **1** : a view of the sea **2** : a picture representing a scene at or of the sea

sea-shell \'sē-ˌshel\ *n* : the shell of a marine animal and esp. a mollusk

sea-shore \-ˌshȯr\ *n* : the shore of a sea

sea-sick \-ˌsik\ *adj* : nauseated by or as if by the motion of a ship — **sea-sick-ness** *n*

sea-side \'sē-ˌsīd\ *n* : SEASHORE

¹**sea-son** \'sē-zən\ *n* [ME *sesoun*, fr. AF *seison* natural season, appropriate time, fr. L *sation-*, *satio* action of sowing, fr. *serere* to sow] **1** : one of the divisions of the year (as spring or summer) **2** : a period of the year associated with a particular activity, event, or holiday ⟨the Easter ~⟩ ⟨hunting ~⟩ — **sea-son-al** \-zə-nəl\ *adj* — **sea-son-al-ly** *adv*

²**season** *vb* **1** : to make pleasant to the taste by use of salt, pepper, or spices **2** : to make (as by aging or drying) suitable for use **3** : to accustom or habituate to something (as hardship) ♦ **Synonyms** HARDEN, INURE, ACCLIMATE, TOUGHEN — **sea-son-er** *n*

sea-son-able \'sē-zə-nə-bəl\ *adj* : occurring at a good or proper time ♦ **Synonyms** TIMELY, PROPITIOUS, OPPORTUNE — **sea-son-ably** \-blē\ *adv*

seasonal affective disorder *n* : depression that recurs as the days grow shorter during the fall and winter

sea·son·ing *n* : something that seasons : CONDIMENT

¹seat \'sēt\ *n* **1** : a chair, bench, or stool for sitting on **2** : a place which serves as a capital or center

²seat *vb* **1** : to place in or on a seat **2** : to provide seats for

seat belt *n* : straps designed to hold a person in a seat

SEATO \'sē-ˌtō\ *abbr* Southeast Asia Treaty Organization

seat–of–the–pants *adj* : employing or based on personal experience, judgment, and effort rather than technological aids ⟨~ navigation⟩

sea turtle *n* : any of two families of marine turtles that have the feet modified into paddles

sea urchin *n* : any of numerous spiny marine echinoderms having thin brittle globular shells

sea·wall \'sē-ˌwȯl\ *n* : an embankment to protect the shore from erosion

¹sea·ward \'sē-wərd\ *n* : the direction or side away from land and toward the open sea

²seaward *also* **sea·wards** \-wərdz\ *adv* : toward the sea

³seaward *adj* **1** : directed or situated toward the sea **2** : coming from the sea

sea·wa·ter \'sē-ˌwȯ-tər, -ˌwä-\ *n* : water in or from the sea

sea·way \-ˌwā\ *n* : an inland waterway that admits ocean shipping

sea·weed \-ˌwēd\ *n* : a marine alga (as a kelp); *also* : a mass of marine algae

sea·wor·thy \-ˌwər-thē\ *adj* : fit for a sea voyage ⟨a ~ ship⟩

se·ba·ceous \si-'bā-shəs\ *adj* : of, relating to, or secreting fatty material

sec *abbr* **1** second; secondary **2** secretary **3** section **4** [L *secundum*] according to

SEC *abbr* Securities and Exchange Commission

se·cede \si-'sēd\ *vb* **se·ced·ed; se·ced·ing** : to withdraw from an organized body and esp. from a political body

se·ces·sion \si-'se-shən\ *n* : the act of seceding — **se·ces·sion·ist** *n*

se·clude \si-'klüd\ *vb* **se·clud·ed; se·clud·ing** : to keep or shut away from others

se·clu·sion \si-'klü-zhən\ *n* : the act of or state of being secluded — **se·clu·sive** \-siv\ *adj*

¹sec·ond \'se-kənd\ *adj* [ME, fr. AF *secund,*fr. L *secundus* second, following, favorable, fr. *sequi* to follow] **1** : being number two in a countable series **2** : next after the first **3** : ALTERNATE ⟨every ~ year⟩ — **second** *or* **sec·ond·ly** *adv*

²second *n* **1** : one that is second **2** : one who assists another (as in a duel) **3** : an inferior or flawed article (as of) **4** : the second forward gear in a motor vehicle

³second *n* [ME *secounde*, fr. ML *secunda*, fr. L, fem. of *secundus* second; fr. its being the second division of a unit into 60 parts, as a minute is the first] **1** : the 60th part of a minute of time or angular measure **2** : an instant of time

⁴second *vb* **1** : to encourage or give support to **2** : to act as a second to **3** : to support (a motion) by adding one's voice to that of a proposer

¹sec·ond·ary \'se-kən-ˌder-ē\ *adj* **1** : second in rank, value, or occurrence : LESSER **2** : belonging to a second or later stage of development **3** : coming after the primary or elementary ⟨~ schools⟩
♦ *Synonyms* SUBORDINATE, COLLATERAL, DEPENDENT

²secondary *n, pl* **-ar·ies** : the defensive backfield of a football team

secondary sex characteristic *n* : a physical characteristic that appears in members of one sex at puberty or in seasonal breeders at breeding season and is not directly concerned with reproduction

second fiddle *n* : one that plays a supporting or subservient role

sec·ond–guess \ˌse-kənd-'ges\ *vb* **1** : to think out other strategies or explanations for after the event **2** : to seek to anticipate or predict

sec·ond·hand \-'hand\ *adj* **1** : not original **2** : not new : USED ⟨~ clothes⟩ **3** : dealing in used goods

secondhand smoke *n* : tobacco smoke that is exhaled by smokers or is given off by burning tobacco and is inhaled by persons nearby

second lieutenant *n* : a commissioned officer (as in the army) ranking next below a first lieutenant

sec·ond–rate \ˌse-kənd-'rāt\ *adj* : INFERIOR

sec·ond–string \'se-kənd-'striŋ\ *adj* : being a substitute (as on a team)

se·cre·cy \'sē-krə-sē\ *n, pl* **-cies 1** : the habit or practice of being secretive **2** : the condition of being hidden or concealed

¹se·cret \'sē-krət\ *adj* **1** : HIDDEN, CONCEALED ⟨a ~ staircase⟩ **2** : COVERT, STEALTHY; *also* : engaged in detecting or spying ⟨a ~ agent⟩ **3** : kept from general knowledge — **se·cret·ly** *adv*

²secret *n* **1** : MYSTERY **2** : something kept from the knowledge of others

sec·re·tar·i·at \ˌse-krə-'ter-ē-ət\ *n* **1** : the office of a secretary **2** : the secretarial staff in an office **3** : the administrative department of a governmental organization ⟨the UN ~⟩

sec·re·tary \'se-krə-ˌter-ē\ *n, pl* **-tar·ies 1** : a person employed to handle records, correspondence, and routine work for another person **2** : an officer of a corporation or business who is in charge of correspondence and records **3** : an official at the head of a department of government **4** : a writing desk — **sec·re·tar·i·al** \ˌse-krə-'ter-ē-əl\ *adj* — **sec·re·tary·ship** \'se-krə-ˌter-ē-ˌship\ *n*

¹se·crete \si-'krēt\ *vb* **se·cret·ed; se·cret·ing** : to form and give off (a secretion)

²se·crete \si-'krēt, 'sē-krət\ *vb* **se·cret·ed; se·cret·ing** : HIDE, CONCEAL

se·cre·tion \si-'krē-shən\ *n* **1** : the process of secreting something **2** : a product of glandular activity; *esp* : one (as a hormone) useful in the organism **3** : the act of hiding something — **se·cre·to·ry** \'sē-krə-ˌtȯr-ē\ *adj*

se·cre·tive \'sē-krə-tiv, si-'krē-\ *adj* : tending to keep secrets or to act secretly — **se·cre·tive·ly** *adv* — **se·cre·tive·ness** *n*

¹**sect** \'sekt\ *n* **1** : a dissenting religious body **2** : a religious denomination **3** : a group adhering to a distinctive doctrine or to a leader

²**sect** *abbr* section; sectional

¹**sec·tar·i·an** \sek-'ter-ē-ən\ *adj* **1** : of or relating to a sect or sectarian **2** : limited in character or scope — **sec·tar·i·an·ism** *n*

²**sectarian** *n* **1** : an adherent of a sect **2** : a narrow or bigoted person

sec·ta·ry \'sek-tə-rē\ *n, pl* **-ries** : a member of a sect

¹**sec·tion** \'sek-shən\ *n* **1** : a part cut off or separated **2** : a distinct part **3** : the appearance that a thing has or would have if cut straight through

²**section** *vb* **1** : to separate or become separated into sections **2** : to represent in sections

sec·tion·al \'sek-shə-nəl\ *adj* **1** : of, relating to, or characteristic of a section **2** : local or regional rather than general in character **3** : divided into sections — **sec·tion·al·ism** *n*

sec·tor \'sek-tər\ *n* **1** : a part of a circle between two radii **2** : an area assigned to a military leader to defend **3** : a subdivision of society

sec·u·lar \'se-kyə-lər\ *adj* **1** : not sacred or ecclesiastical **2** : not bound by monastic vows ⟨a ~ priest⟩

sec·u·lar·ise *Brit var of* SECULARIZE

sec·u·lar·ism \'se-kyə-lə-ˌri-zəm\ *n* : indifference to or exclusion of religion — **sec·u·lar·ist** \-rist\ *n* — **secularist** *also* **sec·u·lar·is·tic** \ˌse-kyə-lə-'ris-tik\ *adj*

sec·u·lar·ize \'se-kyə-lə-ˌrīz\ *vb* **-ized; -iz·ing 1** : to make secular **2** : to transfer from ecclesiastical to civil or lay use, possession, or control — **sec·u·lar·i·za·tion** \ˌse-kyə-lə-rə-'zā-shən\ *n* — **sec·u·lar·iz·er** \'se-kyə-lə-ˌrī-zər\ *n*

¹**se·cure** \si-'kyu̇r\ *adj* **se·cur·er; -est** [L *securus* safe, secure, fr. *se* without + *cura* care] **1** : easy in mind : free from fear **2** : free from danger or risk of loss : SAFE **3** : CERTAIN, SURE — **se·cure·ly** *adv*

²**secure** *vb* **se·cured; se·cur·ing 1** : to make safe : GUARD **2** : to assure payment of by giving a pledge or collateral **3** : to fasten safely ⟨~ a door⟩ **4** : GET, ACQUIRE

se·cu·ri·ty \si-'kyu̇r-ə-tē\ *n, pl* **-ties 1** : SAFETY **2** : freedom from worry **3** : something given as pledge of payment ⟨a ~ deposit⟩ **4** *pl* : bond or stock certificates **5** : PROTECTION

secy *abbr* secretary

se·dan \si-'dan\ *n* **1** : a covered chair borne on poles by two men **2** : an automobile seating four or more people and usu. having a permanent top

¹**se·date** \si-'dāt\ *adj* : quiet and dignified in behavior ✦ *Synonyms* STAID, SOBER, SERIOUS, SOLEMN — **se·date·ly** *adv*

²**sedate** *vb* **se·dat·ed; se·dat·ing** : to dose with sedatives — **se·da·tion** \si-'dā-shən\ *n*

¹**sed·a·tive** \'se-də-tiv\ *adj* : serving or tending to relieve tension

²**sedative** *n* : a sedative drug

sed·en·tary \'se-dᵊn-ˌter-ē\ *adj* : characterized by or requiring much sitting

sedge \'sej\ *n* : any of a family of plants esp. of marshy areas that differ from the related grasses esp. in having solid stems — **sedgy** \'se-jē\ *adj*

sed·i·ment \'se-də-mənt\ *n* **1** : the material that settles to the bottom of a liquid **2** : material (as stones and sand) deposited by water, wind, or a glacier — **sed·i·men·ta·ry** \ˌse-də-'men-tə-rē\ *adj* — **sed·i·men·ta·tion** \-mən-'tā-shən, -ˌmen-\ *n*

se·di·tion \si-'di-shən\ *n* : the causing of discontent, insurrection, or resistance against a government — **se·di·tious** \-shəs\ *adj*

se·duce \si-'düs, -'dyüs\ *vb* **se·duced; se·duc·ing 1** : to persuade to disobedience or disloyalty **2** : to lead astray **3** : to entice to sexual intercourse ✦ *Synonyms* TEMPT, ENTICE, INVEIGLE, LURE — **se·duc·er** *n* — **se·duc·tion** \-'dək-shən\ *n* — **se·duc·tive** \-tiv\ *adj*

sed·u·lous \'se-jə-ləs\ *adj* [L *sedulus,* fr. *sedulo* sincerely, diligently, fr. *se* without + *dolus* guile] : DILIGENT, PAINSTAKING

¹**see** \'sē\ *vb* **saw** \'sȯ\; **seen** \'sēn\; **see·ing 1** : to perceive by the eye; *also* : to have the power of sight **2** : EXPERIENCE **3** : UNDERSTAND **4** : to make sure ⟨~ that order is kept⟩ **5** : to meet with **6** : to keep company with esp. in dating **7** : ACCOMPANY, ESCORT ⟨~ the guests to the door⟩ ✦ *Synonyms* BEHOLD, DESCRY, ESPY, VIEW, OBSERVE, NOTE, DISCERN — **see red** : to become very angry — **see the light** : to realize an obscured truth

²**see** *n* : the authority or jurisdiction of a bishop

¹**seed** \'sēd\ *n, pl* **seed** *or* **seeds 1** : the grains of plants used for sowing **2** : a ripened ovule of a flowering plant that may develop into a new plant; *also* : a plant structure (as a spore or small dry fruit) capable of producing a new plant **3** : DESCENDANTS **4** : SOURCE, ORIGIN **5** : a competitor seeded in a tournament — **seed·less** *adj* — **go to seed** *or* **run to seed 1** : to develop seed **2** : DECAY, DETERIORATE

²**seed** *vb* **1** : SOW, PLANT ⟨~ land with grass⟩ **2** : to bear or shed seeds **3** : to remove seeds from **4** : to rank or schedule (contestants) in a tournament — **seed·er** *n*

seed·bed \-ˌbed\ *n* : soil or a bed of soil prepared for planting seed

seed·ling \'sēd-liŋ\ *n* **1** : a young plant grown from seed **2** : a young tree before it becomes a sapling

seed·time \'sēd-ˌtīm\ *n* : the season for sowing

seedy \\'sē-dē\\ *adj* **seed·i·er; -est 1** : containing or full of seeds **2** : SHABBY

seek \\'sēk\\ *vb* **sought** \\'sȯt\\; **seek·ing 1** : to search for **2** : to try to reach or obtain **3** : ATTEMPT — **seek·er** *n*

seem \\'sēm\\ *vb* **1** : to appear to the observation or understanding **2** : to give the impression of being : APPEAR

seem·ing *adj* : outwardly apparent — **seem·ing·ly** *adv*

seem·ly \\'sēm-lē\\ *adj* **seem·li·er; -est 1** : conventionally proper **2** : FIT

seep \\'sēp\\ *vb* : to flow or pass slowly through fine pores or cracks — **seep·age** \\'sē-pij\\ *n*

seer \\'sir\\ *n* : a person who foresees or predicts events : PROPHET

seer·suck·er \\'sir-ˌsə-kər\\ *n* [Hindi *śīrśakar*, fr. Pers *shīr-o-shakar*, lit., milk and sugar] : a light fabric of linen, cotton, or rayon usu. striped and slightly puckered

see·saw \\'sē-ˌsȯ\\ *n* **1** : a contest in which each side assumes then relinquishes the lead **2** : a children's sport of riding up and down on the ends of a plank supported in the middle; *also* : the plank so used — **seesaw** *vb*

seethe \\'sēth\\ *vb* **seethed; seeth·ing** [archaic *seethe* boil] : to become violently agitated ⟨∼ with jealousy⟩

seg·ment \\'seg-mənt\\ *n* **1** : a part cut off from a geometrical figure (as a circle) by one or more points, lines, or planes **2** : a division of a thing : SECTION — **seg·men·tal** \\seg-'men-tᵊl\\ *adj* — **seg·men·ta·tion** \\ˌseg-mən-'tā-shən\\ *n* — **seg·ment·ed** \\'seg-ˌmen-təd\\ *adj*

seg·re·gate \\'se-gri-ˌgāt\\ *vb* **-gat·ed; -gat·ing** [L *segregare*, fr. *se-* apart + *greg-, grex* herd, flock] : to cut off from others; *esp* : to separate esp. by races or ethnic groups — **seg·re·ga·tion** \\ˌse-gri-'gā-shən\\ *n*

seg·re·ga·tion·ist \\ˌse-gri-'gā-shə-nist\\ *n* : one who believes in or practices the segregation of races

sei·gneur \\sān-'yər\\ *n, often cap* [MF, fr. ML *senior*, fr. L, adj., elder] : a feudal lord

¹seine \\'sān\\ *n* : a large weighted fishing net

²seine *vb* **seined; sein·ing** : to fish or catch with a seine — **sein·er** *n*

seis·mic \\'sīz-mik, 'sīs-\\ *adj* : of, relating to, resembling, or caused by an earthquake — **seis·mi·cal·ly** \\-mi-k(ə-)lē\\ *adv* — **seis·mic·i·ty** \\sīz-'mi-sə-tē, sīs-\\ *n*

seis·mo·gram \\'sīz-mə-ˌgram, 'sīs-\\ *n* : the record of an earth tremor made by a seismograph

seis·mo·graph \\-ˌgraf\\ *n* : an apparatus to measure and record seismic vibrations — **seis·mo·graph·ic** \\ˌsīz-mə-'gra-fik, ˌsīs-\\ *adj* — **seis·mog·ra·phy** \\sīz-'mä-grə-fē\\ *n*

seis·mol·o·gy \\sīz-'mä-lə-jē, sīs-\\ *n* : a science that deals with earthquakes — **seis·mo·log·i·cal** \\ˌsīz-mə-'lä-ji-kəl, ˌsīs-\\ *adj* — **seis·mol·o·gist** \\sīz-'mä-lə-jist, sīs-\\ *n*

seis·mom·e·ter \\sīz-'mä-mə-tər, sīs-\\ *n* : a seismograph measuring the actual movement of the ground

seize \\'sēz\\ *vb* **seized; seiz·ing 1** : to lay hold of or take possession of by force **2** : ARREST **3** : UNDERSTAND **4** : to attack or overwhelm physically : AFFLICT
♦ **Synonyms** TAKE, GRASP, CLUTCH, SNATCH, GRAB

sei·zure \\'sē-zhər\\ *n* **1** : the act of seizing ; the state of being seized **2** : a sudden attack (as of disease)

sel *abbr* select; selected; selection

sel·dom \\'sel-dəm\\ *adv* : not often : RARELY

¹se·lect \\sə-'lekt\\ *adj* **1** : CHOSEN, PICKED; *also* : CHOICE **2** : judicious or restrictive in choice : DISCRIMINATING

²select *vb* : to choose from a number or group : pick out

se·lec·tion \\sə-'lek-shən\\ *n* **1** : the act or process of selecting **2** : something selected : CHOICE **3** : a natural or artificial process that tends to favor the survival and reproduction of individuals with certain traits but not those with others

se·lec·tive \\sə-'lek-tiv\\ *adj* : of or relating to selection : selecting or tending to select ⟨∼ shoppers⟩

selective service *n* : a system for calling men up for military service : DRAFT

se·lect·man \\si-'lekt-ˌman, -mən\\ *n* : one of a board of officials elected in towns of most New England states to administer town affairs

se·le·ni·um \\sə-'lē-nē-əm\\ *n* : a photosensitive chemical element

self \\'self\\ *n, pl* **selves** \\'selvz\\ **1** : the essential person distinct from all other persons in identity **2** : a particular side of a person's character **3** : personal interest : SELFISHNESS

self- *comb form* **1** : oneself : itself **2** : of oneself or itself **3** : by oneself or itself; *also* : automatic **4** : to, for, or toward oneself

self–cen·tered \\'self-'sen-tərd\\ *adj* : concerned only with one's own self — **self–cen·tered·ness** *n*

self–com·posed \\ˌself-kəm-'pōzd\\ *adj* : having control over one's emotions

self–con·scious \\'self-'kän-chəs\\ *adj* : uncomfortably conscious of oneself as an object of observation by others —

self–abasement	self–advancement	self–assertion	self–conceit
self–absorbed	self–aggrandize-	self–assertive	self–concern
self–absorption	ment	self–assurance	self–condemned
self–acceptance	self–aggrandizing	self–assured	self–confessed
self–accusation	self–analysis	self–awareness	self–confidence
self–acting	self–anointed	self–betrayal	self–confident
self–addressed	self–appointed	self–cleaning	self–congratulation
self–adjusting	self–appraisal	self–closing	self–congratulatory
self–administer	self–asserting	self–complacent	

self-con·scious·ly *adv* — **self-con·scious·ness** *n*

self-con·tained \ˌself-kən-ˈtānd\ *adj* 1 : complete in itself 2 : showing self-control; *also* : reserved in manner

self-de·fense \ˈself-di-ˈfens\ *n* 1 : a plea of justification for the use of force or for homicide 2 : the act of defending oneself, one's property, or a close relative

self-ef·fac·ing \-ə-ˈfā-siŋ\ *adj* : RETIRING, SHY

self-ev·i·dent \ˌself-ˈe-və-dənt\ *adj* : evident without proof or reasoning

self-fer·til·i·za·tion \ˌself-ˌfər-tə-lə-ˈzā-shən\ *n* : fertilization of a plant or animal by its own pollen or sperm

self-ful·fill·ing \ˌself-fûl-ˈfi-liŋ\ *adj* : becoming real or true by virtue of having been predicted or expected ⟨a ~ prophecy⟩

self-help \ˈself-ˈhelp\ *n* : the process of bettering oneself or coping with one's problems without the aid of others — **self-help** *adj*

self-ish \ˈsel-fish\ *adj* : concerned with one's own welfare excessively or without regard for others — **self-ish·ly** *adv* — **self-ish·ness** *n*

self-less \ˈself-ləs\ *adj* : UNSELFISH — **self-less·ness** *n*

self-made \ˈself-ˈmād\ *adj* : having achieved success or prominence by one's own efforts ⟨a ~ man⟩

self-pol·li·na·tion \ˌself-ˌpä-lə-ˈnā-shən\ *n* : pollination of a flower by its own pollen or sometimes by pollen from another flower on the same plant

self-reg·u·lat·ing \ˈself-ˈre-gyə-ˌlā-tiŋ\ *adj* : AUTOMATIC

self-righ·teous \-ˈrī-chəs\ *adj* : strongly convinced of one's own righteousness — **self-righ·teous·ly** *adv*

self·same \ˈself-ˌsām\ *adj* : precisely the same : IDENTICAL

self-seal·ing \ˈself-ˈsē-liŋ\ *adj* : capable of sealing itself (as after puncture)

self-seek·ing \ˈself-ˈsē-kiŋ\ *adj* : seeking only to further one's own interests — **self-seeking** *n*

self-start·er \-ˈstär-tər\ *n* : a person who has initiative

self-will \ˈself-ˈwil\ *n* : OBSTINACY

sell \ˈsel\ *vb* **sold** \ˈsōld\; **sell·ing** 1 : to transfer(property) in return for money or something else of value 2 : to deal in as a business 3 : to be sold ⟨cars are ~ing well⟩ — **sell·er** *n*

sell out *vb* 1 : to dispose of entirely by sale; *esp* : to sell one's business 2 : BETRAY — **sell-out** \ˈsel-ˌaüt\ *n*

selt·zer \ˈselt-sər\ *n* [modif. of G *Selterser (Wasser)* water of Selters, fr. Nieder *Selters,* Germany] : artificially carbonated water

sel·vage *or* **sel·vedge** \ˈsel-vij\ *n* : the edge of a woven fabric so formed as to prevent raveling

selves *pl of* SELF

sem *abbr* 1 semicolon 2 seminar 3 seminary

se·man·tic \si-ˈman-tik\ *also* **se·man·ti·cal** \-ti-kəl\ *adj* : of or relating to meaning in language

se·man·tics \si-ˈman-tiks\ *n sing or pl* : the study of meanings in language

sema·phore \ˈse-mə-ˌför\ *n* 1 : a visual signaling apparatus with movable arms 2 : signaling by hand-held flags

sem·blance \ˈsem-bləns\ *n* 1 : outward appearance 2 : IMAGE, LIKENESS

se·men \ˈsē-mən\ *n* [NL, fr. L, seed] : a sticky whitish fluid of the male reproductive tract that contains the sperm

se·mes·ter \sə-ˈmes-tər\ *n* [G, fr. L *semestris* half-yearly, fr. *sex* six + *mensis* month] 1 : half a year 2 : one of the two terms into which many colleges divide the school year

---

self-constituted	self-discipline	self-indulgence	self-regard
self-contempt	self-distrust	self-indulgent	self-reliance
self-contradiction	self-doubt	self-inflicted	self-reliant
self-contradictory	self-educated	self-instruction	self-renewing
self-control	self-employed	self-interest	self-reproach
self-correcting	self-employment	self-knowledge	self-respect
self-created	self-enhancement	self-limiting	self-respecting
self-criticism	self-esteem	self-love	self-restraint
self-cultivation	self-examination	self-lubricating	self-revelation
self-deceit	self-explaining	self-luminous	self-rule
self-deception	self-explanatory	self-operating	self-sacrifice
self-defeating	self-expression	self-perception	self-sacrificing
self-definition	self-forgetful	self-perpetuating	self-satisfaction
self-delusion	self-giving	self-pity	self-satisfied
self-denial	self-governing	self-portrait	self-service
self-denying	self-government	self-possessed	self-serving
self-deprecating	self-hate	self-possession	self-starting
self-deprecation	self-hypnosis	self-preservation	self-styled
self-depreciation	self-identity	self-proclaimed	self-sufficiency
self-described	self-image	self-professed	self-sufficient
self-despair	self-importance	self-promotion	self-supporting
self-destruct	self-important	self-propelled	self-sustaining
self-destruction	self-imposed	self-propelling	self-taught
self-destructive	self-improvement	self-protection	self-torment
self-determination	self-incrimination	self-realization	self-winding
self-directed	self-induced	self-referential	self-worth

semi \'se-,mī\ *n, pl* **sem·is** : SEMITRAILER

semi- \'se-mi, -,mī\ *prefix* **1** : precisely half of **2** : half in quantity or value; *also* : half of or occurring halfway through a specified period **3** : partly : incompletely **4** : partial : incomplete **5** : having some of the characteristics of

semi·au·to·mat·ic \,se-mē-,ó-tə-'ma-tik\ *adj, of a firearm* : able to fire repeatedly but requiring release and another press of the trigger for each successive shot

semi·co·lon \'se-mi-,kō-lən\ *n* : a punctuation mark; used esp. to separate major sentence elements

semi·con·duc·tor \,se-mi-kən-'dək-tər\ *n* : a substance whose electrical conductivity is between that of a conductor and an insulator — **semi·con·duct·ing** *adj*

¹semi·fi·nal \,se-mi-'fī-n²l\ *adj* : being next to the last in an elimination tournament

²semi·fi·nal \'se-mi-,fī-n²l\ *n* : a semifinal round or match — **semi·fi·nal·ist** \-ist\ *n*

semi·lu·nar \-'lü-nər\ *adj* : LUNATE

sem·i·nal \'se-mə-n²l\ *adj* **1** : of, relating to, or consisting of seed or semen **2** : containing or contributing the seeds of later development : CREATIVE, ORIGINAL — **sem·i·nal·ly** *adv*

sem·i·nar \'se-mə-,när\ *n* **1** : a course of study pursued by a group of advanced students doing original research under a professor **2** : CONFERENCE

sem·i·nary \'se-mə-,ner-ē\ *n, pl* **-nar·ies** [ME, seedbed, nursery, fr. L *seminarium*, fr. *semen* seed] : an educational institution; *esp* : one that gives theological training — **sem·i·nar·i·an** \,se-mə-'ner-ē-ən\ *n*

Sem·i·nole \'se-mə-,nōl\ *n, pl* **Seminoles** *or* **Seminole** : a member of an American Indian people of Florida

semi·per·me·able \,se-mi-'pər-mē-ə-bəl\ *adj* : partially but not freely or wholly permeable; *esp* : permeable to some usu. small molecules but not to other usu. larger particles ⟨a ~ membrane⟩ — **semi·per·me·abil·i·ty** \-,pər-mē-ə-'bi-lə-tē\ *n*

Sem·ite \'se-,mīt\ *n* : a member of any of a group of peoples (as the Hebrews or Arabs) of southwestern Asia — **Se·mit·ic** \sə-'mi-tik\ *adj*

semi·trail·er \'se-mi-,trā-lər, -,mī-\ *n* : a freight trailer that when attached is supported at its forward end by the truck tractor; *also* : a semitrailer with attached tractor

sem·o·li·na \,se-mə-'lē-nə\ *n* : the purified hard grains produced from the milling of wheat and used esp. for pasta

semp·stress *var of* SEAMSTRESS

¹sen \'sen\ *n, pl* **sen** — see *yen* at MONEY table

²sen *n, pl* **sen** — see *dollar, ringgit, rupiah* at MONEY table

³sen *n, pl* **sen** — see *riel* at MONEY table

⁴sen *abbr* **1** senate; senator **2** senior

sen·ate \'se-nət\ *n* : the second of two chambers of a legislature

sen·a·tor \'se-nə-tər\ *n* : a member of a senate — **sen·a·to·ri·al** \,se-nə-'tór-ē-əl\ *adj*

send \'send\ *vb* **sent** \'sent\; **send·ing** **1** : to cause to go **2** : EMIT **3** : to propel or drive esp. with force **4** : to put or bring into a certain condition ⟨*sent* them into a rage⟩ **5** : to convey or transmit by an agent — **send·er** *n*

send–off \'send-,óf\ *n* : a demonstration of goodwill and enthusiasm at the start of a new venture (as a trip)

send–up \'send-,əp\ *n* : PARODY, TAKE-OFF

se·ne \'sā-(,)nā\ *n, pl* **sene** — see *tala* at MONEY table

Sen·e·ca \'se-ni-kə\ *n, pl* **Seneca** *or* **Senecas** : a member of an American Indian people of western New York

Sen·e·ga·lese \,se-ni-gə-'lēz, -'lēs\ *n, pl* **Senegalese** : a native or inhabitant of Senegal — **Senegalese** *adj*

se·nes·cence \si-'ne-s²ns\ *n* : the state of being old; *also* : the process of becoming old — **se·nes·cent** \-²nt\ *adj*

se·nile \'sē-,nī(-ə)l, 'se-\ *adj* : OLD, AGED; *esp* : exhibiting a loss of cognitive abilities associated with old age — **se·nil·i·ty** \si-'ni-lə-tē\ *n*

¹se·nior \'sē-nyər\ *n* **1** : a person older or of higher rank than another **2** : a member of the graduating class of a high school or college

²senior *adj* [ME, fr. L, older, elder, compar. of *senex* old] **1** : ELDER **2** : more advanced in dignity or rank **3** : belonging to the final year of a school or college course

senior chief petty officer *n* : a petty officer in the navy or coast guard ranking next below a master chief petty officer

senior citizen *n* : an elderly person; *esp* : one who has retired

senior high school *n* : a school usu. including grades 10 to 12

se·nior·i·ty \sēn-'yòr-ə-tē\ *n* **1** : the quality or state of being senior **2** : a privileged status owing to length of continuous service

senior master sergeant *n* : a noncommissioned officer in the air force ranking next below a chief master sergeant

sen·i·ti \'se-nə-tē\ *n, pl* **seniti** — see *pa'anga* at MONEY table

sen·na \'se-nə\ *n* **1** : CASSIA 2; *esp* : one used medicinally **2** : the dried leaflets or pods of a cassia used as a purgative

semiannual	semidarkness	semiofficial	semiskilled
semiarid	semidivine	semipermanent	semisoft
semicentennial	semiformal	semipolitical	semisolid
semicircle	semigloss	semiprecious	semisweet
semicircular	semi–independent	semiprivate	semitransparent
semicivilized	semiliquid	semiprofessional	semiweekly
semiclassical	semiliterate	semireligious	semiyearly
semiconscious	semimonthly	semiretired	

sen·sa·tion \sen-'sā-shən\ n 1 : awareness (as of noise or heat) or a mental process (as seeing or hearing) due to stimulation of a sense organ; also : an indefinite bodily feeling 2 : a condition of excitement; also : the thing that causes this condition

sen·sa·tion·al \-shə-nəl\ adj 1 : of or relating to sensation or the senses 2 : arousing an intense and usu. superficial interest or emotional reaction — **sen·sa·tion·al·ly** adv

sen·sa·tion·al·ise Brit var of SENSATIONALIZE

sen·sa·tion·al·ism \-nə-ˌli-zəm\ n : the use or effect of sensational subject matter or treatment — **sen·sa·tion·al·ist** \-nə-list\ adj or n — **sen·sa·tion·al·is·tic** \-ˌsā-shə-nə-'lis-tik\ adj

sen·sa·tion·al·ize \-nə-ˌlīz\ vb -ized; -iz·ing : to present in a sensational manner

¹**sense** \'sens\ n 1 : semantic content : MEANING 2 : the faculty of perceiving by means of sense organs; also : a bodily function or mechanism (as sight, hearing, or smell) involving the action and effect of a stimulus on a sense organ 3 : SENSATION, AWARENESS 4 : INTELLIGENCE, JUDGMENT 5 : OPINION ⟨the ~ of the meeting⟩ — **sense·less** adj — **sense·less·ly** adv — **sense·less·ness** n

²**sense** vb sensed; sens·ing 1 : to be or become aware of ⟨~ danger⟩; also : to perceive by the senses 2 : to detect (as radiation) automatically

sense organ n : a bodily structure (as an eye or ear) that receives stimuli (as heat or light) which excite neurons to send information to the brain

sen·si·bil·i·ty \ˌsen-sə-'bi-lə-tē\ n, pl -ties : delicacy of feeling : SENSITIVITY

sen·si·ble \'sen-sə-bəl\ adj 1 : capable of being perceived by the senses or the mind; also : capable of receiving sense impressions 2 : AWARE, CONSCIOUS 3 : REASONABLE, RATIONAL — **sen·si·bly** \-blē\ adv

sen·si·tive \'sen-sə-tiv\ adj 1 : subject to excitation by or responsive to stimuli 2 : having power of feeling 3 : of such a nature as to be easily affected 4 : TOUCHY ⟨a ~ issue⟩ — **sen·si·tive·ly** adv — **sen·si·tive·ness** n — **sen·si·tiv·i·ty** \ˌsen-sə-'ti-və-tē\ n

sensitive plant n : any of several mimosas with leaves that fold or droop when touched

sen·si·tize \'sen-sə-ˌtīz\ vb -tized; -tiz·ing : to make or become sensitive or hypersensitive — **sen·si·ti·za·tion** \ˌsen-sə-tə-'zā-shən\ n

sen·sor \'sen-ˌsȯr, -sər\ n : a device that responds to a physical stimulus

sen·so·ry \'sen-sə-rē\ adj 1 : of or relating to sensation or the senses 2 : AFFERENT

sen·su·al \'sen-shə-wəl\ adj 1 : relating to gratification of the senses 2 : devoted to the pleasures of the senses — **sen·su·al·ist** n — **sen·su·al·i·ty** \ˌsen-shə-'wa-lə-tē\ n — **sen·su·al·ly** adv

sen·su·ous \'sen-shə-wəs\ adj 1 : relating to the senses or to things that can be perceived by the senses 2 : VOLUPTUOUS — **sen·su·ous·ly** adv — **sen·su·ous·ness** n

¹**sent** past and past part of SEND

²**sent** \'sent\ n, pl **sen·ti** \'sen-tē\ — see kroon at MONEY table

sen·te \'sen-tē\ n, pl **li·cen·te** or **li·sen·te** \li-'sen-tē\ — see loti at MONEY table

¹**sen·tence** \'sen-t°ns, -t°nz\ n [ME, fr. AF, fr. L sententia, lit., feeling, opinion, fr. sentire to feel] 1 : the punishment set by a court 2 : a grammatically self-contained speech unit that expresses an assertion, a question, a command, a wish, or an exclamation

²**sentence** vb sen·tenced; sen·tenc·ing : to impose a sentence on

sen·ten·tious \sen-'ten-chəs\ adj : using wise sayings or proverbs; also : using pompous language — **sen·ten·tious·ly** adv — **sen·ten·tious·ness** n

sen·tient \'sen-chənt, -chē-ənt\ adj : capable of feeling : having perception

sen·ti·ment \'sen-tə-mənt\ n 1 : FEELING; also : thought and judgment influenced by feeling : emotional attitude 2 : OPINION, NOTION

sen·ti·men·tal \ˌsen-tə-'men-t°l\ adj 1 : influenced by tender feelings 2 : affecting the emotions ◆ **Synonyms** BATHETIC, MAUDLIN, MAWKISH, MUSHY — **sen·ti·men·tal·ism** n — **sen·ti·men·tal·ist** n — **sen·ti·men·tal·i·ty** \-ˌmen-'ta-lə-tē, -mən-\ n — **sen·ti·men·tal·ly** adv

sen·ti·men·tal·ise Brit var of SENTIMENTALIZE

sen·ti·men·tal·ize \-'men-tə-ˌlīz\ vb -ized; -iz·ing 1 : to indulge in sentiment 2 : to look upon or imbue with sentiment — **sen·ti·men·tal·i·za·tion** \-ˌmen-tə-lə-'zā-shən\ n

sen·ti·mo \sen-'tē-(ˌ)mō\ n, pl -mos — see peso at MONEY table

sen·ti·nel \'sen-t°n-əl\ n [MF sentinelle, fr. It sentinella, fr. sentina vigilance, fr. sentire to perceive, fr. L] : SENTRY

sen·try \'sen-trē\ n, pl **sentries** : a guard at a point of passage

sep abbr separate, separated

Sep abbr September

SEP abbr simplified employee pension

se·pal \'sē-pəl, 'se-\ n : one of the modified leaves comprising a flower calyx

sep·a·ra·ble \'se-pə-rə-bəl\ adj : capable of being separated — **sep·a·ra·bil·i·ty** \ˌse-pə-rə-'bi-lə-tē\

¹**sep·a·rate** \'se-pə-ˌrāt\ vb -rat·ed; -rat·ing 1 : to set or keep apart : DISCONNECT, SEVER 2 : to keep apart by something intervening 3 : to cease to be together : PART

²**sep·a·rate** \'se-prət, -pə-rət\ adj 1 : not connected 2 : divided from each other 3 : SINGLE, PARTICULAR ⟨the ~ pieces of the puzzle⟩ — **sep·a·rate·ly** adv

³**sep·a·rate** \'se-prət, -pə-rət\ n : an article of dress designed to be worn interchangeably with others to form various combinations

sep·a·ra·tion \ˌse-pə-'rā-shən\ n 1 : the act or process of separating : the state of being separated 2 : a point, line, means, or area of division 3 : a formal separating of a married couple by agreement but without divorce

sep·a·rat·ist \'se-prə-tist, 'se-pə-ˌrā-\ n : an advocate of separation (as from a political body) — **sep·a·rat·ism** \'se-prə-ˌti-zəm\ n

sep·a·ra·tive \'se-pə-ˌrā-tiv, 'se-prə-tiv\ adj : tending toward, causing, or expressing separation

sep·a·ra·tor \'se-pə-ˌrā-tər\ n : one that separates; esp : a device for separating cream from milk

se·pia \'sē-pē-ə\ n : a brownish gray to dark brown color

sep·sis \'sep-səs\ n, pl **sep·ses** \'sep-ˌsēz\ : a toxic condition due to spread of bacteria or their toxic products in the body

Sept abbr September

Sep·tem·ber \sep-'tem-bər\ n [ME Septembre, fr. AF & OE, both fr. L September (seventh month), fr. septem seven] : the 9th month of the year having 30 days

sep·tic \'sep-tik\ adj 1 : PUTREFACTIVE 2 : relating to or involving sepsis 3 : of, relating to, or used for sewage treatment and disposal

sep·ti·ce·mia \ˌsep-tə-'sē-mē-ə\ n : BLOOD POISONING

septic tank n : a tank in which sewage is disintegrated by bacteria

sep·tu·a·ge·nar·i·an \ˌsep-ˌtü-ə-jə-'ner-ē-ən, -ˌtyü-\ n : a person whose age is in the seventies — **septuagenarian** adj

Sep·tu·a·gint \sep-'tü-ə-jənt, -'tyü-\ n : a Greek version of the Old Testament prepared in the 3d and 2d centuries B.C. by Jewish scholars

sep·tum \'sep-təm\ n, pl **sep·ta** \-tə\ : a dividing wall or membrane esp. between bodily spaces or masses of soft tissue

se·pul·chral \sə-'pəl-krəl\ adj 1 : relating to burial or the grave 2 : GLOOMY

¹**sep·ul·chre** or **sep·ul·cher** \'se-pəl-kər\ n : a burial vault : TOMB

²**sepulchre** or **sepulcher** vb -**chred** or -**chered**; -**chring** or -**chering** : BURY, ENTOMB

sep·ul·ture \'se-pəl-ˌchúr\ n 1 : BURIAL 2 : SEPULCHRE

se·quel \'sē-kwəl\ n 1 : logical consequence 2 : a literary or cinematic work continuing a story begun in a preceding one

¹**se·quence** \'sē-kwəns\ n 1 : SERIES 2 : chronological order of events 3 : RESULT, SEQUEL ✦ **Synonyms** SUCCESSION, CHAIN, PROGRESSION, TRAIN — **se·quen·tial** \si-'kwen-chəl\ adj — **se·quen·tial·ly** adv

²**sequence** vb **se·quenced; se·quenc·ing** 1 : to arrange in a sequence 2 : to determine the sequence of chemical constituents in ⟨∼ DNA⟩

se·quent \'sē-kwənt\ adj 1 : SUCCEEDING, CONSECUTIVE 2 : RESULTANT

se·ques·ter \si-'kwes-tər\ vb : to set apart : SEGREGATE ⟨∼ a jury⟩

se·ques·trate \'sē-kwəs-ˌtrāt, si-'kwes-\ vb -**trat·ed; -trat·ing** : SEQUESTER — **se·ques·tra·tion** \ˌsē-kwəs-'trā-shən, ˌse-\ n

se·quin \'sē-kwən\ n 1 : an old gold coin of Turkey and Italy 2 : a small metal or plastic plate used for ornamentation esp. on clothing — **se·quined** or **se·quinned** \-kwənd\ adj

se·quoia \si-'kwói-ə\ n : either of two huge California coniferous trees

ser abbr 1 serial 2 series 3 service

sera pl of SERUM

se·ra·glio \sə-'ral-yō\ n, pl -**glios** [It serraglio] : HAREM

se·ra·pe \sə-'rä-pē\ n : a colorful woolen shawl worn over the shoulders esp. by Mexican men

ser·aph \'ser-əf\ n, pl **ser·a·phim** \-ə-ˌfim, -ˌfēm\ or **seraphs** : one of the 6-winged angels standing in the presence of God

ser·a·phim \'ser-ə-ˌfim, -ˌfēm\ n pl 1 : the highest order of angels 2 sing, pl **seraphim** : SERAPH — **se·raph·ic** \sə-'ra-fik\ adj

Ser·bi·an \'sər-bē-ən\ n 1 : SERB 2 : a south Slavic language spoken by the Serbian people — **Serbian** adj

Ser·bo-Cro·a·tian \ˌsər-(ˌ)bō-krō-'ā-shən\ n : the Serbian and Croatian languages together with the Slavic speech of Bosnia, Herzegovina, and Montenegro taken as a single language with regional variants

sere \'sir\ adj : DRY, WITHERED

¹**ser·e·nade** \ˌser-ə-'nād\ n [F, fr. It serenata, fr. sereno clear, calm (of weather) fr. L serenus] : music sung or played as a compliment esp. outdoors at night for a woman being courted

²**serenade** vb -**nad·ed; -nad·ing** : to entertain with or perform a serenade

ser·en·dip·i·ty \ˌser-ən-'di-pə-tē\ n [fr. its possession by the heroes of the Persian fairy tale The Three Princes of Serendip] : the gift of finding valuable or agreeable things not sought for — **ser·en·dip·i·tous** \-təs\ adj — **ser·en·dip·i·tous·ly** adv

se·rene \sə-'rēn\ adj 1 : CLEAR ⟨∼ skies⟩ 2 : QUIET, CALM ✦ **Synonyms** TRANQUIL, PEACEFUL, PLACID — **se·rene·ly** adv — **se·ren·i·ty** \sə-'re-nə-tē\ n

serf \'sərf\ n : a member of a servile class bound to the land and subject to the will of the landowner — **serf·dom** \-dəm\ n

serge \'sərj\ n : a twilled woolen cloth

ser·geant \'sär-jənt\ n [ME, servant, attendant, sergeant, fr. AF sergant, serjant, fr. L servient-, serviens, prp. of servire to serve] 1 : a noncommissioned officer (as in the army) ranking next below a staff sergeant 2 : an officer in a police force

sergeant at arms : an officer of an organization who preserves order and executes commands

sergeant first class n : a noncommissioned officer in the army ranking next below a master sergeant

sergeant major n, pl **sergeants major**

or **sergeant majors 1** : a noncommissioned officer in the army or marine corps serving as chief administrative assistant in a headquarters **2** : a noncommissioned officer in the marine corps ranking above a first sergeant

¹**se·ri·al** \'sir-ē-əl\ *adj* **1** : appearing in parts that follow regularly ⟨a ~ story⟩ **2** : performing a series of similar acts over a period of time ⟨a ~ killer⟩; *also* : occurring in such a series — **se·ri·al·ly** *adv*

²**serial** *n* : a serial story or other writing — **se·ri·al·ist** \-ə-list\ *n*

se·ries \'sir-ēz\ *n, pl* **series** : a number of things or events arranged in order and connected by being alike in some way
♦ **Synonyms** SUCCESSION, PROGRESSION, SEQUENCE, CHAIN, TRAIN, STRING

seri·graph \'ser-ə-ˌgraf\ *n* : an original silk-screen print — **se·rig·ra·pher** \sə-'ri-grə-fər\ *n* — **se·rig·ra·phy** \-fē\ *n*

se·ri·ous \'sir-ē-əs\ *adj* **1** : thoughtful or subdued in appearance or manner : SOBER **2** : requiring much thought or work **3** : EARNEST, DEVOTED **4** : DANGEROUS, HARMFUL **5** : excessive or impressive in quantity or degree ⟨making ~ money⟩ ♦ **Synonyms** GRAVE, SEDATE, STAID — **se·ri·ous·ly** *adv* — **se·ri·ous·ness** *n*

ser·mon \'sər-mən\ *n* [ME, fr. AF *sermun*, fr. ML *sermon, sermo*, fr. L, speech, conversation, fr. *serere* to link together] **1** : a religious discourse esp. as part of a worship service **2** : a lecture on conduct or duty

ser·mon·ize \'sər-mə-ˌnīz\ *vb* **-ized; -izing 1** : to compose or deliver a sermon **2** : to preach to or on at length

se·rol·o·gy \sə-'rä-lə-jē\ *n* : a science dealing with serums and esp. their reactions and properties — **se·ro·log·i·cal** \ˌsir-ə-'lä-ji-kəl\ *or* **se·ro·log·ic** \-jik\ *adj* — **se·ro·log·i·cal·ly** \-ji-k(ə-)lē\ *adv*

se·ro·to·nin \ˌsir-ə-'tō-nən, ˌser-\ *n* : a neurotransmitter that is a powerful vasoconstrictor

se·rous \'sir-əs\ *adj* : of, relating to, resembling, or producing serum; *esp* : of thin watery constitution

ser·pent \'sər-pənt\ *n* : SNAKE

¹**ser·pen·tine** \'sər-pən-ˌtēn, -ˌtīn\ *adj* **1** : SLY, CRAFTY **2** : WINDING, TURNING

²**ser·pen·tine** \-ˌtēn\ *n* : a dull-green mineral having a mottled appearance

ser·rate \'ser-ˌāt\ *adj* : having a saw-toothed edge ⟨a ~ leaf⟩

ser·ried \'ser-ēd\ *adj* : crowded together

se·rum \'sir-əm\ *n, pl* **serums** *or* **se·ra** \-ə\ [L, whey, wheylike fluid] : the clear yellowish antibody-containing fluid that can be separated from blood when it clots; *also* : a preparation of animal serum containing specific antibodies and used to prevent or cure disease

serv *abbr* service

ser·vant \'sər-vənt\ *n* : one that serves others; *esp* : a person employed for domestic or personal work

¹**serve** \'sərv\ *vb* **served; serv·ing 1** : to work as a servant **2** : to render obedience and worship to (God) **3** : to comply with the commands or demands of **4** : to work through or perform a term of service (as in the army) **5** : PUT IN ⟨*served* five years in jail⟩ **6** : to be of use : ANSWER ⟨pine boughs *served* for a bed⟩ **7** : BENEFIT **8** : to prove adequate or satisfactory for ⟨a pie that ~*s* eight people⟩ **9** : to make ready and pass out ⟨~ drinks⟩ **10** : to furnish or supply with something ⟨one power company *serving* the whole state⟩ **11** : to wait on ⟨~ a customer⟩ **12** : to treat or act toward in a specified way **13** : to put the ball in play (as in tennis)

²**serve** *n* : the act of serving a ball (as in tennis)

serv·er \'sər-vər\ *n* **1** : one that serves **2** : a computer in a network that is used to provide services (as access to files) to other computers in the network

¹**ser·vice** \'sər-vəs\ *n* **1** : the occupation of a servant **2** : HELP, BENEFIT **3** : a meeting for worship; *also* : a form followed in worship or in a ceremony ⟨burial ~⟩ **4** : the act, fact, or means of serving **5** : performance of official or professional duties **6** : SERVE **7** : a set of dishes or silverware **8** : a branch of public employment; *also* : the persons in it ⟨civil ~⟩ **9** : military or naval duty

²**service** *vb* **ser·viced; ser·vic·ing** : to do maintenance or repair work on or for

ser·vice·able \'sər-və-sə-bəl\ *adj* : prepared for service : USEFUL, USABLE

ser·vice·man \'sər-vəs-ˌman, -mən\ *n* **1** : a man who is a member of the armed forces **2** : a man employed to repair or maintain equipment

service mark *n* : a mark or device used to identify a service (as transportation or insurance) offered to customers

service station *n* : GAS STATION

ser·vice·wom·an \'sər-vəs-ˌwu̇-mən\ *n* : a woman who is a member of the armed forces

ser·vile \'sər-vəl, -ˌvī(-ə)l\ *adj* **1** : befitting a slave or servant **2** : behaving like a slave : SUBMISSIVE — **ser·vile·ly** *adv* — **ser·vil·i·ty** \ˌsər-'vi-lə-tē\ *n*

serv·ing \'sər-viŋ\ *n* : HELPING

ser·vi·tor \'sər-və-tər\ *n* : a male servant

ser·vi·tude \'sər-və-ˌtüd, -ˌtyüd\ *n* : SLAVERY, BONDAGE

ser·vo \'sər-vō\ *n, pl* **servos 1** : SERVOMOTOR **2** : SERVOMECHANISM

ser·vo·mech·a·nism \'sər-vō-ˌme-kə-ˌni-zəm\ *n* : a device for automatically correcting the performance of a mechanism

ser·vo·mo·tor \-ˌmō-tər\ *n* : a mechanism that supplements a primary control

ses·a·me \'se-sə-mē\ *n* : a widely cultivated annual herb of warm regions; *also* : its seeds that yield an edible oil (**sesame oil**) and are used in flavoring

ses·qui·cen·ten·ni·al \ˌses-kwi-sen-'te-nē-əl\ *n* [L *sesqui-* one and a half, half again] : a 150th anniversary or its celebration — **sesquicentennial** *adj*

ses·qui·pe·da·lian \ˌses-kwə-pə-'dāl-yən\ *adj* **1** : having many syllables : LONG **2** : using long words

ses·sile \'se-ˌsī(-ə)l, - səl\ *adj* : permanently attached and not free to move about

ses·sion \'se-shən\ *n* 1 : a meeting or series of meetings of a body (as a court or legislature) for the transaction of business 2 : a meeting or period devoted to a particular activity

¹**set** \'set\ *vb* **set; set·ting** 1 : to cause to sit 2 : PLACE 3 : ARRANGE, ADJUST 4 : to cause to be or do 5 : SETTLE, DECREE 6 : to fix in a frame 7 : to fix at a certain amount 8 : WAGER, STAKE 9 : to make or become fast or rigid 10 : to adapt (as words) to something (as music) 11 : to become fixed or firm or solid 12 : to be suitable : FIT 13 : BROOD 14 : to have a certain direction 15 : to pass below the horizon 16 : to defeat in bridge — **set about** : to begin to do — **set forth** : to begin a trip — **set off** 1 : to start out on a course or a trip 2 : to cause to explode — **set out** : to begin a trip or undertaking — **set sail** : to begin a voyage — **set upon** : to attack usu. with violence

²**set** *n* 1 : a setting or a being set 2 : DIRECTION, COURSE; *also* : TENDENCY 3 : FORM, BUILD 4 : the fit of something (as a coat) 5 : an artificial setting for the scene of a play or motion picture 6 : a group of tennis games in which one side wins at least six 7 : a group of persons or things of the same kind or having a common characteristic usu. classed together 8 : a collection of things and esp. of mathematical elements (as numbers or points) 9 : an electronic apparatus ⟨a television ~⟩

³**set** *adj* 1 : DELIBERATE, INTENT 2 : fixed by authority or custom 3 : RIGID 4 : PERSISTENT

set·back \'set-ˌbak\ *n* : a temporary defeat : REVERSE

set back *vb* 1 : HINDER, DELAY; *also* : REVERSE 2 : COST

set piece 1 : a composition (as in literature or music) executed in fixed or ideal form often with brilliant effect 2 : a scene, depiction, speech, or event obviously designed to have an imposing effect

set·screw \'set-ˌskrü\ *n* : a screw screwed through one part tightly upon or into another part to prevent relative movement

set·tee \se-'tē\ *n* : a bench or sofa with a back and arms

set·ter \'se-tər\ *n* : a large long-coated hunting dog

set·ting \'se-tiŋ\ *n* 1 : the frame in which a gem is set 2 : the time, place, and circumstances in which something occurs or develops; *also* : SCENERY 3 : music written for a text (as of a poem) 4 : the eggs that a fowl sits on for hatching at one time

set·tle \'se-t°l\ *vb* **set·tled; set·tling** [ME *settlen* to seat, bring to rest, come to rest, fr. OE *setlan*, fr. *setl* seat] 1 : to place so as to stay 2 : to establish in residence; *also* : COLONIZE 3 : to make compact 4 : QUIET, CALM 5 : to establish or secure permanently 6 : to direct one's efforts 7 : to fix by agreement 8 : to give legally 9 : ADJUST, ARRANGE 10 : DECIDE, DETERMINE 11 : to make a final disposition of ⟨~ an account⟩ 12 : to come to rest 13 : to reach an agreement on 14 : to sink gradually to a lower level 15 : to become clear by depositing sediment — **set·tler** *n*

set·tle·ment \'se-t°l-mənt\ *n* 1 : the act or process of settling 2 : BESTOWAL ⟨a marriage ~⟩ 3 : payment or adjustment of an account 4 : COLONY 5 : a small village 6 : an institution providing various community services esp. to large city populations 7 : adjustment of doubts and differences

set-to \'set-ˌtü\ *n*, *pl* **set-tos** : FIGHT

set·up \'set-ˌəp\ *n* 1 : the manner or act of arranging 2 : glass, ice, and nonalcoholic beverage for mixing served to patrons who supply their own liquor 3 : something (as a plot) that has been constructed or contrived; *also* : FRAME-UP

set up *vb* 1 : to place in position; *also* : ASSEMBLE 2 : CAUSE 3 : FOUND, ESTABLISH 4 : FRAME 5

sev·en \'se-vən\ *n* 1 : one more than six 2 : the 7th in a set or series 3 : something having seven units — **seven** *adj or pron* — **sev·enth** \-vənth\ *adj or adv or n*

sev·en·teen \ˌse-vən-'tēn\ *n* : one more than 16 — **seventeen** *adj or pron* — **sev·en·teenth** \-'tēnth\ *adj or n*

seventeen–year locust *n* : a cicada of the U.S. that has in the North a life of 17 years and in the South of 13 years of which most is spent underground as a nymph and only a few weeks as a winged adult

sev·en·ty \'se-vən-tē\ *n*, *pl* **-ties** : seven times 10 — **sev·en·ti·eth** \-tē-əth\ *adj or n* — **seventy** *adj or pron*

sev·er \'se-vər\ *vb* **sev·ered; sev·er·ing** : DIVIDE; *esp* : to separate by or as if by cutting — **sev·er·ance** \'sev-rəns, 'se-və-\ *n*

sev·er·al \'sev-rəl, 'se-və-\ *adj* [ME, fr. AF, fr. ML *separalis*, fr. L *separ* separate, fr. *separare* to separate] 1 : INDIVIDUAL, DISTINCT ⟨federal union of the ~ states⟩ 2 : consisting of an indefinite number but yet not very many — **sev·er·al·ly** *adv*

severance pay *n* : extra pay given an employee on termination of employment

se·vere \sə-'vir\ *adj* **se·ver·er; -est** 1 : marked by strictness or sternness : AUSTERE 2 : strict in discipline 3 : causing distress and esp. physical discomfort or pain ⟨~ weather⟩ ⟨a ~ wound⟩ 4 : hard to endure ⟨~ trials⟩ 5 : SERIOUS ⟨~ depression⟩ ✦ **Synonyms** STERN, ASCETIC, ASTRINGENT — **se·vere·ly** *adv* — **se·ver·i·ty** \-'ver-ə-tē\ *n*

sew \'sō\ *vb* **sewed; sewn** \'sōn\ *or* **sewed; sew·ing** 1 : to unite or fasten by stitches 2 : to engage in sewing

sew·age \'sü-ij\ *n* : waste materials carried off by sewers

¹**sew·er** \'sō-ər\ *n* : one that sews

²**sew·er** \'sü-ər\ *n* : an artificial pipe or channel to carry off waste matter

sew·er·age \'sü-ə-rij\ n 1 : a system of sewers 2 : SEWAGE

sew·ing n 1 : the activity of one who sews 2 : material that has been or is to be sewed

sex \'seks\ n 1 : either of the two major forms that occur in many living things and are designated male or female according to their role in reproduction; also : the qualities by which these sexes are differentiated and which directly or indirectly function in reproduction involving two parents 2 : sexual activity or behavior; also : SEXUAL INTERCOURSE — **sexed** \'sekst\ adj — **sex·less** adj

sex·a·ge·nar·i·an \,sek-sə-jə-'ner-ē-ən\ n : a person whose age is in the sixties — **sexagenarian** adj

sex appeal n : personal appeal or physical attractiveness esp. for members of the opposite sex

sex cell n : an egg cell or sperm cell

sex chromosome n : one of usu. a pair of chromosomes that are usu. similar in one sex but different in the other sex and are concerned with the inheritance of sex

sex hormone n : a steroid hormone (as estrogen or testosterone) that is produced esp. by the gonads or adrenal cortex and chiefly affects the growth or function of the reproductive organs

sex·ism \'sek-,si-zəm\ n : prejudice or discrimination based on sex; esp : discrimination against women — **sex·ist** \'sek-sist\ adj or n

sex·ol·o·gy \sek-'sä-lə-jē\ n : the study of sex or of the interactions of the sexes — **sex·ol·o·gist** \-jist\ n

sex·pot \'seks-,pät\ n : a conspicuously sexy woman

sex symbol n : a usu. renowned person (as an entertainer) noted and admired for conspicuous attractiveness

sex·tant \'sek-stənt\ n [NL sextant-, sextans sixth part of a circle, fr. L, sixth part, fr. sextus sixth] : a navigational instrument for determining latitude

sex·tet \sek-'stet\ n 1 : a musical composition for six voices or instruments; also : the performers of such a composition 2 : a group or set of six

sex·ton \'sek-stən\ n : one who takes care of church property

sex·u·al \'sek-shə-wəl\ adj : of, relating to, or involving sex or the sexes ⟨a ~ spore⟩ ⟨~ relations⟩ — **sex·u·al·i·ty** \,sek-shə-'wa-lə-tē\ n — **sex·u·al·ly** \'sek-shə-wə-lē\ adv

sexual intercourse n 1 : intercourse between a male and a female in which the penis is inserted into the vagina 2 : intercourse between individuals involving genital contact other than insertion of the penis into the vagina

sexually transmitted disease n : a disease (as syphilis, gonorrhea, AIDS, or the genital form of herpes simplex) that is caused by a microorganism or virus usu. or often transmitted by direct sexual contact

sexual relations n pl : SEXUAL INTERCOURSE

sexy \'sek-sē\ adj **sex·i·er; -est** : sexually suggestive or stimulating : EROTIC — **sex·i·ly** \-sə-lē\ adv — **sex·i·ness** \-sē-nəs\ n

SF abbr 1 sacrifice fly 2 science fiction 3 square feet

SFC abbr sergeant first class

¹SG abbr 1 sergeant 2 solicitor general 3 surgeon general

²SG symbol seaborgium

sgd abbr signed

Sgt abbr sergeant

Sgt Maj abbr sergeant major

sh abbr share

shab·by \'sha-bē\ adj **shab·bi·er; -est** 1 : dressed in worn clothes 2 : threadbare and faded from wear 3 : DESPICABLE, MEAN; also : UNFAIR ⟨~ treatment⟩ — **shab·bi·ly** \'sha-bə-lē\ adv — **shab·bi·ness** \-bē-nəs\ n

shack \'shak\ n : HUT, SHANTY

¹shack·le \'sha-kəl\ n 1 : something (as a manacle or fetter) that confines the legs or arms 2 : a check on free action made as if by fetters 3 : a device for making something fast or secure

²shackle vb **shack·led; shack·ling** : to bind or fasten with shackles

shad \'shad\ n, pl **shad** : any of several sea fishes related to the herrings that swim up rivers to spawn and include some important food fishes

¹shade \'shād\ n 1 : partial obscurity 2 : space sheltered from the light esp. of the sun 3 : PHANTOM 4 : something that shelters from or intercepts light or heat; also, pl : SUNGLASSES 5 : a dark color or a variety of a color 6 : a small difference

²shade vb **shad·ed; shad·ing** 1 : to shelter from light and heat 2 : DARKEN, OBSCURE 3 : to mark with degrees of light or color 4 : to show slight differences esp. in color or meaning

shad·ing n : the color and lines representing darkness or shadow in a drawing or painting

¹shad·ow \'sha-dō\ n 1 : partial darkness in a space from which light rays are cut off 2 : SHELTER 3 : shade cast upon a surface by something intercepting rays from a light ⟨the ~ of a tree⟩ 4 : PHANTOM 5 : a shaded portion of a picture 6 : a small portion or degree : TRACE ⟨a ~ of doubt⟩ 7 : a source of gloom or unhappiness — **shad·owy** adj

²shadow vb 1 : to cast a shadow on 2 : to represent faintly or vaguely 3 : to follow and watch closely : TRAIL

shad·ow·box \'sha-dō-,bäks\ vb : to box with an imaginary opponent esp. for training

shady \'shā-dē\ adj **shad·i·er; -est** 1 : affording shade 2 : of questionable honesty or reputation

¹shaft \'shaft\ n, pl **shafts** 1 : the long handle of a spear or lance 2 : SPEAR, LANCE 3 or pl **shaves** \'shavz\ : POLE; esp : one of two poles between which a horse is hitched to pull a vehicle 4 : something (as a column) long and slender 5 : a bar to support a rotating piece or to transmit power by rotation **6** : an inclined opening in the ground (as for finding or mining ore) **7** : a vertical opening (as for an elevator) through the floors of a building **8** : harsh or unfair treatment — usu. used with *the*

²shaft *vb* **1** : to fit with a shaft **2** : to treat unfairly or harshly

shag \'shag\ *n* : a shaggy tangled mass or covering (as of wool) : long coarse or matted fiber, nap, or pile

shag·gy \'sha-gē\ *adj* **shag·gi·er; -est 1** : rough with or as if with long hair or wool **2** : tangled or rough in surface

shah \'shä, 'shó\ *n, often cap* : a sovereign of Iran

Shak *abbr* Shakespeare

¹shake \'shāk\ *vb* **shook** \'shúk\; **shak·en** \'shā-kən\; **shak·ing 1** : to move or cause to move jerkily or irregularly **2** : BRANDISH, WAVE ⟨*shaking* his fist⟩ **3** : to disturb emotionally ⟨*shaken* by her death⟩ **4** : WEAKEN ⟨*shook* his faith⟩ **5** : to bring or come into a certain position, condition, or arrangement by or as if by moving jerkily **6** : to clasp (hands) in greeting or as a sign of goodwill or agreement ◆ *Synonyms* TREMBLE, QUAKE, QUAVER, SHIVER, QUIVER — **shak·able** *or* **shake·able** \'shā-kə-bəl\ *adj*

²shake *n* **1** : the act or a result of shaking **2** : DEAL, TREATMENT ⟨a fair ∼⟩

shake·down \'shāk-,daún\ *n* **1** : an improvised bed **2** : EXTORTION **3** : a process or period of adjustment **4** : a test (as of a new ship or airplane) under operating conditions

shake down *vb* **1** : to take up temporary quarters **2** : to occupy a makeshift bed **3** : to become accustomed esp. to new surroundings or duties **4** : to settle down **5** : to give a shakedown test to **6** : to obtain money from in a deceitful or illegal manner **7** : to bring about a reduction of

shak·er \'shā-kər\ *n* **1** : one that shakes ⟨pepper ∼⟩ **2** *cap* : a member of a religious sect founded in England in 1747

Shake·spear·ean *or* **Shake·spear·ian** \shāk-'spir-ē-ən\ *adj* : of, relating to, or having the characteristics of Shakespeare or his writings

shake–up \'shāk-,əp\ *n* : an extensive often drastic reorganization

shaky \'shā-kē\ *adj* **shak·i·er; -est** : UNSOUND, WEAK — **shak·i·ly** \'shā-kə-lē\ *adv* — **shak·i·ness** \-kē-nəs\ *n*

shale \'shāl\ *n* : a finely layered rock formed from clay, mud, or silt

shall \'shal, 'shal\ *vb, past* **should** \'shəd, 'shúd\ *pres sing & pl* **shall** — used as an auxiliary to express a command, what seems inevitable or likely in the future, simple futurity, or determination

shal·lop \'sha-ləp\ *n* : a light open boat

shal·lot \shə-'lät, 'sha-lət\ *n* [modif. of F *échalote*] : a small clustered bulb that is used in seasoning and is produced by a perennial herb belonging to a subspecies of the onion; *also* : this herb **2** : GREEN ONION

¹shal·low \'sha-lō\ *adj* **1** : not deep **2** : not intellectually profound

²shallow *n* : a shallow place in a body of water — usu. used in pl.

¹sham \'sham\ *n* **1** : an ornamental covering for a pillow **2** : COUNTERFEIT, IMITATION **3** : a person who shams

²sham *vb* **shammed; sham·ming** : FEIGN, PRETEND — **sham·mer** *n*

³sham *adj* : not genuine : FALSE, FEIGNED

sha·man \'shä-mən, 'shā-\ *n* [ultim. fr. Evenki (a language of Siberia) *šamān*] : a priest or priestess who uses magic to cure the sick, to divine the hidden, and to control events

sham·ble \'sham-bəl\ *vb* **sham·bled; sham·bling** : to shuffle along — **shamble** *n*

sham·bles \'sham-bəlz\ *n* **1** : a scene of great slaughter **2** : a scene or state of great destruction or disorder; *also* : MESS

¹shame \'shām\ *n* **1** : a painful sense of having done something wrong, improper, or immodest **2** : DISGRACE, DISHONOR **3** : a cause of feeling shame **4** : something to be regretted ⟨it's a ∼ you'll miss the party⟩ — **shame·ful** \-fəl\ *adj* — **shame·ful·ly** *adv* — **shame·less** *adj* — **shame·less·ly** *adv*

²shame *vb* **shamed; sham·ing 1** : DISGRACE **2** : to make ashamed

shame·faced \'shām-'fāst\ *adj* : ASHAMED, ABASHED — **shame·faced·ly** \-,fā-səd-lē, -,fāst-lē\ *adv*

¹sham·poo \sham-'pü\ *vb* [Hindi *cãpo*, imper. of *cãpnā* to press, shampoo] : to wash (as the hair) with soap and water or with a special preparation; *also* : to clean (as a rug) similarly

²shampoo *n, pl* **shampoos 1** : the act or an instance of shampooing **2** : a preparation for use in shampooing

sham·rock \'sham-,räk\ *n* [Ir *seamróg*, dim. of *seamar* clover] : a plant of folk legend with leaves composed of three leaflets that is associated with St. Patrick and Ireland

shang·hai \shaŋ-'hī\ *vb* **shang·haied; shang·hai·ing** [*Shanghai*, China] : to force aboard a ship for service as a sailor; *also* : to trick or force into an undesirable position

Shan·gri–la \,shaŋ-gri-'lä\ *n* [*Shangri-La*, imaginary land depicted in the novel *Lost Horizon* (1933) by James Hilton] : a remote idyllic hideaway

shank \'shaŋk\ *n* **1** : the part of the leg between the knee and the human ankle or a corresponding part of a quadruped **2** : a cut of meat from the leg **3** : the narrow part of the sole of a shoe beneath the instep **4** : the part of a tool or instrument (as a key or anchor) connecting the functioning part with a part by which it is held or moved

shan·tung \shan-'təŋ\ *n* : a fabric in plain weave having a slightly irregular surface

shan·ty \'shan-tē\ *n, pl* **shanties** [prob. fr. CanF *chantier* lumber camp, hut, fr. F, builder's yard, ways, support for barrels, fr. OF, support, fr. L *cantherius* rafter, trellis] : a small roughly built shelter or dwelling

¹**shape** \'shāp\ *vb* **shaped; shap·ing 1** : to form esp. in a particular shape **2** : DESIGN **3** : ADAPT, ADJUST **4** : REGULATE ✦ *Synonyms* MAKE, FASHION, FABRICATE, MANUFACTURE, FRAME, MOLD

²**shape** *n* **1** : APPEARANCE **2** : surface configuration : FORM **3** : bodily contour apart from the head and face : FIGURE **4** : PHANTOM **5** : CONDITION — **shaped** *adj*

shape·less \'shā-pləs\ *adj* **1** : having no definite shape **2** : not shapely — **shape·less·ly** *adv* — **shape·less·ness** *n*

shape·ly \'shā-plē\ *adj* **shape·li·er; -est** : having a pleasing shape — **shape·li·ness** *n*

shape–shift·er \'shāp-,shif-tər\ *n* : one that seems able to change form or identity at will

shard \'shärd\ *also* **sherd** \'shərd\ *n* : a broken piece : FRAGMENT

¹**share** \'sher\ *n* : PLOWSHARE

²**share** *n* **1** : a portion belonging to one person or group **2** : any of the equal interests into which the capital stock of a corporation is divided

³**share** *vb* **shared; shar·ing 1** : APPORTION **2** : to use or enjoy with others **3** : PARTICIPATE — **shar·er** *n*

share·crop·per \-,krä-pər\ *n* : a farmer who works another's land in return for a share of the crop — **share·crop** *vb*

share·hold·er \-,hōl-dər\ *n* : STOCKHOLDER

share·ware \'sher-,wer\ *n* : software available for usu. limited trial use at little or no cost but that can be upgraded for a fee

¹**shark** \'shärk\ *n* : any of various active, usu. predatory, and mostly large marine cartilaginous fishes

²**shark** *n* : a greedy crafty person

shark·skin \-,skin\ *n* **1** : the hide of a shark or leather made from it **2** : a fabric woven from strands of many fine threads and having a sleek appearance and silky feel

¹**sharp** \'shärp\ *adj* **1** : having a thin cutting edge or fine point : not dull or blunt **2** : COLD, NIPPING ⟨a ~ wind⟩ **3** : keen in intellect, perception, or attention **4** : BRISK, ENERGETIC **5** : IRRITABLE ⟨a ~ temper⟩ **6** : causing intense distress ⟨a ~ pain⟩ **7** : HARSH, CUTTING ⟨a ~ rebuke⟩ **8** : affecting the senses as if cutting or piercing ⟨a ~ sound⟩ ⟨a ~ smell⟩ **9** : not smooth or rounded ⟨~ features⟩ **10** : involving an abrupt or extreme change ⟨a ~ turn⟩ **11** : CLEAR, DISTINCT ⟨mountains in ~ relief⟩; *also* : easy to perceive ⟨a ~ contrast⟩ **12** : higher than the true pitch; *also* : raised by a half step **13** : STYLISH ⟨a ~ dresser⟩ ✦ *Synonyms* KEEN, ACUTE, QUICK-WITTED, PENETRATIVE — **sharp·ly** *adv* — **sharp·ness** *n*

²**sharp** *adv* **1** : in a sharp manner **2** : EXACTLY, PRECISELY ⟨left at 8 ~⟩

³**sharp** *n* **1** : a sharp edge or point **2** : a character # which indicates that a specified note is to be raised by a half step; *also* : the resulting note **3** : SHARPER

⁴**sharp** *vb* : to raise in pitch by a half step

shar–pei \,shä-'pā, ,shär-\ *n, pl* **shar-peis** *often cap* S&P [Chin (Guangdong dial.) sà sand + péi fur] : any of a Chinese breed of dogs that have loose wrinkled skin esp. when young

sharp·en \'shär-pən\ *vb* : to make or become sharp — **sharp·en·er** *n*

sharp·er \'shär-pər\ *n* : SWINDLER; *esp* : a cheating gambler

sharp·ie *or* **sharpy** \'shär-pē\ *n, pl* **sharp·ies 1** : SHARPER **2** : a person who is exceptionally keen or alert

sharp·shoot·er \'shärp-,shü-tər\ *n* : a proficient marksman — **sharp·shoot·ing** *n*

shat·ter \'sha-tər\ *vb* : to dash or burst into fragments — **shat·ter·proof** \'sha-tər-,prüf\ *adj*

¹**shave** \'shāv\ *vb* **shaved; shaved** *or* **shav·en** \'shā-vən\; **shav·ing 1** : to slice in thin pieces **2** : to make bare or smooth by cutting the hair from **3** : to cut or pare off by the sliding movement of a razor **4** : to skim along or near the surface of

²**shave** *n* **1** : any of various tools for cutting thin slices **2** : an act or process of shaving

shav·er \'shā-vər\ *n* **1** : an electric razor **2** : BOY, YOUNGSTER

shaves *pl of* SHAFT

shaving *n* **1** : the act of one that shaves **2** : something shaved off

shawl \'shól\ *n* : a square or oblong piece of fabric used esp. by women as a loose covering for the head or shoulders

Shaw·nee \shȯ-'nē, shä-\ *n, pl* **Shawnee** *or* **Shawnees** : a member of an American Indian people orig. of the central Ohio valley; *also* : their language

shd *abbr* should

she \'shē\ *pron* : that female one ⟨who is ~⟩; *also* : that one regarded as feminine ⟨~'s a fine ship⟩

sheaf \'shēf\ *n, pl* **sheaves** \'shēvz\ **1** : a bundle of stalks and ears of grain **2** : a group of things bound together

¹**shear** \'shir\ *vb* **sheared; sheared** *or* **shorn** \'shórn\; **shear·ing 1** : to cut the hair or wool from : CLIP, TRIM **2** : to deprive by or as if by cutting **3** : to cut or break sharply

²**shear** *n* **1** : any of various cutting tools that consist of two blades fastened together so that the edges slide one by the other — usu. used in pl. **2** *chiefly Brit* : the act, an instance, or the result of shearing **3** : an action or stress caused by applied forces that causes two parts of a body to slide on each other

shear·wa·ter \'shir-,wȯ-tər, -,wä-\ *n* : any of several seabirds related to the petrels that often skim along waves in flight

sheath \'shēth\ *n, pl* **sheaths** \'shēthz, 'shēths\ **1** : a case for a blade (as of a knife); *also* : an anatomical covering suggesting such a case   **2** : a close-fitting dress usu. worn without a belt

sheathe \'shēth\ *also* **sheath** \'shēth\ *vb* **sheathed; sheath·ing**   **1** : to put into a sheath   **2** : to cover with something that guards or protects

sheath·ing \'shē-thiŋ, -thiŋ\ *n* : material used to sheathe something; *esp* : the first covering of boards or of waterproof material on the outside wall of a frame house or on a timber roof

sheave \'shiv, 'shēv\ *n* : a grooved wheel or pulley (as on a pulley block)

she-bang \shi-'baŋ\ *n* : everything involved in what is under consideration ⟨sold the whole ~⟩

¹**shed** \'shed\ *vb* **shed; shed·ding**   **1** : to cause to flow from a cut or wound ⟨~ blood⟩   **2** : to pour down in drops ⟨~ tears⟩   **3** : to give out (as light) : DIF·FUSE   **4** : to throw off (as a natural covering) : DISCARD ⟨~ skin⟩

²**shed** *n* : a slight structure built for shelter or storage

sheen \'shēn\ *n* : a subdued luster

sheep \'shēp\ *n, pl* **sheep**   **1** : any of various cud-chewing mammals that are stockier than the related goats and lack a beard in the male; *esp* : one raised for meat or for its wool or skin   **2** : a timid or defenseless person   **3** : SHEEPSKIN

sheep·dog \'shēp-,dȯg\ *n* : a dog used to tend, drive, or guard sheep

sheep·fold \'shēp-,fōld\ *n* : a pen or shelter for sheep

sheep·herd·er \-,hər-dər\ *n* : a worker in charge of sheep esp. on open range — **sheep·herd·ing** *n*

sheep·ish \'shē-pish\ *adj* : BASHFUL, TIMID; *esp* : embarrassed by consciousness of a fault — **sheep·ish·ly** *adv*

sheep·skin \'shēp-,skin\ *n*   **1** : the hide of a sheep or leather prepared from it; *also* : PARCHMENT   **2** : DIPLOMA

¹**sheer** \'shir\ *vb* : to turn from a course

²**sheer** *adj*   **1** : very thin or transparent   **2** : UNQUALIFIED ⟨~ folly⟩   **3** : very steep ⟨~ cliff⟩   **4** : very thin   ♦ **Synonyms** PURE, SIMPLE, ABSOLUTE, UNADULTERATED, UNMITIGATED — **sheer** *adv*

¹**sheet** \'shēt\ *n*   **1** : a broad piece of cloth (as for a bed); *also* : SAIL   **2** : a single piece of paper   **3** : a broad flat surface ⟨a ~ of ice⟩   **4** : something broad and long and relatively thin

²**sheet** *n* : a rope used to trim a sail

sheet·ing \'shē-tiŋ\ *n* : material in the form of sheets or suitable for forming into sheets

sheikh *or* **sheik** \'shēk, 'shāk\ *n* : an Arab chief — **sheikh·dom** *or* **sheik·dom** \-dəm\ *n*

shek·el \'she-kəl\ *n* — see MONEY table

shelf \'shelf\ *n, pl* **shelves** \'shelvz\   **1** : a thin flat usu. long and narrow structure fastened horizontally (as on a wall) above the floor to hold things   **2** : something (as a sandbar) that suggests a shelf

shelf life *n* : the period of storage time during which a material will remain useful

¹**shell** \'shel\ *n*   **1** : a hard or tough often thin outer covering of an animal (as a beetle, turtle, or mollusk) or of an egg or a seed or fruit (as a nut); *also* : something that resembles a shell ⟨a pastry ~⟩   **2** : a light narrow racing boat propelled by oarsmen   **3** : a case holding an explosive and designed to be fired from a cannon; *also* : a case holding the charge of powder and shot or bullet for small arms   **4** : a plain usu. sleeveless blouse or sweater — **shelled** \'sheld\ *adj* — **shelly** \'she-lē\ *adj*

²**shell** *vb*   **1** : to remove from a shell or husk   **2** : BOMBARD — **shell·er** *n*

¹**shel·lac** \shə-'lak\ *n*   **1** : a purified lac   **:** lac dissolved in alcohol and used as a wood filler or finish

²**shellac** *vb* **shel·lacked; shel·lack·ing**   **1** : to coat or treat with shellac   **2** : to defeat decisively

shellacking *n* : a sound drubbing

shell bean *n* : a bean grown esp. for its edible seeds; *also* : its edible seed

shell·fish \-,fish\ *n* : an invertebrate water animal (as an oyster or lobster) with a shell

shell out *vb* : PAY

shell shock *n* : COMBAT FATIGUE — **shell–shocked** \'shel-,shäkt\ *adj*

¹**shel·ter** \'shel-tər\ *n* : something that gives protection : REFUGE

²**shelter** *vb* **shel·tered; shel·ter·ing** : to give protection or refuge to

shelve \'shelv\ *vb* **shelved; shelv·ing**   **1** : to slope gradually   **2** : to store on shelves   **3** : to dismiss from service or use   **4** : to put aside : DEFER ⟨~ a proposal⟩

shelv·ing \'shel-viŋ\ *n* : material for shelves; *also* : SHELVES

she·nan·i·gan \shə-'na-ni-gən\ *n*   **1** : an underhand trick   **2** : questionable conduct — usu. used in pl.   **3** : high-spirited or mischievous activity — usu. used in pl.

¹**shep·herd** \'she-pərd\ *n*   **1** : one who tends sheep   **2** : GERMAN SHEPHERD

²**shepherd** *vb* : to tend as or in the manner of a shepherd

shep·herd·ess \'she-pər-dəs\ *n* : a woman who tends sheep

shepherd's pie *n* : a meat pie with a mashed potato crust

sheqel *n, pl* **sheqalim** *var of* SHEKEL

sher·bet \'shər-bət\ *n* [Turk *şerbet,* fr. Pers *sharbat,* fr. Ar *sharba* drink]   **1** : a drink of sweetened diluted fruit juice   **2** *also* **sher·bert** \-bərt\ : a frozen dessert of fruit juices, sugar, milk or water, and egg whites or gelatin

sherd *var of* SHARD

sher·iff \'sher-əf\ *n* [ME *shirreve,* fr. OE *scīrgerēfa,* lit., shire reeve (local official)] : a county officer charged with the execution of the law and the preservation of order

sher·ry \'sher-ē\ *n, pl* **sherries** [alter. of earlier *sherris* (taken as pl.), fr. *Xeres* (now *Jerez*), Spain] : a fortified wine with a nutty flavor

Shet·land pony \'shet-lənd-\ *n* : any of a breed of small stocky hardy ponies

shew \'shō\ *Brit var of* SHOW

shi·at·su *also* **shi·at·zu** \shē-'ät-sü\ *n* : a form of acupressure originating in Japan

shib·bo·leth \'shi-bə-ləth\ *n* [Heb *shibbōleth* stream; fr. the use of this word as a test to distinguish the men of Gilead from members of the tribe of Ephraim (Judges 12:5, 6)] **1** : CATCHPHRASE **2** : language that is a criterion for distinguishing members of a group

¹shield \'shēld\ *n* **1** : a broad piece of defensive armor carried on the arm **2** : something that protects or hides **3** : a police officer's badge

²shield *vb* : to protect or hide with a shield ✦ *Synonyms* PROTECT, GUARD, SAFEGUARD

shier *comparative of* SHY

shiest *superlative of* SHY

¹shift \'shift\ *vb* **1** : EXCHANGE, REPLACE **2** : to change place, position, or direction : MOVE; *also* : to change gears **3** : GET BY, MANAGE

²shift *n* **1** : SCHEME, TRICK **2** : a woman's slip or loose-fitting dress **3** : a change in direction, emphasis, or attitude **4** : a group working together alternating with other groups **5** : TRANSFER **6** : GEARSHIFT

shift·less \'shift-ləs\ *adj* : LAZY, INEFFICIENT — **shift·less·ness** *n*

shifty \'shif-tē\ *adj* **shift·i·er; -est** **1** : TRICKY; *also* : ELUSIVE **2** : indicative of a tricky nature ⟨~ eyes⟩

shih tzu \'shēd-'zü, 'shēt-'sü\ *n, pl* **shih tzus** *also* **shih tzu** *often cap S&T* [Chin (Beijing) *shīzi* (gŏu), fr. *shīzi* lion + gŏu dog] : any of a breed of small short-legged dogs of Chinese origin that have a short muzzle and a long dense coat

shii·ta·ke \shē-'tä-kē\ *n* [Jp] : a dark Asian mushroom widely cultivated for its edible cap

shill \'shil\ *n* : one who acts as a decoy (as for a pitchman) — **shill** *vb*

shil·le·lagh *also* **shil·la·lah** \shə-'lā-lē\ *n* [*Shillelagh*, town in Ireland] : CUDGEL, CLUB

shil·ling \'shi-liŋ\ *n* — see MONEY TABLE

shil·ly–shal·ly \'shi-lē-,sha-lē\ *vb* **shillyshall·ied; shil·ly–shal·ly·ing** **1** : to show hesitation or lack of decisiveness **2** : to waste time

shim \'shim\ *n* : a thin often tapered piece of wood, metal, or stone used (as in leveling) to fill in space

shim·mer \'shi-mər\ *vb* : to shine waveringly or tremulously : GLIMMER ✦ *Synonyms* FLASH, GLEAM, GLINT, SPARKLE, GLITTER — **shimmer** *n* — **shim·mery** *adj*

shim·my \'shi-mē\ *n, pl* **shimmies** : an abnormal vibration esp. in the front wheels of a motor vehicle — **shimmy** *vb*

¹shin \'shin\ *n* : the front part of the leg below the knee

²shin *vb* **shinned; shin·ning** : to climb (as a pole) by gripping alternately with arms or hands and legs

shin·bone \'shin-,bōn\ *n* : TIBIA

¹shine \'shīn\ *vb* **shone** \'shōn\ *or* **shined; shin·ing** **1** : to give or cause to give light **2** : GLEAM, GLITTER **3** : to be eminent, conspicuous, or distinguished ⟨gave her a chance to ~⟩ **4** : POLISH ⟨~ your shoes⟩

²shine *n* **1** : BRIGHTNESS, RADIANCE **2** : LUSTER, BRILLIANCE **3** : fair weather : SUNSHINE ⟨rain or ~⟩ **4** : LIKING, FANCY ⟨took a ~ to them⟩ **5** : a polish given to shoes

shin·er \'shī-nər\ *n* **1** : a silvery fish; *esp* : any of numerous small freshwater American fishes related to the carp **2** : BLACK EYE

¹shin·gle \'shiŋ-gəl\ *n* **1** : a small thin piece of building material used in overlapping rows for covering a roof or outside wall **2** : a small sign

²shingle *vb* **shin·gled; shin·gling** : to cover with shingles

³shingle *n* : a beach strewn with gravel; *also* : coarse gravel (as on a beach)

shin·gles \'shiŋ-gəlz\ *n* : an acute inflammation of the spinal and cranial nerves caused by reactivation of the chicken pox virus and associated with eruptions and pain along the course of the affected nerves

shin·ny \'shi-nē\ *vb* **shin·nied; shin·ny·ing** : SHIN

shin splints *n sing or pl* : a condition marked by pain and sometimes tenderness and swelling in the shin caused by repeated small injuries to muscles and associated tissue esp. from running

Shin·to \'shin-,tō\ *n* : the indigenous religion of Japan consisting esp. in reverence of the spirits of natural forces and imperial ancestors — **Shin·to·ism** *n* — **Shin·to·ist** *n or adj*

shiny \'shī-nē\ *adj* **shin·i·er; -est** **1** : BRIGHT, RADIANT; *also* : POLISHED

¹ship \'ship\ *n* **1** : a large oceangoing boat **2** : a ship's officers and crew **3** : AIRSHIP, AIRCRAFT, SPACECRAFT

²ship *vb* **shipped; ship·ping** **1** : to put or receive on board a ship for transportation **2** : to have transported by a carrier **3** : to take or draw into a boat ⟨~ oars⟩ **4** : to engage to serve on a ship — **ship·per** *n*

-ship \,ship\ *n suffix* **1** : state : condition : quality ⟨friend*ship*⟩ **2** : office : dignity : profession ⟨lord*ship*⟩ ⟨clerk*ship*⟩ **3** : art : skill ⟨horseman*ship*⟩ **4** : something showing, exhibiting, or embodying a quality or state ⟨town*ship*⟩ **5** : one entitled to a (specified) rank, title, or appellation ⟨his Lord*ship*⟩ **6** : the body of persons engaged in a specified activity ⟨reader*ship*⟩

ship·board \'ship-,bōrd\ *n* : SHIP

ship·build·er \-,bil-dər\ *n* : one who designs or builds ships

ship·fit·ter \-,fi-tər\ *n* **1** : one who constructs ships **2** : a naval enlisted man who works as a plumber

ship·mate \-,māt\ *n* : a fellow sailor

ship·ment \-mənt\ *n* : the process of shipping; *also* : the goods shipped

shipping n 1 : SHIPS; esp : ships in one port or belonging to one country 2 : transportation of goods

ship·shape \'ship-ˌshāp\ adj : TRIM, TIDY ⟨kept the garage ∼⟩

ship·worm \-ˌwərm\ n : any of various wormlike marine clams that have a shell used for burrowing in wood and damage wooden ships and wharves

¹**ship·wreck** \-ˌrek\ n 1 : a wrecked ship 2 : destruction or loss of a ship 3 : total loss or failure : RUIN

²**shipwreck** vb : to cause or meet disaster at sea through destruction or foundering

ship·wright \'ship-ˌrīt\ n : a carpenter skilled in ship construction and repair

ship·yard \-ˌyärd\ n : a place where ships are built or repaired

shire \'shī(-ə)r, in place-name compounds ˌshir, shər\ n : a county in Great Britain

shirk \'shərk\ vb : to avoid performing (duty or work) — **shirk·er** n

shirr \'shər\ vb 1 : to make shirring in 2 : to bake (eggs removed from the shell) until set

shirr·ing \'shər-iŋ\ n : a decorative gathering in cloth made by drawing up parallel lines of stitches

shirt \'shərt\ n 1 : a loose cloth garment usu. having a collar, sleeves, a front opening, and a tail long enough to be tucked inside pants or a skirt 2 : UNDERSHIRT — **shirt·less** adj

shirt·ing \'shər-tiŋ\ n : cloth suitable for making shirts

shish ke·bab \'shish-kə-ˌbäb\ n [Turk şiş kebabı, fr. şiş spit + kebap roast meat] : kebab cooked on skewers

shiv \'shiv\ n, slang : KNIFE

¹**shiv·er** \'shi-vər\ vb : TREMBLE, QUIVER
   ◆ **Synonyms** SHUDDER, QUAVER, SHAKE, QUAKE

²**shiver** n : an instance of shivering — **shiv·ery** adj

shlemiel var of SCHLEMIEL

shlub var of SCHLUB

shmooze var of SCHMOOZE

Sho·ah \'shō-ə, -ˌä\ n : HOLOCAUST 2

¹**shoal** \'shōl\ n 1 : SHALLOW 2 : a sandbank or bar creating a shallow

²**shoal** n : a large group (as of fish)

shoat \'shōt\ n : a weaned young pig

¹**shock** \'shäk\ n : a pile of sheaves of grain or cornstalks set up in a field

²**shock** n [MF choc, fr. choquer to strike against] 1 : a sharp impact or violent shake or jar 2 : a sudden violent mental or emotional disturbance 3 : a state of bodily collapse that is often marked by a drop in blood pressure and volume and that is caused esp. by crushing wounds, blood loss, or burns 4 : the effect of a charge of electricity passing through the body 5 : SHOCK ABSORBER — **shock·proof** \-ˌprüf\ adj

³**shock** vb 1 : to strike with surprise, horror, or disgust 2 : to subject to the action of an electrical discharge

⁴**shock** n : a thick bushy mass (as of hair)

shock absorber n : any of several devices for absorbing the energy of sudden shocks in machinery

shock·er \'shä-kər\ n : one that shocks; esp : a sensational work of fiction or drama

shock·ing \'shä-kiŋ\ adj : extremely startling and offensive — **shock·ing·ly** adv

shock therapy n : the treatment of mental disorder by induction of coma or convulsions by drugs or electricity

shock wave n : a wave formed by the sudden violent compression of the medium through which it travels

¹**shod·dy** \'shä-dē\ n 1 : wool reclaimed from old rags; also : a fabric made from it 2 : inferior or imitation material

²**shoddy** adj **shod·di·er; -est** 1 : made of shoddy 2 : poorly done or made — **shod·di·ly** \'shä-də-lē\ adv — **shod·di·ness** \-dē-nəs\ n

¹**shoe** \'shü\ n 1 : a covering for the human foot 2 : HORSESHOE 3 : the part of a brake that presses on the wheel

²**shoe** vb **shod** \'shäd\ also **shoed** \'shüd\; **shoe·ing** : to put a shoe or shoes on

shoe·horn \-ˌhȯrn\ n : a curved implement (as of horn or plastic) used in putting on a shoe

shoe·lace \'shü-ˌlās\ n : a lace or string for fastening a shoe

shoe·mak·er \-ˌmā-kər\ n : one who makes or repairs shoes

shoe·string \-ˌstriŋ\ n 1 : SHOELACE 2 : a small sum of money

sho·gun \'shō-gən\ n [Jp shōgun general] : any of a line of military governors ruling Japan until the revolution of 1867–68 — **sho·gun·ate** \'shō-gə-nət, -ˌnāt\ n

shone past and past part of SHINE

shook past of SHAKE

shook–up \(ˌ)shùk-'əp\ adj : nervously upset : AGITATED

¹**shoot** \'shüt\ vb **shot** \'shät\; **shoot·ing** 1 : to drive (as an arrow or bullet) forward quickly or forcibly 2 : to hit, kill, or wound with a missile 3 : to cause a missile to be driven forth or forth from ⟨∼ a gun⟩ 4 : to send forth (as a ray of light) 5 : to thrust forward or out 6 : to pass rapidly along ⟨∼ the rapids⟩ 7 : PHOTOGRAPH, FILM 8 : to move swiftly : DART 9 : to grow by or as if by sending out shoots; also : MATURE, DEVELOP — **shoot·er** n

²**shoot** n 1 : a plant stem with its leaves and branches esp. when not yet mature 2 : an act of shooting 3 : a shooting match

shooting iron n : FIREARM

shooting star n : METEOR 2

shoot up vb : to inject a narcotic into a vein

¹**shop** \'shäp\ n [ME shoppe, fr. OE sceoppa booth] 1 : a place where things are made or worked on : FACTORY, MILL 2 : a retail store ⟨dress ∼⟩

²**shop** vb **shopped; shop·ping** : to visit stores for purchasing or examining goods — **shop·per** n

shop·keep·er \'shäp-ˌkē-pər\ n : a retail merchant

shop·lift \-ˌlift\ vb : to steal goods on display from a store — **shop·lift·er** n

shop·talk \-ˌtȯk\ n : talk about one's business or special interests

shop·worn \-ˌwȯrn\ adj : soiled or frayed from much handling in a store

¹**shore** \'shȯr\ n : land along the edge of a body of water — **shore·less** adj

²**shore** vb **shored; shor·ing** : to give support to : BRACE

³**shore** n : ¹PROP

shore·bird \-ˌbərd\ n : any of a suborder of birds (as the plovers and sandpipers) found mostly along the seashore

shore patrol n : a branch of a navy that exercises guard and police functions

shor·ing \'shȯr-iŋ\ n : a group of things that shore something up

shorn past part of SHEAR

¹**short** \'shȯrt\ adj 1 : not long or tall 2 : not great in distance 3 : brief in time 4 : not coming up to standard or to an expected amount 5 : CURT, ABRUPT 6 : insufficiently supplied ⟨~ of cash⟩ 7 : made with shortening : FLAKY 8 : consisting of or relating to a sale of securities or commodities that the seller does not possess or has not contracted for at the time of the sale ⟨~ sale⟩ — **short·ness** n

²**short** adv 1 : ABRUPTLY, CURTLY 2 : at some point before a goal aimed at

³**short** n 1 : something shorter than normal or standard 2 pl : drawers or pants of less than knee length 3 : SHORT CIRCUIT

⁴**short** vb : SHORT-CIRCUIT

short·age \'shȯr-tij\ n : LACK, DEFICIT

short·cake \'shȯrt-ˌkāk\ n : a dessert consisting of short biscuit spread with sweetened fruit

short·change \-'chānj\ vb : to cheat esp. by giving less than the correct amount of change

short circuit n : a connection made between points in an electric circuit where current is not intended to flow — **short-circuit** vb

short·com·ing \'shȯrt-ˌkə-miŋ\ n : FAULT 1, FLAW

short·cut \-ˌkət\ n 1 : a route more direct than that usu. taken 2 : a quicker way of doing something

short·en \'shȯr-tᵊn\ vb : to make or become short ♦ **Synonyms** CURTAIL, ABBREVIATE, ABRIDGE, RETRENCH

short·en·ing \'shȯr-tᵊn-iŋ\ n : a substance (as lard or butter) that makes pastry tender and flaky

short·hand \'shȯrt-ˌhand\ n : a method of writing rapidly by using symbols and abbreviations for letters, words, or phrases : STENOGRAPHY

short·hand·ed \ˌshȯrt-'han-dəd\ adj : short of the needed number of people

short·horn \'shȯrt-ˌhȯrn\ n, often cap : any of a breed of red, roan, or white cattle of English origin

short hundredweight n — see WEIGHT table

short–lived \'shȯrt-ˌlivd, -'līvd\ adj : of short life or duration

short·ly \'shȯrt-lē\ adv 1 : in a few words 2 : in a short time : SOON

short–or·der \'shȯrt-ˌȯr-dər\ adj : preparing or serving food that can be quickly cooked

short shrift n 1 : a brief respite from death 2 : little consideration

short·sight·ed \'shȯrt-ˌsī-təd\ adj 1 : lacking foresight 2 : NEARSIGHTED — **short·sight·ed·ness** n

short·stop \-ˌstäp\ n : a baseball player defending the area between second and third base

short story n : a short work of fiction usu. dealing with a few characters and a single event

short–tem·pered \ˌshȯrt-'tem-pərd\ adj : having a quick temper

short–term \'shȯrt-ˌtərm\ adj 1 : occurring over or involving a relatively short period of time 2 : of or relating to a financial transaction based on a term usu. of less than a year

short ton n — see WEIGHT table

short·wave \'shȯrt-ˌwāv\ n : a radio wave with a wavelength between 10 and 100 meters

Sho·sho·ne or **Sho·sho·ni** \shə-'shō-nē\ n, pl **Shoshones** or **Shoshoni** : a member of an American Indian people orig. ranging through California, Idaho, Nevada, Utah, and Wyoming

¹**shot** \'shät\ n 1 : an act of shooting 2 : a stroke or throw in some games 3 : something that is shot : MISSILE, PROJECTILE; esp : small pellets forming a charge for a shotgun 4 : a metal sphere that is thrown for distance in the shot put 5 : RANGE, REACH 6 : MARKSMAN 7 : a single photographic exposure 8 : a single sequence of a motion picture or a television program made by one camera 9 : an injection (as of medicine) into the body 10 : a small serving of undiluted liquor or other beverage

²**shot** past and past part of SHOOT

shot·gun \'shät-ˌgən\ n : a gun with a smooth bore used to fire shot at short range

shot put n : a field event in which a shot is heaved for distance

should \'shud, shəd\ past of SHALL — used as an auxiliary to express condition, obligation or propriety, probability, or futurity from a point of view in the past

¹**shoul·der** \'shōl-dər\ n 1 : the part of the body of a person or animal where the arm or foreleg joins the body 2 : either edge of a roadway 3 : a rounded or sloping part (as of a bottle) where the neck joins the body

²**shoulder** vb 1 : to push or thrust with the shoulder 2 : to bear on the shoulder 3 : to take the responsibility of

shoulder belt n : an automobile safety belt worn across the torso and over the shoulder

shoulder blade n : a flat triangular bone at the back of each shoulder

shout \'shaut\ vb : to utter a sudden loud cry — **shout** n

shove \'shəv\ *vb* **shoved; shov·ing** : to push along, aside, or away — **shove** *n*

¹**shov·el** \'shə-vəl\ *n* **1** : a broad long-handled scoop used to lift and throw material **2** : the amount a shovel will hold — **shov·el·ful** \'shə-vəl-ˌfu̇l\ *n*

²**shovel** *vb* **-eled** *or* **-elled; -el·ing** *or* **-el·ling 1** : to take up and throw with a shovel **2** : to dig or clean out with a shovel

¹**show** \'shō\ *vb* **showed** \'shōd\; **shown** \'shōn\ *or* **showed; show·ing 1** : to cause or permit to be seen : EXHIBIT ⟨~ anger⟩ **2** : CONFER, BESTOW ⟨~ mercy⟩ **3** : REVEAL, DISCLOSE ⟨~ed courage in battle⟩ **4** : INSTRUCT ⟨~ me how⟩ **5** : PROVE ⟨~s he was guilty⟩ **6** : APPEAR **7** : to be noticeable **8** : to be third in a horse race

²**show** *n* **1** : a demonstrative display **2** : outward appearance ⟨a ~ of resistance⟩ **3** : SPECTACLE **4** : a theatrical presentation **5** : a radio or television program **6** : third place in a horse race

¹**show·case** \'shō-ˌkās\ *n* : a cabinet for displaying items (as in a store)

²**showcase** *vb* **show·cased; show·cas·ing** : EXHIBIT

show·down \'shō-ˌdau̇n\ *n* : a decisive confrontation or contest; *esp* : the showing of poker hands to determine the winner of a pot

¹**show·er** \'shau̇(-ə)r\ *n* **1** : a brief fall of rain **2** : a party given by friends who bring gifts **3** : a bath in which water is showered on the person; *also* : a facility (as a stall) for such a bath — **show·ery** *adj*

²**shower** *vb* **1** : to rain or fall in a shower **2** : to bathe in a shower

show·man \'shō-mən\ *n* : a notably spectacular, dramatic, or effective performer — **show·man·ship** *n*

show—off \'shō-ˌȯf\ *n* : one that seeks to attract attention by conspicuous behavior

show off *vb* **1** : to display proudly **2** : to act as a show-off

show·piece \'shō-ˌpēs\ *n* : an outstanding example used for exhibition

show·place \-ˌplās\ *n* : an estate or building that is a showpiece

show up *vb* : ARRIVE

showy \'shō-ē\ *adj* **show·i·er; -est** : superficially impressive or striking ⟨a ~ orchid⟩ — **show·i·ly** \'shō-ə-lē\ *adv* — **show·i·ness** \-ē-nəs\ *n*

shpt *abbr* shipment

shrap·nel \'shrap-nəl\ *n, pl* **shrapnel** [Henry *Shrapnel* †1842 Eng. artillery officer] : bomb, mine, or shell fragments

¹**shred** \'shred\ *n* : a narrow strip cut or torn off : a small fragment

²**shred** *vb* **shred·ded; shred·ding** : to cut or tear into shreds

shrew \'shrü\ *n* **1** : any of a family of very small mammals with short velvety fur that are related to the moles **2** : a scolding woman

shrewd \'shrüd\ *adj* : CLEVER, ASTUTE — **shrewd·ly** *adv* — **shrewd·ness** *n*

shrew·ish \'shrü-ish\ *adj* : having an irri-

table disposition : ILL-TEMPERED — **shrew·ish·ly** *adv* — **shrew·ish·ness** *n*

shriek \'shrēk\ *n* : a shrill cry : SCREAM, YELL — **shriek** *vb*

shrift \'shrift\ *n, archaic* : the act of shriving : CONFESSION

shrike \'shrīk\ *n* : any of numerous usu. largely grayish or brownish birds that often impale their usu. insect prey upon thorns before devouring it

¹**shrill** \'shril\ *vb* : to make a high-pitched piercing sound

²**shrill** *adj* : high-pitched : PIERCING ⟨~ whistle⟩ — **shril·ly** *adv*

shrimp \'shrimp\ *n, pl* **shrimps** *or* **shrimp 1** : any of various small marine crustaceans related to the lobsters **2** : a small or puny person

shrine \'shrīn\ *n* [ME, receptacle for the relics of a saint, fr. OE *scrīn*, fr. L *scrinium* case, chest] **1** : the tomb of a saint; *also* : a place where devotion is paid to a saint or deity **2** : a place or object hallowed by its associations

¹**shrink** \'shriŋk\ *vb* **shrank** \'shraŋk\ *or* **shrunk** \'shrəŋk\; **shrunk** *or* **shrunk·en** \'shrəŋ-kən\; **shrink·ing 1** : to draw back or away **2** : to become smaller or more compact **3** : to lessen in value ♦ *Synonyms* CONTRACT, CONSTRICT, COMPRESS, CONDENSE — **shrink·able** *adj*

²**shrink** *n* : a clinical psychiatrist or psychologist

shrink·age \'shriŋ-kij\ *n* **1** : the act of shrinking **2** : the amount lost by shrinkage

shrive \'shrīv\ *vb* **shrived** *or* **shrove** \'shrōv\; **shriv·en** \'shri-vən\ *or* **shrived** [ME, fr. OE *scrīfan* to prescribe, allot, shrive, fr. L *scrībere* to write] : to administer the sacrament of reconciliation to

shriv·el \'shri-vəl\ *vb* **-eled** *or* **-elled; -el·ing** *or* **-el·ling** : to shrink and draw into wrinkles : DWINDLE

¹**shroud** \'shrau̇d\ *n* **1** : something that covers or screens **2** : a cloth placed over a dead body **3** : any of the ropes leading from the masthead of a ship to the side to support the mast

²**shroud** *vb* : to veil or screen from view

shrub \'shrəb\ *n* : a low usu. several-stemmed woody plant — **shrub·by** *adj*

shrub·bery \'shrə-bə-rē\ *n, pl* **-ber·ies** : a planting or growth of shrubs

shrug \'shrəg\ *vb* **shrugged; shrug·ging** : to hunch (the shoulders) up to express aloofness, indifference, or uncertainty — **shrug** *n*

shrug off *vb* **1** : to brush aside : MINIMIZE **2** : to shake off **3** : to remove (a garment) by wriggling out

shtick *also* **schtick** *or* **shtik** \'shtik\ *n* [Yiddish *shtik* pranks, lit., piece] **1** : a usu. comic or repetitious performance or routine **2** : one's special trait, interest, or activity

¹**shuck** \'shək\ *n* : SHELL, HUSK

²**shuck** *vb* : to strip of shucks

shud·der \'shə-dər\ *vb* : TREMBLE, QUAKE — **shudder** *n*

shuf·fle \'shə-fəl\ vb **shuf·fled; shuf·fling** **1** : to mix in a disorderly mass **2** : to rearrange the order of (cards in a pack) by mixing two parts of the pack together **3** : to shift from place to place **4** : to move with a sliding or dragging gait **5** : to dance in a slow lagging manner — **shuffle** n

shuf·fle·board \'shə-fəl-,bòrd\ n : a game in which players use long-handled cues to shove disks into scoring areas marked on a smooth surface

shun \'shən\ vb **shunned; shun·ning** : to avoid deliberately or habitually ◆ *Synonyms* EVADE, ELUDE, ESCAPE, DUCK

¹**shunt** \'shənt\ vb [ME, to turn away] : to turn off to one side : *esp* : to switch (a train) from one track to another

²**shunt** n **1** : a method or device for turning or thrusting aside **2** : a conductor joining two points in an electrical circuit forming an alternate path through which a portion of the current may pass

shut \'shət\ vb **shut; shut·ting** **1** : CLOSE **2** : to forbid entrance into **3** : to lock up **4** : to fold together ⟨~ a penknife⟩ **5** : to cease or suspend activity ⟨~ down an assembly line⟩

shut·down \-,daùn\ n : a temporary cessation of activity (as in a factory)

shut–in \'shət-,in\ n : a person confined to home, a room, or bed because of illness or incapacity

shut·out \'shət-,aùt\ n : a game or contest in which one side fails to score

shut out vb **1** : EXCLUDE **2** : to prevent (an opponent) from scoring in a game or contest

shut·ter \'shə-tər\ n **1** : a movable cover for a door or window : BLIND **2** : the part of a camera that opens and closes to allow light to enter

shut·ter·bug \'shə-tər-,bəg\ n : a photography enthusiast

¹**shut·tle** \'shə-t³l\ n **1** : an instrument used in weaving for passing the horizontal threads between the vertical threads **2** : a vehicle traveling back and forth over a short route ⟨a ~ bus⟩ **3** : SPACE SHUTTLE

²**shuttle** vb **shut·tled; shut·tling** : to move back and forth frequently

shut·tle·cock \'shə-t³l-,käk\ n : a light conical object (as of cork or plastic) used in badminton

shut up vb : to cease or cause to cease talking

¹**shy** \'shī\ adj **shi·er** or **shy·er** \'shī-ər\; **shi·est** or **shy·est** \'shī-əst\ **1** : easily frightened : TIMID **2** : WARY **3** : BASHFUL **4** : DEFICIENT, LACKING — **shy·ly** adv — **shy·ness** n

²**shy** vb **shied; shy·ing** **1** : to show a dislike : RECOIL **2** : to start suddenly aside through fright ⟨the horse *shied*⟩

shy·ster \'shīs-tər\ n : an unscrupulous lawyer or politician

Si *symbol* silicon

SI *abbr* [F *Système International d'Unités*] International System of Units

Si·a·mese \,sī-ə-'mēz, -'mēs\ n, pl **Siamese 1** : THAI — **Siamese** adj

Siamese cat n : any of a breed of slender blue-eyed short-haired domestic cats of Asian origin

Siamese twin n [fr. Chang †1874 and Eng †1874 twins born in Siam with bodies united] : one of a pair of twins with bodies joined together at birth

Siberian husky n : any of a breed of thick-coated compact dogs orig. developed in Siberia to pull sleds

¹**sib·i·lant** \'si-bə-lənt\ adj : having, containing, or producing the sound of or a sound resembling that of the *s* or the *sh* in *sash* — **sib·i·lant·ly** adv

²**sibilant** n : a sibilant speech sound (as English \s\, \z\, \sh\, \zh\, \ch (=tsh)\, or \j (=dzh)\)

sib·ling \'si-bliŋ\ n : a brother or sister considered irrespective of sex; *also* : one of two or more offspring having one common parent

sib·yl \'si-bəl\ n, *often cap* : PROPHETESS — **sib·yl·line** \-bə-,līn, -,lēn\ adj

sic \'sik, 'sēk\ adv : intentionally so written — used after a printed word or passage to indicate that it exactly reproduces an original ⟨said he seed [~] it all⟩

sick \'sik\ adj **1** : not in good health : ILL; *also* : of, relating to, or intended for use in sickness ⟨~ pay⟩ **2** : NAUSEATED **3** : DISGUSTED **4** : PINING **5** : mentally or emotionally unsound **6** : MACABRE, SADISTIC ⟨~ jokes⟩ — **sick·ly** adv

sick·bed \'sik-,bed\ n : a bed on which one lies sick

sick·en \'si-kən\ vb : to make or become sick — **sick·en·ing·ly** adv

sick·le \'si-kəl\ n : a cutting tool consisting of a curved metal blade with a short handle

sickle–cell anemia n : an inherited anemia in which red blood cells tend to become crescent-shaped and clog small blood vessels and which occurs esp. in individuals of African, Mediterranean, or southwest Asian ancestry

sick·ness \'sik-nəs\ n **1** : ill health; *also* : a specific disease **2** : NAUSEA

side \'sīd\ n **1** : the right or left part of the trunk of a body **2** : a place away from a central point or line **3** : a border of an object; *esp* : one of the longer borders as contrasted with an end **4** : an outer surface of an object **5** : a position regarded as opposite to another **6** : a body of contestants — **side** adj — **on the side** : in addition to the main portion

side·arm \-,ärm\ adj : made with a sideways sweep of the arm ⟨a ~ pitch⟩ — **sidearm** adv

side arm n : a weapon worn at the side or in the belt

side·bar \'sīd-,bär\ n : a short news story accompanying a major story and presenting related information

side·board \-,bòrd\ n : a piece of dining-room furniture for holding articles of table service

side·burns \-,bərnz\ n pl : whiskers on the side of the face in front of the ears

side by side adv **1** : beside one another **2** : in the same place, time, or circumstance — **side–by–side** adj

side-car \-ˌkär\ n : a one-wheeled passenger car attached to the side of a motorcycle

side effect n : a secondary and usu. adverse effect (as of a drug)

side-kick \ˈsīdˌkik\ n : PAL, PARTNER

side-line \ˈsīdˌlīn\ n **1** : an activity pursued in addition to one's regular occupation **2** : the space immediately outside the lines of an athletic field or court **3** : a sphere of little or no participation — usu. used in pl.

¹side-long \ˈsīdˌloŋ\ adv : in the direction of or along the side : OBLIQUELY

²sidelong adj : directed to one side ⟨~ look⟩

side-man \ˈsīdˌman\ n : a member of a jazz or swing orchestra

side-piece \-ˌpēs\ n : a piece forming or contained in the side of something

si-de-re-al \sīˈdir-ē-əl, sə-\ adj [L sidereus, fr. sider-, sidus star, constellation] **1** : of or relating to the stars **2** : measured by the apparent motion of the stars

side-sad-dle \ˈsīdˌsa-dᵊl\ n : a saddle for women on which the rider sits with both legs on the same side of the horse — **sidesaddle** adv

side-show \ˈsīdˌshō\ n **1** : a minor show offered in addition to a main exhibition (as of a circus) **2** : an incidental diversion

side-step \-ˌstep\ vb **1** : to step aside **2** : AVOID, EVADE

side-stroke \-ˌstrōk\ n : a swimming stroke which is executed on the side and in which the arms are swept backward and downward and the legs do a scissors kick

side-swipe \-ˌswīp\ vb : to strike with a glancing blow along the side — **side-swipe** n

¹side-track \-ˌtrak\ n : SIDING 1

²sidetrack vb **1** : to switch from a main railroad line to a siding **2** : to turn aside from a purpose

side-walk \ˈsīdˌwok\ n : a paved walk at the side of a road or street

side-wall \-ˌwol\ n **1** : a wall forming the side of something **2** : the side of an automobile tire

side-ways \-ˌwāz\ adv or adj **1** : from the side **2** : with one side to the front **3** : to, toward, or at one side

side-wind-er \-ˌwīn-dər\ n : a small pale-colored desert rattlesnake of the southwestern U.S.

sid-ing \ˈsī-diŋ\ n **1** : a short railroad track connected with the main track **2** : material (as boards) covering the outside of frame buildings

si-dle \ˈsī-dᵊl\ vb **si-dled; si-dling** : to move sideways with one side foremost

SIDS abbr sudden infant death syndrome

siege \ˈsēj\ n **1** : the placing of an army around or before a fortified place to force its surrender **2** : a persistent attack (as of illness)

sie-mens \ˈsē-mənz, ˈzē-\ n : a unit of conductance equivalent to one ampere per volt

si-er-ra \sē-ˈer-ə\ n [Sp, lit., saw, fr. L serra] : a range of mountains esp. with jagged peaks

si-es-ta \sē-ˈes-tə\ n [Sp, fr. L sexta (hora) noon, lit., sixth hour] : a midday rest or nap

sieve \ˈsiv\ n : a utensil with meshes or holes to separate finer particles from coarser or solids from liquids

sift \ˈsift\ vb **1** : to pass through a sieve **2** : to separate with or as if with a sieve **3** : to examine carefully **4** : to scatter by or as if by passing through a sieve — **sift-er** n

sig abbr signature

SIG abbr special interest group

sigh \ˈsī\ vb **1** : to let out a deep audible breath (as in weariness or sorrow) **2** : GRIEVE, YEARN — **sigh** n

¹sight \ˈsīt\ n **1** : something seen or worth seeing **2** : the process or power of seeing; esp : the sense of which the eye is the receptor and by which qualities of appearance (as position, shape, and color) are perceived **3** : INSPECTION **4** : a device (as a small bead on a gun barrel) that aids the eye in aiming **5** : VIEW, GLIMPSE **6** : the range of vision — **sight-less** adj

²sight vb **1** : to get sight of **2** : to aim by means of a sight

sight-ed \ˈsī-təd\ adj : having sight

sight-ly \-lē\ adj : pleasing to the sight

sight-see-ing \ˈsīt-ˌsē-iŋ\ adj : engaged in or used for seeing sights of interest — **sight-seer** \-ˌsē-ər\ n

sig-ma \ˈsig-mə\ n : the 18th letter of the Greek alphabet — Σ or σ or ς

¹sign \ˈsīn\ n **1** : a gesture expressing a command, wish, or thought **2** : SYMBOL **3** : a notice publicly displayed for advertising purposes or for giving direction or warning **4** : OMEN, PORTENT **5** : TRACE, VESTIGE

²sign vb **1** : to mark with a sign **2** : to represent by a sign **3** : to make a sign or signal **4** : to write one's name on in token of assent or obligation **5** : to assign legally **6** : to use sign language — **sign-er** n

¹sig-nal \ˈsig-nəl\ n **1** : a sign agreed on as the start of some joint action **2** : a sign giving warning or notice of something **3** : the message, sound, or image transmitted in electrical communication (as radio)

²signal vb **-naled** or **-nalled; -nal-ing** or **-nal-ling 1** : to notify by a signal **2** : to communicate by signals

³signal adj : DISTINGUISHED ⟨a ~ honor⟩ — **sig-nal-ly** adv

sig-nal-ize \ˈsig-nə-ˌlīz\ vb **-ized; -iz-ing** : to point out or make conspicuous — **sig-nal-i-za-tion** \ˌsig-nə-lə-ˈzā-shən\ n

sig-nal-man \ˈsig-nəl-mən, -ˌman\ n : a person who signals or works with signals

sig-na-to-ry \ˈsig-nə-ˌtor-ē\ n, pl **-ries** : a person or government that signs jointly with others — **signatory** adj

sig·na·ture \'sig-nə-ˌchùr\ *n* 1 : the name of a person written by himself or herself 2 : the sign placed after the clef to indicate the key or the meter of a piece of music

sign·board \'sīn-ˌbòrd\ *n* : a board bearing a sign or notice

sig·net \'sig-nət\ *n* : a small intaglio seal (as in a ring)

sig·nif·i·cance \sig-'ni-fi-kəns\ *n* 1 : something signified : MEANING 2 : SUGGESTIVENESS 3 : CONSEQUENCE, IMPORTANCE

sig·nif·i·cant \-kənt\ *adj* 1 : having meaning; *esp* : having a hidden or special meaning 2 : having or likely to have considerable influence or effect : IMPORTANT — **sig·nif·i·cant·ly** *adv*

sig·ni·fy \'sig-nə-ˌfī\ *vb* **-fied; -fy·ing** 1 : to show by a sign 2 : MEAN, IMPORT 3 : to have significance — **sig·ni·fi·ca·tion** \ˌsig-nə-fə-'kā-shən\ *n*

sign in *vb* : to make a record of arrival (as by signing a register)

sign language *n* : a formal system of hand gestures used for communication (as by the deaf)

sign off *vb* : to announce the end (as of a program or broadcast)

sign of the cross : a gesture of the hand forming a cross (as to invoke divine blessing)

sign on *vb* 1 : ENLIST 2 : to announce the start of broadcasting for the day

sign out *vb* : to make a record of departure (as by signing a register)

sign·post \'sīn-ˌpōst\ *n* : a post bearing a sign

sign up *vb* : to sign one's name in order to obtain, do, or join something

Sikh \'sēk\ *n* : an adherent of a religion of India marked by rejection of caste — **Sikh·ism** *n*

si·lage \'sī-lij\ *n* : fodder fermented (as in a silo) to produce a rich moist animal feed

¹si·lence \'sī-ləns\ *n* 1 : the state of being silent 2 : STILLNESS 3 : SECRECY

²silence *vb* **si·lenced; si·lenc·ing** 1 : to reduce to silence : STILL 2 : to cause to cease hostile firing or criticism

si·lenc·er \'sī-lən-sər\ *n* : a device for muffling the noise of a gunshot

si·lent \'sī-lənt\ *adj* 1 : not speaking : MUTE; *also* : TACITURN 2 : STILL, QUIET 3 : performed or borne without utterance ◆ *Synonyms* RETICENT, RESERVED, CLOSEMOUTHED, CLOSE — **si·lent·ly** *adv*

¹sil·hou·ette \ˌsi-lə-'wet\ *n* [F] 1 : a representation of the outlines of an object filled in with black or some other uniform color 2 : OUTLINE (~ of a ship)

²silhouette *vb* **-ett·ed; -ett·ing** : to represent by a silhouette; *also* : to show against a light background

sil·i·ca \'si-li-kə\ *n* : a mineral that consists of silicon and oxygen

sil·i·cate \'si-lə-ˌkāt, 'si-li-kət\ *n* : a chemical salt that consists of a metal combined with silicon and oxygen

si·li·ceous *also* **si·li·cious** \sə-'li-shəs\ *adj* : of, relating to, or containing silica or a silicate

sil·i·con \'si-li-kən, 'si-lə-ˌkän\ *n* : a nonmetallic chemical element that occurs in combination as the most abundant element next to oxygen in the earth's crust and is used esp. in alloys and semiconductors

sil·i·cone \'si-lə-ˌkōn\ *n* : an organic silicon compound used esp. for lubricants and varnishes

sil·i·co·sis \ˌsi-lə-'kō-səs\ *n* : a lung disease caused by prolonged inhaling of silica dusts

silk \'silk\ *n* 1 : a fine strong lustrous protein fiber produced by insect larvae usu. for their cocoons; *esp* : one from moth larvae (**silk·worms** \-ˌwərmz\) used for cloth 2 : thread or cloth made from silk — **silk·en** \'sil-kən\ *adj* — **silky** *adj*

silk screen *n* : a stencil process in which coloring matter is forced through the meshes of a prepared silk or organdy screen; *also* : a print made by this process — **silk–screen** *vb*

sill \'sil\ *n* : a heavy crosspiece (as of wood or stone) that forms the bottom member of a window frame or a doorway; *also* : a horizontal supporting piece at the base of a structure

sil·ly \'si-lē\ *adj* **sil·li·er; -est** [ME *sely, silly* happy, innocent, pitiable, feeble, fr. OE *sǣlig,* fr. *sǣl* happiness] : FOOLISH, ABSURD, STUPID — **sil·li·ness** *n*

si·lo \'sī-lō\ *n, pl* **silos** [Sp] 1 : a trench, pit, or esp. a tall cylinder for making and storing silage 2 : an underground structure for housing a guided missile

¹silt \'silt\ *n* 1 : fine earth; *esp* : particles of such soil floating in rivers, ponds, or lakes 2 : a deposit (as by a river) of silt — **silty** *adj*

²silt *vb* : to obstruct or cover with silt — **silt·ation** \sil-'tā-shən\ *n*

Si·lu·ri·an \sī-'lùr-ē-ən\ *adj* : of, relating to, or being the period of the Paleozoic era between the Ordovician and the Devonian marked by the appearance of the first land plants — **Silurian** *n*

¹sil·ver \'sil-vər\ *n* 1 : a white ductile metallic chemical element that takes a high polish and is a better conductor of heat and electricity than any other substance 2 : coin made of silver 3 : FLATWARE 4 : a grayish white color — **silvery** *adj*

²silver *adj* 1 : relating to, made of, or coated with silver 2 : SILVERY

³silver *vb* **sil·vered; sil·ver·ing** : to coat with or as if with silver — **sil·ver·er** *n*

silver bromide *n* : a light-sensitive compound used esp. in photography

sil·ver·fish \'sil-vər-ˌfish\ *n* : any of various small wingless insects found in houses and sometimes injurious esp. to sized paper and starched clothes

silver iodide *n* : a light-sensitive compound used in photography, rainmaking, and medicine

silver maple *n* : a No. American maple with deeply cut leaves that are green above and silvery white below

silver nitrate *n* : a soluble compound used in photography and as an antiseptic

sil·ver·ware \'sil-vər-,wer\ *n* : FLATWARE

sim *abbr* simulation; simulator

sim·i·an \'si-mē-ən\ *n* : MONKEY, APE — **simian** *adj*

simian immunodeficiency virus *n* : SIV

sim·i·lar \'si-mə-lər\ *adj* : marked by correspondence or resemblance ♦ *Synonyms* ALIKE, AKIN, COMPARABLE, PARALLEL — **sim·i·lar·i·ty** \,si-mə-'ler-ə-tē\ *n* — **sim·i·lar·ly** *adv*

sim·i·le \'si-mə-(,)lē\ *n* [ME, fr. L, like, similar, fr. neut. of *similis* like, similar] : a figure of speech in which two dissimilar things are compared by the use of *like* or *as* (as in "cheeks like roses")

si·mil·i·tude \sə-'mi-lə-,tüd, -,tyüd\ *n* : LIKENESS, RESEMBLANCE

sim·mer \'si-mər\ *vb* **sim·mered; sim·mer·ing 1** : to stew at or just below the boiling point **2** : to be on the point of bursting out with violence or emotional disturbance — **simmer** *n*

simmer down *vb* : to become calm or peaceful

si·mo·nize \'sī-mə-,nīz\ *vb* **-nized; -niz·ing** : to polish with or as if with wax

si·mo·ny \'sī-mə-nē, 'si-\ *n* [ME *symonie*, fr. AF *simonie*, fr. LL *simonia*, fr. Simon Magus sorcerer of Samaria in Acts 8:9–24] : the buying or selling of a church office

sim·pat·i·co \sim-'pä-ti-,kō, -'pa-\ *adj* : CONGENIAL, LIKABLE

sim·per \'sim-pər\ *vb* : to smile in a silly manner — **simper** *n*

sim·ple \'sim-pəl\ *adj* **sim·pler** \-pə-lər\; **sim·plest** \-pə-ləst\ [ME, fr. AF, plain, uncomplicated, artless, fr. L *simplus*, alter. of *simplex*, lit., single; L *simplus* fr. *sim-* one + *-plus* multiplied by; L *simplex* fr. *sim-* + *-plex* -fold] **1** : free from dishonesty or vanity : INNOCENT **2** : free from ostentation **3** : of humble origin or modest position **4** : STUPID **5** : not complex : PLAIN ⟨a ~ melody⟩ ⟨~ directions⟩ **6** : lacking education, experience, or intelligence **7** : developing from a single ovary ⟨a ~ fruit⟩ ♦ *Synonyms* EASY, FACILE, LIGHT, EFFORTLESS — **sim·ple·ness** *n* — **sim·ply** *adv*

simple interest *n* : interest paid or computed on the original principal only of a loan or on the amount of an account

sim·ple·ton \'sim-pəl-tən\ *n* : FOOL

sim·plic·i·ty \sim-'pli-sə-tē\ *n, pl* **-ties 1** : lack of complication : CLEARNESS **2** : CANDOR, ARTLESSNESS **3** : plainness in manners or way of life **4** : SILLINESS, FOLLY

sim·pli·fy \'sim-plə-,fī\ *vb* **-fied; -fy·ing** : to make less complex — **sim·pli·fi·ca·tion** \,sim-plə-fə-'kā-shən\ *n*

sim·plis·tic \sim-'plis-tik\ *adj* : excessively simple : tending to overlook complexities ⟨a ~ solution⟩

sim·u·late \'sim-yə-,lāt\ *vb* **-lat·ed; -lat·**

ing : to give or create the effect or appearance of : IMITATE; *also* : to make a simulation of — **sim·u·la·tor** \'sim-yə-,lā-tər\ *n*

sim·u·la·tion \,sim-yə-'lā-shən\ *n* **1** : the act or process of simulating **2** : an object that is not genuine **3** : the imitation by one system or process of the way in which another system or process works

si·mul·ta·ne·ous \,sī-məl-'tā-nē-əs, ,si-\ *adj* : occurring or operating at the same time — **si·mul·ta·ne·ous·ly** *adv* — **si·mul·ta·ne·ous·ness** *n*

¹sin \'sin\ *n* **1** : an offense esp. against God **2** : FAULT **3** : a weakened state of human nature in which the self is estranged from God — **sin·less** *adj*

²sin *vb* **sinned; sin·ning** : to commit a sin — **sin·ner** *n*

³sin *abbr* sine

¹since \'sins\ *adv* **1** : from a past time until now **2** : backward in time : AGO **3** : after a time in the past

²since *conj* **1** : from the time when **2** : seeing that : BECAUSE

³since *prep* **1** : in the period after ⟨changes made ~ the war⟩ **2** : continuously from ⟨has been here ~ 1980⟩

sin·cere \sin-'sir\ *adj* **sin·cer·er; sin·cer·est 1** : free from hypocrisy : HONEST **2** : GENUINE, REAL — **sin·cere·ly** *adv* — **sin·cer·i·ty** \-'ser-ə-tē\ *n*

sine \'sīn\ *n* [ML *sinus*, fr. L, curve] : the trigonometric function that is the ratio between the side opposite an acute angle in a right triangle and the hypotenuse

si·ne·cure \'sī-ni-,kyùr, 'si-\ *n* : a paying job that requires little or no work

si·ne die \,sī-ni-'dī-,ē, ,si-nā-'dē-,ā\ *adv* [L, without day] : INDEFINITELY ⟨the meeting adjourned *sine die*⟩

si·ne qua non \,si-ni-,kwä-'nän, -,'nōn\ *n, pl* **sine qua nons** *also* **sine qui·bus non** \-,kwi-(,)bùs-\ [LL, without which not] : something indispensable or essential

sin·ew \'sin-yü\ *n* **1** : TENDON **2** : physical strength — **sin·ewy** *adj*

sin·ful \'sin-fəl\ *adj* : marked by or full of sin : WICKED — **sin·ful·ly** *adv* — **sin·ful·ness** *n*

¹sing \'siŋ\ *vb* **sang** \'saŋ\ *or* **sung** \'səŋ\; **sung; sing·ing 1** : to produce musical tones with the voice; *also* : to utter with musical tones **2** : to make a prolonged shrill sound ⟨locusts ~ing⟩ **3** : to produce harmonious sustained sounds ⟨birds ~ing⟩ **4** : CHANT, INTONE **5** : to write poetry; *also ;* to celebrate in song or verse **6** : to give information or evidence — **sing·er** *n*

²sing *abbr* singular

singe \'sinj\ *vb* **singed; singe·ing** : to scorch lightly the outside of; *esp* : to remove the hair or down from usu. by passing over a flame

¹sin·gle \'siŋ-gəl\ *adj* **1** : UNMARRIED **2** : being alone : being the only one **3** : having only one feature or part **4** : made for one person ♦ *Synonyms* SOLE, UNIQUE, LONE, SOLITARY, SEPA-

RATE, PARTICULAR — **sin·gle·ness** n — **sin·gly** adv

²**single** n **1** : a separate person or thing; also : an unmarried person **2** : a hit in baseball that enables the batter to reach first base **3** pl : a tennis match with one player on each side

³**single** vb **sin·gled; sin·gling 1** : to select (one) from a group **2** : to hit a single

single bond n : a chemical bond in which one pair of electrons is shared by two atoms in a molecule

single–lens reflex n : a camera having a single lens that forms an image which is reflected to the viewfinder or recorded on film

sin·gle–mind·ed \ˌsiŋ-gəl-ˈmīn-dəd\ adj : having one driving purpose or resolve — **sin·gle–mind·ed·ly** adv — **sin·gle–mind·ed·ness** n

sing·song \ˈsiŋ-ˌsȯŋ\ n **1** : verse with marked and regular rhythm and rhyme **2** : a voice delivery marked by monotonous rhythm — **sing·songy** \-ˌsȯŋ-ē\ adj

sin·gu·lar \ˈsiŋ-gyə-lər\ adj **1** : of, relating to, or constituting a word form denoting one person, thing, or instance **2** : OUTSTANDING, EXCEPTIONAL **3** : of unusual quality **4** : ODD, PECULIAR — **singular** n — **sin·gu·lar·i·ty** \ˌsiŋ-gyə-ˈler-ə-tē\ n — **sin·gu·lar·ly** adv

sin·is·ter \ˈsi-nəs-tər\ adj [ME sinistre, fr. AF senestre on the left, fr. L sinister on the left side, inauspicious] **1** : singularly evil or productive of evil **2** : accompanied by or leading to disaster ◆ **Synonyms** BALEFUL, MALIGN, MALEFIC, MALEFICENT — **sin·is·ter·ly** adv

¹**sink** \ˈsiŋk\ vb **sank** \ˈsaŋk\ or **sunk** \ˈsəŋk\; **sunk; sink·ing 1** : SUBMERGE **2** : to descend lower and lower **3** : to grow less in volume or height **4** : to slope downward **5** : to penetrate downward **6** : to fail in health or strength **7** : LAPSE, DEGENERATE **8** : to cause (a ship) to descend to the bottom **9** : to make (a hole or shaft) by digging, boring, or cutting **10** : INVEST — **sink·able** adj

²**sink** n **1** : DRAIN, SEWER **2** : a basin connected with a drain **3** : an extensive depression in the land surface

sink·er \ˈsiŋ-kər\ n : a weight for sinking a fishing line or net

sink·hole \ˈsiŋk-ˌhōl\ n : a hollow place in which drainage collects

si·nol·o·gy \sī-ˈnä-lə-jē\ n, often cap : the study of the Chinese and esp. their language, history, and culture — **si·no·log·i·cal** \ˌsī-nə-ˈlä-ji-kəl\ adj, often cap — **si·nol·o·gist** \sī-ˈnä-lə-jist\ n, often cap

sin tax n : a tax on substances or activities considered sinful or harmful

sin·u·ous \ˈsin-yə-wəs\ adj : bending in and out : WINDING — **sin·u·os·i·ty** \ˌsin-yə-ˈwä-sə-tē\ n — **sin·u·ous·ly** adv

si·nus \ˈsī-nəs\ n [ME, fr. ML, fr. L, curve, hollow] **1** : any of several cavities of the skull usu. connecting with the nostrils **2** : a space forming a channel (as for the passage of blood)

si·nus·itis \ˌsī-nə-ˈsī-təs\ n : inflammation of a sinus of the skull

Sioux \ˈsü\ n, pl **Sioux** \same or ˈsüz\ [AmerF, short for Nadouessioux, fr. Ojibwa naˈtowɛˈssiw-, prob. fr. Algonquian *aˈtowɛˈ- speak another language] : DAKOTA

sip \ˈsip\ vb **sipped; sip·ping** : to drink in small quantities — **sip** n

¹**si·phon** also **sy·phon** \ˈsī-fən\ n **1** : a bent tube through which a liquid can be transferred by means of air pressure up and over the edge of one container and into another container placed at a lower level **2** usu **sy·phon** : a bottle that ejects soda water through a tube when a valve is opened

²**siphon** also **sypon** vb **si·phoned** also **sy·phoned; si·phon·ing** also **sy·phon·ing** : to draw off by means of a siphon

sir \ˈsər\ n [ME sir, sire, fr. AF, lord, feudal superior, fr. VL *seior, alter. of L senior, compar. of senex old, old man] **1** : a man of rank or position — used as a title before the given name of a knight or baronet **2** — used as a usu. respectful form of address

Si·rach \ˈsī-rak, sə-ˈräk\ n — see BIBLE table

¹**sire** \ˈsī(-ə)r\ n, **1** : FATHER; also, archaic : FOREFATHER **2** archaic : LORD — used as a form of address and a title **3** : the male parent of an animal (as a horse or dog)

²**sire** vb **sired; sir·ing** : BEGET

si·ren \ˈsī-rən\ n **1** : a seductive or alluring woman **2** : an electrically operated device for producing a loud shrill warning signal — **siren** adj

sir·loin \ˈsər-ˌlȯin\ n [alter. of earlier surloin, modif. of MF surlonge, fr. sur over (fr. L super) + longe loin] : a cut of beef taken from the part in front of the round

sirup var of SYRUP

si·sal \ˈsī-səl, -zəl\ n : a strong cordage fiber from an agave; also : this agave

sis·sy \ˈsi-sē\ n, pl **sissies** : an effeminate boy or man; also : a timid or cowardly person

sis·ter \ˈsis-tər\ n, **1** : a female having one or both parents in common with another individual **2** : a member of a religious order of women : NUN **3** chiefly Brit : NURSE **4** a : a girl or woman regarded as a comrade **b** : a girl or woman who shares with another a common national or racial origin — **sis·ter·ly** adj

sis·ter·hood \-ˌhu̇d\ n **1** : the state of being a sister **2** : a community or society of sisters **3** : the solidarity of women based on shared conditions

sis·ter–in–law \ˈsis-tə-rən-ˌlȯ\ n, pl **sis·ters–in–law** : the sister of one's spouse; also : the wife of one's brother

sit \ˈsit\ vb **sat** \ˈsat\; **sit·ting 1** : to rest upon the buttocks or haunches **2** : ROOST, PERCH **3** : to occupy a seat **4** : to hold a session **5** : to cover eggs for hatching : BROOD **6** : to pose for a portrait **7** : to remain quiet or inactive **8** : FIT **9** : to cause (oneself) to be seated **10** : to place in position **11** : to keep one's seat on ⟨~ a horse⟩ **12** : BABYSIT — **sit·ter** n

si·tar \si-'tär\ n [Hindi & Urdu *sitār*] : an Indian lute with a long neck and a varying number of strings

sit·com \'sit-ˌkäm\ n : SITUATION COMEDY

site \'sīt\ n **1** : LOCATION **2** : WEB SITE

sit–in \'sit-ˌin\ n : an act of sitting in the seats or on the floor of an establishment as a means of organized protest

sit·u·at·ed \'si-chə-ˌwā-təd\ adj : LOCATED, PLACED

sit·u·a·tion \ˌsi-chə-'wā-shən\ n **1** : LOCATION, SITE **2** : JOB **3** : CONDITION, CIRCUMSTANCES — **sit·u·a·tion·al** \-shə-nəl\ adj

situation comedy n : a radio or television comedy series that involves a continuing cast of characters in a succession of episodes

sit–up \'sit-ˌəp\ n : an exercise performed from a supine position by raising the torso to a sitting position and returning to the original position without lifting the feet

SIV \ˌes-ˌī-'vē\ n [simian *i*mmunodeficiency *v*irus] : a retrovirus related to HIV that causes a disease in monkeys similar to AIDS

six \'siks\ n **1** : one more than five **2** : the 6th in a set or series **3** : something having six units — **six** adj or pron — **sixth** \'siksth\ adj or adv or n

six–gun \'siks-ˌgən\ n : a 6-chambered revolver

six–pack \-ˌpak\ n : six bottles or cans (as of beer) packaged and purchased together; *also* : the contents of a six-pack

six·pence \-pəns, *US also* -ˌpens\ n : the sum of six pence; *also* : an English silver coin of this value

six–shoot·er \'siks-ˌshü-tər\ n : SIX-GUN

six·teen \ˌsiks-'tēn\ n : one more than 15 — **sixteen** adj or pron — **six·teenth** \-'tēnth\ adj or n

six·ty \'siks-tē\ n, pl **sixties** : six times 10 — **six·ti·eth** \'siks-tē-əth\ adj or n — **sixty** adj or pron

siz·able or **size·able** \'sī-zə-bəl\ adj : quite large — **siz·ably** \-blē\ adv

¹size \'sīz\ n [ME *sise* assize, judgment, quantity, fr. AF, short for *assise* assize] : physical extent or bulk : DIMENSIONS; *also* : considerable proportions — **sized** \'sīzd\ adj

²size vb **sized**; **siz·ing** **1** : to grade or classify according to size **2** : to form a judgment of ⟨~ up the situation⟩

³size n : a gluey material used for filling the pores in paper, plaster, or textiles — **siz·ing** n

⁴size vb **sized**; **siz·ing** : to cover, stiffen, or glaze with size

siz·zle \'si-zəl\ vb **siz·zled**; **siz·zling** : to fry or shrivel up with a hissing sound — **sizzle** n

SJ abbr Society of Jesus

SK abbr Saskatchewan

ska \'skä\ n : popular music of Jamaican origin combining traditional Caribbean rhythms and jazz

¹skate \'skāt\ n, pl **skates** also **skate** : any of a family of rays with thick broad winglike fins

²skate n **1** : a metal frame and runner attached to a shoe and used for gliding over ice **2** : ROLLER SKATE; *esp* : IN-LINE SKATE — **skate** vb — **skat·er** n

skate·board \'skāt-ˌbȯrd\ n : a short board mounted on small wheels — **skateboard** vb — **skate·board·er** n

skeet \'skēt\ n : trapshooting in which clay targets are thrown in such a way that their angle of flight simulates that of a flushed game bird

skein \'skān\ n : a loosely twisted quantity of yarn or thread wound on a reel

skel·e·ton \'ske-lə-t³n\ n **1** : a usu. bony supporting framework of an animal body **2** : a bare minimum **3** : FRAMEWORK — **skel·e·tal** \-lə-t³l\ adj

skep·tic \'skep-tik\ n **1** : one who believes in skepticism **2** : a person disposed to skepticism esp. regarding religion — **skep·ti·cal** \-ti-kəl\ adj — **skep·ti·cal·ly** \-k(ə-)lē\ adv

skep·ti·cism \'skep-tə-ˌsi-zəm\ n **1** : a doubting state of mind **2** : a doctrine that certainty of knowledge cannot be attained **3** : doubt concerning religion

sketch \'skech\ n [D *schets*, fr. It *schizzo*, lit., splash] **1** : a rough drawing or outline **2** : a short or light literary composition (as a story or essay); *also* : a short comedy piece — **sketch** vb — **sketchy** adj

¹skew \'skyü\ vb : TWIST, SWERVE

²skew n : SLANT

skew·er \'skyü-ər\ n : a long pin for holding small pieces of meat and vegetables for broiling — **skewer** vb

¹ski \'skē\ n, pl **skis** [Norw, fr. ON *skīth* stick of wood, ski] : one of a pair of long strips (as of wood, metal or plastic) curving upward in front that are used for gliding over snow or water

²ski vb **skied** \'skēd\; **ski·ing** : to glide on skis — **ski·able** \'skē-ə-bəl\ adj — **ski·er** n

¹skid \'skid\ n **1** : a plank for supporting something above the ground **2** : a device placed under a wheel to prevent turning **3** : a timber or rail over or on which something is slid or rolled **4** : the act of skidding **5** : a runner on the landing gear of an aircraft **6** : ²PALLET

²skid vb **skid·ded**; **skid·ding** **1** : to slide without rotating ⟨a *skidding* wheel⟩ **2** : to slide sideways on the road ⟨the car *skidded* on ice⟩ **3** : SLIDE, SLIP

skid row n : a district of cheap saloons frequented by vagrants and alcoholics

skiff \'skif\ n : a small boat

ski jump n : a jump made by a person wearing skis; *also* : a course or track prepared for such jumping — **ski jump** vb — **ski jumper** n

ski·ful *chiefly Brit var of* SKILLFUL

ski lift n : a mechanical device (as a chairlift) for carrying skiers up a long slope

skill \'skil\ n **1** : ability to use one's knowledge effectively in doing some-

thing **2** : developed or acquired ability
♦ *Synonyms* ART, CRAFT, CUNNING, DEXTERITY, EXPERTISE, KNOW-HOW — **skilled** \'skild\ *adj*

skil·let \'ski-lət\ *n* : a frying pan

skill·ful \'skil-fəl\ *adj* **1** : having or displaying skill : EXPERT **2** : accomplished with skill — **skill·ful·ly** *adv* — **skill·ful·ness** *n*

¹**skim** \'skim\ *vb* **skimmed; skim·ming 1** : to take off from the top of a liquid; *also* : to remove (scum or cream) from ⟨∼ milk⟩ **2** : to read rapidly and superficially **3** : to pass swiftly over — **skim·mer** *n*

²**skim** *adj* : having the cream removed

skimp \'skimp\ *vb* : to give insufficient attention, effort, or funds; *also* : to save by skimping

skimpy \'skim-pē\ *adj* **skimp·i·er; -est** : deficient in supply or execution — **skimp·i·ly** \-pə-lē\ *adv*

¹**skin** \'skin\ *n* **1** : the outer limiting layer of an animal body; *also* : the usu. thin tough tissue of which this is made **2** : an outer or surface layer (as a rind or peel) — **skin·less** *adj* — **skinned** *adj*

²**skin** *vb* **skinned; skin·ning** : to free from skin : remove the skin of

³**skin** *adj* : devoted to showing nudes ⟨∼ magazines⟩

skin diving *n* : the sport of swimming under water with a face mask and flippers and esp. without a portable breathing device — **skin·dive** *vb* — **skin diver** *n*

skin·flint \'skin-,flint\ *n* : a very stingy person

skin graft *n* : a piece of skin surgically removed from one area to replace skin in another area — **skin grafting** *n*

skin·head \'skin-,hed\ *n* : a person whose hair is cut very short

¹**skin·ny** \'ski-nē\ *adj* **skin·ni·er; -est 1** : resembling skin **2** : very thin

²**skinny** *n* : inside information

skin·ny–dip \'ski-nē-,dip\ *vb* : to swim in the nude — **skin·ny–dip·per** \-,di-pər\ *n*

skin·tight \'skin-'tīt\ *adj* : closely fitted to the figure ⟨∼ pants⟩

¹**skip** \'skip\ *vb* **skipped; skip·ping 1** : to move with leaps and bounds **2** : to leap lightly over **3** : to pass from point to point (as in reading) disregarding what is in between **4** : to pass over without notice or mention

²**skip** *n* : a light bouncing step; *also* : a gait of alternate hops and steps

skip·jack \'skip-,jak\ *n* : a small sailboat with vertical sides and a bottom similar to a flat V

skip·per \'ski-pər\ *n* [ME, fr. MD *schipper*, fr. *schip* ship] : the master of a ship; *also* : the manager of a baseball team — **skipper** *vb*

skir·mish \'skər-mish\ *n* : a minor engagement in war; *also* : a minor dispute or contest — **skirmish** *vb*

¹**skirt** \'skərt\ *n* : a free-hanging garment or part of a garment extending from the waist down

²**skirt** *vb* **1** : to pass around the outer edge of **2** : BORDER **3** : EVADE

skit \'skit\ *n* : a brief dramatic sketch

ski tow *n* : SKI LIFT

skit·ter \'ski-tər\ *vb* : to glide or skip lightly or quickly : skim along a surface

skit·tish \'ski-tish\ *adj* **1** : CAPRICIOUS **2** : easily frightened ⟨a ∼ horse⟩; *also* : WARY

ski·wear \'skē-,wer\ *n* : clothing suitable for wear while skiing

skosh \'skōsh\ *n* [Jp *sukoshi*] : a small amount : BIT

skul·dug·gery *or* **skull·dug·gery** \,skəl-'də-gə-rē\ *n, pl* **-ger·ies** : underhanded or unscrupulous behavior

skulk \'skəlk\ *vb* : to move furtively : SNEAK, LURK — **skulk·er** *n*

skull \'skəl\ *n* : the skeleton of the head of a vertebrate that protects the brain and supports the jaws

skull and crossbones *n, pl* **skulls and crossbones** : a depiction of a human skull over crossbones usu. indicating a danger

skull·cap \'skəl-,kap\ *n* : a close-fitting brimless cap

¹**skunk** \'skəŋk\ *n, pl* **skunks** *also* **skunk 1** : any of various black-and-white New World mammals related to the weasels that can forcibly eject an ill-smelling fluid when startled **2** : a contemptible person

²**skunk** *vb* : to defeat decisively; *esp* : to prevent entirely from scoring in a game

skunk cabbage *n* : either of two No. American perennial herbs related to the arums that occur in shaded wet to swampy areas and have a fetid odor suggestive of a skunk

sky \'skī\ *n, pl* **skies** [ME, sky, cloud, fr. ON *skȳ* cloud] **1** : the upper air **2** : HEAVEN — **sky·ey** \'skī-ē\ *adj*

sky·cap \-,kap\ *n* : a person employed to carry luggage at an airport

sky·div·ing \-,dī-viŋ\ *n* : the sport of jumping from an airplane and executing various body maneuvers before opening a parachute — **skydiver** *n*

sky·jack \-,jak\ *vb* : to commandeer an airplane in flight by threat of violence — **sky·jack·er** *n* — **sky·jack·ing** *n*

¹**sky·lark** \-,lärk\ *n* : a European lark noted for singing during flight

²**skylark** *vb* : FROLIC, SPORT

sky·light \'skī-,līt\ *n* : a window in a roof or ceiling — **sky·light·ed** \-,lī-təd\ *adj*

sky·line \-,līn\ *n* **1** : HORIZON **2** : an outline (as of buildings) against the sky

¹**sky·rock·et** \-,rä-kət\ *n* : ROCKET 1

²**skyrocket** *vb* : ROCKET 2

sky·scrap·er \-,skrā-pər\ *n* : a very tall building

sky·surf·ing \-,sər-fiŋ\ *n* : skydiving with a short modified surfboard attached to the feet — **sky·surf·er** \-fər\ *n*

sky·walk \-,wȯk\ *n* : an aerial walkway connecting two buildings

sky·ward \-wərd\ *adv* : toward the sky

sky·writ·ing \-,rī-tiŋ\ *n* : writing in the sky formed by smoke emitted from an airplane — **sky·writ·er** *n*

sl *abbr* **1** slightly **2** slip **3** slow

slab \'slab\ *n* : a thick flat piece or slice

¹**slack** \'slak\ *adj* **1** : CARELESS, NEGLI-GENT **2** : SLUGGISH, LISTLESS **3** : not taut **4** : not busy or active ◆ **Synonyms** LAX, REMISS, NEGLECTFUL, DELINQUENT, DERELICT — **slack-ly** *adv* — **slack-ness** *n*

²**slack** *vb* **1** : to make or become slack : LOOSEN, RELAX **2** : SLAKE 2

³**slack** *n* **1** : cessation of movement or flow : LETUP **2** : a part that hangs loose without strain ⟨∼ of a rope⟩ **3** : pants esp. for casual wear — usu. used in pl.

slack-en \'sla-kən\ *vb* : to make or become slack

slack-er \'sla-kər\ *n* **1** : one that shirks work or evades military duty **2** : a young person perceived to be disaffected, apathetic, cynical, or lacking ambition

slag \'slag\ *n* : the waste left after the melting of ores and the separation of metal from them

slain *past part of* SLAY

slake \'slāk, *for 2 also* 'slak\ *vb* **slaked**; **slak-ing** **1** : to relieve or satisfy with or as if with refreshing drink ⟨∼ thirst⟩ **2** : to cause (lime) to crumble by mixture with water

sla-lom \'slä-ləm\ *n* [Norw *slalam*, lit., sloping track] : skiing in a zigzag course between obstacles

¹**slam** \'slam\ *n* : the winning of every trick or of all tricks but one in bridge

²**slam** *n* **1** : a heavy jarring impact : BANG **2** : harsh criticism **3** : a poetry competition

³**slam** *vb* **slammed**; **slam-ming** **1** : to shut violently and noisily **2** : to throw or strike with a loud impact **3** : to criticize harshly

slam-mer \'sla-mər\ *n* : JAIL, PRISON

¹**slan-der** \'slan-dər\ *vb* : to utter slander against : DEFAME — **slan-der-er** *n*

²**slander** *n* [ME *sclaundre*, *slaundre*, fr. AF *esclandre*, alter. of *escandle*, fr. LL *scandalum* stumbling block, offense] : a false report maliciously uttered and tending to injure the reputation of a person — **slan-der-ous** *adj*

slang \'slaŋ\ *n* : an informal nonstandard vocabulary composed typically of invented words, arbitrarily changed words, and extravagant figures of speech — **slangy** *adj*

¹**slant** \'slant\ *n* **1** : a sloping direction, line, or plane **2** : a particular or personal viewpoint — **slant** *adj* — **slant-wise** \-,wīz\ *adv or adj*

²**slant** *vb* **1** : SLOPE **2** : to interpret or present in accordance with a special viewpoint or bias ◆ **Synonyms** INCLINE, LEAN, LIST, TILT, HEEL — **slant-ing-ly** *adv*

slap \'slap\ *vb* **slapped**; **slap-ping** **1** : to strike sharply with the open hand **2** : REBUFF, INSULT — **slap** *n*

slap-stick \-,stik\ *n* : comedy stressing horseplay

¹**slash** \'slash\ *vb* **1** : to cut with sweeping strokes **2** : to cut slits in (a garment) **3** : to reduce sharply — **slash-er** \'sla-shər\ *n*

²**slash** *n* **1** : GASH **2** : an ornamental slit in a garment **3** : a mark / used to denote "or" (as in *and/or*), "and or" (as in *straggler/deserter*), or "per" (as in *feet/second*)

slat \'slat\ *n* : a thin narrow flat strip

¹**slate** \'slāt\ *n* **1** : a dense fine-grained rock that splits into thin layers **2** : a roofing tile or a writing tablet made from this rock **3** : a written or unwritten record ⟨start with a clean ∼⟩ **4** : a list of candidates for election

²**slate** *vb* **slat-ed**; **slat-ing** **1** : to cover with slate **2** : to designate for action or appointment

slath-er \'sla-thər\ *vb* : to spread with or on thickly or lavishly

slat-tern \'sla-tərn\ *n* : a slovenly woman — **slat-tern-ly** *adj*

¹**slaugh-ter** \'slo-tər\ *n* **1** : the butchering of livestock for market **2** : great destruction of lives esp. in battle

²**slaughter** *vb* **1** : to kill (animals) for food : BUTCHER **2** : to kill in large numbers or in a bloody way : MASSACRE

slaugh-ter-house \-,haüs\ *n* : an establishment where animals are butchered

Slav \'släv, 'slav\ *n* : a person speaking a Slavic language

¹**slave** \'slāv\ *n* [ME *sclave*, fr. AF or ML; AF *esclave*, fr. ML *sclavus*, fr. *Sclavus* Slav; fr. the enslavement of Slavs in central Europe in the Middle Ages] **1** : a person held in servitude as property **2** : a device (as the printer of a computer) that is directly responsive to another — **slave** *adj*

²**slave** *vb* **slaved**; **slav-ing** : to work like a slave : DRUDGE

¹**sla-ver** \'sla-vər, 'slā-\ *n* : SLOBBER — **slaver** *vb*

²**slav-er** \'slā-vər\ *n* : a ship or a person engaged in transporting slaves

slav-ery \'slā-v(ə-)rē, 'slāv-rē\ *n* **1** : wearisome drudgery **2** : the condition of being a slave **3** : the practice of owning slaves ◆ **Synonyms** SERVITUDE, BONDAGE, ENSLAVEMENT

¹**Slav-ic** \'sla-vik, 'slä-\ *n* : a branch of the Indo-European language family including various languages (as Russian or Polish) of eastern Europe

²**Slavic** *adj* : of or relating to the Slavs or their languages

slav-ish \'slā-vish\ *adj* **1** : SERVILE **2** : obeying or imitating with no freedom of judgment or choice — **slav-ish-ly** *adv*

slaw \'slö\ *n* : COLESLAW

slay \'slā\ *vb* **slew** \'slü\; **slain** \'slān\; **slay-ing** : KILL — **slay-er** *n*

SLBM *abbr* submarine-launched ballistic missile

sleaze \'slēz\ *n* : a sleazy quality, appearance, or behavior

slea-zy \'slē-zē\ *adj* **slea-zi-er**; **-est** **1** : FLIMSY, SHODDY **2** : marked by low character or quality

¹**sled** \'sled\ *n* : a vehicle usu. on runners adapted esp. for sliding on snow

²**sled** *vb* **sled-ded**; **sled-ding** : to ride or carry on a sled

¹**sledge** \'slej\ *n* : SLEDGEHAMMER

²sledge *n* : a strong heavy sled

sledge·ham·mer \'slej-,ha-mər\ *n* : a large heavy hammer wielded with both hands — **sledgehammer** *adj or vb*

¹sleek \'slēk\ *vb* 1 : to make smooth or glossy 2 : to gloss over

²sleek *adj* 1 : having a smooth well-groomed look 2 : trim and graceful in design ⟨a ~ car⟩

¹sleep \'slēp\ *n* 1 : the natural periodic suspension of consciousness during which bodily powers are restored 2 : a state (as death or coma) suggesting sleep — **sleep·less** *adj* — **sleep·less·ness** *n*

²sleep *vb* **slept** \'slept\; **sleep·ing** 1 : to rest or be in a state of sleep; *also* : to spend in sleep 2 : to have sexual intercourse — usu. used with *with* 3 : to provide sleeping space for

sleep·er \'slē-pər\ *n* 1 : one that sleeps 2 : a horizontal beam to support something on or near ground level 3 : SLEEPING CAR 4 : someone or something unpromising or unnoticed that suddenly attains prominence or value

sleeping bag *n* : a warmly lined bag for sleeping esp. outdoors

sleeping car *n* : a railroad car with berths for sleeping

sleeping pill *n* : a drug in tablet or capsule form taken to induce sleep

sleeping sickness *n* : a serious disease of tropical Africa that is marked by fever, lethargy, confusion, and sleep disturbances and is caused by protozoans transmitted by the tsetse fly

sleep·over \'slēp-,ō-vər\ *n* : an overnight stay (as at another's home)

sleep·walk·er \'slēp-,wȯ-kər\ *n* : one that walks while or as if while asleep — **sleep·walk** \-,wȯk\ *vb*

sleepy \'slē-pē\ *adj* **sleep·i·er; -est** 1 : ready for sleep 2 : quietly inactive — **sleep·i·ly** \'slē-pə-lē\ *adv* — **sleep·i·ness** \-pē-nəs\ *n*

sleet \'slēt\ *n* : frozen or partly frozen rain — **sleet** *vb* — **sleety** *adj*

sleeve \'slēv\ *n* 1 : a part of a garment covering an arm 2 : a tubular part designed to fit over another part — **sleeved** *adj* — **sleeve·less** *adj*

¹sleigh \'slā\ *n* : an open usu. horse-drawn vehicle on runners for use on snow or ice

²sleigh *vb* : to drive or travel in a sleigh

sleight \'slīt\ *n* 1 : TRICK 2 : DEXTERITY

sleight of hand : a trick requiring skillful manual manipulation

slen·der \'slen-dər\ *adj* 1 : SLIM, THIN 2 : WEAK, SLIGHT 3 : MEAGER, INADEQUATE

slen·der·ize \-də-,rīz\ *vb* **-ized; -iz·ing** : to make slender

sleuth \'slüth\ *n* [short for *sleuthhound* bloodhound, fr. ME (Sc) *sleuth hund*, fr. ME *sleuth, slouth, sloth* track of an animal or person, fr. ON *slōth*] : DETECTIVE

¹slew \'slü\ *past of* SLAY

²slew *vb* : TURN, VEER, SKID

¹slice \'slīs\ *vb* **sliced; slic·ing** 1 : to cut a slice from; *also* : to cut into slices 2 : to hit (a ball) so that a slice results

²slice *n* 1 : a thin flat piece cut from something 2 : a flight of a ball (as in golf) that curves in the direction of the dominant hand of the player hitting it

¹slick \'slik\ *vb* : to make smooth or sleek

²slick *adj* 1 : very smooth : SLIPPERY 2 : CLEVER, SMART ⟨a ~ salesperson⟩

³slick *n* 1 : a smooth patch of water covered with a film of oil 2 : a popular magazine printed on coated paper

slick·er \'sli-kər\ *n* 1 : a long loose raincoat 2 : a sly tricky person 3 : a city dweller esp. of natty appearance or sophisticated mannerisms

¹slide \'slīd\ *vb* **slid** \'slid\; **slid·ing** \'slī-diṅ\ 1 : to move smoothly along a surface 2 : to fall by a loss of support 3 : to pass unobtrusively 4 : to move or pass smoothly; *also* : to pass unnoticed ⟨let it ~ by⟩ 5 : to fall or dive toward a base in baseball

²slide *n* 1 : an act or instance of sliding 2 : something (as a cover or fastener) that operates by sliding 3 : a fall of a mass of earth or snow down a hillside 4 : a surface on which something slides 5 : a glass plate on which a specimen is mounted for examination under a microscope 6 : a small transparent photograph that can be projected on a screen

slid·er \'slī-dər\ *n* 1 : one that slides 2 : a baseball pitch that looks like a fastball but curves slightly

slide rule *n* : a manual device for calculation consisting of a ruler and a movable middle piece graduated with logarithmic scales

slier *comparative of* SLY

sliest *superlative of* SLY

¹slight \'slīt\ *adj* 1 : SLENDER; *also* : FRAIL 2 : UNIMPORTANT 3 : small of its kind or in amount ⟨a ~ odor⟩ — **slight·ly** *adv*

²slight *vb* 1 : to treat as unimportant 2 : to ignore discourteously 3 : to perform or attend to carelessly

³slight *n* : a humiliating discourtesy

¹slim \'slim\ *adj* **slim·mer; slim·mest** [D, bad, inferior, fr. MD, *slimp* crooked, bad] 1 : SLENDER, SLIGHT, THIN 2 : SMALL, SLIGHT ⟨a ~ chance⟩

²slim *vb* **slimmed; slim·ming** : to make or become slender

slime \'slīm\ *n* 1 : sticky mud 2 : a slippery substance (as on the skin of a slug or catfish) — **slimy** *adj*

¹sling \'sliṅ\ *vb* **slung** \'sləṅ\; **sling·ing** 1 : to throw forcibly : FLING 2 : to hurl with or as if with a sling

²sling *n* 1 : a short strap with strings attached for hurling stones or shot 2 : something (as a rope or chain) used to hoist, lower, support, or carry; *esp* : a bandage hanging from the neck to support an arm or hand

sling·shot \'sliṅ-,shät\ *n* : a forked stick with elastic bands for shooting small stones or shot

slink \'sliṅk\ *vb* **slunk** \'sləṅk\ *also* **slinked** \'sliṅkt\; **slink·ing** 1 : to move stealthily or furtively **2** : to move sinuously — **slinky** *adj*

¹**slip** \'slip\ *vb* **slipped; slip·ping** **1** : to escape quietly or secretly **2** : to slide along or cause to slide along smoothly **3** : to make a mistake **4** : to pass unnoticed or undone **5** : to fall off from a standard or level

²**slip** *n* **1** : a ramp for repairing ships **2** : a ship's berth between two piers **3** : secret or hurried departure, escape, or evasion **4** : BLUNDER **5** : a sudden mishap **6** : a woman's one-piece garment worn under a dress **7** : PILLOWCASE

³**slip** *n* **1** : a shoot or twig from a plant for planting or grafting **2** : a long narrow strip; *esp* : one of paper used for a record ⟨deposit ∼⟩

⁴**slip** *vb* **slipped; slip·ping** : to take slips from (a plant)

slip·knot \'slip-ˌnät\ *n* : a knot that slips along the rope around which it is made

slipped disk *n* : a protrusion of one of the disks of cartilage between vertebrae with pressure on spinal nerves resulting esp. in low back pain

slip·per \'sli-pər\ *n* : a light low shoe that may be easily slipped on and off

slip·pery \'sli-pə-rē\ *adj* **slip·per·i·er; -est** **1** : icy, wet, smooth, or greasy enough to cause one to fall or lose one's hold **2** : not to be trusted : TRICKY — **slip·per·i·ness** *n*

slip·shod \'slip-ˈshäd\ *adj* : SLOVENLY, CARELESS ⟨∼ work⟩

slip·stream \'slip-ˌstrēm\ *n* : a stream (as of air) driven aft by a propeller

slip-up \'slip-ˌəp\ *n* **1** : MISTAKE **2** : ACCIDENT

¹**slit** \'slit\ *vb* **slit; slit·ting** **1** : SLASH **2** : to cut off or away

²**slit** *n* : a long narrow cut or opening

slith·er \'sli-thər\ *vb* : to slip or glide along like a snake — **slith·ery** *adj*

sliv·er \'sli-vər\ *n* : SPLINTER

slob \'släb\ *n* : a slovenly or boorish person

slob·ber \'slä-bər\ *vb* **slob·bered; slob·ber·ing** : to dribble saliva — **slobber** *n*

sloe \'slō\ *n* : the fruit of the blackthorn

slog \'släg\ *vb* **slogged; slog·ging** **1** : to hit hard : BEAT **2** : to work hard and steadily

slo·gan \'slō-gən\ *n* [alter. of earlier *slogorn*, fr. ScGael *sluagh-ghairm*, fr. *sluagh* army, host + *gairm* cry] : a word or phrase expressing the spirit or aim of a party, group, or cause

slo-mo \'slō-ˌmō\ *n* : SLOW MOTION — **slo-mo** *adj*

sloop \'slüp\ *n* [D *sloep*] : a single-masted sailboat with a jib and a fore-and-aft mainsail

¹**slop** \'släp\ *n* **1** : thin tasteless drink or liquid food — usu. used in pl. **2** : food waste for animal feed : SWILL **3** : excreted body waste — usu. used in pl.

²**slop** *vb* **slopped; slop·ping** **1** : SPILL **2** : to feed with slop ⟨∼ hogs⟩

¹**slope** \'slōp\ *vb* **slop·ing** : SLANT, INCLINE

²**slope** *n* **1** : upward or downward slant or degree of slant **2** : ground that forms an incline **3** : the part of a landmass draining into a particular ocean

slop·py \'slä-pē\ *adj* **slop·pi·er; -est** **1** : MUDDY, SLUSHY **2** : SLOVENLY, MESSY

sloppy joe \-ˈjō\ *n* : ground beef cooked in a thick spicy sauce and usu. served on a bun

slosh \'släsh\ *vb* **1** : to flounder through or splash about in or with water, mud, or slush **2** : to move with a splashing motion

slot \'slät\ *n* **1** : a long narrow opening or groove **2** : a position in a sequence

slot car *n* : an electric toy racing car that runs on a grooved track

sloth \'slȯth\ *n, pl* **sloths** \'slȯths, 'slȯthz\ **1** : LAZINESS, INDOLENCE **2** : any of several slow-moving plant-eating arboreal mammals of So. and Central America — **sloth·ful** *adj*

slot machine *n* **1** : a machine whose operation is begun by dropping a coin into a slot **2** : a coin-operated gambling machine that pays off according to the matching of symbols on wheels spun by a handle

¹**slouch** \'slau̇ch\ *n* **1** : a lazy or incompetent person **2** : a loose or drooping gait or posture

²**slouch** *vb* : to walk, stand, or sit with a slouch : SLUMP

¹**slough** \'slü, 2 usu 'slau̇\ *n* **1** : a wet and marshy or muddy place (as a swamp) **2** : a discouraged state of mind

²**slough** \'sləf\ *also* **sluff** *n* : something that has been or may be shed or cast off

³**slough** \'sləf\ *also* **sluff** *vb* : to cast off

Slo·vak \'slō-ˌväk, -ˌvak\ *n* **1** : a member of a Slavic people of Slovakia **2** : the language of the Slovaks — **Slovak** *adj* — **Slo·va·ki·an** \slō-ˈvä-kē-ən, -ˈva-\ *adj or n*

slov·en \'slə-vən\ *n* [ME *sloveyn* slut, rascal, perh. fr. MD *slof* negligent] : an untidy person

Slo·vene \'slō-ˌvēn\ *n* **1** : a member of a Slavic people living largely in Slovenia **2** : the language of the Slovenes — **Slovene** *adj* — **Slo·ve·nian** \slō-ˈvē-nē-ən\ *adj or n*

slov·en·ly \'slə-vən-lē\ *adj* **1** : untidy in dress or person **2** : lazily or carelessly done : SLIPSHOD

¹**slow** \'slō\ *adj* **1** : SLUGGISH; *also* : dull in mind : STUPID **2** : moving, flowing, or proceeding at less than the usual speed **3** : taking more than the usual time **4** : registering behind the correct time **5** : not lively : BORING ♦ *Synonyms* DILATORY, LAGGARD, DELIBERATE, LEISURELY — **slow** *adv* — **slow·ly** *adv* — **slow·ness** *n*

²**slow** *vb* **1** : to make slow : hold back **2** : to go slower

slow motion *n* : motion-picture action photographed so as to appear much slower than normal — **slow-motion** *adj*

SLR *abbr* single-lens reflex

sludge \'sləj\ *n* : a slushy mass : OOZE; *esp* : solid matter produced by sewage treatment processes

slue *var of* ²SLEW

¹**slug** \\'sləg\\ *n* **1** : a small mass of metal; *esp* : BULLET **2** : a metal disk for use (as in a slot machine) in place of a coin **3** : any of numerous wormlike mollusks related to the snails **4** : a quantity of liquor drunk

²**slug** *vb* **slugged; slug·ging** : to strike forcibly and heavily — **slug·ger** *n*

slug·gard \\'slə-gərd\\ *n* : a lazy person

slug·gish \\'slə-gish\\ *adj* **1** : SLOTHFUL, LAZY **2** : slow in movement or flow **3** : STAGNANT, DULL — **slug·gish·ly** *adv* — **slug·gish·ness** *n*

¹**sluice** \\'slüs\\ *n* [ME *sluse, scluse,* fr. AF *escluse,* fr. LL *exclusa,* fr. L, fem. of *exclusus,* pp. of *excludere* to shut out, exclude] **1** : an artificial passage for water with a gate for controlling the flow; *also* : the gate so used **2** : a channel that carries off surplus water **3** : an inclined trough or flume for washing ore or floating logs

²**sluice** *vb* **sluiced; sluic·ing** **1** : to draw off through a sluice **2** : to wash with running water : FLUSH

¹**slum** \\'sləm\\ *n* : a thickly populated area marked by poverty and dirty or deteriorated houses — **slum·my** \\'slə-mē\\ *adj*

²**slum** *vb* **slummed; slum·ming** : to visit slums esp. out of curiosity; *also* : to go somewhere or do something that might be considered beneath one's station

¹**slum·ber** \\'sləm-bər\\ *vb* **slum·bered; slum·ber·ing** **1** : DOZE; *also* : SLEEP **2** : to be in a sluggish or torpid state

²**slumber** *n* : SLEEP

slum·ber·ous \\'sləm-bə-rəs\\ *or* **slum·brous** \\-brəs\\ *adj* **1** : SLUMBERING, SLEEPY **2** : PEACEFUL, INACTIVE

slum·lord \\'sləm-ˌlȯrd\\ *n* : a landlord who receives unusually large profits from substandard properties

slump \\'sləmp\\ *vb* **1** : to sink down suddenly : COLLAPSE **2** : SLOUCH **3** : to decline sharply — **slump** *n*

slung *past and past part of* SLING

slunk *past and past part of* SLINK

¹**slur** \\'slər\\ *n* : a slighting remark : ASPERSION — **slur** *vb*

²**slur** *vb* **slurred; slur·ring** **1** : to slide or slip over without due mention or emphasis **2** : to perform two or more successive notes of different pitch in a smooth or connected way

³**slur** *n* : a curved line connecting notes to be slurred; *also* : a group of slurred notes

slurp \\'slərp\\ *vb* : to eat or drink noisily — **slurp** *n*

slur·ry \\'slər-ē\\ *n, pl* **slur·ries** : a watery mixture of insoluble matter

slush \\'sləsh\\ *n* **1** : partly melted or watery snow **2** : soft mud — **slushy** *adj*

slush fund *n* : an unregulated fund often for illicit purposes

slut \\'slət\\ *n* **1** : a slovenly woman **2** : a promiscuous woman — **slut·tish** *adj*

sly \\'slī\\ *adj* **sly·er** *also* **sli·er** \\'slī-ər\\; **sly·est** *also* **sli·est** \\'slī-əst\\ **1** : CRAFTY, CUNNING **2** : SECRETIVE, FURTIVE **3** : ROGUISH ♦ *Synonyms* TRICKY, WILY, ARTFUL, FOXY, GUILEFUL — **sly·ly** *also* **sli·ly** *adv* — **sly·ness** *n*

sm *abbr* small

Sm *symbol* samarium

SM *abbr* **1** master of science **2** sergeant major **3** service mark **4** stage manager

SMA *abbr* sergeant major of the army

¹**smack** \\'smak\\ *n* : characteristic flavor; *also* : a slight trace

²**smack** *vb* **1** : to have a taste **2** : to have a trace or suggestion ⟨~*s* of treason⟩

³**smack** *vb* **1** : to move (the lips) so as to make a sharp noise **2** : to kiss or slap with a loud noise

⁴**smack** *n* **1** : a sharp noise made by the lips **2** : a loud kiss or slap

⁵**smack** *adv* : squarely and sharply

⁶**smack** *n* : a sailing ship used in fishing

⁷**smack** *n, slang* : HEROIN

SMaj *abbr* sergeant major

¹**small** \\'smȯl\\ *adj* **1** : little in size or amount **2** : operating on a limited scale **3** : little or close to zero (as in number or value) **4** : made up of little things **5** : TRIFLING, UNIMPORTANT **6** : MEAN, PETTY ♦ *Synonyms* DIMINUTIVE, PETITE, WEE, TINY, MINUTE — **small·ish** *adj* — **small·ness** *n*

²**small** *n* : a small part or product ⟨the ~ of the back⟩

small·pox \\'smȯl-ˌpäks\\ *n* : a contagious virus disease of humans formerly common but now eradicated

small talk *n* : light or casual conversation

small–time \\'smȯl-ˈtīm\\ *adj* : insignificant in performance and standing : MINOR — **small–tim·er** *n*

smarmy \\'smär-mē\\ *adj* **smarm·i·er; -est** : marked by a smug ingratiating, or false earnestness

¹**smart** \\'smärt\\ *adj* **1** : making one smart ⟨a ~ blow⟩ **2** : mentally quick : BRIGHT **3** : WITTY, CLEVER **4** : STYLISH **5** : being a guided missile **6** : containing a microprocessor for limited computing capability ⟨~ terminal⟩ ♦ *Synonyms* KNOWING, QUICK-WITTED, INTELLIGENT, BRAINY, SHARP — **smart·ly** *adv* — **smart·ness** *n*

²**smart** *vb* **1** : to cause or feel a stinging pain **2** : to feel or endure distress — **smart** *n*

smart al·eck \\'smärt-ˌa-lik\\ *n* : a person given to obnoxious cleverness

smart card *n* : a small plastic card that has a built-in microprocessor to store and handle data

smart·en \\'smär-tᵊn\\ *vb* : to make smart or smarter — usu. used with *up*

¹**smash** \\'smash\\ *n* **1** : a smashing blow **2** : a hard, overhand stroke in tennis **3** : the act or sound of smashing **4** : collision of vehicles : CRASH **5** : COLLAPSE, RUIN; *esp* : BANKRUPTCY **6** : a striking success : HIT — **smash** *adj*

²**smash** *vb* **1** : to break or be broken into pieces **2** : to move forward with force and shattering effect **3** : to destroy utterly : WRECK

smat·ter·ing \\'sma-tə-riŋ\\ *n* **1** : superficial knowledge **2** : a small scattered number or amount

¹**smear** \'smir\ n **1** : a spot left by an oily or sticky substance **2** : material smeared on a surface (as of a microscope slide)

²**smear** vb **1** : to overspread esp. with something oily or sticky **2** : SMUDGE, SOIL **3** : to injure by slander or insults

¹**smell** \'smel\ vb **smelled** \'smeld\ or **smelt** \'smelt\; **smell·ing** **1** : to perceive the odor of by sense organs of the nose; also : to detect or seek with or as if with these organs **2** : to have or give off an odor

²**smell** n **1** : ODOR, SCENT **2** : the process or power of perceiving odor; also : the sense by which one perceives odor **3** : an act of smelling — **smelly** adj

smelling salts n pl : an aromatic preparation used as a stimulant and restorative (as to relieve faintness)

¹**smelt** \'smelt\ n, pl **smelts** or **smelt** : any of a family of small food fishes of coastal or fresh waters that are related to the trouts and salmons

²**smelt** vb : to melt or fuse (ore) in order to separate the metal; also : REFINE

smelt·er \'smel-tər\ n **1** : one that smelts **2** : an establishment for smelting

smid·gen or **smid·geon** or **smid·gin** \'smi-jən\ n : a small amount : BIT

smi·lax \'smī-,laks\ n **1** : any of various mostly climbing and prickly plants related to the lilies **2** : an ornamental plant related to the asparagus

¹**smile** \'smī(-ə)l\ vb **smiled; smil·ing** **1** : to look with a smile **2** : to be favorable **3** : to express by a smile

²**smile** n : a change of facial expression to express amusement, pleasure, or affection — **smile·less** \'smī(-ə)l-ləs\ adj

smil·ey \'smī-lē\ adj : exhibiting a smile : frequently smiling

smirch \'smərch\ vb **1** : to make dirty or stained **2** : to bring disgrace on — **smirch** n

smirk \'smərk\ vb : to smile in an affected or smug manner : SIMPER — **smirk** n

smite \'smīt\ vb **smote** \'smōt\; **smit·ten** \'smi-t²n\ or **smote; smit·ing** \'smī-tiŋ\ **1** : to strike heavily; also : to kill by striking **2** : to affect as if by a heavy blow

smith \'smith\ n : a worker in metals; esp : BLACKSMITH

smith·er·eens \,smi-thə-'rēnz\ n pl [perh. fr. Ir smidiríní] : FRAGMENTS, BITS

smithy \'smi-thē\ n, pl **smith·ies** **1** : a smith's workshop **2** : BLACKSMITH

¹**smock** \'smäk\ n : a loose garment worn over other clothes as a protection

²**smock** vb : to gather (cloth) in regularly spaced tucks — **smock·ing** n

smog \'smäg, 'smȯg\ n [blend of smoke and fog] : a thick haze caused by the action of sunlight on air polluted by smoke and automobile exhaust fumes — **smog·gy** adj

¹**smoke** \'smōk\ n **1** : the gas from burning material (as coal, wood, or tobacco) in which are suspended particles of soot **2** : a mass or column of smoke **3** : something (as a cigarette) to smoke; also : the act of smoking — **smoke·less** adj — **smoky** adj

²**smoke** vb **smoked; smok·ing** **1** : to emit smoke **2** : to inhale and exhale the fumes of burning tobacco; also : to use in smoking (~ a pipe) **3** : to stupefy or drive away by smoke **4** : to discolor with smoke **5** : to cure (as meat) with smoke — **smok·er** n

smoke detector n : an alarm that sounds automatically when it detects smoke

smoke jumper n : a forest firefighter who parachutes to locations otherwise difficult to reach

smoke screen n **1** : a screen of smoke to hinder enemy observation **2** : something designed to obscure, confuse, or mislead

smoke·stack \'smōk-,stak\ n : a pipe or funnel through which smoke and gases are discharged

smol·der or **smoul·der** \'smōl-dər\ vb **smol·dered** or **smoul·dered; smol·der·ing** or **smoul·der·ing** **1** : to burn and smoke without flame **2** : to burn inwardly — **smolder** n

smooch \'smüch\ vb : KISS, PET — **smooch** n

¹**smooth** \'smüth\ adj **1** : not rough or uneven **2** : not jarring or jolting **3** : BLAND, MILD **4** : fluent in speech and agreeable in manner — **smooth·ly** adv — **smooth·ness** n

²**smooth** vb **1** : to make smooth **2** : to free from trouble or difficulty

smooth muscle n : muscle with no cross striations that is typical of visceral organs (as the stomach and bladder) and is not under voluntary control

smoothy or **smooth·ie** \'smü-thē\ n, pl **smooth·ies** **1** : an artfully suave person **2** smoothie : a creamy beverage of fruit blended with juice, milk, or yogurt

s'more \'smȯr\ n : a dessert of marshmallow and pieces of chocolate sandwiched between graham crackers

smor·gas·bord \'smȯr-gas-,bȯrd\ n [Sw smörgasbord, fr. smörgas open sandwich + bord table] : a luncheon or supper buffet consisting of many foods

smote past and past part of SMITE

¹**smoth·er** \'smə-thər\ n **1** : thick stifling smoke **2** : a dense cloud (as of fog or dust) **3** : a confused multitude of things

²**smother** vb **smoth·ered; smoth·er·ing** **1** : to be overcome by or die from lack of air **2** : to kill by depriving of air **3** : SUPPRESS **4** : to cover thickly

SMSgt abbr senior master sergeant

¹**smudge** \'sməj\ vb **smudged; smudg·ing** : to soil or blur by rubbing or smearing

²**smudge** n : a dirty or blurred spot — **smudgy** adj

smug \'sməg\ adj **smug·ger; smug·gest** : conscious of one's virtue and importance : SELF-SATISFIED — **smug·ly** adv — **smug·ness** n

smug·gle \'smə-gəl\ vb **smug·gled; smug·gling** **1** : to import or export secretly, illegally, or without paying the duties required by law   **2** : to convey secretly — **smug·gler** \\'smə-glər\\ *n*

smut \\'smət\\ *n*   **1** : something (as soot) that smudges; *also* : SMUDGE, SPOT   **2** : any of various destructive diseases of plants caused by fungi; *also* : a fungus causing smut   **3** : indecent language or matter — **smut·ty** *adj*

smutch \\'sməch\\ *n* : SMUDGE

Sn *symbol* [LL *stannum*] tin

SN *abbr* seaman

snack \\'snak\\ *n* : a light meal : BITE — **snack** *vb*

snaf·fle \\'sna-fəl\\ *n* : a simple jointed bit for a horse's bridle

¹snag \\'snag\\ *n*   **1** : a stump or piece of a tree esp. when under water   **2** : an unexpected difficulty ♦ *Synonyms* OBSTACLE, OBSTRUCTION, IMPEDIMENT, BAR

²snag *vb* **snagged; snag·ging**   **1** : to become caught on or as if on a snag   **2** : to seize quickly : SNATCH

snail \\'snāl\\ *n* : any of numerous small gastropod mollusks with a spiral shell into which they can withdraw

snail mail *n* : mail delivered by a postal system   **2** : MAIL 2

snake \\'snāk\\ *n*   **1** : any of numerous long-bodied limbless reptiles   **2** : a treacherous person   **3** : something that resembles a snake — **snake·like** \\-,līk\\ *adj* — **snaky** *adj*

snake·bite \\-,bīt\\ *n* : the bite of a snake and esp. a venomous snake

¹snap \\'snap\\ *vb* **snapped; snap·ping**   **1** : to grasp or slash at something with the teeth   **2** : to get or buy quickly   **3** : to utter sharp or angry words   **4** : to break suddenly with a sharp sound   **5** : to give a sharp cracking noise   **6** : to throw with a quick motion   **7** : FLASH ⟨her eyes *snapped*⟩   **8** : to put a football into play — **snap·per** *n* — **snap·pish** *adj*

²snap *n*   **1** : the act or sound of snapping   **2** : something very easy to do : CINCH   **3** : a short period of cold weather   **4** : a catch or fastening that closes with a click   **5** : a thin brittle cookie   **6** : ENERGY, VIM; *also* : smartness of movement   **7** : the putting of the ball into play in football

snap bean *n* : a bean grown primarily for its long pods that are cooked as a vegetable when young and tender

snap·drag·on \\'snap-,dra-gən\\ *n* : any of a genus of herbs with long spikes of showy flowers

snapping turtle *n* : either of two large American turtles with powerful jaws and a strong musky odor

snap·py \\'sna-pē\\ *adj*   **1** : quickly made or done   **2** : marked by vigor   **3** : STYLISH

snap·shot \\'snap-,shät\\ *n* : a photograph taken usu. with an inexpensive hand-held camera

snare \\'sner\\ *n* : a trap often consisting of a noose for catching birds or mammals — **snare** *vb*

¹snarl \\'snärl\\ *vb* : to cause to become knotted and intertwined

²snarl *n* : TANGLE — **snarly** \\'snär-lē\\ *adj*

³snarl *vb* : to growl angrily or threateningly

⁴snarl *n* : an angry ill-tempered growl

¹snatch \\'snach\\ *vb*   **1** : to try to grasp something suddenly   **2** : to seize or take away suddenly ♦ *Synonyms* CLUTCH, SEIZE, GRAB, NAB

²snatch *n*   **1** : a short period   **2** : an act of snatching   **3** : something brief or fragmentary ⟨∼es of song⟩

¹sneak \\'snēk\\ *vb* **sneaked** \\'snēkt\\ *or* **snuck** \\'snək\\; **sneak·ing** : to move, act, or take in a furtive manner — **sneak·ing·ly** *adv*

²sneak *n*   **1** : one who acts in a furtive or shifty manner   **2** : a stealthy or furtive move or escape — **sneak·i·ly** \\'snē-kə-lē\\ *adv* — **sneaky** *adj*

sneak·er \\'snē-kər\\ *n* : a sports shoe with a pliable rubber sole

sneer \\'snir\\ *vb* : to show scorn or contempt by curling the lip or by a jeering tone — **sneer** *n*

sneeze \\'snēz\\ *vb* **sneezed; sneez·ing** [ME *snesen*, alter. of *fnesen*, fr. OE *fnēosan*] : to force the breath out suddenly and violently as a reflex act — **sneeze** *n*

SNF *abbr* skilled nursing facility

snick·er \\'sni-kər\\ *n* : a partly suppressed laugh — **snicker** *vb*

snide \\'snīd\\ *adj*   **1** : MEAN, LOW ⟨a ∼ trick⟩   **2** : slyly disparaging ⟨a ∼ remark⟩ — **snide·ly** *adv* — **snide·ness** *n*

sniff \\'snif\\ *vb*   **1** : to draw air audibly up the nose esp. for smelling   **2** : to show disdain or scorn   **3** : to detect by or as if by smelling — **sniff** *n*

snif·fle \\'sni-fəl\\ *n*   **1** *pl* : a head cold marked by nasal discharge   **2** : SNUFFLE — **sniffle** *vb*

¹snip \\'snip\\ *n*   **1** : a fragment snipped off   **2** : a simple stroke of the scissors or shears

²snip *vb* **snipped; snip·ping** : to cut off by bits : CLIP; *also* : to remove by cutting off

¹snipe \\'snīp\\ *n, pl* **snipes** *or* **snipe** : any of several long-billed game birds esp. of marshy areas that belong to the same family as the sandpipers

²snipe *vb* **sniped; snip·ing** : to shoot at an exposed enemy from a concealed position — **snip·er** *n*

snip·py \\'sni-pē\\ *adj* **snip·pi·er; -est** : CURT, SNAPPISH — **snip·pi·ly** \\'sni-pə-lē\\ *adv*

snips \\'snips\\ *n pl* : hand shears used esp. for cutting sheet metal ⟨tin ∼⟩

snitch \\'snich\\ *vb*   **1** : INFORM, TATTLE   **2** : PILFER, SNATCH — **snitch** *n*

sniv·el \\'sni-vəl\\ *vb* **-eled** *or* **-elled; -el·ing** *or* **-el·ling**   **1** : to have a running nose; *also* : SNUFFLE   **2** : to whine in a snuffling manner — **snivel** *n*

snob \\'snäb\\ *n* : one who seeks association with persons of higher social position and looks down on those considered inferior — **snob·bish** *adj* — **snob·bish·ly** *adv* — **snob·bish·ness** *n* — **snob·by** \\'snä-bē\\ *adj*

snob·bery \'snä-bə-rē\ *n, pl* **-ber·ies** : snobbish conduct

¹snoop \'snüp\ *vb* [D *snoepen* to buy or eat on the sly] : to pry in a furtive or meddlesome way

²snoop *n* : a prying meddlesome person

snoopy \'snü-pē\ *adj* **snoop·i·er; -est** : given to snooping

snooty \'snü-tē\ *adj* **snoot·i·er; -est** : DISDAINFUL, SNOBBISH — **snoot·i·ly** \'snü-tə-lē\ *adv*

snooze \'snüz\ *vb* **snoozed; snooz·ing** : to take a nap : DOZE — **snooze** *n*

snore \'snȯr\ *vb* **snored; snor·ing** : to breathe with a rough hoarse noise while sleeping — **snore** *n*

snor·kel \'snȯr-kəl\ *n* [G *Schnorchel*] : a tube projecting above the water used by swimmers for breathing with the face under water — **snorkel** *vb*

snort \'snȯrt\ *vb* **1** : to force air violently and noisily through the nose ⟨his horse ~ed⟩ **2** : to inhale (a drug) through the nostrils — **snort** *n*

snot \'snät\ *n* : nasal mucus

snot·ty \'snä-tē\ *adj* **snot·ti·er; -est** **1** : soiled with snot **2** : meanly contemptible

snout \'snaȯt\ *n* **1** : a long projecting muzzle (as of a pig) **2** : a usu. large or grotesque nose

¹snow \'snō\ *n* **1** : crystals of ice formed from water vapor in the air **2** : a descent or shower of snow crystals

²snow *vb* **1** : to fall or cause to fall in or as snow **2** : to cover or shut in with or as if with snow

¹snow·ball \'snō-ˌbȯl\ *n* : a round mass of snow pressed into shape in the hand for throwing

²snowball *vb* **1** : to throw snowballs at **2** : to increase or expand at a rapidly accelerating rate

snow·bank \-ˌbaŋk\ *n* : a mound or slope of snow

snow·belt \-ˌbelt\ *n, often cap* : a region that receives an appreciable amount of annual snowfall

snow·blow·er \-ˌblō-ər\ *n* : a machine in which a rotating spiral blade picks up and propels snow aside

snow·board \-ˌbȯrd\ *n* : a board like a wide ski ridden in a surfing position downhill over snow

snow·drift \-ˌdrift\ *n* : a bank of drifted snow

snow·drop \-ˌdräp\ *n* : a plant with narrow leaves and a nodding white flower that blooms early in the spring

snow·fall \-ˌfȯl\ *n* : a fall of snow

snow fence *n* : a fence across the path of prevailing winds to protect something (as a road) from drifting snow

snow·field \-ˌfēld\ *n* : a mass of perennial snow at the head of a glacier

snow·mo·bile \'snō-mō-ˌbēl\ *n* : any of various automotive vehicles for travel on snow — **snow·mo·bil·er** \-ˌbē-lər\ *n* — **snow·mo·bil·ing** \-liŋ\ *n*

snow pea *n* : a cultivated pea with flat edible pods

snow·plow \'snō-ˌplaȯ\ *n* **1** : a device for clearing away snow **2** : a skiing maneuver in which the heels of both skis are slid outward for slowing down or stopping

¹snow·shoe \-ˌshü\ *n* : a lightweight platform for the foot designed to enable a person to walk on soft snow without sinking

²snowshoe *vb* **snow·shoed; snow·shoe·ing** : to travel on snowshoes

snow·storm \-ˌstȯrm\ *n* : a storm of falling snow

snow thrower *n* : SNOWBLOWER

snowy \'snō-ē\ *adj* **snow·i·er; -est** **1** : marked by snow **2** : white as snow

snowy egret *n* : a white American egret with a slender black bill

snub \'snəb\ *vb* **snubbed; snub·bing** : to treat with disdain : SLIGHT — **snub** *n*

snub–nosed \'snəb-ˌnōzd\ *adj* : having a nose slightly turned up at the end

snuck *past and past part of* SNEAK

¹snuff \'snəf\ *vb* **1** : to pinch off the charred end of (a candle) **2** : to put out (a candle) — **snuff·er** *n*

²snuff *vb* : to draw forcibly into or through the nose : SMELL

³snuff *n* : SNIFF

⁴snuff *n* : pulverized tobacco

snuf·fle \'snə-fəl\ *vb* **snuf·fled; snuf·fling** **1** : to snuff or sniff audibly and repeatedly **2** : to breathe with a sniffing sound — **snuf·fle** *n*

snug \'snəg\ *adj* **snug·ger; snug·gest** **1** : fitting closely and comfortably **2** : CONCEALED — **snug·ly** *adv* — **snug·ness** *n*

snug·gle \'snə-gəl\ *vb* **snug·gled; snug·gling** : to curl up or draw close comfortably : NESTLE

¹so \'sō\ *adv* **1** : in the manner indicated **2** : in the same way ⟨he's hungry and ~ am I⟩ **3** : THUS **4** : FINALLY **5** : to an indicated or great extent ⟨I'm ~ bored⟩ **6** : THEREFORE

²so *conj* : for that reason ⟨he wanted it, ~ he took it⟩

³so *pron* **1** : the same ⟨became chairman and remained ~⟩ **2** : approximately that ⟨a dozen or ~⟩

⁴so *abbr* south; southern

SO *abbr* strikeout

¹soak \'sōk\ *vb* **1** : to remain in a liquid **2** : WET, SATURATE **3** : to draw in by or as if by absorption ⟨~ up the sunshine⟩
♦ **Synonyms** DRENCH, STEEP, IMPREGNATE

²soak *n* **1** : the act of soaking **2** : the liquid in which something is soaked **3** : DRUNKARD

soap \'sōp\ *n* : a cleansing substance made usu. by action of alkali on fat — **soap** *vb* — **soapy** *adj*

soap·box \'sōp-ˌbäks\ *n* : an improvised platform used for delivering informal speeches

soap opera *n* [fr. its sponsorship by soap manufacturers] : a radio or television daytime serial drama

soap·stone \'sōp-ˌstōn\ *n* : a soft talc–containing stone with a soapy feel

soar \ˈsȯr\ vb : to fly upward or at a height on or as if on wings

sob \ˈsäb\ vb **sobbed; sob·bing** : to weep with convulsive heavings of the chest or contractions of the throat — **sob** n

so·ba \ˈsō-bə\ n [Jp] : a Japanese noodle made from buckwheat flour

so·ber \ˈsō-bər\ adj **so·ber·er** \-bər-ər\; **so·ber·est** \-bə-rəst\ **1** : temperate in the use of liquor **2** : not drunk **3** : serious or grave in mood or disposition **4** : having a quiet tone or color ♦ Synonyms SOLEMN, EARNEST, STAID, SEDATE — **so·ber·ly** adv — **so·ber·ness** n

so·bri·ety \sō-ˈbrī-ə-tē\ n : the quality or state of being sober

so·bri·quet \ˈsō-bri-ˌkā, -ˌket\ n [F] : NICKNAME

soc abbr **1** social; society **2** sociology

so·ca \ˈsō-kə, -ˌkä\ n : soul music blended with calypso

so–called \ˈsō-ˈkȯld\ adj : commonly but often inaccurately so termed

soc·cer \ˈsä-kər\ n [by shortening & alter. fr. association football] : a game played on a field by two teams with a round inflated ball that is kicked or hit with any body part other than the hands or arms

¹so·cia·ble \ˈsō-shə-bəl\ adj **1** : liking companionship : FRIENDLY **2** : characterized by pleasant social relations ♦ Synonyms GRACIOUS, CORDIAL, AFFABLE, GENIAL — **so·cia·bil·i·ty** \ˌsō-shə-ˈbi-lə-tē\ n — **so·cia·bly** \ˈsō-shə-blē\ adv

²sociable n : SOCIAL

¹so·cial \ˈsō-shəl\ adj **1** : marked by pleasant companionship with one's friends **2** : naturally living and breeding in organized communities ⟨~ insects⟩ **3** : of or relating to human society ⟨~ institutions⟩ **4** : of, relating to, or based on rank in a particular society ⟨~ circles⟩; also : of or relating to fashionable society — **so·cial·ly** adv

²social n : a social gathering

so·cial·ise Brit var of SOCIALIZE

so·cial·ism \ˈsō-shə-ˌli-zəm\ n : any of various social systems based on shared or government ownership and administration of the means of production and distribution of goods — **so·cial·ist** \ˈsō-shə-list\ n or adj — **so·cial·is·tic** \ˌsō-shə-ˈlis-tik\ adj

so·cial·ite \ˈsō-shə-ˌlīt\ n : a person prominent in fashionable society

so·cial·ize \ˈsō-shə-ˌlīz\ vb **-ized; -iz·ing** **1** : to regulate according to the theory and practice of socialism **2** : to adapt to social needs or uses **3** : to participate actively in a social gathering — **so·cial·i·za·tion** \ˌsō-shə-lə-ˈzā-shən\ n

social science n : a science (as economics or political science) dealing with a particular aspect of human society — **social scientist** n

social work n : services, activities, or methods providing social services esp. to the economically or socially disadvantaged — **social worker** n

so·ci·e·ty \sə-ˈsī-ə-tē\ n, pl **-ties** [MF societé, fr. L societat-, societas, fr. socius companion] **1** : COMPANIONSHIP **2** : a voluntary association of persons for common ends **3** : a part of a community bound together by common interests and standards; esp : the group or set of fashionable people

so·cio·eco·nom·ic \ˌsō-sē-ō-ˌe-kə-ˈnä-mik, ˌsō-shē-, -ˌē-kə-\ adj : of, relating to, or involving both social and economic factors

sociol abbr sociologist; sociology

so·ci·ol·o·gy \ˌsō-sē-ˈä-lə-jē, ˌsō-shē-\ n : the science of society, social institutions, and social relationships — **so·ci·o·log·i·cal** \ˌsō-sē-ə-ˈlä-ji-kəl, ˌsō-shē-\ adj — **so·ci·ol·o·gist** \-ˈä-lə-jist\ n

so·cio·path \ˈsō-sē-ə-ˌpath, ˈsō-sh(ē-)ə-\ n : a person exhibiting antisocial behavior : PSYCHOPATH — **so·cio·path·ic** \ˌsō-sē-ə-ˈpa-thik, ˌsō-sh(ē-)ə-\ adj

¹sock \ˈsäk\ n, pl **socks** or **sox** \ˈsäks\ : a stocking with a short leg

²sock vb : to hit, strike, or apply forcefully

³sock n : a vigorous blow : PUNCH

sock·et \ˈsä-kət\ n : an opening or hollow that forms a holder for something

socket wrench n : a wrench usu. in the form of a bar and removable socket made to fit a bolt or nut

sock·eye salmon \ˈsäk-ˌī-\ n : a commercially important Pacific salmon

¹sod \ˈsäd\ n : TURF 1

²sod vb **sod·ded; sod·ding** : to cover with sod

so·da \ˈsō-də\ n **1** : SODIUM CARBONATE **2** : SODIUM BICARBONATE **3** : SODIUM **4** : SODA WATER **5** : SODA POP **6** : a sweet drink of soda water, flavoring, and often ice cream

soda pop n : a carbonated, sweetened, and flavored soft drink

soda water n : a beverage of water charged with carbon dioxide

sod·den \ˈsä-dᵊn\ adj **1** : lacking spirit : DULLED **2** : SOAKED, DRENCHED **3** : heavy or doughy from being improperly cooked ⟨~ biscuits⟩

so·di·um \ˈsō-dē-əm\ n : a soft waxy silver white metallic chemical element occurring in nature in combined form (as in salt)

sodium bicarbonate n : a white weakly alkaline salt used esp. in baking powders, fire extinguishers, and medicine

sodium carbonate n : a carbonate of sodium used esp. in washing and bleaching textiles

sodium chloride n : SALT 1

sodium fluoride n : a salt used chiefly in tiny amounts (as in fluoridation) to prevent tooth decay

sodium hydroxide n : a white brittle caustic substance used in making soap and rayon and in bleaching

sodium nitrate n : a crystalline salt used as a fertilizer and in curing meat

sodium thiosulfate n : a hygroscopic crystalline salt used as a photographic fixing agent

sod·omy \ˈsä-də-mē\ n : anal or oral sexual intercourse with a member of the same or opposite sex; also : sexual intercourse with an animal — **sod·om·ize** \'sä-də-ˌmīz\ *vb*

so·ev·er \sō-'e-vər\ *adv* **1** : in any degree or manner ⟨how bad ~⟩ **2** : at all : of any kind ⟨any help ~⟩

so·fa \'sō-fə\ *n* [earlier, raised carpeted floor, fr. It *sofa*, fr. Turk *sofa*, fr. Ar *suffa* carpet, divan] : a couch usu. with upholstered back and arms

soft \'sȯft\ *adj* **1** : not hard or rough : NONVIOLENT **2** : RESTFUL, GENTLE, SOOTHING **3** : emotionally susceptible **4** : not prepared to endure hardship **5** : not containing certain salts that prevent lathering ⟨~ water⟩ **6** : occurring at such a speed as to avoid destructive impact ⟨~ landing of a spacecraft on the moon⟩ **7** : BIODEGRADABLE ⟨a ~ pesticide⟩ **8** : not alcoholic ⟨~ drinks⟩ **9** : less detrimental than a hard narcotic ⟨~ drugs⟩ — **soft·ly** *adv* — **soft·ness** *n*

soft·ball \'sȯft-ˌbȯl\ *n* : a game similar to baseball played with a ball larger and softer than a baseball; *also* : the ball used in this game

soft·bound \-ˌbau̇nd\ *adj* : not bound in hard covers ⟨~ books⟩

soft coal *n* : BITUMINOUS COAL

soft·en \'sȯ-fən\ *vb* : to make or become soft — **soft·en·er** *n*

soft palate *n* : the fold at the back of the hard palate that partially separates the mouth from the pharynx

soft·ware \'sȯft-ˌwer\ *n* : the entire set of programs, procedures, and related documentation associated with a system; *esp* : computer programs

soft·wood \-ˌwu̇d\ *n* **1** : the wood of a coniferous tree as compared to that of a broad-leaved deciduous tree **2** : a tree yielding softwood — **softwood** *adj*

sog·gy \'sä-gē\ *adj* **sog·gi·er**; **-est** : heavy with water or moisture — **sog·gi·ly** \'sä-gə-lē\ *adv* — **sog·gi·ness** \-gē-nəs\ *n*

soi·gné *or* **soi·gnée** \swän-'yā\ *adj* : elegantly maintained; *esp* : WELL-GROOMED

¹soil \'sȯi(-ə)l\ *vb* **1** : CORRUPT, POLLUTE **2** : to make or become dirty **3** : STAIN, DISGRACE ⟨~ed his reputation⟩

²soil *n* **1** : STAIN, DEFILEMENT **2** : EXCREMENT, WASTE

³soil *n* **1** : firm land : EARTH **2** : the upper layer of earth in which plants grow **3** : COUNTRY, REGION

soi·ree *or* **soi·rée** \swä-'rā\ *n* [F *soirée* evening period, evening party, fr. MF, fr. *soir* evening, fr. L *sero* at a late hour] : an evening party

so·journ \'sō-ˌjərn, sō-'jərn\ *vb* : to dwell in a place temporarily — **so·journ** *n* — **so·journ·er** *n*

¹sol \'säl, 'sȯl\ *n* — see MONEY table

²sol *n* : a fluid colloidal system

³sol *abbr* **1** solicitor **2** soluble **3** solution

Sol \'säl\ *n* : SUN

¹sol·ace \'sä-ləs\ *n* : COMFORT

²solace *vb* **so·laced**; **so·lac·ing** : to give solace to : CONSOLE

so·lar \'sō-lər\ *adj* **1** : of, derived from,

or relating to the sun **2** : measured by the earth's course in relation to the sun ⟨the ~ year⟩ **3** : operated by or using the sun's light or heat ⟨~ energy⟩

solar cell *n* : a photoelectric cell used as a power source

solar collector *n* : a device for the absorption of solar radiation for the heating of water or buildings or the production of electricity

solar flare *n* : a sudden temporary outburst of energy from a small area of the sun's surface

so·lar·i·um \sō-'ler-ē-əm\ *n, pl* **-ia** \-ē-ə\ *also* **-i·ums** : a room exposed to the sun; *esp* : a room (as in a hospital) for exposure of the body to sunshine

solar mass *n* : a unit of mass equal to the mass of the sun or about 2×10^{30} kilograms

solar plexus *n* : the general area of the stomach below the sternum

solar system *n* : the sun together with the group of celestial bodies that revolve around it

solar wind *n* : plasma continuously ejected from the sun's surface

sold *past and past part of* SELL

sol·der \'sä-dər, 'sȯ-\ *n* : a metallic alloy used when melted to mend or join metallic surfaces — **solder** *vb*

soldering iron *n* : a metal device for applying heat in soldering

¹sol·dier \'sōl-jər\ *n* [ME *soudeour*, fr. AF, mercenary, fr. *soudee* shilling's worth, wage, fr. *sou, soud* shilling, fr. LL *solidus* a Roman coin, fr. L, solid] : a person in military service; *esp* : an enlisted man or woman — **sol·dier·ly** *adj or adv*

²soldier *vb* **sol·diered**; **sol·dier·ing** **1** : to serve as a soldier **2** : to pretend to work while actually doing nothing

soldier of fortune *n* : ADVENTURER 2

sol·diery \'sōl-jə-rē\ *n* : a body of soldiers

¹sole \'sōl\ *n* : any of various flatfishes including some used for food

²sole *n* **1** : the undersurface of the foot **2** : the bottom of a shoe

³sole *vb* **soled**; **sol·ing** : to furnish (a shoe) with a sole

⁴sole *adj* : SINGLE, ONLY ⟨the ~ survivor⟩ — **sole·ly** \'sōl-lē\ *adv*

so·le·cism \'sä-lə-ˌsi-zəm, 'sō-\ *n* **1** : a mistake in grammar **2** : a breach of etiquette

sol·emn \'sä-ləm\ *adj* **1** : marked by or observed with full religious ceremony ⟨a ~ oath⟩ **2** : FORMAL, CEREMONIOUS **3** : highly serious : GRAVE ⟨a ~ gathering⟩ **4** : SOMBER, GLOOMY ⟨a ~ city⟩ — **so·lem·ni·ty** \sə-'lem-nə-tē\ *n* — **sol·emn·ly** \'sä-ləm-lē\ *adv*

sol·em·nize \'sä-ləm-ˌnīz\ *vb* **-nized**; **-niz·ing** **1** : to observe or honor with solemnity **2** : to celebrate (a marriage) with religious rites — **sol·em·ni·za·tion** \ˌsä-ləm-nə-'zā-shən\ *n*

so·le·noid \'sō-lə-ˌnȯid, 'sä-\ *n* : a coil of wire usu. in cylindrical form that when carrying a current acts like a magnet

so·lic·it \sə-'li-sət\ *vb* **1** : ENTREAT, BEG

2 : to approach with a request or plea **3** : TEMPT, LURE **4** : to try to obtain by request ⟨~ donations⟩ — **so·lic·i·ta·tion** \-,li-sə-'tā-shən\ *n*

so·lic·i·tor \sə-'li-sə-tər\ *n* **1** : one that solicits **2** : LAWYER; *esp* : a legal official of a city or state

so·lic·i·tous \sə-'li-sə-təs\ *adj* **1** : WORRIED, CONCERNED **2** : EAGER, WILLING
♦ **Synonyms** AVID, IMPATIENT, KEEN, ANXIOUS — **so·lic·i·tous·ly** *adv*

so·lic·i·tude \sə-'li-sə-,tüd, -,tyüd\ *n* : CONCERN, ANXIETY

¹sol·id \'sä-ləd\ *adj* **1** : not hollow; *also* : written as one word without a hyphen ⟨a ~ compound⟩ **2** : having, involving, or dealing with three dimensions or with solids ⟨~ geometry⟩ **3** : not loose or spongy : COMPACT ⟨a ~ mass of rock⟩; *also* : neither gaseous nor liquid : HARD, RIGID ⟨~ ice⟩ **4** : of good substantial quality or kind ⟨~ comfort⟩ **5** : thoroughly dependable : RELIABLE ⟨a ~ citizen⟩; *also* : serious in purpose or character ⟨~ reading⟩ **6** : UNANIMOUS, UNITED ⟨~ for pay increases⟩ **7** : of one substance or character — **solid** *adv* — **so·lid·i·ty** \sə-'li-də-tē\ *n* — **sol·id·ly** *adv* — **sol·id·ness** *n*

²solid *n* **1** : a geometrical figure (as a cube or sphere) having three dimensions **2** : a solid substance

sol·i·dar·i·ty \,sä-lə-'der-ə-tē\ *n* : unity based on shared interests, objectives, or standards

so·lid·i·fy \sə-'li-də-,fī\ *vb* **-fied; -fy·ing** : to make or become solid — **so·lid·i·fi·ca·tion** \-,li-də-fə-'kā-shən\ *n*

solid–state *adj* **1** : relating to the structure and properties of solid material **2** : using semiconductor devices rather than vacuum tubes

so·lil·o·quize \sə-'li-lə-,kwīz\ *vb* **-quized; -quiz·ing** : to talk to oneself : utter a soliloquy

so·lil·o·quy \sə-'li-lə-kwē\ *n, pl* **-quies** [LL *soliloquium*, fr. L *solus* alone + *loqui* to speak] **1** : the act of talking to oneself **2** : a dramatic monologue that represents unspoken reflections by a character

sol·i·taire \'sä-lə-,ter\ *n* **1** : a single gem (as a diamond) set alone **2** : a card game for one person

sol·i·tary \'sä-lə-,ter-ē\ *adj* **1** : being or living apart from others **2** : LONELY, SECLUDED **3** : SOLE, ONLY

sol·i·tude \'sä-lə-,tüd, -,tyüd\ *n* **1** : the state of being alone : SECLUSION **2** : a lonely place

soln *abbr* solution

¹so·lo \'sō-lō\ *n, pl* **solos** [It, fr. *solo* alone, fr. L *solus*] **1** : a piece of music for a single voice or instrument with or without accompaniment **2** : an action in which there is only one performer — **solo** *adj or vb* — **so·lo·ist** *n*

²solo *adv* : without a companion : ALONE

so·lon \'sō-lən\ *n* **1** : a wise and skillful lawgiver **2** : a member of a legislative body

sol·stice \'säl-stəs, 'sōl-\ *n* [ME, fr. L *solstitium*, fr. *sol* sun + *-stit-, -stes* standing] : the time of the year when the sun is farthest north of the equator **(summer solstice)** about June 22 or farthest south **(winter solstice)** about Dec. 22 — **sol·sti·tial** \säl-'sti-shəl, sōl-\ *adj*

sol·u·ble \'säl-yə-bəl\ *adj* **1** : capable of being dissolved in or as if in a liquid **2** : capable of being solved or explained — **sol·u·bil·i·ty** \,säl-yə-'bi-lə-tē\ *n*

sol·ute \'säl-,yüt\ *n* : a dissolved substance

so·lu·tion \sə-'lü-shən\ *n* **1** : an action or process of solving a problem; *also* : an answer to a problem **2** : an act or the process by which one substance is homogenously mixed with another usu. liquid substance; *also* : a mixture thus formed

solve \'sälv\ *vb* **solved; solv·ing** : to find the answer to or a solution for — **solv·able** *adj*

sol·ven·cy \'säl-vən-sē\ *n* : the condition of being solvent

¹sol·vent \-vənt\ *adj* **1** : able or sufficient to pay all legal debts **2** : dissolving or able to dissolve

²solvent *n* : a usu. liquid substance capable of dissolving or dispersing one or more other substances

som \'sōm\ *n, pl* **som** — see MONEY table

so·mat·ic \sō-'ma-tik\ *adj* : of, relating to, or affecting the body in contrast to the mind or the sex cells and their precursors

som·ber *or* **som·bre** \'säm-bər\ *adj* **1** : DARK, GLOOMY **2** : GRAVE, MELANCHOLY — **som·ber·ly** *adv*

som·bre·ro \səm-'brer-ō\ *n, pl* **-ros** [Sp, fr. *sombra* shade] : a broad-brimmed felt hat worn esp. in the Southwest and in Mexico

¹some \'səm\ *adj* **1** : one unspecified ⟨~ man called⟩ **2** : an unspecified or indefinite number of ⟨~ berries are ripe⟩ **3** : at least a few or a little ⟨~ years ago⟩

²some *pron* : a certain number or amount ⟨~ of the berries are ripe⟩ ⟨~ of it is missing⟩

¹-some \səm\ *adj suffix* : characterized by a (specified) thing, quality, state, or action ⟨awe*some*⟩ ⟨burden*some*⟩

²-some *n suffix* : a group of (so many) members and esp. persons ⟨four*some*⟩

¹some·body \'səm-,bä-dē, -bə-\ *pron* : some person

²somebody *n* : a person of importance

some·day \'səm-,dā\ *adv* : at some future time

some·how \-,hau̇\ *adv* : by some means

some·one \-(,)wən\ *pron* : some person

som·er·sault *also* **sum·mer·sault** \'sə-mər-,sȯlt\ *n* [MF *sombresaut* leap, ultim. fr. L *super* over + *saltus* leap, fr. *salire* to jump] : a leap or roll in which a person turns heels over head — **somersault** *vb*

som·er·set \-,set\ *n or vb* : SOMERSAULT

some·thing \'səm-thiŋ\ *pron* : some undetermined or unspecified thing

some·time \-,tīm\ *adv* **1** : at a future time **2** : at an unknown or unnamed time

some·times \-,tīmz\ *adv* : OCCASIONALLY

¹some·what \-ˌhwät, -ˌhwət\ *pron* : SOMETHING

²somewhat *adv* : in some degree

some·where \-ˌhwer\ *adv* : in, at, or to an unknown or unnamed place

som·nam·bu·lism \säm-ˈnam-byə-ˌli-zəm\ *n* : performance of motor acts (as walking) during sleep; *also* : an abnormal condition of sleep characterized by this — **som·nam·bu·list** \-list\ *n*

som·no·lent \ˈsäm-nə-lənt\ *adj* : SLEEPY, DROWSY — **som·no·lence** \-ləns\ *n*

so·mo·ni \ˌsō-mō-ˈnē\ *n, pl* **somoni** — see MONEY table

son \ˈsən\ *n* **1** : a male offspring or descendant **2** *cap* : Jesus Christ **3** : a person deriving from a particular source (as a country, race, or school)

so·nar \ˈsō-ˌnär\ *n* [*so*und *na*vigation *ra*nging] : a method or device for detecting and locating submerged objects (as submarines) by sound waves

so·na·ta \sə-ˈnä-tə\ *n* [It] : an instrumental composition with three or four movements differing in rhythm and mood but related in key

son·a·ti·na \ˌsä-nə-ˈtē-nə\ *n* [It, dim. of *sonata*] : a short usu. simplified sonata

song \ˈsȯŋ\ *n* **1** : vocal music; *also* : a short composition of words and music **2** : poetic composition **3** : a distinctive or characteristic sound (as of a bird) **4** : a small amount ⟨sold for a ∼⟩

song·bird \ˈsȯŋ-ˌbərd\ *n* : a bird that utters a series of musical tones

Song of Sol·o·mon \-ˈsä-lə-mən\ — see BIBLE table

Song of Songs — see BIBLE table

song·ster \ˈsȯŋ-stər\ *n* : one that sings

song·stress \-strəs\ *n* : a girl or woman who is a singer

son·ic \ˈsä-nik\ *adj* : of or relating to sound waves or the speed of sound

sonic boom *n* : an explosive sound produced by an aircraft traveling at supersonic speed

son–in–law \ˈsən-ən-ˌlȯ\ *n, pl* **sons–in–law** : the husband of one's daughter

son·net \ˈsä-nət\ *n* : a poem of 14 lines usu. in iambic pentameter with a definite rhyme scheme

son of a gun *n* : an offensive or disagreeable person

so·no·rous \sə-ˈnȯr-əs, ˈsä-nə-rəs\ *adj* **1** : giving out sound when struck **2** : loud, deep, or rich in sound : RESONANT **3** : high-sounding : IMPRESSIVE — **so·nor·i·ty** \sə-ˈnȯr-ə-tē\ *n*

soon \ˈsün\ *adv,* **1** : before long **2** : PROMPTLY, QUICKLY **3** *archaic* : EARLY **4** : WILLINGLY, READILY

soot \ˈsut, ˈsȯt, ˈsüt\ *n* : a fine black powder consisting chiefly of carbon that is formed when something burns and that colors smoke — **sooty** *adj*

sooth \ˈsüth\ *n, archaic* : TRUTH

soothe \ˈsüth\ *vb* **soothed; sooth·ing 1** : to please by flattery or attention **2** : RELIEVE, ALLEVIATE ⟨∼ a burn⟩ **3** : to calm down : COMFORT ⟨∼ a child⟩ — **sooth·er** *n* — **sooth·ing·ly** *adv*

sooth·say·er \ˈsüth-ˌsā-ər\ *n* : one who foretells events — **sooth·say·ing** *n*

¹sop \ˈsäp\ *n* : a conciliatory bribe, gift, or concession

²sop *vb* **sopped; sop·ping 1** : to steep or dip in or as if in a liquid **2** : to wet thoroughly : SOAK; *also* : to mop up (a liquid)

SOP *abbr* standard operating procedure; standing operating procedure

soph *abbr* sophomore

soph·ism \ˈsä-ˌfi-zəm\ *n* **1** : an argument correct in form but embodying a subtle fallacy **2** : SOPHISTRY

soph·ist \ˈsä-fist\ *n* : PHILOSOPHER; *esp* : a captious or casuistical reasoner

so·phis·tic \sä-ˈfis-tik, sə-\ *or* **so·phis·ti·cal** \-ti-kəl\ *adj* : of or characteristic of sophists or sophistry ♦ *Synonyms* FALLACIOUS, ILLOGICAL, UNREASONABLE, SPECIOUS

so·phis·ti·cat·ed \sə-ˈfis-tə-ˌkā-təd\ *adj* **1** : COMPLEX ⟨∼ instruments⟩ **2** : made worldly-wise by wide experience **3** : intellectually appealing ⟨a ∼ novel⟩ — **so·phis·ti·ca·tion** \-ˌfis-tə-ˈkā-shən\ *n*

soph·ist·ry \ˈsä-fə-strē\ *n* : subtly deceptive reasoning or argument

soph·o·more \ˈsäf-ˌmȯr, ˈsä-fə-\ *n* : a student in the second year of high school or college

soph·o·mor·ic \ˌsäf-ˈmȯr-ik, ˌsä-fə-\ *adj* **1** : being overconfident of knowledge but poorly informed and immature ⟨∼ reasoning⟩ **2** : of, relating to, or characteristic of a sophomore ⟨∼ humor⟩

So·pho·ni·as \ˌsä-fə-ˈnī-əs, ˌsō-\ *n* : ZEPHANIAH

sop·o·rif·ic \ˌsä-pə-ˈri-fik\ *adj* **1** : causing sleep or drowsiness **2** : LETHARGIC

so·pra·no \sə-ˈpra-nō, -ˈprä-\ *n, pl* **-nos** [It, fr. *sopra* above, fr. L *supra*] **1** : the highest singing voice; *also* : a singer with this voice **2** : the highest part in a 4-part chorus — **soprano** *adj*

sor·bet \sȯr-ˈbā\ *n* : a usu. fruit-flavored ice served for dessert or between courses as a palate refresher

sor·cery \ˈsȯr-sə-rē\ *n* [ME *sorcerie,* fr. AF, fr. *sorcer* sorcerer, fr. ML *sortiarius,* fr. L *sort-, sors* chance, lot] : the use of magic : WITCHCRAFT — **sor·cer·er** \-rər\ *n* — **sor·cer·ess** \-rəs\ *n*

sor·did \ˈsȯr-dəd\ *adj* **1** : marked by baseness or grossness : VILE **2** : DIRTY, SQUALID — **sor·did·ly** *adv* — **sor·did·ness** *n*

¹sore \ˈsȯr\ *adj* **sor·er; sor·est 1** : causing pain or distress ⟨a ∼ bruise⟩ **2** : painfully sensitive ⟨∼ muscles⟩ **3** : SEVERE, INTENSE **4** : IRRITATED, ANGRY — **sore·ly** *adv* — **sore·ness** *n*

²sore *n* **1** : a sore spot on the body; *esp* : one (as an ulcer) with the tissues broken and usu. infected **2** : a source of pain or vexation

sore·head \ˈsȯr-ˌhed\ *n* : a person easily angered or discontented

sore throat *n* : painful throat due to inflammation of the fauces and pharynx

sor·ghum \ˈsȯr-gəm\ *n* : a tall variable Old World tropical grass grown widely for its edible seed, for forage, or for its sweet juice which yields a syrup

so·ror·i·ty \sə-'rȯr-ə-tē\ n, pl **-ties** [ML *sororitas* sisterhood, fr. L *soror* sister] : a club or organization usu. of female students for social purposes

¹sor·rel \'sȯr-əl\ n : a brownish orange to light brown color; *also* : a sorrel-colored animal (as a horse)

²sorrel n : any of various herbs having a sour juice

sor·row \'sär-ō\ n 1 : deep distress, sadness, or regret; *also* : resultant unhappy or unpleasant state 2 : a cause of grief or sadness 3 : a display of grief or sadness — **sorrow** vb — **sor·row·ful** \-fəl\ adj — **sor·row·ful·ly** \-f(ə-)lē\ adv

sor·ry \'sär-ē\ adj **sor·ri·er; -est** 1 : feeling sorrow, regret, or penitence ⟨~ for yelling at her⟩ 2 : MOURNFUL, SAD 3 : causing sorrow, pity, or scorn : PITIFUL ⟨a ~ lot of ragamuffins⟩

¹sort \'sȯrt\ n 1 : a group of persons or things that have similar characteristics : CLASS 2 : QUALITY, NATURE 3 : an instance of sorting — **all sorts of** : many different — **out of sorts** 1 : somewhat ill 2 : GROUCHY, IRRITABLE

²sort vb 1 : to put in a certain place according to kind, class, or nature 2 : to be in accord : AGREE 3 : SEARCH ⟨~ through this mess⟩ — **sort·er** n

sor·tie \'sȯr-tē, sȯr-'tē\ n 1 : a sudden issuing of troops from a defensive position against the enemy 2 : one mission or attack by one airplane

sort of adv : to a moderate degree

SOS \ˌes-(ˌ)ō-'es\ n : a call or request for help or rescue

so–so \'sō-'sō\ adv or adj : PASSABLY

sot \'sät\ n : a habitual drunkard — **sot·tish** adj — **sot·tish·ly** adv

souf·flé \sü-'flā\ n [F, fr. *soufflé*, pp. of *souffler* to blow, puff up, fr. OF *esouffler*, fr. L *sufflare*, fr. *sub-* up + *flare* to blow] : a spongy dish made light in baking by stiffly beaten egg whites

sough \'sau̇, 'səf\ vb : to make a moaning or sighing sound — **sough** n

sought past and past part of SEEK

¹soul \'sōl\ n 1 : the immaterial essence of an individual life 2 : the spiritual principle embodied in human beings or the universe 3 : an active or essential part 4 : the moral and emotional nature of human beings 5 : spiritual or moral force 6 : PERSON ⟨a kindly ~⟩ 7 : a strong, positive feeling (as of intense sensitivity and emotional fervor) conveyed esp. by black American performers; *also* : NEGRITUDE 8 : SOUL MUSIC — **souled** \'sōld\ adj — **soul·less** \'sōl-ləs\ adj

²soul adj 1 : of, relating to, or characteristic of black Americans or their culture ⟨~ food⟩ 2 : designed for or controlled by blacks ⟨~ radio stations⟩

soul brother n : a black male

soul·ful \'sōl-fəl\ adj : full of or expressing deep feeling ⟨a ~ ballad⟩ — **soul·ful·ly** adv

soul music n : music that is closely related to rhythm and blues and characterized by intensity of feeling

¹sound \'sau̇nd\ adj 1 : not diseased or sickly 2 : free from flaw or defect ⟨a ~ structure⟩ 3 : FIRM, STRONG 4 : free from error or fallacy : RIGHT ⟨~ logic⟩ 5 : LEGAL, VALID 6 : THOROUGH 7 : UNDISTURBED ⟨~ sleep⟩ 8 : showing good judgment — **sound·ly** adv — **sound·ness** n

²sound n 1 : the sensation of hearing; *also* : mechanical energy transmitted by longitudinal pressure waves (**sound waves**) (as in air) that is the stimulus to hearing 2 : something heard : NOISE, TONE; *also* : hearing distance : EARSHOT 3 : a musical style — **sound·less** adj — **sound·less·ly** adv — **sound·proof** \-ˌprüf\ adj or vb

³sound vb 1 : to make or cause to make a sound 2 : to order or proclaim by a sound ⟨~ the alarm⟩ 3 : to convey a certain impression : SEEM ⟨that ~s like fun⟩ 4 : to examine the condition of by causing to give out sounds — **sound·able** \'sau̇n-də-bəl\ adj

⁴sound n : a long passage of water wider than a strait often connecting two larger bodies of water

⁵sound vb 1 : to measure the depth of (water) esp. by a weighted line dropped from the surface : FATHOM 2 : PROBE 3 : to dive down suddenly ⟨the hooked fish ~ed⟩ — **sound·ing** n

sound bite n : a brief recorded statement broadcast esp. on a news program — **sound–bite** adj

sound card n : a circuit board in a computer system designed to produce or reproduce sound

sound·er \'sau̇n-dər\ n : one that sounds; *esp* : a device for making soundings

sound·stage \'sau̇nd-ˌstāj\ n : the part of a motion-picture studio in which a production is filmed

sound·track \'sau̇n(d)-ˌtrak\ n : music recorded to accompany a film or videotape

soup \'süp\ n 1 : a liquid food with stock as its base and often containing pieces of solid food 2 : something having the consistency of soup 3 : an unfortunate predicament ⟨in the ~⟩

soup·çon \süp-'sōⁿ\ n [F, lit., suspicion] : a little bit : ¹TRACE 2

soup up vb : to increase the power of — **souped–up** \'süpt-'əp\ adj

soupy \'sü-pē\ adj **soup·i·er; -est** 1 : having the consistency of soup 2 : densely foggy or cloudy

¹sour \'sau̇(-ə)r\ adj 1 : having an acid or tart taste ⟨~ as vinegar⟩ 2 : SPOILED, PUTRID ⟨a ~ odor⟩ 3 : UNPLEASANT, DISAGREEABLE ⟨~ disposition⟩ — **sour·ish** adj — **sour·ly** adv — **sour·ness** n

²sour vb : to become or make sour

source \'sȯrs\ n 1 : ORIGIN, BEGINNING 2 : a supplier of information 3 : the beginning of a stream of water

source code n : a computer program in its original programming language and before translation (as by a compiler)

¹**souse** \ˈsaůs\ *vb* **soused; sous·ing 1**
: PICKLE **2** : to plunge into a liquid **3**
: DRENCH **4** : to make drunk

²**souse** *n* **1** : something (as pigs' feet)
steeped in pickle **2** : a soaking in liquid
3 : DRUNKARD

¹**south** \ˈsaůth\ *adv* : to or toward the
south; *also* : into a state of decline

²**south** *adj* : **1** situated toward or at the
south **2** : coming from the south

³**south** *n* **1** : the direction to the right of
one facing east **2** : the compass point directly opposite to north **3** *cap* : regions
or countries south of a specified or implied point; *esp* : the southeastern part
of the U.S. — **south·er·ly** \ˈsə-thər-lē\
adj or adv — **south·ern** \ˈsə-thərn\ *adj*
— **South·ern·er** *n* — **south·ern·most**
\-ˌmōst\ *adj* — **south·ward** \ˈsaůth-
wərd\ *adv or adj* — **south·wards**
\-wərdz\ *adv*

south·east \saů-ˈthēst, *naut* saů-ˈēst\ *n* **1**
: the general direction between south and
east **2** : the compass point midway between south and east **3** *cap* : regions or
countries southeast of a specified or implied point — **southeast** *adj or adv* —
south·east·er·ly *adv or adj* — **south·
east·ern** \-ˈēs-tərn\ *adj*

south·paw \ˈsaůth-ˌpȯ\ *n* : a left-handed
person; *esp* : a left-handed baseball pitcher — **southpaw** *adj*

south pole *n, often cap* S&P : the south-
ernmost point of the earth

south·west \saůth-ˈwest, *naut* saů-ˈwest\
n **1** : the general direction between south
and west **2** : the compass point midway
between south and west **3** *cap* : regions
or countries southwest of a specified or
implied point — **southwest** *adj or adv* —
south·west·er·ly *adv or adj* — **south·
west·ern** \-ˈwes-tərn\ *adj*

sou·ve·nir \ˌsü-və-ˈnir\ *n* [F] : something
serving as a reminder

sou'·west·er \saů-ˈwes-tər\ *n* : a long waterproof coat worn at sea in stormy
weather; *also* : a waterproof hat

¹**sov·er·eign** \ˈsä-vrən, -və-rən\ *n* **1** : one
possessing the supreme power and authority in a state **2** : a gold coin of the
United Kingdom

²**sovereign** *adj* **1** : EXCELLENT, FINE **2**
: supreme in power or authority **3**
: CHIEF, HIGHEST **4** : having independ-
ent authority ✦ *Synonyms* DOMINANT,
PREDOMINANT, PARAMOUNT, PREPON-
DERANT

sov·er·eign·ty \-tē\ *n, pl* **-ties 1** : supremacy in rule or power **2** : power to
govern without external control **3** : the
supreme political power in a state

so·vi·et \ˈsō-vē-ˌet, ˈsä-, -ət\ *n* **1** : an
elected governmental council in a Communist country **2** *pl, cap* : the people
and esp. the leaders of the U.S.S.R. — **so·
viet** *adj, often cap* — **so·vi·et·ize** *vb,
often cap*

¹**sow** \ˈsaů\ *n* : an adult female swine

²**sow** \ˈsō\ *vb* **sowed; sown** \ˈsōn\ *or*
sowed; sow·ing 1 : to plant seed for
growing esp. by scattering **2** : to strew

with seed **3** : to scatter abroad — **sow·
er** \ˈsō-ər\ *n*

sow bug \ˈsaů-\ *n* : WOOD LOUSE

sox *pl of* SOCK

soy \ˈsȯi\ *n* : a sauce made from soybeans
fermented in brine

soy·bean \ˈsȯi-ˌbēn\ *n* : an Asian legume
widely grown for forage and for its edible
seeds that yield a valuable oil (**soybean
oil**); *also* : its seed

sp *abbr* **1** special **2** species **3** specimen **4** spelling **5** spirit

Sp *abbr* Spain

SP *abbr* **1** shore patrol; shore patrol-
man **2** shore police **3** specialist

spa \ˈspä\ *n* [*Spa*, watering place in Bel-
gium] **1** : a mineral spring; *also* : a resort
with mineral springs **2** : a health and fitness facility **3** : a hot tub with a
whirlpool device

¹**space** \ˈspās\ *n* **1** : a period of time **2**
: some small measurable distance, area,
or volume **3** : the limitless area in which
all things exist and move **4** : an empty
place **5** : the region beyond the earth's
atmosphere **6** : a definite place (as a seat
on a train or ship) **7** : the distance from
others that a person needs for comfort

²**space** *vb* **spaced; spac·ing** : to place at
intervals — **spac·er** *n*

space–age \ˈspās-ˌāj\ *adj* : of or relating
to the age of space exploration

space·craft \-ˌkraft\ *n* : a vehicle for travel beyond the earth's atmosphere

space·flight \-ˌflīt\ *n* : flight beyond the
earth's atmosphere

space heater *n* : a usu. portable device
for heating a relatively small area

space·man \ˈspās-ˌman, -mən\ *n* : one
who travels outside the earth's atmosphere

space out *vb* : to become distracted or
inattentive

space·ship \-ˌship\ *n* : a vehicle used for
space travel

space shuttle *n* : a reusable spacecraft
designed to transport people and cargo
between earth and space

space station *n* : a large artificial satellite
serving as a base (as for scientific observation)

space suit *n* : a suit equipped to make life
in space possible for its wearer

space walk *n* : a period of activity outside
a spacecraft by an astronaut in space —
space·walk \ˈspās-ˌwȯk\ *vb* — **space·
walk·er** *n*

spa·cious \ˈspā-shəs\ *adj* : very large in
extent : ROOMY ✦ *Synonyms* COMMODI-
OUS, CAPACIOUS, AMPLE — **spa·cious·ly**
adv — **spa·cious·ness** *n*

¹**spade** \ˈspād\ *n* : a shovel with a blade for
digging — **spade·ful** *n*

²**spade** *vb* **spad·ed; spad·ing** : to dig
with a spade — **spad·er** *n*

³**spade** *n* : any of a suit of playing cards
marked with a black figure resembling an
inverted heart with a short stem at the
bottom

spa·dix \ˈspā-diks\ *n, pl* **spa·di·ces** \ˈspā-
də-ˌsēz\ : a floral spike with a fleshy or
succulent axis usu. enclosed in a spathe

spa·ghet·ti \spə-'ge-tē\ n [It, fr. pl. of *spaghetto*, dim. of *spago* cord, string] : pasta made in thin solid strings

spam \'spam\ n : unsolicited usu. commercial e-mail sent to a large number of addresses — **spam** vb

¹**span** \'span\ n 1 : an English unit of length equal to nine inches (about 23 centimeters) 2 : a limited portion of time 3 : the spread (as of an arch) from one support to another

²**span** vb **spanned**; **span·ning** 1 : MEASURE 2 : to extend across

³**span** n : a pair of animals (as mules) driven together

Span abbr Spanish

span·dex \'span-ˌdeks\ n : any of various elastic synthetic textile fibers

span·gle \'span-gəl\ n : a small disk of shining metal or plastic used esp. on a dress for ornament — **spangle** vb

Span·glish \'span-glish\ n : Spanish with many English words included; *also* : a combination of Spanish and English

Span·iard \'span-yərd\ n : a native or inhabitant of Spain

span·iel \'span-yəl\ n [ME *spaynel*, *spaniell*, fr. AF *espainnel*, alter. of *espaignol*, Spaniard] : a dog of any of several breeds of mostly small and short-legged dogs usu. with long wavy hair and large drooping ears

Span·ish \'spa-nish\ n 1 : the chief language of Spain and of the countries colonized by the Spanish 2 **Spanish** pl : the people of Spain — **Spanish** adj

Spanish American n : a resident of the U.S. whose native language is Spanish; *also* : a native or inhabitant of one of the countries of America in which Spanish is the national language — **Spanish–American** adj

Spanish fly n : a toxic preparation of dried green European beetles that causes the skin to blister and is thought to be an aphrodisiac

Spanish moss n : a plant related to the pineapple that grows in pendent tufts of grayish green filaments on trees from the southern U.S. to Argentina

Spanish onion n : a large mild-flavored onion

spank \'spank\ vb : to hit on the buttocks with the open hand — **spank** n

spank·ing \'span-kin\ adj : BRISK, LIVELY ⟨~ breeze⟩ — **spanking** adv

¹**spar** \'spär\ n : a rounded wood or metal piece (as a mast, yard, boom, or gaff) for supporting sail rigging

²**spar** vb **sparred**; **spar·ring** : to box for practice without serious hitting; *also* : SKIRMISH, WRANGLE

¹**spare** \'sper\ vb **spared**; **spar·ing** 1 : to refrain from punishing or injuring : show mercy to 2 : to exempt from something 3 : to get along without 4 : to use frugally or rarely

²**spare** adj **spar·er**; **spar·est** 1 : held in reserve 2 : SUPERFLUOUS 3 : not liberal or profuse 4 : LEAN, THIN 5 : SCANTY

◆ **Synonyms** MEAGER, SPARSE, SKIMPY, EXIGUOUS, SCANT — **spare·ness** n

³**spare** n 1 : a duplicate kept in reserve; *esp* : a spare tire 2 : the knocking down of all the bowling pins with the first two balls

sparing adj : SAVING, FRUGAL ◆ **Synonyms** THRIFTY, ECONOMICAL, PROVIDENT — **spar·ing·ly** adv

¹**spark** \'spärk\ n 1 : a small particle of a burning substance or a hot glowing particle struck from a mass (as by steel on flint) 2 : a short bright flash of electricity between two points 3 : SPARKLE 4 : a particle capable of being kindled or developed : GERM

²**spark** vb 1 : to emit or produce sparks 2 : to stir to activity : INCITE

³**spark** vb : WOO, COURT

¹**spar·kle** \'spär-kəl\ vb **spar·kled**; **spar·kling** 1 : FLASH, GLEAM 2 : to perform brilliantly 3 : EFFERVESCE — **spar·kler** n

²**sparkle** n 1 : GLEAM 2 : ANIMATION

spark plug n : a device that produces a spark to ignite the fuel mixture in an engine cylinder

spar·row \'spa-rō\ n : any of several small dull-colored singing birds

sparse \'spärs\ adj **spars·er**; **spars·est** : thinly scattered : SCANTY ◆ **Synonyms** MEAGER, SPARE, SKIMPY, EXIGUOUS, SCANT — **sparse·ly** adv — **sparse·ness** n

¹**Spar·tan** \'spär-tᵊn\ n 1 : a native or inhabitant of ancient Sparta 2 : a person of great courage and self-discipline

²**Spartan** adj 1 : of or relating to Sparta or Spartans 2 *often not cap* : marked by simplicity, frugality, or avoidance of luxury and comfort ⟨a ~ room⟩

spasm \'spa-zəm\ n 1 : an involuntary and abnormal muscular contraction 2 : a sudden, violent, and temporary effort, emotion, or sensation — **spas·mod·ic** \spaz-'mä-dik\ adj — **spas·mod·i·cal·ly** \-di-k(ə-)lē\ adv

spas·tic \'spas-tik\ adj : of, relating to, marked by, or affected with muscular spasm ⟨~ paralysis⟩ — **spastic** n

¹**spat** \'spat\ past and past part of SPIT

²**spat** n, pl **spat** or **spats** : a young bivalve mollusk (as an oyster)

³**spat** n : a gaiter covering instep and ankle

⁴**spat** n : a brief petty quarrel : DISPUTE

⁵**spat** vb **spat·ted**; **spat·ting** : to quarrel briefly

spate \'spāt\ n : a sudden outburst

spathe \'spāth\ n : a sheathing bract or pair of bracts enclosing an inflorescence (as of the calla lily) and esp. a spadix on the same axis

spa·tial \'spā-shəl\ adj : of or relating to space or to the facility to perceive objects in space — **spa·tial·ly** adv

spat·ter \'spa-tər\ vb 1 : to splash with drops of liquid 2 : to sprinkle around — **spatter** n

spat·u·la \'spa-chə-lə\ n : a flexible knifelike implement for scooping, spreading, or mixing soft substances

spav·in \'spa-vən\ n : a bony enlargement of the hock of a horse — **spav·ined** \-vənd\ adj

¹**spawn** \'spȯn\ vb [ME, fr. AF espandre to spread out, shed, scatter, spawn, fr. L expandere, fr. ex- out + pandere to spread] **1** : to produce eggs or offspring esp. in large numbers **2** : GENERATE ⟨~ed much protest⟩ — **spawn·er** n

²**spawn** n **1** : the eggs of water animals (as fishes or oysters) that lay many small eggs **2** : offspring esp. when produced in great numbers

spay \'spā\ vb **spayed; spay·ing** : to remove the ovaries of (a female animal)

SPCA abbr Society for the Prevention of Cruelty to Animals

SPCC abbr Society for the Prevention of Cruelty to Children

speak \'spēk\ vb **spoke** \'spōk\; **spo·ken** \'spō-kən\; **speak·ing** **1** : to utter words **2** : to express orally **3** : to mention in speech or writing **4** : to address an audience **5** : to use or be able to use (a language) in talking — **to speak of** : worthy of mention ⟨no progress to speak of⟩

speak·easy \'spēk-,ē-zē\ n, pl **-eas·ies** : an illicit drinking place

speak·er \'spē-kər\ n **1** : one that speaks **2** : the presiding officer of a deliberative assembly **3** : LOUDSPEAKER

¹**spear** \'spir\ n **1** : a long-shafted weapon with a sharp point for thrusting or throwing **2** : a sharp-pointed instrument with barbs used in spearing fish — **spear·man** \-mən\ n

²**spear** vb : to strike or pierce with or as if with a spear — **spear·er** n

³**spear** n : a usu. young blade, shoot, or sprout (as of asparagus)

spear·head \-,hed\ n : a leading force, element, or influence — **spearhead** vb

spear·mint \-,mint\ n : a common highly aromatic garden mint

¹**spec** abbr **1** special **2** specifically

²**spec** \'spek\ n : SPECIFICATION 2 — usu. used in pl.

spe·cial \'spe-shəl\ adj **1** : UNCOMMON, NOTEWORTHY **2** : particularly favored **3** : INDIVIDUAL, UNIQUE **4** : EXTRA, ADDITIONAL **5** : confined to or designed for a definite field of action, purpose, or occasion — **special** n

special delivery n : delivery of mail by messenger for an extra fee

special effects n pl : visual or sound effects introduced into a motion picture, video recording, or taped television production

Special Forces n pl : a branch of the army composed of soldiers specially trained in guerrilla warfare

spe·cial·ise Brit var of SPECIALIZE

spe·cial·ist \'spe-shə-list\ n **1** : a person who specializes in a particular branch of learning or activity **2** : any of four enlisted ranks in the army corresponding to the grades of corporal through sergeant first class

spe·cial·ize \'spe-shə-,līz\ vb **-ized; -iz-**

ing : to concentrate one's efforts in a special activity or field; also : to change in an adaptive manner — **spe·cial·i·za·tion** \,spe-shə-lə-'zā-shən\ n

spe·cial·ly \'spe-shə-lē\ adv **1** : in a special manner **2** : for a special purpose : in particular

spe·cial·ty \'spe-shəl-tē\ n, pl **-ties** **1** : a particular quality or detail **2** : a product of a special kind or of special excellence **3** : a skill or discipline in which one specializes

spe·cie \'spē-shē, -sē\ n : money in coin

spe·cies \'spē-shēz, -sēz\ n, pl **spe·cies** [ME, fr. L, appearance, kind, species, fr. specere to look] **1** : SORT, KIND **2** : a category of biological classification ranking just below the genus or subgenus and comprising closely related organisms potentially able to breed with one another

specif abbr specific; specifically

¹**spe·cif·ic** \spi-'si-fik\ adj **1** : having a unique effect or influence or reacting in only one way or with only one thing ⟨~ antibodies⟩ ⟨~ enzymes⟩ **2** : DEFINITE, EXACT ⟨a ~ agreement⟩ **3** : of, relating to, or constituting a species — **spe·cif·i·cal·ly** \-fi-k(ə-)lē\ adv — **spec·i·fic·i·ty** \,spe-sə-'fi-sə-tē\ n

²**specific** n : something specific : DETAIL, PARTICULAR — usu. used in pl.

spec·i·fi·ca·tion \,spe-sə-fə-'kā-shən\ n **1** : the act or process of specifying **2** : a description of work to be done and materials to be used (as in building) — usu. used in pl.

specific gravity n : the ratio of the density of a substance to the density of some substance (as water) taken as a standard when both densities are obtained by weighing in air

spec·i·fy \'spe-sə-,fī\ vb **-fied; -fy·ing** : to mention or name explicitly

spec·i·men \'spe-sə-mən\ n : an item or part typical of a group or whole

spe·cious \'spē-shəs\ adj : seeming to be genuine, correct, or beautiful but not really so ⟨~ reasoning⟩

speck \'spek\ n **1** : a small spot or blemish **2** : a small particle — **speck** vb

speck·le \'spe-kəl\ n : a little speck — **speckle** vb

specs \'speks\ n pl : GLASSES

spec·ta·cle \'spek-ti-kəl\ n **1** : an unusual or impressive public display **2** pl : GLASSES — **spec·ta·cled** \-kəld\ adj

spec·tac·u·lar \spek-'ta-kyə-lər\ adj : exciting to see : SENSATIONAL

spec·ta·tor \'spek-,tā-tər\ n : a person who looks on (as at a sports event) ♦ Synonyms OBSERVER, WITNESS, BYSTANDER, ONLOOKER, EYEWITNESS

spec·ter or **spec·tre** \'spek-tər\ n : a visible disembodied spirit : GHOST

spec·tral \'spek-trəl\ adj **1** : of, relating to, or resembling a specter **2** : of, relating to, or made by a spectrum

spec·tro·gram \'spek-trə-,gram\ n : a photograph, image, or diagram of a spectrum

spec·tro·graph \-,graf\ n : an instrument for dispersing radiation into a spectrum and recording or mapping the spectrum — **spec·tro·graph·ic** \ˌspek-trə-'gra-fik\ *adj* — **spec·tro·graph·i·cal·ly** \-fi-k(ə-)lē\ *adv*

spec·trom·e·ter \spek-'trä-mə-tər\ *n* : an instrument for measuring spectra — **spec·tro·met·ric** \ˌspek-trə-'me-trik\ *adj* — **spec·trom·e·try** \spek-'trä-mə-trē\ *n*

spec·tro·scope \'spek-trə-ˌskōp\ *n* : an instrument that produces spectra esp. of visible electromagnetic radiation — **spec·tro·scop·ic** \ˌspek-trə-'skä-pik\ *adj* — **spec·tro·scop·i·cal·ly** \-pi-k(ə-)lē\ *adv* — **spec·tros·co·pist** \spek-'träs-kə-pist\ *n* — **spec·tros·co·py** \-pē\ *n*

spec·trum \'spek-trəm\ *n, pl* **spec·tra** \-trə\ *or* **spectrums** [NL, fr. L, appearance, fr. *specere* to look] **1** : a series of colors formed when a beam of white light is dispersed (as by a prism) so that its parts are arranged in the order of their wavelengths **2** : a series of radiations arranged in regular order **3** : a continuous sequence or range ⟨a wide ∼ of political opinions⟩

spec·u·late \'spe-kyə-ˌlāt\ *vb* **-lat·ed; -lat·ing** [L *speculari* to spy out, examine, fr. *specula* lookout post, fr. *specere* to look, look at] **1** : to think or wonder about a subject **2** : to take a business risk in hope of gain ♦ *Synonyms* REASON, THINK, DELIBERATE, COGITATE — **spec·u·la·tion** \ˌspe-kyə-'lā-shən\ *n* — **spec·u·la·tive** \'spe-kyə-ˌlā-tiv\ *adj* — **spec·u·la·tive·ly** *adv* — **spec·u·la·tor** \-ˌlā-tər\ *n*

speech \'spēch\ *n* **1** : the act of speaking **2** : TALK, CONVERSATION **3** : a public talk or lecture **4** : LANGUAGE, DIALECT **5** : an individual manner of speaking **6** : the power of speaking — **speech·less** *adj*

¹speed \'spēd\ *n,* **1** *archaic* : SUCCESS **2** : SWIFTNESS, RAPIDITY **3** : rate of motion or performance **4** : a transmission gear (as of a bicycle) **5** : METHAMPHETAMINE; *also* : a related drug ♦ *Synonyms* HASTE, HURRY, DISPATCH, CELERITY — **speed·i·ly** \'spē-də-lē\ *adv* — **speedy** *adj*

²speed *vb* **sped** \'sped\ *or* **speed·ed; speed·ing 1** *archaic* : PROSPER; *also* : GET ALONG, FARE **2** : to go fast; *esp* : to go at an excessive or illegal speed **3** : to cause to go faster — **speed·er** *n*

speed·boat \-ˌbōt\ *n* : a fast motorboat

speed bump *n* : a low raised ridge across a roadway (as in a parking lot) to limit vehicle speed

speed of light : a fundamental physical constant that is the speed of electromagnetic radiation propagation in a vacuum and has the value of 299,792,458 meters per second

speed·om·e·ter \spi-'dä-mə-tər\ *n* : an instrument for indicating speed

speed-up \'spēd-ˌəp\ *n* : ACCELERATION

speed·way \-ˌwā\ *n* : a racecourse for motor vehicles

speed·well \'spēd-ˌwel\ *n* : VERONICA

¹spell \'spel\ *vb* **spelled** \'speld, 'spelt\;

spell·ing [ME, to signify, read by spelling out, fr. AF *espeleir,* of Gmc origin] **1** : to name, write, or print in order the letters of a word **2** : MEAN ⟨another drought may ∼ famine⟩

²spell *n* [ME, talk, tale, fr. OE] **1** : a magic formula : INCANTATION **2** : a controlling influence

³spell *n* **1** : one's turn at work or duty **2** : a stretch of a specified kind of weather **3** : a period of bodily or mental distress or disorder : ATTACK

⁴spell *vb* **spelled** \'speld\; **spell·ing** : to take the place of for a time in work or duty : RELIEVE

spell·bind·er \-ˌbīn-dər\ *n* : a speaker of compelling eloquence; *also* : one that compels attention

spell·bound \-ˌbau̇nd\ *adj* : held by or as if by a spell : FASCINATED

spell-check·er \'spel-ˌche-kər\ *n* : a computer program that identifies possible misspellings in a block of text — **spell-check** \-ˌchek\ *vb*

spell·er \'spe-lər\ *n* **1** : one who spells words **2** : a book with exercises for teaching spelling

spelt \'spelt\ *chiefly Brit past and past part of* ¹SPELL

spe·lunk·er \spi-'lən-kər, 'spē-ˌlən-kər\ *n* [L *spelunca* cave, fr. Gk *spēlynx*] : one who makes a hobby of exploring caves — **spe·lunk·ing** *n*

spend \'spend\ *vb* **spent** \'spent\; **spend·ing 1** : to pay out : EXPEND **2** : WEAR OUT, EXHAUST; *also* : to consume wastefully **3** : to cause or permit to elapse : PASS — **spend·er** *n*

spend·thrift \'spend-ˌthrift\ *n* : one who spends wastefully or recklessly

spent \'spent\ *adj* : drained of energy

sperm \'spərm\ *n, pl* **sperm** *or* **sperms 1** : SEMEN **2** : a male gamete

sper·ma·to·zo·on \(ˌ)spər-ˌma-tə-'zō-ˌän, -'zō-ən\ *n, pl* **-zoa** \-'zō-ə\ : a motile male gamete of an animal usu. with a rounded or elongated head and a long posterior flagellum

sperm cell *n* : SPERM 2

sper·mi·cide \'spər-mə-ˌsīd\ *n* : a preparation or substance used to kill sperm — **sper·mi·cid·al** \ˌspər-mə-'sī-dəl\ *adj*

sperm whale *n* : a large whale with a massive square-shaped head containing a fluid-filled cavity

spew \'spyü\ *vb* : VOMIT

SPF *abbr* sun protection factor

sp gr *abbr* specific gravity

sphag·num \'sfag-nəm\ *n* : any of a genus of atypical mosses that grow in wet acid areas where their remains become compacted with other plant debris to form peat; *also* : a mass of these mosses

sphere \'sfir\ *n* [ME *spere* globe, celestial sphere, fr. AF *espere,* fr. L *sphaera,* fr. Gk *sphaira,* lit., ball] **1** : a globe-shaped body : BALL **2** : a celestial body **3** : a solid figure so shaped that every point on its surface is an equal distance from the center **4** : range of action or influence

— **spher·i·cal** \'sfir-i-kəl, 'sfer-\ *adj* —
spher·i·cal·ly \-i-k(ə-)lē\ *adv*

spher·oid \'sfir-,öid, 'sfer-\ *n* : a figure
similar to a sphere but not perfectly
round — **sphe·roi·dal** \sfir-'öi-dəl\ *adj*

sphinc·ter \'sfiŋk-tər\ *n* : a muscular ring
that closes a bodily opening

sphinx \'sfiŋks\ *n*, *pl* **sphinx·es** or
sphin·ges \'sfin-jēz\ **1** : a winged monster in Greek mythology having a woman's head and a lion's body and noted for
killing anyone unable to answer its riddle **2** : an enigmatic or mysterious person **3** : an ancient Egyptian image having the body of a lion and the head of a
man, ram, or hawk

spice \'spīs\ *n* **1** : any of various aromatic plant products (as pepper or nutmeg)
used to season or flavor foods **2** : something that adds interest and relish —
spice *vb* — **spicy** *adj*

spick–and–span or **spic–and–span**
\,spik-ənd-'span\ *adj* : quite new; *also*
: spotlessly clean

spic·ule \'spi-kyül\ *n* : a slender pointed
body esp. of calcium or silica ⟨sponge
~s⟩

spi·der \'spī-dər\ *n* **1** : any of an order of
arachnids that have a 2-part body, eight
legs, and two or more pairs of abdominal
organs for spinning threads of silk used
esp. in making webs for catching prey **2**
: a cast-iron frying pan — **spi·dery** *adj*

spider mite *n* : any of various small web-
spinning mites that feed on and are pests
of plants

spider plant *n* : a houseplant of the lily
family having long green leaves usu.
striped with white and producing tufts of
small plants on long hanging stems

spi·der·web \'spī-dər-,web\ *n* : the web
spun by a spider

spiel \'spēl\ *vb* : to talk in a fast, smooth,
and usu. colorful manner — **spiel** *n*

spig·ot \'spi-gət, -kət\ *n* : FAUCET

¹spike \'spīk\ *n* **1** : a very large nail **2**
: any of various pointed projections (as
on the sole of a shoe to prevent slipping)
— **spiky** *adj*

²spike *vb* **spiked; spik·ing 1** : to fasten
with spikes **2** : to put an end to : QUASH
⟨~ a rumor⟩ **3** : to pierce with or impale on a spike **4** : to add alcoholic
liquor to (a drink)

³spike *n* **1** : an ear of grain **2** : a long
cluster of usu. stemless flowers

¹spill \'spil\ *vb* **spilled** \'spild, 'spilt\ *also*
spilt \'spilt\; **spill·ing 1** : to cause or
allow to fall, flow, or run out esp. unintentionally **2** : to cause (blood) to be lost
by wounding **3** : to run out or over with
resulting loss or waste **4** : to let out : DI-
VULGE — **spill·able** *adj*

²spill *n* **1** : an act of spilling; *also* : a fall
from a horse or vehicle or an erect posi-
tion **2** : something spilled

spill·way \-,wā\ *n* : a passage for surplus
water to run over or around an obstruction (as a dam)

¹spin \'spin\ *vb* **spun** \'spən\; **spin·ning**
1 : to draw out (fiber) and twist into
thread; *also* : to form (thread) by such

means **2** : to form thread by extruding a
sticky quickly hardening fluid; *also* : to
construct from such thread ⟨spiders ~
their webs⟩ **3** : to produce slowly and by
degrees ⟨~ a story⟩ **4** : TWIRL **5**
: WHIRL, REEL ⟨my head is *spinning*⟩ **6**
: to move rapidly along **7** : to present (as
information) with a particular spin —
spin·ner *n*

²spin *n* **1** : a rapid rotating motion **2** : an
excursion in a wheeled vehicle **3** : a particular point of view, emphasis, or interpretation

spi·na bi·fi·da \,spī-nə-'bi-fə-də\ *n* : a
birth defect in which the spinal column
has a fissure

spin·ach \'spi-nich\ *n* : a dark green herb
grown for its edible leaves

spi·nal \'spī-nᵊl\ *adj* : of or relating to the
backbone or spinal cord — **spi·nal·ly**
adv

spinal column *n* : BACKBONE 1

spinal cord *n* : the thick cord of nervous
tissue that extends from the brain along
the back in the cavity of the backbone
and carries nerve impulses to and from
the brain

spinal nerve *n* : any of the paired nerves
which arise from the spinal cord and pass
to various parts of the body and of which
there are normally 31 pairs in human beings

spin control *n* : the act or practice of attempting to manipulate the way an event
is interpreted

spin·dle \'spin-dᵊl\ *n* **1** : a round tapering stick or rod by which fibers are twisted in spinning **2** : a turned part of a
piece of furniture ⟨the ~s of a chair⟩ **3**
: a slender pin or rod which turns or on
which something else turns

spin·dling \'spind-liŋ\ *adj* : SPINDLY

spin·dly \'spind-lē\ *adj* : being long or tall
and thin and usu. weak

spin·drift \'spin-,drift\ *n* : spray blown
from waves

spine \'spīn\ *n* **1** : BACKBONE **2** : a stiff
sharp process esp. on a plant or animal **3**
: the part of a book where the pages are
attached — **spiny** *adj*

spi·nel \spə-'nel\ *n* : a hard crystalline
mineral of variable color used as a gem

spine·less \'spīn-ləs\ *adj* **1** : having no
spines, thorns, or prickles **2** : lacking a
backbone **3** : lacking courage or determination

spin·et \'spi-nət\ *n* **1** : an early harpsichord having a single keyboard and only
one string for each note **2** : a small upright piano

spin·na·ker \'spi-ni-kər\ *n* : a large triangular sail set on a long light pole

spinning jen·ny \-'je-nē\ *n* : an early
multiple-spindle machine for spinning
wool or cotton

spinning wheel *n* : a small machine for
spinning thread or yarn in which a large
wheel drives a single spindle

spin–off \'spin-,öf\ *n* **1** : a usu. useful by-
product **2** : something (as a TV show)
derived from an earlier work — **spin off**
vb

spin·ster \'spin-stər\ *n* : an unmarried woman past the common age for marrying — **spin·ster·hood** \-ˌhùd\ *n*

spiny lobster *n* : any of several edible crustaceans differing from the related lobsters in lacking the large front claws and in having a spiny carapace

¹**spi·ral** \'spī-rəl\ *adj* : winding or coiling around a center or axis and usu. getting closer to or farther away from it — **spi·ral·ly** *adv*

²**spiral** *n* **1** : something that has a spiral form; *also* : a single turn in a spiral object **2** : a continuously spreading and accelerating increase or decrease

³**spiral** *vb* **-raled** *or* **-ralled; -ral·ing** *or* **-ral·ling 1** : to move and esp. to rise or fall in a spiral course **2** : to form into a spiral

spi·rant \'spī-rənt\ *n* : a consonant (as \f\, \s\, \sh\) uttered with decided friction of the breath against some part of the oral passage — **spirant** *adj*

spire \'spī(-ə)r\ *n* **1** : a slender tapering stalk (as of grass) **2** : a pointed tip (as of an antler) **3** : STEEPLE — **spiry** *adj*

spi·rea *or* **spi·raea** \spī-'rē-ə\ *n* : any of a genus of shrubs related to the roses with dense clusters of small usu. white or pink flowers

¹**spir·it** \'spir-ət\ *n* [ME, fr. AF or L; AF, fr. L *spiritus*, lit., breath, fr. *spirare* to blow, breathe] **1** : a life-giving force; *also* : the animating principle : SOUL **2** *cap* : HOLY SPIRIT **3** : SPECTER, GHOST **4** : PERSON ⟨a bold ∼⟩ **5** : DISPOSITION, MOOD ⟨in good ∼s⟩ **6** : VIVACITY, ARDOR **7** : essential or real meaning : INTENT **8** : distilled alcoholic liquor **9** : LOYALTY ⟨school ∼⟩ — **spir·it·less** *adj*

²**spirit** *vb* : to carry off secretly or mysteriously

spir·it·ed \'spir-ə-təd\ *adj* : full of energy, animation, or courage

¹**spir·i·tu·al** \'spir-i-chəl, -chə-wəl\ *adj* **1** : of, relating to, consisting of, or affecting the spirit : INCORPOREAL **2** : of or relating to sacred matters **3** : ecclesiastical rather than lay or temporal — **spir·i·tu·al·i·ty** \ˌspir-i-chə-'wa-lə-tē\ *n* — **spir·i·tu·al·ize** \'spir-i-chə-ˌlīz, -chə-wə-\ *vb* — **spir·i·tu·al·ly** *adv*

²**spiritual** *n* : a religious song originating among blacks of the southern U.S.

spir·i·tu·al·ism \'spir-i-chə-ˌli-zəm, -chə-wə-\ *n* : a belief that spirits of the dead communicate with the living usu. through a medium — **spir·i·tu·al·ist** \-list\ *n*, *often cap* — **spir·i·tu·al·is·tic** \ˌspir-i-chə-'lis-tik, -chə-wə-\ *adj*

spir·i·tu·ous \'spir-i-chəs, -chə-wəs; 'spir-ə-təs\ *adj* : containing alcohol

spi·ro·chete *also* **spi·ro·chaete** \'spī-rə-ˌkēt\ *n* : any of an order of spirally undulating bacteria including those causing syphilis and Lyme disease

spirt *var of* SPURT

¹**spit** \'spit\ *n* **1** : a thin pointed rod for holding meat over a fire **2** : a point of land that runs out into the water

²**spit** *vb* **spit·ted; spit·ting** : to pierce with or as if with a spit

³**spit** *vb* **spit** *or* **spat** \'spat\; **spit·ting 1** : to eject (saliva) from the mouth **2** : to express by or as if by spitting **3** : to rain or snow lightly

⁴**spit** *n* **1** : SALIVA **2** : perfect likeness ⟨∼ and image of his father⟩

spit·ball \'spit-ˌbòl\ *n* **1** : paper chewed and rolled into a ball to be thrown as a missile **2** : a baseball pitch delivered after the ball has been moistened with saliva or sweat

¹**spite** \'spīt\ *n* : ill will with a wish to annoy, anger, or frustrate : petty malice ♦ *Synonyms* MALIGNITY, SPLEEN, GRUDGE, MALEVOLENCE — **spite·ful** \-fəl\ *adj* — **spite·ful·ly** *adv* — **spite·ful·ness** *n* — **in spite of** : in defiance or contempt of : NOTWITHSTANDING

²**spite** *vb* **spit·ed; spit·ing** : to treat maliciously : ANNOY, OFFEND

spit·tle \'spi-t²l\ *n* : SALIVA

spit·tle·bug \-ˌbəg\ *n* : any of a family of leaping insects with froth-secreting larvae that are related to aphids

spit·toon \spi-'tün\ *n* : a receptacle for spit

splash \'splash\ *vb* **1** : to dash a liquid about **2** : to scatter a liquid on : SPATTER **3** : to fall or strike with a splashing noise ♦ *Synonyms* SPRINKLE, BESPATTER, DOUSE, SPLATTER — **splash** *n*

splash·down \'splash-ˌdaùn\ *n* : the landing of a manned spacecraft in the ocean — **splash down** *vb*

splashy \'spla-shē\ *adj* **splash·i·er; -est** : conspicuously showy : OSTENTATIOUS

¹**splat·ter** \'spla-tər\ *vb* : SPATTER — **splatter** *n*

²**splatter** *adj* : extremely gory or violent ⟨a ∼ movie⟩

¹**splay** \'splā\ *vb* : to spread outward or apart — **splay** *n*

²**splay** *adj* **1** : spread out : turned outward **2** : AWKWARD, CLUMSY

spleen \'splēn\ *n* **1** : a vascular organ located near the stomach in most vertebrates that is concerned esp. with the filtration and storage of blood, destruction of red blood cells, and production of lymphocytes **2** : SPITE, MALICE ♦ *Synonyms* MALIGNITY, GRUDGE, MALEVOLENCE, ILL WILL, SPITEFULNESS

splen·did \'splen-dəd\ *adj* [L *splendidus*, fr. *splendēre* to shine] **1** : SHINING, BRILLIANT **2** : SHOWY, GORGEOUS **3** : ILLUSTRIOUS **4** : EXCELLENT ⟨a ∼ opportunity⟩ ♦ *Synonyms* RESPLENDENT, GLORIOUS, SUBLIME, SUPERB — **splen·did·ly** *adv*

splen·dor \'splen-dər\ *n* **1** : BRILLIANCE ⟨the ∼ of the sun⟩ **2** : POMP, MAGNIFICENCE

splen·dour \'splen-dər\ *chiefly Brit var of* SPLENDOR

sple·net·ic \spli-'ne-tik\ *adj* : marked by bad temper or spite

splen·ic \'sple-nik\ *adj* : of, relating to, or located in the spleen

splice \'splīs\ *vb* **spliced; splic·ing 1** : to unite (as two ropes) by weaving the strands together **2** : to unite (as two lengths of film) by connecting the ends together — **splice** *n*

splint \'splint\ *n* 1 : a thin strip of wood interwoven with others to make something (as a basket) 2 : material or a device used to protect and keep in place an injured body part (as a broken arm)

¹**splin·ter** \'splin-tər\ *n* : a thin piece of something split off lengthwise : SLIVER

²**splinter** *vb* : to split into splinters

split \'split\ *vb* **split**; **split·ting** 1 : to divide lengthwise or along a grain or seam 2 : to burst or break in pieces 3 : to divide into parts or sections 4 : LEAVE ⟨∼ the party⟩ ♦ *Synonyms* REND, CLEAVE, RIP, TEAR — **split** *n*

split–lev·el \'split-'le-vəl\ *n* : a house divided so that the floor in one part is about halfway between two floors in the other

split personality *n* : SCHIZOPHRENIA; *also* : MULTIPLE PERSONALITY DISORDER

split–second \'split-'se-kənd\ *adj* 1 : occurring in a very brief time 2 : extremely precise ⟨∼ timing⟩

split·ting *adj* : causing a piercing sensation ⟨a ∼ headache⟩

splotch \'spläch\ *n* : BLOTCH

splurge \'splərj\ *vb* **splurged**; **splurg·ing** : to spend more than usual esp. on oneself — **splurge** *n*

splut·ter \'splə-tər\ *n* : SPUTTER — **splutter** *vb*

¹**spoil** \'spȯi(-ə)l\ *n* : PLUNDER ⟨∼s of war⟩

²**spoil** *vb* **spoiled** \'spȯi(-ə)ld, 'spȯi(-ə)lt\ *or* **spoilt** \'spȯi(-ə)lt\; **spoil·ing** 1 : ROB, PILLAGE 2 : to damage seriously : RUIN 3 : to impair the quality or effect of 4 : to damage the disposition of by pampering; *also* : INDULGE, CODDLE 5 : DECAY, ROT 6 : to have an eager desire ⟨∼ing for a fight⟩ ♦ *Synonyms* INJURE, HARM, HURT, MAR — **spoil·age** \'spȯi-lij\ *n*

spoil·er \'spȯi-lər\ *n* 1 : one that spoils 2 : a device (as on an airplane or automobile) used to disrupt airflow and decrease lift

spoil·sport \'spȯi(-ə)l-,spȯrt\ *n* : one who spoils the fun of others

¹**spoke** \'spōk\ *past & archaic past part of* SPEAK

²**spoke** *n* : any of the rods extending from the hub of a wheel to the rim

spo·ken \'spō-kən\ *past part of* SPEAK

spokes·man \'spōks-mən\ *n* : a person who speaks as the representative of another or others

spokes·mod·el \-,mä-dᵊl\ *n* : a model who is a spokesman or spokeswoman

spokes·per·son \-,pər-sən\ *n* : SPOKESMAN

spokes·wom·an \-,wu̇-mən\ *n* : a woman who speaks as the representative of another or others

spo·li·a·tion \,spō-lē-'ā-shən\ *n* : the act of plundering : the state of being plundered

¹**sponge** \'spənj\ *n* 1 : an elastic porous water-absorbing mass of fibers that forms the skeleton of various primitive sea animals; *also* : any of a phylum of chiefly marine sea animals that are the source of

natural sponges 2 : a spongelike or porous mass or material — **spongy** \'spən-jē\ *adj*

²**sponge** *vb* **sponged**; **spong·ing** 1 : to bathe or wipe with a sponge 2 : to live at another's expense 3 : to gather sponges — **spong·er** *n*

sponge cake *n* : a light cake made without shortening

sponge rubber *n* : a cellular rubber resembling natural sponge

spon·sor \'spän-sər\ *n* [LL, fr. L, guarantor, surety, fr. *spondēre* to promise] 1 : one who takes the responsibility for some other person or thing : SURETY 2 : GODPARENT 3 : a business firm that pays the cost of a radio or television program usu. in return for advertising time during its course — **sponsor** *vb* — **spon·sor·ship** *n*

spon·ta·ne·ous \spän-'tā-nē-əs\ *adj* [LL *spontaneus*, fr. L *sponte* of one's free will, voluntarily] 1 : done or produced freely or naturally 2 : acting or taking place without external force or cause ♦ *Synonyms* IMPULSIVE, INSTINCTIVE, AUTOMATIC, UNPREMEDITATED — **spon·ta·ne·ity** \,spän-tə-'nē-ə-tē, -'nā-\ *n* — **spon·ta·ne·ous·ly** *adv*

spontaneous combustion *n* : a bursting into flame of material through heat produced within itself by chemical action (as oxidation)

spoof \'spüf\ *vb* 1 : DECEIVE, HOAX 2 : to make good-natured fun of — **spoof** *n*

¹**spook** \'spük\ *n* 1 : GHOST, APPARITION 2 : SPY 2 — **spooky** *adj*

²**spook** *vb* : FRIGHTEN

¹**spool** \'spül\ *n* : a cylinder on which flexible material (as thread) is wound

²**spool** *vb* 1 : to wind on a spool 2 : to regulate data flow by means of a spooler

spool·er \'spü-lər\ *n* : a computer program or routine for regulating data flow

spoon \'spün\ *n* [ME, fr. OE *spōn* splinter, chip] 1 : an eating or cooking implement consisting of a small shallow bowl with a handle 2 : a metal piece used on a fishing line as a lure — **spoon** *vb* — **spoon·ful** *n*

spoon·bill \'spün-,bil\ *n* : any of several wading birds related to the ibises that have a bill with a broad flat tip

spoon–feed \-,fēd\ *vb* **-fed** \-,fed\; **-feed·ing** : to feed by means of a spoon

spoor \'spu̇r, 'spȯr\ *n, pl* **spoor** *or* **spoors** : a track, a trail, a scent, or droppings esp. of a wild animal

spo·rad·ic \spə-'ra-dik\ *adj* : occurring now and then ⟨∼ outbreaks of disease⟩ ♦ *Synonyms* OCCASIONAL, RARE, SCARCE, INFREQUENT, UNCOMMON — **spo·rad·i·cal·ly** \-di-k(ə-)lē\ *adv*

spore \'spȯr\ *n* : a primitive usu. one-celled often environmentally resistant dormant or reproductive body produced by plants, fungi, and some microorganisms

¹**sport** \'spȯrt\ *vb* [ME, to divert, amuse, short for *disporten*, fr. AF *desporter*, to carry away, comfort, entertain, fr. *des-*

(fr. L *dis-* apart) + *porter* to carry, fr. L *portare*] **1** : to amuse oneself : FROLIC **2** : SHOW OFF **1** ⟨∼*ing* new shoes⟩ — **sport·ive** *adj*

²**sport** *n* **1** : a source of diversion : PASTIME **2** : physical activity engaged in for pleasure **3** : JEST **4** : MOCKERY ⟨make ∼ of his efforts⟩ **5** : BUTT, LAUGHINGSTOCK **6** : one who accepts results cheerfully whether favorable or not **7** : an individual exhibiting marked deviation from its normal type esp. as a result of mutation ◆ *Synonyms* PLAY, FROLIC, FUN, RECREATION — **sporty** *adj*

³**sport** *or* **sports** *adj* : of, relating to, or suitable for sport or casual wear ⟨∼ coats⟩

sport fish *n* : a fish noted for the sport it affords anglers

sports·cast \'sports-ˌkast\ *n* : a broadcast dealing with sports events — **sports·cast·er** \-ˌkas-tər\ *n*

sports·man \'sports-mən\ *n* **1** : a person who engages in sports (as in hunting or fishing) **2** : one who plays fairly and wins or loses gracefully — **sports·man·like** \-ˌlīk\ *adj* — **sports·man·ship** *n*

sports medicine *n* : a field of medicine dealing with the prevention and treatment of sports-related injuries

sports·wom·an \-ˌwu̇-mən\ *n* : a woman who engages in sports

sports·writ·er \-ˌrī-tər\ *n* : one who writes about sports esp. for a newspaper — **sports·writ·ing** *n*

sport–util·ity vehicle \'sport-yü-'ti-lə-tē-\ *n* : SUV

¹**spot** \'spät\ *n* **1** : STAIN, BLEMISH **2** : a small part different (as in color) from the main part **3** : LOCATION, SITE — **spot·less** *adj* — **spot·less·ly** *adv* — **on the spot 1** : at the place of action **2** : in difficulty or danger

²**spot** *vb* **spot·ted; spot·ting 1** : to mark or disfigure with spots **2** : to pick out : RECOGNIZE, IDENTIFY

³**spot** *adj* **1** : being, done, or originating on the spot ⟨a ∼ broadcast⟩ **2** : paid upon delivery **3** : made at random or at a few key points ⟨a ∼ check⟩

spot–check \'spät-ˌchek\ *vb* : to make a spot check of

spot·light \-ˌlīt\ *n* **1** : a circle of brilliant light projected upon a particular area, person, or object (as on a stage); *also* : the device that produces this light **2** : public notice — **spotlight** *vb*

spot–on \'spät-'än\ *adj* : exactly correct ⟨a ∼ forecast⟩

spotted owl *n* : a rare large dark brown dark-eyed owl of humid old growth forests and thickly wooded canyons from British Columbia to southern California and central Mexico

spot·ter \'spä-tər\ *n* **1** : one that keeps watch : OBSERVER **2** : one that removes spots

spot·ty \'spä-tē\ *adj* **spot·ti·er; -est** : uneven in quality; *also* : sparsely distributed ⟨∼ attendance⟩

spou·sal \'spau̇-zəl, -səl\ *n* : MARRIAGE 2, WEDDING — usu. used in pl.

spouse \'spau̇s\ *n* : one's husband or wife — **spou·sal** \'spau̇-zəl, -səl\ *adj*

¹**spout** \'spau̇t\ *vb* **1** : to eject or issue forth forcibly and freely ⟨wells ∼ing oil⟩ **2** : to speak pompously

²**spout** *n* **1** : a pipe or hole through which liquid spouts **2** : a jet of liquid; *esp* : WATERSPOUT 2

spp *abbr, pl* species

¹**sprain** \'sprān\ *n* : a sudden or severe twisting of a joint with stretching or tearing of ligaments; *also* : a sprained condition

²**sprain** *vb* : to subject to sprain

sprat \'sprat\ *n* **1** : a small European fish related to the herring; *also* : SARDINE

sprawl \'sprȯl\ *vb* **1** : to lie or sit with limbs spread out awkwardly **2** : to spread out irregularly — **sprawl** *n*

¹**spray** \'sprā\ *n* : a usu. flowering branch; *also* : a decorative arrangement of flowers and foliage

²**spray** *n* **1** : liquid flying in small drops like water blown from a wave **2** : a jet of fine vapor (as from an atomizer) **3** : an instrument (as an atomizer) for scattering fine liquid

³**spray** *vb* **1** : to discharge spray on or into **2** : to scatter or let fall in a spray — **spray·er** *n*

spray can *n* : a pressurized container from which aerosols are sprayed

spray gun *n* : a device for spraying liquids (as paint or insecticide)

¹**spread** \'spred\ *vb* **spread; spread·ing 1** : to scatter over a surface **2** : to flatten out : open out **3** : to distribute over a period of time or among many persons **4** : to cover something with ⟨∼ rugs on the floor⟩ **5** : to prepare for a meal ⟨a ∼ table⟩ **6** : to pass on from person to person **7** : to stretch, force, or push apart — **spread·er** *n*

²**spread** *n* **1** : the act or process of spreading **2** : EXPANSE, EXTENT **3** : a prominent display in a periodical **4** : a food to be spread on bread or crackers **5** : a cloth cover for a bed **6** : distance between two points : GAP

spread·sheet \'spred-ˌshēt\ *n* : an accounting program for a computer

spree \'sprē\ *n* : an unrestrained outburst ⟨buying ∼⟩; *also* : a drinking bout

sprig \'sprig\ *n* : a small shoot or twig

spright·ly \'sprīt-lē\ *adj* **spright·li·er; -est** : LIVELY, SPIRITED ⟨a ∼ musical⟩ ◆ *Synonyms* ANIMATED, VIVACIOUS, GAY — **spright·li·ness** *n*

¹**spring** \'spriŋ\ *vb* **sprang** \'spraŋ\ *or* **sprung** \'sprəŋ\; **sprung; spring·ing 1** : to move suddenly upward or forward **2** : to grow quickly ⟨weeds *sprang* up overnight⟩ **3** : to come from by birth or descent **4** : to move quickly by elastic force **5** : WARP **6** : to develop (a leak) through the seams **7** : to cause to close suddenly ⟨∼ a trap⟩ **8** : to make known suddenly ⟨∼ a surprise⟩ **9** : to make lame : STRAIN

²**spring** *n* **1** : a source of supply; *esp* : an issuing of water from the ground **2**

: SOURCE, ORIGIN; *also* : MOTIVE **3** : the season between winter and summer **4** : an elastic body or device that recovers its original shape when it is released after being distorted **5** : the act or an instance of leaping up or forward **6** : RESILIENCE — **springy** *adj*

spring·board \'spriŋ-ˌbȯrd\ *n* : a springy board used in jumping or vaulting or for diving

spring fever *n* : a lazy or restless feeling often associated with the onset of spring

spring tide *n* : a tide of greater-than-average range that occurs at each new moon and full moon

spring·time \'spriŋ-ˌtīm\ *n* : the season of spring

¹**sprin·kle** \'spriŋ-kəl\ *vb* **sprin·kled; sprin·kling** : to scatter in small drops or particles — **sprin·kler** *n*

²**sprinkle** *n* : a light rainfall

sprin·kling *n* : SMATTERING

¹**sprint** \'sprint\ *vb* : to run at top speed esp. for a short distance — **sprint·er** *n*

²**sprint** *n* **1** : a short run at top speed **2** : a short distance race

sprite \'sprīt\ *n* **1** : GHOST, SPIRIT **2** : ELF, FAIRY

spritz *vb* : SPRAY

sprock·et \'sprä-kət\ *n* : a toothed wheel whose teeth engage the links of a chain

¹**sprout** \'spraȯt\ *vb* : to send out new growth ⟨∼*ing* seeds⟩

²**sprout** *n* : a usu. young and growing plant shoot (as from a seed)

¹**spruce** \'sprüs\ *vb* **spruced; spruc·ing** : to make or become spruce

²**spruce** *adj* **spruc·er; spruc·est** : neat and smart in appearance ✦ **Synonyms** STYLISH, FASHIONABLE, MODISH, DAPPER, NATTY

³**spruce** *n*, *pl* **spruc·es** *also* **spruce** : any of a genus of evergreen pyramid-shaped trees related to the pines and having soft light wood; *also* : the wood of a spruce

sprung *past and past part of* SPRING

spry \'sprī\ *adj* **spri·er** *or* **spry·er** \'sprī-ər\; **spri·est** *or* **spry·est** \'sprī-əst\ : NIMBLE, ACTIVE ⟨a ∼ 75-year-old⟩ ✦ **Synonyms** AGILE, BRISK, LIVELY, SPRIGHTLY

spud \'spəd\ *n* **1** : a sharp narrow spade **2** : POTATO

spume \'spyüm\ *n* : frothy matter on liquids : FOAM — **spumy** \'spyü-mē\ *adj*

spu·mo·ni *also* **spu·mo·ne** \spú-'mō-nē\ *n* [It *spumone*, fr. *spuma* foam] : ice cream in layers of different colors, flavors, and textures often with candied fruits and nuts

spun *past and past part of* SPIN

spun glass *n* : FIBERGLASS

spunk \'spəŋk\ *n* [fr. *spunk* tinder, fr. ScGael *spong* sponge, tinder, fr. Middle Irish *spongc*, fr. L *spongia* sponge] : PLUCK, COURAGE — **spunky** *adj*

¹**spur** \'spər\ *n* **1** : a pointed device fastened to a rider's boot and used to urge on a horse **2** : something that urges to action **3** : a stiff sharp spine (as on the leg of a cock); *also* : a hollow projecting appendage of a flower (as a columbine)

4 : a ridge extending sideways from a mountain **5** : a branch of railroad track extending from the main line ✦ **Synonyms** GOAD, MOTIVE, IMPULSE, INCENTIVE, INDUCEMENT — **spurred** \'spərd\ *adj* — **on the spur of the moment** : on hasty impulse

²**spur** *vb* **spurred; spur·ring 1** : to urge a horse on with spurs **2** : INCITE

spurge \'spərj\ *n* : any of a family of herbs and woody plants with a bitter milky juice

spu·ri·ous \'spyúr-ē-əs\ *adj* [LL *spurius* false, fr. L, *spurius*, n., son of an unknown father] : not genuine : FALSE ⟨∼ eminence⟩

spurn \'spərn\ *vb* **1** : to kick away or trample on **2** : to reject with disdain

¹**spurt** \'spərt\ *vb* : to gush out : SPOUT

²**spurt** *n* : a sudden gushing or spouting

³**spurt** *n* **1** : a sudden brief burst of effort, speed, or development **2** : a sharp increase of activity ⟨∼ in sales⟩

⁴**spurt** *vb* : to make a spurt

sput·ter \'spə-tər\ *vb* **1** : to spit small scattered particles : SPLUTTER **2** : to utter words hastily or explosively in excitement or confusion **3** : to make small popping sounds — **sputter** *n*

spu·tum \'spyü-təm\ *n*, *pl* **spu·ta** \-tə\ [L] : material (as phlegm) that is spit out or coughed up esp. during illness

¹**spy** \'spī\ *vb* **spied; spy·ing 1** : to watch or search for information secretly : act as a spy **2** : to get a momentary or quick glimpse of : SEE

²**spy** *n*, *pl* **spies 1** : one who secretly watches others **2** : a secret agent who tries to get information for one country in the territory of an enemy

spy·glass \'spī-ˌglas\ *n* : a small telescope

sq *abbr* **1** squadron **2** square

squab \'skwäb\ *n*, *pl* **squabs** *or* **squab** : a young bird and esp. a pigeon

squab·ble \'skwä-bəl\ *n* : a noisy altercation : WRANGLE ✦ **Synonyms** QUARREL, SPAT, ROW, TIFF — **squabble** *vb*

squad \'skwäd\ *n* **1** : a small organized group of military personnel **2** : a small group engaged in a common effort

squad car *n* : a police car connected by two-way radio with headquarters

squad·ron \'skwä-drən\ *n* : any of several units of military organization

squal·id \'skwä-ləd\ *adj* **1** : filthy or degraded through neglect or poverty **2** : SORDID, DEBASED ⟨a ∼ political ploy⟩ ✦ **Synonyms** NASTY, FOUL, DIRTY, GRUBBY

squall \'skwȯl\ *n* : a sudden violent gust of wind often with rain or snow — **squally** *adj*

squa·lor \'skwä-lər\ *n* : the quality or state of being squalid

squa·mous cell \'skwä-məs-\ *n* : a scalelike cell of the outer layers of the skin from which a type of carcinoma arises

squan·der \'skwän-dər\ *vb* : to spend wastefully or foolishly

¹**square** \'skwer\ *n* **1** : an instrument used to lay out or test right angles **2** : a rect-

angle with all four sides equal **3** : something square **4** : the product of a number multiplied by itself **5** : an area bounded by four streets **6** : an open area in a city where streets meet **7** : a highly conventional person

²**square** adj **squar·er; squar·est 1** : having four equal sides and four right angles **2** : forming a right angle ⟨cut a ~ corner⟩ **3** : multiplied by itself : SQUARED ⟨x^2 is the symbol for x ~⟩ **4** : being a unit of square measure equal to a square each side of which measures one unit ⟨a ~ foot⟩ **5** : being of a specified length in each of two dimensions ⟨an area 10 feet ~⟩ **6** : exactly adjusted **7** : JUST, FAIR ⟨a ~ deal⟩ **8** : leaving no balance ⟨make accounts ~⟩ **9** : SUBSTANTIAL ⟨a ~ meal⟩ **10** : highly conservative or conventional — **square·ly** adv

³**square** vb **squared; squar·ing 1** : to form with four equal sides and right angles or with flat surfaces ⟨~ a timber⟩ **2** : to multiply (a number) by itself **3** : CONFORM, AGREE **4** : BALANCE, SETTLE ⟨~ an account⟩

square dance n : a dance for four couples arranged to form a square

square measure n : a unit or system of units for measuring area — see METRIC SYSTEM table, WEIGHT table

square–rigged \'skwer-'rigd\ adj : having the chief sails extended on yards that are fastened to the masts horizontally and at their center

square–rig·ger \-,ri-gər\ n : a square-rigged craft

square root n : either of the two numbers whose squares are equal to a given number ⟨the square root of 9 is +3 or −3⟩

¹**squash** \'skwäsh, 'skwȯsh\ vb **1** : to beat or press into a pulp or flat mass **2** : QUASH, SUPPRESS ⟨~ a revolt⟩

²**squash** n **1** : the impact of something soft and heavy; also : the sound of such impact **2** : a crushed mass **3** : a game played on a 4-wall court with a racket and rubber ball

³**squash** n, pl **squash·es** or **squash** : any of various fruits of plants of the gourd family that are used esp. as vegetables; also : a plant and esp. a vine bearing squashes

squash racquets n : SQUASH 3

¹**squat** \'skwät\ vb **squat·ted; squat·ting** [ME squatten to crush, crouch in hiding, fr. MF (dial. of Picardy) esquatir, escuater, fr. OF es- ex- + quatir to hide, fr. VL *coactire to squeeze, alter. of L coactare to compel, fr. cogere to compel] **1** : to sit down upon the hams or heels **2** : to settle on land without right or title; also : to settle on public land with a view to acquiring title — **squat·ter** n

²**squat** adj **squat·ter; squat·test** : low to the ground; also : short and thick in stature ♦ **Synonyms** THICKSET, STOCKY, HEAVYSET, STUBBY

³**squat** n : the act or posture of squatting

squawk \'skwȯk\ n : a harsh loud cry; also : a noisy protest — **squawk** vb

squeak \'skwēk\ vb **1** : to utter or speak in a weak shrill tone **2** : to make a thin high-pitched sound — **squeak** n — **squeaky** adj

¹**squeal** \'skwēl\ vb **1** : to make a shrill sound or cry **2** : to betray a secret or turn informer **3** : COMPLAIN, PROTEST

²**squeal** n : a shrill sharp cry or noise

squea·mish \'skwē-mish\ adj **1** : easily nauseated; also : NAUSEATED **2** : easily disgusted ♦ **Synonyms** FUSSY, NICE, DAINTY, FASTIDIOUS, PERSNICKETY — **squea·mish·ness** n

squee·gee \'skwē-jē\ n : a blade set crosswise on a handle and used for spreading or wiping liquid on, across, or off a surface — **squeegee** vb

¹**squeeze** \'skwēz\ vb **squeezed; squeez·ing 1** : to exert pressure on the opposite sides or parts of **2** : to obtain by pressure ⟨~ juice from a lemon⟩ **3** : to force, thrust, or cause to pass by pressure — **squeez·er** n

²**squeeze** n **1** : an act of squeezing **2** : a quantity squeezed out

squeeze bottle n : a flexible plastic bottle that dispenses its contents when it is squeezed

squelch \'skwelch\ vb **1** : to suppress completely : CRUSH ⟨~ resistance⟩ **2** : to move in soft mud — **squelch** n

squib \'skwib\ n : a brief witty writing or speech

squid \'skwid\ n, pl **squid** or **squids** : any of an order of long-bodied sea mollusks having eight short arms and two longer tentacles and usu. a slender internal shell

squint \'skwint\ vb **1** : to look or aim obliquely **2** : to look or peer with the eyes partly closed **3** : to be cross-eyed — **squint** n or adj

¹**squire** \'skwī(-ə)r\ n [ME squier, fr. AF esquier, fr. LL scutarius, fr. L scutum shield] **1** : an armor-bearer of a knight **2** : a man gallantly devoted to a lady **3** : a member of the British gentry ranking below a knight and above a gentleman; also : a prominent landowner **4** : a local magistrate

²**squire** vb **squired; squir·ing** : to attend as a squire or escort

squirm \'skwərm\ vb : to twist about like a worm : WRIGGLE

¹**squir·rel** \'skwər-əl\ n, pl **squirrels** also **squirrel** [ME squirel, fr. AF escurel, esquirel, fr. VL *scuriolus, dim. of *scurius, alter. of L sciurus, fr. Gk skiouros, prob. fr. skia shadow + oura tail] : any of various rodents usu. with a long bushy tail and strong hind legs; also : the fur of a squirrel

²**squirrel** vb **-reled** or **-relled; -rel·ing** or **-rel·ling** : to store up for future use

¹**squirt** \'skwərt\ vb : to eject liquid in a thin spurt

²**squirt** n **1** : an instrument (as a syringe) for squirting **2** : a small forcible jet of liquid

¹**Sr** abbr **1** senior **2** sister

²**Sr** symbol strontium

SR *abbr* seaman recruit

¹**SRO** _es-(,)är-'ō\ *n* [*single-room occupancy*] : a house or apartment building in which low-income tenants live in single rooms

²**SRO** *abbr* standing room only

SS *abbr* 1 saints 2 Social Security 3 steamship 4 sworn statement

SSA *abbr* Social Security Administration

SSE *abbr* south-southeast

SSG *or* **SSgt** *abbr* staff sergeant

SSI *abbr* supplemental security income

SSM *abbr* staff sergeant major

SSN *abbr* Social Security Number

ssp *abbr* subspecies

SSR *abbr* Soviet Socialist Republic

SSS *abbr* Selective Service System

SST _es-(,)es-'tē\ *n* [*supersonic transport*] : a supersonic passenger airplane

SSW *abbr* south-southwest

st *abbr* 1 stanza 2 state 3 stitch 4 stone 5 street

St *abbr* saint

ST *abbr* 1 short ton 2 standard time

-st — see -EST

sta *abbr* station; stationary

¹**stab** \'stab\ *n* 1 : a wound produced by a pointed weapon 2 : a quick thrust 3 : a brief attempt

²**stab** *vb* **stabbed**; **stab·bing** : to pierce or wound with or as if with a pointed weapon; *also* : THRUST, DRIVE

sta·bile \'stā-,bēl\ *n* : an abstract sculpture or construction similar to a mobile but made to be stationary

sta·bi·lize \'stā-bə-,līz\ *vb* **-lized**; **-liz·ing** 1 : to make stable 2 : to hold steady ⟨~ prices⟩ — **sta·bi·li·za·tion** \,stā-bə-lə-'zā-shən\ *n* — **sta·bi·liz·er** \'stā-bə-,lī-zər\ *n*

¹**sta·ble** \'stā-bəl\ *n* : a building in which domestic animals are sheltered and fed — **sta·ble·man** \-mən, -,man\ *n*

²**stable** *vb* **sta·bled**; **sta·bling** : to put or keep in a stable

³**stable** *adj* **sta·bler**; **sta·blest** 1 : firmly established; *also* : mentally and emotionally healthy 2 : steady in purpose : CONSTANT 3 : DURABLE, ENDURING ⟨~ civilizations⟩ 4 : resistant to chemical or physical change ♦ *Synonyms* LASTING, PERMANENT, PERPETUAL, PERDURABLE — **sta·bil·i·ty** \stə-'bi-lə-tē\ *n*

stac·ca·to \stə-'kä-tō\ *adj or adv* [It] : cut short so as not to sound connected ⟨~ notes⟩

¹**stack** \'stak\ *n* 1 : a large pile (as of hay or grain) 2 : an orderly pile (as of poker chips) 3 : a large quantity 4 : a vertical pipe : SMOKESTACK 5 : a rack with shelves for storing books

²**stack** *vb* 1 : to pile up 2 : to arrange (cards) secretly for cheating

stack up *vb* : MEASURE UP ⟨how do they *stack up* against the competition?⟩

sta·di·um \'stā-dē-əm\ *n, pl* **-dia** \-dē-ə\ *or* **-di·ums** : a structure with tiers of seats for spectators built around a field for sports events

¹**staff** \'staf\ *n, pl* **staffs** \'stafs, 'stavz\ *or* **staves** \'stavz, 'stāvz\ 1 : a pole, stick, rod, or bar used for supporting, for measuring, or as a symbol of authority; *also* : CLUB, CUDGEL 2 : something that sustains ⟨bread is the ~ of life⟩ 3 : the five horizontal lines on which music is written 4 : a body of assistants to an executive 5 : a group of officers holding no command but having duties concerned with planning and managing

²**staff** *vb* : to supply with a staff or with workers

staff·er \'sta-fər\ *n* : a member of a staff (as of a newspaper)

staff sergeant *n* : a noncommissioned officer ranking in the army next below a sergeant first class, in the air force next below a technical sergeant, and in the marine corps next below a gunnery sergeant

¹**stag** \'stag\ *n, pl* **stags** *or* **stag** : an adult male of various large deer

²**stag** *adj* : restricted to or intended for men ⟨a ~ party⟩ ⟨~ movies⟩

³**stag** *adv* : unaccompanied by a date

¹**stage** \'stāj\ *n* [ME, fr. AF *estage* abode, story of a building, stage, fr. VL **staticum*, fr. L *stare* to stand] 1 : a raised platform on which an orator may speak or a play may be presented 2 : the acting profession : THEATER 3 : the scene of a notable action or event 4 : a station or resting place on a traveled road 5 : STAGECOACH 6 : a degree of advance in an undertaking, process, or development 7 : a propulsion unit in a rocket — **stagy** \'stā-jē\ *adj*

²**stage** *vb* **staged**; **stag·ing** : to produce or perform on or as if on a stage — **stage·able** *adj*

stage·coach \'stāj-,kōch\ *n* : a horse-drawn coach that runs regularly between stations

stage manager *n* : one who supervises the physical aspects of a stage production

stag·fla·tion \,stag-'flā-shən\ *n* : inflation with stagnant economic activity and high unemployment

¹**stag·ger** \'sta-gər\ *vb* 1 : to reel from side to side : TOTTER 2 : to begin to doubt : WAVER 3 : to cause to reel or waver 4 : to arrange in overlapping or alternating positions or times ⟨~ working hours⟩ 5 : ASTONISH — **stag·ger·ing·ly** *adv*

²**stagger** *n* 1 *sing or pl* : an abnormal condition of domestic animals associated with damage to the central nervous system and marked by lack of coordination and a reeling unsteady gait 2 : a reeling or unsteady gait or stance

stag·ing \'stā-jiŋ\ *n* 1 : SCAFFOLDING 2 : the assembling of troops and matériel in transit in a particular place

staging post *n* : STOPOVER 2

stag·nant \'stag-nənt\ *adj* 1 : not flowing : MOTIONLESS ⟨~ water in a pond⟩ 2 : DULL, INACTIVE ⟨~ business⟩

stag·nate \'stag-,nāt\ *vb* **stag·nat·ed**; **stag·nat·ing** : to be or become stagnant — **stag·na·tion** \stag-'nā-shən\ *n*

staid \'stād\ *adj* : SOBER, SEDATE ♦ *Synonyms* GRAVE, SERIOUS, EARNEST

¹**stain** \'stān\ *vb* 1 : DISCOLOR, SOIL 2

: TAINT, CORRUPT **3** : DISGRACE **4** : to color (as wood, paper, or cloth) by processes affecting the material itself

²**stain** n **1** : a small soiled or discolored area **2** : a taint of guilt : STIGMA **3** : a preparation (as a dye or pigment) used in staining — **stain·less** adj

stainless steel n : steel alloyed with chromium that is highly resistant to stain, rust, and corrosion

stair \'ster\ n **1** : a series of steps or flights of steps for passing from one level to another — often used in pl. **2** : one step of a stairway

stair·case \-,kās\ n : a flight of steps with their supporting framework, casing, and balusters

stair·way \-,wā\ n : one or more flights of stairs with connecting landings

stair·well \-,wel\ n : a vertical shaft in which stairs are located

¹**stake** \'stāk\ n **1** : a pointed piece of material (as of wood) driven into the ground as a marker or a support **2** : a post to which a person is bound for death by burning; also : execution by burning at the stake **3** : something that is staked for gain or loss **4** : the prize in a contest

²**stake** vb **staked**; **stak·ing 1** : to mark the limits of by or as if by stakes **2** : to tie to a stake **3** : to support or secure with stakes **4** : BET, WAGER

stake·out \'stāk-,aut\ n : a surveillance by police (as of a suspected criminal)

sta·lac·tite \sta-'lak-,tīt\ n [NL stalactites, fr. Gk stalaktos dripping, fr. stalassein to let drip] : an icicle-shaped deposit hanging from the roof or sides of a cavern

sta·lag·mite \sta-'lag-,mīt\ n [NL stalagmites, fr. Gk stalagma drop or stalagmos dripping, fr. stalassein to let drip] : a deposit resembling an inverted stalactite rising from the floor of a cavern

stale \'stāl\ adj **stal·er**; **stal·est 1** : having lost good taste and quality from age ⟨~ bread⟩ **2** : used or heard so often as to be dull ⟨~ news⟩ **3** : not as strong or effective as before ⟨~ from lack of practice⟩ — **stale·ness** n

stale·mate \'stāl-,māt\ n : a drawn contest : DEADLOCK — **stalemate** vb

¹**stalk** \'stok\ n : a plant stem; also : any slender usu. upright supporting or connecting part — **stalked** \'stokt\ adj

²**stalk** vb **1** : to pursue (game) stealthily **2** : to walk stiffly or haughtily

¹**stall** \'stol\ n, **1** : a compartment in a stable or barn for one animal **2** : a booth or counter where articles may be displayed for sale **3** : a seat in a church choir; also : a church pew **4** chiefly Brit : a front orchestra seat in a theater

²**stall** vb : to bring or come to a standstill unintentionally ⟨~ an engine⟩

³**stall** n : the condition of an airfoil or aircraft in which lift is lost and the airfoil or aircraft tends to drop

⁴**stall** n [alter. of stale lure] : a ruse to deceive or delay

⁵**stall** vb : to hold off, divert, or delay by evasion or deception

stal·lion \'stal-yən\ n : a male horse

stal·wart \'stol-wərt\ adj : STOUT, STRONG; also : BRAVE, VALIANT

sta·men \'stā-mən\ n : an organ of a flower that produces pollen

stam·i·na \'sta-mə-nə\ n [L, pl. of stamen warp, thread of life spun by the Fates] : VIGOR, ENDURANCE

sta·mi·nate \'stā-mə-nət, 'sta-mə-, -,nāt\ adj **1** : having or producing stamens **2** : having stamens but no pistils

stam·mer \'sta-mər\ vb : to hesitate or stumble in speaking — **stammer** n — **stam·mer·er** n

¹**stamp** \'stamp; for 2 also 'stamp or 'stomp\ vb **1** : to pound or crush with a heavy instrument **2** : to strike or beat with the bottom of the foot **3** : IMPRESS, IMPRINT ⟨~ "paid" on the bill⟩ **4** : to cut out or indent with a stamp or die **5** : to attach a postage stamp to

²**stamp** n **1** : a device or instrument for stamping **2** : the mark made by stamping; also : a distinctive mark or quality **3** : the act of stamping **4** : a stamped or printed paper affixed to show that a charge has been paid ⟨postage ~⟩ ⟨tax ~⟩

¹**stam·pede** \stam-'pēd\ n : a wild headlong rush or flight esp. of frightened animals

²**stampede** vb **stam·ped·ed**; **stam·ped·ing 1** : to flee or cause to flee in panic **2** : to act or cause to act together suddenly and heedlessly

stance \'stans\ n : a way of standing

¹**stanch** \'stonch, 'stänch, 'stanch\ or **staunch** \'stonch, 'stänch\ vb : to check the flowing of (as blood); also : to cease flowing or bleeding

²**stanch** var of ²STAUNCH

stan·chion \'stan-chən\ n : an upright bar, post, or support

¹**stand** \'stand\ vb **stood** \'stud\; **standing 1** : to take or be at rest in an upright or firm position **2** : to assume a specified position **3** : to remain stationary or unchanged **4** : to be steadfast **5** : to act in resistance ⟨~ against a foe⟩ **6** : to maintain a relative position or rank **7** : to gather slowly and remain ⟨tears stood in her eyes⟩ **8** : to set upright **9** : ENDURE, TOLERATE ⟨I won't ~ for that⟩ **10** : to submit to ⟨~ trial⟩ — **stand pat** : to oppose or resist change

²**stand** n **1** : an act of standing, staying, or resisting **2** : a stop made to give a performance **3** : POSITION, VIEWPOINT **4** : a place taken by a witness to testify in court **5** pl : tiered seats for spectators **6** : a raised platform (as for speakers) **7** : a structure for a small retail business **8** : a structure for supporting or holding something upright ⟨music ~⟩ **9** : a group of plants growing in a continuous area

stand–alone \'stan-də-,lōn\ adj : SELF-CONTAINED; esp : capable of operation independent of a computer system

¹**stan·dard** \'stan-dərd\ n **1** : a figure adopted as an emblem by a people **2** : the personal flag of a ruler; also : FLAG

3 : something set up as a rule for measuring or as a model to be followed **4** : an upright support ⟨lamp ∼⟩

²**standard** *adj* **1** : used as or meeting a standard established by law or custom **2** : regularly and widely used ⟨a ∼ practice⟩ **3** : well established by usage in speech or writing

stan·dard–bear·er \-,ber-ər\ *n* : the leader of a cause

standard deviation *n* : a measure of dispersion in a set of data

stan·dard·ise *Brit var of* STANDARDIZE

stan·dard–is·sue \'stan-dərd-'i-shü\ *adj* : STANDARD, TYPICAL ⟨a ∼ blue suit⟩

stan·dard·ize \'stan-dər-,dīz\ *vb* **-ized; -iz·ing** : to make standard or uniform — **stan·dard·i·za·tion** \,stan-dər-də-'zā-shən\ *n*

standard of living : the necessities, comforts, and luxuries that a person or group is accustomed to

standard time *n* : the time established by law or by general usage over a region or country

¹**stand·by** \'stand-,bī\ *n, pl* **stand·bys** \-,bīz\ **1** : one that can be relied on **2** : a substitute in reserve — **on standby** : ready or available for immediate action or use

²**standby** *adj* **1** : ready for use **2** : relating to. airline travel in which the passenger must wait for an available unreserved seat — **standby** *adv*

stand–in \'stan-,din\ *n* **1** : someone employed to occupy an actor's place while lights and camera are readied **2** : SUBSTITUTE

¹**stand·ing** \'stan-diŋ\ *adj* **1** : ERECT ⟨∼ timber⟩ **2** : not flowing : STAGNANT **3** : remaining at the same level or amount for an indefinite period ⟨∼ offer⟩ **4** : PERMANENT ⟨a ∼ army⟩ **5** : done from a standing position ⟨a ∼ jump⟩

²**standing** *n* **1** : length of service; *also* : relative position in society or in a profession : RANK **2** : DURATION ⟨a custom of long ∼⟩

stand·off \-,dȯf\ *n* : TIE, DRAW

stand·off·ish \stan-'dȯ-fish\ *adj* : somewhat cold and reserved

stand·out \'stan-,daut\ *n* : something conspicuously excellent

stand·pipe \'stand-,pīp\ *n* : a high vertical pipe or reservoir for water used to produce a uniform pressure

stand·point \-,pȯint\ *n* : a position from which objects or principles are judged

stand·still \-,stil\ *n* : a state of rest

stand–up \'stan-,dəp\ *adj* : done or performing in a standing position ⟨a ∼ comic⟩ ⟨∼ comedy⟩

stank *past of* STINK

stan·za \'stan-zə\ *n* [It] : a group of lines forming a division of a poem

sta·pes \'stā-,pēz\ *n, pl* **stapes** *or* **sta·pe·des** \'stā-pə-,dēz\ : the innermost bone of the middle ear of mammals

staph \'staf\ *n* : STAPHYLOCOCCUS

staph·y·lo·coc·cus \,sta-fə-lō-'kä-kəs\ *n, pl* **-coc·ci** \-'kä-,kī, -'käk-,sī\ : any of a genus of spherical bacteria including

some pathogens of skin and mucous membranes — **staph·y·lo·coc·cal** \-'kä-kəl\ *adj*

sta·ple \'stā-pəl\ *n* : a U-shaped piece of metal or wire with sharp points to be driven into a surface or through thin layers (as paper) for attaching or holding together — **staple** *vb* — **sta·pler** *n*

²**staple** *n* **1** : a chief commodity or product **2** : a chief part of something ⟨a ∼ of their diet⟩ **3** : unmanufactured or raw material **4** : a textile fiber suitable for spinning into yarn

³**staple** *adj* **1** : regularly produced in large quantities **2** : PRINCIPAL, MAIN ⟨the ∼ crop⟩

¹**star** \'stär\ *n* **1** : a celestial body that appears as a fixed point of light; *esp* : such a body that is gaseous, self-luminous, and of great mass **2** : a planet or configuration of planets that is held in astrology to influence one's fortune — usu. used in pl. **3** *obs* : DESTINY **4** : a conventional figure representing a star; *esp* : ASTERISK **5** : an actor or actress playing the leading role **6** : a brilliant performer — **star·dom** \'stär-dəm\ *n* — **star·less** *adj* — **star·like** *adj* — **star·ry** *adj*

²**star** *vb* **starred; star·ring** **1** : to adorn with stars **2** : to mark with an asterisk **3** : to play the leading role

star anise *n* : the small brown star-shaped fruit of an Asian tree used as a spice esp. in Chinese cooking

star·board \'stär-bərd\ *n* [ME *sterbord*, fr. OE *stēorbord*, fr. *stēor-* steering oar + *bord* ship's side] : the right side of a ship or airplane looking forward — **starboard** *adj*

star·burst \'stär-bərst\ *n* : a pattern that resembles diverging rays of light

¹**starch** \'stärch\ *vb* : to stiffen with or as if with starch

²**starch** *n* : a complex carbohydrate that is stored in plants, is an important foodstuff, and is used in adhesives and sizes, in laundering, and in pharmacy — **starchy** *adj*

stare \'ster\ *vb* **stared; star·ing** : to look fixedly with wide-open eyes — **stare** *n* — **star·er** *n*

star·fish \'stär-,fish\ *n* : any of a class of echinoderms that have usu. five arms arranged around a central disk and feed largely on mollusks

star fruit *n* : CARAMBOLA 1

¹**stark** \'stärk\ *adj* **1** : rigid as if in death; *also* : STRICT **2** *archaic* : STRONG, ROBUST **3** : SHEER, UTTER ⟨∼ nonsense⟩ **4** : BARREN, DESOLATE ⟨∼ landscape⟩; *also* : UNADORNED ⟨∼ realism⟩ **5** : sharply delineated — **stark·ly** *adv*

²**stark** *adv* : WHOLLY, ABSOLUTELY ⟨∼ naked⟩

star·light \'stär-,līt\ *n* : the light given by the stars

star·ling \'stär-liŋ\ *n* : a dark brown or in summer glossy greenish black European bird related to the crows that is naturalized nearly worldwide and often considered a pest

¹**start** \'stärt\ *vb* **1** : to give an involuntary

twitch or jerk (as from surprise) **2** : BEGIN, COMMENCE **3** : to set going ⟨~ an engine⟩ **4** : to enter or cause to enter a game or contest; *also* : to be in the starting lineup — **start·er** *n*

²**start** *n* **1** : a sudden involuntary motion : LEAP **2** : a spasmodic and brief effort or action **3** : BEGINNING; *also* : the place of beginning

start·er \'stär-tər\ *adj* : being an item acquired with the expectation that a more elaborate one will be acquired in the future ⟨a ~ home⟩

star·tle \'stär-t°l\ *vb* **star·tled; star·tling** : to frighten or surprise suddenly : cause to start

star·tling *adj* : causing sudden fear, surprise, or anxiety — **star·tling·ly** *adv*

starve \'stärv\ *vb* **starved; starv·ing** [ME *sterven* to die, fr. OE *steorfan*] **1** : to die or cause to die from hunger **2** : to suffer extreme hunger or deprivation ⟨*starving* for affection⟩ **3** : to subdue by famine — **star·va·tion** \stär-'vā-shən\ *n*

starve·ling \'stärv-liŋ\ *n* : one that is thin from lack of nourishment

stash \'stash\ *vb* : to store in a secret place for future use — **stash** *n*

sta·sis \'stā-səs, 'sta-\ *n, pl* **sta·ses** \'stā-ˌsēz, 'sta-\ **1** : a stoppage or slowing of the normal flow of a bodily fluid (as blood) **2** : a state of static balance : STAGNATION

¹**stat** \'stat\ *adv* [L *statim*] : without delay : IMMEDIATELY

²**stat** *abbr* statute

¹**state** \'stāt\ *n* [ME *stat*, fr. AF & L; AF *estat*, fr. L *status*, fr. *stare* to stand] **1** : mode or condition of being ⟨the four ~*s* of matter⟩ **2** : condition of mind **3** : social position **4** : a body of people occupying a territory and organized under one government; *also* : the government of such a body of people **5** : one of the constituent units of a nation having a federal government — **state·hood** \-ˌhu̇d\ *n*

²**state** *vb* **stat·ed; stat·ing** **1** : to set by regulation or authority **2** : to express in words

state·craft \'stāt-ˌkraft\ *n* : the art of conducting state affairs

state·house \-ˌhau̇s\ *n* : the building in which a state legislature meets

state·ly \'stāt-lē\ *adj* **state·li·er; -est** **1** : having lofty dignity : HAUGHTY **2** : IMPRESSIVE, MAJESTIC ⟨~ homes⟩ ♦ **Synonyms** MAGNIFICENT, IMPOSING, AUGUST — **state·li·ness** *n*

state·ment \'stāt-mənt\ *n* **1** : the act or result of presenting in words **2** : a summary of a financial account

state·room \'stāt-ˌrüm, -ˌru̇m\ *n* : a private room on a ship or railroad car

state·side \'stāt-ˌsīd\ *adj* : of or relating to the U.S. as regarded from outside its continental limits — **stateside** *adv*

states·man \'stāts-mən\ *n* : a person engaged in fixing the policies and conducting the affairs of a government; *esp* : one wise and skilled in such matters — **states·man·like** *adj* — **states·man·ship** *n*

¹**stat·ic** \'sta-tik\ *adj* **1** : acting by mere weight without motion ⟨~ pressure⟩ **2** : relating to bodies at rest or forces in equilibrium **3** : showing little change **4** : not moving : not active **5** : of or relating to stationary charges of electricity **6** : of, relating to, or caused by radio static

²**static** *n* : noise produced in a radio or television receiver by atmospheric or other electrical disturbances

stat·in \'sta-t°n\ *n* : any of a group of drugs that inhibit the synthesis of cholesterol

¹**sta·tion** \'stā-shən\ *n* **1** : the place where a person or thing stands or is assigned to remain **2** : a regular stopping place on a transportation route : DEPOT **3** : a place where a fleet is assigned for duty **4** : a stock farm or ranch esp. in Australia or New Zealand **5** : social standing **6** : a complete assemblage of radio or television equipment for sending or receiving

²**station** *vb* : to assign to a station

sta·tion·ary \'stā-shə-ˌner-ē\ *adj* **1** : fixed in a station, course, or mode **2** : unchanging in condition ⟨a ~ population⟩

stationary front *n* : the boundary between two air masses neither of which is advancing

station break *n* : a pause in a radio or television broadcast to announce the identity of the network or station

sta·tio·ner \'stā-shə-nər\ *n* : one that sells stationery

sta·tio·nery \'stā-shə-ˌner-ē\ *n* : materials (as paper, pens, or ink) for writing; *esp* : letter paper with envelopes

station wagon *n* : an automobile having a long interior, one or more folding or removable rear seats, and usu. a door at the rear

sta·tis·tic \stə-'tis-tik\ *n* **1** : a single term or datum in a collection of statistics **2** : a quantity (as the mean) that is computed from a sample

sta·tis·tics \-tiks\ *n sing or pl* [G *Statistik* study of political facts and figures, fr. NL *statisticus* of politics, fr. L *status* state] : a branch of mathematics dealing with the collection, analysis, and interpretation of masses of numerical data; *also* : a collection of such numerical data — **sta·tis·ti·cal** \-ti-kəl\ *adj* — **sta·tis·ti·cal·ly** \-ti-k(ə-)lē\ *adv* — **stat·is·ti·cian** \ˌsta-tə-'sti-shən\ *n*

stat·u·ary \'sta-chə-ˌwer-ē\ *n, pl* **-ar·ies** **1** : the art of making statues **2** : STATUES

stat·ue \'sta-chü\ *n* : a likeness (as of a person or animal) sculptured, modeled, or cast in a solid substance

stat·u·esque \ˌsta-chə-'wesk\ *adj* : tall and shapely

stat·u·ette \ˌsta-chə-'wet\ *n* : a small statue

stat·ure \'sta-chər\ *n* **1** : natural height (as of a person) **2** : quality or status gained (as by achievement)

sta·tus \'stā-təs, 'sta-\ *n* **1** : the condition of a person in the eyes of others or of the law **2** : state or condition with respect to circumstances

sta·tus quo \-'kwō\ *n* [L, state in which] : the existing state of affairs

stat·ute \'sta-chüt\ *n* : a law enacted by a legislative body

stat·u·to·ry \'sta-chə-,tȯr-ē\ *adj* : imposed by statute : LAWFUL

statutory rape *n* : sexual intercourse with a person who is below the statutory age of consent

¹**staunch** *var of* ¹STANCH

²**staunch** \'stȯnch, 'stänch\ *adj* **1** : WATERTIGHT ⟨a ~ ship⟩ **2** : FIRM, STRONG; *also* : STEADFAST, LOYAL ♦ *Synonyms* RESOLUTE, CONSTANT, TRUE, FAITHFUL — **staunch·ly** *adv*

¹**stave** \'stāv\ *n* **1** : CUDGEL, STAFF **2** : any of several narrow strips of wood placed edge to edge to make something (as a barrel) **3** : STANZA

²**stave** *vb* **staved** *or* **stove** \'stōv\; **staving 1** : to break in the staves of; *also* : to break a hole in **2** : to drive or thrust away

staves *pl of* STAFF

¹**stay** \'stā\ *n* **1** : a strong rope or wire used to support a mast **2** : ¹GUY

²**stay** *vb* **stayed** \'stād\ *also* **staid** \'stād\; **stay·ing 1** : PAUSE, WAIT **2** : REMAIN **3** : to stand firm **4** : LIVE, DWELL, **5** : DELAY, POSTPONE **6** : to last out (as a race) **7** : STOP, CHECK **8** : to satisfy (as hunger) for a time ♦ *Synonyms* REMAIN, ABIDE, LINGER, TARRY

³**stay** *n* **1** : STOP, HALT **2** : a residence or sojourn in a place

⁴**stay** *n* **1** : PROP, SUPPORT **2** : CORSET — usu. used in pl.

⁵**stay** *vb* : to hold up : PROP

staying power *n* : STAMINA

stbd *abbr* starboard

std *abbr* standard

STD \,es-(,)tē-'dē\ *n* : SEXUALLY TRANSMITTED DISEASE

Ste *abbr* [F *sainte*] saint (female)

stead \'sted\ *n* **1** : ADVANTAGE ⟨stood him in good ~⟩ **2** : the place or function ordinarily occupied or carried out by another ⟨acted in her brother's ~⟩

stead·fast \'sted-,fast\ *adj* **1** : firmly fixed in place **2** : not subject to change **3** : firm in belief, determination, or adherence : LOYAL ♦ *Synonyms* RESOLUTE, TRUE, FAITHFUL, STAUNCH — **stead·fast·ly** *adv* — **stead·fast·ness** *n*

¹**steady** \'ste-dē\ *adj* **steadi·er; -est 1** : direct or sure in movement; *also* : CALM **2** : FIRM, FIXED ⟨held the pole ~⟩ **3** : STABLE ⟨~ prices⟩ **4** : not easily disturbed **5** : RELIABLE ⟨~ friends⟩ **6** : temperate in character or demeanor ♦ *Synonyms* UNIFORM, EVEN — **steadi·ly** \-də-lē\ *adv* — **steadi·ness** \-dē-nəs\ *n* — **steady** *adv*

²**steady** *vb* **stead·ied; steady·ing** : to make or become steady

steak \'stāk\ *n* : a slice of meat and esp. beef; *also* : a slice of a large fish

¹**steal** \'stēl\ *vb* **stole** \'stōl\; **sto·len** \'stō-lən\; **steal·ing 1** : to take and carry away without right or permission **2** : to come or go secretly or gradually **3** : to get for oneself slyly or by skill and daring

⟨~ a kiss⟩ ⟨~ the ball in basketball⟩ **4** : to gain or attempt to gain a base in baseball by running without the aid of a hit or an error ♦ *Synonyms* PILFER, FILCH, PURLOIN, SWIPE

²**steal** *n* **1** : an act of stealing **2** : BARGAIN

¹**stealth** \'stelth\ *n* **1** : secret or unobtrusive procedure **2** : an aircraft design intended to produce a weak radar return

²**stealth** *adj* : STEALTHY ⟨a ~ campaign⟩

stealthy \'stel-thē\ *adj* **stealth·i·er; -est** : done by stealth : FURTIVE, SLY ♦ *Synonyms* SECRET, COVERT, CLANDESTINE, SURREPTITIOUS, UNDERHANDED — **stealth·i·ly** \'stel-thə-lē\ *adv*

¹**steam** \'stēm\ *n* **1** : the vapor into which water is changed when heated to the boiling point **2** : water vapor when compressed so that it supplies heat and power **3** : POWER, FORCE, ENERGY — **steamy** *adj*

²**steam** *vb* **1** : to pass off as vapor **2** : to emit vapor **3** : to move by or as if by the agency of steam — **steam·er** *n*

steam·boat \'stēm-,bōt\ *n* : a boat driven by steam

steam engine *n* : a reciprocating engine having a piston driven by steam

steam·fit·ter \'stēm-,fi-tər\ *n* : a worker who puts in or repairs equipment (as steam pipes) for heating, ventilating, or refrigerating systems

steam·roll·er \-,rō-lər\ *n* : a machine for compacting roads or pavements — **steam·roll·er** *also* **steam·roll** \-,rōl\ *vb*

steam·ship \-,ship\ *n* : a ship driven by steam

steed \'stēd\ *n* : HORSE

¹**steel** \'stēl\ *n* **1** : iron treated with intense heat and mixed with carbon to make it hard and tough **2** : an article made of steel **3** : a quality (as hardness of mind) that suggests steel — **steel** *adj* — **steely** *adj*

²**steel** *vb* : to fill with courage or determination

steel wool *n* : long fine steel shavings used esp. for cleaning and polishing

¹**steep** \'stēp\ *adj* **1** : having a very sharp slope : PRECIPITOUS **2** : too high ⟨~ prices⟩ — **steep·ly** *adv* — **steep·ness** *n*

²**steep** *n* : a steep slope

³**steep** *vb* **1** : to soak in a liquid; *esp* : to extract the essence of by soaking ⟨~ tea⟩ **2** : SATURATE ⟨~ed in learning⟩

stee·ple \'stē-pəl\ *n* : a tall tapering structure built on top of a church tower; *also* : a church tower

stee·ple·chase \-,chās\ *n* [fr. the use of church steeples as landmarks to guide the riders] : a horse race across country; *also* : a race over a course obstructed by hurdles

¹**steer** \'stir\ *n* : a male bovine animal castrated before sexual maturity and usu. raised for beef

²**steer** *vb* **1** : to direct the course of (as by a rudder or wheel) **2** : GUIDE, CONTROL **3** : to pursue a course of action **4** : to be

subject to guidance or direction — **steers·man** \'stirz-mən\ *n*

steer·age \'stir-ij\ *n* **1** : DIRECTION, GUIDANCE **2** : a section in a passenger ship for passengers paying the lowest fares

stego·sau·rus \ˌste-gə-'sȯr-əs\ *n* : any of a genus of plant-eating armored dinosaurs with a series of bony plates along the backbone

stein \'stīn\ *n* : an earthenware mug

stel·lar \'ste-lər\ *adj* : of or relating to stars : resembling a star

¹stem \'stem\ *n* **1** : the main stalk of a plant; *also* : a plant part that supports another part (as a leaf or fruit) **2** : the bow of a ship **3** : a line of ancestry : STOCK **4** : that part of an inflected word which remains unchanged throughout a given inflection **5** : something resembling the stem of a plant — **stem·less** *adj* — **stemmed** \'stemd\ *adj*

²stem *vb* **stemmed; stem·ming** : to have a specified source : DERIVE

³stem *vb* **stemmed; stem·ming** : to make headway against ⟨~ the tide⟩

⁴stem *vb* **stemmed; stem·ming** : to stop or check by or as if by damming

stem cell *n* : an undifferentiated cell that may give rise to many different types of cells

stench \'stench\ *n* : STINK

sten·cil \'sten-səl\ *n* [prob. ultim. fr. ME *stanseld* brightly ornamented, fr. AF *estencelé* spangled, pp. of *estenceler* to sparkle, fr. *estencele* spark, fr. VL *stincilla*, alter. of L *scintilla*] : an impervious material (as metal or paper) perforated with lettering or a design through which a substance (as ink or paint) is applied to a surface to be printed — **stencil** *vb*

ste·nog·ra·phy \stə-'nä-grə-fē\ *n* : the art or process of writing in shorthand — **ste·nog·ra·pher** \-fər\ *n* — **steno·graph·ic** \ˌste-nə-'gra-fik\ *adj*

ste·no·sis \stə-'nō-səs\ *n, pl* **-no·ses** \-ˌsēz\ : a narrowing of a bodily passage or orifice

stent \'stent\ *n* : a short narrow tube inserted into an anatomical vessel esp. to keep a passage open

sten·to·ri·an \sten-'tȯr-ē-ən\ *adj* : extremely loud ⟨~ tones⟩

¹step \'step\ *n* **1** : a rest for the foot in ascending or descending : STAIR **2** : an advance made by raising one foot and putting it down elsewhere **3** : manner of walking **4** : a small space or distance **5** : a degree, rank, or plane in a series **6** : a sequential measure leading to a result

²step *vb* **stepped; step·ping 1** : to advance or recede by steps **2** : to go on foot : WALK **3** : to move along briskly **4** : to press down with the foot **5** : to measure by steps **6** : to construct or arrange in or as if in steps

step aerobics *n sing or pl* : aerobics that involves repeatedly stepping on and off a raised platform

step aside *vb* : STEP DOWN 1

step·broth·er \'step-ˌbrə-thər\ *n* : the son of one's stepparent by a former marriage

step·child \-ˌchī(-ə)ld\ *n* : a child of one's husband or wife by a former marriage

step·daugh·ter \-ˌdȯ-tər\ *n* : a daughter of one's wife or husband by a former marriage

step down *vb* **1** : to give up a position : RETIRE, RESIGN **2** : to lower (a voltage) by means of a transformer

step·fa·ther \-ˌfä-thər\ *n* : the husband of one's mother when distinct from one's natural or legal father

step·lad·der \'step-ˌla-dər\ *n* : a light portable set of steps in a hinged frame

step·moth·er \-ˌmə-thər\ *n* : the wife of one's father when distinct from one's natural or legal mother

step·par·ent \-ˌper-ənt\ *n* : a person who is a stepfather or stepmother

steppe \'step\ *n* [Russ *step'*] : dry level grass-covered treeless land in regions of wide temperature range esp. in southeastern Europe and Asia

step·sis·ter \'step-ˌsis-tər\ *n* : the daughter of one's stepparent by a former marriage

step·son \-ˌsən\ *n* : a son of one's wife or husband by a former marriage

step up *vb* **1** : to increase (a voltage) by means of a transformer **2** : INCREASE, ACCELERATE **3** : to come forward — **step–up** \'step-ˌəp\ *n*

ster *abbr* sterling

ste·reo \'ster-ē-ˌō, 'stir-\ *n, pl* **ste·re·os 1** : stereophonic reproduction **2** : a stereophonic sound system — **stereo** *adj*

ste·reo·phon·ic \ˌster-ē-ə-'fä-nik, ˌstir-\ *adj* : of or relating to sound reproduction designed to create the effect of listening to the original — **ste·reo·phon·i·cal·ly** \-'fä-ni-k(ə-)lē\ *adv*

ster·e·o·scope \'ster-ē-ə-ˌskōp, 'stir-\ *n* [Gk *stereos* solid + *-skopion* means for viewing] : an optical instrument that blends two slightly different pictures of the same subject to give the effect of depth

ste·reo·scop·ic \ˌster-ē-ə-'skä-pik, ˌstir-\ *adj* **1** : of or relating to the stereoscope **2** : characterized by the seeing of objects in three dimensions ⟨~ vision⟩ — **stereo·scop·i·cal·ly** \-'skä-pi-k(ə-)lē\ *adv* — **ste·re·os·co·py** \ˌster-ē-'äs-kə-pē, ˌstir-\ *n*

ste·reo·type \'ster-ē-ə-ˌtīp, 'stir-\ *n* **1** : a metal printing plate cast from a mold made from set type **2** : something agreeing with a pattern; *esp* : an idea that many people have about a thing or a group and that may often be untrue or only partly true — **stereotype** *vb* — **ste·reo·typ·i·cal** \ˌster-ē-ə-'ti-pi-kəl\ *adj* — **ste·reo·typ·i·cal·ly** \-pi-k(ə-)lē\ *adv*

ste·reo·typed \-ˌtīpt\ *adj* : lacking originality or individuality ✦ Synonyms TRITE, CLICHÉD, COMMONPLACE, HACKNEYED, STALE, THREADBARE

ster·ile \'ster-əl\ *adj* **1** : unable to bear fruit, crops, or offspring **2** : free from living things and esp. germs — **ste·ril·i·ty** \stə-'ri-lə-tē\ *n*

ster·il·ize \'ster-ə-ˌlīz\ *vb* **-ized; -iz·ing** : to make sterile; *esp* : to free from germs

— **ster·il·i·za·tion** \ˌster-ə-lə-ˈzā-shən\ n
— **ster·il·iz·er** \ˈster-ə-ˌlī-zər\ n

¹**ster·ling** \ˈstər-liŋ\ n **1** : British money **2** : sterling silver

²**sterling** adj **1** : of, relating to, or calculated in terms of British sterling **2** : having a fixed standard of purity represented by an alloy of 925 parts of silver with 75 parts of copper **3** : made of sterling silver **4** : EXCELLENT ⟨a ~ record of achievement⟩

¹**stern** \ˈstərn\ adj **1** : SEVERE, AUSTERE ⟨~ taskmasters⟩ **2** : STOUT, STURDY ⟨~ resolve⟩ — **stern·ly** adv — **stern·ness** n

²**stern** n : the rear end of a boat

ster·num \ˈstər-nəm\ n, pl **sternums** or **ster·na** \-nə\ : a long flat bone or cartilage at the center front of the chest connecting the ribs of the two sides

ste·roid \ˈstir-ˌȯid, ˈster-\ n : any of various compounds including numerous hormones (as anabolic steroids) and sugar derivatives — **steroid** or **ste·roi·dal** \stə-ˈrȯi-dᵊl\ adj

stetho·scope \ˈste-thə-ˌskōp\ n : an instrument used to detect and listen to sounds produced in the body

ste·ve·dore \ˈstē-və-ˌdȯr\ n [Sp estibador, fr. estibar to pack, fr. L stipare to press together] : one who works at loading and unloading ships

¹**stew** \ˈstü, ˈstyü\ n **1** : a dish of stewed meat and vegetables served in gravy **2** : a state of agitation, worry, or resentment

²**stew** vb **1** : to boil slowly : SIMMER **2** : to be in a state of agitation, worry, or resentment

stew·ard \ˈstü-ərd, ˈstyü-\ n [ME, fr. OE stīweard, fr. stī, stig hall, sty + weard ward] **1** : one employed on a large estate to manage domestic concerns **2** : one who supervises the provision and distribution of food ⟨also⟩ : an employee on a ship or airplane who serves passengers **3** : one actively concerned with the direction of the affairs of an organization — **stew·ard·ship** n

stew·ard·ess \ˈstü-ər-dəs, ˈstyü-\ n : a woman who is a steward esp. on an airplane

stg abbr sterling

¹**stick** \ˈstik\ n **1** : a cut or broken branch or twig; also : a long slender piece of wood **2** : ROD, STAFF **3** : something resembling a stick **4** : a dull uninteresting person **5** pl : remote usu. rural areas

²**stick** vb **stuck** \ˈstək\; **stick·ing** **1** : STAB, PRICK **2** : IMPALE **3** : ATTACH, FASTEN **4** : to thrust or project in some direction or manner **5** : to be unable to proceed or move freely **6** : to hold fast to or as if by gluing : ADHERE **7** : to hold to something firmly or closely : CLING **8** : to become jammed or blocked

stick·er \ˈsti-kər\ n : one that sticks (as a bur) or causes sticking (as glue); esp : an adhesive label

sticker shock n : astonishment and dismay on being informed of a product's unexpectedly high price

stick insect n : any of various usu. wing-

less insects with a long round body resembling a stick

stick·ler \ˈsti-klər, -kə-lər\ n : one who insists on exactness or completeness

stick shift n : a manually operated automobile gearshift usu. mounted on the floor

stick-to-it-ive·ness \stik-ˈtü-ə-tiv-nəs\ n : dogged perseverance : TENACITY

stick up vb : to rob at gunpoint — **stick-up** \ˈstik-ˌəp\ n

sticky \ˈsti-kē\ adj **stick·i·er**; **-est** **1** : ADHESIVE **2** : VISCOUS, GLUEY **3** : tending to stick ⟨~ valve⟩ **4** : DIFFICULT

¹**stiff** \ˈstif\ adj **1** : not pliant : RIGID **2** : not limber ⟨~ joints⟩; also : TENSE, TAUT **3** : not flowing or working easily ⟨~ paste⟩ **4** : not natural and easy : FORMAL **5** : STRONG, FORCEFUL ⟨~ breeze⟩ **6** : HARSH, SEVERE ⟨a ~ penalty⟩ ♦ **Synonyms** INFLEXIBLE, INELASTIC — **stiff·ly** adv — **stiff·ness** n

²**stiff** vb : to refuse to pay or tip

stiff-arm \ˈstif-ˌärm\ vb : to treat with disdain or neglect ⟨~ed her advice⟩

stiff·en \ˈsti-fən\ vb : to make or become stiff — **stiff·en·er** n

stiff-necked \ˈstif-ˈnekt\ adj : STUBBORN, HAUGHTY

sti·fle \ˈstī-fəl\ vb **sti·fled**; **sti·fling** **1** : to kill by depriving of or die from lack of oxygen or air : SMOTHER **2** : to keep in check by effort : SUPPRESS ⟨~ a sneeze⟩ — **sti·fling·ly** adv

stig·ma \ˈstig-mə\ n, pl **stig·ma·ta** \stig-ˈmä-tə, ˈstig-mə-tə\ or **stigmas** [L] **1** : a mark of disgrace or discredit **2** stigmata pl : bodily marks resembling the wounds of the crucified Jesus **3** : the upper part of the pistil of a flower that receives the pollen in fertilization — **stig·mat·ic** \stig-ˈma-tik\ adj

stig·ma·tize \ˈstig-mə-ˌtīz\ vb **-tized**; **-tizing** **1** : to mark with a stigma **2** : to characterize as disgraceful

stile \ˈstī(-ə)l\ n : steps used for crossing a fence or wall

sti·let·to \stə-ˈle-tō\ n, pl **-tos** or **-toes** [It, dim. of stilo stylus, dagger] : a slender dagger

¹**still** \ˈstil\ adj **1** : MOTIONLESS **2** : making no sound : SILENT — **still·ness** n

²**still** vb : to make or become still

³**still** adv **1** : without motion ⟨sit ~⟩ **2** : up to and during this or that time **3** : in spite of that : NEVERTHELESS **4** : EVEN ⟨ran ~ faster⟩ **5** : YET ⟨has ~ to be recognized⟩

⁴**still** n **1** : STILLNESS, SILENCE **2** : a static photograph esp. from a motion picture

⁵**still** n **1** : DISTILLERY **2** : apparatus used in distillation

still-birth \ˈstil-ˌbərth\ n : the birth of a dead fetus

still-born \-ˈbȯrn\ adj : born dead

still life n, pl **still lifes** : a picture of inanimate objects

stilt \ˈstilt\ n : one of a pair of poles for walking with each having a step or loop for the foot to elevate the wearer above the ground; *also* : a polelike support of a structure above ground or water level

stilt·ed \'stil-təd\ *adj* : not easy and natural ⟨~ language⟩

Stil·ton \'stil-t²n\ *n* : a blue cheese of English origin

stim·u·lant \'sti-myə-lənt\ *n* **1** : an agent (as a drug) that temporarily increases the activity of an organism or any of its parts **2** : STIMULUS **3** : an alcoholic beverage — **stimulant** *adj*

stim·u·late \-ˌlāt\ *vb* **-lat·ed; -lat·ing** : to make active or more active : ANIMATE, AROUSE ✦ *Synonyms* EXCITE, PROVOKE, MOTIVATE, QUICKEN — **stim·u·la·tion** \ˌsti-myə-'lā-shən\ *n* — **stim·u·la·tive** \'sti-myə-ˌlā-tiv\ *adj* — **stim·u·la·tor** \-ˌlā-tər\ *n* — **stim·u·la·to·ry** \-lə-ˌtȯr-ē\ *adj*

stim·u·lus \'sti-myə-ləs\ *n, pl* **-li** \-ˌlī\ [L] **1** : something that moves to activity **2** : an agent that directly influences the activity of a living organism or one of its parts

¹**sting** \'stiŋ\ *vb* **stung** \'stəŋ\; **sting·ing 1** : to prick painfully esp. with a sharp or poisonous process **2** : to cause to suffer acutely — **sting·er** *n*

²**sting** *n* **1** : an act of stinging; *also* : a resultant wound, sore, or pain **2** : a pointed often venom-bearing organ (as of a bee) : STINGER **3** : an elaborate confidence game; *esp* : one worked by undercover police to trap criminals

sting·ray \'stiŋ-ˌrā\ *n* : any of numerous rays with sharp stinging spines on a whiplike tail

stin·gy \'stin-jē\ *adj* **stin·gi·er; -est** : not generous : giving or spending as little as possible — **stin·gi·ness** *n*

stink \'stiŋk\ *vb* **stank** \'staŋk\ *or* **stunk** \'stəŋk\; **stunk; stink·ing** : to give forth a strong and offensive smell; *also* : to be extremely bad in quality or repute — **stink** *n* — **stink·er** *n*

stink·bug \'stiŋk-ˌbəg\ *n* : any of various true bugs that emit a disagreeable odor

¹**stint** \'stint\ *vb* **1** : to be sparing or frugal **2** : to cut short in amount

²**stint** *n* **1** : an assigned amount of work **2** : RESTRAINT, LIMITATION **3** : a period of time spent at a particular activity

sti·pend \'stī-ˌpend, -pənd\ *n* [ME, alter. of *stipendy*, fr. L *stipendium*, fr. *stips* gift + *pendere* to weigh, pay] : a fixed sum of money paid periodically for services or to defray expenses

stip·ple \'sti-pəl\ *vb* **stip·pled; stip·pling 1** : to engrave by means of dots and light strokes **2** : to apply (as paint or ink) with small short touches — **stipple** *n*

stip·u·late \'sti-pyə-ˌlāt\ *vb* **-lat·ed; -lat·ing** : to make an agreement; *esp* : to make a special demand for something as a condition in an agreement — **stip·u·la·tion** \ˌsti-pyə-'lā-shən\ *n*

¹**stir** \'stər\ *vb* **stirred; stir·ring 1** : to move slightly **2** : AROUSE, EXCITE **3** : to mix, dissolve, or make by continued circular movement ⟨~ eggs into cake bat-

ter⟩ **4** : to move to activity (as by pushing, beating, or prodding)

²**stir** *n* **1** : a state of agitation or activity **2** : an act of stirring

stir-fry \'stər-ˌfrī\ *vb* : to fry quickly over high heat while stirring continuously — **stir-fry** *n*

¹**stir·ring** \'stər-iŋ\ *adj* **1** : ACTIVE, BUSTLING **2** : ROUSING, INSPIRING ⟨a ~ speech⟩

²**stirring** *n* : a beginning of activity ⟨the first ~s of revolution⟩

stir·rup \'stər-əp\ *n* [ME *stirop*, fr. OE *stigrāp*, lit., mounting rope] **1** : a light frame hung from a saddle to support the rider's foot **2** : STAPES

¹**stitch** \'stich\ *n* **1** : a sudden sharp pain esp. in the side **2** : one of the series of loops formed by or over a needle in sewing

²**stitch** *vb* **1** : to fasten or join with stitches **2** : to decorate with stitches **3** : SEW

stk *abbr* stock

stoat \'stōt\ *n, pl* **stoats** *also* **stoat** : the common Old and New World ermine esp. in its brown summer coat

¹**stock** \'stäk\ *n* **1** *archaic* : a block of wood **2** : a stupid person **3** : a wooden part of a thing serving as its support, frame, or handle **4** *pl* : a device for publicly punishing offenders consisting of a wooden frame with holes in which the feet and hands can be locked **5** : the original from which others derive; *also* : a group having a common origin : FAMILY **6** : LIVESTOCK **7** : a supply of goods **8** : the ownership element in a corporation divided to give the owners an interest and usu. voting power **9** : a company of actors playing at a particular theater and presenting a series of plays **10** : liquid in which meat, fish, or vegetables have been simmered that is used as a basis for soup, gravy, or sauce

²**stock** *vb* : to provide with stock

³**stock** *adj* : kept regularly for sale or use; *also* : commonly used : STANDARD

stock·ade \stä-'kād\ *n* [Sp *estacada*, fr. *estaca* stake, pale, of Gmc origin] : an enclosure (as of posts and stakes) for defense or confinement

stock·bro·ker \-ˌbrō-kər\ *n* : one who executes orders to buy and sell securities

stock car *n* : a racing car that is similar to a regular car

stock exchange *n* : a place where the buying and selling of securities is conducted

stock·hold·er \'stäk-ˌhōl-dər\ *n* : one who owns corporate stock

stock·i·nette *or* **stock·i·net** \ˌstä-kə-'net\ *n* : an elastic knitted fabric used esp. for infants' wear and bandages

stock·ing \'stä-kiŋ\ *n* : a close-fitting knitted covering for the foot and leg

stock market *n* **1** : STOCK EXCHANGE **2** : a market for stocks

stock·pile \'stäk-ˌpī(-ə)l\ *n* : a reserve supply esp. of something essential — **stock·pile** *vb*

stocky \'stä-kē\ *adj* **stock·i·er; -est** : being short and relatively thick : STUR-

DY ✦ *Synonyms* THICKSET, SQUAT, HEAVYSET, STUBBY

stock·yard \'stäk-ˌyärd\ *n* : a yard for stock; *esp* : one for livestock about to be slaughtered or shipped

stodgy \'stä-jē\ *adj* **stodg·i·er; -est** **1** : thick in texture : HEAVY ⟨~ bread⟩ **2** : not interesting : DULL ⟨a ~ accountant⟩ **3** : extremely old-fashioned

¹sto·ic \'stō-ik\ *n* [ME, fr. L *stoicus*, fr. Gk *stōikos*, lit., of the portico, fr. *Stoa* (*Poikilē*) the Painted Portico, portico at Athens where the philosopher Zeno taught] : one who suffers without complaining

²stoic *or* **sto·i·cal** \-i-kəl\ *adj* : not affected by passion or feeling; *esp* : showing indifference to pain ✦ *Synonyms* IMPASSIVE, PHLEGMATIC, APATHETIC, STOLID — **sto·i·cal·ly** \-i-k(ə-)lē\ *adv* — **sto·icism** \'stō-ə-ˌsi-zəm\ *n*

stoke \'stōk\ *vb* **stoked; stok·ing** **1** : to stir up a fire **2** : to tend and supply fuel to a furnace — **stok·er** *n*

STOL *abbr* short takeoff and landing

¹stole *past of* STEAL

²stole \'stōl\ *n* **1** : a long narrow band worn round the neck by some members of the clergy **2** : a long wide scarf or similar covering worn by women

stolen *past part of* STEAL

stol·id \'stä-ləd\ *adj* : not easily aroused or excited : showing little or no emotion ✦ *Synonyms* PHLEGMATIC, APATHETIC, IMPASSIVE, STOIC — **sto·lid·i·ty** \stä-'li-də-tē\ *n* — **stol·id·ly** *adv*

sto·lon \'stō-lən, -ˌlän\ *n* : RUNNER 6

¹stom·ach \'stə-mək\ *n* **1** : a saclike digestive organ of a vertebrate into which food goes from the mouth by way of the throat and which opens below into the intestine **2** : a cavity in an invertebrate animal that is analogous to a stomach **3** : ABDOMEN **4** : desire for food caused by hunger : APPETITE **5** : INCLINATION, DESIRE ⟨had no ~ for an argument⟩

²stomach *vb* : to bear without open resentment : put up with

stom·ach·ache \-ˌāk\ *n* : pain in or in the region of the stomach

stom·ach·er \'stə-mi-kər, -chər\ *n* : the front of a bodice often appearing between the laces of an outer garment (as in 16th century costume)

stomp \'stämp, 'stômp\ *vb* : STAMP — **stomp** *n*

¹stone \'stōn\ *n* **1** : hardened earth or mineral matter : ROCK **2** : a small piece of rock **3** : a precious stone : GEM **4** : CALCULUS **3** **5** : a hard stony seed (as of a date) or one (as of a plum) with a stony covering **6** *pl usu* **stone** : a British unit of weight equal to 14 pounds — **stony** *also* **ston·ey** \'stō-nē\ *adj*

²stone *vb* **stoned; ston·ing** **1** : to pelt or kill with stones **2** : to remove the stones of (a fruit)

Stone Age *n* : the first known period of prehistoric human culture characterized by the use of stone tools

stoned \'stōnd\ *adj* **1** : DRUNK **2** : being under the influence of a drug

stone·wall \'stōn-ˌwôl\ *vb* : to refuse to comply or cooperate with

stone·washed \'stōn-ˌwôsht, -ˌwäsht\ *adj* : having been washed with stones during manufacture to create a softer fabric ⟨~ jeans⟩

stood *past and past part of* STAND

stooge \'stüj\ *n* **1** : a person who plays a subordinate or compliant role to a principal **2** : STRAIGHT MAN

stool \'stül\ *n* **1** : a seat usu. without back or arms **2** : FOOTSTOOL **3** : a seat used while urinating or defecating **4** : a discharge of fecal matter

stool pigeon *n* : DECOY, INFORMER

¹stoop \'stüp\ *vb* **1** : to bend forward and downward **2** : CONDESCEND **3** : to lower oneself morally

²stoop *n* **1** : an act of bending forward **2** : a bent position of head and shoulders

³stoop *n* [D *stoep*] : a porch, platform, or entrance stairway at a house door

¹stop \'stäp\ *vb* **stopped; stop·ping** **1** : to close (an opening) by filling or covering closely **2** : BLOCK, HALT **3** : to cease to go on **4** : to bring activity or operation to an end **5** : STAY, TARRY ✦ *Synonyms* QUIT, DISCONTINUE, DESIST, CEASE

²stop *n* **1** : END, CESSATION **2** : a set of organ pipes of one tone quality; *also* : a control knob for such a set **3** : OBSTRUCTION **4** : PLUG, STOPPER **5** : an act of stopping : CHECK **6** : a delay in a journey : STAY **7** : a place for stopping **8** *chiefly Brit* : any of several punctuation marks **9** : a function of an electronic device that stops a recording

stop–ac·tion \'stäp-'ak-shən\ *n* : STOP-MOTION

stop·gap \'stäp-ˌgap\ *n* : something that serves as a temporary expedient

stop·light \-ˌlīt\ *n* : TRAFFIC LIGHT

stop–mo·tion \'stäp-'mō-shən\ *n* : a filming technique in which successive positions of objects are photographed to produce the appearance of movement

stop·over \'stäp-ˌō-vər\ *n* **1** : a stop at an intermediate point in one's journey **2** : a stopping place on a journey

stop·page \'stä-pij\ *n* : the act of stopping : the state of being stopped

stop·per \'stä-pər\ *n* : something (as a cork) for sealing an opening

stop·watch \'stäp-ˌwäch\ *n* : a watch that can be started or stopped at will for exact timing

stor·age \'stór-ij\ *n* **1** : space for storing; *also* : cost of storing **2** : MEMORY 6 **3** : the act of storing; *esp* : the safekeeping of goods (as in a warehouse)

storage battery *n* : a group of connected rechargeable electrochemical cells used to provide electric current

¹store \'stór\ *vb* **stored; stor·ing** **1** : to place or leave in a safe location for preservation or future use **2** : to provide esp. for a future need

²store *n* **1** : something accumulated and kept for future use **2** : a large or ample quantity **3** : STOREHOUSE **4** : a retail business establishment

store·house \-ˌhau̇s\ *n* : a building for storing goods or supplies; *also* : an abundant source or supply

store·keep·er \-ˌkē-pər\ *n* : one who operates a retail store

store·room \-ˌrüm, -ˌru̇m\ *n* : a room for storing goods or supplies

sto·ried \'stȯr-ēd\ *adj* : celebrated in story or history

stork \'stȯrk\ *n* : any of various large stout-billed Old World wading birds related to the herons and ibises

¹**storm** \'stȯrm\ *n* **1** : a heavy fall of rain, snow, or hail with high wind **2** : a violent outbreak or disturbance **3** : a mass attack on a defended position — **storm·i·ly** \'stȯr-mə-lē\ *adv* — **storm·i·ness** \-mē-nəs\ *n* — **stormy** *adj*

²**storm** *vb* **1** : to blow with violence; *also* : to rain, snow, or hail heavily **2** : to make a mass attack against **3** : to be violently angry : RAGE **4** : to rush along furiously

¹**sto·ry** \'stȯr-ē\ *n, pl* **stories 1** : NARRATIVE, ACCOUNT **2** : REPORT, STATEMENT **3** : ANECDOTE **4** : SHORT STORY **5** : LIE, FALSEHOOD **6** : a news article or broadcast ✦ *Synonyms* UNTRUTH, TALE, CANARD

²**story** *also* **sto·rey** \'stȯr-ē\ *n, pl* **stories** *also* **storeys** : a floor of a building or the space between two adjacent floor levels

sto·ry·tell·er \-ˌte-lər\ *n* : a teller of stories

sto·tin \stō-'tēn\ *n, pl* **sto·ti·nov** \stō-'tē-ˌnȯv\ — see *tolar* at MONEY table

sto·tin·ka \stō-'tin-kə\ *n, pl* **-tin·ki** \-kē\ — see *lev* at MONEY table

¹**stout** \'stau̇t\ *adj* **1** : BRAVE **2** : FIRM ⟨a ~ refusal⟩ **3** : STURDY **4** : STAUNCH, ENDURING ⟨~ loyalty⟩ **5** : SOLID **6** : FORCEFUL, VIOLENT ⟨a ~ attack⟩ **7** : BULKY, THICKSET ✦ *Synonyms* FLESHY, FAT, PORTLY, CORPULENT, OBESE, PLUMP — **stout·ly** *adv* — **stout·ness** *n*

²**stout** *n* : a dark heavy ale

¹**stove** \'stōv\ *n* : an apparatus that burns fuel or uses electricity to provide heat (as for cooking or heating)

²**stove** *past and past part of* STAVE

stow \'stō\ *vb* **1** : HIDE, STORE **2** : to pack in a compact mass

stow·away \'stō-ə-ˌwā\ *n* : one who hides on a vehicle to ride free

STP *abbr* standard temperature and pressure

strad·dle \'stra-dᵊl\ *vb* **strad·dled; strad·dling 1** : to stand, sit, or walk with legs spread apart **2** : to favor or seem to favor two apparently opposite sides — **straddle** *n*

strafe \'strāf\ *vb* **strafed; straf·ing** [G *Gott strafe England* may God punish England, propaganda slogan during World War I] : to fire upon with machine guns from a low-flying airplane

strag·gle \'stra-gəl\ *vb* **strag·gled; straggling 1** : to wander from the direct course : ROVE, STRAY **2** : to become separated from others of the same kind —

strag·gler *n* — **strag·gly** \'stra-g(ə-)lē\ *adj*

¹**straight** \'strāt\ *adj* **1** : free from curves, bends, angles, or irregularities **2** : not wandering from the main point or proper course ⟨~ thinking⟩ **3** : HONEST ⟨a ~ answer⟩ **4** : having the elements in correct order **5** : UNMIXED, UNDILUTED ⟨~ whiskey⟩ **6** : CONVENTIONAL, SQUARE **7** : HETEROSEXUAL

²**straight** *adv* : in a straight manner

³**straight** *n* **1** : a straight line, course, or arrangement **2** : the part of a racetrack between the last turn and the finish **3** : a sequence of five cards in a poker hand

straight–arm \'strāt-ˌärm\ *n* : an act of warding off a person with the arm fully extended — **straight–arm** *vb*

straight·away \'strā-tə-ˌwā\ *n* : a straight stretch (as at a racetrack)

straight·edge \'strāt-ˌej\ *n* : a piece of material with a straight edge for testing straight lines and surfaces or for cutting along or drawing straight lines

straight·en \'strā-tᵊn\ *vb* : to make or become straight

straight flush *n* : a poker hand containing five cards of the same suit in sequence

straight·for·ward \strāt-'fȯr-wərd\ *adj* **1** : FRANK, CANDID, HONEST ⟨a ~ account⟩ **2** : proceeding in a straight course or manner

straight man *n* : an entertainer who feeds lines to a comedian who replies with usu. humorous quips

straight shooter *n* : a thoroughly upright straightforward person

straight·way \'strāt-'wā, -ˌwā\ *adv* : IMMEDIATELY ⟨get ~ to work⟩

¹**strain** \'strān\ *n* [ME *streen* progeny, lineage, fr. OE *strēon* gain, acquisition] **1** : LINEAGE, ANCESTRY **2** : a group (as of people or plants) of presumed common ancestry **3** : an inherited or inherent character or quality ⟨a ~ of madness in the family⟩ **4** : STREAK, TRACE ⟨a ~ of fanaticism⟩ **5** : MELODY **6** : the general style or tone

²**strain** *vb* [ME, fr. AF *estreindre*, fr. L *stringere* to bind or draw tight, press together] **1** : to draw taut **2** : to exert to the utmost **3** : to strive violently **4** : to injure by improper or excessive use **5** : to filter or remove by filtering **6** : to stretch beyond a proper limit — **strain·er** *n*

³**strain** *n* **1** : excessive tension or exertion (as of body or mind) **2** : bodily injury from excessive tension, effort, or use; *esp* : one in which muscles or ligaments are unduly stretched usu. from a wrench or twist **3** : deformation of a material body under the action of applied forces

¹**strait** \'strāt\ *adj* [ME, fr. AF *estreit*, fr. L *strictus* strait, strict, fr. pp. of *stringere*] **1** *archaic* : STRICT **2** *archaic* : NARROW **3** *archaic* : CONSTRICTED **4** : DIFFICULT, STRAITENED

²**strait** *n* **1** : a narrow channel connecting two bodies of water **2** *pl* : DISTRESS

strait·en \'strā-tᵊn\ *vb* **1** : to hem in : CONFINE **2** : to make distressing or difficult

strait·jack·et also **straight·jack·et** \'strāt-ja-kət\ n : a cover or garment of strong material (as canvas) used to bind the body and esp. the arms closely in restraining a violent prisoner or patient — **straitjacket** vb

strait·laced or **straight·laced** \-'lāst\ adj : strict in manners, morals, or opinion

¹**strand** \'strand\ n : SHORE, BEACH

²**strand** vb 1 : to run, drift, or drive upon the shore ⟨a ~ed ship⟩ 2 : to place or leave in a helpless position

³**strand** n 1 : one of the fibers twisted or plaited together into a cord, rope, or cable; also : a cord, rope, or cable made up of such fibers 2 : a twisted or plaited ropelike mass ⟨a ~ of pearls⟩ — **strand·ed** \'stran-dəd\ adj

¹**strange** \'strānj\ adj **strang·er**; **strang·est** [ME, fr. AF estrange, fr. L extraneus, lit., external, fr. extra outside] 1 : of external origin, kind, or character 2 : NEW, UNFAMILIAR ⟨moved to a ~ neighborhood⟩ 3 : DISTANT 6 4 : UNACCUSTOMED, INEXPERIENCED ⟨she was ~ to his ways⟩ ♦ **Synonyms** SINGULAR, PECULIAR, ECCENTRIC, ERRATIC, ODD, QUEER, QUAINT, CURIOUS — **strange·ly** adv — **strange·ness** n

²**strange** n : a quark with a charge of −⅓ and a measured energy of approximately 150 million electron volts

strang·er \'strān-jər\ n 1 : FOREIGNER 2 : INTRUDER 3 : a person with whom one is unacquainted

stran·gle \'straŋ-gəl\ vb **stran·gled**; **stran·gling** 1 : to choke to death : THROTTLE 2 : STIFLE, SUPPRESS ⟨repression ~s free speech⟩ — **stran·gler** n

strangler fig n : any of several figs that begin life atop a host tree and then send down roots that surround it

stran·gu·late \'straŋ-gyə-ˌlāt\ vb **-lat·ed**; **-lat·ing** 1 : STRANGLE, CONSTRICT 2 : to become so constricted as to stop circulation

stran·gu·la·tion \ˌstraŋ-gyə-'lā-shən\ n : the act or process of strangling or strangulating; also : the state of being strangled or strangulated

¹**strap** \'strap\ n : a narrow strip of flexible material used esp. for fastening, holding together, or wrapping

²**strap** vb **strapped**; **strap·ping** 1 : to secure with a strap 2 : BIND, CONSTRICT 3 : to flog with a strap 4 : STROP

strap·less \-ləs\ adj : having no straps; esp : having no shoulder straps

¹**strap·ping** adj : LARGE, STRONG, HUSKY

²**strapping** n : material for a strap

strat·a·gem \'stra-tə-jəm, -ˌjem\ n 1 : a trick to deceive or outwit the enemy; also : a deceptive scheme 2 : skill in deception

strat·e·gy \'stra-tə-jē\ n, pl **-gies** [Gk stratēgia generalship, fr. stratēgos general, fr. stratos camp, army + agein to lead] 1 : the science and art of military command aimed at meeting the enemy under conditions advantageous to one's own force 2 : a careful plan or method esp. for achieving an end — **stra·te·gic** \strə-'tē-jik\ adj — **strat·e·gist** \'stra-tə-jist\ n

strat·i·fy \'stra-tə-ˌfī\ vb **-fied**; **-fy·ing** : to form or arrange in layers — **strat·i·fi·ca·tion** \ˌstra-tə-fə-'kā-shən\ n

stra·tig·ra·phy \strə-'ti-grə-fē\ n : geology that deals with rock strata — **stratigraph·ic** \ˌstra-tə-'gra-fik\ adj

strato·sphere \'stra-tə-ˌsfir\ n : the part of the earth's atmosphere between about 7 miles (11 kilometers) and 31 miles (50 kilometers) above the earth — **strato·spher·ic** \ˌstra-tə-'sfir-ik, -'sfer-\ adj

stra·tum \'strā-təm, 'stra-\ n, pl **stra·ta** \'strā-tə, 'stra-\ [NL, fr. L, spread, bed, fr. neut. of stratus, pp. of sternere to spread out] 1 : a bed, layer, or sheetlike mass (as of one kind of rock lying between layers of other kinds of rock) 2 : a level of culture; also : a group of people representing one stage in cultural development

¹**straw** \'strȯ\ n 1 : stalks of grain after threshing; also : a single coarse dry stem (as of a grass) 2 : a thing of small worth : TRIFLE 3 : a tube (as of paper or plastic) for sucking up a beverage

²**straw** adj 1 : made of straw 2 : having no real force or validity ⟨a ~ vote⟩

straw·ber·ry \'strȯ-ˌber-ē, -bə-rē\ n : an edible juicy usu. red pulpy fruit of any of several low herbs with white flowers and long slender runners; also : one of these herbs

straw boss n : a foreman of a small group of workers

straw·flow·er \'strȯ-ˌflau̇(-ə)r\ n : any of several plants whose flowers can be dried with little loss of form or color

¹**stray** \'strā\ n 1 : a domestic animal wandering at large or lost 2 : WAIF

²**stray** vb 1 : to wander or roam without purpose 2 : DEVIATE

³**stray** adj 1 : having strayed : separated from the group or the main body 2 : occurring at random ⟨~ remarks⟩

¹**streak** \'strēk\ n 1 : a line or mark of a different color or texture from its background 2 : a narrow band of light; also : a lightning bolt 3 : a slight admixture : TRACE 4 : a brief run (as of luck); also : an unbroken series

²**streak** vb 1 : to form streaks in or on 2 : to move very swiftly

¹**stream** \'strēm\ n 1 : a body of water (as a river) flowing on the earth; also : any body of flowing fluid (as water or gas) 2 : a continuous procession ⟨a ~ of traffic⟩

²**stream** vb 1 : to flow in or as if in a stream 2 : to pour out streams of liquid 3 : to trail out in length 4 : to move forward in a steady stream

stream·bed \'strēm-ˌbed\ n : the channel occupied by a stream

stream·er \'strē-mər\ n 1 : a long narrow ribbonlike flag 2 : a long ribbon on a dress or hat 3 : a newspaper headline that runs across the entire sheet 4 pl : AURORA

stream·ing \'strē-miŋ\ adj : relating to or being the transfer of data (as music) in a continuous stream esp. for immediate processing or playback

stream·let \'strēm-lət\ *n* : a small stream

stream-lined \-,līnd\ *adj* **1** : made with contours to reduce resistance to motion through water or air **2** : SIMPLIFIED **3** : MODERNIZED — **stream-line** *vb*

street \'strēt\ *n* [ME *strete*, fr. OE *strǣt*, fr. LL *strata* paved road, fr. L, fem. of *stratus*, pp. of *sternere* to spread out] **1** : a thoroughfare esp. in a city, town, or village **2** : the occupants of the houses on a street

street·car \-,kär\ *n* : a passenger vehicle running on rails on city streets

street fighter *n* : a tough belligerent person

street hockey *n* : a game resembling ice hockey played on a hard surface with hockey sticks and a small ball

street railway *n* : a company operating streetcars or buses

street·walk·er \'strēt-,wȯ-kər\ *n* : PROSTITUTE

strength \'streṅth\ *n* **1** : the quality of being strong : ability to do or endure : POWER **2** : TOUGHNESS, SOLIDITY **3** : power to resist attack **4** : INTENSITY **5** : force as measured in numbers ⟨the ∼ of an army⟩

strength·en \'streṅ-thən\ *vb* : to make or become stronger — **strength·en·er** *n*

stren·u·ous \'stren-yə-wəs\ *adj* **1** : VIGOROUS, ENERGETIC **2** : requiring energy or stamina — **stren·u·ous·ly** *adv*

strep \'strep\ *n* : STREPTOCOCCUS

strep throat *n* : an inflammatory sore throat caused by streptococci and marked by fever, prostration, and toxemia

strep·to·coc·cus \,strep-tə-'kä-kəs\ *n*, *pl* **-coc·ci** \-'kä-,kī, -'käk-,sī, -'kä-,kē, -'käk-,sē\ : any of various spherical bacteria that usu. grow in chains and include some causing serious diseases — **strep·to·coc·cal** \-kəl\ *adj*

strep·to·my·cin \-'mī-sᵊn\ *n* : an antibiotic produced by soil bacteria and used esp. in treating tuberculosis

¹stress \'stres\ *n* **1** : PRESSURE, STRAIN; *esp* : a force that tends to distort a body **2** : a factor that induces bodily or mental tension; *also* : a state induced by such a stress **3** : EMPHASIS **4** : relative prominence of sound **5** : ACCENT; *also* : any syllable carrying the accent — **stress·ful** \'stres-fəl\ *adj*

²stress *vb* **1** : to put pressure or strain on **2** : to put emphasis on : ACCENT

¹stretch \'strech\ *vb* **1** : to spread or reach out : EXTEND ⟨∼ed out her arm⟩ **2** : to draw out in length or breadth : EXPAND **3** : to make tense : STRAIN **4** : EXAGGERATE **5** : to become extended without breaking ⟨rubber ∼es easily⟩ — **stretchy** \'stre-chē\ *adj*

²stretch *n* **1** : an act of extending or drawing out beyond ordinary or normal limits **2** : a continuous extent in length, area, or time **3** : the extent to which something may be stretched **4** : either of the straight sides of a racecourse

³stretch *adj* : easily stretched ⟨∼ pants⟩

¹stretch·er \'stre-chər\ *n* **1** : one that stretches **2** : a device for carrying a sick, injured, or dead person

²stretcher *vb* : to carry or transport on a stretcher

stretch marks *n pl* : striae on the skin (as of the abdomen) due to excessive stretching and rupture of elastic fibers (as from pregnancy)

strew \'strü\ *vb* **strewed**; **strewed** *or* **strewn** \'strün\; **strew·ing 1** : to spread by scattering **2** : to cover by or as if by scattering something over or·on **3** : DISSEMINATE

stria \'strī-ə\ *n*, *pl* **stri·ae** \'strī-,ē\ **1** : STRIATION **3 2** : a stripe or line (as in the skin)

stri·at·ed muscle \'strī-,ā-təd-\ *n* : muscle tissue made up of long thin cells with many nuclei and alternate light and dark stripes that includes esp. the muscle of the heart and muscle that moves the vertebrate skeleton and is mostly under voluntary control

stri·a·tion \strī-'ā-shən\ *n* **1** : the state of being marked with stripes or lines **2** : arrangement of striations or striae **3** : a minute groove, scratch, or channel esp. when one of a parallel series

strick·en \'stri-kən\ *adj* **1** : afflicted by or as if by disease, misfortune, or sorrow **2** : WOUNDED

strict \'strikt\ *adj* **1** : allowing no evasion or escape : RIGOROUS ⟨∼ discipline⟩ **2** : ACCURATE, PRECISE ⟨the ∼ sense of the word⟩ ◆ *Synonyms* STRINGENT, RIGID — **strict·ly** *adv* — **strict·ness** *n*

stric·ture \'strik-chər\ *n* **1** : an abnormal narrowing of a bodily passage; *also* : the narrowed part **2** : hostile criticism : a critical remark

¹stride \'strīd\ *vb* **strode** \'strōd\; **strid·den** \'stri-dᵊn\; **strid·ing** : to walk or run with long regular steps — **strid·er** *n*

²stride *n* **1** : a long step **2** : a stage of progress **3** : manner of striding : GAIT

stri·dent \'strī-dᵊnt\ *adj* : harsh sounding : GRATING, SHRILL

strife \'strīf\ *n* : CONFLICT, FIGHT, STRUGGLE ◆ *Synonyms* DISCORD, CONTENTION, DISSENSION

¹strike \'strīk\ *vb* **struck** \'strək\; **struck** *also* **strick·en** \'stri-kən\; **strik·ing 1** : to take a course : GO ⟨*struck* off through the brush⟩ **2** : to touch or hit sharply; *also* : to deliver a blow **3** : to produce by or as if by a blow ⟨*struck* terror in the foe⟩ **4** : to lower (as a flag or sail) **5** : to collide with; *also* : to injure or destroy by collision **6** : DELETE, CANCEL **7** : to produce by impressing ⟨*struck* a medal⟩; *also* : COIN ⟨∼ a new cent⟩ **8** : to cause to sound ⟨∼ a bell⟩ **9** : to afflict suddenly : lay low ⟨*stricken* with a high fever⟩ **10** : to appear to; *also* : to appear to as remarkable : IMPRESS **11** : to reach by reckoning ⟨∼ an average⟩ **12** : to stop work in order to obtain a change in conditions of employment **13** : to cause (a match) to ignite by rubbing **14** : to come upon ⟨~ gold⟩ **15** : TAKE ON, ASSUME ⟨~ a pose⟩ — **strik·er** *n*

²strike *n* **1** : an act or instance of striking **2** : a sudden discovery of rich ore or oil deposits **3** : a pitched baseball that is swung at but not hit **4** : the knocking down of all the bowling pins with the 1st ball **5** : a military attack

strike·break·er \-ˌbrā-kər\ *n* : a person hired to replace a striking worker

strike·out \-ˌaut\ *n* : an out in baseball as a result of a batter's being charged with three strikes

strike out *vb* **1** : to enter upon a course of action **2** : to start out vigorously **3** : to make an out in baseball by a strikeout

strike–slip \ˈstrīk-ˌslip\ *n* : a fault about which movement is predominantly horizontal

strike up *vb* **1** : to begin or cause to begin to sing or play **2** : BEGIN ⟨~ a conversation⟩

strike zone *n* : the area over home plate through which a pitched baseball must pass to be called a strike

striking *adj* : attracting attention : very noticeable ♦ *Synonyms* ARRESTING, SALIENT, CONSPICUOUS, OUTSTANDING, REMARKABLE, PROMINENT — **strik·ing·ly** *adv*

¹string \ˈstriŋ\ *n* **1** : a line usu. composed of twisted threads **2** : a series of things arranged as if strung on a cord **3** : a plant fiber (as a leaf vein) **4** *pl* : the stringed instruments of an orchestra ♦ *Synonyms* SUCCESSION, PROGRESSION, SEQUENCE, CHAIN, TRAIN

²string *vb* **strung** \ˈstrəŋ\; **string·ing 1** : to provide with strings ⟨~ a racket⟩ **2** : to make tense **3** : to thread on or as if on a string ⟨~ pearls⟩ **4** : to hang, tie, or fasten by a string **5** : to take the strings out of ⟨~ beans⟩ **6** : to extend like a string

string bean *n* : a bean of one of the older varieties of kidney bean that have stringy fibers on the lines of separation of the pods; *also* : SNAP BEAN

string bikini *n* : a scanty bikini

string cheese *n* : cheese that can be pulled apart in narrow strips

stringed \ˈstriŋd\ *adj* **1** : having strings ⟨~ instruments⟩ **2** : produced by strings

strin·gen·cy \ˈstrin-jən-sē\ *n* **1** : STRICTNESS, SEVERITY **2** : SCARCITY ⟨~ of money⟩ — **strin·gent** \-jənt\ *adj*

string·er \ˈstriŋ-ər\ *n* **1** : a long horizontal member in a framed structure or a bridge **2** : a news correspondent paid by the amount of copy

stringy \ˈstriŋ-ē\ *adj* **string·i·er; -est 1** : resembling string esp. in tough, fibrous, or disordered quality ⟨~ meat⟩ ⟨~ hair⟩ **2** : lean and sinewy in build

¹strip \ˈstrip\ *vb* **stripped** \ˈstript\ *also* **stript; strip·ping 1** : to take the covering or clothing from **2** : to take off one's clothes **3** : to pull or tear off **4** : to make bare or clear (as by cutting or grazing) **5** : PLUNDER, PILLAGE ♦ *Syno-*

nyms DIVEST, DENUDE, DEPRIVE, DISMANTLE — **strip·per** *n*

²strip *n* **1** : a long narrow flat piece **2** : AIRSTRIP

¹stripe \ˈstrīp\ *vb* **striped** \ˈstrīpt\; **strip·ing** : to make stripes on

²stripe *n* **1** : a line or long narrow division having a different color from the background **2** : a strip of braid (as on a sleeve) indicating military rank or length of service **3** : TYPE, CHARACTER — **striped** \ˈstrīpt, ˈstrī-pəd\ *adj*

striped bass *n* : a large black-striped marine bony fish that occurs along the Atlantic and Pacific coasts of the U.S. and is an excellent food and sport fish

strip·ling \ˈstri-pliŋ\ *n* : YOUTH, LAD

strip mall *n* : a long building or group of buildings housing several retail stores or service establishments

strip mine *n* : a mine that is worked from the earth's surface by the stripping of the topsoil — **strip–mine** *vb*

strip-tease \ˈstrip-ˌtēz\ *n* : a burlesque act in which a performer removes clothing piece by piece — **strip-teas·er** *n*

strive \ˈstrīv\ *vb* **strove** \ˈstrōv\ *also* **strived** \ˈstrīvd\; **striv·en** \ˈstri-vən\ *or* **strived; striv·ing 1** : to make effort : labor hard **2** : to struggle in opposition : CONTEND ♦ *Synonyms* ENDEAVOR, ATTEMPT, TRY, ASSAY

strobe \ˈstrōb\ *n* **1** : STROBOSCOPE **2** : a device for high-speed intermittent illumination (as in photography)

stro·bo·scope \ˈstrō-bə-ˌskōp\ *n* : an instrument for studying rapid motion by means of a rapidly flashing light

strode *past of* STRIDE

¹stroke \ˈstrōk\ *vb* **stroked; strok·ing 1** : to rub gently **2** : to flatter in a manner designed to persuade

²stroke *n* **1** : the act of striking : BLOW, KNOCK **2** : a sudden action or process producing an impact ⟨~ of lightning⟩; *also* : an unexpected result **3** : sudden weakening or loss of consciousness or the power to move or feel caused by rupture or obstruction (as by a clot) of a blood vessel of the brain **4** : one of a series of movements against air or water to get through or over it ⟨the ~ of a bird's wing⟩ **5** : a rower who sets the pace for a crew **6** : a vigorous effort **7** : the sound of striking (as of a clock) **8** : a single movement with or as if with a tool or implement (as a pen)

stroll \ˈstrōl\ *vb* : to walk in a leisurely or idle manner — **stroll** *n* — **stroll·er** *n*

strong \ˈstroŋ\ *adj* **stron·ger** \ˈstroŋ-gər\; **stron·gest** \ˈstroŋ-gəst\ **1** : POWERFUL, VIGOROUS **2** : HEALTHY, ROBUST **3** : of a specified number ⟨an army 10 thousand ~⟩ **4** : not mild or weak **5** : VIOLENT ⟨~ wind⟩ **6** : ZEALOUS ⟨a ~ supporter⟩ **7** : not easily broken **8** : FIRM, SOLID ⟨~ beliefs⟩ ♦ *Synonyms* STOUT, STURDY, STALWART, TOUGH — **strong·ly** *adv*

strong–arm \ˈstroŋ-ˈärm\ *adj* : having or using undue force ⟨~ operatives⟩

strong force *n* : the physical force responsible for binding together nucleons in the atomic nucleus

strong·hold \-ˌhōld\ *n* : a fortified place : FORTRESS

strong·man \-ˌman\ *n* : one who leads or controls by force of will and character or by military strength

stron·tium \'strän-chē-əm, 'strän-tē-əm\ *n* : a soft malleable metallic chemical element

¹**strop** \'sträp\ *n* : STRAP; *esp* : one for sharpening a razor

²**strop** *vb* **stropped; strop·ping** : to sharpen a razor on a strop

stro·phe \'strō-fē\ *n* [Gk *strophē*, lit., act of turning] : a division of a poem — **stroph·ic** \'strä-fik\ *adj*

strove *past of* STRIVE

struck *past and past part of* STRIKE

¹**struc·ture** \'strək-chər\ *n* [ME, fr. L *structura*, fr. *structus*, pp. of *struere* to heap up, build] **1** : the action of building : CONSTRUCTION **2** : something built (as a house or a dam); *also* : something made up of interdependent parts in a definite pattern of organization **3** : arrangement or relationship of elements (as particles, parts, or organs) in a substance, body, or system — **struc·tur·al** *adj*

²**structure** *vb* **struc·tured; struc·tur·ing** : to make into a structure

stru·del \'strü-dᵊl, 'shtrü-\ *n* [G, lit., whirlpool] : a pastry made of a thin sheet of dough rolled up with filling and baked ⟨apple ∼⟩

¹**strug·gle** \'strə-gəl\ *vb* **strug·gled; strug·gling** **1** : to make strenuous efforts against opposition : STRIVE **2** : to proceed with difficulty or with great effort ♦ *Synonyms* ENDEAVOR, ATTEMPT, TRY, ASSAY

²**struggle** *n* **1** : CONTEST, STRIFE **2** : a violent effort or exertion

strum \'strəm\ *vb* **strummed; strumming** : to play on a stringed instrument by brushing the strings with the fingers ⟨∼ a guitar⟩

strum·pet \'strəm-pət\ *n* : PROSTITUTE

strung \'strəŋ\ *past and past part of* STRING

¹**strut** \'strət\ *vb* **strut·ted; strut·ting** : to walk with an affectedly proud gait

²**strut** *n* **1** : a bar or rod for resisting lengthwise pressure **2** : a haughty or pompous gait

strych·nine \'strik-ˌnīn, -nən, -ˌnēn\ *n* : a bitter poisonous plant alkaloid used as a poison (as for rats) and medicinally as a stimulant of the central nervous system

¹**stub** \'stəb\ *n* **1** : STUMP 2 **2** : a short blunt end **3** : a small part of each leaf (as of a checkbook) kept as a memorandum of the items on the detached part

²**stub** *vb* **stubbed; stub·bing** : to strike (as one's toe) against something

stub·ble \'stə-bəl\ *n* **1** : the cut stem ends of herbs and esp. grasses left in the soil after harvest **2** : a rough surface or growth resembling stubble — **stub·bly** \-b(ə-)lē\ *adj*

stub·born \'stə-bərn\ *adj* **1** : FIRM, DETERMINED **2** : done or continued in a willful, unreasonable, or persistent manner **3** : not easily controlled or remedied ⟨a ∼ cold⟩ — **stub·born·ly** *adv* — **stub·born·ness** *n*

stub·by \'stə-bē\ *adj* : short, blunt, and thick like a stub

stuc·co \'stə-kō\ *n*, *pl* **stuccos** *or* **stuccoes** [It] : plaster for coating exterior walls — **stuc·coed** \'stə-kōd\ *adj*

stuck *past and past part of* STICK

stuck–up \'stək-'əp\ *adj* : CONCEITED

¹**stud** \'stəd\ *n* : a male animal and esp. a horse ⟨**stud·horse** \-ˌhȯrs\⟩ kept for breeding

²**stud** *n* **1** : one of the smaller uprights in a building to which the wall materials are fastened **2** : a removable device like a button used as a fastener or ornament ⟨shirt ∼s⟩ **3** : a projecting nail, pin, or rod

³**stud** *vb* **stud·ded; stud·ding** **1** : to supply with or adorn with studs : DOT ⟨the sky was *studded* with stars⟩

⁴**stud** *abbr* student

stud·book \'stəd-ˌbúk\ *n* : an official record of the pedigree of purebred animals (as horses or dogs)

studding *n* : the studs in a building or wall

stu·dent \'stü-dᵊnt, 'styü-\ *n* : SCHOLAR, PUPIL; *esp* : one who attends a school

stud·ied \'stə-dēd\ *adj* : INTENTIONAL ⟨a ∼ insult⟩ ♦ *Synonyms* DELIBERATE, CONSIDERED, PREMEDITATED, DESIGNED

stu·dio \'stü-dē-ˌō, 'styü-\ *n*, *pl* **-dios** **1** : a place where an artist works; *also* : a place for the study of an art **2** : a place where motion pictures are made **3** : a place equipped for the transmission of radio or television programs

stu·di·ous \'stü-dē-əs, 'styü-\ *adj* : devoted to study — **stu·di·ous·ly** *adv*

¹**study** \'stə-dē\ *n*, *pl* **stud·ies** **1** : the use of the mind to gain knowledge **2** : the act or process of learning about something **3** : careful examination **4** : INTENT, PURPOSE **5** : a branch of learning **6** : a room esp. for reading and writing

²**study** *vb* **stud·ied; study·ing** **1** : to engage in study or the study of **2** : to consider attentively or in detail ♦ *Synonyms* CONSIDER, CONTEMPLATE, WEIGH

¹**stuff** \'stəf\ *n* [ME, fr. AF *estuffes* goods, fr. *estuffer* to fill in (with rubble), furnish, equip, of Gmc origin] **1** : personal property **2** : raw material **3** : a finished textile fabric; *esp* : a worsted fabric **4** : writing, talk, or ideas of little or transitory worth **5** : an unspecified material substance or aggregate of matter **6** : fundamental material **7** : special knowledge or capability

²**stuff** *vb* **1** : to fill by packing things in : CRAM **2** : to eat greedily : GORGE **3** : to prepare (as meat) by filling with a stuffing **4** : to fill (as a cushion) with a soft material **5** : to stop up : PLUG

stuffed shirt \'stəft-\ *n* : a smug, conceited, and usu. pompous and inflexibly conservative person

stuff·ing *n* : material used to fill tightly; *esp* : a mixture of bread crumbs and spices used to stuff food

stuffy \'stə-fē\ *adj* **stuff·i·er; -est** **1** : STODGY **2** : lacking fresh air : CLOSE; *also* : blocked up ⟨a ∼ nose⟩

stul·ti·fy \'stəl-tə-ˌfī\ *vb* **-fied; -fy·ing** **1** : to cause to appear foolish or stupid **2** : to impair, invalidate, or make ineffective **3** : to have a dulling effect on — **stul·ti·fi·ca·tion** \ˌstəl-tə-fə-'kā-shən\ *n*

stum·ble \'stəm-bəl\ *vb* **stum·bled; stum·bling** **1** : to blunder morally **2** : to trip in walking or running **3** : to walk unsteadily; *also* : to speak or act in a blundering or clumsy manner **4** : to happen by chance — **stumble** *n*

stumbling block *n* : an obstacle to belief, understanding, or progress

¹stump \'stəmp\ *n* **1** : the base of a bodily part (as a leg or tooth) left after the rest is removed **2** : the part of a plant and esp. a tree remaining with the root after the trunk is cut off **3** : a place or occasion for political public speaking — **stumpy** *adj*

²stump *vb* **1** : BAFFLE, PERPLEX **2** : to clear (land) of stumps **3** : to tour (a region) making political speeches **4** : to walk clumsily and heavily

stun \'stən\ *vb* **stunned; stun·ning** **1** : to make senseless or dizzy by or as if by a blow **2** : BEWILDER, STUPEFY ⟨*stunned* by the news⟩

stung *past and past part of* STING

stunk *past and past part of* STINK

stun·ning *adj* **1** : causing astonishment or disbelief **2** : strikingly beautiful — **stun·ning·ly** *adv*

¹stunt \'stənt\ *vb* : to hinder the normal growth or progress of

²stunt *n* : an unusual or spectacular feat

stu·pe·fy \'stü-pə-ˌfī, 'styü-\ *vb* **-fied; -fy·ing** **1** : to make stupid, groggy, or insensible **2** : ASTONISH — **stu·pe·fac·tion** \ˌstü-pə-'fak-shən, ˌstyü-\ *n*

stu·pen·dous \stü-'pen-dəs, styü-\ *adj* : causing astonishment esp. because of great size or height ♦ **Synonyms** TREMENDOUS, PRODIGIOUS, MONUMENTAL, MONSTROUS — **stu·pen·dous·ly** *adv*

stu·pid \'stü-pəd, 'styü-\ *adj* [MF *stupide*, fr. L *stupidus*, fr. *stupēre* to be numb, be astonished] **1** : very dull in mind **2** : showing or resulting from dullness of mind — **stu·pid·i·ty** \stü-'pi-də-tē, styü-\ *n* — **stu·pid·ly** *adv*

stu·por \'stü-pər, 'styü-\ *n* **1** : a condition of greatly dulled or completely suspended sense or feeling **2** : a state of extreme apathy or torpor often following stress or shock — **stu·por·ous** *adj*

stur·dy \'stər-dē\ *adj* **stur·di·er; -est** [ME, brave, stubborn, fr. AF *esturdi* stunned, fr. pp. of *esturdir* to stun, fr. VL *exturdire*, fr. L *ex-* + VL *turdus* simpleton, fr. L *turdus* thrush] **1** : STRONG, ROBUST **2** : RESOLUTE, UNYIELDING ♦ **Synonyms** STOUT, STALWART, TOUGH,

TENACIOUS — **stur·di·ly** \-də-lē\ *adv* — **stur·di·ness** \-dē-nəs\ *n*

stur·geon \'stər-jən\ *n* : any of a family of large bony fishes including some whose roe are made into caviar

stut·ter \'stə-tər\ *vb* : to speak with involuntary disruption or blocking of sounds — **stutter** *n* — **stut·ter·er** *n*

stutter step *n* : a move made by a runner (as in football) done to fake a defender out of position

¹sty \'stī\ *n, pl* **sties** : PIGPEN

²sty *or* **stye** *n, pl* **sties** *or* **styes** : an inflamed swelling of a skin gland on the edge of an eyelid

¹style \'stī(-ə)l\ *n* **1** : mode of address : TITLE **2** : a way of speaking or writing; *esp* : one characteristic of an individual, period, school, or nation ⟨ornate ∼⟩ **3** : manner or method of acting, making, or performing; *also* : a distinctive or characteristic manner **4** : a slender pointed instrument or process; *esp* : STYLUS **5** : a fashionable manner or mode **6** : overall excellence, skill, or grace in performance, manner, or appearance **7** : the custom followed in spelling, capitalization, punctuation, and typography — **sty·lis·tic** \stī-'lis-tik\ *adj*

²style *vb* **styled; styl·ing** **1** : NAME, DESIGNATE **2** : to make or design in accord with a prevailing mode

styling *n* : the way in which something is styled

styl·ise *Brit var of* STYLIZE

styl·ish \'stī-lish\ *adj* : conforming to current fashion ♦ **Synonyms** MODISH, SMART, CHIC — **styl·ish·ly** *adv* — **styl·ish·ness** *n*

styl·ist \'stī-list\ *n* **1** : one (as a writer) noted for a distinctive style **2** : a developer or designer of styles

styl·ize \'stī-ˌlīz, 'stī-ə-\ *vb* **styl·ized; styl·iz·ing** : to conform to a style; *esp* : to represent or design according to a pattern or style rather than according to nature or tradition — **styl·i·za·tion** \ˌstī-lə-'zā-shən\ *n*

sty·lus \'stī-ləs\ *n, pl* **sty·li** \'stī-ˌlī\ *also* **sty·lus·es** \'stī-lə-səz\ [L *stylus, stilus* spike, stylus] **1** : a pointed implement used by the ancients for writing on wax **2** : a phonograph needle **3** : a pen-shaped pointing device for entering data into a computer

sty·mie \'stī-mē\ *vb* **sty·mied; sty·mie·ing** : BLOCK, FRUSTRATE ⟨managed to ∼ the opposition⟩

styp·tic \'stip-tik\ *adj* : tending to check bleeding — **styptic** *n*

suave \'swäv\ *adj* [F, fr. MF, pleasant, sweet, fr. L *suavis*] : persuasively pleasing : smoothly agreeable ♦ **Synonyms** URBANE, SMOOTH, BLAND — **suave·ly** *adv* — **sua·vi·ty** \'swä-və-tē\ *n*

¹sub \'səb\ *n* : SUBSTITUTE — **sub** *vb*

²sub *n* : SUBMARINE

³sub *abbr* **1** subtract **2** suburb

sub- \'səb\ *prefix* **1** : under : beneath **2** : subordinate : secondary **3** : subordinate portion of : subdivision of **4** : with repetition of a process described in a simple verb so as to form, stress, or deal with subordinate parts or relations **5** : somewhat **6** : falling nearly in the category of : bordering on

sub·al·pine \ˌsəb-ˈal-ˌpīn\ *adj* **1** : of or relating to the region about the foot and lower slopes of the Alps **2** : of, relating to, or inhabiting high upland slopes esp. just below the timberline

sub·al·tern \sə-ˈbȯl-tərn\ *n* : SUBORDINATE; *esp* : a junior officer (as in the British army)

sub·as·sem·bly \ˌsəb-ə-ˈsem-blē\ *n* : an assembled unit to be incorporated with other units in a finished product

sub·atom·ic \ˌsəb-ə-ˈtä-mik\ *adj* : of or relating to the inside of the atom or to particles smaller than atoms

sub·clin·i·cal \ˌsəb-ˈkli-nə-kəl\ *adj* : not detectable by the usual clinical tests ⟨a ~ infection⟩

sub·com·pact \ˈsəb-ˈkäm-ˌpakt\ *n* : an automobile smaller than a compact

¹**sub·con·scious** \ˌsəb-ˈkän-chəs, ˈsəb-\ *adj* : existing in a mind without entering conscious awareness — **sub·con·scious·ly** *adv* — **sub·con·scious·ness** *n*

²**subconscious** *n* : mental activities just below the threshold of consciousness

sub·con·ti·nent \ˌsəb-ˈkän-tə-nənt\ *n* : a major subdivision of a continent — **sub·con·ti·nen·tal** \ˌsəb-ˌkän-tə-ˈnen-tᵊl\ *adj*

sub·di·vide \ˌsəb-də-ˈvīd, ˈsəb-də-ˌvīd\ *vb* : to divide the parts of into more parts; *esp* : to divide (a tract of land) into building lots — **sub·di·vi·sion** \-ˈvi-zhən, -ˌvi-\ *n*

sub·duc·tion \səb-ˈdək-shən\ *n* : the descent of the edge of one crustal plate beneath the edge of an adjacent plate

sub·due \səb-ˈdü, -ˈdyü\ *vb* **sub·dued; sub·du·ing 1** : to bring into subjection : VANQUISH **2** : to bring under control : CURB **3** : to reduce the intensity of

subj *abbr* **1** subject **2** subjunctive

¹**sub·ject** \ˈsəb-jikt\ *n* [ME *suget, subget,* fr. AF, fr. L *subjectus* one under authority & *subjectum* subject of a proposition, fr. *subicere* to subject, lit., to throw under, fr. *sub-* under + *jacere* to throw] **1** : a person under the authority of another **2** : a person subject to a sovereign **3** : an individual that is studied or experimented on **4** : the person or thing discussed or treated : TOPIC, THEME **5** : a word or word group denoting that of which something is predicated

²**subject** *adj* **1** : being under the power or rule of another **2** : LIABLE, EXPOSED ⟨~ to floods⟩ **3** : dependent on some act or condition ⟨appointment ~ to senate ap-

proval⟩ **✦ Synonyms** SUBORDINATE, SECONDARY, TRIBUTARY, COLLATERAL, DEPENDENT

³**sub·ject** \səb-ˈjekt\ *vb* **1** : to bring under control : CONQUER **2** : to make liable **3** : to cause to undergo or endure — **sub·jec·tion** \-ˈjek-shən\ *n*

sub·jec·tive \(ˌ)səb-ˈjek-tiv\ *adj* **1** : of, relating to, or constituting a subject **2** : of, relating to, or arising within one's self or mind in contrast to what is outside : PERSONAL ⟨~ judgments⟩ ⟨a ~ sensation⟩ — **sub·jec·tive·ly** *adv* — **sub·jec·tiv·i·ty** \ˌjek-ˈti-və-tē\ *n*

subject matter *n* : matter presented for consideration, discussion, or study

sub·join \(ˌ)səb-ˈjȯin\ *vb* : APPEND ⟨~ed a statement of expenses to her report⟩

sub ju·di·ce \(ˌ)sùb-ˈyü-di-ˌkā, ˈsəb-ˈjü-də-(ˌ)sē\ *adv* [L] : before a judge or court : not yet legally decided

sub·ju·gate \ˈsəb-ji-ˌgāt\ *vb* **-gat·ed; -gat·ing** : CONQUER, SUBDUE; *also* : ENSLAVE **✦ Synonyms** REDUCE, OVERCOME, OVERTHROW, VANQUISH, DEFEAT, BEAT — **sub·ju·ga·tion** \ˌsəb-ji-ˈgā-shən\ *n*

sub·junc·tive \səb-ˈjəŋk-tiv\ *adj* : of, relating to, or constituting a verb form that represents an act or state as contingent or possible or viewed emotionally (as with desire) ⟨the ~ mood⟩ — **subjunctive** *n*

sub·lease \ˈsəb-ˈlēs, -ˌlēs\ *n* : a lease by a lessee of part or all of leased premises to another person with the original lessee retaining some right under the original lease — **sublease** *vb*

¹**sub·let** \ˈsəb-ˈlet\ *vb* **-let; -let·ting** : to let all or a part of (a leased property) to another; *also* : to rent (a property) from a lessee

²**sublet** \-ˌlet\ *n* : property and esp. housing obtained by or available through a sublease

sub·li·mate \ˈsə-blə-ˌmāt\ *vb* **-mat·ed; -mat·ing 1** : SUBLIME **2** : to direct the expression of (as a desire or impulse) from a primitive to a more socially and culturally acceptable form — **sub·li·ma·tion** \ˌsə-blə-ˈmā-shən\ *n*

¹**sub·lime** \sə-ˈblīm\ *vb* **sub·limed; sub·lim·ing** : to pass or cause to pass directly from the solid to the vapor state

²**sublime** *adj* **1** : EXALTED, NOBLE **2** : having awe-inspiring beauty or grandeur **✦ Synonyms** GLORIOUS, SPLENDID, SUPERB, RESPLENDENT, GORGEOUS — **sub·lime·ly** *adv* — **sub·lim·i·ty** \-ˈbli-mə-tē\ *n*

sub·lim·i·nal \(ˌ)səb-ˈli-mə-nᵊl, ˈsəb-\ *adj* [*sub-* + L *limin-, limen* threshold] **1** : inadequate to produce a sensation or mental awareness ⟨~ stimuli⟩ **2** : existing or functioning below the threshold of consciousness ⟨the ∼ mind⟩ ⟨∼ advertising⟩

sub·ma·chine gun \ˌsəb-mə-ˈshēn-ˌgən\ *n* : an automatic firearm fired from the shoulder or hip

¹**sub·ma·rine** \ˈsəb-mə-ˌrēn, ˌsəb-mə-ˈrēn\ *adj* : UNDERWATER; *esp* : UNDERSEA

²**submarine** *n* **1** : a naval vessel designed to operate underwater **2** : a large sandwich made from a long split roll with any of a variety of fillings

sub·merge \səb-ˈmərj\ *vb* **sub·merged; sub·merg·ing 1** : to put or plunge under the surface of water **2** : INUNDATE — **sub·mer·gence** \-ˈmər-jəns\ *n*

sub·merse \səb-ˈmərs\ *vb* **sub·mersed; sub·mers·ing** : SUBMERGE — **sub·mer·sion** \-ˈmər-zhən\ *n*

¹**sub·mers·ible** \səb-ˈmər-sə-bəl\ *adj* : capable of being submerged

²**submersible** *n* : something that is submersible; *esp* : a small underwater craft used for deep-sea research

sub·mi·cro·sco·pic \ˌsəb-ˌmī-krə-ˈskä-pik\ *adj* : too small to be seen in an ordinary light microscope

sub·min·ia·ture \ˌsəb-ˈmi-nē-ə-ˌchùr, ˈsəb-, -ˈmi-ni-ˌchùr, -chər\ *adj* : very small

sub·mit \səb-ˈmit\ *vb* **sub·mit·ted; sub·mit·ting 1** : to commit to the discretion or decision of another or of others **2** : YIELD, SURRENDER **3** : to put forward as an opinion — **sub·mis·sion** \-ˈmi-shən\ *n* — **sub·mis·sive** \-ˈmi-siv\ *adj*

sub·nor·mal \ˌsəb-ˈnór-məl\ *adj* : falling below what is normal; *also* : having less of something and esp. intelligence than is normal — **sub·nor·mal·i·ty** \ˌsəb-nór-ˈma-lə-tē\ *n*

sub·or·bit·al \ˌsəb-ˈòr-bə-t³l, ˈsəb-\ *adj* : being or involving less than one orbit

¹**sub·or·di·nate** \sə-ˈbór-də-nət\ *adj* **1** : of lower class or rank ⟨a ∼ officer⟩ **2** : INFERIOR **3** : submissive to authority **4** : subordinated to other elements in a sentence : DEPENDENT ⟨∼ clause⟩ ✦ *Synonyms* SECONDARY, SUBJECT, TRIBUTARY, COLLATERAL

²**subordinate** *n* : one that is subordinate

³**sub·or·di·nate** \sə-ˈbór-də-ˌnāt\ *vb* **sub·or·di·nat·ed; -nat·ing 1** : SUBDUE **2** : to place in a lower rank or class — **sub·or·di·na·tion** \-ˌbór-də-ˈnā-shən\ *n*

sub·orn \sə-ˈbórn\ *vb* **1** : to induce secretly to do an unlawful thing **2** : to induce to commit perjury — **sub·or·na·tion** \ˌsə-ˌbór-ˈnā-shən\ *n*

¹**sub·poe·na** \sə-ˈpē-nə\ *n* [ME *suppena*, fr. L *sub poena* under penalty] : a writ commanding the person named in it to attend court under penalty for failure to do so

²**subpoena** *vb* **-naed; -na·ing** : to summon with a subpoena

sub–Sa·ha·ran \ˌsəb-sə-ˈher-ən\ *adj* : of, relating to, or being the part of Africa south of the Sahara

sub·scribe \səb-ˈskrīb\ *vb* **sub·scribed; sub·scrib·ing 1** : to sign one's name to a document **2** : to give consent by or as if by signing one's name **3** : to promise to contribute by signing one's name with the amount promised **4** : to place an order by signing **5** : to receive a periodical or service regularly on order **6** : FAVOR, APPROVE ✦ *Synonyms* AGREE, ACQUIESCE, ASSENT, ACCEDE — **sub·scrib·er** *n*

sub·script \ˈsəb-ˌskript\ *n* : a symbol (as a letter or number) immediately below or below and to the right or left of another written character — **subscript** *adj*

sub·scrip·tion \səb-ˈskrip-shən\ *n* **1** : the act of subscribing : SIGNATURE **2** : a purchase by signed order

sub·se·quent \ˈsəb-si-kwənt, -sə-ˌkwent\ *adj* : following after : SUCCEEDING ⟨∼ events⟩ — **sub·se·quent·ly** *adv*

sub·ser·vi·ence \səb-ˈsər-vē-əns\ *n* **1** : a subordinate place or condition **2** : SERVILITY — **sub·ser·vi·en·cy** \-ən-sē\ *n* — **sub·ser·vi·ent** \-ənt\ *adj*

sub·set \ˈsəb-ˌset\ *n* : a set each of whose elements is an element of an inclusive set

sub·side \səb-ˈsīd\ *vb* **sub·sid·ed; sub·sid·ing** [L *subsidere*, fr. *sub-* under + *sidere* to sit down, sink] **1** : to settle to the bottom of a liquid **2** : to tend downward : DESCEND **3** : SINK, SUBMERGE ⟨*subsided* into a chair⟩ **4** : to become quiet and tranquil ✦ *Synonyms* ABATE, WANE, MODERATE, SLACKEN — **sub·sid·ence** \səb-ˈsī-d³ns, ˈsəb-sə-dəns\ *n*

¹**sub·sid·iary** \səb-ˈsi-dē-ˌer-ē\ *adj* **1** : furnishing aid or support **2** : of secondary importance **3** : of or relating to a subsidy ✦ *Synonyms* AUXILIARY, CONTRIBUTORY, SUBSERVIENT, ACCESSORY

²**subsidiary** *n, pl* **-iar·ies** : one that is subsidiary; *esp* : a company controlled by another

sub·si·dise *Brit var of* SUBSIDIZE

sub·si·dize \ˈsəb-sə-ˌdīz\ *vb* **-dized; -diz·ing** : to aid or furnish with a subsidy

sub·si·dy \ˈsəb-sə-dē\ *n, pl* **-dies** [ME, *subsidie*, fr. AF, fr. L *subsidium* reserve troops, support, assistance, fr. *sub-* near + *sedēre* to sit] : a gift of public money to a private person or company or to another government

sub·sist \səb-ˈsist\ *vb* **1** : EXIST, PERSIST **2** : to have the means (as food and clothing) of maintaining life; *esp* : to nourish oneself

sub·sis·tence \səb-ˈsis-təns\ *n* **1** : EXISTENCE **2** : means of subsisting : the minimum (as of food and clothing) necessary to support life

sub·son·ic \ˌsəb-ˈsä-nik, ˈsəb-\ *adj* : being or relating to a speed less than that of sound; *also* : moving at such a speed

sub·species \ˈsəb-ˌspē-shēz, -ˌsēz\ *n* : a subdivision of a species; *esp* : a category in biological classification ranking just below a species that designates a geographic population genetically distinct from other such populations and potentially able to breed with them where its range overlaps theirs

sub·stance \'səb-stəns\ *n* **1** : essential nature : ESSENCE ⟨divine ∼⟩; *also* : the fundamental or essential part or quality ⟨the ∼ of the speech⟩ **2** : physical material from which something is made or which has discrete existence; *also* : matter of particular or definite chemical constitution **3** : something (as drugs or alcohol) deemed harmful and usu. subject to legal restriction ⟨∼ abuse⟩ **4** : material possessions : PROPERTY, WEALTH

sub·stan·dard \,səb-'stan-dərd\ *adj* : falling short of a standard or norm

sub·stan·tial \səb-'stan-chəl\ *adj* **1** : existing as or in substance : MATERIAL; *also* : not illusory : REAL **2** : IMPORTANT, ESSENTIAL ⟨a ∼ difference in the stories⟩ **3** : NOURISHING, SATISFYING ⟨∼ meal⟩ **4** : having means : WELL-TO-DO **5** : CONSIDERABLE ⟨∼ profit⟩ **6** : STRONG, FIRM — **sub·stan·tial·ly** *adv*

sub·stan·ti·ate \səb-'stan-chē-ˌāt\ *vb* **-at·ed; -at·ing 1** : to give substance or body to **2** : VERIFY, PROVE ⟨∼ a charge⟩ — **sub·stan·ti·a·tion** \-ˌstan-chē-'ā-shən\ *n*

¹sub·stan·tive \'səb-stən-tiv\ *n* : NOUN; *also* : a word or phrase used as a noun

²substantive *adj* : having substance : REAL

¹sub·sti·tute \'səb-stə-ˌtüt, -ˌtyüt\ *n* : a person or thing replacing another — **substitute** *adj*

²substitute *vb* **-tut·ed; -tut·ing 1** : to put or use in the place of another **2** : to serve as a substitute — **sub·sti·tu·tion** \,səb-stə-'tü-shən, -'tyü-\ *n*

sub·strate \'səb-ˌstrāt\ *n* **1** : the base on which a plant or animal lives **2** : a substance acted upon (as by an enzyme)

sub·stra·tum \'səb-ˌstrā-təm, -ˌstra-\ *n, pl* **-stra·ta** \-tə\ : the layer or structure (as subsoil) lying underneath

sub·struc·ture \'səb-ˌstrək-chər\ *n* : FOUNDATION, GROUNDWORK

sub·sume \səb-'süm\ *vb* **sub·sumed; sub·sum·ing** : to include or place within something larger or more comprehensive

sub·sur·face \'səb-ˌsər-fəs\ *n* : earth material near the surface of the ground — **subsurface** *adj*

sub·ter·fuge \'səb-tər-ˌfyüj\ *n* : a trick or device used in order to conceal, escape, or evade ♦ *Synonyms* FRAUD, DECEPTION, TRICKERY

sub·ter·ra·nean \,səb-tə-'rā-nē-ən\ *adj* **1** : lying or being underground **2** : SECRET, HIDDEN ⟨a ∼ network of criminals⟩

sub·tile \'sə-t°l\ *adj* **sub·til·er** \'sə-t°l-ər\; **sub·til·est** \'sə-t°l-əst\ : SUBTLE ⟨a ∼ aroma⟩

sub·ti·tle \'səb-ˌtī-t°l\ *n* **1** : a secondary or explanatory title (as of a book) **2** : printed matter projected on a motion-picture screen during or between the scenes

sub·tle \'sə-t°l\ *adj* **sub·tler** \'sə-t°l-ər\; **sub·tlest** \'sə-t°l-əst\ **1** : hardly noticeable ⟨∼ differences⟩ **2** : SHREWD, PERCEPTIVE ⟨a ∼ mind⟩ **3** : CLEVER, SLY ⟨a ∼ rogue⟩ — **sub·tle·ty** \-tē\ *n* — **subtly** \'sə-t°l-ē\ *adv*

sub·tract \səb-'trakt\ *vb* : to take away (as one part or number) from another; *also* : to perform the operation of deducting one number from another — **sub·trac·tion** \-'trak-shən\ *n*

sub·tra·hend \'səb-trə-ˌhend\ *n* : a number that is to be subtracted from another

sub·trop·i·cal \,səb-'trä-pi-kəl, 'səb-\ *also* **sub·trop·ic** \-'pik\ *adj* : of, relating to, or being regions bordering on the tropical zone ⟨a ∼ environment⟩ — **sub·trop·ics** \-piks\ *n pl*

sub·urb \'sə-ˌbərb\ *n* **1** : an outlying part of a city; *also* : a small community adjacent to a city **2** *pl* : a residential area adjacent to a city — **sub·ur·ban** \sə-'bər-bən\ *adj or n* — **sub·ur·ban·ite** \sə-'bər-bə-ˌnīt\ *n*

sub·ur·bia \sə-'bər-bē-ə\ *n* **1** : SUBURBS **2** : suburban people or customs

sub·ven·tion \səb-'ven-chən\ *n* : SUBSIDY, ENDOWMENT

sub·vert \səb-'vərt\ *vb* **1** : OVERTHROW, RUIN **2** : CORRUPT — **sub·ver·sion** \-'vər-zhən\ *n* — **sub·ver·sive** \-'vər-siv\ *adj*

sub·way \'səb-ˌwā\ *n* : an underground way; *esp* : an underground electric railway

sub·woof·er \'səb-ˌwu̇-fər\ *n* : a loudspeaker responsive only to the lowest acoustic frequencies

suc·ceed \sək-'sēd\ *vb* **1** : to follow next in order or next after another; *esp* : to inherit sovereignty, rank, title, or property **2** : to attain a desired object or end : be successful

suc·cess \sək-'ses\ *n* **1** : favorable or desired outcome **2** : the gaining of wealth and fame **3** : one that succeeds — **suc·cess·ful** \-fəl\ *adj* — **suc·cess·ful·ly** *adv*

suc·ces·sion \sək-'se-shən\ *n* **1** : the order, act, or right of succeeding to a property, title, or throne **2** : the act or process of following in order **3** : a series of persons or things that follow one after another ♦ *Synonyms* PROGRESSION, SEQUENCE, CHAIN, TRAIN, STRING

suc·ces·sive \sək-'se-siv\ *adj* : following in order : CONSECUTIVE — **suc·ces·sive·ly** *adv*

suc·ces·sor \sək-'se-sər\ *n* : one that succeeds (as to a throne, title, estate, or office)

suc·cinct \(ˌ)sək-'siŋkt, sə-'siŋkt\ *adj* : BRIEF, CONCISE ⟨a ∼ description⟩

◆ **Synonyms** TERSE, LACONIC, SUMMARY, CURT, SHORT — **suc·cinct·ly** adv — **suc·cinct·ness** n

suc·cor \'sə-kər\ n [ME socour, sucurs (taken as pl.), fr. AF socour, sucors, fr. ML succursus, fr. L succurrere to run to the rescue, bring aid] : AID, HELP, RELIEF — **succor** vb

suc·co·tash \'sə-kə-ˌtash\ n [Narragansett msíckquatash boiled corn kernels] : beans and corn kernels cooked together

suc·cour chiefly Brit var of SUCCOR

¹**suc·cu·lent** \'sə-kyə-lənt\ adj 1 : full of juice : JUICY; also : having fleshy tissues that conserve moisture ⟨~ plants⟩ — **suc·cu·lence** \-ləns\ n

²**succulent** n : a succulent plant (as a cactus or an aloe)

suc·cumb \sə-'kəm\ vb 1 : to yield to superior strength or force or overpowering appeal or desire 2 : DIE ◆ **Synonyms** SUBMIT, CAPITULATE, RELENT, DEFER

¹**such** \'səch, 'sich\ adj 1 : of this or that kind 2 : having a quality just specified or to be specified

²**such** pron 1 : such a one or ones ⟨he's a star, and acted as ~⟩ 2 : that or those similar or related thereto ⟨boards and nails and ~⟩

³**such** adv : to that degree : so

such·like \'səch-ˌlīk\ adj : SIMILAR

¹**suck** \'sək\ vb 1 : to draw in liquid and esp. mother's milk with the mouth 2 : to draw liquid from by action of the mouth ⟨~ an orange⟩ 3 : to take in or up or remove by or as if by suction 4 slang : to be objectionable

²**suck** n 1 : a sucking movement or force 2 : the act of sucking

suck·er \'sə-kər\ n 1 : one that sucks 2 : a part of an animal's body used for sucking or for clinging 3 : any of numerous freshwater fishes with thick soft lips for sucking in food 4 : a shoot from the roots or lower part of a plant 5 : a person easily deceived 6 — used as a generalized term of reference ⟨see if you can get that ~ working again⟩

suck·le \'sə-kəl\ vb **suck·led; suck·ling** : to give or draw milk from the breast or udder; also : NURTURE

suck·ling \'sə-kliŋ\ n : a young unweaned mammal

suck–up \'sək-ˌəp\ n : a person who seeks to gain favor by flattery ⟨a ~ to the teacher⟩

su·cre \'sü-(ˌ)krā\ n — see MONEY table

su·crose \'sü-ˌkrōs, -ˌkrōz\ n : a sweet sugar obtained commercially esp. from sugarcane or sugar beets

suc·tion \'sək-shən\ n 1 : the act of sucking 2 : the act or process of drawing something (as liquid or dust) into a space (as in a vacuum cleaner or a pump) by partially exhausting the air in the space — **suc·tion·al** \-shə-nəl\ adj

suction cup n : a cup-shaped device in which a partial vacuum is produced when applied to a surface

sud·den \'sə-dᵊn\ adj [ME sodain, fr. AF sudain, fr. L subitaneus, fr. subitus sudden, fr. pp. of subire to come up] 1 : happening or coming unexpectedly ⟨~ shower⟩; also : changing angle or character all at once ⟨~ turn⟩ ⟨~ descent⟩ 2 : HASTY, RASH ⟨~ decision⟩ 3 : made or brought about in a short time : PROMPT ⟨~ cure⟩ ◆ **Synonyms** PRECIPITATE, HEADLONG, IMPETUOUS — **sud·den·ly** adv — **sud·den·ness** n

sudden infant death syndrome n : death due to unknown causes of an apparently healthy infant usu. before one year of age and esp. during sleep

suds \'sədz\ n pl : soapy water esp. when frothy — **sudsy** \'səd-zē\ adj

sue \'sü\ vb **sued; su·ing** [ME sewen, siuen to follow, strive for, petition, fr. AF sivre, siure, fr. VL *sequere, fr. L sequi to follow] 1 : PETITION, SOLICIT 2 : to seek justice or right by bringing legal action

suede also **suède** \'swād\ n [F gants de Suède Swedish gloves] 1 : leather with a napped surface 2 : a fabric with a suedelike nap

su·et \'sü-ət\ n : the hard fat from beef and mutton that yields tallow

suff abbr 1 sufficient 2 suffix

suf·fer \'sə-fər\ vb **suf·fered; suf·fer·ing** 1 : to feel or endure pain 2 : EXPERIENCE, UNDERGO ⟨~ a defeat⟩ 3 : to bear loss, damage, or injury 4 : ALLOW, PERMIT ◆ **Synonyms** ENDURE, ABIDE, TOLERATE, STAND, BROOK, STOMACH — **suf·fer·able** \'sə-fə-rə-bəl\ adj — **suf·fer·er** n

suf·fer·ance \'sə-frəns, -fə-rəns\ n 1 : consent or approval implied by lack of interference or resistance 2 : ENDURANCE, PATIENCE

suf·fer·ing \'sə-friŋ, -fə-riŋ\ n : PAIN, MISERY, HARDSHIP

suf·fice \sə-'fīs\ vb **suf·ficed; suf·fic·ing** 1 : to satisfy a need : be sufficient 2 : to be capable or competent

suf·fi·cien·cy \sə-'fi-shən-sē\ n 1 : a sufficient quantity to meet one's needs 2 : ADEQUACY

suf·fi·cient \sə-'fi-shənt\ adj : adequate to accomplish a purpose or meet a need — **suf·fi·cient·ly** adv

¹**suf·fix** \'sə-ˌfiks\ n : an affix occurring at the end of a word

²**suf·fix** \'sə-ˌfiks, (ˌ)sə-'fiks\ vb : to attach as a suffix — **suf·fix·ation** \ˌsə-ˌfik-'sā-shən\ n

suf·fo·cate \'sə-fə-ˌkāt\ vb **-cat·ed; -cat·ing** : STIFLE, SMOTHER, CHOKE — **suf·fo·cat·ing·ly** adv — **suf·fo·ca·tion** \ˌsə-fə-'kā-shən\ n

suf·fra·gan \'sə-fri-gən\ n : an assistant bishop; esp : one not having the right of succession — **suffragan** adj

suf·frage \'sə-frij\ n [L suffragium] 1 : VOTE 2 : the right to vote : FRANCHISE

suf·frag·ette \ˌsə-fri-'jet\ n : a woman who advocates suffrage for women

suf·frag·ist \'sə-fri-jist\ n : one who advocates extension of the suffrage esp. to women

suf·fuse \sə-'fyüz\ vb **suf·fused; suf-**

fus·ing : to spread over or through in the manner of a fluid or light ✦ *Synonyms* INFUSE, IMBUE, INGRAIN, STEEP — **suf·fu·sion** \-ˈfyü-zhən\ n

¹**sug·ar** \ˈshu̇-gər\ n 1 : a sweet substance that is colorless or white when pure and is chiefly sucrose from sugarcane or sugar beets 2 : a water-soluble compound (as glucose) similar to sucrose — **sug·ary** adj

²**sugar** vb **sug·ared; sug·ar·ing** 1 : to mix, cover, or sprinkle with sugar 2 : SWEETEN ⟨~ advice with flattery⟩ 3 : to form sugar ⟨a syrup that ~s⟩ 4 : GRANULATE

sugar beet n : a large beet with a white root from which sugar is made

sug·ar·cane \ˈshu̇-gər-ˌkān\ n : a tall grass widely grown in warm regions for the sugar in its stalks

sugar daddy n 1 : a well-to-do usu. older man who supports or spends lavishly on a mistress or girlfriend 2 : a generous benefactor of a cause

sugar maple n : a maple with a sweet sap; esp : one of eastern No. America with sap that is the chief source of maple syrup and maple sugar

sugar pea n : SNOW PEA

sug·ar·plum \ˈshu̇-gər-ˌpləm\ n : a small ball of candy

sug·gest \səg-ˈjest, sə-\ vb 1 : to put (as a thought, plan, or desire) into a person's mind 2 : to remind or evoke by association of ideas ✦ *Synonyms* IMPLY, HINT, INTIMATE, INSINUATE, CONNOTE

sug·gest·ible \səg-ˈjes-tə-bəl, sə-\ adj : easily influenced by suggestion

sug·ges·tion \-ˈjes-chən\ n 1 : an act or instance of suggesting; also : something suggested 2 : a slight indication

sug·ges·tive \-ˈjes-tiv\ adj : tending to suggest something; esp : suggesting something improper or indecent — **sug·ges·tive·ly** adv — **sug·ges·tive·ness** n

¹**sui·cide** \ˈsü-ə-ˌsīd\ n 1 : the act of killing oneself purposely 2 : one that commits or attempts suicide — **sui·cid·al** \ˌsü-ə-ˈsī-dᵊl\ adj

²**suicide** adj : being or performing a deliberate act resulting in the voluntary death of the person who does it ⟨a ~ mission⟩ ⟨a ~ bomber⟩

sui ge·ner·is \ˌsü-ˌī-ˈje-nə-rəs; ˌsü-ē-\ adj [L, of its own kind] : being in a class by itself : UNIQUE

¹**suit** \ˈsüt\ n 1 : an action in court to recover a right or claim 2 : an act of suing or entreating; esp : COURTSHIP 3 : a number of things used together ⟨~ of clothes⟩ 4 : all the playing cards in a pack bearing the same symbol

²**suit** vb 1 : to be appropriate or fitting 2 : to be becoming to 3 : to meet the needs or desires of : PLEASE

suit·able \ˈsü-tə-bəl\ adj : FITTING, PROPER, APPROPRIATE ⟨~ dress⟩ ✦ *Synonyms* FIT, MEET, APT, HAPPY — **suit·abil·i·ty** \ˌsü-tə-ˈbi-lə-tē\ n — **suit·able·ness** \ˈsü-tə-bəl-nəs\ n — **suit·ably** \-tə-blē\ adv

suit·case \ˈsüt-ˌkās\ n : a portable case designed to hold a traveler's clothing and personal articles

suite \ˈswēt, for 4 also ˈsüt\ n 1 : RETINUE 2 : a group of rooms occupied as a unit 3 : a modern instrumental composition in several movements of different character; also : a long orchestral concert arrangement in suite form of material drawn from a longer work 4 : a set of matched furniture for a room

suit·ing \ˈsü-tiŋ\ n : fabric for suits of clothes

suit·or \ˈsü-tər\ n 1 : one who sues or petitions 2 : one who courts a woman or seeks to marry her

su·ki·ya·ki \ˌskē-ˈyä-kē, ˌsu̇-kē-ˈyä-\ n : thin slices of meat, tofu, and vegetables cooked in soy sauce and sugar

sul·fa drug \ˈsəl-fə-\ n : any of various synthetic organic bacteria-inhibiting drugs

sul·fate \ˈsəl-ˌfāt\ n : a salt or ester of sulfuric acid

sul·fide \ˈsəl-ˈfīd\ n : a compound of sulfur

sul·fur also **sul·phur** \ˈsəl-fər\ n : a nonmetallic chemical element used esp. in the chemical and paper industries and in vulcanizing rubber

sulfur di·ox·ide \-dī-ˈäk-ˌsīd\ n : a heavy pungent toxic gas that is used esp. in bleaching, as a preservative, and as a refrigerant, and is a major air pollutant

sul·fu·ric \ˌsəl-ˈfyu̇r-ik\ adj : of, relating to, or containing sulfur

sulfuric acid or **sul·phu·ric acid** \ˌsəl-ˈfyu̇r-ik-\ n : a heavy corrosive oily strong acid

sul·fu·rous also **sul·phu·rous** \ˈsəl-fə-rəs, -fyə-, also esp for 1 ˌsəl-ˈfyu̇r-əs\ adj 1 : of, relating to, or containing sulfur 2 : of or relating to brimstone or the fire of hell : INFERNAL 3 : FIERY, INFLAMED ⟨~ sermons⟩

¹**sulk** \ˈsəlk\ vb : to be or become moodily silent or irritable

²**sulk** n : a sulky mood or spell

¹**sulky** \ˈsəl-kē\ adj **sulk·i·er; -est** : inclined to sulk : MOROSE, MOODY ✦ *Synonyms* GLUM, SURLY, SULLEN, GLOOMY — **sulk·i·ly** \ˈsəl-kə-lē\ adv — **sulk·i·ness** \-kē-nəs\ n

²**sulky** n, pl **sulkies** : a light 2-wheeled horse-drawn vehicle with a seat for the driver and usu. no body

sul·len \ˈsə-lən\ adj 1 : gloomily silent : MOROSE 2 : DISMAL, GLOOMY ⟨a ~ sky⟩ ✦ *Synonyms* GLUM, SURLY, DOUR, SATURNINE — **sul·len·ly** adv — **sul·len·ness** n

sul·ly \ˈsə-lē\ vb **sul·lied; sul·ly·ing** : SOIL, SMIRCH, DEFILE

sul·tan \ˈsəl-tᵊn\ n : a sovereign esp. of a Muslim state — **sul·tan·ate** \-ˌāt\ n

sul·ta·na \ˌsəl-ˈta-nə\ n 1 : a female member of a sultan's family 2 : a pale seedless grape; also : a raisin of this grape

sul·try \ˈsəl-trē\ adj **sul·tri·er; -est** [obs. E sulter to swelter, alter. of E swelter] : very hot and moist : SWELTERING; also : exciting sexual desire

¹**sum** \'səm\ n [ME summe, fr. AF sume, somme, fr. L summa, fr. fem. of summus highest] **1** : a quantity of money **2** : the whole amount **3** : GIST ⟨the ∼ of an argument⟩ **4** : the result obtained by adding numbers **5** : a problem in arithmetic

²**sum** vb **summed; sum·ming** : to find the sum of by adding or counting

su·mac also **su·mach** \'shü-ˌmak, 'shü-\ n : any of a genus of trees, shrubs, and woody vines having spikes or loose clusters of red or whitish berries

sum·ma·rise Brit var of SUMMARIZE

sum·ma·rize \'sə-mə-ˌrīz\ vb **-rized; -riz·ing** : to tell in a summary

¹**sum·ma·ry** \'sə-mə-rē\ adj **1** : covering the main points briefly : CONCISE **2** : done without delay or formality ⟨∼ punishment⟩ ♦ **Synonyms** TERSE, SUCCINCT, LACONIC — **sum·mar·i·ly** \(ˌ)sə-'mer-ə-lē, 'sə-mə-rə-lē\ adv

²**summary** n, pl **-ries** : a concise statement of the main points

sum·ma·tion \(ˌ)sə-'mā-shən\ n : a summing up; esp : a speech in court summing up the arguments in a case

sum·mer \'sə-mər\ n : the season of the year in a region in which the sun shines most directly : the warmest period of the year — **sum·mery** adj

sum·mer·house \'sə-mər-ˌhaús\ n : a covered structure in a garden or park to provide a shady retreat

summersault var of SOMERSAULT

summer squash n : any of various squashes (as zucchini) used as a vegetable while immature

sum·mit \'sə-mət\ n **1** : the highest point **2** : a conference of highest-level officials ⟨an economic ∼⟩

sum·mon \'sə-mən\ vb [ME somnen, somonen, fr. AF somondre, fr. VL *summonere, alter. of L summonēre to remind secretly] **1** : to call to a meeting : CONVOKE **2** : to send for; also : to order to appear in court **3** : to evoke esp. by an act of the will ⟨∼ up courage⟩ — **sum·mon·er** n

sum·mons \'sə-mənz\ n, pl **sum·mons·es 1** : an authoritative call to appear at a designated place or to attend to a duty **2** : a warning or citation to appear in court at a specified time to answer charges

sump·tu·ous \'səmp-shə-wəs, -chə-\ adj : LAVISH, LUXURIOUS ⟨a ∼ banquet⟩ ⟨a ∼ residence⟩

sum up vb : SUMMARIZE

¹**sun** \'sən\ n **1** : the shining celestial body around which the earth and other planets revolve and from which they receive light and heat **2** : a celestial body like the sun **3** : SUNSHINE — **sun·less** adj — **sun·ny** adj

²**sun** vb **sunned; sun·ning 1** : to expose to or as if to the rays of the sun **2** : to sun oneself

Sun abbr Sunday

sun·bath \'sən-ˌbath, -ˌbäth\ n : an exposure to sunlight or a sunlamp — **sun·bathe** \-ˌbāth\ vb

sun·beam \-ˌbēm\ n : a ray of sunlight

sun·block \'sən-ˌbläk\ n : a preparation used on the skin to prevent sunburn (as by blocking ultraviolet radiation)

sun·bon·net \-ˌbä-nət\ n : a bonnet with a wide brim to shield the face and neck from the sun

¹**sun·burn** \-ˌbərn\ vb **-burned** \-ˌbərnd\ or **-burnt** \-ˌbərnt\; **-burn·ing** : to cause or become affected with sunburn

²**sunburn** n : a skin inflammation caused by overexposure to ultraviolet radiation esp. from sunshine

sun·dae \'sən-(ˌ)dā, -dē\ n : ice cream served with topping

Sun·day \'sən-ˌdā, -dē\ n : the 1st day of the week : the Christian Sabbath

sun·der \'sən-dər\ vb : to force apart ♦ **Synonyms** SEVER, PART, DISJOIN, DISUNITE

sun·di·al \'sən-ˌdī(-ə)l\ n : a device for showing the time of day from the shadow cast on a plate by an object with a straight edge

sun·down \-ˌdaún\ n : SUNSET 2

sun·dries \'sən-drēz\ n pl : various small articles or items

sun·dry \'sən-drē\ adj : SEVERAL, DIVERS, VARIOUS ⟨for ∼ reasons⟩

sun·fish \'sən-ˌfish\ n **1** : a large marine fish with a deep flattened body **2** : any of numerous often brightly colored No. American freshwater fishes related to the perches and usu. having the body flattened from side to side

sun·flow·er \-ˌflaú-(ə)r\ n : any of a genus of tall New World plants related to the daisies and often grown for the oil-rich seeds of their yellow-petaled dark-centered flower heads

sung past and past part of SING

sun·glasses \'sən-ˌgla-səz\ n pl : glasses to protect the eyes from the sun

sunk past and past part of SINK

sunk·en \'sən-kən\ adj **1** : SUBMERGED ⟨∼ ships⟩ **2** : fallen in : HOLLOW ⟨∼ cheeks⟩ **3** : lying in a depression ⟨∼ garden⟩; also : constructed below the general floor level ⟨a ∼ living room⟩

sun·lamp \'sən-ˌlamp\ n : an electric lamp designed to emit radiation of wavelengths from ultraviolet to infrared

sun·light \-ˌlīt\ n : SUNSHINE

sun·lit \-ˌlit\ adj : lighted by or as if by the sun

sun protection factor n : a number that is the factor by which the time required for unprotected skin to become sunburned is increased when a sunscreen is used

sun·rise \-ˌrīz\ n **1** : the apparent rising of the sun above the horizon **2** : the time at which the sun rises

sun·roof \-ˌrüf, -ˌrúf\ n : a panel in an automobile roof that can be opened

sun·screen \-ˌskrēn\ n : a preparation on the skin to prevent sunburn (as by absorbing ultraviolet radiation)

sun·set \-ˌset\ n **1** : the apparent descent of the sun below the horizon **2** : the time at which the sun sets

sun·shade \'sən-ˌshād\ n : something (as a parasol or awning) used as a protection from the sun's rays

sun·shine \-ˌshīn\ n : the direct light of the sun — **sun·shiny** adj

sun·spot \-ˌspät\ n : any of the dark spots that appear at times on the sun's surface

sun·stroke \-ˌströk\ n : heatstroke caused by direct exposure to the sun

sun·tan \-ˌtan\ n : a browning of the skin from exposure to the sun's rays

sun-up \-ˌəp\ n : SUNRISE 2

¹sup \'səp\ vb **supped; sup·ping** : to take or drink in swallows or gulps

²sup n : a mouthful esp. of liquor or broth; also : a small quantity of liquid

³sup vb **supped; sup·ping** 1 : to eat the evening meal 2 : to make one's supper ⟨supped on roast beef⟩

⁴sup abbr 1 superior 3 supplement; supplementary 3 supply 4 supra

¹su·per \'sü-pər\ adj 1 : very fine : EXCELLENT 2 : EXTREME, EXCESSIVE ⟨~ secrecy⟩

²super n : SUPERINTENDENT

super- \sü-pər\ prefix 1 : over and above : higher in quantity, quality, or degree than : more than 2 : in addition : extra 3 : exceeding a norm 4 : in excessive degree or intensity 5 : surpassing all or most others of its kind 6 : situated above, on, or at the top of 7 : next above or higher 8 : more inclusive than 9 : superior in status or position

su·per·abun·dant \ˌsü-pər-ə-'bən-dənt\ adj : more than ample — **su·per·abun·dance** \-dən(t)s\ n

su·per·an·nu·ate \ˌsü-pər-'an-yə-ˌwāt\ vb **-at·ed; -at·ing** 1 : to make out-of-date 2 : to retire and pension because of age or infirmity — **su·per·an·nu·at·ed** adj

su·perb \sü-'pərb\ adj [L superbus excellent, proud, fr. super above] : marked to the highest degree by excellence, brilliance, or competence ✦ **Synonyms** RESPLENDENT, GLORIOUS, GORGEOUS, SUBLIME — **su·perb·ly** adv

su·per·charg·er \'sü-pər-ˌchär-jər\ n : a device for increasing the amount of air supplied to an internal combustion engine

su·per·cil·ious \ˌsü-pər-'si-lē-əs\ adj [L superciliosus, fr. supercilium eyebrow, haughtiness] : haughtily contemptuous ✦ **Synonyms** DISDAINFUL, OVERBEARING, ARROGANT, LORDLY, SUPERIOR

su·per·com·put·er \'sü-pər-kəm-ˌpyü-tər\ n : a large very fast mainframe

su·per·con·duc·tiv·i·ty \ˌsü-pər-ˌkän-ˌdək-'ti-və-tē\ n : a complete disappearance of electrical resistance in a substance esp. at very low temperatures — **su·per·con·duc·tive** \-kən-'dək-tiv\ adj — **su·per·con·duc·tor** \-'dək-tər\ n

su·per·con·ti·nent \'sü-pər-ˌkän-tə-nənt\ n : a former large continent from which

other continents are held to have broken off and drifted away

su·per·ego \ˌsü-pər-'ē-gō\ n : the one of the three divisions of the psyche in psychoanalytic theory that functions to reward and punish through a system of moral attitudes, conscience, and a sense of guilt

su·per·fi·cial \ˌsü-pər-'fi-shəl\ adj 1 : of or relating to the surface or appearance only 2 : not thorough : SHALLOW — **su·per·fi·ci·al·i·ty** \-ˌfi-shē-'a-lə-tē\ n — **su·per·fi·cial·ly** adv

su·per·flu·ous \sü-'pər-flə-wəs\ adj : exceeding what is sufficient or necessary : SURPLUS ✦ **Synonyms** EXTRA, SPARE, SUPERNUMERARY — **su·per·flu·i·ty** \ˌsü-pər-'flü-ə-tē\ n

su·per·high·way \ˌsü-pər-'hī-ˌwā\ n : a broad highway designed for high-speed traffic

su·per·im·pose \-im-'pōz\ vb : to lay (one thing) over or above something else

su·per·in·tend \ˌsü-pə-rin-'tend\ vb : to have or exercise the charge and oversight of : DIRECT — **su·per·in·ten·dence** \-'ten-dəns\ n — **su·per·in·ten·den·cy** \-dən-sē\ n — **su·per·in·ten·dent** \-dənt\ n

¹su·pe·ri·or \sü-'pir-ē-ər\ adj 1 : situated higher up, over, or near the top; also : higher in rank or numbers 2 : of greater value or importance 3 : courageously indifferent (as to pain or misfortune) 4 : better than most others of its kind 5 : ARROGANT, HAUGHTY — **su·pe·ri·or·i·ty** \-ˌpir-ē-'ȯr-ə-tē\ n

²superior n 1 : one who is above another in rank, office, or station; esp : the head of a religious house or order 2 : one higher in quality or merit

¹su·per·la·tive \sü-'pər-lə-tiv\ adj 1 : of, relating to, or constituting the degree of grammatical comparison that denotes an extreme or unsurpassed level or extent 2 : surpassing others : SUPREME ✦ **Synonyms** PEERLESS, INCOMPARABLE, SUPERB — **su·per·la·tive·ly** adv

²superlative n 1 : the superlative degree or a superlative form in a language 2 : the utmost degree : ACME

su·per·mar·ket \'sü-pər-ˌmär-kət\ n : a self-service retail market selling foods and household merchandise

su·per·mod·el \'sü-pər-ˌmä-dᵊl\ n : a famous and successful fashion model

su·per·mom \'sü-pər-ˌmäm\ n : an exemplary mother; also : a woman who performs the duties of housekeeping and raising children while also having a full-time job

su·per·nal \sü-'pər-nəl\ adj 1 : being or coming from on high 2 : of heavenly or spiritual character

su·per·nat·u·ral \ˌsü-pər-'na-chə-rəl\ adj : of or relating to phenomena beyond or

superabsorbent	supercity	superheat	superhumanly
superachiever	superclean	superheavy	superindividual
superagency	superexpensive	superhero	superliner
superblock	superfast	superhuman	superman
superbomb	superfine		

outside of nature; *esp* : relating to or attributed to a divinity, ghost, or devil —
su·per·nat·u·ral·ly *adv*

su·per·no·va \ˌsü-pər-ˈnō-və\ *n* : the explosion of a very large star

¹**su·per·nu·mer·ary** \-ˈnü-mə-ˌrer-ē, -ˈnyü-\ *adj* : exceeding the usual or required number : EXTRA ♦ *Synonyms* SURPLUS, SUPERFLUOUS, SPARE

²**supernumerary** *n, pl* **-ar·ies** : an extra person or thing; *esp* : an actor hired for a nonspeaking part

su·per·pose \ˌsü-pər-ˈpōz\ *vb* **-posed; -pos·ing** : SUPERIMPOSE — **su·per·po·si·tion** \-pə-ˈzi-shən\ *n*

su·per·pow·er \ˈsü-pər-ˌpaù(-ə)r\ *n* 1 : excessive or superior power 2 : one of a few politically and militarily dominant nations

su·per·sat·u·rat·ed \-ˈsa-chə-ˌrā-təd\ *adj* : containing an amount of a substance greater than that required for saturation

su·per·scribe \ˈsü-pər-ˌskrīb, ˌsü-pər-ˈskrīb\ *vb* **-scribed; -scrib·ing** : to write on the top or outside : ADDRESS — **su·per·scrip·tion** \ˌsü-pər-ˈskrip-shən\ *n*

su·per·script \ˈsü-pər-ˌskript\ *n* : a symbol (as a numeral or letter) written immediately above or above and to one side of another character

su·per·sede \ˌsü-pər-ˈsēd\ *vb* **-sed·ed; -sed·ing** [ME (Sc) *superceden* to defer, fr. MF *superceder*, fr. L *supersedēre* to be superior to, refrain from, fr. *super-* above + *sedēre* to sit] : to take the place of : REPLACE

su·per·son·ic \-ˈsä-nik\ *adj* 1 : ULTRASONIC 2 : being or relating to speeds from one to five times the speed of sound; *also* : capable of moving at such a speed ⟨a ∼ airplane⟩

su·per·sti·tion \ˌsü-pər-ˈsti-shən\ *n* 1 : beliefs or practices resulting from ignorance, fear of the unknown, or trust in magic or chance 2 : an unreasoning fear of nature, the unknown, or God resulting from superstition — **su·per·sti·tious** \-shəs\ *adj*

su·per·struc·ture \ˈsü-pər-ˌstrək-chər\ *n* : something built on a base or as a vertical extension

su·per·ti·tle \ˈsü-pər-ˌtī-t³l\ *n* : a translation of foreign-language dialogue displayed above a screen or performance

su·per·vene \ˌsü-pər-ˈvēn\ *vb* **-vened; -ven·ing** : to occur as something additional or unexpected

su·per·vise \ˈsü-pər-ˌvīz\ *vb* **-vised; -vis·ing** : OVERSEE, SUPERINTEND — **su·per·vi·sion** \ˌsü-pər-ˈvi-zhən\ *n* — **su·per·vi·sor** \ˈsü-pər-ˌvī-zər\ *n* — **su·per·vi·so·ry** \ˌsü-pər-ˈvī-zə-rē\ *adj*

su·pine \sü-ˈpīn\ *adj* 1 : lying on the back or with the face upward 2 : LETHARGIC, SLUGGISH; *also* : ABJECT

♦ *Synonyms* INACTIVE, INERT, PASSIVE, IDLE

supp *or* **suppl** *abbr* supplement; supplementary

sup·per \ˈsə-pər\ *n* : the evening meal esp. when dinner is taken at midday — **sup·per·time** \-ˌtīm\ *n*

sup·plant \sə-ˈplant\ *vb* 1 : to take the place of (another) esp. by force or trickery 2 : REPLACE

sup·ple \ˈsə-pəl\ *adj* **sup·pler; sup·plest** 1 : COMPLIANT, ADAPTABLE ⟨a ∼ soprano⟩ 2 : capable of bending without breaking or creasing : LIMBER ♦ *Synonyms* RESILIENT, ELASTIC, FLEXIBLE

¹**sup·ple·ment** \ˈsə-plə-mənt\ *n* 1 : something that supplies a want or makes an addition 2 : DIETARY SUPPLEMENT 3 : a continuation (as of a book) containing corrections or additional material — **sup·ple·men·tal** \ˌsə-plə-ˈmen-t³l\ *adj* — **sup·ple·men·ta·ry** \-ˈmen-tə-rē\ *adj*

²**sup·ple·ment** \ˈsə-plə-ˌment\ *vb* : to fill up the deficiencies of : add to — **sup·ple·men·ta·tion** \ˌsə-plə-ˌmen-ˈtā-shən, -mən-\ *n*

sup·pli·ant \ˈsə-plē-ənt\ *n* : one who supplicates : PETITIONER, PLEADER

sup·pli·cant \ˈsə-pli-kənt\ *n* : SUPPLIANT

sup·pli·cate \ˈsə-plə-ˌkāt\ *vb* **-cat·ed; -cat·ing** 1 : to make a humble entreaty; *esp* : to pray to God 2 : to ask earnestly and humbly : BESEECH ♦ *Synonyms* IMPLORE, BEG, ENTREAT, PLEAD — **sup·pli·ca·tion** \ˌsə-plə-ˈkā-shən\ *n*

¹**sup·ply** \sə-ˈplī\ *vb* **sup·plied; sup·ply·ing** [ME *supplien*, to complete, compensate for, fr. MF *souplier* fr. L *supplēre* to fill up, supplement, supply, fr. *sub-* under, up to + *plēre* to fill] 1 : to add as a supplement 2 : to satisfy the needs of 3 : FURNISH, PROVIDE — **sup·pli·er** *n*

²**supply** *n, pl* **supplies** 1 : the quantity or amount (as of a commodity) needed or available; *also* : PROVISIONS, STORES — usu. used in pl. 2 : the act or process of filling a want or need : PROVISION 3 : the quantities of goods or services offered for sale at a particular time or at one price

sup·ply-side \sə-ˈplī-ˌsīd\ *adj* : of, relating to, or being an economic theory that recommends the reduction of tax rates to expand economic activity

¹**sup·port** \sə-ˈpōrt\ *vb* 1 : BEAR, TOLERATE 2 : to take sides with : BACK, ASSIST 3 : to provide with food, clothing, and shelter 4 : to hold up or serve as a foundation for ♦ *Synonyms* UPHOLD, ADVOCATE, CHAMPION — **sup·port·able** *adj* — **sup·port·er** *n* — **sup·port·ive** \-ˈpōr-tiv\ *adj*

²**support** *n* 1 : the act of supporting : the state of being supported 2 : one that supports : PROP, BASE

supernormal	supersalesman	superspy	superstrong
superpatriot	supersecret	superstar	supersubtle
superpatriotic	supersize	superstate	supersystem
superpatriotism	supersized	superstore	supertanker
superpremium	supersmart	superstratum	superthin
superrich	supersophisticated	superstrength	superwoman

support group *n* : a group of people with common experiences and concerns who provide emotional and moral support for one another

sup·pose \sə-'pōz\ *vb* **sup·posed; sup·pos·ing** **1** : to assume to be true (as for the sake of argument) **2** : EXPECT ⟨I am *supposed* to go⟩ **3** : to think probable — **sup·pos·al** *n*

sup·posed \sə-'pōzd, -'pō-zəd\ *adj* : BELIEVED; *also* : mistakenly believed — **sup·pos·ed·ly** \-'pō-zəd-lē, -'pōzd-lē\ *adv*

sup·pos·ing *conj* : if by way of hypothesis : on the assumption that ⟨∼ I did agree with you⟩

sup·po·si·tion \ˌsə-pə-'zi-shən\ *n* **1** : something that is supposed : HYPOTHESIS **2** : the act of supposing

sup·pos·i·to·ry \sə-'pä-zə-ˌtór-ē\ *n, pl* **-ries** [ME *suppositorie*, fr. AF, fr. ML *suppositorium*, fr. LL, neut. of *suppositorius* placed beneath] : a small easily melted mass of usu. medicated material for insertion (as into the rectum)

sup·press \sə-'pres\ *vb* **1** : to put down by authority or force : SUBDUE ⟨∼ a revolt⟩ **2** : to keep from being known; *also* : to stop the publication or circulation of **3** : to hold back : REPRESS ⟨∼ anger⟩ ⟨∼ a cough⟩ — **sup·press·ible** \-'pre-sə-bəl\ *adj* — **sup·pres·sion** \-'pre-shən\ *n* — **sup·pres·sor** \-'pre-sər\ *n*

sup·pres·sant \sə-'pre-sᵊnt\ *n* : an agent (as a drug) suppressing rather than eliminating something ⟨a cough ∼⟩

sup·pu·rate \'sə-pyə-ˌrāt\ *vb* **-rat·ed; -rat·ing** : to form or give off pus — **sup·pu·ra·tion** \ˌsə-pyə-'rā-shən\ *n*

su·pra \'sü-prə, -ˌprä\ *adv* : earlier in this writing : ABOVE

su·pra·na·tion·al \ˌsü-prə-'na-shə-nəl, -ˌprä-\ *adj* : going beyond national boundaries, authority, or interests ⟨∼ organizations⟩

su·prem·a·cist \su̇-'pre-mə-sist\ *n* : an advocate of group supremacy

su·prem·a·cy \su̇-'pre-mə-sē\ *n, pl* **-cies** : supreme rank, power, or authority

su·preme \su̇-'prēm\ *adj* [L *supremus*, superl. of *superus* upper, fr. *super* over, above] **1** : highest in rank or authority **2** : highest in degree or quality ⟨∼ among poets⟩ **3** : ULTIMATE ⟨the ∼ sacrifice⟩ ♦ *Synonyms* SUPERLATIVE, SURPASSING, PEERLESS, INCOMPARABLE — **su·preme·ly** *adv* — **su·preme·ness** *n*

Supreme Being *n* : GOD 1

supt *abbr* superintendent

sur·cease \'sər-ˌsēs\ *n* : CESSATION, RESPITE

¹**sur·charge** \'sər-ˌchärj\ *vb* **1** : to fill to excess : OVERLOAD **2** : to apply a surcharge to (postage stamps)

²**surcharge** *n* **1** : an extra fee or cost **2** : an excessive load or burden **3** : something officially printed on a postage stamp esp. to change its value

sur·cin·gle \'sər-ˌsiŋ-gəl\ *n* : a band put around a horse's body to make something (as a saddle) fast

¹**sure** \'shu̇r\ *adj* **sur·er; sur·est** [ME, *seur, sure*, fr. AF *seur*, fr. L *securus* secure] **1** : firmly established **2** : TRUSTWORTHY, RELIABLE ⟨a ∼ friend⟩ **3** : CONFIDENT ⟨I'm ∼ I'm right⟩ **4** : not to be disputed : UNDOUBTED **5** : bound to happen **6** : careful to remember or attend to something ⟨be ∼ to lock the door⟩ ♦ *Synonyms* CERTAIN, COCKSURE, POSITIVE — **sure·ness** *n*

²**sure** *adv* : SURELY

sure-fire \'shu̇r-ˌfī(-ə)r\ *adj* : certain to get results : DEPENDABLE

sure·ly \'shu̇r-lē\ *adv* **1** : in a sure manner **2** : without doubt **3** : INDEED, REALLY ⟨∼, you don't believe that⟩

sure·ty \'shu̇r-ə-tē\ *n, pl* **-ties** **1** : SURENESS, CERTAINTY **2** : something that makes sure : GUARANTEE **3** : one who is a guarantor for another person

¹**surf** \'sərf\ *n* : waves that break upon the shore; *also* : the sound or foam of breaking waves

²**surf** *vb* **1** : to ride the surf (as on a surfboard) **2** : to scan the offerings of (as television or the Internet) for something of interest — **surf·er** *n* — **surf·ing** *n*

¹**sur·face** \'sər-fəs\ *n* **1** : the outside of an object or body **2** : outward aspect or appearance — **surface** *adj*

²**surface** *vb* **sur·faced; sur·fac·ing** **1** : to give a surface to : make smooth **2** : to rise to the surface

surf·board \'sərf-ˌbȯrd\ *n* : a buoyant board used in surfing

¹**sur·feit** \'sər-fət\ *n* **1** : EXCESS, SUPERABUNDANCE **2** : excessive indulgence (as in food or drink) **3** : disgust caused by excess

²**surfeit** *vb* : to feed, supply, or indulge to the point of surfeit : CLOY

surg *abbr* surgeon; surgery; surgical

¹**surge** \'sərj\ *vb* **surged; surg·ing** **1** : to rise and fall actively : TOSS **2** : to move in waves **3** : to rise suddenly to an excessive or abnormal value

²**surge** *n* **1** : a sweeping onward like a wave of the sea ⟨a ∼ of emotion⟩ **2** : a large billow **3** : a transient sudden increase of current or voltage in an electrical circuit

sur·geon \'sər-jən\ *n* : a physician who specializes in surgery

sur·gery \'sər-jə-rē\ *n, pl* **-ger·ies** [ME *surgerie*, fr. AF *cirurgerie, surgerie*, fr. L *chirurgia*, fr. Gk *cheirourgia*, fr. *cheirourgos* surgeon, fr. *cheirourgos* doing by hand, fr. *cheir* hand + *ergon* work] **1** : a branch of medicine concerned with the correction of physical defects, the repair of injuries, and the treatment of disease esp. by operations **2** : a room or area where surgery is performed **3** : the work done by a surgeon

sur·gi·cal \'sər-ji-kəl\ *adj* : of, relating to, or associated with surgeons or surgery — **sur·gi·cal·ly** \-k(ə-)lē\ *adv*

sur·ly \'sər-lē\ *adj* **sur·li·er; -est** [alter. of ME *serreli* lordly, imperious, prob. fr. *sire, ser* sire] : having a rude unfriendly disposition ♦ *Synonyms* MOROSE, GLUM,

SULLEN, SULKY, GLOOMY — **sur·li·ness**
\-lē-nəs\ *n*

sur·mise \sər-ˈmīz\ *vb* **sur·mised; sur·mis·ing** : to form a notion of from scanty evidence ◆ **Synonyms** CONJECTURE, PRESUME, SUPPOSE — **surmise** *n*

sur·mount \sər-ˈmaůnt\ *vb* **1** : to prevail over : OVERCOME **2** : to get to or lie at the top of

sur·name \ˈsər-ˌnām\ *n* **1** : NICKNAME **2** : the name borne in common by members of a family

sur·pass \sər-ˈpas\ *vb* **1** : to be superior to in quality, degree, or performance : EXCEL **2** : to go beyond the reach or powers of ◆ **Synonyms** TRANSCEND, OUTDO, OUTSTRIP, EXCEED — **sur·pass·ing·ly** *adv*

sur·plice \ˈsər-pləs\ *n* : a loose white outer vestment usu. of knee length

sur·plus \ˈsər-(ˌ)pləs\ *n* **1** : quantity left over : EXCESS **2** : the excess of assets over liabilities ◆ **Synonyms** SUPERFLUITY, OVERABUNDANCE, SURFEIT

¹sur·prise \sər-ˈprīz\ *n* **1** : an attack made without warning **2** : a taking unawares **3** : something that surprises **4** : AMAZEMENT, ASTONISHMENT

²surprise *vb* **sur·prised; sur·pris·ing 1** : to come upon and attack unexpectedly **2** : to take unawares **3** : AMAZE ⟨his conduct *surprised* me⟩ **4** : to cause astonishment or surprise ⟨her success didn't ~⟩ ◆ **Synonyms** ASTONISH, ASTOUND, DUMBFOUND — **sur·pris·ing** *adj*

sur·pris·ing·ly \-ˈprī-ziŋ-lē\ *adv* **1** : in a surprising manner or degree **2** : it is surprising that ⟨~, voter turnout was high⟩

sur·re·al \sə-ˈrē-əl, -ˈrēl\ *adj* **1** : having the intense irrational reality of a dream **2** : of or relating to surrealism — **sur·re·al·ly** *adv*

sur·re·al·ism \sə-ˈrē-ə-ˌli-zəm\ *n* : art, literature, or theater characterized by fantastic or incongruous imagery or effects produced by unnatural juxtapositions and combinations — **sur·re·al·ist** \-list\ *n or adj* — **sur·re·al·is·tic** \-ˌrē-ə-ˈlis-tik\ *adj* — **sur·re·al·is·ti·cal·ly** \-ti-k(ə-)lē\ *adv*

¹sur·ren·der \sə-ˈren-dər\ *vb* **1** : to yield to the power of another : give up under compulsion **2** : RELINQUISH

²surrender *n* : the act of giving up or yielding oneself or the possession of something to another

sur·rep·ti·tious \ˌsər-əp-ˈti-shəs\ *adj* : done, made, or acquired by stealth : CLANDESTINE ◆ **Synonyms** UNDERHAND, COVERT, FURTIVE — **sur·rep·ti·tious·ly** *adv*

sur·rey \ˈsər-ē\ *n, pl* **surreys** : a 2-seated horse-drawn carriage

sur·ro·ga·cy \ˈsər-ə-gə-sē\ *n* : SURROGATE MOTHERHOOD

sur·ro·gate \ˈsər-ə-ˌgāt, -gət\ *n* **1** : DEPUTY, SUBSTITUTE **2** : a law officer in some states with authority in the probate of wills, the settlement of estates, and the appointment of guardians **3** : SURROGATE MOTHER

surrogate mother *n* : a woman who becomes pregnant (as by surgical implantation of a fertilized egg) in order to carry the fetus for another woman — **surrogate motherhood** *n*

sur·round \sə-ˈraůnd\ *vb* **1** : to enclose on all sides : ENCIRCLE **2** : to enclose so as to cut off retreat or escape

sur·round·ings \sə-ˈraůn-diŋz\ *n pl* : conditions by which one is surrounded

surround sound *n* : sound reproduction that uses three or more transmission channels

sur·tax \ˈsər-ˌtaks\ *n* : an additional tax over and above a normal tax

sur·tout \(ˌ)sər-ˈtü\ *n* [F, fr. *sur* over + *tout* all] : a man's long close-fitting overcoat

surv *abbr* survey; surveying; surveyor

sur·veil·lance \sər-ˈvā-ləns\ *n* [F] : close watch; *also* : SUPERVISION

¹sur·vey \sər-ˈvā\ *vb* **sur·veyed; sur·vey·ing** [ME, fr. AF *surveer* to look over, fr. *sur-* over + *veer* to see, fr. L *vidēre*] **1** : to look over and examine closely **2** : to find and represent the contours, measurements, and position of a part of the earth's surface (as a tract of land) **3** : to view or study something as a whole ◆ **Synonyms** SCRUTINIZE, EXAMINE, INSPECT, STUDY — **sur·vey·or** \-ər\ *n*

²sur·vey \ˈsər-ˌvā\ *n, pl* **surveys** : the act or an instance of surveying; *also* : something that is surveyed

sur·viv·al·ism \sər-ˈvī-və-ˌli-zəm\ *n* : an attitude, policy, or practice based on the primacy of survival as a value — **sur·viv·al·ist** \-və-list\ *n or adj*

sur·vive \sər-ˈvīv\ *vb* **sur·vived; sur·viv·ing 1** : to remain alive or existent **2** : OUTLIVE, OUTLAST — **sur·viv·al** *n* — **sur·vi·vor** \-ˈvī-vər\ *n*

sus·cep·ti·ble \sə-ˈsep-tə-bəl\ *adj* **1** : of such a nature as to permit ⟨words ~ of being misunderstood⟩ **2** : having little resistance to a stimulus or agency ⟨~ to colds⟩ **3** : IMPRESSIONABLE, RESPONSIVE ⟨a ~ mind⟩ ◆ **Synonyms** SENSITIVE, SUBJECT, EXPOSED, PRONE, LIABLE, OPEN — **sus·cep·ti·bil·i·ty** \-ˌsep-tə-ˈbi-lə-tē\ *n*

su·shi \ˈsü-shē\ *n* [Jp] : cold rice formed into various shapes and garnished esp. with bits of raw fish or seafood

¹sus·pect \ˈsəs-ˌpekt, sə-ˈspekt\ *adj* : regarded with suspicion; *also* : QUESTIONABLE

²sus·pect \ˈsəs-ˌpekt\ *n* : one who is suspected (as of a crime)

³sus·pect \sə-ˈspekt\ *vb* **1** : to have doubts of : MISTRUST **2** : to imagine to be guilty without proof **3** : SURMISE

sus·pend \sə-ˈspend\ *vb* **1** : to bar temporarily from a privilege, office, or function **2** : to stop temporarily : make inactive for a time **3** : to withhold (judgment) for a time **4** : HANG; *esp* : to hang so as to be free except at one point **5** : to put or hold in suspension **6** : to keep from falling or sinking by some invisible support

sus·pend·er \sə-ˈspen-dər\ *n* : one of two supporting straps which pass over the shoulders and to which the pants are fastened

sus·pense \sə-'spens\ n 1 : SUSPENSION 2 : mental uncertainty : ANXIETY 3 : excitement as to an outcome — **suspense·ful** adj

sus·pen·sion \sə-'spen-chən\ n 1 : the act of suspending : the state or period of being suspended 2 : the state of a substance when its particles are mixed with but undissolved in a fluid or solid; also : a substance in this state 3 : something suspended 4 : the system of devices supporting the upper part of a vehicle on the axles

sus·pen·so·ry \sə-'spen-sə-rē\ adj 1 : SUSPENDED; also : fitted or serving to suspend something 2 : temporarily leaving undetermined

sus·pi·cion \sə-'spi-shən\ n 1 : the act or an instance of suspecting something wrong without proof 2 : TRACE, SOUPÇON ⟨a ~ of garlic⟩ ✦ Synonyms MISTRUST, UNCERTAINTY, DOUBT, SKEPTICISM

sus·pi·cious \sə-'spi-shəs\ adj 1 : open to or arousing suspicion 2 : inclined to suspect 3 : showing suspicion — **sus·pi·cious·ly** adv

sus·tain \sə-'stān\ vb 1 : to provide with nourishment 2 : to keep going : PROLONG ⟨~ed effort⟩ 3 : to hold up : PROP 4 : to hold up under : ENDURE 5 : SUFFER ⟨~ a broken arm⟩ 6 : to support as true, legal, or valid 7 : PROVE, CORROBORATE — **sus·tain·able** \sə-'stā-nə-bəl\ adj

sus·te·nance \'səs-tə-nəns\ n 1 : FOOD, NOURISHMENT 2 : a supplying with the necessities of life 3 : something that sustains or supports

su·ture \'sü-chər\ n 1 : material or a stitch for sewing a wound together 2 : a seam or line along which two things or parts are joined or as if by sewing

SUV \,es-,yü-'vē\ n [sport-utility vehicle] : a vehicle similar to a station wagon but built on a light-truck chassis

su·zer·ain \'sü-zə-rən, -,rān\ n [F] 1 : a feudal lord 2 : a nation that has political control over the foreign relations of another nation — **su·zer·ain·ty** \-tē\ n

svc or **svce** abbr service

svelte \'sfelt\ adj **svelt·er**; **svelt·est** [F, fr. It svelto, fr. pp. of svellere to pluck out, modif. of L evellere, fr. e- out + vellere to pluck] : SLENDER, LITHE

svgs abbr savings

SW abbr 1 shortwave 2 southwest

¹**swab** \'swäb\ n 1 : MOP 2 : a wad of absorbent material esp. for applying medicine or for cleaning; also : a sample taken with a swab 3 : SAILOR

²**swab** vb **swabbed**; **swab·bing** : to use a swab on : MOP

swad·dle \'swä-d³l\ vb **swad·dled**; **swad·dling** 1 : to bind (an infant) in bands of cloth 2 : to wrap up : SWATHE

swaddling clothes n pl : bands of cloth wrapped around an infant

swag \'swag\ n : stolen goods : LOOT

swag·ger \'swa-gər\ vb 1 : to walk with a conceited swing or strut 2 : BOAST, BRAG — **swagger** n

Swa·hi·li \swä-'hē-lē\ n : a language that is a trade and governmental language over much of eastern Africa and the Congo region

swain \'swān\ n [ME swein boy, servant, fr. ON sveinn] 1 : RUSTIC; esp : SHEPHERD 2 : ADMIRER, SUITOR

SWAK abbr sealed with a kiss

¹**swal·low** \'swä-lō\ n : any of numerous small long-winged migratory birds that often have a deeply forked tail

²**swallow** vb 1 : to take into the stomach through the throat 2 : to envelop or take in as if by swallowing 3 : to accept or believe without question, protest, or anger

³**swallow** n 1 : an act of swallowing 2 : an amount that can be swallowed at one time

swal·low·tail \'swä-lō-,tāl\ n 1 : a deeply forked and tapering tail like that of a swallow 2 : TAILCOAT 3 : any of various large butterflies with the border of each hind wing usu. drawn out into a process resembling a tail — **swal·low–tailed** \-,tāld\ adj

swam past of SWIM

swa·mi \'swä-mē\ n [Hindi svāmī, fr. Skt svāmin owner, lord] : a Hindu ascetic or religious teacher

¹**swamp** \'swämp\ n : a spongy wetland — **swamp** adj — **swampy** adj

²**swamp** vb 1 : to fill or become filled with or as if with water 2 : OVERWHELM 3

swamp·land \-,land\ n : SWAMP

swan \'swän\ n, pl **swans** also **swan** : any of various heavy-bodied long-necked mostly pure white swimming birds related to the geese

¹**swank** \'swaŋk\ or **swanky** \'swaŋ-kē\ adj **swank·er** or **swank·i·er**; **-est** : showily smart and dashing; also : fashionably elegant

²**swank** n 1 : PRETENTIOUSNESS 2 : ELEGANCE

swans·down \'swänz-,daún\ n 1 : the very soft down of a swan used esp. for trimming 2 : a soft thick cotton flannel

swan song n : a farewell appearance, act, or pronouncement

swap \'swäp\ vb **swapped**; **swap·ping** : TRADE, EXCHANGE — **swap** n

sward \'sword\ n : the grassy surface of land

¹**swarm** \'sworm\ n 1 : a great number of honeybees leaving together from a hive with a queen to start a new colony; also : a hive of bees 2 : a large crowd

²**swarm** vb 1 : to form in a swarm and depart from a hive 2 : to throng together : gather in great numbers

swart \'swort\ adj : SWARTHY

swar·thy \'swor-thē, -thē\ adj **swar·thi·er**; **-est** : dark in color or complexion : dark-skinned

swash \'swäsh\ vb : to move about with a splashing sound — **swash** n

swash·buck·ler \-,bə-klər\ n : a swaggering or daring soldier or adventurer — **swash·buck·ling** adj

swas·ti·ka \'swäs-ti-kə\ n [Skt svastika, fr. svasti well-being, fr. su- well + as- to be] : a symbol or ornament in the form of a cross with the ends of the arms bent at right angles

swat \'swät\ vb **swat·ted; swat·ting** : to hit sharply 〈~ a fly〉 〈~ a ball〉 — **swat** n — **swat·ter** n

SWAT abbr Special Weapons and Tactics

swatch \'swäch\ n : a sample piece (as of fabric) or a collection of samples

swath \'swäth, 'swóth\ or **swathe** \'swäth, 'swóth, 'swäth\ n [ME, fr. OE swæth footstep, trace] 1 : a row of cut grass or grain 2 : the sweep of a scythe or mowing machine or the path cut in mowing

swathe \'swäth, 'swóth, 'swäth\ vb **swathed; swath·ing** : to bind or wrap with or as if with a bandage

¹**sway** \'swä\ n 1 : a gentle swinging from side to side 2 : controlling influence or power : DOMINION

²**sway** vb 1 : to swing gently from side to side 2 : RULE, GOVERN 3 : to cause to swing from side to side 4 : BEND, SWERVE; also : INFLUENCE ♦ **Synonyms** OSCILLATE, FLUCTUATE, VIBRATE, WAVER

sway·backed \'swä-,bakt\ also **sway·back** \-,bak\ adj : having an abnormally sagging back 〈a ~ mare〉 — **swayback** n

swear \'swer\ vb **swore** \'swór\; **sworn** \'sworn\; **swear·ing** 1 : to make a solemn statement or promise under oath 2 : to assert or promise emphatically or earnestly 3 : to administer an oath to 4 : to bind by or as if by an oath 5 : to use profane or obscene language — **swear·er** n

swear in vb : to induct into office by administration of an oath

sweat \'swet\ vb **sweat** or **sweat·ed; sweat·ing** 1 : to excrete salty moisture from glands of the skin : PERSPIRE 2 : to form drops of moisture on the surface 3 : to work so that one sweats : TOIL 4 : to cause to sweat 5 : to draw out or get rid of by or as if by sweating 6 : to make a person overwork — **sweat** n — **sweaty** adj

sweat·er \'swe-tər\ n 1 : one that sweats 2 : a knitted or crocheted jacket or pullover

sweat·shirt \'swet-,shərt\ n : a loose collarless pullover or jacket usu. of heavy cotton jersey

sweat·shop \'swet-,shäp\ n : a shop or factory in which workers are employed for long hours at low wages and under unhealthy conditions

Swed abbr Sweden

swede \'swed\ n, 1 cap : a native or inhabitant of Sweden 2 chiefly Brit : RUTABAGA

Swed·ish \'swe-dish\ n 1 : the language of Sweden 2 **Swedish** pl : the people of Sweden — **Swedish** adj

¹**sweep** \'swep\ vb **swept** \'swept\; **sweep·ing** 1 : to remove or clean by or as if by brushing 2 : to destroy completely; also : to remove or take with a single swift movement 3 : to remove from sight or consideration 4 : to move over with speed and force 〈the tide swept over the shore〉 5 : to win an overwhelming victory in; also : to win all the games or contests of 6 : to move or extend in a wide curve — **sweep·er** n

²**sweep** n 1 : something (as a long oar) that operates with a sweeping motion 2 : a clearing off or away 3 : a winning of all the contests or prizes in a competition 4 : a sweeping movement 5 : CURVE, BEND 6 : RANGE, SCOPE

sweeping adj : EXTENSIVE 〈~ reforms〉; also : indiscriminately inclusive 〈~ generalities〉

sweep·ings \'swe-piŋz\ n pl : things collected by sweeping

sweep–sec·ond hand \'swep-,se-kənd-\ n : a hand marking seconds on a timepiece

sweep·stakes \'swep-,stäks\ also **sweep·stake** \-,stäk\ n, pl **sweepstakes** 1 : a race or contest in which the entire prize may go to the winner 2 : any of various lotteries

¹**sweet** \'swet\ adj 1 : being or causing the one of the four basic taste sensations that is caused esp. by table sugar and is identified esp. by the taste buds at the front of the tongue; also : pleasing to the taste 2 : AGREEABLE 〈how ~ it is〉 3 : pleasing to a sense other than taste 〈a ~ smell〉 〈~ music〉 4 : not stale or spoiled : WHOLESOME 〈~ milk〉 5 : not salted 〈~ butter〉 — **sweet·ish** adj — **sweet·ly** adv — **sweet·ness** n

²**sweet** n 1 : something sweet : CANDY 2 : DARLING

sweet·bread \'swet-,bred\ n : the pancreas or thymus of an animal (as a calf or lamb) used for food

sweet·bri·ar or **sweet·bri·er** \-,brī-ər\ n : a thorny Old World rose with fragrant white to deep pink flowers

sweet clover n : any of a genus of erect legumes widely grown for soil improvement or hay

sweet corn n : an Indian corn with wrinkled translucent kernels that are rich in sugar

sweet·en \'swe-tᵊn\ vb **sweet·ened; sweet·en·ing** : to make sweet — **sweet·en·er** n — **sweet·en·ing** n

sweet·heart \'swet-,härt\ n : one who is loved

sweet·meat \-,met\ n : CANDY 1

sweet pea n : a garden plant of the legume family with climbing stems and fragrant flowers of many colors; also : its flower

sweet pepper n : any of various large mild thick-walled fruits of a pepper; also : a plant bearing sweet peppers

sweet potato n : a tropical vine related to the morning glory; also : its large sweet edible root

sweet–talk \'swēt-ˌtȯk\ vb : FLATTER, COAX — **sweet talk** n

sweet tooth n : a craving or fondness for sweet food

sweet wil·liam \ˌswēt-'wil-yəm\ n, often cap W : a widely cultivated Old World pink with small white to deep red or purple flowers often showily spotted, banded, or mottled

¹**swell** \'swel\ vb **swelled**; **swelled** or **swol·len** \'swō-lən\; **swell·ing 1** : to grow big or make bigger **2** : to expand or distend abnormally or excessively ⟨a *swollen* joint⟩; also : BULGE **3** : to fill or be filled with emotion (as pride) ♦ **Synonyms** EXPAND, AMPLIFY, DISTEND, INFLATE, DILATE — **swell·ing** n

²**swell** n **1** : a long crestless wave or series of waves in the open sea **2** : the condition of being protuberant **3** : a person dressed in the height of fashion; also : a person of high social position

³**swell** adj **1** : STYLISH; also : socially prominent **2** : EXCELLENT

swelled head n : an exaggerated opinion of oneself : SELF-CONCEIT

swel·ter \'swel-tər\ vb [ME *sweltren*, fr. *swelten* to die, be overcome by heat, fr. OE *sweltan* to die] **1** : to be faint or oppressed with the heat **2** : to become exceedingly hot — **swel·ter·ing** \-tə-riŋ\ adj

swept past and past part of SWEEP

swerve \'swərv\ vb **swerved**; **swerv·ing** : to move abruptly aside from a straight line or course — **swerve** n

¹**swift** \'swift\ adj **1** : moving or capable of moving with great speed **2** : occurring suddenly **3** : READY, ALERT — **swift·ly** adv — **swift·ness** n

²**swift** n : any of numerous small insect-eating birds with long narrow wings

swig \'swig\ vb **swigged**; **swig·ging** : to drink in long drafts — **swig** n

¹**swill** \'swil\ vb **1** : to swallow greedily : GUZZLE **2** : to feed (as hogs) on swill

²**swill** n **1** : food for animals composed of edible refuse mixed with liquid **2** : GARBAGE

¹**swim** \'swim\ vb **swam** \'swam\; **swum** \'swəm\; **swim·ming 1** : to propel oneself along in water by natural means (as by hands and legs, by tail, or by fins) **2** : to glide smoothly along **3** : FLOAT **4** : to be covered with or as if with a liquid **5** : to be dizzy ⟨his head *swam*⟩ **6** : to cross or go over by swimming — **swim·mer** n

²**swim** n **1** : an act of swimming **2** : the main current of activity ⟨in the ∼⟩

swim·ming n : the action, art, or sport of swimming and diving

swimming pool n : a tank (as of concrete or plastic) designed for swimming

swim·suit \'swim-ˌsüt\ n : a suit for swimming or bathing

swim·wear \'swim-ˌwer\ n : clothing for wear while swimming or bathing

swin·dle \'swin-dᵊl\ vb **swin·dled**; **swin·dling** [fr. *swindler*, fr. G *Schwindler* giddy person, fr. *schwindeln* to be dizzy] : CHEAT, DEFRAUD — **swindle** n — **swin·dler** n

swine \'swīn\ n, pl **swine 1** : any of a family of stout short-legged hoofed mammals with bristly skin and a long flexible snout; esp : one widely raised as a meat animal **2** : a contemptible person — **swin·ish** adj

¹**swing** \'swiŋ\ vb **swung** \'swəŋ\; **swing·ing 1** : to move or cause to move rapidly in an arc **2** : to sway or cause to sway back and forth **3** : to hang so as to move freely back and forth or in a curve **4** : to be executed by hanging **5** : to move or turn on a hinge or pivot **6** : to manage or handle successfully **7** : to march or walk with free swaying movements **8** : to have a steady pulsing rhythm; also : to play swing music **9** : to be lively and up-to-date; also : to engage freely in sex ♦ **Synonyms** WIELD, MANIPULATE, PLY, MANEUVER — **swing·er** n — **swing·ing** adj

²**swing** n **1** : the act of swinging **2** : a swinging blow, movement, or rhythm **3** : the distance through which something swings : FLUCTUATION **4** : progression of an activity or process ⟨in full ∼⟩ **5** : a seat suspended by a rope or chain for swinging back and forth for pleasure **6** : jazz music played esp. by a large band and marked by a steady lively rhythm, simple harmony, and a basic melody often submerged in improvisation

³**swing** adj **1** : of or relating to musical swing **2** : that may swing decisively either way (as on an issue) ⟨∼ voters⟩

¹**swipe** \'swīp\ n : a strong sweeping blow

²**swipe** vb **swiped**; **swip·ing 1** : to strike or wipe with a sweeping motion **2** : PILFER, SNATCH **3** : to slide (a card having a magnetic code) through a reading device

swirl \'swərl\ vb : to move or cause to move with a whirling motion — **swirl** n — **swirly** \'swər-lē\ adj

swish \'swish\ n **1** : a prolonged hissing sound **2** : a light sweeping or brushing sound — **swish** vb

Swiss \'swis\ n **1** pl **Swiss** : a native or inhabitant of Switzerland **2** : a hard cheese with large holes — **Swiss** adj

Swiss chard n : a beet having large leaves and succulent stalks often cooked as a vegetable

¹**switch** \'swich\ n **1** : a slender flexible whip, rod, or twig **2** : a blow with a switch **3** : a shift from one thing to another; also : change from the usual **4** : a device for adjusting the rails of a track so that a locomotive or train may be turned from one track to another; also : a railroad siding **5** : a device for making, breaking, or changing the connections in an electrical circuit **6** : a heavy strand of hair often used in addition to a person's own hair for some coiffures

²**switch** vb **1** : to punish or urge on with a switch **2** : WHISK ⟨a cow ∼ing her tail⟩ **3** : to shift or turn by operating a switch **4** : CHANGE, EXCHANGE

switch·back \'swich-ˌbak\ *n* : a zigzag road, trail, or section of railroad tracks for climbing a steep hill

switch·blade \-ˌblād\ *n* : a pocket-knife with a spring-operated blade

switch·board \-ˌbōrd\ *n* : a panel for controlling the operation of a number of electric circuits; *esp* : one used to make and break telephone connections

switch–hit·ter \-'hi-tər\ *n* : a baseball player who bats either right-handed or left-handed — **switch–hit** \'hit\ *vb*

switch·man \'swich-mən\ *n* : one who attends a railroad switch

Switz *abbr* Switzerland

¹**swiv·el** \'swi-vəl\ *n* : a device joining two parts so that one or both can turn freely

²**swivel** *vb* **-eled** *or* **-elled; -el·ing** *or* **-el·ling** : to swing or turn on or as if on a swivel

swiv·et \'swi-vət\ *n* : an agitated state

swiz·zle stick \'swi-zəl-\ *n* : a stick used to stir mixed drinks

swollen *past part of* SWELL

swoon \'swün\ *vb* : FAINT — **swoon** *n*

swoop \'swüp\ *vb* : to move with a sweep ⟨the eagle ~ed down on its prey⟩ — **swoop** *n*

swoopy \'swü-pē\ *adj* : having lines that extend in a wide curve ⟨a ~ silhouette⟩

swop *chiefly Brit var of* SWAP

sword \'sōrd\ *n* **1** : a weapon with a long blade for cutting or thrusting **2** : the use of force

sword·fish \-ˌfish\ *n* : a very large ocean fish used for food that has the upper jaw prolonged into a long swordlike beak

sword·play \-ˌplā\ *n* : the art or skill of wielding a sword

swords·man \'sōrdz-mən\ *n* : one skilled in swordplay; *esp* : FENCER

sword·tail \'sōrd-ˌtāl\ *n* : a small brightly marked Central American fish often kept in aquariums

swore *past of* SWEAR

sworn *past part of* SWEAR

swum *past part of* SWIM

swung *past and past part of* SWING

syb·a·rite \'si-bə-ˌrīt\ *n* : a lover of luxury : VOLUPTUARY — **syb·a·rit·ic** \ˌsi-bə-'ri-tik\ *adj*

syc·a·more \'si-kə-ˌmòr\ *n* : a large spreading tree chiefly of the eastern and central U.S. that has light brown flaky bark and small round fruits hanging on long stalks

sy·co·phant \'si-kə-fənt\ *n* : a servile flatterer — **sy·co·phan·cy** \'si-kə-fən-sē\ *n* — **sy·co·phan·tic** \ˌsi-kə-'fan-tik\ *adj*

syl *or* **syll** *abbr* syllable

syl·lab·i·ca·tion \sə-ˌla-bə-'kā-shən\ *n* : the division of words into syllables

syl·lab·i·fy \sə-'la-bə-ˌfī\ *vb* **-fied; -fy·ing** : to form or divide into syllables — **syl·lab·i·fi·ca·tion** \-ˌla-bə-fə-'kā-shən\ *n*

syl·la·ble \'si-lə-bəl\ *n* [ME, fr. AF *sillabe, silable*, fr. L *syllaba*, fr. Gk *syllabē*, fr. *syllambanein* to gather together, fr. *syn-* with + *lambanein* to take] : a unit of spoken language consisting of an uninterrupted utterance and forming either a whole word (as *cat*) or a commonly

recognized division of a word (as *syl* in *syl-la-ble*); *also* : one or more letters representing such a unit — **syl·lab·ic** \sə-'la-bik\ *adj*

syl·la·bus \'si-lə-bəs\ *n, pl* **-bi** \-ˌbī\ *or* **-bus·es** : a summary containing the heads or main topics of a speech, book, or course of study

syl·lo·gism \'si-lə-ˌji-zəm\ *n* : a logical scheme of a formal argument consisting of a major and a minor premise and a conclusion which must logically be true if the premises are true — **syl·lo·gis·tic** \ˌsi-lə-'jis-tik\ *adj*

sylph \'silf\ *n* **1** : an imaginary being inhabiting the air **2** : a slender graceful woman

syl·van \'sil-vən\ *adj* **1** : living or located in a wooded area; *also* : of, relating to, or characteristic of forest **2** : abounding in woods or trees

sym *abbr* **1** symbol **2** symmetrical

sym·bi·o·sis \ˌsim-ˌbī-'ō-səs, -bē-\ *n, pl* **-o·ses** \-ˌsēz\ : the living together in close association of two dissimilar organisms esp. when mutually beneficial — **sym·bi·ot·ic** \-'ä-tik\ *adj*

sym·bol \'sim-bəl\ *n* **1** : something that stands for something else; *esp* : something concrete that represents or suggests another thing that cannot in itself be pictured ⟨the lion is a ~ of bravery⟩ **2** : a letter, character, or sign used in writing or printing to represent operations, quantities, elements, sounds, or other ideas — **sym·bol·ic** \sim-'bä-lik\ *also* **sym·bol·i·cal** \-li-kəl\ *adj* — **sym·bol·i·cal·ly** \-k(ə-)lē\ *adv*

sym·bol·ise *Brit var of* SYMBOLIZE

sym·bol·ism \'sim-bə-ˌli-zəm\ *n* : representation of abstract or intangible things by means of symbols

sym·bol·ize \'sim-bə-ˌlīz\ *vb* **-ized; -iz·ing 1** : to serve as a symbol of **2** : to represent by symbols — **sym·bol·i·za·tion** \ˌsim-bə-lə-'zā-shən\ *n*

sym·me·try \'si-mə-trē\ *n, pl* **-tries 1** : an arrangement marked by regularity and balanced proportions **2** : correspondence in size, shape, and position of parts that are on opposite sides of a dividing line or center — **sym·met·ri·cal** \sə-'me-tri-kəl\ *or* **sym·met·ric** \sə-'me-trik\ *adj* — **sym·met·ri·cal·ly** \-k(ə-)lē\ *adv*

sympathetic nervous system *n* : the part of the autonomic nervous system that is concerned esp. with the body's repsonse to stress and that tends to decrease the tone and contractility of smooth muscle and increase blood pressure and the activity of the heart

sym·pa·thise *chiefly Brit var of* SYMPATHIZE

sym·pa·thize \'sim-pə-ˌthīz\ *vb* **-thized; -thiz·ing** : to feel or show sympathy — **sym·pa·thiz·er** *n*

sym·pa·thy \'sim-pə-thē\ *n, pl* **-thies 1** : a relationship between persons or things wherein whatever affects one similarly affects the other **2** : harmony of interests and aims **3** : FAVOR, SUPPORT **4** : the capacity for entering into and sharing the feelings or interests of another; *also* : COMPASSION, PITY **5** : an expression of sorrow for another's loss, grief, or misfortune — **sym·pa·thet·ic** \ˌsim-pə-'the-tik\ *adj* — **sym·pa·thet·i·cal·ly** \-ti-k(ə-)lē\ *adv*

sym·pho·ny \'sim-fə-nē\ *n, pl* **-nies 1** : harmony of sounds **2** : a large and complex composition for a full orchestra **3** : a large orchestra of a kind that plays symphonies — **sym·phon·ic** \sim-'fä-nik\ *adj*

sym·po·sium \sim-'pō-zē-əm\ *n, pl* **-sia** \-zē-ə\ *or* **-siums** : a conference at which a particular topic is discussed by various speakers; *also* : a collection of opinions about a subject

symp·tom \'simp-təm\ *n* [LL *symptoma*, fr. Gk *symptōma* happening, attribute, symptom, fr. *sympiptein* to happen, fr. *syn-* with + *piptein* to fall] **1** : something that indicates the presence of disease or abnormality; *esp* : something (as a headache) that can be sensed only by the individual affected **2** : SIGN, INDICATION 〈~s of inner turmoil〉 — **symp·tom·at·ic** \ˌsimp-tə-'ma-tik\ *adj*

syn *abbr* synonym; synonymous; synonymy

syn·a·gogue *also* **syn·a·gog** \'si-nə-ˌgäg\ *n* [ME *synagoge*, fr. AF, fr. LL *synagoga*, fr. Gk *synagōgē* assembly, synagogue, fr. *synagein* to bring together] **1** : a Jewish congregation **2** : the house of worship of a Jewish congregation

syn·apse \'si-ˌnaps, sə-'naps\ *n* : the point at which a nervous impulse passes from one neuron to another — **syn·ap·tic** \sə-'nap-tik\ *adj*

¹sync *also* **synch** \'siŋk\ *vb* **synced** *also* **synched** \'siŋkt\; **sync·ing** *also* **synch·ing** \'siŋ-kiŋ\ : SYNCHRONIZE

²sync *also* **synch** *n* : SYNCHRONIZATION, SYNCHRONISM — **sync** *adj*

syn·chro·ni·sa·tion, syn·chro·nise *Brit var of* SYNCHRONIZATION, SYNCHRONIZE

syn·chro·nize \'siŋ-krə-ˌnīz, 'sin-\ *vb* **-nized; -niz·ing 1** : to occur or cause to occur at the same instant **2** : to represent, arrange, or tabulate according to dates or time **3** : to cause to agree in time **4** : to make synchronous in operation — **syn·chro·nism** \-ˌni-zəm\ *n* — **syn·chro·ni·za·tion** \ˌsiŋ-krə-nə-'zā-shən, ˌsin-\ *n* — **syn·chro·niz·er** *n*

syn·chro·nous \'siŋ-krə-nəs, 'sin-\ *adj* **1** : happening at the same time : CONCURRENT **2** : working, moving, or occurring together at the same rate and at the proper time

syn·co·pa·tion \ˌsiŋ-kə-'pā-shən, ˌsin-\ *n* : a shifting of the regular musical accent : occurrence of accented notes on the weak beat — **syn·co·pate** \'siŋ-kə-ˌpāt, 'sin-\ *vb*

syn·co·pe \'siŋ-kə-(ˌ)pē, 'sin-\ *n* : the loss of one or more sounds or letters in the interior of a word (as in *fo'c'sle* for *forecastle*)

¹syn·di·cate \'sin-di-kət\ *n* **1** : a group of persons who combine to carry out a fi-

nancial or industrial undertaking **2** : a loose association of racketeers **3** : a business concern that sells materials for publication in many newspapers and periodicals at the same time

²syn·di·cate \-də-ˌkāt\ *vb* **-cat·ed; -cat·ing 1** : to combine into or manage as a syndicate **2** : to publish through a syndicate — **syn·di·ca·tion** \ˌsin-də-'kā-shən\ *n*

syn·drome \'sin-ˌdrōm\ *n* : a group of signs and symptoms that occur together and characterize a particular abnormality or condition

syn·er·gism \'sin-ər-ˌji-zəm\ *n* : interaction of discrete agencies (as industrial firms), agents (as drugs), or conditions such that the total effect is greater than the sum of the individual effects — **syn·er·gist** \-jist\ *n* — **syn·er·gis·tic** \ˌsi-nər-'jis-tik\ *adj* — **syn·er·gis·ti·cal·ly** \-ti-k(ə-)lē\ *adv*

syn·er·gy \'si-nər-je\ *n, pl* **-gies** : SYNERGISM

syn·fuel \'sin-ˌfyül\ *n* [*synthetic*] : a fuel derived esp. from a fossil fuel

syn·od \'si-nəd\ *n* : COUNCIL, ASSEMBLY; *esp* : a religious governing body — **syn·od·al** \-nə-dᵊl, -ˌnä-dᵊl\ *adj* — **syn·od·ic** \sə-'nä-dik\ *or* **syn·od·i·cal** \-di-kəl\ *adj*

syn·onym \'si-nə-ˌnim\ *n* : one of two or more words in the same language which have the same or very nearly the same meaning — **syn·on·y·mous** \sə-'nä-nə-məs\ *adj* — **syn·on·y·mous·ly** *adv* — **syn·on·y·my** \-mē\ *n*

syn·op·sis \sə-'näp-səs\ *n, pl* **-op·ses** \-ˌsēz\ : a condensed statement or outline (as of a treatise) : ABSTRACT

syn·op·tic \sə-'näp-tik\ *also* **syn·op·ti·cal** \-ti-kəl\ *adj* : characterized by or affording a comprehensive view

syn·tax \'sin-ˌtaks\ *n* : the way in which words are put together to form phrases, clauses, or sentences — **syn·tac·tic** \sin-'tak-tik\ *or* **syn·tac·ti·cal** \-ti-kəl\ *adj*

syn·the·sis \'sin-thə-səs\ *n, pl* **-the·ses** \-ˌsēz\ : the combination of parts or elements into a whole; *esp* : the production of a substance by union of chemically simpler substances — **syn·the·size** \-ˌsīz\ *vb* — **syn·the·siz·er** *n*

syn·thet·ic \sin-'the-tik\ *adj* : produced artificially esp. by chemical means; *also* : not genuine — **synthetic** *n* — **syn·thet·i·cal·ly** \-ti-k(ə-)lē\ *adv*

syph·i·lis \'si-fə-ləs\ *n* [NL, fr. *Syphilus*, hero of the poem *Syphilis sive Morbus Gallicus* (*Syphilis or the French disease*) (1530) by Girolamo Fracastoro †1553 Ital. physician] : an infectious usu. venereal disease caused by a spirochete — **syph·i·lit·ic** \ˌsi-fə-'li-tik\ *adj or n*

syphon *var of* SIPHON

Sy·rah \sē-'rä\ *n* : a red wine

¹sy·ringe \sə-'rinj\ *n* : a device used esp. for injecting liquids into or withdrawing them from the body

²syringe *vb* **sy·ringed; sy·ring·ing** : to flush or cleanse with or as if with a syringe

syr·up \'sər-əp, 'sir-əp\ *n* **1** : a thick sticky solution of sugar and water often flavored or medicated **2** : the concentrated juice of a fruit or plant — **syr·upy** *adj*

syst *abbr* system

sys·tem \'sis-təm\ *n* **1** : a group of units so combined as to form a whole and to operate in unison **2** : the body as a functioning whole; *also* : a group of bodily organs (as the nervous system) that together carry on some vital function **3** : a definite scheme or method of procedure or classification **4** : regular method or order — **sys·tem·at·ic** \ˌsis-tə-'ma-tik\ — **sys·tem·at·i·cal·ly** \-ti-k(ə-)lē\ *adv*

sys·tem·a·tise *Brit var of* SYSTEMATIZE

sys·tem·a·tize \'sis-tə-mə-ˌtīz\ *vb* **-tized; -tiz·ing** : to make into a system : arrange methodically

¹sys·tem·ic \sis-'te-mik\ *adj* **1** : of, relating to, or affecting the whole body ⟨∼ disease⟩ **2** : of, relating to, or being a

pesticide that when absorbed into the sap or bloodstream makes the entire plant or animal toxic to a pest (as an insect or fungus)

²systemic *n* : a systemic pesticide

systemic lupus er·y·the·ma·to·sus \ˌer-ə-ˌthē-mə-'tō-səs\ *n* : a systemic disease esp. of women characterized by fever, skin rash, and arthritis, often by anemia, by small hemorrhages of the skin and mucous membranes, and in serious cases by involvement of internal organs

sys·tem·ize \'sis-tə-ˌmīz\ *vb* **-ized; -iz·ing** : SYSTEMATIZE

systems analyst *n* : a person who studies a procedure or business to determine its goals or purposes and to discover the best ways to accomplish them — **systems analysis** *n*

sys·to·le \'sis-tə-(ˌ)lē\ *n* : a rhythmically recurrent contraction of the heart — **sys·tol·ic** \sis-'tä-lik\ *adj*

T

¹t \'tē\ *n, pl* **t's** *or* **ts** \'tēz\ *often cap* : the 20th letter of the English alphabet

²t *abbr, often cap* **1** tablespoon **2** teaspoon **3** temperature **4** ton **5** transitive **6** troy **7** true

T *abbr* **1** toddler **2** T-shirt

Ta *symbol* tantalum

TA *abbr* teaching assistant

¹tab \'tab\ *n* **1** : a short projecting flap, loop, or tag; *also* : a short insert or addition **2** : close surveillance : WATCH ⟨keep ∼s on him⟩ **3** : BILL, CHECK **4** : a key on a keyboard esp. for putting data in columns

²tab *vb* **tabbed; tab·bing** : DESIGNATE

tab·by \'ta-bē\ *n, pl* **tabbies** : a usu. striped or mottled domestic cat; *also* : a female domestic cat

tab·er·na·cle \'ta-bər-ˌna-kəl\ *n* [ME, fr. AF, fr. LL *tabernaculum*, fr. L, tent, fr. *taberna* hut] **1** *often cap* : a tent sanctuary used by the Israelites during the Exodus **2** : a receptacle for the consecrated elements of the Eucharist **3** : a house of worship

¹ta·ble \'tā-bəl\ *n* **1** : TABLET 1 **2** : a piece of furniture consisting of a smooth flat top fixed on legs **3** : a supply of food : BOARD, FARE **4** : a group of people assembled at or as if at a table **5** : an orderly arrangement of data usu. in rows and columns **6** : a short list ⟨∼ of contents⟩ — **ta·ble·top** \-ˌtäp\ *n*

²table *vb* **ta·bled; ta·bling** **1** *Brit* : to place on the agenda **2** : to remove (a parliamentary motion) from consideration indefinitely

tab·leau \'ta-ˌblō\ *n, pl* **tab·leaux** \-ˌblōz\ *also* **tableaus** [F] : a scene or event usu. presented on a stage by silent and motionless costumed participants

ta·ble·cloth \'tā-bəl-ˌklȯth\ *n* : a covering spread over a dining table before the table is set

ta·ble d'hôte \ˌtä-bəl-'dōt\ *n* [F, lit., host's table] : a complete meal of several courses offered at a fixed price

ta·ble·land \'tā-bəl-ˌland\ *n* : PLATEAU

ta·ble·spoon \-ˌspün\ *n* **1** : a large spoon used esp. for serving **2** : a unit of measure equal to ½ fluid ounce (15 milliliters)

ta·ble·spoon·ful \-ˌfül\ *n, pl* **-spoonfuls** \-ˌfülz\ *also* **-spoons·ful** \-ˌspünz-ˌfül\ : TABLESPOON 2

tab·let \'ta-blət\ *n* **1** : a flat slab suited for or bearing an inscription **2** : a collection of sheets of paper glued together at one edge **3** : a compressed or molded block of material; *esp* : a usu. disk-shaped medicated mass

table tennis *n* : a game resembling tennis played on a tabletop with wooden paddles and a small hollow plastic ball

ta·ble·ware \'tā-bəl-ˌwer\ *n* : utensils (as of china or silver) for table use

¹tab·loid \'ta-ˌblȯid\ *adj* : condensed into small scope

²tabloid *n* : a newspaper marked by small pages, condensation of the news, and usu. many photographs

¹ta·boo *also* **ta·bu** \tə-'bü, ta-\ *adj* [Tongan (a Polynesian language) *tabu*] : prohibited by a taboo

²taboo *also* **tabu** *n, pl* **taboos** *also* **tabus** **1** : a prohibition against touching, saying, or doing something for fear of immediate harm from a supernatural force **2** : a prohibition imposed by social custom

ta·bor *also* **ta·bour** \'tā-bər\ *n* : a small drum used to accompany a pipe or fife played by the same person

tab·u·lar \'ta-byə-lər\ *adj* **1** : having a flat

surface **2** : arranged in a table; *esp* : set up in rows and columns **3** : computed by means of a table

tab·u·late \-ˌlāt\ *vb* **-lat·ed; -lat·ing** : to put into tabular form — **tab·u·la·tion** \ˌta-byə-ˈlā-shən\ *n* — **tab·u·la·tor** \ˈta-byə-ˌlā-tər\ *n*

TAC \ˈtak\ *abbr* Tactical Air Command

tach \ˈtak\ *n* : TACHOMETER

ta·chom·e·ter \ta-ˈkä-mə-tər, tə-\ *n* [ultim. fr. Gk *tachos* speed] : a device to indicate speed of rotation

tachy·car·dia \ˌta-ki-ˈkär-dē-ə\ *n* : relatively rapid heart action

tachy·on \ˈta-kē-ˌän\ *n* : a hypothetical particle held to travel faster than light

tac·it \ˈta-sət\ *adj* [F or L; F *tacite*, fr. L *tacitus* silent, fr. *tacēre* to be silent] **1** : expressed without words or speech **2** : implied or indicated but not actually expressed ⟨∼ consent⟩ — **tac·it·ly** *adv* — **tac·it·ness** *n*

tac·i·turn \ˈta-sə-ˌtərn\ *adj* : disinclined to talk ♦ **Synonyms** UNCOMMUNICATIVE, RESERVED, RETICENT, CLOSEMOUTHED — **tac·i·tur·ni·ty** \ˌta-sə-ˈtər-nə-tē\ *n*

¹tack \ˈtak\ *vb* **1** : to fasten with tacks; *also* : to add on **2** : to change the direction of (a sailing ship) from one tack to another **3** : to follow a zigzag course

²tack *n* **1** : a small sharp nail with a broad flat head **2** : the direction toward the wind that a ship is sailing ⟨starboard ∼⟩; *also* : the run of a ship on one tack **3** : a change of course from one tack to another **4** : a zigzag course **5** : a course of action

³tack *n* : gear for harnessing a horse

¹tack·le \ˈta-kəl, *naut often* ˈtā-\ *n* **1** : GEAR, APPARATUS, EQUIPMENT **2** : the rigging of a ship **3** : an arrangement of ropes and pulleys for hoisting or pulling heavy objects **4** : the act or an instance of tackling; *also* : a football lineman playing between guard and end

²tackle *vb* **tack·led; tack·ling 1** : to attach and secure with or as if with tackle **2** : to seize, grapple with, or throw down with the intention of subduing or stopping **3** : to set about dealing with ⟨∼ a problem⟩ — **tack·ler** *n*

¹tacky \ˈta-kē\ *adj* **tack·i·er; -est** : sticky to the touch

²tacky *adj* **tack·i·er; -est 1** : SHABBY, SEEDY **2** : marked by lack of style or good taste; *also* : cheaply showy ⟨a ∼ publicity stunt⟩ ⟨a ∼ outfit⟩

ta·co \ˈtä-kō\ *n, pl* **tacos** \-kōz\ [MexSp] : a usu. fried tortilla rolled up with or folded over a filling

tact \ˈtakt\ *n* [F, sense of touch, fr. L *tactus*, fr. *tangere* to touch] : a keen sense of what to do or say to keep good relations with others — **tact·ful** \-fəl\ *adj* — **tact·ful·ly** *adv* — **tact·less** *adj* — **tact·less·ly** *adv*

tac·tic \ˈtak-tik\ *n* : a planned action for accomplishing an end

tac·tics \ˈtak-tiks\ *n sing or pl* **1** : the science of maneuvering forces in combat **2** : the skill of using available means to ac-

complish an end — **tac·ti·cal** \-ti-kəl\ *adj* — **tac·ti·cian** \tak-ˈti-shən\ *n*

tac·tile \ˈtak-tᵊl, ˈtak-ˌtī(-ə)l\ *adj* : of, relating to, or perceptible through the sense of touch

tad·pole \ˈtad-ˌpōl\ *n* [ME *taddepol*, fr. *tode* toad + *polle* head] : an aquatic larva of a frog or toad that has a tail and gills

tae kwon do \ˈtī-ˈkwän-ˈdō\ *n* : a Korean martial art of self-defense

taf·fe·ta \ˈta-fə-tə\ *n* : a crisp lustrous fabric (as of silk or rayon)

taff·rail \ˈtaf-ˌrāl, -rəl\ *n* : the rail around a ship's stern

taf·fy \ˈta-fē\ *n, pl* **taffies** : a candy usu. of molasses or brown sugar stretched until porous and light-colored

¹tag \ˈtag\ *n* **1** : a metal or plastic binding on an end of a shoelace **2** : a piece of hanging or attached material **3** : a hackneyed quotation or saying **4** : a descriptive or identifying epithet

²tag *vb* **tagged; tag·ging 1** : to provide or mark with or as if with a tag; *esp* : IDENTIFY **2** : to attach as an addition **3** : to follow closely and persistently ⟨∼s along everywhere we go⟩ **4** : to hold responsible for something

³tag *n* : a game in which one player chases others and tries to touch one of them

⁴tag *vb* **tagged; tag·ging 1** : to touch in or as if in a game of tag **2** : SELECT

TAG *abbr* the adjutant general

tag sale *n* : GARAGE SALE

Ta·hi·tian \tə-ˈhē-shən\ *n* **1** : a native or inhabitant of Tahiti **2** : the Polynesian language of the Tahitians — **Tahitian** *adj*

tai·ga \ˈtī-gə\ *n* [Russ *taĭga*] : a moist coniferous subarctic forest extending south from the tundra

¹tail \ˈtāl\ *n* **1** : the rear end or a process extending from the rear end of an animal **2** : something resembling an animal's tail **3** *pl* : full evening dress for men **4** : the back, last, lower, or inferior part of something; *esp* : the reverse of a coin — usu. used in pl. ⟨∼s, I win⟩ **5** : one who follows or keeps watch on someone — **tailed** \ˈtāld\ *adj* — **tail·less** \ˈtāl-ləs\ *adj*

²tail *vb* : FOLLOW; *esp* : to follow for the purpose of surveillance

tail·coat \-ˈkōt\ *n* : a coat with tails; *esp* : a man's full-dress coat with two long tapering skirts at the back

¹tail·gate \-ˌgāt\ *n* : a board or gate at the back end of a vehicle that can be let down (as for loading)

²tailgate *vb* **tail·gat·ed; tail·gat·ing 1** : to drive dangerously close behind another vehicle **2** : to hold a tailgate picnic

³tailgate *adj* : relating to or being a picnic set up on a tailgate

tail·light \-ˌlīt\ *n* : a usu. red warning light mounted at the rear of a vehicle

¹tai·lor \ˈtā-lər\ *n* [ME *taillour*, fr. AF *taillur*, fr. *tailler* to cut, fr. LL *taliare*, fr. L *talea* twig, cutting] : a person whose occupation is making or altering garments

²tailor *vb* **1** : to make or fashion as the work of a tailor **2** : to make or adapt to suit a special purpose

tail·pipe \'tāl-ˌpīp\ *n* : an outlet by which engine exhaust gases are expelled from a vehicle (as an automobile)

tail·spin \'tāl-ˌspin\ *n* : a rapid descent or downward spiral

tail·wind \'tāl-ˌwind\ *n* : a wind blowing in the same general direction as a course of movement (as of an aircraft)

¹taint \'tānt\ *vb* 1 : CORRUPT, CONTAMINATE 2 : to affect or become affected with something bad (as putrefaction)

²taint *n* : a contaminating mark or influence

ta·ka \'tä-kə\ *n* — see MONEY table

¹take \'tāk\ *vb* **took** \'tuk\; **tak·en** \'tā-kən\; **tak·ing** [ME, fr. OE *tacan*, fr. ON *taka*] 1 : to get into one's hands or possession : GRASP, SEIZE 2 : CAPTURE; *also* : DEFEAT 3 : to obtain or secure for use 4 : to catch or attack through the effect of a sudden force or influence ⟨*taken* ill⟩ 5 : CAPTIVATE, DELIGHT 6 : to bring into a relation ⟨∼ a wife⟩ 7 : REMOVE, SUBTRACT ⟨∼ three from eight⟩ 8 : to pick out : CHOOSE 9 : ASSUME, UNDERTAKE 10 : RECEIVE, ACCEPT 11 : to use for transportation ⟨∼ a bus⟩ 12 : to become impregnated with : ABSORB ⟨∼s a dye⟩ 13 : to receive into one's body (as by swallowing) ⟨∼ a pill⟩ 14 : ENDURE, UNDERGO ⟨∼ a cut in pay⟩ 15 : to lead, carry, or cause to go along to another place 16 : NEED, REQUIRE ⟨∼s a size nine shoe⟩ 17 : to obtain as the result of a special procedure ⟨∼ a snapshot⟩ 18 : to undertake and do, make, or perform ⟨∼ a walk⟩ 19 : to take effect : ACT, OPERATE **♦ Synonyms** GRAB, CLUTCH, SNATCH, SEIZE, NAB, GRAPPLE — **tak·er** *n* — **take advantage of** 1 : to profit by 2 : EXPLOIT — **take after** : RESEMBLE — **take care** : to be careful — **take care of** : to attend to — **take effect** : to become operative — **take exception** : OBJECT — **take for** : to suppose to be; *esp* : to mistake for — **take place** : HAPPEN — **take to** 1 : to go to 2 : to apply or devote oneself to 3 : to conceive a liking for

²take *n* 1 : the number or quantity taken; *also* : PROCEEDS, RECEIPTS 2 : an act or the action of taking 3 : a television or movie scene filmed or taped at one time; *also* : a sound recording made at one time 4 : a distinct or personal point of view

take·off \'tāk-ˌȯf\ *n* 1 : IMITATION; *esp* : PARODY 2 : an act or instance of taking off

take off *vb* 1 : REMOVE 2 : DEDUCT 3 : to set out : go away 4 : to begin flight

take on *vb* 1 : to begin to perform or deal with; *also* : to contend with as an opponent 2 : ENGAGE, HIRE 3 : to assume or acquire as or as if one's own 4 : to make an unusual show of one's feelings esp. of grief or anger

take over *vb* : to assume control or possession of or responsibility for — **take·over** \'tāk-ˌō-vər\ *n*

take up *vb* 1 : PICK UP 2 : to begin to

occupy (land) 3 : to absorb or incorporate into itself ⟨plants *taking* up nutrients⟩ 4 : to begin to engage in ⟨*took* up jogging⟩ 5 : to make tighter or shorter ⟨*take* up the slack⟩

tak·ings \'tā-kiŋz\ *n pl, chiefly Brit* : receipts esp. of money

ta·la \'tä-lə\ *n, pl* **tala** — see MONEY table

talc \'talk\ *n* : a soft mineral with a soapy feel used esp. in making a soothing powder (**tal·cum powder** \'tal-kəm-\) for the skin

tale \'tāl\ *n* 1 : a relation of a series of events 2 : a report of a confidential matter 3 : idle talk; *esp* : harmful gossip 4 : a usu. imaginative narrative 5 : FALSEHOOD 6 : COUNT, TALLY

tal·ent \'ta-lənt\ *n* 1 : an ancient unit of weight and value 2 : the natural endowments of a person 3 : a special often creative or artistic aptitude 4 : mental power : ABILITY 5 : a person of talent **♦ Synonyms** GENIUS, GIFT, FACULTY, APTITUDE, KNACK — **tal·ent·ed** *adj*

ta·ler \'tä-lər\ *n* : any of numerous silver coins issued by German states from the 15th to the 19th centuries

tales·man \'tālz-mən\ *n* : a person summoned for jury duty

tal·is·man \'ta-ləs-mən, -ləz-\ *n, pl* **-mans** [F *talisman* or Sp *talismán* or It *talismano*, fr. Ar *ṭilsam*, fr. MGk *telesma*, fr. Gk, consecration, fr. *telein* to initiate into the mysteries, complete, fr. *telos* end] : an object thought to act as a charm

¹talk \'tȯk\ *vb* 1 : to express in speech : utter words : SPEAK 2 : DISCUSS ⟨∼ business⟩ 3 : to influence or cause by talking ⟨∼ed him into going⟩ 4 : to use (a language) for communicating 5 : CONVERSE 6 : to reveal confidential information; *also* : GOSSIP 7 : to give a talk : LECTURE — **talk·er** *n* — **talk back** : to answer impertinently

²talk *n* 1 : the act of talking 2 : a way of speaking 3 : a formal discussion 4 : REPORT, RUMOR 5 : the topic of comment or gossip ⟨the ∼ of the town⟩ 6 : an informal address or lecture

talk·ative \'tȯ-kə-tiv\ *adj* : given to talking **♦ Synonyms** LOQUACIOUS, CHATTY, GABBY, GARRULOUS — **talk·ative·ly** *adv* — **talk·ative·ness** *n*

talk·ing-to \'tȯ-kiŋ-ˌtü\ *n* : REPRIMAND, REPROOF

talk radio *n* : radio programming consisting of call-in shows

tall \'tȯl\ *adj* 1 : high in stature; *also* : of a specified height ⟨six feet ∼⟩ 2 : LARGE, FORMIDABLE ⟨a ∼ order⟩ 3 : UNBELIEVABLE, IMPROBABLE ⟨a ∼ story⟩ — **tall·ness** *n*

tal·low \'ta-lō\ *n* : a hard white fat rendered usu. from cattle or sheep tissues and used esp. in candles

¹tal·ly \'ta-lē\ *n, pl* **tallies** 1 : a device for visibly recording or accounting esp. business transactions 2 : a recorded account 3 : a corresponding part; *also* : CORRESPONDENCE

²tally *vb* **tal·lied; tal·ly·ing** 1 : to mark on

or as if on a tally **2** : to make a count of :~RECKON; *also* : SCORE **3** : CORRESPOND, MATCH ✦ *Synonyms* SQUARE, ACCORD, HARMONIZE, CONFORM, JIBE

tal·ly·ho \ˌta-lē-ˈhō\ *n, pl* **-hos** : a call of a huntsman at sight of the fox

Tal·mud \ˈtäl-ˌmu̇d, ˈtal-məd\ *n* [Late Heb *talmūdh*, lit., instruction] : the authoritative body of Jewish tradition — **Tal·mu·dic** \tal-ˈmü-dik, -ˈmyü-, -ˈmə-; täl-ˈmu̇-\ *adj* — **Tal·mud·ist** \ˈtäl-ˌmü-dist, ˈtal-mə-\ *n*

tal·on \ˈta-lən\ *n* : the claw of an animal and esp. of a bird of prey

ta·lus \ˈtā-ləs, ˈta-\ *n* : rock debris at the base of a cliff

tam \ˈtam\ *n* : TAM-O'-SHANTER

ta·ma·le \tə-ˈmä-lē\ *n* [MexSp *tamales*, pl. of *tamal* tamale, fr. Nahuatl *tamalli* steamed cornmeal dough] : ground meat seasoned with chili, rolled in cornmeal dough, wrapped in corn husks, and steamed

tam·a·rack \ˈta-mə-ˌrak\ *n* : a larch of northern No. America; *also* : its hard resinous wood

tam·a·rin \ˈta-mə-rən\ *n* : any of several small So. American monkeys related to the marmosets

tam·a·rind \ˈta-mə-rənd, -ˌrind\ *n* [Sp & Pg *tamarindo*, fr. Ar *tamr hindī*, lit., Indian date] : a tropical tree of the legume family with hard yellowish wood and feathery leaves; *also* : its acid fruit

tam·ba·la \täm-ˈbä-lə\ *n, pl* **-la** *or* **-las** — see *kwacha* at MONEY table

tam·bou·rine \ˌtam-bə-ˈrēn\ *n* : a small shallow drum with loose disks at the sides played by shaking or striking with the hand

¹tame \ˈtām\ *adj* **tam·er; tam·est** **1** : reduced from a state of native wildness esp. so as to be useful to humans : DOMESTICATED **2** : made docile : SUBDUED **3** : lacking spirit or interest : INSIPID ✦ *Synonyms* SUBMISSIVE, DOMESTIC, DOMESTICATED — **tame·ly** *adv* — **tame·ness** *n*

²tame *vb* **tamed; tam·ing** **1** : to make or become tame; *also* : to subject (land) to cultivation **2** : HUMBLE, SUBDUE — **tam·able** *or* **tame·able** \ˈtā-mə-bəl\ *adj* — **tame·less** *adj* — **tam·er** *n*

tam-o'–shan·ter \ˈta-mə-ˌshan-tər\ *n* [fr. poem *Tam o' Shanter* (1790) by Robert Burns †1796 Scot. poet] : a Scottish woolen cap with a wide flat circular crown and usu. a pom-pom in the center

ta·mox·i·fen \tə-ˈmäk-sə-ˌfen\ *n* : a drug used esp. to treat breast cancer

tamp \ˈtamp\ *vb* : to drive down or in by a series of light blows

tam·per \ˈtam-pər\ *vb* **1** : to carry on underhand negotiations (as by bribery) ⟨~ with a witness⟩ **2** : to interfere so as to weaken or change for the worse ⟨~ with a document⟩ **3** : to try foolish or dangerous experiments

tam·pon \ˈtam-ˌpän\ *n* [F, lit., plug] : a plug (as of cotton) introduced into a body cavity usu. to absorb secretions (as from menstruation) or to arrest bleeding

¹tan \ˈtan\ *vb* **tanned; tan·ning** **1** : to change (hide) into leather esp. by soaking in a liquid containing tannin **2** : to make or become brown (as by exposure to the sun) **3** : WHIP, THRASH

²tan *n* **1** : a brown skin color induced by sun or weather **2** : a light yellowish brown color

³tan *abbr* tangent

tan·a·ger \ˈta-ni-jər\ *n* : any of numerous American birds that are often brightly colored

tan·bark \ˈtan-ˌbärk\ *n* : bark (as of oak or sumac) that is rich in tannin and used in tanning

¹tan·dem \ˈtan-dəm\ *n* [L, at last, at length (taken to mean "lengthwise"), fr. *tam* so] **1** : a 2-seated carriage with horses hitched tandem; *also* : its team **2** : a bicycle for two persons sitting one behind the other — **in tandem** : in a tandem arrangement

²tandem *adv* : one behind another

³tandem *adj* **1** : consisting of things arranged one behind the other **2** : working in conjunction with each other

tang \ˈtaŋ\ *n* **1** : a part in a tool that connects the blade with the handle **2** : a sharp distinctive flavor; *also* : a pungent odor — **tangy** *adj*

¹tan·gent \ˈtan-jənt\ *adj* [L *tangent-, tangens*, prp. of *tangere* to touch] : TOUCHING; *esp* : touching a circle or sphere at only one point

²tangent *n* **1** : the trigonometric function that is the ratio between the side opposite and the side adjacent to an acute angle in a right triangle **2** : a tangent line, curve, or surface **3** : an abrupt change of course

tan·gen·tial \tan-ˈjen-chəl\ *adj* **1** : TANGENT **2** : touching lightly : INCIDENTAL ⟨~ involvement⟩ — **tan·gen·tial·ly** *adv*

tan·ger·ine \ˈtan-jə-ˌrēn, ˌtan-jə-ˈrēn\ *n* : a deep orange loose-skinned citrus fruit; *also* : a tree that bears tangerines

¹tan·gi·ble \ˈtan-jə-bəl\ *adj* **1** : perceptible esp. by the sense of touch : PALPABLE **2** : substantially real : MATERIAL ⟨~ rewards⟩ **3** : capable of being appraised ⟨~ assets⟩ ✦ *Synonyms* APPRECIABLE, PERCEPTIBLE, SENSIBLE, DISCERNIBLE — **tan·gi·bil·i·ty** \ˌtan-jə-ˈbi-lə-tē\ *n*

²tangible *n* : something tangible; *esp* : a tangible asset

¹tan·gle \ˈtaŋ-gəl\ *vb* **tan·gled; tan·gling** **1** : to involve so as to hamper or embarrass; *also* : ENTRAP **2** : to unite or knit together in intricate confusion : ENTANGLE

²tangle *n* **1** : a tangled twisted mass **2** : a confusedly complicated state : MUDDLE

tan·go \ˈtaŋ-gō\ *n, pl* **tangos** : a dance of Latin-American origin — **tango** *vb*

tank \ˈtaŋk\ *n* **1** : a large artificial receptacle for liquids **2** : a heavily armed and armored combat vehicle that moves on tracks — **tank·ful** *n*

tan·kard \ˈtan-kərd\ *n* : a tall one-handled drinking vessel

tank·er \ˈtaŋ-kər\ *n* : a vehicle equipped for transporting a liquid

tank top *n* : a sleeveless collarless pullover shirt with shoulder straps

tank town *n* : a small town

tan·ner \\'ta-nər\\ *n* : one that tans hides

tan·nery \\'ta-nə-rē\\ *n, pl* **-ner·ies** : a place where tanning is carried on

tan·nic acid \\'ta-nik-\\ *n* : TANNIN

tan·nin \\'ta-nən\\ *n* : any of various plant substances used esp. in tanning and dyeing, in inks, and as astringents

tan·sy \\'tan-zē\\ *n, pl* **tansies** : a common weedy herb related to the daisies with an aromatic odor and bitter-tasting finely divided leaves

tan·ta·lise *Brit var of* TANTALIZE

tan·ta·lize \\'tan-tə-ˌlīz\\ *vb* **-lized; -liz·ing** [fr. *Tantalus*, king of Greek myth punished in Hades by having to stand up to his chin in water that receded as he bent to drink] : to tease or torment by presenting something desirable but keeping it out of reach — **tan·ta·liz·er** *n* — **tan·ta·liz·ing·ly** *adv*

tan·ta·lum \\'tan-tə-ləm\\ *n* : a gray-white ductile metallic chemical element

tan·ta·mount \\'tan-tə-ˌmaůnt\\ *adj* : equivalent in value or meaning ⟨a relationship ~ to marriage⟩

tan·trum \\'tan-trəm\\ *n* : a fit of bad temper

Tao·ism \\'taů-ˌi-zəm, 'daů-\\ *n* : a Chinese mystical philosophy; *also* : a religion developed from Taoist philosophy and Buddhism — **Tao·ist** \\-ist\\ *adj or n*

¹tap \\'tap\\ *n* **1** : FAUCET, COCK **2** : liquor drawn through a tap **3** : the removing of fluid from a container or cavity by tapping **4** : a tool for forming an internal screw thread **5** : a point in an electric circuit where a connection may be made

²tap *vb* **tapped; tap·ping 1** : to release or cause to flow by piercing or by drawing a plug from a container or cavity **2** : to pierce so as to let out or draw off a fluid **3** : to draw from ⟨~ resources⟩ **4** : to cut in on (as a telephone signal) to get information **5** : to form an internal screw thread in by means of a tap **6** : to connect (as a gas or water main) with a local supply — **tap·per** *n*

³tap *vb* **tapped; tap·ping 1** : to rap lightly **2** : to bring about by repeated light blows **3** : SELECT; *esp* : to elect to membership

⁴tap *n* **1** : a light blow or stroke; *also* : its sound **2** : a small metal plate for the sole or heel of a shoe

ta·pa \\'tä-pə, 'ta-\\ *n* [Sp, lit., cover, lid] : an hors d'oeuvre served with drinks esp. in Spanish bars — usu. used in pl.

¹tape \\'tāp\\ *n* **1** : a narrow flexible band or strip (as of woven fabric) **2** : MAGNETIC TAPE; *also* : CASSETTE

²tape *vb* **taped; tap·ing 1** : to fasten or support with tape **2** : to record on magnetic tape

tape deck *n* : a device used to play back cassette tapes that usu. has to be connected to an audio system

tape measure *n* : a tape marked off in units (as inches) for measuring

¹ta·per \\'tā-pər\\ *n* **1** : a slender wax candle; *also* : a long waxed wick **2** : a gradual lessening of thickness or width in a long object

²taper *vb* **ta·pered; ta·per·ing 1** : to make or become gradually smaller toward one end **2** : to diminish gradually

tape—re·cord \\ˌtāp-ri-ˈkȯrd\\ *vb* : to make a recording of on magnetic tape — **tape recorder** *n* — **tape recording** *n*

tap·es·try \\'ta-pə-strē\\ *n, pl* **-tries** : a heavy reversible textile that has designs or pictures woven into it and is used esp. as a wall hanging

tape·worm \\'tāp-ˌwərm\\ *n* : any of a class of long flat segmented worms parasitic esp. in vertebrate intestines

tap·i·o·ca \\ˌta-pē-ˈō-kə\\ *n* : a usu. granular preparation of cassava starch used esp. in puddings; *also* : a dish (as pudding) that contains tapioca

ta·pir \\'tā-pər\\ *n, pl* **tapirs** *also* **tapir** [Pg *tapir, tapira*, fr. Tupinambá (American Indian language of Brazil) *tapi'ïra*] : any of a genus of large herbivorous hoofed mammals of tropical America and southeastern Asia

tap·pet \\'ta-pət\\ *n* : a lever or projection moved by some other piece (as a cam) or intended to move something else

tap·room \\'tap-ˌrüm, -ˌrům\\ *n* : BARROOM

tap·root \\-ˌrüt, -ˌrůt\\ *n* : a large main root growing straight down and giving off small side roots

taps \\'taps\\ *n sing or pl* : the last bugle call at night blown as a signal that lights are to be put out; *also* : a similar call blown at military funerals and memorial services

tap·ster \\'tap-stər\\ *n* : BARTENDER

¹tar \\'tär\\ *n* **1** : a thick dark sticky liquid distilled from organic material (as wood or coal) **2** : SAILOR, SEAMAN

²tar *vb* **tarred; tar·ring** : to cover or smear with or as if with tar

tar·an·tel·la \\ˌta-rən-ˈte-lə\\ *n* : a lively folk dance of southern Italy in 6/8 time

ta·ran·tu·la \\tə-ˈran-chə-lə, -tə-lə\\ *n, pl* **tarantulas** *also* **ta·ran·tu·lae** \\-ˈran-chə-ˌlē, -tə-ˌlē\\ : any of a family of large hairy American spiders with a sharp bite that is not very poisonous to human beings

tar·dy \\'tär-dē\\ *adj* **tar·di·er; -est 1** : moving slowly : SLUGGISH **2** : LATE
  ✦ **Synonyms** BEHINDHAND, OVERDUE, BELATED — **tar·di·ly** \\-də-lē\\ *adv* — **tar·di·ness** \\-dē-nəs\\ *n*

¹tare \\'ter\\ *n* : a weed of grain fields

²tare *n* : a deduction from the gross weight of a substance and its container made in allowance for the weight of the container — **tare** *vb*

¹tar·get \\'tär-gət\\ *n* [ME, fr. MF *targette*, dim. of *targe* light shield, fr. Gmc origin] **1** : a mark to shoot at **2** : an object of ridicule or criticism **3** : a goal to be achieved

²target *vb* : to make a target of

tar·iff \\'ta-rəf\\ *n* [It *tariffa*, fr. Ar *ta'rīf* notification] **1** : a schedule of duties imposed by a government esp. on imported goods; *also* : a duty or rate of duty imposed in such a schedule **2** : a schedule of rates or charges

tar·mac \'tär-ˌmak\ n : a surface paved with crushed stone covered with tar

tarn \'tärn\ n : a small mountain lake

tar·nish \'tär-nish\ vb : to make or become dull or discolored — **tarnish** n

ta·ro \'tär-ō, 'ter-\ n, pl **taros** : a large-leaved tropical plant related to the arums that is grown for its edible starchy corms; also : its corms

tar·ot \'ter-ō, 'ter-ō\ n : one of a set of usu. 78 playing cards used esp. for fortune-telling

tar·pau·lin \tär-'pȯ-lən, 'tär-pə-\ n : a piece of material (as durable plastic) used for protecting exposed objects

tar·pon \'tär-pən\ n, pl **tarpon** or **tar·pons** : a large silvery bony fish often caught for sport in the warm coastal waters of the Atlantic esp. off Florida

tar·ra·gon \'ter-ə-gän\ [MF targon, ultim. fr. Ar ṭarḵhūn] : a small widely cultivated perennial wormwood with aromatic leaves used as a seasoning; also : its leaves

¹**tar·ry** \'ta-rē\ vb **tar·ried; tar·ry·ing** **1** : to be tardy : DELAY; esp : to be slow in leaving **2** : to stay in or at a place : SOJOURN ♦ **Synonyms** REMAIN, WAIT, LINGER, ABIDE

²**tar·ry** \'tär-ē\ adj : of, resembling, or smeared with tar

tar sand n : sand or sandstone that is naturally soaked with the heavy sticky portions of petroleum

tar·sus \'tär-səs\ n, pl **tar·si** \-ˌsī\ [NL] : the part of a vertebrate foot between the metatarsus and the leg; also : the small bones that support this part — **tar·sal** \-səl\ adj or n

¹**tart** \'tärt\ adj **1** : agreeably sharp to the taste : PUNGENT **2** : BITING, CAUSTIC — **tart·ly** adv — **tart·ness** n

²**tart** n **1** : a small pie or pastry shell containing jelly, custard, or fruit **2** : PROSTITUTE

tar·tan \'tärt-ᵊn\ n : a plaid textile design of Scottish origin usu. distinctively patterned to designate a particular clan

tar·tar \'tär-tər\ n **1** : a substance in the juice of grapes deposited (as in wine casks) as a reddish crust or sediment **2** : a crust on the teeth formed from plaque hardened by calcium salts

tar·tar sauce or **tar·tare sauce** \'tär-tər-\ n : mayonnaise with chopped pickles, olives, or capers

¹**task** \'task\ n [ME taske, fr. MF dial. tasque, fr. ML tasca tax or service imposed by a feudal superior, fr. taxare to tax] : a piece of assigned work ♦ **Synonyms** JOB, DUTY, CHORE, STINT, ASSIGNMENT

²**task** vb : to oppress with great labor

task force n : a temporary grouping to accomplish a particular objective

task·mas·ter \'task-ˌmas-tər\ n : one that imposes a task or burdens another with labor

¹**tas·sel** \'ta-səl, 'tä-\ n **1** : a hanging ornament made of a bunch of cords of even

length fastened at one end **2** : something suggesting a tassel; esp : a male flower cluster of Indian corn

²**tassel** vb **-seled** or **-selled; -sel·ing** or **-sel·ling** : to adorn with or put forth tassels

¹**taste** \'tāst\ vb **tast·ed; tast·ing** **1** : EXPERIENCE, UNDERGO **2** : to try or determine the flavor of by taking a bit into the mouth **3** : to eat or drink esp. in small quantities : SAMPLE **4** : to have a specific flavor

²**taste** n **1** : a small amount tasted **2** : BIT; esp : a sample of experience **3** : the special sense that perceives and identifies sweet, sour, bitter, or salty qualities and is mediated by taste buds on the tongue **4** : a quality perceptible to the sense of taste; also : the sensation obtained from a substance in the mouth : FLAVOR **5** : individual preference **6** : critical judgment, discernment, or appreciation; also : aesthetic quality ♦ **Synonyms** TANG, RELISH, FLAVOR, SAVOR — **taste·ful** \-fəl\ adj — **taste·ful·ly** adv — **taste·less** adj — **taste·less·ly** adv — **tast·er** n

taste bud n : a sense organ mediating the sensation of taste

tasty \'tā-stē\ adj **tast·i·er; -est** : pleasing to the taste : SAVORY ♦ **Synonyms** PALATABLE, APPETIZING, TOOTHSOME, FLAVORSOME — **tast·i·ness** \'tā-stē-nəs\ n

tat \'tat\ vb **tat·ted; tat·ting** : to work at or make by tatting

¹**tat·ter** \'ta-tər\ vb : to make or become ragged

²**tatter** n **1** : a part torn and left hanging **2** pl : tattered clothing

tat·ter·de·ma·lion \ˌta-tər-di-'māl-yən\ n : one that is ragged or disreputable

tat·ter·sall \'ta-tər-ˌsȯl, -səl\ n : a pattern of colored lines forming squares on solid background; also : a fabric in a tattersall pattern

tat·ting \'ta-tiŋ\ n : a delicate handmade lace formed usu. by looping and knotting with a single thread and a small shuttle; also : the act or process of making such lace

tat·tle \'ta-tᵊl\ vb **tat·tled; tat·tling** **1** : CHATTER, PRATE **2** : to tell secrets; also : to inform against another — **tat·tler** n

tat·tle·tale \'ta-tᵊl-ˌtāl\ n : one that tattles : INFORMER

¹**tat·too** \ta-'tü\ n, pl **tattoos** [alter. of earlier taptoo, fr. D taptoe, fr. the phrase tap toe! taps shut!] **1** : a call sounded before taps as notice to go to quarters **2** : a rapid rhythmic rapping

²**tattoo** vb : to mark (the skin) with tattoos

³**tattoo** n, pl **tattoos** [Tahitian tatau] : an indelible figure fixed upon the body esp. by insertion of pigment under the skin

tau \'taü, 'tȯ\ n : the 19th letter of the Greek alphabet — T or τ

taught past and past part of TEACH

¹**taunt** \'tȯnt\ n : a sarcastic challenge or insult

²**taunt** vb : to reproach or challenge in a

mocking manner : jeer at ✦ *Synonyms*
MOCK, DERIDE, RIDICULE, TWIT —
taunt·er n

taupe \'tōp\ n : a brownish gray

Tau·rus \'tȯr-əs\ n [L, lit., bull] 1 : a zodiacal constellation between Aries and Gemini usu. pictured as a bull 2 : the 2d sign of the zodiac in astrology; *also* : one born under this sign

taut \'tȯt\ adj 1 : tightly drawn : not slack 2 : extremely nervous : TENSE 3 : TRIM, TIDY ⟨a ~ ship⟩ — **taut·ly** adv — **taut·ness** n

tau·tol·o·gy \tȯ-'tä-lə-jē\ n, pl **-gies** : needless repetition of an idea, statement, or word; *also* : an instance of such repetition — **tau·to·log·i·cal** \ˌtȯt-ə-'lä-ji-kəl\ adj — **tau·to·log·i·cal·ly** \-ji-k(ə-)lē\ adv — **tau·tol·o·gous** \tȯ-'tä-lə-gəs\ adj — **tau·tol·o·gous·ly** adv

tav·ern \'ta-vərn\ n [ME *taverne*, fr. AF, fr. L *taberna* hut, shop] 1 : an establishment where alcoholic liquors are sold to be drunk on the premises 2 : INN

taw \'tȯ\ n 1 : a marble used as a shooter 2 : the line from which players shoot at marbles

taw·dry \'tȯ-drē\ adj **taw·dri·er; -est** [*tawdry lace* a tie of lace for the neck, fr. St. Audrey (St. Etheldreda) †679 queen of Northumbria] : cheap and gaudy in appearance and quality ✦ *Synonyms* GARISH, FLASHY, CHINTZY, MERETRICIOUS — **taw·dri·ly** adv

taw·ny \'tȯ-nē\ adj **taw·ni·er; -est** : of a brownish orange color

¹tax \'taks\ vb 1 : to levy a tax on 2 : CHARGE, ACCUSE 3 : to put under pressure — **tax·able** \'tak-sə-bəl\ adj — **tax·a·tion** \tak-'sā-shən\ n

²tax n 1 : a charge usu. of money imposed by authority on persons or property for public purposes 2 : a heavy charge : STRAIN

¹taxi \'tak-sē\ n, pl **tax·is** \-sēz\ *also* **tax·ies** : TAXICAB; *also* : a similarly operated boat or aircraft

²taxi vb **tax·ied; taxi·ing** or **taxy·ing; tax·is** or **tax·ies** 1 : to move along the ground or on the water under an aircraft's own power when starting or after a landing 2 : to go by taxicab

taxi·cab \'tak-sē-ˌkab\ n : an automobile that carries passengers for a fare usu. based on the distance traveled

taxi·der·my \'tak-sə-ˌdər-mē\ n : the skill or occupation of preparing, stuffing, and mounting skins of animals — **taxi·der·mist** \-mist\ n

tax·on \'tak-ˌsän\ n, pl **taxa** \-sə\; *also* **taxons** : a taxonomic group or entity

tax·on·o·my \tak-'sä-nə-mē\ n : classification esp. of animals or plants according to natural relationships — **tax·o·nom·ic** \ˌtak-sə-'nä-mik\ adj — **tax·on·o·mist** \tak-'sä-nə-mist\ n

tax·pay·er \'taks-ˌpā-ər\ n : one who pays or is liable for a tax — **tax·pay·ing** adj

Tay–Sachs disease \'tā-'saks-\ n : a hereditary disorder caused by the absence of an enzyme needed to break down fatty material, marked by buildup of lipids in nervous tissue, and causing death in childhood

tb abbr tablespoon; tablespoonful

Tb symbol terbium

TB \ˌtē-'bē\ n : TUBERCULOSIS

TBA abbr, often not cap to be announced

T–bar \'tē-ˌbär\ n : a ski lift with a series of T-shaped bars

tbs or **tbsp** abbr tablespoon; tablespoonful

Tc symbol technetium

TC abbr teachers college

T cell n : any of several lymphocytes (as a helper T cell) specialized esp. for activity in and control of immunity and the immune response

TCP/IP \ˌtē-(ˌ)sē-ˌpē-ˌī-'pē\ n [*transmission control protocol/Internet protocol*] : a set of communications protocols used over networks and esp. the Internet

TD abbr 1 touchdown 2 Treasury Department

TDD abbr telecommunications device for the deaf

TDY abbr temporary duty

Te symbol tellurium

tea \'tē\ n [Chin (dialect of Fujian province) *dé*] 1 : the cured leaves and leaf buds of a shrub grown chiefly in China, Japan, India, and Sri Lanka; *also* : this shrub 2 : a drink made by steeping tea in boiling water 3 : refreshments usu. including tea served in late afternoon; *also* : a reception at which tea is served

teach \'tēch\ vb **taught** \'tȯt\; **teach·ing** 1 : to cause to know something : act as a teacher 2 : to show how ⟨~ a child to swim⟩ 3 : to make to know the disagreeable consequences of an action 4 : to guide the studies of 5 : to impart the knowledge of ⟨~ algebra⟩ — **teach·able** adj — **teach·er** n

teach·ing n 1 : the act, practice, or profession of a teacher 2 : something taught; *esp* : DOCTRINE

tea·cup \'tē-ˌkəp\ n : a small cup used with a saucer for hot beverages

teak \'tēk\ n : the hard durable yellowish brown wood of a tall tropical Asian timber tree related to the vervains; *also* : this tree

tea·ket·tle \'tē-ˌke-t°l\ n : a covered kettle with a handle and spout for boiling water

teal \'tēl\ n, pl **teal** or **teals** 1 : any of various small short-necked wild ducks 2 : a dark greenish blue color

¹team \'tēm\ n [ME *teme*, fr. OE *tēam* offspring, lineage, group of draft animals] 1 : two or more draft animals harnessed to the same vehicle or implement 2 : a number of persons associated in work or activity; *esp* : a group on one side in a match

²team adj : of or performed by a team; *also* : marked by devotion to teamwork ⟨a ~ player⟩

³team vb 1 : to haul with or drive a team 2 : to form a team : join forces

team·mate \-ˌmāt\ n : a fellow member of a team

team·ster \'tēm-stər\ *n* : one who drives a team or truck

team·work \-,wərk\ *n* : the work or activity of a number of persons acting in close association as members of a unit

tea·pot \'tē-,pät\ *n* : a vessel with a spout for brewing and serving tea

¹tear \'tir\ *n* : a drop of the salty liquid that moistens the eye and inner side of the eyelids; *also, pl* : an act of weeping or grieving — **tear·ful** \-fəl\ *adj* — **tear·ful·ly** *adv* — **teary** \'tir-ē\ *adj*

²tear \'tir\ *vb* : to fill with or shed tears ⟨eyes ∼*ing* in the wind⟩

³tear \'ter\ *vb* **tore** \'tōr\; **torn** \'tōrn\; **tear·ing** **1** : to separate parts of or pull apart by force : RENT **2** : LACERATE **3** : to disrupt by the pull of contrary forces **4** : to remove by force : WRENCH **5** : to move or act with violence, haste, or force ◆ *Synonyms* RIP, SPLIT, CLEAVE, REND

⁴tear \'ter\ *n* **1** : the act of tearing **2** : a hole or flaw made by tearing : RENT

tear gas \'tir-\ *n* : a substance that on dispersion in the atmosphere blinds the eyes with tears — **tear gas** *vb*

tear·jerk·er \'tir-,jər-kər\ *n* : an extravagantly pathetic story, song, play, movie, or broadcast

¹tease \'tēz\ *vb* **teased**; **teas·ing** **1** : to disentangle and lay parallel by combing or carding ⟨∼ wool⟩ **2** : to scratch the surface of (cloth) so as to raise a nap **3** : to annoy persistently esp. in fun by goading, coaxing, or tantalizing **4** : to comb (hair) by taking a strand and pushing the short hairs toward the scalp with the comb ◆ *Synonyms* HARASS, WORRY, PESTER, ANNOY

²tease *n* **1** : the act of teasing or state of being teased **2** : one that teases

tea·sel \'tē-zəl\ *n* : a prickly herb or its flower head covered with stiff hooked bracts and used to raise the nap on cloth; *also* : an artificial device used for this purpose

tea·spoon \'tē-,spün\ *n* **1** : a small spoon suitable for stirring beverages **2** : a unit of measure equal to ⅙ fluid ounce (5 milliliters)

tea·spoon·ful \-,fùl\ *n, pl* **-spoonfuls** *also* **-spoons·ful** \-,spünz-,fùl\ : TEASPOON 2

teat \'tit, 'tēt\ *n* : the protuberance through which milk is drawn from an udder or breast

tech *abbr* **1** technical; technically; technician **2** technological; technology

tech·ne·tium \tek-'nē-shē-əm\ *n* : a radioactive metallic chemical element

tech·nic \'tek-nik, tek-'nēk\ *n* : TECHNIQUE 1

tech·ni·cal \'tek-ni-kəl\ *adj* [Gk *technikos* of art, skillful, fr. *technē* art, craft, skill] **1** : having special knowledge esp. of a mechanical or scientific subject ⟨∼ experts⟩ **2** : of or relating to a particular and esp. a practical or scientific subject ⟨∼ training⟩ **3** : according to a strict interpretation of the rules **4** : of or relating

to technique — **tech·ni·cal·ly** \-k(ə-)lē\ *adv*

tech·ni·cal·i·ty \,tek-nə-'ka-lə-tē\ *n, pl* **-ties** **1** : a detail meaningful only to a specialist **2** : the quality or state of being technical

technical sergeant *n* : a noncommissioned officer in the air force ranking next below a master sergeant

tech·ni·cian \tek-'ni-shən\ *n* : a person who has acquired the technique of a specialized skill or subject

tech·nique \tek-'nēk\ *n* [F] **1** : the manner in which technical details are treated or basic physical movements are used **2** : technical methods

tech·no \'tek-nō\ *n* : dance music featuring a fast beat and electronically created sounds usu. without vocals

tech·noc·ra·cy \tek-'nä-krə-sē\ *n* : management of society by technical experts — **tech·no·crat** \'tek-nə-,krat\ *n* — **tech·no·crat·ic** \,tek-nə-'kra-tik\ *adj*

tech·nol·o·gy \tek-'nä-lə-jē\ *n, pl* **-gies** : ENGINEERING; *also* : a manner of accomplishing a task using technical methods or knowledge — **tech·no·log·i·cal** \,tek-nə-'lä-ji-kəl\ *adj*

tec·ton·ics \tek-'tä-niks\ *n sing or pl* **1** : geological structural features **2** : geology dealing esp. with the faulting and folding of a planet or moon — **tec·ton·ic** \-nik\ *adj*

ted·dy bear \'te-dē-,ber\ *n* [*Teddy* Roosevelt; fr. a cartoon depicting the president sparing the life of a bear cub while hunting] : a stuffed toy bear

te·dious \'tē-dē-əs\ *adj* : tiresome because of length or dullness ◆ *Synonyms* BORING, TIRING, IRKSOME — **te·dious·ly** *adv* — **te·dious·ness** *n*

te·di·um \'tē-dē-əm\ *n* : TEDIOUSNESS; *also* : BOREDOM

¹tee \'tē\ *n* : a small mound or peg on which a golf ball is placed to be hit at the beginning of play on a hole; *also* : the area from which the ball is hit to begin play

²tee *vb* **teed**; **tee·ing** : to place (a ball) on a tee

teem \'tēm\ *vb* : to become filled to overflowing : ABOUND ◆ *Synonyms* SWARM, CRAWL, FLOW

teen *adj* : TEENAGE

teen·age \'tēn-,nāj\ *or* **teen·aged** \-,nājd\ *adj* : of, being, or relating to people in their teens — **teen·ag·er** \-,nā-jər\ *n*

teens \'tēnz\ *n pl* : the numbers 13 to 19 inclusive; *esp* : the years 13 to 19 in a person's life

tee·ny \'tē-nē\ *adj* **tee·ni·er**, **-est** : TINY

teepee *var of* TEPEE

tee shirt *var of* T-SHIRT

tee·ter \'tē-tər\ *vb* **1** : to move unsteadily **2** : SEESAW — **teeter** *n*

teeth *pl of* TOOTH

teethe \'tēth\ *vb* **teethed**; **teeth·ing** : to experience the rising of one's teeth through the gums : to grow teeth

teething *n* : growth of the first set of teeth through the gums with its accompanying phenomena

tee·to·tal·er *or* **tee·to·tal·ler** \'tē-'tō-t°l-ər\ *n* : a person who practices complete abstinence from alcoholic drinks — **tee·to·tal** \'tē-'tō-t°l, -₁tō-\ *adj* — **tee·to·tal·ism** \-t°l-₁i-zəm\ *n*

TEFL *abbr* teaching English as a foreign language

Te·ja·no \tā-'hä-(₁)nō\ *n, pl* **-nos** [Mex Sp, fr. *Tejas* Texas] : a Texan of Hispanic descent

tek·tite \'tek-₁tīt\ *n* : a glassy body of probably meteoric origin

tel *abbr* **1** telegram **2** telegraph **3** telephone

tele·cast \'te-li₁kast\ *vb* **-cast** *also* **-casted; -cast·ing** : to broadcast by television — **telecast** *n* — **tele·cast·er** *n*

tele·com \'te-li₁käm\ *n* : TELECOMMUNICATION; *also* : the telecommunications industry

tele·com·mu·ni·ca·tion \₁te-li-kə-₁myü-nə-'kā-shən\ *n* : communication at a distance (as by telephone or radio)

tele·com·mute \'te-li-kə-₁myüt\ *vb* : to work at home by the use of an electronic linkup with a central office

tele·con·fer·ence \'te-li-₁kän-fə-rəns\ *n* : a conference among people remote from one another held using telecommunications — **tele·con·fer·enc·ing** *n*

teleg *abbr* telegraphy

tele·gen·ic \₁te-lə-'je-nik, -'jē-\ *adj* : markedly attractive to television viewers

tele·gram \'te-lə-₁gram\ *n* : a message sent by telegraph

¹tele·graph \-₁graf\ *n* : an electric apparatus or system for sending messages by a code over wires — **tele·graph·ic** \₁te-lə-'gra-fik\ *adj*

²telegraph *vb* : to send or communicate by or as if by telegraph — **te·leg·ra·pher** \tə-'le-grə-fər\ *n*

te·leg·ra·phy \tə-'le-grə-fē\ *n* : the use or operation of a telegraph apparatus or system

tele·mar·ket·ing \₁te-lə-'mär-kə-tiŋ\ *n* : the marketing of goods or services by telephone — **tele·mar·ket·er** \-tər\ *n*

tele·med·i·cine \₁te-lə-'me-də-sən\ *n* : the practice of medicine using two-way voice and visual communication

te·lem·e·try \tə-'le-mə-trē\ *n* : the transmission esp. by radio of measurements made by automatic instruments to a distant station — **tele·me·ter** \'te-lə-₁mē-tər\ *n*

te·lep·a·thy \tə-'le-pə-thē\ *n* : apparent communication from one mind to another by extrasensory means — **tele·path·ic** \₁te-lə-'pa-thik\ *adj* — **tele·path·i·cal·ly** \-thi-k(ə-)lē\ *adv*

¹tele·phone \'te-lə-₁fōn\ *n* : an instrument for sending and receiving sounds over long distances by electricity

²telephone *vb* **-phoned; -phon·ing** **1** : to send or communicate by telephone **2** : to speak to (a person) by telephone — **tele·phon·er** *n*

te·le·pho·ny \tə-'le-fə-nē, 'te-lə-₁fō-\ *n* : use or operation of an apparatus for transmission of sounds as electrical sig-

nals between distant points — **tel·e·phon·ic** \₁te-lə-'fä-nik\ *adj*

tele·pho·to \₁te-lə-'fō-tō\ *adj* : being a camera lens giving a large image of a distant object — **tele·pho·tog·ra·phy** \-fə-'tä-grə-fē\ *n*

tele·play \'te-li-₁plā\ *n* : a story prepared for television production

tele·print·er \'te-lə-₁prin-tər\ *n* : TELETYPEWRITER

tele·promp·ter \'te-lə-₁prämp-tər\ *n* : a device for displaying prepared text to a speaker or performer

¹tele·scope \'te-lə-₁skōp\ *n* **1** : a cylindrical instrument equipped with lenses or mirrors for viewing distant objects **2** : RADIO TELESCOPE

²telescope *vb* **-scoped; -scop·ing** **1** : to slide or pass or cause to slide or pass one within another like the sections of a collapsible hand telescope **2** : COMPRESS, CONDENSE

tele·scop·ic \₁te-lə-'skä-pik\ *adj* **1** : of or relating to a telescope **2** : seen only by a telescope **3** : able to discern objects at a distance **4** : having parts that telescope — **tele·scop·i·cal·ly** \-pi-k(ə-)lē\ *adv*

tele·text \'te-lə-₁tekst\ *n* : a system for broadcasting text over a television signal and displaying it on a decoder-equipped television

tele·thon \'te-lə-₁thän\ *n* : a long television program usu. to solicit funds for a charity

tele·type·writ·er \₁te-lə-'tīp-₁rī-tər\ *n* : a printing device resembling a typewriter used to send and receive signals over telephone lines

tele·vise \'te-lə-₁vīz\ *vb* **-vised; -vis·ing** : to broadcast by television

tele·vi·sion \'te-lə-₁vi-zhən\ *n* [F *télévision*, fr. Gk *tēle* far, at a distance + F *vision* vision] : a system for transmitting images and sound by converting them into electrical or radio waves which are converted back into images and sound by a receiver; *also* : a television receiving set

tell \'tel\ *vb* **told** \'tōld\; **tell·ing** **1** : COUNT, ENUMERATE **2** : to relate in detail : NARRATE ⟨*told* us what happened⟩ **3** : SAY, UTTER **4** : to make known : REVEAL **5** : to report to : INFORM ⟨*told* me her name⟩ **6** : ORDER, DIRECT **7** : to find out by observing ⟨can ~ the difference⟩ **8** : to have a marked effect **9** : to serve as evidence ◆ **Synonyms** DISCLOSE, DISCOVER, BETRAY

tell·er \'te-lər\ *n* **1** : one that relates : NARRATOR **2** : one that counts **3** : a bank employee handling money received or paid out

tell·ing \'te-liŋ\ *adj* : producing a marked effect : EFFECTIVE ⟨~ evidence⟩ ◆ **Synonyms** COGENT, CONVINCING, SOUND

tell off *vb* : REPRIMAND, SCOLD

tell·tale \'tel-₁tāl\ *n* **1** : INFORMER, TATTLETALE **2** : something that serves to disclose : INDICATION — **telltale** *adj*

tel·lu·ri·um \tə-'lur-ē-əm\ *n* : a chemical element used esp. in alloys

tel·net \'tel-₁net\ *n* : a telecommunications protocol for accessing and using a remote computer via a local computer — **telnet** *vb*

tem·blor \'tem-blər\ *n* [Sp, lit., trembling] : EARTHQUAKE

te·mer·i·ty \tə-'mer-ə-tē\ *n, pl* **-ties** : rash or presumptuous daring : BOLDNESS ◆ *Synonyms* AUDACITY, EFFRONTERY, GALL, NERVE, CHEEK

¹**temp** \'temp\ *n* **1** : TEMPERATURE **2** : a temporary worker

²**temp** *abbr* temporary

¹**tem·per** \'tem-pər\ *vb* **1** : to dilute or soften by the addition of something else ⟨∼ justice with mercy⟩ **2** : to bring (as steel) to a desired hardness by reheating and cooling **3** : to toughen (glass) by gradual heating and cooling **4** : TOUGHEN : TUNE

²**temper** *n* **1** : characteristic tone : TENDENCY **2** : the hardness or toughness of a substance ⟨the ∼ of a knife blade⟩ **3** : a characteristic frame of mind : DISPOSITION **4** : calmness of mind : COMPOSURE **5** : state of feeling or frame of mind at a particular time **6** : heat of mind or emotion ◆ *Synonyms* TEMPERAMENT, CHARACTER, PERSONALITY, MAKEUP — **tem·pered** \'tem-pərd\ *adj*

tem·pera \'tem-pə-rə\ *n* [It] : a painting process using an albuminous or colloidal medium as a vehicle; *also* : a painting done in tempera

tem·per·a·ment \'tem-prə-mənt, -pər-mənt\ *n* **1** : characteristic or habitual inclination or mode of emotional response : DISPOSITION ⟨nervous ∼⟩ **2** : excessive sensitiveness or irritability ◆ *Synonyms* CHARACTER, PERSONALITY, NATURE, MAKEUP — **tem·per·a·men·tal** \ˌtem-prə-'men-tᵊl, -pər-'ment-\ *adj*

tem·per·ance \'tem-prəns, -pə-rəns\ *n* : habitual moderation in the indulgence of the appetites or passions; *esp* : moderation in or abstinence from the use of alcoholic beverages

tem·per·ate \'tem-prət, -pə-rət\ *adj* **1** : not extreme or excessive : MILD **2** : moderate in indulgence of appetite or desire **3** : moderate in the use of alcoholic beverages **4** : having a moderate climate ◆ *Synonyms* SOBER, CONTINENT, ABSTEMIOUS

temperate zone *n, often cap T&Z* : the region between the Tropic of Cancer and the arctic circle or between the Tropic of Capricorn and the antarctic circle

tem·per·a·ture \'tem-pər-ˌchúr, -prə-ˌchúr, -chər\ *n* **1** : degree of hotness or coldness of something (as air, water, or the body) as shown by a thermometer **2** : FEVER 1

tem·pest \'tem-pəst\ *n* [ME *tempeste*, fr. AF, ultim. fr. L *tempestas* season, weather, storm, fr. *tempus* time] : a violent storm

tempest in a teapot : a great commotion over an unimportant matter

tem·pes·tu·ous \tem-'pes-chə-wəs\ *adj* : of, involving, or resembling a tempest : STORMY — **tem·pes·tu·ous·ly** *adv* — **tem·pes·tu·ous·ness** *n*

tem·plate \'tem-plət\ *n* : a gauge, mold, or pattern that functions as a guide to the form or structure of something being made

¹**tem·ple** \'tem-pəl\ *n* **1** : a building reserved for religious practice **2** : a place devoted to a special or exalted purpose ⟨a ∼of cuisine⟩

²**temple** *n* : the flattened space on each side of the forehead esp. of humans

tem·po \'tem-pō\ *n, pl* **tem·pi** \-ˌ(ˌ)pē\ *or* **tempos** [It, lit., time] **1** : the rate of speed of a musical piece or passage **2** : rate of motion or activity : PACE

¹**tem·po·ral** \'tem-pə-rəl\ *adj* **1** : of, relating to, or limited by time ⟨∼ and spatial bounds⟩ **2** : of or relating to earthly life or secular concerns ⟨∼ power⟩

²**temporal** *adj* : of or relating to the temples or the sides of the skull

¹**tem·po·rary** \'tem-pə-ˌrer-ē\ *adj* : lasting for a time only : TRANSITORY ◆ *Synonyms* TRANSIENT, EPHEMERAL, MOMENTARY, IMPERMANENT — **tem·po·rar·i·ly** \ˌtem-pə-'rer-ə-lē\ *adv*

²**temporary** *n, pl* **-rar·ies** : one serving for a limited time

tem·po·rise *Brit var of* TEMPORIZE

tem·po·rize \'tem-pə-ˌrīz\ *vb* **-rized; -riz·ing** **1** : to adapt one's actions to the time or the dominant opinion : COMPROMISE **2** : to draw out matters so as to gain time — **tem·po·riz·er** *n*

tempt \'tempt\ *vb* **1** : to entice to do wrong by promise of pleasure or gain **2** : PROVOKE ⟨∼ fate⟩ **3** : to risk the dangers of **4** : to induce to do something : INCITE ◆ *Synonyms* INVEIGLE, DECOY, SEDUCE, LURE — **tempt·er** *n* — **tempt·ing·ly** *adv*

temp·ta·tion \temp-'tā-shən\ *n* **1** : the act of tempting : the state of being tempted **2** : something that tempts

tempt·ress \'temp-trəs\ *n* : a woman who tempts

ten \'ten\ *n* **1** : one more than nine **2** : the 10th in a set or series **3** : something having 10 units — **ten** *adj or pron* — **tenth** \'tenth\ *adj or adv or n*

ten·a·ble \'te-nə-bəl\ *adj* : capable of being held, maintained, or defended — **ten·a·bil·i·ty** \ˌte-nə-'bi-lə-tē\ *n*

te·na·cious \tə-'nā-shəs\ *adj* **1** : not easily pulled apart : COHESIVE, TOUGH ⟨a ∼ metal⟩ **2** : holding fast ⟨∼ of his rights⟩ **3** : RETENTIVE ⟨a ∼ memory⟩ — **te·na·cious·ly** *adv* — **te·nac·i·ty** \tə-'na-sə-tē\ *n*

ten·an·cy \'te-nən-sē\ *n, pl* **-cies** : the temporary possession or occupancy of something (as a house) that belongs to another; *also* : the period of a tenant's occupancy

ten·ant \'te-nənt\ *n* **1** : one who rents or leases (as a house) from a landlord **2** : DWELLER, OCCUPANT — **tenant** *vb* — **ten·ant·less** *adj*

tenant farmer *n* : a farmer who works land owned by another and pays rent either in cash or in shares of produce

ten·ant·ry \'te-nən-trē\ *n, pl* **-ries** : the body of tenants esp. on an estate

Ten Commandments *n pl* : the commandments of God given to Moses on Mount Sinai

¹tend \'tend\ *vb* **1** : to apply oneself ⟨~ to your affairs⟩ **2** : to take care of ⟨~ a plant⟩ **3** : to manage the operations of ⟨~ a machine⟩

²tend *vb* **1** : to move or develop one's course in a particular direction **2** : to show an inclination or tendency

ten·den·cy \'ten-dən-sē\ *n, pl* **-cies** **1** : DRIFT, TREND **2** : a proneness to or readiness for a particular kind of thought or action : PROPENSITY ♦ **Synonyms** BENT, LEANING, DISPOSITION, INCLINATION

ten·den·tious \ten-'den-chəs\ *adj* : marked by a tendency in favor of a particular point of view : BIASED — **ten·den·tious·ly** *adv* — **ten·den·tious·ness** *n*

¹ten·der \'ten-dər\ *adj* [ME, fr. AF *tendre*, fr. L *tener*] **1** : having a soft texture : easily broken, chewed, or cut **2** : physically weak : DELICATE; *also* : IMMATURE **3** : expressing or responsive to love or sympathy : LOVING, COMPASSIONATE **4** : SENSITIVE, TOUCHY ⟨a ~ ego⟩ ♦ **Synonyms** SYMPATHETIC, WARM, WARMHEARTED — **ten·der·ly** *adv* — **ten·der·ness** *n*

²tender *n* [AF *tendre*, fr. *tendre*, v., to stretch, hold out, offer, fr. L *tendere* to stretch, direct] **1** : an offer or proposal made for acceptance; *esp* : an offer of a bid for a contract **2** : something (as money) that may be offered in payment

³tender *vb* : to present for acceptance

⁴tend·er \'ten-dər\ *n* **1** : one that tends or takes care **2** : a boat carrying passengers and freight to a larger ship **3** : a car attached to a steam locomotive for carrying fuel and water

⁵tender *n* [prob. short for *tenderloin*] : a strip of meat (as chicken) often breaded

ten·der·foot \'ten-dər-ˌfu̇t\ *n, pl* **-feet** \-ˌfēt\ *also* **-foots** \-ˌfu̇ts\ **1** : one not hardened to frontier or rough outdoor life **2** : an inexperienced beginner

ten·der·heart·ed \ˌten-dər-'här-təd\ *adj* : easily moved to love, pity, or sorrow

ten·der·ize \'ten-də-ˌrīz\ *vb* **-ized**; **-iz·ing** : to make (meat) tender — **ten·der·iz·er** \'ten-də-ˌrī-zər\ *n*

ten·der·loin \'ten-dər-ˌlȯin\ *n* **1** : a tender strip of beef or pork from near the backbone **2** : a district of a city largely devoted to vice

ten·di·ni·tis *or* **ten·don·itis** \ˌten-də-'nī-təs\ *n* : inflammation of a tendon

ten·don \'ten-dən\ *n* : a tough cord of dense white fibrous tissue uniting a muscle with another part (as a bone) — **ten·di·nous** \-də-nəs\ *adj*

ten·dril \'ten-drəl\ *n* : a slender coiling organ by which some climbing plants attach themselves to a support

ten·e·brous \'te-nə-brəs\ *adj* : shut off from the light : GLOOMY, OBSCURE

ten·e·ment \'te-nə-mənt\ *n* **1** : a house used as a dwelling **2** : a building divided into apartments for rent to families; *esp*

: one meeting only minimum standards of safety and comfort **3** : APARTMENT, FLAT

te·net \'te-nət\ *n* [L, he holds, fr. *tenēre* to hold] : one of the principles or doctrines held in common by members of a group (as a church or profession) ♦ **Synonyms** DOCTRINE, DOGMA, BELIEF

ten·fold \'ten-ˌfōld, -'fōld\ *adj* : being 10 times as great or as many — **ten·fold** \-'fōld\ *adv*

tenge \'teŋ-ˌgä\ *n, pl* **tenge** — see MONEY table

ten—gallon hat *n* : a wide-brimmed hat with a large soft crown

Tenn *abbr* Tennessee

ten·nis \'te-nəs\ *n* : a game played with a ball and racket on a court divided by a net

ten·on \'te-nən\ *n* : a projecting part in a piece of material (as wood) for insertion into a mortise to make a joint

ten·or \'te-nər\ *n* **1** : the general drift of something spoken or written **2** : the highest natural adult male voice; *also* : a singer having this voice **3** : a continuing in a course, movement, or activity ⟨the ~ of my life⟩

tenpenny nail *n* : a nail three inches (about 7.6 centimeters) long

ten·pin \'ten-ˌpin\ *n* : a bottle-shaped bowling pin set in groups of 10 and bowled at in a game (tenpins)

¹tense \'tens\ *n* [ME *tens* time, tense, fr. AF, fr. L *tempus*] : distinction of form of a verb to indicate the time of the action or state

²tense *adj* **tens·er**; **tens·est** [L *tensus*, fr. pp. of *tendere* to stretch] **1** : stretched tight : TAUT **2** : feeling or showing nervous tension ⟨a ~ smile⟩ ♦ **Synonyms** STIFF, RIGID, INFLEXIBLE — **tense·ly** *adv* — **tense·ness** *n* — **ten·si·ty** \'ten-sə-tē\ *n*

³tense *vb* **tensed**; **tens·ing** : to make or become tense

ten·sile \'ten-səl, -ˌsī(-ə)l\ *adj* : of or relating to tension ⟨~ strength⟩

ten·sion \'ten-chən\ *n* **1** : the act of straining or stretching; *also* : the condition of being strained or stretched **2** : a state of mental unrest often with signs of bodily stress **3** : a state of latent hostility or opposition

ten·speed \'ten-ˌspēd\ *n* : a bicycle with a derailleur having 10 possible combinations of gears

¹tent \'tent\ *n* **1** : a collapsible shelter of material stretched and supported by poles **2** : a canopy placed over the head and shoulders to retain vapors or oxygen given for medical reasons

²tent *vb* **1** : to lodge in tents **2** : to cover with or as if with a tent

ten·ta·cle \'ten-ti-kəl\ *n* : any of various long flexible projections about the head or mouth (as of an insect, mollusk, or fish) — **ten·ta·cled** \-kəld\ *adj* — **ten·tac·u·lar** \ten-'ta-kyə-lər\ *adj*

ten·ta·tive \'ten-tə-tiv\ *adj* **1** : not fully worked out or developed ⟨~ plans⟩ **2** : HESITANT, UNCERTAIN ⟨a ~ smile⟩ — **ten·ta·tive·ly** *adv* — **ten·ta·tive·ness** *n*

ten·u·ous \'ten-yə-wəs\ adj 1 : not dense : RARE ⟨a ~ fluid⟩ 2 : not thick : SLENDER ⟨a ~ rope⟩ 3 : having little substance : FLIMSY, WEAK ⟨~ influences⟩ 4 : lacking stability : SHAKY ⟨~ reasoning⟩ — te·nu·i·ty \te-'nü-ə-tē, tə-, -'nyü-\ n — ten·u·ous·ly adv — ten·u·ous·ness n

ten·ure \'ten-yər\ n : the act, right, manner, or period of holding something (as a landed property, an office, or a position)

ten·ured \'ten-yərd\ adj : having tenure ⟨~ faculty members⟩

te·o·sin·te \tā-ō-'sin-tē\ n : a tall annual grass of Mexico that is closely related to Indian corn

te·pee or **tee·pee** \'tē-(.)pē\ n [Dakota t-ípi, fr. t-í- to dwell] : an American Indian conical tent usu. of skins

tep·id \'te-pəd\ adj 1 : moderately warm : LUKEWARM 2 : HALFHEARTED

te·qui·la \tə-'kē-lə, tā-\ n : a Mexican liquor distilled from an agave's sap

ter abbr 1 terrace 2 territory

tera·byte \'ter-ə-.bīt\ n [tera- trillion (10¹²), fr. Gk terat-, teras monster] : 1024 gigabytes; also : one trillion bytes

ter·bi·um \'tər-bē-əm\ n : a metallic chemical element

ter·cen·te·na·ry \.tər-.sen-'te-nə-rē, tər-'sen-tə-.ner-ē\ n, pl -ries : a 300th anniversary or its celebration — **tercentenary** adj

ter·cen·ten·ni·al \.tər-.sen-'te-nē-əl\ adj or n : TERCENTENARY

te·re·do \tə-'rē-dō, -'rā-\ n, pl **-dos** [L] : SHIPWORM

ter·i·ya·ki \.ter-ē-'yä-kē\ n [Jp] : a Japanese dish of meat or fish soaked in a soy marinade and cooked

¹term \'tərm\ n 1 : END, TERMINATION : DURATION; esp : a period of time fixed esp. by law or custom 2 : a mathematical expression connected with another by a plus or minus sign; also : an element (as a numerator) of a fraction or proportion 3 : a word or expression that has a precise meaning in some uses or is limited to a particular subject or field 4 pl : PROVISIONS, CONDITIONS ⟨~s of a contract⟩ 5 pl : mutual relationship ⟨on good ~s⟩ 6 : AGREEMENT, CONCORD 7 : a state of acceptance ⟨come to ~s with his grief⟩

²term vb : to apply a term to : CALL

ter·ma·gant \'tər-mə-gənt\ n : an overbearing or nagging woman : SHREW

¹ter·mi·nal \'tər-mə-nᵊl\ adj 1 : of, relating to, or forming an end, limit, or terminus 2 : FATAL 2 ⟨~ cancer⟩; also : being in or relating to the final stages of a fatal disease ⟨a ~ patient⟩ ♦ Synonyms FINAL, CONCLUDING, LAST, LATEST — **ter·mi·nal·ly** adv

²terminal n 1 : EXTREMITY, END 2 : a device at the end of a wire or on electrical equipment for making a connection 3 : either end of a transportation line (as a railroad) with its offices and freight and passenger stations; also : a freight or passenger station 4 : a device (as in a computer system) for data entry and display

ter·mi·nate \'tər-mə-.nāt\ vb **-nat·ed; -nat·ing** : to bring or come to an end ♦ Synonyms CONCLUDE, FINISH, COMPLETE — **ter·mi·na·ble** \-nə-bəl\ adj — **ter·mi·na·tion** \.tər-mə-'nā-shən\ n — **ter·mi·na·tor** \'tər-mə-.nā-tər\ n

ter·mi·nol·o·gy \.tər-mə-'nä-lə-jē\ n, pl **-gies** : the technical or special terms used in a business, art, science, or special subject

ter·mi·nus \'tər-mə-nəs\ n, pl **-ni** \-.nī\ or **-nus·es** [L] 1 : final goal : END 2 : either end of a transportation line or travel route; also : the station or city at such a place

ter·mite \'tər-.mīt\ n : any of numerous pale soft-bodied social insects that feed on wood

tern \'tərn\ n : any of various chiefly marine birds with narrow wings and often a forked tail

ter·na·ry \'tər-nə-rē\ adj 1 : of, relating to, or proceeding by threes 2 : having three elements or parts

terr abbr territory

¹ter·race \'ter-əs\ n 1 : a flat roof or open platform 2 : a level area next to a building 3 : an embankment with level top 4 : a bank or ridge on a slope to conserve moisture and soil 5 : a row of houses on raised land; also : a street with such a row of houses 6 : a strip of park in the middle of a street

²terrace vb **ter·raced; ter·rac·ing** : to form into a terrace or supply with terraces

ter·ra-cot·ta \.ter-ə-'kä-tə\ n [It terra cotta, lit., baked earth] : a reddish brown earthenware

terra fir·ma \-'fər-mə\ n [NL] : solid ground

ter·rain \tə-'rān\ n : the surface features of an area of land ⟨a rough ~⟩

ter·ra in·cog·ni·ta \'ter-ə-.in-.käg-'nē-tə\ n, pl **ter·rae in·cog·ni·tae** \'ter-.ī-.in-.käg-'nē-.tī\ [L] : an unexplored area or field of knowledge

ter·ra·pin \'ter-ə-pən\ n : any of various turtles of fresh or brackish water

ter·rar·i·um \tə-'rer-ē-əm\ n, pl **-ia** \-ē-ə\ or **-i·ums** : a usu. transparent enclosure for keeping or raising plants or small animals indoors

ter·res·tri·al \tə-'res-trē-əl\ adj 1 : of or relating to the earth or its inhabitants 2 : living or growing on land ⟨~ plants⟩ ♦ Synonyms MUNDANE, EARTHLY, WORLDLY

ter·ri·ble \'ter-ə-bəl\ adj 1 : exciting terror : FEARFUL, DREADFUL ⟨~ weapons⟩ 2 : hard to bear : DISTRESSING ⟨a ~ situation⟩ 3 : extreme in degree : INTENSE ⟨~ heat⟩ 4 : of very poor quality : AWFUL ⟨a ~ play⟩ ♦ Synonyms FRIGHTFUL, HORRIBLE, SHOCKING, APPALLING — **ter·ri·bly** \-blē\ adv

ter·ri·er \'ter-ē-ər\ n [ME terryer, terrer, fr. AF (chen) terrer, lit., earth dog, fr. terre earth, fr. L terra] : any of various usu. small energetic dogs orig. used by hunters to drive small game animals from their holes

ter·rif·ic \tə-ˈri-fik\ adj **1** : exciting terror **2** : EXTRAORDINARY, ASTOUNDING ⟨~ speed⟩ **3** : MAGNIFICENT ⟨makes ~ chili⟩

ter·ri·fy \ˈter-ə-ˌfī\ vb **-fied; -fy·ing** : to fill with terror : FRIGHTEN ♦ **Synonyms** SCARE, TERRORIZE, STARTLE, ALARM — **ter·ri·fy·ing·ly** adv

ter·ri·to·ri·al·i·ty \ˌter-ə-ˌtȯr-ē-ˈa-lə-tē\ n : persistent attachment to a specific territory

ter·ri·to·ry \ˈter-ə-ˌtȯr-ē\ n, pl **-ries 1** : a geographic area belonging to or under the jurisdiction of a governmental authority **2** : a part of the U.S. not included within any state but organized with a separate legislature **3** : REGION, DISTRICT; also : a region in which one feels at home **4** : a field of knowledge or interest **5** : an assigned area **6** : an area occupied and defended by one or a group of animals — **ter·ri·to·ri·al** \ˌter-ə-ˈtȯr-ē-əl\ adj — **go with the territory** or **come with the territory** : to accompany a situation naturally

ter·ror \ˈter-ər\ n **1** : a state of intense fear : FRIGHT **2** : one that inspires fear **3** : violent or destructive acts committed to intimidate a people or government ♦ **Synonyms** PANIC, CONSTERNATION, DREAD, ALARM, DISMAY, HORROR, TREPIDATION

ter·ror·ism \ˈter-ər-ˌi-zəm\ n : the systematic use of terror esp. as a means of coercion — **ter·ror·ist** \-ist\ adj or n

ter·ror·ize \ˈter-ər-ˌīz\ vb **-ized; -iz·ing 1** : to fill with terror : SCARE **2** : to coerce by threat or violence ♦ **Synonyms** TERRIFY, FRIGHTEN, ALARM, STARTLE

ter·ry \ˈter-ē\ n, pl **terries** : an absorbent fabric with a loose pile of uncut loops

terse \ˈtərs\ adj **ters·er; ters·est** [L tersus clean, neat, fr. pp. of tergēre to wipe off] : effectively brief : CONCISE — **terse·ly** adv — **terse·ness** n

ter·tia·ry \ˈtər-shē-ˌer-ē\ adj **1** : of third rank, importance, or value **2** cap : of, relating to, or being the earlier period of the Cenozoic era **3** : occurring in or being the third stage

Tertiary n : the Tertiary period

TESL abbr teaching English as a second language

TESOL abbr Teachers of English to Speakers of Other Languages

¹test \ˈtest\ n [ME, vessel in which metals were assayed, potsherd, fr. AF, pot, fr. L testum earthen vessel] **1** : a critical examination or evaluation : TRIAL **2** : a means or result of testing

²test vb **1** : to put to test : TRY, EXAMINE **2** : to undergo or score on tests

³test adj : relating to or used in testing ⟨a ~ group⟩

tes·ta·ment \ˈtes-tə-mənt\ n **1** cap : either of two main divisions of the Bible **2** : EVIDENCE, WITNESS **3** : CREED **4** : the legal instructions for the disposition of one's property after death : WILL — **tes·ta·men·ta·ry** \ˌtes-tə-ˈmen-tə-rē\ adj

tes·tate \ˈtes-ˌtāt, -tət\ adj : having left a valid will

tes·ta·tor \ˈtes-ˌtā-tər, tes-ˈtā-\ n : a person who dies leaving a valid will

tes·ta·trix \tes-ˈtā-triks\ n : a woman who is a testator

¹tes·ter \ˈtes-tər, ˈtes-\ n : a canopy over a bed, pulpit, or altar

²test·er \ˈtes-tər\ n : one that tests

tes·ti·cle \ˈtes-ti-kəl\ n : TESTIS; esp : one of a mammal usu. with its enclosing structures — **tes·tic·u·lar** adj

tes·ti·fy \ˈtes-tə-ˌfī\ vb **-fied; -fy·ing 1** : to make a statement based on personal knowledge or belief : bear witness **2** : to serve as evidence or proof

tes·ti·mo·ni·al \ˌtes-tə-ˈmō-nē-əl\ n **1** : a statement testifying to benefits received; also : a character reference **2** : an expression of appreciation : TRIBUTE — **testimonial** adj

tes·ti·mo·ny \ˈtes-tə-ˌmō-nē\ n, pl **-nies 1** : evidence based on observation or knowledge **2** : an outward sign : SYMBOL **3** : a solemn declaration made by a witness under oath esp. in a court ♦ **Synonyms** EVIDENCE, CONFIRMATION, PROOF, TESTAMENT

tes·tis \ˈtes-təs\ n, pl **tes·tes** \ˈtes-ˌtēz\ [L, witness, testis] : a typically paired male reproductive gland that produces sperm and testosterone and that in most mammals is contained within the scrotum at sexual maturity

tes·tos·ter·one \te-ˈstäs-tə-ˌrōn\ n : a male sex hormone causing development of the male reproductive system and secondary sex characteristics

test–tube adj **1** : IN VITRO ⟨~ experiments⟩ **2** : produced by in vitro fertilization ⟨~ babies⟩

test tube n : a glass tube closed at one end and used esp. in chemistry and biology

tes·ty \ˈtes-tē\ adj **tes·ti·er; -est** [ME testif, fr. AF, headstrong, fr. teste head, fr. LL testa skull, fr. L, shell] : easily annoyed; also : marked by ill humor

tet·a·nus \ˈte-tə-nəs\ n : an infectious disease caused by bacterial poisons and marked by muscle stiffness and spasms esp. of the jaws — **tet·a·nal** \-nəl\ adj

tetchy \ˈte-chē\ adj **tetchi·er; -est** : irritably or peevishly sensitive

¹tête–à–tête \ˈtāt-ə-ˌtāt\ n [F, lit., head to head] : a private conversation between two persons

²tête–à–tête \ˌtāt-ə-ˈtāt\ adv : in private

³tête–à–tête \ˈtāt-ə-ˌtāt\ adj : being face-to-face : PRIVATE

¹teth·er \ˈte-thər\ n **1** : something (as a rope) by which an animal is fastened **2** : the limit of one's strength or resources

²tether vb : to fasten or restrain by or as if by a tether

tet·ra·eth·yl lead \ˌte-trə-ˈe-thəl-\ n : a heavy oily poisonous liquid used esp. formerly as an antiknock agent in gasoline

tet·ra·he·dron \ˌte-trə-ˈhē-drən\ n, pl **-drons** or **-dra** \-drə\ : a polyhedron that has four faces — **tet·ra·he·dral** \-drəl\ adj

tet·ra·hy·dro·can·nab·i·nol \ˌte-trə-ˌhī-drə-kə-ˈna-bə-ˌnȯl, -ˌnōl\ n : THC

te·tram·e·ter \te-ˈtra-mə-tər\ n : a line of verse consisting of four metrical feet

tet·ri \'te-trē\ *n, pl* **tetri** — see *lari* at MONEY table

Teu·ton·ic \tü-'tä-nik, tyü-\ *adj* : GERMANIC

Tex *abbr* Texas

Tex–Mex \'teks-'meks\ *adj* : characteristic of Mexican-American culture and esp. that of southern Texas

text \'tekst\ *n* 1 : the actual words of an author's work 2 : the main body of printed or written matter on a page 3 : a scriptural passage chosen as the subject esp. of a sermon 4 : THEME, TOPIC 5 : TEXTBOOK — **tex·tu·al** \'teks-chə-wəl\ *adj*

text·book \'tekst-,bùk\ *n* : a book used in the study of a subject

tex·tile \'tek-,stī(-ə)l, 'teks-t³l\ *n* : CLOTH; *esp* : a woven or knit cloth

tex·ture \'teks-chər\ *n* 1 : the visual or tactile surface characteristics and appearance of something ⟨a coarse ~⟩ 2 : essential part 3 : basic structure or structure : FABRIC 4 : overall structure — **tex·tur·al** \-chə-rəl\ *adj*

TGIF *abbr* thank God it's Friday

¹**Th** *abbr* Thursday

²**Th** *symbol* thorium

¹**-th** — see ¹ETH

²**-th** *or* **-eth** *adj suffix* — used in forming ordinal numbers ⟨hundred*th*⟩

³**-th** *n suffix* 1 : act or process 2 : state or condition ⟨dear*th*⟩

Thai \'tī\ *n, pl* **Thai** *or* **Thais** 1 : a native or inhabitant of Thailand 2 : the official language of Thailand — **Thai** *adj*

thal·a·mus \'tha-lə-məs\ *n, pl* **-mi** \-,mī\ [NL] : a subdivision of the brain that serves as a relay station to and from the cerebral cortex and functions in arousal and the integration of sensory information — **tha·lam·ic** \thə-'la-mik\ *adj*

thal·as·se·mia \,tha-lə-'sē-mē-ə\ *n* : any of a group of inherited disorders of hemoglobin synthesis

tha·las·so·ther·a·py \thə-,la-sō-'ther-ə-pē\ *n* [Gk *thalassa* sea] : the use of seawater or sea products (as seaweed) for the benefit of health or beauty

thal·li·um \'tha-lē-əm\ *n* : a poisonous metallic chemical element

¹**than** \'thən, 'than\ *conj* 1 — used after a comparative adjective or adverb to introduce the second part of a comparison expressing inequality ⟨older ~ I am⟩ 2 — used after *other* or a word of similar meaning to express a difference of kind, manner, or identity ⟨adults other ~ parents⟩

²**than** *prep* : in comparison with ⟨older ~ me⟩

thane \'thān\ *n* 1 : a free retainer of an Anglo-Saxon lord 2 : a Scottish feudal lord

thank \'thaŋk\ *vb* : to express gratitude to ⟨~ed them for the present⟩

thank·ful \'thaŋk-fəl\ *adj* 1 : conscious of benefit received 2 : expressive of thanks : GLAD — **thank·ful·ness** *n*

thank·ful·ly \-fə-lē\ *adv* 1 : in a thankful manner 2 : as makes one thankful

thank·less \'thaŋ-kləs\ *adj* 1 : UNAPPRECIATED 2 : UNGRATEFUL

thanks \'thaŋks\ *n pl* : an expression of gratitude

thanks·giv·ing \thaŋks-'gi-viŋ\ *n* 1 : the act of giving thanks 2 : a prayer expressing gratitude 3 *cap* : the 4th Thursday in November observed as a legal holiday for giving thanks for divine goodness

¹**that** \'that, thət\ *pron, pl* **those** \'thōz\ 1 : the one indicated, mentioned, or understood ⟨~ is my house⟩ 2 : the one farther away or first mentioned ⟨this is an elm, ~'s a maple⟩ 3 : what has been indicated or mentioned ⟨after ~, we left⟩ 4 : the one or ones : IT, THEY ⟨*those* who wish to leave may do so⟩

²**that** \thət, 'that\ *conj* 1 : the following, namely ⟨he said ~ he would⟩; *also* : which is, namely ⟨there's a chance ~ it may fail⟩ 2 : to this end or purpose ⟨shouted ~ all might hear⟩ 3 : as to result in the following, namely ⟨so heavy ~ it can't be moved⟩ 4 : for this reason, namely : BECAUSE ⟨we're glad ~ you came⟩

³**that** *adj, pl* **those** 1 : being the one mentioned, indicated, or understood ⟨~ boy⟩ ⟨*those* people⟩ 2 : being the one farther away or less immediately under discussion ⟨this chair or ~ one⟩

⁴**that** \thət, 'that\ *pron* 1 : WHO, WHOM, WHICH ⟨the man ~ saw you⟩ ⟨the man ~ you saw⟩ ⟨the money ~ was spent⟩ 2 : in, on, or at which ⟨the way ~ he drives⟩ ⟨the day ~ it rained⟩

⁵**that** \'that\ *adv* : to such an extent or degree ⟨I like it, but not ~ much⟩

¹**thatch** \'thach\ *vb* : to cover with or as if with thatch — **thatch·er** *n*

²**thatch** *n* 1 : plant material (as straw) for use as roofing 2 : a mat of grass clippings accumulated next to the soil on a lawn 3 : a covering of or as if of thatch ⟨a ~ of white hair⟩

thaw \'thò\ *vb* 1 : to melt or cause to melt 2 : to become as warm as to melt ice or snow 3 : to abandon aloofness or hostility — **thaw** *n*

THC \,tē-(,)āch-'sē\ *n* [*t*etra*h*ydro*c*annabinol] : a physiologically active chemical from hemp plant resin that is the chief intoxicant in marijuana

¹**the** \thə, *before vowel sounds usu* thē\ *definite article* 1 : that in particular 2 — used before adjectives functioning as nouns ⟨a word to ~ wise⟩

²**the** *adv* 1 : to what extent ⟨~ sooner, the better⟩ 2 : to that extent ⟨the sooner, ~ better⟩

theat *abbr* theater; theatrical

the·ater *or* **the·atre** \'thē-ə-tər\ *n* [ME *theatre*, fr. MF, fr. L *theatrum*, fr. Gk *theatron*, fr. *theasthai* to view, fr. *thea* act of seeing] 1 : a building or area for dramatic performances; *also* : a building or area for showing motion pictures 2 : a place of enactment of significant events ⟨~ of war⟩ 3 : a place (as a lecture room) resembling a theater 4 : dramatic literature or performance

theater–in–the–round *n* : a theater with the stage in the center of the auditorium

the·at·ri·cal \thē-'a-tri-kəl\ *also* **the·at·ric** \-trik\ *adj* **1** : of or relating to the theater **2** : marked by artificiality of emotion : HISTRIONIC **3** : marked by extravagant display : SHOWY

the·at·ri·cals \-kəlz\ *n pl* : the performance of plays

the·at·rics \thē-'a-triks\ *n pl* **1** : THEATRICALS **2** : staged or contrived effects

the·be \'thä-bā\ *n, pl* **thebe** — see *pula* at MONEY table

thee \'thē\ *pron, archaic objective case of* THOU

theft \'theft\ *n* : the act of stealing

thegn \'thān\ *n* : THANE 1

their \thər, 'ther\ *adj* : of or relating to them or themselves

theirs \'therz\ *pron* : their one : their ones

the·ism \'thē-,i-zəm\ *n* : belief in the existence of a god or gods — **the·ist** \-ist\ *n or adj* — **the·is·tic** \thē-'is-tik\ *adj*

them \thəm, 'them\ *pron, objective case of* THEY

theme \'thēm\ *n* **1** : a subject or topic of discourse or of artistic representation **2** : a written exercise : COMPOSITION **3** : a melodic subject of a musical composition or movement — **the·mat·ic** \thi-'ma-tik\ *adj*

them·selves \thəm-'selvz, them-\ *pron pl* : THEY, THEM — used reflexively, for emphasis, or in absolute constructions ⟨they govern ∼⟩ ⟨they ∼ came⟩ ⟨∼ busy, they sent me⟩

¹then \'then\ *adv* **1** : at that time **2** : soon after that : NEXT **3** : in addition : BESIDES **4** : in that case **5** : CONSEQUENTLY

²then *n* : that time ⟨since ∼⟩

³then *adj* : existing or acting at that time ⟨the ∼ attorney general⟩

thence \'thens, 'thens\ *adv* **1** : from that place **2** *archaic* : THENCEFORTH **3** : from that fact : THEREFROM

thence·forth \-,fôrth\ *adv* : from that time forward : THEREAFTER

thence·for·ward \thens-'fôr-wərd, thens-\ *also* **thence·for·wards** \-wərdz\ *adv* : onward from that place or time

the·oc·ra·cy \thē-'ä-krə-sē\ *n, pl* **-cies** **1** : government by officials regarded as divinely inspired **2** : a state governed by a theocracy — **the·o·crat·ic** \,thē-ə-'kra-tik\ *adj*

theol *abbr* theological; theology

the·ol·o·gy \thē-'ä-lə-jē\ *n, pl* **-gies** **1** : the study of religious faith, practice, and experience; *esp* : the study of God and of God's relation to the world **2** : a theory or system of theology — **the·o·lo·gian** \,thē-ə-'lō-jən\ *n* — **the·o·log·i·cal** \-'lä-ji-kəl\ *adj*

the·o·rem \'thē-ə-rəm, 'thir-əm\ *n* **1** : a statement esp. in mathematics that has been or is to be proved **2** : an idea accepted or proposed as a demonstrable truth : PROPOSITION

the·o·ret·i·cal \,thē-ə-'re-ti-kəl\ *also* **the·o·ret·ic** \-tik\ *adj* **1** : relating to or having the character of theory **2** : existing only in theory : HYPOTHETICAL — **the·o·ret·i·cal·ly** \-ti-k(ə-)lē\ *adv*

the·o·rise *Brit var of* THEORIZE

the·o·rize \'thē-ə-,rīz\ *vb* **-rized; -riz·ing** : to form a theory : SPECULATE — **the·o·rist** \-rist\ *n*

the·o·ry \'thē-ə-rē, 'thir-ē\ *n, pl* **-ries** **1** : abstract thought **2** : the general principles of a subject **3** : a plausible or scientifically acceptable general principle offered to explain observed facts **4** : HYPOTHESIS, CONJECTURE

theory of games : GAME THEORY

the·os·o·phy \thē-'ä-sə-fē\ *n* : belief about God and the world held to be based on mystical insight — **theo·soph·i·cal** \,thē-ə-'sä-fi-kəl\ *adj* — **the·os·o·phist** \thē-'ä-sə-fist\ *n*

ther·a·peu·tic \,ther-ə-'pyü-tik\ *adj* [Gk *therapeutikos,* fr. *therapeuein* to attend, treat, fr. *theraps* attendant] : of, relating to, or dealing with healing and esp. with remedies for diseases — **ther·a·peu·ti·cal·ly** \-ti-k(ə-)lē\ *adv*

ther·a·peu·tics \,ther-ə-'pyü-tiks\ *n* : a branch of medical or dental science dealing with the use of remedies

ther·a·py \'ther-ə-pē\ *n, pl* **-pies** : treatment of bodily, mental, or behavioral disorders — **ther·a·pist** \-pist\ *n*

¹there \'ther\ *adv* **1** : in or at that place — often used interjectionally **2** : to or into that place : THITHER **3** : in that matter or respect

²there \'ther, thər\ *pron* — used as a function word to introduce a sentence or clause ⟨∼'s a pen here⟩

³there \'ther\ *n* **1** : that place ⟨get away from ∼⟩ **2** : that point ⟨you take it from ∼⟩

there·abouts \,thr-ə-'baùts, 'ther-ə-,baùts\ *or* **there·about** \-'baùt, -,baùt\ *adv* **1** : near that place or time **2** : near that number, degree, or quantity

there·af·ter \ther-'af-tər\ *adv* : after that : AFTERWARD

there·at \-'at\ *adv* **1** : at that place **2** : at that occurrence : on that account

there·by \ther-'bī, 'ther-,bī\ *adv* **1** : by that : by that means **2** : connected with or with reference to that

there·for \ther-'fôr\ *adv* : for or in return for that

there·fore \'ther-,fôr\ *adv* : for that reason : CONSEQUENTLY

there·from \ther-'frəm\ *adv* : from that or it

there·in \ther-'in\ *adv* **1** : in or into that place, time, or thing **2** : in that respect

there·of \-'əv, -'äv\ *adv* **1** : of that or it **2** : from that : THEREFROM

there·on \-'ón, -'än\ *adv* **1** : on that **2** *archaic* : THEREUPON 3

there·to \ther-'tü\ *adv* : to that

there·un·to \ther-'ən-(,)tü, ,ther-ən-'tü\ *adv, archaic* : THERETO

there·upon \'ther-ə-,pón, -,pän; ,ther-ə-'pón, -'pän\ *adv* **1** : on that matter **2** : THEREFORE **3** : immediately after that : at once

there·with \ther-'with -with\ *adv* **1** : with

that **2** *archaic* : THEREUPON, FORTH-
WITH

there·with·al \'ᵗher-wi-ˌt͟hȯl, -ˌt͟hȯl\ *adv*
1 *archaic* : BESIDES **2** : THEREWITH

therm *abbr* thermometer

ther·mal \'t͟hər-məl\ *adj* **1** : of, relating
to, or caused by heat **2** : designed to prevent the loss of body heat ⟨∼ under-
wear⟩ — **ther·mal·ly** *adv*

thermal pollution *n* : the discharge of
heated liquid (as waste water from a factory) into natural waters at a temperature
harmful to the environment

therm·is·tor \'t͟hər-ˌmis-tər\ *n* : an electrical resistor whose resistance varies
sharply with temperature

ther·mo·cline \'t͟hər-mə-ˌklīn\ *n* : the region in a thermally stratified body of
water that separates warmer surface
water from cold deep water

ther·mo·cou·ple \'t͟hər-mə-ˌkə-pəl\ *n* : a
device for measuring temperature by
measuring the temperature-dependent
potential difference created at the junction of two dissimilar metals

ther·mo·dy·nam·ics \ˌt͟hər-mə-dī-'na-
miks\ *n* : physics that deals with the mechanical action or relations of heat —
ther·mo·dy·nam·ic \-mik\ *adj* — **ther-
mo·dy·nam·i·cal·ly** \-mi-k(ə-)lē\ *adv*

ther·mom·e·ter \t͟hər-'mä-mə-tər\ *n* [F
thermomètre, fr. Gk *thermē* heat + *metron*
measure] : an instrument for measuring
temperature typically by the rise or fall of
a liquid (as mercury) in a thin glass tube
— **ther·mo·met·ric** \ˌt͟hər-mə-'me-trik\
adj — **ther·mo·met·ri·cal·ly** \-tri-
k(ə-)lē\ *adv*

ther·mo·nu·cle·ar \ˌt͟hər-mō-'nü-klē-ər,
-'nyü-\ *adj* **1** : of or relating to changes
in the nucleus of atoms of low atomic
weight (as hydrogen) that require a very
high temperature (as in the hydrogen
bomb) **2** : utilizing or relating to a ther-
monuclear bomb ⟨∼ war⟩

ther·mo·plas·tic \ˌt͟hər-mə-'plas-tik\ *adj*
: capable of softening when heated and
hardening again when cooled ⟨∼ resins⟩
— **thermoplastic** *n*

ther·mos \'t͟hər-məs\ *n* : a cylindrical
container with a vacuum between an
inner and an outer wall used to keep liquids hot or cold

ther·mo·sphere \'t͟hər-mə-ˌsfir\ *n* : the
part of the earth's atmosphere that lies
above the mesosphere and that is characterized by steadily increasing temperature with height

ther·mo·stat \'t͟hər-mə-ˌstat\ *n* : a device
that automatically controls temperature
— **ther·mo·stat·ic** \ˌt͟hər-mə-'sta-tik\ *adj*
— **ther·mo·stat·i·cal·ly** \-ti-k(ə-)lē\ *adv*

the·sau·rus \thi-'sȯr-əs\ *n, pl* **-sau·ri**
\-'sȯr-ˌī\ *or* **-sau·rus·es** \-'sȯr-ə-səz\ [NL,
fr. L, treasure, collection, fr. Gk
thēsauros] : a book of words and their
synonyms — **the·sau·ral** \-'sȯr-əl\ *adj*

these *pl of* THIS

the·sis \'thē-səs\ *n, pl* **the·ses** \'thē-ˌsēz\
1 : a proposition that a person advances
and offers to maintain by argument **2**
: an essay embodying results of original

research; *esp* : one written for an academic degree

¹thes·pi·an \'thes-pē-ən\ *adj, often cap* [fr.
Thespis, 6th cent. B.C. Greek poet and reputed originator of tragedy] : relating to
the drama : DRAMATIC

²thespian *n* : ACTOR

Thess *abbr* Thessalonians

Thes·sa·lo·nians \ˌthe-sə-'lō-nyənz, -nē-
ənz\ *n* — see BIBLE table

the·ta \'thā-tə\ *n* : the 8th letter of the
Greek alphabet — Θ or θ

thew \'thü, 'thyü\ *n* : MUSCLE, SINEW —
usu. used in pl.

they \'t͟hā\ *pron* **1** : those individuals
under discussion : the ones previously
mentioned or referred to **2** : unspecified
persons : PEOPLE

thi·a·mine \'thī-ə-mən, -ˌmēn\ *also* **thi·a-
min** \-mən\ *n* : a vitamin of the vitamin B
complex essential to normal metabolism
and nerve function

¹thick \'thik\ *adj* **1** : having relatively
great depth or extent from one surface to
its opposite ⟨a ∼ plank⟩; *also* : heavily
built : THICKSET **2** : densely massed
: CROWDED; *also* : FREQUENT, NUMER-
OUS **3** : dense or viscous in consistency
⟨∼ syrup⟩ **4** : marked by haze, fog, or
mist ⟨∼ weather⟩ **5** : measuring in
thickness ⟨one meter ∼⟩ **6** : imperfectly
articulated : INDISTINCT ⟨∼ speech⟩ **7**
: STUPID, OBTUSE **8** : associated on close
terms : INTIMATE **9** : EXCESSIVE ♦ *Synonyms* COMPACT, CLOSE, TIGHT —
thick·ly *adv*

²thick *n* **1** : the most crowded or active
part **2** : the part of greatest thickness

thick and thin *n* : every difficulty and obstacle ⟨was loyal through *thick and thin*⟩

thick·en \'thi-kən\ *vb* : to make or become thick — **thick·en·er** *n*

thick·et \'thi-kət\ *n* : a dense growth of
bushes or small trees

thick·ness \-nəs\ *n* **1** : the smallest of
three dimensions ⟨length, width, and
∼⟩ **2** : the quality or state of being
thick **3** : LAYER, SHEET ⟨a single ∼ of
canvas⟩

thick·set \'thik-'set\ *adj* **1** : closely
placed or planted **2** : having a thick
body : BURLY

thick–skinned \-'skind\ *adj* **1** : having a
thick skin **2** : not easily bothered by criticism or insult

thief \'thēf\ *n, pl* **thieves** \'thēvz\ : one
that steals esp. secretly

thieve \'thēv\ *vb* **thieved; thiev·ing**
: STEAL, ROB ♦ *Synonyms* FILCH, PIL-
FER, PURLOIN, SWIPE

thiev·ery \'thē-və-rē\ *n, pl* **-er·ies** : the act
of stealing : THEFT

thigh \'thī\ *n* : the part of the vertebrate
hind or lower limb between the knee and
the hip

thigh·bone \'thī-ˌbōn\ *n* : FEMUR

thim·ble \'thim-bəl\ *n* : a cap or guard
worn on the finger to push the needle in
sewing — **thim·ble·ful** *n*

¹thin \'thin\ *adj* **thin·ner; thin·nest 1**
: having little extent from one surface
through to its opposite : not thick : SLEN-

DER **2** : not closely set or placed : SPARSE ⟨~ hair⟩ **3** : not dense or not dense enough : more fluid or rarefied than normal ⟨~ air⟩ ⟨~ syrup⟩ **4** : lacking substance, fullness, or strength ⟨~ broth⟩ **5** : FLIMSY ⟨a ~ excuse⟩ — **thin·ly** adv — **thin·ness** n

²**thin** vb **thinned; thin·ning** : to make or become thin

thine \ˈthīn\ pron, archaic : one or the ones belonging to thee

thing \ˈthiŋ\ n **1** : a matter of concern : AFFAIR ⟨~s to do⟩ **2** pl : state of affairs ⟨~s are improving⟩ **3** : EVENT, CIRCUMSTANCE ⟨the crime was a terrible ~⟩ **4** : DEED, ACT ⟨expected great ~s of him⟩ **5** : a distinct entity : OBJECT **6** : an inanimate object distinguished from a living being **7** pl : POSSESSIONS, EFFECTS **8** : an article of clothing **9** : DETAIL, POINT ⟨checks every little ~⟩ **10** : IDEA, NOTION ⟨says the first ~ he thinks of⟩ **11** : something one likes to do : SPECIALTY ⟨doing her ~⟩

think \ˈthiŋk\ vb **thought** \ˈthȯt\; **thinking** **1** : to form or have in the mind **2** : to have as an opinion : BELIEVE **3** : to reflect on : PONDER **4** : to call to mind : REMEMBER **5** : REASON **6** : to form a mental picture of : IMAGINE **7** : to devise by thinking ⟨thought up a plan to escape⟩ ✦ **Synonyms** CONCEIVE, FANCY, REALIZE, ENVISAGE — **think·er** n

think tank n : an institute, corporation, or group organized for interdisciplinary research (as in technological or social problems)

thin·ner \ˈthi-nər\ n : a volatile liquid (as turpentine) used to thin paint

thin-skinned \ˈthin-ˈskind\ adj **1** : having a thin skin or rind **2** : extremely sensitive to criticism or insult

¹**third** \ˈthərd\ adj : next after the second — **third** or **third·ly** adv

²**third** n **1** : one of three equal parts of something **2** : one that is number three in a countable series **3** : the 3d forward gear in an automotive vehicle

third degree n : the subjection of a prisoner to mental or physical torture to force a confession

third dimension n **1** : thickness, depth, or apparent thickness or depth that confers solidity on an object **2** : a quality that confers reality ⟨third–dimensional adj

third world n, often cap T&W : the aggregate of the underdeveloped nations of the world

¹**thirst** \ˈthərst\ n **1** : a feeling of dryness in the mouth and throat associated with a desire to drink; also : a bodily condition producing this **2** : an ardent desire : CRAVING ⟨a ~ for knowledge⟩ — **thirsty** adj

²**thirst** vb **1** : to need drink : suffer thirst **2** : to have a strong desire : CRAVE

thir·teen \ˌthər-ˈtēn\ n : one more than 12 — **thirteen** adj or pron — **thir·teenth** \-ˈtēnth\ adj or n

thir·ty \ˈthər-tē\ n, pl **thirties** : three times

10 — **thir·ti·eth** \-tē-əth\ adj or n — **thirty** adj or pron

¹**this** \ˈthis\ pron, pl **these** \ˈthēz\ **1** : the one close or closest in time or space ⟨~ is your book⟩ **2** : what is in the present or under immediate observation or discussion ⟨~ is a mess⟩; also : what is happening or being done now ⟨after ~ we'll leave⟩

²**this** adj, pl **these** **1** : being the one near, present, just mentioned, or more immediately under observation ⟨~ book⟩ **2** : constituting the immediate past or future ⟨friends all these years⟩

³**this** adv : to such an extent or degree ⟨didn't expect to wait ~ long⟩

this·tle \ˈthi-səl\ n : any of various tall prickly composite plants with often showy heads of tightly packed tubular flowers

this·tle·down \-ˌdau̇n\ n : the down from the ripe flower head of a thistle

¹**thith·er** \ˈthi-thər\ adv : to that place

²**thither** adj : being on the farther side

thith·er·ward \-wərd\ adv : toward that place : THITHER

thong \ˈthȯŋ\ n **1** : a strip esp. of leather or hide **2** : a sandal held on the foot by a thong between the toes **3** : a narrow strip of swimwear or underwear that passes between the thighs

tho·rax \ˈthȯr-ˌaks\ n, pl **tho·rax·es** or **tho·ra·ces** \ˈthȯr-ə-ˌsēz\ **1** : the part of the body of a mammal between the neck and the abdomen; also : its cavity containing the heart and lungs **2** : the middle of the three main divisions of the body of an insect — **tho·rac·ic** \thə-ˈra-sik\ adj

tho·ri·um \ˈthȯr-ē-əm\ n : a radioactive metallic chemical element

thorn \ˈthȯrn\ n **1** : a woody plant bearing sharp processes **2** : a sharp rigid plant process that is usu. a modified leafless branch **3** : something that causes distress — **thorny** adj

thor·ough \ˈthər-ō\ adj **1** : COMPLETE, EXHAUSTIVE ⟨a ~ search⟩ **2** : very careful : PAINSTAKING ⟨a ~ scholar⟩ **3** : having full mastery — **thor·ough·ly** adv — **thor·ough·ness** n

thor·ough·bred \ˈthər-ə-ˌbred\ adj **1** : bred from the best blood through a long line **2** cap : of or relating to the Thoroughbred breed of horses **3** : marked by high-spirited grace

²**thoroughbred** n **1** cap : any of an English breed of light speedy horses kept chiefly for racing **2** : one (as a pedigreed animal) of excellent quality

thor·ough·fare \-ˌfer\ n : a public road or street

thor·ough·go·ing \ˌthər-ə-ˈgō-iŋ\ adj : marked by thoroughness or zeal

thorp \ˈthȯrp\ n, archaic : VILLAGE

those pl of THAT

¹**thou** \ˈthau̇\ pron, archaic : the person addressed

²**thou** \ˈthau̇\ n, pl **thou** : a thousand of something (as dollars)

¹**though** \ˈthō\ conj **1** : despite the fact that ⟨~ the odds are hopeless, they fight

on⟩ **2** : granting that ⟨∼ it may look bad, still, all is not lost⟩
²**though** *adv* : HOWEVER, NEVERTHELESS ⟨not for long. ∼⟩
¹**thought** \ˈthȯt\ *past and past part of* THINK
²**thought** *n* **1** : the process of thinking **2** : serious consideration : REGARD **3** : reasoning power **4** : the power to imagine : CONCEPTION **5** : IDEA, NOTION **6** : OPINION, BELIEF ⟨spoke his ∼s freely⟩
thought·ful \ˈthȯt-fəl\ *adj* **1** : absorbed in thought **2** : marked by careful thinking ⟨a ∼ essay⟩ **3** : considerate of others ⟨a ∼ host⟩ — **thought·ful·ly** *adv* — **thought·ful·ness** *n*
thought·less \-ləs\ *adj* **1** : insufficiently alert : CARELESS ⟨a ∼ worker⟩ **2** : RECKLESS ⟨a ∼ act⟩ **3** : lacking concern for others : INCONSIDERATE ⟨∼ remarks⟩ — **thought·less·ly** *adv* — **thought·less·ness** *n*
thou·sand \ˈthau̇-ᶻnd\ *n, pl* **thousands** *or* **thousand** : 10 times 100 — **thousand** *adj* — **thou·sandth** \-ᶻnth\ *adj or n*
thousands place *n* : the place four to the left of the decimal point in an Arabic number
thrall \ˈthrȯl\ *n* **1** : SLAVE, BONDMAN **2** : a state of servitude — **thrall·dom** *or* **thral·dom** \ˈthrȯl-dəm\ *n*
¹**thrash** \ˈthrash\ *vb* **1** : THRESH 1 **2** : BEAT, WHIP; *also* : DEFEAT **3** : to move about violently **4** : to go over again and again ⟨∼ over the matter⟩; *also* : to hammer out ⟨∼ out a plan⟩
²**thrash** *n* : rock music that is extremely fast and loud
¹**thrash·er** \ˈthra-shər\ *n* : one that thrashes or threshes
²**thrasher** *n* : any of various long-tailed American songbirds related to the mockingbird
¹**thread** \ˈthred\ *n* **1** : a thin continuous strand of spun and twisted textile fibers **2** : something resembling a textile thread **3** : the ridge or groove that winds around a screw **4** : a line of reasoning or train of thought **5** : a continuing element **6** : a tenuous or feeble support
²**thread** *vb* **1** : to pass a thread through the eye of (a needle) **2** : to pass (as film) through something **3** : to make one's way through or between **4** : to put together on a thread ⟨∼ beads⟩ **5** : to form a screw thread on or in
thread·bare \-ˌber\ *adj* **1** : having the nap worn off so that the thread shows : SHABBY **2** : TRITE
thready \ˈthre-dē\ *adj* **1** : consisting of or bearing fibers of filaments ⟨a ∼ bark⟩ **2** : lacking in fullness, body, or vigor ⟨a ∼ voice⟩
threat \ˈthret\ *n* **1** : an expression of intent to do harm **2** : one that threatens
threat·en \ˈthre-tᵊn\ *vb* **1** : to utter threats against **2** : to give signs or warning of : PORTEND **3** : to hang over as a threat : MENACE **4** : to cause to feel insecure or anxious — **threat·en·ing·ly** *adv*

threat·ened \-t²nd\ *adj* : having an uncertain chance of continued survival; *esp* : likely to become an endangered species
three \ˈthrē\ *n* **1** : one more than two **2** : the 3d in a set or series **3** : something having three units — **three** *adj or pron*
3–D \ˈthrē-ˈdē\ *n* : a three-dimensional form or picture
three–dimensional *adj* **1** : relating to or having three dimensions **2** : giving the illusion of varying distances ⟨a ∼ picture⟩
three·fold \ˈthrē-ˌfōld, -ˈfōld\ *adj* **1** : having three parts : TRIPLE **2** : being three times as great or as many — **three·fold** \-ˈfōld\ *adv*
three·pence \ˈthre-pəns, ˈthri-, ˈthrə-, *US also* ˈthrē-pens\ *n* **1** *pl* **threepence** *or* **three·penc·es** : a coin worth three pennies **2** : the sum of three British pennies
three·score \ˈthrē-ˈskȯr\ *adj* : being three times twenty : SIXTY
three·some \ˈthrē-səm\ *n* : a group of three persons or things
thren·o·dy \ˈthre-nə-dē\ *n, pl* **-dies** : a song of lamentation : ELEGY
thresh \ˈthresh, ˈthrash\ *vb* **1** : to separate (as grain from straw) mechanically **2** : THRASH — **thresh·er** *n*
thresh·old \ˈthresh-ˌhōld\ *n* **1** : the sill of a door **2** : a point or place of beginning or entering : OUTSET **3** : a point at which a physiological or psychological effect begins to be produced
threw *past of* THROW
thrice \ˈthrīs\ *adv* **1** : three times **2** : in a threefold manner or degree
thrift \ˈthrift\ *n* [ME, fr. ON, prosperity, fr. *thrīfask* to thrive] : careful management esp. of money : FRUGALITY — **thrift·i·ly** \ˈthrif-tə-lē\ *adv* — **thrift·less** *adj* — **thrifty** *adj*
thrill \ˈthril\ *vb* [ME *thirlen, thrillen* to pierce, fr. OE *thyrlian,* fr. *thyrel* hole, fr. *thurh* through] **1** : to have or cause to have sudden sharp feeling of excitement; *also* : TINGLE, SHIVER **2** : TREMBLE, VIBRATE — **thrill** *n* — **thrill·er** *n* — **thrill·ing·ly** *adv*
thrips \ˈthrips\ *n, pl* **thrips** : any of an order of minute sucking insects including many plant-feeding pests
thrive \ˈthrīv\ *vb* **thrived** *or* **throve** \ˈthrōv\; **thrived** *also* **thriv·en** \ˈthri-vən\; **thriv·ing** **1** : to grow luxuriantly : FLOURISH **2** : to gain in wealth or possessions : PROSPER
throat \ˈthrōt\ *n* : the part of the neck in front of the spinal column; *also* : the passage through it to the stomach and lungs — **throat·ed** *adj*
throaty \ˈthrō-tē\ *adj* **throat·i·er; -est** **1** : uttered or produced from low in the throat ⟨a ∼ voice⟩ **2** : heavy, thick, or deep as if from the throat ⟨∼ notes of a horn⟩ — **throat·i·ly** \-tə-lē\ *adv* — **throat·i·ness** \-tē-nəs\ *n*
¹**throb** \ˈthräb\ *vb* **throbbed; throb·bing** : to pulsate or pound esp. with abnormal force or rapidity : BEAT, VIBRATE
²**throb** *n* : BEAT, PULSE

throe \'thrō\ *n* **1** : PANG, SPASM ⟨death ~*s*⟩ **2** *pl* : a hard or painful struggle

throm·bo·lyt·ic \ˌthräm-bə-'li-tik\ *adj* : destroying or breaking up a thrombus — **thrombolytic** *n*

throm·bo·sis \thräm-'bō-səs\ *n, pl* **-bo·ses** \-ˌsēz\ : the formation or presence of a clot in a blood vessel — **throm·bot·ic** \-'bä-tik\ *adj*

throm·bus \'thräm-bəs\ *n, pl* **throm·bi** \-ˌbī\ [NL, fr. Gk *thrombos* lump, clot] : a clot of blood formed within a blood vessel and remaining attached to its place of origin

throne \'thrōn\ *n* **1** : the chair of state of a sovereign or high dignitary **2** : royal power : SOVEREIGNTY

¹throng \'throŋ\ *n* **1** : MULTITUDE **2** : a crowding together of many persons

²throng *vb* **thronged; throng·ing** : CROWD

¹throt·tle \'thrä-t°l\ *vb* **throt·tled; throt·tling** [ME *throtlen*, fr. *throte* throat] **1** : CHOKE, STRANGLE **2** : SUPPRESS ⟨policies that ~ creativity⟩ **3** : to reduce the speed of (an engine) by closing the throttle — **throt·tler** *n*

²throttle *n* : a valve regulating the flow of steam or fuel to an engine; *also* : the lever controlling this valve

¹through \'thrü\ *prep* **1** : into at one side and out at the other side of ⟨go ~ the door⟩ **2** : by way of ⟨entered ~ a skylight⟩ **3** : in the midst of ⟨a path ~ the trees⟩ **4** : by means of ⟨succeeded ~ hard work⟩ **5** : over the whole of ⟨rumors swept ~ the office⟩ **6** : during the whole of ⟨~ the night⟩ **7** : to and including ⟨Monday ~ Friday⟩

²through *adv* **1** : from one end or side to the other **2** : from beginning to end : to completion ⟨see it ~⟩ **3** : to the core : THOROUGHLY ⟨he was wet ~⟩ **4** : into the open : OUT ⟨break ~⟩

³through *adj* **1** : permitting free passage ⟨a ~ street⟩ **2** : going from point of origin to destination without change or transfer ⟨a ~ train⟩ **3** : coming from or going to points outside a local area ⟨~ traffic⟩ **4** : FINISHED ⟨~ with the job⟩

¹through·out \thrü-'aut\ *adv* **1** : EVERYWHERE **2** : from beginning to end

²throughout *prep* **1** : in or to every part of **2** : during the whole period of

through·put \'thrü-ˌput\ *n* : OUTPUT, PRODUCTION ⟨the ~ of a computer⟩

throve *past of* THRIVE

¹throw \'thrō\ *vb* **threw** \'thrü\; **thrown** \'thrōn\; **throw·ing** [ME, to cause to twist, throw, fr. OE *thrāwan* to cause to twist] **1** : to propel through the air esp. with a forward motion of the hand and arm ⟨~ a ball⟩ **2** : to cause to fall or fall off **3** : to put suddenly in a certain position or condition ⟨~ into panic⟩ **4** : to put on or take off hastily ⟨~ on a coat⟩ **5** : to lose intentionally ⟨~ a game⟩ **6** : to move (a lever) so as to connect or disconnect parts of something (as a clutch) **7** : to put (an automobile) into a different gear **8** : to act as host for ⟨~ a party⟩

♦ *Synonyms* TOSS, FLING, PITCH, SLING — **throw·er** *n*

²throw *n* **1** : an act of throwing, hurling, or flinging; *also* : CAST **2** : the distance a missile may be thrown **3** : a light coverlet **4** : a woman's scarf or light wrap

throw-away \'thrō-ə-ˌwā\ *n* : something that is or is designed to be thrown away esp. after one use

throwaway *adj* : overly wasteful ⟨a ~ society⟩

throw-back \-ˌbak\ *n* : reversion to an earlier type or phase; *also* : an instance or product of this

throw up *vb* **1** : to build hurriedly **2** : VOMIT

thrum \'thrəm\ *vb* **thrummed; thrumming** : to play or pluck a stringed instrument idly : STRUM

thrush \'thrəsh\ *n* : any of numerous small or medium-sized songbirds that are mostly of a plain color often with spotted underparts

¹thrust \'thrəst\ *vb* **thrust; thrust·ing** **1** : to push or drive with force : SHOVE **2** : STAB, PIERCE **3** : INTERJECT **4** : to press the acceptance of upon someone

²thrust *n* **1** : a lunge with a pointed weapon **2** : ATTACK **3** : the pressure of one part of a construction against another (as of an arch against an abutment) **4** : the force produced by a propeller or jet or rocket engine that drives a vehicle (as an aircraft) forward **5** : a violent push : SHOVE **6** : prominent or essential element

thrust·er *also* **thrust·or** \'thrəs-tər\ *n* : one that thrusts; *esp* : a rocket engine

thru·way \'thrü-ˌwā\ *n* : EXPRESSWAY

¹thud \'thəd\ *n* **1** : ²BLOW **2** : a dull sound

²thud *vb* **thud·ded; thud·ding** : to move or strike so as to make a thud

thug \'thəg\ *n* [Hindi & Urdu *thag*, lit., thief] : a brutal ruffian or assassin — **thug·gish** *adj*

thu·li·um \'thü-lē-əm, 'thyü-\ *n* : a rare metallic chemical element

¹thumb \'thəm\ *n* **1** : the short thick first digit of the human hand or a corresponding digit of a lower animal **2** : the part of a glove or mitten that covers the thumb

²thumb *vb* **1** : to leaf through (pages) with the thumb **2** : to wear or soil with the thumb by frequent handling **3** : to request or obtain (a ride) in a passing automobile by signaling with the thumb

¹thumb·nail \'thəm-ˌnāl\ *n* : the nail of the thumb

²thumbnail *adj* : BRIEF, CONCISE ⟨a ~ description⟩ ⟨a ~ picture⟩

thumb·print \-ˌprint\ *n* : an impression made by the thumb

thumb·screw \-ˌskrü\ *n* **1** : a device of torture for squeezing the thumb **2** : a screw with a head that may be turned by the thumb and index finger

thumb·tack \-ˌtak\ *n* : a tack with a broad flat head for pressing with one's thumb into a board or wall

¹thump \'thəmp\ *vb* **1** : to strike with or as

if with something thick or heavy so as to cause a dull sound **2** : POUND

²**thump** *n* : a blow with or as if with something blunt or heavy; *also* : the sound made by such a blow

¹**thun-der** \'thən-dər\ *n* **1** : the sound following a flash of lightning; *also* : a noise like such a sound **2** : a loud utterance or threat

²**thunder** *vb* **1** : to produce thunder **2** : ROAR, SHOUT

thun-der-bolt \-‚bōlt\ *n* : a flash of lightning with its accompanying thunder

thun-der-clap \-‚klap\ *n* : a crash of thunder

thun-der-cloud \-‚klaůd\ *n* : a cloud charged with electricity and producing lightning and thunder

thun-der-head \-‚hed\ *n* : a large cumulus or cumulonimbus cloud often appearing before a thunderstorm

thun-der-ous \'thən-də-rəs\ *adj* : producing thunder; *also* : making a noise like thunder — **thun-der-ous-ly** *adv*

thun-der-show-er \'thən-dər-‚shaů(-ə)r\ *n* : a shower accompanied by thunder and lightning

thun-der-storm \-‚störm\ *n* : a storm accompanied by thunder and lightning

thun-der-struck \-‚strək\ *adj* : stunned as if struck by a thunderbolt

Thurs *or* **Thu** *abbr* Thursday

Thurs-day \'thərz-‚dā, -dē\ *n* [ME, fr. OE *thursdæg*, fr. ON *thōrsdagr*, lit., day of Thor (Norse god)] : the 5th day of the week

thus \'thəs\ *adv* **1** : in this or that manner **2** : to this degree or extent : SO **3** : because of this or that : HENCE

¹**thwack** \'thwak\ *vb* : to strike with or as if with something flat or heavy

²**thwack** *n* : a heavy blow : WHACK

¹**thwart** \'thwört\ *vb* **1** : FOIL, BAFFLE **2** : BLOCK, DEFEAT ✦ **Synonyms** BALK, OUTWIT, FRUSTRATE

²**thwart** \'thwört, *naut often* 'thört\ *adv* : ATHWART

³**thwart** *adj* : situated or placed across something else

⁴**thwart** *n* : a seat extending across a boat

thy \'thī\ *adj, archaic* : of, relating to, or done by or to thee or thyself

thyme \'tīm, 'thīm\ *n* [ME, fr. AF *time*, fr. L *thymum*, fr. Gk *thymon*, prob. fr. *thyein* to make a burnt offering, sacrifice] : a garden mint with small aromatic leaves used esp. in seasoning; *also* : its leaves so used

thy-mine \'thī-‚mēn\ *n* : a pyrimidine base that is one of the four bases coding genetic information in the molecular chain of DNA

thy-mus \'thī-məs\ *n, pl* **thy-mus-es** : a glandular organ of the neck region that is composed largely of lymphoid tissue, functions esp. in the development of the immune system, and tends to atrophy in the adult

thy-ris-tor \thī-'ris-tər\ *n* : a semiconductor device that acts as a switch, rectifier, or voltage regulator

thy-roid \'thī-‚ròid\ *n* [NL *thyroides*, fr. Gk *thyreoeidēs* shield-shaped, thyroid, fr. *thyreos* shield shaped like a door, fr. *thyra* door] : a large 2-lobed endocrine gland that lies at the base of the neck and produces several iodine-containing hormones that affect growth, development, and metabolism — **thy-roid** *also* **thy-roi-dal** \thī-'ròi-d⁰l\ *adj*

thy-rox-ine *or* **thy-rox-in** \thī-'räk-‚sēn, -sən\ *n* : an iodine-containing hormone that is produced by the thyroid gland, increases metabolic rate, and is used to treat thyroid disorders

thy-self \thī-'self\ *pron, archaic* : YOURSELF

Ti *symbol* titanium

ti-ara \tē-'er-ə, -'är-\ *n* **1** : a 3-tiered crown worn by the pope **2** : a decorative headband or semicircle for formal wear by women

Ti-bet-an \tə-'be-t⁰n\ *n* **1** : the language of the Tibetan people **2** : a native or inhabitant of Tibet — **Tibetan** *adj*

tib-ia \'ti-bē-ə\ *n, pl* **-i-ae** \-bē-‚ē\ *also* **-i-as** [L] : the inner of the two bones of the vertebrate hind or lower limb between the knee and the ankle

tic \'tik\ *n* : a local and habitual twitching of muscles esp. of the face

ti-cal \ti-'käl, 'ti-kəl\ *n, pl* **ticals** *or* **tical** : BAHT

¹**tick** \'tik\ *n* : any of a large group of small bloodsucking arachnids

²**tick** *n* : the fabric case of a mattress or pillow; *also* : a mattress consisting of a tick and its filling

³**tick** *n* **1** : a light rhythmic audible tap or beat **2** : a small mark used to draw attention to or check something

⁴**tick** *vb* **1** : to make the sound of a tick or series of ticks **2** : to mark, count, or announce by or as if by ticking beats **3** : to mark or check with a tick **4** : to function as an operating mechanism : RUN

⁵**tick** *n, chiefly Brit* : CREDIT; *also* : a credit account

tick-er \'ti-kər\ *n,* **1** : something (as a watch) that ticks **2** : a telegraph instrument that prints information (as stock prices) on paper tape **3** *slang* : HEART

ticker tape *n* : the paper ribbon on which a telegraphic ticker prints

¹**tick-et** \'ti-kət\ *n* [MF *etiquet, estiquette* notice attached to something, fr. MF dial. *estiquier* to attach, fr. MD *steken* to stick] **1** : CERTIFICATE, LICENSE, PERMIT; *esp* : a certificate or token showing that a fare or admission fee has been paid **2** : TAG, LABEL **3** : SLATE **4** : a summons issued to a traffic offender

²**ticket** *vb* **1** : to attach a ticket to **2** : to furnish or serve with a ticket

tick-ing \'ti-kiŋ\ *n* : a strong fabric used in upholstering and as a mattress covering

tick-le \'ti-kəl\ *vb* **tick-led; tick-ling** **1** : to excite or stir up agreeably : PLEASE, AMUSE **2** : to have a tingling sensation **3** : to touch (as a body part) lightly so as to cause uneasiness, laughter, or spasmodic movements — **tickle** *n* — **tick-ler** *n*

tick·lish \-kə-lish\ *adj* **1** : OVERSENSI-TIVE, TOUCHY **2** : UNSTABLE ⟨a ~ foothold⟩ **3** : requiring delicate handling ⟨~ subject⟩ **4** : sensitive to tickling — **tick·lish·ly** *adv* — **tick·lish·ness** *n*

tidal wave *n* **1** : an unusually high sea wave that sometimes follows an earthquake **2** : an unusual rise of water alongshore due to strong winds

tid·bit \'tid-ˌbit\ *n* : a choice morsel

¹tide \'tīd\ *n* [ME, time, fr. OE *tīd*] **1** : the alternate rising and falling of the surface of the ocean **2** : something that fluctuates like the tides of the sea — **tid·al** \'tī-dᵊl\ *adj*

²tide *vb* **tid·ed; tid·ing** : to carry through or help along as if by the tide ⟨a loan to ~ us over⟩

tide·land \'tīd-ˌland, -lənd\ *n* **1** : land overflowed during flood tide **2** : land under the ocean within a nation's territorial waters — often used in pl.

tide·wa·ter \-ˌwȯ-tər, -ˌwä-\ *n* **1** : water overflowing land at flood tide **2** : low-lying coastal land

tid·ings \'tī-diŋz\ *n pl* : NEWS, MESSAGE

¹ti·dy \'tī-dē\ *adj* **ti·di·er; -est 1** : well ordered and cared for : NEAT **2** : LARGE, SUBSTANTIAL ⟨a ~ sum⟩ — **ti·di·ness** \'tī-dē-nəs\ *n*

²tidy *vb* **ti·died; ti·dy·ing 1** : to put in order **2** : to make things tidy

³tidy *n, pl* **tidies** : a decorated covering used to protect the back or arms of a chair from wear or soil

¹tie \'tī\ *n* **1** : a line, ribbon, or cord used for fastening, uniting, or closing **2** : a structural element (as a beam or rod) holding two pieces together **3** : one of the cross supports to which railroad rails are fastened **4** : a connecting link : BOND ⟨family ~s⟩ **5** : an equality in number (as of votes or scores); *also* : an undecided or deadlocked contest **6** : NECKTIE

²tie *vb* **tied; ty·ing** *or* **tie·ing 1** : to fasten, attach, or close by means of a tie **2** : to bring together firmly : UNITE **3** : to form a knot or bow in ⟨~ a scarf⟩ **4** : to restrain from freedom of action : CONSTRAIN **5** : to make or have an equal score with

tie·back \'tī-ˌbak\ *n* : a decorative strip for draping a curtain to the side of a window

tie-dye·ing \'tī-ˌdī-iŋ\ *n* : a method of producing patterns in textiles by tying parts of the fabric so that they will not absorb the dye — **tie-dyed** \-ˌdīd\ *adj*

tie-in \'tī-ˌin\ *n* : CONNECTION

tier \'tir\ *n* : ROW, LAYER; *esp* : one of two or more rows arranged one above another — **tiered** \'tird\ *adj*

tie-rod \'tī-ˌräd\ *n* : a rod used as a connecting member or brace

tie-up \-ˌəp\ *n* **1** : a slowing or stopping of traffic or business **2** : CONNECTION

tiff \'tif\ *n* : a petty quarrel — **tiff** *vb*

Tif·fa·ny \'ti-fə-nē\ *adj* : made of pieces of stained glass ⟨a ~ lamp⟩

ti·ger \'tī-gər\ *n* : a very large tawny black-striped Asian cat — **ti·ger·ish** *adj*

¹tight \'tīt\ *adj* **1** : so close in structure as to prevent passage of a liquid or gas **2** : strongly fixed or held : SECURE **3** : TAUT **4** : fitting usu. too closely ⟨~ shoes⟩ **5** : set close together : COMPACT ⟨a ~ formation⟩ **6** : DIFFICULT, TRYING ⟨get in a ~ spot⟩ **7** : STINGY, MISERLY **8** : evenly contested : CLOSE **9** : INTOXICATED **10** : low in supply : hard to get ⟨money is ~⟩ — **tight·ly** *adv* — **tight·ness** *n*

²tight *adv* **1** : TIGHTLY, FIRMLY **2** : SOUNDLY ⟨sleep ~⟩

tight·en \'tī-tᵊn\ *vb* : to make or become tight

tight-fist·ed \'tīt-'fis-təd\ *adj* : STINGY

tight·rope \-ˌrōp\ *n* : a taut rope or wire for acrobats to perform on

tights \'tīts\ *n pl*, : skintight garments covering the body esp. below the waist; *also*, *Brit* : PANTY HOSE

tight·wad \'tīt-ˌwäd\ *n* : a stingy person

ti·gress \'tī-grəs\ *n* : a female tiger

ti·la·pia \tə-'lä-pē-ə, -'lā-\ *n, pl* **tilapia** *also* **ti·la·pi·as** : any of numerous chiefly African freshwater fishes widely raised for food

til·de \'til-də\ *n* [Sp, fr. ML *titulus* tittle] : a mark ~ placed esp. over the letter *n* (as in Spanish *señor* sir) to denote the sound \nʸ\ or over vowels (as in Portuguese *irmã* sister) to indicate nasal quality

¹tile \'tī(-ə)l\ *n* **1** : a flat or curved piece of fired clay, stone, or concrete used for roofs, floors, or walls; *also* : a pipe of earthenware or concrete used for a drain **2** : a thin piece (as of linoleum) used for covering walls or floors — **til·ing** \'tī-liŋ\ *n*

²tile *vb* **tiled; til·ing** : to cover with tiles — **til·er** *n*

¹till \'til\ *prep or conj* : UNTIL

²till *vb* : to work by plowing, sowing, and raising crops : CULTIVATE — **till·able** *adj*

³till *n* : DRAWER; *esp* : a money drawer in a store or bank

till·age \'ti-lij\ *n* **1** : the work of tilling land **2** : cultivated land

¹til·ler \'ti-lər\ *n* [OE *telgor, telgra* twig, shoot] : a sprout or stalk esp. from the base or lower part of a plant

²till·er \'ti-lər\ *n* : one that tills

³til·ler \'ti-lər\ *n* [ME *tiler* stock of a crossbow, tiller, fr. AF *teiler* stock of a crossbow] : a lever used for turning a boat's rudder from side to side

¹tilt \'tilt\ *n* **1** : a contest in which two combatants charging usu. with lances try to unhorse each other : JOUST; *also* : a tournament of tilts **2** : a verbal contest : DISPUTE **3** : a sloping surface : SLANT

²tilt *vb* **1** : to move or shift so as to incline : TIP **2** : to engage in or as if in combat with lances : JOUST, ATTACK

tilth \'tilth\ *n* **1** : TILLAGE 2 **2** : the state of a soil esp. in relation to the suitability of its particle size and structure for growing crops

Tim *abbr* Timothy

tim·ber \'tim-bər\ *n* [ME, fr. OE, building, wood] **1** : growing trees or their wood — often used interjectionally to warn of a falling tree **2** : wood for use in making something **3** : a usu. large squared or dressed piece of wood

tim·bered \'tim-bərd\ adj : having walls framed by exposed timbers

tim·ber·land \'tim-bər-,land\ n : wooded land

tim·ber·line \'tim-bər-,līn\ n : the upper limit of tree growth in mountains or high latitudes

timber rattlesnake n : a widely distributed rattlesnake of the eastern U.S.

timber wolf n : GRAY WOLF

tim·bre also **tim·ber** \'tam-bər, 'tim-\ n [F, fr. MF, bell struck by a hammer, fr. OF, drum, fr. MGk tymbanon kettle-drum, fr. Gk tympanon] : the distinctive quality given to a sound by its overtones

tim·brel \'tim-brəl\ n : a small hand drum or tambourine

¹**time** \'tīm\ n **1** : a period during which an action, process, or condition exists or continues ⟨gone a long ∼⟩ **2** : LEISURE ⟨found ∼ to read⟩ **3** : a point or period when something occurs : OCCASION ⟨the last ∼ we met⟩ **4** : a set or customary moment or hour for something to occur ⟨arrived on ∼⟩ **5** : AGE, ERA **6** : state of affairs : CONDITIONS ⟨hard ∼s⟩ **7** : a rate of speed : TEMPO **8** : a moment, hour, day, or year as indicated by a clock or calendar ⟨what ∼ is it⟩ **9** : a system of reckoning time ⟨solar ∼⟩ **10** : one of a series of recurring instances; also, pl : added or accumulated quantities or examples ⟨five ∼s greater⟩ **11** : a person's experience during a particular period ⟨had a good ∼⟩ **12** : the hours or days of one's work; also : an hourly pay rate ⟨straight ∼⟩ **13** : TIME-OUT 1

²**time** vb **timed; tim·ing** **1** : to arrange or set the time of : SCHEDULE ⟨∼s his calls conveniently⟩ **2** : to set the tempo or duration of ⟨∼ a performance⟩ **3** : to cause to keep time with **4** : to determine or record the time, duration, or rate of ⟨∼ a sprinter⟩ — **tim·er** n

time bomb n **1** : a bomb so made as to explode at a predetermined time **2** : something with a potentially dangerous delayed reaction

time clock n : a clock that records the time workers arrive and depart

time frame n : a period of time esp. with respect to some action or project

time–hon·ored \'tīm-,ä-nərd\ adj : honored because of age or long usage

time·keep·er \-,kē-pər\ n **1** : a clerk who keeps records of the time worked by employees **2** : one appointed to mark and announce the time in an athletic game or contest

time·less \-ləs\ adj **1** : ETERNAL **2** : not limited or affected by time ⟨∼ works of art⟩ — **time·less·ly** adv — **time·less·ness** n

time·ly \-lē\ adj **time·li·er; -est 1** : coming early or at the right time ⟨a ∼ decision⟩ ⟨∼ payment⟩ **2** : appropriate to the time ⟨a ∼ book⟩ — **time·li·ness** n

time–out \'tīm-'aút\ n **1** : a brief suspen-sion of activity esp. in an athletic game **2** : a quiet period used esp. as a disciplinary measure for a child

time·piece \-,pēs\ n : a device (as a clock) to show the passage of time

times \'tīmz\ prep : multiplied by ⟨2 ∼ 2 is 4⟩

time–shar·ing \'tīm-,sher-iŋ\ n **1** : simultaneous use of a computer by many users **2** or **time–share** \-,sher\ : joint ownership or rental of a vacation lodging by several persons with each taking turns using the place

times sign n : the symbol × used to indicate multiplication

time·ta·ble \'tīm-,tā-bəl\ n **1** : a table of the departure and arrival times (as of trains) **2** : a schedule showing a planned order or sequence

time warp n : an anomaly, discontinuity, or suspension held to occur in the progress of time

time·worn \-,wórn\ adj **1** : worn by time **2** : HACKNEYED, STALE ⟨a ∼ joke⟩

tim·id \'ti-məd\ adj : lacking in courage or self-confidence : FEARFUL — **ti·mid·i·ty** \tə-'mi-də-tē\ n — **tim·id·ly** adv

tim·o·rous \'ti-mə-rəs\ adj : of a timid disposition : AFRAID — **tim·o·rous·ly** adv — **tim·o·rous·ness** n

tim·o·thy \'ti-mə-thē\ n : a perennial grass with long cylindrical spikes widely grown for hay in the U.S.

Tim·o·thy \'ti-mə-thē\ n — see BIBLE table

tim·pa·ni \'tim-pə-nē\ n sing or pl [It] : a set of kettledrums played by one performer in an orchestra — **tim·pa·nist** \-nist\ n

¹**tin** \'tin\ n **1** : a soft white crystalline metallic chemical element malleable at ordinary temperatures that is used esp. in solders and alloys **2** : a container (as a can) made of metal (as tinplate)

²**tin** vb **tinned; tin·ning 1** : to cover or plate with tin **2** : to pack in tins

TIN abbr taxpayer identification number

tinct \'tiŋkt\ n : TINCTURE, TINGE

¹**tinc·ture** \'tiŋk-chər\ n, **1** archaic : a substance that colors **2** : a slight admixture : TRACE **3** : an alcoholic solution of a medicinal substance ♦ **Synonyms** TOUCH, SUGGESTION, SUSPICION, TINGE

²**tincture** vb **tinc·tured; tinc·tur·ing 1** : COLOR, TINGE **2** : AFFECT

tin·der \'tin-dər\ n **1** : a very flammable substance used as kindling **2** : something serving to incite or inflame

tin·der·box \'tin-dər-,bäks\ n **1** : a metal box for holding tinder and usu. flint and steel for striking a spark **2** : a highly flammable object or place

tine \'tīn\ n : a slender pointed part (as of a fork or an antler) : PRONG

tin·foil \'tin-,fói(-ə)l\ n : a thin metal sheeting usu. of aluminum or tin-lead alloy

¹**tinge** \'tinj\ vb **tinged; tinge·ing** or **ting·ing 1** : to color slightly : TINT **2** : to affect or modify esp. with a slight odor or taste

²**tinge** n : a slight coloring, flavor, or quality : TRACE ◆ **Synonyms** TOUCH, SUGGESTION, SUSPICION, TINCTURE, SOUPÇON

tin·gle \'tiŋ-gəl\ vb **tin·gled; tin·gling** : to feel a prickling or thrilling sensation 2 : TINKLE — **tingle** n

¹**tin·ker** \'tiŋ-kər\ n 1 : a usu. itinerant mender of household utensils 2 : an unskillful mender : BUNGLER

²**tinker** vb : to repair or adjust something in an unskillful or experimental manner — **tin·ker·er** n

¹**tin·kle** \'tiŋ-kəl\ vb **tin·kled; tin·kling** : to make or cause to make a tinkle

²**tinkle** n : a series of short high ringing or clinking sounds

tin·ni·tus \'ti-nə-təs, tə-'nī-təs\ n : a sensation of noise (as ringing or roaring) in the ears

tin·ny \'ti-nē\ adj **tin·ni·er; -est** 1 : abounding in or yielding tin 2 : resembling tin; also : LIGHT, CHEAP 3 : thin in tone ⟨a ~ voice⟩ — **tin·ni·ly** \-nə-lē\ adv — **tin·ni·ness** \-nē-nəs\ n

tin·plate \'tin-'plāt\ n : thin sheet iron or steel coated with tin — **tin–plate** vb

tin·sel \'tin-səl\ n [ME tyneseyle cloth interwoven with metallic thread, prob. fr. AF tencelé, pp. of tenceler, estenceler to sparkle] 1 : threads, strips, or sheets of metal, paper, or plastic used to produce a glittering appearance 2 : something superficially attractive but of little worth

tin·smith \'tin-ˌsmith\ n : one that works with sheet metal (as tinplate)

¹**tint** \'tint\ n 1 : a slight or pale coloration : HUE 2 : any of various shades of a color

²**tint** vb : to impart a tint to : COLOR

tin·tin·nab·u·la·tion \ˌtin-tə-ˌna-byə-'lā-shən\ n 1 : the ringing of bells 2 : a tingling sound as if of bells

tin·ware \'tin-ˌwer\ n : articles and esp. utensils made of tinplate

ti·ny \'tī-nē\ adj **ti·ni·er; -est** : very small : MINUTE ◆ **Synonyms** MINIATURE, DIMINUTIVE, WEE, LILLIPUTIAN

¹**tip** \'tip\ vb **tipped; tip·ping** 1 : OVERTURN, UPSET 2 : LEAN, SLANT; also : to raise and tilt forward ⟨tipped his hat⟩

²**tip** n : the act or an instance of tipping

³**tip** vb **tipped; tip·ping** 1 : to furnish with a tip 2 : to cover or adorn the tip of

⁴**tip** n 1 : the usu. pointed end of something 2 : a small piece or part serving as an end, cap, or point

⁵**tip** n : a light touch or blow

⁶**tip** vb **tipped; tip·ping** : to strike lightly : TAP

⁷**tip** n : a piece of advice or expert or confidential information : HINT

⁸**tip** vb **tipped; tip·ping** : to impart a piece of information about or to

⁹**tip** vb **tipped; tip·ping** : to give a gratuity to — **tip·per** n

¹⁰**tip** n : a gift or small sum given for a service performed or anticipated

tip–off \'tip-ˌȯf\ n : WARNING, TIP

tip·pet \'ti-pət\ n : a long scarf or shoulder cape

tip·ple \'ti-pəl\ vb **tip·pled; tip·pling** : to drink intoxicating liquor esp. habitually or excessively — **tipple** n — **tip·pler** n

tip·ster \'tip-stər\ n : a person who gives or sells tips esp. for gambling

tip·sy \'tip-sē\ adj **tip·si·er; -est** : unsteady or foolish from the effects of alcohol — **tip·si·ly** \-sə-lē\ adv — **tip·si·ness** \-sē-nəs\ n

¹**tip·toe** \'tip-ˌtō\ n : the position of being balanced on the balls of the feet and toes with the heels raised; also : the ends of the toes

²**tiptoe** adv or adj : on or as if on tiptoe

³**tiptoe** vb **tip·toed; tip·toe·ing** : to walk or proceed on or as if on tiptoe ⟨~ around the issue⟩

¹**tip–top** \'tip-ˌtäp\ n : the highest point

²**tip–top** adj : EXCELLENT, FIRST-RATE

ti·rade \'tī-ˌrād\ n [F, shot, tirade, fr. MF, fr. It tirata, fr. tirare to draw, shoot] : a prolonged speech of abuse or condemnation

tir·a·mi·su \ˌtir-ə-'mē-sü, -mē-'sü\ n [It tiramisù] : a dessert made with ladyfingers, mascarpone, and espresso

¹**tire** \'tī(-ə)r\ vb **tired; tir·ing** 1 : to make or become weary : FATIGUE 2 : to wear out the patience of : BORE

²**tire** n 1 : a metal hoop that forms the tread of a wheel 2 : a rubber cushion usu. containing compressed air that encircles a wheel (as of a bike)

tired adj 1 : WEARY, FATIGUED 2 : HACKNEYED — **tired·ness** n

tire·less \'tī(-ə)r-ləs\ adj : not tiring : UNTIRING, INDEFATIGABLE — **tire·less·ly** adv — **tire·less·ness** n

tire·some \-səm\ adj : tending to bore : WEARISOME, TEDIOUS — **tire·some·ly** adv — **tire·some·ness** n

ti·ro chiefly Brit var of TYRO

tis·sue \'ti-shü\ n [ME tyssshewe, tyssew, a rich fabric, fr. AF, fr. tistre to weave, fr. L texere] 1 : a fine lightweight often sheer fabric 2 : NETWORK, WEB ⟨a ~ of lies⟩ 3 : a soft absorbent paper 4 : a mass or layer of cells forming a basic structural material of an animal or plant

¹**tit** \'tit\ n : TEAT

²**tit** n : any of various small plump Old World songbirds related to the titmice

Tit abbr Titus

ti·tan \'tī-t³n\ n 1 cap : one of a family of giants overthrown by the gods in Greek mythology 2 : one gigantic in size or power

ti·tan·ic \tī-'ta-nik\ adj : enormous in size, force, or power ◆ **Synonyms** IMMENSE, GIGANTIC, GIANT, COLOSSAL, MAMMOTH

ti·ta·ni·um \tī-'tā-nē-əm\ n : a gray light strong metallic chemical element used esp. in alloys

titbit var of TIDBIT

tithe \'tīth\ n [ME, fr. OE teogotha tenth] : a 10th part paid or given esp. for the support of a church — **tithe** vb — **tith·er** n

tit·il·late \'ti-t³l-ˌāt\ vb **-lat·ed; -lat·ing** 1 : to excite pleasurably 2 : TICKLE 3 — **tit·il·la·tion** \ˌti-t³l-'ā-shən\ n

tit·i·vate *or* **tit·ti·vate** \'ti-tə-ˌvāt\ *vb* **-vat·ed; -vat·ing** : to dress up : spruce up — **tit·i·va·tion** \ˌti-tə-'vā-shən\ *n*

ti·tle \'tī-t³l\ *n* **1** : CLAIM, RIGHT; *esp* : a legal right to the ownership of property **2** : the distinguishing name of a written, filmed, or musical production or a work of art **3** : an appellation of honor, rank, or office **4** : CHAMPIONSHIP ♦ *Synonyms* DESIGNATION, DENOMINATION, APPELLATION

ti·tled \'tī-t³ld\ *adj* : having a title esp. of nobility

title page *n* : a page of a book bearing the title and usu. the names of the author and publisher

tit·mouse \'tit-ˌmaůs\ *n, pl* **tit·mice** \-ˌmīs\ : any of several small long-tailed No. American songbirds related to the chickadees

ti·tra·tion \tī-'trā-shən\ *n* : a process of finding the concentration of a solution (as of an acid) by adding small portions of a second solution of known concentration (as of a base) to a fixed amount of the first until an expected change (as in color) occurs

tit·ter \'ti-tər\ *vb* : to laugh in an affected or in a nervous or half-suppressed manner : GIGGLE — **titter** *n*

tit·tle \'ti-t³l\ *n* : a tiny part

tit·tle–tat·tle \'ti-t³l-ˌta-t³l\ *n* : idle talk : GOSSIP — **tittle–tattle** *vb*

tit·u·lar \'ti-chə-lər\ *adj* **1** : existing in title only : NOMINAL ⟨~ ruler⟩ **2** : of, relating to, or bearing a title ⟨~ role⟩

Ti·tus \'tī-təs\ *n* — see BIBLE table

tiz·zy \'ti-zē\ *n, pl* **tizzies** : a highly excited and distracted state of mind

tk *abbr* **1** tank **2** truck

TKO \ˌtē-ˌkā-'ō\ *n* [*technical knockout*] : the termination of a boxing match when a boxer is declared unable to continue the fight

tkt *abbr* ticket

Tl *symbol* thallium

TLC *abbr* tender loving care

T lymphocyte *n* : T CELL

Tm *symbol* thulium

TM *abbr* trademark

T–man \'tē-ˌman\ *n* : a special agent of the U.S. Treasury Department

tn *abbr* **1** ton **2** town

TN *abbr* Tennessee

tng *abbr* training

tnpk *abbr* turnpike

TNT \ˌtē-(ˌ)en-'tē\ *n* : a flammable toxic compound used as a high explosive and in chemical synthesis

¹to \tə, 'tü\ *prep* **1** : in the direction of and reaching ⟨drove ~ town⟩ **2** : in the direction of : TOWARD **3** : ON, AGAINST ⟨apply salve ~ a burn⟩ **4** : as far as ⟨can pay up ~ a dollar⟩ **5** : so as to become or bring about ⟨beaten ~ death⟩ ⟨broken ~ pieces⟩ **6** : BEFORE ⟨it's five minutes ~ six⟩ **7** : UNTIL ⟨from May ~ December⟩ **8** : fitting or being a part of : FOR ⟨key ~ the lock⟩ **9** : with the accompaniment of ⟨sing ~ the music⟩ **10** : in relation or comparison with ⟨similar

~ that one⟩ ⟨won 10 ~ 6⟩ **11** : in accordance with ⟨add salt ~ taste⟩ **12** : within the range of ⟨~ my knowledge⟩ **13** : contained, occurring, or included in ⟨two pints ~ a quart⟩ **14** : as regards ⟨agreeable ~ everyone⟩ **15** : affecting as the receiver or beneficiary ⟨whispered ~ her⟩ ⟨gave it ~ me⟩ **16** : for no one except ⟨a room ~ myself⟩ **17** : into the action of ⟨we got ~ talking⟩ **18** — used for marking the following verb as an infinitive ⟨wants ~ go⟩ and often used by itself at the end of a clause in place of an infinitive suggested by the preceding context ⟨goes to town whenever he wants ~⟩ ⟨can leave if you'd like ~⟩

²to \'tü\ *adv* **1** : in a direction toward ⟨run ~ and fro⟩ **2** : into contact esp. with the frame of a door ⟨the door slammed ~⟩ **3** : to the matter in hand ⟨fell ~ and ate heartily⟩ **4** : to a state of consciousness or awareness ⟨came ~ hours after the accident⟩

TO *abbr* turn over

toad \'tōd\ *n* : any of numerous tailless leaping amphibians differing typically from the related frogs in having a shorter stockier build, rough dry warty skin, and less aquatic habits

toad·stool \-ˌstül\ *n* : MUSHROOM; *esp* : one that is poisonous or inedible

toady \'tō-dē\ *n, pl* **toad·ies** : a person who flatters in the hope of gaining favors : SYCOPHANT — **toady** *vb*

to–and–fro \ˌtü-ən-'frō\ *adj* : forward and backward — **to–and–fro** *n*

¹toast \'tōst\ *vb* **1** : to warm thoroughly **2** : to make (as bread) crisp, hot, and brown by heat **3** : to become toasted

²toast *n* **1** : sliced toasted bread **2** : someone or something in whose honor persons drink **3** : an act of drinking in honor of a toast

³toast *vb* : to propose or drink to as a toast

toast·er \'tō-stər\ *n* : an electrical appliance for toasting

toaster oven *n* : a portable electrical appliance that bakes, broils, and toasts

toast·mas·ter \'tōst-ˌmas-tər\ *n* : a person who presides at a banquet and introduces the after-dinner speakers

toast·mis·tress \-ˌmis-trəs\ *n* : a woman who acts as toastmaster

toasty \'tō-stē\ *adj* **toast·i·er; -est** : pleasantly warm

Tob *abbr* Tobit

to·bac·co \tə-'ba-kō\ *n, pl* **-cos** [Sp *tabaco*] **1** : a tall broad-leaved herb related to the potato; *also* : its leaves prepared for smoking or chewing or as snuff **2** : manufactured tobacco products; *also* : smoking as a practice

to·bac·co·nist \tə-'ba-kə-nist\ *n* : a dealer in tobacco

To·bi·as \tō-'bī-əs\ *n* : TOBIT

To·bit \'tō-bət\ *n* — see BIBLE table

¹to·bog·gan \tə-'bä-gən\ *n* : a long flat-bottomed light sled made of thin boards curved up at one end

²toboggan *vb* **1** : to coast on or as if on a

toboggan 2 : to decline suddenly (as in value) — **to·bog·gan·er** *n*

toc·sin \'täk-sən\ *n* **1** : an alarm bell **2** : a warning signal

¹to·day \tə-'dā\ *adv* **1** : on or for this day **2** : at the present time

²today *n* : the present day, time, or age

tod·dle \'tä-d³l\ *vb* **tod·dled; tod·dling** : to walk with short tottering steps in the manner of a young child — **toddle** *n* — **tod·dler** *n*

tod·dy \'tä-dē\ *n*, *pl* **toddies** [Hindi & Urdu *tāṛī* juice of a palm, fr. *tāṛ* a palm, fr. Skt *tāla*] : a drink made of liquor, sugar, spices, and hot water

to-do \tə-'dü\ *n*, *pl* **to-dos** \-'düz\ : BUSTLE, STIR, FUSS

¹toe \'tō\ *n* **1** : one of the jointed parts of the front end of the vertebrate foot **2** : the front part of a foot or hoof

²toe *vb* **toed; toe·ing** : to touch, reach, or drive with the toes

toea \'tói-ə\ *n* — see *kina* at MONEY table

toe·hold \'tō-,hōld\ *n* **1** : a place of support for the toes **2** : a slight footing

toe·nail \'tō-,nāl\ *n* : a nail of a toe

tof·fee *or* **tof·fy** \'tó-fē, 'tä-\ *n*, *pl* **toffees** *or* **toffies** : candy of brittle but tender texture made by boiling sugar and butter together

to·fu \'tō-(,)fü\ *n* [Jp *tōfu*] : a soft white food product made from soybeans

tog \'täg, 'tóg\ *vb* **togged; tog·ging** : to put togs on : DRESS

to·ga \'tō-gə\ *n* : the loose outer garment worn in public by citizens of ancient Rome — **to·gaed** \-gəd\ *adj*

¹to·geth·er \tə-'ge-thər\ *adv* **1** : in or into one place or group **2** : in or into contact or association ⟨mix ∼⟩ **3** : at one time : SIMULTANEOUSLY ⟨talk and work ∼⟩ **4** : in succession ⟨for days ∼⟩ **5** : in or into harmony or coherence ⟨get ∼ on a plan⟩ **6** : as a group : JOINTLY — **to·geth·er·ness** *n*

²together *adj* : composed in mind or manner

together with *prep* : in addition to : in association with

tog·gery \'tä-gə-rē, 'tó-\ *n* : CLOTHING

tog·gle \'tä-gəl\ *vb* : to switch between two options esp. of an electronic device

toggle switch *n* : an electric switch operated by pushing a projecting lever through a small arc

togs \'tägz, 'tógz\ *n pl* : CLOTHING; *esp* : clothes for a specified use ⟨riding ∼⟩

¹toil \'tói(-ə)l\ *n* **1** : laborious effort **2** : long fatiguing labor : DRUDGERY — **toil·ful** \-fəl\ *adj* — **toil·some** *adj*

²toil *vb* [ME, to argue, struggle, fr. AF *toiller* to make dirty, fight, wrangle, fr. L *tudiculare* to crush, grind, fr. *tudicula* machine for crushing olives, dim. of *tudes* hammer] **1** : to work hard and long **2** : to proceed with great effort : PLOD — **toil·er** *n*

³toil *n* [ME *toile* cloth, net, fr. OF *teile*, fr. L *tela* cloth on a loom] : NET, TRAP — usu. used in pl. ⟨caught in the ∼s of the law⟩

toi·let \'tói-lət\ *n* **1** : the act or process of dressing and grooming oneself **2** : BATH-

ROOM 3 : a fixture for use in urinating and defecating; *esp* : one consisting essentially of a water-flushed bowl and seat — **toilet** *vb*

toi·let·ry \'tói-lə-trē\ *n*, *pl* **-ries** : an article or preparation used in cleaning or grooming oneself — usu. used in pl.

toi·lette \twä-'let\ *n* **1** : TOILET 1 **2** : formal attire; *also* : a particular costume

toilet training *n* : the process of training a child to control bladder and bowel movements and to use the toilet — **toilet train** *vb*

toil·worn \'tói(-ə)l-,wórn\ *adj* : showing the effects of toil

To·kay \tō-'kā\ *n* : naturally sweet wine from Hungary

toke \'tōk\ *n*, *slang* : a puff on a marijuana cigarette or pipe

¹to·ken \'tō-kən\ *n* **1** : an outward sign **2** : SYMBOL, EMBLEM **3** : SOUVENIR, KEEPSAKE **4** : a small part representing the whole **5** : a piece resembling a coin issued as money or for use by a particular group on specified terms

²token *adj* **1** : done or given as a token esp. in partial fulfillment of an obligation **2** : representing only a symbolic effort : MINIMAL, PERFUNCTORY

to·ken·ism \'tō-kə-,ni-zəm\ *n* : the policy or practice of making only a symbolic effort (as to desegregate)

to·lar \'tō-lär\ *n*, *pl* **to·lar·jev** \'tō-lär-,yev\ *or* **tolars** — see MONEY table

told *past and past part of* TELL

tole \'tōl\ *n* : sheet metal and esp. tinplate for use in domestic and ornamental wares

tol·er·a·ble \'tä-lə-rə-bəl\ *adj* **1** : capable of being borne or endured **2** : moderately good : PASSABLE — **tol·er·a·bly** \-blē\ *adv*

tol·er·ance \'tä-lə-rəns\ *n* **1** : the act or practice of tolerating; *esp* : sympathy or indulgence for beliefs or practices differing from one's own **2** : the allowable deviation from a standard (as of size) **3** : the body's capacity to become less responsive over time to something (as a drug used repeatedly) — **tol·er·ant** *adj* — **tol·er·ant·ly** *adv*

tol·er·ate \'tä-lə-,rāt\ *vb* **-at·ed; -at·ing 1** : to exhibit physiological tolerance for (as a drug) **2** : to allow to be or to be done without hindrance ♦ *Synonyms* ABIDE, BEAR, SUFFER, STAND, BROOK — **tol·er·a·tion** \,tä-lə-'rā-shən\ *n*

¹toll \'tōl\ *n* **1** : a tax paid for a privilege (as for passing over a bridge) **2** : a charge for a service (as for a long-distance telephone call) **3** : the cost in life, health, loss, or suffering

²toll *vb* **1** : to cause the slow regular sounding of (a bell) esp. by pulling a rope **2** : to give signal of : SOUND **3** : to sound with slow measured strokes **4** : to announce by tolling

³toll *n* : the sound of a tolling bell

toll·booth \'tōl-,büth\ *n* : a booth where tolls are paid

toll·gate \-,gāt\ *n* : a point where vehicles stop to pay a toll

toll·house \-,haús\ *n* : a house or booth where tolls are paid

tol·u·ene \'täl-yə-ˌwēn\ *n* : a liquid hydrocarbon used esp. as a solvent

tom \'täm\ *n* : the male of various animals (as a cat or turkey)

¹**tom·a·hawk** \'tä-mə-ˌhȯk\ *n* : a light ax used as a missile and as a hand weapon esp. by No. American Indians

²**tomahawk** *vb* : to strike or kill with a tomahawk

to·ma·til·lo \ˌtō-mə-'tē-(ˌ)yō\ *n*, *pl* **-los** : a small round usu. pale green edible fruit of a Mexican herb related to the tomato; *also* : this herb

to·ma·to \tə-'mā-tō, -'mä-\ *n*, *pl* **-toes** [alter. of earlier *tomate*, fr. Sp, fr. Nahuatl *tomatl*] : a usu. large, rounded, and red or yellow pulpy edible berry of a widely grown tropical herb related to the potato; *also* : this herb

tomb \'tüm\ *n* **1** : a place of burial : GRAVE **2** : a house, chamber, or vault for the dead — **tomb** *vb*

tom·boy \'täm-ˌbȯi\ *n* : a girl who behaves in a manner usu. considered boyish — **tom·boy·ish** *adj*

tomb·stone \'tüm-ˌstōn\ *n* : a stone marking a grave

tom·cat \'täm-ˌkat\ *n* : a male domestic cat

Tom Col·lins \'täm-'kä-lənz\ *n* : a tall iced drink with a base of gin

tome \'tōm\ *n* : BOOK; *esp* : a large or weighty one

tom·fool·ery \täm-'fü-lə-rē\ *n* : playful or foolish behavior

tom·my gun \'tä-mē-ˌgən\ *n* : SUBMACHINE GUN — **tommy-gun** *vb*

to·mog·ra·phy \tō-'mä-grə-fē\ *n* : a method of producing a three-dimensional image of the internal structures of a solid object (as the human body or the earth) — **to·mo·graph·ic** \ˌtō-mə-'gra-fik\ *adj*

to·mor·row \tə-'mär-ō\ *adv* : on or for the day after today — **tomorrow** *n*

tom–tom \'täm-ˌtäm\ *n* : a small-headed drum beaten with the hands

ton \'tən\ *n*, *pl* **tons** *also* **ton 1** — see WEIGHT table **2** : a unit equal to the volume of a long ton weight of seawater used in reckoning the displacement of ships and equal to 35 cubic feet

to·nal·i·ty \tō-'na-lə-tē\ *n*, *pl* **-ties** : tonal quality

¹**tone** \'tōn\ *n* [ME, fr. L *tonus* tension, tone, fr. Gk *tonos*, lit., act of stretching; fr. the dependence of the pitch of a musical string on its tension] **1** : vocal or musical sound; *esp* : sound quality **2** : a sound of definite pitch **3** : WHOLE STEP **4** : accent or inflection expressive of an emotion **5** : the pitch of a word often used to express differences of meaning **6** : style or manner of expression **7** : color quality; *also* : SHADE, TINT **8** : the effect in painting of light and shade together with color **9** : healthy and vigorous condition of a living body or bodily part; *also* : the state of partial contraction characteristic of normal muscle **10** : general character, quality, or trend ♦ *Synonyms* ATMOSPHERE, FEELING, MOOD, VEIN — **ton·al** \'tō-nᵊl\ *adj*

²**tone** *vb* **toned; ton·ing 1** : to give a particular intonation or inflection to **2** : to impart tone to **3** : SOFTEN, MELLOW **4** : to harmonize in color : BLEND

tone·arm *n* : the movable part of a record player that carries the pickup and the needle

toney *var of* TONY

tong \'täŋ, 'tȯŋ\ *n* : a Chinese secret society in the U.S.

tongs \'täŋz, 'tȯŋz\ *n pl* : a grasping device consisting of two pieces joined at one end by a pivot or hinged like scissors — **tong** *vb*

¹**tongue** \'təŋ\ *n* **1** : a fleshy movable process of the floor of the mouth used in tasting and in taking and swallowing food and in humans as a speech organ **2** : the flesh of a tongue (as of the ox) used as food **3** : the power of communication **4** : LANGUAGE **1 5** : manner or quality of utterance; *also* : intended meaning **6** : ecstatic usu. unintelligible utterance accompanying religious excitation — usu. used in pl. **7** : something resembling an animal's tongue esp. in being elongated and fastened at one end only — **tongued** \'təŋd\ *adj* — **tongue·less** *adj*

²**tongue** *vb* **tongued; tongu·ing 1** : to touch or lick with the tongue **2** : to articulate notes on a wind instrument

tongue–in–cheek *adj* : characterized by insincerity, irony, or whimsical exaggeration — **tongue in cheek** *adv*

tongue–lash \'təŋ-ˌlash\ *vb* : CHIDE, REPROVE — **tongue–lash·ing** \-iŋ\ *n*

tongue–tied \-ˌtīd\ *adj* : unable or disinclined to speak clearly or freely (as from shyness or a tongue impairment)

tongue twister *n* : an utterance that is difficult to articulate because of a succession of similar consonants

¹**ton·ic** \'tä-nik\ *adj* **1** : of, relating to, or producing a healthy physical or mental condition : INVIGORATING **2** : relating to or based on the 1st tone of a scale — **ton·ic·i·ty** \tō-'ni-sə-tē\ *n*

²**tonic** *n* **1** : the 1st degree of a musical scale **2** : something that invigorates, restores, or refreshes

tonic water *n* : a carbonated beverage flavored with a bit of quinine, lemon, and lime

¹**to·night** \tə-'nīt\ *adv* : on this present night or the coming night

²**tonight** *n* : the present or the coming night

ton·nage \'tə-nij\ *n* **1** : a duty on ships based on tons carried **2** : ships in terms of the number of tons registered or carried **3** : total weight in tons shipped, carried, or mined

ton·sil \'tän-səl\ *n* : either of a pair of oval masses of lymphoid tissue that lie one on each side of the throat at the back of the mouth

ton·sil·lec·to·my \ˌtän-sə-'lek-tə-mē\ *n*, *pl* **-mies** : the surgical removal of the tonsils

ton·sil·li·tis \-'lī-təs\ *n* : inflammation of the tonsils

ton·so·ri·al \tän-'sȯr-ē-əl\ *adj* : of or relating to a barber or a barber's work

ton·sure \'tän-chər\ *n* [ME, fr. AF, ML *tonsura*, fr. L, act of shearing, fr. *tonsus*, pp. of *tondēre* to shear] **1** : the rite of admission to the clerical state by the clipping or shaving of the head **2** : the shaven crown or patch worn by clerics (as monks) — **tonsure** *vb*

tony *also* **ton·ey** \'tō-nē\ *adj* **ton·i·er;** **-est** : marked by an aristocratic manner or style

too \'tü\ *adv* **1** : in addition : ALSO **2** : EXCESSIVELY **3** : to such a degree as to be regrettable **4** : VERY ⟨didn't seem ~ interested⟩

took *past of* TAKE

¹tool \'tül\ *n* **1** : a hand instrument that aids in accomplishing a task **2** : the cutting or shaping part in a machine; *also* : a machine for shaping metal in any way **3** : something used in doing a job ⟨a scholar's books are his ~s⟩; *also* : a means to an end **4** : a person used by another : DUPE **5** *pl* : natural ability

²tool *vb* **1** : to shape, form, or finish with a tool; *esp* : to letter or decorate (as a book cover) by means of hand tools **2** : to equip a plant or industry with machines and tools for production **3** : DRIVE, RIDE ⟨~*ing* along at 60 miles per hour⟩

tool bar *n* : a strip of icons on a computer display providing quick access to the pictured functions

¹toot \'tüt\ *vb* **1** : to sound or cause to sound in short blasts **2** : to blow an instrument (as a horn) — **toot·er** *n*

²toot *n* : a short blast (as on a horn)

tooth \'tüth\ *n, pl* **teeth** \'tēth\ **1** : one of the hard bony structures borne esp. on the jaws of vertebrates and used for seizing and chewing food and as weapons; *also* : a hard sharp structure esp. around the mouth of an invertebrate **2** : something resembling an animal's tooth **3** : any of the projections on the edge of a wheel that fits into corresponding projections on another wheel **4** *pl* : effective means of enforcement — **toothed** \'tütht\ *adj* — **tooth·less** *adj*

tooth·ache \'tüth-ˌāk\ *n* : pain in or about a tooth

tooth·brush \-ˌbrəsh\ *n* : a brush for cleaning the teeth

tooth·paste \-ˌpāst\ *n* : a paste for cleaning the teeth

tooth·pick \-ˌpik\ *n* : a pointed instrument for removing food particles caught between the teeth

tooth powder *n* : a powder for cleaning the teeth

tooth·some \'tüth-səm\ *adj* **1** : AGREEABLE, ATTRACTIVE **2** : pleasing to the taste : DELICIOUS ♦ *Synonyms* PALATABLE, APPETIZING, SAVORY, TASTY

toothy \'tü-thē\ *adj* **tooth·i·er; -est** : having or showing prominent teeth

¹top \'täp\ *n* **1** : the highest part, point, or level of something **2** : the part of a plant with edible roots lying above the ground ⟨beet ~s⟩ **3** : the upper end, edge, or surface ⟨the ~ of a page⟩ **4** : an upper piece, lid, or covering **5** : the highest degree, pitch, or rank **6** : a quark with a charge of +⅔ and a measured energy of approximately 175 billion electron volts

²top *vb* **topped; top·ping 1** : to remove or trim the top of : PRUNE ⟨~ a tree⟩ **2** : to cover with a top or on the top : CROWN, CAP **3** : to be superior to : EXCEL, SURPASS **4** : to go over the top of **5** : to strike (a ball) above the center **6** : to make an end or conclusion ⟨~ off a meal with coffee⟩

³top *adj* **1** : of, relating to, or being at the top : HIGHEST **2** : CHIEF

⁴top *n* : a toy that has a tapering point on which it is made to spin

to·paz \'tō-ˌpaz\ *n* : a hard silicate of aluminum; *esp* : a yellow transparent topaz used as a gem

top·coat \'täp-ˌkōt\ *n* **1** : a lightweight overcoat **2** : a protective coating (as of paint)

top dollar *n* : the highest amount being paid for a commodity or service

top-dress \-ˌdres\ *vb* : to apply material to (as land) without working it in; *esp* : to scatter fertilizer over

top-dress·ing \-ˌdre-siŋ\ *n* : a material used to top-dress soil

top-end \'täp-'end\ *adj* : TOPFLIGHT

top·flight \'täp-'flīt\ *adj* : of, relating to, or being the highest level of excellence or rank — **top flight** *n*

top hat *n* : a tall-crowned hat usu. of beaver or silk

top-heavy \'täp-ˌhe-vē\ *adj* : having the top part too heavy for the lower part

to·pi·ary \'tō-pē-ˌer-ē\ *n, pl* **-ar·ies** : the art of training and trimming trees or shrubs with decorative shapes — **topiary** *adj*

top·ic \'tä-pik\ *n* **1** : a heading in an outlined argument **2** : the subject of a discourse or a section of it : THEME

top·i·cal \-pi-kəl\ *adj* **1** : of, relating to, or arranged by topics ⟨a ~ outline⟩ **2** : relating to current or local events **3** : designed to be applied to or to work on a part (as of the body) — **top·i·cal·ly** \-k(ə-)lē\ *adv*

top·knot \'täp-ˌnät\ *n* **1** : an· ornament (as a knot of ribbons) forming a headdress **2** : a crest of feathers or tuft of hair on the top of the head

top·less \-ləs\ *adj* **1** : wearing no clothing on the upper body **2** : featuring topless waitresses or entertainers

top·mast \'täp-ˌmast, -məst\ *n* : the 2d mast above a ship's deck

top·most \'täp-ˌmōst\ *adj* : highest of all : UPPERMOST

top-notch \-'näch\ *adj* : of the highest quality : FIRST-RATE

top-of-the-line *adj* : being or belonging to the highest or most expensive class

to·pog·ra·phy \tə-'pä-grə-fē\ *n* **1** : the art of showing in detail on a map or chart the physical features of a place or region **2** : the outline of the form of a place showing its relief and the position of features (as rivers, roads, or cities) — **to-pog·ra·pher** \-fər\ n — **top·o·graph·ic** \ˌtä-pə-ˈgra-fik\ or **top·o·graph·i·cal** \-fi-kəl\ adj

topping n : a food served on top of another to make it look or taste better

top·ple \ˈtä-pəl\ vb **top·pled**; **top·pling** **1** : to fall from or as if from being top-heavy **2** : to push over : OVERTURN; also : OVERTHROW

¹tops \ˈtäps\ adj : topmost in quality or importance ⟨∼ in his field⟩

²tops adv : at the very most

top·sail \ˈtäp-ˌsäl, -səl\ also **top·s'l** \-səl\ n : the sail next above the lowest sail on a mast in a square-rigged ship

top secret adj : demanding complete secrecy among those concerned

top·side \ˈtäp-ˈsīd\ adv or adj **1** : to or on the top or surface **2** : on deck

top·sides \-ˈsīdz\ n pl : the top portion of the outer surface of a ship on each side above the waterline

top·soil \ˈtäp-ˌsȯi(-ə)l\ n : surface soil usu. including the organic layer in which plants have most of their roots

top·sy–tur·vy \ˌtäp-sē-ˈtər-vē\ adv **1** : in utter confusion **2** : UPSIDE DOWN — **topsy–turvy** adj

toque \ˈtōk\ n : a woman's small hat without a brim

tor \ˈtȯr\ n : a high craggy hill

To·rah \ˈtȯr-ə\ n **1** : a scroll of the first five books of the Old Testament used in a synagogue; also : these five books **2** : the body of divine knowledge and law found in the Jewish scriptures and tradition

¹torch \ˈtȯrch\ n, **1** : a flaming light made of something that burns brightly and usu. carried in the hand **2** : something that resembles a torch in giving light, heat, or guidance **3** : a portable burner for producing a hot flame **4** chiefly Brit : FLASHLIGHT

²torch vb : to set fire to

torch·bear·er \ˈtȯrch-ˌber-ər\ n **1** : a person who carries a torch **2** : one in the forefront (as of a political campaign)

torch·light \-ˌlīt\ n : light given by torches

torch song n : a popular sentimental song of unrequited love

tore past of TEAR

to·re·ador \ˈtȯr-ē-ə-ˌdȯr\ n : BULL-FIGHTER

to·re·ro \tə-ˈrer-ō\ n, pl **-ros** [Sp] : BULL-FIGHTER

¹tor·ment \ˈtȯr-ˌment\ n **1** : extreme pain or anguish of body or mind **2** : a source of vexation or pain

²tor·ment \tȯr-ˈment\ vb **1** : to cause severe suffering of body or mind to **2** : DISTORT, TWIST ✦ Synonyms RACK, AFFLICT, TRY, TORTURE — **tor·men·tor** \-ˈmen-tər\ n

torn past part of TEAR

tor·na·do \tȯr-ˈnā-dō\ n, pl **-does** or **-dos** [modif of Sp tronada thunderstorm, fr. tronar to thunder, fr. L tonare] : a violent destructive whirling wind accompanied by a funnel-shaped cloud that moves over a narrow path

¹tor·pe·do \tȯr-ˈpē-dō\ n, pl **-does** : a thin cylindrical self-propelled underwater weapon

²torpedo vb **tor·pe·doed**; **tor·pe·do·ing** : to hit or destroy with or as if with a torpedo

torpedo boat n : a small very fast boat for firing torpedoes

tor·pid \ˈtȯr-pəd\ adj **1** : having lost motion or the power of exertion : DORMANT **2** : SLUGGISH **3** : lacking vigor — **tor·pid·i·ty** \tȯr-ˈpi-də-tē\ n

tor·por \ˈtȯr-pər\ n **1** : DULLNESS, APATHY **2** : extreme sluggishness : STAGNATION ✦ Synonyms STUPOR, LETHARGY, LANGUOR, LASSITUDE

¹torque \ˈtȯrk\ n : a force that produces or tends to produce rotation or torsion

²torque vb **torqued**; **torqu·ing** : to impart torque to : cause to twist (as about an axis)

tor·rent \ˈtȯr-ənt\ n [F, fr. L torrent-, torrens, fr. torrent-, torrens burning, seething, rushing, fr. prp. of torrēre to parch, burn] **1** : a tumultuous outburst **2** : a rushing stream (as of water)

tor·ren·tial \tȯ-ˈren-chəl\ adj : relating to or resembling a torrent ⟨∼ rains⟩

tor·rid \ˈtȯr-əd\ adj **1** : parched with heat esp. of the sun : HOT **2** : ARDENT

torrid zone n : the region of the earth between the Tropic of Cancer and the Tropic of Capricorn

tor·sion \ˈtȯr-shən\ n **1** : a wrenching by which one part of a body is under pressure to turn about a longitudinal axis while the other part is held fast or is under pressure to turn in the opposite direction **2** : a twisting of a bodily organ or part on its own axis — **tor·sion·al** \ˈtȯr-shə-nəl\ adj — **tor·sion·al·ly** adv

tor·so \ˈtȯr-sō\ n, pl **torsos** or **tor·si** \ˈtȯr-ˌsē\ [It, lit., stalk] : the trunk of the human body

tort \ˈtȯrt\ n : a wrongful act which does not involve a breach of contract and for which the injured party can recover damages in a civil action

tor·ti·lla \tȯr-ˈtē-ə\ n : a round thin cake of unleavened cornmeal or wheat flour bread

tor·toise \ˈtȯr-təs\ n : TURTLE; esp : any of a family of land turtles

tor·toise·shell \-ˌshel\ n : the mottled horny substance of the shell of some turtles used in inlaying and in making various ornamental articles — **tortoiseshell** adj

tor·to·ni \tȯr-ˈtō-nē\ n : rich ice cream often made with minced almonds and chopped cherries and flavored with rum

tor·tu·ous \ˈtȯr-chə-wəs\ adj **1** : marked by twists or turns : WINDING **2** : DEVIOUS, TRICKY

¹tor·ture \ˈtȯr-chər\ n **1** : anguish of body or mind **2** : the infliction of severe pain esp. to punish or coerce — **tor·tur·ous** \ˈtȯrch-rəs, ˈtȯr-chə-\ adj

²torture vb **tor·tured**; **tor·tur·ing** **1** : to cause intense suffering to : TORMENT **2** : to punish or coerce by inflicting severe pain **3** : TWIST, DISTORT ✦ *Synonyms* RACK, HARROW, AFFLICT, TRY — **tor·tur·er** *n*

To·ry \'tȯr-ē\ *n, pl* **Tories 1** : a member of a chiefly 18th century British party upholding the established church and the traditional political structure **2** : an American supporter of the British during the American Revolution **3** *often not cap* : an extreme conservative — **Tory** *adj*

¹**toss** \'tȯs, 'täs\ *vb* **1** : to fling to and fro or up and down **2** : to throw with a quick light motion; *also* : BANDY **3** : to fling or lift with a sudden motion ⟨—*ed* her head angrily⟩ **4** : to move restlessly or turbulently ⟨—*es* on the waves⟩ **5** : to twist and turn repeatedly **6** : FLOUNCE **7** : to accomplish readily ⟨— off an article⟩ **8** : to decide an issue by flipping a coin

²**toss** *n* : an act or instance of tossing; *esp* : TOSS-UP 1

toss–up \-ˌəp\ *n* **1** : a deciding by flipping a coin **2** : an even chance **3** : something that offers no clear basis for choice

¹**tot** \'tät\ *n* **1** : a small child **2** : a small drink of alcoholic liquor : SHOT

²**tot** *vb* **tot·ted; tot·ting** : to add up

³**tot** *abbr* total

¹**to·tal** \'tōt-ᵊl\ *adj* **1** : making up a whole : ENTIRE ⟨— amount⟩ **2** : COMPLETE, UTTER ⟨a — failure⟩ ⟨a — stranger⟩ **3** : involving a complete and unified effort esp. to achieve a desired effect — **to·tal·ly** *adv*

²**total** *n* **1** : SUM **4 2** : the entire amount ✦ *Synonyms* AGGREGATE, WHOLE, GROSS, TOTALITY

³**total** *vb* **to·taled** *or* **to·talled; to·tal·ing** *or* **to·tal·ling 1** : to add up : COMPUTE **2** : to amount to : NUMBER **3** : to make a total wreck of (a car)

to·tal·i·tar·i·an \ˌtō-ˌta-lə-'ter-ē-ən\ *adj* : of, relating to, or advocating a political regime based on subordination of the individual to the state and strict control of all aspects of life esp. by coercive measures — **totalitarian** *n* — **to·tal·i·tar·i·an·ism** \-ē-ə-ˌni-zəm\ *n*

to·tal·i·ty \tō-'ta-lə-tē\ *n, pl* **-ties 1** : an aggregate amount : SUM, WHOLE **2** : ENTIRETY, WHOLENESS

to·tal·iza·tor *or* **to·tal·isa·tor** \'tō-t°l-ə-ˌzā-tər\ *n* : a machine for registering and indicating the number of bets and the odds on a horse or dog race

¹**tote** \'tōt\ *vb* **tot·ed; tot·ing** : CARRY

²**tote** *vb* **tot·ed; tot·ing** : ADD, TOTAL — usu. used with *up*

to·tem \'tō-təm\ *n* [Ojibwa *oto·te·man* his totem] : an object (as an animal or plant) serving as the emblem of a family or clan and often as a reminder of its ancestry; *also* : something usu. carved or painted to represent such an object

totem pole *n* : a pole that is carved with a series of totems and is erected before the houses of some northwest American Indians

tot·ter \'tä-tər\ *vb* **1** : to tremble or rock as if about to fall : SWAY **2** : to move unsteadily : STAGGER

tou·can \'tü-ˌkan\ *n* [F, fr. Pg *tucano*, fr. Tupinambá (American Indian language of Brazil) *tukána*] : any of a family of chiefly fruit-eating birds of tropical America with brilliant coloring and a very large bill

¹**touch** \'təch\ *vb* **1** : to bring a bodily part (as the hand) into contact with so as to feel **2** : to be or cause to be in contact **3** : to strike or push lightly esp. with the hand or foot **4** : DISTURB, HARM **5** : to make use of ⟨never —*es* alcohol⟩ **6** : to induce to give or lend **7** : to get to : REACH **8** : to refer to in passing : MENTION **9** : to affect the interest of : CONCERN **10** : to leave a mark on; *also* : BLEMISH **11** : to move to sympathetic feeling **12** : to come close : VERGE **13** : to have a bearing : RELATE **14** : to make a usu. brief or incidental stop in port ✦ *Synonyms* AFFECT, INFLUENCE, IMPRESS, STRIKE, SWAY

²**touch** *n* **1** : a light stroke or tap **2** : the act or fact of touching or being touched **3** : the sense by which pressure or traction on the skin or mucous membrane is perceived; *also* : a particular sensation conveyed by this sense **4** : mental or moral sensitiveness : TACT **5** : a small quantity : HINT ⟨a — of spring in the air⟩ **6** : a manner of striking or touching esp. the keys of a keyboard instrument **7** : an improving detail ⟨add a few —*es* to the painting⟩ **8** : distinctive manner or skill ⟨the — of a master⟩ **9** : the state of being in contact ⟨keep in —⟩ ✦ *Synonyms* SUGGESTION, SUSPICION, TINCTURE, TINGE

touch-down \'təch-ˌdaùn\ *n* : the act of scoring six points in American football by being lawfully in possession of the ball on, above, or behind an opponent's goal line

tou·ché \tü-'shā\ *interj* [F] — used to acknowledge a hit in fencing or the success of an argument, an accusation, or a witty point

touch football *n* : football in which touching is substituted for tackling

touch·ing \'tə-chin\ *adj* : capable of stirring emotions ✦ *Synonyms* MOVING, IMPRESSIVE, POIGNANT, AFFECTING

touch off *vb* **1** : to describe with precision **2** : to start by or as if by touching with fire

touch·stone \'təch-ˌstōn\ *n* : a test or criterion of genuineness or quality ✦ *Synonyms* STANDARD, GAUGE, BENCHMARK, YARDSTICK

touch–tone \'təch-'tōn\ *adj* : of, relating to, or being a telephone having push buttons that produce tones corresponding to numbers

touch up *vb* : to improve or perfect by small additional strokes or alterations — **touch–up** \'tə-ˌəp\ *n*

touchy \'tə-chē\ *adj* **touch·i·er; -est 1** : easily offended : PEEVISH **2** : calling for tact in treatment ⟨a ∼ subject⟩ ◆ *Synonyms* IRASCIBLE, CRANKY, CROSS, TETCHY, TESTY

¹tough \'təf\ *adj* **1** : strong or firm in texture but flexible and not brittle **2** : not easily chewed **3** : characterized by severity and determination ⟨a ∼ policy⟩ **4** : capable of enduring strain or hardship : ROBUST **5** : hard to influence : STUBBORN **6** : difficult to accomplish, resolve, or cope with ⟨a ∼ problem⟩ **7** : ROWDYISH ◆ *Synonyms* TENACIOUS, STOUT, STURDY, STALWART — **tough·ly** *adv* — **tough·ness** *n*

²tough *n* : a tough person : ROWDY

tough·en \'tə-fən\ *vb* **tough·ened; tough·en·ing** : to make or become tough

tou·pee \tü-'pā\ *n* [F *toupet* forelock] : a small wig for a bald spot

¹tour \'tùr, *1 is also* 'taù(-ə)r\ *n* **1** : one's turn : SHIFT **2** : a journey in which one returns to the starting point

²tour *vb* : to make a tour

tour de force \ˌtùr-də-'fórs\ *n, pl* **tours de force** *same*\ [F] : a feat or display of strength, skill, or ingenuity

Tou·rette's syndrome \tü-'rets\ *n* : a familial neurological disorder marked by recurrent involuntary tics and vocal sounds

tour·ism \'tùr-ˌi-zəm\ *n* **1** : the practice of traveling for recreation **2** : promotion of touring **3** : accommodation of tourists — **tour·ist** \-ist\ *n*

tourist class *n* : economy accommodations (as on a ship)

tour·ma·line \'tùr-mə-lən, -ˌlēn\ *n* : a mineral that when transparent is valued as a gem

tour·na·ment \'tùr-nə-mənt, 'tər-\ *n* **1** : a medieval sport in which mounted armored knights contended with blunted lances or swords **2** : a championship series of games or athletic contests

tour·ney \-nē\ *n, pl* **tourneys** : TOURNAMENT

tour·ni·quet \'tùr-ni-kət, 'tər-\ *n* : a device (as a tight bandage) to check bleeding or blood flow

tou·sle \'taù-zəl\ *vb* **tou·sled; tou·sling** : to disorder by rough handling : DISHEVEL, MUSS

tout \'taùt, *2 is also* 'tüt\ *vb* **1** : to give a tip or solicit bets on a racehorse **2** : to praise or publicize loudly — **tout** *n*

¹tow \'tō\ *vb* : to draw or pull along behind

²tow *n* **1** : an act of towing or condition of being towed **2** : something (as a barge) that is towed

³tow *n* : short or broken fiber (as of flax or hemp) used esp. for yarn, twine, or stuffing

to·ward \'tórd, 'tō-ərd, tə-'wórd\ *or* **towards** \'tórdz, 'tō-ərdz, tə-'wórdz\ *prep* **1** : in the direction of ⟨heading ∼ the river⟩ **2** : along a course leading to ⟨efforts ∼ reconciliation⟩ **3** : in regard to ⟨tolerance ∼ minorities⟩ **4** : so as to face ⟨turn the chair ∼ the window⟩ **5** : close upon ⟨it was getting along ∼ sun-

down⟩ **6** : for part payment of ⟨here's $100 ∼ your tuition⟩

tow·boat \'tō-ˌbōt\ *n* : TUGBOAT

tow·el \'taù(-ə)l\ *n* : an absorbent cloth or paper for wiping or drying

tow·el·ing *or* **tow·el·ling** *n* : a cotton or linen fabric for making towels

¹tow·er \'taù(-ə)r\ *n* **1** : a tall structure either isolated or built upon a larger structure ⟨an observation ∼⟩ **2** : a towering citadel **3** : a personal computer case that stands in an upright position — **tow·ered** *adj*

²tower *vb* : to reach or rise to a great height

tow·er·ing \'taù(-ə)-riŋ\ *adj* **1** : LOFTY ⟨∼ pines⟩ **2** : reaching high intensity ⟨a ∼ rage⟩ **3** : EXCESSIVE ⟨∼ ambition⟩

tow·head \'tō-ˌhed\ *n* : a person having whitish blond hair — **tow·head·ed** \-ˌhe-dəd\ *adj*

to·whee \'tō-ˌhē, 'tō-(ˌ)ē, tō-'hē\ *n* : a common finch of eastern No. America having the male black, white, and reddish; *also* : any of several closely related finches

to wit *adv* : NAMELY

town \'taùn\ *n* **1** : a compactly settled area usu. larger than a village but smaller than a city **2** : CITY **3** : the inhabitants of a town **4** : a New England territorial and political unit usu. containing both rural and urban areas; *also* : a New England community in which matters of local government are decided by a general assembly (**town meeting**) of qualified voters

town house *n* **1** : the city residence of a person having a country home **2** : a single-family house of two or sometimes three stories connected to another house by a common wall

town·ie *or* **towny** \'taù-nē\ *n, pl* **townies** : a permanent resident of a town as distinguished from a member of another group

towns·folk \'taùnz-ˌfōk\ *n pl* : TOWNSPEOPLE

town·ship \'taùn-ˌship\ *n* **1** : TOWN 4 **2** : a unit of local government in some states **3** : an unorganized subdivision of a county **4** : a division of territory in surveys of U.S. public land containing 36 square miles **5** : an area in the Republic of South Africa segregated for occupation by persons of non-European descent

towns·man \'taùnz-mən\ *n* **1** : a native or resident of a town or city **2** : a fellow citizen of a town

towns·peo·ple \-ˌpē-pəl\ *n pl* **1** : the inhabitants of a town or city **2** : town-bred persons

towns·wom·an \-ˌwù-mən\ *n* **1** : a woman who is a native or resident of a town or city **2** : a woman who is a fellow citizen of a town

tow·path \'tō-ˌpath, -ˌpäth\ *n* : a path (as along a canal) traveled esp. by draft animals towing boats

tow truck *n* : a truck equipped for towing vehicles

tox·emia \täk-'sē-mē-ə\ *n* : a bodily disorder associated with the presence of toxic substances in the blood

tox·ic \'täk-sik\ *adj* [LL *toxicus*, fr. L *toxicum* poison, fr. Gk *toxikon* arrow poison, fr. neut. of *toxikos* of a bow, fr. *toxon* bow, arrow] : of, relating to, or caused by poison or a toxin : POISONOUS — **tox·ic·i·ty** \täk-'si-sə-tē\ *n*

tox·i·col·o·gy \ˌtäk-si-'kä-lə-jē\ *n* : a science that deals with poisons and esp. with problems of their use and control — **tox·i·co·log·i·cal** \-kə-'lä-ji-kəl\ *also* **tox·i·co·log·ic** \-kə-'lä-jik\ *adj* — **tox·i·col·o·gist** \-'kä-lə-jist\ *n*

toxic shock syndrome *n* : an acute disease associated with the presence of a bacterium that is characterized by fever, diarrhea, nausea, diffuse erythema, and shock and occurs esp. in menstruating females using tampons

tox·in \'täk-sən\ *n* : a poisonous substance produced by metabolic activities of a living organism that is usu. unstable, very toxic when introduced into the tissues, and usu. capable of inducing antibodies

¹**toy** \'tói\ *n* 1 : something trifling 2 : a small ornament : BAUBLE 3 : something for a child to play with

²**toy** *vb* 1 : to deal with something lightly : TRIFLE 2 : FLIRT 3 : to amuse oneself as if with a plaything

³**toy** *adj* 1 : DIMINUTIVE ⟨a ~ dog⟩ 2 : designed for use as a toy

tp *abbr* 1 title page 2 township

tpk *or* **tpke** *abbr* turnpike

tr *abbr* 1 translated; translation; translator 2 transpose 3 troop

¹**trace** \'trās\ *n* 1 : a mark (as a footprint or track) left by something that has passed 2 : a minute or barely detectable amount

²**trace** *vb* **traced; trac·ing** 1 : to mark out : SKETCH 2 : to form (as letters) carefully 3 : to copy (a drawing) by marking lines on transparent paper laid over the drawing to be copied 4 : to follow the trail of : track down 5 : to study out and follow the development of — **trace·able** *adj*

³**trace** *n* : either of two lines of a harness for fastening a draft animal to a vehicle

trac·er \'trā-sər\ *n* 1 : one that traces 2 : ammunition containing a chemical to mark the flight of projectiles by a trail of smoke or light

trac·ery \'trā-sə-rē\ *n, pl* **-er·ies** : ornamental work having a design with branching or interlacing lines

tra·chea \'trā-kē-ə\ *n, pl* **-che·ae** \-kē-ˌē\ *also* **-che·as** *or* **-chea** : the main tube by which air passes from the larynx to the lungs of vertebrates — **tra·che·al** \-kē-əl\ *adj*

tra·che·ot·o·my \ˌtrā-kē-'ä-tə-mē\ *n, pl* **-mies** : the surgical operation of cutting into the trachea esp. through the skin

tracing *n* 1 : the act of one that traces 2 : something that is traced 3 : a graphic record made by an instrument for measuring vibrations or pulsations

¹**track** \'trak\ *n* 1 : a mark left in passing 2 : PATH, ROUTE, TRAIL 3 : a course laid out for racing; *also* : track-and-field sports 4 : one of a series of paths along which material (as music) is recorded (as on a CD or magnetic tape) 5 : the course along which something moves; *esp* : a way made by two parallel lines of metal rails 6 : awareness of a fact or progression ⟨lost ~ of time⟩ 7 : either of two endless metal belts on which a vehicle (as a bulldozer) travels

²**track** *vb* 1 : to follow the tracks or traces of : TRAIL 2 : to observe the moving path of (as a missile) 3 : to make tracks on 4 : to carry (as mud) on the feet and deposit — **track·er** *n*

track·age \'tra-kij\ *n* : lines of railway track

track–and–field *adj* : of or relating to athletic contests held on a running track or on the adjacent field

¹**tract** \'trakt\ *n* 1 : an area without precise boundaries ⟨huge ~s of land⟩ 2 : a defined area of land 3 : a system of body parts or organs that act together to perform some function ⟨the digestive ~⟩

²**tract** *n* : a pamphlet of political or religious propaganda

trac·ta·ble \'trak-tə-bəl\ *adj* : easily controlled : DOCILE ♦ **Synonyms** AMENABLE, OBEDIENT, BIDDABLE

tract house *n* : any of many similar houses built on a tract of land

trac·tion \'trak-shən\ *n* 1 : the act of drawing : the state of being drawn 2 : the drawing of a vehicle by motive power; *also* : the particular form of motive power used 3 : the adhesive friction of a body on a surface on which it moves 4 : a pulling force applied to a skeletal structure (as a broken bone) by means of a special device; *also* : a state of tension created by such a pulling force ⟨a leg in ~⟩ — **trac·tion·al** \-shə-nəl\ *adj* — **trac·tive** \'trak-tiv\ *adj*

trac·tor \'trak-tər\ *n* 1 : an automotive vehicle used esp. for drawing farm equipment 2 : a truck for hauling a trailer

¹**trade** \'trād\ *n* 1 : one's regular business or work : OCCUPATION 2 : an occupation requiring manual or mechanical skill 3 : the persons engaged in a business or industry 4 : the business of buying and selling or bartering commodities 5 : an act of trading : TRANSACTION

²**trade** *vb* **trad·ed; trad·ing** 1 : to give in exchange for another commodity : BARTER 2 : to engage in the exchange, purchase, or sale of goods 3 : to deal regularly as a customer — **trade on** : EXPLOIT ⟨*trades on* his family name⟩

trade–in \'trād-ˌin\ *n* : an item of merchandise traded in

trade in *vb* : to turn in as part payment for a purchase

¹**trade·mark** \'trād-ˌmärk\ *n* : a device (as a word or mark) that points distinctly to the origin or ownership of merchandise to which it is applied and that is legally reserved for the exclusive use of the owner; *also* : something that identifies a person or thing

²trademark *vb* : to secure the trademark rights for

trade name *n* : a name that is given by a manufacturer or merchant to a product to distinguish it as made or sold by him and that may be used and protected as a trademark

trad·er \'trā-dər\ *n* 1 : a person whose business is buying or selling 2 : a ship engaged in trade

trades·man \'trādz-mən\ *n* 1 : one who runs a retail store : SHOPKEEPER 2 : CRAFTSMAN

trades·peo·ple \-ˌpē-pəl\ *n pl* : people engaged in trade

trade union *n* : LABOR UNION

trade wind *n* : a wind blowing almost constantly in one direction

trading stamp *n* : a printed stamp given as a premium to a retail customer that when accumulated may be redeemed for merchandise

tra·di·tion \trə-'di-shən\ *n* 1 : an inherited, established, or customary pattern of thought or action 2 : the handing down of beliefs and customs by word of mouth or by example without written instruction; *also* : a belief or custom thus handed down — **tra·di·tion·al** \-ˌdi-shə-nəl\ *adj* — **tra·di·tion·al·ly** *adv*

tra·duce \trə-'düs, -'dyüs\ *vb* **tra·duced; tra·duc·ing** : to lower the reputation of : DEFAME, SLANDER ♦ *Synonyms* MALIGN, LIBEL, CALUMNIATE — **tra·duc·er** *n*

¹traf·fic \'tra-fik\ *n* 1 : the business of bartering or buying or selling 2 : communication or dealings between individuals or groups 3 : the movement (as of vehicles) along a route; *also* : the vehicles, people, ships, or planes moving along a route 4 : the passengers or cargo carried by a transportation system

²traffic *vb* **traf·ficked; traf·fick·ing** 1 : to carry on business dealings 2 : DEAL, TRADE — **traf·fick·er** *n*

traffic circle *n* : ROTARY 2

traffic light *n* : a visual signal (as a system of lights) for controlling traffic

tra·ge·di·an \trə-'jē-dē-ən\ *n* 1 : a writer of tragedies 2 : an actor who plays tragic roles

tra·ge·di·enne \trə-ˌjē-dē-'en\ *n* [F] : an actress who plays tragic roles

trag·e·dy \'tra-jə-dē\ *n, pl* **-dies** [ME *tragedie*, fr. MF, fr. L *tragoedia*, fr. Gk *tragōidia*, fr. *tragos* goat + *aeidein* to sing] 1 : a serious drama with a sorrowful or disastrous conclusion 2 : a disastrous event : CALAMITY; *also* : MISFORTUNE 3 : tragic quality or element ⟨the ~ of life⟩

trag·ic \'tra-jik\ *also* **trag·i·cal** \-ji-kəl\ *adj* 1 : of, relating to, or expressive of tragedy 2 : appropriate to tragedy 3 : LAMENTABLE, UNFORTUNATE — **trag·i·cal·ly** \-ji-k(ə-)lē\ *adv*

¹trail \'trāl\ *vb* 1 : to hang down so as to drag along or sweep the ground 2 : to draw or drag along behind 3 : to extend over a surface in a straggling manner 4 : to lag behind 5 : to follow the track of : PURSUE 6 : DWINDLE ⟨her voice ~ed off⟩

²trail *n* 1 : something that trails or is trailed ⟨a ~ of smoke⟩ 2 : a trace or mark left by something that has passed or been drawn along : SCENT, TRACK ⟨a ~ of blood⟩ 3 : a beaten path; *also* : a marked path through woods

trail bike *n* : a small motorcycle for off-road use

trail·blaz·er \-ˌblā-zər\ *n* : PATHFINDER, PIONEER — **trail·blaz·ing** *adj or n*

trail·er \'trā-lər\ *n* 1 : one that trails; *esp* : a creeping plant (as an ivy) 2 : a vehicle that is hauled by another (as a tractor) 3 : a vehicle equipped to serve wherever parked as a dwelling or place of business 4 : PREVIEW 3

trailer park *n* : a site equipped to accommodate mobile homes

trailing arbutus *n* : a creeping spring-flowering plant of the heath family with fragrant pink or white flowers

¹train \'trān\ *n* [ME, fr. AF, fr. *trainer* to draw, drag] 1 : a part of a gown that trails behind the wearer 2 : RETINUE 3 : a moving file of persons, vehicles, or animals 4 : a connected series ⟨a ~ of thought⟩ 5 : AFTERMATH 6 : a connected line of railroad cars usu. hauled by a locomotive ♦ *Synonyms* SUCCESSION, SEQUENCE, PROCESSION, CHAIN

²train *vb* [ME, to trail, drag, train, fr. AF *trainer*] 1 : to cause to grow as desired ⟨~ a vine on a trellis⟩ 2 : to form by instruction, discipline, or drill 3 : to make or become prepared (as by exercise) for a test of skill 4 : to aim or point at an object ⟨~ guns on a fort⟩ ♦ *Synonyms* DISCIPLINE, SCHOOL, EDUCATE, INSTRUCT — **train·er** *n*

train·ee \trā-'nē\ *n* : one who is being trained esp. for a job

train·ing \'trā-niŋ\ *n* 1 : the act, process, or method of one who trains 2 : the skill, knowledge, or experience gained by one who trains

train·man \-mən\ *n* : a member of a train crew

traipse \'trāps\ *vb* **traipsed; traips·ing** : TRAMP, WALK ⟨~ the countryside⟩

trait \'trāt\ *n* 1 : a distinguishing quality (as of personality) 2 : an inherited characteristic

trai·tor \'trā-tər\ *n* [ME *traytour*, fr. AF *traitre*, fr. L *traditor*, fr. *tradere* to hand over, deliver, betray, fr. *trans-* across + *dare* to give] 1 : one who betrays another's trust or is false to an obligation 2 : one who commits treason — **trai·tor·ous** *adj*

tra·jec·to·ry \trə-'jek-tə-rē\ *n, pl* **-ries** : the curve that a body (as a planet in its orbit) describes in space

tram \'tram\ *n,* 1 : a boxlike car running on rails (as in a mine) 2 *chiefly Brit* : STREETCAR 3 : an overhead cable car

¹tram·mel \'tra-məl\ *n* [ME *tramayle*, a kind of net, fr. OF *tramail*, fr. LL *tremaculum*, fr. L *tres* three + *macula* mesh, spot] : something impeding activity, progress, or freedom — usu. used in pl.

²**trammel** *vb* **-meled** *or* **-melled; -mel·ing** *or* **-mel·ling** 1 : to catch and hold in or as if in a net 2 : HAMPER ♦ **Synonyms** CLOG, FETTER, SHACKLE, HOBBLE

¹**tramp** \'tramp, *1 & 3 are also* 'trämp, 'tromp\ *vb* 1 : to walk, tread, or step heavily 2 : to walk about or through; *also* : HIKE 3 : to tread on forcibly and repeatedly

²**tramp** \'tramp, *5 is also* 'trämp, 'tromp\ *n* 1 : a begging or thieving vagrant 2 : a foot traveler 3 : an immoral woman; *esp* : PROSTITUTE 4 : a walking trip : HIKE 5 : the succession of sounds made by the beating of feet on a road 6 : a ship that does not follow a regular course but takes cargo to any port — **trampy** \'tram-pē\ *adj*

tram·ple \'tram-pəl\ *vb* **tram·pled; tram·pling** 1 : to tread heavily so as to bruise, crush, or injure 2 : to inflict injury or destruction 3 : to press down or crush by or as if by treading — **trample** *n* — **tram·pler** *n*

tram·po·line \ˌtram-pə-'lēn, 'tram-pə-ˌlēn\ *n* [It *trampolino* springboard] : a resilient sheet or web (as of nylon) supported by springs in a metal frame and used as a springboard in tumbling — **tram·po·lin·ist** \-'lē-nist, -ˌlē-\ *n*

trance \'trans\ *n* [ME, fr. AF *transe*, death, coma, rapture, fr. *transir* to depart, die, fr. L *transire* to cross, pass by, fr. *trans-* across + *ire* to go] 1 : STUPOR, DAZE 2 : a sleeplike state of altered consciousness (as of deep hypnosis) 3 : a state of very deep absorption — **trance·like** \-ˌlīk\ *adj*

tran·quil \'traŋ-kwəl, 'tran-\ *adj* : free from agitation or disturbance : QUIET ♦ **Synonyms** SERENE, PLACID, PEACEFUL — **tran·quil·li·ty** *or* **tran·quil·i·ty** \traŋ-'kwi-lə-tē, tran-\ *n* — **tran·quil·ly** *adv*

tran·quil·ize *also* **tran·quil·lize** \'traŋ-kwə-ˌlīz, 'tran-\ *vb* **-ized** *also* **-lized; -iz·ing** *also* **-liz·ing** : to make or become tranquil; *esp* : to relieve of mental tension and anxiety by means of drugs

tran·quil·iz·er *also* **tran·quil·liz·er** \-ˌlī-zər\ *n* : a drug used to relieve mental disturbance (as tension and anxiety)

trans *abbr* 1 transaction 2 transitive 3 translated; translation; translator 4 transmission 5 transportation 6 transverse

trans·act \tran-'zakt, -'sakt\ *vb* : CARRY OUT, PERFORM; *also* : CONDUCT

trans·ac·tion \-'zak-shən, -'sak-\ *n* 1 : something transacted; *esp* : a business deal 2 : an act or process of transacting 3 *pl* : the records of the proceedings of a society or organization — **trans·ac·tion·al** \-shnəl, -shə-nᵊl\ *adj*

trans·at·lan·tic \ˌtrans-ət-'lan-tik, ˌtranz-\ *adj* : crossing or extending across or situated beyond the Atlantic Ocean ⟨a ~ flight⟩

trans·ax·le \trans-'ak-səl\ *n* : a unit combining the transmission and differential gear of a front-wheel-drive automobile

trans·ceiv·er \tran-'sē-vər\ *n* : a radio transmitter-receiver that uses many of the same components for both transmission and reception

tran·scend \tran-'send\ *vb* 1 : to rise above the limits of 2 : SURPASS ♦ **Synonyms** EXCEED, OUTDO, OUTSHINE, OUTSTRIP

tran·scen·dent \-'sen-dənt\ *adj* 1 : exceeding usual limits : SURPASSING 2 : transcending material existence ♦ **Synonyms** SUPERLATIVE, SUPREME, PEERLESS, INCOMPARABLE

tran·scen·den·tal \ˌtran-ˌsen-'den-tᵊl, -sən-\ *adj* 1 : TRANSCENDENT 2 2 : of, relating to, or characteristic of transcendentalism; *also* : ABSTRUSE

tran·scen·den·tal·ism \-tə-ˌli-zəm\ *n* : a philosophy holding that ultimate reality is unknowable or asserting the primacy of the spiritual over the material and empirical — **tran·scen·den·tal·ist** \-tə-list\ *adj or n*

trans·con·ti·nen·tal \ˌtrans-ˌkän-tə-'nen-tᵊl\ *adj* : extending or going across a continent ⟨a ~ railroad⟩

tran·scribe \tran-'skrīb\ *vb* **tran·scribed; tran·scrib·ing** 1 : to write a copy of 2 : to make a copy of (dictated or recorded matter) in longhand or on a typewriter 3 : to represent (speech sounds) by means of phonetic symbols; *also* : to make a musical transcription of

tran·script \'tran-ˌskript\ *n* 1 : a written, printed, or typed copy 2 : an official copy esp. of a student's educational record

tran·scrip·tion \tran-'skrip-shən\ *n* 1 : an act or process of transcribing 2 : COPY, TRANSCRIPT 3 : an arrangement of a musical composition for some instrument or voice other than the original 4 : the process of constructing a messenger RNA molecule using a DNA molecule as a template

tran·scrip·tion·ist \-shə-nist\ *n* : one that transcribes; *esp* : a typist who transcribes medical reports

trans·der·mal \trans-'dər-məl, 'tranz-\ *adj* : relating to, being, or supplying a medication in a form for absorption through the skin ⟨~ nicotine patch⟩

trans·duc·er \trans-'dü-sər, tranz-, -'dyü-\ *n* : a device that is actuated by power from one system and supplies power usu. in another form to a second system

tran·sept \'tran-ˌsept\ *n* : the part of a cruciform church that crosses at right angles to the greatest length; *also* : either of the projecting ends

trans fat \'tran(t)s-, 'tranz-\ *n* : a fat containing unsaturated fatty acids (**trans fatty acids**) that have been linked to an increase in blood cholesterol

¹**trans·fer** \trans-'fər, 'trans-ˌfər\ *vb* **trans·ferred; trans·fer·ring** 1 : to pass or cause to pass from one person, place, or situation to another : MOVE, TRANSMIT

2 : to make over the possession of : CONVEY 3 : to print or copy from one surface to another by contact 4 : to change from one vehicle or transportation line to another — **trans·fer·able** \trans-'fər-ə-bəl\ adj — **trans·fer·al** \-'əl-\ n

²**trans·fer** \'trans-ˌfər\ n 1 : conveyance of right, title, or interest in property from one person to another 2 : an act or process of transferring 3 : one that transfers or is transferred 4 : a ticket entitling a passenger to continue a trip on another route

trans·fer·ence \trans-'fər-əns\ n : an act, process, or instance of transferring

trans·fig·ure \trans-'fi-gyər\ vb **-ured**; **-ur·ing** 1 : to change the form or appearance of 2 : EXALT, GLORIFY — **trans·fig·u·ra·tion** \ˌtrans-ˌfi-gyə-'rā-shən, -gə-\ n

trans·fix \trans-'fiks\ vb 1 : to pierce through with or as if with a pointed weapon 2 : to hold motionless by or as if by piercing ⟨stood ~ed by her gaze⟩

trans·form \trans-'fôrm\ vb : to change in structure, appearance, or character ◆ Synonyms TRANSMUTE, TRANSFIGURE, TRANSMOGRIFY — **trans·for·ma·tion** \ˌtrans-fər-'mā-shən\ n — **trans·for·ma·tive** \trans-'fôr-mə-tiv\ adj

trans·form·er \trans-'fôr-mər\ n : one that transforms; esp : a device for converting variations of current in one circuit into variations of voltage and current in another circuit

trans·fuse \trans-'fyüz\ vb **trans·fused**; **trans·fus·ing** 1 : to cause to pass from one to another 2 : to diffuse into or through 3 : to transfer (as blood) into a vein or an artery of a person or animal — **trans·fu·sion** \-'fyü-zhən\ n

trans·gen·der \tranz-'jen-dər\ adj : having physical or behavioral characteristics transcending traditional gender boundaries

trans·gen·ic \ˌtran(t)s-'je-nik\ adj : being or used to produce an organism or cell with genes introduced from another species of organism ⟨~ crops⟩

trans·gress \trans-'gres, tranz-\ vb [ME, fr. MF transgresser, fr. L transgressus, pp. of transgredi to step beyond or across, fr. trans- across + gradi to step] 1 : to go beyond the limits set by ⟨~ the divine law⟩ : to go beyond : EXCEED 3 : SIN — **trans·gres·sion** \-'gre-shən\ n — **trans·gres·sor** \-'gre-sər\ n

¹**tran·sient** \'tran-shənt, -sē-ənt, -shē-, -zē-\ adj 1 : not lasting long : SHORT-LIVED ⟨~ optimism⟩ 2 : passing through a place with only a brief stay ⟨~visitors⟩ ◆ Synonyms TRANSITORY, PASSING, MOMENTARY, FLEETING — **tran·sient·ly** adv

²**transient** n : one that is transient; esp : a transient guest

tran·sis·tor \tran-'zis-tər, -'sis-\ n [transfer + resistor; fr. its transferring an electrical signal across a resistor] 1 : a small electronic semiconductor device used in electronic equipment 2 : a radio having transistors

tran·sis·tor·ized \-tə-ˌrīzd\ adj : having or using transistors

tran·sit \'tran-sət, -zət\ n 1 : a passing through, across, or over : PASSAGE 2 : conveyance of persons or things from one place to another 3 : usu. local transportation esp. of people by public conveyance 4 : a surveyor's instrument for measuring angles

tran·si·tion \tran-'si-shən, -'zi-\ n : passage from one state, place, stage, or subject to another : CHANGE — **tran·si·tion·al** \-'si-shə-nəl, 'zi-\ adj

tran·si·tive \'tran-sə-tiv, -zə-\ adj 1 : having or containing an object required to complete the meaning 2 : TRANSITIONAL — **tran·si·tive·ly** adv — **tran·si·tive·ness** n — **tran·si·tiv·i·ty** \ˌtran-sə-'ti-və-tē, -zə-\ n

tran·si·to·ry \'tran-sə-ˌtôr-ē, -zə-\ adj : of brief duration : SHORT-LIVED, TEMPORARY ◆ Synonyms TRANSIENT, PASSING, MOMENTARY, FLEETING

transl abbr translated; translation

trans·late \trans-'lāt, tranz-\ vb **trans·lat·ed**; **trans·lat·ing** 1 : to change from one place, state, or form to another 2 : to convey to heaven without death 3 : to turn into one's own or another language — **trans·lat·able** adj — **trans·la·tor** \-'lā-tər\ n

trans·la·tion \tran(t)s-'lā-shən, tranz-\ n 1 : an act, process, or instance of translating 2 : the process of forming a protein molecule from information in messenger RNA — **trans·la·tion·al** \-shnəl, -shə-nᵊl\ adj

trans·lit·er·ate \trans-'li-tə-ˌrāt, tranz-\ vb **-at·ed**; **-at·ing** : to represent or spell in the characters of another alphabet — **trans·lit·er·a·tion** \ˌtrans-ˌli-tə-'rā-shən, ˌtranz-\ n

trans·lu·cent \trans-'lü-sᵊnt, tranz-\ adj : not transparent but clear enough to allow light to pass through — **trans·lu·cence** \-sᵊns\ n — **trans·lu·cen·cy** \-sᵊn-sē\ n — **trans·lu·cent·ly** adv

trans·mi·grate \-'mī-ˌgrāt\ vb : to pass at death from one body or being to another — **trans·mi·gra·tion** \ˌtrans-mī-'grā-shən, ˌtranz-\ n — **trans·mi·gra·to·ry** \trans-'mī-grə-ˌtôr-ē\ adj

trans·mis·sion \-'mi-shən\ n 1 : an act or process of transmitting 2 : the passage of radio waves between transmitting stations and receiving stations 3 : the gears by which power is transmitted from the engine of an automobile to the axle that propels the vehicle 4 : something transmitted

trans·mit \-'mit\ vb **trans·mit·ted**; **trans·mit·ting** 1 : to transfer from one person or place to another : FORWARD 2 : to pass on by or as if by inheritance 3 : to cause or allow to spread abroad or to another ⟨~ a disease⟩ 4 : to cause (as light, electricity, or force) to pass through space or a medium 5 : to send out (radio or television signals) ◆ Synonyms CONVEY, COMMUNICATE, IMPART — **trans·mis·si·ble** \-'mi-sə-bəl\ adj — **trans-**

mit·ta·ble \-'mi-tə-bəl\ *adj* — **trans·mit·tal** \-'mi-t^əl\ *n*

trans·mit·ter \-'mi-tər\ *n* : one that transmits; *esp* : an apparatus for transmitting telegraph, radio, or television signals

trans·mog·ri·fy \trans-'mä-grə-ˌfī, tranz-\ *vb* **-fied; -fy·ing** : to change or alter often with grotesque or humorous effect — **trans·mog·ri·fi·ca·tion** \-ˌmä-grə-fə-'kā-shən\ *n*

trans·mute \-'myüt\ *vb* **trans·mut·ed; trans·mut·ing** : to change or alter in form, appearance, or nature ✦ *Synonyms* TRANSFORM, CONVERT, TRANSFIGURE, METAMORPHOSE — **trans·mu·ta·tion** \ˌtrans-myü-'tā-shən, ˌtranz-\ *n*

trans·na·tion·al \-'na-shə-nəl\ *adj* : extending beyond national boundaries

trans·oce·an·ic \ˌtrans-ˌō-shē-'a-nik, ˌtranz-\ *adj* **1** : lying or dwelling beyond the ocean **2** : crossing or extending across the ocean

tran·som \'tran-səm\ *n* **1** : a piece (as a crossbar in the frame of a window or door) that lies crosswise in a structure **2** : a window above an opening (as a door) built on and often hinged to a horizontal crossbar

tran·son·ic *also* **trans·son·ic** \trans-'sä-nik\ *adj* : being or relating to speeds near that of sound in air or about 741 miles (1185 kilometers) per hour

trans·pa·cif·ic \ˌtrans-pə-'si-fik\ *adj* : crossing, extending across, or situated beyond the Pacific Ocean

trans·par·ent \trans-'per-ənt\ *adj* **1** : clear enough to be seen through **2** : SHEER, DIAPHANOUS ⟨a ∼ fabric⟩ **3** : readily understood : CLEAR; *also* : easily detected ⟨a ∼ lie⟩ ✦ *Synonyms* LUCID, TRANSLUCENT, LUCENT — **trans·par·en·cy** \-ən-sē\ *n* — **trans·par·ent·ly** *adv*

tran·spire \trans-'pī(-ə)r\ *vb* **tran·spired; tran·spir·ing** [MF *transpirer*, fr. ML *transpirare*, fr. L *trans-* across + *spirare* to breathe] **1** : to pass or give off (as water vapor) through pores or a membrane **2** : to become known **3** : to take place : HAPPEN — **tran·spi·ra·tion** \ˌtrans-pə-'rā-shən\ *n*

¹trans·plant \trans-'plant\ *vb* **1** : to dig up and plant elsewhere **2** : to remove from one place and settle or introduce elsewhere : TRANSPORT **3** : to transfer (an organ or tissue) from one part or individual to another — **trans·plan·ta·tion** \ˌtrans-ˌplan-'tā-shən\ *n*

²trans·plant \'trans-ˌplant\ *n* **1** : a person or thing transplanted **2** : the act or process of transplanting

trans·po·lar \trans-'pō-lər\ *adj* : going or extending across either of the polar regions

transponder \tran-'spän-dər\ *n* [*transmitter* + *responder*] : a radio or radar set that upon receiving a certain signal emits a radio signal and that is used to locate and identify objects and in satellites to relay communications signals

¹trans·port \trans-'pōrt\ *vb* **1** : to convey from one place to another : CARRY **2** : to carry away by strong emotion : ENRAP-

TURE **3** : to send to a penal colony overseas ✦ *Synonyms* BEAR, FERRY — **trans·por·ta·tion** \ˌtrans-pər-'tā-shən\ *n* — **trans·port·er** *n*

²trans·port \'trans-ˌpōrt\ *n* **1** : an act of transporting **2** : strong or intensely pleasurable emotion ⟨∼s of joy⟩ **3** : a ship used in transporting troops or supplies; *also* : a vehicle (as a truck or plane) used to transport persons or goods

trans·pose \trans-'pōz\ *vb* **trans·posed; trans·pos·ing 1** : to change the position or sequence of ⟨∼ the letters in a word⟩ **2** : to write or perform (a musical composition) in a different key — **trans·po·si·tion** \ˌtrans-pə-'zi-shən\ *n*

trans·sex·u·al \(ˌ)trans-'sek-shə-wəl\ *n* : a person who psychologically identifies with the opposite sex and may seek to live as a member of this sex esp. by undergoing surgery to modify the external sex organs

trans·ship \tran-'ship, trans-\ *vb* : to transfer for further transportation from one ship or conveyance to another — **trans·ship·ment** *n*

tran·sub·stan·ti·a·tion \ˌtran-səb-ˌstan-chē-'ā-shən\ *n* : the change in the eucharistic elements from the substance of bread and wine to the substance of the body of Christ with only the appearances of bread and wine remaining

trans·verse \trans-'vərs, tranz-\ *adj* : lying across : set crosswise — **transverse** \'trans-ˌvərs, 'tranz-\ *n* — **trans·verse·ly** *adv*

trans·ves·tite \trans-'ves-ˌtīt, tranz-\ *n* : a person and esp. a male who adopts the dress and often the behavior of the opposite sex — **transvestite** *adj* — **trans·ves·tism** \-ˌti-zəm\ *n*

¹trap \'trap\ *n* **1** : a device for catching animals **2** : something by which one is caught unawares; *also* : a situation from which escape is difficult or impossible **3** : a machine for throwing clay pigeons into the air; *also* : SAND TRAP **4** : a light one-horse carriage on springs **5** : a device to allow some one thing to pass through while keeping other things out ⟨a ∼ in a drainpipe⟩ **6** *pl* : a group of percussion instruments (as in a dance orchestra)

²trap *vb* **trapped; trap·ping 1** : to catch in or as if in a trap; *also* : CONFINE **2** : to provide or set (a place) with traps **3** : to set traps for animals esp. as a business ✦ *Synonyms* SNARE, ENTRAP, ENSNARE, BAG, LURE, DECOY — **trap·per** *n*

trap·door \'trap-'dȯr\ *n* : a lifting or sliding door covering an opening in a floor or roof

tra·peze \tra-'pēz\ *n* : a gymnastic apparatus consisting of a horizontal bar suspended by two parallel ropes

trap·e·zoid \'tra-pə-ˌzȯid\ *n* [NL *trapezoides*, fr. Gk *trapezoeidēs* trapezoidal, fr. *trapeza* table, fr. *tra-* four + *peza* foot] : a 4-sided polygon with exactly two sides parallel — **trap·e·zoi·dal** \ˌtra-pə-'zȯid-^əl\ *adj*

trap·pings \'tra-piŋz\ *n pl* 1 : CAPARISON 1 2 : outward decoration or dress; *also* : outward sign ⟨~ of success⟩

traps \'traps\ *n pl* : personal belongings : LUGGAGE

trap·shoot·ing \'trap-ˌshü-tiŋ\ *n* : shooting at clay pigeons sprung from a trap into the air away from the shooter

¹**trash** \'trash\ *n* 1 : something of little worth : RUBBISH 2 : empty or disparaging talk 3 : a worthless person; *also* : such persons as a group : RIFFRAFF — **trashy** *adj*

²**trash** *vb* 1 : to dispose of : DISCARD ⟨~ed the plans⟩ 2 : VANDALIZE, DESTROY 3 : ATTACK 4 : SPOIL, RUIN 5 : to criticize or disparage harshly

trau·ma \'traù-mə, 'trò-\ *n, pl* **traumas** *also* **trau·ma·ta** \-mə-tə\ [Gk, wound] : a bodily or mental injury esp. caused by an external agent; *also* : a cause of trauma — **trau·mat·ic** \trə-'ma-tik, trò-, traù-\ *adj*

trau·ma·tize \-ˌtīz\ *vb* **-tized; -tiz·ing** : to inflict trauma upon

¹**tra·vail** \trə-'vāl, 'tra-ˌvāl\ *n* 1 : painful work or exertion : TOIL 2 : AGONY, TORMENT 3 : CHILDBIRTH, LABOR

²**travail** *vb* : to labor hard : TOIL

¹**trav·el** \'tra-vəl\ *vb* **-eled** *or* **-elled; -el·ing** *or* **-el·ling** [ME *travailen* to torment, labor, journey, fr. AF *travailler* strive, fr. VL *trepaliare* to torture, fr. LL *trepalium* instrument of torture] 1 : to go on or as if on a trip or tour : JOURNEY 2 : to move as if by traveling ⟨news ~s fast⟩ 3 : ASSOCIATE 4 : to go from place to place as a sales representative 5 : to move from point to point ⟨light waves ~ very fast⟩ 6 : to journey over or through ⟨~ing the highways⟩ 7 : to take excessive steps while holding a basketball — **trav·el·er** *or* **trav·el·ler** *n*

²**travel** *n* 1 : the act of traveling : PASSAGE 2 : JOURNEY, TRIP — often used in pl. 3 : the number traveling : TRAFFIC 4 : the motion of a piece of machinery and esp. when to and fro

traveler's check *n* : a check paid for in advance that is signed when bought and signed again when cashed

traveling bag *n* : SUITCASE

trav·el·ogue *or* **trav·el·og** \'tra-və-ˌlòg, -ˌläg\ *n* : a usu. illustrated lecture on travel

¹**tra·verse** \'tra-vərs\ *n* : something that crosses or lies across

²**tra·verse** \trə-'vərs, tra-'vərs *or* 'tra-vərs\ *vb* **tra·versed; tra·vers·ing** 1 : to go or travel across or over 2 : to move or pass along or through 3 : to extend over 4 : SWIVEL

³**tra·verse** \'tra-ˌvərs\ *adj* : TRANSVERSE

trav·er·tine \'tra-vər-ˌtēn, -tən\ *n* : a crystalline mineral formed by deposition from spring waters

¹**trav·es·ty** \'tra-və-stē\ *vb* **-tied; -ty·ing** : to make a travesty of

²**travesty** *n, pl* **-ties** [obs. E *travesty* disguised, parodied, fr. F *travesti*, pp. of *travestir* to disguise, fr. It *travestire*, fr. *tra-* across (fr. L *trans-*) + *vestire* to dress] : an imitation that makes crude fun of something; *also* : an inferior imitation

¹**trawl** \'tròl\ *vb* : to fish or catch with a trawl — **trawl·er** *n*

²**trawl** *n* 1 : a large conical net dragged along the sea bottom in fishing 2 : a long heavy fishing line equipped with many hooks in series

tray \'trā\ *n* : an open receptacle with flat bottom and low rim for holding, carrying, or exhibiting articles

treach·er·ous \'tre-chə-rəs\ *adj* 1 : characterized by treachery 2 : UNTRUSTWORTHY, UNRELIABLE 3 : providing insecure footing or support ⟨a ~ slope⟩ ◆ *Synonyms* TRAITOROUS, FAITHLESS, FALSE, DISLOYAL — **treach·er·ous·ly** *adv*

treach·ery \'tre-chə-rē\ *n, pl* **-er·ies** : violation of allegiance or trust

trea·cle \'trē-kəl\ *n* [ME *triacle* a medicinal compound, fr. AF, fr. L *theriaca*, fr. Gk *thēriakē* antidote against a poisonous bite, fr. *thērion* wild animal] *chiefly Brit* : MOLASSES — **trea·cly** \-k(ə-)lē\ *adj*

¹**tread** \'tred\ *vb* **trod** \'träd\; **trod·den** \'trä-dᵊn\ *or* **trod; tread·ing** 1 : to step or walk on or over 2 : to move on foot : WALK; *also* : DANCE 3 : to beat or press with the feet — **tread water** : to stay afloat and upright in water by sustaining a walking motion

²**tread** *n* 1 : a mark made by or as if by treading 2 : the manner or sound of stepping 3 : the part of a wheel that makes contact with a road 4 : the horizontal part of a step

trea·dle \'tre-dᵊl\ *n* : a lever device pressed by the foot to drive a machine — **treadle** *vb*

tread·mill \'tred-ˌmil\ *n* 1 : a mill worked by persons who tread on steps around the edge of a wheel or by animals that walk on an endless belt 2 : a device with an endless belt on which a person walks or runs in place 3 : a wearisome routine

treas *abbr* treasurer; treasury

trea·son \'trē-zᵊn\ *n* : the offense of attempting to overthrow the government of one's country or of assisting its enemies in war — **trea·son·able** \-zᵊn-ə-bəl\ *adj* — **trea·son·ous** \-zᵊn-əs\ *adj*

¹**trea·sure** \'tre-zhər, 'trā-\ *n* [ME *tresor*, fr. AF, fr. L *thesaurus*, fr. Gk *thēsauros*] 1 : wealth stored up or held in reserve 2 : something of great value

²**treasure** *vb* **trea·sured; trea·sur·ing** 1 : HOARD 2 : to keep as precious : CHERISH ◆ *Synonyms* PRIZE, VALUE, APPRECIATE, ESTEEM

trea·sur·er \'tre-zhə-rər, 'trā-\ *n* : an officer of a club, business, or government who has charge of money taken in and paid out

treasure trove \-ˌtrōv\ *n* 1 : treasure of unknown ownership found buried or hidden 2 : a valuable discovery

trea·sury \'tre-zhə-rē, 'trā-\ *n, pl* **-sur·ies** 1 : a place in which stores of wealth are kept 2 : the place where collected funds are stored and paid out 3 *cap* : a governmental department in charge of finances

¹treat \'trēt\ *vb* **1** : NEGOTIATE **2** : to deal with esp. in writing; *also* : HANDLE **3** : to pay for the food or entertainment of **4** : to behave or act toward ⟨~ them well⟩ **5** : to regard in a specified manner ⟨~ as inferiors⟩ **6** : to give medical or surgical care to **7** : to subject to some action ⟨~ soil with lime⟩

²treat *n* **1** : an entertainment given free to those invited; *also* : food; drink, or entertainment provided at another's expense **2** : a source of joy or amusement

trea·tise \'trē-təs\ *n* : a systematic written exposition or argument

treat·ment \'trēt-mənt\ *n* : the act or manner or an instance of treating someone or something; *also* : a substance or method used in treating

trea·ty \'trē-tē\ *n, pl* **treaties** : an agreement made by negotiation or diplomacy esp. between two or more states or governments

¹tre·ble \'tre-bəl\ *n* **1** : the highest of the four voice parts in vocal music : SOPRANO **2** : a high-pitched or shrill voice or sound **3** : the upper half of the musical pitch range

²treble *adj* **1** : triple in number or amount **2** : relating to or having the range of a musical treble **3** : high-pitched : SHRILL — **tre·bly** *adv*

³treble *vb* **tre·bled; tre·bling** : to make or become three times the size, amount, or number

¹tree \'trē\ *n* **1** : a woody perennial plant usu. with a single main stem and a head of branches and leaves at the top **2** : a piece of wood adapted to a particular use ⟨a shoe ~⟩ **3** : something resembling a tree ⟨a genealogical ~⟩ — **tree·less** *adj*

²tree *vb* **treed; tree·ing** : to drive to or up a tree ⟨~ a raccoon⟩

tree farm *n* : an area of forest land managed to ensure continuous commercial production

tree frog *n* : any of numerous small usu. tree-dwelling amphibians with adhesive disks on the toes

tree line *n* : TIMBERLINE

tree of heaven : a Chinese ailanthus widely grown as an ornamental tree

tree surgery *n* : operative treatment of diseased trees esp. for control of decay — **tree surgeon** *n*

tre·foil \'trē-ˌfȯi(-ə)l, 'tre-\ *n* **1** : an herb (as a clover) with leaves that have three leaflets **2** : a decorative design with three leaflike parts

¹trek \'trek\ *vb* **trekked; trek·king** **1** *chiefly southern Africa* : to travel or migrate by ox wagon **2** : to make one's way arduously

²trek *n, 1 chiefly southern Africa* : a migration esp. of settlers by ox wagon **2** : a slow or difficult journey

trel·lis \'tre-ləs\ *n* [ME *trelis*, fr. AF *treleis*, fr. OF *treille* arbor, fr. L *trichila* summerhouse] : a frame of latticework used esp. to support climbing plants

²trellis *vb* : to provide with a trellis; *esp* : to train (as a vine) on a trellis

trem·a·tode \'tre-mə-ˌtōd\ *n* : any of a class of parasitic worms

¹trem·ble \'trem-bəl\ *vb* **trem·bled; trem·bling** **1** : to shake involuntarily (as with fear or cold) : SHIVER **2** : to move, sound, pass, or come to pass as if shaken or tremulous **3** : to be affected with fear or doubt

²tremble *n* : a spell of shaking or quivering

tre·men·dous \tri-'men-dəs\ *adj* **1** : causing dread, awe, or terror : TERRIFYING **2** : unusually large, powerful, great, or excellent ♦ **Synonyms** STUPENDOUS, MONUMENTAL, MONSTROUS — **tre·men·dous·ly** *adv*

trem·o·lo \'tre-mə-ˌlō\ *n, pl* **-los** [It] : a rapid fluttering of a tone or alternating tones

trem·or \'tre-mər\ *n* **1** : a trembling or shaking esp. from weakness, emotional stress, or disease **2** : a quivering motion of the earth (as during an earthquake)

trem·u·lous \'trem-yə-ləs\ *adj* **1** : marked by trembling or tremors : QUIVERING **2** : TIMOROUS, TIMID — **trem·u·lous·ly** *adv*

¹trench \'trench\ *n* [ME *trenche* track cut through a wood, fr. AF, act of cutting, fr. *trencher* to cut, prob. fr. VL **trinicare* to cut in three, fr. L *trini* three each] **1** : a long narrow cut in the ground : DITCH; *esp* : a ditch protected by banks of earth and used to shelter soldiers **2** *pl* : a place or situation likened to warfare conducted from trenches **3** : a long narrow steep-sided depression in the ocean floor

²trench *vb* **1** : to cut or dig trenches in **2** : to protect (troops) with trenches **3** : to come close : VERGE

tren·chant \'tren-chənt\ *adj* **1** : vigorously effective; *also* : CAUSTIC **2** : sharply perceptive : KEEN **3** : CLEAR-CUT, DISTINCT

tren·cher \'tren-chər\ *n* : a wooden platter for serving food

tren·cher·man \'tren-chər-mən\ *n* : a hearty eater

trench foot *n* : a painful foot disorder resembling frostbite and resulting from exposure to cold and wet

trench mouth *n* : a progressive painful bacterial infection of the mouth and adjacent parts marked by ulceration, bleeding gums, and foul breath

¹trend \'trend\ *vb* **1** : to have or take a general direction : TEND **2** : to show a tendency : INCLINE

²trend *n* **1** : a general direction taken (as by a stream or mountain range) **2** : a prevailing tendency : DRIFT **3** : a current style or preference : VOGUE

trendy \'tren-dē\ *adj* **trend·i·er; -est** : very fashionable; *also* : marked by superficial or faddish appeal or taste

trep·i·da·tion \ˌtre-pə-'dā-shən\ *n* : nervous agitation : APPREHENSION ♦ **Synonyms** HORROR, TERROR, PANIC, CONSTERNATION, DREAD, FRIGHT, DISMAY

¹tres·pass \'tres-pəs, -ˌpas\ *n* **1** : SIN, OF-

FENSE 2 : unlawful entry on someone else's land ✦ **Synonyms** TRANSGRESSION, VIOLATION, INFRACTION, INFRINGEMENT

²**tres·pass** \vb 1 : to commit an offense : ERR, SIN 2 : INTRUDE, ENCROACH; *esp* : to enter unlawfully upon the land of another — **tres·pass·er** n

tress \'tres\ n : a long lock of hair — usu. used in pl.

tres·tle *also* **tres·sel** \'tre-səl\ n 1 : a supporting framework consisting usu. of a horizontal piece with spreading legs at each end 2 : a braced framework of timbers, piles, or steel for carrying a road or railroad over a depression

T. rex \'tē-'reks\ n : TYRANNOSAUR

trey \'trā\ n, pl **treys** : a card or the side of a die with three spots

tri·ad \'trī-,ad, -əd\ n : a union or group of three usu. closely related persons or things

tri·age \trē-'äzh, 'trē-,äzh\ n [F, sorting] : the sorting of and allocation of treatment to patients and esp. battle or disaster victims according to a system of priorities designed to maximize the number of survivors

tri·al \'trī-əl\ n 1 : the action or process of trying or putting to the proof : TEST 2 : the hearing and judgment of a matter in issue before a competent tribunal 3 : a source of vexation or annoyance 4 : an experiment to test quality, value, or usefulness 5 : EFFORT, ATTEMPT ✦ **Synonyms** CROSS, ORDEAL, TRIBULATION, AFFLICTION — **trial** adj

tri·an·gle \'trī-,aŋ-gəl\ n 1 : a polygon that has three sides 2 : something shaped like a triangle — **tri·an·gu·lar** \trī-'aŋ-gyə-lər\ adj — **tri·an·gu·lar·ly** adv

tri·an·gu·la·tion \(,)trī-,aŋ-gyə-'lā-shən\ n : a method using trigonometry to find the location of a point using bearings from two fixed points a known distance apart — **tri·an·gu·late** \trī-'aŋ-gyə-,lāt\ vb

Tri·as·sic \trī-'a-sik\ adj : of, relating to, or being the earliest period of the Mesozoic era marked by the first appearance of the dinosaurs — **Triassic** n

tri·ath·lon \trī-'ath-lən, -,län\ n : an athletic contest consisting of three phases (as swimming, bicycling, and running)

trib abbr tributary

tribe \'trīb\ n 1 : a social group comprising numerous families, clans, or generations 2 : a group of persons having a common character, occupation, or interest 3 : a group of related plants or animals ⟨the cat ∼⟩ — **trib·al** \'trī-bəl\ adj

tribes·man \'trībz-mən\ n : a member of a tribe

trib·u·la·tion \,tri-byə-'lā-shən\ n [ME *tribulacion*, fr. AF, fr. L *tribulatio*, fr. *tribulare* to press, oppress, fr. *tribulum* drag used in threshing] : distress or suffering resulting from oppression or persecution; *also* : a trying experience ✦ **Synonyms** TRIAL, AFFLICTION, CROSS, ORDEAL

tri·bu·nal \trī-'byü-nᵊl, tri-\ n 1 : the seat

of a judge 2 : a court of justice 3 : something that decides or determines ⟨the ∼ of public opinion⟩

tri·bune \'tri-,byün, tri-'byün\ n 1 : an official in ancient Rome with the function of protecting the interests of plebeian citizens from the patricians 2 : a defender of the people

¹**trib·u·tary** \'tri-byə-,ter-ē\ adj 1 : paying tribute : SUBJECT 2 : flowing into a larger stream or a lake ✦ **Synonyms** SUBORDINATE, SECONDARY, DEPENDENT

²**tributary** n, pl **-tar·ies** 1 : a ruler or state that pays tribute 2 : a tributary stream

trib·ute \'tri-(,)byüt, -byət\ n 1 : a payment by one ruler or nation to another as an act of submission or price of protection 2 : a usu. excessive tax, rental, or levy exacted by a sovereign or superior 3 : a gift or service showing respect, gratitude, or affection; *also* : PRAISE ✦ **Synonyms** EULOGY, CITATION, ENCOMIUM, PANEGYRIC

trice \'trīs\ n : INSTANT, MOMENT

tri·ceps \'trī-,seps\ n, pl **triceps** : a large muscle along the back of the upper arm that is attached at its upper end by three main parts and acts to extend the forearm at the elbow joint

tri·cer·a·tops \(,)trī-'ser-ə-,täps\ n, pl **-tops** *also* **-tops·es** [NL, fr. Gk *tri-* three + *kerat-, keras* horn + *ōps* face] : any of a genus of large plant-eating Cretaceous dinosaurs with three horns, a bony crest on the neck, and hoofed toes

tri·chi·na \tri-'kī-nə\ n, pl **-nae** \-(,)nē\ *also* **-nas** : a small slender nematode worm that in the larval state is parasitic in the striated muscles of flesh-eating mammals (as humans)

trich·i·no·sis \,tri-kə-'nō-səs\ n : infestation with or disease caused by trichinae and marked esp. by muscular pain, fever, and swelling

¹**trick** \'trik\ n 1 : a crafty procedure meant to deceive 2 : a mischievous action : PRANK 3 : a childish action 4 : a deceptive or ingenious feat designed to puzzle or amuse 5 : PECULIARITY, MANNERISM 6 : a quick or artful way of getting a result : KNACK ⟨∼s of the trade⟩ 7 : the cards played in one round of a card game 8 : a tour of duty : SHIFT ✦ **Synonyms** RUSE, MANEUVER, ARTIFICE, WILE, FEINT

²**trick** vb 1 : to deceive by cunning or artifice : CHEAT 2 : to dress ornately

trick·ery \'tri-kə-rē\ n : deception by tricks and stratagems

trick·le \'tri-kəl\ vb **trick·led**; **trick·ling** 1 : to run or fall in drops 2 : to flow in a thin gentle stream — **trickle** n

trick·ster \'trik-stər\ n : one who tricks or cheats

tricky \'tri-kē\ adj **trick·i·er**; **-est** 1 : inclined to trickery 2 : requiring skill or caution ⟨a ∼ situation to handle⟩ 3 : UNRELIABLE ⟨a ∼ lock⟩

tri·col·or \'trī-,kə-lər\ n : a flag of three colors ⟨the French ∼⟩

tri·cy·cle \'trī-(,)si-kəl\ n : a 3-wheeled vehicle usu. propelled by pedals

tri·dent \'trī-d°nt\ n [L *trident-, tridens,* fr. *tri-* three + *dent-, dens* tooth] : a 3-pronged spear

tried \'trīd\ adj 1 : found trustworthy through testing 2 : subjected to trials

tri·en·ni·al \trī-'e-nē-əl\ adj 1 : occurring or being done every three years 2 : lasting for three years — **triennial** n

¹**tri·fle** \'trī-fəl\ n 1 : something of little value or importance 2 : a dessert of cake soaked with liqueur and served with toppings (as fruit or cream)

²**trifle** vb **tri·fled; tri·fling** 1 : to talk in a jesting or mocking manner 2 : to treat someone or something as unimportant 3 : DALLY, FLIRT 4 : to handle idly : TOY — **tri·fler** n

tri·fling \'trī-fliŋ\ adj 1 : FRIVOLOUS 2 : TRIVIAL, INSIGNIFICANT ✦ *Synonyms* PETTY, PALTRY, MEASLY, INCONSEQUENTIAL

tri·fo·cals \trī-'fō-kəlz\ n pl : eyeglasses with lenses having one part for close focus, one for intermediate focus, and one for distant focus

tri·fo·li·ate \trī-'fō-lē-ət\ adj : having three leaves or leaflets

¹**trig** \'trig\ adj : stylishly trim : SMART

²**trig** n : TRIGONOMETRY

¹**trig·ger** \'tri-gər\ n [alter. of earlier *tricker,* fr. D *trekker,* fr. MD *trecker* one that pulls, fr. *trecken* to pull] : a movable lever that activates a device when it is squeezed; *esp* : the part of a firearm lock moved by the finger to fire a gun — **trigger** adj — **trig·gered** adj

²**trigger** vb 1 : to fire by pulling a trigger 2 : to initiate, actuate, or set off as if by a trigger ⟨remarks that ∼ed a fight⟩

tri·glyc·er·ide \trī-'gli-sə-ˌrīd\ n : any of a group of lipids that are formed from glycerol and fatty acids and are widespread in animal tissue

trig·o·nom·e·try \ˌtri-gə-'nä-mə-trē\ n : the branch of mathematics dealing with the properties of triangles and esp. with finding unknown angles or sides given the size or length of some angles or sides — **trig·o·no·met·ric** \-nə-'me-trik\ also **trig·o·no·met·ri·cal** \-tri-kəl\ adj

trike \'trīk\ n : TRICYCLE

¹**trill** \'tril\ n 1 : the alternation of two musical tones a scale degree apart : WARBLE 3 : the rapid vibration of one speech organ against another (as of the tip of the tongue against the teeth)

²**trill** vb : to utter as or with a trill

tril·lion \'tril-yən\ n, 1 : a thousand billions 2 *Brit* : a million billions — **trillion** adj — **tril·lionth** \-yənth\ adj or n

tril·li·um \'tri-lē-əm\ n : any of a genus of spring-blooming herbs that are related to the lilies and have an erect stem bearing a whorl of three leaves and a solitary flower

tril·o·gy \'tri-lə-jē\ n, pl **-gies** : a series of three dramas or literary or musical compositions that are closely related and develop one theme

¹**trim** \'trim\ vb **trimmed; trim·ming** [OE *trymian, trymman* to strengthen, arrange, fr. *trum* strong, firm] 1 : to put orna-

ments on : ADORN 2 : to defeat esp. resoundingly 3 : to make trim, neat, regular, or less bulky by or as if by cutting ⟨∼ a beard⟩ ⟨∼ a budget⟩ 4 : to cause (a boat) to assume a desired position in the water by arrangement of the load; *also* : to adjust (as a submarine or airplane) esp. for horizontal motion 5 : to adjust (a sail) to a desired position 6 : to change one's views for safety or expediency — **trim·ly** adv — **trim·mer** n — **trim·ness** n

²**trim** adj **trim·mer; trim·mest** : showing neatness, good order, or compactness ⟨a ∼ figure⟩ ✦ *Synonyms* TIDY, TRIG, SMART, SPRUCE, SHIPSHAPE

³**trim** n 1 : good condition : FITNESS 2 : material used for ornament or trimming; *esp* : the woodwork in the finish of a house esp. around doors and windows 3 : the position of a ship or boat esp. with reference to the horizontal; *also* : the relation between the plane of a sail and the direction of a ship 4 : the position of an airplane at which it will continue in level flight with no adjustments to the controls 5 : something that is trimmed off

tri·ma·ran \'trī-mə-ˌran, ˌtrī-mə-'ran\ n : a sailboat with three hulls

tri·mes·ter \trī-'mes-tər, 'trī-ˌmes-tər\ n 1 : a period of three or about three months (as in pregnancy) 2 : one of three terms into which an academic year is sometimes divided

trim·e·ter \'tri-mə-tər\ n : a line of verse consisting of three metrical feet

trim·ming \'tri-miŋ\ n 1 : DEFEAT 2 : the action of one that trims 3 : something that trims, ornaments, or completes

tri·month·ly \trī-'mənth-lē\ adj : occurring every three months

trine \'trīn\ adj : THREEFOLD, TRIPLE

Trin·i·da·di·an \ˌtri-nə-'dā-dē-ən, -'da-\ n : a native or inhabitant of the island of Trinidad — **Trinidadian** adj

Trin·i·tar·i·an \ˌtri-nə-'ter-ē-ən\ n : a believer in the doctrine of the Trinity — **Trin·i·tar·i·an·ism** \-ē-ə-ˌni-zəm\ n

Trin·i·ty \'tri-nə-tē\ n 1 : the unity of Father, Son, and Holy Spirit as three persons in one Godhead 2 *not cap* : TRIAD

trin·ket \'triŋ-kət\ n 1 : a small ornament (as a jewel or ring) 2 : TRIFLE 1

trio \'trē-ō\ n, pl **tri·os** 1 : a musical composition for three voices or three instruments 2 : the performers of a trio 3 : a group or set of three

¹**trip** \'trip\ vb **tripped; trip·ping** 1 : to move with light quick steps 2 : to catch the foot against something so as to stumble or cause to stumble 3 : to make a mistake : SLIP; *also* : to detect in a misstep : EXPOSE 4 : to release (as a spring or switch) by moving a catch; *also* : ACTIVATE ⟨∼ an alarm⟩ 5 : to get high on a usu. hallucinatory drug

²**trip** n 1 : JOURNEY, VOYAGE 2 : a quick light step 3 : a false step : STUMBLE; *also* : ERROR 4 : the action of tripping mechanically; *also* : a device for tripping 5 : an intense experience; *esp* : one trig-

gered by a hallucinatory drug **6** : absorption in an attitude or state of mind ⟨an ego ~⟩

tri·par·tite \trī-'pär-ˌtīt\ *adj* **1** : divided into three parts **2** : having three corresponding parts or copies **3** : made between three parties ⟨a ~ treaty⟩

tripe \'trīp\ *n* **1** : stomach tissue esp. of a ruminant (as an ox) used as food **2** : something poor, worthless, or offensive : TRASH

¹tri·ple \'tri-pəl\ *vb* **tri·pled; tri·pling** **1** : to make or become three times as great or as many **2** : to hit a triple

²triple *n* **1** : a triple quantity **2** : a group of three **3** : a hit in baseball that lets the batter reach third base

³triple *adj* **1** : being three times as great or as many **2** : having three units or members **3** : repeated three times

triple bond *n* : a chemical bond in which three pairs of electrons are shared by two atoms in a molecule

triple point *n* : the condition of temperature and pressure under which the gaseous, liquid, and solid forms of a substance can exist in equilibrium

trip·let \'tri-plət\ *n* **1** : a unit of three lines of verse **2** : a group of three of a kind **3** : one of three offspring born at one birth

tri·plex \'tri-ˌpleks, 'trī-\ *adj* : THREE-FOLD, TRIPLE

¹trip·li·cate \'tri-pli-kət\ *adj* : made in three identical copies

²trip·li·cate \-plə-ˌkāt\ *vb* **-cat·ed; -cat·ing** **1** : TRIPLE **2** : to provide three copies of ⟨~ a document⟩

³trip·li·cate \-pli-kət\ *n* : three copies all alike — used with *in* ⟨typed in ~⟩

tri·ply \'tri-plē, 'tri-pə-lē\ *adv* : in a triple degree, amount, or manner

tri·pod \'trī-ˌpäd\ *n* : something (as a caldron, stool, or camera stand) that rests on three legs — **tripod** *or* **tri·po·dal** \'tri-pə-dᵊl, 'trī-ˌpä-\ *adj*

trip·tych \'trip-tik\ *n* : a picture or carving in three panels side by side

tri·reme \'trī-ˌrēm\ *n* : an ancient galley having three banks of oars

tri·sect \'trī-ˌsekt, trī-'sekt\ *vb* : to divide into three usu. equal parts — **tri·sec·tion** \'trī-ˌsek-shən\ *n*

trite \'trīt\ *adj* **trit·er; trit·est** [L *tritus*, fr. pp. of *terere* to rub, wear away] : used so commonly that the novelty is worn off : STALE ♦ **Synonyms** HACKNEYED, STEREOTYPED, COMMONPLACE, CLICHÉD

tri·ti·um \'tri-tē-əm, 'tri-shē-\ *n* : a radioactive form of hydrogen with one proton and two neutrons in its nucleus and three times the mass of ordinary hydrogen

tri·ton \'trī-tᵊn\ *n* : any of various large marine gastropod mollusks with a heavy elongated conical shell; *also* : the shell of a triton

trit·u·rate \'tri-chə-ˌrāt\ *vb* **-rat·ed; -rat·ing** : to rub up or grind to a fine powder

¹tri·umph \'trī-əmf\ *n* **1** : the joy or exultation of victory or success **2** : VICTORY, CONQUEST — **tri·um·phal** \trī-'əm-fəl\ *adj*

²triumph *vb* **1** : to obtain victory : PREVAIL **2** : to celebrate victory or success exultantly — **tri·um·phant** \trī-'əm-fənt\ *adj* — **tri·um·phant·ly** *adv*

tri·um·vir \trī-'əm-vər\ *n, pl* **-virs** *also* **-vi·ri** \-və-ˌrī\ : a member of a triumvirate

tri·um·vi·rate \-və-rət\ *n* : a ruling body of three persons

tri·une \'trī-ˌün, -ˌyün\ *adj* : being three in one ⟨the ~ God⟩

triv·et \'tri-vət\ *n* **1** : a 3-legged stand : TRIPOD **2** : a usu. metal stand with short feet for use under a hot dish

triv·ia \'tri-vē-ə\ *n sing or pl* : unimportant matters : obscure facts or details ⟨movie ~⟩

triv·i·al \'tri-vē-əl\ *adj* [L *trivialis* found everywhere, commonplace, fr. *trivium* crossroads, fr. *tri-* three + *via* way] : of little importance — **triv·i·al·i·ty** \ˌtri-vē-'a-lə-tē\ *n*

triv·i·um \'tri-vē-əm\ *n, pl* **triv·ia** \-vē-ə\ : the three liberal arts of grammar, rhetoric, and logic in a medieval university

tri·week·ly \trī-'wē-klē\ *adj* **1** : occurring or appearing three times a week **2** : occurring or appearing every three weeks — **triweekly** *adv*

tro·che \'trō-kē\ *n* : LOZENGE 2

tro·chee \'trō-(ˌ)kē\ *n* : a metrical foot of one accented syllable followed by one unaccented syllable — **tro·cha·ic** \trō-'kā-ik\ *adj*

trod *past and past part of* TREAD

trodden *past part of* TREAD

troi·ka \'trȯi-kə\ *n* [Russ *troĭka*, fr. *troe* three] : a group of three; *esp* : an administrative or ruling body of three

¹troll \'trōl\ *vb* **1** : to sing the parts of (a song) in succession **2** : to fish by trailing a lure or baited hook from a moving boat **3** : to sing or play jovially

²troll *n* : a lure used in trolling; *also* : the line with its lure

³troll *n* : a dwarf or giant in Scandinavian folklore inhabiting caves or hills

trol·ley *also* **trol·ly** \'trä-lē\ *n, pl* **trolleys** *also* **trollies** **1** : a device (as a grooved wheel on the end of a pole) to carry current from a wire to an electrically driven vehicle **2** : a streetcar powered electrically by overhead wires **3** : a wheeled carriage running on an overhead rail or track

trol·ley·bus \'trä-lē-ˌbəs\ *n* : a bus powered electrically by overhead wires

trolley car *n* : TROLLEY 2

trol·lop \'trä-ləp\ *n* : a disreputable woman; *esp* : one who engages in sex promiscuously

trom·bone \träm-'bōn, 'träm-ˌbōn\ *n* [It, fr. *tromba* trumpet] : a brass wind instrument that consists of a long metal tube with two turns and a flaring end and that usu. has a movable slide to vary the pitch — **trom·bon·ist** \-'bō-nist, -ˌbō-\ *n*

tromp \'trämp, 'trȯmp\ *vb* **1** : TRAMP, MARCH **2** : to stamp with the foot **3** : to defeat decisively

trompe l'oeil \(₁)trômp-'lə-ē, trōⁿp-'lœi\ n [F *trompe-l'oeil*, lit., deceives the eye] : a style of painting in which objects are depicted with photographic detail

¹**troop** \'trüp\ n **1** : a cavalry unit corresponding to an infantry company **2** pl : armed forces : SOLDIERS **3** : a collection of people, animals, or things **4** : a unit of Girl Scouts or Boy Scouts under an adult leader

²**troop** vb : to move or gather in crowds

troop·er \'trü-pər\ n **1** : an enlisted cavalryman; *also* : a cavalry horse **2** : a mounted or a state police officer

troop·ship \'trüp-₁ship\ : a ship or aircraft for carrying troops

trope \'trōp\ n : a word or expression used in a figurative sense

tro·phic \'trō-fik\ adj : of or relating to nutrition

tro·phy \'trō-fē\ n, pl **trophies** : something gained or given in conquest or victory esp. when preserved or mounted as a memorial

trop·ic \'trä-pik\ n [ME *tropik*, fr. L *tropicus* of the solstice, fr. Gk *tropikos*, fr. *tropē* turn] **1** : either of the two parallels of latitude approximately 23½ degrees north (**Tropic of Can·cer**) or south (**Tropic of Cap·ri·corn**) of the equator where the sun is directly overhead when it reaches its most northerly or southerly point in the sky **2** pl, often cap : the region lying between the tropics — **trop·i·cal** \-pi-kəl\ or **tropic** adj

tro·pism \'trō-₁pi-zəm\ n : an automatic movement by an organism in response to a source of stimulation; *also* : a reflex reaction involving this

tro·po·sphere \'trō-pə-₁sfir, 'trä-\ n : the part of the atmosphere between the earth's surface and the stratosphere in which most weather changes occur — **tro·po·spher·ic** \₁trō-pə-'sfir-ik, ₁trä-, -'sfer-\ adj

¹**trot** \'trät\ n **1** : a moderately fast gait of a 4-footed animal (as a horse) in which the legs move in diagonal pairs **2** : a human jogging gait between a walk and a run

²**trot** vb **trot·ted; trot·ting 1** : to ride, drive, or go at a trot **2** : to proceed briskly : HURRY — **trot·ter** n

troth \'träth, 'trōth, 'trōth\ n **1** : pledged faithfulness **2** : one's pledged word; *also* : BETROTHAL

trou·ba·dour \'trü-bə-₁dór\ n [F, fr. Old Occitan *trobador*, fr. *trobar* to compose] : any of a class of poet-musicians flourishing esp. in southern France and northern Italy during the 11th, 12th, and 13th centuries

¹**trou·ble** \'trə-bəl\ vb **trou·bled; trou·bling 1** : to agitate mentally or spiritually : DISTURB, WORRY **2** : to produce physical disorder in : AFFLICT ⟨~ to put to inconvenience **4** : RUFFLE ⟨~ the waters⟩ **5** : to make an effort ♦ *Synonyms* DISTRESS, AIL, UPSET — **trou·ble·some** adj — **trou·ble·some·ly** adv — **trou·blous** \-bələs\ adj

²**trouble** n **1** : the quality or state of being troubled esp. mentally **2** : an instance of distress or annoyance **3** : DISEASE, AILMENT ⟨heart ~⟩ **4** : EXERTION, PAINS ⟨took the ~ to phone⟩ **5** : a cause of disturbance or distress

trou·ble·mak·er \-₁mā-kər\ n : a person who causes trouble

trou·ble·shoot·er \-₁shü-tər\ n **1** : a worker employed to locate trouble and make repairs in equipment **2** : an expert in resolving disputes or problems — **trou·ble·shoot** vb

trough \'tróf, 'tróth\ n, pl **troughs** \'tröfs, 'tróvz; 'tröths, 'tröthz\ **1** : a long shallow open boxlike container esp. for water or feed for livestock **2** : a gutter along the eaves of a house **3** : a long channel or depression (as between waves or hills) **4** : an elongated area of low barometric pressure

trounce \'traüns\ vb **trounced; trouncing 1** : to thrash or punish severely **2** : to defeat decisively

troupe \'trüp\ n : COMPANY; *esp* : a group of performers on the stage — **troup·er** n

trou·sers \'traü-zərz\ n pl [alter. of earlier *trouse*, fr. Scot & Ir Gael *triubhas*] : PANTS — **trouser** adj

trous·seau \'trü-sō, trü-'sō\ n, pl **trousseaux** \-₁sōz, -'sōz\ or **trous·seaus** [F] : the personal outfit of a bride

trout \'traüt\ n, pl **trout** also **trouts** [ME, fr. OE *trüht*, fr. LL *tructa*, a fish with sharp teeth, fr. Gk *trōktēs*, lit., gnawer] : any of various mostly freshwater food and game fishes usu. smaller than the related salmons

trow \'trō\ vb, archaic : THINK, SUPPOSE

trow·el \'traü-(ə)l\ n **1** : a hand tool used for spreading, shaping, or smoothing loose or plastic material (as mortar or plaster) **2** : a scoop-shaped tool used in gardening — **trowel** vb

troy \'tròi\ adj : expressed in troy weight ⟨~ ounce⟩

troy weight n : a system of weights based on a pound of 12 ounces and an ounce of 480 grains (31 grams) — see WEIGHT table

tru·ant \'trü-ənt\ n [ME, vagabond, idler, fr. AF, of Celt origin] : a student who stays out of school without permission — **tru·an·cy** \-ən-sē\ n — **truant** adj

truce \'trüs\ n **1** : ARMISTICE **2** : a respite esp. from something unpleasant

¹**truck** \'trak\ vb **1** : EXCHANGE, BARTER **2** : to have dealings : TRAFFIC

²**truck** n **1** : BARTER **2** : DEALINGS **3** : small goods or merchandise; *esp* : vegetables grown for market

³**truck** n **1** : a wheeled vehicle (as a strong heavy automobile) designed for carrying heavy articles or hauling a trailer **2** : a swiveling frame with springs and one or more pairs of wheels used to carry and guide one end of a locomotive or railroad car

⁴**truck** vb **1** : to transport on a truck **2** : to be employed in driving a truck — **truck·er** n

truck farm *n* : a farm growing vegetables for market — **truck farmer** *n*

truck·le \'trə-kəl\ *vb* **truck·led; truck·ling** : to yield slavishly to the will of another : SUBMIT ♦ *Synonyms* FAWN, TOADY, CRINGE, COWER

truc·u·lent \'trə-kyə-lənt\ *adj* **1** : feeling or showing ferocity : SAVAGE **2** : aggressively self-assertive : BELLIGERENT — **truc·u·lence** \-ləns\ *n* — **truc·u·len·cy** \-lən-sē\ *n* — **truc·u·lent·ly** *adv*

trudge \'trəj\ *vb* **trudged; trudg·ing** : to walk or march steadily and usu. laboriously

¹true \'trü\ *adj* **tru·er; tru·est** **1** : STEADFAST, LOYAL **2** : agreeing with facts or reality ⟨a ~ description⟩ **3** : CONSISTENT ⟨~ to expectations⟩ **4** : properly so called ⟨~ love⟩ **5** : RIGHTFUL ⟨~ and lawful king⟩ **6** : conformable to a standard or pattern; *also* : placed or formed accurately ♦ *Synonyms* CONSTANT, STAUNCH, RESOLUTE, STEADFAST

²true *adv* **1** : TRUTHFULLY **2** : ACCURATELY ⟨the bullet flew straight and ~⟩; *also* : without variation from type ⟨breed ~⟩

³true *n* **1** : TRUTH, REALITY — usu. used with *the* **2** : the state of being accurate (as in alignment) ⟨out of ~⟩

⁴true *vb* **trued; tru·ing** *also* **tru·ing** : to bring or restore to a desired precision

true–blue *adj* : marked by unswerving loyalty

true bug *n* : BUG 2

true–heart·ed \'trü-'här-təd\ *adj* : FAITHFUL, LOYAL ⟨a ~ soldier⟩

truf·fle \'trə-fəl, 'trü-\ *n* **1** : the dark or light edible spore-bearing organ of any of several European fungi that grow underground; *also* : one of these fungi **2** : a candy made of chocolate, butter, and sugar shaped into balls and coated with cocoa

tru·ism \'trü-,i-zəm\ *n* : an undoubted or self-evident truth ♦ *Synonyms* COMMONPLACE, PLATITUDE, CLICHÉ

tru·ly \'trü-lē\ *adv* **1** : in all sincerity **2** : in agreement with fact **3** : ACCURATELY **4** : in a proper or suitable manner

¹trump \'trəmp\ *n* : TRUMPET

²trump *n* : a card of a designated suit any of whose cards will win over a card that is not of this suit; *also* : the suit itself — often used in pl.

³trump *vb* : to take with a trump

trumped–up \'trəmpt-'əp\ *adj* : fraudulently concocted : SPURIOUS

trum·pery \'trəm-pə-rē\ *n* **1** : NONSENSE **2** : trivial articles : JUNK

¹trum·pet \'trəm-pət\ *n* **1** : a wind instrument consisting of a long curved metal tube flaring at one end and with a cup-shaped mouthpiece at the other **2** : something that resembles a trumpet or its tonal quality **3** : a funnel-shaped instrument for collecting, directing, or intensifying sound

²trumpet *vb* **1** : to blow a trumpet **2** : to proclaim on or as if on a trumpet ⟨~ the news⟩ — **trum·pet·er** *n*

¹trun·cate \'trəŋ-,kāt, 'trən-\ *adj* : having the end square or blunt

²truncate *vb* **trun·cat·ed; trun·cat·ing** : to shorten by or as if by cutting : LOP — **trun·ca·tion** \,trəŋ-'kā-shən\ *n*

trun·cheon \'trən-chən\ *n* : a police officer's billy club

trun·dle \'trən-dᵊl\ *vb* **trun·dled; trun·dling** : to roll along : WHEEL

trundle bed *n* : a low bed that can be stored under a higher bed

trunk \'trəŋk\ *n* **1** : the main stem of a tree **2** : the body of a person or animal apart from the head and limbs **3** : the main or central part of something **4** : a box or chest used to hold usu. clothes or personal effects (as of a traveler); *also* : the enclosed luggage space in the rear of an automobile **5** : the long muscular nose of an elephant **6** *pl* : men's shorts worn chiefly for sports ⟨swimming ~s⟩ **7** : a usu. major channel or passage

trunk line *n* : a transportation system handling long-distance through traffic

¹truss \'trəs\ *vb* **1** : to secure tightly : BIND **2** : to arrange for cooking by binding close the wings or legs of (a fowl) **3** : to support, strengthen, or stiffen by or as if by a truss

²truss *n* **1** : a collection of structural parts (as beams) forming a rigid framework (as in bridge or building construction) **2** : a device worn to reduce a hernia by pressure

¹trust \'trəst\ *n* **1** : assured reliance on the character, strength, or truth of someone or something **2** : a basis of reliance, faith, or hope **3** : confident hope **4** : financial credit **5** : a property interest held by one person for the benefit of another **6** : a combination of firms formed by a legal agreement; *esp* : one that reduces competition **7** : something entrusted to one to be cared for in the interest of another **8** : CARE, CUSTODY ♦ *Synonyms* CONFIDENCE, DEPENDENCE, FAITH, RELIANCE

²trust *vb* **1** : to place confidence : DEPEND **2** : to be confident : HOPE **3** : ENTRUST **4** : to permit to stay or go or to do something without fear or misgiving **5** : to rely on or on the truth of : BELIEVE **6** : to extend credit to

trust·ee \,trəs-'tē\ *n* **1** : a person to whom property is legally committed in trust **2** : a country charged with the supervision of a trust territory

trust·ee·ship \,trəs-'tē-,ship\ *n* **1** : the office or function of a trustee **2** : supervisory control by one or more nations over a trust territory

trust·ful \'trəst-fəl\ *adj* : full of trust : CONFIDING — **trust·ful·ly** *adv* — **trust·ful·ness** *n*

trust territory *n* : a non-self-governing territory placed under a supervisory authority by the Trusteeship Council of the United Nations

trust·wor·thy \-,wər-thē\ *adj* : worthy of

confidence : DEPENDABLE ✦ **Synonyms** TRUSTY, TRIED, RELIABLE — **trust·wor·thi·ness** n

¹trusty \'trəs-tē\ adj **trust·i·er; -est** : TRUSTWORTHY, DEPENDABLE ⟨a ∼ friend⟩

²trusty \'trəs-tē, ˌtrəs-'tē\ n, pl **trust·ies** : a trusted person; esp : a convict considered trustworthy and allowed special privileges

truth \'trüth\ n, pl **truths** \'trüthz, 'trüths\ 1 : TRUTHFULNESS, HONESTY 2 : the real state of things : FACT 3 : the body of real events or facts : ACTUALITY 4 : a true or accepted statement or proposition ⟨the ∼s of science⟩ 5 : agreement with fact or reality : CORRECTNESS ✦ **Synonyms** VERACITY, VERITY

truth·ful \'trüth-fəl\ adj : telling or disposed to tell the truth — **truth·ful·ly** adv — **truth·ful·ness** n

truth serum n : a drug held to induce a subject under questioning to talk freely

¹try \'trī\ vb **tried; try·ing** [ME trien, fr. AF trier to select, sort, examine, prob. fr. LL tritare to grind] 1 : to examine or investigate judicially 2 : to conduct the trial of 3 : to put to test or trial 4 : to subject to strain, affliction, or annoyance 5 : to extract or clarify (as lard) by melting 6 : to make an effort to do something : ATTEMPT, ENDEAVOR ✦ **Synonyms** ESSAY, ASSAY, STRIVE, STRUGGLE

²try n, pl **tries** : an experimental trial

try·ing adj : severely straining the powers of endurance

try on vb : to put on (a garment) to test the fit and looks

try out vb : to participate in competition esp. for a position on an athletic team or a part in a play — **try·out** \'trī-ˌaut\ n

tryp·to·phan \'trip-tə-ˌfan\ n : a crystalline essential amino acid that is widely distributed in proteins

tryst \'trist\ n 1 : an agreement (as between lovers) to meet 2 : an appointed meeting or meeting place — **tryst** vb — **tryst·er** n

tsar, tsarist var of CZAR, CZARIST

tsarina var of CZARINA

tset·se fly \'tset-sē-, 'tsēt-, 'tet-, 'tēt-, 'set-, 'sēt-\ n : any of several sub-Saharan African dipteran flies including the vector of sleeping sickness

TSgt abbr technical sergeant

T-shirt \'tē-ˌshərt\ n : a collarless shortsleeved or sleeveless cotton undershirt; also : an outer shirt of similar design — **T-shirt·ed** \-ˌshər-təd\ adj

tsk \a click; often read as 'tisk\ interj — used to express disapproval

tsp abbr teaspoon; teaspoonful

T square n : a ruler with a crosspiece at one end for making parallel lines

tsu·na·mi \su̇-'nä-mē, tsu̇-\ n [Jp] : a tidal wave caused esp. by an underwater earthquake or volcanic eruption

TT abbr Trust Territories

TTY abbr teletypewriter

Tu abbr Tuesday

tub \'təb\ n 1 : a wide low bucketlike vessel 2 : BATHTUB; also : BATH 3 : the amount that a tub will hold

tu·ba \'tü-bə, 'tyü-\ n : a large low-pitched brass wind instrument

tub·al \'tü-bəl, 'tyü-\ adj : of, relating to, or involving a tube and esp. a fallopian tube ⟨∼ infection⟩

tube \'tüb, 'tyüb\ n 1 : any of various usu. cylindrical structures or devices; esp : one to convey fluids 2 : a slender hollow anatomical part (as a fallopian tube) functioning as a channel in a plant or animal body : DUCT 3 : a soft round container from which a paste is squeezed 4 : a tunnel for vehicular or rail travel 5 : INNER TUBE 6 : ELECTRON TUBE 7 : TELEVISION — **tubed** \'tübd, 'tyübd\ adj — **tube·less** adj — **tube·like** \'tüb-ˌlīk, 'tyüb-\ adj

tu·ber \'tü-bər, 'tyü-\ n : a short fleshy usu. underground stem (as of a potato plant) bearing minute scalelike leaves each with a bud at its base

tu·ber·cle \'tü-bər-kəl, 'tyü-\ n 1 : a small knobby prominence or outgrowth esp. on an animal or plant 2 : a small abnormal lump in an organ or on the skin; esp : one caused by tuberculosis

tubercle bacillus n : a bacterium that is the cause of tuberculosis

tu·ber·cu·lar \tü-'bər-kyə-lər, tyü-\ adj 1 : TUBERCULOUS 2 : of, resembling, or being a tubercle

tu·ber·cu·lin \tü-'bər-kyə-lən, tyü-\ n : a sterile liquid extracted from the tubercle bacillus and used in the diagnosis of tuberculosis esp. in children and cattle

tu·ber·cu·lo·sis \tü-ˌbər-kyə-'lō-səs, tyü-\ n, pl **-lo·ses** \-ˌsēz\ : a communicable bacterial disease that affects esp. the lungs and is typically marked by fever, cough, difficulty in breathing, and formation of tubercles — **tu·ber·cu·lous** \-'bər-kyə-ləs\ adj

tube·rose \'tüb-ˌrōz, 'tyüb-\ n : a bulbous herb related to the agaves and often grown for its spike of fragrant waxy-white flowers

tu·ber·ous \'tü-bə-rəs, 'tyü-\ adj : of, resembling, or being a tuber

tub·ing \'tü-biŋ, 'tyü-\ n 1 : material in the form of a tube; also : a length of tube 2 : a series or system of tubes

tu·bu·lar \'tü-byə-lər, 'tyü-\ adj : having the form of or consisting of a tube; also : made with tubes

tu·bule \'tü-byül, 'tyü-\ n : a small tube

¹tuck \'tək\ vb 1 : to pull up into a fold ⟨∼ed up her skirt⟩ 2 : to make tucks in 3 : to put into a snug often concealing place ⟨∼ a book under the arm⟩ 4 : to secure in place by pushing the edges under ⟨∼ in a blanket⟩ 5 : to cover by tucking in bedclothes

²tuck n 1 : a fold stitched into cloth to shorten, decorate, or control fullness 2 : a cosmetic surgical operation for the removal of excess skin or fat ⟨a tummy ∼⟩

tuck·er \'tə-kər\ vb **tuck·ered; tuck·er·ing** : EXHAUST, FATIGUE ⟨was ∼ed out after a long day's work⟩

Tues or **Tue** abbr Tuesday

Tues·day \'tüz-dē, 'tyüz-, -dā\ n : the 3d day of the week

tu·fa \'tü-fə, 'tyü-\ n : a porous rock (as travertine) formed as a deposit from springs or streams

tuff \'təf\ n : a rock composed of volcanic detritus

¹**tuft** \'təft\ n 1 : a small cluster of long flexible outgrowths (as hairs); *also* : a bunch of soft fluffy threads cut off short and used as ornament 2 : CLUMP, CLUSTER — **tuft·ed** adj

²**tuft** vb 1 : to provide or adorn with a tuft 2 : to make (as a mattress) firm by stitching at intervals and sewing on tufts — **tuft·er** n

¹**tug** \'təg\ vb **tugged; tug·ging** 1 : to pull hard 2 : to struggle in opposition : CONTEND 3 : to move by pulling hard : HAUL 4 : to tow with a tugboat

²**tug** n 1 : a harness trace 2 : an act of tugging : PULL 3 : a straining effort 4 : a struggle between opposing people or forces 5 : TUGBOAT

tug·boat \-,bōt\ n : a strongly built boat used for towing or pushing

tug–of–war \,təg-əv-'wȯr\ n, pl **tugs–of–war** 1 : a struggle for supremacy 2 : an athletic contest in which two teams pull against each other at opposite ends of a rope

tu·grik or **tu·ghrik** \'tü-grik\ n — see MONEY table

tu·ition \tu̇-'i-shən, tyu̇-\ n : money paid for instruction 〈college ~〉

tu·la·re·mia \,tü-lə-'rē-mē-ə, ,tyü-\ n : an infectious bacterial disease esp. of wild rabbits, rodents, humans, and some domestic animals that in humans is marked by symptoms (as fever) similar to those of influenza

tu·lip \'tü-ləp, 'tyü-\ n [NL *tulipa*, fr. Turk *tülbent* turban] : any of a genus of Eurasian bulbous herbs related to the lilies and grown for their large showy erect cup-shaped flowers; *also* : a flower or bulb of a tulip

tulip tree n : a tall No. American timber tree that is related to the magnolias and has greenish tulip-shaped flowers and soft white wood

tulle \'tül\ n : a sheer often stiffened silk, rayon, or nylon net 〈a veil of ~〉

¹**tum·ble** \'təm-bəl\ vb **tum·bled; tum·bling** [ME, fr. *tumben* to dance, fr. OE *tumbian*] 1 : to fall or cause to fall suddenly and helplessly 2 : to fall into ruin 3 : to perform gymnastic feats of rolling and turning 4 : to roll over and over : TOSS 5 : to issue forth hurriedly and confusedly 6 : to come to understand 7 : to throw together in a confused mass

²**tumble** n 1 : a disorderly state 2 : an act or instance of tumbling

tum·ble–down \'təm-bəl-,dau̇n\ adj : DILAPIDATED, RAMSHACKLE

tum·bler \'təm-blər\ n 1 : one that tumbles; *esp* : ACROBAT 2 : a drinking glass without foot or stem 3 : a movable obstruction in a lock that must be adjusted

to a particular position (as by a key) before the bolt can be thrown

tum·ble·weed \'təm-bəl-,wēd\ n : a plant that breaks away from its roots in autumn and is driven about by the wind

tum·brel or **tum·bril** \'təm-brəl\ n 1 : CART 2 : a vehicle carrying condemned persons (as during the French Revolution) to a place of execution

tu·mid \'tü-məd, 'tyü-\ adj 1 : SWOLLEN, DISTENDED 2 : BOMBASTIC, TURGID

tum·my \'tə-mē\ n, pl **tummies** : BELLY, ABDOMEN, STOMACH

tu·mor \'tü-mər, 'tyü-\ n : an abnormal and functionless new growth of tissue that arises from uncontrolled cellular proliferation — **tu·mor·ous** adj

tu·mour chiefly Brit var of TUMOR

tu·mult \'tü-,məlt, 'tyü-\ n 1 : UPROAR 2 : violent agitation of mind or feelings

tu·mul·tu·ous \tu̇-'məl-chə-wəs, tyu̇-, -chəs\ adj 1 : marked by tumult 2 : tending to incite a tumult 3 : marked by violent upheaval

tun \'tən\ n : a large cask

tu·na \'tü-nə, 'tyü-\ n, pl **tuna** or **tunas** : any of several mostly large marine fishes related to the mackerels and caught for food and sport; *also* : the flesh of a tuna

tun·able \'tü-nə-bəl, 'tyü-\ adj : capable of being tuned — **tun·abil·i·ty** \,tü-nə-'bi-lə-tē, ,tyü-\ n

tun·dra \'tən-drə\ n [Russ] : a treeless plain of arctic and subarctic regions

¹**tune** \'tün, 'tyün\ n 1 : a succession of pleasing musical tones : MELODY 2 : correct musical pitch 3 : harmonious relationship : AGREEMENT 〈in ~ with the times〉 4 : general attitude 〈changed his ~〉 5 : AMOUNT, EXTENT 〈in debt to the ~ of millions〉

²**tune** vb **tuned; tun·ing** 1 : to adjust in musical pitch 2 : to bring or come into harmony : ATTUNE 3 : to put in good working order 4 : to adjust a radio or television receiver so as to receive a broadcast 5 : to adjust the frequency of the output of (a device) to a chosen frequency — **tun·er** n

tune·ful \-fəl\ adj : MELODIOUS, MUSICAL 〈a ~ ballad〉 — **tune·ful·ly** adv — **tune·ful·ness** n

tune·less \-ləs\ adj 1 : UNMELODIOUS 2 : not producing music — **tune·less·ly** adv

tune–up \'tün-,əp, 'tyün-\ n : an adjustment to ensure efficient functioning 〈an engine ~〉

tung·sten \'təŋ-stən\ n [Sw, fr. *tung* heavy + *sten* stone] : a gray-white hard heavy ductile metallic chemical element used esp. in carbide materials, electrical components, and alloys

tu·nic \'tü-nik, 'tyü-\ n 1 : a usu. knee-length belted garment worn by ancient Greeks and Romans 2 : a hip-length or longer blouse or jacket

tuning fork n : a 2-pronged metal implement that gives a fixed tone when struck and is useful for tuning musical instruments

¹**tun·nel** \\'tə-nᵊl\\ *n* : an enclosed passage (as a tube or conduit); *esp* : one underground (as in a mine)

²**tunnel** *vb* **-neled** *or* **-nelled; -nel·ing** *or* **-nel·ling** : to make a tunnel through or under — **tun·nel·er** \\'tən-lər, 'tə-nᵊl-ər\\ *n*

tun·ny \\'tə-nē\\ *n, pl* **tunnies** *also* **tunny** : TUNA

tuque \\'tük, 'tyük\\ *n* [CanF] : a warm knitted cone-shaped cap

tur·ban \\'tər-bən\\ *n* **1** : a headdress worn esp. by Muslims and made of a cap around which is wound a long cloth **2** : a headdress resembling a turban; *esp* : a woman's close-fitting hat without a brim

tur·bid \\'tər-bəd\\ *adj* [L *turbidus* confused, turbid, fr. *turba* confusion, crowd] **1** : cloudy or discolored by suspended particles ⟨a ~ stream⟩ **2** : CONFUSED, MUDDLED — **tur·bid·i·ty** \\tər-'bi-də-tē\\ *n*

tur·bine \\'tər-bən, -₂bīn\\ *n* [F, fr. L *turbin-, turbo* top, whirlwind, whirl] : an engine whose central driveshaft is fitted with curved vanes spun by the pressure of water, steam, or gas

tur·bo·fan \\'tər-bō-₂fan\\ *n* : a jet engine having a fan driven by a turbine for supplying air for combustion

tur·bo·jet \\-₂jet\\ *n* : an airplane powered by a jet engine (**turbojet engine**) having a turbine-driven air compressor supplying compressed air to the combustion chamber

tur·bo·prop \\-₂präp\\ *n* : an airplane powered by a jet engine (**turboprop engine**) having a turbine-driven propeller

tur·bot \\'tər-bət\\ *n, pl* **turbot** *also* **turbots** : a European flatfish that is a popular food fish; *also* : any of several similar flatfishes

tur·bu·lence \\'tər-byə-ləns\\ *n* : the quality or state of being turbulent

tur·bu·lent \\-lənt\\ *adj* **1** : causing violence or disturbance **2** : marked by agitation or tumult : TEMPESTUOUS ⟨a ~ marriage⟩ — **tur·bu·lent·ly** *adv*

tu·reen \\tə-'rēn, tyü-\\ *n* [F *terrine*, fr. MF, fr. fem. of *terrin* of earth] : a deep bowl from which foods (as soup) are served at the table

¹**turf** \\'tərf\\ *n, pl* **turfs** \\'tərfs\\ *also* **turves** \\'tərvz\\ **1** : the upper layer of soil bound by grass and roots into a close mat; *also* : a piece of this **2** : an artificial substitute for turf (as on a playing field) **3** : a piece of peat dried for fuel **4** : a track or course for horse racing; *also* : horse racing as a sport or business

²**turf** *vb* : to cover with turf

tur·gid \\'tər-jəd\\ *adj* **1** : being in a swollen state **2** : excessively embellished in style or language : BOMBASTIC — **tur·gid·i·ty** \\tər-'ji-də-tē\\ *n*

tur·key \\'tər-kē\\ *n, pl* **turkeys** [*Turkey*, country in western Asia and southeastern Europe; fr. confusion with the guinea fowl, supposed to be imported from Turkish territory] : a large No. American bird related to the domestic chicken and widely raised for food

turkey buzzard *n* : TURKEY VULTURE

turkey vulture *n* : an American vulture with a red head and whitish bill

Turk·ish \\'tər-kish\\ *n* : the language of Turkey — **Turkish** *adj*

tur·mer·ic \\'tər-mə-rik\\ *n* : a spice or dyestuff obtained from the large aromatic deep-yellow rhizome of an Indian perennial herb related to the ginger; *also* : this herb

tur·moil \\'tər-₂moi(-ə)l\\ *n* : an extremely confused or agitated condition

¹**turn** \\'tərn\\ *vb* **1** : to move or cause to move around an axis or center : ROTATE, REVOLVE ⟨~ a wheel⟩ **2** : to effect a desired end by turning something ⟨~ the oven on⟩ **3** : WRENCH ⟨~ an ankle⟩ **4** : to change or cause to change position by moving through an arc of a circle ⟨~ed her chair to the fire⟩ **5** : to cause to move around a center so as to show another side of ⟨~ a page⟩ **6** : to revolve mentally : PONDER **7** : to become dizzy : REEL **8** : to reverse the sides or surfaces of ⟨~ a pancake⟩ **9** : UPSET, DISORDER ⟨things were ~ed topsy-turvy⟩ **10** : to set in another esp. contrary direction **11** : to change one's course or direction **12** : to go around ⟨~ a corner⟩ **13** : BECOME ⟨my hair ~ed gray⟩ ⟨~ twenty-one⟩ **14** : to direct toward or away from something; *also* : DEVOTE, APPLY **15** : to have recourse **16** : to become or make hostile **17** : to cause to become of a specified nature or appearance ⟨~s the leaves yellow⟩ **18** : to make or become spoiled : SOUR **19** : to pass from one state to another ⟨water ~s to ice⟩ **20** : CONVERT, TRANSFORM **21** : TRANSLATE, PARAPHRASE **22** : to give a rounded form to; *esp* : to shape by means of a lathe **23** : to gain by passing in trade ⟨~ a quick profit⟩ — **turn·able** \\'tər-nə-bəl\\ *adj* — **turn color 1** : BLUSH **2** : to become pale — **turn loose** : to set free

²**turn** *n* **1** : a turning about a center or axis : REVOLUTION, ROTATION **2** : the action or an act of giving or taking a different direction ⟨make a left ~⟩ **3** : a change of course or tendency ⟨a ~ for the better⟩ **4** : a place at which something turns : BEND, CURVE **5** : a short walk or trip round about ⟨take a ~ around the block⟩ **6** : an act affecting another ⟨did him a good ~⟩ **7** : a place, time, or opportunity accorded in a scheduled order ⟨waited his ~ in line⟩ **8** : a period of duty : SHIFT **9** : a short act esp. in a variety show **10** : a special purpose or requirement ⟨the job serves his ~⟩ **11** : a skillful fashioning ⟨neat ~ of phrase⟩ **12** : a single round (as of rope passed around an object) **13** : natural or special aptitude **14** : a usu. sudden and brief disorder of body or spirits; *esp* : a spell of nervous shock or faintness

turn·about \\'tərn-ə-₂baût\\ *n* **1** : a reversal of direction, trend, or policy **2** : RETALIATION

turn·buck·le \\'tərn-₂bə-kəl\\ *n* : a link with a screw thread at one or both ends for tightening a rod or stay

turn·coat \-,kōt\ n : one who switches to an opposing side or party : TRAITOR

turn down vb : to decline to accept : REJECT — **turn-down** \'tərn-,daůn\ n

turn·er \'tər-nər\ n 1 : one that turns or is used for turning 2 : one that forms articles with a lathe

turn·ery \'tər-nə-rē\ n, pl -er·ies : the work, products, or shop of a turner

turn in vb 1 : to deliver up 2 : to inform on 3 : to acquit oneself of ⟨turn in a good job⟩ 4 : to go to bed

turn·ing \'tər-niŋ\ n 1 : the act or course of one that turns 2 : a place of a change of direction

tur·nip \'tər-nəp\ n 1 : a garden herb related to the cabbage with a thick edible usu. white root 2 : RUTABAGA 3 : the root of a turnip

turn·key \'tərn-,kē\ n, pl **turnkeys** : one who has charge of a prison's keys

turn·off \'tərn-,óf\ n : a place for turning off esp. from an expressway

turn off vb 1 : to deviate from a straight course or a main road 2 : to stop the functioning or flow of 3 : to cause to lose interest; also : to evoke a negative feeling in

turn on vb 1 : to cause to flow, function, or operate 2 : to get high or cause to get high as a result of taking a drug (as marijuana) 3 : EXCITE, STIMULATE

turn·out \'tərn-,aůt\ n 1 : an act of turning out 2 : the number of people who participate or attend an event 3 : a widened place in a highway for vehicles to pass or park 4 : manner of dress 5 : net yield : OUTPUT

turn out vb 1 : EXPEL, EVICT 2 : PRODUCE 3 : to cause to stop functioning by turning a switch 4 : to come forth and assemble 5 : to get out of bed 6 : to prove to be in the end

¹**turn·over** \'tərn-,ō-vər\ n 1 : UPSET 2 : SHIFT, REVERSAL 3 : a filled pastry made by turning half of the crust over the other half 4 : the volume of business done 5 : movement (as of goods or people) into, through, and out of a place 6 : the number of persons hired within a period to replace those leaving or dropped 7 : an instance of a team's losing possession of the ball esp. through error

²**turnover** adj : capable of being turned over

turn over vb : TRANSFER ⟨turn the job over to her⟩

turn·pike \'tərn-,pīk\ n [ME turnepike revolving frame bearing spikes and serving as a barrier, fr. turnen to turn + pike] 1 : TOLLGATE; also : an expressway on which tolls are charged 2 : a main road

turn·stile \-,stī(-ə)l\ n : a post with arms pivoted on the top set in a passageway so that persons can pass through only on foot one by one

turn·ta·ble \-,tā-bəl\ n : a circular platform that revolves (as for turning a locomotive or a phonograph record)

turn to vb : to apply oneself to work

turn up vb 1 : to come to light or bring to light : DISCOVER, APPEAR 2 : to raise or increase by or as if by turning a control 3 : to arrive at an appointed time or place 4 : to happen unexpectedly

tur·pen·tine \'tər-pən-,tīn\ n 1 : a mixture of oil and resin obtained from various cone-bearing trees (as pines) 2 : an oil distilled from turpentine or pine wood and used as a solvent and paint thinner

tur·pi·tude \'tər-pə-,tüd, -,tyüd\ n : inherent baseness : DEPRAVITY

tur·quoise also **tur·quois** \'tər-,kòiz, -,kwòiz\ n [ME turkeys, fr. AF turkeise, fr. fem. of turkeis Turkish; fr. Turc Turk] 1 : a blue, bluish green, or greenish gray mineral that is valued as a gem 2 : a light greenish blue color

tur·ret \'tər-ət\ n 1 : a little ornamental tower often at a corner of a building 2 : a low usu. revolving structure (as on a tank or warship) in which one or more guns are mounted — **tur·ret·ed** \'tər-ə-təd\ adj

¹**tur·tle** \'tər-t²l\ n, archaic : TURTLEDOVE

²**turtle** n, pl **turtles** also **turtle** : any of an order of horny-beaked land, freshwater, or sea reptiles with the trunk enclosed in a bony shell

tur·tle·dove \'tər-t²l-,dəv\ n : any of several small pigeons noted for plaintive cooing

tur·tle·neck \-,nek\ n : a high close-fitting turnover collar (as on a sweater); also : a sweater or shirt with a turtleneck — **tur·tle·necked** \-,nekt\ adj

turves pl of TURF

Tus·ca·ro·ra \,təs-kə-'ròr-ə\ n, pl **Tuscarora** or **Tuscaroras** : a member of an American Indian people of No. Carolina and later of New York and Ontario

tusk \'təsk\ n : a long enlarged protruding tooth (as of an elephant, walrus, or boar) used esp. to dig up food or as a weapon — **tusked** \'təskt\ adj

tusk·er \'təs-kər\ n : an animal with tusks; esp : a male elephant with two normally developed tusks

¹**tus·sle** \'tə-səl\ n 1 : a physical struggle : SCUFFLE 2 : an intense argument, controversy, or struggle

²**tussle** vb **tus·sled; tus·sling** : to struggle roughly

tus·sock \'tə-sək\ n : a dense tuft esp. of grass or sedge; also : a hummock in a marsh or bog bound together by roots — **tus·socky** adj

tu·te·lage \'tü-t²l-ij, 'tyü-\ n 1 : an act of guarding or protecting 2 : the state of being under a guardian or tutor 3 : instruction esp. of an individual

tu·te·lary \'tü-t²-,ler-ē, 'tyü-\ adj : acting as a guardian ⟨~ deity⟩

¹**tu·tor** \'tü-tər, 'tyü-\ n 1 : a person charged with the instruction and guidance of another 2 : a private teacher

²**tutor** vb 1 : to have the guardianship of 2 : to teach or guide individually : COACH ⟨~ed her in Latin⟩ 3 : to receive instruction esp. privately

tu·to·ri·al \tü-'tòr-ē-əl, tyü-\ n : a class

conducted by a tutor for one student or a small number of students

tut·ti \'tü-tē, 'tù-, -ˌtē\ *adj or adv* [It, pl. of *tutto* all] : with all voices and instruments playing together — used as a direction in music

tut·ti-frut·ti \ˌtü-ti-'frü-tē, ˌtù-\ *n* [It, lit., all fruits] : a confection or ice cream containing chopped usu. candied fruits

tu·tu \'tü-(ˌ)tü\ *n* [F] : a short projecting skirt worn by a ballerina

tux·e·do \ˌtək-'sē-dō\ *n, pl* **-dos** *or* **-does** [*Tuxedo* Park, N.Y.] **1** : a usu. black or blackish blue jacket **2** : a semiformal evening suit for men

TV \'tē-'vē\ *n* : TELEVISION

TVA *abbr* Tennessee Valley Authority

TV dinner *n* : a frozen packaged dinner that needs only heating before serving

twad·dle \'twä-d²l\ *n* : silly idle talk : DRIVEL — **twaddle** *vb*

twain \'twān\ *n* **1** : TWO **2** : PAIR

¹twang \'twaŋ\ *n* **1** : a harsh quick ringing sound like that of a plucked bowstring **2** : nasal speech or resonance **3** : the characteristic speech of a region

²twang *vb* **twanged; twang·ing 1** : to sound or cause to sound with a twang **2** : to speak with a nasal twang

tweak \'twēk\ *vb* **1** : to pinch and pull with a sudden jerk and twitch **2** : to make small adjustments to — **tweak** *n*

tweed \'twēd\ *n* **1** : a rough woolen fabric made usu. in twill weaves **2** *pl* : tweed clothing; *esp* : a tweed suit

tweedy \'twē-dē\ *adj* **tweed·i·er; -est 1** : of or resembling tweed **2** : given to wearing tweeds **3** : suggestive of the outdoors in taste or habits

tween \'twēn\ *prep* : BETWEEN

tweet \'twēt\ *n* : a chirping note — **tweet** *vb*

tweet·er \'twē-tər\ *n* : a small loudspeaker that reproduces sounds of high pitch

twee·zers \'twē-zərz\ *n pl* [obs. E *tweeze* n., case for small implements, short for obs. E *etweese*, fr. pl. of obs. E *etwee*, fr. F *étui*] : a small pincerlike implement usu. held between the thumb and index finger and used for grasping something

twelve \'twelv\ *n* **1** : one more than 11 **2** : the 12th in a set or series **3** : something having 12 units — **twelfth** \'twelfth\ *adj or n* — **twelve** *adj or pron*

twelve·month \-ˌmənth\ *n* : YEAR

12–step \'twelv-ˌstep\ *adj* : of, relating to, or being a program designed esp. to help someone overcome a problem (as an addiction) by following 12 tenets

twen·ty \'twen-tē\ *n, pl* **twenties** : two times 10 — **twen·ti·eth** \-tē-əth\ *adj or n* — **twenty** *adj or pron*

twenty–twenty *or* **20/20** \ˌtwen-tē-'twen-tē\ *adj* : characterized by a visual capacity for seeing detail that is normal for the human eye ⟨∼ vision⟩

twice \'twīs\ *adv* **1** : on two occasions **2** : two times ⟨twice is four⟩

¹twid·dle \'twi-d²l\ *vb* **twid·dled; twid·dling 1** : to be busy with trifles; *also* : to play idly with something **2** : to rotate lightly or idly

²twiddle *n* : TURN, TWIST

twig \'twig\ *n* : a small branch — **twig·gy** *adj*

twi·light \'twī-ˌlīt\ *n* **1** : the light from the sky between full night and sunrise or between sunset and full night **2** : a state of imperfect clarity **3** : a period of decline

twilight zone *n* **1** : an area just beyond ordinary legal or ethical limits **2** : TWILIGHT 2 **3** : a world of fantasy or unreality

twill \'twil\ *n* [ME *twyll*, fr. OE *twilic* having a double thread, part trans. of L *bilic-, bilix*, fr. *bi-* two + *licium* thread] **1** : a fabric with a twill weave **2** : a textile weave that gives an appearance of diagonal lines

twilled \'twild\ *adj* : made with a twill weave

¹twin \'twin\ *n* **1** : either of two offspring produced at a birth **2** : one of two persons or things closely related to or resembling each other

²twin *vb* **twinned; twin·ning 1** : to be coupled with another **2** : to bring forth twins

³twin *adj* **1** : born with one other or as a pair at one birth ⟨∼ brother⟩ ⟨∼ girls⟩ **2** : made up of two similar or related members or parts **3** : being one of a pair ⟨∼ city⟩

¹twine \'twīn\ *n* **1** : a strong thread of two or three strands twisted together **2** : an act of entwining or interlacing — **twiny** *adj*

²twine *vb* **twined; twin·ing 1** : to twist together; *also* : to form by twisting **2** : INTERLACE, WEAVE **3** : to coil about a support **4** : to stretch or move in a sinuous manner — **twin·er** *n*

¹twinge \'twinj\ *vb* **twinged; twing·ing** *or* **twinge·ing** : to affect with or feel a sharp sudden pain

²twinge *n* : a sudden sharp stab (as of pain or distress)

¹twin·kle \'twiŋ-kəl\ *vb* **twin·kled; twin·kling 1** : to shine or cause to shine with a flickering or sparkling light **2** : to appear bright with merriment **3** : to flutter or flit rapidly — **twin·kler** *n*

²twinkle *n* **1** : a wink of the eyelids; *also* : the duration of a wink **2** : an intermittent radiance **3** : a rapid flashing motion — **twin·kly** \'twiŋ-klē\ *adj*

twin·kling \'twiŋ-kliŋ\ *n* : the time required for a wink : INSTANT

¹twirl \'twərl\ *vb* : to turn or cause to turn rapidly ⟨∼ a baton⟩ ◆ *Synonyms* REVOLVE, ROTATE, CIRCLE, SPIN, SWIRL, PIROUETTE — **twirl·er** *n*

²twirl *n* **1** : an act of twirling **2** : COIL, WHORL — **twirly** \'twər-lē\ *adj*

twist \'twist\ *vb* **1** : to unite by winding one thread or strand round another **2** : WREATHE, TWINE **3** : to turn so as to hurt : SPRAIN ⟨∼ed my ankle⟩ **4** : to twirl into spiral shape **5** : to subject (as a shaft) to torsion **6** : to turn from the true form or meaning **7** : to pull off or break by torsion **8** : to follow a winding course **9** : to turn around

²**twist** *n* **1** : something formed by twisting or winding **2** : an act of twisting : the state of being twisted **3** : a spiral turn or curve; *also* : SPIN **4** : a turning aside **5** : ECCENTRICITY **6** : a distortion of meaning **7** : an unexpected turn or development **8** : DEVICE, TRICK **9** : a variant approach or method

twist·er \'twis-tər\ *n* **1** : one that twists; *esp* : a ball with a forward and spinning motion **2** : TORNADO; *also* : WATERSPOUT 2

¹**twit** \'twit\ *n* : FOOL

²**twit** *vb* **twit·ted; twit·ting** : to ridicule as a fault; *also* : TAUNT ✦ **Synonyms** DERIDE, MOCK, RAZZ

¹**twitch** \'twich\ *vb* **1** : to move or pull with a sudden motion : JERK **2** : to move jerkily : QUIVER **3** : to have a twitch

²**twitch** *n* **1** : an act or movement of twitching **2** : a brief spasmodic contraction of muscle fibers

¹**twit·ter** \'twi-tər\ *vb* **1** : to make a succession of chirping noises **2** : to talk in a chattering fashion **3** : to tremble with agitation : FLUTTER

²**twitter** *n* **1** : a slight agitation of the nerves **2** : a small tremulous intermittent noise (as made by a swallow) **3** : a light chattering

twixt \'twikst\ *prep* : BETWEEN 〈∼ the two extremes〉

two \'tü\ *n, pl* **twos** **1** : one more than one **2** : the second in a set or series **3** : something having two units — **two** *adj or pron*

two cents *n* **1** *or* **two cents' worth** : an opinion offered on a topic under discussion **2** : a sum or object of very small value

two–faced \'tü-'fāst\ *adj* **1** : DOUBLE-DEALING, FALSE **2** : having two faces

two·fold \'tü-,fōld, -'fōld\ *adj* **1** : having two units or members **2** : being twice as much or as many — **twofold** \-'fōld\ *adv*

2,4–D \,tü-,fôr-'dē\ *n* : an irritant compound used esp. as a weed killer

2,4,5–T \-,fiv-'tē\ *n* : an irritant compound used esp. as an herbicide and defoliant

two·pence \'tə-pəns, *US also* 'tü-,pens\ *n* : the sum of two pence

two·pen·ny \'tə-pə-nē, *US also* 'tü-,pe-nē\ *adj* : of the value of or costing twopence

two·ply \'tü-'plī\ *adj* **1** : woven as a double cloth **2** : consisting of two strands or thicknesses

two·some \'tü-səm\ *n* **1** : a group of two persons or things : COUPLE **2** : a golf match between two players

two·step \'tü-,step\ *n* : a ballroom dance performed with a sliding step in march or polka time; *also* : a piece of music for this dance — **two·step** *vb*

two·time \'tü-,tīm\ *vb* : to betray (a spouse or lover) by secret lovemaking with another — **two·tim·er** *n*

two·way *adj* : involving two elements or allowing movement or use in two directions or manners

2WD *abbr* two-wheel drive

twp *abbr* township

TWX *abbr* teletypewriter exchange

TX *abbr* Texas

ty·coon \tī-'kün\ *n* [Jp *taikun* feudal lord] **1** : a masterful leader (as in politics) **2** : a powerful businessman or industrialist

tyin \'tēn\ *n, pl* **tyin** — see *tenge* at MONEY table

tying *pres part of* TIE

ty·iyn \tē-'en\ *n, pl* **tyiyn** — see *som* at MONEY table

tyke \'tīk\ *n* : a small child

tym·pan·ic membrane \tim-'pa-nik-\ *n* : EARDRUM

tym·pa·num \'tim-pə-nəm\ *n, pl* **-na** \-nə\ *also* **-nums** : EARDRUM; *also* : MIDDLE EAR — **tym·pan·ic** \tim-'pa-nik\ *adj*

¹**type** \'tīp\ *n* [ME, fr. LL *typus*, fr. L & Gk; L *typus* image, fr. Gk *typos* blow, impression, model, fr. *typtein* to strike, beat] **1** : a person, thing, or event that foreshadows another to come : TOKEN, SYMBOL **2** : MODEL, EXAMPLE **3** : a distinctive stamp, mark, or sign : EMBLEM **4** : rectangular blocks usu. of metal each having a face so shaped as to produce a character when printed **5** : the letters or characters printed from or as if from type **6** : general character or form common to a number of individuals and setting them off as a distinguishable class 〈horses of draft ∼〉 **7** : a class, kind, or group set apart by common characteristics 〈a seedless ∼ of orange〉; *also* : something distinguishable as a variety 〈reactions of this ∼〉 ✦ **Synonyms** SORT, NATURE, CHARACTER, DESCRIPTION

²**type** *vb* **typed; typ·ing** **1** : to represent beforehand as a type **2** : to produce a copy of; *also* : REPRESENT, TYPIFY **3** : to write with a typewriter or computer keyboard **4** : to identify as belonging to a type **5** : TYPECAST

type A *adj* : relating to, having, or being a personality marked esp. by impatience and aggressiveness

type·cast \-,kast\ *vb* **-cast; -cast·ing** **1** : to cast (an actor) in a part calling for characteristics possessed by the actor **2** : to cast repeatedly in the same type of role

type·face \-,fās\ *n* : all type of a single design

type 1 diabetes \'tīp-'wən-\ *n* : a form of diabetes mellitus usu. developing before adulthood and marked by severe insulin deficiency

type·script \'tīp-,skript\ *n* : typewritten matter

type·set \-,set\ *vb* **-set; -set·ting** : to set in type : COMPOSE — **type·set·ter** *n*

type 2 diabetes \-'tü-\ *n* : a form of diabetes mellitus developing esp. in adults and usu. in obese individuals and marked by excess sugar in the blood

type·write \-,rīt\ *vb* **-wrote** \-,rōt\; **-writ·ten** \-,ri-t²n\ : TYPE 3

type·writ·er \-,rī-tər\ *n* **1** : a machine for writing in characters similar to those produced by printers' type by means of types striking a ribbon to transfer ink or carbon impressions onto paper **2** : TYPIST

type·writ·ing \-,rī-tiṇ\ *n* : the use of a typewriter ⟨teach ∼⟩; *also* : writing produced with a typewriter

¹ty·phoid \'tī-,fȯid, tī-'fȯid\ *adj* : of, relating to, or being a communicable bacterial disease (**typhoid fever**) marked by fever, diarrhea, prostration, and intestinal inflammation

²typhoid *n* : TYPHOID FEVER

ty·phoon \tī-'fün\ *n* : a hurricane occurring esp. in the region of the Philippines or the China sea

ty·phus \'tī-fəs\ *n* : a severe infectious disease transmitted esp. by body lice, caused by a rickettsia, and marked by high fever, stupor and delirium, intense headache, and a dark red rash

typ·i·cal \'ti-pi-kəl\ *adj* **1** : being or having the nature of a type **2** : exhibiting the essential characteristics of a group **3** : conforming to a type — **typ·i·cal·i·ty** \,ti-pə-'ka-lə-tē\ *n* — **typ·i·cal·ness** *n*

typ·i·cal·ly \-pi-k(ə-)lē\ *adv* **1** : in a typical manner **2** : in typical circumstances

typ·i·fy \'ti-pə-,fī\ *vb* **-fied; -fy·ing 1** : to represent by an image, form, model, or resemblance **2** : to embody the essential or common characteristics of

typ·ist \'tī-pist\ *n* : a person who types esp. as a job

ty·po \'tī-pō\ *n, pl* **typos** : an error (as of spelling) in typed or typeset material

ty·pog·ra·pher \tī-'pä-grə-fər\ *n* : one who designs or arranges printing

ty·pog·ra·phy \tī-'pä-grə-fē\ *n* : the art of printing with type; *also* : the style, arrangement, or appearance of printed matter — **ty·po·graph·ic** \,tī-pə-'gra-fik\ *or* **ty·po·graph·i·cal** \-fi-kəl\ *adj* — **ty·po·graph·i·cal·ly** *adv*

ty·ran·ni·cal \tə-'ra-ni-kəl, tī-\ *also* **ty·ran·nic** \-nik\ *adj* : of or relating to a tyrant : DESPOTIC ◆ **Synonyms** ARBITRARY, ABSOLUTE, AUTOCRATIC — **ty·ran·ni·cal·ly** \-ni-k(ə-)lē\ *adv*

tyr·an·nise *Brit var of* TYRANNIZE

tyr·an·nize \'tir-ə-,nīz\ *vb* **-nized; -niz·ing** : to act as a tyrant : rule with unjust severity — **tyr·an·niz·er** *n*

ty·ran·no·saur \tə-'ra-nə-,sȯr\ *n* : a massive American flesh-eating dinosaur of the Cretaceous that had small forelegs and walked on its hind legs

ty·ran·no·sau·rus \tə-,ra-nə-'sȯr-əs\ *n* : TYRANNOSAUR

tyr·an·nous \'tir-ə-nəs\ *adj* : unjustly severe — **tyr·an·nous·ly** *adv*

tyr·an·ny \'tir-ə-nē\ *n, pl* **-nies 1** : oppressive power **2** : the rule or authority of a tyrant : government in which absolute power is vested in a single ruler **3** : a tyrannical act

ty·rant \'tī-rənt\ *n* **1** : an absolute ruler : DESPOT **2** : a ruler who governs oppressively or brutally **3** : one who uses authority or power harshly

tyre *chiefly Brit var of* ²TIRE

ty·ro \'tī-rō\ *n, pl* **tyros** [ML, fr. L *tiro* young soldier, tyro] : a beginner in learning : NOVICE

tzar, tzarist *var of* CZAR, CZARIST

¹u \'yü\ *n, pl* **u's** *or* **us** \'yüz\ *often cap* : the 21st letter of the English alphabet

²u *abbr, often cap* unit

¹U \'yü\ *adj* : characteristic of the upper classes

²U *abbr* **1** [abbr. of *Union of Orthodox Hebrew Congregations*] kosher certification — often enclosed in a circle **2** university **3** unsatisfactory

³U *symbol* uranium

UAE *abbr* United Arab Emirates

UAR *abbr* United Arab Republic

UAW *abbr* United Automobile Workers

ubiq·ui·tous \yü-'bi-kwə-təs\ *adj* : existing or being everywhere at the same time : OMNIPRESENT — **ubiq·ui·tous·ly** *adv* — **ubiq·ui·ty** \-kwə-tē\ *n*

U-boat \'yü-,bōt\ *n* [trans. of G *U-boot*, short for *Unterseeboot*, lit., undersea boat] : a German submarine

UC *abbr* uppercase

ud·der \'ə-dər\ *n* : an organ (as of a cow) consisting of two or more milk glands enclosed in a large hanging sac and each provided with a nipple

UFO \,yü-(,)ef-'ō\ *n, pl* **UFO's** *or* **UFOs** \-'ōz\ : an unidentified flying object; *esp* : FLYING SAUCER

ug·ly \'ə-glē\ *adj* **ug·li·er; -est** [ME, fr. ON *ugligr*, fr. *uggr* fear] **1** : FRIGHTFUL, DIRE **2** : offensive to the sight : HIDEOUS **3** : offensive or unpleasant to any sense **4** : morally objectionable : REPULSIVE **5** : likely to cause inconvenience or discomfort **.6** : SURLY, QUARRELSOME ⟨an ∼ disposition⟩ — **ug·li·ness** \-glē-nəs\ *n*

UHF *abbr* ultrahigh frequency

UK *abbr* United Kingdom

ukase \yü-'kās, -'kāz\ *n* [F & Russ; F, fr. Russ *ukaz*, fr. *ukazat'* to show, order] : an edict esp. of a Russian emperor or government

uku·le·le *also* **uke·le·le** \,yü-kə-'lā-lē\ *n* [Hawaiian *'ukulele*, fr. *'uku* flea + *lele* jumping] : a small usu. 4-stringed guitar popularized in Hawaii

ul·cer \'əl-sər\ *n* **1** : an open eroded sore of skin or mucous membrane often discharging pus **2** : something that festers and corrupts like an open sore — **ul·cer·ous** *adj*

ul·cer·ate \'əl-sə-ˌrāt\ vb -at·ed; -at·ing : to become affected with an ulcer — **ul·cer·a·tive** \'əl-sə-ˌrā-tiv\ adj

ul·cer·a·tion \ˌəl-sə-'rā-shən\ n 1 : the process of forming or state of having an ulcer 2 : ULCER 1

ul·na \'əl-nə\ n : the bone on the little-finger side of the human forearm; also : a corresponding bone of the forelimb of vertebrates above fishes

ul·ster \'əl-stər\ n : a long loose overcoat

ult abbr 1 ultimate 2 ultimo

ul·te·ri·or \ˌəl-'tir-ē-ər\ adj 1 : lying farther away : more remote 2 : situated beyond or on the farther side 3 : going beyond what is openly said or shown : HIDDEN ⟨~ motives⟩

¹**ul·ti·mate** \'əl-tə-mət\ adj 1 : most remote in space or time : FARTHEST 2 : last in a progression : FINAL 3 : the best or most extreme of its kind 4 : arrived at as the last resort 5 : FUNDAMENTAL, ABSOLUTE, SUPREME ⟨~ reality⟩ 6 : incapable of further analysis or division : ELEMENTAL 7 : MAXIMUM ♦ **Synonyms** CONCLUDING, EVENTUAL, LATEST, TERMINAL — **ul·ti·mate·ly** adv

²**ultimate** n : something ultimate

ul·ti·ma·tum \ˌəl-tə-'mā-təm, -'mä-\ n, pl -tums or -ta \-tə\ : a final condition or demand whose rejection will bring about a resort to forceful action

ul·ti·mo \'əl-tə-ˌmō\ adj [L ultimo mense in the last month] : of or occurring in the month preceding the present

¹**ul·tra** \'əl-trə\ adj : going beyond others or beyond due limits : EXTREME

²**ultra** n : EXTREMIST

ul·tra·con·ser·va·tive \-kən-'sər-və-tiv\ adj : extremely conservative

ul·tra·high frequency \-'hī-\ n : a radio frequency between 300 and 3000 megahertz

¹**ul·tra·light** \'əl-trə-ˌlīt\ adj : extremely light esp. in weight

²**ultralight** n : a very light recreational aircraft typically carrying only one person

ul·tra·ma·rine \ˌəl-trə-mə-'rēn\ n 1 : a deep blue pigment 2 : a very bright deep blue color

ul·tra·mi·cro·scop·ic \-ˌmī-krə-'skä-pik\ adj : too small to be seen with an ordinary microscope

ul·tra·mod·ern \-'mä-dərn\ adj : extremely or excessively modern in idea, style, or tendency

ul·tra·mon·tane \-'män-ˌtān, -ˌmän-'tān\ adj 1 : of or relating to countries or peoples beyond the mountains (as the Alps) 2 : favoring greater or absolute supremacy of papal over national or diocesan authority in the Roman Catholic Church — **ultramontane** n, often cap — **ul·tra·mon·tan·ism** \-'män-tə-ˌni-zəm\ n

ul·tra·pure \-'pyu̇r\ adj : of the utmost purity

ul·tra·short \-'shȯrt\ adj 1 : having a wavelength below 10 meters 2 : very short in duration

ul·tra·son·ic \ˌəl-trə-'sä-nik\ adj : having a frequency too high to be heard by the human ear — **ul·tra·son·i·cal·ly** \-ni-k(ə-)lē\ adv

ul·tra·son·ics \-'sä-niks\ n sing or pl 1 : ultrasonic vibrations 2 : the science of ultrasonic phenomena

ul·tra·sound \-ˌsau̇nd\ n 1 : ultrasonic vibrations 2 : the diagnostic or therapeutic use of ultrasound and esp. a technique involving the formation of a two-dimensional image of internal body structures 3 : a diagnostic examination using ultrasound

ul·tra·vi·o·let \-'vī-ə-lət\ adj : having a wavelength shorter than those of visible light and longer than those of X-rays ⟨~ radiation⟩; also : producing or employing ultraviolet radiation — **ultraviolet** n

ul·tra vi·res \ˌəl-trə-'vī-rēz\ adv or adj [NL, lit., beyond power] : beyond the scope of legal power or authority

ul·u·late \'əl-yə-ˌlāt\ vb -lat·ed; -lat·ing : HOWL, WAIL

uma·mi \ü-'mä-mē\ n [Jp, flavor] : a meaty or savory taste sensation produced esp. by monosodium glutamate

um·bel \'əm-bəl\ n : a flat-topped or rounded flower cluster in which the individual flower stalks all arise near one point on the main stem

um·ber \'əm-bər\ n : a brown earthy substance valued as a pigment either in its raw state or burnt — **umber** adj

umbilical cord n : a cord containing blood vessels that connects the navel of a fetus with the placenta of its mother

um·bi·li·cus \ˌəm-'bi-li-kəs, ˌəm-bə-'lī-\ n, pl **um·bi·li·ci** \ˌəm-'bi-lə-ˌkī, ˌəm-bə-'lī-ˌkī, -ˌsī\ or **um·bi·li·cus·es** : NAVEL — **um·bil·i·cal** \ˌəm-'bi-li-kəl\ adj

um·bra \'əm-brə\ n, pl **umbras** or **um·brae** \-(ˌ)brē, -ˌbrā\ 1 : SHADE, SHADOW 2 : the conical part of the shadow of a celestial body from which the sun's light is completely blocked

um·brage \'əm-brij\ n 1 : SHADE; also : FOLIAGE 2 : RESENTMENT, OFFENSE ⟨take ~ at a remark⟩

um·brel·la \ˌəm-'bre-lə\ n 1 : a collapsible shade for protection against weather consisting of fabric stretched over hinged ribs radiating from a center pole 2 : something that provides protection 3 : something that covers a range of elements

umi·ak \'ü-mē-ˌak\ n : an open Eskimo boat made of a wooden frame covered with skins

ump \'əmp\ n : UMPIRE

um·pire \'əm-ˌpī(-ə)r\ n [ME oumpere, alter. of noumpere (the phrase a noumpere being understood as an oumpere), fr. AF nounpier single, odd, fr. non not + per equal, fr. L par] 1 : one having authority to decide finally a controversy or question between parties 2 : an official in a sport who rules on plays — **umpire** vb

ump·teen \'əmp-ˌtēn\ adj : very many : indefinitely numerous — **ump·teenth** \-ˌtēnth\ adj

UN abbr United Nations

un- \ˌən, ˈən\ *prefix* **1** : not : IN-, NON- **2** : opposite of : contrary to

un·able \ˌən-ˈā-bəl\ *adj* **1** : not able **2** : UNQUALIFIED, INCOMPETENT

un·abridged \ˌən-ə-ˈbrijd\ *adj* **1** : not abridged ⟨an ∼ edition of Shakespeare⟩ **2** : complete of its class : not based on one larger ⟨an ∼ dictionary⟩

un·ac·com·pa·nied \ˌən-ə-ˈkəm-pə-nēd\ *adj* : not accompanied; *esp* : being without instrumental accompaniment

un·ac·count·able \ˌən-ə-ˈkaún-tə-bəl\ *adj* **1** : not to be accounted for : INEXPLICABLE **2** : not responsible — **un·ac·count·ably** \-blē\ *adv*

un·ac·count·ed \-ˈkaún-təd\ *adj* : not accounted ⟨the loss was ∼ for⟩

un·ac·cus·tomed \ˌən-ə-ˈkəs-təmd\ *adj* **1** : not customary : not usual or common **2** : not accustomed or habituated ⟨∼ to noise⟩

un·adul·ter·at·ed \ˌən-ə-ˈdəl-tə-ˌrā-təd\ *adj* : PURE, UNMIXED ✦ *Synonyms* ABSOLUTE, SHEER, SIMPLE, UNALLOYED, UNDILUTED, UNMITIGATED

un·af·fect·ed \ˌən-ə-ˈfek-təd\ *adj* **1** : not influenced or changed mentally, physically, or chemically **2** : free from affectation : NATURAL, GENUINE — **un·af·fect·ed·ly** *adv*

un·alien·able \-ˈāl-yə-nə-bəl, -ˈā-lē-ə-\ *adj* : INALIENABLE

un·aligned \ˌən-ə-ˈlīnd\ *adj* : not associated with any one of competing international blocs ⟨∼ nations⟩

un·al·loyed \ˌən-ə-ˈlóid\ *adj* : UNMIXED, UNQUALIFIED, PURE ⟨∼ happiness⟩

un·al·ter·able \ˌən-ˈól-tə-rə-bəl\ *adj* : not capable of being altered or changed — **un·al·ter·ably** \-blē\ *adv*

un—Amer·i·can \ˌən-ə-ˈmer-ə-kən\ *adj* : not characteristic of or consistent with American customs or principles

unan·i·mous \yú-ˈna-nə-məs\ *adj* [L *unanimus*, fr. *unus* one + *animus* mind] **1** : being of one mind : AGREEING **2** : formed with or indicating the agreement of all — **una·nim·i·ty** \ˌyü-nə-ˈni-mə-tē\ *n* — **unan·i·mous·ly** *adv*

un·arm \ˌən-ˈärm\ *vb* : DISARM

un·armed \-ˈärmd\ *adj* : not armed or armored ⟨∼ civilians⟩

un·as·sail·able \ˌən-ə-ˈsā-lə-bəl\ *adj* : not liable to doubt, attack, or question ⟨an ∼ argument⟩

un·as·sum·ing \ˌən-ə-ˈsü-miŋ\ *adj* : MODEST ⟨an ∼ librarian⟩ ⟨an ∼ manner⟩ ⟨an ∼ neighborhood⟩ ✦ *Synonyms* HUMBLE, LOWLY, MEEK

un·at·tached \ˌən-ə-ˈtacht\ *adj* **1** : not married or engaged **2** : not joined or united

un·avail·ing \ˌən-ə-ˈvā-liŋ\ *adj* : being of no avail — **un·avail·ing·ly** *adv*

un·avoid·able \ˌən-ə-ˈvói-də-bəl\ *adj* : not avoidable : INEVITABLE ✦ *Synonyms* CERTAIN, INELUCTABLE, INESCAPABLE, NECESSARY — **un·avoid·ably** \-blē\ *adv*

¹**un·aware** \ˌən-ə-ˈwer\ *adv* : UNAWARES

²**unaware** *adj* : not aware : IGNORANT — **un·aware·ness** *n*

un·awares \-ˈwerz\ *adv* **1** : without knowing : UNINTENTIONALLY **2** : without warning : by surprise ⟨taken ∼⟩

un·bal·anced \ˌən-ˈba-lənst\ *adj* **1** : not in a state of balance **2** : mentally disordered **3** : not adjusted so as to make credits equal to debits

un·bar \-ˈbär\ *vb* : UNBOLT, OPEN

un·bear·able \ˌən-ˈber-ə-bəl\ *adj* : greater than can be borne ⟨∼ pain⟩ ✦ *Synonyms* INSUFFERABLE, INSUPPORTABLE, INTOLERABLE, UNENDURABLE, UNSUPPORTABLE — **un·bear·ably** \-blē\ *adv*

un·beat·able \-ˈbē-tə-bəl\ *adj* : not capable of being defeated ✦ *Synonyms* INDOMITABLE, INVINCIBLE, INVULNERABLE, UNCONQUERABLE

un·beat·en \-ˈbē-t°n\ *adj* **1** : not pounded, beaten, or whipped **2** : UNTRODDEN **3** : UNDEFEATED

un·be·com·ing \ˌən-bi-ˈkə-miŋ\ *adj* : not becoming : UNSUITABLE, IMPROPER ✦ *Synonyms* INDECOROUS, INDECENT, INDELICATE, UNSEEMLY — **un·be·com·ing·ly** *adv*

un·be·knownst \ˌən-bi-ˈnōnst\ *also* **un·be·known** \-ˈnōn\ *adj* : happening or existing without one's knowledge

un·be·lief \ˌən-bə-ˈlēf\ *n* : the withholding or absence of belief : DOUBT — **un·be·liev·ing** \-ˈlē-viŋ\ *adj*

un·be·liev·able \-ˈlē-və-bəl\ *adj* : too improbable for belief; *also* : of such a superlative degree as to be hard to believe ⟨an ∼ catch for a touchdown⟩ ✦ *Synonyms* INCONCEIVABLE, UNIMAGINABLE, UNTHINKABLE — **un·be·liev·ably** \-blē\ *adv*

---

unabashed	unadventurous	unanticipated	unasked
unabated	unadvertised	unapologetic	unassertive
unabsorbed	unaesthetic	unapparent	unassisted
unabsorbent	unaffiliated	unappealing	unathletic
unacademic	unafraid	unappeased	unattainable
unaccented	unaggressive	unappetizing	unattended
unacceptable	unaided	unappreciated	unattested
unacclimatized	unalike	unappreciative	unattractive
unaccommodat-	unaltered	unapproachable	unauthentic
ing	unambiguous	unappropriated	unauthorized
unaccredited	unambiguously	unapproved	unavailable
unacknowledged	unambitious	unarguable	unavowed
unacquainted	unanchored	unarguably	unawakened
unadapted	unannounced	unarmored	unbaked
unadjusted	unanswerable	unartistic	unbaptized
unadorned	unanswered	unashamed	

un·be·liev·er \-'lē-vər\ n 1 : INFIDEL 2 : DOUBTER

un·bend \-'bend\ vb **-bent** \-'bent\; **-bend·ing** 1 : to free from being bent : make or become straight 2 : UNTIE 3 : to make or become less stiff or more affable : RELAX

un·bend·ing adj : formal and distant in manner : INFLEXIBLE

un·bi·ased \ˌən-'bī-əst\ adj : free from bias; esp : UNPREJUDICED ⟨an ~ opinion⟩ ✦ *Synonyms* DISINTERESTED, DISPASSIONATE, IMPARTIAL, NONDISCRIMINATORY, NONPARTISAN, OBJECTIVE, UNCOLORED

un·bid·den \-'bi-dᵊn\ also **un·bid** \-'bid\ adj : not bidden : UNASKED

un·bind \-'bīnd\ vb **-bound** \-'baůnd\; **-bind·ing** 1 : to remove bindings from : UNTIE 2 : RELEASE

un·blessed also **un·blest** \ˌən-'blest\ adj 1 : not blessed 2 : EVIL

un·block \-'bläk\ vb : to free from being blocked

un·blush·ing \ˌən-'blə-shiŋ\ adj 1 : not blushing 2 : SHAMELESS ⟨~ greed⟩ — **un·blush·ing·ly** adv

un·bod·ied \-'bä-dēd\ adj 1 : having no body; also : DISEMBODIED 2 : FORMLESS

un·bolt \ˌən-'bōlt\ vb : to open or unfasten by withdrawing a bolt

un·bolt·ed \-'bōl-təd\ adj : not fastened by bolts

un·born \-'bórn\ adj : not yet born

un·bos·om \-'bů-zəm, -'bü-\ vb 1 : DISCLOSE, REVEAL 2 : to disclose the thoughts or feelings of oneself

un·bound·ed \-'baůn-dəd\ adj : having no bounds or limits ⟨~ enthusiasm⟩ ✦ *Synonyms* BOUNDLESS, ENDLESS, IMMEASURABLE, LIMITLESS, MEASURELESS, UNLIMITED

un·bowed \ˌən-'baůd\ adj 1 : not bowed down 2 : UNSUBDUED

un·bri·dled \-'brī-dᵊld\ adj 1 : UNRESTRAINED ⟨~ enthusiasm⟩ 2 : not confined by a bridle

un·bro·ken \-'brō-kən\ adj 1 : not damaged 2 : not subdued or tamed 3 : not interrupted : CONTINUOUS

un·buck·le \-'bə-kəl\ vb : to loose the buckle of : UNFASTEN ⟨~ a belt⟩

un·bur·den \-'bər-dᵊn\ vb 1 : to free or relieve from a burden 2 : to relieve oneself of (as cares or worries)

un·but·ton \-'bə-tᵊn\ vb : to unfasten the buttons of ⟨~ your coat⟩

un·called–for \ˌən-'kóld-ˌfór\ adj : not called for, needed, or wanted

un·can·ny \-'ka-nē\ adj 1 : GHOSTLY, MYSTERIOUS, EERIE 2 : suggesting superhuman or supernatural powers ✦ *Synonyms* SPOOKY, UNEARTHLY, WEIRD — **un·can·ni·ly** \-'ka-nə-lē\ adv

un·ceas·ing \-'sē-siŋ\ adj : never ceasing ✦ *Synonyms* CEASELESS, CONTINUOUS, ENDLESS, INTERMINABLE, UNENDING, UNREMITTING — **un·ceas·ing·ly** adv

un·cer·e·mo·ni·ous \ˌən-ˌser-ə-'mō-nē-əs\ adj : acting without or lacking ordinary courtesy : ABRUPT — **un·cer·e·mo·ni·ous·ly** adv

un·cer·tain \ˌən-'sər-tᵊn\ adj 1 : not determined or fixed ⟨an ~ quantity⟩ 2 : subject to chance or change : not dependable ⟨~ weather⟩ 3 : not definitely known 4 : not sure ⟨~ of the truth⟩ — **un·cer·tain·ly** adv

un·cer·tain·ty \-'tᵊn-tē\ n 1 : lack of certainty : DOUBT 2 : something that is uncertain ✦ *Synonyms* CONCERN, DOUBT, DUBIETY, INCERTITUDE, SKEPTICISM, SUSPICION

un·chain \ˌən-'chān\ vb : to free by or as if by removing a chain

un·charged \ˌən-'chärjd\ adj : having no electrical charge

un·char·i·ta·ble \-'cha-rə-tə-bəl\ adj : not charitable; esp : severe in judging others — **un·char·i·ta·ble·ness** n — **un·char·i·ta·bly** \-blē\ adv

un·chart·ed \-'chär-təd\ adj 1 : not recorded on a map, chart, or plan 2 : UNKNOWN ⟨discussion moving into ~ territory⟩

un·chris·tian \-'kris-chən\ adj 1 : not of the Christian faith 2 : contrary to the Christian spirit

un·churched \-'chərcht\ adj : not belonging to or connected with a church

un·cial \'ən-shəl, -chəl; 'ən-sē-əl\ adj : relating to or written in a form of script with rounded letters used esp. in early Greek and Latin manuscripts — **uncial** n

un·cir·cu·lat·ed \ˌən-'sər-kyə-ˌlā-təd\ adj : issued for use as money but kept out of circulation

un·cir·cum·cised \ˌən-'sər-kəm-ˌsīzd\ adj 1 : not circumcised 2 : HEATHEN

un·civ·il \ˌən-'si-vəl\ adj 1 : not civilized : BARBAROUS 2 : DISCOURTEOUS, ILL-MANNERED, IMPOLITE ⟨~ remarks⟩

un·civ·i·lized \-'si-və-ˌlīzd\ adj 1 : not civilized : BARBAROUS 2 : remote from civilization : WILD

un·clasp \-'klasp\ vb : to open by or as if by loosing the clasp

un·cle \'əŋ-kəl\ n [ME, fr. AF, fr. L *avunculus* mother's brother] 1 : the brother of one's father or mother 2 : the husband of one's aunt

un·clean \ˌən-'klēn\ adj 1 : morally or

unbeloved	unbrushed	uncaught	unchastely
unbleached	unbudging	uncensored	unchasteness
unblemished	unburied	uncensured	unchastity
unblinking	unburned	unchallenged	unchecked
unbound	uncanceled	unchangeable	unchivalrous
unbranched	uncanonical	unchanged	unchristened
unbranded	uncap	unchanging	unclad
unbreakable	uncapitalized	unchaperoned	unclaimed
unbridgeable	uncared–for	uncharacteristic	unclassified
unbruised	uncataloged	unchaste	

spiritually impure **2** : prohibited by ritual law for use or contact **3** : DIRTY, SOILED — **un·clean·li·ness** \-lē-nəs\ *n* — **un·clean·ly** *adj* — **un·clean·ness** *n*

un·clench \-'klench\ *vb* : to open from a clenched position : RELAX

Uncle Tom \-'täm\ *n* [fr. *Uncle Tom*, faithful slave in Harriet Beecher Stowe's novel *Uncle Tom's Cabin* (1851-52)] : a black who is eager to win the approval of whites

un·cloak \ˌən-'klōk\ *vb* **1** : to remove a cloak or cover from **2** : UNMASK, REVEAL ⟨~ an impostor⟩

un·clog \-'kläg\ *vb* : to remove an obstruction from

un·close \-'klōz\ *vb* : OPEN — **un·closed** \-'klōzd\ *adj*

un·clothe \-'klōth\ *vb* : to strip of clothes or a covering — **un·clothed** \-'klōthd\ *adj*

un·coil \ˌən-'kȯi(-ə)l\ *vb* : to release or become released from a coiled state

un·com·fort·able \ˌən-'kəmf-tə-bəl, -'kəm-fər-tə-\ *adj* **1** : causing discomfort **2** : feeling discomfort — **un·com·fort·ably** *adv*

un·com·mit·ted \ˌən-kə-'mi-təd\ *adj* : not committed; *esp* : not pledged to a particular belief, allegiance, or program ⟨~ voters⟩

un·com·mon \ˌən-'kä-mən\ *adj* **1** : not ordinarily encountered : UNUSUAL, RARE **2** : REMARKABLE, EXCEPTIONAL ⟨a soldier of ~ courage⟩ ✦ *Synonyms* EXTRAORDINARY, PHENOMENAL, SINGULAR, UNIQUE — **un·com·mon·ly** *adv*

un·com·mu·ni·ca·tive \ˌən-kə-'myü-nə-ˌkā-tiv, -ni-kə-\ *adj* : not inclined to talk or impart information : RESERVED ✦ *Synonyms* CLOSEMOUTHED, RETICENT, SILENT, TACITURN

un·com·pro·mis·ing \ˌən-'käm-prə-ˌmī-ziŋ\ *adj* : not making or accepting a compromise : UNYIELDING ✦ *Synonyms* ADAMANT, INFLEXIBLE, OBDURATE, RIGID, UNBENDING

un·con·cern \ˌən-kən-'sərn\ *n* **1** : lack of care or interest : INDIFFERENCE **2** : freedom from excessive concern

un·con·cerned \-'sərnd\ *adj* **1** : not having any part or interest **2** : not anxious or upset : free of worry ✦ *Synonyms* ALOOF, DETACHED, INCURIOUS, REMOTE, UNCURIOUS, UNINTERESTED — **un·con·cern·ed·ly** \-'sər-nəd-lē\ *adv*

un·con·di·tion·al \ˌən-kən-'di-shə-nəl\ *adj* : not limited in any way ⟨~ surrender⟩ — **un·con·di·tion·al·ly** *adv*

un·con·di·tioned \-'di-shənd\ *adj* **1** : not

subject to conditions **2** : not acquired or learned : NATURAL ⟨~ responses⟩ **3** : producing an unconditioned response ⟨~ stimuli⟩

un·con·quer·able \ˌən-'käŋ-kə-rə-bəl\ *adj* : incapable of being conquered or overcome : INDOMITABLE

un·con·scio·na·ble \-'kän-shə-nə-bəl\ *adj* **1** : not guided or controlled by conscience **2** : not in accordance with what is right or just ⟨~ sales practices⟩ ✦ *Synonyms* UNREASONABLE, UNDUE, UNJUSTIFIABLE, UNWARRANTABLE, UNWARRANTED — **un·con·scio·na·bly** \-blē\ *adv*

¹**un·con·scious** \ˌən-'kän-chəs, -shəs\ *adj* **1** : not knowing or perceiving : not aware **2** : not done consciously or on purpose **3** : having lost consciousness **4** : of or relating to the unconscious — **un·con·scious·ly** *adv* — **un·con·scious·ness** *n*

²**unconscious** *n* : the part of one's mental life of which one is not ordinarily aware but which is often a powerful force in influencing behavior

un·con·sti·tu·tion·al \ˌən-ˌkän-stə-'tü-shə-nəl, -'tyü-\ *adj* : not according to or consistent with the constitution of a state or society — **un·con·sti·tu·tion·al·i·ty** \-ˌtü-shə-ˈna-lə-tē, -ˌtyü-\ *n* — **un·con·sti·tu·tion·al·ly** \-'tü-shə-nə-lē, -ˌtyü-\ *adv*

un·con·trol·la·ble \ˌən-kən-'trō-lə-bəl\ *adj* : incapable of being controlled : UNGOVERNABLE — **un·con·trol·la·bly** \-blē\ *adv*

un·con·ven·tion·al \-'ven-chə-nəl\ *adj* : not conventional : being out of the ordinary — **un·con·ven·tion·al·i·ty** \-ˌven-chə-'na-lə-tē\ *n* — **un·con·ven·tion·al·ly** \-'ven-chə-nə-lē\ *adv*

un·cork \ˌən-'kȯrk\ *vb* **1** : to draw a cork from **2** : to release from a sealed or pent-up state; *also* : to let go

un·count·ed \-'kaun-təd\ *adj* **1** : not counted **2** : INNUMERABLE

un·cou·ple \-'kə-pəl\ *vb* : DISCONNECT ⟨~ railroad cars⟩

un·couth \-'küth\ *adj* [ME, unfamiliar, fr. OE *uncūth*, fr. *un-* + *cūth* known] **1** : strange, awkward, and clumsy in shape or appearance **2** : vulgar in conduct or speech : RUDE ✦ *Synonyms* DISCOURTEOUS, ILL-MANNERED, IMPOLITE, UNGRACIOUS, UNMANNERED, UNMANNERLY

un·cov·er \-'kə-vər\ *vb* **1** : to make known : DISCLOSE, REVEAL **2** : to expose to view by removing some covering

uncleaned	uncommercial	uncongenial	uncontroversial
unclear	uncompensated	unconnected	unconverted
uncleared	uncomplaining	unconquered	unconvincing
unclouded	uncompleted	unconsecrated	uncooked
uncluttered	uncomplicated	unconsidered	uncooperative
uncoated	uncomplimentary	unconsolidated	uncoordinated
uncollected	uncompounded	unconstrained	uncorrected
uncolored	uncomprehending	unconsumed	uncorroborated
uncombed	unconcealed	unconsummated	uncountable
uncombined	unconfined	uncontaminated	
uncomely	unconfirmed	uncontested	
uncomic	unconformable	uncontrolled	

3 : to take the cover from **4** : to remove the hat from; *also* : to take off the hat as a token of respect — **un·covered** *adj*

un·crit·i·cal \ˌən-'kri-ti-kəl\ *adj* **1** : not critical : lacking in discrimination **2** : showing lack or improper use of critical standards or procedures — **un·crit·i·cal·ly** \-k(ə-)lē\ *adv*

un·cross \-'krȯs\ *vb* : to change from a crossed position ⟨∼ed his legs⟩

unc·tion \'əŋk-shən\ *n* **1** : the act of anointing as a rite of consecration or healing **2** : exaggerated or insincere earnestness of language or manner

unc·tu·ous \'əŋk-chə-wəs\ *adj* [ME, fr. MF or ML; MF *unctueus*, fr. ML *unctuosus*, fr. L *unctus* act of anointing, fr. *unguere* to anoint] **1** : FATTY, OILY **2** : insincerely smooth in speech and manner — **unc·tu·ous·ly** *adv*

un·curl \ˌən-'kərl\ *vb* : to make or become straightened out from a curled or coiled position

un·cut \ˌən-'kət\ *adj* **1** : not cut down or into **2** : not shaped by cutting ⟨an ∼ diamond⟩ **3** : not having the folds of the leaves slit ⟨an ∼ book⟩ **4** : not abridged or curtailed ⟨the ∼ version of the film⟩ **5** : not diluted ⟨∼ heroin⟩

un·daunt·ed \-'dȯn-təd\ *adj* : not daunted : not discouraged or dismayed ♦ *Synonyms* BOLD, BRAVE, DAUNTLESS, FEARLESS, INTREPID, VALIANT — **un·daunt·ed·ly** *adv*

un·de·ceive \ˌən-di-'sēv\ *vb* : to free from deception, illusion, or error

un·de·mon·stra·tive \ˌən-di-'män-strə-tiv\ *adj* : restrained in expression of feeling : RESERVED

un·de·ni·able \ˌən-di-'nī-ə-bəl\ *adj* **1** : plainly true : INCONTESTABLE **2** : unquestionably excellent or genuine ♦ *Synonyms* INCONTROVERTIBLE, INDISPUTABLE, INDUBITABLE, UNQUESTIONABLE. — **un·de·ni·ably** \-blē\ *adv*

¹un·der \'ən-dər\ *adv* **1** : in or into a position below or beneath something **2** : below some quantity, level, or limit ⟨$10 or ∼⟩ **3** : in or into a condition of subjection, subordination, or unconsciousness ⟨the ether put him ∼⟩

²un·der \ˌən-dər, 'ən-\ *prep* **1** : lower than and overhung, surmounted, or sheltered by ⟨∼ a tree⟩ **2** : subject to the authority or guidance of ⟨served ∼ him⟩ ⟨was ∼ contract⟩ **3** : subject to the action or effect of ⟨∼ the influence of alcohol⟩ **4** : within the division or grouping of ⟨items ∼ this heading⟩ **5** : less or lower than (as in size, amount, or rank) ⟨earns ∼ $5000⟩

³under \'ən-dər\ *adj* **1** : lying below, beneath, or on the ventral side **2** : facing or protruding downward **3** : SUBORDI-

NATE **4** : lower than usual, proper, or desired in amount, quality, or degree

un·der·achiev·er \ˌən-dər-ə-'chē-vər\ *n* : one (as a student) who performs below an expected level of proficiency

un·der·act \-'akt\ *vb* : to perform feebly or with restraint

un·der·ac·tive \-'ak-tiv\ *adj* : characterized by abnormally low activity ⟨an ∼ thyroid gland⟩ — **un·der·ac·tiv·i·ty** \-ˌak-'ti-və-tē\ *n*

un·der·age \-'āj\ *adj* : of less than mature or legal age

un·der·arm \-ˌärm\ *adj* **1** : UNDERHAND **2** ⟨an ∼ throw⟩ **2** : placed under or on the underside of the arms ⟨∼ seams⟩ — **underarm** *adv or n*

un·der·bel·ly \'ən-dər-ˌbe-lē\ *n* **1** : a vulnerable area **2** : the underside of a body or mass

un·der·bid \ˌən-dər-'bid\ *vb* **-bid; -bidding 1** : to bid less than another **2** : to bid too low

un·der·body \'ən-dər-ˌbä-dē\ *n* : the lower parts of the body of a vehicle

un·der·bred \ˌən-dər-'bred\ *adj* : marked by lack of good breeding

un·der·brush \'ən-dər-ˌbrəsh\ *n* : shrubs, bushes, or small trees growing beneath large trees

un·der·car·riage \-ˌka-rij\ *n* **1** : a supporting framework or underside (as of an automobile) **2** : the landing gear of an airplane

un·der·charge \ˌən-dər-'chärj\ *vb* : to charge (as a person) too little — **undercharge** \'ən-dər-ˌchärj\ *n*

un·der·class \'ən-dər-ˌklas\ *n* : LOWER CLASS

un·der·class·man \ˌən-dər-'klas-mən\ *n* : a member of the freshman or sophomore class

un·der·clothes \'ən-dər-ˌklō(th)z\ *n pl* : UNDERWEAR

un·der·cloth·ing \-ˌklō-thiŋ\ *n* : UNDERWEAR

un·der·coat \-ˌkōt\ *n* **1** : a coat worn under another **2** : a growth of short hair or fur partly concealed by the longer and usu. coarser hairs of a mammal **3** : a coat of paint under another

un·der·coat·ing \-ˌkō-tiŋ\ *n* : a special waterproof coating applied to the underside of a vehicle

un·der·cov·er \ˌən-dər-'kə-vər\ *adj* : acting or executed in secret; *esp* : employed or engaged in secret investigation ⟨an ∼ agent⟩

un·der·croft \'ən-dər-ˌkrȯft\ *n* [ME, fr. *under* + *crofte* crypt, fr. MD, fr. ML *crupta*, fr. L *crypta*] : a vaulted chamber under a church

un·der·cur·rent \-ˌkər-ənt\ *n* **1** : a current below the surface **2** : a hidden ten-

uncreative	uncultured	undated	undefiled
uncredited	uncured	undecided	undefinable
uncropped	uncurious	undecipherable	undefined
uncrowded	uncurtained	undeclared	undemanding
uncrowned	uncustomary	undecorated	undemocratic
uncrystallized	undamaged	undefeated	undenominational
uncultivated	undamped	undefended	undependable

dency of feeling or opinion ⟨an ∼ of dread⟩

un·der·cut \ˌən-dər-ˈkət\ *vb* **-cut;** **-cutting 1** : to cut away the underpart of **2** : to offer to sell or to work at a lower rate than **3** : to strike (the ball) obliquely downward so as to give a backward spin or elevation to the shot — **un·der·cut** \ˈən-dər-ˌkət\ *n*

un·der·de·vel·oped \ˌən-dər-di-ˈve-ləpt\ *adj* **1** : not normally or adequately developed ⟨∼ muscles⟩ **2** : having a relatively low level of economic development ⟨the ∼ nations⟩

un·der·dog \ˈən-dər-ˌdȯg\ *n* : the loser or predicted loser in a struggle

un·der·done \ˌən-dər-ˈdən\ *adj* : not thoroughly done or cooked : RARE

un·der·draw·ers \ˈən-dər-ˌdrȯrz, -ˌdrȯ-ərz\ *n pl* : UNDERPANTS

un·der·draw·ing \ˈən-dər-ˌdrȯ-iŋ\ *n* : a preliminary sketch made prior to painting

un·der·em·pha·size \ˌən-dər-ˈem-fə-ˌsīz\ *vb* : to emphasize inadequately — **un·der·em·pha·sis** \-səs\ *n*

un·der·em·ployed \-im-ˈplȯid\ *adj* : having less than full-time or adequate employment

un·der·es·ti·mate \-ˈes-tə-ˌmāt\ *vb* : to set too low a value on

un·der·ex·pose \-ik-ˈspōz\ *vb* : to expose (a photographic plate or film) for less time than is needed — **un·der·ex·po·sure** \-ˈspō-zhər\ *n*

un·der·feed \ˌən-dər-ˈfēd\ *vb* **-fed** \-ˈfed\; **-feed·ing** : to feed with too little food

un·der·foot \-ˈfu̇t\ *adv* **1** : under the feet ⟨flowers trampled ∼⟩ **2** : close about one's feet : in the way

un·der·fur \ˈən-dər-ˌfər\ *n* : an undercoat of fur esp. when thick and soft

un·der·gar·ment \-ˌgär-mənt\ *n* : a garment to be worn under another

un·der·gird \ˌən-dər-ˈgərd\ *vb* : to brace up : STRENGTHEN

un·der·go \ˌən-dər-ˈgō\ *vb* **-went** \-ˈwent\; **-gone** \-ˈgȯn, -ˈgän\; **-go·ing 1** : to submit to : ENDURE **2** : to go through : EXPERIENCE ⟨∼ a change⟩

un·der·grad \ˈən-dər-ˌgrad\ *n* : UNDERGRADUATE

un·der·grad·u·ate \ˌən-dər-ˈgra-jə-wət, -jə-ˌwāt\ *n* : a student at a university or college who has not received a first degree

¹un·der·ground \ˌən-dər-ˈgrau̇nd\ *adv* **1** : beneath the surface of the earth **2** : in or into hiding or secret operation

²un·der·ground \ˈən-dər-ˌgrau̇nd\ *n* **1** : a space under the surface of the ground; *esp* : SUBWAY **2** : a secret political movement or group; *esp* : an organized body working in secret to overthrow a government or an occupying power **3** : an avant-garde group or movement that operates outside the establishment

³underground \ˈən-dər-ˌgrau̇nd\ *adj* **1** : being, growing, operating, or located below the surface of the ground ⟨∼ stems⟩ **2** : conducted by secret means **3** : produced or published by the under-

ground ⟨∼ publications⟩; *also* : of or relating to the avant-garde underground

un·der·growth \ˈən-dər-ˌgrōth\ *n* : low growth (as of herbs and shrubs) on the floor of a forest

¹un·der·hand \ˈən-dər-ˌhand\ *adv* **1** : in an underhanded or secret manner **2** : with an underhand motion

²underhand *adj* **1** : UNDERHANDED **2** : made with the hand kept below the level of the shoulder ⟨an ∼ pitch⟩

¹un·der·hand·ed \ˌən-dər-ˈhan-dəd\ *adv* : UNDERHAND

²underhanded *adj* : marked by secrecy and deception — **un·der·hand·ed·ly** *adv* — **un·der·hand·ed·ness** *n*

un·der·lie \-ˈlī\ *vb* **-lay** \-ˈlā\; **-lain** \-ˈlān\; **-ly·ing** \-ˈlī-iŋ\ **1** : to lie or be situated under **2** : to be at the basis of : form the foundation of : SUPPORT

un·der·line \ˈən-dər-ˌlīn\ *vb* **1** : to draw a line under **2** : EMPHASIZE, STRESS — **underline** *n*

un·der·ling \ˈən-dər-liŋ\ *n* : SUBORDINATE, INFERIOR

un·der·lip \ˌən-dər-ˈlip\ *n* : the lower lip

un·der·ly·ing \ˌən-dər-ˌlī-iŋ\ *adj* **1** : lying under or below **2** : FUNDAMENTAL, BASIC ⟨∼ principles⟩

un·der·mine \-ˈmīn\ *vb* **1** : to excavate beneath **2** : to weaken or wear away secretly or gradually

un·der·most \ˈən-dər-ˌmōst\ *adj* : lowest in relative position — **undermost** *adv*

¹un·der·neath \ˌən-dər-ˈnēth\ *prep* **1** : directly under **2** : under subjection to

²underneath *adv* **1** : below a surface or object : BENEATH **2** : on the lower side

un·der·nour·ished \ˌən-dər-ˈnər-isht\ *adj* : supplied with insufficient nourishment — **un·der·nour·ish·ment** \-ˈnər-ish-mənt\ *n*

un·der·pants \ˈən-dər-ˌpants\ *n pl* : a usu. short undergarment for the lower trunk : DRAWERS

un·der·part \-ˌpärt\ *n* : a part lying on the lower side (as of a bird or mammal)

un·der·pass \-ˌpas\ *n* : a crossing of a highway and another way (as a road) at different levels; *also* : the lower level

un·der·pay \ˌən-dər-ˈpā\ *vb* : to pay less than what is normal or required

un·der·pin·ning \ˈən-dər-ˌpi-niŋ\ *n* : the material and construction (as a foundation) used for support of a structure — **un·der·pin** \ˌən-dər-ˈpin\ *vb*

un·der·play \ˌən-dər-ˈplā\ *vb* : to treat or handle with restraint; *esp* : to play a role with subdued force

un·der·pop·u·lat·ed \ˌən-dər-ˈpä-pyə-ˌlā-təd\ *adj* : having a lower than normal or desirable density of population

un·der·priv·i·leged \-ˈpriv-lijd, -ˈpri-və-lijd\ *adj* : having fewer esp. economic and social privileges than others

un·der·pro·duc·tion \ˌən-dər-prə-ˈdək-shən\ *n* : the production of less than enough to satisfy the demand or of less than the usual supply

un·der·rate \-ˈrāt\ *vb* : to rate or value too low

un·der·rep·re·sent·ed \-ˌre-pri-ˈzen-təd\ *adj* : inadequately represented

un·der·score \ˈən-dər-ˌskȯr\ *vb* **1** : to draw a line under : UNDERLINE **2** : EMPHASIZE — **underscore** *n*

¹**un·der·sea** \ˌən-dər-ˈsē\ *adj* : being, carried on, or used beneath the surface of the sea

²**undersea** *or* **un·der·seas** \-ˈsēz\ *adv* : beneath the surface of the sea

un·der·sec·re·tary \ˌən-dər-ˈse-krə-ˌter-ē\ *n* : a secretary immediately subordinate to a principal secretary ⟨~ of state⟩

un·der·sell \-ˈsel\ *vb* **-sold** \-ˈsōld\; **-sell·ing** : to sell articles cheaper than

un·der·sexed \-ˈsekst\ *adj* : deficient in sexual desire

un·der·shirt \ˈən-dər-ˌshərt\ *n* : a collarless undergarment with or without sleeves

un·der·shoot \ˌən-dər-ˈshüt\ *vb* **-shot** \-ˈshät\; **-shoot·ing** **1** : to shoot short of or below (a target) **2** : to fall short of (a runway) in landing an airplane

un·der·shorts \ˈən-dər-ˌshȯrts\ *n pl* : underpants for men or boys

un·der·shot \ˈən-dər-ˌshät\ *adj* **1** : moved by water passing beneath ⟨an ~ waterwheel⟩ **2** : having the lower front teeth projecting beyond the upper when the mouth is closed

un·der·side \ˈən-dər-ˌsīd, ˌən-dər-ˈsīd\ *n* : the side or surface lying underneath

un·der·signed \ˈən-dər-ˌsīnd\ *n, pl* **undersigned** : one whose name is signed at the end of a document

un·der·sized \ˌən-dər-ˈsīzd\ *also* **un·der·size** \-ˈsīz\ *adj* : of a size less than is common, proper, or normal

un·der·skirt \ˈən-dər-ˌskərt\ *n* : a skirt worn under an outer skirt; *esp* : PETTICOAT

un·der·staffed \ˌən-dər-ˈstaft\ *adj* : inadequately staffed

un·der·stand \ˌən-dər-ˈstand\ *vb* **-stood** \-ˈstud\; **-stand·ing** **1** : to grasp the meaning of : COMPREHEND **2** : to have thorough or technical acquaintance with or expertness in ⟨~ finance⟩ **3** : to have reason to believe ⟨I ~ you are leaving tomorrow⟩ **4** : INTERPRET ⟨we ~ this to be a refusal⟩ **5** : to have a sympathetic attitude **6** : to accept as settled ⟨it is *understood* that he will pay the expenses⟩ — **un·der·stand·able** \-ˈstan-də-bəl\ *adj*

un·der·stand·ably \-blē\ *adv* : as can be easily understood

¹**un·der·stand·ing** \ˌən-dər-ˈstan-diŋ\ *n* **1** : knowledge and ability to judge : INTELLIGENCE ⟨a person of ~⟩ **2** : agreement of opinion or feeling **3** : a mutual agreement informally or tacitly entered into

²**understanding** *adj* : endowed with understanding : TOLERANT, SYMPATHETIC

un·der·state \ˌən-dər-ˈstāt\ *vb* **1** : to represent as less than is the case **2** : to state with restraint esp. for effect — **un·der·state·ment** *n*

un·der·stood \ˌən-dər-ˈstud\ *adj* **1** : agreed upon **2** : IMPLICIT

un·der·sto·ry \ˈən-dər-ˌstȯr-ē\ *n* : the vegetative layer between the top layer of a forest and the ground cover

un·der·study \ˈən-dər-ˌstə-dē\ *n* : one who is prepared to act another's part or take over another's duties — **understudy** \ˈən-dər-ˌstə-dē, ˌən-dər-ˈstə-dē\ *vb*

un·der·sur·face \ˈən-dər-ˌsər-fəs\ *n* : UNDERSIDE

un·der·take \ˌən-dər-ˈtāk\ *vb* **-took** \-ˈtuk\; **-tak·en** \-ˈtā-kən\; **-tak·ing 1** : to take upon oneself : set about ⟨~ a task⟩ **2** : to put oneself under obligation **3** : GUARANTEE, PROMISE

un·der·tak·er \ˈən-dər-ˌtā-kər\ *n* : one whose business is to prepare the dead for burial and to arrange and manage funerals

un·der·tak·ing \ˈən-dər-ˌtā-kiŋ, ˌən-dər-ˈtā-kiŋ; *2 is* ˌən-dər-ˌtā-kiŋ *only*\ *n* **1** : the act of one who undertakes or engages in any project **2** : the business of an undertaker **3** : something undertaken **4** : PROMISE, GUARANTEE

under–the–counter *adj* : UNLAWFUL, ILLICIT ⟨~ sale of drugs⟩

un·der·tone \ˈən-dər-ˌtōn\ *n* **1** : a low or subdued tone or utterance **2** : a subdued color (as seen through and modifying another color)

un·der·tow \-ˌtō\ *n* : the current beneath the surface that flows seaward when waves are breaking upon the shore

un·der·val·ue \ˌən-dər-ˈval-yü\ *vb* **1** : to value or estimate below the real worth **2** : to esteem lightly

un·der·wa·ter \ˌən-dər-ˈwȯ-tər, -ˈwä-\ *adj* : lying, growing, worn, or operating below the surface of the water — **un·der·wa·ter** *adv*

under way \-ˈwā\ *adv* **1** : into motion from a standstill **2** : in progress

un·der·wear \ˈən-dər-ˌwer\ *n* : clothing or a garment worn next to the skin and under other clothing

un·der·weight \ˌən-dər-ˈwāt\ *adj* : weighing below what is normal, average, or necessary — **underweight** *n*

un·der·wire \ˈən-dər-ˌwī(-ə)r\ *n* : a wire running through the bottom of a brassiere to aid in support

un·der·world \ˈən-dər-ˌwərld\ *n* **1** : the place of departed souls : HADES **2** : the side of the world opposite to one **3** : the world of organized crime

un·der·write \ˈən-dər-ˌrīt, ˌən-dər-ˈrīt\ *vb* **-wrote** \-ˌrōt, -ˈrōt\; **-writ·ten** \-ˌri-tᵊn, -ˈri-tᵊn\; **-writ·ing 1** : to write under or at the end of something else **2** : to set one's name to an insurance policy and thereby become answerable for a designated loss or damage **3** : to subscribe to : agree to **4** : to guarantee financial support of — **un·der·writ·er** *n*

un·de·sign·ing \ˌən-di-ˈzī-niŋ\ *adj* : having no artful, ulterior, or fraudulent purpose : SINCERE

un·de·sir·able \-ˈzī-rə-bəl\ *adj* : not desirable — **undesirable** *n*

un·de·vi·at·ing \ˌən-ˈdē-vē-ˌā-tiŋ\ *adj* : keeping a true course

un·dies \ˈən-dēz\ *n pl* : UNDERWEAR; *esp* : women's underwear

un·do \ˌən-ˈdü\ vb **-did** \-ˈdid\; **-done** \-ˈdən\; **-do·ing** 1 : to make or become unfastened or loosened : OPEN 2 : to make null or as if not done : REVERSE 3 : to bring to ruin; also : UPSET

un·doc·u·ment·ed \ˌən-ˈdä-kyə-ˌmen-təd\ adj 1 : not supported by documentary evidence 2 : lacking documents required for legal immigration

un·do·ing n : a cause of ruin

un·doubt·ed \-ˈdau̇-təd\ adj : not doubted or called into question : CERTAIN — **un·doubt·ed·ly** adv

¹un·dress \ˌən-ˈdres\ vb : to remove the clothes or covering of : STRIP, DISROBE

²undress n 1 : informal dress; esp : a loose robe or dressing gown 2 : ordinary dress 3 : NUDITY

un·due \-ˈdü, -ˈdyü\ adj 1 : not due 2 : exceeding or violating propriety or fitness : EXCESSIVE 〈~ force〉

un·du·lant \ˈən-jə-lənt, ˈən-də-, -dyə-\ adj : rising and falling in waves

undulant fever n : a human disease caused by bacteria from infected domestic animals or their products and marked by intermittent fever, chills, headache, weakness, and weight loss

un·du·late \-ˌlāt\ vb **-lat·ed**; **-lat·ing** [LL undula small wave, fr. L unda wave] 1 : to have a wavelike motion or appearance 2 : to rise and fall in pitch or volume

un·du·la·tion \ˌən-jə-ˈlā-shən, ˌən-də-, -dyə-\ n 1 : wavy or wavelike motion 2 : pulsation of sound 3 : a wavy appearance or outline — **un·du·la·to·ry** \ˈən-jə-lə-ˌtȯr-ē, ˈən-də-, -dyə-\ adj

un·du·ly \ˌən-ˈdü-lē, ˈən-, -ˈdyü-\ adv : in an undue manner : EXCESSIVELY

un·dy·ing \-ˈdī-iŋ\ adj : not dying : IMMORTAL, PERPETUAL

un·earned \-ˈərnd\ adj : not earned by labor, service, or skill 〈~ income〉

un·earth \ˌən-ˈərth\ vb 1 : to dig up out of or as if out of the earth 〈~ buried treasure〉 2 : to bring to light : DISCOVER 〈~ a secret〉

un·earth·ly \-lē\ adj 1 : not of or belonging to the earth 2 : SUPERNATURAL, WEIRD; also : ABSURD

un·easy \ˌən-ˈē-zē\ adj 1 : AWKWARD,

EMBARRASSED 〈~ among strangers〉 2 : disturbed by pain or worry; also : RESTLESS 3 : UNSTABLE 〈an ~ truce〉 — **un·eas·i·ly** \-ˈē-zə-lē\ adv — **un·eas·i·ness** \-ˈē-zē-nəs\ n

un·em·ployed \ˌən-im-ˈplȯid\ adj : not being used; also : having no job

un·em·ploy·ment \-ˈplȯi-mənt\ n 1 : lack of employment 2 : money paid at regular intervals (as by a government agency) to an unemployed person

un·end·ing \ˌən-ˈen-diŋ\ adj : having no ending : ENDLESS

un·equal \ˌən-ˈē-kwəl\ adj 1 : not alike (as in size, amount, number, or value) 2 : not uniform : VARIABLE 3 : badly balanced or matched 4 : INADEQUATE, INSUFFICIENT 〈~ to the task〉 — **un·equal·ly** adv

un·equaled or **un·equalled** \-kwəld\ adj : not equaled : UNPARALLELED 〈an artist of ~ talent〉

un·equiv·o·cal \ˌən-i-ˈkwi-və-kəl\ adj : leaving no doubt : CLEAR — **un·equiv·o·cal·ly** adv

un·err·ing \ˌən-ˈer-iŋ, ˌən-ˈər-\ adj : making no errors : CERTAIN, UNFAILING 〈~ accuracy〉 — **un·err·ing·ly** adv

UNES·CO \yü-ˈnes-kō\ abbr United Nations Educational, Scientific, and Cultural Organization

un·even \ˌən-ˈē-vən\ adj 1 : ODD 3 2 : not even : not level or smooth : RUGGED, RAGGED 3 : IRREGULAR; also : varying in quality — **un·even·ly** adv — **un·even·ness** n

un·event·ful \ˌən-i-ˈvent-fəl\ adj : lacking interesting or noteworthy incidents — **un·event·ful·ly** adv

un·evolved \ˌən-i-ˈvälvd\ adj 1 : not fully developed 〈an ~ wine〉 2 : lacking cultural refinement

un·ex·am·pled \ˌən-ig-ˈzam-pəld\ adj : UNPRECEDENTED, UNPARALLELED 〈fought with ~ passion〉

un·ex·cep·tion·able \ˌən-ik-ˈsep-shə-nə-bəl\ adj : not open to exception or objection : beyond reproach

un·ex·pect·ed \ˌən-ik-ˈspek-təd\ adj : not expected : UNFORESEEN — **un·ex·pect·ed·ly** adv

un·fail·ing \ˌən-ˈfā-liŋ\ adj 1 : not failing,

undeserved	undisguised	undyed	unenthusiastic
undeserving	undismayed	uneager	unenviable
undesired	undisputed	uneatable	unequipped
undetected	undissolved	uneaten	unessential
undetermined	undistinguished	uneconomic	unethical
undeterred	undistributed	uneconomical	unexamined
undeveloped	undisturbed	unedifying	unexcelled
undifferentiated	undivided	unedited	unexceptional
undigested	undogmatic	uneducated	unexcited
undignified	undomesticated	unembarrassed	unexciting
undiluted	undone	unemotional	unexpired
undiminished	undoubled	unemphatic	unexplained
undimmed	undramatic	unenclosed	unexploded
undiplomatic	undraped	unencumbered	unexplored
undirected	undreamed	unendurable	unexposed
undisciplined	undressed	unenforceable	unexpressed
undisclosed	undrinkable	unenforced	unexpurgated
undiscovered	undulled	unenlightened	unfading
undiscriminating	undutiful	unenterprising	

flagging, or waning : CONSTANT **2** : IN-
EXHAUSTIBLE ⟨a subject of ~ interest⟩
3 : INFALLIBLE, SURE ⟨an ~ test⟩ — **un-
fail·ing·ly** adv
un·fair \-'fer\ adj **1** : marked by injustice,
partiality, or deception : UNJUST **2** : not
equitable in business dealings — **un·fair-
ly** adv — **un·fair·ness** n
un·faith·ful \,ən-'fāth-fəl\ adj **1** : not
observant of vows, allegiance, or duty
: DISLOYAL **2** : INACCURATE, UNTRUST-
WORTHY ⟨an ~ copy of a document⟩ —
un·faith·ful·ly adv — **un·faith·ful·ness**
n
un·fa·mil·iar \,ən-fə-'mil-yər\ adj **1** : not
well-known : STRANGE ⟨an ~ place⟩ **2**
: not well acquainted ⟨~ with the sub-
ject⟩ — **un·fa·mil·iar·i·ty** \-,mi-lē-'er-,
-'yer-\ n
un·fas·ten \,ən-'fa-sᵊn\ vb : to make or
become loose : UNDO, DETACH
un·feel·ing \-'fē-liŋ\ adj **1** : lacking feeling : INSENSATE **2** : HARDHEARTED,
CRUEL — **un·feel·ing·ly** adv
un·feigned \-'fānd\ adj : not feigned : not
hypocritical : GENUINE
un·fet·ter \-'fe-tər\ vb **1** : to free from
fetters **2** : LIBERATE
un·fil·ial \,ən-'fi-lē-əl, -'fil-yəl\ adj : not
observing the obligations of a child to a
parent : UNDUTIFUL
un·fin·ished \,ən-'fi-nisht\ adj **1** : not
brought to an end **2** : being in a rough or
unpolished state
¹un·fit \-'fit\ adj : not fit or suitable; esp
: physically or mentally unsound — **un·
fit·ness** n
²unfit vb : to make unfit : DISQUALIFY
un·fix \-'fiks\ vb **1** : to loosen from a fastening : DETACH **2** : UNSETTLE
un·flap·pa·ble \-'fla-pə-bəl\ adj : not easily upset or panicked — **un·flap·pa·bly**
adv
un·fledged \,ən-'flejd\ adj : not feathered
or ready for flight; also : IMMATURE, CAL-
LOW
un·flinch·ing \-'flin-chiŋ\ adj : not flinch-
ing or shrinking : STEADFAST — **un·
flinch·ing·ly** adv
un·fold \-'fōld\ vb **1** : to open the folds of
: open up **2** : to lay open to view : DIS-
CLOSE **3** : BLOSSOM, DEVELOP
un·for·get·ta·ble \,ən-fər-'ge-tə-bəl\ adj
: incapable of being forgotten — **un·for-
get·ta·bly** \-blē\ adv
un·formed \-'fȯrmd\ adj : not regularly
formed or ordered : UNDEVELOPED
un·for·tu·nate \-'fȯr-chə-nət\ adj **1** : not
fortunate : UNLUCKY **2** : attended with

misfortune **3** : UNSUITABLE ⟨an ~
choice of words⟩ — **unfortunate** n
un·for·tu·nate·ly \-nət-lē\ adv **1** : in an
unfortunate manner **2** : it is unfortunate
un·found·ed \,ən-'faùn-dəd\ adj : lacking
a sound basis : GROUNDLESS
un·freeze \-'frēz\ vb **-froze** \-'frōz\, **-fro-
zen** \-'frō-zᵊn\; **-freez·ing 1** : to cause
to thaw **2** : to remove from a freeze ⟨~
prices⟩
un·fre·quent·ed \,ən-frē-'kwen-təd; ,ən-
'frē-kwən-\ adj : seldom visited or traveled over
un·friend·ly \,ən-'frend-lē\ adj **1** : not
friendly or kind : HOSTILE **2** : UNFA-
VORABLE ⟨~ to new business⟩ — **un-
friend·li·ness** \-lē-nəs\ n
un·frock \-'fräk\ vb : DEFROCK
un·fruit·ful \-'früt-fəl\ adj **1** : not producing fruit or offspring : BARREN **2**
: yielding no valuable result : UNPROF-
ITABLE — **un·fruit·ful·ness** n
un·furl \-'fərl\ vb : to loose from a furled
state : UNFOLD
un·gain·ly \-'gān-lē\ adj [un- + obs. gainly
proper, becoming, fr. gain direct, handy,
fr. ME geyn, fr. OE gēn, fr. ON gegn
against] : CLUMSY, AWKWARD — **un·
gain·li·ness** \-lē-nəs\ n
un·gen·er·ous \,ən-'je-nə-rəs\ adj : not
generous or liberal : STINGY
un·glued \,ən-'glüd\ adj : UPSET, DISOR-
DERED
un·god·ly \,ən-'gäd-lē, -'gȯd-\ adj **1** : IM-
PIOUS, IRRELIGIOUS **2** : SINFUL,
WICKED **3** : OUTRAGEOUS ⟨an ~ hour⟩
— **un·god·li·ness** \-lē-nəs\ n
un·gov·ern·able \-'gə-vər-nə-bəl\ adj
: not capable of being governed, guided,
or restrained : UNRULY
un·gra·cious \-'grā-shəs\ adj **1** : not
courteous : RUDE **2** : not pleasing : DIS-
AGREEABLE ⟨an ~ task⟩
un·grate·ful \,ən-'grāt-fəl\ adj **1** : not
thankful for favors **2** : DISAGREEABLE;
also : THANKLESS — **un·grate·ful·ly** adv
— **un·grate·ful·ness** n
un·guard·ed \-'gär-dəd\ adj **1** : UNPRO-
TECTED **2** : DIRECT, INCAUTIOUS ⟨~ re-
marks⟩
un·guent \'əŋ-gwənt, 'ən-\ n : a soothing
or healing salve : OINTMENT
¹un·gu·late \'əŋ-gyə-lət, -ən-, -,lāt\ adj [LL
ungulatus, fr. L ungula hoof, fr. unguis
nail, hoof] : having hoofs
²ungulate n : a hoofed mammal (as a cow,
horse, or rhinoceros)
un·hal·lowed \,ən-'ha-lōd\ adj **1** : not
consecrated : UNHOLY **2** : IMPIOUS,

unfaltering	unfiltered	unformulated	unglamorous
unfashionable	unfitted	unfortified	unglazed
unfashionably	unflagging	unframed	ungoverned
unfathomable	unflattering	unfree	ungraceful
unfavorable	unflavored	unfulfilled	ungracefully
unfavorably	unfocused	unfunded	ungraded
unfeasible	unfolded	unfunny	ungrammatical
unfeminine	unforced	unfurnished	unground
unfenced	unforeseeable	unfussy	ungrudging
unfermented	unforeseen	ungentle	unguided
unfertilized	unforgivable	ungentlemanly	unhackneyed
unfilled	unforgiving	ungerminated	

PROFANE **3** : contrary to accepted standards : IMMORAL

un·hand \ˌən-ˈhand\ *vb* : to remove the hand from : let go

un·hand·some \-ˈhan-səm\ *adj* **1** : not beautiful or handsome : HOMELY **2** : UNBECOMING **3** : DISCOURTEOUS, RUDE

un·handy \-ˈhan-dē\ *adj* : INCONVENIENT; *also* : AWKWARD

un·hap·py \-ˈha-pē\ *adj* **1** : UNLUCKY, UNFORTUNATE ⟨an ~ coincidence⟩ **2** : SAD, MISERABLE **3** : INAPPROPRIATE ⟨an ~ choice⟩ — **un·hap·pi·ly** \-ˈha-pə-lē\ *adv* — **un·hap·pi·ness** \-pē-nəs\ *n*

un·har·ness \-ˈhär-nəs\ *vb* : to remove the harness from (as a horse)

un·healthy \-ˈhel-thē\ *adj* **1** : not conducive to health : UNWHOLESOME **2** : SICKLY, DISEASED

un·heard \-ˈhərd\ *adj* **1** : not heard **2** : not granted a hearing

unheard–of *adj* : previously unknown; *esp* : UNPRECEDENTED ⟨moving at ~ speeds⟩

un·hinge \ˌən-ˈhinj\ *vb* **1** : to make unstable esp. mentally **2** : to take from the hinges

un·hitch \-ˈhich\ *vb* : UNFASTEN, LOOSE

un·ho·ly \-ˈhō-lē\ *adj* **1** : not holy : PROFANE, WICKED **2** : very unpleasant ⟨an ~ mess⟩ — **un·ho·li·ness** \-lē-nəs\ *n*

un·hook \-ˈhu̇k\ *vb* : to loose from a hook

un·horse \-ˈhȯrs\ *vb* : to dislodge from or as if from a horse

uni·cam·er·al \ˌyü-ni-ˈka-mə-rəl\ *adj* : having a single legislative house or chamber

UNI·CEF \ˈyü-nə-ˌsef\ *abbr* [*United Nations International Children's Emergency Fund*, its former name] United Nations Children's Fund

uni·cel·lu·lar \ˌyü-ni-ˈsel-yə-lər\ *adj* : having or consisting of a single cell

uni·corn \ˈyü-nə-ˌkȯrn\ *n* [ME *unicorne*, fr. AF, fr. LL *unicornis*, fr. L, having one horn, fr. *unus* one + *cornu* horn] : a mythical animal with one horn in the middle of the forehead

uni·cy·cle \ˈyü-ni-ˌsī-kəl\ *n* : a vehicle that has a single wheel and is usu. propelled by pedals

uni·di·rec·tion·al \ˌyü-ni-də-ˈrek-shə-nəl, -dī-\ *adj* : having, moving in, or responsive in a single direction

uni·fi·ca·tion \ˌyü-nə-fə-ˈkā-shən\ *n* : the act, process, or result of unifying : the state of being unified

¹uni·form \ˈyü-nə-ˌfȯrm\ *adj* **1** : not varying ⟨~ procedures⟩ **2** : of the same form with others — **uni·form·ly** *adv*

²uniform *vb* : to clothe with a uniform

³uniform *n* : distinctive dress worn by members of a particular group (as an army or a police force)

uni·for·mi·ty \ˌyü-nə-ˈfȯr-mə-tē\ *n, pl* **-ties** : the state of being uniform

uni·fy \ˈyü-nə-ˌfī\ *vb* **-fied; -fy·ing** : to make into a coherent whole : UNITE

uni·lat·er·al \ˌyü-nə-ˈla-tə-rəl\ *adj* : of, having, affecting, or done by one side only — **uni·lat·er·al·ly** *adv*

un·im·peach·able \ˌən-im-ˈpē-chə-bəl\ *adj* : not liable to accusation : IRREPROACHABLE ⟨an ~ reputation⟩

un·in·hib·it·ed \ˌən-in-ˈhi-bə-təd\ *adj* : free from inhibition; *also* : boisterously informal — **un·in·hib·it·ed·ly** *adv*

un·in·stall \ˌən-in-ˈstȯl\ *vb* : to remove (software) from a computer system

un·in·tel·li·gent \-ˈte-lə-jənt\ *adj* : lacking intelligence

un·in·tel·li·gi·ble \-jə-bəl\ *adj* : not intelligible : OBSCURE — **un·in·tel·li·gi·bly** \-blē\ *adv*

un·in·ter·est·ed \ˌən-ˈin-trəs-təd, -tə-rəs-, -tə-ˌres-\ *adj* : not interested : not having the mind or feelings engaged or aroused

un·in·ter·rupt·ed \ˌən-ˌin-tə-ˈrəp-təd\ *adj* : not interrupted : CONTINUOUS

union \ˈyün-yən\ *n* **1** : an act or instance of uniting two or more things into one : the state of being so united : COMBINATION, JUNCTION **2** : a uniting in marriage **3** : something formed by a combining of parts or members; *esp* : a confederation of independent individuals (as nations or persons) for some common purpose **4** : an organization of workers (as a labor union or a trade union) formed to advance its members' interests esp. in respect to wages and working conditions **5** : a device emblematic of union used on or as a national flag; *also* : the upper inner corner of a flag **6** : a device for connecting parts (as of a machine); *esp* : a coupling for pipes

union·ise *Brit var of* UNIONIZE

union·ism \ˈyün-yə-ˌni-zəm\ *n* **1** : the principle or policy of forming or adhering to a union; *esp*, *cap* : adherence to the policy of a firm federal union before or during the U.S. Civil War **2** : the principles or system of trade unions — **union·ist** *n*

union·ize \ˈyün-yə-ˌnīz\ *vb* **-ized; -iz·ing**

unhampered	unhistorical	unimportant	uninspired
unhardened	unhonored	unimposing	uninstructed
unharmed	unhoused	unimpressed	uninstructive
unharvested	unhurried	unimpressive	uninsured
unhatched	unhurt	unimproved	unintelligent
unhealed	unhygienic	unincorporated	unintelligible
unhealthful	unidentifiable	uninfected	unintelligibly
unheated	unidentified	uninfluenced	unintended
unheeded	unidiomatic	uninformative	unintentional
unhelpful	unimaginable	uninformed	unintentionally
unheralded	unimaginative	uninhabitable	uninteresting
unheroic	unimpaired	uninhabited	uninterrupted
unhesitating	unimpassioned	uninitiated	uninvited
unhindered	unimpeded	uninjured	uninviting

: to form into or cause to join a labor union — **un·ion·i·za·tion** \ˌyün-yə-nə-ˈzā-shən\

union jack n 1 : a flag consisting of the part of a national flag that signifies union 2 cap U&J : the national flag of the United Kingdom

unique \yü-ˈnēk\ adj 1 : being the only one of its kind : SINGLE, SOLE 2 : very unusual : NOTABLE — **unique·ly** adv — **unique·ness** n

uni·sex \ˈyü-nə-ˌseks\ adj : not distinguishable as male or female; also : suitable or designed for both males and females — **unisex** n

uni·sex·u·al \ˌyü-nə-ˈsek-shə-wəl\ adj 1 : having only male or only female sex organs 2 : UNISEX

uni·son \ˈyü-nə-sən, -zən\ n [ME unisoun, fr. MF unisson, fr. ML unisonus having the same sound, fr. L unus one + sonus sound] 1 : sameness or identity in musical pitch 2 : the condition of being tuned or sounded at the same pitch or in octaves ⟨sing in ∼⟩ 3 : harmonious agreement or union : ACCORD

unit \ˈyü-nət\ n 1 : the smallest whole number greater than zero : ONE 2 : a definite amount or quantity used as a standard of measurement 3 : a single thing, person, or group that is a constituent of a whole; also : a part of a military establishment that has a prescribed organization — **unit** adj

Uni·tar·i·an \ˌyü-nə-ˈter-ē-ən\ n : a member of a religious denomination stressing individual freedom of belief — **Uni·tar·i·an·ism** n

uni·tary \ˈyü-nə-ˌter-ē\ adj 1 : of or relating to a unit 2 : not divided — **uni·tar·i·ly** \ˌyü-nə-ˈter-ə-lē\ adv

unite \yü-ˈnīt\ vb **unit·ed; unit·ing** 1 : to put or join together so as to make one : COMBINE, COALESCE 2 : to join by a legal or moral bond; also : to join in interest or fellowship 3 : AMALGAMATE, CONSOLIDATE 4 : to act in concert

unit·ed \yü-ˈnī-təd\ adj 1 : made one : COMBINED 2 : relating to or produced by joint action 3 : being in agreement : HARMONIOUS

unit·ize \ˈyü-nə-ˌtīz\ vb **-ized; -iz·ing** 1 : to form or convert into a unit 2 : to divide into units

uni·ty \ˈyü-nə-tē\ n, pl **-ties** 1 : the quality or state of being or being made one : ONENESS 2 : a definite quantity or combination of quantities taken as one or for which 1 is made to stand in calculation 3 : CONCORD, ACCORD, HARMONY 4 : continuity without change ⟨∼ of purpose⟩ 5 : reference of all the parts of a literary or artistic composition to a single main idea 6 : totality of related parts ♦ **Synonyms** SOLIDARITY, UNION, INTEGRITY

univ abbr 1 universal 2 university

uni·valve \ˈyü-ni-ˌvalv\ n : a mollusk having a shell with only one piece; esp : GASTROPOD — **univalve** adj

uni·ver·sal \ˌyü-nə-ˈvər-səl\ adj 1 : including, covering, or affecting the whole without limit or exception : available or applying to everyone ⟨∼ privileges⟩ ⟨a ∼ rule⟩ 2 : present or occurring everywhere 3 : used or for use among all ⟨a ∼ language⟩ 4 : adaptable for various purposes ⟨a ∼ remote control⟩ — **uni·ver·sal·ly** adv

uni·ver·sal·i·ty \-vər-ˈsa-lə-tē\ n : the quality or state of being universal

uni·ver·sal·ize \-ˈvər-sə-ˌlīz\ vb **-ized; -iz·ing** : to make universal : GENERALIZE — **uni·ver·sal·i·za·tion** \-ˌvər-sə-lə-ˈzā-shən\ n

universal joint n : a shaft coupling for transmitting rotation from one shaft to another not in a straight line with it

Universal Product Code n : a combination of a bar code and numbers by which a scanner can identify a product and usu. assign a price

uni·verse \ˈyü-nə-ˌvərs\ n [ME, fr. L universum, fr. neut. of universus entire, whole, fr. unus one + versus turned toward, fr. pp. of vertere to turn] : the whole body of things observed or assumed : COSMOS

uni·ver·si·ty \ˌyü-nə-ˈvər-sə-tē\ n, pl **-ties** : an institution of higher learning authorized to confer degrees in various special fields (as theology, law, and medicine) as well as in the arts and sciences generally

un·just \ˌən-ˈjəst\ adj : characterized by injustice — **un·just·ly** adv

un·kempt \-ˈkempt\ adj 1 : lacking order or neatness; also : ROUGH, UNPOLISHED 2 : not combed : DISHEVELED

un·kind \-ˈkīnd\ adj : not kind or sympathetic ⟨an ∼ remark⟩ — **un·kind·ly** adv — **un·kind·ness** n

un·kind·ly \-ˈkīnd-lē\ adj : UNKIND — **un·kind·li·ness** n

un·know·ing \ˌən-ˈnō-iŋ\ adj : not knowing — **un·know·ing·ly** adv

un·known \-ˈnōn\ adj : not known or not well-known — **unknown** n

un·lace \ˌən-ˈlās\ vb : to loose by undoing a lace

un·lade \-ˈlād\ vb **lad·ed; -laded** or **-laden** \-ˈlā-dᵊn\; **-lad·ing** : to take the load or cargo from : UNLOAD

un·latch \-ˈlach\ vb 1 : to open or loose by lifting the latch 2 : to become loosed or opened

un·law·ful \ˌən-ˈlö-fəl\ adj 1 : not lawful : ILLEGAL 2 : ILLEGITIMATE — **un·law·ful·ly** adv

un·lead·ed \-ˈle-dəd\ adj : not treated or mixed with lead or lead compounds

un·learn \-ˈlərn\ vb : to put out of one's knowledge or memory; also : to discard the habit of

un·learned \-ˈlər-nəd for 1; -ˈlərnd for 2\ adj 1 : UNEDUCATED, ILLITERATE 2 : not gained by study or training

unjointed	unkept	unknowledgeable	unladylike
unjustifiable	unknowable	unlabeled	unlamented
unjustified			

un·leash \-ˈlēsh\ *vb* : to free from or as if from a leash : let loose

un·less \ən-ˈles, ˈən-ˌles\ *conj* : except on condition that 〈won't go ∼ you do〉

un·let·tered \ən-ˈle-tərd\ *adj* : not educated : ILLITERATE

¹un·like \-ˈlīk\ *adj* 1 : not like : DISSIMILAR, DIFFERENT 2 : UNEQUAL — **un·like·ness** *n*

²unlike *prep* 1 : different from 〈she's quite ∼ her sister〉 2 : unusual for 〈it's ∼ you to be late〉 3 : differently from 〈behaves ∼ his brother〉

un·like·li·hood \ˌən-ˈlī-klē-ˌhu̇d\ *n* : IMPROBABILITY

un·like·ly \-ˈlī-klē\ *adj* 1 : not likely : IMPROBABLE 2 : likely to fail

un·lim·ber \ən-ˈlim-bər\ *vb* : to get ready for action

un·list·ed \ˌən-ˈlis-təd\ *adj* 1 : not appearing on a list; *esp* : not appearing in a telephone book 2 : not listed on a stock exchange

un·load \-ˈlōd\ *vb* 1 : to take away or off : REMOVE 〈∼ cargo from a hold〉; *also* : to get rid of 2 : to take a load from 〈∼ the ship〉; *also* : to relieve or set free : UNBURDEN 〈∼ one's mind of worries〉 3 : to draw the charge from 〈∼ed the gun〉 4 : to sell in volume

un·lock \-ˈläk\ *vb* 1 : to open or unfasten through release of a lock 2 : RELEASE 〈∼ a flood of emotions〉 3 : DISCLOSE, REVEAL 〈∼ nature's secrets〉

un·looked–for \-ˈlu̇kt-ˌfȯr\ *adj* : UNEXPECTED

un·loose \ən-ˈlüs\ *vb* : to relax the strain of : set free; *also* : UNTIE

un·loos·en \-ˈlü-sᵊn\ *vb* : UNLOOSE

un·love·ly \-ˈləv-lē\ *adj* : having no charm or appeal : not amiable

un·luck·i·ly \-ˈlə-kə-lē\ *adv* : UNFORTUNATELY

un·lucky \-ˈlə-kē\ *adj* 1 : UNFORTUNATE, ILL-FATED 2 : likely to bring misfortune : INAUSPICIOUS 3 : REGRETTABLE

un·man \ˌən-ˈman\ *vb* 1 : to deprive of manly courage 2 : CASTRATE

un·man·ly \-ˈman-lē\ *adj* : not manly : COWARDLY; *also* : EFFEMINATE

un·man·ner·ly \-ˈma-nər-lē\ *adj* : RUDE, IMPOLITE — **unmannerly** *adv*

un·mask \ˌən-ˈmask\ *vb* 1 : to strip of a mask or a disguise : EXPOSE 2 : to remove one's mask

un·mean·ing \-ˈmē-niŋ\ *adj* : having no meaning : SENSELESS

un·me·di·at·ed \ˌən-ˈmē-dē-ˌā-təd\ *adj* : not mediated : not communicated or transformed by an intervening agency

un·meet \-ˈmēt\ *adj* : not meet or fit : UNSUITABLE, IMPROPER

un·men·tion·able \-ˈmen-chə-nə-bəl\ *adj* : not fit or proper to be talked about 〈an ∼ topic〉

un·mer·ci·ful \-ˈmər-si-fəl\ *adj* : not merciful : CRUEL, MERCILESS — **un·mer·ci·ful·ly** *adv*

un·mind·ful \-ˈmīnd-fəl\ *adj* : not mindful : CARELESS, UNAWARE

un·mis·tak·able \ˌən-mə-ˈstā-kə-bəl\ *adj* : not capable of being mistaken or misunderstood : CLEAR, OBVIOUS — **un·mis·tak·ably** \-blē\ *adv*

un·mit·i·gat·ed \ˌən-ˈmi-tə-ˌgā-təd\ *adj* 1 : not softened or lessened 2 : ABSOLUTE, DOWNRIGHT 〈an ∼ liar〉

un·moor \-ˈmu̇r\ *vb* : to loose from or as if from moorings

un·mor·al \-ˈmȯr-əl\ *adj* : having no moral perception or quality : AMORAL — **un·mo·ral·i·ty** \ˌən-mə-ˈra-lə-tē\ *n*

un·muz·zle \-ˈmə-zəl\ *vb* : to remove a muzzle from

un·nat·u·ral \ˌən-ˈna-chə-rəl\ *adj* : contrary to or acting contrary to nature or natural instincts; *also* : ABNORMAL — **un·nat·u·ral·ly** *adv* — **un·nat·u·ral·ness** *n*

un·nec·es·sar·i·ly \ˌən-ˌne-sə-ˈser-ə-lē\ *adv* 1 : not by necessity 2 : to an unnecessary degree 〈∼ harsh〉

un·nerve \ˌən-ˈnərv\ *vb* : to deprive of courage, strength, or steadiness; *also* : UPSET

un·num·bered \ˌən-ˈnəm-bərd\ *adj* : not numbered or counted : INNUMERABLE

un·ob·tru·sive \ˌən-əb-ˈtrü-siv\ *adj* : not obtrusive or forward : not bold : INCONSPICUOUS — **un·ob·tru·sive·ly** *adv*

un·oc·cu·pied \ˌən-ˈä-kyə-ˌpīd\ *adj* 1 : not busy : UNEMPLOYED 2 : not occupied : EMPTY, VACANT

un·or·ga·nized \-ˈȯr-gə-ˌnīzd\ *adj* 1 : not formed or brought into an integrated or ordered whole 2 : not organized into unions 〈∼ labor〉

un·pack \ˌən-ˈpak\ *vb* 1 : to separate and remove things packed 2 : to open and remove the contents of

unleavened	unmapped	unmodified	unobserved
unlicensed	unmarked	unmolested	unobstructed
unlighted	unmarketable	unmotivated	unobtainable
unlikable	unmarred	unmounted	unofficial
unlimited	unmarried	unmovable	unofficially
unlined	unmasculine	unmoved	unopened
unlit	unmatched	unmusical	unopposed
unliterary	unmeant	unnameable	unoriginal
unlivable	unmeasurable	unnamed	unorthodox
unlovable	unmeasured	unnecessary	unorthodoxy
unloved	unmelodious	unneeded	unostentatious
unloving	unmentioned	unnewsworthy	unowned
unmade	unmerited	unnoticeable	unpaged
unmalicious	unmilitary	unnoticed	unpaid
unmanageable	unmilled	unobjectionable	unpainted
unmanned	unmixed	unobservant	unpaired

un·par·al·leled \ˌən-'pa-rə-ˌleld\ *adj* : having no parallel; *esp* : having no equal or match

un·par·lia·men·ta·ry \ˌən-ˌpär-lə-'men-tə-rē\ *adj* : contrary to parliamentary practice

un·peg \ˌən-'peg\ *vb* **1** : to remove a peg from **2** : to unfasten by or as if by removing a peg

un·per·son \'ən-'pər-sᵊn, -ˌpər-\ *n* : a person who usu. for political or ideological reasons is removed from recognition or consideration

un·pile \ˌən-'p(-ə)l\ *vb* : to take or disentangle from a pile

un·pin \-'pin\ *vb* : to remove a pin from : UNFASTEN

un·pleas·ant \-'ple-zᵊnt\ *adj* : not pleasant : DISAGREEABLE — **un·pleas·ant·ly** *adv* — **un·pleas·ant·ness** *n*

un·plug \ˌən-'pləg\ *vb* **1** : UNCLOG **2** : to remove (a plug) from a receptacle; *also* : to disconnect from an electric circuit by removing a plug

un·plumbed \-'pləmd\ *adj* **1** : not tested or measured with a plumb line **2** : not thoroughly explored

un·pop·u·lar \ˌən-'pä-pyə-lər\ *adj* : not popular : looked upon or received unfavorably — **un·pop·u·lar·i·ty** \ˌən-ˌpä-pyə-'la-rə-tē\ *n*

un·prec·e·dent·ed \ˌən-'pre-sə-ˌden-təd\ *adj* : having no precedent : NOVEL

un·pre·ten·tious \ˌən-pri-'ten-chəs\ *adj* : not pretentious : MODEST

un·prin·ci·pled \ˌən-'prin-sə-pəld\ *adj* : lacking sound or honorable principles : UNSCRUPULOUS

un·print·able \-'prin-tə-bəl\ *adj* : unfit or too offensive to be printed ⟨~ remarks⟩

un·prof·it·able \ˌən-'prä-fə-tə-bəl\ *adj* : not profitable : USELESS, VAIN

un·pro·tect·ed \ˌən-prə-'tek-təd\ *adj* **1** : lacking protection **2** : performed without measures to prevent pregnancy or sexually transmitted disease ⟨~ sex⟩

un·qual·i·fied \ˌən-'kwä-lə-ˌfīd\ *adj* **1** : not having requisite qualifications **2** : not modified or restricted by reservations : COMPLETE — **un·qual·i·fied·ly** \-ˌfī-əd-lē\ *adv*

un·ques·tion·able \-'kwes-chə-nə-bəl\ *adj* : not questionable : INDISPUTABLE — **un·ques·tion·ably** \-blē\ *adv*

un·ques·tion·ing \-chə-niŋ\ *adj* : not questioning : accepting without examination or hesitation — **un·ques·tion·ing·ly** *adv*

un·qui·et \-'kwī-ət\ *adj* **1** : not quiet : AGITATED, DISTURBED **2** : physically, emotionally, or mentally restless : UNEASY

un·quote \'ən-ˌkwōt\ *n* — used orally to indicate the end of a direct quotation

un·rav·el \ˌən-'ra-vəl\ *vb* **1** : to separate the threads of **2** : SOLVE ⟨~ a mystery⟩ **3** : to become unraveled

un·read \-'red\ *adj* **1** : not read; *also* : left unexamined **2** : lacking the benefits or the experience of reading

un·re·al \-'rēl\ *adj* : lacking in reality, substance, or genuineness — **un·re·al·i·ty** \ˌən-rē-'a-lə-tē\ *n*

un·rea·son·able \-'rē-zᵊn-ə-bəl\ *adj* **1** : not governed by or acting according to reason; *also* : not conformable to reason : ABSURD **2** : exceeding the bounds of reason or moderation — **un·rea·son·able·ness** *n* — **un·rea·son·ably** *adv*

un·rea·soned \-'rē-zᵊnd\ *adj* : not based on reason or reasoning ⟨~ fears⟩

un·rea·son·ing \-'rē-zᵊn-iŋ\ *adj* : not using or showing the use of reason as a guide or control

un·re·con·struct·ed \ˌən-ˌrē-kən-'strək-təd\ *adj* : not reconciled to some political, economic, or social change; *esp* : holding stubbornly to a particular belief, view, place, or style

un·reel \ˌən-'rēl\ *vb* **1** : to unwind from or as if from a reel **2** : to perform successfully

un·re·gen·er·ate \ˌən-ri-'je-nə-rət\ *adj* : not regenerated or reformed

un·re·lent·ing \-'len-tiŋ\ *adj* **1** : not yielding in determination : STERN ⟨~ leader⟩ **2** : not letting up or weakening in vigor or pace : CONSTANT — **un·re·lent·ing·ly** *adv*

un·re·mit·ting \-'mi-tiŋ\ *adj* : CONSTANT, INCESSANT ⟨~ pain⟩ — **un·re·mit·ting·ly** *adv*

unpalatable	unpolluted	unprogressive	unrealized
unpardonable	unposed	unpromising	unrecognizable
unpasteurized	unpractical	unprompted	unrecognized
unpatriotic	unpredictability	unpronounceable	unrecorded
unpaved	unpredictable	unpropitious	unrecoverable
unpeeled	unprejudiced	unproven	unredeemable
unperceived	unpremeditated	unprovided	unrefined
unperceptive	unprepared	unprovoked	unreflecting
unperformed	unpreparedness	unpublished	unreflective
unpersuaded	unprepossessing	unpunished	unregistered
unpersuasive	unpressed	unquenchable	unregulated
unperturbed	unpretending	unquestioned	unrehearsed
unplanned	unpretty	unraised	unrelated
unplanted	unprivileged	unrated	unreliable
unpleasing	unprocessed	unratified	unrelieved
unplowed	unproductive	unreachable	unremarkable
unpoetic	unprofessed	unreadable	unremembered
unpolished	unprofessional	unready	unremovable
unpolitical	unprogrammed	unrealistic	

un·re·quit·ed \,ən-ri-ˈkwī-təd\ adj : not requited : not reciprocated or returned in kind ⟨∼ love⟩

un·re·served \-ˈzərvd\ adj : not limited or partial ⟨∼ enthusiasm⟩ 2 : not cautious or reticent : FRANK, OPEN 3 : not set aside for special use — **un·re·serv·ed·ly** \-ˈzər-vəd-lē\ adv

un·rest \ˌən-ˈrest\ n : a disturbed or uneasy state : TURMOIL

un·re·strained \ˌən-ri-ˈstrānd\ adj 1 : IMMODERATE, UNCONTROLLED ⟨∼ anger⟩ 2 : SPONTANEOUS

un·re·straint \-ˈstrānt\ n : lack of restraint

un·rid·dle \ˌən-ˈri-dᵊl\ vb : to find the explanation of : SOLVE

un·righ·teous \-ˈrī-chəs\ adj 1 : SINFUL, WICKED 2 : UNJUST — **un·righ·teous·ness** n

un·ripe \-ˈrīp\ adj : not ripe : IMMATURE

un·ri·valed or **un·ri·valled** \ˌən-ˈrī-vəld\ adj : having no rival : SUPREME

un·robe \-ˈrōb\ vb : DISROBE, UNDRESS

un·roll \-ˈrōl\ vb 1 : to unwind a roll of : open out 2 : DISPLAY, DISCLOSE 3 : to become unrolled or spread out

un·roof \-ˈrüf, -ˈruf\ vb : to strip off the roof or covering of

un·ruf·fled \ˌən-ˈrə-fəld\ adj 1 : not agitated or upset 2 : not ruffled : SMOOTH ⟨∼ water⟩

un·ruly \-ˈrü-lē\ adj [ME unreuly, fr. un- + reuly disciplined, fr. reule rule, fr. AF, fr. L regula straightedge, rule, fr. regere to direct] : not submissive to rule or restraint : TURBULENT ⟨∼ passions⟩ — **un·rul·i·ness** \-ˈrü-lē-nəs\ n

un·sad·dle \ˌən-ˈsa-dᵊl\ vb 1 : to remove the saddle from a horse 2 : UNHORSE

un·sat·u·rat·ed \-ˈsa-chə-ˌrā-təd\ adj 1 : capable of absorbing or dissolving more of something 2 : containing double or triple bonds between carbon atoms ⟨∼ fat⟩ — **un·sat·u·rate** \-rət\ n

un·saved \ˌən-ˈsāvd\ adj : not saved; esp : not rescued from eternal punishment

un·sa·vory \-ˈsā-və-rē\ adj 1 : TASTELESS 2 : unpleasant to taste or smell 3 : morally offensive ⟨∼ characters⟩

un·say \-ˈsā\ vb -said \-ˈsed\; -say·ing : to take back (something said) : RETRACT, WITHDRAW

un·scathed \-ˈskāthd\ adj : wholly unharmed : not injured

un·schooled \-ˈsküld\ adj : not schooled : UNTAUGHT, UNTRAINED

un·sci·en·tif·ic \ˌən-ˌsī-ən-ˈti-fik\ adj : not

scientific : not in accord with the principles and methods of science

un·scram·ble \ˌən-ˈskram-bəl\ vb 1 : RESOLVE, CLARIFY 2 : to restore (as a radio message) to intelligible form

un·screw \-ˈskrü\ vb 1 : to draw the screws from 2 : to loosen by turning

un·scru·pu·lous \-ˈskrü-pyə-ləs\ adj : not scrupulous : UNPRINCIPLED — **un·scru·pu·lous·ly** adv — **un·scru·pu·lous·ness** n

un·seal \-ˈsēl\ vb : to break or remove the seal of : OPEN

un·search·able \-ˈsər-chə-bəl\ adj : not capable of being searched or explored ⟨∼ forests⟩

un·sea·son·able \-ˈsē-zⁿn-ə-bəl\ adj : not seasonable : happening or coming at the wrong time : UNTIMELY — **un·sea·son·ably** \-blē\ adv

un·seat \-ˈsēt\ vb 1 : to throw from one's seat esp. on horseback 2 : to remove from political office

un·seem·ly \-ˈsēm-lē\ adj : not according with established standards of good form or taste; also : not suitable — **un·seem·li·ness** n

un·seen \ˌən-ˈsēn\ adj : not seen : INVISIBLE ⟨∼ dangers⟩

un·seg·re·gat·ed \-ˈse-gri-ˌgā-təd\ adj : not segregated; esp : free from racial segregation

un·self·ish \-ˈsel-fish\ adj : not selfish : GENEROUS — **un·self·ish·ly** adv — **un·self·ish·ness** n

un·set·tle \ˌən-ˈse-tᵊl\ vb : to move or loosen from a settled position : DISPLACE, DISTURB

un·set·tled \-ˈse-tᵊld\ adj 1 : not settled : not fixed (as in position or character) 2 : not calm : DISTURBED 3 : not decided in mind : UNRESOLVED 4 : not paid ⟨∼ accounts⟩ 5 : not occupied by settlers

un·shack·le \-ˈsha-kəl\ vb : to free from shackles

un·shaped \-ˈshāpt\ adj : not shaped; esp : not being in finished, final, or perfect form ⟨∼ ideas⟩ ⟨∼ timber⟩

un·sheathe \ˌən-ˈshēth\ vb : to draw from or as if from a sheath

un·ship \-ˈship\ vb 1 : to remove from a ship 2 : to remove or become removed from position ⟨∼ an oar⟩

un·shod \ˌən-ˈshäd\ adj : not wearing or provided with shoes

un·sight·ly \ˌən-ˈsīt-lē\ adj : unpleasant to the sight : UGLY ⟨an ∼ mess⟩

un·skilled \-ˈskild\ adj 1 : not skilled; esp

unrepentant	unrewarding	unsatisfied	unserviceable
unreported	unrhymed	unscented	unsexual
unrepresentative	unrhythmic	unscheduled	unshaded
unrepresented	unripened	unscholarly	unshakable
unrepressed	unromantic	unsealed	unshaken
unresistant	unromantically	unseasoned	unshapely
unresisting	unsafe	unseaworthy	unshaven
unresolved	unsaid	unsegmented	unshorn
unresponsive	unsalable	unself–conscious	unsifted
unresponsiveness	unsalted	unself–consciously	unsigned
unrestful	unsanctioned	unsensational	unsinkable
unrestricted	unsanitary	unsentimental	
unreturnable	unsatisfactory	unserious	

: not skilled in a specified branch of work **2** : not requiring skill

un·skill·ful \-'skil-fəl\ *adj* : lacking in skill or proficiency — **un·skill·ful·ly** *adv*

un·sling \-'sliŋ\ *vb* **-slung** \-'sləŋ\; **-sling·ing** : to remove from being slung

un·snap \-'snap\ *vb* : to loosen or free by or as if by undoing a snap

un·snarl \-'snärl\ *vb* : to remove snarls from : UNTANGLE

un·so·phis·ti·cat·ed \,ən-sə-'fis-tə-,kā-təd\ *adj* **1** : not worldly-wise : lacking sophistication **2** : SIMPLE

un·sought \,ən-'sȯt\ *adj* : not sought : not searched for or asked for : not obtained by effort ⟨~ honors⟩

un·sound \-'saund\ *adj* **1** : not healthy or whole; *also* : not mentally normal ⟨of ~ mind⟩ **2** : not valid **3** : not firmly made or fixed ⟨structurally ~⟩. — **un·sound·ly** *adv* — **un·sound·ness** *n*

un·spar·ing \-'sper-iŋ\ *adj* **1** : HARD, RUTHLESS ⟨~ criticism⟩ **2** : not frugal : LIBERAL, PROFUSE ⟨~ generosity⟩

un·speak·able \-'spē-kə-bəl\ *adj* **1** : impossible to express in words **2** : extremely bad ⟨~ offenses⟩ — **un·speak·ably** \-blē\ *adv*

un·spool \,ən-'spül\ *vb* **1** : to unwind from a spool **2** : to present artfully ⟨~ a new film⟩

un·spot·ted \-'spä-təd\ *adj* : not spotted or stained; *esp* : free from moral stain

un·sprung \-'sprəŋ\ *adj* : not sprung; *esp* : not equipped with springs

un·sta·ble \-'stā-bəl\ *adj* **1** : not stable **2** : FICKLE, VACILLATING; *also* : lacking effective emotional control **3** : readily changing (as by decomposing) in chemical or physical composition or in biological activity ⟨an ~ atomic nucleus⟩

un·steady \,ən-'ste-dē\ *adj* : not steady : UNSTABLE — **un·stead·i·ly** \-'ste-də-lē\ *adv* — **un·stead·i·ness** \-'ste-dē-nəs\ *n*

un·stint·ing \-'stin-tiŋ\ *adj* **1** : not restricting or holding back **2** : giving or being given freely or generously ⟨~ praise⟩

un·stop \-'stäp\ *vb* **1** : UNCLOG **2** : to remove a stopper from

un·stop·pa·ble \,ən-'stä-pə-bəl\ *adj* : incapable of being stopped

un·strap \-'strap\ *vb* : to remove or loose a strap from

un·stressed \,ən-'strest\ *adj* : not

stressed; *esp* : not bearing a stress or accent ⟨~ syllables⟩

un·strung \-'strəŋ\ *adj* **1** : having the strings loose or detached **2** : made weak, disordered, or unstable

un·stud·ied \-'stə-dēd\ *adj* **1** : not acquired by study **2** : NATURAL, UNFORCED ⟨moved with ~ grace⟩

un·sub·stan·tial \,ən-səb-'stan-chəl\ *adj* : INSUBSTANTIAL

un·sung \,ən-'səŋ\ *adj* **1** : not sung **2** : not celebrated in song or verse ⟨~ heroes⟩

un·swerv·ing \,ən-'swər-viŋ\ *adj* **1** : not swerving or turning aside **2** : STEADY

un·tan·gle \,ən-'taŋ-gəl\ *vb* **1** : DISENTANGLE **2** : to straighten out : RESOLVE ⟨~ a problem⟩

un·taught \-'tȯt\ *adj* **1** : not instructed or taught : IGNORANT **2** : NATURAL, SPONTANEOUS ⟨~ kindness⟩

un·think·able \-'thiŋ-kə-bəl\ *adj* : not to be thought of or considered as possible ⟨~ cruelty⟩

un·think·ing \,ən-'thiŋ-kiŋ\ *adj* : not thinking; *esp* : THOUGHTLESS, HEEDLESS — **un·think·ing·ly** *adv*

un·thought \,ən-'thȯt\ *adj* : not anticipated : UNEXPECTED — often used with *of* ⟨unthought-of-development⟩

un·tie \-'tī\ *vb* **-tied; -ty·ing** *or* **-tie·ing** **1** : to free from something that ties, fastens, or restrains : UNBIND **2** : DISENTANGLE, RESOLVE **3** : to become loosened or unbound

¹un·til \,ən-'til\ *prep* : up to the time of ⟨worked ~ 5 o'clock⟩

²until *conj* **1** : up to the time that ⟨wait ~ he calls⟩ **2** : to the point or degree that ⟨ran ~ she was breathless⟩

¹un·time·ly \,ən-'tīm-lē\ *adv* : at an inopportune time : UNSEASONABLY; *also* : PREMATURELY

²untimely *adj* : PREMATURE ⟨~ death⟩; *also* : INOPPORTUNE, UNSEASONABLE

un·tir·ing \,ən-'tī-riŋ\ *adj* : not becoming tired : INDEFATIGABLE ⟨an ~ worker⟩ — **un·tir·ing·ly** *adv*

un·to \'ən-,tü\ *prep* : TO

un·told \,ən-'tōld\ *adj* **1** : too great or numerous to count **2** : not told : not revealed

¹un·touch·able \,ən-'tə-chə-bəl\ *adj* : forbidden to the touch

²untouchable *n* : a member of the lowest social class in India having in traditional

unsmiling	unsportsmanlike	unsupportable	untalented
unsociable	unstained	unsupported	untamed
unsoiled	unstated	unsure	untanned
unsold	unsterile	unsurpassed	untapped
unsoldierly	unstructured	unsurprising	untarnished
unsolicited	unstylish	unsurprisingly	untaxed
unsolvable	unsubdued	unsuspected	unteachable
unsolved	unsubstantiated	unsuspecting	untenable
unsorted	unsubtle	unsuspicious	untenanted
unspecified	unsuccessful	unsweetened	untended
unspectacular	unsuccessfully	unsymmetrical	untested
unspent	unsuitable	unsympathetic	unthrifty
unspiritual	unsuited	unsystematic	untidy
unspoiled	unsullied	untactful	untilled
unspoken	unsupervised	untainted	untitled

Hindu belief the quality of defiling by contact with a member of a higher caste

un·touched \,ən-'təcht\ *adj* **1** : not subjected to touching **2** : not described or dealt with **3** : not tasted **4** : being in a primeval state or condition **5** : UNAFFECTED ⟨~ by scandals⟩

un·tow·ard \,ən-'tórd, -'tō-ərd; ,ən-tə-'wórd\ *adj* **1** : difficult to manage : STUBBORN, WILLFUL ⟨an ~ child⟩ **2** : INCONVENIENT, TROUBLESOME ⟨an ~ encounter⟩

un·tried \,ən-'trīd\ *adj* : not tested or proved by experience or trial; *also* : not tried in court

un·true \-'trü\ *adj* **1** : not faithful : DISLOYAL **2** : not according with a standard of correctness **3** : FALSE

un·truth \,ən-'trüth, 'ən-,trüth\ *n* **1** : lack of truthfulness **2** : FALSEHOOD

un·tune \-'tün, -'tyün\ *vb* **1** : to put out of tune **2** : DISARRANGE, DISCOMPOSE

un·tu·tored \-'tü-tərd, -'tyü-\ *adj* : UNTAUGHT, UNLEARNED, IGNORANT

un·twine \-'twīn\ *vb* : UNWIND, DISENTANGLE

un·twist \,ən-'twist\ *vb* **1** : to separate the twisted parts of : UNTWINE **2** : to become untwined

un·used \-'yüst, -'yüzd *for 1;* -'yüzd *for 2*\ *adj* **1** : UNACCUSTOMED ⟨~ to such treatment⟩ **2** : not used

un·usu·al \-'yü-zhə-wəl\ *adj* : not usual : UNCOMMON, RARE — **un·usu·al·ly** *adv*

un·ut·ter·able \,ən-'ə-tə-rə-bəl\ *adj* : being beyond the powers of description : INEXPRESSIBLE ⟨~ shame⟩ — **un·ut·ter·ably** \-blē\ *adv*

un·var·nished \-'vär-nisht\ *adj* **1** : not varnished **2** : not embellished : PLAIN ⟨the ~ truth⟩

un·veil \,ən-'vāl\ *vb* **1** : to remove a veil or covering from : DISCLOSE **2** : to remove a veil : reveal oneself

un·voiced \-'vóist\ *adj* **1** : not verbally expressed : UNSPOKEN **2** : VOICELESS 2

un·war·rant·able \-'wòr-ən-tə-bəl\ *adj* : not justifiable : INEXCUSABLE — **un·war·rant·ably** \-blē\ *adv*

un·weave \-'wēv\ *vb* **-wove** \-'wōv\; **-wo·ven** \-'wō-vən\; **-weav·ing** : DISENTANGLE, RAVEL

un·well \,ən-'wəl\ *adj* : SICK, AILING

un·whole·some \-'hōl-səm\ *adj* **1** : harmful to physical, mental, or moral well-being ⟨~ food⟩ **2** : CORRUPT, UNSOUND ⟨~ deals⟩; *also* : offensive to the senses : LOATHSOME ⟨an ~ stench⟩

un·wieldy \-'wēl-dē\ *adj* : not easily managed, handled, or used (as because of

bulk, weight, or complexity) : AWKWARD ⟨an ~ tool⟩

un·wind \-'wīnd\ *vb* **-wound** \-'waúnd\; **-wind·ing** **1** : to undo something that is wound : loose from coils **2** : to become unwound : be capable of being unwound **3** : RELAX

un·wise \,ən-'wīz\ *adj* : not wise : FOOLISH — **un·wise·ly** *adv*

un·wit·ting \-'wi-tiŋ\ *adj* **1** : not knowing : UNAWARE **2** : not intended : INADVERTENT ⟨~ mistake⟩ — **un·wit·ting·ly** *adv*

un·wont·ed \-'wòn-təd, -'wōn-\ *adj* **1** : RARE, UNUSUAL **2** : not accustomed by experience — **un·wont·ed·ly** *adv*

un·world·ly \-'world-lē\ *adj* **1** : not of this world; *esp* : SPIRITUAL **2** : NAIVE **3** : not swayed by worldly considerations — **un·world·li·ness** \-lē-nəs\ *n*

un·wor·thy \,ən-'wər-thē\ *adj* **1** : BASE, DISHONORABLE **2** : not meritorious : not worthy : UNDESERVING **3** : not deserved : UNMERITED ⟨~ treatment⟩ — **un·wor·thi·ly** \-thə-lē\ *adv* — **un·wor·thi·ness** \-thē-nəs\ *n*

un·wrap \-'rap\ *vb* : to remove the wrapping from : DISCLOSE

un·writ·ten \-'ri-t²n\ *adj* **1** : not in writing : ORAL, TRADITIONAL ⟨an ~ law⟩ **2** : containing no writing : BLANK

un·yield·ing \,ən-'yēl-diŋ\ *adj* **1** : characterized by lack of softness or flexibility **2** : characterized by firmness or obduracy

un·yoke \-'yōk\ *vb* : to remove a yoke from; *also* : SEPARATE, DISCONNECT

un·zip \-'zip\ *vb* : to zip open : open by means of a zipper

¹up \'əp\ *adv* **1** : in or to a higher position or level; *esp* : away from the center of the earth **2** : from beneath a surface (as ground or water) **3** : from below the horizon **4** : in or into an upright position; *esp* : out of bed **5** : with greater intensity ⟨speak ~⟩ **6** : to or at a greater rate or amount ⟨prices went ~⟩ **7** : in or into a better or more advanced state or a state of greater intensity or activity ⟨stir ~ a fire⟩ **8** : into existence, evidence, or knowledge ⟨the missing book turned ~⟩ **9** : into consideration ⟨brought the matter ~⟩ **10** : to or at bat **11** : into possession or custody ⟨gave himself ~⟩ **12** : ENTIRELY, COMPLETELY ⟨eat it ~⟩ **13** — used for emphasis ⟨clean ~ a room⟩ **14** : ASIDE, BY ⟨lay ~ supplies⟩ **15** : so as to arrive or approach ⟨ran ~ the path⟩ **16** : in a direction opposite to down **17** : in or into parts ⟨tear ~ paper⟩ **18** : to a stop ⟨pull ~ at the

untraceable	untrodden	unversed	unwed
untraditional	untroubled	unvisited	unwelcome
untrained	untrustworthy	unwanted	unwilling
untrammeled	untruthful	unwarranted	unwillingly
untranslatable	untypical	unwary	unwillingness
untranslated	unusable	unwashed	unwomanly
untraveled	unvaried	unwavering	unworkable
untraversed	unvarying	unweaned	unworn
untreated	unventilated	unwearable	unworried
untrimmed	unverifiable	unwearied	unwounded
untrod	unverified	unweathered	unwoven

curb⟩ **19** : for each side ⟨the score was 15 ∼⟩

²up *adj* **1** : risen above the horizon ⟨the sun is ∼⟩ **2** : being out of bed ⟨∼ by 6 o'clock⟩ **3** : relatively high ⟨prices are ∼⟩ **4** : RAISED, LIFTED ⟨windows are ∼⟩ **5** : BUILT, CONSTRUCTED ⟨the house is ∼⟩ **6** : grown above a surface ⟨the corn is ∼⟩ **7** : moving, inclining, or directed upward **8** : marked by agitation, excitement, or activity **9** : READY; *esp* : highly prepared **10** : going on : taking place ⟨find out what is ∼⟩ **11** : EXPIRED, ENDED ⟨the time is ∼⟩ **12** : extensively aware or informed ⟨∼ on the news⟩ **13** : being ahead or in advance of an opponent ⟨one hole ∼ in a match⟩ **14** : presented for or being under consideration ⟨∼ for promotion⟩ **15** : charged before a court ⟨∼ for robbery⟩

³up *prep* **1** : to, toward, or at a higher point of ⟨∼ a ladder⟩ **2** : to or toward the source of ⟨∼ the river⟩ **3** : to or toward the northern part of ⟨∼ the coast⟩ **4** : to or toward the interior of ⟨traveling ∼ the country⟩ **5** : ALONG ⟨walk ∼ the street⟩

⁴up *n* **1** : an upward course or slope **2** : a period or state of prosperity or success ⟨he had his ∼s and downs⟩ **3** : a quark with a charge of +⅔ that is one of the constituents of the proton and neutron

⁵up *vb* **upped** \'əpt\ *or in 2* **up; upped; upping; ups** *or in 2* **up 1** : to rise from a lying or sitting position **2** : to act abruptly or surprisingly ⟨she *upped* and left home⟩ **3** : to move or cause to move upward ⟨*upped* the prices⟩

Upa·ni·shad \ü-'pän-i-ˌshäd\ *n* : one of a set of Vedic philosophical treatises

¹up·beat \'əp-ˌbēt\ *n* : an unaccented beat in a musical measure; *esp* : the last beat of the measure

²upbeat *adj* : OPTIMISTIC, CHEERFUL

up·braid \ˌəp-'brād\ *vb* : to criticize, reproach, or scold severely

up·bring·ing \'əp-ˌbriŋ-iŋ\ *n* : the process of bringing up and training

UPC *abbr* Universal Product Code

up·chuck \'əp-ˌchək\ *vb* : VOMIT

up·com·ing \'əp-ˌkə-miŋ\ *adj* : FORTHCOMING, APPROACHING ⟨the ∼ election⟩

up–coun·try \'əp-ˌkən-trē\ *adj* : of or relating to the interior of a country or a region — **up–country** \'əp-'kən-\ *adv*

up·date \ˌəp-'dāt\ *vb* : to bring up to date — **update** \'əp-ˌdāt\ *n*

up·draft \'əp-ˌdraft, -ˌdräft\ *n* : an upward movement of gas (as air)

up·end \ˌəp-'end\ *vb* : to set, stand, or rise on end; *also* : OVERTURN

up–front \'əp-ˌfrənt, ˌəp-'frənt\ *adj* **1** : HONEST, CANDID ⟨an ∼ answer⟩ **2** : ADVANCE ⟨∼ payment⟩

up front *adv* : in advance ⟨paid *up front*⟩

¹up·grade \'əp-ˌgrād\ *n* **1** : an upward grade or slope **2** : INCREASE, RISE

²up·grade \'əp-ˌgrād, ˌəp-'grād\ *vb* **1** : to raise to a higher grade or position; *esp* : to advance to a job requiring a higher level of skill **2** : to improve or replace (as software or a device) for increased usefulness

up·growth \'əp-ˌgrōth\ *n* : the process of growing upward : DEVELOPMENT; *also* : a product or result of this

up·heav·al \ˌəp-'hē-vəl\ *n* **1** : the action or an instance of uplifting esp. of part of the earth's crust **2** : a violent agitation or change

¹up·hill \'əp-'hil\ *adv* : upward on a hill or incline; *also* : against difficulties

²up·hill \-ˌhil\ *adj* **1** : situated on elevated ground **2** : ASCENDING **3** : DIFFICULT, LABORIOUS ⟨an ∼ struggle⟩

up·hold \ˌəp-'hōld\ *vb* **-held** \-'held\; **-hold·ing 1** : to give support to **2** : to support against an opponent **3** : to keep elevated — **up·hold·er** *n*

up·hol·ster \ˌəp-'hōl-stər\ *vb* : to furnish with or as if with upholstery — **up·hol·ster·er** *n*

up·hol·stery \-stə-rē\ *n, pl* **-ster·ies** [ME *upholdester* upholsterer, fr. *upholden* to uphold, fr. *up* + *holden* to hold] : materials (as fabrics, padding, and springs) used to make a soft covering esp. for a seat

UPI *abbr* United Press International

up·keep \'əp-ˌkēp\ *n* : the act or cost of keeping up or maintaining; *also* : the state of being maintained

up·land \'əp-lənd, -ˌland\ *n* : high land esp. at some distance from the sea — **upland** *adj*

¹up·lift \ˌəp-'lift\ *vb* **1** : to lift or raise up : ELEVATE **2** : to improve the condition of esp. morally, socially, or intellectually

²up·lift \'əp-ˌlift\ *n* **1** : a lifting up; *esp* : an upheaval of the earth's surface **2** : moral or social improvement ⟨spiritual ∼⟩; *also* : a movement to make such improvement

up·mar·ket \ˌəp-'mär-kət\ *adj* : appealing to wealthy consumers

up·most \'əp-ˌmōst\ *adj* : UPPERMOST

up·on \ə-'pón, -'pän\ *prep* : ON

¹up·per \'ə-pər\ *adj* **1** : higher in physical position, rank, or order ⟨∼ management⟩ **2** : constituting the smaller and more restricted branch of a bicameral legislature **3** *cap* : being a later part or formation of a specific geological period **4** : being toward the interior ⟨the ∼ Amazon⟩ **5** : NORTHERN ⟨∼ Minnesota⟩

²upper *n* : one that is upper; *esp* : the parts of a shoe or boot above the sole

up·per·case \ˌəp-ər-'kās\ *adj* : CAPITAL 1 — **uppercase** *n*

upper class *n* : a social class occupying a position above the middle class and having the highest status in a society — **upper–class** *adj*

up·per·class·man \ˌə-pər-'klas-mən\ *n* : a junior or senior in a college or high school

upper crust *n* : the highest social class or group; *esp* : the highest circle of the upper class

up·per·cut \'ə-pər-ˌkət\ *n* : a short swinging punch delivered (as in boxing) in an upward direction usu. with a bent arm

upper hand *n* : MASTERY, ADVANTAGE

up·per·most \'ə-pər-ˌmōst\ *adv* : in or

into the highest or most prominent position — **uppermost** adj

up·pish \'ə-pish\ adj : UPPITY

up·pi·ty \'ə-pə-tē\ adj : ARROGANT, PRESUMPTUOUS

up·raise \,əp-'rāz\ vb : to lift up : ELEVATE

¹**up·right** \'əp-,rīt\ adj 1 : PERPENDICULAR, VERTICAL 2 : erect in carriage or posture 3 : morally correct : JUST — **up·right** adv — **up·right·ly** adv — **up·right·ness** n

²**upright** n 1 : the state of being upright : a vertical position 2 : something that stands upright

upright piano n : a piano whose strings run vertically

up·ris·ing \'əp-,rī-ziŋ\ n : INSURRECTION, REVOLT, REBELLION

up·riv·er \'əp-'ri-vər\ adv or adj : toward or at a point nearer the source of a river

up·roar \'əp-,rȯr\ n [D oproer, fr. MD, fr. op up + roer motion] : a state of commotion, excitement, or violent disturbance

up·roar·i·ous \,əp-'rȯr-ē-əs\ adj 1 : marked by uproar 2 : extremely funny — **up·roar·i·ous·ly** adv

up·root \,əp-'rüt, -'ru̇t\ vb 1 : to remove by or as if by pulling up by the roots 2 : DISPLACE 1 ⟨families were ~ed⟩

¹**up·set** \,əp-'set\ vb -set; -set·ting 1 : to force or be forced out of the usual upright, level, or proper position 2 : to disturb emotionally : WORRY; also : to make somewhat ill 3 : UNSETTLE, DISARRANGE 4 : to defeat unexpectedly

²**up·set** \'əp-,set\ n 1 : an upsetting or being upset; esp : a minor illness 2 : a derangement of plans or ideas 3 : an unexpected defeat

³**up·set** \(,)əp-'set\ adj : emotionally disturbed or agitated

up·shot \'əp-,shät\ n : the final result

¹**up·side** \'əp-,sīd\ n 1 : the upper side 2 : a positive aspect 3 : PROMISE ⟨rookies with much ~⟩

²**up·side** \,əp-'sīd\ prep : up on or against the side of ⟨knocked him ~ the head⟩

up·side down \,əp-,sīd-'daun\ adv 1 : with the upper and the lower parts reversed in position 2 : in or into confusion or disorder — **upside-down** adj

up·si·lon \'ü̇p-sə-,län, 'yü̇p-, 'əp-\ n : the 20th letter of the Greek alphabet — Y or υ

¹**up·stage** \'əp-'stāj\ adv or adj : toward or at the rear of a theatrical stage

²**up·stage** \,əp-'stāj\ vb : to draw attention away from (as an actor)

¹**up·stairs** \,əp-'sterz\ adv 1 : up the stairs : to or on a higher floor 2 : to or at a higher position

²**up·stairs** \,əp-'sterz\ adj : situated above the stairs esp. on an upper floor ⟨~ bedroom⟩

³**up·stairs** \'əp-'sterz, 'əp-,sterz\ n sing or pl : the part of a building above the ground floor

up·stand·ing \,əp-'stan-diŋ, 'əp-\ adj 1 : ERECT 2 : STRAIGHTFORWARD, HONEST

¹**up·start** \,əp-'stärt\ vb : to jump up suddenly

²**up·start** \'əp-,stärt\ n : one that has risen suddenly; esp : one that claims more personal importance than is warranted — **up·start** \-'stärt\ adj

up·state \'əp-'stāt\ adj : of, relating to, or characteristic of a part of a state away from a large city and esp. to the north — **upstate** adv — **upstate** n

up·stream \'əp-'strēm\ adv : at or toward the source of a stream — **upstream** adj

up·stroke \'əp-,strōk\ n : an upward stroke (as of a pen)

up·surge \-,sərj\ n : a rapid or sudden rise ⟨an ~ in interest⟩

up·swept \'əp-,swept\ adj : swept upward ⟨~ hairdo⟩

up·swing \'əp-,swiŋ\ n : an upward swing; esp : a marked increase or rise (as in activity)

up·take \'əp-,tāk\ n 1 : UNDERSTANDING, COMPREHENSION ⟨quick on the ~⟩ 2 : an act or instance of absorbing and incorporating esp. into a living organism, tissue, or cell

up·thrust \'əp-,thrəst\ n : an upward thrust (as of the earth's crust) — **up·thrust** vb

up·tight \'əp-'tīt\ adj 1 : TENSE, NERVOUS, UNEASY; also : ANGRY, INDIGNANT 2 : rigidly conventional

up-to-date adj 1 : extending up to the present time 2 : abreast of the times : MODERN — **up-to-date·ness** n

up·town \'əp-,taun\ n : the upper part of a town or city; esp : the residential district — **up·town** \'əp-'taun\ adj or adv

¹**up·turn** \'əp-,tərn, ,əp-'tərn\ vb 1 : to turn (as earth) up or over 2 : to turn or direct upward

²**up·turn** \'əp-,tərn\ n : an upward turn esp. toward better conditions or higher prices

¹**up·ward** \'əp-wərd\ or **up·wards** \-wərdz\ adv 1 : in a direction from lower to higher 2 : toward a higher or better condition 3 : toward a greater amount or higher number, degree, or rate

²**upward** adj : directed or moving toward or situated in a higher place or level : ASCENDING — **up·ward·ly** adv

upwards of also **upward** of adv : more than : in excess of ⟨they cost upwards of $25 each⟩

up·well \,əp-'wel\ vb : to move or flow upward

up·well·ing \-'we-liŋ\ n : a rising or an appearance of rising to the surface and flowing outward; esp : the movement of deep cold usu. nutrient-rich ocean water to the surface

up·wind \'əp-'wind\ adv or adj : in the direction from which the wind is blowing

ura·cil \'yu̇r-ə-,sil\ n : a pyrimidine base that is one of the four bases coding genetic information in the molecular chain of RNA

ura·ni·um \yu̇-'rā-nē-əm\ n : a silvery heavy radioactive metallic chemical element used as a source of atomic energy

Ura·nus \'yu̇r-ə-nəs, yu̇-'rā-\ n [LL, the sky personified as a god, fr. Gk Ouranos, fr. ouranos sky, heaven] : the planet 7th in order from the sun

ur·ban \'ər-bən\ adj : of, relating to, characteristic of, or constituting a city

ur·bane \ˌər-'bān\ adj [L urbanus urban, urbane, fr. urbs city] : very polite and polished in manner : SUAVE

ur·ban·ite \'ər-bə-ˌnīt\ n : a person who lives in a city

ur·ban·i·ty \ˌər-'ba-nə-tē\ n, pl **-ties** : the quality or state of being urbane

ur·ban·ize \'ər-bə-ˌnīz\ vb **-ized; -iz·ing** : to cause to take on urban characteristics — **ur·ban·i·za·tion** \ˌər-bə-nə-'zā-shən\ n

ur·chin \'ər-chən\ n [ME, hedgehog, fr. AF heriçun, hirechoun, ultim. fr. L ericius] : a pert or mischievous youngster

Ur·du \'ûr-dü, 'ər-\ n [Hindi & Urdu urdū, fr. Pers zabān-e-urdū-e-muallā language of the Exalted Comp (the imperial bazaar in Delhi)] : an Indo-Aryan language that is the official language of Pakistan and that is widely used by Muslims in urban areas of India

urea \yu̇-'rē-ə\ n : a soluble nitrogenous compound that is the chief solid constituent of mammalian urine

ure·mia \yu̇-'rē-mē-ə\ n : accumulation in the blood of materials normally passed off in the urine resulting in a poisoned condition — **ure·mic** \-mik\ adj

ure·ter \'yu̇r-ə-tər\ n : a duct that carries the urine from a kidney to the bladder

ure·thra \yu̇-'rē-thrə\ n, pl **-thras** or **-thrae** \-(ˌ)thrē\ : the canal that in most mammals carries off the urine from the bladder and in the male also serves to carry semen from the body — **ure·thral** \-thrəl\ adj

ure·thri·tis \ˌyu̇r-i-'thrī-təs\ n : inflammation of the urethra

¹urge \'ərj\ vb **urged; urg·ing 1** : to present, advocate, or demand earnestly **2** : to try to persuade or sway ⟨~ a guest to stay⟩ **3** : to serve as a motive or reason for **4** : to impress or impel to some course or activity ⟨the dog urged the sheep onward⟩

²urge n **1** : the act or process of urging **2** : a force or impulse that urges or drives

ur·gent \'ər-jənt\ adj **1** : calling for immediate attention : PRESSING **2** : urging insistently — **ur·gen·cy** \-jən-sē\ n — **ur·gent·ly** adv

uric \'yu̇r-ik\ adj : of, relating to, or found in urine

uric acid n : a nearly insoluble acid that is the chief nitrogenous excretory product of birds but is present in only small amounts in mammalian urine

uri·nal \'yu̇r-ə-nᵊl\ n **1** : a receptacle for urine **2** : a place for urinating

uri·nal·y·sis \ˌyu̇r-ə-'na-lə-səs\ n : chemical analysis of urine

uri·nary \'yu̇r-ə-ˌner-ē\ adj **1** : relating to, occurring in, or being organs for the formation and discharge of urine **2** : of, relating to, or for urine

urinary bladder n : a membranous sac in many vertebrates that serves for the temporary retention of urine and discharges by the urethra

uri·nate \'yu̇r-ə-ˌnāt\ vb **-nat·ed; -nat·ing** : to release or give off urine — **uri·na·tion** \ˌyu̇r-ə-'nā-shən\ n

urine \'yu̇r-ən\ n : a waste material from the kidneys that is usu. a yellowish watery liquid in mammals but is semisolid in birds and reptiles

URL \ˌyü-(ˌ)är-'el, 'ər(-ə)l\ n [uniform (or universal) resource locator] : a series of usu. alphanumeric characters that specifies the storage location of a resource on the Internet

urn \'ərn\ n **1** : a vessel that typically has the form of a vase on a pedestal and often is used to hold the ashes of the dead **2** : a closed vessel usu. with a spout for serving a hot beverage

uro·gen·i·tal \ˌyu̇r-ō-'je-nə-tᵊl\ adj : of, relating to, or being the excretory and reproductive organs or functions

urol·o·gy \yu̇-'rä-lə-jē\ n : a branch of medical science dealing with the urinary or urogenital tract and its disorders — **uro·log·i·cal** \ˌyu̇r-ə-'lä-ji-kəl\ also **uro·log·ic** \-jik\ adj — **urol·o·gist** \yu̇-'rä-lə-jist\ n

Ur·sa Ma·jor \ˌər-sə-'mā-jər\ n [L, lit., greater bear] : the northern constellation that contains the stars which form the Big Dipper

Ursa Mi·nor \-'mī-nər\ n [L, lit., lesser bear] : the constellation including the north pole of the heavens and the stars that form the Little Dipper with the North Star at the tip of the handle

ur·sine \'ər-ˌsīn\ adj : of, relating to, or resembling a bear

ur·ti·car·ia \ˌər-tə-'ker-ē-ə\ n [NL, fr. L urtica nettle] : HIVES

us \'əs\ pron objective case of WE

US abbr United States

USA abbr **1** United States Army **2** United States of America

us·able also **use·able** \'yü-zə-bəl\ adj : suitable or fit for use — **us·abil·i·ty** \ˌyü-zə-'bi-lə-tē\ n

USAF abbr United States Air Force

us·age \'yü-sij, -zij\ n **1** : habitual or customary practice or procedure **2** : the way in which words and phrases are actually used **3** : the action or mode of using **4** : manner of treating

USB \ˌyü-(ˌ)es-'bē\ n [universal serial bus] : a standardized computer interface for attaching peripherals

USCG abbr United States Coast Guard

USDA abbr United States Department of Agriculture

¹use \'yüs\ n **1** : the act or practice of using or employing something : EMPLOYMENT, APPLICATION **2** : the fact or state of being used **3** : the way of using **4** : USAGE, CUSTOM **5** : the privilege or benefit of using something **6** : the ability or power to use something (as a limb) **7** : the legal enjoyment of property that consists in its employment, occupation, or exercise; also : the benefit or profit esp. from property held in trust **8** : USEFULNESS, UTILITY; also : the end served : OBJECT, FUNCTION **9** : something useful or beneficial ⟨it's no ~ arguing⟩ **10** : the occasion or need to employ ⟨he had no more ~ for it⟩ **11** : ESTEEM, LIKING ⟨had no ~ for modern art⟩

²**use** \'yüz\ *vb* **used** \'yüzd; *"used to"* usu '*yüs-tə*; **us·ing 1** : to put into action or service : EMPLOY **2** : to consume or take (as drugs) regularly **3** : UTILIZE ⟨~ tact⟩; *also* : MANIPULATE ⟨*used* his friends to get ahead⟩ **4** : to expend or consume by putting to use **5** : to behave toward : TREAT ⟨*used* the horse cruelly⟩ **6** : to benefit from ⟨house could ~ a coat of paint⟩ **7** — used in the past with *to* to indicate a former practice, fact, or state ⟨we *used* to work harder⟩ — **us·er** *n*

used \'yüzd\ *adj* **1** : having been used by another : SECONDHAND ⟨~ cars⟩ **2** : ACCUSTOMED, HABITUATED ⟨~ to the heat⟩

use·ful \'yüs-fəl\ *adj* : capable of being put to use : ADVANTAGEOUS; *esp* : serviceable for a beneficial end — **use·ful·ly** *adv* — **use·ful·ness** *n*

use·less \-ləs\ *adj* : having or being of no use : WORTHLESS, INEFFECTUAL — **use·less·ly** *adv* — **use·less·ness** *n*

USES *abbr* United States Employment Service

use up *vb* : to consume completely

¹**ush·er** \'ə-shər\ *n* [ME *ussher,* fr. AF *ussier, usscher,* fr. VL **ustiarius* doorkeeper, fr. L *ostium, ustium* door, mouth of a river] **1** : an officer who walks before a person of rank **2** : one who escorts people to their seats (as in a church or theater)

²**usher** *vb* **1** : to conduct to a place **2** : to precede as an usher, forerunner, or harbinger **3** : INAUGURATE, INTRODUCE ⟨~ in a new era⟩

ush·er·ette \,ə-shə-'ret\ *n* : a girl or woman who is an usher (as in a theater)

USIA *abbr* United States Information Agency

USMC *abbr* United States Marine Corps

USN *abbr* United States Navy

USO *abbr* United Service Organizations

USP *abbr* United States Pharmacopeia

USPS *abbr* United States Postal Service

USS *abbr* United States ship

USSR *abbr* Union of Soviet Socialist Republics

usu *abbr* usual; usually

usu·al \'yü-zhə-wəl\ *adj* **1** : accordant with usage, custom, or habit : NORMAL **2** : commonly or ordinarily used **3** : ORDINARY ♦ **Synonyms** CUSTOMARY, HABITUAL, ACCUSTOMED, ROUTINE — **usu·al·ly** \'yü-zhə-wə-lē, 'yü-zhə-lē\ *adv*

usu·fruct \'yü-zə-,frəkt\ *n* [L *ususfructus,* fr. *usus et fructus* use and enjoyment] : the legal right to use and enjoy the benefits and profits of something belonging to another

usu·rer \'yü-zhər-ər\ *n* : one that lends money esp. at an exorbitant rate

usu·ri·ous \yü-'zhùr-ē-əs\ *adj* : practicing, involving, or constituting usury ⟨a ~ rate of interest⟩

usurp \yù-'sərp, -'zərp\ *vb* [ME, fr. AF *usorper,* fr. L *usurpare,* to take possession

of without legal claim, fr. *usu* (abl. of *usus* use) + *rapere* to seize] : to seize and hold by force or without right ⟨~ a throne⟩ — **usur·pa·tion** \,yü-sər-'pā-shən, -zər-\ *n* — **usurp·er** \yù-'sər-pər, -'zər-\ *n*

usu·ry \'yü-zhə-rē\ *n, pl* **-ries 1** : the lending of money with an interest charge for its use **2** : an excessive rate or amount of interest charged; *esp* : interest above an established legal rate

UT *abbr* Utah

Ute \'yüt\ *n, pl* **Ute** or **Utes** : a member of an American Indian people orig. ranging through Utah, Colorado, Arizona, and New Mexico

uten·sil \yù-'ten-səl\ *n* [ME, vessels for domestic use, fr. MF *utensile,* fr. L *utensilia,* fr. neut. pl. of *utensilis* useful, fr. *uti* to use] **1** : an instrument or vessel used in a household and esp. a kitchen **2** : a useful tool

uter·us \'yü-tə-rəs\ *n, pl* **uter·us·es** or **uteri** \'yü-tə-,rī\ : the muscular organ of a female mammal in which the young develop before birth — **uter·ine** \-,rīn, -rən\ *adj*

utile \'yüt-ªl, 'yü,tī(-ə)l\ *adj* : USEFUL

uti·lise *Brit var of* UTILIZE

¹**util·i·tar·i·an** \yù-,ti-lə-'ter-ē-ən\ *n* : a person who believes in utilitarianism

²**utilitarian** *adj* **1** : of or relating to utilitarianism **2** : of or relating to utility : aiming at usefulness rather than beauty; *also* : serving a useful purpose

util·i·tar·i·an·ism \yù-,ti-lə-'ter-ē-ə-,ni-zəm\ *n* : a theory that the greatest good for the greatest number should be the main consideration in making a choice of actions

¹**util·i·ty** \yü-'ti-lə-tē\ *n, pl* **-ties 1** : USEFULNESS **2** : something useful or designed for use **3** : a business organization performing a public service and subject to special governmental regulation **4** : a public service or a commodity (as electricity or water) provided by a public utility; *also* : equipment to provide such or a similar service

²**utility** *adj* **1** : capable of serving esp. as a substitute in various uses or positions ⟨a ~ outfielder⟩ ⟨a ~ cord⟩ **2** : being of a usable but poor quality ⟨~ beef⟩

utility knife *n* : a knife designed for general use; *esp* : one with a retractable blade

uti·lize \'yü-tə-,līz\ *vb* **-lized; -liz·ing** : to make use of : turn to profitable account or use — **uti·li·za·tion** \,yü-tə-lə-'zā-shən\ *n*

ut·most \'ət-,mōst\ *adj* **1** : situated at the farthest or most distant point : EXTREME **2** : of the greatest or highest degree, quantity, number, or amount — **utmost** *n*

uto·pia \yù-'tō-pē-ə\ *n* [*Utopia,* imaginary island described in Sir Thomas More's *Utopia,* fr. Gk *ou* not, no + *topos* place] **1** *often cap* : a place of ideal perfection esp. in laws, government, and social conditions **2** : an impractical scheme for social improvement

¹**uto·pi·an** \-pē-ən\ *adj, often cap* **1** : of, re-

lating to, or resembling a utopia **2** : proposing ideal social and political schemes that are impractical **3** : VISIONARY

²**utopian** *n* **1** : a believer in the perfectibility of human society **2** : one who proposes or advocates utopian schemes

¹**ut-ter** \'ə-tər\ *adj* [ME, remote, fr. OE *ūtera* outer, compar. adj. fr. *ūt* out, adv.] : ABSOLUTE, TOTAL ⟨~ ruin⟩ — **ut-ter-ly** *adv*

²**utter** *vb* [ME *uttren*, fr. *utter* outside, adv., fr. OE *ūtor*, compar. of *ūt* out] **1** : to send forth as a sound : express in usu. spoken words : PRONOUNCE, SPEAK **2** : to put (as currency) into circulation — **ut-ter-er** *n*

ut-ter-ance \'ə-tə-rəns\ *n* **1** : something uttered; *esp* : an oral or written state-

ment **2** : the action of uttering with the voice : SPEECH **3** : power, style, or manner of speaking

ut-ter-most \'ə-tər-ˌmōst\ *adj* : EXTREME, UTMOST ⟨the ~ parts of the earth⟩ — **ut-termost** *n*

U-turn \'yü-ˌtərn\ *n* : a turn resembling the letter U; *esp* : a 180-degree turn made by a vehicle in a road

UV *abbr* ultraviolet

uvu-la \'yü-vyə-lə\ *n, pl* **-las** *or* **-lae** \-ˌlē, -ˌlī\ : the fleshy lobe hanging at the back of the roof of the mouth — **uvu-lar** \-lər\ *adj*

UW *abbr* underwriter

ux-o-ri-ous \ˌək-'sȯr-ē-əs, ˌəg-'zȯr-\ *adj* : excessively devoted or submissive to a wife

¹**v** \'vē\ *n, pl* **v's** *or* **vs** \'vēz\ *often cap* : the 22d letter of the English alphabet

²**v** *abbr, often cap* **1** vector **2** velocity **3** verb **4** versus **5** very **6** very **7** victory **8** vide **9** voice **10** voltage **11** volume **12** vowel

V *symbol* **1** vanadium **2** volt

Va *abbr* Virginia

VA *abbr* **1** Veterans Administration **2** vice admiral **3** Virginia

va-can-cy \'vā-kən-sē\ *n, pl* **-cies** **1** : a vacating esp. of an office, position, or piece of property **2** : a vacant office, position, or tenancy; *also* : the period during which it stands vacant **3** : empty space : VOID **4** : the state of being vacant

va-cant \'vā-kənt\ *adj* **1** : not occupied ⟨~ seat⟩ ⟨~ room⟩ **2** : EMPTY ⟨~ space⟩ **3** : free from business or care ⟨a few ~ hours⟩ **4** : devoid of thought, reflection, or expression ⟨a ~ smile⟩ — **va-cant-ly** *adv*

va-cate \'vā-ˌkāt\ *vb* **va-cat-ed; va-cating** **1** : to make void : ANNUL **2** : to make vacant (as an office or house); *also* : to give up the occupancy of

¹**va-ca-tion** \vā-'kā-shən, və-\ *n* : a period of rest from work : HOLIDAY

²**vacation** *vb* : to take or spend a vacation — **va-ca-tion-er** *n*

va-ca-tion-ist \-shə-nist\ *n* : a person taking a vacation

va-ca-tion-land \-shən-ˌland\ *n* : an area with recreational attractions and facilities for vacationists

vac-ci-nate \'vak-sə-ˌnāt\ *vb* **-nat-ed; -nat-ing** : to administer a vaccine to usu. by injection

vac-ci-na-tion \ˌvak-sə-'nā-shən\ *n* **1** : the act of vaccinating **2** : the scar left by vaccinating

vac-cine \vak-'sēn, 'vak-ˌsēn\ *n* [F *vaccin*, fr. *vaccine* cowpox, fr. NL *vaccina* (in *variolae vaccinae* cowpox), fr. L, fem. of *vaccinus* of or from cows, fr. *vacca* cow] : a preparation of material (as of killed or

weakened viruses or bacteria) used in vaccinating to produce or increase immunity to a disease

vac-cin-ia \vak-'si-nē-ə\ *n* : COWPOX

vac-il-late \'va-sə-ˌlāt\ *vb* **-lat-ed; -lating** **1** : SWAY, TOTTER; *also* : FLUCTUATE **2** : to incline first to one course or opinion and then to another : WAVER — **vac-il-la-tion** \ˌva-sə-'lā-shən\ *n*

va-cu-ity \va-'kyü-ə-tē\ *n, pl* **-ities** **1** : an empty space **2** : the state, fact, or quality of being vacuous **3** : something that is vacuous

vac-u-ole \'va-kyə-ˌwōl\ *n* : a usu. fluid-filled cavity esp. in the cytoplasm of an individual cell — **vac-u-o-lar** \ˌva-kyə-'wō-lər, -ˌlär\ *adj*

vac-u-ous \'va-kyə-wəs\ *adj* **1** : EMPTY, VACANT, BLANK **2** : DULL, STUPID, INANE ⟨~ movies⟩ — **vac-u-ous-ly** *adv* — **vac-u-ous-ness** *n*

¹**vac-u-um** \'va-(ˌ)kyüm, -kyəm\ *n, pl* **vac-uums** *or* **vac-ua** \-kyə-wə\ [L, fr. neut. of *vacuus* empty] **1** : a space entirely empty of matter **2** : a space from which most of the air has been removed (as by a pump) **3** : VOID, GAP **4** : VACUUM CLEANER — **vacuum** *adj*

²**vacuum** *vb* : to use a vacuum device (as a vacuum cleaner) on ⟨~ the den⟩

vacuum bottle *n* : THERMOS

vacuum cleaner *n* : a household appliance for cleaning (as floors or rugs) by suction

vacuum-packed *adj* : having much of the air removed before being hermetically sealed ⟨~ fish⟩

vacuum tube *n* : an electron tube from which most of the air has been removed

va-de me-cum \ˌvā-dē-'mē-kəm, ˌvä-dē-'mā-\ *n, pl* **vade mecums** [L, go with me] : something (as a handbook or manual) regularly carried about

VADM *abbr* vice admiral

¹**vag-a-bond** \'va-gə-ˌbänd\ *adj* **1** : WANDERING, HOMELESS **2** : of, characteristic

of, or leading the life of a vagrant or
tramp **3** : leading an unsettled or irresponsible life

²**vagabond** *n* : one leading a vagabond life;
esp : TRAMP

va·gar·i·ous \va-ˈger-ē-əs\ *adj* : marked
by vagaries : CAPRICIOUS ⟨~ leadership⟩
— **va·gar·i·ous·ly** *adv*

va·ga·ry \ˈvā-gə-rē, və-ˈger-ē\ *n, pl* **-ries**
: an odd or eccentric idea or action
: WHIM, CAPRICE

va·gi·na \və-ˈjī-nə\ *n, pl* **-nae** \-(ˌ)nē\ *or*
-nas [L, lit., sheath] : a canal that leads
from the uterus to the external opening
of the female sex organs — **vag·i·nal**
\ˈva-jə-nᵊl\ *adj* — **vag·i·nal·ly** \-nᵊl-ē\
adv

vag·i·ni·tis \ˌva-jə-ˈnī-təs\ *n* : inflammation of the vagina

va·gran·cy \ˈvā-grən-sē\ *n, pl* **-cies** **1**
: the quality or state of being vagrant;
also : a vagrant act or notion **2** : the offense of being a vagrant

¹**va·grant** \ˈvā-grənt\ *n* : a person who has
no job and wanders from place to place

²**vagrant** *adj* **1** : of, relating to, or characteristic of a vagrant **2** : following no
fixed course : RANDOM, CAPRICIOUS ⟨~
thoughts⟩ — **va·grant·ly** *adv*

vague \ˈvāg\ *adj* **vagu·er; vagu·est** [MF,
fr. L *vagus*, lit., wandering] **1** : not clear,
definite, or distinct ⟨a ~ plan⟩ ⟨~ sil-
houettes⟩ **2** : not clearly felt or analyzed
⟨a ~ unrest⟩ ✦ *Synonyms* OBSCURE,
DARK, ENIGMATIC, AMBIGUOUS, EQUIVO-
CAL — **vague·ly** *adv* — **vague·ness** *n*

vain \ˈvān\ *adj* [ME, fr. AF, empty, futile,
fr. L *vanus*] **1** : of no real value : IDLE,
WORTHLESS **2** : FUTILE, UNSUCCESS-
FUL **3** : proud of one's looks or abilities
✦ *Synonyms* CONCEITED, NARCISSISTIC,
VAINGLORIOUS — **vain·ly** *adv* — **in
vain** **1** : without success ⟨her efforts
were *in vain*⟩ **2** : in a blasphemous manner ⟨took the Lord's name *in vain*⟩

vain·glo·ri·ous \ˌvān-ˈglōr-ē-əs\ *adj*
: marked by vainglory : BOASTFUL

vain·glo·ry \ˈvān-ˌglōr-ē\ *n* **1** : excessive
or ostentatious pride esp. in one's own
achievements **2** : vain display : VANITY

val *abbr* value; valued

va·lance \ˈva-ləns, ˈvā-\ *n* **1** : drapery
hanging from an edge (as of an altar,
table, or bed) **2** : a drapery or a decorative frame across the top of a window

vale \ˈvāl\ *n* : VALLEY, DALE

vale·dic·tion \ˌva-lə-ˈdik-shən\ *n* [L *vale-
dicere* to say farewell, fr. *vale* farewell +
dicere to say] : an act or utterance of
leave-taking : FAREWELL

vale·dic·to·ri·an \-ˌdik-ˈtòr-ē-ən\ *n* : the
student usu. of the highest rank in a graduating class who delivers the valedictory
address at commencement

vale·dic·to·ry \-ˈdik-tə-rē\ *adj* : bidding
farewell : delivered as a valediction ⟨a ~
address⟩ — **valedictory** *n*

va·lence \ˈvā-ləns\ *n* [LL *valentia* power,
capacity, fr. L *valēre* to be strong] : the
combining power of an atom as shown by
the number of its electrons that are lost,

gained, or shared in the formation of
chemical bonds

Va·len·ci·ennes \və-ˌlen-sē-ˈen, ˌva-lən-
sē-, -ˈenz\ *n* : a fine handmade lace

val·en·tine \ˈva-lən-ˌtīn\ *n* : a sweetheart
chosen or complimented on Valentine's
Day; *also* : a gift or greeting given on this
day

Valentine's Day *also* **Valentine Day** *n*
: February 14 observed in honor of St.
Valentine and as a time for exchanging
valentines

¹**va·let** \ˈva-lət, -(ˌ)lā; va-ˈlā\ *n* **1** : a male
servant who takes care of a man's clothes
and performs personal services **2** : an attendant in a hotel or restaurant who performs personal services (as parking cars)
for customers

²**valet** *vb* : to serve as a valet

val·e·tu·di·nar·i·an \ˌva-lə-ˌtü-də-ˈner-ē-
ən, -ˌtyü-\ *n* : a person of a weak or sickly constitution; *esp* : one whose chief
concern is his or her ill health — **val·e·
tu·di·nar·i·an·ism** \-ē-ə-ˌni-zəm\ *n*

val·iant \ˈval-yənt\ *adj* : having or show-
ing valor : BRAVE, HEROIC ✦ *Synonyms*
VALOROUS, DOUGHTY, COURAGEOUS,
BOLD, AUDACIOUS, DAUNTLESS, UN-
DAUNTED, INTREPID — **val·iant·ly** *adv*

val·id \ˈva-ləd\ *adj* **1** : having legal force
⟨a ~ contract⟩ **2** : founded on truth or
fact : capable of being justified or defended : SOUND ⟨a ~ argument⟩ ⟨~
reasons⟩ — **va·lid·i·ty** \və-ˈli-də-tē\ *n* —
val·id·ly *adv*

val·i·date \ˈva-lə-ˌdāt\ *vb* **-dat·ed; -dat·
ing** **1** : to make legally valid **2** : to
confirm the validity of **3** : VERIFY —
val·i·da·tion \ˌva-lə-ˈdā-shən\ *n*

va·lise \və-ˈlēs\ *n* [F] : SUITCASE

val·ley \ˈva-lē\ *n, pl* **valleys** : a long depression between ranges of hills or mountains

val·or \ˈva-lər\ *n* [ME *valour*, worth, worthiness, bravery, fr. AF fr. ML *valor*, fr. L
valēre to be strong] : personal bravery
✦ *Synonyms* HEROISM, PROWESS, GAL-
LANTRY — **val·or·ous** \ˈva-lə-rəs\ *adj*

val·o·ri·za·tion \ˌva-lə-rə-ˈzā-shən\ *n* : the
support of commodity prices by any of
various forms of government subsidy —
val·o·rize \ˈva-lə-ˌrīz\ *vb*

val·our *chiefly Brit var of* VALOR

¹**valu·able** \ˈval-yə-bəl, -yə-wə-bəl\ *adj* **1**
: having money value **2** : having great
money value **3** : of great use or service
✦ *Synonyms* INVALUABLE, PRICELESS,
COSTLY, EXPENSIVE, DEAR, PRECIOUS

²**valuable** *n* : a usu. personal possession of
considerable value ⟨their ~s were stolen⟩

val·u·ate \ˈval-yə-ˌwāt\ *vb* **-at·ed; -at·ing**
: to place a value on : APPRAISE — **val·u·
a·tor** \-ˌwā-tər\ *n*

val·u·a·tion \ˌval-yə-ˈwā-shən\ *n* **1** : the
act or process of valuing; *esp* : appraisal
of property **2** : the estimated or determined market value of a thing

¹**val·ue** \ˈval-yü\ *n* **1** : a fair return or
equivalent in money, goods, or services
for something exchanged **2** : the monetary worth of a thing; *also* : relative
worth, utility, or importance ⟨nothing of

~ to say⟩ **3** : an assigned or computed numerical quantity ⟨the ~ of *x* in an equation⟩ **4** : relative lightness or darkness of a color : LUMINOSITY **5** : the relative length of a tone or note **6** : something (as a principle or ideal) intrinsically valuable or desirable ⟨human rather than material ~s⟩ — **val·ue·less** *adj*

²**value** *vb* **val·ued; valu·ing 1** : to estimate the monetary worth of : APPRAISE **2** : to rate in usefulness, importance, or general worth **3** : to consider or rate highly : PRIZE, ESTEEM ⟨*valued* your opinions⟩ — **val·u·er** *n*

val·ue–add·ed tax *n* : an incremental excise tax that is levied on the value added at each stage of the processing of a raw material or the production and distribution of a commodity

valve \'valv\ *n* **1** : a structure (as in a vein) that temporarily closes a passage or that permits movement in one direction only **2** : a device by which the flow of a fluid material may be regulated by a movable part; *also* : the movable part of such a device **3** : a device in a brass wind instrument for quickly varying the tube length in order to change the fundamental tone by some definite interval **4** : one of the separate usu. hinged pieces of which the shell of some animals and esp. bivalve mollusks consists **5** : one of the pieces into which a ripe seed capsule or pod separates — **valved** \'valvd\ *adj* — **valve·less** *adj*

val·vu·lar \'val-vyə-lər\ *adj* : of, relating to, or affecting a valve esp. of the heart ⟨~ heart disease⟩

va·moose \və-'müs, va-\ *vb* **va·moosed; va·moos·ing** [Sp *vamos* let us go] : to leave or go away quickly

¹**vamp** *n* **1** : the part of a boot or shoe upper covering esp. the front part of the foot **2** : a short introductory musical passage often repeated

²**vamp** \'vamp\ *vb* **1** : to provide with a new vamp **2** : to patch up with a new part **3** : INVENT, IMPROVISE ⟨~ up an excuse⟩

³**vamp** *n* : a woman who uses her charm or wiles to seduce and exploit men

⁴**vamp** *vb* : to practice seductive wiles on : to act like a vamp

vam·pire \'vam-ˌpī(-ə)r\ *n* [F, fr. G *Vampir*, fr. Serbian *vampir*] **1** : a night-wandering bloodsucking ghost **2** : a person who preys on other people; *esp* : a woman who exploits and ruins her lover **3** : VAMPIRE BAT

vampire bat *n* : any of various bats of Central and South America that feed on the blood of animals; *also* : any of several other bats that do not feed on blood but are sometimes reputed to do so

¹**van** \'van\ *n* : VANGUARD

²**van** *n* : a usu. enclosed wagon or motor-truck for moving goods or animals; *also* : a versatile enclosed box-like motor vehicle

va·na·di·um \və-'nā-dē-əm\ *n* : a soft grayish ductile metallic chemical element used esp. to form alloys

Van Al·len belt \van-'a-lən-\ *n* : a belt of intense radiation in the magnetosphere composed of charged particles trapped by earth's magnetic field

van·co·my·cin \ˌvan-kə-'mī-sᵊn\ *n* : an antibiotic used esp. against staphylococci

van·dal \'van-dᵊl\ *n* **1** *cap* : a member of a Germanic people who sacked Rome in A.D. 455 **2** : a person who willfully mars or destroys property

van·dal·ise *Brit var of* VANDALIZE

van·dal·ism \'van-də-ˌli-zəm\ *n* : willful or malicious destruction or defacement of public or private property

van·dal·ize \-ˌlīz\ *vb* **-ized; -iz·ing** : to subject to vandalism : DAMAGE

Van·dyke \van-'dīk\ *n* : a trim pointed beard

vane \'vān\ *n* [ME, fr. OE *fana* banner] **1** : a movable device attached to a high object for showing wind direction **2** : a thin flat or curved object that is rotated about an axis by a flow of fluid or that rotates to cause a fluid to flow or that redirects a flow of fluid ⟨the ~s of a windmill⟩ **3** : a feather fastened near the back end of an arrow for stability in flight

van·guard \'van-ˌgärd\ *n* **1** : the troops moving at the front of an army **2** : the forefront of an action or movement

va·nil·la \və-'ni-lə\ *n* [NL, genus name, fr. Sp *vainilla* vanilla (plant and fruit), dim. of *vaina* sheath, fr. L *vagina*] : a flavoring extract made synthetically or obtained from the long beanlike pods (**vanilla beans**) of a tropical American climbing orchid; *also* : this orchid

van·ish \'va-nish\ *vb* : to pass from sight or existence : disappear completely — **van·ish·er** *n*

van·i·ty \'va-nə-tē\ *n, pl* **-ties 1** : something that is vain, empty, or useless **2** : the quality or fact of being useless or futile : FUTILITY **3** : undue pride in oneself or one's appearance : CONCEIT **4** : a small case for cosmetics : COMPACT

vanity plate *n* : an automobile license plate bearing distinctive letters or numbers designated by the owner

van·quish \'van-kwish, 'van-\ *vb* **1** : to overcome in battle or in a contest **2** : to gain mastery over (as an emotion)

van·tage \'van-tij\ *n* **1** : superiority in a contest **2** : a position giving a strategic advantage or a commanding perspective

va·pid \'va-pəd, 'vā-\ *adj* : lacking spirit, liveliness, or zest : FLAT, INSIPID ⟨~ gossip⟩ — **va·pid·i·ty** \va-'pi-də-tē\ *n* — **vap·id·ly** *adv* — **vap·id·ness** *n*

va·por \'vā-pər\ *n* **1** : fine separated particles (as fog or smoke) floating in the air and clouding it **2** : a substance in the gaseous state; *esp* : one that is liquid under ordinary conditions **3** : something insubstantial or fleeting **4** *pl* : a depressed or hysterical nervous condition

va·por·ing \'vā-pə-riŋ\ *n* : an idle, boastful, or high-flown expression or speech — usu. used in pl.

va·por·ise *Brit var of* VAPORIZE

va·por·ize \'vā-pə-ˌrīz\ *vb* **-ized; -iz·ing**

1 : to convert into vapor 2 : to destroy as if by converting to vapor ⟨*vaporized* enemy tanks⟩ — **va·por·i·za·tion** \ˌvā-pə-rə-ˈzā-shən\ *n*

va·por·iz·er \-ˌrī-zər\ *n* : a device that vaporizes something (as a medicated liquid)

vapor lock *n* : an interruption of flow of a fluid (as fuel in an engine) caused by the formation of vapor in the feeding system

va·por·ous \ˈvā-pə-rəs\ *adj* 1 : full of vapors : FOGGY, MISTY 2 : UNSUBSTANTIAL, VAGUE ⟨~ speculations⟩ — **va·por·ous·ly** *adv* — **va·por·ous·ness** *n*

va·pory \ˈvā-pə-rē\ *adj* : MISTY

va·pour *chiefly Brit var of* VAPOR

va·que·ro \vä-ˈker-ō\ *n, pl* **-ros** [Sp, fr. *vaca* cow, fr. L *vacca*] : a ranch hand : COWBOY

var *abbr* 1 variable 2 variant; variation 3 variety 4 various

¹**var·i·able** \ˈver-ē-ə-bəl\ *adj* 1 : able or apt to vary : CHANGEABLE 2 : FICKLE 3 : not true to type : ABERRANT ⟨a ~ wheat⟩ — **var·i·abil·i·ty** \ˌver-ē-ə-ˈbi-lə-tē, ˌvar-\ *n* — **var·i·ably** \-blē\ *adv*

²**variable** *n* 1 : a quantity that may take on any of a set of values; *also* : a mathematical symbol representing a variable 2 : something that is variable

var·i·ance \ˈver-ē-əns\ *n* 1 : variation or a degree of variation : DEVIATION 2 : DISAGREEMENT, DISPUTE 3 : a license to do something contrary to the usual rule ⟨a zoning ~⟩ 4 : the square of the standard deviation ✦ *Synonyms* DISCORD, CONTENTION, DISSENSION, STRIFE, CONFLICT

¹**var·i·ant** \ˈver-ē-ənt\ *adj* 1 : differing from others of its kind or class 2 : varying usu. slightly from the standard or type

²**variant** *n* 1 : one that exhibits variation from a type or norm 2 : one of two or more different spellings or pronunciations of a word

var·i·a·tion \ˌver-ē-ˈā-shən\ *n* 1 : the act, process, or an instance of varying : a change in form, position, or condition : MODIFICATION, ALTERATION 2 : extent of change or difference 3 : divergence in the characteristics of an organism from those typical or usual for its group; *also* : one exhibiting such variation 4 : repetition of a musical theme with modifications in rhythm, tune, harmony, or key

vari·col·ored \ˈver-i-ˌkə-lərd\ *adj* : having various colors : VARIEGATED

var·i·cose \ˈva-rə-ˌkōs\ *adj* : abnormally swollen and dilated ⟨~ veins⟩ — **var·i·cos·i·ty** \ˌva-rə-ˈkä-sə-tē\ *n*

var·ied \ˈver-ēd\ *adj* 1 : having many forms or types : DIVERSE 2 : VARIEGATED — **var·ied·ly** *adv*

var·ie·gat·ed \ˈver-ē-ə-ˌgā-təd\ *adj* 1 : having patches, stripes, or marks of different colors ⟨~ flowers⟩ 2 : VARIED 1 — **var·ie·gate** \-ˌgāt\ *vb* — **var·ie·ga·tion** \ˌver-ē-ə-ˈgā-shən\ *n*

¹**va·ri·etal** \və-ˈrī-ə-tᵊl\ *adj* : of or relating to a variety; *esp* : of, relating to, or producing a varietal

²**varietal** *n* : a wine bearing the name of the principal grape from which it is made

va·ri·ety \və-ˈrī-ə-tē\ *n, pl* **-et·ies** 1 : the state of being varied or various : DIVERSITY 2 : a collection of different things : ASSORTMENT 3 : something varying from others of the same general kind 4 : any of various groups of plants or animals within a species distinguished by characteristics insufficient to separate species : SUBSPECIES 5 : entertainment such as is given in a stage presentation comprising a series of performances (as songs, dances, or acrobatic acts)

var·i·o·rum \ˌver-ē-ˈȯr-əm\ *n* : an edition or text of a work containing notes by various persons or variant readings of the text

var·i·ous \ˈver-ē-əs\ *adj* 1 : VARICOLORED 2 : of differing kinds : MULTIFARIOUS 3 : UNLIKE ⟨animals as ~ as the jaguar and the sloth⟩ 4 : having a number of different aspects 5 : NUMEROUS, MANY 6 : INDIVIDUAL, SEPARATE ✦ *Synonyms* DIVERGENT, DISPARATE, DIFFERENT, DISSIMILAR, DIVERSE, UNALIKE — **var·i·ous·ly** *adv*

var·let \ˈvär-lət\ *n* 1 : ATTENDANT 2 : SCOUNDREL, KNAVE

var·mint \ˈvär-mənt\ *n* [alter. of *vermin*] 1 : an animal considered a pest; *esp* : one classed as vermin and unprotected by game law 2 : a contemptible person : RASCAL

¹**var·nish** \ˈvär-nish\ *n* 1 : a liquid preparation that is applied to a surface and dries into a hard glossy coating; *also* : the glaze of this coating 2 : something suggesting varnish by its gloss 3 : outside show : deceptive or superficial appearance

²**varnish** *vb* 1 : to cover with varnish 2 : to cover or conceal with something that gives a fair appearance : GLOSS

var·si·ty \ˈvär-sə-tē\ *n, pl* **-ties** [by shortening & alter. fr. *university*] 1 *Brit* : UNIVERSITY 2 : the principal team representing a college, school, or club

vary \ˈver-ē\ *vb* **var·ied; vary·ing** 1 : ALTER, CHANGE 2 : to make or be of different kinds : introduce or have variety : DIVERSIFY, DIFFER 3 : DEVIATE, SWERVE 4 : to change in bodily structure or function away from what is usual for members of a group

vas·cu·lar \ˈvas-kyə-lər\ *adj* [NL *vascularis*, fr. L *vasculum* small vessel, dim. of *vas* vase, vessel] : of or relating to a channel or system of channels for the conveyance of a body fluid (as blood or sap); *also* : supplied with or containing such vessels and esp. blood vessels ⟨the ~ system⟩

vascular plant *n* : a plant having a specialized system for carrying fluids that includes xylem and phloem

vas def·er·ens \ˈvas-ˈde-fə-rənz\ *n, pl* **va·sa def·er·en·tia** \ˈvā-zə-ˌde-fə-ˈren-shē-ə\ : a sperm-carrying duct of the testis

vase \ˈvās, ˈvāz\ *n* : a usu. round vessel of greater depth than width used chiefly for ornament or for flowers

va·sec·to·my \və-ˈsek-tə-mē, vā-ˈzek-\ *n*,

pl **-mies** : surgical excision of all or part of the vas deferens usu. to induce sterility

va·so·con·stric·tion \ˌvā-zō-kən-ˈstrik-shən\ *n* : narrowing of the interior diameter of blood vessels

va·so·con·stric·tor \-tər\ *n* : an agent (as a nerve fiber or a drug) that initiates or induces vasoconstriction

vas·sal \ˈva-səl\ *n* **1** : a person under the protection of a feudal lord to whom he owes homage and loyalty : a feudal tenant **2** : one occupying a dependent or subordinate position — **vassal** *adj*

vas·sal·age \-sə-lij\ *n* **1** : the state of being a vassal **2** : the homage and loyalty due from a vassal **3** : SERVITUDE, SUBJECTION

¹**vast** \ˈvast\ *adj* : very great in size, amount, degree, intensity, or esp. extent ⟨~ plains⟩ ⟨~ knowledge⟩ ✦ **Synonyms** ENORMOUS, HUGE, GIGANTIC, COLOSSAL, MAMMOTH — **vast·ly** *adv* — **vast·ness** *n*

²**vast** *n* : a great expanse : IMMENSITY

vasty \ˈvas-tē\ *adj* : VAST, IMMENSE

vat \ˈvat\ *n* : a large vessel (as a tub or barrel) esp. for holding liquids in manufacturing processes

VAT *abbr* value-added tax

vat·ic \ˈva-tik\ *adj* : PROPHETIC, ORACULAR

Vat·i·can \ˈva-ti-kən\ *n* **1** : the papal headquarters in Rome **2** : the papal government

va·tu \ˈvä-ˌtü\ *n, pl* **vatu** — see MONEY table

vaude·ville \ˈvȯd-vəl, ˈväd-, ˈvȯd-, -ˌvil\ *n* [F, fr. MF, satirical song, alter. of *vaudevire*, fr. *vau-de-Vire* valley of Vire, town in northwest France where such songs were composed] : a stage entertainment consisting of unrelated acts (as of acrobats, comedians, dancers, or singers)

¹**vault** \ˈvȯlt\ *n* **1** : an arched masonry structure usu. forming a ceiling or roof; *also* : something (as the sky) resembling a vault **2** : a room or space covered by a vault esp. when underground **3** : a room or compartment for the safekeeping of valuables **4** : a burial chamber; *also* : a usu. metal or concrete case in which a casket is enclosed at burial — **vaulty** *adj*

²**vault** *vb* : to form or cover with a vault

³**vault** *vb* : to leap vigorously esp. by aid of the hands or a pole — **vault·er** *n*

⁴**vault** *n* : an act of vaulting : LEAP

vault·ed \ˈvȯl-təd\ *adj* **1** : built in the form of a vault : ARCHED **2** : covered with a vault

vault·ing \-tiŋ\ *adj* : reaching for the heights ⟨~ ambition⟩

vaunt \ˈvȯnt\ *vb* [ME, fr. AF *vanter*, fr. LL *vanitare*, ultim. fr. L *vanus* vain] : BRAG, BOAST — **vaunt** *n*

vaunt·ed \ˈvȯn-təd\ *adj* : much praised or boasted of

vb *abbr* verb; verbal

V–chip \ˈvē-ˌchip\ *n* : a computer chip in a television set used to block based on content the viewing of certain programs

VCR \ˌvē-(ˌ)sē-ˈär\ *n* [videocassette recorder] : a device that records and plays back videotapes

VD *abbr* venereal disease

VDT *abbr* video display terminal

veal \ˈvēl\ *n* : the flesh of a young calf

vec·tor \ˈvek-tər\ *n* **1** : a quantity that has magnitude and direction **2** : an organism (as a fly or tick) that transmits a pathogen

Ve·da \ˈvā-də\ *n* [Skt, lit., knowledge] : any of a class of Hindu sacred writings — **Ve·dic** \ˈvā-dik\ *adj*

Ve·dan·ta \vā-ˈdän-tə, və-, -ˈdan-\ *n* : an orthodox Hindu philosophy based on the Upanishads

vee·jay \ˈvē-jā\ *n* : an announcer of a program featuring music videos

veep \ˈvēp\ *n* : VICE PRESIDENT

veer \ˈvir\ *vb* : to shift from one direction or course to another ✦ **Synonyms** TURN, AVERT, DEFLECT, DIVERT — **veer** *n*

veg·an \ˈvē-gən, ˈvā-; ˈve-jən, -ˌjan\ *n* : a strict vegetarian who consumes no animal food or dairy products — **veg·an·ism** \ˈvē-gə-ˌni-zəm, ˈvā-, ˈve-\ *n*

¹**veg·e·ta·ble** \ˈvej-tə-bəl, ˈve-jə-\ *adj* [ME, fr. ML *vegetabilis* vegetative, fr. *vegetare* to grow, fr. L, to animate, fr. *vegetus* lively, fr. *vegēre* to enliven] **1** : of, relating to, or growing like plants ⟨the ~ kingdom⟩ **2** : made from, obtained from, or containing plants or plant products ⟨~ oils⟩ **3** : suggesting that of a plant (as in inertness) ⟨a ~ existence⟩

²**vegetable** *n* **1** : PLANT 1 **2** : a usu. herbaceous plant grown for an edible part that is usu. eaten as part of a meal; *also* : such an edible part

veg·e·tal \ˈve-jə-t°l\ *adj* **1** : VEGETABLE **2** : VEGETATIVE

veg·e·tar·i·an \ˌve-jə-ˈter-ē-ən\ *n* : one that believes in or practices living on a diet of vegetables, fruits, grains, nuts, and sometimes animal products (as milk and cheese) — **vegetarian** *adj* — **veg·e·tar·i·an·ism** \-ē-ə-ˌni-zəm\ *n*

veg·e·tate \ˈve-jə-ˌtāt\ *vb* **-tat·ed; -tat·ing** : to live or grow in the manner of a plant; *esp* : to lead a dull inert life

veg·e·ta·tion \ˌve-jə-ˈtā-shən\ *n* **1** : the act or process of vegetating; *also* : inert existence **2** : plant life or cover (as of an area) — **veg·e·ta·tion·al** \-shə-nəl\ *adj*

veg·e·ta·tive \ˈve-jə-ˌtā-tiv\ *adj* **1** : of or relating to nutrition and growth esp. as contrasted with reproduction **2** : of, relating to, or composed of vegetation **3** : VEGETABLE 3

veg out \ˈvej-\ *vb* **vegged out; vegging out** [short for *vegetate*] : to spend time idly or passively

ve·he·ment \ˈvē-ə-mənt\ *adj* **1** : marked by great force or energy **2** : marked by strong feeling or expression : PASSIONATE, FERVID — **ve·he·mence** \-məns\ *n* — **ve·he·ment·ly** *adv*

ve·hi·cle \ˈvē-ə-kəl, ˈvē-ˌhi-\ *n* **1** : a medium by which a thing is applied or administered ⟨linseed oil is a ~ for pigments⟩ **2** : a medium through or by means of which something is conveyed or expressed **3** : a means of transporting persons or goods ✦ **Synonyms** INSTRUMENT, AGENT, AGENCY, ORGAN, CHANNEL — **ve·hic·u·lar** \vē-ˈhi-kyə-lər\ *adj*

¹**veil** \ˈvāl\ *n* **1** : a piece of often sheer or diaphanous material used to screen or curtain something or to cover the head or face **2** : the life of a nun ⟨take the ∼⟩ **3** : something that hides or obscures like a veil ⟨a ∼ of secrecy⟩

²**veil** *vb* : to cover with or as if with a veil : wear a veil

¹**vein** \ˈvān\ *n* **1** : a fissure in rock filled with mineral matter; *also* : a bed of useful mineral matter **2** : any of the tubular branching vessels that carry blood from the capillaries toward the heart **3** : any of the bundles of vascular vessels forming the framework of a leaf **4** : any of the thickened ribs that stiffen the wings of an insect **5** : something (as a wavy variegation in marble) suggesting veins **6** : a distinctive style of expression **7** : a distinctive element or quality : STRAIN **8** : MOOD, HUMOR — **veined** \ˈvānd\ *adj*

²**vein** *vb* : to pattern with or as if with veins — **vein·ing** *n*

vel *abbr* velocity

ve·lar \ˈvē-lər\ *adj* : of or relating to a velum and esp. that of the soft palate

veld *or* **veldt** \ˈvelt, ˈfelt\ *n* [Afrikaans *veld*, fr. D, field] : an open grassland esp. in southern Africa usu. with scattered shrubs or trees

vel·lum \ˈve-ləm\ *n* [ME *velym*, fr. AF *velim, veeslin*, fr. *veelin*, adj., of a calf, fr. *veel* calf] **1** : a fine-grained lambskin, kidskin, or calfskin prepared for writing on or for binding books **2** : a strong cream-colored paper — **vellum** *adj*

ve·loc·i·pede \və-ˈlä-sə-ˌpēd\ *n* : an early bicycle

ve·loc·i·rapt·or \və-ˈlä-sə-ˌrap-tər\ *n* : any of a genus of agile flesh-eating bipedal dinosaurs of the Cretaceous having a sickle-shaped claw on each foot

ve·loc·i·ty \və-ˈlä-sə-tē\ *n, pl* **-ties** : quickness of motion : SPEED ⟨the ∼ of light⟩

ve·lour *or* **ve·lours** \və-ˈlu̇r\ *n, pl* **ve·lours** \-ˈlu̇rz\ : any of various textile fabrics with pile like that of velvet

ve·lum \ˈvē-ləm\ *n, pl* **ve·la** \-lə\ : a membranous body part (as the soft palate) resembling a veil

vel·vet \ˈvel-vət\ *n* [ME *veluet, velvet*, fr. AF, fr. *velu* shaggy, ultim. fr. L *villus* shaggy hair] **1** : a fabric having a short soft dense warp pile **2** : something resembling or suggesting velvet (as in softness or luster) **3** : the soft skin covering the growing antlers of deer — **velvet** *adj* — **velvety** *adj*

vel·ve·teen \ˌvel-və-ˈtēn\ *n* **1** : a fabric woven usu. of cotton in imitation of velvet **2** *pl* : clothes made of velveteen

Ven *abbr* venerable

ve·nal \ˈvē-nᵊl\ *adj* : capable of being bought or bribed : MERCENARY, CORRUPT — **ve·nal·i·ty** \vi-ˈna-lə-tē\ *n* — **ve·nal·ly** \ˈvē-nᵊl-ē\ *adv*

ve·na·tion \ve-ˈnā-shən, vē-\ *n* : an

arrangement or system of veins ⟨the ∼ of the hand⟩ ⟨leaf ∼⟩

vend \ˈvend\ *vb* : SELL; *esp* : to sell as a hawker or peddler — **vend·ible** *adj*

vend·ee \ven-ˈdē\ *n* : one to whom a thing is sold : BUYER

ven·det·ta \ven-ˈde-tə\ *n* : a feud marked by acts of revenge

vending machine *n* : a coin-operated machine for selling merchandise

ven·dor \ˈven-dər, *for 1 also* ven-ˈdȯr\ *n* **1** : one that vends : SELLER **2** : VENDING MACHINE

¹**ve·neer** \və-ˈnir\ *n* [G *Furnier*, fr. *furnieren* to veneer, fr. F *fournir* to furnish] **1** : a thin usu. superficial layer of material ⟨brick ∼⟩; *esp* : a thin layer of fine wood glued over a cheaper wood **2** : superficial display : GLOSS

²**veneer** *vb* : to overlay with a veneer

ven·er·a·ble \ˈve-nə-rə-bəl\ *adj* **1** : deserving to be venerated — often used as a religious title **2** : made sacred by association

ven·er·ate \ˈve-nə-ˌrāt\ *vb* **-at·ed; -at·ing** : to regard with reverential respect ✦ **Synonyms** ADORE, REVERE, REVERENCE, WORSHIP — **ven·er·a·tion** \ˌve-nə-ˈrā-shən\ *n*

ve·ne·re·al \və-ˈnir-ē-əl\ *adj* : of or relating to sexual intercourse or to diseases transmitted by it ⟨a ∼ infection⟩

venereal disease *n* : a contagious disease (as gonorrhea or syphilis) usu. acquired by having sexual intercourse with someone who already has it

ve·ne·tian blind \və-ˈnē-shən-\ *n* : a blind having thin horizontal parallel slats that can be adjusted to admit a desired amount of light

ven·geance \ˈven-jəns\ *n* : punishment inflicted in retaliation for an injury or offense : REVENGE

venge·ful \ˈvenj-fəl\ *adj* : filled with a desire for revenge : VINDICTIVE — **venge·ful·ly** *adv*

ve·nial \ˈvē-nē-əl\ *adj* : capable of being forgiven : EXCUSABLE ⟨∼ sin⟩

ve·ni·re \və-ˈnī-rē\ *n* : a panel from which a jury is drawn

ve·ni·re fa·ci·as \-ˈfā-shē-əs\ *n* [ME, fr. ML, you should cause to come] : a writ summoning persons to appear in court to serve as jurors

ve·ni·re·man \və-ˈnī-rē-mən, -ˈnir-ē-\ *n* : a member of a venire

ven·i·son \ˈve-nə-sən, -zən\ *n, pl* **venisons** *also* **venison** [ME, fr. AF *veneisun* game, venison, fr. L *venatio*, fr. *venari* to hunt, pursue] : the edible flesh of a deer

ven·om \ˈve-nəm\ *n* [ME *venim*, fr. AF, ultim. fr. L *venenum* magic charm, drug, poison] **1** : poisonous material secreted by some animals (as snakes, spiders, or bees) and transmitted usu. by biting or stinging **2** : ILL WILL, MALEVOLENCE

ven·om·ous \ˈve-nə-məs\ *adj* **1** : full of venom : POISONOUS **2** : SPITEFUL, MALEVOLENT **3** : secreting and using venom ⟨∼ snakes⟩ — **ven·om·ous·ly** *adv*

ve·nous \'vē-nəs\ *adj* **1** : of, relating to, or full of veins **2** : being purplish red oxygen-deficient blood rich in carbon dioxide that is present in most veins

¹vent \'vent\ *vb* **1** : to provide with a vent **2** : to serve as a vent for **3** : EXPEL, DISCHARGE **4** : to relieve oneself by vigorous or emotional expression

²vent *n* **1** : an opportunity or way of escape or passage : OUTLET **2** : an opening for the escape of a gas or liquid or for the relief of pressure

³vent *n* : a slit in a garment esp. in the lower part of a seam (as of a jacket or skirt)

ven·ti·late \'ven-tə-ˌlāt\ *vb* **-lat·ed; -lat·ing** **1** : to discuss freely and openly ⟨~ a question⟩ **2** : to give vent to ⟨~ one's grievances⟩ **3** : to cause fresh air to circulate through (as a room or mine) so as to replace foul air **4** : to provide with a vent or outlet ♦ *Synonyms* EXPRESS, VENT, AIR, UTTER, VOICE, BROACH — **ven·ti·la·tor** \-lā-tər\ *n*

ven·ti·la·tion \ˌven-tə-ˈlā-shən\ *n* **1** : the act or process of ventilating **2** : circulation of air (as in a room) **3** : a system or means of providing fresh air

ven·tral \'ven-trəl\ *adj* **1** : of or relating to the belly : ABDOMINAL **2** : of, relating to, or located on or near the surface of the body that in humans is the front but in most other animals is the lower surface — **ven·tral·ly** *adv*

ven·tri·cle \'ven-tri-kəl\ *n* **1** : a chamber of the heart that receives blood from the atrium of the same side and pumps it into the arteries **2** : any of the communicating cavities of the brain that are continuous with the central canal of the spinal cord — **ven·tric·u·lar** \ven-ˈtri-kyə-lər\ *adj*

ven·tril·o·quism \ven-ˈtri-lə-ˌkwi-zəm\ *n* [LL *ventriloquus* ventriloquist, fr. L *venter* belly + *loqui* to speak; fr. the belief that the voice is produced from the ventriloquist's stomach] : the production of the voice in such a manner that the sound appears to come from a source other than the speaker — **ven·tril·o·quist** \-kwist\ *n*

ven·tril·o·quy \-kwē\ *n* : VENTRILOQUISM

¹ven·ture \'ven-chər\ *vb* **-tured; -tur·ing** **1** : to expose to hazard : RISK **2** : to undertake the risks of : BRAVE **3** : to offer at the risk of rebuff, rejection, or censure ⟨~ an opinion⟩ **4** : to proceed despite danger : DARE

²venture *n* **1** : an undertaking involving chance or risk; *esp* : a speculative business enterprise **2** :ʼsomething risked in a speculative venture : STAKE

ven·ture·some \'ven-chər-səm\ *adj* **1** : involving risk : DANGEROUS, HAZARDOUS **2** : inclined to venture : BOLD, DARING ♦ *Synonyms* ADVENTUROUS, VENTUROUS, RASH, RECKLESS, FOOLHARDY — **ven·ture·some·ly** *adv* — **ven·ture·some·ness** *n*

ven·tur·ous \'ven-chə-rəs\ *adj* : VENTURESOME — **ven·tur·ous·ly** *adv* — **ven·tur·ous·ness** *n*

ven·ue \'ven-yü\ *n* [AF, alter. of *vinné, visné*, lit., neighborhood, neighbors, ultim. fr. L *vicinitas* vicinity] **1** : the place from which the jury is taken and where the trial is held **2** : the place in which the alleged events from which a legal action arises took place **3** : a place where events are held ⟨music ~s⟩

Ve·nus \'vē-nəs\ *n* : the planet 2d in order from the sun

Ve·nu·sian \vi-ˈnü-zhən, -ˈnyü-\ *adj* : of or relating to the planet Venus

Venus fly·trap *or* **Ve·nus's–fly·trap** \'vē-nə-səz-ˈflī-ˌtrap\ *n* : an insect-eating plant of the Carolina coast that has the leaf tip modified into an insect trap

ve·ra·cious \və-ˈrā-shəs\ *adj* **1** : TRUTHFUL, HONEST **2** : TRUE, ACCURATE ⟨~ details⟩ — **ve·ra·cious·ly** *adv*

ve·rac·i·ty \və-ˈra-sə-tē\ *n, pl* **-ties** **1** : devotion to truth : TRUTHFULNESS **2** : conformity with fact : ACCURACY **3** : something true

ve·ran·da *or* **ve·ran·dah** \və-ˈran-də\ *n* : a long open usu. roofed porch

verb \'vərb\ *n* : a word that is the grammatical center of a predicate and expresses an act, occurrence, or mode of being

¹ver·bal \'vər-bəl\ *adj* **1** : of, relating to, or consisting of words; *esp* : having to do with words rather than with the ideas to be conveyed **2** : expressed in usu. spoken words : not written : ORAL ⟨a ~ contract⟩ **3** : of, relating to, or formed from a verb **4** : LITERAL, VERBATIM — **ver·bal·ly** *adv*

²verbal *n* : a word that combines characteristics of a verb with those of a noun or adjective

verbal auxiliary *n* : an auxiliary verb

ver·bal·ize \'vər-bə-ˌlīz\ *vb* **-ized; -iz·ing** **1** : to speak or write in wordy or empty fashion **2** : to express something in words : describe verbally **3** : to convert into a verb — **ver·bal·i·za·tion** \ˌvər-bə-lə-ˈzā-shən\ *n*

verbal noun *n* : a noun derived directly from a verb or verb stem and in some uses having the sense and constructions of a verb

ver·ba·tim \(ˌ)vər-ˈbā-təm\ *adv or adj* : in the same words : word for word

ver·be·na \(ˌ)vər-ˈbē-nə\ *n* : VERVAIN; *esp* : any of several garden vervains of hybrid origin with showy spikes of bright often fragrant flowers

ver·biage \'vər-bē-ij, -bij\ *n* **1** : superfluity of words usu. of little or obscure content **2** : DICTION, WORDING

ver·bose \(ˌ)vər-ˈbōs\ *adj* : using more words than are needed : WORDY ♦ *Synonyms* PROLIX, DIFFUSE, REDUNDANT, WINDY — **ver·bos·i·ty** \-ˈbä-sə-tē\ *n*

ver·bo·ten \vər-ˈbō-tᵊn, fer-\ *adj* [G] : forbidden usu. by dictate

ver·dant \'vər-dᵊnt\ *adj* : green with growing plants — **ver·dant·ly** *adv*

ver·dict \'vər-(ˌ)dikt\ *n* [ME *verdit, verdict*, fr. AF *veirdit*, fr. *veir* true (fr. L *verus*) + *dit* saying, dictum, fr. L *dictum*, fr. *dicere* to say] **1** : the finding or decision of a jury **2** : DECISION, JUDGMENT

ver·di·gris \'vər-də-ˌgrēs, -ˌgris\ *n* : a green or bluish deposit that forms on copper, brass, or bronze surfaces

ver·dure \'vər-jər\ *n* : the greenness of growing vegetation; *also* : such vegetation

¹**verge** \'vərj\ *n* [[ME, rod, measuring rod, margin, fr. AF, rod, area of jurisdiction, fr. L *virga* twig, rod, line] **1** : a staff carried as an emblem of authority or office **2** : something that borders or bounds : EDGE, MARGIN **3** : BRINK, THRESHOLD ⟨on the ∼ of collapse⟩

²**verge** *vb* **verged; verg·ing** **1** : to be contiguous **2** : to be on the verge

³**verge** *vb* **verged; verg·ing** **1** : to move or extend in some direction or toward some condition : INCLINE **2** : to be in transition or change

verg·er \'vər-jər\ *n,* **1** *chiefly Brit* : an attendant who carries a verge (as before a bishop) **2** : SEXTON

ve·rid·i·cal \və-'ri-di-kəl\ *adj* **1** : TRUTHFUL **2** : not illusory : GENUINE

ver·i·fy \'ver-ə-ˌfī\ *vb* **-fied; -fy·ing 1** : to confirm in law by oath **2** : to establish the truth, accuracy, or reality of ⟨∼ the claim⟩ ◆ *Synonyms* AUTHENTICATE, CORROBORATE, SUBSTANTIATE, VALIDATE — **ver·i·fi·able** *adj* — **ver·i·fi·ca·tion** \ˌver-ə-fə-'kā-shən\ *n*

ver·i·ly \'ver-ə-lē\ *adv* **1** : in very truth : CERTAINLY **2** : TRULY, CONFIDENTLY

ver·i·si·mil·i·tude \ˌver-ə-sə-'mi-lə-ˌtüd, -ˌtyüd\ *n* : the quality or state of appearing to be true or real

ver·i·ta·ble \'ver-ə-tə-bəl\ *adj* : ACTUAL, GENUINE, TRUE — **ver·i·ta·bly** *adv*

ver·i·ty \'ver-ə-tē\ *n, pl* **-ties 1** : the quality or state of being true or real : TRUTH, REALITY **2** : something (as a statement) that is true **3** : HONESTY, VERACITY

ver·meil *n* [MF] **1** \'vər-məl, -ˌmāl\ : VERMILION **2** \ver-'mā\ : gilded silver

ver·mi·cel·li \ˌvər-mə-'che-lē, -'se-\ *n* [It, fr. pl. of *vermicello,* dim. of *verme* worm] : a pasta made in thinner strings than spaghetti

ver·mic·u·lite \vər-'mi-kyə-ˌlīt\ *n* : any of various lightweight water-absorbent minerals derived from mica

ver·mi·form appendix \'vər-mə-ˌform-\ *n* : APPENDIX 2

ver·mil·ion *also* **ver·mil·lion** \vər-'mil-yən\ *n* : a bright reddish orange color; *also* : any of various red pigments

ver·min \'vər-mən\ *n, pl* **vermin 1** : small common harmful or objectionable animals (as lice or mice) that are difficult to get rid of **2** : birds and mammals that prey on game — **ver·min·ous** *adj*

ver·mouth \vər-'müth\ *n* [F *vermout,* fr. G *Wermut* wormwood] : a dry or sweet wine flavored with herbs and often used in mixed drinks

¹**ver·nac·u·lar** \vər-'na-kyə-lər\ *adj* [L *vernaculus* native, fr. *verna* slave born in the master's house, native] **1** : of, relating to, or being a language or dialect native to a region or country rather than to a literary,

cultured, or foreign language **2** : of, relating to, or being the normal spoken form of a language **3** : applied to a plant or animal in common speech as distinguished from biological nomenclature ⟨∼ names⟩

²**vernacular** *n* **1** : a vernacular language **2** : the mode of expression of a group or class **3** : a vernacular name of a plant or animal

ver·nal \'vər-nᵊl\ *adj* : of, relating to, or occurring in the spring

ver·ni·er \'vər-nē-ər\ *n* : a short scale made to slide along the divisions of a graduated instrument to indicate parts of divisions

ve·ron·i·ca \və-'rä-ni-kə\ *n* : any of a genus of herbs related to the snapdragons that have small usu. bluish flowers

ver·sa·tile \'vər-sə-tᵊl\ *adj* : turning with ease from one thing or position to another; *esp* : having many aptitudes — **ver·sa·til·i·ty** \ˌvər-sə-'ti-lə-tē\ *n*

¹**verse** \'vərs\ *n* **1** : a line of poetry; *also* : STANZA **2** : metrical writing distinguished from poetry esp. by its lower level of intensity **3** : POETRY **4** : POEM **5** : one of the short divisions of a chapter in the Bible

²**verse** *vb* **versed; vers·ing** : to familiarize by experience, study, or practice ⟨well *versed* in the theater⟩

ver·si·cle \'vər-si-kəl\ *n* : a verse or sentence said or sung by a leader in public worship and followed by a response from the people

ver·si·fi·ca·tion \ˌvər-sə-fə-'kā-shən\ *n* **1** : the making of verses **2** : metrical structure

ver·si·fy \'vər-sə-ˌfī\ *vb* **-fied; -fy·ing 1** : to write verse **2** : to turn into verse — **ver·si·fi·er** \-ˌfī-ər\ *n*

ver·sion \'vər-zhən\ *n* **1** : TRANSLATION; *esp* : a translation of the Bible **2** : an account or description from a particular point of view esp. as contrasted with another **3** : a form or variant of a type or original

vers li·bre \ver-'lēbrᵊ\ *n, pl* **vers li·bres** *same*\ [F] : FREE VERSE

ver·so \'vər-sō\ *n, pl* **versos** : a left-hand page

ver·sus \'vər-səs\ *prep* **1** : AGAINST 1 ⟨the champion ∼ the challenger⟩ **2** : in contrast or as an alternative to ⟨free trade ∼ protection⟩

vert *abbr* vertical

ver·te·bra \'vər-tə-brə\ *n, pl* **-brae** \-ˌbrā, -(ˌ)brē\ *or* **-bras** [L] : one of the segments of bone or cartilage making up the backbone

ver·te·bral \(ˌ)vər-'tē-brəl, 'vər-tə-\ *adj* : of, relating to, or made up of vertebrae : SPINAL

vertebral column *n* : BACKBONE 1

¹**ver·te·brate** \'vər-tə-brət, -ˌbrāt\ *adj* **1** : having a backbone **2** : of or relating to the vertebrates

²**vertebrate** *n* : any of a large group of animals (as mammals, birds, reptiles, amphibians, or fishes) that have a backbone or in some primitive forms (as a lamprey)

a flexible rod of cells and that have a tubular nervous system arranged along the back and divided into a brain and spinal cord

ver·tex \'vər-ˌteks\ n, pl **ver·ti·ces** \'vər-tə-ˌsēz\ also **ver·tex·es** [ME, top of the head, fr. L vertex, vortex whirl, whirlpool, top of the head, summit, fr. vertere to turn] **1** : the point opposite to and farthest from the base of a geometrical figure **2** : the point where the sides of an angle or three or more edges of a polyhedron (as a cube) meet **3** : the highest point : TOP, SUMMIT

ver·ti·cal \'vər-ti-kəl\ adj **1** : of, relating to, or located at the vertex : directly overhead **2** : rising perpendicularly from a level surface : UPRIGHT — **vertical** n — **ver·ti·cal·i·ty** \ˌvər-tə-'ka-lə-tē\ n — **ver·ti·cal·ly** \-k(ə-)lē\ adv

ver·tig·i·nous \(ˌ)vər-'ti-jə-nəs\ adj : marked by, affected with, or tending to cause dizziness

ver·ti·go \'vər-ti-ˌgō\ n, pl **-goes** or **-gos** : DIZZINESS, GIDDINESS

vertu var of VIRTU

ver·vain \'vər-ˌvān\ n : any of a genus of chiefly American herbs or low woody plants with often showy heads or spikes of tubular flowers

verve \'vərv\ n : liveliness of imagination; also : VIVACITY

¹very \'ver-ē\ adj **veri·er; -est** [ME verray, verry, fr. AF verai, ultim. fr. L verax truthful, fr. verus true] **1** : EXACT, PRECISE ⟨the ~ heart of the city⟩ **2** : exactly suitable ⟨the ~ tool for the job⟩ **3** : ABSOLUTE, UTTER ⟨the veriest nonsense⟩ **4** — used as an intensive esp. to emphasize identity ⟨before my ~ eyes⟩ **5** : MERE, BARE ⟨the ~ idea scared him⟩ **6** : SELFSAME, IDENTICAL ⟨the ~ man I saw⟩

²very adv **1** : in actual fact : TRULY **2** : to a high degree : EXTREMELY

very high frequency n : a radio frequency of between 30 and 300 megahertz

ves·i·cant \'ve-si-kənt\ n : an agent that causes blistering — **vesicant** adj

ves·i·cle \'ve-si-kəl\ n : a membranous and usu. fluid-filled cavity in a plant or animal; also : BLISTER — **ve·sic·u·lar** \və-'si-kyə-lər\ adj

¹ves·per \'ves-pər\ n, **1** cap, archaic : EVENING STAR **2** : a vesper bell **3** archaic : EVENING, EVENTIDE

²vesper adj : of or relating to vespers or the evening

ves·pers \-pərz\ n pl, often cap : a late afternoon or evening worship service

ves·sel \'ve-səl\ n **1** : a container (as a barrel, bottle, bowl, or cup) for holding something **2** : a person held to be the recipient of a quality (as grace) **3** : a craft bigger than a rowboat **4** : a tube in which a body fluid (as blood or sap) is contained and circulated

¹vest \'vest\ vb **1** : to place or give into the possession or discretion of some person or authority **2** : to grant or endow with a particular authority, right, or property **3** : to become legally vested **4** : to clothe

with or as if with a garment; esp : to garb in ecclesiastical vestments

²vest n, **1** : a sleeveless garment for the upper body usu. worn over a shirt **2** chiefly Brit : a man's sleeveless undershirt **3** : a front piece of a dress resembling the front of a vest

ves·tal \'ves-tᵊl\ adj : CHASTE

²vestal n : VESTAL VIRGIN

vestal virgin n **1** : a virgin consecrated to the Roman goddess Vesta and to the service of watching the sacred fire perpetually kept burning on her altar **2** : a chaste woman

vest·ed \'ves-təd\ adj : fully and unconditionally guaranteed as a legal right, benefit, or privilege

vested interest n : an interest (as in an existing political, economic, or social arrangement) to which the holder has a strong commitment; also : one (as a corporation) having a vested interest

ves·ti·bule \'ves-tə-ˌbyül\ n **1** : a passage or room between the outer door and the interior of a building **2** : any of various bodily cavities forming or suggesting an entrance to some other cavity or space — **ves·tib·u·lar** \ve-'sti-byə-lər\ adj

ves·tige \'ves-tij\ n [F, fr. L vestigium footprint, track, vestige] : a trace or visible sign left by something lost or vanished; also : a minute remaining amount — **ves·ti·gial** \ve-'sti-jē-əl, -jəl\ adj — **ves·ti·gial·ly** adv

vest·ing \'ves-tiŋ\ n : the conveying to an employee of inalienable rights to share in a pension fund; also : the right so conveyed

vest·ment \'vest-mənt\ n **1** : an outer garment; esp : a ceremonial or official robe **2** pl : CLOTHING, GARB **3** : a garment or insignia worn by a cleric when officiating or assisting at a religious service

vest–pocket adj : very small ⟨a ~ park⟩

ves·try \'ves-trē\ n, pl **vestries 1** : a room in a church for vestments, altar linens, and sacred vessels **2** : a room used for church meetings and classes **3** : a body administering the temporal affairs of an Episcopal parish

ves·try·man \-mən\ n : a member of a vestry

ves·ture \'ves-chər\ n **1** : a covering garment **2** : CLOTHING, APPAREL

¹vet \'vet\ n : VETERINARIAN

²vet adj or n : VETERAN

³vet vb : to evaluate for appraisal or acceptance ⟨~ a manuscript⟩

vetch \'vech\ n : any of a genus of twining leguminous herbs including some grown for fodder and green manure

vet·er·an \'ve-trən, -tə-rən\ n [L veteranus, fr. veteranus old, of long experience, fr. veter-, vetus old] **1** : an old soldier of long service **2** : a former member of the armed forces **3** : a person of long experience usu. in an occupation or skill — **veteran** adj

Veterans Day n : November 11 observed as a legal holiday in commemoration of the end of hostilities in 1918 and 1945

vet·er·i·nar·i·an \ˌve-trə-ˈner-ē-ən, ˌve-tə-rə-\ *n* : one qualified and authorized to practice veterinary medicine

¹vet·er·i·nary \ˈve-trə-ˌner-ē, ˈve-tə-rə-\ *adj* : of, relating to, or being the medical care of animals and esp. domestic animals

²veterinary *n, pl* **-nar·ies** : VETERINARIAN

¹ve·to \ˈvē-tō\ *n, pl* **vetoes** [L, I forbid] **1** : an authoritative prohibition **2** : a power of one part of a government to forbid the carrying out of projects attempted by another part; *esp* : a power vested in a chief executive to prevent the carrying out of measures adopted by a legislature **3** : the exercise of the power of veto

²veto *vb* **1** : FORBID, PROHIBIT **2** : to refuse assent to (a legislative bill) so as to prevent enactment or cause reconsideration — **ve·to·er** *n*

vex \ˈveks\ *vb* **vexed** *also* **vext; vex·ing** **1** : to bring trouble, distress, or agitation to **2** : to annoy continually with little irritations

vex·a·tion \vek-ˈsā-shən\ *n* **1** : the act of vexing **2** : the quality or state of being vexed : IRRITATION **3** : a cause of trouble or annoyance

vex·a·tious \-shəs\ *adj* **1** : causing vexation : ANNOYING **2** : full of distress or annoyance : TROUBLED — **vex·a·tious·ly** *adv* — **vex·a·tious·ness** *n*

vexed \ˈvekst\ *adj* : fully debated or discussed ⟨a ~ question⟩

VF *abbr* **1** video frequency **2** visual field

VFD *abbr* volunteer fire department

VFW *abbr* Veterans of Foreign Wars

VG *abbr* **1** very good **2** vicar-general

VHF *abbr* very high frequency

VI *abbr* Virgin Islands

via \ˈvī-ə, ˈvē-ə\ *prep* **1** : by way of **2** : by means of

vi·a·ble \ˈvī-ə-bəl\ *adj* **1** : capable of living; *esp* : sufficiently developed as to be capable of surviving outside the mother's womb ⟨a ~ fetus⟩ **2** : capable of growing and developing ⟨~ seeds⟩ **3** : capable of being put into practice : WORKABLE **4** : having a reasonable chance of succeeding ⟨a ~ candidate⟩ — **vi·a·bil·i·ty** \ˌvī-ə-ˈbi-lə-tē\ *n* — **vi·a·bly** \ˈvī-ə-blē\ *adv*

via·duct \ˈvī-ə-ˌdəkt\ *n* : a long elevated roadway usu. consisting of a series of short spans supported on arches, piers, or columns

vi·al \ˈvī-əl\ *n* : a small vessel for liquids

vi·and \ˈvī-ənd\ *n* : an article of food

vi·at·i·cum \vī-ˈa-ti-kəm, vē-\ *n, pl* **-cums** *or* **-ca** \-kə\ *n* **1** : the Christian Eucharist given to a person in danger of death **2** : an allowance esp. in money for traveling needs and expenses

vibes \ˈvībz\ *n pl* **1** : VIBRAPHONE **2** : VIBRATIONS

vi·brant \ˈvī-brənt\ *adj* **1** : VIBRATING, PULSATING **2** : pulsating with vigor or activity ⟨a ~ personality⟩ **3** : readily set in vibration : RESPONSIVE **4** : sounding from vibration **5** : BRIGHT ⟨~ colors⟩ — **vi·bran·cy** \-brən-sē\ *n*

vi·bra·phone \ˈvī-brə-ˌfōn\ *n* : a percussion instrument like the xylophone but with metal bars and motor-driven resonators

vi·brate \ˈvī-ˌbrāt\ *vb* **vi·brat·ed; vi·brat·ing** **1** : OSCILLATE **2** : to set in vibration **3** : to be in vibration **4** : WAVER, FLUCTUATE **5** : to respond sympathetically : THRILL

vi·bra·tion \vī-ˈbrā-shən\ *n* **1** : a rapid to-and-fro motion of the particles of an elastic body or medium (as a stretched cord) that produces sound **2** : an act of vibrating : a state of being vibrated : OSCILLATION **3** : a trembling motion **4** : VACILLATION **5** : a feeling or impression that someone or something gives off — usu. used in pl. ⟨good ~s⟩ — **vi·bra·tion·al** \-shə-nəl\ *adj*

vi·bra·to \vi-ˈbrä-tō\ *n, pl* **-tos** [It] : a slightly tremulous effect imparted to vocal or instrumental music

vi·bra·tor \ˈvī-ˌbrā-tər\ *n* : one that vibrates or causes vibration; *esp* : a vibrating electrical device used in massage or for sexual stimulation

vi·bra·to·ry \ˈvī-brə-ˌtōr-ē\ *adj* : consisting of, capable of, or causing vibration

vi·bur·num \vī-ˈbər-nəm\ *n* : any of a genus of widely distributed shrubs or small trees related to the honeysuckle and bearing small usu. white flowers in broad clusters

vic *abbr* vicinity

Vic *abbr* Victoria

vic·ar \ˈvi-kər\ *n* **1** : an administrative deputy **2** : a minister in charge of a church who serves under the authority of another minister — **vi·car·i·ate** \vī-ˈker-ē-ət\ *n*

vic·ar·age \ˈvi-kə-rij\ *n* : a vicar's home

vicar–general *n, pl* **vicars–general** : an administrative deputy (as of a Roman Catholic or Anglican bishop)

vi·car·i·ous \vī-ˈker-ē-əs\ *adj* [L *vicarius*, fr. *vicis* change, alternation, stead] **1** : acting for another **2** : done or suffered by one person on behalf of another or others ⟨a ~ sacrifice⟩ **3** : sharing in someone else's experience through the use of the imagination or sympathetic feelings — **vi·car·i·ous·ly** *adv* — **vi·car·i·ous·ness** *n*

¹vice \ˈvīs\ *n* **1** : DEPRAVITY, WICKEDNESS **2** : a moral fault or failing **3** : a habitual usu. trivial fault **4** : an undesirable behavior pattern in a domestic animal

²vice *chiefly Brit var of* VISE

³vi·ce \ˈvī-sē\ *prep* : in the place of; *also* : rather than

vice admiral *n* : a commissioned officer in the navy or coast guard ranking above a rear admiral

vice·ge·rent \ˈvīs-ˈjir-ənt\ *n* : an administrative deputy of a king or magistrate — **vice·ge·ren·cy** \-ən-sē\ *n*

vi·cen·ni·al \vī-ˈse-nē-əl\ *adj* : occurring once every 20 years

vice presidency *n* : the office of vice president

vice president *n* **1** : an officer ranking next to a president and usu. empowered to act for the president during an absence or disability **2** : any of several of a president's deputies

vice·re·gal \'vīs-'rē-gəl\ *adj* : of or relating to a viceroy

vice·roy \'vīs-,rói\ *n* : the governor of a country or province who rules as representative of the sovereign — **vice·roy·al·ty** \-əl-tē\ *n*

vice ver·sa \,vī-si-'vər-sə, 'vīs-'vər-\ *adv* : with the order reversed

vi·chys·soise \,vi-shē-'swäz, ,vē-\ *n* [F] : a soup made esp. from leeks or onions and potatoes, cream, and chicken stock and usu. served cold

vic·i·nage \'vi-sə-nij\ *n* : a neighboring or surrounding district : VICINITY

vi·cin·i·ty \və-'si-nə-tē\ *n, pl* **-ties** [MF *vicinité*, fr. L *vicinitas*, fr. *vicinus* neighboring, fr. *vicus* row of houses, village] **1** : NEARNESS, PROXIMITY **2** : a surrounding area : NEIGHBORHOOD

vi·cious \'vi-shəs\ *adj* **1** : having the quality of vice : WICKED, DEPRAVED **2** : DEFECTIVE, FAULTY; *also* : INVALID **3** : IMPURE, FOUL **4** : having a savage disposition; *also* : marked by violence or ferocity **5** : MALICIOUS, SPITEFUL ⟨~ gossip⟩ **6** : worsened by internal causes that augment each other ⟨~ wage-price spiral⟩ — **vi·cious·ly** *adv* — **vi·cious·ness** *n*

vi·cis·si·tude \və-'si-sə-,tüd, vī-, -,tyüd\ *n* : an irregular, unexpected, or surprising change

vic·tim \'vik-təm\ *n* **1** : a living being offered as a sacrifice in a religious rite **2** : an individual injured or killed (as by disease or accident) **3** : a person cheated, fooled, or injured ⟨a ~ of circumstances⟩

vic·tim·ise *Brit var of* VICTIMIZE

vic·tim·ize \'vik-tə-,mīz\ *vb* **-ized; -iz·ing** : to make a victim of — **vic·tim·i·za·tion** \,vik-tə-mə-'zā-shən\ *n* — **vic·tim·iz·er** \'vik-tə-,mī-zər\ *n*

vic·tim·less \'vik-təm-ləs\ *adj* : having no victim ⟨considered gambling to be a ~ crime⟩

vic·tor \'vik-tər\ *n* : WINNER, CONQUEROR

vic·to·ria \vik-'tòr-ē-ə\ *n* : a low 4-wheeled carriage with a folding top and a raised driver's seat in front

¹**Vic·to·ri·an** \vik-'tòr-ē-ən\ *adj* **1** : of or relating to the reign of Queen Victoria of England or the art, letters, or tastes of her time **2** : typical of the standards, attitudes, or conduct of the age of Victoria esp. when considered prudish or narrow

²**Victorian** *n* **1** : a person and esp. an author of the Victorian period **2** : a typically large ornate house built during Queen Victoria's reign

vic·to·ri·ous \vik-'tòr-ē-əs\ *adj* : having won a victory **2** : of, relating to, or characteristic of victory ⟨~ exuberance⟩ — **vic·to·ri·ous·ly** *adv*

vic·to·ry \'vik-tə-rē\ *n, pl* **-ries** : the overcoming of an enemy or an antago-

nist **2** : achievement of mastery or success in a struggle or endeavor

¹**vict·ual** \'vi-t²l\ *n* [ME *vitaille, vituayle*, fr. AF, fr. LL *victualia*, pl., provisions, food, fr. neut. pl. of *victualis* of nourishment, fr. L *victus* nourishment, way of living, fr. *vivere* to live] **1** : food fit for humans **2** *pl* : food supplies

²**victual** *vb* **-ualed** *or* **-ualled; -ual·ing** *or* **-ual·ling** **1** : to supply with food **2** : to store up provisions

vict·ual·ler *or* **vict·ual·er** \'vi-t²l-ər\ *n* : one that supplies provisions (as to an army or a ship)

vi·cu·ña *or* **vi·cu·na** \vi-'kün-yə, vī-; vī-'kü-nə, -'kyü-\ *n* **1** : a So. American wild mammal related to the llama and alpaca; *also* : its wool **2** : a soft fabric woven from the wool of the vicuña; *also* : a sheep's wool imitation of this

vi·de \'vī-dē, 'vē-,dā\ *vb imper* [L] : SEE — used to direct a reader to another item

vi·de·li·cet \və-'de-lə-,set, vī-; vi-'dā-li-,ket\ *adv* [ME, fr. L, fr. *vidēre* to see + *licet* it is permitted] : that is to say : NAMELY

¹**vid·eo** \'vi-dē-,ō\ *n* **1** : TELEVISION **2** : VIDEOTAPE; *also* : a recording similar to a videotape but stored in digital form **3** : a videotaped performance ⟨music ~s⟩

²**video** *adj* **1** : relating to or used in transmission or reception of the television image **2** : relating to or being images on a television screen or computer display ⟨a ~ terminal⟩

video camera *n* : a camera that records visual images and usu. sound; *esp* : CAMCORDER

vid·eo·cas·sette \,vi-dē-ō-kə-'set\ *n* **1** : a case containing videotape for use with a VCR **2** : a recording (as of a movie) on a videocassette

videocassette recorder *n* : VCR

vid·eo·disc *or* **vid·eo·disk** \'vi-dē-ō-,disk\ *n* **1** : OPTICAL DISK **2** : a recording (as of a movie) on a videodisc

video game *n* : an electronic game played on a video screen

vid·e·o·gen·ic \,vi-dē-ō-'je-nik\ *adj* : TELEGENIC

vid·eo·phone \'vid-ē-ə-,fōn\ *n* : a telephone for transmitting both audio and video signals

¹**vid·eo·tape** \'vid-ē-ō-,tāp\ *n* : a recording of visual images and sound made on magnetic tape; *also* : the magnetic tape used for such a recording

²**videotape** *vb* : to make a videotape of

videotape recorder *n* : a device for recording and playing back videotapes

vie \'vī\ *vb* **vied; vy·ing** \'vī-in\ : to compete for superiority : CONTEND — **vi·er** \'vī-ər\ *n*

Viet·cong \vē-'et-'käŋ, ,vē-ət-, -'kóŋ\ *n, pl* **Vietcong** : a guerrilla member of the Vietnamese communist movement

¹**view** \'vyü\ *n* **1** : the act of seeing or examining : INSPECTION; *also* : SURVEY **2** : a way of looking at or regarding something **3** : ESTIMATE, JUDGMENT ⟨stated his ~s⟩ **4** : a sight (as of a landscape) regarded for its pictorial quality **5** : extent

or range of vision ⟨within ∼⟩ **6** : OBJECT, PURPOSE ⟨done with a ∼ to promotion⟩ **7** : a picture of a scene

²view *vb* **1** : to look at attentively : EXAMINE **2** : SEE, WATCH ⟨∼ a film⟩ **3** : to examine mentally : CONSIDER — **view·er** *n*

view·er·ship \'vyü-ər-₁ship\ *n* : a television audience esp. with respect to size or makeup

view·find·er \'vyü-₁fīn-dər\ *n* : a device on a camera for showing the view to be included in the picture

view·point \-₁point\ *n* : POINT OF VIEW, STANDPOINT

vi·ges·i·mal \vī-'je-sə-məl\ *adj* : based on the number 20

vig·il \'vi-jəl\ *n* **1** : a religious observance formerly held on the night before a religious feast **2** : the day before a religious feast observed as a day of spiritual preparation **3** : evening or nocturnal devotions or prayers — usu. used in pl. **4** : an act or a time of keeping awake when sleep is customary; *esp* : WATCH 1

vigilance committee *n* : a committee of vigilantes

vig·i·lant \'vi-jə-lənt\ *adj* : alertly watchful esp. to avoid danger — **vig·i·lance** \-ləns\ *n* — **vig·i·lant·ly** *adv*

vig·i·lan·te \₁vi-jə-'lan-tē\ *n* : a member of a volunteer committee organized to suppress and punish crime summarily (as when the processes of law are viewed as inadequate); *also* : a self-appointed doer of justice — **vig·i·lan·tism** \-'lan-₁ti-zəm\ *n*

¹vi·gnette \vin-'yet\ *n* [F, fr. MF *vignete*, fr. dim. of *vigne* vine] **1** : a small decorative design **2** : a picture (as an engraving or a photograph) that shades off gradually into the surrounding ground **3** : a short descriptive literary sketch

²vignette *vb* **vi·gnett·ed; vi·gnett·ing 1** : to finish (as a photograph) like a vignette **2** : to describe briefly

vig·or \'vi-gər\ *n* **1** : active strength or energy of body or mind **2** : INTENSITY, FORCE ⟨the ∼ of their quarrel⟩

vig·or·ous \'vi-gə-rəs\ *adj* **1** : having vigor : ROBUST **2** : done with force and energy — **vig·or·ous·ly** *adv* — **vig·or·ous·ness** *n*

vig·our *chiefly Brit var of* VIGOR

Vi·king \'vī-kiŋ\ *n* [ON *vīkingr*] : any of the pirate Norsemen who raided or invaded the coasts of Europe in the 8th to 10th centuries

vile \'vī(-ə)l\ *adj* **vil·er; vil·est 1** : morally despicable or abhorrent **2** : physically repulsive : FOUL **3** : of little worth **4** : DEGRADING, IGNOMINIOUS **5** : utterly bad or contemptible ⟨∼ weather⟩ — **vile·ly** \'vī(-ə)l-lē\ *adv* — **vile·ness** *n*

vil·i·fy \'vi-lə-₁fī\ *vb* **-fied; -fy·ing** : to blacken the character of with abusive language : DEFAME ◆ *Synonyms* MALIGN, CALUMNIATE, SLANDER, LIBEL, TRADUCE — **vil·i·fi·ca·tion** \₁vi-lə-fə-'kā-shən\ *n* — **vil·i·fi·er** \'vi-lə-₁fī-ər\ *n*

vil·la \'vi-lə\ *n* **1** : a country estate **2**

: the rural or suburban residence of a wealthy person

vil·lage \'vi-lij\ *n* [ME, fr. AF *vilage*, fr. *vile* manorial estate, farmstead, fr. L *villa*] **1** : a settlement usu. larger than a hamlet and smaller than a town **2** : an incorporated minor municipality **3** : the people of a village

vil·lag·er \'vi-li-jər\ *n* : an inhabitant of a village

vil·lain \'vi-lən\ *n* **1** : VILLEIN **2** : an evil person : SCOUNDREL

vil·lain·ess \-lə-nəs\ *n* : a woman who is a villain

vil·lain·ous \-lə-nəs\ *adj* **1** : befitting a villain : WICKED, EVIL **2** : highly objectionable : DETESTABLE ◆ *Synonyms* VICIOUS, INIQUITOUS, NEFARIOUS, INFAMOUS, CORRUPT, DEGENERATE — **vil·lain·ous·ly** *adv* — **vil·lain·ous·ness** *n*

vil·lainy \-lə-nē\ *n, pl* **-lain·ies 1** : villainous conduct; *also* : a villainous act **2** : villainous character or nature

vil·lein \'vi-lən, -₁lān\ *n* **1** : a free villager of Anglo-Saxon times **2** : an unfree peasant having the status of a slave to a feudal lord

vil·len·age \'vil-ə-nij\ *n* **1** : the holding of land at the will of a feudal lord **2** : the status of a villein

vil·lous \'vi-ləs\ *adj* : covered with fine hairs or villi

vil·lus \'vi-ləs\ *n, pl* **vil·li** \-₁lī, -(₁)lē\ **1** : a slender usu. vascular process; *esp* : one of the tiny projections of the mucous membrane of the small intestine that function in the absorption of food

vim \'vim\ *n* : robust energy and enthusiasm : VITALITY

VIN *abbr* vehicle identification number

vin·ai·grette \₁vi-ni-'gret\ *n* [F] : a sauce made typically of oil, vinegar, and seasonings

vin·ci·ble \'vin-sə-bəl\ *adj* : capable of being overcome or subdued

vin·di·cate \'vin-də-₁kāt\ *vb* **-cat·ed; -cat·ing 1** : AVENGE **2** : EXONERATE, ABSOLVE **3** : CONFIRM, SUBSTANTIATE **4** : to provide defense for : JUSTIFY **5** : to maintain a right to : ASSERT — **vin·di·ca·tor** \-₁kā-tər\ *n*

vin·di·ca·tion \₁vin-də-'kā-shən\ *n* : the act of vindicating or the state of being vindicated; *esp* : justification against denial or censure : DEFENSE

vin·dic·tive \vin-'dik-tiv\ *adj* **1** : disposed to revenge **2** : intended for or involving revenge **3** : VICIOUS, SPITEFUL — **vin·dic·tive·ly** *adv* — **vin·dic·tive·ness** *n*

vine \'vīn\ *n* [ME, fr. AF *vigne*, fr. L *vinea* vine, vineyard, fr. fem. of *vineus* of wine, fr. *vinum* wine] **1** : GRAPE 2 **2** : a plant whose stem requires support and which climbs (as by tendrils) or trails along the ground; *also* : the stem of such a plant

vin·e·gar \'vi-ni-gər\ *n* [ME, fr. AF *vin egre*, lit., sour wine] : a sour liquid obtained by fermentation (as of cider, wine, or malt) and used to flavor or preserve foods

vin·e·gary \-gə-rē\ *adj* **1** : resembling vinegar : SOUR **2** : disagreeable in manner or disposition : CRABBED

vine·yard \'vin-yərd\ *n* **1** : a field of grapevines esp. to produce grapes for wine production **2** : a sphere of activity : field of endeavor

vi·nous \'vī-nəs\ *adj* **1** : of, relating to, or made with wine 〈~ medications〉 **2** : showing the effects of the use of wine 〈~ bloodshot eyes〉

¹**vin·tage** \'vin-tij\ *n* **1** : a season's yield of grapes or wine **2** : WINE; *esp* : a usu. superior wine which comes from a single year **3** : the act or period of gathering grapes or making wine **4** : a period of origin 〈clothes of 1890 ~〉

²**vintage** *adj* **1** : of, relating to, or produced in a particular vintage **2** : of old, recognized, and enduring interest, importance, or quality : CLASSIC 〈~ cars〉 **3** : of the best and most characteristic — used with a proper noun

vint·ner \'vint-nər\ *n* : a dealer in wines

vi·nyl \'vīⁿ-nᵊl\ *n* **1** : a chemical derived from ethylene by the removal of one hydrogen atom **2** : a polymer of a vinyl compound or a product (as a textile fiber) made from one

vinyl chloride *n* : a flammable gaseous carcinogenic compound used esp. to make vinyl resins

vi·ol \'vī-əl\ *n* : a bowed stringed instrument chiefly of the 16th and 17th centuries having a fretted neck and usu. six strings

¹**vi·o·la** \vī-'ō-lə, 'vī-ə-lə\ *n* : VIOLET 1; *esp* : any of various hybrid garden plants with white, yellow, purple, or variously colored flowers that resemble but are smaller than those of the related pansies

²**vi·o·la** \vē-'ō-lə-lə\ *n* : an instrument of the violin family slightly larger and tuned lower than a violin — **vi·o·list** \-list\ *n*

vi·o·la·ble \'vī-ə-lə-bəl\ *adj* : capable of being violated

vi·o·late \'vī-ə-ˌlāt\ *vb* **-lat·ed; -lat·ing** **1** : BREAK, DISREGARD 〈~ a law〉 〈~ a frontier〉 **2** : RAPE **3** : PROFANE, DESECRATE **4** : INTERRUPT, DISTURB 〈*violated* his privacy〉 — **vi·o·la·tor** \-ˌlā-tər\ *n*

vi·o·la·tion \ˌvī-ə-'lā-shən\ *n* : an act or instance of violating : the state of being violated ♦ *Synonyms* BREACH, INFRACTION, TRESPASS, INFRINGEMENT, TRANSGRESSION

vi·o·lence \'vī-ləns, 'vī-ə-ləns\ *n* **1** : exertion of physical force so as to injure or abuse **2** : injury by or as if by infringement or profanation **3** : intense or furious often destructive action or force **4** : vehement feeling or expression : INTENSITY **5** : jarring quality : DISCORDANCE ♦ *Synonyms* COMPULSION, COERCION, DURESS, CONSTRAINT

vi·o·lent \-lənt\ *adj* **1** : marked by extreme force or sudden intense activity **2** : caused by or showing strong feeling 〈~ words〉 **3** : EXTREME, INTENSE 〈~ pain〉 〈~ colors〉 **4** : emotionally agitated to the point of loss of self-control **5**

: caused by force : not natural 〈~ death〉 — **vi·o·lent·ly** *adv*

vi·o·let \'vī-ə-lət\ *n* **1** : any of a genus of herbs or small shrubs usu. with heart-shaped leaves and both aerial and underground flowers; *esp* : one with small usu. solid-colored flowers **2** : a reddish blue color

vi·o·lin \ˌvī-ə-'lin\ *n* : a bowed stringed instrument with four strings that has a shallow body, a fingerboard without frets, and a curved bridge — **vi·o·lin·ist** \-'li-nist\ *n*

vi·o·lon·cel·lo \ˌvī-ə-lən-'che-lō\ *n* [It] : CELLO — **vi·o·lon·cel·list** \-list\ *n*

VIP \ˌvē-ˌī-'pē\ *n, pl* **VIPs** \-'pēz\ [*very important person*] : a person of great influence or prestige; *esp* : a high official with special privileges

vi·per \'vī-pər\ *n* **1** : a common stout-bodied Eurasian venomous snake having a bite only rarely fatal to humans; *also* : any snake (as a pit viper) of the same family as the viper **2** : any venomous or reputedly venomous snake **3** : a vicious or treacherous person — **vi·per·ine** \-pə-ˌrīn\ *adj*

vi·ra·go \və-'rä-gō, -'rā-\ *n, pl* **-goes** *or* **-gos** [ME, fr. L, strong or heroic woman, fr. *vir* man] **1** : a loud overbearing woman **2** : a woman of great strength and courage

vi·ral \'vī-rəl\ *adj* : of, relating to, or caused by a virus 〈a ~ infection〉 — **vi·ral·ly** *adv*

vir·eo \'vir-ē-ˌō\ *n, pl* **-e·os** [L, a small bird, fr. *virēre* to be green] : any of various small insect-eating American songbirds mostly olive green and grayish in color

¹**vir·gin** \'vər-jən\ *n* **1** : an unmarried woman devoted to religion **2** : an unmarried girl or woman **3** *cap* : the mother of Jesus **4** : a person who has not had sexual intercourse

²**virgin** *adj* **1** : free from stain : PURE, SPOTLESS **2** : CHASTE **3** : befitting a virgin : MODEST **4** : FRESH, UNSPOILED; *esp* : not altered by human activity 〈~ forest〉 **5** : INITIAL, FIRST

¹**vir·gin·al** \'vər-jə-nᵊl\ *adj* : of, relating to, or characteristic of a virgin or virginity — **vir·gin·al·ly** *adv*

²**virginal** *n* : a small rectangular spinet without legs popular in the 16th and 17th centuries

Vir·gin·ia creeper \vər-'jin-yə-\ *n* : a No. American vine related to the grapes that has leaves with five leaflets and bluish-black berries

Virginia reel *n* : an American country-dance

vir·gin·i·ty \vər-'ji-nə-tē\ *n, pl* **-ties** **1** : the quality or state of being virgin; *esp* : MAIDENHOOD **2** : the unmarried life : CELIBACY

Vir·go \'vər-gō\ *n* [L, lit., virgin] : a zodiacal constellation between Leo and Libra usu. pictured as a young woman **2** : the 6th sign of the zodiac in astrology; *also* : one born under this sign

vir·gule \'vər-gyül\ *n* : ²SLASH 3

vir·i·des·cent \,vir-ə-'de-s³nt\ *adj* : slightly green : GREENISH

vir·ile \'vir-əl\ *adj* **1** : having the nature, powers, or qualities of a man **2** : MASCULINE, MALE **3** : MASTERFUL, FORCEFUL — **vi·ril·i·ty** \və-'ri-lə-tē\ *n*

vi·ri·on \'vī-rē-,än, 'vir-ē-\ *n* : a complete virus particle consisting of an RNA or DNA core with a protein coat

vi·rol·o·gy \vī-'rä-lə-jē\ *n* : a branch of science that deals with viruses and viral diseases — **vi·rol·o·gist** \-jist\ *n*

vir·tu \vər-'tü, ,vir-\ *or* **ver·tu** \vər-, ,ver-\ *n* [It *virtù*, lit., virtue] **1** : a love of or taste for objects of art **2** : objects of art (as curios and antiques)

vir·tu·al \'vər-chə-wəl\ *adj* **1** : being in essence or in effect though not formally recognized or admitted ⟨a ~ dictator⟩ **2** : being on or simulated on a computer or computer network

vir·tu·al·ly \'vər-chə-wə-lē\ *adv* **1** : almost entirely : NEARLY **2** : for all practical purposes ⟨~ unknown⟩

virtual reality *n* : an artificial environment that is experienced through sensory stimuli (as sights and sounds) provided by an interactive computer program; *also* : the technology used to create or access a virtual reality

vir·tue \'vər-chü\ *n* [ME *vertu*, fr. AF, fr. L *virtus* strength, manliness, virtue, fr. *vir* man] **1** : conformity to a standard of right : MORALITY **2** : a particular moral excellence **3** : manly strength or courage : VALOR **4** : a commendable quality : MERIT **5** : active power to accomplish a given effect : POTENCY, EFFICACY **6** : chastity esp. in a woman

vir·tu·os·i·ty \,vər-chə-'wä-sə-tē\ *n, pl* **-ties** : great technical skill in the practice of a fine art

vir·tu·o·so \,vər-chə-'wō-sō, -zō\ *n, pl* **-sos** *or* **-si** \-sē, -zē\ [It] **1** : one skilled in or having a taste for the fine arts **2** : one who excels in the technique of an art; *esp* : a highly skilled musical performer ♦ **Synonyms** EXPERT, ADEPT, ARTIST, DOYEN, MASTER — **virtuoso** *adj*

vir·tu·ous \'vər-chə-wəs\ *adj* **1** : having or showing virtue and esp. moral virtue **2** : CHASTE — **vir·tu·ous·ly** *adv*

vir·u·lent \'vir-ə-lənt, 'vir-yə-\ *adj* **1** : highly infectious ⟨a ~ germ⟩; *also* : marked by a rapid, severe, and often deadly course ⟨a ~ disease⟩ **2** : extremely poisonous or venomous : NOXIOUS **3** : full of malice : MALIGNANT — **vir·u·lence** \-ləns\ *n* — **vir·u·lent·ly** *adv*

vi·rus \'vī-rəs\ *n, pl* **vi·rus·es** [L, venom, poisonous emanation] **1** : any of a large group of submicroscopic infectious agents that have an outside coat of protein around a core of RNA or DNA, that can grow and multiply only in living cells, and that cause important diseases in human beings, lower animals, and plants; *also* : a disease caused by a virus **2** : something (as a corrupting influence) that poisons the mind or spirit **3** : a computer program that is usu. hidden within

another program and that reproduces itself and inserts the copies into other programs and usu. performs a malicious action (as destroying data)

vis *abbr* **1** visibility **2** visual

vi·sa \'vē-zə, -sə\ *n* [F] **1** : an endorsement by the proper authorities on a passport to show that it has been examined and the bearer may proceed **2** : a signature by a superior official signifying approval of a document

²**visa** *vb* **vi·saed** \-zəd, -səd\; **vi·sa·ing** \-zə-iŋ, -sə-\ : to give a visa to (a passport)

vis·age \'vi-zij\ *n* : the face or countenance of a person or sometimes an animal; *also* : LOOK, APPEARANCE

¹**vis-à-vis** \,vēz-ə-'vē, ,vēs-\ *prep* [F, lit., face-to-face] **1** : face-to-face with : OPPOSITE **2** : in relation to **3** : as compared with

²**vis-à-vis** *n, pl* **vis-à-vis** *same or* -'vēz\ **1** : one that is face-to-face with another **2** : ESCORT **3** : COUNTERPART **4** : TÊTE-À-TÊTE

³**vis-à-vis** *adv* : in company : TOGETHER

viscera *pl of* VISCUS

vis·cer·al \'vi-sə-rəl\ *adj* **1** : felt in or as if in the viscera **2** : not intellectual : INSTINCTIVE **3** : of or relating to the viscera — **vis·cer·al·ly** *adv*

vis·cid \'vi-səd\ *adj* : VISCOUS — **vis·cid·i·ty** \vi-'si-də-tē\ *n*

vis·cos·i·ty \vis-'kä-sə-tē\ *n, pl* **-ties** : the quality of being viscous; *esp* : the property of resistance to flow in a fluid

vis·count \'vī-,kaůnt\ *n* : a member of the British peerage ranking below an earl and above a baron

vis·count·ess \-,kaůn-təs\ *n* **1** : the wife or widow of a viscount **2** : a woman who holds the rank of viscount in her own right

vis·cous \'vis-kəs\ *adj* [ME *viscouse*, fr. AF *viscos*, fr. LL *viscosus* full of birdlime, viscous, fr. L *viscum* mistletoe, birdlime] **1** : having the sticky consistency of glue **2** : having or characterized by viscosity

vis·cus \'vis-kəs\ *n, pl* **vis·cera** \'vi-sə-rə\ : an internal organ of the body; *esp* : one (as the heart or liver) located in the cavity of the trunk

vise \'vīs\ *n* [ME *vys, vice* screw, fr. AF *vyz*, fr. L *vitis* vine] : a tool with two jaws for holding work that typically close by a screw or lever

vis·i·bil·i·ty \,vi-zə-'bi-lə-tē\ *n, pl* **-ties** **1** : the quality, condition, or degree of being visible **2** : the degree of clearness of the atmosphere

vis·i·ble \'vi-zə-bəl\ *adj* : capable of being seen ⟨~ stars⟩; *also* : MANIFEST, APPARENT ⟨has no ~ means of support⟩ — **vis·i·bly** \-blē\ *adv*

¹**vi·sion** \'vi-zhən\ *n* **1** : something seen otherwise than by ordinary sight (as in a dream or trance) **2** : a vivid picture created by the imagination **3** : the act or power of imagination **4** : unusual wisdom in foreseeing what is going to happen **5** : the act or power of seeing : SIGHT **6** : something seen; *esp* : a lovely sight

²vision *vb* : IMAGINE, ENVISION

¹vi·sion·ary \ˈvi-zhə-ner-ē\ *adj* **1** : of the nature of a vision : ILLUSORY, UNREAL **2** : not practical : UTOPIAN **3** : seeing or likely to see visions : given to dreaming or imagining ◆ *Synonyms* IMAGINARY, FANTASTIC, CHIMERICAL, QUIXOTIC

²visionary *n, pl* **-ar·ies 1** : one whose ideas or projects are impractical : DREAMER **2** : one who sees visions

¹vis·it \ˈvi-zət\ *vb* **1** : to go to see in order to comfort or help **2** : to call on either as an act of courtesy or friendship **3** : to dwell with for a time as a guest **4** : to come to or upon as a reward, affliction, or punishment **5** : INFLICT ⟨*~ed* his wrath upon them⟩ **6** : to make a visit or regular or frequent visits **7** : CHAT, CONVERSE ⟨enjoys *~ing* with the neighbors⟩ — **vis·it·able** *adj*

²visit *n* **1** : a short stay : CALL **2** : a brief residence as a guest **3** : a journey to and stay at a place **4** : a formal or professional call (as by a doctor)

vis·i·tant \ˈvi-zə-tənt\ *n* : VISITOR

vis·i·ta·tion \ˌvi-zə-ˈtā-shən\ *n* **1** : VISIT; *esp* : an official visit **2** : a special dispensation of divine favor or wrath; *also* : a severe trial

visiting nurse *n* : a nurse employed to visit sick persons or perform public health services in a community

vis·i·tor \ˈvi-zə-tər\ *n* : one that visits

vi·sor \ˈvī-zər\ *n* **1** : the front piece of a helmet; *esp* : a movable upper piece **2** : VIZARD **3** : a projecting part (as on a cap) to shade the eyes — **vi·sored** \-zərd\ *adj*

vis·ta \ˈvis-tə\ *n* **1** : a distant view through or along an avenue or opening **2** : an extensive mental view over a series of years or events

VISTA *abbr* Volunteers in Service to America

¹vi·su·al \ˈvi-zhə-wəl\ *adj* **1** : of, relating to, or used in vision ⟨*~* organs⟩ **2** : perceived by vision ⟨a *~* impression⟩ **3** : VISIBLE ⟨*~* objects⟩ **4** : done by sight only ⟨*~* navigation⟩ **5** : of or relating to instruction by means of sight ⟨*~* aids⟩ — **vi·su·al·ly** *adv*

²visual *n* : something (as a graphic) that appeals to the sight and is used for illustration, demonstration, or promotion — usu. used in pl.

vi·su·al·ize \ˈvi-zhə-wə-ˌlīz\ *vb* **-ized; -iz·ing** : to make visible; *esp* : to form a mental image of — **vi·su·al·i·za·tion** \ˌvi-zhə-wə-lə-ˈzā-shən\ *n* — **vi·su·al·iz·er** *n*

vi·ta \ˈvē-tə, ˈvī-\ *n, pl* **vi·tae** \ˈvē-ˌtī, ˈvī-ˌtē\ [L, lit., life] : a brief autobiographical sketch

vi·tal \ˈvī-t³l\ *adj* **1** : concerned with or necessary to the maintenance of life **2** : full of life and vigor : ANIMATED **3** : of, relating to, or characteristic of life or living beings **4** : FATAL, MORTAL ⟨*~* wound⟩ **5** : FUNDAMENTAL, INDISPENSABLE — **vi·tal·ly** *adv*

vi·tal·i·ty \vī-ˈta-lə-tē\ *n, pl* **-ties 1** : the property distinguishing the living from

the nonliving **2** : mental and physical vigor **3** : enduring quality **4** : ANIMATION, LIVELINESS

vi·tal·ize \ˈvī-tə-ˌlīz\ *vb* **-ized; -iz·ing** : to impart life or vigor to : ANIMATE — **vi·tal·i·za·tion** \ˌvī-tə-lə-ˈzā-shən\ *n*

vi·tals \ˈvī-t³lz\ *n pl* **1** : vital organs (as the heart and brain) **2** : essential parts

vital signs *n pl* : the pulse rate, respiratory rate, body temperature, and often blood pressure of a person

vital statistics *n pl* : statistics dealing with births, deaths, marriages, health, and disease

vi·ta·min \ˈvī-tə-mən\ *n* : any of various organic substances that are essential in tiny amounts to the nutrition of most animals and some plants and are mostly obtained from foods

vitamin A *n* : any of several vitamins (as from egg yolk or fish-liver oils) required esp. for good vision

vitamin B *n* **1** : VITAMIN B COMPLEX **2** *or* **vitamin B₁** : THIAMINE

vitamin B complex *n* : a group of vitamins that are found widely in foods and are essential for normal function of certain enzymes and for growth

vitamin B₆ \-ˈbē-ˈsiks\ *n* : any of several compounds that are considered essential to vertebrate nutrition

vitamin B₁₂ \-ˈbē-ˈtwelv\ *n* : a complex cobalt-containing compound that occurs esp. in liver and is essential to normal blood formation, neural function, and growth; *also* : any of several compounds of similar action

vitamin C *n* : a vitamin found esp. in fruits and vegetables that is needed by the body to prevent scurvy

vitamin D *n* : any or all of several vitamins that are needed for normal bone and tooth structure and are found esp. in fish-liver oils, egg yolk, and milk or are produced by the body in response to ultraviolet light

vitamin E *n* : any of various oily fat-soluble liquid vitamins whose absence in the body is associated with such ailments as infertility, the breakdown of muscles, and vascular problems and which are found esp. in leaves and in seed germ oils

vitamin K *n* : any of several vitamins needed for blood to clot properly

vi·ti·ate \ˈvi-shē-ˌāt\ *vb* **-at·ed; -at·ing 1** : CONTAMINATE, POLLUTE; *also* : DEBASE, PERVERT **2** : to make legally ineffective : INVALIDATE ⟨*~* a contract⟩ — **vi·ti·a·tion** \ˌvi-shē-ˈā-shən\ *n* — **vi·ti·a·tor** \ˈvi-shē-ˌā-tər\ *n*

vi·ti·cul·ture \ˈvi-tə-ˌkəl-chər\ *n* : the growing of grapes — **vi·ti·cul·tur·al** \ˌvi-tə-ˈkəl-chə-rəl\ *adj* — **vi·ti·cul·tur·ist** \-rist\ *n*

vit·re·ous \ˈvi-trē-əs\ *adj* **1** : of, relating to, or resembling glass : GLASSY ⟨*~* rocks⟩ **2** : of, relating to, or being the clear colorless transparent jelly (**vitreous humor**) behind the lens in the eyeball

vit·ri·ol \ˈvi-trē-əl\ *n* : something resembling acid in being caustic, corrosive, or biting — **vit·ri·ol·ic** \ˌvi-trē-ˈä-lik\ *adj*

vit·tles \ˈvi-t³lz\ *n pl* : VICTUALS

vi·tu·per·ate \vī-ˈtü-pə-ˌrāt, və-, -ˈtyü-\ *vb* **-at·ed; -at·ing** : to abuse in words : SCOLD ◆ *Synonyms* REVILE, BERATE, RATE, UPBRAID, RAIL, LASH — **vi·tu·per·a·tive** \-ˈtü-pə-rə-tiv, -ˈtyü-, -ˌrā-\ *adj* — **vi·tu·per·a·tive·ly** *adv*

vi·tu·per·a·tion \(ˌ)vī-tü-pə-ˈrā-shən, və-, -tyü-\ *n* : lengthy harsh criticism or abuse

vi·va \ˈvē-və\ *interj* [It & Sp, long live] — used to express goodwill or approval

vi·va·ce \vē-ˈvä-chä\ *adv or adj* [It] : in a brisk spirited manner — used as a direction in music

vi·va·cious \və-ˈvā-shəs, vī-\ *adj* : lively in temper, conduct, or spirit : SPRIGHTLY — **vi·va·cious·ly** *adv* — **vi·va·cious·ness** *n*

vi·vac·i·ty \-ˈva-sə-tē\ *n* : the quality or state of being vivacious

vi·va vo·ce \ˌvī-və-ˈvō-sē, ˌvē-və-ˈvō-chä\ *adj* [ML, with the living voice] : expressed or conducted by word of mouth : ORAL — **viva voce** *adv*

viv·id \ˈvi-vəd\ *adj* **1** : BRILLIANT, INTENSE ⟨a ~ red⟩ **2** : having the appearance of vigorous life **3** : producing a strong impression on the senses; *esp* : producing distinct mental pictures ⟨a ~ description⟩ — **viv·id·ly** *adv* — **viv·id·ness** *n*

viv·i·fy \ˈvi-və-ˌfī\ *vb* **-fied; -fy·ing 1** : to put life into : ANIMATE **2** : to make vivid — **viv·i·fi·ca·tion** \ˌvi-və-fə-ˈkā-shən\ *n* — **viv·i·fi·er** *n*

vi·vip·a·rous \vī-ˈvi-pə-rəs, və-\ *adj* : producing living young from within the body rather than from eggs — **vi·vi·par·i·ty** \ˌvī-və-ˈpa-rə-tē, ˌvi-\ *n*

viv·i·sec·tion \ˌvi-və-ˈsek-shən, ˈvi-və-ˌsek-\ *n* : the cutting of or operation on a living animal; *also* : animal experimentation esp. if causing distress to the subject

vix·en \ˈvik-sən\ *n* **1** : an ill-tempered scolding woman **2** : a female fox

viz *abbr* videlicet

viz·ard \ˈvi-zərd\ *n* : a mask for disguise or protection

vi·zier \və-ˈzir\ *n* : a high executive officer of many Muslim countries

VJ *abbr* veejay

VOA *abbr* Voice of America

voc *abbr* **1** vocational **2** vocative

vocab *abbr* vocabulary

vo·ca·ble \ˈvō-kə-bəl\ *n* : TERM, NAME; *esp* : a word as such without regard to its meaning

vo·cab·u·lary \vō-ˈka-byə-ˌler-ē\ *n, pl* **-lar·ies 1** : a list or collection of words usu. alphabetically arranged and defined or explained : LEXICON **2** : a stock of words in a language used by a class or individual or in relation to a subject

vocabulary entry *n* : a word (as the noun *book*), hyphenated or open compound (as the verb *cross-refer* or the noun *boric acid*), word element (as the affix *-an*), abbreviation (as *agt*), verbalized symbol (as *Na*), or term (as *master of ceremonies*) entered alphabetically in a dictionary for the purpose of definition or identification or expressly included as an inflected form (as the noun *mice* or the verb *saw*) or as a derived form (as the noun *godlessness* or the adverb *globally*) or related phrase (as *in spite of*) run on at its base word and usu. set in a type (as boldface) readily distinguishable from that of the lightface running text which defines, explains, or identifies the entry

¹vo·cal \ˈvō-kəl\ *adj* **1** : uttered by the voice : ORAL **2** : relating to, composed or arranged for, or sung by the human voice ⟨~ music⟩ **3** : given to expressing oneself freely or insistently : OUTSPOKEN **4** : of or relating to the voice

²vocal *n* **1** : a vocal sound **2** : a vocal composition or its performance

vocal cords *n pl* : either of two pairs of elastic folds of mucous membrane that project into the cavity of the larynx and function in the production of vocal sounds

vo·cal·ic \vō-ˈka-lik\ *adj* : of, relating to, or functioning as a vowel

vo·cal·ise *Brit var of* VOCALIZE

vo·cal·ist \ˈvō-kə-list\ *n* : SINGER

vo·cal·ize \-ˌlīz\ *vb* **-ized; -iz·ing 1** : to give vocal expression to : UTTER; *esp* : SING **2** : to make voiced rather than voiceless — **vo·cal·iz·er** *n*

vo·ca·tion \vō-ˈkā-shən\ *n* **1** : a summons or strong inclination to a particular state or course of action ⟨religious ~⟩ **2** : regular employment : OCCUPATION, PROFESSION — **vo·ca·tion·al** \-shə-nəl\ *adj*

vo·ca·tion·al·ism \-shə-nə-ˌli-zəm\ *n* : emphasis on vocational training in education

voc·a·tive \ˈvä-kə-tiv\ *adj* : of, relating to, or constituting a grammatical case marking the one addressed — **vocative** *n*

vo·cif·er·ate \vō-ˈsi-fə-ˌrāt\ *vb* **-at·ed; -at·ing** [L *vociferari*, fr. *voc-, vox* voice + *ferre* to bear] : to cry out loudly : CLAMOR, SHOUT — **vo·cif·er·a·tion** \-ˌsi-fə-ˈrā-shən\ *n*

vo·cif·er·ous \vō-ˈsi-fə-rəs\ *adj* : making or given to loud outcry — **vo·cif·er·ous·ly** *adv* — **vo·cif·er·ous·ness** *n*

vod·ka \ˈväd-kə\ *n* [Russ, fr. *voda* water] : a colorless liquor distilled from a mash (as of rye or wheat)

vogue \ˈvōg\ *n* [MF, action of rowing, course, fashion, fr. *voguer* to sail, fr. OF, fr. OIt *vogare* to row] **1** : popular acceptance or favor : POPULARITY **2** : a period of popularity **3** : one that is in fashion at a particular time ◆ *Synonyms* MODE, FAD, RAGE, CRAZE, TREND, FASHION

vogu·ish \ˈvō-gish\ *adj* **1** : FASHIONABLE, SMART **2** : suddenly or temporarily popular

¹voice \ˈvȯis\ *n* **1** : sound produced through the mouth by vertebrates and esp. by human beings (as in speaking or singing) **2** : musical sound produced by the vocal cords : the power to produce such sound; *also* : one of the melodic parts in a vocal or instrumental composition **3** : the vocal organs as a means of tone production ⟨train the ∼⟩ **4** : sound produced by vibration of the vocal cords as heard in vowels and some consonants **5** : the power of speaking **6** : a sound suggesting a voice ⟨the ∼ of the sea⟩ **7** : an instrument or medium of expression **8** : a choice, opinion, or wish openly expressed; *also* : right of expression **9** : distinction of form of a verb to indicate the relation of the subject to the action expressed by the verb

²**voice** *vb* **voiced; voic·ing** : to give voice or expression to : UTTER ⟨∼ a complaint⟩ ✦ **Synonyms** EXPRESS, VENT, AIR, VENTILATE

voice box *n* : LARYNX

voiced \'vòist\ *adj* **1** : having a voice ⟨soft-*voiced*⟩ **2** : uttered with voice ⟨a ∼ consonant⟩ — **voiced·ness** \'vòist-nəs, 'vòi-səd-nəs\ *n*

voice·less \'vòis-ləs\ *adj* **1** : having no voice **2** : not pronounced with voice — **voice·less·ly** *adv* — **voice·less·ness** *n*

voice mail *n* : an electronic communication system in which spoken messages are recorded for later playback to the intended recipient; *also* : such a message

voice–over *n* : the voice in a film or television program of a person who is heard but not seen or not seen talking

voice·print \'vòis-ˌprint\ *n* : an individually distinctive pattern of voice characteristics that is spectrographically produced

¹**void** \'vòid\ *adj* **1** : UNOCCUPIED, VACANT ⟨a ∼ bishopric⟩ **2** : containing nothing : EMPTY **3** : LACKING, DEVOID ⟨proposals ∼ of sense⟩ **4** : VAIN, USELESS **5** : of no legal force or effect : NULL

²**void** *n* **1** : empty space : EMPTINESS, VACUUM **2** : a feeling of want or hollowness

³**void** *vb* **1** : to make or leave empty; *also* : VACATE, LEAVE **2** : DISCHARGE, EMIT ⟨∼ urine⟩ **3** : to render void : ANNUL, NULLIFY ⟨∼ a contract⟩ — **void·able** *adj* — **void·er** *n*

voi·là \vwä-'lä\ *interj* [F] — used to call attention or to express satisfaction or approval

voile \'vòi(-ə)l\ *n* : a sheer fabric used for women's clothing and curtains

vol *abbr* **1** volume **2** volunteer

vol·a·tile \'vä-lə-t²l\ *adj* **1** : readily becoming a vapor at a relatively low temperature ⟨a ∼ liquid⟩ **2** : tending to erupt into violence **3** : likely to change suddenly — **vol·a·til·i·ty** \ˌvä-lə-'ti-lə-tē\ *n* — **vol·a·til·ize** \'vä-lə-tə-ˌlīz\ *vb*

vol·ca·nic \väl-'ka-nik\ *adj* **1** : of, relating to, or produced by a volcano **2** : explosively violent ⟨∼ emotions⟩

vol·ca·nism \'väl-kə-ˌni-zəm\ *n* : volcanic action or activity

vol·ca·no \väl-'kā-nō\ *n, pl* **-noes** *or* **-nos** [It *or* Sp; It *vulcano*, fr. Sp *vulcán*, ultim. fr. L *Volcanus*, Roman god of fire and metalworking] : an opening in the crust of the earth, a planet, or a moon from which molten rock and steam issue; *also* : a hill or mountain composed of the ejected material

vol·ca·nol·o·gy \ˌväl-kə-'nä-lə-jē\ *n* : a branch of geology that deals with volcanic phenomena — **vol·ca·nol·o·gist** \-kə-'nä-lə-jist\ *n*

vole \'vōl\ *n* : any of various small rodents that are closely related to the lemmings and muskrats

vo·li·tion \vō-'li-shən\ *n* **1** : the act or the power of making a choice or decision : WILL **2** : a choice or decision made — **vo·li·tion·al** \-'li-shə-nəl\ *adj*

¹**vol·ley** \'vä-lē\ *n, pl* **volleys** **1** : a flight of missiles (as arrows) **2** : simultaneous discharge of a number of missile weapons **3** : an act of volleying **4** : a burst of many things at once ⟨a ∼ of angry letters⟩

²**volley** *vb* **vol·leyed; vol·ley·ing** **1** : to discharge or become discharged in or as if in a volley **2** : to hit an object of play (as a ball) in the air before it touches the ground

vol·ley·ball \-ˌbȯl\ *n* : a game played by volleying an inflated ball over a net; *also* : the ball used in this game

volt \'vōlt\ *n* : the meter-kilogram-second unit of electrical potential difference and electromotive force equal to the difference in potential between two points in a wire carrying a constant current of one ampere when the power dissipated between the points is equal to one watt

volt·age \'vōl-tij\ *n* : potential difference measured in volts

vol·ta·ic \väl-'tā-ik, vōl-\ *adj* : of, relating to, or producing direct electric current by chemical action

volte–face \vȯlt-'fäs, ˌvȯl-tə-\ *n* : a reversal in policy : ABOUT-FACE

volt·me·ter \'vōlt-ˌmē-tər\ *n* : an instrument for measuring in volts the difference in potential between different points of an electrical circuit

vol·u·ble \'väl-yə-bəl\ *adj* : fluent and smooth in speech : GLIB ✦ **Synonyms** GARRULOUS, LOQUACIOUS, TALKATIVE — **vol·u·bil·i·ty** \ˌväl-yə-'bi-lə-tē\ *n* — **vol·u·bly** \'väl-yə-blē\ *adv*

vol·ume \'väl-yəm, -(ˌ)yüm\ *n* [ME, fr. AF, fr. L *volumen* roll, scroll, fr. *volvere* to roll] **1** : a series of printed sheets bound typically in book form; *also* : an arbitrary number of issues of a periodical **2** : space occupied as measured by cubic units ⟨the ∼ of a cylinder⟩ **3** : sufficient matter to fill a book ⟨her glance spoke ∼s⟩ **4** : AMOUNT ⟨increasing ∼ of business⟩ **5** : the degree of loudness of a sound ✦ **Synonyms** BODY, BULK, MASS

vo·lu·mi·nous \və-'lü-mə-nəs\ *adj* : having or marked by great volume or bulk : LARGE — **vo·lu·mi·nous·ly** *adv* — **vo·lu·mi·nous·ness** *n*

¹**vol·un·tary** \'vä-lən-ˌter-ē\ *adj* **1** : done, made, or given freely and without compulsion ⟨a ∼ sacrifice⟩ **2** : done on purpose : INTENTIONAL ⟨∼ manslaughter⟩ **3** : of, relating to, or regulated by the will ⟨∼ behavior⟩ **4** : having power of free choice **5** : provided or supported by voluntary action ⟨a ∼ organization⟩ ✦ **Syn-**

onyms DELIBERATE, WILLFUL, WILLING, WITTING — **vol·un·tar·i·ly** \,vä-lən-'ter-ə-lē\ *adv*

²**voluntary** *n, pl* **-tar·ies** : an organ solo played in a religious service

voluntary muscle *n* : muscle (as most striated muscle) under voluntary control

¹**vol·un·teer** \,vä-lən-'tir\ *n* **1** : a person who voluntarily undertakes a service or duty **2** : a plant growing spontaneously esp. from seeds lost from a previous crop

²**volunteer** *vb* **1** : to offer or give voluntarily **2** : to offer oneself as a volunteer

vo·lup·tu·ary \və-'ləp-chə-,wer-ē\ *n, pl* **-ar·ies** : a person whose chief interest in life is the indulgence of sensual appetites

vo·lup·tu·ous \-chə-wəs\ *adj* **1** : giving sensual gratification **2** : given to or spent in enjoyment of luxury or pleasure ♦ *Synonyms* LUXURIOUS, EPICUREAN, SENSUOUS — **vo·lup·tu·ous·ly** *adv* — **vo·lup·tu·ous·ness** *n*

vo·lute \və-'lüt\ *n* : a spiral or scroll-shaped decoration

¹**vom·it** \'vä-mət\ *n* : an act or instance of throwing up the contents of the stomach through the mouth; *also* : the matter thrown up

²**vomit** *vb* **1** : to throw up the contents of the stomach through the mouth **2** : to belch forth : GUSH

voo·doo \'vü-dü\ *n, pl* **voodoos 1** : a religion that is derived from African polytheism and is practiced chiefly in Haiti **2** : a person who deals in spells and necromancy; *also* : ¹SPELL **1 3** : a charm used in voodoo — **voodoo** *adj*

voo·doo·ism \-,i-zəm\ *n* **1** : VOODOO 1 **2** : the practice of witchcraft

vo·ra·cious \vo-'rā-shəs, və-\ *adj* **1** : having a huge appetite : RAVENOUS **2** : very eager ⟨a ~ reader⟩ ♦ *Synonyms* GLUTTONOUS, RAVENING, RAPACIOUS — **vo·ra·cious·ly** *adv* — **vo·ra·cious·ness** *n* — **vo·rac·i·ty** \-'ra-sə-tē\ *n*

vor·tex \'vor-,teks\ *n, pl* **vor·ti·ces** \'vor-tə-,sēz\ *also* **vor·tex·es** \'vor-,tek-səz\ : WHIRLPOOL; *also* : something resembling a whirlpool

vo·ta·ry \'vō-tə-rē\ *n, pl* **-ries 1** : ENTHUSIAST, DEVOTEE; *also* : a devoted adherent or admirer **2** : a devout or zealous worshiper

¹**vote** \'vōt\ *n* [ME (Sc), fr. L *votum* vow, wish, fr. *vovēre* to vow] **1** : a choice or opinion of a person or body of persons expressed usu. by a ballot, spoken word, or raised hand; *also* : the ballot, word, or gesture used to express a choice or opinion **2** : the decision reached by voting **3** : the right of suffrage **4** : a group of voters with some common characteristics ⟨the big city ~⟩ — **vote·less** *adj*

²**vote** *vb* **vot·ed; vot·ing 1** : to cast a vote **2** : to elect, decide, pass, defeat, grant, or make legal by a vote **3** : to declare by general agreement **4** : to offer as a suggestion : PROPOSE **5** : to cause to vote esp. in a given way — **vot·er** *n*

vo·tive \'vō-tiv\ *adj* : consisting of or expressing a vow, wish, or desire

vou *abbr* voucher

vouch \'vaüch\ *vb* **1** : PROVE, SUBSTANTIATE **2** : to verify by examining documentary evidence **3** : to give a guarantee **4** : to supply supporting evidence or testimony; *also* : to give personal assurance

vouch·er \'vaü-chər\ *n* **1** : an act of vouching **2** : one that vouches for another **3** : a documentary record of a business transaction **4** : a written affidavit or authorization **5** : a form indicating a credit against future purchases or expenditures

vouch·safe \vaüch-'sāf\ *vb* **vouch·safed; vouch·saf·ing** : to grant or give as or as if a privilege or a special favor

¹**vow** \'vaü\ *n* : a solemn promise or statement; *esp* : one by which a person is bound to an act, service, or condition ⟨marriage ~s⟩

²**vow** *vb* **1** : to make a vow or as a vow **2** : to bind or commit by a vow — **vow·er** *n*

vow·el \'vaü(-ə)l\ *n* **1** : a speech sound produced without obstruction or friction in the mouth **2** : a letter representing such a sound

vox po·pu·li \'väks-'pä-pyə-,li\ *n* [L, voice of the people] : popular sentiment

¹**voy·age** \'voi-ij\ *n* [ME, *viage, veyage*, fr. AF *veiage*, fr. LL *viaticum*, fr. L, traveling money, fr. neut. of *viaticus* of a journey, fr. *via* way] : a journey esp. by water from one place or country to another

²**voyage** *vb* **voy·aged; voy·ag·ing** : to take or make a voyage — **voy·ag·er** *n*

voya·geur \,voi-ə-'zhər, ,vwä-yä-\ *n* [CanF] : a person employed by a fur company to transport goods to and from remote stations esp. in the Canadian Northwest

voy·eur \vwä-'yər, voi-'ər\ *n* **1** : one who obtains sexual pleasure from viewing esp. covertly the nudity or sexual activity of others **2** : an observer of the sordid — **voy·eur·ism** \-,i-zəm\ *n* — **voy·eur·is·tic** \,vwä-(,)yər-'is-tik, ,voi-ər-\ *adj*

VP *abbr* **1** verb phrase **2** vice president

vs *abbr* **1** versus

vss *abbr* **1** verses **2** versions

V/STOL *abbr* vertical or short takeoff and landing

Vt *or* **VT** *abbr* Vermont

VTOL *abbr* vertical takeoff and landing

VTR *abbr* videotape recorder

vul·ca·nize \'vəl-kə-,nīz\ *vb* **-nized; -niz·ing** : to treat rubber or rubberlike material chemically to give useful properties (as elasticity and strength)

Vulg *abbr* Vulgate

vul·gar \'vəl-gər\ *adj* [ME, fr. L *vulgaris* of the mob, vulgar, fr. *vulgus* mob, common people] **1** : VERNACULAR ⟨the ~ tongue⟩ **2** : of or relating to the common people : GENERAL, COMMON **3** : lacking cultivation or refinement : BOORISH; *also* : offensive to good taste or refined feelings ♦ *Synonyms* GROSS, OBSCENE, RIBALD, DIRTY, INDECENT, PROFANE — **vul·gar·ly** *adv*

vul·gar·i·an \,vəl-'ger-ē-ən\ *n* : a vulgar person

vul·gar·ism \'vəl-gə-ˌri-zəm\ *n* **1** : VULGARITY **2** : a word or expression originated or used chiefly by illiterate persons **3** : a coarse expression : OBSCENITY

vul·gar·i·ty \ˌvəl-'ga-rə-tē\ *n, pl* **-ties 1** : something vulgar **2** : the quality or state of being vulgar

vul·gar·ize \'vəl-gə-ˌrīz\ *vb* **-ized; -iz·ing** : to make vulgar — **vul·gar·i·za·tion** \ˌvəl-gə-rə-'zā-shən\ *n* — **vul·gar·iz·er** \'vəl-gə-ˌrī-zər\ *n*

Vul·gate \'vəl-ˌgāt\ *n* [ML *vulgata,* fr. LL *vulgata editio* edition in general circulation] : a Latin version of the Bible used by the Roman Catholic Church

vul·ner·a·ble \'vəl-nə-rə-bəl\ *adj* **1** : capable of being wounded : susceptible to wounds **2** : open to attack : liable to increased penalties in contract bridge —

vul·ner·a·bil·i·ty \ˌvəl-nə-rə-'bi-lə-tē\ *n* — **vul·ner·a·bly** \'vəl-nə-rə-blē\ *adv*

vul·pine \'vəl-ˌpīn\ *adj* : of, relating to, or resembling a fox esp. in cunning ⟨∼ charms⟩

vul·ture \'vəl-chər\ *n* **1** : any of various large birds (as a turkey vulture) related to the hawks, eagles, and falcons but having weaker claws and the head usu. naked and living chiefly on carrion **2** : a rapacious person

vul·va \'vəl-və\ *n, pl* **vul·vae** \-ˌvē\ [ME, fr. ML, fr. L *volva, vulva* womb, female genitals] : the external parts of the female genital organs — **vul·val** \'vəl-vəl\ *or* **vul·var** \-vər, -ˌvär\ *adj*

vv *abbr* **1** verses **2** vice versa

VX \'vē-ˌeks\ *n* : an extremely toxic chemical weapon

vying *pres part of* VIE

¹w \'də-bəl-(ˌ)yü\ *n, pl* **w's** *or* **ws** *often cap* : the 23d letter of the English alphabet

²w *abbr, often cap* **1** water **2** watt **3** week **4** weight **5** west; western **6** wide; width **7** wife **8** with

W *symbol* [G *Wolfram*] tungsten

WA *abbr* **1** Washington **2** Western Australia

wacky \'wa-kē\ *adj* **wack·i·er; -est** : ECCENTRIC, CRAZY

¹wad \'wäd\ *n* **1** : a little mass, bundle, or tuft ⟨∼s of clay⟩ **2** : a soft mass of usu. light fibrous material **3** : a pliable plug (as of felt) used to retain a powder charge (as in a cartridge) **4** : a considerable amount (as of money) **5** : a roll of paper money

²wad *vb* **wad·ded; wad·ding 1** : to push a wad into ⟨∼ a gun⟩ **2** : to form into a wad **3** : to hold in by a wad ⟨∼ a bullet in a gun⟩ **4** : to stuff or line with a wad : PAD

wad·ding \'wä-diŋ\ *n* **1** : WADS; *also* : material for making wads **2** : a soft mass or sheet of short loose fibers used for stuffing or padding

wad·dle \'wä-dᵊl\ *vb* **wad·dled; wad·dling** : to walk with short steps swaying from side to side like a duck — **waddle** *n*

wade \'wād\ *vb* **wad·ed; wad·ing 1** : to step in or through a medium (as water) more resistant than air **2** : to move or go with difficulty or labor and often with determination ⟨∼ through a dull book⟩ — **wad·able** *or* **wade·able** \'wā-də-bəl\ *adj* — **wade** *n*

wad·er \'wā-dər\ *n* **1** : one that wades **2** : SHOREBIRD; *also* : WADING BIRD **3** *pl* : a waterproof garment consisting of pants with attached boots for wading

wa·di \'wä-dē\ *n* [Ar *wādī*] : a streambed of southwest Asia and northern Africa that is dry except in the rainy season

wading bird *n* : any of an order of long-

legged birds (as sandpipers, cranes, or herons) that wade in water in search of food

wa·fer \'wā-fər\ *n* **1** : a thin crisp cake or cracker **2** : a thin round piece of unleavened bread used in the Eucharist **3** : something (as a piece of candy) that resembles a wafer

¹waf·fle \'wä-fəl\ *n* : a soft but crisped cake of batter cooked in a special hinged metal ütensil (**waffle iron**)

²waffle *vb* **waf·fled; waf·fling** \-f(ə)liŋ\ : to speak or write in a vague or evasive manner

¹waft \'wäft, 'waft\ *vb* : to cause to move or go lightly by or as if by the impulse of wind or waves

²waft *n* **1** : a slight breeze : PUFF **2** : the act of waving

¹wag \'wag\ *vb* **wagged; wag·ging 1** : to sway or swing shortly from side to side or to-and-fro ⟨the dog *wagged* his tail⟩ **2** : to move in chatter or gossip ⟨scandal caused tongues to ∼⟩

²wag *n* : an act of wagging : a wagging movement

³wag *n* : WIT, JOKER

¹wage \'wāj\ *n* **1** : payment for labor or services usu. according to contract **2** *pl* : RECOMPENSE, REWARD

²wage *vb* **waged; wag·ing 1** : to engage in : CARRY ON ⟨∼ a war⟩ **2** : to be in process of being waged

¹wa·ger \'wā-jər\ *n* **1** : BET, STAKE **2** : something on which bets are laid : GAMBLE

²wager *vb* : BET — **wa·ger·er** *n*

wag·gery \'wa-gə-rē\ *n, pl* **-ger·ies 1** : mischievous merriment : PLEASANTRY **2** : JEST, TRICK

wag·gish \'wa-gish\ *adj* **1** : resembling or characteristic of a wag : MISCHIEVOUS **2** : SPORTIVE, HUMOROUS

wag·gle \'wa-gəl\ *vb* **wag·gled; wag-**

gling : to move backward and forward or from side to side : WAG — **waggle** n

wag·gon \\'wag-ən\\ *chiefly Brit var of* WAGON

wag·on \\'wa-gən\\ n **1** : a 4-wheeled vehicle; *esp* : one drawn by animals and used for freight or merchandise **2** : PADDY WAGON **3** : a child's 4-wheeled cart **4** : STATION WAGON

wag·on·er \\'wa-gə-nər\\ n : the driver of a wagon

wag·on·ette \\,wa-gə-'net\\ n : a light wagon with two facing seats along the sides behind a cross seat in front

wa·gon–lit \\vä-gōⁿ-'lē\\ n, pl **wagons–lits** *or* **wagon–lits** \\same or -'lēz\\ [F, fr. *wagon* railroad car + *lit* bed] : a railroad sleeping car

wagon train n : a column of wagons traveling overland

wag·tail \\'wag-,tāl\\ n : any of various slender-bodied mostly Old World birds with a long tail that jerks up and down

wa·hi·ne \\wä-'hē-nē, -,nä\\ n **1** : a Polynesian woman **2** : a female surfer

wa·hoo \\'wä-,hü\\ n, pl **wahoos** : a large vigorous food and sport fish related to the mackerel and found in warm seas

waif \\'wāf\\ n **1** : something found without an owner and esp. by chance **2** : a stray person or animal; *esp* : a homeless child

wail \\'wāl\\ vb **1** : LAMENT, WEEP **2** : to make a sound suggestive of a mournful cry **3** : COMPLAIN — **wail** n

wail·ful \\-fəl\\ adj : SORROWFUL, MOURNFUL ♦ *Synonyms* MELANCHOLY, DOLEFUL, LUGUBRIOUS, LAMENTABLE, PLAINTIVE, WOEFUL — **wail·ful·ly** adv

wain \\'wān\\ n : a usu. large heavy farm wagon

wain·scot \\'wān-skət, -,skōt, -,skät\\ n **1** : a usu. paneled wooden lining of an interior wall of a room **2** : the lower part of an interior wall when finished differently from the rest — **wainscot** vb

wain·scot·ing *or* **wain·scot·ting** \\-,skō-tiŋ, -,skä-, -sko-\\ n : material for a wainscot; *also* : WAINSCOT

waist \\'wāst\\ n **1** : the narrowed part of the body between the chest and hips **2** : a part resembling the human waist esp. in narrowness or central position ⟨the ∼ of a ship⟩ **3** : a garment or part of a garment (as a blouse or bodice) for the upper part of the body

waist·band \\-,band\\ n : a band (as on pants or a skirt) that fits around the waist

waist·coat \\'wes-kət, 'wāst-,kōt\\ n, *chiefly Brit* : VEST 1

waist·line \\'wāst-,līn\\ n **1** : a line around the waist at its narrowest part; *also* : the length of this **2** : the line at which the bodice and skirt of a dress meet

¹wait \\'wāt\\ vb **1** : to remain inactive in readiness or expectation : AWAIT ⟨∼ for orders⟩ **2** : to delay serving (a meal) **3** : to act as attendant or servant ⟨∼ on customers⟩ **4** : to attend as a waiter : SERVE ⟨∼ tables⟩ ⟨∼ at a banquet⟩ **5** : to be ready

²wait n **1** : a position of concealment usu.

with intent to attack or surprise ⟨lie in ∼⟩ **2** : an act or period of waiting

wait·er \\'wā-tər\\ n **1** : one that waits on another; *esp* : a person who waits tables **2** : TRAY

waiting game n : a strategy in which one or more participants withhold action in the hope of an opportunity for more effective action later

waiting room n : a room (as at a doctor's office) for the use of persons who are waiting

wait·per·son \\'wāt-,pər-sən\\ n : a waiter or waitress

wait·ress \\'wā-trəs\\ n : a woman who waits tables

waive \\'wāv\\ vb **waived**; **waiv·ing** [ME *weiven* to decline, reject, give up, fr. AF *waiver, gaiver*, fr. *waif* lost, stray] **1** : to give up claim to ⟨*waived* his right to a trial⟩ **2** : POSTPONE

waiv·er \\'wā-vər\\ n : the act of waiving right, claim, or privilege; *also* : a document containing a declaration of such an act

¹wake \\'wāk\\ vb **woke** \\'wōk\\ *also* **waked** \\'wākt\\; **wo·ken** \\'wō-kən\\ *also* **waked** *or* **woke**; **wak·ing** **1** : to be or remain awake; *esp* : to keep watch (as over a corpse) **2** : AWAKE, AWAKEN ⟨the baby *woke* up early⟩

²wake n **1** : the state of being awake **2** : a watch held over the body of a dead person prior to burial

³wake n : the track left by a ship in the water; *also* : a track left behind

wake·board \\'wāk-,bȯrd\\ n : a short board with foot bindings on which a rider is towed by a motorboat across its wake — **wake·board·er** n — **wake·board·ing** n

wake·ful \\'wāk-fəl\\ adj : not sleeping or able to sleep : SLEEPLESS, ALERT — **wake·ful·ness** n

wak·en \\'wā-kən\\ vb : WAKE

wake–rob·in \\'wāk-,rä-bən\\ n : TRILLIUM

wak·ing \\'wā-kiŋ\\ adj : passed in a conscious or alert state ⟨every ∼ hour⟩

wale \\'wāl\\ n : a ridge esp. on cloth; *also* : the texture esp. of a fabric

¹walk \\'wȯk\\ vb [partly fr. ME *walken*, fr. OE *wealcan* to roll, toss and partly fr. ME *walkien*, fr. OE *wealcian* to roll up, muffle up] **1** : to move or cause to move on foot usu. at a natural unhurried gait ⟨∼ to town⟩ ⟨∼ a horse⟩ **2** : to pass over, through, or along by walking ⟨∼ the streets⟩ **3** : to perform or accomplish by walking ⟨∼ guard⟩ **4** : to follow a course of action or way of life ⟨∼ humbly in the sight of God⟩ **5** : WALK OUT **6** : to receive a base on balls; *also* : to give a base on balls to — **walk·er** n

²walk n **1** : a going on foot ⟨go for a ∼⟩ **2** : a place, path, or course for walking **3** : distance to be walked ⟨a quarter-mile ∼ from here⟩ **4** : manner of living : CONDUCT, BEHAVIOR **5** : social or economic status ⟨various ∼s of life⟩ **6** : manner of walking : GAIT; *esp* : a slow 4-beat gait of a horse **7** : BASE ON BALLS

walk·a·way \'wȯ-kə-ˌwā\ *n* : an easily won contest

walk·ie–talk·ie \ˌwȯ-kē-ˈtȯ-kē\ *n* : a small portable radio transmitting and receiving set

¹**walk–in** \'wȯk-ˌin\ *adj* : large enough to be walked into ⟨a ~ refrigerator⟩

²**walk–in** *n* 1 : an easy election victory 2 : one that walks in

walking papers *n pl* : DISMISSAL, DISCHARGE

walking stick *n* 1 : a stick used in walking 2 : STICK INSECT; *esp* : one of the U.S. and Canada

walk–on \'wȯk-ˌȯn, -ˌän\ *n* : a small part in a dramatic production

walk·out \-ˌau̇t\ *n* 1 : a labor strike 2 : the action of leaving a meeting or organization as an expression of disapproval

walk out *vb* 1 : to leave suddenly often as an expression of disapproval 2 : to go on strike

walk·over \-ˌō-vər\ *n* : a one-sided contest : an easy victory

walk–up \'wȯk-ˌəp\ *n* : a building or apartment house without an elevator — **walk–up** *adj*

walk·way \-ˌwā\ *n* : a passage for walking

¹**wall** \'wȯl\ *n* [ME, fr. OE *weall*, fr. L *vallum* rampart, fr. *vallus* stake, palisade] 1 : a structure (as of stone or brick) intended for defense or security or for enclosing something 2 : one of the upright enclosing parts of a building or room 3 : the inside surface of a cavity or container ⟨the ~ of a boiler⟩ 4 : something like a wall in appearance, function, or effect ⟨a tariff ~⟩ — **walled** \'wȯld\ *adj*

²**wall** *vb* 1 : to provide, separate, or surround with or as if with a wall ⟨~ in a garden⟩ 2 : to close (an opening) with or as if with a wall ⟨~ up a door⟩

wal·la·by \'wä-lə-bē\ *n, pl* **wallabies** *also* **wallaby** : any of various small or medium-sized kangaroos

wall·board \'wȯl-ˌbȯrd\ *n* : a structural material (as of wood pulp or plaster) made in large sheets and used for sheathing interior walls and ceilings

wal·let \'wä-lət\ *n* 1 : a bag or sack for carrying things on a journey 2 : a pocketbook with compartments (as for personal papers and usu. unfolded money) : BILLFOLD

wall·eye \'wȯl-ˌī\ *n* 1 : an eye with a whitish iris or an opaque white cornea 2 : a large vigorous No. American food and sport fish related to the perches — **wall·eyed** \-ˌlīd\ *adj*

wall·flow·er \'wȯl-ˌflau̇(-ə)r\ *n* 1 : any of several Old World herbs related to the mustards; *esp* : one with showy fragrant flowers 2 : a person who usu. from shyness or unpopularity remains alone (as at a dance)

Wal·loon \wä-ˈlün\ *n* : a member of a people of southern and southeastern Belgium and adjacent parts of France — **Walloon** *adj*

¹**wal·lop** \'wä-ləp\ *vb* 1 : to beat soundly

: TROUNCE 2 : to hit hard : SOCK ♦ **Synonyms** BATTER, BEAT, LAMBASTE, POUND, PUMMEL, THRASH

²**wallop** *n* 1 : a powerful blow or impact 2 : the ability to hit hard 3 : emotional, sensory, or psychological force : IMPACT ⟨a story with a ~⟩

wal·lop·ing \'wä-lə-piŋ\ *adj* 1 : LARGE, WHOPPING 2 : exceptionally fine or impressive

¹**wal·low** \'wä-lō\ *vb* 1 : to roll oneself about sluggishly in or as if in deep mud ⟨hogs ~ing in the mire⟩ 2 : to indulge oneself excessively ⟨~ in luxury⟩ 3 : to become or remain helpless ⟨~ in ignorance⟩ ♦ **Synonyms** BASK, INDULGE, LUXURIATE, REVEL, WELTER

²**wallow** *n* : a muddy or dust-filled area where animals wallow

wall·pa·per \'wȯl-ˌpā-pər\ *n* : decorative paper for the walls of a room — **wallpaper** *vb*

wall–to–wall *adj* 1 : covering the entire floor ⟨wall-to-wall carpeting⟩ 2 : covering or filling one entire space or time ⟨crowds of wall-to-wall people⟩

wal·nut \'wȯl-(ˌ)nət\ *n* [ME *walnot*, fr. OE *wealhhnutu*, lit., foreign nut, fr. *Wealh* Welshman, foreigner + *hnutu* nut] 1 : a nut with a furrowed usu. rough shell and an adherent husk from any of a genus of trees related to the hickories; *esp* : the large edible nut of a Eurasian tree 2 : a tree that bears walnuts 3 : the usu. reddish to dark brown wood of a walnut used esp. in cabinetwork and veneers

wal·rus \'wȯl-rəs, 'wäl-\ *n, pl* **walrus** *or* **wal·rus·es** : a large mammal of arctic waters that is related to the seals and has long ivory tusks

¹**waltz** \'wȯlts\ *n* [G *Walzer*, fr. *walzen* to roll, dance] 1 : a gliding dance done to music having three beats to the measure 2 : music for or suitable for waltzing

²**waltz** *vb* 1 : to dance a waltz 2 : to move or advance easily, successfully, or conspicuously ⟨he ~ed off with the championship⟩ — **waltz·er** *n*

wam·ble \'wäm-bəl\ *vb* **wam·bled; wam·bling** : to progress unsteadily or with a lurching shambling gait

Wam·pa·no·ag \ˌwäm-pə-ˈnō-(ˌ)ag; ˌwȯm-\ *n, pl* **Wampanoag** *or* **Wampanoags** [Narragansett, lit., easterners] : a member of an American Indian people of parts of Rhode Island and Massachusetts

wam·pum \'wäm-pəm\ *n* [short for *wampumpeag*, fr. Massachuset (an Algonquian Indian language) *wampompeag*, fr. *wampan* white + *api* string + *-ag*, pl. suffix] 1 : beads made of shells strung in strands, belts, or sashes and used by No. American Indians as money and ornaments 2 *slang* : MONEY

wan \'wän\ *adj* **wan·ner; wan·nest** 1 : SICKLY, PALLID; *also* : FEEBLE 2 : DIM, FAINT 3 : LANGUID ⟨a ~ smile⟩ ♦ **Synonyms** ASHEN, BLANCHED, DOUGHY, LIVID, PALE, WAXEN — **wan·ly** *adv* — **wan·ness** *n*

wand \'wänd\ *n* 1 : a slender staff carried

in a procession **2** : the staff of a fairy, diviner, or magician

wan·der \'wän-dər\ vb **1** : to move about aimlessly or without a fixed course or goal : RAMBLE **2** : to go astray in conduct or thought; esp : to become delirious ✦ **Synonyms** GAD, GALLIVANT, MEANDER, RANGE, ROAM, ROVE — **wan·der·er** n

wandering Jew n : either of two trailing or creeping plants cultivated for their showy and often white-striped foliage

wan·der·lust \'wän-dər-ˌləst\ n : strong longing for or impulse toward wandering

¹wane \'wän\ vb **waned; wan·ing 1** : to grow gradually smaller or less ⟨the full moon ∼s to new⟩ ⟨his strength waned⟩ **2** : to lose power, prosperity, or influence **3** : to draw near an end ⟨summer is waning⟩ ✦ **Synonyms** ABATE, EBB, MODERATE, RELENT, SLACKEN, SUBSIDE

²wane n : a waning (as in size or power); also : a period in which something is waning

wan·gle \'waŋ-gəl\ vb **wan·gled; wan·gling 1** : to obtain by sly or devious means; also : to use trickery or questionable means to achieve an end **2** : MANIPULATE; also : FINAGLE

wan·na·be also **wan·na·bee** \'wä-nə-ˌbē\ n : a person who wants or aspires to be someone or something else or who tries to look or act like someone else

¹want \'wònt, 'wänt\ vb **1** : to fail to possess : LACK ⟨they ∼ the necessities of life⟩ **2** : to feel or suffer the need of **3** : NEED, REQUIRE ⟨the house ∼s painting⟩ **4** : to desire earnestly : WISH

²want n **1** : a lack of a required or usual amount : SHORTAGE **2** : dire need : DESTITUTION **3** : something wanted : DESIRE **4** : personal defect : FAULT

¹want·ing \'wòn-tiŋ, 'wän-\ adj **1** : not present or in evidence : ABSENT **2** : falling below standards or expectations **3** : lacking in ability or capacity : DEFICIENT ⟨∼ in common sense⟩

²wanting prep **1** : LESS, MINUS ⟨a month ∼ two days⟩ **2** : WITHOUT ⟨a book ∼ a cover⟩

¹wan·ton \'wòn-tᵊn, 'wän-\ adj [ME, undisciplined, fr. wan- deficient, wrong + towen, pp. of teen to draw, train, discipline] **1** : UNCHASTE, LEWD, LUSTFUL; also : SENSUAL **2** : having no regard for justice or for other persons' feelings, rights, or safety : MERCILESS, INHUMANE ⟨∼ cruelty⟩ **3** : having no just cause ⟨a ∼ attack⟩ — **wan·ton·ly** adv — **wan·ton·ness** n

²wanton n : a wanton individual; esp : a lewd or immoral person

³wanton vb **1** : to be wanton : act wantonly **2** : to pass or waste wantonly

wa·pi·ti \'wä-pə-tē\ n, pl **wapiti** or **wapitis** : ELK 2

¹war \'wòr\ n **1** : a state or period of usu. open and declared armed fighting between states or nations **2** : the art or science of warfare **3** : a state of hostility, conflict, or antagonism **4** : a struggle between opposing forces or for a particular

end ⟨∼ against disease⟩ — **war·less** \-ləs\ adj

²war vb **warred; war·ring** : to engage in warfare : be in conflict

³war abbr warrant

¹war·ble \'wòr-bəl\ n **1** : a melodious succession of low pleasing sounds **2** : a musical trill

²warble vb **war·bled; war·bling 1** : to sing or utter in a trilling manner or with variations **2** : to express by or as if by warbling

³warble n : a swelling under the skin esp. of the back of cattle, horses, and wild mammals caused by the maggot of a fly (**warble fly**); also : its maggot

war·bler \'wòr-blər\ n **1** : SONGSTER **2** : any of various small slender-billed chiefly Old World songbirds related to the thrushes and noted for their singing **3** : any of numerous small bright-colored insect-eating American birds with a usu. weak and unmusical song

war·bon·net \'wòr-ˌbä-nət\ n : a feathered American Indian ceremonial headdress

war crime n : a crime (as genocide) committed during or in connection with war

war cry n **1** : a cry used by fighters in war **2** : a slogan used esp. to rally people to a cause

¹ward \'wòrd\ n **1** : a guarding or being under guard or guardianship; esp : CUSTODY **2** : a body of guards **3** : a division of a prison **4** : a division in a hospital **5** : a division of a city for electoral or administrative purposes **6** : a person (as a child) under the protection of a guardian or a law court **7** : a person or body of persons under the protection or tutelage of a government **8** : a means of defense : PROTECTION

²ward vb : to turn aside : DEFLECT — usu. used with off ⟨∼ off a blow⟩

¹-ward also **-wards** adj suffix **1** : that moves, tends, faces, or is directed toward ⟨windward⟩ **2** : that occurs or is situated in the direction of ⟨seaward⟩

²-ward or **-wards** adv suffix **1** : in a (specified) direction ⟨upwards⟩ ⟨afterward⟩ **2** : toward a (specified) point, position, or area ⟨skyward⟩

war dance n : a dance performed (as by American Indians) before going to war or in celebration of victory

war·den \'wòr-dᵊn\ n **1** : GUARDIAN, KEEPER **2** : the governor of a town, district, or fortress **3** : an official charged with special supervisory or enforcement duties ⟨game ∼⟩ ⟨air raid ∼⟩ **4** : an official in charge of the operation of a prison **5** : one of two ranking lay officers of an Episcopal parish **6** : any of various British college officials

ward·er \'wòr-dər\ n : WATCHMAN, WARDEN

ward heel·er \-ˌhē-lər\ n : a local worker for a political boss

ward·robe \'wòr-ˌdrōb\ n [ME warderobe, fr. AF *warderobe, garderobe, fr. warder, garder to guard + robe robe] **1** : a room or closet where clothes are kept; also

: CLOTHESPRESS 2 : a collection of wearing apparel ⟨his summer ∼⟩

ward·room \-ˌdrüm, -ˌdrúm\ n : the dining area for officers aboard a warship

ward·ship \ˈwórd-ˌship\ n 1 : GUARDIANSHIP 2 : the state of being under care of a guardian

ware \ˈwer\ n 1 : manufactured articles or products of art or craft : GOODS ⟨glass*ware*⟩ 2 : an article of merchandise ⟨a peddler hawking his ∼s⟩ 3 : items (as dishes) of fired clay : POTTERY

ware·house \-ˌhaús\ n : a place for the storage of merchandise or commodities : STOREHOUSE — **warehouse** vb — **ware·house·man** \-mən\ n — **ware·hous·er** \-ˌhaú-zər, -sər\ n

ware·room \ˈwer-ˌrüm, -ˌrúm\ n : a room in which goods are exhibited for sale

war·fare \ˈwór-ˌfer\ n 1 : military operations between enemies : WAR; *also* : an activity undertaken by one country to weaken or destroy another ⟨economic ∼⟩ 2 : STRUGGLE, CONFLICT

war·fa·rin \ˈwór-fə-rən\ n : an anticoagulant compound used as a rodent poison and in medicine

war·head \ˈwór-ˌhed\ n : the section of a missile containing the charge

war·horse \-ˌhórs\ n 1 : a horse for use in war 2 : a veteran soldier or public person (as a politician) 3 : a musical composition that is often performed

war·like \-ˌlīk\ adj 1 : fond of war ⟨∼ peoples⟩ 2 : of, relating to, or useful in war : MILITARY, MARTIAL ⟨∼ supplies⟩ 3 : befitting or characteristic of war or of soldiers ⟨∼ attitudes⟩

war·lock \-ˌläk\ n [ME *warloghe*, fr. OE *wǣrloga* one that breaks faith, the Devil, fr. *wǣr* faith, troth + *-loga* (fr. *lēogan* to lie)] : SORCERER, WIZARD

war·lord \-ˌlórd\ n 1 : a high military leader 2 : a military commander exercising local civil power by force ⟨former Chinese ∼s⟩

¹**warm** \ˈwórm\ adj 1 : having or giving out heat to a moderate or adequate degree ⟨∼ milk⟩ ⟨a ∼ stove⟩ 2 : serving to retain heat ⟨∼ clothes⟩ 3 : feeling or inducing sensations of heat ⟨∼ from exercise⟩ ⟨a ∼ climb⟩ 4 : showing or marked by strong feeling : ARDENT ⟨∼ support⟩ 5 : marked by tense excitement or hot anger ⟨a ∼ campaign⟩ 6 : giving a pleasant impression of warmth, cheerfulness, or friendliness ⟨∼ colors⟩ ⟨a ∼ tone of voice⟩ 7 : marked by or tending toward injury, distress, or pain ⟨made things ∼ for the enemy⟩ 8 : newly made : FRESH ⟨a ∼ scent⟩ 9 : near to a goal ⟨getting ∼ in a search⟩ — **warm·ly** adv

²**warm** vb 1 : to make or become warm 2 : to give a feeling of warmth or vitality to 3 : to experience feelings of affection or pleasure ⟨she ∼ed to her guest⟩ 4 : to reheat for eating ⟨∼ed over the roast⟩ 5 : to make ready for operation or performance by preliminary exercise or operation ⟨∼ up the motor⟩ 6 : to become increasingly ardent, interested,

or competent ⟨the speaker ∼ed to his topic⟩ — **warm·er** n

warm–blood·ed \-ˈbləd-dəd\ adj : able to maintain a relatively high and constant body temperature relatively independent of that of the surroundings

warmed–over \ˈwórmd-ˈō-vər\ adj 1 : REHEATED ⟨∼ cabbage⟩ 2 : not fresh or new ⟨∼ ideas⟩

warm front n : an advancing edge of a warm air mass

warm·heart·ed \ˈwórm-ˈhär-təd\ adj : marked by warmth of feeling : CORDIAL — **warm·heart·ed·ness** n

warming pan n : a long-handled covered pan filled with live coals and formerly used to warm a bed

war·mon·ger \ˈwór-ˌmən-gər, -ˌmän-\ n : one who urges or attempts to stir up war — **war·mon·ger·ing** \-g(ə-)riŋ\ n

warmth \ˈwórmth\ n 1 : the quality or state of being warm 2 : ZEAL, ARDOR, FERVOR

warm up vb : to engage in exercise or practice esp. before entering a game or contest — **warm–up** \ˈwórm-ˌəp\ n

warn \ˈwórn\ vb 1 : to put on guard : CAUTION; *also* : ADMONISH, COUNSEL 2 : to notify esp. in advance : INFORM 3 : to order to go or keep away

¹**warn·ing** \ˈwór-niŋ\ n 1 : the act of warning : the state of being warned 2 : something that warns or serves to warn ⟨a tornado ∼⟩

²**warning** adj : serving as an alarm, signal, summons, or admonition ⟨a ∼ bell⟩ — **warn·ing·ly** adv

¹**warp** \ˈwórp\ n 1 : the lengthwise threads on a loom or in a woven fabric 2 : a twist out of a true plane or straight line ⟨a ∼ in a board⟩

²**warp** vb [ME, fr. OE *weorpan* to throw] 1 : to turn or twist out of shape; *also* : to become so twisted 2 : to lead astray : PERVERT; *also* : FALSIFY, DISTORT

war paint n : paint put on the face and body by American Indians as a sign of going to war

war·path \ˈwór-ˌpath, -ˌpäth\ n : the course taken by a party of American Indians going on a hostile expedition — **on the warpath** : ready to fight or argue

war·plane \-ˌplān\ n : a military airplane; *esp* : one armed for combat

warp speed n : the highest possible speed

¹**war·rant** \ˈwór-ənt, ˈwär-\ n 1 : AUTHORIZATION; *also* : JUSTIFICATION, GROUND 2 : evidence (as a document) of authorization; *esp* : a legal writ authorizing an officer to take action (as in making an arrest, seizure, or search) 3 : a certificate of appointment issued to an officer of lower rank than a commissioned officer

²**warrant** vb 1 : to guarantee security or immunity to : SECURE 2 : to declare or maintain positively ⟨I ∼ this is so⟩ 3 : to assure (a person) of the truth of what is said 4 : to guarantee to be as it appears or as it is represented ⟨∼ goods as of the first quality⟩ 5 : SANCTION, AUTHORIZE 6 : to give proof of : ATTEST; *also* : GUAR-

ANTEE 7 : JUSTIFY ⟨his need ∼s the expenditure⟩

warrant officer *n* 1 : an officer in the armed forces ranking next below a commissioned officer 2 : a commissioned officer ranking below an ensign in the navy or coast guard and below a second lieutenant in the marine corps

war·ran·ty \'wȯr-ən-tē, 'wär-\ *n, pl* **-ties** : an expressed or implied statement that some situation or thing is as it appears to be or is represented to be; *esp* : a usu. written guarantee of the integrity of a product and of the maker's responsibility for the repair or replacement of defective parts

war·ren \'wȯr-ən, 'wär-\ *n* 1 : an area where rabbits breed; *also* : a structure where rabbits are bred or kept 2 : a crowded tenement or district

war·rior \'wȯr-yər; 'wär-ē-ər, 'wär-\ *n* : a man engaged or experienced in warfare

war·ship \'wȯr-,ship\ *n* : a naval vessel

wart \'wȯrt\ *n* 1 : a small usu. horny projecting growth on the skin; *esp* : one caused by a virus 2 : a protuberance resembling a wart (as on a plant) — **warty** *adj*

wart·hog \'wȯrt-,hȯg, -,häg\ *n* : a wild African hog that has large tusks and in the male two pairs of rough warty protuberances below the eyes

war·time \'wȯr-,tīm\ *n* : a period during which a war is in progress

wary \'wer-ē\ *adj* **war·i·er; -est** : very cautious; *esp* : careful in guarding against danger or deception — **war·i·ly** \'wer-ə-lē\ *adv* — **war·i·ness** \'wer-ē-nəs\ *n*

was *past 1st & 3d sing of* BE

wa·sa·bi \'wä-sə-bē; wä-'sä-\ *n* [Jp] : a condiment prepared from the ground greenish root of an Asian herb and similar in flavor and use to horseradish; *also* : the herb or its root

¹**wash** \'wȯsh, 'wäsh\ *vb* 1 : to clean with water and usu. soap or detergent ⟨∼ clothes⟩ ⟨∼ your hands⟩ 2 : to wet thoroughly : DRENCH 3 : to flow along the border of ⟨waves ∼ the shore⟩ 4 : to pour or flow in a stream or current 5 : to move or remove by or as if by the action of water 6 : to cover or daub lightly with a liquid (as whitewash) 7 : to run water over (as gravel or ore) in order to separate valuable matter from refuse ⟨∼ sand for gold⟩ 8 : to undergo laundering ⟨a dress that doesn't ∼ well⟩ 9 : to stand a test ⟨that story will not ∼⟩ 10 : to be worn away by water

²**wash** *n,* 1 : the act or process or an instance of washing or being washed 2 : articles to be washed or being washed 3 : a thin coat of paint (as watercolor) 4 : the flow or action of a mass of water (as a wave) 5 : worthless esp. liquid waste : REFUSE, SWILL 6 : erosion by waves (as of the sea) 7 : a disturbance in a fluid (as water or the air) caused by the passage of a wing or propeller 8 *West* : the dry bed of a stream

³**wash** *adj* : WASHABLE

wash·able \'wȯ-shə-bəl, 'wä-\ *adj* : capable of being washed without damage — **wash·abil·i·ty** \,wȯ-shə-'bi-lə-tē, ,wä-\ *n*

wash–and–wear *adj* : of, relating to, or being a fabric or garment that needs little or no ironing after washing

wash·ba·sin \'wȯsh-,bā-sᵊn, 'wäsh-\ *n* : WASHBOWL

wash·board \-,bȯrd\ *n* : a grooved board to scrub clothes on

wash·bowl \-,bōl\ *n* : a large bowl for water for washing hands and face

wash·cloth \-,klȯth\ *n* : a cloth used for washing one's face and body

washed–out \'wȯsht-'aut, 'wäsht-\ *adj* 1 : faded in color 2 : EXHAUSTED ⟨felt ∼ after working all night⟩

washed–up \-'əp\ *adj* : no longer successful, popular, skillful, or needed

wash·er \'wȯ-shər, 'wä-\ *n* 1 : a ring or perforated plate used around a bolt or screw to ensure tightness or relieve friction 2 : one that washes; *esp* : a machine for washing

wash·er·wom·an \-,wu̇-mən\ *n* : a woman whose occupation is washing clothes

wash·ing \'wȯ-shiŋ, 'wä-\ *n* 1 : material obtained by washing 2 : articles washed or to be washed

washing soda *n* : SODIUM CARBONATE

Wash·ing·ton's Birthday \'wȯ-shiŋ-tənz-, 'wä-\ *n* : the 3d Monday in February observed as a legal holiday

wash·out \'wȯsh-,aut, 'wäsh-\ *n* 1 : the washing away of earth (as from a road); *also* : a place where earth is washed away 2 : a complete failure

wash·room \-,rüm, -,ru̇m\ *n* : BATHROOM

wash·stand \-,stand\ *n* 1 : a stand holding articles needed for washing face and hands 2 : LAVATORY 1

wash·tub \-,təb\ *n* : a tub for washing or soaking clothes

wash·wom·an \'wȯsh-,wu̇-mən, 'wäsh-\ *n* : WASHERWOMAN

washy \'wȯ-shē, 'wä-\ *adj* **wash·i·er; -est** 1 : WEAK, WATERY 2 : PALLID 3 : lacking in vigor, individuality, or definiteness

wasp \'wäsp, 'wȯsp\ *n* : any of numerous social or solitary winged insects related to the bees and ants with biting mouthparts and in females and workers an often formidable sting

WASP *or* **Wasp** *n* [*w*hite *A*nglo-*S*axon *P*rotestant] : an American of northern European and esp. British ancestry and of Protestant background

wasp·ish \'wäs-pish, 'wȯs-\ *adj* 1 : SNAPPISH, IRRITABLE 2 : resembling a wasp in form; *esp* : slightly built ♦ **Synonyms** FRACTIOUS, FRETFUL, HUFFY, PEEVISH, PETULANT, QUERULOUS

wasp waist *n* : a very slender waist

¹**was·sail** \'wä-səl, wä-'säl\ *n* [ME *wæs hæil, washayl,* fr. ON *ves heill* be well] 1 : an early English toast to someone's health 2 : a hot drink made with wine, beer, or cider, spices, sugar, and usu. baked apples and traditionally served at

Christmas **3** : riotous drinking : REVEL-RY

²**wassail** vb **1** : CAROUSE **2** : to drink to the health of — **was·sail·er** n

Was·ser·mann test \'wä-sər-mən-, 'vä-\ n : a blood test for the detection of syphilis

wast·age \'wā-stij\ n : WASTE 3

¹**waste** \'wāst\ n **1** : a sparsely settled or barren region : DESERT; *also* : uncultivated land **2** : the act or an instance of wasting : the state of being wasted **3** : gradual loss or decrease by use, wear, or decay **4** : material left over, rejected, or thrown away; *also* : an unwanted by-product of a manufacturing or chemical process **5** : refuse (as garbage) that accumulates about habitations **6** : material (as feces) produced but not used by a living organism — **waste·ful** \-fəl\ adj — **waste·ful·ly** adv — **waste·ful·ness** n

²**waste** vb **wast·ed; wast·ing 1** : DEVASTATE **2** : to wear away or diminish gradually : CONSUME **3** : to spend or use carelessly or uselessly : SQUANDER **4** : to lose or cause to lose weight, strength, or energy ⟨*wasting* away from fever⟩ **5** : to become diminished in bulk or substance : DWINDLE ✦ *Synonyms* DEPREDATE, DESOLATE, DESPOIL, RAVAGE, SPOIL, STRIP — **wast·er** n

³**waste** adj **1** : being wild and uninhabited : BARREN, DESOLATE; *also* : UNCULTIVATED **2** : being in a ruined condition **3** : discarded as worthless after being used ⟨∼ water⟩ **4** : excreted from or stored in inert form in a living organism as a byproduct of vital activity ⟨∼ matter from birds⟩

waste·bas·ket \'wāst-₁bas-kət\ n : a receptacle for refuse

waste·land \-₁land, -lənd\ n : land that is barren or unfit for cultivation

waste·pa·per \-'pā-pər\ n : paper thrown away as used, not needed, or not fit for use

wast·rel \'wā-strəl\ n : a person who wastes resources : SPENDTHRIFT

¹**watch** \'wäch, 'wöch\ vb **1** : to be or stay awake intentionally : keep vigil ⟨∼*ed* by the patient's bedside⟩ ⟨∼ and pray⟩ **2** : to be on the lookout for danger : be on one's guard **3** : to keep guard ⟨∼ outside the door⟩ **4** : OBSERVE ⟨∼ a game⟩ **5** : to keep in view so as to prevent harm or warn of danger ⟨∼ a brush fire carefully⟩ **6** : to keep oneself informed about ⟨∼ his progress⟩ **7** : to lie in wait for esp. so as to take advantage of ⟨∼*ed* her opportunity⟩ — **watch·er** n

²**watch** n **1** : the act of keeping awake to guard, protect, or attend; *also* : a state of alert and continuous attention **2** : a public weather alert ⟨a winter storm ∼⟩ **3** : close observation **4** : LOOKOUT, WATCHMAN, GUARD **5** : a period during which a part of a ship's crew is on duty; *also* : the part of a crew on duty during a watch **6** : a portable timepiece carried on the person

watch·band \'wäch-₁band, 'wöch-\ n : the bracelet or strap of a wristwatch

watch·dog \-₁dog\ n **1** : a dog kept to guard property **2** : one that guards or protects

watch·ful \-fəl\ adj : steadily attentive and alert esp. to danger : VIGILANT — **watch·ful·ly** adv — **watch·ful·ness** n

watch·mak·er \-₁mā-kər\ n : a person who makes or repairs watches — **watch·mak·ing** \-₁mā-kiŋ\ n

watch·man \-mən\ n : a person assigned to watch : GUARD

watch night n : a devotional service lasting until after midnight esp. on New Year's Eve

watch·tow·er \'wäch-₁taú(-ə)r, 'wöch-\ n : a tower for a lookout

watch·word \-₁wərd\ n **1** : a secret word used as a signal or sign of recognition **2** : a word or motto used as a slogan or rallying cry

¹**wa·ter** \'wö-tər, 'wä-\ n **1** : the liquid that descends as rain and forms rivers, lakes, and seas **2** : a natural mineral water — usu. used in pl. **3** pl : the water occupying or flowing in a particular bed; *also* : a band of seawater bordering on and under the control of a country **4** : any of various liquids containing or resembling water; *esp* : a watery fluid (as tears, urine, or sap) formed or circulating in a living organism **5** : a specified degree of thoroughness or completeness ⟨a scoundrel of the first ∼⟩

²**water** vb **1** : to supply with or get or take water ⟨∼ horses⟩ ⟨the ship ∼*ed* at each port⟩ **2** : to treat (as cloth) so as to give a lustrous appearance in wavy lines **3** : to dilute by or as if by adding water to **4** : to form or secrete water or watery matter ⟨her eyes ∼*ed*⟩ ⟨my mouth ∼*ed*⟩

water bed n : a bed whose mattress is a watertight bag filled with water

wa·ter·borne \-₁börn\ adj : supported, carried, or transmitted by water

water buffalo n : a common oxlike often domesticated Asian bovine

water chestnut n : a whitish crunchy vegetable used esp. in Chinese cooking that is the peeled tuber of a widely cultivated Asian plant; *also* : the tuber or the sedge itself

water closet n : a compartment or room with a toilet bowl : BATHROOM; *also* : a toilet bowl along with its accessories

wa·ter·col·or \'wö-tər-₁kə-lər, 'wä-\ n **1** : a paint whose liquid part is water **2** : the art of painting with watercolors **3** : a picture made with watercolors

wa·ter·course \-₁körs\ n : a stream of water; *also* : the bed of a stream

wa·ter·craft \-₁kraft\ n : a craft for water transport : SHIP, BOAT

wa·ter·cress \-₁kres\ n : an aquatic perennial Eurasian cress that is naturalized in the U.S. and has edible leaves used esp. in salads

wa·ter·fall \-₁föl\ n : a very steep descent of the water of a stream

wa·ter·fowl \'wö-tər-₁faú(-ə)l, 'wä-\ n, pl **-fowl** *also* **-fowls** : a bird that frequents water; *esp* : a swimming bird (as a duck) hunted as game

wa·ter·front \-ˌfrənt\ n : land or a section of a town fronting or abutting on a body of water

water gap n : a pass in a mountain ridge through which a stream runs

water glass n : a drinking glass

water hyacinth n : a showy floating aquatic plant of tropical America that often clogs waterways (as in the southern U.S.)

watering hole n : a place (as a bar) where people gather socially

watering place n : a resort that features mineral springs or bathing

water lily n : any of various aquatic plants with floating roundish leaves and showy, solitary flowers

wa·ter·line \ˈwȯ-tər-ˌlīn, ˈwä-\ n : a line that marks the level of the surface of water on something (as a ship or the shore)

wa·ter·logged \-ˌlȯgd, -ˌlägd\ adj : so filled or soaked with water as to be heavy or unmanageable ⟨a ∼ boat⟩

wa·ter·loo \ˌwȯ-tər-ˈlü, ˌwä-\ n, pl **-loos** [Waterloo, Belgium, scene of Napoleon's defeat in 1815] : a decisive or final defeat or setback

¹**wa·ter·mark** \ˈwȯ-tər-ˌmärk, ˈwä-\ n 1 : a mark indicating height to which water has risen 2 : a marking in paper visible when the paper is held up to the light

²**watermark** vb : to mark (paper) with a watermark

wa·ter·mel·on \-ˌme-lən\ n : a large roundish or oblong fruit with sweet juicy usu. red pulp; also : a widely grown African vine related to the squashes that produces watermelons

water moccasin n : a venomous pit viper chiefly of the southeastern U.S. that is related to the copperhead

water ou·zel \-ˈü-zəl\ n : DIPPER 1

water park n : an amusement park with a pool and wetted slides

water pill n : DIURETIC

water pipe n : a pipe for smoking that has a long flexible tube whereby the smoke is cooled by passing through water

water pistol n : a toy pistol for squirting a jet of liquid

water polo n : a team game played in a swimming pool with a ball resembling a soccer ball

wa·ter·pow·er \ˈwȯ-tər-ˌpau̇(-ə)r, ˈwä-\ n : the power of moving water used to run machinery

¹**wa·ter·proof** \ˈwȯ-tər-ˌprüf, ˈwä-\ adj : not letting water through; esp : covered or treated with a material to prevent permeation by water — **wa·ter·proof·ing** n

²**waterproof** n 1 : a waterproof fabric 2 chiefly Brit : RAINCOAT

³**waterproof** vb : to make waterproof

wa·ter–re·pel·lent \ˌwȯ-tər-ri-ˈpe-lənt, ˌwä-\ adj : treated with a finish that is resistant to water penetration

wa·ter–re·sis·tant \-ri-ˈzis-tənt\ adj : WATER-REPELLENT

wa·ter·shed \ˈwȯ-tər-ˌshed, ˈwä-\ n 1 : a dividing ridge between two drainage ar-

eas 2 : the region or area drained by a particular body of water

wa·ter·side \-ˌsīd\ n : the land bordering a body of water

water ski n : a ski used on water when the wearer is towed — **wa·ter–ski** vb — **wa·ter–ski·er** \-ˌskē-ər\ n

water snake n : any of various snakes found in or near freshwater and feeding largely on aquatic animals

wa·ter·spout \ˈwȯ-tər-ˌspau̇t, ˈwä-\ n 1 : a pipe for carrying water from a roof 2 : a funnel-shaped cloud extending from a cloud down to a spray torn up by whirling winds from an ocean or lake

water strider n : any of various long-legged bugs that move about swiftly on the surface of water

water table n : the upper limit of the portion of the ground wholly saturated with water

wa·ter·tight \ˌwȯ-tər-ˈtīt, ˌwä-\ adj 1 : constructed so as to keep water out 2 : allowing no possibility for doubt or uncertainty ⟨a ∼ case against the accused⟩

wa·ter·way \ˈwȯ-tər-ˌwā, ˈwä-\ n : a navigable body of water

wa·ter·wheel \-ˌhwēl, -ˌwēl\ n : a wheel made to turn by water flowing against it

water wings n pl : an air-filled device to give support to a person's body esp. when learning to swim

wa·ter·works \ˈwȯ-tər-ˌwərks, ˈwä-\ n pl : a system for supplying water (as to a city)

wa·tery \ˈwȯ-tə-rē, ˈwä-\ adj 1 : containing, full of, or giving out water ⟨∼ clouds⟩ 2 : being like water : THIN, WEAK ⟨∼ lemonade⟩; also : being soft and soggy ⟨∼ turnips⟩

WATS \ˈwäts\ abbr Wide-Area Telecommunications Service

watt \ˈwät\ n [James Watt †1819 Scottish engineer and inventor] : the metric unit of power equal to the work done at the rate of one joule per second or to the power produced by a current of one ampere across a potential difference of one volt

watt·age \ˈwä-tij\ n : amount of power expressed in watts

wat·tle \ˈwä-tᵊl\ n 1 : a framework of rods with flexible branches or reeds interlaced used esp. formerly in building; also : material for this framework 2 : a naked fleshy process hanging usu. from the head or neck (as of a bird) — **wat·tled** \-tᵊld\ adj

W Aust abbr Western Australia

¹**wave** \ˈwāv\ vb **waved**; **wav·ing** 1 : FLUTTER ⟨flags waving in the breeze⟩ 2 : to motion with the hands or with something held in them in signal or salute 3 : to become moved or brandished to-and-fro; also : BRANDISH, FLOURISH ⟨∼ a sword⟩ 4 : to move before the wind with a wavelike motion ⟨fields of waving grain⟩ 5 : to curve up and down like a wave : UNDULATE

wave n 1 : a moving ridge or swell on the surface of water 2 : a wavelike formation or shape ⟨a ∼ in the hair⟩ **3** : the action or process of making wavy or curly **4** : a waving motion; *esp* : a signal made by waving something **5** : FLOW, GUSH ⟨a ∼ of anger swept over her⟩ **6** : a peak of activity ⟨a ∼ of selling⟩ **7** : a disturbance that transfers energy progressively from point to point in a medium ⟨light travels in ∼s⟩ ⟨a sound ∼⟩ **8** : a period of hot or cold weather — **wave-like** *adj*

wave·length \'wāv-,leŋkth\ *n* **1** : the distance in the line of advance of a wave from any one point (as a crest) to the next corresponding point **2** : a line of thought that reveals a common understanding

wave·let \-lət\ *n* : a little wave : RIPPLE

wa·ver \'wā-vər\ *vb* **1** : to fluctuate in opinion, allegiance, or direction **2** : REEL, TOTTER; *also* : QUIVER, FLICKER ⟨∼ing flames⟩ **3** : FALTER **4** : to give an unsteady sound : QUAVER ♦ *Synonyms* FALTER, HESITATE, SHILLY-SHALLY, VACILLATE — **waver** *n* — **wa·ver·er** *n* — **wa·ver·ing·ly** *adv*

wavy \'wā-vē\ *adj* **wav·i·er; -est** : having waves : moving in waves

¹wax \'waks\ *n* **1** : a yellowish plastic substance secreted by bees for constructing the honeycomb **2** : any of various substances like beeswax

²wax *vb* : to treat or rub with wax — **wax·er** *n*

³wax *vb* **1** : to increase in size, numbers, strength, volume, or duration **2** : to increase in apparent size ⟨the moon ∼es toward the full⟩ **3** : to take on a quality or state : BECOME ⟨∼ed indignant⟩ ⟨the party ∼ed merry⟩

wax bean *n* : a kidney bean with pods that turn creamy yellow to bright yellow when mature enough to use as snap beans

wax·en \'wak-sən\ *adj* **1** : made of or covered with wax **2** : resembling wax (as in color or consistency)

wax museum *n* : a place where wax effigies are exhibited

wax myrtle *n* : any of a genus of shrubs or trees with aromatic leaves; *esp* : an evergreen shrub or small tree of the eastern U.S. that produces small hard berries with a thick coating of bluish-white wax used for candles

wax·wing \'waks-,wiŋ\ *n* : any of a genus of chiefly brown to gray singing birds with a showy crest and red waxy material on the tips of some wing feathers

wax·work \-,wərk\ *n* **1** : an effigy usu. of a person in wax **2** *pl* : an exhibition of wax figures

waxy \'wak-sē\ *adj* **wax·i·er; -est** **1** : made of or full of wax **2** : WAXEN 2

way \'wā\ *n* **1** : a thoroughfare for travel or passage : ROAD, PATH, STREET **2** : ROUTE ⟨knew the ∼ home⟩ **3** : a course of action ⟨chose the easy ∼⟩; *also* : opportunity, capability, or fact of doing as one pleases ⟨always had your own ∼⟩ **4** : a possible course : POSSIBILITY ⟨no two ∼s about it⟩ **5** : METHOD, MODE ⟨this ∼ of thinking⟩ ⟨a new ∼ of

painting⟩ **6** : FEATURE, RESPECT ⟨a good worker in many ∼s⟩ **7** : the usual or characteristic state of affairs ⟨as is the ∼ with old people⟩; *also* : individual characteristic or peculiarity ⟨used to her ∼s⟩ **8** : DISTANCE ⟨a short ∼ from here⟩ ⟨a long ∼ from success⟩ **9** : progress along a course ⟨working my ∼ through college⟩ **10** : something having direction : LOCALITY ⟨out our ∼⟩ **11** : STATE, CONDITION ⟨the ∼ things are⟩ **12** *pl* : an inclined structure upon which a ship is built or is supported in launching **13** : CATEGORY, KIND ⟨get what you need in the ∼ of supplies⟩ **14** : motion or speed of a boat through the water — **by the way** : by way of interjection or digression — **by way of 1** : for the purpose of ⟨*by way of* illustration⟩ **2** : by the route through : VIA — **out of the way 1** : WRONG, IMPROPER **2** : SECLUDED, REMOTE

way·bill \'wā-,bil\ *n* : a paper that accompanies a freight shipment and gives details of goods, route, and charges

way·far·er \'wā-,fer-ər\ *n* : a traveler esp. on foot — **way·far·ing** \-,fer-iŋ\ *adj*

way·lay \'wā-,lā\ *vb* **-laid** \-,lād\; **-lay·ing** : to lie in wait for or attack from ambush

way–out \'wā-'aút\ *adj* : FAR-OUT

-ways *adv suffix* : in (such) a way, course, direction, or manner ⟨side*ways*⟩

ways and means *n pl* : methods and resources esp. for raising revenues needed by a state; *also* : a legislative committee concerned with this function

way·side \'wā-,sīd\ *n* : the side of or land adjacent to a road or path

way station *n* : an intermediate station on a line of travel (as a railroad)

way·ward \'wā-wərd\ *adj* [ME, short for *awayward* turned away, fr. *away*, adv. + *-ward* directed toward] **1** : following one's own capricious or wanton inclinations ⟨∼ children⟩ **2** : UNPREDICTABLE, IRREGULAR ⟨a ∼ act⟩

WBC *abbr* white blood cells

WC *abbr* **1** water closet **2** without charge

WCTU *abbr* Women's Christian Temperance Union

we \'wē\ *pron* **1** — used of a group that includes the speaker or writer **2** — used for the singular *I* by a monarch, editor, or writer

weak \'wēk\ *adj* **1** : lacking strength or vigor : FEEBLE **2** : not able to sustain or resist much weight, pressure, or strain **3** : deficient in vigor of mind or character; *also* : resulting from or indicative of such deficiency ⟨a ∼ policy⟩ ⟨a ∼ will⟩ **4** : not supported by truth or logic ⟨a ∼ argument⟩ **5** : lacking skill or proficiency; *also* : indicative of a lack of skill or aptitude **6** : lacking vigor of expression or effect **7** : of less than usual strength ⟨∼ tea⟩ **8** : not having or exerting authority ⟨∼ government⟩; *also* : INEFFECTIVE, IMPOTENT ⟨∼ measures to control crime⟩ **9** : of, relating to, or constituting a verb or verb conjugation that forms the past tense and past participle by adding *-ed* or *-d* or *-t* — **weak·ly** *adv*

weak·en \'wē-kən\ *vb* : to make or become weak ✦ *Synonyms* ENFEEBLE, DEBILITATE, UNDERMINE, SAP, CRIPPLE, DISABLE

weak·fish \'wēk-ˌfish\ *n* [obs. D *weekvis*, fr. D *week* soft + *vis* fish] : a common marine fish of the Atlantic coast of the U.S. caught for food and sport; *also* : any of several related food fishes

weak force *n* : the physical force responsible for particle decay processes in radioactivity

weak–kneed \'wēk-'nēd\ *adj* : lacking willpower or resolution

weak·ling \'wē-kliŋ\ *n* : a person who is physically, mentally, or morally weak

weak·ly \'wē-klē\ *adj* : FEEBLE, WEAK

weak·ness \'wēk-nəs\ *n* **1** : the quality or state of being weak; *also* : an instance or period of being weak ⟨in a moment of ~ he agreed to go⟩ **2** : FAULT, DEFECT **3** : an object of special desire or fondness ⟨chocolate is her ~⟩

¹weal \'wēl\ *n* : WELL-BEING, PROSPERITY

²weal *n* : WELT

weald \'wēld\ *n* [The *Weald,* wooded district in England, fr. ME *Weeld,* fr. OE *weald* forest] **1** : FOREST **2** : WOLD

wealth \'welth\ *n* [ME *welthe* welfare, prosperity, fr. *wele* weal] **1** : abundance of possessions or resources : AFFLUENCE, RICHES **2** : abundant supply : PROFUSION ⟨a ~ of detail⟩ **3** : all property that has a money or an exchange value; *also* : all objects or resources that have economic value ✦ *Synonyms* FORTUNE, PROPERTY, SUBSTANCE, WORTH

wealthy \'wel-thē\ *adj* **wealth·i·er; -est** : having wealth : RICH

wean \'wēn\ *vb* **1** : to accustom (a young mammal) to take food by means other than nursing **2** : to free from a source of dependence; *also* : to free from a usu. unwholesome habit or interest

weap·on \'we-pən\ *n* **1** : something (as a gun, knife, or club) used to injure, defeat, or destroy **2** : a means of contending against another — **weap·on·less** \-ləs\ *adj*

weap·on·ry \-rē\ *n* : WEAPONS

¹wear \'wer\ *vb* **wore** \'wȯr\; **worn** \'wȯrn\; **wear·ing 1** : to use as an article of clothing or adornment ⟨~ a coat⟩ ⟨~s earrings⟩; *also* : to carry on the person ⟨~ a gun⟩ **2** : EXHIBIT, PRESENT ⟨~ a smile⟩ **3** : to impair, diminish, or decay by use or by scraping or rubbing ⟨clothes *worn* to shreds⟩; *also* : to produce gradually by friction, rubbing, or wasting away ⟨~ a hole in the rug⟩ **4** : to exhaust or lessen the strength of : WEARY, FATIGUE ⟨*worn* by care and toil⟩ **5** : to endure use : last under use or the passage of time ⟨this cloth ~s well⟩ **6** : to diminish or fail with the passage of time ⟨the day ~s on⟩ ⟨the effect of the drug *wore* off⟩ **7** : to grow or become by attrition, use, or age ⟨the coin was *worn*

thin⟩ — **wear·able** \'wer-ə-bəl\ *adj* — **wear·er** *n*

²wear *n* **1** : the act of wearing : the state of being worn ⟨clothes for everyday ~⟩ **2** : clothing usu. of a particular kind or for a special occasion or use ⟨children's ~⟩ **3** : wearing or lasting quality ⟨the coat still has lots of ~ in it⟩ **4** : the result of wearing or use : impairment due to use ⟨the suit shows ~⟩

wear and tear *n* : the loss, injury, or stress to which something is subjected in the course of use; *esp* : normal depreciation

wear down *vb* : to weary and overcome by persistent resistance or pressure

wea·ri·some \'wir-ē-səm\ *adj* : causing weariness : TIRESOME — **wea·ri·some·ly** *adv* — **wea·ri·some·ness** *n*

wear out *vb* **1** : TIRE **2** : to make or become useless by wear

¹wea·ry \'wir-ē\ *adj* **wea·ri·er; -est 1** : worn out in strength, energy, or freshness **2** : expressing or characteristic of weariness ⟨a ~ sigh⟩ **3** : having one's patience, tolerance, or pleasure exhausted ⟨~ of war⟩ — **wea·ri·ly** \'wir-ə-lē\ *adv* — **wea·ri·ness** \-ē-nəs\ *n*

²weary *vb* **wea·ried; wea·ry·ing** : to become or make weary : TIRE

¹wea·sel \'wē-zəl\ *n, pl* **weasels** : any of various small slender flesh-eating mammals related to the minks — **wea·sel·ly** *also* **wea·sely** \'wēz-lē, 'wē-zə-lē\ *adj*

²weasel *vb* **wea·seled; wea·sel·ing 1** : to use weasel words : EQUIVOCATE **2** : to escape from or evade a situation or obligation — often used with *out*

weasel word *n* [fr. the weasel's reputed habit of sucking the contents out of an egg while leaving the shell intact] : a word used to avoid a direct or forthright statement or position

¹weath·er \'we-thər\ *n* **1** : the state of the atmosphere with respect to heat or cold, wetness or dryness, calm or storm, clearness or cloudiness **2** : a particular and esp. a disagreeable atmospheric state : RAIN, STORM

²weather *vb* **1** : to expose to or endure the action of weather; *also* : to alter (as in color or texture) by such exposure **2** : to bear up against successfully ⟨~ a storm⟩ ⟨~ troubles⟩

³weather *adj* : WINDWARD

weath·er–beat·en \'we-thər-ˌbē-tən\ *adj* : worn or damaged by exposure to the weather; *also* : toughened or tanned by the weather ⟨~ face⟩

weath·er·cock \-ˌkäk\ *n* : a weather vane shaped like a rooster

weath·er·ing \'we-thə-riŋ\ *n* : the action of the weather in altering the color, texture, composition, or form of exposed objects; *also* : alteration thus effected

weath·er·ize \'we-thə-ˌrīz\ *vb* **-ized; -iz·ing** : to make (as a house) better protected against winter weather (as by adding insulation)

weath·er·man \-ˌman\ *n* : one who reports and forecasts the weather : METEOROLOGIST

weath·er·per·son \-ˌpər-sən\ n : a person who reports and forecasts the weather : METEOROLOGIST

weath·er·proof \ˈwe-thər-ˌprüf\ adj : able to withstand exposure to weather — **weatherproof** vb

weath·er·strip·ping \ˈwe-thər-ˌstri-piŋ\ n : material used to seal a door or window at the edges — **weath·er·strip** vb — **weather strip** n

weather vane n : VANE 1

weath·er·worn \ˈwe-thər-ˌwȯrn\ adj : worn by exposure to the weather

¹**weave** \ˈwēv\ vb wove \ˈwōv\ or weaved; wo·ven \ˈwō-vən\ or weaved; weav·ing 1 : to form by interlacing strands of material; esp : to make on a loom by interlacing warp and filling threads ⟨~ cloth⟩ 2 : to interlace (as threads) into a fabric and esp. cloth 3 : SPIN 2 4 : to make as if by weaving together parts 5 : to insert as a part : work in 6 : to move in a winding or zigzag course esp. to avoid obstacles ⟨we wove our way through the crowd⟩ — **weav·er** n

²**weave** n : something woven; also : a pattern or method of weaving ⟨a loose ~⟩

¹**web** \ˈweb\ n 1 : a fabric on a loom or coming from a loom 2 : COBWEB; also : SNARE, ENTANGLEMENT ⟨caught in a ~ of deceit⟩ 3 : an animal or plant membrane; esp : one uniting the toes (as in many birds) 4 : NETWORK ⟨a ~ of highways⟩ 5 : the series of barbs on each side of the shaft of a feather 6 : WORLD WIDE WEB — **webbed** \ˈwebd\ adj

²**web** vb webbed; web·bing 1 : to make a web 2 : to cover or provide with webs or a network 3 : ENTANGLE, ENSNARE

web·bing \ˈwe-biŋ\ n : a strong closely woven tape designed for bearing weight and used esp. for straps, harness, or upholstery

web·cam \ˈweb-ˌkam\ n : a camera used in transmitting live images over the World Wide Web

web·cast \ˈweb-ˌkast\ n : a transmission of sound and images via the World Wide Web — **webcast** vb

web·foot·ed \ˈweb-ˈfu̇-təd\ adj : having webbed feet

web·mas·ter \ˈweb-ˌmas-tər\ n, often cap : a person responsible for the creation or maintenance of a Web site

Web site n : a group of World Wide Web pages made available online (as by an individual or business)

wed \ˈwed\ vb wed·ded also wed; wed·ding 1 : to take, give, enter into, or join in marriage : MARRY 2 : to unite firmly

Wed abbr Wednesday

wed·ding \ˈwe-diŋ\ n 1 : a marriage ceremony usu. with accompanying festivities : NUPTIALS 2 : a joining in close association 3 : a wedding anniversary or its celebration

¹**wedge** \ˈwej\ n 1 : a piece of wood or metal that tapers to a thin edge and is used to split logs or rocks or to raise heavy weights 2 : something (as an action or policy) that serves to open up a way for a breach, change, or intrusion 3 : a wedge-shaped object or part ⟨a ~ of pie⟩

²**wedge** vb wedged; wedg·ing 1 : to hold firm by or as if by driving in a wedge 2 : to force (something) into a narrow space

wed·lock \ˈwed-ˌläk\ n [ME wedlok, fr. OE wedlāc marriage bond, fr. wedd pledge + -lāc, suffix denoting activity] : the state of being married : MARRIAGE, MATRIMONY

Wednes·day \ˈwenz-(ˌ)dā, -dē\ n [ME, fr. OE wōdnesdæg, lit., day of Woden (supreme god of the pagan Anglo-Saxons)] : the 4th day of the week

wee \ˈwē\ adj [ME (Sc) we, fr. we, n., little bit, fr. OE wǣge weight] 1 : very small : TINY 2 : very early ⟨~ hours of the morning⟩

¹**weed** \ˈwēd\ n 1 : a plant that tends to grow thickly where it is not wanted and to choke out more desirable plants 2 : MARIJUANA

²**weed** vb 1 : to clear of or remove weeds or something harmful, inferior, or superfluous ⟨~ a garden⟩ 2 : to get rid of ⟨~ out the troublemakers⟩ — **weed·er** n

³**weed** n : mourning clothes — usu. used in pl. ⟨widow's ~s⟩

weedy \ˈwē-dē\ adj 1 : full of weeds 2 : resembling a weed esp. in vigor of growth or spread 3 : noticeably lean and scrawny : LANKY

week \ˈwēk\ n 1 : seven successive days; esp : a calendar period of seven days beginning with Sunday and ending with Saturday 2 : the working or school days of the calendar week

week·day \ˈwēk-ˌdā\ n : a day of the week except Sunday or sometimes except Saturday and Sunday

¹**week·end** \-ˌend\ n : the period between the close of one working or business or school week and the beginning of the next

²**weekend** vb : to spend the weekend

¹**week·ly** \ˈwē-klē\ adj 1 : occurring, appearing, or done every week 2 : computed in terms of one week ⟨~ rental rates⟩ — **weekly** adv

²**weekly** n, pl weeklies : a weekly publication

ween \ˈwēn\ vb, archaic : SUPPOSE 3

wee·ny \ˈwē-nē\ also ween·sy \ˈwēn-sē\ adj : exceptionally small

weep \ˈwēp\ vb wept \ˈwept\; weep·ing 1 : to express emotion and esp. sorrow by shedding tears : BEWAIL, CRY 2 : to give off fluid slowly : OOZE — **weep·er** n

weeping adj 1 : TEARFUL ⟨~ gratitude⟩ 2 : having slender drooping branches

weeping willow n : a willow with slender drooping branches

weepy \ˈwē-pē\ adj : inclined to weep

wee·vil \ˈwē-vəl\ n : any of a large group of beetles having a long head usu. curved into a snout and including many whose larvae are destructive plant-feeding pests — **wee·vily** or **wee·vil·ly** \ˈwē-və-lē\ adj

weft \ˈweft\ n 1 : a filling thread or yarn

in weaving **2** : WEB, FABRIC; *also* : something woven

¹weigh \'wā\ *vb* [ME *weyen*, fr. OE *wegan* to move, carry, weigh] **1** : to find the heaviness of **2** : to have weight or a specified weight **3** : to consider carefully : PONDER **4** : to merit consideration as important : COUNT ⟨evidence ∼*ing* against him⟩ **5** : to raise before sailing ⟨∼ anchor⟩ **6** : to press down with or as if with a heavy weight

²weigh *n* [alter. of *way*] : WAY — used in the phrase *under weigh*

¹weight \'wāt\ *n* **1** : the amount that something weighs; *also* : the standard amount that something should weigh **2** : a quantity or object weighing a usu. specified amount **3** : a unit (as a pound or kilogram) of weight or mass; *also* : a system of such units **4** : a heavy object for holding or pressing something down; *also* : a heavy object for throwing or lifting in an athletic contest **5** : a mental or emotional burden **6** : IMPORTANCE; *also* : INFLUENCE ⟨threw his ∼ around⟩ **7** : overpowering force **8** : relative thickness (as of a textile) ⟨summer-*weight* clothes⟩ ♦ **Synonyms** SIGNIFICANCE, MOMENT, CONSEQUENCE, IMPORT, AUTHORITY, PRESTIGE, CREDIT

☞ the WEIGHTS table is on page 826

²weight *vb* **1** : to oppress with a burden ⟨∼*ed* down with cares⟩ **2** : to load with or as if with a weight

weight·less \'wāt-ləs\ *adj* : having little weight : lacking apparent gravitational pull — **weight·less·ly** *adv* — **weight·less·ness** *n*

weighty \'wā-tē\ *adj* **weight·i·er; -est** **1** : of much importance or consequence : MOMENTOUS, SERIOUS ⟨∼ problems⟩ **2** : SOLEMN ⟨a ∼ manner⟩ **3** : HEAVY **4** : POWERFUL, TELLING ⟨∼ arguments⟩

weiner *var of* WIENER

weir \'wer, 'wir\ *n* **1** : a fence set in a waterway for catching fish **2** : a dam in a stream to raise the water level or divert its flow

weird \'wird\ *adj* [ME *wird, werd* fate, destiny, fr. OE *wyrd*] **1** : MAGICAL **2** : ODD, UNUSUAL ♦ **Synonyms** EERIE, UNCANNY, SPOOKY — **weird·ly** *adv* — **weird·ness** *n*

weirdo \'wir-(₁)dō\ *n, pl* **weird·os** : a person who is extraordinarily strange or eccentric

Welch *var of* WELSH

¹wel·come \'wel-kəm\ *vb* **wel·comed; wel·com·ing** **1** : to greet cordially or courteously **2** : to accept, meet, or face with pleasure ⟨he ∼s criticism⟩

²welcome *adj* **1** : received gladly into one's presence ⟨a ∼ visitor⟩ **2** : giving pleasure : PLEASING ⟨∼ news⟩ **3** : willingly permitted or admitted ⟨all are ∼ to use the books⟩ **4** — used in the phrase "You're welcome" as a reply to an expression of thanks

³welcome *n* **1** : a cordial greeting or reception **2** : the state of being welcome ⟨overstayed their ∼⟩

¹weld \'weld\ *vb* **1** : to unite (metal or plastic parts) either by heating and allowing the parts to flow together or by hammering or pressing together **2** : to unite closely or intimately ⟨∼*ed* together in friendship⟩ — **weld·er** *n*

²weld *n* **1** : a welded joint **2** : union by welding

wel·fare \'wel-₁fer\ *n* **1** : the state of doing well esp. in respect to happiness, well-being, or prosperity **2** : aid in the form of money or necessities for those in need; *also* : the agency through which the aid is given

welfare state *n* : a nation or state that assumes primary responsibility for the individual and social welfare of its citizens

wel·kin \'wel-kən\ *n* : SKY; *also* : AIR

¹well \'wel\ *n* **1** : a spring with its pool : FOUNTAIN; *also* : a source of supply ⟨a ∼ of information⟩ **2** : a hole sunk in the earth to obtain a natural deposit (as of water, oil, or gas) **3** : an open space (as for a staircase) extending vertically through floors of a structure **4** : something suggesting a well

²well *vb* : to rise up and flow out

³well *adv* **bet·ter** \'be-tər\; **best** \'best\ **1** : in a good or proper manner : RIGHTLY; *also* : EXCELLENTLY, SKILLFULLY **2** : SATISFACTORILY, FORTUNATELY ⟨the party turned out ∼⟩ **3** : ABUNDANTLY ⟨eat ∼⟩ **4** : with reason or courtesy : PROPERLY ⟨I cannot ∼ refuse⟩ **5** : COMPLETELY, FULLY, QUITE ⟨∼ worth the price⟩ ⟨*well*-hidden⟩ **6** : INTIMATELY, CLOSELY ⟨I know him ∼⟩ **7** : CONSIDERABLY, FAR ⟨∼ over a million⟩ ⟨∼ ahead⟩ **8** : without trouble or difficulty ⟨we could ∼ have gone⟩ **9** : EXACTLY, DEFINITELY ⟨remember it ∼⟩

⁴well *adj* **1** : PROSPEROUS; *also* : being in satisfactory condition or circumstances **2** : SATISFACTORY, PLEASING ⟨all is ∼⟩ **3** : ADVISABLE, DESIRABLE ⟨it is not ∼ to anger him⟩ **4** : free or recovered from ill health : HEALTHY **5** : FORTUNATE ⟨it is ∼ that this has happened⟩

well–ad·just·ed \₁wel-ə-'jəs-təd\ *adj* : WELL-BALANCED 2

well–ad·vised \-əd-'vīzd\ *adj* **1** : PRUDENT ⟨∼ restraint⟩ **2** : resulting from, based on, or showing careful deliberation or wise counsel ⟨∼ plans⟩

well–ap·point·ed \-ə-'pȯin-təd\ *adj* : properly fitted out ⟨a ∼ house⟩

well–ba·lanced \'wel-'ba-lənst\ *adj* **1** : nicely or evenly balanced or arranged **2** : emotionally or psychologically untroubled

well–be·ing \-'bē-iŋ\ *n* : the state of being happy, healthy, or prosperous

well–born \-'bȯrn\ *adj* : born of noble or wealthy lineage

well–bred \-'bred\ *adj* : having or indicating good breeding : REFINED

well–de·fined \-di-'fīnd\ *adj* : having clearly distinguishable limits or boundaries

well–dis·posed \-di-'spōzd\ *adj* : disposed to be friendly, favorable, or sympathetic

well–done \'wel-'dən\ *adj* **1** : rightly or

U.S. WEIGHTS AND MEASURES

LENGTH

UNIT	SYMBOL	U.S. EQUIVALENT	METRIC EQUIVALENT
mile	mi	5280 feet, 1760 yards	1.609 kilometers
rod	rd	5.50 yards, 16.5 feet	5.029 meters
yard	yd	3 feet, 36 inches	0.9144 meter
foot	ft *or* '	12 inches, 0.333 yard	30.48 centimeters
inch	in *or* "	0.083 foot, 0.028 yard	2.54 centimeters

AREA

UNIT	SYMBOL	U.S. EQUIVALENT	METRIC EQUIVALENT
square mile	sq mi *or* mi^2	640 acres	2.590 square kilometers
acre	ac	4840 square yards, 43,560 square feet	4047 square meters
square rod	sq rd *or* rd^2	30.25 square yards	25.293 square meters
square yard	sq yd *or* yd^2	9 square feet	0.836 square meter
square foot	sq ft *or* ft^2	144 square inches	0.093 square meter
square inch	sq in *or* in^2	0.0069 square foot	6.452 square centimeter

VOLUME

UNIT	SYMBOL	U.S. EQUIVALENT	METRIC EQUIVALENT
cubic yard	cu yd *or* yd^3	27 cubic feet	0.765 cubic meter
cubic foot	cu ft *or* ft^3	1728 cubic inches	0.028 cubic meter
cubic inch	cu in *or* in^3	0.00058 cubic foot	16.387 cubic centimeter

WEIGHT—AVOIRDUPOIS

UNIT	SYMBOL	U.S. EQUIVALENT	METRIC EQUIVALENT
ton			
short ton		2000 pounds	0.907 metric ton
long ton		2240 pounds	1.016 metric tons
hundredweight	cwt		
short hundredweight		100 pounds	45.359 kilograms
long hundredweight		112 pounds	50.802 kilograms
pound	lb *also* #	16 ounces	0.454 kilogram
ounce	oz	16 drams, 437.5 grains	28.350 grams
dram	dr	27.344 grains	1.772 grams
grain	gr	0.037 dram	0.0648 gram

CAPACITY

UNIT	SYMBOL	U.S. EQUIVALENT	METRIC EQUIVALENT
		LIQUID MEASURE	
gallon	gal	4 quarts	3.785 liters
quart	qt	2 pints	0.946 liter
pint	pt	4 gills	473.176 milliliters
gill	gi	4 fluid ounces	118.294 milliliters
fluid ounce	fl oz *or* f℥	8 fluid drams	29.573 milliliters
fluid dram	fl dr *or* fℨ	60 minims	3.697 milliliters
minim	min *or* ♏	⅟₆₀ fluid dram	0.061610 milliliter
		DRY MEASURE	
bushel	bu	4 pecks	35.239 liters
peck	pk	8 quarts	8.810 liters
quart	qt	2 pints	1.101 liters
pint	pt	½ quart	0.551 liter

properly performed   **2** : cooked thoroughly

well-en·dowed \'wel-in-'daủd\ *adj*   **1** : having plenty of money or property   **2** : having large breasts

well-fa·vored \-'fā-vərd\ *adj* : GOOD-LOOKING, HANDSOME ⟨a ~ face⟩

well-fixed \-'fikst\ *adj* : WELL-HEELED

well-found·ed \-'faủn-dəd\ *adj* : based on good reasons

well-groomed \-'grümd, -'grủmd\ *adj* : neatly dressed or cared for

well-ground·ed \-'graủn-dəd\ *adj*   **1** : having a firm foundation   **2** : WELL-FOUNDED

well·head \-,hed\ *n*   **1** : the source of a spring or a stream   **2** : principal source   **3** : the top of or a structure built over a well

well-heeled \-'hēld\ *adj* : financially well-off

well-known \-'nōn\ *adj* : fully or widely known

well-mean·ing \-'mē-niŋ\ *adj* : having or based on good intentions

well·ness \-nəs\ *n* : good health esp. as an actively sought goal ⟨~ clinics⟩ ⟨lifestyles that promote ~⟩

well-nigh \-'nī\ *adv* : ALMOST, NEARLY ⟨~ impossible⟩

well-off \-'of\ *adj* : being in good condition or circumstances; *esp* : WELL-TO-DO

well-or·dered \-'or-dərd\ *adj* : having an orderly procedure or arrangement

well-placed \-'plāst\ *adj* : appropriately or advantageously directed or positioned

well-read \-'red\ *adj* : well informed through reading

well-round·ed \-'raủn-dəd\ *adj*   **1** : broadly trained, educated, and experienced   **2** : COMPREHENSIVE ⟨a ~ program of activities⟩

well-spo·ken \'wel-'spō-kən\ *adj*   **1** : speaking well and esp. courteously   **2** : spoken with propriety ⟨~ words⟩

well·spring \-,spriŋ\ *n* : a source of continuous supply

well-timed \-'tīmd\ *adj* : TIMELY ⟨a ~ announcement⟩

well-to-do \,wel-tə-'dü\ *adj* : having more than adequate financial resources : PROSPEROUS

well-turned \'wel-'tərnd\ *adj*   **1** : pleasingly shaped ⟨a ~ ankle⟩   **2** : pleasingly expressed ⟨a ~ phrase⟩

well-wish·er \'wel-,wi-shər\ *n* : an admiring supporter or fan — **well-wish·ing** *adj or n*

welsh \'welsh, 'welch\ *vb*   **1** : to avoid payment   **2** : to break one's word ⟨~ed on his promises⟩

Welsh \'welsh\ *also* **Welch** \'welch\ *n* [ME *walisch, welisch,* adj., Welsh, fr. OE *wælisc* foreign, British, Welsh, fr. *Wealh* foreigner, Briton, Welshman]   **1** Welsh *pl* : the people of Wales   **2** : the Celtic language of Wales — **Welsh** *adj* — **Welsh·man** \-mən\ *n*

Welsh cor·gi \-'kór-gē\ *n* [W *corgi,* fr. *cor* dwarf + *ci* dog] : a short-legged long-backed dog with foxy head of either of two breeds of Welsh origin

Welsh rabbit *n* : melted often seasoned cheese served over toast or crackers

Welsh rare·bit \-'rer-bət\ *n* : WELSH RABBIT

¹welt \'welt\ *n*   **1** : the narrow strip of leather between a shoe upper and sole to which other parts are stitched   **2** : a doubled edge, strip, insert, or seam for ornament or reinforcement   **3** : a ridge or lump raised on the skin usu. by a blow; *also* : a heavy blow

²welt *vb*   **1** : to furnish with a welt   **2** : to hit hard

¹wel·ter \'wel-tər\ *vb*   **1** : WRITHE, TOSS; *also* : WALLOW   **2** : to rise and fall or toss about in or with waves   **3** : to become deeply sunk, soaked, or involved   **4** : to be in turmoil

²welter *n*   **1** : TURMOIL   **2** : a chaotic mass or jumble

wel·ter·weight \'wel-tər-,wāt\ *n* : a boxer weighing more than 135 but not over 147 pounds

wen \'wen\ *n* : an abnormal growth or a cyst protruding from a surface esp. of the skin

wench \'wench\ *n* [ME *wenche,* short for *wenchel* child, fr. OE *wencel*]   **1** : a young woman   **2** : a female servant

wend \'wend\ *vb* : to direct one's course : proceed on (one's way)

went *past of* GO

wept *past and past part of* WEEP

were *past 2d sing, past pl, or past subjunctive of* BE

were·wolf \'wer-,wủlf, 'wir-, 'wər-\ *n, pl* **were·wolves** \-,wủlvz\ [ME, fr. OE *werwulf,* fr. *wer* man + *wulf* wolf] : a person transformed into a wolf or capable of assuming a wolf's form

wes·kit \'wes-kət\ *n* : VEST 1

¹west \'west\ *adv* : to or toward the west

²west *adj*   **1** : situated toward or at the west   **2** : coming from the west

³west *n*   **1** : the general direction of sunset   **2** : the compass point directly opposite to east   **3** *cap* : regions or countries west of a specified or implied point   **4** *cap* : Europe and the Americas — **wes·ter·ly** \'wes-tər-lē\ *adv or adj* — **westward** *adv or adj* — **west·wards** *adv*

¹west·ern \'wes-tərn\ *adj*   **1** : lying toward or coming from the west   **2** *cap* : of, relating to, or characteristic of a region conventionally designated West   **3** *cap* : of or relating to the Roman Catholic or Protestant segment of Christianity — **West·ern·er** *n*

²western *n, often cap* : a novel, story, film, or radio or television show about life in the western U.S. during the latter half of the 19th century

west·ern·ize \'wes-tər-,nīz\ *vb* **-ized; -iz·ing** : to give western characteristics to — **west·ern·i·za·tion** \,wes-tər-nə-'zā-shən\ *n*

West Nile virus \-'nī(-ə)l-\ *n* [*West Nile* province of Uganda] : a virus that is transmitted to humans by mosquitoes and causes an illness marked by fever, headache, muscle ache, and sometimes encephalitis or meningitis; *also* : this illness

¹**wet** \'wet\ *adj* **wet·ter; wet·test** **1** : consisting of or covered or soaked with liquid (as water) **2** : RAINY ⟨~ days⟩ **3** : not dry ⟨~ paint⟩ **4** : permitting or advocating the manufacture and sale of alcoholic beverages ⟨a ~ town⟩ ⟨a ~ candidate⟩
✦ *Synonyms* DAMP, DANK, MOIST, HUMID — **wet·ly** *adv* — **wet·ness** *n*

²**wet** *n* **1** : WATER; *also* : WETNESS, MOISTURE **2** : rainy weather : RAIN **3** : an advocate of a wet liquor policy

³**wet** *vb* **wet** *or* **wet·ted; wet·ting** : to make or become wet

wet blanket *n* : one that quenches or dampens enthusiasm or pleasure

weth·er \'we-thər\ *n* : a castrated male sheep or goat

wet·land \'wet-,land, -lənd\ *n* : land or areas (as swamps) containing much soil moisture — usu. used in pl.

wet nurse *n* : a woman who cares for and suckles children not her own

wet suit *n* : a rubber suit for swimmers that acts to retain body heat by keeping a layer of water against the body as insulation

wh *abbr* **1** which **2** white

¹**whack** \'hwak\ *vb* **1** : to strike with a smart or resounding blow **2** : to cut with or as if with a whack

²**whack** *n* **1** : a smart or resounding blow; *also* : the sound of such a blow **2** : PORTION, SHARE ⟨must each pay our ~⟩ **3** : CONDITION, STATE ⟨the machine is out of ~⟩ **4** : an opportunity or attempt to do something : CHANCE **5** : a single action or occasion ⟨made three pies at a ~⟩

¹**whale** \'hwāl\ *n, pl* **whales 1** *or pl* **whale** : CETACEAN; *esp* : one (as a sperm whale or killer whale) of large size **2** : a person or thing impressive in size or quality ⟨a ~ of a story⟩

²**whale** *vb* **whaled; whal·ing** : to fish or hunt for whales

³**whale** *vb* **whaled; whal·ing 1** : THRASH **2** : to strike or hit vigorously

whale·boat \-,bōt\ *n* : a long narrow rowboat originally used by whalers

whale·bone \-,bōn\ *n* : BALEEN

whal·er \'hwā-lər\ *n* **1** : a person or ship that hunts whales **2** : WHALEBOAT

whale shark *n* : a shark of warm waters that is the largest known fish

wham·my \'hwa-mē\ *n, pl* **wham·mies** : JINX, HEX

wharf \'hworf\ *n, pl* **wharves** \'hworvz\ *also* **wharfs** : a structure alongside which ships lie to load and unload

¹**what** \'hwät, 'hwət\ *pron* **1** — used to inquire about the identity or nature of a being, an object, or some matter or situation ⟨~ is he, a salesman⟩ ⟨~'s that⟩ ⟨~ happened⟩ **2** : that which ⟨I know ~ you want⟩ **3** : WHATEVER 1 ⟨take ~ you want⟩

²**what** *adv* **1** : in what respect : HOW ⟨~ does he care⟩ **2** — used with *with* to introduce a prepositional phrase that expresses cause ⟨kept busy ~ with school and work⟩

³**what** *adj* **1** — used to inquire about the identity or nature of a person, object, or matter ⟨~ books do you read⟩ **2** : how remarkable or surprising ⟨~ an idea⟩ **3** : WHATEVER

¹**what·ev·er** \hwät-'e-vər, hwət-\ *pron* **1** : anything or everything that ⟨does ~ he wants to⟩ **2** : no matter what ⟨~ you do, don't cheat⟩ **3** : WHAT 1 — used as an intensive ⟨~ do you mean⟩

²**whatever** *adj* : of any kind at all ⟨no food ~⟩

³**whatever** *adv* : in any case : whatever the case may be — often used to suggest the unimportance of an issue or choice ⟨see a movie, watch TV,—~⟩

¹**what·not** \'hwät-,nät, 'hwət-\ *pron* : any of various other things that might also be mentioned ⟨needles, pins, and ~⟩

²**whatnot** *n* : a light open set of shelves for small ornaments

what·so·ev·er \,hwät-sō-'e-vər, ,hwət-\ *pron or adj* : WHATEVER

wheal \'hwēl\ *n* : a rapidly formed flat slightly raised itching or burning patch on the skin; *also* : WELT

wheat \'hwēt\ *n* : a cereal grain that yields a fine white flour used chiefly in breads, baked goods, and pastas; *also* : any of several widely grown grasses yielding wheat — **wheat·en** *adj*

wheat germ *n* : the vitamin-rich wheat embryo separated in milling

whee·dle \'hwē-dᵊl\ *vb* **whee·dled; whee·dling 1** : to entice by flattery **2** : to gain or get by wheedling

¹**wheel** \'hwēl\ *n,* **1** : a disk or circular frame that turns on a central axis **2** : a device whose main part is a wheel **3** : something resembling a wheel in shape or motion **4** : a curving or circular movement **5** : machinery that imparts motion : moving power ⟨the ~s of government⟩ **6** : a person of importance **7** *pl, slang* : AUTOMOBILE — **wheeled** \'hwēld\ *adj* — **wheel·less** *adj*

²**wheel** *vb* **1** : ROTATE, REVOLVE **2** : to change direction as if turning on a pivot **3** : to convey or move on wheels or in a vehicle

wheel·bar·row \-,ber-ō\ *n* : a vehicle with handles and usu. one wheel for carrying small loads

wheel·base \-,bās\ *n* : the distance in inches between the front and rear axles of an automotive vehicle

wheel·chair \-,cher\ *n* : a chair mounted on wheels esp. for the use of disabled persons

wheel·er \'hwē-lər\ *n* **1** : one that wheels **2** : WHEELHORSE **3** : something that has wheels — used in combination ⟨a side-*wheeler*⟩

wheel·er–deal·er \,hwē-lər-'dē-lər\ *n* : a shrewd operator esp. in business or politics

wheel·horse \'hwēl-,hors\ *n* **1** : a horse in a position nearest the front wheels of a wagon **2** : a steady and effective worker esp. in a political body

wheel·house \-,haus\ *n* : PILOTHOUSE

wheel–thrown \'hwēl-ˌthrōn\ adj : made on a potter's wheel

wheel·wright \-ˌrīt\ n : a maker and repairer of wheels and wheeled vehicles

¹**wheeze** \'hwēz\ vb **wheezed; wheez·ing** : to breathe with difficulty usu. with a whistling sound

²**wheeze** n 1 : a sound of wheezing 2 : an often repeated and well-known joke 3 : a trite saying

wheezy \'hwē-zē\ adj **wheez·i·er; -est** 1 : inclined to wheeze 2 : having a wheezing sound — **wheez·i·ly** \-zə-lē\ adv — **wheez·i·ness** \-zē-nəs\ n

whelk \'hwelk\ n : a large sea snail; esp : one much used as food in Europe

whelm \'hwelm\ vb : to overcome or engulf completely : OVERWHELM

¹**whelp** \'hwelp\ n : any of the young of various carnivorous mammals (as a dog)

²**whelp** vb : to give birth to (whelps); also : bring forth young

¹**when** \'hwen\ adv 1 : at what time ⟨~ will you return⟩ 2 : at or during which time ⟨a time ~ things were better⟩

²**when** conj 1 : at or during the time that ⟨leave ~ I do⟩ 2 : every time that ⟨they all clapped ~ he sang⟩ 3 : in the event that : IF ⟨disqualified ~ you cheat⟩ 4 : ALTHOUGH ⟨quit politics ~ he might have had a great career in it⟩

³**when** pron : what or which time ⟨since ~ have you been the boss⟩

⁴**when** n : the time of a happening

whence \'hwens\ adv or conj : from what place, source, or cause

when·ev·er \hwe-'ne-vər, hwə-\ conj or adv : at whatever time

when·so·ev·er \ˌhwen-sō-ˌe-vər\ conj : at any or every time that

¹**where** \'hwer\ adv 1 : at, in, or to what place ⟨~ is it⟩ 2 : at, in, or to what situation, position, direction, circumstances, or respect ⟨~ does this road lead⟩

²**where** conj 1 : at, in, or to what place ⟨knows ~ the house is⟩ 2 : at, in, or to what situation, position, direction, circumstances, or respect ⟨shows ~ the road leads⟩ 3 : WHEREVER ⟨goes ~ she likes⟩ 4 : at, in, or to what place ⟨the town ~ we live⟩ 5 : at, in, or to the place at, in, or to which ⟨stay ~ you are⟩ 6 : in a case, situation, or respect in which ⟨outstanding ~ endurance is called for⟩

³**where** n : PLACE, LOCATION ⟨the ~ and how of the accident⟩

¹**where·abouts** \-ə-ˌbauts\ also **where·about** \-ˌbaut\ adv : about where : near what place ⟨~ does he live⟩

²**whereabouts** n sing or pl : the place where a person or thing is ⟨his present ~ are unknown⟩

where·as \hwer-'az\ conj 1 : while on the contrary; also : ALTHOUGH 2 : in view of the fact that : SINCE

where·at \-'at\ conj 1 : at or toward which 2 : in consequence of which : WHEREUPON

where·by \-'bī\ conj : by, through, or in accordance with which ⟨the means ~ we achieved our goals⟩

¹**where·fore** \'hwer-ˌfȯr\ adv 1 : for what reason or purpose : WHY 2 : THEREFORE

²**wherefore** n : an answer or statement giving an explanation : REASON

¹**where·in** \hwer-'in\ adv : in what : in what respect ⟨~ was I wrong⟩

²**wherein** conj 1 : in which : WHERE ⟨the city ~ we live⟩ 2 : during which 3 : in what way : HOW ⟨showed me ~ I was wrong⟩

where·of \-'əv, -'äv\ conj 1 : of what ⟨knows ~ he speaks⟩ 2 : of which or whom ⟨books ~ the best are lost⟩

where·on \-'ȯn, -'än\ conj : on which ⟨the base ~ it rests⟩

where·so·ev·er \'hwer-sō-ˌe-vər\ conj : WHEREVER

where·to \'hwer-ˌtü\ conj : to which

where·up·on \'hwer-ə-ˌpȯn, -ˌpän\ conj 1 : on which 2 : closely following and in consequence of which

¹**wher·ev·er** \hwer-'e-vər\ adv : where in the world ⟨~ did he get that tie⟩

²**wherever** conj 1 : at, in, or to whatever place ⟨thrives ~ he goes⟩ 2 : in any circumstance in which

where·with \'hwer-ˌwith, -ˌwith\ conj : with or by means of which ⟨lack the tools ~ to repair the damage⟩

where·with·al \'hwer-wi-ˌthȯl, -ˌthȯl\ n : MEANS, RESOURCES; esp : MONEY

wher·ry \'hwer-ē\ n, pl **wherries** : a long light rowboat sharp at both ends

whet \'hwet\ vb **whet·ted; whet·ting** 1 : to sharpen by rubbing on or with something abrasive (as a whetstone) 2 : to make keen : STIMULATE ⟨~ the appetite⟩

wheth·er \'hwe-thər\ conj 1 : if it is or was true that ⟨ask ~ he is going⟩ 2 : if it is or was better ⟨uncertain ~ to go or stay⟩ 3 : whichever is or was the case, namely that ⟨~ we succeed or fail, we must try⟩ 4 : EITHER ⟨turned out well ~ by accident or design⟩

whet·stone \'hwet-ˌstōn\ n : a stone for sharpening blades

whey \'hwā\ n : the watery part of milk that separates after the milk sours and thickens

¹**which** \'hwich\ adj 1 : being what one or ones out of a group ⟨~ shirt should I wear⟩ 2 : WHICHEVER

²**which** pron 1 : which one or ones ⟨~ is yours⟩ ⟨~ are his⟩ ⟨it's in May or June, I'm not sure ~⟩ 2 : WHICHEVER ⟨we have all kinds; take ~ you like⟩ 3 — used to introduce a relative clause and to serve as a substitute therein for the noun modified by the clause ⟨the money ~ is coming to me⟩

¹**which·ev·er** \hwich-'e-vər\ adj : no matter which ⟨~ way you go⟩

²**whichever** pron : whatever one or ones

which·so·ev·er \ˌhwich-sō-'e-vər\ pron or adj, archaic : WHICHEVER

whick·er \'hwi-kər\ vb : NEIGH, WHINNY — **whicker** n

¹**whiff** \'hwif\ n 1 : a quick puff or slight gust (as of air) 2 : an inhalation of odor,

gas, or smoke **3** : a slight trace ⟨a ∼ of scandal⟩ **4** : STRIKEOUT

²**whiff** vb **1** : to expel, puff out, or blow away in or as if in whiffs **2** : to inhale an odor **3** : STRIKE OUT 3

Whig \ˈhwig\ n [short for *Whiggamore*, member of a Scottish group that marched to Edinburgh in 1648 to oppose the court party] **1** : a member or supporter of a British political group of the late 17th through early 19th centuries seeking to limit royal authority and increase parliamentary power **2** : an American favoring independence from Great Britain during the American Revolution **3** : a member or supporter of an American political party formed about 1834 to oppose the Democrats

¹**while** \ˈhwī(-ə)l\ n **1** : a period of time ⟨stay a ∼⟩ **2** : the time and effort used : TROUBLE ⟨worth your ∼⟩

²**while** conj **1** : during the time that ⟨she called ∼ you were out⟩ **2** : AS LONG AS ⟨∼ there's life there's hope⟩ **3** : ALTHOUGH ⟨∼ he's respected, he's not liked⟩

³**while** vb whiled; whil·ing : to cause to pass esp. pleasantly ⟨∼ away an hour⟩

¹**whi·lom** \ˈhwī-ləm\ adv [ME, lit., at times, fr. OE *hwīlum*, dat. pl. of *hwīl* time, while] archaic : FORMERLY

²**whilom** adj : FORMER ⟨his ∼ friends⟩

whilst \ˈhwīlst\ conj, chiefly Brit : WHILE

whim \ˈhwim\ n : a sudden wish, desire, or change of mind

whim·per \ˈhwim-pər\ vb : to make a low whining plaintive or broken sound — **whimper** n

whim·si·cal \ˈhwim-zi-kəl\ adj **1** : full of whims : CAPRICIOUS **2** : resulting from or characterized by whim or caprice : ERRATIC — **whim·si·cal·i·ty** \ˌhwim-zə-ˈka-lə-tē\ n — **whim·si·cal·ly** \ˈhwim-zi-k(ə-)lē\ adv

whim·sy also **whim·sey** \ˈhwim-zē\ n, pl whimsies also whimseys **1** : WHIM, CAPRICE **2** : a fanciful or fantastic device, object, or creation esp. in writing or art

whine \ˈhwīn\ vb whined; whin·ing [ME, fr. OE *hwīnan* to whiz] **1** : to utter a usu. high-pitched plaintive or distressed cry; also : to make a sound similar to such a cry **2** : to complain with or as if with a whine — **whine** n — **whin·er** n — **whiny** also **whin·ey** \ˈhwī-nē\ adj

¹**whin·ny** \ˈhwi-nē\ vb whin·nied; whin·ny·ing : to neigh usu. in a low or gentle manner

²**whinny** n, pl whinnies : NEIGH

¹**whip** \ˈhwip\ vb whipped; whip·ping **1** : to move, snatch, or jerk quickly or forcefully ⟨∼ out a gun⟩ **2** : to strike with a slender lithe implement (as a lash) esp. as a punishment; also : SPANK **3** : to drive or urge on by or as if by using a whip **4** : to bind or wrap (as a rope or rod) with cord in order to protect and strengthen; also : to wind or wrap around something **5** : DEFEAT **6** : to stir up : INCITE ⟨∼ up enthusiasm⟩ **7** : to pro-

duce in a hurry ⟨∼ up a meal⟩ **8** : to beat (as eggs or cream) into a froth **9** : to proceed nimbly or briskly; also : to flap about forcefully ⟨flags *whipping* in the wind⟩ — **whip·per** n — **whip into shape** : to bring forcefully to a desired state or condition

²**whip** n **1** : a flexible instrument used for whipping **2** : a stroke or cut with or as if with a whip **3** : a dessert made by whipping a portion of the ingredients ⟨prune ∼⟩ **4** : a person who handles a whip **5** : a member of a legislative body appointed by a party to enforce party discipline **6** : a whipping or thrashing motion

whip·cord \-ˌkȯrd\ n **1** : a thin tough braided cord **2** : a strong cloth with fine diagonal cords or ribs

whip hand n : positive control : ADVANTAGE

whip·lash \ˈhwip-ˌlash\ n **1** : the lash of a whip **2** : injury resulting from a sudden sharp movement of the neck and head (as of a person in a vehicle that is struck from the rear)

whip·per·snap·per \ˈhwi-pər-ˌsna-pər\ n : a small, insignificant, or presumptuous person

whip·pet \ˈhwi-pət\ n : any of a breed of small swift slender dogs that are used for racing

whipping boy n : SCAPEGOAT

whip–poor–will \ˈhwi-pər-ˌwil\ n : an American insect-eating bird with dull variegated plumage whose call at nightfall and just before dawn is suggestive of its name

whip·saw \ˈhwip-ˌsȯ\ vb : to beset with two or more adverse conditions or situations at once

¹**whir** also **whirr** \ˈhwər\ vb whirred; whir·ring : to move, fly, or revolve with a whir

²**whir** also **whirr** n : a continuous fluttering or vibratory sound made by something in rapid motion

¹**whirl** \ˈhwərl\ vb **1** : to move or drive in a circle or curve esp. with force or speed **2** : to turn or cause to turn rapidly in circles **3** : to turn abruptly : WHEEL **4** : to move or go quickly **5** : to become dizzy or giddy : REEL

²**whirl** n **1** : a rapid rotating or circling movement; also : something whirling **2** : COMMOTION, BUSTLE ⟨the social ∼⟩ **3** : a state of mental confusion **4** : TRY ⟨gave it a ∼⟩

whirl·i·gig \ˈhwər-li-ˌgig\ n [ME *whirlegigg*, fr. *whirlen* to whirl + *gigg* top] **1** : a child's toy having a whirling motion **2** : something that continuously whirls or changes

whirl·pool \ˈhwərl-ˌpül\ n : water moving rapidly in a circle so as to produce a depression in the center into which floating objects may be drawn

whirl·wind \-ˌwind\ n **1** : a small whirling windstorm **2** : a confused rush **3** : a violent or destructive force

whirly·bird \ˈhwər-lē-ˌbərd\ n : HELICOPTER

¹**whish** \ˈhwish\ vb : to move with a whish or swishing sound

²**whish** n : a rushing sound : SWISH

¹**whisk** \'hwisk\ n **1** : a quick light sweeping or brushing motion **2** : a usu. wire kitchen implement for beating food by hand **3** : WHISK BROOM

²**whisk** vb **1** : to move nimbly and quickly **2** : to move or convey briskly ⟨~ed the children off to bed⟩ **3** : to beat or whip lightly ⟨~ eggs⟩ **4** : to brush or wipe off lightly ⟨~ a coat⟩

whisk broom n : a small broom with a short handle used esp. as a clothes brush

whis·ker \'hwis-kər\ n **1** : one hair of the beard **2** pl : the part of the beard that grows on the sides of the face or on the chin **3** : one of the long bristles or hairs growing near the mouth of an animal (as a cat or mouse) — **whis·kered** \-kərd\ adj

whis·key or **whis·ky** \'hwis-kē\ n, pl **whiskeys** or **whiskies** [Ir uisce beatha & ScGael uisge beatha, lit., water of life] : a liquor distilled from fermented wort (as that obtained from rye, corn, or barley mash)

¹**whis·per** \'hwis-pər\ vb **1** : to speak very low or under the breath; also : to tell or utter by whispering ⟨~ a secret⟩ **2** : to make a low rustling sound — **whis·per·er** \-pər-ər\ n

²**whisper** n **1** : something communicated by or as if by whispering : HINT, RUMOR **2** : an act or instance of whispering

whist \'hwist\ n : a card game played by four players in two partnerships with a deck of 52 cards

¹**whis·tle** \'hwi-səl\ n **1** : a device by which a shrill sound is produced ⟨steam ~⟩ ⟨tin ~⟩ **2** : a shrill clear sound made by forcing breath out or air in through the puckered lips **3** : the sound or signal produced by a whistle or as if by whistling **4** : the shrill clear note of an animal (as a bird)

²**whistle** vb **whis·tled**; **whis·tling 1** : to utter a shrill clear sound by blowing or drawing air through the puckered lips **2** : to utter a shrill note or call resembling a whistle **3** : to make a shrill clear sound esp. by rapid movements ⟨the wind whistled⟩ **4** : to blow or sound a whistle **5** : to signal or call by a whistle **6** : to produce, utter, or express by whistling ⟨~ a tune⟩ — **whis·tler** n

whis·tle–blow·er \'hwi-səl-ˌblō-ər\ n : IN-FORMER

whis·tle–stop \-ˌstäp\ n : a brief personal appearance by a political candidate orig. on the rear platform of a touring train

whit \'hwit\ n [prob. alter. of ME wiht, wight creature, thing, fr. OE wiht] : the smallest part or particle : BIT

¹**white** \'hwīt\ adj **whit·er**; **whit·est 1** : free from color **2** : of the color of new snow or milk; esp : of the color white **3** : light or pallid in color ⟨lips ~ with fear⟩ **4** : SILVERY; also : made of silver **5** : of, relating to, or being a member of a group or race characterized by light-colored skin **6** : free from spot or blemish : PURE, INNOCENT **7** : BLANK **2** ⟨~

space in printed matter⟩ **8** : not intended to cause harm ⟨a ~ lie⟩ **9** : wearing white ⟨~ friars⟩ **10** : marked by snow ⟨~ Christmas⟩ **11** : consisting of a wide range of frequencies ⟨~ light⟩ — **white·ness** \-nəs\ n — **whit·ish** \'hwī-tish\ adj

²**white** n **1** : the color of maximal lightness that characterizes objects which both reflect and transmit light : the opposite of black **2** : a white or light-colored part or thing ⟨the ~ of an egg⟩; also, pl : white garments **3** : the light-colored pieces in a 2-player board game; also : the person by whom these are played **4** : one that is or approaches the color white **5** : a person of a light-skinned race

white ant n : TERMITE

white blood cell n : any of the colorless blood cells (as lymphocytes) that do not contain hemoglobin but do have a nucleus

white–bread \'hwīt-'bred\ adj : being, typical of, or having qualities (as blandness) associated with the white middle class

white·cap \'hwīt-ˌkap\ n : a wave crest breaking into white foam

white chocolate n : a whitish confection chiefly of cocoa butter, milk, and sugar

white–col·lar \'hwīt-'kä-lər\ adj : of, relating to, or constituting the class of salaried workers whose duties do not require the wearing of work clothes or protective clothing

white dwarf n : a small very dense whitish star of low luminosity

white elephant n **1** : an Indian elephant of a pale color that is sometimes venerated in India, Sri Lanka, Thailand, and Myanmar **2** : something requiring much care and expense and giving little profit or enjoyment

white feather n [fr. the superstition that a white feather in the plumage of a gamecock is a mark of a poor fighter] : a mark or symbol of cowardice

white·fish \'hwīt-ˌfish\ n : any of various freshwater food fishes related to the salmons and trouts

white flag n : a flag of pure white used to signify truce or surrender

white gold n : a pale alloy of gold resembling platinum in appearance

white goods n pl : white fabrics or articles (as sheets or towels) typically made of cotton or linen

White·hall \'hwīt-ˌhȯl\ n : the British government

white hat n **1** : an admirable and honorable person **2** : a mark or symbol of goodness

white·head \-ˌhed\ n : a small whitish lump in the skin due to retention of secretion in an oil gland duct

white heat n : a temperature higher than red heat at which a body becomes brightly incandescent

white–hot adj **1** : being at or radiating white heat **2** : FERVID ⟨~ enthusiasm⟩

White House \-ˌhaus\ n **1** : a residence of the president of the U.S. **2** : the executive department of the U.S. government

white lead *n* : a heavy white poisonous carbonate of lead used esp. formerly as a pigment in exterior paints

white matter *n* : whitish nerve tissue esp. of the brain and spinal cord that consists largely of neuron processes enclosed in a fatty material and that typically lies under the cortical gray matter

whit·en \'hwī-t'n\ *vb* : to make or become white ♦ **Synonyms** BLANCH, BLEACH — **whit·en·er** *n*

white oak *n* : any of various oaks with acorns that take one year to mature; *also* : its hard durable wood

white pepper *n* : a spice that consists of the berry of a pepper plant ground after removal of its black husk

white pine *n* : a tall-growing pine of eastern No. America with needles in clusters of five; *also* : its wood

white sale *n* : a sale on white goods

white shark *n* : GREAT WHITE SHARK

white slave *n* : a woman or girl held unwillingly for purposes of prostitution — **white slavery** *n*

white·tail \'hwīt-,tāl\ *n* : WHITE-TAILED DEER

white–tailed deer *n* : a No. American deer with a rather long tail white on the underside and the males of which have forward-arching antlers

white–tie \-'tī\ *adj* : characterized by or requiring formal evening clothes consisting of usu. white tie and tailcoat for men and a formal gown for women

white·wall \'hwit-,wȯl\ *n* : an automobile tire having a white band on the sidewall

¹**white·wash** \-,wȯsh, -,wäsh\ *vb* 1 : to whiten with whitewash 2 : to clear of a charge of wrongdoing by offering excuses, hiding facts, or conducting a perfunctory investigation 3 : SHUT OUT 2

²**whitewash** *n* 1 : a liquid mixture (as of lime and water) for whitening a surface 2 : a clearing of wrongdoing by whitewashing

white water *n* : frothy water (as in breakers, rapids, or falls)

white·wood \-,wu̇d\ *n* : any of various trees and esp. a tulip tree having light-colored wood; *also* : such wood

¹**whith·er** \'hwi-thər\ *adv* 1 : to what place 2 : to what situation, position, degree, or end ⟨~ will this drive him⟩

²**whither** *conj* 1 : to the place at, in, or to which; *also* : to which place 2 : to whatever place

whith·er·so·ev·er \,hwi-thər-sō-'e-vər\ *conj* : to whatever place

¹**whit·ing** \'hwi-tiŋ\ *n, pl* **whiting** *also* **whit·ings** : any of several usu. light or silvery food fishes (as a hake) found mostly near seacoasts

²**whiting** *n* : calcium carbonate in powdered form used esp. as a pigment and in putty

whit·low \'hwit-,lō\ *n* : a deep inflammation of a finger or toe with pus formation

Whit·sun·day \'hwit-'sən-dē, -sən-,dā\ *n* [ME *Whitsonday*, fr. OE *hwīta sunnandæg*, lit., white Sunday; prob. fr. the custom of wearing white robes by those

newly baptized at this season] : PENTECOST

whit·tle \'hwi-t'l\ *vb* **whit·tled**; **whit·tling** 1 : to pare or cut off chips from the surface of (wood) with a knife; *also* : to cut or shape by such paring 2 : to reduce as if by paring down ⟨~ down expenses⟩

¹**whiz** *or* **whizz** \'hwiz\ *vb* **whizzed**; **whiz·zing** : to hum, whir, or hiss like a speeding object (as an arrow or ball) passing through air

²**whiz** *or* **whizz** *n, pl* **whiz·zes** : a hissing, buzzing, or whizzing sound

³**whiz** *n, pl* **whiz·zes** : WIZARD 2

who \'hü\ *pron* 1 : what or which person or persons ⟨~ did it⟩ ⟨~ is he⟩ ⟨~ are they⟩ 2 : the person or persons that ⟨knows ~ did it⟩ 3 — used to introduce a relative clause and to serve as a substitute therein for the substantive modified by the clause ⟨the person ~ lives there is rich⟩

WHO *abbr* World Health Organization

whoa \'wō, 'hwō, 'hō\ *vb imper* 1 — a command to an animal to stand still 2 : cease or slow a course of action or a line of thought

who·dun·it *also* **who·dun·nit** \hü-'də-nət\ *n* : a detective or mystery story

who·ev·er \hü-'e-vər\ *pron* : whatever person : no matter who

¹**whole** \'hōl\ *adj* [ME *hool* healthy, unhurt, entire, fr. OE *hāl*] 1 : being in healthy or sound condition : free from defect or damage 2 : having all its proper parts or elements ⟨~ milk⟩ 3 : constituting the total sum of : ENTIRE ⟨owns the ~ island⟩ 4 : each or all of the ⟨the ~ family⟩ 5 : not scattered or divided : CONCENTRATED ⟨gave me his ~ attention⟩ 6 : seemingly complete or total ⟨the ~ idea is to help, not hinder⟩ ♦ **Synonyms** PERFECT, INTACT, SOUND — **whole·ness** *n*

²**whole** *n* 1 : a complete amount or sum 2 : something whole or entire — **on the whole** 1 : in view of all the circumstances or conditions 2 : in general

³**whole** *adv* : COMPLETELY, WHOLLY, ENTIRELY ⟨a ~ new term⟩

whole food *n* : a food eaten in its natural state with little or no artificial additives

whole·heart·ed \'hōl-'här-təd\ *adj* : undivided in purpose, enthusiasm, will, or commitment

whole hog *adv* : to the fullest extent : COMPLETELY ⟨accepted the proposals whole hog⟩

whole note *n* : a musical note equal to one measure of four beats

whole number *n* : any of the set of nonnegative integers; *also* : INTEGER

¹**whole·sale** \'hōl-,sāl\ *n* : the sale of goods in quantity usu. for resale by a retail merchant

²**wholesale** *adj* 1 : performed on a large scale without discrimination ⟨~ slaughter⟩ 2 : of, relating to, or engaged in wholesaling — **wholesale** *adv*

³**wholesale** *vb* **whole·saled**; **whole·sal-**

ing : to sell at wholesale — **whole·sal·er** n

whole·some \'hōl-səm\ adj **1** : promoting mental, spiritual, or bodily health or well-being ⟨a ~ environment⟩ **2** : sound in body, mind, or morals : HEALTHY **3** : PRUDENT ⟨~ respect for the law⟩ — **whole·some·ness** n

whole wheat adj : made of ground entire wheat kernels

whol·ly \'hōl-lē\ adv **1** : COMPLETELY, TOTALLY **2** : SOLELY, EXCLUSIVELY

whom \'hüm\ pron, objective case of WHO

whom·ev·er \hü-'me-vər\ pron, objective case of WHOEVER

whom·so·ev·er \hüm-sō-'e-vər\ pron, objective case of WHOSOEVER

¹whoop \'hwüp, 'hwup, 'hüp, 'hup\ vb **1** : to shout or call loudly and vigorously **2** : to make the characteristic whoop of whooping cough **3** : to go or pass with a loud noise **4** : to utter or express with a whoop; also : to urge, drive, or cheer with a whoop

²whoop n **1** : a whooping sound or utterance : SHOUT, HOOT **2** : a crowing intake of breath after a fit of coughing in whooping cough

¹whoop·ee \'hwü-(ˌ)pē, 'hwü-\ interj — used to express exuberance

²whoopee n **1** : boisterous fun **2** : sexual play — usu. used with make

whooping cough n : an infectious bacterial disease esp. of children marked by convulsive coughing fits often followed by a shrill gasping intake of breath

whooping crane n : a large white nearly extinct No. American crane noted for its loud whooping call

whoop·la \'hwüp-ˌlä, 'hwup-\ n **1** : HOOPLA **2** : boisterous merrymaking

whop·per \'hwä-pər\ n : something unusually large or extreme of its kind; esp : a monstrous lie

whop·ping \'hwä-piŋ\ adj : extremely large ⟨a ~ increase⟩

whore \'hȯr\ n : PROSTITUTE

whorl \'hwȯrl, 'hwərl\ n **1** : a group of parts (as leaves or petals) encircling an axis and esp. a plant stem **2** : something that whirls or coils around a center : COIL, SPIRAL **3** : one of the turns of a snail shell

whorled \'hwȯrld, 'hwərld\ adj : having or arranged in whorls

¹whose \'hüz\ adj : of or relating to whom or which esp. as possessor or possessors, agent or agents, or object or objects of an action ⟨asked ~ bag it was⟩

²whose pron : whose one or ones ⟨~ is this car⟩ ⟨~ are those books⟩

who·so \'hü-ˌsō\ pron : WHOEVER

who·so·ev·er \hü-sō-'e-vər\ pron : WHOEVER

whs or **whse** abbr warehouse

whsle abbr wholesale

¹why \'hwī\ adv : for what reason, cause, or purpose ⟨~ did you do it⟩

²why conj **1** : the cause, reason, or purpose for which ⟨that is ~ you did it⟩ **2** : for which : on account of which ⟨knows the reason ~ you did it⟩

³why n, pl **whys** : REASON, CAUSE ⟨the ~s of racial prejudice⟩

⁴why \'wī, 'hwī\ interj — used to express surprise, hesitation, approval, disapproval, or impatience ⟨~, here's what I was looking for⟩

WI abbr **1** West Indies **2** Wisconsin

WIA abbr wounded in action

Wic·ca \'wi-kə\ n [prob. fr. OE wicca wizard] : a religion that affirms the existence of supernatural power (as magic) and of deities who inhere in nature and that ritually observes seasonal and life cycles

wick \'wik\ n : a loosely bound bundle of soft fibers that draws up oil, tallow, or wax to be burned in a candle, oil lamp, or stove

wick·ed \'wi-kəd\ adj **1** : morally bad : EVIL, SINFUL **2** : FIERCE, VICIOUS **3** : ROGUISH ⟨a ~ glance⟩ **4** : REPUGNANT, VILE ⟨a ~ odor⟩ **5** : HARMFUL, DANGEROUS ⟨a ~ attack⟩ **6** : impressively excellent ⟨throws a ~ fastball⟩ — **wick·ed·ly** adv — **wick·ed·ness** n

wick·er \'wi-kər\ n **1** : a small pliant branch (as an osier or a withe) **2** : WICKERWORK — **wicker** adj

wick·er·work \-ˌwərk\ n : work made of osiers, twigs, or rods : BASKETRY

wick·et \'wi-kət\ n **1** : a small gate or door; esp : one forming a part of or placed near a larger one **2** : a windowlike opening usu. with a grille or grate (as at a ticket office) **3** : a set of three upright rods topped by two crosspieces bowled at in cricket **4** : an arch or hoop in croquet

wick·i·up \'wi-kē-ˌəp\ n : a hut used by nomadic Indians of the western and southwestern U.S. with a usu. oval base and a rough frame covered with reed mats, grass, or brushwood

wid abbr widow, widower

¹wide \'wīd\ adj **wid·er; wid·est** **1** : covering a vast area **2** : measured across or at right angles to the length **3** : not narrow : BROAD; also : ROOMY **4** : opened to full width ⟨eyes ~ with wonder⟩ **5** : not limited : EXTENSIVE ⟨~ experience⟩ **6** : far from the goal, mark, or truth ⟨was ~ of the truth⟩ — **wide·ly** adv

²wide adv **wid·er; wid·est** **1** : over a great distance or extent : WIDELY ⟨searched far and ~⟩ **2** : over a specified distance, area, or extent **3** : so as to leave a wide space between ⟨~ apart⟩ **4** : so as to clear by a considerable distance ⟨ran ~ around left end⟩ **5** : COMPLETELY, FULLY ⟨opened her eyes ~⟩

wide area network n : a computer network (as the Internet) over a large area (as a country or the globe) for sharing resources or exchanging data

wide–awake \ˌwīd-ə-'wāk\ adj : fully awake; also : KNOWING, ALERT

wide–body \'wīd-ˌbä-dē\ n : a large jet aircraft having a wide cabin

wide–eyed \'wīd-'īd\ adj **1** : having the

eyes wide open esp. with wonder or astonishment 2 : NAIVE

wide·mouthed \-'maůthd, -'maůtht\ *adj* 1 : having one's mouth opened wide (as in awe) 2 : having a wide mouth ⟨~ jars⟩

wid·en \'wī-dᵊn\ *vb* : to increase in width, scope, or extent

wide·spread \'wīd-'spred\ *adj* 1 : widely scattered or prevalent 2 : widely extended or spread out ⟨~ wings⟩

widgeon *var of* WIGEON

¹**wid·ow** \'wi-dō\ *n* : a woman who has lost her husband by death and has not married again — **wid·ow·hood** *n*

²**widow** *vb* : to cause to become a widow or widower

wid·ow·er \'wi-də-wər\ *n* : a man who has lost his wife by death and has not married again

width \'width\ *n* 1 : a distance from side to side : the measurement taken at right angles to the length : BREADTH 2 : largeness of extent or scope; *also* : FULLNESS 3 : a measured and cut piece of material ⟨a ~ of calico⟩

wield \'wēld\ *vb* 1 : to use or handle esp. effectively ⟨~ a broom⟩ 2 : to exert authority by means of : EMPLOY ⟨~ influence⟩ — **wield·er** *n*

wie·ner *also* **wei·ner** \'wē-nər\ *n* [short for *wienerwurst*, fr. G., lit., Vienna sausage] : FRANKFURTER

wife \'wīf\ *n, pl* **wives** \'wīvz\ 1 *dial* : WOMAN 2 : a woman acting in a specified capacity — used in combination ⟨fish*wife*⟩ 3 : a female partner in a marriage — **wife·hood** *n* — **wife·less** *adj* — **wife·ly** *adj*

wig \'wig\ *n* [short for *periwig*, modif. of MF *perruque*, fr. It *parrucca, perrucca* hair, wig] : a manufactured covering of natural or synthetic hair for the head; *also* : TOUPEE

wi·geon *or* **wid·geon** \'wi-jən\ *n, pl* **wigeon** *or* **wigeons** *or* **widgeon** *or* **widgeons** : any of several medium-sized freshwater ducks

wig·gle \'wi-gəl\ *vb* **wig·gled; wig·gling** 1 : to move to and fro with quick jerky or shaking movements : JIGGLE 2 : WRIGGLE — **wiggle** *n*

wig·gler \'wi-glər, -gə-lər\ *n* 1 : a larva or pupa of a mosquito 2 : one that wiggles

wig·gly \'wi-glē, -gə-lē\ *adj* 1 : tending to wiggle ⟨a ~ worm⟩ 2 : WAVY ⟨~ lines⟩

wight \'wīt\ *n* : a living being : CREATURE

wig·let \'wi-glət\ *n* : a small wig used esp. to enhance a hairstyle

¹**wig·wag** \'wig-,wag\ *vb* 1 : to signal by or as if by a flag or light waved according to a code 2 : to make or cause to make a signal (as with the hand or arm)

²**wigwag** *n* : the art or practice of wigwagging

wig·wam \'wig-,wäm\ *n* : a hut of the Indians of the eastern U.S. having typically an arched framework of poles overlaid with bark, rush mats, or hides

¹**wild** \'wī(-ə)ld\ *adj* 1 : living in a state of nature and not ordinarily tamed ⟨~ ducks⟩ 2 : growing or produced without human aid or care ⟨~ honey⟩ ⟨~ plants⟩

3 : WASTE, DESOLATE ⟨~ country⟩ 4 : UNCONTROLLED, UNRESTRAINED, UNRULY ⟨~ passions⟩ ⟨a ~ young stallion⟩ 5 : TURBULENT, STORMY ⟨a ~ night⟩ 6 : EXTRAVAGANT, FANTASTIC, CRAZY ⟨~ ideas⟩ 7 : indicative of strong passion, desire, or emotion ⟨a ~ stare⟩ 8 : UNCIVILIZED, SAVAGE 9 : deviating from the natural or expected course : ERRATIC ⟨a ~ throw⟩ 10 : able to represent any playing card designated by the holder ⟨deuces ~⟩ — **wild·ly** *adv* — **wild·ness** *n*

²**wild** *adv* 1 : WILDLY 2 : without regulation or control ⟨running ~⟩

³**wild** *n* 1 : WILDERNESS 2 : a natural or undomesticated state or existence

wild boar *n* : an Old World wild hog from which most domestic swine have been derived

wild card *n* 1 : an unknown or unpredictable factor 2 : one picked to fill a leftover play-off or tournament position 3 *usu* **wild-card** : a symbol (as ? or *) used in a keyword search to represent the presence of unspecified characters

wild carrot *n* : QUEEN ANNE'S LACE

¹**wild·cat** \'wī(-ə)ld-,kat\ *n, pl* **wildcats** 1 : any of various small or medium-sized cats (as a lynx or ocelot) 2 : a quick-tempered hard-fighting person

²**wildcat** *adj* 1 : not sound or safe ⟨~ schemes⟩ 2 : initiated by a group of workers without formal union approval ⟨~ strike⟩

³**wildcat** *vb* **wild·cat·ted; wild·cat·ting** : to drill an oil or gas well in a region not known to be productive

wil·de·beest \'wil-də-,bēst\ *n, pl* **wildebeests** *also* **wildebeest** [Afrikaans *wildebees*, fr. *wilde* wild + *bees* ox] : either of two large African antelopes with an ox-like head and horns and a horselike mane and tail

wil·der·ness \'wil-dər-nəs\ *n* [ME, fr. *wildern* wild, fr. OE *wilddēoren* of wild beasts] : an uncultivated and uninhabited region

wild·fire \'wī(-ə)ld-,fī(-ə)r\ *n* : an uncontrollable fire — **like wildfire** : very rapidly

wild·flow·er \-,flaů(-ə)r\ *n* : the flower of a wild or uncultivated plant or the plant bearing it

wild·fowl \-,faů(-ə)l\ *n* : a bird and esp. a waterfowl hunted as game

wild–goose chase *n* : the pursuit of something unattainable

wild·life \'wī(-ə)ld-,līf\ *n* : nonhuman living things and esp. wild animals living in their natural environment

wild oat *n* 1 : any of several Old World wild grasses 2 *pl* : offenses and indiscretions attributed to youthful exuberance — usu. used in the phrase *sow one's wild oats*

wild rice *n* : a No. American aquatic grass; *also* : its edible seed

wild type *n* : a gene or trait that is typical of a natural population of organisms in contrast to that of mutant forms; *also* : an organism with such a gene or trait

wild·wood \'wī(-ə)ld-ˌwu̇d\ *n* : a wood unaltered or unfrequented by humans

¹wile \'wī(-ə)l\ *n* **1** : a trick or stratagem intended to ensnare or deceive; *also* : a playful trick **2** : TRICKERY, GUILE

²wile *vb* **wiled; wil·ing** : LURE, ENTICE

¹will \'wil\ *vb, past* **would** \'wu̇d\ *pres sing & pl* **will 1** : WISH, DESIRE ⟨call it what you ~⟩ **2** — used as an auxiliary verb to express (1) desire, willingness, or in negative constructions refusal ⟨~ you have another⟩ ⟨he *won't* do it⟩, (2) customary or habitual action ⟨~ get angry over nothing⟩, (3) simple futurity ⟨tomorrow we ~ go shopping⟩, (4) capability or sufficiency ⟨the back seat ~ hold three⟩, (5) determination or willfulness ⟨I ~ go despite them⟩, (6) probability ⟨that ~ be the mailman⟩, (7) inevitability ⟨accidents ~ happen⟩, or (8) a command ⟨you ~ do as I say⟩

²will *n* **1** : wish or desire often combined with determination ⟨the ~ to win⟩ **2** : something desired; *esp* : a choice or determination of one having authority or power **3** : the act, process, or experience of willing : VOLITION **4** : the mental powers manifested as wishing, choosing, desiring, or intending **5** : a disposition to act according to principles or ends **6** : power of controlling one's own actions or emotions ⟨a leader of iron ~⟩ **7** : a legal document in which a person declares to whom his or her possessions are to go after death

³will *vb* **1** : to dispose of by or as if by a will : BEQUEATH **2** : to determine by an act of choice; *also* : DECREE, ORDAIN **3** : INTEND, PURPOSE; *also* : CHOOSE

will·ful *or* **wil·ful** \'wil-fəl\ *adj* **1** : governed by will without regard to reason : OBSTINATE **2** : INTENTIONAL ⟨~ murder⟩ — **will·ful·ly** *adv*

wil·lies \'wi-lēz\ *n pl* : a fit of nervousness : JITTERS — used with *the*

will·ing \'wi-liŋ\ *adj* **1** : inclined or favorably disposed in mind : READY ⟨~ to go⟩ **2** : prompt to act or respond ⟨~ workers⟩ **3** : done, borne, or accepted voluntarily or without reluctance **4** : of or relating to the will : VOLITIONAL — **will·ing·ly** *adv* — **will·ing·ness** *n*

wil·li·waw \'wi-lē-ˌwȯ\ *n* : a sudden violent gust of cold land air common along mountainous coasts of high latitudes

will-o'-the-wisp \ˌwil-ə-thə-'wisp\ *n* **1** : a light that appears at night over marshy grounds **2** : a misleading or elusive goal or hope

wil·low \'wi-lō\ *n* **1** : any of a genus of quick-growing shrubs and trees with tough pliable shoots **2** : an object made of willow wood

wil·low·ware \-ˌwer\ *n* : dinnerware that is usu. blue and white and that is decorated with a story-telling design featuring a large willow tree by a little bridge

wil·lowy \'wi-lə-wē\ *adj* : PLIANT; *also* : gracefully tall and slender

will-pow·er \'wil-ˌpau̇-(ə)r\ *n* : energetic determination : RESOLUTENESS

wil·ly-nil·ly \ˌwi-lē-'ni-lē\ *adv or adj* [alter. of *will I nill I* or *will ye nill ye* or *will he nill he; nill* fr. archaic *nill* to be unwilling, fr. ME *nilen,* fr. OE *nyllan,* fr. *ne* not + *wyllan* to wish] : without regard to one's choice : by compulsion ⟨they rushed us along ~⟩

¹wilt \'wilt\ *vb* **1** : to lose or cause to lose freshness and become limp esp. from lack of water : DROOP **2** : to grow weak or faint : LANGUISH

²wilt *n* : any of various plant disorders marked by wilting and often shriveling

wily \'wī-lē\ *adj* **wil·i·er; -est** : full of guile : TRICKY — **wil·i·ness** \-lē-nəs\ *n*

wimp \'wimp\ *n* : a weak, cowardly, or ineffectual person — **wimpy** \'wim-pē\ *adj*

¹wim·ple \'wim-pəl\ *n* : a cloth covering worn over the head and around the neck and chin by women esp. in the late medieval period and by some nuns

²wimple *vb* **wim·pled; wim·pling 1** : to cover with or as if with a wimple **2** : to ripple or cause to ripple

¹win \'win\ *vb* **won** \'wən\; **win·ning** [ME *winnen,* fr. OE *winnan* to struggle] **1** : to get possession of esp. by effort : GAIN; *also* : to obtain by work : EARN **2** : to gain in or as if in battle or contest; *also* : to be the victor in ⟨*won* the war⟩ **3** : to solicit and gain the favor of; *esp* : to induce to accept oneself in marriage

²win *n* : VICTORY; *esp* : 1st place at the finish (as of a horse race)

wince \'wins\ *vb* **winced; winc·ing** : to shrink back involuntarily (as from pain) : FLINCH — **wince** *n*

winch \'winch\ *n* : a machine that has a drum on which is wound a rope or cable for hauling or hoisting — **winch** *vb*

¹wind \'wind\ *n* **1** : a movement of the air **2** : a prevailing force or influence : TENDENCY, TREND **3** : BREATH ⟨he had the ~ knocked out of him⟩ **4** : gas produced in the stomach or intestines **5** : something insubstantial; *esp* : idle words **6** : air carrying a scent (as of game) **7** : INTIMATION ⟨they got ~ of our plans⟩ **8** : WIND INSTRUMENTS; *also, pl* : players of wind instruments

²wind *vb* **1** : to get a scent of ⟨the dogs ~*ed* the game⟩ **2** : to cause to be out of breath ⟨he was ~*ed* from the climb⟩ **3** : to allow (as a horse) to rest so as to recover breath

³wind \'wind, 'wind\ *vb* **wind·ed** \'wīn-dəd, 'win-\ *or* **wound** \'wau̇nd\; **wind·ing** : to sound by blowing ⟨~ a horn⟩

⁴wind \'wind\ *vb* **wound** \'wau̇nd\ *also* **wind·ed; wind·ing 1** : ENTANGLE, INVOLVE **2** : to introduce stealthily : INSINUATE **3** : to encircle or cover with something pliable : WRAP, COIL, TWINE ⟨~ a bobbin⟩ **4** : to hoist or haul by a rope or chain and a winch **5** : to tighten the spring of; *also* : CRANK **6** : to raise to a high level (as of excitement) **7** : to cause to move in a curving line or path **8** : to have a curving course or shape ⟨a river ~*ing* through the valley⟩ **9** : to move or lie so as to encircle

⁵**wind** \'wīnd\ *n* : COIL, TURN

wind·age \'win-dij\ *n* : the influence of the wind in deflecting the course of a projectile through the air; *also* : the amount of such deflection

wind·bag \'wind-ˌbag\ *n* : an overly talkative person

wind·blown \-ˌblōn\ *adj* : blown by the wind; *also* : having the appearance of being blown by the wind

wind·break \-ˌbrāk\ *n* : a growth of trees or shrubs serving to break the force of the wind; *also* : a shelter from the wind

wind·burned \-ˌbərnd\ *adj* : irritated and inflamed by exposure to the wind — **wind·burn** \-ˌbərn\ *n*

wind·chill \-ˌchil\ *n* : a still-air temperature that would have the same cooling effect on exposed human skin as a given combination of temperature and wind speed

windchill factor *n* : WINDCHILL

wind down *vb* **1** : to draw toward an end **2** : RELAX, UNWIND

wind·er \'wīn-dər\ *n* : one that winds

wind·fall \'wind-ˌfȯl\ *n* **1** : something (as a tree or fruit) blown down by the wind **2** : an unexpected or sudden gift, gain, or advantage

wind·flow·er \-ˌflau̇-ər\ *n* : ANEMONE

¹**wind·ing** \'wīn-diŋ\ *n* : material (as wire) wound or coiled about an object

²**winding** *adj* **1** : having a pronounced curve or spiral ⟨∼ stairs⟩ **2** : having a course that winds ⟨a ∼ road⟩

wind·ing–sheet \-ˌshēt\ *n* : SHROUD

wind instrument *n* : a musical instrument (as a flute or horn) sounded by wind and esp. by the breath

wind·jam·mer \'wind-ˌja-mər\ *n* : a sailing ship; *also* : one of its crew

wind·lass \'win-dləs\ *n* [ME *wyndlas*, alter. of *wyndase*, fr. OF *guindas, windas*, fr. ON *vindāss*, fr. *vinda* to wind + *āss* pole] : a winch used esp. on ships for hoisting or hauling

wind·mill \'wind-ˌmil\ *n* : a mill or machine worked by the wind turning sails or vanes that radiate from a central shaft

win·dow \'win-dō\ *n* [ME *windowe*, fr. ON *vindauga*, fr. *vindr* wind + *auga* eye] **1** : an opening in the wall of a building to let in light and air; *also* : the framework with fittings that closes such an opening **2** : WINDOWPANE **3** : an opening resembling or suggesting that of a window in a building **4** : an interval of time during which certain conditions or an opportunity exists **5** : a rectangular box appearing on a computer screen on which information (as files or program output) is displayed — **win·dow·less** *adj*

window box *n* : a box for growing plants in or by a window

window dressing *n* **1** : display of merchandise in a store window **2** : a showing made to create a deceptively favorable impression

win·dow·pane \'win-dō-ˌpān\ *n* : a pane in a window

win·dow–shop \-ˌshäp\ *vb* : to look at the displays in store windows without going inside the stores to make purchases — **win·dow–shop·per** *n*

win·dow·sill \-ˌsil\ *n* : the horizontal member at the bottom of a window

wind·pipe \'wind-ˌpīp\ *n* : TRACHEA

wind·proof \-'prüf\ *adj* : impervious to wind ⟨a ∼ jacket⟩

wind·row \'wind-ˌrō\ *n* **1** : hay raked up into a row to dry **2** : a row of something (as dry leaves) swept up by or as if by the wind

wind shear *n* : a radical shift in wind speed and direction that occurs over a very short distance

wind·shield \'wind-ˌshēld\ *n* : a transparent screen (as of glass) in front of the occupants of a vehicle

wind sock *n* : an open-ended truncated cloth cone mounted in an elevated position to indicate wind direction

wind·storm \-ˌstȯrm\ *n* : a storm with high wind and little or no rain

wind·surf·ing \-ˌsər-fiŋ\ *n* : the sport or activity of riding a sailboard — **wind·surf** \-ˌsərf\ *vb* — **wind·surf·er** *n*

wind·swept \'wind-ˌswept\ *adj* : swept by or as if by wind ⟨∼ plains⟩

wind tunnel *n* : an enclosed passage through which air is blown to investigate air flow around an object

wind·up \'wīn-ˌdəp\ *n* **1** : CONCLUSION, FINISH **2** : a series of regular and distinctive motions made by a pitcher preliminary to delivering a pitch

wind up *vb* **1** : to bring or come to a conclusion : END **2** : to put in order for the purpose of bringing to an end **3** : to arrive in a place, situation, or condition at the end or as a result of a course of action ⟨*wound up* as paupers⟩ **4** : to make a pitching windup

¹**wind·ward** \'win-dwərd\ *n* : the side or direction from which the wind is blowing

²**windward** *adj* : being in or facing the direction from which the wind is blowing

windy \'win-dē\ *adj* **wind·i·er; -est** **1** : having wind : exposed to winds ⟨a ∼ day⟩ ⟨a ∼ prairie⟩ **2** : STORMY **3** : FLATULENT **4** : indulging in or characterized by useless talk : VERBOSE

¹**wine** \'wīn\ *n* [ME *win*, fr. OE *wīn*, ultim. fr. L *vinum*] **1** : fermented grape juice used as a beverage **2** : the usu. fermented juice of a plant product (as fruit) used as a beverage ⟨rice ∼⟩

²**wine** *vb* **wined; win·ing** : to treat to or drink wine

wine cellar *n* : a room for storing wines; *also* : a stock of wines

wine·grow·er \-ˌgrō-ər\ *n* : one that cultivates a vineyard and makes wine

wine·press \-ˌpres\ *n* : a vat in which juice is pressed from grapes

win·ery \'wī-nə-rē, 'wīn-rē\ *n, pl* **-eries** : a wine-making establishment

¹**wing** \'wiŋ\ *n* **1** : one of the movable feathered or membranous paired appendages by means of which a bird, bat, or insect flies **2** : something suggesting a wing; *esp* : an airfoil that develops the lift which supports an aircraft in flight **3** : a plant or animal appendage or part lik-

ened to a wing **4** : a turned-back or extended edge on an article of clothing **5** : a means of flight or rapid progress **6** : the act or manner of flying : FLIGHT **7** *pl* : the area at the side of the stage out of sight **8** : one of the positions or players on either side of a center position or line **9** : either of two opposing groups within an organization : FACTION **10** : a unit in military aviation consisting of two or more squadrons — **wing·less** *adj* — **wing·like** \-,līk\ *adj* — **on the wing** : in flight : FLYING — **under one's wing** : in one's charge or care

²**wing** *vb* **1** : to fit with wings; *also* : to enable to fly easily **2** : to pass through in flight : FLY ⟨~ the air⟩ ⟨swallows ~*ing* southward⟩ **3** : to let fly : DISPATCH **4** : to wound in the wing ⟨~ a bird⟩; *also* : to wound without killing **5** : to perform without preparation : IMPROVISE ⟨~*ing* it⟩

wing·ding \'wiŋ-,diŋ\ *n* : a wild, lively, or lavish party

winged \'wiŋd, 'wiŋ-əd, *in compounds* 'wiŋd\ *adj* **1** : having wings esp. of a specified character **2** : soaring with or as if with wings : ELEVATED **3** : SWIFT, RAPID

wing nut *n* : a nut with winglike extensions that can be gripped with the thumb and finger

wing·span \'wiŋ-,span\ *n* : the distance between the tips of a pair of wings

wing·spread \-,spred\ *n* : the spread of the wings; *esp* : the distance between the tips of the fully extended wings of a winged animal

¹**wink** \'wiŋk\ *vb* **1** : to close and open one eye quickly as a signal or hint **2** : to close and open the eyes quickly : BLINK **3** : to avoid seeing or noticing something ⟨~ at a traffic violation⟩ **4** : TWINKLE, FLICKER — **wink·er** \'wiŋ-kər\ *n*

²**wink** *n* **1** : a brief period of sleep : NAP **2** : an act of winking; *esp* : a hint or sign given by winking **3** : INSTANT ⟨dries in a ~⟩

win·ner \'wi-nər\ *n* : one that wins

¹**win·ning** \'wi-niŋ\ *n* **1** : VICTORY **2** : something won; *esp* : money won at gambling ⟨large ~*s*⟩

²**winning** *adj* **1** : successful esp. in competition **2** : ATTRACTIVE, CHARMING

win·now \'wi-nō\ *vb* **1** : to remove (as chaff) by a current of air; *also* : to free (as grain) from waste in this manner **2** : to sort or separate as if by winnowing

wino \'wī-nō\ *n, pl* **win·os** : one who is addicted to drinking wine

win·some \'win-səm\ *adj* [ME *winsum*, fr. OE *wynsum*, fr. *wynn* joy] **1** : generally pleasing and engaging **2** : CHEERFUL, GAY — **win·some·ly** *adv* — **win·some·ness** *n*

¹**win·ter** \'win-tər\ *n* : the season of the year in any region in which the noonday sun shines most obliquely : the coldest period of the year

²**winter** *vb* **1** : to pass the winter ⟨~*ed* in Florida⟩ **2** : to feed or find food during the winter ⟨~*ed* on hay⟩

³**winter** *adj* : sown in autumn for harvesting in the following spring or summer ⟨~ wheat⟩

win·ter·green \'win-tər-,grēn\ *n* **1** : a low evergreen plant of the heath family with white bell-shaped flowers and spicy red berries **2** : an aromatic oil or its flavor from the wintergreen

win·ter·ize \'win-tə-,rīz\ *vb* **-ized; -iz·ing** : to make ready for winter

win·ter·kill \'win-tər-,kil\ *vb* : to kill or die by exposure to winter weather

winter squash *n* : any of various hard-shelled squashes that keep well in storage

win·ter·tide \-,tīd\ *n* : WINTER

win·ter·time \-,tīm\ *n* : WINTER

win·try \'win-trē\ *adj* **win·tri·er; -est 1** : of, relating to, or characteristic of winter ⟨~ weather⟩ **2** : CHILLING, CHEERLESS ⟨a ~ welcome⟩

¹**wipe** \'wīp\ *vb* **wiped; wip·ing 1** : to clean or dry by rubbing ⟨~ dishes⟩ **2** : to remove by or as if by rubbing ⟨~ away tears⟩ **3** : to erase completely : OBLITERATE **4** : to pass or draw over a surface ⟨*wiped* his hand across his face⟩ — **wip·er** *n*

²**wipe** *n* **1** : an act or instance of wiping; *also* : BLOW, STRIKE, SWIPE **2** : something used for wiping

wipe out *vb* : to destroy completely

¹**wire** \'wī-(-ə)r\ *n* **1** : metal in the form of a thread or slender rod; *also* : a thread or rod of metal **2** : hidden or secret influences controlling the action of a person or organization — usu. used in pl. ⟨pull ~*s*⟩ **3** : a line of wire for conducting electric current **4** : a telegraph or telephone wire or system **5** : TELEGRAM, CABLEGRAM **6** : the finish line of a race

²**wire** *vb* **wired; wir·ing 1** : to provide or equip with wire ⟨~ a house⟩ **2** : to bind, string, or mount with wire **3** : to send or send word to by telegraph

wired *adj* **1** : furnished with wires **2** : connected to the Internet **3** : feverishly excited

wire·hair \'wī-(-ə)r-,her\ *n* : a wirehaired dog or cat

wire·haired \-'herd\ *adj* : having a stiff wiry outer coat of hair

¹**wire·less** \-ləs\ *adj* **1** : having no wire or wires **2** : RADIO **3** : of or relating to data communications using radio waves

²**wireless** *n*, **1** : telecommunication involving signals transmitted by radio waves; *also* : the technology used in radio telecommunication **2** *chiefly Brit* : RADIO

wire–pull·er \-,pu̇-lər\ *n* : one who uses secret or underhanded means to influence the acts of a person or organization — **wire–pull·ing** *n*

wire service *n* : a news agency that sends out syndicated news copy to subscribers by wire or satellite

wire·tap \-,tap\ *n* : the act or an instance of tapping a telephone or telegraph wire to get information; *also* : an electrical connection used for such tapping — **wiretap** *vb* — **wire·tap·per** \-ˌta-pər\ *n*

wire·worm \-ˌwərm\ *n* : any of various slender hard-coated beetle larvae esp. destructive to plant roots

wir·ing \ˈwī(-ə)r-iŋ\ *n* : a system of wires

wiry \ˈwī(-ə)r-ē\ *adj* **wir·i·er** \ˈwī-rē-ər\; **-est 1** : made of or resembling wire **2** : slender yet strong and sinewy — **wir·i·ness** \ˈwī-rē-nəs\ *n*

Wis *or* **Wisc** *abbr* Wisconsin

Wisd *abbr* Wisdom

wis·dom \ˈwiz-dəm\ *n* [ME, fr. OE *wīsdōm*, fr. *wīs* wise] **1** : accumulated philosophic or scientific learning : KNOWLEDGE; *also* : INSIGHT **2** : good sense : JUDGMENT **3** : a wise attitude or course of action

Wisdom *n* — see BIBLE table

Wisdom of Sol·o·mon \-ˈsä-lə-mən\ — see BIBLE table

wisdom tooth *n* : the last tooth of the full set on each side of the upper and lower jaws of humans

¹wise \ˈwīz\ *n* : WAY, MANNER, FASHION ⟨in no ∼⟩ ⟨in this ∼⟩

²wise *adj* **wis·er; wis·est 1** : having wisdom : SAGE **2** : having or showing good sense or good judgment **3** : aware of what is going on : KNOWING ⟨got ∼ to his secrets⟩; *also* : CRAFTY, SHREWD **4** : possessing inside information **5** : INSOLENT, FRESH ⟨a ∼ retort⟩ — **wise·ly** *adv*

-wise \ˌwīz\ *adv comb form* : in the manner or direction of ⟨slantwise⟩

wise·acre \ˈwīz-ˌā-kər\ *n* [MD *wijssegger* soothsayer] : SMART ALECK

¹wise·crack \ˈwīz-ˌkrak\ *n* : a clever, smart, or flippant remark

²wisecrack *vb* : to make a wisecrack

wise guy *n* : SMART ALECK

¹wish \ˈwish\ *vb* **1** : to have a desire : long for ⟨∼ you were here⟩ ⟨∼ for a puppy⟩ **2** : to form or express a wish concerning ⟨∼ed him a happy birthday⟩ **3** : BID ⟨he ∼ed me good morning⟩ **4** : to request by expressing a desire ⟨I ∼ you to go now⟩

²wish *n* **1** : an act or instance of wishing or desire : WANT; *also* : GOAL **2** : an expressed will or desire

wish·bone \-ˌbōn\ *n* : a forked bone in front of the breastbone in most birds

wish·ful \ˈwish-fəl\ *adj* **1** : expressive of a wish; *also* : having a wish **2** : according with wishes rather than fact ⟨∼ thinking⟩

wishy–washy \ˈwi-shē-ˌwȯ-shē, -ˌwä-\ *adj* : WEAK, INSIPID; *also* : morally feeble

wisp \ˈwisp\ *n* **1** : a small handful (as of hay or straw) **2** : a thin strand, strip, or fragment ⟨a ∼ of hair⟩; *also* : a thready streak ⟨a ∼ of smoke⟩ **3** : something frail, slight, or fleeting ⟨a ∼ of a smile⟩ — **wispy** *adj*

wis·te·ria \wis-ˈtir-ē-ə\ *also* **wis·tar·ia** \-ˈtir-ē-ə also -ˈter-\ *n* : any of a genus of chiefly Asian mostly woody vines related to the peas and widely grown for their long showy clusters of blue, white, purple, or rose flowers

wist·ful \ˈwist-fəl\ *adj* : feeling or showing a timid desire — **wist·ful·ly** *adv* — **wist·ful·ness** *n*

wit \ˈwit\ *n* **1** : reasoning power : INTELLIGENCE **2** : mental soundness : SANITY — usu. used in pl. **3** : RESOURCEFULNESS, INGENUITY; *esp* : quickness and cleverness in handling words and ideas **4** : a talent for making clever remarks; *also* : a person noted for making witty remarks — **wit·ted** \ˈwi-təd\ *adj* — **at one's wit's end** : at a loss for a means of solving a problem

¹witch \ˈwich\ *n* **1** : a person believed to have magic power; *esp* : SORCERESS **2** : an ugly old woman : HAG **3** : a charming or alluring girl or woman

²witch *vb* : BEWITCH

witch·craft \ˈwich-ˌkraft\ *n* : the power or practices of a witch : SORCERY

witch doctor *n* : a person in a primitive society who uses magic to treat sickness and to fight off evil spirits

witch·ery \ˈwi-chə-rē\ *n, pl* **-er·ies 1** : SORCERY **2** : FASCINATION, CHARM

witch·grass \ˈwich-ˌgras\ *n* : any of several grasses that are weeds in cultivated areas

witch ha·zel \ˈwich-ˌhā-zəl\ *n* **1** : a shrub of eastern No. America bearing small yellow flowers in the fall **2** : a soothing alcoholic lotion made from witch hazel bark

witch–hunt \ˈwich-ˌhənt\ *n* **1** : a searching out and persecution of persons accused of witchcraft **2** : the searching out and deliberate harassment esp. of political opponents

witch·ing \ˈwi-chiŋ\ *adj* : of, relating to, or suitable for sorcery or supernatural occurrences

with \ˈwith, ˈwith\ *prep* **1** : AGAINST ⟨a fight ∼ his brother⟩ **2** : FROM ⟨parting ∼ friends⟩ **3** : in mutual relation to ⟨talk ∼ a friend⟩ **4** : in the company of ⟨went there ∼ her⟩ **5** : AS REGARDS, TOWARD ⟨is patient ∼ children⟩ **6** : compared to ⟨on equal terms ∼ another⟩ **7** : in support of ⟨I'm ∼ you all the way⟩ **8** : in the presence of : CONTAINING ⟨tea ∼ sugar⟩ **9** : in the opinion of : as judged by ⟨their arguments had weight ∼ her⟩ **10** : BECAUSE OF, THROUGH ⟨pale ∼ anger⟩; *also* : by means of ⟨hit him ∼ a club⟩ **11** : in a manner indicating ⟨work ∼ a will⟩ **12** : GIVEN, GRANTED ⟨∼ your permission I'll leave⟩ **13** : HAVING ⟨came ∼ good news⟩ ⟨stood there ∼ his mouth open⟩ **14** : characterized by ⟨boys ∼ good morals⟩ **15** : at the time of : right after ⟨∼ that we left⟩ **16** : DESPITE ⟨∼ all her cleverness, she failed⟩ **17** : in the direction of ⟨swim ∼ the tide⟩

with·al \wi-ˈthȯl, -ˈthäl\ *adv* **1** : together with this : BESIDES **2** : on the other hand : NEVERTHELESS

with·draw \with-ˈdrȯ, with-\ *vb* **-drew** \-ˈdrü\; **-drawn** \-ˈdrȯn\; **-draw·ing** \-ˈdrȯ-iŋ\ **1** : to take back or away : REMOVE **2** : to call back (as from consideration); *also* : RETRACT **3** : to go away : RETREAT, LEAVE **4** : to terminate one's participation in or use of something

with·draw·al \-'drȯ-əl\ *n* **1** : an act or instance of withdrawing **2** : the discontinuance of the use or administration of a drug and esp. an addicting drug; *also* : the period following such discontinuance marked by often painful physiological and psychological symptoms **3** : a pathological retreat from the real world (as in some schizophrenic states)

with·drawn \with-'drȯn\ *adj* **1** : ISOLATED, SECLUDED **2** : socially detached and unresponsive

withe \'with\ *n* : a slender flexible twig or branch

with·er \'wi-thər\ *vb* **1** : to shrivel from or as if from loss of bodily moisture and esp. sap **2** : to lose or cause to lose vitality, force, or freshness ⟨their enthusiasm ~ed⟩ **3** : to cause to feel shriveled ⟨~ed him with a glance⟩

with·ers \'wi-thərz\ *n pl* : the ridge between the shoulder bones of a horse; *also* : the corresponding part in other 4-footed animals

with·hold \with-'hōld, with-\ *vb* **-held** \-'held\; **-hold·ing 1** : to hold back : RESTRAIN; *also* : RETAIN **2** : to refrain from granting, giving, or allowing ⟨~ permission⟩ ⟨~ names⟩

withholding tax *n* : a tax on income withheld at the source

¹**with·in** \with-'thin, -'thin-\ *adv* **1** : in or into the interior : INSIDE **2** : inside oneself : INWARDLY

²**within** *prep* **1** : inside the limits or influence of ⟨~ call⟩ **2** : in the limits or compass of ⟨~ a mile⟩ **3** : in or to the inner part of ⟨~ the room⟩

with–it \'wi-thət, -thət\ *adj* : socially or culturally up-to-date

¹**with·out** \wi-'thaut, -'thaut\ *prep* **1** : OUTSIDE **2** : LACKING ⟨~ hope⟩; *also* : not accompanied by or showing ⟨spoke ~ thinking⟩

²**without** *adv* **1** : on the outside : EXTERNALLY **2** : with something lacking or absent ⟨has learned to do ~⟩

with·stand \with-'stand, with-\ *vb* **-stood** \-'stud\; **-stand·ing** : to stand against : RESIST; *esp* : to oppose (as an attack) successfully

wit·less \'wit-ləs\ *adj* : lacking wit or understanding : FOOLISH — **wit·less·ly** *adv* — **wit·less·ness** *n*

¹**wit·ness** \'wit-nəs\ *n* [ME *witnesse*, fr. OE *witnes* knowledge, testimony, witness, fr. *wit* mind, intelligence] **1** : TESTIMONY ⟨bear ~ to the fact⟩ **2** : one that gives evidence; *esp* : one who testifies in a cause or before a court **3** : one present at a transaction so as to be able to testify that it has taken place **4** : one who has personal knowledge or experience of something **5** : something serving as evidence or proof : SIGN

²**witness** *vb* **1** : to bear witness : TESTIFY **2** : to act as legal witness of **3** : to furnish proof of : BETOKEN **4** : to be a witness

of **5** : to be the scene of ⟨this region has ~ed many wars⟩

wit·ti·cism \'wi-tə-ˌsi-zəm\ *n* : a witty saying or phrase

wit·ting \'wi-tiŋ\ *adj* : done knowingly : INTENTIONAL — **wit·ting·ly** *adv*

wit·ty \'wi-tē\ *adj* **wit·ti·er; -est** : marked by or full of wit : AMUSING ⟨a ~ writer⟩ ⟨a ~ remark⟩ ✦ **Synonyms** HUMOROUS, FACETIOUS, JOCULAR, JOCOSE — **wit·ti·ly** \-tə-lē\ *adv* — **wit·ti·ness** \-tē-nəs\ *n*

wive \'wīv\ *vb* **wived; wiv·ing** : to take a wife

wives *pl of* WIFE

wiz·ard \'wi-zərd\ *n* [ME *wysard* wise man, fr. *wys* wise] **1** : MAGICIAN, SORCERER **2** : a very clever or skillful person ⟨a ~ at chess⟩

wiz·ard·ry \'wi-zər-drē\ *n, pl* **-ries 1** : magic skill : SORCERY **2** : great skill or cleverness in an activity

wiz·en \'wi-zᵊn, 'wē-\ *vb* : to become or cause to become dry, shrunken, or wrinkled ⟨a face ~ed by age⟩

wk *abbr* **1** week **2** work

WL *abbr* wavelength

wmk *abbr* watermark

WNW *abbr* west-northwest

WO *abbr* warrant officer

w/o *abbr* without

woad \'wōd\ *n* : a European herb related to the mustards; *also* : a blue dyestuff made from its leaves

wob·ble \'wä-bəl\ *vb* **wob·bled; wob·bling 1** : to move or cause to move with an irregular rocking or side-to-side motion **2** : TREMBLE, QUAVER **3** : WAVER, VACILLATE — **wobble** *n* — **wob·bly** \-b(ə-)lē\ *adj*

woe \'wō\ *n* **1** : deep suffering from misfortune, affliction, or grief **2** : TROUBLE, MISFORTUNE ⟨economic ~s⟩

woe·be·gone \'wō-bi-ˌgȯn\ *adj* : exhibiting woe, sorrow, or misery; *also* : being in a sorry condition

woe·ful *also* **wo·ful** \'wō-fəl\ *adj* **1** : full of woe : AFFLICTED **2** : involving, bringing, or relating to woe ⟨~ stories⟩ **3** : DEPLORABLE ⟨~ test scores⟩ — **woe·ful·ly** *adv*

wok \'wäk\ *n* [Chin (Guangzhou & Hong Kong dial.) *wohk*] : a bowl-shaped cooking utensil used esp. in stir-frying

woke *past and past part of* WAKE

woken *past part of* WAKE

wold \'wōld\ *n* : an upland plain or stretch of rolling land without woods

¹**wolf** \'wulf\ *n, pl* **wolves** \'wulvz\ **1** : any of several large erect-eared bushy-tailed doglike predatory mammals that live and hunt in packs; *esp* : GRAY WOLF **2** : a fierce or destructive person — **wolf·ish** *adj* — **wolf in sheep's clothing** : one who hides a hostile intention with a friendly manner

²**wolf** *vb* : to eat greedily : DEVOUR

wolf·hound \-ˌhaund\ *n* : any of several large dogs orig. used in hunting wolves

wol·fram \'wul-frəm\ *n* : TUNGSTEN

wol·ver·ine \ˌwul-və-'rēn\ *n, pl* **wolver-**

ines *also* **wolverine** : a dark shaggy-coated flesh-eating mammal of northern forests and associated tundra that is related to the weasels

wom·an \'wu̇-mən\ *n, pl* **wom·en** \'wi-mən\ [ME, fr. OE *wīfman*, fr. *wīf* woman, wife + *man* human being, man] **1** : an adult female person **2** : WOMANKIND **3** : feminine nature : WOMANLINESS **4** : a female servant or attendant

wom·an·hood \'wu̇-mən-,hu̇d\ *n* **1** : the state of being a woman : the distinguishing qualities of a woman or of womankind **2** : WOMEN, WOMANKIND

wom·an·ish \'wu̇-mə-nish\ *adj* **1** : associated with or characteristic of women rather than men **2** : suggestive of a weak character : EFFEMINATE

wom·an·ize \'wu̇-mə-,nīz\ *vb* : to pursue casual sexual relationships with numerous women — **wom·an·iz·er** *n*

wom·an·kind \'wu̇-mən-,kīnd\ *n* : the females of the human race : WOMEN

wom·an·like \-,līk\ *adj* : WOMANLY

wom·an·ly \-lē\ *adj* : having qualities characteristic of a woman — **wom·an·li·ness** \-lē-nəs\ *n*

woman suffrage *n* : possession and exercise of suffrage by women

womb \'wüm\ *n* **1** : UTERUS **2** : a place where something is generated

wom·bat \'wäm-,bat\ *n* : any of several stocky burrowing Australian marsupials that resemble small bears

wom·en·folk \'wi-mən-,fōk\ *also* **wom·en·folks** \-,fōks\ *n pl* : WOMEN

¹won \'wən\ *past and past part of* WIN

²won \'wän\ *n, pl* **won** — see MONEY table

¹won·der \'wən-dər\ *n* **1** : a cause of astonishment or surprise : MARVEL; *also* : MIRACLE **2** : the quality of exciting wonder ⟨the charm and ∼ of the scene⟩ **3** : a feeling (as of awed astonishment or uncertainty) aroused by something extraordinary or affecting

²wonder *vb* **1** : to feel surprise or amazement **2** : to feel curiosity or doubt ⟨∼ about the future⟩

wonder drug *n* : MIRACLE DRUG

won·der·ful \'wən-dər-fəl\ *adj* **1** : exciting wonder : MARVELOUS, ASTONISHING **2** : unusually good : ADMIRABLE ⟨did a ∼ job⟩ — **won·der·ful·ly** \-f(ə-)lē\ *adv* — **won·der·ful·ness** *n*

won·der·land \-,land, -lənd\ *n* **1** : an imaginary place of delicate beauty or magical charm **2** : a place that excites admiration or wonder ⟨a scenic ∼⟩

won·der·ment \-mənt\ *n* **1** : ASTONISHMENT, SURPRISE **2** : a cause of or occasion for wonder **3** : curiosity about something

won·drous \'wən-drəs\ *adj* : WONDERFUL, MARVELOUS ⟨a ∼ feat⟩ — **won·drous·ly** *adv* — **won·drous·ness** *n*

wonk \'wäŋk, 'wȯŋk\ *n* : one who works in a specialized usu. intellectual field ⟨computer ∼s⟩

¹wont \'wȯnt, 'wōnt\ *adj* [ME *woned, wont*, fr. pp. of *wonen* to dwell, be used to, fr.

OE *wunian*] **1** : ACCUSTOMED, USED ⟨as we are ∼ to do⟩ **2** : INCLINED, APT

²wont *n* : CUSTOM, USAGE, HABIT ⟨according to her ∼⟩

won't \'wōnt\ : will not

wont·ed \'wȯn-təd, 'wōn-\ *adj* : ACCUSTOMED, CUSTOMARY ⟨his ∼ courtesy⟩

woo \'wü\ *vb* **1** : to try to gain the love of : COURT **2** : SOLICIT, ENTREAT **3** : to try to gain or bring about ⟨∼ public favor⟩ — **woo·er** *n*

¹wood \'wu̇d\ *n* **1** : a dense growth of trees usu. larger than a grove and smaller than a forest — often used in pl. **2** : a hard fibrous substance that is basically xylem and forms the bulk of trees and shrubs beneath the bark; *also* : this material fit or prepared for some use (as burning or building) **3** : something made of wood

²wood *adj* **1** : WOODEN **2** : suitable for holding, cutting, or working with wood **3** *or* **woods** \'wu̇dz\ : living or growing in woods

³wood *vb* **1** : to supply or load with wood esp. for fuel **2** : to cover with a growth of trees

wood alcohol *n* : METHANOL

wood·bine \'wu̇d-,bīn\ *n* : any of several honeysuckles; *also* : VIRGINIA CREEPER

wood·block \-,bläk\ *n* : WOODCUT

wood·chop·per \-,chä-pər\ *n* : one engaged esp. in chopping down trees

wood·chuck \-,chək\ *n* : a thickset grizzled marmot of Alaska, Canada, and the northeastern U.S.

wood·cock \'wu̇d-,käk\ *n, pl* **wood·cocks** : a brown eastern No. American game bird with a short neck and long bill that is related to the snipe; *also* : a related and similar Old World bird

wood·craft \-,kraft\ *n* **1** : skill and practice in matters relating to the woods and esp. in how to take care of oneself in them **2** : skill in shaping or constructing articles from wood

wood·cut \-,kət\ *n* **1** : a relief printing surface engraved on a block of wood **2** : a print from a woodcut

wood·cut·ter \-,kə-tər\ *n* : a person who cuts wood

wood duck *n* : a showy crested American duck of which the male has iridescent multicolored plumage

wood·ed \'wu̇-dəd\ *adj* : covered with woods or trees ⟨∼ slopes⟩

wood·en \'wu̇-d³n\ *adj* **1** : made of wood **2** : lacking flexibility : awkwardly stiff — **wood·en·ly** *adv* — **wood·en·ness** *n*

wood·en·ware \'wu̇-d³n-,wer\ *n* : articles made of wood for domestic use

wood·land \'wu̇d-lənd, -,land\ *n* : land covered with trees : FOREST — **woodland** *adj*

wood·lot \'wu̇d-,lät\ *n* : a restricted area of woodland usu. privately kept to meet fuel and timber needs

wood louse *n* : any of various small flat crustaceans that live esp. in ground litter and under stones and bark

wood·man \'wùd-mən\ n : WOODSMAN

wood·note \-,nōt\ n : verbal expression that is natural and artless

wood nymph n : a nymph living in the woods

wood·peck·er \'wùd-,pe-kər\ n : any of numerous usu. brightly marked climbing birds with stiff spiny tail feathers and a chisellike bill used to drill into trees for insects

wood·pile \-,pī(-ə)l\ n : a pile of wood and esp. firewood

wood rat n : PACK RAT

wood·shed \-,shed\ n : a shed for storing wood and esp. firewood

woods·man \'wùdz-mən\ n : a person who frequents or works in the woods; esp : one skilled in woodcraft

woodsy \'wùd-zē\ adj **woods·i·er; -est** : relating to or suggestive of woods ⟨a ∼ odor⟩

wood·wind \'wùd-,wind\ n : one of a group of wind instruments including flutes, clarinets, oboes, bassoons, and sometimes saxophones

wood·work \-,wərk\ n : work made of wood; esp : interior fittings (as moldings or stairways) of wood

woody \'wù-dē\ adj **wood·i·er; -est 1** : abounding or overgrown with woods ⟨a ∼ trail⟩ **2** : of or containing wood or wood fibers ⟨∼ plants⟩ **3** : characteristic or suggestive of wood — **wood·i·ness** \'wù-dē-nəs\ n

woof \'wùf\ n [alter. of ME oof, fr. OE ōwef, fr. ō- (fr. on on) + wefan to weave] **1** : WEFT **1 2** : a woven fabric; also : its texture

woof·er \'wù-fər\ n : a loudspeaker that reproduces sounds of low pitch

wool \'wùl\ n : the soft wavy or curly hair of some mammals and esp. the domestic sheep; also : something (as a textile or garment) made of wool **2** : material that resembles a mass of wool — **wooled** \'wùld\ adj

¹wool·en or **wool·len** \'wù-lən\ adj **1** : made of wool **2** : of or relating to the manufacture or sale of woolen products ⟨∼ mills⟩

²woolen or **woollen** n **1** : a fabric made of wool **2** : garments of woolen fabric — usu. used in pl.

wool·gath·er·ing \-,ga-thə-riŋ\ n : idle daydreaming

¹wool·ly also **wooly** \'wù-lē\ adj **wool·li·er; -est 1** : of, relating to, or bearing wool **2** : consisting of or resembling wool **3** : mentally confused ⟨∼ thinking⟩ **4** : marked by a lack of order or restraint ⟨the wild and ∼ West⟩

²wool·ly also **wool·ie** or **wooly** \'wù-lē\ n, pl **wool·lies** : a garment made from wool; esp : underclothing of knitted wool — usu. used in pl.

woolly adel·gid \-ə-'del-jəd\ n : either of two aphids accidentally introduced into No. America where they are serious pests of firs and hemlocks

woolly bear n : any of numerous very hairy moth caterpillars

woolly mammoth n : a heavy-coated mammoth formerly inhabiting colder parts of the northern hemisphere

woo·zy \'wü-zē\ adj **woo·zi·er; -est 1** : BEFUDDLED **2** : somewhat dizzy, nauseated, or weak **3** : somewhat indistinct or unfocused : FUZZY — **woo·zi·ness** \'wü-zē-nəs\ n

¹word \'wərd\ n **1** : something that is said; esp : a brief remark **2** : a speech sound or series of speech sounds that communicates a meaning; also : a graphic representation of such a sound or series of sounds **3** : ORDER, COMMAND **4** often cap : the 2d person of the Trinity; also : GOSPEL **5** : NEWS, INFORMATION **6** : PROMISE **7** pl : QUARREL, DISPUTE **8** : a verbal signal : PASSWORD — **word·less** adj

²word vb : to express in words : PHRASE

word·age \'wər-dij\ n **1** : WORDS **2** : number of words **3** : WORDING

word·book \'wərd-,bùk\ n : VOCABULARY, DICTIONARY

word·ing \'wər-diŋ\ n : verbal expression : PHRASEOLOGY

word of mouth : oral communication

word·play \'wərd-,plā\ n : playful use of words

word processing n : the production of typewritten documents with automated and usu. computerized text-editing equipment — **word process** vb

word processor n : a keyboard-operated terminal for use in word processing; also : software to perform word processing

wordy \'wər-dē\ adj **word·i·er; -est** : using many words : VERBOSE ♦ **Synonyms** PROLIX, DIFFUSE, REDUNDANT — **word·i·ness** \-dē-nəs\ n

wore past of WEAR

¹work \'wərk\ n **1** : TOIL, LABOR; also : EMPLOYMENT ⟨out of ∼⟩ **2** : TASK, JOB ⟨have ∼ to do⟩ **3** : the energy used when a force is applied over a given distance **4** : DEED, ACHIEVEMENT **5** : a fortified structure **6** pl : engineering structures **7** pl : a place where industrial labor is done : PLANT, FACTORY **8** pl : the moving parts of a mechanism **9** : something produced by mental effort or physical labor; esp : an artistic production (as a book or needlework) **10** : WORKMANSHIP ⟨careless ∼⟩ **11** : material in the process of manufacture **12** pl : everything possessed, available, or belonging ⟨the whole ∼s went overboard⟩; also : drastic treatment ⟨gave him the ∼s⟩ ♦ **Synonyms** OCCUPATION, EMPLOYMENT, BUSINESS, PURSUIT, CALLING — **in the works** : in process of preparation

²work adj **1** : used for work ⟨∼ elephants⟩ **2** : suitable or styled for wear while working ⟨∼ clothes⟩

³work vb **worked** \'wərkt\ or **wrought** \'ròt\; **work·ing 1** : to bring to pass : EFFECT **2** : to fashion or create a useful or desired product through labor or exertion **3** : to prepare for use (as by kneading) **4** : to bring into a desired form by a manufacturing process ⟨∼ cold steel⟩ **5** : to set or keep in operation : OPERATE ⟨a pump ∼ed by hand⟩ **6** : to solve by reasoning or calculation ⟨∼ out a problem⟩ **7** : to cause to toil or labor ⟨∼ed the men hard⟩; *also* : to make use of ⟨∼ a mine⟩ **8** : to pay for with labor or service ⟨∼ off a debt⟩ **9** : to bring or get into some position or condition by stages ⟨the stream ∼ed itself clear⟩ ⟨the knot ∼ed loose⟩ **10** : CONTRIVE, ARRANGE ⟨∼ it so you can leave early⟩ **11** : to practice trickery or cajolery on ⟨∼ed the management for a free ticket⟩ **12** : EXCITE, PROVOKE ⟨∼ed himself into a rage⟩ **13** : to exert oneself physically or mentally; *esp* : to perform work regularly for wages **14** : to function according to plan or design **15** : to produce a desired effect : SUCCEED ⟨the plan ∼ed⟩ **16** : to make way slowly and with difficulty ⟨he ∼ed forward through the crowd⟩ **17** : to permit of being worked ⟨this wood ∼s easily⟩ **18** : to be in restless motion; *also* : FERMENT 1 — **work on 1** : AFFECT **2** : to try to influence or persuade — **work upon** : to have effect upon : operate on : INFLUENCE

work·able \'wər-kə-bəl\ *adj* **1** : capable of being worked ⟨∼ clay⟩ **2** : PRACTICABLE, FEASIBLE — **work·able·ness** *n*

work·a·day \'wər-kə-ˌdā\ *adj* **1** : relating to or suited for working days **2** : PROSAIC, ORDINARY ⟨∼ chores⟩

work·a·hol·ic \ˌwər-kə-'hȯ-lik, -'hä-\ *n* : a compulsive worker

work·bench \-ˌbench\ *n* : a bench on which work esp. of mechanics, machinists, and carpenters is performed

work·book \-ˌbu̇k\ *n* **1** : a worker's manual **2** : a student's book of problems to be answered directly on the pages

work·day \'wərk-ˌdā\ *n* **1** : a day on which work is done as distinguished from a day off **2** : the period of time in a day when work is performed

work·er \'wər-kər\ *n* **1** : one that works; *esp* : a person who works for wages **2** : any of the sexually undeveloped individuals of a colony of social insects (as bees, ants, or termites) that perform the work of the community

workers' compensation *n* : a system of insurance that reimburses an employer for damages paid to an employee who was injured while working

work ethic *n* : belief in work as a moral good

work farm *n* : a farm on which persons guilty of minor law violations are confined

work·horse \'wərk-ˌhȯrs\ *n* **1** : a horse used for hard work **2** : a person who does most of the work of a group task **3** : something that is useful, durable, or dependable

work·house \-ˌhau̇s\ *n*, **1** *Brit* : POORHOUSE **2** : a house of correction for persons guilty of minor law violations

¹work·ing \'wər-kiŋ\ *n* **1** : manner of functioning — usu. used in pl. **2** *pl* : an excavation made in mining or tunneling

²working *adj* **1** : engaged in work ⟨a ∼ journalist⟩ **2** : adequate to allow work to be done ⟨a ∼ majority⟩ ⟨a ∼ knowledge of French⟩ **3** : adopted or assumed to help further work or activity ⟨a ∼ draft⟩ **4** : spent at work ⟨∼ life⟩

work·ing·man \'wər-kiŋ-ˌman\ *n* : WORKER 1

work·man \'wərk-mən\ *n* **1** : WORKER 1 **2** : ARTISAN, CRAFTSMAN

work·man·like \-ˌlīk\ *adj* : worthy of a good workman : SKILLFUL

work·man·ship \-ˌship\ *n* : the art or skill of a workman : CRAFTSMANSHIP; *also* : the quality of a piece of work ⟨a vase of exquisite ∼⟩

work·out \'wərk-ˌau̇t\ *n* **1** : a practice or exercise to test or improve one's fitness, ability, or performance **2** : a test or trial to determine ability or capacity or suitability

work out *vb* **1** : to bring about esp. by resolving difficulties **2** : DEVELOP, ELABORATE **3** : to prove effective, practicable, or suitable ⟨our plan didn't *work out*⟩ **4** : to amount to a total or calculated figure — used with *at* **5** : to engage in a workout

work·place \'wərk-ˌplās\ *n* : a place (as an office) where work is done

work·room \'wərk-ˌrüm, -ˌru̇m\ *n* : a room used for work

work·shop \-ˌshäp\ *n* **1** : a shop where manufacturing or handicrafts are carried on **2** : a seminar emphasizing exchange of ideas and practical methods

work·sta·tion \-ˌstā-shən\ *n* : an area with equipment for the performance of a specialized task; *also* : a personal computer usu. connected to a computer network

world \'wərld\ *n* [ME, fr. OE *woruld* human existence, this world, age, fr. a prehistoric compound whose first constituent is represented by OE *wer* man and whose second constituent is akin to OE *eald* old] **1** : the earth with its inhabitants and all things upon it **2** : people in general : MANKIND **3** : human affairs ⟨withdraw from the ∼⟩ **4** : UNIVERSE, CREATION **5** : a state of existence : scene of life and action ⟨the ∼ of the future⟩ **6** : a distinctive class of persons or their sphere of interest ⟨the musical ∼⟩ **7** : a part or section of the earth or its inhabitants by itself **8** : a great number or quantity ⟨a ∼ of troubles⟩ **9** : a celestial body

world—beat·er \-ˌbē-tər\ *n* : one that excels all others of its kind : CHAMPION

world—class *adj* : of the highest caliber in the world ⟨a ∼ athlete⟩

world·ling \-liŋ\ *n* : a person absorbed in the concerns of the present world

world·ly \-lē\ *adj* **1** : of, relating to, or devoted to this world and its pursuits rather than to religion or spiritual affairs **2** : WORLDLY-WISE, SOPHISTICATED — **world·li·ness** \-lē-nəs\ *n*

world·ly—wise \-ˌwīz\ *adj* : possessing a practical and often shrewd understanding of human affairs

world·wide \'wərld-'wīd\ *adj* : extended throughout the entire world — **worldwide** *adv*

World Wide Web *n* : a part of the Internet usu. accessed through a browser and containing files connected by hyperlinks

¹**worm** \'wərm\ *n* **1** : any of various small long usu. naked and soft-bodied round or flat invertebrate animals (as an earthworm, nematode, tapeworm, or maggot) **2** : a human being who is an object of contempt, loathing, or pity : WRETCH **3** : something that inwardly torments or devours **4** *pl* : infestation with or disease caused by parasitic worms **5** : a spiral or wormlike thing (as the thread of a screw) — **worm·like** \-,līk\ *adj* — **wormy** *adj*

²**worm** *vb* **1** : to move or cause to move or proceed slowly and deviously **2** : to insinuate or introduce (oneself) by devious or subtle means **3** : to obtain or extract by artful or insidious pleading, asking, or persuading ⟨∼ed the truth out of him⟩ **4** : to treat (an animal) with a drug to destroy or expel parasitic worms

worm–eat·en \'wərm-,ē-t°n\ *adj* : eaten or burrowed by worms

worm gear *n* : a mechanical linkage consisting of a short rotating screw whose threads mesh with the teeth of a gear wheel

worm·hole \'wərm-,hōl\ *n* : a hole or passage burrowed by a worm

worm·wood \-,wu̇d\ *n* **1** : any of a genus of aromatic woody plants (as a sagebrush); *esp* : one of Europe used in absinthe **2** : something bitter or grievous : BITTERNESS

worn *past part of* WEAR

worn–out \'wōrn-'au̇t\ *adj* : exhausted or used up by or as if by wear

wor·ri·some \'wər-ē-səm\ *adj* **1** : causing distress or worry ⟨∼ news⟩ **2** : inclined to worry or fret ⟨a ∼ mother⟩

¹**wor·ry** \'wər-ē\ *vb* **wor·ried; wor·ry·ing 1** : to shake and mangle with the teeth ⟨a terrier ∼ing a rat⟩ **2** : to make anxious or upset ⟨her poor health *worries* me⟩ **3** : to feel or express great care or anxiety : FRET ⟨∼ing about his health⟩ — **wor·ri·er** *n*

²**worry** *n, pl* **worries 1** : ANXIETY **2** : a cause of anxiety : TROUBLE

wor·ry·wart \'wər-ē-,wȯrt\ *n* : one who is inclined to worry unduly

¹**worse** \'wərs\ *adj, comparative of* BAD *or of* ILL **1** : bad or evil in a greater degree : less good **2** : more unfavorable, unpleasant, or painful; *also* : SICKER

²**worse** *n* **1** : one that is worse **2** : a greater degree of ill or badness ⟨a turn for the ∼⟩

³**worse** *adv, comparative of* BAD *or of* ILL : in a worse manner : to a worse extent or degree

wors·en \'wər-s°n\ *vb* : to make or become worse ⟨the rash ∼ed⟩

¹**wor·ship** \'wər-shəp\ *n* [ME *worshipe* worthiness, respect, reverence paid to a divine being, fr. OE *weorthscipe* worthiness, respect, fr. *weorth* worthy, worth + -*scipe* -ship, suffix denoting quality or

condition] **1** *chiefly Brit* : a person of importance — used as a title for officials **2** : reverence toward a divine being or supernatural power; *also* : the expression of such reverence **3** : extravagant respect or admiration or devotion ⟨∼ of the dollar⟩

²**worship** *vb* **-shipped** *also* **-shiped; -ship·ping** *also* **-ship·ing 1** : to honor or reverence as a divine being or supernatural power **2** : IDOLIZE ⟨∼s his brother⟩ **3** : to perform or take part in worship — **wor·ship·er** *or* **wor·ship·per** *n*

wor·ship·ful \'wər-shəp-fəl\ *adj* **1** *archaic* : NOTABLE, DISTINGUISHED **2** *chiefly Brit* — used as a title for various persons or groups of rank or distinction **3** : VENERATING, WORSHIPING

¹**worst** \'wərst\ *adj, superlative of* BAD *or of* ILL **1** : most bad, evil, ill, or corrupt ⟨the ∼ criminals⟩ **2** : most unfavorable, unpleasant, or painful ⟨the ∼ scenario⟩; *also* : most unsuitable, faulty, or unattractive **3** : least skillful or efficient ⟨her ∼ students⟩

²**worst** *adv, superlative of* ILL *or of* BAD *or* BADLY **1** : to the extreme degree of badness or inferiority ⟨the ∼ dressed person⟩ : in the worst manner **2** : MOST ⟨those who need help ∼⟩

³**worst** *n* : one that is worst

⁴**worst** *vb* : DEFEAT

wor·sted \'wu̇s-təd, 'wər-stəd\ *n* [ME, fr. *Worsted* (now *Worstead*), England] : a smooth compact yarn from long wool fibers; *also* : a fabric made from such yarn

wort \'wərt, 'wȯrt\ *n* : a sweet liquid drained from mash and fermented to form beer and whiskey

¹**worth** \'wərth\ *n* **1** : monetary value; *also* : the equivalent of a specified amount or figure ⟨$5 ∼ of gas⟩ **2** : the value of something measured by its qualities **3** : MERIT, EXCELLENCE

²**worth** *prep* **1** : equal in value to; *also* : having possessions or income equal to **2** : deserving of ⟨well ∼ the effort⟩

worth·less \'wərth-ləs\ *adj* **1** : lacking worth : VALUELESS; *also* : USELESS **2** : LOW, DESPICABLE — **worth·less·ness** *n*

worth·while \'wərth-'hwī(-ə)l\ *adj* : being worth the time or effort spent

¹**wor·thy** \'wər-thē\ *adj* **wor·thi·er; -est 1** : having worth or value : ESTIMABLE ⟨a ∼ cause⟩ **2** : HONORABLE, MERITORIOUS ⟨my ∼ opponent⟩ **3** : having sufficient worth ⟨∼ of the honor⟩ — **wor·thi·ly** \'wər-thə-lē\ *adv* — **wor·thi·ness** \-thē-nəs\ *n*

²**worthy** *n, pl* **worthies** : a worthy person

would \'wu̇d\ *past of* WILL **1** *archaic* : wish for : WANT **2** : strongly desire : WISH ⟨I ∼ I were young again⟩ **3** — used as an auxiliary to express (1) preference ⟨∼ rather run than fight⟩, (2) wish, desire, or intent ⟨those who ∼ forbid gambling⟩, (3) habitual action ⟨we ∼ meet often for lunch⟩, (4) a contingency or possibility ⟨if he were coming, he ∼ be here by now⟩, (5) probability ⟨∼ have won if he hadn't tripped⟩, or (6) a request ⟨~ you help us⟩ 4 : COULD 5 : SHOULD

would-be \'wu̇d-ˌbē\ *adj* : desiring or pretending to be ⟨a ~ artist⟩

¹**wound** \'wu̇nd\ *n* 1 : an injury involving cutting or breaking of bodily tissue (as by violence, accident, or surgery) 2 : an injury or hurt to feelings or reputation

²**wound** *vb* : to inflict a wound to or in

³**wound** \'wau̇nd\ *past and past part of* WIND

wove *past of* WEAVE

woven *past part of* WEAVE

¹**wow** \'wau̇\ *n* : a striking success : HIT

²**wow** *vb* : to arouse enthusiastic approval ⟨~ed the critics⟩

WP *abbr* word processing; word processor

WPM *abbr* words per minute

wpn *abbr* weapon

wrack \'rak\ *n* [ME, fr. OE *wræc* misery, punishment, something driven by the sea] : violent or total destruction

wraith \'rāth\ *n, pl* **wraiths** \'rāths, 'rāthz\ 1 : GHOST, SPECTER 2 : an insubstantial appearance : SHADOW

¹**wran·gle** \'raŋ-gəl\ *vb* **wran·gled; wran·gling** 1 : to quarrel angrily or peevishly : BICKER 2 : ARGUE 3 : to obtain by persistent arguing 4 : to herd and care for (livestock) on the range — **wran·gler** *n*

²**wrangle** *n* : an angry, noisy, or prolonged dispute; *also* : CONTROVERSY

¹**wrap** \'rap\ *vb* **wrapped; wrap·ping** 1 : to cover esp. by winding or folding 2 : to envelop and secure for transportation or storage 3 : to enclose wholly : ENFOLD 4 : to coil, fold, draw, or twine about something 5 : SURROUND, ENVELOP ⟨*wrapped* in mystery⟩ 6 : INVOLVE, ENGROSS ⟨*wrapped* up in a hobby⟩ 7 : to complete filming or recording

²**wrap** *n* 1 : WRAPPER, WRAPPING 2 : an article of clothing that may be wrapped around a person 3 *pl* : SECRECY ⟨kept under ~s⟩ 4 : completion of filming or recording

wrap·around \'ra-pə-ˌrau̇nd\ *n* : a garment (as a dress) adjusted to the figure by wrapping around

wrap·per \'ra-pər\ *n* 1 : that in which something is wrapped 2 : one that wraps 3 : an article of clothing worn wrapped around the body

wrap·ping \'ra-piŋ\ *n* : something used to wrap an object : WRAPPER

wrap—up \'rap-ˌəp\ *n* : SUMMARY

wrap up *vb* 1 : SUMMARIZE, SUM UP 2 : to bring to a usu. successful conclusion

wrasse \'ras\ *n* : any of a large family of usu. brightly colored marine fishes including many food fishes

wrath \'rath\ *n* 1 : violent anger : RAGE 2 : divine punishment ♦ **Synonyms** INDIGNATION, IRE, FURY, ANGER

wrath·ful \-fəl\ *adj* 1 : filled with wrath : very angry 2 : showing, marked by, or arising from anger — **wrath·ful·ly** *adv* — **wrath·ful·ness** *n*

wreak \'rēk\ *vb* [ME *wreken*, fr. OE *wrecan* to drive, punish, avenge] 1 : to exact as a punishment : INFLICT ⟨~ vengeance on an enemy⟩ 2 : to give free scope or rein to ⟨~ed his wrath⟩ 3 : BRING ABOUT, CAUSE ⟨~ havoc⟩

wreath \'rēth\ *n, pl* **wreaths** \'rēthz, 'rēths\ : a circular band of flowers or leaves usu. for decoration; *also* : something having a circular or coiling form ⟨a ~ of smoke⟩

wreathe \'rēth\ *vb* **wreathed; wreath·ing** 1 : to shape or take on the shape of a wreath 2 : to crown, decorate, or cover with or as if with a wreath ⟨a face *wreathed* in smiles⟩

¹**wreck** \'rek\ *n* 1 : something (as goods) cast up on the land by the sea after a shipwreck 2 : SHIPWRECK 3 : a destructive crash ⟨a car ~⟩ 4 : the action of breaking up or destroying something 5 : broken remains (as of a vehicle after a crash) 6 : something disabled or in a state of ruin; *also* : an individual broken in health or strength, or spirits ⟨he's a nervous ~⟩

²**wreck** *vb* 1 : SHIPWRECK 2 : to ruin or damage by breaking up : involve in disaster or ruin

wreck·age \'re-kij\ *n* 1 : the act of wrecking : the state of being wrecked : RUIN 2 : the remains of a wreck

wreck·er \'re-kər\ *n* 1 : one that searches for or works upon the wrecks of ships 2 : TOW TRUCK 3 : one that wrecks; *esp* : one whose work is the demolition of buildings

wren \'ren\ *n* : any of a family of small mostly brown singing birds with short wings and often a tail that points upward

¹**wrench** \'rench\ *vb* 1 : to move with a violent twist 2 : to pull, strain, or tighten with violent twisting or force 3 : to injure or disable by a violent twisting or straining ⟨~ed her back⟩ 4 : to snatch forcibly : WREST

²**wrench** *n* 1 : a forcible twisting; *also* : an injury (as to one's ankle) by twisting 2 : a tool for holding, twisting, or turning (as nuts or bolts)

¹**wrest** \'rest\ *vb* 1 : to pull or move by a forcible twisting movement 2 : to gain with difficulty by or as if by force or violence ⟨~ control of the government from the dictator⟩

²**wrest** *n* : a forcible twist : WRENCH

¹**wres·tle** \'re-səl, 'ra-\ *vb* **wres·tled; wres·tling** 1 : to grapple with and try to throw down an opponent 2 : to compete against in wrestling 3 : to struggle for control (as of something difficult) ⟨~ with a problem⟩ — **wres·tler** \'res-lər, 'ras-\

²**wrestle** *n* : the action or an instance of wrestling : STRUGGLE

wres·tling \'res-liŋ\ *n* : the sport in which two opponents wrestle each other

wretch \'rech\ *n* [ME *wrecche*, fr. OE *wrecca* outcast, exile] 1 : a miserable unhappy person 2 : a base, despicable, or vile person

wretch·ed \'re-chəd\ *adj* **1** : deeply afflicted, dejected, or distressed : MISERABLE **2** : WOEFUL, GRIEVOUS ⟨a ~ accident⟩ **3** : DESPICABLE ⟨a ~ trick⟩ **4** : poor in quality or ability : INFERIOR ⟨~ workmanship⟩ — **wretch·ed·ly** *adv* — **wretch·ed·ness** *n*

wrig·gle \'ri-gəl\ *vb* **wrig·gled; wrig·gling 1** : to twist or move to and fro like a worm : SQUIRM ⟨wriggled in his chair⟩ ⟨~ your toes⟩; *also* : to move along by twisting and turning ⟨a snake wriggled along the path⟩ **2** : to extricate oneself as if by wriggling ⟨~ out of difficulty⟩ — **wriggle** *n*

wrig·gler *n* **1** : one that wriggles **2** : WIGGLER 1

wring \'riŋ\ *vb* **wrung** \'rəŋ\; **wring·ing** \'riŋ-iŋ\ **1** : to squeeze or twist esp. so as to make dry or to extract moisture or liquid ⟨~ wet clothes⟩ **2** : to get by or as if by twisting or pressing ⟨~ the truth out of him⟩ **3** : to twist so as to strain or sprain : CONTORT ⟨~ his neck⟩ **4** : to twist together as a sign of anguish ⟨wrung her hands⟩ **5** : to affect painfully as if by wringing : TORMENT ⟨her plight wrung my heart⟩

wring·er \'riŋ-ər\ *n* : one that wrings; *esp* : a device for squeezing out liquid or moisture ⟨clothes ~⟩

¹wrin·kle \'riŋ-kəl\ *n* **1** : a crease or small fold on a smooth surface (as in the skin or in cloth) **2** : a clever or new method, trick, or·idea — **wrin·kly** \-k(ə-)lē\ *adj*

²wrinkle *vb* **wrin·kled; wrin·kling** : to develop or cause to develop wrinkles

wrist \'rist\ *n* : the joint or region between the hand and the arm; *also* : a corresponding part in a lower animal

wrist·band \-,band\ *n* : a band or the part of a sleeve encircling the wrist

wrist·let \-lət\ *n* : WRISTBAND; *esp* : a close-fitting knitted band attached to the top of a glove or the end of a sleeve

wrist·watch \-,wäch\ *n* : a small watch attached to a bracelet or strap to fasten about the wrist

writ \'rit\ *n* **1** : something written **2** : a written legal order signed by a court officer

writ·able \'rī-tə-bəl\ *adj* : being an electronic storage medium on which it is possible to introduce new data ⟨a ~ DVD⟩

write \'rīt\ *vb* **wrote** \'rōt\; **writ·ten** \'ri-tᵊn\ *also* **writ** \'rit\; **writ·ing** \'rī-tiŋ\ [ME, fr. OE *wrītan* to scratch, draw, inscribe] **1** : to form characters, letters, or words on a surface ⟨learn to read and ~⟩ **2** : to form the letters or the words of ⟨~ your name⟩ ⟨~ a check⟩ **3** : to put down on paper : express in writing **4** : to make up and set down for others to read ⟨~ a book⟩ ⟨~ music⟩ **5** : to write a letter to **6** : to communicate by letter : CORRESPOND

write-in \'rīt-,in\ *n* : a vote cast by writing in the name of a candidate; *also* : a candidate whose name is written in

write in *vb* : to insert (a name not listed on a ballot) in an appropriate space; *also* : to cast (a vote) in this manner

write off *vb* : to eliminate (an asset) from a bookkeeping record : enter as a loss or expense

writ·er \'rī-tər\ *n* : one that writes esp. as a business or occupation : AUTHOR

writer's cramp *n* : a painful spasmodic contraction of muscles of the hand or fingers brought on by excessive writing

write-up \'rīt-,əp\ *n* : a written account (as in a newspaper); *esp* : a flattering article

writhe \'rīth\ *vb* **writhed; writh·ing 1** : to twist and turn this way and that ⟨~ in pain⟩ **2** : to suffer with shame or confusion

writing *n* **1** : the act of one that writes; *also* : HANDWRITING **2** : something that is written or printed **3** : a style or form of composition **4** : the occupation of a writer

Writings \'rī-tiŋz\ *n pl* : the third part of the Jewish scriptures

wrnt *abbr* warrant

¹wrong \'ròŋ\ *n* **1** : an injurious, unfair, or unjust act **2** : a violation of the legal rights of another person **3** : something that is wrong : wrong principles, practices, or conduct ⟨know right from ~⟩ **4** : the state, position, or fact of being wrong

²wrong *adj* **wrong·er** \'ròŋ-ər\; **wrong·est** \'ròŋ-əst\ **1** : SINFUL, IMMORAL **2** : not right according to a standard or code : IMPROPER **3** : INCORRECT ⟨a ~ solution⟩ **4** : UNSATISFACTORY **5** : UNSUITABLE, INAPPROPRIATE **6** : constituting a surface that is considered the back, bottom, inside, or reverse of something ⟨iron only on the ~ side of the fabric⟩ ✦ *Synonyms* FALSE, ERRONEOUS, INCORRECT, INACCURATE, UNTRUE — **wrong·ly** *adv*

³wrong *adv* **1** : INCORRECTLY **2** : in a wrong direction, manner, or relation

⁴wrong *vb* **wronged; wrong·ing** \'ròŋ-iŋ\ **1** : to do wrong to : INJURE, HARM **2** : to treat unjustly : DISHONOR, MALIGN ✦ *Synonyms* OPPRESS, PERSECUTE, AGGRIEVE

wrong·do·er \'ròŋ-,dü-ər\ *n* : a person who does wrong and esp. moral wrong — **wrong·do·ing** \-,dü-iŋ\ *n*

wrong·ful \'ròŋ-fəl\ *adj* **1** : WRONG, UNJUST **2** : UNLAWFUL — **wrong·ful·ly** *adv* — **wrong·ful·ness** *n*

wrong·head·ed \-'he-dəd\ *adj* : stubborn in clinging to wrong opinion or principles — **wrong·head·ed·ly** *adv* — **wrong·head·ed·ness** *n*

wrote *past of* WRITE

wroth \'ròth, 'rōth\ *adj* : filled with wrath : ANGRY

wrought \'ròt\ *adj* [ME, fr. pp. of *worken* to work] **1** : FASHIONED, FORMED ⟨carefully ~ essays⟩ **2** : ORNAMENTED **3** : beaten into shape by tools : HAMMERED ⟨~ metals⟩ **4** : deeply stirred : EXCITED ⟨gets easily ~ up⟩

wrung *past and past part of* WRING

wry \'rī\ *adj* **wry·er** \'rī-ər\; **wry·est** \'rī-əst\ **1** : having a bent or twisted shape ⟨a ~ smile⟩; *also* : turned abnormally to one side : CONTORTED ⟨a ~ neck⟩ **2**

: cleverly and often ironically humorous — **wry·ly** adv — **wry·ness** n

wry·neck \'rī-ˌnek\ n **1** : either of two Old World woodpeckers that differ from typical woodpeckers in having a peculiar manner of twisting the head and neck **2** : an abnormal twisting of the neck and head to one side caused by muscle spasms

WSW abbr west-southwest

wt abbr weight

wurst \'wərst, 'wurst\ n : SAUSAGE

wuss \'wus\ n : WIMP — **wussy** \'wu-sē\ adj

WV or **W Va** abbr West Virginia

WW abbr World War

w/w abbr wall-to-wall

WY or **Wyo** abbr Wyoming

WYS·I·WYG \'wi-zē-ˌwig\ adj [what you see is what you get] : of, relating to, or being a computer display that shows a document exactly as it will appear when printed out

¹x \'eks\ n, pl **x's** or **xs** \'ek-səz\ often cap **1** : the 24th letter of the English alphabet **2** : an unknown quantity

²x vb **x-ed** also **x'd** or **xed** \'ekst\; **x-ing** or **x'ing** \'ek-siŋ\ : to cancel or obliterate with a series of x's — usu. used with out

³x abbr **1** ex **2** experimental **3** extra

⁴x symbol **1** times ⟨3 x 2 is 6⟩ **2** by ⟨a 3 x 5 index card⟩ **3** often cap power of magnification

Xan·a·du \'za-nə-ˌdü, -ˌdyü\ n [fr. Xanadu, locality in Kubla Khan (1798), poem by Eng. poet Samuel Taylor Coleridge †1834] : an idyllic, exotic, or luxurious place

Xan·thip·pe \zan-'thi-pē, -'ti-\ or **Xan·tip·pe** \-'ti-pē\ n [Gk Xanthippē, shrewish wife of Socrates] : an ill-tempered woman

x-ax·is \'eks-ˌak-səs\ n : the axis of a graph or of a system of coordinates in a plane parallel to which abscissas are measured

X–C abbr cross-country

X chromosome n : a sex chromosome that usu. occurs paired in each female cell and single in each male cell in organisms (as humans) in which the male normally has two unlike sex chromosomes

Xe symbol xenon

xe·non \'zē-ˌnän, 'ze-\ n [Gk, neut. of xenos strange] : a heavy gaseous chemical element occurring in minute quantities in air

xe·no·pho·bia \ˌze-nə-'fō-bē-ə, ˌzē-\ n : fear and hatred of strangers or foreigners or of what is strange or foreign — **xe·no·phobe** \'ze-nə-ˌfōb, 'zē-\ n — **xe·no·pho·bic** \ˌze-nə-'fō-bik, ˌzē-\ adj

xe·ric \'zir-ik, 'zer-\ adj : characterized by or requiring only a small amount of moisture ⟨a ~ habitat⟩

xeri·scape \'zir-ə-ˌskāp, 'zer-\ n, often cap : a landscaping method utilizing water-conserving techniques

xe·rog·ra·phy \zə-'rä-grə-fē\ n : a process

for copying printed matter by the action of light on an electrically charged surface in which the latent image is developed with a powder — **xe·ro·graph·ic** \ˌzir-ə-'gra-fik\ adj

xe·ro·phyte \'zir-ə-ˌfīt\ n : a plant adapted for growth with a limited water supply — **xe·ro·phyt·ic** \ˌzir-ə-'fi-tik\ adj

xi \'zī, 'ksī\ n : the 14th letter of the Greek alphabet — Ξ or ξ

XL abbr **1** extra large **2** extra long

Xmas \'kris-məs also 'eks-məs\ n [X (symbol for Christ, fr. the Gk letter chi (X), initial of Christos Christ) + -mas (in Christmas)] : CHRISTMAS

XML \ˌeks-(ˌ)em-'el\ n : a markup language that indicates the structural type of data

XO abbr executive officer

x-ra·di·a·tion \ˌeks-ˌrā-dē-'ā-shən\ n, often cap **1** : exposure to X-rays **2** : radiation consisting of X-rays

x-ray \'eks-ˌrā\ vb, often cap : to examine, treat, or photograph with X-rays

X-ray \'eks-ˌrā\ n **1** : a radiation with an extremely short wavelength of less than 100 angstroms that is able to penetrate through various thicknesses of solids and to act on photographic film **2** : a photograph taken with X-rays — **X-ray** adj

XS abbr extra small

xu \'sü\ n, pl **xu** — see dong at MONEY table

xy·lem \'zī-ləm, -ˌlem\ n : a woody tissue of vascular plants that transports water and dissolved materials upward, functions in support and storage, and lies central to the phloem

xy·lo·phone \'zī-lə-ˌfōn\ n [Gk xylon wood + phōnē voice, sound] : a musical instrument consisting of a series of wooden bars graduated in length to produce the musical scale, supported on belts of straw or felt, and sounded by striking with two small wooden hammers — **xy·lo·phon·ist** \-ˌfō-nist\ n

¹y \'wī\ *n, pl* y's *or* ys \'wīz\ *often cap* : the 25th letter of the English alphabet

²y *abbr* 1 yard 2 year

¹Y \'wī\ *n* : YMCA, YWCA

²Y *symbol* yttrium

¹-y *also* -ey \ē\ *adj suffix* 1 : characterized by : full of ⟨dirty⟩ ⟨clayey⟩ 2 : having the character of : composed of ⟨icy⟩ 3 : like : like that of ⟨homey⟩ ⟨wintry⟩ ⟨stagy⟩ 4 : tending or inclined to ⟨sleepy⟩ ⟨chatty⟩ 5 : giving occasion for (specified) action ⟨teary⟩ 6 : performing (specified) action ⟨curly⟩

²-y \ē\ *n suffix, pl* -ies 1 : state : condition : quality ⟨beggary⟩ 2 : activity, place of business, or goods dealt with ⟨laundry⟩ 3 : whole body or group ⟨soldiery⟩

³-y *n suffix, pl* -ies : instance of a (specified) action ⟨entreaty⟩ ⟨inquiry⟩

YA *abbr* young adult

¹yacht \'yät\ *n* [obs. D *jaght*, fr. Middle Low German *jacht*, short for *jachtschip*, lit., hunting ship] : a usu. large recreational watercraft

²yacht *vb* : to race or cruise in a yacht

yacht·ing \'yä-tiŋ\ *n* : the sport of racing or cruising in a yacht

yachts·man \'yäts-mən\ *n* : a person who owns or sails a yacht

ya·hoo \'yā-hü, 'yä-\ *n, pl* yahoos [fr. *Yahoo*, one of a race of brutes having the form of men in Jonathan Swift's *Gulliver's Travels*] : a boorish, crass, or stupid person

Yah·weh \'yä-,wā\ *also* Yah·veh \-,vä\ *n* : GOD 1 — used esp. by the Hebrews

¹yak \'yak\ *n, pl* yaks *also* yak : a large long-haired wild or domesticated ox of Tibet and adjacent Asian uplands

²yak *also* yack \'yak\ *n* : persistent or voluble talk — yak *also* yack *vb*

yam \'yam\ *n* 1 : the edible starchy root of various twining plants used as a staple food in tropical areas; *also* : a plant that produces yams 2 : a usu. deep orange sweet potato

yam·mer \'ya-mər\ *vb* [ME *yameren*, alter. of *yomeren* to murmur, be sad, fr. OE *gēomran*] 1 : WHIMPER 2 : CHATTER — yammer *n*

¹yank \'yaŋk\ *vb* : to pull with a quick vigorous movement

²yank *n* : a strong sudden pull : JERK

Yank \'yaŋk\ *n* : YANKEE

Yan·kee \'yaŋ-kē\ *n* 1 : a native or inhabitant of New England; *also* : a native or inhabitant of the northern U.S. 2 : AMERICAN 2

yan·qui \'yäŋ-kē\ *n, often cap* [Sp] : a citizen of the U.S. as distinguished from a Latin American

¹yap \'yap\ *vb* yapped; yap·ping 1 : BARK, YELP 2 : GAB

²yap *n* 1 : a quick sharp bark 2 : CHATTER

¹yard \'yärd\ *n* [ME, fr. OE *geard* enclosure, yard] 1 : a small enclosed area open to the sky and adjacent to a building 2 : the grounds of a building 3 : the grounds surrounding a house usu. covered with grass 4 : an enclosure for livestock 5 : an area set aside for a particular business or activity 6 : a system of railroad tracks for storing cars and making up trains

²yard *n* [ME *yarde*, fr. OE *gierd* twig, measure, yard] 1 — see WEIGHT table 2 : a long spar tapered toward the ends that supports and spreads the head of a sail — the whole nine yards : all of a set of circumstances, conditions, or details

yard·age \'yär-dij\ *n* : an aggregate number of yards; *also* : the length, extent, or volume of something as measured in yards

yard·arm \'yärd-,ärm\ *n* : either end of the yard of a square-rigged ship

yard·man \-mən, -,man\ *n* : a person employed in or about a yard

yard·mas·ter \-,mas-tər\ *n* : the person in charge of a railroad yard

yard·stick \-,stik\ *n* 1 : a graduated measuring stick three feet long 2 : a standard for making a critical judgment : CRITERION ♦ Synonyms GAUGE, TOUCHSTONE, BENCHMARK, MEASURE

yar·mul·ke \'yä-mə-kə, 'yär-, -məl-\ *n* [Yiddish *yarmlke*] : a skullcap worn esp. by Jewish males in the synagogue and the home

yarn \'yärn\ *n* 1 : a continuous often plied strand composed of fibers or filaments and used in weaving and knitting to form cloth 2 : STORY; *esp* : a tall tale

yar·row \'ya-rō\ *n* : a strong-scented herb related to the daisies that has white or pink flowers in flat clusters

yaw \'yo\ *vb* : to deviate erratically from a course ⟨the ship ~ed in the heavy seas⟩ — yaw *n*

yawl \'yol\ *n* : a 2-masted sailboat with the shorter mast aft of the rudder

¹yawn \'yon\ *vb* : to open wide; *esp* : to open the mouth wide and take a deep breath usu. as an involuntary reaction to fatigue or boredom — yawn·er *n*

²yawn *n* : the act of yawning

yawp *or* yaup \'yop\ *vb* 1 : to make a raucous noise : SQUAWK 2 : CLAMOR, COMPLAIN — yawp·er *n*

yaws \'yoz\ *n pl* : a contagious tropical disease caused by a spirochete closely resembling the causative agent of syphilis and marked by skin lesions

y-ax·is \'wī-,ak-səs\ *n* : the axis of a graph or of a system of coordinates in a plane parallel to which the ordinates are measured

Yb *symbol* ytterbium

YB *abbr* yearbook

Y chromosome *n* : a sex chromosome that is characteristic of male cells in organisms (as humans) in which the male typically has two unlike sex chromosomes

yd abbr yard

¹ye \'yē\ pron : YOU 1

²ye \yē, yə, originally same as THE\ definite article, archaic : THE — used by early printers to represent the manuscript word þe (the)

¹yea \'yā\ adv 1 : YES — used in oral voting 2 : INDEED, TRULY

²yea n : an affirmative vote; also : a person casting such a vote

yeah \'yeə, 'yaə\ adv : YES

year \'yir\ n 1 : the period of about 365¼ solar days required for one revolution of the earth around the sun; also : the time in which a planet completes a revolution about the sun 2 : a cycle of 365 or 366 days beginning with January 1; also : a calendar year specified usu. by a number 3 pl : a time of special significance ⟨their glory ∼s⟩ 4 pl : AGE ⟨advanced in ∼s⟩ 5 : a period of time other than a calendar year ⟨the school ∼⟩

year·book \-ˌbŭk\ n 1 : a book published annually esp. as a report 2 : a school publication recording the history and activities of a graduating class

year·ling \'yir-liŋ, 'yər-lən\ n 1 : one that is a year old 2 : a racehorse between January of the year after the year in which it was born and the next January

year·long \'yir-'lȯŋ\ adj : lasting through a year

¹year·ly \'yir-lē\ adj : ANNUAL

²yearly adv : every year

yearn \'yərn\ vb 1 : to feel a longing or craving 2 : to feel tenderness or compassion ♦ Synonyms LONG, PINE, HANKER, HUNGER, THIRST

yearn·ing n : a tender or urgent longing

year–round \'yir-'raùnd\ adj : effective, employed, or operating for the full year : not seasonal ⟨a ∼ resort⟩

yeast \'yēst\ n, 1 : a surface froth or a sediment in sugary liquids (as fruit juices) that consists largely of cells of a tiny fungus and is used in making alcoholic liquors and as a leaven in baking 2 : a commercial product containing yeast fungi in a moist or dry medium 3 : a minute one-celled fungus present and functionally active in yeast that reproduces by budding; also : any of several similar fungi 4 archaic : the foam of waves : SPUME 5 : something that causes ferment or activity

yeast infection n : infection of the vagina with an excess growth of a normally present fungus that resembles a yeast

yeasty \'yē-stē\ adj yeast·i·er; -est 1 : of, relating to, or resembling yeast 2 : UNSETTLED 3 : full of vitality; also : FRIVOLOUS

yegg \'yeg\ n : one that breaks open safes to steal; also : ROBBER

¹yell \'yel\ vb : to utter a loud cry or scream : SHOUT — **yell·er** n

²yell n 1 : SHOUT 2 : a cheer used esp. to encourage an athletic team (as at a college)

¹yel·low \'ye-lō\ adj 1 : of the color yellow 2 : having a yellow complexion or skin 3 : SENSATIONAL ⟨∼ journalism⟩ 4 : COWARDLY — **yel·low·ish** \'ye-lə-wish\ adj

²yellow n 1 : a color between green and orange in the spectrum : the color of ripe lemons or sunflowers 2 : something yellow; esp : the yolk of an egg 3 pl : any of several plant diseases marked by stunted growth and yellowing of foliage

³yellow vb : to make or turn yellow

yellow birch n : a No. American birch with thin lustrous gray or yellow bark; also : its strong hard wood

yellow fever n : an acute infectious viral disease marked by prostration, jaundice, fever, and often hemorrhage and transmitted by a mosquito

yellow jack n : YELLOW FEVER

yellow jacket n : any of various small social wasps having the body barred with bright yellow

yel·low·tail \'ye-lō-ˌtāl\ n : any of various fishes with a yellow or yellowish tail including several valuable food fishes

yelp \'yelp\ vb [ME, to boast, cry out, fr. OE gielpan to boast, exult] : to utter a sharp quick shrill cry — **yelp** n

Ye·me·ni \'ye-mə-nē\ n : YEMENITE — **Yemeni** adj

Ye·men·ite \'ye-mə-ˌnīt\ n : a native or inhabitant of Yemen — **Yemenite** adj

¹yen \'yen\ n, pl yen — see MONEY table

²yen n [obs. E argot yen-yen craving for opium, fr. Chin (Guangdong dial.) yīn= yáhn, fr. yīn opium + yáhn craving] : a strong desire : LONGING

yeo·man \'yō-mən\ n 1 : an attendant or officer in a royal or noble household 2 : a naval petty officer who performs clerical duties 3 : a person who owns and cultivates a small farm; esp : one of a class of English freeholders below the gentry — **yeo·man·ly** \-lē\ adj

yeo·man·ry \-rē\ n : the body of yeomen and esp. of small landed proprietors

-yer — see -ER

¹yes \'yes\ adv — used as a function word esp. to express assent or agreement or to introduce a more emphatic or explicit phrase

²yes n : an affirmative reply

ye·shi·va also **ye·shi·vah** \yə-'shē-və\ n, pl yeshivas or ye·shi·voth \-ˌshē-'vōt, -'vōth\ : a Jewish school esp. for religious instruction

yes–man \'yes-ˌman\ n : a person who endorses uncritically every opinion or proposal of a superior

¹yes·ter·day \'yes-tər-dē, -ˌdā\ adv 1 : on the day preceding today 2 : only a short time ago

²yesterday n 1 : the day last past 2 : time not long past

yes·ter·year \'yes-tər-ˌyir\ n 1 : last year 2 : the recent past

¹yet \'yet\ adv 1 : in addition : BESIDES; also : EVEN 6 2 : up to now; also : STILL 3 : so soon as now ⟨not time to go ∼⟩ 4 : EVENTUALLY 5 : NEVERTHELESS, HOWEVER

²**yet** *conj* : but nevertheless : BUT

ye·ti \'ye-tē, 'yā-\ *n* : ABOMINABLE SNOWMAN

yew \'yü\ *n* **1** : any of a genus of evergreen trees and shrubs with dark stiff poisonous needles and fleshy fruits **2** : the wood of a yew; *esp* : that of an Old World yew

Yid·dish \'yi-dish\ *n* [Yiddish *yidish,* short for *yidish daytsh,* lit., Jewish German] : a language derived from medieval German and spoken by Jews esp. of eastern European origin — **Yiddish** *adj*

¹**yield** \'yēld\ *vb* **1** : to give as fitting, owed, or required **2** : GIVE UP; *esp* : to give up possession of on claim or demand **3** : to bear as a natural product **4** : PRODUCE, SUPPLY **5** : to bring in : RETURN **6** : to give way (as to force or influence) **7** : to give place ♦ *Synonyms* RELINQUISH, CEDE, WAIVE, SURRENDER

²**yield** *n* : something yielded; *esp* : the amount or quantity produced or returned

yield·ing \'yēl-diŋ\ *adj* **1** : not rigid or stiff : FLEXIBLE **2** : SUBMISSIVE, COMPLIANT

yikes \'yīks\ *interj* — used to express fear or astonishment

yip \'yip\ *vb* **yipped; yip·ping** : YAP

YK *abbr* Yukon Territory

YMCA \,wī-,em-(,)sē-'ā\ *n* : Young Men's Christian Association

YMHA \,wī-,em-,āch-'ā\ *n* : Young Men's Hebrew Association

yo \'yō\ *interj* — used to call attention, indicate attentiveness, or express affirmation

YOB *abbr* year of birth

yo·del \'yō-dəl\ *vb* **yo·deled** *or* **yo·delled; yo·del·ing** *or* **yo·del·ling** : to sing by suddenly changing from chest voice to falsetto and back; *also* : to shout or call in this manner — **yodel** *n* — **yo·del·er** *n*

yo·ga \'yō-gə\ *n* [Skt, lit., yoking, fr. *yunakti* he yokes] **1** *cap* : a Hindu theistic philosophy teaching the suppression of all activity of body, mind, and will in order that the self may realize its distinction from them and attain liberation **2** : a system of exercises for attaining bodily or mental control and well-being — **yo·gic** \-gik\ *adj, often cap*

yo·gi \'yō-gē\ *also* **yo·gin** \-gən, -,gin\ *n* **1** : a person who practices yoga **2** *cap* : an adherent of the Yoga philosophy

yo·gurt *also* **yo·ghurt** \'yō-gərt\ *n* [Turk *yoğurt*] : a soured slightly acid often flavored semisolid food made of milk and milk solids to which cultures of bacteria have been added

¹**yoke** \'yōk\ *n, pl* **yokes** **1** : a wooden bar or frame by which two draft animals (as oxen) are coupled at the heads or necks for working together; *also* : a frame fitted to a person's shoulders to carry a load in two equal portions **2** : a clamp that embraces two parts to hold or unite them in position **3** *pl usu* **yoke** : two animals yoked together **4** : SERVITUDE, BONDAGE **5** : TIE, LINK ⟨the ~ of matrimo-

ny⟩ **6** : a fitted or shaped piece esp. at the shoulder of a garment ♦ *Synonyms* COUPLE, PAIR, BRACE

²**yoke** *vb* **yoked; yok·ing** **1** : to put a yoke on : couple with a yoke **2** : to attach a draft animal to ⟨~ a plow⟩ **3** : JOIN; *esp* : MARRY

yo·kel \'yō-kəl\ *n* : a naive or gullible country person

yolk \'yōk\ *n* **1** : the yellow rounded inner mass of the egg of a bird or reptile **2** : the stored food material of an egg that supplies nutrients (as proteins and cholesterol) to the developing embryo — **yolked** \'yōkt\ *adj*

Yom Kip·pur \,yōm-ki-'pu̇r, ,yäm-, -'ki-pər\ *n* [Heb *yōm kippūr,* lit., day of atonement] : a Jewish holiday observed in September or October with fasting and prayer as a day of atonement

¹**yon** \'yän\ *adj* : YONDER

²**yon** *adv* **1** : YONDER **2** : THITHER ⟨ran hither and ~⟩

¹**yon·der** \'yän-dər\ *adv* : at or to that place

²**yonder** *adj* **1** : more distant ⟨the ~ side of the river⟩ **2** : being at a distance within view ⟨~ hills⟩

yore \'yȯr\ *n* [ME, fr. *yore,* adv., long ago, fr. OE *geāra,* fr. *gēar* year] : time long past ⟨in days of ~⟩

York·ie \'yȯr-kē\ *n* : YORKSHIRE TERRIER

York·shire terrier \'yȯrk-,shir-, -shər-\ *n* : any of a breed of compact toy terriers with long straight silky hair

you \'yü\ *pron* **1** : the person or persons addressed ⟨~ are a nice person⟩ ⟨~ are nice people⟩ **2** : ONE **2** ⟨~ turn this knob to open it⟩

¹**young** \'yəŋ\ *adj* **youn·ger** \'yəŋ-gər\; **youn·gest** \'yəŋ-gəst\ **1** : being in the first or an early stage of life, growth, or development **2** : having little experience **3** : recently come into being **4** : YOUTHFUL **5** *cap* : belonging to or representing a new or revived usu. political group or movement — **young·ish** \'yəŋ-ish\ *adj*

²**young** *n, pl* **young** : young persons; *also* : young animals

young·ling \'yəŋ-liŋ\ *n* : one that is young — **youngling** *adj*

young·ster \-stər\ *n* **1** : a young person **2** : CHILD

your \'yu̇r, 'yȯr, yər\ *adj* : of or relating to you or yourself

yours \'yu̇rz, 'yȯrz\ *pron* : one or the ones belonging to you

your·self \yər-'self\ *pron, pl* **yourselves** \-'selvz\ : YOU — used reflexively, for emphasis, or in absolute constructions ⟨you'll hurt ~⟩ ⟨do it ~⟩

youth \'yüth\ *n, pl* **youths** \'yüthz, 'yüths\ **1** : the period of life between childhood and maturity **2** : a young man; *also* : young persons **3** : YOUTHFULNESS

youth·ful \'yüth-fəl\ *adj* **1** : of, relating to, or appropriate to youth **2** : being young and not yet mature **3** : FRESH, VIGOROUS — **youth·ful·ly** *adv* — **youth·ful·ness** *n*

youth hostel *n* : HOSTEL 2

yowl \'yaủ(-ə)l\ *vb* : to utter a loud long mournful cry : WAIL — **yowl** *n*

yo-yo \'yō-(,)yō\ *n, pl* **yo-yos** [prob. fr. Ilocano (a Philippine language) *yóyó*] : a thick grooved double disk with a string attached to its center that is made to fall and rise to the hand by unwinding and rewinding on the string — **yo-yo** *vb*

yr *abbr* **1** year **2** your

yrbk *abbr* yearbook

YT *abbr* Yukon Territory

yt-ter-bi-um \i-'tər-bē-əm\ *n* : a rare metallic chemical element

yt-tri-um \'i-trē-əm\ *n* : a rare metallic chemical element

yu-an \'yü-ən, yü-'än\ *n, pl* **yuan 1** — see MONEY table **2** : the dollar of the Republic of China (Taiwan)

yuc-ca \'yə-kə\ *n* : any of a genus of plants related to the agaves that grow esp. in warm dry regions and bear large clusters of white cup-shaped flowers atop a long stiff stalk

yuck *also* **yuk** \'yək\ *interj* — used to express rejection or disgust

yule \'yül\ *n, often cap* : CHRISTMAS

Yule log *n* : a large log formerly put on the hearth on Christmas Eve as the foundation of the fire

yule-tide \'yül-,tīd\ *n, often cap* : CHRISTMASTIDE

yum-my \'yə-mē\ *adj* **yum-mi-er; -est** : highly attractive or pleasing

yup-pie \'yə-pē\ *n* [prob. fr. *y*oung *u*rban *p*rofessional + *-ie* (as in hippie)] : a young college-educated adult employed in a well-paying profession and living and working in or near a large city — **yup-pie-dom** \-dəm\ *n*

yurt \'yủrt\ *n* : a light round tent of skins or felt stretched over a lattice framework used by pastoral peoples of inner Asia

YWCA \,wī-,də-bəl-yü-(,)sē-'ā\ *n* : Young Women's Christian Association

YWHA \-,äch-'ā\ *n* : Young Women's Hebrew Association

¹z \'zē\ *n, pl* **z's** *or* **zs** \'zēz\ *often cap* : the 26th letter of the English alphabet

²z *abbr* **1** zero **2** zone

Z *symbol* atomic number

Zach *abbr* Zacharias

Zach-a-ri-as \,zak-ə-'rī-əs\ *n* : ZECHARIAH

¹za-ny \'zā-nē\ *n, pl* **zanies** [It *zanni*, a traditional masked clown, fr. It dial. *Zanni*, nickname for It *Giovanni* John] **1** : CLOWN, BUFFOON **2** : a silly or foolish person

²zany *adj* **za-ni-er; -est 1** : characteristic of a zany **2** : CRAZY, FOOLISH ⟨a ~ movie⟩ — **za-ni-ly** \'zā-nə-lē\ *adv* — **za-ni-ness** \'zā-nē-nəs\ *n*

zap \'zap\ *vb* **zapped; zap-ping 1** : DESTROY, KILL **2** : to irradiate esp. with microwaves

zeal \'zēl\ *n* : eager and ardent interest in the pursuit of something : FERVOR
◆ **Synonyms** ENTHUSIASM, PASSION, ARDOR

zeal-ot \'ze-lət\ *n* : a zealous person; *esp* : a fanatical partisan ⟨a religious ~⟩
◆ **Synonyms** ENTHUSIAST, BIGOT

zeal-ous \'ze-ləs\ *adj* : filled with, characterized by, or due to zeal — **zeal-ous-ly** *adv* — **zeal-ous-ness** *n*

ze-bra \'zē-brə\ *n, pl* **zebras** *also* **zebra** : any of several African mammals related to the horse but conspicuously striped with black or dark brown and white or buff

zebra mussel *n* : a freshwater Eurasian mollusk introduced into U.S. waterways where it colonizes and clogs water intake pipes

ze-bu \'zē-bü, -byü\ *n* : any of various breeds of domestic oxen developed in India that have a large fleshy hump over the shoulders, a dewlap, drooping ears,

and marked resistance to heat and to insect attack

Zech *abbr* Zechariah

Zech-a-ri-ah \,zek-ə-'rī-ə\ *n* — see BIBLE table

zed \'zed\ *n, chiefly Brit* : the letter *z*

zeit-geist \'tsīt-,gīst, 'zīt-\ *n* [G, fr. *Zeit* time + *Geist* spirit] : the general intellectual, moral, and cultural state of an era

Zen \'zen\ *n* : a Japanese Buddhist sect that teaches self-discipline, meditation, and attainment of enlightenment through direct intuitive insight

ze-na-na \zə-'nä-nə\ *n* : HAREM

ze-nith \'zē-nəth\ *n* **1** : the point in the heavens directly overhead **2** : the highest point : ACME ⟨the ~ of her career⟩
◆ **Synonyms** CULMINATION, PINNACLE, APEX

ze-o-lite \'zē-ə-,līt\ *n* : any of various feldsparlike silicates used esp. as water softeners

Zeph *abbr* Zephaniah

Zeph-a-ni-ah \,zef-ə-'nī-ə\ *n* — see BIBLE table

zeph-yr \'ze-fər\ *n* : a breeze from the west; *also* : a gentle breeze

zep-pe-lin \'ze-plən, -pə-lən\ *n* [Count Ferdinand von *Zeppelin* †1917 Ger. airship manufacturer] : a cylindrical rigid blimplike airship

¹ze-ro \'zē-rō, 'zir-ō\ *n, pl* **zeros** *also* **ze-roes** [ultim. fr. Ar *şifr*] **1** : the numerical symbol 0 : the number represented by the symbol 0 **3** : the point at which the graduated degrees or measurements on a scale (as of a thermometer) begin **4** : the lowest point

²zero *adj* **1** : of, relating to, or being a zero **2** : having no magnitude or quantity **3** : ABSENT, LACKING; *esp* : having no modified inflectional form

³**zero** *vb* : to adjust the sights of a firearm to hit the point aimed at — usu. used with *in*

zero hour *n* : the time at which an event (as a military operation) is scheduled to begin

zest \'zest\ *n* **1** : a quality of enhancing enjoyment : PIQUANCY **2** : keen enjoyment : GUSTO — **zest·ful** \-fəl\ *adj* — **zest·ful·ly** *adv* — **zest·ful·ness** *n* — **zesty** \'zes-tē\ *adj*

ze·ta \'zā-tə, 'zē-\ *n* : the 6th letter of the Greek alphabet — Z or ζ

zi·do·vu·dine \zi-'dō-vyü-,dēn\ *n* : AZT

¹**zig·zag** \'zig-,zag\ *n* : one of a series of short sharp turns, angles, or alterations in a course; *also* : something marked by such a series

²**zigzag** *adj* : in or by a zigzag path

³**zigzag** *adj* : having short sharp turns or angles

⁴**zigzag** *vb* **zig·zagged; zig·zag·ging** : to form into or proceed along a zigzag

zil·lion \'zil-yən\ *n* : a large indeterminate number

zinc \'ziŋk\ *n* : a bluish-white metallic chemical element that is commonly found in minerals and is used esp. in alloys and as a protective coating for iron and steel

zinc oxide *n* : a white solid used esp. as a pigment, in compounding rubber, and in ointments and sunblocks

zine \'zēn\ *n* : a noncommercial publication usu. devoted to specialized subject matter

zin·fan·del \'zin-fən-,del\ *n, often cap* : a dry red table wine made chiefly in California

zing \'ziŋ\ *n* **1** : a shrill humming noise **2** : VITALITY **4** — **zing** *vb*

zing·er \'ziŋ-ər\ *n* : a pointed witty remark or retort

zin·nia \'zi-nē-ə, 'zēn-yə\ *n* : any of a genus of tropical American herbs or low shrubs related to the daisies and widely grown for their showy long-lasting flowers

Zi·on \'zī-ən\ *n* **1** : the Jewish people **2** : the Jewish homeland as a symbol of Judaism or of Jewish national aspiration **3** : HEAVEN **4** : UTOPIA

Zi·on·ism \'zī-ə-,ni-zəm\ *n* : an international movement orig. for the establishment of a Jewish national or religious community in Palestine and later for the support of modern Israel — **Zi·on·ist** \-nist\ *adj or n*

¹**zip** \'zip\ *vb* **zipped; zip·ping** : to move, act, or function with speed or vigor

²**zip** *n* **1** : a sudden sharp hissing sound **2** : ENERGY, VIM

³**zip** *n* : NOTHING, ZERO ⟨the score was 27 to ∼⟩

⁴**zip** *vb* **zipped; zip·ping** : to close or open with a zipper

zip code *n, often cap Z&I&P* [*zone improvement* *p*lan] : a number that identifies each postal delivery area in the U.S.

zip·per \'zi-pər\ *n* : a fastener consisting of two rows of metal or plastic teeth on strips of tape and a sliding piece that closes an opening by drawing the teeth together

zip·py \'zi-pē\ *adj* **zip·pi·er; -est 1** : very speedy ⟨a ∼ car⟩ **2** : strikingly appealing ⟨∼ clothes⟩

zir·con \'zər-,kän\ *n* : a zirconium-containing mineral transparent varieties of which are used as gems

zir·co·ni·um \,zər-'kō-nē-əm\ *n* : a gray corrosion-resistant metallic chemical element used esp. in alloys and ceramics

zit \'zit\ *n* : PIMPLE

zith·er \'zi-thər, -thər\ *n* : a musical instrument having 30 to 40 strings played with plectrum and fingers

zi·ti \'zē-tē\ *n, pl* **ziti** [It] : medium-size tubular pasta

zlo·ty \'zlȯ-tē\ *n, pl* **zlo·tys** \-tēz\ *or* **zloty** — see MONEY table

Zn *symbol* zinc

zo·di·ac \'zō-dē-,ak\ *n* [ME, fr. AF, fr. L *zodiacus*, fr. Gk *zōidiakos*, fr. *zōidion* carved figure, sign of the zodiac, fr. dim. of *zōion* living being, figure] **1** : an imaginary belt in the heavens that encompasses the paths of most of the planets and is divided into 12 constellations or ,signs **2** : a figure representing the signs of the zodiac and their symbols — **zo·di·a·cal** \zō-'dī-ə-kəl\ *adj*

zom·bie *also* **zom·bi** \'zäm-bē\ *n* : a person who is believed to have died and been brought back to life without speech or free will

zon·al \'zō-nᵊl\ *adj* : of, relating to, or having the form of a zone — **zon·al·ly** *adv*

¹**zone** \'zōn\ *n* [ME, fr. AF, fr. L *zona* belt, zone, fr. Gk *zōnē*] **1** : any of five great divisions of the earth's surface made according to latitude and temperature including the torrid zone, two temperate zones, and two frigid zones **2** : something that forms an encircling band ⟨a ∼ of tissue⟩ **3** : a region or area set off as distinct from surrounding parts ⟨business ∼⟩ ⟨postal ∼⟩

²**zone** *vb* **zoned; zon·ing 1** : ENCIRCLE **2** : to arrange in or mark off into zones; *esp* : to divide (as a city) into sections reserved for different purposes

zonked \'zäŋkt\ *adj* : being or acting as if under the influence of alcohol or a drug : HIGH

zoo \'zü\ *n, pl* **zoos** : a park where wild animals are kept for exhibition

zoo·ge·og·ra·phy \,zō-ə-jē-'ä-grə-fē\ *n* : a branch of biogeography concerned with the geographical distribution of animals — **zoo·ge·og·ra·pher** \-fər\ *n* — **zoo·geo·graph·ic** \-,jē-ə-'gra-fik\ *also* **zoo·geo·graph·i·cal** \-fi-kəl\ *adj*

zoo·keep·er \'zü-,kē-pər\ *n* : a person who cares for animals in a zoo

zool *abbr* zoological; zoology

zoological garden *n* : ZOO

zo·ol·o·gy \zō-'ä-lə-jē\ *n* : a branch of biology that deals with the classification and the properties and vital phenomena of animals — **zo·o·log·i·cal** \ˌzō-ə-'lä-ji-kəl\ adj — **zo·ol·o·gist** \zō-'ä-lə-jist\ n

zoom \'züm\ vb **1** : to move with a loud hum or buzz **2** : to gain altitude quickly **3** : to focus a camera or microscope using a special lens that permits the apparent distance of the object to be varied — **zoom** n

zoom lens n : a camera lens in which the image size can be varied continuously while the image remains in focus

zoo·mor·phic \ˌzō-ə-'mȯr-fik\ adj **1** : having the form of an animal **2** : of, relating to, or being the representation of a deity in the form or with the attributes of an animal

zoo·plank·ton \ˌzō-ə-'plaŋk-tən, -ˌtän\ n : plankton composed of animals

zoo·spore \'zō-ə-ˌspȯr\ n : a motile spore

zoot suit \'züt-\ n : a flashy suit of extreme cut typically consisting of a thigh-length jacket with wide padded shoulders and pants that are wide at the top and narrow at the bottom — **zoot-suit·er** \-ˌsü-tər\ n

Zo·ro·as·tri·an·ism \ˌzȯr-ə-'was-trē-ə-ˌni-zəm\ n : a religion founded by the Persian prophet Zoroaster — **Zo·ro·as·tri·an** \-trē-ən\ adj or n

zounds \'zaúndz\ interj [euphemism for God's wounds] — used as a mild oath

zoy·sia \'zȯi-shə, -zhə, -sē-ə, -zē-ə\ n : any of a genus of creeping perennial grasses having fine wiry leaves and including some used as lawn grasses

ZPG abbr zero population growth

Zr symbol zirconium

zuc·chet·to \zü-'ke-tō, tsü-\ n, pl **-tos** [It] : a small round skullcap worn by Roman Catholic ecclesiastics

zuc·chi·ni \zü-'kē-nē\ n, pl **-ni** or **-nis** [It] : a smooth cylindrical usu. dark green summer squash; also : a plant that bears zucchini

Zu·lu \'zü-ˌlü\ n, pl **Zulu** or **Zulus** : a member of a Bantu-speaking people of South Africa; also : the Bantu language of the Zulus

Zu·ni \'zü-nē\ or **Zu·ñi** \-nyē\ n, pl **Zuni** or **Zunis** or **Zuñi** or **Zuñis** : a member of an American Indian people of western New Mexico; also : the language of the Zuni people

zwie·back \'swē-ˌbak, 'swī-, 'zwē-, 'zwī-, -ˌbäk\ n [G, lit., twice baked, fr. zwie- twice + backen to bake] : a usu. sweetened bread that is baked and then sliced and toasted until dry and crisp

Zwing·li·an \'zwiŋ-glē-ən, 'swiŋ-, -lē-; 'tsfiŋ-lē-\ adj : of or relating to the Swiss religious reformer Ulrich Zwingli or his teachings — **Zwinglian** n

zy·de·co \'zī-də-ˌkō\ n : popular music of southern Louisiana that combines tunes of French origin with elements of Caribbean music and the blues

zy·gote \'zī-ˌgōt\ n : a cell formed by the union of two sexual cells; also : the developing individual produced from such a cell — **zy·got·ic** \zī-'gä-tik\ adj

Foreign Words & Phrases

Biographical Names

Geographical Names

FOREIGN WORDS & PHRASES

These words and phrases occur frequently enough in English context to be included in a general English dictionary, but they merit a special section because they have not become a part of the English vocabulary.

---

ab·eunt stu·dia in mo·res \'ä-be-ˌùnt-ˈstü-dē-ˌä-ˌin-ˈmō-ˌrās\ [L] : practices zealously pursued pass into habits

à bien·tôt \ä-byäⁿ-tō\ [F] : so long

ab in·cu·na·bu·lis \ˌäb-ˌiŋ-kù-ˈnä-bù-ˌlēs\ [L] : from the cradle : from infancy

à bon chat, bon rat \ä-bōⁿ-ˈshä bōⁿ-ˈrä\ [F] : to a good cat, a good rat : retaliation in kind

à bouche ou·verte \ä-bü-shü-vert\ [F] : with open mouth : eagerly : uncritically

ab ovo us·que ad ma·la \äb-ˈō-vō-ˌùs-kwe-ˌäd-ˈmä-lä\ [L] : from egg to apples : from soup to nuts : from beginning to end

à bras ou·verts \ä-brä-zü-ver\ [F] : with open arms : cordially

ab·sit in·vi·dia \'äb-ˌsit-in-ˈwi-dē-ˌä\ [L] : let there be no envy or ill will

ab uno dis·ce om·nes \äb-ˈü-nō-ˌdis-ke-ˈòm-ˌnäs\ [L] : from one learn to know all

ab ur·be con·di·ta \äb-ˈùr-be-ˈkòn-di-ˌtä\ [L] : from the founding of the city (Rome, founded 753 B.C.) — used by the Romans in reckoning dates

ab·usus non tol·lit usum \'ä-ˌbü-sùs-ˌnōn-ˌtò-lit-ˈü-sùm\ [L] : abuse does not take away use, i.e., is not an argument against proper use

à compte \ä-ˈkōⁿt\ [F] : on account

à coup sûr \ä-kü-sœr\ [F] : with sure stroke : surely

acte gra·tuit \äk-tə-grä-twᵉē\ [F] : gratuitous impulsive act

ad ar·bi·tri·um \ˌad-är-ˈbi-trē-ùm\ [L] : at will : arbitrarily

ad as·tra per as·pe·ra \ˌad-ˈas-trə-ˌpər-ˈas-pə-rə\ [L] : to the stars by hard ways — motto of Kansas

ad ex·tre·mum \ˌäd-ek-ˈsträ-ˌmùm, ˌad-ik-ˈstrē-məm\ [L] : to the extreme : at last

ad ka·len·das Grae·cas \ˌäd-kä-ˈlen-däs-ˈgrī-ˌkäs\ [L] : at the Greek calends : never (since the Greeks had no calends)

ad ma·jo·rem Dei glo·ri·am \äd-mä-ˈyòr-ˌem-ˈde-ˌē-ˈglòr-ē-ˌäm\ [L] : to the greater glory of God — motto of the Society of Jesus

ad pa·tres \ˈäd-ˈpä-ˌträs\ [L] : (gathered) to his fathers : deceased

ad re·fe·ren·dum \ˌäd-ˌre-fe-ˈren-dùm\ [L] : for reference : for further consideration by one having the authority to make a final decision

à droite \ä-drwät\ [F] : to or on the right hand

ad un·guem \äd-ˈùŋ-ˌgwem\ [L] : to the fingernail : to a nicety : exactly (from the use of the fingernail to test the smoothness of marble)

ad utrum·que pa·ra·tus \ˌäd-ù-ˈtrùm-kwe-pä-ˈrä-tùs\ [L] : prepared for either (event)

ad vi·vum \äd-ˈwē-ˌwùm\ [L] : to the life

ae·gri som·nia \ˌī-grē-ˈsòm-nē-ˌä\ [L] : a sick man's dreams

ae·quam ser·va·re men·tem \ˈī-ˌkwäm-ser-ˌwä-rä-ˈmen-ˌtem\ [L] : to preserve a calm mind

ae·quo ani·mo \ˌī-ˌkwō-ˈä-ni-ˌmō\ [L] : with even mind : calmly

ae·re per·en·ni·us \ˈī-rä-pe-ˈre-nē-ˌùs\ [L] : more lasting than bronze

à gauche \ä-gōsh\ [F] : to or on the left hand

age quod agis \ˈä-ge-ˌkwòd-ˈä-gis\ [L] : do what you are doing : to the business at hand

à grands frais \ä-gräⁿ-fre\ [F] : at great expense

à huis clos \ä-wᵉē-klō\ [F] : with closed doors : behind closed doors

aide–toi, le ciel t'ai·dera \ed-twä lə-ˈsyel-te-drä\ [F] : help yourself (and) heaven will help you

aî·né \e-nä\ [F] : elder : senior (masc.)

aî·née \e-nä\ [F] : elder : senior (fem.)

à l'aban·don \ä-lä-bäⁿ-dōⁿ\ [F] : carelessly : in disorder

à la belle étoile \ä-lä-bel-ä-twäl\ [F] : under the beautiful star : in the open air at night

à la bonne heure \ä-lä-bò-nœr\ [F] : at a good time : well and good : all right

à la fran·çaise \ä-lä-fräⁿ-sez\ [F] : in the French manner

à l'amé·ri·caine \ä-lä-mä-rē-ken\ [F] : in the American manner : of the American kind

à l'an·glaise \ä-läⁿ-glez\ [F] : in the English manner

à la page \ä-lä-päzh\ [F] : at the page : up-to-the-minute

à la russe \ä-lä-rœs\ [F] : in the Russian manner

alea jac·ta est \ˈä-lē-ˌä-ˌyäk-tä-ˈest\ [L] : the die is cast

à l'im·pro·viste \ä-laⁿ-pró-vēst\ [F] : unexpectedly

ali·quan·do bo·nus dor·mi·tat Ho·me·rus \ˌä-li-ˌkwän-dō-ˈbò-nùs-dòr-ˈmē-ˌtät-hō-ˈmer-ùs\ [L] : sometimes (even) good Homer nods

alis vo·lat pro·pri·is \ˈä-ˌlēs-ˌwò-ˌlät-ˈprō-prē-ˌ ēs\ [L] : she flies with her own wings — motto of Oregon

al·ki \ˈal-ˌkī, -kē\ [Chinook Jargon] : by and by — motto of Washington

alo·ha oe \ä-ˌlō-hä-ˈói, -ˈō-ē\ [Hawaiian] : love to you : greetings : farewell

al·ter idem \ˌòl-tər-ˈī-ˌdem, ˌäl-ter-ˈē-\ [L] : second self

à mer·veille \ä-mer-vā\ [F] : marvelously : wonderfully

ami·cus hu·ma·ni ge·ne·ris \ä-ˈmē-kùs-hü-ˌmä-nē-ˈge·ne-ris\ [L] : friend of the human race

ami·cus us·que ad aras \-ˌùs-kwe-ˌäd-ˈär-ˌäs\ [L] : a friend as far as to the altars, i.e., except in what is contrary to one's religion; *also* : a friend to the last extremity

ami de cour \ä-ˌmē-də-ˈkúr\ [F] : court friend : insincere friend

amor pa·tri·ae \ˈä-ˌmòr-ˈpä-trē-ˌī\ [L] : love of one's country

amor vin·cit om·nia \ˈä-ˌmòr-ˌwiŋ-kit-ˈòm-nē-ä\ [L] : love conquers all things

an·cienne no·blesse \äⁿ-syen-nò-bles\ [F] : old-time nobility : the French nobility before the Revolution of 1789

an·guis in her·ba \ˌäŋ-gwis-in-ˈher-ˌbä\ [L] : snake in the grass

ani·mal bi·pes im·plu·me \ˈä-ni-ˌmäl-ˌbi-ˌpäs-im-ˈplü-me\ [L] : two-legged animal without feathers (i.e., the human race)

ani·mis opi·bus·que pa·ra·ti \ˈä-ni-ˌmēs-ˌó-pi-ˈbùs-kwe-pä-ˈrä-tē\ [L] : prepared in mind and resources — one of the mottoes of South Carolina

an·no ae·ta·tis su·ae \ˈä-nō-ī-ˌtä-tis-ˈsü-ˌī\ [L] : in the (specified) year of his (or her) age

an·no mun·di \ˌä-nō-ˈmún-dē\ [L] : in the year of the world — used in reckoning dates from the supposed period of the creation of the world, esp. as fixed by James Ussher at 4004 B.C., or by the Jews at 3761 B.C.

an·no ur·bis con·di·tae \ˌä-nō-ˌùr-bis-ˈkòn-di-ˌtī\ [L] : in the year of the founded city : in the year that the city was founded (Rome, founded 753 B.C.)

an·nu·it coep·tis \ˌä-nü-ˌit-ˈkòip-ˌtēs\ [L] : He (God) has approved our beginnings — motto on the reverse of the Great Seal of the United States

à peu près \ä-pœ-pre\ [F] : nearly : approximately

à pied \ä-pyä\ [F] : on foot

à point \ä-pwäⁿ\ [F] : at the right time

après moi le dé·luge \ä-pre-mwä-lə-dā-lüezh\ *or* **après nous le déluge** \ä-prenü-\ [F] : after me the deluge — attributed to Louis XV

à pro·pos de bottes \ä-prə-pō-də-bòt\ [F] : apropos of boots — used to change the subject

à pro·pos de rien \-ryaⁿ\ [F] : apropos of nothing

aqua et ig·ni in·ter·dic·tus \ˌä-kwä-et-ˈig-nē-ˌin-ter-ˈdik-tùs\ [L] : forbidden to be furnished with water and fire : outlawed

Ar·ca·des am·bo \ˈär-kä-ˌdes-ˈäm-bō\ [L] : both Arcadians : two persons of like occupations or tastes; *also* : two rascals

ar·rec·tis au·ri·bus \ä-ˈrek-ˌtēs-ˈaú-ri-ˌbùs\ [L] : with ears pricked up : attentively

ar·ri·ve·der·ci \ˌär-ē-vä-ˈder-chē\ [It] : till we meet again : farewell

ars lon·ga, vi·ta bre·vis \ärs-ˈlòŋ-ˌgä-ˌwē-ˌtä-ˈbre-wis\ [L] : art is long, life is short : human life span limits all that might be accomplished

as—sa·laam alai·kum \əs-sə-ˈläm-ə-ˈlī-kùm\ [Ar *as-salāmu 'alaykum*] : peace to you — used as a traditional greeting among Muslims

a ter·go \ä-ˈter-(ˌ)gō\ [L] : from behind

à tort et à tra·vers \ä-tòr-ä-ä-trä-verˈ\ [F] : wrong and crosswise : at random : without rhyme or reason

au bout de son la·tin \ō-büd-sōⁿ-lä-taⁿ, -bü-də-\ [F] : at the end of one's Latin : at the end of one's mental resources

au con·traire \ō-kōⁿ-trer\ [F] : on the contrary

au·de·mus ju·ra nos·tra de·fen·de·re \aù-ˈdä-mús-ˌyúr-ä-ˈnò-strä-dä-ˈfen-de-rä\ [L] : we dare defend our rights — motto of Alabama

au·den·tes for·tu·na ju·vat \aù-ˈden-ˌtäs-fòr-ˌtü-nä-ˈyù-ˌwät\ [L] : fortune favors the bold

au·di al·te·ram par·tem \ˈaú-dē-ˌäl-te-ˌräm-ˈpär-ˌtem\ [L] : hear the other side

au fait \ō-fet, -feˈ\ [F] : to the point : fully competent : fully informed : socially correct

au fond \ō-fōⁿ\ [F] : at bottom : fundamentally

au grand sé·rieux \ō-gräⁿ-sä-ryœ\ [F] : in all seriousness

au mieux \ō-myœ\ [F] : on the best terms : on intimate terms

au pays des aveugles les borgnes sont rois \ō-pä-ē-dä-zä-vœglə-lä-bòrnʸə-sōⁿ-rwä\ [F] : in the country of the blind the one-eyed men are kings

au·rea me·di·o·cri·tas \ˈaú-rē-ä-ˌme·dē-ˈò-kri-ˌtäs\ [L] : the golden mean

au reste \ō-rest\ [F] : for the rest : besides

au sé·rieux \ō-sä-ryœ\ [F] : seriously

aus·si·tôt dit, aus·si·tôt fait \ō-sē-tō-dē ō-sē-tō-feˈ\ [F] : no sooner said than done

aut Cae·sar aut ni·hil \aút-ˈkī-sär-ˌaút-ˈni-ˌhil\ [L] : either a Caesar or nothing

au·tres temps, au·tres mœurs \ō-trə-täⁿ ō-trə-mœrs\ [F] : other times, other customs

aut vin·ce·re aut mo·ri \aut-'win-ke-rä-,aut-'mó-,rē\ [L] : either to conquer or to die

aux armes \ō-zärm\ [F] : to arms

avant la lettre \ä-vän-lä-letr³\ [F] : before the letter : before a (specified) name or entity existed

ave at·que va·le \'ä-,wä-,ät-kwe-'wä-,lā\ [L] : hail and farewell

à vo·tre san·té \ä-vót-sän-tā, -vò-trə-\ [F] : to your health — used as a toast

ax·is mun·di \'ak-səs-'mún-dē\ [L] : turning point of the world : line through the earth's center around which the universe revolves

bel·la fi·gu·ra \'bel-lə-fē-'gü-rä\ [It] : fine appearance or impression

belle laide \bel-led\ [F] : beautiful ugly woman : woman who is attractive though not conventionally beautiful

bel·lum om·ni·um con·tra om·nes \'bel-lúm-'òm-nē-ùm-,kòn-trä-'òm-,nās\ [L] : war of all against all

bien en·ten·du \byaⁿ-nän-tän-due\ [F] : well understood : of course

bien–pen·sant \byaⁿ-pän-säⁿ\ [F] : rightminded : one who holds orthodox views

bien·sé·ance \byaⁿ-sā-äⁿs\ [F] : propriety

bis dat qui ci·to dat \'bis-,dät-kwē-'ki-tō-,dät\ [L] : he gives twice who gives promptly

bon ap·pé·tit \bò-nä-pā-tē\ [F] : good appetite : enjoy your meal

bon gré, mal gré \'bōⁿ-,grā 'mäl-,grā\ [F] : whether with good grace or bad : willynilly

bon·jour \bōⁿ-zhür\ [F] : good day : good morning

bonne foi \bòn-fwä\ [F] : good faith

bon·soir \bōⁿ-swär\ [F] : good evening

bru·tum ful·men \'brü-tùm-'fúl-men\ [L] : insensible thunderbolt : a futile threat or display of force

ca·dit quae·stio \'kä-dit-'kwī-stē-,ō\ [L] : the question drops : the argument collapses

carte d'iden·ti·té \kärt-dē-däⁿ-tē-tā\ [F] : identity card

cau·sa si·ne qua non \'kaù-,sä-,si-nä-kwä-'nōn\ [L] : an indispensable cause or condition

ça va sans dire \sä-vä-säⁿ-dir\ [F] : it goes without saying

ca·ve ca·nem \,kä-wä-'kä-,nem\ [L] : beware the dog

ce·dant ar·ma to·gae \'kä-,dänt-,är-mə-'tō-,gī\ [L] : let arms yield to the toga : let military power give way to civil power — motto of Wyoming

ce n'est que le pre·mier pas qui coûte \snek-lə-prə-myä-pä-kē-küt\ [F] : it is only the first step that costs

c'est–à–dire \se-tä-dir\ [F] : that is to say : namely

c'est au·tre chose \se-tōt-shōz, -tō-trə-\ [F] : that's a different thing

c'est la guerre \se-lä-ger\ [F] : that's war : it cannot be helped

c'est la vie \se-lä-vē\ [F] : that's life : that's how things happen

c'est plus qu'un crime, c'est une faute \se-plue-kœⁿ-krēm se-tuen-fōt\ [F] : it is worse than a crime, it is a blunder

ce·te·ra de·sunt \,kä-te-,rä-'dā-,sùnt\ [L] : the rest is missing

cha·cun à son goût \shä-kœⁿ-nä-sōⁿ-gü\ [F] : everyone to his taste

châ·teau en Es·pagne \shä-tō-äⁿ-nes-pänʸ\ [F] : castle in Spain : a visionary project

cher·chez la femme \sher-shä-lä-fäm\ [F] : look for the woman

che sa·rà, sa·rà \,kā-sä-,rä sä-'rä\ [It] : what will be, will be

che·val de ba·taille \shə-väl-də-bä-täʸ\ [F] : warhorse : argument constantly relied on : favorite subject

co·gi·to, er·go sum \'kō-gi-,tō ,er-gō-'sùm\ [L] : I think, therefore I exist

co·mé·die hu·maine \kò-mä-dē-ue-men\ [F] : human comedy : the whole variety of human life

comme ci, comme ça \kòm-sē kòm-sä\ [E] : so-so

com·pa·gnon de voy·age \kōⁿ-pä-nyōⁿ-də-vwä-yäzh\ [F] : traveling companion

compte ren·du \kōⁿt-rän-due\ [F] : report (as of proceedings in an investigation)

con·cor·dia dis·cors \kòn-'kòr-dē-ä-'dis-,kòrs\ [L] : discordant harmony

con·fes·sio fi·dei \kòn-'fe-sē-ō-'fi-dē-,ē\ [L] : confession of faith

cor·rup·tio op·ti·mi pes·si·ma \kò-'rùp-tē-,ō-'äp-ti-,mē-'pe-si-,mä\ [L] : the corruption of the best is the worst of all

coup de maî·tre \küd-metr³, kü-də-\ [F] : masterstroke

coup d'es·sai \kü-dä-se\ [F] : experiment : trial

coûte que coûte \küt-kə-küt\ [F] : cost what it may

cre·do quia ab·sur·dum est \,krä-dō-'kwē-ä-äp,sùr-dùm-'est\ [L] : I believe it because it is absurd

cres·cit eun·do \,kres-kit-'eún-dō\ [L] : it grows as it goes — motto of New Mexico

crise de nerfs or **crise des nerfs** \krēz-də-ner\ [F] : crisis of nerves : nervous collapse : hysterical fit

crux cri·ti·co·rum \'krúks-,kri-ti-'kōr-ùm\ [L] : crux of critics

cu·jus re·gio, ej·us re·li·gio \,kü-yùs-'re-gē-,ō ,e-yùs-re-'li-gē-,ō\ [L] : whose region, his or her religion : subjects are to accept the religion of their ruler

cum gra·no sa·lis \,kúm-,grä-nō-'sä-lis\ [L] : with a grain of salt

cur·sus ho·no·rum \'kùr-sùs-hò-'nòr-ùm\ [L] : course of honors : succession of offices of increasing importance

cus·tos mo·rum \,kùs-tòs-'mòr-ùm\ [L] : guardian of manners or morals : censor

d'ac·cord \dä-kȯr\ [F] : in accord : agreed

dame d'hon·neur \däm-dȯ-nœr\ [F] : lady-in-waiting

dam·nant quod non in·tel·li·gunt \'däm-ˌnänt-ˌkwȯd-ˌnōn-in-ˈte-li-ˌgunt\ [L] : they condemn what they do not understand

de bonne grâce \də-bȯn-gräs\ [F] : with good grace : willingly

de gus·ti·bus non est dis·pu·tan·dum \dā-ˈgu̇s-tə-ˌbu̇s-ˌnōn-ˌest-ˌdis-pu̇-ˈtän-ˌdu̇m\ [L] : there is no disputing about tastes

Dei gra·tia \ˌde-ˌē-ˈgrä-tē-ˌä\ [L] : by the grace of God

de in·te·gro \dā-ˈin-te-ˌgrō\ [L] : anew : afresh

de·len·da est Car·tha·go \dā-ˈlen-dä-ˌest-kär-ˈtä-gō\ [L] : Carthage must be destroyed

de·li·ne·a·vit \dā-ˌlē-nä-ˈä-wit\ [L] : he (or she) drew it

de mal en pis \də-mä-läⁿ-pē\ [F] : from bad to worse

de mi·ni·mis non cu·rat lex \dā-ˈmi-ni-ˌmēs-ˌnōn-ˌkü-ˌrät-ˈleks\ [L] : the law takes no account of trifles

de mor·tu·is nil ni·si bo·num \dā-ˈmȯr-tü-ˌēs-ˌnēl-ni-sē-ˈbȯ-ˌnu̇m\ [L] : of the dead (say) nothing but good

de nos jours \də-nō-zhür\ [F] : of our time : contemporary — used postpositively esp. after a proper name

Deo fa·ven·te \dā-ō-fä-ˈven-tā\ [L] : with God's favor

Deo gra·ti·as \dā-ō-ˈgrä-tē-ˌäs\ [L] : thanks (be) to God

de pro·fun·dis \ˌdā-prō-ˈfu̇n-dēs\ [L] : out of the depths

der Geist der stets ver·neint \dər-ˈgīst-dər-ˌshtäts-fer-ˈnīnt\ [G] : the spirit that ever denies — applied originally to Mephistopheles

de·si·pe·re in lo·co \dā-ˈsi-pe-rä-in-ˈlō-kō\ [L] : to indulge in trifling at the proper time

de te fa·bu·la nar·ra·tur \dā-ˌtā-ˈfä-bù-lä-nä-ˈrä-ˌtu̇r\ [L] : the story applies to you

De·us ab·scon·di·tus \ˌdā-u̇s-ˌäp-ˈskȯn-di-ˌtu̇s\ [L] : hidden God : God unknowable by the human mind

De·us vult \ˌdā-u̇s-ˈwu̇lt\ [L] : God wills it — rallying cry of the First Crusade

di·es fau·stus \ˌdē-ˌās-ˈfau̇-stu̇s\ [L] : lucky day

dies in·fau·stus \-ˈin-ˌfau̇-stu̇s\ [L] : unlucky day

dies irae \-ˈē-ˌrī, -ˌrā\ [L] : day of wrath — used of the Judgment Day

Dieu et mon droit \dyœ-ā-mȯⁿ-drwä\ [F] : God and my right — motto on the British royal arms

Dieu vous garde \dyœ-vü-gärd\ [F] : God keep you

di·ri·go \ˈdē-ri-ˌgō\ [L] : I direct — motto of Maine

dis ali·ter vi·sum \ˌdēs-ˌä-li-ˌter-ˈwē-ˌsu̇m\ [L] : the Gods decreed otherwise

di·tat De·us \ˌdē-ˌtät-ˈdā-ˌu̇s\ [L] : God enriches — motto of Arizona

di·vi·de et im·pe·ra \ˈdē-wi-ˌde-ˌet-ˈim-pe-ˌrä\ [L] : divide and rule

do·cen·do dis·ci·mus \dȯ-ˌken-dō-ˈdis-ki-ˌmu̇s\ [L] : we learn by teaching

Do·mi·ne, di·ri·ge nos \ˈdȯ-mi-ˌne-ˈdē-ri-ˌge-ˈnōs\ [L] : Lord, direct us — motto of the City of London

Do·mi·nus vo·bis·cum \ˌdȯ-mi-ˌnu̇s-wō-ˈbēs-ˌku̇m\ [L] : the Lord be with you

dul·ce et de·co·rum est pro pa·tria mo·ri \ˌdu̇l-ˌke-et-de-ˈkȯr-ùm-ˌest-prō-ˌpä-trē-ˌä-ˈmȯ-ˌrē\ [L] : it is sweet and seemly to die for one's country

dum spi·ro, spe·ro \ˌdu̇m-ˈspē-rō-ˈspä-rō\ [L] : while I breathe, I hope — one of the mottoes of South Carolina

dum vi·vi·mus vi·va·mus \ˌdu̇m-ˈwē-wē-ˌmu̇s-wē-ˈwä-mu̇s\ [L] : while we live, let us live

d'un cer·tain âge \dœⁿ-ser-te-näzh\ [F] : of a certain age : no longer young

dux fe·mi·na fac·ti \ˌdu̇ks-ˌfä-mi-nä-ˈfäk-ˌtē\ [L] : a woman was leader of the exploit

ec·ce sig·num \ˌe-ke-ˈsig-ˌnu̇m\ [L] : behold the sign : look at the proof

e con·tra·rio \ˌā-kȯn-ˈträr-ē-ˌō\ [L] : on the contrary

écra·sez l'in·fâme \ā-krä-zä-laⁿ-fäm\ [F] : crush the infamous thing

eheu fu·ga·ces la·bun·tur an·ni \ˌā-ˌheü-fü-ˈgä-ˌkäs-lä-ˈbùn-ˌtùr-ˈä-ˌnē\ [L] : alas! the fleeting years glide on

ein' fes·te Burg ist un·ser Gott \īn-ˌfes-tə-ˈbu̇rk-ist-ˌu̇n-zər-ˈgȯt\ [G] : a mighty fortress is our God

em·bar·ras de choix \äⁿ-bä-rä-də-shwä\ or **embarras du choix** \-du̇-shwä\ [F] : embarrassing variety of choice

em·bar·ras de ri·chesses or **embarras de ri·chesse** \äⁿ-bä-räd-rē-shes, -rä-də-\ [F] : embarrassing surplus of riches : confusing abundance

en ami \äⁿ-nä-mē\ [F] : as a friend

en ef·fet \äⁿ-nä-fe\ [F] : in fact : indeed

en fa·mille \äⁿ-fä-mē\ [F] : in or with one's family : at home : informally

en·fant ché·ri \äⁿ-fäⁿ-shä-rē\ [F] : loved or pampered child : one that is highly favored

en·fant gâ·té \äⁿ-fäⁿ-gä-tā\ [F] : spoiled child

en·fants per·dus \äⁿ-fäⁿ-per-du̇\ [F] : lost children : soldiers sent to a dangerous post

en·fin \äⁿ-faⁿ\ [F] : in conclusion : in a word

en gar·çon \äⁿ-gär-sōⁿ\ [F] : as or like a bachelor

en garde \äⁿ-gärd\ [F] : on guard

en pan·tou·fles \äⁿ-päⁿ-tüflᵊ\ [F] : in slippers : at ease : informally

en plein air \äⁿ-ple-ner\ [F] : in the open air

en plein jour \äⁿ-plaⁿ-zhür\ [F] : in broad day

en règle \äⁿ-reglᵊ\ [F] : in order : in due form

en re·tard \äⁿr-(ə-)tär\ [F] : behind time : late

en re·traite \äⁿr-(ə-)tret\ [F] : in retreat : in retirement

en re·vanche \äⁿr-(ə-)väⁿsh\ [F] : in return : in compensation

en se·condes noces \äⁿs-gōⁿd-nós, äⁿsə-\ [F] : in a second marriage

en·se pe·tit pla·ci·dam sub li·ber·ta·te qui·e·tem \ˌen-se-ˌpe-tit-ˈplä-ki-ˌdäm-sùb-ˌlē-ber-ˌtä-te-kwē-ˈä-ˌtem\ [L] : with the sword she seeks calm repose under liberty : by the sword we seek peace, but peace only under liberty — motto of Massachusetts

eo ip·so \ā-ō-ˈip-(ˌ)sō\ [L] : by that itself : by that fact alone

épa·ter le bour·geois \ā-pä-tä-lə-bür-zhwä\ or **épater les bour·geois** \-lä-bür-\ [F] : to shock the middle classes

e plu·ri·bus unum \ˌē-ˌplùr-ə-bəs-ˈ(y)ü-nəm, ˌā-ˌplúr-i-bùs-ˈü-núm\ [L] : one out of many — used on the Great Seal of the U.S. and on several U.S. coins

ep·pur si muo·ve \äp-ˌpür-sē-ˈmwó-vä\ [It] : and yet it does move — attributed to Galileo after recanting his assertion of the earth's motion

Erin go bragh \ˌer-ən-gə-ˈbró, -gō-ˈbrä\ [Ir go brách or go bráth, lit., till doomsday] : Ireland forever

er·ra·re hu·ma·num est \e-ˈrär̩-ä-hü-ˌmä-nùm-ˈest\ [L] : to err is human

es·prit de l'es·ca·lier \es-ˌprē-də-ˌlä-kä-lyä\ or **es·prit d'es·ca·lier** \-prē-des-\ [F] : wit of the staircase : repartee thought of only too late

es·se quam vi·de·ri \ˈe-sä-ˌkwäm-wi-ˈdä-rē\ [L] : to be rather than to seem — motto of North Carolina

est mo·dus in re·bus \est-ˈmò-ˌdùs-in-ˈrä-ˌbùs\ [L] : there is a proper measure in things, i.e., the golden mean should always be observed

es·to per·pe·tua \ˈes-ˌtō-per-ˈpe-tù-ˌä\ [L] : may she endure forever — motto of Idaho

et hoc ge·nus om·ne \et-ˌhōk-ˌge-nùs-ˈóm-ne\ or **et id genus omne** \et-ˌid-\ [L] : and everything of this kind

et in Ar·ca·dia ego \ˌet-in-är-ˌkä-dē-ä-ˈe-gō\ [L] : I too (lived) in Arcadia

et sic de si·mi·li·bus \et-ˌsēk-dä-si-ˈmi-li-ˌbùs\ [L] : and so of like things

et tu Bru·te \et-ˈtü-ˈbrü-te\ [L] : thou too, Brutus — exclamation attributed to Julius Caesar on seeing his friend Brutus among his assassins

eu·re·ka \yù-ˈrē-kä\ [Gk] : I have found it — motto of California

Ewig–Weib·li·che \ˌä-vik-ˈvīp-li-kə\ [G] : eternal feminine

ex·al·té \eg-zäl-tā\ [F] : emotionally excited or elated : fanatic

ex ani·mo \eks-ˈä-ni-ˌmō\ [L] : from the heart : sincerely

ex·cel·si·or \ik-ˈsel-sē-ər, eks-ˈkel-sē-ˌór\ [L] : still higher — motto of New York

ex·cep·tio pro·bat re·gu·lam de re·bus non ex·cep·tis \eks-ˈkep-tē-ˌō-ˌprō-bät-ˈrä-gù-ˌläm-dä-ˈrä-ˌbùs-ˌnōn-eks-ˈkep-ˌtēs\ [L] : an exception establishes the rule as to things not excepted

ex·cep·tis ex·ci·pi·en·dis \eks-ˈkep-ˌtēs-eks-ˌki-pē-ˈen-ˌdēs\ [L] : with the proper or necessary exceptions

ex·i·tus ac·ta pro·bat \ˈek-si-ˌtùs-ˌäk-tä-ˈpró-ˌbät\ [L] : the outcome justifies the deed

ex li·bris \eks-ˈlē-bris\ [L] : from the books of — used on bookplates

ex me·ro mo·tu \ˌeks-ˌmer-ō-ˈmō-tü\ [L] : out of mere impulse : of one's own accord

ex ne·ces·si·ta·te rei \ˌeks-ne-ˌke-si-ˈtä-te-ˈrä(-ˌē)\ [L] : from the necessity of the case

ex ni·hi·lo ni·hil fit \eks-ˈni-hi-ˌlō-ˌni-ˌhil-ˈfit\ [L] : from nothing nothing is produced

ex pe·de Her·cu·lem \eks-ˌpe-de-ˈher-kù-ˌlem\ [L] : from the foot (we may judge of the size of) Hercules : from a part we may judge of the whole

ex·per·to cre·de \eks-ˌper-tō-ˈkrä-de\ or **experto cre·di·te** \-ˈkrä-di-ˌte\ [L] : believe one who has had experience

ex un·gue le·o·nem \eks-ˌùn-gwe-le-ˈō-ˌncm\ [L] : from the claw (we may judge of) the lion : from a part we may judge of the whole

ex vi ter·mi·ni \eks-ˌwē-ˈter-mə-ˌnē\ [L] : from the force of the term

fa·ci·le prin·ceps \ˌfä-ki-le-ˈpriⁿ-ˌkeps\ [L] : easily first

fa·ci·lis de·scen·sus Aver·no \ˈfä-ki-ˌlis-dä-ˌskän-ˌsùs-ä-ˈwer-nō\ or **facilis de·scensus Aver·ni** \-(ˌ)nē\ [L] : the descent to Avernus is easy : the road to evil is easy

fa·çon de par·ler \fä-sōⁿ-də-pär-lä\ [F] : manner of speaking : figurative or conventional expression

faire suivre \fer-swᵉēvrᵊ\ [F] : have forwarded : please forward

fas est et ab ho·ste do·ce·ri \fäs-ˈest-et-äb-ˈhó-ste-dò-ˈkä-(ˌ)rē\ [L] : it is right to learn even from an enemy

Fa·ta vi·am in·ve·ni·ent \ˌfä-tä-ˈwē-ˌäm-in-ˈwe-nē-ˌent\ [L] : the Fates will find a way

fat·ti mas·chii, pa·ro·le fe·mi·ne \ˌfät-tē-ˈmäs-ˌkē pä-ˌró-lä-ˈfä-mē-ˌnä\ [It] : deeds are males, words are females : deeds are more effective than words — motto of Maryland, where it is generally interpreted as meaning "manly deeds, womanly words"

faux bon·homme \fō-bò-nòm\ [F] : pretended good fellow

faux–naïf \fœ-nä-ēf\ [F] : spuriously or affectedly childlike : artfully simple

fe·lix cul·pa \'fā-liks-'kůl-pä\ [L] : fortunate fault — used esp. of original sin in relation to the consequent coming of Christ

femme de cham·bre \fäm-də-shäⁿbrᵃ\ [F] : chambermaid : lady's maid

fe·sti·na len·te \fe-,stē-nä-'len-,tā\ [L] : make haste slowly

feux d'ar·ti·fice \fœ-där-tē-fēs\ [F] : fireworks : display of wit

fi·at ex·pe·ri·men·tum in cor·po·re vi·li \'fē-,ät-ek-,sper-ē-'men-,tùm-in-,kòr-pò-re-'wē-lē\ [L] : let experiment be made on a worthless body

fi·at ju·sti·tia, ru·at cae·lum \,fē-,ät-'yùs-'ti-tē-ä ,rü-,ät-'kī-,lùm\ [L] : let justice be done though the heavens fall

fi·at lux \,fē-,ät-'lùks\ [L] : let there be light

Fi·dei De·fen·sor \,fi-de-,ē-dä-'fän-,sòr\ [L] : Defender of the Faith — a title of the sovereigns of England

fille de cham·bre \fē-də-shäⁿbrᵃ\ [F] : lady's maid

fille d'hon·neur \fē-dò-nœr\ [F] : maid of honor

fi·nem re·spi·ce \,fē-,nem-'rä-spi-,ke\ [L] : consider the end

fi·nis co·ro·nat opus \,fē-nis-kò-,rō-,nät-'ō-,pùs\ [L] : the end crowns the work

flo·re·at \'flō-re-,ät\ [L] : may (he, she, or it) flourish — usu. followed by a name

fluc·tu·at nec mer·gi·tur \'flùk-tù-,ät-,nek-'mer-gi-,tùr\ [L] : it is tossed by the waves but does not sink — motto of Paris

fo·lie de gran·deur or **fo·lie des gran·deurs** \fò-lē-də-gräⁿ-dœr\ [F] : delusion of greatness : megalomania

force de frappe \fòrs-də-fräp\ [F] : a force equipped to deal a retaliatory blow

fors·an et haec olim me·mi·nis·se ju·va·bit \,fòr-,sän-,et-'hïk-,ō-lim-,me-mi-'ni-se-yù-'wä-bit\ [L] : perhaps this too will be a pleasure to look back on one day

for·tes for·tu·na ju·vat \'fòr-,tās-fòr-,tü-nä-'yù-,wät\ [L] : fortune favors the brave

fron·ti nul·la fi·des \'fròn-,tē-,nù-lä-'fi-,däs\ [L] : no reliance can be placed on appearance

fu·it Ili·um \'fù-it-'i-lē-ùm\ [L] : Troy has been (i.e., is no more)

fu·ror lo·quen·di \,fùr-,òr-lò-'kwen-(,)dē\ [L] : rage for speaking

furor po·e·ti·cus \-pò-'ā-ti-kùs\ [L] : poetic frenzy

furor scri·ben·di \-skrē-'ben-(,)dē\ [L] : rage for writing

Gal·li·ce \'gä-li-,ke\ [L] : in French : after the French manner

gar·çon d'hon·neur \gär-sōⁿ-dò-nœr\ [F] : bridegroom's attendant

garde du corps \gärd-dœ-kòr\ [F] : bodyguard

gar·dez la foi \gär-dā-lä-fwä\ [F] : keep faith

gau·de·a·mus igi·tur \,gaù-dē-'ä-mùs-'i-gi-,tùr\ [L] : let us then be merry

gens d'é·glise \zhäⁿ-dä-glēz\ [F] : church people : clergy

gens de guerre \zhäⁿ-də-ger\ [F] : military people : soldiery

gens du monde \zhäⁿ-dœ-mōⁿd\ [F] : people of the world : fashionable people

gno·thi se·au·ton \'gnō-thē-,se-aù-'tón\ [Gk] : know thyself

goût de ter·roir \gü-də-te-rwär\ [F] : taste of the earth

grand monde \grä-mōⁿd\ [F] : great world : high society

gros·so mo·do \'gròs-(,)sō-'mō-(,)dō\ [It] : roughly

guerre à ou·trance \ger-ä-ü-träⁿs\ [F] : war to the uttermost

gu·ten Tag \,gü-tən-'täk\ [G] : good day

has·ta la vis·ta \,äs-tə-lä-'vēs-tə\ [Sp] : good-bye

haute vul·ga·ri·sa·tion \ōt-vœl-gä-rē-zä-syōⁿ\ [F] : high popularization : effective presentation of a difficult subject to a general audience

haut goût \ō-gü\ [F] : high flavor : slight taint of decay

hic et nunc \'hēk-et-'nùⁿk\ [L] : here and now

hic et ubi·que \,hēk-et-ù-'bē-kwe\ [L] : here and everywhere

hic ja·cet \hik-'jä-sət, hēk-'yä-ket\ [L] : here lies — used preceding a name on a tombstone

hinc il·lae la·cri·mae \,hiŋk-,i-,lī-'lä-kri-,mī\ [L] : hence those tears

hoc age \'hōk-'ä-ge\ [L] : do this : apply yourself to what you are about

homme d'af·faires \òm-dä-fer\ [F] : man of business : business agent

homme d'es·prit \òm-des-prē\ [F] : man of wit

homme moyen sen·suel \òm-mwä-yaⁿ-säⁿ-swᵉel\ [F] : the average nonintellectual man

ho·mo sum: hu·ma·ni nil a me ali·e·num pu·to \'hò-mō-,sùm hü-,mä-nē-'nēl-ä-,mā-,ä-lē-'ä-nùm-'pù-tō\ [L] : I am a human being: I regard nothing of human concern as foreign to my interests

ho·ni soit qui mal y pense \ò-nē-swä-kē-mäl-ē-päⁿs\ [F] : shamed be he who thinks evil of it — motto of the Order of the Garter

hors com·merce \òr-kò-mers\ [F] : outside the trade : not offered through regular commercial channels

hu·ma·num est er·ra·re \hü-,mä-nùm-,est-e-'rär-ä\ [L] : to err is human

ich dien \ik-'dēn\ [G] : I serve — motto of the Prince of Wales

ici on parle fran·çais \ē-sē-ōⁿ-pärl-fräⁿ-se\ [F] : French is spoken here

idées re·çues \ē-dār-(ə-)sœ\ [F] : received ideas : conventional opinions

id est \id-'est\ [L] : that is

ig·no·ran·tia ju·ris ne·mi·nem ex·cu·sat \,ig-nò-,rän-tē-ä-'yùr-is-'nā-mi-,nem-eks-'kü-,sät\ [L] : ignorance of the law excuses no one

ig·no·tum per ig·no·ti·us \ig-'nō-tùm-,per-ig-'nō-tē-,ùs\ [L] : (explaining) the unknown by means of the more unknown

il faut cul·ti·ver no·tre jar·din \ēl-fō-kœl-tē-vā-nòt-zhär-daⁿ, -nò-trə-zhär-\ [F] : we must cultivate our garden : we must tend to our own affairs

in ae·ter·num \,in-ī-'ter-,nùm\ [L] : forever

in du·bio \in-'dù-bē-,ō\ [L] : in doubt : undetermined

in fu·tu·ro \in-fù-'túr-ō\ [L] : in the future

in hoc sig·no vin·ces \in-hōk-'sig-nō-'wiŋ-,kās\ [L] : by this sign (the Cross) you will conquer

in li·mi·ne \in-'lē-mi-,ne\ [L] : on the threshold : at the beginning

in om·nia pa·ra·tus \in-'òm-nē-ä-pä-'rä-,tùs\ [L] : ready for all things

in par·ti·bus in·fi·de·li·um \in-'pär-ti-,bùs-,in-fi-'dā-lē-,ùm\ [L] : in the regions of the infidels — used of a titular bishop having no diocesan jurisdiction, usu. in non-Christian countries

in prae·sen·ti \,in-prī-'sen-,tē\ [L] : at the present time

in sae·cu·la sae·cu·lo·rum \in-'sī-kù-,lä-,sī-kù-'lòr-ùm, -'sä-kù-,lä-,sä-\ [L] : for ages of ages : forever and ever

in·shal·lah \,in-shä-'lä\ [Ar *in shaʼ Allāh*] : if Allah wills : God willing

in sta·tu quo an·te bel·lum \in-,stä-tü-kwō-,än-te-'be-lùm\ [L] : in the same state as before the war

in·te·ger vi·tae sce·le·ris·que pu·rus \,in-te-,ger-'wē-,tī-,ske-le-'ris-kwe-'pū-rùs\ [L] : upright of life and free from wickedness

in·ter nos \,in-ter-'nōs\ [L] : between ourselves

in·tra mu·ros \,in-trä-'mü-,rōs\ [L] : within the walls

in utrum·que pa·ra·tus \,in-ü-'trùm-kwe-pä-'rä-,tùs\ [L] : prepared for either (event)

in·ve·nit \in-'wā-nit\ [L] : he or she devised it

in vi·no ve·ri·tas \in-wē-nō-'wā-ri-,täs\ [L] : there is truth in wine

in·vi·ta Mi·ner·va \in-,wē-,tä-mi-'ner-,wä\ [L] : Minerva being unwilling : without natural talent or inspiration

ip·sis·si·ma ver·ba \ip-'si-si-,mä-'wer-,bä\ [L] : the very words

ira fu·ror bre·vis est \,ē-rä-'fúr-,òr-'bre-wis-,est\ [L] : anger is a brief madness

j'ac·cuse \zhä-kœz\ [F] : I accuse : bitter denunciation

jac·ta alea est \'yäk-,tä-,ä-lē-,ä-'est\ [L] : the die is cast

j'adoube \zhä-düb\ [F] : I adjust — used in chess when touching a piece without intending to move it

ja·nu·is clau·sis \,yä-nù-,ēs-'klaù-,sēs\ [L] : behind closed doors

je main·tien·drai \zhə-maⁿ-tyäⁿ-drā\ [F] : I will maintain — motto of the Netherlands

jeu de mots \zhœd-mō, zhœ-də-\ [F] : play on words : pun

Jo·an·nes est no·men eius \yō-'ä-nās-est-,nō-men-'ā-yùs\ [L] : John is his name — motto of Puerto Rico

jo·lie laide \zhó-lē-led\ [F] : good-looking ugly woman : woman who is attractive though not conventionally pretty

jour·nal in·time \zhür-näl-aⁿ-tēm\ [F] : intimate journal : private diary

jus di·vi·num \,yüs-di-'wē-,nùm\ [L] : divine law

jus·ti·tia om·ni·bus \,yùs-,ti-tē-,ä-'òm-ni-,bùs\ [L] : justice for all — motto of the District of Columbia

j'y suis, j'y reste \zhē-swᵉē zhē-rest\ [F] : here I am, here I remain

Kin·der, Kir·che, Küche \'kin-dər 'kir-kə 'kᵛœ-kə\ [G] : children, church, kitchen

la belle dame sans mer·ci \lä-bel-däm-säⁿ-mer-sē\ [F] : the beautiful lady without mercy

la·bo·ra·re est ora·re \'lä-bō-,rär-ä-,est-'ō-,rär-ä\ [L] : to work is to pray

la·bor om·nia vin·cit \'lä-,bòr-,òm-nē-,ä-'wiŋ-kit\ [L] : labor conquers all things — motto of Oklahoma

la·cri·mae re·rum \,lä-kri-,mī-'rā-,rùm\ [L] : tears for things : pity for misfortune; *also* : tears in things : tragedy of life

lais·sez–al·ler *or* **lais·ser–al·ler** \le-sā-ä-lā\ [F] : letting go : lack of restraint

lap·sus ca·la·mi \,läp-sùs-'kä-lä-,mē\ [L] : slip of the pen

lap·sus lin·guae \-'liŋ-,gwī\ [L] : slip of the tongue

la reine le veut \lä-ren-lə-vœ\ [F] : the queen wills it

la·scia·te ogni spe·ran·za, voi ch'en·tra·te \läsh-'shä-tä-,ō-nᵛē-spä-'rän-tsä ,vō-ē-kän-'trä-tä\ [It] : abandon all hope, ye who enter

lau·da·tor tem·po·ris ac·ti \laù-'dä-,tòr-,tem-pò-ris-'äk-,tē\ [L] : one who praises past times

laus Deo \laùs-'dā-ō\ [L] : praise (be) to God

Le·bens·welt \'lā-bəns-,velt\ [G] : life world : world of lived experience

le cœur a ses rai·sons que la rai·son ne con·naît point \lə-kœr-ä-sä-re-zōⁿk-lä-re-zōⁿ-kò-ne-pwaⁿ\ [F] : the

heart has its reasons. that reason knows
nothing of

le roi est mort, vive le roi \lə-rwä-e-môr
vēv-lə-rwä\ [F] : the king is dead, long
live the king

le roi le veut \lə-rwä-lə-vœ\ [F] : the king
wills it

le roi s'avi·se·ra \lə-rwä-sä-vēz-rä\ [F]
: the king will consider

le style, c'est l'homme \lə-stēl se-lòm\
[F] : the style is the man

l'état, c'est moi \lä-tä se-mwä\ [F] : the
state, it is I

l'étoile du nord \lä-twäl-dœ-nór\ [F] : the
star of the north — motto of Minnesota

Lie·der·kranz \'lē-dər-ˌkränts\ [G]
: wreath of songs : German singing society

lit·tera scrip·ta ma·net \ˌli-te-ˌrä-ˌskrip-
tä-'mä-net\ [L] : the written letter abides

lo·cus in quo \ˌló-kús-in-'kwō\ [L] : place
in which

l'union fait la force \lue-nyōⁿ-fe-lä-fórs\
[F] : union makes strength — motto of
Belgium

lu·sus na·tu·rae \ˌlü-sús-nä-'túr-ē, -'túr-
ˌī\ [L] : freak of nature

ma foi \mä-fwä\ [F] : my faith! : indeed

mag·na est ve·ri·tas et prae·va·le·bit
\ˌmäg-nä,-est-'wä-ri-ˌtäs-et-ˌprī-wä-'lä-bit\
[L] : truth is mighty and will prevail

mag·ni no·mi·nis um·bra \ˌmäg-nē-ˌnō-
mi-nis-'úm-brä\ [L] : the shadow of a
great name

ma·ha·lo \'mä-hä-lō\ [Hawaiian] : thank
you

ma·lade ima·gi·naire \mä-läd-ē-mä-zhē-
ner\ [F] : imaginary invalid : hypochon-
driac

mal de siècle \mäl-də-syeklᵊ\ [F] : illness
from worldly concerns : world-weariness

ma·lis avi·bus \ˌmä-ˌlēs-'ä-wi-ˌbús\ [L]
: under evil auspices

man spricht Deutsch \män-shprikt-
'dòich\ [G] : German spoken

ma·riage de con·ve·nance \mä-ryäzh-
də-kōⁿv-näⁿs\ [F] : marriage of convenience

ma·ri com·plai·sant \mä-rē-kōⁿ-ple-zäⁿ\
[F] : complaisant husband : cuckold who
accepts his wife's infidelity

mau·vaise honte \mò-vez-ōⁿt\ [F] : bad
shame : bashfulness

mau·vais quart d'heure \mò-ve-
kär-dœr\ [F] : bad quarter hour : an uncomfortable though brief experience

me·dio tu·tis·si·mus ibis \'me-dē-ˌō-tü-
ˌti-si-mús-'ē-bis\ [L] : you will go most
safely by the middle course

me ju·di·ce \mä-'yü-di-ke\ [L] : I being
judge : in my judgment

mens sa·na in cor·po·re sa·no \mäns-
'sä-nä-in-ˌkòr-pò-re-'sä-nō\ [L] : a sound
mind in a sound body

me·um et tu·um \ˌmē-əm-ˌet-'tü-əm, ˌme-
úm-ˌet-'tü-úm\ [L] : mine and thine : distinction of private property

mi·ra·bi·le vi·su \mi-ˌrä-bi-lä-'wē-sü\ [L]
: wonderful to behold

mi·ra·bi·lia \ˌmir-ə-'bi-lē-ˌä\ [L] : wonders
: miracles

mœurs \mœr(s)\ [F] : mores : attitudes,
customs, and manners of a society

mo·le ru·it sua \'mō-le-'rú-it-ˌsú-ä\ [L]
: it collapses from its own bigness

monde \mōⁿd\ [F] : world : fashionable
world : society

mon·ta·ni sem·per li·be·ri \mōn-'tä-nē-
ˌsem-per-'lē-be-ˌrē\ [L] : mountaineers
are always free — motto of West Virginia

mo·nu·men·tum ae·re per·en·ni·us
\ˌmò-nú-'men-tùm-ˌī-re-pe-'re-nē-ús\ [L]
: a monument more lasting than bronze
— used of an immortal work of art or literature

mo·re suo \ˌmòr-ā-'sü-ō\ [L] : in his (or
her) own manner

mo·ri·tu·ri te sa·lu·ta·mus \ˌmòr-i-'túr-
ē-ˌtä-sä-lü-'tä-mús\ or **mori·turi te sa·lu·
tant** \-'sä-lù-ˌtänt\ [L] : we (or those) who
are about to die salute thee

mul·tum in par·vo \ˌmùl-tùm-in-'pär-vō,
-'pär-wō\ [L] : much in little

**mu·ta·to no·mi·ne de te fa·bu·la nar·ra·
tur** \mü-ˌtä-tō-'nō-mi-ne-ˌdā-ˌtä-'fä-bù-lä-
nä-'rä-ˌtúr\ [L] : with the name changed
the story applies to you

my·ster·i·um tre·men·dum \mi-'ster-ē-
ˌúm-tre-'men-dúm\ [L] : overwhelming
mystery

**na·tu·ram ex·pel·las fur·ca, ta·men us·
que re·cur·ret** \nä-'tü-ˌräm-ek-ˌspe-läs-
'fúr-ˌkä, ˌtä-men-'ùs-kwe-re-'kúr-et\ [L]
: you may drive nature out with a pitch-
fork, but she will keep coming back

na·tu·ra non fa·cit sal·tum \nä-'tü-rä-
ˌnōn-ˌfä-kit-'säl-ˌtùm\ [L] : nature makes
no leap

ne ce·de ma·lis \nā-ˌkä-de-'mä-ˌlēs\ [L]
: yield not to misfortunes

ne·mo me im·pu·ne la·ces·sit \'nä-mō-
'mä-im-ˌpü-nä-lä-'ke-sit\ [L] : no one attacks me with impunity — motto of Scotland and of the Order of the Thistle

ne quid ni·mis \ˌnä-ˌkwid-'ni-mis\ [L]
: not anything in excess

n'est-ce pas? \nes-pä\ [F] : isn't it so?

nicht wahr? \nikt-'vär\ [G] : not true?
: isn't it so?

nil ad·mi·ra·ri \'nēl-ˌäd-mi-'rär-ē\ [L] : to
be excited by nothing : equanimity

nil de·spe·ran·dum \'nēl-ˌdä-spä-'rän-
dùm\ [L] : never despair

nil si·ne nu·mi·ne \'nēl-ˌsi-nä-'nü-mi-ne\
[L] : nothing without the divine will —
motto of Colorado

n'im·porte \naⁿ-pórt\ [F] : it's no matter

no·lens vo·lens \ˌnō-ˌlenz-'vō-ˌlenz\ [L]
: unwilling (or) willing : willy-nilly

non om·nia pos·su·mus om·nes \nōn-
'óm-nē-ä-ˌpò-sú-mús-'òm-ˌnäs\ [L] : we
can't all (do) all things

non om·nis mo·ri·ar \nōn-ˈȯm-nis-ˈmȯr-ē-ˌär\ [L] : I shall not wholly die

non sans droict \nōⁿ-sä²-drwä\ [OF] : not without right — motto on Shakespeare's coat of arms

non sum qua·lis eram \ˌnōn-ˌsum-ˌkwä-lis-ˈer-ˌäm\ [L] : I am not what I used to be

nos·ce te ip·sum \ˌnȯs-ke-ˌtā-ˈip-ˌsum\ [L] : know thyself

nos·tal·gie de la boue \nȯs-täl-zhēd-lä-bü, -zhē-də-\ [F] : yearning for the mud : attraction to what is unworthy, crude, or degrading

nous avons chan·gé tout ce·la \nü-zä-vō²-shä²-tü-sə-lä\ [F] : we have changed all that

nous ver·rons ce que nous ver·rons \nü-ve-rō²s-kə-nü-ve-rō², -rō²-sə-kə-\ [F] : we shall see what we shall see

no·vus ho·mo \ˌnō-wus-ˈhō-mō\ [L] : new man : man newly ennobled : upstart

novus or·do se·clo·rum \-ˌȯr-ˌdō-sā-ˈklȯr-ùm\ [L] : a new cycle of the ages — motto on the reverse of the Great Seal of the United States

nu·gae \ˈnü-ˌgī\ [L] : trifles

nuit blanche \nwē²-blä²sh\ [F] : white night : a sleepless night

nyet \ˈnyet\ [Russ] : no

ob·iit \ˈȯ-bē-ˌit\ [L] : he or she died

ob·scu·rum per ob·scu·ri·us \ȯb-ˈskyùr-um-per-ȯb-ˈskyùr-ē-us\ [L] : (explaining) the obscure by means of the more obscure

ode·rint dum me·tu·ant \ˈō-de-ˌrint-ˌdum-me-tü-ˌänt\ [L] : let them hate, so long as they fear

odi et amo \ˈō-ˌdē-et-ˈä-(ˌ)mō\ [L] : I hate and I love

omer·tà \ō-ˈmer-tä\ [It] : conspiracy of silence

om·ne ig·no·tum pro mag·ni·fi·co \ˌȯm-ne-ig-ˈnō-ˌtum-prō-mäg-ˈni-fi-ˌkō\ [L] : everything unknown (is taken) as grand : the unknown tends to be exaggerated in importance or difficulty

om·nia mu·tan·tur, nos et mu·ta·mur in il·lis \ˌȯm-nē-ä-mü-ˈtän-ˌtur ˌnōs-et-mü-ˌtä-mur-in-ˈi-ˌlēs\ [L] : all things are changing, and we are changing with them

om·nia vin·cit amor \ˈȯm-nē-ä-ˈwiⁿ-kit-ˈä-ˌmȯr\ [L] : love conquers all

onus pro·ban·di \ˌō-nus-prō-ˈban-ˌdī, -dē\ [L] : burden of proof

ora pro no·bis \ˌō-rä-prō-ˈnō-ˌbēs\ [L] : pray for us

ore ro·tun·do \ˌȯr-ē-rō-ˈtən-dō\ [L] : with round mouth : eloquently

oro y pla·ta \ˌȯr-ō-ē-ˈplä-tə\ [Sp] : gold and silver — motto of Montana

o tem·po·ra! o mo·res! \ō-ˈtem-pȯ-rä ō-ˈmō-ˌräs\ [L] : oh the times! oh the manners!

oti·um cum dig·ni·ta·te \ˈō-tē-ˌum-kùm-ˌdig-ni-ˈtä-te\ [L] : leisure with dignity

où sont les neiges d'an·tan? \ü-sō²-lä-

nezh-dä²-tä² [F] : where are the snows of yesteryear?

outre–mer \ütr³-mer\ [F] : overseas : distant lands

pal·li·da Mors \ˌpa-li-dä-ˈmȯrz\ [L] : pale Death

pa·nem et cir·cen·ses \ˈpä-ˌnem-et-kir-ˈkän-ˌsäs\ [L] : bread and circuses : provision of the means of life and recreation by government to appease discontent

pan·ta rhei \ˌpän-ˌtä-ˈrā\ [Gk] : all things are in flux

par avance \pär-ä-vä²s\ [F] : in advance : by anticipation

par avion \pär-ä-vyō²\ [F] : by airplane — used on airmail

par ex·em·ple \pär-äg-zä²plᵊ\ [F] : for example

pars pro to·to \ˈpärs-(ˌ)prō-ˈtō-(ˌ)tō\ [L] : part (taken) for the whole

par·tu·ri·unt mon·tes, nas·ce·tur ri·di·cu·lus mus \pär-ˈtùr-ē-ˌùnt-ˈmȯn-ˌtäs näs-ˈkä-ˌtùr-ri-ˌdi-kù-lùs-ˈmüs\ [L] : the mountains are in labor, and a ridiculous mouse will be brought forth

pa·ter pa·tri·ae \ˈpä-ˌter-ˈpä-trē-ˌī\ [L] : father of his country

pau·cis ver·bis \ˌpaù-ˌkēs-ˈwer-ˌbēs\ [L] : in a few words

pax vo·bis·cum \ˈpäks-vō-ˈbēs-ˌkùm\ [L] : peace (be) with you

peine forte et dure \pen-fȯr-tä-dᵘer\ [F] : strong and hard punishment : torture

per an·gus·ta ad au·gus·ta \per-ˈän-ˌgus-tä-äd-ˈaù-ˌgus-tä\ [L] : through difficulties to honors

per·fide Al·bion \per-fēd-äl-byō²\ [F] : perfidious Albion (England)

peu à peu \pœ-ä-pœ\ [F] : little by little

peu de chose \pœd-shōz, pœ-də-\ [F] : a trifle

pièce d'oc·ca·sion \pyes-dȯ-kä-zyō²\ [F] : piece for a special occasion

pinx·it \ˈpink-sit\ [L] : he or she painted it

place aux dames \pläs-ō-däm\ [F] : (make) room for the ladies

ple·no ju·re \ˌplä-nō-ˈyúr-e\ [L] : with full right

plus ça change, plus c'est la même chose \plœ-sä-shä²zh plœ-se-lä-mem-shōz\ [F] : the more that changes, the more it's the same thing — often shortened to *plus ça change*

plus roy·a·liste que le roi \plœ-rwä-yä-lēst-kəl-rwä\ [F] : more royalist than the king

po·cas pa·la·bras \ˌpō-käs-pä-ˈlä-vräs\ [Sp] : few words

po·eta nas·ci·tur, non fit \pō-ˌä-tä-ˈnäs-ki-ˌtùr nōn-ˈfit\ [L] : a poet is born, not made

po·ète mau·dit \pō-et-mō-dē\ [F] : accursed poet : a writer dogged by misfortune and lack of recognition

pol·li·ce ver·so \ˌpȯ-li-ke-ˈwer-sō\ [L]

: with thumb turned : with a gesture or expression of condemnation

post hoc, er·go prop·ter hoc \'pòst-,hōk ,er-gō-'pròp-ter-,hōk\ [L] : after this, therefore on account of it (a fallacy of argument)

post ob·itum \pòst-'ò-bi-,tùm\ [L] : after death

pour ac·quit \pür-ä-kē\ [F] : received payment

pour en·cou·ra·ger les autres \pür-än-kü-rä-zhä-lā-zōtr³\ [F] : in order to encourage the others — said ironically of an action (as an execution) carried out in order to compel others to obey

pour le mé·rite \pür-lə-mā-rēt\ [F] : for merit

pri·mum non no·ce·re \prē-mùm-,nōn-nō-'kā-rā\ [L] : the first thing (is) to do no harm

pro aris et fo·cis \prō-,ä-,rēs-et-'fò-,kēs\ [L] : for altars and firesides

pro bo·no pu·bli·co \prō-,bò-nō-'pü-bli-,kō\ [L] : for the public good

pro hac vi·ce \prō-,häk-'wi-ke\ [L] : for this occasion

pro pa·tria \prō-'pä-trē-,ä\ [L] : for one's country

pro re·ge, le·ge, et gre·ge \prō-'rā-,ge 'lā-,ge et-'gre-,ge\ [L] : for the king, the law, and the people

pro re na·ta \prō-,rā-'nä-tä\ [L] : for an occasion that has arisen : as needed — used in medical prescriptions

quand même \kän-mem\ [F] : even so : all the same

quan·tum mu·ta·tus ab il·lo \,kwän-tùm-mü-'tä-tùs-äb-'i-lō\ [L] : how changed from what he once was

quan·tum suf·fi·cit \,kwän-təm-'sə-fə-,kit\ [L] : as much as suffices : a sufficient quantity — used chiefly in medical prescriptions

¿quién sa·be? \kyän-'sä-vä\ [Sp] : who knows?

qui fa·cit per ali·um fa·cit per se \kwē-,fä-kit-,per-'ä-lē-,ùm-,fä-kit-,per-'sä\ [L] : he who does (something) through another does it through himself

quis cus·to·di·et ip·sos cus·to·des? \,kwis-kùs-'tō-dē-,et-,ip-,sōs-kùs-'tō-,dās\ [L] : who will keep the keepers themselves?

qui s'ex·cuse s'ac·cuse \kē-'sek-,skuez-'sä-,kuez\ [F] : he who excuses himself accuses himself

quis se·pa·ra·bit? \,kwis-,sä-pə-'rä-bit\ [L] : who shall separate (us)? — motto of the Order of St. Patrick

qui trans·tu·lit sus·ti·net \kwē-'träns-tù-,lit-'sùs-ti-,net\ [L] : He who transplanted sustains (us) — motto of Connecticut

qui va là? \kē-vä-lä\ [F] : who goes there?

quo·ad hoc \,kwò-,äd-'hōk\ [L] : as far as this : to this extent

quod erat de·mon·stran·dum \,kwòd-

'er-,ät-,de-mən-'stran-dəm, -,dä-,mòn-'strän-,dúm\ [L] : which was to be demonstrated

quod erat fa·ci·en·dum \-,fä-kē-'en-,dúm\ [L] : which was to be done

quod sem·per, quod ubi·que, quod ab om·ni·bus \kwòd-'sem-,per kwòd-'ù-bi-,kwä ,kwòd-äb-'óm-ni-,bùs, -,kwòd-ù-'bē-(,)kwä-\ [L] : what (has been held) always, everywhere, by everybody

quod vi·de \kwòd-'wi-,de\ [L] : which see

quo·rum pars mag·na fui \'kwòr-ùm-,pärs-,mäg-nä-'fù-ē\ [L] : in which I played a great part

quos de·us vult per·de·re pri·us de·men·tat \kwōs-'dä-ùs-,wùlt-'per-de-,rä-,pri-ùs-dä-'men-,tät\ [L] : those whom a god wishes to destroy he first drives mad

quot ho·mi·nes, tot sen·ten·ti·ae \kwòt-'hò-mi-,nās ,tòt-sen-'ten-tē-,ī\ [L] : there are as many opinions as there are men

quo va·dis? \kwō-'wä-dis, -'vä-dəs\ [L] : whither are you going?

rai·son d'état \re-zōn-dā-tä\ [F] : reason of state

re·cu·ler pour mieux sau·ter \rə-kue-lā-pür-myœ-sō-tä\ [F] : to draw back in order to make a better jump

reg·nat po·pu·lus \,reg-,nät-'pò-pù-,lùs\ [L] : the people rule — motto of Arkansas

re in·fec·ta \,rä-in-'fek-,tä\ [L] : the business being unfinished : without accomplishing one's purpose

re·li·gio lo·ci \re-'li-gē-,ō-'lò-,kē\ [L] : religious sanctity of a place

rem acu te·ti·gis·ti \rem-'ä-,kü-,te-ti-'gis-tē\ [L] : you have touched the point with a needle : you have hit the nail on the head

ré·pon·dez s'il vous plaît \rā-pōn-dā-sēl-vü-ple\ [F] : reply, if you please

re·qui·es·cat in pa·ce \,re-kwē-'es-,kät-in-'pä-,ke, ,rä-kwē-'es-,kät-in-'pä-,chä\ [L] : may he or she rest in peace — used on tombstones

re·spi·ce fi·nem \,rā-spi-,ke-'fē-,nem\ [L] : look to the end : consider the outcome

re·sur·gam \re-'sùr-,gäm\ [L] : I shall rise again

re·te·nue \rət-nœ\ [F] : self-restraint : reserve

re·ve·nons à nos mou·tons \rəv-nōn-ä-nō-mü-tōn\ [F] : let us return to our sheep : let us get back to the subject

ruse de guerre \rùez-də-ger\ [F] : war stratagem

rus in ur·be \,rüs-in-'ùr-,be\ [L] : country in the city

sae·va in·dig·na·tio \,sī-wä-,in-dig-'nä-tē-ō\ [L] : fierce indignation

sal At·ti·cum \sal-'a-ti-kəm\ [L] : Attic salt : wit

salle à man·ger \säl-ä-män-zhā\ [F] : dining room

sa·lon des re·fu·sés \sä-lōn-dār-(ə-)fue-zä\ [F] : salon of the refused : exhibition of art that has been rejected by an official body

sa·lus po·pu·li su·pre·ma lex es·to \ˌsä-ˌlüs-ˈpō-pu̇-ˌlē-sü-ˌprā-mä-ˌleks-ˈes-tō\ [L] : let the welfare of the people be the supreme law — motto of Missouri

sanc·ta sim·pli·ci·tas \ˌsaŋk-tä-sim-ˈpli-ki-ˌtäs\ [L] : holy simplicity — often used ironically in reference to another's naïveté

sans doute \sän-ˈdüt\ [F] : without doubt

sans gêne \sän-ˈzhen\ [F] : without embarrassment or constraint

sans peur et sans re·proche \sän-ˈpœr-ä-säⁿ-rə-ˈprȯsh\ [F] : without fear and without reproach

sans sou·ci \sän-sü-sē\ [F] : without worry

sa·yo·na·ra \ˌsī-ə-ˈnär-ə, ˌsä-yə-\ [Jp] : good-bye

sculp·sit \ˈskəlp-sət, ˈskülp-sit\ [L] : he or she carved it

scu·to bo·nae vo·lun·ta·tis tu·ae co·ro·nas·ti nos \ˈskü-ˌtō-ˈbȯ-ˌnī-ˌvȯ-lùn-ˌtä-tis-ˈtü-ˌī-ˈkȯr-ȯ-ˌnäs-tē-ˈnōs\ [L] : Thou hast crowned us with the shield of Thy good will — a motto on the Great Seal of Maryland

se·cun·dum ar·tem \se-ˌkün-dùm-ˈär-ˌtem\ [L] : according to the art : according to the accepted practice of a profession or trade

secundum na·tu·ram \-nä-ˈtü-ˌräm\ [L] : according to nature : naturally

se de·fen·den·do \ˈsä-ˌdā-ˌfen-ˈden-dō\ [L] : in self-defense

se ha·bla es·pa·ñol \sä-ˌäv-lä-ˌäs-pä-ˈnyȯl\ [Sp] : Spanish spoken

sem·per ea·dem \ˌsem-ˌper-ˈe-ä-ˌdem\ [L] : always the same (fem.) — motto of Queen Elizabeth I

sem·per fi·de·lis \ˌsem-pər-fə-ˈdā-ləs\ [L] : always faithful — motto of the U.S. Marine Corps

sem·per idem \ˌsem-ˌper-ˈē-ˌdem\ [L] : always the same (masc.)

sem·per pa·ra·tus \ˌsem-pər-pə-ˈrä-təs\ [L] : always prepared — motto of the U.S. Coast Guard

se non è ve·ro, è ben tro·va·to \sä-ˌnȯn-e-ˈvä-rō e-ˌben-trō-ˈvä-tō\ [It] : even if it is not true, it is well conceived

sha·lom alei·chem \ˌshȯ-lom-ə-ˈlā-kəm, ˌshō-, -kəm\ [Heb *shālôm 'alēkhem*] : peace to you — used as a traditional Jewish greeting

sic itur ad as·tra \sēk-ˈi-ˌtùr-ˌäd-ˈäs-trə\ [L] : thus one goes to the stars : such is the way to immortality

sic sem·per ty·ran·nis \ˌsik-ˌsem-pər-tə-ˈra-nəs\ [L] : thus ever to tyrants — motto of Virginia

sic trans·it glo·ria mun·di \ˌsēk-ˈträn-sit-ˌglȯr-ē-ä-ˈmùn-dē\ [L] : so passes away the glory of the world

si jeu·nesse sa·vait, si vieil·lesse pou·vait! \sē-ˈzhœ-nes-ˈsä-ve sē-ˈvye-yes-ˈpü-ve\ [F] : if youth only knew, if age only could!

si·lent le·ges in·ter ar·ma \ˌsi-ˌlent-ˈlā-ˌgäs-ˌin-ter-ˈär-mä\ [L] : the laws are silent in the midst of arms (i.e., in time of war)

s'il vous plaît \sēl-vü-ple\ [F] : if you please

si·mi·lia si·mi·li·bus cu·ran·tur \si-ˈmi-lē-ä-si-ˈmi-li-bùs-kü-ˈrän-ˌtùr\ [L] : like is cured by like

si·mi·lis si·mi·li gau·det \ˈsi-mi-lis-ˈsi-mi-lē-ˈgaù-det\ [L] : like takes pleasure in like

si mo·nu·men·tum re·qui·ris, cir·cum·spi·ce \ˌsē-ˌmȯ-nù-ˌmen-tùm-re-ˈkwē-ris kir-ˈkùm-spi-ke\ [L] : if you seek his monument, look around — epitaph of Sir Christopher Wren in St. Paul's, London, of which he was architect

sim·pliste \saⁿ-plēst\ [F] : simplistic : overly simple or naïve

si quae·ris pen·in·su·lam amoe·nam, cir·cum·spi·ce \ˌsē-ˈkwī-ris-pä-ˈnin-sə-ˌläm-ä-ˈmȯi-ˌnäm kir-ˈkùm-spi-ke\ [L] : if you seek a beautiful peninsula, look around — motto of Michigan

sis·te vi·a·tor \ˌsis-te-wē-ˈä-ˌtȯr\ [L] : stop, traveler — used on Roman roadside tombs

si vis pa·cem, pa·ra bel·lum \sē-ˈwēs-pä-ˌkem ˈpä-rä-ˈbe-ˌlùm\ [L] : if you wish peace, prepare for war

sol·vi·tur am·bu·lan·do \ˈsȯl-wi-ˌtùr-ˌäm-bù-ˈlän-dō\ [L] : it is solved by walking : the problem is solved by a practical experiment

spo·lia opi·ma \ˌspȯ-lē-ä-ō-ˈpē-mä\ [L] : rich spoils : the arms taken by the victorious from the vanquished general

sta·tus quo an·te bel·lum \ˈstä-tùs-kwō-ˌän-te-ˈbe-lùm\ [L] : the state existing before the war

sua·vi·ter in mo·do, for·ti·ter in re \ˈswä-wi-ˌter-in-ˈmȯ-dō ˈfȯr-ti-ˌter-in-ˈrā\ [L] : gently in manner, strongly in deed

sub ver·bo \sùb-ˈwer-bō, ˌsəb-ˈvər-bō\ *or* **sub vo·ce** \sùb-ˈwȯ-ke, ˌsəb-ˈvō-sē\ [L] : under the word — introducing a cross-reference in a dictionary or index

sunt la·cri·mae re·rum \sùnt-ˌlä-kri-ˌmī-ˈrä-rùm\ [L] : there are tears for things : tears attend trials

suo ju·re \ˌsù-ō-ˈyùr-e\ [L] : in his or her own right

suo lo·co \-ˈlȯ-kō\ [L] : in its proper place

suo Mar·te \-ˈmär-te\ [L] : by one's own exertions

su·um cui·que \ˌsù-ùm-ˈkwi-kwe\ [L] : to each his own

tant mieux \täⁿ-myœ\ [F] : so much the better

tant pis \-pē\ [F] : so much the worse : too bad

tem·po·ra mu·tan·tur, nos et mu·ta·mur in il·lis \ˌtem-pȯ-rä-mü-ˈtän-ˌtùr

,nōs-,et-mü-,tä-mùr-in-'i-,lēs\ [L] : the times are changing, and we are changing with them

tem·pus edax re·rum \'tem-pús-,e-,däks-'rä-rùm\ [L] : time, that devours all things

tem·pus fu·git \,tem-pəs-'fyü-jət, ,tem-pús-'fü-git\ [L] : time flies

ti·meo Da·na·os et do·na fe·ren·tes \,ti-mē-,ō-'dä-nä-,ōs-,et-,dō-nä-fe-'ren-,tās\ [L] : I fear the Greeks even when they bring gifts

to·ti·dem ver·bis \,tō-ti-,dem-'wer-,bēs\ [L] : in so many words

to·tis vi·ri·bus \,tō-,tēs-'wē-ri-,bùs\ [L] : with all one's might

to·to cae·lo \,tō-tō-'kī-lō\ *or* **toto coe·lo** \-'kói-lō\ [L] : by the whole extent of the heavens : diametrically

tou·jours per·drix \tü-zhür-per-drē\ [F] : always partridge : too much of a good thing

tour d'ho·ri·zon \tür-dò-rē-zō^n\ [F] : circuit of the horizon : general survey

tous frais faits \tü-fre-fe\ [F] : all expenses defrayed

tout à fait \tü-tä-fe\ [F] : altogether : quite

tout au con·traire \tü-tō-kō^n-trer\ [F] : quite the contrary

tout à vous \tü-tä-vü\ [F] : wholly yours : at your service

tout bien ou rien \tü-'bya^n-nü-'rya^n\ [F] : everything well (done) or nothing (attempted)

tout com·pren·dre c'est tout par·don·ner \'tü-kō^n-prä^n-drə-se-'tü-pär-dò-nā\ [F] : to understand all is to forgive all

tout court \tü-kür\ [F] : quite short : and nothing else : simply : just; *also* : brusquely

tout de même \tüt-mem\ [F] : all the same : nevertheless

tout de suite \tüt-sw^{y}ēt\ [F] : immediately; *also* : all at once : consecutively

tout en·sem·ble \tü-tä^n-sä^{n}bl$^\circ$\ [F] : all together : general effect

tout est per·du fors l'hon·neur \tü-te-per-dœ-fòr-lò-nœr\ *or* **tout est perdu hors l'honneur** \-dœ-ór-\ [F] : all is lost save honor

tout le monde \tü-lə-mō^{n}d\ [F] : all the world : everybody

tra·hi·son des clercs \trä-ē-zò^n-dä-klerk\ [F] : treason of the intellectuals

tranche de vie \trä^{n}sh-də-'vē\ [F] : slice of life

trist·esse \trē-stes\ [F] : melancholy

tru·di·tur di·es die \'trü-di-,túr-'di-,ās-'di-,ā\ [L] : day is pushed forth by day : one day hurries on another

tu·e·bor \tü-'ā-,bòr\ [L] : I will defend — a motto on the Great Seal of Michigan

ua mau ke ea o ka ai·na i ka po·no \ù-ä-'mä-ù-kā-'ā-ä-ō-kä-'ā-ē-nä-,e-kä-'pō-nō\ [Hawaiian] : the life of the land is perpet-

uated in righteousness — motto of Hawaii

über al·les \,ue-ber-'ä-les\ [G] : above everything else

Über·mensch \'ue-bər-,mench\ [G] : superman

ul·ti·ma ra·tio re·gum \'úl-ti-mä-,rä-tē-ō-'rä-gùm\ [L] : the final argument of kings, i.e., war

und so wei·ter \ùnt-zō-'vī-tər\ [G] : and so on

uno ani·mo \,ü-nō-'ä-ni-,mō\ [L] : with one mind : unanimously

ur·bi et or·bi \,ùr-bē-,et-'òr-bē\ [L] : to the city (Rome) and the world : to everyone

uti·le dul·ci \,ü-ti-le-'dùl-,kē\ [L] : the useful with the agreeable

ut in·fra \ùt-'in-frä\ [L] : as below

ut su·pra \ùt-'sü-prä\ [L] : as above

va·de re·tro me, Sa·ta·na \,wä-de-'rä-trō-,mä 'sä-tä-,nä\ [L] : get thee behind me, Satan

vae vic·tis \wī-'wik-,tēs\ [L] : woe to the vanquished

va·ria lec·tio \,wär-ē-ä-'lek-tē-,ō\ *pl* **va·ri·ae lec·ti·o·nes** \'wär-ē-,ī-,lek-tē-'ō-,nās\ [L] : variant reading

va·ri·um et mu·ta·bi·le sem·per fe·mi·na \,wär-ē-ùm-,et-,mü-'tä-bi-le-,sem-,per-'fä-mi-nä\ [L] : woman is ever a fickle and changeable thing

ve·di Na·po·li e poi mo·ri \,vä-dē-'nä-pō-lē-ä-,pó-ē-'mò-rē\ [It] : see Naples and then die

ve·ni, vi·di, vi·ci \,wä-nē ,wē-dē 'wē-kē, ,vä-nē ,vē-dē 'vē-chē\ [L] : I came, I saw, I conquered

ven·tre à terre \vä^n-trä-ter\ [F] : belly to the ground : at very great speed

ver·ba·tim ac lit·te·ra·tim \wer-'bä-tim-,äk-,li-te-'rä-tim\ [L] : word for word and letter for letter

ver·bum sat sa·pi·en·ti est \,wer-bùm-'sät-,sä-pē-'en-tē-,est\ [L] : a word to the wise is sufficient

via cru·cis \wē-ä-'krü-sis\ [L] : Way of the Cross : path of suffering

vieux jeu \vyœ-zhœ\ [F] : old game : old hat

vin·cit om·nia ve·ri·tas \,wiŋ-kit-'òm-nē-ä-'wā-ri-,täs\ [L] : truth conquers all things

vin·cu·lum ma·tri·mo·nii \,wiŋ-kù-lùm-,mä-tri-'mō-nē-,ē\ [L] : bond of marriage

vin du pays \va^n-dœ-pā-ē\ *or* **vin de pays** \va^n-də-\ [F] : wine of the locality

vir·gi·ni·bus pu·e·ris·que \wir-'gi-ni-bùs-,pù-e-'rēs-kwe\ [L] : for girls and boys

vir·go in·tac·ta \'vir-gō-in-'täk-tä\ [L] : untouched virgin

vir·tu·te et ar·mis \wir-'tü-te-,et-'är-mēs\ [L] : by valor and arms — motto of Mississippi

vis me·di·ca·trix na·tu·rae \\'wēs-ˌme-di-'kä-triks-nä-'tü-ˌrī\ [L] : the healing power of nature

vive la dif·fé·rence \vēv-lä-dē-fā-rä^{n}s\ [F] : long live the difference (between the sexes)

vive la reine \vēv-lä-ren\ [F] : long live the queen

vive le roi \vēv-lə-rwä\ [F] : long live the king

vix·e·re for·tes an·te Aga·mem·no·na \wik-ˌsä-re-'fór-ˌtäs-ˌän-te-ˌä-gä-'mem-nò-ˌnä\ [L] : brave men lived before Agamemnon

vogue la ga·lère \vòg-lä-gä-ler\ [F] : let the galley be kept rowing : keep on, whatever may happen

voi·là tout \vwä-lä-tü\ [F] : that's all

vox et prae·te·rea ni·hil \'wòks-et-prī-'ter-e-ä-'ni-ˌhil\ [L] : voice and nothing more

vox po·pu·li vox Dei \wòks-'pò-pù-ˌlē-ˌwòks-'dā-ē\ [L] : the voice of the people is the voice of God

Wan·der·jahr \'vän-dər-ˌyär\ [G] : year of wandering

wie geht's? \vē-'gāts\ [G] : how goes it? : how is it going? — used as a greeting

wun·der·bar \'vùn-dər-ˌbär\ [G] : wonderful

BIOGRAPHICAL NAMES

This section gives basic information on many notable figures from contemporary culture, history, legend, mythology, and biblical tradition. Figures from the Bible, myth, and legend are clearly identified as such.

In cases where individuals have alternate names, they are entered under the name by which they are best known. Names are generally alphabetized by the main element of the surname, without regard for connectives such as *da, de, van,* or *von* (as **Gama** . . . Vasco da). Names appearing in the entry in italics are original names, maiden names, or nicknames.

The first dates given in the entry are birth/death dates; other dates refer to terms in office, reigns, achievements, or honors. Abbreviations used here are listed in the front section Abbreviations in This Work.

Aar·on \'er-ən\ brother of Moses and 1st high priest of the Hebrews in the Bible

Aaron Hank 1934–   *Henry Louis Aaron* Amer. baseball player

Abel \'ā-bəl\ son of Adam and Eve and brother of Cain in the Bible

Abra·ham \'ā-brə-,ham\ patriarch and founder of the Hebrew people in the Bible; also revered by Muslims

Achil·les \ə-'ki-lēz\ hero of the Trojan War in Greek mythology

Ad·am \'a-dəm\ the 1st man in biblical tradition

Ad·ams \'a-dəmz\ Abigail 1744–1818 née *Smith* Amer. writer; wife of John Adams

Adams Ansel Easton 1902–1984 Amer. photographer

Adams John 1735–1826 2d pres. of the U.S. (1797–1801)

Adams John Quin·cy \'kwin-zē, -sē\ 1767–1848 6th pres. of the U.S. (1825–29); son of John and Abigail Adams

Adams Samuel 1722–1803 patriot in the Amer. Revolution

Ad·dams \'a-dəmz\ Jane 1860–1935 Amer. social worker; Nobel Prize winner (1931)

Ado·nis \ə-'dä-nəs, -'dō-\ youth in Greek mythology loved by Aphrodite

Ae·ne·as \i-'nē-əs\ Trojan hero in Greek and Roman mythology

Ae·o·lus \'ē-ə-ləs\ god of the winds in Greek mythology

Aes·chy·lus \'es-kə-ləs, 'ēs-\ 525–456 B.C. Greek dramatist

Aes·cu·la·pi·us \,es-k(y)ə-'lā-pē-əs\ god of medicine in Roman mythology — compare ASCLEPIUS

Ae·sop \'ē-,säp, -səp\ legendary Greek writer of fables

Ag·a·mem·non \,a-gə-'mem-,nän, -nən\ leader of the Greeks during the Trojan War in Greek mythology

Ag·nes \'ag-nəs\ Saint *died* 304 A.D. Christian martyr

Ahab \'ā-,hab\ king of Israel in the 9th cent. B.C. and husband of Jezebel

Ajax \'ā-jaks\ hero in Greek mythology who kills himself because the armor of Achilles is awarded to Odysseus during the Trojan War

Alad·din \ə-'la-dᵊn\ youth in the *Arabian Nights' Entertainments* who acquires a magic lamp

Al·bright \'ól-,brīt\ Madeleine 1937– née *Korbel* Amer. (Czech-born) diplomat; U.S. secretary of state (1997–2001)

Al·cott \'ól-kət, 'al-, -,kät\ Louisa May 1832–1888 Amer. author

Al·ex·an·der \,a-lig-'zan-dər, ,e-\ name of eight popes: esp. **VI** 1431–1503 (pope 1492–1503)

Alexander the Great 356–323 B.C. *Alexander III* king of Macedonia (336–323)

Al·fred \'al-frəd, -fərd\ 849–899 *Alfred the Great* king of the West Saxons (871–899)

Ali \ä-'lē\ Muhammad 1942–   orig. *Cassius Clay* Amer. boxer

Ali Ba·ba \,a-lē-'bä-bə, ,ä-lē-\ woodcutter in the *Arabian Nights' Entertainments* who enters the cave of the Forty Thieves by using the password *Sesame*

Al·len \'a-lən\ Ethan 1738–1789 Amer. Revolutionary soldier

Amerigo Vespucci — see VESPUCCI

Am·herst \'a-(,)mərst\ Jeffery 1717–1797 Baron *Amherst* Brit. general in America

Amund·sen \'ä-mən-sən\ Roald 1872–1928 Norwegian explorer

An·a·ni·as \,a-nə-'nī-əs\ early Christian in the Bible struck dead for lying

An·der·sen \'an-dər-sən\ Hans Christian 1805–1875 Danish writer of fairy tales

An·der·son \'an-dər-sən\ Marian 1897–1993 Amer. contralto

An·ge·lou \'an-jə-(,)lō, *commonly* -,lü\ Maya 1928–   orig. *Marguerite Johnson* Amer. author

Anne \'an\ 1665–1714 queen of Great Britain (1702–14)

An·tho·ny \'an(t)-thə-nē\ Susan Brownell 1820–1906 Amer. suffragist

An·tig·o·ne \an-'ti-gə-(,)nē\ daughter of Oedipus and Jocasta in Greek mythology

An·to·ny \'an-tə-nē\ Mark *ca* 82–30 B.C.

Marc Anthony; *Marcus An·to·ni·us* \an-ˈtō-nē-əs\ Roman general and triumvir (43–30)

Aph·ro·di·te \ˌa-frə-ˈdī-tē\ goddess of love and beauty in Greek mythology — compare VENUS

Apol·lo \ə-ˈpä-(ˌ)lō\ god of sunlight, prophecy, music, and poetry in Greek and Roman mythology

Ap·ple·seed \ˈap-əl-ˌsēd\ Johnny 1774–1845 orig. *John Chapman* Amer. pioneer

Aqui·nas \ə-ˈkwī-nəs\ Saint Thomas 1224/25–1274 Ital. theologian

Ar·chi·me·des \ˌär-kə-ˈmē-dēz\ *ca* 287–212 B.C. Greek mathematician and inventor

Ares \ˈa-(ˌ)rēz, ˈer-(ˌ)ēz\ god of war in Greek mythology — compare MARS

Ar·is·toph·a·nes \ˌa-rə-ˈstä-fə-ˌnēz\ *ca* 450–*ca* 388 B.C. Greek playwright

Ar·is·tot·le \ˈa-rə-ˌstä-tᵊl\ 384–322 B.C. Greek philosopher

Arm·strong \ˈärm-ˌstroŋ\ Lance 1971– Amer. cyclist

Armstrong Louis 1901–1971 *Satch·mo* \ˈsach-ˌmō\ Amer. jazz musician

Armstrong Neil Alden 1930– Amer. astronaut; 1st man on the moon (1969)

Ar·nold \ˈär-nᵊld\ Benedict 1741–1801 Amer. Revolutionary general and traitor

Ar·te·mis \ˈär-tə-məs\ goddess of the moon, wild animals, and hunting in Greek mythology — compare DIANA

Ar·thur \ˈär-thər\ legendary king of the Britons whose story is based on traditions of a 6th-century military leader — **Ar·thu·ri·an** \är-ˈthur-ē-ən, -ˈthyur-\ *adj*

Arthur Chester Alan 1829–1886 21st pres. of the U.S. (1881–85)

As·cle·pi·us \ə-ˈsklē-pē-əs\ god of medicine in Greek mythology — compare AESCULAPIUS

As·tor \ˈas-tər\ John Jacob 1763–1848 Amer. (Ger.-born) fur trader and capitalist

Athe·na \ə-ˈthē-nə\ *or* **Athe·ne** \-nē\ goddess of wisdom in Greek mythology — compare MINERVA

At·las \ˈat-ləs\ Titan in Greek mythology forced to bear the heavens on his shoulders

At·ti·la \ˈa-tə-lə, ə-ˈti-lə\ 406?–453 A.D. king of the Huns

At·tucks \ˈa-təks\ Crispus 1723?–1770 Amer. patriot

Au·du·bon \ˈo-də-bən, -ˌbän\ John James 1785–1851 Amer. (Haitian-born) artist and naturalist

Au·gus·tine \ˈo-gə-ˌstēn; o-ˈgəs-tən, ə-\ Saint 354–430 A.D. church father; bishop of Hippo (396–430)

Au·gus·tus \o-ˈgəs-təs, ə-\ *or* **Caesar Augustus** *or* **Oc·ta·vi·an** \äk-ˈtā-vē-ən\ 63 B.C.–14 A.D., 1st Roman emperor (27 B.C.–14 A.D.)

Au·ro·ra \ə-ˈrȯr-ə, o-\ goddess of the dawn in Roman mythology — compare EOS

Aus·ten \ˈos-tən, ˈäs-\ Jane 1775–1817 Eng. author

Bac·chus \ˈba-kəs, ˈbä-\ — see DIONYSUS

Bach \ˈbäk, ˈbäk\ Johann Sebastian 1685–1750 Ger. composer

Ba·con \ˈbā-kən\ Francis 1561–1626 Eng. philosopher and author

Ba·den–Pow·ell \ˈbä-dᵊn-ˈpō-əl\ Robert Stephenson Smyth 1857–1941 Baron *Baden-Powell* Brit. general and founder of Boy Scout movement

Baf·fin \ˈba-fən\ William *ca* 1584–1622 Eng. navigator

Bal·boa \bal-ˈbō-ə\ Vasco Núñez de 1475–1519 Span. explorer

Bal·ti·more \ˈbȯl-tə-ˌmȯr, -mər\ Lord — see George CALVERT

Bal·zac \ˈbȯl-ˌzak, ˈbal-\ Honoré de 1799–1850 French author

Ba·rab·bas \bə-ˈra-bəs\ prisoner in the Bible released in preference to Jesus at the demand of the multitude

Bar·num \ˈbär-nəm\ P. T. 1810–1891 *Phineas Taylor Barnum* Amer. showman

Bar·rie \ˈba-rē\ Sir James Matthew 1860–1937 Scot. author

Bar·thol·di \bär-ˈtäl-dē, -ˈtȯl-, -ˈthäl-, -ˈthȯl-\ Frédéric-Auguste 1834–1904 French sculptor of the Statue of Liberty

Bar·ton \ˈbär-tᵊn\ Clara 1821–1912 founder of American Red Cross

Beau·re·gard \ˈbȯr-ə-ˌgärd\ Pierre Gustave Toutant 1818–1893 Amer. Confederate general

Beck·et \ˈbe-kət\ Saint Thomas *ca* 1118–1170 *Thomas à Becket* archbishop of Canterbury (1162–70)

Beck·ett \ˈbe-kət\ Samuel 1906–1989 Irish playwright in France; Nobel Prize winner (1969)

Bee·tho·ven \ˈbā-ˌtō-vən\ Ludwig van 1770–1827 Ger. composer

Bell \ˈbel\ Alexander Graham 1847–1922 Amer. (Scot.-born) inventor of the telephone

Bel·low \ˈbe-(ˌ)lō\ Saul 1915–2005 Amer. (Canad.-born) author

Ben·e·dict \ˈbe-nə-ˌdikt\ name of 15 popes: esp. **XIV** 1675–1758 (pope 1740–58); **XV** 1854–1922 (pope 1914–22)

Be·nét \bə-ˈnā\ Stephen Vincent 1898–1943 Amer. author

Ben·ja·min \ˈben-jə-mən\ youngest son of Jacob and ancestor of one of the 12 tribes of Israel in the Bible

Ben·ton \ˈben-tᵊn\ Thomas Hart 1889–1975 Amer. painter

Be·o·wulf \ˈbā-ə-ˌwulf\ legendary warrior and hero of the Old Eng. poem *Beowulf*

Be·ring \ˈber-iŋ, ˈbir-\ Vitus 1681–1741 Danish navigator and explorer for Russia

Ber·lin \(ˌ)bər-ˈlin\ Irving 1888–1989 Amer. (Russ.-born) composer

Ber·ni·ni \ber-ˈnē-nē\ Gian Lorenzo

Biographical Names

1598–1680 Ital. sculptor, architect, and painter

Bes·se·mer \\'be-sə-mər\ Sir Henry 1813–1898 Eng. engineer and inventor

Be·thune \bə-'thün, -'thyün\ Mary 1875–1955 née *McLeod* Amer. educator

Bi·zet \bē-'zā\ Georges 1838–1875 French composer

Black Hawk \\'blak-ˌhȯk\ 1767–1838 Amer. Indian chief

Black·well \\'blak-ˌwel, -wəl\ Elizabeth 1821–1910 Amer. (Eng.-born) physician

Blair \\'bler\ Tony 1953– *Anthony Charles Lynton Blair* Brit. prime minister (1997–)

Blake \\'blāk\ William 1757–1827 Eng. poet and artist

Bloom·er \\'blü-mər\ Amelia 1818–1894 née *Jenks* Amer. social reformer

Boc·cac·cio \bō-'kä-ch(ē-ˌ)ō\ Giovanni 1313–1375 Ital. author

Bohr \\'bȯr\ Niels 1885–1962 Danish physicist; Nobel Prize winner (1922)

Bo·leyn \bu̇-'lin, -'lēn\ Anne 1507?–1536 2d wife of Henry VIII and mother of Elizabeth I of England

Bo·lí·var \bə-'lē-ˌvär; 'bä-lə-ˌvär, -vər\ Simón \sē-ˌmōn, ˌsī-mən\ 1783–1830 South Amer. liberator

Bon·i·face \\'bä-nə-fəs, -ˌfās\ name of 9 popes: esp. VIII *ca* 1235 (or 1240)–1303 (pope 1294–1303)

Boone \\'bün\ Daniel 1734–1820 Amer. pioneer

Booth \\'büth\ John Wilkes 1838–1865 Amer. actor; assassin of Abraham Lincoln

Bo·re·as \\'bȯr-ē-əs\ god of the north wind in Greek mythology

Bot·ti·cel·li \ˌbä-tə-'che-lē\ Sandro 1445–1510 Ital. painter

Bow·ie \\'bü-ē, 'bō-\ Jim 1796–1836 *James Bowie* Amer. popular hero of the Texas revolution

Boyle \\'bȯi(-ə)l\ Robert 1627–1691 Eng. physicist and chemist

Brad·bury \\'brad-ˌber-ē, -b(ə-)rē\ Ray Douglas 1920– Amer. author

Brad·dock \\'bra-dək\ Edward 1695–1755 Brit. general in America

Brad·ford \\'brad-fərd\ William 1590–1657 Pilgrim leader

Brad·street \\'brad-ˌstrēt\ Anne *ca* 1612–1672 Amer. poet

Bra·dy \\'brā-dē\ Mathew B. 1823?–1896 Amer. photographer

Brahe \\'brä; 'brä-hē, -hə\ Tycho 1546–1601 Danish astronomer

Brah·ma \\'brä-mə\ creator god of the Hindu sacred triad — compare SHIVA; VISHNU

Brahms \\'brämz\ Johannes 1833–1897 Ger. composer

Braille \\'brāl, 'brī\ Louis 1809–1852 French blind teacher of the blind

Brant \\'brant\ Joseph 1742–1807 *Thayendanegea* Mohawk Indian chief

Brant Mary 1736?–1796 *Molly Brant* Mohawk Indian leader; sister of Joseph Brant

Braun \\'brau̇n\ Wernher von 1912–1977 Amer. (Ger.-born) rocket engineer

Brezh·nev \\'brezh-ˌnef\ Leonid Ilich 1906–1982 Soviet leader of the Communist Party (1964–82); pres. of the U.S.S.R. (1960–64; 1977–82)

Bron·të \\'brän-tē, -ˌtä\ family of Eng. writers: Charlotte 1816–1855 and her sisters Emily 1818–1848 and Anne 1820–1849

Brooks \\'bru̇ks\ Gwendolyn Elizabeth 1917–2000 Amer. poet

Brown \\'brau̇n\ John 1800–1859 Amer. abolitionist

Brow·ning \\'brau̇-niŋ\ Elizabeth Barrett 1806–1861 Eng. poet

Browning Robert 1812–1889 Eng. poet; husband of the preceding

Bru·tus \\'brü-təs\ Marcus Junius 85–42 B.C. Roman politician; one of Julius Caesar's assassins

Bry·an \\'brī-ən\ William Jennings 1860–1925 Amer. lawyer and politician

Bu·chan·an \byü-'ka-nən, bə-\ James 1791–1868 15th pres. of the U.S. (1857–61)

Buck \\'bək\ Pearl S. 1892–1973 née *Sydenstricker* Amer. author; Nobel Prize winner (1938)

Bud·dha \\'bü-də, 'bu̇-\ *ca* 563–*ca* 483 B.C. orig. *Siddhartha Gautama* Indian founder of Buddhism

Buffalo Bill — see W. F. CODY

Bun·yan \\'bən-yən\ John 1628–1688 Eng. preacher and author

Bunyan Paul — see PAUL BUNYAN

Bur·bank \\'bər-ˌbaŋk\ Luther 1849–1926 Amer. horticulturist

Bur·goyne \(ˌ)bər-'gȯin, 'bər-ˌ\ John 1722–1792 Brit. general in America

Burns \\'bərnz\ Robert 1759–1796 Scot. poet

Burn·side \\'bərn-ˌsīd\ Ambrose Everett 1824–1881 Amer. general

Burr \\'bər\ Aaron 1756–1836 vice pres. of the U.S. (1801–5)

Bush \\'bu̇sh\ George (Herbert Walker) 1924– 41st pres. of the U.S. (1989–93)

Bush George W. 1946– *George Walker Bush* 43rd pres. of the U.S. (2001–); son of the preceding

By·ron \\'bī-rən\ Lord 1788–1824 *George Gordon Byron*, 6th Baron *Byron* Eng. poet

Cab·ot \\'ka-bət\ John *ca* 1450–*ca* 1499 orig. *Giovanni Ca·bo·to* \kä-'bō-tō\ Ital. navigator; explorer for England

Cabot Sebastian 1476?–1557 Eng. navigator; son of J. Cabot

Ca·bri·ni \kə-'brē-nē\ Saint Frances Xavier 1850–1917 *Mother Cabrini* 1st Amer. (Ital.-born) saint (1946)

Cae·sar \\'sē-zər\ (Gaius) Julius 100?–44 B.C. Roman general, political leader, and writer

Cain \'kān\ son of Adam and Eve and brother of Abel in the Bible

Calamity Jane \kə-'la-mə-tē-\ 1852?–1903 *Martha Jane Burk* \'bərk\ née *Cannary* \'ka-nə-rē\ Amer. frontier figure

Cal·houn \kal-'hün\ John Caldwell 1782–1850 vice pres. of the U.S. (1825–32)

Ca·lig·u·la \kə-'li-gyə-lə\ 12–41 A.D. Roman emperor (37–41)

Cal·li·ope \kə-'lī-ə-(,)pē\ muse of heroic poetry in Greek mythology

Cal·vert \'kal-vərt\ George 1580?–1632 Baron *Baltimore* Eng. colonist in America

Cal·vin \'kal-vən\ John 1509–1564 *Jean Calvin* or *Cau·vin* \kō-'vaⁿ\ French theologian and reformer

Ca·mus \kä-'mue\ Albert 1913–1960 French author; Nobel Prize winner (1957)

Ca·nute \kə-'nüt, -'nyüt\ *died* 1035 *Canute the Great* Danish king of England (1016–35); of Denmark (1018–35); of Norway (1028–35)

Car·ne·gie \kär-'ne-gē, 'kär-nə-gē\ Andrew 1835–1919 Amer. (Scot.-born) industrialist and philanthropist

Car·roll \'ka-rəl\ Lewis 1832–1898 pseud. of *Charles Lutwidge Dodgson* Eng. author and mathematician

Car·son \'kär-sᵊn\ Kit 1809–1868 *Christopher Carson* Amer. frontiersman and guide

Carson Rachel Louise 1907–1964 Amer. scientist and writer

Car·ter \'kär-tər\ Jimmy 1924– orig. *James Earl Carter, Jr.* 39th pres. of the U.S. (1977–81); Nobel Prize winner (2002)

Car·tier \kär-'tyā, 'kär-tē-,ā\ Jacques 1491–1557 French explorer

Ca·ru·so \kə-'rü-(,)sō, -(,)zō\ En·ri·co \en-'rē-kō\ 1873–1921 Ital. tenor

Car·ver \'kär-vər\ George Washington 1861?–1943 Amer. agricultural chemist and agronomist

Ca·sa·no·va \,ka-zə-'nō-və, ,ka-sə-\ Giovanni Giacomo 1725–1798 Ital. adventurer

Cas·san·dra \kə-'san-drə, -'sän-\ daughter of Priam in Greek mythology who is endowed with the gift of prophecy but fated never to be believed

Cas·satt \kə-'sat\ Mary 1845–1926 Amer. painter

Cas·tro \'käs-(,)trō\ **(Ruz)** \'rüs\ Fidel 1926– Cuban premier (1959–)

Cath·er \'ka-thər\ Willa 1873–1947 Amer. author

Cath·er·ine \'ka-th(ə-)rən\ name of 1st, 5th, and 6th wives of Henry VIII of England: Catherine of Aragon 1485–1536; Catherine Howard 1520?–1542; Catherine Parr 1512–1548

Catherine I 1684–1727 wife of Peter the Great; empress of Russia (1725–27)

Catherine II 1729–1796 *Catherine the Great* empress of Russia (1762–96)

Catherine de Mé·di·cis \-də-,mā-dē-'sēs, -'me-də-(,)chē\ 1519–1589 Ital. *Ca·te·ri·na de' Me·di·ci* \,kä-tā-'rē-nä-dā-'me-dē-(,)chē\ queen consort of Henry II of France (1547–59) and regent of France (1560–74)

Cav·en·dish \'ka-vən-(,)dish\ Henry 1731–1810 Eng. scientist

Ce·ci·lia \sə-'sēl-yə, -'sil-\ Saint *fl.* 3d cent. A.D. Christian martyr; patron saint of music

Ce·res \'sir-(,)ēz\ goddess of agriculture in Roman mythology — compare DEMETER

Cer·van·tes \sər-'van-,tēz, -'vän-,tās\ Miguel de 1547–1616 Span. author

Cé·zanne \sā-'zan\ Paul 1839–1906 French painter

Cha·gall \shə-'gäl, -'gal\ Marc 1887–1985 Russ. painter in France

Cham·plain \,sham-'plān, shäⁿ-'plaⁿ\ Samuel de 1567–1635 French explorer in America

Chap·lin \'cha-plən\ Charlie 1889–1977 Sir *Charles Spencer Chaplin* Brit. actor and producer

Chapman \'chap-mən\ John — see Johnny APPLESEED

Char·le·magne \'shär-lə-,mān\ 742–814 A.D. *Charles the Great* or *Charles I* Frankish king (768–814); emperor of the West (800–814)

Charles \'chär(-ə)lz\ name of 10 kings of France: esp. **II** 823–877 A.D. *Charles the Bald* (r. 840–77); Holy Roman emperor (875–77); **IV** 1294–1328 *Charles the Fair* (r. 1322–28); **V** 1337–1380 *Charles the Wise* (r. 1364–80); **VI** 1368–1422 *Charles the Mad* or *the Beloved* (r. 1380–1422); **VII** 1403–1461 *Charles the Well-Served* or *the Victorious* (r. 1422–61); **IX** 1550–1574 (r. 1560–74); **X** 1757–1836 (r. 1824–30)

Charles name of 2 kings of Great Britain: **I** 1600–1649 (r. 1625–49); **II** 1630–1685 (r. 1660–85); son of Charles I

Charles V 1500–1558 Holy Roman emperor (1519–56); king of Spain as *Charles I* (1516–56)

Charles Edward Stuart — see Charles Edward STUART

Charles Mar·tel \-mär-'tel\ *ca* 688–741 A.D. Frankish ruler (719–41); grandfather of Charlemagne

Cha·ryb·dis \kə-'rib-dəs\ whirlpool off the coast of Sicily personified in Greek mythology as a female monster

Chau·cer \'chô-sər\ Geoffrey *ca* 1342–1400 Eng. poet

Che·khov \'che-,kôf, -,kòv\ Anton Pavlovich 1860–1904 Russ. author

Che·ney \'chē-nē, *commonly* 'chā-\ Richard Bruce 1941– vice pres. of the U.S. (2001–)

Cheops — see KHUFU

Ches·ter·ton \'ches-tər-tən\ G. K. 1874–1936 *Gilbert Keith Chesterton* Eng. author

Cho·pin \'shō-ˌpan, -ˌpanⁿ\ Frédéric François 1810–1849 Polish composer

Chou En–lai or Zhou Enlai \'jō-'en-'lī\ 1898–1976 Chinese Communist politician; premier (1949–76)

Chré·tien \krā-'tyanⁿ\ Jean 1934– Canad. prime minister (1993–2003)

Christ Jesus — see JESUS

Chris·tie \'kris-tē\ Dame Agatha 1890–1976 née Miller Eng. author

Chur·chill \'chər-ˌchil, 'chərch-ˌhil\ Sir Winston Leonard Spencer 1874–1965 Brit. prime minister (1940–45; 1951–55) Nobel Prize winner (1953)

Clark \klärk\ George Rogers 1752–1818 Amer. soldier and frontiersman

Clark William 1770–1838 Amer. explorer (with Meriwether Lewis)

Clay \'klā\ Henry 1777–1852 Amer. politician and orator

Clem·ens \'kle-mənz\ Samuel Langhorne — see Mark TWAIN

Cle·o·pa·tra \ˌklē-ə-'pa-trə, -'pä-\ 69–30 B.C. queen of Egypt (51–30)

Cleve·land \'klēv-lənd\ (Stephen) Grover 1837–1908 22nd and 24th pres. of the U.S. (1885–89; 1893–97)

Clin·ton \'klin-tᵊn\ William Jefferson 1946– Bill Clinton 42nd pres. of the U.S. (1993–2001)

Cly·tem·nes·tra \ˌklī-təm-'nes-trə\ wife of Agamemnon in Greek mythology

Cobb \'käb\ Ty 1886–1961 Tyrus Raymond Cobb Amer. baseball player

Co·chise \kō-'chēs\ 1812?–1874 Apache Indian chief

Co·dy \'kō-dē\ William Frederick 1846–1917 Buffalo Bill Amer. hunter, guide, and showman

Co·han \'kō-ˌhan\ George Michael 1878–1942 Amer. composer

Cole·ridge \'kōl-rij, 'kō-lə-rij\ Samuel Taylor 1772–1834 Eng. poet

Co·lette \kȯ-'let\ 1873–1954 orig. Sidonie-Gabrielle Colette French author

Co·lum·bus \kə-'ləm-bəs\ Christopher 1451–1506 Ital. navigator and explorer for Spain

Con·fu·cius \kən-'fyü-shəs\ 551–479 B.C. Chinese philosopher

Con·rad \'kän-ˌrad\ Joseph 1857–1924 Brit. (Polish-born) author

Con·sta·ble \'kən(t)-stə-bəl, 'kän(t)-\ John 1776–1837 Eng. painter

Con·stan·tine I \'kän(t)-stən-ˌtēn, -ˌtīn\ after 280–337 A.D. Constantine the Great Roman emperor (306–37)

Cook \'kůk\ Captain James 1728–1779 Eng. navigator

Coo·lidge \'kü-lij\ (John) Calvin 1872–1933 30th pres. of the U.S. (1923–29)

Coo·per \'kü-pər, 'ků-\ James Fenimore 1789–1851 Amer. author

Co·per·ni·cus \kō-'pər-ni-kəs\ Nicolaus 1473–1543 Polish astronomer

Cop·land \'kō-plənd\ Aaron 1900–1990 Amer. composer

Cop·ley \'kä-plē\ John Singleton 1738–1815 Amer. painter

Corn·plan·ter \'kȯrn-ˌplan-tər\ ca 1732–1836 John O'Bail Seneca Indian leader of partly European ancestry

Corn·wal·lis \kȯrn-'wä-ləs\ Charles 1738–1805 1st Marquess Cornwallis Brit. general in America

Co·ro·na·do \ˌkȯr-ə-'nä-(ˌ)dō, ˌkär-\ Francisco Vásquez de ca 1510–1554 Span. explorer of southwestern U.S.

Cor·tés \kȯr-'tez, 'kȯr-ˌ\ Hernán or Hernando 1485–1547 Span. conqueror of Mexico

Cous·teau \kü-'stō\ Jacques-Yves 1910–1997 French marine explorer

Crane \'krān\ Stephen 1871–1900 Amer. author

Crazy Horse \'krā-zē-ˌhȯrs\ 1842?–1877 Ta-sunko-witko Sioux Indian chief

Crock·ett \'krä-kət\ Davy 1786–1836 David Crockett Amer. frontiersman

Crom·well \'kräm-ˌwel, 'krəm-, -wəl\ Oliver 1599–1658 Eng. general; lord protector of England (1653–58)

Cro·nus \'krō-nəs, 'krä-\ Titan in Greek mythology overthrown by his son Zeus

Cum·mings \'kə-minz\ Edward Estlin 1894–1962 known as e. e. cummings Amer. poet

Cu·pid \'kyü-pəd\ god of love in Roman mythology — compare EROS

Cu·rie \kyů-'rē, 'kyůr-(ˌ)ē\ Marie 1867–1934 née Sklo·dow·ska \sklə-'dȯf-skə\ French (Polish-born) chemist; Nobel Prize winner (1903, 1911)

Curie Pierre 1859–1906 French chemist; husband of M. Curie; Nobel Prize winner (1903)

Cus·ter \'kəs-tər\ George Armstrong 1839–1876 Amer. general

Cy·ra·no de Ber·ge·rac \'sir-ə-ˌnō-də-'ber-zhə-ˌrak\ Savinien 1619–1655 French playwright

Cy·rus II \'sī-rəs\ ca 585–ca 529 B.C. Cyrus the Great king of Persia (ca 550–529)

Dae·da·lus \'de-də-ləs, 'dē-\ builder in Greek mythology of the Cretan labyrinth and inventor of wings by which he and his son Icarus escape imprisonment

Dahl \'däl\ Roald 1916–1990 Brit. writer

Da·lí \'dä-lē, by himself dä-'lē\ Salvador 1904–1989 Span. painter

Dal·ton \'dȯl-tᵊn\ John 1766–1844 Eng. chemist and physicist

Da·na \'dä-nə\ Richard Henry 1815–1882 Amer. author

Dan·iel \'dan-yəl\ prophet in the Bible who is held captive in Babylon and delivered from a den of lions

Dan·te \'dän-(ˌ)tā, 'dan-, -(ˌ)tē\ 1265–1321 Dante Ali·ghie·ri \ˌa-lə-'gyer-ē\ Ital. poet

Dare \'der\ Virginia 1587–? 1st child born in America of Eng. parents

Da·ri·us I \də-'rī-əs\ 550–486 B.C. *Darius the Great* king of Persia (522–486)

Dar·row \'da-(ˌ)rō\ Clarence Seward 1857–1938 Amer. lawyer

Dar·win \'där-wən\ Charles Robert 1809–1882 Eng. naturalist

Da·vid \'dā-vəd\ a youth in the Bible who slays Goliath and succeeds Saul as king of Israel

Da·vis \'dā-vəs\ Jefferson 1808–1889 pres. of the Confederate States of America (1861–65)

Dawes \'dòz\ William 1745–1799 Amer. patriot

Debs \'debz\ Eugene Victor 1855–1926 Amer. socialist and labor organizer

De·bus·sy \ˌde-byü-'sē, ˌdā-\ Claude 1862–1918 French composer

De·ca·tur \di-'kā-tər\ Stephen 1779–1820 Amer. naval officer

De·foe \di-'fō\ Daniel 1660–1731 Eng. author

De·gas \də-'gä\ Edgar 1834–1917 French painter

de Gaulle \di-'gōl, -'gòl\ Charles 1890–1970 French general; pres. of Fifth Republic (1958–69)

De·li·lah \di-'lī-lə\ mistress and betrayer of Samson in the Bible

De·me·ter \di-'mē-tər\ goddess of agriculture in Greek mythology — compare CERES

de Mille \də-'mil\ Agnes 1905–1993 Amer. dancer and choreographer

De·mos·the·nes \di-'mäs-thə-ˌnēz\ 384–322 B.C. Athenian orator and statesman

Demp·sey \'dem(p)-sē\ Jack 1895–1983 orig. *William Harrison Dempsey* Amer. boxer

Des·cartes \dā-'kärt\ René 1596–1650 French mathematician and philosopher

de So·to \thä-'sō-(ˌ)tō, di-\ Hernando *ca* 1496–1542 Span. explorer

Dew·ey \'dü-ē, 'dyü-\ George 1837–1917 Amer. admiral

Dewey John 1859–1952 Amer. philosopher and educator

Dewey Melvil 1851–1931 Amer. librarian

Di·ana \dī-'a-nə\ ancient Ital. goddess of the forest and of childbirth who was identified with Artemis by the Romans

Dick·ens \'di-kənz\ Charles 1812–1870 pseud. *Boz* \'bäz, 'bōz\ Eng. author

Dick·in·son \'di-kən-sən\ Emily Elizabeth 1830–1886 Amer. poet

Di·do \'dī-(ˌ)dō\ legendary queen of Carthage who falls in love with Aeneas and kills herself when he leaves her

Di·Mag·gio \də-'mä-zhē-(ˌ)ō, -'ma-jē-(ˌ)ō\ Joe 1914–1999 *Joseph Paul DiMaggio* Amer. baseball player

Di·o·ny·sus \ˌdī-ə-'nī-səs, -'nē-\ god of wine and ecstasy in classical mythology

Dis·ney \'diz-nē\ Walt 1901–1966 *Walter Elias Disney* Amer. film producer and cartoonist

Dis·rae·li \diz-'rā-lē\ Benjamin 1804–1881 Earl of *Beaconsfield* Brit. prime minister (1868; 1874–80)

Dix \'diks\ Dorothea Lynde 1802–1887 Amer. social reformer

Dodg·son \'däd-sən, 'däj-\ Charles Lutwidge — see Lewis CARROLL

Donne \'dən\ John 1572–1631 Eng. poet and clergyman

Don Qui·xote \ˌdän-kē-'(h)ō-tē, ˌdän-\ hero of Cervantes' *Don Quixote*

Dos·to·yev·sky \ˌdäs-tə-'yef-skē, -'yev-\ Fyodor Mikhaylovich 1821–1881 Russ. novelist

Doug·las \'də-gləs\ Stephen Arnold 1813–1861 Amer. politician

Doug·lass \'də-gləs\ Frederick 1817–1895 Amer. abolitionist

Doyle \'dòi(-ə)l\ Sir Arthur Conan 1859–1930 Brit. physician and author

Drake \'drāk\ Sir Francis *ca* 1540–1596 Eng. navigator, explorer, and admiral

Drei·ser \'drī-sər, -zər\ Theodore 1871–1945 Amer. author

Du·Bois \dü-'bòis, dyü-\ William Edward Burghardt 1868–1963 Amer. educator and writer

Du·mas \dü-'mä, dyü-\ Alexandre 1802–1870 *Dumas père* \'per\ French author

Dumas Alexandre 1824–1895 *Dumas fils* \'fēs\ French author

Dun·can \'dəŋ-kən\ Isadora 1877–1927 Amer. dancer

Dü·rer \'dùr-ər, 'dyùr-, 'dùer-\ Albrecht 1471–1528 Ger. painter and engraver

Ea·kins \'ā-kənz\ Thomas 1844–1916 Amer. artist

Ear·hart \'er-ˌhärt, 'ir-\ Amelia 1897–1937 Amer. aviator

Earp \'ərp\ Wyatt 1848–1929 Amer. frontiersman and lawman

Ed·dy \'e-dē\ Mary Baker 1821–1910 Amer. founder of Christian Science

Ed·i·son \'e-də-sən\ Thomas Alva 1847–1931 Amer. inventor

Ed·ward \'ed-wərd\ name of 8 post-Norman kings of England: I 1239–1307 *Edward Longshanks* (r. 1272–1307); II 1284–1327 (r. 1307–27); III 1312–1377 (r. 1327–77); IV 1442–1483 (r. 1461–70; 1471–83); V 1470–1483 (r. 1483); VI 1537–1553 (r. 1547–53); son of Henry VIII and Jane Seymour; VII 1841–1910 (r. 1901–10); son of Queen Victoria; VIII 1894–1972 (r. 1936; abdicated) *Duke of Windsor*; son of George V

Ein·stein \'īn-ˌstīn\ Albert 1879–1955 Amer. (Ger.-born) physicist; Nobel Prize winner (1921)

Ei·sen·how·er \'ī-zᵊn-ˌhaù(-ə)r\ Dwight David 1890–1969 Amer. general; 34th pres. of the U.S. (1953–61)

Elec·tra \i-'lek-trə\ sister of Orestes in Greek mythology who aids him in avenging their father's murder

Eli·jah \i-'lī-jə\ Hebrew prophet of the 9th cent. B.C.

El·i·on \'e-lē-ən\ Gertrude Belle 1918–1999 Amer. pharmacologist; Nobel Prize winner (1988)

El·iot \'e-lē-ət, 'el-yət\ George 1819–1880 pseud. of *Mary Ann Evans* Eng. author

Eliot T. S. 1888–1965 *Thomas Stearns Eliot* Brit. (Amer.-born) poet; Nobel Prize winner (1948)

Eliz·a·beth I \i-'li-zə-bəth\ 1533–1603 queen of England (1558–1603); daughter of Henry VIII and Anne Boleyn

Elizabeth II 1926–   queen of the United Kingdom (1952–   ); daughter of George VI

El·ling·ton \'e-liŋ-tən\ Duke 1899–1974 *Edward Kennedy Ellington* Amer. bandleader and composer

Em·er·son \'e-mər-sən\ Ralph Waldo 1803–1882 Amer. essayist and poet

En·dym·i·on \en-'di-mē-ən\ beautiful youth in Greek mythology loved by the goddess of the moon

Eos \'ē-,äs\ goddess of the dawn in Greek mythology — compare AURORA

Ep·i·cu·rus \,e-pi-'kyùr-əs\ 341–270 B.C. Greek philosopher

Er·ik the Red \'er-ik\ *fl.* 10th cent. orig. *Erik Thorvaldson* Norwegian explorer; father of Leif Eriksson

Eriksson Leif — see LEIF ERIKSSON

Eros \'er-,äs, 'ir-\ god of love in Greek mythology — compare CUPID

Esau \'ē-(,)sò\ son of Isaac and Rebekah and elder twin brother of Jacob in the Bible

Es·ther \'es-tər\ Hebrew woman in the Bible who as the queen of Persia delivers her people from destruction

Eu·clid \'yü-kləd\ *fl. ca* 300 B.C. Greek mathematician

Eu·rip·i·des \yù-'ri-pə-,dēz\ *ca* 484–406 B.C. Greek playwright

Eu·ro·pa \yù-'rō-pə\ princess in Greek mythology who was carried off by Zeus disguised as a white bull

Eu·ryd·i·ce \yù-'ri-də-(,)sē\ wife of Orpheus in Greek mythology

Eve \'ēv\ the 1st woman in biblical tradition; wife of Adam

Eze·kiel \i-'zē-kyəl, -kē-əl\ Hebrew prophet of the 6th cent. B.C.

Fahr·en·heit \'fa-rən-,hīt, 'fär-ən-\ Daniel Gabriel 1686–1736 Ger. physicist

Far·a·day \'fa-rə-,dā, -dē\ Michael 1791–1867 Eng. chemist and physicist

Far·ra·gut \'fa-rə-gət\ David ˚Glasgow 1801–1870 Amer. admiral

Faulk·ner \'fók-nər\ William 1897–1962 Amer. author; Nobel Prize winner (1949)

Faust \'faùst\ *or* **Fau·stus** \'faù-stəs, 'fò-\ magician in Ger. legend who sells his soul to the devil for knowledge and power

Fawkes \'fòks\ Guy 1570–1606 Eng. conspirator

Fer·di·nand \'fər-də-,nand\ **V** of Castile *or* **II** of Aragon 1452–1516 *Ferdinand the Catholic* king of Castile (1474–1504), of Aragon (1479–1516), of Naples (1504–16); husband of Isabella I

Fer·mi \'fer-(,)mē\ Enrico 1901–1954 Amer. (Ital.-born) physicist; Nobel Prize winner (1938)

Field·ing \'fēl-diŋ\ Henry 1707–1754 Eng. author

Fill·more \'fil-,mòr\ Millard 1800–1874 13th pres. of the U.S. (1850–53)

Fitz·ger·ald \fits-'jer-əld\ Ella 1917–1996 Amer. singer

Fitzgerald F. Scott 1896–1940 *Francis Scott Key Fitzgerald* Amer. author

Flem·ing \'fle-miŋ\ Sir Alexander 1881–1955 Brit. bacteriologist; Nobel Prize winner (1945)

Flo·ra \'flòr-ə\ goddess of flowers in Roman mythology

Flying Dutchman legendary Dutch mariner condemned to sail the seas until Judgment Day

Ford \'fòrd\ Gerald Rudolph 1913–38th pres. of the U.S. (1974–77)

Ford Henry 1863–1947 Amer. automobile manufacturer

Fos·sey \'fò-sē, 'fä-\ Dian 1932–1985 Amer. zoologist

Fos·ter \'fòs-tər, 'fäs-\ Stephen Collins 1826–1864 Amer. songwriter

Fran·cis of As·si·si \'fran(t)-səs-əv-ə-'si-sē, -sē-\ Saint 1181/1182–1226 Ital. friar; founder of Franciscan order

Fran·co \'fräŋ-(,)kō, 'fraŋ-\ Francisco 1892–1975 Span. general, dictator, and head of Span. state (1936–75)

Frank \'fraŋk, 'fräŋk\ Anne 1929–1945 Ger.-born diarist during the Holocaust

Frank·lin \'fraŋ-klən\ Benjamin 1706–1790 Amer. patriot, author, and inventor

Fred·er·ick I \'fre-d(ə-)rik\ *ca* 1123–1190 *Frederick Barbarossa* Holy Roman emperor (1152–90)

Frederick II 1712–1786 *Frederick the Great* king of Prussia (1740–86)

Fré·mont \'frē-,mänt\ John Charles 1813–1890 Amer. general and explorer

French \'french\ Daniel Chester 1850–1931 Amer. sculptor

Freud \'fròid\ Sigmund 1856–1939 Austrian neurologist; founder of psychoanalysis

Frig·ga \'fri-gə\ wife of Odin and goddess of married love and the hearth in Norse mythology

Frost \'fròst\ Robert Lee 1874–1963 Amer. poet

Ful·ler \'fù-lər\ (Richard) Buckminster 1895–1983 Amer. engineer and architect

Fuller (Sarah) Margaret 1810–1850 Amer. author and reformer

Ful·ton \'fùl-tºn\ Robert 1765–1815 Amer. inventor

Ga·bri·el \'gā-brē-əl\ archangel named in

Hebrew tradition — compare MICHAEL; RAPHAEL; URIEL

Ga·ga·rin \gə-ˈgär-ən\ Yury Alekseyevich 1934–1968 Russ. astronaut; 1st man in space (1961)

Gage \ˈgāj\ Thomas 1721–1787 Brit. general in America

Gal·a·had \ˈga-lə-ˌhad\ knight of the Round Table in medieval legend who finds the Holy Grail

Gal·a·tea \ˌga-lə-ˈtē-ə\ female figure sculpted by Pygmalion in Greek mythology and given life by Aphrodite in answer to the sculptor's prayer

Ga·len \ˈgā-lən\ 129–ca 216 A.D. Greek physician and writer

Ga·li·leo \ˌga-lə-ˈlē-(ˌ)ō, -ˈlā-\ 1564–1642 Galileo Galilei Ital. astronomer and physicist

Gall \ˈgȯl\ 1840?–1894 Sioux Indian leader

Ga·ma \ˈga-mə, ˈgä-\ Vasco da ca 1460–1524 Portuguese navigator and explorer

Gan·dhi \ˈgän-dē, ˈgan-\ Indira 1917–1984 Indian prime minister (1966–77; 1980–84); daughter of Jawaharlal Nehru

Gandhi Mohandas Karamchand 1869–1948 Ma·hat·ma \mə-ˈhät-mə, -ˈhat-\ Gandi Indian leader

Gar·field \ˈgär-ˌfēld\ James Abram 1831–1881 20th pres. of the U.S. (1881)

Gar·i·bal·di \ˌga-rə-ˈbȯl-dē\ Giuseppe 1807–1882 Ital. patriot

Gar·ri·son \ˈga-rə-sən\ William Lloyd 1805–1879 Amer. abolitionist

Gates \ˈgāts\ Bill 1955– William Henry Gates III Amer. computer software manufacturer

Gau·guin \gō-ˈgaⁿ\ Paul 1848–1903 French painter

Gau·ta·ma Buddha \ˈgau̇-tə-mə, -ˈgō-\ — see BUDDHA

Geh·rig \ˈger-ig\ Lou 1903–1941 Henry Louis Gehrig Amer. baseball player

Gei·sel \ˈgī-zəl\ Theodor Seuss 1904–1991 pseud. Dr. Seuss Amer. author and illustrator

Gen·ghis Khan \ˌjeŋ-gəs-ˈkän, ˌgeŋ-\ ca 1162–1227 Mongol conqueror

George \ˈjȯrj\ name of 6 kings of Great Britain: I 1660–1727 (r. 1714–27); II 1683–1760 (r. 1727–60); III 1738–1820 (r. 1760–1820); IV 1762–1830 (r. 1820–30); V 1865–1936 (r. 1910–36); VI 1895–1952 (r. 1936–52); father of Elizabeth II

Ge·ron·i·mo \jə-ˈrä-nə-ˌmō\ 1829–1909 Apache Indian leader

Gersh·win \ˈgər-shwən\ George 1898–1937 Amer. composer

Gid·e·on \ˈgi-dē-ən\ Hebrew hero in the Bible

Gil·bert \ˈgil-bərt\ Sir William Schwenck 1836–1911 Eng. librettist and poet; collaborator with Sir Arthur Sullivan

Gins·burg \ˈginz-ˌbərg\ Ruth Bader 1933– Amer. jurist

Glad·stone \ˈglad-ˌstōn, chiefly Brit -stən\ William Ewart 1809–1898 Brit. prime minister (1868–74; 1880–85; 1886; 1892–94)

Glenn \ˈglen\ John Herschel 1921– Amer. astronaut and politician; 1st Amer. to orbit the earth (1962)

Go·di·va \gə-ˈdī-və\ an Eng. gentlewoman who in legend rode naked through Coventry to save its citizens from a tax

Goe·thals \ˈgō-thəlz\ George Washington 1858–1928 Amer. engineer who directed the building of the Panama Canal

Goe·the \ˈgə(r)-tə, ˈgœ-tə\ Johann Wolfgang von 1749–1832 Ger. author

Gogh, van \van-ˈgō, -ˈgäk\ Vincent Willem 1853–1890 Dutch painter

Gol·ding \ˈgōl-diŋ\ William Gerald 1911–1993 Eng. author; Nobel Prize winner (1983)

Go·li·ath \gə-ˈlī-əth\ Philistine giant who is killed by David in the Bible

Gom·pers \ˈgäm-pərz\ Samuel 1850–1924 Amer. (Brit.-born) labor leader

Goo·dall \ˈgu̇-(ˌ)dȯl, -(ˌ)däl\ Jane 1934– Brit. zoologist

Good·year \ˈgu̇d-ˌyir\ Charles 1800–1860 Amer. inventor

Gor·ba·chev \ˌgȯr-bə-ˈchȯf, -ˈchef\ Mikhail Sergeyevich 1931– Soviet leader of Communist party (1985–91); pres. of U.S.S.R. (1990–91); Nobel Prize winner (1990)

Gore \ˈgȯr\ Albert, Jr. 1948– vice pres. of the U.S. (1993–2001)

Gor·gas \ˈgȯr-gəs\ William Crawford 1854–1920 Amer. army surgeon

Gra·ham \ˈgrā-əm, ˈgra(-ə)m\ Martha 1893–1991 Amer. dancer and choreographer

Grant \ˈgrant\ Ulysses S. 1822–1885 orig. Hiram Ulysses Grant Amer. general; 18th pres. of the U.S. (1869–77)

Gre·co, El \el-ˈgre-(ˌ)kō\ 1541–1614 Doménikos Theotokópoulos Span. (Cretan-born) painter

Gree·ley \ˈgrē-lē\ Horace 1811–1872 Amer. journalist and politician

Greene \ˈgrēn\ (Henry) Graham 1904–1991 Brit. author

Greene Nathanael 1742–1786 Amer. Revolutionary general

Greg·o·ry \ˈgre-g(ə-)rē\ name of 16 popes: esp. I Saint ca 540–604 A.D. Gregory the Great (pope 590–604); VII Saint ca 1020–1085 (pope 1073–85); XIII 1502–1585 (pope 1572–85)

Grey \ˈgrā\ Lady Jane 1537–1554 queen of England for 9 days (1553)

Grey Zane 1872–1939 Amer. author

Grieg \ˈgrēg\ Edward Hagerup 1843–1907 Norwegian composer

Grimm \ˈgrim\ Jacob 1785–1863 and his brother Wilhelm 1786–1859 Ger. philologists and folklorists

Guin·e·vere \ˈgwi-nə-ˌvir\ legendary wife of King Arthur and lover of Lancelot

Gu·ten·berg \'gü-t⁹n-,bⲁrg\ Johannes *ca* 1400–1468 Ger. inventor of printing method from movable type

Ha·des \'hā-(,)dēz\ — see PLUTO

Ha·dri·an \'hā-drē-ən\ 76–138 A.D. Roman emperor (117–138)

Ha·gar \'hā-,gär, -gⲁr\ mistress of Abraham and mother of Ishmael in the Bible

Hai·le Se·las·sie \'hī-lē-sə-'la-sē, -'lā-\ 1892–1975 emperor of Ethiopia (1930–36; 1941–74)

Hale \'hāl\ Edward Everett 1822–1909 Amer. minister and author

Hale Nathan 1755–1776 Amer. Revolutionary hero

Hal·ley \'ha-lē\ Edmond *or* Edmund 1656–1742 Eng. astronomer and mathematician

Hal·sey \'hòl-sē, -zē\ William Frederick 1882–1959 Amer. admiral

Ham·il·ton \'ha-mⲁl-tⲁn\ Alexander 1755–1804 Amer. political leader

Ham·mu·ra·bi \,ha-mⲁ-'rä-bē\ *died ca* 1750 B.C. king of Babylon (*ca* 1792–50)

Han·cock \'han-,käk\ John 1737–1793 Amer. Revolutionary patriot

Han·del \'han-d⁹l\ George Frideric 1685–1759 Brit. (Ger.-born) composer

Han·dy \'han-dē\ W. C. 1873–1958 *William Christopher Handy* Amer. blues musician and composer

Han·ni·bal \'ha-nⲁ-bⲁl\ 247–183? B.C. Carthaginian general

Har·ding \'här-diŋ\ Warren Gamaliel 1865–1923 29th pres. of the U.S. (1921–23)

Har·dy \'här-dē\ Thomas 1840–1928 Eng. author

Har·ri·son \'ha-rⲁ-sⲁn\ Benjamin 1833–1901 23rd pres. of the U.S. (1889–93); grandson of W. H. Harrison

Harrison William Henry 1773–1841 Amer. general; 9th pres. of the U.S. (1841)

Harte \'härt\ Bret 1836–1902 orig. *Francis Brett Harte* Amer. author

Har·vey \'här-vē\ William 1578–1657 Eng. physician and anatomist

Haw·thorne \'hò-,thòrn\ Nathaniel 1804–1864 Amer. author

Haydn \'hī-d⁹n\ Franz Joseph 1732–1809 Austrian composer

Hayes \'hāz\ Rutherford Birchard 1822–1893 19th pres. of the U.S. (1877–81)

Hearst \'hⲁrst\ William Randolph 1863–1951 Amer. newspaper publisher

Hec·tor \'hek-tⲁr\ son of Priam and Hecuba; Trojan hero slain by Achilles in Greek mythology

Hec·u·ba \'he-kyⲁ-bⲁ\ wife of Priam in Greek mythology

Hel·en of Troy \,he-lⲁn-ⲁv-'tròi\ wife of Menelaus whose abduction by Paris in Greek mythology causes the Trojan War

He·li·os \'hē-lē-ⲁs, -(,)òs\ god of the sun in Greek mythology — compare SOL

Hem·ing·way \'he-miŋ-,wā\ Ernest Miller 1899–1961 Amer. author; Nobel Prize winner (1954)

Hen·ry \'hen-rē\ name of 8 kings of England: I 1068–1135 (r. 1100–35); II 1133–1189 (r. 1154–89); III 1207–1272 (r. 1216–72); IV 1366–1413 (r. 1399–1413); V 1387–1422 (r. 1413–22); VI 1421–1471 (r. 1422–61; 1470–71); VII 1457–1509 (r. 1485–1509); VIII 1491–1547 (r. 1509–47)

Henry name of 4 kings of France: I *ca* 1008–1060 (r. 1031–60); II 1519–1559 (r. 1547–59); III 1551–1589 (r. 1574–89); IV 1553–1610 *Henry of Navarre* (r. 1589–1610)

Henry O. 1862–1910 pseud. of *William Sydney Porter* Amer. author

Henry Patrick 1736–1799 Amer. patriot and orator

Hen·son \'hen(t)-sⲁn\ Matthew Alexander 1866–1955 Amer. arctic explorer

He·phaes·tus \hi-'fes-tⲁs, -'fēs-\ god of fire and of metalworking in Greek mythology — compare VULCAN

He·ra \'hir-ⲁ, 'he-rⲁ, 'her-ⲁ\ sister and wife of Zeus and goddess of women and marriage in Greek mythology — compare JUNO

Her·cu·les \'hⲁr-kyⲁ-,lēz\ *or* **Her·a·cles** \'her-ⲁ-,klēz-, 'he-rⲁ-\ hero in Greek mythology noted for his strength

Her·maph·ro·di·tus \(,)hⲁr-,ma-frⲁ-'dī-tⲁs\ son of Hermes and Aphrodite who in Greek mythology is joined with a nymph into one body

Her·mes \'hⲁr-(,)mēz\ god of commerce, eloquence, invention, travel, and theft who serves as herald and messenger of the other gods in Greek mythology — compare MERCURY

Her·od \'her-ⲁd\ 73–4 B.C. *Herod the Great* Roman king of Judea (37–4)

Herod An·ti·pas \'an-tⲁ-pⲁs, -,pas\ 21 B.C.–39 A.D., Roman governor of Galilee (4 B.C.–39 A.D.); son of Herod the Great

Hes·se \'he-sⲁ\ Hermann 1877–1962 Ger. author; Nobel Prize winner (1946)

Hey·er·dahl \'hā-ⲁr-,däl\ Thor 1914–2002 Norwegian explorer and author

Hi·a·wa·tha \,hī-ⲁ-'wò-thⲁ, ,hē-ⲁ-, -'wä-\ legendary Iroquois Indian chief

Hick·ok \'hi-,käk\ Wild Bill 1837–1876 orig. *James Butler Hickok* Amer. frontiersman and U.S. marshal

Hil·ton \'hil-t⁹n\ James 1900–1954 Eng. novelist

Hip·poc·ra·tes \hi-'pä-krⲁ-,tēz\ *ca* 460–*ca* 377 B.C. Greek physician

Hi·ro·hi·to \,hir-ō-'hē-(,)tō\ 1901–1989 emperor of Japan (1926–89)

Hit·ler \'hit-lⲁr\ Adolf 1889–1945 Ger. (Austrian-born) chancellor and dictator (1933–45)

Hodg·kin \'häj-kin\ Dorothy Mary 1910–1994 née *Crowfoot* Brit. physicist; Nobel Prize winner (1964)

Holmes \'hōmz, 'hōlmz\ Oliver Wendell 1809–1894 Amer. physician and author

Holmes Oliver Wendell, Jr. 1841–1935 Amer. jurist; son of the preceding

Ho·mer \'hō-mər\ *fl.* 9th *or* 8th cent. B.C. Greek epic poet

Homer Winslow 1836–1910 Amer. painter

Hooke \'huk\ Robert 1635–1703 Eng. scientist

Hook·er \'hu̇-kər\ Thomas 1586?–1647 Eng. colonist; a founder of Connecticut

Hoo·ver \'hü-vər\ Herbert Clark 1874–1964 31st pres. of the U.S. (1929–33)

Hoover John Edgar 1895–1972 Amer. director of the Federal Bureau of Investigation (1924–72)

Hop·per \'hä-pər\ Grace 1906–1992 née *Murray* Amer. admiral, mathematician, and computer scientist

Hou·di·ni \hü-'dē-nē\ Harry 1874–1926 orig. *Erik Weisz* Amer. magician

Hous·ton \'hyü-stən, 'yü-\ Sam 1793–1863 *Samuel Houston* Amer. politician; pres. of the Republic of Texas (1836–38; 1841–44)

Howe \'hau̇\ Elias 1819–1867 Amer. inventor

Howe Julia 1819–1910 née *Ward* Amer. suffragist and reformer

Hud·son \'həd-sən\ Henry *ca* 1565–1611 Eng. explorer

Hughes \'hyüz\ (James) Langston 1902–1967 Amer. author

Hugo \'hyü-(,)gō, 'yü-\ Victor 1802–1885 French author

Hus·sein I \hü-'sān\ 1935–1999 king of Jordan (1952–99)

Hutch·in·son \'hə-chə(n)-sən\ Anne 1591–1643 née *Marbury* Eng. colonist and religious leader in America

Hutchinson Thomas 1711–1780 Amer. colonial administrator

Hux·ley \'həks-lē\ Aldous Leonard 1894–1963 Eng. author

Hy·men \'hī-mən\ god of marriage in Greek mythology

Ib·sen \'ib-sən, 'ip-\ Henrik 1828–1906 Norwegian playwright

Ic·a·rus \'i-kə-rəs\ son of Daedalus who in Greek mythology falls into the sea when the wax of his artificial wings melts as he flies too near the sun

Ig·na·tius \ig-'nā-sh(ē-)əs\ Saint 1491–1556 *Ignatius of Loyola* Span. priest; founder of Society of Jesus (Jesuits)

In·no·cent \'i-nə-sənt\ name of 13 popes: esp. **II** *died* 1143 (pope 1130–43); **III** 1160/61–1216 (pope 1198–1216); **IV** *died* 1254 (pope 1243–54); **XI** 1611–1689 (pope 1676–89)

Ir·ving \'ər-vin\ Washington 1783–1859 Amer. author

Isaac \'ī-zik, -zək\ son of Abraham and father of Jacob in the Bible

Is·a·bel·la I \i-zə-'be-lə\ 1451–1504 queen of Castile (1474–1504) and of Aragon (1479–1504); wife of Ferdinand V

Isa·iah \ī-'zā-ə, *chiefly Brit* -'zī-\ Hebrew prophet of the 8th cent. B.C.

Ish·ma·el \'ish-(,)mā-əl, -mē-\ outcast son of Abraham and Hagar in the Bible

Ives \'īvz\ Charles Edward 1874–1954 Amer. composer

Jack·son \'jak-sən\ Andrew 1767–1845 Amer. general; 7th pres. of the U.S. (1829–37)

Jackson Thomas Jonathan 1824–1863 *Stonewall Jackson* Amer. Confederate general

Ja·cob \'jā-kəb\ son of Isaac and Rebekah and younger twin brother of Esau in the Bible

James \'jāmz\ one of the 12 apostles in the Bible

James *the Less* one of the 12 apostles in the Bible

James name of 2 kings of Great Britain: **I** 1566–1625 (r. 1603–25); king of Scotland as *James VI* (r. 1567–1625); **II** 1633–1701 (r. 1685–88)

James Henry 1843–1916 Brit. (Amer.-born) author

Ja·nus \'jā-nəs\ god of gates and doors and of all beginnings in Roman mythology and that is pictured with two opposite faces

Ja·son \'jā-s°n\ hero in Greek mythology noted for his successful quest of the Golden Fleece

Jay \'jā\ John 1745–1829 Amer. jurist and statesman; 1st chief justice of the U.S. Supreme Court (1789–95)

Jef·fer·son \'je-fər-sən\ Thomas 1743–1826 3d pres. of the U.S. (1801–09)

Jem·i·son \'je-mə-sən\ Mae 1956– Amer. astronaut and physician

Jer·e·mi·ah \jer-ə-'mī-ə\ Hebrew prophet of the 7th–6th cent. B.C.

Je·sus \'jē-zəs, -zəz\ *or* **Jesus Christ** *ca* 6 B.C.–*ca* 30 A.D. source of the Christian religion and Savior in the Christian faith

Jez·e·bel \'je-zə-,bel\ queen of Israel and wife of Ahab who is noted for her wickedness in the Bible

Joan of Arc \jōn-əv-'ärk\ Saint *ca* 1412–1431 *the Maid of Orléans* French national heroine

Job \'jōb\ man in the Bible who has many sufferings but keeps his faith

Jo·cas·ta \jō-'kas-tə\ queen of Thebes in Greek mythology who unknowingly marries her son Oedipus

John \'jän\ one of the 12 apostles believed to be the author of the 4th Gospel, three Epistles, and the Book of Revelation

John name of 23 popes: esp. **XXIII** 1881–1963 (pope 1958–63)

John 1167–1216 *John Lackland* king of England (1199–1216)

John·son \'jän(t)-sən\ Andrew 1808–1875 17th pres. of the U.S. (1865–69)

Johnson Lyndon Baines 1908–1973 36th pres. of the U.S. (1963–69)

Johnson Samuel 1709–1784 *Dr. Johnson* Eng. lexicographer and author

John the Baptist Saint, 1st cent. A.D. prophet and baptizer of Jesus in the Bible

Jol·liet *or* **Jo·liet** \zhōl-ʲyā\ Louis 1645–1700 French-Canad. explorer

Jo·nah \ʲjō-nə\ Hebrew prophet who in the Bible spends three days in the belly of a great fish

Jones \ʲjōnz\ John Paul 1747–1792 Amer. (Scot.-born) naval officer

Jop·lin \ʲjä-plən\ Scott 1868–1917 Amer. pianist and composer

Jor·dan \ʲjȯr-dᵊn\ Michael 1963– Amer. basketball player

Jo·seph \ʲjō-zəf\ son of Jacob in the Bible who rises to high office in Egypt after being sold into slavery by his brothers

Joseph Chief *ca* 1840–1904 Nez Percé Indian chief

Joseph Saint, husband of Mary, the mother of Jesus, in the Bible

Josh·ua \ʲjä-sh(ə-)wə\ Hebrew leader in the Bible who succeeds Moses during the settlement of the Israelites in Canaan

Joyce \ʲjȯis\ James Augustine 1882–1941 Irish author

Juan Car·los \ʲ(h)wän-ʲkär-ˌlōs\ 1938– king of Spain (1975–   )

Ju·dah \ʲjü-də\ son of Jacob and ancestor of one of the 12 tribes of Israel in the Bible

Ju·das \ʲjü-dəs\ *or* **Judas Is·car·i·ot** \-isˈka-rē-ət\ one of the 12 apostles and the betrayer of Jesus in the Bible

Jung \ʲyu̇ŋ\ Carl Gustav 1875–1961 Swiss psychologist

Ju·no \ʲjü-(ˌ)nō\ queen of heaven, wife of Jupiter, and goddess of light, birth, women, and marriage in Roman mythology — compare HERA

Ju·pi·ter \ʲjü-pə-tər\ chief god and god of light, of the sky and weather, and of the state in Roman mythology — compare ZEUS

Kalb \ʲkälp, ʲkalb\ Johann 1721–1780 Baron *de Kalb* \di-ʲkalb\ Ger. general in Amer. Revolutionary army

Ka·me·ha·me·ha I \kə-ˌmā-ə-ʲmā-(ˌ)hä\ 1758?–1819 orig. *Paiea* Hawaiian king (1795–1819)

Keats \ʲkēts\ John 1795–1821 Eng. poet

Kei·ler \ʲke-lər\ Helen Adams 1880–1968 Amer. deaf and blind lecturer and author

Kel·vin \ʲkel-vən\ 1st Baron 1824–1907 *William Thomson* Brit. mathematician and physicist

Ken·ne·dy \ʲke-nə-dē\ John Fitzgerald 1917–1963 35th pres. of the U.S. (1961–63)

Kennedy Robert Francis 1925–1968 attorney general of the U.S. (1961–64); brother of the preceding

Ke·o·kuk \ʲkē-ə-ˌkək\ 1780?–1848 Amer. Indian chief

Key \ʲkē\ Francis Scott 1779–1843 Amer. lawyer; author of "The Star-Spangled Banner"

Khayyám Omar — see OMAR KHAYYÁM

Khru·shchev \krüsh-ʲchȯf, -ʲchȯv\ Nikita Sergeyevich 1894–1971 premier of U.S.S.R. (1958–64)

Khu·fu \ʲkü-(ˌ)fü\ *or Greek* **Che·ops** \ʲkē-ˌäps\ *fl.* 25th cent. B.C. king of Egypt and pyramid builder

Kidd \ʲkid\ William *ca* 1645–1701 *Captain Kidd* Scot. pirate

Kier·ke·gaard \ʲkir-kə-ˌgär(d), -ˌgȯr\ Søren 1813–1855 Danish philosopher

King \ʲkiŋ\ Billie Jean 1943–   Amer. tennis player

King Martin Luther, Jr. 1929–1968 Amer. minister and civil rights leader; Nobel Prize winner (1964)

Kip·ling \ʲkip-liŋ\ Rudyard 1865–1936 Eng. author; Nobel Prize winner (1907)

Kis·sin·ger \ʲki-sᵊn-jər\ Henry Alfred 1923–   Amer. (Ger.-born) government official; U.S. secretary of state (1973–77); Nobel Prize winner (1973)

Knox \ʲnäks\ John *ca* 1514–1572 Scot. religious reformer

Koch \ʲkȯk, ʲkȯk̲, ʲkōk, ʲkōk̲\ Robert 1843–1910 Ger. bacteriologist; Nobel Prize winner (1905)

Koś·ciusz·ko \kȯsh-ʲchüsh-(ˌ)kō, ˌkä-sē-ʲəs-ˌkō\ Tadeusz 1746–1817 Polish patriot and general in Amer. Revolutionary army

Krish·na \ʲkrish-nə, ʲkrēsh-\ god worshipped in later Hinduism

Ku·blai Khan \ʲkü-ˌblə-ʲkän, -ˌblī-\ 1215–1294 Mongol leader; grandson of Genghis Khan

La·fa·yette \ˌlä-fē-ʲet, ˌla-\ Marquis de 1757–1834 French general in Amer. Revolutionary army

La·ius \ʲlā-əs, ʲlī-əs\ king of Thebes who in Greek mythology is killed by his son Oedipus

Lan·ce·lot \ʲlan(t)-sə-ˌlät, ʲlän(t)-, -s(ə-)lət\ legendary knight of the Round Table and lover of Queen Guinevere

Lange \ʲlaŋ\ Dorothea 1895–1965 Amer. photographer

Lao·tzu \ʲlau̇d-ʲzə\ *fl.* 6th cent. B.C. Chinese philosopher

La Salle \lə-ʲsal\ Sieur de 1643–1687 *René-Robert Cavelier* French explorer

La·voi·sier \lə-ˌvˌwä-zē-ˌā\ Antoine-Laurent 1743–1794 French chemist

Law·rence \ʲlȯr-ən(t)s, ʲlär-\ D. H. 1885–1930 *David Herbert Lawrence* Eng. author

Lawrence Thomas Edward 1888–1935 *Lawrence of Arabia* Brit. soldier and author

Laz·a·rus \ʲlaz-rəs, ʲla-zə-\ brother of Mary and Martha who in the Bible is raised by Jesus from the dead

Lazarus beggar in the biblical parable of the rich man and the beggar

Le·da \'lē-də\ Spartan princess in Greek mythology who is courted by Zeus in the form of a swan

Lee \'lē\ Ann 1736–1784 Eng. mystic; founder of Shaker society in the U.S.

Lee Henry 1756–1818 *Light-Horse Harry* Amer. general

Lee Robert Edward 1807–1870 Amer. Confederate general; son of the preceding

Leeu·wen·hoek \'lā-vən-ˌhu̇k\ Antonie van 1632–1723 Dutch naturalist

Leif Er·iks·son *or* **Er·ics·son** \ˌlāv-'er-ik-sən, ˌlēf-\ *fl.* 1000 Norwegian explorer; son of Erik the Red

Le·nin \'le-nən\ 1870–1924 orig. *Vladimir Ilyich Ul·ya·nov* \ül-'yän-əf, -ˌóf, -ˌóv\ Russ. Communist leader

Leo \'lē-(ˌ)ō\ name of 13 popes: esp. **I** Saint *died* 461 A.D. *Leo the Great* (pope 440–61); **III** Saint *died* 816 (pope 795–816); **XIII** 1810–1903 (pope 1878–1903)

Le·o·nar·do da Vin·ci \ˌlē-ə-'när-(ˌ)dō də-'vin-chē, ˌlā-, -'vēn-\ 1452–1519 Ital. painter, sculptor, architect, and engineer

Lew·is \'lü-əs\ C. S. 1898–1963 *Clive Staples Lewis* Brit. author

Lewis John Llewellyn 1880–1969 Amer. labor leader

Lewis Meriwether 1774–1809 Amer. explorer (with William Clark)

Lewis Sinclair 1885–1951 Amer. author; Nobel Prize winner (1930)

Lin·coln \'liŋ-kən\ Abraham 1809–1865 16th pres. of the U.S. (1861–65)

Lind·bergh \'lin(d)-ˌbərg\ Charles Augustus 1902–1974 Amer. aviator

Lin·nae·us \lə-'nē-əs, -'nā-\ Carolus 1707–1778 *Carl von Linné* Swedish botanist

Lis·ter \'lis-tər\ Joseph 1827–1912 Eng. surgeon and medical scientist

Liszt \'list\ Franz 1811–1886 Hungarian pianist and composer

Liv·ing·stone \'li-viŋ-stən\ David 1813–1873 Scot. missionary in Africa

Lon·don \'lən-dən\ Jack 1876–1916 *John Griffith London* Amer. author

Long·fel·low \'lóŋ-ˌfe-(ˌ)lō\ Henry Wadsworth 1807–1882 Amer. poet

Lou·is \'lü-ē, lü-'ē\ name of 18 kings of France: esp. **IX** Saint 1214–1270 (r. 1226–70); **XI** 1423–1483 (r. 1461–83); **XII** 1462–1515 (r. 1498–1515); **XIII** 1601–1643 (r. 1610–43); **XIV** 1638–1715 (r. 1643–1715); **XV** 1710–1774 (r. 1715–74); **XVI** 1754–1793 (r. 1774–92; guillotined); **XVII** 1785–1795 (r. in name 1793–95); **XVIII** 1755–1824 (r. 1814–15; 1815–24)

Lou·is \'lü-əs\ Joe 1914–1981 orig. *Joseph Louis Barrow* Amer. boxer

Low \'lō\ Juliette 1860–1927 née *Gordon* Amer. founder of the Girl Scouts

Low·ell \'lō-əl\ Amy 1874–1925 Amer. poet

Lowell James Russell 1819–1891 Amer. author

Luke \'lük\ physician and companion of the apostle Paul believed to be the author of the 3d Gospel and the Book of Acts

Lu·ther \'lü-thər\ Martin 1483–1546 Ger. Reformation leader

Ly·on \'lī-ən\ Mary 1797–1849 Amer. educator

Mac·Ar·thur \mə-'kär-thər\ Douglas 1880–1964 Amer. general

Ma·cy \'mā-sē\ Anne Sullivan 1866–1936 née *Sullivan* Amer. educator; teacher of Helen Keller

Mad·i·son \'ma-də-sən\ James 1751–1836 4th pres. of the U.S. (1809–17)

Ma·gel·lan \mə-'je-lən, *chiefly Brit* -'ge-\ Ferdinand *ca* 1480–1521 Portuguese navigator and explorer

Mal·colm X \'mal-kəm-'eks\ 1925–1965 Amer. civil rights leader

Man·de·la \man-'de-lə\ Nelson Rolihlahla 1918– pres. of South Africa (1994–99); Nobel Prize winner (1993)

Ma·net \ma-'nā, mä-\ Édouard 1832–1883 French painter

Mann \'man\ Horace 1796–1859 Amer. educator

Mao Tse-tung *or* **Mao Zedong** \'maù-(')dzə-'du̇ŋ, -(')tsə-\ 1893–1976 Chinese Communist leader of People's Republic of China (1949–76)

Mar·co·ni \mär-'kō-nē\ Guglielmo 1874–1937 Ital. physicist and inventor; Nobel Prize winner (1909)

Marco Polo — see POLO

Ma·rie An·toi·nette \ˌan-twə-'net, -tə-\ 1755–1793 wife of Louis XVI of France

Mar·i·on \'mer-ē-ən\ Francis 1732?–1795 *the Swamp Fox* Amer. commander in Revolution

Mark \'märk\ evangelist believed to be the author of the 2d Gospel

Mark Antony — see ANTONY

Mar·quette \mär-'ket\ Jacques 1637–1675 *Père Marquette* French-born Jesuit missionary and explorer in America

Mars \'märz\ god of war in Roman mythology — compare ARES

Mar·shall \'mär-shəl\ George Catlett 1880–1959 Amer. general and diplomat; Nobel Prize winner (1953)

Marshall John 1755–1835 Amer. jurist; chief justice of the U.S. Supreme Court (1801–35)

Mar·tha \'mär-thə\ sister of Lazarus and Mary and friend of Jesus in the Bible

Mar·tin \'mär-tᵊn, mär-'tan\ Saint 316–397 *Martin of Tours* \-'tu̇r\ patron saint of France

Martin \'mär-tᵊn\ Paul (Edgar Phillipe) 1938– Canad. prime minister (2003–)

Marx \'märks\ Karl 1818–1883 Ger. political philosopher and socialist

Mary \'mer-ē, 'ma-rē, 'mä-rē\ *Saint Mary*; *Virgin Mary* mother of Jesus

Mary sister of Lazarus and Martha in the Bible

Mary I 1516–1558 *Mary Tudor*; *Bloody Mary* queen of England (1553–58)

Mary II 1662–1694 joint Brit. sovereign with William III (1689–94)

Mary Mag·da·lene \'mag-də-lən, -ˌlēn\ woman in the Bible who sees the risen Christ

Mary, Queen of Scots 1542–1587 *Mary Stuart* queen of Scotland (1542–67)

Mas·sa·soit \ˌma-sə-'sȯit\ *died* 1661 Amer. Indian chief

Math·er \'ma-thər, -thər\ Cotton 1663–1728 Amer. religious leader and author

Mather Increase 1639–1723 Amer. minister and author; father of Cotton Mather

Ma·tisse \ma-'tēs, mə-\ Henri 1869–1954 French painter

Mat·thew \'ma-(ˌ)thyü\ apostle believed to be the author of the 1st Gospel

Mau·pas·sant \ˌmō-pə-'säⁿ\ Guy de 1850–1893 French author

Mays \'māz\ Willie Howard 1931– Amer. baseball player

Mc·Au·liffe \mə-'kȯl-əf\ Christa 1948–1986 Amer. teacher; 1st private citizen in space (1986)

Mc·Car·thy \mə-'kär-thē\ Joseph Raymond 1908–1957 Amer. politician

Mc·Clel·lan \mə-'kle-lən\ George Brinton 1826–1885 Amer. general

Mc·Clin·tock \mə-'klin-tək\ Barbara 1902–1992 Amer. botanist; Nobel Prize winner (1983)

Mc·Cor·mick \mə-'kȯr-mik\ Cyrus Hall 1809–1884 Amer. inventor

Mc·Kin·ley \mə-'kin-lē\ William 1843–1901 25th pres. of the U.S. (1897–1901)

Mead \'mēd\ Margaret 1901–1978 Amer. anthropologist

Meade \'mēd\ George Gordon 1815–1872 Amer. Civil War general

Mea·ny \'mē-nē\ George 1894–1980 Amer. labor leader

Me·dea \mə-'dē-ə\ woman with magic powers in Greek mythology who helps Jason to win the Golden Fleece and who kills her children when he leaves her

Medici Catherine de' — see CATHERINE DE MÉDICIS

Me·di·ci \'me-də-chē\ Lorenzo de' 1449–1492 *Lorenzo the Magnificent* Florentine statesman, ruler, and patron of the arts

Me·du·sa \mi-'dü-sə, -'dyü-, -zə\ Gorgon in Greek mythology slain by Perseus

Me·ir \mä-'ir\ Golda 1898–1978 prime minister of Israel (1969–74)

Mel·ville \'mel-ˌvil\ Herman 1819–1891 Amer. author

Men·del \'men-dᵊl\ Gregor Johann 1822–1884 Austrian botanist

Men·dels·sohn (–Bar·thol·dy) \'men-

dᵊl-sən(-bär-'tȯl-dē, -'thȯl-)\ Felix 1809–1847 Ger. composer

Men·e·la·us \ˌme-nə-'lā-əs\ king of Sparta, brother of Agamemnon, and husband of Helen of Troy in Greek mythology

Meph·is·toph·e·les \ˌme-fə-'stä-fə-ˌlēz\ chief devil in the Faust legend

Mer·ca·tor \(ˌ)mər-'kā-tər\ Gerardus 1512–1594 orig. *Gerhard Kremer* Flemish cartographer

Mer·cu·ry \'mər-kyə-rē, -k(ə-)rē\ god of commerce, eloquence, travel, and theft who serves as messenger of the other gods in Roman mythology — compare HERMES

Mer·lin \'mər-lən\ prophet and magician in the legend of King Arthur

Met·a·com \'me-tə-ˌkäm\ *or* **King Philip** *ca* 1638–1676 *Met·a·com·et* \ˌme-tə-'käm-ət\ Amer. Indian chief; son of Massasoit

Mi·chael \'mī-kəl\ archangel named in Hebrew tradition — compare GABRIEL; RAPHAEL; URIEL

Mi·chel·an·ge·lo \ˌmī-kə-'lan-jə-ˌlō, ˌmi-, ˌmē-kə-'län-\ 1475–1564 Ital. sculptor, painter, architect, and poet

Mi·das \'mī-dəs\ legendary king having the power to turn everything he touched into gold

Mil·lay \mi-'lā\ Edna St. Vincent 1892–1950 Amer. poet

Mil·ler \'mi-lər\ Arthur 1915– Amer. playwright

Milne \'mil(n)\ A. A. 1882–1956 *Alan Alexander Milne* Eng. author

Mil·ton \'mil-tᵊn\ John 1608–1674 Eng. poet

Mi·ner·va \mə-'nər-və\ goddess of wisdom in Roman mythology — compare ATHENA

Mi·no·taur \'mi-nə-ˌtȯr, 'mī-\ monster in Greek mythology shaped half like a man and half like a bull

Min·u·it \'min-yə-wət\ Peter *ca* 1580–1638 Dutch colonial administrator in America

Mitch·ell \'mi-chəl\ Maria 1818–1889 Amer. astronomer

Mo·lière \mōl-'yer, 'mōl-ˌ\ 1622–1673 orig. *Jean-Baptiste Poquelin* French actor and playwright

Mo·net \mō-'nā\ Claude 1840–1926 French painter

Mon·roe \mən-'rō\ James 1758–1831 5th pres. of the U.S. (1817–25)

Mont·calm \mänt-'kälm-, -'käm-\ Marquis de 1712–1759 *Louis-Joseph de Montcalm-Grozon* French field marshal in Canada

Mon·tes·so·ri \ˌmän-tə-'sȯr-ē\ Maria 1870–1952 Ital. educator

Mon·te·zu·ma II \ˌmän-tə-'zü-mə\ 1466–1520 last Aztec emperor of Mexico (1502–20)

Moore \'mȯr, 'mùr\ Marianne 1887–1972 Amer. poet

More \'mȯr\ Sir Thomas 1478–1535 *Saint*

Thomas More Eng. public official and author

Mor·gan \\'mȯr-gən\\ J. P. 1837–1913 *John Pierpont Morgan* Amer. financier

Mor·ri·son \\'mȯr-ə-sən, 'mär-\\ Toni 1931– orig. *Chloe Anthony Wofford* Amer. author; Nobel Prize winner (1993)

Morse \\'mȯrs\\ Samuel Finley Breese 1791–1872 Amer. artist and inventor

Mo·ses \\'mō-zəz\\ Hebrew prophet and lawgiver in the Bible

Moses Grandma 1860–1961 *Anna Mary Moses née Robertson* Amer. painter

Mott \\'mät\\ Lucretia 1793–1880 Amer. reformer

Mo·zart \\'mōt-ˌsärt\\ Wolfgang Amadeus 1756–1791 Austrian composer

Mu·ham·mad \\mō-'ha-məd, -'hä-\\ *ca* 570–632 A.D. Arab prophet and founder of Islam

Mus·so·li·ni \\ˌmü-sə-'lē-nē, ˌmú-\\ Be·ni·to \\bə-'nēt-ō\\ 1883–1945 *Il Du·ce* \\ēl-'dü-chā\\ Ital. fascist premier (1922–43)

Na·bo·kov \\nə-'bȯ-kəf\\ Vladimir 1899–1977 Amer. (Russ.-born) author

Na·po·leon I \\nə-'pōl-yən, -'pō-lē-ən\\ *or* **Napoleon Bo·na·parte** \\'bō-nə-ˌpärt\\ 1769–1821 French general and emperor of the French (1804–15)

Nar·cis·sus \\när-'si-səs\\ beautiful youth in Greek mythology who pines away for love of his own reflection and is then turned into the narcissus flower

Nash \\'nash\\ Ogden 1902–1971 Amer. poet

Na·tion \\'nā-shən\\ Car·ry \\'kar-ē\\ Amelia 1846–1911 née *Moore* Amer. temperance agitator

Nav·ra·ti·lo·va \\ˌnav-rə-tə-'lō-və\\ Martina 1956– Amer. (Czech-born) tennis player

Neb·u·cha·drez·zar II \\ˌne-byə-kə-'dre-zər, -bə-\\ *or* **Neb·u·chad·nez·zar** \\-kəd-'ne-\\ *ca* 630–*ca* 561 B.C. Chaldean king of Babylon (605–562)

Neh·ru \\'ner-(ˌ)ü, 'nā-(ˌ)rü\\ Ja·wa·har·lal \\jə-'wä-hər-ˌläl\\ 1889–1964 1st prime minister of Republic of India (1947–64)

Nel·son \\'nel-sən\\ Horatio 1758–1805 Viscount *Nelson* Brit. admiral

Nem·e·sis \\'ne-mə-səs\\ goddess of reward and punishment in Greek mythology

Nep·tune \\'nep-ˌtün, -ˌtyün\\ god of the sea in Roman mythology — compare PO·SEIDON

Ne·ro \\'nē-(ˌ)rō, 'nir-(ˌ)ō\\ 37–68 A.D. Roman emperor (54–68)

Nev·el·son \\'ne-vəl-sən\\ Louise 1900?–1988 Amer. sculptor

New·ton \\'nü-tᵊn, 'nyü-\\ Sir Isaac 1642–1727 Eng. mathematician and physicist

Nich·o·las \\'ni-k(ə-)ləs\\ Saint *fl.* 4th cent. A.D. Christian bishop

Nicholas I 1796–1855 czar of Russia (1825–55)

Nicholas II 1868–1918 last czar of Russia (1894–1917)

Nietz·sche \\'nē-chə, -chē\\ Friedrich Wilhelm 1844–1900 Ger. philosopher

Night·in·gale \\'nī-tᵊn-ˌgāl, -tiŋ-\\ Florence 1820–1910 *Lady of the Lamp* Eng. nurse and philanthropist

Ni·ke \\'nī-kē\\ goddess of victory in Greek mythology

Ni·o·be \\'nī-ə-bē\\ bereaved mother in Greek mythology who while weeping for her slain children is turned into a stone from which her tears continue to flow

Nix·on \\'nik-sən\\ Richard Milhous 1913–1994 37th pres. of the U.S. (1969–74)

No·ah \\'nō-ə\\ biblical builder of the ark in which he, his family, and living creatures of every kind survive the biblical Flood

No·bel \\nō-'bel\\ Alfred Bernhard 1833–1896 Swedish manufacturer, inventor, and philanthropist

Nor·man \\'nȯr-mən\\ Jessye 1945– Amer. soprano

Oak·ley \\'ōk-lē\\ Annie 1860–1926 orig. *Phoebe Anne Oakley Moses* Amer. sharpshooter

Oce·anus \\ō-'sē-ə-nəs\\ Titan who rules over a great river encircling the earth in Greek mythology

O'·Con·nor \\ō-'kä-nər\\ (Mary) Flannery 1925–1964 Amer. author

O'Connor Sandra Day 1930– Amer. jurist

Odin \\'ō-dᵊn\\ *or* **Wo·den** \\'wō-dᵊn\\ chief god, god of war, and patron of heroes in Norse mythology

Odys·seus \\ō-'di-sē-əs, -'dis-yəs, -'di-shəs, -'di-ˌshüs\\ *or* **Ulys·ses** \\yü-'li-(ˌ)sēz\\ king of Ithaca and hero in Greek mythology

Oe·di·pus \\'e-də-pəs, 'ē-\\ son of Laius and Jocasta who in Greek mythology kills his father and marries his mother not knowing their identity

Ogle·thorpe \\'ō-gəl-ˌthȯrp\\ James Edward 1696–1785 Eng. general and founder of Georgia

O'·Keeffe \\ō-'kēf\\ Georgia 1887–1986 Amer. painter

Olaf V \\'ō-ləf, -ˌläf, -ˌlaf; 'ü-ˌläf\\ 1903–1991 king of Norway (1957–91)

Omar Khay·yám \\ˌō-ˌmär-ˌkī-'yäm, ˌō-mər-, -'yam\\ 1048–1131 Persian poet and astronomer

O'·Neill \\ō-'nēl\\ Eugene Gladstone 1888–1953 Amer. playwright; Nobel Prize winner (1936)

Or·pheus \\'ȯr-ˌfyüs, -fē-əs\\ poet and musician in Greek mythology

Or·well \\'ȯr-ˌwel, -wəl\\ George 1903–1950 pseud. of *Eric Arthur Blair* Eng. author

Osce·o·la \\ˌä-sē-'ō-lə, ˌō-\\ *ca* 1804–1838 Seminole Indian chief

Otis \\'ō-təs\\ James 1725–1783 Amer. Revolutionary patriot

Ov·id \\'ä-vəd\\ 43 B.C.–17 A.D.? Roman poet

Ow·en \\'ō-ən\\ Robert 1771–1858 Welsh social reformer

Ow·ens \\'ō-ənz\\ Jesse 1913–1980 orig. *James Cleveland Owens* Amer. track-and-field athlete

Paine \\'pān\\ Thomas 1737–1809 Amer. (Eng.-born) political philosopher and author

Pan \\'pan\\ god of pastures, flocks, and shepherds in Greek mythology who is usu. represented as having the legs, ears, and horns of a goat

Pan·do·ra \\pan-'dòr-ə\\ woman in Greek mythology who out of curiosity opens a box and lets loose all of the evils that trouble humans

Pank·hurst \\'paŋk-ˌhərst\\ Emmeline 1858–1928 née *Goulden* Eng. suffragist

Par·is \\'pa-rəs\\ son of Priam whose abduction of Helen of Troy in Greek mythology leads to the Trojan War

Park·man \\'pärk-mən\\ Francis 1823–1893 Amer. historian

Parks \\'pärks\\ Rosa 1913–　née *Mc-Cauley* Amer. civil rights activist

Pas·cal \\pa-'skal, päs-'käl\\ Blaise 1623–1662 French mathematician and philosopher

Pas·ter·nak \\'pas-tər-ˌnak\\ Boris Leonidovich 1890–1960 Russ. author; Nobel Prize winner (1958)

Pas·teur \\pas-'tər\\ Louis 1822–1895 French chemist and microbiologist

Pat·rick \\'pa-trik\\ Saint *fl.* 5th cent. A.D. apostle and patron saint of Ireland

Pat·ton \\'pa-tⁿn\\ George Smith 1885–1945 Amer. general

Paul \\'pòl\\ Saint *died ca* 67 A.D. Christian missionary and author of several New Testament epistles

Paul name of 6 popes: esp. **III** 1468–1549 (pope 1534–49); **V** 1552–1621 (pope 1605–21); **VI** 1897–1978 (pope 1963–78)

Paul Bun·yan \\'bən-yən\\ giant lumberjack in Amer. folklore

Pau·ling \\'pò-liŋ\\ Linus Carl 1901–1994 Amer. chemist; Nobel Prize winner (1954, 1962)

Pav·lov \\'päv-ˌlòf, 'pav-, -ˌlòv\\ Ivan Petrovich 1849–1936 Russ. physiologist; Nobel Prize winner (1904)

Pa·vlo·va \\'pav-lə-və, pav-'lō-\\ Anna 1881–1931 Russ. ballerina

Pea·ry \\'pir-ē\\ Robert Edwin 1856–1920 Amer. arctic explorer

Pe·cos Bill \\ˌpā-kəs-'bil\\ cowboy in Amer. folklore known for his extraordinary feats

Peg·a·sus \\'pe-gə-səs\\ winged horse in Greek mythology

Penn \\'pen\\ William 1644–1718 Eng. Quaker leader and founder of Pennsylvania

Per·i·cles \\'per-ə-ˌklēz\\ *ca* 495–429 B.C. Athenian political leader

Per·ry \\'per-ē\\ Matthew Calbraith 1794–1858 Amer. commodore

Perry Oliver Hazard 1785–1819 Amer. naval officer; brother of the preceding

Per·seph·o·ne \\pər-'se-fə-nē\\ daughter of Zeus and Demeter who in Greek mythology is abducted by Pluto to rule with him over the underworld

Per·shing \\'pər-shiŋ, -zhiŋ\\ John Joseph 1860–1948 Amer. general

Pe·ter \\'pē-tər\\ Saint *died ca* 64 A.D. orig. *Si·mon* \\'sī-mən-\\ one of the 12 apostles in the Bible

Peter I 1672–1725 *Peter the Great* czar of Russia (1682–1725)

Phil·ip \\'fi-ləp\\ Saint, one of the 12 apostles in the Bible

Philip King — see METACOM

Philip name of 6 kings of France: esp. **II** *or* **Philip Augustus** 1165–1223 (r. 1179–1223); **IV** 1268–1314 *Philip the Fair* (r. 1285–1314); **VI** 1293–1350 (r. 1328–50)

Philip name of 5 kings of Spain: esp. **II** 1527–1598 (r. 1556–98); **V** 1683–1746 (r. 1700–46)

Philip II 382–336 B.C. king of Macedon (359–336); father of Alexander the Great

Pi·cas·so \\pi-'kä-(ˌ)sō, -'ka-\\ Pablo 1881–1973 Span. painter and sculptor in France

Pic·card \\pi-'kär, -'kärd\\ Auguste 1884–1962 and his son Jacques 1922–　Swiss scientists and developers of the bathyscaphe

Pick·ett \\'pi-kət\\ George Edward 1825–1875 Amer. Confederate general

Pierce \\'pirs\\ Franklin 1804–1869 14th pres. of the U.S. (1853–57)

Pi·late \\'pī-lət\\ Pon·tius \\'pän-chəs, 'pòn-chəs\\ *died after* 36 A.D. Roman governor of Judea (26–36)

Pinkerton \\'piŋ-kər-tⁿn\\ Allan 1819–1884 Amer. (Scot.-born) detective

Pis·sar·ro \\pə-'sär-(ˌ)ō\\ Camille 1830–1903 French (West Indian-born) painter

Pitt \\'pit\\ William 1759–1806 *the Younger Pitt* Eng. prime minister (1783–1801; 1804–6)

Pi·us \\'pī-əs\\ name of 12 popes: esp. **VII** 1742–1823 (pope 1800–23); **IX** 1792–1878 (pope 1846–78); **X** Saint 1835–1914 (pope 1903–14); **XI** 1857–1939 (pope 1922–39); **XII** 1876–1958 (pope 1939–58)

Pi·zar·ro \\pə-'zär-(ˌ)ō\\ Francisco *ca* 1475–1541 Span. conqueror of Peru

Pla·to \\'plā-(ˌ)tō\\ *ca* 428–348 (*or* 347) B.C. Greek philosopher

Plu·to \\'plü-(ˌ)tō\\ god of the underworld in Greek mythology

Po·ca·hon·tas \\ˌpō-kə-'hän-təs\\ *ca* 1595–1617 Amer. Indian friend of the colonists at Jamestown; daughter of Powhatan

Poe \\'pō\\ Edgar Allan 1809–1849 Amer. author

Polk \\'pōk\\ James Knox 1795–1849 11th pres. of the U.S. (1845–49)

Po·lo \'pō-(ˌ)lō\ Marco *ca* 1254–1324 Venetian merchant and traveler

Poly·phe·mus \ˌpä-lə-'fē-məs\ a one-eyed creature in Greek mythology that is blinded by Odysseus

Ponce de Le·ón \ˌpän(t)s-ə-də-lē-'ōn, ˌpänts-də-, -'lē-ən\ Juan 1460–1521 Span. explorer

Pon·ti·ac \'pän-tē-ˌak\ *ca* 1720–1769 Ottawa Indian chief

Por·ter \'pòr-tər\ Cole Albert 1891–1964 Amer. composer

Porter Katherine Anne 1890–1980 Amer. author

Porter William Sydney — see O. HENRY

Po·sei·don \pə-'sī-dᵊn\ god of the sea in Greek mythology — compare NEPTUNE

Pot·ter \'pä-tər\ (Helen) Beatrix 1866–1943 Brit. author and illustrator

Pound \'paùnd\ Ezra Loomis 1885–1972 Amer. poet

Pound·mak·er \'paùnd-ˌmā-kər\ 1826–1886 Cree Indian chief

Pow·ell \'paù(-ə)l\ Colin Luther 1937– Amer. general; U.S. secretary of state (2001–)

Pow·ha·tan \ˌpaù-ə-'tan, paù-'ha-tᵊn\ 1550?–1618 Amer. Indian chief of a confederacy of Algonquian-speaking tribes; father of Pocahontas

Pres·ley \'pres-lē, 'prez-\ Elvis Aaron 1935–1977 Amer. popular singer

Pri·am \'prī-əm, -ˌam\ king of Troy during the Trojan War in Greek mythology

Price \'prīs\ (Mary) Leontyne 1927– Amer. soprano

Pro·me·theus \prə-'mē-thē-əs, -ˌthyüs\ Titan in Greek mythology who is punished by Zeus for stealing fire from heaven and giving it to humans

Pro·teus \'prō-tyüs, -tē-əs\ sea god in Greek mythology who is capable of assuming different forms

Ptol·e·my \'tä-lə-mē\ *fl.* 2d cent. A.D. Greco-Egyptian astronomer, geographer, and mathematician in Alexandria

Puc·ci·ni \pü-'chē-nē\ Giacomo 1858–1924 Ital. composer

Pu·las·ki \pə-'las-kē, pyü-\ Kazimierz 1747–1779 Polish soldier in Amer. Revolutionary army

Pu·lit·zer \'pù-lət-sər *(family's pron)*, 'pyü-\ Joseph 1847–1911 Amer. (Hungarian-born) journalist

Pu·tin \'pü-tin\ Vladimir Vladimirovich 1952– pres. of Russia (2000–)

Pyg·ma·lion \pig-'māl-yən, -'mā-lē-ən\ sculptor in Greek mythology who creates Galatea

Py·thag·o·ras \pə-'tha-gə-rəs, pī-\ *ca* 580–*ca* 500 B.C. Greek philosopher and mathematician

Ra \'rä\ god of the sun and chief deity of ancient Egypt

Ra·leigh *or* **Ra·legh** \'ró-lē, 'rä- *also* 'ra-\ Sir Walter 1554?–1618 Eng. navigator and writer

Ram·ses \'ram-ˌsēz\ *or* **Ram·e·ses** \'ra-mə-ˌsēz\ name of 12 kings of Egypt: esp. **II** (r. 1279–1213 B.C.,); **III** (r. 1187–1156 B.C.)

Ran·dolph \'ran-ˌdälf\ Asa Philip 1889–1979 Amer. labor and civil rights leader

Ra·pha·el \'ra-fē-əl, 'rä-, -ˌel\ archangel named in Hebrew tradition — compare GABRIEL; MICHAEL; URIEL

Ra·pha·el \'ra-fē-əl, 'rä-, 'rä-\ 1483–1520 orig. *Raffaello Sanzio* or *Santi* Ital. painter

Ras·pu·tin \ra-'spyü-tᵊn, -'spü-, -'spü-\ Grigory Yefimovich 1872–1916 Russ. mystic

Rea·gan \'rā-gən\ Ronald Wilson 1911–2004 40th pres. of the U.S. (1981–89)

Re·bek·ah \ri-'be-kə\ wife of Isaac and mother of Jacob in the Bible

Red Cloud \'red-ˌklaùd\ 1822–1909 Sioux Indian chief

Red Jack·et \'red-ˌja-kət\ 1758?–1830 *Sa-go-ye-wa-tha* \sä-ˌgoi-(y)ə-'wä-thə\ Seneca Indian chief

Reed \'rēd\ Walter 1851–1902 Amer. army surgeon

Rem·brandt \'rem-ˌbrant *also* -ˌbränt\ 1606–1669 *Rembrandt (Harmenszoon) van Rijn* Dutch painter

Rem·ing·ton \'re-miŋ-tən\ Frederic 1861–1909 Amer. painter and sculptor

Re·mus \'rē-məs\ son of Mars who in Roman mythology is killed by his twin brother Romulus

Re·noir \'ren-ˌwär, rən-'\ (Pierre-) Auguste 1841–1919 French painter

Re·vere \ri-'vir\ Paul 1735–1818 Amer. patriot and silversmith

Rich·ard \'ri-chərd\ name of 3 kings of England: **I** 1157–1199 *Richard the Lion-Hearted* (r. 1189–99); **II** 1367–1400 (r. 1377–99); **III** 1452–1485 (r. 1483–85)

Ride \'rīd\ Sally Kristen 1951– Amer. astronaut; 1st Amer. woman in space (1983)

Rob·in Good·fel·low \'rä-bən-'gùd-ˌfe-(ˌ)lō\ mischievous elf in Eng. folklore

Robin Hood \-ˌhùd\ legendary Eng. outlaw who gave to the poor what he stole from the rich

Rob·in·son \'rä-bən-sən\ Edwin Arlington 1869–1935 Amer. poet

Robinson Jackie 1919–1972 *Jack Roosevelt Robinson* Amer. baseball player

Rob·in·son Cru·soe \'rä-bə(n)-sən-'krü-(ˌ)sō\ shipwrecked sailor in Daniel Defoe's *Robinson Crusoe* who lives for many years on a desert island

Ro·cham·beau \ˌrō-ˌsham-'bō\ Comte de 1725–1807 French general in Amer. Revolution

Rocke·fel·ler \'rä-ki-ˌfe-lər\ John Davison 1839–1937 and his son John Davison, Jr. 1874–1960 Amer. oil magnates and philanthropists

Ro·ma·nov \rō-'mä-nəf, 'rō-mə-ˌnäf\ Michael 1596–1645 1st czar (1613–45) of Russ. Romanov dynasty (1613–1917)

Rom·u·lus \'räm-yə-ləs\ son of Mars in Roman mythology who is the twin brother of Remus and the founder of Rome

Rönt·gen *or* **Roent·gen** \'rent-gən, 'rənt-, -jən\ Wilhelm Conrad 1845–1923 Ger. physicist; Nobel Prize winner (1901)

Roo·se·velt \'rō-zə-vəlt, -ˌvelt\ (Anna) Eleanor 1884–1962 Amer. lecturer and writer; wife of F. D. Roosevelt

Roosevelt Franklin Delano 1882–1945 32nd pres. of the U.S. (1933–45)

Roosevelt Theodore 1858–1919 26th pres. of the U.S. (1901–09); Nobel Prize winner (1906)

Ross \'ròs\ Betsy 1752–1836 née *Griscom* reputed maker of 1st Amer. flag

Ros·si·ni \rò-'sē-nē, rə-\ Gioacchino Antonio 1792–1868 Ital. composer

Row·ling \'rō-liŋ\ J. K. 1965–   *Joanne Kathleen Rowling* Brit. author

Ru·bens \'rü-bənz\ Peter Paul 1577–1640 Flemish painter

Ru·dolph \'rü-ˌdòlf, -ˌdälf\ Wilma Glodean 1940–1994 Amer. athlete

Rus·sell \'rə-səl\ Bertrand Arthur William 1872–1970 3d Earl *Russell* Eng. mathematician and philosopher; Nobel Prize winner (1950)

Ruth \'rüth\ woman in the Bible who was one of the ancestors of King David

Ruth Babe 1895–1948 *George Herman Ruth* Amer. baseball player

Ruth·er·ford \'rə-thə(r)-fərd, -thə(r)-\ Ernest 1871–1937 Baron *Rutherford* Brit. physicist; Nobel Prize winner (1908)

Sa·bin \'sā-bin\ Albert Bruce 1906–1993 Amer. (Polish-born) physician and microbiologist

Sac·a·ga·wea \ˌsa-kə-jə-'wē-ə\ 1786?–1812 Shoshone Indian guide to Lewis and Clark

Sa·dat \sə-'dat, -'dät\ Anwar el- 1918–1981 pres. of Egypt (1970–81); Nobel Prize winner (1978)

Sa·gan \'sā-gən\ Carl Edward 1934–1996 Amer. astronomer and science writer

Saint Nicholas — see Saint NICHOLAS; SANTA CLAUS

Sal·in·ger \'sa-lən-jər\ J. D. 1919–   *Jerome David Salinger* Amer. author

Salk \'sò(l)k\ Jonas Edward 1914–1995 Amer. physician and medical researcher

Sa·lo·me \sə-'lō-mē, 'sa-lə-ˌmä\ niece of Herod Antipas who in the Bible is given the head of John the Baptist as a reward for her dancing

Sa·mo·set \'sa-mə-ˌset, sə-'mä-sət\ *died ca* 1653 Amer. Indian leader

Sam·son \'sam(p)-sən\ powerful Hebrew hero in the Bible who fights against the Philistines but is betrayed by Delilah

Sam·u·el \'sam-yə-wəl, -ˌyəl\ Hebrew

judge in the Bible who appoints Saul and then David king

Sand·burg \'san(d)-ˌbərg\ Carl 1878–1967 Amer. author

Sang·er \'saŋ-ər\ Margaret 1883–1966 née *Higgins* Amer. birth-control activist

San·ta Claus \'san-tə-ˌklòz\ plump white=bearded and red-suited old man in modern folklore who delivers presents to good children at Christmastime

Sap·pho \'sa-(ˌ)fō\ *fl. ca* 610–*ca* 580 B.C. Greek poet

Sa·rah \'ser-ə, 'sä-rə\ wife of Abraham and mother of Isaac in the Bible

Sar·gent \'sär-jənt\ John Singer 1856–1925 Amer. painter

Sar·tre \'särtrᵊ\ Jean-Paul 1905–1980 French philosopher and author

Sat·urn \'sa-tərn\ god of agriculture in Roman mythology

Saul \'sòl, 'säl\ 1st king of Israel in the Bible

Saul *or* **Saul of Tarsus** the apostle Paul in the Bible

Sche·her·a·zade \shə-ˌher-ə-'zäd\ fictional wife of a sultan and narrator of the tales in the *Arabian Nights' Entertainments*

Schin·dler \'shind-lər\ Oskar 1908–1974 Ger. humanitarian during the Holocaust

Schu·bert \'shü-bərt, -ˌbert\ Franz Peter 1797–1828 Austrian composer

Schu·mann \'shü-ˌmän, -mən\ Clara 1819–1896 née *Wieck* \'vēk\ Ger. pianist; wife of R. Schumann

Schumann Robert Alexander 1810–1856 Ger. composer

Schweit·zer \'shwīt-sər, 'shvīt-, 'swīt-\ Albert 1875–1965 French theologian, philosopher, physician, and music scholar; Nobel Prize winner (1952)

Scott \'skät\ Dred \'dred\ 1795?–1858 Amer. slave

Scott Robert Falcon 1868–1912 Brit. polar explorer

Scott Sir Walter 1771–1832 Scot. author

Scott Winfield 1786–1866 Amer. general

Scyl·la \'si-lə\ nymph in Greek mythology who is changed into a monster and inhabits a cave opposite the whirlpool Charybdis off the coast of Sicily

Se·at·tle \sē-'a-tᵊl\ 1786?–1866 Amer. Indian chief

Se·le·ne \sə-'lē-nē\ goddess of the moon in classical mythology

Se·quoy·ah *or* **Se·quoia** \si-'kwòi-ə\ *ca* 1760–1843 *George Guess* Cherokee Indian scholar

Ser·ra \'ser-ə\ Junípero 1713–1784 Span. missionary in Mexico and California

Se·ton \'sē-tᵊn\ Saint Elizabeth Ann 1774–1821 *Mother Seton* née *Bayley* Amer. religious leader

Seu·rat \sə-'rä\ Georges 1859–1891 French painter

Sew·ard \'sü-ərd, 'sùrd\ William Henry

1801–1872 Amer. politician; U.S. secretary of state (1861–69)

Shack·le·ton \'sha-kəl-tən\ Sir Ernest Henry 1874–1922 Brit. polar explorer

Shake·speare \'shāk-ˌspir\ William 1564–1616 Eng. playwright and poet

Shaw \'shȯ\ George Bernard 1856–1950 Brit. playwright; Nobel Prize winner (1925)

Shaw Robert Gould 1837–1863 Amer. soldier

Shel·ley \'she-lē\ Mary Wollstonecraft 1797–1851 née *Godwin* Eng. author; wife of P. B. Shelley

Shelley Percy Bysshe \'bish\ 1792–1822 Eng. poet

Shep·ard \'she-pərd\ Alan Bartlett, Jr. 1923–1998 Amer. astronaut; 1st Amer. in space (1961)

Sher·i·dan \'sher-ə-dən\ Philip Henry 1831–1888 Amer. general

Sher·lock Holmes \'shər-ˌläk-'hōmz, -'hōlmz\ detective in stories by Sir Arthur Conan Doyle

Sher·man \'shər-mən\ John 1823–1900 Amer. statesman; brother of W. T. Sherman

Sherman William Tecumseh 1820–1891 Amer. general

Shi·va \'shi-və, 'shē-\ *or* **Si·va** \'si-və, 'shi-, 'sē-, 'shē-\ god of destruction and regeneration in the Hindu sacred triad — compare BRAHMA; VISHNU

Sieg·fried \'sig-ˌfrēd, 'sēg-\ hero in Germanic legend who kills a dragon guarding a gold hoard

Si·mon \'sī-mən\ *or* **Simon the Zealot** one of the 12 apostles in the Bible

Si·na·tra \sə-'nä-trə\ Frank 1915–1998 *Francis Albert Sinatra* Amer. singer and actor

Sind·bad the Sailor \'sin-ˌbad\ citizen of Baghdad whose adventures are narrated in the *Arabian Nights' Entertainments*

Sis·y·phus \'si-sə-fəs\ king of Corinth who in Greek mythology is condemned to roll a heavy stone up a hill in Hades only to have it roll down again as it nears the top

Sit·ting Bull \ˌsi-tiŋ-'bùl\ *ca* 1831–1890 Sioux Indian chief

Siva — see SHIVA

Smith \'smith\ Bessie 1894?–1937 Amer. blues singer

Smith John *ca* 1580–1631 Eng. colonist in America

Smith Joseph 1805–1844 Amer. founder of the Mormon Church

Soc·ra·tes \'sä-krə-ˌtēz\ *ca* 470–399 B.C. Greek philosopher

Sol \'säl\ god of the sun in Roman mythology — see HELIOS

Sol·o·mon \'sä-lə-mən\ 10th-century B.C. king of Israel noted for his wisdom

Soph·o·cles \'sä-fə-ˌklēz\ *ca* 496–406 B.C. Greek playwright

Sou·sa \'sü-zə, 'sü-sə\ John Philip 1854–1932 Amer. bandmaster and composer

Spar·ta·cus \'spär-tə-kəs\ *died* 71 B.C. Roman slave and gladiator

Sphinx \'sfiŋ(k)s\ monster in Greek mythology having a lion's body, wings, and the head and bust of a woman

Spiel·berg \'spēl-ˌbərg\ Steven 1947– Amer. filmmaker

Squan·to \'skwän-tō\ *died* 1622 Amer. Indian friend of the Pilgrims

Sta·lin \'stä-lən, 'sta-, -ˌlēn\ Joseph 1879–1953 Soviet Communist party leader (1922–53), premier (1941–53), and dictator

Stan·dish \'stan-dish\ Myles *or* Miles 1584?–1656 Amer. colonist

Stan·ley \'stan-lē\ Sir Henry Morton 1841–1904 Brit. explorer in Africa

Stan·ton \'stan-t³n\ Elizabeth Cady 1815–1902 Amer. suffragist

Stein \'stīn\ Gertrude 1874–1946 Amer. author

Stein·beck \'stīn-ˌbek\ John Ernst 1902–1968 Amer. author; Nobel Prize winner (1962)

Steu·ben \'stü-bən, 'styü-, 'shtȯi-\ Friedrich Wilhelm von 1730–1794 Prussian-born general in Amer. Revolution

Ste·ven·son \'stē-vən-sən\ Adlai Ewing 1900–1965 Amer. politician

Stevenson Robert Louis 1850–1894 Scot. author

Sto·ker \'stō-kər\ Bram 1847–1912 *Abraham Stoker* Irish author

Stowe \'stō\ Harriet Beecher 1811–1896 Amer. author

Stra·di·va·ri \ˌstra-də-'vär-ē, -'ver-\ Antonio 1644?–1737 Ital. violin maker

Strauss \'shtraús, 'straús\ Johann 1804–1849 and his sons Johann, Jr. 1825–1899 and Josef 1827–1870 Austrian composers

Strauss Richard 1864–1949 Ger. composer

Stra·vin·sky \strə-'vin(t)-skē\ Igor 1882–1971 Amer. (Russ.-born) composer

Stu·art \'stü-ərt, 'styü-; 'st(y)ùrt\ Charles Edward 1720–1788 *the Young Pretender; Bonnie Prince Charlie* claimant to the Brit. throne

Stuart Gilbert Charles 1755–1828 Amer. painter

Stuart Jeb 1833–1864 *James Ewell Brown Stuart* Amer. Confederate general

Stuy·ve·sant \'stī-və-sənt\ Peter *ca* 1610–1672 Dutch colonial administrator in America

Sul·li·van \'sə-lə-vən\ Sir Arthur Seymour 1842–1900 Eng. composer; collaborator with Sir William Gilbert

Sullivan Louis Henri 1856–1924 Amer. architect

Sum·ner \'səm-nər\ Charles 1811–1874 Amer. politician

Sun Yat-sen \'sùn-'yät-'sen\ 1866–1925 Chinese statesman

Biographical Names

Sut·ter \'sə-tər, 'sü-\ John Augustus 1803–1880 Amer. (Ger.-born) pioneer in California

Swift \'swift\ Jonathan 1667–1745 Eng. (Irish-born) author

Synge \'siŋ\ John Millington 1871–1909 Irish playwright

Taft \'taft\ William Howard 1857–1930 27th pres. of the U.S. (1909–13); chief justice of the U.S. Supreme Court (1921–30)

Ta·gore \tə-'gòr\ Ra·bin·dra·nath \rə-'bin-drə-,nät\ 1861–1941 Indian poet; Nobel Prize winner (1913)

Tall·chief \'tòl-,chēf\ Maria 1925– Amer. dancer

Tan \'tan\ Amy 1952– Amer. author

Ta·ney \'tò-nē\ Roger Brooke 1777–1864 Amer. jurist; chief justice of the U.S. Supreme Court (1836–64)

Tan·ta·lus \'tan-tə-ləs\ king in Greek mythology who is condemned to stand up to his chin in a pool of water in Hades and beneath fruit-laden boughs only to have the water or fruit go out of reach at each attempt to drink or eat

Tay·lor \'tā-lər\ Zachary 1784–1850 Amer. general; 12th pres. of the U.S. (1849–50)

Tchai·kov·sky \chī-'kòf-skē, chə-, -'kòv-\ Pyotr Ilich 1840–1893 Russ. composer

Te·cum·seh \tə-'kəm(p)-sə, -sē\ 1768–1813 Shawnee Indian chief

Tek·a·kwitha \,te-kə-'kwi-thə\ Kateri 1656–1680 *Lily of the Mohawks* beatified Mohawk Indian religious

Ten·ny·son \'te-nə-sən\ Alfred 1809–1892 Baron *Tennyson* known as *Alfred, Lord Tennyson* Eng. poet

Te·re·sa \tə-'rā-zə, -'rē-sə\ Mother 1910–1997 beatified Albanian religious in India; Nobel Prize winner (1979)

Teresa of Ávi·la \'ä-vi-lə\ Saint 1515–1582 Span. nun and mystic

Tes·la \'tes-lə\ Nikola 1856–1943 Amer. (Croatian-born) electrical engineer and inventor

Thatch·er \'tha-chər\ Margaret Hilda 1925– Baroness *Thatcher of Kesteven* née *Roberts* Brit. prime minister (1979–90)

The·seus \'thē-,sūs, -sē-əs\ hero in Greek mythology who kills the Minotaur and conquers the Amazons

Thom·as \'tä-məs\ apostle in the Bible who demanded proof of Jesus' resurrection

Thomas à Becket — see Saint Thomas BECKET

Thomas Aquinas Saint — see AQUINAS

Thor \'thòr\ god of thunder, weather, and crops in Norse mythology

Tho·reau \thə-'rō, thò-\ Henry David 1817–1862 Amer. author

Thorpe \'thòrp\ Jim 1888–1953 *James Francis Thorpe* Amer. athlete

Thur·ber \'thər-bər\ James Grover 1894–1961 Amer. author

Ti·be·ri·us \tī-'bir-ē-əs\ 42 B.C.–37 A.D. Roman emperor (14–37)

Tocque·ville \'tōk-,vil, 'tòk-, 'täk-, -,vēl, -vəl\ Alexis de 1805–1859 French politician and author

Tol·kien \'tòl-,kēn\ J. R. R. 1892–1973 *John Ronald Reuel Tolkien* Brit. author

Tol·stoy \tòl-'stòi, tōl-', täl-', 'tòl-,, 'täl-,\ Leo 1828–1910 Count *Lev Nikolayevich Tolstoy* Russ. author

Tou·louse–Lau·trec \tü-,lüz-lō-'trek\ Henri de 1864–1901 French painter

Tri·ton \'trī-t°n\ sea god in Greek mythology who is half man and half fish

Trots·ky \'trät-skē\ Leon 1879–1940 orig. *Lev Davidovich Bronstein* Russ. Communist leader

Tru·deau \'trü-(,)dō, trü-'\ Pierre Elliott 1919–2000 Canad. prime minister (1968–79, 1980–84)

Tru·man \'trü-mən\ Harry S. 1884–1972 33rd pres. of the U.S. (1945–53)

Truth \'trüth\ Sojourner 1797?–1883 Amer. abolitionist

Tub·man \'təb-mən\ Harriet *ca* 1820–1913 Amer. abolitionist

Tut·ankh·a·men \,tü-,taŋ-'kä-mən, -,täŋ-\ originally *Tut·ankh·a·ten* \-'kä-t°n\ *ca* 1370–1352 B.C., king of Egypt (1361–1352 B.C.)

Twain \'kle-mənz\ Mark 1835–1910 pseud. of *Samuel Langhorne Clem·ens* \'klem-ənz\ Amer. author

Tweed \'twēd\ William Marcy 1823–1878 *Boss Tweed* Amer. politician

Ty·ler \'tī-lər\ John 1790–1862 10th pres. of the U.S. (1841–45)

Ulysses — see ODYSSEUS

Ura·nus \'yùr-ə-nəs, yù-'rā-\ the sky personified as a god and father of the Titans in Greek mythology

Ur·ban \'ər-bən\ name of eight popes: esp. **II** *ca* 1035–1099 (pope 1088–99)

Uri·el \'yùr-ē-əl\ archangel named in Hebrew tradition — compare GABRIEL; MICHAEL; RAPHAEL

Val·en·tine \'va-lən-,tīn\ Saint, 3d cent. Christian martyr

Van Bu·ren \van-'byùr-ən, vən-\ Martin 1782–1862 8th pres. of the U.S. (1837–41)

Van Dyck or **Van·dyke** \van-'dīk, vən-\ Sir Anthony 1599–1641 Flemish painter

van Gogh Vincent — see GOGH, VAN

Ve·láz·quez \və-'las-kəs, -'läs-, -kwiz, -(,)käs\ Diego 1599–1660 Span. painter

Ve·nus \'vē-nəs\ goddess of love and beauty in Roman mythology — compare APHRODITE

Ver·di \'ver-dē\ Giuseppe 1813–1901 Ital. composer

Ver·meer \vər-'mer, -'mir\ Jan or Johannes 1632–1675 Dutch painter

Verne \\'vərn, 'vern\ Jules \'jülz\ 1828–1905 French author

Ves·puc·ci \ve-'spü-chē, -'spyü-\ Amer·i·go \ə-'mer-i-,gō\ 1454–1512 Latin *Amer·i·cus Ves·pu·cius* \ə-'mer-ə-kəs-,ves-'pyü-sh(ē-)əs\ Ital. navigator for Spain and namesake of America

Vic·to·ria \vik-'tòr-ē-ə\ 1819–1901 *Alexandrina Victoria* queen of the United Kingdom (1837–1901)

Vinci, da Leonardo — see LEONARDO DA VINCI

Vir·gil *also* **Ver·gil** \'vər-jəl\ 70–19 B.C. Roman poet

Vish·nu \'vish-(,)nü\ god of preservation in the Hindu sacred triad — compare BRAHMA; SHIVA

Vol·ta \vōl-'tar, väl-, vòl-, -'ter\ Alessandro 1745–1827 Ital. physicist

Vol·taire \vōl-'tar, väl-, vòl-, -'ter\ 1694–1778 orig. *François-Marie Arouet* French author

Vul·can \'vəl-kən\ god of fire and metal-working in Roman mythology — compare HEPHAESTUS

Wag·ner \'väg-nər\ Ri·chard \'ri-,kärt, -,kärt\ 1813–1883 Ger. composer

Walk·er \'wò-kər\ Alice Malsenior 1944– Amer. writer

Wal·len·berg \'wä-lən-,bərg\ Raoul 1912–1947? Swedish diplomat and hero of the Holocaust

War·ren \'wòr-ən, 'wär-\ Earl 1891–1974 Amer. jurist; chief justice of the U.S. Supreme Court (1953–69)

Wash·ing·ton \'wò-shiŋ-tən, 'wä-\ Booker Tal·ia·ferro \'tä-lə-vər\ 1856–1915 Amer. educator

Washington George 1732–1799 Amer. general; 1st pres. of the U.S. (1789–97)

Watt \'wät\ James 1736–1819 Scot. inventor

Wayne \'wān\ Anthony 1745–1796 *Mad Anthony* Amer. general

Web·ster \'web-stər\ Daniel 1782–1852 Amer. politician

Webster Noah 1758–1843 Amer. lexicographer

Wel·ling·ton \'we-liŋ-tən\ Duke of 1769–1852 *Arthur Wellesley; the Iron Duke* Brit. general and statesman

Wells \'welz\ H. G. 1866–1946 *Herbert George Wells* Eng. author and historian

Wel·ty \'wel-tē\ Eudora 1909–2001 Amer. author

Wes·ley \'wes-lē, 'wez-\ John 1703–1791 Eng. founder of Methodism

Wes·ting·house \'wes-tiŋ-,haùs\ George 1846–1914 Amer. inventor and industrialist

Whar·ton \'hwòr-tᵊn, 'wòr-\ Edith 1862–1937 née *Jones* Amer. author

Whis·tler \'hwis-lər, 'wis-\ James (Abbott) McNeill 1834–1903 Amer. artist

Whit·man \'hwit-mən, 'wit-\ Walt 1819–1892 Amer. poet

Whit·ney \'hwit-nē, 'wit-\ Eli 1765–1825 Amer. inventor

Whit·ti·er \'hwi-tē-ər, 'wit-\ John Greenleaf 1807–1892 Amer. poet

Wie·sel \vē-'zel, wē-\ Elie 1928– Amer. (Romanian-born) author; Nobel Prize winner (1986)

Wilde \'wī(-ə)ld\ Oscar 1854–1900 Irish author

Wil·der \'wī(-ə)l-dər\ Thornton Niven 1897–1975 Amer. author

Wil·liam \'wil-yəm\ name of 4 kings of England: **I** *ca* 1028–1087 *William the Conqueror* (r. 1066–87); **II** *ca* 1056–1100 *William Rufus* \'rü-fəs\ (r. 1087–1100); **III** 1650–1702 (r. 1689–1702); **IV** 1765–1837 (r. 1830–37)

Wil·liam Tell \,wil-yəm-'tel\ legendary Swiss patriot commanded to shoot an apple off his son's head

Wil·liams \'wil-yəmz\ Roger 1603?–1683 Eng. colonist

Williams Ted 1918–2002 *Theodore Samuel Williams* Amer. baseball player

Williams Tennessee 1911–1983 orig. *Thomas Lanier Williams* Amer. playwright

Williams Venus 1980– and her sister Serena 1981– Amer. tennis players

Wil·son \'wil-sən\ (Thomas) Woodrow 1856–1924 28th pres. of the U.S. (1913–21); Nobel Prize winner (1919)

Win·throp \'win(t)-thrəp\ John 1588–1649 1st governor of Massachusetts Bay Colony

Woden — see ODIN

Woll·stone·craft \'wùl-stən-,kraft\ Mary 1759–1797 Eng. feminist and writer

Woods \'wùdz\ Tiger 1975– *Eldrick Woods* Amer. golfer

Woolf \'wùlf\ Virginia 1882–1941 Eng. author

Words·worth \'wərdz-(,)wərth\ William 1770–1850 Eng. poet

Wo·vo·ka \wō-'vō-kə\ 1858?–1932 *Jack Wilson* Paiute Indian mystic

Wren \'ren\ Sir Christopher 1632–1723 Eng. architect

Wright \'rīt\ Frank Lloyd 1867–1959 Amer. architect

Wright Orville 1871–1948 and his brother Wilbur 1867–1912 Amer. pioneers in aviation

Wright Richard 1908–1960 Amer. author

Wy·eth \'wī-əth\ Andrew Newell 1917– Amer. painter

Yeats \'yāts\ William Butler 1865–1939 Irish author

Yel·tsin \'yelt-sən, 'yel-sin\ Boris Niko·layevich 1931– pres. of Russia (1990–99)

York \'yòrk\ Alvin Cullum 1887–1964 Amer. hero in World War I

Young \\'yəŋ\ Brig·ham \\'brig-əm\ 1801–1877 Amer. Mormon leader

Za·har·i·as \zə-'ha-rē-əs\ Babe Didrikson 1914–1956 *Mildred Ella Zaharias* née *Didrikson* Amer. athlete

Zech·a·ri·ah \ˌze-kə-'rī-ə\ Hebrew prophet of the 6th cent. B.C.

Zeng·er \\'zeŋ-gər, -ər\ John Peter 1697–1746 Amer. (Ger.-born) journalist and printer

Zeph·y·rus \\'ze-fə-rəs\ god of the west wind in Greek mythology

Zeus \\'züs\ chief god and ruler of the sky and weather in Greek mythology — compare JUPITER

GEOGRAPHICAL NAMES

This section gives basic information about the world's countries, regions, cities, and major physical features. The latest population figures are given for nations, cities, and some regions. For many of these entries, derived nouns and adjectives are also listed (as **Iceland . . . Icelander . . . n**). Other derived words not shown here have been separately entered in the main A-Z section, because of the presence of additional senses (as **Chinese**).

Abbreviations used here are listed in the front section Abbreviations in This Work. The capital letters N, E, S, and W, used singly or in combination and without a period, indicate direction. For example, "N India" means "northern India." Where direction is a part of the name, the word is spelled out.

The symbol ✳ denotes a capital. Sizes are given in conventional U.S. units, with metric equivalents following.

Ab·er·deen \,a-bər-'dēn\ city NE Scotland; *pop* 211,080 — **Ab·er·do·ni·an** \,a-bər-'dō-nē-ən\ *adj or n*

Ab·i·djan \,ä-bē-'jän, ,a-bi-\ city, seat of government of Ivory Coast; *pop* 1,934,342

Abilene \'a-bə-,lēn\ city NW *cen* Texas; *pop* 115,930

Abu Dha·bi \,ä-bü-'dä-bē, -'thä-\ city, ✳ of United Arab Emirates; *pop* 347,000

Abu·ja \ä-'bü-jä\ city *cen* Nigeria; its ✳; *pop* 423,391

Ab·ys·sin·ia \,a-bə-'si-nē-ə, -nyə\ — see ETHIOPIA — **Ab·ys·sin·i·an** \-nē-ən, -nyən\ *adj or n*

Aca·dia \ə-'kā-dē-ə\ *or French* **Aca·die** \à-kà-'dē\ NOVA SCOTIA — an early name — **Aca·di·an** \-ē-ən\ *adj or n*

Aca·pul·co \,ä-kä-'pül-(,)kō, ,a-\ city & port S Mexico on the Pacific; *pop* 687,292

Ac·cra \'ä-krə, 'a-; ə-'krä\ city & port, ✳ of Ghana; *pop* 867,459

Acon·ca·gua \,ä-kōn-'kä-gwä\ mountain 22,834 ft. (6960 m.) W Argentina; highest in the Andes & in Western Hemisphere

Ad·dis Aba·ba \'ä-dis-'ä-bä-,bä, ,a-dəs-'a-bə-bə\ city, ✳ of Ethiopia; *pop* 2,646,000

Ad·e·laide \'a-də-,lād\ city S Australia, ✳ of South Australia; *pop* 917,000

Aden \'ä-d°n, 'ā-\ city & port S Yemen; *pop* 240,370

Aden, Gulf of arm of Indian Ocean between Yemen (Arabia) & Somalia (Africa)

Adirondack \,a-də-'rän-,dak\ mountains NE New York; highest Mount Marcy 5344 ft. (1629 m.)

Admiralty \'ad-m(ə-)rəl-tē\ **1** island SE Alaska **2** islands W Pacific N of New Guinea; part of Papua New Guinea

Adri·at·ic Sea \,ä-drē-'a-tik, ,a-\ arm of Mediterranean between Italy & Balkan Peninsula

Ae·ge·an Sea \i-'jē-ən\ arm of Mediterranean between Asia Minor & Greece

Af·ghan·i·stan \af-'ga-nə-,stan, -'gä-nə-,stän\ country W Asia E of Iran; ✳, Kabul; *pop* (est.) 28,717,000

Af·ri·ca \'a-fri-kə\ continent S of the Mediterranean

Aga·na \ä-'gä-nyä\ town, ✳ of Guam; *pop* 1139

Agra \'ä-grə, 'ə-\ city N India SSE of Delhi; *pop* 1,259,979

Aguas·ca·lien·tes \,ä-gwäs-,käl-'yen-,täs\ city *cen* Mexico NE of Guadalajara; metropolitan area *pop* 637,303

Agul·has, Cape \ə-'gə-ləs\ cape Republic of South Africa; most southerly point of Africa, at 34° 52' S latitude

Ahag·gar \ə-'hä-gər, ,ä-hə-'gär\ mountains S Algeria in W *cen* Sahara

Ah·mad·abad \'ä-mə-də-,bäd, -,bad\ city W India N of Bombay; *pop* 3,515,361

Ak·ron \'a-krən\ city NE Ohio; *pop* 217,074

Al·a·bama \,a-lə-'ba-mə\ state SE U.S.; ✳, Montgomery; *pop* 4,447,100 — **Al·a·bam·i·an** \-'ba-mē-ən\ *or* **Al·a·bam·an** \-'ba-mən\ *adj or n*

Alas·ka \ə-'las-kə\ **1** peninsula SW Alaska SW of Cook Inlet **2** state of U.S. in NW North America; ✳, Juneau; *pop* 626,932 **3** mountain range S Alaska extending from Alaska Peninsula to Yukon boundary — **Alas·kan** \-kən\ *adj or n*

Alaska, Gulf of inlet of Pacific off S Alaska between Alaska Peninsula on W & Alexander Archipelago on E

Al·ba·nia \al-'bā-nē-ə, -nyə\ country S Europe in Balkan Peninsula on Adriatic; ✳, Tirane; *pop* 3,069,275

Al·ba·ny \'ól-bə-nē\ city, ✳ of New York; *pop* 95,658

Albemarle Sound \'al-bə-,märl\ inlet of the Atlantic in NE North Carolina

Albert, Lake \'al-bərt\ lake E Africa between Uganda & Democratic Republic of the Congo in course of the Nile

Al·ber·ta \al-'bər-tə\ province W Canada;

✳, Edmonton; *pop* 2,974,807 — **Al·ber·tan** \-'bər-t⁽ə⁾n\ *adj or n*

Al·bu·quer·que \'al-bə-ˌkər-kē\ ˌ*city cen* New Mexico; *pop* 448,607

Al·ca·traz \'al-kə-ˌtraz\ island California in San Francisco Bay

Al·da·bra \äl-'dä-brə\ island NW Indian Ocean N of Madagascar; belongs to Seychelles

Al·der·ney \'ȯl-dər-nē\ — see CHANNEL

Alep·po \ə-'le-(ˌ)pō\ *city* N Syria; *pop* 1,445,000

Aleu·tian \ə-'lü-shən\ islands SW Alaska extending 1700 mi. (2735 km.) W from Alaska Peninsula

Al·ex·an·der \ˌal-ig-'zan-dər, ˌel-\ archipelago SE Alaska

Al·ex·an·dria \ˌa-lig-'zan-drē-ə, ˌe-\ **1** city N Virginia S of District of Columbia; *pop* 128,283 **2** city N Egypt on the Mediterranean; *pop* 3,170,000 — **Al·ex·an·dri·an** \-drē-ən\ *adj or n*

Al·ge·ria \al-'jir-ē-ə\ country NW Africa on Mediterranean; ✳, Algiers; *pop* 22,971,000 — **Al·ge·ri·an** \-ē-ən\ *adj or n*

Al·giers \al-'jirz\ city, ✳ of Algeria; *pop* 1,365,400 — **Al·ge·rine** \ˌal-jə-'rēn\ *adj or n*

Al·lah·a·bad \'ä-lä-hä-ˌbäd, 'a-lə-hə-ˌbad\ city N India on the Ganges; *pop* 990,298

Al·le·ghe·ny \ˌa-lə-'gā-nē\ **1** river 325 mi. (523 km.) long W Pennsylvania & SW New York **2** mountains of Appalachian system E U.S. in Pennsylvania, Maryland, Virginia, & West Virginia

Al·len·town \'a-lən-ˌtaůn\ city E Pennsylvania; *pop* 106,632

Al·maty \äl-'mä-tē\ *or* **Al·ma–Ata** \əl-ˈmä-ə-'tä; ˌal-mə-'ä-tə, -ə-'tä\ city, former ✳ of Kazakhstan; *pop* 1,156,200

Alps \'alps\ mountain system *cen* Europe — see MONT BLANC

Al·tai *or* **Al·tay** \al-'tī\ mountain system *cen* Asia between Mongolia & W China & between Kazakhstan & Russia

Ama·ga·sa·ki \ˌä-mä-gä-'sä-kē\ city Japan in W *cen* Honshu; *pop* 466,187

Am·a·ril·lo \ˌa-mə-'ri-(ˌ)lō, -lə\ city NW Texas; *pop* 173,627

Am·a·zon \'a-mə-ˌzän, -zən\ river 3900 mi. (6436 km.) long N South America flowing from Peruvian Andes into Atlantic in N Brazil

Amer·i·ca \ə-'mer-ə-kə, -'me-rə-\ **1** either continent (**North America** *or* **South America**) of Western Hemisphere **2** *or* **the Amer·i·cas** \-kəz\ lands of Western Hemisphere including North, Central, & South America & West Indies **3** UNITED STATES OF AMERICA — **American** *adj or n*

American Falls — see NIAGARA FALLS

American Samoa *or* **Eastern Samoa** islands SW *cen* Pacific; U.S. territory; ✳, Pago Pago (on Tutuila Island); *pop* 57,291

Am·man \ä-'män, a-, -'man\ city, ✳ of Jordan; *pop* 627,505

Am·ster·dam \'am(p)-stər-ˌdam, 'äm(p)-stər-ˌdäm\ city, official ✳ of the Netherlands; *pop* 735,526

Amur \ä-'múr\ river 1780 mi. (2784 km.) long E Asia flowing into the Pacific & forming part of boundary between China & Russia

An·a·heim \'a-nə-ˌhīm\ city SW California E of Long Beach; *pop* 328,014

An·a·to·lia \ˌa-nə-'tō-lē-ə, -'tōl-yə\ — see ASIA MINOR — **An·a·to·li·an** \-'tō-lē-ən, -'tōl-yən\ *adj or n*

An·chor·age \'aŋ-k(ə-)rij\ city S *cen* Alaska; *pop* 260,283

An·da·man \'an-də-mən, -ˌman\ **1** islands India in Bay of Bengal S of Myanmar & N of Nicobar Islands **2** sea, arm of Bay of Bengal S of Myanmar — **An·da·man·ese** \ˌan-də-mə-'nēz, -'nēs\ *adj or n*

An·des \'an-(ˌ)dēz\ mountain system W South America extending from Panama to Tierra del Fuego — see ACONCAGUA — **An·de·an** \'an-(ˌ)dē-ən, an-'\ *adj* — **An·dine** \'an-ˌdēn, -ˌdīn\ *adj*

An·dor·ra \an-'dȯr-ə, -'där-ə\ country SW Europe in E Pyrenees between France & Spain; ✳, Andorra la Vella; *pop* 57,110 — **An·dor·ran** \-ən\ *adj or n*

Andorra la Vel·la \lä-'vel-yä\ town, ✳ of Andorra; *pop* 21,513

An·dros \'an-drəs\ island, largest of Bahamas

An·gel Falls \'än-jəl\ waterfall 3212 ft. (979 m.) SE Venezuela; world's highest waterfall

Ang·kor \'aŋ-ˌkȯr\ ruins of ancient city NW Cambodia

An·gle·sey \'aŋ-gəl-sē\ island NW Wales

An·go·la \aŋ-'gō-lə, an-\ country SW Africa S of mouth of Congo River; ✳, Luanda; *pop* 10,609,000 — **An·go·lan** \-lən\ *adj or n*

An·i·ak·chak Crater \ˌa-nē-'ak-ˌchak\ volcanic crater SW Alaska on Alaska Peninsula; 6 mi. (10 km.) in diameter

An·ka·ra \'aŋ-kə-rə, 'äŋ-\ city, ✳ of Turkey in *cen* Anatolia; *pop* 2,559,471

An·nap·o·lis \ə-'na-pə-lis\ city, ✳ of Maryland; *pop* 35,838

Ann Ar·bor \(ˌ)an-'är-bər\ city SE Michigan; *pop* 114,024

An·shan \'än-'shän\ city NE China; *pop* 1,203,986

An·ta·nan·a·ri·vo \ˌän-tä-ˌnä-nä-'rē-(ˌ)vō\ city, ✳ of Madagascar; *pop* 958,929

Ant·arc·ti·ca \ant-'ärk-ti-kə, -'är-ti-\ body of land around the South Pole; plateau covered by great ice cap

An·ti·gua \an-'tē-gə, -gwə\ island West Indies in the Leewards; with Barbuda forms independent **Antigua and Barbuda**; ✳, Saint John's; *pop* 83,000

An·til·les \an-'ti-lēz\ the West Indies except for the Bahamas — see GREATER ANTILLES; LESSER ANTILLES — **An·til·le·an** \-lē-ən\ adj

An·trim \'an-trəm\ district E Northern Ireland; pop 44,322

Ant·werp \'ant-,wərp, 'an-,twərp\ city N Belgium; pop 448,709

Aomen — see MACAO

Aorangi — see COOK, MOUNT

Ap·en·nines \'a-pə-,nīnz\ mountain chain Italy extending length of the peninsula; highest peak Monte Corno (NE of Rome) 9560 ft. (2897 m.) — **Ap·en·nine** \'a-pə-,nīnz\ adj

Apia \ä-'pē-ä\ town, ✳ of Samoa; pop 38,000

Apo, Mount \'ä-(,)pō\ volcano Philippines in SE Mindanao 9692 ft. (2954 m.); highest peak in the Philippines

Ap·pa·la·chia \,a-pə-'lā-chə, -'la-chə, -'lā-shə\ region E U.S. including Appalachian Mountains from S cen New York to cen Alabama

Ap·pa·la·chian Mountains \,a-pə-'lā-ch(ē-)ən, -sh(ē-)ən\ mountain system E North America extending from S Quebec to cen Alabama — see MITCHELL, MOUNT

Aqa·ba, Gulf of \'ä-kä-bə\ arm of Red Sea E of Sinai Peninsula

Aquid·neck \ə-'kwid-,nek\ or **Rhode** island SE Rhode Island in Narragansett Bay

Ara·bia \ə-'rā-bē-ə\ peninsula of SW Asia including Saudi Arabia, Yemen, Oman, & Persian Gulf States

Ara·bi·an \ə-'rā-bē-ən\ **1** desert E Egypt between the Nile & Red Sea **2** sea NW section of Indian Ocean between Arabia & India

Ara·fu·ra \,ä-rä-'fü-rä\ sea between N Australia & W New Guinea

Ar·al Sea \'a-rəl\ formerly **Lake Aral** lake W Asia between Kazakhstan & Uzbekistan

Ar·a·rat \'a-rə-,rat\ mountain 16,946 ft. (5165 m.) E Turkey near border of Iran

Arc·tic \'ärk-tik, 'är-tik\ **1** ocean N of Arctic Circle **2** Arctic regions **3** archipelago N Canada in Nunavut & Northwest Territories

Ar·da·bil or **Ar·de·bil** \,är-də-'bēl\ city NW Iran; pop 281,973

Ards \'ärdz\ district E Northern Ireland; pop 64,026

Are·ci·bo \,ä-rä-'sē-(,)bō\ city & port N Puerto Rico; pop 100,131

Ar·gen·ti·na \,är-jən-'tē-nə\ country S South America between the Andes & the Atlantic; ✳, Buenos Aires; pop 33,070,000 — **Ar·gen·tine** \'är-jən-,tīn, -,tēn\ adj or n — **Ar·gen·tin·ean** or **Ar·gen·tin·i·an** \,är-jən-'ti-nē-ən\ adj or n

Ar·gos \'är-,gòs, -gəs\ ancient Greek city-state S Greece

Ar·i·zo·na \,a-rə-'zō-nə\ state SW U.S.; ✳, Phoenix; pop 5,130,632 — **Ar·i·zo·nan** \-nən\ or **Ar·i·zo·nian** \-nē-ən, -nyən\ adj or n

Ar·kan·sas \'är-kən-,sò\ **1** river 1450 mi. (2334 km.) long SW cen U.S. flowing SE into the Mississippi **2** state S cen U.S.; ✳, Little Rock; pop 2,673,400 — **Ar·kan·san** \är-'kan-zən\ adj or n

Ar·ling·ton \'är-liŋ-tən\ city N Texas; pop 332,969

Ar·magh \är-'mä, 'är-,\ **1** district S Northern Ireland; pop 51,331 **2** town cen Armagh district; pop 14,265

Ar·me·nia \är-'mē-nē-ə, -nyə\ **1** region W Asia in mountainous area SE of Black Sea & SW of Caspian Sea divided between Iran, Turkey, & Armenia (country) **2** country E Europe; ✳, Yerevan; pop 3,426,000

Arn·hem Land \'är-nəm\ region N Australia on N coast of Northern Territory

Ar·no \'är-(,)nō\ river 150 mi. (241 km.) long cen Italy flowing through Florence

Aru·ba \ə-'rü-bə\ island Netherlands Antilles off coast of NW Venezuela; pop 69,000

Ar·vada \är-'va-də\ city N cen Colorado NW of Denver; pop 102,153

Ash·ga·bat \'äsh-gə-,bät\ or **Ashkh·a·bad** \'ash-kə-,bad, -,bäd\ city, ✳ of Turkmenistan; pop 412,200

Asia \'ā-zhə, -shə\ continent of Eastern Hemisphere N of the Equator — see EURASIA

Asia Mi·nor \-'mī-nər\ or **An·a·to·lia** \,a-nə-'tō-lē-ə, -'tōl-yə\ peninsula in modern Turkey between Black Sea on N & the Mediterranean on S

As·ma·ra \az-'mä-rə, -'ma-rə\ city, ✳ of Eritrea; pop 342,706

As·syr·ia \ə-'sir-ē-ə\ ancient empire W Asia extending along the middle Tigris & over foothills to the E — **As·syr·i·an** \-ən\ adj or n

As·ta·na \ä-stä-'nä\ city, ✳ of Kazakhstan; pop 319,318

Asun·ción \ä-sün-'syōn\ city, ✳ of Paraguay; pop 502,426

As·wân \ä-'swän, ä-\ city S Egypt on the Nile near site of **Aswân High Dam**; pop 191,461

Ata·ca·ma \,ä-tä-'kä-mä\ desert N Chile

Atchaf·a·laya \ə-),cha-fə-'lī-ə\ river 225 mi. (362 km.) long S Louisiana flowing S into Gulf of Mexico

Ath·a·bas·ca or **Ath·a·bas·ka** \,a-thə-'bas-kə, ,ä-\ river 765 mi. (1231 km.) long NE Alberta flowing into **Lake Athabasca** on Alberta–Saskatchewan border

Ath·ens \'a-thənz\ **1** city NE Georgia; pop 101,489 **2** city, ✳ of Greece; pop 748,110 — **Athe·nian** \ə-'thē-nē-ən, -nyən\ adj or n

At·lan·ta \ət-'lan-tə, at-\ city, ✽ of Georgia; *pop* 416,474

At·lan·tic \ət-'lan-tik, at-\ ocean separating North America & South America from Europe & Africa; often divided into **North Atlantic** and **South Atlantic** — **Atlantic** *adj*

At·las \'at-ləs\ mountains NW Africa extending from SW Morocco to N Tunisia

At·ti·ca \'a-ti-kə\ ancient state E Greece; chief city Athens — **At·tic** \'at-ik\ *adj*

Auck·land \'ȯ-klənd\ city N New Zealand on NW North Island; urban area *pop* 1,074,510

Au·gus·ta \ȯ-'gəs-tə, ə-\ **1** city E Georgia; *pop* 199,775 **2** city, ✽ of Maine; *pop* 18,560

Au·ro·ra \ə-'rȯr-ə, ȯ-\ **1** city NE *cen* Colorado; *pop* 276,393 **2** city NE Illinois; *pop* 142,990

Auschwitz — see OSWIECIM

Aus·tin \'ȯs-tən, 'äs-\ city, ✽ of Texas; *pop* 656,562

Aus·tral·asia \ˌȯs-trə-'lā-zhə, ˌäs-, -'lā-shə\ Australia, Tasmania, New Zealand, & Melanesia — **Aus·tral·asian** \-zhən, -shən\ *adj or n*

Aus·tra·lia \ȯ-'strāl-yə, ä-, ə-\ **1** continent of Eastern Hemisphere SE of Asia **2** country including continent of Australia & island of Tasmania; ✽, Canberra; *pop* 17,562,000 — **Aus·tra·lian** \-yən\ *adj or n*

Australian Alps mountain range SE Australia in E Victoria & SE New South Wales; part of Great Dividing Range

Australian Capital Territory district SE Australia including two areas, one containing Canberra (✽ of Australia) & the other on Jervis Bay (inlet of the South Pacific); surrounded by New South Wales

Aus·tria \'ȯs-trē-ə, 'äs-\ country *cen* Europe; ✽, Vienna; *pop* 7,812,100 — **Aus·tri·an** \-ən\ *adj or n*

Aus·tria–Hun·ga·ry \-'həŋ-gə-rē\ country 1867–1918 *cen* Europe including Bohemia, Moravia, Transylvania, Galicia, and what are now Austria, Hungary, Slovenia, Crotia, & part of NE Italy — **Aus·tro–Hun·gar·i·an** \'ȯs-(ˌ)trō-ˌhəŋ-'ger-ē-ən, ˌäs-\ *adj or n*

Aus·tro·ne·sia \ˌȯs-trə-'nē-zhə, ˌäs-, -'nēshə\ **1** islands of the South Pacific **2** area extending from Madagascar through Malay Peninsula & Malay Archipelago to Hawaii & Easter Island — **Aus·tro·ne·sian** \-zhən, -shən\ *adj or n*

Avon \'ā-vən, 'a-\ river 96 mi. (154 km.) long *cen* England flowing WSW into the Severn

Ayers Rock \'erz\ outcrop *cen* Australia in SW Northern Territory

Ayles·bury \'ālz-b(ə-)rē\ town SE *cen* England; *pop* 41,288

Ayr \'er\ *or* **Ayr·shire** \-ˌshir, -shər\ former county SW Scotland

Azer·bai·jan \ˌa-zər-ˌbī-'jän, ˌä-\ country SE Europe bordering on Caspian Sea; ✽, Baku; *pop* 7,029,000 — **Azer·bai·ja·ni** \ˌa-zər-ˌbī-'jä-nē, ˌä-\ *adj or n*

Azores \'ā-ˌzȯrz, ə-'\ islands Portugal in North Atlantic lying 800 mi. (1287 km.) W of Portuguese coast; *pop* 241,763 — **Azor·e·an** *or* **Azor·i·an** \ā-'zȯr-ē-ən, ə-\ *adj or n*

Bab·y·lon \'ba-bə-lon, -ˌlän\ ancient city, ✽ of Babylonia; site 55 mi. (89 km.) S of Baghdad near the Euphrates — **Bab·y·lo·nian** \ˌba-bə-'lō-nyən, -nē-ən\ *adj or n*

Bab·y·lo·nia \ˌba-bə-'lō-nyə, -nē-ə\ ancient country W Asia in valley of lower Euphrates and Tigris rivers

Bac·tria \'bak-trē-ə\ ancient country W Asia in present NE Afghanistan — **Bac·tri·an** \'bak-trē-ən\ *adj or n*

Bad·lands barren region SW South Dakota & NW Nebraska

Baf·fin \'ba-fən\ **1** bay of the Atlantic between W Greenland & E Baffin Island **2** island NE Canada in Arctic Archipelago N of Hudson Strait

Bagh·dad \'bag-ˌdad, ˌbäg-'däd\ city, ✽ of Iraq on the Tigris; *pop* (est.) 5,949,000

Ba·guio \ˌbä-gē-'ō\ city, former summer ✽ of the Philippines in NW *cen* Luzon; *pop* 183,000

Ba·ha·mas \bə-'hä-məz\ islands in N Atlantic SE of Florida; ✽, Nassau; *pop* 303,611 — **Ba·ha·mi·an** \bə-'hä-mē-ən, -'hä-\ *or* **Ba·ha·man** \-'hä-mən, -'hämən\ *adj or n*

Bahia — see SALVADOR

Bah·rain \bä-'rān\ islands in Persian Gulf off coast of Arabia; country; ✽, Manama; *pop* 485,600 — **Bah·raini** \-'rä-nē\ *adj or n*

Bai·kal, Lake *or* **Lake Bay·kal** \bī-'käl, -'kal\ lake Russia, in mountains N of Mongolia

Ba·ja California \'bä-(ˌ)hä\ peninsula NW Mexico W of Gulf of California

Bakersfield \'bā-kərz-ˌfēld\ city S California; *pop* 247,057

Ba·ku \bä-'kü\ city, ✽ of Azerbaijan on W coast of Caspian Sea; *pop* 1,150,000

Bal·a·ton \'ba-lə-ˌtän, 'bȯ-lȯ-ˌtän\ lake W Hungary

Bal·boa Heights \(ˌ)bal-'bō-ə\ town Panama; formerly the center of administration for Canal Zone

Bal·e·ar·ic Islands \ˌba-lē-'a-rik\ islands E Spain in the W Mediterranean

Ba·li \'bä-lē, 'ba-\ island Indonesia off E end of Java; *pop* 2,777,811 — **Ba·li·nese** \ˌbäl-i-'nēz, ˌbal-, -'nēs\ *adj or n*

Bal·kan \'bȯl-kən\ **1** mountains N Bulgaria extending from Serbia border to Black Sea; highest 7793 ft. (2375 m.) **2** peninsula SE Europe between Adriatic &

Ionian seas on the W & Aegean & Black seas on the E

Bal·kans \\'bȯl-kənz\\ *or* **Balkan States** countries occupying the Balkan Peninsula: Slovenia, Croatia, Bosnia and Herzegovina, independent Macedonia, Serbia and Montenegro, Romania, Bulgaria, Albania, Greece, Turkey (in Europe)

Bal·ly·me·na \\ˌba-lē-'mē-nə\\ district NE *cen* Northern Ireland; *pop* 56,032

Bal·ly·mon·ey \\ˌba-lē-'mə-nē\\ district N *cen* Northern Ireland; *pop* 23,984

Bal·tic Sea \\'bȯl-tik\\ arm of the Atlantic N Europe E of Scandinavian Peninsula

Bal·ti·more \\'bȯl-tə-ˌmȯr, -mər\\ city N *cen* Maryland; *pop* 651,154

Ba·ma·ko \\'bä-mä-ˌkō\\ city, ✳ of Mali on the Niger; *pop* 745,787

Ban·bridge \\ban-'brij\\ district SE *cen* Northern Ireland; *pop* 33,102

Ban·dar Se·ri Be·ga·wan \\ˌbən-dər-ˌser-ē-bə-'gä-wän\\ town, ✳ of Brunei; *pop* 27,285

Ban·dung \\'bän-ˌdu̇ŋ\\ city Indonesia in W Java SE of Jakarta; *pop* 2,057,442

Ban·ga·lore \\'baŋ-gə-ˌlȯr\\ city S India W of Madras; *pop* 4,292,223

Bang·kok \\'baŋ-ˌkäk, baŋ-'\\ city, ✳ of Thailand; *pop* 6,320,200

Ban·gla·desh \\ˌbäŋ-glə-'desh, ˌbaŋ-, ˌbəŋ-, -'däsh\\ country S Asia E of India; ✳, Dhaka; *pop* 115,075,000 — see EAST PAKISTAN — **Ban·gla·deshi** \\-'de-shē, -'dä-\\ *adj or n*

Ban·gor \\'baŋ-ˌgȯr, 'ban-ˌgȯr\\ town E Northern Ireland; *pop* 46,585

Ban·gui \\bäŋ-'gē\\ city, ✳ of Central African Republic; *pop* 300,723

Ban·jul \\'bän-ˌjül\\ *formerly* **Bath·urst** \\'bath-(ˌ)ərst\\ city & port, ✳ of Gambia; *pop* 44,188

Bao·tou *or* **Pao–t'ou** \\'bau̇-'tō\\ city N China; *pop* 983,508

Bar·ba·dos \\bär-'bā-(ˌ)dōs, -dəs, -(ˌ)dōz\\ island West Indies in Lesser Antilles E of Windward Islands; country, ✳, Bridgetown; *pop* 250,010 — **Bar·ba·di·an** \\-'bā-dē-ən\\ *adj or n*

Bar·bu·da \\bär-'bü-də\\ island West Indies; part of independent Antigua and Barbuda

Bar·ce·lo·na \\ˌbär-sə-'lō-nə\\ city NE Spain on the Mediterranean; chief city of Catalonia; *pop* 1,503,884

Bar·king and Dag·en·ham \\'bär-kiŋ-ən(d)-'da-gə-nəm\\ borough of E Greater London, England; *pop* 139,900

Bar·na·ul \\ˌbär-nə-'ül\\ city S Russia; *pop* 606,000

Bar·net \\'bär-nət\\ borough of N Greater London, England; *pop* 283,000

Bar·ran·qui·lla \\ˌbär-än-'kē-yä\\ city N Colombia; *pop* 1,018,800

Barren Grounds treeless plains N Canada W of Hudson Bay

Bar·row, Point \\'ba-(ˌ)rō\\ most northerly point of Alaska & of U.S. at about 71°25′ N latitude

Ba·si·lan \\bä-'sē-ˌlän\\ island S Philippines

Bas·il·don \\'ba-zəl-dən\\ town SE England; *pop* 157,500

Bass \\'bas\\ strait separating Tasmania & continent of Australia

Basse·terre \\bas-'ter, bäs-\\ seaport Saint Kitts, ✳ of Saint Kitts-Nevis; *pop* 14,725

Basutoland — see LESOTHO

Bathurst — see BANJUL

Bat·on Rouge \\ˌba-tᵊn-'rüzh\\ city, ✳ of Louisiana; *pop* 227,818

Ba·var·ia \\bə-'ver-ē-ə\\ *or German* **Bay·ern** \\'bī-ərn\\ state SE Germany bordering on Czech Republic & Austria; *pop* 11,448,800 — **Ba·var·i·an** \\bə-'ver-ē-ən, -'var-\\ *adj or n*

Ba·ya·mon \\ˌbī-ä-'mōn\\ city NE *cen* Puerto Rico; *pop* 224,004

Beau·fort \\'bō-fərt\\ sea consisting of part of Arctic Ocean NE of Alaska & NW of Canada

Beau·mont \\'bō-ˌmänt, bō-'\\ city SE Texas; *pop* 113,866

Bech·u·a·na·land \\ˌbech-'wä-nə-ˌland, ˌbe-chə-\\ **1** region S Africa N of Orange River **2** — see BOTSWANA — **Bech·u·a·na** \\ˌbech-'wä-nə, ˌbe-chə-\\ *adj or n*

Bed·ford·shire \\'bed-fərd-ˌshir, -shər\\ *or* **Bedford** county SE England

Bedloe's — see LIBERTY

Bei·jing \\'bā-'jiŋ\\ *or* **Pe·king** \\'pē-'kiŋ, 'pā-\\ city, ✳ of China; *pop* 10,819,407

Bei·rut \\bā-'rüt\\ city, ✳ of Lebanon; urban area *pop* 1,100,000

Be·la·rus \\ˌbē-lə-'rüs, ˌbye-lə-\\ country *cen* Europe; ✳, Minsk; *pop* 9,899,000 — **Be·la·ru·si·an** \\-'rü-sē-ən, -'rə-shən\\ *or* **Be·la·rus·sian** \\-'rə-shən\\ *adj or n*

Belau — see PALAU

Be·lém \\be-'lem\\ city N Brazil; *pop* 1,280,614

Bel·fast \\'bel-ˌfast, bel-'\\ city, ✳ of Northern Ireland; *pop* 295,100

Bel·gium \\'bel-jəm\\ *or French* **Bel·gique** \\bel-'zhēk\\ *or Flemish* **Bel·gië** \\'bel-kē-ə\\ country W Europe; ✳, Brussels; *pop* 10,309,725 — **Bel·gian** \\'bel-jən\\ *adj or n*

Bel·grade \\'bel-ˌgrād, -ˌgräd, ˌgrad, bel-'\\ *or* **Beo·grad** \\bā-'ȯ-ˌgräd\\ city, ✳ of Serbia and Montenegro on the Danube; *pop* 1,553,854

Be·lize \\bə-'lēz\\ *formerly* **British Honduras** country Central America on the Caribbean; ✳, Belmopan; *pop* 241,000 — **Be·liz·ean** *adj or n*

Belize City seaport E Belize; *pop* 45,158

Belle·vue \\'bel-ˌvyü\\ city W Washington E of Seattle; *pop* 109,569

Bel·mo·pan \\ˌbel-mō-'pän\\ city, ✳ of Belize; *pop* 6500

Be·lo Ho·ri·zon·te \\'bā-lō-ˌȯr-ē-'zȯn-tē\\

city E Brazil N of Rio de Janeiro; *pop* 2,238,526

Be·lo·rus·sia \ˌbe-lō-ˈrə-shə, ˌbye-lō-\ *or* **Bye·lo·rus·sia** \bē-ˌe-lō-, ˌbye-lō-\ former republic of U.S.S.R.; became independent Belarus in 1991 — **Belo·rus·sian** \ˌbe-lō-ˈrə-shən, ˌbye-\ *adj or n*

Ben·gal \ben-ˈgȯl, beŋ-, -ˈgäl\ region S Asia including delta of Ganges & Brahmaputra rivers; divided between Bangladesh & India — **Ben·gal·ese** \ˌbeŋ-gə-ˈlēz, ˌben-, -ˈlēs\ *adj or n*

Bengal, Bay of arm of Indian Ocean between India & Myanmar

Be·nin \bə-ˈnēn, -ˈnin; ˈbe-nin\ *formerly* **Da·ho·mey** \də-ˈhō-mē\ country W Africa on Gulf of Guinea; ✳, Porto-Novo; *pop* 5,074,000 — **Ben·i·nese** \bə-ˌni-ˈnēz, -ˌnē-, -ˈnēs; ˌbe-ni-ˈnēz, -ˈnēs\ *adj or n*

Ben Nev·is \ben-ˈne-vəs\ mountain 4406 ft. (1343 m.) W Scotland in the Grampians; highest in Great Britain

Beograd — see BELGRADE

Ber·gen \ˈbər-gən, ˈber-\ city & port SW Norway; *pop* 209,375

Be·ring \ˈbir-iŋ, ˈber-\ **1** sea, arm of the North Pacific between Alaska & NE Siberia **2** strait at narrowest point 53 mi. (85 km.) wide between North America (Alaska) and Asia (Russia)

Berke·ley \ˈbər-klē\ city W California on San Francisco Bay N of Oakland; *pop* 102,743

Berk·shire \ˈbərk-ˌshir, -shər\ hills W Massachusetts; highest point Mount Greylock 3491 ft. (1064 m.)

Ber·lin \(ˌ)bər-ˈlin, *G* ber-ˈlēn\ city, ✳ of Germany; divided 1945–90 into **East Berlin** (✳ of East Germany) & **West Berlin** (city of West Germany lying within East Germany); *pop* 3,392,900 — **Ber·lin·er** \(ˌ)bər-ˈli-nər\ *n*

Ber·mu·da \(ˌ)bər-ˈmyü-də\ islands W Atlantic ESE of Cape Hatteras; a British colony; ✳, Hamilton; *pop* 62,059 — **Ber·mu·dan** \-dᵊn\ *or* **Ber·mu·di·an** \-dē-ən\ *adj or n*

Bern \ˈbərn, ˈbern\ city, ✳ of Switzerland; *pop* 122,469 — **Ber·nese** \(ˌ)bər-ˈnēz, -ˈnēs\ *adj or n*

Bes·sa·ra·bia \ˌbe-sə-ˈrā-bē-ə\ region SE Europe now chiefly in Moldova — **Bes·sa·ra·bi·an** \-bē-ən\ *adj or n*

Beth·le·hem \ˈbeth-li-ˌhem, -lē-həm, -lē-əm\ town of ancient Palestine in Judaea; the present-day town is SW of Jerusalem in the West Bank; *pop* 34,180

Bev·er·ly Hills \ˈbe-vər-lē\ city SW California within Los Angeles; *pop* 33,784

Bex·ley \ˈbek-slē\ borough of E Greater London, England; *pop* 211,200

Bho·pal \bō-ˈpäl\ city N *cen* India; *pop* 1,433,875

Bhu·tan \bü-ˈtän, -ˈtan\ country S Asia in the Himalayas on NE border of India; ✳,

Thimphu; *pop* 1,546,000 — **Bhu·ta·nese** \ˌbü-tə-ˈnēz, -ˈnēs\ *adj or n*

Bi·ki·ni \bi-ˈkē-nē\ atoll W Pacific in Marshall Islands

Bil·lings \ˈbi-liŋz\ city S *cen* Montana; largest in state; *pop* 89,847

Bi·lox·i \bə-ˈlək-sē, -ˈläk-\ city & port SE Mississippi on Gulf of Mexico; *pop* 50,644

Bi·o·ko \bē-ˈō-(ˌ)kō\ *formerly* **Fer·nan·do Póo** \fer-ˈnän-(ˌ)dō-ˈpō\ island portion of Equatorial Guinea in Gulf of Guinea

Bir·ken·head \ˈbər-kən-ˌhed, ˌbər-kən-ˈ\ borough NW England on the Mersey opposite Liverpool; *pop* 123,907

Bir·ming·ham \ˈbər-miŋ-ˌham\ **1** city N *cen* Alabama; *pop* 242,820 **2** city W *cen* England; *pop* 934,900

Bis·cay, Bay of \ˈbis-ˌkā, -kē\ inlet of the Atlantic between W coast of France & N coast of Spain

Bish·kek \bish-ˈkek\ *formerly 1926–91* **Frun·ze** \ˈfrün-zi\ city, ✳ of Kyrgyzstan; *pop* 641,400

Bis·marck \ˈbiz-ˌmärk\ **1** city, ✳ of North Dakota; *pop* 55,532 **2** archipelago W Pacific N of E end of New Guinea

Bis·sau \bi-ˈsau̇\ city, ✳ of Guinea-Bissau; *pop* 125,000

Bi·thyn·ia \bə-ˈthi-nē-ə\ ancient country NW Asia Minor bordering on Sea of Marmara and Black Sea — **Bi·thyn·i·an** \-nē-ən\ *adj or n*

Bit·ter·root \ˈbi-tə(r)-ˌrüt, -ˌru̇t\ range of the Rockies along Idaho–Montana boundary

Black·burn \ˈblak-(ˌ)bərn\ town NW England; *pop* 132,800

Black Forest forested mountain region Germany along E bank of the upper Rhine

Black Hills mountains W South Dakota & NE Wyoming

Black·pool \ˈblak-ˌpül\ town NW England on Irish Sea; *pop* 144,500

Black Sea sea between Europe & Asia connected with Aegean Sea through the Bosporus, Sea of Marmara, & Dardanelles

Blanc, Mont — see MONT BLANC

Blan·tyre \ˈblan-ˌtī(-ə)r\ city S Malawi; *pop* 554,578

Bloem·fon·tein \ˈblüm-fən-ˌtān, -ˌfän-\ city Republic of South Africa, judicial ✳ of the country; *pop* 149,836

Blue Ridge E range of the Appalachians E U.S. extending from S Pennsylvania to N Georgia

Bodh Gaya \ˈbōd-ˈgī-ä\ village NE India; one of the holiest sites of Buddhism

Boe·o·tia \bē-ˈō-sh(ē-)ə\ ancient state E *cen* Greece NW of Attica; chief ancient city, Thebes — **Boe·o·tian** \bē-ˈō-shən\ *adj or n*

Bo·go·tá \ˌbō-gō-ˈtä, -ˈtȯ, ˈbō-gə-\ city, ✳ of Colombia; *pop* 4,921,300

Bo Hai *or* **Po Hai** \'bō-'hī\ *or* **Gulf of Chih·li** \'chē-'lē, 'jir-\ arm of Yellow Sea NE China

Bo·he·mia \bō-'hē-mē-ə\ region W Czech Republic; chief city, Prague

Bo·hol \bō-'hól\ island S *cen* Philippines

Boi·se \'bói-sē, -zē\ city, ✳ of Idaho; *pop* 185,787

Bo·liv·ia \bə-'li-vē-ə\ country W *cen* South America; administrative ✳, La Paz; constitutional ✳, Sucre; *pop* 8,274,325 — **Bo·liv·i·an** \-vē-ən\ *adj or n*

Bo·lo·gna \bō-'lō-nyä\ city N Italy; *pop* 379,964

Bol·ton \'bōl-t⁸n\ town NW England; *pop* 253,300

Bom·bay \bäm-'bā\ *or* **Mum·bai** \'məm-ˌbī\ city & port W India; *pop* 11,914,398

Bonn \'bän, 'bón\ city Germany on the Rhine SSE of Cologne, formerly (1949–99) ✳ of West Germany; *pop* 296,244

Boo·thia \'bü-thē-ə\ peninsula N Canada W of Baffin Island; its N tip is most northerly point in mainland North America

Bor·ders \'bòr-dərz\ former administrative region SE Scotland

Bor·neo \'bòr-nē-ˌō\ island Malay Archipelago SW of the Philippines; divided between Brunei, Indonesia, and Malaysia

Bos·nia \'bäz-nē-ə, 'bóz\ region S Europe; with Herzegovina forms independent **Bosnia and Her·ze·go·vi·na** \ˌhert-sə-gō-'vē-nə, ˌhərt-, -'gō-və-nə\; ✳, Sarajevo; *pop* 4,422,000 — **Bos·ni·an** \-nē-ən\ *adj or n*

Bos·po·rus \'bäs-p(ə-)rəs\ strait 18 mi. (29 km.) long between Turkey in Europe & Turkey in Asia connecting Sea of Marmara & Black Sea

Bos·ton \'bòs-tən\ city, ✳ of Massachusetts; *pop* 589,141 — **Bos·to·nian** \bò-'stō-nē-ən, -nyən\ *adj or n*

Bot·a·ny Bay \'bä-tə-nē\ inlet of South Pacific SE Australia in New South Wales S of Sydney

Both·nia, Gulf of \'bäth-nē-ə\ arm of Baltic Sea between Sweden & Finland

Bo·tswa·na \bät-'swä-nə\ *formerly* **Bech·u·a·na·land** \ˌbech-'wä-nə-land\ country S Africa; ✳, Gaborone; *pop* 1,611,021

Boul·der \'bōl-dər\ city N *cen* Colorado; *pop* 94,673

Boulder Dam — see HOOVER DAM

Bourne·mouth \'bòrn-məth, 'bùrn-\ town S England on English Channel; *pop* 154,400

Brad·ford \'brad-fərd\ city N England; *pop* 280,691

Brah·ma·pu·tra \ˌbrä-mə-'pü-trə\ river about 1800 mi. (2900 km.) long S Asia flowing from the Himalayas in Tibet to Ganges Delta

Bra·sí·lia \brə-'zil-yə\ city, ✳ of Brazil; *pop* 2,051,146

Bra·ti·sla·va \ˌbra-tə-'slä-və, ˌbrä\ city on the Danube; ✳ of Slovakia; *pop* 428,672

Bra·zil \brə-'zil\ country E & *cen* South America; ✳, Brasília; *pop* 169,799,170 — **Bra·zil·ian** \brə-'zil-yən\ *adj or n*

Braz·za·ville \'bra-zə-ˌvil, 'brä-zə-ˌvēl\ city, ✳ of Republic of the Congo on W bank of lower Congo River; *pop* 937,579

Bre·men \'bre-mən, 'brä-\ city & port NW Germany; *pop* 552,746

Bren·ner \'bre-nər\ pass 4495 ft. (1370 m.) high in the Alps between Austria & Italy

Brent \'brent\ borough of W Greater London, England; *pop* 226,100

Bret·on, Cape \ˌkāp-'bre-t⁸n, kə-'bre-, -'bri-\ cape Canada; most easterly point of Cape Breton Island & of Nova Scotia

Bridge·port \'brij-ˌpòrt\ city SW Connecticut on Long Island Sound; *pop* 139,529

Bridge·town \'brij-ˌtaùn\ city, ✳ of Barbados; *pop* 5996

Brigh·ton \'brī-t⁸n\ town S England on English Channel; *pop* 133,400

Bris·bane \'briz-bən, -ˌbän\ city & port E Australia; ✳ of Queensland; *pop* 751,115

Bris·tol \'bris-t⁸l\ **1** city & port SW England; *pop* 370,300 **2** channel between S Wales & SW England

Brit·ain \'bri-t⁸n\ **1** the island of Great Britain **2** UNITED KINGDOM

British Columbia province W Canada on Pacific coast; ✳, Victoria; *pop* 3,907,738

British Commonwealth — see COMMONWEALTH, THE

British Empire former empire consisting of Great Britain & the British dominions & dependencies

British Guiana — see GUYANA

British Honduras — see BELIZE

British India the part of India formerly under direct British administration

British Indian Ocean Territory British colony in Indian Ocean consisting of Chagos Archipelago

British Isles island group W Europe consisting of Great Britain, Ireland, & nearby islands

British Virgin Islands E islands of Virgin Islands; a British possession; *pop* 14,786

British West Indies islands of the West Indies including Jamaica, Trinidad and Tobago, & the Bahama & Cayman islands, Windward Islands, Leeward Islands, & British Virgin Islands

Brit·ta·ny \'bri-tə-nē\ region NW France SW of Normandy

Brom·ley \'bräm-lē\ borough of SE Greater London, England; *pop* 281,700

Bronx \'bräŋks\ *or* **The Bronx** borough of New York City NE of Manhattan; *pop* 1,332,650

Brook·lyn \'brùk-lən\ borough of New York City at SW end of Long Island; *pop* 2,465,326

Brooks Range \'brúks\ mountains N Alaska

Browns·ville \'braúnz-,vil, -vəl\ city S Texas on the Rio Grande; *pop* 139,722

Bru·nei \brü-'nī, 'brü-,nī\ country NE Borneo; ✳, Bandar Seri Begawan; *pop* 332,844 — **Bru·nei·an** \brü-'nī-ən\ *adj or n*

Brus·sels \'brə-səlz\ city, ✳ of Belgium; *pop* 136,730

Bu·cha·rest \'bü-kə-,rest, 'byü\ city, ✳ of Romania; *pop* 1,921,751

Buck·ing·ham·shire \'bə-kiŋ-əm-,shir\ *or* **Buckingham** county SE *cen* England

Bu·da·pest \'bü-də-,pest\ city, ✳ of Hungary; *pop* 2,008,546

Bue·nos Ai·res \,bwā-nəs-'a-rēz, Sp ,bwā-nōs-'ī-rās\ city, ✳ of Argentina; *pop* 2,960,976

Buf·fa·lo \'bə-fə-,lō\ city NW New York on Lake Erie; *pop* 292,648

Bu·jum·bu·ra \,bü-jəm-'bur-ə\ city, ✳ of Burundi; *pop* 236,334

Bu·ko·vi·na \,bü-kō-'vē-nə\ region E *cen* Europe in foothills of E Carpathians

Bul·gar·ia \,bəl-'ger-ē-ə, bul-\ country SE Europe on Black Sea; ✳, Sofia; *pop* 8,466,000 — **Bul·gar·i·an** \,bəl-'ger-ē-ən, bul-\ *adj or n*

Bull Run \'bul-'rən\ stream NE Virginia

Bun·ker Hill \'bəŋ-kər\ height in Boston, Massachusetts

Bur·bank \'bər-,baŋk\ city SW California; *pop* 100,316

Bur·gun·dy \'bər-gən-dē\ region E France — **Bur·gun·di·an** \(,)bər-'gən-dē-ən\ *adj or n*

Bur·ki·na Fa·so \búr-'kē-nə-'fä-sō, bər-\ *formerly* **Upper Vol·ta** \'vōl-tə, 'vól-\ country W Africa N of Ivory Coast, Ghana, & Togo; ✳, Ouagadougou; *pop* 9,780,000

Bur·ling·ton \'bər-liŋ-tən\ city NW Vermont; largest in state; *pop* 38,889

Bur·ma \'bər-mə\ — see MYANMAR — **Bur·mese** \,bər-'mēz, -'mēs\ *adj or n*

Bu·run·di \bù-'rün-dē, -'rün-\ country E *cen* Africa; ✳, Bujumbura; *pop* 5,665,000 — **Bu·run·di·an** \-dē-ən\ *adj or n*

Busan — see PUSAN

Bute \'byüt\ island SW Scotland in Firth of Clyde

Butte \'byüt\ city SW Montana; county *pop* 34,606

Byelorussia — see BELORUSSIA

By·zan·tine Empire \'bi-zªn-,tēn, 'bī-, -,tīn; bə-'zan-,tēn, -tīn, bī-\ empire of SE & S Europe and W Asia from 4th to 15th century

By·zan·ti·um \bə-'zan-sh(ē-)əm, -'zant-ē-əm\ ancient city on site of modern Istanbul

Caer·nar·von \kär-'när-vən, kə(r)-\ town & seaport NW Wales; *pop* 9506

Ca·guas \'kä-,gwäs\ town E *cen* Puerto Rico; *pop* 140,502

Cai·ro \'kī-(,)rō\ city, ✳ of Egypt; *pop* 6,633,000 — **Cai·rene** \kī-'rēn\ *adj or n*

Ca·la·bria \kə-'lä-brē-ə, -'lä\ district of ancient Italy consisting of area forming heel of Italian Peninsula — **Ca·la·bri·an** \kə-'lä-brē-ən, -'lä-\ *adj or n*

Cal·cut·ta \kal-'kə-tə\ *or* **Kol·ka·ta** \kōl-'kä-tä\ city E India on Hugli River; *pop* 4,580,544 — **Cal·cut·tan** \-'kə-tªn\ *adj or n*

Cal·e·do·nia \,ka-lə-'dō-nyə, -nē-ə\ — see SCOTLAND — **Cal·e·do·nian** \-nyən, -nē-ən\ *adj or n*

Cal·ga·ry \'kal-gə-rē\ city SW Alberta, Canada; *pop* 878,866

Ca·li \'kä-lē\ city W Colombia; *pop* 1,624,400

Cal·i·for·nia \,ka-lə-'fór-nyə\ state SW U.S.; ✳, Sacramento; *pop* 33,871,648 — **Cal·i·for·nian** \-nyən\ *adj or n*

California, Gulf of arm of the Pacific NW Mexico

Cal·va·ry \'kal-v(ə-)rē\ place outside ancient Jerusalem where Jesus was crucified

Cambay, Gulf of — see KHAMBHAT (Gulf of)

Cam·bo·dia \kam-'bō-dē-ə\ *or* **Kam·pu·chea** \,kam-pù-'chē-ə\ country SE Asia in S Indochina; ✳, Phnom Penh; *pop* 11,437,656 — **Cam·bo·di·an** \kam-'bō-dē-ən\ *adj or n*

Cam·bria \'kam-brē-ə\ WALES — an old name

Cam·bridge \'kām-brij\ **1** city E Massachusetts W of Boston; *pop* 101,355 **2** city E England; *pop* 92,772

Cam·bridge·shire \'kām-brij-,shir, -shər\ *or* **Cambridge** county E England

Cam·den \'kam-dən\ borough of N Greater London, England; *pop* 170,500

Cam·er·oon *or* French **Cam·er·oun** \,kam-mə-'rün\ country W Africa; ✳, Yaoundé; *pop* 13,103,000 — **Cam·er·oo·nian** \-'rü-nē-ən, -rü-nyən\ *adj or n*

Ca·mi·guin \,kä-mē-'gēn\ island Philippines, off N coast of Mindanao

Ca·naan \'kä-nən\ ancient region SW Asia; approximately the area later called Palestine — **Ca·naan·ite** \'kä-nə-,nīt\ *adj or n*

Can·a·da \'ka-nə-də\ country N North America; ✳, Ottawa; *pop* 27,296,859 — **Ca·na·di·an** \kə-'nä-dē-ən\ *adj or n*

Canadian Falls — see NIAGARA FALLS

Canadian Shield *or* **Lau·ren·tian Plateau** \lò-'ren(t)-shən\ plateau region E Canada & NE U.S. extending from Mackenzie River basin E to Davis Strait & S to S Quebec, S *cen* Ontario, NE Minnesota, N Wisconsin, NW Michigan, and NE New York including the Adirondacks

Canal Zone *or* **Panama Canal Zone**

strip of territory Panama leased to U.S. (until 1979) for Panama Canal

Ca·nary \kə-ˈner-ē\ islands Spain in the Atlantic off NW coast of Africa; *pop* 1,493,784

Ca·nav·er·al, Cape \kə-ˈnav-rəl, -ˈna-və-\ *or 1963–73* **Cape Ken·ne·dy** \ˈken-ə-dē\ cape E Florida in the Atlantic on **Canaveral Peninsula** E of Indian River

Can·ber·ra \ˈkan-b(ə-)rə, -ˌber-ə\ city, ✻ of Australia in Australian Capital Territory; *pop* 348,600

Cannes \ˈkan, ˈkän\ port SE France; *pop* 69,363

Can·ter·bury \ˈkan-tə(r)-ˌber-ē, -b(ə-)rē\ city SE England; *pop* 34,404

Canton — see GUANGZHOU

Cape Bret·on Island \ˈkāp-ˈbret-tᵊn, kə-ˈbre-, -ˈbri-\ island NE Nova Scotia

Cape Coral city SW Florida; *pop* 102,286

Cape Horn — see HORN, CAPE

Cape of Good Hope — see GOOD HOPE, CAPE OF

Cape Province *or* **Cape of Good Hope** *or before 1910* **Cape Colony** former province S Republic of South Africa

Cape Town \ˈkāp-ˌtaůn\ city, legislative ✻ of Republic of South Africa and formerly ✻ of Cape Province; *pop* 776,617

Cape Verde \ˈvərd\ islands in the North Atlantic off W Africa; country; ✻, Praia; *pop* 350,000 — **Cape Verd·ean** \ˈvər-dē-ən\ *adj or n*

Cape York Peninsula \ˈyórk\ peninsula NE Australia in N Queensland

Ca·pri \kə-ˈprē, kə-; ˈkä-(ˌ)prē, ˈka-\ island Italy S of Bay of Naples; *pop* 7270

Ca·ra·cas \kə-ˈrä-käs\ city, ✻ of Venezuela; *pop* 1,824,892

Car·diff \ˈkär-dif\ city, ✻ of Wales; *pop* 272,600

Ca·rib·be·an Sea \ˌka-rə-ˈbē-ən, kə-ˈri-bē-\ arm of the Atlantic; on N & E are the West Indies, on S is South America, & on W is Central America — **Caribbean** *adj*

Car·lisle \kär-ˈlī(-ə)l, kər-, ˈkär-ˌ\ city NW England; *pop* 99,800

Carls·bad Caverns \ˈkär(-ə)lz-ˌbad\ series of caves SE New Mexico

Car·mar·then \kär-ˈmär-thən, kə(r)-\ port S Wales; *pop* 54,800

Car·o·li·na \ˌka-rə-ˈlī-nə\ English colony on E coast of North America founded 1663 & divided 1729 into North Carolina & South Carolina (the **Carolinas**) — **Car·o·lin·i·an** \ˌka-rə-ˈli-nē-ən, -nyən\ *adj or n*

Ca·ro·li·na \ˌkä-rō-ˈlē-nä\ city NE Puerto Rico; *pop* 186,076

Car·o·line \ˈka-rə-ˌlīn, -lən\ islands W Pacific E of S Philippines; comprising Palau & the Federated States of Micronesia

Car·pa·thi·an \kär-ˈpā-thē-ən\ mountains E *cen* Europe along boundary between Slovakia & Poland & in N & *cen* Roma-

nia; highest Gerlachovksky 8711 ft. (2655 m.)

Car·pen·tar·ia, Gulf of \ˌkär-pən-ˈter-ē-ə\ inlet of Arafura Sea N of Australia

Car·rick·fer·gus \ˌka-rik-ˈfər-gəs\ district E Northern Ireland; *pop* 32,439

Car·roll·ton \ˈka-rəl-tən\ city N Texas; *pop* 109,576

Car·son City \ˈkär-sᵊn\ city, ✻ of Nevada; *pop* 52,457

Car·thage \ˈkär-thij\ ancient city N Africa NE of modern Tunis; ✻ of an empire that once included much of NW Africa, E Spain, & Sicily — **Car·tha·gin·ian** \ˌkär-thə-ˈji-nyən, -nē-ən\ *adj or n*

Ca·sa·blan·ca \ˌka-sə-ˈblaŋ-kə, ˌkä-sə-ˈbläŋ-, -zə-\ city W Morocco on the Atlantic; *pop* 3,102,000

Cas·cade Range \(ˌ)kas-ˈkād\ mountains NW U.S. in Washington, Oregon, & N California — see RAINIER, MOUNT

Cas·per \ˈkas-pər\ city *cen* Wyoming; *pop* 49,644

Cas·pi·an Sea \ˈkas-pē-ən\ salt lake between Europe and Asia about 90 ft. (27 m.) below sea level

Cas·tile \ka-ˈstēl\ *or in full* **Cas·ti·lla** \kä-ˈstēl-yä, -ˈstē-yä\ region & ancient kingdom *cen* & N Spain

Cast·le·reagh \ˈka-səl-(ˌ)rā\ district E Northern Ireland; *pop* 60,649

Cas·tries \ˈkas-ˌtrēz, -ˌtrēs\ seaport, ✻ of Saint Lucia; *pop* 1814

Cat·a·lo·nia \ˌka-tə-ˈlō-nyə, -nē-ə\ region NE Spain bordering on France & the Mediterranean; chief city, Barcelona; *pop* 6,059,494 — **Cat·a·lo·nian** \-ˈō-nyən, -nē-ən\ *adj or n*

Ca·thay \ka-ˈthā\ an old name for China

Cats·kill \ˈkat-ˌskil\ mountains in Appalachian system SE New York W of the Hudson

Cau·ca·sus \ˈkó-kə-səs\ mountain system SE Europe between Black & Caspian seas in Russia, Georgia, Azerbaijan, & Armenia

Cay·enne \kī-ˈen, kā-\ city, ✻ of French Guiana; *pop* 37,097

Cay·man \(ˌ)kā-ˈman, *attributively* ˈkā-mən\ islands West Indies NW of Jamaica; a British colony; *pop* 23,881

Ce·bu \sā-ˈbü\ island E *cen* Philippines

Ce·dar Rapids \ˈsē-dər\ city E Iowa; *pop* 120,758

Cel·tic Sea \ˈkel-tik, ˈsel-\ inlet of the Atlantic in British Isles SE of Ireland, SW of Wales, & W of SW England

Central African Republic country N *cen* Africa; ✻, Bangui; *pop* 2,998,000

Central America narrow portion of North America from S border of Mexico to South America — **Central American** *adj or n*

Central Valley valley of Sacramento &

San Joaquin rivers in California between Sierra Nevada & Coast Ranges

Cey·lon \si-'län, sā-\ **1** island in Indian Ocean off S India **2** — see SRI LANKA — **Cey·lon·ese** \ˌsā-lə-'nēz, ˌsē-, ˌse-, -'nēs\ *adj or n*

Chad \'chad\ country N *cen* Africa; ✱, N'Djamena; *pop* 5,200,000 — **Chad·ian** \'cha-dē-ən\ *adj or n*

Chad, Lake shallow lake N *cen* Africa at junction of boundaries of Chad, Niger, & Nigeria

Cha·gos Archipelago \'chä-gəs\ island group *cen* Indian Ocean; forms British Indian Ocean Territory — see DIEGO GARCIA

Chal·dea \kal-'dē-ə\ ancient region SW Asia on Euphrates River & Persian Gulf — **Chal·de·an** \-'dē-ən\ *adj or n* — **Chal·dee** \'kal-ˌdē\ *n*

Cham·pagne \sham-'pān\ region NE France

Cham·plain, Lake \sham-'plān\ lake between New York & Vermont extending N into Quebec

Chan·di·garh \'chən-dē-gər\ city N India N of Delhi; *pop* 510,565

Chan·dler \'chan(d)-lər\ city SW *cen* Arizona; *pop* 176,581

Chang \'chäŋ\ or **Yang·tze** \'yaŋ-'sē, 'yaŋ(k)t-'sē; 'yäŋ-'tsə\ river 3434 mi. (5525 km.) long *cen* China flowing into East China Sea

Chang·chun \'chäŋ-'chùn\ city NE China; *pop* 1,679,270

Chang·sha \'chäŋ-'shä\ city SE *cen* China; *pop* 1,113,312

Channel islands in English Channel including Jersey, Guernsey, & Alderney & belonging to United Kingdom; *pop* 135,694

Charles \'chär(-ə)lz\ river 47 mi. (76 km.) long E Massachusetts flowing into Boston harbor

Charles, Cape cape E Virginia N of entrance to Chesapeake Bay

Charles·ton \'chär(-ə)l-stən\ **1** seaport SE South Carolina; *pop* 96,650 **2** city, ✱ of West Virginia; *pop* 53,421

Char·lotte \'shär-lət\ city S North Carolina; *pop* 540,828

Charlotte Ama·lie \ə-'mäl-yə, 'a-mə-lē\ city, ✱ of Virgin Islands of the U.S.; on island of Saint Thomas; *pop* 12,331

Char·lottes·ville \'shär-ləts-ˌvil, -vəl\ city *cen* Virginia; *pop* 45,049

Char·lotte·town \'shär-lət-ˌtaùn\ city, ✱ of Prince Edward Island, Canada; *pop* 32,245

Chat·ta·noo·ga \ˌcha-tə-'nü-gə\ city SE Tennessee; *pop* 155,554

Chech·nya \chech-'nyä, 'chech-nyə\ republic of SE Russia in Europe; ✱, Grozny

Chelms·ford \'chemz-fərd\ town SE England; *pop* 150,000

Che·lya·binsk \chel-'yä-bən(t)sk\ city W Russia; *pop* 1,143,000

Cheng–chou — see ZHENGZHOU

Cheng·du or **Ch'eng–tu** \'chəŋ-'dü\ city SW *cen* China; *pop* 1,713,255

Chennai — see MADRAS

Cher·no·byl \chər-'nō-bəl, (ˌ)cher-\ site N Ukraine of town abandoned after 1986 nuclear accident

Ches·a·peake \'che-sə-ˌpēk, 'ches-ˌpēk\ city SE Virginia; *pop* 199,184

Chesapeake Bay inlet of the Atlantic in Virginia & Maryland

Chesh·ire \'che-shər, -ˌshir\ or **Ches·ter** \'ches-tər\ county W England bordering on Wales

Chester \'ches-tər\ city NW England; *pop* 58,436

Chev·i·ot \'chē-vē-ət, 'che-\ hills along English–Scottish border

Chey·enne \shī-'an, -'en\ city, ✱ of Wyoming; *pop* 53,011

Chi·ba \'chē-bä\ city E Japan in Honshu on Tokyo Bay E of Tokyo; *pop* 887,164

Chi·ca·go \shə-'kä-(ˌ)gō, -'kò-, -gə\ city & port NE Illinois on Lake Michigan; *pop* 2,896,016 — **Chi·ca·go·an** \-'kä-gō-ən, -'kò-\ *n*

Chi·chén It·zá \chē-ˌchen-ēt-'sä, -'ēt-sə\ ruined Mayan city SE Mexico in Yucatán Peninsula

Chich·es·ter \'chi-chəs-tər\ city S England; *pop* 24,189

Ch'i–ch'i–ha–erh — see QIQIHAR

Chihli, Gulf of — see BO HAI

Chi·le \'chi-lē, 'chē-(ˌ)lä\ country SW South America; ✱, Santiago; *pop* 15,116,435 — **Chil·ean** \'chi-lē-ən, chə-'lä-ən\ *adj or n*

Chim·bo·ra·zo \ˌchēm-bō-'rä-(ˌ)zō\ mountain 20,561 ft. (6267 m.) W *cen* Ecuador

Chi·na \'chī-nə\ **1** country E Asia; ✱, Beijing; *pop* 1,179,467,000 — see TAIWAN **2** sea section of the W Pacific; divided at Taiwan strait into East China & South China seas

Chin–chou or **Chinchow** — see JINZHOU

Chi·și·nău \ˌkē-shē-'naù\ or **Ki·shi·nev** \ˌki-shi-'nyóf; 'ki-shə-ˌnef, -ˌnev\ city *cen* Moldova; its ✱; *pop* 665,000

Chit·ta·gong \'chi-tə-ˌgäŋ, -ˌgòŋ\ city SE Bangladesh on Bay of Bengal; *pop* 1,566,070

Chong·qing or **Ch'ung–ch'ing** \'chùŋ-'chiŋ\ or **Chung·king** \'chùŋ-'kiŋ\ city SW *cen* China; *pop* 2,266,772

Christ·church \'krīs(t)-ˌchərch\ city New Zealand on E coast of South Island; urban area *pop* 334,107

Christ·mas \'kris-məs\ island E Indian Ocean SW of Java; governed by Australia; *pop* 1000

Chu·la Vis·ta \ˌchü-lə-'vis-tə\ city SW California S of San Diego; *pop* 173,556

Chuuk \\'chŭk\ *or* **Truk** \\'trək, 'trŭk\ islands *cen* Carolines, part of Federated States of Micronesia

Cin·cin·na·ti \\,sin(t)-sə-'na-tē, -'na-tə\ city SW Ohio; *pop* 331,285

Ci·u·dad Juá·rez \syü-'thäth-'hwär-es, 'wär-; ,sē-ü-'dad\ city Mexico on Texas border; urban area *pop* 1,011,786

Ciudad Trujillo — *see* SANTO DOMINGO

Clarks·ville \\'klärks-,vil, -vəl\ city N Tennessee NW of Nashville; *pop* 103,455

Clear·wa·ter \\'klir-,wȯ-tər, -,wä-\ city W Florida NW of St. Petersburg; *pop* 108,787

Cleve·land \\'klēv-lənd\ city & port NE Ohio on Lake Erie; *pop* 478,403

Clyde \\'klīd\ river 106 mi. (171 km.) long SW Scotland flowing into **Firth of Clyde** (estuary)

Coast Mountains mountain range W British Columbia, Canada; the N continuation of Cascade Range

Coast Ranges chain of mountain ranges W North America extending along Pacific coast W of Sierra Nevada & Cascade Range & through Vancouver Island into S Alaska to Kenai Peninsula & Kodiak Island

Cod, Cape \-'käd\ peninsula SE Massachusetts

Coim·ba·tore \\,kȯim-bə-'tȯr\ city S India; *pop* 816,321

Cole·raine \kōl-'rān, 'kōl-,\ **1** district N Northern Ireland; *pop* 51,062 **2** port in Coleraine district

Co·logne \kə-'lōn\ city W Germany on the Rhine; *pop* 956,690

Co·lom·bia \kə-'ləm-bē-ə\ country NW South America; *, Bogotá; *pop* 26,525,670 — **Co·lom·bi·an** \-bē-ən\ *adj or n*

Co·lom·bo \kə-'ləm-(,)bō\ city, * of Sri Lanka; *pop* 615,000

Col·o·ra·do \\,kä-lə-'ra-(,)dō\ **1** river 1450 mi. (2334 km.) long SW U.S. & NW Mexico flowing from N Colorado into Gulf of California **2** desert SE California **3** plateau region SW U.S. W of Rocky Mountains **4** state W U.S.; *, Denver; *pop* 4,301,261 — **Col·o·rad·an** \-'ra-dᵊn, -'rä-\ *or* **Co·lo·ra·do·an** \-'ra-dō-ən, -'rä-\ *adj or n*

Colorado Springs city *cen* Colorado E of Pikes Peak; *pop* 360,890

Co·lum·bia \kə-'ləm-bē-ə\ **1** river 1214 mi. (1953 km.) long SW Canada & NW U.S. flowing S & W from SE British Columbia into the Pacific **2** plateau in Columbia River basin in E Washington, E Oregon, & SW Idaho **3** city, * of South Carolina; *pop* 116,278

Co·lum·bus \kə-'ləm-bəs\ **1** city W Georgia; *pop* 186,291 **2** city, * of Ohio; *pop* 711,470

Com·mon·wealth, the \\'käm-ən-,wel(t)th\ *or* **Commonwealth of Na-** tions *formerly* **British Commonwealth** the United Kingdom & most of the countries formerly dependent on it

Com·o·ros \\'kä-mə-,rōz\ islands off SE Africa NW of Madagascar; country (except for Mayotte Island); *, Moroni; *pop* 519,527

Con·a·kry \\'kä-nə-krē\ city, * of Guinea; *pop* 581,000

Con·cord \\'kän-,kȯrd, 'käŋ-\ **1** city W California; *pop* 121,780 **2** town E Massachusetts NW of Boston; *pop* 16,993 **3** city, * of New Hampshire; *pop* 40,687

Con·go \\'käŋ-(,)gō\ **1** *or* **Zaire** \zä-'ir\ river over 2700 mi. (4344 km.) long W Africa flowing into the Atlantic **2** *officially* **Democratic Republic of the Congo** *formerly 1971–97* **Zaire** country *cen* Africa consisting of most of Congo River basin E of lower Congo River; *, Kinshasa; *pop* 43,775,000 **3** *or officially* **Republic of the Congo** country W *cen* Africa W of lower Congo River; *, Brazzaville; *pop* 2,775,000 — **Con·go·lese** \\,käŋ-gə-'lēz, -'lēs\ *adj or n*

Con·nacht \\'kä-,nȯt\ province W Ireland; *pop* 422,909

Con·nect·i·cut \kə-'ne-ti-kət\ **1** river 407 mi. (655 km.) long NE U.S. flowing S from N New Hampshire into Long Island Sound **2** state NE U.S.; *, Hartford; *pop* 3,405,565

Constantinople — *see* ISTANBUL

Continental Divide line of highest points of land separating the waters flowing W from those flowing N or E and extending SSE from NW Canada across W U.S. through Mexico & Central America to South America where it joins the Andes Mountains

Cook \\'kŭk\ **1** inlet of the Pacific S Alaska W of Kenai Peninsula **2** islands South Pacific SW of Society Islands belonging to New Zealand; *pop* 17,614 **3** strait New Zealand between North Island & South Island

Cook, Mount *formerly* **Ao·rangi** \aú-'räŋ-ē\ mountain 12,349 ft. (3764 m.) New Zealand in W *cen* South Island in Southern Alps; highest in New Zealand

Cooks·town \\'kŭks-,taún\ district *cen* Northern Ireland; *pop* 30,808

Co·pen·ha·gen \\,kō-pən-'hā-gən, -'hä-\ city, * of Denmark; *pop* 501,285

Cor·al Sea \\'kȯr-əl, 'kär-\ arm of the W Pacific NE of Australia

Coral Springs city SE Florida; *pop* 117,549

Cór·do·ba \\'kȯr-də-bə, 'kȯr-thō-,vä\ city N *cen* Argentina; *pop* 1,179,067

Cor·inth \\'kȯr-ən(t)th, 'kär-\ **1** region of ancient Greece **2** ancient city; site SW of present city of Corinth — **Co·rin·thi·an** \kə-'rin(t)-thē-ən\ *adj or n*

Corinth, Gulf of inlet of Ionian Sea *cen* Greece N of the Peloponnese

Cork \'kòrk\ city S Ireland; *pop* 123,062

Corn·wall \'kòrn-ˌwòl, -wəl\ *or since 1974* **Cornwall and Isles of Scilly** \'si-lē\ county SW England

Co·ro·na \kə-'rō-nə\ city SW California E of Los Angeles; *pop* 124,966

Cor·pus Chris·ti \ˌkòr-pəs-'kris-tē\ city & port S Texas; *pop* 277,454

Cor·reg·i·dor \kə-'re-gə-ˌdòr\ island Philippines at entrance to Manila Bay

Cor·si·ca \'kòr-si-kə\ island France in the Mediterranean N of Sardinia; *pop* 260,149 — **Cor·si·can** \'kòr-si-kən\ *adj or n*

Cos·ta Me·sa \'mā-sə\ city SW California; *pop* 108,724

Costa Ri·ca \'rē-kə\ country Central America between Nicaragua & Panama; ✳, San José; *pop* 4,075,863 — **Costa Ri·can** \-kən\ *adj or n*

Côte d'Ivoire — see IVORY COAST

Cots·wold \'kät-ˌswōld, -swəld\ hills SW *cen* England

Cov·en·try \'kə-vən-trē\ city *cen* England; *pop* 292,500

Craig·av·on \krā-'ga-vən\ district *cen* Northern Ireland; *pop* 74,494

Cra·ter \'krā-tər\ lake 1932 ft. (589 m.) deep SW Oregon in Cascade Range

Crete \'krēt\ island Greece in E Mediterranean; *pop* 536,980 — **Cre·tan** \'krē-t⁸n\ *adj or n*

Cri·mea \krī-'mē-ə, krə-\ peninsula SE Europe in S Ukraine, extending into Black Sea — **Cri·me·an** \krī-'mē-ən, krə-\ *adj*

Cro·atia \krō-'ā-sh(ē-)ə\ country SE Europe; ✳, Zagreb; *pop* 4,437,460 — **Croat** \'krō-ˌat\ *n*

Croy·don \'kròi-d⁸n\ borough of S Greater London, England; *pop* 299,600

Cu·ba \'kyü-bə, 'kü-və\ island in the West Indies; country; ✳, Havana; *pop* 10,892,000 — **Cu·ban** \'kyü-bən\ *adj or n*

Cum·ber·land \'kəm-bər-lənd\ river 687 mi. (1106 km.) long S Kentucky & N Tennessee

Cumberland Gap pass through Cumberland Plateau NE Tennessee

Cumberland Plateau mountain region E U.S.; part of S Appalachian Mountains extending from S West Virginia to NE Alabama

Cum·bria \'kəm-brē-ə\ county NW England; *pop* 486,900

Cum·bri·an \'kəm-brē-ən\ mountains NW England chiefly in Cumbria county

Cu·par \'kü-pər\ town E Scotland; *pop* 6642

Cu·ri·ti·ba \ˌkùr-ə-'tē-bə\ city S Brazil SW of São Paulo; *pop* 1,587,315

Cush \'kəsh, 'kùsh\ ancient country NE Africa in upper Nile valley S of Egypt —

Cush·ite \'kə-ˌshīt, 'kù-\ *n* — **Cush·it·ic** \kə-'shi-tik, kù-\ *adj*

Cuz·co \'küs-(ˌ)kō\ city S *cen* Peru; *pop* 316,804

Cymru — see WALES

Cy·prus \'sī-prəs\ island E Mediterranean S of Turkey; country; ✳, Nicosia; *pop* 793,100 — **Cyp·ri·ot** \'si-prē-ət, -ˌät\ *or* **Cyp·ri·ote** \-ˌōt, -ət\ *adj or n*

Cy·re·na·ica \ˌsir-ə-'nā-ə-kə, ˌsī-rə-\ ancient region N Africa on coast W of Egypt — **Cy·re·na·i·can** \-'nā-ə-kən\ *adj or n*

Czecho·slo·va·kia \ˌche-kə-slō-'vä-kē-ə, -slə-, -'va-\ former country *cen* Europe divided into the independent states of the Czech Republic & Slovakia — **Czecho·slo·vak** \'slō-ˌväk, -ˌvak\ *adj or n* — **Czecho·slo·va·ki·an** \-slō-'vä-kē-ən, -slə-, -'va-\ *adj or n*

Czech Republic country *cen* Europe; ✳, Prague; *pop* 10,332,000

Daegu — see TAEGU

Daejeon — see TAEJON

Dahomey — see BENIN

Dairen — see DALIAN

Da·kar \'da-ˌkär, dä-'kär\ city, ✳ of Senegal; *pop* 1,729,823

Da·ko·ta 1 *or* **James** river 710 mi. (1143 km.) long North Dakota & South Dakota flowing S into the Missouri 2 territory 1861–89 NW U.S. divided 1889 into states of North Dakota & South Dakota (the **Dakotas** \-təz\ )

Da·lian \'dä-'lyen\ *or* **Ta·lien** \'dä-'lyen\ *or* **Lü·da** *or* **Lü–ta** \'lü-'dä\ *or* **Dai·ren** \'dī-'ren\ city NE China; *pop* 1,723,302

Dal·las \'da-ləs, -lis\ city NE Texas; *pop* 1,188,580

Dal·ma·tia \dal-'mä-sh(ē-)ə\ region W Balkan Peninsula on the Adriatic — **Dal·ma·tian** \-shən\ *adj or n*

Da·ly City \'dā-lē\ city W California S of San Francisco; *pop* 103,621

Da·mas·cus \də-'mas-kəs\ city, ✳ of Syria; *pop* 1,451,000

Dan·ube \'dan-(ˌ)yüb\ river 1771 mi. (2850 km.) long S Europe flowing from SW Germany into Black Sea — **Da·nu·bi·an** \də-'nü-bē-əs, da-, -'nyü-\ *adj*

Dar·da·nelles \ˌdär-də-'nelz\ *or* **Hel·les·pont** \'he-lə-ˌspänt\ strait NW Turkey connecting Sea of Marmara & the Aegean

Dar es Sa·laam \ˌdär-ˌe(s)-sə-'läm\ city, ✳ of Tanzania; *pop* 1,360,850

Dar·ling \'där-liŋ\ river about 1700 mi. (2735 km.) long SE Australia in Queensland & New South Wales flowing SW into the Murray

Dar·win \'där-wən\ city Australia, ✳ of Northern Territory; *pop* 70,071

Da·vao \dä-'vau, dä-'vaù\ city S Philippines in E Mindanao on Davao Gulf; *pop* 850,000

Dav·en·port \'da-vən-ˌpȯrt\ city E Iowa; pop 98,359

Da·vis \'dā-vəs\ strait between SW Greenland & E Baffin Island connecting Baffin Bay & the Atlantic

Day·ton \'dā-tᵊn\ city SW Ohio; pop 166,169

Dead Sea salt lake between Israel & Jordan; 1312 ft. (400 m.) below sea level

Death Valley dry valley E California & S Nevada containing lowest point in U.S. (282 ft. or 86 m. below sea level)

Dec·can \'de-kən, -ˌkan\ plateau region S India

Del·a·ware \'de-lə-ˌwer, -wər\ **1** river 296 mi. (476 km.) long E U.S. flowing S from S New York into Delaware Bay **2** state E U.S.; ✳, Dover; pop 783,600 — **Del·a·war·ean** or **Del·a·war·ian** \ˌde-lə-'wer-ē-ən\ adj or n

Delaware Bay inlet of the Atlantic between SW New Jersey & E Delaware

Del·hi \'de-lē\ city N India; pop 9,817,439 — see NEW DELHI

De·los \'dē-ˌläs\ island Greece — **De·lian** \'dē-lē-ən, 'dēl-yən\ adj or n

Del·phi \'del-ˌfī\ ancient town cen Greece on S slope of Mt. Parnassus

Democratic Republic of the Congo — see CONGO 2

Denali — see MCKINLEY, MOUNT

Den·mark \'den-ˌmärk\ country N Europe occupying most of Jutland & neighboring islands; ✳, Copenhagen; pop 5,383,507

Den·ver \'den-vər\ city, ✳ of Colorado; pop 554,636

Der·by \'där-bē\ city N cen England; pop 214,000

Der·by·shire \'där-bē-ˌshir, -shər\ or **Derby** county N cen England

Der·ry \'der-ē\ or **Lon·don·der·ry** \ˌlən-dən-'der-ē\ city & port NW Northern Ireland; pop 62,697

Des Moines \di-'mȯin\ city, ✳ of Iowa; pop 198,682

De·troit \di-'trȯit\ **1** river 31 mi. (50 km.) long between SE Michigan & Ontario connecting Lake Saint Clair & Lake Erie **2** city SE Michigan; pop 951,270

Dev·on \'de-vən\ or **De·von·shire** \'de-vən-ˌshir, -shər\ county SW England

Dha·ka \'dä-kə\ city, ✳ of Bangladesh; pop 3,637,892

Die·go Gar·cia \dē-ˌā-gō-ˌgär-'sē-ə\ island in Indian Ocean; chief island of Chagos Archipelago

Dili or **Dilli** \'di-lē\ city & port N Timor, ✳ of East Timor

Di·nar·ic Alps \də-'na-rik\ range of the E Alps in W Slovenia, W Croatia, Bosnia and Herzegovina, & Montenegro

District of Co·lum·bia \kə-'ləm-bē-ə\ federal district E U.S. coextensive with city of Washington; pop 572,059

Djakarta — see JAKARTA

Dji·bou·ti \jə-'bü-tē\ **1** country E Africa on Gulf of Aden; pop 510,000 **2** city, its ✳; pop 300,000

Dni·pro·pe·trovs'k or **Dne·pro·pe·trovsk** \də-ˌnye-prə-pə-'trȯfsk\ city E cen Ukraine; pop 1,189,000

Dodge City \'däj\ city S Kansas on Arkansas River; pop 25,176

Do·do·ma \dō-'dō-(ˌ)mä\ city NE cen Tanzania designated as future national ✳; pop 203,833

Do·ha \'dō-(ˌ)hä\ city & port, ✳ of Qatar on Persian Gulf; pop 217,294

Dom·i·ni·ca \ˌdä-mə-'nē-kə\ island West Indies in the Leeward Islands; country; ✳, Roseau; pop 71,242

Do·min·i·can Republic \də-'mi-ni-kən\ country West Indies in E Hispaniola; ✳, Santo Domingo; pop 8,533,744 — **Dominican** adj or n

Don \'dän\ river 1224 mi. (1969 km.) long SW Russia

Do·nets'k \də-'nyetsk\ city E Ukraine; pop 1,121,000

Dor·ches·ter \'dȯr-chəs-tər, -ˌches-\ town S England; pop 14,049

Dor·set \'dȯr-sət\ or **Dor·set·shire** \-ˌshir, -shər\ county S England on English Channel

Dort·mund \'dȯrt-ˌmunt, -mənd\ city W Germany in the Ruhr; pop 601,007

Dou·a·la \dü-'ä-lä\ seaport W Cameroon; pop 810,000

Dou·ro \'dȯr-(ˌ)ü\ or Spanish **Due·ro** \'dwe(ə)r-ō\ river 556 mi. (895 km.) long N Spain & N Portugal flowing into the Atlantic

Do·ver \'dō-vər\ city, ✳ of Delaware; pop 32,135

Dover, Strait of channel between SE England & N France; the most easterly section of English Channel

Down \'daun\ district SE Northern Ireland; pop 57,511

Downey \'dau̇-nē\ city SW California SE of Los Angeles; pop 107,323

Down·pat·rick \daun-'pa-trik\ town E Northern Ireland; pop 8245

Dra·kens·berg \'drä-kənz-ˌbərg\ mountain range E Republic of South Africa & Lesotho; highest peak Thabana Ntlenyana 11,425 ft. (3482 m.)

Dres·den \'drez-dən\ city E Germany; pop 485,132

Dub·lin \'də-blən\ city, ✳ of Ireland; pop 495,781

Dud·ley \'dəd-lē\ town W cen England; pop 300,000

Duis·burg \'dü-əs-ˌbərg, 'düz-ˌ, 'dyüz-ˌ\ city W Germany at junction of Rhine & Ruhr rivers; pop 537,441

Du·luth \də-'lüth\ city & port NE Minnesota; pop 86,918

Dum·fries \ˌdəm-ˈfrēs, -ˈfrēz\ burgh S Scotland; *pop* 32,084

Dumfries and Gal·lo·way \ˈga-lə-ˌwā\ administrative subdivision of S Scotland

Dun·dee \ˌdən-ˈdē\ city E Scotland; *pop* 172,860

Dun·gan·non \ˌdən-ˈga-nən\ district W Northern Ireland; *pop* 45,322

Dur·ban \ˈdər-bən\ city and seaport E Republic of South Africa; *pop* 736,852

Dur·ham \ˈdər-əm, ˈdə-rəm, ˈdu̇r-əm\ city N *cen* North Carolina; *pop* 187,035

Du·shan·be \dü-ˈsham-bə, dyü-, -ˈshäm-, ˈdyü-ˌ; ˌdyü-shäm-ˈbā\ city, ✳ of Tajikistan; *pop* 595,000

Düs·sel·dorf \ˈdü-səl-ˌdȯrf, ˈdyü-, ˈdu̇-\ city W Germany on the Rhine; *pop* 577,561

Ea·ling \ˈē-liŋ\ borough of W Greater London, England; *pop* 263,300

East An·glia \ˈaŋ-glē-ə\ region E England; *pop* 1,366,300

East China Sea — see CHINA

Eas·ter \ˈē-stər\ island Chile SE Pacific about 2000 mi. (3200 km.) W of Chilean coast

Eastern Cape province SE Republic of South Africa; *pop* 6,504,000

Eastern Ghats \ˈgäts, ˈgȯts, ˈgəts\ chain of low mountains SE India along coast

Eastern Hemisphere the half of the earth E of the Atlantic Ocean including Europe, Asia, Australia, and Africa

Eastern Roman Empire the Byzantine Empire from 395 to 474

Eastern Samoa — see AMERICAN SAMOA

East Germany — see GERMANY

East Indies the Malay Archipelago — **East Indian** *adj or n*

East London city S Republic of South Africa; *pop* 119,727

East Pakistan the former E division of Pakistan consisting of E portion of Bengal; now Bangladesh

East River strait SE New York connecting upper New York Bay & Long Island Sound and separating Manhattan & Long Island

East Sea — see JAPAN, SEA OF

East Sus·sex \ˈsə-siks\ county SE England; *pop* 670,600

East Timor country SE Asia on E Timor; ✳, Dili; *pop* 747,750

Ebro \ˈā-(ˌ)brō\ river 565 mi. (909 km.) long NE Spain flowing into the Mediterranean

Ec·ua·dor \ˈe-kwə-ˌdȯr, ˌe-kwä-ˈthȯr\ country W South America; ✳, Quito; *pop* 12,156,608 — **Ec·ua·dor·an** \ˌe-kwə-ˈdȯr-ən\ *or* **Ec·ua·dor·ean** *or* **Ec·ua·dor·ian** \-ē-ən\ *adj or n*

Ed·in·burgh \ˈe-d⁼n-ˌbərg\ city, ✳ of Scotland; *pop* 434,520

Ed·mon·ton \ˈed-mən-tən\ city, ✳ of Alberta, Canada; *pop* 666,104

Edom \ˈē-dəm\ ancient country SW Asia S of Judaea & Dead Sea — **Edom·ite** \ˈēd-ə-ˌmīt\ *n*

Egypt \ˈē-jipt\ country NE Africa & Sinai Peninsula of SW Asia bordering on Mediterranean & Red seas; ✳, Cairo; *pop* 67,313,000

Eire — see IRELAND

Elam \ˈē-ləm\ ancient country SW Asia at head of Persian Gulf E of Babylonia — **Elam·ite** \ˈē-lə-ˌmīt\ *n*

Elbe \ˈel-bə, ˈelb\ river 720 mi. (1159 km.) long N Czech Republic & NE Germany flowing NW into North Sea

El·bert, Mount \ˈel-bərt\ mountain 14,433 ft. (4399 m.) W *cen* Colorado; highest in Colorado & the Rocky Mountains

El·brus, Mount \el-ˈbrüz, -ˈbrüs\ mountain 18,510 ft. (5642 m.) Russia; highest in the Caucasus & in Europe

El·burz \el-ˈbu̇rz\ mountains N Iran

Eliz·a·beth \i-ˈli-zə-bəth\ city NE New Jersey; *pop* 120,568

Elles·mere \ˈelz-ˌmir\ island N Canada in Nunavut

Ellice — see TUVALU

El·lis Island \ˈe-ləs\ island SE New York S of Manhattan; served as immigration station 1892–1954

El Mon·te \el-ˈmän-tē\ city SW California E of Los Angeles; *pop* 115,965

El Paso \el-ˈpa-(ˌ)sō\ city W Texas on Rio Grande; *pop* 563,662

El Sal·va·dor \el-ˈsal-və-ˌdȯr, -ˌsal-və-ˈ; ˌel-ˌsäl-vä-ˈthȯr\ country Central America bordering on the Pacific; ✳, San Salvador; *pop* 5,517,000

Ely, Isle of \ˈē-lē\ area of high ground amid marshes in East Anglia, England

En·field \ˈen-ˌfēld\ borough of N Greater London, England; *pop* 248,900

En·gland \ˈiŋ-glənd, ˈiŋ-lənd\ country S Great Britain; a division of United Kingdom; ✳, London; *pop* 49,138,831

English Channel arm of the Atlantic between S England & N France

En·nis·kil·len \ˌe-nə-ˈski-lən\ town SW Northern Ireland in Fermanagh district

Ephra·im \ˈē-frē-əm\ **1** hilly region N Jordan E of Jordan River **2** — see ISRAEL — **Ephra·im·ite** \ˈē-frē-ə-ˌmīt\ *n*

Equatorial Guinea *formerly* **Spanish Guinea** country W Africa including Mbini & Bioko; ✳, Malabo; *pop* 376,000

Erie \ˈir-ē\ **1** city & port NW Pennsylvania; *pop* 103,717 **2** canal New York between Hudson River at Albany & Lake Erie at Buffalo; now superseded by New York State Barge Canal

Erie, Lake lake E *cen* North America in U.S. & Canada; one of the Great Lakes

Er·in \ˈer-ən\ poetic name of Ireland

Er·i·trea \ˌer-ə-ˈtrē-ə, -ˈtrā-\ country NE Africa; ✳, Asmara; *pop* 3,317,611 — **Er·i·tre·an** \-ən\ *adj or n*

Es·con·di·do \ˌes-kən-'dē-(ˌ)dō\ city SW California N of San Diego; pop 133,559

Es·fa·han \ˌes-fə-'hän, -'han\ or **Is·fa·han** \ˌis-\ city W cen Iran; pop 986,753

Española — see HISPANIOLA

Es·sen \'e-sᵊn\ city W Germany in the Ruhr; pop 626,989

Es·sex \'e-siks\ county SE England on North Sea

Es·to·nia \e-'stō-nē-ə, -nyə\ country E Europe on Baltic Sea; ✲, Tallinn; pop 1,361,242 — **Es·to·nian** \e-'stō-nē-ən, -nyən\ adj or n

Ethi·o·pia \ˌē-thē-'ō-pē-ə\ formerly **Ab·ys·sin·ia** \ˌa-bə-'si-nē-ə, -nyə\ country E Africa; ✲, Addis Ababa; pop 67,220,000 — **Ethi·o·pi·an** \-pē-ən\ adj or n

Et·na, Mount \'et-nə\ volcano 10,902 ft. (3323 m.) Italy in NE Sicily

Eto·bi·coke \e-'tō-bi-ˌkō\ former city Canada in SE Ontario; now part of Toronto

Etru·ria \i-'trúr-ē-ə\ ancient country cen peninsula of Italy

Eu·gene \yü-'jēn\ city W Oregon; pop 137,893

Eu·phra·tes \yù-'frā-(ˌ)tēz\ river 1700 mi. (2736 km.) long SW Asia flowing from E Turkey & uniting with the Tigris to form the Shatt al Arab

Eur·asia \yú-'rā-zhə, -shə\ landmass consisting of Europe & Asia — **Eur·asian** \-zhən, -shən\ adj or n

Eu·rope \'yúr-əp\ continent of the Eastern Hemisphere between Asia & the Atlantic; pop 498,000,000

European Union economic, scientific, & political organization consisting of Belgium, France, Italy, Luxembourg, Netherlands, Germany, Denmark, Greece, Ireland, United Kingdom, Spain, Portugal, Austria, Finland, & Sweden

Ev·ans·ville \'e-vənz-ˌvil\ city SW Indiana; pop 121,582

Ev·er·est, Mount \'ev-rəst, 'e-və-\ mountain 29,035 ft. (8850 m.) S Asia in the Himalayas on border between Nepal & Tibet; highest in the world

Ev·er·glades \'e-vər-ˌglādz\ swamp region S Florida now partly drained

Ex·e·ter \'ek-sə-tər\ city SW England; pop 101,100

Faer·oe or **Far·oe** \'fer-(ˌ)ō\ islands NE Atlantic NW of the Shetlands belonging to Denmark; pop 47,653 — **Faer·o·ese** \ˌfar-ə-'wēz, ˌfer-, -'wēs\ adj or n

Fair·banks \'fer-ˌbaŋks\ city E cen Alaska; pop 30,224

Fair·field \'fer-ˌfēld\ municipality SE Australia in E New South Wales; pop 175,099

Fai·sa·la·bad \ˌfī-ˌsä-lə-'bäd, -ˌsa-lə-'bad\ formerly **Ly·all·pur** \lē-ˌäl-'púr\ city NE Pakistan W of Lahore; pop 2,008,861

Falk·land Islands \'fó-klənd, 'fòl-\ or *Spanish* **Is·las Mal·vi·nas** \ˌēs-läs-mäl-'vē-näs\ island group SW Atlantic E of S end of Argentina; a British colony; ✲, Stanley; pop 2100

Far East the countries of E Asia & the Malay Archipelago — usually thought to consist of the Asian countries bordering on the Pacific but sometimes including also India, Sri Lanka, Bangladesh, Tibet, & Myanmar — **Far Eastern** adj

Far·go \'fär-(ˌ)gō\ city E North Dakota; largest in state; pop 90,599

Faroe — see FAEROE

Fay·ette·ville \'fā-ət-ˌvil, -vəl\ city SE cen North Carolina; pop 121,015

Fear, Cape \'fir\ cape SE North Carolina at mouth of Cape Fear River

Fer·man·agh \fər-'ma-nə\ district SW Northern Ireland; pop 54,062

Fernando Póo — see BIOKO

Fez \'fez\ city N cen Morocco; pop 774,574

Fife \'fīf\ administrative subdivision of E Scotland

Fi·ji \'fē-(ˌ)jē\ islands SW Pacific; country; ✲, Suva; pop 775,077 — **Fi·ji·an** \'fē-(ˌ)jē-ən, fi-\ adj or n

Fin·land \'fin-lənd\ country NE Europe; ✲, Helsinki; pop 5,058,000 — **Fin·land·er** n

Flan·ders \'flan-dərz\ **1** region W Belgium & N France on North Sea **2** semi-autonomous region W Belgium; pop 5,972,781

Flat·tery, Cape \'fla-tə-rē\ cape NW Washington at entrance to Strait of Juan de Fuca

Flint \'flint\ city SE Michigan; pop 124,943

Flor·ence \'flór-ən(t)s, 'flär-\ or *Italian* **Fi·ren·ze** \fē-'rent-sā\ city cen Italy; pop 374,501 — **Flor·en·tine** \'flór-ən-ˌtēn, 'flär-, -ˌtīn\ adj or n

Flor·i·da \'flór-ə-də, 'flär-\ state SE U.S.; ✲, Tallahassee; pop 15,982,378 — **Flo·rid·i·an** \flə-'ri-dē-ən\ or **Flor·i·dan** \'flór-ə-dən, 'flär-\ adj or n

Florida, Straits of channel between Florida Keys on NW & Cuba & Bahamas on S & E connecting Gulf of Mexico & the Atlantic

Florida Keys chain of islands off S tip of Florida

Foochow — see FUZHOU

For·a·ker, Mount \'fòr-i-kər, 'fär-\ mountain 17,400 ft. (5304 m.) S cen Alaska in Alaska Range

For·mo·sa \fòr-'mō-sə, fər-, -zə\ — see TAIWAN — **For·mo·san** \fòr-'mō-sᵊn, fər-, -zᵊn\ adj or n

For·ta·le·za \ˌfòr-tə-'lā-zə\ city & port NE Brazil on the Atlantic; pop 2,141,402

Fort Col·lins \'kä-lənz\ city N Colorado; pop 118,652

Fort–de–France \ˌfòr-də-'fräⁿs\ city West Indies; ✲ of Martinique on W coast; pop 93,598

Forth \'fȯrth\ river 116 mi. (187 km.) long S *cen* Scotland flowing E into North Sea through **Firth of Forth**

Fort Knox \'näks\ military reservation N *cen* Kentucky SSW of Louisville; location of U.S. Gold Bullion Depository

Fort Lau·der·dale \'lȯ-dər-ˌdāl\ city SE Florida; *pop* 152,397

Fort Wayne \'wān\ city NE Indiana; *pop* 205,727

Fort Worth \'wərth\ city NE Texas; *pop* 534,694

Fox \'fäks\ islands SW Alaska in the E Aleutians

Foxe Basin \'fäks\ inlet of the Atlantic N Canada in E Nunavut W of Baffin Island

France \'fran(t)s, 'fräⁿs\ country W Europe between the English Channel & the Mediterranean; ✳, Paris; *pop* 58,520,688

Frank·fort \'fraŋk-fərt\ city, ✳ of Kentucky; *pop* 27,741

Frank·furt \'fraŋk-fərt, 'fräŋk-ˌfùrt\ *or in full* **Frankfurt am Main** \(ˌ)äm-'mīn\ city W Germany on Main River; *pop* 654,679

Frank·lin \'fraŋ-klən\ former district N Canada in Northwest Territories including Arctic Archipelago & Boothia & Melville peninsulas

Fra·ser \'frā-zər, -zhər\ river 850 mi. (1368 km.) long Canada in S *cen* British Columbia flowing into the Pacific

Fred·er·ic·ton \'fre-drik-tən, 'fre-də-rik-\ city, ✳ of New Brunswick, Canada; *pop* 47,560

Free State *formerly* **Or·ange Free State** \'ȯr-inj, 'är-, -ənj\ province E *cen* Republic of South Africa; *pop* 2,767,000

Free·town \'frē-ˌtaùn\ city, ✳ of Sierra Leone; *pop* 178,600

Fre·mont \'frē-ˌmänt\ city W California; *pop* 203,413

French Guiana country N South America on the Atlantic; an overseas division of France; ✳, Cayenne; *pop* 128,000

French Indochina — *see* INDOCHINA

Fres·no \'frez-ˌnō\ city S *cen* California SE of San Francisco; *pop* 427,652

Frunze — *see* BISHKEK

Fu·ji, Mount \'fü-jē\ *or* **Fu·ji·ya·ma** \ˌfü-jē-'yä-mä\ mountain 12,388 ft. (3776 m.) Japan in S *cen* Honshu; highest in Japan

Fu·ku·o·ka \ˌfü-kü-'ō-kä\ city Japan in N Kyushu; *pop* 1,341,470

Ful·ler·ton \'fù-lər-tən\ city SW California; *pop* 126,003

Fu·na·fu·ti \ˌfü-nä-'fü-tē\ city, ✳ of Tuvalu; *pop* 1328

Fun·dy, Bay of \'fən-dē\ inlet of the Atlantic SE Canada between New Brunswick & Nova Scotia

Fu·shun \'fü-'shùn\ city NE China E of Shenyang; *pop* 1,202,388

Fu·zhou \'fü-'jō\ *or* **Foo·chow** \'fü-'jō, -'chaù\ city & port SE China; *pop* 874,809

Ga·bon \gä-'bōⁿ\ country W Africa on the Equator; ✳, Libreville; *pop* 1,014,976 — **Gab·o·nese** \ˌga-bə-'nēz, -'nēs\ *adj or n*

Ga·bo·rone \ˌgä-bō-'rō-(ˌ)nä, ˌkä-\ city, ✳ of Botswana; *pop* 133,468

Gads·den Purchase \'gadz-dən\ area of land S of Gila River in present Arizona & New Mexico purchased 1853 by the U.S. from Mexico

Ga·la·pa·gos Islands \gə-'lä-pə-gəs, -'la-, -ˌgōs\ island group Ecuador in the Pacific 600 mi. (965 km.) W of South America; *pop* 9785

Ga·la·tia \gə-'lā-sh(ē-)ə\ ancient country *cen* Asia Minor in region around modern Ankara, Turkey — **Ga·la·tian** \-shən\ *adj or n*

Ga·li·cia \gə-'li-sh(ē-)ə\ **1** region E *cen* Europe now divided between Poland & Ukraine **2** region NW Spain on the Atlantic — **Ga·li·cian** \-'li-shən\ *adj or n*

Gal·i·lee \'ga-lə-ˌlē\ hilly region N Israel — **Gal·i·le·an** \ˌga-lə-'lē-ən\ *adj or n*

Galilee, Sea of *or modern* **Lake Ti·be·ri·as** \tī-'bir-ē-əs\ lake N Israel on Syrian border; crossed by Jordan River

Gal·lo·way \'ga-lə-ˌwā\ former administrative district of SW Scotland — *see* DUMFRIES AND GALLOWAY

Gam·bia \'gam-bē-ə, 'gäm-\ country W Africa; ✳, Banjul; *pop* 687,817 — **Gam·bi·an** \-bē-ən\ *adj or n*

Gan·ges \'gan-jēz\ river 1550 mi. (2494 km.) long N India flowing from the Himalayas SE & E to unite with the Brahmaputra and empty into Bay of Bengal through a vast delta — **Gan·get·ic** \gan-'je-tik\ *adj*

Garden Grove city SW California; *pop* 165,196

Gar·land \'gär-lənd\ city NE Texas NNE of Dallas; *pop* 215,768

Ga·ronne \gə-'rän, gä-'rȯn\ river 355 mi. (571 km.) long SE France flowing NW

Gary \'ger-ē\ city NW Indiana on Lake Michigan; *pop* 102,746

Gas·co·ny \'gas-kə-nē\ region SW France — **Gas·con** \'gas-kən\ *adj or n*

Gas·pé \ga-'spā, 'ga-ˌ\ peninsula SE Quebec E of mouth of the Saint Lawrence — **Gas·pe·sian** \ga-'spē-zhən\ *adj or n*

Gaul \'gȯl\ *or Latin* **Gal·lia** \'ga-lē-ə\ ancient country W Europe chiefly consisting of region occupied by modern France & Belgium

Gau·teng \'gaù-ˌteŋ\ province *cen* NE Republic of South Africa; *pop* 6,864,000

Ga·za Strip \'gä-zə, 'ga-\ district NE Sinai Peninsula on the Mediterranean

Ge·ne·va \jə-'nē-və\ city SW Switzerland on Lake Geneva; *pop* 175,998 — **Ge·ne·van** \-vən\ *adj or n* — **Gen·e·vese** \ˌje-nə-'vēz, -'vēs\ *adj or n*

Geneva, Lake lake on border between SW Switzerland & E France

Gen·oa \'je-nō-ə\ *or Italian* **Ge·no·va**

\'je-nō-(,)vä\ city & port NW Italy; *pop* 632,366 — **Gen·o·ese** \,je-nō-'ēz, -'ēs\ *or* **Gen·o·vese** \-nə-'vēz, -'vēs\ *adj or n*

George·town \'jȯrj-,taůn\ **1** a W section of Washington, District of Columbia **2** city & port, ✱ of Guyana; *pop* 162,000

Geor·gia \'jȯr-jə\ **1** state SE U.S.; ✱, Atlanta; *pop* 8,186,453 **2** *or* **Republic of Georgia** country SE Europe on Black Sea S of Caucasus Mountains; ✱, Tbilisi; *pop* 5,493,000 — **Geor·gian** \'jȯr-jən\ *adj or n*

Georgia, Strait of channel Canada & U.S. between Vancouver Island & main part of British Columbia NW of Puget Sound

Georgian Bay inlet of Lake Huron in S Ontario

Ger·man·town \'jər-mən-,taůn\ a NW section of Philadelphia, Pennsylvania

Ger·ma·ny \'jər-mə-nē\ country *cen* Europe bordering on North & Baltic seas; ✱, Berlin; divided 1946–90 into two independent states: the **Federal Republic of Germany** (West Germany; ✱, Bonn) & the **German Democratic Republic** (East Germany; ✱, East Berlin); *pop* 82,440,000

Get·tys·burg \'ge-tēz-,bərg\ town S Pennsylvania; *pop* 7490

Gha·na \'gä-nə, 'ga-\ *formerly* **Gold Coast** country W Africa on Gulf of Guinea; ✱, Accra; *pop* 15,636,000 — **Gha·na·ian** \gä-'nā-ən, ga-, -'nī-ən\ *or* **Gha·ni·an** \'gä-nē-ən, 'ga-, -nyən\ *adj or n*

Ghats \'gȯts\ two mountain chains S India consisting of **Eastern Ghats** & **Western Ghats**

Ghent \'gent\ city NW *cen* Belgium; *pop* 226,220

Gi·bral·tar \jə-'brȯl-tər\ British colony on S coast of Spain including Rock of Gibraltar; *pop* 29,760

Gibraltar, Rock of cape on S coast of Spain in Gibraltar at E end of Strait of Gibraltar; highest point 1396 ft. (426 m.)

Gibraltar, Strait of passage between Spain & Africa connecting the Atlantic & the Mediterranean

Gi·la \'hē-lə\ river 630 mi. (1014 km.) long SW New Mexico & S Arizona flowing W into the Colorado

Gil·bert \'gil-bərt\ town SW *cen* Arizona; *pop* 109,697

Gilbert and El·lice Islands \'e-lis\ island group W Pacific; divided into Kiribati and Tuvalu

Gil·e·ad \'gi-lē-əd\ mountain region of NE ancient Palestine E of Jordan River; now in NW Jordan — **Gil·e·ad·ite** \-lē-ə-,dīt\ *n*

Gi·za \'gē-zə\ city N Egypt on the Nile SW of Cairo; *pop* 2,096,000

Gla·cier Bay \'glā-shər\ inlet SE Alaska at S end of Saint Elias Range

Glas·gow \'glas-(,)kō, 'glas-(,)gō, 'glaz-(,)gō\ city S *cen* Scotland on the Clyde; *pop* 681,470 — **Glas·we·gian** \gla-'swē-jən, glaz-\ *adj or n*

Glen·dale \'glen-,dāl\ **1** city *cen* Arizona NW of Phoenix; *pop* 218,812 **2** city S California NE of Los Angeles; *pop* 194,973

Glouces·ter \'gläs-tər, 'glȯs\ town SW *cen* England; *pop* 91,800

Glouces·ter·shire \'gläs-tər-,shir, -shər, 'glȯs-\ *or* **Gloucester** county SW *cen* England

Goa \'gō-ə\ district W India on Malabar coast

Goat Island island W New York in Niagara River — see NIAGARA FALLS

Go·bi \'gō-(,)bē\ desert E *cen* Asia in Mongolia & N China

Godt·hab — see NUUK

Godwin Austen — see K2

Go·lan Heights \'gō-,län, -lən\ hilly region NE of Sea of Galilee

Gol·con·da \gäl-'kän-də\ ruined city *cen* India W of Hyderabad

Gold Coast 1 — see GHANA **2** coast region W Africa on N shore of Gulf of Guinea E of Ivory Coast

Golden Gate strait W California connecting San Francisco Bay with Pacific Ocean

Good Hope, Cape of \,gůd-'hōp\ cape S Republic of South Africa on SW coast of Western Cape province

Gorki — see NIZHNIY NOVGOROD

Gö·te·borg \,yœ-tə-'bȯr-ē\ city & port SW Sweden; *pop* 474,921

Gram·pi·an \'gram-pē-ən\ hills N *cen* Scotland

Grand Banks shallow area in the W North Atlantic SE of Newfoundland

Grand Canyon gorge of Colorado River NW Arizona

Grand Canyon of the Snake HELLS CANYON

Grande, Rio — see RIO GRANDE

Grand Prairie city NE *cen* Texas W of Dallas; *pop* 127,427

Grand Rapids city SW Michigan; *pop* 197,800

Graz \'gräts\ city S Austria; *pop* 226,244

Great Australian Bight wide bay on S coast of Australia

Great Barrier Reef coral reef Australia off NE coast of Queensland

Great Basin region W U.S. between Sierra Nevada & Wasatch Range including most of Nevada & parts of California, Idaho, Utah, Wyoming, & Oregon; has no drainage to ocean

Great Bear lake Canada in Northwest Territories draining through Great Bear River into Mackenzie River

Great Brit·ain \'bri-t²n\ **1** island W Europe NW of France consisting of England,

Scotland, & Wales; *pop* 53,917,000 **2**
UNITED KINGDOM

Great Dividing Range mountain system
E Australia & Tasmania extending S
from Cape York Peninsula — see
KOSCIUSKO, MOUNT

Greater Antilles group of islands of the
West Indies including Cuba, Hispaniola,
Jamaica, & Puerto Rico — see LESSER
ANTILLES

Greater London metropolitan county SE
England consisting of City of London &
32 surrounding boroughs

Greater Manchester metropolitan county NW England including city of Manchester

Great Lakes chain of five lakes (Superior,
Michigan, Huron, Erie, & Ontario) *cen*
North America in U.S. & Canada

Great Plains elevated plains region W *cen*
U.S. & W Canada E of the Rockies; extending from W Texas to NE British Columbia & NW Alberta

Great Rift Valley basin SW Asia & E
Africa extending with several breaks
from valley of the Jordan S to *cen*
Mozambique

Great Salt Lake lake N Utah having salty
waters & no outlet

Great Slave Lake lake NW Canada in S
Northwest Territories drained by
Mackenzie River

Great Smoky mountains between W
North Carolina & E Tennessee; highest
Clingmans Dome 6643 ft. (2025 m.)

Greece \'grēs\ country S Europe at S end
of Balkan Peninsula — *cap* Athens; *pop*
10,964,020

Green \'grēn\ **1** mountains E North
America in the Appalachians extending
from S Quebec S through Vermont into
W Massachusetts **2** river 730 mi. (1175
km.) long W U.S. flowing from W
Wyoming S into the Colorado in SE Utah

Green Bay 1 inlet of NW Lake Michigan
120 mi. (193 km.) long in NW Michigan &
NE Wisconsin **2** city NE Wisconsin on
Green Bay; *pop* 102,313

Green·land \'grēn-lənd, -ˌland\ island in
the North Atlantic off NE North America
belonging to Denmark; *cap* Nuuk; *pop*
55,171

Greens·boro \'grēnz-ˌbər-ō\ city N *cen*
North Carolina; *pop* 223,891

Green·wich \'gre-nich, 'grēn-nich, 'grin-
ˌwich\ borough of SE Greater London,
England; *pop* 200,800

Greenwich Village \'gre-nich\ section of
New York City in Manhattan on lower W
side

Gre·na·da \grə-'nā-də\ island West Indies
in S Windward Islands; independent
country; *cap* Saint George's; *pop* 102,632

Gren·a·dines, the \ˌgre-nə-'dēnz, 'gre-nə-
ˌ\ islands West Indies in *cen* Windward Is-

lands; N islands part of Saint Vincent and
the Grenadines; S islands dependency of
Grenada

Groz·ny \'grȯz-nē, 'gräz-\ city S Russia in
Europe; *cap* of Chechnya; *pop* 388,000

Gua·da·la·ja·ra \ˌgwä-də-lə-'här-ə, ˌgwä-
thä-lä-'hä-rä\ city W *cen* Mexico; *pop*
2,987,194

Gua·dal·ca·nal \ˌgwä-dºl-kə-'nal, ˌgwä-
də-kə-\ island W Pacific in the SE
Solomons; *pop* 23,922

Gua·dal·qui·vir \ˌgwä-dºl-ki-'vir, -'kwi-
vər\ river 408 mi. (656 km.) long S Spain
flowing into the Atlantic

Gua·de·loupe \'gwä-də-ˌlüp\ two islands
separated by a narrow channel in West
Indies in *cen* Leeward Islands; an overseas
division of France; *pop* 418,000

Gua·lla·ti·ri \ˌgwä-yə-'tir-ē, ˌgwī-ə-\ volcano 19,882 ft. (6060 m.) high N Chile

Guam \'gwäm\ island W Pacific in S Marianas belonging to U.S.; *cap* Agana; *pop*
154,805 — **Gua·ma·ni·an** \gwä-'mä-nē-
ən\ *adj or n*

Gua·na·ba·ra Bay \ˌgwä-nä-'bär-ə\ inlet
of the Atlantic SE Brazil on which city of
Rio de Janeiro is located

Guang·dong \'gwäŋ-'dung\ *or* **Kwang-
tung** \'gwäŋ-'dung, 'kwäŋ-, -'tüŋ\ province SE China bordering on South China
Sea & Gulf of Tonkin; *cap* Guangzhou;
pop 62,829,236

Guang·zhou \'gwäŋ-'jō\ *or* **Can·ton**
\'kan-ˌtän, kan-'\ city & port SE China;
pop 2,914,281

Guan·tá·na·mo Bay \gwän-'tä-nä-ˌmō\
inlet of the Caribbean in SE Cuba; site of
U.S. naval station

Gua·te·ma·la \ˌgwä-tə-'mä-lə, -tä-'mä-lä\
1 country Central America; *pop*
9,713,000 **2** *or* **Guatemala City** city, its
cap; *pop* 1,132,730 — **Gua·te·ma·lan**
\-'mä-lən\ *adj or n*

Gua·ya·quil \ˌgwī-ə-'kēl, -'kil\ city & port
W Ecuador; *pop* 1,508,444

Guay·na·bo \gwī-'nä-(ˌ)bō, -(ˌ)vō\ city NE
cen Puerto Rico; *pop* 100,053

Guern·sey \'gərn-zē\ — see CHANNEL

Gui·a·na \gē-'a-nə, -'ä-nə; gī-'a-nə\ region
N South America on the Atlantic; includes Guyana, French Guiana, Suriname, & nearby parts of Brazil &
Venezuela — **Gui·a·nan** \-nən\ *adj or n*

Guin·ea \'gi-nē\ **1** region W Africa on
the Atlantic extending along coast from
Gambia to Angola **2** country W Africa
N of Sierra Leone & Liberia; *cap* Conakry;
pop 7,300,000 — **Guin·ean** \'gi-nē-ən\
adj or n

Guinea, Gulf of arm of the Atlantic W
cen Africa

Guin·ea–Bis·sau \ˌgi-nē-bi-'saù\ country
W Africa; *cap* Bissau; *pop* 1,036,000

Gui·yang \'gwä-'yäŋ\ *or* **Kuei–yang**
\'gwä-'yäŋ\ city S China; *pop* 1,018,619

Gulf States states of U.S. bordering on Gulf of Mexico: Florida, Alabama, Mississippi, Louisiana, and Texas

Gulf Stream warm current of the Atlantic Ocean flowing from Gulf of Mexico NE along coast of U.S. to Nantucket Island and from there eastward

Guy·ana \gī-'an-ə\ *formerly* **British Guiana** country N South America on the Atlantic; ✳, Georgetown; *pop* 755,000 — **Guy·a·nese** \ˌgī-ə-'nēz, -'nēs\ *adj or n*

Gwangju — see KWANGJU

Gwent \'gwent\ former county SE Wales

Gwyn·edd \'gwi-neth\ former county NW Wales

Hack·ney \'hak-nē\ borough of N Greater London, England; *pop* 164,200

Hague, The \thə-'hāg\ city SW Netherlands; a national ✳; *pop* 457,726

Hai·kou \'hī-'kō\ city & port SE China; *pop* 280,153

Hai·phong \'hī-'fȯŋ, -'fäŋ\ city & port N Vietnam; *pop* 1,726,900

Hai·ti \'hā-tē\ country West Indies in W Hispaniola; ✳, Port-au-Prince; *pop* 6,902,000 — **Haitian** \'hā-shən\ *adj or n*

Ha·le·a·ka·la Crater \ˌhä-lā-ˌä-kä-'lä\ crater over 2500 ft. (762 m.) deep Hawaii in E Maui

Hal·i·fax \'ha-lə-ˌfaks\ municipality & port, ✳ of Nova Scotia, Canada; *pop* 359,111

Ham·burg \'ham-ˌbərg; 'häm-ˌbu̇rg, -ˌbu̇rk\ city N Germany on the Elbe; *pop* 1,668,800 — **Ham·burg·er** \-ˌbər-gər, -ˌbu̇r-\ *n*

Ham·hung \'häm-ˌhu̇ŋ\ city E *cen* North Korea; *pop* 701,000

Ham·il·ton \'ha-məl-tən\ **1** town, ✳ of Bermuda; *pop* 969 **2** city & port, S Ontario, Canada on Lake Ontario; *pop* 490,268

Ham·mer·smith and Ful·ham \'ha-mər-ˌsmith-ənd-'fu̇-ləm\ borough of SW Greater London, England; *pop* 136,500

Hamp·shire \'hamp-ˌshir, -shər\ county S England on English Channel

Hamp·ton \'hamp-tən\ city SE Virginia; *pop* 146,437

Hampton Roads channel SE Virginia through which James River flows into Chesapeake Bay

Hang·zhou \'häŋ-'jō\ *or* **Hang-chow** \'haŋ-'chau̇, 'häŋ-'jō\ *or* **Hang-chou** \'jō\ city E China; *pop* 1,099,660

Han·ni·bal \'ha-nə-bəl\ city NE Missouri on the Mississippi River; *pop* 17,757

Han·no·ver *or* **Han·o·ver** \'ha-ˌnō-vər, -nə-vər, G hä-'nō-fər\ city N *cen* Germany; *pop* 517,746

Ha·noi \ha-'nȯi, hə-, hä-\ city, ✳ of Vietnam; *pop* 2,931,400

Ha·ra·re \hə-'rä-(ˌ)rā\ *formerly* **Salisbury** \'sȯlz-ˌber-ē, -b(ə-)rē\ city, ✳ of Zimbabwe; *pop* 1,184,169

Har·bin \'här-bən, här-'bin\ *or* **Ha-erh-pin** \'hä-'ər-'bin\ city NE China; *pop* 2,443,398

Har·in·gey \'ha-riŋ-ˌgā\ borough of N Greater London, England; *pop* 187,300

Har·lem \'här-ləm\ section of New York City in N Manhattan

Har·ris·burg \'ha-rəs-ˌbərg\ city, ✳ of Pennsylvania; *pop* 48,950

Har·row \'ha-(ˌ)rō\ borough of NW Greater London, England; *pop* 194,300

Hart·ford \'härt-fərd\ city, ✳ of Connecticut; *pop* 121,578

Hat·ter·as, Cape \'ha-tə-rəs\ cape North Carolina on Hatteras Island

Ha·vana \hə-'va-nə\ city, ✳ of Cuba; *pop* 2,096,054

Hav·ant \'ha-vənt\ town S England; *pop* 117,400

Ha·ver·ing \'hāv-riŋ, 'hä-və-riŋ\ borough of NE Greater London, England; *pop* 224,400

Ha·waii \hə-'wä-yē, -'wä-ˌē\ **1** *or* **Ha·wai·ian Islands** *formerly* **Sand·wich Islands** \ˌsan-(d)wich-\ group of islands *cen* Pacific belonging to U.S. **2** island, largest of the group **3** state of U.S., ✳, Honolulu; *pop* 1,211,537

Hay·ward \'hā-wərd\ city W California SE of Oakland; *pop* 140,030

Heb·ri·des \'he-brə-ˌdēz\ islands W Scotland in the North Atlantic consisting of **Outer Hebrides** (to W) and **Inner Hebrides** (to E); *pop* 30,660 — **Heb·ri·de·an** \ˌhe-brə-'dē-ən\ *adj or n*

Hel·e·na \'he-lə-nə\ city, ✳ of Montana; *pop* 25,780

Hellespont — see DARDANELLES

Hells Canyon \'helz\ canyon of Snake River on Idaho–Oregon boundary

Hel·sin·ki \'hel-ˌsiŋ-kē, hel-'\ city, ✳ of Finland; *pop* 559,718

Hen·der·son \'hen-dər-sən\ city S Nevada; *pop* 175,381

Hen·ry, Cape \'hen-rē\ cape E Virginia S of entrance to Chesapeake Bay

Her·e·ford and Wor·ces·ter \'her-ə-fərd-°n-'wu̇s-tər\ former county W England bordering on Wales

Hert·ford·shire \'här-fərd-ˌshir, 'härt-, -shər\ *or* **Hertford** county SE England

Her·ze·go·vi·na \ˌhert-sə-gō-'vē-nə, ˌhərt-, -ˌgō-və-nə\ *or Serb* **Her·ce·go·vi·na** \ˌkert-sə-gō-vē-nä\ region S Europe S of Bosnia & NW of Montenegro; part of Bosnia and Herzegovina — **Her·ze·go·vi·nian** \ˌhert-sə-gō-'vē-nē-ən, ˌhərt-, -nyən\ *n*

Hi·a·le·ah \ˌhī-ə-'lē-ə\ city SE Florida; *pop* 226,419

Hi·ber·nia \hī-'bər-nē-ə\ — see IRELAND — **Hi·ber·ni·an** \-ən\ *adj or n*

Hi·ga·shi·ōsa·ka \hē-ˌgä-shē-'ō-sä-kä\ city Japan in S Honshu E of Osaka; *pop* 515,094

High·land \'hī-lənd\ administrative subdivision of NW Scotland

High·lands \'hī-ləndz\ the mountainous N part of Scotland lying N & W of the Lowlands

High Plains the Great Plains esp. from Nebraska southward

Hil·ling·don \'hi-liŋ-dən\ borough of W Greater London, England; *pop* 225,800

Hi·ma·la·yas, the \,hi-mə-'lā-əz\ *or the* **Himalaya** mountain system S Asia on border between India & Tibet and in Kashmir, Nepal, & Bhutan — see EVER-EST, MOUNT — **Hi·ma·la·yan** \,him-ə-'lā-ən, hə-'mäl-(ə-)ən\ *adj*

Hin·du Kush \'hin-(ˌ)dü-'kùsh, -'kəsh\ mountain range *cen* Asia SW of the Pamirs on border of Kashmir and in Afghanistan

Hin·du·stan \,hin-(ˌ)dü-'stan, -də-, -'stän\ **1** a name for N India **2** the subcontinent of India **3** the country of India

Hi·ro·shi·ma \,hir-ə-'shē-mə, hə-'rō-shə-mə\ city Japan in SW Honshu on Inland Sea; *pop* 1,126,239

His·pan·io·la \,his-pə-'nyō-lə\ *or Spanish* **Es·pa·ño·la** \,es,pä-'nyō-lä\ island West Indies in Greater Antilles; divided between Haiti on W & Dominican Republic on E

Ho·bart \'hō-bərt\ city Australia, ✳ of Tasmania; *pop* 47,106

Ho Chi Minh City \'hō-,chē-'min\ *formerly* **Sai·gon** \sī-'gän, 'sī-,\ city S Vietnam; *pop* 5,479,000

Hoh·hot \'hō-'hōt\ *or* **Hu·he·hot** \'hü-(ˌ)hä-'hōt\ city N China, ✳ of Inner Mongolia; *pop* 652,534

Hok·kai·do \hó-'kī-(ˌ)dō\ island N Japan N of Honshu; *pop* 5,683,062

Hol·land \'hä-lənd\ **1** county of Holy Roman Empire bordering on North Sea & consisting of area now forming part of W Netherlands **2** — see NETHERLANDS — **Hol·land·er** \-lən-dər\ *n*

Hol·ly·wood \'hä-lē-,wùd\ **1** section of Los Angeles, California, NW of downtown district **2** city SE Florida; *pop* 139,357

Holy Roman Empire empire consisting mainly of German & Italian territories & existing from 9th or 10th century to 1806

Hon·du·ras \hän-'dùr-əs, -'dyùr-; ón-'dü-räs\ country Central America; ✳, Tegucigalpa; *pop* 4,604,800 — **Hon·du·ran** \-ən\ *adj or n*

Hong Kong \'häŋ-,käŋ, -'käŋ\ *or Chinese* **Xiang·gang** \'shyäŋ-,gäŋ\ special administrative region China on SE coast including Hong Kong Island & Jiulong Peninsula; chief city Victoria; *pop* 6,843,000

Ho·ni·a·ra \,hō-nē-'är-ə\ town, ✳ of Solomon Islands; *pop* 35,288

Ho·no·lu·lu \,hä-nə-'lü-(ˌ)lü, ,hō-nə-\ city, ✳ of Hawaii on Oahu; *pop* 371,657

Hon·shu \'hän-(ˌ)shü, 'hòn-\ island Japan; largest of the four chief islands; *pop* 102,324,961

Hood, Mount \'hùd\ mountain 11,235 ft. (3424 m.) NW Oregon in Cascade Range

Hoo·ver Dam \'hü-vər\ *or* **Boul·der Dam** \'bōl-dər\ dam 726 ft. (221 m.) high in Colorado River between Arizona & Nevada — see MEAD, LAKE

Hormuz, Strait of \'(h)ór-,məz, (h)ór-'müz\ strait connecting Persian Gulf & Gulf of Oman

Horn, Cape \'hòrn\ cape S Chile on an island in Tierra del Fuego; the most southerly point of South America at 56° S latitude

Horn of Africa the easternmost projection of Africa; variously used to refer to Somalia, SE or all of Ethiopia, & sometimes Djibouti

Horseshoe Falls — see NIAGARA FALLS

Houns·low \'haúnz-(ˌ)lō\ borough of SW Greater London, England; *pop* 193,400

Hous·ton \'hyüs-tən, 'yüs-\ city SE Texas; *pop* 1,953,631

How·rah \'haú-rə\ city E India on Hugli River opposite Calcutta; *pop* 1,008,704

Hsi·an — see XI'AN

Huang *or* **Hwang** \'hwäŋ\ *or* **Yellow** river about 3000 mi. (4828 km.) long N China flowing into Bo Hai

Hud·ders·field \'hə-dərz-,fēld\ town N England NE of Manchester; *pop* 123,888

Hud·son \'həd-sən\ **1** river 306 mi. (492 km.) long E New York flowing S **2** bay, inlet of the Atlantic in N Canada **3** strait NE Canada connecting Hudson Bay & the Atlantic

Hu·gli *or* **Hoo·ghly** \'hü-glē\ river 120 mi. (193 km.) long E India flowing S into Bay of Bengal

Huhehot — see HOHHOT

Hull \'həl\ *or* **Kings·ton upon Hull** \'kiŋ-stən\ city & port N England; *pop* 242,200

Hun·ga·ry \'həŋ-gə-rē\ country *cen* Europe; ✳, Budapest; *pop* 10,142,000

Hunt·ing·ton Beach \'hən-tiŋ-tən\ city SW California; *pop* 189,594

Hunts·ville \'hənts-,vil, -vəl\ city N Alabama; *pop* 158,216

Hu·ron, Lake \'hyùr-,än, 'yùr-\ lake E *cen* North America in U.S. & Canada; one of the Great Lakes

Hy·der·abad \'hī-d(ə-)rə-,bad, -,bäd\ **1** city S *cen* India; *pop* 3,449,878 **2** city SE Pakistan on the Indus; *pop* 1,166,894

Iba·dan \i-'bä-d°n, -'ba-\ city SW Nigeria; *pop* 1,263,000

Ibe·ri·an \ī-'bir-ē-ə\ peninsula SW Europe occupied by Spain & Portugal

Ice·land \'īs-lənd, 'īs-,land\ island SE of Greenland between Arctic & Atlantic oceans; country; ✳, Reykjavik; *pop* 282,849 — **Ice·land·er** \'īs-,lan-dər, 'īs-lən-\ *n*

Ida·ho \'ī-də-,hō\ state NW U.S.; ✳, Boise; *pop* 1,293,953 — **Ida·ho·an** \,ī-də-'hō-ən\ *adj or n*

Igua·çú *or* **Igua·zú** \,ē-gwə-'sü\ river 745 mi. (1199 km.) long S Brazil flowing W

IJs·sel *or* **Ijs·sel** \'ī-səl, 'ā-\ river 70 mi. (113 km.) long E Netherlands flowing out of Rhine N into IJsselmeer

IJs·sel·meer \'ī-səl-,mer, 'ā-\ *or* **Lake Ijs·sel** freshwater lake N Netherlands separated from North Sea by a dike; part of former Zuider Zee (inlet of North Sea)

Ilium — see TROY

Il·li·nois \,i-lə-'nói\ state N *cen* U.S.; ✳, Springfield; *pop* 12,419,293 — **Il·li·nois·an** \,i-lə-'nói-ən\ *adj or n*

Il·lyr·ia \i-'lir-ē-ə\ ancient country S Europe and Balkan Peninsula on the Adriatic — **Il·lyr·i·an** \-ē-ən\ *adj or n*

Im·pe·ri·al Valley \im-'pir-ē-əl\ valley SE corner of California & partly in NE Baja California, Mexico

In·chon \'in-,chən\ city South Korea on Yellow Sea; *pop* 2,466,338

In·de·pen·dence \,in-də-'pen-dən(t)s\ city W Missouri E of Kansas City; *pop* 113,288

In·dia \'in-dē-ə\ **1** subcontinent S Asia S of the Himalayas between Bay of Bengal & Arabian Sea **2** country consisting of major portion of the subcontinent; ✳, New Delhi; *pop* 896,567,000 **3** *or* **Indian Empire** before 1947 those parts of the subcontinent of India under British rule or protection

In·di·an \'in-dē-ən\ ocean E of Africa, S of Asia, W of Australia, & N of Antarctica

In·di·ana \,in-dē-'a-nə\ state E *cen* U.S.; ✳, Indianapolis; *pop* 6,080,485 — **In·di·an·an** \-'a-nən\ *or* **In·di·an·i·an** \-'a-nē-ən\ *adj or n*

In·di·a·nap·o·lis \,in-dē-ə-'na-pə-ləs\ city, ✳ of Indiana; *pop* 791,926

Indian River lagoon 165 mi. (266 km.) long E Florida between main part of the state & coastal islands

Indian Territory former territory S U.S. in present state of Oklahoma

In·dies \'in-(,)dēz\ **1** EAST INDIES **2** WEST INDIES

In·do·chi·na \,in-(,)dō-'chī-nə\ **1** peninsula SE Asia including Myanmar, Malay Peninsula, Thailand, Cambodia, Laos, & Vietnam **2** *or* **French Indochina** former country SE Asia consisting of area now forming Cambodia, Laos, & Vietnam — **In·do·Chi·nese** \-chī-'nēz, -'nēs\ *adj or n*

In·do·ne·sia \,in-də-'nē-zhə, -shə\ country SE Asia in Malay Archipelago consisting of Sumatra, Java, S & E Borneo, Sulawesi, W New Guinea, & many smaller islands; ✳, Jakarta; *pop* 187,468,250 — **In·do·ne·sian** \-zhən, -shən\ *adj or n*

In·dore \in-'dór\ city W *cen* India; *pop* 1,597,441

In·dus \'in-dəs\ river 1800 mi. (2897 km.) long S Asia flowing from Tibet NW & SSW through Pakistan into Arabian Sea

In·gle·wood \'in-gəl-,wùd\ city SW California; *pop* 112,580

In·land Sea \'in-,land, -lənd\ inlet of the Pacific in SW Japan between Honshu on N and Shikoku and Kyushu on S

Inner Hebrides — see HEBRIDES

Inner Mon·go·lia \-,män-'gōl-yə, män-, -'gō-lē-ə\ region N China; *pop* 21,456,798

Inside Passage protected shipping route between Puget Sound, Washington, & the lower part of Alaska

In·ver·ness \,in-vər-'nes\ town NW Scotland; *pop* 63,090

Io·ni·an \ī-'ō-nē-ən\ sea, arm of the Mediterranean between SE Italy & W Greece

Io·wa \'ī-ə-wə\ state N *cen* U.S.; ✳, Des Moines; *pop* 2,926,324 — **Io·wan** \-wən\ *adj or n*

Ips·wich \'ip-(,)swich\ town SE England; *pop* 115,500

Iqa·lu·it \ē-'ka-lü-ət\ town Canada, ✳ of Nunavut on Baffin Island; *pop* 5236

Iran \i-'rän, -'ran\ *formerly* **Per·sia** \'pərzhə\ country SW Asia; ✳, Tehran; *pop* 59,570,000 — **Irani** \-'rä-nē, -'ra-\ *adj or n* — **Ira·nian** \i-'rä-nē-ən, -'ran-ē-, -'rän-ē-\ *adj or n*

Iraq \i-'räk, -'rak\ country SW Asia in Mesopotamia; ✳, Baghdad; *pop* (est.) 24,683,000 — **Iraqi** \-'räk-ē, -'rak-\ *adj or n*

Ire·land \'ī(ə)r-lənd\ **1** *or Latin* **Hi·ber·nia** \hī-'bər-nē-ə\ island W Europe in the North Atlantic; one of the British Isles **2** *or* **Eire** \'er-ə\ country occupying major portion of the Ireland (island); ✳, Dublin; *pop* 3,917,203

Irian Jaya — see WEST PAPUA

Irish Sea arm of the North Atlantic between Great Britain & Ireland

Ir·kutsk \ir-'kütsk, ,ər-\ city S Russia near Lake Baikal; *pop* 639,000

Ir·ra·wad·dy \,ir-ə-'wä-dē\ river 1300 mi. (2092 km.) long Myanmar flowing S into Bay of Bengal

Ir·tysh \ir-'tish, ,ər-\ river over 2600 mi. (4180 km.) long *cen* Asia flowing NW & N from Altay Mountains in China, through Kazakhstan, & into W *cen* Russia

Ir·vine \'ər-,vīn\ city SW California; *pop* 143,072

Ir·ving \'ər-vin\ city NE Texas NW of Dallas; *pop* 191,615

Isfahan — see ESFAHAN

Is·lam·abad \is-'lä-mə-,bäd, iz-, -'la-mə-,bad\ city, ✳ of Pakistan; *pop* 529,180

Islas Malvinas — see FALKLAND ISLANDS

Isle of Man — see MAN, ISLE OF

Isle of Wight \'wīt\ island England in English Channel

Isle Roy·ale \'ī(-ə)l-'roi(-ə)l\ island Michigan in Lake Superior

Isles of Scilly 1 — see CORNWALL AND ISLES OF SCILLY **2** — see SCILLY

Is·ling·ton \'iz-lin-tən\ borough of N Greater London, England; pop 155,200

Ispahan — see ESFAHAN

Is·ra·el \'iz-rē(-ə)l, -(,)rā(-ə)l\ **1** kingdom in ancient Palestine consisting of lands occupied by the Hebrew people **2** or **Ephra·im** \'ē-frē-əm\ the N part of the Hebrew kingdom after about 933 B.C. **3** country SW Asia; ✳, Jerusalem; pop 4,037,620 — **Is·rae·li** \iz-'rā-lē\ adj or n

Is·tan·bul \is-tən-'bül, -,tan-, -,tän-, -'bül, 'is-tən-,, or with m for n\ formerly **Con·stan·ti·no·ple** \kän-,stan-tə-'nō-pəl\ city NW Turkey on the Bosporus & Sea of Marmara; pop 6,620,241

Is·tria \'is-trē-ə\ peninsula in Croatia & Slovenia extending into the N Adriatic — **Is·tri·an** \-trē-ən\ adj or n

It·a·ly \'i-tə-lē\ country S Europe including a boot-shaped peninsula & the islands of Sicily & Sardinia; ✳, Rome; pop 57,844,017

Itas·ca, Lake \ī-'tas-kə\ lake NW cen Minnesota; source of the Mississippi

Ivory Coast or **Côte d'Ivoire** \,kōt-də-'vwär\ country W Africa on Gulf of Guinea; official ✳, Yamoussoukro; seat of government, Abidjan; pop 13,459,000 — **Ivor·i·an** \(,)ī-'vōr-ē-ən\ adj or n — **Ivory Coast·er** \'kō-stər\ n

Iwo Ji·ma \ē-(,)wō-'jē-mə\ island Japan in W Pacific SSE of Tokyo

Izhevsk \'ē-,zhefsk\ or 1985–87 **Usti·nov** \'üs-ti-,nóf, -,nóv\ city W Russia; pop 651,000

Iz·mir \iz-'mir\ formerly **Smyr·na** \'smər-nə\ city W Turkey; pop 1,757,414

Jack·son \'jak-sən\ city, ✳ of Mississippi; pop 184,256

Jack·son·ville \'jak-sən-,vil\ city NE Florida; pop 735,617

Jai·pur \'jī-,púr\ city NW India; pop 2,324,319

James \'jāmz\ **1** — see DAKOTA **2** river 340 mi. (547 km.) long Virginia flowing E into Chesapeake Bay

James Bay the S extension of Hudson Bay between NE Ontario & W Quebec

James·town \'jāmz-,taún\ ruined village E Virginia on James River; first permanent English settlement in America (1607)

Jam·shed·pur \'jäm-,shed-,púr\ city E India; pop 570,349

Ja·pan \jə-'pan, ja-\ country E Asia consisting of Honshu, Hokkaido, Kyushu, Shikoku, & other islands in the W Pacific; ✳, Tokyo; pop 126,925,843

Japan, Sea of or **East Sea** arm of the Pacific between Japan & main part of Asia

Ja·va \'jä-və, 'ja-\ island Indonesia SW of Borneo; chief city, Jakarta; pop 107,581,306 — **Ja·va·nese** \,ja-və-'nēz, jä-, -'nēs\ n

Jef·fer·son City \'je-fər-sən\ city, ✳ of Missouri; pop 39,636

Jer·sey \'jər-zē\ — see CHANNEL

Jersey City NE New Jersey on Hudson River; pop 240,055

Je·ru·sa·lem \jə-'rü-s(ə-)ləm, -'rü-z(ə-)ləm\ city NW of Dead Sea, ✳ of Israel; pop 544,200

Jid·da or **Jid·dah** \'ji-də\ or **Jed·da** or **Jed·dah** \'je-də\ city W Saudi Arabia on Red Sea; pop 561,104

Ji·lin \'jē-'lin\ or **Ki·rin** \'kē-'rin\ city NE China; pop 1,036,858

Ji·nan or **Tsi·nan** \'jē-'nän\ city E China; pop 1,500,000

Jin·zhou or **Chin–chou** or **Chin-chow** \'jin-'jō\ city NE China; pop 400,000

Jiu·long \'jü-'lón\ or **Kow·loon** \'kaú-'lün\ **1** peninsula SE China in Hong Kong opposite Hong Kong Island **2** city on Jiulong Peninsula; pop 1,975,265

Jo·han·nes·burg \jō-'hä-nəs-,bərg, -'ha-\ city NE Republic of South Africa; pop 654,232

Jo·li·et \,jō-lē-'et\ city NE Illinois; pop 106,221

Jor·dan \'jór-dᵊn\ **1** river 200 mi. (322 km.) long Israel & Jordan flowing S from Syria into Dead Sea **2** country SW Asia in NW Arabia; ✳, Amman; pop 5,182,000 — **Jor·da·ni·an** \jór-'dā-nē-ən\ adj or n

Juan de Fu·ca, Strait of \,wän-də-'fyü-kə, ,hwän-də-\ strait 100 mi. (161 km.) long between Vancouver Island, British Columbia, & Olympic Peninsula, Washington

Ju·daea or **Ju·dea** \jü-'dē-ə, -'dā-\ region of ancient Palestine forming its S division under Persian, Greek, & Roman rule — **Ju·dean** \-ən\ adj or n

Ju·neau \'jü-(,)nō, jü-'\ city, ✳ of Alaska; pop 30,711

Ju·ra \'júr-ə\ mountain range extending along boundary between France & Switzerland N of Lake of Geneva

Jut·land \'jət-lənd\ **1** peninsula N Europe extending into North Sea and consisting of main part of Denmark & N portion of Germany **2** the main part of Denmark

Ka·bul \'kä-bəl, -,bül; kə-'bül\ city, ✳ of Afghanistan; pop (est.) 2,272,000

Ka Lae \'kä-'lä-ä\ or **South Cape** or

South Point most southerly point of Hawaii & of U.S.

Kal·a·ha·ri \ˌka-lə-ˈhär-ē, ˌkä-\ desert region S Africa N of Orange River in S Botswana & NW Republic of South Africa

Kalgan — see ZHANGJIAKOU

Ka·li·man·tan \ˌkä-lə-ˈman-ˌtan, ˌkä-lē-ˈmän-ˌtän\ **1** BORNEO — its Indonesian name **2** the S & E portion of Borneo belonging to Indonesia

Ka·li·nin·grad \kə-ˈlē-nən-ˌgrad, -nyən-, -ˌgrät\ *formerly* **Kö·nigs·berg** \ˈkā-nigz-ˌbərg\ city & port W Russia; *pop* 424,000

Kam·chat·ka \kam-ˈchat-kə, -ˈchät-\ peninsula 750 mi. (1207 km.) long E Russia

Kam·pa·la \käm-ˈpä-lä, kam-\ city, ✳ of Uganda; *pop* 773,463

Kampuchea — see CAMBODIA

Kan·da·har \ˈkən-də-ˌhär\ city SE Afghanistan; *pop* (est.) 359,700

Ka·no \ˈkä-(ˌ)nō\ city N cen Nigeria; *pop* 594,800

Kan·pur \ˈkän-ˌpu̇r\ city N India on the Ganges; *pop* 2,532,138

Kan·sas \ˈkan-zəs\ state W cen U.S.; ✳, Topeka; *pop* 2,688,418 — **Kan·san** \ˈkan-zən\ *adj or n*

Kansas City **1** city NE Kansas bordering on Kansas City, Missouri; *pop* 146,866 **2** city W Missouri; *pop* 441,545

Kao–hsiung \ˈkau̇-ˈshyu̇ŋ, ˈgau̇-\ city & port SW Taiwan; *pop* 1,405,860

Ka·ra·chi \kə-ˈrä-chē\ city S Pakistan on Arabian Sea; *pop* 9,339,023

Ka·ra·gan·da \ˌkär-ə-ˈgän-də\ *or* **Qa·ra·ghan·dy** \-dē\ city cen Kazakhstan; *pop* 608,600

Kar·a·ko·ram Pass \ˌkär-ə-ˈkȯr-əm\ mountain pass NE Kashmir in **Karakoram Range** (system connecting the Himalayas with the Pamirs)

Ka·re·lia \kə-ˈrē-lē-ə, -ˈrēl-yə\ region NE Europe in Finland & Russia; *pop* 800,000 — **Ka·re·lian** \kə-ˈrē-lē-ən, -ˈrēl-yən\ *adj or n*

Ka·roo *or* **Kar·roo** \kə-ˈrü\ plateau region W Republic of South Africa W of Drakensberg Mountains

Kash·mir \ˈkash-ˌmir, ˈkazh-, ˈkazh-ˌ, kash-ˈ, kazh-ˈ\ disputed territory N subcontinent of India; claimed by India & Pakistan — **Kash·mi·ri** \kash-ˈmi(ə)r-ē, kazh-\ *adj or n*

Ka·thi·a·war \ˌkä-tē-ə-ˈwär\ peninsula W India N of Gulf of Cambay

Kath·man·du *or* **Kat·man·du** \ˌkat-ˌman-ˈdü, ˌkät-ˌmän-\ city, ✳ of Nepal; metropolitan area *pop* 671,846

Kat·mai, Mount \ˈkat-ˌmī\ volcano 6715 ft. (2047 m.) S Alaska on Alaska Peninsula

Kat·te·gat \ˈka-ti-ˌgat\ arm of North Sea between Sweden & E coast of Jutland Peninsula of Denmark

Kau·ai \kä-ˈwä-ē\ island Hawaii NW of Oahu

Kau·nas \ˈkau̇-nəs, -ˌnäs\ city cen Lithuania; *pop* 378,943

Ka·wa·sa·ki \ˌkä-wä-ˈsä-kē\ city Japan in E Honshu S of Tokyo; *pop* 1,249,905

Ka·zakh·stan *or* **Ka·zak·stan** \ˌka-(ˌ)zak-ˈstan\ country NW cen Asia; ✳, Astana; *pop* 17,186,000 — **Ka·zakh** *also* **Ka·zak** \kə-ˈzak, -ˈzäk\ *n*

Ka·zan \kə-ˈzan\ city W Russia; *pop* 1,098,000

Kee·wa·tin \kē-ˈwā-tᵊn, -ˈwä-\ former district N Canada in E Northwest Territories NW of Hudson Bay; area now part of Nunavut

Ke·me·ro·vo \ˈkye-mə-rə-və\ city S cen Russia; *pop* 521,000

Ke·nai \ˈkē-ˌnī\ peninsula S Alaska E of Cook Inlet

Kennedy, Cape — see CANAVERAL, CAPE

Ken·sing·ton and Chel·sea \ˈken-ziŋ-tən-ənd-ˈchel-sē, ˈken(t)-siŋ-\ borough of W Greater London, England; *pop* 127,600

Kent \ˈkent\ county SE England — **Kent·ish** \ˈken-tish\ *adj*

Ken·tucky \kən-ˈtə-kē\ state E cen U.S.; ✳, Frankfort; *pop* 4,041,769 — **Ken·tuck·i·an** \-kē-ən\ *adj or n*

Ken·ya \ˈke-nyə, ˈkē-\ **1** mountain 17,058 ft. (5199 m.) cen Kenya **2** country E Africa S of Ethiopia; ✳, Nairobi; *pop* 28,662,239 — **Ken·yan** \-nyən\ *adj or n*

Key West \ˈwest\ city SW Florida on Key West (island); *pop* 25,478

Kha·ba·rovsk \kə-ˈbär-əfsk, kə-\ city SE Russia; *pop* 615,000

Kham·bhat, Gulf of \ˈkəm-bət\ *or* **Gulf of Cam·bay** \kam-ˈbā\ inlet of Arabian Sea in India N of Bombay

Khar·kiv \ˈkär-kəf, ˈkär-\ *or* **Khar·kov** \ˈkär-ˌkȯf, ˈkär-, -ˌkȯv, -kəf\ city NE Ukraine; *pop* 1,623,000

Khar·toum \kär-ˈtüm\ city, ✳ of Sudan; *pop* 1,950,000

Khy·ber \ˈkī-bər\ pass 33 mi. (53 km.) long on border between Afghanistan & Pakistan

Ki·bo \ˈkē-(ˌ)bō\ mountain peak 19,340 ft. (5895 m.) NE Tanzania; highest peak of Kilimanjaro & highest point in Africa

Kiel \ˈkēl\ — see NORD-OSTSEE

Ki·ev \ˈkē-ˌef, -ˌev, -if\ *or Ukrainian* **Kyiv** \ˈkyē-ü\ city, ✳ of Ukraine; *pop* 2,587,000

Ki·ga·li \kē-ˈgä-lē\ city, ✳ of Rwanda; *pop* 232,733

Ki·lau·ea \ˌkē-lä-ˈwä-ä\ volcanic crater Hawaii on Hawaii Island on E slope of Mauna Loa

Kil·i·man·ja·ro \ˌki-lə-mən-ˈjär-(ˌ)ō, -ˈja-(ˌ)rō\ mountain NE Tanzania; highest in Africa — see KIBO

Kil·lar·ney, Lakes of \ki-'lär-nē\ three lakes SW Ireland

Kings·ton \'kiŋ-stən\ city & port, ✱ of Jamaica; *pop* 103,771

Kingston upon Hull — see HULL

Kingston upon Thames borough of SW Greater London, England; *pop* 130,600

Kings·town \'kiŋz-ˌtaùn\ seaport, ✱ of Saint Vincent and the Grenadines; *pop* 15,670

Kin·sha·sa \kin-'shä-sə\ city, ✱ of Democratic Republic of the Congo; *pop* 3,804,000

Ki·ri·bati \'kir-ə-ˌbas\ island group W Pacific; country; ✱, Tarawa; *pop* 78,600

Kirin — see JILIN

Kirk·wall \'kər-ˌkwȯl\ town and port N Scotland, ✱ of Orkney Islands; *pop* 5947

Kishinev — see CHIŞINĂU

Ki·ta·kyu·shu \kē-ˌtä-'kyü-(ˌ)shü\ city Japan in N Kyushu; *pop* 1,011,471

Kitch·e·ner \'kich-nər, 'ki-chə-\ city SE Ontario, Canada; *pop* 190,399

Kit·ty Hawk \'kit-ē-ˌhȯk\ town E North Carolina; *pop* 2991

Klon·dike \'klän-ˌdīk\ region NW Canada in *cen* Yukon Territory in valley of Klondike River

Knox·ville \'näks-ˌvil, -vəl\ city E Tennessee; *pop* 173,890

Ko·be \'kō-bē, -ˌbā\ city Japan in S Honshu; *pop* 1,493,398

Ko·di·ak \'kō-dē-ˌak\ island S Alaska E of Alaska Peninsula

Ko·la \'kō-lə\ peninsula NW Russia

Ko·rea \kə-'rē-ə\ peninsula E Asia between Yellow Sea & Sea of Japan (East Sea); divided 1948 into independent countries of North Korea & South Korea — **Ko·re·an** \kə-'rē-ən\ *adj or n*

Ko·ror \'kȯr-ˌȯr\ town, ✱ of Palau; *pop* 13,303

Kos·ci·us·ko, Mount \ˌkä-zē-'əs-(ˌ)kō, ˌkä-sē-\ mountain 7310 ft. (2228 m.) SE Australia in SE New South Wales; highest in Great Dividing Range & in Australia

Ko·so·vo \'kȯ-sə-ˌvō, 'kä-\ autonomous province S Serbia and Montenegro; *pop* (est.) 2,092,000

Kowloon — see JIULONG

Krak·a·tau \ˌkra-kə-'taú\ *or* **Krak·a·toa** \-'tō-ə\ island & volcano Indonesia between Sumatra & Java

Kra·kow \'krä-ˌkaú, 'kra-, 'krä-, -(ˌ)kȯ, Pol 'krä-ˌküf\ city S Poland; *pop* 748,356

Kras·no·dar \ˌkräs-nə-'där\ city SW Russia; *pop* 635,000

Kras·no·yarsk \ˌkräs-nə-'yärsk\ city S *cen* Russia; *pop* 925,000

Kry·vyy Rih \kri-'vē-'riҟ\ *or* **Kri·voy Rog** \ˌkri-ˌvȯi-'rȯg, -'rȯk\ city SE *cen* Ukraine; *pop* 724,000

K2 \ˌkā-'tü\ *or* **God·win Aus·ten** \ˌgäd-wən-'ȯs-tən, ˌgȯ-, -'äs-\ mountain 28,250 ft. (8611 m.) N Kashmir in Karakoram Range; second highest in the world

Kua·la Lum·pur \ˌkwä-lə-'lùm-ˌpùr, -'ləm-, -ˌlùm-'\ city, ✱ of Malaysia; *pop* 1,145,075

Kuei·yang — see GUIYANG

Kun·lun \'kün-'lün\ mountain system W China extending E from the Pamirs; highest peak Ulugh Muztagh 25,340 ft. (7724 m.)

Kun·ming \'kùn-'miŋ\ city S China; *pop* 1,127,411

Kur·di·stan \ˌkùr-də-'stan, ˌkər-, -'stän; 'kər-də-ˌ\ region SW Asia chiefly in E Turkey, NW Iran, & N Iraq — **Kurd** \'kùrd, 'kərd\ *n* — **Kurd·ish** \'kùr-dish, 'kər-\ *adj*

Ku·ril *or* **Ku·rile** \'kyùr-ˌēl, 'kùr-; kyù-'rēl, kü-\ islands Russia in W Pacific between Kamchatka Peninsula & Hokkaido Island

Ku·wait \kù-'wāt\ **1** country SW Asia in Arabia at head of Persian Gulf; *pop* 1,355,827 **2** city, its ✱; *pop* 181,774 — **Ku·waiti** \-'wā-tē\ *adj or n*

Kuybyshev — see SAMARA

Kuz·netsk Basin \kùz-'netsk\ *or* **Kuzbas** *or* **Kuz·bass** \'kùz-ˌbas\ basin S *cen* Russia

Kwa·ja·lein \'kwä-jə-lən, -ˌlān\ island W Pacific in Marshall Islands

Kwang·ju *or* **Gwang·ju** \'gwäŋ-(ˌ)jü\ city SW South Korea; *pop* 1,350,948

Kwa·Zu·lu–Na·tal \kwä-'zü-(ˌ)lü-nə-'täl\ province E Republic of South Africa; *pop* 8,553,000

Kyo·to \kē-'ōt-ō\ city Japan in W *cen* Honshu; *pop* 1,467,785

Kyr·gyz·stan \ˌkir-gi-'stan, -'stän\ country W *cen* Asia; ✱, Bishkek; *pop* 4,526,000

Kyu·shu \'kyü-(ˌ)shü\ island Japan S of W end of Honshu; *pop* 13,445,561

Lab·ra·dor \'la-brə-ˌdȯr\ **1** peninsula E Canada between Hudson Bay & the Atlantic divided between the provinces of Quebec & Newfoundland and Labrador **2** the part of the peninsula belonging to the province of Newfoundland and Labrador — **Lab·ra·dor·ean** *or* **Lab·ra·dor·ian** \ˌla-brə-'dȯr-ē-ən\ *adj or n*

Lac·ca·dive \'la-kə-ˌdēv, -ˌdīv, -div\ islands India in Arabian Sea N of Maldive Islands

La·co·nia \lə-'kō-nē-ə, -nyə\ ancient country S Greece in SE Peloponnese; ✱, Sparta — **La·co·nian** \-nē-ən, -nyən\ *adj or n*

La·fay·ette \ˌla-fē-'et, ˌlä-\ city S Louisiana; *pop* 110,257

La·gos \'lä-ˌgäs, -ˌgōs\ city, former ✱ (1960–91) of Nigeria; *pop* 1,340,000

La·hore \lə-'hȯr\ city E Pakistan; *pop* 5,143,495

Lake District region NW England containing many lakes & mountains

Lake·hurst \'lāk-(,)hərst\ borough E New Jersey; *pop* 2522

Lake·wood \'lāk-,wùd\ city *cen* Colorado; *pop* 144,126

Lam·beth \'lam-bəth, -,beth\ borough of S Greater London, England; *pop* 220,100

La·nai \lə-'nī, lä-\ island Hawaii W of Maui

Lan·ca·shire \'laŋ-kə-,shir, -shər\ *or* **Lan·cas·ter** \'laŋ-kəs-tər\ county NW England — **Lan·cas·tri·an** \laŋ-'kas-trē-ən, lan-\ *adj or n*

Lan·cas·ter \'laŋ-kəs-tər, 'lan-,kas-tər\ city NW England; *pop* 125,600

Land's End \'landz-'end\ cape SW England; most westerly point of England

Lan·sing \'lan-siŋ\ city, ✳ of Michigan; *pop* 119,128

Lan·zhou *or* **Lan·chou** \'län-'jō\ city W China; *pop* 1,194,640

Laos \'laùs, 'lä-(,)ōs, 'lä-,äs\ country SE Asia in Indochina NE of Thailand; ✳, Vientiane; *pop* 4,533,000 — **Lao·tian** \lä-'ō-shən, 'laù-shən\ *adj or n*

La Paz \lä-'päz, -'pas\ city, administrative ✳ of Bolivia; *pop* 711,036

Lap·land \'lap-,land, -lənd\ region N Europe above the Arctic Circle in N Norway, N Sweden, N Finland, & Kola Peninsula of Russia — **Lap·land·er** \-,lan-dər, -lən-\ *n*

La·re·do \lə-'rā-(,)dō\ city S Texas on the Rio Grande; *pop* 176,576

Larne \'lärn\ district NE Northern Ireland; *pop* 29,181

Las·sen Peak \'la-sᵊn\ volcano 10,457 ft. (3187 m.) N California at S end of Cascade Range

Las Ve·gas \läs-'vā-gəs\ city SE Nevada; *pop* 478,434

Latin America **1** Spanish America and Brazil **2** all of the Americas S of the U.S. — **Latin–American** *adj* — **Latin American** *n*

Latin Quarter section of Paris, France S of the Seine

Lat·via \'lat-vē-ə\ country E Europe on Baltic Sea; ✳, Riga; *pop* 2,345,768

Lau·ren·tian Mountains \lò-'ren(t)-shən\ hills E Canada in S Quebec N of the Saint Lawrence on S edge of Canadian Shield

Laurentian Plateau — see CANADIAN SHIELD

La·val \lə-'val\ city S Quebec NW of Montreal; *pop* 343,005

Law·rence \'lòr-ən(t)s, 'lär-\ city NE corner of Massachusetts; *pop* 72,043

League of Nations political organization established at the end of World War I; replaced by United Nations 1946

Leb·a·non \'le-bə-nən\ **1** mountains Lebanon (country) running parallel to coast **2** country SW Asia on the Medi-

terranean; ✳, Beirut; *pop* 2,909,000 — **Leb·a·nese** \,le-bə-'nēz, -'nēs\ *adj or n*

Leeds \'lēdz\ city N England; *pop* 674,400

Lee·ward Islands \'lē-wərd, 'lü-ərd\ **1** islands Hawaii extending WNW from main islands of the group **2** islands South Pacific in W Society Islands **3** islands West Indies in N Lesser Antilles extending from Virgin Islands (on N) to Dominica (on S)

Le Ha·vre \lə-'hävrᵊ, -'häv\ city N France on English Channel; *pop* 190,924

Leh·man Caves \'lē-mən\ limestone caverns E Nevada

Leices·ter \'les-tər\ city *cen* England ENE of Birmingham; *pop* 270,600

Leices·ter·shire \'les-tər-,shir, -shər\ *or* **Leicester** county *cen* England

Lein·ster \'len(t)-stər\ province E Ireland; *pop* 2,105,579

Leip·zig \'līp-sig, -sik\ city E Germany; *pop* 503,191

Le·na \'lē-nə, 'lā-\ river about 2700 mi. (4345 km.) long E Russia, flowing NE & N from mountains W of Lake Baikal into Arctic Ocean

Leningrad — see SAINT PETERSBURG

Le·ón \lā-'ōn\ city *cen* Mexico; metropolitan area *pop* 1,174,180

Ler·wick \'lər-(,)wik, 'ler-\ town and port N Scotland in the Shetlands; *pop* 7223

Le·so·tho \lə-'sō-(,)tō, -'sü-(,)tü\ *formerly* **Ba·su·to·land** \bə-'sü-tō-,land\ country S Africa surrounded by Republic of South Africa; ✳, Maseru; *pop* 1,903,000

Lesser Antilles islands in the West Indies including Virgin Islands, Leeward Islands, & Windward Islands, Barbados, Trinidad, Tobago, & islands in the S Caribbean N of Venezuela — see GREATER ANTILLES

Le·vant \lə-'vant\ the countries bordering on the E Mediterranean — **Lev·an·tine** \'lev-ən-,tīn, -,tēn, lə-'van-\ *adj or n*

Lew·es \'lü-əs\ town S England

Lew·i·sham \'lü-ə-shəm\ borough of SE Greater London, England; *pop* 215,300

Lew·is with Har·ris \'lü-əs-with-'ha-rəs, -with-\ island NW Scotland in Outer Hebrides

Lex·ing·ton \'lek-siŋ-tən\ **1** city NE *cen* Kentucky; county *pop* 260,512 **2** town NE Massachusetts; *pop* 30,355

Ley·te \'lā-tē\ island Philippines S of Samar

Lha·sa \'lä-sə, 'la-\ city SW China, ✳ of Tibet; *pop* 106,885

Li·be·ria \lī-'bir-ē-ə\ country W Africa on the North Atlantic; ✳, Monrovia; *pop* 2,101,628 — **Li·be·ri·an** \-ē-ən\ *adj or n*

Lib·er·ty \'li-bər-tē\ *formerly* **Bed·loe's** \'bed-,lōz\ island SE New York; site of the Statue of Liberty

Li·bre·ville \'lē-brə-,vil, -,vēl\ city, ✳ of Gabon; *pop* 419,596

Lib·ya \'li-bē-ə\ country N Africa on the

Mediterranean W of Egypt; ✳, Tripoli; *pop* 4,573,000 — **Lib·y·an** \'li-bē-ən\ *adj or n*

Libyan desert N Africa W of the Nile in Libya, Egypt, & Sudan

Liech·ten·stein \'lik-tən-ˌstīn, 'lik-tən-ˌshtīn\ country W Europe between Austria & Switzerland; ✳, Vaduz; *pop* 33,525 — **Liech·ten·stein·er** \-ˌstī-nər, -ˌshtī-\ *n*

Lif·fey \'li-fē\ river 50 mi. (80 km.) long E Ireland

Li·gu·ria \lə-'gyur-ē-ə\ region NW on Ligurian Sea — **Li·gu·ri·an** \-ē-ən\ *adj or n*

Ligurian Sea arm of the Mediterranean N of Corsica

Li·lon·gwe \li-'lòn-(ˌ)gwā\ city, ✳ of Malawi; *pop* 498,185

Li·ma \'lē-mə\ city, ✳ of Peru; *pop* 5,825,900

Lim·a·vady \ˌli-mə-'va-dē\ district NW Northern Ireland; *pop* 29,201

Lim·po·po \lim-'pō-(ˌ)pō\ river 1000 mi. (1609 km.) long Africa flowing from Republic of South Africa into Indian Ocean in Mozambique

Lin·coln \'liŋ-kən\ **1** city, ✳ of Nebraska; *pop* 225,581 **2** city E England; *pop* 81,900

Lin·coln·shire \'liŋ-kən-ˌshir, -shər\ *or* **Lincoln** county E England

Line \'līn\ islands Kiribati S of Hawaii; *pop* 4782

Lis·bon \'liz-bən\ *or Portuguese* **Lis·boa** \lēzh-'vō-ə\ city, ✳ of Portugal; *pop* 564,657

Lis·burn \'liz-(ˌ)bərn\ district E Northern Ireland; *pop* 99,162

Lith·u·a·nia \ˌli-thə-'wā-nē-ə, ˌli-thyə-, -nyə\ country E Europe; ✳, Vilnius; *pop* 3,483,972

Lit·tle Rock \'li-t°l-ˌräk\ city, ✳ of Arkansas; *pop* 183,133

Liv·er·pool \'li-vər-ˌpül\ city NW England; *pop* 448,300

Li·vo·nia \lə-'vō-nē-ə, -nyə\ city SE Michigan; *pop* 100,545

Lju·blja·na \lē-ˌü-blē-'ä-nə\ city, ✳ of Slovenia; *pop* 323,291

Lla·no Es·ta·ca·do \'la-(ˌ)nō-ˌes-tə-'kä-(ˌ)dō, 'lä-, 'yä-\ *or* **Staked Plain** \'stäk(t)-\ plateau region SE New Mexico & NW Texas

Lo·bam·ba \lō-'bäm-bə\ town, legislative ✳ of Swaziland; *pop* (est.) 10,000

Lodz \'lüj, 'lädz\ city *cen* Poland WSW of Warsaw; *pop* 851,690

Lo·fo·ten \'lō-ˌfō-t°n\ islands NW Norway

Lo·gan, Mount \'lō-gən\ mountain 19,524 ft. (5951 m.) NW Canada in Saint Elias Range; highest in Canada & second highest in North America

Loire \lə-'wär, 'lwär\ river 634 mi. (1020 km.) long *cen* France flowing NW & W into Bay of Biscay

Lo·mé \lō-'mā\ city, ✳ of Togo; *pop* 229,400

Lo·mond, Loch \'lō-mənd\ lake S *cen* Scotland

Lon·don \'lən-dən\ **1** city SE Ontario, Canada; *pop* 336,539 **2** city, ✳ of England & of United Kingdom on the Thames; consists of **City of London** & **Greater London** metropolitan county; *pop* 6,377,900 — **Lon·don·er** \-də-nər\ *n*

Londonderry — see DERRY

Long Beach city SW California S of Los Angeles; *pop* 461,522

Long Island island 118 mi. (190 km.) long SE New York S of Connecticut

Long Island Sound inlet of the Atlantic between Connecticut & Long Island, New York

Lon·gueuil \lòn-'gāl\ city Canada in S Quebec E of Montreal; *pop* 128,016

Lor·raine \lə-'rān, lò-\ region NE France

Los An·ge·les \lòs-'an-jə-ləs\ city SW California; *pop* 3,694,820

Lou·ise, Lake \lü-'ēz\ lake SW Alberta, Canada

Lou·i·si·ana \lù-ˌē-zē-'a-nə, ˌlü-ə-zē-, ˌlü-zē-\ state S U.S.; ✳, Baton Rouge; *pop* 4,468,976 — **Lou·i·si·an·ian** \-'a-nē-ən, -'a-nyən\ *or* **Lou·i·si·an·an** \-'a-nən\ *adj or n*

Louisiana Purchase area W *cen* U.S. between Rocky Mountains & the Mississippi purchased 1803 from France

Lou·is·ville \'lü-i-ˌvil, -vəl\ city N Kentucky on the Ohio River; *pop* 256,231

Low Countries region W Europe consisting of modern Belgium, Luxembourg, & the Netherlands

Low·ell \'lō-əl\ city NE Massachusetts NW of Boston; *pop* 105,167

Lower 48 the continental states of the U.S. excluding Alaska

Low·lands \'lō-ləndz, -ˌlandz\ the *cen* & E part of Scotland

Lu·an·da \lü-'än-də\ city, ✳ of Angola; *pop* 1,544,400

Lub·bock \'lə-bək\ city NW Texas; *pop* 199,564

Lu·bum·ba·shi \ˌlü-büm-'bä-shē\ city SE Democratic Republic of the Congo; *pop* (est.) 1,138,000

Luck·now \'lək-ˌnaú\ city N India ESE of Delhi; *pop* 2,207,340

Lüda *or* **Lü·ta** — see DALIAN

Lu·ray Caverns \'lü-ˌrā, lü-'\ series of caves N Virginia

Lu·sa·ka \lü-'sä-kä\ city, ✳ of Zambia; *pop* 982,362

Lü·shun \'lü-'shùn, 'lœ-\ *or* **Port Ar·thur** \-'är-thər\ seaport NE China; part of greater Dalian

Lu·ton \'lü-t°n\ town SE *cen* England; *pop* 167,300

Lux·em·bourg *or* **Lux·em·burg** \'lək-səm-ˌbərg, 'lùk-səm-ˌbúrk\ **1** country W

Europe bordered by Belgium, France, & Germany; *pop* 392,000 **2** city, its ✻; *pop* 75,377 — **Lux·em·bourg·er** \-ˌbər-gər, -ˌbùr-\ *n* — **Lux·em·bourg·ian** \ˌlək-səm-ˈbər-gē-ən, ˌlùk-səm-ˈbùr-\ *adj*

Lu·zon \lü-ˈzän\ island N Philippines; *pop* 23,900,796

L'viv \lə-ˈvē-ü, -ˈvēf\ *or* **L'vov** \lə-ˈvóf, -ˈvóv\ *or Polish* **Lwów** \lə-ˈvüf, -ˈvüv\ city W Ukraine; *pop* 802,000

Lyallpur — see FAISALABAD

Lyd·ia \ˈli-dē-ə\ ancient country W Asia Minor on the Aegean — **Lyd·i·an** \-ē-ən\ *adj or n*

Lyon \ˈlyōⁿ\ *or* **Lyons** \lē-ˈōⁿ, ˈlī-ənz\ city SE *cen* France; *pop* 445,274

Ma·cao *or Portuguese* **Ma·cau** \mə-ˈkaù\ *or Chinese* **Ao·men** \ˈaù-ˈmən\ **1** special administrative region on coast of SE China W of Hong Kong; *pop* 488,000 **2** city, its ✻; *pop* 161,252 — **Mac·a·nese** \ˌmä-kə-ˈnēz, -ˈnēs\ *n*

Mac·e·do·nia \ˌma-sə-ˈdō-nē-ə, -nyə\ **1** region S Europe in Balkan Peninsula in NE Greece, the former Yugoslav section & now independent country of Macedonia, & SW Bulgaria including territory of ancient kingdom of Macedonia (**Mac·e·don** \ˈmas-ə-dən, -ə-ˌdän\ ) **2** country S *cen* Balkan Peninsula; ✻, Skopje; a former republic of Yugoslavia; *pop* 2,038,059 — **Mac·e·do·nian** \ˌmas-ə-ˈdō-nyən, -nē-ən\ *adj or n*

Mac·gil·li·cud·dy's Reeks \mə-ˈgi-lə-ˌkə-dēz-ˈrēks\ mountains SW Ireland; highest Carrantuohill 3414 ft. (1041 m.)

Ma·chu Pic·chu \ˌmä-(ˌ)chü-ˈpē-(ˌ)chü, -ˈpēk-\ site SE Peru of ancient Inca city

Mac·ken·zie \mə-ˈken-zē\ river 1120 mi. (1802 km.) long NW Canada flowing from Great Slave Lake NW into Beaufort Sea

Mack·i·nac, Straits of \ˈma-kə-ˌnò, -ˌnak\ channel N Michigan connecting Lake Huron & Lake Michigan

Ma·con \ˈmā-kən\ city *cen* Georgia; *pop* 97,255

Mad·a·gas·car \ˌma-də-ˈgas-kər, -kär\ *formerly* **Mal·a·gasy Re·public** \ˌma-lə-ˈga-sē\ island country W Indian Ocean off SE Africa; ✻, Antananarivo; *pop* 16,694,272 — **Mad·a·gas·can** \ˌma-də-ˈgas-kən\ *adj or n*

Ma·dei·ra \mə-ˈdir-ə, -ˈder-ə\ **1** river 2013 mi. (3239 km.) long W Brazil flowing NE into the Amazon **2** islands Portugal in the North Atlantic N of the Canary Islands; *pop* 245,011 **3** island; chief of the Madeira group — **Ma·dei·ran** \-ˈdir-ən, -ˈder-\ *adj or n*

Mad·i·son \ˈma-də-sən\ city, ✻ of Wisconsin; *pop* 208,054

Ma·dras \mə-ˈdras, -ˈdräs\ *or* **Chen·nai** \ˈche-ˌnī\ city SE India; *pop* 4,216,268

Ma·drid \mə-ˈdrid\ city, ✻ of Spain; *pop* 2,938,723

Ma·du·rai \ˌmä-də-ˈrī\ city S India; *pop* 922,913

Mag·da·len Islands \ˈmag-də-lən\ *or F* **Îles de la Ma·de·leine** \ˌēl-də-lä-mäd-ˈlen, -mä-də-ˈlen\ islands Canada in Gulf of Saint Lawrence between Newfoundland & Prince Edward Island

Ma·gel·lan, Strait of \mə-ˈje-lən, *chiefly Brit* -ˈge-\ strait at S end of South America between mainland & Tierra del Fuego

Magh·er·a·felt \ˈmär-ə-ˌfelt, ˈma-kə-rə-ˌfelt\ district *cen* Northern Ireland; *pop* 35,874

Maid·stone \ˈmād-stən, -ˌstōn\ town SE England; *pop* 133,200

Main \ˈmīn, ˈmän\ river 325 mi. (523 km.) long S *cen* Germany flowing W into the Rhine

Maine \ˈmān\ state NE U.S.; ✻, Augusta; *pop* 1,274,923 — **Main·er** \ˈmä-nər\ *n*

Ma·jor·ca \mä-ˈjór-kə, mə-, -ˈyór-\ *or Spanish* **Ma·llor·ca** \mä-ˈyór-kä\ island Spain in W Mediterranean — **Ma·jor·can** \-ˈjór-kən, -ˈyór\ *adj or n*

Ma·ju·ro \mə-ˈjùr-(ˌ)ō\ atoll, ✻ of Marshall Islands; *pop* (est.) 20,000

Mal·a·bar Coast \ˈma-lə-ˌbär\ region SW India on Arabian Sea

Ma·la·bo \mä-ˈlä-(ˌ)bō\ city, ✻ of Equatorial Guinea; *pop* 37,237

Ma·lac·ca, Strait of \mə-ˈla-kə, -ˈlä-\ channel between S Malay Peninsula & island of Sumatra

Ma·la·wi \mə-ˈlä-wē\ *formerly* **Ny·asa·land** \nī-ˈa-sə-ˌland, nē-\ country SE Africa on Lake Nyasa; ✻, Lilongwe; *pop* 10,475,257 — **Ma·la·wi·an** \-ən\ *adj or n*

Ma·lay \mə-ˈlā, ˈmā-(ˌ)lā\ **1** archipelago SE Asia including Sumatra, Java, Borneo, Sulawesi, Moluccas, & Timor; usu. thought to include the Philippines & sometimes New Guinea **2** peninsula SE Asia divided between Thailand & Malaysia (country)

Ma·laya \mə-ˈlā-ə, mä-\ **1** the Malay Peninsula **2** former country SE Asia on Malay Peninsula; now part of Malaysia

Ma·lay·sia \mə-ˈlā-zh(ē-)ə, -sh(ē-)ə\ **1** the Malay Archipelago **2** the Malay Peninsula & Malay Archipelago **3** country SE Asia; ✻, Kuala Lumpur; *pop* 19,077,000 — **Ma·lay·sian** \mə-ˈlā-zhən, -shən\ *adj or n*

Mal·dives \ˈmól-ˌdēvz, -ˌdīvz\ islands in Indian Ocean SW of Sri Lanka; country; ✻, Male Atoll; *pop* 270,101 — **Mal·div·i·an** \mól-ˈdi-vē-ən, mal-\ *adj or n*

Ma·le \ˈmä-lē\ atoll, ✻ of Maldives; *pop* (est.) 63,000

Ma·li \ˈmä-lē, ˈma-\ country W Africa; ✻, Bamako; *pop* 8,646,000 — **Ma·li·an** \-lē-ən\ *adj or n*

Mal·ta \ˈmól-tə\ islands in the Mediterranean S of Sicily; country since 1964; ✳, Valletta; *pop* 397,296 — **Mal·tese** \mŏl-ˈtēz, -ˈtēs\ *adj or n*

Malvinas, Islas — see FALKLAND IS-LANDS

Mam·moth Cave \ˈma-məth\ limestone caverns SW *cen* Kentucky

Man, Isle of \ˈman\ island British Isles in Irish Sea; has own legislature & laws; *pop* 60,496

Ma·na·gua \mä-ˈnä-gwä\ city, ✳ of Nicaragua; *pop* 552,900

Ma·na·ma \mə-ˈna-mə\ city, ✳ of Bahrain; *pop* 136,999

Man·ches·ter \ˈman-ˌches-tər, -chəs-tər\ 1 city S *cen* New Hampshire; *pop* 107,006 2 city NW England; *pop* 406,900

Man·chu·ria \man-ˈchu̇r-ē-ə\ region NE China S of the Amur — **Man·chu·ri·an** \-ē-ən\ *adj or n*

Man·hat·tan \man-ˈha-tᵊn, mən-\ 1 island SE New York in New York City 2 borough of New York City consisting chiefly of Manhattan Island; *pop* 1,537,195

Ma·nila \mə-ˈni-lə\ city, ✳ of Philippines in W Luzon; *pop* 1,587,000

Man·i·to·ba \ˌma-nə-ˈtō-bə\ province *cen* Canada; ✳, Winnipeg; *pop* 1,150,034 — **Man·i·to·ban** \-bən\ *adj or n*

Man·i·tou·lin \ˌma-nə-ˈtü-lən\ island 80 mi. (129 km.) long S Ontario in Lake Huron

Ma·pu·to \mä-ˈpü-(ˌ)tō, -(ˌ)tü\ city, ✳ of Mozambique; *pop* 966,800

Mar·a·cai·bo \ˌma-rə-ˈkī-(ˌ)bō, ˌmär-ä-\ city NW Venezuela; *pop* 1,207,513

Maracaibo, Lake extension of a gulf of the Caribbean NW Venezuela

Mar·a·thon \ˈma-rə-ˌthän\ plain E Greece NE of Athens

Mar·i·ana \ˌmer-ē-ˈa-nə\ islands W Pacific N of Caroline Islands; comprise Commonwealth of Northern Mariana Islands & Guam

Mariana Trench ocean trench W Pacific extending from SE of Guam to NW of Mariana Islands; deepest in world

Ma·rin·du·que \ˌma-rən-ˈdü-(ˌ)kā, ˌmärēn-\ island *cen* Philippines; *pop* 173,715

Maritime Provinces the Canadian provinces of New Brunswick, Nova Scotia, & Prince Edward Island & sometimes thought to include Newfoundland and Labrador

Ma·ri·u·pol \ˌma-rē-ˈü-ˌpȯl, -pəl\ *or* 1949–89 **Zhda·nov** \zhə-ˈdä-nəf\ city E Ukraine; *pop* 417,000

Mar·ma·ra, Sea of \ˈmär-mə-rə\ sea NW Turkey connected with Black Sea by the Bosporus & with Aegean Sea by the Dardanelles

Marne \ˈmärn\ river 325 mi. (523 km.) long NE France flowing W into the Seine

Mar·que·sas \mär-ˈkā-zəz, -zəs, -səz, -səs\

islands South Pacific; belonging to France; *pop* 7358 — **Mar·que·san** \-zən, -sən\ *adj or n*

Mar·ra·kech \ˌma-rə-ˈkesh, ˈma-rə-, mə-ˈrä-kish\ city *cen* Morocco; *pop* 439,728

Mar·seille \mär-ˈsā\ *or* **Mar·seilles** \mär-ˈsā, -ˈsālz\ city SE France; *pop* 797,491

Mar·shall Islands \ˈmär-shəl\ islands W Pacific E of the Carolines; republic, in association with U.S.; ✳, Majuro; *pop* 70,822

Mar·tha's Vineyard \ˈmär-thəz\ island SE Massachusetts off SW coast of Cape Cod WNW of Nantucket

Mar·ti·nique \ˌmär-tə-ˈnēk\ island West Indies in the Windward Islands; an overseas division of France; ✳, Fort-de-France; *pop* 377,000

Mary·land \ˈmer-ə-lənd\ state E U.S.; ✳, Annapolis; *pop* 5,296,486 — **Mary·land·er** \-lən-dər, -ˌlan-\ *n*

Mas·ba·te \mäz-ˈbä-tē, mäs-\ island *cen* Philippines

Mas·e·ru \ˈma-sə-ˌrü, -zə-\ city, ✳ of Lesotho; *pop* 71,500

Mash·had \mə-ˈshad\ city NE Iran; *pop* 1,463,508

Ma·son–Dix·on Line \ˈmā-sᵊn-ˈdik-sən\ boundary between Maryland & Pennsylvania; often considered the boundary between N & S states

Mas·qat \ˈməs-ˌkät\ *or* **Mus·cat** \-ˌkät, -kət\ town E Arabia, ✳ of Oman; *pop* 100,000

Mas·sa·chu·setts \ˌma-sə-ˈchü-səts, -zəts\ state NE U.S.; ✳, Boston; *pop* 6,349,097

Mat·a·be·le·land \ˌma-tə-ˈbē-lē-ˌland, ˌmä-tä-ˈbā-lä-\ region SW Zimbabwe

Mat·lock \ˈmat-ˌläk\ town N England; *pop* 20,610

Mat·ter·horn \ˈma-tər-ˌhȯrn, ˈmä-\ mountain 14,691 ft. (4478 m.) on border between Switzerland & Italy

Maui \ˈmau̇-ē\ island Hawaii NW of Hawaii Island

Mau·na Kea \ˌmau̇-nä-ˈkä-ä, ˌmȯ-\ extinct volcano 13,796 ft. (4205 m.) Hawaii in N *cen* Hawaii Island

Mau·na Loa \-ˈlō-ə\ volcano 13,680 ft. (4170 m.) Hawaii in S *cen* Hawaii Island

Mau·re·ta·nia *or* **Mau·ri·ta·nia** \ˌmȯr-ə-ˈtā-nē-ə, ˌmär-, -nyə\ ancient country NW Africa in modern Morocco & W Algeria — **Mau·re·ta·ni·an** *or* **Mau·ri·ta·ni·an** \-nē-ən, -nyən\ *adj or n*

Mauritania country NW Africa on the Atlantic N of Senegal River; ✳, Nouakchott; *pop* 2,171,000 — **Mauritanian** *adj or n*

Mau·ri·tius \mȯ-ˈri-sh(ē-)əs\ island in Indian Ocean E of Madagascar; country; ✳, Port Louis; *pop* 1,210,196 — **Mau·ri·tian** \-ˈri-shən\ *adj or n*

May, Cape \ˈmā\ cape S New Jersey at entrance to Delaware Bay

Ma·yon, Mount \mä-ʰyōn\ volcano 8077 ft. (2462 m.) Philippines in SE Luzon

Ma·yotte \mä-ʰyät, -ʰyȯt\ island Comoros group; French dependency; *pop* 90,000 — see COMOROS

Ma·za·ma, Mount \mə-ʰzäm-ə\ prehistoric mountain SW Oregon the collapse of whose top formed Crater Lake

Mba·bane \ˌəm-bä-ʰbä-nä\ *city*, ✳ of Swaziland; *pop* 57,992

Mbi·ni \em-ʰbē-nē\ *formerly* Río Mu·ni \ˌrē-ō-ʰmü-nē\ mainland portion of Equatorial Guinea

Mc·Al·len \mə-ʰka-lən\ city S Texas; *pop* 106,414

Mc·Kin·ley, Mount \mə-ʰkin-lē\ *or* De·na·li \də-ʰnä-lē\ mountain 20,320 ft. (6194 m.) S *cen* Alaska in Alaska Range; highest in U.S. & North America

Mead, Lake \ʰmēd\ reservoir NW Arizona & SE Nevada formed by Hoover Dam in Colorado River

Mec·ca \ʰme-kə\ city W Saudi Arabia containing the Great Mosque of Islam; *pop* 366,801

Me·dan \mä-ʰdän\ city Indonesia, in N Sumatra; *pop* 1,730,752

Me·de·llín \ˌme-də-ʰlēn, ˌmä-thä-ʰyēn\ city NW Colombia; *pop* 1,581,400

Me·di·na \mə-ʰdī-nə\ city W Saudi Arabia; *pop* 608,295

Med·i·ter·ra·nean \ˌme-də-tə-ʰrā-nē-ən, -nyən\ sea 2300 mi. (3700 km.) long between Europe & Africa connecting with the Atlantic through Strait of Gibraltar

Me·kong \ʰmā-ˌkȯŋ, -ʰkäŋ; ʰmä-ˌ\ river 2600 mi. (4184 km.) long SE Asia flowing from E Tibet S & SE into South China Sea in S Vietnam

Mel·a·ne·sia \ˌme-lə-ʰnē-zhə, -shə\ islands of the Pacific NE of Australia & S of Micronesia including Bismarck, the Solomons, Vanuatu, New Caledonia, & the Fijis

Mel·bourne \ʰmel-bərn\ city SE Australia, ✳ of Victoria; metropolitan area *pop* 2,761,995

Melos — see MÍLOS

Mel·ville \ʰmel-ˌvil\ **1** island N Canada, split between Northwest Territories & Nunavut **2** peninsula Canada in Nunavut

Mem·phis \ʰmem(p)-fəs\ **1** city SW Tennessee; *pop* 650,100 **2** ancient city N Egypt S of modern Cairo

Mem·phre·ma·gog, Lake \ˌmem(p)-fri-ʰmä-ˌgäg\ lake on border between Canada (Quebec) & United States (Vermont)

Men·do·ci·no, Cape \ˌmen-də-ʰsē-(ˌ)nō\ cape NW California

Mer·cia \ʰmər-sh(ē-)ə\ ancient Anglo-Saxon kingdom *cen* England — **Mer·cian** \ʰmər-shən\ *adj or n*

Mer·sey \ʰmər-zē\ river 70 mi. (113 km.)

long NW England flowing NW & W into Irish Sea

Mer·sey·side \ʰmər-zē-ˌsīd\ metropolitan county NW England; includes Liverpool

Mer·ton \ʰmər-tᵊn\ borough of SW Greater London, England; *pop* 161,800

Me·sa \ʰmā-sə\ city S *cen* Arizona; *pop* 396,375

Me·sa·bi Range \mə-ʰsä-bē\ region NE Minnesota that contains iron ore

Mes·o·po·ta·mia \ˌme-s(ə-)pə-ʰtä-mē-ə, -myə\ **1** region SW Asia between Euphrates & Tigris rivers **2** the entire Tigris–Euphrates valley — **Mes·o·po·ta·mian** \-mē-ən, -myən\ *adj or n*

Mes·quite \mə-ʰskēt, me-\ city NE Texas E of Dallas; *pop* 124,523

Meuse \ʰmyüz, ʰmə(r)z, ʰmœz\ river 580 mi. (933 km.) long W Europe flowing from NE France into North Sea in the Netherlands

Mex·i·co \ʰmek-si-ˌkō\ **1** country S North America; *pop* 89,995,000 **2** *or* **Mexico City** city, its ✳; metropolitan area *pop* 16,674,160 — **Mex·i·can** \ʰmek-si-kən\ *adj or n*

Mexico, Gulf of inlet of the Atlantic SE North America

Mi·ami \mī-ʰa-mē\ city & port SE Florida; *pop* 362,470

Miami Beach city SE Florida; *pop* 87,933

Mich·i·gan \ʰmi-shi-gən\ state N *cen* U.S.; ✳, Lansing; *pop* 9,938,444 — **Mich·i·gan·der** \ˌmi-shi-ʰgan-dər\ *n* — **Mich·i·ga·ni·an** \ˌmi-shə-ʰgä-nē-ən, -ʰga-\ *n* — **Mich·i·gan·ite** \ʰmi-shi-gə-ˌnīt\ *n*

Michigan, Lake lake N *cen* U.S.; one of the Great Lakes

Mi·cro·ne·sia \ˌmī-krə-ʰnē-zhə, -shə\ islands of the W Pacific E of the Philippines & N of Melanesia including Caroline, Kiribati, Mariana, & Marshall groups — **Mi·cro·ne·sian** \-zhən, -shən\ *adj or n*

Micronesia, Federated States of islands W Pacific in the Carolines; country in association with U.S.; ✳, Palikir; *pop* 134,597

Middle East the countries of SW Asia & N Africa — usually thought to include the countries extending from Libya on the W to Afghanistan on the E — **Middle Eastern** *adj*

Mid·dles·brough \ʰmi-dᵊlz-brə\ town N England; *pop* 141,100

Middle West — see MIDWEST

Mid Gla·mor·gan \ʰmid-glə-ʰmȯr-gən\ former county SE Wales

Mid·i·an \ʰmi-dē-ən\ ancient region NW Arabia E of Gulf of Aqaba — **Mid·i·an·ite** \-ē-ə-ˌnīt\ *n*

Mid·lands \ʰmid-ləndz\ the *cen* counties of England

Mid·way \ʰmid-ˌwā\ islands *cen* Pacific 1300 mi. (2092 km.) WNW of Honolulu belonging to U.S.

Mid·west \,mid-'west\ *or* **Middle West** region N *cen* U.S. including area around Great Lakes & in upper Mississippi valley from Ohio on the E to North Dakota, South Dakota, Nebraska, & Kansas on the W — **Mid·west·ern** \,mid-'wes-tərn\ *or* **Middle Western** *adj* — **Mid·west·ern·er** \,mid-'wes-tə(r)-nər\ *or* **Middle Westerner** *n*

Mi·lan \mə-'lan, -'län\ *or Italian* **Mi·la·no** \mē-'lä-(,)nō\ city NW Italy; *pop* 1,449,403 — **Mil·a·nese** \,mi-lə-'nēz, -'nēs\ *adj or n*

Mí·los *or* **Me·los** \'mē-,läs\ island Greece

Mil·wau·kee \mil-'wö-kē\ city SE Wisconsin on Lake Michigan; *pop* 596,974

Mi·nas Basin \'mī-nəs\ bay *cen* Nova Scotia; NE extension of Bay of Fundy

Min·da·nao \,min-də-'nä-,ō, -'naů\ island S Philippines; *pop* 13,966,000

Min·do·ro \min-'dòr-(,)ō\ island *cen* Philippines; *pop* 473,940

Min·ne·ap·o·lis \,mi-nē-'a-pə-lis\ city SE Minnesota; *pop* 382,618

Min·ne·so·ta \,mi-nə-'sō-tə\ state N *cen* U.S.; *, Saint Paul; *pop* 4,919,479 — **Min·ne·so·tan** \-'sō-t°n\ *adj or n*

Mi·nor·ca \mə-'nòr-kə\ island Spain in W Mediterranean — **Mi·nor·can** \mə-'nòr-kən\ *adj or n*

Minsk \'min(t)sk\ city, * of Belarus; *pop* 1,589,000

Mis·sis·sau·ga \,mi-sə-'sò-gə\ city Canada in S Ontario; *pop* 612,925

Mis·sis·sip·pi \,mi-sə-'si-pē\ **1** river 2340 mi. (3765 km.) long *cen* U.S. flowing into Gulf of Mexico — see ITASCA, LAKE **2** state S U.S.; *, Jackson; *pop* 2,844,658

Mis·sou·ri \mə-'zùr-ē\ **1** river 2466 mi. (3968 km.) long W U.S. flowing from SW Montana to the Mississippi in E Missouri (state) **2** state *cen* U.S.; *, Jefferson City; *pop* 5,595,211 — **Mis·sou·ri·an** \-'zùr-ē-ən\ *adj or n*

Mitch·ell, Mount \'mi-chəl\ mountain 6684 ft. (2037 m.) W North Carolina in the Appalachians; highest in U.S. E of the Mississippi

Mo·bile \mō-'bēl, 'mō-,bēl\ city SW Alabama on Mobile Bay (inlet of Gulf of Mexico); *pop* 198,915

Mo·des·to \mə-'des-(,)tō\ city *cen* California; *pop* 188,856

Mog·a·di·shu \,mä-gə-'di-(,)shü, ,mö-, -'dē-\ *or* **Mog·a·di·scio** \-(,)shō\ city, * of Somalia; *pop* 349,245

Mo·hawk \'mō-,hök\ river E *cen* New York flowing into the Hudson

Mo·hen·jo Da·ro \mō-'hen-(,)jō-'där-(,)ō\ prehistoric city in valley of the Indus NE of modern Karachi, Pakistan

Mo·ja·ve *or* **Mo·ha·ve** \mə-'hä-vē, mō-\ desert S California SE of S end of Sierra Nevada

Mol·da·via \mäl-'dā-vē-ə, -vyə\ region E Europe in NE Romania & Moldova — **Mol·da·vian** \-vē-ən, -vyən\ *adj or n*

Mol·do·va \mäl-'dō-və, mòl-\ country E Europe in E Moldavia region; *, Chişinău; *pop* 4,362,000 — **Mol·do·van** \-vən\ *adj or n*

Mol·o·kai \,mä-lə-'kī, ,mō-lō-'kä-ē\ island Hawaii ESE of Oahu

Mo·luc·cas \mə-'lə-kəz\ islands Indonesia E of Sulawesi; *pop* 1,857,790 — **Mo·luc·ca** \mə-'lə-kə\ *adj* — **Mo·luc·can** \-kən\ *adj or n*

Mom·ba·sa city & port S Kenya; *pop* 665,018

Mo·na·co \'mä-nə-,kō\ country W Europe on Mediterranean coast of France; *, Monaco; *pop* 30,500 — **Mo·na·can** \'mä-nə-kən, mə-'nä-kən\ *adj or n* — **Mon·e·gasque** \,mä-ni-'gask\ *n*

Mon·go·lia \män-'gōl-yə, mäŋ-, -'gō-lē-ə\ **1** region E Asia E of Altay Mountains; includes Gobi Desert **2** country E Asia consisting of major portion of Mongolia region; *, Ulaanbaatar; *pop* 2,182,000

Mo·non·ga·he·la \mə-,nän-gə-'hē-lə, -,näŋ-gə-, -'hä-lə\ river N West Virginia & SW Pennsylvania

Mon·ro·via \(,)mən-'rō-vē-ə\ city, * of Liberia; *pop* 243,243

Mon·tana \män-'ta-nə\ state NW U.S.; *, Helena; *pop* 902,195 — **Mon·tan·an** \-nən\ *adj or n*

Mont Blanc \mōⁿ-'bläⁿ\ mountain 15,771 ft. (4807 m.) SE France on Italian border; highest in the Alps

Mon·te·go Bay \män-'tē-(,)gō\ city & port NW Jamaica on Montego Bay (inlet of the Caribbean); *pop* 83,446

Mon·te·ne·gro \,män-tə-'nē-(,)grō, -'nä-, -'ne-\ republic of S Serbia and Montenegro on the Adriatic Sea; *pop* 616,327

Mon·ter·rey \,män-tə-'rā\ city NE Mexico; metropolitan area *pop* 3,022,268

Mon·te·vi·deo \,män-tə-və-'dā-(,)ō, -'vi-dē-,ō; ,mòn-tä-vē-'thä-ō\ city, * of Uruguay; *pop* 1,260,753

Mont·gom·ery \(,)mən(t)-'gə-mə-rē, män(t)-, -'gä-; -'gəm-rē, -'gäm-\ city, * of Alabama; *pop* 201,568

Mont·pe·lier \mänt-'pēl-yər, -'pil-\ city, * of Vermont; *pop* 8035

Mon·tre·al \,män-trē-'òl, ,mən-\ city S Quebec, Canada on Montreal Island in the Saint Lawrence; *pop* 1,039,534

Mont·ser·rat \,män(t)-sə-'rat\ island British West Indies in the Leeward Islands; *pop* 12,100

Mo·ra·via \mə-'rä-vē-ə\ region E Czech Republic — **Mo·ra·vi·an** \mə-'rä-vē-ən\ *adj or n*

Mo·rea \mə-'rē-ə\ PELOPONNESE — an old name — **Mo·re·an** \-'rē-ən\ *adj or n*

Mo·re·no Valley \mə-'rē-(,)nō\ city S California; *pop* 142,381

Mo·roc·co \mə-'rä-(,)kō\ country NW

Africa; ✳, Rabat; *pop* 29,631,000 — **Mo·roc·can** \-kən\ *adj or n*

Mo·ro·ni \mò-'rō-nē\ city, ✳ of Comoros; *pop* 23,432

Mos·cow \'mäs-(,)kō, -,kaù\ *or Russian* **Mos·kva** \màsk-'vä\ city, ✳ of Russia; *pop* 8,769,000

Mo·selle \mō-'zel\ river about 340 mi. (545 km.) long E France & W Germany

Moyle \'mòi(-ə)l\ district N Northern Ireland; *pop* 14,617

Mo·zam·bique \,mō-zəm-'bēk\ **1** channel SE Africa between Mozambique (country) & Madagascar **2** country SE Africa; ✳, Maputo; *pop* 16,099,246 — **Mo·zam·bi·can** \,mō-zəm-'bē-kən\ *adj or n*

Mpu·ma·lan·ga \əm-,pü-mä-'läŋ-gä\ province NE Republic of South Africa; *pop* 2,911,000

Mukden — see SHENYANG

Mul·tan \mùl-'tän\ city NE Pakistan SW of Lahore; *pop* 1,197,384

Mumbai — see BOMBAY

Mu·nich \'myü-nik\ *or German* **Mün·chen** \'muen-kən\ city S Germany in Bavaria; *pop* 1,229,052

Mun·ster \'mən(t)-stər\ province S Ireland; *pop* 1,100,614

Mur·cia \'mər-sh(ē-)ə\ region & ancient kingdom SE Spain — **Mur·cian** \-shən\ *adj or n*

Mur·ray \'mər-ē, 'mə-rē\ river 1609 mi. (2589 km.) long SE Australia flowing W from E Victoria into Indian Ocean in South Australia

Mur·rum·bidg·ee \,mər-əm-'bi-jē, ,mə-rəm-\ river almost 1000 mi. (1609 km.) long SE Australia in New South Wales flowing W into the Murray

Muscat — see MASQAT

Myan·mar \'myän-,mär\ *or* **Bur·ma** \'bər-mə\ country SE Asia; ✳, Yangon; *pop* 45,573,000

My·ce·nae \mī-'sē-(,)nē\ ancient city S Greece in NE Peloponnese

Myr·tle Beach \'mər-t²l\ city E South Carolina on the Atlantic; *pop* 22,759

My·sore \mī-'sòr\ city S India; *pop* 742,261

Nab·a·taea *or* **Nab·a·tea** \,na-bə-'tē-ə\ ancient Arab kingdom SE of Palestine — **Nab·a·tae·an** *or* **Nab·a·te·an** \-'tē-ən\ *adj or n*

Na·goya \nə-'gòi-ə, 'nä-gò-(,)yä\ city Japan in S cen Honshu; *pop* 2,171,557

Nag·pur \'näg-,pùr\ city E cen India; *pop* 2,051,320

Nai·ro·bi \nī-'rō-bē\ city, ✳ of Kenya; *pop* 2,083,509

Na·mib·ia \nə-'mi-bē-ə\ *formerly* **South–West Africa** country SW Africa on the Atlantic; ✳, Windhoek; *pop* 1,511,600 — **Na·mib·ian** \-bē-ən, -byən\ *adj or n*

Nan·chang \'nän-'chäŋ\ city SE China; *pop* 1,086,124

Nan·jing \'nän-'jiŋ\ *or* **Nan·king** \'nan-'kiŋ, 'nän-\ city E China; *pop* 2,090,204

Nan·tuck·et \nan-'tə-kət\ island SE Massachusetts S of Cape Cod; *pop* 6012

Na·per·ville \'nā-pər-,vil\ city NE Illinois W of Chicago; *pop* 128,358

Na·ples \'nā-pəlz\ *or Italian* **Na·po·li** \'nä-pō-lē\ *ancient* **Ne·ap·o·lis** \nē-'a-pə-ləs\ city S Italy on Bay of Naples; *pop* 1,000,470 — **Ne·a·pol·i·tan** \,nē-ə-'päl-ə-tən\ *adj or n*

Nar·ra·gan·sett Bay \,na-rə-'gan(t)-sət\ inlet of the Atlantic SE Rhode Island

Nash·ville \'nash-,vil, -vəl\ city, ✳ of Tennessee; *pop* 569,891

Nas·sau \'na-,sò\ city, ✳ of Bahamas on New Providence Island; *pop* 172,196

Na·tal \nə-'tal, -'täl\ former province E Republic of South Africa

Na·u·ru \nä-'ü-(,)rü\ island W Pacific S of the Equator; country; ✳, Yaren; *pop* 10,000 — **Na·u·ru·an** \-'ü-rə-wən\ *adj or n*

Naz·a·reth \'na-zə-rəth\ town of ancient Palestine in cen Galilee; now a city of N Israel; *pop* 49,800

N'Dja·me·na \ən-jä-'mä-nä, -'mē-\ city, ✳ of Chad; *pop* 687,800

Neagh, Lough \läk-'nä\ lake Northern Ireland; largest in British Isles

Near East the countries of NE Africa & SW Asia — **Near Eastern** *adj*

Ne·bras·ka \nə-'bras-kə\ state cen U.S.; ✳, Lincoln; *pop* 1,711,263 — **Ne·bras·kan** \-kən\ *adj or n*

Neg·ev \'ne-,gev\ desert region S Israel

Ne·gro \'nä-(,)grō, 'ne-\ river 1400 mi. (2253 km.) long in E Colombia & N Brazil flowing into the Amazon

Ne·gros \'nä-(,)grōs, 'ne-\ island cen Philippines

Ne·pal \nə-'pòl, nä-\ country Asia on NE border of India in the Himalayas; ✳, Kathmandu; *pop* 23,151,423 — **Nep·a·lese** \,ne-pə-'lēz, -'lēs\ *adj or n* — **Ne·pali** \nə-'pòl-ē, -'päl-, -'pal-\ *adj or n*

Ness, Loch \'nes\ lake NW Scotland

Neth·er·lands \'ne-thər-ləndz\ **1** *or Dutch* **Ne·der·land** \'näd-ər-,länt\ *also* **Holland** country NW Europe on North Sea; ✳, Amsterdam; seat of the government, The Hague; *pop* 15,009,000 **2** LOW COUNTRIES — an historical usage — **Neth·er·land** \'ne-thər-lənd\ *adj* — **Neth·er·land·er** \-,lan-dər, -lən-\ *n* — **Neth·er·land·ish** \-,lan-dish, -lən-\ *adj*

Netherlands Antilles islands of the West Indies belonging to the Netherlands; ✳, Willemstad; *pop* 190,566

Ne·va \'nē-və, 'nä-, nye-'vä\ river 40 mi. (64 km.) long W Russia; flows through Saint Petersburg

Ne·vada \nə-'va-də\ state W U.S.; ✳, Carson City; *pop* 1,998,257 — **Ne·vad·an** \-'va-dᵊn, -'vä-\ *adj or* **Ne·vad·i·an** \-'va-dē-ən, -'vä-\ *adj or n*

Ne·vis \'nē-vəs\ island West Indies in the Leeward Islands — see SAINT KITTS

New Amsterdam town founded 1625 on island of Manhattan by the Dutch; renamed New York 1664 by the British

New·ark \'nü-ərk, 'nyü-\ city NE New Jersey; *pop* 273,546

New Britain island W Pacific in Bismarck group; *pop* 263,500

New Bruns·wick \-'brənz-(ˌ)wik\ province SE Canada; ✳, Fredericton; *pop* 757,077

New Caledonia island SW Pacific SW of Vanuatu; an overseas department of France; ✳, Nouméa; *pop* 183,100

New·cas·tle \'nü-ˌka-səl, 'nyü-\ city SE Australia in E New South Wales; metropolitan area *pop* 262,331

Newcastle *or* **Newcastle upon Tyne** \'tīn\ city N England; *pop* 263,000

New Delhi city, ✳ of India S of Delhi; *pop* 294,783

New England section of NE U.S. consisting of states of Maine, New Hampshire, Vermont, Massachusetts, Rhode Island, & Connecticut — **New En·gland·er** \'iŋ-glən-dər\ *n*

New·found·land \'nü-fən(d)-lənd, 'nyü-, -ˌlənd; ˌnü-fən(d)-'lland, ˌnyü-\ island Canada in the Atlantic — **New·found·land·er** \-lən-dər, -ˌlan-\ *n*

Newfoundland and Labrador province E Canada consisting of Newfoundland Island and Labrador; ✳, Saint John's; *pop* 533,761

New France the possessions of France in North America before 1763

New Guinea **1** island W Pacific N of E Australia; divided between West Papua, Indonesia & independent Papua New Guinea **2** the NE portion of the island of New Guinea together with some nearby islands; now part of Papua New Guinea — **New Guinean** *adj or n*

New·ham \'nü-əm, 'nyü-\ borough of E Greater London, England; *pop* 200,200

New Hamp·shire \'hamp-shər, -ˌshir\ state NE U.S.; ✳, Concord; *pop* 1,235,786 — **New Hamp·shire·man** \-mən\ *n* — **New Hamp·shir·ite** \-ˌīt\ *n*

New Ha·ven \'hā-vən\ city S Connecticut; *pop* 123,626

New Hebrides — see VANUATU

New Jersey state E U.S.; ✳, Trenton; *pop* 8,414,350 — **New Jer·sey·an** \-ən\ *n* — **New Jer·sey·ite** \-ˌīt\ *n*

New Mex·i·co \'mek-si-ˌkō\ state SW U.S.; ✳, Santa Fe; *pop* 1,819,046 — **New Mex·i·can** \-si-kən\ *adj or n*

New Neth·er·land \'ne-thər-lənd\ former Dutch colony (1613–64) North America along Hudson & lower Delaware rivers

New Or·leans \'òr-lē-ənz, 'òr-lənz, 'òrl-yənz, (ˌ)òr-'lēnz\ city SE Louisiana; *pop* 484,674

New·port \'nü-ˌpòrt, 'nyü-, -ˌpòrt\ **1** town S England in Isle of Wight; *pop* 23,570 **2** city SE Wales; *pop* 129,900

Newport News \'nü-ˌpòrt-'nüz, 'nyü-ˌpòrt-'nyüz, -pərt-\ city SE Virginia; *pop* 180,150

New Providence island NW *cen* Bahamas; chief town, Nassau; *pop* 210,832

New·ry \'nü-rē, 'nyü-\ urban district S Northern Ireland

New South Wales state SE Australia; ✳, Sydney; *pop* 5,732,032

New Spain former Spanish possessions in North America, Central America, West Indies, & the Philippines

New Sweden former Swedish colony (1638–55) North America on W bank of Delaware River

New·town·ab·bey \ˌnü-tᵊn-'a-bē, ˌnyü-\ district E Northern Ireland; *pop* 73,832

Newtown Saint Bos·wells \'nü-ˌtaún-sənt-'bäz-wəlz, 'nyü-, -ˌsänt-\ village S Scotland

New World the Western Hemisphere including North America and South America

New York **1** state NE U.S.; ✳, Albany; *pop* 18,976,457 **2** *or* **New York City** city SE New York (state); *pop* 8,008,278 — **New York·er** \'yòr-kər\ *n*

New York State Barge Canal — see ERIE

New Zea·land \'zē-lənd\ country SW Pacific ESE of Australia; ✳, Wellington; *pop* 3,737,277 — **New Zea·land·er** \-lən-dər\ *n*

Ni·ag·a·ra Falls \(ˌ)nī-'a-g(ə-)rə\ falls New York & Ontario in **Niagara River** (flowing N from Lake Erie into Lake Ontario); divided by Goat Island into Horseshoe Falls, or Canadian Falls (158 ft. or 48 m. high) & American Falls (167 ft. or 51 m. high)

Nia·mey \nē-'ä-(ˌ)mā, nyä-'mā\ city, ✳ of Niger; *pop* 392,165

Ni·caea \nī-'sē-ə\ *or* **Nice** \'nīs\ ancient city W Bithynia; site at modern village in NW Turkey — **Ni·cae·an** \nī-'sē-ən\ *adj or n* — **Ni·cene** \'nī-ˌsēn, nī-'sēn\ *adj*

Ni·ca·ra·gua \ˌni-kə-'rä-gwə, ˌnē-kä-'rä-gwä\ **1** lake about 100 mi. (160 km.) long S Nicaragua **2** country Central America; ✳, Managua; *pop* 4,265,000 — **Ni·ca·ra·guan** \-'rä-gwən-'rä-gwən\ *adj or n*

Nice \'nēs\ city & port SE France on the Mediterranean; *pop* 345,892

Nic·o·bar \'ni-kə-ˌbär\ islands India in Bay of Bengal S of the Andamans; *pop* 14,563

Nic·o·sia \ˌni-kə-'sē-ə\ city, ✳ of Cyprus; *pop* 206,200

Ni·ger \'nī-jər, nē-'zher\ **1** river 2600 mi. (4184 km.) long W Africa flowing into Gulf of Guinea. **2** country W Africa N of Nigeria; ✻, Niamey; pop 8,516,000 — **Ni·ger·ien** \ˌnī-jir-ē-'en, nē-'zher-ē-ən\ adj or n — **Ni·ger·ois** \ˌnē-zhər-'wä, -zher-\ n

Ni·ge·ria \nī-'jir-ē-ə\ country W Africa on Gulf of Guinea; ✻, Abuja; pop 88,514,501 — **Ni·ge·ri·an** \-ē-ən\ adj or n

Nii·hau \'nē-ˌhau\ island Hawaii WSW of Kauai

Nile \'nī(-ə)l\ river 4160 mi. (6693 km.) long E Africa flowing from Lake Victoria in Uganda N into the Mediterranean in Egypt

Nil·gi·ri \'nil-gə-rē\ hills S India

Nin·e·veh \'ni-nə-və\ ancient city, ✻ of Assyria; ruins in Iraq on the Tigris

Nip·i·gon, Lake \'ni-pə-ˌgän\ lake Canada in W Ontario N of Lake Superior

Nizh·niy Nov·go·rod \'nizh-nē-'näv-gəˌräd, -'nóv-gə-rət\ formerly 1932–89 **Gor·ki** \'gór-kē\ city W Russia; pop 1,433,000

Nord–Ost·see \'nórt-'óst-'zā\ or **Kiel** \'kēl\ canal 61 mi. (98 km.) long N Germany across base of Jutland Peninsula connecting Baltic Sea & North Sea

Nor·folk \'nór-fək\ city & port SE Virginia; pop 234,403

Nor·man·dy \'nór-mən-dē\ region NW France NE of Brittany

North 1 river estuary of the Hudson between NE New Jersey & SE New York **2** sea, arm of the Atlantic E of Great Britain **3** island N New Zealand; pop 2,829,798

North·al·ler·ton \nór-'tha-lər-tən\ town N England; pop 9556

North America continent of Western Hemisphere NW of South America & N of the Equator — **North American** adj or n

North·amp·ton \nór-'tham(p)-tən, nórth-'ham(p)-\ town cen England; pop 145,421

North·amp·ton·shire \-ˌshir, -shər\ or **Northampton** county cen England

North Cape cape New Zealand at N end of North Island

North Car·o·li·na \ˌker(-ə)-'lī-nə, ˌka-rə-\ state E U.S.; ✻, Raleigh; pop 8,049,313 — **North Car·o·lin·ian** \-'li-nē-ən, -'li-nyən\ adj or n

North Da·ko·ta \də-'kō-tə\ state N U.S.; ✻, Bismarck; pop 642,200 — **North Da·ko·tan** \-'kō-t²n\ adj or n

North Down district E Northern Ireland; pop 70,308

Northern Cape province W Republic of South Africa; pop 749,000

Northern Cook islands S cen Pacific N of Cook Islands

Northern Hemisphere the half of the earth that lies N of the Equator

Northern Ireland region N Ireland comprising 26 districts of Ulster; a division of United Kingdom; ✻, Belfast; pop 1,685,267

Northern Mar·i·ana Islands \ˌmer-ē-'a-nə\ islands W Pacific; commonwealth in association with U.S.; ✻ on Saipan; pop 69,221

Northern Rhodesia — see ZAMBIA

Northern Territory territory N & cen Australia; ✻, Darwin; pop 169,300

North Korea or **Democratic People's Republic of Korea** country N half of Korean Peninsula in E Asia; ✻, Pyongyang; pop 22,646,000

North Las Vegas city SE Nevada; pop 115,448

North Slope region N Alaska between Brooks Range & Arctic Ocean

North·um·ber·land \nór-'thəm-bər-lənd\ county N England

North·um·bria \nór-'thəm-brē-ə\ ancient country Great Britain in what is now N England and S Scotland — **North·um·bri·an** \-brē-ən\ adj or n

North Vietnam — see VIETNAM

North West province N Republic of South Africa; pop 3,349,000

Northwest Passage sea passage between the Atlantic and the Pacific along the N coast of North America

Northwest Territories territory NW Canada consisting of the area of the mainland north of 60° between Yukon Territory & Nunavut; ✻, Yellowknife; pop 40,860

North York former city Canada in SE Ontario; now part of Toronto

North Yorkshire county N England

Nor·walk \'nór-ˌwók\ city SW California SE of Los Angeles; pop 103,298

Nor·way \'nór-ˌwā\ country N Europe in Scandinavia; ✻, Oslo; pop 4,552,200

Nor·wich \'nór-(ˌ)wich\ city E England; pop 120,700

Not·ting·ham \'nä-tiŋ-əm\ city N cen England; pop 261,500

Not·ting·ham·shire \'nä-tiŋ-əm-ˌshir, -shər\ or **Nottingham** county N cen England

Nouak·chott \nù-'äk-ˌshät\ city, ✻ of Mauritania; pop 393,325

Nou·méa \nü-'mā-ə\ city, ✻ of New Caledonia; pop 65,110

No·va Sco·tia \ˌnō-və-'skō-shə\ province SE Canada; ✻, Halifax; pop 942,691 — **No·va Sco·tian** \-shən\ adj or n

No·vo·kuz·netsk \ˌnō-(ˌ)vō-küz-'netsk, ˌnó-və-küz-'nyetsk\ city S Russia in Asia; pop 600,000

No·vo·si·birsk \ˌnō-(ˌ)vō-sə-'birsk, ˌnó-və-\ city S Russia in Asia; pop 1,442,000

Nu·bia \'nü-bē-ə, 'nyü-\ region NE Africa in Nile valley in S Egypt & N Sudan — **Nu·bi·an** \'nü-bē-ən, 'nyü-\ adj or n

Nu·ku·a·lo·fa \ˌnü-kü-ä-ˈlō-fä\ seaport, ✻ of Tonga; *pop* 22,400

Nu·mid·ia \nü-ˈmi-dē-ə, nyü-\ ancient country N Africa E of Mauretania in modern Algeria — **Nu·mid·i·an** \-dē-ən\ *adj or n*

Nu·na·vut \ˈnü-nə-ˌvüt\ semiautonomous territory NE Canada; ✻, Iqaluit; *pop* 28,159

Nu·rem·berg \ˈnur-əm-ˌbərg, ˈnyur-\ *or German* **Nürn·berg** \ˈnurn-ˌberk\ city S Germany; *pop* 497,496

Nuuk \ˈnük\ *or* **Godt·håb** \ˈgot-ˌhop\ town, ✻ of Greenland on SW coast; *pop* 12,181

Ny·asa, Lake \nī-ˈas-ə, nē-\ lake SE Africa in Malawi, Mozambique, & Tanzania

Nyasaland — see MALAWI

Oa·hu \ō-ˈä-(ˌ)hü\ island Hawaii; site of Honolulu

Oak·land \ˈō-klənd\ city W California on San Francisco Bay E of San Francisco; *pop* 399,484

Ob' \ˈäb, ˈob\ river over 2250 mi. (3620 km.) long W Russia in Asia flowing NW & N into Arctic Ocean

Oce·a·nia \ˌō-shē-ˈa-nē-ə, -ˈä-\ lands of the *cen* & S Pacific: Micronesia, Melanesia, Polynesia including New Zealand, & sometimes Australia & Malay Archipelago

Ocean·side \ˈō-shən-ˌsīd\ city SW California NNW of San Diego; *pop* 161,029

Oder \ˈō-dər\ *or* **Odra** \ˈo-drə\ river about 565 mi. (909 km.) long *cen* Europe flowing from Silesia NW into Baltic Sea; forms part of boundary between Poland & Germany

Odes·sa \ō-ˈde-sə\ city & port S Ukraine on Black Sea; *pop* 1,101,000

Ohio \ō-ˈhī-(ˌ)ō, ə-, -ə\ **1** river about 981 mi. (1578 km.) long E U.S. flowing from W Pennsylvania into the Mississippi **2** state E *cen* U.S.; ✻, Columbus; *pop* 11,353,140 — **Ohio·an** \-ˈhī-ō-ən\ *adj or n*

Oka·ya·ma \ˌō-kä-ˈyä-mä\ city Japan in W Honshu on Inland Sea; *pop* 626,642

Okee·cho·bee, Lake \ˌō-kə-ˈchō-bē\ lake S *cen* Florida

Oke·fe·no·kee \ˌō-kə-fə-ˈnō-kē, ˌō-kē-\ swamp SE Georgia & NE Florida

Okhotsk, Sea of \ō-ˈkätsk, ə-ˈkotsk\ inlet of the North Pacific E Russia in Asia

Oki·na·wa \ˌō-kə-ˈnä-wə, -ˈnau̇-ə\ **1** islands Japan in *cen* Ryukyus **2** island, chief of group — **Oki·na·wan** \-ˈnä-wən, -ˈnau̇-ən\ *adj or n*

Okla·ho·ma \ˌō-klə-ˈhō-mə\ state S *cen* U.S.; ✻, Oklahoma City; *pop* 3,450,654 — **Okla·ho·man** \-mən\ *adj or n*

Oklahoma City city, ✻ of Oklahoma; *pop* 506,132

Old·ham \ˈōl-dəm\ city NW England; *pop* 211,400

Old Point Comfort cape SE Virginia N of entrance to Hampton Roads

Ol·du·vai Gorge \ˈōl-də-ˌvī\ canyon N Tanzania SE of Serengeti Plain; site of fossil beds

Old World the half of the earth to the E of the Atlantic Ocean including Europe, Asia, and Africa & esp. the continent of Europe

Olym·pia \ə-ˈlim-pē-ə, ō-\ **1** city, ✻ of Washington; *pop* 42,514 **2** plain S Greece in NW Peloponnese

Olym·pic \-pik\ mountains NW Washington on Olympic Peninsula; highest Mt. Olympus 7965 ft. (2428 m.)

Olym·pus \ə-ˈlim-pəs, ō-\ mountains NE Greece

Omagh \ˈō-mə, -(ˌ)mä\ **1** district W Northern Ireland; *pop* 45,343 **2** town in Omagh district; *pop* 17,280

Oma·ha \ˈō-mə, -(ˌ)mä\ **1** beach NW France in Normandy **2** city E Nebraska on Missouri River; *pop* 390,007

Oman \ō-ˈmän, -ˈman\ country SW Asia in SE Arabia; ✻, Masqat; *pop* 2,477,687 — **Omani** \ō-ˈmä-nē, -ˈma-\ *adj or n*

Oman, Gulf of arm of Arabian Sea between Oman & SE Iran

Omsk \ˈom(p)sk, ˈäm(p)sk\ city SW Russia in Asia; *pop* 1,169,000

On·tar·io \än-ˈter-ē-ˌō\ **1** city SW California; *pop* 158,007 **2** province E Canada; ✻, Toronto; *pop* 11,874,436 — **Ontar·i·an** \-ē-ən\ *adj or n*

Ontario, Lake lake E *cen* North America in U.S. & Canada; one of the Great Lakes

Oran \ō-ˈrän\ city & port NW Algeria; *pop* 628,558

Or·ange \ˈär-inj, ˈär(-ə)nj, ˈor-inj, ˈor(-ə)nj\ **1** city SW California; *pop* 128,821 **2** river 1300 mi. (2092 km.) long S Africa flowing W from Drakensberg Mountains into the Atlantic

Orange Free State — see FREE STATE

Or·e·gon \ˈor-i-gon, ˈär-\ state NW U.S.; ✻, Salem; *pop* 3,421,399 — **Or·e·go·nian** \ˌor-i-ˈgō-nē-ən, ˌär-, -ˈnyən\ *adj or n*

Oregon Trail pioneer route to the NW about 2000 mi. (3220 km.) long from Missouri to Washington

Ori·no·co \ˌor-ē-ˈnō-(ˌ)kō\ river 1336 mi. (2150 km.) long Venezuela flowing into the Atlantic

Ork·ney \ˈork-nē\ islands N Scotland; *pop* 19,570

Or·lan·do \or-ˈlan-(ˌ)dō\ city *cen* Florida; *pop* 185,951

Osa·ka \ō-ˈsä-kä, ˈō-sä-ˌkä\ city Japan in S Honshu; *pop* 2,598,774

Osh·a·wa \ˈä-shə-wə, -ˌwä, -ˌwo\ city SE Ontario, Canada on Lake Ontario ENE of Toronto; *pop* 139,051

Os·lo \ˈäz-(ˌ)lō, ˈäs-\ city, ✻ of Norway; *pop* 507,831

Oś·wię·cim \ˌosh-ˈfyen-chēm\ *or German*

Ausch·witz \\'aush-,vits\\ town S Poland W of Krakow; *pop* 45,282

Ot·ta·wa \\'ä-tə-wə, -,wä, -,wò\\ **1** river 696 mi. (1120 km.) E Canada in SE Ontario & S Quebec flowing E into the Saint Lawrence **2** city, ✳ of Canada in SE Ontario on Ottawa River; *pop* 774,072

Ot·to·man Empire \\'ä-tə-mən\\ former Turkish sultanate in SE Europe, W Asia, & N Africa

Oua·ga·dou·gou \\,wä-gä-'dü-(,)gü\\ city, ✳ of Burkina Faso; *pop* 366,000

Outer Hebrides — see HEBRIDES

Over·land Park \\'ō-vər-lənd\\ city NE Kansas; *pop* 149,080

Ox·ford \\'äks-fərd\\ *cen* England; *pop* 109,000

Ox·ford·shire \\'äks-fərd-,shir, -shər\\ *or* **Oxford** county *cen* England

Ox·nard \\'äks-,närd\\ city SW California; *pop* 170,358

Ozark Plateau \\'ō-,zärk\\ *or* **Ozark Mountains** eroded plateau N Arkansas, S Missouri, & NE Oklahoma with E extension into S Illinois

Pa·cif·ic \\pə-'si-fik\\ ocean extending from Arctic Circle to the Equator (**North Pacific**) and from the Equator to the Antarctic regions (**South Pacific**) & from W North America & W South America to E Asia & Australia — **Pacific** *adj*

Pacific Islands, Trust Territory of the grouping of islands in W Pacific formerly under U.S. administration: the Carolines & the Marshalls

Pacific Rim the countries bordering on or located in the Pacific Ocean — used esp. of Asian countries on the Pacific

Pa·dang \\'pä-,daŋ\\ city Indonesia in W Sumatra; *pop* 631,543

Pa·dre \\'pä-drē, -,drä\\ island 113 mi. (182 km.) long S Texas in Gulf of Mexico

Pa·go Pa·go \\,pä-(,)gō-'pä-(,)gō, ,päŋ-(,)ō-'päŋ-(,)ō\\ town, ✳ of American Samoa on Tutuila Island; *pop* 4278

Painted Desert region N *cen* Arizona

Pak·i·stan \\'pa-ki-,stan, ,pä-ki-'stän\\ country S Asia NW of India; ✳, Islamabad; *pop* 131,434,000 — see EAST PAKISTAN — **Pak·i·stani** \\,pa-ki-'sta-nē, ,pä-ki-'stä-\\ *adj or n*

Pa·lau \\pə-'laù\\ *or* **Be·lau** \\bə-\\ island group W Pacific in the W Carolines in association with U.S.; country; ✳, Koror; *pop* 17,225 — **Pa·lau·an** \\pə-'laù-ən\\ *n*

Pa·la·wan \\pə-'lä-wən, -,wän\\ island W Philippines between South China & Sulu seas; *pop* 528,287

Pa·lem·bang \\,pä-ləm-'bäŋ\\ city Indonesia in SE Sumatra; *pop* 1,141,036

Pa·ler·mo \\pä-'ler-(,)mō, pä-'ler-\\ city Italy, ✳ of Sicily; *pop* 679,290

Pal·es·tine \\'pa-lə-,stīn\\ **1** ancient region SW Asia bordering on E coast of the Mediterranean and extending E of Jordan River **2** region bordering on the Mediterranean on W and Dead Sea on E; now approximately coextensive with Israel & the West Bank — **Pal·es·tin·ian** \\,pa-lə-'sti-nē-ən, -nyən\\ *adj or n*

Pa·li·kir \\,pä-lē-'kir\\ town, ✳ of Federated States of Micronesia on Pohnpei Island; *pop* 6227

Pal·i·sades \\,pa-lə-'sädz\\ line of high cliffs 15 mi. (24 km.) long on W bank of the Hudson in SE New York & NE New Jersey

Palm·dale \\'päm-,dāl, 'pälm-\\ city SW California W of Los Angeles; *pop* 116,670

Pa·mirs \\pə-'mirz\\ elevated mountainous region *cen* Asia in E Tajikistan & on borders of China, India, Pakistan, & Afghanistan; many peaks over 20,000 ft. (6096 m.)

Pam·li·co Sound \\'pam-li-,kō\\ inlet of the North Atlantic E North Carolina between main part of the state & offshore islands

Pam·pa \\'pam-pə\\ city NW Texas; *pop* 17,887

Pan·a·ma \\'pan-ə-,mä, -,mò, ,pan-ə-'mä, -'mò\\ **1** country S Central America; *pop* 2,839,177 **2** *or* **Panama City** city, its ✳ on the Pacific; *pop* 411,549 **3** canal 40 mi. (64 km.) long Panama connecting Atlantic & Pacific oceans — **Pan·a·ma·ni·an** \\,pan-ə-'mä-nē-ən\\ *adj or n*

Panama, Isthmus of *formerly* **Isthmus of Dar·i·en** \\,der-ē-'en\\ strip of land *cen* Panama connecting North America & South America

Panama Canal Zone — see CANAL ZONE

Pa·nay \\pə-'nī\\ island *cen* Philippines

Pan·gaea \\pan-'jē-ə\\ hypothetical land area believed to have once connected the landmasses of the Southern Hemisphere with those of the Northern Hemisphere

Pan·mun·jom *or* **Pan·mun·jeom** \\,pän-,mùn-'jəm\\ village on North Korea–South Korea border

Pao–t'ou — see BAOTOU

Pap·ua, Territory of \\'pa-pyü-wə, 'pä-pü-wə\\ former British territory consisting of SE New Guinea & offshore islands; now part of Papua New Guinea

Papua New Guinea country SW Pacific combining former territories of Papua & New Guinea; ✳, Port Moresby; *pop* 5,190,736

Par·a·guay \\'pa-rə-,gwī, -,gwä\\ **1** river 1584 mi. (2549 km.) long *cen* South America flowing from Brazil S into the Paraná in Paraguay **2** country *cen* South America; ✳, Asunción; *pop* 4,643,000 — **Par·a·guay·an** \\,pa-rə-'gwī-ən, -'gwä-\\ *adj or n*

Par·a·mar·i·bo \\,pa-rə-'ma-rə-,bō\\ city, ✳ of Suriname; *pop* 200,000

Pa·ra·ná \\,pär-ə-'nä\\ river about 2500 mi.

(4022 km.) long *cen* South America flowing S from Brazil into Argentina

Pa·ri·cu·tin \pä-,rē-kü-'tēn\ **1** former village Mexico **2** volcano on site of former village of Paricutin

Par·is \'pa-rəs\ city, ✱ of France; *pop* 2,125,851 — **Pa·ri·sian** \pə-'ri-zhən, -'rē-\ *adj or n*

Par·nas·sus \pär-'na-səs\ mountain *cen* Greece

Par·os \'pär-,ós\ island Greece — **Par·i·an** \'par-ē-ən, 'per-\ *adj*

Par·ra·mat·ta \,pa-rə-'ma-tə\ city SE Australia in New South Wales NW of Sydney; *pop* 132,798

Par·thia \'pär-thē-ə\ ancient country SW Asia in NE modern Iran — **Par·thi·an** \-thē-ən\ *adj or n*

Pas·a·de·na \,pa-sə-'dē-nə\ **1** city SW California E of Glendale; *pop* 133,936 **2** city SE Texas; *pop* 141,674

Pat·a·go·nia \,pa-tə-'gō-nyə, -nē-ə\ region South America S of about 40° S latitude in S Argentina & S tip of Chile; sometimes thought to include Tierra del Fuego — **Pat·a·go·nian** \-nyən, -nē-ən\ *adj or n*

Pat·er·son \'pa-tər-sən\ city NE New Jersey; *pop* 149,222

Pat·mos \'pat-məs\ island Greece SSW of Samos

Pat·na \'pət-nə\ city NE India on the Ganges; *pop* 1,376,950

Pearl Harbor inlet Hawaii on S coast of Oahu W of Honolulu

Peking — see BEIJING

Pe·li·on \'pē-lē-ən\ mountain 5089 ft. (1551 m.) NE Greece

Pel·o·pon·nese \'pe-lə-pə-,nēz, -,nēs\ or **Pel·o·pon·ni·sos** \,pe-lə-pə-'nē-səs\ peninsula forming S part of mainland of Greece

Pem·broke Pines \'pem-,brōk\ city SE Florida; *pop* 137,427

Pen·nine Chain \'pe-,nīn\ mountains N England; highest Cross Fell 2930 ft. (893 m.)

Penn·syl·va·nia \,pen(t)-səl-'vā-nyə, -nē-ə\ state E U.S.; ✱, Harrisburg; *pop* 12,281,054

Pe·o·ria \pē-'ôr-ē-ə\ **1** town SW *cen* Arizona; *pop* 108,364 **2** city N *cen* Illinois; *pop* 112,936

Per·ga·mum \'pər-gə-məm\ or **Per·ga·mus** \-məs\ ancient Greek kingdom including most of Asia Minor

Perm \'pərm, 'perm\ city E Russia in Europe; *pop* 1,099,000

Pernambuco — see RECIFE

Persia — see IRAN

Per·sian Gulf \'pər-zhən\ arm of Arabian Sea between Iran & Arabia

Perth \'pərth\ city, ✱ of Western Australia; *pop* 80,517

Pe·ru \pə-'rü, pā-\ country W South America; ✱, Lima; *pop* 22,916,000 — **Pe·ru·vi·an** \-'rü-vē-ən\ *adj or n*

Pe·tra \'pē-trə, 'pe-\ ancient city NW Arabia; site in SW Jordan

Petrograd — see SAINT PETERSBURG

Phil·a·del·phia \,fi-lə-'del-fyə, -fē-ə\ city SE Pennsylvania; *pop* 1,517,550 — **Phil·a·del·phian** \-fyən, -fē-ən\ *adj or n*

Phil·ip·pines \,fi-lə-'pēnz, 'fi-lə-,pēnz\ island group approximately 500 mi. (805 km.) off SE coast of Asia; country; ✱, Manila; *pop* 64,954,000 — **Phil·ip·pine** \,fi-lə-'pēn, 'fi-lə-,\ *adj*

Phnom Penh \(pə-)'näm-'pen, (pə-)'nóm-\ city, ✱ of Cambodia; *pop* 800,000

Phoe·ni·cia \fi-'ni-sh(ē-)ə, -'nē-\ ancient country SW Asia on the Mediterranean in modern Syria & Lebanon

Phoe·nix \'fē-niks\ city, ✱ of Arizona; *pop* 1,321,045

Phry·gia \'fri-j(ē-)ə\ ancient country W *cen* Asia Minor

Pic·ar·dy \'pi-kər-dē\ *or F* **Pi·car·die** \pē-kär-'dē\ region & former province N France bordering on English Channel N of Normandy — **Pi·card** \'pi-,kärd, -kərd\ *adj or n*

Pied·mont \'pēd-,mänt\ plateau region E U.S. E of the Appalachians between SE New York & NE Alabama

Pierre \'pir\ city, ✱ of South Dakota; *pop* 13,876

Pie·ter·mar·itz·burg \,pē-tər-'ma-rəts-,bərg\ city E Republic of South Africa; *pop* 128,598

Pigs, Bay of \'pigz\ *or* **Ba·hía de Co·chi·nos** \bä-'ē-ä-thä-kō-'chē-nōs\ bay W Cuba on S coast

Pikes Peak \'pīks\ mountain 14,110 ft. (4301 m.) E *cen* Colorado in a range of the Rockies

Pin·dus \'pin-dəs\ mountains W Greece; highest point 8136 ft. (2480 m.)

Pi·sa \'pē-zə, *It* -sä\ city W *cen* Italy W of Florence; *pop* 91,977

Pit·cairn \'pit-,kern\ island South Pacific; a British colony; *pop* less than 100

Pitts·burgh \'pits-,bərg\ city SW Pennsylvania; *pop* 334,563

Plac·id, Lake \'pla-səd\ lake NE New York

Pla·no \'plā-(,)nō\ city NE Texas N of Dallas; *pop* 222,030

Plov·div \'plóv-,dif, -,div\ city S Bulgaria; *pop* 379,083

Plym·outh \'pli-məth\ **1** town SE Massachusetts; *pop* 51,701 **2** city & port SW England; *pop* 238,800

Po \'pō\ river 405 mi. (652 km.) N Italy flowing into the Adriatic

Po Hai — see BO HAI

Pohn·pei \'pōn-,pā\ *or* **Po·na·pe** \'pō-nə-,pā\ island W Pacific in the E Carolines; part of Federated States of Micronesia

Po·land \'pō-lənd\ country *cen* Europe on

Baltic Sea; ✳, Warsaw; *pop* 38,038,400 — Pole *n*

Pol·y·ne·sia \ˌpä-lə-'nē-zhə, -shə\ islands of the *cen* & S Pacific including Hawaii, the Line, Tonga, Cook, & Samoa islands, & often New Zealand among others

Pom·er·a·nia \ˌpä-mə-'rä-nē-ə, -nyə\ region N Europe on Baltic Sea; formerly in Germany, now mostly in Poland

Po·mo·na \pə-'mō-nə\ city SW California E of Los Angeles; *pop* 149,473

Pom·peii \päm-'pā, -'pā-ˌē\ ancient city S Italy SE of Naples destroyed 79 A.D. by eruption of Vesuvius — Pom·pe·ian \-'pā-ən\ *adj or n*

Pon·ce \'pȯn(t)-(ˌ)sā\ city S Puerto Rico; *pop* 186,475

Pon·do·land \'pän-(ˌ)dō-ˌland\ region S Republic of South Africa

Pon·ta Del·ga·da \ˌpȯn-tə-del-'gä-də\ city & port Portugal, largest in the Azores; *pop* 65,854

Pont·char·train, Lake \'pänt-shər-ˌträn, ˌpänt-shər-'\ lake SE Louisiana E of the Mississippi & N of New Orleans

Pon·tus \'pän-təs\ ancient country NE Asia Minor — Pon·tic \'pänt-ik\ *adj or n*

Poole \'pül\ town S England on English Channel; *pop* 130,900

Po·po·ca·te·petl \ˌpō-pə-'ka-tə-ˌpe-t⁹l, -ˌka-tə-'\ volcano 17,887 ft. (5452 m.) SE *cen* Mexico

Port Arthur — see LÜSHUN

Port–au–Prince \ˌpȯrt-ō-'prin(t)s, ˌpȯr-(t)ō-'präⁿs\ city, ✳ of Haiti; *pop* 752,600

Port Jack·son \'jak-sən\ inlet of South Pacific SE Australia in New South Wales; harbor of Sydney

Port·land \'pȯrt-lənd\ 1 city SW Maine; largest in state; *pop* 64,249 2 city NW Oregon; *pop* 529,121

Port Lou·is \'lü-əs, 'lü-ē\ city, ✳ of Mauritius; *pop* 146,876

Port Mores·by \'mȯrz-bē\ city, ✳ of Papua New Guinea; *pop* 254,158

Por·to \'pȯr-(ˌ)tü\ city & port NW Portugal; *pop* 310,600

Por·to Ale·gre \'pȯr-(ˌ)tü-ä-'lā-grē\ city & port S Brazil; *pop* 1,360,590

Port of Spain city NW Trinidad, ✳ of Trinidad and Tobago; *pop* 49,031

Por·to–No·vo \ˌpȯr-tō-'nō-(ˌ)vō\ city, ✳ of Benin; *pop* 192,000

Port Phil·lip Bay \'fi-ləp\ inlet of South Pacific SE Australia in Victoria; harbor of Melbourne

Port Said \sä-'ēd, 'sīd\ city & port NE Egypt on the Mediterranean at N end of the Suez Canal; *pop* 262,760

Ports·mouth \'pȯrts-məth\ 1 city SE Virginia; *pop* 100,565 2 city S England; *pop* 174,400

Por·tu·gal \'pȯr-chi-gəl, ˌpür-tü-'gäl\ country SW Europe; ✳, Lisbon; *pop* 10,356,117

Portuguese India former Portuguese possession on W coast of India; became part of India 1962

Port–Vi·la \ˌpȯrt-'vē-lə\ *or* Vila city, ✳ of Vanuatu; *pop* 18,905

Po·to·mac \pə-'tō-mək, -mik\ river 287 mi. (462 km.) long flowing from West Virginia into Chesapeake Bay and forming boundary between Maryland & Virginia

Pough·keep·sie \pə-'kip-sē, pō-\ city & river port SE New York on the Hudson; *pop* 29,871

Po·wys \'pō-əs\ administrative subdivision E *cen* Wales

Prague \'präg\ *or* Czech Pra·ha \'prä-(ˌ)hä\ city, ✳ of Czech Republic; *pop* 1,162,179

Praia \'prī-ə\ town, ✳ of Cape Verde; *pop* 61,797

Prairie Provinces the Canadian provinces of Alberta, Manitoba, & Saskatchewan

Pres·ton \'pres-tən\ town NW England; *pop* 126,200

Pre·to·ria \pri-'tȯr-ē-ə\ city Republic of South Africa, administrative ✳ of the country; *pop* 303,684

Prib·i·lof \'pri-bə-ˌlȯf\ islands Alaska in Bering Sea

Prince Ed·ward Island \'ed-wərd\ island SE Canada in Gulf of Saint Lawrence; a province; ✳, Charlottetown; *pop* 138,514

Prince Ru·pert's Land \'rü-pərts\ historical region N & W Canada consisting of drainage basin of Hudson Bay

Prince·ton \'prin(t)-stən\ borough W *cen* New Jersey; *pop* 14,203

Prín·ci·pe \'prin(t)-si-pē\ island W Africa in Gulf of Guinea — see SÃO TOMÉ AND PRÍNCIPE

Pro·vence \prə-'vän(t)s, prō-'väⁿs\ region SE France on the Mediterranean

Prov·i·dence \'prä-və-dən(t)s, -ˌden(t)s\ city, ✳ of Rhode Island; *pop* 173,618

Pro·vo \'prō-(ˌ)vō\ city N *cen* Utah; *pop* 105,166

Prud·hoe Bay \'prü-(ˌ)dō, 'prə-\ inlet of Beaufort Sea N Alaska

Prus·sia \'prə-shə\ former kingdom, & later, state Germany — Prus·sian \'prə-shən\ *adj or n*

Pueb·lo \'pwe-ˌblō\ city SE *cen* Colorado SSE of Colorado Springs; *pop* 102,121

Puer·to Ri·co \ˌpȯr-tə-'rē-(ˌ)kō, ˌpwer-tō-\ island West Indies E of Hispaniola; a self-governing commonwealth associated with U.S.; ✳, San Juan; *pop* 3,808,610 — Puer·to Ri·can \-'rē-kən\ *adj or n*

Pu·get Sound \'pyü-jət\ arm of the North Pacific W Washington

Pu·ne \'pü-nə\ city W India, ESE of Bombay; *pop* 2,540,069

Pun·jab \ˌpən-'jäb, -'jab, 'pən-ˌ\ region in Pakistan & NW India in valley of the Indus

Pu·san \'pü-ˌsän, 'bü-\ *or* **Bu·san** \'bü-\ city SE South Korea; *pop* 3,655,437

Pyong·yang \'pyòŋ-'yaŋ, 'pyaŋ-, -'yäŋ\ city, ✳ of North Korea; *pop* 2,355,000

Pyr·e·nees \'pir-ə-ˌnēz\ mountains on French–Spanish border extending from Bay of Biscay to the Mediterranean; highest Pico de Aneto 11,168 ft. (3404 m.)

Qaraghandy — see KARAGANDA

Qa·tar \'kä-tər, 'gä-, 'gə-; kə-'tär\ country E Arabia on peninsula extending into Persian Gulf; ✳, Doha; *pop* 539,000 — **Qa·tari** \kə-'tär-ē, gə-\ *adj or n*

Qing·dao \'chiŋ-'daù\ *or* **Tsing·tao** \'chiŋ-'daù, '(t)siŋ-'daù\ city & port E China; *pop* 1,459,195

Qi·qi·har \'chē-'chē-'här\ *or* **Ch'i·ch'i·ha·erh** \'chē-'chē-'hä-'ər\ city NE China; *pop* 1,500,000

Que·bec \kwi-'bek, ki-\ *or French* **Qué·bec** \kā-'bek\ 1 province E Canada; *pop* 7,410,504 2 city, its ✳, on the Saint Lawrence; *pop* 169,076

Queens \'kwēnz\ borough of New York City on Long Island E of Brooklyn; *pop* 2,229,379

Queens·land \'kwēnz-ˌland, -lənd\ state NE Australia; ✳, Brisbane; *pop* 3,116,200 — **Queens·land·er** \-ˌlan-dər, -ˌlən-\ *n*

Que·zon City \'kā-ˌsòn\ city Philippines in Luzon; formerly ✳ of the country; *pop* 1,632,000

Qui·to \'kē-(ˌ)tō\ city, ✳ of Ecuador; *pop* 1,100,847

Ra·bat \rə-'bät\ city, ✳ of Morocco; *pop* 668,000

Rai·nier, Mount \rə-'nir, rā-\ mountain 14,410 ft. (4392 m.) W *cen* Washington; highest in Cascade Range

Raj·pu·ta·na \ˌräj-pə-'tä-nə\ *or* **Ra·ja·sthan** \'räj-ə-ˌstän\ region NW India S of Punjab

Ra·leigh \'rò-lē, 'rä-lē\ city, ✳ of North Carolina; *pop* 276,093

Ran·cho Cu·ca·mon·ga \'ran-(ˌ)chō-ˌkü-kə-'mäŋ-gə, 'rän-, -'mäŋ-\ city SW California; *pop* 127,743

Rand — see WITWATERSRAND

Rand·wick \'ran-(ˌ)dwik\ municipality SE Australia in E New South Wales; *pop* 115,349

Rangoon — see YANGON

Ra·wal·pin·di \ˌrä-wəl-'pin-dē, raùl-'-, ròl-'\ city NE Pakistan NNW of Lahore; *pop* 1,409,768

Read·ing \'re-diŋ\ town S England; *pop* 122,600

Re·ci·fe \ri-'sē-fē\ *formerly* **Per·nam·bu·co** \ˌpər-nəm-'bü-(ˌ)kō, -'byü-\ city NE Brazil; *pop* 1,422,905

Red \'red\ 1 river 1018 mi. (1638 km.) long flowing E on Oklahoma–Texas boundary and into the Atchafalaya & the Mississippi in Louisiana 2 sea between Arabia & NE Africa

Red·bridge \'red-(ˌ)brij\ borough of NE Greater London, England; *pop* 220,600

Re·gi·na \ri-'jī-nə\ city, ✳ of Saskatchewan, Canada; *pop* 178,225

Re·no \'rē-(ˌ)nō\ city NW Nevada; *pop* 180,480

Republic of the Congo — see CONGO 3

Ré·union \rē-'yü-nyən, ˌrā-ə-'nyō⁴\ island W Indian Ocean; an overseas division of France; ✳, Saint-Denis; *pop* 634,000

Reyk·ja·vik \'rā-kyə-ˌvik, -ˌvēk\ city, ✳ of Iceland; *pop* 112,490

Rhine \'rīn\ river 820 mi. (1320 km.) long W Europe flowing from SE Switzerland to North Sea in the Netherlands — **Rhen·ish** \'re-nish, 'rē-\ *adj*

Rhine·land \'rīn-ˌland, -lənd\ *or German* **Rhein·land** \'rīn-ˌlänt\ the part of Germany W of the Rhine — **Rhine·land·er** \'rīn-ˌlan-dər, -lən-\ *n*

Rhode Is·land \rōd-'ī-lənd\ 1 *or officially* **Rhode Island and Providence Plantations** state NE U.S.; ✳, Providence; *pop* 1,048,319 2 — see AQUIDNECK — **Rhode Is·land·er** \-lən-dər\ *n*

Rhodes \'rōdz\ island Greece in the SE Aegean

Rho·de·sia \rō-'dē-zh(ē-)ə\ — see ZIMBABWE — **Rho·de·sian** \-zh(ē-)ən\ *adj or n*

Rhone *or French* **Rhône** \'rōn\ river 505 mi. (813 km.) long Switzerland & SE France

Rich·mond \'rich-mənd\ 1 — see STATEN ISLAND 2 city, ✳ of Virginia; *pop* 197,790

Richmond upon Thames borough of SW Greater London, England; *pop* 154,600

Ri·ga \'rē-gə\ city, ✳ of Latvia; *pop* 747,157

Rio de Ja·nei·ro \ˌrē-(ˌ)ō-dā-zhə-'ner-(ˌ)ō, -dē-\ city SE Brazil on Guanabara Bay; *pop* 5,857,904

Rio Grande \ˌrē-(ˌ)ō-'grand, -'gran-dē\ *or Mexican* **Rio Bra·vo** \ˌrē-(ˌ)ō-'brä-(ˌ)vō\ river 1885 mi. (3034 km.) long SW U.S. forming part of U.S.–Mexico boundary and flowing into Gulf of Mexico

Río Muni — see MBINI

Riv·er·side \'ri-vər-ˌsīd\ city S California; *pop* 255,166

Riv·i·era \ˌri-vē-'er-ə\ coast region SE France & NW Italy

Ri·yadh \rē-'yäd\ city, ✳ of Saudi Arabia; *pop* 4,700,000

Ro·a·noke \'rō-(ə-)ˌnōk\ city W Virginia; *pop* 94,911

Roanoke Island island North Carolina S of entrance to Albemarle Sound

Rob·son, Mount \'räb-sən\ mountain 12,972 ft. (3954 m.) W Canada in E British Columbia; highest in the Canadian Rockies

Roch·es·ter \\'rä-chəs-tər, -₁ches-tər\ city W New York; *pop* 219,773

Rock·ford \\'räk-fərd\ city N Illinois; *pop* 150,115

Rocky Mountains *or* **Rock·ies** \\'rä-kēz\ mountains W North America extending SE from N Alaska to *cen* New Mexico

Roman Empire the empire of ancient Rome

Ro·ma·nia \rù-'mā-nē-ə, rō-, -nyə\ *or* **Ru·ma·nia** \rù-\ country SE Europe on Black Sea; *, Bucharest; *pop* 21,698,181

Rom·blon \räm-'blōn\ island group *cen* Philippines

Rome \\'rōm\ *or Italian* **Ro·ma** \\'rō-mä\ city, * of Italy; *pop* 2,655,970

Ro·sa·rio \rō-'zär-ē-₁ō, -'sär-\ city E *cen* Argentina on the Paraná; *pop* 591,428

Ro·seau \rō-'zō\ seaport, * of Dominica; *pop* 14,847

Ros·tov—on—Don \rə-'stóf-₁än-'dän, -'stóv, -₁ón-\ city S Russia in Europe; *pop* 1,027,000

Ros·well \\'räz-₁wel, -wəl\ city SE New Mexico; *pop* 45,293

Ro·ta \\'rō-tə\ island W Pacific in the Marianas

Rot·ter·dam \\'rä-tər-₁dam, -₁däm\ city & port SW Netherlands; *pop* 598,660

Ru·an·da—Urun·di \rü-'än-dä-ü-'rün-dē\ former trust territory E *cen* Africa bordering on Lake Tanganyika; now divided into Burundi & Rwanda

Rudolf, Lake — see TURKANA, LAKE

Ruhr \\'rùr\ **1** river 146 mi. (235 km.) long W Germany flowing NW & W to the Rhine **2** industrial district W Germany E of the Rhine in valley of Ruhr River

Rumania — see ROMANIA

Rupert's Land PRINCE RUPERT'S LAND

Rush·more, Mount \\'rəsh-₁mór\ mountain 5600 ft. (1707 m.) W South Dakota in Black Hills

Rus·sia \\'rə-shə\ **1** former empire largely having the same boundaries as U.S.S.R. **2** UNION OF SOVIET SOCIALIST REPUBLICS **3** country E Europe & N Asia; *, Moscow; *pop* 148,000,000

Ru·the·nia \rü-'thē-nyə, -nē-ə\ region W Ukraine W of the N Carpathians — **Ru·the·nian** \-'thē-nyən, -nē-ən\ *adj or n*

Ru·wen·zo·ri \₁rü-ən-'zór-ē\ mountain group E *cen* Africa between Uganda & Democratic Republic of the Congo; highest Mount Margherita 16,763 ft. (5109 m.)

Rwan·da *formerly* **Ru·an·da** \rü-'än-dä\ country E *cen* Africa; *, Kigali; *pop* 7,584,000 — **Rwan·dan** \-dən\ *adj or n*

Ryu·kyu \rē-'yü-(₁)kyü, -(₁)kü\ islands Japan extending in an arc from S Japan, to N tip of Taiwan; *pop* 1,222,458 — **Ryu·kyu·an** \-₁kyü-ən, -₁kü-\ *adj or n*

Saar \\'sär, 'zär\ **1** river about 150 mi. (241 km.) long Europe flowing from E France to W Germany **2** *or* **Saar·land** \\'sär-₁land, 'zär-\ region W Europe in valley of Saar River between France & Germany

Sac·ra·men·to \₁sa-krə-'men-(₁)tō\ **1** river 382 mi. (615 km.) long N California flowing S into Suisun Bay **2** city, * of California; *pop* 407,018

Sag·ue·nay \\'sa-gə-₁nā, ₁sa-gə-'\ river 105 mi. (169 km.) long Canada in S Quebec flowing E into the Saint Lawrence

Sa·ha·ra \sə-'her-ə, -'här-\ desert region N Africa extending from Atlantic coast to Red Sea — **Sa·ha·ran** \-ən\ *adj*

Sa·hel \\'sa-hil, sə-'hil\ the S fringe of the Sahara

Saigon — see HO CHI MINH CITY

Saint Al·bans \\'ól-bənz\ city SE England; *pop* 122,400

Saint Cath·a·rines \\'ka-th(ə-)rənz\ city Canada in SE Ontario; *pop* 129,170

Saint Christopher — see SAINT KITTS

Saint Clair, Lake \\'kler\ lake SE Michigan & SE Ontario connected by **Saint Clair River** (40 mi. or 64 km. long) with Lake Huron & draining by Detroit River into Lake Erie

Saint Croix \sānt-'krói, sənt-\ **1** river 129 mi. (208 km.) long Canada & U.S. on border between New Brunswick & Maine **2** island West Indies; largest of Virgin Islands of the U.S.; *pop* 50,139

Saint Eli·as, Mount \i-'lī-əs\ mountain 18,008 ft. (5489 m.) on Alaska–Canada boundary in **Saint Elias Range**

Saint George's \\'jór-jəz\ town, * of Grenada; *pop* 29,400

Saint George's Channel channel British Isles between SW Wales & Ireland

Saint Gott·hard \sānt-'gä-tərd, sənt-, 'gät-hərd\ pass S *cen* Switzerland in Saint Gotthard Range of the Alps

Saint He·le·na \₁sānt-ə-'lē-nə, ₁sänt-hə-'lē-\ island South Atlantic; a British colony; *pop* 5644

Saint Hel·ens, Mount \sānt-'he-lənz, sənt-\ volcano S Washington

Saint John \sānt-'jän, sənt-\ city & port Canada in New Brunswick; *pop* 69,661

Saint John's \sänt-'jänz, sənt-\ **1** city, * of Antigua and Barbuda; *pop* 22,342 **2** city, * of Newfoundland and Labrador, Canada; *pop* 99,182

Saint Kitts \\'kits\ *or* **Saint Chris·to·pher** \\'kris-tə-fər\ island West Indies in the Leeward Islands; with Nevis forms independent **Saint Kitts–Nevis**; *, Basseterre (on Saint Kitts); *pop* 41,800

Saint Law·rence \sānt-'lór-ən(t)s, sənt-, -'lär-\ **1** river 760 mi. (1223 km.) long E Canada in Ontario & Quebec bordering on U.S. in New York and flowing from Lake Ontario NE into the **Gulf of Saint Lawrence** (inlet of the Atlantic) **2** seaway Canada & U.S. in and along the Saint

Lawrence between Lake Ontario & Montreal

Saint Lou·is \sānt-'lü-əs, sənt-\ city E Missouri on the Mississippi; *pop* 348,189

Saint Lu·cia \sānt-'lü-shə, sənt-\ island West Indies in the Windwards S of Martinique; country; ✳, Castries; *pop* 157,775

Saint Mo·ritz \ˌsānt-mə-'rits, ˌsaⁿ-mə-\ or *G* **Sankt Mo·ritz** \ˌzäŋkt-mə-'rits\ town E Switzerland; *pop* 5900

Saint Paul \'pȯl\ city, ✳ of Minnesota; *pop* 287,151

Saint Pe·ters·burg \'pē-tərz-ˌbərg\ **1** city W Florida; *pop* 248,232 **2** *formerly* 1914–24 **Pet·ro·grad** \'pe-trə-ˌgrad, -ˌgrät\ or 1924–91 **Le·nin·grad** \'le-nən-ˌgrad, -ˌgrät\ city W Russia in Europe; *pop* 4,952,000

Saint Thom·as \'tä-məs\ island West Indies, one of Virgin Islands of the U.S.; chief town, Charlotte Amalie

Saint Vin·cent \sānt-'vin(t)-sənt, sənt-\ island West Indies in the *cen* Windward Islands; with N Grenadines forms independent **Saint Vincent and the Grenadines**; ✳, Kingstown (on Saint Vincent); *pop* 109,000

Sai·pan \sī-'pan, -'pän, 'sī-ˌ\ island W Pacific in the Marianas; *pop* 38,896

Sa·kai \(ˌ)sä-'kī\ city Japan in S Honshu; *pop* 792,018

Sa·kha·lin \'sa-kə-ˌlēn, -lən; ˌsä-kä-'lēn\ island SE Russia in W Pacific N of Hokkaido, Japan

Sal·a·mis \'sa-lə-məs\ ancient city Cyprus on E coast

Sa·lem \'sā-ləm\ city, ✳ of Oregon; *pop* 136,924

Sa·li·nas \sə-'lē-nəs\ city W California; *pop* 151,060

Salisbury — see HARARE

Salisbury Plain plateau S England; site of Stonehenge

Salop — see SHROPSHIRE

Salt Lake City city, ✳ of Utah; *pop* 181,743

Sal·ton Sea \'sȯl-t°n\ saline lake about 235 ft. (72 m.) below sea level SE California; formed by diversion of water from Colorado River

Sal·va·dor \'sal-və-ˌdȯr, ˌsal-və-'\ or Ba·hia \bä-'ē-ə\ city NE Brazil on the Atlantic; *pop* 2,443,107 — **Sal·va·dor·an** \ˌsal-və-'dȯr-ən\ or **Sal·va·dor·ean** or **Sal·va·dor·ian** \-ē-ən\ *adj or n*

Sal·ween \'sal-ˌwēn\ river about 1500 mi. (2415 km.) long SE Asia flowing from Tibet S into Bay of Bengal in Myanmar

Sa·mar \'sä-ˌmär\ island *cen* Philippines

Sa·ma·ra \sə-'mär-ə\ or 1935–91 **Kuy·by·shev** \'kwē-bə-ˌshef, 'kü-ē-bə-, -ˌshev\ city W Russia, on the Volga; *pop* 1,239,000

Sa·mar·ia \sə-'mer-ē-ə\ district of ancient Palestine W of the Jordan between Galilee & Judaea

Sam·ar·qand or **Sam·ar·kand** \'sa-mər-ˌkand\ city E Uzbekistan; *pop* 370,500

Sam·ni·um \'sam-nē-əm\ ancient country S *cen* Italy — **Sam·nite** \'sam-ˌnīt\ *adj or n*

Sa·moa \sə-'mō-ə\ **1** islands SW *cen* Pacific N of Tonga; divided at longitude 171° W into American Samoa (or Eastern Samoa) & independent Samoa **2** *formerly* **Western Samoa** islands Samoa W of 171° W; country; ✳ Apia; *pop* 156,349 — **Sa·mo·an** \sə-'mō-ən\ *adj or n*

Sa·mos \'sā-ˌmäs, 'sä-ˌmös\ island Greece in the Aegean off coast of Turkey

San·aa or **Sana** \sa-'nä, 'sa-ˌnä\ city SW Arabia, ✳ of Yemen; *pop* 125,093

San An·dre·as Fault \ˌsan-an-'drā-əs\ zone of faults in California extending from N coast toward head of Gulf of California

San An·to·nio \ˌsan-ən-'tō-nē-ˌō\ city S Texas; *pop* 1,144,646

San Ber·nar·di·no \ˌsan-ˌbər-nə(r)-'dē-(ˌ)nō\ city S California; *pop* 185,401

San Di·ego \ˌsan-dē-'ā-(ˌ)gō\ coastal city SW California; *pop* 1,223,400

San·i·bel Island \'sa-nə-bəl, -ˌbel\ island SW Florida

Sand·wich \'san(d)-(ˌ)wich\ town SE England; *pop* 4227

Sandwich Islands — see HAWAII

San Fran·cis·co \ˌsan-frən-'sis-(ˌ)kō\ city W California on San Francisco Bay & Pacific Ocean; *pop* 776,733

San Joa·quin \ˌsan-wä-'kēn, -wȯ-\ river 350 mi. (563 km.) long *cen* California flowing NW into the Sacramento

San Jo·se \ˌsan-(h)ō-'zā\ city W California SE of San Francisco; *pop* 894,943

San Jo·sé \ˌsän-hō-'sā, ˌsan-(h)ō-'zā\ city, ✳ of Costa Rica; *pop* 330,529

San Juan \san-'wän, ˌsän-'hwän\ city, ✳ of Puerto Rico; *pop* 434,374

San Ma·ri·no \ˌsan-mə-'rē-(ˌ)nō\ **1** small country S Europe surrounded by Italy ENE of Florence near Adriatic Sea; *pop* 24,000 **2** town, its ✳; *pop* 2300 — **Sam·mar·i·nese** \ˌsa(m)-ˌma-rə-'nēz, -'nēs\ *n* — **San Mar·i·nese** \ˌsan-ˌma-\ *adj or n*

San Pe·dro Su·la \ˌsän-'pā-(ˌ)thrō-'sü-lä\ city NW Honduras; *pop* 300,400

San Sal·va·dor \san-'sal-və-ˌdȯr, ˌsän-'säl-vä-ˌthȯr\ **1** island *cen* Bahamas **2** city, ✳ of El Salvador; *pop* 349,333

San·ta Ana \ˌsan-tə-'a-nə, ˌsän-tä-'ä-nä\ city SW California ESE of Long Beach; *pop* 337,977

San·ta Bar·ba·ra \'bär-b(ə-)rə\ or **Chan·nel** islands California off SW coast in the North Pacific

Santa Clara \'kler-ə\ city W California NW of San Jose; *pop* 102,361

Santa Cla·ri·ta \klə-'rē-tə\ city S California N of Los Angeles; *pop* 151,088

San·ta Fe \ˌsan-tə-'fā\ city, * of New Mexico; *pop* 62,203

Santa Fe Trail pioneer route to the SW U.S. about 1200 mi. (1930 km.) long used esp. 1821–80 from vicinity of Kansas City, Missouri, to Santa Fe, New Mexico

Santa Rosa \ˌsan-tə-'rō-zə\ city W California N of San Francisco; *pop* 147,595

San·ti·a·go \ˌsan-tē-'ä-(ˌ)gō, ˌsän-\ city, * of Chile; *pop* 200,792

San·to Do·min·go \ˌsan-tə-də-'min-(ˌ)gō\ *formerly* **Tru·ji·llo** \trü-'hē-(ˌ)yō\ city, * of Dominican Republic; metropolitan area *pop* 2,677,056

São Pau·lo \saủ-'paủ-(ˌ)lü, -(ˌ)lō\ city SE Brazil; *pop* 10,434,252

São To·mé \saủ⁻tə-'mā\ town, * of São Tomé and Príncipe; *pop* 43,420

São Tomé and Príncipe country W Africa; * São Tomé; *pop* 128,000

Sap·po·ro \'sä-pō-ˌrō; sä-'pōr-(ˌ)ō\ city Japan on W Hokkaido; *pop* 1,822,368

Sa·ra·je·vo \ˌsa-rə-'yä-(ˌ)vō, ˌsär-ə-\ city SE *cen* Bosnia and Herzegovina, its *; *pop* (est.) 602,500

Sa·ra·tov \sə-'rä-təf\ city W Russia, on the Volga; *pop* 909,000

Sar·din·ia \sär-'di-nē-ə, -'di-nyə\ island Italy in the Mediterranean S of Corsica; *pop* 1,648,044 — **Sar·din·ian** \sär-'di-nē-ən, -'din-yən\ *adj or n*

Sar·gas·so Sea \sär-'ga-(ˌ)sō\ area of nearly still water in the North Atlantic lying chiefly between 20° & 35° N latitude & 30° & 70° W longitude

Sas·katch·e·wan \sa-'ska-chə-wən, sa-, -ˌwän\ province W Canada; *, Regina; *pop* 1,015,783

Sas·ka·toon \ˌsas-kə-'tün\ city *cen* Saskatchewan, Canada; *pop* 196,811

Sau·di Ara·bia \'saủ-dē, 'sȯ-dē, sä-'ü-dē\ country SW Asia occupying largest part of Arabian Peninsula; *, Riyadh; *pop* 20,800,000 — **Saudi** *adj or n* — **Saudi Arabian** *adj or n*

Sault Sainte Ma·rie Canals \'sü-(ˌ)sänt-mə-'rē\ *or* **Soo Canals** \ˌsü\ three ship canals, two in U.S. (Michigan) & one in Canada (Ontario), at rapids in river connecting Lake Superior & Lake Huron

Sa·vaii \sə-'vī-ˌē\ island, largest in independent Samoa

Sa·van·nah \sə-'va-nə\ city & port E Georgia; *pop* 131,510

Sa·voy \sə-'vȯi\ *or French* **Sa·voie** \sä-'vwä\ region SE France SW of Switzerland bordering on Italy — **Sa·voy·ard** \sə-'vȯi-ˌärd, ˌsa-ˌvȯi-'ärd, ˌsa-ˌvwä-'yär(d)\ *adj or n*

Sca·fell Pike \ˌskȯ-'fel\ mountain 3210 ft. (978 m.) NW England; highest in Cumbrian Mountains & in England

Scan·di·na·via \ˌskan-də-'nā-vē-ə, -vyə\

1 peninsula N Europe occupied by Norway & Sweden **2** Denmark, Norway, Sweden, & sometimes also Iceland & Finland — **Scan·di·na·vian** \ˌskan-də-'nā-vē-ən, -vyən\ *adj or n*

Scar·bor·ough \'skär-ˌbər-ō\ former city Canada in SE Ontario; now part of Toronto

Schel·de \'skel-də\ *or* **Scheldt** \'skelt\ river 270 mi. (434 km.) long W Europe flowing from N France through Belgium into North Sea in Netherlands

Schuyl·kill \'skü-kᵊl, 'skül-ˌkil\ river 131 mi. (211 km.) long SE Pennsylvania flowing SE into the Delaware River at Philadelphia

Scil·ly, Isles of \'si-lē\ island group SW England off Land's End; *pop* 2900

Sco·tia \'skō-shə\ SCOTLAND — the Medieval Latin name

Scot·land \'skät-lənd\ *or Latin* **Cal·e·do·nia** \ˌka-lə-'dō-nyə, -nē-ə\ country N Great Britain; a division of United Kingdom; *, Edinburgh; *pop* 5,062,011

Scotts·dale \'skäts-ˌdāl\ city SW *cen* Arizona E of Phoenix; *pop* 202,705

Scyth·ia \'si-thē-ə, -thē\ ancient area of Europe & Asia N & NE of Black Sea & E of Aral Sea — **Scyth·i·an** \'si-thē-ən, -thē-\ *adj or n*

Se·at·tle \sē-'a-tᵊl\ city & port W Washington; *pop* 563,374

Seine \'sān, 'sen\ river 480 mi. (772 km.) long N France flowing NW into English Channel

Sel·kirk \'sel-ˌkərk\ range of the Rocky Mountains SE British Columbia, Canada; highest peak, 11,555 ft. (3522 m.)

Se·ma·rang \sə-'mär-ˌäŋ\ city Indonesia in *cen* Java; *pop* 1,250,971

Sen·dai \(ˌ)sen-'dī\ city Japan in NE Honshu; *pop* 1,008,130

Sen·e·ca Falls \'se-ni-kə\ village W *cen* New York; *pop* 6861

Sen·e·gal \ˌse-ni-'gȯl, -'gäl, 'se-ni-ˌ\ **1** river 1015 mi. (1633 km.) long W Africa flowing W into the North Atlantic **2** country W Africa; *, Dakar; *pop* 7,899,000 — **Sen·e·ga·lese** \ˌse-ni-gə-'lēz, -'lēs\ *adj or n*

Seoul \'sōl\ city, * of South Korea; *pop* 9,853,972

Ser·bia \'sər-bē-ə\ region in the Balkans comprising a federated republic of Serbia and Montenegro; *pop* 9,823,000

Serbia and Montenegro *formerly* **Yu·go·sla·via** country S Europe on Balkan Peninsula; *, Belgrade; *pop* 10,561,000

Ser·en·ge·ti Plain \ˌser-ən-'ge-tē\ area N Tanzania

Seven Hills the seven hills upon and about which was built the city of Rome, Italy

Sev·ern \'se-vərn\ river 210 mi. (338 km.)

long Wales & England flowing from E *cen* Wales into Bristol Channel

Se·ville \sə-'vil\ *or Spanish* **Se·vi·lla** \sā-'vē-(ˌ)yä\ city SW Spain; *pop* 684,633

Sew·ard Peninsula \'sü-ərd\ peninsula 180 mi. (290 km.) long W Alaska projecting into Bering Sea

Sey·chelles \sā-'shel(z)\ islands W Indian Ocean NE of Madagascar; country; ✻, Victoria; *pop* 72,700 — **Sey·chel·lois** \ˌsā-shəl-'wä, -shel-\ *n*

Shang·hai \shaŋ-'hī\ municipality & port E China; *pop* 7,469,509

Shan·non \'sha-nən\ river 230 mi. (370 km.) long W Ireland flowing S & W into the North Atlantic

Sharon, Plain of \'sher-ən\ region Israel on the coast

Shas·ta, Mount \'shas-tə\ mountain 14,162 ft. (4316 m.) N California in Cascade Range

Shatt al Ar·ab \ˌshat-al-'a-rəb\ river 120 mi. (193 km.) long SE Iraq formed by flowing together of Euphrates & Tigris rivers and flowing SE into Persian Gulf

Shef·field \'she-ˌfēld\ city N England; *pop* 499,700

Shen·an·do·ah \ˌshe-nən-'dō-ə, ˌsha-nə-'dō-ə\ valley Virginia between the Allegheny & Blue Ridge mountains

Shen·yang \'shən-'yäŋ\ *or traditionally* **Muk·den** \'mük-dən, 'mək-; mük-'den\ city NE China; chief city of Manchuria; *pop* 3,603,712

Sher·brooke \'shər-ˌbrük\ city Quebec, Canada E of Montreal; *pop* 75,916

Sher·wood Forest \'shər-ˌwüd\ ancient royal forest *cen* England

Shet·land \'shet-lənd\ islands N Scotland NE of the Orkneys; *pop* 22,270

Shi·jia·zhuang *or* **Shih–chia–chuang** \'shir-'jyä-'jwäŋ, 'shē-\ city NE China; *pop* 1,068,439

Shi·ko·ku \shē-'kō-(ˌ)kü\ island S Japan E of Kyushu; *pop* 4,195,106

Shi·raz \shi-'räz, -'raz\ city SW *cen* Iran; *pop* 848,289

Shreve·port \'shrēv-ˌpȯrt\ city NW Louisiana on Red River; *pop* 200,145

Shrews·bury \'sh(r)üz-ˌber-ē, -b(ə-)rē\ town W England; *pop* 31,640

Shrop·shire \'shräp-shər, -ˌshir\ *or* 1974–80 **Sal·op** \'sal-əp\ county W England bordering on Wales

Shu·ma·gin \'shü-mə-gən\ islands SW Alaska S of Alaska Peninsula

Siam — see THAILAND

Siam, Gulf of — see THAILAND, GULF OF

Si·be·ria \sī-'bir-ē-ə\ region N Asia in Russia between the Urals & the North Pacific — **Si·be·ri·an** \-ən\ *adj or n*

Sic·i·ly \'si-s(ə-)lē\ *or Italian* **Si·ci·lia** \sē-'chēl-yä\ island S Italy SW of toe of peninsula of Italy; ✻, Palermo; *pop* 5,076,700 — **Si·cil·ian** \sə-'sil-yən\ *adj or n*

Si·er·ra Le·one \sē-ˌer-ə-lē-'ōn, sir-ə-, -lē-'ō-nē\ country W Africa on the North Atlantic; ✻, Freetown; *pop* 4,491,000 — **Si·er·ra Le·on·ean** \-'ō-nē-ən\ *adj or n*

Si·er·ra Ma·dre \sē-ˌer-ə-'mä-drā, 'syer-ä-'mä-ṯhrä\ mountain system Mexico including **Sierra Madre Oc·ci·den·tal** \ˌäk-sə-ˌden-'täl, ˌōk-sē-ˌthen-'täl\ range W of the *cen* plateau, **Sierra Madre Ori·en·tal** \ˌȯr-ē-ˌen-'täl\ range E of the plateau, & **Sierra del Sur** \'sur, 'sür\ range to the S

Sierra Ne·va·da \nə-'va-də, -'vä-\ 1 mountain range E California & W Nevada — see WHITNEY, MOUNT 2 mountain range S Spain

Sik·kim \'si-kəm, -ˌkim\ former country SE Asia on S slope of the Himalayas between Nepal & Bhutan; part of India (country); *pop* 406,457

Si·le·sia \sī-'lē-zh(ē-)ə, sə-, -sh(ē-)ə\ region E *cen* Europe in valley of the upper Oder; formerly chiefly in Germany now chiefly in E Czech Republic & SW Poland — **Si·le·sian** \-zh(ē-)ən, -sh(ē-)ən\ *adj or n*

Silk Road *or* **Silk Route** ancient trade route that extended from China to the Mediterranean

Sim·coe, Lake \'sim-(ˌ)kō\ lake Canada in SE Ontario

Si·mi Valley \sē-'mē\ city SW California W of Los Angeles; *pop* 111,351

Sim·plon Pass \'sim-ˌplän\ mountain pass 6590 ft. (2009 m.) between Switzerland & Italy

Si·nai \'sī-ˌnī\ 1 mountain on Sinai Peninsula where according to the Bible the Law was given to Moses 2 peninsula extension of continent of Asia NE Egypt between Red Sea & the Mediterranean

Sin·ga·pore \'siŋ-ə-ˌpȯr\ 1 island off S end of Malay Peninsula; country; *pop* 4,163,700 2 city, its ✻; *pop* 206,500 — **Sin·ga·por·ean** \ˌsiŋ-ə-'pȯr-ē-ən\ *adj or n*

Sinkiang Uighur — see XINJIANG UYGUR

Sioux Falls \'sü\ city SE South Dakota; largest in state; *pop* 123,975

Skag·ge·rak \'ska-gə-ˌrak\ arm of North Sea between S Norway & N Denmark

Skop·je \'skȯp-ye, -pyə\ city, ✻ of independent Macedonia; *pop* 563,301

Sla·vo·nia \slə-'vō-nē-ə, -nyə\ region E Croatia — **Sla·vo·ni·an** \-nē-ən, -nyən\ *adj or n*

Slo·va·kia \slō-'vä-kē-ə, -'va-\ country *cen* Europe; ✻, Bratislava; *pop* 5,379,455

Slo·ve·nia \slō-'vē-nē-ə, -nyə\ country S Europe; ✻, Ljubljana; *pop* 1,975,164

Smyrna — see IZMIR

Snake \'snäk\ river NW U.S. flowing from NW Wyoming into the Columbia in SE Washington

Snow·don \'snō-dᵊn\ massif 3560 ft. (1085 m.) in Snow·do·nia \snō-'dō-nē-ə, -nyə\ (mountainous district) NW Wales; highest point in Wales

So·ci·e·ty \sə-'sī-ə-tē\ islands South Pacific; belonging to France; chief island, Tahiti; *pop* 162,573

So·fia \'sō-fē-ə, 'sò-, sō-'\ city, * of Bulgaria; *pop* 1,141,142

So·ho \'sō-ˌhō\ district of *cen* London, England

So·li·hull \ˌsō-li-'həl\ city *cen* England; *pop* 194,100

Sol·o·mon \'sä-lə-mən\ 1 islands W Pacific E of New Guinea divided between Papua New Guinea & independent Solomon Islands 2 sea, arm of Coral Sea W of the Solomons

Solomon Islands country, SW Pacific E of New Guinea; *, Honiara (on Guadalcanal); *pop* 349,000

So·ma·lia \sō-'mä-lē-ə, sə-, -'mäl-yə\ country E Africa on Gulf of Aden & Indian Ocean; *, Mogadishu; *pop* 8,050,000 — So·ma·li·an \-'mä-lē-ən, -'mäl-yən\ *adj or n*

So·ma·li·land \sō-'mä-lē-ˌland, sə-\ region E Africa consisting of Somalia, Djibouti, & part of E Ethiopia — So·ma·li \sō-'mä-lē, sə-\ *n*

Som·er·set \'sə-mər-ˌset, -sət\ or Som·er·set·shire \-ˌshir, -shər\ county SW England

So·nor·an \sə-'nór-ən\ or So·no·ra \sə-'nór-ə\ desert SW U.S. & NW Mexico

Soo Canals — see SAULT SAINTE MARIE CANALS

South island S New Zealand; *pop* 906,756

South Africa, Republic of *formerly* Union of South Africa country S Africa; administrative *, Pretoria; legislative *, Cape Town; judicial *, Bloemfontein; *pop* 30,193,000 — South African *adj or n*

South America continent of Western Hemisphere SE of North America and chiefly S of the Equator — South American *adj or n*

South·amp·ton \saù-'tham(p)-tən, saùth-'ham(p)-\ city S England; *pop* 194,400

South Australia state S Australia; *, Adelaide; *pop* 1,462,900 — South Australian *adj or n*

South Bend \'bend\ city N Indiana; *pop* 107,789

South Cape or South Point — see KALAE

South Car·o·li·na \ˌker-(ə)-'lī-nə, ˌka-rə-\ state SE U.S.; *, Columbia; *pop* 4,012,012 — South Car·o·lin·i·an \-'li-nē-ən, -'li-nyən\ *adj or n*

South China Sea — see CHINA

South Da·ko·ta \də-'kō-tə\ state NW *cen* U.S.; *, Pierre; *pop* 754,844 — South Da·ko·tan \-'kō-tᵊn\ *adj or n*

South·end–on–Sea \ˌsaù-ˌthend-ˌòn-'sē, -ˌän-\ seaside resort SE England E of London; *pop* 153,700

Southern Alps mountain range New Zealand in W South Island extending almost the length of the island

Southern Hemisphere the half of the earth that lies S of the Equator

South Georgia island S Atlantic E of Tierra del Fuego; administered by United Kingdom

South Korea or Republic of South Korea country S half of Korean Peninsula in E Asia; *, Seoul; *pop* 45,985,289

South Seas the areas of the Atlantic, Indian, & Pacific oceans in the Southern Hemisphere

South Shields \'shēldz\ seaport N England; *pop* 87,203

South Vietnam — see VIETNAM

South·wark \'sə-thərk, 'saùth-wərk\ borough of S Greater London, England; *pop* 196,500

South–West Africa — see NAMIBIA

South Yorkshire metropolitan county N England; *pop* 1,248,500

Soviet Central Asia portion of *cen* & SW Asia formerly belonging to U.S.S.R. and including the former soviet socialist republics of present-day Kyrgyzstan, Tajikistan, Uzbekistan & sometimes Kazakhstan

Soviet Union — see UNION OF SOVIET SOCIALIST REPUBLICS

So·we·to \sō-'wā-tō, -'we-, -tü\ residential area NE Republic of South Africa adjoining SW Johannesburg

Spain \'spān\ country SW Europe on Iberian Peninsula; *, Madrid; *pop* 39,141,000

Spanish America 1 the Spanish-speaking countries of America 2 the parts of America settled and formerly governed by the Spanish

Spanish Guinea — see EQUATORIAL GUINEA

Spanish Sahara — see WESTERN SAHARA

Spar·ta \'spär-tə\ ancient city S Greece in Peloponnese; * of Laconia

Spo·kane \spō-'kan\ city E Washington; *pop* 195,629

Spring·field \'spriŋ-ˌfēld\ 1 city, * of Illinois; *pop* 111,454 2 city SW Massachusetts; *pop* 152,082 3 city SW Missouri; *pop* 151,580

Sri Lan·ka \(ˌ)srē-'läŋ-kə, (ˌ)shrē-, -'laŋ-\ *formerly* Cey·lon \si-'län, sā-\ country having the same boundaries as island of Ceylon; *, Colombo; *pop* 17,829,500 — Sri Lan·kan \-'läŋ-kən, -'laŋ-\ *adj or n*

Sri·na·gar \srē-'nə-gər\ city N India; *pop* 894,940

Staf·ford \'sta-fərd\ town W *cen* England; *pop* 117,000

Staf·ford·shire \'sta-fərd-ˌshir, -shər\ *or* **Stafford** county W *cen* England

Staked Plain — see LLANO ESTACADO

Stam·ford \'stam-fərd\ city SW Connecticut; *pop* 117,083

Stan·ley \'stan-lē\ town, ✳ of Falkland Islands; *pop* 1559

Stat·en Island \'sta-t⁰n\ **1** island SE New York SW of mouth of the Hudson **2** *formerly* **Rich·mond** \'rich-mənd\ borough of New York City including Staten Island; *pop* 443,728

Ster·ling \'stər-liŋ\ city SE Michigan; *pop* 124,471

Stir·ling \'stər-liŋ\ town *cen* Scotland; *pop* 38,638

Stock·holm \'stäk-ˌhō(l)m\ city, ✳ of Sweden; *pop* 758,148

Stock·port \'stäk-ˌpórt\ town NW England; *pop* 276,800

Stock·ton \'stäk-tən\ city *cen* California; *pop* 243,771

Stoke–on–Trent \'stōk-ˌän-'trent, -ˌón-\ city *cen* England; *pop* 244,800

Stone·henge \'stōn-ˌhenj, (ˌ)stōn-'\ prehistoric assemblage of megaliths S England in Wiltshire on Salisbury Plain

Stone Mountain mountain 1686 ft. (514 m.) NW Georgia E of Atlanta

Stor·no·way \'stór-nə-ˌwā\ seaport NW Scotland; chief town of Lewis with Harris Island; *pop* 8660

Stra·bane \strə-'ban\ district W Northern Ireland; *pop* 35,668

Strath·clyde \strath-'klīd\ former region SW Scotland; included Glasgow

Strom·bo·li \'sträm-bō-(ˌ)lē\ volcano 2500 ft. (758 m.) Italy on **Stromboli Island** in Tyrrhenian Sea

Stutt·gart \'shtut-ˌgärt, 'stut-, 'stət-\ city SW Germany; *pop* 591,946

Styx \'stiks\ chief river of the underworld in Greek mythology

Süchow — see XUZHOU

Su·cre \'sü-(ˌ)krā\ city, constitutional ✳ of Bolivia; *pop* 130,952

Su·dan \sü-'dan, -'dän\ **1** region N Africa S of the Sahara between the Atlantic & the upper Nile **2** country NE Africa S of Egypt; ✳, Khartoum; *pop* 25,000,000 — **Su·da·nese** \ˌsüd-ə-'nēz, -'nēs\ *adj or n*

Sud·bury \'səd-ˌber-ē, -b(ə-)rē\ city SE Ontario, Canada; *pop* 155,219

Su·ez, Gulf of \sü-'ez, 'sü-ˌez\ arm of Red Sea

Suez, Isthmus of isthmus NE Egypt between Mediterranean & Red seas connecting Africa & Asia

Suez Canal canal 100 mi. (161 km.) long NE Egypt across the Isthmus of Suez

Suf·folk \'sə-fək\ county E England on North Sea

Sui·sun Bay \sə-'sün\ inlet of San Francisco Bay, W *cen* California

Su·la·we·si \ˌsü-lä-'wä-sē\ island Indonesia E of Borneo; *pop* 12,520,711

Su·lu \'sü-(ˌ)lü\ **1** archipelago SW Philippines SW of Mindanao **2** sea W Philippines

Su·ma·tra \su̇-'mä-trə\ island W Indonesia S of Malay Peninsula — **Su·ma·tran** \-trən\ *adj or n*

Su·mer \'sü-mər\ the S division of ancient Babylonia — **Su·me·ri·an** \sü-'mer-ē-ən, -'mir-\ *adj or n*

Sun·belt \'sən-ˌbelt\ region S & SW U.S.

Sun·da \'sün-də, 'sən-\ strait between Java & Sumatra

Sun·der·land \'sən-dər-lənd\ seaport N England; *pop* 286,800

Sun·ny·vale \'sə-nē-ˌvāl\ city W California; *pop* 131,760

Sun Valley resort center *cen* Idaho

Su·pe·ri·or, Lake \su̇-'pir-ē-ər\ lake E *cen* North America in U.S. & Canada; largest of the Great Lakes

Su·ra·ba·ya \ˌsu̇r-ə-'bī-ə\ city Indonesia in NE Java; *pop* 2,483,871

Su·ri·na·me \ˌsu̇r-ə-'nä-mə\ country N South America between Guyana & French Guiana; ✳, Paramaribo; *pop* 403,000 — **Su·ri·nam·er** \'su̇r-ə-ˌnä-mər, ˌsu̇r-ə-'nä-\ *n* — **Su·ri·nam·ese** \ˌsu̇r-ə-nə-'mēz, -'mēs\ *adj or n*

Sur·rey \'sər-ē, 'sə-rē\ city Canada in SW British Columbia; *pop* 347,825

Sut·ton \'sə-t⁰n\ borough of S Greater London, England; *pop* 164,300

Su·va \'sü-və\ city & port, ✳ of Fiji on Viti Levu Island; *pop* 63,628

Su·wan·nee \sə-'wä-nē, 'swä-\ river 250 mi. (400 km.) SE U.S. flowing SW into Gulf of Mexico

Sverdlovsk — see YEKATERINBURG

Swan·sea \'swän-zē\ city & port SW Wales; *pop* 182,100

Swa·zi·land \'swä-zē-ˌland\ country SE Africa between Republic of South Africa & Mozambique; ✳, Mbabane; *pop* 929,718 — **Swa·zi** \'swä-zē\ *adj or n*

Swe·den \'swē-d⁰n\ country N Europe on Scandinavia (peninsula) bordering on Baltic Sea; ✳, Stockholm; *pop* 8,940,788

Swit·zer·land \'swit-sər-lənd\ country W Europe in the Alps; ✳, Bern; *pop* 6,996,000

Syd·ney \'sid-nē\ city SE Australia, ✳ of New South Wales; metropolitan area *pop* 3,097,956

Syr·a·cuse \'sir-ə-ˌkyüs, -ˌkyüz\ city *cen* New York; *pop* 147,306

Syr·ia \'sir-ē-ə\ **1** ancient region SW Asia bordering on the Mediterranean **2** country S of Turkey; ✳, Damascus; *pop* 13,398,000 — **Syr·i·an** \-ē-ən\ *adj or n*

Syrian Desert desert region between Mediterranean coast & the Euphrates in N Saudi Arabia, SE Syria, W Iraq, & NE Jordan

Table Bay harbor of Cape Town, Republic of South Africa

Ta·briz \tə-ˈbrēz\ city NW Iran; *pop* 971,482

Ta·co·ma \tə-ˈkō-mə\ city & port W Washington S of Seattle; *pop* 193,556

Tae·gu \ˈtā-gü, ˈdā-\ *or* **Dae·gu** \ˈdā-\ city SE South Korea; *pop* 2,473,990

Tae·jon \ˈtā-ˈjən, ˈdā-\ *or* **Dae·jeon** \ˈdā-\ city *cen* South Korea NW of Taegu; *pop* 1,365,961

Ta·gus \ˈtā-gəs\ *or Spanish* **Ta·jo** \ˈtä-(ˌ)hō\ *or Portuguese* **Te·jo** \ˈtä-(ˌ)zhü\ river 626 mi. (1007 km.) long Spain & Portugal flowing W into the North Atlantic

Ta·hi·ti \tə-ˈhē-tē\ island South Pacific in Society Islands; *pop* 131,309

Tai·chung \ˈtī-ˈchu̇ŋ\ city W Taiwan; *pop* 779,370

T'ai–nan \ˈtī-ˈnän\ city SW Taiwan; *pop* 702,237

Tai·pei \ˈtī-ˈpā, -ˈbā\ city, ✳ of (Nationalist) China in N Taiwan; *pop* 2,651,419

Tai·wan \ˈtī-ˈwän\ *formerly* **For·mo·sa** \fȯr-ˈmō-sə, fər-, -zə\ **1** island China off SE coast of mainland; seat of government of (Nationalist) Republic of China; ✳, Taipei; *pop* 20,926,000 **2** strait between Taiwan & mainland of China connecting East China & South China seas — **Tai·wan·ese** \ˌtī-wə-ˈnēz, -ˈnēs\ *adj or n*

Tai·yuan \ˈtī-ˈywen, -ˈywän\ city N China; *pop* 1,533,884

Ta·jik·i·stan \tä-ji-ki-ˈstan, tə-, -ˌjē-, -ˈstän\ country W *cen* Asia bordering on China & Afghanistan; ✳, Dushanbe; *pop* 5,705,000

Ta·kli·ma·kan *or* **Ta·kla Ma·kan** \ˌtä-klə-mə-ˈkän\ desert W China

Ta–lien — see DALIAN

Tal·la·has·see \ˌta-lə-ˈha-sē\ city, ✳ of Florida; *pop* 150,624

Tal·linn \ˈta-lən, ˈtä-\ city, ✳ of Estonia; *pop* 398,434

Tam·pa \ˈtam-pə\ city W Florida on **Tampa Bay** (inlet of Gulf of Mexico); *pop* 303,447

Tan·gan·yi·ka \ˌtan-gə-ˈnyē-kə, ˌtaŋ-gə-, -ˈnē-\ former country E Africa S of Kenya; now part of Tanzania

Tanganyika, Lake lake E Africa between Tanzania & Democratic Republic of the Congo

Tang·shan \ˈdäŋ-ˈshän, ˈtäŋ-\ city NE China; *pop* 1,044,194

Tan·za·nia \ˌtan-zə-ˈnē-ə, ˌtän-\ country E Africa on Indian Ocean, including Zanzibar; designated ✳, Dodoma; seat of government, Dar es Salaam; *pop* 26,542,000 — **Tan·za·ni·an** \-ˈnē-ən\ *adj or n*

Ta·ra·wa \tə-ˈrä-wə, ˈta-rə-,wä\ island *cen* Pacific, contains ✳ of Kiribati; *pop* 28,802

Tar·ry·town \ˈta-rē-,taủn\ village SE New York; *pop* 11,090

Tar·sus \ˈtär-səs\ ancient city of S Asia Minor; now a city in S Turkey

Tash·kent \tash-ˈkent, täsh-\ city, ✳ of Uzbekistan; *pop* 2,073,000

Tas·ma·nia \taz-ˈmā-nē-ə, -nyə\ *or earlier* **Van Die·men's Land** \van-ˈdē-mənz-\ island SE Australia S of Victoria; a state; ✳, Hobart; *pop* 471,400 — **Tas·ma·nian** \taz-ˈmā-nē-ən, -nyən\ *adj or n*

Tas·man Sea \ˈtaz-mən\ the part of the South Pacific between SE Australia & New Zealand

Ta·try \ˈtä-trē\ *or* **Ta·tra** \ˈtä-trə\ mountains N Slovakia & S Poland in *cen* Carpathian Mountains

Taun·ton \ˈtȯn-tən, ˈtän-\ town SW England; *pop* 35,326

Tbi·li·si \tə-ˈbē-lə-sē, tə-bə-ˈlē-sē\ *or* **Tiflis** \ˈti-fləs, tə-ˈflēs\ city, ✳ of Republic of Georgia; *pop* 1,260,000

Te·gu·ci·gal·pa \tə-ˌgü-sə-ˈgäl-pə, tä-ˌgü-sē-ˈgäl-pä\ city, ✳ of Honduras; *pop* 608,100

Teh·ran \ˌtā-(ə-)ˈran, te-ˈran, -ˈrän\ city, ✳ of Iran; at foot of S slope of Elburz Mountains; *pop* 6,042,584

Tel Aviv \ˌtel-ə-ˈvēv\ city W Israel on the Mediterranean; *pop* 353,200

Tem·pe \ˈtem-ˈpē\ city S *cen* Arizona; *pop* 158,625

Ten·nes·see \ˌte-nə-ˈsē, ˈte-nə-ˌ\ **1** river 652 mi. (1049 km.) long in Tennessee, N Alabama, & W Kentucky **2** state E *cen* U.S.; ✳, Nashville; *pop* 5,689,283 — **Ten·nes·se·an** *or* **Ten·nes·see·an** \ˌte-nə-ˈsē-ən\ *adj or n*

Te·noch·ti·tlan \tä-ˌnóch-tēt-ˈlän\ ancient name of Mexico City

Tex·as \ˈtek-səs, -siz\ state S U.S.; ✳, Austin; *pop* 20,851,820 — **Tex·an** \-sən\ *adj or n*

Texas Panhandle the NW projection of land in Texas

Thai·land \ˈtī-ˌland, -lənd\ *formerly* **Si·am** \sī-ˈam\ country SE Asia on Gulf of Thailand; ✳, Bangkok; *pop* 60,617,200 — **Thai·land·er** \-ˌlan-dər, -lən-\ *n*

Thailand, Gulf of *formerly* **Gulf of Siam** arm of South China Sea between Indochina & Malay Peninsula

Thames \ˈtemz\ river over 200 mi. (322 km.) long S England flowing E from the Cotswolds into the North Sea

Thar \ˈtär\ desert E Pakistan & NW India (country) E of Indus River

Thebes \ˈthēbz\ **1** *or* **The·bae** \ˈthē-(ˌ)bē\ ancient city S Egypt on the Nile **2** ancient city E Greece NNW of Athens — **The·ban** \ˈthē-bən\ *adj or n*

Thes·sa·lo·ni·ki \ˌthe-sä-lō-ˈnē-kē\ city N Greece; *pop* 402,443

Thim·phu \tim-ˈpü\ city, ✳ of Bhutan; *pop* 45,000

Thousand Islands island group Canada

& U.S. in the Saint Lawrence River in Ontario & New York

Thousand Oaks city SW California W of Los Angeles; *pop* 117,005

Thrace \'thrās\ *or ancient* **Thra·cia** \'thrā-sh(ē-)ə\ region SE Europe in Balkan Peninsula N of the Aegean now divided between Greece & Turkey; in ancient times extended N to the Danube — **Thra·cian** \'thrā-shən\ *adj or n*

Thunder Bay city SW Ontario, Canada on Lake Superior; *pop* 109,016

Tian·jin \'tyän-'jin\ *or* **Tien·tsin** \'tyen-'tsin, 'tin-\ city NE China SE of Beijing; *pop* 7,764,141

Tian Shan *or* **Tien Shan** \'tyen-'shän, -'shan\ mountain system *cen* Asia extending NE from Pamirs

Ti·ber \'tī-bər\ *or Italian* **Te·ve·re** \'tā-vā-rā\ river 252 mi. (405 km.) long *cen* Italy flowing through Rome into Tyrrhenian Sea

Tiberias, Lake — see GALILEE, SEA OF

Ti·bes·ti \tə-'bes-tē\ mountains N *cen* Africa in *cen* Sahara in NW Chad; highest 11,204 ft. (3415 m.)

Ti·bet \tə-'bet\ *or* **Xi·zang** \'shēd-'zäŋ\ region SW China on high plateau at average altitude 16,000 ft. (4877 m.) N of the Himalayas; *, Lhasa; *pop* 2,196,010

Tier·ra del Fue·go \tē-'er-ə-(,)del-fü-'ā-(,)gō, 'tyer-ā-(,)thel-'fwā-gō\ **1** island group off S South America **2** chief island of the group; divided between Argentina & Chile

Tiflis — see TBILISI

Ti·gris \'tī-grəs\ river 1180 mi. (1899 km.) long Turkey & Iraq flowing SSE and uniting with the Euphrates to form the Shatt al Arab

Ti·jua·na \,tē-ə-'wä-nə, tē-'hwä-nä\ city NW Mexico on the U.S. border; *pop* 991,592

Tim·buk·tu \,tim-,bək-'tü, tim-'bək-(,)tü\ *or* **Tom·bouc·tou** \tōⁿ-bük-'tü\ town Mali near Niger River; *pop* 31,925

Ti·mor \'tē-,mȯr, tē-'\ island S Malay archipelago SE of Sulawesi; W half part of Indonesia, E half independent East Timor

Ti·ra·ne *or* **Ti·ra·na** \ti-'rä-nə, tē-\ city, * of Albania; *pop* 519,720

Ti·rol *or* **Ty·rol** \tə-'rōl\ *or Italian* **Ti·ro·lo** \tē-'rò-(,)lò\ region in E Alps in W Austria & NE Italy — **Ti·ro·le·an** \tə-'rō-lē-ən, tī-\ *or* **Tir·o·lese** \,tir-ə-'lēz, ,tī-rə-, -'lēs\ *adj or n*

Ti·ti·ca·ca, Lake \,ti-ti-'kä-kä, ,tē-tē-\ lake on Bolivia–Peru boundary at altitude of 12,500 ft. (3810 m.)

To·ba·go \tə-'bā-(,)gō\ island West Indies NE of Trinidad; part of independent Trinidad and Tobago; *pop* 54,084 — **To·ba·go·ni·an** \,tō-bə-'gō-nē-ən, -nyən\ *n*

To·go \'tō-(,)gō\ country W Africa on Gulf of Guinea; *, Lomé; *pop* 3,810,000 — **To·go·lese** \,tō-gə-'lēz, -'lēs\ *adj or n*

To·kyo \'tō-kē-,ō, -,kyō\ city, * of Japan in SE Honshu on Tokyo Bay; *pop* 12,064,101 — **To·kyo·ite** \'tō-kē-(,)ō-,īt\ *n*

To·le·do \tə-'lē-(,)dō, -'lē-də\ city NW Ohio; *pop* 313,619

Tol'·yat·ti \tȯl-'yä-tē\ city W Russia; NW of Samara; *pop* 666,000

Ton·ga \'täŋ-gə, 'täŋ-ə, 'tȯŋ-ä\ islands SW Pacific E of Fiji Islands; country; *, Nukualofa; *pop* 101,002 — **Ton·gan** \-(g)ən\ *adj or n*

Tonkin, Gulf of \'täŋ-kən\ arm of South China Sea E of N Vietnam

To·pe·ka \tə-'pē-kə\ city, * of Kansas; *pop* 122,377

Tor·bay \(,)tȯr-'bā\ urban area SW England; *pop* 122,500

To·ron·to \tə-'rän-(,)tō, -'rän-tə\ city, * of Ontario, Canada; *pop* 2,481,494

Tor·rance \'tȯr-ən(t)s, 'tär-\ city SW California; *pop* 137,946

Tor·res \'tȯr-əs\ strait between New Guinea & Cape York Peninsula, Australia

Tou·louse \tü-'lüz\ city SW France; *pop* 390,301

Tower Hamlets borough of E Greater London, England; *pop* 153,500

Trans·vaal \tran(t)s-'väl, tranz-\ former province NE Republic of South Africa

Tran·syl·va·nia \,tran(t)-səl-'vā-nyə, -nē-ə\ region W Romania — **Tran·syl·va·nian** \-nyən, -nē-ən\ *adj or n*

Transylvanian Alps a S extension of Carpathian Mountains in *cen* Romania

Tren·ton \'tren-tᵊn\ city, * of New Jersey; *pop* 85,403

Trin·i·dad \'tri-nə-,dad\ island West Indies off NE coast of Venezuela; with Tobago forms the independent country of **Trinidad and Tobago**; *, Port of Spain; *pop* 1,262,386 — **Trin·i·da·di·an** \,tri-nə-'dä-dē-ən, -'da-\ *adj or n*

Trip·o·li \'tri-pə-lē\ **1** city & port NW Lebanon; *pop* 127,611 **2** city & port, * of Libya; *pop* 591,062

Tris·tan da Cu·nha \,tris-tən-də-'kü-nə, -nyə\ island South Atlantic, chief of the Tristan da Cunha Islands (part of British colony of Saint Helena); *pop* 296

Tri·van·drum \tri-'van-drəm\ city S India; *pop* 744,739

Tro·bri·and \'trō-brē-,änd, -,and\ islands SW Pacific in Solomon Sea belonging to Papua New Guinea

Trond·heim \'trän-,hām\ city & port *cen* Norway; *pop* 137,346

Trow·bridge \'trō-(,)brij\ town S England; *pop* 22,984

Troy \'trȯi\ *or* **Il·i·um** \'i-lē-əm\ *or* **Tro·ja** \'trō-jə, -yə\ ancient city NW Asia Minor SW of the Dardanelles

Truk — see CHUUK

Tru·ro \'trür-(ˌ)ō\ city SW England; *pop* 16,277

Tsinan — see JINAN

Tsingtao — see QINGDAO

Tuc·son \'tü-ˌsän\ city SE Arizona; *pop* 486,699

Tu·la \'tü-lä\ city W Russia S of Moscow; *pop* 541,000

Tul·sa \'təl-sə\ city NE Oklahoma; *pop* 393,049

Tu·nis \'tü-nəs, 'tyü-\ city ✳ of Tunisia; *pop* 620,149

Tu·ni·sia \tü-'nē-zh(ē-)ə, tyü-, -'ni-\ country N Africa on the Mediterranean E of Algeria; ✳, Tunis; *pop* 9,673,600 — **Tu·ni·sian** \-zh(ē-)ən\ *adj or n*

Tu·rin \'tùr-ən, 'tyùr-\ city NW Italy on the Po; *pop* 900,987

Tur·ka·na, Lake \tər-'ka-nə\ *or* **Lake Ru·dolf** \'rü-ˌdolf, -ˌdälf\ lake N Kenya in Great Rift Valley

Tur·key \'tər-kē\ country W Asia & SE Europe between Mediterranean & Black seas; ✳, Ankara; *pop* 50,664,458 — **Turk** \'tərk\

Turk·men·i·stan \(ˌ)tərk-ˌme-nə-'stan, -'stän\ country *cen* Asia; ✳, Ashkhabad; *pop* 3,958,000 — **Turk·me·ni·an** \ˌtərk-'mē-nē-ən\ *adj*

Turks and Cai·cos \'tərks-ənd-'kā-kəs, -ˌkōs\ two groups of islands West Indies at SE end of the Bahamas; a British colony; *pop* 12,350

Tu·tu·i·la \ˌtü-tü-'wē-lä\ island South Pacific, chief of American Samoa group

Tu·va·lu \tü-'vä-(ˌ)lü, -'vär-(ˌ)ü\ *formerly* **El·lice** \'e-lis\ islands W Pacific N of Fiji; country; ✳, Funafuti; *pop* 9700 — see GILBERT AND ELLICE ISLANDS

Tyne and Wear \'tīn-ənd-'wir\ metropolitan county N England

Tyre \'tī(-ə)r\ ancient city ✳ of Phoenicia; now a town of S Lebanon — **Tyr·i·an** \'tir-ē-ən\ *adj or n*

Tyrol — see TIROL — **Ty·ro·le·an** \tə-'rō-lē-ən, tī-\ *adj or n* — **Ty·ro·lese** \ˌtir-ə-'lēz, ˌtī-rə-, -'lēs\ *adj or n*

Tyr·rhe·ni·an Sea \tə-'rē-nē-ən\ the part of the Mediterranean SW of Italy N of Sicily & E of Sardinia & Corsica

Ufa \ü-'fä\ city W Russia NE of Samara; *pop* 1,097,000

Ugan·da \ü-'gän-də, yü-, -'gan-\ country E Africa N of Lake Victoria; ✳, Kampala; *pop* 24,551,021 — **Ugan·dan** \-dən\ *adj or n*

Ukraine \yü-'krān, 'yü-ˌ\ country E Europe on N coast of Black Sea; ✳, Kiev; *pop* 52,344,000 — **Ukrai·ni·an** \yü-'krā-nē-ən\ *adj or n*

Ulaan·baa·tar *or* **Ulan Ba·tor** \ˌü-ˌlän-'bä-ˌtor\ city ✳ of Mongolia; *pop* 548,400

Ul·san \'ül-ˌsän\ city SE South Korea; *pop* 1,012,110

Ul·ster \'əl-stər\ **1** region N Ireland (island) consisting of Northern Ireland & N Ireland (country) **2** province N Ireland (country); *pop* 246,714 **3** NORTHERN IRELAND

Um·bria \'əm-brē-ə\ region *cen* Italy in the Apennines; *pop* 840,482

Un·ga·va \ˌən-'gä-və\ **1** bay inlet of Hudson Strait NE Canada **2** peninsula region NE Canada in N Quebec

Union of South Africa — see SOUTH AFRICA, REPUBLIC OF

Union of Soviet Socialist Republics *or* **U.S.S.R.** *or* **Soviet Union** country 1922–91 E Europe & N Asia; former union of 15 republics comprising present-day countries of Armenia, Azerbaijan, Belarus, Estonia, Georgia, Kazakhstan, Kyrgyzstan, Latvia, Lithuania, Moldova, Russia, Tajikistan, Turkmenistan, Ukraine, & Uzbekistan

United Arab Emir·ates \'e-mə-rət, -ˌräts\ country E Arabia on Persian Gulf; composed of seven emirates; ✳, Abu Dhabi; *pop* 1,986,000

United Kingdom *or in full* **United Kingdom of Great Britain and Northern Ireland** country W Europe in British Isles consisting of England, Scotland, Wales, Northern Ireland, Channel Islands, & Isle of Man; ✳, London; *pop* 58,789,194

United Nations international territory; a small area in New York City in E *cen* Manhattan; seat of permanent headquarters of a political organization established in 1945

United States of America *or* **United States** country North America bordering on Atlantic, Pacific, & Arctic oceans & including Hawaii; ✳, Washington; *pop* 281,421,906

Upper Volta — see BURKINA FASO — **Upper Vol·tan** \'väl-t°n, 'võl-, 'vòl-\ *adj or n*

Ural \'yùr-əl\ **1** mountains Russia & Kazakhstan extending about 1640 mi. (2640 km.); usually thought of as dividing line between Europe & Asia; highest about 6214 ft. (1894 m.) **2** river over 1500 mi. (2414 km.) long Russia & Kazakhstan flowing from S end of Ural Mountains into Caspian Sea

Uru·guay \'ù̇r-ə-ˌgwī, 'yùr-\ **1** river about 1000 mi. (1609 km.) long SE South America **2** country SE South America; ✳, Montevideo; *pop* 3,149,000 — **Uru·guay·an** \ˌù̇r-ə-'gwī-ən, ˌyùr-\ *adj or n*

Ürüm·qi \'ue-'rum-'chē\ *or* **Urum·chi** \ü-'rüm-chē, ˌùr-əm-'\ city NW China; *pop* 1,046,898

Us·pa·lla·ta \ˌüs-pä-'yä-tä, -'zhä-\ mountain pass S South America in the Andes between Argentina & Chile

Ustinov — see IZHEVSK

Utah \'yü-ˌtò, -ˌtä\ state W U.S.; ✳, Salt

Lake City; *pop* 2,233,169 — **Utah·an** \-ˌtȯ(-ə)n, -ˌtä(-ə)n\ *adj or n* — **Utahn** \-ˌtȯ(-ə)n, -ˌtä(-ə)n\ *n*

Uz·bek·i·stan \(ˌ) u̇z-ˌbe-ki-ˈstan, ˌəz-, -ˈstän\ country W *cen* Asia between Aral Sea & Afghanistan; *, Tashkent; *pop* 21,179,000

Va·duz \vä-ˈdüts\ town, * of Liechtenstein; *pop* 4949

Val·dez \val-ˈdēz\ city & port S Alaska; *pop* 4036

Va·len·cia \və-ˈlen(t)-sh(ē-)ə, -sē-ə\ **1** region & ancient kingdom E Spain **2** city, its *, on the Mediterranean; *pop* 738,441

Val·le·jo \və-ˈlā-(ˌ)ō\ city W California; *pop* 116,760

Valley Forge locality SE Pennsylvania

Val·let·ta \və-ˈle-tə\ city, * of Malta; *pop* 9210

Van·cou·ver \van-ˈkü-vər\ **1** city SW Washington on Columbia River opposite Portland, Oregon; *pop* 143,560 **2** island W Canada in SW British Columbia **3** city & port SW British Columbia, Canada; *pop* 545,671

Van Diemen's Land — see TASMANIA

Van·u·atu \ˌvan-wä-ˈtü, ˌvän-\ *formerly* **New Heb·ri·des** \ˈhe-brə-ˌdēz\ islands SW Pacific W of Fiji; country; *, Port-Vila; *pop* 142,419

Va·ra·na·si \və-ˈrä-nə-sē\ city N India; *pop* 1,100,748

Vat·i·can City \ˈva-ti-kən\ independent state within Rome, Italy; *pop* 911

Ven·e·zu·e·la \ˌve-nə-ˈzwä-lə, -zə-ˈwä-, ˌbä-nä-ˈswä-lä\ country N South America; *, Caracas; *pop* 20,609,000 — **Ven·e·zu·e·lan** \-lən\ *adj or n*

Ven·ice \ˈve-nəs\ *or Italian* **Ve·ne·zia** \ve-ˈnet-sē-ä\ city N Italy on islands in Lagoon of Venice; *pop* 275,368 — **Ve·ne·tian** \və-ˈnē-shən\ *adj or n*

Ven·tu·ra \ven-ˈtu̇r-ə, -ˈtyu̇r-\ city & port SW California; *pop* 100,916

Ve·ra·cruz \ˌver-ə-ˈkrüz, -ˈkrüs\ city E Mexico; metropolitan area *pop* 560,200

Ver·mont \vər-ˈmänt\ state NE U.S.; *, Montpelier; *pop* 608,827 — **Ver·mont·er** \-ˈmän-tər\ *n*

Ve·ro·na \ve-ˈrō-nä\ city N Italy W of Venice; *pop* 257,477

Ver·sailles \(ˌ)vər-ˈsī, ver-\ city N France, WSW suburb of Paris; *pop* 91,029

Ve·su·vi·us \və-ˈsü-vē-əs\ volcano about 4190 ft. (1277 m.) S Italy near Bay of Naples

Vicks·burg \ˈviks-ˌbərg\ city W Mississippi; *pop* 26,407

Vic·to·ria \vik-ˈtȯr-ē-ə\ **1** city, * of British Columbia, Canada on Vancouver Island; *pop* 74,125 **2** island N Canada in Arctic Archipelago **3** state SE Australia; *, Melbourne; *pop* 4,244,221 **4** city & port, Hong Kong; *pop* 1,026,870 **5** sea-

port, * of Seychelles; *pop* 28,000 — **Vic·to·ri·an** \vik-ˈtȯr-ē-ən\ *adj or n*

Victoria, Lake lake E Africa in Tanzania, Kenya, & Uganda

Victoria Falls waterfall 355 ft. (108 m.) S Africa in the Zambezi on border between Zambia & Zimbabwe

Vi·en·na \vē-ˈe-nə\ *or German* **Wien** \ˈvēn\ city, * of Austria on the Danube; *pop* 1,550,123 — **Vi·en·nese** \ˌvē-ə-ˈnēz, -ˈnēs\ *adj or n*

Vien·tiane \(ˌ)vyen-ˈtyän\ city, * of Laos; *pop* 132,253

Vie·ques \vē-ˈā-käs\ island Puerto Rico off E end of main island

Viet·nam \vē-ˈet-ˈnäm, vyet-, ˌvē-ət-, vēt-; -ˈnam\ country SE Asia in Indochina; *, Hanoi; divided 1954–75 into the independent states of **North Vietnam** (*, Hanoi) & **South Vietnam** (*, Saigon); *pop* 79,727,400 — **Viet·nam·ese** \vē-ˌet-nə-ˈmēz, ˌvyet-, ˌvē-ət-, ˌvēt-, -na-, -nä-, -ˈmēs\ *adj or n*

Vila — see PORT-VILA

Vi·la No·va de Ga·ia \ˈvē-lə-ˈnȯ-və-dē-ˈgī-ə\ city NW Portugal; *pop* 288,749

Vil·ni·us \ˈvil-nē-əs\ city, * of Lithuania; *pop* 542,287

Vin·land \ˈvin-lənd\ a portion of the coast of North America visited & so called by Norse voyagers about 1000 A.D.; thought to be located along the North Atlantic in what is now E or NE Canada

Vir·gin·ia \vər-ˈji-nyə, -ˈji-nē-ə\ state E U.S.; *, Richmond; *pop* 7,078,515 — **Vir·gin·ian** \-nyən, -nē-ən\ *adj or n*

Virginia Beach city SE Virginia; *pop* 425,257

Virginia City locality W Nevada

Virgin Islands island group West Indies E of Puerto Rico — see BRITISH VIRGIN ISLANDS; VIRGIN ISLANDS OF THE UNITED STATES

Virgin Islands of the United States the W islands of the Virgin Islands; U.S. territory; *, Charlotte Amalie (on Saint Thomas); *pop* 108,612

Vi·sa·yan \və-ˈsī-ən\ islands *cen* Philippines

Vish·a·kha·pat·nam \vi-ˌshä-kə-ˈpət-nəm\ *or* **Vis·a·kha·pat·nam** \vi-ˌsä-\ city E India; *pop* 969,608

Vis·tu·la \ˈvis-chə-lə, ˈvish-chə-, ˈvis-tə-\ river over 660 mi. (1062 km.) long Poland flowing N from the Carpathians

Vi·ti Le·vu \ˌvē-tē-ˈle-(ˌ)vü\ island SW Pacific; largest of the Fiji group

Vlad·i·vos·tok \ˌvla-də-və-ˈstäk, -ˈväs-ˌtäk\ city & port SE Russia on Sea of Japan; *pop* 648,000

Vol·ga \ˈväl-gə, ˈvȯl-, ˈvōl-\ river about 2300 mi. (3700 km.) long W Russia; longest river in Europe

Vol·go·grad \ˈväl-gə-ˌgrad, ˈvȯl-, ˈvōl-,

-ˌgrät\ city S Russia in Europe, on the Volga; *pop* 1,006,000

Vol·ta \ˈväl-tə, ˈvȯl-, ˈvōl-\ river about 300 mi. (485 km.) long Ghana flowing from **Lake Volta** (reservoir) into Gulf of Guinea

Vo·ro·nezh \və-ˈrȯ-nish\ city S *cen* Russia in Europe; *pop* 902,000

Vosges \ˈvōzh\ mountains NE France on W side of Rhine valley; highest 4672 ft. (1424 m.)

Wa·co \ˈwā-(ˌ)kō\ city *cen* Texas; *pop* 113,726

Wad·den·zee \ˌvä-dᵊn-ˈzā\ inlet of the North Sea N Netherlands

Wake \ˈwāk\ island North Pacific N of Marshall Islands; U.S. territory

Wake·field \ˈwāk-ˌfēld\ city N England; *pop* 60,540

Wa·la·chia *or* **Wal·la·chia** \wä-ˈlā-kē-ə\ region S Romania between Transylvanian Alps & the Danube

Wales \ˈwālz\ *or Welsh* **Cym·ru** \ˈkəm-ˌrē\ principality SW Great Britain; a division of United Kingdom; ✱, Cardiff; *pop* 2,903,085

Wal·lo·nia \wä-ˈlō-nē-ə\ semiautonomous region S Belgium; *pop* 3,358,560

Wal·sall \ˈwȯl-ˌsȯl, -səl\ town W *cen* England; *pop* 255,600

Wal·tham Forest \ˈwȯl-thəm\ borough of NE Greater London, England; *pop* 203,400

Wands·worth \ˈwän(d)z-(ˌ)wərth\ borough of SW Greater London, England; *pop* 237,500

War·ley \ˈwȯr-lē\ town W *cen* England; *pop* 152,455

War·ren \ˈwȯr-lē\ city SE Michigan; *pop* 138,247

War·saw \ˈwȯr-ˌsȯ\ *or Polish* **War·sza·wa** \vär-ˈshä-vä\ city, ✱ of Poland; *pop* 1,655,063

War·wick \ˈwär-ik\ town England; *pop* 21,936

War·wick·shire \ˈwär-ik-ˌshir, -shər\ *or* **Warwick** county *cen* England

Wa·satch \ˈwȯ-ˌsach\ range of the Rockies SE Idaho & N *cen* Utah; highest Mount Timpanogos 12,008 ft. (3660 m.), in Utah

Wash·ing·ton \ˈwȯ-shiŋ-tən, ˈwä-\ **1** state NW U.S.; ✱, Olympia; *pop* 5,894,121 **2** city, ✱ of U.S.; having the same boundaries as District of Columbia; *pop* 572,059 — **Wash·ing·to·nian** \ˌwȯ-shiŋ-ˈtō-nē-ən, ˌwä-, -nyən\ *adj or n*

Washington, Mount mountain 6288 ft. (1916 m.) N New Hampshire; highest in White Mountains

Wa·ter·bury \ˈwȯ-tə(r)-ˌber-ē, ˈwä-\ city W *cen* Connecticut; *pop* 107,271

Wa·ver·ley \ˈwā-vər-lē\ municipality SE Australia in E New South Wales; *pop* 59,095

Wei·mar Republic \ˈvī-ˌmär, ˈwī-\ the German republic 1919–33

Wel·land \ˈwe-lənd\ canal 27 mi. (44 km.) long SE Ontario connecting Lake Erie & Lake Ontario

Wel·ling·ton \ˈwe-liŋ-tən\ city, ✱ of New Zealand; urban area *pop* 339,747

Wes·sex \ˈwe-siks\ ancient kingdom S England

West Bank area Middle East W of Jordan River; occupied by Israel since 1967 with parts having been transferred to Palestinian administration since 1993

West Brom·wich \ˈbrä-mich\ town W *cen* England; *pop* 154,930

West Co·vi·na \kō-ˈvē-nə\ city SW California; *pop* 105,080

Western Australia state W Australia; ✱, Perth; *pop* 1,676,400 — **Western Australian** *adj or n*

Western Cape province SW Republic of South Africa; *pop* 3,635,000

Western Ghats — see GHATS

Western Hemisphere the half of the earth lying W of the Atlantic Ocean & comprising North America, South America, & surrounding waters

Western Isles English name for the administrative area of W Scotland consisting of the Outer Hebrides

Western Sahara *formerly* **Spanish Sahara** territory NW Africa; occupied by Morocco

Western Samoa — see SAMOA

West Germany — see GERMANY

West Indies islands lying between SE North America & N South America & consisting of the Greater Antilles, Lesser Antilles, & Bahamas — **West Indian** *adj or n*

West Midlands metropolitan county W *cen* England; includes Birmingham

West·min·ster \ˈwes(t)-ˌmin(t)-stər\ city N *cen* Colorado NW of Denver; *pop* 100,940

West Pakistan the former W division of Pakistan now having the same boundaries as Pakistan

West Papua *or formerly* **Iri·an Ja·ya** \ˈir-ē-ˌän-ˈjī-ä\ *or* **West Irian** territory of Indonesia consisting of the W half of New Guinea; *pop* 1,648,708

West·pha·lia \west-ˈfāl-yə, -ˈfā-lē-ə\ region W Germany E of the Rhine — **West·pha·lian** \west-ˈfāl-yən, -ˈfā-lē-ən\ *adj or n*

West Point U.S. military post SE New York

West Quod·dy Head \ˈkwä-dē\ cape; most easterly point of Maine & of the Lower 48

West Sus·sex \ˈsə-siks\ county SE England

West Valley City city N Utah S of Salt Lake City; *pop* 108,896

West Virginia state E U.S.; *, Charleston; *pop* 1,808,344 — **West Virginian** *adj or n*

West York·shire metropolitan county NW England; includes Wakefield

White sea NW Russia in Europe

White·horse \'hwīt-ˌhȯrs, 'wīt-\ city, * of Yukon Territory, Canada; *pop* 19,058

White Mountains mountains N New Hampshire in the Appalachians — see WASHINGTON, MOUNT

Whit·ney, Mount \'hwit-nē, 'wit-\ mountain 14,495 ft. (4418 m.) SE *cen* California in Sierra Nevada; highest in U.S. outside of Alaska

Wich·i·ta \'wi-chə-ˌtȯ\ city S Kansas; *pop* 344,284

Wichita Falls city N Texas; *pop* 104,197

Wien — see VIENNA

Wight, Isle of — see ISLE OF WIGHT

Wil·lem·stad \'vi-ləm-ˌstät\ city, * of Netherlands Antilles; *pop* 43,547

Wil·liams·burg \'wil-yəmz-ˌbərg\ city SE Virginia; *pop* 11,998

Wil·ming·ton \'wil-miŋ-tən\ city N Delaware; largest in state; *pop* 72,664

Wilt·shire \'wilt-ˌshir, -shər\ county S England

Win·ches·ter \'win-ˌches-tər, -chəs-tər\ city S England; *pop* 30,642

Win·der·mere \'win-də(r)-ˌmir\ lake NW England in Lake District

Wind·hoek \'vint-ˌhu̇k\ city, * of Namibia; *pop* 144,558

Wind·sor \'win-zər\ city S Ontario, Canada on Detroit River; *pop* 208,402

Wind·ward Islands \'wind-wərd\ islands West Indies in the S Lesser Antilles extending S from Martinique but not including Barbados, Tobago, or Trinidad

Win·ni·peg \'wi-nə-ˌpeg\ city, * of Manitoba, Canada; *pop* 619,544

Winnipeg, Lake lake S *cen* Manitoba, Canada

Win·ni·pe·sau·kee, Lake \ˌwi-nə-pə-'sȯ-kē\ lake *cen* New Hampshire

Win·ston–Sa·lem \ˌwin(t)-stən-'sä-ləm\ city N North Carolina; *pop* 185,776

Wis·con·sin \wi-'skän(t)-sən\ state N *cen* U.S.; *, Madison; *pop* 5,363,675 — **Wis·con·sin·ite** \-sə-ˌnīt\ *n*

Wit·wa·ters·rand \'wit-wȯ-tərz-ˌrand, -ˌwä-, -ˌränd, -ˌränt\ *or* **Rand** ridge of gold-bearing rock NE Republic of South Africa

Wol·lon·gong \'wu̇-lən-ˌgäŋ, -ˌgȯŋ\ city SE Australia in E New South Wales S of Sydney; *pop* 211,417

Wol·ver·hamp·ton \ˌwu̇l-vər-'ham(p)-tən\ town W *cen* England NW of Birmingham; *pop* 236,582

Worces·ter \'wu̇s-tər\ city E *cen* Massachusetts; *pop* 172,648

Wran·gell, Mount \'raŋ-gəl\ volcano 14,163 ft. (4317 m.) S Alaska in **Wrangell Mountains**

Wro·claw \'vrȯt-ˌswäf, -ˌsläv\ city SW Poland in Silesia; *pop* 642,334

Wu·han \'wü-'hän\ city E *cen* China; *pop* 3,284,229

Wu·xi *or* **Wu·hsi** \'wü-'shē\ city E China; *pop* 826,833

Wy·o·ming \wī-'ō-miŋ\ state NW U.S.; *, Cheyenne; *pop* 493,782 — **Wy·o·ming·ite** \-miŋ-ˌīt\ *n*

Xi'an *or* **Hsi–an** \'shē-'än\ city E *cen* China; *pop* 1,959,044

Xianggang — see HONG KONG

Xin·jiang Uy·gur *or* **Sin·kiang Ui·ghur** \'shin-'jyäŋ-'wē-gər\ region W China between the Kunlun & Altai mountains; *pop* 15,155,778

Xizang — see TIBET

Xu·zhou \'shü-'jō\ *or* **Sü·chow** \'shü-'jō, 'sü-\ city E China; *pop* 805,695

Yak·i·ma \'ya-kə-ˌmȯ\ city S *cen* Washington; *pop* 71,845

Ya·lu \'yä-(ˌ)lü\ river 500 mi. (804 km.) long SE Manchuria & North Korea

Ya·mous·sou·kro \ˌyä-mə-'sü-krō\ town, official * of Ivory Coast; *pop* 110,000

Yan·gon \'yän-'gōn\ *formerly* **Ran·goon** \ran-'gün, raŋ-\ city, * of Myanmar; *pop* 1,717,649

Yangtze — see CHANG

Yaoun·dé \yau̇n-'dā\ city, * of Cameroon; *pop* 649,000

Yap \'yap, 'yäp\ island W Pacific in the W Carolines

Ya·ren \'yä-ˌrən\ town, * of Nauru; *pop* 1100

Ya·ro·slavl \ˌyär-ə-'slä-vəl\ city *cen* Russia in Europe, NE of Moscow; *pop* 637,000

Yaz·oo \ya-'zü, 'ya-(ˌ)zü\ river W *cen* Mississippi

Ye·ka·te·rin·burg \yi-'ka-tə-rən-ˌbərg, yi-ˌkä-ti-rēm-'bu̇rk\ *formerly* **Sverd·lovsk** \sverd-'lȯfsk\ city W Russia, in *cen* Ural Mountains; *pop* 1,371,000

Yellow 1 — see HUANG **2** sea, section of East China Sea between N China, North Korea, & South Korea

Yel·low·knife \'ye-lō-ˌnīf\ town, * of Northwest Territories, Canada; *pop* 16,541

Ye·men \'ye-mən\ country S Arabia bordering on Red Sea & Gulf of Aden; *, Sanaa; *pop* 12,961,000 — **Ye·me·ni** \'ye-mə-nē\ *adj or n* — **Ye·men·ite** \-mə-ˌnīt\ *adj or n*

Ye·ni·sey *or* **Ye·ni·sei** \ˌyi-ni-'sā\ river over 2500 mi. (4022 km.) long *cen* Russia, flowing N into Arctic Ocean

Ye·re·van \ˌyer-ə-'vän\ city, * of Armenia; *pop* 1,199,000

Yo·ko·ha·ma \ˌyō-kō-'hä-mä\ city Japan in SE Honshu on Tokyo Bay S of Tokyo; *pop* 3,426,651

Yon·kers \'yäŋ-kərz\ city SE New York N of New York City; *pop* 196,086

York \'yȯrk\ city N England; *pop* 100,600

York, Cape cape NE Australia in Queensland at N tip of Cape York Peninsula

York·shire \-ˌshir, -shər\ former county N England

Yo·sem·i·te Falls \yō-'se-mə-tē\ waterfall E California in Yosemite Valley; includes two falls, the upper 1430 ft. (436 m.) & the lower 320 ft. (98 m.)

Youngs·town \'yəŋz-ˌtaůn\ city NE Ohio; *pop* 82,026

Yu·ca·tán \ˌyü-kə-'tan, -kä-'tän\ peninsula SE Mexico & N Central America including Belize & N Guatemala

Yu·go·sla·via \ˌyü-gō-'slä-vē-ə, ˌyü-gə-\ 1 former country S Europe including Serbia, Montenegro, Slovenia, Croatia, Bosnia and Herzegovina, & Macedonia; *, Belgrade 2 — see SERBIA AND MONTENEGRO — **Yu·go·slav** \ˌyü-gō-'släv, -'slav; 'yü-gō-ˌ\ or **Yu·go·sla·vi·an** \ˌyü-gō-'slä-vē-ən, -gə-\ *adj or n*

Yu·kon \'yü-ˌkän\ 1 river 1979 mi. (3185 km.) long NW Canada & Alaska flowing into Bering Sea 2 or **Yukon Territory** territory NW Canada; *, Whitehorse; *pop* 29,885

Yu·ma \'yü-mə\ city SW corner of Arizona on the Colorado; *pop* 77,515

Za·greb \'zä-ˌgreb\ city, * of Croatia; *pop* 779,145

Zaire \zä-'ir\ 1 river in Africa — see CONGO 1 2 country in Africa — see CONGO 2 — **Zair·ean** or **Zair·ian** \zä-'ir-ē-ən\ *adj or n*

Zam·be·zi or **Zam·be·si** \zam-'bē-zē, zäm-'bä-zē\ river about 1700 mi. (2735 km.) long SE Africa flowing from NW Zambia into Mozambique Channel

Zam·bia \'zam-bē-ə\ *formerly* **Northern Rhodesia** country S Africa N of the Zambezi; *, Lusaka; *pop* 9,132,000 — **Zam·bi·an** \'zam-bē-ən\ *adj or n*

Zan·zi·bar \'zan-zə-ˌbär\ island Tanzania off NE Tanganyika coast; united 1964 with Tanganyika forming Tanzania

Za·po·rizh·zhya or **Za·po·ro·zh'ye** \ˌzä-pə-'rēzh-zhyə\ city SE Ukraine; *pop* 897,000

Zhang·jia·kou \'jäŋ-'jyä-'kō\ or **Kal·gan** \'kal-'gan\ city NE China NW of Beijing; *pop* 529,136

Zhdanov — see MARIUPOL

Zheng·zhou or **Cheng·chou** \'jəŋ-'jō\ city NE *cen* China; *pop* 1,159,679

Zim·ba·bwe \zim-'bä-bwē, -(ˌ)bwä\ *formerly* **Rhodesia** country S Africa S of Zambezi River; *, Harare; *pop* 7,550,000 — **Zim·ba·bwe·an** \-ən\ *adj or n*

Zui·der Zee \ˌzī-dər-'zā, -'zē\ — see IJSSELMEER

Zu·lu·land \'zü-(ˌ)lü-ˌland\ territory E Republic of South Africa on Indian Ocean

Zu·rich \'zůr-ik\ city N Switzerland; *pop* 340,873